W9-CGQ-985

American
DRUG INDEX

30th Edition

American DRUG INDEX

1986

30th Edition

NORMAN F. BILLUPS, R.Ph., M.S., Ph.D.

Dean and Professor of Pharmacy
College of Pharmacy
The University of Toledo

Associate Editor
SHIRLEY M. BILLUPS, R.N., B.Ed.

Oncology Nurse
The Toledo Hospital

J. B. LIPPINCOTT COMPANY
Philadelphia

London New York São Paulo
Mexico City St. Louis Sydney

ISBN 0-397-50736-4

Library of Congress Catalog Card Number 55-6286

Printed in the United States of America

Preface

The 30th Edition of the *American Drug Index* (ADI) has been prepared for the identification, explanation, and correlation of the many pharmaceuticals available to the medical, pharmaceutical, and allied health professions. The need for this index has become acute as the variety and number of drugs and drug products have continued to multiply. For this reason the *ADI* should be most useful to pharmacists, nurses, physicians, medical transcriptionists, dentists, sales personnel, students, and teachers in the fields incorporating pharmaceuticals. *Special note to medical transcriptionists:* Although all names in the *ADI* appear in bold capitalized type, trade products are easily identifiable by the manufacturer's name in parentheses immediately following the trade name. The names for official products are preceded by a bullet (•) and should appear in lower case in transcription. The therapeutic and pharmaceutical classes are denoted by a box (■) preceding the name and should be a helpful cross-reference guide.

The organization of the *ADI* falls into the following ten major sections: Monographs of Drug Products, Common Abbreviations Used in Medical Orders, Aproximate Practical Equivalents, Common Systems of Weight and Measure, Glossary, Title Changes For U.S.P. XXI and N.F. XVI Monographs, Container Requirements for U.S.P. XXI Drugs, Container and Storage Requirements for Sterile U.S.P. XXI Drugs, Pharmaceutical Company Labeler Code Index Numbers, and Pharmaceutical Manufacturer and/or Drug Distributor Addresses. The U.S.P. XXI and N.F. XVI Title Changes section has been added to make the *ADI* an even more complete and valuable reference tool.

MONOGRAPHS: The organization of the monograph section of the *ADI* is fundamentally alphabetical with extensive cross-indexing. Names listed are generic (also called non-proprietary, public name, or common name); brand (also called trade-mark, proprietary, or specialty); and chemical. Synonyms that are in general use also are included. All names used for a pharmaceutical appear in alphabetical order with the pertinent data given under the brand name by which it is made available.

The monograph for a typical brand name product consists of the manufacturer, generic and/or chemical names, composition and strength, pharmaceutical forms available, package size, dosage, and use.

Generic names appear in alphabetical order, followed by the corresponding recognition of the drug to the U.S.P. (United States Pharmacopeia), N.F. (National Formulary), and USAN (United States Adopted Names). Each of these officially recognized generic names is preceded by a bullet (•) at the beginning of each entry. The information is in accord with the U.S.P. XXI and N.F. XVI and through Supplement 2, which became official on July 1, 1985; and the USAN-1986.

British Approved Names, indicated by (B.A.N.), are included in this edition with the permission of the Controller of Her Britannic Majesty's Stationery Office.

Because of the multiplicity of specialty names (brand names) used for the same therapeutic agent or the same combination of therapeutic agents, it was apparent that some correlation could be done. As an example of this, please turn to tetracycline HCl. Here under the generic name are listed the various brand names. Following are combinations of tetracycline HCl organized in a manner to point out relationships among the many products. Reference then is made to the specialty name or names having the indicated composition. Under the specialty name are given manufacturer, composition, available forms, sizes, dosage, and use.

The multiplicity of generic names for the same therapeutic agent has complicated the nomenclature of these agents. Examples of multiple generic names for the same chemical substance are (1) parabromdylamine, brompheniramine; (2) acetaminophen, p-hydroxy acetanilid, N-acetyl-p-aminophenol; (3) guaifenesin, glyceryl guaiacolate, glyceryl guaiacol ether, guaianesin, guaifylline, guaiphenesin, guayanesin, methphenoxydiol; (4) pyrilamine, pyranisamine, pyranilamine, pyraminyl, anisopyradamine.

The cross-indexing feature of the *ADI* permits the finding of drugs or drug combinations when only one major ingredient is known. For example, a combination of aluminum hydroxide gel and magnesium trisilicate is available. This combination can be found by looking under the name of either of the two ingredients, and in each case the specialty names are given. A second form of cross-indexing involves the listing of drugs under various therapeutic and pharmaceutical classes (i.e., antacids, antihistamines, diuretics, laxatives, etc.). Each of these classes is preceded by a box (■) at the beginning of each entry.

ABBREVIATIONS: A listing of Common Abbreviations Used in Medical Orders is included as an aid in interpreting medical orders. The Latin or Greek word and abbreviation are both given with the meaning.

CONVERSION FACTORS: The listing of Approximate Practical Equivalents is added as an aid in calculating and converting dosages among the metric, apothecary, and avoirdupois systems.

WEIGHT AND MEASURE: Tables containing the Common Systems of Weight and Measure are included to aid the practitioner in calculating dosages in the metric, apothecary, and avoirdupois systems.

GLOSSARY: A listing of commonly used terms, with brief definitions, is included as an aid in interpreting the use given for drug monographs listed in the *ADI.*

NEW TITLES FOR U.S.P. XXI AND N.F. XVI MONOGRAPHS: 119 new official monographs appeared through Supplement 2 to the 1985 U.S.P. XXI and N.F. XVI, and an additional 535 new monographs have appeared since the 1980 U.S.P. XX and N.F. XV. Since many of these new monographs apply to commonly used drug products, this section has been added to aid the practitioner in identifying drug products.

CONTAINER AND STORAGE REQUIREMENTS FOR U.S.P. XXI COMPENDIAL DRUGS: These sections have been added on container and storage requirements specified by the U.S.P. XXI for compendial drugs, to aid the practitioner in storing and dispensing.

ORAL DOSAGE FORMS THAT SHOULD NOT BE CRUSHED: For the first time this year, a section has been added to alert the health care practitioner about oral dosage forms that should not be crushed, and to serve as an aid in consulting with patients. Examples of products falling into the "non-crush" category are extended-release, enteric-coated, encapsulated beads, wax matrix, sublingual, and encapsulated liquid formulations.

LABELER CODE INDEX: The Pharmaceutical Labeler Code Index is presented to aid the practitioner in the identification of drug products. In this section, the codes are listed in numerical order followed by the name of the manufacturer.

MANUFACTURER ADDRESSES: The name, address, and zip code of virtually every American Pharmaceutical Manufacturer and/or Drug Distributor are listed in alphabetical order in this section. Additionally, a pharmaceutical labeler code number appears before the address of each company as a further aid in the identification of drug products.

A special word of appreciation and acknowledgment is given to my wife, Shirley, who served again this year as my Associate Editor—and helped to compile much of the information that appears in the monograph section of this volume. Special thanks are also extended to the manufacturers who supplied product information and made helpful comments and suggestions for this index, and to Dr. Kenneth S. Alexander, who organized the information on Container and Storage Requirements for U.S.P. XXI Drugs.

Correspondence or communication with reference to a drug or drug products listed in the *American Drug Index* should be directed to Norman F. Billups, Ph.D., Dean, College of Pharmacy; The University of Toledo; Toledo, Ohio 43606, or call 419-537-4235.

Norman F. Billups, R.Ph., Ph.D.

Contents

[•] Denotes official name: Generic name or chemical name approved by F.D.A. or recognized by the U.S.P., N.F., or USAN.

[■] Denotes therapeutic and pharmaceutical classes.

A

-200 PYRINATE. (Norcliff Thayer) **Liquid:** Pyrethrins 0.17%, piperonyl butoxide technical 2.00%, petroleum distillate 5.00%. Bot. 2 fl. oz., 4 fl. oz. **Gel:** Pyrethrins 0.33%, piperonyl butoxide technical 4.00%, petroleum distallate 5.33%. Tube 1 oz.
Use: Topically, pediculosis.

.A.A. OINTMENT. (Jenkins) Ammoniated mercury 2%, acid salicylic 1.25%, acid boric 1%, zinc oxide 15%. Jar 1 oz., 1 lb.
Use: Impetigo, nonspecific eczema & minor skin irritations.

AND D HAND CREAM. (Schering) Emollients isopropyl myristate & squalane. Tube 2 oz.
Use: Dry skin, sunburn, irritations.

AND D OINTMENT. (Kenyon) Vits. A & D in lanolin-petrolatum base. Jar 1 lb.

AND D OINTMENT. (Schering) Petrolatum-lanolin. Tube 1.5 oz., 4 oz.. Jar 1 lb.

& D TABLETS. (Barth's) Vit. A 10,000 I.U., D 400 I.U./Tab. Bot. 100s, 500s.

AND D VITAMIN CAPSULES. (Lannett) Vit. A 5000 I.U., D 400 I.U./Cap. Bot. 500s, 1000s.
Use: Vit. supplement.

AND D VITAMIN CREAM. (Eckerd) Bot. 1.5 oz., 4 oz.

& D VITAMIN OINTMENT. (Quality Generics) Vit. A & D in lanolin-petroleum base Tube 2 oz., Jar 1 lb.
Use: Emollient.

AND D VITAMIN OINTMENT. (Lannett) In a petrolatum-lanolin base. Jar 1, 5 lb.

AND D VITAMIN OINTMENT. (Ulmer) Jar 1 lb., 2 oz.

-A PLUS. (Galen) Al hydroxide gel 400 mg., Mg oxide 175 mg., Na lauryl sulfate 25 mg., Me cellulose 100 mg., hyoscyamine sulfate 0.1037 mg., atropine sulfate 0.0194 mg., hyoscine HBr 0.0065 mg./Tab. Bot. 100s, 1000s. Susp. 1 pt.

AS INFANTIL W/VITAMIN C. (Winthrop Products) Acetylsalicylic acid, Vit. C.
Use: Analgesic, antipyretic.

AS TABLETS. (Winthrop Products) Acetylsalicylic acid.
Use: Analgesic, antipyretic.

BBOCIN. Oxytetracycline, B.A.N.

BBOKINASE. (Abbott) Urokinase 250,000 I.U./5 ml. Lyophilized powder. Vial 5 ml.
Use: Plasminogen activator.

BBOKINASE OPEN-CATH. (Abbott) Urokinase for catheter clearance 5,000 I.U./ml. Univial.
Use: Clearance of fibrin occluded catheters.

BBOTT AFP-EIA. (Abbott) Test Kits 100s.
Use: Enzyme immunoassay for the quantitative measurement of alpha-fetoprotein in human serum to aid in the management of testicular cancer.

BBOTT CMV TOTAL AB EIA. (Abbott) Test kits 100s.
Use: Enzyme immunoassay for the detection of antibody to cytomegalovirus in human serum, plasma, and whole blood.

ABBOTT-HB$_e$ TEST. (Abbott) Test kits 100s.
Use: Radioimmunoassay or enzyme immunoassay for detection of hepatitis B$_e$ antigen and/or antibody to hepatitis B$_e$ antigen.

ABBOTT IgE EIA. (Abbott) Test kits 100s.
Use: Enzyme immunoassay for quantitative determination of IgE in human serum and plasma.

ABC COMPOUND w/CODEINE #3. (Zenith) Aspirin 325 mg., caffeine 40 mg., butalbital 50 mg., codeine phosphate 30 mg./Cap.
Use: Analgesic.

ABCDG VITAMIN CAPSULES. (Lannett) Vit. A 5000 u., D 400 u., B-1 1 mg., B-2 2 mg., C 30 mg./Cap. Bot. 1000s.
Use: Vitamin supplement.

ABDEC BABY VITAMIN DROPS. (Parke-Davis) Vit. A 1500 I.U., D 400 I.U., B-1 0.5 mg., B-2 0.6 mg., B-6 0.4 mg., pantothenic acid 3 mg., niacin 8 mg., C 35 mg./ml. Bot. 1⅔ oz. w/dropper.
Use: Vitamin deficiencies.

ABDEC WITH FLUORIDE BABY VITAMIN DROPS. (Parke-Davis) Vit. A 1500 I.U., D 400 I.U., C 35 mg., B-1 0.5 mg., B-2 0.6 mg., B-6 0.4 mg., niacin 8 mg., pantothenic acid 3 mg./ml. w/fluoride. Bot. 50 ml.
Use: Vitamin therapy with fluoride.

ABDO. (Eastwood) Cap. Bot. 100s.

ABDOL W/MINERALS. (Parke-Davis) Vit. C 50 mg., B-2 2.5 mg., B-12 1 mcg., B-6 0.5 mg., B-1 2.5 mg., niacinamide 20 mg., Vit. A 5000 I.U., D 400 I.U., Ca pantothenate 2.5 mg., folic acid 0.1 mg., iodine 0.15 mg., Mn 1 mg., K 5.0 mg., Fe 15 mg., Cu 1 mg., Zn 0.5 mg., Mg 1 mg., Ca 44 mg., P 34 mg./Cap. Bot. 100s.
Use: Vitamin-mineral deficiency states.

ABSORBABLE CELLULOSE COTTON OR GAUZE.
See: Oxidized Cellulose (Various Mfr.)

• **ABSORBABLE DUSTING POWDER,** U.S.P. XXI.

• **ABSORBABLE GELATIN FILM,** U.S.P. XXI. Sterile nonantigenic, absorbable, water-insoluble, gelatin film.
See: Gelfilm (Upjohn)

• **ABSORBABLE GELATIN SPONGE,** U.S.P. XXI. Gelatin sponge.
Use: Surgical aid.
See: Gelfoam, Preps. (Upjohn)

• **ABSORBABLE SURGICAL SUTURE,** U.S.P. XXI. (Various Mfr.) Surgical Gut, Surgical Catgut, Catgut suture.
Use: Surgical aid.

• **ABSORBENT GAUZE,** U.S.P. XXI.
Use: Surgical aid.

ABSORBINE ARTHRITIC PAIN LOTION. (W.F. Young) Bot. 2 oz., 4 oz.

ABSORBINE FOOT POWDER. (W.F. Young) Zinc stearate, parachloroxylenol, aluminum chlorhydroxy, allantonate, benzethonium chloride, menthol. Plastic bot. 3 oz. w/shaker top.
Use: Athlete's foot treatment.

ABSORBINE, JR. (W.F. Young) Wormwood, thymol, chloroxylenol, menthol, acetone, zinc stearate, parachloroxylenol, aluminum chlorhydroxy, allantonate, benzethonium chloride, menthol. Liq. Bot. 1 oz., 2 oz., 4 oz., 12 oz. w/applicator.

Use: Muscle soreness, stiffness, treatment of athlete's foot.

ABUSCREEN. (Roche Diagnostics) An immunological and radiochemical assay for morphine and morphine glucuronide in nanogram levels. Utilizes ^{3}H labeled morphine assayed with liquid scintillation counters using conventional beta counting procedures and ^{125}I labeled morphine requiring gamma scintillation equipment. 100 tests.

ACABEL. Bevonium Methylsulphate, B.A.N.

• **ACACIA,** N.F. XVI. Syrup N.F. XVI. Acacia senegal, gum arabic. (Penick) pow., 0.25 lb., 1 lb.; tears, 0.25-1 lb.; whole, 0.25-1 lb.
Use: Demulcent, emulsifier, suspending agent.

A-CAINE. (A.V.P.) Rectal ointment. Tube 1.25 oz.
Use: Rectal care, anti-hemorrhoidal.

A CAPSULES. (Stanlabs) Natural Vit. A 5,000 I.U., 10,000 I.U., 25,000 I.U., 50,000 I.U./Cap. Bot. 100s. Synthetic or soluble, 10,000 I.U., 25,000 I.U., 50,000 I.U./Cap. Bot. 100s.

A-CAPS. (Drug Industries) Vit. A 50,000 I.U./Cap. Bot. 100s, 500s.
Use: Vitamin A therapy.

• **ACARBOSE.** USAN.
Use: Inhibitor.

ACCELERASE. (Organon) Pancrelipase: Lipase 4000 U., amylase 15,000 U., protease 15,000 U., other pancreatic enzymes mixed with bile salts 65 mg., cellulase 2 mg., calcium carbonate 20 mg./Cap. Bot. 60s.
Use: Functional digestive disorders.

ACCURBRON. (Merrell Dow) Theophylline, anhydrous 10 mg./ml. Bot. pt.
Use: Bronchial asthma treatment.

ACCUSENS T TASTE FUNCTION KIT. (Westport) Test for ability to distinguish among salty, sweet, sour and bitter tastants. Kit contains 15 bottles (60 ml.) tastants and 30 taste record forms.
Use: Diagnostic taste function kit.

ACCUTANE. (Roche) Isotretinoin 10 mg., or 40 mg./Cap. Bot. 100s.
Use: Treatment of severe recalcitrant cystic acne.

A-C-D SOLUTION, U.S.P. Sod. citrate, citric acid & dextrose in sterile pyrogen-free solution.
Baxter-600 cc. bot. with 70, 120 or 300 cc. of sol.; 1000 cc. with 500 cc. of sol.
Cutter-500 cc. bot. with 75 or 120 cc. of sol.; 650 cc. bot. with 80 or 130 cc. of sol.
Diamond-(Abbo-Vac) 250 cc., 500 cc.
Use: Anticoagulant for preparation of plasma or whole blood.

A-C-D SOLUTION MODIFIED. (Squibb) Acid citrate dextrose anticoagulant solution modified.
Use: Anticoagulant for use in radiolabeling red blood cells.

ACDRILE. Methyl Cysteine, B.A.N.

• **ACEBUTOLOL.** USAN. (±)-1-(2-Acetyl-4-butyramidophenoxy)-3-isopropylaminopropan-2-ol. (Ives) (±)-N-[3-Acetyl-4-[2-hydroxy-3-[(1-methylethyl)amino]propoxy]-phenyl] butamide.
Use: Beta adrenergic receptor blocking agent.
See: Sectral, Cap. (Ives)

• **ACECAINIDE HYDROCHLORIDE.** USAN.
Use: Cardiac depressant.

• **ACECLIDINE.** USAN. 3-Quinuclidinol acetate (ester) Glaucostat. Under study.
Use: Parasympathomimetic.

• **ACEDAPSONE.** USAN. 4′,4″-Sulfonylbis (acetanilide)
Use: Antimalarial; antibacterial (leprostatic).

ACEDOVAL. (Vale) Dover's powder 15 mg., ipecac 1.5 mg., aspirin 162 mg., caffeine anhydrous 8.1 mg./Tab. Bot. 100s, 1000s, 5000s.

ACEDYNE. (Vale) Aspirin 64.8 mg., caffeine anhydrous 3.2 mg., atropine sulfate 0.032 mg./Tab. Bot. 100s, 1000s, 5000s.

ACEFYLLINE PIPERAZINE. Acepifylline, B.A.N.

• **ACEGLUTAMIDE ALUMINUM.** USAN.
Use: Antiulcerative.

ACELAX. (Marcen) Danthron 100 mg., prune concentrate 64 mg., Chondrus drispus 64 mg./Tab. Bot. 100s, 1000s.
Use: Laxative.

ACENOCOUMAROL. 3-(α-Acetonyl-4-nitrobenzyl)-4-hydroxy-coumarin. Nicoumalone, B.A.N.

A'CENOL. (Kay) Acetaminophen 5 gr./Tab. Bot. 1000s
Use: Analgesic.

ACEPHEN. (G&W) **Adult:** Acetaminophen 650 mg./Supp. Box 12s, 100s.**Pediatric:** Acetaminophen 120 mg./Supp. Box 12s, 100s.
Use: Analgesic, antipyretic.

ACEPIFYLLINE. B.A.N. Piperazine theophyllin-7-ylacetate. Acefylline Piperazine (I.N.N.). Etophylate.
Use: Spasmolytic.

ACEPROMAZINE. 10(3-Dimethylaminopropyl)-3-acetyl phenothiazine maleate. Plegicil. (Ayerst) 1-(10-(3-(Dimethylamino)propyl)-10H-phenothiazin-2-yl)ethanon e(Z)-2-butenedioate.
Use: Tranquilizer.

ACEPROMAZINE. B.A.N. 2-Acetyl-10-(3-dimethylaminopropyl)phenothiazine. Notensil maleate
Use: Tranquilizer.

• **ACEPROMAZINE MALEATE.** USAN.
Use: Sedative.

ACEROLA C. (Kirkman) Vit. C 100 mg./Wafer. Bot. 100s

ACEROLA-C. (Barth's) Vit. C 300 mg./Wafer. Bot. 30s 90s, 180s, 360s.

ACEROLA-PLEX. (Barth's) Vit. C 100 mg., bioflavonoids 50 mg./Tab. Bot. 100s, 500s.

ACETA. (Century) Acetaminophen. **Elix.** (120 mg./5 cc) Bot. 4 oz., pint, gal. **Tabs.** (5 gr.) Bot. 100s, 1000s, 3000s, 5000s.
Use: Analgesic.

ACETA W/CODEINE. (Century) Acetaminophen 325 mg., codeine phosphate 0.5 gr./Tab. Bot. 100s.
Use: Analgesic.

ACETAMIDE. N-[5-(Aminosulfonyl)-3-methyl-1,3,4-thiodiazol-2(3H)-ylidene]-. Methazolamide.

ACETAMIDE, 2,2-DICHLORO-N-[2-HYDROXY-1-(HYDROXYMETHYL)-2-(4-NITROPHENYL)ETHYL] Chloramphenicol, U.S.P. XXI.

ACETAMIDE, 2-(DIETHYLAMINO)-N-(2,6-DIMETHYLPHENYL)-. Lidocaine, U.S.P. XXI.

ACETAMIDE, N-[5-(AMINOSULFONYL)-1,3,-4-THIADIAZOL-2-YL]-. Acetazolamide, U.S.P. XXI.

ACETAMIDE, N-(4-HYDROXYPHENYL)-. Acetaminophen, U.S.P. XXI.

ACETAMIDE, N-(5,6,7,9-TETRAHYDRO-1,2,3,10-TETRAMETHOXY-9-OXOBENZO[a]-HEPTALEN-7-YL-. Colchicine, U.S.P. XXI.

-ACETAMIDOBENZOIC ACID SALT of 2-dimethylaminoethanol.
See: Deaner, Tab. (Riker).

-ACETAMIDO-2,4,6-TRIIODO-N-METHYLISOPHTHALAMIC ACID. Iothalamic Acid, U.S.P. XXI.

-ACETAMIDO-2,4,6-TRIIODO-N-METHYLISOPHTHALAMIC ACID, SODIUM SALT. Iothalamate Sodium Injection, U.S.P. XXI.

ACETAMINOPHEN, U.S.P. XXI. Elix., for Effervescent Oral Soln., Tabs, Cap. U.S.P. XXI. N-Acetyl-p-amino-phenol. Acetamide, N-(4-hydroxyphenyl)-. 4′-Hydroxyacetanilide.
Use: Analgesic, antipyretic.
See: Acephen, Supp. (G&W)
Aceta, Tab. Elix., Supp. (Century)
Acetagesic (Kay)
Actamin, Tab. (Buffington)
Acetaminophen Uniserts, Suppos. (Upsher-Smith)
Aminodyne, Elix. (Bowman)
Anapap, Tab. (Fellows)
Anelix, Elix. (Kirkman)
Anuphen, Supp. (Comatic)
Apap, Cap., Tab. (Various Mfr.)
Capital, Tab. (Carnrick)
Chlor-A-Tyl. (Jenkins)
Dapa, Tab. (Ferndale)
Datril 500, Tab. (Bristol-Myers)
Dimindol, Tab., Elix. (Blue Line)
Dolanex, Elix. (Lannett)
Dularin, Syr. (Donner)
Febridol, Elix., Tab. (Amid)
Fendon, Tab. (APC)
G-1 (Hauck)
Janupap, Tab. (Reid-Provident)
Lestemp, Elix. (Reid-Provident)
Liquiprin, Solu. (Norcliff Thayer)
Lyteca, Syr., Tab. (Westerfield)
Medigesic (Medics)
Nebs, Tab., Liq. (Eaton)
Nilprin 7.5, Tab. (AVP)
Parten, Tab. (Parmed)
Phenaphen, Cap., Tab. (Robins)
Proval, Cap., Elix., Drop., Tab. (Reid-Provident)
SK-Apap, Tab., Elix. (SmithKline)
Tapar, Tab. (Parke-Davis)
Temetan, Elix., Tab. (Nevin)
Tempra, Drop, Syr., (Mead Johnson)
Tenlap, Elix. (Merrell Dow)
Tussapap, Tab. (Sutliff & Case)
Tylenol, Drops, Elix., Liq., Tab., Chew. Tab. (McNeil)
Tylenol Extra-Strength, Tab., Cap. (McNeil)
Valadol, Tab., Liq. (Squibb)
Valorin Tab. (Otis Clapp)

ACETAMINOPHEN W/COMBINATIONS
Aceta w/Codeine, Tab. (Century)
Akes-N-Pain, Cap. (Edw. J. Moore)
Al-Ay Modified, Tab. (Bowman)
Algecol, Tab. (Winston)
Allerest Headache Strength, Tab. (Pharmacraft)
Allylgesic W/Ergotamine, Cap. (Elder)
Allylvon, Cap. (Elder)
Alumadrine, Tab. (Fleming)
Amaphen, Cap. (Trimen)
Aminodyne, Elix. (Bowman)
Anaphen, Cap. (Mallard)
Anodynos-DHC, Tab. (Berlex)
Anodynos Forte, Tab. (Buffington)
Apap w/Codeine, Tab. (Central)
Apapalone, Tab. (Amfre-Grant)
Arthol Tabs. (Towne)
Arthralgen, Tab. (Robins)
Bancaps (Westerfield)
Bancaps-C (Westerfield)
Banesin-Forte, Tab. (Westerfield)
Bexahist, Cap. (Bexar)
Biophens-S, Tab. (La Crosse)
Blanex, Cap. (Edwards)
Bowman Cold Tab. (Bowman)
B-Pap., Liq. (Wren)
BQ Cold Tabs (Bristol-Myers)
Bromo-Seltzer, Gran. (Warner-Lambert)
Butigetic, Tab. (McNeil)
Capital w/Codeine, Tab., Susp. (Carnrick)
Cardui, Tab. (Chattem Labs.)
Cerose Comp., Cap. (Ives)
Chexit, Tab. (Dorsey)
Christodyne-DHC, Tab. (Paddock)
Clistin-D, Tab. (McNeil)
Coastaldyne, Tab. (Coastal)
Coastalgesic, Tab. (Coastal)
Codalan, Tab. (Lannett)
Codap (Reid-Provident)
Codimal, Tab. (Central)
Colrex Compound, Elix. (Rowell)
Comtrex, Cap., Liq., Tab. (Bristol-Myers)
Conar-A, Tab., Susp. (Beecham Labs)
Conex, Preps. (Westerfield)
Congesprin, Liq., Tab. (Bristol-Myers)
Contac Jr., Liq. (Menley & James)
Coricidin Sinus Headache Tab. (Schering)
Coryban-D, Syr. (Roerig)
Corzans, Tab. (Moore Kirk)
Co-Tylenol, Liq., Tab. (McNeil)
Dapase, Tab. (Ferndale)
Darvocet-N, Tab. (Lilly)
Darvocet-N 100, Tab. (Lilly)
Daycare, Liq. (Vicks)
Demerol APAP, Tab. (Winthrop-Breon)
Dengesic, Tab. (Scott-Alison)
Desa-Hist AT, Tab. (Pharmics)
Dolene AP-65, Tab. (Lederle)
Dolopar, Liq. (O'Neal)
Drinacet Cap. (Philips Roxane)
Drinophen, Cap. (Lannett)
D-Sinus, Cap. (Laser)
Dularin-TH, Tab. (Dooner)
Duoprin, Tab. (Dunhall)
Duo-3X, Tab. (Med. Spec.)

Dynosal, Tab. (Mallard)
Empracet with Codeine, Tab. (Burroughs Wellcome)
Enz-Cold, Cap. (Edw. J. Moore)
Esemgesic, Tab. (Spencer-Mead)
Esgic, Tab. (Gilbert)
Excedrin, Cap., Tab. (Bristol-Myers)
F.C.A.H. Caps. (Scherer)
Femicin, Tab. (Norcliff Thayer)
Fendol, Tab. (Buffington)
Gemnisyn, Tab. (Rorer)
Guaiamine, Cap. (Sutliff & Case)
Histalets, Tab. (Edw. J. Moore)
Histogesic, Tab. (Century)
Histosal #2, Tab. (Ferndale)
Hi-Temp, Tab. (Saron)
Hycomine Comp., Tab. (Du Pont)
Isomel, Cap. (Reid-Provident)
Kiddies Sialco, Tab. (Foy)
Kleer, Syr. (Scrip)
Koryza Tab. (Fellows-Testagar)
Maxigesic, Cap. (W.F. Merchant)
Midran, Tab. (Quality Generics)
Midrin, Cap. (Carnrick)
Myocalm, Tab. (Parmed)
Myolate, Tab. (Panray)
Naldetuss, Syr. (Bristol)
N-D Gesic, Tab. (Hyrex)
Neo-Pyranistan, Tab. (Standex Labs.)
Nokane, Tab. (Wren)
Novahistine Singlet, Tab. (Merrell Dow)
Novahistine Sinus Tablets, Tab. (Merrell Dow)
Nylorac PB, Tab. (Beard)
Nyquil, Liq. (Vicks)
Opasal, Cap. (Elder)
Ornex, Cap. (Menley & James)
Pamprin, Tab. (Chattem Labs.)
Panitol H.M.B., Tab. (Wesley)
Panritis, Tab. (Pan Amer.)
Parafon Forte, Tab. (McNeil)
Partuss-A, Tab. (Parmed)
Partuss T.D., Tab. (Parmed)
Pavadon Elix. (Coastal)
Pedituss, Liq. (Sutliff & Case)
Pedric, Elix., Wafers (Vale)
Percogesic, Tab. (Du Pont)
Phenahist, Cap., Elix. (Amid)
Phenaphen #2, #3, #4 (Robins)
Phenaphen-650, Tab. (Robins)
Phrenilin, Tab. (Carnrick)
Presalin, Tab. (Mallard)
Prodolor, Tab. (Amfre-Grant)
Proval No. 3, Tab. (Reid-Provident)
Renpap, Tab. (Wren)
Rentuss, Cap., Syr. (Wren)
Repan, Tab. (Everett)
Rhinex, D•Lay, Tab. (Lemmon)
Rhinidrin, Tab. (Central)
Rhinogesic, Tab. (Vale)
Rhinspec, Tab. (Lemmon)
S.A.C. Sinus, Tabs. (Towne)
Salatin w/Codeine, Tab. (Ferndale)
Saleto, Tab. (Mallard)
Saleto-D, Tab. (Mallard)
Salphenyl, Cap., Liq. (Mallard)
Santussin, Prep. (Sandia)
Scotgesic, Cap., Elix. (Scott/Cord)
Scotuss Pediatric Cough Syr. (Scott/Cord)
Sedacane, Cap. (Edw. J. Moore)
Sedalgesic, Tab. (Table Rock)
Sedragesic, Tab. (Lannett)
Sialco, Tab. (Foy)
Sinarest, Tab. (Pharmacraft)
Sine-Aid, Tab. (McNeil)
Sinoze, Tab. (Bowman)
Sinubid, Tab. (Warner Chilcott)
Sinulin, Tab. (Carnrick)
Sinumal, Tab., Liq. (Cook)
Sinus Tab., Tab. (Zenith)
Sinutab, Prods. (Warner-Lambert)
SK-APAP W/codeine, Tab. (SmithKline)
SK-65 APAP, Tab. (SmithKline)
Spantuss, Liq. (Arco)
Spendrisin, Tab. (Spencer-Mead)
Stopain, Tab. (Quality Generics)
Sunril, Cap. (Emko)
Super-Anahist Tablets (Warner-Lambert)
Symptomax, Liq. (Reid-Provident)
Talacen, Cap. (Winthrop-Breon)
T-Caps, Cap. (Burlington)
Tega-Code, Cap. (Ortega)
Tegapap, Liq., Tab. (Ortega)
Teragen, Tab. (O'Neal)
T-Gesic, Cap. (Tennessee)
Triaminicin, Tab. (Dorsey)
Triaprin, Cap. (Dunhall)
Trind, Syr. (Mead Johnson)
Trind-DM, Syr. (Mead Johnson)
Tussagesic, Tab., Susp. (Dorsey)
Two-Dyne, Tab. (Hyrex)
Tylenol Preps. (McNeil)
Tylenol with Codeine, Elixir, Tab. (McNeil)
Tylox, Cap. (McNeil)
Valihist, Cap. (Clapp)
Vicks Daycare, Liq. (Vicks)
Windolor, Tab. (Winston)
Wygesic, Tab. (Wyeth)
Zenex Comp., Cap. (Zenith)

• **ACETAMINOPHEN AND ASPIRIN TABLETS,** U.S.P. XXI.
Use: Analgesic.

• **ACETAMINOPHEN AND DIPHENHYDRAMINE CITRATE TABLETS,** U.S.P. XXI.

• **ACETAMINOPHEN ORAL SUSPENSION,** U.S.P. XXI.
Use: Analgesic.

ACETAMINOPHENOL.
See: Acetaminophen.

ACETAMINOPHEN UNISERTS. (Upsher-Smith) Acetaminophen 120 mg./Supp. Ctn. 12s; 325 mg./Supp. Ctn. 12s, 50s; 650 mg./Supp. Ctn. 12s, 50s, 500s.
Use: Analgesic, antipyretic.

ACETANILID. (Various Mfr.) (Acetylaminobenzene, acetylaniline, antifebrin) N-phenylacetamide cry.
Use: Antipyretic, analgesic.

ETARSOL.
See: Acetarsone, Tabs.
ETARSONE. 3-Acetamido-4-hydroxy-phenylarsonic acid. Acetarsol, Acetphenarsine, Amarsan, Dynarsan, Ehrlich 594, Limarsol, Orarsan, Osarsal, Osvarsan, Paroxyl, Stovarsol.
ETARSONE SALT OF ARECOLINE.
See: Drocarbil.
ETAZIDE. Acetazolamide, B.A.N.
CETAZOLAMIDE, U.S.P. XXI. Tab. U.S.P. XXI. N-5-Sulfamoyl-1,3,4-thiadiazol-2-yl) acetamide. Acetamide, N-[5-(aminosulfonyl)-1,3,4-thiadiazol-2-yl]-.
Use: Carbonic anhydrase inhibitor.
See: Diamox, Tab., Sequels (Lederle)
Hydrazol, Tab. (Softcon)
ETAZOLAMIDE. B.A.N. 5-Acetamido-1,3,4-thiadiazole-2-sulfonamide.
Use: Treatment of glaucoma.
See: Acetazide
Diamox
CETAZOLAMIDE SODIUM, STERILE, U.S.P. XXI.
Use: Carbonic anhydrase inhibitor.
See: Diamox, Inj. (Lederle)
ET-DIA-MER-SULFONAMIDE. Sulfacetamide, sulfadiazine & sulfamerazine.
See: Buffonamide, Susp., Tab. (Reid-Provident)
Buf-Sul, Tabs. & Susp. (Sheryl)
Cetazine, Tab. (Bowman)
Coco-Diazine, Susp. (Lilly)
Sulfadiazine, sulfamerazine & sulfacetamide, Susp.
ETEST REAGENT TABLETS. (Ames) Sod. nitroprusside, disodium phosphate, aminoacetic acid, lactose. Tab. Bot. 100s, 250s.
Use: Test for acetone or diacetic acid in urine.
CETIC ACID, U.S.P. XXI, Glacial, Otic soln., U.S.P. XXI. Diluted, N.F. XVI.
Use: Pharmaceutic aid (acidifying agent).
CETIC ACID IRRIGATION, U.S.P. XXI. 0.25% solution. (Abbott) 250 ml glass cont.; 250 ml.
Use: Irrigating solution
CETIC ACID, POTASSIUM SALT. Potassium Acetate, U.S.P. XXI.
CETICYL.
See: Acetylsalicylic Acid.
CETILUM ACIDULATUM.
See: Acetylsalicylic Acid. (Various Mfr.)
ACETOHEXAMIDE, U.S.P. XXI. Tab. U.S.P. XXI. N-(p-acetylphenylsulfonyl)-N′-cyclo-hexylurea. 1-((p-acetylphenyl)sulfonyl)-3-cyclohexylurea. Benzenesulfonamide, 4-acetyl-N-[[cyclohexylamino]carbonyl].
Use: Blood sugar lowering compound, antidiabetic.
See: Dymelor, Tab. (Lilly)
ACETOHYDROXAMIC ACID, U.S.P. XXI. Tab, U.S.P. XXI.
Use: Enzyme inhibitor.
See: Lithostat (Mission)
CETOJEN, JR. (Jenkins) Acetylsalicylic acid 1.5 gr., phenacetin 1 gr., hyoscyamus ext. 0.0125 gr., (total alkaloids 0.0002 gr.) gelsemium ext. 0.0125 gr./Tab. Bot. 1000s.

ACETOLAX. (Mills) Acetphenylisatin 5 mg., Vit. B-1 1 mg., sod. carboxymethyl cellulose 500 mg./Tab. Bulk Pkg. 1000s.
Use: Laxative.
ACETOL.
See: Acetylsalicylic Acid. (Various Mfr.)
ACETOMEROCTOL. Acetato [2-hydroxy-5-(1,1,-3,3-tetramethylbutyl) phenyl] mercury. Under study.
Use: Topical antiseptic.
• **ACETONE,** N.F. XVI.
ACETONE or DIACETIC ACID TEST.
See: Acetest, Tab. (Ames)
3-(alpha-ACETONYLBENZYL)-4-HYDROXYCOUMARIN SODIUM SALT. Warfarin Sodium.
ACETOPHEN CAPSULE. (Jenkins) Aspirin 3.5 gr., phenacetin 2.5 gr., caffeine 0.5 gr./Cap. Bot. 1000s.
ACETOPHEN C.T. GREEN. (Jenkins) Aspirin 3.5 gr., phenacetin 2.5 gr., caffeine 0.25 gr./Tab. Bot. 1000s.
• **ACETOPHENAZINE MALEATE,** U.S.P. XXI. Tab. U.S.P. XXI. 2-Acetyl-10- {3-[4-(-β-hydroxyethyl)-piperazinyl] propyl} phenothiazine dimaleate. 10-[3-[4-(2-Hydroxyethyl)-1-piperazinyl]-propyl)]-phenothiazin-2-yl methyl ketone maleate (1:2).
Use: Tranquilizer.
See: Tindal Maleate, Tab. (Schering)
ACETOPHENETIDIN. Phenacetin, U.S.P. XXI. Ethoxyacetanilide.
Use: Antipyretic, analgesic.
ACETORPHINE. B.A.N. O^3-Acetyl-7,8-dihydro-7α[1(R)-hydroxy-1-methylbutyl]-O^6-methyl-6,-14-endoethenomorphine.
Use: Narcotic analgesic.
ACETOSAL.
See: Acetylsalicylic Acid. (Various Mfr.)
ACETOSALIC ACID.
See: Acetylsalicylic Acid. (Various Mfr.)
ACETOSALIN.
See: Acetylsalicylic Acid. (Various Mfr.)
ACETOSULFONE. 4,4′-Diaminodiphenylsulfone-2-N-acetylsulfonamide sodium. (N^1-acetyl-6-sulfanilylmetanilamido) sodium.
• **ACETOSULFONE SODIUM.** USAN.
Use: Antibacterial.
ACETOXYPHENYLMERCURY.
See: Phenylmercuric acetate.
ACETPHENARSINE.
See: Acetarsone, Tab. (City Chemical)
ACETPHENOLISATIN.
See: Oxyphenisatin Acetate Prep.
W/D-Calcium pantothenate, sodium sulfosuccinate.
See: Peri-Pantyl, Tab. (McGregor)
W/Docusate sodium, sodium carboxymethylcellulose.
See: Scrip-Lax, Tab. (Scrip)
ACETRIZOATE SODIUM. 3-Acetamido-2,4,6,-triiodobenzoate sodium.
W/Polyvinylpyrrolidone.
See: Salpix, Vial (Ortho)
ACETRIZOIC ACID. 3-Acetylamino-2,4,6,-triiodobenzoic acid.
See: Acetrizoate, Sod.

ACET-THEOCIN SODIUM.
See: Theophylline Sod. acetate (Various Mfr.)
ACETYL ADALIN.
See: Acetylcarbromal. (Various Mfr.)
p-ACETYLAMINOBENZALDEHYDE THIOSEMICARBAZONE. (Amithiozone, Antib, Berculon A, Benzothiozon, Conteben, Myuizone, Neustab, Tebethion, Thiomicid, Thioparamizone, Thiacetazone).
Use: With streptomycin in the treatment of tuberculosis.
ACETYLAMINOBENZENE.
See: Acetanilid. (Various Mfr.)
N-ACETYL-p-AMINOPHENOL. Acetaminophen, U.S.P. XXI.
ACETYLANILINE.
See: Acetanilid. (Various Mfr.)
ACETYL-BETA-METHYLCHOLINE CHLORIDE.
See: Mecholyl Chloride, Amp. (Baker, J.T.)
ACETYL-BROMO-DIETHYLACETYL-CARBAMIDE.
See: Acetylcarbromal. (Various Mfr.)
ACETYLCARBROMAL. (Meyer) Acetyl adalin, acetylbromodiethylacetyl-carbamide. Pow. for mfg.
Use: Sedative.
See: Paxarel, Tab. (Circle)
W/Bromisovalum, scopolamine aminoxide HBr.
See: Tranquinal, Tab. (Barnes-Hind)
• **ACETYLCHOLINE CHLORIDE,** U.S.P. XXI. For Ophth. Soln., U.S.P. XXI. Ethananinium,2-(acetyloxy)-N, N, N-trimethyl-, chloride. Choline chloride acetate.
Use: S.C., I.M., I.V. Parasympathomimetic agent & vasodilator. Paroxysmal tachycardia.
See: Miochol Ophthalmic (CooperVision)
ACETYLCHOLINE-LIKE THERAPEUTIC AGENTS.
See: Cholinergic agents.
• **ACETYLCYSTEINE,** U.S.P. XXI. Sol. U.S.P. XXI. N-Acetyl-L-cysteine.
Use: Mucolytic agent.
See: Mucomyst, Sol. (Mead Johnson)
• **ACETYLCYSTEINE AND ISOPROTERENOL HYDROCHLORIDE INHALATION SOLUTION,** U.S.P. XXI.
Use: Mucolytic agent.
See: Mucomyst with Isoproterenol, Sol. (Mead Johnson)
ACETYLCYSTEINE. B.A.N. N-Acetyl-L-cysteine. Airbron
Use: Liquefaction of bronchial secretion.
ACETYLDIGITOXIN. α-Digitoxin monoacetate. Acetyltridigitoxose. The natural-occurring cardiac glycoside defined as the alpha acetyl ester of digitoxin.
Use: Digitoxin therapy. Cardiotonic.
ACETYLDIHYDROCODEINONE. Thebacon, B.A.N.
ACETYLIN.
See: Acetylsalicylic Acid. (Various Mfr.)
ACETYLMETHADOL, I.N.N. Methadyl acetate, B.A.N.
ACETYLPHENYLISATIN.
See: Oxyphenisatin Acetate.
1-((p-ACETYLPHENYL)SULFONYL)-3-CYCLO-HEXYLUREA. Acetohexamide.
ACETYLRESORCINOL.
See: Resorcinol Monoacetate. (Various Mfr.)

ACETYLSAL.
See: Acetylsalicylic Acid
ACETYLSALICYLATE ALUMINUM.
See: Aluminum Aspirin
ACETYLSALICYLIC ACID. Aspirin, U.S.P. XXI. Acidum acetylsalicylicum, 2-acetoxybenzoic ac Acetilum Acidulatum, Acetophen, Acetol, Acetosa Acetosalic Acid, Acetosalin, Aceticyl, Acetylsal, Acylpryin, Aspro, Helicon, Rhodine, Salacetin, Salcetogen, Saletin.
See: Aspirin Preps. (Various Mfr.)
ACETYLSALICYLIC ACID, ACETOPHENETIDIN AND CAFFEINE.
See: A.P.C., Prep. (Various Mfr.)
ACETYL SULFAMETHOXYPYRIDAZINE. 3-(N-Acet sulfanilamido)-6-methoxypyridazine.
N[1]-ACETYLSULFANILAMIDE. (Albucid; p-Aminobe zenesulfonacetamide; Sulfacet; Sulfacetamide, N-Sulfanilylacetamide.)
Use: Sulfonamide therapy.
ACETYL SULFISOXAZOLE. Sulfisoxazole Acetyl, U.S.P. XXI.
See: Gantrisin Acetyl, Syr., Susp. (Roche)
Lipo-Gantrisin Acetyl, Liq. (Roche)
ACETYLTANNIC ACID. Tannic acid acetate.
Use: Antiperistaltic.
AC EYE DROPS. (Walgreen) Tetrahydrozoline HCl 0.05%, zinc sulfate 0.25%. Bot. 0.75 oz.
Use: Allergy, colds, eye relief.
ACHLORHYDRIA DETERMINATION.
See: Diagnex Blue, Prep. (Squibb)
ACHLORHYDRIA THERAPY.
See: Acidol. (Various Mfr.)
Glutamic Acid HCl (Various Mfr.)
Muripsin, Tab. (Norgine)
Normacid, Tab. (Stuart)
ACHOL. (Enzyme Process) Vit. A 4000 U., ketocholanic acids 62 mg./Tab. Bot. 100s, 250s.
Use: Vitamin A supplement and therapy.
ACHROMYCIN. (Lederle) Tetracycline HCl.
Intramuscular: (100 mg., 250 mg., buffered w/ascorbic acid) Vial. Box 1s, 100s.
Intravenous: (250 mg., 500 mg., buffered w/ascorbic acid) Vial.
Oint. (3%) Tube 0.5 oz. & 1 oz.
Oint. (Ophth.) 1% Tubes ⅛ oz.
Ophth. Susp. 1%, Plastic dropper bot. 4 ml.
ACHROMYCIN-V. (Lederle) Tetracycline HCl. **Cap.:** 25 mg. Bot. 100s, 1000s, Unit dose 10 × 10s, Unit o use 50 × 28s; 500 mg. Bot. 100s, 1000s; Unit of use 50 × 20s; Unit dose 10 × 10s. **Oral Susp.:** 125 mg./5 cc. w/methylparaben 0.12%, propylparaben 0.03%. Bot. 2 oz., 1 pt.
Use: Treatment of infections caused by both gram negative and gram-positive bacteria.
ACID ACRIFLAVINE.
See: Acriflavine Hydrochloride (Various Mfr.)
ACID CITRATE DEXTROSE SOLUTION.
See: A.C.D. Sol. (Various Mfr.)
ACID CITRATE DEXTROSE ANTICOAGULANT SOLUTION MODIFIED.
See: A-C-D Solution Modified (Squibb)

ACID HISTAMINE PHOSPHATE.
See: Histamine Phosphate. (Various Mfr.)

ACID MANTLE CREME. (Dorsey) Aluminum acetate in specially prep. water-soluble hydrophilic cream at pH 4.2. Tube 1 oz., Jar 4 oz., 1 lb.
Use: Skin prophylactic agent in restoring normal skin acidity.

ACID MANTLE LOTION. (Dorsey) Aluminum acetate lotion. pH 4.5 Bot. 4 oz.
Use: Dermatitis.

ACIDOL.
See: Betaine Hydrochloride (Various Mfr.)

ACIDOPHILUS W/PECTIN. (Barth's) *Lactobacillus acidophilus* w/natural citrus pectin 100 mg./Cap. Bot. 100s.
Use: Aid to digestion.

ACID TRYPAFLAVINE.
See: Acriflavine Hydrochloride. (Various Mfr.)

ACIDULATED PHOSPHATE FLUORIDE. (Scherer) Flavored soln. containing 0.31% fluoride ion in 0.1 molar phosphate. Bot. 64 oz. Office Product.
Use: Dental caries prevention.

ACIDULIN. (Lilly) Glutamic acid HCl 340 mg./Pulvule. Bot. 100s, 1000s.
Use: Achlorhydria.

• **ACIFRAN.** USAN.
Use: Antihyperlipoproteinemic.

ACIGLUMIN.
See: Glutamic Acid Hydrochloride. (Various Mfr.)

ACI-JEL. (Ortho) Glacial acetic acid 0.921%, ricinoleic acid 0.70%, oxyquinoline sulfate 0.025%, glycerine 5%. Tube 85 Gm. w/dose applicator.
Use: Vaginal acidifier.

ACINITRAZOLE. B.A.N. 2-Acetamido-5-nitrothiazole, Aminitrozole (I.N.N.)
Use: Treatment of trichomoniasis.
See: Trichorad
Tritheon

• **ACLARUBICIN.** USAN.
Use: Antineoplastic.

ACLOBROM. Propantheline Bromide, B.A.N.

• **ACLOMETASONE DIPROPIONATE,** U.S.P. XXI.
Cream, oint., U.S.P. XXI.

A.C.N. (Person & Covey) Vitamin A palmitate 25M I.U., ascorbic acid 250 mg., niacinamide 25 mg./Tab. Bot. 100s.
Use: Dietary supplement.

ACNAVEEN. (CooperCare)
See: Aveenobar Medicated (CooperCare)

ACNA-VITE. (Cenci) Vit. A 10,000 I.U., C 250 mg., hesperidin 50 mg., niacinamide 25 mg./Cap. Bot. 75s.
Use: Acne vulgaris with Vit. A & C deficiency.

ACNE-5. (Goldline) Benzoyl peroxide 5%. Bot. 1 oz.
Use: Acne treatment.

ACNE-10. (Goldline) Benzoyl peroxide 10%. Bot. 1 oz.
Use: Acne treatment.

ACNE-AID CLEANSING BAR. (Stiefel) Neutral soap of 6.3% surfactant blend. Non-medicated. Bar 4.0 oz., 5.8 oz.
Use: Cleanse oily skin and acne.

ACNE-AID CREAM. (Stiefel) Benzoyl peroxide 10% in special cover-up base. Tube, 1.8 oz.
Use: Absorbs oil, hides blemishes.

ACNE-AID LOTION. (Stiefel) Sulfur 10%, alcohol 10% in a washable base. Clear or Tinted Bot. plastic 2 oz.
Use: Treatment of acne.

ACNEDERM. (Lannett) **Lotion:** Dispersable sulfur 5%, zinc sulfate 1%, zinc oxide 10%, alcohol 21%. Bot. 2 oz. **Soap:** Zinc oxide 2%, zinc sulfate 1%, colloidal sulfur 5%. Cake 3.2 oz.
Use: Skin conditions.

ACNE-DOME CREAM & LOTION. (Miles Pharm) Regular: sulfur 4%, resorcinol monoacetate 3%, in a vehicle buffered to the pH range of normal skin. **Cream:** Tube 1 oz. **Lotion:** Bot. 2 oz.
Use: Treatment of acne.

ACNE-DOME MEDICATED CLEANSER. (Miles Pharm) Sulfur 2%, salicylic acid 2% in a colloidal soybean complex. Medicated w/sponge 4 oz.
Use: Medicated skin cleanser.

ACNE LOTION. (Weeks & Leo) Benzoyl peroxide 10% in odorless, greaseless, vanishing lotion. Bot. 2 oz.
Use: Treatment for acne.

ACNO CLEANSER. (Baker/Cummins) Isopropyl alcohol 60%. Bot. 8 oz.
Use: Antiseptic astringent for the treatment of acne.

ACNO LOTION. (Baker/Cummins) Micronized sulfur 3%, salicylic acid 2%. Bot. 4 oz.
Use: Treatment of acne.

ACNOMEL. (Menley & James) Resorcinol 2%, sulfur 8%, alcohol 11%.
Cream. Tube 1 oz.
Use: Acne therapy.

ACNOPHILL. (Torch) Sulfur 5%, Pot. and zinc sulfides and polysulfides 5%, zinc oxide 10% in hydrophilic vehicle. Plain or tinted. Jar 1 lb. and 2 oz.
Use: Acne treatment.

ACNOTEX. (C & M Pharmacal) Sulfur 8%, salicylic acid 2.25% in lotion base. Bot. 2 oz.
Use: Anti-acne cover-up lotion.

• **ACODAZOLE HYDROCHLORIDE.** USAN.
Use: Antineoplastic.

ACOTUS. (Whorton) Phenylephrine HCl 5 mg., guaiacol glyceryl ether 100 mg., menthol 1 mg., alcohol, by vol. 10%/5 cc. Bot. 4 oz., 12 oz., gal.
Use: Colds, coughs.

ACR. (Western Research) Ammonium chloride 7.5 gr./Tab. Handicount 28s (36 bags of 28 tab.)
Use: Diuretic.

ACRIFLAVINE. Euflavine, Gonacrine, Neutroflavine Acriflavine neutral; a mixture of 2, 8-diamino-10-methylacridinium chloride & 2,8-diaminoacridine. (Lilly) Tab. 1.5 gr. Bot. 100s.
Use: External antiseptic.

ACRIFLAVINE HYDROCHLORIDE. (Various Mfr.) Hydrochloride form of acriflavine. Acid acriflavine, acid trypaflavine, flavine, trypaflavine.
National Aniline—Pow., Bot. (1, 5, 10, 25, & 50 Gm.). Tab. (1.5 gr.) Bot. 50s & 100s.
Use: External bacteriostatic.

• **ACRISORCIN,** U.S.P. XXI. Cream U.S.P. XXI. 9-Aminoacridinium 4-hexylresorcinolate.
See: Akrinol Cream (Schering)
Use: Topical, tinea versicolor. Local antifungal.

• **ACRONINE.** USAN. 3, 12-Dihydro-6-methoxy-3,3,12-trimethyl-7H-pyrano[2,3,-c]acridin-7-one. Under study.
Use: Antineoplastic.

A-C TABLET. (Century) Aspirin 6 gr., caffeine 0.5 gr./Tab.
Bot. 100s, 1000s
Use: Analgesic.

ACTACIN-C SYRUP. (Vangard) Codeine phosphate 10 mg., triprolidine HCl 2 mg., pseudoephedrine HCl 20 mg., guaifenesin 100 mg./ 5 ml. Bot. pt., gal.
Use: Antihistamine, decongestant, cough depressant.

ACTACIN SYRUP. (Vangard) Triprolidine HCl 1.25 mg., pseudoephedrine HCl 30 mg./ 5 ml. Bot. pt., gal.
Use: Antihistamine, decongestant.

ACTACIN TABLETS. (Vangard) Triprolidine HCl 2.5 mg., pseudoephedrine HCl 60 mg./Tab. Bot. 100s, 1000s.
Use: Antihistamine/decongestant.

ACTAGEN. (Generix) Triprolidine HCl 2.5 mg., pseudoephedrine HCl 60 mg. Tab. Bot. 100s, 1000s.
Use: Symptomatic treatment of allergic rhinitis.

ACTAGEN-C COUGH SYRUP. (Goldline) Triprolidine HCl, pseudoephedrine HCl, codeine phosphate/Bot. 4 oz., pt., gal.
Use: Decongestant, cough suppressor.

ACTAGEN TABLETS. (Goldline) Triprolidine HCl, pseudoephedrine HCl. Bot. 100s, 1000s.
Use: Decongestant.

ACTAL SUSPENSION. (Winthrop Products) Aluminum hydroxide.
Use: Antacid.

ACTAL PLUS TABLETS. (Winthrop Products) Aluminum hydroxide, magnesium hydroxide.
Use: Antacid, demulcent.

ACTAL TABLETS. (Winthrop Products) Aluminum hydroxide.
Use: Antacid.

ACTAMIN. (Buffington) Acetaminophen 325 mg./Tab. Sugar, lactose, and salt free. Dispens-A-Kit: 500s, Aidpaks 100s. Unit boxes 20s. Medipaks 200s.
Use: Analgesic, anti-pyretic.

ACTAMIN EXTRA. (Buffington) Acetaminophen 500 mg./Tab. Sugar, lactose, and salt free. Dispens-A-Kit 500s. Medipaks 200s.
Use: Extra strength nonaspirin analgesic and antipyretic.

ACTAMIN SUPER. (Buffington) Acetaminophen 500 mg. Tab. w/caffeine. Sugar, salt, and lactose free. Dispens-A-Kits 500s, Medipaks 200s.
Use: Maximum strength analgesic, antipyretic.

• **ACTAPLANIN.** USAN.
Use: Growth stimulant.

ACTH-ACTEST GEL. (Fellows) Repository corticotropin 40 or 80 u./cc. Vial 5 cc.

ACTH. (Adrenocorticotropic hormone. Adrenocorticotrop(h)in).
See: Corticotropin, U.S.P.
Mallard—(40 u./ml., 5 ml.)
Forest—(40 u. or 80 u./ml., 5 ml.)
Parke, Davis—25 units/Vial; 40 units/Vial.
Pharmex—(40 u. or 80 u./ml., 5 ml.)

ACTH GEL, PURIFIED. Arcum.—40 or 80 units/ml., vial 5 ml. Conal.—40 or 80 units/ml., vial 5 ml. Hart Labs.—40 units/ml., vial 5 ml. Bowman—Adrenocorticotropic hormone 40 u., aqueous gelatin 16%, phenol 0.5%/cc. Vial 5 cc.
Use: Repository corticotropin.
Arcum—(40 u. or 80 u./ml., 5 ml.)
Bell—(40 u. or 80 u./ml., 5 ml.)
Bowman—(40 u./ml., 5 ml.)
Hyrex—(40 u. or 80 u./ml., 5 ml.)
Jenkins—(40 u. or 80 u./ml., 5 ml.)
Vortech—40 units/ml., 80 units/ml., Vial 5 ml.
Rocky Mtn. Pharmacal—40 units/ml., 80 units/ml. Vial 5 ml.
Wesley Pharm.—40 units/ml., vial 5 ml.; 80 units/ml., vial 5 ml.
Wyeth—(40 u. or 80 u./ml. or Tubex)

ACTHAR. (Armour) Corticotropin for Injection. Vial 25, 40 u./Vial. (Lyophilized w/gelatin). Pkg. 10s.
Use: I.M., S.C. or I.V. stimulation of adrenal cortex and diseases related to it.

ACTICORT LOTION 100. (Baker/Cummins) Hydrocortisone alcohol 1% in a specially formulated vehicle. Bot. 2 oz.
Use: Anti-inflammatory & antipruritic.

ACTIDIL. (Burroughs Wellcome) Triprolidine HCl **Tab.** 2.5 mg./Tab. Bot. 100s. **Syr.** 1.25 mg./5 ml. Bot. 1 pt.
Use: Antihistamine.

ACTI-DIONE. (Upjohn) Cycloheximide. (3-[2-(3,5-Dimethyl-2-oxocyclohexyl)-2-hydroxyethyl]-glutarimide) 85-100% w/w.
Not for medicinal use. For professional use only. Bot. 4 Gm.

ACTIDOSE. (Paddock) Activated charcoal solution 25 Gm./120 ml. or 50 Gm./240 ml.
Use: Orally or through gastric tube to adsorb toxins in GI tract in drug overdose or poisoning emergency.

ACTIDOSE-AQUA. (Paddock) Activated charcoal aqueous suspension 25 Gm/120 ml. or 50 Gm/240 ml.
Use: Orally or through gastric tube to absorb toxins in GI tract in drug overdose or poisoning.

ACTIFED. (Burroughs Wellcome) **Tab.:** Triprolidine HCl. 2.5 mg., pseudoephedrine HCl. 60 mg./Tab. Bot. 30s, 100s, 1000s. Boxes 12s, 24s. Unit dose pack 100s. Unit of use 90s. Ctn. 24s. **Cap.:** Triprolidine HCl 2.5 mg., pseudoephedrine HCl 60 mg./Cap. Box 10s, 20s. **Syr.:** Triprolidine HCl 1.25 mg., pseudoephedrine HCl 30 mg./5 ml. Bot. 4 oz., 1 pt., gal.
Use: Common cold, allergic rhinitis.

ACTIFED CAPSULES. (Burroughs Wellcome) Triprolidine HCl 2.5 mg., pseudoephedrine HCl 60 mg.,/Cap. Box 10s, 20s.
Use: Nasal decongestant, antihistamine.

CTIFED WITH CODEINE COUGH SYRUP. (Burroughs Wellcome) Codeine phosphate 10 mg., triprolidine HCl 2 mg., pseudoephedrine HCl 30 mg., dextromethorphan 100 mg./5 ml. Bot. pt., gal.
Use: Treatment of the common cold.

CTINOMYCIN. B.A.N. Antimicrobial substances with antitumor activity produced by Streptomyces antibioticus and Streptomyces chrysomallus. Sanamycin is Actinomycin C.

CTINOMYCIN C. Name previously used for Cactinomycin.

CTINOMYCIN D. Dactinomycin, U.S.P. XXI.
See: Cosmegen (Merck Sharp & Dohme)

ACTINOQUINOL SODIUM. USAN.
Use: Ultraviolet screen.

CTINOSPECTOCIN. Name previously used for Spectinomycin.

CTIVATED ATTAPULGITE.
/Aluminum hydroxide, magnesium carbonate coprecipitate, compressed gel.
See: Hykasil, Cream (Philips Roxane)
/Polysorbate 80, colloidal sulfur, salicylic acid, propylene glycol.
See: Sebasorb Lotion (Summers Labs.)

CTIVATED CHARCOAL TABLETS. (Cowley) 5 gr./Tab. Bot. 1000s.

CTIVATED 7-DEHYDROCHOLESTEROL.
See: Vitamin D-3 (Various Mfr.)

CTIVATED ERGOSTEROL.
See: Calciferol.

CTIVE LIFE CLOSED OSTOMY POUCH. (ConvaTec) One-piece closed-end pouch with skin barrier, picture frame support adhesive, odor proof pouch.

CTIVE LIFE OPEN OSTOMY POUCH. (ConvaTec) One-piece disposable ostomy appliance with stomahesive peristomal skin covering and adhesive support collar. Box 10s.

CTOL EXPECTORANT. (Beecham Labs) Noscapine 30 mg., guaifenesin 200 mg./5 ml. or Tab. **Syr.** W/alcohol 12.5%. Bot. pt. **Tab.** Bot. 100s.
Use: Treatment of symptoms associated with common cold.

CTOMOL. Mebanazine, B.A.N.

CTOQUINOL SODIUM. 8-Ethoxy-5-quinoline-sulfonic acid sodium salt.
Use: Ultraviolet screen.

CTOS 50. Corticotrophin, B.A.N.

CTRAPID HUMAN INSULIN. (Squibb Novo) Human insulin 100 Units/ml. Vial 10 ml.
Use: Human insulin (rapid action).

CTRIOL. Epioestriol, B.A.N.

CTYLATE. (Kinney) Ammonium salicylate 80 mg., pot. salicylate 80 mg., strontium salicylate 80 mg., pot. para-aminobenzoate 0.32 Gm., ascorbic acid 20 mg./Tab. Bot. 100s.
Use: Rheumatoid arthritis.

CUCRON. (Seatrace) Acetaminophen 300 mg., salicylamide 200 mg., phenyltoloxamine 20 mg./Tab. Bot. 100s, 1000s, 5000s.
Use: Antihistaminic, analgesic.

• **ACYCLOVIR.** USAN. 9-(2-hydroxyethoxymethyl)-guanine.
Use: Management of initial herpes genitalis and mucocutaneous herpes simplex virus infections.
See: Zovirax Caps., Oint. (Burroughs Wellcome)

• **ACYCOLOVIR SODIUM.** USAN.
Use: Antiviral.

ACYLPYRIN.
See: Aspirin

ADALAN LANATABS. (Lannett) Amobarbital 50 mg., homatropine methylbromide 7.5 mg., methamphetamine HCl 10 mg./T.D. Tab. Bot. 100s, 1000s.

ADAMANTANAMINE HCl. Amantadine HCl. Anti-flu capsule. This drug is thought to protect cells against entry of the flu virus without actually destroying the virus. Also used in the treatment of Parkinson's disease.
See: Symmetrel, Cap., Syr. (Du Pont)

ADANON. Methadone, B.A.N.

ADAPETTES. (Alcon) EDTA 0.1%., chimerosal 0.004%. Pkg. 15 ml.
Use: Contact lens rewetting and lubricating solution.

ADAPIN. (Pennwalt) Doxepin HCl 10 mg., 25 mg. 50 mg., 75 mg., 100 mg./Cap. Bot. 100s, 1000s. 25 mg., 50 mg./Cap. also available in 5000s.
Use: Antianxiety, antidepressant.

ADAPT. (Alcon) Povidone, EDTA 0.1%, thimerosal 0.004%. Bot. 15 ml.
Use: Contact lens cushioning solution.

ADATUSS. (Merchant) Hydrocodone bitartrate 5 mg., guaifenesin 100 mg., alcohol 5%/5 ml. Syr. Bot. pt., gal.
Use: Cough relief.

A.D.C. DROPS. (CMC) Vit. A 3000 I.U., D 400 I.U., C 60 mg./0.6 cc. Bot. 60 cc.

ADCORTYL. Triamcinolone, B.A.N.

ADEECON. (CMC) Vit. A 5000 I.U., D 1000 I.U./Cap. Bot. 1000s.
Use: Supplement.

ADEFLOR CHEWABLE. (Upjohn) Fluoride 1 mg. & 0.5 mg., Vitamin A 4000 I.U., D 400 I.U., C 75 mg., thiamine monitrate (B-1) 2 mg., B-2 2 mg., niacinamide 18 mg., B-6 1 mg., calcium pantothenate 5 mg., B-12 2 mcg./0.5 or 1 mg. Chewable Tab. Bot. 100s, 500s.
Use: Prevention of dental caries.

ADEFLOR DROPS. (Upjohn) Vit. A 2000 I.U., D 400 I.U., C 50 mg., B-6 1 mg., fluoride (as sodium fluoride) 0.5 mg./0.6 ml. Bot. 50 ml. w/dropper.
Use: Prevention of dental caries.

ADEFLOR M TABLETS. (Upjohn) Vit. A 6000 I.U., D 400 I.U., B-1 1.5 mg., B-2 2.5 mg., C 100 mg., niacinamide 20 mg., Vit. B-6 10 mg., calcium pantothenate 10 mg., Vit. B-12 2 mcg., folic acid 0.1 mg., fluoride (as sodium fluoride) 1 mg., calcium (as calcium carbonate) 250 mg., iron 30 mg./Tab. Bot. 100s, 500s.
Use: Dietary supplement.

• **ADENINE.** U.S.P. XXI. 6-Aminopurine.

ADENO TWELVE GEL INJECTION. (Fellows) Adenosine-5-monophosphate 25 mg., methionine 25 mg., niacin 10 mg./cc. Vial 10 cc.

ADENOCREST. (Nutrition) Adenosine-5-monophosphate sod. 25 mg., nicotinic acid as sod. salt 25 mg., gelatin 100 mg. w/benzyl alcohol 1.5%/cc. Vials 10 cc.
Use: Capillary and arterial vasodilation.

ADENOLIN FORTE. (Lincoln) Adenosine-5-mono-phosphate, 25 mg., methionine 25 mg., niacin 10 mg./cc. Vial 15 cc.
Use: Arthritis, bursitis, tendinitis & other degenerative diseases.

• **ADENOSINE.** F.D.A. 6-Amino-9-beta-D-Ribofuranosyl-9H-purine.

ADENOSINE IN GELATIN. (Fellows) **Forte:** Adenosine-5-monophosphate 50 mg./cc. **Super:** Adenosine-5-monophosphate 100 mg./cc.

ADENOSINE-5-MONOPHOSPHATE AS THE SODIUM SALT.
See: Adenocrest, Amp. (Nutrition)

• **ADENOSINE PHOSPHATE.** USAN. 5-Adenylic acid. B.A.N. Adenosine-5′-(dihydrogen phosphate). Adenosine monophosphate, AMP.
Use: Nutrient.
See: Adenyl
Cobalasine, Inj. (Keene)
My-B-Den (Miles Pharm)

ADENYL. Adenosine Phosphate, B.A.N.

ADEPSINE OIL.
See: Petrolatum Liquid (Various Mfr.)

ADICILLIN. B.A.N. 6-[D(+)-5-Amino-5-carboxyvaleramido]penicillanic acid. Penicillin N.
Use: Antibiotic.

• **ADINAZOLAM.** USAN.
Use: Antidepressant, sedative.

• **ADINAZOLAM MESYLATE.** USAN.
Use: Antidepressant, sedative.

ADIPEX-P. CAPSULES. (Lemmon) Phentermine HCl 37.5 mg./Cap. Bot. 100s, 400s.
Use: Anorectic agent.

ADIPEX-P TABLETS. (Lemmon) Phentermine HCl 37.5 mg./Tab. Bot. 100s, 400s, 1000s.
Use: Anorectic agent.

• **ADIPHENINE HYDROCHLORIDE.** USAN. (2-Diethylaminoethyl diphenylacetate hydrochloride.) Pow. 1 lb. for mfg. use.
Use: Antispasmodic.

ADIPIODONE (I.N.N.). Iodipamide, B.A.N.

3,3′-(ADIPOYLDIIMINO)-BIS[2,4,6-TRI-IODOBENZOIC ACID]. Iodipamide, U.S.P. XXI.

ADIPOST. (Ascher) Phendimetrazine tartrate 105 mg./Slow-rel. Cap. Bot. 100s.
Use: Appetite suppressant.

ADISOL TAB. (Major) Disulfiram 250 mg./Tab. Bot. 100s. 500 mg./Tab. Bot. 50s.
Use: Treatment of alcoholism.

ADLERIKA. (Last) Magnesium sulfate 4.0 Gm./15 ml. Bot. 12 oz.
Use: Laxative.

ADONIDINE. (City Chem.) Bot. 1 Gm.
Use: Cardiac stimulant.

ADPHEN TABLETS. (Ferndale) Phendimetrazine tartrate 35 mg./Tab. Bot. 100s.
Use: Anorexiant.

A-D-R. (Lincoln) dl-Methionine 250 mg., corn starch lubricant 42 mg./Cap. Bot. 100s, 500s.
Use: Amino acid supplement.

ADRENALIN(E).
See: Epinephrine. (Various Mfr.)

ADRENALIN CHLORIDE SOLUTION. (Parke-Davis) Epinephrine HCl. Principle of the medullary portion of suprarenal glands. **Amp.:** 1:1000-1 ml. Epinephrine 1 mg./ml. with not more than 0.1% sodium bisulfite as preservative. Amps. 10s. **Steri-Vial 1:1000**-1 ml Epinephrine in isotonic sodium chloride solution with 0.5% chlorobutanol and not more than 0.15% sodium bisulfite as preservative. Vial 30 ml. **Soln. 1:1000-1** ml. Screw cap Bot. 1 oz. (Same desc. a. Steri-Vial). **Soln. 1:100.** Each 100 ml. contains 1 Gm epinephrine HCl dissolved in sodium chloride-citrate buffer solution with Phemerol chloride 0.2 mg./ml. and sodium bisulfite 0.2% as preservative. Bot. 0.25 oz.
Use: Sympathomimetic agent.

ADRENALINE HYDROCHLORIDE.
See: Epinephrine Hydrochloride. (Various Mfr.)

• **ADRENALONE.** USAN. 3′,4′-Dihydroxy-2-(methylamino)-acetophenone.
Use: Adrenergic (ophthalmic).

ADRENAMINE.
See: Epinephrine (Various Mfr.)

ADRENERGIC AGENTS.
See: Sympathomimetic agents

ADRENERGIC-BLOCKING AGENTS.
See: Sympatholytic agents

ADRENINE.
See: Epinephrine. (Various Mfr.)

ADRENOCHROME.
See: Carbazochrome Salicylate.

ADRENOCHROMAZONE.
See: Carbazochrome Salicylate.

ADRENOCHROME MONOSEMICARBAZONE.
See: Carbazochrome Salicylate

ADRENOCORTICOTROPIC HORMONE. ACTH acts by stimulating the endogenous production of cortisone and the final result is similar whichever substance is administered. The nature of action of each is unknown. Both are necessary in the metabolism of carbohydrates, protein & fat & exert profound effects on neuromuscular metabolism.
See: ACTH gel, Inj. (Bowman)
Corticotropin, U.S.P.
Cortigel (Savage)

ADRENOMIST INHALANT AND NEBULIZERS. (Nephron) Epinephrine 1%, Bot. 0.5 oz., 1.25 oz.
Use: Inhalant for bronchial asthma.

ADRENUCLEO. (Enzyme Process) Vit. C 250 mg., d-cal. pantothenate 12.5 mg., bioflavonoids 62.5 mg./Tab. Bot. 100s, 250s.
Use: Vitamin-C supplement therapy.

ADRIAMYCIN. (Adria) Doxorubicin HCl 10 mg., lactose 50 mg./Vial Pkg. 10s. Doxorubicin HCl 50 mg., lactose 250 mg./Vial Ctn. 1s.
Use: Antineoplastic.

ADRIN TABS. (Major) Nylidrin 6 mg. or 12 mg./Tab. Bot. 100s, 1000s.
Use: Vasodilator.

ADRUCIL. (Adria) Fluorouracil 500 mg./10 ml. Ampule 10 ml.
Use: Antineoplastic agent.

ADSORBOCARPINE. (Alcon) Pilocarpine HCl 1%, 2%, 4% in adsorbobase, water polymers, & polyvinylpyrrolidone. Vials 15 ml.
Use: Miotic.

ADSORBONAC OPHTH. SOLUTION. (Alcon) Sodium chloride 2% or 5% in vehicle of polyvinylpyrrolidone and BP water soluble polymers. Dropper Vial 15 ml.
Use: Reduction of corneal edema and clearing of the cornea for diagnostic examination.

ADSORBOTEAR. (Alcon) Hydroxyethylcellulose 0.44%, w/polyvinylpyrrolidone, thimerosal 0.002%, EDTA 0.5%. Bot. dropper 15 ml.
Use: Artificial tears.

ADSORMONE. (Herring) Complete set of reagents required. Pow. 100 Gm.
Use: Pregnancy test.

ADVANCE. (Ross) **Ready-to-Feed formula:** (16 cal/fl oz). Each liter contains: Protein 20 g, fat 27 g, carbohydrate 55 g, Ca 0.51 g, P 0.39 g, Na 0.30 g max., Mg 64 mg., Fe 12 mg., Zn 5 mg., Cu 6 mg., iodine 60 mcg., Mn 34 mcg., K 900 mg., C 520 mg., Vit. A 2000 IU, D 400 IU, E 20 IU, C 50 mg., B-1 0.75 mg., B-2 0.9 mg., niacin 10 mg., B-6 0.6 mg., pantothenic acid 4 mg., folic acid 0.1 mg., B-12 2.5 mcg. **Conc.liquid:** (32 Cal/fl oz) 13 fl. oz diluted 1:1 with water to give 16 Cal/fl oz "as feed" beverage see ADVANCE ready-to-feed for composition on "as fed" basis.
Use: A nutritional beverage for older infants.

ADVANCE PREGNANCY TEST. (Ortho) Can be used as early as 3 days after a missed period. Gives results in 30 min. Kit of 1 test.
Use: Test for pregnancy.

ADVENT. (Winston) Vit. A 4000 I.U., D 400 I.U., C 200 mg., B-1 2 mg., B-2 1.5 mg., B-6 0.5 mg., B-12 1 mcg., niacinamide 10 mg., Ca. lactate 400 mg., ferrous fumarate 200 mg., iodine 0.01 mg., Pot. 0.835 mg., Cu 0.15 mg., Mn 0.05 mg., Zn 0.085 mg./Tab. Bot. 100s, 1000s.
Use: Pregnancy and lactation.

ADVIL. (Whitehall) Ibuprofen 200 mg. Bot. 8s, 24s, 50s, 100s.
Use: Analgesic.

AERDIL. (Econo Med) Triprolidine HCl 1.25 mg., pseudoephedrine HCl 30 mg./5 ml. Bot. Pts., Gal.
Use: Rhinitis treatment.

AEROBID. (Key) Flunisolide in an inhaler system. 7 Gm. canister of 100 metered inhalations.
Use: Bronchial asthma treatment.

AEROCAINE. (Aeroceuticals) Benzyl alcohol 22.7%, benzocaine 13.6%, benzethonium chloride 0.5%. Spray Bot. 0.5 oz., 2.5 oz.
Use: Topical anesthetic, antiseptic, antipruritic.

AEROCELL. (Aeroceuticals) Exfoliative cytology fixative spray. Bot. 2.25 oz.

AERODINE. (Aeroceuticals) Povidone-iodine aerosol. Bot. 3 oz.
Use: Broad range antiseptic germicide.

AEROFREEZE. (Aeroceuticals) Trichloromonofluoromethane & dichlorodifluoromethane. Aerosol containers 8 oz. (12s).
Use: Topical anesthetic.

AEROLATE-III. (Fleming) Theophylline 65 mg./T. D. Cap. Bot. 100s, 1000s.
Use: Bronchodilation.

AEROLATE SR. & JR. (Fleming) **Caps.** Theophylline 4 gr. for Sr. and 2 gr. for Jr./Cap. Bot. 100s, 1000s. **Syrup:** 160 mg./15 ml., Bot. pt., gal.
Use: Bronchodilation.

AEROPURE. (Aeroceuticals) Isopropanol 7.8%, triethylene glycol 3.9%, essential oils 3%, methyldodecyl benzyl trimethyl ammonium chloride 0.12%, methyldodecylxylene bis (trimethyl ammonium chloride) 0.03%, inert ingredients, 85.15%. Bot. 0.8 oz., 4.5 oz.
Use: Concentrated air sanitizer and deodorizer.

AEROSAN. (Ulmer) Air sanitizer, disinfectant & deodorant. Aerosol Spray Can 16.6 oz.
Use: Disinfectant spray.

AEROSEB-DEX. (Herbert) Dexamethasone 0.01%, alcohol 65.1% w/isopropyl myristate and butane propellant. Aerosol 58 Gm.
Use: Corticosteroid-responsive dermatoses.

AEROSEB-HC. (Herbert) Hydrocortisone 0.5%, alcohol 64.6% w/isopropyl myristate and butane propellant. Aerosol 58 Gm.
Use: Corticosteroid-responsive dermatoses.

AEROSEPT. (Dalin) Lidocaine, cetyltrimethylammonium bromide, hexachlorophene. Aerosol Pkg. 6 oz.
Use: Antiseptic, anesthetic.

AEROSIL. (Aeroceuticals) Dimethylpolysiloxane. Bot. 4.5 oz.
Use: Silicone lubricant and protective spray.

AEROAID MERTHIOLATE. (Aeroceuticals) Merthiolate (Lilly) 1:1000 w/alcohol 72%. Spray Bot. 3 oz.
Use: First aid antiseptic spray.

AEROSOL OT.
See: Docusate Sodium, U.S.P.

AEROSOLV. (Aeroceuticals) Isopropyl alcohol, chlorinated solvent, silicone. Aerosol 5.5 oz.
Use: Adhesive tape remover.

AEROSPORIN STERILE POWDER. (Burroughs Wellcome) Polymixin B sulfate 500,000 u./Vial. Multidose Vials 20 ml.
Use: Antibacterial.

AEROSPORIN SULFATE. (Burroughs Wellcome) Polymyxin B sulfate 50 mg., **Sterile Pow.** (500,000 u.) Vial (20 cc.). **Otic Sol.,** sterile. Bot. 10 cc.
Use: Orally for bacillary dysentery, parenteral form for hospital use only.
See: Polymyxin B sulfate, U.S.P.
W/Bacitracin.
See: Polysporin, Oint. (Burroughs Wellcome)
W/Bacitracin & neomycin sulfate.
See: Neosporin, oint. & Ophth. Oint. (Burroughs Wellcome)
W/Bacitracin, neomycin, hydrocortisone.
See: Cortisporin, Prep. (Burroughs Wellcome)

AEROTHERM. (Aeroceuticals) Benzyl alcohol 22.7%, benzocaine 13.6%. Spray Bot. 5 oz.
Use: First aid spray for burns.

AEROTROL. Isoprenaline, B.A.N.

AEROZOIN. (Aeroceuticals) Comp. tr. of benzoin 30%, isopropyl alcohol 44.8%. Spray Bot. 3.5 oz.
Use: Skin conditioner for tape and cast dressing.

AETHYLIS CHLORIDUM.
See: Ethyl Chloride (Various Mfr.)

AFAXIN CAPSULES. (Winthrop Products) Vit. A Palmitate 50,000 I.U., 10,000 I.U./Cap.
Use: Vitamin A deficiency.

A-FIL. (Rydell) Methyl-anthranilate 5%., titanium dioxide 5% in vanishing cream base. Tube 1.5 oz. Neutral or dark.
Use: Sunscreen.

AFKO-LUBE. (APC) Docusate sodium 100 mg./Cap. Bot. 100s.
Use: Stool softener.

AFKO-LUBE LAX. (APC) Docusate sodium 100 mg., casanthranol 30 mg./Cap. Bot. 100s.
Use: Stool softener.

AFRIKOL. (Citroleum) Suntan lotion w/no cocoa butter or lanolin. Bot. 4 oz.

AFRIN. (Schering) Oxymetazoline HCl 0.5 mg., aminoacetic acid 3.8 mg., sorbitol soln. 57 mg., phenylmercuric acetate 0.02 mg., benzalkonium Cl 0.2 mg./ml. **Nose Drops:** Drop. Bot. 20 ml. **Nasal Spray:** Plastic Spray Bot. 15 ml., 30 ml. **Pediatric Nose Drop:** Oxymetazoline 0.25 mg./ml. Drop. Bot. 20 ml.
Use: Nasal decongestant.

AFRIN MENTHOL NASAL SPRAY. (Schering) Oxymethazoline HCl 0.5 mg./ml. w/menthol. Bot. 15 ml.
Use: Nasal decongestant.

AFRINOL REPETABS. (Schering) Pseudoephedrine sulfate 120 mg./Repeat Action Tab. Box 12s. Bot. 100s.
Use: Nasal decongestant.

AFTATE. (Plough) Tolnaftate 1%. **Gel:** Tube 0.5 oz. **Non-Aerosol Spray:** 1.5 oz. **Spray Liquid:** 4 oz. aerosol can; **Spray Powder:** 3.5 oz. **Powder:** 2.25 oz. Can.
Use: Topical antifungal.

AFTER BITE. (Tender) Ammonium hydroxide 3.6% in aqueous soln. w/mink oil as humectant. Applicator Vials, Towlettes
Use: Anti-pruritic, external analgesic for insect bites.

• **AGAR,** N.F. XVI. (Various Mfr.) Agar-agar, Bengal Gelatin, Ceylon.
Use: Bulk laxative, suspending aid.
W/Mineral oil.
See: Agoral, Emulsion (Warner-Chilcott)
Petrogalar (Wyeth)

AGGREGATED ALBUMIN.
See: Albumotope-LS (Squibb)

AGOBYL. (C.M.C.) Magnesium sulfate 37.0 Gm., succinic acid 2.0 Gm., peptone (bacteriological) 9.0 Gm., citric acid 4.0 Gm., sod. bicarbonate 6.0 Gm., sucrose (mint flavored) 42.0 Gm./100 Gm. Pkg. 125 Gm.

AGOFOLLIN.
See: Estradiol. (Various Mfr.)

AGORAL. W/Phenolphthalein (Parke-Davis) Phenolphthalein & mineral oil in an emulsion containing agar tragacanth, egg-albumin, acacia, glycerin and water Marshmallow flavor. Bot. 8, 16 fl. oz., Raspberry flavored Bot. pint.
Use: Laxative.

AGORAL, PLAIN. (Parke-Davis) Emulsion of mineral oil and an agar-gel. Bot. 16 oz.
Use: Laxative.

A/G-PRO. (Miller) Protein hydrolysate 50 gr. w/essential and nonessential amino acids 45%, l-lysine 50 mg., methionine 12.5 mg. and Fe, Cu, iodine, Mn, K, Zn, Mg./6 Tab. Bot. 180s.
Use: Tissue repair.

AGURIN.
See: Theobromine Sod. Acetate (Various Mfr.)

AHAN. (Eric, Kirk & Gary) Vitamin A acetate 25,000 I.U./Cap. Bot. 100s. 50,000 I.U., 100,000 I.U./Cap. Bot. 100s.

A-HYDROCORT. (Abbott) Hydrocortisone sodium succinate. 100 mg./2 ml. Pkg. 1s, 5s, 25s, 100s; 250 mg./2 ml. Pkg. 1s, 5s, 25s, 100s; 500 mg./4 ml. Pkg. 1s, 5s, 25s, 100s; 1000 mg./8 ml. Pkg. 1s, 5s, 25s.
Use: Anti-inflammatory.

AIR & SURFACE DISINFECTANT. (Aeroceuticals) Dimethylbenzylammonium Cl 0.33%, phenylphenol 0.25%, essential oils 0.10%, ethyl alcohol 44.25%. Aerosol spray.
Use: Air sanitizer, deodorizer..

AIRBRON. Acetylcysteine, B.A.N.

AIR-TABS G.G. (Scrip) Dyphylline 200 mg., guaifenesin 200 mg./Tab. Bot. 100s.
Use: Bronchodilator, expectorant.

AKES-N-PAIN. (Edward J. Moore) Acetaminophen 120 mg., salicylamide 210 mg., caffeine 30 mg., Ca gluconate 60 mg./Cap. Bot. 30s.
Use: Analgesic.

AKES-N-PAIN RUB. (Edward J. Moore) Histamine dihydrochloride, methyl nicotinate, oleoresin capsicum, glycomonosalicylate. Tube 1.25 oz.

AKINETON. (Knoll) Biperiden HCl 2 mg./Tab. Bot. 100s, 1000s.
Use: Anticholinergic and myospasmolytic for Parkinson's disease and drug-induced parkinsonism.

AKINETON LACTATE. (Knoll) Biperiden lactate 5 mg in aqueous 1.4% sodium lactate solution/cc. Amp 1 cc. Box 10s.
Use: Relief of Parkinson-like dystonic crises.

• **AKLOMIDE.** USAN.
Use: Coccidiostat.

AKNE DRYING LOTION. (Alto) Zinc oxide 12%, urea 10%, sulfur 6%, salicylic acid 2%, benzalkonium chloride 0.2%, isopropyl alcohol 70%, in a base containing menthol, silicon dioxide, iron oxide and perfume. Bot. ¾ oz., 2.25 oz.
Use: Acne vulgaris, acne rosacea, seborrhea.

AKNE-MYCIN. (Hermal) Erythromycin. **Oint.:** 20 mg./Gm. in ointment base. Tube 25 Gm. **Soln.:** 20 mg./ml. Bot. 2 oz.
Use: For tropical control of acne vulgaris.

KNE SCRUB. (Alto) Povidone iodine with polyethylene granules. Bot. ¾ oz.
Use: Acne cleanser, antiseptic, microbicidal

KRINOL CREAM. (Schering) Acrisorcin, the hexylresorcinol salt of 9-aminoacridine, 2 mg. in a polyethylene glycol base/Gm. Tube 50 Gm.
Use: Topical treatment of tinea versicolor.

KSHURN. (Seatrace) Danthron 75 mg./Tab. Bot. 100s, 1000s.
Use: Laxative.

LA-BATH. (Del-Ray) Bath oil Bot. 8 oz., 12 oz.
Use: Emollient and skin softener.

LA-CORT. (Del-Ray) Hydrocortisone 1%. **Cream.** Tube 1 oz., 3 oz. **Lotion** 1%, Bot. 4 oz.
Use: Glucocorticoid.

LA-DERM. (Del-Ray) Emollient lotion. Bot 8 oz., 12 oz.
Use: Emollient lotion.

LAGEL. (Century) Aluminum hydroxide gel. Bot. 12 oz.
Use: Antacid.

LA-SEB SHAMPOO. (Del-Ray) Antiseborreic shampoo. Bot. 4 oz., 12 oz.
Use: Antiseborrheic shampoo.

LA-SEB T SHAMPOO. (Del-Ray) Antiseborreic shampoo. Bot. 4 oz., 12 oz.
Use: Antiseborrheic shampoo.

LADRINE. (Scherer) Ephedrine sulfate 8.1 mg., secobarbital sod. 16.2 mg./Tab. Bot. 100s. Ephedrine sulfate 8.1 mg., secobarbital sodium 16.2/5 cc. Bot. pt.
Use: Antiasthmatic.

LAMAG. (Barre) Magnesium-aluminum hydroxide gel. Susp. Bot. pt.
/Belladonna alkaloid, Susp. Bot. 8 oz.

LAMAG ANTACID SUSP. (Goldline) Bot. 12 oz.
Use: Antacid.

ALAMECIN. USAN.
Use: Antibacterial.

LAMINE-C. (Vortech) Codeine phosphate 10 mg., chlorpheniramine maleate 2 mg. phenylpropanolamine HCl 18.75 mg./5 ml. W alcohol 5%. Bot. 4 oz., Gal.
Use: Decongestant, antitussive.

LAMINE EXPECTORANT. (Vortech) Codeine phosphate 10 mg., guaifenesin 100 mg., phenylephrine HCl 10 mg., phenylpropanolamine HCl 18.75 mg./5 ml. W alcohol 7.5% Bot. 4 oz., Gal.
Use: Decongestant, antitussive.

LAMINE LIQUID. (Vortech) Phenylpropranolamine HCl 18.75 mg., chlorpheniramine maleate 2 mg/5ml. W alcohol 5%. Bot. 4 oz., Gal.
Use: Decongestant.

ALANINE, U.S.P. XXI. $C_3H_7NO_2$. L-Alanine.

ALANINE, N-(2,4-DIHYDROXY-3,3-DIMETHYL-1-OXOBUTYL)-, CALCIUM SALT (2:1). Calcium Pantothenate, U.S.P. XXI.

ALAPROCLATE. USAN.
Use: Antidepressant.

LA-QUIN 0.5%. (Del-Ray) Hydrocortisone, iodochlorhydroxyquin cream. Tube 1 oz.

ALA-SCALP HP 2%. (Del-Ray) Hydrocortisone lotion. Bot. 1 oz.

ALA-TET. (Del-Ray) Tetracycline HCl 250 mg./Cap. Bot. 100s, 1000s.
Use: Antibiotic.

ALATONE. (Major) Sprionolactone 25 mg./Tab. Bot. 250s, 1000s.
Use: Antihypertensive.

ALAXIN. (Delta) Oxyethlene oxypropylene polymer 240 mg./Cap. Bot. 100s.
Use: Fecal softener, constipation remedy.

AL-AY. (Bowman)**Green Oblong Tube.:** Phenylephrine HCl 5 mg., chlorpheniramine maleate 2 mg., aspirin 162 mg., caffeine 15 mg., aminoacetic acid 162 mg./Tab. Bot. 100s, 1000s.**Dark Green S.C.:** Phenylephrine HCl 5 mg., chlorpheniramine maleate 2 mg., acetaminophen 160 mg., caffeine 15 mg./Tab. Bot. 100s, 1000s.
Use: Nasal decongestant.

AL-AY MODIFIED. (Bowman) Phenylephrine HCl 5 mg., chlorpheniramine maleate 2 mg., acetaminophen 160 mg., caffeine 15 mg./Tab. Bot. 100s, 1000s.
Use: Nasal decongestant.

ALAZANINE TRICHLORPHATE. 3-Ethyl-2-[3-(3-ethyl-2-benzothiazolinylidene) propenyl]-benzothiazolium 2,4,5-trichlorophenoxide salt with two formula weights of 2,4,5[trichlorophenol].
Use: Anthelmintic.

ALAZIDE TABS. (Major) Spironolactone w/hydrochlorothiazide. Bot. 250s, 1000s.
Use: Antihypertensive.

ALAZINE TABS. (Major) Hydralazine 10 mg., 25 mg. or 50 mg./Cap. Bot. 100s, 1000s
Use: Antihypertensive.

ALBALON-A LIQUIFILM. (Allergan) Naphazoline HCl 0.05%, antazoline phosphate 0.5%, polyvinyl alcohol 1.4%, benzalkonium Cl, edetate disodium, povidone, sodium Cl., sodium acetate, acetic acid and/or sodium hydroxide and purified water. Bot. 5 ml., 15 ml.
Use: Ocular antihistamine, decongestant.

ALBALON LIQUIFILM. (Allergan) Naphazoline HCl 0.1%, polyvinyl alcohol 1.4%, benzalkonium Cl, edetate disodium, citric acid, sodium citrate, sodium Cl, sodium hydroxide and purified water. Bot. 5 ml., 15 ml.
Use: Ocular vasoconstrictor.

ALBAMYCIN. (Upjohn) Novobiocin sod. 250 mg./Cap. Bot. 100s.
Use: Wide-range antibiotic therapy.

• **ALBENDAZOLE.** USAN.
Use: Anthelmintic.

ALBOLENE CREAM. (Norcliff Thayer) Unscented: Jar 6 oz., 12 oz. Scented: Jar 6 oz., 12 oz.

ALBUCID.
See: Sulfacetamide

ALBUCONN 25% SOL. (Cryosan) Normal serum albumin (human) 12.5 Gm. in 50 ml. sol. for IV administration. Vial 50 ml.
Use: Treatment of plasma or blood volume deficit, acute hypoproteinemia, oncotic deficit.

• **ALBUMIN, AGGREGATED.** USAN.
Use: Diagnostic aid.

• **ALBUMIN, AGGREGATED IODINATED 1 131 SERUM,** USAN.
Use: Radioactive agent.

ALBUMINAR 5 AND ALBUMINAR-25. (Armour) Normal serum albumin, Human U.S.P. **5%:** 5% solution with administration set. Bot. 50 ml., 250 ml., 500 ml., 1000 ml. **25%:** 25% solution. Vial 20 ml., 50 ml., 100 ml. with administration set.

• **ALBUMIN, CHROMATED Cr 51 SERUM.** USAN. Radio-Chromated Serum Albumin Human.
See: Chromalbin (Squibb)

• **ALBUMIN HUMAN,** U.S.P. XXI. Normal Human Serum Albumin.
Use: Blood volume supporter
See: Proserum 5, Inj. (Merrell Dow)

ALBUMIN HUMAN SALT-POOR.
Use: Shock, hypoproteinemia, renal diseases & cirrhosis.
See: Pro-Bumin, Vial (Lederle)

• **ALBUMIN, IODINATED I-125 SERUM.** USAN. Radio-iodinated (^{125}I) Serum Albumin Human.
Use: Diagnostic aid.

• **ALBUMIN, IODINATED I-131 SERUM,** U.S.P. XXI. Radio-iodinated (^{131}I) Serum Albumin Human. Aggregated Radio-Iodinated (I-131) Albumin Human.
Use: Diagnostic aid.
See: Albumotope-LS (Squibb)

• **ALBUMIN, IODINATED I-131 AGGREGATED INJECTION,** U.S.P. XXI.
Use: Diagnostic aid.

ALBUMIN-SALINE DILUENT. (Hollister-Stier) Pre-measured vials 1.8 ml., 4 ml., 4.5 ml., 9 ml., or 30 ml. Vials 2 ml., 5 ml., 10 ml., 30 ml.
Use: Dilute allergenic extracts & venom products for patient testing and treating.

ALBUMOTOPE I-131. (Squibb) Albumin, Iodinated I-131 Serum (50 uCi).

ALBUSTIX REAGENT STRIPS. (Ames) Firm paper reagent strips impregnated with tetrabromphenol blue, citrate buffer and a protein-adsorbing agent. Bot. 100s.
Use: Diagnostic, to indicate the presence of albumin in the urine.

• **ALBUTEROL SULFATE,** USAN.
Use: Bronchodilator.
See: Proventil, Tab. (Schering)
Ventolin, Tab. (Glaxo)

• **ALBUTEROL.** USAN.
Use: Bronchodilator.

• **ALBUTOIN.** USAN. 3-Allyl-5-isobutyl-2-thiohydantoin.

ALCAINE. (Alcon) Proparacaine HCl 0.5%, glycerin, sod. chloride, benzalkonium chloride.
Bot. 15 ml.
Use: Ophthalmic topical anesthetic.

ALCLEAR EYE LOTION. (Walgreen) Bot. 8 oz.
Use: Sterile isotonic fluid for eye irritation.

• **ALCLOFENAC.** USAN. 4-Allyloxy-3-chlorophenylacetic acid.
Use: Analgesic; anti-inflammatory.
See: Prinalgin

• **ALCLOMETASONE DIPROPIONATE.** USAN.
Use: Anti-inflammatory.

ALCLOXA. USAN. Tetrahydroxychloro-[(2-hydroxy-5-oxo-2-imidazolin-4-yl)ureato]-dialuminum.
Use: Astringent, keratolytic.

ALCOBON. Flucytosine, B.A.N.

• **ALCOHOL,** U.S.P. XXI. Ethanol, ethyl alcohol.
Use: Topical anti-infective; pharmaceutic aid (sc vent).

• **ALCOHOL, DEHYDRATED,** U.S.P. XXI.

• **ALCOHOL, DEHYDRATED INJECTION,** U.S.P. XX

• **ALCOHOL AND DEXTROSE INJECTION,** U.S.P. XXI.

• **ALCOHOL, DILUTED,** N.F. XVI.

• **ALCOHOL, RUBBING,** U.S.P. XXI. Rubefacient.

ALCOHOL 5% AND DEXTROSE 5%. (Abbott) Alcohol 5 ml., dextrose 5 Gm./100 ml. Bot. 1000 m

ALCOJET. (Alconox) Biodegradable machine washin detergent and wetting agent. Ctn. 9 × 4 lb., 25 lb. 50 lb., 100 lb., 300 lb.
Use: Detergent and wetting agent.

ALCOLEC. (American Lecithin) Lecithin w/choline base, cephalin, lipositol. Caps. 100s. Gran. 8 oz., 1 lb.
Use: Colloid, emulsifier, antioxidant.

ALCONEFRIN 12 AND 50. (Webcon) Phenylephrine HCl 0.16% w/benzalkonium chloride. Dropper Bot. 1 oz.
Use: Nasal decongestant.

ALCONEFRIN 25. (Webcon) Phenylephrine HCl 0.25% plus Benzalkonium chloride. Dropper Bot. 3 cc. Spray Pkg. 1 oz.

ALCON LENS CASE. (Alcon) Ctn. of 12s.
Use: Thermal and chemical disinfection regimens hard gas permeable and soft contact lenses.

ALCONOX. (Alconox) Biodegradable detergent & wetting agent. Box 4 lb., Container 25 lb., 50 lb., 100 lb., 300 lb.
Use: Anionic detergent and wetting agent.

ALCOPAR. Bephenium Hydroxynaphthoate, B.A.N.

ALCOTABS. (Alconox) Tabs., Box 100s, 6s.
Use: Cleaning pipettes and test tubes.

ALCO-VITE. (Galen) Vit. A 6666 I.U., D 333 I.U., B-1 3.3 mg., B-2 2.66 mg., B-6 3.3 mg., B-12 5 mcg., 66.6 mg., E 5 I.U., Ca pantothenate 20 mg., niacinamide 20 mg., biotin 0.053 mg., folic acid 1. mg., PABA 11 mg., inositol 53.3 mg., choline bitartrate 53.3 mg., desoxycholic acid 1.25 mg./Cap. Bot. 100s, 1000s.
Use: Nutritional supplement—lipotropic therapy.

• **ALCURONIUM CHLORIDE.** USAN.
Diallyldinortoxiferin dichloride.
Use: Muscle relaxant.
See: Alloferin (Roche)
Toxiferene (Roche)

ALDACTAZIDE TABLETS. (Searle) Spironolactone and hydrochlorothiazide. **25 mg./25 mg.:** Bot. 100 500s, 1000s, 2500s. Unit Dose 100s. **50 mg./50 mg.:** Bot. 100s. Unit Dose 100s.
Use: Antihypertensive, treatment of edema of cirrhosis & of CHF, nephrotic syndrome.

ALDACTONE TABLETS. (Searle) Spironolactone **25 mg.**/Tab. Bot. 100s, 500s, 1000s, 2500s. Unit Do 100s. **50 mg.**/Tab. Bot. 100s. Unit Dose 100s. **10 mg.**/Tab. Bot. 100s. Unit Dose 100s.

Use: Antihypertensive; treatment of edema of cirrhosis & CHF, nephrotic syndrome; in hypokalemia; primary aldosteronism.

LDERLIN HYDROCHLORIDE. Pronethalol, B.A.N.

LDINAMIDE. 2-Carbamoyl pyrazine.

ALDIOXA. USAN. Aluminum dihydroxy allantoinate. Dihydroxy-[(2-hydroxy-5-oxo-2-imidazolin-4-yl)ureato] aluminum.
Use: Astringent, keratolytic.

LDOCLOR-150. (Merck Sharp & Dohme) Methyldopa 250 mg., chlorothiazide 150 mg./Tab. Bot. 100s.
Use: Antihypertensive agent.

LDOCLOR-250. (Merck Sharp & Dohme) Methyldopa 250 mg., chlorothiazide 250 mg./Tab. Bot. 100s.
Use: Antihypertensive agent.

LDOCORTEN. Aldosterone, B.A.N.

LDOMET. (Merck Sharp & Dohme) Methyldopa Tablets: **125 mg.**/Tab. Bot. 100s. **250 mg.**/Tab. Bot. 100s, 1000s. Unit-dose 100s. Unit-of-use 100s. **500 mg.**/Tab. Bot. 100s, 500s. Unit-dose 100s. Unit of use 60s, 100s.
Use: Antihypertensive agent.
/Chlorothiazide.
See: Aldoclor, Tab. (Merck Sharp & Dohme)
/Hydrochlorothiazide.
See: Aldoril, Tab. (Merck Sharp & Dohme)

LDOMET ESTER HCl. (Merck Sharp & Dohme) Methyldopate HCl 250 mg./5 ml. w/citric acid anhydrous 25 mg., sodium bisulfite 16 mg., disodium edetate 2.5 mg., monothioglycerol 10 mg. sodium hydroxide to adjust pH, methylparaben 0.15%, propylparaben 0.02% w/water for inj. q.s. to 5 ml. Vial 5 ml.
Use: Antihypertensive agent.

LDOMET ORAL SUSPENSION. (Merck Sharp & Dohme) Methyldopa 250 mg./5 ml. w/alcohol 1%., benzoic acid 0.1%., sodium bisulfite 0.2%. Bot. 473 ml.
Use: Antihypertensive agent.

.DORIL-15. (Merck Sharp & Dohme) Methyldopa 250 mg., hydrochlorothiazide 15 mg./Tab. Bot. 100s, 1000s. Unit-dose 100s.
Use: Antihypertensive agent.

.DORIL-25. (Merck Sharp & Dohme) Methyldopa 250 mg., hydrochlorothiazide 25 mg./Tab. Bot. 100s, 1000s. Unit-dose 100s.
Use: Antihypertensive agent.

.DORIL D30. (Merck Sharp & Dohme) Methyldopa 500 mg., hydrochlorothiazide 30 mg./Tab. Bot. 100s.
Use: Antihypertensive agent.

.DORIL D50. (Merck Sharp & Dohme) Methyldopa 500 mg., hydrochlorothiazide 50 mg./Tab. Bot. 100s.
Use: Antihypertensive agent.

.DOSTERONE B.A.N. 11β,21-Dihydroxy-3,-20-dioxopregn-4-en-18-al. Aldocorten. Electrocortin.
Use: Corticosteroid.

.DOSTERONE RIA DIAGNOSTIC KIT. (Abbott) Test kit 50s.
Use: Radioimmunoassay for direct measurement of total aldosterone in serum, plasma or urine.

ALERMINE. (Reid-Provident) Chlorpheniramine maleate 4 mg./Tab. Bot. 100s, 500s, 1000s.

ALERMINE T.D. (Reid-Provident) Chlorpheniramine maleate 8 or 12 mg./Granucap. Bot. 1000s.

ALERSULE CAPSULES. (Misemer) Chlorpheniramine maleate 8 mg., phenylephrine HCl 20 mg./Cap. Bot. 100s.
Use: Symptoms of common cold and hay fever.

ALERT-PEP. (Approved) Caffeine 200 mg./Cap. Bot. 16s.
Use: General alertness.

• **ALETAMINE HYDROCHLORIDE.** USAN.
Use: Antidepressant.

ALEUDRIN. Isoprenaline, B.A.N.

ALEVAIRE SOLUTION. (Winthrop Products) Superinone.
Use: Mucolytic.

• **ALEXIDINE.** USAN. 1,1′-Hexamethylenebis[5-(2-ethylhexyl) biguanide].
Use: Antibacterial.

• **ALFAPROSTOL.** USAN.
Use: Prostaglandin (veterinary).

ALFENTA. (Janssen) Alfentanil
Use: Analgesic.

• **ALFENTANIL HYDROCHLORIDE.** USAN.
Use: Analgesic, narcotic.

ALFICETYN. Chloramphenicol, B.A.N.

ALFLORONE. Fludrocortisone, B.A.N.

• **ALFUZOSIN HYDROCHLORIDE.** USAN.
Use: Antihypertensive.

ALGECOL TABLETS. (Winston) Acetaminophen 5 gr., phenylpropanolamine HCl 25 mg., phenylephrine HCl 10 mg., chlorpheniramine maleate 2 mg./Tab. Bot. 100s, 1000s.
Use: Analgesic, decongestant, antihistaminic.

ALGEL. (Faraday) Magnesium trisilicate 0.5 Gm., aluminum hydroxide 0.25 Gm./Tab. Bot. 100s. Susp., Bot. gal.
Use: Antacid.

ALGELDRATE. (Warner-Lambert) Hydrated aluminum hydroxide.
Use: Antacid.

ALGEMIN. (Thurston) Macrocystis pyrifera alga. Powd. Jar 8 oz. Tabs. Bot. 300s.
Use: Dietary aid.

• **ALGESTONE ACETONIDE.** USAN. 16α,-17α-Isopropylidenedioxypregn-4-ene-3,20-dione;
Use: Progestational steroid.

• **ALGESTONE ACETOPHENIDE.** USAN. (R)-16α, 17-Dihydroxypregn-4-ene-3,20-dione cyclic acetal with acetophenone.
Use: Progestin.

ALGETUSS. (Winston) Dextromethorphan HBr 60 mg., ammonium chloride 300 mg., phenylpropanolamine HCl 50 mg., chlorpheniramine maleate 7.5 mg., sodium citrate 720 mg./fl. oz. Bot. pt.
Use: Antitussive, expectorant.

ALGEX LINIMENT. (Approved) Menthol, camphor, methylsalicylate, eucalyptus. Bot. 4 oz.
Use: Heat therapy.

ALGIN.
See: Sodium Alginate, N.F. XVI.
ALGIN-ALL. (Barth's) Sodium alginate from kelp. Tab. Bot. 100s, 500s.
• **ALGINIC ACID,** N.F. XVI.
Use: Pharmaceutic aid (tablet binder; thickening agent).
ALGINIC ACID. W/Aluminum hydroxide dried gel, magnesium trisilicate, and sod. bicarbonate.
See: Gaviscon Foamtabs (Marion)
• **ALGRELDRATE.** USAN.
Use: Antacid.
ALIDINE DIHYDROCHLORIDE OR PHOSPHATE. Anileridine, N.F.
• **ALIFLURANE.** USAN.
Use: Anesthetic.
ALIKAL POWDER. (Winthrop Products) Sodium bicarbonate, tartaric acid powder.
Use: Antacid.
ALIMEMAZINE (I.N.N.). Trimeprazine, B.A.N.
• **ALIPAMIDE.** USAN. 4-Chloro-3-sulfamoylbenzoic acid 2,2-dimethylhydrazide.
Use: Diuretic, antihypertensive.
ALIPAMIDE. B.A.N. 4-Chloro-2′,2′-dimethyl-3-sulfamoylbenzohydrazide.
Use: Diuretic.
ALIPCO. (Drug Products) Strychnine sulfate 0.5 mg., belladonna lvs. ext. 5.4 mg., phenolphthalein 32 mg., aloin 13 mg., podophyllin 4 mg., ipecac 4 mg./Tab. Bot. 1000s.
Use: Adult laxative.
ALISOBUMAL.
See: Butalbital, U.S.P. XXI.
ALKALOL. (Alkalol Co.) Thymol, eucalyptol, menthol, camphor, benzoin, pot. alum, pot. chlorate, sod. bicarb., sod. chloride, sweet birch oil, spearmint oil, pine & cassia oil, alcohol 0.05%. Bot. 1 pt. Nasal douche cup Pkg. 1s.
Use: Eyes, nose, throat & all inflamed mucous membranes.
ALKA-MED LIQUID. (Blue Cross) Aluminum hydroxide 200 mg., magnesium hydroxide 200 mg./ 5 ml. Bot. 8 oz.
Use: Antacid.
ALKA MED TABLETS. (Blue Cross) Magnesium hydroxide, aluminum hydroxide. Bot. 60s.
Use: Antacid.
ALKA-MINTS. (Miles) Calcium carbonate 850 mg./Tab. Carton 30s, 60s.
Use: Chewable antacid.
ALKA-SELTZER. (Miles) Heat treated sodium bicarbonate 1916 mg., citric acid 1000 mg., acetylsalicylic acid 324 mg./Tab. Bot. 8s, 26s; foil 12s, 36s, 72s, 100s.
Use: Effervescent antacid, analgesic.
ALKA-SELTZER PLUS. (Miles) Chlorpheniramine maleate 2 mg., phenylpropanolamine bitartrate 24 mg., aspirin 324 mg./Tab. Foil Pkgs: 20s, 36s.
Use: Relief of cold symptoms.
ALKA-SELTZER SPECIAL EFFERVESCENT ANTACID. (Miles) Heat treated sodium bicarbonate 958 mg., citric acid 832 mg., potassium bicarbonate 31 mg./Tab. Foil Pkgs: 12s, 20s, 36s.
Use: Antacid.
ALKAVERVIR. Mixture of Veratrum viride alkaloids.
ALKERAN. (Burroughs Wellcome) Melphalan 2 mg./Tab., Bot. 50s.
Use: Treatment of epithial carcinoma of ovary and multiple myeloma.
ALKETS. (Upjohn) Ca carbonate 780 mg., Mg. carbonate 130 mg., Mg. oxide 65 mg./Tab. Bot. 100s.
Use: Antacid.
ALKOHOLA COMPOUND. (Sutliff & Case) Ethyl alcohol 70%. Bot. pt.
Use: Local soothing, cooling and stimulating effec
ALK-PHOSTEL. (Warner-Lambert) Box 100 test sets
ALKYLBENZYLDIMETHYLAMMONIUM CHLORIDE. Benzalkonium Chloride, N.F. XVI.
W/Methylrosaniline chloride, polyoxyethylenenonylphenol, polyethylene glycol tert-dodecylthioether.
See: Hyva, Tab. (Holland-Rantos)
• **ALLANTOIN.** USAN.
Use: Wounds and resistant ulcers to stimulate the growth of healthy tissue.
See: Cutemol, (Summers)
Sebical Cream Shampoo (Reed & Carnrick)
W/Aminacrine, sulfanilamide.
See: Par Cream (Parmed)
Sufamal, Cream (Milex)
Vagidine, Cream (Elder)
Vagitrol, Cream (Syntex)
W/Balsam, Lano-sil, silicone.
See: Balmex Med. Lot. (Macsil)
W/Camphor, menthol, tinct. benzoin.
See: Siltex, Oint. (Edward J. Moore)
W/Cetyl dimethyl ethyl ammonium Br, pramoxine HC pyrilamine maleate.
See: Quad-Creme (Sutliff & Case)
W/p-Chloro-m-xylenol.
See: Cebum, Shampoo (Dermik)
W/Coal tar ext., hexachlorophene, glycerin & lanolin
See: Pso-Rite, Cream (DePree)
W/Coal tar in cream base.
See: Tegrin Cream (Block Drug)
W/Coal tar solution, isopropyl myristate, psorilan.
See: Psorelief, Sol (Quality Generics)
W/Dienestrol, sulfanilamide, aminacrine HCl.
See: AVC/Dienestrol Cream, Suppos. (Merrell Dow
W/Hydrocortisone.
See: Tarcortin, Cream (Reed & Carnrick)
W/Nitrofurazone.
See: Eldezol, Oint. (Elder)
W/Pramoxine HCl, benzalkonium Cl.
See: Perifoam, Aerosol (Rowell Labs.)
W/Resorcinol, hexachlorophene, menthol.
See: Tackle, Gel. (Colgate-Palmolive)
W/Salicylic Acid, sulfur.
See: Neutrogena Disposables (Neutrogena)
W/Sulfanilamide, 9-aminoacridine HCl.
See: Femguard Vaginal, Cream (Reid-Provident)
Nil Vaginal Cream (Century)

Sulfem Vag. Cream (Federal Pharm.)
Triconol Vag. Cream (Coastal)
Vagisan, Creme (Sandia)
Vagisul, Creme (Sheryl)

W/Sulfisoxazole, Aminoacridine.
Use: Topically, aid in the promotion of granulation.
See: Vagilia, Cream, Supp. (Lemmon)

W/Tarbonis.
See: Sebical, Shampoo (Carnrick & Reed)

W/Vit. A, Vit. D.
See: A-D Dressing (LaCrosse)

ALLBEE C-800. (Robins) Vit. E 45 I.U., C 800 mg., B-1 15 mg., B-2 17 mg., niacin 100 mg., B-6 25 mg., B-12 mcg., pantothenic acid 25 mg./Tab. Bot. 60s.
Use: Vitamin supplement.

ALLBEE C-800 PLUS IRON. (Robins) Vit. E 45 I.U., C 800 mg., B-1 15 mg., B-2 17 mg., niacin 100 mg., B-6 25 mg., B-12 12 mcg., pantothenic acid 25 mg., iron 27 mg., folic acid 0.4 mg./Tab. Bot. 60s.
Use: Vitamin supplement with iron.

ALLBEE W/VITAMIN C. (Robins) Vit. B-1 15 mg., B-6 5 mg., B-2 10.2 mg., niacin 50 mg., pantothenic acid 10 mg., Vitamin C 300 mg./Cap. Bot. 30s, 100s, 1000s. Dis-co packs (Caps) 10x100s.
Use: Vitamin supplement.

ALLBEE-T. (Robins) B-1 15.5 mg., B-2 10 mg., B-6 8.2 mg., pantothenic acid 23 mg., niacin 100 mg., Vit. C 500 mg., B-12 5 mcg./Tab. Bot. 100s, 500s.
Use: Vitamin supplement.

ALL BETTER CAPSULES. (Image) Vitamin capsules Bot. 100s.
Use: Supplement.

ALLBEX. (Approved) Vit. B-1 5 mg., B-2 2 mg., B-6 0.25 mg., calcium pantothenate 3 mg., niacinamide 20 mg., ferrous sulfate 194.4 mg., inositol 10 mg., choline 10 mg., Vit. B-12 (conc.) 3 mcg./Cap. Bot. 100s, 1000s.
Use: Vitamin deficiencies.

ALL-DAY B-COMPLEX. (Barth's) Vit. B-12 25 mcg., B-1 7 mg., B-2 14 mg., niacin 4.67 mg., B-6, pantothenic acid, folic acid, choline, aminobenzoic acid, inositol, biotin, Mg, Mn, Cu/Cap. Bot. 30s, 90s, 180s, 360s.

ALL-DAY-C. (Barth's) Vit. C 200 mg./Cap. 500 mg./Tab. with rose hip extract. Bot. 30s, 90s, 180s, 360s.

ALL-DAY IRON YEAST. (Barth's) Iron 20 mg., Vit. B-1 2 mg., B-2 4 mg., niacin 0.57 mg./Cap. Bot. 30s, 90s, 180s.

ALL-DAY-VITES. (Barth's) Vit. A 10,000 I.U., D 400, I.U. B-1 3 mg., B-2 6 mg., niacin 1 mg., C 120 mg., B-12 10 mcg., E 30 I.U./Cap. Bot. 30s, 90s, 180s, 360s.

ALLEGRON. Nortriptyline.

ALLERBEN INJECTION. (Fellows) Diphenhydramine 10 mg./cc. Vial 30 cc.

ALLERCHLOR INJECTION. (Fellows) Chlorpheniramine maleate 10 mg./cc. Vial 30 cc.

ALLERDEC CAPSULES. (Towne) Phenylpropanolamine HCl 25 mg., chlorpheniramine maleate 1 mg., pyrilamine maleate 5 mg./Cap. Bot. 25s, 50s.

ALLEREST. (Pharmacraft) **Tabs:** Phenylpropanolamine HCl 18.7 mg., chlorpheniramine maleate 2 mg./Tab. Sleeve Pack 24s, 48s. Bot. 72s. **Chewable Tablets for Children:** phenylpropanolamine HCl 9.4 mg., chlorpheniramine maleate 1 mg./Tab. Sleeve Pack 24s. **Timed-Release Caps.:** phenylpropanolamine HCl 50 mg., chlorpheniramine maleate 4 mg./Cap. Sleeve Pack 10s. **Nasal Spray:** phenylephrine HCl 0.5%. Bot. 0.5 oz. **Eye Drops:** Naphazoline HCl 0.012%, benzalkonium Cl 0.01%, disodium edetate 0.1% w/boric acid, sodium borate. Bot. 0.5 oz. **Headache Strength Tabs.:** Acetaminophen 325 mg., phenylpropanolamine HC1 18.7 mg., chlorpheniramine maleate 2 mg./Tab. Sleeve Pack 24s.
Use: Hay fever, allergy.

ALLEREST SINUS PAIN FORMULA. (Pharmacraft) Acetaminophen 500 mg., phenlypropanolamine HCl 18.7 mg., chlorpheniramine maleate 2 mg./Tab. Sleeve pack 20s.
Use: Hay fever, allergy, sinus headache.

ALLERGAN HYDROCARE CLEANING & DISINFECTING SOLUTION. (Allergan) Bot. 4 oz., 8 oz., 12 oz.
Use: Clean, disinfect, & store soft (hydrophilic) contact lenses.

ALLERGAN HYDROCARE PRESERVED SALINE SOLUTION. (Allergan) Bot. 8 oz., 12 oz.
Use: Heat disinfection, rinsing, and storage of soft (hydrophilic) contact lenses.and for rinsing in conjunction with chemical disinfection.

ALLERGAN SORBI-CARE SALINE SOLUTION. (Allergan) Saline solution. Bot. 8 oz.
Use: Rinsing, heat disinfection and storage of soft (hydrophilic) contact lenses and for rinsing in conjunction with chemical disinfection.

ALLERGEN EAR DROPS. (Goldline) Bot. 0.5 oz.
Use: Treatment of otitis media, removal cerumen.

ALLERGENIC EXT. (Barry) Poison ivy, oak and sumac ext. triple antigen. In hypo-allergenic oil vehicle. Vial 5 cc.

ALLERGENIC EXTRACTS. (Center) Allergenic extracts of pollen, mold, house dust, inhalants, epidermal & insects in saline 0.9% & phenol 0.4% up to 1:10 w/v or 40,000 PNU/ml. in sets or vials up to 30 ml.
Use: Diagnosis & hyposensitization treatment of allergies.

ALLERGENIC EXTRACTS. (Hollister-Stier) Allergenic extracts of pollens, foods, inhalants, epidermals, fungi, insects, miscellaneous antigens, autogenous extracts. Scratch tests, vials.
Use: Diagnosis and treatment of causative factors in allergy.

ALLERGESIC IMPROVED. (Vitarine) Phenylpropanolamine HCl 18.7 mg., chlorpheniramine maleate 2 mg./Tab. Vial 48s.
Use: Relief of upper respiratory allergy symptoms.

ALLERGEX. (Hollister-Stier) Silicones, polyethylene and triethylene glycol, antioxidants, mineral oil concentrate. Bot. 1 pt. Aerosol Spray, Bot. pt.
Use: Control of house dust allergens.

ALLERGY. (Eckerd) Chlorpheniramine maleate, phenylephrine HCl, ascorbic acid, calcium pantothenate/Tab. Bot. 48s.
ALLERGY II TABLETS. (Eckerd) Chlorpheniramine maleate 4 mg., phenylpropanolamine 37.5 mg./Tab. Bot. 24s., 48s.
Use: Decongestant, antihistamine.
ALLERGY PREPARATIONS.
See: Antihistamine Preparations
ALLERGY TABS. (Weeks & Leo) Phenylpropanolamine HCl 37.5 mg., chlorpheniramine 4 mg./Tab. Vials 30s.
Use: Allergy relief.
ALLERID-D.C. (Trimen) Chlorpheniramine maleate 6 mg., pseudoephedrine HCl 120 mg./Cap. Bot. 100s.
Use: Antihistamine decongestant.
ALLERID-O.D. (Trimen) Chlorpheniramine maleate 8 mg., 12 mg./Cap. Bot. 100s.
ALLERSONE. (Mallard) Hydrocortisone 0.5%, diperodon HCl 0.5%, zinc oxide 5%, sodium lauryl sulfate, propylene glycol, cetyl alcohol, petrolatum, methyl & propyl parabens. Oint. Tube 15 Gm.
Use: Anti-inflammatory, antipruritic & antiallergic.
ALLETORPHINE. B.A.N. N-Allyl-7,8-dihydro-7α-(1(R)-hydroxy-1-methylbutyl)-0^6-methyl-6,14-endoethenonormorphine. N-Allylnoretorphine.
Use: Analgesic.
• **ALLOBARBITAL.** USAN. 5,5-Diallylbarbituric acid.
W/Acetaminophen, salicylamide, caffeine.
See: Allylvon, Cap. (Elder)
W/Aspirin, acetaminophen, aluminum aspirin.
See: Allylgesic, Tab. (Elder)
W/Ergotamine tartrate.
See: Allylgesic w/Ergotamine, Cap. (Elder)
ALLOBARBITONE.
See: Diallylbarbituric Acid (Various Mfr.)
ALLOMETHADIONE. (I.N.N.) Aloxidone, B.A.N.
• **ALLOPURINOL,** U.S.P. XXI. Tablets, U.S.P. XXI. 1 H-Pyrazolo-[3, 4-d] pyrimidin-4-ol.
Use: Antigout, xanthine oxidase inhibitor.
See: Lopurin, Tab. (Boots Pharm)
Zyloprim, Tab. (Burroughs Wellcome)
ALLOPURINOL. B.A.N. 1H-Pyrazolo[3,4-d] pyrimidin-4-ol.
Use: Uricosuric.
ALLPYRAL. (Miles Pharm) Allergenic extracts, alum-precipitated. For subcutaneous inj. pollens, molds, epithelia, house dust, other inhalants, stinging insects.
Use: Allergies.
ALLYLBARBITURIC ACID. Allylisobutyl-barbituric acid, butalbital. Tab. (Various Mfr.)
Use: Sedative.
W/A.P.C.
See: Anti-Ten, Tab. (Century)
Fiorinal, Cap., Tab. (Sandoz)
Marnal, Tab. (Vortech)
Salipral, Tab. (Kenyon)
Tenstan (Standex)
W/Aspirin, acetaminophen, caffeine.
See: Paradol, Tab. (Medics)
W/Acetaminophen, homatropine methylbromide.
See: Panitol H.M.B., Tab. (Wesley)
W/Acetaminophen, salicylamide, caffeine.
See: Renpap, Tab. (Wren)
17-ALLYL-4,5α-EPOXY-3,14-DIHYDROXY-MORPHINAN-6-ONE HCl. Naloxone Hydrochloride, U.S.P. XXI.
ALLYLESTRENOL. 17a-Allyl-17b-hydroxy-4-estrene.
N-ALLYL-14-HYDROXY-NORDIHYDROMORPHINONE HCl. Naloxone Hydrochloride, U.S.P. XXI.
ALLYL-ISOBUTYLBARBITURIC ACID.
See: Allyl Barbituric Acid.
5-ALLYL-5-ISOPROPYLBARBITURIC ACID.
See: Aprobarbital.
ALLYLISOPROPYLMALONYLUREA.
See: Aprobarbital.
ALLYL ISOTHIOCYANATE, Oil of mustard. (Various Mfr.)
Use: Counterirritant in neuralgia.
4-ALLYL-2-METHOXYPHENOL. Eugenol, U.S.P. XXI.
N-ALLYLNORMORPHINE HCl.
Nalorphine HCl
See: Nalline HCl, Amp. (Merck Sharp & Dohme)
N-ALLYLNOROXYMORPHONE HCl. Naloxone Hydrochloride, U.S.P. XXI.
ALLYLOESTRENOL. B.A.N. 17α-Allyloestr-4-en-17β-ol. Gestanin.
Use: Progestational steroid.
5-ALLYL-5-PHENYLBARBITURIC ACID. Alphenal, Aphenate.
Use: Sedative & hypnotic.
ALLYLPRODINE. B.A.N. 3-Allyl-1-methyl-4-phenyl-4-propionyloxypiperidine.
Use: Analgesic.
5-ALLYL-SEC-BUTYLBARBITURIC ACID.
See: Lotusate, Cap. (Winthrop-Breon)
• **ALMADRATE SULFATE.** USAN. Aluminum magnesium hydroxide-oxide-sulfate-hydrate.
Use: Antacid.
ALMAGUCIN. Antacid mix of gastric mucin, dried aluminum hydroxide gel & mag. trisilicate.
ALMATRI. (Robinson) Aluminum hydroxide gel. 4 gr. Mg trisilicate 7.5 gr./Tab. Bot. 100s, 1000s. Bulk Pack 5000s.
Use: Antacid adsorbent.
ALMOCARPINE. (Ayerst) Pilocarpine HCl 1%, 2%, and 4%, Steri-Tainer drop bot. 15 ml. each.
Use: Reduction of intraocular tension.
• **ALMOND OIL,** N.F. XVI. Pharmaceutic aid (emollient and perfume).
ALMORA. (Forest) Magnesium gluconate 0.5 Gm./Tab. Pkg. 100s.
Use: Sedative in dysmenorrhea.
ALNYTE. (Mayer) Scopolamine aminoxide HBr. 0.2 mg., salicylamide 250 mg./Tab. Pkg. 16s.
ALOCASS LAXATIVE. (Western Research) Aloin 0.25 gr., cascara sagrada 0.5 gr., rhubarb 0.5 gr., ginger
1/32 gr., pow. ext. belladonna 1/20 gr./Tab. Bot. 1000s. Paks 28.
Use: Laxative.
• **ALOE,** U.S.P. XXI.
Use: See Compound Benzoin Tincture.

LOE GRANDE CREME. (Gordon) Aloe Vit. E 1500 I.U., A 100,000 u./oz. in cream base. Jar 2 oz.
Use: Skin care cream.

LOE VERA ACTIVE PRINCIPLE.
See: Alvagel, Oint. (Kenyon)

ALOFILCON A. USAN.
Use: Contact lens material.

LOIN.. (Baker, J.T.) A mixture of cryst. Pentosides from various aloes. Bot. 1 oz.
Use: Laxative.
'/Ox bile (desiccated), phenolphthalein, cascara sagrada ext., podophyllin.
See: Bilgon (Reid-Provident)

ALONIMID. USAN.
Use: Sedative.

LOPHEN PILLS. (Parke-Davis) Phenolphthalein 60 mg./Pill Bot. 100s.
Use: Laxative.

LOTONE. (Major) Triamcinolone 4 mg./Tab. Bot. 100s.
Use: Anti-inflammatory steroid.

LO-TUSS IMPROVED. (Vortech) Dextromethorphan HBr. 10 mg., phenylephrine HCl 5 mg., chlorpheniramine maleate 2 mg., salicylamide 227 mg., acetophenetidin 100 mg., caffeine 10 mg./Tab. Bot. 100s, 1000s.
Use: Temporary relief of cold symptoms.

LOXIDONE. B.A.N. 3-Allyl-5-methyloxazolidine-2,4-dione. Allomethadione (I.N.N.) Malidone.
Use: Anticonvulsant.

LOXIPRIN. B.A.N. Polymeric condensation product of aluminum oxide and O-acetylsalicylic acid. Palaprin.
Use: Antirheumatic.

ALPERTINE. USAN.
Use: Antipsychotic.

ALPHA AMYLASE. USAN. A concentrated form of alpha amylase produced by a strain of nonpathogenic bacteria.
See: Kutrase, Cap. (Kremers-Urban)
Ku-Zyme, Cap. (Kremers-Urban)

LPHA-AMYLASE W-100. W/Proteinase W-300, cellase W-100, lipase, estrone, testosterone, vitamins, minerals.
See: Geramine, Tab. (Brown)

LPHA-BEL. (Moore Kirk) Phenobarbital 50 mg., hyoscyamine sulfate 0.3 mg., hyoscine HBr 0.02 mg., atropine sulfate 0.06 mg./timed disintegration Cap. Bot. 100s, 1000s.
Use: Antispasmodic and sedative for pylorospasm, gastritis and colitis, biliary colic.

LPHACETYLMETHADOL. B.A.N. α-4-Dimethylamino-1-ethyl-2,2-diphenylpentyl acetate.
Use: Analgesic.

LPHA CHYMAR. (Barnes-Hind) A lyophilized form of crystallized alpha-chymotrypsin. Vial 1s. (750 USP units) w/10 ml. diluent for ophthalmic solution.
Use: To dissolve the zonule fibers of the lens of the eye.

LPHA-CHYMOTRYPSIN.
See: Alpha Chymar, Vial (Armour)
Zolyse, Vial (Alcon)

α-CYCLOHEXYL-α-PHENYL-1-PYRROLIDINEPROPANOL HCl.
See: Procyclidine HCl (Burroughs Wellcome)

ALPHADERM. (Norwich Eaton) Hydrocortisone 1%, urea 10% in a powder-in-cream base. Tubes 30 Gm, 100 Gm.
Use: Dermatoses treatment.

ALPHADOLONE. B.A.N. 3α,21-Dihydroxy-5α-pregnane-11,20-dione.
Use: Anesthetic component.

ALPHA-E. (Barth's) d-Alpha tocopherol 50 I.U., 100 I.U./Cap. Bot. 100s, 500s, 1000s. 200 I.U./Cap. Bot. 100s, 250s. 400 I.U./Cap. Bot. 100s, 250s, 500s.

ALPHA E OIL & CREAM. (Towne) 2 oz.

ALPHA-ESTRADIOL. Known to be beta-Estradiol.
See: Estradiol (Various Mfr.)

ALPHA-ESTRADIOL BENZOATE.
See: Estradiol benzoate. (Various Mfr.)

ALPHA FAST. (Eastwood) Bath oil. Bot. 16 oz.

ALPHA-HYPOPHAMINE.
See: Oxytocin Injection

ALPHA-KERI. (Westwood) **Bath Oil:** Mineral oil, lanolin oil, PEG-4-dilaurate, benzophenone-3, D & C green #6, fragrance. Bot. 4 oz., 8 oz., 16 oz.; **Spray:** 5 oz. **Cleansing Bar:** bar containing Na tallowate, Na cocoate, water, mineral oil, fragrance, PEG-75, glycerin, titanium dioxide, lanolin oil, NaCl, BHT, EDTA, D&C green # 5, D&C yellow # 10.
Use: Treatment of dry skin.

ALPHAMEPRODINE. B.A.N. α-3-Ethyl-1-methyl-4-propionyloxypiperidine.
Use: Analgesic.

ALPHAMETHADOL. B.A.N. α-6-Dimethyl-amino-4,4-diphenylheptan-3-ol.
Use: Analgesic.

ALPHAMIN. (Vortech) Crystalline hydroxocobalamin 1000 mcg./CC. Vial 10 ml., 30 ml.
Use: Pernicious & megaloblastic anemia.

ALPHA-METHYLDOPA. Name previously used for Methyldopa.

ALPHAMUL. (Lannett) Castor oil 60% w/v, emulsifying agent. Bot. 3 fl. oz., gal.
Use: Laxative.

ALPHA-PHENOXYETHYL PENICILLIN, POTASSIUM.
See: Phenethicillin Potassium.

ALPHAPRODINE. B.A.N. α-1,3-Dimethyl-4-phenyl-4-propionyloxypiperidine.
Use: Analgesic.
See: Nisentil, Inj. (Roche)

• **ALPHAPRODINE HYDROCHLORIDE,** U.S.P. XXI. Inj. U.S.P. XXI. dl-Alpha-1,3-Dimethyl-4-phenyl-4-piperidinol propionate HCl. Inj.
Use: Analgesic.
See: Nisentil HCl, Amp., Vial (Roche)

alphaREDISOL. (Merck Sharp & Dohme) Hydroxocobalamin 1000 mcg./ml. w/sod. chloride 0.82%, anhydrous sod. acetate 0.02%, acetic acid to adjust pH, methylparaben 0.15%, propylparaben 0.02%, and water for injection q.s. Vial 10 ml.
Use: Vitamin B-12 therapy (hematopoietic).

ALPHASONE ACETOPHENIDE. Name previously used for Algestone acetonide.

ALPHA-TOCOPHEROL.
See: Dalfatol, Cap. (Reid-Provident)
Tocopherol, Alpha (Various Mfr.)

dl-ALPHA-TOCOPHEROL SUCCINATE.
See: D'Alpha-E, Cap. (Alto)

ALPHATREX CREAM & OINTMENT. (Savage) Betamethasone dipropionate 0.05%. Tube 15 Gm., 45 Gm.
Use: Relief of inflammatory & pruritic dermatosis.

ALPHA VEE-12. (Schlicksup) Hydroxocobalamin 1000 mcg./ml. Vial 10 ml.

ALPHAXALONE. B.A.N. 3α-Hydroxy-5α-pregnane-11,20-dione.
Use: Anesthetic component.

ALPHENAL.
See: 5-Allyl-5-phenylbarbituric acid. (Var. Mfr.)

ALPHOSYL. (Reed & Carnrick) Allantoin 1.7%, special crude coal tar extracts 5%. **Lot.:** Bot. 8 fl. oz. **Cream** 2 oz.
Use: Psoriasis treatment.

• **ALPRAZOLAM,** U.S.P. XXI. Tab., U.S.P. XXI. 8-Chloro-1-methyl-6-phenyl-4H-s- triazolo (4,3-α)(1,4)benzodiazepine.
Use: Management of anxiety disorders.
See: Xanax, Tab. (Upjohn)

ALPRENOLOL. B.A.N. 1-(2-Allylphenoxy)-3-iso-propylaminopropan-2 ol. Betaptin hydrochloride.
Use: Beta adrenergic receptor blocking agent.

• **ALPROSTADIL,** U.S.P. XXI. Inj., U.S.P. XXI. (11α, 13E,15S)-11,15 dihydroxy-9-oxoprost-13-en-1-oic acid.
Use: Palliative therapy to maintain patency of the ductus arteriosus in neonates with congenital heart defects.
See: Prostin VR, Inj. (Upjohn)

• **ALPRENOLOL HYDROCHLORIDE.** USAN.
Use: Anti-adrenergic.

AL-R. (Saron) Chlorpheniramine maleate 6 mg. or 12 mg./S.R. cap.Bot. 100s.
Use: Antihistamine.

ALRAMUCIL. (Alra) Psullium.
Use: Bulk laxative.

• **ALRESTATIN SODIUM.** USAN.
Use: Enzyme inhibitor.

ALSEROXYLON. A fat-soluble alkaloidal fraction extracted from the root of Rauwolfia serpentina; 1 mg. is equiv. to 0.2 mg. of reserpine.
See: Koglucoid, Tab. (Panray)
Raudolfin, Tabs. (Premo)
Rautensin, Tab. (Dorsey)
Rauwiloid, Tab. (Riker)
Vio-Serpine, Tab. (Rowell)

ALSEROXYLON-ALKAVERVIR. A mixture of partially purified extracts of Rauwolfia serpentina and Veratrum viride.

ALSORB GEL. (Standex) Colloidal suspension of magnesium & aluminum hydroxide.

ALSORB GEL, C.T. (Standex) Calcium carbonate 2 gr., glycine 3 gr., magnesium trisilicate 3 gr./Tab.

ALTACITE. Hydrotalcite, B.A.N.

• **ALTANSERIN TARTRATE.** USAN.
Use: Serotonin antagonist.

ALTERNAGEL. (Stuart) Aluminum hydroxide 600 mg./5 ml. Bot. 5 oz., 12 oz.
Use: High-potency, sodium free antacid.

ALTEX. (Cenci) Spironolactone 25 mg./Tab. Bot. 100s, 1000s.
Use: Diuretic, antihypertensive.

ALTEXIDE. (Cenci) Spironolactone 25 mg., hydrochlorothiazide 25 mg./Tab. Bot. 100s, 1000s
Use: Diuretic, antihypertensive.

ALTHIAZIDE. USAN. 3-Allylthiomethyl-3-4-dihydro-6-chloro-7-sulfamoyl-1,2,4-benzothiadiazine-1-dioxide.
Use: Hypotensive and diuretic.

ALTILEV. Nortriptyline, B.A.N.

• **ALTRENOGEST.** USAN.
Use: Progestin (veterinary).

ALUCAINE. (Jenkins) Benzocaine 5%, carbolic acid 1.39%, ichthammol 1.39%, balsam peru 0.46%, alum exsic. 3.7% w/oil cade, oil eucalyptus in oint base. Oint. Tube 1 oz., 1 lb.
Use: Relief of pain in burns, scalds, cuts.

ALU-CAP. (Riker) Aluminum hydroxide dried gel 47 mg. w/silicon dioxide and talc/Cap. Bot. 100s.
Use: Antacid.

AL-U-CREME. (MacAllister) Aluminum hydroxide equialent to 4% aluminum oxide. Susp.: Bot. 1 pt., 1 gal.
Use: Antacid.

ALUDROX. (Wyeth) **Susp.,** Aluminum hydroxide gel 307 mg., w/magnesium hydroxide 103 mg./5 ml. Bot. 12 fl. oz.: Box 12s. **Tab.** Aluminum hydroxide 233 mg., magnesium hydroxide 83 mg./Tab. Box. 100s.
Use: Antacid.

ALUGAN. Bromocyclen, B.A.N.

ALUKALIN. Activated kaolin.
See: Lusyn, Tab. (Pennwalt)

ALULEX. (Lexington) Magnesium trisilicate 3.25 gr., aluminum hydroxide gel 3.5 gr., phenobarbital 1/8 gr., homatropine methylbromide 1/60 gr./Tab. Bot. 100s.
Use: Treatment of peptic ulcer.

• **ALUM,** U.S.P. XXI. Sulfuric acid, aluminum ammonium salt (2:1:1), dodecahydrate. Sulfuric acid, aluminum potassium salt (2:1:1), dodecahydrate.
Use: Astringent.

• **ALUM, AMMONIUM,** U.S.P. XXI.
Use: Astringent.

• **ALUM, POTASSIUM,** U.S.P. XXI.
Use: Astringent.

ALUMADRINE. (Fleming) Acetaminophen 500 mg., phenylpropanolamine HCl 25 mg., chlorpheniramine maleate 4 mg./Tab. Bot. 100s, 1000s.
Use: Mild upper respiratory infections.

ALUMATE-HC. (Dermco) Hydrocortisone ⅛% & 0.25%, Cream. ⅛% Pkg. 4 oz., 0.25% Pkg. 1 oz., 0.5% Pkg. 0.5 oz., 1 oz.; 1% pkg. 0.5 oz.
Use: Anti-inflammatory agent.

ALUMATE MIXTURE. (Schlicksup) Aluminum hydroxide gel, milk of magnesia/Tsp. Bot. 12 oz., gal.

ALUMID LIQUID. (Vangard) Aluminum hydroxide 225 mg., magnesium hydroxide 200 mg./5 ml. Bot. 12 oz.
Use: Antacid.

ALUMID PLUS LIQUID. (Vangard) Aluminum hydroxide 100 mg., magnesium hydroxide 200 mg., simethicone 20 mg., sodium 0.68 mg./5 ml. Bot. 12 oz.
Use: Antacid, antiflatulent..

ALUMINA HYDRATED POWDER.
W/Activated attapulgite, pectin.
See: Polymagma, Plain, Tabs (Wyeth)

• **ALUMINA AND MAGNESIA ORAL SUSPENSION,** U.S.P. XXI.
Use: Antacid.

• **ALUMINA AND MAGNESIA TABLETS,** U.S.P. XXI.
Use: Antacid.

• **ALUMINA AND MAGNESIUM TRISILICATE ORAL SUSPENSION,** U.S.P. XXI.
Use: Antacid.

• **ALUMINA, MAGNESIA, AND CALCIUM CHLORIDE ORAL SUSPENSION,** U.S.P. XXI.
Use: Antacid.

• **ALUMINA, MAGNESIA, AND CALCIUM CARBONATE TABLETS.** U.S.P. XXI.
Use: Antacid.

ALUMINETT. (Lannett) Aluminum hydroxide 10 gr./Tab. Bot. 1000s.
Use: Antacid.

ALUMINOSTOMY. (Richards Pharm.) Aluminum pow. 18%, with zinc oxide and zinc stearate in a bland water repellent ointment. Jars 2 & 6 oz. and 1 lb.
Use: An occlusive dressing for skin protection; colostomies and ileostomies.

ALUMINUM.
See: Aluminostomy (Richards Pharm.)

ALUMINUM ACETATE.
See: Acid Mantle Creme (Dorsey)
Acid Mantle Lotion (Dorsey)
Buro-Sol, cream & powder (Doak)
W/Phenol, zinc oxide, boric acid, eucalyptol, ichthammol.
See: Lanaburn, Oint. (Lannett)
W/Salicylic acid, boric acid.

• **ALUMINUM ACETATE TOPICAL SOLUTION,** U.S.P. XXI. (Various Mfr.). Burow's Solution.
Use: Astringent.
See: Bluboro Powder (Herbert)
Buro-Sol Pow. Conc. (Doak)
Burotor, Emul. (Torch)
Domeboro, Pow. (Miles Pharm)

ALUMINUM AMINOACETATE, DIHYDROXY.
See: Dihydroxy aluminum aminoacetate (Various Mfr.)

ALUMINUM CARBONATE BASIC.
See: Basaljel, Susp. (Wyeth)

• **ALUMINUM CHLOROHYDRATE.** USAN.
Use: Anhidrotic.

• **ALUMINUM CHLOROHYDREX.** USAN.
Use: Astringent.

ALUMINUM CHLORHYDROXY ALLANTOINATE.
See: Alcloxa (Schuylkill)

• **ALUMINUM CHLORIDE,** U.S.P. XXI. Aluminum chloride hexahydrate.
Use: Astringent.
W/Oxyquinoline sulfate, benzalkonium chloride.
See: Alochor Stypic (Gordon Labs.)

ALUMINUM CLOFIBRATE. B.A.N. Di-[2-(4-chlorophenoxy)-2-methylpropionato]hydroxyaluminum
Use: Treatment of arteriosclerosis.

ALUMINUM DIHYDROXYAMINOACETATE.
See: Dihydroxy Aluminum Aminoacetate, U.S.P. XXI. (Various Mfr.)

ALUMINUM GLYCINATE, BASIC.
See: Dihydroxy Aluminum Aminoacetate, U.S.P. XXI.
W/Aspirin, & Mag. carbonate.
See: Bufferin, Tabs. (Bristol-Myers)

• **ALUMINUM HYDROXIDE GEL,** U.S.P. XXI. Aq. susp. of aluminum hydroxide equiv. to 4% aluminum oxide.
Use: Antacid.
See: ALterna GEL, Gel (Stuart)
Al-U-Creme, Susp. (MacAllister)
Aluminett, Tab. (Lannett)
Alu-Cap, Cap. (Riker)
Alu-Tab., Tab. (Riker)
Amphojel, Susp., Tab. (Wyeth)
Dialume, Cap. (Armour)
Hydroxal, Susp. (Blue Line)
No-Co-Gel, Susp. (Noyes)
Nutrajel, Bot. (Cenci)
W/Aminoacetic acid, mag. trisilicate.
See: Maracid-2, Tab. (Marin)
W/Aminophylline.
See: Asmadrin, Tab. (Jenkins)
W/Amobarbital, homatropine methylbromide, kaolin colloidal.
See: Komal, Tab. (O'Neal)
W/Atropine sulfate, mag. trisilicate, phenobarbital.
See: PAMA, Tab. (Vortech)
W/Belladonna ext., magnesium hydroxide.
See: Trialka, Liq., Tab. (Commerce)
W/Calcium carbonate.
See: Alkalade, Susp., Tab. (DePree)
W/Calcium carbonate, magnesium carbonate, magnesium trisilicate.
See: Marblen, Susp., Tab. (Fleming)
W/Dicyclomine HCl, magnesium hydroxide, methylcellulose.
See: Triactin Liquid, Tab. (Norwich)
W/Gastric mucin, Mg glycinate.
See: Mucogel, Liq., Tab. (Inwood)
W/Homatropine methylbromide.
See: Aloxed, Susp. (Vortech)
W/Clioquinol, methylcellulose, atropine sulf., hyoscine HBr, hyoscyamine sulf.
See: Enterex, Tab. (Person & Covey)

W/Kaolin, pectin.
See: Kenpectin, Syr. (Kenwood)
Metropectin, Liq. (Pennwalt)
W/Magnesium carbonate.
See: Estomul-M Liq., Tabs. (Riker)
W/Magnesium carbonate, calcium carbonate, aminoacetic acid.
See: Glycogel Tab. or Susp. (Central)
W/Magnesium hydroxide.
See: Alsorb Gel (Standex)
Aludrox, Susp., Tab. (Wyeth)
Delcid, Liq. (Merrell Dow)
Kolantyl, Gel, Wafer (Merrell Dow)
Maalox, Susp. (Rorer)
Mylanta, Tab. (Stuart)
Mylanta II, Tab. (stuart)
Neutralox, Susp. (Lemmon)
Nutramag, Liq. (Cenci)
WinGel, Liq., Tab. (Winthrop Consumer Products)
W/Magnesium hydroxide, aspirin.
See: Calciphen, Tab. (Westerfield)
Cama, Tab. (Dorsey)
Cama Inlay-Tabs. (Dorsey)
W/Magnesium hydroxide, belladonna ext.
W/Magnesium hydroxide, calcium carbonate.
See: Camalox, Susp. (Rorer)
W/Mag. hydroxide, glycine, magnesium trisilicate, belladonna ext.
W/Magnesium hydroxide and simethicone.
See: DI-GEL, Liq. (Plough.)
Maalox Plus, Susp. (Rorer)
Mylanta, Liq. (Stuart)
Mylanta-II, Liq. (Stuart)
Silain-Gel, Lig., Tab. (Robins)
Simeco, Liq. (Wyeth)
W/Magnesium trisilicate.
See: Antacid G, Tab. (Walgreen)
Antacid Tablets, Tab. (Panray)
Arcodex Antiacid, Tab. (Arcum)
Barosil, Susp. (Barry-Martin)
Gacid, Tab. (Arcum)
Malcogel, Susp. (Upjohn)
Malcotabs (Upjohn)
Manalum, Tab. (Paddock)
Neutracomp, Liq., Tab. (C.M.C.)
Trilox, Susp., Tab. (Blue Line)
Trisogel, Pulvule, Susp. (Lilly)
W/Magnesium trisilicate, atropine sulf., phenobarbital.
See: Pama, Tab. (Vortech)
W/Paregoric, kaolin (colloidal), bismuth subcarbonate, pectin, aromatics.
See: Kapinal, Tab. (Jenkins)
W/Phenindamine tartrate, phenylephrine HCl, aspirin, caffeine, magnesium carbonate.
See: Dristan, Tab. (Whitehall)
W/Phenol, zinc oxide, camphor, eucalyptol, ichthammol.
See: Almophen, Oint. (Bowman)
W/Prednisolone.
See: Fernisolone-B (Ferndale)
Predoxine, Tab. (Mallard)
W/Sodium salicylate, Acetaminophen, Vit. C.
See: Gaysal-S., Tab. (Geriatric)

• **ALUMINUM HYDROXIDE GEL, DRIED,** U.S.P. XXI. Tabs. U.S.P. XXI.
Use: Antacid.
See: Amphojel, Tab. (Wyeth)

ALUMINUM HYDROXIDE GEL, DRIED W/COMBINATIONS.
Alased, Tab. (Norgine)
Aludrox, Susp., Tab. (Wyeth)
Alurex, Tab. (Rexall)
Ascriptin, Tab. (Rorer)
Ascriptin A/D, Tab. (Rorer)
Ascriptin W/Codeine, Tab. (Rorer)
Aspadine, Tab. (Vortech)
Azolid-A, Cap. (USV Pharm.)
Banacid, Tab. (Buffington)
Buffadyne, Tab. (Lemmon)
Butazolidin Alka, Cap. (Geigy)
Calciphen, Tab. (Westerfield)
Camalox, Tab. (Rorer)
Cimadrox, Tab. (Elder)
Coralsone Modif. Tab. (Zemmer)
Decagesic, Tab. (Merck Sharp and Dohme)
Delcid, Liq. (Merrell Dow)
Estomul, Tab., Liq. (Riker)
Eugel, Tab. (Reid-Provident)
Eulcin, Tab. (Leeds)
Fermalox, Tab. (Rorer)
Gas-Eze, Tab. (Edward J. Moore)
Gaviscon, Foamtabs (Marion)
Gelumina, Tab. (APC)
Gelumina Plus, Liq. (APC)
Gelusil, Preps. (Park-Davis)
Kamadrox, Tab. (Elder)
Kamadrox Jel, Liq. (Elder)
Kao-Lumin, Tab. (Philips Roxane)
Kathmagel, Tab. (Mason)
Kenpectin, Liq. (Kenwood)
Kenpectin-P, Liq. (Kenwood)
Kolantyl, Wafers (Merrell Dow)
Kudrox, Tab., Susp. (Kremers-Urban)
Maalox, Tab. (Rorer)
Maalox Plus, Tab. (Rorer)
Magnatril, Tab., Susp. (Lannett)
Malcotabs, Tab. (Upjohn)
Metropectin, Tab. (Pennwalt)
Mylanta, Tab. and Liq. (Stuart)
Mylanta II, Tab. and Liq. (Stuart)
Neosorb Plus, Tab. (Lemmon)
Neutralox, Tab. (Lemmon)
Pama, Tab. (N. Am. Pharmacal)
Phencaset Improved, Tab. (Elder)
Presalin, Tab. (Mallard)
Silmagel, Tab. (Lannett)
Spasmasorb, Tab. (Hauck)
Syntrogel, Tab. (Block)
Trialatine, Tab. (Bowman)
Trisogel, Pulvules, Liq. (Lilly)

ALUMINUM HYDROXIDE GLYCINE.
See: Dihydroxy aluminum aminoacetate

-UMINUM HYDROXIDE MAGNESIUM CARBONATE.
See: Aloxine (O'Neal)
DI-GEL, Tab. (Plough)
Magnagel, Susp., Tab. (Mallard)
/Aminoacetic acid, calcium carbonate.
See: Eugel, Tab., Liq. (Reid-Provident)
/Dicyclomine HCl, magnesium trisilicate, methylcellulose.
See: Triactin, Liq., Tab. (Norwich)
/Magnesium trisilicate.
See: Escot, Cap. (Reid-Provident)
/Magnesium trisilicate, bismuth aluminate.
See: Escot, Cap. (Reid-Provident)

ALUMINUM MONOSTEARATE, N.F. XVI. Aluminum, dihydroxy(octadecanoato-O-)-,Dihydroxy (stearato)aluminum.

-UMINUM OXIDE.
See: Epi-Clear Scrub Cleanser (Squibb)

-UMINUM PHENOSULFONATE
See: AR-EX Cream Deodorant (Ar-Ex)

ALUMINUM PHOSPHATE GEL, U.S.P. XXI. Aluminum phosphate 4.15%.
See: Phosphajel, Susp. (Wyeth)

-UMINUM SALT OF THE AMINO ACID GLYCINE.
See: Dihydroxy aluminum aminoacetate, Prep. (Various Mfr.)

ALUMINUM SESQUICHLOROHYDRATE. USAN.
Use: Anhidrotic.

-UMINUM SODIUM CARBONATE HYDROXIDE.
See: Dihydroxyaluminum Sodium Carbonate

ALUMINUM SUBACETATE TOPICAL SOLUTION, U.S.P. XXI. (Various Mfr.) Aluminum acetate basic solution, aluminum subacetate solution.
Use: As an astringent wash.

ALUMINUM SULFATE, U.S.P. XXI.
Use: Pharmaceutic necessity for preparation of aluminum subacetate solution.

ALUMINUM ZIRCONIUM TETRACHLOROHYDREX GLY. USAN.
Use: Anhidrotic.

ALUMINUM ZIRCONIUM TRICHLOROHYDREX GLY. USAN.
Use: Anhidrotic.

-LUPENT. (Boehringer Ingelheim) Metaproterenol sulfate. Orciprenaline, B.A.N. **Metered dose inhaler.** 15 cc. **Tab.** 10 mg. or 20 mg. Bot. 100s. **Syr.** 10 mg./5 ml., Bot. pt. **Inhalant Sol.** 5%, Bot. 10 ml. Unit Dose 0.9%, 2 ml. vials.
Use: Bronchodilator.

-LURATE. (Roche) Aprobarbital 40 mg./5 ml. Alcohol 20%. Elixir: Red, Bot. 1 pt.
Use: Sedative.

-LUREX. (Rexall) Magnesium-aluminum hydroxide. **Susp.** (200 mg.-150 mg./5 cc.) Bot. 12 oz. **Tab.** (400 mg.-300 mg.) Box 50s.
Use: Relief of gastric hyperacidity.

-LU-TAB. (Riker) Aluminum hydroxide gel 600 mg./Tab. Bot. 250s.
Use: Antacid.

-LVAGEL. (Kenyon) 55% Aloe vera active principle in oint. base. Tube 2 oz., 4 oz.
Use: Topically, for sunburn, eczema, dermatitis, x-ray & radiation burns.

ALVEDIL CAPS. (Luly-Thomas) Theophylline 4 gr., pseudoephedrine HCl 50 mg., butabarbital 15 mg./Cap. Bot. 100s.
Use: Asthma.

• **ALVERINE CITRATE.** USAN. N-ethyl-3,3′-diphenyl dipropylamine citrate.
Use: Anticholinergic.
See: Spacolin, Tab. (Philips Roxane)

AL-VITE. (Drug Industries) Vit. A 10,000 I.U., D-3 400 I.U., E 25 I.U., C 200 mg., B-1 20 mg., B-2 10 mg., B-6 6 mg., Ca. Pantothenate 20 mg., niacinamide 100 mg., B-12 w/intrinsic factor conc. 0.5 u./Tab. Bot. 100s, 500s.
Use: Vitamin therapy.

AMA. (Wampole-Zeus) Antimitochondrial antibodies test by IFA. Tests 48s.
Use: Diagnostic aid in the identification of primary biliary cirrhosis.

• **AMACETAM SULFATE.** USAN.
Use: Cognition Adjuvant.

AMACID. (Kenyon) An acid protein hydrolysate prepared from casein and lactalbumin by special process which retains l-tryptophan and other essential amino acids. Bot. 4 oz., pt., gal.

• **AMADIMONE ACETATE.** USAN.
Use: Progestin.

AMARIL D SPANTAB. (Vortech) Phenlypropanolamine HC1 40 mg., phenylephrine HC1 10 mg., phenyltoloxamine citrate 15 mg., chlorpheniramine maleate 5 mg./Sustained Release Tab. Bot. 1000s.
Use: Antihistamine, decongestant.

AMARIL D SYRUP. (Vortech) Phenylpropanolamine HCl 20 mg., phenylephrine HCl 5 mg., phenyltoloxamine 7.5 mg., chlorpheniramine maleate 2.5 mg./5 ml. Bot. 4 oz., 128 oz.
Use: Antihistamine, decongestant.

AMANOZINE HCl. 2-Amino-4-anilino-s-triazine HCl.

AMANTADINE. B.A.N. 1-Adamantanamine.
Use: Antiviral agent, treatment of Parkinson's disease.
See: Symmetrel, Cap. (Du Pont)

• **AMANTADINE HYDROCHLORIDE,** U.S.P. XXI. Caps, Syr. U.S.P. XXI. 1-Adamantanamine HCl. Tricylo [3.3.1.1^{3},^{7}] decan-1-amine, HCl.
Use: Antiviral agent, treatment of Parkinson's disease.
See: Symmetrel, Caps, Syr. (Du Pont)

AMAPHEN. (Trimen) Butabarbital 50 mg., caffeine 40 mg., acetaminophen 360 mg./Cap. Bot. 100s.
Use: Analgesic.

AMARANTH. 3-Hydroxy-4-[(4-sulfo-1-naphthyl)azo]-2,7-naphthalene-disulfonic acid trisodium salt. F.D. and C. Red No. 2.
Use: Color (Not for internal use).

AMARGYL. Chlorpromazine, B.A.N.

AMARSAN. See: Acetarsone, Tab.

AMATROL LIQUID. (Vortech) Balanced amounts of levulose and dextrose w/orthophosphoric acid, stabilized at optimal pH. Bot. 3 oz., gal.
Use: Antiemetic.

AMAZONE. 1:4-Benzoquinone amidinohydrazine thiosemicarbazone hydrate. Iversal.

AMBAY. (Bay) Codeine phosphate 10 mg., bromodiphenhydramine HCl 12.5 mg., bromodiphenhydramine HCl 3.75 mg., ammonium Cl. 80 mg., potassium guaicolsulfonate 80 mg., menthol 0.5 mg./5 ml. w/alcohol 5%. Bot. 4 oz., pt., gal.
Use: Antitussive, antihistaminic.

AMBAZONE. B.A.N. 1,4-Benzoquinone amidinohydrazone thiosemicarbazone.
See: Iversal hydrate
Use: Antiseptic.

AMBENONIUM CHLORIDE. N,N'-bis-(2-Diethyl aminoethyl) oxamide bis-2-chlorobenzyl chloride. [Oxalylbis (iminoethylene)] bis [(o-chlorobenzyl)-diethylammonium] dichloride.
Use: Cholinergic for treatment of myasthenia gravis.
See: Mytelase, Cap. (Winthrop-Breon)

AMBENONIUM CHLORIDE. B.A.N. NN'-Di-[2-(N-2-chlorobenzyldiethylammonio) ethyl] oxamide dichloride.
Use: Cholinesterase inhibitor.

AMBENOXAN. B.A.N. 2-(2-Methoxyethoxyethylaminomethyl)-1,4-benzodioxan.
Use: Muscle relaxant.

AMBENYL COUGH SYRUP. (Marion) Codeine phosphate 10 mg., bromodiphendyramine HCl 12.5 mg./5 ml. w/alcohol 5%. Bot. 4 oz. pt., gal.
Use: Relief of upper respiratory symptoms and coughs associated with allergies or common cold.

AMBENYL-D. (Marion) Guaifenesin 200 mg., pseudoephedrine HCl 60 mg., dextromethorphan HBr 30 mg./10 ml. w/alcohol 9.5%. Bot. 4 oz.
Use: Antitussive, expectorant, nasal decongestant.

AMBERLITE, I.R.P.-64. (Rohm and Haas) Polacrilin.

AMBERLITE, I.R.P.-88. (Rohm and Haas) Polacrilin potassium.

AMBILHAR. Niridazole, B.A.N.

• **AMBOMYCIN.** USAN. Isolated from filtrates of *Streptomyces ambofaciens.*
Use: Anti-neoplastic agent.

AMBRAMYCIN. Tetracycline, B.A.N.

AMBROSIACEAE POLLENS.
See: Allergenic Extracts (Ragweed and related pollens) Parke, Davis

• **AMBRUTICIN.** USAN.
Use: Antifungal.

AMBUCAINE. Ambutoxate HCl.

AMBUCETAMIDE. 2-(di-n-Butylamino)-2-(p-methoxyphenyl)acetamide.

AMBUCETAMIDE. B.A.N. α-Dibutylamino-4-methoxyphenylacetamide.
Use: Antispasmodic.

• **AMBUPHYLLINE.** USAN. Theophylline compound with 2-amino-2-methyl-1-propanol. Bufylline
Use: Diuretic, Smooth muscle relaxant.

AMBUSIDE. USAN. 5-Allylsulfamoyl-2-chloro-4-(3-hydroxybut-2-enylideneamino)benzenesulfonamide.
Use: Diuretic.
See: Novohydrin

AMBUTONIUM BROMIDE. Ethyl-dimethylammonium(3-carbamyl-3,3-diphenyl propyl)-ethyl dimethylammonium bromide.

AMBUTONIUM BROMIDE. B.A.N. (3-Carbamoyl-3,3-diphenylpropyl)ethyldimethylammonium bromide.
Use: Antispasmodic.

AMBUTOXATE HYDROCHLORIDE. 2-Diethylaminoethyl-4-amino-2-butoxybenzoate HCl.

AMC. (Schlicksup) Ammonium chloride 7.5 gr./Tab. Bot. 1000s.

AMCAP. (Circle) Ampicillin trihydrate equivalent to 250 mg. ampicillin/Cap. Bot. 100s.
Use: Antibiotic.

AMCILL. (Parke-Davis) **Cap:** Ampicillin trihydrate 250 mg. or 500 mg./Cap. Bot. 100s, 500s, unit dose pkg 100s. **Oral Susp.:** 125 mg. or 250 mg./5 ml. Bot. 100 ml., 200 ml. Bot. 100 ml., 200 ml. **Ped. Drops:** 100 mg./ml. w/sod. benzoate 0.1% as preservative. Bot. 20 ml.
Use: Penicillin therapy.

• **AMCINAFAL.** USAN. 9-Fluoro-11β, 16α,17,21-tetrahydroxypregna-1,4-diene-3, 20-dione cyclic 16, 17-acetal with 3-pentanone.
Use: Anti-inflammatory.

• **AMCINAFIDE.** USAN. (R)-9-Fluoro-11β, 16α,17,21-tetrahydroxypregna-1, 4-diene-3,20-dione cyclic 16, 17-acetal with acetophenone.
Use: Anti-inflammatory.

• **AMCINONIDE,** U.S.P. XXI. Cream, Oint., U.S.P. XXI.
Use: Glucocorticoid.

AMCORT. (Keene) Triamcinolone diacetate 40 mg./ml. Vial 5 ml.
Use: Parenteral steroid.

• **AMDINOCILLIN.** USAN. 6-β-amidinopenicillanic acid.
Use: Antibacterial.
See: Cocatin, Inj. (Roche)

■ **AMEBACIDES.**
See: Acetarsone (Various Mfr.)
Aralen HCl, Inj. (Winthrop-Breon)
Aralen Phosphate, Tab. (Winthrop-Breon)
Carbarsone, Pulvule & Tab. (Lilly)
Chiniofon, Tab. (Various Mfr.)
Diiodohydroxyquin (Various Mfr.)
Diodoquin, Tab. (Searle)
Emetine HCl (Various Mfr.)
Flagyl, Tab. (Searle)
Humatin, Kapseal, Syr. (Parke-Davis)
Yodoxin, Tab. (Glenwood)

AMEBAN.
See: Carbarsone

AMEBAQUIN. (U.S. Products) Iodoquinol 650 mg./Tab.
Bot. 100s.
Use: Amebicidal activity against *Entamoeba histolytica.*

AMECHOL.
See: Methacholine Chloride

• **AMEDALIN HCl.** USAN. 3-Methyl-3-[3-(methylamino)propyl]-1-phenyl-2-indolinone monohydrochloride.
Use: Antidepressant.

MEN. (Carnrick) Medroxyprogesterone acetate 10 mg./Tab. Bot. 50s, 100s, 1000s.
Use: Progestin.

MERICAINE AEROSOL. (American Critical Care) Benzocaine 20% in a water-soluble vehicle. Bot. 0.67 oz., 2 oz, 4 oz.
Use: Topical anesthetic.

MERICAINE ANESTHETIC LUBRICANT. (American Critical Care) Benzocaine 20%, benzethonium chloride 0.1% in a water-sol. polyethylene glycol base. 2.5 Gm. Foil Pack, Pkg. 144s. Tube 1 oz.
Use: Local anesthetic.

MERICAINE FIRST AID SPRAY. (American Critical Care) Benzocaine 10%, benzethonium chloride 0.1%, alcohol 25%. Pump spray 4 oz.
Use: Topical anesthetic.

MERICAINE FIRST AID BURN OINTMENT. (American Critical Care) Benzocaine 20%, benzethonium chloride 0.1%, in a water-soluble polyethylene glycol base. Tube 0.75 oz.
Use: Local anesthetic.

MERICAINE HEMORRHOIDAL OINTMENT. (American Critical Care) Benzocaine 20% and benzethonium chloride 0.1% in a water-soluble polyethylene glycol base. Tube 1 oz. w/rectal applicator.
Use: Hemorrhoidal pain and itching.

MERICAINE OTIC. (American Critical Care) Benzethonium chloride 0.1%, Benzocaine 20% in a water-soluble base of 1% (w/w) glycerin and polyethylene glycol 300. Bot. 0.5 oz.
Use: Pain and inflammation of otitis media.

MERTAN. (Lilly) Tannic acid 5%, Merthiolate 1:5000. Tube 1 oz.
Use: Burns.

MER-TET. (Robinson) Tetracycline HCl 250 mg., 500 mg./Cap. Bot. 100s, 1000s.
Use: Antibiotic.

MER-TET SUSPENSION. (Robinson) Tetracycline HCl oral suspension 125 mg./5 ml. Bot. pt.
Use: Antibiotic.

MESEC CAPSULES. (Glaxo) Aminophylline 130 mg., ephedrine HCl 25 mg./Cap. Bot. 100s, 500s.
Use: Bronchodilator.

AMETANTRONE ACETATE. USAN.
Use: Antineoplastic.

METAZOLE. B.A.N. 3-(2-Aminoethyl)pyrazole. Betazole (I.N.N.). Histalog, hydrochloride.
Use: To stimulate gastric secretion in diagnostic tests.

-METHAPRED UNIVIAL. (Abbott) Methylprednisolone sodium succinate. 40 mg./1 ml. Pkg. 1s, 25s, 50s, 100s; 125 mg./2 ml. Pkg. 1s, 5s, 25s, 50s, 100s; 500 mg./4 ml. Pkg. 1s, 5s, 25s, 100s; 1000 mg./8 ml. Pkg. 1s, 5s, 25s 100s.
Use: Anti-inflammatory.

METHOCAINE HYDROCHLORIDE.
See: Pontocaine HCl (Winthrop-Breon)

METHOPTERIN.
See: Methotrexate (Lederle)

MFECLORAL. B.A.N. α-Methyl-N(2,2,2-trichloroethylidene)-phenethylamine.
Use: Appetite suppressant.

• **AMFENAC SODIUM.** USAN.
Use: Anti-inflammatory.

AMFEPRAMONE (I.N.N.). Diethylpropion, B.A.N.

• **AMFLUTIZOLE.** USAN.
Use: Treatment of gout.

AMFODYNE.
See: Imidecyl Iodine

• **AMFONELIC ACID.** USAN. 7-Benzyl-1-ethyl-4-oxo-1,8-naphthyridine-3-carboxylic acid.
Use: Central nervous system stimulant.

AMFRECIN. (Amfre-Grant) Sodium lauryl sulfate 0.25%, lactose 82%, papain 1%, citric acid 16%, methyl salicylate 0.25%, menthol 0.50%. Bot. 4 oz., 8 oz.
Use: Vaginal douche.

AMGENAL COUGH SYRUP. (Goldline) Bot. pt., gal.
Use: Relief of URI symptoms and coughs.

AMIBIARSON.
See: Carbarsone. (Various Mfr.)

AMICAR. (Lederle) 6-Aminocaproic acid. **Syrup** 250 mg./ml. Bot. pt. **Vial** 250 mg./ml. 20 ml. **Tab.** 500 mg./ml. Tab., Bot. 100s.
Use: Antifibrinolytic agent.

AMICARBALIDE. B.A.N. 3,3′-Diamidino-carbanilide. Diampron, isethionate.
Use: Antiprotozoan, veterinary medicine.

• **AMICLORAL.** USAN. 6-0-(2,2,2-Trichloro-1-hydroxyethyl)-α-D-glucopyranosel-4 polymer with α-D-glucopyranose.
Use: Food additive (veterinary).

• **AMICYCLINE.** USAN.
Use: Antibacterial.

• **AMIDAPSONE.** USAN. p-Sulfanilylphenyl urea.
Use: Antiviral (for poultry).

AMIDATE. (Abbott) Etomidate 2 mg./ml w/propylene glycol 35%. 20 mg./10 ml. single dose Amp.; 40 mg./20 ml. single dose Amp.; 40 mg./20 ml. Abboject syringe.
Use: Anesthesia induction.

AMIDE-VC. (Scrip) Sulfanilamide 15%, 9-aminoacridine HCl 0.2%, allantoin 1.5%. Tube: 4 oz. plus applicator.

AMIDE V/S. (Scrip) Sulfanilamide 500 mg., diiodohydroxyquin 100 mg., diethylstilbestrol 0.1 mg./Insert. Pkg. 12s.
Use: Germicidal; antifungal.

AMIDEPHRINE. B.A.N. 3-(1-Hydroxy-2-methylaminoethyl)methanesulfonanilide. Dricol.
Use: Vasoconstrictor; nasal decongestant.

• **AMIDEPHRINE MESYLATE.** USAN.
Use: Adrengergic.

AMIDOFEBRIN.
See: Aminopyrine (Various Mfr.)

AMIDONE HYDROCHLORIDE.
See: Methadone Hydrochloride (Various Mfr.)

AMIDOPYRAZOLINE.
See: Aminopyrine (Various Mfr.)

AMIDOTRIZOIC ACID. Diatrizoic Acid, B.A.N.

AMIDOTRIZOATE, SODIUM.
See: Diatrizoate Sodium

AMID-SAL. (Glenwood) Salicylamide. 3.5 gr./Tab. Bot. 100s.
Use: Analgesic, antipyretic.

• **AMIFLOXACIN.** USAN.
Use: Antibacterial.

• **AMIFLOXACIN MESYLATE.** USAN.
Use: Antibacterial.

AMIGEN. (Baxter) Protein hydrolysate 5%. Bot. 500, 1000 ml.; 10% 500, 1000 ml.; 5% w/dextrose 5% Bot. 500 ml., 1000 ml.; 5% w/dextrose 5%, alcohol 5% Bot. 1000 ml.; 5% w/fructose 10% Bot. 1000 ml.; 5% w/fructose 12.5%, alcohol 2.4% Bot. 1000 ml.
Use: Provides amino acids and calories.

• **AMIKACIN,** U.S.P. XXI.
Use: Antibacterial.

• **AMIKACIN SULFATE INJECTION.** U.S.P. XXI. 0-3-Amino-3-deoxy-α-D-glucopyranosyl(1-6)-0-(6-amino-6-deoxy-α-D-glucopyranosyl(1-4)-N-[(S)-4-amino-2-hydroxyl-1-oxobutyl]-2-deoxy-D-streptamine sulfate.
Use: Antibacterial.
See: Amikin, Inj. (Bristol)

AMIKAPRON. Tranexamic Acid, B.A.N.

AMIKIN. (Bristol) Amikacin sulfate injection. 100 mg., 500 mg., 1.0 Gm. vials., 500 mg. Disposable Syringes.
Use: Infections from gram-positive & gram-negative bacteria including pseudomonas species.

AMILORIDE. B.A.N. N-Amidino-3,5-diamino-6-chloropyrazine-2-carboxamide.
Use: Diuretic.
See: Midamor, Tab. (Merck Sharp & Dohme)
W/Hydrochlorthiazide
See: Moduretic, Tab. (Merck Sharp & Dohme)

• **AMILORIDE HYDROCHLORIDE,** U.S.P. XXI. Tab., U.S.P. XXI. Pyrazinecarboxamide,3,5-diamino-N-(aminoiminomethyl)-6-chloro-,monochloride.
Use: Antikaliuretic diuretic, antihypertensive.
See: Midamor, Tab. (Merck Sharp & Dohme)

• **AMILORIDE HYDROCHLORIDE AND HYDROCHLORTHIAZIDE TABLETS,** U.S.P. XXI.
Use: Antikaliuretic diuretic, antihypertensive.
See: Moduretic, Tab. (Merck Sharp & Dohme)

AMINA-21. (Miller) L-form amino acids 600 mg./Cap. Bot. 100s, 300s.
Use: Tissue repair.

• **AMINACRINE.** F.D.A. 9-Aminoacridine.

• **AMINACRINE HYDROCHLORIDE.** USAN. 9-Aminoacridine hydrochloride.
W/Dienestrol, sulfanilamide, allantoin.
See: AVC/Dienestrol Cream, Suppos. (Merrell Dow)
Use: Bacteriostatic agent.
W/Oxyquinoline benzoate.
See: Triva, Vag. Jelly (Boyle)
W/Sulfanilamide, allantoin.
See: AVC, Cream, Suppos. (Merrell Dow)
Femguard Vaginal Cream (Reid-Provident)
Sulfem Vag. Cream (Federal Pharm.)
Triconol Vaginal Cream (Coastal)
Vagidine, Cream (Elder)
Vagitrol, Cream, Suppos. (Lemmon)

AMIN-AID. (American McGaw) Instant drinks & puddings.
Use: Dietary aid for renal disease patients.

AMINARSONE.
See: Carbarsone (Various Mfr.)

AMINE RESIN.
See: Polyamine Methylene Resin

AMINESS. (KabiVitrum) Essential aminoacids. 10 Tab. = adult aminoacid MDR. Jar 300s.
Use: Protein restricted diet supplement.

AMINICOTIN.
See: Nicotinamide (Various Mfr.)

AMINITROZOLE. Acinitrazole, B.A.N.

AMINOACETIC ACID. Glycerine U.S.P. XXI. (Various Mfr.) (Glycine, glycocoll) available as elixir, pow. & tab.
Use: Myasthenia gravis, irrigating solution.
W/Aluminum hydroxide, magnesium hydroxide, calcium carbonate.
See: Eugel, Tab. & Liq. (Reid-Provident)
W/Calcium carbonate.
See: Antacid pH, Tab. (Towne)
Eldamint, Tab. (Elder)
W/Calcium carbonate, aluminum hydroxide, magnesium carbonate.
See: Glytabs, Tab. (Pharmics)
W/Calcium carbonate, magnesium carbonate, bismuth subcarbonate, dried aluminum hydroxide gel.
See: Buffer-Tabs (O'Neal)
W/Magnesium trisilicate, aluminum hydroxide.
See: Maracid-2, Tab. (Marin)
W/Phenylephrine HCl, pyrilamine maleate, acetylsalicylic acid, caffeine.
See: Al-Ay, Tabs. (Bowman)
W/Phenylephrine HCl, chlorpheniramine maleate, acetaminophen, caffeine.
See: Codimal, Tab. (Central)
W/Vit. B complex, C and iron.
See: Bironate-B, Cap. (Coastal)

AMINOACETIC ACID & CALCIUM CARBONATE.
W/Lysine.
See: Lycolan, Elix. (Lannett)

AMINO ACID & PROTEIN PREP.
See: Aminoacetic Acid, U.S.P. XXI.
Glutamic Acid
Histidine HCl
Lysine
Phenylalanine
Thyroxine

■ **AMINO ACIDS.**
Use: Amino-acid supplementation.
See: Aminosol, Sol. (Abbott)
Aminosyn, Sol. (Abbott)
Essential-8, Liq. (Medics)
W/Estrone, testosterone, vitamins & minerals.
See: Geramine, Tab. & Inj. (Brown)
W/Vit. B-12.
See: Stuart Amino Acids and B-12, Tab. (Stuart)

AMINOACRIDINE.
Use: Bacteriostatic agent.
See: 9-aminoacridine

9-AMINOACRIDINE HCl. (Various Mfr.)
Aminacrine HCl.
See: Vagisec Plus (J. Schmid)

/Hydrocortisone acetate, tyrothricin, phenylmercuric acetate, polysorbate-80, urea, lactose.
See: Aquacort, Vag. Supp. (Webcon)
/Iodoquinol.
See: Vagitric, Oint. (Elder)
/Phenylmercuric acetate, tyrothricin, urea, lactose.
See: Trinalis, Vag. Supp. (Webcon)
/Polyoxyethylene nonyl phenol, sodium edetate, docusate sodium.
See: Vagisec Plus, Supp. (Schmid)
/Pramoxine HCl, acetic acid, parachlorometa-xylenol, methyl-dodecylbenzyltrimethyl ammonium chloride.
See: Drotic No. 2, Drops (Ascher)
/Sulfanilamide & allantoin.
See: AVC Cream, Supp. (Merrell Dow)
Nil Vaginal Cream (Century)
Par Cream (Parmed)
Vagisan, Creme (Sandia)
Vagisul, Creme (Sheryl)
/Sulfisoxazole, allantoin.
See: Vagilia, Cream (Lemmon)
AMINOBENZENE-SULFONYLACETYLIMIDE.
See: Sulfacetamide
AMINOBENZOATE CALCIUM.
/Salicylamide, Vit. C, mephenesin.
See: Causalin, Tab. (Amfre-Grant)
AMINOBENZOATE POTASSIUM, U.S.P. XXI. Caps., for Oral Soln., Tabs., U.S.P. XXI.
See: Potaba, Pow., Tab. (Glenwood)
/Hydrocortisone, ammonium salicylate & ascorbic acid.
See: Neocylate sodium free, Tab. (Central)
/Potassium salicylate.
See: Pabalate-Sodium Free, Tab. (Robins)
/Pot. salicylate, ascorbic acid.
See: Pabalan, Tab. (Lannett)
AMINOBENZOATE SODIUM, U.S.P. XXI.
See: PABA Sod., Tab. (Various Mfr.)
/Phenobarbital, colchicine salicylate, Vit. B-1 & aspirin.
See: Doloral, Tab. (Alamed)
/Salicylamide, ascorbic acid.
See: Sylapar, Tab. (O'Neal)
/Sodium salicylate.
See: PABA-C, Tab. (Vortech)
Pabalate, Tab. (Robins)
Salpara, Tab. (Reid-Provident)
/Salicylamide, sod. salicylate, ascorbic acid, butabarbital sod.
See: Bisalate, Tab. (Allison Lab.)
AMINOBENZOIC ACID, U.S.P. XXI. Gel., Topical Soln., U.S.P. XXI. Benzoic acid, 4-amino. PABA. Available as cap., bot., pow., sol. & tab. Massengill-Sol. (10%) Bot. 1 pt.
Use: Topical protectant (sun-screening agent).
See: Pabafilm (Owen)
Pabanol, Lot. (Elder)
/Mephenisin, Salicylamide.
See: Sal-Phenesin, Tab. (Marion)
/Sod. salicylate & ascorbic acid.
See: Nucorsal, Tab. (Westerfield)

p-AMINOBENZOIC ACID, SALTS.
See: p-Aminobenzoate potassium p-Aminobenzoate sodium
• **AMINOCAPROIC ACID,** U.S.P. XXI. Syr., Inj., Tab., U.S.P. XXI. 6-Aminohexanoic acid.
Use: Antifibrinolytic, hemostatic.
See: Amicar, Syr., Tab., Vial (Lederle)
• **AMINOCAPROIC ACID.** USAN. 6-Aminohexanoic acid. Amicar. Epsikapron.
Use: Inhibitor of fibrinolytic activity.
AMINOCARDOL.
See: Aminophylline. (Various Mfr.)
AMINO CERV. (Milex) Urea 8.34%, sodium propionate 0.50%, methionine 0.83%, cystine 0.35%, inositol 0.83%, benzalkonium chloride 0.000004%, buffered to pH 5.5. Tube with applicator 2.75 oz.
Use: Mild cervicitis, postpartum cervicitis, cervical tears, post cauterization, post cryosurgery, post conization.
p-AMINO-N-[2-(DIETHYLAMINO)ETHYL]-BENZAMIDE MONOHYDROCHLORIDE. Procainamide Hydrochloride, U.S.P. XXI.
AMINODYNE COMPOUND. (Bowman) Acetaminophen 2.5 gr., aspirin 3.5 gr., caffeine 0.5 gr./Tab. Bot. 100s, 1000s.
2-AMINOETHANOL.
See: Monoethanolamine
(−)-α-(1-AMINOETHYL)-3,4-DIHYDROXYBENZYL ALCOHOL.
See: Levonordefrin
(−)-α-(AMINOETHYL)-3,4-DIHYDROXYBENZYL ALCOHOL TARTRATE. Norepinephrine Bitartrate, U.S.P. XXI.
(±)-α-(1-AMINOETHYL)-2,5-DIMETHOXYBENZYL ALCOHOL HCl. Methoxamine Hydrochloride, U.S.P. XXI.
(-)-α-(1-AMINOETHYL)-m-HYDROXYBENZYL ALCOHOL TARTRATE. Metaraminol Bitartrate, U.S.P. XXI.
AMINO-ETHYL-PROPANOL.
See: Aminoisobutanol
W/Bromotheophyllin
See: Pamabrom (Various Mfr.)
4-(2-AMINOETHYL)IMIDAZOLE BIS(DIHYDROGEN PHOSPHATE). Histamine Phosphate, U.S.P. XXI.
3-AMINO-α-ETHYL-2,4,6-TRIIODOHYDROCINNAMIC ACID. Iopanoic Acid, U.S.P. XXI.
AMINOFEN. (Dover) Acetaminophen 325 mg./Tab. Sugar, lactose and salt free. Unit Dose Box 500s.
Use: Analgesic, antipyretic.
AMINOFEN MAX. (Dover) Acetaminophen 500 mg./Tab. Sugar, lactose and salt free. Unit Dose Box 500s.
Use: Extra strength analgesic, antipyretic.
AMINOFORM.
See: Methenamine. (Various Mfr.)
AMINOGEN. (Christina) Vit. B complex & folic acid. Amp. 2 cc. Box 12s, 24s, 100s.
Vial 10 cc.
Use: Protein hydrolysate therapy.
• **AMINOGLUTETHIMIDE,** U.S.P. XXI. Tab. U.S.P. XXI. 2-(p-Aminophenyl)-2-ethylglutarimide.

Use: Treatment of Cushing's syndrome.
See: Cytadren, Prods. (Ciba)

6-AMINOHEXANOIC ACID. Aminocaprolic acid
See: Amicar, Syr., Tab., Vial (Lederle)

• **AMINOHIPPURATE SODIUM,** U.S.P. XXI. Inj., U.S.P. XXI. Glycine, N-(4-aminobenzoyl)-, monosodium salt. Monosodium p-aminohippurate. (Merck Sharp & Dohme) 2 Gm./10 ml. Amp. 10 ml., 50 ml.
Use: I.V., Diagnostic aid for renal plasma flow.

• **AMINOHIPPURIC ACID,** U.S.P. XXI. Glycine, N-(4-aminobenzoyl)-.
Use: Diagnostic aid (renal function determination).

N-[p-[[(2-AMINO-4-HYDROXY-6-PTERIDINYL)METHYL]AMINO]BENZOYL]- - -GLUTAMIC ACID. Folic Acid, U.S.P. XXI.

AMINOISOBUTANOL. 2-Amino-2-methylpronanol-1
See: Butaphyllamine
Pamabrom for combinations

AMINOISOMETRADINE. DL-2-Amino-4-(methylthio) butyric acid.
See: Methionine

(+)-4-AMINO-3-ISOXAZOLIDINONE. Cycloserine, U.S.P. XXI.

8-[(4-AMINO-1-METHYLBUTYL)AMINO]-6-METHOXYQUINOLINE PHOSPHATE. Primaquine Phosphate, U.S.P. XXI.

AMINOMETRADINE. B.A.N. 1-Allyl-6-amino-3-ethylpyrimidine-2,4-dione. Mictine.
Use: Diuretic.

AMINONAT. Protein hydrolysates (oral)

AMINONITROZOLE. N-(5-Nitro-2-thiazolyl) acetamide.
Use: Antitrichomonal.

AMINOPENTAMIDE SULFATE. 4-(Dimethylamino)-2,2-diphenylvaleramide sulfate.
Use: Anticholinergic.

7-(D-2-AMINO-2-PHENYLACETAMIDO)-3-METHYL-8-OXO-5-THIA-1-AZABICYCLO-[4.2.0.]OCT-2-ENE -2-CARBOXYLIC ACID MONOHYDRATE. Cephalexin, U.S.P. XXI.

AMINOPHYLLIN. (Searle) Trademark for Aminophylline. **100 mg.**/Tab. Bot. 100s, 1000s. Unit Dose 100s. **200 mg.**/Tab. Bot. 100s, 1000s. Unit Dose 100s.
Use: Bronchodilator.

AMINOPHYLLIN INJECTION. (Searle) Trademark for Aminophylline. Amp. **250 mg.:** 10 ml., 25s, 100s; **500 mg.:** 20 ml. 25s, 100s.
Use: Bronchodilator

• **AMINOPHYLLINE,** U.S.P. XXI. Enema, Inj., Suppos., Tabs., U.S.P. XXI. Theophylline compound w/ethylenediamine (2:1). (Aminocardol, Ammophyllin, Cardophyllin, Carena, Diophyllin, Genophyllin, Ionphylline, Metaphyllin, Phyllindon, Teholamine, Theophyldine.)
Use: Smooth muscle relaxant (bronchodilator).
See: Aminodur, Dura-Tab. (Berlex)
Lixaminol, Elix. (Ferndale)
Panamin, Tab. (Panray)
Phyllocontin, Tab. (Purdue Fredrick)
Rectalad-Aminophylline. (Wallace)
Somophyllin Oral Liquid (Fisons)
Somophyllin Rectal Solution (Fisons)

• **AMINOPHYLLINE INJECTION,** U.S.P.XXI. (Abbott) Amp. 250 mg./10 ml., 500 mg./20 ml; Fliptop vial 10 mg./20 ml., 20 mg./50 ml.
Use: Bronchodilator.

AMINOPHYLLINE COMBINATIONS.
Amphedrine Compound, Cap. (Lannett)
Asmadrin (Jenkins)
Asminorel, Tab. (Reid-Provident)
Asthmacon, Cap. (CMC)
B.M.E., Elix. (Brothers)
Bronchovent, Tab. (Mills)
Lixaminol AT/5 cc. (Ferndale)
Mudrane GG-2, Tab. (Poythress)
Orthoxine and Aminophylline, Cap. (Upjohn)
Quinamm, Tab. (Merrell Dow)
Quinite, Tab. (Reid-Provident)
Romaphed, Tab. (Robinson)
Strema, Cap. (Foy)
Theocomp, Cap. (Barry Martin)
Theo-Kaps (Scrip)

AMINOPHYLLINE WITH PHENOBARBITAL COMBINATIONS.
Amodrine, Tab. (Searle)
Mudrane, Tab. (Poythress)
Mudrane GG, Tab. (Poythress)

• **AMINOPHYLLINE INJECTION,** U.S.P. XXI. Theophylline ethylenediamine. Amp. 3¾ gr., 7.5 gr (Various Mfr.).

• **AMINOPHYLLINE SUPPOSITORIES,** U.S.P. XXI. 7.5 gr., 3⅜ gr., (Various Mfr.) Pediatric 0.125 gr. Box 12s (Wyeth).

• **AMINOPHYLLINE TABLETS,** U.S.P. XXI. Plain or enteric coated 1.5 gr., 3 gr. (Various Mfr.)

AMINOPHYLLINE-PHENOBARBITAL. (Robinson) Aminophylline 1.5 gr., phenobarbital 0.25 gr. or 0.5 gr./Tab. Bot. 100s, 1000s. Bulk Pack 5000s. Aminophylline 3 gr., phenobarbital 0.25 gr., or 0.5 gr./Tab. Bot. 100s, 1000s. Bulk Pack 5000s.

AMINOPHYLLINE-PHENOBARBITAL. (Sutliff & Case) Aminophylline 100 mg., phenobarbital 16 mg., aluminum hydroxide 32 mg./Tab. Bot. 100s, 1000s

AMINOPHYLLINE-PHENOBARBITAL No. 1. (Sutliff Case) Aminophylline 1.5 gr., Phenobarbital 0.25 gr./Tab. Bot. 100s, 1000s.

AMINOPREL. (Pasadena Research) Isolated vegetable protein 4500 mg., 1-lysine monohydrochloride 360 mg., di-methionone 90 mg., all essential amino acids, nonessential amino acids, iron 12 mg copper 1.5 mg., zinc 12 mg., iodine 0.015 mg., manganese 10 mg., potassium 20 mg., magnesium 240 mg./6 Tab. Bot. 180s.
Use: Dietary supplement.

AMINOPROMAZINE (I.N.N.). Proquamezine, B.A.N.

AMINOPTERIN SODIUM. B.A.N. Sodium N-[4-(2,4-diaminopteridin-6-ylmethyl)aminobenzoyl]-L-glutamate. Sodium N-[p-[[2,4,-(diamino-6-pteridinyl)methyl]amino]benzoyl]-L-glutamate.
Use: Antineoplastic agent.

4-AMINO-PTEROYLBLUTAMATE SOD. Aminopterin.

2-AMINOPURINE-6-THIOL.
See: Thioguanine

MINOPYRINE. Amidofebrin, Amidopyrazoline, Anafebrina, Novamidon, Pyradone. Dimethylamino-phenyl-dimethylpyrazolone.
Use: Antipyretic, analgesic.
See: Dipyrone, Vial (Maurry)
MINOQUIN NAPHTHOATE.
See: Pamaquine Naphthoate
AMINOQUINOLINE DERIVATIVES.
See: Aralen HCl (Winthrop-Breon)
Chloroquine Phosphate (Various Mfr.)
Plaquenil Sulfate (Winthrop-Breon)
Primaquine Phosphate (Winthrop-Breon)
AMINOQUINOLINE DERIVATIVES.
See: Primaquine Phosphate, U.S.P.
AMINOREX. USAN. 2-Amino-5-phenyl-2-oxazoline.
Use:Appetite suppressant.
See: Apiquel fumarate.
AMINOSALICYLATE CALCIUM, U.S.P. XXI. Cap., Tab., U.S.P. XXI. Calcium 4-Aminosalicylate (1:2) trihydrate. (Dumas-Wilson) 7.5 gr., Bot. 1000s.
Use: Tuberculosis therapy.
See: Teebacin Calcium, Tab. (CMC)
Parasal Calcium (Panray)
'/Isoniazid, pyridoxine HCl.
See: Calpas-Inah-6, Tabs. (Amer. Chem. & Drug)
MINOSALICYLATE POTASSIUM. Monopotassium 4-aminosalicylate.
Use: Antibacterial (tuberculostatic).
See: Parasal Pot., Tab. (Panray)
Paskalium, Tab. & Pow. (Glenwood)
Teebacin Kalium, Tab., Pow. (CMC)
AMINOSALICYLATE SODIUM, U.S.P. XXI. Tab., U.S.P. XXI. Aminosalicyate sodium Benzoic acid, 4-amino-2-hydroxy-, monosodium salt, dihydrate. Monosodium 4-amino-salicylate dihydrate.
Use: Tuberculostatic.
See: Neopasalate, Tab. (Mallincrodt)
Parasal Sodium, Pow., Tab., (Panray)
P.A.S., Pow. (Century)
Pasara Sod., Pow., Tab. (Dorsey)
Pasdium, Tab. (Kasar)
Teebacin, Tab., Pow. (CMC)
AMINOSALICYLIC ACID, U.S.P. XXI. Tablets, U.S.P. XXI. 4-Amino-2-hydroxybenzoic acid. PAS, p-Aminosalicylic acid. (Lilly) 500 mg. Enseal, Bot. 100s.
Use: Adjunct to streptomycin in tuberculosis.
See: Parasal, Tab., Pow. (Panray)
P.A.S. (Lilly)
P.A.S. Acid, Tab. (Kasar)
PASNA (Barnes-Hind)
Teebacin Acid, Tab. (CMC)
W/Isoniazid.
See: Di-Isopacin, Tab. (CMC)
Isopacin, Tab. (CMC)
-AMINOSALICYLIC ACID SALTS.
See: Aminosalicylate Calcium
Aminosalicylate Potassium
Aminosalicylate Sodium
MINOSYN. (Abbott) Crystalline amino acid solution. **3.5% M:** 1,000 ml.; **5%:** 250 ml., 500 ml., 1,000 ml. cont.; **7%:** 500 ml.; 7% kit (cs/3); 7% w/Electrolytes, 500 ml.; 7% w/Electrolytes, TPN kit; 10%, 500 ml.; **8.5%:** 1000 ml. w/Electrolytes 1000 ml. Single dose containers.
Use: I.V., nutritional.
AMINOSYN R.F. (Abbott) Single dose containers, 300 ml.
Use: I.V. source of protein.
AMINO-THIOL. (Marcen) Sulfur 10 mg., casein 50 mg., sod. citrate 5 mg., phenol 5 mg., benzyl alcohol 5 mg./cc. Vial 10 cc., 30 cc.
Use: Treatment of arthritis, neuritis.
AMINOTRATE PHOSPHATE. Trolnitrate phosphate.
See: Triethanolamine, preps.
AMINOXYTROPINE TROPATE HCl. Atropine-N-oxide HCl.
AMIPAQUE. (Winthrop-Breon) Metrizamide 3.75 Gm./20 ml. Vial; 6.75 Gm./50 ml. Vial; 2.5 Gm./20 ml. Vial; 13.5 Gm./100 ml. Vial.
Use: Myleography, C.T. cisternography, pediatric angiocardiography, intravenous digital arteriography.
AMIPHENAZOLE. B.A.N. 2,4-Diamino-5-phenyl-thiazole.
Use: Respiratory stimulant.
See: Daptazole
AMIPHENAZOLE HCl. 2,4-Diamino-5-phenylthiazole HCl. Daptazole.
• **AMIQUINSIN HYDROCHLORIDE.** USAN. 4-Amino-6,7-dimethoxyquinoline hydrochloride monohydrate. Under study.
Use: Antihypertensive.
AMIRON HEMATINIC. (Misemer) Ferrous fumarate 275 mg., ascorbic acid 100 mg., folic acid 1 mg., cyanocobalamine 15 mcg./Cap.
Use: Prevention & treatment of iron & folic acid deficiencies.
AMISOMETRADINE. B.A.N. 6-Amino-1,2-methylallyl-3-methylpyrimidine-2,4-dione. Rolicton.
Use: Diuretic.
AMITIN. (Thurston) Vit. C 200 mg., lemon bioflavonoid 100 mg., niacinamide 60 mg., methionine 100 mg./Tab. Bot. 100s, 500s.
Use: Dietary supplement and therapy.
AMITONE. (Norcliff Thayer) Calcium carbonate 350 mg./Tab. Bot. 100s.
Use: Antacid.
• **AMITRAZ.** USAN.
Use: Scabicide.
AMITRIL. (Parke-Davis) Amitriptyline HCl 10 mg., 25 mg., 50 mg., 75 mg., 100 mg., 150 mg./Tab. Bot. 100s, 1000s. Unit dose 100s.
Use: Antidepressant.
AMITRIPTYLINE. B.A.N. 3-(3-Dimethylamino-propylidene)dibenzo[a,d]cyclohepta-1,4-diene. Amitriptyline hydrochloride. Laroxyl. Lenitzol. Saroten. Tryptizol.
Use: Antidepressant.
See: Elegen-G, Tab. (Grafton)
• **AMITRIPTYLINE HCl.** U.S.P. XXI. Inj., Tab. U.S.P. XXI. 10,11-dihydro-N, N-dimethyl-5H-dibenzo[a,d]cycloheptene-Δ^5,γ-propylamine hydrochloride.
Use: Antidepressant.

See: Elavil HCl, Tab., Inj. (Merck Sharp & Dohme)
Endep, Tab. (Roche)
SK-Amitriptyline, Tab. (SmithKline)
W/Chlordiazepoxide.
See: Limbitrol, Tab. (Roche)
W/Perphenazine.
See: Etrafon, Prod. (Schering)
Triavil, Tabs. (Merck Sharp & Dohme)

AMMENS MEDICATED POWDER. (Bristol-Myers) Boric acid 4.55%, zinc oxide 9.10%, talc and starch. Can. 6.25 oz., 11 oz.
Use: Heat rash, prickly heat or diaper rash.

AMMOIDIN. Methoxsalen.

AMMONIA. Aromatic Ammonia Spirit, U.S.P. XXI. Strong Sol. N.F. XVI. (Lilly) 0.4 ml; pt.; Aspirols 0.4 ml. Pkg. 12s. (Burroughs-Wellcome) Vaporoles 5.41 minims in crushable glass capsule. Box 12s, 100s.
Use: Fainting.

• **AMMONIA SOLUTION, STRONG,** N.F. XVI. (Stanlabs) 28% Bot. pt., gal.
Use: Pharmaceutic aid (source of ammonia).

• **AMMONIATED MERCURY,** U.S.P. XXI. Oint., Ophth. Oint., U.S.P. XXI. (Various Mfr.)
See: Mercuronate 5% Oint. (Bowman)
W/Phenol
See: Pixacreme, Jar (Pixacol)
W/Salicylic acid.
See: Emersal, Liq. (Medco)

AMMONIUM, ALKYLDIMETHYL(PHENYL-METHYL)-, CHLORIDE. Benzalkonium Chloride, U.S.P. XXI.

AMMONIUM BENZOATE.
Use: Urinary antiseptic.

• **AMMONIUM CARBONATE,** N.F. XVI.
Use: Source of ammonia.

• **AMMONIUM CHLORIDE,** U.S.P. XXI. Inj., Tab., U.S.P. XXI. **Tab.** plain or E.C. (5 gr. & 7.5 gr.) (Various Mfr.) **Inj.:** (Cutter) 120 mEq./30 ml. Vial.
Use: Diuretic, expectorant, alkalosis.
See: Nodema Tab. (Towne)

AMMONIUM CHLORIDE, ENSEALS. (Lilly) Ammonium chloride. Timed disintegrating tablets. Enseals 7.5 gr. Bot. 100s.
Use: Acidification of the urine.

AMMONIUM MANDELATE. Ammonium salt of mandelic acid. Syrup, (8 Gm./fl. oz.) Bot pt., gal.
Use: Orally, urinary antiseptic.

• **AMMONIUM MOLYBDATE.** U.S.P. XXI. Inj., U.S.P. XXI.

AMMONIUM NITRATE.
See: Reditemp-C, Cold Pack (Wyeth)

• **AMMONIUM PHOSPHATE,** N.F. XVI. Phosphoric acid diammonium salt. Diammonium phosphate.

AMMONIUM VALERATE.
Use: Sedative.

AMMOPHYLLIN.
See: Aminophylline, U.S.P. XXI. (Various Mfr.)

AMMORID. (Kinney) Benzethonium chloride & zinc oxide in a lanolin absorption base. Tube 2 oz.
Use: Topically, dermatologic ointment.

AMMORID DIAPER RINSE. (Kinney) Methylbenzethonium chloride 5%, plus deionizing & buffering agents in dry powder form, readily solubl in water. Bot. 240 Gm.
Use: Protection against diaper rash.

• **AMOBARBITAL,** U.S.P. XXI. Elixir, Tablets, U.S.P. XXI. (Various Mfr.) 5-Ethyl-5-isoamylbarbituric acid.
Use: Hypnotic of intermediate duration.
See: Amytal, Elix., Pulvule, Tab. (Lilly)

AMOBARBITAL W/COMBINATIONS.
Amobell, Cap. (Bock)
Amodex, Cap. (Fellows)
Amo-Dexules, Cap. (Recsei)
Amoseco, Cap. (Robinson)
Amytal & Aspirin, Pulvule (Lilly)
Aspadine, Tab. (Vortech)
Asthmacon, Cap. (CMC)
Barbeloid, Tab. (Vale)
Bronchovent, Tab. (Mills)
Buffadyne A-S, Tab. (Lemmon)
Buffadyne w/Barbiturates, Tab. (Lemmon)
Butatrax, Cap. (Sutliff & Case)
Dextrobar, Tab. (Lannett)
Ectasule, Cap. (Fleming)
Hydrochol-Plus, Tab. (Elder)
Komal, Tab. (O'Neal)
Milidex, Cap. (Briar)
Monotheamin and Amytal, Pulvule (Lilly)
Obalan Lanatabs, Tab. (Lannett)
Obe-Slim, Tab. (Jenkins)
Penta-E W/Amobarb, Cap. (Recsei)
Phetabar, Cap. (Moore-Kirk)
Scoline-Amobarbital, Tab. (Westerfield)
Spancap No. 2, Cap. (Vortech)
Stim, Prep. (Scrip)
Trimex, Cap. (Mills)
Vasobarb, Cap. (Reid-Provident)

• **AMOBARBITAL SODIUM,** U.S.P. XXI. Capsules, Sterile, XXI. (Various Mfr.) 2,4,6(1H,3H,5H)-Pyrimid netrione, 5-ethyl-5-(3-me-thylbutyl)-, monosodiur salt. Sodium 5-ethyl-5-isopentylbarbiturate.
Amp.: (1⅞ gr.) 6s, 12s, 25s, 100s; (3.25 gr.) 6s, 12s, 25s, 100s; (7.5 gr.) 6s, 12s, 25s, 100s. (Various Mfr.)
Cap.: (3 gr.) Bot. 1000s. (Amer. Drug Prods.)
Pow.: Bot. 4 oz., 0.5 lb., 1 lb. Pkg. 5 lb. (Various Mfr.)
Vial: (15.5 gr.) 10 cc. (Various Mfr.)
Use: Hypnotic of intermediate duration, sedative.
See: Amytal Sod. (Lilly)
W/Ephedrine HCl, theophylline, chlorpheniramine maleate.
See: Theo-Span, Cap. (Scrip)
W/Secobarbital Sod.
See: Amsee, Tab. (Kenyon)
Compobarb, Cap. (Vitarine)
Dusotal, Cap. (Harvey)
Lanabarb, Cap. (Lannett)

AMOBARBITAL-EPHEDRINE CAPSULES. (Lannett) Amobarbital 50 mg., ephedrine sulfate 25 mg./Cap Bot. 500s, 1000s.

AMOBELL. (Bock) Amobarbital 15 mg., belladonna ext. 10 mg./Cap. Bot. 100s, 1000s.
Use: Sedative & antispasmodic.

MOCAL JR. (Jenkins) Pyrilamine maleate 3 mg., phenylephrine HCl 1 mg., tartar emetic 1/136 gr., benzoic acid 1/68 gr., ipecac pow. 1/16 gr., amm. chloride 0.5 gr., iodized Cal. 1/16 gr., licorice ext. 1 gr./Tab. Bot. 1000s.
Use: Expectorant and anodyne.

MOCILLIN. (Vortech) Crystalline penicillin G potassium, buffered w/sod. citrate, 3,000,000 u./60 cc. Bot. 60 cc.
Use: Antibiotic.

MO-DERM. (High) Mineral abrasive, lecith. neut. soap base, 3,4,4′-trichlorocarbanilide 1%, allantoin 2%. Pkg. 3.5 oz. bars.
Use: Skin cleanser.

MODEX. (Fellows) Dextroamphetamine HCl 5 mg., amobarbital 20 mg./Tab. Bot. 100s, 1000s.

AMODIAQUINE, U.S.P. XXI. 7-Chloro-4-(3-diethylaminomethyl-4-hydroxyanilino)quinoline.
Use: Antimalarial.

AMODIAQUINE HYDROCHLORIDE, U.S.P. XXI. Tab. U.S.P. XXI. 4-(7-Chloro-4-quinolylamino)-α-(Diethylamino)-o-cresol-di-HCl.
Use: Antimalarial.

MODIN. (Vortech) Adenosine-5-monophosphoric acid 25 mg., niacin 10 mg., cyanocobalamin 300 mcg., methionine 25 mg./cc. Vial 10 cc.

MODOPA TABS. (Major) Methyldopa 250 mg./Tab. Bot. 100s, 1000s; 500 mg./Tab. Bot. 100s, 500s.
Use: Antihypertensive.

MODRINE. (Searle) Aminophylline 100 mg., racephedrine HCl 25 mg., phenobarbital 8 mg./Tab. Bot. 100s.
Use: Antiasthmatic

M-O-GEL. (Vortech) Kaolin 90 gr., pectin 2 gr./oz. Bot. 4 oz., gal.
Use: Relief of simple diarrhea.

MOGEL PG. (Vortech) Pow. opium 24 mg., phenobarbital 16.2 mg., kaolin 6 Gm., pectin 142.8 mg., hyoscyamine sulfate 0.1037 mg., atropine sulfate 0.0194 mg., hyoscine HBr 0.0065 mg., sod. benzoate 60 mg. 1 oz. w/alcohol 9.1%. Bot. 4 oz., gal.
Use: Antidiarrheal.

MOL. Mono-n-amyl-hydroquinone ether.
See: B-F-I, Pow. (Calgon)

MOLINE. (Major) Aminophylline 1.5 gr./ E.C.Tab. Bot. 250s. 100 mg. or 200 mg/ Tab. Bot. 1000s.
Use: Bronchodilator.

MONIDRIN. (Forest) Ammonium chloride 200 mg., guaifenesin 100 mg./Tab. Bot. 1000s.
Use: Cough preparation.

MOPYROQUIN HCl. 4-(7-Chloro-4-quinolylamino)-a-1-pyrrolidyl-o-cresoldihydrochloride.
See: Propoquin.

MOSAN. (Oral-B) Sodium bitartrate, sodium perborate. Boxes 20, 40 single-dose packets. Liquid Drops 0.5 oz., 2 oz.
Use: Mouth and gum care.

MOSECO. (Robinson) Secobarbital & amobarbital. Bot. 100s, 1000s.
Use: Sedative.

AMOTRIPHENE. 2,3,3-Tris(p-methoxy-phenyl)-N,N-dimethylallylamine, 3-Dimethylamino-1, 1.2-tris(4-methoxyphenyl)-1-propene HCl.
Use: Coronary vasodilator.

AMOXAL. Pentalamide, B.A.N.

• **AMOXAPINE.** USAN. 2-Chloro-II-(I-piperazinyl)-dibenz[b,f][1,4]oxazepine.
Use: Antidepressant.
See: Asendin, Tab. (Lederle)

• **AMOXICILLIN.** U.S.P. XXI. Cap., Oral Susp., Sterile, For Susp., Tab., U.S.P. XXI. 6-[D-(−)2-Amino-2-(p-hydroxyphenyl)acetamido]-3,3-dimethyl-7-oxo-4-thia-1-azabicy-clo[3.2.0]heptane-2-carboxylic acid.
Use: Antibiotic.
See: Amoxil, Preps. (Beecham Labs)
Polymox, Preps. (Bristol)
Sumox, Preps. (Reid-Provident)

AMOXICILLIN TRIHYDRATE.
Use: Antibiotic
See: Amoxil Chewable, Tab. (Beecham Labs)
Augmentin, Tab., Susp. (Beecham Labs)
Polymox, Cap., Susp. (Bristol)
Trimox, Preps. (Squibb)
Utimox, Cap, Susp. (Parke-Davis)
Wymox, Cap, Liq. (Wyeth)

AMOXIL. (Beecham Labs) Amoxicillin, **Cap:** 250 mg. Bot. 100s, 500s. Unit dose 10 × 10. 500 mg. Bot. 100s, 500s. Unit dose 10 × 10. **Oral Suspension:** 125 mg. and 250 mg./5 ml. Bot. 80 ml., 100 ml., 150 ml. Unit dose 5 ml.

AMOXIL CHEWABLE TABLETS. (Beecham Labs) Amoxicillin trihydrate 125 mg./Tab., Bot. 60s. 250 mg./Tab. Bot. 100s.
Use: Antibiotic.

AMOXIL PEDIATRIC DROPS. (Beecham Labs) Amoxicillin 50 mg./ml. Bot. 15 ml., 30 ml.

AMP. Adenosine Phosphate, B.A.N.

AMPERIL. (Geneva) Ampicillin trihydrate 250 mg., 500 mg./Cap.
Bot. 100s, 500s.

• **AMPHECLORAL.** USAN. α-Methyl-N-(2,2,2-trichloroethylidene) phenethylamine.
Use: Sympathomimetic.

AMPHEDRINE COMPOUND CAPSULES. (Lannett) Aminophylline-ephedrine compound. Bot. 1000s.

AMPHENIDONE. I-(m-Aminophenyl)-2-(IH)-pyridone.
Use: Central stimulant.

AMPHETAMINE, LEVO.
See: Levamphetamine

AMPHETAMINE HYDROCHLORIDE. Rac. amphetamine HCl, methylphenethylamine HCl, dl-1-phenyl-2-aminopropane HCl, dl-methylphenethylamine HCl, rac. desoxynorephedrine HCl. **Amp.** 20 mg./cc 1 cc. (Various Mfr.) **Cap.** (Various Mfr.)
Use: Vasoconstrictor, central nervous system stimulant.

AMPHETAMINE WITH DEXTROAMPHETAMINE AS RESIN COMPLEXES.
See: Biphetamine, Cap. (Pennwalt)

AMPHETAMINE PHOSPHATE. Monobasic dl-a-methylphenethylamine phosphate. Monobasic racemic amphetamine phos.

AMPHETAMINE PHOSPHATE, DIBASIC, Racemic amphetamine phosphate. **Cap.** 5 mg., 10 mg. **Tab.** 5 mg., 10 mg. (Various Mfr.)

• **AMPHETAMINE PHOSPHATE, DEXTRO,** U.S.P. XXI. Tab., U.S.P. XXI. Dextro-amphetamine phosphate. (Various Mfr.).

• **AMPHETAMINE SULFATE,** U.S.P. XXI. Tab., U.S.P. XXI. dl-a-Methylphenethylamine sulfate. (Racemic or dl form). Cap. (5, 10 mg.) (Various Mfr.). Tab. (5, 10 mg.) (Various Mfr.). Vials (20 mg./cc.) (Various Mfr.).

AMPHETAMINE SULFATE, DEXTRO.
See: Dextroamphetamine Sulfate, U.S.P. XXI.

d-AMPHETAMINE CARBOXYMETHYLCELLULOSE SALT.
See: Bontril, T.R. Tab. (Carnrick)

d-AMPHETAMINE HYDROCHLORIDE. (Various Mfr.) Dextroamphetamine HCl. **Cap.** 5 mg., 10 mg. (Various Mfr.) **Tab.** 5 mg., 10 mg. (Various Mfr.)
Use: Vasoconstrictor, central nervous system stimulant.

levo-AMPHETAMINE.
See: Levamphetamine.

AMPHOCAPS. (Blue Cross) Ampicillin 250 mg. or 500 mg./Cap. Bot. 100s
Use: Antibiotic.

AMPHODEX. (Jamieson-McKames) d-Amphetamine sulfate 15 mg., amobarbital 45 mg., Vit. A 6,600 I.U., D 400 I.U., B-1 1.6 mg., B-2 2.5 mg., niacinamide 15.5 mg., C 30 mg., Fe sulfate 20 mg., copper sulfate 2.8 mg., sod. molybdate 0.45 mg., zinc sulfate 2.8 mg., pot. iodide 0.13 mg./T.R. Cap. Bot. 100s.
Use: Appetite depressant.

AMPHOJEL. (Wyeth) Aq. susp. of aluminum hydroxide, (320 mg./5 ml.) equivalent to 4% aluminum oxide. Bot. 12 fl. oz. Tab. 5 gr. Bot. 100s. Tab. 10 gr. Ctn. 100s. Suspension without flavor. Bot. 12 fl. oz.
Use: Gastric & duodenal ulcer or hyperacidity.

• **AMPHOMYCIN.** F.D.A. An antibiotic produced by *Streptomyces canus.* Amphocortrin.

• **AMPHOMYCIN.** USAN. An antibiotic produced by *Streptomyces canus.*
See: Ecomytrin

AMPHOTERICIN.
See: Fungizone, Prep. (Squibb)

AMPHOTERICIN. B.A.N. Polyene antibiotics isolated from a strain of a Streptomyces species, referred to as *Streptomyces nodosus.* **Amphotericin B.**
See: Fungilin
Fungizone

• **AMPHOTERICIN B,** U.S.P. XXI. Cream, Inj., Lotion, Oint., U.S.P. XXI. A polyene antibiotic substance obtained from cultures of *Streptomyces nodosus.*
Use: Antifungal.
See: Fungizone, Prep. (Squibb)
W/Tetracycline & K metaphosphate.
See: Mysteclin-F, Prep. (Squibb)

• **AMPICILLIN,** U.S.P. XXI. Caps., Oral Susp., Boluses, Sol. Powd., Sterile Susp., Tab., U.S.P. XXI. 6[(D)-α-Aminophenyl-acetamido) penicillanic acid. 6-(D-2-Amino-2-phenylacetamido)-3, 3-dimethyl-7-oxo 4-thia-1-azabicyclo [3.2.0] heptane-2-carboxylic aci
Use: Antibiotic.
See: Amcill, Prep. (Parke-Davis)
Omnipen, Prep. (Wyeth)
Penbritin, Prep. (Ayerst)
Pfizerpen A, Prep. (Pfipharmecs)
Polycillin, Prep. (Bristol)
Principen, Prep. (Squibb)
Roampicillin, Tab. (Robinson)
Roampicillin Powder, Inj. (Robinson)
Totacillin, Prep. (Beecham Labs)
W/Probenecid
See: Polycillin-PRB, Unit dose (Bristol)
Principen W/Probenecid Cap. (Squibb)
Probampacin (Robinson)
Trojacillin-Plus, Oral Susp. (Young)

• **AMPICILLIN AND PROBENECID CAPSULES,** U.S.P. XXI.

• **AMPICILLIN AND PROBENECID FOR ORAL SUSPENSION,** U.S.P. XXI.

• **AMPICILLIN SODIUM STERILE,** U.S.P. XXI.
Use: Antibiotic.
See: Omnipen-N, Inj. (Wyeth)
Pen A/N, Vial (Pfipharmecs)
Pensyn-N. Sterile (Upjohn)
Polycillin-N (Bristol Labs)
Principen/N, Vial (Squibb)
SK-Ampicillin-N, Vial (SmithKline)
Totacillin-N, Vial (Beecham Labs)

AMPICILLIN TRIHYDRATE. Caps., Oral Susp. marketed by various manufacturers.
Use: Antibiotic.

AMPICILLIN TRIHYDRATE.
See: Amcap, Cap. (Circle)
Ameril, Cap., Susp. (Geneva)
Ampi-Co, Cap. or Susp. (Coastal)
D-Amp, Cap., Susp. (Dunhall)
Pensyn, Preps. (Upjohn)
Polycillin Prep. (Bristol)
Principen, Cap., Susp. (Squibb)
Principen 250 (Squibb)
SK-Ampicillin, Prep. (SmithKline)
Supen, Cap., Susp. (Reid Provident)
Totacillin, Cap., Susp. (Beecham Labs)

AMPI-CO. (Coastal) Ampicillin trihydrate. **Caps.** 25 mg., 500 mg./Cap. Bot. 100s. **Pow. for oral Susp** 125 mg./5 cc. Bot. 80 cc. **Susp.** 250 mg./5 cc., Bot. 80 cc.
Use: Antibiotic.

AMPROL. (MSD AGVET) Amprolium 25% medicated feed; 20% soluble powder; 9.6% solution.
Use: Coccidiostat, veterinary medicine.

AMPROL HI-E. (MSD AGVET) Amprolium 25%, ethop bate 8%, medicated feed.
Use: Coccidiostat, veterinary medicine.

AMPROL PLUS. (MSD AGVET) Amprolium 25%, ethopabate 0.8%., medicated feed.
Use: Coccidiostat, veterinary medicine.

• **AMPROLIUM,** U.S.P. XXI. Oral Powder, Soluble Powder, U.S.P. XXI. 1-(4-Amino-2-propyl-5-pyrimic nylmethyl)-2-picolinium chloride.

Use: Coccidiostat, veterinary medicine.
See: Amprol (MSD AGVET)
Amprol Hi-E (MSD AGVET)
Amprol Plus (MSD AGVET)
Amprolmix (MSD AGVET)
Amprovine (MSD AGVET)
Corid (MSD AGVET)
Pancoxin hydrochloride (MSD AGVET)

MPROTROPINE PHOSPHATE. 2-Diethylamino-2,2-dimethylpropyl tropate.

MPROVINE. (MSD AGVET) Amprolium Sol. 9.6%, premix 25%, medicated feed.
Use: Coccidiostat, veterinary medicine, 20% soluble powder.

AMQUINATE. USAN.
Use: Antimalarial.

AMSACRINE. USAN.
Use: Antineoplastic.

AMRINONE. USAN.
Use: Cardiotonic.
See: Inocor Lactate Inj. (Winthrop-Breon)

MSEE. (Kenyon) Amobarbital sod. ¾ gr., secobarbital sod. ¾ gr./Cap. Bot. 100s, 1000s.
Use: Sedative.

MSEE #2. (Kenyon) Amobarbital sod. 1.5 gr., secobarbital sod. 1.5 gr./Cap. Bot. 100s, 1000s.
Use: Sedative.

M-TUSS ELIXIR. (T.E. Williams) Codeine phosphate 10 mg., phenylephrine HCl 10 mg., phenyl-propanolamine HCl 5 mg., prophenpyridamine maleate 12.5 mg., guaifenesin 44 mg., fl. ext. ipecac 0.17 min., citric acid 60 mg., sodium citrate 197 mg./5 ml. w/alcohol 5%. Bot. pt., gal.
Use: Antitussive, vasoconstrictor, antihistaminic expect.

M-WAX. (Amlab) Urea, benzocaine, propylene glycol and glycerin. Bot. 10 cc.
Use: Ear drops.

MYL. Phenyl phenol, phenyl mercuric nitrate.
See: Lubraseptic Jelly (Guardian)

AMYLASE.
/Calcium carbonate, glycine, belladonna ext.
See: Trialka, Tab. (Commerce)
/Lipase, protease, cellase, hyoscine HBr.
See: Am-Zyme, Tab. (Vortech).
/Pancreatin, protease, lipase.
See: Dizymes, Caps. (Recsei)
/Pepsin, homatropine methyl Br, lipase, protease, bile salts.
See: Digesplen, Tab., Elixir (Med. Prod. Panamericana)
/Pepsin, pancreatin, ox bile extract.
See: Gourmase, Cap. (Rowell)
/Phenobarbital, belladonna, pepsin, amylase, pancreatin, ox bile extract.
See: Gourmase-PB, Cap. (Rowell)
/Protease, lipase, simethicone.
See: Tri-Cone, Cap. (Meyer)

AMYLENE HYDRATE, N.F. XVI. Tertiary amyl alcohol. Tert-pentyl alcohol. 2-Methyl-2-butanol. (Various Mfr.).
Use: Pharmaceutic aid (solvent).

• **AMYL NITRITE,** U.S.P. XXI. Inhalant, U.S.P. XXI. Isoamyl nitrite. Isopentyl nitrite. Burroughs Wellcome—Vaporole (0.18 cc.) (0.3 cc.) Box 12s. Lilly—Aspirols (0.18 cc., 0.3 cc.) Box 12s.
Use: Inhalation, coronary vasodilator in angina pectoris.
W/Sodium nitrite, sodium thiosulfate.
See: Cyanide Antidote Pkg. (Lilly)

AMYLOCHROME TEST. (Roche Diagnostics) Colorimetric test for serum amylase with a built-in chemical standard. Box 60 tests.

AMYLOLYTIC ENZYME.
W/Butabarbital sod., belladonna ext., cellulolytic enzyme, proteolytic enzyme, lipolytic enzyme, iron oxbile.
See: Butibel-Zyme, Tab. (McNeil)
W/Calcium carbonate, glycine, proteolytic and cellulolytic enzymes.
See: Co-Gel, Tab. (Arco)
W/Cellulolytic, proteolytic and lipolytic enzymes, hyoscyamine sulfate.
See: Converspaz, Tab. (Ascher)
W/Lipase, proteolytic, cellulolytic enzymes, phenobarbital, hyoscyamine sulf., atropine sulf.
See: Arco-Lipase Plus, Tab. (Arco)
W/Proteolytic, cellulolytic, lipolytic enzymes, iron, ox bile.
See: Spaszyme, Tab. (Dooner)
W/Proteolytic enzyme. d-sorbitol.
See: Kuzyme, Cap. (Kremers-Urban)
W/Proteolytic, cellulolytic enzymes.
See: Trienzyme, Tab. (Fellows-Testagar)
W/Proteolytic enzyme, cellulolytic enzyme, lipolytic enzyme.
See: Arco-Lase, Tab. (Arco)
Zymme, Tab. (Scrip)
W/Proteolytic enzyme (Papain), homatropine methylbromide, d-sorbitol.
See: Converzyme, Liz. (Ascher)
W/Proteolytic enzyme, lipolytic enzyme, cellulolytic enzyme, & belladonna ext.
See: Mallenzyme improved, Tab. (Mallard)

AMYLOZINE. Trifluoperazine, B.A.N.

AMYTAL. (Lilly) Amobarbital. **Elixir:** 4 gr./fl. oz. w/alcohol 34%. Bot. 16 fl. oz.
Tab.:(15 mg.), Bot. 100s, 500s; (30 mg.), Bot. 100s, 1000s; (50 mg.), Bot. 100s, 500s; (100 mg.), Bot. 100s, 500s.
Use: Hypnotic.
W/Aminophylline & ephedrine HCl.
See: Amesec, Cap. (Lilly)
W/Ephedrine.
See: Ephedrine w/Amytal, Cap. (Lilly)

AMYTAL SODIUM. (Lilly) Amobarbital sodium. **Amp.:** (2 gr.) Pkg. 6s; (4 gr.) Pkg. 6s, 25s; (7.5 gr.) Pkg. 6s, 25s; (4 gr., 7.5 gr.) w/amp. of water for injection. **Pulvules:** (1 gr.) Bot. 100s, 500s (3 gr.) Bot. 100s, 500s. Blister pak 10 × 10s.
Use: Orally, I.M.; I.V., rapid-acting sedative.
W/Seconal sodium.
See: Tuinal, Cap. (Lilly)

AM-ZYME. (Vortech) Pancreatic enzyme concentrate 66 mg., amylase 6666 u., protease 6000 u., lipase

160 u., cellase 1.33 u./inner E.C. Tab.; pancreatic enzyme concentrate 34 mg., amylase 3334 u., protease 3000 u., lipase 80 u., cellase 0.67 mg., hyoscine HBr 0.006 mg. outer Tab. Bot. 100s, 1000s.
Use: Digestive aid.

ANA. (Wampole-Zeus) Antinuclear antibodies test by IFA. Tests 54s.
Use: Aid in the diagnosis of SLE and similar connective tissue disorders.

ANA HEp-2. (Wampole-Zeus) Antinuclear antibodies test by IFA. Tests 50s.
Use: Aid in the diagnosis of SLE and similar connective tissue disorders.

ANABOLEX. Stanolone, B.A.N.

■ **ANABOLIC AGENTS.** These agents stimulate constructive processes leading to retention of nitrogen and increasing the body protein.
See: Adroyd, Tab. (Parke-Davis)
Anabolin-IM, Vial (Alto)
Anadrol, Tab. (Syntex)
Anavar, Tab. (Searle)
Android, Tab. (Brown)
Crestabolic, Vial (Nutrition)
Deca-Durabolin, Amp., Vial (Organon)
Dianabol, Tab. (Ciba)
Di Genik, Vial (Savage)
Drolban, Vial (Lilly)
Durabolin, Amp., Vial (Organon)
Halotestin, Tab. (Upjohn)
Maxibolin, Elix., Tab. (Organon)
Ora-Testryl, Tab. (Squibb)
Os-Cal-Mone, Tab. (Marion)
Winstrol, Tab. (Winthrop-Breon)

W/Vitamins and minerals.
See: Dumogran, Tab. (Squibb).

ANABOLIN. (Sig) Methylandrostenediol dipropionate 50 mg., benzyl alcohol 2%, sesame oil q.s./ml. Vial 10 ml. **Aq. susp.:** Methylandrostenediol 50 mg./ml. in sodium phosphate buffer. Vial 10 ml.

ANABOLIN-IM. (Alto) Nandrolone phenpropionate 50 mg./ml. Vial 2 ml.
Use: Anabolic agent.

ANABOLIN LA-100. (Alto) Nandrolone decanoate 100 mg./ml. Vial 2 ml.
Use: Anabolic, anti-catabolic steroid.

ANACAINE. (Gordon) Benzocaine 10%. Jar. 1 oz., 1 lb.
Use: Anesthetic, antiseptic.

ANACEL. (Softcon) Tetracaine HCl 0.5%, w/Methulose (methylcellulose), preservative-benzalkonium chloride 1:10,000, & sod. chloride. Plastic containers 15 cc.
Use: Topical anesthetic in ophthalmology.

ANACIN-3 CHILDREN'S. (Whitehall) Acetaminophen. **Elixir:** 160 mg./5 ml. Bot. 2 oz., 4 oz. **Chewable Tab.:** 80 mg./Tab. Bot. 30s.
Use: Analgesic.

ANACIN-3 INFANTS. (Whitehall) Acetaminophen 80 mg./0.8 ml. Bot. 0.5 oz.
Use: Analgesic.

ANACIN-3 REGULAR STRENGTH. (Whitehall) Acetaminophen 325 mg./Tab. Bot. 24s, 50s, 100s.
Use: Analgesic.

ANACIN-3 WITH CODEINE. (Ayerst) Acetaminophen and codeine phosphate in 3 strengths: acetaminophen 325 mg., codeine phosphate 15 mg.; or acetaminophen 300 mg., codeine 30 mg.; or acetaminophen 300 mg. codeine phosphate 60 mg./Tab. Bot. 100s.
Use: Aspirin-free analgesic, antipyretic, antitussive.

ANACIN CAPSULES. (Whitehall) Aspirin 400 mg., caffeine 32 mg./Cap. Bot. 20s, 40s, 75s, 125s.
Use: Analgesic.

ANACIN MAXIMUM STRENGTH. (Whitehall) Aspirin 500 mg., caffeine 32 mg. **Tab.:** Bot. 12s, 20s, 40s, 75s, 150s. **Cap.:** 30s, 60s.
Use: Analgesic.

ANACIN-3 MAXIMUM STRENGTH. (Whitehall) Acetaminophen 500 mg., **Cap.:** 36s, 72s. **Tab.:** Tin 12s. Bot. 20s, 40s, 75s, 150s.
Use: Analgesic.

ANACIN TABLETS. (Whitehall) Aspirin 400 mg., caffeine 32 mg./Tab. Tins 12s. Bot. 30s, 50s, 100s, 200s, 300s.
Use: Analgesic.

ANADROL-50. (Syntex) Oxymetholone 50 mg./Tab. Bot. 100s.
Use: Anabolic steroid therapy.

ANAFEBRINA.
See: Aminopyrine. (Various Mfr.)

ANAFED. (Everett) **Cap.:** Chlorpheniramine maleate 8 mg., pseudoephedrine HCl 120 mg./T.R. Cap. Bot.100s. **Liq.:** Chlorpheniramine maleate 2 mg., pseudoephedrine HCl 30 mg./5 ml. Bot. pt.
Use: Antihistamine, decongestant.

ANAFER. (British Drug House) Ferrous sulfate 200 mg., Vit. C 10 mg., menadione as diacetyl derivative 1.5 mg./Tab. Bot. 100s, 1000s.
Use: Treatment of iron-deficiency anemia.

ANAFLEX. Polynoxylin, B.A.N.

ANAFRANIL. (Geigy). Under study.
See: Clomipramine HCl

• **ANAGESTONE ACETATE.** USAN. 17-Hydroxy-6α-methylpregn-4-en-20-one acetate.
See: Progestin

• **ANAGRELIDE HYDROCHLORIDE.** USAN.
Use: Antithrombotic.

ANAIDS. (Forest) Calcium carbonate 300 mg., sodium phenobarbital 9 mg./Tab. Bot. 1000s.
Use: Stomach disorders.

ANA-KIT. (Hollister-Stier) Two dose syringe which allows administration of two measured doses 0.3 ml. each, of epinephrine; four Chol-Amine tablets, each 2 mg. chlorpheniramine maleate; two sterilized swabs, tourniquet, instructions/kit.
Use: For severe potentially anaphylactic insect stings.

ANALATE. (Winston) Magnesium salicylate 600 mg./Tab. Bot. 100s.
Use: Analgesic.

ANALBALM IMPROVED FORMULA. (Central) Methyl salicylate 10%, menthol 1%, camphor 3%. Liq. Bot. 4 oz., pt., gal. Green or pink.
Use: Topically, counterirritant to reduce inflammation.

ANALEPTICS. Usually a term applied to agents with stimulant action particularly on the central nervous system. See also central nervous system stimulants.
See: Amphetamine salts (Various Mfr.)
Coramine, Amp. Liq. (Ciba)
Cylert, Tab. (Abbott)
Deaner, Tab. (Riker)
Dextroamphetamine salts (Various Mfr.)
Dopram, Vial (Robins)
Ephedrine Salts (Various Mfr.)
Methamphetamine salts (Various Mfr.)
Metrazol, Amp. (Knoll)
Nikethamide (Various Mfr.)
Pentylenetetrazol (Various Mfr.)
Picrotoxin, Amp. (Various Mfr.)
Ritalin HCl, Tab. (Ciba)
Sodium Succinate (Various Mfr.)

ANALGESIC BALM. (Various Mfr.) Menthol w/methyl salicylate in a suitable base.
A.P.C., 1.5 oz., 1 lb.
Fougera, 1 oz.
Horton & Converse, 1 oz., 1 lb.
Lilly, 1 oz., 1 lb.
Musterole (Plough)
Stanlabs, 1 oz., pt.
Wisconsin, 1 lb., 5 lb.

ANALGESIC LINIMENT. (C.M.C.) Methyl nicotinate, methyl salicylate, dipropylene glycol salicylate, menthol, camphor, oil of cassia, oleoresins, capsicum, ginger. Plastic Bot. 4 oz.

ANALGESIC LOTION. (Weeks & Leo) Methyl nicotinate 1%, methyl salicylate 10%, camphor 0.1%, menthol 0.1%. Bot. 4 oz.
Use: Relief of symptomatic pain of muscular pain, sprains, & arthritis.

ANALGESIC LIQUID. (Weeks & Leo) Triethanolamine salicylate 10% in an alcohol base. Bot. 4 oz.
Use: Relief for sore aching muscles, neuralgia, arthritis.

ANALGESIC OINTMENT "LANNETT". (Lannett) Camphor, menthol syn., methyl salicylate in lanolin petrolatum base. Tube 1 oz., Jar 1 lb., 5 lb.

ANALGESICS.
See preparations of: Acetanilid-type, Antipyrine-type, Aspirin, Salicylamide.

ANALGESINE.
See: Antipyrine (Various Mfr.)

ANALGETS. (Vale) Aspirin 64.8 mg., magnesium trisilicate 64.8 mg./Tab. Bot. 100s, 1000s, 5000s.
Use: Analgesic.

ANALGIC-C. (Kenyon) Salicylamide 250 mg., acetaminophen 250 mg., ascorbic acid 25 mg./Tab. Bot. 100s, 1000s.
Use: Analgesic.

ANALUCIN. (Lincoln) Pentetrazol 100 mg./cc. Vial 10 cc.
Use: I.M., Subcut. Senile confusion.

ANAMINE T.D. CAPSULES. (Mayrand) Chlorpheniramine maleate 8 mg., pseudoephedrine HCl 20 mg./T.D. Cap. Bot. 100s.

ANAMINE SYRUP. (Mayrand) Chlorpheniramine maleate 2 mg., pseudoephedrine HCl 30 mg./5 cc. Bot. pt.

ANAPAP. (Fellows) Acetaminophen 325 mg./Tab. Bot. 100s, 1000s.
Use: Analgesic.

ANAPOLON. Oxymetholone, B.A.N.

ANAPREL. Rescinnamine, B.A.N.

ANAPROTIN. Stanolone, B.A.N.

ANAPROX. (Syntex) Naproxen sodium 275 mg./Tab. Bot. 100s, 500s. Blister pkg. 100s.
Use: Analgesic.

ANAREL. Guanadrel sulfate.

ANAROL. (Kenyon) Acetaminophen 120 mg./5 cc. Bot. 4 oz.
Use: Analgesic, antipyretic.

ANASPAZ. (Ascher) l-Hyoscyamine sulfate 0.125 mg./Tab. Bot. 100s, 500s.
Use: Antispasmodic, anticholinergic therapy for the hyperactive G.I. tract.

ANASPAZ PB. (Ascher) l-Hyoscyamine sulfate 0.125 mg., phenobarbital 15.0 mg./Tab. Bot. 100s, 500s.
Use: Antispasmodic, anticholinergic therapy with sedative for the hyperactive G.I. tract.

ANATUSS SYRUP. (Mayrand) Acetaminophen 130 mg., dextromethorphan HBr 5 mg., phenylephrine HCl 5 mg., phenylpropanolamine HCl 12.5 mg., chlorpheniramine maleate 2 mg., guaifenesin 25 mg./5 cc w/alcohol 12%. Bot. 4 oz., pt.
Use: Decongestant.

ANATUSS TABS. (Mayrand) Guaifenesin 50 mg., acetaminophen 300 mg., dextromethrorphan HBr 10 mg., phenylephrine HCl 5 mg., phenylpropanolamine HCl 25 mg., chlorpheniramine maleate 2 mg./Tab. Bot. 100s, 500s.
Use: Relief of cough.

ANAVAR. (Searle) Oxandrolone. 2.5 mg./Tab. Bot. 100s.
Use: Anabolic agent.

ANAYODIN.
See: Chiniofon

ANAZOLE TABLETS. (Winthrop Products) Stanozolol.
Use: Anabolic steroid.

• **ANAZOLENE SODIUM.** USAN. 4-[(4-Anilino-5-sulfo-1-naphthyl)azo]-5-hydroxy-2,7-naphthalenedisulfonic acid trisodium salt. (2) C.I. acid blue 92 trisodium salt. Sodium Anoxynaphthonate, B.A.N.
Use: Diagnostic aid (blood volume and cardiac output).
See: Coomassie Blue (Ayerst)

ANBESOL GEL. (Whitehall) Benzocaine 6.3%, phenol 0.5%, alcohol 70%. Tube 0.25 oz.
Use: Antiseptic, anesthetic.

ANBESOL LIQUID. (Whitehall) Benzocaine 6.3%, phenol 0.5%, povidone-iodine 0.04%, alcohol 70%. Bot. 0.31 oz., 0.74 oz.
Use: Antiseptic, anesthetic.

ANCARIS. Thenium Closylate, B.A.N.

ANCEF. (SmithKline) Cefazolin sodium. **Vials** equivalent to 250 mg., 500 mg., or 1 Gm. of cefazolin; **Multi Packs:** 500 mg., or 1 Gm./Pack. 25s.; **Bulk Vials:** 5 Gm., 10 Gm.; **Piggyback Vials:**

500 mg., or 1 Gm./100 ml. **Minibags:** 1 Gm./50 ml. w/5% dextrose injection (D5W).
Use: Antibiotic.

ANCID TABLET AND SUSPENSION. (Sheryl) Calcium aluminum carbonate, di-amino acetate complex. Tab. 100s, Susp. 1 pt.
Use: Antacid.

ANCOBON. (Roche) Flucytosine 250 mg., 500 mg./Cap. Bot. 100s.
Use: Serious Candida and/or Cryptococcus infections.

ANCOLAN DIHYDROCHLORIDE. Meclozine, B.A.N.

ANCOLOXIN. Meclozine, B.A.N.

• **ANCROD.** USAN. An active principle obtained from the venom of the Malayan pitviper Agkistrodon rhodostoma.
Use: Anticoagulant.
See: Arvin

ANDESTERONE SUSPENSION. (Lincoln) Estrone 2 mg., testosterone 6 mg./cc. Vial 15 cc. **Forte:** Estrone 1 mg., Testosterone 20 mg./cc. Inj. vial 15 cc.
Use: I.M. hormone therapy.

ANDOIN. (Ulmer) Allantoin 1% w/vitamin A & D in ointment base. 2 oz., 1 lb.
Use: Topically, stimulates granulation.

ANDRENEX. (Pasadena Research) Adrenal cortex w/biological activity equiv. to hydrocortisone acetate 100 or 200 mcg./cc. Vial 10 cc., 30 cc.
Use: Hypoadrenal conditions.

ANDREST 90–4. (Seatrace) Testosterone enanthate 90 mg., estradiol valerate 4 mg./ml. Vial 10 cc.

ANDRIOL INJECTION. (Reid-Provident) Methandriol dipropionate 50 mg./cc. Vial 10 cc.
Use: Treatment of senile and postmenopausal osteoporosis.

ANDRO 100. (Forest) Testosterone 100 mg./ml. Vial 10 ml.

ANDRO L.A. 200. (Forest) Testosterone enanthate 200 mg./ml. Vial 10 ml.

ANDRO-CYP 100. (Keene) Testosterone cypionate 100 mg./ml. Bot. 10 ml.
Use: I.M. long acting androgen therapy.

ANDRO-CYP 200. (Keene) Testosterone cypionate 200 mg./ml. Bot. 10 ml.
Use: I.M. long acting androgen therapy.

ANDRO FEM. (Pasadena Research) Testosterone cypionate 50 mg., estradiol cypionate 2 mg., chlorobutanol 0.5%, cotton seed oil./ml. Vial ml.
Use: Menopause; osteoporosis.

ANDROGEN-860 INJECTION. (Blue Line) Testosterone cypionate 100 mg., benzyl alcohol 0.9% in cottonseed oil/cc. Vial 10 cc.

■ **ANDROGENS.** Substances which possess masculinizing activities.
See: Methyltestosterone
Testosterone
Testosterone cyclopentylpropionate
Testosterone enanthate
Testosterone heptanoate
Testosterone phenylacetate
Testosterone propionate

■ **ANDROGEN-ESTROGEN THERAPY.**
See: Dienestrol with Methyltestosterone
Duomed-P.A., Vial (Medics)
Estradiol Esters with Methyltestosterone
Estradiol Esters with Testosterone
Estrogenic Substance, Conjugated with Methyltestosterone
Estrogenic Substance Mixed with Methyltestosterone
Estrogenic Substance Mixed with Testosterone
Estrone with Testosterone
Gynetone, Tab. (Schering)

ANDROGYN L.A. (Forest) Testosterone enanthate 9[illegible] mg., estradiol valerate 4 mg./ml. in sesame oil. Via[illegible] 10 ml.

ANDROID-5, 10 and 25. (Brown) Methyltestosterone [illegible] mg./Buccal Tab., 10 mg./Tab. & 25 mg./Tab. Bot. 60s, 250s.
Use: Impotence due to androgenic deficiency.

ANDROID-F. (Brown) Fluoxymeterone 10 mg./Tab. Bo[illegible] 60s.
Use: Impotence due to androgenic deficiency, prevention postpartum breast pain and engorgement.

ANDROID HCG. (Brown) Human chorionic gonadotropin 10,000 u. w/diluent. Vial 10 cc.

ANDROID-T. (Brown) Testosterone 50 mg., 100 mg./cc Aq. susp. Vial 10 cc.

ANDROLAN AQUEOUS. (Lannett) Testosterone 25 mg., 50 mg., 100 mg./cc. susp. Vials 10 cc.
Use: I.M., androgen therapy.

ANDROLAN IN OIL. (Lannett) Testosterone propionate 25 mg., 50 mg., 100 mg./cc. in oil. Vials 10 cc.
Use: I.M. androgen therapy.

ANDROLIN. (Lincoln) Testosterone 100 mg./cc. Vial 10 cc.
Use: I.M., androgen therapy.

ANDROLONE. (Keene) Nandrolone phenpropionate 25 mg./ml. in sesame oil. Vial 5 ml.
Use: Anabolic agent.

ANDROLONE 50. (Keene) Nandrolone phenpropionate 50 mg./ml. in sesame oil. Vial 2 ml
Use: Prolonged anabolic stimulation.

ANDROLONE-D 100. (Keene) Nandrolone decanoate 100 mg./ml. in sesame oil. Vial 2 ml.
Use: I.M. anabolic maintenance.

ANDRONAQ-50. (Central) Testosterone 50 mg., sodium carboxymethylcellulose 2 mg., methylcellulose 0.3 mg., povidone 0.3 mg., docusate sodium 0.15 mg., thimerosal 0.08 mg./ml. Vial 10 ml. Box 12s.
Use: I.M., androgen therapy.

ANDRONAQ LA. (Central)Testosterone cypionate 100 mg. w/benzyl alchohol 0.9% in cottonseed oil. Vial 10 ml. Pkg. 10s.
Use: I.M. androgen therapy.

ANDRONATE. (Pasadena Research) Testosterone cypionate 100 mg., 200 mg., benzyl alcohol 9 mg./cc. 200 mg. also contains benzyl benzoate 0.2 cc., in cotton seed oil. Multi Dose Vial 10 cc.
Use: Androgen therapy.

IDRONE. (Rocky Mtn.) Testosterone 25 mg., estrone 2 mg./cc. Vial 10 cc.

IDRONEX. (Tunex) Methandriol dipropionate 50 mg./ml. Vial 10 cc.
Use: Treatment of senile and post menopausal osteoporosis.

IDROSTALONE. Mestanolone, B.A.N.

NDROSTANAZOLE.
See: Stanozolol.

NDROSTANE-17-(beta)-ol-3one.
See: Stanolone

NDROSTANOLONE. (I.N.N.) Stanolone.

NDROST-4-EN-3-ONE, 17-(3-CYCLOPENTYL-1-OXOPROPOXY)-,(17β)-. Testosterone Cypionate, U.S.P. XXI.

NDROST-4-EN-3-ONE,9-FLUORO-11,17-DIHYDROXY-17-METHYL-,(11β,17β)-. Fluoxymesterone, U.S.P. XXI.

NDROST-4-EN-3-ONE,17-HYDROXY-17-METHYL-,(17β)-. Methyltesterone, U.S.P. XXI.

NDROST-4-EN-3-ONE,17-(1-OXOHEPTYL)-OXY-,(17β)-. Testosterone Enanthate, U.S.P. XXI.

NDROSTENOPYRAZOLE. Anabolic steroid; pending release.

NDROTEST P.
See: Testosterone Propionate.

NDRYL. (Keene) Testosterone enanthate, 200 mg./ml. Vial 10 ml.
Use: Androgen.

NDYLATE FORTE. (Vita Elixir) Acetaminophen 3 gr., salicylamide 3 gr., caffeine 0.25 gr./Tab.
Use: Antipyretic, analgesic, circulatory stimulant.

NDYLATE RUB. (Vita Elixir) Methylnicotinate, methylsalicylate, camphor, dipropyleneglycol salicylate, oil of cassia, oleoresion of capsicum, oleoresin of ginger.
Use: Temporary relief of minor aches and pain.

NDYLATE TABLETS. (Vita Elixir) Sodium salicylate 10 gr.
Use: Antipyretic, analgesic.

NECAL CREAM. (Lannett) Benzocaine 3%, calamine 5%, zinc oxide 5%. Jar 1 lb.

NECTINE. Suxamethonium Chloride, B.A.N.

NECTINE. (Burroughs Wellcome) Succinylcholine chloride. Sterile Sol. (20 mg./ml.) 10 ml. Vials multiple dose Sterile Pow. Flo-Pak. 500 or 1000 mg. Box 12s.
Use: I.V., short-acting skeletal muscle relaxant.

NEFRIN NASAL SPRAY. (Walgreen) Phenylephrine HCl 0.5%, pheniramine maleate 0.2%. Bot. 0.5 oz.
Use: Antihistaminic, decongestant.

NEFRIN NASAL SPRAY, LONG ACTING. (Walgreen) Oxymetazoline HCl 0.05%. Bot. 0.5 oz.
Use: Relief of nasal congestion.

ANELEP-O.D. (Trimen) Phenytoin 250 mg./Cap. Bot. 100s.
Use: Anticonvulsant in epilepsy.

ANERGAN 25. (Forest) Promethazine HCl 25 mg./ml. Vial 10 ml.

ANERGAN 50. (Forest) Promethazine HCl 50 mg./ml. Vial 10 ml.

ANERTAN.
See: Testosterone Propionate.

ANBESOL BABY GEL. (Whitehall) Benzocain 7.5%. Tube 0.25 oz.
Use: For teething pain in infants and small children.

ANESTACON. (Webcon) Lidocaine HCl 20 mg./ml. Bot. 15 ml. 12s., 240 ml.
Use: Anesthesia of urethral mucosa.

ANESTHESIN. Ethyl-p-aminobenzoate.
Use: Local anesthetic.
See: Benzocaine, U.S.P. XXI.

ANETHAINE.
See: Pontocaine Hydrochloride (Winthrop-Breon)

• **ANETHOLE,** N.F. XVI. p-Propenylanisole. Benzene, 1-methoxy-4-(1-propenyl)-.
Use: Flavor.

ANEURINE HYDROCHLORIDE.
See: Thiamine HCl, Prep.
(Various Mfr.)

ANEXSIA W/CODEINE. (Beecham Labs) Codeine phosphate 30 mg., aspirin 325 mg./Tab. Bot. 100s.
Use: Analgesic.

ANEXSIA-D. (Beecham Labs) Hydrocodone bitartrate 7 mg., aspirin 325 mg./Tab. Bot. 100s, 1000s.
Use: Analgesic.

ANGEL SWEET. (Garrett) Cosmetic topical aerosol cream of Vitamins A and D_2. 90 Gm.
Use: Protective cream.

ANGEN. (Davis & Sly) Estrone 2 mg., testosterone 25 mg./cc. Aq. susp. Vial 10 cc.
Use: S. C., estrogen and androgen therapy.

ANGERIN. (Kingsbay) Nitroglycerin 1 mg./Cap. Bot. 60s.
Use: Coronary vasodilator.

ANGEX. (Janssen) Lidoflazine.
Use: Coronary vasodilator.

ANGIJEN GREEN. (Jenkins) Pentaerythritol tetranitrate 10 mg., 20 mg./Tab. Bot. 1000s.
Use: Hypertension.

ANGIJEN S.C. SALMON. (Jenkins) Pentaerythritol tetranitrate 10 mg., phenobarbital 8 mg./Tab. Bot. 1000s.

ANGIJEN NO. 1. (Jenkins) Pentaerythritol tetranitrate 20 mg., phenobarbital 15. mg./Tab. Bot. 1000s.
Use: Hypertension.

ANGIL. (Kenyon) Pentaerythritol tetranitrate 10 mg., mephobarbital 0.25 gr., phenobarbital ⅛ gr./Tab. Bot. 100s, 1000s.
Use: Vasodilation.

ANGINAR. (Pasadena Research) Erythrityl tetranitrate 10 mg./Tab. Bot. 100s, 1000s. 15 mg./Tab. Bot. 100s. 10 mg. w/Phenobarbital 15 mg./Tab. Bot. 100s.
Use: Prophylaxis and long term treatment of angina pectoris.

ANGIOGRAPHIN. Diatrizoic Acid, B.A.N.

ANGIOTENSIN AMIDE. B.A.N. Val^5-hypertensin II-Asp-β-amide.
Use: Hypertensive.
See: Hypertensin (Ciba)

• **ANGIOTENSIN AMIDE.** USAN. 1-L-asparaginyl-5-L-valyl angiotensin octapeptide. 1L-asparagine-5-L-Valine angiotensin.

ANGIOTENSIN IMMUTOPE KIT I-125. (Squibb) 200 test kits.
Use: Diagnostic-radioimmunoassay.

ANGIOVIST 282. (Berlex) Diatrizoate meglumine 600 mg., edetate calcium 0.1 mg./ml. Vial 50 ml., 100 ml., or 150 ml. Box 10s.
Use: Diagnostic radiopaque medium for parenteral use.

ANGIOVIST 292. (Berlex) Diatrizoate meglumine 520 mg., diatrizoate sodium 80 mg., edetate calcium disodium 0.1 mg./ml. Vial 30 ml., 50 ml., or 100 ml. Box 10s.
Use: Diagnostic radiopaque medium for parenteral use.

ANGIOVIST 370. (Berlex) Diatrizoate meglumine 660 mg., diatrizoate sodium 100 mg., edetate calcium disodium 0.1 mg./ml. Vial 50 ml., 100 ml., 150ml. or 200 ml. Box 10s.
Use: Diagnostic radiopaque medium for parenteral use.

ANGITAB. (Moore Kirk) Pentaerythritol tetranitrate 10 mg., triple-barb (phentobarbital sod., butarbital sod., phenobarbital sod. each 33.5%) 8 mg./Tab. Bot. 100s, 1000s.
Use: Coronary vasodilator to prevent attacks of angina pectoris.

ANGITRATE. (Moore Kirk) Pentaerythritol tetranitrate 10 mg., 20 mg./Tab. Bot. 100s, 1000s.
Use: Coronary vasodilator.

ANGOLON HYDROCHLORIDE. Imolamine, B.A.N.

ANG-O-SPAN. (Scrip) Nitroglycerin 2.5 mg./Cap. Bot.: 100s.

ANHYDROHYDROXYPROGESTERONE. Ethisterone.
Use: Corpus luteum hormone deficiency, threatened abortion.

ANHYDRON. (Lilly) Cyclothiazide 2 mg./Tab. Bot. 100s, 1000s.
Use: Diuretic.

• **ANIDOXIME.** USAN. 3-Diethylaminopropiophenone-O-(p-methoxyphenylcarbamoyl)oxime.
Use: Analgesic.
See: Bamoxine (U.S.V. Pharm.)

A-NIL. (Vangard) Codeine phosphate 10 mg., bromodiphenydramine HC1 3.75 mg., diphenhydramine HCl 8.75 mg., ammonium chloride 80 mg., potassium guaiacolsulfonate 80 mg., menthol 0.5 mg./5 ml. w/alcohol 5%. Bot. Pts. Gal.
Use: Antitussive, expectorant.

• **ANILERIDINE,** U.S.P. XXI. Inj., U.S.P. XXI. 4-Piperidinecarboxylic acid, 1-[2-(4-aminophenyl)ethyl]-4-phenyl-ethyl ester. Ethyl 1-(p-amino-phenethyl)-4-phenylisonipecotate. Available as the phosphate salt for injection.
Use: Analgesic.
See: Leritine Injection (Merck Sharp & Dohme)

• **ANILERIDINE HCl,** U.S.P. XXI. Tab., U.S.P. XXI. 1-(4-aminophenethyl)-4-phenylisonipecotic acid ethyl ester.
Use: Analgesic.
See: Leritine HCl, Tab. (Merck Sharp & Dohme).

• **ANILOPAM HYDROCHLORIDE.** USAN.
Use: Analgesic.

ANION EXCHANGE RESINS.
See: Polyamine-Methylene Resin

• **ANIRACETAM.** USAN.
Use: Mental performance enhancer

• **ANIROLAC.** USAN.
Use: Anti-inflammatory, analgesic.

• **ANISE OIL,** N.F. XVI.
Use: Flavor.

ANISINDIONE. 2-p-Anisyl indandione-1,3,2-(p-methoxyphenyl) indane-1,3-dione.
Use: Anticoagulant.

ANISINDIONE. B.A.N. 2-(4-Methoxyphenyl)-indane-1,3-dione.
Use: Anticoagulant.
See: Miradon, Tab. (Schering)

ANISOPYRADAMINE.
See: Pyrilamine Maleate

• **ANISOTROPINE.** F.D.A. Tropine 2-propylvalerate.

• **ANISOTROPINE METHYLBROMIDE.** USAN. Octatropine Methylbromide, B.A.N. 2-Propyl-pentanoyl tropinium methylbromide. 8-Methyltropinium bromide 2 Propylvalerate.
Use: Anticholinergic.
See: Valpin 50, Tab. (Du Pont)
W/Phenobarbital.
See: Valpin 50-PB, Tab. (Du Pont)

2-p-ANISYLINDANDIONE-1,3.
See: Miradon, Tabs. (Schering)

• **ANITRAZAFEN.** USAN.
Use: Anti-inflammatory.

ANOCAINE. (Mallard) Benzocaine, zinc oxide, bismuth subgallate, boric acid, peruvian balsam/Supp. Box 12s.

ANODYNINE. Antipyrine

ANODYNON.
See: Ethyl Chloride

ANODYNOS. (Buffington) Aspirin, salicylamide, caffeine/Tab. Sugar, lactose and salt free. Dispens-A-Kit 500s. Bot. 100s, 500s.
Use: Analgesic, antipyretic, and anti-inflammatory.

ANODYNOS-DHC TABLETS. (Berlex) Hydrocodone bitartrate 5 mg., aspirin 230 mg., acetaminophen 150 mg., caffeine 30 mg./Tab. Bot. 100s.
Use: Narcotic, analgesic, antitussive.

ANODYNOS FORTE. (Buffington) Chlorpheniramine maleate, phenylephrine HCl, salicylamide, acetaminophen, caffeine/Tab. Sugar, lactose and salt free. Dispens-A-Kit 500s. Bot. 100s.
Use: Decongestant, antipyretic, antihistaminic and analgesic for treatment of cold, hay fever and sinusitis relief.

ANOQUAN. (Mallard) Butalbital 50 mg., caffeine 40 mg., acetaminophen 325 mg./Cap. Bot. 100s, 1000s.
Use: Analgesic-sedative.

ANOREX. (Dunhall) Phendimetrazine 35 mg./Tab. Bot. 100s.
Use: Anorectic.

ANOREXIGENIC AGENTS. Appetite depressants.
See: Amphetamine Preps.
Didrex, Tab. (Upjohn)
Plegine, Tab. (Ayerst)
Preludin HCl (Boehringer Ingelheim)
Sanorex, Tab. (Sandoz)
Tenuate (Merrell Dow)
Tepanil, Tab. (Riker)
Wilpo, Tab. (Dorsey)

NOVLAR. Norethindrone plus ethinylestradiol.
Use: Oral contraceptive.

ANOXOMER. USAN.
Use: Pharmaceutic aid.

NOXYNAPHTHONATE SODIUM. Anazolene Sodium.

NQUIL. Benperidol, B.A.N.

NSPOR. (SmithKline) Cephradine (a semisynthetic cephalosporin) **Caps.** 250 mg./Cap. Bot. 100s. Unit dose 100s. 500 mg./Cap. Bot. 20s, 100s. Unit dose 100s. **Oral Susp.** 125 mg., and 250 mg./5 ml. Bot. 100 ml.
Use: Antibiotic.

NTABUSE. (Ayerst) Disulfiram 250 mg./Tab. Bot. 100s; 500 mg./Tab. Bot. 50s, 1000s.
Use: Orally, in alcoholism.

NTACID. (Zenith) Aluminum hydroxide 3¾ gr., Mg trisilicate 7.5 gr./Tab. Bot. 100s.
Use: Antacid.

NTACID #2. (Richlyn) Calcium carbonate 5.5 gr., magnesium carbonate 2.5 gr./Tab. Bot. 100s.
Use: Antacid.

NTACID NO. 6. (Bowman) Ca carbonate 0.42 Gm., glycine 0.18 Gm./Tab. Bot. 100s.

NTACID. (Walgreen) Calcium carbonate 300 mg./Tab. Bot. 100s.
Use: Relief of heartburn, sour stomach and/or acid indigestion.

NTACID M LIQUID. (Walgreen) Aluminum oxide 0.2 g., magnesium hydroxide 0.1 g/1 Tsp. Bot. 12 oz.
Use: Antacid.

NTACID POWDER. (DeWitt) Bot. 4 oz.
Use: For heartburn and acid indigestion.

NTACID RELIEF TABLETS. (Walgreen) Dihydroxyaluminum sodium carbonate 334 mg./Tab. Bot. 75s.
Use: Relief of acid indigestion, heartburn.

NTACID TABLETS. (Sutliff & Case) Ca carbonate 0.42 Gm., glycine 0.18 Gm./Chewable Tab. Bot. 100s, 1000s.

■ **ANTACIDS.** A drug that neutralizes excess gastric acid.
See: Alka-Seltzer, Tab. (Miles)
Alka-Seltzer Plus, Tab. (Miles)
Alka-Seltzer Special Effervescent Antacid, Tab. (Miles)
Alka-2 Chewable Antacid, Tab. (Miles)
Aluminum Hydroxide Gel (Various Mfr.)
Aluminum Hydroxide Gel W/Combinations (Various Mfr.)
Aluminum Hydroxide Gel Dried (Various Mfr.)
Aluminum Hydroxide Gel Dried W/Combinations (Various Mfr.)
Aluminum Hydroxide Magnesium Carbonate, Tab. (Various Mfr.)
Aluminum Phosphate Gel (Wyeth)
Aluminum Proteinate, Tab. (Rowell)
Amitone, Tab. (Norcliff Thayer)
Calcium Carbonate, Precipitated (Various Mfr.)
Calcium Carbonate Tablets (Various Mfr.)
Carbamine (Key Pharm.)
Ceo-Two, Supp. (Beutlich)
Chooz, Gum Tab. (Plough)
Citrocarbonate, Liq. (Upjohn)
Dicarbosil, Tab. (Arch)
Di-Gel, Liq., Tab. (Plough)
Dihydroxyaluminum Aminoacetate (Various Mfr.)
Dihydroxyaluminum Sodium Carbonate, Tab. (Warner-Lambert)
Magaldrate, Tab., Susp. (Ayerst)
Magnesium Carbonate (Various Mfr.)
Magnesium Glycinate, Tab. (Various Mfr.)
Magnesium Hydroxide (Various Mfr.)
Magnesium Oxide, Tab., Cap. (Various Mfr.)
Magnesium Trisilicate (Various Mfr.)
Neutralox, Susp. (Lemmon)
Oxaine, Susp. (Wyeth)
Ratio, Tab. (Adria)
Rolaids, Tab. (Warner-Lambert)
Romach, Tab. (ROR Pharmacal)
Sodium Bicarbonate, Inj., Tab. (Various Mfr.)
Tums, Tab. (Norcliff Thayer)

ANTACID SPECIAL NO. 1. (Jenkins) Mg carbonate 3 gr., Ca carbonate 2 gr., bismuth subcarbonate 1 gr., cerium oxalate 0.5 gr./Tab. Bot. 1000s.

ANTACID TABLETS. (Panray) Mg trisilicate 500 mg., aluminum hydroxide gel 250 mg./Tab. Bot. 500s, 1000s.

ANTACID W/PHENOBARBITAL. (Archer-Taylor) Mg hydroxide 0.3 Gm., Ca carbonate 9.3 Gm., atropine 0.2 mg., phenobarbital 8 mg./Tab. Bot. 1000s.
Use: Antacid and sedative.

ANTA GEL. (Blue Cross) Aluminum hydroxide 200 mg., magnesium hydroxide 200 mg., simethicone 20 mg./5 ml. Bot. 12 oz.
Use: Antacid, antiflatulant.

ANTA-GEL II. (Blue Cross) Aluminum hydroxide 400 mg., magnesium hydroxide 400 mg., simethicone 30 mg./5 ml. Bot. 12 oz.
Use: Antiflatulant, antacid.

■ **ANTAGONISTS OF CURARIFORM DRUGS.**
See: Neostigmine Methylsulfate
Tensilon Chloride (Roche)

ANTASTAN.
See: Antazoline Hydrochloride, U.S.P. XXI.

ANTAZOLINE. B.A.N. N-Phenylbenzylamino-methyl-2-imidazoline.
Use: Antihistamine.
See: Antistin
Histostab

ANTAZOLINE HYDROCHLORIDE. Antastan. 2(N-Benzylanilinomethyl)-2-imidazoline HCl.
See: Arithmin, Tab. (Lannett)

• **ANTAZOLINE PHOSPHATE,** U.S.P. XXI. 2-[(N-Benzylanilino)methyl]-2-imidazoline dihydrogen phosphate.
Use: Antihistaminic.
See: Arithmin, Inj. (Lannett)
W/Naphazoline, boric acid, phenylmercuric acetate sod. chloride, sod. carbonate anhydrous.
See: Vasocon-A Ophthalmic, Sol. (Smith, Miller & Patch)
W/Naphazoline HCl, polyvinyl alcohol.
See: Albalon-A Liquifilm, Ophth. Sol. (Allergan)

ANTEPAR. (Burroughs Wellcome) Piperazine citrate. **Syr.** equiv. to 100 mg. of piperazine hexahydrate/ml. Bot. 1 pt. **Tab.** (500 mg.) Bot. 100s.
Use: Orally; anthelmintic, to eradicate pinworms and roundworms.

ANTERIOR PITUITARY.
See: Pituitary, Anterior.

ANTHATEST. (Kay) Testosterone enanthate, oil sol. 200 mg./ml. Vial 10 ml.
Use: Testosterone supplement.

ANTHELMINTIC. A remedy for worms.
See: Alcopara, Granules (Burroughs Wellcome)
Antepar, Preps. (Burroughs Wellcome)
Antiminth, Susp. (Roerig)
Atabrine, Tab. (Winthrop-Breon)
Betanaphthol Benzoate (Various Mfr.)
Carbon Tetrachloride (Various Mfr.)
Gentian Violet
Hetrazan, Tab. (Lederle)
Jayne's PW Vermifuge (Glenbrook)
Jayne's RW, Tab. (Glenbrook)
Mintezol, Tab., Susp. (Merck Sharp & Dohme)
Piperazine Prep. (Various Mfr.)
Povan, Tab., Susp. (Parke-Davis)
Terramycin (Various Mfr.)
Tetrachloroethylene

■ **ANTHELMINTICS, VETERINARY USE.** (MSD AGVET)
See: Camvet (MSD AGVET)
Equizole (MSD AGVET)
Equizole A (MSD AGVET)
Equizole B (MSD AGVET)
Omnizole (MSD AGVET)
TBZ (MSD AGVET)
TBZ-2 (MSD AGVET)
TBZ-6 (MSD AGVET)
Thibenzole (MSD AGVET)
Thibenzole 100 (MSD AGVET)
Thibenzole 200 (MSD AGVET)

• **ANTHELMYCIN.** USAN.
Use: Anthelmintic.

ANTHELVET. Tetramisole HCl.

ANTHICAL. Mepyramine, B.A.N.

ANTHIPHEN. Dichlorophen, B.A.N.

ANTHISAN. Mepyramine, B.A.N.
See: Pyrilamine Maleate

ANTHRA-DERM. (Dermik) Anthralin 0.1%, 0.25%,0.-5%, 1.0% in petrolatum ointment base. Tube 1.5 oz.
Use: Psoriasis.

• **ANTHRALIN,** U.S.P. XXI. Ointment. U.S.P. XXI. 1,8,9-Anthracenetriol. Cignolin, Dithranol, Dihydroxy Anthranol.
Use: Treatment of psoriasis.
See: Anthra-Derm Ointment (Dermik)
Lasan, Cream (Stiefel)
W/Mineral oil
See: Lasan Pomade (Stiefel)

ANTHRALIN PASTE 0.2%. (Durel) Anthralin 0.2%, salicylic acid 0.2%, paraffin 5.0%, Lassar's paste q.s. Jars 1 oz., 1 lb.
Use: Enzyme metabolism inhibition and reduction of mitotic turnover.

ANTHRALIN POMADE 0.4%. (Durel) Anthralin 0.4% salicylic acid 0.4%, sodium lauryl sulfate, 2.1%, cetyl alcohol 21.9%, mineral oil q.s. Bot. 4 oz., 1 oz.
Use: Enzyme metabolism inhibition and reduction of mitotic turnover.

• **ANTHRAMYCIN.** USAN.
Use: Antineoplastic.

ANTHRAQUINONE OF CASCARA.
See: Cascara Sagrada products

ARTHROTRIN TABLETS. (Whiteworth) Enteric coated aspirin 325 mg./Tab. Bot. 100s.
Use: Analgesic.

ANTIACID. (Hillcrest North) Aluminum hydroxide, Mg trisilicate, Ca carbonate. Tab. Bot. 100s.

ANTI-ACID NO. 1. (Vortech) Ca carbonate 3.5 gr., M carbonate 2.5 gr., bismuth subnitrate 0.5 gr., aromatics q.s./Tab. Bot. 100s, 1000s.
Use: Antacid.

ANTI-ALLERGY CAPSULES. (Robinson) Phenylephrine HCl 2.5 mg., phenylpropanolamine HCl 25 mg. pyrilamine maleate 10 mg., chlorpheniramine maleate 2 mg., phenylpyridine HCl 10 mg./Cap. Bot. 100s, 1000s.
Use: Antihistamine.

ANTI-ALLERGY TABLET. (Walgreen) Phenylpropanolamine HCl 18.7 mg., chlorpheniramine maleate 2 mg./Tab. Bot. 24s.
Use: Decongestant, antihistamine.

■ **ANTIARTHRITIC HORMONES.**
See: Alphadrol, Tab. (Upjohn)
Aristocort, Prep. (Lederle)
Celestone, Prep. (Schering)
Decadron, Tab., Inj. (Merck Sharp & Dohme)
Dexamethasone (Various Mfr.)
Fluprednisolone (Various Mfr.)
Haldrone, Tab. (Lilly)
Kenacort, Prep. (Squibb)
Medrol, Prep. (Upjohn)
Methylprednisolone, Prep. (Upjohn)
Prednisolone (Various Mfr.)
Prednisone (Various Mfr.)
Pregnenolone Acetate (Various Mfr.)
Thiodyne, Inj. (Savage)

ANTI-ASTHMA TABLETS. (Panray) Theophylline 130 mg., ephedrine HCl 25 mg., phenobarbital 8 mg./Tab. Bot. 1000s.

ANTIASTHMATIC COMBINATIONS.
See: Cromolyn Sodium, Cap. (Various Mfr.)
Decadron Respihaler, Aer. (Merck Sharp & Dohme)
Ephedrine HCl (Various Mfr.)
Ephedrine Sulfate (Various Mfr.)
Isoephedrine HCl (Various Mfr.)
Isoetharine (Winthrop-Breon)
Isoetharine HCl (Winthrop-Breon)
Isoetharine Mesylate (Winthrop-Breon)
Isoproterenol HCl (Various Mfr.)
Isoproterenol Sulfate (Various Mfr.)
Methoxyphenamine HCl (Various Mfr.)
Phenylephrine HCl (Various Mfr.)
Phenylpropanolamine HCl (Various Mfr.)
Pseudoephedrine HCl (Various Mfr.)
Racephedrine HCl (Various Mfr.)

NTIASTHMATIC INHALANT.
See: AsthmaHaler (Norcliff Thayer)
AsthmaNefrin, Sol. (Norcliff Thayer)

NTI-B. (Eckerd) Phenylephrine HCl 0.5%, pyrilamine maleate 0.5%. **Nasal Spray.** Xylometazoline HCl 0.1%. Bot. 20 cc., 40 cc. **Troches** cetylpyridinium Cl, benzocaine 10 mg., d-methorphan. Bot. 10s, 20s.
Use: Nasal decongestant.

NTI-B MIST. (Eckerd) Phenylephrine HCl 0.5%, pyrilamine maleate 0.5%, cetalkonium chloride 0.02%, thimerosal 0.002%.

NTIBACTERIAL SERUMS.
See: Hypertussis Serum
Influenzae Antihaemophilus Type B Serum

NTIBASON.
See: Methylthiouracil (Various Mfr.)

NTIBIOPTO. (Softcon) Chloramphenicol 0.5% **Ophthalmic soln.** Bot. 7.5 cc. **Sterile Ophthalmic Oint.** Chloramphenicol 10 mg. (1.0%) in a special base of liquid petrolatum and polyethylene/Gm. Tube 3.5 Gm.
Use: Antibiotic for eye infections.

ANTIBIOTICS
See: Amoxicillin (Various Mfr.)
Amphotericin B (Squibb)
Ampicillin (Various Mfr.)
Ampicillin Sodium (Various Mfr.)
Ampicillin Trihydrate (Various Mfr.)
Anspor, Cap., Susp. (SmithKline)
Bacitracin (Various Mfr.)
Benzathine Penicillin G (Various Mfr.)
Carbenicillin Disodium, Inj., (Various Mfr.)
Carbenicillin Idanyl Sodium, Tab. (Roerig)
Cefadroxil (Bristol, Mead Johnson)
Cefazolin Sodium, Vial (Various Mfr.)
Cephalexin (Lilly)
Cephalexin Monohydrate, Pulvule, Susp. (Lilly)
Cephaloglycin Dihydrate, Pulvule (Lilly)
Cephaloridine (Lilly)
Cephalothin, Sodium, Vial (Lilly)
Chloramphenicol (Various Mfr.)
Chloramphenicol Sodium Succinate, Inj. (Various Mfr.)
Chlortetracycline HCl (Lederle)
Clindamycin (Upjohn)
Cloxpan, Cap. (Beecham Labs)
Colistimethate Sodium, Inj. (Parke-Davis)
Colistin Sulfate, Ophth., Susp. (Various Mfr.)
Demecycline (Lederle)
Demethylchlortetracycline HCl (Lederle)
Dicloxacillin, Cap., Susp. (Various Mfr.)
Doxycycline (Various Mfr.)
Duricef, Cap. (Mead Johnson)
Erythromycin (Various Mfr.)
Erythromycin Ethylsuccinate (Abbott, Ross)
Erythromycin Lactobionate for Injection (Abbott)
Erythromycin Stearate, Tab. (Various Mfr.)
Flucytosine, Cap. (Roche)
Gentamicin Sulfate (Schering)
Griseofulvin, Tab., Susp. (Various Mfr.)
Griseofulvin Microcry., Tab., Cap. (Various Mfr.)
Hetacillin (Bristol-Myers)
Kanamycin Sulfate, Cap., Inj. (Bristol-Myers)
Ledercillin VK, Prod. (Lederle)
Lincomycin (Upjohn)
Mefoxin, Inj. (Merck Sharp & Dohme)
Methacycline HCl, Cap., Syr. (Wallace)
Methicillin Sodium, Vial, Pow. (Various Mfr.)
Minocycline, Cap. (Lederle)
Nafcillin, Sodium, Vial, Cap., Pow. (Wyeth)
NegGram, Prod. (Winthrop-Breon)
Nalidixic Acid, N.F.
Neomycin Sulfate, Tab., Sol. (Various Mfr.)
Novobiocin (Various Mfr.)
Novobiocin Calcium (Upjohn)
Novobiocin Sodium, Cap. (Upjohn)
Nystatin (Various Mfr.)
Oxacillin, Sodium (Various Mfr.)
Oxytetracycline (Pfizer)
Paromomycin, Cap., Syr. (Parke-Davis)
Penicillin G, Potassium (Various Mfr.)
Penicillin G, Potassium W/Comb. (Various Mfr.)
Penicillin G, Procaine (Various Mfr.)
Penicillin G, Procaine W/Comb. (Various Mfr.)
Penicillin G, Sodium (Various Mfr.)
Penicillin V Potassium (Various Mfr.)
Phenethicillin Potassium, Tab., Pow., Sol. (Various Mfr.)
Phenoxymethyl Penicillin (Various Mfr.)
Polymyxin B Sulfate (Various Mfr.)
Rifampin, Cap. (Various Mfr.)
Rolitetracycline (Various Mfr.)
Seromycin, Pulvule (Lilly)
Sodium Cloxacillin, Cap., Sol. (Bristol-Myers)
Streptomycin Sulfate (Various Mfr.)
Tetracycline (Various Mfr.)
Tetracycline HCl (Various Mfr.)
Tetracycline Phosphate Complex (Various Mfr.)
Triacetyloleandomycin (Various Mfr.)
Troleandomycin, Cap., Susp. (Various Mfr.)
Vancomycin HCl (Lilly)

■ **ANTIBIOTICS, VETERINARY USE.**
See: Oxytetracycline (Merck Animal Health)
Penstrep (Merck Animal Health)
Pro-Penstrep (Merck Animal Health)
Sulfastrep w/sulfonamides (Merck Animal Health)

Tresaderm w/thiabendazole, dexamethasone & neomycin. (Merck Animal Health)
Vetstrep (Merck Animal Health)

ANTICEPHALGICS. Agents used to prevent or cure a headache usually of the recurring type over the region of the external carotid artery.
See: Cafergot, Supp., Tab. (Sandoz)
DHE-45, Inj. (Sandoz)
Gynergen, Amp., Tab. (Sandoz)
Sansert, Tab. (Sandoz)
Wigraine, Tab., Supp. (Organon)

ANTI-CHLOR. (Galen) Chlorprophenpyridamine maleate 4 mg./Tab. Bot. 100s, 1000s.
Use: Hay fever, urticaria, allergic eczema, drug sensitivity, serum sickness.

■ **ANTICHOLINERGIC AGENTS.** Parasympatholytic agents.
See: Akineton (Knoll)
Antrenyl Bromide (Ciba)
Artane HCl (Lederle)
Atropine preps.
Banthine Bromide (Searle)
Belladonna preps.
Cantil Preps. (Merrell Dow)
Cogentin (Merck Sharp & Dohme)
Daricon, Tab. (Beecham Labs)
Dicyclomine HCl (Various Mfr.)
Disipal (Riker)
Donabarb Sr., Cap. (Elder)
Homatropine methylbromide
Hybephen, Prods. (Beecham Labs)
Kemadrin, Tab. (Burroughs Wellcome)
Kinesed, Tab. (Stuart)
L-Hyoscyamine, Tab. (Kremers-Urban)
Murel, Amp. (Ayerst)
Norflex, Inj., Tab. (Riker)
Oxyphencyclimine HCl (Various Mfr.)
Pagitane HCl, Tab. (Lilly)
Pamine Bromide, Tab., Sol. (Upjohn)
Panparnit HCl
Parsidol HCl, Tab. (Parke-Davis)
Pathilon (Lederle)
Phenoxene HCl (Merrell Dow)
Prantal Methylsulfate, Tab. (Schering)
Pro-Banthine Bromide, Preps. (Searle)
Robinul, Tab., Inj. (Robins)
Scopolamine methylbromide
Scopolamine methylbromide HBr.
Spasmate, Tab. (Spencer-Mead)
Spasmolin, Tab., Cap. (Spencer-Mead)
Spasmolin TDC, Cap. (Spencer-Mead)
Tral, Preps. (Abbott)
Trihexyphenidyl HCl (Various Mfr.)
Trocinate, Tab. (Polythress)
Valpin 50, Tab. (Du Pont)
Valpin 50-PB, Tab. (Du Pont)

ANTICHOLINESTERASE TOXICITY ANTIDOTE.
See: Protopam Chloride, vial (Ayerst)

• **ANTICOAGULANT CITRATE DEXTROSE SOLUTION,** U.S.P. XXI.
Use: Anticoagulant for storage of whole blood.
See: A.C.D. Solution. (Various Mfr.)

• **ANTICOAGULANT CITRATE PHOSPHATE DEXTROSE ADENINE SOLUTION,** U.S.P. XXI.
Use: Anticoagulant for storage of whole blood.

• **ANTICOAGULANT CITRATE PHOSPHATE DEXTROSE SOLUTION,** U.S.P. XXI.
Use: Anticoagulant for storage of whole blood.

• **ANTICOAGULANT HEPARIN SOLUTION,** U.S.P. XXI.
Use: Anticoagulant for storage of whole blood.

■ **ANTICOAGULANTS.**
See: Acenocoumarin
Anisindione
Bishydroxycoumarin (Various Mfr.)
Calciparine, Inj. (American Critical Care)
Coumadin, Amp., Tab. (Du Pont)
Depo-Heparin, Sod. (Upjohn)
Dicumarol (Various Mfr.)
Dipaxin, Tab. (Upjohn)
Diphenadione
Eridione, Tab. (Eric, Kirk & Gary)
Ethyl Biscoumacetate, Tab.
Hedulin, Tab. (Merrell Dow)
Hemostatics
Heparin, Sod. (Various Mfr.)
Liquamar, Tab. (Organon)
Liquaemin Sod., Vial (Organon)
Miradon, Tab. (Schering)
Panheprin, Amp., Vial (Abbott)
Panwarfin, Tab. (Abbott)
Phenindione, Tab. (Various Mfr.)
Warfarin (Various Mfr.)

• **ANTICOAGULANT SODIUM CITRATE SOLUTION** U.S.P. XXI. Anticoagulant (plasma and blood, fractionation).

■ **ANTICONVULSANTS.** Agents that inhibit muscular spasms originating in the central nervous system.
See: Amytal Sodium, Ampul (Lilly)
Celontin, Cap. (Parke-Davis)
Depakene, Liq., Tab. (Abbott)
Dilantin, Preps. (Parke-Davis)
Gemonil, Tabs. (Abbott)
Glutamic Acid (Various Mfr.)
Magnesium sulf.
Mephobarbital
Mesantoin, Tab. (Sandoz)
Milontin, Cap. (Parke-Davis)
Paradione, Cap., Sol. (Abbott)
Peganone, Tab. (Abbott)
Phenurone, Tab. (Abbott)
Phenytoin, Susp., Tab. (Various Mfr.)
Phenytoin Sodium, Cap. (Various Mfr.)
Phenobarbital (Various Mfr.)
Tegretol, Tab. (Geigy)
Tridione, Cap., Dulcet, Sol., Tab. (Abbott)
Valium, Tab. (Roche)
Zarontin, Cap., Syrup (Parke-Davis)

■ **ANTIDEPRESSANTS.**
See: Amitid, Tab. (Squibb)
Amitriptyline HCl (Various Mfr.)
Aventyl HCl Pulv., Liq. (Lilly)
Deaner, Tab. (Riker)
Deprol, Tab., (Wallace)

Desipramine HCl, Cap., Tab. (Var. Mfr.)
Elavil Tab., Injection (Merck Sharp & Dohme)
Imipramine HCl, Amp., Tab. (Var. Mfr.)
Imipramine Pamoate, Cap. (Geigy)
Marplan, Tab. (Roche)
Mono-amine oxidase inhibitors
Nardil, Tab. (Parke-Davis)
Niamid, Tab. (Pfizer)
Norpramin, Preps. (Merrell Dow)
Pamelor, Cap., Liq. (Sandoz)
Parnate Sulf., Tab. (SmithKline)
Pertofrane, Cap. (USV)
Presamine, Tab. (USV)
Protriptyline HCl (Merck Sharp & Dohme)
Ritalin, Tab., Vial (Ciba)
Sinequan, Caps. (Pfizer)
Tofranil, Amp., Tab. (Geigy)
Tofranil-PM, Cap. (Geigy)
Triavil, Tab. (Merck Sharp & Dohme)
Vivactil, Tab. (Merck Sharp & Dohme)

ANTIDIARRHEICS.
See: Attapulgite, Activated (Various Mfr.)
B.K.Z., Elix., Tab. (Sutliff & Case)
Cantil, Liq., Tab. (Merrell Dow)
Coly-Mycin S, Oral Susp., (Parke-Davis)
Corrective Mixture, Liq. (Beecham Labs)
Corrective Mixture with Paregoric, Liq. (Beecham Labs)
DIA-Quel Liq. (Inter. Pharm. Corp.)
Diastay, Tab. (Elder)
Diastop, Liq. (Elder)
Diatrol, Tab. (Otis-Clapp)
Donnagel, Susp. (Robins)
Donnagel-PG (Robins)
Furoxone Liq., Tab. (Eaton)
Homapin, Preps. (Mission)
Infatol Pink, Liq. (Scherer)
Kaolin (Various Mfr.)
Kaolin Colloidal (Various Mfr.)
Kaomin, Pow. (Lilly)
Kaopectate, Susp. (Upjohn)
Keotin, Susp. (Blue Line)
Lactinex, Tab., Granule (Hynson, Westcott & Dunning)
Lactobacillus acidophilus & *bulgaricus* mixed culture, Tab. (Hynson, Westcott & Dunning)
Lactobacillus acidophilus, viable culture (Various Mfr.)
Lomotil, Liq., Tab., (Searle & Co.)
Milk of Bismuth. (Various Mfr.)
Mycifradin Sulfate, Sol., Tab. (Upjohn)
Palsorb Improved, Liq. (Hauck)
Paocin, Susp. (Massengill)
Paregel, Liq. (Ferndale)
Parelixer, Liq. (Purdue-Fredericks)
Parepectolin, Susp. (Rorer)
Pectocel, Susp. (Lilly)
Pektamalt, Susp. (Warren-Teed)
Pepto-Bismol, Liq. & Tab. (Norwich)
Polymagma, Susp., Tab. (Wyeth)
Sorboquel, Tab. (Schering)

■ **ANTIDIURETICS.**
See: Pitressin, Amp. (Parke-Davis)
Pitressin Tannate In Oil, Amp. (Parke-Davis)
Pituitary Post. Inj. (Various Mfr.)

ANTIDOL. Ethosalamide, B.A.N.

ANTIDOTE, NARCOTIC.
See: Nalline Prods (Merck Sharp & Dohme)

■ **ANTIEMETICS.**
See: Antinauseants

ANTIEPILEPTIC AGENT.
See: Anticonvulsants

ANTIFEBRIN.
See: Acetanilid (Various Mfr.)

■ **ANTIFLATULENTS.**
See: Di-Gel, Prods. (Plough)
Silain, Tab., Gel (Robins)
Simethicone Prods.

ANTIFOAM A COMPOUND. (Merrell Dow)
Use: Antiflatulent.
See: Simethicone, U.S.P. XXI.

ANTIFOLIC ACID.
See: Methotrexate, Tab. (Lederle)

ANTIFORMIN. Alkaline solution of sod. hypochlorite in sod. hydroxide 7.5%; available chlorine 5.2%; may be colored with meta cresol purple.

■ **ANTIFUNGAL AGENTS.**
See: Fungicides

• **ANTIHEMOPHILIC FACTOR,** U.S.P. XXI. Human antihemophilic factor. (Hyland & Alpha Therapeutics) Antihemophilic Factor, human. Method for Syringe Adm. 10 ml. 450 A.H.F. or 300 A.H.F. units/Pkg. W/Syringe 30 ml. or 900 A.H.F. u/Pkg.
Use: Antihemophilic.
See: Factorate, Vial (Armour)
Hemofil, Vial (Hyland)
Humafac, Vial (Parke-Davis)
Koate, Vial (Cutter)

ANTIHEPARIN. Protamine Sulfate.

ANTIHISTAMINE CREAM. (Towne) Methapyrilene HCl 10 mg., pyrilamine maleate 5 mg., allantoin 2 mg., diperodon HCl 2.5 mg., benzocaine 10 mg., menthol 2 mg./Gm. Cream. Jar 2 oz.
Use: Skin rashes and itching.

■ **ANTIHISTAMINES.**
See: Actidil, Tab., Syr. (Burroughs Wellcome)
Ambodryl, Kapseal (Parke-Davis)
Benadryl HCl, Preps. (Parke-Davis)
Chlorpheniramine Maleate (Various Mfr.)
Chlorpheniramine Maleate W/Comb. (Various Mfr.)
Clistin, Elix., Tabs. (McNeil)
Co-Pyronil, Pulvule, Susp. (Lilly)
Diafen, Tab. (Riker)
Dimetane, Preps. (Robins)
Diphenhydramine HCl (Various Mfr.)
Diphenylpyraline HCl (Various Mfr.)
Disophrol, Prod. (Schering)
Doxylamine Succinate (Merrell Dow)
Drixoral, Prod. (Schering)
Forhistal Maleate, Syr., Tab. (Ciba)
Inhiston, Tab. (Plough)

Methapyrilene Salts (Various Mfr.)
Novahistine LP, Tab. (Merrell Dow)
Optimine, Prod. (Schering)
PBZ, Tab. (Geigy)
PPZ-SR, Tab. (Geigy)
Periactin, Syr., Tab. (Merck Sharp & Dohme)
Promethazine HCl (Various Mfr.)
Prophenpyridamine Maleate (Various Mfr.)
Pyrilamine Maleate (Various Mfr.)
Tripelennamine HCl (Various Mfr.)
Triprolidine HCl (Various Mfr.)

■ **ANTIHYPERTENSIVES.**
See: Hypertension Therapy.

ANTI-ITCH CREAM. (Spencer-Mead) Burow's solution 5%, phenol 0.5%, menthol 0.5%, camphor 1% in washable base. Tube 1 oz.

ANTI-ITCH LOTION. (Towne) Diphenhydramine HCl 1%, pramoxine HCl 0.5%, titanium dioxide 1%, zinc oxide 4%. Lot. Bot. 4 oz.

ANTILEPROTICS.
See: Hansen's disease.

ANTILERGE. (Metz) Chlorpheniramine maleate 8 mg., phenylephrine HCl 12 mg./Tab. Bot. 30s.
Use: Antihistamine, decongestant.

ANTILEUKEMIA.
See: Antineoplastic Agents

ANTILIRIUM. (Forest) Physostigmine salicylate 2 mg./2 ml. Amp. Box. 12s.
Use: Parasympathomimetic.

ANTILUSIN. Pentamethonium Iodide, B.A.N.

■ **ANTIMALARIAL AGENTS.**
See: Amodiaquin HCl
Aralen HCl, Tab. (Winthrop-Breon)
Aralen Phosphate and Aralen Phosphate W/Primaquine (Winthrop-Breon)
Atabrine Hydrochloride, Tab. (Winthrop-Breon)
Chloroguanide Hydrochloride.
Chloroquine Phosphate (Winthrop-Breon)
Daraprim Tab. (Burroughs Wellcome)
Hydroxychloroquine Sulfate
Paludrine HCl, Tab. (Ayerst)
Pamaquine Naphthoate.
Plaquenil Sulfate, Tab. (Winthrop-Breon)
Plasmochin Naphthoate.
Primaquine Phosphate, Tab. (Winthrop-Breon)
Pyrimethamine
Quinacrine Hydrochloride, Tab.
Quinine Salts (Various Mfr.)
Quinine Sulfate (Various Mfr.)
Totaquine, Pow.

ANTIME. (Rand) Pentaerythritol tetranitrate 30 mg. or 80 mg./Cap. Bot. 60s, 500s.
Use: Smooth muscle relaxant.

ANTIME FORTE. (Rand) Pentaerythritol tetranitrate 30 mg., secobarbital 50 mg./Cap. Bot. 60s, 500s.
Use: Smooth muscle relaxant.

ANTIMINTH. (Pfipharmecs) Pyrantel pamoate 250 mg./5 ml. Bot. 5 ml.
Use: Anthelminitic.

• **ANTIMONY POTASSIUM TARTRATE,** U.S.P. XXI. Antimonate (2-), bis[u-[2,3-dihydroxybutanedioato (4-)-0,0:0,0]]-di-, dipotassium, trihydrate, stereoisomer. Dipotassium bis[u-tar-trato(4-)] diantimonate (2-) trihydrate. Tartar emetic. (Various Mfr.)
Use: Schistosomiasis, leishmaniasis, expectorant & emetic.
W/Cocillana, euphorbia pilulifera, squill, senega.
See: Cylana, Syr. (Bowman)
W/Guaifensin, codeine phosphate.
See: Cheracol, Syr. (Upjohn)
W/Guaifenesin, dextromethorphan HBr.
See: Cheracol-D, Syr. (Upjohn)
W/Paregoric, glycyrrhiza fl. ext.
See: Brown Mixture (Lilly)
W/Thenylpyramine HCl, ammonium chloride, sod. citrate, menthol, aromatics.
See: Histacomp, Syr., Tab. (Approved Pharm.)

■ **ANTIMONY PREPARATIONS.**
See: Antimony Potassium Tartrate (Various Mfr.)
Antimony Sodium Thioglycollate (Various Mfr.)
Tartar Emetic (Various Mfr.)

ANTIMONY SODIUM THIOGLYCOLLATE. (Various Mfr.)
Use: Schistosomiasis, leishmaniasis & filariasis.

• **ANTIMONY TRISULFIDE COLLOID.** USAN.
Use: Pharmaceutic aid.

ANTIMONYL POTASSIUM TARTRATE.
See: Antimony Potassium Tartrate, U.S.P. XXI.

■ **ANTINAUSEANTS.**
See: Antinauseants Supprettes "WANS" (Webcon)
Atarax, Tab., Syr. (Roerig)
Bendectin, Tab. (Merrell Dow)
Bucladin-S, Softab Tab. (Stuart)
Compazine, Preps. (SmithKline)
Dramamine, and Dramamine-D, Preps. (Searle)
Emesert, Rectal Insert (American Critical Care)
Emetrol, Liq. (Rorer)
Marezine, Preps. (Burroughs Wellcome)
Matropinal, Preps (Comatic)
Meclizine HCl, Tab. (Various Mfr.)
Mepergan, Inj. (Wyeth)
Naus-A-Tories, Supp. (Table Rock)
Nausetrol, Syr. (Medical Chemicals)
Phenergan, Preps. (Wyeth)
Pyridoxine HCl Preparations (Various Mfr.)
Thorazine, Preps. (SmithKline)
Tigan, Preps. (Beecham Labs)
Torecan Amp., Supp., Tab. (Sandoz)
Trilafon, Preps. (Schering)
Vistaril, Cap., Susp., Sol. (Pfizer)

ANTINAUSEA SUPRETTES "WANS." (Webcon) **Child:** pyrilamine maleate 25 mg., pentobarbital sodium 30 mg./Supp. **No. 1:** Pyrilamine maleate 50 mg., pentobarbital sodium 45 mg./Supp. **No. 2:** Pyrilamine maleate 50 mg., pentobarbital sodium 100 mg./Supp. Box 12s
Use: Nausea, vomiting.

■ **ANTINEOPLASTIC AGENTS.**
See: Adriamycin, Vial (Adria)
Alkeran, Tab. (Burroughs Wellcome)
Blenoxane, Amp. (Bristol)
Cosmegen, Inj. (Merck Sharp & Dohme)
Cytosar, sterile (Upjohn)
Cytoxan, Tab., Vials. (Mead Johnson)
Dicorvin, Tab. (Amfre-Grant)

Drolban, Inj. (Lilly)
Elspar, Inj. (Merck Sharp & Dohme)
Estinyl, Tab. (Schering)
Estradurin, Inj. (Ayerst)
5-Fluorouracil, Amp. (Roche)
FUDR, Vials (Roche)
Hydrea, Cap. (Squibb)
Leukeran, Tab. (Burroughs Wellcome)
Lysodren, Tab. (Calbio)
Matulane, Cap. (Roche)
Medroxyprogesterone Acetate Tab., Vials (Various Mfr.)
Megace, Tab. (Mead Johnson)
Methosarb, Tab. (Upjohn)
Mercaptopurine, Tab. (Burroughs Wellcome)
Methotrexate, Tab. (Lederle)
Methotrexate Sod., Vial (Lederle)
Meticorten, Tab. (Schering)
Mithracin, Vial (Pfizer)
Mustargen, Inj. (Merck Sharp & Dohme)
Myleran, Tab. (Burroughs Wellcome)
Oncovin, Amp. (Lilly)
Progynon, Pellets, Susp. (Schering)
Purinethol, Tab. (Burroughs Wellcome)
TACE, Cap. (Merrell Dow)
Teslac, Tab., Vial (Squibb)
Thioguanine, Tab. (Burroughs Wellcome)
Thio-Tepa, Vial (Lederle)
Triethylene Melamine, Tab. (Lederle)
Uracil Mustard, Cap. (Upjohn)
Velban, Amp. (Lilly)
Verceyte, Tab. (Abbott)

NTI 5-NITRO-2-FURALDEHYDE OXIME. Nifuroxime.

ANTI-OBESITY AGENTS.
See: Thyroid
Amphetamine Preparations (Various Mfr.)
Dextro-amphetamine Preparations (Various Mfr.)
Diethylpropion HCl
Fastin, Cap. (Beecham Labs)
Ionamin, Cap. (Pennwalt)
Levo-Amphetamine
Methamphetamine Preparations (Various Mfr.)
Plegine, Tab. (Ayerst)
Preludin, Tab. (Boehringer Ingelheim)
Sanorex, Tab. (Sandoz)
Statobex, Tab. (Lemmon)
Tenuate (Merrell Dow)
Tepanil, Tab. (Riker)

NTI-PAK COMPOUND. (Lowitt) Phenylephrine HCl 5 mg., salicylamide 0.23 Gm., acetophenetidin 0.15 gr., caffeine 0.03 Gm., ascorbic acid 50 mg., hesperidin complex 50 mg., chlorprophenpyridamine maleate 2 mg./Tab. Bot. 30s, 100s.
Use: Cold therapy.

NTIPARASYMPATHOMIMETICS.
See: Parasympatholytic agents.

NTI-PELLAGRA VITAMIN.
See: Nicotinic acid.

NTI-PERNICIOUS ANEMIA PRINCIPLE.
See: Vitamin B-12

NTIPHEN. Dichlorophen, B.A.N.

ANTIPHLOGISTINE. (Denver) Medicated poultice. Jar 5 oz., 1 lb., Tube 8 oz., Hosp. can 5 lb.

■ **ANTIPROTOZOAN AGENTS.**
See: Antimony Preparations
Arsenic Preparations
Bismuth Preparations
Chiniofon (Various Mfr.)
Diiodohydroxyquinoline
Emetine Hydrochloride (Various Mfr.)
Furazolidone
Iodohydroxyquinoline Sulfonate Sodium
Iodocholohydroxyquinoline
Levofuraltadone
Quinoxyl
Suramin Sodium

• **ANTIPYRINE,** U.S.P. XXI. 2,3-Dimethyl-1-phenyl-3-pyrazolin-5-one. (Various Mfr.) Analgesine, anodynine, dimethyloxyquinazine, oxydimethylquinizine, parodyne, phenazone, phenylone, pyrazoline, sedatine.
Use: Analgesic, antipyretic.
W/Benzocaine, glycerin.
See: Aurotis, Liq. (Research Pharmacal Lab.) Ear Drops, Liq. (Sutliff & Case)
W/Benzocaine, chlorobutanol.
See: G.B.A., Drops (Scrip)
W/Carbamide, benzocaine, cetyldimethylbenzylammonium HCl.
See: Auralgesic, Liq. (Elder)
W/Phenylephrine HCl, benzocaine.
See: Tympagesic, Liq. (Adria)
W/Pyrilamine maleate, phenylephrine, benzalkonium.
See: Prefrin-A Ophthalmic (Allergan)

• **ANTIPYRINE AND BENZOCAINE OTIC SOLUTION,** U.S.P. XXI.
Use: Local anesthetic.
See: Auro Ear Drops (Commerce)
Lanaurine, Drop (Lannett)
Pyrocaine Eardrop, Liq. (Med. Chem.)

■ **ANTIRHEUMATIC PREPARATIONS.**
See: p-Aminobenzoic Acid and salts (cal., pot., sod.)
Ammonium Salicylate
Anti-arthritic Hormones
Colchicine preps.
Gentisate Sodium
Gold Sod. Thiosulfate, Preps. (Various Mfr.)
Myochrysine, Inj. (Merck Sharp & Dohme)
Salicylamide preps.
Sodium Salicylate
Solganal, Vial (Schering)

■ **ANTIRICKETTSIAL AGENTS.**
See: p-Aminobenzoic Acid (Various Mfr.)
p-Aminobenzoate, Sod. (Various Mfr.)
Aureomycin, Preps. (Lederle)
Chloromycetin, Preps. (Parke-Davis)
Rocky Mountain Spotted Fever Serum (Rabbit), Vial (Lederle)
Terramycin, Preps. (Pfizer)

ANTI-RUST TABLETS. (Lannett) Not for medicinal use; anticorrosive for use with benzalkonium aqueous sterilizing solution. Sodium carbonate monohydrate 1.15 Gm., sodium nitrate 0.50 Gm.for a total of 1.66 Gm./Tab. Bot. 500s.

ANTI-RUST TABLETS. (Winthrop-Breon) Sodium nitrite 0.50 Gm., sodium bicarbonate 1.16 Gm. for a total of 1.66 Gm./Tab. Bot. 50s, 500s.
Use: Rust preventive.

ANTISCORBUTIC VITAMIN.
See: Ascorbic Acid

ANTISEPTIC, CHLORINE, ACTIVE.
See: Antiseptic, N-Chloro Compounds, Hypochlorite Preps.

■ **ANTISEPTIC, DYES.**
See: Acriflavine (Various Mfr.)
Aminoacridine, HCl
Bismuth Violet, Prep. (Table Rock)
Brilliant Green
Crystal Violet
Fuchsin
Gentian Violet (Various Mfr.)
Methylrosaniline Chloride (Various Mfr.)
Methyl Violet
Pyridium, Tab. (Parke-Davis)
Serenium, Tab. (Squibb)

■ **ANTISEPTIC, MERCURIALS.**
See: Mercresin (Upjohn)
Mercurochrome, Preps. (Hynson, Wescott & Dunning)
Merthiolate, Preps. (Lilly)
Phenylmercuric Acetate (Various Mfr.)
Phenylmercuric Borate (Various Mfr.)
Phenylmercuric Nitrate (Various Mfr.)
Phenylmercuric Picrate (Various Mfr.)
Thimerosal

■ **ANTISEPTIC, N-CHLORO COMPOUNDS.**
See: Chloramine-T (Various Mfr.)
Chlorazene, Powd., Tab. (Badger)
Dichloramine-T (Various Mfr.)
Halazone, Tab. (Abbott)

■ **ANTISEPTIC, PHENOLS.**
See: Anthralin (Various Mfr.)
Bithionol
Coal Tar Products (Various Mfr.)
Creosote (Various Mfr.)
Cresols (Various Mfr.)
Guaiacol (Various Mfr.)
Hexachlorophene (Various Mfr.)
Hexylresorcinol (Var. Mfr.)
Methylparaben (Various Mfr.)
o-Phenylphenol (Various Mfr.)
Oxyquinoline Salts (Various Mfr.)
Parachlorometaxylenol (Various Mfr.)
Phenol (Various Mfr.)
Picric Acid (Various Mfr.)
Propylparaben (Various Mfr.)
Pyrogallol (Various Mfr.)
Resorcinol (Various Mfr.)
Resorcinol Monoacetate (Various Mfr.)
Thymol (Various Mfr.)
Trinitrophenol (Various Mfr.)

■ **ANTISEPTIC, SURFACE-ACTIVE AGENTS.**
See: Bactine, Preps. (Miles)
Benzalkonium Chloride (Var. Mfr.)
Benzethonium Chloride (Var. Mfr.)
Ceepryn (Merrell Dow)
Cēpacol Preps. (Merrell Dow)
Cetylpyridinium Chloride (Var. Mfr.)
Diaparene Chloride, Preps. (Glenbrook)
Methylbenzethonium Chloride (Various Mfr.)
Zephiran Chloride, Preps. (Winthrop-Breon)

■ **ANTISEPTICS.**
See: Furacin, Preps. (Eaton)
Iodine Products
Mercurials
N-Chloro Compounds
Phenols
Surface Active Agents

ANTISPAS. (Keene) Dicyclomine HCl 10 mg./ml. Vial 10 ml.
Use: Antispasmodic.

■ **ANTISPASMODICS.** Usually refers to agents that combat the muscarinic effect of liberated acetylcholine. The relief of smooth muscle spasms. Parasympatholytic agents.
See: Anticholinergic Agents.
Spasmolytic Agents

ANTISPASMODIC CAPSULES. (Lemmon) Phenobarbital 16.2 mg., hyoscyamine sulfate 0.1037 mg., atropine sulfate 0.0194 mg., scopolamine HBr 0.0065 mg./Cap. Bot. 1000s.
Use: Antispasmodic.

ANTISTEREPTOLYSIN-O. Titration procedure.
See: Aslo (Wampole Labs)

ANTISTERILITY VITAMIN.
See: Vitamin E

ANTISTIN HYDROCHLORIDE OR MESYLATE.
Antazoline, B.A.N.

ANTI-TEN. (Century) Allylisobutylbarbituric acid ¾ gr., aspirin 3 gr., phenacetin 2 gr., caffeine ⅔ gr./Tab. Bot. 100s, 1000s.
Use: Analgesic-sedative.

ANTI-THERM. (Scrip) Sod. chloride 7 gr., dextrose 3 gr., Vit. C 20 mg./Tab. Bot. 1000s.
Use: Sodium chloride deficiency.

■ **ANTITHYROID AGENTS.**
See: Iothiouracil Sodium
Methimazole
Methylthiouracil (Various Mfr.)
Propylthiouracil (Various Mfr.)
Tapazole, Tab. (Lilly)

■ **ANTITOXINS.**
See: Botulism Antitoxin
Diphtheria Antitoxin
Gas Gangrene Antitoxin
Tetanus Antitoxin

■ **ANTITUBERCULOSIS AGENTS.**
See: Aminosalicylates (Na, Ca, K) (Various Mfr.)
Benzapas, Pow., Tab. (Dorsey)
Calcium Benzoylpas (Various Mfr.)
Capastat Sulfate, Amp. (Lilly)
Cycloserine, Pulvule (Lilly)
Diasone Sod., Tab. (Abbott)
Dihydrosteptomycin (Various Mfr.)
Di-Isopacin, Tab. (CMC)
Isoniazid (Various Mfr.)
Myambutol, Tab. (Lederle)
Natri-Pas, Pow., Tab. (Glenwood)

Niadox, Tab. (Barnes-Hind)
Niconyl, Tab. (Parke-Davis)
Pasara Sod., Pow., Tab. (Dorsey)
Pasdium, Tab. (Kasar)
P.A.S. Acid, Tab. (Kasar)
Pyrazinamide, Tab. (Lederle)
Rifadin, Cap. (Merrell Dow)
Rimactane, Cap. (Ciba)
Seromycin, Pulvule (Lilly)
Streptomycin (Various Mfr.)
Teebacin, Prep. (CMC)
Trecator-SC, Tab. (Ives)
Triniad, Tab. (Kasar)
Uniad, Tab. (Kasar)
Uniad-Plus 5,10, Tab. (Kasar)

ITI-TUSS. (Century) Guaifenesin 100 mg./5 cc. Bot. 4 oz., pint, gal.
Use: Cough suppressant.

ITI-TUSS D.M. (Century) Guaifenesin 100 mg., dextromethorphan HBr 15 mg./5 cc. Bot. 4 oz., pint, gal.
Use: Cough suppressant.

ITI-TUSSIVE. (Canright) Dextromethorphan HBr 10 mg., potassium guaiacol sulfonate 125 mg., terpin hydrate 100 mg., phenylpropanolamine HCl 12.5 mg., pyrilamine maleate 12.5 mg./Tab. Bot. 60's.
Use: Cough suppressor & nasal decongestant.

ITITUSSIVE COUGH SYRUP. (Weeks & Leo) Chlorpheniramine 2 mg., phenylephrine HCl 5 mg., dextromethorphan 15 mg., ammonium Cl 50 mg./5 ml.
Use: Decongestant, antihistaminic, antitussive, expectorant.

ITITUSSIVE COUGH SYRUP WITH CODEINE. (Weeks & Leo) Chlorpheniramine maleate 2 mg., phenylephrine HCl 5 mg., codeine phosphate 10 mg., ammonium Cl 50 mg./5 ml. Bot. 4 oz.
Use: Nasal decongestant, antihistaminic, analgesic, expectorant.

NTITUSSIVE-DECONGESTANT.
See: St. Joseph Cough Syrup for Children (Plough)
Tussend, Tab., Liq. (Merrell Dow).

ANTIVENIN (CROTALIDAE) POLYVALENT, U.S.P. XXI. Polyvalent crotaline antivenin. Rattlesnake antivenin for four species of pit vipers.
Use: passive immunizing agent for treatment of rattlesnake bite.

ANTIVENIN (LATRODECTUS MACTANS), U.S.P. XXI. (Merck Sharp & Dohme) Black widow spider antivenin. Each vial contains not less than 6000 antivenin units. Thimerosal (mercury derivative) 1:10,000 added as preservative. Vial 2.5 ml.
Use: Treatment of black widow spider bite symptoms.

ANTIVENIN (MICRUS FULVIUS), U.S.P. XXI. (Wyeth) Lyophilized antivenin of animal origin (micrurus fulvius) with phenol 0.25% and thimerosal 0.005% as preservatives. Bacteriostatic water w/phenylmercuric nitrate 1:100,000 as preservative. Combination package. Vial 10 ml.
Use: Bites of North American Coral Snake and Texas Coral Snake.

ANTIVENIN, SNAKE, POLYVALENT. (Wyeth) Antivenin Crotalidae, Polyvalent, U.S.P. XXI. (Crotalidae) Rattlesnake, copperhead & moccasin antitoxic serum. Pkg., Combination w/Phenol 0.25%, thimerosal 1:20,000 as preservatives. One disposable syringe, 10 cc. of bacteriostatic water for inj. w/preservative phenyl mercuric nitrate 1:100,000; one applicator vial iodine tinct. Normal horse serum 1:10, as sensitivity testing material.
Use: Bites by crotalid snakes of the United States.

ANTIVERT. (Roerig) Meclizine HCl 12.5 mg., 25 mg. or 50 mg./Tab. **12.5 mg.:** Bot. 100s, 1000s. Unit Dose 100s; **25 mg.:** Bot. 100s, 1000s. Unit dose 100s. **50 mg.:** Bot. 100s.
Use: Vertigo & motion sickness.

ANTIXEROPHTHALMIC VITAMIN.
See: Vitamin A

ANTRENYL. (Ciba) Oxyphenonium bromide 5 mg./Tab. Bot. 100s.
Use: Anticholinergic activity.

ANTRIZINE TABS. (Major) Meclizine 12.5 mg./Tab. Bot. 100s, 1000s, 3000s. 25 mg./Tab. Bot. 100s, 1000s.
Use: Vertigo, motion sickness.

ANTROCOL. (Poythress) Atropine sulfate 0.195 mg., phenobarbital 16 mg., bensulfoid 65 mg./Tab. or Cap. Bot. 100s, 500s.
Use: Sedative, antispasmodic.

ANTROCOL ELIXIR. (Poythress) Atropine sulfate 0.039 mg., phenobarbital 3 mg., alcohol 20%. Bot. 1 oz. w/dropper. Bot. pt.
Use: Treatment of a variety of gastro-intestinal disturbances in infants and children.

ANTURAN. Sulphinpyrazone, B.A.N.

ANTURANE. (Ciba) Sulfinpyrazone, U.S.P. 100 mg./Tab. Bot 100s. 200 mg./Cap. Bot. 100s.
Use: Treatment of chronic gout.

ANUCAINE. (Calvin) Procaine 50 mg., butyl-p-aminobenzoate 200 mg., benzyl alcohol 265 mg., in sweet almond oil/5 ml. Amp. 5 ml.
Box 6s, 24s, 100s.
Use: I.M., anesthetic for rectal treatment.

ANUGARD HC. (Vangard) Bismuth subgallate 2.25%, bismuth resorcin compund 1.75%, benzyl benzoate 1.2%, peruvian balsam 1.8%, zinc oxide 11.0%, pramoxine HCl 10 mg./Supp. Bot. 12s.
Use: Hemorrhoid treatment.

ANUJECT. (Hauck) Procaine solution. Vial 5 ml., 10 ml.
Use: Proctologic conditions.

ANULAN SUPPOSITORIES. (Lannett) Bismuth resorcin compound, bismuth subgallate, zinc oxide, boric acid, balsam peru. Box 12s.

ANUPHEN. (Comatic) Acetaminophen 125 mg. 300 mg., 600 mg. In a polyethylene glycol base/Supp. Box 12s.
Use: Analgesic.

ANUSOL. (Parke-Davis) Bismuth subgallate (2.25%), bismuth resorcin compound (1.75%), Peruvian balsam (1.8%), zinc oxide (11.00%), benzyl benzoate (1.2%), dibasic Ca phosphate in

hydrogenated vegetable oil. Supp. Boxes 12s, 24s, 48s.
Use: Hemorrhoidal.

ANUSOL-HC. (Parke-Davis) Same as Anusol plus hydrocortisone acetate 10 mg./Supp. Box 12s, 24s.

ANUSOL-HC CREAM. (Parke-Davis) Hydrocortisone acetate 5 mg., bismuth subgallate 22.5 mg., bismuth resorcin compound 17.5 mg., benzyl benzoate 12 mg., propylparaben, methylparaben, polysorbate 60, sorbitan monostearate/Gm. Tube 1 oz.

ANUSOL OINTMENT. (Parke-Davis) Peruvian balsam 18mg., zinc oxide 110mg./Gm. w/bismuth subiodide and pramoxine HCl 1% in a mineral oil glyceryl stearate and water base. Tube 1 oz., 2 oz.
Use: Topically, irritative & inflammatory disorders of the skin.

ANXANIL. (Econo Med) Hydroxyzine HCl 25 mg./Tab. Bot. 100s.
Use: Relief of anxiety and tension.

ANYAGE. (Morton) Vit. A 5000 I.U., D 400 I.U., B-1 3 mg., B-2 3 mg., B-6 1 mg., C 50 mg., niacinamide 20 mg., B-12 2.5 mcg., Ca pantothenate 5 mg./Cap. Bot. 1000s.
Use: Multi-vitamin.

AORACILLIN-B. (Vita Elixir) Penicillin G 200,000 u. and 500,000 u./Tab. Bot. 50s.
Use: Antibiotic.

APAC. (Vortech) Aspirin 325 mg., caffeine 16 mg.,/Tab. Bot 1000s.
Use: Analgesic.

APAC-IMPROVED. (Vortech) Aspirin 400 mg., caffeine 32 mg./Tab. Bot. 1000s.
Use: Analgesic.

APACOMP TABLETS. (Lannett) Bot. 1000s.

APAP. (Stanlabs) Acetaminophen 5 gr./Tab. Bot. 100s, 1000s.

APAP ACETAMINOPHEN TAB. (Towne) 350 mg. Bot. 100s.

APA-SAN. (Bowman) Acetaminophen 324 mg., aspirin 324 mg./Tab. Bot. 100s, 1000s.
Use: Analgesic, antipyretic.

APATATE. (Kenwood) Thiamine HCl 15 mg., Vit. B-12 25 mcg., Vit. B-6 0.5 mg./cc. Bot. Liq. 4 oz., 8 oz.
Use: Orally; nutritional supplement.

• **APAZONE.** USAN. 5-(Dimethylamino)-9-methyl-2-propyl-IH-pyrazolo[1,2,-a][1,2,4] benzotriazine-1,-3(2H)-dione.
Use: Anti-inflammatory.

A.P.C. (Various Mfr.) Aspirin, phenacetin & caffeine. Cap., Tab.
Use: Analgesic.
See: A.S.A. Compound, Preps. (Lilly)
Aspodyne, Tab. (Blue Line)
Gelsodyne, Tab. (Blue Line)
P.A.C. Compound, Cap. or Tab. (Upjohn)
Pan-APC, Tab. (Panray)
Phensal, Tab. (Merrell Dow)
W/Aluminum hydroxide gel, magnesium hydroxide.
See: Buffadyne, Tab. (Lemmon)
W/Aluminum hydroxide gel, methapyrilene HCl, magnesium hydroxide.
See: Buffadyne 25, Tab. (Lemmon)
W/Codeine phosphate. (Various Mfr.)
See: Anexsia w/Codeine, Tab. (Beecham Labs)
Anexsia D, Tab. (Beecham Labs)
Aspodyne w/Codeine, Tab. (Blue Line)
W/Codeine phosphate, phenolphthalein.
See: Phenodyne, w/Codeine, Cap. (Blue Line)
W/Phenolphthalein.
See: Phenodyne, Tab., Blue Line

APC W/ANTIHISTAMINE TABLET. (Sutliff & Case) Salicylamide 227 mg., acetophenetidin 160 mg., caffeine 32.5 mg., pyrilamine maleate 6.25 mg., methapyriline fumarate 6.25 mg./Tab. Bot 100s, 1000s.

APC WITH CODEINE TABLOIDS. (Burroughs Wellcome) Aspirin 227 mg., phenacetin 162 mg. caffeine 32 mg./Tab. w/codeine. **#3:** codeine phosphate 30 mg./Tab. **#4:** codeine phosphate 6 mg./Tab. Bot: 100s, 1000s.
Use: Narcotic analgesic.

A.P.C. W/GELSEMIUM COMBINATIONS
See: Aidant, Tab. (Noyes)
Ansemco, No. 2, Tab. (Elder)
Asphac-G, Tab. (Central)
Valacet, Tab. (Vale)

APC & GEL #2. (Scrip) Aspirin 3.5 gr., acetaminophen 2.5 gr., caffeine 0.25 gr., tr. gelsemium 3 min./Tab. Bot. 100s.

APCOGESIC. (Apco) Sod. salicylate 5 gr., colchicine 1/320 gr., Ca carbonate 65 mg., dried aluminum hydroxide gel 130 mg., phenobarbital ⅛ gr./Tab. Bot. 100s.
Use: Arthritis, rheumatoid involvement.

APCOHIST. (APC) Phenylpropanolamine HCl 25 mg, chlorpheniramine maleate 1 mg.,/Tab. Bot. 100s.
Use: Antihistaminic; decongestant.

APCORETIC. (APC) Caffeine anhydrous 100 mg., ammonium chloride 325 mg./Tab. Bot. 90s.
Use: Diuretic.

APHCO HEMORRHOIDAL COMBINATION. (APC) Combination package of Aphco Hemorrhoidal Ointment 1.5 oz. tube, Aphco Hemorrhoidal Suppositories, box 12s, 1000s.
Use: Relief of discomfort of piles.

APEHN TABS. (Major) Trihexyphenidyl 2 mg./or 5 mg./Tab. Bot. 250s, 1000s.
Use: Parkinsonism treatment.

APHONAL TABLETS. (Panray) Isobutyl-allyl-barbitu acid 50 mg., caffeine 40 mg., aspirin 200 mg., acetophenetidin 130 mg./Tab. Bot. 1000s.
Use: Sedative with analgesics.

APICILLIN. D-(-)-α-Aminobenzyl penicillin.
See: Ampicillin

APIQUEL FUMARATE. Aminorex, B.A.N.

APISATE. Diethylpropion, B.A.N.

A.P.L. (Ayerst) Chorionic Gonadotropin for Injection. Dry form, package provides one vial containing 5000 U.S.P. Units, 10,000 U.S.P. Units, or 20,000 U.S.P. Units, and one 10 ml. Amp. w/sterile diluer w/benzyl alcohol, phenol, lactose, sod. hydroxide or HCl.
Use: Chorionic gonadotropin therapy.

APLISOL. (Parke-Davis) Tuberculin purified protein d rivative diluted 5 u./0.1 ml, w/polysorbate 80, pot.

& sod phosphates, phenol. Vial 1 ml. (10 tests), 5 ml. (50 tests)

LITEST. (Parke-Davis) Purified tuberculin protein fraction buffered with pot. & sod. phosphates, phenol 0.5%/Single-use, multipuncture unit. 25s.

ODOL. Anileridine dihydrochloride.
Use: Relief of pain.

POMORPHINE HYDROCHLORIDE. U.S.P. XXI. Tablets, U.S.P. XXI. 4H-Dibenzo[de,g] quinoline-10,-11-diol, 5,6,6a,7-tetrahydro-6-methyl HCl hemihydrate. 6α,β-Aporphine-10,11-diol HCl, hemihydrate. Pow., Bot. 5 gr., 15 gr., 1/8 oz., 1 oz. (Various Mfr.) Lilly. H.T. (1/10 gr.) 100s.
Use: Emetic.

ORPHINE-10, 11-DIOL HYDROCHLORIDE.
See: Apomorphine Hydrochloride

PEDRINE. (Thompson Medical) Phenylpropanolamine HCl 25 mg., multivitamins, caffeine 100 mg./Tab.
Use: Appetite depressant.

PETITE-DEPRESSANT.
See: Anorexigenic agents

APRAMYCIN. USAN. B.A.N. An antibiotic produced by Streptomyces tenebrarius.
Use: Antibacterial, veterinary medicine.

PRAZONE CAPS. (Major) Sulfinpyrazone 200 mg./Cap. Bot. 500s.
Use: Treatment of chronic gout.

PRAZONE TABS. (Major) Sulfinpyrazone 100 mg./Tab. Bot. 100s.
Use: Treatment of chronic gout.

PRESAZIDE. (Ciba) **25/25 Cap.** Hydralazine HCl 25 mg., hydrochlorothiazide 25 mg. Cap. **50/50 Cap.** Hydralazine HCl 50 mg., hydrochlorothiazide 50 mg./Cap. **100/50 Cap.** Hydralazine 100 mg., hydrochlorothiazide 50 mg./Cap.
Use: Antihypertensive.

PRESOLINE. (Ciba) Hydralazine hydrochloride. **Amp.** 20 mg. w/propylene glycol, methyl- & propylp hydroxy benzoate. 1 ml. Pkg. 5s. **Tab.** 10 mg. Bot. 100s, 1000s, Consumer pack 100s.; 25 mg., 50 mg. Bot. 100s, 500s, 1000s. Consumer pack 100s. Accu-Pak, blister units of 100s.; 100 mg. Bot. 100s. Consumer pack 100s.
Use: Hypertensive disorders.
/Serpasil.
See: Serpasil Prod., Preps. (Ciba)

PRESOLINE-ESIDRIX. (Ciba) Hydralazine HCl 25 mg., Hydrochlorothiazide 15 mg./Tab. Bot. 100s.
Use: Hypertension.

APRINDINE. USAN. 3-[N-(Indan-2-yl)-N-phenylamino]propyldiethylamine. (Lilly) N-(2,3-Dihydro-1H-inden-2-yl)-N′,N′-diethyl-N-phenyl-1,3-propanediamine.
Use: Anti-arrhythmic.

PRINOX. Bendrofluazide, B.A.N.

PROBARBITAL. 5-Allyl-5-isopropylbarbituric acid, Allylisopropylmalonylurea) Pow.
Use: Long acting hypnotic.
See: A.P.B., Tab. (Lemmon)

PROBEE W/C. (Approved) Vit. B-1 15 mg., B-2 10 mg., B-6 5 mg., niacinamide 50 mg., Calc. pantothenate 10 mg., Vit. C 250 mg./Cap. or Tab. **Caps.** Bot. 100s, 1000s. **Tab.** Bot. 50s, 100s, 1000s.
Use: Vitamin deficiencies.

APROZIDE CAPS. (Major) 25/25: Hydralazine 25 mg., hydrochlorothiazide 25 mg./Cap. Bot. 250s. 50/50: hydralazine 50 mg., hydrochlorothiazide 50 mg./Cap. Bot. 250s, 500s.
Use: Antihypertensive.

• **APROTININ.** USAN. A polypeptide proteinase inhibitor.
See: Trasylol

A.P.S. Aspirin, phenacetin and salicylamide

APSIN VK. Phenoxymethylpenicillin, B.A.N.

• **APTAZAPINE MALEATE.** USAN.
Use: Antidepressant.

APTOCAINE. B.A.N. 2-Pyrrolidin-1-ylpropiono-o-toluidide.
Use: Local anesthetic.
See: Pirothesin hydrochloride

APYRON.
See: Magnesium acetylsalicylate

AQ-4B. (Western Research) Trichlormethiazide 4 mg./Tab. Bot. 1000s.
Use: Diuretic.

AQUA-BAN. (Thompson Medical) Caffeine, ammonium chloride/Tab. Bot. 80s.
Use: Pre-menstrual water retention.

AQUA BAN PLUS. (Thompson Medical) Ammonium Cl 650 mg., caffeine 200 mg., bran 6 mg./Tab.
Use: Mild diuretic for pre-menstrual water retention.

AQUABASE. (Vale) Cetyl alcohol, propylene glycol, sodium lauryl sulfate, white wax, purified water. Jar 1 lb.
Use: Hydrophilic ointment base.

AQUACARE CREAM. (Herbert) Emollients, moisturizers, benzyl alcohol, oleth-3 phosphate, imidazolidinyl urea, and fragance. Tube 2.5 oz.
Use: Dry skin treatment.

AQUACARE/HP. (Herbert) Emollients, moisturizers, urea 10%, benzyl alcohol. **Cream** 2.5 oz. **Lotion** 8 oz., 16 oz.
Use: Dry skin treatment.

AQUACHLOR. (Geneva) Chlortetracycline.
Use: Antibiotic.

AQUACHLORAL. (Webcon) Chloral hydrate w/polyethylene glycol and a spreading agent. Supp. (5 gr., 10 gr.) Strip 12s.
Use: (Rectal) sedative.

AQUA-CILLIN 250. (Kenyon) Crystalline penicillin G pot. 3 million u. buffered w/sod. citrate./60 cc. Vial.

AQUACILLIN G. (Geneva) Penicillin G.
Use: Antibiotic.

AQUACYCLINE. (Geneva) Tetracycline HCl.
Use: Antibiotic.

AQUADERM. (C & M Pharmacal) Purified water, glycerin 25%, salicylic acid 0.1%, octoxynol-9 0.03%, 0.0001% FD&C red #40. Bot. 2 oz.
Use: Moisturizer for dry & aging skin.

AQUAFUREN. (Geneva) Nitrofurantoin.
Use: Antibacterial for urinary infections.

AQUA IVY. (Miles Pharm) Poison ivy extract 1:5 dil. Vial 10 cc.
Use: Hyposensitization.

AQUAKAY.
See: Menadione (Var. Mfr.)

AQUA LACTEN LOTION. (Herald Pharmacal) Demineralized water, urea, petrolatum, propylene glycol monostearat sorbitan monosterate, lactic acid. Bot. 8 oz.
Use: Dry Skin.

AQUALIN-PLUS SUPPRETTES. (Webcon) Theophylline and sod. pentobarbital:-Child: 120 mg. & 24 mg./Cream Supp. 12s; No. 2A: 480 mg. & 48 mg./White Supp. 12s; No. 2: 480 mg. & 100 mg./Light Yellow Supp. Jar 12s.

AQUALOSE. Poloxyl Lanolin, B.A.N.

AQUA MENSE W/IRON. (Stanlabs) Herbal water pill. Bot. 40s.
Use: Diuretic.

AQUAMEPHYTON INJECTION. (Merck Sharp & Dohme) Phytonadione 2 mg. or 10 mg./ml. as an aqueous colloidal solution of Vitamin K-1, w/polyoxyethylated fatty acid derivative 70 mg., dextrose 37.5 mg., benzyl alcohol 0.9%, water for injection q.s. to 1 ml. For injection by I.V., I.M., or subcutaneous routes. Amp. 1 mg./0.5 ml. Box 25s; 10 mg./1 ml. 6s, 25s. Vial 10 mg./ml. 2.5 ml. & 5 ml.
Use: Control of hemorrhage, coagulation disorders.

AQUA MIST. (Faraday) Nasal spray. Squeeze Bot. 20 cc.

AQUAMOX. Quinethazone, B.A.N.

AQUAMUCIL. (Cenci) Psyllium hydrophilic mucilloid. Bot. 7 oz., 14 oz.

AQUAMYCIN. (Geneva) Erythromycin.
Use: Antibiotic.

AQUANIL. (Sig) Mersalyl 100 mg., theophylline (hydrate) 50 mg., methyl paraben 0.18%, propyl paraben 0.02%. Vial 10 cc.

AQUANINE. (Geneva) Quinine HCl.
Use: Antimalarial.

AQUAOXY. (Geneva) Oxytetracycline HCl.
Use: Antibiotic.

AQUAPHENICOL. (Geneva) Chloramphenicol.
Use: Antibiotic.

AQUAPHILIC OINTMENT. (Medco Lab) Hydrated hydrophillic ointment. Jar 16 oz.
Use: Dry skin conditioner and an ointment base.

AQUAPHILIC OINTMENT WITH CARBAMIDE 10% and 20%. (Medco Lab) Stearyl alcohol, white petrolatum, sorbitol, propylene glycol, urea, ionic emulsifier, lactic acid, methylparaben, propylparaben.
Use: Prescription compounding and dry skin.

AQUAPHOR. (Beiersdorf, Germany) Xipamide
Use: Diuretic used to treat edema and hypertension.

AQUAPHOR. Water-miscible ointment base. Jar 1 lb., 5 lb., 45 lb.
Use: Water-miscible ointments.
See: Eucerin, Emulsion (Duke).

AQUAPHYLLIN SYRUP. (Ferndale) Theophylline anhydrous 80 mg./15 ml. Unit dose pks. 15 ml., 3[illegible] ml. Bot. 16 oz., gal.
Use: Bronchodilator.

AQUAPOOL CONCENTRATE. (Parker) Color additiv[e] for hydrotherapy therapy to control foaming. Bot. pt., gal.

AQUAPRES. (Coastal) Benzthiazide 50 mg./Tab. Bo[t.] 100s, 1000s.
Use: Diuretic.

■ **AQUARIUM DRUGS.** (Geneva) Various antibiotic, antifungal, vitamin & antibacterial drugs for aquarium use.

AQUASEC. (Pasadena Research) Benzthiazide 50 mg./Tab. Bot. 100s, 1000s.
Use: Diuretic.

AQUASOL A. (Armour) Water-miscible Vitamin A. **Pa[r]enteral** 50,000 U.S.P. Units./ml. Vial 2 ml. Box 10 **Caps:** 25,000 U.S.P. Units./Cap. Bot. 100s. 50,00[0] U.S.P. Units./Cap. Bot. 100s, 500s. **Drops:** 5000 U.S.P. Units./0.1 ml. Bot. 30 ml. w/dropper.
Use: Vitamin A therapy and supplement.

AQUASOL E. (Armour) Vitamin E. **Caps.:** 100 I.U./Cap. Bot. 100s. 400 I.U./Cap. Bot. 30s.**Drops:** 15 I.U./0.3 ml. Bot. 12 ml., 30 ml. w/dropper.
Use: Vitamin E supplement.

AQUASONIC 100. (Parker) Water-soluble contact me[-]dium gel for ultrasonic and electrical transmission. Bot. 250 ml., 1 L, 4 L.

AQUASONIC 100 STERILE. (Parker) Water-solubl[e] sterile gel for ultrasonic & electrical transmission. Foil Pouches 15 Gm.
Use: Contact medium gel for medical ultrasound when sterility is indicated.

AQUASULF. (Geneva) Triple sulfa tablet.
Use: Antibacterial.

AQUATAG. (Reid-Provident) Benzthiazide 25 mg., 5[0] mg./Tab.
Bot. 100s, 1000s.
Use: Antihypertensive, diuretic.

AQUATENSEN. (Wallace) Methyclothiazide 5 mg./Tab. Bot. 100s., 500s.
Use: Diuretic and antihypertensive agent.

AQUAVITE. (Geneva) Soluble multivitamin.
Use: Multivitamin.

AQUAZOL. (Geneva) Sulfisoxazole.
Use: Antibacterial.

AQUEOUS ALLERGENS. (Miles Pharm)
Use: Hyposensitization.

AQUEST. (Dunhall) Estrone (20,000 I.U.) 2 mg./ml. Vial 30 ml.
Use: Estrogen replacement.

AQUEX TABLETS. (Lannett) Trichlormethiazide 4 mg./Tab. Bot. 100s. 1000s.
Use: Diuretic.

AQUINONE.
See: Menadione, U.S.P. XXI.

AQUOL BATH OIL. (Lamond) Vegetable oil, olive oi[l]. Bot. 4 oz., 6 oz., 16 oz., qt., gal.
Use: Dry skin, eczema, pruritic conditions.

1-β-D-ARABINOFURANOSYLCYTOSINE. Cytarabin[e] U.S.P. XXI.

-3. (Stanlabs) Bot. 100s.
Use: Antacid tablets.

RALEN HYDROCHLORIDE (Winthrop-Breon) Chloroquine HCl 50 mg./ml. 5 ml. Amps. Box 5s.
Use: Malaria; extraintestinal amebiasis.

ALEN PHOSPHATE. (Winthrop-Breon) Chloroquine phosphate. 500 mg./Tab. Bot. 25s.
Use: Malaria, extraintestinal amebiasis.

RALEN PHOSPHATE W/PRIMAQUINE PHOSPHATE. (Winthrop-Breon) Aralen phosphate 500 mg., primaquine phosphate 79 mg./Tab. Bot. 100s.
Use: Prophylaxis of malaria.

ALIS TABLETS. (Winthrop Products) Glycobiarsol, chloroquine phosphate.
Use: Intestinal amebicide.

RAMINE (Merck Sharp & Dohme) Metaraminol bitartrate (equivalent to metaraminol) 10.0 mg./ml. w/sodium chloride 4.4 mg., water for injection q.s. ad. 1.0 ml., methylparaben 0.15%, propylparaben 0.02%, & sodium bisulfite 0.2%. Vial 10 ml.
Use: Sympathomimetic amine (Vasopressor).

RANOTIN. USAN.
Use: Antiviral.

RBAPROSTIL. USAN.
Use: Antisecretory.

RBOLIC. (Burgin-Arden) Methandriol dipropionate 50 mg./cc. Vial 10 cc.

RBON INJECTION. (Forest) Cyanocobalamine 200 mcg., thiamine HCl 5 mg., riboflavin-5 sodium phosphate 2.86 mg., pyridoxine HCl 10 mg., panthenol 2 mg., niacinamide 50 mg./ml. Vial 30 ml.
Use: multivitamin.

RBON PLUS SC. (Forest) Vit. A 5000 I.U., D 400 I.U., E 30 I.U., C 90 mg., folic acid 400 mcg., B-1 2.25 mg., B-2 2.6 mg., niacinamide 20 mg., B-6 3 mg., B-12 9 mcg., pantothenic acid 10 mg., biotin 150 mcg., calcium 162 mg., phosphorus 125 mg., iodine 150 mcg., magnesium 100 mg., copper 3 mg., manganese 7.5 mg., potasium 7.5 mg., zinc 22.5 mg./Tab. Bot. 100s, 1000s.
Use: Vitamin, mineral supplement.

RBUTAL. (Arcum) Butalbital ¾ gr., phenacetin 2 gr., aspirin 3 gr., caffeine ⅔ gr./Tab. Bot. 100s, 1000s.
Use: Sedative analgesic for tension headache.

RCLOFENIN. USAN.
Use: Diagnostic aid for hepatic function determination.

RCOBAN TABLETS. (Arcum) Meprobamate 400 mg./Tab. Bot. 50s, 1000s.
Use: Anxiety and tension states.

RCOBEX EXTRA STRENGTH CAPS. (Arcum) Vits. B-1 100 mg., B-2 2 mg., B-6 5 mg., niacinamide 125 mg., panthenol 10 mg., B-12 30 mcg., benzyl alcohol 1%, genistic acid ethanolamide 2.5%/cc. Vial 30 cc.
Use: B Vitamin therapy.

RCOCEE. (Arco) Vit. C 750 mg./Tab. Bot. 30s, 100s, 500s.
Use: Vitamin C deficiency.

ARCOCILLIN. (Arcum) Crystalline penicillin G pot. 400,000 u./Tab. Bot. 100s, 1000s. Powder 400,000 u./5 cc. Bot. 80 cc.

ARCODEX ANTACID TABLETS. (Arcum) Magnesium trisilicate 500 mg., aluminum hydroxide 250 mg./Tab. Bot. 100s, 1000s.
Use: Antacid.

ARCO-LASE. (Arco) Trizyme 38 mg. (Amylolytic 30 mg., proteolytic 6 mg., celluloytic 2 mg.), lipase 25 mg./Tab. Bot. 50s.
Use: Digestive disorders.

ARCO-LASE PLUS. (Arco) Phenobarbital 8 mg., hyoscyamine sulfate 0.10 mg, atropine sulfate 0.02 mg., trizyme 38 mg., lipase 25 mg./Tab. Bot. 50s.
Use: Treatment of gastrointestinal disturbances.

ARCORET. (Arco) Protease 30 mg., B-12 100 mcg., B-1 30 mg./Tab. Bot. 60s.
Use: Nutritional supplement, protamine appetite, weight gain.

ARCORT W/IRON. (Arco) Elemental iron 150 mg., protease 30 mg., B-12 100 mcg., B-1 30 mg./Tab. Bot. 60s.
Use: Prevention and treatment of iron deficiency anemia.

ARCOSTERONE. (Arcum) Methyltestosterone Oral: 10 mg., 25 mg./Tab. Bot. 100s, 1000s. Subling.: 10 mg./Tab. Bot. 100s, 1000s.
Use: Hormone therapy.

ARCO-THYROID. (Arco) Thyroid 1.5 gr./Tab. Bot. 1000s.

ARCOTINIC. (Arco) Ferrous fumarate 5 gr., ferrous sulfate 5 gr., Vit. C 500 mg., desiccated liver 400 mg./Tab. Bot. 100s.

ARCOTINIC LIQUID. (Arco) Ferrous gluconate 9 gr., liver fraction 1 gr., Vit. B-1 4.5 mg., B-2 4.5 mg., B-6 1.5 mg., d-panthenol 4 mg., niacinamide 30 mg./Tbsp. Bot. pt.
Use: Iron-deficiency anemia.

ARCOTRATE. (Arcum) Pentaerythritol tetranitrate 10 mg./Tab. **No. 2.** Pentaerythritol tetranitrate 20 mg./Tab. **No. 3.** Pentaerythritol tetranitrate 20 mg., phenobarbital ⅛ gr./Tab. Bot. 100s, 1000s.

ARCOVAL IMPROVED. (Arcum) Vit. A palmitate 10,000 I.U., D 400 I.U., thiamine mononitrate 15 mg., B-2 10 mg., nicotinamide 150 mg., B-6 5 mg., Ca pantothenate 10 mg., Vit. B-12 5 mcg., C 150 mg., E 5 I.U./Cap. Bot. 100s, 1000s.
Use: Dietary supplement.

ARCUM R-S. (Arcum) Reserpine 0.25 mg./Tab. Bot. 100s, 1000s.

ARCUM V-M. (Arcum) Vit. A palmitate 5000 I.U., D 400 I.U., B-1 2.5 mg., B-2 2.5 mg., B-6 0.5 mg., B-12 2 mcg., C 50 mg., niacinamide 20 mg., Ca pantothenate 5 mg., Fe 18 mg./Cap. Bot. 100s, 1000s.
Use: Dietary supplement.

A-R-D. (Birchwood) Anatomically shaped dressing for anorectal wounds, treatment of pruritus ani and other perianal irritations. Dispenser 24s.

ARDEBEN. (Burgin-Arden) Diphenhydramine HCl 10 mg., chlorobutanol 0.5%. Inj. 30 cc. vial.

ARDECAINE 1%. (Burgin-Arden) Lidocaine HCl 1%. Inj. 30 cc. vial.

ARDECAINE 2%. (Burgin-Arden) Lidocaine HCl 2%. Inj. 30 cc. vial.

ARDECAINE 1% W/EPINEPHRINE. (Burgin-Arden) Lidocaine HCl 1% w/epinephrine. Inj. 30 cc. vial.

ARDECAINE 2% W/EPINEPHRINE. (Burgin-Arden) Lidocaine HCl 2% w/Epinephrine. Inj. 30 cc. vial.

ARDEFEM 10. (Burgin-Arden) Estradiol valerate 10 mg./cc. 10 cc. vial.

ARDEFEM 20. (Burgin-Arden) Estradiol valerate 20 mg./cc. 10 cc. vial.

ARDEFEM 40. (Burgin-Arden) Estradiol valerate 40 mg./cc. Vial 10cc.

ARDEPRED SOLUBLE. (Burgin-Arden) Prednisolone 20 mg., niacinamide 25 mg., disodium edetate 0.5 mg., sodium bisulfite 1 mg., phenol 5 mg./cc. Vial 10cc.

ARDERONE 100. (Burgin-Arden) Testosterone enanthate 100 mg./cc. 10 cc. vial.

ANDERONE 200. (Burgin-Arden) Testosterone enanthate 200 mg./cc. 10 cc. vial.

ARDEVILA TABLETS. (Winthrop Products) Inositol hexanicotinate.
Use: Peripheral vasodilator.

ARDIOL 90/4. (Burgin-Arden) Testosterone enanthate 90 mg., estradiol valerate 4 mg./cc. 10 cc. vial.

ARECA. 0.35% of Ether soluble alkaloids, as arecoline.
Use: Anthelmintic (veterinary).

ARECOLINE ACETARSONE SALT.
See: Drocarbil.

Ar-EX BATH OIL. (Ar-Ex) Unscented only. Cholesterol base, mineral oil, isopropyl-myristate, polyethylene glycol 400 dilaurate. Bot. 8 oz.

AR-EX BODY LOTION. (Ar-Ex) Unscented only. Stearic acid, glycerol monostearate, cholesterol base, oil of sesame, sorbitan monooleate, triethanolamine, isopropyl myristate, mineral oil, oxyquinoline benzoate, carbonyl diamide. Bot. 8 oz.

AR-EX BRUSH-ON BROW. (Ar-Ex) Unscented only. Talc, titanium dioxide, microcrystalline wax, butylated hydroxyanisole, cosmetic colors. Tortoise shell compact with mirror and brush.

AR-EX BRUSH-ON COMPLEXION COLORING. (Ar-Ex) Unscented only. Talc, colloidal kaolin, zinc stearate, propyl parahydroxybenzoate, mineral oil, titanium dioxide, cosmetic color. Tortoise shell compact with mirror and hypo-allergenic nylon brush.

AR-EX BRUSH-ON EYESHADOW. (Ar-Ex) Unscented only. Talc, calcium carbonate, magnesium stearate, isopropyl palmitate, cosmetic colors. Tortoise shell compact with mirror and sponge and brush applicator.

AR-EX CAKE EYELINER. (Ar-Ex) Unscented only. Zinc stearate, calcium carbonate, talc, polyoxyethylene sorbitan monooleate, sorbitan sesquioleate, cetyl alcohol, butylated hydroxyanisole, inorganic pigments. Tortoise shell compact with mirror and brush.

AR-EX CHAP CREAM. (Ar-Ex) Scented or unscented. Diethylene glycol stearate, beeswax, lecithin, cholesterol, carbonyl diamide. Jar. 4 oz., 9 oz., 8 lbs. Tubes 1.5 oz.

AR-EX CLEANSING CREAM. (Ar-Ex) Scented or unscented. Liquid petrolatum, beeswax, ozokerite. Scented 4 oz. Unscented 4 oz., 8 oz.

AR-EX COLD CREAM. (Ar-Ex) Scented or unscente[d]. Liquid petrolatum, beeswax, ozokerite. Scented 4 oz. Unscented 4 oz., 8 oz., 7 lbs.

AR-EX COMPACT FACE POWDER. (Ar-Ex) Face po[w]der in compressed cakes, unscented only. Same composition as AR-EX Face Powder, but compress[ed] into cakes. Tortoise shell compact with mirror and 7 oz. cake. Refills available.

AR-EX CREAM DEODORANT. (Ar-Ex) Unscented on[ly]. Glyceryl monostearate, cholesterol absorption bas[e], spermaceti, glycerine, sorbitol, propylene glycol. Preservatives: methyl and propyl parahydroxybenzoates, aluminum phenolsulfonate. Jar. 1.25 oz. Tube 1 oz.

AR-EX CREAM FOR DRY SKIN. (Ar-Ex) Scented or unscented. Liquid petrolatum, beeswax, ozokerite, cholesterol base. Scented 4 oz., 8 oz. Unscented 4 oz., 8 oz.

AR-EX CREAM FOR OILY SKIN. (Ar-Ex) Unscent[ed] only. Ozokerite, cetyl alcohol, petrolatum, petrolatum liquidum. Jar. 3.75 oz.

AR-EX DISAPPEAR-BLEMISH STICK. (Ar-Ex) Unscented only. Carnauba wax, white petrolatum, mi[n]eral oil, ozokerite, titanium dioxide, butylated hydroxyanisole, cosmetic colors. Available in combination gold and silver swivel case.

AR-EX EYE CREAM. (Ar-Ex) Unscented only. Chole[s]terol base, petrolatum, glycerol monostearate, paraffin, oil of sesame, liquid petrolatum, white beeswax. Jar. 0.5 oz.

AR-EX EYE MAKEUP REMOVER PADS. (Ar-Ex) Un[s]cented only. 100% cotton, specially refined white oil. Jar. 50 Pads.

AR-EX EYE PENCIL. (Ar-Ex) Unscented only, Sp[er]maceti, petrolatum, paraffin wax, japan-wax subs[ti]tute, zinc stearate, cosmetic grade iron oxide, cosmetic grade carbon black.

AR-EX EYESHADOW STICK. (Ar-Ex) Unscented on[ly]. Paraffin wax, petrolatum, liquid petrolatum, cosmetic grade pigments. Swivel container.

Ar-EX FACE POWDER. (Ar-Ex) A hypo-allergenic fa[ce] powder. Unscented only. Talc, colloidal kaolin, zi[nc] stearate, titanium dioxide, cosmetic colors. Box 2.25 oz.

AR-EX FOUNDATION LOTION. (Ar-Ex) A hypo-all[er]genic liquid make-up, unscented only. Cetyl alcoh[ol], cholesterol, aluminum magnesium silicate, sodium lauryl sulfate, glycerine, titanium dioxide, triethanolamine stearate, cosmetic iron oxide pigments, Bot. 2 oz.

AR-EX HAIR SPRAY. (Ar-Ex) Unscented only. Polyvi[n...] plasticizers, polyethoxylated cholesterol, anhydrou[s] alcohol, fluorocarbon propellants. Aerosol cans 7 oz., 14 oz.

AR-EX HAND LOTION. (Ar-Ex) Unscented only. Stea[ric] acid in quince seed extract, glycerin, liquid petrolatum, cholesterol base. Bot. 8 oz.

AR-EX LIP GLOSS & SUN SCREEN STICK. (Ar-E[x]) Unscented only. Isopropyl fatty-acid esters, homo menthyl salicylate, mineral oil, candelilla wax, butylated hydroxyanisole. In gold and silver swivel case.

AR-EX A MAN'S HAIR SPRAY. (Ar-Ex) Unscented only. Polyvinyl plasticizers, polyethoxylated cholesterol, anhydrous alcohol, fluorocarbon propellants. Aerosol can 7 oz.

AR-EX MASCARA. (Ar-Ex) Unscented only. Roll-on. Liquid petrolatum, beeswax, carnauba wax, sorbitan sesquioleate, polyoxyethylene sorbitan monostearate, borax, propyl and methyl para-hydroxymenzoate, inorganic cosmetic pigments. Roll-on applicurler cake in tortoise shell compact with mirror and spiral brush.

AR-EX MOISTURE CREAM. (Ar-Ex) Unscented only. Glyceryl monostearate, cetyl alcohol, cetyl lactate, depollenized beeswax, isopropyl myristate, sesame oil, glycerine, polyoxyethylene sorbitan monostearate. Jar. 2 oz.

AR-EX MOISTURE LOTION. (Ar-Ex) Scented or unscented. Saturated cholesterol absorption base, stearic acid, glycerol monostearate, oil of sesame, glycerine, triethanolamine. Vial. 2 oz.

AR-EX MULTIBASE. (Ar-Ex) Aliphatic alcohols, polyhydric alcohols, lauric acid esters, petrolatum. Jar 16 oz., 7 lb.

AR-EX NAIL POLISH. (Ar-Ex) Unscented only. Butyl acetate, ethyl acetate, Cellosolve acetate, xylol cellulose acetate, camphor, plasticizer, resin, cosmetic colors. Bot 0.5 fl. oz. with applicator

AR-EX NAIL POLISH REMOVER. (Ar-Ex) Butyl acetate, ethyl acetate, Cellosolve acetate, xylol. Bot. 2 fl. oz.

AR-EX NIGHT CREAM. (Ar-Ex) Scented or unscented. Cholesterol absorption base, lecithin, beeswax, liquid petrolatum. Jar. Scented or unscented, 2 oz. Unscented only, 4 oz.

AR-EX REGULAR LIPSTICK. (Ar-Ex) Unscented only. Beeswax, castor oil, candelilla wax, butyl stearate, lake colors, certified, tetrabromfluorescein, in brass swivel containers.

AR-EX SAFE-SUDS. (Ar-Ex) Unscented only. A synthetic organic detergent. Alkyl sulfonates. Container 22 oz.

AR-EX SHAMPOO (SOAPLESS). (Ar-Ex) Unscented only. Protein, buffered to a pH of 6.7 approaching the natural pH of the scalp. Bot. 8 oz.

AR-EX SPECIAL FORMULA LIPSTICK. (Ar-Ex) Unscented only. Lipstick without the dye. Composition is the same as AR-EX Indelible Lipstick except contains no Bromofluorescein compounds. Available in silveroid swivel cases.

AR-EX SPRAY DEODORANT. (Ar-Ex) Unscented only. Glycerine, Tween, urea, aluminum phenolsulfonate. Bot. 1.5 oz.

AR-EX SUN SCREEN. (Ar-Ex) Unscented only. Glyceryl monostearate, stearic acid, cetyl alcohol, mineral oil, isopropyl myristate, cholesterol absorption base, propylene glycol, homo menthyl salicylate, polyoxyethylene sorbitan monooleate. Bot. 8 oz.

AR-EX SUPERFATTED SOAP. (Ar-Ex) Unscented only. Titanium dioxide, beta methyl umbelliferone, mineral oil, cholesterol absorption base, tallow, coconut oil. Toilet size, Bath size 5.5 oz.

AR-EX TALC. (Ar-Ex) Unscented only. Talc, zinc stearate, boric acid, iron oxide pigment. Shaker can 3 oz.

AR-EX WAVE SET. (Ar-Ex) Unscented only. Quince seed base, plasticized, glycerine, lake color. Bot. 8 fl. oz.

ARFONAD. (Roche) Trimethaphan camsylate 50 mg./ml. w/sod. acetate 0.013%. Amp. 10 ml. Box 10s.
Use: Short-acting vasodilator for control of hypertension.
Note: Refrigerate between 2° and 8° C.

ARGESIC CREAM. (Econo Med) Triethanolamine, methylsalicylate in cream base. Tube 2 oz.
Use: Arthritis, muscular aches and pains.

ARGESIC TABLETS. (Econo Med) Phenyltoloxamine citrate 30 mg., magnesium salicylate 600 mg./Tab. Bot. 100s.
Use: Analgesic, antiinflammatory.

• **ARGININE,** U.S.P. XXI. $C_6H_{14}N_4O_2$. L-Arginine.

• **ARGININE GLUTAMATE.** USAN. L(+)-arginine salt of L(+)-glutamic acid.
Use: Aid in ammonia intoxication due to hepatic failure.

ARGININE GLUTAMATE. B.A.N. L-Arginine salt of L-glutamic acid.
Use: Nutrient.
See: Modumate.

• **ARGININE HYDROCHLORIDE,** U.S.P. XXI. Inj., U.S.P. XXI.

ARGIPRESSIN. B.A.N. 8-Argininevasopressin.
Use: Antidiuretic hormone.

• **ARGIPRESSIN TANNATE.** USAN.
Use: Antidiuretic.

ARGYN.
See: Mild Silver Protein (Various Mfr.)

ARGYROL S.S. 20%. (CooperVision) Mild silver protein 20%. Dropperettes in 1 ml. Box 12s.
Use: Local anti-infective.

ARGYROL S.S. 10%. (CooperVision) Stabilized solution of mild silver protein 10%. Bot. 0.5 oz., 1 oz.
Use: Local anti-infective.

ARIDOL. (MPL) Pamabrom 52 mg., pyrilamine maleate 30 mg., homatropine methylbromide 1.2 mg., hyoscyamine sulfate 0.10 mg., scopolamine HBr 0.02 mg., methamphetamine HCl 1.5 mg./Tab. Bot. 100s.
Use: Dysmenorrhea, premenstrual tension.

• **ARILDONE.** USAN.
Use: Antiviral.

ARISTOCORT. (Lederle) Triamcinolone. **Tab.** 1 mg. Bot. 50s. 2 mg. 100s. 4 mg. Bot. 30s, 100s, 500s. 8 mg. Bot. 50s. 16 mg. Bot. 30s. **Tab. Aristo-Pk.** 4 mg. Pkg. 16s. **Syr.** (diacetate w/methylparaben 0.08%, propylparaben 0.02%). 2 mg./5 cc. Bot. 4 oz.
Use: Anti-inflammatory steroid.

ARISTOCORT A CREAM. (Lederle) Triamcinolone acetonide w/emulsifying wax, isopropyl palmitate, glycerin, sorbitol, lactic acid & benzyl alcohol.

0.025% w/Aquatain. Tube 15 Gm., 60 Gm. **0.1%.** Tube 15 Gm., 60 Gm. Jar 240 Gm. **0.5%.** Tube 15 Gm. Jar 240 Gm.
Use: Anti-inflammatory steroid.

ARISTOCORT ACETONIDE, SODIUM PHOSPHATE SALT. (Lederle).
Use: Glucosteroid.
See: Aristocort preps.
Sodium Phosphate Triamcinolone Acetonide

ARISTOCORT CREAM. (Lederle) Triamcinolone acetonide w/emulsifying wax, polysorbate 80, polysorbate 60, mono and diglycerides, squalane, sorbitol soln., sorbic acid, pot. sorbate. **LP: 0.025%:** Tube 15 Gm. 60 Gm. Jar 240 Gm., 5.25 lb.; **R: 0.1%:** Tube 15 Gm., 60 Gm., Jar 240 Gm., 5.25 lb.; **HP: 0.5%:** Tube 15 Gm. Jar 240 Gm.
Use: Anti-inflammatory steroid.

ARISTOCORT DIACETATE FORTE. (Lederle) Triamcinolone diacetate 40 mg./ml. Vials 1 & 5 ml.
Use: Parenteral steroid, depository.

ARISTOCORT DIACETATE INTRALESIONAL. (Lederle) Triamcinolone diacetate 25 mg./ml. Vial 5 ml.

ARISTOCORT A OINTMENT. (Lederle) Triamcinolone acetonide **0.1%.** Tube 15, 60 Gm. **0.5%.** Tube 15 Gm.

ARISTOCORT OINTMENT. (Lederle) Triamcinolone acetonide. **0.1%:** Tube 15 Gm., 60 Gm. Jar 240 Gm., 5 lb. **0.5%:** Tube 15 Gm. Jar 240 Gm.
Use: Adrenocortical steroid.

ARISTO-PAK. (Lederle) Triamcinolone 4 mg./Tab. 16s.
Use: Glucocorticoid; anti-inflammatory.

ARISTOSPAN INTRALESIONAL. (Lederle) Triamcinolone hexacetonide 5 mg./ml. w/polysorbate 80 0.20% w/v, sorbitol sol. 50% w/v, water q.s., benzyl alcohol 0.90% w/v. Vial 5 ml.

ARISTOSPAN PARENTERAL. (Lederle) Triamcinolone hexacetonide 20 mg./ml. micronized susp. w/polysorbate 80 0.40% w/v, sorbitol sol. 50% w/v, water q.s., benzyl alcohol 0.90% w/v. Vial 1 ml., 5 ml.
Use: Anti-inflammatory.

ARITHMIN INJECTABLE. (Lannett) Antazoline phosphate 100 mg./2 cc. Amp. 12s, 100s.
Use: Antihistaminic.

ARITHMIN TABLETS. (Lannett) Antazoline HCl 100 mg., 200 mg./Tab. Bot. 100s.
Use: Antihistaminic.

ARLACEL 83. (ICI Americas) Sorbitan Sesquioleate.

ARLACEL 165. (ICI Americas) Glyceryl monostearate and PEG-100 stearane nonionic self-emulsifying.

ARLACEL C. (ICI Americas) Sorbitan Sesquioleate. Mixture of oleate esters of sorbitol and its anhydrides.
Use: Surface-active agent.

ARLAMOL E. (ICI Americas) Polyoxypropylene (15), stearyl ether, BHT 0.1%.
Use: Emollient

ARLATONE 507. (ICI Americas) Padimate O.
Use: Ultra-violet absorber.

ARLEF. Flufenamic Acid, B.A.N.

ARLIDIN. (USV Labs.) Nylidrin HCl 6 mg., 12 mg./Tab. Bot. 100s, 1000s. Strip dispenser 100s.
Use: Orally, vasodilator, increases peripheral circulation and cardiac output.

ARLIX. (Hoechst) Piretanide HCl.
Use: Diuretic, hypotensive.

ARM-A-CHAR. (Armour) Activated charcoal suspensi 30 Gm. in 4 oz. water. Bot. 4 oz.
Use: Adsorbent for use in poisonings or in drug overdosages.

ARM-A-MED ISOETHADRINE HCl. (Armour) Isoeth drine HCl 0.062%, 0.125%, 0.167 %, 0.2%, or 0.25%. Boxes 100s. Plastic vials 2 ml., 2.5 ml., 3 ml., or 4 ml.
Use: Respiratory therapy.

ARM-A-MED ISOPROTERENOL HCl. (Armour) Is proterenol HCl 0.031% or 0.062%. Box 100s. Via 4 ml.
Use: Respiratory therapy.

ARM-A-VIAL. (Armour) Sodium chloride 0.45% or 0.9 w/sterile water. Box 100s. Plastic vials 3 ml. or 5 ml.
Use: Small volume respiratory therapy.

ARM-A-VIAL LV. (Armour) Sterile water for inhalatic sodium chloride 0.45%, or 0.9%. Bot. 250 ml., 50 ml., 1000 ml., 2000 ml.
Use: Large volume respiratory therapy.

ARMOUR THYROID. (USV Labs.) Desiccated anima thyroid glands (active thyroid hormones: T-4 thyrc ine, T-3 thyronine 0.25 gr., 0.5 gr., 1.0 gr., 1.5 gr., 2 g 3 gr., 4 gr., 5 gr./Tab. Most strengths available in several package sizes including: Bot. 100s, 1000s Handy Hundreds, Carton Strip 100s.
Use: Treatment thyroid deficiency.

A.R.M. (Menley & James) Chlorpheniramine maleate 4.0 mg., phenylpropanolamine HCl 25.0 mg. Tab. Pkgs. 20s, 40s.
Use: Hay fever, allergy, sinus congestion.

ARMYL. Lymecycline, B.A.N.

ARNE TIMESULES. (Haag) Ferrous fumarate 330 mg., thiamine 5 mg./Cap. Bot. 30s, 100s, 300s, 1000s.
Use: Anemia.

ARNE-C. (Haag) Ferrous fumarate 104 mg., ascort acid 60 mg./Tab. Chewable, Bot. 100s, 1000s.

ARNICA TINCTURE. (Lilly) Arnica in alcohol 66%. Bot. 4 fl. oz.

AROMATIC AMMONIA SPIRIT.
See: Ammonia, Aromatic Spirit, U.S.P. XXI.

AROMATIC AMMONIA VAPOROLE. (Burroughs Wellcome) Inhalent. Vial 5 minims.
Use: Inhalent for faintness.

• **AROMATIC ELIXIR,** N.F XVI. (Lilly) Alcohol. 22%. Bot. 16 fl. oz.
Use: Flavored vehicle.

AROXINE. Forminitrazole, B.A.N.

• **ARPRINOCID.** USAN.
Use: Coccidiostat.

ARSAMBIDE.
See: Carbarsone (Various Mfr.)

ARSANILIC ACID. B.A.N. p-Aminophenylarsonic acid.
Use: Treatment of enteritis; growth promotion, veterinary medicine.
See: Maize Pro-Gen

ARSECLOR.
See: Dichlorophenarsine hydrochloride (Var. Mfr.)

ARSENIC COMPOUNDS.
Use: Rarely employed in modern medicine; there are no longer any official compounds.
See: Acetarson.
Arsphenamine
Carbarsone (Various Mfr.)
Dichlorophenarsine HCl
Ferric Cacodylate
Glycobiarsol
Neoarsphenamine
Oxophenarsine HCl
Sodium Cacodylate (Various Mfr.)
Tryparsamide

ARSENOBENZENE.
See: Arsphenamine

ARSENPHENOLAMINE.
See: Arsphenamine

ARSPHENAMINE. 3, 3′-diamino-4, 4′ dihydroxy-arsenobenzene dihydrochloride. Arsenobenzene, arsenobenzol, arsenphenolamine, Ehrlich 606, salvarsan.
Use: Formerly used as antisyphilitic.

ARSTHINOL. Cyclic (hydroxymethyl) ethylene-3-acetamido-4-hydroxydithiobenzenearsonite.
Use: Antiprotozoal.

ARTANE. (Lederle) Trihexyphenidyl HCl. Benzhexol, B.A.N. **Elixir.** Methylparaben 0.08%, propylparaben 0.02% (2 mg./5 ml.), Bot. 1 pt.; **Tab.** (2 mg. & 5 mg.), Bot. 100s, 1000s. Unit dose 10×10 in 10s. **Sequels:** 5 mg., Bot. 60s, 500s.
Use: Parkinsonism.

ARTARAU. (Archer-Taylor) Rauwolfia serpentina 50 mg. or 100 mg./Tab. Bot. 100s, 1000s.

ARTASE. (Jamieson-McKames) Prednisone 0.75 mg., salicylamide 5 gr., C 20 mg., aluminum hydroxide 75 mg./Tab. Bot. 100s.

ARTA-VI-C. (Archer-Taylor) Multivitamins with Vit. C 100 mg./Tab. Bot. 100s.
Use: Supplement.

ARTAZYME. (Archer-Taylor) Autolyzed proteolytic enzyme. Bot. 13 cc.

ARTEGRAFT. USAN. Arterial graft composed of a section of bovine carotid artery that has been subjected to enzymatic digestion with ficin and tanned with dialdehyde starch.

ARTERENOL.
See: Levophed, Amp. (Winthrop-Breon)

ARTERIAL GRAFT. (Johnson & Johnson) Bovine origin.
Use: Arterial grafting.

ARTHOL. (Towne) Acetaminophen 250 mg., salicylamide 250 mg./Tab. Bot. 60s, 100s.
Use: Analgesic.

ARTHRALGEN. (Robins) Salicylamide 250 mg., acetaminophen 250 mg./Tab. Bot. 30s, 100s, 500s.
Use: Analgesic.

ARTHRITIC PAIN LOTION. (Walgreen) Triethanolamine salicylate 10%. Bot. 6 oz.
Use: Relief from aches and pains of arthritis and rheumatism.

ARTHRITIS BAYER TIMED RELEASE ASPIRIN. (Glenbrook) Aspirin 650 mg./TR Tab. Bot. 30s, 72s, 125s.
Use: Analgesic, antipyretic, antiinflammatory.

ARTHRITIS PAIN FORMULA. (Whitehall) Aspirin 7.5 gr., aluminum hydroxide gel 20 mg., magnesium hydroxide 60 mg./Tab. Bot. 10s, 40s, 100s, 175s.
Use: Analgesic.

ARTHRITIS PAIN FORMULA, ASPIRIN FREE. (Whitehall) Acetaminophen 500 mg./Tab. Bot. 30s., 75s.
Use: Analgesic.

ARTHRITIS STRENGTH BUFFERIN. (Bristol-Myers) Aspirin 486 mg./Tab. w/Dialminate (basic aluminum glycinate and magnesium carbonate.) Bot. 40s, 100s.
Use: Analgesic.

ARTHRITIS VACCINES.
See: Streptococcus Vaccine (Lilly)

ARTHROPAN LIQUID. (Purdue Frederick) Choline salicylate 870 mg./tsp. Bot. 8, 16 oz.
Use: Analgesic or antipyretic, pain of rheumatoid arthritis and other painful conditions.

ARTICULOSE-50. (Seatrace) Prednisolone acetate 50 mg./ml. Vial 10 cc.

ARTICULOSE L. A. (Seatrace) Triamcinolone diacetate 40 mg./ml. Vial 5 cc.

■ **ARTIFICIAL TANNING AGENT.**
See: QT, Prods, (Plough)
Sudden Tan, Prods. (Plough)

ARTIFICIAL TEARS. (Maurry) Hydroxyethylcellulose 0.5%, with NaCl, benzalkonium Cl 0.01% as preservative, EDTA and purified water. Bot. 15 cc.
Use: Lubricant.

ARTOSIN. Tolbutamide, B.A.N.

ARTRA BEAUTY BAR. (Plough) Triclocarban 1% in soap base. Cake 3.6 oz.
Use: Dermatologic.

ARTRA SKIN TONE CREAM. (Plough) Hydroquinone 2% ointment. Tube 0.33 oz., 1 oz. (normal only), 2 oz., 4 oz. For normal skin, for dry skin and for oily skin.
Use: Skin lightener.

ARVIN. Ancrod, B.A.N.

ARVYNOL. Ethchlorvynol, B.A.N.

ASA. (Wampole-Zeus) Anti-skin antibodies test by IFA. Tests 48s.
Use: Aid in the diagnosis of pemphigus vulgaris and bullous pemphigoid.

A.S.A.. (Lilly) Aspirin. Acetylsalicylic acid. **Enseals** (5 & 10 gr.) Bot. 100s, 1000s. **Pulvules** (5 gr.) Bot. 100s. **Supp.** (5 & 10 gr.) Pkg. 6s; 144s; **Tab.** (5 gr.) Bot. 100s, 1000s. Blisterpak (10 × 10s).

A.S.A. AND CODEINE COMPOUND. (Lilly) Acetylsalicylic acid 380 mg., caffeine 30 mg., codeine phosphate 30 mg./Pulvule or Tab. Bot. 100s.
Use: Analgesic, antipyretic.

ASAFETIDA, EMULSION OF. Milk of Asafetida.

ASALCO NO. 1. (Jenkins) Acetylsalicylic acid 3.5 gr., acetophenetidin 2.5 gr., caffeine 0.5 gr./Tab. or Cap. Bot. 1000s.
Use: Colds, neuralgia, muscular soreness.

ASALCO NO. 2. (Jenkins) Dover's powder 0.25 gr., acid acetylsalicylic 3.5 gr., acetophenetidin 2.5 gr., caffeine 0.5 gr., tinct. gelsemium 2 mg./Tab. or Cap. Bot. 1000s.
Use: Anodyne, analgesic with sedative effects.

ASAPED TABLETS. (Winthrop Products) Acetylsalicylic acid.
Use: Analgesic antipyretic.

ASAWIN TABLETS. (Winthrop Products) Acetylsalicylic acid.
Use: Analgesic, antipyretic.

ASAFEN TABLETS. (Winthrop Products) Paracetamol with other products.
Use: Colds.

A.S.B. (Femco) Calcium carb., magnesium carb., bismuth subcarb., sod. bicarb. & kaolin. Pow., Can 3 oz. Tabs. 50s.
Use: Antacid.

ASBRON G. (Sandoz) Theophylline sodium glycinate 300 mg., guaifenesin 100 mg., alcohol 15% (Elixir only) Tab. Bot. 100s; Elix. Bot. 1 pt.
Use: Relief of acute bronchial asthma & for reversible bronchospasm associated with chronic bronchitis & emphysema.

ASCLEROL. (Spanner) Liver injection crude (2 mcg./cc.) 50%, Vit. B-1 20 mg., B-2 3 mg., B-6 1 mg., B-12 30 mcg., niacinamide 100 mg., panthenol 2.8 mg., choline chloride 20 mg., inositol 10 mg./cc. Multiple dose vial 10 cc.

ASCORVITE. (Vitarine) Vit. C 1000 mg./Gradual Release Tab.
Use: Dietary supplement.

ASCO SOLU-CAPS AND TABLETS. (Sutliff & Case) Aspirin 3 gr., Dover's powder 0.25 gr., acetophenetidin 1.5 gr., camphor monobromated 0.25 gr., atropine sulfate 1/500 gr./Cap. or Tab. Bot. 100s, 1000s.

ASCORBAJEN. (Jenkins) Ascorbic acid and Sodium ascorbate equiv. to 100 mg. of Vit. C/Tab. Bot. 1000s.
Use: Dietary adjuvant.

ASCORBATE SODIUM. Antiscorbutic vitamin.

• **ASCORBIC ACID,** U.S.P. XXI. Injection, Oral Solution, U.S.P. XXI. Tablets, U.S.P. XXI. 3-Oxo-L-gulofuranolactone (enol form). Antiscorbic vitamin; vitamin C.
Cap. (Various Mfr.) 25 mg., 100 mg., 250 mg., 500 mg. **Injection.** (Various Mfr.) Amp. (100 mg./cc.) 1 cc., 2 cc., 5 cc., (200 mg./cc.) 5 cc., (500 mg.) 2 cc., 5 cc., 10 cc., 30 cc. (250 mg./cc.) 10 cc., (1000 mg.) 10 cc. **Tab.** (25 mg., 50 mg., 100 mg., 250 mg., 500 mg.) (Various Mfr.)
Use: Vitamin C therapy
See: Ascorbajen, Tab. (Jenkins)
Ascorbicap, Cap. (ICN)
Ascorbineed, Cap. (Hanlon)
C-Caps 500 (Drug Industries)
Cecon, Sol. (Abbott)
Cenolate, Amp. (Abbott)
Cetane, Cap., Vial (Fellows)
Cevalin, Tab., Amp. (Lilly)
Cevi-Bid, Cap. (Geriatric)
Ce-Vi-Sol, Drops (Mead Johnson)
C-Long, Cap., (Reid-Provident)
C-Syrup-500 (Ortega)
Duoscorb, Powd. (Upsher-Smith)
Neo-Vadrin, Preps. (Scherer)
Solucap C, Cap. (Jamieson-McKames)
Synchro-C, Caps. (Carnrick)
Tega-C Tab. (Oretega)

• **ASCORBIC ACID INJECTION,** U.S.P. XXI.
See: Cevalin, Amp, (Lilly)

ASCORBIC ACID SALTS.
See: Bismuth Ascorbate
Calcium Ascorbate
Sodium Ascorbate

ASCORBICAP. (ICN) Ascorbic acid 500 mg./Cap. Bot. 50s, 250s.
Use: Treatment of Vit. C deficiency.

ASCORBINEED. (Hanlon) Vit. C 500 mg./T-Cap. B[illegible] 100s.

ASCORBOCIN POWDER. (Paddock) Vit. C 500 mg., niacin 500 mg., B-1 50 mg., B-6 50 mg., d-αtocophe[illegible] polyethylene glycol 1000 succinate 50 I.U., w/lactose/3 Gm. Bot. 1 lb.
Use: Vitamin supplement.

• **ASCORBYL PALMITATE,** N.F. XVI. L-Ascorbic acid palmitate.
Use: Preservative; antioxidant.

ASCORVITE S.R. (Vitarine) Vit. C 500 mg./Sus. Re[illegible] Cap.
Use: Dietary supplement.

ASCRIPTIN. (Rorer) Aspirin 325 mg., magnesium ar[illegible] aluminum hydroxide (Maalox) 150 mg./Tab. Bot. 50s, 100s, 225s, 500s, also available w/Codeine 15 mg., Bot. 100s. 30 mg. Bot. 100s.
Use: Analgesic, antipyretic, anti-inflammatory.

ASCRIPTIN A/D. (Rorer) Aspirin 325 mg., magnesiu[illegible] and aluminum hydroxides (Maalox) 300 mg./Tab. Bot. 100s, 225s, 500s.
Use: Analgesic, antipyretic, anti-inflammatory.

ASCRIPTIN W/CODEINE No. 2, (Rorer) Codeine phosphate 15 mg., aspirin 325 mg., magnesium and aluminum hydroxides (Maalox) 150 mg./Tab. Bot. 100s.
Use: Orally, analgesic, antipyretic, anti-inflammato[illegible]

ASCRIPTIN W/CODEINE No. 3. (Rorer) Codeine phosphate 30 mg., aspirin 325 mg., magnesium and aluminum hydroxides (Maalox) 150 mg./Tab. Bot. 100s.
Use: Orally, analgesic, antipyretic, anti-inflammato[illegible]

ASELLACRIN. (Serono) Human growth hormone (somatropin) 10 I.U./Vial. plus/vial NaCl diluent; 2[illegible] I.U./Vial plus 1 amp. NaCl diluent. Ctn. 1s, 2,s, 4s[illegible]
Use: Growth hormone replacement.

ASENDIN. (Lederle) Amoxapine 25 mg., 50 mg., 10[illegible] mg., or 150 mg./Tab.
Use: Antidepressant.

ASEPTICHROME.
See: Merbromin (Various Mfr.)
ASLUM. (Drug Products) Carbolic acid 1%, aluminum acetate, ichthammol, zinc oxide, aromatic oils in a petrolatum-stearin base. **Tube** 1 oz. **Jar** 1 lb.
Use: Astringent & soothing dressing.
ASMA. (Wampole-Zeus) Anti-smooth muscle antibody test by IFA. Tests 48.
Use: Diagnostic aid in identifying specific autoimmune disorders.
ASMABAR. (Blue Line) Ephedrine sulfate 25 mg., theophylline 130 mg., butabarbital 20 mg./Tab. Bot. 100s, 1000s.
Use: Treatment of bronchial asthma.
ASMADRIN. (Jenkins) Aminophylline 4 gr., aluminum hydroxide gel, dried, 4 gr., ephedrine HCl ⅜ gr., "trio-bar" 0.25 gr. (Representing 33⅓% each of pentobarbital sod., butabarbital sod., and phenobarbital sod)/Tab. Bot. 100s.
ASMA-LIEF. (Quality Generics) Theophylline 2 gr., ephedrine HCl ⅜ gr., phenobarbital ⅛ gr./Tab. Bot. 50s, 100s, 1000s.
Use: Bronchial asthma and hay fever.
ASMALIX. (Century) Theophylline 80 mg., alcohol 20%, /15 ml. Bot. qt., gal.
Use: Bronchodilator.
ASMASADINA. (Panray) Aminophylline 130 mg., ephedrine HCl 25 mg., amobarbital 25 mg./Cap. Bot. 100s.
ASMA SYRUP. (Coastal) Theophylline 150 mg., guaifenesin 90 mg., alcohol 15%/15 cc. Bot. 16 oz., gal.
ASMATEX. (Kenyon) Chlorpheniremine 1.25 mg., phenylephrine HCl 2.5 mg., acetylsalicylic acid 150 mg. buffered w/aluminum and magnesium hydroxide/Tab. Bot. 100s.
ASMA-TUSS. (Blue Cross) Phenobarbital 4 mg., theophylline 15 mg., ephedrine sulfate 12 mg., guaifenesin 50 mg./5 ml. Bot. 4 oz.
Use: Bronchial asthma treatment.
ASMOLIN. (Lincoln) l-Epinephrine 2.5 mg./cc. w/a glycerin solution 25%. Multiple dose vial 10 cc.
Use: For bronchial asthma.
ASOLECTIN. (Associated Conc.) Chemical lecithin 25%, chemical cephalin 22%, inositol phosphatides 16%, soybean oil 2.5%, other miscellaneous sterols and lipids 34.5%.
Use: As a diet supplement and aid in lipid metabolism.
ASPARAGINASE. USAN. L-asparagine amidohydrolase.
Use: Antineoplastic.
See: Elspar, Inj. (Merck Sharp & Dohme)
L-ASPARAGINE-5-L-VALINEANGIOTENSIN II.
See: Angiotensin amide.
ASPARTAME, N.F. XVI. 3-Amino-N-(α-methoxycarbonyl-phenethyl)succinamic acid. L-Aspartyl-L-phenylalanine methyl ester.
Use: Sweetening agent.
ASPARTIC ACID. USAN. Aspartic acid; aminosuccinic acid.
Use: Management of fatigue.

• **ASPARTOCIN.** USAN.
Use: Antibacterial.
A-SPAS. (Hyrex) Dicyclomine HCl 10 mg./ml. Vial 10 ml.
Use: Antispasmodic for I.M. administration.
ASPERBUF. (Bowman) Aspirin 324 gr., aluminum hydroxide dried gel 2 gr./Tab. Bot. 100s, 1000s.
Use: Analgesic.
ASPERCIN. (Otis Clapp) Aspirin 325 mg./Tab. Sugar, lactose, and salt free. Safety packs 500s.
Use: Analgesic, antipyretic, anti-inflammatory.
ASPERCIN EXTRA. (Otis Clapp) Aspirin 500 mg./Tab. Sugar, lactose, and salt free. Safety packs 500s.
Use: Extra strength analgesic, antipyretic, anti-inflammatory.
ASPERCREME. (Stanlabs) Triethanolamine salicylate 10% in a neutral cream base. Bot. 6 oz., Travelettes 5 gm.
ASPERCREME. (Thompson Medical) Triethanolamine salicylate 10% in cream base.
Use: Relief of minor arthritic, rheumatic and muscular aches and pains.
ASPERGILLUS ORYZAE ENZYME. Diastase
See: Taka-Diastase, Preps. (Parke-Davis)
ASPERGUM. (Plough) Aspirin 3.5 gr./1 Gum tablet. Tab. Orange or Cherry flavor. Box 16s, 40s.
Use: Analgesic.
ASPERKINASE. Proteolytic enzyme mixture derived from *aspergillus oryzae.*
• **ASPERLIN.** USAN.
Use: Antibacterial, antineoplastic.
ASPERMIN. (Buffington) Aspirin 325 mg./Tab. Sugar, lactose, and salt free. Dispens-A-Kits 500s.
Use: Analgesic, antipyretic, anti-inflammatory.
ASPERMIN EXTRA. (Buffington) Aspirin 500 mg./Tab. Sugar, lactose, and salt free. Dispens-A-Kit 500s.
Use: Analgesic, antipyretic, anti-inflammatory.
ASPIRBAR. (Lannett) Phenobarbital 0.25 gr., aspirin 10 gr./Tab. Bot. 1000s.
ASPIR-D COMPOUND CAPSULES. (Lannett) Cap. Bot. 100s.
ASPIR-CODE. (Robinson) Salicylamide 3.5 gr., phenacetin 2.5 gr., caffeine 0.5 gr., codeine phosphate 2 mg./Tab. Bot. 36s, 100s.
• **ASPIRIN,** U.S.P. XXI. Caps, Suppos, Tab., U.S.P. XXI. A.S.A., Acetophen, Acetol, Acetosal, Acetosalin, Aceticyl, Acetylin, Acetylsal, Empirin, Saletin. Acetylsalicylic acid, Benzoic acid, 2-(acetyloxy)-., Salicyclic acid acetate.
Use: Analgesic, antipyretic, & antirheumatic.
See: A.S.A., Prep. (Lilly)
Aspergum, Gum, Tab. (Plough)
Aspirjen Jr., Tab. (Jenkins)
BC Tablets (Block Drug)
Buffinol, Tab. (Otis Clapp)
Ecotrin, Tab. (SmithKline)
Empirin, Tab. (Burroughs Wellcome)
Measurin, Tab. (Winthrop-Breon)
Norwich Aspirin, Tab. (Norwich Eaton)
St. Joseph, Prods. (Plough)

W/Acetophenetidin & caffeine.
See: A.P.C. preparations (Various Mfg.)
• **ASPIRIN, ALUMINA, AND MAGNESIA TABLETS,** U.S.P. XXI.
Use: Analgesic, antacid.
ASPIRIN-BARBITURATE COMBINATIONS.
See: Acetabar, Cap., Tab. (Philips Roxane)
Amytal w/Acetylsal., Cap. (Lilly)
Anaphen, Cap. (Mallard)
Aspirbar, Tab. (Lannett)
Aspirin Uniserts,Suppos. (Upsher-Smith)
Axotal, Tab. (Warren-Teed)
Brogesic, Tab. (Brothers)
Bufabar, Tab. (Philips Roxane)
Buff-A Comp., Cap., Tabs. (Mayrand)
Cefinal, Tab. (Alto)
Doloral, Tab. (Alamed)
Fiorinal, Cap., Tab. (Sandoz)
Marnal, Tab., Cap. (Vortech)
Nipirin, Cap. (Elder)
Palgesic, Tab., Cap. (Pan Amer.)
Percobarb, Cap. (Du Pont)
Rotense, Tab. (Robinson)
Salibar Jr., Tab. (Jenkins)
Sedagesic, Tabs. (Kay)
Sedalgesic, Tab. (Table Rock)
ASPIRIN ENTERIC COATED.
See: A.S.A., Prep. (Lilly)
Ecotrin, Tab. (Menley & James)
ASPIRIN PLUS. (Walgreen) Aspirin 400 mg., caffeine 32 mg./Tab. Bot. 100s.
Use: Analgesic.
ASPIRIN SALTS.
See: Calcium Acetylsalicylate
ASPIRIN W/O.T.C. COMBINATIONS.
See: A.C.A., Caps., Tabs. (Scrip)
Alka Seltzer, Tab. (Miles)
Alka Seltzer Plus, Tab. (Miles)
Anacin, Tab. (Whitehall)
Analgestine Forte, Cap. (Mallard)
Anaphen, Cap. (Mallard)
Anodynos, Tab. (Buffington)
A.P.C., Tab. & Cap. (Various Mfr.)
A.S.A. Comp., Cap., Tab. (Lilly)
Ascriptin, Tab. (Rorer)
Ascriptin A/D, Tab. (Rorer)
Bayer Aspirin Preps. (Glenbrook)
Bayer Prods. (Glenbrook)
BC Powder (Block Drug)
Bexophene, Cap. (Mallard)
Buffaprin, Tab. (Buffington)
Bufferin, Tab. (Bristol-Myers)
Buffinol, Tab. (Otis Clapp)
Cama, Tab. (Dorsey)
Capathyn, Cap. (Scrip)
Capron, Cap. (Vitarine)
Congespirin, Tab. (Bristol-Myers)
Coralsone Modified, Tab. (Zemmer)
Counterpain, Tube (Squibb)
Damason, Prep. (Mason)
Derfort, Cap. (Cole)
Derfule, Cap. (Cole)
Dolor, Tab. (Geriatric Pharm.)
Dynosal, Tab. (Mallard)
Emagrin, Tab. (Otis Clapp)
Emagrin Forte, Tab. (Otis Clapp)
Excedrin, Cap., Tab. (Bristol-Myers)
Excedrin P.M., Tab. (Bristol-Myers)
4-Way, Tab., Spray (Bristol-Myers)
Gemnisyn, Tab. (Rorer)
Liquiprin, Tab. (Mitchum-Thayer)
Midol, Cap., Spray (Glenbrook)
PAC, Cap., Tab. (Upjohn)
Pap, Cap. (Zenith)
Phenacaps, Cap. (Scrip)
Phensal, Tab. (Merrell Dow)
Presalin, Tab. (Mallard)
Saleto, Prep. (Mallard)
Salocol, Tab. (Mallard)
Scrip-Dyne Comp., Cap. (Scrip)
Sine-Off Tablets (Menley & James)
Stanback, Pow., Tab. (Stanback)
St. Joseph Cold Tablets For Children (Plough)
Trigesic, Tab. (Squibb)
Vanquish, Cap. (Glenbrook)
ASPIRIN UNISERTS. (Upsher-Smith) Aspirin 12 mg./Supp. Ctn. 12s, 50s; 300 mg./Supp. Ctn. 12s, 50s; 600 mg/Supp. Ctn. 12s, 50s.
Use: Analgesic, antipyretic.
ASPIRJEN Jr. (Jenkins) Aspirin 2.5 gr./Tab. Bot. 1000s.
Use: Analgesic.
ASPIR-PHEN. (Robinson) Aspirin 5 gr., phenobarbit 0.5 gr./Tab. Bot. 100s, 1000s. Bulk Pack 5000s.
Use: Pediatric.
ASPIRTAB. (Dover) Aspirin 325 mg./Tab. Sugar, lactose, and salt free. Unit dose Box 500s.
Use: Analgesic, antipyretic, anti-inflammatory.
ASPIRTAB MAX. (Dover) Aspirin 500 mg./Tab. Sugar, lactose, and salt free. Unit dose Box 500s.
Use: Extra strength analgesic, antipyretic, anti-inflammatory.
ASPODYNE. (Blue Line) Aspirin 3.5 gr., acetophenetidin 2.5 gr., caffeine 0.5 gr./Tab. Bot. 1000s.
W/Codeine phosphate 0.25 gr. Bot. 1000s.
Use: Analgesic-antipyretic.
ASPOGEN. Dihydroxyaluminum aminoacetate.
ASPRO.
See: Acetylsalicylic acid.
ASPROJECT. (Mayrand) Sodium thiosalicylate 50 mg./ml. Vial 30 ml.
Use: Analgesic, antipyretic. **0.5mg.:** Bot. 100s, 500s. Redipak 25s. **1.0 mg.:** Bot. 100s, 500s, 1000s. Redipak 25s. **2 mg.:**
ASTARIL TABLETS. (Winthrop Products) Theophylline anhydrous, ephedrine sulphate.
Use: Antiasthmatic.
• **ASTEMIZOLE.** USAN.
Use: Antihistaminic.
ASTEROL. 6-(2-Diethylaminoethoxy)-2-dimethylaminobenzothiazole dihydrochloride. Diamthazole Dihydrochloride, B.A.N.
Use: Antifungal drug.

STHMACON. (CMC) Aminophylline 130 mg., ephedrine HCl 25 mg., amobarbital 25 mg./Cap. Bot. 100s, 500s, 1000s.
Use: Antiasthmatic.

STHMA METER. (Rexall) Epinephrine 0.2 mg./dose. Aerosol nebulizer w/measured dose valve 15 cc. or 300 doses.

STHMAHALER. (Norcliff Thayer) Epinephrine bitartrate 7 mg./ml. in an inert propellant. Oral inhaler, 15 ml. with mouthpiece; refills.
Use: Bronchial asthma.

STHMANEFRIN SOLUTION & NEBULIZER. (Norcliff Thayer) Racepin (racemic epinephrine) as HCl equivalent to 2.25% epinephrine base, chlorobutanol 0.5%. Bot. 0.5 fl. oz., 1 fl. oz.
Use: Bronchial asthma.

ASTROMICIN SULFATE. USAN.
Use: Antibacterial.

STRO-VITES. (Faraday) Vit. A 3500 I.U., D 400 I.U., C 60 mg., B-1 0.8 mg., B-2 1.3 mg., niacinamide 14 mg., B-6 1 mg., B-12 2.5 mcg., folic acid 0.05 mg., pantothenic acid 5 mg., Fe 12 mg./Tab. Bot. 100s, 250s.

ST/SGOT REAGENT STRIPS. Seralyzer reagent strip. Bot. 25 strips.
Use: A quantitative strip test for aspartate transaminase/serum glutamicoxaloacetic transaminase in serum or plasma.

SUNTOL. Coumaphos, B.A.N.

SUPIRIN. (Suppositoria) Aspirin 60 mg., 120 mg., 200 mg., 300 mg., 600 mg./1.2 Gm./Suppository. Box 12s, 100s, 1000s.
Use: Alternate route of administration for aspirin.

.T. 10.
See: Dihydrotachysterol

TABEE TD. (Defco) Vit. C 500 mg., B-1 15 mg., B-2 10 mg., B-6 2 mg., nicotinamide 50 mg., calcium pantothenate 10 mg./Cap. Bot. 30s, 1000s.
Use: Water-soluble B-complex and ascorbic acid vitamin deficiencies.

TABRINE HYDROCHLORIDE. (Winthrop-Breon) Quinacrine hydrochloride. **Tab.** (0.1 Gm.) Bot. 100s.
Use: Malaria of all types, giardiasis and tapeworm.

TARAX. (Roerig) Hydroxyzine HCl **Tab.** 10 mg. or 25 mg. Bot. 100s, 500s. Unit dose 10 × 10s. Unit of use 40s; 50mg. Bot. 100s, 500s. Unit dose 10 × 10s; 100 mg. Bot. 100s. Unit dose 10 × 10s. **Syr.** 10 mg./5 cc. w/alcohol 0.5% Bot. 1 pt.
Use: Treatment of tension, antianxiety & allergic dermatoses.

/Ephedrine sulfate, theophylline.
See: Marax, Tab., Syr. (Roerig)

/Penta-erythrityltetranitrate.
See: Cartrax, Tab. (Roerig)

ATARAXIC AGENTS.
See: Tranquilizers

TARVET. Acepromazine.

TEMPOL. Methylpentynol, B.A.N.

TENOLOL. USAN. 4-(2-Hydroxy-3-isopropylamino-propoxy) phenylacetamide.
Use: Beta adrenergic blocking agent.
See: Tenormin, Tab. (Stuart)

ATENSINE. Diazepam, B.A.N.

AT-EZE. (Faraday) Caps. Vial 30s. Bot. 1000s.
Use: Sleep aid.

ATGAM. (Upjohn) Lymphocyte immune globulin, antithymocyte globulin 250 mg. protein (50 mg./ml.). Amp. 5 ml.
Use: Management of allograft rejection in renal transplant patients.

ATGARD. Dichlorvos, B.A.N.

ATHLETE'S FOOT OINTMENT. (Walgreen) Zinc Undecylenate 20%, undecylenic acid 5%. Tube 1.5 oz.
Use: Antifungal.

ATHROMBIN.
See: Warfarin Sod.

ATHROMBIN-K TABLETS. (Purdue Frederick) Warfarin potassium 5 mg./Tab. Bot. 100s.
Use: Anticoagulant.

ATIVAN INJECTION. (Wyeth) Lorazepam 2 mg., 4 mg./ml. Vials 1 ml., 10 ml. Tubex. Pkg. 10s.
Use: Preanesthesia.

ATIVAN TABLETS. (Wyeth) Lorazepam 0.5 mg., 1 mg. or 2 mg./Tab. **0.5 mg.:** Bot. 100s, 500s. Redipak 25s. **1.0 mg.:** Bot. 100s, 500s, 1000s. Redipak 25s. **2 mg.:** Bot. 100s, 500s, 1000s. Redipak 25s.
Use: Minor tranquilizer for use in treatment of anxiety and tension.

• **ATOLIDE.** USAN. 2-Amino-4′-(diethylamino)-o-benzotoluidide. Under study.
Use: Anticonvulsant.

ATOZINE TABS. (Major) Hydroxyzine HC1 10 mg., 25 mg. or 50 mg./Tab. Bot. 250s, 1000s.
Use: Antianxiety, tension.

ATPEG. (ICI Americas) Polyethylene glycol available as 300, 400, 600, 4000.
Use: Surfactant and humectant.

• **ATRACURIUM BESYLATE.** USAN.
Use: Skeletal muscle relaxant.

ATRIDINE. (Interstate) Tripolidine 2.5 mg., pseudoephedrine HCl 60 mg./Tab. Bot. 100s, 1000s.
Use: Antihistimine, nasal decongestant.

ATROBARB NO. 1 (Jenkins) Phenobarbital sod. $\frac{1}{8}$ gr., atropine sulfate $\frac{1}{1000}$ gr./Tab. Bot. 1000s.
Use: Sedative.

ATROBARB NO. 2 (Jenkins) Phenobarbital sod. 0.25 gr., atropine sulfate $\frac{1}{500}$ gr./Tab. Bot. 1000s.
Use: Antispasmodic, antiemetic

ATROBARB NO. 3 (Jenkins) Phenobarbital sod. 0.25 gr., atropine sulfate $\frac{1}{250}$ gr./Tab. Bot. 1000s.
Use: Antispasmodic, antiemetic.

ATROCAP. (Freeport) Atropine sulfate 0.06 mg., hyoscyamine sulfate 0.3 mg., hyoscine hydrobromide 0.02 mg., phenobarbital 50 mg./T.R. Cap. Bot. 1000s.
Use: Sedative, anti-spasmodic, anticholinergic.

ATROCHOLIN. (Glaxo) Dehydrocholic acid 2 gr., homatropine methylbromide $\frac{1}{100}$ gr./Tab. Bot. 100s, 1000s, 5000s.
Use: Antispasmodic & hydrocholeretic.

ATROMID-S. (Ayerst) Clofibrate 500 mg./Cap. Bot. 100s.
Use: Hypercholesterolemia and/or hypertriglyceridemia.

ATROPHYSINE. (Lannett) Physostigmine salicylate 0.6 mg., atropine sulf. 0.6 mg./cc. Vials 30 cc.
Use: I.M., antispasmodic for skeletal muscle.

• **ATROPINE,** U.S.P. XXI. 1αH, 5αH-Tropan-3α-ol dl-Tropate (Ester) (dl-Hyoscyamine)dl-Tropyltropate.
See: Atropine Combinations

ATROPINE AND DEMEROL INJECTION. (Winthrop-Breon) Atropine sulfate 0.4 mg., meperidine HCl 50 mg. or 75 mg./Carpuject.
Use: Preoperative sedation.

ATROPINE BUFOPTO. (Softcon) Atropine sulf. 0.5%, 1% in methulose w/Benzalkonium chloride. Bot. 15 cc.
Use: Mydriasis and cycloplegia.

■ **ATROPINE-HYOSCINE-HYOSCYAMINE COMBINATIONS. (See also Belladonna Products)**
See: Almezyme, Cap. (Glaxo)
Barbella, Tab., Elix. (Fellows)
Barbeloid, Tab. (Vale)
Bar-Cy-Amine, Elix. (Sutliff & Case)
Bar-Cy-A-Tab, Tab. (Sutliff & Case)
Bar-Don, Tab., Elix. (Warren-Teed)
Belakoids TT, Tab. (Philips Roxane)
Belbutal No. 2 Kaptabs. (Churchill)
Brobella-P.B., Tab. (Brothers)
Buren, Tab. (Ascher)
Donnacin, Elix., Tab. (Pharmex)
Donnagel, Susp. (Robins)
Donnamine, Elix., Tab. (Tennessee Pharm.)
Donnatal, Cap., Elix., Tab. (Robins)
Donnatal #2, Tab. (Robins)
Donnatal Extentabs, Tab. (Robins)
Donnazyme, Tab. (Robins)
Eldonal, Prep. (Canright)
Haponal, Cap. (Jenkins)
Hyatal, Elix. (Winsale)
Hybephen, Preps. (Beecham Labs)
Hyonal, Prep. (Paddock)
Hyonatol B, Preps. (Bowman)
Hytrona, Tab. (Webcon)
Kinesed, Tab. (Stuart)
Koryza Tab. (Fellows)
Levamine, Tab. (Glaxo)
Maso-Donna, Elix., Tab. (Mason)
Nilspasm, Tab. (Parmed)
Renalgin, Tab. (Meyer)
Sedamine, Tab. (Dunhall)
Sedapar, Tab. (Parmed)
Sedralex, Elix., Tab. (Kay)
Seds, Tab. (Pasadena Research)
Spabelin, Elix. (Arcum)
Spasdel, Cap. (Marlop)
Spasloids, Tab. (G.F. Harvey)
Spasmolin, Tab. (Bell)
Spasquid, Elix. (Geneva)
Spastolate, Elix., Tab. (Barry-Martin)
Uriseptin, Tab. (Blaine)
Urogesic, Tab. (Edwards)
Zemarine Elix., Cap., Tab. (Zemmer)

ATROPINE METHYLNITRATE. (Various Mfr.) dl-Hyoscyamine methylnitrate.
See: Harvatrate, Tab. (O'Neal)
Thitrate W.P., Tab. (Blaine)
W/Hyoscine HBr, hyoscyamine sulfate, amobarbital sodium.
See: Amocine, Tab. (Mallard)
W/Methenamine mandelate & Phenylazodiaminopyridine HCl.
See: Uritral, Cap. (Central)
W/Oxidized bile acids, ox and hog bile ext., phenobarbital.
See: G.B.S., Tab. (O'Neal)
W/Phenobarbital & dihydroxy aluminum aminoacetate
See: Atromal, Tab. (Blaine)
Harvatrate A, Tab. (O'Neal)
W/Sulfaguanidine, sulfacetamide, neomycin sulf., carob flour.
See: Neogel W/Sulf, Tab. (Vortech)

ATROPINE-N-OXIDE HCl.
See: Atropine Oxide HCl.

• **ATROPINE OXIDE HYDROCHLORIDE.** USAN. Atropine N-oxide hydrochloride.
See: X-Tro. (Xttrium)

• **ATROPINE SULFATE,** U.S.P. XXI. Inj. Ophth. Oint. Ophth. Soln., Tablets, U.S.P. XXI. (Various Mfr.) Benzeneacetic acid, α-(hydroxymethyl-,8-methyl-8-azabicyclo-[3.2.1.]oct-3-yl ester, endo-(±)-, sulfat (2:1) (salt), monohydrate. l-αH, 5-α-H-Tropan-3-α-ol (±)-tropate (ester), sulfate (2:1) (salt) monohydrate. **Pediatric Inj.:** (Abbott) 0.05 mg./ml. 5 ml. Abboject.**Tab-Hypodermic,** 1/500, 1/200, 1/100, 1/ gr./Tab. **Tab-Oral,** 1/500, 1/250, 1/200, 1/150, 1/100 gr./Tab. **In** (Abbott) 0.1 mg./ml. 10 ml. Abboject syringe. **Lyophilized.** Lyopine (Hyrex)
Use: Anticholinergic, antidote to cholinesterase inhibitors.
See: Isopto-Atropine (Alcon)
Lyopine, Inj. (Hyrex)
Parasympatholytic & antispasmodic agent
W/Chlorpheniramine.
See: Histunex, Inj. (Tunex)
W/Ephedrine sulfate.
See: Enuretrol, Tab. (Berlex)

ATROPINE SULFATE W/PHENOBARBITAL.
See: Alised, Tab. (Elder)
Antrocol, Tab., Cap. (Poythress)
Arco-Lase Plus, Tab. (Arco)
Barbeloid, Tab. (Vale)
Bar-Tropin, Tab. (Fellows-Testagar)
Bioxatphen, Tab. (Zemmer)
Briabell, Tab. (Briar)
Briaspaz, Tab. (Briar)
Brobella-P.B., Tab. (Brothers)
Cerebel, Liq. (Xttrium)
Copin, Tab. (Bluco)
Donnatal, Cap., Extentabs, Tab., Elix. (Robins)
Donnatal #2, Tab. (Robins)
Haponal, Cap. (Jenkins)
Histacon, Tab., Syr. (Marsh-Emory)
Hyatal Elix. (Winsale)
Magnased, Tab. (Century)
Magnox, Tabs. (Bowman)

P & A, Tab. (Scrip)
Palbar No. 2, Tab. (Hauck)
PAMA, Tab. (N. Am. Pharm.)
Peece, Cap., Tab. (Scrip)
Ro Trim, Cap. (Rocky Mtn.)
Sedatabs, Tab. (Parkdale)
Seds, Tab. (Pasadena Research)
Spabelin, Elix. (Arcum)
Spasaid, Cap. (Century)
Spasdel, Cap. (Marlop)
Spasidon, Tab. (Haag)
Spasmate, Tab. (Spencer-Mead)
Spasmolin, Tab. (Kenyon)
Spastosed, Tab. (N. Am. Pharm.)
Stannitol (Standex)

TROPISOL. (CooperVision) Atropine sulfate solution. **Dropperettes** 0.5%, 1%, 2%. 1 ml. 12s. **Dropper Bot.** 1%, 5 ml. **Bot.** 1%, 15 ml.
Use: Mydriasis, cycloplegia.

TROSED. (Freeport) Atropine sulfate 0.0195 mg., hyoscine HBr 0.0065 mg., hyoscyamine sulfate 0.1040 mg. phenobarbital 0.25 gr./Tab. Bot. 1000s, 5000s.
Use: Sedative, anti-spasmodic, anticholinergic.

TROVENT.
See: Ipratropium bromide, B.A.N.

T-SOLUTION. (Winthrop Products) Dihydrotachysterol solution.
Use: Hypocalcemic tetany.

/T/S TOPICAL SOLUTION. (Hoechst) Erythromycin 2% topical sol. Bot. 60 ml. W/applicator.
Use: Acne treatment, topical.

TTAPULGITE, ACTIVATED.
See: Quintess, Susp. (Lilly)
V/Pectin, hydrated alumina powder.
See: Polymagma Plain Tablets (Wyeth)
V/Polysorbate 80, salicylic acid, propylene glycol.
See: Sebasorb Lotion (Summer)

TTENUVAX. (Merck Sharp & Dohme) Measles virus vaccine, live, attenuated w/neomycin 25 mcg./Vial. Single-dose vial w/diluent. Box of 10 single-dose vials.
Use: Immunization against measles.
V/Meruvax.
See: M-R-Vax-II, Vial (Merck Sharp & Dohme)
V/Mumpsvax, Meruvax.
See: M-M-R II, Vial (Merck Sharp & Dohme)

TURBANE HYDROCHLORIDE. Phenglutarimide, B.A.N.

TUSSIN EXPECTORANT. (Amfre-Grant) Chlorpheniramine maleate 2 mg., phenylephrine HCl 5 mg., phenylpropanolamine HCl 5 mg., guaifenesin 100 mg./5 cc Bot. 4 oz., pt., gal.
Use: Coughs

TUSSIN-D.M. EXPECTORANT. (Amfre-Grant) Chlorpheniramine maleate 2 mg., phenylephrine HCl 5 mg., phenylpropanolamine HCl 5 mg., guaifenesin 100 mg., d-methorphan HBr 15 mg./5 cc. Syr. Bot. 4 oz., pt., gal.
Use: Coughs.
W/Pentobarbital sodium, 2-diethylaminoethyl diphenylacetate hydrochloride, aluminum hydroxide.
See: Spasmasorb, Tab. (Hauck)

A.T.V. VAGINAL SUPPOSITORIES. (Amfre-Grant) Estrone 0.2 mg. lactose 50.0 mg./supp. Pkg. 12s with inserter.
Use: Hormone-estrogen therapy.

AUDINORM. Dioctyl Sodium Sulphosuccinate, B.A.N.

AUGMENTIN ORAL SUSPENSION. (Beecham Labs) **125:** Amoxicillian 125 mg., clavulanic acid (as potassium salt) 31.25 mg./5 ml. Bot. 75 ml., 150 ml. **250**: Amoxicillin 250 mg., clavulanic acid (as potassium salt) 62.5 mg./5 ml. Bot. 75 ml., 150 ml.
Use: Antibiotic.

AUGMENTIN TABLETS. (Beecham Labs) Amoxicillin trihydrate 250 mg. or 500 mg., clavulanic acid (as potassium salt) 125mg./Tab. Bot. 30s.
Use: Antibiotic.

AURA-BELL. (Metro Med) Bot. 0.5 oz.
Use: Ear solution.

AURAL ACUTE. (Saron) Polymyxin B sulfate 10,000 u., neomycin sulfate 5 mg., hydrocortisone 10 mg./10 cc w/alcohol 0.1%.
Use: Antibiotic ear drops.

AURALGAN OTIC SOLUTION. (Ayerst) Antipyrine 54 mg., benzocaine 14 mg./ml. w/oxyquinoline sulfate in dehyd. glycerin. (contains not more than 0.6% moisture). Bot. w/dropper 0.5 fl. oz.
Use: Treatment otitis media (acute), removal of cerumen.

AURALGESIC. (Wesley) Carbamide 10%, antipyrine 5%, benzocaine 2.5%, cetyldimethylbenzyl-ammonium HCl 0.2%. Bot. 0.5 oz.

• **AURANOFIN.** USAN.
Use: Antirheumatic.

AUREOMYCIN PREPARATIONS. (Lederle) Chlortetracycline HCl.
Oint. Ophth.: 1%. (10 mg./Gm.) Tube ⅛ oz.
Oint. Topical: 3% in white petrolatum, anhydrous lanolin base. Tube 20 Gm., 0.5 oz., 1 oz.
Use: Broad spectrum antibiotic.

AUREOQUIN DIAMATE. Name previously used for Quinetolate.

AURINOL EAR DROPS. (CMC) Benzocaine, antipyrene, glycerol. Bot. 0.5 oz., pt., gal.
Use: Removal of wax.

AURISPORIN. (Vortech) Polymyxin B sulfate 10,000 units, neomycin sulfate 3.5 mg., hydrocortisone 10 mg./ml. w/potassium metabisulfite 0.1%, hydrochloric acid, propylene glycol. Bot. 10 ml. dropper.
Use: Otic antibiotic.

AURISTIL. (Blue Line) Benzocaine 9%, hexylresorcinol 0.1%, menthol 4%, camphor 2%. Dropules 50 min., rubber-cap droppers, 12s.
Use: Analgesic for ear-ache.

AURI-TUSS. (Zemmer) Dextromethorphan HBr 15 mg., chlorpheniramine maleate 1 mg., guaifenesin 90 mg., phenylephrine HCl 5 mg., alcohol 10%/5 cc. Syrup. Bot. 3 oz., pt., gal.
Use: Control of cough.

AUROCAINE. (Vita Elixir) Benzocaine 0.15 Gm., antipyrine 0.70 Gm., glycerol q.s.
Use: Otic analgesic.

AUROCEIN. (Christina) Gold naphthyl sulfhydryl derivative. Amp. (5% or 12.5%) 10 cc.
Use: Antirheumatic gold therapy.

AURO-DRI. (Commerce) Boric acid 2.75% in isopropyl alcohol. Bot. 1 oz.
Use: Relief of swimmer's ear.

AURO EAR DROPS. (Commerce) Carbamide peroxide 6.5% in a specially prepared base. Tube 0.5 oz.
Use: For softening wax.

AUROLIN.
See: Gold sodium thiosulfate.

AUROMID EARDROPS. (Vangard) Antipyrine 54 mg., benzocaine 14 mg./ml. w/glycerin dehydrated q.s. to 1 ml. Bot. 15 ml.
Use: Decongestant, analgesic.

AUROPIN.
See: Gold sodium thiosulfate.

AUROSAN.
See: Gold sodium thiosulfate.

AUROTHIOBLYCANIDE. 2-Mercaptoacetanilide S-gold (1+) salt.
Use: Antirheumatic.

AUROTHIOGLUCOSE INJECTION.
See: Sterile aurothioglucose suspension.

AUROTHIOMALATE, SODIUM.
See: Gold Sodium Thiomalate, U.S.P. XXI.

AUROTIS. (Research Pharmacal Lab.) Antipyrine 4%, benzocaine 1%, glycerine 95%. 15 cc.
Use: Acute otitis media.

AURTO. (CMC)
Use: Treatment of acute otitis media

AUSAB. (Abbott) Test kit 100s.
Use: Radioimmunoassay or enzyme immunoassay for detection of antibody to hepatitis B surface antigen.

AUSCELL. (Abbott) Test kit 110s, 450s, 1800s.
Use: Reverse passive hemagglutination test for hepatitis B surface antigen.

AUSRIA II-125. (Abbott) Antibody to test for hepatitis B surface antigen. Test kit 100s, 500s, 600s, 700s, 800s, 900s, 1000s.
Use: Radioimmunoassay for detection of hepatitis B antigen.

AUSZYME II. (Abbott) Test kit 100s, 500s.
Use: Enzyme immunoassay for detection of hepatitis B surface antigen.

AUTOANTIBODY SCREEN. (Wampole-Zeus) Autoantibody screening system. Tests 48s.
Use: To screen serum for the presence of a variety of autoantibodies.

AUTOLET KIT. (Ames) Automatic blood letting spring-loaded device.
Use: Obtaining capillary blood samples from fingertips, earlobes or heels.

AUTOPLEX. (Hyland) Anti-inhibitor coagulant complex prepared from pooled human plasma. Vial 30 ml.
Use: Anti-inhibitor coagulant complex.

AUTRINIC. Intrinsic factor concentrate.
Use: Increase absorption of Vit. B-12.

AUXOTAB ENTERIC 1 & 2. (Colab) Rapid identification of enteric bacteria and pseudomonas. Test contains capillary units with selective biochemical reagents.

A-VAN. (Stewart-Jackson) Dimenhydrinate 25 mg., niacin 50 mg./Cap. Bot. 100s.
Use: Treatment of vertigo, dizziness, Meniere's syndrome, labyrinthitis.

AVAZYME. (Wallace) Crystalline chymotrypsin (20,000 units) 20 mg./Enteric coated tab. Bot. 48s, 250s.
Use: Anti-inflammatory agent, enzyme preparation chymotrypsin preparation.

AVAZYME-100. (Wallace) Crystalline chymotrypsin (100,000 units) 40 mg./Enteric coated Tab. Bot. 48s, 250s.
Use: Anti-inflammatory agent, enzyme preparation chymotrypsin preparation.

AVC CREAM. (Merrell Dow) Sulfanilamide 15%, aminacrine HCl 0.2%, allantoin 2% with lactose, in a water-miscible base made from propylene glycol stearic acid, diglycol stearate to acid pH. Tube 4 oz. w/applicator.
Use: Vulvovaginitis when responsible organism not known *(Trichomonas vaginalis, Candida albicans,* o *Hemophilus vaginitis).*

AVC SUPPOSITORIES. (Merrell Dow) Sulfanilamide 1.05 Gm., aminacrine HCl 0.014 Gm., allantoin 0.14 Gm. with lactose, in a base made from polyethlene glycol 400, polysorbate 80, polyethylene glycol 3350, glycerin, inert glycerin-gelatin covering. Box of 16s w/inserter.
Use: Vulvovaginitis when responsible organism not known *(Trichomonas vaginalis, Candida albicans,* or *Hemophilus vaginalis).*

AVC/DIENESTROL CREAM. (Merrell Dow) Dienestrol 0.01%, sulfanilamide 15%, aminacrine HCl 0.2%, allantoin 2% with lactose, in a water-miscible base made from propylene glycol, stearic acid, diglycol stearate, triethanolamine, butylated hydroxytoluene. Tube 4 oz., w/applicator.
Use: Atrophic vaginitis and kraurosis vulvae associated with menopause and complicated by infection.

AVC/DIENESTROL SUPPOSITORIES. (Merrell Dow) Dienestrol 0.7 mg., sulfanilamide 1.05 Gm., aminacrine HCl 0.014 Gm., allantoin 0.14 Gm. with lactose, in a base made from polyethylene glycol 400, polysorbate 80, polyethylene glycol 3350, glycerin, butylated hydroxytoluene, inert glycerin-gelatin covering. Box of 16s w/inserter.
Use: Atrophic vaginitis and kraurosis vulvae associated with menopause and complicated by infection.

AVEENOBAR MEDICATED. (Rydell) Aveeno colloidal oatmeal 50%, sulfur 2%, salicylic acid 2%, in soap-free cleansing bar. Formerly Acnaveen. Bar 3.5 oz.
Use: Antipruritic cleanser and shampoo.

AVEENO BATH. (Rydell) Colloidal oatmeal. Box 1 lb., 4 lb.
Use: Antipruritic bath.

AVEENOBAR OILATED. (Rydell) Vegetable oils, lanolin derivative, glycerine 29%, Aveeno colloidal oatmeal 30% in soap-free base. Formerly Emulave Bar. 3 oz.

Use: Lubricates, protects and helps remoisturize dry skin.

/EENOBAR REGULAR. (Rydell) A soap-free cleansing bar containing 50% colloidal oatmeal, anionic sulfonate and hypo-allergenic lanolin. Formerly Aveeno Bar. Bar 3.2 oz., 4.4 oz.
Use: Hypoallergenic cleansing agent.

/EENO COLLOIDAL OATMEAL. (Rydell) Colloidal oatmeal. Box 1 lb., 4 lb.
Use: Acute, inflammatory "wet" dermatoses.

/EENO LOTION. (Rydell) Colloidal oatmeal (A demulcent) in a soothing mildly drying aqueous lotion base. Bot. 6 oz.
Use: Relief of sunburn, poison ivy and oak, diaper rash and other minor skin problems.

/EENO OILATED. (CooperCare) Aveeno colloidal oatmeal impregnated with a high percentage (35%) of liquid petrolatum and refined olive oil. Box. 8 oz., 2 lb.
Use: Dry skin conditions.

/ENTYL HCl. (Lilly) Nortriptyline HCl equiv. to 10 mg. base/5 ml. **Liq.** Bot. 16 fl. oz. **Pulvule:** equiv. to 10 mg. base or 25 mg. base/Cap. Bot. 100s, 500s. Blisterpak 10 × 10s.
Use: Mental depression and anxiety-tension states.

/ERTIN. Tribromoethanol (Var. Mfr.)

/ICALM HCl. Metoserpate, B.A.N.

/INAR. Uredepa.
Use: Anti-neoplastic agent.

/ITENE. (Alcon) Hydrochloric acid salt of purified bovin corium collagen. Fibrous Form: Jars. 1 Gm., 6 Gm. Webb Form: Blister Paks. Sheets of 70 mm × 70 mm, 70 mm × 35 mm.
Use: Absorbable topical hemostat.

/LOCLOR. Chloroquine, B.A.N.

/LOSULFON. (Ayerst) Dapsone Tab. 100 mg. Bot. 100s.
Use: Treatment of all forms of leprosy.

/OMINE. Promethazine Theoclate, B.A.N.

/ONIQUE. (Geneva) Vit. A 4000 I.U., D 400 I.U., B-1 1 mg., B-2 1.2 mg., B-6 2 mg., B-12 2 mcg., Ca pantothenate 5 mg., B-3 10 mg., C 30 mg., Ca 100 mg., P 76 mg., Fe 10 mg., Mn 1 mg., Mg. 1 mg. Zn 1 mg.
Use: Multiple vitamin.

AVOPARCIN. USAN.
Use: Antibacterial.

.V.P. CILLIN TABS AND POWDER FOR SYRUP. (A.V.P.) Potassium Penicillin G. **Syr.:** (400,000 u) 250 mg./5 cc. Bot. 80 cc. **Tab.:** 250 mg./Tab. Bot. 100s.
Use: Anti-infective.

.V.P. NATAL-FA. (A.V.P.) Vitamin A 5000 I.U., iron, elemental from 200 mg., ferrous fumarate 65 mg., calcium 165 mg., phosphorus 75 mg., C 100 mg., B-6 10 mg., folic acid 1 mg./Tab. Bot. 100s.
Use: Dietary supplement during pregnancy or lactation.

AVRIDINE. USAN.
Use: Antiviral.

/R PADS. (Birchwood) Witch hazel-glycerin impregnated flannel pad. 40 pads/Jar.
Use: Personal hygiene.

AWAKE. (Walgreen) Caffeine 100 mg./Tab. Bot. 36s.
Use: Stimulant.

AXEROPHTHOL.
See: Vitamin A

AXON THROAT SPRAY. (McKesson) Bot. 5.0 gm.
Use: Sore throat remedy.

AXOTAL. (Adria) Butalbital 50 mg., aspirin 650 mg./Tab. Bot. 100s, 500s. Stat-Pak 100s.
Use: Relief of symptomatic complex of tension headaches.

AXSINATE. (Lannett) Styramate 200 mg., salicylamide 210 mg., acetophenetidin 150 mg., caffeine 30 mg./Tab. Bot. 50s.
Use: Analgesic.

AYDS APPETITE SUPPRESSANT CANDY. (Jeffrey Martin) Benzocaine 5 mg. in chewy candy base w/25 cal./Cube candy. Ctn. 12s, 48s, 96s.
Use: Appetite suppressant.

AYGESTIN. (Ayerst) Norethindrone acetate 5 mg./Tab. Bot. 50s. cycle packs 10s.
Use: Progestin hormone therapy.

AYR SALINE NASAL DROPS. (Ascher) Sodium chloride 0.65% adjusted with phosphate buffers to proper tonicity and pH to prevent nasal irritation. Bot. 20 ml.
Use: In babies & children to loosen and remove mucus secretions, etc.

AYR SALINE NASAL MIST. (Ascher) Sodium chloride 0.65% in isotonic spray. Bot. 50 ml.
Use: Dry, congested nasal membranes due to overuse of decongestant nasal sprays and drops.

8-AZABICYCLO[3.2.1.]OCTANE-2-CARBOXYLIC ACID, 3-(BENZOYLOXY)-8-METHYL-, METHYL ESTER, HCl. Cocaine Hydrochloride, U.S.P. XXI.

8-AZABICYCLO[3.2.1]OCTANE, 3-(DIPHENYL-METHOXY)-,endo-, METHANE-SULFONATE. Benztropine Mesylate, U.S.P. XXI.

• **AZABON.** USAN.
Use: Stimulant.

• **AZACITIDINE.** USAN.
Use: Antineoplastic.

• **AZACHLORZINE HYDROCHLORIDE.** USAN.
Use: Vasodilator.

AZACYCLONOL HCl. Alpha, alpha-diphenyl-4-piperidine-methanol HCl.

AZACYCLONOL. B.A.N. α-4-Piperidylbenzhydrol. Frenquel hydrochloride.
Use: Tranquilizer.

AZALINE TABS. (Major) Sulfasalazine 500 mg./Tab. Bot. 100s, 1000s.
Use: Ulcerative colitis treatment.

AZALINE EC TABS. (Major) Sulfasalazine 500 mg./EC Tab. Bot. 100s.
Use: Ulcerative colitis treatment.

AZALOMYCIN. B.A.N. A mixture of related antibiotics produced by Streptomyces hygroscopicus var. azalomyceticus.

AZAMETHONIUM BROMIDE. (Ciba) 3-Methyl-3-aza-pentamethylenebis (ethyldimethyl-ammonium) dibromide. Pendiomide, Pentamin.
Use: Ganglionic blocking agent.

• **AZALOXAN FUMARATE.** USAN.
Use: Antidepressant.

AZAMETHONIUM BROMIDE. B.A.N. 3-Methyl-3-aza-pentamethylenedi(ethyldimethylammonium bromide). Pendiomide.
Use: Ganglionic blocking agent.

• **AZANATOR MALEATE.** USAN.
Use: Bronchodilator.

• **AZANIDAZOLE.** USAN.
Use: Antiprotozoal.

• **AZAPERONE.** USAN. 4′-Fluoro-4-[4-(2-pyridyl)-piperazin-l-yl]butyrophenone. Stresnil. Suicalm.
Use: Tranquilizer, veterinary medicine.

AZAPETINE. B.A.N. 6-Allyl-5,7-dihydrodibenz-[c,e]azepine. Ilidar phosphate.
Use: Vasodilator.

AZAPETINE PHOSPHATE. 6-Allyl-6,7-dihydro-5H-dibenz(c,e)azepine, azephine.

AZAPROPAZONE. A fazone.

AZAPROPAZONE. B.A.N. 5-Dimethylamino-9-methyl-2-propyl-1H-pyrazolo[1,2-α][1,2,4]-benzotriazine-1,3 (2H)-dione.
Use: Analgesic; anti-inflammatory.

• **AZARIBINE.** USAN. 2-β-D-Ribofuranosyl-1,2,4-triazine-3,5-(2H,4H)dione2,3′,5′-triacetate. 6-Azauridine 2′,3′,5′-triacetate. Triazure.
Use: Treatment of psoriasis.

• **AZAROLE.** USAN.
Use: Immunoregulator.

• **AZASERINE.** USAN.
Use: Antifungal.

• **AZATADINE MALEATE,** U.S.P. XXI. 5-H-Benzo (5-6) cyclohepta (1,2-b) pyridine, 6,11-dihydro-11-(1-methyl-4-piperidylidene)-5H-benzo(5,6)-cyclohepta (1,2-b) pyridine maleate (1:2)
Use: Antihistaminic.
See: Optimine, Tab. (Schering)
Trinalin, Tab. (Schering)

• **AZATHIOPRINE,** U.S.P. XXI. Tab., U.S.P. XXI. (Burroughs Wellcome) 6-(1-Methyl-4-nitroimidazol-5-ylthio) purine. IH-Purine, 6-[(l-methyl-4-nitro-IH-imidazol-5-yl)thio]-.6-[(l-Methyl-4-nitroimidazol-5-yl)thio]purine.
Use: Anti-leukemic compound.
See: Imuran, Inj., Tab. (Burroughs Wellcome)

AZATHIOPRINE. B.A.N. 6-(1-Methyl-4-nitroimidazol-5-ylthio)purine.
Use: Antimetabolite.

AZATHIOPRINE SODIUM, U.S.P. XXI.
Use: Anti-leukemic compound.

• **AZELASTINE HYDROCHLORIDE.** USAN.
Use: Anti-allergic, anti-asthmatic.

• **AZEPINDOLE.** USAN.
Use: Antidepressant.

• **AZETEPA.** USAN. PP-Diaziridin-1-yl-N-ethyl-1,3,4-thiadiazol-2-ylphosphinamide.
Use: Antimetabolite.

AZIDOCILLIN. B.A.N. 6-[D(—)-α-Azidophenyl-acetamido]penicillanic acid.
Use: Antibiotic.

• **AZIPRAMINE HYDROCHLORIDE.** USAN.
Use: Antidepressant.

AZLIN. (Miles Pharm) Azlocillin sodium. Vials 2 Gm., 3 Gm., or 4 Gm.
Use: Broad spectrum antibiotic.

• **AZLOCILLIN.** USAN.
Use: Antibacterial.
See: Azlin, Inj. (Miles)

• **AZLOCILLIN SODIUM, STERILE,** U.S.P. XXI.
Use: Antibacterial.

AZLYTAL. (U.S. Ethicals) Phenobarbital 16.2 mg., hyoscyamine sulfate 0.1037 mg., atropine sulfate 0.0194 mg., scopolamine HBr 0.0065 mg./Tab. Bc 1000s.
Use: Intestinal anti-spasmodic.

AZMA-AID. (Purepac) Theophylline 2 gr., ephedrine ³ gr., phenobarbital ⅛ gr./Tab. Bot. 100s, 250s, 1000s.
Use: Bronchodilator.

AZMACORT INHALER. (Rorer) Triamcinolone acetonide 200 mcg. actuation of which approximately 100 mcg. are delivered from the collapasible expansion chamber activator. 20 Gm. canister contains 60 mg. triamcinolone acetonide w/oral adapter.
Use: Treatment of chronic bronchial asthma.

AZMADRINE. (U.S. Ethicals) Aminophylline compound Caps. Bot. 50s, 100s. Tab. 24s.
Use: Bronchial dilator

AZMADRINE PEDIATRIC SUSPENSION. (U.S. Ethicals) Theophylline 65 mg., ephedrine HCl phenobarbital 4 mg./5 ml.
Bot. 120 ml., 480 ml.
Use: Bronchial dilator.

AZMA-EZE. (Eckerd) Theophylline 100 mg., ephedrin HCl 25 mg., guaifenesin 100 mg., chlorpheniramin maleate 2 mg./Tab. Bot. 48s.
Use: Bronchial asthma.

AZO-100. (Scruggs) Phenylazodiaminopyridine HCl 1C mg./Tab. Bot. 100s, 1000s.
Use: Urinary tract analgesic.

• **AZOCONAZOLE.** USAN.
Use: Antifungal.

AZO-CYST. (Moore Kirk) Phenylazodiaminopyridine H 50 mg., calcium mandelate 120 mg., acid sod. phosphate 120 mg., methenamine 120 mg., hyoscyamine HBr 0.1037 mg., hyoscine HBr 0.006 mg., atropine sulfate 0.0194 mg./Tab. Bot. 100s, 1000s.
Use: Urinary tract sterilization.

AZODINE. (Vortech) Phenylazodiaminopyridine HCl 1.5 gr./Tab. Bot. 1000s.
Use: Urinary anti-infective, analgesic.

AZODYNE.
W/Sulfadiazine, sulfamethizole
See: Suladyne, Tab. (Stuart)

AZODYNE HCl
See: Pyridium, Tab. (Parke-Davis)

AZO-GAMAZOLE TABS. (Major) Bot. 100s, 1000s.
Use: Urinary tract infections.

AZO GANTANOL. (Roche) Sulfamethoxazole 500 mg., phenazopyridine HCl 100 mg./Tab. Bot. 100s 500s.

Use: Treatment of urinary tract infections complicated by pain.

ZO GANTRISIN. (Roche) Sulfisoxazole 500 mg., phenazopyridine HCl 50 mg./Tab. Bot. 100s, 500s.
Use: Treatment of urinary tract infections complicated by pain.

ZOLID. (USV Labs.) Phenylbutazone 100 mg./Tab. or Caps. Bot. 100s, 1000s.
Use: Anti-inflammatory.

AZOLIMINE. USAN.
Use: Diuretic.

ZOMAN. Hexazole, B.A.N.

ZO NEGACIDE TABLETS. (Winthrop Products) Nalidixic acid, phenazopyridine HCl.
Use: Painful lower urinary tract infection.

AZOSEMIDE. USAN.
Use: Diuretic.

ZO-SOXAZOLE. (Quality Generics) Sulfisoxazole 500 mg., phenylazodiaminopyridine HCl 50 mg./Tab. Bot. 100s, 1000s.

ZO-STANDARD. (Webcon) Phenazopyridine HCl 95 mg./Tab. Bot. 30s.
Use: Urinary tract infections.

ZOSTIX REAGENT STRIPS. (Ames) Bromthymol blue, urease, buffers. Bot. 25 strips.
Use: A colorimetric test for blood urea nitrogen level.

ZO-SULFISOXAZOLE. (Century) Sulfisoxazole 500 mg., phenylazopyridine HCl 50 mg./Tab. Bot. 1000s.

ZO-SULFISOXAZOLE. (Vortech) Sulfisoxazole 500 mg., phenylazodiaminopyridine HCl 50 mg./Tab. Bot. 1000s.
Use: Urinary tract infections.

ZO-SULFISOXAZOLE. (Richlyn) Sulfisoxazole 500 mg., phenylazopyridine HCl 50 mg./Tab. Bot. 1000s.

ZO-SULFISOXAZOLE. (Fellows) Azo-sulfisoxazole 500 mg., phenylazodiaminopyridine 50 mg./Tab. Bot. 100s, 1000s.

AZOTOMYCIN. USAN. Antibiotic isolated from broth filtrates of *Streptomyces ambofaciens.*
Use: Anti-neoplastic agent.

ZO-URIZOLE. (Jenkins) Sulfisoxazole 0.5 Gm., phenazopyridine HCl 50 mg./Tab. Bot. 1000s.

ZOVAN BLUE. Tetrasodium salt of 4:4′-di-[7-(1-amino-8-hydroxy-2:4-disulpho)-naphthylazo]-3:3′-bitolyl.
See: Evans Blue Dye, Amp. (City Chemical; Harvey)

ZOVAN BLUE. B.A.N. Tetrasodium salt of 4,4′-di-(8-amino-1-hydroxy-5,7-disulfo-2-naphthylazo)-3,3′-bitolyl.
Use: Diagnostic aid.
See: Evans Blue

ZO WINTOMYLON. (Winthrop Products) Nalidixic acid, phenazopyridine HCl.
Use: Painful lower urinary tract infection.

ZPAN. (Zenith) Phenobarbital 8 mg., theophylline 130 mg., ephedrine HCl 24 mg./Tab.
Use: Bronchodilator used in treatment of asthma.

AZTREONAM. USAN.
Use: Antimicrobial.

AZUDIMIDINE. Salazosulphadimidine, B.A.N.

AZULFIDINE ORAL SUSPENSION. (Pharmacia) Sulfasalazine 250 mg./5 ml. Bot. pt.
Use: Mild to moderate ulcerative colitis. Adjunctive therapy in severe ulcerative colitis.

AZULFIDINE TABLETS and EN-TABS. (Pharmacia) Sulfasalazine (salicylazosulfapyridine) 500 mg./En-tab or Tab. Bot. 100s, 500s. Unit dose 100s, 1000s.
Use: Mild to moderate ulcerative colitis and adjunctive therapy in severe ulcerative colitis.

AZURESIN. B.A.N. Prepared from carbacrylic cation exchange resin and azure A dye (3-amino-7-dimethylaminophenazathionium chloride). Diagnex Blue.
Use: Diagnostic aid.

B

B-1. Thiamine hydrochloride.

B-1 50. (Western Research) Vitamin B-1 50 mg./Tab. Bot. 1000s.
Use: Vitamin deficiency supplement.

B-2. Riboflavin.

B-3. Niacinamide.

B-6. Pyridoxine hydrochloride.

B-6 50. (Western Research) Vitamin B-6 50 mg./Tab. Bot. 1000s.
Use: Vitamin deficiency supplement.

B-12. Cyanocobalamin.

B-12 PLEX W/C. (Vortech) Univial 10 ml.
Use: Vitamin B complex with vitamin C.

B & A. (Eastern Research) Sod. bicarbonate, pot. alum., borax. Hygienic pow. Jar. 8 oz., 5 lb.
Use: Vaginal douche.

B.A. GRADUAL. (Federal) Theophylline 260 mg., pseudo-ephedrine HCl 50 mg., butabarbital 15 mg./Gradual. Bot. 50s, 1000s.

BABY COUGH. (DeWitt) Bot. 3 oz.
Use: Anti-cough for infants and children.

BABY COUGH SYRUP. (Towne) Amm. chloride 300 mg., sod. citrate 600 mg./oz. w/citric acid. Bot. 4 oz.
Use: Antitussive (pediatric).

• **BACAMPICILLIN HYDROCHLORIDE,** U.S.P. XXI. for Oral Soln., Tab., U.S.P. XXI.
Use: Antibiotic.

BACARATE. (Reid-Provident) Phendimetrazine tartrate 35 mg./Tab. Bot. 100s, 1000s.
Use: Appetite suppressant.

BACCO-RESIST. (Vita Elixir) Lobeline sulfate 1/64 gr.
Use: Antismoking lozenge.

BACDIP. Quintiofos, B.A.N.

BACID. (Fisons) A specially cultured strain of human *Lactobacillus acidophilus,* sodium carboxymethylcellulose 100 mg./Cap. Bot. 50s, 100s.
Use: Functional diarrhea.

BACIGUENT ANTIBIOTIC OINTMENT. (Upjohn) Bacitracin 500 u./Gm. Oint Tube 0.5 oz., 1 oz., 4 oz.
Use: Topically, pyogenic skin infections.

BACIGUENT OPHTHALMIC OINTMENT. (Upjohn) Bacitracin 500 u./Gm., in a base of white petrolatum, anhydrous lanolin, mineral oil, & chlorobutanol. Tube 3.5 Gm.

• **BACITRACIN,** U.S.P. XXI. Oint., Ophth., Oint., Sterile, U.S.P. XXI. An antibiotic produced by a strain of *Bacillus subtilis.*
Available forms (Various Mfr.)
Diagnostic Tabs.
Ointment
Ophthalmic Oint.
Soluble Tabs.
Systemic Use, Vial.
Topical Use, Vial.
Troches
Vaginal Tabs.
Use: Antibacterial.
See: baciquent, Oint. (Upjohn)
W/Neomycin sulfate.
See: Bacimycin, Oint. (Merrell Dow)
Bacitracin-Neomycin, Oint, Ophth. Oint. (Various Mfr.)
W/Neomycin, polymyxin B sulfate.
See: Baximin, Oint. (Quality Generics)
BPN Ointment (Norwich Eaton)
Mycitracin, Oint. & Ophth. Oint. (Upjohn)
Neosporin, Oint. & Ophth. Oint., Aerosol, Pwd. (Burroughs Wellcome)
Neo-Thrycex, Oint. (Commerce)
P.B.N., Oint. (Jenkins)
Tigo, Oint. (Burlington)
Tri-Biotic Oint. (Burgin-Arden)
Tri-Biotic, Oint. (Standex)
Tri-Bow Oint. (Bowman)
Triple Antibiotic Oint. (Kenyon, North American Pharmacal, Towne)
W/Neomycin sulf., polymyxin B sulf., hydrocortisone acetate.
See: Neopolycin-HC, Oint., Ophth. Oint. (Merrell Dow)
W/Neomycin sulfate, polymyxin B sulfate, diperodon HCl.
See: Epimycin A, Oint. (Delta)
Mity-Mycin, Oint. (Reid-Provident)
W/Polymyxin B sulfate.
See: Polysporin, Oint. & Ophth. Oint. (Burroughs Wellcome)
W/Polymyxin B sulfate and neomycin sulfate.
See: Trimixin, Oint. (Hance)
W/Polymyxin B. sulfate, neomycin sulfate & hydrocortisone free alcohol.
See: Biotic-Ophth. W/HC, Oint. (Scrip)
Cortisporin, Preps. (Burroughs Wellcome)

BACITRACIN. B.A.N. An antibiotic produced by a strain of *Bacillus subtilis.*

• **BACITRACIN METHYLENE DISALICYLATE,** U.S.P. XXI. Soluble, Soluble Powd., U.S.P. XXI.
Use: Antibiotic.

BACITRACIN-NEOMYCIN OINTMENT. (Various Mfr.) Neomycin sulfate equiv. to 3.5 mg. of base, bacitracin 500 u./Gm. Topical Oint. Tube 0.5 oz., 1 oz., Ophth. Oint. ⅛ oz.
Use: Treatment of infectious due to gram-positive or gram-negative bacteria.

• **BACITRACIN ZINC,** U.S.P. XXI. Sterile, Soluble Powd., U.S.P. XXI.(Upjohn) Stevil powder 10,000 u or 50,000 u./Vial.
Use: Antibiotic.
W/Neomycin sulfate, polymyxin B sulfate.
See: Neomixin B sulfate.
See: Neomixin, Oint. (Mallard)
Neo-polycin, Oint. (Merrell Dow)
Neosporin, Prods. (Burroughs Wellcome)
Neotal, Oint. (Mallard)
W/Neomycin sulfate, polymyxin B, benzalkonium chloride.
See: Biotres, Oint. (Central Pharmacal)
W/Neomycin sulfate, polymyxin B sulfate, hydrocortisone acetate.
See: Biotres HC, Cream (Central)
Coracin, Oint. (Mallard)
W/Polymyxin B sulfate, neomycin sulfate.
See: Ophthel, Ophth. Oint. (Elder)
Polycin, Oint. (Merrell Dow)

• **BACITRACIN ZINC OINTMENT,** U.S.P. XXI. Bacitracin Zinc in an anhydrous ointment base.
Use: Antibiotic ointment.

• **BACITRACIN ZINC AND POLYMIXIN B SULFATE OINTMENT,** U.S.P. XXI. Ophthalmic Oint., U.S.P. XXI.
Use: Antibiotic.

BACIT-WHITE. (Whiteworth) Bacitracin ointment. Tub 0.5 oz., 1 oz.
Use: Antibiotic ointment.

• **BACLOFEN.** USAN. 4-Amino-3-(4-chloropheny butyric acid. β-Aminomethyl-p-chlorohydrocinnam acid.
Use: Muscle relaxant.
See: Lioresal, Tab. (Geigy)

BAC-NEO-POLY OINTMENT. (Burgin-Arden) Bacitracin 400 u., neomycin sulfate 5 mg., polymyxin B sulfate 5000 u./Gm. Tube 0.5 oz.

BACTAL 1%. (La Crosse) Bar and liquid surgical soap. Bar. 1 doz. Liq. 8 oz., gal.

BACTALIN. (La Crosse) Cetylpyridinium chloride, phosphate buffers. Plastic Bot. 8 oz., 0.5 gal.
Use: Mouth wash.
B.A.C. Gram-Negative: *Pseudomonas aeruginosa, Escherichia coli, and Aerobacter aerogenes.* Vial 3.5 cc.
B.A.C. Pooled Stock #1: *Diplococcus pneumoniae* Types I, II, V, VII, and XIV; *Streptococcus pyogenes,* Group A, Types 3, 10, 1 and Granger; *Staphylococcus aureus* and *albus; Streptococcus viridans* strains R1551, R1822, and R353; *Neisseria catarrhalis, Escherichia coli,* and *Haemophilus influenzae* Types a and b. Vial 3.5 cc
B.A.C. Pooled Stock #2: *Diplococcus pneumoniae* Types III, VI, and XIX; *Klebsiella pneumoniae* Type A, *Streptococcus pyogenes* Types 14, 18, and 19; *Pseudomonas aeruginosa, Escherichia coli,* and *Aerobacter aerogenes.* Vial 3.5 cc.
B.A.C. Staphylococcal: *Staphylococcus aureus* and *albus* phage types 42B/52/80/81 obtained from skin lesions, eye, ear, sinus and respiratory tract infections. Vial 3.5 cc.

B.A.C. Pooled Skin: *Staphylococcus aureus* and *albus,* and *Proteus vulgaris* isolated from skin lesions in patients with boils, carbuncles, furuncles and acne, Vial 3.5 cc.

BACTERIOSTATIC WATER FOR INJECTION. U.S.P. XXI. (Abbott) 30 ml. multiple-dose Fliptop Vial (plastic).
Use: Pharmaceutic acid for diluting and dissolving drugs for injection.

BACTIGEN H. INFLUENZAE. (Wampole) Rapid latex agglutination slide test for the qualitative detection of *Hemophilus influenzae,* type b antigen in cerebrospinal fluid, serum, and urine. Patient kits 15s, 30s.
Use: Aid in the differential diagnosis of bacterial meningitis.

BACTIGEN MENINGITIS PANEL. (Wampole) Rapid latex agglutination slide test for the qualitative detection of Hemophilus influenzae type b, Neisseria meningitidis A/B/C/Y/W135 and Streptococcus pneumoniae antigens in cerebrospinal fluid, serum and urine. Patient kit 18s.
Use: Aid in the differential diagnosis of bacterial meningitis.

BACTIGEN N. MENINGITIDIS. (Wampole) Rapid latex agglutination slide test for the qualitative detection of Neisseria meningitidis, serogroups A,B,C,Y & W 135 antigens in cerebrospinal fluid, serum & urine. Patient kits 15s, 30s.
Use: Aid in the differential diagnosis of bacterial meningitis.

BACTIGEN S. PNEUMONIAE. (Wampole) Rapid latex agglutination slide test for the qualitative detection of *streptococcus pneumoniae* antigens in cerebrospinal fluid, serum and urine. Patient kits 15s, 30s.
Use: Aid in the differential diagnosis of bacterial meningitis.

BACTINE ANTISEPTIC/ANESTHETIC FIRST AID SPRAY. (Miles) Benzalkonium Cl 0.13%, lidocaine 2.5%. **Squeeze Bot.:** 2 oz., 4 oz., 16 oz. **Liquid:** 3 oz. aerosol.
Use: Antiseptic, anesthetic.

BACTINE HYDROCORTISONE SKIN CREAM. (Miles) Hydrocortisone 0.5% Tube 0.5 oz.
Use: Antipruritic, antiinflammatory.

BACLOFEN, U.S.P. XXI. Tab., U.S.P. XXI.

BACTOCILL. (Beecham Labs) Oxacillin Sodium **Caps.:** 250 mg. Bot. 100s. 500 mg. Bot. 100s. **Vial:** (w/dibasic sod. phosphate 40 mg., methylparaben 3.6 mg., propylparaben 0.4 mg., sodium 3.1 mEq/Gm.) 500 mg., 1 Gm., 2 Gm., 4 Gm./Vial; 10s. Piggyback vial 1 Gm., 2 Gm., 25s. Bulk pharm pkg 10 Gm. Box 25s.
Use: Antibiotic.

BACTRIM. (Roche) Sulfamethoxazole 400 mg., trimethoprim 80 mg./Tab. Bot. 100s, 500s. Teledose 100s. Prescription Paks 40s, 400s.
Use: Urinary infections, otitis media, pneumonitis.

BACTRIM ORAL SUSP. (Roche) Sulfamethoxazole 200 mg., trimethoprim 40 mg./5 ml. Bot. pt.
Use: Urinary infections, otitis media, pneumonitis.

BACTRIM PEDIATRIC SUSPENSION. (Roche) Trimethorprim 40 mg., sulfamethoxyole 200 mg./5 ml. Bot. 16 oz.
Use: Urinary tract infections.

BACTRIM DS. (Roche) Trimethoprim 160 mg., sulfamethoxazole 800 mg./Tab. Bot. 100s. Teledose 100s. Paks of 20s.
Use: Urinary infections, otitis media, pneumonitis.

BACTURCULT. (Wampole) A urinary bacteria culture medium diagnostic urine culture system for urine collection, for bacteriuria screening and presumptive bacterial identification. Kits 10s, 100s.
Use: Diagnosis of bacteriuria.

BADIONAL. Sulphathiourea, B.A.N.

BAFIL CREAM. (Scruggs) Hydrocortisone 0.5%, clioquinol 3%, lidocaine 3%, pH adjusted to 6.0 Tube 1 oz.
Use: Broad control of dermatologic disorders.

B.A. GRADUALS. (Amfre-Grant) Theophylline 260 mg., pseudoephedrine HCl 50 mg., butabarbital 15 mg./Tab. Bot. 50s, 1000s.
Use: Bronchial dilators.

BAKERS BEST. (Scherer) Water, alcohol 38%, propylene glycol, ext. capsicum, glycerin, boric acid, Tween 80, diethylphthalate, rose oil, pyrilamine maleate, glacial acetic acid, Uvinul MS 40, hexetidine, benzalkonium chloride 50%, Supercel Hyflo, sodium hydroxide 76%. Bot. 8 oz.
Use: Antipruritic and antiseborrheic.

BAL. (Hynson, Westcott & Dunning) 2,3-Dimercapto-propanol 100 mg., benzyl benzoate 210 mg., peanut oil 680 mg./ml. Amp. 3 ml. Box 10s.
Use: Treatment of arsenic, gold & mercury poisoning, and also acute lead poisoning in combination with edetate calcium disodium injection.

BALANCED SALT SOLUTION. (Alcon) Sod. chloride 0.46%, pot. chloride, 0.075%, cal. chloride 0.036%, mag. chloride 0.03% in sod. acetate-sod. citrate buffer system. Drop-Trainer 15 ml., 30 ml., 250 ml., 500 ml.
Use: Intraocular irrigating solution.

BALMEX BABY POWDER. (Macsil) Specially purified balsam Peru, zinc oxide, talc, starch, calcium carbonate. Shaker top cans. 4 oz.
Use: Adsorbent, emollient, & soothing powder.

BALMEX EMOLLIENT LOTION. (Macsil) Fraction of lanolin, allantoin, specially purified balsam Peru, silicone in a non-mineral oil base.
Bot. 6 fl. oz.
Use: Emollient, antibacterial and protective lotion.

BALMEX OINTMENT.(Macsil) Specially purified balsam Peru, Vit. A & D, zinc oxide, & bismuth subnitrate in a base w/silicone. Tubes 1, 2, 4 oz., plastic jars 1 lb.
Use: Emollient, protective, anti-inflammatory, & healing ointment.

BALNEOL. (Rowell) Water, mineral oil, propylene glycol, glyceryl stearate PEG-100 stearate, PEG-40 stearate, laureth-4, PEG-4-dilaurate, lanolin oil, sodium acetate, carbomer-934, triethanolamine, methyl paraben, docusate sodium, acetic acid, fragrance. Bot. 1 oz., 4 oz.

Use: Emollient cleansing of irritated perianal & external vaginal area.

BALNETAR. (Westwood) Tar equivalent to 2.5% Coal Tar, U.S.P. Bot. 8 oz.
Use: Temporary relief of itching & scaling due to psoriasis, eczema and other tar-responsive dermatoses.

BALSAN. Specially purified balsam Peru.
See: Balmex Prod. (Macsil)

BALTRON R. (Reid-Provident) Peptonized iron 59 mg., folic acid 0.8 mg., liver injection USP (equiv. in Vit. B-12 activity to 5 mcg. cyanocobalamin), procaine HCl 1%, phenol 0.5%, sodium citrate 1%/2 cc., water q.s. Vials 30 cc.

BAMATE. (Century) Meprobamate 400 mg./Tab. Bot. 50s, 100s, 500s, 1000s, 5000s.
Use: Minor tranquilizer.

• **BABMERMYCINS.** USAN.
Use: Antibacterial.

BAMETHAN. B.A.N. 2-Butylamino-1-(4-hydroxyphenyl) ethanol.
Use: Vasodilator.
See: Vasculit sulfate

• **BAMETHAN SULFATE.** USAN. α-[(Butylamino) methyl]-p-hydroxybenzyl alcohol sulfate.
Use: Vasodilator.

BAMIFYLLINE. B.A.N. 8-Benzyl-7-[2-(N-ethyl-2-hydroxy-ethylamino)ethyl]theophylline. Trentadil hydrochloride.
Use: Bronchodilator.

BAMIFYLLINE HYDROCHLORIDE. USAN. 8-Benzyl-7-[2-[ethyl (2-hydroxyethyl) amino]ethyl]-theophylline HCl.
Use: Bronchodilator.

BAMIPINE. B.A.N. 4-(N-Benzylanilino)-1-methyl-piperidine.
Use: Antihistamine.
See: Soventol.

• **BAMNIDAZOLE.** USAN.
Use: Antiprotozoal.

BANACID. (Buffington) Aluminum hydroxide, Mg hydroxide, Mg trisilicate/Tab. Sugar, lactose, and salt free. Dispens-A-Kit 500s, Medipaks 200s. Unit boxes 8s, 16s.
Use: Antacid.

BANALG. (Forest) Menthol, camphor, methyl salicylate & eucalyptus oil in a greaseless base. Regular liniment and hospital strength. Bot. 2 oz., 1 pt., gal.
Use: Topically, a counterirritant.

BANATIL. (Trimen) Butabarbital 32.4 mg., hyoscyamine sulfate 0.25 mg., scopolamine methylnitrate 0.05 mg., atropine sulfate 0.086 mg./D.R. Tab. Bot. 100s. Elix. pt.
Use: G. I. hypermotility & spasm.

BANCAPS. (Forest) Acetaminophen 325 mg., butalbital 50 mg./Cap. Bot. 100s, 500s.
Use: Analgesic, muscle relaxant and sedative.

BANCAP HC. (Forest) Acetaminophen 500 mg., hydrocodone bitratrate 5 mg./Cap. Bot. 100s, 500s.
Use: Analgesic.

• **BANDAGE, ADHESIVE,** U.S.P. XXI.
Use: Surgical aid.

• **BANDAGE, GAUZE,** U.S.P. XXI.
Use: Surgical aid.

BANESIN. (Forest) Acetaminophen 500 mg./Tab.
Use: Analgesic.

BANFLEX. (Forest) Orphenadrine citrate 30 mg./ml. IM or IV. Vials 10 ml.
Use: Skeletal muscle relaxant.

BANGESIC. (H.L. Moore) Menthol, camphor, methyl salicylate, eucalyptus oil in nongreasy base. Bot. 2 oz., gal.
Use: Local analgesic.

BANOCIDE.
See: Diethylcarbamazine Citrate, U.S.P.

BANTHINE. (Searle) Methantheline bromide 50 mg./Tab. Bot. 100s.
Use: Orally, anticholinergic preparation.

BANTRON BRAND SMOKING DETERRENT TABLETS. (Jeffrey Martin) Magnesium carbonate, 129.6 mg., lobeline sulfate alkaloids 2mg., tribasic calcium phosphate 129.6 mg./Tab. Carton 18s, 36s.
Use: Smoking deterrent.

BARACHLOR TABLETS. (Barry-Martin) Chlorpropher pyridamine maleate 4 mg./Tab. Bot. 1000s.

BARACHLOR T.D. CAPSULES. (Barry-Martin) Chlor pheniramine maleate 8 mg. or 12 mg./Cap. Bot. 100s, 500s, 1000s.

BARACOL EAR DROPS. (Barry-Martin) Antipyrine 1. Gm., benzocaine 0.46 Gm., propylene glycol 0.926 fl. oz./fl. oz. Bot. 15 cc., pt., gal.
Use: Ear pain and wax softening.

BARAGESIC SPRAY. (Barry-Martin) Methol, methylsal cylate, camphor, isopropanol, trichloro-fluorome thane, dichlorodifluoromethane, plus essential oils. Can 6 oz.
Use: Relief of aches and pains.

BARAMINE CAPSULES(Barry-Martin) Diphenhydra mine HCl 50 mg./Cap. Bot. 100s.

BARAMINE ELIXIR. (Barry-Martin) Diphenhydramin HCl 10 mg./4 cc. Bot., pt., gal.

BARAMINE EXPECTORANT. (Barry-Martin) Diphenhy dramine HCl 80 mg., ammonium chloride 12 gr., sod. citrate 5 gr., menthol 0.1 gr./fl. oz. Bot. pt., gal.

BARAZOLE TABLETS. (Barry-Martin) Sulfisoxazole 0. Gm./Tab. Bot. 100s, 1000s.

BARAZOLE-AZO TABLETS. (Barry-Martin) Sulfisox azole 0.5 Gm., phenazopyridine 50 mg./Tab. Bot. 100s, 1000s.

BARBASED TABS. (Major) Butabarbital 0.25 gr. or 0.5 gr./Tab. Bot. 1000s.
Use: Sedative, hypnotic.

BARBELLA ELIXIR. (Fellows) Phenobarbital 0.25 gr., hyoscyamine sulfate 0.1037 mg., atropine sulfate 0.0194 mg., scopolamine HBr 0.0065 mg./alcohol 23%/tsp. Bot. 4 oz., gal.

BARBELLA TABLETS. (Fellows) Phenobarbital 16.2 mg., atropine sulfate 0.0194 mg., hyoscyamine sulfate 0.1037 mg., hyoscine HBr 0.0065 mg./Tab. Bot. 100s, 1000s, 5000s.

.RBELOID. (Vale) Phenobarbital 16.2 mg., hyoscyamine sulfate 0.1037 mg., atropine sulfate 0.0194 mg., scopolamine hydrobromide 0.0065 mg./Tab. Bot. 100s, 500s, 1000s.
Use: Orally, antispasmodic & sedative.

RBENYL.
See: Phenobarbital.

RBIDONNA. (Wallace) **Elixir:** phenobarbital 21.6 mg. hyoscyamine sulfate 0.174 mg., atropine sulfate 0.034 mg., scopolamine HBr 0.01 mg., alcohol 15%/5 ml. Bot. 1 pt.; **Tab.:** phenobarbital 16 mg., hyoscyamine sulfate 0.1286 mg., atropine sulfate 0.0250 mg., scopolamine HBr 0.0074 mg./Tab. Bot. 100s, 500s.
Use: Antispasmodic and sedative. Combination for G.I. disorders.

RBIDONNA NO. 2. (Wallace) Phenobarbital 32 mg., hyoscyamine sulfate 0.1286 mg., atropine sulfate 0.0250 mg., scopolamine HBr 0.0074 mg./Tab. Bot. 100s.
Use: Antispasmodic & sedative combination for G.I. disorders.

ARBINAL CAPSULES. (Fellows) Phenobarbital 0.5 gr., acetophenetidin 2 gr., aspirin 3 gr., hyoscyamus 0.25 gr./Cap. Bot. 100s, 500s.

ARBINAL NO. 3. (Fellows) Phenobarbital 0.25 gr., codeine phosphate 0.5 gr., acetophenetidin 2 mg., aspirin 3 gr., hyoscyamine sulfate .031 mg./Cap. Bot. 100s, 500s.

ARBIPHENYL.
See: Phenobarbital.

ARBITA. (Vortech) Phenobarbital 16 mg./Tab. Bot. 1000s.
Use: Orally, sedative.

ARBITAL. Barbitone, Deba, Dormonal, Hypnogene, Malonal, Sedeval, Uronal, Veronal, Vesperal, Diethylbarbituric acid, diethylmalonylurea.
Use: Orally, sedative, hypnotic.
/Aspirin, caffeine, niacinamide.
See: Mentran, Tab. (Pasadena Research)

ARBITAL SODIUM. Barbitone Sodium, Diethylbarbiturate Monosodium, Diethylmalonylurea Sodium, Embinal, Medinal, Veronal Sodium.
Use: Hypnotic, sedative.

ARBITONE.
See: Barbital.

ARBITONE SODIUM.
See: Barbital Sodium.

ARBITURATE-ASPIRIN COMBINATIONS.
See: Aspirin-Barbiturate Combination.

ARBITURATES, INTERMEDIATE DURATION.
See: Butabarbital (Various Mfr.)
Butethal (Various Mfr.)
Diallylbarbituric Acid (Various Mfr.)
Lotusate, Caps. (Winthrop-Breon)
Vinbarbital. (Various Mfr.)

■ **BARBITURATES, LONG DURATION.**
See: Barbital (Various Mfr.)
Mebaral, Tab. (Winthrop-Breon)
Mephobarbital (Var. Mfr.)
Phenobarbital (Various Mfr.)
Phenobarbital Sod. (Various Mfr.)

■ **BARBITURATES, SHORT DURATION.**
See: Amobarbital (Various Mfr.)
Amobarbital Sod. (Various Mfr.)
Butalbital (Var. Mfr.)
Butallylonal (Various Mfr.)
Cyclobarbital (Var. Mfr.)
Cyclopal
Pentobarbital Salts (Var. Mfr.)
Sandoptal
Secobarbital (Various Mfr.)

BARBITURATES, TRIPLE.
See: Butseco, S.C.T., Tab. (Bowman)
Ethobral, Cap. (Wyeth)

BARBITURATES, ULTRASHORT DURATION.
See: Hexobarbital
Neraval
Pentothal Sod., Amp. (Abbott)
Surital Sod., Amp., Vials (Parke-Davis)
Thiopental Sod. (Var. Mfr.)

BARBO COMPOUND LIQUID. (Guild) Bot. 8 oz.

BARBO COMPOUND POWDER. (Guild) Pkg. 0.25 oz.

BARBO COMPOUND INSTANT NO. 1, NO. 2 and NO. 3. (Guild) Bot. 1 oz.

BARC GEL. (Commerce) Pyrethrins, piperonyl butoxide technical and petroleum distillate in gel base. Tube 1 oz.
Use: Direct application pediculicide. Kills head lice, crab and eggs on contact.

BARC LIQUID. (Commerce) Pyrethrins, piperonyl butoxide technical, petroleum distillate. Bot. 2 oz.
Use: Kills and controls lice, nits and crab lice.

BARC NON-BODY LICE CONTROL SPRAY. (Commerce) Resmethrin-5-(phenylmethyl)-3-furanyl] methyl-2, 2-dimethyl-3-(2-methyl-1-propanyl) cyclopropanecarboxylate. Spray can 5 oz.
Use: Control of lice and louse eggs on inanimate objects.

BAR-CY-AMINE. (Sutliff & Case) Phenobarbital 16.0 mg., hyoscyamine sulfate 0.0856 mg., atropine sulfate 0.0171 mg., hyoscine hydrobromide 0.0068 mg., alcohol 20%/5 cc. Bot. 1 pt., 1 gal.
Use: Orally, antispasmodic & sedative.

BAR-CY-A-TAB. (Sutliff & Case) Phenobarbital 0.25 gr., hyoscyamine sulfate 0.0856 mg., atropine sulfate 0.0171 mg., hyoscine hydrobromide 0.0068 mg./Tab. Bot. 100s, 1000s, 5000s.
Use: Antispasmodic-sedative.

BARHOMA ELIXIR. (Blue Line) Phenobarbital 400 mg., homatropine methylbromide 33.8 mg., alcohol 13.5%/100 cc. Bot. pt., gal.
Use: Sedative.

BARHOMA TABLETS. (Blue Line) Phenobarbital 0.25 gr., homatropine methylbromide $\frac{1}{48}$ gr./Tab. Bot. 100s, 1000s.
Use: Sedative.

BARIDIUM TABLETS. (Barry-Martin) Phenylazopyridine HCl 1.5 gr./Tab. 24s, 100s, 500s, 1000s.

BARI-STRESS M. (Barre) Vit. B-1 10 mg., B-2 10 mg., niacinamide 100 mg., Vit. C 300 mg., B-6 2 mg., B-12 4 mcg., folic acid 1.5 mg., cal. pantothenate 20

mg./Cap. or Tab. **Cap:** Bot. 30s, 100s, 1000s. **Tab.** Bot. 100s, 1000s.
Use: Stress vitamin therapy.

BARITRATE. (Barry-Martin) Pentaerythritol tetranitrate 10 mg. or 20 mg./Tab. Bot. 1000s.

BARITRATE PHENOBARBITAL TABLETS. (Barry-Martin) Pentaerythritol tetranitrate 10 mg., or 20 mg., phenobarbital 15 mg./Tab. Bot. 1000s.

• **BARIUM HYDROXIDE LIME,** U.S.P. XXI.
Use: Carbon dioxide absorbant.

■ **BARIUM SULFATE PREPARATION.**
See: Baroflave, Pow. (Lannett)
Barotrast, Pow., Cream (Barnes-Hind)
Fleet Barobag, Liq. (Fleet)
Raybar, Susp. (Fleet)
Redi-Flow, Susp. (Berlex)
Rugar, Susp. (McKesson)

BARLEVITE. (Barth's) Vit. B-6 0.6 mg., B-12 3 mcg., pantothenic acid 0.6 mg., D 3 I.U., l-lysine 20 mg./0.6 ml. 100-Day Supply.

BARNES-HIND CLEANING AND SOAKING SOLUTION. (Barnes-Hind) Cleaning and buffering agents, benzalkonium chloride 0.01%, disodium edetate 0.2%. Bot. 4 fl. oz.
Use: Hard contact lens cleaner and disinfectant.

BARNES-HIND GERMICIDAL SOLUTION. (Barnes-Hind) Benzalkonium Cl (1:750) 0.13%, disodium edetate 0.1%. Bot. gal.
Use: Anti-rust disinfectant for medical and dental instruments.

BARNES-HIND WETTING SOLUTION. (Barnes-Hind) Polyvinyl alcohol with disodium edetate 0.02%, benzalkonium chloride 0.004%. Bot. 35 ml., 2 fl. oz.
Use: Hard contact lens wetting solution.

BAROBAG. (Lafayette) Disposable prefilled barium enema bag. 12 oz., 16 oz. w/or w/o retention catheter.
Use: Barium enema.

BARODENSE. (Lafayette) Contains 97% colloidal microbarium sulfate. Drum 100 lb.
Use: Alimentary tract radiography.

BAROFLAVE POWDER. (Lannett) Barium sulfate for diagnostic X-ray use. Bot. 5 lb., Fibre drum 25 lb.

BAROGEL SUSPENSION. (Barry-Martin) Amphoteric aluminum hydroxide gel. Bot. qt., gal.

BAROLOID. (Lafayette) Microbarium sulfate. Drum 100 lbs.
Use: Contrast medium for radiography of the alimentary tract.

BAROPECTIN SUSPENSION. (Barry-Martin) Kaolin 90 gr., pectin 2 gr./fl. oz. Bot. qt., gal.

BAROSIL SUSPENSION. (Barry-Martin) Magnesium trisilicate 0.5 Gm., aluminum hydroxide 0.25 Gm./tsp. Bot. qt., gal.

BAROSMIN.
See: Diosmin.

BAROTRAST. (Armour) Barium sulfate. Cartons 25 lb.
Use: Gastrointestinal x-ray diagnosis.

BAROTUSSIN SYRUP. (Barry-Martin) Guaifenesin 100 mg., desoxyephedrine HCl 1 mg./5 cc. Bot. qt., gal.

BAROVITE LIQUID. (Barry-Martin) Vit. B-1 10 mg., B-12 25 mcg./5 cc. Bot. 4 oz., pt., qt.
Use: Appetite stimulant.

W/Iron. Ferric pyrophosphate 250 mg./5 cc. plus Barovite liquid formula.

BARSEB HC SCALP LOTION. (Barnes-Hind) Hydrocortisone 1%, isopropyl alcohol 45%, isopropyl myristate, propylene glycol. Bot. 1.75 oz.
Use: Anti-seborrheic for dermatitis of the scalp.

BARSEB THERA-SPRAY. (Barnes-Hind) Hydrocortisone alcohol 360 mg., salicylic acid 288 mg., benzalkonium chloride 14 mg., propylene glycol, isopropyl myristate, ethanol, butane (propellant). W/plastic applicator 184 Gm.
Use: Anti-seborrheic for dermatitis of the scalp.

BAR-TEST. (Vitarine) Barium sulfate 10 gr./Tab.
Use: Diagnostic agent.

BARTONE. (Rand) Phenobarbital 16.2 mg., scopolamine HBr 0.0065 mg., atropine sulfate 0.0194 mg., hyoscyamine sulfate 0.1037 mg./Tab. or 5 cc. **Tab.** Bot. 100s, 1000s. **Elixir** 1 pt., 1 gal.
Use: Antispasmodic.

BASA. (Freeport) Acetylsalicylic acid 324 mg./Tab. Bot. 1000s.
Use: Headache and minor aches.

BASALJEL. (Wyeth) Aluminum carbonate gel. **Susp.:** Equiv. to 400 mg./5 cc. Extra strength, aluminum carbonate gel equiv. to 1000 mg. aluminum hydroxide gel. Bot. 12 fl. oz.,**Cap.:** equivalent to 500 mg. aluminum hydroxide. Bot. 100s, 500s. **Tab.:** equivalent to 500 mg. aluminum hydroxide. Bot. 100s.
Use: Orally, prophylaxis of renal stone.

BASELAN. (Metro Med) Jar 1 lb.
Use: Ointment base, emollient.

BASIC ALUMINUM AMINOACETATE.
See: Dihydroxy Aluminum Aminoacetate.

BASIC ALUMINUM CARBONATE.
See: Basaljel, Susp. (Wyeth)

BASIC ALUMINUM GLYCINATE.
See: Dihydroxyaluminum aminoacetate.

BASIC BISMUTH CARBONATE.
See: Bismuth Subcarbonate.

BASIC BISMUTH GALLATE.
See: Bismuth Subgallate (Various Mfr.)

BASIC BISMUTH NITRATE.
See: Bismuth Subnitrate (Various Mfr.)

BASIC BISMUTH SALICYLATE.
See: Bismuth Subsalicylate.

BASIC FUCHSIN.
See: Carbol-Fuchsin Topical Solution, U.S.P. XXI.

BAUMODYNE GEL. (Vortech) Methyl salicylate, menthol, eucalyptus oil, and preservatives in 70% isopropyl alcohol gel.
Use: Relief of joint and muscle pain.

BAMODYNE OINTMENT. (Vortech) Methyl salicylate, menthol, eucalyptus oil, and preservatives in non-greasy base.
Use: Relief of joint and muscle pain.

BAXIMIN OINTMENT. (Quality Generics) Polymyxin B sulfate 5000 u., bacitracin 400 u., neomycin sulfate 5 mg./Gm. Tube 0.5 oz.
Use: Antibiotic.

AYAMINIC EXPECTORANT. (Bay) Phenlypropanolamine HCl 12.5 mg., guaifenesin 100 mg./5 ml. w/alcohol 5%. Bot. 4 oz., pt. gal.
Use: Decongestant, expectorant.

AYAMINIC SYRUP. (Bay) Phenylpropanolamine HCl 12.5 mg., chlorpheniramine maleate 2 mg./5 ml. Bot. 4 oz., pt., gal.
Use: Decongestant, antihistaminic.

AYAMINICOL. (Bay) Phenlypropanolamine HCl 12.5 mg., chlorpheniramine maleate 2 mg., dextromethorphan HBr 10 mg./5 ml. Bot. 4 oz., pt., gal.
Use: Decongestant, antitussive, antihistaminic.

AYAPAP. (Bay) Acetaminophen 160 mg./5 ml. w/alcohol 7% Bot. 2 oz., 4 oz., pt., gal.
Use: Pain relief, anti-pyretic.

AYAPAP DROPS. (Bay) Acetaminophen 80 mg./0.8 ml. w/alcohol 7%. Bot. 15 ml.
Use: Pain relief, anti-pyretic.

AYAPAP W/CODEINE. (Bay) Codeine phosphate 12 mg., acetaminophen 120 mg./5 ml. w/alcohol 7%. Bot. 4 oz., pt., gal.
Use: Pain relief.

AY-ASE. (Bay) Phenobarbital gr. 0.25, hyoscyamine sulfate 0.1037 mg., atropine sulfate 0.0194 mg., hyosine HBr 0.0065 mg./5 ml. w/alcohol 23%. Bot. 4 oz., pt., gal.
Use: Antispasmodic, sedative.

AYCODAN SYRUP. (Bay) Hydrocodone bitartrate 5 mg., homatropine MBr 1.5 mg./5 ml. Bot. 4 oz., pt., gal.
Use: Antitussive.

AYCOMINE PEDIATRIC. (Bay) Phenylpropanolamine HCl 12.5 mg., hydrocodone bitartrate 2.5 mg./5 ml. Bot. 4 oz., pt., gal.
Use: Antitussive.

AYCOMINE SYRUP. (Bay) Phenylpropanolamine HCl 25.0 mg., hydrocodone bitartrate 5 mg./5 ml. Bot. 4 oz., pt., gal.
Use: Antitussive.

AYCOTUSSEND EXPECTORANT. (Bay) Pseudoephedrine HCl 60 mg., hydrocodone bitartrate 5 mg., guaifenesin 200 mg./5 ml. w/alcohol 12.5%. Bot. 4 oz., pt., gal.
Use: Antitussive, expectorant.

AYCOTUSSEND LIQUID. (Bay) Pseudoephedrine HCl 60 mg., hydrocodone bitartrate 5 mg./5 ml. w/alcohol 5%. Bot. 4 oz., pt., gal.
Use: Antitussive, decongestant.

AYDEC DM DROPS. (Bay) Pseudoephedrine HCl 25 mg., dextromethorphan HBr 4 mg., carbinoxamine maleate 2 mg./1 ml. Bot. 30 ml.
Use: Decongestant, antitussive, antihistaminic.

AYDEC DM SYRUP. (Bay) Carbinoxamine maleate 4 mg., pseudoephedrine HCl 60 mg., dextromethorphan HBr 15 mg./5 ml. w/alcohol 0.6%. Bot. 4 oz., pt., gal.
Use: Decongestant, antitussive, antihistaminic.

AYER ASPIRIN, GENUINE. (Glenbrook) Aspirin 5 gr. (325 mg.)/Tab. Film coated (non-enteric). Bot. 24s, 50s, 100s, 200s, 300s. Plastic 12s.
Use: Analgesic, antipyretic, anti-inflammatory.

BAYER ASPIRIN, MAXIMUM. (Glenbrook) Aspirin 500 mg./Tab. Film coated. Bot. 30s, 60s, 100s.
Use: Analgesic, antipyretic, antiinflammatory, antiplatelet.

BAYER CHILDREN'S CHEWABLE ASPIRIN. (Glenbrook) Aspirin 1.25 gr. (81 mg.)/Tab. Bot. 36s.
Use: Analgesic, antipyretic, anti-inflammatory.

BAYER CHILDREN'S COLD TABLETS. (Glenbrook) Phenylpropanolamine HCl 3.125 mg., Aspirin 1.25 gr. (81 mg.)/Tab. Bot. 30s.
Use: Analgesic, decongestant.

BAYER COUGH SYRUP FOR CHILDREN. (Glenbrook) Phenylpropanolamine HCl 9 mg., dextromethorphan HBr 7.5 mg./5 ml. w/alcohol 5%. Bot. 3 oz.
Use: Decongestant, antitussive.

BAYER TIMED-RELEASE ASPIRIN, ARTHRITIS. (Glenbrook) Aspirin 10 gr. (650 mg.)/T.R. Tab. Bot. 30s, 72s, 125s.
Use: Analgesic, antipyretic, anti-inflammatory.

BAYER 205.
See: Suramin Sodium. (No Mfr. currently listed.)

BAYFRIN NASAL SPRAY. (Bay) Oxymetazoline HCl 0.05%. Spray Bot. 15 ml.
Use: Decongestant.

BAYHISTINE DH. (Bay) Codeine phosphate 10 mg., chlorpheniramine maleate 2 mg., pseudoephedrine HCl 30 mg./5 ml. w/alcohol 5%. Bot. 4 oz., pt., gal.
Use: Decongestant, antitussive, antihistaminic.

BAYHISTINE ELIXIR. (Bay) Chlorpheniramine maleate 2 mg., phenylpropanolamine HCl 18.75 mg./5 ml. w/alcohol 5%. Bot. 4 oz., pt., gal.
Use: Decongestant, antihistaminic.

BAYHISTINE EXPECTORANT. (Bay) Codeine phosphate 10 mg., guaifenesin 100 mg., pseudoephedrine HCl 30 mg./5 ml. w/alcohol 7.5% Bot. 4 oz., pt., gal.
Use: Expectorant, antitussive, decongestant.

BAYIDYL SYRUP. (Bay) Triprolidine HCl 1.25 mg./5 ml. w/alcohol 4%. Bot. 4 oz., Pt., Gal.
Use: Antihistamine.

BAYLOCAINE 2% VISCOUS SOLUTION. (Bay) Lidocaine HCl 2%. Bot. 100 ml.
Use: Local anesthetic.

BAYLOCAINE 4% SOLUTION. (Bay) Lidocaine HCl 4%. Bot. 50 ml. or 100 ml.
Use: Local anesthetic.

BAYLOX. (Bay) Magnesia and alumina oral susp. Bot. 12 oz., gal.
Use: Antacid.

BAYMETHAZINE SYRUP FORTIS. (Bay) Promethazine HCl 25 mg./5 ml. w/alcohol 1.5%. Bot. 4 oz., pt.
Use: Antihistamine.

BAYON ELIXIR. (Bay) Potassium 20 meq./15 ml. Bot. 4 oz., pt., gal.
Use: Supplement.

BAYORINADE. (Bay) Phenylpropanolamine HCl 125 mg., caramiphen edisylate 6.7 mg./5 ml. w/alcohol 5%. Bot. 4 oz., pt., gal.
Use: Decongestant, antitussive.

BAYTUSSIN. (Bay) Guaifenesin 100 mg./5 ml. w/alcohol 3.5%. Bot. 4 oz., pt., gal.
Use: Expectorant.

BAYTUSSIN AC. (Bay) Guaifenesin 100 mg., codeine phosphate 10 mg./5 ml. w/alcohol 3.5%. Bot. 4 oz., pt., gal.
Use: Antitussive, expectorant.

BAYTUSSIN DM. (Bay) Guaifenesin 100 mg., dextromethorphan HBr 15 mg./5 ml. w/alcohol 1.4%. Bot. 4 oz., pt., gal.
Use: Antitussive, expectorant.

B-BALM. (Vortech) Phenol 65 mg., zinc oxide 10%, comp. benzoin tr. 0.15 cc., methyl salicylate 20 mg., denatured alcohol 0.45 cc./oz. Jar 1 oz., 2 oz., 1 lb.
Use: Antiseptic.

B-BETTER CAPS. (Image) B-complex 50 mg./Cap. Bot. 100s.
Use: Supplement.

B-BEX T. (Image) Bot. 100s.
Use: Supplement.

BBR. (Western Research) Vit. B-1 10 mg., B-12 25 mcg./Tab. 28 Pack, 1000s.
Use: Vit. B deficiency.

BC-1000. (Reid-Provident) Vit. B-1 50 mg., B-2 5 mg., B-12 1000 mcg., B-6 5 mg., d-panthenol 6 mg., niacinamide 125 mg., ascorbic acid 50 mg., benzyl alcohol 1%/ml. Vial 10 ml.
Use: Vitamin supplement.

b-CAPSA I VACCINE. (Mead Johnson) Haemophilus & Polysaccharide Vaccine purified from *Haemophilius influenzae* type b, strain Eag. Pkg. of one 10 dose Vial of lypholized vaccine and one Vial of 6.5 ml. diluent.
Use: Immunization of children 24 mo. to 6 yrs. of age against *Haemophilus influenzae* b.

B-C-BID CAPSULES. (Geriatric) Vit. B-1 15 mg., B-2 10 mg., B-6 5 mg., niacinamide 50 mg., Ca pantothenate 10 mg., Vit. C 300 mg., B-12 5 mcg./Cap. Bot. 30s, 100s, 500s.

• **BCG VACCINE,** U.S.P. XXI. (Lilly) Prepared from a Glaxo substrain of a Danish strain of BCG bacillus. Vial 1 cc. 10 doses.
Use: Immunization against tuberculosis.

BCG VACCINE. (Glaxo) Living BCG bacillus (Danish 1077 substrain) 8-26 million CFU's/lcc. Powder for reconstitution. Amp. 1 ml.
Use: Immunization against tuberculosis.

BCNU. 1,3-bis(2-Chloroethyl)-1-nitrosourea.
Use: Antineoplastic agent.
See: BiCNU, Inj. (Bristol)

BCO. (Western Research) Vit. B-1 10 mg., B-2 2 mg., B-6 1.5 mg., B-12 25 mcg., niacinamide 50 mg./Tab. Bot. 1000s.

B-COM. (Century) Vit. B-1 3 mg., B-2 3 mg., B-6 0.5 mg., niacinamide 20 mg., Ca pantothenate 5 mg., B-12 1 mcg., liver desic. (undefatted) 60 mg., debittered brewer's dried yeast 60 mg./Cap. Bot. 100s, 1000s.

B-COMPLEX. (Reid-Provident) Vit. B-1 100 mg., niacinamide 100 mg., B-2 2 mg., B-6 4 mg., calcium pantothenate 10 mg./cc. Vials 30 cc.

B-COMPLEX 2. (Kenyon) Vit. B-1 3 mg., B-2 3 mg., B-6 0.5 mg., Ca pantothenate 5 mg., niacinamide 2 mg., dried yeast N.F. 60 mg./Cap. Bot. 100s.

B-COMPLEX NO. 5. (Pharmex) Vit. B-1 100 mg., B- 2 mg., B-6 4 mg., panthenol 10 mg., niacinamide 10 mg., benzyl alcohol 1%, propylparaben 0.02%, methylparaben 0.18%/cc. Vial 30 cc.

B-COMPLEX 25-25 INJ. (Fellows) Niacinamide 10 mg., B-1 25 mg., B-2 1 mg., B-6 2 mg., pantothen acid 2 mg./cc. Vial 30 cc.

B-COMPLEX 100 (Kenyon) Vit. B-1 100 mg., B-2 2 mg B-6 4 mg., d-panthenol 4 mg., niacinamide 10 mg./cc. Vial 30 cc.

B COMPLEX #100 (Medical Chem; CMC) B-1 100 mg Vit. B-2 2 mg., B-6 4 mg., d-panthenol 4 mg., niacinamide 100 mg./cc. Vial 30 cc.

B COMPLEX 100. (Rabin-Winters) Vit. B-1 100 mg., B-2 2 mg., B-6 2 mg., niacinamide 125 mg., panthen 10 mg./cc. Vial 30 cc.

B-COMPLEX 100/100. (Sandia) Vit. B-1 100 mg., B-2 2 mg., B-6 2 mg., niacinamide 100 mg./cc. Vial 3 cc. Inj.

B COMPLEX CAPSULES. (Arcum) Vit. B-1 1.5 mg., B-2 2 mg., niacinamide 10 mg., B-6 0.1 mg., Ca pantothenate 1.0 mg., liver desic. 70 mg., dried yeast 100 mg./Cap. Bot. 100s, 1000s.

B-COMPLEX CAPSULES. (Vortech) Vit. B-1 1.5 mg., B-2 2 mg., B-6 0.1 mg., Ca pantothenat 1 mg., dried yeast 100 mg., niacinamide 10 mg., desiccated liver 70 mg./Cap. Bot. 100s.

B COMPLEX CAPSULES J.F. (Bryant) Vit. B-1 1 mg. B-2 0.3 mg., nicotinic acid 0.3 mg., B-6 0.25 mg., live desic. 0.15 Gm., yeast powder, dried 0.15 Gm./Cap. Bot. 100s, 1000s.

B COMPLEX INJECTION WITH VITAMIN C.
See: Cplex Cap. (Arcum)

B COMPLEX WITH B-12 CAPSULES. (Bryant) Vit. B-1 2 mg., B-2 2 mg., B-6 0.5 mg., niacinamide 1 mg., B-12 2 mcg., biotin 10 mcg., Ca pantothenate 1. mg., choline dihydrogen citrate 40 mg., inositol 30 mg., liver, desic. 1 gr., brewer's yeast 3 gr./Cap. Bot. 100s, 1000s.

B-COMPLEX W/C. (Towne) Vit. C 300 mg., B-1 15 mg B-2 10 mg., B-6 5 mg., niacinamide 50 mg., calciur pantothenate 10 mg./Cap. Bot. 100s.

B-COMPLEX WITH C. (Sutliff & Case) Vit. B-1 3 mg., B-2 3 mg., C 30 mg., B-6 1.5 mg., pantothenic acid mg., niacin 15 mg., yeast 5 mg./Tab. Bot. 100s, 1000s
Use: Orally, vitamin B complex w/Vit. C.

B-COMPLEX W/C. (Zenith) Vit. B-1 15 mg., B-2 10 mg B-6 5 mg., nicotinamide 50 mg., Ca pantothenate 1 mg., Vit. C 300 mg./Cap. Bot. 100s.

BC POWDER. (Block) Aspirin 10 gr., salicylamide 3 gr., caffeine 0.5 gr./Powder. Pkg. 2s, 6s, 24s, 50s, 100s.
Use: Analgesic, antipyretic.

BC TABLETS. (Block) Aspirin 5 gr., Salicylamide 1.5 gr., caffeine 0.25 gr./Tab. Bot. 12s, 50s, 100s.
Use: Analgesic.

-VITE. (Drug Industries) Vit. B-1 25 mg., B-2 5 mg., B-6 1 mg., B-12 2 mcg., C 150 mg., pantothenate 10 mg., niacinamide 50 mg./Tab. Bot. 100s, 500s.
Use: Stress therapy.

DAY TABLETS. (Barth's) Vit. B-1 7 mg., B-2 14 mg., niacin 4.67 mg., B-12 5 mcg./Tab. Bot. 100s, 500s.

EP. Same as Benzathine Penicillin G.

DOX. (Lannett) Vit. B-1 100 mg., B-6 100 mg./cc. Vials 10 cc.
Use: I.M. or I.V. nausea and vomiting.

OZEN. (Standex) Vit. B-12 25 mcg./Tab. Bot. 1000s.

DRAM w/C COMPUTABS. (Dram) Vit. B-2 10 mg., B-6 5 mg., nicotinamide 50 mg., Ca pantothenate 20 mg., B-1 5 mg./Tab. Bot. 100s.
Use: Vitamin deficiencies.

ACH GLO. (Eckerd) Ethyl dihydroxypropyl PABA. Bot. 4 oz. Lotion & oil Bot. 4 oz., 8 oz.
Use: Sunscreen.

ACH GLO ULTRA 21. (Eckerd) Padimate O, oxybenzone. Bot. 4 oz.
Use: Maximum protection sunblock lotion.

BATAB NO. 2. (Freeport) Belladonna 1/6 gr., phenobarbital 0.25 gr./Tab. Bot. 1000s.
Use: Sedative, anti-spasmodic.

BECANTHONE HYDROCHLORIDE. USAN.
Use: Antischistosomal.

CEEVITE CAPSULES. (Blue Cross) Vit. C 300 mg., B-1 15 mg., B-2 10 mg., niacin 50 mg., B-6 5 mg., pantothenic acid 10 mg./Tab. Bot. 100s.
Use: Vitamin supplement.

-CE FORTE. (Kenyon) B-1 15 mg., B-2 10 mg., niacinamide 80 mg., B-6 20 mg., d-panthenol 23 mg., C 100 mg./2 cc. Vial 20 cc.

-CE-PLEX. (CMC) B-6 6 mg., B-1 10 mg., B-2 10 mg., niacinamide 80 mg., panthenol 6 mg., sodium ascorbate 100 mg./2 cc. Vials 30 cc.

ECLAMIDE. B.A.N. N-Benzyl-3-chloropropionamide.
Use: Anticonvulsant.
See: Nydrane

ECLOMETHASONE. B.A.N. 9α-Chloro-11β, 17α, 21-trihydroxy-16β-methylpregna-1, 4-diene-3,20-dione. 9 α-Chloro-16β-methylprednisolone.
Use: Corticosteroid.

BECLOMETHASONE DIPROPIONATE. USAN.
Use: Corticosteroid.
See: Beclovent Inhaler (Glaxo)
Beconase Nasal Inhaler (Glaxo)
Vancenase Nasal Inhaler (Schering)
Vanceril Inhaler (Schering)

BECLOMYCIN DIPROPIONATE, U.S.P. XXI.
Use: Corticosteriod.

ECLOVENT INHALER. (Glaxo) Beclomethasone diproprionate 42 mcg./dose. Aerosol canister (16.8 Gm.) containing 200 metered inhalations. Canister 16.8 Gm. w/oral adapter. Refill canister 16.8 Gm.
Use: Treatment of chronic bronchial asthma.

ECOMP-C. (Cenci) Vit. C 250 mg., B-1 25 mg., B-2 10 mg., nicotinamide 50 mg., B-6 2 mg., Ca pantothenate 10 mg., hesperidin complex 50 mg./Cap. Bot. 100s, 500s.
Use: Deficiencies of the water-soluble vitamins.

BECONASE NASAL INHALER. (Glaxo) Beclomethasone dipropionate 42 mcg./acuation. Aerosol canister (16.8 Gm.) containing 200 metered inhalations. Canister 16.8 Gm w/nasal adapter.
Use: Corticosteroid.

BECOPLEX. (Blue Line) Vit. B-1 3 mg., B-2 3 mg., B-6 0.25 mg., Ca pantothenate 5 mg., niacinamide 10 mg., dried brewer's yeast 2 gr., liver extract (fraction II) 1 gr./Tab. Bot. 100s.

BECOPLEX FORTIFIED. (Blue Line) Vit. B-1 1 mg., B-2 2 mg., B-12 1 mcg., exc. ferrous sulfate 136 mg., des. liver 200 mg./Cap. Bot. 100s, 1000s.
Use: Orally, vitamin with liver & iron therapy.

BECOTIN. (Dista) Vit. B-1 10 mg., B-2 10 mg., B-6 4.1 mg., niacinamide 50 mg., pantothenic acid 25 mg., Vit. B-12 1 mcg./Pulvule. Bot. 100s.
Use: Orally, vitamin B complex deficiencies.

BECOTIN-T. (Dista) Vit. B-1 15 mg.; B-2 10 mg.; B-6 5 mg., niacinamide 100 mg., pantothenic acid 20 mg.; B-12 4 mcg.; C 300 mg./Tab. Bot. 100s, 1000s. Blister pkg. 10 × 10s.
Use: Vit. B-complex and Vit. C deficiencies.

BECOTIN W/VIT. C. (Dista) Vit. B-1 10 mg., B-2 10 mg., B-6 4.1 mg., niacinamide 50 mg., pantothenic acid 25 mg., Vit. B-12 1 mcg., C 150 mg./Pulvule. Bot. 100s, 500s, 1000s. Blister pkg. 10 × 10s.
Use: Orally, vitamin B complex and vitamin C deficiencies.

BEDOCE. (Lincoln) Crystalline anhydrous B-12 1000 mcg./cc. Vial 10 cc.
Use: I.M., vitamin B-12 therapy.

BEDOCE-GEL. (Lincoln) Vit. B-12 1000 mcg./cc. in 17% gelatin solution. Vial 10 cc.

BEDSORE SPRAY. (Century) Silicone, tincture of benzoin compound. Bot. 7 oz.
Use: Bedsore treatment.

BEECHWOOD CREOSOTE.
See: Creosote, N.F.

BEECOMP. (Vitarine) Vit. B-1 1.5 mg., B-2 2 mg., B-6 1 mg., Ca pantothenate 5 mg., niacinamide 10 mg./Cap. Bot. 50s, 1000s.
Use: Supplement.

BEEF PEPTONES. (Sandia) Water soluble peptones derived from beef 20 mg./2 cc. Vial 30 cc. Inj.

BEEKAPS. (Pharmics) Vit. C 400 mg., lemon bio-flavonoid 200 mg., B-1 25 mg., B-2 10 mg., Ca pantothenate 10 mg., B-6 10 mg., niacinamide 50 mg./Cap. Bot. 100s, 500s, 1000s.
Use: Dietary supplement.

BEELITH. (Beach) Pyridoxine HCl 25 mg., magnesium oxide 600 mg./Tab. Bot. 100s, 500s.
Use: Dietary supplement.

BEEPEN-VK. (Beecham Labs) Penicillin VK. **Tab.:** 250 mg./Tab. Bot. 1000s; 500 mg./Tab. Bot. 500s. **Syrup:** 125 mg./5 cc. Bot. 100 cc, 200 cc; 250 mg./5 cc. Bot. 100 cc, 200 cc.
Use: Antibiotics.

BEESIX INJECTION. (Fellows) Pyridoxine HCl 100 mg./cc. Vial 10 cc.

BEE-THI. (Burgin-Arden) Cyanocobalamin 1000 mcg., thiamine HCl 100 mg. in isotonic solution of sodium chloride/cc. Vial 10 cc., 20 cc.

BEE-TWELVE 1000. (Burgin-Arden) Cyanocobalamin 1000 mcg./cc. Vial 10 cc., 30 cc.

BEEZE W/VITAMIN C. (Quality Generics) Vit. B-1 15 mg., B-2 10 mg., B-6 5 mg., C 300 mg., niacinamide 50 mg., ca pantothenate 10 mg./Cap. Bot. 100s, 1000s.

BEFERRIC. (Kenyon) Ferric ammonium citrate 500 mg., B-1 12 mg., B-2 6 mg., B-6 0.6 mg., folic acid 0.5 mg., Cal. pantothenate 6 mg., niacinamide 15 mg., Mg 2 mg., Mg 1 mg., Co 0.1 mg., Zn 2 mg./Fl. oz. Bot. 4 oz.

BEHEPAN.
See: Vitamin B-12

BEJECTAL. (Abbott) Voluntarily withdrawn from the market.

BEJECTAL W/ VIT. C. (Abbott) Voluntary withdrawn from the market.

BELAP. (Lemmon) Phenobarbital 16.2 mg., belladonna extract 10.8 mg./Tab. Bot. 100s, 1000s.
Use: Anticholinergic, sedative.

BELATOL NO. 1; NO. 2. (Cenci) **No. 1:** Belladonna leaf extract ⅛ gr., phenobarbital 0.25 gr./Tab. 100s, 1000s. **No. 2:** Belladonna leaf extract ⅛ gr., phenobarbital 0.5 gr./Tab. Bot. 100s, 1000s.
Use: Antispasmodic and sedative.

BELATOL ELIXIR. (Cenci) Phenobarbital 20 mg., belladonna 6.75 min., alcohol 45%/5 cc. Elix. Bot. pt., gal.
Use: Antispasmodic.

BELBUTAL NO. 2 KAPTABS. (Churchill) Phenobarbital 32.4 mg., hyoscyamine sulfate 0.1092 mg., atropine sulfate 0.0215 mg., hyoscine HBr 0.0065 mg./Tab. Bot. 100s.
Use: Antispasmodic sedative.

BELDIN. (Blue Cross) Diphenhydramine HCl 12.5 mg./5 ml. w/alcohol 5%. Bot. gal.
Use: Antitussive.

BELEXAL. (Vale) Vit. B-1 1.5 mg., B-2 2 mg., B-6 0.167 mg., Ca pantothenate 1 mg., niacinamide 10 mg./Tab. w/brewer's yeast. Bot. 100s, 1000s, 5000s.
Use: Vitamin supplement.

BELEXON FORTIFIED IMPROVED. (APC) Liver fraction No. 2 3 gr., yeast ext. 3 gr., B-1 5 mg., B-2 6 mg., niacinamide 10 mg., Ca pantothenate 2 mg., cyanocobalamin 1 mcg., iron 10 mg./Cap. Bot. 100s.

BELFER. (Forest) Vit. B-1 2 mg., B-2 2 mg., B-12 10 mcg., B-6 2 mg., C 50 mg., iron gluconate 17 mg., sorbitol 100 mg./Tab. Bot. 100s.
Use: Anemia.

BELIVRON. (Vitarine) Vit. B-1 1 mg., B-2 1 mg., B-12 3 mcg., liver powder 7 gr., iron & ammonium citrates (green) 3 gr./Cap. Bot. 100s, 250s.
Use: Supplement.

BELIVRON TONIC ELIXIR. (Vitarine) Vit. B-1 6 mg., B-2 3 mg., B-6 2 mg., B-12 6 mcg., niacinamide 30 mg., folic acid 0.05 mg., pantothenic acid 6 mg., iron ammon. citrates 1.3 mg., Mn cit. 130 mg., Cu sulfate 1.6 mg., Mg sulfate 200 mg., pot. sulfate 20 mg., Zn sulfate 20 mg., liver fraction No. 1 175 mg., beef peptone 175 mg./Fl. oz. Bot. 8 oz., pt.
Use: High-potency tonic.

BELLACHAR. (Wolins) Phenobarbital 20 mg., activated charcoal 120 mg., belladonna ext. 5 mg./Tab. Bot. 1000s.

BELLADENAL. (Sandoz) Bellafoline 0.25 mg., phenobarbital 50 mg./Tab. Bot. 100s.
Use: Antispasmodic & anticholinergic.

BELLADENAL S. (Sandoz) Bellafoline 0.25 mg., phenobarbital 50 mg./Tab. Bot. 100s.
Use: Antispasmodic & anticholinergic.

■ **BELLADONNA ALKALOIDS.**
Use: Intestinal antispasmodic.
W/Combinations.
See: Accelerase-PB, Cap. (Organon)
Belladenal, Preps. (Sandoz)
Bellophen, Tab. (Vortech)
Belphen, Tab. (Robinson)
Belphen Elixir (Robinson)
Belphen Timed Caps. (Robinson)
Coryztime, Cap. (Elder)
Decobel, Lanacaps (Lannett)
Fitacol Stankaps (Standex)
Kamabel Liq. (Towne)
Nilspasm, Tab. (Parmed)
Ultabs, Tab. (Burlington)
Urised, Tab. (Webcon)
U-Tract, Tab. (Bowman)
Wigraine, Tab., Supp. (Organon)
Woltac, Cap. (Wolins)
Wyanoids, Supp., Oint. w/applic. (Wyeth)

• **BELLADONNA EXTRACT,** U.S.P. XXI. Tab. U.S.P. XXI.

■ **BELLADONNA EXTRACT COMBINATIONS.**
See: Amobell, Cap. (Bock)
Amsodyne, Tab. (Elder)
B & O Supprettes (Webcon)
Belap, Tab. (Lemmon)
Bellachar, Tab. (Wolins)
Bellafedrol A-H. Tab. (Lannett)
Bello-phen, Tab. (Wolins)
Bellkatal, Tab. (Ferndale)
Butibel, Tab., Elix. (McNeil)
Butibel-Zyme, Tab. (McNeil)
Gelcomul, Liq. (Commerce)
Hycoff Cold, Caps (Saron)
Lanothal, Pills (Lannett)
Phebe (Western Research)
Rectacort, Supp. (Century)

• **BELLADONNA LEAF,** U.S.P. XXI.
W/Phenobarbital & benzocaine.
Use: Anticholinergic.
See: Gastrolic, Tab. (Mallard)

■ **BELLADONNA PRODUCTS AND PHENOBARBITAL COMBINATIONS.**
See: Accelerase-PB, Cap. (Organon)
Alised, Tab. (Elder)
Atrocap, Cap. (Freeport)
Atrosed, Tab. (Freeport)
Bebatab, Tab. (Freeport)
Belap, Elix., Tab. (Lemmon)

Belatol, Tab., Elix. (Cenci)
Belbarb, Tab. (Arnar-Stone)
Belladenal, Elixir, Spacetab, and Tab. (Sandoz)
Bellergal, Spacetab., Tab. (Dorsey)
Bellkatal, Tab. (Ferndale)
Bellophen, Tab. (Richlyn)
B-Sed, Tab. (Scrip)
Chardonna, Tab. (Rorer)
Donabarb, Elix., Tab. (Elder)
Donnafed Jr., Tab. (Jenkins)
Donnatal, Cap., Elixir, Tab., Extentab (Robins)
Donnatal #2, Tab. (Robins)
Donnazyme, Tab. (Robins)
Gastrolic, Tab. (Mallard)
Hypnaldyne, Tab. (North American Pharm.)
Kinesed, Tab. (Stuart)
Mallenzyme, Tab. (Mallard)
Medi-Spas, Elix. (Medical Chemicals)
Phenobarbital and Belladonna Tab. (Lilly)
Phen-o-bel, Tab. (Coastal)
Phen-o-bel-T, T.R. Cap. (Coastal)
Sedapar, Tab. (Parmed)
Sedatromine, Tab. (Sutliff & Case)
Spabelin, Tab. (Arcum)
Spabelin No. 2, Tab. (Arcum)
Spasnil, Tab. (Rhode)

ELLADONNA TINCTURE, U.S.P. XXI.

LLAFEDROL A-H TABLETS. (Lannett) Pyrilamine naleate 12.5 mg., chlorpheniramine maleate 1 mg., henylephrine HCl 2.5 mg., ext. belladonna 6 ng./Tab. Bot. 100s, 500s, 1000s.
Jse: Antihistamine w/antispasmodic.

LLAFOLINE. (Sandoz) Levorotatory alkaloids of elladonna as malates. **Amp.** 0.5 mg./cc. SandoPak Pkg. 20s. **Tab.** 0.25 mg./Tab. Bot. 100s.
Jse: Antispasmodic for spastic conditions of smooth muscles and excessive secretions.

LLALPHEN. (CMC) Atropine sulfate 0.0194 mg., hyoscyamine sulfate 0.1037 mg., hyoscine HBr).0065 mg., phenobarbital 16.2 mg./Tab. Bot. 100s, 500s, 1000s.
Jse: Visceral spasms and hyperirritability.

LLANEED. (Hanlon) Belladonna & phenobarbital 16 mg./Cap. Bot. 100s.
Jse: Antispasmodic.

LL-ANS. (C.S. Dent) Sodium bicarbonate 264 mg., willow charcoal 38.8 mg., gingerine 0.0003 ml./Tab. Vial 60s, 120s. Also available in double strength. Vial 60s, 120s.
Jse: Antacid.

LLASTAL CAPSULES. (U.S. Ethicals) Phenobarbital 16.2 mg., hyoscyamine sulfate).1037 mg., atropine sulfate 0.0194 mg., scopolamine HBr 0.0065 mg./Cap. Bot. 1000s.
Jse: Intestinal antispasmodic.

LLASTAL ELIXIR. (U.S. Ethicals) Belladonna alkaloids, phenobarbital 16.2 mg., hyoscyamine sulfate 0.1037 mg., atropine sulfate 0.0194 mg., scopolamine HBr 0.0065 mg./5 ml. Bot. 120 ml., 3840 ml.
Jse: Adjunctive therapy in treatment of irritable bowel syndrome.

BELLERGAL. (Sandoz) Bellafoline 0.1 mg., ergotamine tartrate 0.3 mg., phenobarbital 20.0 mg./Tab. Bot. 100s.
Use: Orally, sedative w/antispasmodic.

BELLERGAL-S. (Sandoz) Ergotamine Tartrate 0.6 mg., Bellafoline 0.2 mg., Phenobarbital 40.0 mg./Spacetab. Bot. 100s.
Use: Menopausal disorders.

BELLKATAL. (Ferndale) Phenobarbital 1/8 gr., Pow. Ext. belladonna leaves 4/25 gr., kaolin colloidal 7.5 gr./Tab. Bot. 100s, 1000s.
Use: Sedative, antiparasympathomimetic, antispasmodic, absorbent.

• **BELOXAMIDE.** USAN.
Use: Antihyperlipoproteinemic.

BELPHEN. (Robinson) Belladonna alkaloids, phenobarbital. Tab. Bot. 100s, 1000s.
Use: Antispasmodic, sedative.

BELPHEN ELIXIR. (Robinson) Belladonna alkaloids w/phenobarbital elixir. Bot. pt., gal.

BELPHEN TABLETS. (Stanlabs) #1 Belladonna leaf ext. 1/8 gr., phenobarbital 0.25 gr./Tab. #2 Belladonna leaf ext. 1/8 gr., phenobarbital 0.5 gr./Tab. Bot. 1000s.
Use: Antispasmodic.

BELPHEN TIMED CAPS. (Robinson) Belladonna alkaloids, phenobarbital time disintegration. Bot. 100s, 500s, 1000s.
Use: Antispasmodic, sedative.

BEMEGRIDE. B.A.N. 3-Ethyl-3-methylglutarimide.
See: Megimide
Use: Medullary respiratory stimulant.

BEMINAL 500. (Ayerst) Vit. B-1 25 mg., B-2 12.5 mg., niacinamide 100 mg., B-6 10 mg., calcium pantothenate 20 mg., C 500 mg. cyanocobalamin 5 mcg./Tab. Bot. 100s.
Use: Vitamin B therapy.

BEMINAL FORTE W/VIT. C. (Ayerst) Vit. B-1 25 mg., B-2 12.5 mg., niacinamide 50 mg., B-6 3 mg., calcium pantothenate 10 mg., C 250 mg., B-12 2.5 mcg./Cap. Bot. 100s.
Use: Vitamins B & C therapy.

BEMINAL STRESS PLUS IRON. (Ayerst) Vit. B-1 25 mg., B-2 12.5 mg., B-3 100 mg., B-5 20 mg., B-6 10 mg., B-12 25 mcg., folic acid 400 mcg., C 700 mg., E 45 I.U., iron 27 mg./Tab. Bot. 60s.
Use: Dietary supplement.

BEMINAL STRESS PLUS ZINC. (Ayerst) Vit. B-1 25 mg., B-2 12.5 mg., B-3 100 mg., B-5 20 mg., B-6 10 mg., B-12 25 mcg., C 700 mg., E 45 I.U. Zn 45 mg./Tab. Bot. 60s.
Use: Dietary supplement.

BENACEN. (Cenci) Probenecid 0.5 gm./Tab. Bot. 100s, 1000s.

BENACHLOR. (Jenkins) Diphenhydramine HCl 12.5 mg., ammonium chloride 130 mg., sod. citrate 55 mg., menthol 1.11 mg., alcohol 5%/5 cc. Syr. Bot. 3 oz., 4 oz., gal.

BENACOL. (Cenci) Dicyclomine HCl 20 mg./Tab. Bot. 100s, 1000s.
Use: Smooth muscle spasm.

BENACTYZINE. B.A.N. 2-Diethylaminoethyl benzilate.
Use: Tranquilizer.
See: Suavitil hydrochloride.

BENACTYZINE HYDROCHLORIDE. 2-Diethylaminoethyl benzilate HCl.
W/Meprobamate.
See: Deprol, Tab. (Wallace)

BENA-D-10. (Seatrace) Diphenhydramine HCl 10 mg./ml. Vial 30 cc.

BENA-D-50. (Seatrace) Diphenhydramine HCl 50 mg./ml. Vial 10 cc.

BENADRYL COUGH PREPARATION.
See: Benylin Cough Syrup (Parke-Davis)

BENADRYL HYDROCHLORIDE. (Parke-Davis) Diphenhydramine hydrochloride.
Use: Antihistaminic.
Amp.: (50 mg./ml.) 1 ml. Box 10s.
Cap.: (25 mg.) Bot. 100s, 1000s. Unit dose 100s.
Cream: (2%) Tube 1 & 2 oz.
Elixir (w/alcohol 14%): (12.5 mg./5 ml.) Bot. 4 oz., 1 pt., 1 gal. Unit dose 5 ml × 100s.
Kapseals: (50 mg.) Bot. 100s, 1000s. Unit dose 100s.
Steri-Dose: (50 mg./ml., pH adjusted w/HCl or sod. hydroxide) Amp. 1 ml. Box 10s. Disposable syringes 1 ml. **Steri-Vial:** (10 mg./ml. Phemerol benzethonium chloride as germicidal agent. pH adjusted w/sod. hydroxide or HCl) 10 ml., 30 ml. (50 mg./ml.) 10 ml.
W/Ammonium chloride, sod. citrate, menthol.
See: Benylin Cough Syrup (Parke-Davis)
W/Ephedrine sulfate. (Parke-Davis) Benadryl hydrochloride 50 mg., ephedrine sulfate 25 mg./Cap. Bot. 100s.
Use: Provides the complementary effects of the original antihistaminic & the sympathomimetic.
W/Zinc oxide, alcohol.
See: Ziradryl, Lot. (Parke-Davis)

BENADRYL HCl LOTION OR CREAM.
See: Caladryl, Cream, Lot. (Parke-Davis)

BENAHIST 10. (Keene) Diphenhydramine 10 mg./ml. Vial 30 ml.
Use: Antihistaminic.

BENAHIST 50. (Keene) Diphenhydramine 50 mg./ml. Vial 10 ml.
Use: Antihistaminic.

BENANEERIN HCl. 3-(2-Aminoethyl)-1-benzyl-5-methoxy-2-methylindole HCl.

BENANSERIN HYDROCHLORIDE. 3-(2-Aminoethyl)-1-benzyl-5-methoxy-2-methylindole monohydrochloride.
Use: Serotonin antagonist.

BENAPEN.
See: Benethamine

BENAPHEN CAPS. (Major) Diphenyhdramine 25 mg. or 50 mg./Cap. Bot. 100s, 1000s.
Use: Antihistamine.

BENAPRYZINE. B.A.N. 2-(N-Ethylpropylamino)-ethyl benzilate.
Use: Treatment of the parkinsonian syndrome.

• **BENAPRYZINE HYDROCHLORIDE.** USAN.
Use: Anticholingeric.

BENASE. (Ferndale) Proteolytic enzymes extracted from Carica papaya 20,000 u. enzyme activity/Ta Bot. 1000s.
Use: Reduction of edema and relief of episiotomy

BENASEPT. (Blue Line) Benzalkonium chloride **Concentrate** 17%. Bot. 4 oz., gal. **Sol.** 1:1000, stainless. Bot. 1 gal. **Vaginal Jelly** 1:3000, sod. lactate-lactic acid buffer, tragacanth-pectin-glyceri water base, methylparaben, propylparaben, coloring, perfume, w/applicator, Tube 1.5 oz.
Use: Topically, cationic germicidal.

BENAT-12. (Hauck) Cyanocobalamine 30 mcg., liver jection 0.5 ml., B-1 10 mg., B-2 2 mg., niacinamide mg., d-panthenol 1 mg., B-6 1 mg./ml. w/benzyl alc hol 4%, phenol 0.5%. Vial 10 ml.
Use: Anti-anemic.

• **BENDAZAC.** USAN. [l-Benzyl-(H-indazol-3yl)ox acetic acid.
Use: Anti-inflammatory.

BENDROFLUAZIDE. B.A.N. 3-Benzyl-3,4-dihydro-6-trifluoromethylbenzo-1,2,4-thiadiazine-7-sulfonamic 1,1-dioxide. Bendroflumethiazide (I.N.N.)
Use: Diuretic.
See: Aprinox
Berkozide
Centyl
Neo-Naclex

• **BENDROFLUMETHIAZIDE,** U.S.P. XXI. Tab., U.S. XXI. 3-Benzyl-3:4-dihydro-7-sulphamoly-6-trifluoromethylbenzo-1:2:4-thiadiazine 1:1-dioxide. 6-(Trifluoromethyl)-2H-1,2,4-benzothiadiazine-7-sulfo amide 1, 1-dioxide.
Use: Diuretic; antihypertensive.
See: Naturetin, Tab. (Squibb)
Naturetin-10, Tab. (Squibb)
W/Potassium Chloride.
See: Naturetin W-K, Tab. (Squibb)
W/Rauwolfia serpentina
See: Rauzide, Tab.
W/Rauwolfia serpentina, potassium chloride.
See: Rautrax-N, Tab. (Squibb)
Rautrax-N Modified, Tab. (Squibb)

BENDYLATE CAP. (Reid-Provident) Diphenhydrami HCl 25 mg. & 50 mg./Cap. Bot. 100s, 1000s.

BENDYLATE INJ. (Reid-Provident) Diphenhydrami HCl 10 mg. in water for inj. w/benzethonium chloride 1:10,000/cc. Vials 30 cc.

BENEGYN CREAM. (Vortech) Tube. 96 Gm. w/applicator.
Use: Trichomoniasis, moniliasis & mixed infection

BENEMID. (Merck Sharp & Dohme) Probenecid 0.5 Gm./Tab. Bot. 100s, 1000s. Unit-dose 100s.
Use: Uricosuric, adjuvant to antibiotic therapy for elevation and prolongation of plasma levels.
W/Colchicine.
See: Colbenemid, Tab. (Merck Sharp & Dohme)

BENEPHEN ANTISEPTIC MEDICATED POWDER. (Halsted) Methylbenzethonium chloride 1:1800,

ıagnesium carbonate, in cornstarch base. Shaker ans 3.56 oz.
Jse: Deodorant, antiseptic.

ɴEPHEN ANTISEPTIC OINTMENT W/COD IVER OIL. (Halsted) Methylbenzethonium chloride :1000, water-repellent base of zinc oxide and corn- tarch. Tubes 1.5 oz., jars 1 lb.
Jse: Antiseptic.

ɴEPHEN ANTISEPTIC VITAMIN A & D CREAM. Halsted) Methylbenzethonium chloride 1:1000, cod ver oil w/vit. A & D in petrolatum & glycerin base. ubes 2 oz., jars 1 lb.
Jse: Antiseptic.

ɴEPRO TABS. (Major) Probenecid 500 mg./Tab. 3ot. 100s, 1000s.
Jse: Uricosuric.

ɴETHAMINE PENICILLIN. B.A.N. N-Benzyl-phene- ıylammonium 6-phenylacetamidopenicillanate. N- 3enzylphenethylamine salt of benzylpenicillin. 3enapen.
Jse: Antibiotic.

ɴGAL GELATIN.
See: Agar.

N-GAY CHILDREN'S VAPORIZING RUB. (Leeming) Camphor, menthol, w/oils of turpentine, eucalyptus, edar leaf, nutmeg and thyme in stainless white ase. Jar 1.125 oz.
Jse: Chest colds.

N-GAY EXTRA STRENGTH BALM. (Leeming) Men- hol & methylsalicylate. Jars 3.75 oz.
Jse: External analgesic.

N-GAY GEL. (Leeming) Methyl salicylate, menthol, lcohol 40%. Tube 1.25 oz., 3.0 oz.
Jse: External analgesic.

N-GAY GREASELESS OINTMENT. (Leeming) Methyl salicylate, menthol. Tube 1.25 oz., 3.0 oz., .0 oz.
Jse: External analgesic.

N-GAY LOTION. (Leeming) Methyl salicylate, men- hol in lotion base. Bot. 2 oz., 4 oz.
Jse: External analgesic.

N-GAY OINTMENT. (Leeming) Methyl salicylate, nenthol in ointment base. Tube 1.25 oz., 3 oz., 5 z.
Jse: External analgesic.

NISONE. (Rydell) Betamethasone benzoate .025% **Cream:** 15 Gm., 60 Gm. **Gel:** 15 Gm., 60 Gm. **Lotion:** 15 ml., 60 ml., **Oint.:** 15 Gm., 60 Gm.
Jse: Anti-inflammatory agent.

NN. (Scrip) Probenecid 500 mg./Tab. Bot. 1000s.
Jse: Orally, increase excretion of uric acid.

NN-C. (Scrip) Probenecid 500 mg., colchicine 0.5 ng./Tab. Bot. 1000s.
Jse: Chronic gout and gouty arthritis.

NOJECT. (Mayrand) Diphenhydramine HCl 50 ng./ml. Vial 10 ml.
Jse: Antihistamine, anticholingergic.

NOQUIN. (Elder) Monobenzone 20% in cream ase. Tube 1.25 oz.

NORAL CAPSULES. (Winthrop Products) 3enorylate.
Jse: Analgesic, antipyretic.

BENORAL SUSPENSION. (Winthrop Products)
Benorylate.
Use: Analgesic, antipyretic.

BENORAL TABLETS. (Winthrop Products)
Benorylate.
Use: Analgesic, antipyretic.

• **BENORTERONE.** USAN. 17 β-Hydroxy-17-methyl-β-norandrost-4-en-3-one.
Use: Antiandrogen.

BENORYLATE. B.A.N. 4-Acetamidophenyl O-acetyl-salicylate. Benoral.
Use: Analgesic.

• **BENOXAPROFEN.** USAN. 2-(2-p-Chlorophenyl-ben-zoxazol-5-yl)propionic acid.
Use: Anti-inflammatory; analgesic.

• **BENOXINATE HYDROCHLORIDE,** U.S.P. XXI. Ophth. Soln., U.S.P. XXI. 2-(Diethylaminoethyl)4-amino-3-butoxybenzoate HCl.
See: Dorsacaine, Sol. (Dorsey)
W/Fluorescein sod.
See: Flurless, Sol. (Barnes-Hind)

BENOXYL LOTION. (Stiefel) Benzoyl peroxide 5% or 10% in mild lotion base. Bot. 1 oz., 2 oz.
Use: Acne therapy.

• **BENPERIDOL.** USAN. 1-{1-[3-(4-Fluorobenzoyl)-pro-pyl]-4-piperidyl}benzimidazolin-2-one.
Use: Tranquilizer.
See: Anquil

• **BENSALAN.** USAN. 3,5-Dibromo-N-p-bromo-benzyl)-salicylamide. Under study.
Use: Germicide.

• **BENSERAZIDE.** USAN. DL-2-Amino-3-hydroxy-2′-(2,-3,4-trihydroxybenzyl)propionohydrazide.
Use: Treatment of the parkinsonian syndrome.

BENSULDAZIC ACID. B.A.N. (5-Benzyl-6-thioxo-1,3,5-thiadiazin-3-yl)acetic acid. Defungit sodium salt.
Use: Fungicide, veterinary medicine.

BENSULFOID. (Poythress) Colloidal sulfur 33%**Tabs.** Elemental sulfur 130 mg. by weight, fused on colloidal bentonite. 2 gr. Bot. 100s. **Pow.:** 1 oz.
Use: Prescription compounding.
W/Phenobarbital
See: Solfoton, Tab. or Cap. (Poythress)

BENSULFOID LOTION. (Poythress) Bensulfoid 6% (33% colloidal sulfur), thymol 0.5%, resorcinol 2% w/alcohol (by vol.) 12%, perfume, cosmetic colors, emulsifiers/Lotion Bot. 2 oz.
Use: Topical treatment of acne.

• **BENTAZEPAM.** USAN.
Use: Sedative.

BENTICAL. (Lamond) Bentonite, zinc oxide, zinc carbonate, titanium dioxide. Bot. 4 oz., 6 oz., 8 oz., 16 oz., 32 oz., 0.5 gal., gal.
Use: Bland lotion.

• **BENTIROMIDE.** USAN.
Use: Diagnostic aid.
See: Chymex, Sol. (Adria)

• **BENTONITE,** N.F. XVI.
Use: Pharmaceutical aid (suspending agent).

• **BENTONITE, PURIFIED,** N.F. XVI.
Use: Pharmaceutical aid.

• **BENTONITE MAGMA,** N.F. XVI.
Use: Pharmaceutical aid (suspending agent).

BENTRAC 25, 50. (Kenyon) Diphenhydramine HCl 25 mg., 50 mg./Cap. Bot. 100s.

BENTRAC-ELIXIR. (Kenyon) Diphenhydramine HCl 10 mg., alcohol 14%/4 cc. Bot. 4 oz.

BENTRAC EXPECTORANT. (Kenyon) Diphenhydramine HCl 80 mg., ammonium chloride 12 gr., sod. citrate 5 gr., chloroform 2 gr., menthol 1/10 gr., alcohol 5%/Fl. oz. Bot. 4 oz.

BENTYL. (Merrell Dow) Dicyclomine HCl.**Caps.** 10 mg. Bot. 100s, 500s, 1000s. Unit dose 100s.**Tab.** 20 mg., Bot. 100s, 500s, 1000s. Unit dose 100s. **Syr.** 10 mg./5 ml. Bot. 1 pt. **Inj.** 10 mg./ml. Amp. 2 ml.,syringe 2 ml. (both contain sod. chloride). Vial 10 ml. (also contains sod. chloride, chlorobutanol hydrous).
Use: Antispasmodic for irritable bowel syndrome.

• **BENURESTAT.** USAN.
Use: Enzyme inhibitor.

BENYLIN COUGH SYRUP. (Parke-Davis) Diphenhydramine HCl 12.5 mg. w/alcohol 5%. Bot. 4 oz., 8 oz., 1 pt., 1 gal. Unit dose 5 ml., 10 ml., Box 100s.
Use: Orally, coughs.

BENYLIN DM COUGH SYRUP. (Parke-Davis) Dextromethorphan HBr 10 mg./5 ml. w/alcohol 5% Bot. 4 oz., 8 oz.
Use: Cough suppressant.

BENZA. (Century) Benzalkonium chloride 1:5000 and 1:750. Bot. 2 oz., 4 oz.
Use: Antiseptic, germicide.

BENZAC 5 & 10. (Owen) Benzoyl peroxide 5% or 10%w/polyoxyethylene lauryl ether 6%, alcohol 12%, dimethicone, carbomer 940, fragrance & purified water; may contain sodium hydroxide and/or citric acid to adjust pH. Tube 60 Gm.
Use: Acne vulgaris treatment.

BENZAC w 2.5. (Owen) Benzoyl peroxide 2.5%, in gel base of dioctyl sodium sulfosuccinate, edetate disodium, poloxamer 182, carbomer 940, propylene glycol, silicon dioxide, purified water. Tubes 60 Gm., 90 Gm.
Use: Acne vulgaris treatment.

BENZAC w 5 & 10. (Owen) Benzoyl peroxide 5% or 10% w/docusate sodium, edetate disodium, poloxamer 182, carbomer 940, propylene glycol, silicon dioxide purified water and buffer. Tube 60, 90 Gm.
Use: Acne vulgaris treatment.

BENZAC w WASH. (Owen) Benzoyl peroxide 5% in vehicle of sodium C14-16 olefin sulfonate, carbomer 940, purified water. Bot. 4 oz.
Use: Adjunct to primary acne regimens.

BENZAGEL. (Dermik) Benzoyl peroxide 5% or 10% in gel base of water, carbomer 940, alcohol 14%, sodium hydroxide, docusate sodium, fragrance. Tube 1.5 oz., 3 oz.
Use: Treatment of acne.

• **BENZALDEHYDE,** N.F. XVI. Cpd. Elix., N.F. XVI.
Use: Pharm. aid (flavor).

• **BENZALKONIUM CHLORIDE,** N.F. XVI. Sol., N.F. XVI. Alkyldimethylbenzylammonium chloride. Zephirol. Sol. 1:5000. ammonium, alkyldimethyl(phenylmethyl)-, chloride.
Use: Surface antiseptic and antimicrobial preservative.
See: Benasept, Sol. & Tr., Vaginal Jelly (Blue Lin
Benz-All, Liq. (Xxtrium)
Econopred, Susp. (Alcon)
Eye-Stream (Alcon)
Germicin, Sol. (Consolidated Mid.)
Hyamine 3500 (Rohm & Haas)
Otrivin Spray (Geigy)
Ultra Tears (Alcon)
Zalkon Conc., Liq. (Gordon)
Zephiran Chloride Preps. (Winthrop-Breon)
W/Aluminum Cl, oxyquinoline sulfate.
See: Alochor Styptic, Liq. (Gordon)
W/Bacitracin zinc, polymyxin B, neomycin sulf.
See: Biotres, Oint. (Central)
W/Benzocaine, benzyl alcohol.
See: Aerocain, Oint. (Aeroceuticals)
W/Benzocaine, orthohydroxyphenyl-mercuric chlor parachlorometaxylenol
See: Unguentine, Aerosol (Norwich)
W/Berberine HCl, sodium borate, phenylephrine H(sodium chloride, boric acid.
See: Ocusol, Eye Lotion, Drops (Norwich)
W/Boric acid, potassium chloride, sodium carbonat anhydrous, disodium edetate.
See: Swim-Eye, Drops (Savage)
W/Chlorophyll.
See: Mycomist, Spray Liq. (Gordon)
W/Hydrocortisone.
See: Barseb Thera-Spray, Sol. (Barnes-Hind)
W/Diperodon HCl, carbolic acid, ichthammol, thym camphor, juniper tar.
See: Boro Oint. (Scrip)
W/Disodium edetate, pot. chloride, isotonic boric a
See: Dacriose (Smith, Miller & Patch)
W/Epinephrine.
See: Epinal, Sol. (Alcon)
W/Epinephrine bitartrate, pilocarpine HCl, mannitol.
See: E-Pilo Ophthalmic, Preps. (Smith, Miller & Patch)
W/Ethoxylated lanolin, methylparaben, hamamelis water, & glycerin.
See: Mediconet, cloth wipes. (Medicone)
W/Gentamicin sulfate, disodium phosphate, monosodium, phosphate, sodium chloride.
See: Garamycin Ophthalmic Sol., Preps. (Scherir
W/Hydroxypropyl methylcellulose.
See: Isopto Plain & Tears (Alcon)
W/Hydroxypropyl methycellulose, disodium edetate
See: Goniosol (Smith, Miller & Patch)
W/Isopropyl alcohol, methyl salicylate.
See: Cydonol Massage Lotion (Gordon)
W/Lidocaine, phenol.
See: Unguentine, spray (Norwich)
W/Methylcellulose.
See: Tearisol (Smith, Miller & Patch)
W/Methylcellulose, phenylephrine HCl.
See: Efricel ⅛% (Professional Pharmacal)

Oxyquinolin sulfate, distilled water.
See: Oxyzal Wet Dressing, Sol. (Gordon)
Phenylephrine, pyrilamine maleate, antipyrine.
See: Prefrin-A, Ophthalmic (Allergan)
Phenylephrine HCl
See: S.A.C. Nasal Spray (Towne)
Pilocarpine HCl, epinephrine bitartrate, mannitol.
See: E-Pilo Ophthalmic, Preps. (Smith, Miller & Patch)
Polymyxin B, neomycin sulfate, zinc bacitracin.
See: Biotres, Oint. (Central)
Polyoxyethylene ethers.
See: Ionax, Aerosol Can. (Owen)
Polyvinyl alcohol.
See: Contique Artificial Tears (Alcon)
Potassium alum.
See: Hygefem Douche, Liq., Pwd., Tab. (Blue Line)
Pramoxine HCl, allantoin.
See: Perifoam, Aerosol (Rowell)
Pramoxine HCl, hydrocortisone.
parachlorometaxylenol, acetic acid.
See: My Cort Otic #2, Ear Drops (Scrip)
Steramine Otic, Drop. (Mayrand)
Pramoxine HCl, hydrocortisone.
parachlorometaxylenol, acetic acid, propylene glycol.
See: Otostan H.C. (Standex)
Pyrilamine maleate, pheniramine maleate, chlorpheniramine maleate, menthol.
See: Trigelamine, Oint. (Edward J. Moore)
Sod. borate, sod. bicarbonate, sod. chloride.
See: Zalkon Wet Dressing, Liq. (Gordon)
Tripelennamine HCl, methapyrilene.
See: Didelamine, Cream (Commerce Drug)
Zinc oxide, urea, sulfur, salicylic acid, isopropyl alcohol in a base containing menthol, silicon dioxide, iron oxide and perfume.
See: Akne Drying Lotion, Bot. (Alto)

NZ-ALL. (Xttrium) Benzalkonium Cl 12.9%. Packets 10 cc., 10 cc. 15s.
Use: Germicidal concentrate with anti-rust factor.

NZALOIDS. (Jenkins) Benzocaine 5.0 mg., cal. iodized 12.0 mg., eucalyptol 0.35 mg., methenamine 6.5 mg., menthol 0.2 mg./Loz. Bot. 1000s.

NZAMIDE, 4-AMINO-N-[2-(DIETHYL-AMINO)-ETHYL]-,MONOHYDROCHLORIDE. Procainamide Hydrochloride, U.S.P. XXI.

NZAMIDE, N-(1-METHYLETHYL)-4-[(2-METHYL-HYDRAZINO)METHYL]-, MONOHYDROCHLORIDE. Procarbazine Hydrochloride, U.S.P. XXI.

ENZATHINE PENCILLIN G, U.S.P. XXI. Oral Susp. Sterile, Tab., U.S.P. XXI. N,N′-Dibenzylethylenediamine di(benzylpenicillin) Benzethacil. 3,3-Dimethyl-7-oxo-6-(2-phenylacetamido)-4-thia-1-azabicyclo [3.2.0] heptaine-2-carboxylic acid compound with N,N-Dibenzylethylene-diamine (2:1). Dibencil, Penidural.
Use: Antibiotic.
See: Permapen, Disp. Syr. (Pfipharmecs)
Isoject Permapen, Aq. Susp. (Pfizer)
Procaine penicillin G.
See: Bicillin P.A.B., Disp. Syr. (Wyeth)

BENZAMYCIN TOPICAL GEL. (Dermik) Erythromycin 3%, benzoyl peroxide 5%. Jar 23.3 Gm.
Use: Treatment of acne vulgaris.

BENZATHINE PENICILLIN. B.A.N. NN′-Dibenzylethylenedi(ammonium 6-phenylacetamido-penicillanate). NN′-Dibenzylethylenediamine di-(benzylpenicillin).
Use: Antibiotic.
See: Dibencil
Neolin
Penidural
Permapen

BENZAZOLINE HYDROCHLORIDE.
See: Tolazoline HCl

• **BENZBROMARONE.** USAN.
Use: Uricosuric.

BENZCHLORPROPAMID.
Used in Europe under:
Nydrane
Posedrine

BENZ-EASE. (Novocol) Benzocaine, oil of clove, oxyquinoline benzoate. Tube 0.25 oz., 6s, 36s.
Use: Anesthetic antiseptic adhesive ointment.

BENZEDREX INHALER. (Menley & James) Propylhexedrine, 250 mg., w/menthol and lavender oil. Single plastic tubes, 12s.
Use: Relieves nasal congestion in colds and hay fever; ear block and pressure pain during air travel.

BENZEHIST. (Pharmex) Diphenhydramine HCl 10 mg./cc. Vial 30 cc.
Use: Antihistaminic.

BENZENAMINIUM, 3-[[(DIMETHYLAMINO)-CARBONYL]OXY]-N,N,N-TRIMETHYL-, Bromide or Methyl Sulfate.
See: Neostigmine Bromide, U.S.P. XXI. or Methyl Sulfate, U.S.P. XXI.

BENZENE, 1-CHLORO-2-[2,2-DICHLORO-1-(4-CHLOROPHENYL)ETHYL]-.
See: Mitotane, U.S.P. XXI.

BENZENEACETIC ACID, α-HYDROXY, 8-METHYL-8-AZABICYCLO[3.2.1.]-OCT-3-YL ESTER; HYDROBROMIDE, ENDO-($\pm$)-. Homatropine Hydrobromide, U.S.P. XXI.

BENZENECARBOXIMIDAMIDE, 4-[2-[4-(AMINOIMINOMETHYL)-PHENYL]ETHENYL]-3-HYDROXY-, BIS(2-HYDROXYETHANE-SULFONATE)(SALT). Hydroxystilbamidine Isethionate, U.S.P. XXI.

BENZENEDECANOIC ACID, IODO-t-METHYL-, ETHYL ESTER. Iophendylate, U.S.P. XXI.

1,3-BENZENEDIOL. Resorcinol, U.S.P. XXI.

1,4-BENZENEDIOL. Hydroquinone, U.S.P. XXI.

BENZENE HEXACHLORIDE, GAMMA.
See: Lindane, U.S.P. XXI.

BENZENEMETHANOL, α-(1-AMINOETHYL)-2,5-DIMETHOXY-, HCl. Methoxamine Hydrochloride, U.S.P. XXI.

BENZENEMETHANOL, α-(1-AMINOETHYL)-3-HYDROXY-[R-(R*,R*)]-2,3-DIHYDROXY-BUTANE-DIOATE (1:1) (salt). Metaraminol Bitartrate.

BENZENEMETHANOL, 3-HYDROXY-α-[(METHYLAMINO)METHYL]-, HYDROCHLORIDE(S)-. Phenylephrine Hydrochloride, U.S.P. XXI.

BENZENEPROPANOIC ACID, 3-AMINO-α-ETHYL-2,4,6-TRIIODO-., CALCIUM OR SODIUM SALTS. Iopanoic Acid, Calcium or Sodium, U.S.P. XXI.

BENZENETHANOL, α-[2-(DIMETHYLAMINO)-1-METHYLETHYL]-α-PHENYL-, PROPANOATE (ESTER), HCl. Propoxyphene Hydrochloride, U.S.P. XXI.

BENZESTROL 4,4′-(1,2-Diethyl-3-methyltrimethylene) diphenol.

BENZETHACIL. Dibenzylethylenediamine dipenicillin G DBED.
See: Penicillin G Benzathine, U.S.P. XXI.

BENZETHIDINE. B.A.N. Ethyl 1-(2-benzyloxyethyl)-4-phenylpiperidine-1-carboxylate.
Use: Narcotic analgesic.

• **BENZETHONIUM CHLORIDE,** U.S.P. XXI. Tincture, Topical Sol. U.S.P. XXI. Benzyldimethyl [2-[2-[p-(1,-1,3,3-tetramethylbutyl)phenoxy]ethoxy]ethyl]ammonium chloride.
Use: Surface antiseptic and antimicrobial preservative.
See: Ammorid Diaper Rinse, Oint. (Kinney)
Hyacide, Sol. (Niltig)
Hyamine 1622 (Rohm & Haas)
Phemerol Chloride, Sol. & Tr. (Parke-Davis)
Phemithyn, Liq. (Davis & Sly)
W/Benzocaine.
See: Americaine, Oint., Aerosol (Arnar-Stone)
Dermoplast, Spray (Ayerst)
W/Nonyl phenoxypolyoxyethylene ethanol.
See: Dalkon Foam (Robins)
Emko Pre-Fil, Foam (Emko)
W/Zinc oxide.
See: Ammorid, Oint. (Kinney)

BENZETHONIUM CHLORIDE. B.A.N. Benzyldimethyl-2-{2-[4-(1,1,3,3-tetramethylbutyl)-phenoxy]ethoxy}ethylammonium chloride.
Use: Antibacterial.
See: Phemeride

• **BENZETIMIDE HCl.** USAN. (1)2-(l-Benzyl-4-piperidyl)-2-phenylglutarimide monohydrochloride.
Use: Anticholinergic.

BENZHEXOL. B.A.N. 1-Cyclohexyl-1-phenyl-3-piperidinopropan-1-ol. Trihexyphenidyl (I.N.N.)
Use: Treatment of the Parkinsonian syndrome.
See: Artane
Trinol

N-BENZHYDRYL-N-METHYLPIPERAZINE HCl. Cyclizine Hydrochloride, U.S.P. XXI.

alpha-BENZHYDROL HCl. Diphenylhydroxy-carbinol.

BENZIDE. (Canright) Benzthiazide 50 mg./Tab. Bot. 100s, 1000s.
Use: Diuretic and antihypertensive.

• **BENZILONIUM BROMIDE.** USAN. 1-Ethyl-3-pyrrolidinyl benzilate ethylbromide.
Use: Anticholinergic.

BENZILONIUM BROMIDE. B.A.N. 3-Benziloyloxy-1, 1-diethylpyrrolidinium bromide.
Use: Inhibition of gastric secretion.
See: Portyn

BENZINDAMINE HCl. Benzydamine HCl.

1H-BENZ[E]INDOLIUM, 2-[7-[1,3-dihydro-1,1-dimeth 3-(4-sulfobutyl)-2h-benz[e]indol-2-ylidene]-1,3,5-he atrienyl]-1,1-dimethyl-3-(4-sulfobutyl) hydroxide, in salt, sodium salt.
See: Indocyanine Green, U.S.P. XXI.

• **BENZINDOPYRINE HYDROCHLORIDE.** USAN. 1 Benzyl-3-[2-(4-pyridyl)-ethyl] indole hydrochlori Pyrbenzindole
Use: Tranquilizer.

BENZIODARONE. B.A.N. 2-Ethyl-3-(4-hydroxy-3,5-d iodobenzoyl-benzofuran.
Use: Coronary vasodilator.
See: Cardivix

1,2-BENZISOTHIAZOLIN-3-ONE 1,1-DIOXIDE CA CIUM SALT.
See: Saccharin Calcium, U.S.P. XXI.

1,2-BENZISOTHIAZOLIN-3-ONE 1,1-DIOXIDE S DIUM SALT.
See: Saccharin Sodium, U.S.P. XXI.

BENZO-C. (Freeport) Benzocaine 5 mg., cetalkoni Cl. 5 mg., ascorbic acid 50 mg./Troche. Bot. 1000s, or cello-packed boxes 1000s.
Use: Relief of minor sore throat.

• **BENZOCAINE,** U.S.P. XXI. Cream, Oint., Otic Sol Topical Aerosol, Topical Soln., U.S.P. XXI. Ethyl-p aminobenzoate. Anesthesin, orthesin, parathesin.
Use: Local anesthetic.
W/Combinations.
See: Aerotherm, Oint. (Aeroceuticals)
Aerocaine, Oint. (Aeroceuticals)
Americaine, Oint., Aerosol (American Critical Care)
Aminophylline W/Pentobarbital, Tab. (Searle)
Anacaine, Oint. (Gordon)
Anecal, Cream (Lannett)
Aura-Aid, Liq. (Edward J. Moore)
Auralgan, Otic Drops (Ayerst)
Auralgesic, Liq. (Elder)
Auristel, Dropules (Blue Line)
Aurotis, Liq. (Research Pharmacal Lab.)
Benadex, Oint. (Fuller)
Benzo-C, Troche (Freeport)
Benzocol, Oint. (Mallard)
Benzodent, Oint. (Vicks)
Biscolan, Supp. (Lannett)
Boilaid, Oint. (Edward J. Moore)
Bonal Itch Cream, Cream (Edward J. Moore)
Bowman Drawing Paste, Oint. (Bowman)
Boil-Ease Anesthetic Drawing Salve (Commerc
Burn Gon, Oint. (Edward J. Moore)
20-Cain Burn Relief, Bot. (Alto)
Calamatum, Preps. (Blair)
Caloxide cream W/benzocaine, (Blue Line)
Calsarbain, Tab. (Sutliff & Case)
Cēpacol, Troches (Merrell Dow)
Cetacaine, Preps. (Cetylite)
Chiggerex, Oint. (Scherer)

Chiggertox, Liq. (Scherer)
Chloraseptic Children's Lozenges, (Norwich Eaton)
CPI Hemorrhoidal, Supp. (Century)
Culminal, Cream (Culminal)
D.D.D. Cream (Campana)
Dent's Dental Poultice (C.S. Dent)
Dent's Lotion, Jel (C.S. Dent)
Dent's Toothache Gum (C.S. Dent)
Derma Medicone (Medicone)
Derma Medicone-HC (Medicone)
Dermoplast, Spray (Ayerst)
Diplan, Cap. (Reid-Provident)
Doctient, Supp. (Suppositoria)
Doctient H.C., Supp. (Suppositoria)
Dulzit, Cream (Commerce)
Ear Drops. Liq. (Sutliff & Case)
Epinephricaine, Oint. (Upjohn)
Erase, Supp. (LaCrosse)
E.R.O. Forte, Liq. (Scherer)
Extend, Tab. (Edward J. Moore)
Foille, Preps. (Carbisulphoil)
Formula 44 Cough Control Discs, Loz. (Vicks)
Fung-O-Spray (Scrip)
G.B.A. Drops (Scrip)
Hemocaine, Oint. (Mallard)
Hurricaine, Liq. or Gel (Beutlich)
Isodettes Loz. (Norcliff-Thayer)
Jiffy, Drops (Block Drug)
Kanalka, Tab. (Lannett)
Kankex, Liq. (Edward J. Moore)
Lanaurine, Drop. (Lannett)
Lanazets, Loz. (Lannett)
Listerine Cough Control Lozenges (Warner-Lambert)
Medicone Dressing (Medicone)
Meditrating Throat Lozenge, Loz. (Vicks)
My-Cort Drops (Scrip)
Myringacaine, Liq. (Upjohn)
Neo-Cutone, Lot. (Sutliff & Case)
Nilatus, Loz. (Bowman)
Off-Ezy Corn Remover, Liq. (Commerce)
Oracin, Loz. (Vicks)
Oradex-C, Troche (Commerce)
Ora-Jel, Gel. (Commerce)
Otolgesic, Dropules (Blue Line)
Pain-Eze, Oint. (Edward J. Moore)
Pazo, Oint. & Supp. (Bristol-Myers)
Pyrogallic Acid Oint. (Gordon)
Pytosin, Sol. (Blue Line)
Rectal Medicone (Medicone)
Rectal Medicone-HC, Supp. (Medicone)
Rectal Medicone Unguent (Medicone)
Ridupois Capsule (Elder)
Rite-Diet, Cap. (Edward J. Moore)
Robitussets, Troches (Robins)
S.A.C. Throat Lozenges (Towne)
Salicide, Oint. (Gordon)
Scrip, Preps. (Scrip)
Sepo, Loz. (Otis Clapp)
Solarcaine, Lot. (Plough)
Soretts, Loz. (Lannett)
Spec-T Sore Throat-Cough Suppressant Loz. (Squibb)
Spec-T Sore Throat-Decongestant Loz. (Squibb)
Sucrets Cold Decongestant Lozenge (Calgon)
Sucrets Cough Control Lozenge (Calgon)
Tanac, Liq. (Commerce)
Thorzetts Lozenges (Towne)
Trocaine Lozenges, Loz. (Vortech)
Tympagesic, Liq. (Adria)
Tyro-Loz, Loz. (Kenyon)
Tyzomint, Loz. (Blue Line)
Unguentine Aerosol (Norwich)
Vicks Cough Silencers, Loz. (Vicks)
Vicks Formula 44 Cough Control Discs, Loz. (Vicks)
Vicks Medi-Trating Throat Lozenges, Loz. (Vicks)
Vicks Oracin, Loz. (Vicks)

BENZOCHLOROPHENE SODIUM. The sodium salt of ortho-benzyl-para-chlorophenol.

BENZOCOL. (Mallard)Benzocaine 5%, Tubes 1 oz.
Use: Surface anesthetic.

BENZOCTAMINE. B.A.N. N-Methyl-9,10-ethanoanthracene-9(10H)-methylamine.
Use: Tranquilizer.
See: Tacitin

• **BENZOCTAMINE HYDROCHLORIDE.** USAN. N-Methyl-9,10-ethanoanthracene-9(10H)-methylamine HCl.
Under study.
Use: Muscle relaxant.

BENZODENT. (Vicks Prods) Benzocaine 20%, eugenol 0.4%, hydroxyquinoline sulfate 0.1%, in an adhesive ointment base. Tube 0.25 oz., 1 oz.
Use: Analgesic in adjustment to dentures.

BENZODEPA. USAN. Benzyl[bis(aziridinyl)-phosphinyl] carbamate.
Use: Antineoplastic.

1,4-BENZODIAZEPINE SERIES.
See: Dalmane, Cap. (Roche)
Librium, Prep. (Roche)
Serax, Prep. (Wyeth)
Tranxene, Cap. (Abbott)
Valium, Preps. (Roche)

BENZODYNE IMPROVED. (Kay) Camphor, menthol, thymol, propylene glycol, glycerine. Bot. 0.5 oz.
Use: Softening ear wax.

BENZODYNE-R. (Kay) Ear drops w/dropper. Bot. 15 ml.
Use: Ear drops.

BENZOIC ACID. (Various Mfr.) Pkg. 0.25 lb., 1 lb.
Use: Fungistatic & fungicidal.
W/Boric acid, zinc oxide, zinc stearate.
See: Ting, Cream, Pow. (Pharmacraft)
W/Salicylic acid.
See: Whitfield's Oint. (Var. Mfr.)

BENZOIC ACID, 2-HYDROXY. Salicylic Acid, U.S.P. XXI.

• **BENZOIC AND SALICYLIC ACIDS OINTMENT,** U.S.P. XXI.
Use: Antifungal (topical).
See: Whitfield's Oint. (Var. Mfr.)

• **BENZOIN,** U.S.P. XXI. Tincture, Compound U.S.P. XXI.

Use: Topical protectant, expectorant-.
See: Arcum—Bot. 2 oz., 4 oz., pt., gal.
Lilly—Bot. 4 fl. oz., pt.
Rals—Aerosol 12 oz.
Stanlabs—Bot. 2 oz., 4 oz., pt., Cmpnd. Bot. 1 oz., 4 oz., pt.
W/Methyl salicylate, guaiacol.
See: Methagul, Oint. (Gordon)
W/Podophyllum resin.
See: Podoben, Liq. (Maurry)
W/Polyoxyethylene dodecanol, aromatics.
See: Vicks Vaposteam, Liq. (Vicks)

BENZOL. Usually refers to benzene.

• **BENZONATATE.** U.S.P. XXI. Caps., U.S.P. XXI. ω-Meth-oxypoly-(ethyleneoxy)ethyl-p-butylaminobenzoate. 2,5,8,11,14,17,20,23,26-Nonaoxaoctacosan-28-yl p-(butylamino)benzoate. B.A.N.: 3,6,9,12,15,18,21, 24,27-non-aoxaoctacosyl 4-N-butylaminobenzoate.
Use: Cough suppressant.
See: Tessalon, Perles (Du Pont)

BENZOPHENONE.
See: Pan Ultra, Lot. & Lipstick (Cummins)
W/Oxybenzone, dioxybenzone.
See: Solbar Lotion (Person & Covey)

BENZOPYRROLATE.
See: Benzopyrronium

BENZOQUINOLIMINE.
See: Emete-Con (Pfizer)

BENZOQUINONIUM CHLORIDE.
Use: Skeletal muscle relaxant (No mfr. listed)

BENZOSULFIMIDE.
See: Saccharin U.S.P. XXI.

BENZOSULPHINIDE SODIUM. Name previously used for Saccharin Sodium.

2H-1,2,4-BENZOTHIADIAZINE-7-SULFONAMIDE, 6-CHLORO-3,4-DIHYDRO-, 1,1,-DIOXIDE. Hydrochlorothiazide, U.S.P. XXI.

2-BENZOTHIAZOLESULFONAMIDE, 6-ETHOXY-. Ethoxzolamide, U.S.P. XXI.

• **BENZOXIQUINE.** USAN.
Use: Disinfectant.

BENZOYL p-AMINOSALICYLIC
See: Benzapas, Pow., Tab. (Dorsey)

BENZOYLPAS CALCIUM Benzoic acid, 4-(benzoylamino)-2-hydroxy-calcium salt (2:1), pentahydrate. Calcium 4-benzamidosalicylate (1:2) pentahydrate.
Use: Antitubercular.
See: Benzapas, Tab., Pow. (Dorsey)

• **BENZOYL PEROXIDE, HYDROUS,** U.S.P. XXI. Gel., Lot., U.S.P. XXI. Peroxide, dibenzoyl.
Use: Keratolytic.
See: Benzagel-5&10, Oint. (Dermik)
Benoxyl, Lot. (Stiefel)
Clearasil Acne Treatment, Cream (Vicks)
Clearasil Antibacterial Acne Lotion (Vicks)
Epi-Clear Antiseptic Lotion, Scrub (Squibb)
Oxy-5 Acne Pimple Medication (Norcliff Thayer)
Oxy-10 Maximum Strength acne-pimple medication (Norcliff Thayer)
Oxy Wash Antibacterial Skin Wash (Norcliff Thayer)
Panoxyl, Bar (Stiefel)
Persadox, Cream, Lot. (Ortho)
Persadox HP Cream, Lot. (Owen)
Persa-Gel, Gel (Ortho)
Topex, Lot. (Vicks)
W/Chlorhydroxyquinoline, hydrocortisone.
See: Loroxide-HC, Lot. (Dermik)
Vanoxide-HC, Lotion (Dermik)
W/Polyoxyethylene lauryl ether
See: Benzac 5&10, Gel (Owen)
Desquam-X, Gels (Westwood)
W/Sulfur.
See: Sulfoxyl Lotion (Stiefel)

N'-BENZOYLSULFANILAMIDE.
See: Sulfabenzamide
W/Sulfacetamide, sulfathiazole, urea.
See: Sultrin, Tab, Cream (Ortho)

BENZPHETAMINE HCl. N-Benzyl-N-α-dimethylphethylamine HCl, dextro.
Use: Anorexiant.
See: Didrex, Tab. (Upjohn)

BENZPYRINIUM BROMIDE. 1-Benzyl-3-hydroxypyridinium bromide dimethylcarbamate.

• **BENZQUINAMIDE.** USAN. N,N-diethyl-1,3,4,6,7,1 hexahydro-2-hydroxy-9,10-dimethoxy-2H-benzo[a]quinolizine-3-carboxamide acetate.
Use: Antiemetic agent.
See: Emete-Con, Vial (Roerig)
Quantril (Roerig)

BENZQUINAMIDE. B.A.N. 2-Acetoxy-3-diethylcarboyl-1,3,4,6,7,11b-hexahydro-9,10-dimethoxy-2H-bzo[a]quinolizine.
Use: Tranquilizer.

BENZTHIANIDE. 3-Benzylthiomethyl-6-chloro-7-sumyl-2H-1,2,4-benzothiadiazine-1,1-di-oxide. Ure

• **BENZTHIAZIDE,** U.S.P. XXI. Tabs., U.S.P. XXI. 3-Benzylthiomethyl-6-chloro-7-sulfamyl-1,2,4-benzoadiazine 1,1-dioxide. 3-((benzylthio)-methyl)-6-chlc 2H-1,2,4,benzothiadiazine-7-sulfonamide 1,1-dioxi 6-chloro-3[(phenylmethyl) thio] methyl -2H-1,2,4, bzothiadiazine-7-sulfonamide 1,1-dioxide.
Use: Diuretic, antihypertensive.
See: Aquapres, Tab. (Coastal)
Aqua-Scrip, Tab. (Scrip)
Aquasec, Tabs. (Pasadena Research)
Aquatag, Tab. (Reid-Provident)
Diucen, Tab. (Central)
Hy-Drine, Tab. (Zemmer)
Lemazide, Tab. (Lemmon)
Marazide, Tab. (Vortech)
Proaqua, Tab. (Reid-Provident)
Urazide, Tab. (Mallard)
W/Reserpine
See: Exna-R, Tab. (Robins)

BENZTHIAZIDE. B.A.N. 3-Benzylthiomethyl-6-chlc benzo-1,2,4-thiadiazine-7-sulfonamide 1,1-dioxide
Use: Diuretic.
See: Fovane.

BENZTROPINE. B.A.N. 3-Benzhydryloxytropane.
Use: Treatment of the Parkinsonian syndrome.
See: Cogentin mesylate.

ENZTROPINE MESYLATE, U.S.P. XXI., Inj., Tab. .S.P. XXI., Methanesulfonate, 3α-(Diphenylmethox-)-1αH,5αH-tropane methanesulfonate.
se: Parasympatholytic; antiparkinsonian.
Sodium Chloride.
ee: Cogentin, Tab., Amp. (Merck Sharp & Dohme)
NZTROPINE METHANESULFONATE.
ee: Benztropine Mesylate.
NZYDAMINE. B.A.N. 1-Benzyl-3-(3-dimethyl-amino-ropoxy)indazole.
Jse: Anti-inflammatory; analgesic.
NZYDAMINE HCl. USAN. 1-Benzyl-3-3-(dimethylamino)-propoxyl]-1H-indazole hydro-hloride. Tantum.
Jse: Analgesic, anti-inflammatory, antipyretic.
NZYDROFLUMETHIAZIDE. 3-Benzyl-3,4-dihydro--(trifluoromethyl)-1,2,4-benzthiadiazine-7-sulfonami-e, 1,1-dioxide.
ee: Bendroflumethiazide
ENZYL ALCOHOL, N.F. XVI. Phenylcarbinol.
Jse: Antiseptic, local anesthetic.
ee: Topic, Gel (Ingram)
Vicks Blue Mint, Regular & Wild Cherry Medicated Cough Drops (Vicks)
ENZYHYDRYL-N-METHYLPIPERAZINE HCl. Cy-lizine Hydrochloride, U.S.P. XXI.
N-BENZYLANILINO)METHYL)-2-IMIDAZOLINE HOSPHATE.
ee: Antazoline phosphate, U.S.P. XXI.
ENZYL BENZOATE, U.S.P. XXI. Lot., U.S.P. XXI. enzoic acid, phenylmethyl ester.
Jse: 10 to 30% emulsion in scabies; pharm. ecessity.
NZYL BENZOATE SAPONATED. Triethanolamine 0 Gm., oleic acid 80 Gm., benzyl benzoate q.s. 000 cc.
NZYL CARBINOL.
ee: Phenylethyl Alcohol, U.S.P. XXI.
NZYLDIETHYL((2,6-XYLYLCARBAMOYL)METHY-)AMMONIUM BENZOATE.
ee: Denatonium Benzoate
BENZYL[2-(DIMETHYLAMINO)ETHYL]AMINO]-YRIDINE CITRATE (1:1). Tripelennamine Citrate, J.S.P. XXI.
-N-BENZYL-N,α-DIMETHYLPHENETHYLAMINE HYDROCHLORIDE.
ee: Benzphetamine hydrochloride
NZYLDIMETHYL(2-PHENOXYETHYL)-AMMO-IUM 3-HYDROXY-2-NAPHTHOATE (1:1). Be-henium Hydroxynaphthoate, U.S.P. XXI.
BENZYLOXY)PHENOL. Monobenzone, U.S.P. XXI.
NZYLPENICILLIN-C-14. (Nuclear-Chicago) Carbon-4 labelled penicillin; prepared from phenyl-(acetic cid-1-C-14), 6-aminopenicillanic acid as the potas-ium salt. 23.4 mc/mM (62.9 mc/mg); adiochemical purity is 100%. Vacuum-sealed glass ials 50 microcuries, 0.5 millicuries.
Jse: Radioisotope.
NZYLPENICILLIN 2-DIETHYLAMINO-ETHYL STER HI. Neopenil, Estopen. (None listed)
NZYL PENICILLIN G, POTASSIUM.
ee: Penicillin G Potassium.

• **BENZYLPENICILLOYL POLYLYSINE CONCENTRATE,** U.S.P. XXI. Inj., U.S.P. XXI.
Use: Antibiotic.
BENZYL PENICILLIN G, SODIUM.
See: Penicillin G Sodium
BEPANTHEN.
See: Panthenol.
BEPHEDIN. Benzyl ephedrine.
BEPHENIUM BROMIDE. N-Benzyl-N, N-dimethyl-N-(2-phenoxyethyl)ammonium bromide.
• **BEPHENIUM HYDROXYNAPHTHOATE,** U.S.P. XXI. For Oral Susp., U.S.P. XXI. Benzyldimethyl (2-phenoxy-ethyl)ammonium-3-hydroxy-2-naphthoate. Ben-zenemethanaminium,N,N-dimethyl-N-(2-phenox-y-ethyl)-, salt with 3-hydroxy-2-naphthalenecarboxylic acid (1:1).
Use: Anthelmintic (hookworms).
BEPHENIUM HYDROXYNAPHTHOATE. B.A.N. Benzyldimethyl-2-phenoxyethylammonium 3-hydroxy-2-naphthoate.
Use: Treatment of ancylostomiasis and ascariasis.
See: Alcopar.
• **BEPRIDIL HYDROCHLORIDE.** USAN.
Use: Vasodilator.
BERBERINE.
W/Hydrastine, glycerin.
See: Murine, Ophth. Sol.
BERBERINE HYDROCHLORIDE.
W/Borax, sodium chloride, boric acid, camphor water, cherry laurel water, rose water, thimerosol.
See: Lauro, Eye irrigator and drops. (Otis Clapp)
BER-EX. (Dolcin) Cal. succinate 2.8 gr., acetylsalicylic acid 3.7 gr./Tab. Bot. 100s, 500s.
Use: Orally, for treatment of arthritic & rheumatic disorders.
BEROCCA. (Roche) Vit. B-1 15 mg., B-2 15 mg., B-6 5 mg., niacinamide 100 mg., Ca pantothenate 20 mg., B-12 5 mcg., folic acid 0.5 mg., C 500 mg./Tab. Bot. 100s, 500s.
Use: Vitamin B-complex and C.
BEROCCA-C. (Roche) Vit. B-1 10 mg., B-2 10 mg., niacinamide 80 mg., B-6 20 mg., panthenol 20 mg., C 100 mg. & d-Biotin 0.2 mg. benzyl alcohol 1%, sod. hydroxide/2 ml. Amp. 2 ml. Box 10s. Vial 20 ml.
Use: I.V., I.M., water-soluble vitamin therapy.
BEROCCA-C 500. (Roche) In addition to Berocca formula, this product contains 400 mg., Vit. C, methyl and propyl parabens 0.2%, sod. bicarb. Amp. 2 ml. Duplex Amps. 2 × 2 ml.
BEROCCA-C PLUS INJECTABLE. (Roche) Vit. B-1 3 mg., biotin 60 mcg., B-2 3.6 mg., niacinamide 40 mg., B-6 4 mg., d-pantethenol 15 mg., C 100 mg./ml. Amp.: Duplex pkg. containing 1 ml. concentrate plus 1 ml. solvent. Box 25s.; Vials: Duplex pkg. containing 20 ml. vial concentrate plus 20 ml. solvent. Box 1s.
Use: I.M. water soluble vitamin therapy.
BEROCCA PLUS TABLETS. (Roche) Vit. A 5000 I.U., E 30 I.U., C 500 mg., B-1 20 mg., B-2 20 mg., niacinamide 100 mg., B-6 25 mg., biotin 0.15 mg., pantothenic acid 25 mg., folic acid 0.8 mg., B-12 50 mcg.,

iron 27 mg., Cr 0.1 mg., Mg. 50 mg., Mn 5 mg., Cu 3 mg., Zn 22.5 mg./Tab. Bot. 100s. Prescription only.
Use: Multivitamin and mineral supplement for use in physiologic stress.

BEROCCA-WS. (Roche) **Solution No. 1:** Vit. B-1 3 mg., B-2 3.6 mg., biotin 60 mcg., niacinamide 40 mg., B-6 4 mg., C 100 mg., panthenol 15 mg./ml. **Solution No. 2:** Vit. B-12 5 mcg., folic acid 400 mg./ml. Multiple dose vials, duplex pckg.
Use: Parenteral dietary supplement of water soluble vitamins.

BEROVITE PLUS TABLETS. (Everett) Vitamin B Complex with minerals. Bot.100s.
Use: Dietary supplement.

BERPLEX-C. (Alton) B & C vitamins. Bot. 100s, 1000s.
Use: Dietary supplement.

BERSOTRIN. (Kenyon) Vit. B-1 15 mg., B-2 10 mg., C 300 mg., Ca pantothenate 10 mg., niacinamide 50 mg., B-6 5 mg./Cap. Bot. 100s.

BERUBIGEN. (Upjohn) Vit. B-12. I.M.; 1000 mcg., benzyl alcohol 15 mg., NaCl 9 mg. water q.s. to 1 ml. 10 ml. vial 5s.
Use: Hematopoietic.

BERVITE. (Alton) Multiple vitamin. Bot. 100s, 1000s.
Use: Dietary supplement.

• **BERYTHROMYCIN.** USAN. (1) 12-Deoxyery-thromycin; (2) Erythromycin B.
Use: Anti-amebic, antibacterial.

BESAPRIN TABLETS. (Winthrop Products) Aspirin, chlormezanone.
Use: Analgesic, tranquilizer, muscle relaxant.

BESEROL TABLETS. (Winthrop Products) Acetaminophen, chlormezanone.
Use: Analgesic, tranquilizer, muscle relaxant.

BESITEX B1. (Mills) Ephedrine ethylenediamine HCl 6 mg./Tab. Bot. 100s.
Use: Appetite depression.

BESITEX B3. (Mills) Ephedrine ethylenediamine HCl 6 mg./Tab. Bot. 100s.
Use: Appetite depression.

BESTA CAPSULES. (Hauck) Vit. B-1 20 mg., B-2 15 mg., niacinamide 100 mg., calcium pantothenate 20 mg., E 50 units, magnesium sulfate 70 mg., zinc sulfate 80 mg., B-12 4 mcg., B-6 25 mg., Vit. C 300 mg./Tab. Bot. 100s, 1000s.
Use: Vitamin supplement.

BEST C CAPS. (Hauck) Ascorbic acid 500 mg./Cap. Timed released. Bot. 100s.

BESTRONE INJECTION. (Bluco) Estrone in aqueous susp. 2 mg. or 5 mg./cc.

BETA-2. (Nephron) Isoetharine HCl 1%. Bot. 10 ml., 30 ml.
Use: Respiratory.

BETA-B-PLEX INJECTION. (Hauck) High potency B-complex. (100-100) Vial 30 ml.
Use: Vitamin B deficiency.

• **BETA CAROTENE,** U.S.P. XXI. Cap., U.S.P. XXI. β, β-Carotene. All-trans-B-Carotene. (All-E)-1,1-(3,7,-12,16-Tetramethyl-1,3,5,7,9,11,13,15,17-octadecanonaene-1,18-diyl) bis (2,6,6-trimethylcyclohexene).

BETACETYLMETHADOL. B.A.N. β-4-Dimethylamin 1-ethyl-2,2-diphenylpentyl acetate.
Use: Narcotic analgesic.

BETACREST. (Nutrition) Vit. B-1 15 mg., B-2 10 mg. 6 5 mg., B-12 4 mcg., Ca pantothenate 20 n niacinamide 100 mg., Vit. C 600 mg., liver 125 mg./Kapule. Bot. 60s. B-1 100 mg., B-2 2 mg., B-6 5 mg., B-12 30 mcg., niacinamide 125 mg., p thenol 10 mg., with benzyl alcohol 1.5%/cc. Vial 30 cc., I.M. or I.V.
Use: Vitamin therapy.

BETACREST KAPULE. (Nutrition) Vit. B-1 30 mg., 2 20 mg., B-6 10 mg., B-12 8 mcg., Cal. pantothen 40 mg., niacinamide 200 mg., Vit. C 600 mg., live desicc. 250 mg./2 Caps. Bot. 60s.
Use: Therapeutic B-Complex w/Vit. C

BETADINE. (Purdue Frederick) **Povidone-iodine.**
Aerosol Spray, Bot. 3 oz.
Antiseptic Gauze Pads 12s.
Antiseptic Gel, Tube 3 oz., 18 Gm. w/vaginal applicator.
Antiseptic Lubricating Gel, Pkg. 1/6 oz. Box 200s.
Disposable Medicated Douche, concentrated packette w/cannula and 6 oz. water.
Douche, Bot. 1 oz., 8 oz., gal.
Douche Kit w/dispenser 8 oz.
Douche Packette, 0.5 oz. (6 per carton)
Helafoam Solution Canister 9 oz.
Mouthwash/Gargle, Bot. 6 oz.
Oint., Tube 1 oz., Jar 1 lb., 5 lb.
Oint., packette 1/32 oz., 1/8 oz.
Perineal Wash Conc. Kit, Bot. 8 oz. w/dispenser
Shampoo, Bot. 4 oz.
Skin Cleanser, Bot. 1 oz., 4 oz.
Skin Cleanser Foam, Canister 6 oz.
Solution, 0.5 oz., 4 oz., 8 oz., 16 oz., 32 oz., gal.
Solution Packette, 1 oz.
Solution Swab Aid, 100s.
Solution Swabsticks, 1s, 3s.
Surgical Scrub, Bot. 1 pt., 1 pt. w/dispenser, 1 q 1 gal., packette 0.5 oz.
Surgi-prep Sponge-Brush 36s.
Vaginal Suppositories, Box 7s w/vaginal applicat
Viscous Formula Antiseptic Gauze Pads: 3" × 9 Box 12s.
Whirlpool Concentrate, Bot. gal.
Use: As an antiseptic for uses indicated in produ labeling.

BETA-ESTRADIOL.
See: Estradiol, U.S.P. XXI.

BETAEUCAINE HCl. Name previously used for Eucaine HCl.

BETAGEN. (Enzyme Process) Vit. B-1 1 mg., B-2 mg., niacin 15 mg., B-6 18 mg., pantothenic acid mg., choline 1.8 Gm., betaine 96 mg./6 Tab. Bot 100s, 250s.
Use: Dietary supplement.

BETAGEN OINTMENT. (Goldline) Povidone iodine ointment. Tube 1 oz. Jar 1 lb.
Use: Antiseptic.

TAGEN SOLUTION. (Goldline) Povidone iodine. Bot. pt. gal.,
Use: Antiseptic.

TAGEN SURGICAL SCRUB. (Goldline) Povidone iodine. Bot. pt., gal.
Use: Antiseptic.

TA-HCG. (Abbott) Test kit 100s.
Use: Enzyme immunoassay for detection of beta subunit of human chorionic gonadotropin.

ETAHISTINE HYDROCHLORIDE. USAN. 2-(2-Methylaminoethyl) pyridine dihydrochloride.
Use: Meniere's disease. A diamine oxidase inhibitor. Increase microcirculation.
See: Serc dihydrochloride.

TA-HYPOPHAMINE.
See: Vasopressin

ETAINE HYDROCHLORIDE, U.S.P. XXI. Acidol HCl, lycine HCl.
Ferrous fumarate, docusate sodium, desic. liver, vitamins, minerals.
See: Hemaferrin, Tab. (Western Research)
Pancreatin, pepsin, and ammonium chloride.
See: Zypan, Tab. (Standard Process)
Pepsin.
See: Normacid, Tab. (Stuart)

TALIN S. (Lilly) Thiamine hydrochloride.
Amp.: (100 mg./ml.) 100s.
Elixir: 2.25 mg./5 ml. w/alcohol 10%. Bot. 1 pt., 1 gal.
Tab.: (25, 50 & 100 mg.) Bot. 100s.
Vial: (100 mg./ml.) 10 ml., 30 ml.
Use: I.M., I.V., orally; Vit. B-1 deficiency.

TALIN 12 CRYSTALLINE. (Lilly) B-12 1000 mcg./1 ml. Also with sod. chloride 0.25%, benzyl alcohol 2%. Vial 10 ml.
Use: B-12 therapy, pernicious anemia.

ETAXOLOL HYDROCHLORIDE. USAN.

TAMEPRODINE. B.A.N. β-3-Ethyl-1-methyl-4-phenyl-4-propionyloxypiperidine.
Use: Narcotic analgesic.

TAMETHADOL. B.A.N. β-6-Dimethylamino-4,4-diphenylheptan-3-ol.
Use: Narcotic analgesic.

ETAMETHASONE, U.S.P. XXI. Cream, Syrup, Tabs., U.S.P. XXI. 9-α-Fluoro-11β, 17,21-trihydroxy16β-methylpregna-1,4-diene-3,20-dione. 9α-Fluoro16β-methylprednisolone. Acetate and sodium phosphate.
Use: Glucocorticoid.
See: Celestone, Cream, Inj., Syr., Tab. (Schering)

ETAMETHASONE ACETATE, U.S.P. XXI. Pregna-1,4-diene-3,20-dione, 9-fluoro-11, 17-dihydroxy-16-methyl-21-(acetyloxy)-, (11β, 16β)-. 9-Fluoro-11β, 17,21-trihydroxy-16β-methylpregna-1,4-diene-3,20-dione 21-acetate.

TAMETHASONE ACIBUTATE. B.A.N. 21-Acetoxy-9α-fluoro-11β-hydroxy-16β-methyl-17-(2-methylpropionyloxy)pregna-1,4-diene-3,20-dione.
Use: Corticosteroid.

ETAMETHASONE BENZOATE, U.S.P. XXI. Gel, U.S.P. XXI. 9-Fluoro-11β 17,21-trihydroxy-16β-methylpregna-1,4-diene-3,20-dione 17 benzoate.
Use: Glucocorticoid.
See: Benisone. (Warner-Chilcott)
Flurobate (Texas Pharmacal)
Uticort, Prods. (Parke-Davis)

• **BETAMETHASONE DIPROPIONATE,** U.S.P. XXI. Topical Aerosol, Cream, Lotion, Oint., U.S.P. XXI.
See: Diprosone Prods. (Schering) Diprolene, Oint. (Schering)

• **BETAMETHASONE SODIUM PHOSPHATE,** U.S.P. XXI. Pregna-1,4-diene-3,20-dione, 9-fluoro-11,17-dihydroxy-16-methyl-21-(phosphonoxy)-, disodium salt, (11β, 16β). 9-Fluoro-11β,17,21-trihydroxy-16β-methylpregna-1,4-diene-3,20-dione 21-(disodium phosphate).
See: Celestone Phosphate Inj. (Schering)

• **BETAMETHASONE SODIUM PHOSPHATE AND BETAMETHASONE ACETATE SUSPENSION, STERILE,** U.S.P. XXI.
See: Celestone Soluspan (Schering)

• **BETAMETHASONE VALERATE,** U.S.P. XXI. Topical Aerosol, Cream, Lotion, Oint. U.S.P. XXI. Pregna-1,4-diene-3,20-dione,9-fluoro-11,21-dihydroxy-16-methyl-17-[(1-oxopentyl)oxy]-,(11β,16β)-. 9-Fluoro-11β,17,21-trihydroxy-16β-methylpregna-1,4-diene-3,20-
dione 17-valerate.
See: Betatrex Prods. (Savage)

• **BETAMICIN SULFATE.** USAN.
Use: Antibacterial.

BETANAPHTHOL. 2-Naphthol.
Use: Parasiticide.

BETANAPHTHOL BENZOATE. (Amend) Pow. 1 oz., 0.25 lb., 1 lb. Merck-Pow. 1 oz., 0.25 lb., 1 lb.
Use: Antiseptic & parasiticide.

BETAPEN-VK. (Bristol) Penicillin V potassium.
Oral Solution: 125 mg., 250 mg./5 ml. Bot. 100 ml., 200 ml. **Tab:** 250 mg./Tab. Bot. 100s, 1000s; 500 mg./Tab. Bot. 100s.
Use: Treatment of infections where penicillin is effective.

BETAPRODINE. B.A.N. β-1,3-Dimethyl-4-phenyl-4-propionyloxypiperidine.
Use: Narcotic analgesic.

BETAPRONE. (Forest) Beta-propiolactone. Pkg. 100 cc. Amp. 5 cc., 12s.
Use: Sterilization of vaccines and tissue grafts.

BETA-PROPIOLACTONE.
See: Betaprone, Vial (Forest)

BETA-PYRIDYL-CARBINOL. Nicotinyl alcohol. Alcohol corresponding to nicotinic acid.
See: Roniacol, Elixir & Tab. (Roche Lab.)

BETA-TEC. (Wampole) Double antibody radioimmunoassay for the qualitative detection and quantitative determination of B-hCG/hCG in serum. Kits 125s.
Use: Aid in the diagnosis of pregnancy.

BETA-TEC QUALITATIVE. (Wampole) Double antibody radioimmunoassay for the qualitative detection of B-hCG/hCG in serum. Kits 125s.
Use: Aid in the diagnosis of pregnancy.

BETATREX. (Savage) Betamethasone valerate 0.1%. Cream and Ointment. Tubes 15 Gm., 45 Gm.; Lotion Bot. 60 cc.
Use: Relief of inflammatory and pruritic manifestations.

BETA-VAL CREAM. (Lemmon) Betamethasone valerate equivalent to 0.1% betamethasone base in cream base. Tube 15 Gm., 45 Gm.
Use: Topical anti-inflammatory, anti-pruritic.

BETA-VAL LOTION. (Lemmon) Betamethasone valerate equivalent to 0.1% betamethasone in lotion base. Bot. 60 ml.
Use: Topical anti-infective, anti-pruritic.

BETA-VAL OINTMENT. (Lemmon) Beta-methasone valerate equivalent to 0.1% betamethasone base in ointment base. Tube 15 Gm., 45 Gm.
Use: Anti-inflammatory; anti-pruritic.

BETA-VITE LIQUID ELIXIR. (Vortech) Vit. B-1 10 mg., B-12 25 mcg./5 cc. Bot. 4 oz., gal.
Use: Appetite stimulant.

BETA-VITE W/IRON LIQUID. (Vortech) Vit. B-12 25 mcg., B-1 10 mg., ferric pyrophosphate 250 mg./5 cc. Bot. 4 oz., gal.
Use: Appetite stimulant.

• **BETAXOLOL HYDROCHLORIDE.** USAN.
Use: Anti-anginal, antihypertensive.

BETAZOLE HCl. XXI. 1H-Pyrazole-3-ethanamine, dihydrochloride. 3-(2-Aminoethyl)pyrazole diHCl.
Use: Diagnostic aid (gastric secretion indicator).
See: Histalog, Amp. (Lilly).

BETAZYME. (Inwood) Vit. B-1 2.5 mg., B-1 (Cocarboxylase from yeast) 2.5 mg., B-2 10 mg., niacinamide 50 mg., calcium pantothenate 25 mg., B-6 2.5 mg., menadione (2 methyl-1-4-naphthoquinone) 2 mg., choline HCl 10 mg., high potency yeast concentrate 200 mg., Brewer's type yeast 200 mg., yeast protein hydrolysate 1 Gm., sodium nucleate 100 mg., glutamic acid 50 mg., glycine 50 mg., cysteine HCl 25 mg., iron 50 mg., manganese 50 mg., magnesium 50 mg., zinc 5 mg./3 Tabs. Bot. 100s, 1000s.
Use: Vitamin, mineral, enzyme supplement.

• **BETHANECHOL CHLORIDE,** U.S.P. XXI. Inj., Tabs., U.S.P. XXI. (2-Hydroxypropyl) trimethylammonium Chloride Carbamate. Carbamylmethylcholine chloride.
Use: Parasympathomimetic.
See: Duvoid, Tab. (Norwich Eaton)
Myotonachol, Tab., Amp. (Glenwood)
Urecholine, Amp. & Tab. (Merck Sharp & Dohme)
Vesicholine, Tab. (Star)

• **BETHANIDINE.** USAN. 2-Benzyl-1,3-dimethylguanidine.
Use: Hypotensive.
See: Bethanid
Esbatal sulfate.

BETHAPRIM DS TABS. (Major) Trimethoprim w/sulfamethoxazole DS/Tab. Bot. 100s, 500s.
Use: Urinary tract infections, otitis media, pneumonia.

BETHAPRIM SS TABS. (Major) Trimethoprim w/sulfamethoxazole. Bot. 100s.
Use: Urinary tract infections, otitis media, pneumonia.

BETTER GEN M. (Image) multiple vitamin. Bot. 100 250s.
Use: Supplement.

• **BEVANTOLOL HYDROCHLORIDE.** USAN.
Use: Antianginal, antihypertensive, cardiac depressant.

BEVONIUM METHYLSULFATE. B.A.N. 2-Benziloylo methyl-1,1-dimethylpiperidinium methylsulfate.
Use: Antispasmodic.
See: Acabel

BEXIBEE. (Vortech) Vit. B-1 100 mg., cyanocobalar 1000 mcg., benzyl alcohol 1.5%/ml. Vial 10 ml.
Use: Vitamin B therapy.

• **BEZAFIBRATE.** USAN.
Use: Antihyperlipoproteinemic.

BEZITRAMIDE. B.A.N. 4-[4-(2-Oxo-3-propionylb zimidazolin-1-yl)piperidino]-2,2-diphenylbutyronitril
Use: Narcotic analgesic.

BEZON. (Whittier) Vits. B-1 5 mg., B-2 3 mg., niaci mide 20 mg., pantothenic acid 3 mg., B-6 0.5 mg. 50 mg., B-12 1 mcg./Cap.
Bot. 30s, 100s.

BEZON FORTE. (Whittier) Vits. B-1 25 mg., B-2 1 mg., niacinamide 50 mg., pantothenic acid 10 mg B-6 5 mg., C 250 mg./Cap. Bot. 30s, 100s.

B-F-I POWDER. (Beecham Products) Bismuth-form iodide, zinc phenolsulfonate, bismuth subgallate, amol, pot. alum, boric acid, menthol, eucalyptol, thymol & inert diluents. Can 0.25 oz., 1.25 oz., 8 oz.
Use: Antiseptic first aid powder.

B-GEN WITH C. (Image) Vitamin B and C Bot. 10 250s.
Use: Supplement.

B.G.O. (Calotabs) Iodoform, salicylic acid, sulfur, zi oxide, phenol (liquefied) 1%, calamine, menthol, petrolatum, lanolin and mineral oil, undecylenic a 1%. Jar ⅞ oz., Tube 1⅛ oz.
Use: Antiseptic, antifungal.

B-HCG. (Roche) Rapid RIA assay for beta-human c rionic gonadotropin. 100 test kit.

• **BIALAMICOL.** F.D.A. 5,5′-Diallyl-alpha,alpha′-bis-(thylamino) m,m′-bitolyl-4,4′-diol.

BIALAMICOL. 6,6′-Dially-α,α'-bisdiethylaminomethy 4,4′-dihydroxydiphenyl, dihydrochloride. Biallylami
Use: Antiamebic.

BIALAMICOL. B.A.N. 3,3′-Diallyl-5,5′-bisdiethylaminomethyl-4,4′-dihydroxybiphenyl.
Use: Treatment of amebiasis.
See: Camoform dihydrochloride

• **BIALAMICOL HCl.** USAN. 5,5′-Diallyl-α,α'-bis-(thylamino)-m,m′-bitolyl-4,4′-diol HCl.
Use: Antiamebic.

BIAMINE. (Forest) Thiamine HCl 100 mg./ml. Vial cc.

BI-AMINE. (Ulmer) n-alkyl dimethyl benzyl ammon chloride 4.5%, n-alkyl dimethyl ethylbenzyl

nonium chloride 4.5%, tetrasodium ethylenediamine tetraacetate 2%, Na carbonate 4%. Bot. gal.
Use: Quaternary germicide, detergent, deodorant solution.

APHASIC INSULIN INJECTION. A suspension of insulin crystals in a solution of insulin buffered at pH 7. Insulin Novo Rapitard.

AVAX-II. (Merck Sharp & Dohme) Rubella & mumps virus vaccine, live. See details under Meruvax-II and Mumpsvax. Single-dose vial w/diluent-containing disposable syringe. Box of 10 single-dose vials; Box of 10 single-dose vials w/diluent-containing disposable syringes.
Use: Immunization against rubella and mumps.

BENZONIUM BROMIDE. B.A.N. 2-(1,2-Diphenylethoxy)ethyltrimethylammonium bromide.
Use: Cough suppressant.
See: Thoragol

CALPHO IN-A-TAB. (Blue Line) Vitamin A acetate 1000 I.U., D-2 100 I.U., B-1 0.25 mg., B-2 0.33 mg., C 16.67 mg., niacinamide 3.33 mg., calcium 250 mg., iron 2.5 mg./Tab. Bot. 100s, 175s, 1000s.

CHLORACETIC ACID. (Kahlenberg) Dichloroacetic acid full strength. Treatment kit. 0.5 oz. ea. 10 ml.
Use: Escharotic.

CHOLAN. (Galen) Ox bile extract 1.5 gr., cascara ext. 5 gr., phenolphthalein 5 gr., oleoresin capsicum 0.05 gr./Tab. Bot. 100s, 1000s.
Use: Choleretic-Laxative.

CHOLATE. (Blue Line) Desic. ox gall 2.25 gr., phenophthalein 0.5 gr., cascarin 0.5 gr./Tab. Bot. 100s, 1000s.
Use: Orally, choleretic & cholagogue.

CILLIN. (Wyeth) Penicillin G benzathine 200,000 u./Tab. Bot. 36s.
Use: Antibiotic.

CILLIN C-R. (Wyeth) Penicillin G benzathine 150,000 u., procaine penicillin G 150,000 u./cc. w/sod. citrate, lecithin, povidone, C.M.C., sorbitan monopalmitate, polyoxyethylene sorbitan monopalmitate, methyl- and propylparaben. Vial 10 cc. Bicillin 300,000 u., procaine penicillin G 300,000 u./1 cc. w/sod. citrate, lecithin, C.M.C. povidone, methyl- and propylparaben. Tubex cartridge. Pkg. 10s, 50s. Bicillin 600,000 u., procaine penicillin G 600,000 u./2 cc. Tubex cartridge. Pkg. 10s, 50s, and 2 cc. single dose syringe, 10s. Bicillin 1,200,000 u., procaine penicillin G 1,200,000 u./4 cc. single-dose syringe, 2,400,000 u./single-dose disp. syringe, 10s, 4 cc.
Use: Antibiotic.

CILLIN C-R 900/300 INJECTION. (Wyeth) Penicillin G benzathine 900,000 u., penicillin G procaine 300,000 u./2 ml. Tubex. Pkg. 10s.
Use: Antibiotic.

CILLIN LONG-ACTING. (Wyeth) Penicillin G benzathine 300,000 U./cc. w/sod. citrate, lecithin, povidone, C.M.C., sorbitan monopalmitate, polyoxyethylene sorbitan monopalmitate, methyl- and propylparaben. 300,000 U/ml. Vial 10 cc. 600,000 u./Tubex., 900,000 u./Tubex. Pkg. 10s. Tubex w/sod. citrate, lecithin, C.M.C. povidone, methyl- and propylparaben. 10s.
1,200,000 u./2 cc. Tubex 10s. Single dose disp. syringe, 10s. 2,400,000 U./4 cc. single dose disp. syringe, 10s.

BICITRA. (Willen) Sodium citrate dihydrate 500 mg., citric acid monohydrate 334 mg., 5 mEq sodium ion/5 ml. Shohl's Solution. Bot. 4 oz., 1 pt., 1 gal. Unit dose 15 ml.
Use: Systemic alkalizer potassium free and sugar free.

• **BICLODIL HYDROCHLORIDE.** USAN.
Use: Antihypertensive (Vasodilator).

BiCNU. (Bristol) Carmustine (BCNU) 100 mg., sterile diluent (absolute ethanol) 3 ml./Vial.
Use: Antineoplastic injection.

BICOZENE CREAM. (Creighton) Benzocaine 6%, resorcinol 1.66% in cream base. Tube 1 oz.
Use: External itching or irritation of vaginal and rectal areas.

BICYCLINE. (Knight) Tetracycline HCl 250 mg./Cap. Bot. 100s.
Use: Broad-spectrum antibiotic.

BICYCLO[2.2.1]HEPTANE-2-ONE, 1,7,7-TRI-METHYL-. Camphor, U.S.P. XXI.

[BICYCLOHEXYL]-1-CARBOXYLIC ACID, 2-(DIETHYLAMINO)-ETHYL ESTER HCl. Dicyclomine Hydrochloride, U.S.P. XXI.

BIDIMAZIUM IODIDE. B.A.N. 4-(Biphenyl-4-yl)-2-(4-dimethylaminostyryl)-3-methylthiazolium iodide.
Use: Anthelmintic.

BIDROLAR. (Forrest) Docusate sodium ⅔ gr., ox bile 1 gr./Tab. Bot. 30s, 100s.
Use: Treatment of constipation.

BIFE. (Jenkins) Thiamine HCl 1 mg., ferrous sulfate, exsic. 3 gr./Tab. Bot. 1000s.
Use: Iron deficiency anemias and B-1 avitaminosis.

BIFLURANOL. B.A.N. erythro-4,4′-(1-Ethyl-2-methylethylene)di-(2-fluorophenol).
Use: Benign hypertrophy of the prostate.

• **BIFONAZOLE.** USAN.
Use: Antifungal.

BIG LEAGUE RUB. (Eckerd) Bot. pt.

BIHISTOL. (Sutliff & Case) Pyrilamine maleate 25 mg./Tab. Bot. 100s, 1000s.
Use: Antihistaminic.

BI-K. (USV Labs.) Liquid potassium supplement. Bot. 16 oz.
Use: Treatment of hypokalemia.

BILAMIDE. (Norgine) Ox bile 200 mg., homatropine methylbromide 1.4 mg., phenobarbital 8 mg./Tab. Bot. 50s, 250s.
Use: Management of symptoms in hypermotility of the GI tract. Management of symptoms in hypermotility of the GI tract.

BILAX. (Drug Industries) Dehydrocholic acid 50 mg., docusate sodium 100 mg./Cap. Bot. 100s, 500s.
Use: Fecal softener.

BILE ACIDS, OXIDIZED. Note also dehydrocholic acid.

W/Atropine methyl nitrate, ox & hog bile ext., phenobarbital.
See: G.B.S., Tab. (O'Neal)
W/Bile whole (desiccated), dessicated whole pancreas, homatropine methylbromide.
See: Pancobile, Tab. (Reid-Provident)
W/Ox bile, steapsin, phenobarbital & homatropine methylbromide.
See: Oxacholin, Tab. (Philips Roxane)

BILECHOL. (Manne) Atropine sulfate 0.12 mg., nitroglycerin 0.12 mg., magnesium sulfate 0.3 Gm., ext. ox bile/Tab.
Bot. 1000s.
Use: Biliary stimulant & laxative.

BILE EXTRACT. (Various Mfr.) Pow. 0.25 lb., 1 lb.
W/Cascara sagrada, dandelion root, podophyllin, tr. nux vomica.
See: Oxachol, Liq. (Philips Roxane)
W/Dehydrocholic acid, homatropine methylbromide, phenobarbital.
See: Neocholan, Tab. (Merrell Dow)
W/Pancreatic substance, dl-methionine, choline bitartrate.
See: Licoplex, Tab. (Mills)

BILE EXTRACT, OX. Purified oxgall.
Lilly—Enseal 5 gr., Bot. 100s, 500s, 1000s.
C. D. Smith—Tab. 5 gr., Bot. 1000s.
Stoddard—Tab. 3 gr., Bot. 100s, 500s, 1000s.
W/Cellulase, pepsin, glutamic acid HCl, pancreatin
See: Kanulase, Tab. (Dorsey)
W/Cellulase, pepsin, glutamic acid HCl, pancreatin, methscopolamine nitrate, & pentobarbital.
See: Kanumodic, Tab. (Dorsey)
W/Colcynth comp. ext., cascara sagrada ext., podophyllin & hyoscyamus ext.
See: Bileo-Secrin Compound Tablets (First Texas)
W/Dehydrocholic acid, homatropine methylbromide, phenobarbital.
See: Bilamide, Tab. (Norgine)
W/Dehydrocholic acid, pepsin, & homatropine methylbromide.
See: Biloric, Cap. (Arcum)
W/Desoxycholic acid, oxidized bile acids, pancreatin.
See: Bilogen, Tab. (Organon)
W/Enzyme conc., pepsin & dehydrocholic acid, belladonna ext.
See: Ro-Bile, Tab. (Rowell)
W/Oxidized bile acids, steapsin, phenobarbital & homatropine methylbromide.
See: Oxacholin, Tab. (Philips Roxane)
W/Pepsin, pancreatic enzyme concentrate.
See: Konzyme, Tab. (Brunswick)
Nu'Leven, Tab. (Lemmon)
Nu'Leven Plus, Tab. (Lemmon)
W/Phenolphthalein, cascarin.
See: Bicholate, Tab. (Blue Line)
W/Sod. salicylate, phenolphthalein, chionanthus ext., cascara sagrada ext., sod. glycocholate, sod. taurocholate.
See: Glycols, Tab. (Bowman)

BILEIN. Bile salts obtained from ox bile.

BILE-LIKE PRODUCTS.
See: Zanchol, Tab. (Searle)

■ **BILE PRODUCTS.**
See: Bile Salts
Dehydrocholic Acid
Desoxycholic Acid
Ketocholanic Acid

■ **BILE SALTS.** Sod. glycocholate & taurocholate. Note also Bile Ext., Ox, and oxidized bile acids.
Lilly—Enseal 5 gr., Bot. 100s.
See: Bilein
Bisol, Tab. (Paddock)
Ox Bile Extract
Oxidized Bile Acids
W/Belladonna & nux vomica comp. Bile salts 60 mg, belladonna leaf ext. 5 mg., nux vomica ext. 2 mg. phenolphthalein 30 mg., Sod. salicylate 15 mg., aloin 15 mg./Tab. Bot. 1000s.
Use: Orally, laxative w/antispasmodic.
W/Cascara, phenophthalein, aloin.
See: Amlax, Tab. (Vortech)
W/Cascara ext., phenolphthalein, oleoresin capsicum
See: Bilocomp, Tab. (Lannett)
W/Cascara sagrada, phenolphthalein, capsicum oleoresin & peppermint oil.
See: Torocol, Tab. (Plessner)
W/Cellulase, calcium carbonate & pancrelipase.
See: Accelerase, Cap. (Organon)
W/Cellulase, pancrelipase, cal. carbonate, belladonna alkaloids, phenobarbital.
See: Accelerase-PB, Cap. (Organon)
W/Dehydrocholic acid & pancreatic substance.
See: Depancol, Tab. (Parke-Davis)
W/Dehydrocholic acid, pepsin, pancreatin.
See: Progestive, Tab. (NCP)
W/Iron.
See: Bilron, Pulvule (Lilly)
W/Pancreatin, pepsin, dehydrocholic acid, desoxycholic acid.
See: Enzylax, Tab. (Kay)
Pepsatal, Tab. (Kenyon)
W/Pancrelipase, cellulase.
See: Cotazym-B, Tab. (Organon)
W/Papain, cascara sagrada ext., phenolphthalein & capsicum oleoresin.
See: Torocol Compound, Tab. (Plessner)
W/Pepsin, homatropine, methylBr, amylase, lipase, protease.
See: Digesplen, Tab., Elixir, Drops (Med. Prod. Panamericana)
W/Phenophthalein, ext. chionanthus.
See: Bile Anthus Comp., Cap. (Scrip)
W/Sod. salicylate, phenolphthalein, chionanthus ext. bile ext., cascara sagrada ext.
See: Glycols, Tab. (Bowman)

BILE, WHOLE DESICCATED.
W/Pancreatin, mycozyme diastase, pepsin, ext. nux vomica.
See: Enzobile, Tab. (Mallard)

BILEZYME. (Geriatric) Amylolytic enzyme 30 mg., proteolytic enzyme 6 mg., dehydrocholic acid 200

g., desoxycholic acid 50 mg./Tab. Bot. 42s, 100s,)0s.
se: Digestive aid.

:ZYME PLUS. (Geriatric) Phenobarbital 8 mg., ɔmatropine methylbromide 2.5 mg., gerilase 30 ıg., geriprotase 6 mg., dehydrocholic acid 200 mg., ɘsoxycholic acid 50 mg./Tab. Bot. 42s, 100s,)0s.
se: Constipation, liver, gallbladder disease, colic.

I-LABSTIX REAGENT STRIPS. (Ames) Reagent trips. Bot. 100s.
se: Diagnostic test for pH, protein, glucose, etones, bilirubin and blood in urine.

IRUBIN REAGENT STRIPS. (Ames) Seralyzer ɜagent strip. Bot. 25s.
lse: A quantitative strip test for total bilirubin in ɘrum or plasma.

IVIST. (Berlex) Ipodate sodium 500 mg./Cap. 'atch cover Box 6s, 20s.
lse: Oral radiopaque medium for cholecystography nd cholangiography.

OCOMP TABLETS. (Lannett) Bile salts 1.5 gr., xt. cascara 0.5 gr., phenolphthalein 0.5 gr., leoresin capsicum 1/20 min./Tab. Bot. 1000s.
Jse: Laxative.

OGEN. (Organon) Ox bile ext. 120 mg., oxidized nixed ox bile acids 75 mg. (equiv. to 75 mg. lehydrocholic acid), desoxycholic acid 30 mg., ancreatin 250 mg./Tab. Bot. 100s.
Jse: Orally, choleretic & digestant.

OGEST. (Mills) Mixed oxidized bile acids 65 mg., lesoxycholic acid 60 mg., ext. ox bile 40 mg., epsin 100 mg., pancreatin 100 mg., inositol 40 ng., dimethionine 120 mg., betaine HCl 75 mg., holine bitartrate 100 mg., diazyme 10 mg./Tab. 3ot. 100s.
Jse: Gallbladder disorders, indigestion, cirrhosis,)besity.

OPAQUE. (Winthrop-Breon) Tyropanoate sodium 750 mg./Cap. Envelopes of 4 caps. Box 25s.
Jse: Cholecystography.

ORIC. (Arcum) Pepsin 9.0 mg., ox bile 160 ng./Cap. Bot. 100s, 1000s.
Jse: Antispasmodic.

RON. (Lilly) Iron bile salts. Pulvule 150mg./Cap. 3ot. 100s. 300 mg./Cap Bot. 100s, 500s.
Use: Orally, physiologic laxative.

STAN. (Standex) Bile salts 0.5 gr., cascara sagrada pow. ext. 0.5 gr., phenolphthalein 0.5 gr., aloin 1/8 gr., podophyllin 1/20 gr./Tab. Bot. 100s.

TRICIDE. (Miles) Praziquantel 600 mg./Tab. Bot. 6s.
Use: Trematodicide.

METHOXYCAINE LACTATE. Bis-[b-(o-methoxy-phenyl) isopropyl] amine lactate. Isocaine Lactate.

NATE. (Tunex) Testosterone enanthate 90 mg., estradiol valerate 4 mg./ml. in sesame oil. Vial 10 cc.
Use: Androgen & estrogen therapy.

NAZINE. Todrazoline, B.A.N.

BINDAZAC. B.A.N. 1-Benzylindazol-3-yloxyacetic acid. Bendazac (I.N.N.)
Use: Anti-inflammatory.

BINEX-C. (Scruggs) B complex formula with C vitamins. Tab. Bot. 100s, 1000s.

• **BINIRAMYCIN.** USAN.
Use: Antibiotic.

BINTRON TABLETS. (Madland) Liver fraction 4.6 gr., ferrous sulfate 5 gr., Vit. B-1 3 mg., B-2 0.5 mg., B-6 0.15 mg., C 20.0 mg., Ca pantothenate 0.3 mg., niacinamide 10 mg./Tab. Bot. 100s, 1000s.
Use: Hematinic.

BIOCAL 250. (Miles) Calcium 250 mg./Chewable Tab. Bot. 60s.
Use: Calcium supplement.

BIOCAL 500. (Miles) Calcium 500 mg./Tab. Bot. 60s.
Use: Calcium supplement.

BIOCEPT-G. (Wampole) Radioreceptor assay for the qualitative detection of hCG in serum. Kits 30s, 150s.
Use: Aid in the diagnosis of pregnancy.

BIO-CREST. (Nutrition) Citrus bioflavonoid complex 200 mg., Vit. C 250 mg., rutin 50 mg./Tabseal. Bot. 100s.
Use: Abnormal capillary permeability, fragility, & bleeding.

BIO/DOPA. (DDR Pharm.) Levodopa 125 mg., 250 mg., 500 mg./Cap. Bot. 100s.
Use: Parkinsonism.

BIO-FLAVONOID COMPOUNDS. Vit. P.

BIO-FLAVONOID COMPOUND, CITRUS.
W/Vit. C.
See: C.V.P. Syr. & Cap. (USV Pharm.)
Mevanin-C, Cap. (Beutlich)
Mevatinic-C, Tab. (Beutlich)
Peridin-C, Tab. (Beutlich)
Pregent, Tab. (Beutlich)

BIOGASTRONE:
See: Carbenoxolone.

• **BIOLOGICAL INDICATOR FOR DRY-HEAT STERILIZATION, PAPER STRIP,** U.S.P. XXI.
Use: Indicator.

• **BIOLOGICAL INDICATOR FOR ETHYLENE OXIDE STERILIZATION, PAPER STRIP,** U.S.P. XXI.
Use: Indicator.

• **BIOLOGICAL INDICATOR FOR STEAM STERILIZATION,** U.S.P. XXI.
Use: Indicator.

BIO-MEDI-PEC. (Medi-Rx) Neomycin sulfate 300 mg., kaolin 6 Gm., pectin 0.13 Gm./Fl. oz. Bot. pt., gal.
Use: Diarrhea therapy.

BIONATE 50-2. (Seatrace) Testosterone cypionate 50 mg., estradiol cypionate 2 mg./ml. Vial 10 ml.

BIOPAR, FORTE. (USV Labs.) Vit. B-12 w/intrinsic factor concentrate 0.5u., Cobalamin 25 mcg./Tab. Bot. 30s.

BIORAL.
See: Carbenoxolone.

BIOS I.
See: Inositol.

BIOSONE. (Kay) Hydrocortisone acetate 50 mg., methylparaben, propylparaben, sodium chloride 9 mg./cc. Vial 5 cc.
Use: Hydrocortisone therapy.

BIO-STIK. (Commerce) Benzocaine, allantoin, octyl dimethyl PABA, camphor, menthol in special base and core. Swivel stick 0.1 oz.
Use: Relief of chapped, dry lips.

BIOTEXIN.
See: Novobiocin.

BIOTIC-OPH. (Scrip) Bacitracin 400 u., polymyxin B sulfate 5000 u., neomycin sulfate 5 mg., in a petroleum and mineral oil base 3 mg. ophthalmic/Gm. Tube ⅛ oz.

BIOTIC-T-400. (Scrip) Penicillin G (buffered w/calcium carb.)400,000 u./Tab. Bot. 100s.

BIOTRUM. (Vitarine) Vitamin and mineral replacement.
Use: Dietary supplement.

BIO-TYTRA. (Approved) Neomycin sulfate 2.5 mg., gramicidin 0.25 mg., benzocaine 10 mg./Troche. Box 10s.
Use: Antibiotic.

BIOXATPHEN. (Zemmer) Phenobarbital ⅛ gr., atropine sulfate 1/1000 gr., bismuth subnitrate 2 gr., cerium oxalate 2 gr./Tab.
Bot. 100s, 1000s.
Use: Orally, antispasmodic & sedative.

BIOZYME-C. (Armour) Collagenase 250 units/Gm. in white petrolatum base.
Use: Debriding chronic dermal ulcers and severely burned areas.

• **BIPENAMOL HYDROCHLORIDE.** USAN.
Use: Antidepressant.

• **BIPERIDEN,** U.S.P. XXI. 1-Piperidinepropanol,α-bicyclo[2.2.1]hept-5-en-2-yl-α-phenyl-.α-5-Norbornen-2-yl-α-phenyl-1-piperidinepropanol.
Use: Anticholinergic.

BIPERIDEN. B.A.N. 1-(Bicyclo[2.2.1]hept-5-en-2-yl)-1-phenyl-3-piperidinopropan-1-ol.
Use: Treatment of the Parkinsonian syndrome.
See: Akineton (hydrochloride or lactate)

• **BIPERIDEN HYDROCHLORIDE,** U.S.P. XXI. Tabs., U.S.P. XXI. 1-Piperidinepropanol, -α-bicyclo[2.2.1]-hept-5-en-2-yl-α-phenyl-, hydrochloride. α-5-Norbornen-2-yl-α-phenyl-1-piperidinepropanol hydrochloride.

• **BIPERIDEN LACTATE INJECTION,** U.S.P. XXI. 1-Piperidinepropanol, α-bicyclo[2.2.1]hept-5-en-2-yl-α-phenol, compound with 2-hydroxypropanoic acid (1:1). α-5-Norbornen-2-yl-α-phenyl-1-piperidinepropanol lactate (salt).

BIPERIDEN HCl and LACTATE. (Alpha-(Bicyclo[2,2,1] hept-5-en-2-yl)-alpha-phenyl-1-piperidine propanol.
See: Akineton, Amp., Tab. (Knoll)

BIPHASIC INSULIN INJECTION. B.A.N. A suspension of insulin crystals in a solution of insulin buffered at pH 7.
Use: Hypoglycemic agent.
See: Insulin Novo Rapitard

• **BIPHENAMINE HYDROCHLORIDE.** USAN. 2-Diethylaminoethyl-3-phenylsalicylate hydrochloride.

BIPHETAMINE 12.5. (Pennwalt) Dextroamphetami (as resin complex) 6.25 mg., amphetamine (as resin complex) 6.25 mg./Cap. Bot. 100s
Use: Appetite suppressant.

BIPHETAMINE 20. (Pennwalt) Dextroamphetamine (as resin complex) 10 mg., amphetamine (as res complex) 10 mg./Cap. Bot. 100s.
Use: Appetite suppressant.

BIPHETANE DC. (Bay) Codeine phosphate 10 mg brompheniramine maleate 2 mg., phenylpropanolamine HCl 12.5 mg./5 ml. w/alc 0.95%. Bot. 4 oz., Pt., Gal.
Use: Antitussive, antihistaminic, decongestant, expectorant.

BIPHETANE DX. (Bay) Brompheniramine maleate mg., dextromethorphan HBr 10 mg., pseudoephedrine HCl 30 mg./5 ml. w/alcohol 0.95% Bot. 4 oz., Pt. Gal.
Use: Antihistaminic, decongestant, antitussive.

BIPHETAP ELIXIR. (Bay) Brompheniramine malea 4 mg., phenylpropanolamine HCl 25 mg./ 5 ml. w/alcohol 2.3%. Bot. 4 oz., Pt., Gal.
Use: Antihistaminic, decongestant.

BIPOLE-S. (Spanner) Testosterone 25 mg., estron mg./cc. Vial 10 cc.

BIRONATE-B. (Coastal) Fe sulfate exs. 100 r aminoacetic acid (glycine) 175 mg., Vit. B-1 5 mg. 2 1 mg., desiccated liver 150 mg., B-12 0.85 m folic acid 0.25 mg., niacinamide 5 mg., Vit. C 12(mg./Cap. Bot. 100s.
Use: Dietary supplement.

■ **BIRTH CONTROL.**
See: Oral Contraceptive.

BIS (ACETOXYPHENYL) OXINDOL.
See: Oxyphenisatin.

• **BISACODYL,** U.S.P. XXI. Suppos., Tabs.: U.S.P. XXI. Phenol, 4,4′-(2-pyridinylmethylene)bis-,diacet (ester). Di-(p-acetoxyphenyl)-2-pyridylmethane. 4-4′-(2-pyridylmethylene) diphenol diacetate (ester).
Use: Cathartic.
See: Bisacodyl Uniserts, Suppos. (Upsher-Smith)
Deficol, Tab., Supp. (Vangard)
Delco-Lax, Tab. (Delco)
Dulcolax, Tab., Supp. (Boehringer Ingelheim)
Theralax, Tab. & Supp. (Beecham Labs)

• **BISACODYL TANNEX.** USAN. Water-soluble cc plex of bisacodyl and tannic acid.
Use: Contact laxative.
See: Clysodrast, packet (Barnes-Hind)

BISACODYL UNISERTS. (Upsher-Smith) Bisacodyl mg./Suppos. Carton 12s, 50s, 500s.
Use: Laxative.

BISALATE. (Allison) Sod. salicylate 5 gr., salicylami 2.5 gr., Sod. paraminobenzoate 5 gr., ascorbic ac 50 mg., butabarbital sod. ⅛ gr./Tab. Bot. 100s, 1000s.
Use: Rheumatic disorders.

• **BISANTRENE HYDROCHLORIDE.** USAN.
Use: Antineoplastic.

SARSONATE. (Marcen) Arsenic 3 mg., bismuth 7 mg., benzyl alcohol 5 mg., phenol 5 mg., sod. citrate 5 mg./cc. Vial 30 cc.
Use: Syphilis.

SATIN.
See: Oxyphenisatin.

4-BIS(3-BROMOPROPIONYL)PIPERAZINE.
See: Pipobroman

[BIS(2-CHLOROETHYL)AMINO]TETRAHYDRO-2H-1,3,2-OXAZAPHOSPHORINE 2-OXIDE MONOHYDRATE. Cyclophosphamide, U.S.P. XXI.

SCOLAN SUPPOSITORIES. (Lannett) Bismuth subgallate, benzocaine, resorcin, cod liver oil, lanolin, zinc oxide/Supp. Box 12s.

SCOLAN HC SUPPOSITORIES. (Lannett) Same as Biscolan Supp. w/hydrocortisone acetate 10 mg./Supp. Box 12s.

N'-BIS(p-ETHOXYPHENYL)ACETAMIDINE MONOHYDROCHLORIDE.
See: Phenacaine Hydrochloride, U.S.P. XXI.

4-BIS(2-ETHYLHEXYL)SULFOSUCCINATE, CALCIUM SALT. Docusate Sodium, U.S.P. XXI.

IS 5-[3-(DIMETHYLAMINO)PROPYL]-10,11-DIHYDRO-5H-DIBENZ[b,f] AZEPINE COMPOUND (2:1) WITH 4,4-METHYLENE-BIS-[3-HYDROXY-2-NAPHTHOIC ACID].
See: Imipramine Pamoate (Geigy)

ISHYDROXYCOUMARIN.
See: Dicumarol, U.S.P. XXI.

3-BIS(p-HDROXYPHENYL)PHTHALIDE. Phenolphthalein, U.S.P. XXI.

ISMOSALICATE COMPOUND. (Blue Line) Cal. carb. 48 gr., mag. trisilicate 40 gr., bismuth subcarb. 8 gr., zinc phenolsulphonate 4 gr. Bot. 14 oz., 1 gal.
Use: Orally, antacid.

ISMU-KINO. (Denver) Bismuth oxycarb. 10 gr., eucalyptus gum 6 gr., phenyl salicylate, camphor, menthol & carminative oils of nutmeg & clove in soothing, demulcent base, w/alcohol 2%/fl. oz. Bot. 4 oz., 1 pt.
Use: Stomach and intestinal upset.

ISMUTH ALUMINATEW/Magnesium trisilicate, aluminum hydroxide and magnesium carbonate coprecipitate.
See: Escot, Cap. (Reid-Provident)

ISMUTH BETANAPHTHOL. (Amend) Bi_2O_3 75%, betanaphthol 18%. Bot. 1 oz., 0.25 lb.
Use: Intestinal astringent.

ISMUTH GLYCOLLYLARSANILATE. B.A.N. Bismuthyl N-glycoloylarsanilate. Glycobiarsol (I.N.N.)
Use: Treatment of amebiasis.

ISMUTH GLYCOLYLARSANILATE. Bismuthyl N-glycollylarsanilate.
Use: Antiamebic.
See: Glycobiarsol, N.F. XVI.

ISMUTH HYDROXIDE.
See: Milk of Bismuth, U.S.P. XXI.

ISMUTH, INSOLUBLE PRODUCTS.
See: Bismuth Subgallate (Various Mfr.)
Bismuth Subsalicylate (Various Mfr.)
Bismuth Tribromophenate (N.Y. Quinine)

BISMUTH, MAGMA. Name previously used for Milk of Bismuth.

• **BISMUTH, MILK OF,** N.F. XVI.
Use: Astringent, antacid.

BISMUTH OXYCARBONATE.
See: Bismuth Subcarbonate

BISMUTH POTASSIUM TARTRATE. Basic bismuth pot. bismuthotartrate.
Brewer—25 mg./cc. Amp. 2 cc.
Miller—Amp. (0.016 Gm./cc.) 2 cc., Box 12s, 100s; Bot. 30 cc., 60 cc.
Raymer—(2.5%) Amp. 2 cc., Box 12s, 100s.
Use: I.M.; syphilis.

BISMUTH RESORCIN COMPOUND.
W/Bismuth subgallate, balsam peru, benzocaine, Zn oxide, boric acid.
See: Bonate, Supp. (Suppositoria)
W/Bismuth subgallate, balsam peru, Zn oxide, boric acid.
See: Versal, Supp. (Suppositoria)
W/Bismuth subgallate, zinc oxide, boric acid, balsam peru.
See: Anulan, Supp. (Lannett)

BISMUTH SODIUM TARTRATE.
Use: I.M.; syphilis.

BISMUTH SUBBENZOATE. (N.Y. Quinine)
Use: Dusting powder for wounds.

BISMUTH SUBCARBONATE.
Use: Gastroenteritis, diarrhea.
W/Benzocaine, cod liver oil, lanolin, zinc oxide, resorcin, balsam Peru.
See: Doctient, Supp. (Suppositoria)
W/Benzocaine, zinc oxide, boric acid.
See: Aracain Rectal Supp. (Commerce)
W/Calcium carbonate, magnesium carbonate.
See: Dimacid, Tab. (Otis Clapp)
W/Calcium carbonate, magnesium carbonate, aminoacetic acid, dried aluminum hydroxide gel.
See: Buffertabs, Tab. (O'Neal)
W/Charcoal and ginger.
See: Harv-a-carbs, Tab. (O'Neal)
W/Hydrocortisone acetate, belladonna extract, ephedrine sulfate, zinc oxide, boric acid, balsam peru, cocoa butter.
See: Rectacort, Supp. (Century)
W/Kaolin, pectin.
See: B-K-P Mixture, Liq. (Sutliff & Case) K-C, Liq. (Century)
W/Paregoric, Kaolin (colloidal), aluminum hydroxide, Pectin.
See: Kapinal, Tab. (Jenkins)
W/Paregoric, phenyl salicylate, zinc phenolsulfonate, pepsin.
See: Bismuth, salol, zinc and paregoric. (Bowman)
W/Pectin, kaolin, opium pow.
See: KBP/O, Cap. (Cole)
W/Phenyl salicylate, zinc phenolsulfonate, pepsin.
See: Bismuth, salol, zinc compound (Bowman)
W/Phenyl salicylate, chloroform, eucalyptus gum, camphor.
See: Bismu-Kino, Liq. (Denver Chem.)

W/Ephedrine sulfate, ext. belladonna, zinc oxide, boric acid, bismuth oxyiodide, peruvian balsam.
See: Wyanoids, Preps. (Wyeth)
W/Sodium salicylate, phenolphthalein, bismuth subgallate.
See: Laxogen, Tab. (Vortech)
BISMUTH SUBGALLATE. (Various Mfr.) Dermatol.
Use: Topically for skin conditions; Orally as an antidiarrheal.
W/Balsam of peru, Zn oxide, cod liver oil.
See: Pile-Gon, Oint. (Edward J. Moore)
W/Benzocaine, resorcin, cod liver oil, lanolin, zinc oxide.
See: Biscolan, Supp. (Lannett)
W/Benzocaine, zinc oxide, boric acid, peruvian balsam.
See: Anocaine, Supp. (Mallard)
W/Bismuth oxyiodide, bismuth resorcin comp, benzocaine, boric acid.
See: Bonate, Supp. (Suppositoria)
W/Bismuth resorcin comp., balsam peru, benzocaine, Zn oxide, boric acid.
See: Bonate, Supp. (Suppositoria)
W/Bismuth resorcin compound, zinc oxide, boric acid, balsam peru.
See: Anulan, Supp. (Lannett)
Versal, Supp. (Suppositoria)
W/Cod liver oil, benzocaine, lanolin, zinc oxide, resorcin, balsam Peru, hydrocortisone.
See: Doctient HC, Supp. (Suppositoria)
W/Hydrocortisone acetate, bismuth resorcin comp., zinc oxide, peruvian balsam, benzyl benzoate.
See: Anusol-HC, Cream, Supp. (Parke-Davis)
W/Diethylaminoacet-2, 6-xylidide, zinc oxide, aluminum subacetate, & peruvian balsam.
See: Xylocaine Suppositories (Astra)
W/Kaolin, colloidal.
See: Diastop, Liq. (Elder)
W/Kaolin colloidal, calcium carbonate, magnesium trisilicate, papain, atropine sulphate.
See: Kaocasil, Tab. (Jenkins)
W/Kaolin, opium, zinc phenolsulfonate, pectin.
See: Cholactabs, Tab. (Philips Roxane)
W/Kaolin, pectin, zinc phenolsulfonate, opium pow.
See: Diastay, Tab. (Elder)
W/Kaolin, zinc phenolsulfonate, opium pow.
See: B-K-Z, Tab. (Sutliff & Case)
W/Nux vomica, activated charcoal, pepsin, berberis, diastase, pancreatin, hydrastis, papain.
See: Digestalin, Tab. (Vortech)
W/Opium pow., pectin, kaolin, and zinc phenolsulfonate.
See: Amogel, Tab. (Vortech)
Bismuth, Pectin & Paregoric (Lemmon)
B.K.Z., Tab. (Sutliff & Case)
W/Sodium salicylate, bismuth subcarbonate, phenolphthalein.
See: Laxogen, Tab. (Vortech)
W/Zinc oxide, bis. resorcin comp., peruvian bal., benzyl benzoate.
See: Anugesic, Supp., Oint. (Parke-Davis)
Anusol, Supp., Oint. (Parke-Davis)

BISMUTH SUBIODIDE.
See: Bismuth oxyiodide.
• **BISMUTH SUBNITRATE,** U.S.P. XXI.
Use: Gastroenteritis, amebic dysentery & locally f wounds.
W/Atropine sulfate, phenobarbital & cerium oxalate.
See: Bioxatphen, Tab. (Zemmer)
W/Calcium carbonate, magnesium carbonate.
See: Antacid No. 2, Tab. (Bowman)
Maygel, Tab. (Century)
W/Sodium bicarbonate, Mg carbonate.
See: Bismatesia, Can (Noyes)
W/Sod. bicarbonate, magnesium carbonate, diastase papain.
Panacarb, Tab. (Lannett)
BISMUTH SUBSALICYLATE. Basic bismuth salicyla
Use: I.M., to treat syphilis.
W/Calcium carbonate, glycocoll
See: Pepto-Bismol, Tab. (Norwich)
W/Calcium carbonate, Ca phenolsulfonate.
See: Pan-Bis-Cal, Liq. (Noyes)
W/Pectin, salol, kaolin, zinc sulfocarbolate, aluminum hydroxide.
See: Wescola Antidiarrheal-Stomach Upset (Weste Research)
W/Phenylsalicylate, zinc phenolsulfonate, methylcellulose, magnesium aluminum silicate.
See: Pepto-Bismol, Liq. (Norwich)
BISMUTH TANNATE. (Various Mfr.) Tanbismuth.
Use: Astringent & protective in G.I. disorders.
BISMUTH TRIBROMOPHENATE. (N.Y. Quinine).
Use: Intestinal antiseptic.
BISMUTH VIOLET. (Table Rock) Bismuth Violet. **Oint.** 1%, Jar 1 oz., 1 lb. **Sol.** 0.5%, Bot. 0.5 oz., oz., pt., gal. **Tr.** 0.5%, Bot. 6 oz., 1 pt., also 1% w/benzoic and salicylic acid Bot. 0.5 oz., 6 oz., 1 pt.
Use: Bactericidal & fungicidal.
BISMUTH, WATER-SOLUBLE PRODUCTS.
See: Bismuth Potassium Tartrate (Various Mfr.)
• **BISOBRIN LACTATE.** USAN. Meso-1,1′-tetramet lenebis[1,2,3,4-tetrahydro-6,7-dimethoxyisoquinoline dilactate.
Use: Fibrinolytic.
BISODOL POWDER. (Whitehall) Sodium bicarbonate 644 mg., magnesium carbonate 475 mg./Tsp. Bot. 3 oz., 5 oz.
Use: Antacid.
BISODOL TABLETS. (Whitehall) Calcium carbonate 194 mg., magnesium hydroxide 178 mg./Tab. Bot. 30s, 100s.
Use: Antacid.
BISOXATIN. B.A.N. 2,3-Dihydro-2,2-di(4-hydroxyphenyl)-1,4-benzoxazin-3-one.
Use: Laxative.
See: Laxonalin diacetate
• **BISOXATIN ACETATE.** USAN.
Use: Cathartic.
BISQUADINE. (Sterwin) Alexidine.
BIS(2,2,2-TRIFLUOROETHYL) ETHER.
See: Fluorthyl.

-TROPAMIDE, Tropicamide.
See: Mydriacyl, Sol. (Alcon)
TE & ITCH LOTION. (Weeks & Leo) Pramoxine HCl 1%, pyrilamine maleate 2%, pheniramine maleate 0.2%, chlorpheniramine maleate 0.2%. Bot. 4 oz.
Use: First aid lotion for sunburn, minor burns, cuts, insect bites & irritations.
THIONOL. 2,2′-Thiobis(4,6-dichlorophenol)
Use: Local anti-infective.
See: Actamer (Monsanto Chem.)
/Allantoin salicylic acid.
See: Domerine, Shampoo (Miles Pharm)
/Resorcinol monoacetate, sulfur.
See: Acne-Dome, Preps. (Miles Pharm)
THIONOL. B.A.N. 2,2′-Thiobis-(4,6-dichlorophenol).
Use: Antiseptic.
BITHIONOLATE SODIUM. USAN. Disodium 2,2′-thiobis-(4,6-dichlorophenoxide).
BITOLTEROL MESYLATE. USAN.
Use: Bronchodilator.
TRATE. (Arco) Phenobarbital 15 mg., pentaerythritol tetranitrate 20 mg./Tab. Bot. 100s.
Use: Angina pectoris.
K-P MIXTURE. (Sutliff & Case) Kaolin 40 gr., bismuth subcarbonate 20 gr., pectin 10 gr./fl. oz. Bot. 1 pt., 1 gal.
K-Z TABLETS, CHEWABLE. (Sutliff and Case) Kaolin 370 mg., bismuth subgallate 60 mg., Zn phenolsulfonate 16 mg., powd. opium 5 mg./Tab. Bot. 100s, 1000s.
Use: Diarrhea.
LACK AND WHITE BLEACHING CREAM. (Plough) Hydroquinone 2%. 0.75 oz., Tube 1.5 oz.
Use: Skin lightener.
LACK AND WHITE OINTMENT. (Plough) Resorcinol 3%. Tube 0.75 oz., 2.25 oz.
Use: Antiseptic-antipruritic dressing.
LACK DRAUGHT SYRUP. (Chattem) Casanthrol 90 mg./Tablespoonful. Bot. 2 oz., 4 oz.
Use: Laxative.
LACK DRAUGHT TABLETS. (Chattem) Powdered Senna extract 200 mg./Tab. Bot. 30s.
Use: Laxative
LACK WIDOW SPIDER, ANTIVENIN.
See: Antivenin, Inj. (Merck Sharp & Dohme)
LAINE P.N.F. (Blaine) Tab. 100s.
Use: Vitamin mineral prenatal.
LANEX. (Edwards) Chlorzoxazone 250 mg., acetaminophen 300 mg./Cap. Bot. 100s.
Use: Relief of pain and muscle spasm.
LAUD STRUBEL. (Strubel) Ferrous sulfate 190 mg./Cap. Bot. 100s.
Use: Treatment of iron deficiency anemia.
LASTOMYCIN.
Use: Diagnostic aid (dermal reactivity).
LEFCON. (Madland) Sod. sulfacetamide 30% ointment, ophthalmic. Tube ⅛ oz.
LENOXANE. (Bristol) Bleomycin sulfate 15 u./Vial. in 10s; Single units in 1s.
Use: Antineoplastic injection.

BLEOMYCIN. (B.A.N.) Antibiotic obtained from cultures of Streptomyces verticillus.
Use: Antineoplastic.
• **BLEOMYCIN SULFATE, STERILE,** U.S.P. XXI.
See: Blenoxane, Inj., (Bristol)
BLEPH-10 LIQUIFILM. (Allergan) Sulfacetamide sodium 10%, polyvinyl alcohol 1.4%, thimerosal 0.005%, polysorbate 80, sod. thiosulfate, pot. phosphate monobasic, edetate disodium, sod. phosphate dibasic (anhydrous), hydrochloric acid and purified water. Plastic dropper bot. 5 ml., 15 ml. Unit Dose 2.5 ml.
Use: Topical anti-infective agent for ophthalmic use.
BLEPH-10 S.O.P. STERILE OPHTHALMIC OINTMENT. (Allergan) Sulfacetamide sodium 10%, phenylmercuric acetate 0.0008% w/white petrolatum, mineral oil, nonionic lanolin derivatives. Tube 3.5 Gm.
Use: Topical anti-infective agent for ophthalmic use.
BLEPHAMIDE LIQUIFILM. (Allergan) Sulfacetamide sodium 10%, prednisolone acetate 0.2%, polyvinyl alcohol 1.4%. Dropper Bot. 5 ml. & 10 ml. Unit Dose 2.5 ml.
Use: Topical anti-inflammatory and anti-infective for ophthalmic use.
BLEPHAMIDE S.O.P. STERILE OPHTHALMIC OINTMENT. (Allergan) Prednisolone acetate 0.2%, sulfacetamide sodium 10%. Tube 3.5 Gm.
Use: Topical anti-inflammatory and anti-infective for ophthalmic use.
BLINK-N-CLEAN. (Allergan) Polyoxyl 40 stearate and polyethylene glycol 300 with 0.5% chlorobutanol. Bot. 7.5 ml., 15 ml. Unit dose 1 ml.
Use: Hard contact lens cleaning and rewetting solution.
BLINX. (Barnes-Hind) Sterile, isotonic, alkaline borate buffer containing boric acid and sodium borate, phenylmercuric acetate 0.004%. Bot. 1 oz. & 4 oz.
Use: Ophthalmic Irrigation and eye wash.
BLIS. (Commerce) Bot. 7 oz.
Use: Foot bath.
BLIS-TO-SOL. (Chattem) **Liquid:** Salicylic acid, undecylenic acid. Bot. 1 oz., 2 oz. **Powder:** Benzoic acid, salicylic acid. Bot. 2 oz.
Use: Topical anti-fungal.
BLOCADREN. (Merck Sharp & Dohme) Timolol maleate 10 mg. or 20 mg./Tab. Bot. 100s.
Use: Antihypertensive, prevention of recurrent myocardial infarction.
BLOOD, ANTICOAGULANTS.
See: Anticoagulants.
• **BLOOD CELLS, RED,** U.S.P. XXI.
Use: Blood replenisher.
BLOOD COAGULATION.
See: Hemostatics
BLOOD CULTURE PREP KIT. (Marion) Isopropyl alcohol 70%, acetone 10%, FREPP, povidone iodine 10%, SEPP, Isopropyl alcohol wipe. Ctn. 20s.
Use: Skin prep kit.
BLOOD FRACTIONS.
See: Albumin (Human) Salt-Poor (Armour; Hyland)

BLOOD GLUCOSE CONCENTRATOR.
See: Glucagon (Lilly)

• **BLOOD GROUPING SERUMS,** U.S.P. XXI. Anti-Rh. (Anti-D) 85%-Tubes, 10 tests; Vial, with pipette, 5 cc. Anti-Rh. (Anti C plus D) 17%-Tube, 10 tests; Vial, with pipette, 5 cc.
Use: Diagnostic aid in the determination of Rh. (D) and Rh. (C plus D) factors in red blood cells.

• **BLOOD GROUPING SERUM, ANTI-A,** U.S.P. XXI.
Use: Diagnostic aid (in vitro, blood).

• **BLOOD GROUPING SERUM, ANTI-B,** U.S.P. XXI.
Use: Diagnostic aid (invitro, blood).

• **BLOOD GROUP SPECIFIC SUBSTANCES A, B AND AB,** U.S.P. XXI. Blood neutralizer (isoagglutinins, group O blood).

BLOOD PLASMA.
See: Normal Human Plasma

BLOOD PLASMA SUBSTITUTES.
See: Dextran (Cutter; Pharmachem)

BLOOD VOLUME DETERMINATION.
See: Evans Blue, dye (Harvey; City)

• **BLOOD, WHOLE HUMAN,** U.S.P. XXI.
Use: Blood replenisher.

BLU-6. (Bluco) Pyridoxine HCl 100 mg./ml. Vial 10 ml.
Use: Vitamin B-6 supplement.

BLU-12 100. (Bluco) Cyanocobalamin 100 mcg./ml. Vial 30 ml.
Use: Vitamin B-12 injectable.

BLU-12 1000. (Bluco) Cyanocobalamin 1000 mcg./ml. Vial 30 ml.
Use: Vitamin B-12 injectable.

BLUDEX. (Burlington) Methenamine 40.8 mg., methylene blue 5.4 mg., phenyl salicylate 18.1 mg., atropine sulfate 0.03 mg. hysocyamine 0.03 mg., benzoic acid 4.5 mg./Tab. Bot. 100s, 1000s.
Use: Urinary antiseptic and antispasmodic.

BLUE-GRAY (HEMORRHOIDAL) SUPPOSITORIES. (Quality Generics) Bismuth subiodide, bismuth subcarbonate, zinc oxide, boric acid, benzocaine. Boxes 12s.
Use: Treatment of hemorrhoids.

BLUTENE CHLORIDE. Tolonium chloride, Toluidine blue O chloride, 3-amino-7-dimethylamino-2-methyl-phenazathonium salt.

B-MAJOR. (Barth's) Vit. B-1 7 mg., B-2 14 mg., niacin 2.35 mg., B-12 7.5 mcg., B-6 0.15 mg., pantothenic acid 0.37 mg., choline 85 mg., inositol 6 mg., biotin, folic acid, aminobenzoic acid./Cap. Bot. 1s, 3s, 6s, 12s.

B.M.E. (Brothers) Aminophylline 32 mg., ephedrine sulfate 8 mg., phenobarbital 8 mg., chlorpheniramine maleate 2 mg., alcohol 15%/5 cc. Bot. pt.

B-N. (Eric, Kirk & Gary). Bacitracin 500 units; neomycin sulfate, 5 mg./Oint. 0.5 oz.
Use: Dermatitis, impetigo, burns.

B-NUTRON TABLETS. (Nion) Vit. B-1 2 mg., niacinamide 18 mg., B-6 2.2 mg., cyanocobalamine 3 mcg., folic acid 0.4 mg., iron 6 mg., pantothenic acid 3.3 mg., plus vit. B complex as provided by 150 mg. Brewer's yeast/Tab. Bot. 100s, 500s.
Use: Dietary supplement.

B and O SUPPRETTES NO. 15A & NO. 16A. (Webcon) Opium 30 mg. or 60 mg., belladonna e 15 mg./Supp. Jars 12s.
Use: Analgesic, antispasmodic, sedative.

BOBID. (Boyd) Phenylpropanolamine HCl 50 mg., chlorpheniramine maleate 8 mg., methscopolamir bromide 2.5 mg./Cap. Bot. 100s.

BOILAID. (Edward J. Moore) Benzocaine, tetracaine ichtchammol, resin cerate, thymol iodide. Jar 1 oz
Use: Anesthetic drawing salve.

BOIL-EASE ANESTHETIC DRAWING SALVE. (Co merce) Benzocaine, ichthammol, sulfur, camphor, juniper tar. Tube. 1 oz.
Use: Boils.

BOILnSOAK. (Alcon) Sodium chloride 0.7%, thimerosal 0.001%, disodium edetate 0.1%. Bot. oz., 8 oz.
Use: Soft contact lenses care.

• **BOLANDIOL DIPROPIONATE.** USAN.
Use: Anabolic.

• **BOLASTERONE.** USAN.
Use: Anabolic.

BOLAX. (Boyd) Docusate sodium 240 mg., phenolphthalein 30 mg., dihydrocholic acid ¾ gr./Cap. Bot. 100s.

BOLDENONE. B.A.N. 17β-Hydroxyandrosta-1,4-dien 3-one.
Use: Anabolic steroid.

• **BOLDENONE UNDECYLENATE.** USAN. 17β Hydroxyandrosta-1,4-dien-3-one 10 undecenoate. Parenabol. Under study.
Use: Anabolic.

• **BOLENOL.** USAN. 19-Nor-17-α-pregn-5-en-17-ol. α-ethyl-5-estren-17-ol. Under study.
Use: Anabolic.

BOLINE HOUDE, BOLDINE. (C.M.C.) Bot. 40s.

• **BOLMANTALATE.** USAN. 17β-Hydroxyestr-4-en-3-one adamantane-1-carboxylate.
Use: Anabolic steroid.

BON-A-DAY, IMPROVED. (Inwood) Vit. A 5000 I.U., 400 I.U., B-1 1.5 mg., B-2 1.7 mg., niacinamide 2 mg., C 60 mg., B-6 2 mg., folic acid 0.1 mg., pant thenic acid 10 mg., B-12 5 mcg./Tab. Bot. 100s, 250 365s.

BON-A-DAY w/IRON, IMPROVED. (Inwood) Same fo mula as above with iron 18 mg./Tab. Bot. 100s, 250s, 365s.

BONAL ITCH CREAM. (Edward J. Moore) Benzocaine, dibucaine, tetracaine in water-washab base. Tube 1 oz.
Use: Itching; anesthetic.

BON-A-LETS. (Inwood) Vit. A 10,000 I.U., D 1000 I.U B-1 5 mg., B-2 5 mg., nicotinamide 25 mg., B-6 2 mg B-12 2 mcg., Ca pantothenate 5 mg., C 100 mg./Ta Bot. 100s, 250s.

BON-A.M. (Inwood) Vit. A 5000 I.U., D 500 I.U., C 75 mg B-1 3 mg., B-2 3 mg., B-6 2 mg., Ca pantothenate mg., B-12 1 mcg., E 3 I.U., niacinamide 20 mg., iro 10 mg./Tab. Bot. 100s.

BONATE. (Suppositoria) Bismuth subgallate, Peru balsam, benzocaine, zinc oxide/Suppository. Box 12s, 100s, 1000s.
Use: Antihemorrhoidal.

ON-BEE W/C CAPSULES. (Inwood) Vit. B-1 15 mg., B-2 10 mg., B-6 5 mg., nicotinamide 50 mg., Ca pantothenate 10 mg., C 300 mg./Cap. Bot. 100s.

ON-BEE FORTE W/C CAPSULES. (Inwood) Vit. B-1 25 mg., B-2 12.5 mg., nicotinamide 50 mg., B-6 3 mg., Ca pantothenate 10 mg., C 250 mg., B-12 2.5 mcg./Cap. Bot. 100s, 250s.

ONINE. (Pfipharmecs) Meclizine HCl 25 mg./Chewable Tab. Bot. 100s, 500s.
Use: Motion sickness.

ONINE OTC. (Pfipharmecs) Meclizine HCl 25 mg./Chewable Tab. Pkg. 8 tabs.
Use: Motion sickness.

ON-O-TIN W/C CAPSULES. (Inwood) Vit. B-1 10 mg., B-12 10 mg., B-6 5 mg., niacinamide 50 mg., Ca pantothenate 25 mg., liver des. & def. 350 mg., B-12 1 mcg., C 150 mg./Cap. Bot. 100s, 250s.

ONTRIL PDM. (Carnrick) Phendimetrazine tartrate 35 mg./3 layer Tab. Bot. 100s, 1000s.
Use: Anorexiant.

ONTRIL SLOW RELEASE CAPSULES. (Carnrick) Phendimetrazine tartrate 105 mg./Cap. Bot. 100s.
Use: Anorexiant.

OPEN-VK. (Boyd) Pot. phenoxymethyl penicillin 400,000 u./Tab. Bot. 100s.

ORAX. Sodium Borate, N.F. XVI.

ORGHESE LA RIVIERA SUN PRODUCTS. (Revlon) Padimate O, Oxybenzone in cream & gel bases giving sun protection factors of 2, 4, 6, and 8..
Use: Sunburn prevention.

BORIC ACID, N.F. XVI. Cryst. or Pow.
Use: Mild antiseptic.
See: Borofax, Oint. (Burroughs Wellcome)
'/Combinations.
See: Saratoga Ointment (Blair)

ORIC ACID OINTMENT. (Various Mfr.) 5% to 10%.

·BORNANONE. Camphor, U.S.P. XXI.

ORNAPRINE. B.A.N. 3-Diethylaminopropyl 2-phenylbicyclo[2.2.1]-heptane-2-carboxylate.
Use: Spasmolytic.
See: Sormodren

BORNELONE. USAN.
Use: Ultraviolet screen.

OROFAX OINTMENT. (Burroughs Wellcome) Boric acid 5%. Tube 1.75 oz.
Use: Topically, for chafed and chapped skin.

OROGLYCERIN. Glycerol borate. (Emerson) Bot. pt.

OROGLYCERIN GLYCERITE. Boric acid 31 parts & glycerin 96 parts.
Use: Externally, in dermatitis.

OROTANNIC COMPLEX. Boric Acid 31 mg., Tannic acid 50 mg.
'/Salicylic acid, ethyl alcohol.
See: Onycho-Phytex, Liq. (Unimed)

BOTULISM ANTITOXIN, U.S.P. XXI.
Use: Prophylaxis & treatment of the toxins of C. botulinum, Types A or B; passive immunizing agent.

OURBONAL.
See: Ethyl Vanillin, N.F. XVI.

OWMAN COLD TABS. (Bowman) Acetaminophen 324 mg., phenylpropanolamine HCl 24.3 mg., caffeine 16.2 mg./Tab. Bot. 100s, 1000s, 5000s.
Use: Decongestant, analgesic.

BOWMAN'S POISON ANTIDOTE KIT. (Bowman) Syrup ipecac 1 oz., 1 Bottle; activated charcoal liquid 2 oz., 3 Bottles.
Use: First aid for accidental poisoning.

BOWSTERAL. (Bowman) Isopropanol 60%. Bot. pt., gal.
Use: Anti-rust disinfectant for surgical instruments.

BOWTUSSIN D.M.. (Bowman) Guaifenesin 100 mg., dextromethorphan HBr 15 mg./ 5 ml. w/alcohol 15%. Bot. 3 oz., pt., gal.
Use: Coughs.

• BOXIDINE. USAN. 1-[2-[[4'-(Trifluoromethyl)-4-biphenylyl]-oxy]ethyl]pyrrolidine.
Use: Adrenal steroid blocker.

BOYLEX. (Approved) Diperodon, hexachlorophene, rosin cerate, ichtchammol, carbolic acid, thymol, camphor, juniper tar. Tube 1 oz.
Use: Drawing salve.

B-PAP. (Wren) Acetaminophen 120 mg., sod. butabarbital 15 mg./5 cc. Bot. pt., gal.

B-PAS.
See: Calcium Benzoylpas

B-PLEX 100, INJECTABLE. (Jenkins) Vit. B-1 100 mg., B-2 2 mg., B-6 2 mg., panthenol 10 mg., niacinamide 125 mg., ethanolamide of gentisic acid 2.5%/cc. Vial 30 cc.
Use: Vitamin B therapy.

B-PLEX 100 W/B-12. (Jenkins) Vit. B-1 100 mg., B-2 2 mg., B-6 5 mg., niacinamide 125 mg., panthenol 10 mg., B-12 30 mcg., ethanolamide of gentisic acid 2.5%/cc. Vial 30 cc. 12s.

B-PLUS. (Enzyme Process) Vit. B-1 5 mg., B-2 mg., niacin 20 mg., B-6 4 mg., pantothenic acid 15 mg., B-12 15 mcg./4 Tab. Bot. 100s, 250s.
Use: Dietary supplement.

B-P-M CREAM. (Durel) Burow's solution 5%, phenol 0.5%, menthol 0.5%, camphor 1% in Duromantel cream. Jars 1 oz., lb., 6 lb.
Use: Generalized, widespread eczematous eruptions.

BPP LEMMON. (Lemmon) Powd. opium 1.2 mg. (Equiv. to 0.3 ml. paregoric), bismuth subgallate 120 mg., pectin 15 mg., kaolin 120 mg., zinc phenolsulfonate 15 mg./Tab. Bot. 1000s.
Use: Antidiarrheal.

BP-PAPAVERINE. (Burlington) Papaverine HCl 150 mg./Sus. Rel. Cap. Bot. 50s.
Use: For relief of cerebral & peripheral ischemia associated with arterial spasm & myocardial ischemia complicated by arrhythmias.

BQ COLD TABLETS. (Bristol-Myers) Acetaminophen 325 mg., phenylpropanolamine HCl 12.5 mg., chlorpheniramine maleate 2.0 mg./Tab. Card 16s; Bot. 30s, 50s.
Use: Cold treatment.

B.Q.R. (Calotabs) Fl. extract Cascara sagrada aromatic, sodium salicylate, syrup of ipecac, menthol, balsam peru in elix. lactated pepsin base w/Alcohol 8.5%. Bot. 2 fl. oz.
Use: Cold discomforts.

BRACE. (Norcliff Thayer) Denture adhesive. Tube 1.4 oz., 2.4 oz.

BRADOSOL BROMIDE. (Ciba) Domiphen bromide.

BRANCHAMIN 4%. (Travenol) Isoleucine 1.38 Gm., leucine 1.38 Gm., valine 1.25 Gm./100 ml. Bot. 500 ml.
Use: Adjunct to regular TPN therapy for highly stressed or traumatized patients.

BRAN FIBER WAFERS. (Nion) Unprocessed wheat bran 1000 mg., celery, parsley, watercress, lecithin. Six wafers daily with a glass of water at mealtime. Bot. 180s.
Use: Dietary supplement.

BRASIVOL FINE, MEDIUM AND ROUGH. (Stiefel) Aluminum oxide scrub particles in a surfactant cleansing base. **Fine**—Jar 5.1 oz. **Medium**—Jar 6 oz. **Rough**—Jar 6.5 oz.
Use: Scrub cleanser.

BRASIVOL BASE. (Stiefel) Cleansing paste containing polyoxyethylene lauryl ether and a surfactant cleanser. Jar 4.1 oz.
Use: Degreasing skin cleanser.

BREACOL DECONGESTANT COUGH MEDICATION. (Glenbrook) Dextromethorphan HBr 10 mg., phenylpropanolamine HCl 37.5 mg., alcohol 10%, chlorpheniramine maleate 4 mg./Tsp. Bot. 3 oz., 6 oz.
Use: Antitussive, decongestant antihistaminic.

BREATHEASY. (Pascal Co.) Racemic epinephrine HCl sol. 2.2% inhaled by use of nebulizer. Bot. 0.25 oz., 0.5 oz., 1 oz.
Use: Relief of bronchial congestion due to asthma or related respiratory allergies.

BREEZEE MIST. (Pedinol) Aluminum chlorohydroxide complex, undecylenic acid, menthol. Aerosol Bot. 4 oz.
Use: Antifungal, deodorant, anti-perspirant, foot powder.

BREONESIN. (Winthrop-Breon) Guaifenesin 200 mg./Cap. Bot. 100s.
Use: Expectorant.

BRETHAIRE. (Geigy) Terbutaline sulfate inhaler 7.5 ml. (10.5 Gm.) w/mouthpiece
Use: Bronchodilator.

BRETHINE. (Geigy) Terbutaline sulfate. **Tab.:** 2.5 mg./Tab. Bot. 100s, 1000s, unit dose 100s; Gy-Pak 100s. 5 mg./Tab. Bot. 100s, 1000s, unit dose 100s; Gy-Pak 100s. **Amp.:** 1 mg./ml. Box 10s, 100s.
Use: Bronchodilator.

• **BRETYLIUM TOSYLATE.** USAN. 2-Bromobenzyl-ethyldimethylammonium toluene-p-sulfonate.
Use: Hypotensive.
See: Bretylate
Bretylol, Inj. (American Critical Care)
Darenthin

BRETYLOL. (American Critical Care) Bretylium tosylate 50 mg./ml. Amp. 10 ml.
Use: Anti-arrythmic, antifibrillatory agent.

BREVICON. (Syntex) Norethindrone 0.5 mg., ethinyl estradiol 0.035 mg./Tab. 21 & 28 day (7 inert tabs) Wallette.
Use: Oral contraceptive.

BREVITAL SODIUM. (Lilly) Methohexital sodium. **Powder:** (anhydrous Na carbonate) 500 mg., 50 **Vial:** 1s, 25s, w/diluent 50 ml. 1s, 2.5 Gm. 1s, 25 250 ml. 1s, 25s. 5.0 Gm. 1s, 500 ml. 1s, 25s.
Use: (1%) Ultrashort-acting intravenous anestheti

BREWER'S YEAST. (Various Mfr.) Pow., Tab. 6 gr., 7.5 gr., 1 lb.
W/Docusate sodium.
See: Doss or Super Doss, Tab., Cap. (Ferndale)
W/Psyllium seed, plantago ovata, karaya gum.
See: Plantamucin Granules, (Elder)

BREXIN. (Savage) Pseudoephedrine HCl 60 mg., carbinoxamine maleate 4 mg., guaifenesin 100 mg./Cap. Bot. 100s, 500s.
Use: Decongestant.

BREXIN L.A. (Savage) Chlorpheniramine maleate 8 mg., pseudoephedrine HCl 120 mg./L.A. Bot. 100
Use: Temporary relief of cold symptoms.

BREXIN LIQUID. (Savage) Pseudoephedrine HCl 3C mg., carbinoxamine maleate 2 mg., guaifenesin 1C mg./5 ml. Bot. Pts.
Use: Temporary relief of cough, cold symptoms.

BRIABELL. (Vortech) Phenobarbital 16.2 mg., hyoscyamine sulfate 0.104 mg., atropine sulfate 0.0195 mg., scopolamine hydrobromide 0.0065 mg./Tab. Bot. 1000s.
Use: Antispasmodic & sedative.

BRICANYL INJECTION. (Merrell Dow) Terbutaline sulfate 1 mg., sod. chloride 8.9 mg., hydrochloric acid to adjust pH to 3.0-5.0/Amp. 1 ml. 10s.
Use: Bronchodilator.

BRICANYL TABLETS. (Merrell Dow) Terbutaline sulfate 2.5 or 5 mg./Tab. **2.5 mg.** Bot. 100s, 100C unit dose 100s; **5 mg.** Bot. 100s, 1000s, unit dose 100s.
Use: Bronchodilator.

BRIGEN-G. (Grafton) Chlordiazepoxide 5 mg., 10 m or 25 mg./Tab. Bot. 500s.
Uses: Emotional disturbances, sedative.

BRIJ 96 and 97. (ICI Americas) Polyoxyl 10 oleyl ether available as 96 & 97.
Use: Surface active agent.

BRIJ-721. (ICI Americas) Polyoxyethylene 21 stea ether (100% active).
Use: Surface active agent.

• **BRINOLASE.** USAN. Fibrinolytic enzyme produced by *Aspergillus oryzae.*
Use: Fibrinolytic.

BRIREL W/SUPERINONE. (Winthrop Products) Hexahydropyrazine, hexahydrate.
Use: Anthelmintic.

BRISTOJECT. (Bristol) Prefilled disposable syringes w/needle.
Aminophylline: 250 mg./10 ml.
Atropine Sulf: 5 mg./5 ml. or 1 mg./ml. 10s.
Ca Chloride: 10%. 10 ml. 10s.
Dexamethasone 20 mg./5 ml.
Dextrose: 50%. 50 ml. 10s.
Diphenhydramine 50 mg./5 ml.
Dopamine HCl: 200 mg./5 ml., 400 mg./10 ml.
Ephedrine 50 mg./10 ml.
Epinephrine: 1:10,000 10 ml. 10s.

Lidocaine HCl. 1%: 5 ml., 10 ml.; 2%: 5 ml.; 4%: 25 ml., 50 ml.; 20%: 5 ml., 10 ml.
Magnesium Sulf: 5 Gm./10 ml. 10s.
Metaraminol: 1%, 10 ml.
Sod. Bicarbonate: 7.5% 50 ml., 8.4% 50 ml. 10s.

ITISH ANTI-LEWISITE. Dimercaprol
See: BAL

OBELLA-P.B. (Brothers) Atropine sulfate 0.0195 mg., hyoscine HBr 0.0065 mg., hyoscyamine sulfate 0.1040 mg., phenobarbital 0.25 gr./Tab. Bot. 100s, 1000s.

OCILLIN. (Brothers) Pot. penicillin G 400,000 u./Tab. or 5 cc. Bot. 100s. Bot. 80 cc.

OCON C.R. (Forest) Brompheniramine maleate 12 mg., phenylephrine HCl 15 mg., phenylpropanolamine HCl 15 mg./Tab. Bot. 100s.
Use: Antihistamine, decongestant.

ROCRESINE. USAN. 0-(4-Bromo-3-hydroxybenzyl)-hydroxylamine. Alpha(amino-oxy)-6-bromo-m-cresol.
Use: Histidine decarboxylase inhibitor.
See: Contramine phosphate

ROCRINAT. USAN.
Use: Diuretic.

OCYCLINE. (Brothers) Tetracycline HCl 250 mg./Cap. Bot. 100s, 1000s.

OFEZIL. B.A.N. 2-(4-p-Bromophenylthiazol-2-yl)propionic acid.
Use: Anti-inflammatory.

ROFOXINE. USAN.
Use: Antipsychotic.

OGESIC. (Brothers) Isobutylalkylbarbituric acid ¾ gr., aspirin 5 gr., caffeine ¾ gr., phenacetin 3.75 gr./Tab. Bot. 100s, 500s. W/Codeine/Tab. Bot. 100s.

OHEMBIONE. (Brown) Vit. B-12 100 mcg., liver inj. USP (10 mcg. B-12/cc.), B-1 25 mg., B-2 2 mg., B-6 10 mg., w/benzyl alcohol 1.5% & procaine HCl 1%/cc. Vial 10 cc.
Use: Liver plus Vit. B complex.

OLADE. (Brothers) Chlorpheniramine maleate 8 mg., phenylephrine HCl 20 mg., methscopolamine nitrate 2.5 mg./Cap. Bot. 50s, 500s.

OMACRYLIDE. N-(acrylamidomethyl)-3-bromopropionamide.

BROMADOLINE MALEATE. USAN.
Use: Analgesic.

OMALEATE. A mixture of 2-amino-2-methyl-1-propanol and 8-bromotheophylline.
See: Pamabrom.

OMALIX. (Century) Bromphenramine maleate 4 mg., phenylephrine HCl 5 mg., phenylpropanolamine HCl 5 mg., alcohol 2.3%/5 ml. Bot. 4 oz., pt., gal.
Use: Antihistaminic, decongestant.

OMANYL. (National Pharm) Codeine phosphate 10 mg., bromodiphenhydramine HCl 12.5 mg./ 5 ml. w/alcohol 5%.
Use: Antitussive, antihistaminic.

OMAPAPP. (Zenith) Brompheniramine maleate 4 mg., phenylephrine HCl 5 mg., phenylpropanolamine HCl 5 mg./Tab. Bot. 100s.
Use: Antihistamine.

BROMATANE D.C. COUGH SYRUP. (Goldline) Brompheniramine maleate, phenylpropanolamine HCl, codeine phosphate. Bot. gal.
Use: Antihistaminic, nasal decongestant.

BROMATAPP ELIXIR. (Goldline) Brompheniramine maleate, phenylephrine HCl, phenylephrine HCl, phenylpropanolamine HCl. Bot. 4 oz., pt., gal.
Use: Antihistaminic, nasal decongestant.

BROMATAPP T.D. TAB. (Goldline) Brompheniramine maleate, phenylephrine HCl, phenylpropanolamine HCl extend tabs. Bot. 100s, 1000s
Use: Antihistaminic, nasal decongestant.

BROMAURIC ACID. Hydrogen tetrabromoaurate.

• **BROMAZEPAM.** USAN. 7-Bromo-1,3-dihydro-5-(2-Pyridyl)-2H-1,4-benzodiazepin-2-one.
Use: Minor tranquilizer.

BROMAZINE.
See: Ambodryl HCl, Elix., Kapseal (Parke-Davis)

BROMBAY ELIXIR. (Bay) Brompheniramine maleate 2 mg./5 ml. w/alcohol 3%. Bot. 4 oz., pt., gal.
Use: Antihistamine.

• **BROMCHLORENONE.** USAN. 6-Bromo-5-chloro-2-benzoxazolinone. (Maumee) Vinyzene.
Use: Local anti-infective.

BROMEBRIC ACID. B.A.N. cis-3-Bromo-3-p-anisoylacrylic acid.
Use: Cytotoxic agent.
See: Cytembena sodium salt

• **BROMELAINS.** USAN. A concentrate of proteolytic enzymes derived from pineapple plant, *Ananas comosus*.
Use: Oral depolymerizing enzyme; anti-inflammatory, antiedema.
See: Ananase, Tab. (Rorer)

BROMENZYME. (Barth's) Bromelain 40 mg./Tab. Bot. 100s, 250s, 500s.
Use: Digestive aid.

BROMEPAPH ELIXIR. (Quality Generics) Brompheniramine maleate 4 mg., phenylephrine HCl 5 mg., phenylpropanolamine HCl 5 mg., alcohol 2.3%/5 cc. Bot. pt., gal.

BROMEPAPH EXTENDED-ACTION TABLETS. (Quality Generics) Brompheniramine maleate 12 mg., phenylephrine HCl 15 mg., phenylpropanolamine HCl 15 mg./Tab. Bot. 100s, 1000s.

BROMETHOL.
See: Avertin

BROMEZYME. (Barth's) Bromelain 40 mg., papaya fruit, papain enzyme/Tab. Bot. 100s, 250s, 500s.

BROMFED CAPSULES. (Muro) Brompheniramine maleate 12 mg., pseudoephedrine HCl 120 mg./TR Cap. Bot. 100s, 500s.
Use: Nasal antihistamine, decongestant.

BROMFED-PD CAPSULES. (Muro) Brompheniramine maleate 6 mg., pseudoephedrine HCl 60 mg./TR Cap. Bot. 100s.
Use: Nasal antihistamine, decongestant.

BROMFED TABLETS. (Muro) Brompheniramine maleate 4 mg., pseudoephedrine HCl 60 mg./Tab. Bot. 100s.
Use: Nasal antihistamine, decongestant.

BROMHEXINE. B.A.N. N-(2-Amino-3,5-dibromobenzyl)-N-cyclohexylmethylamine.
Use: Bronchial mucolytic.
See: Bisolvon hydrochloride.

• **BROMHEXINE HCl.** USAN. (1) 3,5-Dibromo-Nα-cyclohexyl-Nα-methyltoluene-α,2-diamine monohydrochloride. (2) N-cyclohexyl-N-methyl-(2-amino-3,-5-dibromobenzyl) ammonium chloride.
Use: Expectorant; mucolytic.
See: Bisolvon (Boehringer Ingelheim)

BROMIDES.
See: Lanabrom, Elix. (Lannett)
Neurosine, Liq., Tab. (Dios)
Peacocks Bromides, Liq. (Natcon)

■ **BROMIDE SALTS.**
See: Calcium Bromide
Ferrous Bromide
Potassium Bromide
Sodium Bromide
Strontium Bromide

BROMI-LOTION. (Gordon) Aluminum hydroxychloride 20%. in emollient base. Bot. 1.5 oz., 4 oz.
Use: Antiperspirant.

• **BROMINDIONE.** USAN. 2-(4-Bromophenyl)(2)2-(p-Bromophenyl)-1,3-indandione.
Use: Anticoagulant.
See: Circladin

BROMISOVALUM. α-Bromoisovaleryl urea. (Premo) Pow. Bot. 1 oz., 0.25 & 1 lb. Tab. (5 gr.) Bot. 100s, 1000s.
W/Acetaminophen, salicylamide.
See: Sedalgesic Tablets (Table Rock)
W/Acetylcarbromal, acetaminophen.
See: Isomel, Cap. (Reid-Provident)
Vannor, Cap. (Vortech)
W/Acetylcarbromal, scopolamine aminoxide HBr.
See: Tranquinal, Tab. (Barnes-Hind)
W/Carbromal.
See: Bro-T's, Tab. (Brothers)

BROMI-TALC. (Gordon) Pot. alum, bentonite, talc. Shaker can 3.5 oz., 1 lb., 15 lb.
Use: Bromidrosis, hyperhidrosis.

2-BROMO-2-CHLORO-1,1,1-TRIFLUOROETHANE.
See: Halothane, U.S.P. XXI.

• **BROMOCRIPTINE.** USAN. 2-Bromo-α-ergocryptine.
Use: Prolactin inhibitor.
See: Parlodel, Tab. (Sandoz)

• **BROMOCRIPTINE MESYLATE.** USAN.
Use: Enzyme inhibitor.

• **BROMOCRIPTINE MESYLATE,** U.S.P. XXI. Tab., U.S.P. XXI.
Use: Prolactin inhibitor.

BROMOCYCLEN. B.A.N. 5-Bromomethyl-1,2,3,4,7,7-hexachloronorborn-2-ene.
Use: Insecticide; acaricide, veterinary medicine.
See: Alugan.

BROMODIETHYLACETYLUREA.
See: Carbromal.

2-(p-BROMO-α-(2-(DIMETHYLAMINO)-ETHYL BENZYL)PYRIDINE MALEATE (1:1)
See: Brompheniramine Maleate, U.S.P. XXI.
Dexbrompheniramine Maleate, U.S.P. XXI.

BROMODIPHENHYDRAMINE. B.A.N. N-2-(4-Bromobenzhydryloxy)ethyldimethylamine. Bromazine (I.N.N.)
Use: Antihistamine.

• **BROMODIPHENHYDRAMINE HCl,** U.S.P. XXI. Caps., Elix., U.S.P. XXI. 2-[(4-Bromophenyl)phenmethoxy]-N,N-dimethyl-, hydrochloride. 2-(p-Bromo-α-phenylbenzyl)oxy)-N,N-dimethylethylamine hydrochloride. Ethanamine.
W/Combinations.
See: Ambenyl Prods. (Marion)

BROMOFROM. Tribromomethane.

BROMOISOVALERYL UREA. Alpha, bromoisovaleryl urea.
See: Bromisovalum

2-((p-BROMO-α-PHENYLBENZYL)OXY)-N,N-DIMETHYLETHYLAMINE HYDROCHLORIDE
Bromodiphenhydramine hydrochloride, U.S.P. XXI.

BROMOPHIN.
See: Apomorphine HCl (Various Mfr.)

BROMO QUININE COLD TABLETS.
See: BQ Cold Tablets (Bristol-Myers)

BROMO-SELTZER. (Warner-Lambert) Acetaminophen 325 mg., sodium bicarbonate 2.78 Gm. and citric acid 2.22 Gm. which when dissolved, forms sodium citrate 2.85 Gm./Dose. Lg. (2⅝ oz.), King (4.25 oz.), Giant (9 oz.), Foil pack, single dose 48s.
Use: Effervescent antacid, analgesic.

8-BROMOTHEOPHYLLINE W/2-amino-2-methyl-1-propanol.
See: Pamabrom

BROMOTHEOPHYLLINATE AMINOISOBUTANOL.
See: Pamabrom

BROMOTHEOPHYLLINATE PYRILAMINE.
See: Pyrabrom

BROMOTHEOPHYLLINATE PYRANISAMINE.
See: Pyrabrom

• **BROMOXANIDE.** USAN.
Use: Anthelmintic.

• **BROMPERIDOL.** USAN.
Use: Antipsychotic.

BROMPHENIRAMINE. B.A.N. 3-(4-Bromophenyl)-3-(2-pyridyl)propyldimethylamine.
Use: Antihistamine.
See: Dimotane hydrogen maleate

BROMPHENIRAMINE EXPECTORANT. (Quality Generics) Brompheniramine maleate 2 mg., guaifenesin 100 mg., phenylephrine HCl 5 mg., phenylpropanolamine HCl 5 mg., alcohol 3.5%/5 ml. Syr. Bot. pint, gal.
Use: Expectorant.

• **BROMPHENIRAMINE MALEATE,** U.S.P. XXI. Elix., Inj., Tabs., U.S.P. XXI. 2-{p-Bromo-α-[2-di-methylamino)ethyl]-benzyl]}-pyridine maleate.
Use: Antihistaminic.
See: Dimetane, Tab., Elixir, Inj. (Robins)
Histapp Prods. (Upsher-Smith)
Rolabromophen, Tab. (Robinson)
Rolabromophen Decongestant Elixir (Robinson)
Rolabromophen Elixir (Robinson)
Rolabromophen Expectorant (Robinson)
Rolabromophen Forte, Tab. (Robinson)

Rolabromophen Injection (Robinson)
Rolabromophen Timed, Tab. (Robinson)
Symptom 3, Liq. (Parke-Davis)
Veltane (Lannett)

)MPHENIRAMINE MALEATE /COMBINATIONS.
ee: Bro-Expectorant W/Codeine, Liq. (Reid-Provient)
Bromapapp, Cap. (Zenith)
Bromepaph, Preps. (Quality Generics)
Brompheniramine Expect. Syr. (Quality Generics)
Bro-Tane, Liq. (Scrip)
Bro-Tapp, Liq. (Scrip)
Cortane, Preps. (Standex)
Cortapp, Elix. (Standex)
Dimetane Decongestant, Tab., Elix. (Robins)
Dimetane Expectorant, Liq. (Robins)
Dimetane Expectorant-DC, Liq. (Robins)
Dimetapp Extentabs, Elix. (Robins)
Eldatapp, Tab., Liq. (Elder)

OMTAPP. (Blue Cross) Brompheniramine maleate mg., phenylephrine HCl 5 mg., henylpropanolamine HCl 5 mg./5 ml. Bot. 16 oz., al.
Jse: Antihistaminic, decongestant.

ONCAJEN. (Jenkins) Pyrilamine maleate 10 mg., henylephrine HCl 2 mg., potassium guaiacol sulfonate 2 gr., ammonium chloride 2 gr., ipecac 1/8 r./Tab. Bot. 1000s.

ONCHIAL SYRUP. (Eckerd) Potassium uaiacolsulfonate 200 mg., alcohol 5%./5 cc. **DM:** otassium guaiacol sulfonate 200 mg., dextronethorphan HBr 15 mg./5 cc. Bot. pt. Bot. 8 oz.

ONCHIAL SYRUP DM. (Eckerd) Guaifenesin 150 ng., dextromethorphan H Br 15 mg./Dose. Bot. 4 oz., 8 oz.
Jse: Expectorant, cough syrup.

ONCHOHIST. (Sutliff & Case) Guaifenesin 250 ng., phenylephrine HCl 25 mg., chlorpheniramine maleate 6 mg., Sod. citrate 280 mg./Fl. Oz. Bot. 1 pt., 1 gal.
Use: Orally, non-narcotic antihistamine expectorant.

ONCHOLATE CAPSULES. (Bock) Ephedrine HCl 12.5 mg., guaifenesin 200 mg./Cap.
Use: Expectorant, bronchodilator.

ONCHOLATE SYRUP. (Bock) Ephedrine HCl 6.25 mg., guaifenesin 100 mg./5 ml.
Use: Bronchodilator.

ONCHOVENT. (Mills) Aminophylline 90 mg., guaifenesin 50 mg., amobarbital 16 mg./coated Tab. Bot. 100s.
Use: Bronchodilator, expectorant, sedative.

ONCOL. (Pasadena Research) Guaiacol 0.1 Gm., iodoform 0.02 Gm. camphor 0.05 Gm., eucalyptol 0.08 Gm., benzyl alcohol 2%/ 2 cc. Vial 30 cc.
Use: Liquefacient expectorant for intramuscular injection.

ONDECON. (Parke-Davis) **Tab.:** Oxtriphylline 200 mg., guaifenesin 100 mg./Tab. Bot. 100s. **Elix.** Oxtriphylline 100 mg., guaifenesin 50 mg./5 ml., w/alcohol 20%. Bot. 8 oz., 16 oz.
Use: Expectorant-bronchodilator.

BRONICOF. (Jenkins) Ethylmorphine HCl 2.5 mg., syrup hydriodic acid 50%, pot. citrate 438 mg., sod. benzoate 10 mg., aromatics/5 cc. Bot. 3 oz., 4 oz., gal.
Use: Cough sedative and expectorant.

BRONITIN. (Whitehall) Theophylline hydrous 130 mg., guiafenesin 100 mg., ephedrine HCl 24.3 mg., pyrilamine maleate 16.6 mg./Tab. Bot. 18s, 50s.
Use: Bronchodilator.

BRONKAID MIST. (Winthrop Consumer Products) Epinephrine 0.5%. Each spray releases 0.25 mg. epinephrine. Bot. 0.5 oz., 3/4 oz.
Use: Treatment of bronchial asthma.

BRONKAID MIST SUSPENSION. (Winthrop Consumer Products) Epinephrine bitartrate 0.7%. Each spray releases 0.3 mg. epinephrine bitartrate equiv. to 0.16 mg. epinephrine base. Bot. 10cc.
Use: Treatment of bronchial asthma.

BRONKAID TABLETS. (Winthrop Consumer Products) Ephedrine sulfate 24 mg., guaifenesin 100 mg., theophylline 100 mg./Tab. Box 24s, 60s.
Use: Bronchial congestion and bronchial asthma.

BRONKASMA TABLETS. (Winthrop Products) Theophylline anhydrous, ephedrine sulphate, thenyldiamine.
Use: Antiasthmatic.

BRONKEPHRINE. (Winthrop-Breon) Ethylnorepinephrine HCl 2 mg./ml. in a sterile isotonic sol. sod. chloride 0.7% w/sod. acetone bisulfite 0.2% and sod. hydroxide or HCl to adjust pH to 2.9-4.5. Amp., 1. ml. Box, 25s.
Use: S.C., I.M., bronchodilator in bronchial asthma.

BRONKODYL. (Winthrop-Breon) Theophylline 100 mg., 200 mg./Cap. Bot. 100s.
Use: Bronchodilator.

BRONKOLATE "G". (Parmed) Dyphylline 200 mg., guaifenesin 200 mg./Tab. Bot. 100s, 1000s.
Use: Bronchodilator, expectorant.

BRONKOLIXIR. (Winthrop-Breon) Guaifenesin 50 mg., ephedrine sulfate 12 mg., theophylline 15 mg., phenobarbital 4 mg./5 cc. Bot. pt.
Use: Bronchodilater.

BRONKOMETER. (Winthrop-Breon) Isoetharine mesylate 0.61% w/ saccharin, menthol and alcohol 30%. Metered dose in fluoro hydrocarbon propellant. Bot. w/nebulizer 10 ml., 15 ml., 20 ml. Refill 10 ml. 15 ml., 20 ml.
Use: Bronchodilator.

BRONKOSOL. (Winthrop-Breon) Isoetharine HCl 1% in aqueous glycerin sol. for oral inhalation. Bot. 10 ml., 30 ml.
Use: Bronchodilator.

BRONKOSOL UNIJET. (Winthrop-Breon) Isoetharine HCl inhalation 0.25% in sterile aqueous sol. for oral inhalation w/sodium Cl., citric acid, sodium hydroxide, acetone sodium bisulfite. Unijet 2 ml. Box 10s.
Use: Bronchodilator.

BRONKOTABS. (Winthrop-Breon) Ephedrine sulf. 24 mg., theophylline 100 mg., guaifenesin 100 mg., phenobarb. 8 mg./Tab. Bot. 100s, 1000s.
Use: Bronchodilator.

BRONKOTUSS. (Hyrex) Chlorpheniramine maleate 4 mg., guaifenesin 100 mg., ephedrine sulfate 8.216 mg., hydriodic acid syrup 1.67 mg./5 ml. W/alcohol 5% Bot. 16 oz., 128 oz.
Use: Expectorant.

BRONOPOL. B.A.N. 2-Bromo-2-nitropropane-1,3-diol.
Use: Antiseptic; preservative.

BRON-SED. (Southern Pharm.) Ephedrine HCl 20 mg., pyrilamine maleate 12.5 mg., pot. iodide 15 mg., fl. ext. Ipecac 0.25 min., phenobarbital 1/6 gr./5 cc. Elixir. Bot. pt.
Use: Bronchodilator.

• **BROPERAMOLE.** USAN.
Use: Anti-inflammatory.

BROSERPINE. (Brothers) Reserpine 0.25 mg./Tab. Bot. 250s, 1000s.

BRO-T'S. (Brothers) Bromisovalum 0.12 Gm., carbromal 0.2 Gm./Tab. Bot. 100s, 1000s.
Use: Sedative, tranquilizer.

BROTANE EXPECTORANT. (Blue Cross) Guaifenesin 100 mg., brompheniramine maleate 2 mg., phenylephrine HCl 5 mg., phenylpropanolamine HCl 5 mg./5 ml. w/alcohol 3.5% Bot. 16 oz.
Use: Expectorant, antihistaminic, decongestant.

BRO-TANE EXPECTORANT. (Scrip) Brompheniramine maleate 2 mg., guaifenesin 100 mg., phenylephrine HCl 5 mg., phenylpropanolamine HCl 5 mg./5 ml. Bot. 4 oz.

BRO-TAPP ELIXIR. (Scrip) Brompheniramine maleate 4 mg., phenylephrine HCl 5 mg., phenylpropanolamine 5 mg./5 ml. Bot. 4 oz.

BROTIANIDE. B.A.N. 2-Bromo-4-chloro-6-(4-bromophenylthiocarbamoyl)phenyl acetate.
Use: Anthelmintic, veterinary medicine.

• **BROTIZOLAM.** USAN.
Use: Hypnotic.

BRO-TUSS. (Brothers) Dextromethorphan HBr 15 mg., chlorpheniramine maleate 2 mg., phenylephrine HCl 5 mg., ammonium Cl 100 mg., sod. citrate 150 mg., Vit. C 30 mg./10 cc. Bot. 4 oz., pt., gal.

BRO-TUSS A.C. (Brothers) Acetaminophen 120 mg., codeine phosphate 10 mg., phenylephrine HCl 5 mg., chlorpheniramine maleate 2 mg., menthol 1 mg., alcohol 10%/5 cc. Bot. pt., gal.

BRUCELLA VACCINE. Undulant fever vaccine.
Use: I.M., S.C., undulant fever.

BRYAN'S ELIXIR. (Howze) Multivitamin and mineral supplement. Bot. 4 oz., pt.
Use: For vitamin deficiency.

BRYREL SYRUP. (Winthrop Products) Piperazine citrate anhydrous 110 mg./ml. Bot. 1 oz.
Use: Anthelmintic.

B-SCORBIC. (Pharmics) Vit. C 400 mg., B-1 25 mg., B-2 10 mg., B-12 2 mcg., calcium pantothenate 10 mg., nicotinamide 50 mg., hesperidin 200 mg./Ta Bot. 100s, 1000s.
Use: Vitamin supplement.

BSS PLUS. (Alcon) Balanced salt solution with bicarbonate dextrose, glutathione. Two part solution: Part I contains 480 ml., Part II (20 ml. V mixed within 6 hrs. of surgery.
Use: Intraocular irrigating solution

• **BUCAINIDE MALEATE.** USAN.
Use: Cardiac depressant.

BUCETIN. B.A.N. N-3-Hydroxybutyryl-p-phenetidine.
Use: Analgesic.

BUCHU.
See: Barosmin

• **BUCINDOLOL HYDROCHLORIDE.** (USAN) A Me Johnson investigational drug.
Use: Investigative: antihypertensive.

BUCLADIN-S. (Stuart) Buclizine HCl 50 mg., Soft Tab. Bot. 100s.
Use: Prevention and treatment of nausea, vomitin and dizziness associated with motion sickness.

BUCLIZINE. B.A.N. 1-(4-t-Butylbenzyl)-4-(4-chlorobe hydryl)piperazine.
Longifene and Vibazine dihydrochloride.
Use: Antiemetic.

• **BUCLIZINE HYDROCHLORIDE.** USAN. 1-(p-t Butylbenzyl)-4-(p-chloro-alpha-phenylbenzyl) pipe zine dihydrochloride.
See: Bucladin-S, Tab. (Stuart)

BUCLOSAMIDE. B.A.N. N-Butyl-4-chlorosalicyl-amid
Use: Antimycotic.

• **BUCRYLATE.** USAN.
Use: Surgical aid.

• **BUDESONIDE.** USAN.
Use: Anti-inflammatory.

• **BUFACET.** (Jenkins) Acetylsalicylic acid 3.5 gr., acetophenetidin 2.5 gr., caffeine alkaloid 0.5 gr., aromatics and buffered w/alum. hydroxide gel./Tab. Bot. 1000s.
Use: Analgesic.

BUF ACNE CLEANSING BAR. (3M Products) Salicylic acid 1%, sulfur 1%, in detergent cleansin bar, 3.5 oz.
Use: Acne treatment.

BUF BODY SCRUB. (3M Products) Round cleansing sponge on plastic handles.
Use: Cleansing hard to reach parts of the body.

BUFEXAMAC. B.A.N. 4-Butoxyphenylacetohydroxam acid.
Use: Anti-inflammatory.
See: Droxaryl.

BUFF-A. (Mayrand) Aspirin acid 5 gr./Tab. buffered mixture of magnesium hydroxide and aluminum hydroxide dried gel. Bot. 100s, 1000s.
Use: Analgesic.

BUFFACETIN. (Kay) Aspirin 3.5 gr., phenacetin 2.5 gr., caffeine 0.5 gr./Tab. Bot. 100s, 500s, 1000s.
Use: Analgesic.

BUFF-A-COMP. (Mayrand) **Tab.:** Aspirin 648 mg., ca feine 40 mg., butalbital 50 mg./Tab. **Cap.:** Butalbit

50 mg., aspirin 325 mg., caffeine 40 mg./Cap. Bot. 100s.
Use: Analgesic, antipyretic.

FF-A-COMP NO. 3. (Mayrand) Butalbital 50 mg., aspirin 325 mg., caffeine 40 mg., codeine phosphate 30 mg./Tab. Bot. 100s.
Use: Analgesic.

FFAPRIN. (Buffington) Aspirin 325 mg./Tab. Buffered with magnesium oxide. Sugar, lactose and salt free. Dispens-A-Kit 500s.
Use: Buffered analgesic, antipyretic, anti-inflammatory.

FFAPRIN EXTRA. (Buffington) Aspirin 500 mg./Tab. Buffered with magnesium oxide. Sugar, lactose and salt free. Dispens-A-Kit 500s.
Use: Extra strength buffered aspirin analgesic, antipyretic, anti-inflammatory.

JFFASAL. (Dover) Aspirin 325 mg./Tab. w/ magnesium oxide. Sugar, lactose and salt free. Unit dose Box 500s.
Use: Buffered analgesic, antipyretic, anti-inflammatory.

JFFASAL MAX. (Dover) Aspirin 500 mg./Tab. w/ magnesium oxide. Sugar, lactose and salt free.
Use: Extra strength buffered analgesic, antipyretic, anti-inflammatory.

UFFERIN CAPSULES. (Bristol-Myers) Aspirin 325 mg./Cap. buffered with magnesium carbonate, magnesium oxide, calcium carbonate. Bot 30s, 50s, 75s.
Use: Analgesic.

UFFERIN EXTRA STRENGTH CAPSULES. (Bristol-Myers) Aspirin 500 mg./Cap buffered with magnesium carbonate, magnesium oxide, calcium carbonate. Bot. 24s.,50s., 75s.
Use: Analgesic.

UFFERIN EXTRA STRENGTH TABLETS. (Bristol-Myers) Aspirin 500 mg./Tab. buffered with magnesium carbonate, aluminum glycinate. Bot. 30s, 60s, 100s.
Use: Analgesic.

UFFERIN TABLETS. (Bristol-Myers) Aspirin 325 mg./Tab. buffered with aluminum glycinate, magnesium carbonate. Bot. 12s, 36s, 60s, 100s, 165s, 225s, 375s. Industrial 200 × 2s, 1000s.
Use: Mild analgesic.

UFFERIN WITH CODEINE. (Bristol) Codeine phosphate 30 mg., aspirin 325 mg., aluminum glycinate 48.6 mg., magnesium carbonate 97.2 mg./Tab. Bot. 100s.
Use: Analgesic.

UFFETS II. (Bowman) Aspirin 226 mg., acetaminophen 162 mg., caffeine 32.4 mg./Tab. Bot. 100s, 1000s.
Use: Analgesic, antipyretic.

UFFINOL. (Otis Clapp) Aspirin 325 mg./Tab. buffered with magnesium oxide. Sugar, lactose and salt free. Safety packs 500s. Bot. 100s. Aidpaks 100s. Unit boxes 20s. Medipaks 200s.
Use: Buffered analgesic, antipyretic.

BUFFINOL EXTRA. (Otis Clapp) Aspirin 500 mg./Tab. Sugar, lactose and salt free. Safety packs 500s.
Use: Extra strength buffered analgesic, anti-pyretic, anti-inflammatory agent.

BUF FOOT CARE KIT. (3M Products) Cleansing system for the feet.
Use: Cleansing and moisturizing feet.

BUF FOOT CARE LOTION. (3M Products) Moisturizing lotion for feet.
Use: Foot moisturizer.

BUF FOOT CARE SOAP. (3M Products) Bar 3.5 oz.
Use: Foot cleanser.

• **BUFILCON A.** USAN.
Use: Contact lens material.

BUF KIT FOR ACNE. (3M Products) Cleansing sponge, cleansing bar 3.5 oz. w/booklet, holding tray.
Use: Cleansing system for acne.

BUF LOTION. (3M Products) Moisturizing lotion.
Use: Moisturizer.

BUFOPTO ATROPINE. (Softcon) Atropine 0.5%, 1% in a vehicle (Methulose) methylcellulose, benzalkonium chloride 1:10,000 as preservative, w/monobasic sod. phosphate, dibasic sod. phosphate, & sod. chloride. Dropper Bot. 15 ml.

BUFOPTO ZINC SULFATE. (Softcon) Zinc sulfate 0.25% in benzalkonium chloride solution, 1:25,000 as preservative. Dropper Bot. 0.5 oz., 1 oz.
Use: Eye anti-infective.

• **BUFORMIN.** USAN. 1-Butylbiguanide. Silubin.
Use: Oral hypoglycemic agent.

BUFOSAL. (Table Rock) Sod. salicylate 15 gr./Dr. w/cal. carb. & sod. bicarb. as granulated effer. Bot. 4 oz.
Use: Orally, analgesic & antipyretic.

BUF-OXAL. (3M Products) Benzoyl peroxide 5% or 10%. Tube 2 oz.
Use: Topical treatment of acne, pimples, blemishes.

BUF-PED NON MEDICATED CLEANSING SPONGE. (3M Products) Abrasive cleansing sponge.
Use: Cleansing skin on feet.

BUF PUF BODYMATE. (3M Products) Oval two-sided cleansing sponge. Abrasive/gentle.
Use: Cleansing all areas of the body.

BUF-PUF NON MEDICATED CLEANSING SPONGE. (3M Products) Abrasive cleansing sponge.
Use: Skin cleansing.

BUFROLIN. B.A.N. 6-Butyl-1,4,7,10-tetrahydro-4,10-dioxo-1,7-phenanthroline-2,8-dicarboxylic acid.
Use: Treatment of allergic airway obstruction.

BUFS. (Moore Kirk) Acetylsalicylic acid 3.5 gr., phenacetin 2.5 gr., caffeine 0.5 gr./Tab. Bot. 100s, 1000s.
Use: Relief of pain in simple headache, neuralgia, and common cold.

BUF-SUL TABLETS AND SUSPENSION. (Sheryl) 167 mg. of each sulfacetamide, sulfadiazine & sulfamerazine. Tab. 100s, Susp. pt.
Use: Antibacterial.

BUF-TABS. (Blue Cross) Aspirin 5 gr./Tab. w/aluminum hydroxide, glycine magnesium carbonate. Bot. 100s.
Use: Analgesic.

BUFURALOL. B.A.N. 2-tert-Butylamino-1-(7-ethylbenzofuran-2-yl)ethanol.
Use: Beta adrenergic blocking agent.

BUFYLLINE. B.A.N. Theophylline compound with 2-amino-2-methylpropan-1-ol (1:1).
Use: Bronchodilator.
See: Ambuphylline

BUGS BUNNY. (Miles) Vit. A 2500 I.U., E 15 I.U., C 60 mg., folic acid 0.3 mg., B-1 1.05 mg., B-2 1.2 mg., niacin 13.5 mg., B-6 1.05 mg., B-12 4.5 mcg., D 400 I.U./Tab. Bot. 60s, 100s.
Use: Multivitamin supplement.

BUGS BUNNY CHEWABLE VITAMINS AND MINERALS. (Miles) Vit. A 5000 I.U., D 400 I.U., E 30 I.U., C 60 mg., folic acid 0.4 mg., B-1 1.5 mg., B-2 1.7 mg., niacin 20 mg., B-6 2 mg., B-12 6 mcg., biotin 40 mcg., pantothenic acid 10 mg., iron 18 mg., calcium 100 mg., phosphorus 100 mg., iodine 150 mcg., magnesium 20 mg., manganese 2.5 mg., zinc 15 mg./Tab. Bot 60s.
Use: Chewable multivitamin with minerals.

BUGS BUNNY PLUS IRON. (Miles) Vit. A 2500 I.U., E 15 I.U., C 60 mg., folic acid 0.3 mg., B-1 1.05 mg., B-2 1.2 mg., niacin 13.5 mg., B-6 1.05 mg., B-12 4.5 mcg., D 400 I.U., iron 15 mg./Tab. Bot. 60s, 100s.
Use: Multivitamin supplement with iron.

BUGS BUNNY WITH EXTRA C. (Miles) Vit. A 2500 I.U., D 400 I.U., E 15 I.U., C 250 mg., folic acid 0.3 mg., B-1 1.05 mg., B-2 1.20 mg., niacin 13.50 mg., B-6 1.05 mg., B-12 4.5 mcg./Tab. Bot. 60s.
Use: Chewable multivitamin supplement with extra vitamin C.

BU LBORO POWDER. (Herbert) Aluminum sulfate, calcium acetate 1.9 Gm./Pkt. Ctn. 12s, 100s.
Use: Astringent soaking solution.

BULKOGEN. A mucin extracted from the seeds of *Cyanopsis tetragonaloba.*

• **BUMETANIDE.** USAN. 3-Butylamino-4-phenoxy-5-sulfamoylbenzoic acid.
Use: Diuretic.
See: Bumex, Tab. (Roche)

• **BUMETRIZOLE.** USAN.
Use: Ultraviolet screen.

BUMEX. (Roche) Bumetanide 0.5 mg. or 0.1 mg./Tab. Bot. 100s, 500s. Tel-E-Dose 30s. Ampuls 2 ml., 0.25 mg./ml. Box 10s.
Use: Potent diuretic.

BUMINATE. (Hyland) Normal serum Albumin (Human) **25%** solution in 20 ml. w/o administration set, 50 ml. and 100 ml. w/administration set; **5%** sol in 250 ml. and 500 ml. with administration set.

BUMINTEST REAGENT TABLETS. (Ames) Sulfosalicylic acid in effer. tab. Tab., Bot. 100s.
Use: Test for albumin in urine.

BUN REAGENT STRIPS. (Ames) Seralyzer reagent strips. Bot. 25s.
Use: A quantitative strip test for BUN in serum or plasma.

BUNAMIDINE. B.A.N. NN-Dibutyl-4-hexyloxy-1-naphthamidine
Use: Anthelmintic, veterinary medicine.
See: Buban hydroxynaphthoate
Scolaban hydrochloride

• **BUNAMIDE HYDROCHLORIDE.** USAN.
Use: Anthelmintic.

BUNAMIODYL SODIUM. Sodium 3-butyramido-α-eth-2,4,6-triiodocinnamate.
Use: Diagnostic aid (radiopaque medium).

BUNIODYL. B.A.N. 3-(3-Butyramido-2,4,6-triiodophenyl)-2-ethylacrylic acid. Bunamiodyl (I.N.N.)
Use: Radio-opaque substance.
See: Orabilix sodium salt

• **BUNOLOL HCl.** USAN. (±)-5-[3-(tert)-butylamino)-2-hydroxypropoxy]-3,4-dihydro-1-(2H)-naphthalenone hydrochloride.
Use: Antiadrenergic (β-receptors).

BUPHENINE. B.A.N. 1-(4-Hydroxyphenyl)-2-(1-methyl-3-phenylpropylamino)propan-1-ol.
Use: Peripheral vasodilator.
See: Perdilatal hydrochloride

• **BUPICOMIDE.** USAN.
Use: Antihypertensive.

BUPIVACAINE. B.A.N. 1-Butyl-2-(2,6-xylylcarbamoyl)piperidide. 1-Butyl-2′,6′-pipecoloxylidide. (Abbott) 0.5% Soln. Amp 20 ml.
Use: Local anesthetic.

• **BUPIVACAINE AND EPINEPHRINE INJECTION,** U.S.P. XXI.
See: Marcaine w/Epinephrine, Inj. (Winthrop-Breon)

• **BUPIVACAINE HYDROCHLORIDE,** U.S.P. XXI. Inj. U.S.P. XXI. 2-piperidinecarboxamide, 1-butyl-N-(2, 6-dimethylphenyl)-, monohydrochloride, monohydrate.
Use: Local anesthetic.
See: Marcaine, Injectable (Winthrop-Breon)
Sensorcaine, Inj. (Astra)

BUPRENEX INJECTION. (Norwich Eaton) Buprenorphine HCl 0.3 mg./ml. Amp. 1.0 ml.
Use: Parenteral opiate analgesic.

BUPRENORPHINE. B.A.N. N-Cyclopropylmethyl-7,8-dihydro-7α-(1-(S)-hydroxy-1,2,2-trimethylpropyl)-O^6-methyl-6,14-endoethanonormorphine.
Use: Analgesic.
See: Buprenex, Inj. (Norwich Eaton)

• **BUPRENORPHINE HYDROCHLORIDE.** USAN.
Use: Analgesic.

• **BUPROPION HYDROCHLORIDE.** USAN.
Use: Antidepressant.

• **BUQUINOLATE.** USAN. Ethyl 4-hydroxy-6,7-diisobutoxy-3-quinolinecarboxylate.
Use: Coccidiostat for poultry.

• **BURAMATE.** USAN. 2-Hydroxyethyl benzylcarbamate. Hyamate.
Use: Anti-convulsant, tranquilizer.
See: Hyamate (Xttrium)

BURDEO. (Hill) Aluminum subacetate 100 mg., boric acid 300 mg./Oz. Bot. 3 oz. Roll-on 8 oz.
Use: Deodorant.

ıLESON RECTAL OINTMENT. (Burleson) Phenol, nc oxide, zinc stearate, boric acid, eucalyptol, ınolin, white petrolatum. Tube 2 oz.
'se: Temporary relief of itching and discomfort due) hemorrhoids and rectal problems.

ꟼNATE. (Burlington) Vit. A 4000 I.U., D-2 400 I.U., ıiamine HCl 3 mg., riboflavin 2 mg., niacinamide 0 mg., pyridine HCl 2 mg., cyanocobalamin 5 ıcg., calcium pantothenate 0.5 mg., folic acid 0.4 ıg., ascorbic acid 50 mg., ferrous fumarate 300 ıg., calcium 200 mg., iodine 0.15 mg., copper 1 ıg., magnesium 5 mg., zinc 1.5 mg. Tab. Bot. 00s.
Jse: Prenatal Vitamin.

RN GON. (Edward J. Moore) Benzocaine, cod liver ıil, boric acid, lanolin. Tube 1.25 oz.
Jse: Burn and first aid ointment.

URN THERAPY.
See: Americaine, Prep. (Arnar-Stone)
Amertan, Jelly (Lilly)
Burn-A-Lay, Cream (Ken-Gate)
Burnicin, Oint. (Quality Generics)
Burn-Quel, Aerosol (Halperin)
Butesin Picrate Oint. (Abbott)
Foille, Prep. (Carbisulphoil)
Kip, Prep. (Youngs Drug Prod.)
Nupercainal, Oint. (Ciba)
Silvadene, Cream (Marion)
Solarcaine, Prep. (Plough)
Sulfamylon, Cream (Winthrop-Breon)
Unguentine, Prep. (Norwich)

RN-A-LAY. (Ken-Gate) Chlorobutanol 0.75%, oxy-quinoline benzoate 0.025%, zinc oxide 2%, thymol).5%. Cream. Tube 1 oz.
Jse: Burn remedy.

RN-QUEL. Halperin Aerosol dispenser. 1 oz., 2 oz.
Jse: Burn therapy.

RNTAME SPRAY. (Otis Clapp) Benzocaine, 8-hy-droxyquinoline. Aerosol can 2.5 oz.
Use: Anethetic/antiseptic burn spray.

R-OIL-ZINC. (Durel) Zinc oxide, talcum, lanolin, olive oil, Burow's solution. Bot. 4 oz., pt., gal.
Use: Generalized and widespread eczematous eruptions, acute and subacute inflammatory processes, exfoliative dermatitis.

R-OIL-ZINC LOTION PLUS. (Durel) Menthol 0.25%, phenol 0.5% added to Bur-oil-zinc comp. Bot. 4 oz., pt., gal.
Use: Antipruritic.

RO-SOL ANTISEPTIC POWDER. (Doak) Contents make a dilute Burow's Sol.—aluminum acetate topical sol. plus benzethonium chloride. Pkg. (2.36 Gm.) 12s, 100s. Bot. Pow. 4 oz., 1 & 5 lb.

ROW'S SOLUTION. Aluminum Acetate Topical Solution, U.S.P. XXI.
See: Buro-Sol, Cream, Pow. (Doak)
Domeboro, Pow., Tab. (Miles Pharm)
/Boric acid, acetic acid.
See: Star-Otic, Drops (Star)

BURSUL. (Burlington) Sulfamethiazole 500 mg./Tab. Bot. 100s.
Use: Sulfa-specific urinary inf.

BUR-TUSS. (Burlington) Chlorpheniramine maleate 2 mg., phenylepherine HCl 5 mg., phenylpropanolamine HCl 5 mg., guaifenesin 100 mg., alcohol 2.5%/5 cc. Bot. Pt., Gal.
Use: Expectorant.

BUR-ZIN. (Lamond) Aluminum acetate solution 2%, zinc oxide 10%. Bot. 4 oz., 8 oz., pt., qt., gal. Also w/o lanolin.
Use: Treatment of eczema, pruritic conditions, irritated skin.

• **BUSERELIN ACETATE.** USAN.
Use: Gonad-stimulating principle.

• **BUSPAR TABLETS.** (Mead Johnson) Buspirone HCl 5 mg. or 10 mg./Tab.
Use: Anti-anxiety.

• **BUSPIRONE HYDROCHLORIDE.** USAN.
Use: Anti-anxiety.
See: BuSpar, Tab. (Mead Johnson)

• **BUSULFAN,** U.S.P. XXI. Tabs. U.S.P. XXI. Tetramethylene dimethanesulfonate. 1-4-Dimethanesulphonyloxybutane. 1,4-Butanediol dimethane-sulfonate.
Use: Chronic myeloid leukemia.
See: Myleran, Tab. (Burroughs Wellcome)

BUSULPHAN. B.A.N. Tetramethylene di(methanesulphonate).
Use: Antineoplastic agent.
See: Myleran

• **BUTABARBITAL,** U.S.P. XXI 5-sec-Butyl-5-ethylbarbituric acid.
Use: Sedative, hypnotic.
See: BBS, Tab. (Reid-Provident)
Butisol, Prods. (McNeil)
Da-Sed, Tab. (Sheryl)
Expansatol, Caps. (Merit)
Medarsed, Elixir, Tab. (Medar)
W/Acetaminophen.
See: Coastalgesic, Tab. (Coastal)
G-3, Tab. (Hauck)
Sedapap, Elixir (Mayrand)
Sedapap-10, Tab. (Mayrand)
W/Acetaminophen, & codeine phosphate.
See: Coastaldyne, Tab. (Coastal)
G-3, Cap. (Hauck)
W/Acetaminophen, mephenesin.
See: T-Caps, Cap. (Burlington)
W/Acetaminophen, phenacetin, caffeine.
See: Windolor, Tab. (Winston)
W/Acetaminophen, salicylamide, phenyltoloxamine citrate.
See: Dengesic, Tab. (Scott-Alison)
Scotgesic, Cap., Elixir (Scott/Cord)
W/Acetysalicylic acid, phenacetin, caffeine, hyoscyamine sulfate, codeine phosphate.
See: Butadeine, Cap. (Sutliff & Case)
W/Ambutonium bromide, aluminum hydroxide, mag. hydroxide.
See: Aludrox, Susp., Tab. (Wyeth)

W/Aminophylline, phenylpropanolamine HCl, chlorpheniramine maleate, aluminum hydroxide, magnesium trisilicate.
See: Asmacol, Tabs. (Vale)
W/Amobarbital.
See: Butatrax, Caps. (Sutliff & Case)
W/Carboxyphen.
See: Bontril Timed No. 2, Tab. (G. W. Carnrick)
W/Chlorpheniramine maleate, hyoscine hydrobromide.
See: Pedo-Sol, Tab., Elixir (Warren Pharmacal)
W/Dihydroxypropyl theophylline, ephedrine HCl.
See: Airet R, Tabs. (Baylor Labs.)
W/Ephedrine sulfate, theophylline.
See: Asmabar, Tabs. (Bluline)
W/Ephedrine sulfate, theophylline.
See: Airet Y, Tab., Elix. (Baylor)
W/Ephedrine HCl, theophylline, guaifenesin.
See: Quibron Plus, Cap., Elix. (Mead Johnson)
W/Ephedrine HCl, theophylline, isoproterenol.
W/Ephedrine sulfate, theophylline, guaifenesin.
See: Broncholate, Cap., Elix. (Bock)
W/l-Hyoscyamine.
See: Cystospaz-SR, Caps. (Webcon)
Levamine, Tabs., Caps. (Meyer)
W/Hyoscyamine sulfate, atropine sulfate, hyoscine HBr, homatropine methylbromide.
See: Butabell HMB, Tabs., Elix. (Saron)
W/Hyoscyamine sulfate, scopolamine methylnitrate, atropine sulfate.
See: Banatil, Cap., Elixir (Trimen)
W/Nitroglycerin.
See: Nitrodyl-B, Cap. (Bock)
W/Pentaerythritol tetranitrate.
See: Petn Plus (Saron)
W/Pentobarbital & phenobarbital.
See: Quiess, Tab. (O'Neal)
Triple Barbiturate Elixir (CMC)
W/Phenazopyridine & hyoscyamine HBr.
See: Pyridium Plus, Tab. (Parke-Davis)
W/Phenazopyridine, scopolamine HBr, atropine sulfate, hyoscyamine sulfate.
See: Buren, Tab. (Ascher)
W/Phenobarbital, pentobarbital, hyoscyamine sulfate, hyoscine hydrobromide, atropine sulfate.
See: Neoquess, Tab. (O'Neal)
W/Salicylamide.
See: Dapco, Tab. (Mericon)
W/Secobarbital.
See: Monosyl, Tab. (Arcum)
W/Secobarbital, pentobarbital phenobarbital.
See: Quad-Set, Tab. (Kenyon)
W/Theophylline.
See: Theobid, Cap. (Meyer)
W/Theophylline, pseudoephedrine HCl.
See: Asmadil, Cap. (Reid-Provident)
Ayr, Liq. (Ascher)
Ayrcap, Cap. (Ascher)
Az-Kap, Cap. (Keene)
B. A., Prods. (Federal)
Bronchobid, Duracap (Meyer)

• **BUTABARBITAL SODIUM.** U.S.P. XXI. Caps., Elix., Tabs., U.S.P. XXI. Sod. 5-sec-butyl-5-ethylbarbiturate.
Use: Sedative & hypnotic.
See: BBS, Tab. (Reid-Provident)
Butalan, Elix. (Lannett)
Butazem, Tab., Elix. (Zemmer)
Buticaps, Cap. (McNeil)
Butisol Sodium, Elixir, Tab. (McNeil)
Expansatol, Cap. (Merit)
Quiebar, Spantab, Tab (Nevin)
Renbu, Tab. (Wren)
Soduben Tab., Elxr. (Arcum)
W/Acetaminophen.
See: Amino-Bar, Tab. (Bowman)
Minotal, Tabs. (Carnrick)
W/Acetaminophen, aspirin, caffeine.
See: Dolor Plus, Tab. (Geriatric)
W/Acetaminophen, caffeine.
See: Dularin-TH, Tab. (Donner)
Phrenilin, Tab. (Carnrick)
W/Acetaminophen, mephenesin, codeine phosphate
See: Bancaps-C, Cap. (Westerfield)
W/Acetaminophen, phenacetin, caffeine anydrous
See: Butigetic, Tab. (McNeil)
W/Acetaminophen, salicylamide.
See: Banesin Forte, Tab. (Westerfield)
Indogesic, Tab. (Century)
W/Acetaminophen, salicylamide, d-amphetamine sulfate, hexobarbital, secobarbital sod., phenobarbital.
See: Sedragesic, Tab. (Lannett)
W/Aluminum hydroxide dried gel, Mg glycinate, Pow ext. belladonna leaf.
See: Bellabarbital Buffered, Cap. (Consol.-Midland
W/d-Amphetamine sulfate.
See: Bontril, Tab. (Carnrick)
W/Ascorbic acid, Sod. p-aminobenzoate, salicylamic Sod. salicylate.
See: Bisalate, Tab. (Allison)
W/Atropine sulfate, hyoscyamine HBr, alcohol, hyoscine HBr.
See: Hyonatol Tab., Hyonatol B Elixir, Hexett, Tab (Bowman)
W/Belladonna ext.
See: Butibel, Tab., Elix. (McNeil)
Quiebel, Elixir, Cap. (Nevin)
W/Belladonna ext., enzymes, & iron oxbile.
See: Butibel-zyme, Tab. (McNeil)
W/Dehydrocholic acid, belladonna extract.
See: Decholin-BB, Tabs. (Miles Pharm)
W/Hyoscine HBr, hyoscyamine sulfate, atropine sulfate.
See: Zemarine, Elix., Tab., Cap. (Zemmer)
W/Methscopolamine bromide, aluminum hydroxide g dried & Mag. trisilicate.
See: Eulcin, Tab. (Leeds)
W/Pentaerythritol tetranitrate.
See: Covap, Tab. (Blue Line)
Perbuzem, Tab. (Zemmer)
W/Pentobarbital sod., phenobarbital sod.
See: Trio-Bar, Tab. (Jenkins)
W/Phenobarbital sod. acetaminophen, phenacetin, caffeine.
See: Two-Dyne, Tab. (Key)

Salicylamide, mephenesin.
See: Metrogesic, Tab. (Metro)
Secobarbital sodium.
See: Monosyl, Tab. (Arcum)
Secobarbital sod., pentobarbital sod. & phenobarbital.
See: Nidar, Tab. (Armour)
Quadrabarb, Tab. (Vortech)
Secobarbital Sodium & phenobarbital.
See: S.B.P., Tab. (Lemmon)
Simethicone, hyoscyamine sulfate, atropine sulfate, hyoscine HBr.
See: Sidonna, Tab. (Reed & Carnrick)
Theophylline, pseudoephedrine HCl.
See: Dilorbron, Cap. (Hauck)
TABELL HMB. (Saron) Butabarbital 15 mg., hyoscyamine sulfate 0.1037 mg., atropine sulfate 0.0194 mg., hyoscine HBr 0.0065 mg./Tab. Bot. 100s, 1000s.
TACAINE.
Use: Surface anesthetic.
See: Butyn Dental Oint. (Abbott).
TACAINE SULFATE. 1-Propanol,3-(dibutylamino)-,4-aminobenzoate (ester), sulfate (salt) (2:1). 3-(Dibutylamino)-1-propanol, p-aminobenzoate (ester) sulfate (2:1). Various manufacturers.
Use: Surface anesthetic.
BUTACETIN. USAN. 4'-Tert-butoxyacetanilide.
Use: Analgesic.
BUTACLAMOL HYDROCHLORIDE. USAN.
Use: Antipsychotic.
BUTAGEN CAPS. (Goldline) Phenylbutazone 100 mg./Cap. Bot. 100s, 500s.
Use: Analgesic, anti-inflammatory agent.
TALAMINE. B.A.N. 5-(2-Dibutylaminoethyl)-amino-3-phenyl-1,2,4-oxadiazole.
Use: Vasodilator.
BUTALBITAL, U.S.P. XXI. 5-Allyl-5-isobutyl-barbituric acid. Allylbarbituric Acid.
Use: Sedative.
See: Buff-A-Comp #3 (Mayrand)
Lotusate, Cap. (Winthrop-Breon)
Sandoptal, Prep. (Sandoz)
W/Acetaminophen, caffeine.
See: Esgic, Tab. (Gilbert)
W/Acetaminophen, phenacetin, caffeine.
See: Arbutal, Tab. (Arcum)
Buff-A-Comp, Tab.-Cap. (Mayrand)
Cefinal, Tab. (Alto)
Protension, Tab. (Blaine)
Repan, Tab. (Everett)
W/Aspirin, phenacetin, caffeine.
See: Duogesic, Cap. (Western Research)
Fiorinal, Cap., Tab. (Sandoz)
W/Aspirin, phenacetin, caffeine, codeine phosphate.
See: Buff-A-Comp, Tab w/Codeine. (Mayrand)
Fiorinal With Codeine, Cap. (Sandoz)
W/Caffeine, aspirin, acetaminophen.
See: Anaphen, Cap. (Mallard)
W/Caffeine, aspirin, aluminum hydroxide.
See: Kengesin, Tab. (Kenwood)
W/Phenacetin, aspirin, caffeine.
See: Arbutal, Tab. (Arcum)
• **BUTALBITAL AND ASPIRIN TABLETS,** U.S.P. XXI.
Use: Analgesic, sedative.
BUTALGIN.
See: Methadone HCl (Various Mfr.)
BUTALAN ELIXIR. (Lannett) Sodium butabarbital 0.2 Gm./30 cc. Bot. pt., gal.
Use: Sedative.
BUTALIX. (Vale) Alcohol 10%, sod. butabarbital 200 mg./Fl. oz. Bot. pt., gal.
BUTALLYLONAL. 5-(2-Bromoallyl)-5-sec-butylbarbituric acid. (Pernocton)
Use: Hypnotic.
• **BUTAMBEN,** U.S.P. XXI. Benzoic acid, 4-amino-,butyl ester. Butyl p-aminobenzoate.
Use: Anesthetic, local.
• **BUTAMBEN PICRATE.** USAN.
Use: Topical anesthetic.
See: Butesin Picrate, Oint. (Abbott)
• **BUTAMIRATE CITRATE.** USAN.
Use: Antitussive.
• **BUTAMISOLE HYDROCHLORIDE.** USAN.
Use: Anthelmintic.
BUTAMYRATE. B.A.N. 2-(2-Diethylaminoethoxy)-ethyl 2-phenylbutyrate.
Use: Cough suppressant.
See: Sinecod citrate
• **BUTANE,** N.F. XVI.
BUTANEDIOIC ACID, MONO[2-[(2,2-DICHLOROACETYL) AMINO]-3-HYDROXY-3-(4-NITROPHENYL)PROPYL]ESTER, MONOSODIUM SALT. Chloramphenicol Sodium Succinate, U.S.P. XXI.
BUTANEDIOIC ACID,SULFO-, 1-4-BIS(2-ETHYLHEXYL)ESTER, SODIUM SALT. Docusate Sodium, U.S.P. XXI.
1,4-BUTANEDIOL DIMETHANESULFONATE. Busulfan, U.S.P. XXI.
BUTANILICAINE. B.A.N. 2-Butylamino-6'-chloroacet-o-toluidide.
Use: Local anesthetic.
BUTANISAMIDE. 1-Butyl-1-(o-methoxyphenyl) urea.
1-BUTANONE,4-[4-(4-CHLOROPHENYL-4-HYDROXYL-1-PIPERIDINYL]-1-(4-FLUOROPHENYL)-. Haloperidol, U.S.P. XXI.
• **BUTAPERAZINE.** USAN. 1-{ 10-[3-(4-Methyl-1-piperazinyl)propyl]phenothiazin-2-yl }-1-butanone.
Use: Psychotropic agent.
See: Repoise (Robins)
• **BUTAPERAZINE MALEATE.** USAN.
Use: Antipsychotic.
BUTAPHYLLAMINE. Ambuphylline. Theophylline aminoisobutanol. Theophylline with 2-amino-2-methyl-1-propanol.
BUTAPRO ELIXIR. (Approved) Butabarbital sod. 0.2 Gm./30 cc. Bot. pt., gal.
BUTATRAN. (Hauck) Butabarbital 0.5 gr./Tab. Bot. 100s.
Use: Sedative.
BUTATRAX. (Sutliff & Case) Amobarbital 20 mg., butabarbital 30 mg./Cap. Bot. 100s, 1000s.
Use: Sedative.

BUTAZEM. (Zemmer) Butabarbital sodium **Tab.:** 15 mg., 30 mg. 0.1 Gm./Tab. Bot. 100s, 1000s. **Elix.:** Bot. 3 oz., pt. gal.
Use. Sedative.

BUTAZOLIDIN CAPSULES. (Geigy) Phenylbutazone 100 mg./Cap. Bot. 100s, 1000s. Unit Dose 100s. Gy-Pak 100s.
Use: Analgesic, anti-inflammatory, antiarthritic and antipyretic.

BUTAZOLIDIN TABLETS. (Geigy) Phenylbutazone 100 mg./Tab. Bot. 100s, 1000s, Unit Dose 100s.
Use: Anti-inflammatory, analgesic, antipyretic and antiarthritic.

BUTAZONE. (Major) Phenylbutazone. **Cap.:** 100 mg./Cap. Bot. 100s, 500s. **Tab.:** 100 mg./Tab. Bot. 500s.
Use: Anti-inflammatory, analgesic.

BUTELLINE.
See: Butacaine Sulfate (Various Mfr.)

2-BUTENEDIOIC ACID,(E)-,IRON(2+)-SALT. Ferrous Fumarate, U.S.P. XXI.

• **BUTERIZINE.** USAN.
Use: Vasodilator.

BUTESIN PICRATE. n-Butyl-p-aminobenzoate. Butamben picrate.

BUTESIN PICRATE OINTMENT. (Abbott) Contains 1% butamben picrate. Tube 1 oz.
Use: Minor burns of various kinds—electrical, steam, hot metal & scalds.

BUTETHAL. (Various Mfr.) 5-Ethyl-5-butylbarbituric acid.
Use: Sedative & hypnotic.

BUTETHAMATE. B.A.N. 2-Diethylaminoethyl 2-phenylbutyrate.
Use: Antispasmodic.

BUTETHAMINE FORMATE. 2-Isobutyl aminoethyl-p-aminobenzoate formate.

BUTETHAMINE HYDROCHLORIDE. 2-(Isobutylamino) ethyl-p-amino benzoate HCl.
See: Dentocaine (Amer. Chem. & Drug)

BUTETHANOL.
See: Pontocaine Phydrochloride, Preps. (Winthrop-Breon)

BUTHALITONE SODIUM. B.A.N. A mixture of 100 parts by weight of the monosodium derivative of 5-allyl-5-isobutyl-2-thiobarbituric acid and 6 parts by weight of dried sodium carbonate.
Use: Hypnotic; sedative.
See: Transithal
Ulbreval

• **BUTHIAZIDE.** USAN. 6-Chloro-3, 4-dihydro-3-isobutyl-2H-1,2,4-benzothiadiazine-7-sulfonamide 1,1-dioxide.
Use: Diuretic, antihypertensive

BUTIBEL Tab. and Elixir. (Wallace) Butabarbital sod. 15 mg., belladonna ext. 15 mg./Tab. or 5 cc. **Tab.** Bot. 100s. **Elixir** (alcohol 7%), Bot. pt.
Use: Antispasmodic and sedative combination for G.I. disorders.

BUTIBEL-ZYME. (McNeil Pharm) Butabarbital Sod. 15 mg., belladonna ext. 15 mg., proteolytic enzyme 10 mg., amylolytic enzyme 20 mg., cellulolytic enzyme 5 mg., lipolytic enzyme 100 mg., iron ox bile 30 mg./Tab. Bot. 100s.
Use: Digestive aid.

BUTICAPS. (Wallace) Butabarbital sodium 15 mg., mg./Cap. Bot. 100s.
Use: Sedative and hypnotic.

• **BUTIKACIN.** USAN.
Use: Antibacterial.

• **BUTIFENIN.** USAN.
Use: Diagnostic aid.

• **BUTIROSIN SULFATE.** USAN. A mixture of the sulfates of the A and B forms of an antibiotic produced by *Bacillus circularis.*
Use: Antibacterial.

BUTISOL SODIUM. (Wallace) Butabarbital sodium. **Elixir:** 30 mg/5cc. Bot pt., gal. **Tab:** 15 mg., 30 mg., 50mg. or 100mg. Bot. 100s, 1000s.
Use: Intermediate sedative & hypnotic.
See: Buticaps, Cap. (Wallace)
W/Belladonna ext.
See: Butibel, Tab. and Elixir. (Wallace)
W/Belladonna ext., digestive enzymes & iron oxbile
See: Butibel-Zyme, Tab. (McNeil)

• **BUTIXIRATE.** USAN.
Use: Analgesic, antirheumatic.

• **BUTOCONAZOLE NITRATE.** USAN.
Use: Antifungal.

BUTOLAN. Benzylphenyl carbamate.

• **BUTONATE.** USAN.
Use: Anthelmintic.

• **BUTOPAMINE.** USAN.
Use: Cardiotonic.

BUTOPYRONOXYL. (Indalone) Butyl mesityl oxide.
Use: Insect repellant, used in Comp. Dimethyl Phthalate Solution.

• **BUTORPHANOL.** USAN.
Use: Analgesic, antitussive.

• **BUTORPHANOL TARTRATE,** U.S.P. XXI. Inj., U.S.P. XXI.
Use: Analgesic.
See: Stadol, Inj., (Bristol)

BUTOXAMINE. B.A.N. (±)-erythro-1-(2,5-Dimethoxphenyl)-2-t-butylaminopropan-1-ol.
Use: Inhibitor of fatty acid mobilization.

• **BUTOXAMINE HCl.** USAN. α-[1-(Tertbutylamino thyl]-2,5-dimethoxybenzyl alcohol HCl.
Use: Oral hypoglycemic; antilipemic.

2-BUTOXY-N-(2-(DIETHYLAMINO)ETHYL)-CINCHONINAMIDE. Dibucaine, U.S.P. XXI.

BUTRIPTYLINE. B.A.N.DL-3-(10,11-Dihydro-5H-dibenzo[a,d]cycloheptene-5-yl)-2-methyl-propyldimethylamine.
Use: Antidepressant.

• **BUTRIPTYLINE HYDROCHLORIDE.** USAN. dl-11-Dihydro-N, N, β-trimethyl-5H-dibenzo (a,d)cycloheptene-5-propylamine hydrochloride.
Use: Antidepressant.

• **BUTYL ALCOHOL,** N.F. XVI. Butyl alcohol is *n*-bu alcohol.

BUTYL AMINOBENZOATE. n-Butyl p-Aminobenzoate. Scuroforme.
Use: Surface anesthetic.

enzocaine, tetracaine HCl.
ee: Cetacaine, Preps. (Cetylite)
enzyl alcohol, phenylmercuric borate, benzocaine.
ee: Dermathyn, Oint. (Davis & Sly)
rocaine, benzyl alcohol, in sweet almond oil
ee: Anucaine, Amp. (Calvin)
etracaine
ee: Pontocaine, Oint. (Winthrop-Breon)
TYLATED HYDROXYANISOLE, N.F. XVI. tert-
utyl-4-methoxyphenol.
se: Pharmaceutic aid (antioxidant).
YLATED HYDROXYANISOLE. B.A.N. 2-t-Butyl-
methoxyphenol.
se: Antioxidant.
TYLATED HYDROXYTOLUENE, N.F. XVI. 2.6-
-tert-butyl-P-cresol.
se: Pharmaceutic aid (antioxidant).
YLATED HYDROXYTOLUENE. B.A.N. 2,6-Di-t-
utyl-p-cresol.
se: Antioxidant.
JTYL-1,2-DIPHENYLPYRAZOLIDINE-3,5-DIONE.
henylbutazone, U.S.P. XXI.
YL p-HYDROXYBENZOATE. Butylparaben, N.F.
VI.
TYLPARABEN, N.F. XVI. Butyl p-Hydroxy-benzo-
e.
se: Pharmaceutical aid (antifungal preservative).
YLPHENAMIDE. N-n-butyl-3-phenyl-salicylamide.
YLPHENYLSALICYLAMIDE.
ee: Butylphenamide
JTYL-3-(p-TOLYLSULFONYL)UREA. Tolbut-
nide, U.S.P. XXI.
YN DENTAL OINTMENT. (Abbott) Butacaine 4%
nt. Tube 0.25 oz., 1 oz.
se: Relief of pain due to dentures.
TE. (Bluco) B-1 100 mg., B-2 2 mg., B-6 4 mg.,
acinamide 100 mg., d-penthenol 4 mg./cc. Vial 30
:.
se: B vitamin deficiency.
.
ee: Bromisovalum.
LOMINE. (Major) Dicyclomine. **Cap:** 10 mg./Cap.
ot. 250s, 1000s. **Tab.:** 20 mg./Tab. Bot. 250s,
00s.
se: Antispasmodic for irritable bowel.
A'S. (C.M.C.) Musculosine. Bot. 4¾ oz.

C

BADON-M. (Reid-Provident) Cyanocobalamin 1000
cg./cc. Vials 10 cc, 30 cc. I.M. or S.C.
ABUFOCON B. USAN.
se: Contact lens material.
CODYLIC ACID SALTS.
Ferric Salt
Iron Salt
Sodium Salt
ACTINOMYCIN. USAN. Dactinomycin 10%;
ctinomycin C_2 45% and actinomycin C_3 45%.
ctinomycin C.
se: Antineoplastic agent.
ee: Sanamycin (FBA Pharm.)

CADE OIL.
See: Juniper Tar

CADE OIL CREAM NO. 26. (Durel) Cade oil 3%, ammoniated mercury 2%, in Duromantel cream. Jars 1 oz., lb., 6 lb.
Use: Psoriasis vulgaris.

CADE OIL CREAM NO. 27. (Durel) Cade oil 5%, sulfur 5%, salicylic acid 3%, added to Duromantel cream. Jars 1 oz., lb., 6 lb.
Use: Psoriasis vulgaris, hyperkeratotic eczemas of the palms and soles.

CAD-O-BATH. (Durel) Oil of cade 35%, polysorbate "20" 35%. Bot. 8 oz., pt., gal.
Use: Generalized pruritus, pruritic dermatoses, psoriasis.

CAFATINE TABS. (Major) Ergotamine and caffeine. Bot. 250s.
Use: Migraine with tension & GI disturbances.

CAFEDRINE. B.A.N. L-7-[2-(β-Hydroxy-α-methylphenethylamino)ethyl]-theophylline.
Use: Analeptic.

CAFENOL. (Winthrop Products) Aspirin, caffeine.
Use: Analgesic.

CAFERGOT P-B SUPPOSITORIES. (Sandoz) Ergotamine tartrate 2 mg., caffeine 100 mg., bellafoline 0.25 mg., pentobarbital 60 mg./Suppos. Box 12s.
Use: Treatment of migraine with tension & gastrointestinal disturbances.

CAFERGOT P-B TABLETS. (Sandoz) Ergotamine tartrate 1 mg., caffeine 100 mg., bellafoline 0.125 mg., pentobarbital sodium 30 mg./Tab. SigPak dispensing pkg. of 90s, 250s.
Use: Migraine with tension & gastrointestinal disturbances.

CAFERGOT SUPPOSITORIES. (Sandoz) Ergotamine tartrate 2 mg., caffeine 100 mg. in cocoa butter base. Box 12s.
Use: Treatment of migraine.

CAFERGOT TABLETS. (Sandoz) Ergotamine tartrate 1 mg., caffeine 100 mg./S.C. Tab. Bot. 250s. SigPak dispensing pkg. of 90s.
Use: Treatment of migraine.

CAFERMINE P-B SUPPOSITORIES. (Goldline) Ergotamine tartrate, caffeine. Box 10s.
Use: Treatment of migraine headaches.

• **CAFFEINE,** U.S.P. XXI. 1H-Purine-2,6-dione, 3,-7-dihydro-1,3,7-trimethyl-xanthine. (Various Mfr.) Guaranine; Methyltheobromine; Thein.
Use: Cardiac, respiratory & psychic stimulant.
See: Enerjets, Loz. (Chilton)
Femicin, Tab. (Norcliff Thayer)
Nodoz, Tabs. (Bristol-Myers)
Stim 250, Cap. (Scrip)
Tirend (Norcliff-Thayer)
Vivarin, Tab. (J.B. Williams)

CAFFEINE CITRATED.
Use: Central nervous system stimulant.

CAFFEINE SODIO-BENZOATE.
See: Caffeine sod. benzoate

• **CAFFEINE SODIUM BENZOATE INJECTION,** U.S.P. XXI. Approximately equal parts of caffeine and sod. benzoate. (Various Mfr.) Amp. (3¾ & 7.5

gr.) 2 cc., Box 12s, 100s. Hypo Tab. (1 gr.) Tube 20s, 100s & Pow.
Use: Orally & I.M. Central nervous system stimulant.

CAFFEINE SODIUM SALICYLATE. (Various Mfr.) Bot. 1 oz.; Pkg. 0.25 lb., 1 lb.
Use: See caffeine.

CAFFEINE-THEOPHYLLINE COMPOUND, w/Nux Vomica Ext.
See: Xanthinux, Tab. (Cole)

CAFFIN-T.D. (Kenyon) Caffeine 250 mg./Cap. Bot. 100s.

CAG. (Western Research) Calcium gluconate 1004 mg./Tab. Bot. 1000s.
Use: Supplement.

CAGOL. (Harvey) Guaiacol 0.1 Gm., eucalyptol 0.08 Gm., iodoform 0.2 Gm., camphor 0.05 Gm./2 cc. in olive oil. Vial 30 ml.
Use: I.M., expectorant.

20-CAIN BURN RELIEF. (Alto) Benzocaine 20%, benzyl alcohol 2.3%, urea 5.38%, p-chloro-m-xylenol 0.51%, propylene glycol 71.81%. Spray Bot. 6 oz.
Use: Relief from sunburn, minor burns, nonvenomous insect bites, and itching from minor skin irritations.

CALADRYL. (Parke-Davis) 1% Benadryl HCl in specially prepared calamine base. **Cream;** tube, 1.5 oz., Bot. 6 oz. Plastic Squeeze Bot. 2.5 oz.
Use: Antihistaminic & antipruritic.

CALAFORMULA. (Eric, Kirk & Gary) Ferrous gluconate 130 mg., calcium lactate 130 mg., Vit. A 1000 I.U., D 400 I.U., B-1 2 mg., B-2 2 mg., niacinamide 5 mg., ascorbic acid 20 mg., folic acid 0.130 mg., Mg 0.250 mg., Cu 0.250 mg., Zn 0.250 mg., Mn 0.250 mg., K 0.075 mg./Cap. Bot. 50s, 100s, 500s, 1000s, 5000s.
Use: Prenatal dietary supplement.

CALAFORMULA WITH AMPHETAMINE. (Eric, Kirk & Gary) Calaformula with amphetamine sulfate 5 mg./Cap. Bot. 100s.
Use: Control appetite.

CALAFORMULA F. (Eric, Kirk & Gary) Calaformula plus fluorine 0.333 mg./Tab. Bot. 100s.
Use: Protect against decay of teeth.

CALAHIST LOTION. (Walgreen) Diphenhydramine HCl 1%, calamine 8.1%, camphor 0.1%. Bot. 6 oz.
Use: Antihistamine & antipruritic.

CALAMATUM. (Blair) **Lotion** Zinc oxide, calamine, benzocaine 3%. Bot. 3¾ oz. **Oint.** Zinc oxide, calamine, phenol, camphor, benzocaine. Tube 1.5 oz.
Use: Relief of minor skin irritations.

CALAMATUM AEROSOL SPRAY. (Blair) Benzocaine 3% w/zinc oxide, calamine, phenol, camphor. Spray Can 3 oz.
Use: Relief of minor skin irritations.

• **CALAMINE,** U.S.P. XXI. Lotion, Phenolated Lotion, U.S.P. XXI. (Various Mfr.) Iron oxide mixture with zinc oxide.
Use: Astringent and mild antiseptic.

CALAN. (Searle) Verapamil HCl 80 mg. or 120 mg./Tab. Bot. 100s, Unit Dose 100s. mg./Tab. Bot. 100s, 500s, 1000s. Unit Dose 100s.
Use: Calcium antagonist, antianginal, antiarrhythmic.

CALAN I.V. (Searle) Verapamil HCl. **Amp.:** 5 mg./2 ml. Ctn. 10s. **Vial:** 5 mg./2 ml. 10 mg./4 ml. Ctn. 5s, 10s. **Syringe:** 5 mg./2 ml. 10 mg./4 ml. Ctn. 5s, 10s.
Use: Antiarrhythmic.

CALBRODEX. (Pasadena Research) Calcium gluconate 0.5 Gm., strontium Br 0.5 Gm., dextro 1 Gm./10 cc. Amp. for IV use. 25s, 100s.

CAL-C-BATE. (Kay) Calcium gluconate 700 mg., cium lactate 300 mg., dextrose 500 mg., Vit. C 1 gm./10 cc. 25/10 ml. ampules. I.V.
Use: Calcium deficiencies.

CALCEE. (Pasadena Research) Calcium gluconate 350 mg., calcium lactate 150 mg., dextrose 250 mg., ascorbic acid 500 mg./5 cc. amp. 25s, 100s Amp. 10 cc. 25s, 100s.

CALCET. (Mission) Calcium lactate 240 mg. calcium gluconate 240 mg., calcium carbonate 240 mg., calcium 152.8 mg., Vit. D-2 100 u./Tab. Bot. 100
Use: Dietary supplement.

CALCIBIND. (Mission) Sodium cellulose phosphate 2.5 Gm./Packet. Box 90s.
Use: Absorptive hypercalciuria.

CALCICAPS. (Nion) Calcium 750 mg., phosphorus 360 mg., Vit. D 300 I.U./6 Tab. Bot. 100s, 500s.
Use: Dietary supplement.

CALCICAPS-FOUR. (Nion) Sugar free. Calcium [illegible] mg., Vit D 400 I.U./4 Tab. Bot. 100s.
Use: Dietary supplement.

CALCICAPS WITH IRON. (Nion) Calcium 750 mg., phosphorus 360 mg., Vit. D 400 I.U., ferrous gluconate 384 mg./6 Tab. Bot. 100s, 500s.
Use: Dietary supplement.

CALCICAPS, SUPER. (Nion) Calcium 334 mg., phosphorus 41.7 mg., Vit. D 133 I.U./Tab. Bot. 100s.
Use: Dietary supplement.

CALCIDE. (Blue Line) Available iodine in combinati with lime and starch 0.2 gr./Tab. Bot. 1000s.

CALCIDRINE SYRUP. (Abbott) Codeine 8.4 mg., c iodide anh. 152 mg. alcohol 6%/5 ml. Bot. 4 oz. pt., gal.
Use: Treatment of cough due to colds.

• **CALCIFEDIOL,** U.S.P. XXI. Caps., U.S.P. XXI.
Use: Calcium regulator.

CALCIFEROL. Ergocalciferol, U.S.P. XXI. Vitamin D-2, viosterol, synthetic vitamin D, irradiated erg terol, activated ergosterol.
Use: Vitamin D (Antirachitic).
See: Calciferol, Tab., Inj. (Kremers-Urban)
Calderol, Tab. (Upjohn)
Deltalin, Gelseal (Lilly)
Drisdol, Cap., Sol. (Winthrop-Breon)

CALCIFEROL DROPS. (Rorer) Ergocalciferol 8000 (0.2 mg.)/ml. or 200 U (0.5 mcg.)/drop. Bot. 60 w/dropper.
Use: Prevention Vit. D deficiency in infants, child & adults.

CALCIFEROL INJECTION. (Rorer) Ergocalciferol 500,000 U (12.5 mg.)/ml. Amp. 1 ml. Box 5s.
Use: Hypoparathyroidism & refractory rickets.

:IFEROL TABLETS. (Rorer) Ergocalciferol ,000 U (1.25 mg./Tab. Bot. 100s.
e: Hypoparathyroidism and refractory rickets.
:IGARDS. (Eckerd) Bot. 300s.
:IMAR INJECTION, SYNTHETIC. (USV Labs.) A lcitonin solution (Salmon origin) containing 200 ./ml. Vial 2 ml.
e: To lower bone reabsorption in Paget's ease, hypercalcemia and post menopausal teoporosis.
:IPARINE. (American Critical Care) Heparin lcium Injection. **5000** u/0.2 ml. prefilled syringe. x 10s. **12500** u/0.5 ml. Amp w/disposable ringe & needle. Box 10s. **20000** u/0.8 ml. Amp disposable syringe & needle. Box 10s.
e: IM, IV, or SC anticoagulant.
LCITONIN. USAN. Hormone from thyroid gland.
e: Plasma hypocalcemic hormone.
CITONIN SALMON.
e: Calcimar, Inj. (Armour)
LCITRIOL. USAN. 9, 10-seco (5Z, 7E)-5, 7, 10 (19)-olestatriene-1a, 3b, 25-triol.
e: Management of hypocalcemia in chronic renal alysis patients.
e: Rocaltrol, Cap. (Roche)
CIUM ACETYLSALICYLATE. Kalmopyrin, lsetal, soluble aspirin, tylcalsin.
e: As aspirin.
CIUM ALUMINUM CARBONATE.
l-Amino Acetate Complex.
e: Ancid Tablet and Suspension (Sheryl)
CIUM AMINOSALICYLATE. Aminosalicylate alcium, N.F. XVI.
CIUM AMPHOMYCIN.
e: Amphomycin.
LCIUM AND MAGNESIUM CARBONATES ABLETS, U.S.P. XXI.
e: Antacid.
CIUM 4-BENZAMIDOSALICYLATE. Calcium ninacyl B-PAS. Benzoylpas Calcium.
e: Benzapas, Pow., Tab. (Dorsey)
CIUM BENZAMIDOSALICYLATE. B.A.N. Calcium benzamido-2-hydroxybenzoate.
e: Treatment of tuberculosis.
CIUM BENZOYL-p-AMINOSALICYLATE.
e: Benzoylpas calcium
CIUM BENZOYLPAS.
e: Benzoylpas Calcium
CIUM BIS-DIOCTYL SULFOSUCCINATE.
e: Dioctyl Calcium Sulfosuccinate
CIUM CARBASPIRIN. F.D.A. Calcium salicylate acetate compound with urea.
riaminic.
e: Ursinus, Tab. (Dorsey)
LCIUM CARBONATE AND MAGNESIA ABLETS, U.S.P. XXI.
e: Antacid.
CIUM CARBONATE, AROMATIC. (Lilly) Calcium rbonate 10 gr./Tab. Bot. 100s, 1000s.
LCIUM CARBONATE, PRECIPITATED, U.S.P. XI. (Various Mfr.) Precipitated chalk; carbonic acid, lcium salt (1:1).
Use: Antacid.
See: Amitone, Tab. (Norcliff Thayer)
Biocal Prods. (Miles)
Cal-Sup, Tab. (Riker)
Dicarbosil, Tab. (Arch)
Mallamint, Tab. (Mallard)
Tums, Tab. (Norcliff Thayer)

CALCIUM CARBONATE W/COMB.
See: Accelerase, Cap. (Organon)
Alised, Tab. (Elder)
Alka-2, Tab. (Miles)
Alkalade, Susp., Tab. (DePree)
Alkets, Tab. (Upjohn)
Anti-Acid No. 1, Tab. (N. Amer. Pharm.)
Antacid pH, Tab. (Towne)
Antacin, Tab. (Reid-Provident)
Calsarbain, Tab. (Sutliff & Case)
Camalox, Tab., Susp. (Rorer)
Ca-Plus, Tab. (Miller)
Carbonates No. 3, Tab. (Noyes)
Co-Gel, Tab. (Arco)
Diatrol, Tab. (Otis Clapp)
Dimacid, Tab. (Otis Clapp)
Equilets, Tab. (Mission Pharm.)
Eugel, Susp., Tab. (Reid-Provident)
Gas-Eze, Tab. (Edward J. Moore)
Glytabs, Chew. Tab. (Pharmics)
Hycidol, Pow. (Mallard)
Iodized Lime, Tab. (Elder)
Kanalka, Tab. (Lannett)
Kaocasil, Tab. (Jenkins)
Lactocal, Tab. (Laser)
Marbien, Susp., Tab. (Fleming)
Maygel, Tab. (Century)
Natabec, Prep. (Parke-Davis)
Os-Cal 500, Tab. (Marion)
Os-Cal-Mone, Tab. (Marion)
Pan-Bis-Cal, Susp. (Noyes)
P.H. Tablets, Chewable (Scrip)
Pregent, Tab. (Beutlich)
Ratio, Tab. (Adria)
Spastosed, Tab. (N. Amer. Pharm.)
Titralac, Liq., Tab. (Riker)

• **CALCIUM CARBONATE ORAL SUSPENSION,** U.S.P. XXI.
Use: Antacid.
• **CALCIUM CARBONATE TABLETS,** U.S.P. XXI.
Use: Antacid.
CALCIUM CARBIMIDE. Calcium cyanamide.
CALCIUM CASEINATE.
See: Casec, Pow. (Mead Johnson)
CALCIUM CHEL 330. (Geigy).
Use: Heavy metal antagonist.
See: Calcium Trisodium Pentetate.
• **CALCIUM CHLORIDE,** U.S.P. XXI. Inj., U.S.P. XXI.
Use: Calcium replenisher.
• **CALCIUM CHLORIDE CA 45.** USAN.
Use: Radioactive agent.
• **CALCIUM CHLORIDE CA 47.** USAN.
Use: Radioactive agent.
• **CALCIUM CHLORIDE INJECTION.** U.S.P. XXI. (Upjohn) 1 Gm. Amp. 10 ml., 25s. (Torigian)1 Gm.

Amp. 10 ml. 12s, 25s, 100s. (Trent) 10% Amp. 10 ml. (Cutter) 13.6 mEq./10 ml. Vial.
Use: I.V., hypocalcemic tetany.
CALCIUM CYCLAMATE. Calcium cyclohexanesulfamate.
CALCIUM CYCLOBARBITAL. Calcium 5-(l-cyclohexen-l-yl)-5-ethylbarbiturate.
Use: Central depressant.
CALCIUM CYCLOHEXANESULFAMATE.
See: Calcium Cyclamate
CALCIUM DL-PANTOTHENATE. Calcium Pantothenate, Racemic, U.S.P. XXI.
CALCIUM 3-((DIMETHYLAMINO)METHYLENE)-AMINO)-2,4,6-TRIIODOHYDROCINNAMATE,
See: Calcium Ipodate.
CALCIUM DIOCTYL SULFOSUCCINATE. Docusate Calcium, U.S.P. XXI.
See: Surfak (Hoechst)
CALCIUM DISODIUM EDATHAMIL.
See: Edetate Calcium Disodium, U.S.P. XXI.
CALCIUM DISODIUM EDETATE. Edetate Calcium Disodium, U.S.P. XXI.
CALCIUM DISODIUM VERSENATE. (Riker) Calcium Disodium Edetate U.S.P. Amp. 1 gm./5 ml. in water for injection. Box 6s.
Use: I.V.; lead poisoning.
CALCIUM EDETATE SODIUM. Edetate Calcium Disodium, U.S.P. XXI.
CALCIUM EDTA.
See: Calcium Disod. Versenate, Amp., Tab. (Riker)
CALCIUM FOLINATE. B.A.N. Calcium N-[4-(2-amino-5-formyl-5,6,7,8-tetrahydro-4-hydroxy-pteridin-6-ylmethyl-aminobenzoyl]-L-glutamate.
Use: Antidote to folic acid antagonists.
See: Leucovorin Calcium
• **CALCIUM GLUBIONATE.** USAN. (1) (D-Gluconato) (lactobionato) calcium monohydrate; (2) Calcium D-gluconate lactobionate monohydrate.
Use: Calcium replenisher.
• **CALCIUM GLUCEPTATE,** U.S.P. XXI. (Lilly) Calcium salt of d-glucoheptonic acid represents 0.09 Gm. calcium (4.5 mEq.)/5 cc. Amp. 5 cc. 25s.
Use: Treatment of hypocalcemia.
• **CALCIUM GLUCEPTATE INJECTION,** U.S.P. XXI. (Abbott) Calcium gluceptate 1.1 Gm. containing 90 mg. Ca/5 ml. Abboject Syringe (22G × 1.5") 5 ml., Ampul 5 ml.
Use: Calcium therapy.
CALCIUM GLUCOHEPTONATE. (Various Mfr.) Cal. D-glucoheptonate O.
Use: Uncontrolled muscular spasms due to lack of calcium in blood.
• **CALCIUM GLUCONATE,** U.S.P. XXI. Injection, Tab., U.S.P. XXI. D-Gluconic acid, calcium salt.(2:1) **Inj.:** (Upjohn) Each 10 ml. provides 94.68 mg. (4.72 mEq.) of Ca. **Amp.** 10 ml.; **Tab.** 5 gr., 7.5 gr., 10 gr. or 15 gr.; **Wafers** 15 gr. (Various Mfr.)
W/Calcium ascorbate, benzyl alcohol, sodium bisulfite.
See: Cal-C-Bate, Amps. (Kay)
W/Vit. D (Lilly) Vit. D 660 u., cal. gluconate 1 Gm./Tab., Cal. gluconate 5 gr., Vit. D 330 u./Pulvule. Bot. 100s.
Use: Calcium and vitamin-D supplement.

CALCIUM GLYCEROPHOSPHATE. Neurosin. (Various Mfr.)
• **CALCIUM HYDROXIDE,** U.S.P. XXI. Topical Solution U.S.P. XXI.
Use: Astringent; pharm. necessity for calamine lotion.
CALCIUM HYPOPHOSPHITE. (N.Y. Quinine & Ch Works)
CALCIUM IODIDE.
W/Codeine phosphate.
See: Calcidrine Syrup (Abbott)
W/Chloral hydrate, ephedrine HCl.
See: Iophed, Syr. (Marsh-Emory)
CALCIUM IODIZED.
Cal-Lime #1, Tab. (Scrie)
W/Calcium creosotate.
See: Niocrese, Tab. (Noyes)
W/Ipecac, ext. hyoscyamus, ext. licorice.
See: Kaldifane, Tab. (Noyes)
CALCIUM IODOBEHENATE. Calioben. (Various M
CALCIUM IPODATE, Ipodate Calcium, U.S.P. XXI
See: Oragrafin Calcium, Granules (Squibb)
CALCIUM KINATE GLUCONATE. Kinate is hexahydrotetrahydroxybenzoate. Calcium Quina
• **CALCIUM LACTATE,** U.S.P. XXI. Tab., U.S.P. X Propanoic acid, 2-hydroxy-, calcium salt (2:1), drate. Tab. (Upjohn) 650 mg. (4.2 mEq.) Ca/Ta Bot. 100s.
Use: Calcium deficiency and prophylaxis.
W/Calcium glycerophosphate.
See: Calphosan, Amp., Vial (Carlton)
W/Ca glycerophosphate, phenol, sod. chloride solution.
See: Calpholac, Vial (Century)
Calphosan, Inj. (Brown)
W/Niacinamide, folic acid, ferrous gluconate, vitamins.
See: Pergrava No. 2, Cap. (Arcum)
W/Phenobarbital, ext. hyoscyamus, terpin hydrate guaifenesin.
See: Gylanphen, Tab. (Lannett)
W/Theobromine sodium salicylate, phenobarbital.
See: Theolaphen, Tab. (Elder)
W/Thiamine HCl.
See: Nycralan, Tab. (Lannett)
W/Zinc sulfate.
See: Zinc-220, Cap. (Alto)
CALCIUM LACTOPHOSPHATE. Lactic acid hydrc phosphate calcium salt.
CALCIUM LEUCOVORIN. Leucovorin Calcium, U. XXI.
Use: Overdosage folic acid antagonists.
• **CALCIUM LEVULINATE,** U.S.P. XXI. Inj., U.S.P. XXI. Pentanoic acid, 4-oxo-,calcium salt (2:1), drate. Amp. 10%.
Use: Calcium replenisher.
See: Calcium Levulinate, Pow. (City Chemical)
Levucal, Amp. (Kay)
CALCIUM MANDELATE. (Various Mfr.). Urisept (Grail)
Use: Orally, urinary antiseptic & acidifier.

CIUM NOVOBIOCIN. Calcium salt of an ıtibacterial substance produced by *Streptomyces veus.*
se: Antibiotic.
.CIUM OROTATE.
ee: Calora, Tab. (Miller)
.CIUM OXYTETRACYCLINE. Oxytetracycline alcium, N.F. XIV.
LCIUM PANTOTHENATE, U.S.P. XXI. Tab., .S.P. XXI. β-Alanine, N-(2,4-dihydroxy-3,3-dimethyl-oxobutyl)-,calcium salt (2:1). Vit. B-5. D(+)-N-lpha, gamma dihydroxy-beta,beta-dimethyl-butyryl)-eta aminopropionic acid, calcium salt, dextro form.
se: Vitamin B (enzyme co-factor).
ee: Liver-Iron B Complex With Vitamin B-12, inj. Maurry)
antholin, Tab. (Lilly)
Ascorbic acid, niacinamide, Vits. B-1, B-2, B-6, -12, A, D, E.
ee: Tota-Vi-Caps Gelatin Capsule, Cap. (Elder)
Calcium carbonate.
ee: Ilomel, Pow. (Warren-Teed)
Calcium carbonate, ferrous fumarate, niacinamide.
ee: Prenatag, Tab. (Reid-Provident)
Danthron.
ee: Modane, Tab., Liq. (Warren-Teed)
Parlax, Tab. (Parmed)
Docusate sodium.
ee: Pantyl, Tab. (McGregor)
Docusate sodium, acetphenolisatin.
ee: Android-Plus, Tab. (Brown)
Peri-Pantyl, Tab. (McGregor)
Methoscopolamine nitrate, mephobarbital.
ee: Ilocalm, Tabs. (Warren-Teed)
Niacin, vitamins.
ee: Hi-Bee, Cap. (Vortech)
Niacinamide and vitamins.
ee: Allbee C-800, Prods. (Robins)
Allbee T, Caps. (Robins)
Allbee with C, Caps. (Robins)
Ferrovite, Tab. (Laser)
Fumatinic, Tab. (Laser)
Maintenance Vitamin Formula, Tab. (Burgin-Arden)
Mulvidren, Tab. (Stuart)
OB-Tabs, Tab. (Laser)
Probec, Tab. (Stuart)
Probec-T, Tab. (Stuart)
Stuart Hematinic, Tab. (Stuart)
Stuart Therapeutic Multivitamin, Tab. (Stuart)
Therapeutic Vitamin Tablets, Tab. (Vortech)
Vita Cebus, Tab. (Cenci)
Niacinamide, B-1, B-2, B-6.
ee: Noviplex Capsules, Cap. (Elder)
B-1, niacinamide, B-2, B-6, B-12, Vit. B-12, choline hloride, inositol, dl-methionine, testosterone, es-rone, procaine.
ee: Gerihorm, Inj. (Burgin-Arden)
Vitamin complex, ferrous fumarate, folic acid.
alcium lactate, niacinamide.
ee: Vitanate, Tab. (Century)
W/Vit. A, D, B-1, B-2, C, niacinamide, calcium. phosphorus, iron, Vit. B-6, B-12, E, magnesium, manganese, potassium, zinc, choline bitartrate, inositol.
See: Geriatric Vitamin Formula, Tab. (Burgin-Arden)
W/Vitamin C, niacin zinc sulf., Vit. E, B-1, B-2, B-6, B-12.
See: Z-Bec, Tab. (Robins)
W/Vitamin complex and iron.
See: Vita-iron, Tab. (Century)
W/Vitamins and minerals, niacinamide.
See: Arcum-VM, Cap. (Arcum)
Capre, Tab. (Marion)
Orovimin, Tab. (Reid-Provident)
Os-Cal Forte, Tab. (Marion)
Os-Vim, Tab. (Marion)
Stuartinic, Tab. (Stuart)
Theramin, Tab. (Arcum)
Theron, Tab. (Stuart)
Uplex, Cap. (Arcum)
Vit-Min-I-Fact, Tab. (Sutliff & Case)
W/Vitamins, minerals, methyl testosterone, ethinyl estradiol, niacinamide.
See: Geritag, Cap. (Reid-Provident)
W/Vitamin complex, yeast, niacinamide, desiccated liver.
See: B-Complex, Cap. (Vortech)
W/Vit. C, niacinamide, zinc sulf., magnesium sulf., Vit. B-1, B-2, B-6.
See: Vicon-C, Cap. (Meyer)
W/Zinc sulf., niacinamide, magnesium sulf., manganese Cl, Vitamin complex.
See: Vicon Plus, Cap. (Meyer)
• **CALCIUM PANTOTHENATE, RACEMIC,** U.S.P. XXI. β-Alanine, N-(2,4-dihydroxy-3,3-dimethyl-1-oxo-butylO-, calcium salt (2:1), (±-Calcium DL-pantothenate (1:2).
Use: Vitamin B (enzyme co-factor).
See: Pantholin (Lilly)
• **CALCIUM PHOSPHATE, DIBASIC,** U.S.P. XXI. Tab., U.S.P. XXI.
See: Dicalcium Phosphate
Diostate D, Tab. (Upjohn)
CALCIUM PHOSPHATE, MONOCALCIUM.
See: Dicalcium Phosphate
• **CALCIUM PHOSPHATE, TRIBASIC,** N.F. XVI. (Various Mfr.)
CALCIUM-PHOSPHORUS-FREE.
See: Fosfree, Tab. (Mission)
• **CALCIUM POLYCARBOPHOL,** U.S.P. XXI.
Use: Cathartic.
CALCIUM PROPIONATE.
See: Propionate-caprylate mixtures.
CALCIUM QUINATE.
See: Calcium Kinate Gluconate
• **CALCIUM SACCHARATE,** U.S.P. XXI.
Use: Sweetening agent.
CALCIUM SACCHARIN. Saccharin Calcium, U.S.P. XXI.
Use: Sweetening agent.
CALCIUM SALICYLATE, THEOBROMINE.
See: Theocalcin, Tab., Pow. (Knoll)
CALCIUM SALTS OF SUGAR ACIDS.
See: Gluco-Calcium, Vial (Lilly)

• **CALCIUM SILICATE,** N.F. XVI. A compound of calcium oxide and silicon dioxide.

• **CALCIUM STEARATE,** N.F. XVI.
Use: Pharmaceutic aid (tablet lubricant).

CALCIUM SUCCINATE.
W/Aspirin.
See: Ber-Ex, Tab. (Dolcin)
Dolcin, Tab. (Dolcin)
W/Phenobarbital, salicylamide, Vit. C.
See: Calsuxaphen, Cap., Tab. (Lannett)

• **CALCIUM SULFATE,** N.F. XVI.
Use: Pharmaceutic aid (tablet diluent).

CALCIUM TRISODIUM PENTETATE. Calcium trisodium (carboxymethylimino)-bis(ethyl-enenitrilo) tetra-acetic acid.
Use: Heavy metal antagonist.
See: Calcium Chel 330 (Geigy)

CALCIUM TRISODIUM PENTETATE. B.A.N. Calcium chelate of the trisodium salt of diethylenetriamine-NNN′N″N″-penta-acetic acid.
Use: Chelating agent.

CALCIUM UNDECYLENATE.
See: Caldesene, Pow. (Pharmacraft)
Cruex Squeeze Pow. (Pharmacraft)

CALCIWAFERS. (Nion) Calcium 165 mg., Vit. D. 66.7 I.U./Wafer. Bot. 96s.
Use: Dietary supplement.

CALDECORT CREAM. (Pharmacraft) Hydrocortisone acetate equivalent to hydrocortisone 0.5% in cream base. Tube 0.5 oz., 1 oz.
Use: Antipruritic.

CALDECORT SPRAY. (Pharmacraft) Hydrocortisone acetate 0.5%. Aerosol can 1.5 oz.
Use: Antipruritic.

CALDEE. (Jenkins) Ascorbic acid (sodium ascorbate equiv. to 10 mg. Vit. C) 10 mg., Vit. D 200 I.U., dicalcium phosphate 7.5 gr., irradiated yeast/Tab. Bot. 1000s.
Use: Calcium deficiencies.

CALDEROL. (Organon) Calcifediol 20 mcg. or 50 mcg./Tab. Bot. 60s.
Use: Treatment of metabolic bone disease or hypercalcemia associated with chronic renal failure in renal dialysis patients.

CALDESENE. (Pharmacraft) **Oint:** Petrolatum 53.9%, zinc oxide 15%. Tube 1.25 oz. **Pow.:** calcium undecylenate 10%. Bot. 2 oz., 4 oz.
Use: Diaper rash, prickly heat, chafing.

CAL-D-MINT. (Enzyme Process) Calcium 800 mg., magnesium 150 mg., iron 18 mg., iodine 0.10 mg., copper 2 mg., Vit. D 200 I.U./2 Tab. Bot. 100s, 250s.
Use: Dietary mineral supplement.

CAL-D-PHOS. (Archer-Taylor) Dicalcium phosp. 4.5 gr., cal. gluconate 3 gr. w/D/Tab. Bot. 1000s.

CALEL-D. (USV Labs.) Calcium 500 mg., Vit. D 200 I.U./Tab. Bot. 60s.
Use: Dietary supplement.

CALFER-VITE. (Drug Industries) Ca 250 mg., iron 30 mg., Mn 2 mg., Cu 0.2 mg., Zn 1 mg., iodine 0.15 mg., niacinamide 20 mg., lemon bioflavonoid complex 25 mg., A 5000 I.U., D 400 I.U., C 75 mg., B-1 3 mg., B-2 3 mg., B-6 2 mg., B-12 2 mcg., pantothenate 5 mg./Tab. Bot. 100s, 500s, 1000s.
Use: Prenatal vitamin and mineral supplement.

CALICARB. (Jenkins) Calcium carbonate 0.25 Gm., magnesium carbonate 0.15 Gm., bismuth subnitr 60 mg., powd. ipecac 0.25 mg., aromatics/Tab. Bot. 1000s.
Use: Gastric hyperacidity.

CALICYLIC CREME. (Gordon) Salicylic acid 10% cream base. Jar. 2 oz.
Use: Removal of heavy callus.

CAL-IM. (Standex; Kenyon) Calcium glycerophosph 1%, calcium levulinate 1.5%. Vial 30 cc.

CALINATE-FA. (Reid-Provident) Calcium 250 mg., V 4000 I.U., D 400 I.U., B-1 3 mg., B-2 3 mg., B-6 5 B-12 1 mcg., folic acid 1 mg., C 50 mg., niacinam 20 mg., d-panthenol 1 mg., iron 60 mg., iodine (mg., manganese 0.2 mg., magnesium 0.2 mg., z 0.1 mg., copper 0.15 mg./Tab. Bot. 100s, 1000s.
Use: Prenatal dietary supplement.

CALIOBEN.
See: Calcium Iodobehenate

CALIVITE. (Apco) Ca carbonate 885 mg., Fe sulfa 199 mg., Vit. A 3600 I.U., D 400 I.U., C 75 mg., 1 1.5 mg., B-2 1.95 mg., B-6 0.75 mg., nicotinic 15 mg., Vit. B-12 activity 0.025 mcg., choline 1 mcg., inositol 2500 mcg., pantothenic acid 75 m folic acid 25 mcg., p-aminobenzoic acid 12 mcg., mg., Mg 1.0 mg., Zn 0.075 mg., Mn 0.02 mg., C 0.01 mg., Co 0.02 mcg./Tab. Bot. 100s.
Use: Dietary supplement and prenatal vitamin.

CAL-LIME-1. (Scrip) Calcium iodized 1 gr./Tab. 1000s.

CALMOL 4-SUPPOSITORIES. (Mentholatum) Z oxide in a cocoa butter-lanolin alcohol base. Box 24s.
Use: Rectal suppository that protects against irritation and trauma.

CALMOSIN. (Spanner) Cal. gluconate, strontium bromide. Ampul 10 cc. 100s.

CALOMEL. Mercurous chloride.
Use: Cathartic.

CALOR-AID. (American McGaw) Instant drink, high orie, protein-free dietetic aid.
Use: Dietary supplement.

CALOTABS, Reformulated. (Calotabs) Docusate sodium 100 mg., casanthranol 30 mg./Tab. Box 10s.
Use: Laxative.

CALOXIDE CREAM W/BENZOCAINE. (Blue Line) Calamine 10%, zinc oxide 10%, ethyl aminobenzoate (benzocaine) 3% in a water miscible base. Tube 1.5 oz.
Use: Topically, protective & antiseptic.

CALOXIDINE (IODIZED CALCIUM).
See: Calcium Iodized

CAL-NOR. (Vortech) Ca glycerophosphate 1%, levulinate 1.5%. Vial 100 ml.
Use: Calcium deficiency.

CALPHOSAN. (Brown) Cal. lactate 50 mg. & cal. glycerophosphate 50 mg., phenol 0.25% (preservative), physiological solution of sodium

loride q.s./10 cc. Amp. 10 cc. Box 10s, 100s; l 60 cc.
e: Therapy for calcium deficiency.
PHOSAN-B-12. (Brown) Calphosan plus Vit. B-12 0 mcg./10 cc. Vials 60 cc.
e: Therapy for calcium deficiency.
SAN. (Burgin-Arden) Calcium glycerophosphate 10 ., calcium levulinate 15 mg., chlorobutanol %/cc. Inj. Vial, 100 cc.
e: Calcium therapy.
SARBAIN TABLETS. (Sutliff & Case) enobarbital 0.25 gr., Ca carbonate 3 gr., sod. arbonate 3 gr., papain 1 gr., pancreatin 1 gr., nzocaine 0.25 gr./Tab. Bot. 100s, 1000s.
SCORBATE. (Forest) Vit. D 50 I.U., C 89.5 mg., lcium 262 mg., phosphorus 194 mg./Tab. Bot. 0s.
e: Multivitamin.
SUP. (Riker) Calcium carbonate 750 mg./Tab. Bot. 0s.
e: Calcium supplement.
SUXAPHEN. (Lannett) Calcium succinate 2.5 gr., licylamide 4 gr., phenobarbital ⅛ gr., Vitamin C mg./Cap., Tab. Bot. 250s, 500s, 1000s.
e: Sedative.
TRATE 600. (Lederle) Calcium carbonate 600 ./Tab. Bot. 60s.
e: High potency calcium supplement.
TRATE 600 + D. (Lederle) Calcium carbonate 0 mg., Vit. D 125 I.U./Tab. Bot. 60s.
e: High potency calcium supplement with Vitamin
LUSTERONE. USAN. (1) 17β-Hydroxy-7β, 17-di- ethylandrost-4-ene-3-one; (2) 7β, 17α-dimethyl stosterone.
e: Antineoplastic.
A ARTHRITIS PAIN RELIEVER. (Dorsey) Aspirin 0 mg., magnesium oxide 150 mg., aluminum droxide gel 150 mg./Tab. Bot. 100s, 250s.
e: Temporary relief of minor arthritic pain.
ALOX. (Rorer) Suspension of aluminum droxide 225 mg., magnesium hydroxide 200 mg., cium carbonate 250 mg./5 ml. Sodium content 05 mEq) 1.2 mg./5 ml. Bot. 12 oz.
e: Antacid.
ALOX TABLETS. (Rorer) Magnesium hydroxide 0 mg., aluminum hydroxide 225 mg., calcium rbonate 250 mg./Tab. Sodium content (0.04 Eq) 1.0 mg./Tab. Bot. 50s.
e: Antacid.
MBENDAZOLE. USAN. Isopropyl 2-(4-thiazolyl)- benzi-midazolecarbamate.
e: Anthelmintic, veterinary medicine.
e: Camvet (MSD AGVET).
ELLIA LOTION. (O'Leary) Moisturizer lotion for ce, hands and body. Bot. 4 oz.
EO OIL. (Medco Lab) Mineral oil base, synthetic reading oil, de-waxed oil-soluble principle of lanolin, d proper surfactants. Pl. bot. 8 oz., 16 oz., 32 oz.
e: Emollient, antipruritic and cleansing agent as th oil.

CAMPHO-PHENIQUE. (Winthrop Consumer Products) **Liq.:** Phenol 4.7%, camphor 10.8%. Bot. 0.75 oz., 1.5 oz., 4 oz. **Gel.:** 0.23 oz., 0.5 oz.
Use: Topical antiseptic.

CAMPHO-PHENIQUE LIP BALM. (Winthrop Consumer Products) Padimate O, hydrogenated vegetable oil, microcrystalline wax, mineral oil, cetyl esters, wax, lanolin oil, camphor, phenol. Stick 0.15 oz.
Use: Antiseptic.

• **CAMPHOR,** U.S.P. XXI. Spirit U.S.P. XXI. Bicyclo-[2.2.1.]heptane-2-one, 1,7,7-trimethyl. 2-Bornanone.
Use: Topical antipruritic; anti-infective; pharm. necessity for camphorated phenol, paregoric and flexible collodion, antitussive, expectorant, local counterirritant, nasal decongestant.
See: Vicks Inhaler (Vicks)
Vicks Regular and Wild Cherry Medicated Cough Drops (Vicks)
Vicks Medi-Trating Throat Lozenges (Vicks)
Vicks Sinex, Nasal Spray (Vicks)
Vicks Vaporub, Oint. (Vicks)
Vicks Vaposteam, Liq. (Vicks)
Vicks Va-Tro-Nol, Nose Drops (Vicks)

CAMPHOR, MONOBROMATED. 3-Bromo-2-bornanone.

• **CAMPHORATED, PARACHLOROPHENOL,** U.S.P. XXI.
Use: Anti-infective (dental).

CAMPHORIC ACID. 1,2,2-Trimethyl-1,3-cyclopentanedicarboxylic acid.

CAMPHORIC ACID ESTER. Ester of p-Tolylmethylcarbinal as Diethanolamine Salt.

CAMPTROPIN. (Jenkins) Caffeine alkaloid 5 mg., camphor 12 mg., atropine sulfate 0.1 mg./Tab. Bot. 1000s.
Use: Common cold and hay fever.

CAMVET. (MSD AGVET) Cambendazole
Paste: 45% cambendazole;
Pellets: 5.3% cambendazole;
Susp.: 3%.
Use: Anthelmintic, veterinary medicine.

CANDEX LOTION. (Miles Pharm) Nystatin 100,000 u./ml. Bot. 30 ml.
Use: Treatment moniliasis.

• **CANDICIDIN,** U.S.P. XXI. Oint., Vag. Tab., U.S.P. XXI. An antifungal antibiotic derived from *Strep. griseus.*
Use: Local antifungal.
See: Candeptin, Vag. Tabs, Oint. (Julius Schmid)
Vanobid, Oint. & Vag. Tab. (Merrell Dow)

CANDICIDIN. B.A.N. One or more of a mixture of heptanes with antifungal activity produced by *Streptomyces griseus* and other *Streptomyces* species.

C & T. (Hyrex) Vit B-12 1000 mg., thiamine 100 mg./ml. Vial 10 ml.
Use: Vitamin B deficiencies.

CANDYCON. (Allison) Chlorprophenpyridamine maleate 2 mg., phenylephrine HCl 5 mg./Tab. Bot. 50s.
Use: Antihistamine-Decongestant.

CANNABINOL. B.A.N. 6,6,9-Trimethyl-3-pentyl-benzo[c]chromen-l-ol.

CANOPAR. (Burroughs Wellcome).
See: Thenium closylate

• **CANRENOATE POTASSIUM.** USAN.
Use: Aldosterone antagonist.

• **CANRENONE.** USAN.
Use: Aldosterone antagonist.

CANTHARIDIN.
Use: Treatment for removal of warts.

CANTIL. (Merrell Dow) Mepenzolate bromide. 25 mg./Tab. Bot. 100s.
Use: Adjunctive treatment of peptic ulcer.

CANTRI. (Hauck) Sulfisoxazole 10%, aminacrine HCl 0.2%, allantoin 2%/Tube. Tube 90 Gm.
Use: Treatment of vaginitis and cervicitis.

CANZ. (Forest) Pepsin 260 mg., pancreatin 260 mg., dehydrocholic acid 40 mg./Tab. Bot. 100s, 500s, 1000s.
Use: Digestive aid.

CA-OROTATE. (Miller) Calcium (as calcium orotate) 65 mg./3 Tab. Bot. 100s.

C-A-P. (Eastman) Cellulose acetate phthalate.

CAPA. (U.S. Ethicals) Acetaminophen 432 mg./Tab. Bot. 20s, 100s, 500s.
Use: Antipyretic, analgesic.

CAPAHIST-DMH. (Freeport) Chlorpheniramine maleate 8 mg., phenylpropanolamine HCl 50 mg., atropine sulfate 1/180 gr., dextromethorphan HBr 20 mg./T.R. Cap.
Use: Relief from coughing and URI congestion.

CAPASTAT SULFATE. (Lilly) Capreomycin sulfate 1 Gm./10 ml. Vial 10 ml. Box 10s.
Use: Antituberculostatic.

CAPILLARISXOINTMENT. (Guild) Pkg. 1 oz., 3.5 oz.

CAPILLARIS X SHAMPOO. (Guild) Pkg. 6 oz.

CAPITAL W/CODEINE. (Carnrick) Codeine phosphate 30 mg., acetaminophen 325 mg./Tab. Bot. 100s.
Use: Analgesic.

CAPITAL WITH CODEINE SUSPENSION. (Carnrick) Acetaminophen 120 mg., codeine phosphate 12 mg./5 ml. Bot. 16 oz.
Use: Analgesic.

CAPITROL CREAM SHAMPOO. (Westwood) 5,7-dichloro-8-hydroxyquinoline. Chloroxine 2% in a shampoo base containing: Sodium octoxynol-3 sulfonate, PEG-6 lauramide, dextrin, stearyl alcohol/ceteareth-20, sodium lauryl sulfoacetate, docusate sodium, magnesium aluminum silicate, PEG-14M, EDTA, benzyl alcohol 1%, citric acid, water, color, fragrance. Tube 85 Gm.
Use: Treatment of dandruff & mild to moderately severe seborrheic dermatitis of the scalp.

Ca-PLUS-PROTEIN. (Miller) Calcium (as contained in a calcium-protein complex made with specially isolated soy protein and torula yeast) 280 mg./Tab. Bot. 100s.
Use: Calcium deficiency.

CAPNITRO. (Freeport) Nitroglycerin 6.5 mg./T.R. Cap. Bot. 100s.
Use: Peripheral vasodilator.

• **CAPOBENATE SODIUM.** USAN. Sodium 6-(3,4,5-trimethoxybenzamido) Hexanoate.
Use: Cardiac depressant (antiarrhythmic).

• **CAPOBENIC ACID.** USAN. 6-(3,4,5-Trimethoxybenzamido)-hexanoic acid.
Use: Cardiac depressant (antiarrhythmic).

CAPOTEN. (Squibb) Captopril 12.5 mg., 25 mg., 5[0] mg., or 100 mg./Tab. Bot 100s.
Use: Antihypertensive agent, treatment conges[tive] heart failure.

CAPOZIDE. (Squibb) Captopril/hydrochlorothiazid[e] 25/15, 25/25, 50/15, 50/25/Tab. Bot. 100s
Use: Antihypertensive agent.

CAPREOMYCIN. B.A.N. An antibiotic produced by *Streptomyces capreolus.*
See: Capastat sulfate

• **CAPREOMYCIN SULFATE STERILE,** U.S.P. XX[I]. An antibiotic derived from *Streptomyces caprec[olus]*. Caprocin.
Use: Antibiotic (tuberculostatic).
See: Capastat Sulfate, Amp. (Lilly)

CAPROCHLORONE. Levo-gamma-(o-chlorobenzy[l])-delta-oxo-gamma-phenylcaproic acid.

CAPRON. (Vitarine) Acetaminophen 227 mg., asp[irin] 227 mg., caffeine anh., 32.4 mg./Cap. Bot. 18s, 1000s.
Use: Analgesic.

CAPROXAMINE. B.A.N. (E)-3′-Amino-4′-methyl[...]anophenone O-(2-aminoethyl)oxime.
Use: Antidepressant.

CAPRYLATE-PROPIONATE MIXTURES.
See: Sopronol, Preps. (Wyeth)

CAPRYLATE, SALTS.
See: Sodium Caprylate
Zinc Caprylate

CAPRYLATE SODIUM, INJECTION.
Ingram—Amp. 33%, 1 cc. Pkg. 12s, 25s, 10[0]
Use: Fungus infections of skin.
See: Sodium Caprylate Preps.

CAPSICUM OLEORESIN.

W/Alcohol, benzocaine, oxyquinoline, thymol, capsicum oleoresin.
See: Dent's Dental Poultice (C. S. Dent)

W/Alcohol, chlorobutanol hydrous (chloroform derivative), phenol, eugenol, cresol.
See: Dent's Toothache Drops Treatment (C. S. Dent)

W/Benzocaine, phenol.
See: Dent's Toothache Gum (C. S. Dent)

W/Camphor, corn oil, cajuput oil and turpentine o[il].
See: Capsolin, Oint. (Parke-Davis)

W/Methyl salicylate, oil of camphor, oil of pine, turpentine oil.
See: Sloan's Liniment, Liq. (Warner-Lambert)

CAPSULES, EMPTY GELATIN. (Lilly) Lilly market[s] clear empty gelatin capsules in sizes 000,00,0,1,2,3,4,5.

• **CAPTAMINE HYDROCHLORIDE.** USAN. N-(2-[mer]captoethyl)dimethylamine hydrochloride.
Use: Cutaneous depigmenting activity.

CAPTODIAME. B.A.N. 4-Butylthiobenzhydryl 2-d[ime]thylaminoethyl sulfide.

Jse: Tranquilizer.
See: Covatin hydrochloride.
PTODIAME HCl. 4-Butylthio-a-phenylbenzyl 2-dimethylaminoethyl sulfide. Covatin hydrochloride.
APTOPRIL. USAN. Angiotensin I converting nzyme inhibitor.
Jse: Antihypertensive agent.
See: Capoten, Tab. (Squibb)
PULETS. (Vitarine) Vit. A 5000 I.U., D 400 I.U., B-1 2.5 mg., B-2 2.5 mg., B-6 0.5 mg., C 50 mg., cal. antothenate 5 mg., niacinamide 20 mg., cobalamin mcg./Cap. Bot. 100s, 250s, 1000s.
PULETS M CAPTABS. (Vitarine) Vit. A 5000 I.U., D 400 I.U., B-1 2.5 mg., B-2 2.5 mg., C 50 mg., niacinamide 20 mg., B-6 0.5 mg., Ca. pantothenate 5 mg., B-12 2 mcg., Fe 10 mg., iodine 0.05 mg., Cu 0.5 mg., Mn 0.5 mg., Mg 6 mg., Zn 0.5 mg., Ca 50 mg./Tab. Bot. 00s.
APURIDE. USAN.
Jse: Hypnotic.
QUIN. (Forest) Hydrocortisone 1%, clioquinol 3%. Cream. Tube 20 Gm.
Jse: Derma-steroid.
ARACEMIDE. USAN.
Jse: Antineoplastic.
RAFATE. (Marion) Sucralfate 1 Gm./Tab. Bot. 00s. Unit dose, Ctn. 100s.
Jse: Treatment of duodenal ulcers.
ARAMEL, N.F. XVI.
Jse: Pharm. aid (Color).
RAMIPHEN. B.A.N. 2-Diethylaminoethyl 1-phenylcyclopentane-1-carboxylate.
Jse: Treatment of the parkinsonian syndrome.
See: Parpanit hydrochloride
Taoryi edisylate
RAMIPHEN EDISYLATE.
Phenylpropanolamine.
See: Tuss-Ornade, Prods. (SmithKline)
RAMIPHEN ETHANEDISULFONATE.
Phenylephrine hydrochloride, phenindamine artrate.
See: Dondril, Tab. (Whitehall)
RAMIPHEN HYDROCHLORIDE. 1-Phenylcyclopentanecarboxylic acid 2-diethyl-aminoethyl ester hydrochloride.
Jse: Proposed for muscular spasm & tremor in Parkinson's disease.
ARAWAY, N.F. XVI. Oil, N.F. XVI.
Jse: Flavor.
RBACEL. (Softcon) Sterile buffered aqueous nethulose solution containing carbachol U.S.P. in ¾%, 1.5%, 3% strengths, with benzalkonium hloride. 15 cc. plastic direct-application bots.
Jse: Glaucoma.
ARBACHOL, U.S.P. XXI. Intraocular Sol., Ophth. Soln., U.S.P. XXI. Ethanaminium, 2-(aminocarbonyl)-oxy-N,N,N-trimethyl-, chloride. Carbamycholine chlode. Choline chloride carbamate, Lentin, Carbolin.
Jse: Parasympathomimetic agent; cholinergic.
See: Carbacel, Sol. (Softcon)
Miostat Intraocular, Solution (Alcon)
Murocarb, Soln. (Muro)
W/Methylcellulose.
See: Isopto Carbachol, Soln. (Alcon)
CARBACRYLAMINE RESINS.
Use: Cation-exchange resin.
• **CARBADOX.** USAN. Methyl 3-quinoxalin-2-ylmethylenecarbazate N^1N^4-dioxide.
Use: Antibacterial, veterinary medicine.
See: Mecadox.
CARBAMATE.
See: Valmid, Tab. (Lilly)
CARBAMAZEPINE. B.A.N. Dibenz[b,f]azepine-5-carboxamide.
Use: Treatment of trigeminal neuralgia.
See: Tegretol
• **CARBAMAZEPINE,** U.S.P. XXI. Tab., U.S.P. XXI. 5H-dibenz[b,f]azepine-5-carboxamide.
Use: Treatment epilepsy & trigeminal neuralgia.
See: Tegretol, Tab. (Geigy)
CARBAMIDE.
See: Urea U.S.P. XXI. (Various Mfr.)
CARBAMIDE COMPOUNDS.
See: Acetylcarbromal (Various Mfr.)
Bromisovalum (Various Mfr.)
Bromural, Tab. (Knoll)
Carbrital, Elix. & Kap. (Parke-Davis)
Carbromal (Various Mfr.)
Carbropent, Tab. (Blue Line)
Iotis, Liq. (Research Pharmacal Lab.)
Sedamyl, Tab. (Riker)
• **CARBAMIDE PEROXIDE TOPICAL SOLUTION,** U.S.P. XXI. Urea compound w/hydrogen peroxide (1:1).
Use: Local anti-infective (dental).
See: Clear Drops. (Internat. Pharm.)
Urea-Peroxide (Various Mfr.)
CARBAMIDE PEROXIDE, 6.5% IN GLYCERIN.
Use: Softening hardened ear wax
See: Murine Ear Drops (Abbott)
Murine Ear Wax Removal System (Abbott)
N-CARBAMOYLARSANILIC ACID.
See: Carbarsone, U.S.P. XXI. (Var. Mfr.)
CARBAMINO PHENYL-ARSONIC ACID.
See: Carbarsone (Various Mfr.)
(3-CARBAMOYL-3,3-DIPHENYLPROPYL)-DIISOPROPYLMETHYLAMMONIUM IODIDE.
See: Isopropamide Iodide
CARBAMYLCHOLINE CHLORIDE.
See: Carbachol
CARBAMYLMETHYLCHOLINE CHLORIDE.
See: Urecholine, Tab., Inj. (Merck Sharp & Dohme)
• **CARBANTEL LAURYL SULFATE.** USAN.
Use: Anthelmintic.
• **CARBARSONE,** U.S.P. XXI. Caps., U.S.P. XXI. (Var. Mfr.) N-carbamoylarsanilic acid. Amabevan, ameban, amibiarson, arsambide, fenarsone, leucarsone, aminarsone, amebarsone. p-Ureidobenzenearsonic acid.
Pulvule (Lilly) (250 mg.) Bot. 20s.
Use: Acute & chronic amebiasis & trichomoniasis.
CARBARYL. B.A.N. 1-Naphthyl methylcarbamate.
Use: Insecticide, veterinary medicine.
See: Sevin

• **CARBASPIRIN CALCIUM.** USAN.
Use: Analgesic.
• **CARBAZERAN.** USAN.
Use: Cardiotonic.
CARBAZOCHROME SALICYLATE. Adrenochrome Monosemicarbazone Sod. Salicylate Complex.
See: Adrenosem Salicylate, Amp, Syr., Tab. (Beecham-Massengill)
CARBAZOCINE. (Warner-Lambert) cis-14-(Cyclopropylmethyl)-1,2,3,4,4a,5,6,11-octa-hydro-5-11b-iminoethano-11bH-benzo(a)carbazole.
Use: Analgesic.
CARBENICILLIN. B.A.N. 6-(α-Carboxyphenyl-acetamido)penicillanic acid.
Use: Antibiotic.
See: Pyopen.
• **CARBENICILLIN DISODIUM, STERILE,** U.S.P. XXI. Sterile, U.S.P. XXI. 4-Thia-1-azabicyclo[3.2.0]-heptane-2-carboxylic acid, 6-[(carboxyphenylacetyl)-amino]-3,3-dimethyl-7-oxo-, disodium salt. N-(2-Carboxy-3,3-dimethyl-7-oxo-4-thia-1-azabicyclo-[3.2.0]-hept-6-yl)-2-phenylmalonamic acid disodium salt.
Use: Antibacterial.
See: Geopen disodium, Vial (Roerig)
Pyopen, Inj. (Beecham Labs)
• **CARBENICILLIN INDANYL SODIUM,** U.S.P. XXI. Tabs., U.S.P. XXI.
See: Geocillin, Tab. (Roerig)
• **CARBENICILLIN PHENYL SODIUM.** USAN.
Use: Antibacterial.
• **CARBENICILLIN POTASSIUM.** USAN.
Use: Antibacterial.
CARBENOXOLONE. B.A.N. 3β-(3-Carboxypropionyloxy)-11-oxo-olean-12-en-30-oic acid.
Use: Treatment of peptic ulcer.
See: Biogastrone
Bioral
Duogastrone disodium salt
• **CARBENOXOLONE SODIUM.** USAN.
Use: Glucocorticoid.
CARBENZIDE. (Warner-Lambert) Ethyl 3-(a-methylbenyl) carbazate. Under study.
Use: Anti-depressant, monoamine oxidase inhibitor.
CARBETAPENTANE CITRATE. 2-[2-(Diethylamino)ethoxy] ethyl 1-phenyl-cyclopentyl-1-carboxylate dihydrogen citrate.
Use: Antitussive.
W/Codeine phosphate, chlorpheniramine maleate, guaifenesin.
See: Tussar-2, Syr. (Armour)
W/Terpin hydrate, menthol, alcohol, sod. citrate, citric acid, glycerin.
See: Toclonol Expectorant, Liq. (Cenci)
W/Terpin hydrate, sod. citrate, citric acid, menthol glycerin, alcohol, codeine.
See: Toclonol W/Codeine, Liq. (Cenci)
CARBETHOXYSYRINGOYL METHYLRESERPATE.
See: Singoserp, Tab. (Ciba)
CARBETHYL SALICYLATE.
See: Sal-Ethyl Carbonate, Tab. (Parke-Davis)
• **CARBETIMER.** USAN.
Use: Antineoplastic.
• **CARBIDOPA,** U.S.P. XXI. 2-(3,4-Dihydroxybenzyl)-2-hydrazinopropionic acid; (-)-Lα-hydrazino-α-methyl-β-(3,4-dihydroxybenzene) propanoic acid monohydrate.
Use: Decarboxylase inhibitor.
W/Levodopa
See: Sinemet, Tab. (Merck Sharp & Dohme)
• **CARBIDOPA AND LEVODOPA TABLETS,** U.S.P. XXI.
Use: Treatment of parkinsonian syndrome.
See: Sinemet, Tab (Merck Sharp & Dohme)
CARBIMAZOLE. B.A.N. Ethyl 3-methyl-2-thioimidazline-1-carboxylate.
Use: Antithyroid substance.
See: Bimazol
Neo-Mercazole.
CARBIMAZOLE. 1-Ethoxycarbonyl-2:3-di-hydro-3-methyl-2-thioimidazole. Neo-Mercazole.
CARBINOXAMINE. B.A.N. 2-(4-Chloro-α-2-pyridylbezyloxy-ethyldimethylamine. Davenol. Extil hydrog maleate.
Use: Antihistamine.
See: Clistin, Tab. (McNeil)
CARBINOXAMINE HCl.
W/acetaminophen, phenylephrine HCl.
• **CARBINOXAMINE MALEATE,** U.S.P. XXI. Tabs., U.S.P. XXI. 2-[p-Chloro-alpha-[(2-(dimethyl-amino-ethoxy]benzyl]pyridine bimaleate.
Use: Antihistaminic.
See: Clistin Elix., Tab. (McNeil)
W/Acetaminophen.
See: Clistin-D, Tab. (McNeil)
W/Ammonium chloride, pot. guaiacol sulfonate, sod citrate.
See: Clistin Expectorant (McNeil)
W/Pseudoephedrine HCl.
See: Rondec Prods. (Ross)
W/Pseudoephedrine HCl, dextromethorphan HBr.
See: Rondec DM, Drops and Syrup (Ross)
CARBIPHENE. B.A.N. α-Ethoxy-N-methyl-N [2-(N-methylphenethylamino)ethyl]diphenyl-acetamide.
See: Jubalon hydrochloride.
Use: Analgesic.
• **CARBIPHENE HCl.** USAN. 2-Ethoxy-N-methyl-n-[2 (methylphenethylamino)ethyl]-2, 2-diphenyl-ace mide HCl.
Use: Analgesic.
CARBOCAINE. (Cook-Waite) Mepivacaine HCl 30 m NaCl 3 mg./1.8 ml. Cartridge. Mepivacaine HCl 2 mg., levonordefrin 0.05 mg., NaCl 4 mg., acetone sodium bisulfite not more than 2 mg./1.8 ml. Cartrige.
Use: Local anesthetic (dental).
CARBOCAINE HCl. (Winthrop-Breon) Mepivaca HCl. **1%**: Single Dose Vial 30 ml. Multiple Dose Vial 50 ml.; **1.5%**: Single Dose Vial 30 ml.; **2%**: Single Dose Vial 20 ml. Multiple Dose Vial 50 ml.
Use: Nerve block, caudal, epidural, and infiltratior
• **CARBOCLORAL.** USAN. Ethyl (2,2,2,-trichloro-1-droxyethyl)carbamate.

se: Hypnotic.
ee: Chloralurethane.
Prodorm (Parke-Davis)
RBOCYSTEINE. USAN.
se: Mucolytic.
BOL-FUCHSIN PAINT. Original fuchsin formula
own as Castellani's Paint. Fuchsin 0.3%, boric
id 1%, phenol 4.5%, resorcinol 10%, acetone
%, alcohol 10%, water q.s. 1 oz., 4 oz., 1 pt.
se: Local antifungal.
e: Carfusin, Sol. (Rorer)
Castaderm, Lot. (Lannett)
Castellani's Paint (Various Mfr.)
RBOL-FUCHSIN TOPICAL SOLUTION, U.S.P.
XI.
se: Topical antifungal.
BOLONIUM BROMIDE. B.A.N.
examethylenedi(carbamoylcholine bromide).
excarbacholine Bromide (I.N.N.)
se: Muscle relaxant.
e: Imbretil.
RBOMER, N.F. XVI. A polymer of acrylic acid,
osslinked with a polyfunctional agent.
se: Pharmaceutic aid (suspending agent);
nulsifying agent.
e: Carbopol 934 P (Goodrich)
BOMER. B.A.N. A polymer of acrylic acid
osslinked with allyl sucrose.
se: Pharmaceutical aid.
e: Carbopol 934.
RBOMER 910. USAN.
se: Pharmaceutic aid.
RBOMER 934. USAN.
se: Pharmaceutic aid.
RBOMER 934P. USAN.
e: Pharmaceutic aid.
RBOMER 940. USAN.
se: Pharmaceutic aid.
RBOMER 941. USAN.
e: Pharmaceutic aid.
BOMYCIN. An antibiotic from *Streptomyces*
lstedii.
RBON DIOXIDE, U.S.P. XXI.
se: Inhalation, respiratory stimulant.
e: Ceo-Two, Supp. (Beutlich)
RBON TETRACHLORIDE, N.F. XVI.
nzinoform. (Var. Mfr.)
se: Pharm. aid (solvent).
BONATES NO. 3. (Noyes) Calcium carbonate 3.5
., Mg carbonate 2.5 gr., bismuth subcarbonate
5 gr./Tab. Bot. 100s, 1000s.
BONIC ACID, DILITHIUM SALT. Lithium
rbonate, U.S.P. XXI.
BONIC ACID, DISODIUM SALT. Sodium
rbonate, N.F. XVI.
BONIC ACID, MONOSODIUM SALT. Sodium
carbonate, U.S.P. XXI.
BONIC ANHYDRASE INHIBITOR.
e: Daranide, Tab. (Merck Sharp & Dohme)
Diamox, Tab., Sequel, Vial (Lederle)
Hydrazol, Tab. (Softcon)
Neptazane, Tab. (Lederle)

CARBONIS DETERGENS, LIQUOR.
See: Coal Tar Solution.
CARBONYL DIAMIDE.
See: Chap Cream (Ar-Ex)
CARBOPHENOTHION. B.A.N. S-(4)Chlorophenylthiomethyl)00)diethyl phosphorodithioate.
Use: Insecticide, veterinary medicine.
See: Garrathion
Trithion
• **CARBOPLATIN.** USAN.
Use: Antineoplastic.
• **CARBOPROST.** USAN.
Use: Oxytocic.
• **CARBOPROST TROMETHAMINE,** U.S.P. XXI. Inj., U.S.P. XXI.
Use: Oxytocic.
See: Prostin, Amp. (Upjohn)
CARBOSE D.
See: Carboxymethylcellulose sodium, Prep. (Various Mfr.)
CARBOTABS. (Jenkins) Sodium bicarbonate 3⅓ gr., magnesium carbonate 1 gr., calcium carbonate ¾ gr., papain 1/32 gr., pancreatin 1/32 gr./Tab. Bot. 1000s.
Use: Effervescent antacid.
CARBOWAX, 300, 400, 1540, 4000. Polyethylene glycol 300, 400, 1540, 4000.
CARBOXIN. (Kay) Methocarbamol 500 mg., or 750 mg./Tab. Bot. 100s, 500s.
Use: Musculoskeletal conditions.
CARBOXYMETHYLCELLULOSE SALT OF DEXTROAMPHETAMINE. Carboxyphen.
See: Bontril Timed Tab. (Carnrick)
• **CARBOXYMETHYLCELLULOSE SODIUM,** U.S.P. XXI. Paste, Tab., U.S.P. XXI. Cellulose, carboxymethyl ester, sod. salt. Carbose D, C.M.C. (Hercules Pow. Co.)
Use: Pharm. aid (suspending agent; tablet excipient; viscosity-increasing agent); cathartic.
W/Acetphenolisatin, docusate sodium.
See: Scrip-Lax, Tab. (Scrip)
W/Alginic acid, sodium bicarbonate.
See: Pretts, Tabs. (Marion)
W/Belladonna ext., kaolin, pectin, zinc phenosulfonate.
See: Gelcomul, Liq. (Commerce)
W/Danthron, Vit. B-1, oxyethylene oxpropylene polymer.
See: Evactol, Cap. (Delta)
W/Digitoxin.
See: Foxalin, Cap. (Standex)
Thegitoxin (Standex)
W/Docusate sodium.
See: Dialose, Cap. (Stuart)
W/Docusate sodium, casanthranol.
See: Dialose Plus, Cap. (Stuart)
Disolan Forte, Cap. (Lannett)
Tri-Vac, Cap. (Rhode)
W/Docusate sodium, oxyphenisatin acetate.
See: Dialose Plus, Cap. (Stuart)
W/Methylcellulose.
See: Ex-Caloric, Wafer (Eastern Research)

W/Testosterone, estrone, sod. chloride.
See: Tostestro, Inj. (Bowman)
• **CARBOXYCELLULOSE SODIUM 12,** N.F. XVI.
CARBOXYMETHYLCYSTEINE. B.A.N. S-Carboxymethylcysteine.
Use: Mucolytic agent.
See: Mucodyne
Thiodril
3,3-CARBOXYMETHYLENE Bis-(4-Hydroxycoumarin)ethyl ester. Tromexan.
CARBOXYPHEN
W/Butabarbital.
See: Bontril, Timed Tab. (G. W. Carnrick)
CARBROMAL. (Various Mfr.) Bromodiethylacetylurea, bromadel, nyctal, planadalin, uradal.
Use: Sedative & mild hypnotic.
W/Bromisovalum (Bromural).
See: Bro-T's, Tab. (Brothers)
W/Pentobarbital sod.
See: Carbropent, Tab. (Blue Line)
CARBROPENT. (Blue Line) Pentobarbital sod. 1.5 gr., carbromal 4 gr./Tab. Bot. 100s, 1000s.
Use: Sedative & hypnotic.
CARBUTAMIDE. B.A.N. 1-Butyl-3-sulphanilylurea.
Use: Hypoglycemic agent.
See: Bucrol
Invenol
Nadisan
CARBUTAMIDE. N-Butyl-N'-sulfanilyl-urea. BZ. 55; Invenol; Nadisan.
Use: Oral hypoglycemic agent.
• **CARBUTEROL HYDROCHLORIDE.** USAN.
Use: Bronchodilator.
CARDABID. (Saron) Nitroglycerine 2.5 mg./S.R.Tab. Bot. 60s, 100s.
Use: Antianginal.
• **CARDAMON** N.F. XVI. Oil, seed, Cpd. Tincture; N.F. XVI.
Use: Flavor.
CARDEC DM SYRUP. (Goldline) Carbinoxamine maleate, pseudoephedrine HCl, dextromethorphan HBr. Bot. 4 oz., pt., gal.
Use: Non-narcotic cough mixture.
CARDEC DM DROPS. (Goldline) Carbinoxamine maleate, pseudoephedrine HCl, dextromethorphan HBr. Bot. 30 ml.
Use: Decongestant, antitussive.
CARDENZ. (Miller) Vit. C 25 mg., E 5 mg., inositol 30 mg., p-aminobenzoic acid 9 mg., A 2000 I.U., B-6 1.5 mg., B-12 1 mcg., D 100 I.U., niacinamide 20 mg., Mg 23 mg., I 0.05 mg. K. 8 mg./Tab. Bot. 100s.
Use: Adults dietary supplement.
CARDIAMID.
See: Nikethamide. (Various Mfr.)
CARDIAZOL.
See: Metrazol, Preps. (Knoll)
CARDILATE. (Burroughs Wellcome) Erythrityl tetranitrate. **Tab.** 5 mg. 100s, 10 mg. 100s, 1000s. **Chewable Tab.** 10 mg., Bot. 100s.
Use: Prophylaxis and long-term treatment of patients with recurrent anginal pain.
CARDIOGRAFIN. (Squibb) Diatrizoate methylglucamine 85% in a sterile, aqueous solution. Vial 50 cc.
Use: Diagnostic agent.
CARDIO-GREEN. (Hynson, Westcott & Dunning) St Indocyanine Green. Vials 25 mg. and 50 mg.
Use: For indicator dilution, hepatic function and ophthalmic angiography studies.
CARDIO-GREEN DISPOSABLE UNIT. (Hynson, W cott & Dunning) Vial Cardio-Green, ampule aque solvent & calibrated syringe. 10 mg., 40 mg.
Use: For indicator dilution, hepatic function and ophthalmic angiography studies.
CARDIOQUIN TABLETS. (Purdue Frederick) Quinidine polygalacturonate 275 mg. equivalent quinidine sulfate 200 mg./Tab. Bot. 100s, 500s.
Use: Cardiac arrhythmias.
CARDIOTROL-CK. (Roche) Lyophilized human se containing three CK isoenzymes from human tis source. 10x2 ml.
Use: Suitable for use as a quality control for immunochemical or electrophoretic assays.
CARDIOTROL-LD. (Roche) Lyophilized human se containing all LD isoenzymes from human tissue source. 10x1ml.
Use: Suitable for use as a quality control for immunochemical or electrophoretic assays.
CARDIZEM. (Marion) Diltiazem HCl 30 mg. or 60 mg./Tab. Bot. 100s. Unit Dose 100s.
Use: Treatment of angina.
CARDOPHYLLIN.
See: Aminophylline. (Various Mfr.)
CARDOXIN. (Vita Elixir) Digoxin 0.25 mg./Tab.
Use: Cardiotonic.
CARENA.
See: Aminophylline (Various Mfr.)
CARFECILLIN. B.A.N. 6-(α-Phenoxycarbonylphenylacetamido) penicillanic acid.
Use: Antibiotic.
• **CARFENTANIL CITRATE.** USAN.
Use: Analgesic, narcotic.
CARFIN TABS. (Major) Warfarin sodium 2.5 mg. c mg./Tab. Bot. 100s; 5 mg./Tab. Bot. 250s.
Use: Anticoagulant.
CARGENTOS.
See: Silver Protein, Mild
CARGESIC. (Rand) Bot. 2 oz.
Use: Analgesic, counterirritant.
CARICA PAPAYA ENZYME.
See: Papain (Various Mfr.)
W/Diastase.
See: Caripeptic, Liq. (Upjohn)
CARINDACILLIN. B.A.N. 6-(α-Indan-5-yloxycarb phenylacetamido)penicillanic acid.
Use: Antibiotic.
CARISOPRODOL, U.S.P. XXI. N-isopropyl mepr mate. Isomeprobamate, N-isopropyl-2-methyl-2- pyl-1, 3 propanediol dicarbamate. B.A.N. 2- bamoyloxymethyl-2-N-isopropylcarbamoyloxyme pentane.

se: Muscle relaxant.
ee: Rela, Tab. (Schering)
Soma, Tab. (Wallace)
ARISOPRODOL AND ASPIRIN TABLETS, U.S.P. XI.
se: Analgesic, muscle relaxant.
ee: Soma Compound Tab. (Wallace)
ARISOPRODOL, ASPIRIN, AND CODEINE HOSPHATE TABLETS, U.S.P. XXI.
se: Analgesic, muscle relaxant.
ee: Soma Compound w/Codeine Tab. (Wallace)
RI-TAB. (T.E. Williams) Fluoride 0.5 mg., Vitamin A 000 U., D 200 U., C 75 mg./Softab. Bot. 100s.
se: Aid in development of caries-resistant teeth and rophylaxis of vitamin A, D & C deficiencies.
ARMANTADINE. USAN.
se: Antiparkinsonian.
RMOL 10. (Syntex) Urea (carbamide) 10% in ypoallergenic water-washable lotion base. Bot. fl. oz.
se: Dry skin.
RMOL 20. (Syntex) Urea (carbamide) 20% in ypoallergenic vanishing cream base. Tube 3 oz., ar 1 lb.
se: Dry & hyperkeratotic skin.
RMOL-HC CREAM 1%. (Syntex) Micronized hy-rocortisone acetate 1%, in water-washable base ontaining urea. Tube 1 oz. Jar 4 oz.
Jse: Topical corticosteroid.
ARMUSTINE. USAN. 1,3bis-(2-chloroethyl)-1-ni-rosourea.
Jse: Antineoplastic.
ee: Bicnu, Inj. (Bristol)
RNATION INSTANT BREAKFAST. (Carnation) Non-fat instant breakfast containing 280 K cal. w/15 Gm. protein and 8 oz. whole milk. Pkt. 35 Gm. Ctn. s. Six flavors.
se: Nutritionally complete enteral meal upplement.
ARNIDAZOLE. USAN. Methyl-nitro-imidazole.
se: Antiparasitic, antiprotozoal.
AROXAZONE. USAN.
Jse: Antidepressant.
RPERIDINE. B.A.N. Ethyl 1-(2-carbamoylethyl)-4-henylpiperidine-4-carboxylate.
RPHENAZINE. B.A.N. 10- {3-[4-(2-Hydroxyethyl)pip-razin-1-yl]propyl}-2-propionylphenothiazine.
Jse: Tranquilizer.
ARPHENAZINE MALEATE, U.S.P. XXI. Oral Sol., J.S.P. XXI. 1-{10-(3-[4-(2-Hydroxyethyl)-1-piperazi-yl]-propyl) phenothiazin-2-yl}-1-propanone bis maleate).
Jse: Chronic psychosis.
See: Proketazine, Tab., Liq. (Wyeth)
ARRAGEENAN, N.F. XVI.
RSALAM. B.A.N. 1,3-Benzoxazine-2,4-dione. O-Car-amoylsalicylic acid lactam
Jse: Analgesic.
ARTAZOLATE. USAN.
Jse: Antidepressant.
ARTEOLOL HYDROCHLORIDE. USAN.
Jse: Anti-adrenergic.

CARTER'S LITTLE PILLS. (Carter Products) Bisacodyl 5 mg./Pill. Vial 30s, 85s.
Use: Laxative.
CARTICAINE. B.A.N. Methyl 4-methyl-3-(2-propylaminopropionamido)thiophene-2-carboxylate.
See: Ultracain hydrochloride.
Use: Local anesthetic.
CARTUCHO COOK WITH RAVOCAINE. (Winthrop Products) Ravocaine, novocain and levophed or neo-cobefrin.
Use: Dental anesthetic.
• **CARUBICIN.** USAN.
Use: Antineoplastic.
• **CARUMONAM SODIUM.** USAN.
Use: Antibacterial.
CAR-VIT. (Mericon) Ascorbic acid 60 mg., vitamin A acetate 4000 I.U., D-2 400 I.U., ferrous fumarate 90 mg. (iron 30 mg.), oyster shell 600 mg. (calcium 230 mg.)/Cap. Bot. 90s, 1000s.
CARZENIDE. p-Sulfoamoylbenozoic acid.
Use: Carbonic anhydrase inhibitor.
CASA-DICOLE. (Blue Cross) Docusate sodium 100 mg., casanthrol 30 mg./Cap. Bot. 100s.
Use: Laxative, stool softeners.
• **CASANTHRANOL.** USAN. A purified mixture of the anthranol glycosides derived from Cascara sagrada.
Use: Cathartic.
See: Black Draught, Prods. (Chattem Labs.)
W/Bile of ox, phenolphthalein.
See: Bicholate, Tab., (Blue Line)
W/Docusate sodium
See: Bu-Lax-Plus, Cap. (Ulmer)
Calotabs, Tabs. (Calotabs)
Comfolax-Plus, Cap. (Rorer)
Comfolax-Plus, Cap. (Searle)
Comfula-Plus (Searle)
Constiban, Cap. (Quality Generics)
Diolax, Cap. (Century)
Dio-Soft (Standex)
Diothron, Cap. (Vortech)
Disanthrol, Cap. (Lannett)
Disulans, Cap. (Noyes)
D-S-S W/Casanthranol, Cap. (Wolins)
Easy-Lax Plus, Cap. (Walgreen)
Genericace, Cap. (Fellows-Testagar)
Neo-Vardin D-S-S-C, Cap. (Scherer)
Nuvac, Cap. (LaCrosse)
Peri-Colace, Cap., Syr. (Mead Johnson)
Sodex, Cap. (Mallard)
Sofflax, Cap. (Medics)
Stimulax, Cap. (Geriatric)
Syncelax, Cap. (Blue Line)
Tonelax Plus, Cap. (A.V.P.)
W/Docusate sodium, sod. carboxymethylcellulose.
See: Dialose Plus, Cap. (Stuart)
Disolan Forte, Cap. (Lannett)
Tri-Vac, Cap. (Rhode)
W/Mineral oil and irish moss.
See: Neo-Kondremul, Liq. (Fisons)
CASCARA. (Lilly) Cascara 150 mg./Tab. Bot. 100s.
Use: Cathartic.

CASCARA, AROMATIC (Lilly) Alcohol 19%. Bot. 16 fl. oz.
Use: Cathartic.

• **CASCARA FLUIDEXTRACT, AROMATIC,** U.S.P. XXI.
Use: Cathartic.
W/Psyllium husk pow. & prune pow.
See: Casyllium, Pow. (Upjohn)

CASCARA GLYCOSIDES.
Use: Cathartic.

• **CASCARA SAGRADA,** U.S.P. XXI. Extract, Fluidextract, U.S.P. XXI. (Various Mfr.)
Use: Pharmaceutical necessity for Aromatic Cascara Fluidextract.

• **CASCARA SAGRADA EXTRACT,** U.S.P. XXI.
Use: Cathartic.
W/Bile salts, phenolphthalein, aloin.
See: Amlax, Tab. (Vortech)
W/Bile salts, phenolphthalein, aloin, papain, ext. nux vomica.
See: Taurocolate, Tab. (Vortech)
W/Bile salts, papain, phenolphthalein, capsicum oleoresin.
See: Torocol Compound, Tab. (Plessner)
W/Bile salts, phenolphthalein, capsicum oleoresin & peppermint oil.
See: Torocol, Tab. (Plessner)
W/Capsicum, ginger.
See: Flatulence, Tab. (Wolins)
W/Docusate sodium.
See: Dioctyl-Zem, Tab. (Zemmer)
W/Ox bile (desiccated), phenolphthalein, aloin, podophyllin.
See: Bilgon, Tab. (Reid-Provident)
W/Oxgall, dandelion root, podophyllin, tr. nux vomica.
See: Oxachol, Liq. (Philips Roxane)
W/Pancreatin, pepsin, sod. salicylate.
See: Bocresin, Liq. (Scrip)
W/Phenolphthalein, sodium glycocholate, sodium taurocholate, aloin.
See: Bicholax, Tab. (Elder)
Oxiphen, Tab. (Webcon)
W/Sod. salicylate, phenoiphthalein, chionanthus ext., bile ext., sod. glycocholate, sod. taurocholate.
See: Glycols, Tab. (Bowman)

• **CASCARA SAGRADA FLUID EXTRACT,** U.S.P. XXI. (Parke-Davis) Alcohol 18% Bot. 1 pt., 1 gal., Unit dose 5 ml..
Use: Cathartic.
See: Cas-Evac, Liq. (Parke-Davis)
Bilstan (Standex)

CASCARA SAGRADA FLUID EXTRACT AROMATIC. Aromatic Cascara Fluidextract, U.S.P. XXI.
W/Psyllium husk pow., prune pow.
See: Casyllium, Granules (Upjohn)

• **CASCARA TABLETS,** U.S.P. XXI.
Use: Cathartic.

CASCARIN.
See: Casanthranol (Various Mfr.)

CASEC. (Mead Johnson) Calcium caseinate (derived from skim milk curd and calcium carbonate). Pow. Can 3.33 oz.
Use: Provides extra protein for infants, children o adults.

CASOATE-A. (Marcen) Hydrolyzed casein 100 mg., h tidine monohydrochloride 4 mg., benzyl alcohol 5 mg., phenol 5 mg./cc. Vial 10 cc.
Use: Gastroduodenal ulcer therapy.

CASTADERM. (Lannett) A lotion of boric acid, resorcinol, acetone & soln. of carbol fuchsin. Bot 1, 4 & 16 oz.
Use: Eczematoid conditions of epidermatophytic origin.

CASTEL-MINUS. (Syosset) Resorcinl 8%, alcohol 8. w/acetone, fuchsin. Bot. 1 oz.
Use: Antifungal.

CASTELLANI PAINT. (Pedinol) Fuchsin, phenol resorcinol, acetone, alcohol. Bot. 1 oz., 16 oz./w color; colorless 1 oz., 16 oz.
Use: Local antifungal drying agent.

CASTELLANI'SPAINT. (Archer-Taylor) Bot. 4 oz., oz.
Use: Fungicide solution.

CASTELLANI'S PAINT. (Penta) Carbol-fuchsin s Fuchsin 0.3%, phenol 4.5%, resorcinol 10.0%, acetone 1.5%, alcohol 13%. Bot. 1 oz., 4 oz., pt.
Use: Dermatological formulation, for external use only under direct supervision of a physician.

• **CASTOR OIL,** U.S.P. XXI. Aromatic, Caps., U.S.P. XXI. (Squibb) Bot. 2 oz., 4 oz.
Use: Cathartic; pharmaceutic aid (plasticizer).
See: Neoloid (Lederle)

CASTOR OIL ELASTIC FILLED CAPSULES (Lilly) Castor oil 10 min./Cap. Bot 100s.
Use: Cathartic.

• **CASTOR OIL EMULSION,** U.S.P. XXI.
Use: Cathartic.

• **CASTOR OIL, HYDROGENATED,** N.F. XVI.
Use: Cathartic.

CATAPRES. (Boehringer Ingelheim) Clonidine HCl mg., 0.2 mg. or 0.3 mg./Tab. **0.1mg.:** Bot. 100s, 1000s. Unit Dose 100s. **0.2 mg.:** Bot. 100s, 1000 Unit Dose 100s. **0.3 mg.:** Bot. 100s, 1000s.
Use: Antihypertensive.

CATARASE. (CooperVision) Chymotrypsin 1:5,000 (300 units) in a 2 chamber vial with 2 ml. sterile diluent; Chymotrypsin 1:10,000 (150 units) in a 2 chamber vial with 2 ml. sterile diluent.
Use: Enzymatic zonulysis prior to intracapsular le extraction.

CATARRHALIS, KILLED NEISSERIA.
W/*Klebsiella pneumoniae, Diplococcus pneumoniae* Streptococci, staphylococci.
See: Combined Vaccine No. 4 W/Catarrhalis, Inj. (Lilly)

CATHOMYCIN CALCIUM. Calcium novobiocin.

CATHOMYCIN SODIUM. Novobiocin sod.

■ **CATIONIC RESINS.**
See: Resins, Sodium Removing

CAUSALIN. (Amfre-Grant) Magnesium salicylate 6 mg./Tab. Bot. 100s 1000s.
Use: Analgesic, anti-inflammatory.

CAVACAINE. (Graham) Mepivacaine HCl 3%. Vial ml.
Use: Anesthetic.

BIO. (Barth's) Vit. C. 150 mg., citrus bioflavonoid complex 100 mg., rutin 50 mg./Tab. Bot. 100s, 500s, 1000s.

B-PLEX CAPSULES. (Barry-Martin) Vit. B-1 15 mg., B-2 10 mg., niacinamide 50 mg., Ca pantothenate 10 mg., C 250 mg., B-6 5 mg./Cap. Bot. 100s, 500s.
Use: Vitamin supplement.

B TIME. (Arco) Ascorbic acid 200 mg., Vit. B-1 10 mg., B-2 10 mg., B-6 5 mg., B-12 10 mcg., niacinamide 50 mg., calcium pantothenate 10 mg./Cap. Vit. C 300 mg., B-1 15 mg., B-2 10 mg., B-6 5 mg., cobalamin concentrate 5 mcg., niacinamide 100 mg., D-panthenol 20 mg./5 cc. **Caps.** Bot. 40s, 120s, 500s. **Liq.,** Bot. 4 oz.
Use: Vitamin supplements.

B TIME 500. (Arco) Vit. C 500 mg., B-1 10 mg., B-2 10 mg., B-6 5 mg., cyanocobalamin 10 mg., niacinamide 50 mg., Ca pantothenate 10 mg./Tab. Bot. 30s, 100s, 500s.

B VONE CAPSULES. (Armour) Vitamin B Complex and C supplement. Bot. 100s.
Use: Vitamins B and C supplement.

CAPS 500. (Drug Industries) Vitamin C 500 mg./Cap. Bot. 100s.
Use: Vitamin C supplement.

:NU. Lomustine.
See: CeeNu, Tab. (Bristol)

D.M. EXPECTORANT. (Lannett) Dextromethorphan HBr 10 mg., chlorpheniramine maleate 1 mg., phenylephrine HCl 5 mg., sodium citrate 15 mg., guaifenesin 25 mg./5 cc. Bot. pt., gal.
Use: Antihistaminic, antitussive cough expectorant.

D.P. CAPS. (Goldline) Chlordiazepoxide HCl 5 mg., 10 mg., or 25 mg./Cap. Bot. 100s, 500s, 1000s.
Use: Relief of anxiety and tension.

:A. (Abbott) Test kits 100s.
Use: Radioimmunoassay or enzyme immunoassay for quantitative measurement of carcinoembryonic antigen in human serum or plasma.

:A-ROCHE. (Roche) Radioimmunoassay capable of detecting and measuring plasma levels of CEA in the nanogram range. Sensitivity-0.5 ng./ml. of CEA.

:A-ROCHE TEST KIT. (Roche) Carcinoembryonic antigen, a glycoprotein which is a constituent of the glycocalyx of embryonic entodermal epithelium. Test Kit.
Use: Diagnostic agent.

:B NUGGETS. (Scott/Cord) Vit. B-1 15 mg., B-2 15 mg., B-6 5 mg., B-12 5 mcg., C 600 mg., niacinamide 100 mg., E 40 I.U., calcium pantothenate 20 mg., folic acid 0.1 mg./Nugget. Bot. 60s.

:BENASE. (Upjohn) Intrinase 0.167 N.F. unit (oral), Sod. ascorbate 150 mg., B-1 10 mg., B-2 10 mg., B-6 2.5 mg., Cal. pantothenate 10 mg., niacinamide 75 mg./Tab. Bot. 50s.
Use: Hematinic.

:BO-CAPS. (Forest) Placebo timed capsules.

:BRALAN-M TABLETS. (Lannett) B-1 10 mg., Cap. Bot. 50s, 500s.
Use: Relief of cerebral and peripheral ischemia.
niacinamide 30 mg., B-12 3 mcg., C 100 mg., E 5 I.U., A 10,000 I.U., D 1000 I.U., Fe 15 mg., Cu 1 mg., iodine 0.15 mg., Mn 1 mg., Mg 5 mg., Zn 1.5 mg./Tab. Bot. 100s, 1000s.
Use: Mineral-vitamin supplement.

CEBRALAN M.T. TABLETS. (Lannett) Vit. B-1 15 mg., B-2 10 mg., B-6 2 mg., pantothenic acid 10 mg., niacinamide 100 mg., B-12 7.5 mcg., C 150 mg., E 5 I.U., A 25,000 I.U., Cu 1 mg., Fe 15 mg., iodine 0.15 mg., Mn 1 mg., Mg 5 mg., Zn 1.5 mg./Tab. Bot. 100s, 1000s.
Use: High potency mineral-vitamin tablet.

CECLOR. (Lilly) **Pulvules:** Cefaclor 250 or 500 mg./Pulvule. Bot. 15s,100s. Blister pkg. 10 × 10s. **Oral Susp.:** Cefaclor 125 or 250 mg./5 ml. Bot. 75 ml., 150 ml.
Use: Antibiotic.

CECON SOLUTION. (Abbott) Ascorbic acid 10% in propylene glycol. Each drop from enclosed dropper supplies 2.5 mg. ascorbic acid; each ml. contains 100 mg. Bot. w/dropper 50 ml.
Use: Vitamin-C therapy.

CEDILANID-D. (Sandoz) Deslanoside, desacetyl lanatoside C. 0.4 mg./2 ml. w/citric acid, sodium phosphate, alcohol 9.8%, glycerin 15%, Water for injection qs 2 ml./Amp. SandoPak Pkg. 20s.
Use: Parenterally, digitalization.

CEEAMIDE. (Image) Vitamin Tab. Bot. 100s. Liquid Bot. 16 oz.
Use: Supplement.

CEEBATE. (Mallard) Ascorbic acid 250 mg./ml. Vial 30 ml.
Use: Scurvy treatment and prevention.

CeeNU. (Bristol) Lomustine (CCNU) 10 mg., 40 mg., 100 mg./Cap. Bot. 20s. Dose pk. of two cap. each of three strengths.
Use: Antineoplastic agent.

CEEPA. (Geneva) Theophylline 130 mg., ephedrine HCl 24 mg., phenobarbital 8 mg./Tab. Bot. 100s, 1000s.

CEEPRYN. Cetylpyridinium chloride.
Use: Antiseptic.
See: Cēpacol Lozenges, Sol., Troches (Merrell Dow)

CEETOLAN CONCENTRATE. (Lannett) Cetyldimethylbenzyl ammonium chloride 1:5500/2 oz. Bot. diluted w/1 gal. water. Bot. 2 oz.
Use: Mouthwash.

• **CEFACLOR,** U.S.P. XXI. Capsules, For Oral Susp., For Oral Susp., U.S.P. XXI.
Use: Antibacterial.
See: Ceclor, Cap. (Lilly)

• **CEFACTOR.** USAN.
Use: Antibacterial.

• **CEFADROXIL,** U.S.P. XXI. Caps., Tabs., Oral Susp., U.S.P. XXI. 7-[[D-2-amino-2-(4 hydroxyphenyl) acetyl] amino]-3-methyl-8-oxo-5-thia-1-azabicyclo [4.2.0] Oct-2-ene-2-carboxylic acid monohydrate.
Use: Antibiotic
See: Duricef, Cap., Tab., Susp. (Mead Johnson)
Ultracef, Cap. (Bristol)

CEFADYL. (Bristol) Cephapirin sodium 500 mg., 1 Gm., 2 Gm./Vial.; Piggyback vials 1 Gm., 2 Gm., 4 Gm.; Bulk vial 20 Gm.
Use: Antibiotic, IM & IV.

• **CEFAMANDOLE.** USAN.
Use: Antibacterial.

• **CEFAMANDOLE NAFATE, STERILE,** U.S.P. XXI. For Inj. U.S.P. XXI. 5-Thia-1-azabicyco (4.2.0) oct-2-ene-2-carboxylic acid, 7-(((formyloxy,) phenylacetyl) amino) -3- (((1-methyl-1H-tetrazol -5-yl)thio)methyl) - 8- oxo-, monosodium salt, (6R-(6α, 7 β (R)))—.
Use: Antibiotic
See: Mandol, Amp. (Lilly)

• **CEFAMANDOLE SODIUM,** U.S.P. XXI. For Inj., U.S.P., Sterile, U.S.P. XXI.
Use: Antibiotic.

• **CEFAPAROLE.** USAN.
Use: Antibacterial.

CEFAPIRIN. B.A.N. 7-[α-(4-Pyridylthioacetamido)]-cephalosporanic acid.
Use: Antibiotic.
See: Cefatrex
Cefatrexyl sodium salt.

• **CEFATRIZINE.** USAN.
Use: Antibacterial.

• **CEFAZAFLUR SODIUM.** USAN.
Use: Antibacterial.

• **CEFAZOLIN,** U.S.P. XXI.
Use: Antibiotic.

• **CEFAZOLIN SODIUM, STERILE,** U.S.P. XXI. Inj., U.S.P. XXI. Sodium salt of 3-[(5-methyl-1, 3, 4-thiadiazol-2-yl) thio]-methyl -8-oxo 7-[2-(1H-tetrazol-1-yl) acetanido]-5-thia-1-azabicyclo[4-2.0]oct-2-ene-2-carboxylic acid.
Use: Antibiotic.
See: Ancef, Vial (SmithKline)
Kefzol, Amp. (Lilly)

• **CEFBUPERAZONE.** USAN.
Use: Antibacterial.

CEFERA. (Haag) Ferrous fumarate 200 mg. (equiv. to 60 mg. Iron), ascorbic acid 100 mg./Tab. Bot. 100s, 1000s.
Use: Treatment of iron deficiency.

CEFERA PLUS. (Haag) Ferrous fumarate 194 mg., Vit. C 50 mg., B-1 2 mg., B-2 2 mg., niacinamide 15 mg., B-6 0.5 mg., B-12 5 mcg./Tab. Bot. 100s, 500s, 1000s.
Use: Iron and vitamin deficiency.

• **CEFETAMET.** USAN.
Use: Antibacterial.

CEFINAL II. (Alto) Salicymide 150 mg., acetaminophen 250 mg., doxylamine succinate 25 mg./Tab. Bot. 100s.
Use: Nighttime analgesic.

CEFIZOX. (SmithKline) Semisynthetic cephalosporin equivalent to: **Vials:** 1 Gm. or 2 Gm. of ceftizoxime/Vial. **Piggyback Vials:** 1 Gm. or 2 Gm./100 ml. ml. **Minibags:** 1 Gm. or 2 Gm./50ml. w/dextrose injection (D5W).
Use: Antibiotic.

• **CEFMENOXINE HYDROCHLORIDE.** USAN.
Use: Antibacterial.
See: Takeda (Abbott)

CEFOBID. (Roerig) Cefoperazone sodium 1 Gm. or 2 Gm./Vial 1 Gm. or 2 Gm. PBU 10 pack.
Use: Antibiotic for I.V. or I.M. administration.

CEFOL FILMTAB. (Abbott) Vit. B-1 15 mg., B-2 10 m B-6 5 mg., B-12 6 mcg., C 750 mg., E 30 I.U., pantothenate 20 mg., niacinamide 100 mg., folic acid 500 mcg./Tab. Bot. 100s.

• **CEFONICID MONOSODIUM.** USAN.
Use: Antibacterial.
See: Monicid (SmithKline)

• **CEFONICID SODIUM.** USAN.
Use: Antibacterial.

• **CEFOPERAZONE SODIUM, STERILE,** U.S.P. XXI
Use: Antibacterial.
See: Cefobid, Inj. (Roerig)

• **CEFORANIDE.** USAN.
Use: Antibacterial.
See: Precef, Inj. (Bristol)

• **CEFOTAXIME SODIUM.** USAN.
Use: Antibacterial.
See: Claforan, Inj. (Hoechst)

• **CEFOTETAN.** USAN.
Use: Antibacterial.

• **CEFOTETAN DISODIUM.** USAN.
Use: Antibacterial.

• **CEFOTIAM HYDROCHLORIDE.** USAN.
Use: Antibacterial.

• **CEFOXITIN.** USAN.
Use: Antibacterial.

• **CEFOXITIN SODIUM, STERILE,** U.S.P. XXI. 5-Thia-1-azabicyclo (4.2.0) oct-2-ene-2-carboxylic acid, 3-((aminocarbonyl) oxy) methyl)-7-methoxy-8-oxo-7-((2-thienylacetyl)-amino)-, sodium salt (6R-cis)-.
Use: Antibiotic.
See: Mefoxin, Inj. (Merck Sharp & Dohme)

• **CEFPIMIZOLE.** USAN.
Use: Antibacterial.

• **CEFPIMIZOLE SODIUM.** USAN.
Use: Antibacterial.

• **CEFROXADINE.** USAN.
Use: Antibacterial.

• **CEFSULODIN SODIUM, STERILE,** U.S.P. XX1.
Use: Antibacterial.

• **CEFTAZIDIME.** USAN.
Use: Antibacterial.

• **CEFTIZOXIME SODIUM.** USAN.
Use: Antibacterial.

• **CEFTRIAXONE SODIUM.** USAN.
Use: Antibacterial.
See: Rocephin, Inj. (Roche)

• **CEFUROXIME.** USAN (6R, 7R)-3-Carbamoyloxymethyl-7-[(2Z)-2-(2-furyl)-2-methoxyiminoacetamido]-cep -3-em-1-carboxylic acid.
Use: Antibiotic.

• **CEFUROXIME AXETIL.** USAN.
Use: Antibiotic.

CELESTONE. (Schering) Betamethasone 0.6 mg./ **Tab.** Bot. 100s, 500s. Tab-Pack 21s. **Syr.:** 0.6 mg./ cc. Alcohol $<1\%$. Bot. 4 oz.
Use: Anti-inflammatory steroid.

CELESTONE CREAM. (Schering) Betamethasone (0.2%) 2 mg./Gm. Tubes 15 Gm.
Use: Dermatoses.

CELESTONE PHOSPHATE INJECTION. (Schering) Betamethasone sodium phosphate 4 mg./ml.

quivalent to betamethasone alcohol 3 mg./ml. mpules 1 ml. Multidose vials, 5 ml.
se: Anti-inflammatory.
ESTONE SOLUSPAN. (Schering) Betamethasone odium phosphate 3 mg., betamethasone acetate 3 g., dibasic sod. phosphate 7.1 mg., monobasic od. phosphate 3.4 mg., edetate disodium 0.1 mg., enzalkonium chloride 0.2 mg./ml. Vial 5 ml.
se: Anti-inflammatory.
LABURATE. (Eastman) Cellulose acetate utyrate.
se: Pharmaceutic aid (plastic filming agent).
LIPROLOL HYDROCHLORIDE. USAN.
se: Anti-adrenergic.
LACEPHATE. B.A.N. A partial mixed acetate and ydrogen phthalate ester of cellulose.
se: Enteric coating.
LASE W-100. W/Alpha-amylase W-100, proteinase -300, lipase, estrone, testosterone, vitamins, miner- ls.
ee: Geramine, Tab. (Brown)
mylase, protease, lipase, hyoscine HBr.
ee: Am-Zyme, Tab. (Vortech)
LEPACBIN. (Arthrins) Vit. A 1200 I.U., B-1 1.5 mg., -2 1.5 mg., B-6 0.75 mg., niacinamide 7.5 mg., pan- henol 3 mg., C 20 mg., B-12 2 mcg., E 1 I.U./Cap. Bot. 80s.
se: Dietary supplement.
LOTHYL. (C-D Consumer Products) Methylcel- llose 0.5 Gm./Tab. 100s, 1000s.
se: Bulk laxative.
ELLULASE. USAN. A concentrate of cellulose-split- ng enzymes derived from *Aspergillus niger* and ther sources.
se: Digestive Aid.
Bile salts, mixed conjugated, pancrelipase.
ee: Cotazym-B, Tab. (Organon)
Mylase, prolase, calcium carbonate, magnesium lycinate.
ee: Zylase, Tabs. (Vitarine)
Mylase, prolase & lipase.
ee: Ku-Zyme, Cap. (Kremers-Urban)
Pepsin, glutamic acid, pancreatin, ox bile ext.
See: Kanulase, Tab. (Dorsey)
Pepsin, pancreatin enz. conc., dehydrocholic acid.
See: Gastroenterase, Tabs. (Wallace)
LLULOSE.
Hexachlorophene.
See: ZeaSorb, Pow. (Stiefel)
ELLULOSE ACETATE, N.F. XVI.
LLULOSE, ACETATE, 1,2-BENZENEDICARBOXY- ATE. Cellulose Acetate Phthalate, N.F. XVI.
ELLULOSE ACETATE PHTHALATE, N.F. XVI.
Cellulose, acetate, 1,2-benzenedicarboxylate.
Use: Pharm. aid (tablet-coating agent).
LLULOSE, CARBOXYMETHYL, SODIUM SALT.
Carboxymethylcellulose Sodium, U.S.P. XXI.
LLULOSE, HYDROXYPROPYL METHYL ETHER.
Hydroxypropyl Methylcellulose, U.S.P. XXI.
LLULOSE METHYL ETHER.
See: Methylcellulose, Prep. (Various Mfr.)

• **CELLULOSE MICROCRYSTALLINE,** N.F. XVI.
Use: Tablet diluent.
CELLULOSE, NITRATE. Pyroxylin, U.S.P. XXI.
CELLULOSE, OXIDIZED. Oxidized Cellulose, U.S.P. XXI.
Use: Local hemostatic.
CELLULOSE, OXIDIZED REGENERATED, U.S.P. XXI.
• **CELLULOSE, POWDERED,** N.F. XVI.
• **CELLULOSE SODIUM PHOSPHATE,** U.S.P. XXI.
Use: Antiurolithic.
CELLULOSIC ACID.
See: Oxidized Cellulose. (Various Mfr.)
CELLULOLYTIC.
W/Amylolytic, proteolytic.
See: Trienzyme, Tabs. (Fellows-Testagar)
CELLULOLYTIC ENZYME.
See: Cellulase (Various Mfr.)
W/Amylolytic, proteolytic enzymes, lipase, phenobarbital, hyoscyamine sulf., atropine sulf.
See: Arco-Lipase Plus, Tab. (Arco)
W/Amylolytic enzyme, proteolytic enzyme, lipolytic enzyme, butisol sodium, belladonna.
See: Butibel-zyme Tabs (McNeil)
W/Calcium carbonate, glycine, amylolytic and proteolytic enzymes.
See: Co-Gel, Tab. (Arco)
W/Proteolytic enzyme, amylolytic enzyme, lipolytic enzyme.
See: Ku-Zyme, Cap. (Kremers-Urban)
Zymme, Cap. (Scrip)
W/Proteolytic, amylolytic, lipolytic enzymes, iron, ox bile.
See: Spaszyme., Tab. (Dooner)
CELOID. (Xttrium) Lemon bioflavonoid complex 100 mg., ascorbic acid 100 mg./Cap. Bot. 100s, 1000s.
CELONTIN. (Parke-Davis) Methsuximide. Kapseal 150 mg., 300 mg. Bot. 100s.
Use: Petit mal and psychomotor attacks.
CENAFED. (Century) Pseudoephedrine HCl 60 mg./Tab. Bot. 100s, 1000s.
Use: Bronchodilator.
CENAFED SYRUP. (Century) Pseudoephedrine HCl 30 mg./5 cc. Bot. 4 oz., pint, gal.
Use: Bronchodilator.
CENAHIST. (Century) Chlorpheniramine maleate 8 mg., phenylephrine HCl 20 mg., methscopolamine nitrate 2.5 mg./Cap. Bot. 100s, 500s, 1000s.
Use: Relief from allergic conditions.
CENAID. (Century) Salicylamide 227 mg., phenacetin 100 mg., caffeine 10 mg., ascorbic acid 20 mg., phenylephrine HCl 5 mg., chlorpheniramine maleate 2 mg./Tab. Bot. 100s, 1000s.
Use: Analgesic.
CENA-K. (Century) Potassium chloride 20%. Bot. pt., gal.
CENALAX. (Century) Bisacodyl. **Tab.:** 5 mg./Tab. Bot. 100s, 1000s. **Supp.:** 10 mg./Supp. Pkgs. 12s, 1000s.
Use: Laxative.

CENALONE. (Kay) Triamcinolone acetonide 40 mg./ml. Vial 5 ml.
Use: Glucocorticoid.

CENALONE INJECTION. (Century) Prednisolone sod. phosphate 20 mg./cc. Vial 10 cc.

CENALONE L.A. (Century) Prednisone sodium phosphate and prednisolone acetate 80 mg.

CEN-E. (Century) Vitamin E 100 I.U./Cap., 200 I.U./ Cap., 400 I.U./Cap. Bot. 100s, 1000s.

CENOCORT A-40. (Central) Triamcinolone acetate 40 mg./ml. Vials 5 ml. Box 12s.
Use: Glucocorticoid.

CENOCORT FORTE. (Central) Triamcinolone diacetate 40 mg./ml. Vials 5 ml. Box 12s.
Use: Glucocorticoid.

CENOLATE. (Abbott)
Use: Treatment of Vitamin C deficiency.

CENTER-AL. (Center) Allergenic extracts, alum precipitated 10,000 PNU/ml. or 20,000 PNU/ml. Vials 10 ml.
Use: Treatment of allergy due to pollens or house dust.

■ **CENTRAL NERVOUS SYSTEM DEPRESSANTS.**
See: Sedatives

■ **CENTRAL NERVOUS SYSTEM STIMULANTS.**
See: Amphetamine (Various Mfr.)
D-Amphetamine (Various Mfr.)
Anorexigenic agents
Benzedrine, Cap., Tab. (SmithKline)
Caffeine (Various Mfr.)
Coramine, Liq., Inj. (Ciba)
Deaner, Tab. (Riker)
Desoxyephedrine HCl, Tab. (Various Mfr.)
Desoxyn HCl, Tab. Gradumet. (Abbott)
Dexedrine, Preps. (SmithKline)
Methamphetamine HCl (Various Mfr.)
Metrazol, Preps. (Knoll)
Nikethamide (Various Mfr.)
Pentylenetetrazol (Various Mfr.)
Picrotoxin
Ritalin HCl, Tab., Inj. (Ciba)

CENTRAX. (Parke-Davis) Prazepam. **Cap.**: 5 mg., 10 mg., or 20 mg./Cap. Bot. 100s, 500s. **Tab.** 10 mg./Tab. Bot. 100s. Unit dose 100s.
Use: Symptomatic relief of anxiety and tension associated with anxiety disorders, transient situational disorders, functional or organic disorders.

CENTRUM. (Lederle) Vit A 5000 I.U., E 30 I.U., C 90 mg., folic acid 400 mcg., B-1 2.25 mg., B-2 2.6 mg., B-6 3 mg., niacinamide 20 mg., B-12 9 mcg., D 400 I.U., biotin 45 mcg., pantothenic acid 10 mg., Ca 162 mg., phosphorus 125 mg., iodine 150 mcg., iron 27 mg., Mg. 100 mg., K 30 mg., Mn 5 mg., Cr 25 mcg., Se 25 mcg., molybdenum 25 mcg., zinc 15 mg., Cu 2 mg., Vit. K 25 mcg., Cl 27.2 mg./Tab.
Use: Vitamin & Mineral supplement.

CENTRUM JR. (Lederle) Vit. A 5000 I.U., D 400 I.U., E 30 I.U., C 60 mg., folic acid 400 mcg., B-1 1.5 mg., B-6 2 mg., B-12 6 mcg., riboflavin 1.7 mg., niacinamide 20 mg., iron 18 mg., magnesium 40 mg., copper 2 mg., zinc 15 mg., manganese 1 mg./Tab. Bot.60s.
Use: Vitamin, mineral, iron supplement for children.

CENTRUM JR. + EXTRA C. (Lederle) Vit. A 5,000 I.U. D 400 I.U., E 30 I.U., C 300 mg., folic acid 4 mcg., biotin 45 mcg., B-1 1.5 mg., pantothenic acid mg., B-2 1.7 mg., nicacinamide 20 mg., B-6 2 mg. 12 6 mcg., K-1 10 mcg., iron 18 mg., magnesium mg., iodine 150 mcg., copper 2 mg. phosphorous 50 mg., calcium 108 mg., zinc 15 mg., manganese 1 mg., molebdenum 20 mcg., chromium 20 mcg./Chewable Tab. Cherry, orange, grape, lem lime flavors. Bot. 60s
Use: Childrens dietary supplement.

CENTURY HOSPITAL RUB. (Century) Lanolins, menthol, allantoin in soothing base. Bot. 8 oz.
Use: Emollient lotion.

CENTUSS. (Century) Dextromethorphan HBr 10 mg salicylamide 227 mg., phenacetin 100 mg., caffei 10 mg., ascorbic acid 20 mg., phenylephrine HCl mg., chlorpheniramine maleate 2 mg./MLT Tab. Bot. 100s, 1000s.
Use: Antitussive and analgesic.

CEO-TWO. (Beutlich) Potassium bitartrate and sod. carbonate in polyethylene glycol base. Supp. 10s
Use: Laxative.

CEPACOL. (Merrell Dow) Ceepryn (brand of cetylpyridinium chloride) 1:2000, alcohol 14%, phosphate buffers and aromatics.Bot. 12 oz., 18 oz., 24 oz., 32oz., 4 × 2 qt.
Use: Mouthwash and gargle for oral hygiene.

CEPACOL ANESTHETIC LOZENGES. (Merrell Dow) Benzocaine,cetylpyridinium chloride 1:1500, aromatics in citrus flavored hard candy base. Pkg 18s, 324s.
Use: Temporary relief of minor throat & mouth pa

CEPACOL THROAT LOZENGES. (Merrell Dow) Cetylpyridinium chloride 1:1500, benzyl alcohol 0.3%, aromatics in mint flavored hard candy base Pkg. 18s, 648s.
Use: Temporary relief of dryness and minor mout & throat irritations.

CEPASTAT LOZENGES. (Merrell Dow) Phenol 1.45%, menthol 0.12%/Lozenge w/sorbitol, eucalyptus oil. Pkg. 18s, 300s, 648s.
Use: Temporary relief of minor sore throat pain.

CEPASTAT CHERRY FLAVOR LOZENGES. (Merre Dow) Phenol 0.73%, menthol 0.12% in sorbitol base. Box 18s.
Use: Temporary relief of sore throats in children and older.

CEPHACETRILE SODIUM. Sodium 7-(2-cyanoaceta do)-3-(hydroxy-methyl)-8-oxo-5-thia-1-aza-bicyclo [4.3.0]oct-2-ene-2-carboxylate acetate (ester).
Use: Antibacterial.

• **CEPHADRINE TABLETS,** U.S.P. XXI.

• **CEPHALEXIN,** U.S.P. XXI. Caps., Oral Susp., Tab U.S.P. XXI. 7-(D-2-Amino-2-phenyl-acetamido) methyl-8-oxo-5-thia-1-azabicyclo-[4.2.0]oct-2-3n3-2-carboxylic acid. 5-Thia-1-azabicyclo[4.2.0.]oct-2 ene-2-carboxylic acid,7-[(aminophenylacetyl)amin 3-methyl-8oxo-, monohydrate.
Use: Antibiotic.

CEPHALEXIN. B.A.N. 7-(D-α-Aminophenylacetamid 3-cephem-4-carboxylic acid.

Jse: Antibiotic.
See: Ceporex
Keflex
PHALEXIN MONOHYDRATE.
See: Keflex, Pulvule & Susp. (Lilly)
PHALIN.
Lechithin with choline base, lipositol.
See: Alcolec, Cap., Granules (American Lecithin)
PHALOGLYCIN. 7-(D-2-Amino-2-phenyl-acetamido)-3-(hydroxymethyl)-8-oxo-5-thia-1-azabicyclo[4.2.0]oc-2-ene-2-carboxylic acid, acetate(ester) dihydrate.
Use: Antibiotic.
PHALOGLYCIN. B.A.N. 7-[(—)-α-Amino-phenylacetamido]cephalosporanic acid.
Use: Antibiotic.
See: Kefglycin
PHALOGLYCIN DIHYDRATE.
See: Kafocin, Pulvule (Lilly)
PHALONIUM. B.A.N. 3-(4-Carbamoyl-1-pyridinio-methyl)-7-(2-thienylacetamido)-3-cephem-4-carboxylate.
Use: Antibiotic.
PHALORAM. B.A.N. 7-Phenylacetamidocephalosporanic acid.
Use: Antibiotic.
PHALORIDINE. B.A.N. 7-[(2-Thienyl)acetamido]-3-(1-pyridylmethyl)-3-cephem-4-carboxylic acid betaine.
Use: Antibiotic.
See: Ceporin
PHALORIDINE, STERILE. 1-[[2-Carboxy-8-oxo-7-[2-(2-thienyl)acetamido]-5-thia-1-azabicyclo[4.2.0]oct-2-en-3-yl]methyl]pyridinium hydroxide inner salt.
Use: Antibacterial.
See: Loridine, Amp. (Lilly)
PHALOSPORIN C. B.A.N. 7-(5-Amino-5-carboxy-valeramido)cephalosporanic acid.
Use: Antibiotic.
PHALOTHIN. B.A.N. 7-(2-Thienylacetamido) cephalosporanic acid. A semisynthetic antibiotic using the fungus Cephalosporium. Not inactivated by penicillinase.
Use: Antibiotic.
See: Keflin Prods (Lilly) Seffin, Inj. (Glaxo)
CEPHALOTHIN SODIUM, STERILE, U.S.P. XXI. Inj., Sterile, For Inj., U.S.P. XXI. (Lilly) 7-(2-Thienyl acetamido) cephalosporanic acid sod. salt. 5-Thia-1-azabicyclo[4.2.0]oct-2-ene-2-carboxylic acid,3-[(acetyloxy)methyl]-8-oxo-7-[(2-thienylacetyl)-amino]-,monosodium salt.
Use: Antibacterial, antibiotic.
See: Keflin, Vial (Lilly)
PHAMANDOLE. B.A.N. 7-D-Mandelamido-3-[(1-methyltetrazol-5-yl)thiomethyl]-3-cephem-4-carboxylic acid.
Use: Antibiotic.
CEPHAPIRIN SODIUM, STERILE, U.S.P. XXI. Sodium 3-(hydroxymethyl)-8-oxo-7-[2-(4-pyridylthio) acetamido]-5-thia-1-azabicyclo[4.2.0]oct-2-ene-2-carboxylate acetate (ester).
Use: Antibiotic.
See: Cefadyl, Vial (Bristol)

CEPHAZOLIN. B.A.N. 3-[(5-Methyl-1,3,4-thiadiazol-2-yl)thiomethyl]-7-(tetrazol-1-ylacetamido)-3-cephem-4-carboxylic acid.
Use: Antibiotic.
CEPHAZOLIN SODIUM.
See: Ancef (SmithKline)
Kefzol (Lilly)
CEPHOXAZOLE. B.A.N. 7-(3-o-Chlorophenyl-5-methylisoxazole-4-carboxamido)-cephalosporanic acid.
Use: Antibiotic.
• **CEPHRADINE,** U.S.P. XXI. Cap., Inj., Oral Susp., Sterile U.S.P. XXI. 7-[D-2-Amino-2-(1,4-cyclohexadien-1-yl-acetamido]-3-methyl-8-oxo-5-thia-1-azabicyclo[4.2.0]oct-2-ene-2-carboxylic acid monohydrate.
Use: Antibiotic.
See: Anspor, Cap., Susp. (SmithKline)
Eskacef
Velosef, Cap., Inj., Susp. (Squibb)
CEPHULAC. (Merrell Dow) Lactulose syrup 10 G./15 ml. Bot. pt., 2 qt. Unit dose 30 ml. Box 100s.
Use: Prevention & treatment of portal-systemic encephalopathy.
CERABEX-T. (Vitarine) Vit. C 500 mg., with high potency vitamins.
Use: Dietary supplement.
CERAPON. Triethanolamine Polypeptide Oleate-Condensate. (Purdue-Frederick)
See: Cerumenex, Drops (Purdue-Frederick)
CEREBEL. (Xttrium) Phenobarbital elix. 2.02 ml., milk of bismuth 2.5 ml., cerium oxalate 300 mg., hyoscyamine sulfate 5.2 mcg., atropine sulfate 0.01 mg., hyoscine HBr 3 mcg., alcohol 6%/5 cc. Bot. pt.
Use: Antidiarrheal.
CEREBID-150. (Saron) Papaverine HCl 150 mg./Sus. Rel. Cap. Bot. 100s, 1000s.
Use: Cerebral and peripheral ischemia.
CEREBID-200. (Saron) Papaverine HCl 200 mg./Sus. Rel. Tab. Bot. 100s, 1000s.
Use: Cerebral and peripheral ischemia.
CERELOSE.
See: Glucose (Various Mfr.)
CERESPAN. (USV Labs.) Papaverine HCl 150 mg./Sustained release cap. Bot. 100s, 1000s.
Use: Cerebral and peripheral ischemia.
CERETEX. (Enzyme Process) iron 15 mg., B-12 10 mcg., B-1 2 mg., B-6 1 mg., niacinamide 1 mg., pantothenic acid 0.15 mg., B-2 2 mg., iodine 15mg./2 cc. Bot. 60 cc., 8 0z.
Use: Supplement.
CEROSE COMPOUND. (Ives) Chlorpheniramine maleate 4 mg., phenylephrine HCl 10 mg., acetaminophen 325 mg./Cap. Bot. 100s.
Use: Relief of allergy, common cold, pain, fever, sinusitis, nasal congestion.
CEROSE, DM. (Ives) Dextromethorphan HBr 10 mg., phenindamine tartrate 5 mg., phenylephrine HCl 5 mg., fl. ex. ipecac 0.17 min., glycerin 40 min., pot. guaiacolsulfonate 86 mg., sod. citrate 3 gr., citric acid 1 gr. & alcohol 2.5%/5 cc. Sugar free. Bot. 4 oz., 1 pt.
Use: Symptomatic relief of coughs due to colds, nasal congestion, sinusitis.

CERTANE. (Ladco) Vaginal cones 6s. Vaginal jelly tube 12s.
Use: Contraceptive.

CERTANE DOUCHE POWDER. (Ladco) Oxyquinoline sulfate, boric acid, sod. chloride & sod. sulfo-dioctyl succinate. Can 4 oz., 12 oz. Packettes 9s, 18s.
Use: Vaginal cleanser.

CERTANE JELLY. (Ladco) Phenylmercuric acetate 0.02%, w/oxyquinoline sulfate, boric acid, sod. sulfo-dioctyl succinate. Tube 2.25 oz., 4.25 oz.
Use: Contraceptive jelly.

CERUBIDINE. (Ives) Daunorubicin HCl 5 mg./ml. once reconstituted w/4 ml. water for injection. Vial 20 mg.
Use: Antineoplastic.

• **CERULETIDE.** USAN.
Use: Stimulant.

CERUMENEX DROPS. (Purdue Frederick) Triethanolamine polypeptide oleate-condensate. Dropper bot. 6 cc., 12 cc.
Use: Removal of cerumen (ear wax).

CERVO. (Sutliff & Case) Sod. citrate 560 mg., ammonium chloride 520 mg., pot. guaiacol sulfonate 520 mg., antimony pot. tartrate 5.4 mg./Fl. oz. Bot. pt., gal.
Use: Cough due to sore throat or colds.

CES. (I.C.N.) Conjugated estrogens, 0.625 mg., 1.25 mg., 2.5 mg./Tab.
Use: Hormone.

• **CESIUM CHLORIDE.** USAN.
Use: Myocardial scanning.

• **CETABEN SODIUM.** USAN.
Use: Antihyperlipoproteinemic.

CETACAINE. (Cetylite) Benzocaine 14%, butyl aminobenzoate 2%, tetracaine HCl 2%, benzalkonium Cl 0.5%, cetyl dimethyl ethyl ammonium bromide 0.005%, **Aerosol Spray** 56 Gm. 50 cc. **Liquid:** 56 Gm.**Oint.:** Jar 37 Gm., flavored. **Hosp. Gel:** 29 Gm.
Use: Topical anesthetic.

CETACIN. (Jenkins) Cetylpyridinium Cl 4 mg., sodium propionate 10 mg., benzocaine 6 mg./Tab. Bot. 1000s.
Use: Anesthetic throat lozenge.

CETACORT LOTION. (Owen) Hydrocortisone in concentrations of 0.25%, 0.5%, or 1% w/cetyl alcohol, propylene glycol, stearyl alcohol, sodium lauryl sulfate, butylparaben, methylparaben, propylparaben and purified water. Bot. 2 oz., 4 oz.
Use: Relief of inflammatory manifestations of corticosteroid-responsive dermatoses.

• **CETALKONIUM.** F.D.A.
Benzylhexadecyldimethylammonium ion.

• **CETALKONIUM CHLORIDE.** USAN.
Cetyldimethylbenzyl ammonium chloride.
Use: Antibacterial agent.
W/Phenylephrine, pyrilamine maleate, thimerosal.
See: Anti-B Mist (DePree)

CETALKONIUM CHLORIDE. B.A.N.
Benzylhexadecyldimethylammonium chloride.
Use: Anti-infective.

CETAMIDE. (Alcon) Sulfacetamide sod. 10%. Sterile ophthalmic oint. Tube 3.5 Gm.

• **CETAMOLOL HYDROCHLORIDE.** USAN.
Use: Anti-adrenergic

CETANE CAPSULES. (Forest) Ascorbic acid 500 mg./Cap. Bot. 100s, 1000s.
Use: Vit. C deficiency.

CETAPHIL CREAM. (Owen) Purified water, cetyl alcohol, propylene glycol, sodium lauryl sulfate, stearyl alcohol, methylparaben, propylparaben, butylparaben. Jar 1 lb.
Use: Skin cleanser for soap intolerant people.

CETAPHIL LOTION. (Owen) Cetyl alcohol, stearyl alcohol, propylene glycol, sod. lauryl sulfate, methylparaben, propylparaben, butylparaben, purified water. Bot. 8 fl. oz., 16 fl. oz.
Use: Lipid-free skin cleanser.

CETAPRED. (Alcon) Sulfacetamide sodium 10%, prednisolone 0.25% in a methylcellulose vehicle. Soln. Ophth. Oint. Tube 3.5 Gm.
Use: Inflammatory and infectious conditions of the eye.

CETAZOL. (Professional Pharmacal) Acetazolamide 250 mg./Tab. Bot. 100s.
Use: Glaucoma treatment, carbonic anhydrase inhibitor.

• **CETIEDIL CITRATE.** USAN.
Use: Vasodilator.

• **CETIRIZINE HYDROCHLORIDE.** USAN.
Use: Antihistaminic.

• **CETOCYCLINE HYDROCHLORIDE.** USAN.
Use: Antibacterial.

CETOMACROGOL 1000. B.A.N. Polyethylene glycol 1000 monocetyl ether. Polyoxyethylene glycol 100 monocetyl ether.
Use: Pharmaceutical aid.

• **CETOPHENICOL.** USAN. D-threo-N- {p-[acetyl-β-hydroxy-α-(hydroxymethyl)-phenethyl]}-2,2-dichloroacetamide.
Use: Antibacterial agent.

• **CETOSTEARYL ALCOHOL,** N.F. XVI.
Use: Pharmaceutic aid (emulsifying agent).

CETOXIME. B.A.N. N-Benzylanilinoacetamidoxime.
Use: Antihistamine.
See: Febramine

• **CETRAXATE HYDROCHLORIDE.** USAN.
Use: Anti-ulcerative.

CETRIMONIUM CHLORIDE. B.A.N.
Hexadecyltrimethylammonium chloride.
Use: Antiseptic detergent.

CETRO-CIROSE. (Ives) Codeine phosphate 30 mg., potassium guaiacolsulfonate 8 gr., glycerin 240 minim ipecac flext. 1 min., sod. citrate 18 gr., citric acid 6 gr./5 cc w/alcohol 1.5% Bot. 1 pt., 1 gal.
Use: Narcotic cough preparation.

CETYBEN TROCHES. (Sutliff & Case) Cetylpyridinium chloride (1:1000) 1 mg., diperodon HCl 1 mg./Troche. Box 100s, 1000s.
Use: Throat irritations.

• **CETYL ALCOHOL,** N.F. XVI. 1-Hexadecanol.
Use: Emulsifying & stiffening agent.

• **CETYL ESTERS WAX,** N.F. XVI.

CETYLCIDE SOLUTION. (Cetylite) Cetyldimethylethyl ammonium Br 6.5%, benzalkonium Cl 6.5%,

sopropyl alcohol 13%. Inert ingredients 74%, ncluding sodium nitrite. Amp. 15 cc., Bot. 32 oz., 16 oz.
Jse: Disinfectant.
TYLDIMETHYL BENZYL AMMONIUM CHLORIDE.
See: Ceetolan Concentrate, Liq. (Lannett)
Benzocaine, ascorbic acid.
See: Locane, Troches (Reid-Provident)
Trocaine Lozenges (Vortech)
Phenylephrine HCl, pyrilamine maleate.
See: Dalihist, Nasal Spray (Dalin)
ETYLPYRIDINIUM CHLORIDE, U.S.P. XXI.
Topical Soln., Loz., U.S.P. XXI. 1-Hexadecylpyridinium chloride.
Jse: Local anti-infective.
See: Bactalin, Bot. (LaCrosse)
Benzocaine.
See: Axon Throat Loz. (McKesson)
Cēpacol, Throat Lozenges, (Merrell Dow)
Coirex, Preps. (Rowell)
Lanazets, Loz. (Lannett)
Oradex-C, Troches (Commerce)
Semets, Troches (Beecham Labs)
Spec-T Sore Throat Loz. (Squibb)
Tyro-Loz. (Kenyon)
Vicks Medi-Trating Throat Lozenges (Vicks)
Benzocaine.
See: Cepacol Anticeptic Lozenges (Merrell Dow)
Benzocaine, Menthol, camphor, eucalyptus oil.
See: Vicks Medi-Trating Throat Lozenges (Vicks)
Dextromethorphan HBr, benzocaine.
See: Thorzettes Logenes (Towne)
Methapyrilene HCl, naphazoline.
See: Korizol, Spray (Sutliff & Case)
d-Methorphan HBr, phenyltoloxamine dihydrogen citrate, and sodium citrate.
See: Exo-Kol, Cough Syrup, Spray, Tab. (Inwood)
Phenylephrine HCl, methapyrilene HCl, menthol, eucalyptol, camphor, methyl salicylate.
See: Vicks Sinex Nasal Spray (Vicks)
Phenylpropanolamide HCl, benzocaine, terpin hydrate.
See: S.A.C. Throat Lozenges (Towne)
TYLPYRIDINIUM CHLORIDE. B.A.N. 1-Hexadecylpyridinium chloride.
Use: Antiseptic detergent.
See: Ceepryn
Merocet
TYLTRIMETHYL AMMONIUM BROMIDE. (Bio Labs.) Cetrimide B.P., Cetavlon, CTAB.
Use: Antiseptic, Surface-active agent.
Hydrocortisone, phenylephrine, methapyrilene, chlorobutanol.
See: T-Spray (Saron)
Lidocaine, hexachlorophene.
See: Aerosept, Aerosol (Dalin)
VALIN. (Lilly) Ascorbic acid. **Amp.:** (100 mg.) 2 cc. pkg. 6s, 100s. (500 mg.) 1 cc. Pkg. 25s. (1 Gm.) 10 cc. Pkg. 25s. **Tab.:** (100 mg.) Bot. 100s, (250 mg.) Bot. 100s. (500 mg.) Bot. 100s, 500s.
Use: I.M., I.V., S.C. & orally, Vitamin C deficiency.

CEVI-BID. (Geriatric) Ascorbic acid 500 mg./Cap. Bot. 30s, 100s, 500s.
Use: Vitamin C therapy.
CEVI-FER. (Geriatric) Ascorbic acid 300 mg., ferrous fumarate 60 mg., folic acid 1 mg./Cap. Bot. 30s.
Use: Treatment secondary anemias.
CE-VI-SOL. (Mead Johnson) Ascorbic acid 35 mg./0.6 ml. Bot. w/dropper 50 ml.
Use: Vitamin C supplementation.
CEVITA. (Kay) **Chewable Tabs.** Ascorbic acid 100 mg. or 250 mg./Chewable Tab. Bot. 100s, 1000s. **Tabs.** 500 mg. 100s, 1000s. Kaykaps T.D. 500 mg., Bot. 60s, 250s, 500s, 1000s.
Use: Vitamin supplement.
CEVITA INJECTION. (Kay) Sodium ascorbate 250 mg./ml. Vial 30 ml.; 10 Gm./50 ml. Vial 50 ml.; 200 mg./ml. Amp. 5 ml.
Use: Vitamin C supplement.
CEVITAMIC ACID.
See: Ascorbic acid.
CEVITAN.
See: Ascorbic acid.
CEWIN TABLETS. (Winthrop Products) Ascorbic acid.
Use: Vitamin C supplement.
CEYLON GELATIN.
See: Agar.
CEZ. (Dattel) Vit. A 2,000 I.U., C 250 mg., E 100 I.U., zinc sulfate 25 mg./Cap. Bot. 60s.
Use: Vitamin supplement.
C.G. (Sig) Choronic gonadotropin (lyophilized) 10,000 u., mannitol 100 mg., supplied with diluent. Univial 10 ml.
CG DISPOSABLE UNIT.
See: Cardio Green, Vial (Hynson, Westcott & Dunning)
CG RIA. (Abbott) Test kit 100s.
Use: Diagnostic kit for cholyglycine.
CHAP CREAM. (Ar-Ex) Carbonyl diamide. Tubes 1.5 oz., 3.25 oz. Jar 4 oz., 9 oz., 18 oz.
Use: Hypoallergenic hand cream.
CHAPOLINE CREAM LOTION. (Wade) Glycerine, boric acid, chlorobutanol 0.5%, alcohol 10%. Bot. 4 oz., pt., gal.
Use: Skin irritation.
CHARCOAID. (Requa) Activated charcoal in sorbital slurry. Bot. 6 oz.
Use: Antidote for acute toxic ingestion.
CHARCOAL.
See: Requa's Charcoal, Prods. (Requa)
• **CHARCOAL, ACTIVATED,** U.S.P. XXI.
Use: Antidote: pharmaceutic aid (Adsorbent).
See: Kerr Charcodote, Pow. (Panray)
Kerr Insta-Char, Susp. (Kerr)
W/Nux vomica, bismuth subgallate, pepsin, berberis, diastase, pancreatin, hydrastis, papain.
See: Charcocaps, Cap. (Requa)
Charcotabs, Tab. (Requa)
Digestalin, Tab. (Vortech)
CHARCOAL ANTIDOTE. (U.S. Products) Activated charcoal 15 Gm., 30 Gm. Box 12s.
Use: Poison antidote.

CHARCOCAPS. (Requa) Activated charcoal 260 mg./Cap. Bot. 36s, 300s.
Use: G.I. Detoxicant, antiflatulent, antidiarrheal, indigestion.

CHARCODOTE. (Panray) Activated charcoal. 15 Gm., 30 Gm./unit dose.
Use: Antidote, poison control.

CHARDONNA-2. (Rorer) Phenobarbital 15 mg., belladonna extract 15 mg./Tab. Bot. 100s.
Use: Antispasmodic, antisecretory, sedative.

CHARDOSE POWDER. (Upsher-Smith) Activated charcoal USP 20 gm. or 30 gm./Unit Dose Bottle.
Use: Oral adsorbent.

CHARGERS. (Eckerd) Caffeine 100 mg.
Use: CNS stimulant. Tab. Bot. 40s.

CHARO SCATTER-PAKS. (Requa) Activated charcoal 5 Gm./Packet.
Use: Odor absorber.

CHAZ SCALP TREATMENT DANDRUFF SHAMPOO. (Revlon) Zinc pyrithione 1% in liquid shampoo.
Use: Dandruff shampoo.

CHECKMATE. (Oral-B) Acidulated phosphate fluoride 1.23%. Bot. 2 oz., 16 oz.
Use: Topical application to aid in dental caries prevention.

CHEK-STIX URINALYSIS CONTROL STRIPS. (Ames) Bot. 25s.
Use: Control strips for visual urinalysis.

CHELAFRIN.
See: Epinephrine.

CHELAMIDE INJECTION. (Vortech) Disodium edetate 150 mg./ml. Vial 20 ml.
Use: Chelating agent.

CHELATING AGENT.
See: Bal, Amp. (Hynson, Westcott & Dunning)
Calcium Disodium Versenate, Amp., Tab. (Riker)
Desferal, Amp. (Ciba)
Endrate Disodium, Amp. (Abbott)
Magora, Tab. (Miller)

CHELEN.
See: Ethyl Chloride.

CHEL-IRON. (Kinney) Ferrocholinate, Iron choline citrate complex 0.33 Gm. equiv. to 40 mg. of elemental iron/Tab. Bot. 100s.
Use: Iron deficiency anemias.

CHEL-IRON LIQUID. (Kinney) 0.417 Gm. ferrocholinate equiv. to 50 mg. of elemental iron per teaspoonful. Bot. 8 fl. oz.
Use: Pediatric oral iron therapy.

CHEL-IRON PEDIATRIC DROPS. (Kinney) 0.208 Gm. Ferrocholinate, equiv. to 25 mg. of elemental iron/cc. Bot. 60 cc. with calibrated dropper.
Use: Pediatric oral iron therapy.

CHEL-IRON PLUS. (Kinney) Ferrocholinate 200 mg. (equiv. to 24 mg. elemental iron) Vit. B-12 with intrinsic factor concentrate ⅓ u., Vit. C 50 mg., B-1 2 mg., B-2 2 mg., B-6 HCl 2 mg., niacin 25 mg./Tab. Bot. 100s.
Use: Iron deficiency anemias.

CHEMIPEN. Pot. phenethicillin.
Use: Infections amenable to therapy with oral penicillin.

CHEMOVAG SUPPS. (Fellows) Sulfisoxazole 0.5 Gm./Supp. Bot. 12s w/applicators.
Use: Cervicitis, vaginitis, vulvitis and related gynecologic disorders.

CHEMOZINE. (Tennessee Pharm.) Sulfadiazine, 0.1 Gm., sulfamerazine, 0.167 Gm., sulfamethazine, 0.167 Gm./Tab. Bot. 100s, 1000s. Susp. Bot. 1 p 1 gal.

CHENATAL. (Miller) Ca 580 mg., Mg 200 mg., Vit. 100 mg., lemon bioflavonoid complex 30 mg., fol acid 0.4 mg., A 5000 I.U., D 400 I.U., B-1 3 mg., 2 3 mg., B-6 5 mg., B-12 9 mcg., niacinamide 30 m pantothenic acid 5 mg., tocopherols (mixed) 10 mg., Fe 20 mg., Cu 1 mg., Mn 2 mg., K 10 mg., 25 mg., iodine 0.1 mg./2 Tabs. Bot. 100s.
Use: Prenatal vitamin-mineral combination.

CHENIX. (Rowell) Chenodiol 250 mg./Tab. Bot. 10
Use: Cholesterol gallstone disolution.

• **CHENODIOL.** USAN.
Use: Anticholelithogenic.
See: Chenix, Tab. (Rowell)

CHERACOL D. (Upjohn) Dextromethorphan HBr 10 mg., guaifenesin 100 mg./ 5 ml. w/alcohol 4.75% Bot. 2 oz., 4 oz., 6 oz.
Use: Coughs due to colds.

CHERACOL. (Upjohn) Codeine phosphate 10 mg., guaifenesin 100 mg./5 ml. w/alcohol 4.75%. Bot. oz., 4 oz., pt.
Use: Narcotic-containing cough mixture.

CHERACOL PLUS. (Upjohn) Phenylpropanolamine HCl 25 mg., dextromethorphan HBr 20 mg., chlorpheniramine maleate 4 mg./15 ml. Bot. 4 oz 6 oz.
Use: Treatment of head cold symptoms.

CHERALIN SYRUP. (Lannett) Pot. guaiacol sulfona 8 gr., ammonium chloride 8 gr., antimony and pot tartrate 1/12 gr. in white pine & wild cherry/Fl. oz. Bot. pt., gal.; also with codeine 1 gr./Oz. Bot. pt., gal.
Use: Cough preparation.

CHERAPAS. (Kay) Hydrochlorothiazide 15 mg., reserpine 0.1 mg., hydralazine 25 mg./Tab. Bot. 1000s.
Use: Treat hypertension.

CHERASULFA PEDIATRIC. (Cenci) Triple sulfa. (5 gr.): Sulfadiazine, 1.67 gr., sulfamethazine, 1.67 g sulfamerazine 1.67 gr., sodium citrate 6 gr./5 cc. Bot. 16 oz. **F.S. Liq.**: (7.5 gr.) Bot. 16 oz. **Tab.**: 7 gr. Bot. 100s, 1000s, 5000s.
Use: Infections caused by sulfonamide-suscepti organisms.

CHERASULFA SUSPENSION. (Sutliff & Case) Sulfadiazine 167 mg., sulfamethazine 167 mg., sulfamerazine 167 mg., sod. citrate 51 mg./5 cc. Susp. Bot. pt., gal.
Use: Triple sulfonamide therapy.

CHERATUSSIN COUGH SYRUP. (Towne) Dextromethorphan HBr 45 mg., ammon. chloride 575 mg., citrate sodium 280 mg.,/Fl. oz. Bot. 4 o

CHERI-APRO. (Approved) Codeine phos. 1 gr., p guaicolsulfonate 8 gr., tartar emetic 1/12 gr./fl. oz. Bot. 4 oz., gal.

ERIJEN MORPHINE SULFATE. (Jenkins) Alcohol %, morphine sulfate 2.5 mg., ammonium chloride 8 mg., potassium guaiacolsulfonate 88 mg., tartar metic 0.9 mg./5 cc. Syr. 4 oz., gal.
ERO-TRISULFA-V. (Vita Elixir) Sulfadiazine 0.166 im., sulfacetamide 0.166 Gm., sulfamerazine .166 Gm., sodium citrate 0.500 Gm./5 cc. Susp. ot. pt.
se: Multiple sulfonamide therapy.
ERRALEX. (Barre) Pot. guiacolsulfonate 8 gr., mmonium chloride 3 gr., tartar emetic 1/12 gr., lcohol 3%/Fl. oz. Also w/codeine phosphate 1 gr. ot. pt., gal.
se: Coughs due to colds.
ERRY-B. (Vortech) Nicotinamide 10 mg., Vit. B-1 2.5 ng., B-2 0.5 mg., B-6 0.15 mg., d-pantothenyl alcohol .20 mg./cc. Bot. 1 oz., pt., Gal.
Jse: B-complex therapy.
HERRY JUICE, N.F. XVI.
Jse: Flavor.
HERRY SYRUP, N.F. XVI.
Jse: Pharmaceutic aid (Vehicle)
ESTAMINE. (Leeds) Chlorpheniramine maleate 8 r 12 mg./Cap. Bot. 50s.
Jse: Allergic states responsive to antihistamines.
EW HIST. (Kenyon) Phenylephrine HCl 7.5 mg., hlorpheniramine maleate 2 mg., C 50 mg./Wafer. lot. 100s.
EWIES TABLETS. (Barry-Martin) Vit. A 5000 I.U., D 00 I.U., B-1 3 mg., B-2 2.5 mg., B-6 1 mg., -12 1 mcg., C 50 mg., niacinamide 20 mg./Tab. Bot. 00s, 250s. Also available w. minerals.
Jse: Multivitamin.
Fluoride. Chewies Tab. formula plus fluoride 0.5 ng./Tab.
Jse: Vitamin supplement
EW-VIMS. (Barth's) Vit. A 5000 I.U., D 400 I.U., B-1 3 mg., -2 6 mg., niacin 1.71 mg., C 100 mg., B-12 mcg., E 5 I.U./Tab. Bot. 30s, 90s, 180s, 360s.
Jse: Multivitamin.
EW-VI-TAB. (Blue Cross) Vit A 2,500 I.U., D 400 I.U., 15 I.U., C 60 mg., folic acid 0.3 mg., B-1 1.05 mg., -2 1.2 mg., niacin 13.5 mg., B-6 1.05 mg., B-12 4.5 ncg./Tab. Bot. 100s.
Jse: Vitamin supplement.
EW-VI-TAB WITH IRON. (Blue Cross) Vit. A 5,000 .U., C 60 mg., E 15 I.U., folic acid 0.4 mg., B-1 1.5 mg., -2 1.7 mg., niacin 20 mg., B-6 2 mg., B-12 6 mcg., D 00 I.U., iron 18 mg./Tab. Bot. 100s.
Jse: Vitamin and iron supplement.
EW-VITE. (Vortech) Vit. A. 5000 I.U., D 500 I.U., C 50 ng., B-1 3 mg., B-2 2.5 mg., B-6 1 mg., Niacinamide 0 mg., B-12 1 mcg./Tab. Bot. 100s, 1000s
Jse: Multiple vitamin.
EWVITES. (Zenith) Vit. A 3,500 I.U., D 400 I.U., B-1 1.1 mg., B-2 1.2 mg., niacinamide 15 mg., C 40 mg., -6 1.2 mg., B-12 5 mcg., folic acid 0.1 mg., pantohenic acid 5 mg./Tab. Bot. 100s.
Jse: Chewable vitamins.
EW VITES. (Kenyon) Vit. A 5000 I.U., D 500 I.U., -1 2 mg., B-2 2 mg., B-6 1 mg., B-12 2 mcg. Ca pantothenate 2 mg., C 50 mg., niacinamide 10 mg., fluoride 0.05 mg./Tab. Bot. 100s.
CHEXIT. (Dorsey) Pheniramine maleate 12.5 mg., pyrilamine maleate 12.5 mg., phenylpropanolamine 25 mg., dextromethorphan HBr 30 mg., terpin hydrate 180 mg., acetaminophen 325 mg./Tab. Dispenser 12s.
Use: Decongestant & antitussive.
CHIGGEREX. (Scherer) Benzocaine 0.02% w/camphor, menthol, peppermint oil, olive oil, clove oils, pegosperse, methylparaben, distilled water. Oint. Jar 50 Gm.
Use: Chigger bites.
CHIGGERTOX. (Scherer) Benzocaine 2.1%, benzyl benzoate 21.4%, soft soap, isopropyl alcohol. Liq. Bot. 1 oz.
Use: Chigger, tick, and mosquito bites.
CHILDREN'S CONGEST-AFED DM SYRUP. (Eckerd) Pseudoephedrine HCl 30 mg., guaifenesin 100 mg., dextromethorphan HBr 10 mg./5 ml. w/alcohol 10%. Bot. 4 oz.
Use: Decongestant, expectorant, antitussive.
CHILDREN'S COUGH SYRUP. (Eckerd) Phenylpropanolamine HCl 6.25 mg., guaifenesin 75 mg., dextromethorphan 5 mg.,/5 ml. w/alcohol 5%. Bot. 4 oz.
Use: Expectorant, decongestant, antitussive.
CHILDREN'S HOLD 4-HOUR COUGH SUPPRESSANT & DECONGESTANT. (Beecham Products) Dextromethorphan HBr 3.75 mg., phenylpropanolamine HCl. 6.25 mg./Loz. 10s.
Use: Antitussive & decongestant.
CHILDREN'S NO ASPIRIN ELIXIR. (Walgreen) Acetaminophen 80 mg./2.5 ml. Bot. 4 oz.
Use: Analgesic.
CHILDREN'S NO-ASPIRIN TABLETS. (Walgreen) Acetaminophen 80 mg./Tab. Bot. 30s.
Use: Analgesic.
CHINESE GELATIN.
See: Agar
CHINESE ISINGLASS. 7-Iodo-8-hydroxyquinoline-5-sulfonic acid sodium salt. Yatren.
Use: Amebic dysentery.
CHINIOFON. 7-Iodo-8-hydroxyquinoline-5-sulfonic acid, anayodin, yatren, quinoxyl. (CMC) Chiniofon 250 mg., 8-hydroxy-7-iodoquinoline-5-sulfonic acid 80%, sod. bicarbonate 20%/Tab. Bot. 100s, 1000s.
Use: Intestinal amebiasis.
CHINOSOL. (Vernon) 8-Hydroxyquinoline sulfate. Tab. 7.5 gr. Vial 6s. Trit. Tabs. (3/5 gr.) Bot. 50s. Vial 110s. Pow. 1 oz.
Use: Antiseptic sol.
CHLAMYDIAZYME. (Abbott) Test kits 100s.
Use: Enzyme immunoassay for detection of *Chlamydia trachomatis* from urethral or urogenital swabs.
CHLO-AMINE. (Hollister-Stier) Chlorpheniramine maleate 2 mg./Chewable Tab. Box 24x4 mg. Tab. Packages.
Use: Antihistaminic.
• **CHLOPHEDIANOL.** F.D.A. 2-Chloro-alpha-[2-(dimethylamino)ethyl] benzhydrol.

CHLOPHEDIANOL. B.A.N. 2-Chloro-α-(2-dimethylaminoethyl)benzhydrol.
Use: Cough suppressant.
See: Detigon Hydrochloride

• **CHLOPHEDIANOL HCl.** USAN. a-(2-Dimethylaminoethyl)-o-chlorobenzyhydrol HCl.
See: Ulo, Syr. (Riker)
W/Diphenylpyraline HCl, phenylephrine HCl, gualifenesin, alcohol.
See: Acutuss Expectorant (Philips Roxane)

CHLOR-4. (Mills) Chlorpheniramine maleate 4 mg./Tab. Bot. 100s.

CHLOR-100. (Vortech) Chlorpheniramine maleate 100 mg./ml. Vial 10 ml.
Use: Antihistaminic.

CHLORACET CAP. (Jenkins) Chlorpheniramine maleate 4 mg., salicylamide 3 gr., phenacetin 2 gr., caffein 0.5 gr., ascorbic acid 50 mg./Cap. Bot. 1000s.

CHLORAFED. (Hauck) Chlorpheniramine maleate 2 mg., pseudoephedrine HCl 30 mg./5 ml. Alcohol, dye, sugar and corn free. Bot. Pts.
Use: Allergy and common cold treatment.

CHLORAFED TIMECELLES. (Hauck) Chlorpheniramine maleate 8 mg., pseudoephedrine HCl 120 mg./Sustained action timeceles. Bot. 100s, 500s. Unit dose 100s.
Use: Allergy and common cold treatment.

CHLORAFED H.S. TIMECELLES. (Hauck) Chlorpheniramine maleate 4 mg., pseudoephedrine HCl 60 mg./S.R. Cap. Bot. 100s, 500s.
Use: Allergy & common cold treatment.

CHLORAHIST. (Evron) Chlorpheniramine maleate 4 mg./Tab. Bot. 100s, 1000s. Chlorpheniramine maleate 8 or 12 mg./Cap. Bot. 250s, 1000s. Syr. 2 mg./4 cc. Bot. qt.
Use: Symptomatic relief of allergic manifestations.

• **CHLORAL BETAINE.** USAN.
Use: Sedative.

CHLORALFORMAMIDE. N-(2,2,2-trichloro-l-hydroxyethyl) formamide.

• **CHLORAL HYDRATE,** U.S.P. XXI. Caps., Syr. U.S.P. XXI. 1,1-Ethanediol, 2,2,2-trichloro-ethanol. Chloral.
Use: Hypnotic and sedative.
See: Aquachloral Supprettes, Supp. (Webcon)
Cohidrate, Cap. (Coastal)
Felsules, Cap. (Fellows-Testagar)
H.S. Need, Cap. (Hanlon)
Maso-Chloral, Cap. (Mason)
Noctec, Cap. & Syr. (Squibb)
Oradrate, Cap. (Coast Labs.)
Rectules, Supp. (Fellows-Testagar)
SK-Chloral Hydrate, Cap. (SmithKline)
Somnos, Elixir. (Merck Sharp & Dohme)
Generic Products:
Fellows-Cap. (3¾ gr.) Bot. 100s, 500s, 1000s.
Quality Generics- (7.5 gr.) Bot. 100s.
G.F. Harvey-Cap. (3¾ gr.) Bot. 100s; (7.5 gr.) Bot. 100s.
Lederle-Cap. 500 mg. 100s.
Pacific Pharm. Corp.-Cap. (7.5 gr.) Bot. 100s, 1000s.
Parke, Davis—Cap. (500 mg.) Bot. 100s, unit dc 100s.
Stayner-Cap. (250 mg. and 500 mg.) Bot. 100s, 500 mg. Bot. 1000s, Crystals Bot. 1 lb. and 5
West-Ward-Cap. (3¾ gr., 7.5 gr.) Bot. 100s.

CHLORAL HYDRATE BETAINE (1:1) COMPOUN Chloral Betaine.

CHLORAL-METHYLOL OINTMENT. (Ulmer) Me salicylate, methol. Jar. 2 oz., 1 lb.
Use: Analgesic ointment.

CHLORALPYRINE DICHLORALPYRINE.
See: Dichloralantipyrine

CHLORALURETHANE. Name used for Carbochlor

CHLORAMAN. (Rasman) Chlorpheniramine malea 12 mg./Tab. Bot. 100s, 500s, 1000s.
Use: Antihistaminic.

• **CHLORAMBUCIL,** U.S.P. XXI. Tab. U.S.P. XXI. 4-{p-[Bis(2-chlorethyl)-amino]-phenyl} butyric acid. Benzenebutanoic acid. 4-[bis(2-chloroethyl)-amino]-.
Use: Antineoplastic.
See: Leukeran, Tab. (Burroughs-Wellcome)

CHLORAMBUCIL. B.A.N. 4-[4-Di-(2-chloroethyl) ami phenyl]butyric acid.
Use: Antineoplastic agent.
See: Leukeran

CHLORAMINE-T. Sod. paratoluenesulfan chloram chloramine & chlorozone.
Lilly-Tab. (0.3 Gm.), Bot. 100s, 1000s.
Robinson, Pow., 1 oz.
Use: Antiseptic, deodorant.
See: Chlorazene, Prep. (Badger)

• **CHLORAMPHENICOL.** U.S.P. XXI. Caps., Cream, Oral Soln., Tab., Otic Soln., Sterile, Ophth. Sol., Ophth. Oint., for Ophth. Sol. Inj., U.S.P. XXI. D(-)-threo-2, 2-Dichloro-N[Beta-hydroxy-alpha-(hydroxymethyl)-p-nitrophenethyl]acetamide.
Use: Antibacterial, antirickettsial.
See: Antibiopto, Soln. Oint. (Softcon)
Chlorcetin
Chloromycetin, Prep. (Parke-Davis)
Chloroptic Ophth. Oint. (Allergan)
Chloroptic S.O.P. Ophth. Oint. (Allergan)
Econochlor, Soln., Oint. (Alcon)
Kemicetine
Mychel, Cap. (Rachelle)
Ophthochlor, Sol. (Parke-Davis)
Paraxin
W/Polymixin B.
Use: Treatment of superficial ocular infections involving the conjunctivia and/or cornea caused b susceptible organisms.
See: Chloromyxin Ophthalmic Oint. (Parke-Davis)
W/Polymyxin B, Hydrocortisone.
See: Ophthocort, Oint. (Parke-Davis)
W/Prednisolone alcohol.
See: Chloroptic-P S.O.P. Ophth. Oint. (Allergan)

CHLORAMPHENICOL. B.A.N. D-threo-2-Dichloroacetamido-1-(4-nitrophenyl)propane-1, 3-diol.
Use: Antiseptic; antibiotic.

CHLORAMPHENICOL AND HYDROCORTISONE ACETATE FOR OPHTHALMIC SUSPENSION, U.S.P. XXI.
Use: Antibiotic, anti-inflammatory.
See: Chloromycetin, Prods. (Parke-Davis)

CHLORAMPHENICOL AND POLYMYXIN B SULFATE OPHTHALMIC OINTMENT, U.S.P. XXI.
Use: Antibiotic.

CHLORAMPHENICOL, POLYMIXIN B SULFATE, AND HYDROCORTISONE ACETATE OPHTHALMIC OINTMENT, U.S.P. XXI.
Use: Antibiotic, anti-inflammatory.
See: Chloromycetin, Prods. (Parke-Davis).

CHLORAMPHENICOL AND PREDNISOLONE OPHTHALMIC OINTMENT, U.S.P. XXI.
Use: Antibiotic, steroid combination.
See: Chloromycetin, Prods. (Parke-Davis)

CHLORAMPHENICOL PALMITATE, U.S.P. XXI.
Oral Susp. U.S.P. XXI.
Use: Antibacterial, antirickettsial.
See: Chloromycetin Palmitate, Oral Susp. (Parke-Davis)

CHLORAMPHENICOL PANTOTHENATE COMPLEX. USAN. A complex consisting of 4 parts of chloramphenicol to one part of calcium pantothenate. Pantofenicol
Use: Antibiotic.

CHLORAMPHENICOL SODIUM SUCCINATE, STERILE, U.S.P. XXI.
Use: Antibacterial, antirickettsial.
See: Chloromycetin Succinate, Inj., (Parke-Davis)
Mychel-S, IV. (Rachelle)

CHLORANIL. 2,3,5,6-Tetrachloro-1,4-benzoquinone.

CHLORASEPTIC CHILDREN'S LOZENGES. (Procter & Gamble) Benzocaine 5 mg./Loz. Pkg. 18s.
Use: Anesthetic for temporary relief of minor sore throat pain.

CHLORASEPTIC LIQUID. (Procter & Gamble) Total phenol 1.4% as phenol and sodium phenolate. Menthol and cherry flavors. Bot. 6 oz. w/pump sprayer. Bot. 8 oz., 12 oz. Aerosol Spray 1.5 oz. Spray also contains compressed nitrogen.
Use: Antiseptic and anesthetic mouthwash and gargle for temporary relief of sore throat pain.

CHLORASEPTIC LOZENGE. (Procter & Gamble) Total phenol 32.5 mg./lozenge as phenol and sodium phenolate. Menthol and cherry flavors. Pkg. 18s, 36s.
Use: Anesthetic and antiseptic lozenge for temporary relief of minor sore throat pain.

CHLOR-A-TYL. (Jenkins) Acetyl-p-aminophenol 160 mg., chlorpheniramine maleate 1 mg., phenylephrine HCl 7.5 mg., ascorbic acid 15 mg./Tab. Bot. 1000s.

CHLORAZANIL HCl. 2-Amino-4-(p-chloroanilino)-s-triazine HCl. Daquim

CHLORAZENE. (Badger) Chloramine-T, sod. p-toluenesulfonchloramide. Pow., Pkg. No. 1 & No. 2; Bot. 1 lb., 5 lb. Aromatic Pow. (5%), Bot. 1 lb., 5 lb. Tab. (0.3 Gm.), Bot. 20s, 100s, 1000s, 5000s.
Use: Topically; antiseptic, deodorant.

CHLORAZEPATE DIPOTASSIUM.
Use: Minor tranquilizer.
See: Tranxene Prods. (Abbott)

CHLORAZEPTATE MONOPOTASSIUM.
Use: Minor tranquilizer

CHLORAZINE TABS. . (Major) Prochlorperazine 5 mg. or 10 mg./Tab. Bot. 100s.
Use: Treatment nausea and vomiting.

CHLORAZONE.
See: Chloramine-T

CHLOR BENZO MOR, A AND D OINTMENT. (Wade) Vitamins A and D fortified, chlorobutanol 3%, benzocaine 2%, benzyl alcohol 3%, actamer 1%, in lanolin and petrolatum base. Tube 1 oz., Jar 1 oz., lb.
Use: Antiseptic, anesthetic.

CHLOR BENZO MOR SPRAY. (Wade) Vitamin A and D fortified, chlorabutanol 3%, benzocaine 2%, benzyl alcohol 3%, and actamer 1%, in lanolin and mineral oil base. Bot. 2 oz., 11 oz.
Use: Antiseptic, anesthetic.

CHLORBETAMIDE. B.A.N. Dichloro-N-(2,4-dichlorobenzyl)-N-(2-hydroxyethyl)acetamide.
Use: Treatment of amebiasis.
See: Mantomide
Pontalin

CHLORBUTANOL.
See: Chlorobutanol, N.F. XVI.

CHLORBUTOL.
See: Chlorobutanol, N.F. XVI.

CHLORCYCLIZINE. B.A.N. 1-(4-Chlorobenzhydryl)-4-methylpiperazine.
Use: Antihistamine.
See: Di-paralene Histantin hydrochloride

• **CHLORCYCLIZINE HYDROCHLORIDE,** N.F. XVI. 1-(p-Chloro-α-phenylbenzyl)-4-methylpiperazine HCl. 1-(p-Chlorobenzhydryl)-4-methylpiperazine HCl. Histantin.
Use: Antihistaminic.
W/Hydrocortisone acetate.
See: Mantadil, Cream (Burroughs Wellcome)
W/Pseudoephedrine HCl.
See: Fedrazil, Tab. (Burroughs Wellcome)

• **CHLORDANTOIN.** F.D.A. 5-(1-Ethylpentyl)-3-[(trichloromethyl) thio] hydantoin.

• **CHLORDANTOIN.** USAN. 5-(1-Ethylamyl)-3-trichloromethyl thiohydantoin.
Use: Antifungal.
See: Sporostacin Cr. (Ortho)

• **CHLORDIAZEPOXIDE,** U.S.P. XXI. Tab., U.S.P. XXI. 3H-1, 4-Benzodiazepin-2-amine, 7-chloro-N-methyl-5-phenyl-, 4-oxide; 7-chloro-2-(methylamino)-5-phenyl-3H-1, 4-benzodiazepine 4-oxide.
Use: Tranquilizer.
See: A-poxide, Cap. (Abbott)
Brigen-G, Tab. (Grafton)
Libritabs, Tab. (Roche)
Menrium, Tab. (Roche)
W/Amitriptyline
See: Limbitrol, Tab. (Roche)

• **CHLORDIAZEPOXIDE HCl,** U.S.P. XXI., Caps, Sterile U.S.P. XXI. 7-Chloro-2-methylamino-5-phenyl-

3H-1, 4-benzodiazepine-4-oxide HCl. Methaminodiazepine HCl.
Use: Emotional disturbance, sedative.
See: A-poxide, Cap. (Abbott)
Chlordiazachel, Cap. (Rachelle)
Librium, Cap., Inj. (Roche)
Screen, Cap. (Foy)
SK-Lygen, Cap. (SmithKline)
Zetran, Cap. (Hauck)
W/Clidinium bromide
See: Chlordinium Sealets, Cap. (Lemmon)
Librax, Cap. (Roche)

• **CHLORDIAZEPOXIDE AND AMITRIPTPTYLINE HCL TABLETS,** U.S.P. XXI.
Use: Tranquilizer.
See: Limbitrol, Tab. (Roche)

CHLORDIMORPHINE HCl. γ-Morpholino-propyl-2-chloro-4-phenylphenyl ether HCl.

CHLORDINIUM SEALETS. (Lemmon) Chlordiazepoxide HCl 5 mg., clidinium Br 2.5 mg./Cap. Bot. 100s, 500s, 1000s.
Use: Gastrointestinal disorders.

CHLOREN 4. (Wren) Chlorpheniramine maleate 4 mg./Tab. Bot. 100s, 1000s.

CHLOREN 8 T.D. (Wren) Chlorpheniramine maleate 8 mg./Tab. Bot. 100s, 1000s.

CHLOREN 12 T.D. (Wren) Chlorpheniramine maleate 12 mg./Tab. Bot. 100s, 1000s.

CHLORESIUM OINTMENT. (Rystan) Water soluble chlorophyll "a" (0.5%) in specially prepared water-soluble base. Tube 1 oz., 4 oz. Jar 1 lb.
Use: Promote tissue growth and deodorize.

CHLORESIUM SOLUTION. (Rystan) Water-soluble chlorophyll "a" (0.2%) in isotonic saline solution. Bot. 8 oz., 32 oz.
Use: Cleansing and deodorization of purulent wounds.

CHLORESIUM TOOTH PASTE. (Rystan) Purified chlorophyllin (water-soluble). Tube 3.25 oz.

CHLORETHYL.
See: Ethyl Chloride

CHLORFENVINPHOS. B.A.N. 2-Chloro-1-(2,4-dichlorophenyl)vinyl diethyl phosphate.
Use: Insecticide, veterinary medicine.
See: Birlane

CHLORGUANIDE HYDROCHLORIDE.
See: Chloroguanide HCl (Various Mfr.)

CHLORHEXADOL. 2-Methyl-4-(2′,2′,2′,-trichlor-1′-hydroxyethoxy)-2-pentanol. Lora

CHLORHEXADOL. B.A.N. 2-Methyl-4-(2,2,2-trichloro-1-hydroxyethoxy)pentan-2-ol.
Use: Hypnotic; sedative.
See: Chloralodol (I.N.N.)
Medodorm

• **CHLORHEXIDINE.** F.D.A. 1,1′-Hexamethylenebis-[5-(ρ-chlorophenyl) biguanide]
Use: Antiseptic.
See: Hibiclens
Hibiscrub
Hibitane
Lisium
Rotersept

• **CHLORHEXIDINE GLUCONATE.** USAN. 1,1′-Hexamethylenebis[5-(ρ-chlorophenyl)biguanide] dihydrochloride.
Use: Antimicrobial skin cleanser.
See: Hibiclens, Liq. (Stuart)
Hibistat, Liq. (Stuart)

• **CHLORHEXIDINE HYDROCHLORIDE.** USAN.
Use: Anti-infective, topical.

CHLORHYDROXYQUINOLIN.
See: Quinolor Comp., Oint. (Squibb)

CHLORINATED AND IODIZED PEANUT OIL.
Chloriodized Oil.

• **CHLORINDANOL.** USAN. 7-Chloro-4-indanol.
Use: Antiseptic, spermaticide.

CHLORINE COMPOUND, ANTISEPTIC. Antiseptics, Chlorine.

CHLORIODIZED OIL. Chlorinated and iodized peanut oil.

CHLORISONDAMINE CHLORIDE. 4,5,6,7-Tetrachloro-2-(2-dimethylaminoethyl)-isoindoline dimethchloride.

CHLORISONDAMINE CHLORIDE. B.A.N. 4,5,6,7-Tetrachloro-2-(2-trimethylammonioethyl)-isoindolinium dichloride.
Use: Hypotensive.
See: Ecolid

CHLORMADINONE. B.A.N. 6-Chloro-17α-hydroxypregna-4,6-diene-3,20-dione.
Use: Progestational steroid.
See: Clordion
Normenon
Verton

• **CHLORMADINONE ACETATE.** USAN. 6-Chloro-6-dehydro-17α-acetoxyprogesterone. 6-Chloro-17-hydroxypregna-4,6-diene-3,20 dione Acetate.

CHLOR MAL w/SAL + APAP S.C. (Richlyn) Chlorpheneramine maleate 2 mg., acetaminophen 150 mg., salicylamide 175 mg./Tab. Bot. 1000s.
Use: Antihistamine, analgesic.

CHLORMENE. (Robinson) Chlorpheniramine maleate 4 mg./Tab.
Bot. 100s, 1000s.
Use: Antihistamine.

CHLORMENE INJECTION. (Robinson) Chlorpheniramine maleate injection. 10 mg., 30 cc. Vial; 100 mg. 10 cc. Vial.

CHLORMENE REPEAT ACTION. (Robinson) Chlorpheniramine 8 mg., 12 mg./Tab. Bot. 100s, 1000s.

CHLORMENE TIMECAPS. (Robinson) Chlorpheniramine maleate time disintegration 8 mg., 12 mg./Tab. Bot. 100s, 500s, 1000s.

CHLORMERODRIN. 3-Chloro-mercuri-2-methoxypropylurea. Chloro (2-methoxy-3-ureidopropyl) mercury. Mercloran.
Use: Diuretic.

CHLORMERODRIN Hg 197 INJECTION. Mercury ^{197}HG, [3-[(aminocarbonyl)amino]-2-methoxypropyl]-chloro-. Chloro(2-methoxy-3-ureidopropyl)mercury-^{197}Hg.
Use: Diagnostic aid (renal scanning).

LORMERODRIN Hg 203 INJECTION. Mercury-^{203}Hg,[3-[(aminocarbonyl)amino]-ureidopropyl)mercury-^{203}Hg.
Jse: Diagnostic aid (tumor localization).
LORMETHIAZOLE. B.A.N. 5-(2-Chloroethyl)-4-methylthiazole.
Jse: Hypnotic; sedative.
See: Heminevrin (base or the edisylate)
LORMEZANONE. Chlormethazanone. 2-(4-Chlorophenyl)-3-methyl-4-methathiazanone-1-2-dioxide
Use: Tranquilizer.
See: Trancopal, Cap. (Winthrop-Breon)
LORMIDAZOLE. B.A.N. 1-(4-Chlorobenzyl)-2-methylbenzimidazole.
Use: Antifungal agent.
LOR-NIRAMINE ALLERGY TABS. (Whiteworth) Chlorpheniramine maleate 4 mg./Tab. Bot. 24s, 100s.
Use: Antihistaminic.
LOROAZODIN. Alpha, alpha, Azobis-(chloroformamidine).
CHLORO-H-1,2,4-BENZOTHIADIAZINE-7-SULFONAMIDE 1,1-DIOXIDE.
See: Chlorothiazide
(γ-(ρ-CHLOROBENZYL) CINNAMYL) PYRROLIDINE PHOSPHATE (1:2).
See: Pyrrobutamine Phosphate
CHLOROBUTANOL, N.F. XVI. 1,1,1-Trichloro-2-methyl-2-propanol. Sedaform. (Various Mfr.)
Use: Anesthetic, antiseptic & hypnotic; pharmaceutic aid (antimicrobial preservative).
See: Cerumenex, Drops. (Purdue-Frederick)
Pre-Sert(Allergan)
/Atropine sulfate, chlorpheniramine maleate, phenylpropanolamine HCl.
See: Decongestant, Inj. (Century)
/Benzocaine and camphor.
See: Eardro, Liq. (Jenkins)
/Calcium glycerophosphate, calcium levulinate.
See: Cal San, Inj. (Burgin-Arden)
/Cetyltrimethylammonium Br, methapyrilene HCl, phenylephrine HCl, hydrocortisone.
See: T-Spray, Liq. (Saron)
/Diphenhydramine HCl.
See: Ardeben, Inj. (Burgin-Arden)
/Ephedrine hydrochloride, sodium chloride.
See: Efedron HCl Nasal Jelly (Hart)
/Estradiol cypionate, testosterone cypionate.
See: Depo-Testadiol, Vial (Upjohn)
Depotestogen, Vial (Hyrex)
Testadiate-Depo, Vial (Kay)
/Glycerin, anhydrous.
See: Ophthalgan, Liq. (Ayerst)
/Liquifilm.
See: Liquifilm Tears (Allergan)
/Methylcellulose.
See: Lacril (Allergan)
/Myristyl-gamma-picolinium chloride.
See: Wet Tone, Soln. (Riker)
/Nonionic lanolin derivative.
See: Lacri-Lube, Ophthalmic Ointment (Allergan)
W/Polyethylene glycol, polyoxyl 40 stearate.
See: Blink-N-Clean (Allergan)
W/Sod. chloride.
See: Ocean, Liq. (Fleming)
W/Tannic acid, isopropyl alcohol.
See: Outgro, Sol. (Whitehall)
W/Testosterone enanthate.
See: Anthatest, Vial (Kay)
W/Vit. B-1, B-2, B-6, niacinamide, calcium pantothenate, benzyl alcohol.
See: Lanoplex, Inj. (Lannett)
CHLOROCON. (CMC) Chloroquine phosphate 250 mg./Tab. Bot. 100s, 500s, 1000s.
Use: Antimalarial.
• **CHLOROCRESOL.** USAN.
Use: Antiseptic, disinfectant.
7-CHLORO-6-DEMETHYLTETRACYCLINE HYDROCHLORIDE.
See: Demeclocycline Hydrochloride
7-CHLORO-1,3-DIHYDRO-3-HYDROXY-5-PHENYL-2H-1,4-BENZODIAZEPIN-2-ONE.
See: Oxazepam
7-CHLORO-1,3-DIHYDRO-1-METHYL-5-PHENYL-2H-1,4-BENZODIAZEPIN-2-ONE.
See: Diazepam
7-CHLORO-4,6-DIMETHOXYCOUMARAN-3-ONE-2-SPIRO-1′-(2′-METHOXY-6′-METHYLCYCLOHEX-2′-EN-4′-ONE). Griseofulvin.
2-(ρ-CHLORO-α-(2-(DIMETHYLAMINO)-ETHOXY) BENZYL)PYRIDINE MALEATE (1:1).
See: Carbinoxamine Maleate
(+)-2-(ρ-CHLORO-α-(2-(DIMETHYLAMINO)-ETHYL) BENZYL) PYRIDINE MALEATE (1:1).
See: Dexchlorpheniramine Maleate
2-CHLORO-10-[3-(DIMETHYLAMINO)-PROPYL]PHENOTHIAZINE. Chlorpromazine, U.S.P. XXI.
(E)-2-CHLORO-N,N-DIMETHYLTHIOZANTHENE-Δ-9 γ-PROPYLAMINE.
See: Chlorprothixene
CHLOROETHANE.
See: Ethyl Chloride
CHLORODRI. (Kenyon) Chlorpheniramine maleate 5 mg., phenylpropanolamine HCl 12.5 mg., atropine sulfate 0.2 mg./cc. Vial 10 cc.
1-CHLORO-3-ETHYL-1-PENTEN-4-YN-3-OL.
See: Ethchlorvynol, U.S.P. XXI.
• **CHLOROFORM,** N.F. XVI. Bot. 1 lb., 5 lb.
Use: Inhalation anesthetic: solvent.
4-CHLORO-N-FURFURYL-5-SULFAMOYL-ANTHRANILIC ACID. Furosemide, U.S.P. XXI.
CHLOROGUANIDE HYDROCHLORIDE. (Various Mfr.) (Proguanil HCl) 1-(p-Chlorophenyl)-5-isopropylbiguanidine HCl. Guanatol HCl.
Use: Antimalarial.
CHLOROHYDRATES. Same as Hydrochloride.
6-CHLORO-17-HYDROXYPREGNA-4,6-DIENE-3, 20-DIONE ACETATE.
See: Chlormadinone Acetate
CHLORO-IODOHYDROXYQUINOLINE.
See: Clioquinol, U.S.P. XXI.
5-CHLORO-7-IODO-8-QUINOLINOL.
See: Clioquinol, U.S.P. XXI.

p-CHLOROMETAXYLENOL.
W/Benzocaine,.benzyl alcohol, propylene glycol.
See: 20-Cain Burn Relief, Bot. (Alto)
W/Hydrocortisone, pramoxine HCl.
See: Orlex HC, Otic (Baylor)

CHLOROMETHAPYRILENE CITRATE.
See: Chlorothen Citrate.

CHLORO(2-METHOXY-3-UREIDOPROPYL)-MERCURY.
See: Chlormerodin

7-CHLORO-2-(METHYLAMINO)-5-PHENYL-3H-1,4-BENZODIAZEPINE 4-OXIDE.
See: Chlordiazepoxide, U.S.P. XXI.

2-CHLORO-10-(3-(4-METHYL-1-PIPER-AZINYL)-PROPYL)PHENOTHIAZINE.
See: Prochlorperazine, U.S.P. XXI.

CHLOROMYCETIN. (Parke-Davis) Chloramphenicol.
Cream: (1%) w/cetyl alcohol, sod. lauryl sulfate, liq. petrolatum, buffered with sod. phosphate, and propylparaben. Tube 1 oz.
Kapseal: (250 mg.) Bot. 16s, 100s. Unit dose 100s.
Ophth. Oint.: (1%) in base of petrolatum and polyethylene. Tube 3.5 Gm.
Ophth. Sol.: (25 mg.) Bot. w/dropper 15 cc. (dry). Sol. 5 mg./ml. Plastic dropper Bot. 5 ml.
Otic Drops: (0.5%) 5 mg./ml. w/propylene glycol Bot. 15 ml.
Palmitate, Oral Susp. (150 mg./5 ml.) w/Sodium benzoate 0.5% Bottles 60 ml.
Use: Antibiotic.

CHLOROMYCETIN-CORTISOL OPHTHALMIC. (Parke-Davis) Chloromycetin 12.5 mg., hydrocortisone acetate 25 mg., borate buffer, phemerol. Vial 5 ml. Stable at room temperature for 10 days after reconstitution with water.
Use: Inflammatory infections.

CHLOROMYCETIN SODIUM SUCCINATE I.V. (Parke-Davis) Chloramphenicol sodium succinate dried powder which when reconstituted contains chloromycetin 100 mg./ml. Steri-vials 1 Gm. 10s.
Use: I.V. treatment of salmonella typhi infections.

CHLOROMYXIN. (Parke-Davis) Chloramphenicol 10 mg., polymixin B 5000 units/Gm. in base of liquid petrolatum & polyethylene. Tube 3.5 Gm.
Use: Treatment of ocular infections.

CHORON 10. (Forest) Chorionic gonadotropin 1000 units. Vial 10 ml.

CHLOROPHEN. (C.M.C.) Chlorpheniramine maleate 20 mg./cc. Vial 10 cc. 100 mg./cc. Vial 10 cc.
Use: Antihistamine therapy.

CHLOROPHEN. (Robinson) Chlorphentermine HCl 65 mg./Tab. Bot. 100s, 1000s.

p-CHLOROPHENOL.
See: Parachlorophenol

CHLOROPHENOTHANE. 1,1,1-Trichloro-2,2-bis(p-chlorophenyl) ethane. Gesarol, Neocid, Dicophane
Use: Pediculicide.

4-(3-(2-CHLOROPHENOTHIAZIN-1-yl)-PROPYL)-1-PIPERAZINEETHANOL.
See: Perphenazine, U.S.P. XXI.

1-(p-CHLORO-α-PHENYLBENZYL)-4-METHYL-PIPERAZINE MONOHYDROCHLORIDE.
See: Chlorcyclizine Hydrochloride, U.S.P. XXI.

4-(4-(p-CHLOROPHENYL)-4-HYDROXYPIPERIDIN-4-FLUOROBUTYROPHENONE.
See: Haloperidol, U.S.P. XXI.

CHLOROPHYLL. W/Formalin, benzalkonium chlori
See: Mycomist, Spray Liq. (Gordon)

CHLOROPHYLL "a" OINTMENT.
See: Chloresium Oint. (Rystan)

CHLOROPHYLL "a" SOLUTION (Chlorophyllin).
See: Chloresium Sol. (Rystan)

CHLOROPHYLL COMPLEX PERLES. (Standard Process) Natural chlorophyll extracted from alfalf and tillandsia. Vit. K 3.3 mg./6 Perles. Bot. 60s, 350s. Oint. Tube 1.5 oz., Jar 3 oz.

CHLOROPHYLL TABLETS.
See: Derifil, Tab. (Rystan)
Nullo, Tab. (Depree)

CHLOROPHYLL, WATER-SOLUBLE. (Various M Chlorophyllin.
See: Chloresium Prep. (Rystan)
Derifil, Pow. (Rystan)

CHLOROPHYLLIN.
Use: Healing agent & deodorizer.

• **CHLOROPHYLLIN COPPER COMPLEX.** USAN.
Use: Deodorant.

• **CHLOROPROCAINE HCl,** U.S.P. XXI. Inj., U.S.P. XXI. beta, Diethylamino-ethyl 2-chloro-4-amino-be zoate HCl. 4-amino-2-chloro-, 2-(diethylamino) et ester, HCl. 2-(Diethylamino) ethyl 4-amino-2-chlo benzoate HCl. (Abbott) 2% or 3%. Concentration Abboject Syringe, Ampul or Vial.
See: Nesacaine, Vial (Pennwalt)
Nescaine-CE, Vial (Pennwalt)

CHLOROPTIC-P S.O.P. STERILE OPHTHALM OINTMENT. (Allergan) Chloramphenicol 1%, pre nisolone alcohol 0.5%. Ophth. Oint. Tube 3.5 Gm
Use: Topical anti-inflammatory and anti-infective ophthalmic use.

CHLOROPTIC STERILE OPHTHALMIC SOLUTION (Allergan) Chloramphenicol 0.5%, chlorobutanol 0.5%. Dropper bot. 7.5 ml. Unit dose 2.5 ml.
Use: Topical anti-infective for treatment of ocular fections.

• **CHLOROQUINE,** U.S.P. XXI. 7-Chloro-4-[[4-(diethylamino)-1-methyl butyl]amino]quinoline.
Use: Pharmaceutic necessity for chloroquine HCl.
See: Aralen HCl Prods. (Winthrop-Breon)

CHLOROQUINE. B.A.N. 7-Chloro-4-(4-diethyl-amino-1-methylbutylamino)-quinoline.
Use: Antimalarial.
See: Aralen
Avloclor
Bemasulph
Nivaquine
Resochin
Roquine, Tab. (Robinson)

• **CHLOROQUINE HYDROCHLORIDE, INJ.,** U.S.P. XXI.
Use: Antiamebic, antimalarial.

HLOROQUINE PHOSPHATE, U.S.P. XXI. Tab. J.S.P. XXI. Nivaquine.
Jse: Febrile attacks of malaria; antiamebic; lupus erythematosus suppressant.
See: Aralen Phosphate, Tab. (Winthrop-Breon)
Chlorocon, Tab. (C.M.C.)

(7-CHLORO-4-QUINOLYL)AMINO)-α-(DIETHYLAMINO)-0-CRESOL DIHYDROCHLORIDE. Amodiaquine Hydrochloride U.S.P. XXI.

CHLORO-SALICYLANILIDE.

CHLOROTETRACYCLINE HYDROCHLORIDE.
Use: Antibacterial, antiprotozoan.
See: Chlortetracycline Hydrochloride, U.S.P. XXI.

LOROTHEN. 2-[(5-Chloro-2-thenyl)(2-dimethylaminoethyl)amino]pyridine hydrochloride & citrate salts (Chlorothenylpyramine, chloromethapyrilene, Pyrithen).
Use: Symptomatic relief in allergic disorders.

LOROTHEN CITRATE. (Whittier) 2-[-(5-Chloro-2-thenyl)]2-dimethylamino)-ethyl]amino]pyridine dihydrogen citrate. Chloromethapyrilene, Chlorothenylpyramine, pyrithen. Tab., Bot. 100s.
Use: (Oral 25 to 50 mg.) Antihistaminic in relief of allergic disorders.
/Pyrilamine, thenylpyramine.
See: Derma-Pax, Liq. (Recsei)

(5-CHLORO-2-THENYL)(2-DIMETHYLAMINO)ETHYL)AMINO)PYRIDINE CITRATE (1:1).
See: Chlorothen Citrate

LOROTHENYLPYRAMINE. Chlorothen, Prep.

LOROTHEOPHYLLINATE W/BENADRYL.
See: Dramamine, Prep. (Searle)

CHLOROTHIAZIDE, U.S.P. XXI. Oral Susp., Tabs., U.S.P. XXI. 6-Chloro-2H-1,2,4-benzothiadiazine-7-sulfonamide 1,1-dioxide.
Use: Diuretic.
See: Diuril, Tab., Susp. (Merck Sharp & Dohme)
/Methyldopa
See: Aldoclor, Tab. (Merck Sharp & Dohme)
/Reserpine
See: Diupres, Tab. (Merck Sharp & Dohme)

HLOROTHIAZIDE. B.A.N. 6-Chlorobenzo-1,2,4-thiadiazine-7-sulphonamide 1,1-dioxide.
Use: Diuretic.
See: Chlotride
Diuril, Prods. (Merck Sharp & Dohme)
Saluric

CHLOROTHIAZIDE SODIUM FOR INJECTION, U.S.P. XXI.
See: Sodium Diuril, Vial (Merck Sharp & Dohme)

HLOROTHYMOL. 6-Chlorothymol.
Use: Antibacterial.

CHLOROTRIANISENE, U.S.P. XXI. Cap., U.S.P. XXI. Chlorotris (p-methoxyphenyl)ethylene.
Use: Estrogen.
See: TACE, Cap. (Merrell Dow)

HLOROTRIANISENE. B.A.N. Chlorotri-(4-methoxyphenyl)ethylene.
Use: Estrogen.
See: TACE, Cap. (Merrell Dow)

HLOROTRIS(p-METHOXYPHENYL)ETHYLENE,
See: Chlorotrianisene, U.S.P. XXI.

β-CHLOROVINYL ETHYNYL CARBINOL.
See: Placidyl, Cap. (Abbott)

• **CHLOROXINE.** USAN.
Use: Antiseborrheic.

• **CHLOROXYLENOL.** USAN. 4-Chloro-3,5-xylenol. p-Chloro-m-xylenol; parachloro-metaxylenol; benzytol.
Use: Antiseptic.
W/Benzocaine, menthol, lanolin.
See: Unburn, Spray, Cream, Lot. (Leeming-Pacquin)
W/Hexachlorophene.
See: Desitin, Preps. (Leeming-Pacquin)
W/Methyl salicylate, menthol, camphor, thymol, eucalyptus oil, isopropyl alcohol.
See: Gordobalm, Balm (Gordon)

CHLORPHED INJECTION. (Hauck) Brompheniramine maleate 10 mg./ml. Vial 10 ml.
Use: Allergy & common cold treatment.

CHLORPHEN. (Wolins) Chlorpheniramine maleate 0.75 mg., salicylamide 80 mg., phenacetin 16 mg./Tab. Bot. 1000s.

CHLORPHENADE. (Wolins) Atropine sulfate 1/180 gr., chlorpheniramine maleate 8 mg., phenylpropanolamine HCl 50 mg./T.D. Cap. Bot. 100s, 1000s.

• **CHLORPHENESIN.** F.D.A. 3-(p-Chlorophenoxy)-1,2-propanediol.

CHLORPHENESIN. B.A.N. 3-(4-Chlorophenoxyl)-propane-1,2-diol.
Use: Antifungal agent.
See: Mycil

• **CHLORPHENESIN CARBAMATE.** USAN. 3-(p-Chlorophenoxy)-2-hydroxypropyl carbamate.
Use: Muscle relaxant.
See: Maolate, Tab. (Upjohn)

CHLORPHENEX CAPS. (Wolins) Acetaminophen 325 mg., phenylpropanolamine HCl 18 mg./Cap. Bot. 100s, 1000s.

CHLORPHENIRAMINE. B.A.N. 1-(4-Chlorophenyl)-3-dimethylamino-1-(2-pyridyl)propane. 3-(4-Chlorophenyl)-3-(2-pyridyl)propyldimethylamine.
Use: Antihistamine.
See: Chlorphenamine (I.N.N.)
Chlorprophenpyridamine
Haynon
W/Atropine sulfate.
See: Histunex, Inj. (Tunex)
W/Phenylephrine HCl, phenylpropanolamine HCl, phenyltoloxamine citrate.
See: Naldecon, Tab., Drops, Syr. (Bristol-Myers)
W/Phenylephrine, analgesics, and Vitamin C.
See: Corico, Caps. (Haag)

• **CHLORPHENIRAMINE MALEATE,** U.S.P. XXI. Inj., Syr., Tab., U.S.P. XXI. 2-[p-Chloro-alpha(2-dimethylaminoethyl)benzyl]pyridine maleate, chlorprophenpyridamine maleate. 2-Pyridinepropanamine, gamma-(4-chlorophenyl)-N,N-dimethyl-,(Z)-2-butenedioate(1:1).
Use: Antihistaminic.
See: Alermine, Tab. (Reid-Provident)
Barachlor T.D., Cap., Tab. (Barry Martin)
Chestamine, Cap. (Leeds)

Chlo-Amine, Tab. (Hollister-Stier)
Chloraman, Tab. (Rasman)
Chloren, Preps. (Wren)
Chlor-4, Tab. (Mills)
Chlormene, Tab. (Robinson)
Chlormene Injection (Robinson)
Chlormene Repeat Action, Tab. (Robinson)
Chlormene Timecaps, Tab. (Robinson)
Chlor-Niramine, Tab. (Whiteworth)
Chlorophen, Vial (Medical Chem.)
Chlor-pen, Vial, Tab. (Amer. Chem. & Drug)
Chlor-Span, Cap. (Burlington)
Chlortab, Tab., Cap., Inj. (North American Pharmacal)
Chlor-Trimeton Maleate, Prep. (Schering)
Cosea, Preps. (Center)
Histacon, Tab., Syr. (Marsh-Emory)
Histaspan, Cap. (USV Labs.)
Histex, Cap. (Mallard)
Nasahist (Keene)
Panahist, Tab. (Panray)
Phenetron, Preps. (Lannett)
Polaramine, Tab., Syr. (Schering)
Pyranistan Tab. (Standex)
Rhinihist, Elix. (Central)
Teldrin, Spansule, Cap. (Menley & James)
Trymegen (Medco)

CHLORPHENIRAMINE MALEATE W/COMBINATIONS

See: Al-Ay, Preps (Bowman)
Alclear Anti-allergy, Tab. (Walgreen)
Alcon Decongestant, Tab., Liq. (Webcon)
Algetuss, Syr. (Winston)
Alka-Seltzer Plus, Tab. (Miles)
Allercomp, Tab. (Wolins)
Allerdec, Cap. (Towne)
Allerest Prods. (Pharmacraft)
Allergesic, Tab. (Vitarine)
Allergy (Eckerd)
Alo-Tuss, Tab. (North Amer. Pharm.)
Alumadrine, Tab. (Fleming)
Amohist, Tab. (Vortech)
A.R.M., Tab. (Menley & James)
Atussin Expectorant, Liq. (Federal)
Atussin-D.M. Expectorant, Liq. (Federal)
Bayer Prods. (Glenbrook)
Bellafedrol A-H, Tab. (Lannett)
B.M.E., Liq. (Brothers)
Bobid, Cap. (Boyd)
Breacol Cough Medication, Liq. (Glenbrook)
Brolade, Cap. (Brothers)
Bronchohist, Syr. (Sutliff & Case)
Bur-Tuss Expectorant (Burlington)
CDM, Expect. (Lannett)
Cenahist, Caps. (Century)
Cenaid, Tabs. (Century)
Centuss, Tab. (Century)
Cerose Comp., Liq. (Ives)
Chew-Hist, Wafer (Kenyon)
Chlorodri, Vial (Kenyon)
Chlorpel, Caps. (Santa)
Chlorphen, Vial (Kenyon)
Chlorphen, Tab. (Wolins)
Chlorphenade, T.D. Cap. (Wolins)
Chlorphenwol, Cap. (Wolins)
Chlor-Trimeton, Preps. (Schering)
Chlor-Trimeton Expect. (Schering)
Codimal, Tab. (Central)
Co-Histine DH, Elix. (Kay)
Col-Decon, Tab. (Quality Generics)
Colrex Compound, Preps. (Rowell)
Comtrex, Cap., Liq., Tab. (Bristol-Myers)
Conalsyn Croncap, Cap. (Cenci)
Conhist, Cap. (Mallard)
Conjec, Inj., (Mallard)
Contac, Cap. (Menley & James)
Cophene No. 2, Cap. (Dunhall)
Cophene-S, Syr. (Dunhall)
Coricidin, Prep. (Schering)
Coriforte, Cap. (Schering)
Corilin, Liq. (Schering)
Corizahist, Preps. (Mason)
Coryban-D, Cap., Syrup (Roerig)
Coryzaid, Tab. (Elder)
Coryztime, Cap., Vial (Elder)
Corzone, Syr. (Xttrium)
Co-Sansprin, Tab. (Wolins)
Cotrol-D, Tab. (Beecham Labs)
Co-Tylenol, Preps. (McNeil)
C3 Capsules (Menley & James)
Dallergy, Cap., Tab., Syr. (Laser)
Dasikon, Cap. (Beecham Labs)
Decobel, Cap. (Lannett)
Decojen, Tab., Vial (Jenkins)
Deconamine, Cap., Tab., Elxr., Syrup (Berlex)
Decongestant, Tab. (Panray)
Decongestant, Vial (Century)
Dehist, Cap. (Forest)
Demazin, Tab., Syr. (Schering)
Derma-Pax, Lot. (Recsei)
Desa-Hist AT, Tab., Syr. (Pharmics)
Desa-Hist PF Elixir, PF-8, Cap. (Pharmics)
Dextromal, Liq. (Mallard)
Dezest, Cap. (Geneva Drugs)
Dodamin, Tab. (Reid-Provident)
Donatussin, Liq., Syr. (Laser)
Dri-Drip, Cap., Liq. (Coastal)
Dri-Hist Meta-Kaps, Cap. (Sutliff & Case)
Drinus, Syr., Cap., (Amfre-Grant)
Drinus-M, Cap. (Amfre-Grant)
Dristan, Preps. (Whitehall)
Drucon, Elix. (Standard Drug)
Drynal (Blaine)
Efricon Expectorant, (Lannett)
Expectico, Syr. (Coastal)
Expecto Hist, Tab. (Wolins)
Extendryl, Cap., Syr., Tab. (Fleming)
F.C.A.H., Caps (Scherer)
Fedahist, Prods. (Donner)
Fitacol (Standex)
Forcold, Syr. (Lemmon)
Formadrin, Liq. (Kenyon)
Gomahist, Liq. (Burgin-Arden)
Guahist (Hickam)

Guaiamine, Cap. (Sutliff & Case)
Guaiodol-Plus, Vial (Kenyon)
Guistrey Fortis, Tab. (Bowman)
Hista-Compound #5, Tab. (Vortech)
Histacon, Syr., Tab. (Marsh-Emory)
Histapco, Tabs. (Apco)
Hista-Vadrin, Cap., Syrup, Tab. (Scherer)
Histine Prods. (Freeport)
Histogesic, Tab. (Century)
Histone, Tab. (Blaine)
Historal, Cap., Liq. (W.F. Merchant)
Histussinol, Syr. (Bock)
Hycoff, Cap., Syr. (Saron)
Hycoff-X, Expect. (Saron)
Hycomine Comp., Tab. (Du Pont)
Infantuss, Liq. (Scott/Cord)
Kiddi-Koff, Liq. (Reid-Provident)
Kiddisan, Tab. (O'Neal)
Koldeze, Cap. (Scrip)
Koryza, Tabs. (Fellows-Testagar)
Kronofed-A, Cap. (Ferndale)
Lanatuss, Expect. (Lannett)
Marhist (Marlop)
Medcohist, Tabs. (Hauck)
Midran, Tab. (Quality Generics)
Naldecon, Preps. (Bristol)
Napril, Cap. (Marion)
Narine, T.R. Cap. (Dooner)
Narspan, Cap. (Coast Labs.)
Naso-Dex, Cap. (Commerce)
Neo-Pyranistan, Tab. (Standex)
Nilcol, Tabs. and Elix. (Parke-Davis)
Nolamine, Tab. (Carnrick)
Novafed A, Cap., Liq. (Merrell Dow)
Novahistine, Preps. (Merrell Dow)
Oraminic, Prep. (Vortech)
Oriphan, Tab. (Panray)
Ornade, Prods. (SmithKline)
Para-Hist, Cap., Syr. (Pharmics)
Partuss, Liq. (Parmed)
Partuss T.D., Tab. (Parmed)
Pectorine, Liq. (Scrip)
Pertussin Plus Night-Time Cold Medicine, Syr. (Chesebrough-Pond's)
Phenahist, Preps (Amid)
Phenchlor Prods. (Freeport)
Phenetron Comp., Tab. (Lannett)
Phenylin, Cap. (Mallard)
Polytuss-DM, Liq. (Rhode)
P.R. Syrup, Liq. (Fleming)
Pyma, Cap., Vial (Fellows-Testagar)
Pyristan, Cap., Elix. (Arcum)
Pyranistan (Standex)
Quartets, Cap. (DePree)
Quelidrine, Syr. (Abbott)
Rentuss, Cap., Syr. (Wren)
Resclor, Tab. (Dunhall)
Rhinex D M, Syr., Tab. (Lemmon)
Rhinogesic, Tab. (Vale)
Rhinosyn, Cap, Liq. (Comatic)
Rid-A-Col, Tab. (Panray)
Rid-A-Col D, Tab. (Panray)
Rinocidin, Cap., Liq. (Cenci)
Rohist-D, Cap. (Rocky Mtn.)
Rolanade, Cap. (Robinson)
Romilar CF, Syr. (Block)
Ryna, Liq. (Wallace)
Ryna-tussadine, Tab., Liq. (Wallace)
Salphenyl, Cap. (Mallard)
Scotcof, Liq. (Scott/Cord)
Scotuss Liq. (Scott/Cord)
Scotnord (Scott/Cord)
Shertus, Liq. (Sheryl)
Sialco, Tab. (Foy)
Sinaprel, Cap. (Pasadena Research)
Sinarest, Tab., (Pharmacraft)
Sine-Off, Tab. (Menley & James)
Sino-Comp., Tab. (Bio-Factor)
Sinodec, Cap. (Primedics)
Sinovan Timed, Cap. (Drug Ind.)
Sinucol, Cap., Vial (Tennessee)
Sinulin, Tab. (Carnrick)
Sinutab Extra Strength, Cap. (Warner-Lambert)
Spantuss, Liq., Tab. (Arco)
Spectab, Tab. (Reid-Provident)
Statomin Maleate CC, Tab. (Bowman)
Sudafed Plus, Tab., Syr. (Burroughs Wellcome)
Supercitin, Syr. & Sugar-Free, Cap. (Vitarine)
Symptrol, Cap. (Saron)
T.A.C. Cap. (Towne)
Tercol, Liq. (Commerce)
Thor, Cap. (Towne)
Tonecol, Syr., Tab. (A.V.P.)
Triamincin Chewables, (Dorsey)
Trigelamine, Oint. (Edward J. Moore)
Trisohist, Cap. (Riker)
Turbilixir, Liq. (Burlington)
Turbispan Leisurecaps, Cap. (Burlington)
Tusquelin, Syr. (Circle)
Tussar-2, Syr. (Armour)
Tusscaps, Cap. (Martin-Phillips)
U-R-D, Prods. (Hickam)
Valihist, Cap. (Otis Clapp)
Vernate, Inj. (Reid-Provident)
Wesade, Cap. (Western Research)

d-CHLORPHENIRAMINE MALEATE.
See: Polarmine Expect., Syr., Tab. (Schering)

CHLORPHENIRAMINE RESIN W/COMBINATIONS.
See: Omni-Tuss, Liq. (Pennwalt)

CHLORPHENIRAMINE TANNATE.
W/Carbetapentane tannate, ephedrine tannate, phenylephrine tannate.
See: Rynatuss Tabs., Susp. (Wallace)
W/Phenylephrine tannate, pyrilamine tannate.
See: Rynatan, Tab., Susp. (Wallace)

CHLORPHENOCTIUM AMSONATE. B.A.N. 2,4-Dichlorophenoxymethyldimethyloctylammonium 4,4′-diaminostilbene-2,2′-disulfonate.
Use: Antifungal agent.

CHLORPHENOXAMINE. B.A.N. N-2-(4-Chloro-α-methylbenzhydryloxy)ethyldimethylamine.
Use: Treatment of the parkinsonian syndrome.
See: Clorevan

• **CHLORPHENOXAMINE HCl,** U.S.P. XXI. Tab., U.S.P. XXI. beta-Dimethylaminoethyl (p-chlor-alpha-methyl-benzhydryl-ether HCl.

• **CHLORPHENTERMINE.** F.D.A. 4-Chloro-alpha, alpha-dimethylphenethylamine.

CHLORPHENTERMINE. B.A.N. 4-Chloro-$\alpha\alpha$-dimethylphenethylamine.
Use: Appetite suppressant.
See: Lucofen

• **CHLORPHENTERMINE HCl.** USAN. p-Chloro-α, α-dimethylphenethylamine HCl.
Use: Anorexic.
See: Chlorophen, Tab. (Robinson)

CHLORPHTHALIDONE. 1-Oxo-3-(3′-sulfanyl-4′-chlorphenyl)-3-hydroxy-isoindoline.
See: Chlorthalidone

CHLORPROGUANIL. B.A.N. 1-(3,4-Dichlorophenyl)-5-isopropylbiguanide.
Use: Antimalarial.
See: Lapudrine

• **CHLORPROMAZINE,** U.S.P. XXI. Supp. U.S.P. XXI. 2-Chloro-10-[3-(dimethylamino)propyl]-phenothiazine. 10H-Phenothiazine-10-propanamine,2-chloro-N,N-dimethyl-
Use: Anti-emetic; tranquilizer.
See: Chloractil
Largactil

• **CHLORPROMAZINE HCl,** U.S.P. XXI. Inj., Syr., Tab. U.S.P. XXI.
Use: Anti-emetic; tranquilizer.
See:
Chlorzine, Inj. (Mallard)
Promachlor, Tab. (Geneva)
Promapar, Tab. (Parke-Davis)
Promaz, Inj. (Keene)
Sonazine, Tab. (Reid-Provident)
Terpium, Tab. (Scrip)
Thorazine, Amp., Supp., Syr., Tab., Cap., Liq. (SmithKline)

• **CHLORPROPAMIDE,** U.S.P. XXI. Tabs. U.S.P. XXI. 1-[(p-Chlorophenyl)-sulfonyl]-3-propylurea.Benzenesulfonamide, 4-chloro-N-[(propylamino)carbonyl]-.
Use: Hypoglycemic agent.
See: Diabinese, Tab. (Pfizer Laboratories)

CHLORPROPAMIDE. B.A.N. 1-(4-Chlorobenezenesulphonyl)-3-propylurea.
Use: Oral hypoglycemic agent.
See: Diabinese
Glucamide, Tab. (Lemmon)

CHLORPROPHENPYRIDAMINE MALEATE.
See: Chlorpheniramine Maleate, U.S.P. XXI.

• **CHLORPROTHIXENE,** U.S.P. XXI. Inj., Oral Susp., Tab., U.S.P. XXI. 1-Propanamine, 3-(2-chloro-9H-thioxanthene-9-ylidene)-N,N-dimethyl-,(Z)-; (Z)-2-Chloro-N,N-dimethylthioxanthene-$\Delta^9\gamma$-propylamine.
Use: Tranquilizer; antiemetic.
See: Taractan, Tab., Conc., Inj. (Roche)

CHLORQUINALDOL. 5,7-Dichloro-8-hydroxyquinaldine.

CHLORQUINALDOL. B.A.N. 5,7-Dichloro-8-hydroxy-2-methylquinoline.
Use: Antiseptic; fungicide.
See: Steroxin

CHLORQUINOL. A mixture of the chlorinated products of 8-hydroxyquinoline containing about per cent of 5,7-dichloro-8-hydroxyquinoline. Quix.

CHLOR-SPAN. (Burlington) Chlorpheniramine male 8 mg./Sus. Rel. Cap. Bot. 60s.
Use: Antihistaminic.

CHLORSPAN-12. (Vortech) Chlorpheniramine male 12 mg./Cap. Bot. 1000s.
Use: Antihistaminic.

CHLORTAB. (Vortech) Chlorpheniramine maleate mg. or 8 mg./Tab.
Bot. 1000s.
Vial 100 mg./cc., 10 cc.; Spancap: 12 mg./Cap.
Use: Antihistaminic.

• **CHLORTETRACYCLINE HCl,** U.S.P. XXI. Caps., Oint., Ophth. Oint., Sterile, Tab., U.S.P. XXI. 7-Chl tetracycline hydrochloride.
Use: Antibiotic.
See: Aureomycin, Prep. (Lederle)

• **CHLORTHALIDONE,** U.S.P. XXI. Tabs. U.S.P. XX 2-Chloro-5-(1-hydroxy-3-oxo-1-isoindolinyl)benzenesulfonamide. Benzenesulfonamide, 2-chloro-5-(2,3-dihydro-1-hydroxy-3-oxo-1H-isoindol-1-yl)-.
Use: Diuretic, antihypertensive.
See: Combipres, Tab. (Boehringer-Ingelheim)
Hygroton, Tab. (USV Labs.)
W/Reserpine.
See: Demi-Regroton, Tab. (USV Labs.)
Regroton, Tab. (USV Labs.)

CHLORTHENOXAZIR. B.A.N. 2-(2-Chloroethyl)-2,3-dihydro-1,3-benzoxazin-4-one.
Use: Anti-inflammatory; analgesic.

CHLOR-TRIMETON. (Schering) Chlorpheniramine maleate **Inj.** 10 mg./ml. Amp. 1 ml. 100s. **Allerg Tab.** 4 mg./Tab. Box 24s, 48s. Bot. 100s, 1000s 5000s. **Long Acting Allergy Repetabs:** 8 mg./Tab. Box 24s., 48s. Bot. 100s, 1000s, 5000s (12 mg.) Bot. 100s, 1000s. **Syr.** 2 mg./5 ml. Bot. oz., gal.
Use: Antihistaminic.

CHLOR-TRIMETON W/COMBINATIONS. (Scheri Chlorpheniramine maleate.
W/Aspirin
See: Coricidin, Tab., Medilets (Schering)
Coricidin Medilets, Tab. (Schering)
W/Aspirin, phenylpropanolamine.
See: Coricidin "D", Prods. (Schering)
W/Aspirin, phenylephrine.
See: Coricidin Demilets (Schering)
W/Aspirin, chlorpheniramine maleate, phenylephrine HCl.
See: Coricidin Demilets, Tab. (Schering)
W/Phenylephrine HCl.
See: Demazin, Prods. (Schering)
W/Pseudoephedrine sulfate.
See: Chlor-Trimeton Long-Acting Decongestant Repetabs (Schering)
W/Salicylamide, phenacetin, caffeine, Vit. C.
See: Coriforte, Cap. (Schering)
W/Sod. salicylate, amino acetic acid.
See: Corilin, Liq. (Schering)

HLOR-TRIMETON DECONGESTANT TABLETS. (Schering) Chlorpheniramine maleate 4 mg., pseudoephedrine sulfate 60 mg./Tab. Box 24s, 48s.
Use: Decongestant, antihistaminic.

HLOR-TRIMETON EXPECTORANT. (Schering) Chlorpheniramine maleate 2 mg., phenylephrine HCl 10 mg., ammonium chloride 100 mg., sod. citrate 50 mg., guaifenesin 50 mg./5 ml. Alcohol < 1%. Bot. 16 oz.
Use: Antihistaminic, antitussive, decongestant.

HLOR-TRIMETON LONG-ACTING DECONGESTANT REPETABS. (Schering) Chlorpheniramine maleate 8 mg., pseudoephedrine sulfate 120 mg./S.R. Tab. Box 12s, 36s.
Use: Antihistamine, nasal decongestant.

HLORTRON. (Pharmex) Chlorpheniramine maleate 10 mg./Vial. Vial 30 cc.

HLORULAN TABLETS "500" (Lannett) 500 mg. Bot. 100s, 1000s.

HLORZIDE. (Foy) Hydrochlorothyazide 50 mg./Tab. Bot. 1000s.
Use: Diuretic.

HLORZOXAZONE, U.S.P. XXI. Tab., U.S.P. XXI. 5-Chlorobenzoxazolin-2-one. 5-Chlorobenzoxazolinone.
Use: Muscle relaxant.
See: Paraflex, Tab. (McNeil)
/Acetaminophen.
See: Blanex, Cap. (Edwards)
Parafon Forte, Tab. (McNeil)

HLORZOXAZONE AND ACETAMINOPHEN CAPSULES, U.S.P. XXI.
Use: Muscle relaxant, analgesic.

HLORZOXAZONE AND ACETAMINOPHEN TABLETS, U.S.P. XXI.
Use: Muscle relaxant, analgesic.

HOICE 10. (Whiteworth) Potassium Cl 10% solution, unflavored. Bot. Gal.
Use: Replacement therapy for potassium deficiency states.

HOICE 20. (Whiteworth) Potassium Cl 20% solution, unflavored. Bot. Gal.
Use: Replacement therapy for potassium deficiency states.

HOLACRYLAMINE RESIN. An anion exchange resin consisting of a water soluble polymer having a molecular weight equivalent between 350 and 360 in which aliphatic quaternary amine groups are attached to an acrylic backbone by ester linkages.

HOLAJEN. (Jenkins) Ox bile ext. 3.5 gr., desoxycholic acid ⅛ gr., dehydrocholic acid ⅛ gr., pancreatin 1.0 gr., betaine HCl 1.0 gr. Bot. 1000s.
Use: Cholagogue laxative.

HOLALIC ACID.
See: Cholic Acid

HOLAN-DH. (Pennwalt) Dehydrocholic acid 250 mg./Tab. Bot. 100s.
Use: Laxative.

HOLAN-HMB. (Pennwalt) Dehydrocholic acid 250 mg./Tab. Bot. 100s.
Use: Laxative.

CHOLANIC ACID. Dehydrodesoxycholic acid.

CHOLA-ZEM. (Zemmer) Atropine sulfate 1/500 gr., sod. glycocholate 1 gr., taurocholate 1 gr., nitroglycerin 1/500 gr., mag. sulfate 5 gr./Tab. Bot. 100s, 1000s.
Use: Choleretic & cholagogue with antispasmodic.

• **CHOLECALCIFEROL,** U.S.P. XXI. Vit. D-3, Activated 5,7-Cholestadien-3β-ol. 9,10-Secocholesta-5,7,-10(19)-trien-3-ol.
Use: Antirachitic vitamin.
See: Decavitamin Cap. & Tab.

CHOLECALCIFEROL. B.A.N. 9,10-Secocholesta-5,7,-10(19)-trien-3β-ol.
Use: Treatment of vitamin D deficiency.
See: Vitamin D-3

■ **CHOLECYSTOGRAPHY AGENTS.**
See: Bilopaque, Cap., (Winthrop-Breon)
Iodized Oil (Various Mfr.)
Iophendylate Inj.
Pantopaque, Amp. (LaFayette)
Telepaque, Tab. (Winthrop-Breon)

CHOLEDYL. (Parke-Davis) Oxtriphylline. **Tab.** (100 mg.) Bot. 100s, (200 mg.) Bot. 100s, 1000s. Unit dose 100s. **Elix.** 100 mg./5 ml., alcohol 20%. Bot. pt. **Pediatric Syrup**: 50 mg./5 ml. Bot. pt.
Use: Theophylline therapy.

CHOLEDYL SA. (Parke-Davis) Oxtriphylline 400 mg. or 600 mg./Tab. Bot. 100s. Unit dose 100s.
Use: Relief of acute and chronic bronchial asthma.

• **CHOLERA VACCINE,** U.S.P. XXI. (Lederle) India Strains, Vials 1.5 cc. (Lilly) Vials 1.5 cc. (Wyeth) Vials 1.5 cc., 20 cc.
Use: Active immunizing agent.

CHOLERETIC.
See: Bile Preps. and Forms
Dehydrocholic Acid
Desoxycholic Acid
Tocamphyl, Tab. (Various Mfr.)

CHOLESTERIN.
See: Cholesterol.

• **CHOLESTEROL,** N.F. XVI. Cholest-5-en-3β-ol. 5,6-Cholesten-3-Ol(Cholesterin). (Various Mfr.)
Use: Pharmaceutic aid (emulsifying agent).

CHOLESTEROL REAGENT STRIPS (Ames) Seralyzer reagent strips. Bot. 25s.
Use: A quantitative strip test for cholesterol in serum.

• **CHOLESTYRAMINE RESIN,** U.S.P. XXI. A styryl-divinyl-benzene copolymer (about 2% divinylbenzene) containing quaternary ammonium groups.
Use: Resin producing insoluble bile acid complexes.
See: Questran (Mead Johnson)

• **CHOLESTYRAMINE FOR ORAL SUSPENSION,** U.S.P. XXI.

CHOLIC ACID. 3,7,12-Trihydroxycholanic acid. Cholalic acid. Dehydrocholic Acid.

CHOLINATE. (Cenci) Choline dihydrogen citrate 1 Gm./4 cc. Bot. 16 oz., gal.
Use: Liver disorders.

CHOLINE BITARTRATE.
W/Bile extract, pancreatic substance, dl-methionine.
See: Licoplex, Tab. (Mills)

W/Hesperidin, niacinamide, protein hydrolysate, methionine, inositol, vitamins, minerals.
See: Norimex-Plus, Cap. (Vortech)
W/Inositol, B-Vitamins.
See: Lipotriad Cap., (Smith, Miller & Patch)
W/Lemon bioflavonoid complex, inositol, Vit. C, B-Vitamins.
See: Lipoflavonoid, Cap. (Smith, Miller & Patch)
W/Methionine, inositol, liver desiccated, Vitamin B-12.
See: Limvic, Tab. (Briar)
W/Mucopolysaccharide, epinephrine neutralizing factor, pancreatic lipotropic fraction, dl-methionine, inositol, bile ext.
See: Lipo-K, Cap. (Marcen)
W/d-Pantothenyl alcohol.
See: Ilopan-Choline, Tab. (Adria)
W/Pentylenetetrazol, nicotinic acid, methyl-testosterone, ethinyl estradiol, Vit. B-1, B-2, B-6, B-12, C, panthenol, inositol.
See: Benizol Plus, Elixir, Tab. (ICN)
W/Safflower oil, whole liver, soybean, lecithin, inositol, methionine, natural tocopherols, B-6, B-12, panthenol.
See: Nutricol, Cap., Vial (Nutrition Control)

CHOLINE CHLORIDE. (Various Mfr.)
Use: Liver disorders.
W/Inositol, methionine, Vit. B-12.
See: Cho-Meth, Vial (Kenyon)
Lychol-B, Inj. (Burgin-Arden)
W/Methionine, vitamins, niacinamide, panthenol.
See: Minoplex, Vial (Savage)
W/Panthenol, inositol, vitamins, minerals, estrone, testosterone.
See: Geramine, Inj. (Brown)
W/Panthenol, inositol, vitamins, minerals, estrone, testosterone, polydigestase.
See: Geramine, Tab. (Brown)
W/B-1, niacinamide, B-2, B-6, calcium pantothenate, cyanocobalamin, Vit. B-12, inositol, dl-methionine, testosterone, estrone, procaine.
See: Gerihorm, Inj. (Burgin-Arden)

CHOLINE CHLORIDE, CARBAMATE. Carbachol, U.S.P. XXI.

CHOLINE CHLORIDE SUCCINATE.
See: Succinylcholine Chloride, U.S.P. XXI.

CHOLINE CITRATE, TRICHOLINE CITRATE.
W/Inositol, methionine, B-12.
See: Cholimeth Tab. (Central)

CHOLINE DIHYDROGEN CITRATE. 2-Hydroxy-ethyl trimethylammonium citrate-U.S. Vit. 0.5 Gm. Bot. 100s, 500s.
Use: Liver disorders.
See: Cholinate, Liq. (Cenci)

CHOLINE SALICYLATE.
See: Arthropan, Liq. (Purdue Frederick)

CHOLINE MAGNESIUM TRISALICYLATE.
Use: Anti-inflammatory agent.
See: Trilisate, Tab. (Purdue Fredrick)

CHOLINE SALICYLATE. B.A.N. Choline salt of salicylic acid.
Use: Analgesic; antipyretic.

CHOLINE THEOPHYLLINATE.
See: Oxtriphylline.

CHOLINE THEOPHYLLINATE. B.A.N. Choline salt o theophylline.
Use: Bronchodilator.
See: Choledyl

■ **CHOLINERGIC AGENTS,**
(Parasympathomimetic Agents).
See: Mecholyl Chloride, Inj. (Baker)
Mestinon, Tab., Amp., Syr. (Roche)
Mytelase, Cap. (Winthrop-Breon)
Pilocarpine Nitrate (Var. Mfr.)
Prostigmin Bromide, Tab. (Roche)
Prostigmin Methylsulfate, Inj. (Roche)
Tensilon, Inj. (Roche)
Urecholine, Inj., Tab. (Merck Sharp & Dohme)

■ **CHOLINERGIC BLOCKING AGENTS.**
See: Parasympatholytic agents

CHO-LIV-12. (Jenkins) Choline 100 mg., cyanocob lamin 200 mcg., liver equal to Vit. B-12 10 mcg./c Vial 10 cc., 12s.

CHOL METH IN B. (Esco) Choline bitartrate 235 mg inositol 112 mg., methionine 70 mg., betaine anhydrous 50 mg., Vit. B-12 6 mcg., Vit. B-1 6 mg., V B-6 3 mg., niacin 10 mg./Cap. Bot. 500s, 1000s.
Use: Vitamin supplement.

CHOLOGRAFIN MEGLUMINE. (Squibb) Iodipamide methylglucamine (52%) 0.52 Gm./10 ml. Amp. 10.3% 100 ml.
Use: I.V., Cholangiography and cholecystography.

CHOLOGRAFIN SODIUM. Disodium salt of N,N'-adip bis-(3-amino-2:4:6 triodobenzoic acid).

CHOLOXIN. (Flint) Sodium dextrothyroxine 1 mg., 2 mg., 4mg., 6 mg./Tab. 2 mg., 4 mg. Bot. 100s, 250s; 1 mg., 6 mg. Bot. 100s.
Use: Hypocholesterolemic.

CHOLYGLYCINE.
See: CG RIA, Kit (Abbott)

CHO-METH. (Kenyon) Methionine 30 mg., choline chl ride 200 mg., inositol 100 mg., Vit. B-12, 12 mcg./2 c Vial 30 cc.

CHONDODENDRON TOMENTOSUM.
See: Curare

CHONDRUS. Irish Moss
W/Petrolatum, Liq.
See: Kondremul, Liq. (Fisons)

CHOO E PLUS C. (Stayner) Vit. E 100 I.U., Vit. C 25 mg./Tab. Bot. 100s.

CHOOZ ANTACID GUM. (Plough) Calcium carbonat 360 mg./Gum tablet. Pkg. 16s.
Use: Antacid.

CHOREX 5. (Hyrex) Chorionic gonadotropin 5,000 I.U., urea 100 mg., thimerosal 1.0 mg., sodium phosphate buffer/Vial. Vial 10 ml.
Use: Hormone therapy.

CHOREX 10. (Hyrex) Chorionic gonadotropin 10,000 I.U., urea 100 mg., thimerosal 1.0 mg., sodium phosphate buffer/Vial 10 cc.
Use: Hormone therapy.

CHORIGON. (Dunhall) Chorionic gonadotropin (dried 1000 I.U./ml. Vial 10 ml.
Use: Cryptorchidism, functional uterine bleeding.

ORION-PLUS. (Pharmex) Chorionic gonadotropin 10,000 u./Vial. Diluent: Glutamic acid 52 mcg., B- 25 mg., procaine 1%/cc. Vial 10 cc.
HORIONIC GONADOTROPIN, U.S.P. XXI. Inj. J.S.P. XXI. 5,000 I.U./Vial w/diluent 10 cc., 10,000 .U./Vial w/diluent 10 cc. (Serono) 10,000 I.U. of ıCG, mannitol 100 mg., benzyl alcohol 0.9%/10 ml. vial.
Jse: Prepubertal cryptorchidism, hypogonadotropic ypogonadism, & induction of ovulation & regnancy in anovulatory women.
See: Antuitrin-S (Parke-Davis)
A.P.L., Inj. (Ayerst)
C-G-10, Vial. (Scrip)
Chorigon, Amp. (Dunhall)
Chorex 5, Vial. (Hyrex)
Chorex 10, Vial. (Hyrex)
Chorion-Plus, Vial (Pharmex)
Follutein, Vial (Squibb)
Gonadex (Continental Dist.)
Khorion (Hickam)
Neovital-Diluent, Inj. (Pasadena Research)
Pre-Ine, Inj. (Kay)
Rochoric, Inj. (Rocky Mtn.)
RISTODYNE-DHC. (Paddock) Acetyl-p-amino-phenol 150 mg., aspirin 230 mg., caff. 30 mg., dihydrocodeinone bitartrate 5 mg./Tab. Bot. 100s, 500s.
Jse: Analgesic, antitussive.
IROMAGEN. (Savage) **Cap:** Ferrous fumarate 200 mg., Vit. C 250 mg., B-12 activity 10 mcg., desiccated stomach substances 100 mg./soft gelatin cap. Bot. 100s, 500s. **Injectable:** Iron peptonized 100 mg., B-12 5 mcg., cyanocobalamin 25 mcg. lidocaine HCl 1%/2 cc. Vials 10 cc., 30 cc.
Jse: Hematinic.
IROMAGEN OB CAPSULES. (Savage) Prenatal vitamin & mineral. Bot. 100s.
Jse: Pregnancy and lactation.
IROMALBIN. (Squibb) 100 uCi containing chromium CR 51 and human albumin.
IROMARGYRE.
See: Merbromin (Var. Mfr.)
HROMATE Cr-51, SODIUM FOR INJECTION, J.S.P. XXI.
IROMATED (Cr-51) SERUM ALBUMIN (HUMAN).
IROMATED SOLUTION (51Cr).
See: Chromitope sodium (Squibb)
IROMELIN COMPLEXION BLENDER. (Summers) Dihydroxyacetone 5%, alcohol 50%. Bot. 1 oz.
Use: Cosmetic darkening of whitened skin areas.
IROMIC ACID, DISODIUM SALT. Sodium Chromate Cr 51 Injection, U.S.P. XXI.
HROMIC CHLORIDE, U.S.P. XXI. Inj., U.S.P. XXI. Chromium chloride (CrCl3) hexahydrate. Chromium (3+) chloride hexahydrate.
Use: Chromium deficiency treatment.
See: Chrometrace, Inj. (Armour)
HROMIC CHLORIDE Cr 51. USAN.
Use: Radioactive agent.
See: Chromitope Chloride (Squibb)

• **CHROMIC PHOSPHATE Cr 51.** USAN.
Use: Radioactive agent.
• **CHROMIC PHOSPHATE P 32 SUSPENSION,** U.S.P.XXI.
Use: Radioactive agent.
CHROMETRACE. (Armour) Chromic chloride injection containing Chromium 4 mcg./ml. Vial 10 ml. Box 25s.
Use: Supplement to I.V. Solutions for chromium deficiency.
CHROMITOPE SODIUM. (Squibb) Chromate Cr 51, Sodium for Injection 0.25 mCi.
• **CHROMONAR HCl.** USAN. Ethyl[[3-[-2-(diethylamino)-ethyl]-4-methyl-2-oxo-2H-1-benzopyran-7-yl]oxy]acetate HCl. Intensain
Use: Recommended as coronary vasodilator, upon release.
CHRONULAC. (Merrell Dow) Lactulose 10 Gm./15 ml. Bot. 8 oz., 32 oz. Unit dose 30 ml. Box 100s.
Use: Treatment of constipation.
CHRYSAZIN.
See: Danthron, N.F. XVI.
CHUR-HIST. (Churchill) Chlorpheniramine 4 mg./Kaptab. Bot. 100s.
Use: Antihistamine.
CHYMEX. (Adria) Bentiromide 500 mg./7.5 ml. w/propylene glycol 40%.
Use: Screening test for pancreatic exocrine insufficiency. Monitoring the adequacy of supplemental pancreatic activity.
CHYMODIACTIN. (Smith) Chymodiactin 10,000 units, sodium L-cysteinate HCl. Vial 10,000 units.
Use: Treatment of herniated lumbar intervertebral discs.
• **CHYMOPAPAIN.** USAN. Proteolytic enzyme isolated from papaya latex, differing from papain in electrophoretic mobility, solubility, and substrate specificity.
Use: Proteolytic enzyme.
CHYMORAL. (USV Labs.) Trypsin and chymotrypsin, 50,000 Armour units (activity in ratio of approximately 6 to 1)/Tab. Bot. 48s.
Use: Oral anti-inflammatory.
CHYMORAL-100. (USV Labs.) Trypsin and chymotrypsin 100,000 Armour units/Tab. (Activity ratio approximately 6 to 1). Bot. 48s, 250s.
Use: Oral enzymes for treatment of inflammation.
• **CHYMOTRYPSIN,** U.S.P. XXI. Ophth. Sol. U.S.P. XXI. An enzyme, α-Chymotrypsin obtained in crystalline form from mammalian pancreas by aqueous acid extraction of its proenzyme, chymotrypsinogen, and subsequent conversion with trypsin to chymotrypsin.
Use: Proteolytic enzyme.
See: Avazyme, Tab. (Wallace)
Catarase, Sol. (CooperVision)
W/Trypsin.
Chymoral, Tab. (Armour)
Orenzyme, Tab. (Merrell Dow)
W/Trypsin, neomycin palmitate.
See: Biozyme, Oint. (Armour)

CHYMOTRYPSIN. B.A.N. An enzyme obtained from chymotrypsinogen by activation with trypsin.
Use: Proteolytic enzyme.
See: α-Chymotrypsin
Chymar
Chymar-Zon

CIBALITH-S. (Ciba) Lithium 8 mEq./5 ml. in sugar-free, raspberry-flavored syrup. Bot. 480 ml.
Use: Manic-depressive states.

C.I. BASIC VIOLET 3. Gentian Violet, U.S.P. XXI.

• **CIBENZOLINE.** USAN.
Use: Cardiac depressant (anti-arrhythmic).

• **CICLAFRINE HYDROCHLORIDE.** USAN.
Use: Antihypotensive.

CICLAZINDOL. B.A.N. 10-m-Chlorophenyl-2,3,4,-10-tetrahydropyrimido[1,2-α]-indol-10-ol.
Use: Antidepressant.

CICLOPIROX. B.A.N. 6-Cyclohexyl-1-hydroxy-4-methyl-2-pyridone.
Use: Fungicide.
See: Batrafen (ethanolamine salt).

• **CICLOPIROX OLAMINE,** U.S.P. XXI. Cream, U.S.P. XXI.
Use: Antifungal.
See: Loprox, Cream (Hoechst)

• **CICLOPROFEN.** USAN. 2-(2-Fluorenyl)propionic acid.
Use: Anti-inflammatory.

• **CICLOPROLOL HYDROCHLIRIDE.** USAN.
Use: Anti-adrenergic (beta receptor).

CICLOXOLONE. B.A.N. 3β-(cis-2-Carboxycyclo-hexyl-carbonyloxy)-11-oxo-olean-12-en-30-oic acid.
Use: Treatment of gastric ulcers.

CIDEX. (Surgikos) Activated dialdehyde solution. Bot. qt., gal., 5 gal.
Use: Sterilizing & disinfecting solution.

C.I. DIRECT BLUE 53 TETRASODIUM SALT. Evans Blue, U.S.P. XXI.

• **CIDOXIEPIN HCl.** USAN.
Use: Psychotherapeutic.

• **CIGLITAZONE.** USAN.
Use: Antidiabetic.

CIGNOLIN.
See: Anthralin (Var. Mfr.)

• **CILADOPA HYDROCHLORIDE.** USAN.
Use: Antiparkinsonian, dopaminergic agent.

• **CILASTATIN SODIUM.** USAN.
Use: Enzyme inhibitor.

CILFOMIDE TABLETS. (Winthrop Products) Inositol hexanicotinate.
Use: Hypolipidimic, peripheral vasodilator.

CILLIUM. (Whiteworth) Psyllium hydrophilic mucilloid. Bot. 14 oz. 21 oz.
Use: Bulk laxative.

• **CIMETIDINE,** U.S.P. XXI. Tab. U.S.P. XXI. 1-Methyl-3-[2-(5-methylimidazol-4-ylmethylthio)ethyl]guanidine -2-carbonitrile.
Use: H-2-receptor histamine antagonist.
See: Tagamet, Tab., Inj. (SmithKline)

CINACORT SPAN. (Foy) Triamcinolone acetonide 40 mg./ml. Vial 5 ml.
Use: Adrenocortical steroid replacement therapy.

• **CINANSERIN HYDROCHLORIDE.** USAN. 2′-[[3-(Dimethylamino)-propyl]thio]cinnamanilide HCl.
Use: Serotonin antagonist.

CINCHONA BARK. (Various Mfr.)
Use: Antimalarial & tonic.
W/Anhydrous quinine, cinchonidine, cinchonine, quinidine & quinine.
See: Totaquine, Pow. (Various Mfr.)
W/Iron oxide, nux vomica, Vitamin B-1, alcohol.
See: Briatonic, Liq. (Briar)

CINCHONAN-9-OL, 6′-METHOXY-, (9S)-, MONO-D GLUCONATE (SALT), OR SULFATE (SALT). Quinidine Gluconate, Sulfate.

CINCHONIDINE SULFATE.

CINCHONINE SALTS. (Various Mfr.)
Use: As quinine dihydrochloride.

CINCHOPHEN. 2-Phenylcinchoninic acid.
Use: Analgesic.

CINEPAZATE. B.A.N. Ethyl 4-(3,4,5-trimethoxy-c namoyl)piperazin-1-ylacetate.
Vascoril hydrogen maleate.
Use: Treatment of angina.

• **CINEPAZET MALEATE.** USAN.
Use: Anti-anginal.

CINEPAZIDE. B.A.N. 1-Pyrrolidin-1-ylcarbonyl-methy 4-(3,4,5-trimethoxycinnamoyl)-piperazine.
Use: Peripheral vasodilator.
See: Vasodistal hydrogen maleate.

CINEX-40. (Tunex) Triamcinolone diacetate 40 mg./ Vial 5cc.
Use: Parenteral steroid, depository.

• **CINFLUMIDE.** USAN.
Use: Muscle relaxant.

• **CINGESTOL.** USAN. 19-Nor-17α-pregn-5-en-20-y 17-ol.
Use: Progestogen.

CINNAMALDEHYDE.

• **CINNAMEDRINE.** USAN. a-[1-(Cinnamyl-methylamine)-ethyl] benzyl alcohol.
Use: Uterine antispasmodic.
See: Midol, Tab. (Glenbrook)

CINNAMIC ALDEHYDE. Name previously used for Cinnamaldehyde.

• **CINNAMON,** N.F. XVI.
Use: Flavoring agent.

• **CINNAMON OIL,** N.F. XVI. (Various Mfr.)
Use: Pharmaceutic aid. (flavor)

CINNAMYL EPHEDRINE HCl.
W/Acetaminophen, homatropine methylbromide.
See: Periodic, Cap. (Towne)

• **CINNARIZINE.** USAN. 1-Diphenylmethyl-4-trans-c namylpiperazine; 1-Benzhydryl-4-cinnamylpiperazi F.D.A. 1-Cinnamyl-4-diphenyl-methylpiperazine.
See: Mitronal
Stugeron

CINNASIL. (Amfre-Grant) Rescinnamine Tab. 0.5 Graduals 0.5 mg. Bot. 100s.
Use: Treatment of hypertension.

CINNOPENTAZONE. INN for Cintazone.

CINO-40. (Reid-Provident) Triamcinolone diacetate mg./ml. Vial. 5 ml.
Use: Glucocorticoid.

OBAC. (Dista) Cinoxacin. 250 mg./Pulvule. Bot. 0s. 500 mg./Pulvule. Bot. 50s.
se: Treatment of urinary tract infections.
NODINE HYDROCHLORIDE. USAN.
se: Antibacterial.
NOXACIN, U.S.P. XXI. Caps. U.S.P. XXI. 1-Ethyl--oxo[1,3]dioxolo-,5-g]cinnoline-3-carboxylic acid.
se: Antibacterial.
ee: Cinobac, Cap. (Dista).
NOXATE., U.S.P. XXI. Lotion, U.S.P. XXI. 2-Ethoxethyl p-methoxycinnamate.
se: Ultraviolet screen.
ee: Sundare Prods. (Cooper).
Methyl anthranilate.
ee: Maxafil Cream (Cooper).
OXOLONE. B.A.N. Cinnamyl 3β-acetoxy-11-oxo-lean-12-en-30-oate.
se: Treatment of gastric ulcers.
NPERENE. USAN. 1-Cinnamyl-4-(2,6-dioxo-3-pheyl-3-piperidyl)piperidine.
se: Tranquilizer.
-QUIN. (Rowell) Quinidine sulfate. **Tab:** 100 mg., 200 ng., 300 mg./Tab. Bot. 100s, 1000s, Unit dose 00s. **Cap.:** 200 mg./Cap. Bot. 100s, 1000s; 300 ng./Cap. Bot. 100s, 500s. Unit dose 100s.
Jse: Cardiac depressant.
NTAZONE. USAN. 2-Pentyl-6-phenyl-1H-pyrazolo 1,2-a] cinnoline-1,3(2H)-dione.
Jse: Anti-inflammatory.
NTRIAMIDE. USAN.
Jse: Antipyschotic.
PREFADOL SUCCINATE. USAN.
Jse: Analgesic.
NROMIDE. USAN.
Jse: Anticonvulsant.
IPROCINONIDE. USAN.
Jse: Adrenocortical steroid.
IPROFIBRATE. USAN.
Jse: Antihyperlipoproteinemic.
IPROSTENE CALCIUM. USAN.
Jse: Platelet anti-aggregatory agent.
IRAMADOL. USAN.
Jse: Analgesic.
IRAMADOL HYDROCHLORIDE. USAN.
Jse: Analgesic.
RAMINE. (Zemmer) Chlorpheniramine maleate. **Elixir:** 3 oz., pt., gal. **Parenteral:** (100 mg./cc.) Vial 10 cc. **Tab.:** 4 mg., Bot. 100s, 1000s. **Tab. T.R.:** 8 mg., Bot. 100s, 1000s, 12 mg., Bot. 100s, 1000s.
Jse: Antihistaminic.
RBED. (Boyd) Papaverine HCl 150 mg./Cap. Bot. 100s.
Jse: Antispasmodic effect on smooth muscle.
RCANOL. (Riker) **0.5 mg. Sublingual Tab.:** Dihydroergocornine 0.167 mg., dihydroergocristine 0.167 mg., dihydroergocryptine 0.167 mg. (alpha-beta ratio 2:1) mesylates/0.5 mg. Tab.; **1.0 mg. Tab.:** dihydroergocornine 0.333 mg., dihydroergocristine 0.333 mg., dihydroergocryptine (alkpha-beta ratio 2:1) mesylates/1 mg. Tab. Bot. 100s, 1000s.
Use: To improve performance of self-care in elderly, mood elevator.

CIRCAVITE T. (Circle) Vit. A acetate 25,000 I.U, D-2 400 I.U., B-1 15 mg., B-2 10 mg., B-6 5 mg., C 300 mg., B-12 10 mcg., E 5 I.U., niacinamide 100 mg., pantothenic acid 20 mg., ferrous sulfate 15 mg., calcium 110 mg./Tab. w/KI, Cu, Mg, Zn Bot. 100s.
Use: Vitamin and mineral supplement.

CIRCUBID. (Merchant) Ethaverine HCl 150 mg./Cap. Bot. 100s, 1000s.
Use: Peripheral and cerebral vascular insufficiency.

CIRIN. (Zemmer) Aspirin 300 mg., ascorbic acid 50 mg./Tab. Bot. 100s, 1000s.
Use: Analgesic.

• **CIROLEMYCIN.** USAN.
Use: Antibacterial, antineoplastic.

• **CISAPRIDE.** USAN.
Use: Peristaltic stimulant.

CISPLATIN. USAN.
Use: Antineoplastic agent.
See: Platinol, Inj. (Bristol)

CITANEST. (Astra) Prilocaine HCl w/sod. chloride, sod. hydroxide. Vial 30 cc., 1%, 2%. Ampul 1% 30 cc.; 2% 30 cc.; 3% 20 cc.
Use: Local anesthetic.

• **CITENAMIDE.** USAN.
Use: Anticonvulsant.

CITHAL CAPSULES. (Table Rock) Ext. watermelon seed 2 gr., theobromine 4 gr., phenobarbital 0.25 gr./Cap. Bot. 100s, 500s.
Use: Hypertension.

CITRA CAPSULES. (Boyle) Phenylephrine HCl 10 mg., ascorbic acid 50 mg., pheniramine maleate 6.25 mg., pyrilamine maleate 8.33 mg., salicylamide 227 mg., phenacetin 120 mg., caffeine alk. 30 mg. chlorpheniramine maleate 1 mg./Cap. Bot. 16s, 100s.
Use: Antihistamine, decongestant, analgesic.

CITRAMIN-500. (Thurston) Vit. C 500 mg., rose hips, acerola with mixed bioflavonoids/Loz. Bot. 100s, 250s, 1000s.
Use: Trauma, corticotropin therapy, pregnancy and lactation.

CITRASAN B. (Sandia) Lemon bioflavonoid complex 300 mg., Vit. C 300 mg., B-1 30 mg., B-2 10 mg., B-6 5 mg., B-12 4 mcg., cal. pantothenate 10 mg., niacinamide 50 mg./Tab. Bot. 100s, 1000s.

CITRASAN K LIQUID. (Sandia) Vit. C 125 mg., Vit. K 0.66 mg., lemon bioflavonoid complex 125 mg./5 cc. Bot. pt., gal.

CITRASAN K-250. (Sandia) Vit. C 250 mg., Vit. K 1 mg., lemon bioflavonoid 250 mg./Tab. Bot. 100s, 1000s.

CITRATED CAFFEINE.
See: Caffeine Citrate

CITRATED NORMAL HUMAN PLASMA.
See: Plasma, Normal Human.

CITRESCO-K. (Esco) Vit. C 100 mg., citrus bioflavonoid complex 100 mg., vit. K 0.7 mg./Cap. Bot. 100s, 500s, 1000s.
Use: Treatment of vit. K deficiencies.

• **CITRIC ACID,** U.S.P. XXI. 1,2,3-Propanetricarboxylic acid, 2-hydroxy-.

• **CITRIC ACID, MAGNESIUM OXIDE, AND SODIUM CARBONATE IRRIGATION,** U.S.P. XXI.
Use: Irrigating solution.

CITRIN.
See: Vitamin P

CITRIN CAPSULES. (Table Rock) Ext. watermelon seed 4 gr./Cap. Bot. 100s, 500s.
Use: Hypertension.

CITROBIC. (Blue Line) Hesperidin 100 mg., ascorbic acid 100 mg./Tab. Bot. 100s, 1000s.
Use: Fragile capillaries.

CITRO-C CAPSULES. (Barry-Martin) Bioflavonoids 100 mg., Vit. C 100 mg./Cap. Bot. 100s, 500s.

CITROCARBONATE. (Upjohn) Sod. bicarbonate 0.78 Gm., sod. citrate anhydrous 1.82 Gm./teaspoon. Bot. 4 oz., 8 oz.
Use: Increase alkali reserve.

CITROHIST. (Robinson) Prophenpyridamine 6.75 mg., pyrilamine maleate 8.33 mg., hesperidin 50 mg., C 50 mg., ephedrine sulfate 16.2 mg., salicylamide 3.5 gr., phenacetin 2 gr., caffeine alkaloid 0.5 gr., atropine sulfate 1/600 gr./Cap. Bot. 100s, 1000s. Bulk Pack 5000s. Vial 20s.
Use: Cold symptoms.

CITROLEUM SUNBURN CREME. (Citroleum) Bot. 4 oz.

CITROLITH. (Beach) Potassium citrate 50 mg., sodium citrate 950 mg./Tab. Bot. 100s.
Use: Urinary alkalizer.

CITROMA. (National Magnesia) Magnesium citrate oval soln. Bot. 10 oz.
Use: Laxative and bowel evacument.

CITROMA LOW SODIUM. (National Magnesia) Magnesium citrate oral soln. w/lemon or cherry flavor in sugar free vehicle. Bot. l0 oz.
Use: Laxative and bowel evacument.

CITROPAM. (Jenkins) No. 1 Ammonium chloride 0.5 Gm., citric acid 0.5 Gm., potassium quaiacolsulfonate 0.5 Gm./fl. oz. Bot. 3 oz., 4 oz., gal. Also Citropam No. 2 w./codeine phosphate 30 mg./fl., oz.
Bot. 3 oz., 4 oz., gal.
Use: Cough syrup.

CITROTEIN. (Sandoz Nutrition) Orange Flavor: Sucrose, pasteurized egg white solids, maltodextrin, citric acid, natural & artificial flavors, mono & diglycerides, partially hydrogenated soybean oil, vitamins & minerals, FD&C yellow No. 5 and No. 6. Powder 1.57 oz./packet, Cans 14.16 oz. Orange, grape and punch flavors.
Use: Supplementary oral feeding.

CITROVORUM FACTOR. Leucovorin Calcium, U.S.P. XXI.
See: Leucovorin Calcium (Lederle) Folinic Acid.

CITRUS BIOFLAVONOID COMPOUND.
See: Bioflavonoid Cpds. (Various Mfr.)
C.V.P., Syr. (USV Pharm.)
Vitamin P

W/Ascorbic acid, phenyltoloxamine dihydrogen citrate, salicylamide, acetyl p-aminophenol, caffeine, racemic amphetamine sulf.
See: Euphenex, Tab. (Westerfield)

CK(CPK) REAGENT STRIPS. (Ames) Seralyzer reagent strips. Bot. 25s.
Use: A quantitative strip test for creatine phosphokinase in serum or plasma.

C-JECT. (Lincoln) Ascorbic acid 2,000 mg., sodium sulfite 0.1%, disodium sequestrene 0.01%, 10 cc Ampule 10 cc. "Score-Break" Box 25s.

C-JECT WITH B. (Lincoln) When mixed with 10 cc. Diluent each vial contains: Vit. C 2,000 mg., B-1 mg., B-2 5 mg., B-6 10 mg., nicotinamide 100 mg., w methylparaben 0.89 mg., propyparaben 0.22 mg., sodium bisulfite 10 mg., disodium sequestrene 1 mg. Box of 6 lyophilized plugs and 6 10-cc. vials Sterile Diluent.

CKA CANKER AID. (Pannett Prod.) Benzocaine, aluminum hydrate, mag. trisilicate, sod. acid carbonate. Pow.
Use: Cold-canker sore.

CLAFORAN. (Hoechst) Cefotaxime sodium 1.0 Gm. 2.0, and 10 Gm./Vial. Infusion Bottles 1.0 Gm. ar 2.0 Gm.
Use: Broad spectrum antibiotic.

CLAMIDOXIC ACID. B.A.N. [2-(3,4-Dichlorobenzamido)phenoxy]acetic acid.
Use: Antirheumatic.

CLAMOXYQUIN. B.A.N. 5-Chloro-7-(3-diethylaminopropylaminomethyl)-8-hydroxyquinoline.
Use: Treatment of amebiasis.

• **CLAMOXYQUIN HYDROCHLORIDE.** USAN. 5-Chro-7-(((3-(diethylamino)propyl)-amino)methyl)-8-quilinol dihydrochloride.
Use: Amebicide.

CLARETIN-12.
See: Vitamin B-12

• **CLAZOLAM.** USAN.
Use: Tranquilizer.

• **CLAZOLIMINE.** USAN.
Use: Diuretic.

CLEANING & SOAKING SOLUTION. (Barnes-Hir Benzalkonium chloride 0.01%, EDTA 0.2%. Bot. oz.
Use: Hard contact lens cleaner and disinfectant.

CLEAN-N-SOAK. (Allergan) Phenyl mercuric nitrate 0.004% in a sterile buffered solution. Bot. 4 oz.
Use: Hard contact lens cleaning & soaking solutic cleaning agent.

CLEARASIL ACNE TREATMENT CREAM. (Vicks Prods) Benzoyl peroxide 10% in tinted or vanishi base. Tube 0.65 oz., 1.0 oz.
Use: Topical acne medication.

CLEARASIL ANTIBACTERIAL ACNE LOTION. (Vicks Prods) Benzoyl peroxide 5%, Bot. 1 oz.
Use: Topical acne medication.

CLEARASIL ANTIBACTERIAL SOAP. (Vicks Prods Triclosan 0.75% in soap cake 3.25 oz.
Use: Skin cleanser.

CLEARASIL PORE DEEP CLEANSER. (Vicks Prod Salicylic acid 0.5%, alcohol 43%. Bot. 4 oz., 8 oz
Use: Medicated skin cleanser.

CLEARASIL STICK. (Vicks Prods) Sulfur 8%, resorcinol 1%. Stick. 1/8 oz.
Use: Topical acne medication.

EAR BY DESIGN. (Herbert) Benzoyl peroxide .5% in an invisible, greaseless gel base. Tubes, .5 oz., 3 oz.
Jse: Acne skin medication.

EAREX ACNE CREAM. (Approved) Allantoin, sulfur, resorcinol, d-panthenol, isopropanol. Tube 1.5 oz.

EAR EYES EYE DROPS. (Ross) Naphazoline HCl).012%, w/benzalkonium chloride 0.01%, disodium edetate 0.1%, boric acid, sodium borate. Bot. 0.5 oz.,1.5 oz.
Jse: Ophthalmic decongestant.

EFAMIDE. B.A.N. $\alpha\alpha$-Dichloro-N-(2-hydroxy-ethyl)-N-[4-(4-nitrophenoxy)benzyl]acetamide.
Jse: Treatment of amebiasis.
See: Mebinol

LEMASTINE. USAN. (+)-2-[2-(4-Chloro-α-methyl-benzhydryloxy)ethyl]-1-methylpyrrolidine.
Jse: Antihistamine.
See: Tavegil hydrogen fumarate
Tavist, Tab. (Dorsey)

LEMASTINE FUAMARATE. USAN.
Jse: Antihistaminic.

LEMASTINE FUMARATE TABLETS, U.S.P. XXI.
Jse: Antihistaminic.

EMIZOLE. B.A.N. 1-(4-chlorobenzyl)-2-pyrrolidin-1-ylmethylbenzimidazole.
Jse: Antipruritic.

EMIZOLE HCl. 1-p-Chlorobenzyl-2-pyrrolidyl-methyl benzimidazole. Reactrol.

EMIZOLE PENICILLIN. B.A.N. Benzylpenicillin combined with 1-(4-chlorobenzyl)-2-pyrrolidin-1-ylmethylbenzimidazole. Neopenyl.
Jse: Antibiotic.

ENPYRIN. B.A.N. 1-Butyl-2-(3,4-dichloro-phenylimino)pyrrolidine.
Jse: Insecticide, veterinary medicine.

EOCIN HCl. (Upjohn) Clindamycin HCl equiv. to clindamycin base 75 mg./Cap. Bot. 100s; 150 mg./Cap. Bot. 16s, 100s. Unit-Dose 100s.
Jse: Antibiotic.

EOCIN PEDIATRIC, (Upjohn) Clindamycin palmitate HCl equivalent to 75 mg., clindamycin/5 ml. when reconstituted as directed. Bot. 100 ml.
Jse: Antibiotic.

EOCIN PHOSPHATE. (Upjohn) Clindamycin phosphate equivalent to 150 mg. clindamycin/ml. **300 mg.**: Amp. 2 ml. w/disodium edetate 1 mg., benzyl alcohol 18.9 mg. Pack 25s, 100s. Vial 2 ml. Pack 25s, 100s. **600 mg.:** Amp. 4 ml. w/disodium edetate 2 mg., benzyl alcohol 37.8 mg. Pack 25s, 100s. Vial 4 ml. Pack 25s, 100s.**900 mg:** Vial 6 ml. Pack 25s, 100s
Jse: Antibiotic.

EOCIN T. (Upjohn) Clindamycin phosphate 1%. Bot. 30 ml., 60 ml.; pt.
Use: Antibiotic for treatment of acne vulgaris.

ERZ. (CooperVision) A neutral hypertonic balanced salt soln. Lubricating and rewetting eye drops. Bot. 25 ml. w/dropper.
Use: For hard and soft contact lenses.

CLERZ 2. (CooperVision) Lubricating/rewetting eye drops. A neutral isotonic balanced salt sol. Bot. 15 ml. w/Dropper.
Use: For hard and soft contact lenses.

C-LEST. (Tunex) Betamethasone sodium phosphate equivalent to betamethasone 3 mg., sodium phosphate 10 mg./ml. Vial 5 cc.
Use: Anti-inflammatory.

CLETOQUINE. B.A.N. 7-Chloro-4-[4-(2-hydroxy-ethylamino)-1-methylbutyl]aminoquinoline.
Use: Anti-inflammatory.

• **CLIDINIUM BROMIDE,** U.S.P. XXI. Caps., U.S.P. XXI. 1-Methyl-3-benzil-oyloxy-quinuclidinium bromide. 3-Hydroxy-1-methyl-quinuclidinium bromide benzilate.
Use: Anticholinergic.
See: Quarzan, Cap. (Roche)
W/Chlordiazepoxide.
See: Chloridinium Sealets, Cap. (Lemmon)
Librax, Cap. (Roche)

CLIMESCO. (Esco) Methyl testosterone 5 mg., yohimbine HCl 5 mg., ext. nux vomica 5 mg., thiamine HCl 25 mg./Cap. Bot. 100s, 500s, 1000s.
Use: Male climacteric and hypogonadal impotence; neurasthenia.

• **CLINDAMYCIN.** USAN. Methyl 7-chloro-6,7,8-tri-deoxy-6-(trans-1-methyl-4-propyl-L-2-pyrrolidine-carboxamido)-1-thio-L-threo-α-D-galactooctopy-ranoside.
Use: Antibiotic.
See: Dalacin C

• **CLINDAMYCIN HYDROCHLORIDE,** U.S.P. XXI. Caps. U.S.P. XXI.
Use: Antibacterial.
See: Cleocin HCl A.D.T., Cap. (Upjohn)

• **CLINDAMYCIN PALMITATE HYDROCHLORIDE,** U.S.P. XXI. Oral Soln., U.S.P. XXI.
Use: Antibacterial.
See: Cleocin Pediatric (Upjohn)
Cleocin T, Liq. (Upjohn)

• **CLINDAMYCIN PHOSPHATE,** U.S.P. XXI. Inj., Topical Sol., Sterile, U.S.P. XXI.
Use: Antibacterial.
See: Cleocin phosphate, Inj. (Upjohn)

CLINISTIX REAGENT STRIPS. (Ames) Glucose oxidase, peroxidase and orthotolidine. Diagnostic test for glucose in urine. Bot. 50s.
Use: Diagnostic agent: glucosuria.

CLINITAR CREAM. (Ulmer) Coal tar extract 2%. Tube 4 oz.
Use: Anti-dermatitis, topical anti-pruritic, anti-psoriasis, anti-seborrhea agent.

CLINITAR SHAMPOO. (Ulmer) Coal tar extract 2%. Tube 4 oz.
Use: Anti-dandruff, anti-dermatitis, topical anti-pruritic, anti-psoriasis, anti-seborrhea agent.

CLINITAR STICK. (Ulmer) Crude coal tar 5%. Stick 20 ml.
Use: Anti-dermatitis, anti-pruritic, anti-psoriasis, anti-seborrhea agent.

CLINITEST. (Ames) Reagent tablets containing copper sulfate, sod. hydroxide & heat-producing

agents. Patient's plastic set; Tab. refills, **Bot.** 36s, 100s, 250s, **Box** 100s, 500s, sealed in foil. **Child-resistant Bot.** 36s, 100s.
Use: For urine-sugar determination.

CLINITEST DROPPERS. (Ames) Pkgs. 3s.
Use: Droppers for use with Clinitest reagent tablets.

CLINITEST REAGENT TABLETS 2-DROP METHOD. (Ames) Bot. 36s, 100s. Pt. plastic set.
Use: Test for urine sugar.

CLINITEST SET. (Ames) Urine-sugar analysis set with bottle of 36 tablets and 2 foil wrapped tablets.

CLINITEST TEST TUBES. (Ames) Carton 6s.

CLINOCAINE HCl.
See: Procaine HCl

CLINORIL. (Merck Sharp & Dohme) Sulindac 150 mg. and 200 mg./Tab. Bot. 100s. Unit-dose 100s. Unit-of-use 60s, 100s.
Use: Nonsteroidal anti-inflammatory and analgesic for treatment of osteoarthritis, rheumatoid arthritis, ankylosing spondylitis, acute painful shoulder, and acute gouty arthritis

• **CLIOQUINOL,** U.S.P. XXI. Comp. Pow., Cream, Oint., U.S.P. XXI. 5-Chloro-7-iodo-8-quinolinol. Quinambicide, Rometin. Iodohydroxyquin.
Use: Antiamebic; local anti-infective.
See: HCV Creame (Saron)
Quin III, Cream (Lemmon)
Quinoform, Oint., Cream, Lot. (C & M Pharmacal)
Torofor, Cream, Oint. (Torch)
Vioform, Prep. (Ciba)
W/Aluminum acetate solution, hydrocortisone.
See: Hydrelt, Cream, Oint. (Elder)
W/Hydrocortisone.
See: Bafil, Cream (Skruggs)
Caquin Cream (O'Neal, Jones, Feldman)
Coidocort Cream (Coast)
Corticoid, Cream (Jenkins)
Cort Nib V, Cream (Cenci)
Domeform-HC, Cream (Miles Pharm)
Durel-Cort 'V,' Cream, Oint., Lot. (Durel)
Hi-Form Cream (Blaine)
Hydrelt, Cream (Elder)
Hysone, Cream, Oint. (Mallard)
Ido-Cortistan Ointment (Standex)
Iodocort, Cream (Ulmer)
Iohydro, Cream (Freeport)
Kencort, Cream (Kenyon)
Lanvisone, Cream (Lannett)
Maso-Form, Cream (Mason)
Mity-Quin Cream (Reid-Provident)
Racet, Cream (Lemmon)
Racet Forte, Cream (Lemmon)
Vioform-Hydrocortisone, Cream, Oint., Lotion (Ciba)
Vio-Hydrocort, Cr. and Oint. (Quality Generics)
W/Hydrocortisone acetate.
See: Quinsone, Oint. (Sutliff & Case)
Viotag Cream (Reid-Provident)
W/Hydrocortisone acetate, lidocaine.
See: Lidaform-HC, Creme, Lot. (Miles Pharm)
W/Hydrocortisone, coal tar solution.
See: Tar-Quin-HC, Oint. (Jenkins)
W/Hydrocortisone, lidocaine.
See: Bafil Lotion (Scruggs)
HIL-20 Lotion (Reid-Provident)
W/Hydrocortisone, chlorobutanol.
See: Hc-Form, Jelly (Recsei)
W/Hydrocortisone, coal tar extract.
See: Racet LCD, Cream (Lemmon)
W/Hydrocortisone and pramoxine HCl.
See: Dermarex Cream (Hyrex)
Quinsone, Cream (Sutliff & Case)
Sherform-HC, Oint. (Sheryl)
Stera-Form Creme (Mayrand)
V-Cort, Cream (Scrip)
Vio-Hydrosone, Cream (Vortech)
W/Methylcellulose, aluminum hydroxide, atropine su hyoscine HBr, hyoscyamine sulf.
See: Enterex, Tab. (Person & Covey)
W/Nystatin.
See: Nystaform, Oint. (Miles Pharm)

• **CLIOXANIDE.** USAN. 2-(4-Chlorophenylcarbamoyl 4,6-di-iodophenylacetate.
Use: Anthelmintic, veterinary medicine.
See: Tremerad

• **CLIPROFEN.** USAN.
Use: Anti-inflammatory.

CLISTIN. (McNeil Pharm) Carbinoxamine maleate 4 mg./Tab. Bot. 100s.
Use: Antihistamine.

CLISTIN-D. (McNeil Pharm) Carbinoxamine maleate mg., Acetaminophen 300 mg., phenylephrine HCl 10 mg./Tab. Bot. 100s.
Use: Common cold.

• **CLOBAMINE MESYLATE.** USAN.
Use: Antidepressant.

• **CLOBAZAM.** USAN. 7-Chloro-1-methyl-5-phenyl-1, benzodiazepine-2,4-dione.
Use: Tranquilizer.

CLOBENZTROPINE. 3-(p-Chloro-a-phenylbenzyl-ox tropane.

CLOBETASOL. B.A.N. 21-Chloro-9α-fluoro-11β, 17α dihydroxy-16β-methylpregna-1,4-diene-3,20-dione.
Use: Corticosteroid.

• **CLOBETASOL PROPIONATE.** USAN.
Use: Corticosteroid.

CLOBETASONE. B.A.N. 21-Chloro-9α-fluoro-17α-h droxy-16β-methylpregna-1,4-diene-3,11,20-trione.
Use: Corticosteroid.

• **CLOBETASONE BUTYRATE.** USAN.
Use: Corticosteroid.

CLOCIGUANIL. B.A.N. 4,6-Diamino-1-(3,4-dichlorobe zyloxy)-1,2-dihydro-2,2-dimethyl-1,3,5-triazine.
Use: Antimalarial.

• **CLOCORTOLONE ACETATE.** USAN.
Use: Glucocorticoid.

• **CLOCORTOLONE PIVALATE,** U.S.P. XXI. Cream, U.S.P. XXI.
Use: Glucocorticoid.

CLOCREAM. (Upjohn) Vit. A & D in vanishing base. Tube 1 oz.
Use: Relief of minor skin irritations.

• **CLODANOLENE.** USAN.
Use: Relaxant.

,ODAZON HYDROCHLORIDE. USAN.
se: Antidepressant.
DERM. (Ortho) Clocortolone pivalate cream 1%. Tube 15 Gm., 45 Gm.
se: Steroid responsive dermatoses.
ODRONIC ACID. USAN.
se: Regulator.
,OFAZIMINE. USAN. 3-(p-Chloroanilino) 10-(p-chlophenyl)-2,10-dihydro-2-(isopropylimino)-phenane.
se: Tuberculostatic; leprostatic.
FAZIMINE. B.A.N. 3-(4-Chloroanilino)-10-(4-chloroenyl)-2,10-dihydro-2-isopropylimino-phenazine.
se: Treatment of leprosy.
ee: Lamprene
OFIBRATE, U.S.P. XXI. Caps., U.S.P. XXI. Ethyl (p-chlorophenoxy-2-methyl-propionate. Propanoic cid, 2-(4-chlorophenoxy)-2-methyl-, methyl ster.
se: Cardiovascular disorders; antihyperlipidemic.
ee: Atromid S., Caps. (Ayerst)
,OFILIUM PHOSPHATE. USAN.
se: Cardiac depressant.
,OFLUCARBAN. USAN. 4,4′-Dichloro-3-(trifluoroethyl)-carbanilide. Irgasan, CF3.
se: Recommended as antiseptic, on release.
FLUPEROL. B.A.N. 4-(4-Chloro-3-trifluoro-methylhenyl)-1-[3-(4-fluorobenzoyl)propyl]piperidin-4-ol.
se: Neuroleptic.
GESTONE. B.A.N. 6-Chloro-3β, 17-dihydroxypreg-a-4,6-diene-20-one.
se: Progestational steroid.
,OGESTONE ACETATE. USAN. 6-Chloro-3β, 17-hydroxypregna-4,6-dien-20-one diacetate. Under udy.
se: Progestogen.
GUANAMILE. B.A.N. 1-Amidino-3-(3-chloro-4-yanophenyl)urea.
se: Antimalarial.
MACRAN. B.A.N. NN-Dimethyl-3-(2-chloro-9, 10-hydroacridin-9-yl)propylamine.
se: Tranquilizer.
,OMACRAN PHOSPHATE. USAN. 2-Chloro-9-[3-methyl-amino)propyl] acridan phosphate (1:1). nder study.
se: Tranquilizer.
,OMEGESTONE ACETATE. USAN. 6-Chloro-7-acetoxy-1,6α-methyl-4,6-pregnadiene-3,20-one. Under study.
se: Progestogen.
,OMETHERONE. USAN. 6α-Chloro-16α-ethyl-pregn-4-ene-3,20-dione.
se: Anti-estrogen.
MID. (Merrell Dow) Clomiphene citrate) mg./Tab. Carton 30s.
se: Ovulatory failure (dysfunction) in patient esiring pregnancy.
,OMINOREX. USAN.
se: Anorexic.
,OMIPHENE CITRATE. U.S.P. XXI. Tabs., U.S.P. XI. 2-[p-(2-Chloro-1,2-diphenyl-vinyl)phenoxy]trieylamine dihydrogen citrate. Ethanamine, 2-[4-(2-chloro-1,2-diphenylethenyl)-phenoxy]-N,N-diethyl-, 2-hydroxy-1,2,3-propanetricarboxylate(1:1).
Use: Fertility agent.
See: Clomid, Tab. (Merrell Dow)
Serophene, Tab. (Serono)
CLOMIPRAMINE. B.A.N. 3-Chloro-5-(3-dimethylamino-propyl-10,11-dihydrodibenz[b,f]azepine.
Use: Antidepressant.
See: Anafranil hydrochloride
CLOMIPRAMINE HCl. USAN. 3-Chloro-5-[3-(dimethyl-amino)propyl]-10, 11-dihydro-5H-dibenz-[b,f] azepine monohydrochloride.
Use: Antidepressant.
CLOMOCYCLINE. B.A.N. N^2-(Hydroxymethyl)-chlortetracycline.
Use: Antibiotic.
See: Chlormethylencycline Megaclor
• **CLONAZEPAM,** U.S.P. XXI. Tab. U.S.P. XXI. 5-(o-Chlorophenyl)-1,3-dihydro-7-nitro-2H-1,4-benzodiazepin-2-one. B.A.N. 5-(2-Chlorophenyl)-1,3-dihydro-7-nitro-2H-1,4-benzodiazepin-2-one. Rivotril.
Use: Anticonvulsant.
See: Clonopin, Tab. (Roche)
C-LONG. (Reid-Provident) Ascorbic acid 500 mg./long-acting Cap. Bot. 100s.
• **CLONIDINE.** USAN. 2-(2,6-Dichloroanilino)-2-imidazoline.
Use: Hypotensive.
See: Catapres
Dixarit
• **CLONIDINE HYDROCHLORIDE,** U.S.P. XXI. Tabs., U.S.P. XXI. Benzamine, 2,6-dichloro-N-2-imidazolidinyl-idene-, monochloride. (1)2-(2,6-Dichloranilino)-2-imidazoline monohydrochloride. (2)2-(2,6-Dichlorophenylamino)-2-imidazoline HCl.
Use: Antihypertensive.
See: Catapres, Tab. (Boehringer Ingelheim)
• **CLONIDINE HYDROCHLORIDE AND CHLORTHALIDONE TABLETS,** U.S.P. XXI.
Use: Antihypertensive, diuretic.
See: Combipres, Tab. (Boehringer Ingelheim)
CLONITAZENE. B.A.N. 2-(4-Chlorobenzyl)-1-(2-diethylaminoethyl)-5-nitrobenzimidazole.
Use: Narcotic analgesic.
• **CLONITRATE.** USAN. 3-Chloro-1,2-propanediol dinitrate. Dylate
Use: Coronary vasodilator.
• **CLONIXERIL.** USAN.
Use: Analgesic.
• **CLONIXIN.** USAN.
Use: Analgesic.
CLONOPIN. (Roche) Clonazepam 0.5 mg., 1 mg., 2.0 mg./Tab. Pkg. 100s.
Use: Anticonvulsant (petit mal).
• **CLOPAMIDE.** USAN. (1) 4-Chloro-N-(2,6-dimethyl-piperidino)-3-sulfamoylbenzamide; (2)4-chloro-3-sulfamoylbenzoic acid 1,5-dimethylpentamethylenehydrazide.
Use: Antihypertensive; diuretic.
See: Aquex, Tab. (Lannett)
Brinaldix

• **CLOPENTHIXOL.** USAN. 4-[3-(2-Chlorothioxanthen-9-ylidene)propyl]-1-piperazine-ethanol.
Use: Antipsychotic.
See: Sordinol (Ayerst)

• **CLOPERIDONE HYDROCHLORIDE.** USAN. 3-[3-[4-(m-Chlorophenyl)-1-piperazinyl] propyl]-2,-4-(IH, 3H)-quinazolinedione HCl.
Use: Sedative; tranquilizer.

CLOPHEDIANOL HCl.
See: Acutuss, Tab., Expect. (Philips Roxane)

CLOPHENOXATE HCl. 2-Dimethylamino-ethyl p-chlorphenoxyacetate HCl.
Use: Cerebral stimulant.

CLOPENTHIXOL. B.A.N. 2-Chloro-9- 3-[4-(2-hydroxyethyl)piperazin-1-yl]-propylidene thiaxanthene.
Use: Psychotropic.
See: Sordinol dihydrochloride

• **CLOPIDOL.** USAN. 3,5-Dichloro-4-hydroxy-2,6-dimethylpyridine.
Use: Antiprotozoan, veterinary medicine.
See: Coyden 25

• **CLOPIMOZIDE.** USAN.
Use: Antipsychotic.

• **CLOPIPAZAN MESYLATE.** USAN.
Use: Antipsychotic.

CLOPIRAC. USAN. 1-p-Chlorophenyl-2,5-dimethylpyrrol-3-ylacetic acid.
Use: Anti-inflammatory.

CLOPONONE. B.A.N. β,4-Dichloro-α-dichloroacetamidopropiophenone.
Use: Antiseptic.

• **CLOPREDNOL.** USAN.
Use: Glucocorticoid.

CLOPROSTENOL. B.A.N. ($\pm$)-7- (1R,2R,3R,5S)-2-[(3R)-4-(3-Chlorophenoxy)-3-hydroxybut-1-(E)-enyl]-3,5-dihydroxycyclopent-1-yl hept-5-(Z) enoic acid.
Use: Synchronization of estrus; infertility, veterinary medicine.

• **CLOPROSTENOL SODIUM.** USAN.
Use: Prostaglandin.

CLOQUINATE. B.A.N. Chloroquine di-(8-hydroxy-7-iodoquinoline-5-sulfonate).
Use: Treatment of amebiasis.
See: Resotren

• **CLORAZEPATE DIPOTASSIUM.** USAN. 7-Chloro-2,3-dihydro-2,2-dihydroxy-5-phenyl-IH-1,4-benzodiazepine-3-carboxylic acid dipotassium salt.
Use: Minor tranquilizer.
See: Tranxene, Cap. (Abbott)

• **CLORAZEPATE MONOPOTASSIUM.** USAN.
Use: Minor tranquilizer.

CLORAZEPIC ACID. B.A.N. 7-Chloro-2,3-dihydro-2,2-dihydroxy-5-phenyl-1H-1,4-benzodiazepine-3-carboxylic acid.
Use: Sedative.
See: Azene, monopotassiuim salt (Du Pont)
Tranxene dipotassium salt (Abbott)

• **CLORETHATE.** USAN.
Use: Sedative, hypnotic.

CLOREXOLONE. USAN. 5-Chloro-2-cyclohexyl-6-sulfamoylisoindolin-1-one.
Use: Diuretic.
See: Nefrolan

CLORFED II. (Stewart-Jackson) Chlorpheniramin mg., pseudoephedrine 60 mg./Tab. Bot. 100s.
Use: Decongestant, antihistamine.

CLORFED CAPSULES. (Stewart-Jackson) Cl pheniramine 8 mg., pseudoephedrine 120 mg./C Bot. 100s.
Use: Antihistamine, decongestant.

CLORFED EXPECTORANT. (Stewart-Jack Pseudoephedrine 30 mg., guaifensen 100 mg., codeine 10 mg. Bot. pt.
Use: Decongestant, expectorant, antitussive.

CLORFED LIQUID. (Stewart-Jackson) Chlorphe mine 2 mg., pseudoephedrine 30 mg. w/alcohol volume 5%. Bot. pt.
Use: Decongestant, antihistamine.

CLORGYLINE. B.A.N. N-3-(2,4-Dichlorophenoxy) pyl-N-methylprop-2-ynylamine.
Use: Monoamine oxidase inhibitor; antidepressa

CLORINDIONE. B.A.N. 2-(4-Chlorophenyl)indane-1 dione.
Use: Anticoagulant.
See: Indalitan

• **CLOROPERONE HYDROCHLORIDE.** USAN.
Use: Antipsychotic.

CLORPACTIN WCS-90. (Guardian) Sodium oxychl sene. Bot. 2 Gm. 5s.
Use: Topical antiseptic for irrigation of infected areas.

• **CLOROPHENE.** USAN. 4-Chloro-alpha-phenyl-o-sol.
Use: Disinfectant.
See: Santophen 1 (Monsanto)

CLORPRENALINE. B.A.N. 1-(2-Chlorophenyl)-2-propylaminoethanol.
Use: Sympathomimetic.

• **CLORPRENALINE HYDROCHLORIDE.** USAN. (formerly Isoprophenamine HCl) 1-(α-Chlorophe 2-isopropyl-aminoethanol hydrochloride hydrate. tel
Use: Bronchodilator.

• **CLORSULON.** USAN.
Use: Antiparasitic, fasciolicide.

• **CLORTERMINE HCl.** USAN. o-Chloro-α,α-dime phenethylamine HCl.
Use: Anorexic.
See: Voranil (USV Labs.)

• **CLOSANTEL.** USAN.
Use: Anthelmintic.

• **CLOSIRAMINE ACETURATE.** USAN.
Use: Antihistaminic.

CLOSTEBOL ACETATE. B.A.N. 17β-Acetoxy-4-c roandrost-4-en-3-one.
Use: Anabolic steroid.

• **CLOTHIAPINE.** USAN. 2-Chloro-11-(4-methyl-pip zin-1-yl)dibenzo[b,f][1,4]thiazepine.
Use: Tranquilizer.

• **CLOTHIXAMIDE MALEATE.** USAN. 4-[3-(2-Chl thioxanthen-9-ylidene)propyl]-N-methyl-1-piperaz propionamide dimaleate.
Use: Tranquilizer.

.**OTICASONE PROPIONATE.** USAN.
se: Anti-inflammatory.
.**OTRIMAZOLE,** U.S.P. XXI. Cream, Lotion,
opical Soln., Vaginal Tabs., U.S.P. XXI. l-(o-Chloro-
,α-diphenylbenzyl)-imidazole.
se: Antifungal.
ee: Gyne-Lotrimin, Cream, Vaginal Tab. (Schering)
Lotrimin, Cream, Sol. (Schering)
Myclex, Cream, Sol. (Miles Pharm)
Myclex-G, Vag. Suppos. (Miles Pharm)
.**OVE OIL,** N.F. XVI.
se: Pharmaceutic aid (flavor).
VERINE. (Medtech) White salve. Tin 1 oz.
se: Temporary relief of minor skin irritations &
urns.
VOCAIN. (Vita Elixir) Benzocaine, oil of cloves.
se: Dental medicine, surface anesthetic.
XACILLIN. B.A.N. 6-[3-(2-Chlorophenyl)-5-
ethylisoxazole-4-carboxamido]penicillanic acid.
(2-Chlorophenyl)-5-methylisoxazol-4-ylpenicillin.
se: Antibiotic.
ee: Orbenin sodium salt
.**OXACILLIN BENZATHINE,** U.S.P. XXI.
tramammary Sol., Sterile, U.S.P. XXI.
se: Antibiotic.
.**OXACILLIN SODIUM,** U.S.P. XXI., Caps.,
tramammary Sol., Sterile, For Oral Soln., U.S.P.
XI. 4-Thia-1-azabicyclo[3.2.0]heptane-2-carboxylic
cid,6-[[[3-(2-chlorophenyl)-
methyl-4-isoxazoly]carbonyl]amino]-3,3-dimethyl-
oxo-,monosodium salt, monohydrate. Monosodium
[3-(o-chlorophenyl)-5-methyl-4-isoxazolecarboxami-
o]-3,3-dimethyl-7-oxo-4-thia-1-azabicyclo[3.2.0]hept-
ne-2-carboxylate monohydrate.
se: Antibiotic for resistant staph infections.
ee: Cloxapen, Cap. (Beecham Labs)
Tegopen, Cap., Granules (Bristol)
XAPEN. (Beecham Labs) Cloxacillin sodium 250
g. & 500 mg./Cap. Bot. 100s.
se: Antibiotic.
.**OXYQUIN.** USAN.
se: Antibacterial.
.**OZAPINE.** USAN. 8-Chloro-11-(4-methylpiperazin-
-yl)-5H-dibenzo[b,e][1,4]-diazepine.
se: Sedative.
SIVOL CAPSULES. (Ayerst) Vit. A 10,000 U.S.P.
nits, D-2 400 U.S.P. Units, C 150 mg., B-1 10 mg.,
-2 5 mg., B-6 0.5 mg., d-panthenol 1 mg., B-12 2.5
cg., niacinamide 50 mg., E 0.5 I.U., Fe 15 mg.,
a 120 mg., Mn 0.5 mg., Zn 0.6 mg., Mg 3
g./Cap. 100s.
se: Nutritional supplement.
SIVOL SYRUP. (Ayerst) Vit. A 2500 U.S.P. Units,
-2 400 U.S.P. Units, C 15 mg., B-12 2 mcg., B-1 1
g., B-2 1 mg., niacinamide 5 mg., d-panthenol 3 mg.,
-6 0.6 mg., manganese, 0.5 mg., zinc. 0.5 mg., mag-
esium, 3 mg./5 ml. Bot. 8, 16 fl. oz.
se: Nutritional supplement.
SIVOL TABLETS. (Ayerst) Vit. A 10,000 U.S.P.
nits, D-2 400 U.S.P. Units, C 150 mg., B-1 10 mg.,
-2 5 mg., B-6 0.5 mg., d-panthenol 1 mg., B-12 2.5
cg., niacinamide 50 mg., E 0.5 I.U., Fe 15 mg.,
Ca 120 mg., Mn 0.5 mg., Zn 0.6 mg., Mg 3 mg./Tab. Bot. 130s.
Use: Nutritional supplement.

CLYSODRAST. (Armour) Bisacodyl 1.5 mg., tannic acid 2.5 Gm./packet. 25s, 50s.
Use: Colonic laxative.

C.M.C. CELLULOSE GUM.
See: Carboxymethylcellulose Sodium, Preps.

CMV. (Wampole-Zeus) Cytomegalovirus antibody test system. Tests 100s.
Use: For the qualitative and semi-quantitative detection of CMV antibody in human serum.

COACTIN. (Roche) Amdinocillin 500 mg. or 1 Gm./Vial to be re-constituted for IV or IM administration. Box 10s.
Use: Urinary tract infections.

COAGULANTS.
See: Hemostatics

• **COAL TAR,** U.S.P. XXI. Oint., Sol., U.S.P. XXI.
Use: Topical antieczematic; antipsoriatic.
See: Balnetar, Liq. (Westwood)
Estar, Gel (Westwood)
L.C.D. Comp., Oint., Sol. (Almay)
Polytar Bath, Liq. (Stiefel)
Tarbonis, Cream (Reed & Carnrick)
Zetar, Preps. (Dermik)
W/Allantoin, hydrocortisone.
See: Alphosyl-HC, Lot., Cream (Reed & Carnrick)
W/Hydrocortisone.
See: Doak Oil Forte, Liq. (Doak)
Tarcortin, Cream (Reed & Carnrick)
W/Iodoquinol, hydrocortisone.
See: ZeTar-Quin, Cream (Dermik)
W/Mercury oleate, salicylic acid, phenol, p-nitrophenol.
See: Prosol, Emulsion (Torch)
W/Zinc oxide.
See: Tarpaste, Paste (Doak)

COAL TAR BATH. (Durel) Coal tar solution 20%, polysorbate "20" 5%, isopropanol 75%. Bot. 8 oz., pt., gal.
Use: Generalized pruritus, pruritic dermatoses, psoriasis.

COAL TAR CREAM COTASOL. (Durel) Coal tar solution 5% in Duromantel cream. Jars 1 oz., 1 lb., 6 lb.
Use: Atopic dermatitis, mild forms of contact dermatitis, seborrheic dermatitis.

COAL TAR, DISTILLATE.
See: Lavatar, Liq. (Doak)
Syntar, Cream (Elder)
W/Sulfur & salicylic acid.
See: Pragmatar, Oint. (Menley & James)

COAL TAR EXTRACT
W/Allantoin, hexachlorophene.
See: Sebical Cream (Reed & Carnrick)
W/Allantoin, hexachlorophene, glycerin, lanolin.
See: Pso-Rite, Cream (DePree)
W/Allantoin, salicylic acid & perhydrosqualine.
See: Skaylos Cream (Ambix)
Skaylos Lotion (Ambix)
W/Salicylic acid, resorcinol, benzoic acid.
See: Mazon Cream (Norcliff-Thayer)

COAL TAR PASTE.
W/Zinc paste.
See: Tarpaste, Paste (Doak)
• **COAL TAR TOPICAL SOLUTION,** U.S.P. XXI.
Liquor Carbonis Detergens. L.C.D.
See: Balnetar, Liq. (Westwood)
Estar, Gel (Westwood)
L.C.D. Compound Oint., Sol. (Almay)
Psorigel, Gel (Owen)
Wright's Soln. (Fougera)
Zetar, Emuls., Shampoo (Dermik)
W/Allantoin, psorilan, myristate.
See: Iocon, Shampoo (Owen)
Psorelief, Cream (Quality Generics)
W/Hydrocortisone, iodoquinol.
See: Cor-Tar-Quin, Cream, Lotion (Miles Pharm)
W/Hydrocortisone alcohol, clioquinololine and diperodon HCl, Vit. A, D.
See: Pentarcort, Cream (Dalin)
W/Robane (perhydrosqualene).
See: Skaylos Shampoo (Ambix)
W/Salicylic acid.
See: Epidol, Sol. (Spirt)
Ionil T, Shampoo (Owen)
W/Salicylic acid, sulfur, protein.
See: Vanseb-T Tar Shampoo (Herbert)
COASTALDYNE. (Coastal) Codeine phosphate 30 mg., acetaminophen 500 mg./Tab. Bot. 100s, 1000s.
Use: Analgesic.
COASTALGESIC. (Coastal) Acetaminophen 7.5 gr., caffeine 0.5 gr., butabarbital 0.25 gr./Tab. Bot. 100s, 1000s.
Use: Analgesic.
• **COBALAMINE CONCENTRATE,** U.S.P. XXI.
Use: Hematopoietic vitamin.
See: Vitamin B-12 (Var. Mfr.)
COBALT CHLORIDE.
W/Ferrous gluconate, Vit. B-12, duodenum whole desic.
See: Bitrinsic-E, Cap. (Elder)
COBALT GLUCONATE.
W/Ferrous gluconate, B-12 activity, desiccated stomach substance, folic acid.
See: Chromagen, Cap., Inj. (Savage)
COBALT-LABELED VITAMIN B-12.
See: Rubratope-57 (Squibb)
• **COBALTOUS CHLORIDE Co 57.** USAN.
Use: Radioactive agent.
• **COBALTOUS CHLORIDE Co 60.** USAN.
Use: Radioactive agent.
COBALT STANDARDS FOR VITAMIN B-12.
See: Cobatope-57, and Cobatope-60 (Squibb)
COBAN SODIUM SALT.
See: Monensin, B.A.N.
COBATOPE-57. (Squibb) Cobaltous Chloride Co 57.
COBEX 100. (Standex) Vit. B-12 100 mcg.
COBEX 1000. (Standex) Vit. B-12 1000 mcg./10 cc. Vial 30 cc.
CO-BILE. (Western Research) Hog bile 64.8 mg., pancreas sub. 64.8 mg., papain-pepsin complex 97.2 mg., diatase malt 16.2 mg., papain 48.6 mg., pepsin 48.6 mg./Tab. Bot. 1000s.
Use: Digestant.

COBIONE.
Contains Vit. B-12.
COBIRON. (Pharmex) Cyanocobalamin 100 mcg., hydroxycobalamine 50 mcg., ferrous gluconate 6[illegible] mg., liver injection 5 mcg./2 cc.; procaine HCl 2[illegible] phenol 0.5%. Vial 30 cc.
COBRA VENOM.
See: Cobroxin, Amp. (Hynson, Westcott & Dunni[illegible]
Nyloxin, Inj. (Hynson, Westcott & Dunning)
• **COCAINE,** U.S.P. XXI. Methyl 3β-Hydroxy-1αH,-5[illegible] tropane-2β-carboxylate Benzoate (Ester) Alkaloi[illegible]
• **COCAINE HYDROCHLORIDE,** U.S.P. XXI. Tab., [illegible] Topical Sol., U.S.P. XXI. 8-Azabicyclo[3.2.1]octan[illegible] 2-carboxylic acid, 3-(benzoyloxy)-8-methyl-, me[illegible] ester, hydrochloride. Methyl 3β-hydroxy-1αH,5αH[illegible] tropan-2β-carboxylate, benzoate (ester) hydroc[illegible] ride.
CO-CARBOXYLASE. B.A.N. Pyrophosphoric ester aneurine.
Use: Co-enzyme.
■ **COCCIDIOSTATS, VETERINARY USE.**
See: Amprol (MSD AGVET)
Amprol Hi-E (MSD AGVET)
Amprol Plus (MSD AGVET)
Amprovine (MSD AGVET)
Corid (MSD AGVET)
Nicarb (MSD AGVET)
S.Q. (MSD AGVET)
COCCULIN.
See: Picrotoxin, Inj. (Various Mfr.)
COCILAN SYRUP. (Approved) Euphorbia, wild lettuce, cocillana, squill, senega and cascarin (bitterless). Bot. gal. Available w/codeine. Bot. g[illegible]
COCILLANA.
W/Euphorbia pilulifera, squill, antimony potassium tartrate, senega.
See: Cylana Syr. (Bowman)
COCILLIN V-K. (Coastal) Pot. phenoxymethyl penic[illegible] 250 mg. (400,000 u.)/Tab. Bot. 100s, 1000s.
• **COCOA,** N.F. XVI. Syr., N.F. XVI.
Use: Pharm. Aid (Flavor; flavored vehicle).
• **COCOA BUTTER,** N.F. XVI.
Use: Pharm. Aid (Suppository base).
CODACTIDE. B.A.N. D-Ser^{1}-Lys^{17,18}-β^{1-18}-cortico[illegible] phin amide.
Use: Corticotrophic peptide.
CODAHIST THROAT LOZENGES. (Towne) Bot. 1[illegible]
CODALAN NO. 1. (Lannett) Codeine phosphate 8 mg., salicylamide 230 mg., acetaminophen 150 [illegible] caffeine 30 mg./Tab. Bot. 100s, 500s, 1000s. **Codalan No. 2** contains codeine phosphate 15 mg./Tab; Bot. 100s, 500s, 1000s. **Codalan No.** [illegible] contains codeine phosphate 30 mg./Tab. Bot. 100s, 500s, 1000s.
CODAMINE PEDIATRIC. (Quality Generics) Hydrocodone bitartrate 2.5 mg., phenylpropanolamine HCl 12.5 mg./5 ml. Bot. pt gal.
Use: Antitussive, antihistaminic.
CODAMINE PEDIATRIC SYRUP. (Goldline) Hydrocodone bitartrate. Bot. pt.
Use: Antitussive.

DAMINE SYRUP. (Quality Generics) Hydrocodone itartrate 5.0 mg., phenylpropanolamine HCl 25 ng./5 ml. Bot. pt., gal.
Use: Antitussive, Antihistaminic.

DAMINE SYRUP. (Goldline) Hydrocodone itartrate w/phenylpropanolamine. Bot. pt.
Jse: Antitussive.

DANOL OINTMENT. (A.P.C.) Vit. A, Vit. D, exachlorophene, zinc oxide.
ube 1.5 oz., 4 oz.
ar 1 lb.
Use: Diaper rash, minor burns, skin irritations.

DAP. (Reid-Provident) Codeine phosphate 32 mg., cetaminophen 325 mg./Tab. Bot. 500s.
Jse: Analgesic.

DAPRIN. (Cenci) APC w/codeine **No. 2:** (0.25 gr.), **No. 3:** (0.5 gr.), **No. 4:** (1 gr.). Bot. 100s, 1000s.

DASA I. (Stayner) Codeine phosphate 0.25 gr., aspirin 5 gr./Cap. Bot. 100s, 500s.
Jse: Analgesic.

DASA II. (Stayner) Codeine phosphate 0.5 gr., aspirin 5 gr./Cap. Bot. 100s, 500s.

DASA FORTE. (Stayner) Codeine phosphate 0.5 gr., aspirin 10 gr./Cap. Bot. 100s, 500s.

DASA TABS. (Stayner) Codeine phosphate 0.5 gr. or 0.25 gr., aspirin 5 gr./Tab. Bot. 100s, 1000s.

ODEINE, U.S.P. XXI. 7,8-Didehydro-4,5α-epoxy-3-methoxy-17-methylmorphinan-6α-ol monohydrate.
Cryst. or Pow. Bot. ⅛ oz., & 1 oz.
Jse: analgesic (Narcotic); antitussive.

DEINE COMBINATIONS.
See: Actifed-C, Exp., Syr. (Burroughs-Wellcome)
- Anexsia w/Cod., Tab. (Beecham Labs)
- APAP w/Codeine, Tab. (Central)
- A.P.C. w/Cod., Tab. (Various Mfr.)
- Ascriptin W/Codeine No. 2, Tab. (Rorer)
- Ascriptin W/Codeine No. 3, Tab. (Rorer)
- Asphac-G w/Codeine, Tab. (Central)
- Aspodyne w/Cod., Tab. (Blue Line)
- Bancap w/Codeine, Cap. (Westerfield)
- Bri-Stan, Liq. (Briar)
- Buff-A-Comp., Tab. (Mayrand)
- Butadeine, Cap. (Sutliff & Case)
- Calcidrine Syr. (Abbott)
- Capital w/Codeine, Tab., Susp. (Carnrick)
- Cerose, Liq. (Ives)
- Cetro-Cirose, Liq. (Ives)
- Cheracol, Syr. (Upjohn)
- Chlor-Trimeton Expect. (Schering)
- Coastaldyne, Tab. (Coastal)
- Codalan, Tab. (Lannett)
- Codap, Tab. (Reid-Provident)
- Codasa I & II, Cap. (Stayner)
- Codel, Exp., Syr. (Elder)
- Colrex Compound, Cap., Elix. (Rowell)
- Cosanyl Cough Syrup (Health Care Ind.)
- Co-Xan, Liq. (Central)
- Drucon w/Codeine, Liq. (Standard Drug)
- Empirin, No. 1, No. 2, No. 3, No. 4, Tab. (Burroughs-Wellcome)
- Fedahist-C, Expect. (Dooner)
- Fiorinal w/Codeine, Cap. (Sandoz)
- G-3, Cap. (Hauck)
- Golacol, Syr. (Arcum)
- Guialyn W/Codeine, Liq. (Scrip)
- Histussinol W/C, Syr. (Bock)
- Isoclor, Expect. (Arnar-Stone)
- Kiddi-Koff, Liq. (Republic)
- Mallergan, Liq. (Mallard)
- Maxigesic, Cap. (W.F. Merchant)
- Novahistine, Expect. (Merrell Dow)
- Nucofed, Liq. (Beecham)
- Partuss AC (Parmed)
- Pavadon Elix. (Coastal)
- Pediacof, Syr. (Winthrop-Breon)
- Percogesic-C, Tab. (Du Pont)
- Phenaphen, #2, #3, #4 Cap. (Robins)
- Phenaphen-650, Cap. (Robins)
- Phenatuss, Liq. (Dalin)
- Phenergan Expectorant w/Codeine, Troches (Wyeth)
- Phenodyne w/Codeine Phos., Cap. (Blue Line)
- Poly-histine Expectorant, Liq. (Bock)
- Proval No. 3, Tab. (Reid-Provident)
- Prunicodeine, Syr. (Lilly)
- Respi-Sed, Liq. (Vortch)
- Robitussin A-C, DAC (Robins)
- SK-APAP W/Codeine, Tab. (SmithKline)
- Syrcodate, Syr. (Blue Line)
- Tega-Code, Cap. (Ortega)
- Tolu-Sed, Elix. (Scherer)
- TSG Croup Liquid, Liq. (Elder)
- Tussar-2, Syr. (Armour)
- Tussi-Organidin, Liq. (Wallace)
- Tylenol w/Codeine, No. 1, No. 2, No. 3, No. 4 Tab. (McNeil)
- Tylenol w/Codeine Elixir (McNeil)
- Vasotus, Liq. (Sheryl)

CODEINE RESIN COMPLEX COMBINATIONS.
See: Omni-Tuss, Liq. (Pennwalt)

CODEINE METHYLBROMIDE. Eucodin.
Use: Narcotic cough depressant.

• **CODEINE PHOSPHATE,** U.S.P. XXI. Inj., Tablets, U.S.P. XXI. (Various Mfr.) Pow. Bot. ⅛ oz., 0.25 oz., 0.5 oz. & 1 oz.
Use: Narcotic analgesic antitussive.

• **CODEINE SULFATE,** U.S.P. XXI. Tab., U.S.P. XXI. 7,8-Didehydro-4,5α-epoxy-3-methoxy-17-methyl-morphinan-6α-ol sulfate.

CODELCORTONE.
See: Prednisolone.

CODICLEAR DH SYRUP. (Central) Hydrocodone bitartrate 5 mg., potassium guaiaco/sulfonate 300 mg./5 ml. Bot. 4 oz., pts.
Use: Antitussive-expectorant.

CODIMAL-A. (Central) Brompheniramine maleate 10 mg./ml. w/methylparaben 0.18%, propylparaben 0.02%. I.M. Vial 10 ml.
Use: Antihistaminic.

CODIMAL CAPSULES (Central) Chlorpheniramine maleate 2 mg., pseudoephedrine HCl 30 mg., acetaminophen 325 mg./Cap. Bot. 24s, 100s, 1000s.
Use: Temporary relief of cold symptoms.

CODIMAL DH SYRUP. (Central) Hydrocodone bitartrate 1.66 mg., phenylephrine HCl 5 mg.,

pyrilamine maleate 8.33 mg./5 ml. Bot. 4 oz., pt., gal.
Use: Antihistaminic expectorant.

CODIMAL DM. (Central) Dextromethorphan HBr 10 mg., phenylephrine HCl 5 mg., pyrilamine maleate 8.33 mg./5 ml. w/ alcohol 4%. Sugar Free. Bot. 4 oz., pt., gal.

CODIMAL EXPECTORANT. (Central) Phenylpropanolamine HCl 25 mg., guaifenesin 100 mg./5 ml. Bot. 4 oz., Pt.
Use: Temporary relief of coughs due to common cold.

CODIMAL-L.A. (Central) Chlorpheniramine maleate 8 mg., pseudoephedrine HCl 120 mg./Cap. Bot. 100s, 1000s.
Use: Antihistamine, decongestant.

CODIMAL PH SYRUP. (Central) Codeine phosphate 10 mg., phenylephrine HCl 5 mg., pyrilamine maleate 8.33 mg./5 ml. Bot. 4 oz., pt., gal.
Use: Sedative expectorant for coughs due to colds.

CODIMAL TABLETS. (Central) Chlorpheniramine maleate 2 mg., pseudoephedrine HCl 30 mg., acetaminophen 325 mg./Tab. Bot. 24s, 100s, 1000s.
Use: Relief symptoms of common cold.

CODISTAN NO. 1. (Vortech) Guaifenesin 100 mg., dextromethorphan HBr 15 mg./5ml. w/alcohol 1.4%. Syr. Bot. 4 oz.
Use: Treatment of coughs and colds.

• **COD LIVER OIL,** U.S.P. XXI. Emulsion, emulsion w/malt.
Use: Vitamin A & D therapy.

W/Anesthesin, zinc oxide, hydroxyquinoline.
See: Medicone Dressing. (Medicone)

W/Benzocaine.
See: Morusan, Oint. (Beecham Labs)

W/Creosote. (Bryant) Cod liver oil 9 min., creosote 1 min./Cap. Bot. 100s.

W/Malt ext. (Burroughs Wellcome) Vit. A 6450 I.U., Vit. D 645 I.U. Bot. 10 fl. oz., 20 fl. oz.

W/Methylbenzethonium Cl.
See: Benephen, Prods. (Halsted)

W/Viosterol.
Abbott-Vit. A 2800 I.U., Vit. D 255 I.U./Gm. Bot. 12 fl. oz.
Squibb-Vit. A 2000 I.U., Vit. D 440 I.U./Gm. Bot. 4 & 12 fl. oz.

W/Zinc oxide.
See: Desitin, Prep. (Leeming)

COD LIVER OIL CONCENTRATE. (Schering) Concentrate of cod liver oil with vitamins A and D added. **Cap.** Bot. 40s, 100s. **Tab.** Bot. 100s, 240s. Also W/Vit. C. Bot. 100s.

COD LIVER OIL OINTMENT.
See: Moruguent, Oint. (Beecham Labs)

• **CODORPHONE HYDROCHLORIDE.** USAN.
Use: Analgesic.

• **CODOXIME.** USAN.
Use: Antitussive.

• **CODOXY.** (Halsey) Oxycodone HCl 4.50 mg., oxycodone terephthalate 0.38 mg., aspirin 325 mg./Tab. Bot. 100s.
Use: Pain relief.

CODROXOMIN INJECTION. (Fellows) Crystalline hydroxocobalamin 1000 mcg./cc. Vial 10 cc.

COENZYME-B. (Inwood) Diphosphothiamin (Co-carboxylase) 25 mg./Cap. Bot. 50s. Amp. (50 mg./2 cc.). Bot. 12s, 25s, 50s, 100s.
Use: Coenzyme for Vitamin B-1.

CO-ESTRO. (Robinson) Conjugated estrogen 0.6 mg., 1.25 mg., 2.5 mg./Tab. Bot. 100s, 500s, 1000s.
Use: Estrogen therapy.

CO-GEL. (Arco) Calcium carbonate 300 mg., glycine [illegible] mg., Trizyme (amylolytic enzyme 3 mg., proteolytic enzyme 0.6 mg., cellulolytic enzyme 0.2 mg.) 3.8 mg./Tab. Bot. 100s.
Use: Hyperacidity.

COGENTIN. (Merck Sharp & Dohme) Benztropine Mesylate **Tab.:** 0.5 mg. Bot. 100s; 1 mg. Bot. 100s, Unit-dose 100s; 2 mg. Bot. 100s, 1000s, Unit-dose 100s. **Inj.:** benztropine mesylate 1 mg./1 ml. w/sodium chloride 9 mg. and water for injection q.s. to 1 ml. Amp. 2 ml., Box 6s.
Use: Parkinsonism, extrapyramidal disorders due to neuroleptic drugs.

CO-GESIC. (Central) Hydrocodone bitartrate 5 mg., acetaminophen 500 mg./Tab. Bot. 100s.
Use: Analgesic.

COHEMA. (Sutliff & Case) Manganese 5 mg., copper 0.2 mg., molybdenum 0.2 mg., cobalt 0.5 mg., zinc 1 mg., Vit. B-1 1 mg., niacinamide 10 mg., Vit. B-12 1 mcg. Vit. C 60 mg., ferrous fumarate 3[illegible] mg./Tab. Bot. 100s, 1000s.
Use: Hematinic

CO-HEP-TRAL. (Davis & Sly) Folic acid 10 mg., B-[illegible] 100 mcg., liver injection, q.s./cc. Vial 10 cc.
Use: Anemias and sprue.

COHIDRATE. (Coastal) Chloral hydrate 500 mg./Cap. Bot. 100s, 1000s.
Use: Sedative.

CO-HISTINE DH. (Kay) Codeine phosphate 10 mg., phenylpropanolamine HCl 18.75 mg., chlorpheniramine maleate 2 mg./5 ml. w/alcohol 5%. Bot. 1 Gal.
Use: Decongestant, antitussive, antihistamine.

CO-HISTINE EXPECTORANT. (Kay) Codeine phosphate 10 mg., phenylpropanolamine HCl 18.75 mg., guaifenesin 100 mg./5 ml w/alcohol 7.5%. Bot. Gal.
Use: Relief of cough and nasal congestion.

COLABID TABS. (Major) Probenecil w/colchicine. Bot. 100s, 1000s.
Use: Uricosuric.

COLACE. (Mead Johnson) Docusate sodium. **Cap.** (50 mg. or 100 mg.) Bot. 30s, 60s, 250s, 1000s. Single unit pack 10s, (100 mg. only), 100s. **Liq.** 1%, Bot. 30 cc., pt. Syr. (20 mg./5 cc.) Bot. 8 oz., 1 pt.
Use: Orally, fecal softener.

;asanthrol.
ee: Peri-Colace, Cap., Syr. (Mead Johnson)
.AGYN. (Smith) Zinc sulfocarbolate, pot,
cyquinoline sulfate, lactic acid and boric acid,
elly. Tube w/applicator & refill 6 oz. Douche Pow.
oz., 7 oz., 14 oz.
se: Contraceptive.
.ANA SYRUP. (Hance) Tinct. euphorbia pilulifera
cc., syr. wild lettuce 8 cc., tinct. cocillana 2.5 cc.,
r. squill cmpd. 1.5 cc., cascara 0.25 Gm.,
enthol 4.8 mg./fl. oz. Bot. 4 fl. oz., gal. Also w.
ionin 15 mg./fl. oz. Bot. gal.
se: Cough preparation.
.ASPASE B.A.N. L-Asparagine amidohydrolase ob-
ined from cultures of Escherichia coli.
ee: Crasnitin
.BENEMID. (Merck Sharp & Dohme) Probenecid
5 Gm., colchicine 0.5 mg./Tab. Bot. 100s.
se: Uricosuric for chronic gouty arthritis.
.BENI-MOR. (H.L. Moore) Probenecid 0.5 mg./Tab.
ot. 100s, 1000s.
se: Chronic gouty arthritis.
)LCHICINE, U.S.P. XXI. Tab., Inj. U.S.P. XXI.
cetamide, N-(5,6,7,9-tetrahydro-1,2,3,10-
etrame-thoxy-9-oxobenzo[a]heptalen-7-yl)-.
/arious Mfr.)
se: Gout suppressant.
Benemid.
ee: Colbenemid, Tab. (Merck Sharp & Dohme)
Methyl salicylate. (Parke-Davis) Colchicine 1/250 gr.,
ethyl salicylate 3 min./Cap. Bot. 100s, 500s,
000s.
se: Orally, gout therapy.
Probenecid
ee: Benn-C, Tab. (Scrip)
Colbenemid, Tab. (Merck Sharp & Dohme)
Robenecid with colchicine, Tab. (Robinson)
Sod. salicylate.
ee: Salcoce, Tab. (Cole)
Sod. salicylate, calcium carbonate, dried aluminum
ydroxide gel, phenobarbital.
ee: Apcogesic, Tabs. (Apco)
Sod. salicylate & pot. iodide.
ee: Bricolide, Tab. (Briar)
Colsalide, Tab. (Vortech)
LCHICINE SALICYLATE.
Phenobarbital, Sod. p-aminobenzoate, Vit. B-1 & as-
irin.
See: Doloral, Tab. (Alamed)
LD-CAPS TIMED RELEASE. (Stayner) Replaces
Super-Polyhist Cold Capsules. Pack of 12.
OLD CREAM, U.S.P. XXI.
Jse: Emollient; water-in-oil emulsion ointment base.
LD CREAM FOR COMPOUNDING ESCRIPTIONS. (Lilly) Ointment (Not U.S.P.) Bot.
6 oz.
L-DECON. (Quality Generics) Chlorpheniramine
naleate 5 mg., phenylephrine HCl 10 mg.,
phenylpropanolamine HCl 40 mg., phenyltoloxamine
citrate 15 mg./Tab. Bot. 100s, 1000s.
Jse: Decongestant.

COLD FACTOR 12 CAPSULES. (Pharmacraft) Phenylpropanolamine HCl 75 mg., chlorpheniramine maleate 8 mg./Cap. Sleeve pack 10s.
Use: Treatment of colds, allergy, nasal congestion.

COLD FACTOR 12 LIQUID. (Pharmacraft) Phenylpropanolamine HCl 37.5, chlorpheniramine maleate 4 mg./5 ml. Bot. 1.7 oz., 3 oz.
Use: colds, allergy, nasal congestion.

COLDONYL. (Dover) Acetaminophen, phenylephrine HCl and atropine sulfate tablets. Sugar, lactose and salt free. Unit dose Box 500s.
Use: Cold, hay fever and allergy relief.

COLDRAN. (Blue Cross) Phenelephrine HCl 5 mg., chlorpheniramine maleate 2 mg., salisylamide 1.5 gr., acetaminophen 0.5 gr., caffeine/ Tab. Bot. 30s.
Use: Colds, allergies, sinus congestion.

COLDRINE. (Mallard) Acetaminophen 200 mg., pseudoephedrine HCl 30 mg./Tab. Bot. 1000s. Sani-Pak 1000s.
Use: Analgesic, decongestant.

COLD SORE LOTION. (DeWitt) Camphor 3.7%, Tr. benzoin 4.1%, phenol 0.3%, menthol 0.3% w/alcohol 90%. Bot. 0.5 oz.
Use: Cold sore, fever blister and cracked lip relief.

COLD SORE LOTION. (McKesson) Bot. 0.25 oz.
Use: Treatment of cold sores.

COLD SORE LOTION. (Purepac) Camphor, benzoin, aluminum chloride. Bot. 0.5 oz.
Use: Astringent, analgesic, protectant for cold sores and fever blisters.

COLD TABLETS. (Walgreen) Phenylephrine HCl 5 mg., chlorpheniramine maleate 2 mg., acetaminophen 325 mg./Tab. Bot. 50s.
Use: Decongestant, antihistamine, analgesic.

COLD TABLETS MULTIPLE SYMPTOM. (Walgreen) Acetaminophen 325 mg., phenylpropanolamine HCl 12.5 mg., chlorpheniramine maleate 1 mg., dextromethorphan HBr 10 mg./Tab. Bot. 50s.
Use: Symptomatic relief of colds; decongestant.

COLD VACCINES, ORAL. Sherman—Oral Tabs.
See: Entoral, Pulvule (Lilly)

COLESTID. (Upjohn) Colestipol HCl 5 Gm./pkt. Box 30s, Bot. 500 Gm.
Use: Adjunctive therapy to diet for reduction of elevated serum cholesterol in hypercholesterolemic patients.

• **COLESTIPOL HYDROCHLORIDE.** USAN.
Use: Antihyperlipoproteinemic.

COL-EVAC. (Fellows) Pot. bitartrate, bicarbonate of soda and a blended base of polyethylene glycols. Supps. 2s, 12s.

COLEXUSS. (Jenkins) White pine 56.7 mg., wild cherry 56.7 mg., American spikenard 6 mg., poplar bud 6 mg., sanguinaria 5 mg., menthol 0.5 mg./fldr. Bot. 3 oz., 4 oz., gal.
Use: Cough syrup.

COLFANT. (Jenkins) Paregoric 2 min. (pow. opium 1/125 gr.), sod. bicarbonate 1 gr., Mg trisilicate 5/8 gr.,

ext. catnip 1/50 gr., ext. chamomile 1/100 gr. (Matricaria), oil fennel q.s./Tab. Bot. 1000s.
Use: Antacid, analgesic.

COLICELL. (Sutliff & Case) Whole bile ext. 227 mg., ketocholanic acids 97 mg., methyl cellulose 130 mg., homatropine methylbromide 2.5 mg./Tab. Bot. 100s, 1000s.
Use: Laxative w/antispasmatic.

COLIMYCIN SODIUM METHANESULFONATE. (Parke-Davis)
See: Colistimethate Sod.

COLIMYCIN SULFATE. (Parke-Davis)
See: Coly-Mycin, Preps. (Parke-Davis)

• **COLISTIMETHATE SODIUM, STERILE,** U.S.P. XXI. Sod. Colistin Methanesulfonate. Colistinmethanesulfonic acid, pentasodium salt. Pentasodium colistinmethanesulfonate.
Use: Antibiotic.
See: Coly-Mycin-M, Injectable (Parke-Davis)

COLISTIN. B.A.N. A mixture of polypeptides produced by strains of Bacillus polymyxa var. colistinus.
Use: Antibiotic.
See: Colomycin sulfate

COLISTIN BASE.
W/Neomycin base, hydrocortisone acetate, thonzonium bromide, polysorbate 80, acetic acid, sodium acetate.
See: Coly-Mycin Otic W/Neomycin and Hydrocortisone, Liq. (Parke-Davis)

COLISTIN AND NEOMYCIN SULFATES AND HYDROCORTISONE ACETATE OTIC SUSPENSION, U.S.P. XXI.
Use: Antibiotic, anti-inflammatory.

COLISTIN METHANESULFONATE.
See: Colistimethate Sodium

• **COLISTIN SULFATE,** U.S.P. XXI. Oral Susp., U.S.P. XXI. The sulfate salt of an antibiotic substance elaborated by Aerobacillus colistinus.
Use: Antibacterial.
See: Colymycin-S Ophthalmic (Softcon)
Coly-Mycin S Susp. (Parke-Davis)

COLISTIN SULFOMETHATE. B.A.N. An antibiotic obtained from colistin sulfate by sulfomethylation with formaldehyde and sodium bisulfite.

COLITUSSIN. (Dalin) Bot. 4 oz. Pediatric. Bot. 4 oz.

CO-LIVER. (Standex) Folic acid 1 mg., Vit. B-12 100 mcg., liver 10 mcg./cc. Vial 10 cc.

COLLADERM. (C & M Pharmacal) Purified water, glycerin, soluble collagen, hydrolysed elastin, allantoin, ethylhydroxycellulose, sorbic, octoxynol-9. Bot. 2.3 oz.
Use: Moisturizer & protein replenisher for dry & aging skin.

COLLAGENASE.
See: Santyl (Knoll)

COLLAGENASE ABC OINTMENT. (Advance Biofactures) Collagenase 250 u./Gm. in white petrolatum. 25 Gm., 50 Gm.
Use: Debridement of dermal ulcers and burned areas.

• **COLLODION,** U.S.P. XXI. Flexible, U.S.P. XXI.
Use: Topical protectant.

COLLOIDAL ALUMINUM HYDROXIDE.
See: Aluminum Hydroxide Gel, U.S.P. XXI.

COLLOIDAL GOLD.
See: Aureotope (Squibb)

COLLOIDAL SILVER IODIDE.
See: Neo-Silvol, Sol. (Parke-Davis)

COLLYRIUM. (Wyeth) Neutral borate sol. with bori acid, sodium borate, thimerosal 0.002% and wa Bot. 6 fl. oz. with eyecup.
Use: Eye lotion.

COLLYRIUM 2. (Wyeth) Tetrahydrozoline hydrochloride 0.05%. zinc sulfate 0.25%, glyceri 1%, boric acid, sodium borate, benzalkonium Cl 0.02%. Bot. 0.5 oz.
Use: Relieve minor irritation burning, dryness of eyes.

COLOCTYL. (Vitarine) Docusate sodium 100 mg./Cap. Bot. 100s, 1000s. Unit dose 1000s.
Use: Stool softener.

COLOGEL. (Lilly) Methylcellulose 9 Gm./100 ml. w/alcohol 5% Bot. 16 fl. oz.
Use: Constipation.

COLREX. (Rowell) Chlorpheniramine maleate 2 mg phenylephrine HCl 5 mg., acetaminophen 325 mg./Cap. Bot. 24s, 100s.

COLREX COMPOUND. (Rowell) Codeine phospha 16 mg., acetaminophen 325 mg., phenylephrine HCl 10 mg., chlorpheniramine maleate 2 mg./Ca Bot. 100s, 1000s.
Use: Relief of symptoms from common cold.

COLREX COMPOUND ELIXIR. (Rowell) Codeine phosphate 8 mg., acetaminophen 120 mg., chlorpheniramine maleate 1 mg., phenylephrine H 5 mg./5 ml. Alcohol 9.5%. Sugar free elixer. Bot 60 ml., 480 ml., gal.
Use: Relief of cough, congestion.

COLREX DECONGESTANT. (Rowell) Chlorpheniramine maleate 4 mg., tripelennamine HCl 50 mg., phenylpropanolamine HCl 25 mg., phenylephrine HCl 10 mg./Tab. Bot. 100s.
Use: Decongestant.

COLREX EXPECTORANT. (Rowell) Guaifenesin 1(mg./5 cc. w/alcohol 4.7%. Bot. 120 ml., 480 ml. Sugar free base
Use: Bronchial secretions.

COLREX SYRUP. (Rowell) Dextromethorphan HBr mg., phenylephrine HCl 5 mg., chlorpheniramine maleate 2 mg./5 cc. w/alcohol 4.5% Bot. Sugar free base. 120 ml.
Use: Relief of cough.

COLREX TROCHES. (Rowell) Benzocaine 10 mg., cetylpyridinium chloride 2.5 mg./Troche. 20s.
Use: Relief of sore throat due to the common cold.

COLSALIDE. (Vortech) Colchicine 0.65 mg./Tab. B 1000s.
Use: Gout & gouty arthritis & neuritis.

COLSPAN. (Zenith) Chlorpheniramine maleate 1 mg phenylpropanolamine HCl 50 mg., belladonna alkaloids 0.16 mg., pheniramine maleate 12.5 mg./Cap. Bot. 10s, 1000s.

OLTEROL MESYLATE. USAN.
Use: Bronchodilator.
LY-MYCIN M PARENTERAL. (Parke-Davis) Colistimethate sodium equivalent 150 mg. colistin base per vial.
Use: Urinary tract infections.
LY-MYCIN S OTIC DROPS W/NEOMYCIN AND HYDROCORTISONE. (Parke-Davis) Colistin base as the sulfate 3 mg., neoymycin base as the sulfate 3.3 mg., hydrocortisone acetate 10 mg., thonzonium bromide, polysorbate 80, acetic acid, sodium acetate/cc. 5 ml. w/dropper. 10 ml. Bot. 5 cc.
Use: Acute and chronic external otitis.
LY-MYCIN S. (Parke-Davis) Colistin sulfate 300 mg./60 ml. For oral susp. Bot. 300 mg.
Use: Acute bacterial diarrhea.
MBAGEN T.D. CAPS. (Goldline) Prochlorperazine, isopropamide. Bot. 100s, 500s, 1000s.
Use: Antinausea.
MBICAL D. (Mills) Calcium 375 mg., Vit. D 400 I.U., phosphorus 180 mg., magnesium 144 mg./3 Tab. Bot. 1000s.
Use: Vitamin, nutrition therapy.
MBICHOLE. (Trout) Dehydrocholic acid 2 gr., desoxycholic acid 1 gr./Tab. Bot. 100s, 1000s.
Use: Stimulate bile flow.
MBID. (SmithKline) 'Darbid' (isopropamide) as the iodide 5 mg., 'Compazine' (prochlorperazine) as the maleate 10 mg./Spansule. Bot. 50s, 500s. Unit pkg. 100s.
Use: Gastrointestinal disorders.
MBIPRES TABLETS. (Boehringer Ingelheim) Clonidine HCl 0.1 or 0.2 mg., chlorthalidone 15 mg./Tab. Bot. 100s, 1000s.
Use: Antihypertensive.
MBISTIX REAGENT STRIPS. (Ames) Protein test-tetrabromphenol blue, citrate buffer, protein-absorbing agent; glucose test area-glucose oxidase, orthotolidin and a catalyst; pH test area methyl red and bromthymol blue. Box, strips, 100s.
Use: Diagnostic agent. Proteinuria, glucosuria, pH.
OMFORT DROPS. (Barnes-Hind) Naphazoline HCl 0.03% with disodium edetate 0.02% and benzalkonium chloride 0.005%. Plastic dropper bot. 15 ml., 30 ml.
Use: Ophthalmic decongestant.
OMFORT GEL LIQUID. (Walgreen) Aluminum hydroxide compressed gel 200 mg., magnesium hydroxide 200 mg., simethicone 20 mg./5 ml. Bot. 12 oz.
Use: Antacid-antiflatulent.
OMFORT GEL TABLETS. (Walgreen) Magnesium hydroxide 85 mg., simethicone 25 mg., aluminum hydroxide-magnesium carbonate codried gel 282 mg./Tab. Bot. 100s.
Use: Antacid-antiflatulent.
OMFORTINE. (Dermik) Zinc oxide 12%, Vit. A & D, lanolin in protective base. Oint. Tube 1.5 oz. 4 oz.
Use: Antiseptic & protective ointment.
OMHIST L.A. CAPSULES. (Norwich Eaton) Phenylephrine HCl 20 mg., chlorpheniramine maleate 4 mg., phenyltoloxamine citrate 50 mg./Cap. Bot. 100s.
Use: Relief of allergies and congestion.
COMHIST TABLETS. (Norwich Eaton) Phenylephrine HCl 10 mg., chlorpheniramine maleate 2 mg., phenyltoloxamine citrate 25 mg./Tab. Bot. 100s.
Use: For the relief of allergies and congestion.
COMPAL. (Reid-Provident) Dihydrocodeine 16 mg., acetaminophen 356.4 mg., Caffeine 30 mg./Cap. Bot. 100s.
Use: Analgesic.
COMPAT NUTRITION ENTERAL DELIVERY SYSTEM. (Sandoz Nutrition) Bot. 600 ml., 1400 ml.
Use: Enteral delivery set for administration of tube feeding.
COMPAZINE. (SmithKline) Prochlorperazine as the maleate. **Tab.:** 5 mg., 10 mg., 25 mg., Bot. 100s, 1000s. Unit dose 100s. except for 25 mg. **Inj.,** Edisylate salt 2 ml. (5 mg./ml.) Boxes 10s, 100s, 500s. Multiple-dose vials-Edisylate salt 10 ml. (5 mg./ml.) 1s, 20s., 100s.; Disposable Syringe 5 mg./ml. Syringe 2 ml. Box 10s, 100s. **Spansule** Maleate Salt 10 mg., 15 mg., 30 mg., Bot. 50s, 500s. Unit dose 100s. **Supp.:** 2.5 mg., 5 mg., 25 mg., Box 12s. **Syrup:** Edisylate salt 5 mg./5 ml. Bot. 4 fl. oz.
Use: Treatment of mental & emotional disturbances; also nausea & vomiting.
COMPLEAT-B. (Sandoz Nutrition) Deionized water, beef puree, hydrolyzed cereal solids, green bean puree, pea puree, nonfat milk, corn oil, maltodextrin, peach puree, orange juice, mono & diglycerides, carrageenan, vitamins & minerals. Bot. 250 ml. Cans 250 ml.
Use: Tube feeding.
COMPLEAT-MODIFIED FORMULA. (Sandoz Nutrition) Deionized water, hydrolyzed cereal solids, beef puree, pea puree, green bean puree, corn oil, peach puree, mono and diglycerides, orange juice, carrageenan, vitamins & minerals. Cans 250 ml.
Use: Lactose free, low sodium, isotonic blenderized tube feeding.
COMPLETONE ELIXIR FORT. (Winthrop Products) Ferrous gluconate.
Use: Hematinic.
COMPLEX 15 CREAM. (Baker/Cummins) Jar. 4 oz.
Use: Moisturizing cream.
COMPLEX 15 LOTION. (Baker/Cummins) Bot. 8 oz.
Use: Moisturizing lotion.
COMPOUND 42.
See: Warfarin (Various Mfr.)
COMPOUND B.
See: Corticosterone (Various Mfr.)
COMPOUND CB3025.
See: Alkeran, Tabs. (Burroughs Wellcome)
COMPOUND E. (Kendall)
See: Cortisone Acetate. (Various Mfr.)
COMPOUND F.
See: Hydrocortisone (Various Mfr.)

COMPOUND W. (Whitehall) Salicylic acid 17% w/w in flexible collodion vehicle W/ether 63.5%. Bot. 0.31 oz.
Use: Wart remover.

COMPOZ. (Jeffrey Martin) Diphenhydramine HCl 50 mg./Tab. Ctn. 24s.
Use: Night-time sleep aid.

COMPRELETS. (Quality Generics) Vit. A 10,000 I.U., B-1 25 mg., B-2 12 mg., B-3 75 mg., B-5 3 mg., B-6 1.2 mg., B-12 mcg., C 150 mg., D 400 I.U., E 3.3 I.U., biotin 2 mcg., Ca 40 mg., iron 3 mg., K 0.5 mg., Cu 1.25 mg., Mn 1.0 mg., Mg 0.8 mg., Zn 1.25 mg., & amino acid factors/Tab. Bot. 100s, 1000s.
Use: Vitamin, mineral, amino acid therapy.

COM-PRO-SPAN. (Quality Generics) Prochlorperazine 10 mg., isopropamide 5 mg./Cap. Bot. 100s, 500s.
Use: Gastointestinal disorders.

COMTREX CAPSULES MULTI-SYMPTOM COLD RELIEVER. (Bristol-Myers) Acetaminophen 325 mg., phenylpropanolamine HCl 12.5 mg., chlorpheniramine maleate 1.0 mg., dextromethorphan HBr 10 mg./Cap. Bot. 16s, 36s.
Use: Analgesic, decongestant, antihistamine, cough reliever.

COMTREX LIQUID MULTI-SYMPTOM COLD RELIEVER. (Bristol-Myers) Acetaminiophen 650 mg., phenylpropanolamine HCl 25 mg., chlorpheniramine maleate 2 mg., dextromethorphan HBr 20 mg./30 ml. w/alcohol 20%. Bot. 6 oz., 10 oz.
Use: Analgesic, decongestant, antihistamine, cough reliever.

COMTREX NIGHTIME. (Bristol-Myers) Acetaminophen 1000 mg., pseudoephedrine HCl 60 mg., chlorpheniramine maleate 4 mg., dextromethorphan HBr 30 mg./30 ml. w/alcohol 25%. Bot. 6 oz., 10 oz.
Use: Analgesic, decongestant, antihistamine, cough reliever.

COMTREX TABLETS MULTI-SYMPTOM COLD RELIEVER. (Bristol-Myers) Acetaminophen 325 mg., phenylpropanolamine HCl 12.5 mg., chlorphemiramine maleate 1.0 mg., dextromethorphan HBr 10 mg./Tab. w/F D and C Yellow #5. Bot. 24s, 50s, 100s.
Use: Analgesic, decongestant antihistamine, cough reliever.

CONACETOL. (CMC) Acetaminophen 5 gr./Tab. **Tabs.** Bot. 50s, 100s, 1000s. **Elix:** 120 mg., Bot. pt., gal.
Use: Analgesic antipyretic.

CONACETON ELIXIR. (CMC) Acetaminophen elixir.
Use: Analgesic.

CONALSYN. (Cenci) Chlorpheniramine maleate 8 mg., phenylephrine HCl 20 mg., methscopolamine nitrate 2.5 mg./T.R. Cap. Bot. 30s, 250s, 500s.
Use: Hay fever and similar allergies.

CONAR. (Beecham Labs) Noscapine 15 mg., phenylephrine HCl 10 mg./5 ml. Bot. pt.

CONAR-A SUSPENSION. (Beecham Labs) Noscapine 7.5 mg., phenylephrine HCl 5.0 mg., acetaminophen 150.0 mg., guaifenesin 50.0 mg./cc. Bot. pt.

CONAR-A TAB. (Beecham Labs) Noscapine 15 m phenylephrine HCl 10 mg., acetaminophen 300 m guaifenesin 100 mg./Tab. Bot. 100s. Unit dose 2

CONAR EXPECTORANT. (Beecham Labs) Noscapine 15 mg., phenylephrine HCl 10 mg., guaifenesin 100 mg.,/5 cc. Bot. 4 oz. in 12s, pt.

CONCENTRATED OLEOVITAMIN A & D.
See: Oleovitamin A & D, Concentrated, Cap. (Various Mfr.)

CONCENTRATED TUBERCULIN.

CONCEPTROL CONTRACEPTIVE GEL. (Advance Care) Nonoxynol-9 in 4% concentration. Tube 70 G w/applicator.
Use: Contraceptive jelly.

CONCEPTROL CREAM. (Advanced Care) Nonoxyn 9 5%, in an oil-in-water emulsion at pH 4.5. Tube Gm. with applicator.
Use: Contraceptive cream.

CONCEPTROL DISPOSABLE CONTRACEPTIVE GEL. (Advanced Care) Nonoxynol-9 in 4% concen tion. Pkg. 6 or 10 disposable applicators.
Use: Contraceptive jelly.

CONDOL SUSPENSION. (Winthrop Products) Dipyrone, chlormezanone.
Use: Analgesic, muscle relaxant.

CONDOL TABLETS. (Winthrop Products) Dipyrone, Chlormezanone.
Use: Analgesic, muscle relaxant.

CONEST. (Grafton) Conjugated estrogens 0.625 mg 1.25 mg., or 2.5 mg./Tab. Bot. 100s, 1000s.
Use: Female hormone supplement.

CONESTORAL. (Galen) Sodium estrone sulfate 0.6 mg./Tab. Bot. 100s, 1000s.
Use: Treatment of menopausal syndrome, hypogenitalism, functional uterine bleeding.

CONEX-DA. (Forest) Phenylpropanolamine HCl 3 mg., chlorpheniramine maleate 4 mg./Dual action Tab. Bot. 100s, 1000s.
Use: Orally, relief of nasal congestion.

CONEX LOZENGE CT. (Forest) Benzocaine 5 mg., methylparaben 2 mg., propylparaben 0.5 mg., cetylpyridinium chloride 0.5 mg./Bot. 1000s.
Use: Topical anesthetic, antibacterial.

CONEX PLUS. (Forest) Phenylpropanolamine HCl 12.5 mg., chlorpheniramine maleate 4 mg., acetaminophen 325 mg./Tab. Bot. 100s, 1000s.
Use: Orally, analgesic and relief of nasal congestion.

CONEX SYRUP. (Forest) Phenylpropanolamine HCl 12 mg., guaifenesin 100 mg./10 cc. Bot. 4 oz., 1 pt.
Use: Treatment of cough due to colds.

CONEX WITH CODEINE. (Forest) Codeine phosphate 10 mg., guaifenesin 100 mg., phenylpropanolamine HCl 12.5 mg./5 ml. Bot. 4 c

CONFIDENT. (Block) Carboxymethylcellulose gum, ethylene oxide polymer, petrolatum/mineral oil base. Tube 0.7 oz., 1.4 oz., 2.4 oz.
Use: Denture adhesive cream.

CONGESPIRIN COUGH SYRUP. (Bristol-Myers) Dextromethorphan hydrobromide 5 mg./5 ml. Bot 3 oz.
Use: Children's antitussive.

IGESPIRIN FOR CHILDREN, ASPIRIN FREE. ristol-Myers) Acetaminophen 81 mg., phenyleph-e HCl 1.25 mg./Tab. Bot. 24s.
se: Analgesic, nasal decongestant, antipyretic.
IGESPIRIN LIQUID COLD MEDICINE. (Bristol-yers) Acetaminophen 130 mg., enylpropanolamine HCl 6.25 mg., alcohol 10%/5 . Bot. 3 oz.
se: Children's analgesic, decongestant.
IGESPIRIN TABLETS. (Bristol-Myers) Aspirin 81 g., phenylephrine HCl 1.25 mg./Tab. Bot. 36s.
se: Children's analgesic decongestant.
IGESTAC. (Menley & James) Pseudoephedrine Cl 60 mg., quaifenesin 400 mg./Tab. Bot. 12s, 4s, 50s.
se: Decongestant/expectorant.
IGEST-AFED DM SYRUP. (Eckerd) Pseudoephe-ine HCl 30 mg., guaifenesin 150 mg., extromethorphan HBr 10 mg./ 5 ml. w/alcohol)%. Bot. 4 oz.
se: Decongestant, expectorant, antitussive.
IGESTERONE. (Kenyon) Conjugated estrogens .625 mg., 1.25 mg., or 2.5 mg./tab. Bot. 100s.
IGO RED. Injection.
se: Hemostatic in hemorrhagic disorders.
IGESS. (Fleming) **Sr.:** Guaifenesin 250 mg., seudoephedrine HCl 120 mg./Cap. **Jr.:** uaifenesin 125 mg., pseudoephedrine HCl 60 ıg./Cap. Bot. 100s, 1000s.
se: Expectorant/bronchodilator.
NIB OINTMENT. (Guild) 0.25 oz.
NJEC. (Mallard) Atropine sulfate 0.2 mg., hlorpheniramine maleate 5 mg./cc. Vial 10 ml.
NJUGATED ESTROGENS.
ee: Estrogens, Conjugated (Various Mfr.)
NJUGENS. (Coastal) Conjugated estrogens 1.25 ıg./Tab. Bot. 100s.
NJUTABS. (Rand) Conjutabs 62: estrogens, 0.625 ıg./Tab. Conjutabs 125: estrogens, 1.25 mg./Tab. onjutabs 250: estrogens, 2.50 mg./Tab. (Enteric oated) Bot. 100s, 500s.
se: Estrogen therapy and supplementation.
NMEL. (Winthrop Products) Dipyrone as drops, yrup, suppositories (adult and child strength), ıjection and tablets.
Jse: Analgesic, antipyretic, anti-inflammatory.
NSIN COUMOUND SALVE. (Wisconsin) Carbolic cid ointment. Jar 2 oz., 1 lb.
Jse: Minor cuts, burns, skin irritations.
NSIN WHITE IODINE. (Wisconsin) Decolorized odine Bot. 0.5 oz, 16 oz.
Jse: Antiseptic, nail hardener.
NSTAB-100. (Kenyon) Docusate sodium 100 ng./Tab. Bot. 100s, 1000s.
NSTANT-T. (Geigy) Theophylline (anhydrous) 200 ng., or 300 mg./Sus. Rel. Tab. Bot. 100s. Unit lose 100s. Gy-Pak 60s.
Jse: Asthma and reversible bronchospasm.
NSTIBAN. (Quality Generics) Casanthranol 30 ng., docusate sodium 100 mg./Cap. Bot. 30s, 100s, 1000s.
Jse: Constipation.

CONSTONATE 60. Docusate sodium 100 mg., 250 mg./Cap. Bot. 100s, 1000s.
Use: Fecal softener.
CONTAC. (Menley & James) Phenylpropanolamine HCl 75 mg.; chlorpheniramine maleate 8 mg./Continuous action capsule. Pkg. 10s, 20s, 30s, 40s.
Use: Treatment of nasal congestion due to common cold, hay fever and sinusitis.
CONTAC COUGH CAPSULES. (Menley & James) Dextromethorphan HBr 30 mg., pseudoephedrine HCl 60 mg./Cap. Pkg. 10s, 20s.
Use: For coughing and nasal congestion due to common cold.
CONTAC JR. (Menley & James) Phenylpropanolamine HCl 9.375 mg., acetaminophen 162.5 mg., dextromethorphan HBr 5.0 mg./5cc w/alcohol 10%. Bot. 4 oz.
Use: Congestion, aches, fever & cough due to colds.
CONTAC SEVERE COLD FORMULA. (Menley & James) Pseudoephedrine HCl 30 mg., acetaminophen 500 mg., dextromethorphan HBr. 15 mg., chlorpheniramine maleate 2 mg./Cap. Pkg. 10s, 20s.
Use: Colds with flu-like symptoms.
CONTAC SEVERE COLD FORMULA NIGHT STRENGTH. (Menley & James) Acetaminophen 1000 mg., dextromethorphan HBr 30 mg., pseudoephedrine HCl 60 mg., doxylamine succinate 7.5 mg./oz. w/alcohol 2.5% Bot. 5 oz.
Use: Treatment of colds with flu-like symptoms.
CONTACTISOL. (CooperVision) Sterile buffered isotonic soln. preserved with benzalkonium chloride 0.01%, edetate disodium 0.01%. Bot. 1.9 oz.
Use: Cleaning and wetting solution for hard contact lenses.
CONTIQUE. (Alcon) Family of contact lens products.
Wetting Solution 2 oz.
Soaking Solution 4 oz.
Cleaning Solution 1 oz.
Flow-Thru Contact Lens Case
Swirl Clean Hard Lens Cleaner
■ **CONTRACEPTIVES.**
See: Oral Contraceptives (Var. Mfr.)
Foams, Vaginal.
See: Delfen, Vaginal Foam (Ortho Pharm.)
Emko, Vaginal Foam (Emko)
Jellies & Creams, Vaginal.
See: Colagyn, Jel (Smith)
Colagyn, Jel (Smith)
Conceptrol, Cream, Gel (Ortho)
Gynol II, Gel (Ortho)
Immolin, Cream-Jel (Schmid)
Koromex-A, Jelly (Holland-Rantos)
Koromex, Cream or Jelly (Holland-Rantos)
Ortho-Creme (Ortho)
Ortho-Gynol, Jelly (Ortho)
Suppositories, Vaginal.
See: Intercept, Inserts (Ortho)
Lorophyn, Supp., Jelly (Eaton)
CONTRAPAR. (Wellcome; Gloxazone. (B.A.N.)

CONVERSPAZ. (Ascher) Cellulase 5 mg., protease 10 mg., amylase 30 mg., lipase 13 mg., l-hyoscyamine sulfate 0.0625 mg./Cap. Bot. 100s.
Use: To aid digestion of food.

CONVERZYME CAPS. (Ascher) Cellulase 5 mg., protease 10 mg., amylase 30 mg., lipase 13 mg./Cap. Bot. 100s.
Use: Aid for digestion of food.

COOPERVISION BALANCED SALT SOLUTION. (CooperVision) Sterile intraocular irrigation sol. Bot. 15 ml., 500 ml.
Use: Intraocular irrigating solution during intraocular surgical procedures.

COPAVIN. (Lilly) Caps. Bot. 100s.

COPE. (Glenbrook) Aspirin 421.2 mg., magnesium hydroxide 50 mg., dried aluminum hydroxide gel 25 mg., caffeine 32 mg./Tab. Bot. 15s, 36s, 60s.
Use: Tension headaches, muscular aches, neuritic pain, fevers.

COPENE. (Kenyon) Chlorphentermine HCl 65 mg./Tab. Bot. 100s.

COPHENE #2. (Dunhall) Chlorpheniramine maleate 12 mg., phenylpropanolamine HCl 50 mg., phenylephrine HCl 25 mg./Time Cap. Bot. 100s, 500s.
Use: Decongestant, antihistaminic.

COPHENE INJECTABLE. (Dunhall) Atropine sulf. 0.2 mg., phenylpropanolamine HCl 12.5 mg., chlorpheniramine maleate 5 mg./ml. Pkg. 10 ml.
Use: Decongestant, antihistaminic.

COPHENE-PL. (Dunhall) Phenylephrine HCl 20 mg., phenylpropanolamine HCl 20 mg., chlorpheniramine maleate 5 mg./5 cc. Bot. 16 oz.
Use: Cough due to colds and allergy.

COPHENE-S. (Dunhall) Dihydrocodone bitartrate 3 mg., phenylephrine HCl 20 mg., phenylpropanolamine HCl 20 mg., chlorpheniramine maleate 5 mg./5 cc. Bot. pt.
Use: Antitussive.

COPHENE-X. (Dunhall) Carbetapentane citrate 20 mg., phenylephrine HCl 10 mg., phenylpropanolamine HCl 20 mg., chlorpheniramine maleate 2.5 mg., potassium guaiacolsulfonate 45 mg./Cap. Bot. 100s, 500s.
Use: Antihistamine, decongestant, expectorant, antitussive.

COPHENE-XP SYRUP. (Dunhall) Carbetapentane citrate 20 mg., phenylephrine HCl 10 mg., phenylpropanolamine HCl 20 mg., chlorpheniramine maleate 2.5 mg. potassium guaiacolsulfonate 45 mg./5 ml. Bot. pt.
Use: Antihistamine, decongestant, antitussive.

COPPERHEAD BITE THERAPY.
See: Antivenin, Snake Polyvalent Inj. (Wyeth)

COPPERIN. (Vernon) Iron ammonium citrate w/copper (6 gr.). "A" adult dose, "B" children dose. Bot. 30s, 100s, 500s.
Use: Treatment of secondary anemias.

COPPERTONE. (Plough) A series of products marketed under the coppertone name including: Waterproof Lotions SPF 4, 6, 8, and 15 (Bot. 4 fl. oz.); Lite Formula Oil SPF 2 (Bot. 4 fl. oz.); Lite Lotion SPF 4 (Bot. 4 fl. oz.). Contain one or mo of the following ingredients:: Padimate O, oxybenzone, homosalate.
Use: Ultraviolet sunscreen.

COPPERTONE NOSKOTE. (Plough) Homosalate and Oxybenzone 3% sunscreen ointment. (SPF Jar. 1 oz. Tube 7/16 oz.
Use: Ultraviolet sunscreen.

COPPERTRACE. (Armour) Cupric chloride injectio containing copper 0.4 mg./ml. Vial 10 ml. Box 2
Use: Supplement to I.V. solutions for copper deficiency.

COPPER UNDECYLENATE.
W/Sod. propionate, Sod. caprylate, propionic acid, undecylenic acid, salicylic acid.

COPROBATE. (Coastal) Meprobamate 400 mg./T Bot. 100s, 1000s.
Use: Muscle relaxant and tranquilizer.

CO-PYRONIL 2. (Dista) Chlorpheniramine malea mg., pseudoephedrine HCl 60 mg./Pulvule. Bot. 100s, 1000s.
Use: Allergic symptoms, antihistaminic.

CO-PYRONIL 2 PEDIATRIC. (Dista) Chlorphenira maleate 2 mg., pseudoephedrine HCl 30 mg./Pulvule. Bot. 100s. Liquid 16 fl. oz.
Use: Allergic symptoms, antihistaminic.

CORAB. (Abbott) Test kit 100s.
Use: Radioimmunoassay for detection of antibo to hepatitis B core antigen.

CORACE INJECTION. (Fellows) Cortisone acetate mg./cc. Vial 10 cc.

CORAL. (Lorvic) Fluroide ion 1.23%, 0.1 molar phosphate. Jar 250 Gm., Coral II: 180 disposabl cup units/carton.
Use: Phosphate/fluoride prophylaxis paste.

CORAL/PLUS. (Lorvic) Free fluoride ion 2.2%, recrystallized kaolinite. Tube 250 Gm.

CORALSONE MODIFIED. (Zemmer) Aspirin 300 m ascorbic acid 50 mg., aluminum hydroxide 35 mg./Tab. Bot. 100s, 1000s.

CORAMINE. (Ciba) Nikethamide, Liq. 25%. Bot. 3 Amp. 25% 1.5 cc. Pkg. 20s.
Use: Respiratory stimulant.

CORANE CAPSULES. (Fellows) Pyrilamine maleat 25 mg., pheniramine maleate 10 mg., phenylpropanolamine HCl 25 mg., phenylephrine HCl 10 mg./Cap. Bot. 100s, 500s, 1000s.

CORBICIN-125. (Arthrins) Vit. C 125 mg./Cap. B 100s.
Use: Vitamin C supplement.

CORDRAN LOTION. (Dista) Flurandrenolide 0.05% w/cetyl alcohol, benzyl alcohol, stearic acid, glyceryl monostearate, polyoxyl 40 stearate, glycerin, mineral oil, menthol and purified water. Squeeze bot. 15 ml. and 60 ml.
Use: Dermatologic steroid.

CORDRAN OINTMENT. (Dista) Flurandrenolide 0.025%, 0.05%; emulsified petrolatum base/Gm. 0.05% Tube 15 Gm., 30 Gm., 60 Gm. Jar 225 G. 0.025%. Tube 30 Gm., 60 Gm. Jar 225 Gm.
Use: Dermatologic steroid.

ꞮDRAN-N CREAM & OINTMENT. (Dista) Fluran-
'enolide 0.5 mg.; neomycin sulfate 5 mg./Gm.
ube 15 Gm., 30 Gm., 60 Gm.
se: Dermatologic steroid.
ꞮDRAN SP. (Dista) Flurandrenolide 0.025% and
05%, in emulsified base w/cetyl alcohol, stearic
cid, polyoxyl 40 stearate, mineral oil, propylene
ycol, sodium citrate, citric acid, purified water.
.05%, Tube 15 Gm., 30 Gm., 60 Gm., Jar 225
m.; 0.025%, Tube 30 Gm., 60 Gm. Jar 225 Gm.
se: Dermatologic steroid.
ꞮDRAN TAPE. (Dista) Flurandrenolide 4 mcg./sq.
m. Roll 7.5 cm. × 60 cm., 7.5 cm. × 200 cm.
ꞮDROL. (Vita Elixir) Prednisolone 5 mg. or 20
ig./Tab. Bot. 100s
se: Treatment of inflammatory conditions.
REGA POWDER. (Block) Denture adhesive
ontaining polyethyleneoxide polymer w/peppermint
il, karaya gum. Pkg.: pocket 0.7 oz.; medium 1.15
z.; economy 3.55 oz.
se: Denture adhesive powder.
RGARD. (Squibb) Nadolol 40 mg., 80 mg., 120 mg.
r 160 mg./Tab. Bot 100s, 1000s. Unit Dose 100s.
se: Antihypertensive and antiangina beta-blocker.
RGONJECT-5. (Mayrand) Human chorionic gonado-
opin 500 u./ml. Vial 10 ml.
ORIANDER OIL, N.F. XVI.
se: Pharm. Aid (flavor).
RIBAN. Diamphenethide, B.A.N.
RICIDIN. (Schering) Chlorpheniramine maleate 2
ig., aspirin 325 mg./Tab. Bot. 12s, 24s, 60s, 100s,
000s. Box 100 x 4 Tab. packets.
Jse: Common cold.
RICIDIN COUGH SYRUP. (Schering) Guaifenesin
00 mg., phenylpropanolamine HCl 12.5 mg.,
extromethorphan HBr. 10 mg./5 ml. w/alcohol <
.5%. Bot. 4 oz.
se: Antitussive.
RICIDIN 'D' DECONGESTANT TABLETS.
Schering) Chlorpheniramine maleate 2 mg., aspirin
25 mg., phenylpropanolamine HCl 12.5 mg./Tab.
ot. 12s, 24s, 50s, 100s. Box 100 x 4 Tab packets.
Jse: Nasal decongestant & treatment of common
old.
RICIDIN DEMILETS. (Schering) Acetaminophen
0 mg. (1.25 gr.), chlorpheniramine maleate 1.0
ng., phenylpropanolamine HCl 6.25 mg./Chewable
ab. Box 24s, 36s.
Jse: Decongestant.
**RICIDIN EXTRA STRENGTH SINUS HEADACHE
TABLETS.** (Schering) Acetaminophen 500 mg.,
henylpropanolamine HCl 12.5 mg.,
hlorpheniramine maleate 2 mg/Tab. Box 24s.
Jse: Antihistaminic, decongestant and analgesic.
RICIDIN MEDILETS. (Schering) Chlorpheniramine
naleate 1.0 mg., phenylpropanolamine HCl 6.25
ng./Chewable tab. Box 24s, 36s.
Jse: Antihistaminic, decongestant.
RICIDIN NASAL MIST. (Schering) Phenylephrine
HCl 5 mg./ml. Bot. 20 ml.
Jse: Decongestant.

CORICO. (Haag) Phenylephrine, chlorpheniramine, analgesics and Vitamin C. Capsules, Bot. 100s, 500, 1000s.
Use: Common cold treatment.
CORID. (MSD AGVET) Amprolium: 20% sol. powder; 9.6% solution, 1.25% crumbles.
Use: Coccidiostat, veterinary medicine.
CORILIN INFANT LIQUID. (Schering) Chlorpheniramine maleate 0.75 mg., sod. salicylate 80 mg./ml. w/alcohol < 1% Bot. 30 ml.
Use: Antihistamine, analgesic, antipyretic.
CORMED.
See: Nikethamide (Various Mfr.)
• **CORMETHASONE ACETATE.** USAN.
Use: Anti-infammatory.
CORN FIX. (Last) Turpentine oil 2.4%, liquefied phenol 2.25%. Bot. 0.3 oz.
Use: Corn remedy.
CORN HUSKERS LOTION. (Warner-Lambert) Glycerin 6.7%, alcohol 5.7%. Bot. 4 oz., 7 oz.
Use: Moisturizing skin lotion.
• **CORN OIL,** N.F. XVI.
Use: Pharm. Aid (solvent: oleaginous vehicle).
See: G. B. Prep Emulsion (Gray)
Lipomul-Oral, Liq. (Upjohn)
CORNS-O-POPPIN. (Ries-Hamly) Salicylic acid 6.5%, benzoic acid 12%.
Use: Treatment of corns
CORON IRON TABLETS. (Jamieson-McKames) Cobalt gluconate 25 mg., ferrous gluconate 200 mg./Tab. Bot. 100s.
COR-OTICIN. (Maurry) Hydrocortisone acetate 15 mg., neomycin sulf. 5 mg., sod. cit., polysorbate 80, carboxymethylcellulose, sod. metabisulf., sodium chloride, chlorobutanol 0.5%, sod. hydr./cc. Aq. susp. 5 cc.
Use: Anti-inflammatory, antibiotic.
COROVAS TYMCAPS. (Amfre-Grant) Pentaerythritol tetranitrate 30 mg., secobarbituric acid 50 mg./Cap. Bot. 60s, 120s, 500s, 1000s.
Use: Prolonged action coronary vasodilator.
CORPUS LUTEUM, EXTRACT (WATER SOLUBLE).
See: Progesterone, Preps. (Var. Mfr.)
CORRECTIVE MIXTURE W/PAREGORIC. (Beecham Labs) Zinc sulfocarbolate 10 mg., phenyl salicylate 22 mg., bismuth subsalicylate 85 mg., pepsin 45 mg., paregoric 0.6 ml./5cc. w/alcohol 2%. Bot. Gal.
Use: Antidiarrheal.
CORRECTOL LIQUID. (Plough) Yellow phenolphthalein 65 mg./15 ml. Bot. 8 oz., 16 oz.
Use: Laxative.
CORSALONE MODIFIED. (Zemmer) Aspirin 300 mg., ascorbic acid 50 mg., aluminum hydroxide 35 mg./E.C. Tab., Bot. 100s.
CORSYM CAPSULES. (Pennwalt) Phenylpropanolamine HCl 75 mg., chlorpheniramine maleate 8 mg./Cap. Sleeve pack 12s.
Use: Treatment of colds, allergy, nasal congestion.
CORSYM SYRUP. (Pennwalt) Phenylpropanolamine HCl 37.5, chlorpheniramine maleate 4 mg./5 ml. Bot. 3 oz.
Use: Treatment of colds, allergy, nasal congestion.

CORTAID. (Upjohn) Hydrocortisone acetate equivalent to hydrocortisone 5 mg./Gm.**Cream:** 0.5 oz., 1 oz. tube. **Lotion:** 1 oz., 2 oz. Bot. **Ointment:** 0.5 oz., 1 oz. tube. **Spray:** 1.5 fl. oz.
Use: Anti-inflammatory, antipruritic.

CORTAN. (Blue Cross) Presnisone 5 mg./Tab. Bot. 1000s.
Use: Anti-inflammatory.

CORTANE D.C. EXPECTORANT. (Standex) Brompheniramine maleate 2 mg., guaifenesin 100 mg., phenylephrine HCl 5 mg., phenylpropanolamine HCl 5 mg., codeine phosphate 10 mg., alcohol 3.5%/5 cc. Bot. pt.

CORTANE EXPECTORANT. (Standex) Brompheniramine maleate 2 mg., guaifenesin 100 mg., phenylephrine 5 mg., phenylpropanolamine HCl 5 mg., alcohol 3.5%/5 ml. Bot. pt.

CORTAPP ELIXIR. (Standex) Brompheniramine maleate 5 mg., phenylephrine HCl 5 mg., phenylpropanolamine HCl 5 mg., alcohol 2.3%/5 cc. Bot. pt.

CORTATRIGEN EAR SUSPENSION. (Goldline) Bot. 10 ml.
Use: External ear infections.

CORTATRIGEN MODIFIED EAR DROPS. (Goldline) Bot. 10 ml.
Use: External ear infections.

CORT-DOME. (Miles Pharm) Hydrocortisone alcohol; **Cream:** ⅛%—1 oz., 4 oz. 0.25%, 1 oz., 4 oz., 1 lb. 0.5%—0.5 oz., 1 oz. Jar 4 oz., 1 lb.; 1%—0.5 oz., 1 oz. **Lotion:** ⅛%, 6 oz.; 0.25%,-4 oz.; 0.5%—0.5 oz., 1 oz., 4 oz., 1%—0.5 oz., 1 oz. **Supp.** (25 mg., 15 mg.) Box 12s.
Use: Topically; dermatitis.

CORTEF ACETATE OINTMENT. (Upjohn) Hydrocortisone acetate 10 mg./Gm. w/lanolin (anhydrous), white petrolatum, and mineral oil. Tube 20 Gm. (10 mg./Gm.)
Use: Anti-inflammatory corticosteroid for topical application.

CORTEF ACETATE STERILE SUSPENSION. (Upjohn) Hydrocortisone acetate 50 mg., sodium carboxymethylcellulose 4.8 mg., polysorbate 80 3.9 mg. sod. chloride 8.7 mg., benzyl alcohol 8.83 mg./ml. Vial 5 ml.
Use: Anti-inflammatory corticosteriod for local injection.

CORTEF FEMININE ITCH CREAM. (Upjohn) Hydrocortisone acetate equivalent to hydrocortisone 5 mg./Gm. Tube 0.5 oz.
Use: Anti-inflammatory, antipruritic.

CORTEF ORAL SUSPENSION. (Upjohn) Hydrocortisone 10 mg./5 ml. (as 13.4 mg. hydrocortisone cypionate). Oral susp. Bot. 4 oz.
Use: Anti-inflammatory corticosteriod for oral administration.

CORTEF TABLETS. (Upjohn) Hydrocortisone. Tab. 5 mg., Bot. 50s; 10 mg. & 20 mg., Bot. 100s.
Use: Anti-inflammatory corticosteriod.

CORTENEMA. (Rowell) Hydrocortisone 100 mg., in aqueous solution w/carboxypolymethylene, polysorbate 80, & methylparaben 0.18%/60 ml. Bot. w/applicator. Pkg. 7s. Unit dose 1s.
Use: Idiopathic nonspecific ulcerative colitis.

CORTENIL.
See: Desoxycorticosterone Acetate, Preps. (Vari Mfr.)

CORTICAINE CREAM. (Glaxo) Hydrocortisone acetate 0.5%, dibucaine 0.5%. Tube 1 oz.
Use: Topical anti-inflammatory and anesthetic, tihemorrhoidal.

CORTICAINE SUPPOSITORIES. (Glaxo) Hydrocortisone acetate 10 mg./Supp. Box 12s.
Use: Corticosteroid, antihemorrhoidal.

■ **CORTICAL HORMONE PRODUCTS.**
See: Adrenal Cortex Ext. (Various Mfr.)
Aristocort, Preps. (Lederle)
Corticotropin, Preps. (Var. Mfr.)
Hydrocortisone, Preps. (Var. Mfr.)
Cortisone Acetate, Preps. (Var. Mfr.)
Decadron LA, Inj. (Merck Sharp & Dohme)
Decadron, Tab., Elixir, Inj. (Merck Sharp & Dohme)
Desoxycorticosterone Acetate, Preps. (Var. Mf
Dexamethasone, Tab. (Var. Mfr.)
Fludrocortisone (Var. Mfr.)
Hydeltrasol, Inj. (Merck Sharp & Dohme)
Hydrocortone Acetate, Inj. (Merck Sharp & Dohme)
Hydrocortone Phosphate, Inj. (Merck Sharp & Dohme)
Kenacort, Prep. (Squibb)
Lipo-Adrenal Cortex, Inj. (Upjohn)
Medrol, Preps. (Upjohn)
Methylprednisolone, Tab. (Var. Mfr.)
Prednisolone, Tab. (Var. Mfr.)
Prednisone, Tab. (Var. Mfr.)
Triamcinolone, Tab. (Var. Mfr.)

CORTICAL OINT. (Jenkins) Hydrocortisone 0.33%, calamine 5.0%, pyrilamine maleate 0.25%, petrolatum, stearyl alcohol, mineral oil, propylene glycol, polyoxyl 40 stearate, methyl and propyl parabens (preservatives), purified water. Tube 0.5 oz.

CORTICOID. (Jenkins) Hydrocortisone alcohol 10 mg., clioquinol 30 mg., methyl paraben 0.5 mg., propyl paraben 0.5 mg./Gm. Tube 20 Gm.

CORTICOSTERONE. Kendall's Compound B (Vario Mfr.)

CORTICOTROPHIN. B.A.N. Adrenocorticotrophic hormone.
Use: Adrenocorticotrophin; ACTH
See: Acthar
Actos 50
Cortic-Gel
Cortrophin ZN

CORTICOTROPIN-GEL PURIFIED. (Wilson) Corticotropin in gelatin menstruum, Vial (40 u./cc. & 80 u./cc.) 5 cc.
Use: I.M., S.C.; corticotropin therapy.

CORTICOTROPIN HIGHLY PURIFIED.
See: H. P. Acthar Gel. Vial. (Armour)

CORTICOTROPIN INJECTION, U.S.P. XXI. ACTH, Adrenocorticotropic hormone or adrenocorticotrop(h)in or corticotropin.
Use: Adrenocorticotropic hormone; adrenocortical steroid (anti-inflammatory): diagnostic aid (adrenocortical insufficiency).
See: Cortrophin Gel, Vial, Amp. (Organon)

CORTICOTROPIN FOR INJECTION, U.S.P. XXI.
Use: Adrenocorticotropic hormone; adrenocortical steroid (anti-inflammatory); diagnostic aid (adrenocortical insufficiency).

CORTICOTROPIN INJECTION, REPOSITORY, U.S.P. XXI. (Various Mfr.)
Use: I.M. anterior pituitary hormone therapy: adrenocortical steroid (anti-inflammatory); diagnostic aid (adrenocortical insufficiency).
See: Acthar Gel, Vial (Armour)
ACTH Gel. Purified (Var. Mfr.)
Cortigel, Vial (Savage)
Cortrophin Gel Amp., Vial (Organon)
H.P. Acthar Gel, Vial (Armour)

CORTICOTROPIN ZINC.
See: Cortrophin-Zinc, Vials (Organon)

CORTICOTROPIN-ZINC HYDROXIDE SUSPENSION, STERILE, U.S.P. XXI. Absorbed on zinc hydroxide.
Use: Adrenocorticotropic hormone; adrenocortical steroid (anti-inflammatory); diagnostic aid (adrenocortical insufficiency).

CORTIFOAM. (Reed & Carnrick) Hydrocortisone acetate 10% in an aerosol foam w/propylene glycol, emulsifying wax, steareth 10, cetyl alcohol, methylparaben propylparaben, trolamine, water and inert propellants. Container 20 Gm. w/rectal applicator for 14 applicatorfuls.
Use: Rectal foam, glucocorticoid therapy.

CORTIGEL. (Savage) Purified corticotropin 40 or 80 u./cc. in 16% gelatin solution. Vial 5 cc.
Use: Adrenocorticosteroid.

CORTIGESTIC OTIC DROPS. (Century) Bot. 10 cc.
Use: Ear drops.

CORTIKAY CREAM. (Kay) Dubicaine w/hydrocortisone 0.5% in cream base Bot. 1 oz.
Use: Topical anti-inflammatory, anesthetic.

CORTIN 1% CREAM. (C & M Pharmacal) Hydrocortisone 1%, clioquinol 3%. Tube 20 Gm.
Use: Allergic & atopic eczemas.

CORTINAL. (Kenyon) Micronized hydrocortisone alcohol in a nonallergenic water washable base 5 mg./Gm. Tube 1 oz.

CORTIPREL CREAM. (Pasadena Research) Hydrocortisone acetate 0.5%, 1% in special base. 0.5% Tube 1 oz., 1% Tube 0.5 oz.

CORTISOL.
See: Hydrocortisone, U.S.P.XXI.
Note: Cortisol was the official published name for hydrocortisone in U.S.P.XXI. The name was changed back to Hydrocortisone, U.S.P. in Supplement 1 to the U.S.P.XXI.

CORTISOL CYCLOPENTYLPROPIONATE.
See: Cortef Fluid, Susp., Tab. (Upjohn)

CORTISONE. B.A.N. 17α,21-Dihydroxypregn-4-ene-3,11,20-trione. 17-Hydroxy-11-dehydrocorticosterone.
Adreson, Cortelan, Cortistab, and Cortisyl are the 21-acetate
Use: Corticosteroid.

• **CORTISONE ACETATE,** U.S.P. XXI. Sterile Susp., Tab., U.S.P. XXI. 17,21-Dihydroxypregn-4-ene 3,11,-20-trione 21 acetate. (Kendall's Comp. E) Tab. (Upjohn) 5 mg., 10 mg., or 25 mg./Tab. Bot. 50s, 100s, 500s.
Use: Adrenocortical steroid (anti-inflammatory).
See: Cortistan (Standex)
Cortone Acetate, Tab., Inj. (Merck Sharp & Dohme)
Pantisone, Tab. (Panray)

CORTISPORIN CREAM. (Burroughs Wellcome) Polymyxin B sulfate 10,000 u., neomycin sulfate 5 mg., gramicidin 0.25 mg., hydrocortisone acetate 5 mg./Gm. w/methylparaben 0.25%. Tube 7.5 Gm.
Use: Anti-inflammatory.

CORTISPORIN OINTMENT. (Burroughs Wellcome) Polymyxin B sulfate 5,000 u., bacitracin zinc 400 u., neomycin sulfate 5 mg., hydrocortisone (1%) 10 mg./Gm. in petrolatum base. Tube 0.5 oz.
Use: Anti-inflammatory and antibacterial.

CORTISPORIN OPHTHALMIC OINTMENT. (Burroughs Wellcome) Polymyxin B sulfate 10,000 u., bacitracin 400 u., neomycin sulfate 5 mg., hydrocortisone (1%) 10 mg./Gm. in petrolatum base. Tube ⅛ oz. Sterile.
Use: Anti-inflammatory & antibacterial.

CORTISPORIN OPHTHALMIC SUSPENSION. (Burroughs Wellcome) Polymyxin B sulfate 10,000 u., neomycin sulfate 5 mg., hydrocortisone (1%) 10 mg., in sterile, saline, isotonic/ml. W/thimerosal, cetyl alcohol, glyceryl monostearate, liq. petrolatum, polyoxyl 40 stearate, propylene glycol. Drop bot. 7.5 ml. Sterile.
Use: Optic, inflammation.

CORTISPORIN OTIC SOLUTION STERILE. (Burroughs Wellcome) Polymixin B sulf. 10,000 u., neomycin sulf. 5 mg., hydrocortisone 10 mg./ml. w/glycerin, HCl, propylene glycol, & K metabisulfite 0.1%. Bot. W/dropper 10 ml. Sterile.
Use: External ear infections.

CORTISPORIN OTIC SUSPENSION. (Burroughs Wellcome) Polymyxin B sulf. 10,000 u., neomycin sulf. 5 mg., hydrocortisone free alcohol 10 mg./ml. W/cetyl alcohol, propylene glycol, polysorbate 80, thimerosal. Bot. w/dropper 10 ml. Sterile.
Use: Ear infections.

CORTISTAN. (Standex) Cortisone 25 mg./10 cc.

• **CORTIVAZOL.** USAN. 11B,17,21-trihydroxy-6, 16α-dimethyl-2′-phenyl-2′H-pregna-2,4,6-trieno[3,2-c]-pyrazol-20-one 21-acetate.
Use: Anti-inflammatory.

CORTIZONE-S, MAXIMUM STRENGTH. (Thompson Medical) Hydrocortisone 0.5%. Tubes.
Use: Relief of dermatitis, itch, rash.

CORT-NIB CREAM. (Cenci) Hydrocortisone alcohol, 0.-25%, 0.5%, 1.0%. **Cream:** Tube 1 oz. Jar 1 lb.
Use: Anti-inflammatory agent.

CORT-NIB V CREAM. (Cenci) Hydrocortisone alcohol 0.5%, clioquinol 3%. Tube 1 oz.
Use: Anti-inflammatory agent.

• **CORTODOXONE.** USAN. 17,21-Dihydroxy-pregn-4-ene-3,20-dione. Cortexolone.
Use: Anti-inflammatory.

CORTOGEN ACETATE. Cortisone acetate.

CORTONE ACETATE. (Merck Sharp & Dohme) Cortisone acetate. **Tab.** 25 mg., Bot. 100s. **Saline Susp.,** 25 mg./ml. and 50 mg./ml. W/sod. chloride 9 mg., polysorbate 80-4 mg., sodium carboxymethyl-cellulose 5 mg., benzyl alcohol 9 mg./ml., water for injection q.s. 1 ml. **25 mg.**/ml. Vial, 20 ml.; **50 mg.**/ml. Vial, 10 ml.
Use: Anti-inflammatory corticosteroid.

CORTOXIDE GEL. (Syosset) Hydrocortisone 0.5% or 1% in gel base. Bot. 1.5 oz.
Use: Treatment of dermatoses.

CORT-QUIN. (Miles Pharm) Hydrocortisone alcohol 0.25%, iodoquinol 1% in vehicle buffered to the pH range of normal skin. Hydrocortisone alcohol 0.5%, iodoquinol 1% in Acid Mantle vehicle of cetyl alcohol, stearyl alcohol, sod. lauryl sulfate, beeswax, white petrolatum, liquid petrolatum glycerin methylparaben. Tube 0.5 oz., 1 oz.
Use: Antibacterial, antiprotozoal, antifungal.

CORTRIL TOPICAL OINTMENT 1%. (Pfipharmecs) Hydrocortisone 1% W/cetyl and stearyl alcohol, propylene glycol, sod. lauryl sulfate, petrolatum, cholesterol, mineral oil, methyl and propyl parabens in ointment base. Tube 0.5 oz.
Use: Anti-inflammatory.

CORTROPHIN GEL. (Organon) Corticotropin, Gel. **40 U/cc.** Vial 5 ml. **80 U./cc.** Vial 5 ml. Box 1s.
Use: Hormone (ACTH).

CORTROPHIN-ZINC. (Organon) Corticotropin zinc 40 u./ml. Vial 5 cc.
Use: Hormone (ACTH).

CORTROSYN INJECTION. (Organon) Cosyntropin 0.25 mg., mannitol 10 mg., lyophilized pow./1 ml. Vial. Pkg. w/1 ml. amp. diluent. Box 10s. Vial.

CORT-TOP OINTMENT. (Standex) Topical hydrocortisone 1%. Tube 20 Gm.

CORUBEEN. (Spanner) B-12 crystalline 1000 mcg./cc. Vial 10 cc.

CORYBAN-D. (Pfipharmecs) Phenylpropanolamine 25 mg., chlorpheniramine maleate 2 mg., caffeine 30 mg./Cap. Bot. 24s.
Use: Common cold.

CORYBAN-D SYRUP. (Pfipharmecs) Phenylephrine HCl 5 mg., acetaminophen 120 mg., guaifenesin 50 mg., d-methorphan HBr 7.5 mg., and alcohol 7.5%/5 cc. tsp. Bot. 4 oz. 12s
Use: Common cold, allergies.

CORYZEX. (Vitarine) Acetaminophen 325 mg., phenylpropanolamine HCl 12.5 mg., chlorpheniramine maleate 1 mg., dextromethorphan HBr. 10 mg./Cap.
Use: Symptomatic relief of discomforts of cold.

CORZANS. (Moore Kirk) Acetaminophen 160 mg., chlorpheniramine maleate 1 mg., phenylephrine H 7.5 mg., ascorbic acid 15 mg./Tab. Bot. 100s, 1000s.
Use: Treatment of common cold and hay fever.

CORZIDE. (Squibb) Nadolol 40 mg., Bendrolumethiazide 5 mg./Tab or Nadolol 80 mg bendroflumethiazide 5 mg./Tab. Bot. 100s.
Use: Antihypertensive, B-blocker diuretic combination.

CORZONE. (Xttrium) Dextromethorphan HBr 15 mg chlorpheniramine maleate 1.8 mg., phenyltoloxamine dihydrogen citrate 8 mg., phenylpropanolamine HCl 12.5 mg., ammonium C 90 mg./5 cc. Bot. pt., gal.
Use: Relief of coughs due to colds.

CORZYME. (Abbott) Test kit 100s.
Use: Enzyme immunoassay for detection of antibody to hepatitis B core antigen.

CORZYME-M. (Abbott) Test kits 100s.
Use: Enzyme immunoassay for the detection of I antibody to hepatitis B core antigen.

COSALDON. Pentifylline, B.A.N.

CO-SANSPRIN. (Wolins) Acetaminophen 325 m chlorpheniramine maleate 1 mg., phenylephrine H 5 mg./Tab. Bot. 1000s.

COSANYL. (Health Care Industries) Codeine sulfate 10 mg., d-pseudoephedrine HCl 30 mg./5 ml. w/ cohol 6% in peach flavored base. Bot. 4 oz., 1 pt 1 gal.

COSANYL-DM. (Health Care Industries) Dextrometh phan HBr 15 mg., d-pseudoephedrine HCl 30 mg. ml. w/alcohol 6% in a peach flavored base. Bot. oz., gal.
Use: Sedative, expectorant.

COSMEGEN. (Merck Sharp & Dohme) Actinomycin (dactinomycin) 0.5 mg. (lyophilized powder), mannitol 20 mg./Vial.
Use: Antineoplastic.

COSMOLINE.
See: Petrolatum

COSPRIN. (Glenbrook) Aspirin 325 mg. or 650 mg./Tab. **650 mg.**/Tab. Bot. 36s, 72s; **325 mg** ./Tab. Bot. 60s, 125s.
Use: Analgesic, anti-inflammatory.

COSULID. (Ciba) Sulfachloropyridazine.

• **COSYNTROPIN.** USAN.
Use: Adrenocorticotropic hormone.
See: Cortrosyn, Vial (Organon)

COTAPHYLLINE TABS. (Major) Oxtriphylline 100 m or 200 mg./Tab. Bot. 100s, 500s.
Use: Theophylline therapy.

COTARNINE CHLORIDE. Cotarnine hydrochloride.

COTARNINE HYDROCHLORIDE.
See: Cotarnine Chloride

COTAZYM. (Organon) Pancrelipase, Lipase 8,000 u., protease 30,000 u., amylase 30,000 u. having digestive power for 17 Gm. dietary fat, trypsin, having digestive power for 34 Gm. dietary protein; amylase, having digestive power for 40 Gm. dietar starch, plus other enzymes from whole hog

ancreas/Cap. Bot. 100s, 500s. Cherry flavored.
:ap. Bot. 100s.
Jse: Pancreatic enzyme deficiency.
TAZYM-B. (Organon) Mixed conjugated bile salts 65 ng., pancrelipase 165 mg., cellulase 2 mg./Tab. Bot. 60s.
Jse: Enzyme digestant.
RTAZYM-S. (Organon) Pancrelipase spheres, lipase ,000 U., protease 20,000 U., amylase 20,000 J./Tab.
Jse: Pancreatic enzyme deficiency.
TIN. (Pasadena Research) Pepsin 250 mg., pancreatin 300 mg., bile salts 150 mg., dehydrocholic acid 25 mg./Tab. Bot. 100s, 1000s.
-TINIC INJECTION. (Vortech) Iron peptonized 59 ng., folic acid 5 mg., liver injection equiv. to B-12 5 ncg., procaine HCl 1%, sod. citrate 1%, pheno .5%/2 cc. Vial 30 ml.
Jse: Hematinic.
TININE FUMARATE. (-)-1-Methyl-5-(3-pyridyl)-2 pyrolidinone compound (2:1) with fumaric acid.
Jse: Psychomotor stimulant.
TOLATE TABS. (Major) Benztropine 1 mg. or 2 ng./Tab. Bot. 100s, 1000s.
Jse: Parkinsonism.
TRIM. (Lemmon) Sulfamethoxazole 400 mg., trimethoprim 80 mg./Tab. Bot. 100s, 500s. Unit Dose 100s.
Jse: Antibacterial.
TRIM D.S. (Lemmon) Sulfamethoxazole 800 mg., trimethoprim 160 mg./Tab. Bot. 100s, 500s. Unit Dose 100s.
Use: Anti-infective.
TRIM PEDIATRIC. (Lemmon) Sulfamethoxazole 200 mg., trimethoprim 40 mg./5 ml. Bot. pt.
Use: Anti-infective.
TRIM S.S.. (Lemmon) Sulfamethoxazole 400 mg., trimethoprim 800 mg./Tab. Bot. 100s.
Use: Anti-infective.
-TRIMOXAZOLE. B.A.N. Compounded preparations of trimethoprim and sulfamethoxazole in the proportions of 1 part to 5 parts.
Use: Antibacterial.
See: Bactrim Prods (Roche)
Septra (Burroughs Wellcome)
Septrin
COTTON, PURIFIED, U.S.P. XXI.
Use: Surgical aid.
COTTONSEED OIL, N.F. XVI.
Use: Pharm. aid, solvent, oleaginous vehicle.
TYLENOL CHEWABLE COLD TABLET. (McNeil Prods) Acetaminophen 80 mg., phenylpropanolamine HCl 3.125 mg., chlorpheniramine maleate 0.5 mg./Tab. Bot. 24s.
Use: Analgesic, antipyretic, relief of cold and flu symptoms.
TYLENOL CHILDREN'S LIQUID COLD FORMULA. (McNeil Prods) Acetaminophen 160 mg., chlorpheniramine maleate 1 mg., pseudoephedrine HCl 15 mg./5 ml. Bot. 4 oz.
Use: Analgesic, antipyretic, decongestant.

COTYLENOL COLD FORMULA CAPSULES. (McNeil Prods) Acetaminophen 325 mg., chlorpheniramine maleate 2 mg., pseudoephedrine HCl 30 mg., dextromethorphan HBr 15 mg./Cap. Box. 20s. Bot. 40s.
Use: Multisymptom cold and cough formula.
COTYLENOL COLD FORMULA TABLETS. (McNeil Prods) Chlorpheniramine maleate 2 mg., dextromethorphan HBr 15 mg., pseudoephedrine HCl 30 mg., acetaminophen 325 mg./Tab. Vial 10s; Box 24s; Bot. 50s, 100s.
Use: Multisymptom cough and cold formula.
COTYLENOL LIQUID COLD FORMULA. (McNeil Prods) Acetaminophen 650 mg., chlorpheniramine maleate 4 mg., pseudoephedrine HCl 60 mg., dextromethorphan HCl 30 mg./30 ml. w/alcohol 7.5% Bot. 5 oz.
Use: Multisymptom cough and cold formula.
COUGH EEZ. (Kay) Dextromethorphan 15 mg., benzocaine 3 mg./Cap. Bot.
Use: Cough & minor sore throat.
COUGH WAFERS. (Wolins) Benzocaine ⅛ gr., plant ext. licorice 1/16 gr., anise oil q.s., eucalyptol q.s., menthol q.s./Tab. Bot. 1000s.
COUMADIN. (Du Pont) Warfarin sodium crystalline. 2 mg., 2.5 mg., 5 mg., 7.5 mg., 10 mg./Tab. Bot. 1000s. Hospital pack Box. 100s. **Inj.** 50 mg./Vial w/diluent sod. chloride, thimerosal, and sod. hydroxide to adjust pH. Box 6s.
Use: Anticoagulant.
COUMAPHOS. B.A.N. 0-3-Chloro-4-methylcoumarin-7-y100-diethylphosphorothioate.
Use: Insecticide, veterinary medicine.
See: Asuntol
COUMARIN.
Use: Pharmaceutic aid.
• **COUMERMYCIN.** USAN. Antibiotic derived from *Streptomyces rishiriensis.*
Use: Antibiotic.
• **COUMERMYCIN SODIUM.** USAN.
Use: Antibiotic.
COUNTERPAIN RUB. (Squibb) Methyl salicylate, eugenol, menthol. Oint. Tube 1 oz.
Use: External analgesic.
COVAP. (Blue Line) Pentaerythritol tetranitrate 15 mg., sod. butabarbital 20 mg./Tab. Bot. 100s, 1000s.
Use: Angina pectoris.
COVERMARK. (O'Leary) Neutral cream, hypoallergenic, opaque, greaseless. Jars 1 oz., 3.25 oz., avail. in eight shades.
Use: Conceals birthmarks and skin discolorations.
COVERMARK CREAM ROUGE. (O'Leary) Same basic formulation as Covermark: Regular and waterproof formulas. Shades: Blonde, medium and brunette. Bot. Waterproof ¾ oz., 2¾ oz. Regular 1.24 oz., 4 oz.
Use: To conceal birthmarks and skin discolorations.
COVICONE CREAM. (Abbott) Silicone, nitrocellulose, castor oil suspended in vanishing cream base. Tube 1 oz.
Use: Topically for protecting skin from irritation.

CO-XAN SYRUP. (Central) Theophylline anhydrous 150 mg., ephedrine HCl 25 mg., Guaifenesin 100 mg., codeine phosphate 15 mg., alcohol 10%/15 ml. Bot. 1 pt.
Use: Bronchial spasms.

COYDEN 25. Clopidol, B.A.N.

COZ OINTMENT. (Sentinel) Zinc oxide, cod liver oil, menthol, phenol. Jar 2 oz., 1 lb.
Use: Skin irritation.

CP. (Western Research) Phenylpropanolamine 75 mg., caffeine 140 mg./Cap. Bot. 1000s.
Use: Anorectic-decongestant.

CP-2. (Century) Aspirin 4 gr., phenacetin 2 gr., caffeine 0.25 gr./Tab. Bot. 100s, 1000s, 5000s.

C.P.C. PLUS. (Coastal) Phenylephrine HCl 5 mg., phenylpropanolamine HC1 25 mg., chlorpheniramine maleate 2 mg., vit. C 60 mg./Tab. Bot. 50s, 100s, 500s.
Use: Antihistaminic and decongestant.

CPI HEMORRHOIDAL SUPPS. (Century) Bismuth subgallate, bismuth oxyiodide, bismuth resorcin comp., balsam Peru, benzocaine, Zn oxide, boric acid. 12s.
Use: Antihemorrhoidal.

CPLEX. (Arcum) Vit. B-1 10 mg., B-2 10 mg., B-6 5 mg., B-12 10 mcg., niacinamide 100 mg., calcium pantothenate 25 mg., Vit. C 150 mg., liver 50 mg., dried yeast 50 mg./Cap. Bot. 100s, 1000s.
Use: Dietary supplement.

C.P.M. TABLETS. (Goldline)
Chlorpheniramine 4 mg./Tab. Bot. 1000s.
Use: Antihistaminic.

CREATININE REAGENT STRIPS.
(Ames) Seralyzer reagent strips. Bot. 25s.
Use: A quantitative strip test for creatinine in serum or plasma.

CREMACOAT 1. (Vicks) Dextromethorphan HBr 30 mg./15 ml. w/alcohol 10%. Bot. 3 oz., 6 oz.
Use: Cough suppressant.

CREMACOAT 2. (Vicks) Guaifenesin 200 mg./15 ml. w/alcohol 10%. Bot. 3 oz., 6 oz.
Use: Expectorant.

CREMACOAT 3. (Vicks) Dextromethorphan HBr 20 mg., phenylpropanolamine HCl 37.5 mg., guaifenesin 200 mg./15 ml. w/alcohol 10%. Bot. 3 oz., 6 oz.
Use: Cough suppressant, nasal decongestant, expectorant.

CREMACOAT 4. (Vicks) Dextromethorphan HBr 20 mg., phenylpropanolamine HCl 37.5 mg., doxylamine succinate 7.5 mg./15 ml. Bot. 3 oz, 6 oz.
Use: Cough suppressant, nasal decongestant, antihistaminic.

CREMAGOL. (Cremagol) Emulsion of liq. petrolatum, agar agar, acacia, glycerin. Bot. 14 oz. Also w/cascara 11 gr./oz. Bot. 14 oz., also w/phenolphthalein 2 gr./oz. Bot. 14 oz.
Use: Laxative.

CREMESONE. (Dalin) Hydrocortisone alcohol 5 mg./Gm. Tube 1 oz.
Use: Inflammatory skin diseases or allergic dermatitis.

CREOMULSION COUGH MEDICINE. (Creomulsior Beechwood creosote, cascara, ipecac, menthol, white pine, wild cherry w/alcohol. For Adults. Bo & 8 fl. oz.
Use: Coughs and bronchial irritations due to cold

CREOMULSIN FOR CHILDREN. (Creomulsion) Beechwood creosote, cascara, ipecac, menthol, white pine, wild cherry w/alcohol. For Children. B 4 fl. oz., 8 fl. oz.
Use: Coughs and bronchial irritations due to cold

CREOSANT COUGH SYRUP. (DeWitt) Ammonium chloride, beechwood creosote, menthol, w/alcoh 3%. Bot. 4 oz.
Use: Cough relief.

CREOSOTE. Wood creosote, creosote, beechwood creosote.
W/Ipecac, menthol, licorice, white pine, wild cherry, cascara, Vitamin C.
See: Creozets, Loz. (Creomulsion)

CREOSOTE CARBONATE.

CREOTERP. (Jenkins) Terpin hydrate 2 gr., potassi iodide 1/8 gr., creosote 1/10 min., eucalyptol 1/10 mir Tab. Bot. 1000s.
Use: Antitussive.

CREO-TERPIN. (Denver) Creosote 0.12 ml., s glycerophosphate 259 mg., terpin hydrate 130 mg chloroform 0.06 ml., alcohol 25%/30 ml. Bot. 3 o 6 oz.
Use: Antitussive.

■ **CRESCORMON.** (Kabi) Somatotropin 4 I.U./Vial. I.M. administration.
Use: Long-term therapy for children who have grow failure secondary to somatropin deficiency.
Note: Crescormon will be available only for patients who qualify for treatment; full documentation for prospective patients to be submitted to Kabi Group Inc. for approval.

CRESCORMON. (Pharmacia) Somatropin 4 I.U./Vial + 2 ml. NaCl injection.
Use: Long term treatment of children with growth failure secondary to somatropin deficiency.

• **CRESOL,** N.F. XVI. Mixture of 3 isomeric cresols. Phenol, methyl cresol.
Use: Antiseptic & disinfectant.

CRESOL PREPARATIONS.
Use: Antibacterial (inanimate objects).
See: Cresol, Sol. (Various Mfr.)
Cresylone, Liq. (Parke-Davis)
Saponated Cresol Sol.

CRESTABOLIC. (Nutrition) Protein anabolic steroid, methandriol dipropionate 50 mg./ml. w/benzyl alcohol 5% in sesame oil. Vial 10 cc.
Use: Treatment of conditions where tissue building action is desired.

m-CRESYL-ACETATE.
See: Cresylate, Liq. (Recsei)

CRESYLATE. (Recsei) M-cresyl-acetate. Otic sol. 0 oz. dropper bot., Pts.
Use: Otomycosis due to *Aspergillus niger* & *furunculosis*.

ESYLIC ACID. Same as Cresol.

ITICARE HN. (Mead Johnson) High nitrogen elemental diet. Protein 14%, fat 3%, carbohydrate 83%. Bot. 8 oz.
Use: Complete, high-quality elemental nutrition.

OFERRIN. (Fellows) Iron peptonate 50 mg., liver inj. 2.5 mcg., Vit. B-12 12.5 mcg., lidocaine HCl 1%, phenol 0.5%, Na citrate 0.125%, Na bisulfite 0.009%/ml. Vial 10 ml., 30 ml.
Use: Iron deficiency anemia.

ROFILCON A. USAN
Use: Contact lens material.

ROMITRILE SODIUM. USAN.
Use: Antihistaminic.

ROMOGLYCIC ACID. B.A.N. 1,3-Di-(2-car-boxy-4-oxochromen-5-yloxy)propan-2-ol.
Use: Treatment of allergic airway obstruction.

CROMOLYN SODIUM, U.S.P. XXI. For Inhalation, Inhalation Nasal Sol. U.S.P. XXI. Disodium 5,5'-[(2-hydroxytrimethylene)dioxy]bis[4-oxo-4H-1-benzopyran-2-carboxylate].
Use: Treatment of allergic airway obstruction.
See: Intal, Cap. (Fisons)
Opticrom, Soln. (Fisons)

-RON. (Rowell) Ascorbic acid 100 mg., ferrous fumarate 200 mg./Tab. Bot. 100s, 1000s.
Use: Anemias.

-RON F.A. (Rowell) Ferrous fumarate 200 mg., Vit. C 600 mg., folic acid 0.5 mg./Tab. Bot. 100s.
Use: Iron-deficiency and megaloblastic anemias of pregnancy.

-RON FORTE. (Rowell) Ferrous fumarate 200 mg., ascorbic acid 600 mg./Tab. Bot. 100s, 1000s.
Use: Iron deficiency anemia.

-RON FRECKLES. (Rowell) Vitamin C 50 mg., ferrous fumarate 100 mg./Chewable Tab. Bot. 100s,
Use: Iron deficiency in children.

RONETAL.
See: Disulfiram

ROPROPAMIDE. B.A.N. NN-Dimethyl-2-(N-propylcrotonamido)butyramide.
Use: Respiratory stimulant.

ROSE HIPS. (Robinson) 100 mg., 250 mg., 500 mg./Tab. Bot. 100s, 250s, 1000s.

CROSCARMELLOSE SODIUM, N.F. XVI.
Use: Tablet disintegrant.

CROSPOVIDONE, N.F. XVI.
Use: Pharmaceutic aid (tablet excipient).

ROSS ASPIRIN. (Cross) Aspirin 325 mg./Tab. Sugar, salt and lactose free. Bot. 100s, 1000s
Use: Analgesic, antipyretic, anti-inflammatory.

ROTALINE ANTIVENIN, POLYVALENT. Antivenin Crotalidae Polyvalent, U.S.P. XXI. North and South American Antisnakebite serum.
Use: Passive immunizing agent.

• **CROTAMITON,** U.S.P. XXI. Cream, U.S.P. XXI. N-Crotonyl-N-ethyl-o-toluidine.
Use: Antipruritic.
See: Eurax, Cream, Lot. (Geigy)

CROTETHAMIDE. B.A.N. 2-(N-Ethylcrotonamido)-NN-dimethylbutyramide.
Use: Respiratory stimulant.

CRPA, CRPA LATEX TEST. (Laboratory Diagnostics) CRPA, 1 ml.—CRP Positest Control, 0.5 ml. CRPA Latex Test Kit.
Use: Rapid latex agglutination test for the qualitative determination of C reactive protein.

CRUDE TUBERCULIN.
See: Tuberculin, Old, Vial (Parke-Davis)

CRUEX CREAM. (Pharmacraft) Total undecylenate 20% as undecylenic acid and zinc undecylenate. Tube 1.5 oz.
Use: Antifungal, jock itch.

CRUEX SPRAY POWDER. (Pharmacraft) Total undecylenate 19% as undecylenic acid and zinc undecylenate. Aerosol can 1.8 oz., 3.5 oz., 5.5 oz.,
Use: Antifungal, jock itch.

CRUEX SQUEEZE POWDER. (Pharmacraft) Calcium undecylenate 10%. Plastic squeeze Bot. 1.5 oz.
Use: Antifungal, jock itch.

• **CRUFOMATE.** USAN. 4-tert-Butyl-2-chlorophenyl methyl methylphosphoramidate.
Use: Insecticide; anthelmintic, veterinary medicine.
See: Ruelene.

CRYPTENAMINE ACETATE & TANNATE. Esters of alkaloids of veratrum viride.

CRYPTOLIN. (Hoechst) Gonadorelin in nasal spray.
Use: Cryptorchism treatment.

CRYSPEN-400. (Knight) Buffered penicillin G potassium 400,000 u./Tab. Bot. 100s.
Use: Anti-infective.

CRYSTALLINE TRYPSIN. Highly purified prep. of enzyme as derived from mammalian pancreas glands.
See: Tryptar, Inj. (Armour)

CRYSTALLOSE. (Jamieson-McKames) Saccharin sodium. Crystals, Box 0.25 oz., ¾ oz. Liquid, plas. squeeze bot. ¾ oz., 2 oz.
Use: Sweetening agent.

CRYSTAL VIOLET.
See: Methylrosaniline Chloride, U.S.P.

CRYSTAMINE. (Dunhall) Cyanocobalamin 1,000 mcg./ml. Vial 10 ml, or 30 ml.
Use: Vitamin B-12 deficiency.

CRYSTI-12. (Hauck) Vitamin B-12 1000 mcg./ml. Vial 10 ml., 30 ml.
Use: B-12 parenteral.

CRYSTICILLIN 300 A.S. (Squibb) Sterile procaine penicillin G suspension U.S.P. 300,000 u./ml. w/lecithin, povidone, sod. citrate, sod. formaldehyde sulfoxylate, sod. carboxymethylcellulose, methylparaben & propylparaben. Vial 10 cc.
Use: Bactericidal agent against penicillin-sensitive microorganisms during the stage of active multiplication.

CRYSTICILLIN 600 A.S. (Squibb) Sterile procaine penicillin G suspension 600,000 u./1.2 cc. w/lecithin, phenol, povidone, sod. citrate, sod. carboxymethylcellulose, sod. formaldehyde sufoxylate, methylparaben, & propylparaben. Vial 12 ml.

Use: Bactericidal agent against penicillin-sensitive microorganisms during the stage of active multiplication.

CRYSTODIGIN TABLETS. (Lilly) Crystalline digitoxin **0.05 mg.**/Tab. Bot. 100s; **0.1 mg.**/Tab. Bot. 100s, 5000s. Blister pkg. 10 × 10s; 0.15 mg./Tab. Bot. 100s, 500s, **0.2 mg.**/Tab. Bot. 100s, 500s.
Use: Congestive heart failure.

CRYSTOGRAFIN. Meglumine diatrizoate.
Use: Contrast medium.

C-SPAN. (Edwards) Ascorbic acid 500 mg./Timed Release Cap. Bot. 100s.
Use: Treatment of Vit. C deficiency.

C SPERIDIN. (Marlyn) Bioflavanoids with Vitamin C. Bot. 100s, 1000s.

C.S.R. UNIT. Unit represents the amount of veratrum viride extract per Kg. of body weight which will just abolish the pressor response to the carotid sinus reflex resulting from occlusion of the carotid arteries in dogs.
See: Cryptenamine

C-SYRUP-500. (Ortega) Ascorbic acid 500 mg./5 ml. Bot. pt., gal.

CTAB.
See: Cetyl Trimethyl Ammonium Bromide

CTD COMPLEX TABLETS. (Image) Vitamin C. Bot. 100s.
Use: Supplement.

C-TUSSIN. (Century) Codeine phosphate 10 mg., phenylpropanolamine HCl 18.72 mg., guaifenesin 100 mg./5 ml. w/alcohol 7.5%. Bot. 10 cc., gal.
Use: Expectorant.

CULMINAL. (Culminal) Benzocaine 3% in water miscible ointment base. Tube 1 oz.
Use: Prevention of premature ejaculation.

CUMETHAROL. B.A.N. 4,4′-Dihydroxy-3,3′-(2-methoxyethylidene)dicoumarin.
Use: Anticoagulant.
See: Dicumoxane

CUPREX. (Beecham Products) Tetrahydronaphthalene, copper oleate. Bot. 3 oz., 1 pt.
Use: Topically, pediculocide.

• **CUPRIC ACETATE Cu 64.** USAN.
Use: Radioactive agent.

• **CUPRIC CHLORIDE,** U.S.P. XXI., Inj., U.S.P. XXI.
Use: Copper deficiency treatment.
See: Coppertrace, Inj. (Armour)

• **CUPRIC SULFATE,** U.S.P. XXI. Inj., U.S.P. XXI.
Use: Antidote to phosphorus.
W/Zinc sulfate & camphor.
See: Dalibour, Pow. (Doak)

CUPRIMINE. (Merck Sharp & Dohme) Penicillamine 125 mg., 250 mg./Cap. Bot. 100s.
Use: Wilson's disease, cystinuria, rheumatoid arthritis.

• **CUPRIMYXIN.** USAN.
Use: Antibacterial.

CURARE.
Use: Muscle relaxant.
See: d-Tubocurarine Salts (Various Mfr.)

CURARE ANTAGONIST.
See: Neostigmine Methylsulfate Inj. (Various Mfr.)
Tensilon, Amp. (Roche)

CURBAN. (Pasadena Research) Dextroamphetamine sulfate 10, 15 mg./Tab. Bot. 100s, 1000s.
Use: Central stimulant.

CURRAL.
See: Diallyl Barbituric Acid, Tab. (Various Mfr.)

CURRETAB. (Reid-Provident) Medroxyprogesterone acetate 10 mg./Tab. Bot. 50s.
Use: Progestin.

CUTAR. (Summers) Coal tar solution 7.5% w/Liquid petrolatum, isopropyl myristate, acetylated lanolin, lanolin alcohols extract. Bot. 6 oz.
Use: Bath oil emulsion.

CUTEMOL EMOLLIENT CREAM. (Summers) Allantoin 0.2%, hypoallergenic lanolin fractions, with additional emollient agents and a nonionic emulsifier in a high-aqueous content water-in-cream base. Tube 2 oz., Bath Oil 6 oz.
Use: Dermatologic.

CUTICURA ACNE CREAM. (Jeffrey Martin) Benzoyl peroxide 5%, allantoin, phenoxyethanol, alcohol 1%.
Use: Dermatologic, acne.

CUTICURA ANTIBACTERIAL MEDICATED SOAP. (Jeffrey Martin) Triclocarban 1%. Bars 3.25 oz., 5 oz.
Use: Cleaning combination for the skin.

CUTICURA MEDICATED SHAMPOO. (Jeffrey Martin) Sodium lauryl sulfate, sodium stearate, salicylic acid, protein, sulfur. Tube 3 oz.
Use: Antidandruff shampoo.

CUTICURA MEDICATED SOAP. (Jeffrey Martin) Triclocarban 1%, petrolatum, emollients. Bars 3.5 oz. 5.5 oz.
Use: Antibacterial skin care.

CUTICURA OINTMENT. (Jeffrey Martin) Beeswax synthetic, isopropyl palmitate, mineral wax, mineral oil, oxyquinoline, pine oil phenol, petrolatum, precipitated sulfur, rose geranium oil. Tin ¾ oz., 1¾ oz. Jar. 4.25 oz.
Use: Skin care.

CUTTER INSECT REPELLENT. (Miles) N,N-Diethyl-meta-toluamide 28.5%, other isomers 1.5% Vial 1 oz. Foam, Can 2 oz.; Spray 7 oz., 14 oz. aerosol can; Assortment Pack; First Aid Kits, Trial Pack, 6s; Marine Pack, 3s; Camp Pack, 4s. Pocket Pack, Travel Pack.
Use: Insect repellent.

C VITAMIN.
See: Ascorbic Acid, Prep.

C.V.P. CAPSULES. (Armour) Bioflavonoids 100 mg./Cap Bot. 100s.
Use: Vitamin supplement.

CYACETAZIDE. B.A.N. Cyanoacetohydrazide.
Use: Anthelmintic, veterinary medicine.

CYADE-GEL. (Kenyon) Adenosine-5-monophosphate 100 mg., Vit. B-12 100 mcg./cc. Vial 10 cc.

CYANIDE ANTIDOTE PACKAGE. (Lilly) 2 Amp. (300 mg./10 ml.) sodium nitrite; 2 Amp. (12.5 Gm./50 ml.) w/sodium thiosulfate; 12 aspirols amyl nitrite 5

in./Pkg. Check exact dosage before dministration.
se: Treatment of cyanide poisoning.
NOCOB. (Paddock) Vit. B-12 1000 mcg./cc. Bot. 00 cc. Vials 10 cc.
se: Vitamin B-12 deficiency.
ANOCOBALAMIN, U.S.P. XXI. Inj. U.S.P. XXI.α- ,6-Dimethyl-benzimidazol-1-yl)cobamide cyanide. itamin B-12.
se: Vitamin B-12.
ee: Cobastab
Cytacon
Cytamen
Redisol, Inj., Tab. (Merck Sharp & Dohme)
ANOCOBALAMIN CO 57, USP XXI. Cap., Oral oln., U.S.P. XXI.
se: Diagnostic aid (pernicious anemia)
ANOCOBALAMIN CO 60, U.S.P. XXI. Cap., Oral oln., U.S.P. XXI.
se: Diagnostic aid (pernicious anemia).
NOJECT 10 AND 30. (Mayrand) Vit. B-12 1000 cg./ml. Vial 10 ml.
NOVER. (Research Supplies) Cyanocobalamin 00 mcg., liver inj. 10 mcg., folic acid 10 mg./cc. yo-layer vials 10 cc. with 10 cc. vials of diluent.
se: Treatment of pernicious anemia.
CLACILLIN, U.S.P. XXI. For Oral Susp., Tab., .S.P. XXI. 6-(1-Aminocyclohexanecarbox- mide)-3,3-dimethyl-7-oxo-4-thia-1-azabicyclo-[3.2.0] eptane-2-carboxylic acid.
se: Antibacterial.
ee: Cyclapen-W, Liq., Tab. (Wyeth)
LAMATE SODIUM. Cyclohexanesulfamate ihydrate salt.
YCLAMIC ACID. USAN. N-Cyclohexylsulfamic acid. lexamic Acid. Cyclohexanesulfamic acid. Currently anned in U.S.
Jse: Sweetening agent.
CLAN CAPS. (Major) Cyclandelate 200 mg./Cap. ot. 250s.
se: Vasodilator.
CLANDELATE. 3,3,5-Trimethylcyclohexyl mande- ate.
Jse: Vasodilator.
ee: Cyclan, Cap. (Major)
Cyclospasmol, Tab., Cap. (Ives)
CLANDELATE. B.A.N. 3,3,5-Trimethylcyclohexyl nandelate.
Jse: Treatment of vascular disorders.
ee: Cyclospasmol
CLAPEN-W. (Wyeth) Cyclacillin 250 mg. or 500 ng./Tab. Bot. 100s.
Jse: Antibiotic.
CLAPEN-W FOR ORAL SUSPENSION. (Wyeth) Cy- lacillin 125 mg./5 ml. or 250 mg./5 ml. Bot. to nake 100 ml., 150 ml., 200 ml.
Jse: Antibiotic.
CLARBAMATE. B.A.N. 1,1-Di(phenylcarbamoyl- xymethyl)cyclopentane.
Jse: Muscle relaxant; tranquilizer.
ee: Casmalon

• **CYCLAZOCINE.** USAN. 3-(Cyclopropylmethyl)-1,2,3,- 4,5,6-hexahydro-6, 11-dimethyl-2,6-methano-3- benzazocin-8-ol. This product is under study.
Use: Analgesic.
• **CYCLINDOLE.** USAN.
Use: Antidepressant.
• **CYCLIRAMINE MALEATE.** USAN.
Use: Antihistaminic.
• **CYCLIZINE,** U.S.P. XXI. Piperazine, 1-(diphenylme- thyl)-4-methyl-1-(Diphenylmethyl)-4-methyl pipera- zine.
Use: Antihistamine.
See: Marzine (hydrochloride)
Valoid (hydrochloride or lactate)
• **CYCLIZINE HYDROCHLORIDE,** U.S.P. XXI. Tab. U.S.P. XXI. 1-Diphenylmethyl-4-methylpiperazine. N- Benzhydryl-N-methyl piperazine.
Piperazine, 1-(diphenylmethyl)-4- methyl-,monohydrochloride.
Use: Antiemetic.
See: Marezine Hydrochloride and lactate, Preps. (Burroughs Wellcome)
W/Ergotamine tartrate, caffeine.
See: Migral, Tab. (Burroughs Wellcome)
• **CYCLIZINE LACTATE INJECTION,** U.S.P. XXI. A sterile soln. of cyclizine lactate in water for injection.
Use: Antihistamine, antiemetic.
CYCLOBARBITAL. 5-(1-Cyclohexen-1-yl)-5-ethylbar- bituric acid.
Use: Central depressant.
CYCLOBARBITAL CALCIUM. Cyclobarbitone, namuron, palinum, cyclobarbital Cal. 5-(1-Cyclohex- enyl)-5-Ethylbarbituric Acid.
Use: Hypnotic & sedative w/intermediate action.
CYCLOBARBITONE. B.A.N. 5-(Cyclohex-1-enyl)-5- ethylbarbituric acid.
Use: Hypnotic; sedative.
See: Phanodorm
Rapidal (calcium salt)
CYCLO-BELL. (Moore Kirk) Scopolamine HBr 0.0065 mg., hyoscyamine HBr 0.1037 mg., atropine sulfate 0.0194 mg., Triple Barb 5.4 mg., each of phenobarbital sodium, butabarbital sodium, pentobarbital sodium, 16.2 mg./Tab. Bot. 100s, 1000s.
Use: Antispasmodic and sedative.
• **CYCLOBENDAZOLE.** USAN.
Use: Anthelmintic.
CYCLOBENZAPRINE HCl. U.S.P. XXI. Tab., U.S.P. XXI. 5-(3-Dimethylamino-propylidene)-dibenzo(a.e.)- cycloheptatriene HCl.
Use: Relief of muscle spasm associated with acute, painful musculoskeletal conditions.
See: Flexeril, Tab. (Merck Sharp & Dohme)
CYCLOGEN. (Central) Dicyclomine HCl 10 mg. sodium Cl 0.9%, chlorobutanol hydrate 0.5%. Vial 10 ml.
Box 12's.
Use: Antispasmotic.

CYCLOCORT. (Lederle) Amcinonide in Aquatain hydrophilic base 0.1%. Tubes 15 Gm., 30 Gm., 60 Gm.
Use: Topical corticosteroid.

CYCLOCUMAROL. 3,4-Dihydro-2-methoxy-2-methyl-4-phenyl-2H,5H-pyrano[3,2c][1]benzopyran-5-one.
Use: Anticoagulant.

CYCLOCOUMAROL. B.A.N. 3,4-Dihydro-2-methoxy-2-methyl-4-phenylpyrano[3,2-c]coumarin.
Use: Anticoagulant.
See: Cumopyran

CYCLOFENIL. B.A.N. 4,4′-Diacetoxybenzhydrylidenecyclohexane.
Use: Treatment of infertility.
See: Ondonid
Sexovid

• **CYCLOFILCON A.** USAN.
Use: Contact lens material.

CYCLOGUANIL EMBONATE. B.A.N. 4,6-Diamino-1-(4-chlorophenyl)-1,2-dihydro-2,2-dimethyl-1,3,5-triazine compound with 4,4′-methylenedi-(3-hydroxy-2-naphthoic acid) (2:1).
Use: Antimalarial.

• **CYCLOGUANIL PAMOATE.** USAN. 4,6-Diamino-1-(p-chlorophenyl)-1,2-dihydro-2,2-dimethyl-s-triazine compound (2:1) with 4,4′-methylenebis-[3-hydroxy-2-naphthoic acid].
Use: Antimalarial.

CYCLOGYL. (Alcon) Cyclopentolate HCl. Sol. 0.5%, 1% & 2%. Droptainer 2 ml., 5 ml., 15 ml.
Use: Cycloplegic & mydriatic.

CYCLOHEPTENYLETHYL BARBITURIC ACID. Heptabarbital.

CYCLOHEXANE, 1,2,3,4,6,6-HEXACHLORO-. Benzene Hexachloride, Gamma.

• **CYCLOHEXIMIDE.** USAN.
Use: Antipsoriatic.

1-(CYCLOHEXYLAMINO)-2-PROPANOL BENZOATE (ESTER) HYDROCHLORIDE.
See: Hexylcaine Hydrochloride, U.S.P. XXI.

(3-CYCLOHEXYL-3-HYDROXY-3-PHENYLPROPYL)-TRIETHYLAMMONIUM CHLORIDE.
See: Tridihexethyl Chloride, U.S.P. XXI.

α-CYCLOHEXYL-α-PHENYL-1-PIPERIDINEPROPANOL HYDROCHLORIDE. Trihexyphenidyl Hydrochloride, U.S.P. XXI.

• **CYCLOMETHICONE,** N.F. XVI.

CYCLOMETHYCAINE. B.A.N. 3-(2-Methylpiperidino)-propyl 4-cyclohexyloxybenzoate.
Use: Local anesthetic.
See: Surfathesin sulfate

CYCLOMETHYCAINE AND METHAPYRILENE.
See: Surfadil Cream, Lot. (Lilly)

• **CYCLOMETHYCAINE SULFATE,** U.S.P. XXI. Creme, Jelly, Oint., Supp., U.S.P. XXI. 3-(2-Methylpiperidino) propyl p-(cyclohexyloxy) benzoate sulfate.
Use: Topical anesthesia.
See: Surfacaine, Prep. (Lilly)
W/Methapyrilene.
See: Surfadil, Cream, Lot. (Lilly)

CYCLOMETHYCAINE AND THENYLPYRAMINE.
See: Surfadil Cream, Lot. (Lilly)

CYCLOMINE. (Tunex) Dicyclomine HCl 10 mg./ml. Vial 10 cc.
Use: Antispasmodic.

CYCLOMYDRIL. (Alcon) Phenylephrine HCl 1%, cyclopentolate HCl 0.2% in a sterile ophthalmic solution. Bot. 7.5 ml. Droptainer 2 ml. & 5 ml.
Use: Mydriatic.

CYCLONIL. (Seatrace) Dicyclomine HCl 10 mg./ml. Vial 10 cc.

CYCLOPAL. 5-Allyl-5(2-cyclopenten-1-yl)-barbituric acid. Cyclopentenyl allylbarbituric acid.

CYCLOPAR. (Parke-Davis) Tetracycline HCl
250 mg. Cap. Bot. 100s, 1000s.
500 mg. Cap. Bot. 100s.
Use: Antibiotic.

CYCLOPENTAMINE. B.A.N. 1-Cyclopentyl-2-methylaminopropane.
Use: Vasoconstrictor.
See: Clopane (hydrochloride)

• **CYCLOPENTAMINE HYDROCHLORIDE,** U.S.P. XXI. Nasal Soln., U.S.P. XXI. N-a-Dimethylcyclopentaneethylamine HCl.
Use: Adrenergic (vasoconstrictor).
See: Clopane hydrochloride, nasal sol. (Dista)
W/Aludrine.
See: Aerolone Compound, Sol. (Lilly)
W/Chlorpheniramine.
See: Hista-Clopane, Pulvule (Lilly)

CYCLOPENTENYL - ALLYL - BARBITURIC ACID.
See: Cyclopal

• **CYCLOPENTHIAZIDE.** USAN. 6-Chloro-3-(cyclopentylmethyl)-3,4-dihydro-2H-1,2,4-benzothiadiazine-sulfonamide 1,1-dioxide.
Use: Diuretic, anti-hypertensive.
See: Navidrex

CYCLOPENTOLATE. B.A.N. 2-Dimethylaminoethyl (1-hydrocyclopentyl)-2-phenylacetate.
Use: Mydriatic.
See: Cyclogyl
Mydrilate (hydrochloride)

• **CYCLOPENTOLATE HYDROCHLORIDE,** U.S.P. XXI. Ophth. Soln., U.S.P. XXI. β-Di-methyl-aminoe (1-hydroxycyclopentyl) phenylacetate HCl. 2-(Dimethylamino)ethyl 1-Hydroxy-α-phenylcyclopentane-acetate HCl. Benzeneacetic acid, α-(1-hydroxy-cyclopentyl)-,2-(dimethylamino)ethyl ester, hydrochloride.
Use: Anticholinergic (ophthalmic).
See: Cyclogyl, Sol. (Alcon)
W/Phenylephrine HCl.
See: Cyclomydril, Sol. (Alcon)

α-CYCLOPENTYL-α-PHENYL-1-PIPERIDINEPROPANOL HYDROCHLORIDE.
See: Cycrimine Hydrochloride, U.S.P. XXI.

CYCLOPENTYLPROPIONATE.
See: Depo-Testosterone, Vial (Upjohn)

• **CYCLOPHENAZINE HYDROCHLORIDE.** USAN.
Use: Antipsychotic.

• **CYCLOPHOSPHAMIDE,** U.S.P. XXI. Inj., Tabs., U.S.P. XXI. N,N-bis(2-Chloroethyl)-tetrahydro-,2-oxide, monodydrate. 2 H-1,3,2-Oxazaphosphorin-amine. phordiamidic acid cyclic ester monohydra

2-[bis(2-Chloroethyl) amino] tetrahydro-2H-1,3,2-oxazaphosphorine-2-Oxide.
Use: Antineoplastic; Immunosuppressive.
See: Cytoxan, Tab., Vial (Bristol Oncology).
:YCLOPROPANE, U.S.P. XXI. Trimethylene.
Use: Inhalation anesthetic.
'CLOPYRRONIUM BROMIDE. (Robins) 1-Ethyl-3-pyrrolidyl a-phenylcyclo-pentane-acetate methobromide.
Use: Anticholinergic.
'CLORPHAN. (Roche) On trial.
Use: Morphine antagonist.
'CLOSERINE. B.A.N. D-4-Aminoisoxazolid-3-one.
Use: Antibiotic.
See: Seromycin
:YCLOSERINE, U.S.P. XXI. Caps., U.S.P. XXI. D-(+)-4-Amino-3-isoxazolidinone. 3-Isoxazolidinone, 4-amino-, (R)-. An antibiotic produced by *Streptomycin orchidaceus.* Oxamycin.
Use: Antibacterial (tuberculostatic).
See: Seromycin, Cap. (Lilly)
'CLOSPASMOL CAPSULES. (Ives) Cyclandelate. 200 mg. or 400 mg./Cap. **200 mg.:** Bot. 100s, 500s, 1000s. Clinipak. **400 mg.:** Bot. 100s, 500s. Clinipak.
Use: Vasodilator.
'CLOSPASMOL TABLETS. (Ives) Cyclandelate 100 mg./Tab. Bot. 100s, 500s.
Use: Vasodilator.
:YCLOSPORINE. USAN.
Use: Immunosuppressive.
See: Sandimmune, Inj., Oral Soln. (Sandoz)
'CLO-TAB. (Jenkins) Butabarbital sod. 5.4 mg., pentobarbital sod. 5.4 mg., phenobarbital sod. 5.4 mg., hyoscyamine HBr 0.1037 mg., scopolamine HBr 0.0065 mg., atropine sulfate 0.0194 mg./Tab. Bot. 1000s.
:YCLOTHIAZIDE, U.S.P. XXI. Tabs., U.S.P. XXI. 6-Chloro-3-(2-norbornenyl-5)-7-sulfamyl-3,4-dihydro-1,2,4-benzothiadiazine-1, 1-dioxide,-6-Chloro-3,4-dihydro-3-(5-norbornen-2-yl)-2H-1,2,4-benzothiadiazine-7-sulfonamide-1,-1-Dioxide. Bot. 100s, 1000s.
Use: Diuretic.
See: Anhydron, Tab. (Lilly)
Fluidil, Tab. (Adria)
'COSTAT HCl. Robenidine, B.A.N.
'CRIMINE. B.A.N. 1-Cyclopentyl-1-phenyl-3-piperidinopropan-1-ol.
Use: Treatment of the parkinsonian syndrome.
'CRIMINE HYDROCHLORIDE. a-Cyclopentyl-a-phenyl-1-piperidine propanol HCl.
See: Pagitane Hydrochloride, Tab. (Lilly)
'DONOL MASSAGE LOTION. (Gordon) Isopropyl alcohol 14%, methyl salicylate, benzalkonium chloride. Bot. 4 oz., gal.
Use: Massage lotion for feet.
CYHEPTAMIDE. USAN.
Use: Anticonvulsant.
'LERT CHEWABLE TABLETS. (Abbott) Pemoline 37.5 mg./Tab. Bot. 100s.
Use: Childhood attention-deficit syndrome (hyperkinetic syndrome)
CYLERT TABLETS. (Abbott) Pemoline 18.75, 37.5, 75 mg./Tab. Bot. 100s.
Use: Childhood attention-defecit syndrome (hyperkinetic syndrome).
p-CYMEN-3-OL. Thymol, N.F. XVI.
CYNOBAL. (Arcum) Cyanocobalamin injection Vial 100 mcg./cc. 30 cc. 1000/mcg./cc. 10 cc. 30 cc.
CYOMIN. (Forest) Cyanocobalamin 1000 mcg./ml. Vial 30 ml.
• **CYPENAMINE HCL.** USAN. 2-Phenylcyclopentylamine Hydrochloride.
Use: Antidepressant.
• **CYPOTHRIN.** USAN.
Use: Insecticide.
• **CYPRAZEPAM.** USAN.
Use: Sedative.
CYPRENORPHINE. B.A.N. N-Cyclopropylmethyl-7,8-dihydro-7α-(1-hydroxy-1-methylethyl)-O^6-methyl-6,14-endoethenonormorphine.
Use: Narcotic antagonist.
CYPROHEPTADINE. B.A.N. 4-(1,2:5,6-Dibenzocycloheptatrienylidene)-1-methylpiperidine.
Use: Antihistamine.
See: Periactin, Tab., Syrup (Merck Sharp & Dohme).
• **CYPROHEPTADINE HYDROCHLORIDE,** U.S.P. XXI. Syrup, Tabs., U.S.P. XXI. 4-(5H-Dibenzo-[a,d]cyclohepten-5-ylidene)-1-methylpiperidene Hydrochloride. 1-Methyl-4-(5-dibenzo-[a,e]cycloheptatrienylidene) piperidine HCl monohydrate.
Use: Antihistaminic; antipruritic.
See: Periactin, Tab., Syr. (Merck Sharp & Dohme)
• **CYPROLIDOL HYDROCHLORIDE.** USAN. Diphenyl (2-(4-pyridyl)cyclo-propyl)-methanol hydrochloride.
Use: Psychotherapeutic drug.
• **CYPROQUINATE.** USAN.
Use: Coccidiostat (for poultry)
CYPROTERONE. B.A.N. 6-Chloro-17α-hydroxy-1α,2α-methylenepregna-4,6-diene-3,20-dione.
Use: Anti-androgen.
• **CYPROTERONE ACETATE.** USAN. 6-Chloro-17-hydroxy-1α-2α-methylenepregna-4,6-diene-3, 20-dione acetate.
Use: Anti-androgen.
• **CYPROXIMIDE.** USAN.
Use: Antidepressant.
CYREN A.
See: Diethylstilbestrol Prep. (Various Mfr.)
CYRIMINE HCl. 1-Phenyl-1-cyclopentyl-3-piperidino-1-propanol HCl.
Use: Antispasmodic.
See: Pagitane HCl, Tab. (Lilly)
CYSTAMIN.
See: Methenamine, Tab. (Various Mfr.)
CYSTAMINE. (Tennessee) Methenamine 2 gr., phenyl salicylate 0.5 gr., phenazopyridine HCl 10 mg., benzoic acid 1/8 gr., hyoscyamine sulfate 1/2000 gr., atropine sulfate 1/2000 gr./S.C. Tab. Bot. 100s, 1000s.
Use: Urinary tract infections.
CYSTEX. (CooperVision) Methenamine, salicylamide, sodium salicylate, benzoic acid/Tab. Bot. 40s, 100s.

Use: Antibacterial and analgesic for relief of symptoms of bladder and kidney irritation.

• **CYSTINE.** USAN. An essential amino acid. Delta—Bot. 100 Gm.; Mann—Bot. 25 Gm.; Abbott—50 mg./ml. HCl salt solution.
Use: Amino acid replacement therapy, an additive for infants on TPN.

• **CYSTEINE HCL,** U.S.P. XXI. Lotion, U.S.P. XXI. L-Cysteine hydrochloride monohydrate.
Use: Amino acid for replacement therapy.

CYSTISED (IMPROVED). (Jenkins) Atropine sulfate 0.03 mg., hyoscyamine 0.03 mg., gelsemium 6.1 mg., methenamine 40.8 mg., salol 18.1 mg., benzoic acid 4.5 mg., methylene blue 5.4 mg./Tab. Bot. 1000s.

CYSTITOL. (Vortech) Atropine sulfate 0.03 mg., hyoscyamine 0.03 mg., gelsemium 6.1 mg., methenamine 40.8 mg., salol 18.1 mg., benzoic acid 4.5 mg./Tab. Bot. 1000s.

CYSTO. (Freeport) Methenamine 40.8 mg., methylene blue 5.4 mg., phenyl salicylate 18.1 mg., atropine sulfate 0.03 mg., hyoscyamine 0.03 mg., benzoic acid 4.5 mg./Tab. Bot. 1000s.
Use: Cystitis, pyelitis, trigonitis in pregnancy, urethritis.

CYSTOGRAFIN. (Squibb) Meglumine diatrizoate 30%, bound iodine 14%, EDTA 0.04%. Bot. 100 cc. Box 10s. 300 cc. Box 10s.
Use: Retrograde cystourethrography.

CYSTOGRAFIN-DILUTE. (Squibb) Diatrizoate, meglumine 18% organically-bound iodine 85 mg./ml. Vial 300 ml, 500 ml.
Use: Contrast agent, retrograde cystourethrography.

CYSTOSOL. (Travenol) **Pre-diluted:** sorbitol 2.5 Gm., mannitol 0.5 Gm., hexitols 3%/100 ml. Bot. 1500 ml. **Conc.:** sorbitol 50 Gm., mannitol 10 Gm., hexitols 60%/100 ml. Bot. 150 ml., 500 ml.

CYSTO-SPAZ. (Webcon) l-Hyoscyamine 0.15 mg./Tab. Bot. 100s.
Use: Antispasmodic.

CYSTO-SPAZ-M. (Webcon) Hyoscyamine sulfate 375 mcg./Cap. Bot. 100s.

CYSTREA. (Moore Kirk) Methenamine 2 gr., phenyl salicylate 0.5 gr., methylene blue 1/5 gr., benzoic acid 1/10 gr., hyoscyamine alkaloid 1/2000 gr., atropine sulfate 1/2000 gr./Tab. Bot. 100s, 1000s.
Use: Urinary antiseptic.

CYTADREN. (Ciba) Aminoglutethimide 250 mg./Tab. Bot. 100s.
Use: Cushing's syndrome.

CYTAL, PRE-DILUTED. (Cutter) Sorbitol 2-7 Gm., mannitol 0.54 Gm./100 ml. Bot. 1500 ml.
Use: Urological irrigant.

• **CYTARABINE,** U.S.P. XXI. Sterile, U.S.P. XXI. 2(1H)-Pyrimidihone, 4-amino-1-β- -arabinofuranosyl-. 1-β- -Arabinofuranosylcytosine.
Use: Antineoplastic.
See: Cytosar, Inj. (Upjohn)

• **CYTARABINE HYDROCHLORIDE.** USAN. 1-Arabinoluranosylcytosine hydrochloride.
Use: Management of acute leukemias.
See: Cytosar-U, Vial (Upjohn)

CYRONINE TABS. (Major) Liothyronine sodium 25 mcg. or 50 mcg./Tab. Bot. 100s.
Use: Treatment of inadequate endogenous thyroi production.

CYTOMEL. (SmithKline) Liothyronine sodium. Tab. 5 mcg., 25 mcg., 50 mcg. Bot. 100s. 25 mcg. Bot. 1000s.
Use: Treatment of inadequate endogenous thyroi production.

CYTOSAR-U. (Upjohn) Cytarabine (**20 mg./ml.**) 1 mg./5 ml. Vial 5 ml. w/5 ml. amp. diluent; (**50 mg./ml.**) 500 mg./10 ml. w/10 ml. amp. diluent.
Use: Management of acute granulocytic leukemia

CYTOSINE ARABINOSIDE HCl. Cytarabine HCl.

CYTOSINE, 5-FLUORO-. Flucytosine, U.S.P. XIX.

CYTOX. (MPL) Cyanocobalamin 500 mcg., B-6 20 m B-1 100 mg., benzyl alcohol 2% in isotonic solution sod. chloride./ml. Inj. Vial 10 cc.
Use: Treatment of polyneuritis, osteoarthritis, alcohol neuritis, migraine headache.

CYTOXAN. (Bristol Oncology) Cyclophosphamide. **Vial.** 100 mg., 10 cc., 200 mg., 20 cc., 500 mg., 2 cc., 12s., 1 Gm., 2 Gm. **Tab.** 25 mg. or 50 mg. B 100s, single unit pack 100s and Bot. 1000s 50 m only.
Use: Certain forms of cancer.

D

DAA.
See: Dihydroxy Aluminum Aminoacetate

• **DACARBAZINE,** U.S.P. XXI. For Inj., U.S.P. XXI. 5 (3,3-Dimethyltriazeno)-imidazole-4-carboxamide.
Use: Antineoplastic.
See: Dtic-Dome, Inj. (Miles Pharm)

DACODYL TABS. (Major) Bisacodyl 5 mg./Tab. Bo 100s, 1000s.
Use: Laxative.

DACRIOSE. (CooperVision) Isotonic, buffered soluti of purified water, sodium chloride, potassium chloride, sodium hydroxide, sodium phosphate, ar preserved with benzalkonium chloride 0.01% and edetate disodium 0.03%. Bot. 0.5 oz., 1 oz., 4 oz.
Use: Ophthalmic irrigating solution.

• **DACTINOMYCIN,** U.S.P. XXI. Inj., U.S.P. XXI. Actinomycin D.
Use: Antineoplastic.
See: Cosmegen, Vial (Merck Sharp & Dohme)

DACURONIUM BROMIDE. B.A.N. 3α-Acetoxy-17β-hydroxy-5α-androstan-2β,16β-di-(1-methyl-1-piperi nium) dibromide.
Use: Neuromuscular blocking agent.

DAILY/JET. (Kirkman) Multiple vitamins. Bot. 100s.

DAILY VITAMIN LIQUID. (Bay) Vit. A 2500 I.U., D 400 I.U., E 15 I.U., C 60 mg., B-1 1.2 mg., B-2 1.2 m B-6 1.05 mg., B-12 4.5 mcg., nicainamide 13.5 mg. ml. Bot. 8 oz., pt., gal.
Use: Multivitamins.

DAILY VITAMINS. (Kirkman) Vit. A 5,000 I.U., D 40 I.U., C 50 mg., B-1 3 mg., B-2 2.5 mg., B-6 1 mg.,

2 1 mcg., niacinamide 20 mg., d-calcium pantothe-ate 1 mg./Tab. Bot. 100s.
Jse: Multivitamins.

ILY VITAMINS W/IRON. (Kirkman) Vit. A 5,000 .U., D 400 I.U., B-1 2 mg., B-2 2.5 mg., B-6 1 mg., 3-12 1 mcg., niacinamide 20 mg., d-calcium pantothe-ate 1 mg., iron 18 mg./Tab. Bot. 100s.
Jse: Multivitamins with iron.

ILY VITES. (Image) Multiple vitamin. Bot. 100s, 365s.
Jse: Supplement.

INITE TABLETS. (Wallace) Aminophylline 200 ng., pentobarbital sodium 16 mg., ephedrine HCl 6 mg., dried aluminum hydroxide gel 160 mg., enzocaine 16 mg./Tab. Bot. 100s.
Jse: Bronchodilator for treatment of bronchial asthma.

INITE-KI. (Wallace) Aminophylline 200 mg., pheno-arbital 16 mg., ephedrine HCl 16 mg., potassium odide 325 mg., dried aluminum hydroxide gel 160 ng., benzocaine 16 mg./Tab. Bot. 100s.
Jse: Bronchodilator and expectorant combination or treatment of bronchial asthma.

ISY 2 PREGNANCY TEST KIT. (Advanced Care) 2 tests per kit.
Jse: Accurate pregnancy test result in 45 minutes, or use 3 days after a missed period.

KIN'S SOLUTION.
See: Sodium Hypochlorite Solution Diluted.

LALONE. (Forest) Dexamethasone sodium hosphate 4 mg./ml. Vial 5 ml.

LALONE L.A. (Forest) Dexamethasone 8 mg./ml. Vial 5 cc.
Jse: Adrenocortical steroid therapy.

LALONE D.P. (Forest) Dexamethasone acetate 16 ng./ml. Vial 1 ml. Box 5s; 2 ml. Box 10s.

LCAINE. (Forest) Lidocaine HCl 2%. Vial 5 ml. Box 6s.

LEDALIN TOSYLATE. USAN. 3-Methyl-3-[3-(me-hylamino)propyl]-1-phenylindoline mono-p-toluene sulfonate.
Jse: Antidepressant.

LEX. (Dalin) Dextromethorphan HBr 45 mg., henylephrine HCl 15 mg., chlorpheniramine naleate 6 mg., guaifenesin 180 mg., ammonium chloride 600 mg./Fl. oz. Syr., Bot. 4 oz., pt. Throat ozenge 10s, 18s. Cap. 20s. Pediatric, Bot. 4 oz. T.R. 15s.
Jse: Coughs and colds.

LICOTE. (Dalin) Hexachlorophene, pyrilamine naleate, diperodon HCl, 0.25%, dimethyl olysiloxane, silicone, zinc oxide, camphor. Lot. Bot. 4 fl. oz.
Jse: Antihistaminic, antipruritic, anesthetic for chickenpox, pityriasis rosea, and allergic pruritus.

LICREME. (Dalin) Vit. A 750 I.U., D 75 I.U., diperodon HCl 0.25%, quaternary ammonium cpd. Tubes: 1.5 and 4 oz. Jar, 16 oz.
Jse: Vit. A & D therapy.

LIDERM LIQUID. (Dalin) Night applic. Ethyl alc, 36%, quat. ammonium cpd., carbolic acid, benzoic acid, salicylic acid, resorcin, camphor, tannic acid, soln. coal tar and chlorthymol. Bot. 0.5 oz., 1 oz.
Use: Antipruritic, fungicidal, deodorant liq.

DALIDERM POWDER. (Dalin) Zinc undecylenate, sod. propionate, quat. ammonium cpd., salicylic acid, boric acid, aluminum acetate, alum. Can 2 oz., 3.5 oz.
Use: Antipruritic, fungicidal, deodorant pwdr.

DALIDYNE. (Dalin) Methylbenzethonium chloride, tannic acid, benzocaine, ethyl alcohol, benzyl alcohol, camphor, menthol, & chlorothymol. Lot. Bot. 0.25, 0.5, 1 fl. oz.
Use: Cancrum, stomatitis, thrush, painful gums.

DALIDYNE JEL. (Dalin) Benzocaine, cherry-flavored base. Tube 10 Gm.

DALIDYNE THROAT SPRAY. (Dalin) Lidocaine, cetyldimethylbenzyl ammonium chloride, ethyl alcohol. Aerosol ⅓ oz.
Use: Anesthetic, antiseptic.

DALIFORT. (Dalin) Vit. A 25,000 I.U., D 400 I.U., C 500 mg., B-1 10 mg., B-2 5 mg., B-6 5 mg., B-12 5 mcg., niacinamide 100 mg., d-calcium pantothenate 20 mg., iron 10 mg., magnesium oxide 5 mg., zinc sulfate 1.5 mg., copper sulfate 1 mg./Tab. Bot. 30s, 100s.
Use: Vitamin-mineral dietary supplement.

DALIHIST. (Dalin) Phenylephrine HCl 0.5%, pyrilamine maleate 0.15%, cetyl benzyldimethyl ammon. chloride 0.04% in aq. isotonic sol. Nasal Spray 20 cc
Use: Decongestant, antihistaminic.

DALIMYCIN. (Dalin) Oxytetracycline HCl 250 mg./Cap. Bot. 24s, 100s.
Use: Broad spectrum antibiotic.

DALISEPT. (Dalin) Vit. A 750 I.U., D 75 I.U., diperodon HCl 1%, methylbenzethonium Cl 0.1%. Tubes, 2 & 4 oz. Jar, 16 oz.
Use: Antiseptic, anesthetic, Vit. A & D ointment.

DALIVIM FORTE. (Dalin) Iron ammonium citrate 18 gr., liver fraction 3 gr., Vit. B-12 60 mcg., A palmitate 10,000 I.U., D 1000 I.U., B-1 12 mg., B-2 4 mg., niacinamide 20 mg., Vit. B-6 2 mg., Ca pantothenate 12 mg., mixed tocopherols 30 mg., Ca glycerophosphate 65 mg., manganese glycerophosphate 17.5 mg./Oz. Bot. 4 oz., 8 oz., 16 oz.
Use: Hematinic and dietary supplement.

DALIVIM FORTE TABLETS. (Dalin) Fe fumarate 100 mg., liver desic. 150 mg., B-12 10 mcg., Vit. A palmi-tate 1667, D 167 I.U., C 50 mg., B-1 3 mg., B2 3 mg., niacinamide 10 mg., B-6 0.5 mg., cal. pantothenate 2 mg., cal. glycerophosphate 11 mg., manganese glycerophosphate 3 mg./Tab. Bot. 50s, 100s.
Use: Vitamin and mineral supplement.

DALLERGY CAPSULES. (Laser) Chlorpheniramine maleate 8 mg., phenylephrine HCl 20 mg., methscopolamine nitrate 2.5 mg./Cap. Bot. 100s, 1000s.
Use: Antihistaminic, decongestant, antisecretory.

DALLERGY SYRUP. (Laser) Chlorpheniramine maleate 2 mg., phenylephrine HCl 10 mg.,

methscopolamine nitrate 0.625 mg./5 ml. Bot. pt., gal.
Use: Antihistaminic, decongestant, antisecretory.

DALLERGY TABLETS. (Laser) Chlorpheniramine maleate 4 mg., phenylephrine HCl 10 mg., methscopolamine nitrate 1.25 mg./Tab. Bot. 100s, 1000s.
Use: Antihistaminic, decongestant, antisecretory.

DALMANE. (Roche) Flurazepam HCl 15 mg., 30 mg./Cap. Bot. 100s, 500s. Tel-E-Dose pkg. 100s. Prescription Pak 30s, 300s. Teledose 100s (4 rolls x 25 Caps.), RNP (Reverse Numbered Packages).
Use: Hypnotic agent.

D-ALPHA-E CAP. (Alto) di-Alpha-tocopherol acetate 100 mg. I.U./Cap. Bot. 100s.
Use: Vit. E therapy.

DAMASON-P. (Mason) Hydrocodone bitartrate 5 mg., aspirin 224 mg., caffeine 32 mg./Tab. Bot. 100s, 500s.
Use: Analgesic, antitussive.

DAMBOSE.
See: Inositol, Tabs.

D-AMP. (Dunhall) Ampicillin trihydrate 500 mg./Cap. Bot. 100s. **Susp.** 250 mg./5 cc. Bot. 200 cc.
Use: Antibiotic.

DANATROL CAPSULES. (Winthrop Products) Danazol.
Use: Gonadotropin inhibitor.

• **DANAZOL,** U.S.P. XXI. Caps., U.S.P. XXI. 17α-Pregna-2,4-dien-20-yno-[2,3-d]isoxazol-17-ol.
Use: Pituitary gonadotropin suppressant.
See: Danocrine, Cap. (Winthrop-Breon)

DANDRUFF SHAMPOO. (Walgreen) Zinc pyrithione. 2 Gm./100 ml. Bot. 11 oz. Tube 7 oz.
Use: Dandruff control.

DANEX PROTEIN ENRICHED DANDRUFF SHAMPOO. (Herbert) Pyrithione zinc 1%. Bot. 4 oz.
Use: Antidandruff.

DANIVAC. (Fellows) 1, 8-Dihydroxyanthraquinone (Danthron) 75 mg./Tab. Bot. 1000s.
Use: Constipation.

DANOCRINE. (Winthrop-Breon) Danazol 50 mg., 100 mg., or 200 mg./Cap. Bot. 100s.
Use: Treatment of endometriosis, fibrocystic breast disease, hereditary angioedema.

DANOGAR TABLETS. (Winthrop Products) Danazol.
Use: Gonadotropin inhibitor.

DANOL CAPSULES. (Winthrop Products) Danazol.
Use: Gonadotropin inhibitor.

DANTHANE. (Western Research) Danthron 75 mg./Tab. Handicount 28 (36 bags of 28s)
Use: Cathartic

• **DANTHRON,** U.S.P. XXI. Tabs., U.S.P. XXI. 1,8-Dihydroxy-anthraquinone, dioxyanthraquinone, Chrysazin.
Use: Cathartic.
See: Danivac, Tab. (Fellows-Testagar)
Danthane. Tab. (Western Research)
Dorbane, Tab. (Riker)
Modane, Prod. (Adria)
W/d-Calcium pantothenate.
See: Dantrolax, Tab. (Wolins)
Danvac, Tab. (Kenyon)
Parlax, Tab. (Parmed)
Weslax, Tab. (Western Research)
W/Calcium docusate.
See: Doxidan, Cap. (Hoechst)
W/Chondrus drispus, prune concentrate.
See: Acelax, Tab. (Marcen)
W/Docusate sodium.
See: Doctate-P, Cap. (Glaxo)
Dorbantyl, Cap. (Riker)
Dorbantyl Forte, Cap., (Riker)
Doxan, Tab. (Hoechst)
Doxate-D, Tab. (Dunhall)
Guarsol, Tab. (Western Research)
W/Oxyethylene oxpropylene polymer, B-1, carb ymethyl cellulose.
See: Evactol, Cap. (Delta)
W/Sod. lauryl sulfate.

DANTRIUM. (Norwich Eaton) Dantrolene sodium 25 mg./Cap. Bot. 100s, 500s, & Unit dose 100s; 50 mg./Cap. Bot. 100s; 100 mg./Cap. Bot. 100s, un dose 100s.
Use: Skeletal muscle relaxant, prophylaxis of malignant hyperthermia.

DANTRIUM I.V. (Norwich Eaton) Dantrolene sodiur 20 mg./Vial.
Use: Treatment of malignant hyperthermia.

DANTROLAX. (Wolins) Danthron 75 mg., D-calci pantothenate 25 mg./Tab. Bot. 1000s.

• **DANTROLENE.** USAN. 1(((5-(4-nitrophenyl) -2-fu nyl) methylene) amino)-2, 4- nidazolidinedione.
Use: Skeletal muscle relaxant.

• **DANTROLENE SODIUM.** USAN.
See: Dantrium, Cap. (Norwich Eaton)

DANVAC. (Kenyon) Danthron 37.5 mg., 75 mg., d-calcium pantothenate 12.5 mg., 25 mg./Tab. B 100s.
Use: Laxative.

DAPA TABLETS. (Ferndale) Acetaminophen 324 mg./Tab. Bot. 100s.
Use: Analgesic.

DAPCO. (Schlicksup) Salicylamide 300 mg., butabarbital 15 mg./Tab. Bot. 100s, 1000s.
Use: Analgesic w/sedative.

DAPEX. (Ferndale) Phentermine HCl 37.5 mg./Cap Bot. 100s.
Use: Anorectic.

• **DAPSONE,** U.S.P. XXI. Tabs., U.S.P. XXI. Benzenamine, 4,4′-sulfonyl-bis-. Diaminodiphenyls fone. 4,4′-Sulfonyldianiline.
Use: Treatment of leprosy; dermatitis herpetiform suppressant.
See: Avlosulfon, Tab. (Ayerst)

DAPTAZOLE. Amiphenazole, B.A.N.

DARAGEN. (Owen) Collagen polypeptide and benzalkonium chloride in a mild amphoteric base Bot. 8 oz.
Use: Hair repair shampoo.

DARA SOAPLESS SHAMPOO. (Owen) Purified wat potassium coco hydrolyzed protein, sulfated cast

oil, pentasodium triphosphate, sodium benzoate, sodium lauryl sulfate, fragrance. Bot. 8 oz., 16 oz.
Use: For people with sensitive scalp.

RANIDE. (Merck Sharp & Dohme) Dichlorphenamide. 50 mg./Tab. Bot. 100s.
Use: Carbonic anhydrase inhibitor for reduction of intraocular pressure in glaucoma.

RAPRIM. (Burroughs Wellcome) Pyrimethamine 25 mg./Tab. Bot. 100s.
Use: Orally, antimalarial.

RBID. (SmithKline) Isopropamide Iodide 5 mg./Tab. Bot. 50s.
Use: Anticholinergic, gastrointestinal antispasmodic.
Compazine.
See: Combid, Cap. (SmithKline)

RCO G-60. (ICI Americas) Activated carbon from lignite.
Use: Purifier.

RENTHIN. Bretylium Tosylate, B.A.N.

RICON. (Beecham Labs) Oxyphencyclimine HCl 10 mg./Tab. Bot. 60s, 500s.
Use: G-I & G-U disorders.

RICON-PB. (Beecham Labs) Oxyphencyclimine HCl 5 mg., phenobarbital 15 mg./Tab. Bot. 100s.
Use: Anticholinergic with sedative.

RO TABLETS-C.T. (Fellows) Dextroamphetamine HCl 5 mg./Tri-tab. Bot. 100s, 1000s, 5000s.

RO TIMED CAPSULES. (Fellows) d-Amphetamine HCl 15 mg./Cap. Bot. 100s, 1000s.

RVISUL. Diaveridine, B.A.N.

RVOCET-N 50. (Lilly) Propoxyphene napsylate 50 mg., acetaminophen 325 mg./Tab. Bot. 100s (Rx Pak), 500s; Blister pkg. 10 × 10s; Rx Pak 20 × 50s.
Use: Analgesic.

RVOCET-N 100. (Lilly) Propoxyphene napsylate 100 mg., acetaminophen 650 mg./Tab. Bot. 100s (Rx Pak), 500s; Blister pkg. 10 × 10s; 500 single cut blisters; Unit dose rolls 20 × 25s
Use: Relief of mild to moderate pain.

RVON. (Lilly) Propoxyphene HCl **32** mg./Pulvule. Bot. 100s (Rx Pak), 500s; Blister pkg. 10 × 10s. **65 mg.**/Pulvule. Bot. 100s (Rx Pak), 500s; Blister pkg. 10 × 10s; 500 single-cut individually labeled blisters; Unit dose 20 rolls × 25s; Rx Pak 25 × 30s, 20 × 50s.
Use: Analgesic.

RVON COMPOUND. (Lilly) Propoxyphene HCl 32 mg., aspirin 389 mg., caffeine 32.4 mg./Pulvule. Bot. 100s (Rx Pak), 500s.
Use: Antipyretic and analgesic.

RVON COMPOUND-65. (Lilly) Propoxyphene HCl 65 mg., aspirin 389 mg., caffeine 32.4 mg./Pulvule Bot. 100s (Rx Pak), 500s; Blister pkg. 10 × 10s;
Use: Acute, chronic or recurrent pain.

RVON-N. (Lilly) Propoxyphene napsylate **Tabs.**: 100 mg./Tab. Bot. 100s (Rx Pak), 500s; Blister pkg. 10 × 10s; Rx Pak 20 × 50s. **Susp.** 50 mg./5 ml. Bot. 16 fl oz.
W/A.S.A. Propoxyphene napsylate 100 mg., aspirin 325 mg./Tab. Bot. 100s (Rx Pak), 500s.
Use: Analgesic.

DARVON WITH A.S.A. (Lilly) Darvon 65 mg., A.S.A. 325 mg./Pulvule. Bot. 100s (Rx Pak), 500s.
Use: Analgesic without caffeine.

DA-SED TABLET. (Sheryl) Butabarbital 0.5 gr./Tab. Tab. 100s.
Use: For mild, prolonged "daytime" sedation.

DASIKON. (Beecham Labs) Chlorpheniramine maleate 2 mg., caffeine 32 mg., acetylsalicylic acid 195 mg., phenacetin 130 mg., atropine sulfate 0.065 mg./Cap. Bot. 500s.
Use: Colds.

DASIN. (Beecham Labs) Ipecac 3 mg., acetylsalicylic acid 130 mg., camphor 15 mg., caffeine 8 mg., atropine sulfate 0.13 mg./Cap. Bot. 100s, 500s.
Use: Analgesic, antipyretic, diaphoretic.

D-ASMA-S. (Dunhall) Secobarbitol sodium 16.2 mg., ephedrine sulfate 8.1 mg./5 ml. w/alcohol 9%. Bot. Pt.
Use: Anti-asthmatic.

DATRIL EXTRA STRENGTH CAPSULES. (Bristol-Myers) Acetaminophen 500 mg./Cap. Bot. 24s, 50s.
Use: Analgesic.

DATRIL EXTRA STRENGTH TABLETS. (Bristol-Myers) Acetaminophen 500 mg./Tab. Bot. 30s, 60s, 100s.
Use: Analgesic.

DATURINE HBr.
See: Hyoscyamine Salts (Var. Mfr.)

DAUNORUBICIN. B.A.N.
Use: Antineoplastic.

• **DAUNORUBICIN HCL,** U.S.P. XXI. For Inj., U.S.P. XXI. An antibiotic produced by *Streptomyeces ceruleorubidus.* 3-Acetyl-1,2,3,-4,6,11-hexahydro-3,5,12-trihydroxy-10-methoxy-6,11-dioxonaphthacen-1-yl-3-amino-2,3,6-trideoxy-β-D-galactopyranoside.
Use: Antineoplastic.
See: Cerubidin, Inj. (Ives)

• **DAUNORUBICIN HYDROCHLORIDE.** USAN.
Use: Antineoplastic.

DAVITAMON K.
See: Menadione Inj., Tab. (Various Mfr.)

DAVOSIL. (Hoyt) Silicon carbide in glycerin base. Jar 8 oz., 10 oz.
Use: Clean and polish teeth.

DAYALETS. (Abbott) Vit. B-1 1.5 mg., B-2 1.7 mg., A 5000 I.U., C 60 mg., D 400 I.U. niacinamide 20 mg., B-6 2 mg., B-12 6 mcg., E 30 I.U., folic acid 0.4 mg./Filmtab. Bot. 100s.
Use: Vitamin.

DAYALETS PLUS IRON. (Abbott) Vit. B-1 1.5 mg., B-2 1.7 mg., niacinamide 20 mg., B-6 2 mg., C 60 mg., A 5000 I.U., D 400 I.U., E 30 I.U., B-12 6 mcg., iron 18 mg., folic acid 0.4 mg./Filmtab. Bot. 100s.
Use: Dietary supplement.

DAY CAPS. (Towne) Vit. A 5,500 I.U., D 400 I.U., B-1 3 mg., B-2 3 mg., B-6 0.5 mg., B-12 4 mcg., C 50 mg., Ca pantothenate 5 mg., niacinamide 20 mg./Cap. Bot. 120s, 300s.

DAY CAP TABS-M. (Towne) Vit. A 5,500 I.U., D 400 I.U., B-1 3 mg., B-2 3 mg., B-6 0.5 mg., B-12 4 mcg., C 50 mg., niacinamide 20 mg., Ca pantothenate 5 mg., l-Lysine HCl 15 mg., Fe 10 mg., Zn 1.5 mg., Mn 1 mg., iodine 0.1 mg., Cu 1 mg., K 5 mg., Mg 6 mg./Captab Bot. 100s, 250s.

DAY-TAB. (Towne) Vit. A 5000 I.U., D 400 I.U., B-1 15 mg., B-2 10 mg., C 600 mg., niacinamide 20 mg., B-6 5 mg., folic acid 400 mcg., pantothenic acid 10 mg., zinc 15 mg. Cu 2 mg., B-12 5 mcg./Tab. Bot. 100s, 200s.

DAY TAB ESSENTIAL. (Towne) Vit. A 5000 I.U., D 400 I.U., E 15 I.U., C 60 mg., folic acid 0.4 mg., B-1 1.5 mg., B-2 1.7 mg., niacin 20 mg., B-6 2 mg., B-12 6 mcg./Tab. Bot. 200s.
Use: Dietary supplement.

DAY TABS, NEW. (Towne) Vit A 5000 I.U., E 15 I.U., D 400 I.U., C 60 mg., folic acid 0.4 mg., B-1 1.5 mg., B-2 1.7 mg., niacin 20 mg., B-6 20 mg., B-12 6 mcg./Tab. Bot 100s, 250s.
Use: Dietary supplement.

DAY-TAB PLUS IRON. (Towne) Iron 18 mg., Vit. A 5000 I.U., D 400 I.U., B-1 1.5 mg., B-2 1.7 mg., niacinamide 20 mg., C 60 mg., B-6 2 mg., pantothenic acid 10 mg., B-12 6mcg., folic acid 0.1 mg./Tab. Bot. 100s.

DAY TAB STRESS COMPLEX. (Towne) Vit. A 5000 I.U., C 600 mg., B-1 15 mg., B-2 10 mg., niacin 100 mg., D 400 I.U., E 30 I.U., B-6 5 mg., folic acid 400 mcg., B-12 6 mcg. pantothenic acid 20 mg., iron 18 mg., zinc 15 mg., copper 2 mg./Tab. Bot. 60s.
Use: Dietary supplement.

DAY TABS PLUS IRON, NEW. (Towne) Vit. A 5000 I.U., E 15 I.U., D 400 I.U., C 60 mg., folic acid 0.4 mg., B-1 1.5 mg., B-2 1.7 mg., niacin 20 mg., B-6 20 mg., B-12 6 mcg., iron 18 mcg./Tab. Bot. 250s.
Use: Dietary supplement.

DAY TAB WITH IRON. (Towne) Vit. A 5000 I.U., D 400 I.U., E 15 I.U., C 60 mg., folic acid 1.5 mg., B-1 15 mg., B-2 1.7 mg., niacin 20 mg., B-6 2 mg., B-12 6 mcg., iron 18 mg./Tab. Bot. 200s.
Use: Daily as a dietary supplement.

DAY-VITE. (Drug Industries) Vit. A 10,000 I.U., D-3 1000 I.U., E 10 I.U., C 100 mg., B-1 5 mg., B-2 5 mg., B-6 2 mg., B-12 2 mcg., niacinamide 25 mg., Ca pantothenate 10 mg./Tab. Bot. 100s, 500s.
Use: Dietary supplement.

DAZAMIDE TABS. (Major) Acetazolamide 250 mg./Tab. Bot. 250s, 1000s.
Use: Diuretic.

• **DAZANDROL MALEATE.** USAN.
Use: Antidepressant.

• **DAZMEGREL.** USAN.
Use: Inhibitor (thromboxane synthetase).

• **DAZOPRIDE FUMARATE.** USAN.
Use: Peristaltic stimulant.

• **DAZOXIBEN HYDROCHLORIDE.** USAN.
Use: Antithrombotic.

DB ELECTRODE PASTE. (Day-Baldwin) Tube 5%.

DBED. Dibenzylethylenediamine dipenicillin G.
See: Benzathine penicillin G Susp.

DCA
See: Desoxycorticosterone acetate Preps. (Various Mfr.)

D-CAINE. (Century) Dibucaine 1%, with rectal tube. oz.
Use: Local anesthetic.

DCP. (Towne) Calcium 180 mg., phosphorus 105 mg., Vit. D 66.7 I.U./Tab. Bot. 100s.
Use: Dietary supplement.

DDAVP. (Centerchem) Desmopressin acetate 0.1 mg./ml. Vial 2.5 ml. w/applicator tubes.
Use: Antidiuretic therapy.

DDAVP. (USV Labs.) Desmopressin acetate 0.1 mg. chlorobutanol 5.0 mg., sodium chloride 9.0 mg./m Vial 2.5 ml. w/applicator tubes for nasal administration.
Use: Antidiuretic therapy in central diabetes insipidus.

DDAVP INJECTION. (USV Labs.) Desmopressin acetate 4.0 mcg., ml/ Amp. 1 ml.
Use: Antidiuretic therapy for central diabetes insipidus.

D-DIOL. (Burgin-Arden) Testosterone cypionate 50 m estradiol cypionate 2 mg./cc. Vial 10 cc.

DDS.
See: Dapsone Tab., U.S.P. XXI.

DDT.
See: Chlorophenothane.

DEACETYLLANATOSIDE C.
See: Deslanoside, U.S.P. XXI.

DEADLY NIGHTSHADE LEAF, U.S.P.
See: Belladonna Leaf, U.S.P. XXI.

DEANOL. B.A.N. 2-Dimethylaminoethanol.
Use: Central nervous system stimulant.
See: Deaner, Tab. (Riker)

DEANOL ACETAMIDOBENZOATE. (2-Dimethylaminoethanol as the p-acetamido-benzoic acid salt).
See: Deaner, Tab. (Riker)

DEAPRIL-ST. (Mead Johnson) Dihydrogenated erg alkaloids (ergoloid mesylates): dihydroergocornine, dihydroergocristine, & dihydroergokryptine as the mesylates, 1:1:1 ratio. Bot. 100s 1 mg. sublingual Tab.
Use: Selected symptoms in elderly patients.

DEBA.
See: Barbital (Various Mfr.)

DEBRISAN. Dextranomer, B.A.N.

DEBRISAN. (Pharmacia) Spherical hydrophilic beads 0.1-0.3 mm diameter. Bot. 60 Gm., 120 Gm. Pks. 7 4g, 14 × 14g. U.S. distributor Johnson & Johnson Products.
Use: Cleansing exuding lesions such as venous stasis ulcers, decubitus ulcers, infected traumatic and surgical wounds, and infected burns.

• **DEBRISOQUIN SULFATE.** USAN. 3,4-Dihydro-2(IH isoquinolinecarboxamidine sulfate. Formerly Isocaramidine Sulfate
Use: Hypotensive agent.

DEBRISOQUINE. B.A.N. 2-Amidino-1,2,3,4-tetrahydroisoquinoline.
Use: Hypotensive.
See: Declinax (sulfate)

DEBROX. (Marion) Carbamide peroxide 6.5% in anh drous glycerol. Plastic Squeeze Bot. 0.5 oz., 1 c
Use: Excess ear wax.

CA-BON. (Barrows) Vit. A 3000 I.U., D 400 I.U., C 60 ng., B-1 1 mg., B-2 1.2 mg., niacinamide 8 mg., 3-6 1 mg., panthenol 3 mg., B-12 1 mcg., biotin 30 ncg./0.6 cc. Drops Bot. 50 cc. Chewable Tabs. 3ot. 100s, 250s.
Jse: Vitamin supplement.

CADERM IN ESTERGEL. (Merck Sharp & Dohme))examethasone 0.1% w/isopropyl myristate gel, vood alcohols, refined lanolin alcohol, nicrocrystalline wax, anhydrous citric acid, anhydrous sod. phosphate dibasic. Tube 30 Gm.
Jse: Corticosteroid (glucocorticoid).

CADROL. (Paddock) Dexamethasone sodium phosphate 4 mg./cc. Vial 5 cc.
Jse: Corticosteroid.

CADROL L.A. INJECTION. (Goldline))examethasone 8 mg. Vial 5 ml.
Jse: Corticosteroid.

CADRON. (Merck Sharp & Dohme))examethasone. **Tabs.** 0.25 mg., Bot. 100s; 0.5 ng., Bot. 100s, Unit-dose 100s; 0.75 mg., 5-12 Pak, 12s, Bot. 100s, 1000s Unit-dose 100s; 1.5 mg. Bot. 50s. Unit-dose 100s; 4 mg. Bot. 50s Unit-dose 100s. **Elixir** 0.5 mg./5 ml., w/benzoic acid 0.1%, alcohol 5% Bot. w/dropper 100 ml., Bot. w/out dropper 237 ml.
Neomycin sulfate.
See: NeoDecadron, Ophth. Soln., Ophth. Oint., Topical., Cream (Merck Sharp & Dohme)

CADRON-LA SUSPENSION. (Merck Sharp & Dohme) Dexamethasone acetate equiv. to 8 mg. dexamethasone/1ml. w/sod. chloride 6.67 mg., creatinine 5 mg., disodium edetate 0.5 mg., sodium carboxymethylcellulose 5 mg., polysorbate 80 0.75 mg., sod. hydroxide to adjust pH, benzyl alcohol 9 mg., sod. bisulfite 1 mg., water for injection, q.s. 1 ml. Vials 1 ml., 5 ml.
Jse: Corticosteroid (glucocorticoid).

CADRON PHOSPHATE. (Merck Sharp & Dohme) Dexamethasone sod. phosphate equivalent in various forms:
Ophth. Sol. 0.1% w/creatinine, sod. citrate, sod. borate, polysorbate 80, hydrochloric acid to adjust pH, disodium edetate, sodium bisulfite 0.1%, water for inj., phenylethanol 0.25%, benzalkonium Cl 0.02%. Ocumeter dispenser 5 ml.
Use: Corticosteroid responsive inflammatory conditions of the eye and ear.
Ophth. Oint. 0.05% w/white petrolatum and mineral oil. Tube 3.5 gm.
Use: Corticosteroid responsive inflammatory conditions of the eye or ear.
Topical Cream 0.1% w/stearyl alcohol, cetyl alcohol, mineral oil, polyoxyl 40 stearate, sorbitol sol., methyl polysilicone emul., creatinine, purified water, sod. citrate, disod. edetate, sod. hydroxide to adjust pH, methylparaben 0.15%, sorbic acid 0.1%. Tube 15 Gm., 30 Gm.
Use: Corticosteroid responsive dermatoses.
Turbinaire Each metered spray dispenses 0.1 mg. dexamethasone sodium phosphate equivalent to 0.084 mg. dexamethasone w/fluorochlorohydrocarbons as propellants and alcohol 2%. Aerosol w/nasal applicator Container 170 sprays; refill package without nasal applicator.
Use: Allergic or inflammatory nasal conditions.
W/Neomycin
Use: Corticosteroid, antibiotic.
See: NeoDecadron, Ophth. Soln., Ophth. Oint., Topical Cream (Merck Sharp & Dohme)
W/Xylocaine **Inj.** Dexamethasone sodium phosphate equivalent to dexamethasone phosphate 4 mg., lidocaine HCl 10 mg., citric acid 10 mg., creatinine 8 mg., sodium bisulfite 0.5 mg., disodium edetate 0.5 mg., sod. hydroxide to adjust pH, water for injection, methylparaben 1.5 mg., propylparaben 0.2 mg./ml. Vial 5 ml.
Use: Corticosteriod (glucocorticoid) for local injection.

DECADRON PHOSPHATE INJECTION. (Merck Sharp & Dohme) Dexamethasone sod. phosphate 4 mg./ml. and 24 mg./ml., with creatinine 8 mg., sod. citrate 10 mg., disodium edetate 0.5 mg. (24 mg./ml, only), sod. hydroxide to adjust pH, sod. bisulfite 1 mg., methylparaben 1.5 mg., propylparaben 0.2 mg./ml. **4 mg./ml.:** Disposable syringe 1 ml., 2.5 ml., 1s.; Vial 1 ml., 25s.; Vial 5 ml. 1s.; Vial 25 ml. 1s. **24 mg./ml.** (for I.V. use only): Vial 5 ml., 1s; 10 ml., 1s.
Use: Corticosteroid (glucocorticoid).

DECADRON PHOSPHATE RESPIHALER. (Merck Sharp & Dohme) Each metered spray dispenses dexamethasone sodium phosphate equivalent to 0.1 mg. dexamethasone phosphate (approximately 0.084 mg. dexamethasone) w/fluorochlorohydrocarbons as propellants, alcohol 2%. Aerosol for oral inhalation, 170 sprays in pressurized container.
Use: Bronchial asthma treatment.

DECA-DURABOLIN. (Organon) Nandrolone decanoate injection w/benzyl alcohol 10%. **50 mg./ml.** Amp. 1 ml. Box 4s; Multidose Vial 2 ml. **100 mg./ml.** Multidose Vial 2 ml. Box 1s, 25s. 200 mg./ml. Multidose vial 1 ml. Box 1s, 25s.
Use: I.M. depot-anabolic.

DECA-DURABOLIN REDIJECT SYRINGES. (Organon) Nandrolone decanoate. 200 mg./ml., 100 mg./ml., 50 mg./ml. Syringes 1 ml. Box 25s.
Use: Depot-anabolic.

DECAHYDRO-4α,7,9-TRIHYDROXY-2-METHYL-6,8-BIS(METHYLAMINO)-4H-PYRANO 2,3-β[1,4]BENZODIOXIN-4-ONE DIHYDROCHLORIDE PENTAHYDRATE. Sterile Spectinomycin Hydrochloride, U.S.P. XXI.

DECAJECT 5 AND 10. (Mayrand) Dexamethasone sod. phosphate 4 mg./ml. Vial 10 ml.
Use: Anti-inflammatory corticosteroid.

DECAJEST LA. (Mayrand) Dexamethasone acetate 8 mg./ml. Vial 5 ml.
Use: Anti-inflammatory corticosteroid.

DE-CAL. (Vortech) Calcium 250 mg., Vit. D 1.25 u./Tab. Bot. 100s, 1000s.
Use: Calcium and Vitamin D therapy.

DECALIX. (Pharmed) Dexamethasone 0.5 mg./5 ml. Bot. 100 ml.
Use: Adrenocortical steroid therapy.

DECAMETH. (Foy) Dexamethasone sodium phosphate inj. 4 mg./5cc vial.
Use: Adrenocortical steroid therapy.

DECAMETH L.A. (Foy) Dexamethasone sodium phosphate injection. 8 mg./ml.; 5 ml. vials.
Use: Steroid therapy.

DECAMETH TABLETS. (Foy) Dexamethasone 0.75 mg./Tab. Bot. 1000s.
Use: Steroid therapy.

DECAMETHONIUM BROMIDE.
Use: Muscle relaxant.
See: Syncurine, Vial (Burroughs Wellcome)

DECAMETHONIUM IODIDE. B.A.N.
Decamethylenedi(trimethylammonium iodide).
Use: Muscle relaxant.
See: Eulissin

DECAPRYN. (Merrell Dow) Doxylamine succinate. 12.5 mg./Tab. Bot. 100s.
Use: Antihistamine.
W/Pyridoxine HCl.
See: Bendectin, Tab. (Merrell Dow)

DECASONE INJECTION. (Fellows) Dexamethasone sod. phosphate equiv. to dexamethasone phosphate 4 mg./cc. Vial 5 cc.

DECASPRAY. (Merck Sharp & Dohme) Topical dexamethasone aerosol. Every second of spray dispenses approximately 0.075 mg. of dexamethasone. Dexamethasone 10 mg., isopropyl myristate, isobutane in pressurized container 25 Gm.
Use: Corticosteroid responsive dermatoses.

• **DECAVITAMIN CAPSULES AND TABLETS,** U.S.P. XXI. Vit. A 4000 I.U., D 400 I.U., C 70 mg., calcium pantothenate 10 mg., B-12 5 mcg., folic acid 100 mcg., nicotinamide 20 mg., B-6 2 mg., B-2 2 mg., B-1 2 mg./Cap. or Tab.
Use: Vitamin therapy.

DECCASOL-T. (Kenyon) Vit. B-1 10 mg., B-2 5 mg., B-6 2 mg., pantothenic acid 10 mg., niacinamide 30 mg., B-12 3 mcg., C 100 mg., E 5 I.U., A 10,000 I.U., D 1000 I.U., Fe 15 mg., Cu 1 mg., Mn 1 mg., Mg 5 mg., Zn 1.5 mg./Tab. Bot. 100s.

DECCOX. Decoquinate, B.A.N.

DECHOLIN. (Miles Pharm) Dehydrocholic acid 250 mg./Tab. Bot. 100s, 500s, 1000s.
Use: Laxative.

DECHCOLIN SODIUM. (Miles Pharm) Sodium dehydrocholate 20% aqueous sol. Amp. 5cc, Boxes 20 amps.
Use: Diagnostic.

DECHLORISON ACETATE. 9-alpha, 11-beta, di-chloro-1,4-pregnadiene-17-alpha, 21-diol-3,20-dione-21 acetate. Diloderm.

DECICAIN. Tetracaine HCl.

• **DECLENPERONE.** USAN.
Use: Sedative.

DECLOFEN SR CAPSULES. (U.S. Ethicals) Theophylline 250 mg./S.R. Cap. Bot. 100s.
Use: Prolonged relief and/or prevention of symptoms of asthma and reversible bronchospasm.

DECLOMYCIN HCl. (Lederle) **Cap.** Demeclocycine HCl 150 mg./Cap. Bot. 100s. **Tab.** 150 mg./Tab., Bot. 100s; 300 mg./Tab. Bot. 12s, 48s
Use: Broad spectrum antibiotic.

DECOBEL LANACAPS. (Lannett) Belladonna alkaloids 0.128 mg., phenylpropanolamine HCl 50 mg., chlorpheniramine maleate 1 mg., pheniramin maleate 12.5 mg./Cap. Bot. 100s, 1000s.
Use: Decongestant.

DECOHIST CAPSULES. (Towne) Chlorpheniramine maleate 1 mg., phenylpropanolamine HCl 12.5 mg salicylamide 180 mg., caffeine 15 mg./Cap. Bot. 18s.
Use: Antihistaminic.

DECOJEN. (Jenkins) Aspirin 2.5 gr., chlorpheniramir maleate 1.25 mg., phenylephrine HCl 2.5 mg./Tal Bot. 1000s.
Use: Nasal decongestant.

DECOJEN INJECTION. (Jenkins) Atropine sulfate 0 mg., phenylpropanolamine HCl 12.5 mg., chlorpheniramine maleate 5 mg., water for injectic q.s./cc. Vials 10 cc. 12s.

DECOLONE-50. (Kay) Nandrolone decanoate 50 m or 100 mg./ml. Vial 2 ml.
Use: Anabolic.

DECONAMINE ELIXIR. (Berlex) Chlorpheniramine maleate 2 mg., d-pseudoephedrine HCl 30 mg., alc hol 15%/5 ml. Bot. 473 ml.
Use: Antihistaminic, decongestant.

DECONAMINE SR CAPSULES. (Berlex) Chlorpheniramine maleate 8 mg., d-pseudoeph drine HCl 120 mg./Cap. Bot. 100s, 500s.
Use: Antihistaminic, decongestant.

DECONAMINE SYRUP. (Berlex) Chlorpheniramine maleate 2 mg., d-pseudoephedrine HCl 30 mg./ 5 r Bot. 473 ml.
Use: Antihistaminic, decongestant.

DECONAMINE TABLETS, DYE-FREE. (Berlex) Chl pheniramine maleate 4 mg., d-pseudoephedrine H 60 mg./Tab. Bot. 100s, 500s.
Use: Antihistaminic, decongestant.

DECONGESTANT. (Century) Atropine sulfate 0.2 mg chlorpheniramine maleate 5 mg., phenylpropanolamine HCl 12.5 mg., chlorobutanol 0.5%, water for inj./cc. Inj. Vial 10 cc.

DECONGESTANT CAPSULES. (Zenith) Chlorpheniramine maleate 12 mg., phenylpropanolamine HCl 75 mg./Cap.
Use: Decongestant, antihistaminic.

DECONGESTANT NA. (Vitarine) Acetaminophen 32 mg., phenylpropanolamine HCl 18 mg./Cap.
Use: Decongestant.

DECONGESTANT TABLETS. (Panray) Chlorpheniramine maleate 2 mg., aspirin 388.8 mg caffeine 32.4 mg., phenylephrine 10 mg./Tab. Bot 1000s.

DECONTABS. (Zenith) Phenylpropanolamine HCl 40 mg., phenlephrine HCl 10 mg., phenylteoloxamine citrate 15 mg., chlorpheniramine maleate 5 mg./S Tab.
Use: Decongestant, antihistaminic.

• **DECOQUINATE.** USAN. Ethyl 6-decyloxy-7-ethoxy 4-hydroxyquinoline-3-carboxylate.
Use: Antiprotozoan, veterinary medicine.
See: Deccox.

• **DECTAFLUR.** USAN.
Use: Dental caries prophylactic.

UBITEX. (Merchant) Scarlet red modified 1%, ruvian balsam, castor oil, zinc oxide in an ntment base containing starch, white petrolatum, uid petrolatum & plasticized hydrocarbon gel. rs 4 oz., 16 oz.
se: Decubitus care.
URITIS. (Sween) Cream, Jar 2 oz. Pads, Jar 80s.
se: Bed sores treatment.
P DOWN PAIN RELIEF RUB. (Beecham oducts) Methyl salicylate 15%, menthol 5%, ethyl nicotinate 0.7%, camphor 0.5%.
ibes 1.25 oz., 3 oz.
se: Relieve pain of minor arthritis, sore joints, uscle aches, sprains, backaches, lumbago.
P STRENGTH MUSTEROLE. (Plough) Methyl licylate 30%, menthol 3%, methyl nicotinate 5% Tube 1.25 oz., 3 oz.
se: Analgesic rub.
FEROXAMINE. USAN.
se: Chelating agent for iron.
FEROXAMINE HYDROCHLORIDE. USAN.
se: Chelating agent for iron.
FEROXAMINE MESYLATE, U.S.P. XXI. Sterile, S.P. XXI. *N*-[5-[3-[(5-aminopentyl)-hydroxycar-amoyl]propionamido]-pentyl]-3-[[5-(*N*-hydroxyaceta-ido)pentyl]-carbamoyl]-propionohydroxamic acid.
se: Iron depleter.
ee: Desferal, Amp. (Ciba)
ICOL. (Vangard) **Tab.:** Bisacodyl 5 mg./Tab. Bot. 0s, 1000s. **Supp.:** Bisacodyl 10 mg./supp. Box 2s.
se: Laxative.
INATE. (Fellows) Docusate sodium 100 mg./Tab. ot. 1000s.
UNGIT SODIUM SALT. Bensuldazic acid, B.A.N.
EST-2. (Barnes-Hind) Naphazoline HCl 0.012%, enzalkonium chloride 0.0067%, disodium edetate 02% Bot. 15 ml.
se: Ophthalmic decongestant for eye irritations.
IST CAPSULES. (Forest) Phenylpropanolamine Cl 75 mg., chlorpheniramine maleate 12 mg./Cap. R. Bot. 100s.
se: Decongestant, antihistaminic.
HYDROACETIC ACID. N.F. XVI.
se: Pharmaceutic aid (preservative).
HYDROCHOLATE SODIUM INJ., U.S.P. XXI. odium 3,7,12-trioxo-5B-Cholan-24-oate.
se: Relief of liver congestion; diagnosis of cardiac ilure.
ee: Decholine Sodium, Inj. (Miles Pharm)
EHYDROCHOLESTEROL, ACTIVATED. (Various fr.) Vitamin D-3.
YDROCHOLIC ACID. B.A.N. 3,7,12-Trioxo-5β-holanic acid.
se: Laxative.
ee: Bilostat
Decholin, Tab. (Miles Pharm)
Dehydrocholin
HYDROCHOLIC ACID, U.S.P. XXI. Tabs., U.S.P. XI. 3,7,12-Trioxo-5β-cholan-24-oic acid.
etocholanic acid, oxidized cholic acid, bile acids xidized.
Use: Orally, hydrocholeretic & choleretic.
See: Cholan-DH, Tab. (Pennwalt)
Ketocholanic acid
Neocholan, Tab. (Merrell Dow)
W/Amyloytic and proteolytic enzymes, desoxycholic acid.
See: Bilezyme, Tab. (Geriatric)
W/Bile, homatropine methylbromide, pepsin.
See: Biloric, Caps. (Arcum)
W/Bile, homatropine methylbromide, phenobarbital.
See: Bilamide, Tab. (Norgine)
W/Bile ext., methyl cellulose, homatropine methylbromide.
See: Colicell, Tab. (Sutliff & Case)
W/Bile ext., pepsin, pancreatin.
See: Progestive, Tab. (NCP)
W/Desoxycholic acid.
See: Combichole, Tab. (F. Trout)
Ketosox, Tab. (Ascher)
W/Docusate sodium.
See: Dubbalax-B, Cap. (Redford)
Dubbalax-N, Cap. (Redford)
Neolax, Tab. (Central)
W/Docusate sodium, phenolphthalein.
See: Bolax, Cap. (Boyd)
Sarolax (Saron)
Tripalax, Cap. (Redford)
W/Homatropine methylbromide.
See: Atrocholin. Tab. (Blue Line)
Cholan V, Tab. (Pennwalt)
Dranochol, Tab. (Marin)
Hepahydrin, Tab. (Comatic)
W/Homatropine methylbromide, sod. pentobarbital.
See: Homachol, Tab. (Lemmon)
W/Methscopolamine, ox bile, amobarbital.
See: Hydrochol Plus, Tab. (Elder)
W/Ox bile, homatropine methylbromide, phenobarbital.
See: Bilamide, Tab. (Norgine)
W/Pancreatin, pepsin, bile salts, desoxycholic acid.
See: Enzylax, Tab. (Kay)
Pepsatal, Tab. (Kenyon)
W/Pancreatin, pepsin, ox bile, belladonna ext.
See: Ro-Bile, Tab. (Rowell)
W/Pepsin, pancreatin.
See: Digestozyme, Tab. (Wolins)
W/Pepsin, pancreatin, ox bile ext. papain.
See: Canz, Tab. (Cole)
W/Pepsin, pancreatin enz. conc., cellulase.
See: Gastroenterase, Tab (Wallace)
W/Phenobarbital & homatropine methylbromide.
See: Cholan-HMB, Tab. (Pennwalt)
W/Phenobarbital, homatropine methylbromide, gerilase, geriprotase, desoxycholic acid.
See: Bilezyme Plus, Tabs. (Geriatric)
W/Phenolphthalein, docusate sodium.
See: Sarolax, Cap. (Saron)
W/Prolase-300, Mylase-100, hyoscine HBr, atropine sulfate.
See: Almezyme, Cap. (Meyer)
DEHYDROCHOLIN.
See: Dehydrocholic acid.

11-DEHYDRO-17-HYDROXYCORTICOSTERONE. See: Cortisone.

DEHYDRODESOXYCHOLIC ACID. See: Cholanic acid

DEHYDROEMETINE. B.A.N. 3-Ethyl-1,6,7,11b-tetrahydro-9,10-dimethoxy-2-(1,2,3,4-tetrahydro-6,7-dimethoxy-1-isoquinolylmethyl)-4H-benzo[a]-quinolizine. 2,3-Dehydroemetine.
Use: Treatment of amebiasis.
See: Mebadin

DEKASOL. (Seatrace) Dexamethasone phosphate 4 mg./ml. Vial 5 cc or 10 cc.

DEKASOL L.A. (Seatrace) Dexamethasone acetate 8 mg./ml. Vial 5 cc.

DEKA-VITES TABLETS. (Barry-Martin) Vit. A 5000 I.U., D 1000 I.U., B-1 2.5 mg., B-2 2.5 mg., B-6 0.5 mg., B-12 2 mcg., niacinamide 20 mg., Ca pantothenate 5 mg., C 50 mg., dicalcium phosphate 69.45 mg., ferrous sulfate, dried 51 mg., potassium iodide 0.2 mg., manganese sulfate 3.2 mg., copper sulfate monohydrate 2.8 mg., zinc sulfate, dried 2.77 mg., magnesium sulfate 21.58 mg., potassium sulfate 1.2 mg./Tab.Bot. 100s, 250s.
Use: Vitamin supplement w. minerals.

DEKEN'S OINTMENT. (Guild) Bot. 4 oz.

DE-KOFF. (Whiteworth) Terpin hydrate w/dextromethorphan elixir. Bot 4 oz.
Use: Antitussive.

DELACORT LOTION. (Mericon) Hydrocortisone 0.5%. Bot. 1 oz., 4 oz.

DELADIOL-40. (Dunhall) Estradiol valerate 40 mg./ml. Vial 10 ml.
Use: Long-acting estrogen.

DELADUMONE. (Squibb) Testosterone enanthate 90 mg., estradiol valerate 4 mg. in sesame oil/ml., chlorobutanol 0.5%. Vial 5 ml., 1 dose (1 cc.).
Use: Androgen and estrogen therapy.

DELADUMONE OB. (Squibb) Testosterone enanthate 180 mg., estradiol valerate 8 mg. in sesame oil/cc. Vial w/benzyl alcohol 2%. 2 cc./dose. Unimatic disp. syringe w/needle. (2 cc.) Pkg. 1s, 10s.

DELALUTIN. (Squibb) 17-α-Hydroxyprogesterone caproate 125 mg./cc., in sesame oil, benzyl benzoate 30%, benzyl alcohol 2%; 250 mg./cc., in castor oil, benzyl benzoate 46%, benzyl alcohol 2%. 125 mg./cc. Vial 10 cc. 250 mg./cc. Vial 5 cc. Unimatic 1-dose syringe 1 cc.
Use: I.M., long-acting progestational agent.

DELANEX. (Tunex) Hydroxyprogestrone caproate 250 mg./ml. w/benzyl benzoate 46%, benzyl alcohol 2% as preservative. Vial 5 cc.
Use: Long-acting progestational agent.

DEL-ANTHRA OINTMENT. (Del-Ray) Anthralin 0.03% Jar 4 oz.
Use: Treatment of psoriasis.

DELAPAV. (Dunhall) Papaverine HCl 150 mg./Time Cap. Bot. 100s, 1000s.
Use: Vasodilator.

DEL-AQUA-5. (Del-Ray) Benzoyl peroxide 5%. Tube 1.5 oz.
Use: Topical aid for acne vulgaria.

DEL-AQUA-10. (Del-Ray) Benzoyl peroxide 10%. Tu 1.5 oz.
Use: Topical aid for acne vulgaria.

DELAQUIN LOTION. (Schlicksup) Hydrocortisone 0.5%, Iodoquin 3%. Bot. 3 oz.

DELATEST. (Dunhall) Testosterone enanthate 100 mg./ml. Amp. 10 ml.
Use: Androgen therapy.

DELATESTADIOL. (Dunhall) Testosterone enantha 90 mg., estradiol valerate 4 mg./ml. Amp. 10 ml.
Use: Androgen and estrogen therapy.

DELATESTRYL. (Squibb) Testosterone enanthate 200 mg./cc. in sesame oil, chlorobutanol 0.5%. 5 cc. 1-dose Unimatic syringe (1 cc.) 1s, 10s.
Use: I.M., androgen therapy.

DELAXIN. (Ferndale) Methocarbamol 500 mg./Tab Bot. 100s, 500s.
Use: Musculoskeletal conditions.

DELCID. (Merrell Dow) Aluminum hydroxide 600 m magnesium hydroxide 665 mg./5 ml. Bot. plastic 8 oz.
Use: Antacid.

DEL-CLENS, (Del-Ray) Soapless cleanser. Bot. 8 c

DELCOBESE. (Delco), d-Amphetamine sulfate 25% amphetamine adipate 25%, amphetamine adip 25%, amphetamine sulfate 25%, Cap., Time Cap 5, 10, 15, 20 mg. Bot. 1000s. Tab.,
Use: Anorexiant, CNS stimulant.

DELCO-LAX. (Delco) Bisacodyl 5 mg./Tab. Bot. 100
Use: Laxative.

DELCOPLEX. (Delco) Multivitamin & multimineral Tab. Bot 1000s, 5000s, 10,000s.
Use: Sugar free vit. & mineral replacement.

DELCO-RETIC. (Delco) Hydrochlorothiazide 25 mg., mg./Tab. Bot. 1000s.
Use: Diuretic and antihypertensive.

DELCOZINE. (Delco) Phendimentrazine tartrate. 70 mg/Tab. Bot. 1000s, 5000s.
Use: Anorexiant, CNS stimulant.

DELESTREC. Estradiol 17-undecanoate.
Use: Estrogen.

DELESTROGEN. (Squibb) Estradiol valerate 10 mg./cc., in sesame oil, chlorobutanol 0.5%. Vial cc. 20 mg./cc., in castor oil, benzyl benzoate 20 benzyl alcohol 2%. Vial 5 cc. 40 mg./cc., in cast oil, benzyl benzoate 40%, benzyl alcohol 2%. Vi 5 cc. Unimatic single dose syringe: 20 mg., 1 cc. 1s, 10s.
Use: I.M., amenorrhea, menopausal syndrome.

DELFEN CONTRACEPTIVE FOAM. (Advanced Ca Nonoxynol-9 12.5% in an oil-in-water emulsion at 4.5 to 5.0. Can with applicator 20 Gm. Can only Gm. 50 Gm.
Use: Contraceptive foam.

DELINAL. Propenzolate Hydrochloride.

DELMADINONE. B.A.N. 6-Chloro-17α-hydroxypregı 1,4,6-triene-3,20-dione.
Use: Progestational steroid.

• **DELMADINONE ACETATE.** USAN. 6-Chloro-17-droxypregna-1, 4, 6-triene-3, 20-dione acetate.
Use: Progestin.
See: Delmate (Syntex)

LNAV. Dioxathion, B.A.N.

LSYM. (Pennwalt) Dextromethorphan polisterex equivalent to dextromethorphan HBr 30 mg./5 ml. Bot. 3 oz.
Use: Antitussive.

LTA-CORTEF. (Upjohn) Prednisolone 5 mg./Tab. Bot. 100s, 500s.
Use: Orally, rheumatoid arthritis & intractable bronchial asthma.

LTA-CORTRIL.
Prednisolone.

LTA-1-CORTISONE.
See: Deltasone, Tab. (Upjohn)

LTACORTONE.
Prednisone.

ELTAFILCON A. USAN.
Use: Contact lens material.

ELTAFILCON B. USAN.
Use: Contact lens material.

LTA-1-HYDROCORTISONE.
See: Prednisolone (Var. Mfr.)

LTA¹, 6-METHYL-HYDROCORTISONE.
See: Medrol, Preps. (Upjohn)

LTAPEN. (Trimen) Potassium penicillin G, U.S.P. 00,000 u./5 cc. Oral Susp. Bot. "16 dose." Tab. Bot. 100s.
Use: Antibiotic.

LTASONE. (Upjohn) Prednisone. **2.5 mg.**/Tab. Bot. 100s, **5 mg.**/Tab. Bot. 100s, 500s. Unit-Dose 00s. Dosepak 21s. **10 mg., 20 mg.**/Tab. Bot. 00s, 500s. Unit-Dose 100s. **50 mg.**/Tab. 100s, Unit Dose 100s.
Use: Orally, rheumatoid arthritis & intractable bronchial asthma.

L-TRAC. (Del-Ray) Acne lotion. Bot. 2 oz.
Use: Topical aid for acne.

LTRA-STAB.
See: Prednisolone (Var. Mfr.)

L-STAT. (Del-Ray) Abradent cleaner. Jar 2 oz.
Use: Topical aid for acne.

LYSID. Lysergic acid diethylamide.
Use: Potent psychotogenic.

MAZIN. (Schering) **Syr.:** Chlorpheniramine maleate mg., phenylephrine HCl 2.5 mg./5 ml., alcohol .5%. Bot. 4 oz. **Repetab:** Outer and inner layers: chlorpheniramine maleate 2 mg./layer, phenylephrine 10 mg./layer. Box 24s. Bot. 100s, 000s.
Use: Antihistamine, decongestant.

EMECARIUM BROMIDE, U.S.P. XXI. Ophth. Sol. U.S.P. XXI.
Use: Cholinergic (ophthalmic).
See: Humorsol, Sol. (Merck Sharp & Dohme)

EMECLOCYCLINE, U.S.P. XXI. Oral Susp., U.S.P. XXI. 7-Chloro-4-(dimethylamino)-1,4,4α,5,5α,6,11,12-octahydro-3,6,10,-12,12α-pentahydroxy-1,11-dioxo-2-naphthacene-carboxamide.
Use: Antibacterial.
See: Declomycin Prods (Lederle)
Ledermycin Prods (Lederle)

EMECLOCYCLINE HYDROCHLORIDE, U.S.P. XI. Caps., Tabs., U.S.P. XXI.
Use: Antibacterial.
See: Declomycin, HCl, Preps. (Lederle)

• **DEMECLOCYCLINE HYDROCHLORIDE AND NYSTATIN CAPSULES,** U.S.P. XXI.
Use: Antibacterial.
See: Declostatin, Cap.(Lederle)

• **DEMECLOCYCLINE HYDROCHLORIDE AND NYSTATIN TABLETS,** U.S.P. XXI.
Use: Antibacterial
See: Declostatin, Tab. (Lederle)

DEMECOLCINE. B.A.N. N-Methyl-N-deacetyl-colchicine.
Use: Antimitotic, leukemia therapy.
See: Colcemid

• **DEMECYCLINE.** USAN.
Use: Antibacterial.

DEMEROL APAP. (Winthrop-Breon) Meperidine HCl 50 mg., acetaminophen 300 mg./Tab. Bot. 100s.
Use: Analgesic.

DEMEROL HYDROCHLORIDE. (Winthrop-Breon) Meperidine HCL. **Syrup:** (50 mg./tsp.) Bot. 16 fl. oz. **Inj.: Detecto-Seal, Carpuject, Sterile Cartridge-Needle Units.2.5%:** (25 mg./ml.), **5%:** (50 mg./ml.), **7.5%:** (75 mg./ml.), **10%:** (100 mg./ml.), Boxes 10s. **Uni-Amp. 5%:** 0.5 ml (25 mg.)/Amp., 1 ml. (50 mg.)/Amp., 1.5 ml. (75 mg.)/Amp., and 2 ml. (100 mg.)/Amp. Box 25s; **10%:** 1 ml. (100 mg.)/Amp. Box 25s. **Uni-Nest 5%:** 0.5 ml (25 mg.)/Amp., 1 ml. (50 mg.)/Amp., 1.5 ml (75 mg.)/Amp. and 2 ml. (100 mg.)/Amp. Box 25s; **10%:** 1 ml./Amp. Box 25s. **Vials: 5%** multiple-dose vials/30 ml. Box 1s; **10%** multiple dose vials/20 ml. Box 1s.**Tab.:** (50 mg.) Bot. 100s, 500s. Hospital blister pack 25s. (100 mg.) Bot. 100s, 500s. Hospital blister pack 25s.
Use: Analgesic.

DEMETHYL CHLORTETRACYCLINE HCl.
See: Demeclocycline HCl, U.S.P. XXI.

DEMI-REGROTON. (USV Labs.) Chlorthalidone 25 mg., reserpine 0.125 mg./Tab. Bot. 100s., 1000s.
Use: Antihypertensive.

• **DEMOXEPAM.** USAN. 7-Chloro-1, 3-dihydro-5-phenyl-2H-1, 4-benzodiazepin-2-one-4-oxide.
Use: Minor tranquilizer.

DEMSER. (Merck Sharp & Dohme) Metyrosine 250 mg./Cap. Bot. 100s.
Use: Treatment of patients with pheochromocytoma.

DEMULEN 1/50-21. (Searle) Ethynodiol diacetate 1 mg., ethinyl estradiol 50 mcg./Tab. Compack Disp. 21s, 6×21., 24 × 21. Refills 21s, 12×21.
Use: Oral contraceptive.

DEMULEN 1/35-21. (Searle) Ethynodiol diacetate 1 mg., ethinyl estradiol 35 mcg./Tab. Compack disp. 21s, 6 ×21s, 24 × 21. Refill 21s, 12 × 21.
Use: Low-estrogen oral contraceptives.

DEMULEN 1/35-28. (Searle) Ethynodiol diacetate 1 mg., ethinyl estradiol 35 mcg./Tab. Compack 28s: 21 active tabs, 7 placebo tabs. Compack 6×28, 24 × 28. Refills 28s, 12 × 28.
Use: Low-estrogen oral contraceptive.

DEMULEN 1/50-28. (Searle) Ethynodiol diacetate 1 mg., ethinyl estradiol 50 mcg./Tab. Compack 28s: 21 active tabs, 7 placebo tabs. Compack Disp. of 28, 6×28, 24×28. Refills 28s, 12×28.
Use: Oral contraceptive.

DENALAN DENTURE CLEANSER. (Whitehall) Sodium percarbonate 30%. Bot. 7 oz., 13 oz.
Use: Denture cleanser.

• **DENATONIUM BENZOATE,** N.F. XVI. Bitrex (MacFarlan Smith, Ltd. Scotland) Benzyldiethyl [(2, 6-xylylcarbamoyl) methyl] ammonium benzoate.
Use: Denaturant for ethyl alcohol.
See: Bitrex

DENCORUB. (Last) Methyl salicylate 20%, menthol 0.75%, camphor 1%, oil eucalyptus 0.5%. Tube 1.25 oz., 2.75 oz.
Use: Greaseless analgesic rub.

DENGESIC. (Scott-Alison) Salicylamide 100 mg., acetaminophen 240 mg., phenyltoloxamine dihydrogen citrate 30 mg., butabarbital ⅛ gr./Tab. Bot. 60s, 500s.
Use: Analgesic w/sedative.

• **DENOFUNGIN.** USAN.
Use: Antifungal, antibacterial.

DENOREX. (Whitehall) Coal tar solution 9.0%, menthol 1.5%. Bot. 4 oz., 8 oz.
Use: Medicated shampoo.

DENOREX GEL. (Whitehall) Coal tar solution 9%, menthol 1.5%. Tube 2 oz., 4 oz.
Use: Medicated shampoo.

DENOREX MOUNTAIN FRESH. (Whitehall) Coal tar sol. 9%, menthol 1.5%. Bot. 4 oz., 8 oz.
Use: Medicated shampoo.

DENOREX WITH CONDITIONERS. (Whitehall) Coal tar sol. 9%, menthol 1.5%. Bot 4 oz., 8 oz.
Use: Medicated shampoo.

DENQUEL. (Vicks Prods) Potassium nitrate 5%. Tube 1.6 oz., 3 oz., 4.5 oz.
Use: Sensitive teeth toothpaste.

DENTAL CARIES PREVENTIVE. (Hoyt) Fluoride ion 1.2%, alumina abrasive. 2 Gm. Box 200s, Jars 9 oz.
Use: Clean and polish teeth.

DENTAVITE CHEWABLE TABLETS. (Reid-Provident) Vit. A 3000 I.U., D 400 I.U., C 60 mg., B-1 1 mg., B-2 1.2 mg., B-6 1 mg., niacinamide 8 mg., calcium pantothenate 3 mg., fluoride 1 mg./Tab. Bot. 100s.
Use: Fluoride with vitamin supplement.

DENTROL. (Block) Carboxymethylcellulose, polyethelyne oxide homopolymer, peppermint & spearmint in mineral oil base. Bot. 0.9 oz., 1.8 oz.
Use: Liquid denture adhesive.

DENT'S DENTAL POULTICE. (C.S. Dent) Alcohol 64%, benzocaine, oxyquinoline, thymol, capsicum oleoresin. Box 6s, 12s.

DENT'S EAR WAX DROPS. (C.S. Dent) Glycerine, propylene glycol, mineral oil, chloroform 1%, polyoxyethylene sorbitan monooleate. Bot. ⅛, 0.25 oz.

DENT'S LOTION-JEL. (C.S. Dent) Benzocaine in special base. Tube 3/16 oz.
Use: Toothache, teething pain, denture irritation.

DENT'S TOOTHACHE DROPS TREATMENT. (C.S. Dent) Alcohol 60%, chlorobutanol hydrous (chloroform derivative) 0.09%, phenol, eugenol, cresol and capsicum oleoresin. Bot. ⅛ fl. oz.

DENT'S TOOTHACHE GUM. (C.S. Dent) Benzocain phenol, capsicum oleoresin in base of cotton and wax. Box 21 grs.

DENYL SODIUM.
See: Diphenylhydantoin Sodium, Cap (Various Mf

DEOXYCHOLIC ACID.
See: Desoxycholic Acid, Tab. (Various Mfr.)

11-DEOXYCORTICOSTERONE ACETATE. Desoxycorticosterone Acetate, U.S.P XXI.

DEOXYCORTICOSTERONE ACETATE.
See: Desoxycorticosterone acetate, U.S.P. XXI.

2-DEOXY-5-FLUOROURIDINE.
See: FUDR, Vial (Roche)

2-DEOXY-5-IODOURIDINE. Idoxuridine, U.S.P. XXI.

1-DEOXY-1-(METHYLAMINO)-d-GLUCITOL. Meg mine, U.S.P. XXI.

1-DEOXY-1-(METHYLAMINO)-D-GLUCITOL 5/8 — ACETAMIDO-2,4,6,-TRIIODO-N-METHYLISOPHT ALAMATE (SALT). Iothalamate Meglumine Injection, U.S.P. XXI.

1-DEOXY-1-(METHYLAMINO)-D-GLUCITOL 3,3′-(ADIPOYLDIIMINO) BIS[2,4,6-TRI-IODOBENZOATE] (2:1) (SALT). Iodipamide Meglumine Injection, U.S.P. XXI.

1-DEOXY-1-(METHYLAMINO)-D-GLUCITOL 3, 5-DIACETAMIDO-2,4,6-TRIIODOBENZOATE (SAL Diatrizoate Meglumine, U.S.P. XXI.

D.E.P.-75. (Merchant) Diethylpropion HCl 75 mg./C Bot. 100s.
Use: Anorexant.

DEPAKENE. (Abbott) Valproic acid **Cap.:** 250 mg./Cap. Bot. 100s. Unit dose 100s. **Syrup:** 250 mg./5 ml. Bot. pt.
Use: Anticonvulsant.

DEPAKOTE. (Abbott) Divalproex sodium 125 mg., 250 mg. or 500 mg./Enteric Coated Tab. Bot. 10 Unit dose 100s.
Use: Antiepileptic agent.

dep ANDRO 100. (Forest) Testosterone cypionate cottonseed oil 100 mg./ml. Vial 10 ml.

dep ANDROGYN. (Forest) Testosterone cypionate mg., estradiol cypionate 2 mg./ml. Vial 10 ml.

dep ANDRO 200. (Forest) Testosterone cypionate cottonseed oil 200 mg./ml. Vial 10 ml.

DEPEN TITRATABLE TABLETS. (Wallace) Penicillamine 250 mg./Tab. Bot. 100s.
Use: Disease modifying anti-rheumatoid agent for vere active rheumatoid arthritis unresponsive to conventional therapy.

DEPEPSEN. Amylosulfate sodium.
Use: Peptic ulcer therapy.

DEP-ESTRADIOL. (Rocky Mtn.) Estradiol cypionate mg./cc. Vial 10 cc.
Use: Female hormone therapy.

DEPESTRO. (Kay) Estradiol cypionate 5 mg./ml. Vi 10 ml.
Use: Hormone supplement.

GYNOGEN. (Forest) Estradiol cypionate in ttonseed oil 5 mg./ml. Vial 10 ml.

MEDALONE 40. (Forest) Methylprednisolone etate in aqueous suspension 40 mg./ml. Vial 5 .

MEDALONE 80. (Forest) Methylprednisolone etate 80 mg./ml. Vial 5 ml.

OESTRA. (Tennessee Pharm.) Estradiol pionate 5 mg./cc. Vial 10 cc.
se: Estrogen therapy.

O-ESTRADIOL. (Upjohn) Estradiol cypionate 1 mg., mg./ml. chlorobutanol anhydrous 5.4 mg./ml. 'cottonseed oil. Estradiol cypionate **1 mg./ml.** al 10 ml. **5 mg./ml.** Vial 5 ml.
se: Estrogen therapy.

OGEN. (Sig) Estradiol valerate 10 mg., 20 g./ml. in oil. Vial 10 ml.
se: Estrogen therapy.

OGEN. (Hyrex) Estradiol cypionate 5 mg., Vial cc.
se: Long acting estrogen.

O-MED 40. (Tunex) Methylprednisolone acetate 40 g./ml. Vial 5 cc.
se: Anti-infammatory.

O-MED 80. (Tunex) Methylprednisolone acetate 80 g./ml. Vial 5 cc.
se: Anti-inflammatory.

O-MEDROL. (Upjohn) Methylprednisolone acetate mg., 40 mg., or 80 mg./ml. suspended in lyethylene glycol 3350 (29.6 mg., 29 mg., or 28 g./ml), sod. chloride (8.9 mg., 8.7 mg. or 8.5 g./ml.), myristyl-gamma-picolinium chloride 0.19 . **20 mg./ml.:** Vials 5 ml. Box 1s, 5s, 25s, 50s, 0s. **40 mg./ml.:** Vials 1 ml., 5 ml., 10 ml. Box 1s, , 25s, 50s, 100s. 25 pack 25, 50, 100 or more. **mg./ml.:** Vials 1 ml., 5 ml. 1s, 5s, 25s, 50s, 0s. Unit-Dose 1 ml. U-Ject. 5s, 25s, 50s, 100s. 25 ck 25, 50, 100 or more.
e: Anti-inflammatory.

O-PRED. (Hyrex) Methylprednisolone acetate susnsion 40 mg./ml. Vial 5 ml., 10 ml. 80 mg./ml. al 5 ml.
e: Steroid-anti-inflammatory.

O-PRED 100. (Vortech) Prednisolone acetate 100 g., sodium chloride 0.65%, pectin 0.2%, cinamide 25 mg./ml. w/preservative and buffer. al 10 ml.
se: Adrenocortical steroid.

O-PROVERA. (Upjohn) Medroxyprogesterone acee 100 mg. and 400 mg./ml. **100 mg./ml.:** spended in polyethylene glycol 3350, 27.6 mg., lysorbate 80, 1.84 mg., sod. chloride, 8.3 mg., ethylparaben, 1.75 mg., propylparaben 0.194 g./ml. Vial 5 ml. 1s, 5s, 25s. **400 mg./ml.:** spended in polyethylene glycol 3350, 20.3 mg. d. sulfate (anhydrous), 11 mg., myristyl-gammaolinium chloride, 1.69 mg./ml. Vial 2.5 ml., 10ml. ml. U-Ject. 1s, 5s, 25s.
se: Adunctive therapy and palliative treatment of perable, recurrent, and metastic endometrial or al carcinoma.

DEPOTEST. (Hyrex) Testosterone cypionate 100 mg. and 200 mg. Vial 10 cc.
Use: Male hormone, long acting.

DEPOTEST. (Kay) Testosterone cypionate 100 mg. or 200 mg./ml. Vial 10 ml.
Use: Androgen.

DEPO-TESTADIOL. (Upjohn) Sterile sol. testosterone cypionate 50 mg., estradiol cypionate 2 mg., chlorobutanol 5.4 mg./ml. w/cottonseed oil 874 mg./ml. Vial 1 ml., 10 ml. Box 1s, 5s, 25s.
Use: Androgen-estrogen therapy.

DEPOTESTOGEN. (Hyrex) Testosterone cypionate 50 mg., estradiol cypionate 2 mg., chlorobutanol 5 mg., in cottonseed oil/cc. Vial 10 cc.
Use: Androgen-estrogen therapy, long acting.

DEPO-TESTOSTERONE. (Upjohn) Testosterone cypionate 50 mg., 100 mg., or 200 mg./ml. **50 mg./ml.:** testosterone cypionate in chlorobutanol (anhydrous), 5.4 mg. cottonseed oil, 874 mg./ml. Vial 10 ml. 1s, 5s, 25s. **100 mg./ml.:** testosterone cypionate in benzyl alcohol 9.45 mg., cottonseed oil, 736 mg./ml. Vial 1 ml., 10 ml. 1s, 5s, 25s. **200 mg./ml.:** testosterone cypionate in benzyl benzoate, 0.2 ml., benzyl alcohol, 9.45 mg., cottonseed oil, 560 mg./ml. Vial 1 ml., 10 ml. 1s, 5s, 25s.
Use: I.M., long-acting androgen therapy.

DEPRODONE. B.A.N. 11 β 17α-Dihydroxypregna-1, 4-diene-3,20-dione.
Use: Corticosteroid.

DEPROL TABLETS. (Wallace) Meprobamate 400 mg., benactyzine HCl 1 mg./Tab. Bot. 100s, 500s. Unit dose 500s, 1000s.
Use: Antidepressant.

• **DEPROSTIL.** USAN.
Use: Antisecretory.

DEP-TEST. (Sig) Testosterone cypionate 100 mg./ml. Vial 10 ml.
Use: Androgenic.

DEP-TESTOSTERONE. (Rocky Mtn.) Testosterone cypionate 200 mg. /cc. Vial 10 cc. 100 mg./cc. 1 cc.
Use: Male hormone therapy.

DEP-TESTRADIOL. (Rocky Mtn.) Estradiol cypionate 2 mg., testosterone cypionate 50 mg./cc. Vial 10 cc.

DEPTROPINE. B.A.N. 3-(10, 11-Dihydrodibenzo-[a, d]cycloheptadien-5-yloxy)tropane.
Use: Bronchodilator.
See: Brontina (dihydrogen citrate)

DEQUALINIUM CHLORIDE. B.A.N. Decamethylenedi-(4-aminoquinaldinium chloride).
Use: Antiseptic.
See: Dequadin

DEQUIBOLIN-100. (Vortech) Nandrolone decandate 100 mg./ml. Vial 2 ml.
Use: I.M. androgen, anabolic, anti-catabolic steroid.

DERIFIL. (Rystan) Water-soluble derivatives of chlorophyll 100 mg./Tab. or 5 ml. of prepared sol. Bot. 30s, 100s, 1000s. Pow. 1 oz., 10 oz.
Use: Designed to control colostomy or ileostomy odors; odor of incontinent patients.

DERISOL. (Wolins) Amobarbital 0.5 gr., aspirin 2.5 gr., N-acety-p-aminophenol 2.5 gr./Tab. Bot. 1000s.
Use: Analgesic.

DERMACARE. (Jenkins) Hexachlorophene, camphor, menthol, lanolin. Bot. 2 oz. , 6 oz., pt., gal.
Use: Antiseptic skin lotion.

DERMACOAT AEROSOL SPRAY. (Century) Benzocaine 4.5%. Bot. 7 oz.
Use: Topical anesthetic.

DERMACON. (Paddock) Dermal contact ionogenic catalytic emulsoid. Bot. gal.

DERMACORT CREAM. (Rowell) Hydrocortisone 1% in a water soluble cream of stearyl alcohol, cetyl alcohol, isopropyl palmitate, citric acid, polyoxethylene 40 stearate, sod. phosphate, propylene glycol, water, benzyl alcohol & buffered to pH 5.0. Jar 1 lb.
Use: Inflammatory skin disorders.

DERMACORT LOTION. (Rowell) Hydrocortisone 0.5% or 1% in lotion base, buffered to pH 5.0 Paraben free. Bot. 120 ml.
Use: Topical corticosteroid cream.

DERMA-COVER. (Scrip) Sulfur, salicylic acid, hyamine 10x, isopropyl alcohol 22%, in powder film forming base. Bot. 2 oz.

DERMA-GUARD. (Greer) Protective adhesive pow. Can w/sifter top, 4 oz. Spray top Bot. 4 oz., pkg. 1 lb. Rings. Pkg. 5s, 10s.
Use: Protective powder for skin.

DERMAL-RUB. (Mallard) Menthol racemic 7%, camphor 1%, methyl salicylate 1%, cajuput oil 1%. Cream. Jar 1 oz., 1 lb.
Use: Analgesic.

DERMA-MEDICONE. (Medicone) Benzocaine 20 mg., oxyquinoline sulfate 10.5 mg., menthol 4.8 mg., ichthammol 10 mg., zinc oxide 137 mg./Gm. w/petrolatum, lanolin, perfume, certified color. Oint., Tube 1 oz.; Jar 1 lb.
Use: Antipruritic & vasoconstrictor.

DERMA MEDICONE-HC. (Medicone) Hydrocortisone acetate 10 mg., benzocaine 20 mg., oxyquinoline sulfate 10.5 mg., ephedrine HCl 1.1 mg., menthol 4.8 mg., ichthammol 10 mg., zinc oxide 137 mg./Gm. w/petrolatum, lanolin, perfume. Oint., Tube 7 Gm. & 20 Gm.
Use: Dermatoses.

DERMANEED. (Hanlon) Zirconium oxide 4.5%, calamine 6%, zinc oxide 4%, actamer 0.1% in bland lotionized base. Bot. 4 oz.
Use: Poison ivy.

DERMA-PAX. (Recsei) Methapyrilene HCl 0.22%, chlorothenylpyramine maleate 0.06%, pyrilamine maleate 0.22%, benzyl alcohol 1%, chlorobutanol 1%, isopropyl alcohol 40%. Liq. 4 oz., pt.
Use: Topically, antipruritic w/antihistamine.

DERMAPHILL. (Torch) Aluminum acetate 1%, phenol 1%, menthol 0.5%, camphor 3%, in hydrophilic vehicle. Jar 1 lb., 2 oz.
Use: General soothing and cooling applications.

DERMA-pH SKIN LOTION. (Day-Baldwin) pH 4.6 to 4.9. Mentholated or plain. Plastic Squeeze Bot. 4 oz., 8 oz. Plastic Bot. gal.

DERMAREX. (Hyrex) Hydrocortisone 1%, clioquinc 3%, pramoxine HCl 0.5%. Cream Tubes, 0.5 oz.
Use: Antifungal and antibacterial agent.

DERMA-SMOOTHE/FS OIL. (Hill) Fluocinolone ac nide 0.01% topical oil. Bot. 4 oz.
Use: Psoriasis, seborrheic dermatitis & atopic dermatitis.

DERMA-SMOOTHE OIL. (Hill) Refined peanut oil, r eral oil in lipophilic base.
Use: Relieves itching, softens skin.

DERMA-SONE 1%. (Hill) Hydrocortisone 1%, pran ine HCl 1%, cetyl alcohol, glyceryl monosterate, isopropyl myristate, potassium sorbate, furcellera
Use: Relief of the inflammatory manifestations o corticosteroid responsive dermatoses.

DERMASSAGE. (Colgate) Mineral oil, TEA-stea propylene glycol, stearic acid, menthol, diammonium phosphate, methylparaben, lanolin, oxyquinoline sulfate, urea, propylparaben. Lot. 6, 12, 16 oz., Cream 3.5 oz.

DERMA SOAP. (Ferndale) Dowicil 0.1%. 4 oz. w/dispenser.

DERMA-SOFT. (Vogarell) Medicated cream. Sali acid, castor oil, triethanolamine. Tube ¾ oz.
Use: Removal of corns, calluses, warts.

DERMASORCIN. (Lamond) Resorcin 2%, sulfur 5 Bot. 1 oz., 2 oz., 4 oz., 8 oz., pt., 32 oz., 0.5 gal
Use: Treatment of acne and seborrhea.

DERMASTRINGE. (Lamond) Bot. 4 oz., 6 oz., 8 oz pt., 32 oz., gal.
Use: Skin cleansing solution.

DERMASUL. (Lamond) Sulfur 5%. Bot. 1 oz., 2 oz oz., 8 oz., pt., 32 oz., 0.5 gal., gal.
Use: Treatment of acne and seborrhea.

DERMATHYN. (Davis & Sly) Benzyl alcohol 3%, benzocaine 3.5%, butyl-p-aminobenzoate 1% & p nylmercuric borate. Tube 1 oz.
Use: Topical local anesthetic.

DERMATIC BASE. (Whorton) Compounding crean base. Bot. 16 oz.
Use: Preparing creams and lotions with water-ba materials.

DERMATOL.
See: Bismuth subgallate, Preps. (Various Mfr.)

DERMAX. (Dermco) Methphenoxydiol 100 mg., (3- methosyphenoxy)-1, 2-propanediol) Bot. 100s, 10
Use: Tension states.

DERMEZE. (Premo) Thenylpyramine HCl 2%, benzocaine 2%, tyrothricin 0.25 mg./Gm. Massa Lotion 5¾ oz.
Use: Topically; antihistaminic, antibiotic & anesthetic.

DERMIDON ANTI-ITCH CREAM. (Republic) Pyrilar maleate 0.5%, phenyltoloxamine dihydrogen citr 0.5%, diperidon HCl 0.25%, benzalkonium chlor 0.1%, menthol, camphor, water washable crean Tube 1.25 oz.
Use: Relief of itching.

DERMOLATE ANTI-ITCH CREAM. (Schering) drocortisone 0.5% in a greaseless, vanishing cream. Tube 15 gm., 30 gm.
Use: Antipruritic.

RMOLATE ANTI-ITCH SPRAY. (Schering) Hydrocortisone 0.5%, alcohol 24%. Pump spray bot. 45 ml.
Use: Antipruritic.
RMOLATE ANAL-ITCH OINTMENT. (Schering) Hydrocortisone 0.5%. Tube 30 gm.
Use: Antipruritic.
RMOLATE SCALP-ITCH LOTION. (Schering) Hydrocortisone 0.5%, alcohol 47%. Squeeze Bot. 30 ml.
Use: Antipruritic.
RMOLIN. (Mallard) Menthol racemic, methyl salicylate, camphor, mustard oil, isopropyl alcohol 3%. Liniment. Bot. 3 oz., pt., gal.
Use: Topically, for pain.
RMO PEDIC ELBOW LOTION. (CMC) Bot. 4 oz.
Use: Soothing elbow lotion.
RMO PEDIC FOOT LOTION. (CMC) Bot. 4 oz.
Use: Soothing foot lotion.
RMOPLAST AEROSOL SPRAY. (Ayerst) Benzocaine 20%, menthol 0.5%, in water-dispersible base of Tween 85, PEG 400 monolaurate, methylparaben as preservative, and propellants. Spray 2.75 oz., 6 oz.
Use: Topically as anesthetic, antipruritic.
RMOVAN. (Owen) Glyceryl stearate, spermaceti, mineral oil, glycerin, cetyl alcohol, butylparaben, methylparaben, propylparaben, & purified water. Vanishing-type base, Jar 1 lb.
Use: Cream base (lanolin free).
SACCHROMIN. A nonprotein bacterial colloidal dispersion of polysaccharide.
SA-HIST AT. (Pharmics) Phenylpropanolamine HCl 50 mg., chlorpheniramine maleate 6 mg., dextromethorphan HBr 30 mg., terpin hydrate 180 mg., acetaminophen 325 mg./Tab. **Tabs.** Bot. 100s. **Syr.** Bot. pt., gal.
Use: Decongestant, antihistamine, antitussive, expectorant and analgesic.
SA-HIST PF CAPSULES. (Pharmics) Chlorpheniramine maleate 8 mg., phenylpropanolamine HCl 50 mg./Cap. Bot. 100s, 500s.
Use: Decongestant, antihistaminic combination for nasal congestion due to allergies.
SA-HIST PF ELIXIR. (Pharmics) Chlorprophenpyridamine maleate 2 mg., 1-phenylephrine HCl 3 mg., alcohol 7.5% in a syrup base/5 cc. Bot. pts., gal.
Use: Systemic nasal decongestant.
SAMYCIN. (Pharmics) Tetracycline HCl 250 mg./Cap. Bot. 100s.
Use: Tetracycline therapy.
ESCINOLONE ACETONIDE. USAN.
Use: Glucocorticoid.
SENEX. (Pharmacraft) **Cream:** Total undecylenate 20% as undecylenic acid and zinc undecylenic . Tube 1.5 oz. **Oint.**: Total undecylenate 20% as undecylencic acid and zinc undecylenate. Tube 0.9 oz., 1.8 oz. Can 1 lb. **Pow.** Total undecylenate 19% as undecylenic acid and zinc undecylenate. Can 1.5 oz., 3 oz. Carton 1 lb. **Liquid:** Undecylenic acid 10%, isopropyl alcohol 47.1%. Pump Spray Bot. 1.5 oz. **Spray Powder:** Total undecylenate 19% as undecylenic acid and zinc undecylenate. Aerosol can 2.7 oz., 5.5. oz., **Penetrating Foam:** Undecylenic acid 10% isopropyl alchol 35.2%. Can 1.5 oz.
Use: Antifungal, athlete's foot treatment.
DESENEX FOOT & SNEAKER SPRAY. (Pharmacraft) Aluminum chlorhydrex w/alcohol 89.3%. Aerosol Can 2.7 oz.
Use: Foot deodorant, antiperspirant.
DE SERPA. (de Leon) Reserpine, Tab. 0.25, 0.5 mg., Bot. 100s, 500s. Tab. 0.25 mg. Bot. 1000s.
Use: Tranquilizer and hypotensor.
DESERPIDINE. B.A.N. 11-Demethoxyreserpine.
Use: Tranquilizer.
DESERPIDINE. An alkaloid derived from *Rauwolfia canescens.* 11-Desmethoxyreserpine (Raunormine)
Use: Treatment of hypertension.
See: Harmonyl, Tab. (Abbott)
W/Hydrochlorothiazide
See: Oreticyl, Tab. (Abbott)
W/Methyclothiazide.
See: Enduronyl and Enduronyl Forte, Tabs. (Abbott)
DESFERAL. (Ciba) Deferoxamine mesylate 500 mg./5 ml. Amp. 4s.
Use: Iron salt poisoning.
DESFERRIOXAMINE. B.A.N. 30-Amino-3,14,25-trihydroxy-3,9,14,20,25-penta-azatriacontane-2,10,-13,21,24-pentaone. Deferoxamine (I.N.N.)
Use: Chelating agent.
See: Desferal, Amp. (Ciba)
• **DESIPRAMINE HYDROCHLORIDE,** U.S.P. XXI. Caps., Tab., U.S.P. XXI. 10, 11-Dihydro-5-[3-(methylamino)propyl]-5H-dibenz[b,f]azepine hydrochloride.
Use: Antidepressant.
See: Norpramin, Tab. (Merrell Dow)
Pertofrane, Cap. (USV Labs.)
DESITIN. (Leeming) **Pow.** Talc. Can 3 oz., 7 oz., 10 oz. **Oint.** Cod liver oil, zinc oxide, talc, petrolatum, lanolin. Tube 1.25 oz., 2.25 oz., 4.25 oz., 8 oz. Jar 1 lb.
Use: Diaper rash remedy.
• **DESLANOSIDE,** U.S.P. XXI. Inj., U.S.P. XXI. Deacetyllanatoside C.
Use: Cardiotonic.
See: Cedilanid-D, Amp. (Sandoz)
DESMA. (Tablicaps) Diethylstilbesterol 25 mg./Tab. Patient dispensers 10s.
Use: Estrogen therapy.
11-DESMETHOXY RESERPINE. Deserpidine.
See: Harmonyl, Tab. (Abbott)
DESMOPRESSIN. B.A.N. 1-Desamino-8-D-arginine-vasopressin.
Use: Treatment of diabetes insipidus.
• **DESMOPRESSIN ACETATE.** USAN.
Use: Treatment of diabetes insipidus.
See: DDVAP, Liq. (Centerchem)
DESO-CREME. (Quality Generics) Zinc undecylenate 20%, caprylic acid 5%, sod. propionate 2%. Tubes 1 oz.
Use: Athlete's foot, ringworn and fungus infections.

DESOMORPHINE. B.A.N. 7,8-Dihydro-6-deoxymorphine.
Use: Narcotic analgesic.

• **DESONIDE.** USAN. 16-alpha-Hydroxyprednisolone-16, 17 acetonide. B.A.N. 11 β,21-Dihydroxy-16α, 17 α-isopropylidenedioxypregna-1,4-diene-3,20-dione.
Use: Anti-inflammatory.
See: Desowen Cream (Owen)
Tridesilon, Cream (Miles Pharm)

DESOWEN CREAM. (Owen) Desonide 0.5 mg./Gm. Tube 15 Gm, 60 Gm.
Use: Anti-inflammatory for dermatoses.

• **DESOXIMETASONE GEL,** U.S.P. XXI.

DESOXYCHOLIC ACID. (Various Mfr.) Deoxycholic acid, 3,12-Dihydroxycholanic acid. Tab. 1.5 gr.
Use: Choleretic.
See: Droxolan, Tab. (O'Neal)
W/Dehydrocholic acid.
See: Combichole, Tab. (Trout)
Foydox, Tab. (Foy)
Ketosox, Tab. (Ascher)
W/Dehydrocholic acid, ox bile extract, phenobarbital.
See: Oxsorbil PB, Cap. (Ives)
W/Dehydrocholic acid, bile ext., sorbitan mono-oleate, oleic acid.
See: Oxsorbil, Cap. (Ives)
W/Dehydrocholic acid, choline methionine tartrate, & adiphenine HCl.
See: Desacholine, Tab. (Mallard)
W/Ox bile ext., mixed ox bile acids, pancreatin.
See: Bilogen Tabs. (Organon)
W/Pancreatin, pepsin, bile salts, dehydrocholic acid.
See: Enzylax, Tab. (Kay)
Pepsatal, Tab. (Kenyon)
W/Phenobarbital, homatropine methylbromide, gerilase, geriprotase, dehydrocholic acid.
See: Bilezyme Plus, Tabs. (Geriatric)

• **DESOXIMETASONE,** U.S.P. XXI. Cream, U.S.P. XXI.
Use: Adrenocortical steroid.

• **DESOXYCORTICOSTERONE ACETATE,** U.S.P. XXI. Inj., Pellets, U.S.P. XXI. Pregn-4-ene-3,20-dione, 21-(acetyloxy)-. 11-Deoxycorticosterone acetate. (Various Mfr.) (DCA, Deoxycostone acetate, Cortate, Cortiron, Cortenil, Cortigen, Syncort, Syncortyl.) Aq. susp., 5 mg./cc. Vial 10 cc.; in sesame oil, 5 mg./cc. Vial 10 cc.
Uses: I.M. or S.C. (2-5 mg.) adrenal cortical insufficiency; (salt-regulating).
See: Doca Acetate, Inj. (Organon)
Percorten, Amp., Pellet & Vial (Ciba)

• **DESOXYCORTICOSTERONE PIVALATE,** U.S.P. XXI. Sterile Susp. U.S.P. XXI. Pregn-4-ene-3,20-dione, 21-(2,2-dimethyl-1-oxopropoxy)-11-deoxycorticosterone pivalate.
Use: Salt-regulator; adrenocortical steroid.
See: Percorten Privalate, Vial (Ciba)

• **DESOXYCORTICOSTERONE TRIMETHYLACETATE.** 11-Deoxycorticosterone pivalate.
Use: Adrenocortical steroid (salt-regulating).

DESOXYCORTONE ACETATE.
See: Desoxycorticosterone Acetate, Prep. (Various Mfr.)

DESOXYEPHEDRINE HYDROCHLORIDE. (Various Mfr.) Dextro-l-phenyl-2-methylaminopropane, d-phenylisopropylmethylamine, d-N-methylamphetamine.
See: Methamphetamine HCl, Prep.

dl-DESOXYEPHEDRINE HYDROCHLORIDE.
See: dl-Methamphetamine HCl

DESOXYMETHASONE. B.A.N. 9α-Fluoro-11β,-21-dihydroxy-16α-methylpregna-1,4-diene-3,20-dione.
Use: Topical corticosteroid.
See: Esperson

DESOXYN. (Abbott) Methamphetamine HCl.
Tab.: 5 mg., Bot. 100s, 1000s.
Gradumets: 5 mg., Bot. 100s, 10 & 15 mg. Bot. 100s, 500s.
Use: Central nervous system stimulant.

DESOXY NOREPHEDRINE.
Use: Central nervous system stimulant.
See: Amphetamine HCl, Preps. (Various Mfr.)

DESOXYRIBONUCLEASE.
W/Fibrinolysin.
See: Elase, prep. (Parke-Davis)

DESQUAM-X 5% or 10% GEL. (Westwood) Benzoyl peroxide 5% or 10%, laureth-4 6% in a gel base w/water, carbomer 940, diisopropanolamine, disodium edetate. Tube. 1.5 oz., 3 oz.
Use: Antibacterial and drying lotion for control of acne.

DESQUAM-X 4% or 10% WASH. (Westwood) Benzoyl peroxide 4% or 10% in a lathering base of sodium oxtoxynol-3 sulfonate, docusate sodium, magnesium aluminum silicate, methylcellulose, EDTA. Bot. 5 oz.
Use: Topical antibacterial and skin cleanser for the control of acne vulgaris.

D-EST. (Burgin-Arden) Estradiol cypionate 5 mg./cc. cc. vial.

DESYREL. (Mead Johnson) Trazodone HCl 50 mg., 100 mg./Tab. Unit dose 100s.
Use: Antidepressant.

DESYREL DIVIDOSE. (Mead Johnson) trazodone HCl 150 mg./Dividose Tab. Bot. 100s.
Use: Antidepressant.

DETACHOL. (Ferndale) Bland, nonirritating liquid for removing adhesive tape. Pkg. 4 oz.

DE TAL. (de Leon) Phenobarbital 0.25 gr., hyoscyamine sulfate 0.1037 mg., atropine sulfate 0.0194 mg., hyoscine HBr 0.0065 mg./Tab. or 5 cc. **Tab.** Bot. 100s; **Elix.** alcohol 20%, Bot. pt.

DETANE. (Commerce) Tube 0.5 oz.
Use: Desensitizing lubricant.

• **DETERENOL HYDROCHLORIDE.** USAN.
Use: Adrenergic.

DETERGENTS, Surface-Active.
See: pHisoDerm, Liq. (Winthrop Products)
pHisoHex, Liq. (Winthrop Consumer Products)
Zephiran, Prods. (Winthrop-Breon)

DETIGON HYDROCHLORIDE.
See: Chlophedianol HCl. (Var. Mfr.)

EUTIERIUM OXIDE. USAN.
Use: Radioactive agent.
TUSS. (Zenith) Caramiphen edisylate 40 mg., henylpropanolamine HCl 75 mg., isopropamide odide equiv. to 2.5 mg. of isopropamide/S.R. Cap.
Use: Allergy, cold treatment.
TUSSIN EXPECTORANT. (Quality Generics) Pseudoephedrine HCl 60 mg., hydrocodone itartrate 5 mg., guaifenesin 200 mg./5 ml. Bot. pt., al.
Use: Antitussive, decongestant, expectorant.
TUSSIN LIQUID. (Quality Generics) Hydrocodone itartrate 5 mg., pseudoephedrine HCl 60 mg./5 ml. w/alcohol 57. Bot. pt., gal.
Use: Antitussive, decongestant.
WITT'S COUGH CONTROL MEDICINE. (DeWitt) Dextromethorphan HBr 8 mg., ammonium chloride 0 mg., pot. guaiacolsulfonate 75 mg., glycerin, alcohol 3%/5 ml. Bot. 4 oz.
Use: Antitussive.
WITT'S PILLS. (DeWitt) Analgesic and mild diuretic pills. Blister Packs 20s, 40s, 80s.
Use: Backache and joint pain relief.
XACEN-4. (Central) Dexamethasone phosphate (furnished as dexamethasone sodium phosphate) 4 mg./ml. w/sodium citrate 10 mg., sodium bisulfite 1 mg., methylparaben 1.5 mg., propylparaben 0.2 mg., creatinine 8 mg./ml. and sodium hydroxide to adjust pH. Vial 10 ml. Box 12s.
Use: Corticosteroid therapy by I.M. and soft tissue injection.
XACEN-LA-8. (Central) Dexamethasone acetate equivalant to dexamethasone 8 mg./ml. w/sodium Cl 6.67 mg., creatinine 5 mg., disodium edetate 0.5 mg., sodium carboxymethylcellulose 5 mg., polysorbate-80 0.75 mg., benzyl alcohol 9 mg., sodium bisulfite 1 mg./ml. Vial 5 ml. Box 12s.
Use: Corticosteroid therapy by I. M. and soft tissue injection.
XACIDIN OPHTHALMIC SUSPENSION. (CooperVision) Neomycin 3.5 mg., polymyxin B sulfate 10,000 u., dexamethosone 1 mg./ml. Bot. 5 ml.
Use: Anti-infective/steroid combination for inflammatory ocular conditions.
XACILLIN. Epicillin, B.A.N.
X-A-DIET ORIGINAL FORMULA. (O'Connor) Phenylpropanolamine HCL 75 mg., caffeine 200 mg./Cap. Pkg. 3s, 6s, 10s, 24s, 48s.
Use: Appetite suppressant/diuretic.
X-A-DIET CAFFEINE FREE. (O'Connor) Phenylpropanolamine HCl 75 mg./Cap. Pkg. 3s, 6s, 20s, 40s.
Use: Appetite suppressant.
XAMETH. (Major) Dexamethasone 0.5 mg., 0.75 mg., 1.5 mg. or 4 mg./Tab. Bot. 100s.
Use: Corticosteroid.
• **DEXAMETHASONE,** U.S.P. XXI. Tab., Elix., Gel, Ophth. Susp., Topical Aerosol, U.S.P. XXI. Pregna-1,4-diene-3,20-dione,9-fluoro-11,17,21-trihydroxy-16-methyl-, (11β,16α). 9-fluoro-11β, 17,21-trihydroxy-16α-methyl-, pregna-1,4-diene-3,20-dione.
Use: Adrenocortical steroid (anti-inflammatory); Same as for prednisone or prednisolone; Dose: Individualized according to disease, 0.75 mg. is equivalent to 4 mg. triamcinolone, 5 mg. prednisone/prednisolone, 20 mg. hydrocortisone or 25 mg. cortisone.
See: Aeroseb-Dex, Aerosol (Herbert)
Decaderm in Estergel (Merck Sharp & Dohme)
Decadron, Tab., Elxr. (Merck Sharp & Dohme)
Decameth, Inj. (Foy)
Decameth L.A., Inj. (Foy)
Decaspray, Aerosol (Merck Sharp & Dohme)
Dexaport, Tab. (Freeport)
Dezone, Tab. (Reid-Provident)
Dexone TM, Tab. (Rowell)
Hexadrol, Tab. Elxr., Cream. (Organon)
Maxidex Ophth. liq. (Alcon)
SK-Dexamethasone, Tab. (SmithKline)
W/Neomycin Sulf.
See: NeoDecadron, Prep. (Merck Sharp & Dohme)
NeoDecaspray, Aerosol (Merck Sharp & Dohme)
W/Neomycin sulf., polymyxin B sulf.
See: Maxitrol Ophth. Susp., Oint. (Alcon)
• **DEXAMETHASONE ACETATE,** U.S.P. XXI. Sterile Susp.., U.S.P. XXI.
Use: Adrenocortical steroid (anti-inflammatory)
See: Dexzone LA, Ind. (Tunex)
Tendron, Inj. (Amfre-Grant)
• **DEXAMETHASONE SODIUM PHOSPHATE.** U.S.P. XXI. Inhalation Aerosol, Cream, Ophth. Oint., Ophth. Soln., Inj., U.S.P. XXI. Pregn-4-ene-3,20-dione, 9-fluoro-11, 17-dihydroxy-16-methyl-21-(phosphonooxy)-disodium salt, (11β, 16α)-9-Fluoro-11β, 17,21-trihydroxy-16α-methylpregna-1,4-diene-3,20-dione-21-(dihydrogen phosphate) disodium salt.
Use: Adrenocortical steroid (anti-inflammatory).
See: Dexzone, Inj. (Tunex)
Decadron Phosphate, Preps. (Merck Sharp & Dohme)
Decadron Phosphate Respihaler (Merck Sharp & Dohme)
Decaject, Vial (Mayrand)
Decameth, Inj. (Foy)
Dexone, Inj. (Keene, Mallard)
Dezone, Inj. (Reid-Provident)
Hexadrol Phosphate, Inj. (Organon)
Savacort D, Inj. (Savage)
Solurex, Inj. (Hyrex)
Tendron, Inj. (Amfre-Grant)
W/Lidocaine (Xylocaine)
See: Decadron Phos w/Xylocaine, Inj. (Merck Sharp & Dohme)
W/Neomycin sulfate.
See: NeoDecadron, Prep. (Merck Sharp & Dohme)
• **DEXAMISOLE.** USAN.
Use: Antidepressant.
DEXAMPEX. (Lemmon) Dextroamphetamine sulfate.
Tab.: 5 mg./Tab. Bot. 1000s, 5000s,. 10 mg./Tab. 1000s, 5000s. **Cap.**: 15mg./Cap. Bot. 1000s, 5000s.
Use: Central stimulant, narcolepsy treatment.

DEXAMPHETAMINE. B.A.N. (+)-α-Methyl-phenethylamine. (+)-Amphetamine.
Use: Central nervous system stimulant; appetite supressant.
See: Dexamed
Dexedrine

DEXAMPHETAMINE.
See: Dextroamphetamine (Var. Mfr.)

DEXA-PED CHEWABLE VITAMINS. (Xttrium) Vit. A 5000 I.U., D 400 I.U., B-1 2 mg., B-2 2 mg., B-6 1.5 mg., B-12 5 mcg., C 75 mg., niacinamide 10 mg., Ca pantothenate 2 mg., E 1 I.U./Tab. Bot. 150s, 250s.

DEXA-PED VITAMIN DROPS. (Xttrium) Vit. A 3000 I.U., D 400 I.U., C 60 mg., B-1 1 mg., B-2 1.2 mg., niacinamide 8 mg., B-6 1 mg., panthenol 3 mg., B-12 1 mcg., biotin 30 mcg./0.6 cc. Bot. 60 cc.

DEXAPHEN S.A. TABS. (Major) Bot. 100s, 1000s.
Use: Antihistamine, nasal decongestant.

DEXAPORT. (Freeport) Dexamethasone 0.75 mg.,/Tab. Bot. 1000s.
Use: Anti-inflammatory.

DEXASONE. (Ferndale) Dexamethasone sodium phosphate 4 mg./ml. Vial 10 cc.
Use: Adrenocortical steroid therapy.

DEXASONE INJECTION. (Hauck) Dexamethasone sodium phosphate 4 mg./ml. Vial 5 ml, 30 ml.
Use: Advenocortical steroid.

DEXASONE-L.A. INJECTION. (Hauck) Dexamethasone acetate 8 mg./ml. Vial 5 ml., 30 ml.
Use: Adrenocortical steroid.

DEXASPORIN OPHTHALMIC SUSPENSION. (Quality Generics) Dexamethasone 0.1%, neomycin 3.5 mg., polymyxin B sulfate 10,000 u./ml. Bot. 5 ml.
Use: Anti-inflammatory, antibiotic.

DEXATRIM. (Thompson Medical)
Phenylpropanolamine HCl, caffeine. Available in Regular, Extra Strength, Caffeine Free and Caffeine Free plus Vitamins.
Use: Appetite suppressant.

DEXBROM. (Zenith) Dexbrompheniramine maleate 6 mg., pseudoephedrine sulfate 120 mg./Time Release Tab.
Use: Antihistaminic, decongestant.

• **DEXBROMPHENIRAMINE MALEATE,** U.S.P. XXI. (+)-2-[p-Bromo-α-[2-(dimethylamino) ethyl]-[benzyl]-pyridine maleate. Dextro form of brompheniramine. Dextroparabromdylamine 1-(p-bromophenyl-1-(2-pyridyl)-3-dimethylamino propane maleate. (+)-2-(p-Bromo-α-(2-(dimethylamino)ethyl)benzyl)-pyridine-Maleate (1:1)
Use: Antihistaminic.
W/Pseudoephedrine sulfate.
See: Disophrol Chronotab, Tab. (Schering)
Drixoral S.A., Tab. (Schering)

• **DEXCHLORPHENIRAMINE MALEATE,** U.S.P. XXI. Syrup, Tabs., U.S.P. XXI. d-2-[p-Chloroalpha(2-dimethyl-amino-ethyl)benzyl] pyridine bimaleate. (+)-2-(p-Chloro-α-(2-dimethylamino)-ethyl)benzyl)pyridine-Maleate (1:1) Dextro-Chlorpheniramine Maleate.
Use: Antihistaminic.
See: Polaramine, Repetabs Tab., Tab., Syr. (Schering)
W/Pseudoephedrine sulfate, guaifenesin, alcohol.
See: Polaramine Expect. (Schering)

• **DEXCLAMOL HYDROCHLORIDE.** USAN.
Use: Sedative.

DEXEDRINE. (SmithKline) Dextroamphetamine sulfate. **Elixir:** 5 mg./5 ml. (Alcohol 10%.) Bot. 16 oz. **Tab.:** (5 mg.) Bot. 100s, 1000s. **Spansule:** 5 mg. Bot. 50s; 10 mg., 15 mg. Bot. 50s, 500s.
Use: Central nervous system stimulant.

• **DEXETIMIDE.** USAN. (+)-3-(1-Benzyl-4-piperidyl)-3-phenylpiperidine-2,6-dione.
Use: Treatment of the parkinsonian syndrome.

• **DEXIMAFEN.** USAN.
Use: Antidepressant.

• **DEXIVACAINE.** USAN.
Use: Anesthetic.

DEXO-LA. (Mallard) Dexamethasone 8 mg./ml. Vial ml.
Use: Adrenocortical steroid.

DEXON. (Kay) Dexamethasone sodium phosphate 4 mg./ml. Vial 10 ml.
Use: Anti-inflammatory.

DEXON. (Pasadena Research) Desoxycorticosterone acetate 5 mg./ml. Vial 10 cc. (In sesame oil).

DEXON L.A. (Kay) Dexamethasone acetate 8 mg./r Vial 5 ml.
Use: Anti-inflammatory.

DEXONE. (Mallard) Dexamethasone sodium phosphate. 4 mg./ml. Amp. 5 ml.
Use: Anti-inflammatory.

DEXONE. (Keene) Dexamethasone sodium phosphate 4 mg./ml. Vial 5 ml., 10 ml.
Use: Anti-inflammatory.

DEXONE L.A.. (Keene) Dexamethasone acetate suspension equiv. to 8 mg. dexamethasone. Vial 5 ml.

DEXONE TM. (Rowell) Dexamethasone 0.5 mg., 0.7 mg., 1.5 mg., 4 mg. Tab. Bot. 100s. Unit dose 100s.

• **DEXOXADROL HYDROCHLORIDE.** USAN. d-2-(2 Diphenyl-1,3-dioxolan-4-yl) piperidine hydrochloric Dextro form of dioxadrol HCl.
Use: Antidepressant.

• **DEXPANTHENOL,** U.S.P. XXI. Preparation, U.S.P. XXI. (+)-2,4-Dihydroxy-N-(3-hydroxypropyl)-3,3-dimethylbutyramide.
Use: Treatment of paralytic ileus and postoperativ distention.
See: Bepanthen
Ilopan, Inj. (Adria)
Intrapan, Vial (Intra; Arcum)
Panthoderm Lotion, Cream (USV Labs.)
Tonestat, Inj. (A.V.P.)

DEXPROPRANOLOL. B.A.N. (+)-1-Isopropylamino-3-(1-naphthyloxy)propan-2-ol.
Use: Antiarrhythmic.

• **DEXPROPANOLOL HCl.** USAN. (±)-l-(Isopropylamino)-3-(l-naphthyloxy)-2-propanol HCl.
Use: Cardiac depressant (antiarrhythmic).

DEX-SALT. (Quality Generics) Sodium chloride 7 gr., v B-1 1 mg., dextrose 3 gr./Tab. Bot. 100s, 1000s.

:XSONE INJECTION (Vortech) Dexamethasone sod. phosphate equiv. to dexmethasone phos. 4 mg., creatinine 8 mg., sod. citrate 10 mg., sod. bisulfite 1 mg., methyl paraben 1.5 mg., propyl paraben 0.2 mg./cc. Vial 5 cc.
Use: Adrenocortical steroid (Anti-inflammatory).

:XTRAN. B.A.N. Polyanhydroglucose.
Use: Restoration of blood volume.
See: Dextraven
Intradex

EXTRAN.
Use: Blood volume expander.
See: LMWD-Dextran 40 (Pharmchem)
Macrodex, Sol. (Pharmacia)

EXTRAN 6%. (Abbott)
See: Dextran 75, I.V. (Abbott)

DEXTRAN 40. USAN. Polysaccharide (m.w. 40,000) produced by the action of Leuconostoc mesenteroides on saccharose.
Use: Blood suspension stabilizer.
See: LMD 10% (Abbott)
Rheomacrodex, Sol. (Pharmacia)

EXTRAN 45, 75. Polysaccharide (m.w. 45,000 & 75,000) produced by the action of Leuconostoc mesenteroides on saccharose. Rheotran (45).
Use: Blood plasma volume extender, antithrombogenic agent.

DEXTRAN 70. USAN. A polysaccharide.
Macrodex, Sol. (Pharmacia)
Use: Blood volume expander.

DEXTRAN 75. USAN. Dextran 75 6% in 0.9% saline. Flask 500 ml.; Dextran 75 6% in 5% dextrose. Flask 500 ml.
Use: Blood plasma expander.

EXTRANOMER. B.A.N. Dextran cross-linked with epichlorohydrin.
Use: Promoter of wound-healing.
See: Debrisan.

DEXTRATES, N.F. XVI. Mixture of sugars (approximately 92% dextrose monohydrate and 8% higher saccharides; dextrose equivalent is 95 to 97%) resulting from the controlled enzymatic hydrolysis of starch.
Use: Pharmaceutic aid (tablet binder and diluent).

EXTRIFERRON. B.A.N. A colloidal solution of ferric hydroxide in complex with partially hydrolyzed dextrin.
Use: Treatment of iron-deficiency anemia.
See: Astrafer

EXTRIFERRON. The hematinic preparation of a colloidal solution of ferric hydroxide in complex with partially hydrolyzed dextrin.
See: Imferon, Amps. (Merrell Dow)

DEXTRIN, N.F. XVI.
Use: Pharmaceutical aid.

DEXTROAMPHETAMINE. USAN.
Use: Stimulant.

EXTROAMPHETAMINE WITH AMPHETAMINE AS RESIN COMPLEX.
See: Biphetamine 12.5, 20, Cap. (Pennwalt)

DEXTROAMPHETAMINE HYDROCHLORIDE.
(Various Mfr.) d-Amphetamine HCl. (+)-2-Aminopropylbenzene.
See: Daro, Preps. (Fellows- Testagar)

DEXTROAMPHETAMINE PHOSPHATE. Monobasic d-a-methylphenethlyamine phosphate. (+)-α-Methylphenethylamine phosphate.
Use: Central stimulant.
See: d-Amphetamine Phos. for combinations

• **DEXTROAMPHETAMINE SULFATE,** U.S.P. XXI. Caps., Elix., Tabs, U.S.P. XXI. Benzeneethanamine, α-methyl-, sulfate (2:1). (+)-α-Methylphenethylamine sulfate (2:1). d-Amphetamine sulfate, d-Methylphenylamine sulfate.
Use: Central stimulant.
See: Amphedex, Cap. (Paddock)
Dexampex, Cap., Tab. (Lemmon)
Dexedrine, Prep. (SmithKline)
Diphylets, Granucaps (Reid-Provident)
Oxydess, Tab. (Vortech)
Robese P., Tab., Vial (Rocky Mtn.)
Spancap #1, #4. (Vortech)
Tidex Tabs. (Allison)

DEXTROAMPHETAMINE SULFATE W/COMBINATIONS.
See: Amphodex, Cap. (Jamieson-McKames)
Delcobese (Delco)
Dextrobar, Tab. (Lannett)
Min-Gera, Tab. (Scrip)
Ro Trim, Cap. (Rocky Mtn.)
Trimex, Trimex #2, Cap. (Mills)

DEXTROBAR. (Lannett) Dextroamphetamine sulfate 5 mg., amobarbital 32 mg./Tab. Bot. 500s, 1000s.
Use: Central stimulant.

DEXTROCAINE. (Wolins) Dextromethorphan HBr 5 mg., benzocaine 1 mg./Loz. Bot. 1000s.

DEXTROCELL. (Jones) Dextroamphetamine sulfate 2.5 mg., methylcellulose 5 gr./Tab. Bot. 100s, 1000s.

DEXTRO-CHEK CALIBRATORS. (Ames) Clear liquid sol. containing measured amounts of glucose. Low calibrator contains 0.05% w/v glucose. High calibrator contains 0.30% w/v glucose.
Use: Dextrostix to perform calibration procedure with glucometer reflectance photometer.

DEXTRO-CHLORPHENIRAMINE MALEATE.
See: Polaramine, Repetab, Tab., Expect., Syr. (Schering)

DEXTRO DESOXYEPHEDRINE HCl.
See: Dee-10, Tab. (Scrip)

• **DEXTROMETHORPHAN,** U.S.P. XXI. (+)-3-Methoxy-N-methylmorphinan.
Use: Cough suppressant.
See: Benylin DM Cough Syrup (Parke-Davis)
Delsym, Liq. (Pennwalt)
Extend-12, Liq. (Robins)
Romilar (hydrobromide)
W/Benzocain, menthol, peppermint oil.
See: Vicks Formula 44 Cough Control Discs, Loz. (Vicks)

• **DEXTROMETHORPHAN HYDROBROMIDE,** U.S.P. XXI. Syrup, U.S.P. XXI. d-3-Methoxy-N-methylmorphi-

nan. (+)-3-Methoxy-17-methyl-9α, 13α,-14α-morphinan HBr. Dormethan. d-Methorphan.
Use: Antitussive.
See: Benylin DM Cough Syrup, Syr. (Parke-Davis)
Dicodethal, Elix. (Lannett)
Maxefed, Tab. (Noyes)
Mediquell, Tab (Warner-Lambert)
Romilar, Loz., Syr., Cap., Tab. (Block)
St. Joseph Cough Syrup (Plough)
Symptom 1, Liq. (Parke-Davis)
Tus-F, Liq. (Orbit)
Tussade Tab. (Westerfield)

DEXTROMETHORPHAN HBr W/COMBINATIONS
See: Algetuss, Syr. (Winston)
Alo-Tuss, Tab. (Vortech)
Ambenyl-D, Liq. (Marion)
Anti-Tuss D.M., Liq. (Century)
Anti-Tussive, Tab. (Canright)
Bayer Prods. (Glenbrook)
Breacol cough Medication, Liq. (Glenbrook)
Capahist-DMH, Cap. (Freeport)
C.D.M., Expect. (Lannett)
Centuss, MLT, Tabs. (Century)
Cerose Compound, Cap. (Ives)
Cerose DM, Liq. (Ives)
Cheracol-D, Cough Syr. (Upjohn)
Cheratussin, Cough Syr. (Towne)
Chexit, Tab. (Dorsey)
Children's Hold 4-Hour Cough Suppressant & Decongestant, Loz. (Calgon)
Chloraseptic DM Cough Control Lozenges (Eaton)
Codimal DM, Liq. (Central)
Colchek, Tab. (Creomulsion)
Colrex, Syr. (Rowell)
Combi-Tuss, Syr. (Table Rock)
Comtrex, Cap., Liq. Tab. (Bristol-Myers)
Congespirin Cough Syrup (Bristol-Myers)
Consin-DM, Syr. (Wisconsin)
Consotuss Antitussive, Syr. (Merrell Dow)
Contac Jr., Liq. (Menley & James)
Coricidin Childrens Cough Syrup (Schering)
Corzone, Syr. (Xttrium)
C3 Capsules (Menley & James
Daycare, Liq. (Vicks)
Dextrocaine, Loz. (Wolins)
Dextro-Tuss GG, Liq. (Ulmer)
Dextro-Tussin, Liq. (Ulmer)
Dimacol, Cap. (Robins)
Donatussin, Syr. (Laser)
Dorcol Ped. Cough Syr. (Dorsey)
Dristan Cough Formula, Syr. (Whitehall)
End-A-Koff, Jr. Syr. (Quality Generics)
Endotussin-N N, Syr. (Du Pont)
Formula 44 Prods. (Vicks)
G-100/DM, Syr. (Bock)
Halls Mentho-Lyptus Decongestant Cough Formula, Liq. (Warner-Lambert)
Histalets, DM, Syr. (Reid Provident)
Histivite-D, Syr. (Vitarine)
Hold 4-Hour Cough Suppressant, Loz. (Calgon)
Hycoff, Prep. (Seton)
Infantuss, Liq. (Scott/Cord)
Ipsatol, Syr. (Lakeside)
Listerine Cough Control Lozenges (Warner-Lambert)
Naldetuss, Syr. (Bristol)
Niltuss, Syr. (Minn. Pharm.)
N-N Cough Syrup (Vitarine)
Nyquil, Liq. (Vicks)
Ornacol, Cap., Liq. (Menley & James)
Orthoxicol, Syr. (Upjohn)
Para-Hist DM, Tab. (Pharmics)
Partuss, Liq. (Parmed)
Phenergan, Pediatric, Liq. (Wyeth)
Propahist-DM, Syr. (Blue Line)
Polytuss-DM, Liq. (Rhode)
Quartets, Cap. (DePree)
Quelidrine, Syr. (Abbott)
Queltuss, Syr., Tab. (Westerfield)
Rentuss, Tab., Syr. (Wren)
Rentuss, Tab. (Wren)
Rhinex DM, Liq., Tab. (Lemmon)
Robitussin-DM, Syr., Loz. (Robins)
Robitussin-CF (Robins)
Romilar Prods. (Block)
Rondec DM, Drops and Syrup (Ross)
S.A.C. Cough Formula (Towne)
Scotcof Liq. (Scott/Cord)
Scotuss, Pediatric Cough Syr. (Scott/Cord)
Shertus, Liq. (Sheryl)
Silence Is Golden Children's Cough Lozenges (Bristol-Myers)
Silence Is Golden Cough Lozenges (Bristol-Myers)
Silexin, Syr. (Clapp)
Sorbase Cough Syr. (Fort David)
Spantuss, Liq., Tab. (Arco)
Spec-T Sore Throat-Cough Suppressant Lozenges (Squibb)
Sucrets Cough Control Lozenge (Calgon)
Sudafed Cough Syrup (Burroughs Wellcome)
Synatuss-One, Liq. (Freeport)
Tercol, Liq. (Commerce)
Thor, Cough Syr. (Towne)
Thor Capsules (Towne)
Thorzettes Lozenges (Towne)
Tolu-Sed DM, Liq. (Scherer)
Tonecol, Syr., Tab. (A.V.P.)
Triaminic-DM Cough Formula (Dorsey)
Triaminicol, Syr. (Dorsey)
Trihista-Cod, Tab. (Recsei)
Tri-Medicol, Syr. (Medical Chemical)
Trind-DM, Syr. (Mead Johnson)
Tusquelin, Syr. (Circle)
Tussagesic, Tab., Susp. (Dorsey)
Tusscaps, Cap. (Martin-Phillips)
Tuss-Chlorphenade, Cap. (Wolins)
Tusscidin Expectorant D, Liq. (Cenci)
Unproco, Cap. (Reid-Provident)
Vicks Cough Prods. (Vicks)
Vicks Daycare, Liq. (Vicks)
Vicks Formula 44 Prods. (Vicks)

Vicks Nyquil, Liq. (Vicks)
Wal-Tussin DM, Syr. (Walgreen)

:XTROMORAMIDE. B.A.N. (+)-1-(3-Methyl-4-morpholino-2, 2-diphenylbutyryl) pyrrolidine.
Use: Narcotic analgesic.
See: Jetrium
Palfium [hydrogen tartrate]

:XTROMORAMIDE TARTRATE. dl-(3-Methyl-4-morpholino-2, 2-d-phenyl-butyryl) pyrrolidine.

:XTRO-PANTOTHENYL ALCOHOL.
See: Panthenol (Var. Mfr.)

:XTROPROPOXYPHENE. B.A.N. α-(+)-4-Dimethylamino-3-methyl-1, 2-diphenyl-2-propionyl-oxy-butane. α-(+)-1-Benzyl-3-dimethylamino-2-methyl-1-phenylpropyl propionate.
Use: Analgesic.
See: Darvon Prods. (Lilly)
Depronal SA [hydrochloride]
Doxolene [napsylate]

:XTRO PROPOXYPHENE HCl.
See: Propoxyphene HCl, Caps. (Var. Mfr.)
/Acetylsalicylic acid, phenaglycodol.
See: Darvo-Tran, Pulvule (Lilly)

:XTRORPHAN. B.A.N. (+)-3-Hydroxy-N-methylmorphinan.
Use: Narcotic analgesic.
See: Dextromethorphan HBr (Var. Mfr.)

DEXTROSE, U.S.P. XXI. Inj., U.S.P. XXI. d-Glucose. -Glucose, monohydrate.
Use: Fluid and nutrient replenisher.
/Cal. ascorbate & benzyl alcohol inj.
See: Calscorbate, Amp. (Cole)
/Psyllium mucilloid.
See: V-lax, Pow. (Century)

DEXTROSE EXCIPIENT, N.F. XVI.
Use: Pharmaceutic aid (tablet excipient)

DEXTROSE & SODIUM CHLORIDE INJECTION, U.S.P. XXI. (Abbott) 10% Dextrose and 0.225% Sodium Chloride Injection. Single dose container 500 ml.
Use: Fluid and electrolyte replenisher.

EXTROSE LARGE VOLUME PARENTERALS. (Abbott)
extrose 2 0.5% in Water-1000 ml.
extrose 2 0.5% in 0.5 Str. Lact. Ringer's or in 0.5 Str. Saline-1000 ml.
extrose 5% in Water-150, 250, 500, 1000 ml. in Abbo-Vac glass or LifeCare flexible plastic cont.; partial-fill glass: 50 in 200 ml., 50 in 300 ml., 100 in 300 ml., 400 in 500 ml.; partial-fill plastic: 50 in 150 ml., 100 in 150 ml.
extrose 5% in Lact. Ringer's-250, 1000 ml. glass; 1000 ml. plastic cont.
extrose 5% in Ringer's-500, 1000 ml.
extrose 5% in Saline 0.9% or in 0.25, ⅓ or 0.5 Str. Saline-250, 500, 1000 ml. glass or plastic cont.
extrose 10% in Water-250, 500, 1000 ml. cont.
extrose 20% in Water-500 ml.
extrose 50% in Water-500 ml.
Dextrose 20%, 30%, 40%, 50%, 60% and 70% Injections, U.S.P. in partial-fill cont., 500 ml. in 1000 ml.
Dextrose Injection 50%. Bot. 1000 ml
Dextrose 50% and Injection w/Electrolytes in partial-fill cont., 500 ml. in 1000 ml.
Dextrose Injection 70%. Bot. 1000 ml.
Use: Fluid, calorie and electrolyte source.

DEXTROSE SMALL VOLUME PARENTERALS. (Abbott) Dextrose 10%, 5 ml. ampul; Dextrose 50%, 50 ml. Abboject Syr. (18 G × 1.5")
Use: Caloric source.

DEXTROSTIX. (Ames) A cellulose strip containing glucose oxidase and indicator system. Bot. 25s, 100s. Box 10s foil wrapped.
Use: Blood-glucose test.

DEXTROTHYROXINE. B.A.N. 3-[4-(4-Hydroxy-3,5-di-iodophenoxy)-3, 5-di-iodophenyl]-D-alanine.
Use: Treatment of hypercholesterolemia.
See: Choloxin [sodium derivative]

DEXTROTHYROXINE SODIUM, U.S.P. XXI. Tab., U.S.P. XXI. D-Tyrosine, 0-(4-hydroxy-3, 5-diiodophenyl)- 3, 5-diiod-, monosodium salt hydrate.
Use: Anticholesteremic.
See: Choloxin, Tab. (Flint)

DEXULE. (Approved) Vit. A 1333 I.U., D 133 I.U., B-1 0.33 mg., B-2 0.4 mg., C 10 mg., niacinamide 3.3 mg., Fe 3.3 mg., Ca 29 mg., P 15 mg., methylcellulose 100 mg., benzocaine 3 mg./Cap. Bot. 21s, 90s.
Use: Reducing aid.

DEXYL. (Pinex) Dextromethorphan HBr 15 mg., Vit. C 20 mg./Tab. Box 20s.
Use: Cough due to cold.

• **DEZAQUANINE.** USAN.
Use: Antineoplastic.

• **DEZAQUANINE MESYLATE.** USAN.
Use: Antineoplastic.

DEXZONE. (Tunex) Dexamethasone sod. phosphate equiv. to 4 mg./ml. Vial 5 cc.
Use: Corticosteroid.

DEXZONE LA. (Tunex) Dexamethasone acetate equiv. to 8 mg./ml. Vial 5 cc.
Use: Corticosteroid.

DEZEST. (Geneva) Atropine sulfate, phenylpropanolamine HCl, chlorphenaramine maleate. Bot. 100s.
Use: Decongestant.

• **DEZOCINE.** USAN.
Use: Analgesic.

DEZONE. (Reid-Provident) Dexamethasone 0.75 mg./Tab. Bot. 100s **Inj.,** Dexamethasone sodium phosphate 4 mg./ml. Vial 5 ml.
Use: Synthetic adrenocortical steroid.

D-FILM. (CooperVision) Cleaning gel. Poloxamer 407, benzalkonium chloride 0.025%, edetate trisodium 0.25%. 25 Gm.
Use: Cleaning gel for hard contact lenses.

DFP. Diisopropyl fluorophosphate (Var. Mfr.)

D.H.E. 45. (Sandoz) Dihydroergotamine mesylate. Amp. 1 mg./ml., methanesulfonic acid/sod. hydroxide, alcohol 6.1%, glycerin 15%, Water for

Injection U.S.P., q.s. to 1 ml. SandoPak Pkg. 20s.
Use: Parenterally, treatment of migraine.

DHS CONDITIONING RINSE. (Person & Covey) Conditioning ingredients. Bot. 8 oz.
Use: Dermatalogical hair care.

D.H.S. SHAMPOO. (Person & Covey) Blend of cleansing surfactants and emulsifiers. Plastic Bot. w/dispenser 8 oz., 16 oz.
Use: Dermatological hair and scalp shampoo.

DHS TAR GEL SHAMPOO. (Person & Covey) Coal Tar, U.S.P. 0.5% Bot. 8 oz.
Use: Treatment of Seborrhea & psoriasis of scalp.

DHS TAR SHAMPOO. (Person & Covey) Coal tar 0.5% in DHS shampoo. Bot. 4 oz., 8 oz.
Use: Seborrhea and psoriasis of the scalp.

DHS ZINC SHAMPOO. (Person & Covey) Zinc pyrithione 2% in DHS shampoo. Bot. 6 oz., 12 oz.
Use: Anti-dandruff shampoo.

DHT. (Roxane) Dihydrotachysterol. **Tab.:** 0.125, 0.2 or 0.4 mg./Tab. **Oral Sol.:** 0.2 mg./5 ml. Bot. 500 ml. **Intensol:** Dihydrotachysterol 0.2 mg./ml. w/alcohol 20%. Bot. 30 ml. w/dropper
Use: Calcium regulator.

DIABETA. (Hoechst) Glyburide. 1.25 mg., 2.5 mg. or 5.0 mg./Tab. Bot. 100s.
Use: Oral antidiabetic agent.

DIABETUSSIN EXPECTORANT. (Research Pharmacal Lab.) Guaifenesin 100 mg., pot. citrate, glycerine, citric acid, menthol/5 cc. sugar free. Bot. 4 oz., pt., gal.
Use: Expectorant.

DIABINESE. (Pfizer Laboratories) Chlorpropamide 100 mg./Tab. Bot. 100s, 500s. Unit dose 100s; 250 mg./Tab. 100s, 250s, 1000s. Unit dose 100s.
Use: Hypoglycemic agent.

DIABISMUL LIQUID. (Forest) Opium 7 mg., pectin 80 mg., kaolin 2500 mg./15 ml. Bot. 8 oz.
Use: Anidiarrheal.

DIABISMUL TABLETS. (Forest) Bismuth subcarbonate 125 mg., powdered opium 1.23 mg., calcium carbonate 125 mg./Tab. Bot. 1000s.
Use: Antidiarrheal.

DIACETAMATE. B.A.N. 4-Acetamidophenyl acetate.
Use: Analgesic.

3, 5-DIACETAMIDO-2, 4, 6-TRIIODOBENZOIC ACID. Diatrizoic Acid, U.S.P. XXI.

DIACETIC ACID TEST.
See: Acetest, Tab. (Ames)

DIACETO. (Archer-Taylor) Aspirin 3.5 gr., acetophenetidin 2.5 gr., caffeine 0.5 gr./Tab. Bot. 100s, 1000s.

DIACETO W/CODEINE. (Archer-Taylor) Codeine 0.25 gr. or 0.5 gr./Tab. or Cap. Bot. 500s, 1000s.

DIACETO W/GELSEMIUM. (Archer-Taylor) Phenobarbital 0.5 gr. gelsemium 3 min./Tab. Bot. 1000s.

• **DIACETOLOL HYDROCHLORIDE.** USAN.
Use: Anti-adrenergic.

DIACETRIZOATE, SODIUM.
See: Diatrizoate (Var. Mfr.)

• **DIACETYLATED MONOGLYCERIDES,** N.F. XVI. Glycerin esterfied with edible fat-forming fatty acids and acetic acid.

DIACETYLCHOLINE CHLORIDE. Succinyl-choline Chloride.
See: Anectine Chloride, Inj., Pow. (Burroughs-Wellcome)

DIACETYL-DIHYDROXYDIPHENYLISATIN.
See: Oxyphenisatin acetate (Var. Mfr.)

DIACETYLDIOXYPHENYLISATIN.
See: Oxyphenisatin acetate (Var. Mfr.)

DIACETYLMORPHINE SALTS. Heroin. Forbidden in U.S.A. by Federal statute because of its addiction causing nature.

DIACETYLNALORPHINE. B.A.N. O[3]O[6]-Diacetyl-N-allylnormorphine.
Use: Narcotic analgesic.

DIACHLOR TABS. (Major) Chlorothiazide 250 mg. or 500 mg./Tab. Bot. 250s., 1000s.
Use: Diuretic.

DIACTION. (Boots) Diphenoxylate HCl 2.5 mg., atropine sulfate 0.025 mg./Tab. Bot. 100s, 500s.
Use. Antidiarrheal.

DIADAX CAPSULES. (O'Connor) Phenylpropanolamine HCl 50 mg./Cap. Bot. 14s, 30s, 40s.
Use: Appetite suppressant.

DIADAX TABLETS. (O'Connor) Phenylpropanolamine HCl 25 mg./Tab. Bot. 21s, 100s.
Use: Appetite suppressant.

DI-ADEMIL.
See: Hydroflumethiazide, Tab. (Var. Mfr.)

DIA-EAZ. (Central) Bismuth subgallate 0.15 Gm., kaolin 5.5 Gm./15 ml. w/preservatives and aromatics. Bot. 8 oz.
Use: Antidiarrheal.

DIAGARD. (Vitarine) Cassanthranol 30 mg., docusate sodium 100 mg./Cap.
Use: Fecal softener.

DIA-GESIC. (Central) Hydrocodone bitartrate 5 mg., acetaminophen 150 mg., aspirin 230 mg., caffeine 30 mg./Tab. Bot. 100s, 1000s.
Use: Analgesic.

DIAGNIOL.
See: Sodium Acetrizoate

DIAGNOSTIC 50+. (Barry) Allergenic extracts scratch test kit 3% (1:30 dilution w/v). Vial 1.5 cc/w dropper.
Use: Testing for common allergies to dust, molds; and various tree, grass and weed pollens.

■ **DIAGNOSTIC AGENTS.**
See: Acholest, Kit. (Fougera)
Baroflave, Pow. (Lannett)
Cardio-Green, Vial (Hynson Westcott & Dunning)
Cardiografin, Vial (Squibb)
Cea-Roche, Kit (Roche)
Chografin, Prep. (Squibb)
Coccidioidin, Vial (Cutter)
Dextrostix, Strips (Ames)
Diptheria Toxin for Schick Test (Var. Mfr.)
Evans Blue, Amp. (Harvey)
Fertility Tape (Weston Labs.)
Fluorescein Sodium Ophth. Sol. (Various Mfr.)
Fluor-I-Strip (Ayerst)
Fluor-I-Strip A.T. (Ayerst)

Fluress, Ophth. Sol. (Barnes-Hind)
Glucola, Sol. (Ames)
Hema-Combistix Strips (Ames)
Hemastix Strips (Ames)
Histalog, Amp. (Lilly)
Histoplasmin, Vial (Parke-Davis)
Indigo Carmine (Var. Mfr.)
Mannitol Sol., Inj. (Merck Sharp & Dohme)
Phenolsulfonphthalein (Var. Mfr.)
Phentolamine Methanesulfonate, Inj. (Var. Mfr.)
Regitine, Amp. & Tab. (Ciba)
Rheumanosticon Slide Test (Organon)
Rocky Mountain Spotted Fever Antigen, Vial (Lederle)
Sodium Dehydrocholate, Inj. (Var. Mfr.)
Tes-Tape (Lilly)
See also: Cholecystography Agents
Kidney Function Agents
Liver Function Agents
Urography Agents

)IAGNOSTIC AGENTS FOR URINE.
See: Acetest, Tab. (Ames)
Albustix, Strips (Ames)
Bumintest, Tab. (Ames)
Clinistix, Strips (Ames)
Clinitest, Tab. (Ames)
Hema-Combistix, Strip (Ames)
Hemastix, Strip (Ames)
Hematest, Tab. (Ames)
Icotest, Tab. (Ames)
Ketostix, Strips (Ames)
Pheniplate, Preps. (Ames)
Phenistix, Strips (Ames)
Uristix, Strips (Ames)

AGNOSTIC '10' KIT. (Panray) 10-2 cc. A.T.V. vials. Mxd molds Vial 2 cc., mxd inhalants-D Vial 2 cc., mxd insects Vial 2 cc., mxd epidermals Vial 2 cc., house dust Vial 2 cc., mxd ragweed Vial 2 cc., mxd trees Vial 2 cc., mxd grasses Vial 2 cc., mxd weeds Vial 2 cc., control vial Vial 2 cc.

AHIST ELIXIR. (Century) Diphenhydramine HCl 12.5 mg./ml. Bot. gal.
Use: Antihistaminic.

ALLYLAMICOL. Diallyl-diethylaminoethyl phenol di HCl.

ALLYBARBITURIC ACID. Allobarbital, Allobarbitone, Curral.
'Acetaminophen, aluminum aspirin, aspirin.
See: Allylgesic, Tab. (Elder)
'Atropine sulfate, Mag. carb., Cal. carb. precipitated & bismuth subcarb.
See: Dia-Tropine, Tab. (O'Neal)

ALLYLNORTOXIFERINE.
See: Alloferin (Roche)

ALMINATE. Mixture mag. carb. and (alminate) dihydroxyaluminum glycinate.
'Aspirin.
See: Bufferin, Preps. (Bristol-Myers)

ALONE TABS. (Major) Methandrostenolone 5 mg./Tab. Bot. 100s.
Use: Anabolic steroid.

DIALOSE. (Stuart) Docusate potassium 100 mg./Cap.
Bot. 36s, 100s, 500s,
Unit Dose 100s.
Use: Stool softener for treatment of constipation due to lack of moisture in stool.

DIALOSE PLUS. (Stuart) Docusate potassium 100 mg., casanthranol 30 mg./Cap.
Bot. 36s, 100s, 500s,
Unit Dose 100s.
Use: Stool softener with peristaltic activator for constipation caused by decreased intestinal motility.

DIALUME. (Armour) Aluminum hydroxide gel 500 mg./Cap. Bot. 100s, 500s.
Use: Antacid.

DIA-MER-SULFONAMIDES. Sulfadiazine, Sulfamerazine.
See: Aldiazol-M, Susp. (Beecham-Massengill)
Sulfonamide Duplex, Susp. (Lilly)
W/Alkaline agents.
See: Aldiazol-M, Susp. (Beecham-Massengill)

DIAMETHINE.
See: Dimethyl tubocurarine (Var. Mfr.)

DIAMINE DIPENICILLIN G.
See: Benzethacil (Var. Mfr.)

DI-AMINO ACETATE COMPLEX W/Calcium Aluminum Carbonate.
See: Ancid Tab. & Susp. (Sheryl)

4,6-DIAMINO-1(P-CHLOROPHENYL)-1,2-DIHYDRO-2,2-DIMETHYL-S-TRIAZINE COMPOUND (2:1) WITH 4,4′-METHYLENEBIS-[3-HYDROXY-2-NAPHTHOIC ACID]. Camolar

2,4-DIAMINO-5-(p-CHLOROPHENYL)-6-ETHYLPYRIMIDINE. Pyrimethamine, U.S.P. XXI.

DIAMINODIPHENYLSULFONE. Dapsone, U.S.P. XXI.
Use: Treatment of malaria.
See: Avlosulfon, Tab. (Ayerst)
Diasone Sod., Tab. (Abbott)
Glucosulfone Sod., Inj. (Var. Mfr.)

2,6-DIAMINO-3-PHENYLAZOPYRIDINE HYDROCHLORIDE.
Use: Urogenital antiseptic.
See: Phenazopyridine HCl (Var. Mfr.)
Phenylazo-diaminopyridine hydrochloride

DIAMINOPROPYL TETRAMETHYLENE.
See: Spermine

L-(+)-N-[p][2,4-DIAMINO-6-PYERIDINYL)METHYL] METHYLAMINO[BENZOYL]-GLUTAMIC ACID. Methotrexate, U.S.P. XXI.

DIAMOCAINE. B.A.N. 1-(2-Anilinoethyl)-4-(2-diethylaminoethoxy)-4-phenylpiperidine.
Use: Local anesthetic.

• **DIAMOCAINE CYCLAMATE.** USAN. (1) 1-(2-Anilinoethyl)-4-[2-(diethylamino)-ethoxy]-4-phenylpiperidine bis(cyclohexanesulfamate); (2) Cyclohexanesulfamic acid compound with 1-(2-anilinoethyl)-4-[2-(diethylamino)ethoxy]-4-phenylpiperidine (2:1).
Use: Local anesthetic.

DIAMOX. (Lederle) Acetazolamide (2-acetylamino-1,-3,4-thiadiazole-5-sulfonamide). **Tab.** 125 mg., Bot. 100s; 250 mg. Bot. 100s, 1000s. **Parenteral Vial** sod. salt 500 rng., (sod. hydroxide to adjust pH).

Use: Diuretic. Carbonic anhydrase inhibitor, glaucoma therapy.

DIAMOX SEQUELS. (Lederle) Acetazolamide 500 mg./Cap. Bot. 30s, 100s.
Use: Diuretic, glaucoma therapy.

DIAMPHENETHIDE. B.A.N. $\beta\beta'$-Oxydi(aceto-p-phenetidide).
Use: Anthelmintic, veterinary medicine.
See: Coriban

DIAMPROMIDE. B.A.N. N-[2-(N-Methylphenethylamino)propyl]propionanilide.
Use: Analgesic.

DIAMPRON ISETHIONATE. Amicarbalide, B.A.N.

DIAMTHAZOLE. B.A.N. 6-(2-Diethylaminoethoxy)-2-dimethylaminobenzothiazole.
Dimazole (I.N.N.)
Use: Antifungal agent.
See: Asterol (dihydrochloride)

DIAMTHAZOLE DIHYDROCHLORIDE. Asterol.

DIANEAL. (Travenol) Na 141 mEq, Ca 3.5 mEq, Mg 1.5 mEq, Cl 101 mEq, lactate 45 mEq/Liter. w/Dextrose 1.5% or 4.25%. Bot. 1000 ml., 2000 ml.
Use: Peritoneal dialysis solution.

DIANEAL 137. (Travenol) Na 132 mEq, Ca 3.5 mEq, Mg 1.5 mEq, Cl 102 mEq, lactate 35 mEq/Liter W/Dextrose 1.5% or 4.25%. Bot. 2000 ml.
Use: Peritoneal dialysis solution.

DIANEAL 137 WITH DEXTROSE. (Travenol) Na 132, Ca 3.5, Mg 1.5, Cl 102, lactate 35 mEq/liter w/dextrose 1.5%, 2.5%, 4.25%. Viaflex or Ambuflex III plastic Bot. 500 ml., 1000 ml., 1500 ml., 2000 ml.
Use: Peritoneal dialysis.

DIANEAL K-141. (Travenol) Na 132 mEq, Ca 3.5 mEq, Mg 1.5 mEq, Cl 106 mEq, lactate 35 mEq, K 4 mEq/Liter. W/Dextrose 1.5% or 4.25%. Bot. 2000 ml.

DIANEAL PD-2 WITH DEXTROSE. (Travenol) Na 132, Ca 3.5, Mg 0.5, Cl 96, lacate 40 mEq./Liter. Viaflex or Ambu-flex Bot. 250 ml., 500 ml., 750 ml., 1000 ml., 1500 ml., 2000 ml., 3000 ml., 5000 ml.,
Use: Peritoneal dialysis.

1,4:3,6-DIANHYDRO-D-GLUCITOL DINITRATE. Diluted Isosorbide Dinitrate, U.S.P. XXI.

1,4:3,6-DIANHYDRO-SORBITOL-2,5-DINITRATE. Diluted Isosorbide Dinitrate, U.S.P. XXI.

DIAPAKARE. (Paddock) Antibacterial agent. Cans 9 oz. (Powd.)
Use: Diaper rash, prickly heat.

DIAPAKARE ANTIBACTERIAL POWDER. (Paddock) Diaphene, corn starch, sod. bicarbonate.

• **DIAPAMIDE.** USAN.
Use: Diuretic, antihypertensive.

DIAPANTIN. (Janssen) Isoprofamide bromide.
Use: Anticholinergic.

DIAPARENE. (Glenbrook) Methylbenzethonium chloride. **Pow.** 1:1000, Bot. 4 oz., 9 oz., 12.5 oz. **Oint.,** 1:1000, Tube 1 oz., 2 oz., 4 oz.
Use: Surface-active disinfectant.

DIAPARENE CRADOL EMULS. (Glenbrook) Methylbenzethonium chloride in pet. and lanolin Base. Plast. Bot. 3 oz.
Use: Seborrhea capitis.

DIAPARENE OINTMENT. (Glenbrook) Methylbenzethonium Cl. 0.1% w/petrolatum & glycerin. Tubes 1 oz., 2 oz., 4 oz.
Use: Soothe, soften, protect irritated areas.

DIAPARENE PERI-ANAL CREAM. (Glenbrook) Methybenzethonium chloride 1:1000, zinc oxide, starch, cod liver oil & casein. Cream, Tube 1 oz., 2 oz., 4 oz.
Use: Rectally, dermatitis.

DIAPER RASH CREAM. (Eckerd) Bot. 4 oz.
Use: Protective and emollient.

DIAPHENYLSULFONE. Dapsone, U.S.P. XXI.

DIAPID. (Sandoz) Lypressin synthetic lysine-8 vasopressin. Equiv. to 50 U.S.P. units posterior pituitary/cc. (0.185 mg./cc.). Nasal spray. Bot. Plastic squeeze 8 ml.
Use: Diabetes insipidus.

DIAPARESS. (Jenkins) Cod liver oil, diperodon HCl 0.25%, Zinc oxide, starch, aluminum acetate, Peruvian balsam. Tubes 1.5 oz.
Use: Minor skin irritations.

DI-AP-TROL. (Foy) Phendimetrazine tartrate 35 mg./Tab. Bot. 100s, 1000s.

DIAQUA. (Hauck) Hydrochlorthiazide 50 mg./Tab. Bot. 100s, 1000s. Unit dose 100s.
Use: Diuretic.

DIAR AID. (Thompson Medical) Activated attapulgate and pectin.
Use: Antidiarrheal.

DIARREST. (Dover) Calcium carbonate, pectin/Tab. Sugar, lactose and salt free. Unit dose box 500s.
Use: Antidiarrheal.

DIARRHEA RELIEF WITH PAREGORIC. (Weeks & Leo) Bismuth subsalicylate 63 mg., kaolin 675 mg., pectin 27 mg. paregoric 0.6 ml./5 ml. Bot. 4 oz.
Use: Relief of diarrhea and nausea.

DIARRHEA THERAPY.
See: Antidiarrheics

DIASERP TABS. (Major) Chlorothiazide 250 mg. or 500 mg./Tab. w/reserpine. Bot. 100s.
Use: Antihypertensive.

DIASPORAL. (Doak) Formerly Sulfur Salicyl Diasporal. Sulfur 3%, salicylic acid 2%, isopropyl alcohol in diasporal base. Cream: Jar 3¾ oz.
Use: Topical antiseptic.

DIASTASE.
See: Aspergillus oryzae enzyme
W/Bismuth subnitrate, sod. bicarb., magnesium carbonate, papain.
See: Panacarb, Tab. (Lannett)
W/Carica papaya enzyme.
See: Caripeptic, Liq. (Upjohn)
W/Sod. bicarbonate, magnesium carbonate, bismuth subnitrate, papain.

DIASTIX REAGENT STRIPS. (Ames) Broad range test for glucose in urine. Containing glucose

oxidase, peroxidase, potassium iodide/w blue background dye. Tab. Pkg. 50s, 100s.
Use: Dip-and-Read test for urine glucose.

DIATRIC. (Pasadena Research) Methyl testosterone 5 mg., ethinyl estradiol 0.02 mg./Tab. Bot. 100s, 1000s.
Use: Anabolic.

DIATRIZOATE. 3,5-diacetamido-2,4,6-triiodobenzoic acid.

• **DIATRIZOATE MEGLUMINE,** U.S.P. XXI. Inj., U.S.P. XXI. Benzoic acid, 3,5-bis(acetylamino)-2,4,6-tri-iodo-, compound with 1-deoxy-1-(methylamino)--glucitol (1:1).
Use: Diagnostic aid (radiopaque medium).
See: Angiovist 282, Inj. (Berlex)
Cardiografin, Vial (Squibb)
Cystographin, Inj. (Squibb)
Gastrografin, Liq. (Squibb)
Hypaque-Cysto, Liq. (Winthrop-Breon)
Hypaque Meglumine (Winthrop-Breon)
Renografin, Inj. (Squibb)
Reno-M-DIP, Inj. (Squibb)
Reno-M-30, Inj. (Squibb)
Reno-M-60, Inj. (Squibb)
Urovist, Prods. (Berlex)
W/Iodipamide methylglucamine.
See: Sinografin, Vial (Squibb)
W/Sod. Diatrizoate.
See: Renovist, Inj. (Squibb)

• **DIATRIZOATE MEGLUMINE AND DIATRIZOATE SODIUM INJECTION,** U.S.P. XXI.
Use: Diagnostic aid (radiopaque medium).
See: Angiorist 292, Inj. (Berlex)
Angiovist 370, Inj. (Berlex)
Gastrovist, Sol. (Berlex)
Hypaque-M Prods. (Winthrop-Breon)

• **DIATRIZOATE MEGLUMINE AND DIATRIZOATE SODIUM SOLUTION,** U.S.P. XXI.
See: Gastrografini Sol. (Squibb)
Renografin-60, Sol. (Squibb)
Renografin-76, Sol. (Squibb)
Rénovist, Sol. (Squibb)

DIATRIZOATE METHYLGLUCAMINE.
See: Diatrizoate Meglumine, U.S.P. XXI.

DIATRIZOATE METHYLGLUCAMINE SODIUM. Sod. salt of N-methylglucamine salt of 3,5-diacetamido-2,4,6-triiodobenzoate.

• **DIATRIZOATE SODIUM,** U.S.P. XXI. Inj., Sol., U.S.P. XXI. Benzoic acid, 3,5-bis(acetylamino)-2,4,6-triiodo-, monosodium salt.
Use: Diagnostic aid (radiopaque medium).
See: Hypaque Prods. (Winthrop-Breon)
Urovist Sodium, Inj. (Berlex)
W/Meglumine diatrizoate.
See: Gastrografin, Liq. (Squibb)
Renografin-60, -76, Vial (Squibb)
Renovist II, Vial (Squibb)
W/Methylglucamine diatrizoate, sodium citrate, disodium ethylenediamine tetra-acetate dihydrate, methylparaben, propylparaben.
See: Renovist, Vial (Squibb)

• **DIATRIZOATE SODIUM I-125.** USAN.
Use: Radioactive agent.

• **DIATRIZOATE SODIUM I-131.** USAN.
Use: Radioactive agent.

• **DIATRIZOIC ACID.** USAN. 3,5-Diacetamido-2,4,6-tri-iodobenzoic acid.
Use: Radio-opaque substance.
See: Amidotrizoic Acid
Hypaque sodium salt

• **DIATRIZOIC ACID,** U.S.P. XXI. Benzoic acid, 3,5-bis(acetylamino)-2,4,6-triiodo-. 3,5-Diacetamido-2,-4,6-triiodobenzoic acid.
Use: Radiopaque medium (urographic).

DIATROL. (Otis Clapp) Pectin, calcium carbonate/Tab. Safety Pack 500s; Bot. 100s. Aidpaks 100s. Unit boxes 20s.
Use: Antidiarrheal.

• **DIAVERIDINE.** USAN. 2,4-Diamino-5-(3,4-dimethoxybenzyl)pyrimidine. Present in Darvisul
Use: Antiprotozoan, veterinary medicine.

• **DIAZEPAM,** U.S.P. XXI. Cap., Extended-Release Cap., Inj., Tabs: U.S.P. XXI. 2H-1,4-Benzodiazepin-2-one, 7-chloro-1,3-dihydro-1-methyl-5-phenyl-. 7-Chloro-1,3-dihydro-1-methyl-5-phenyl-2H-1,4-benzodiazepin-2-one. B.A.N. 7-Chloro-1,3-dihydro-1-methyl-5-phenyl-2H-1,4-benzodiazepin-2-one.
Use: Agent for control of emotional disturbances; sedative; tranquilizer.
See: Valcaps, Cap. (Roche)
Valium, Tab. (Roche)
Valrelease, S.R. Cap. (Roche)

DIAZINON.
See: Dimpylate, B.A.N.

• **DIAZIQUONE.** USAN.
Use: Antineoplastic.

DIAZMA. (Pharmex) Diphylline 250 mg./cc. Vial 10 cc.

DI-AZO. (Kay) Phenazopyridine HC1 100 mg./Tab. Bot. 50s, 100s, 1000s.
Use: Urinary analgesic.

DIAZOMYCINS A, B, & C. Antibiotic obtained from Streptomyces ambofaciens. Under study.

6-DIAZO-5-OXO-L-NORLEUCINE.

DIAZO-TEL TEST SYSTEM. (Warner-Lambert) A bilirubin test system.
Use: Aid in the diagnosis of red blood cell breakdown, liver disease or blockage of the bile duct.

• **DIAZOXIDE,** U.S.P. XXI. Cap., Oral Susp., Inj., U.S.P. XXI. 7-Chloro-3-methyl-2H-1,-2, 4-benzothiadiazine-1, 1-dioxide.
Use: Antihypertensive.
See: Hyperstat, Inj. (Schering)
Proglycem Capsules (Schering)
Proglycem Suspension (Schering)

• **DIBASIC CALCIUM PHOSPHATE,** U.S.P. XXI.
See: D.C.P. 340, Tabs. (Parke-Davis)
Diostate D, Tab. (Upjohn)

DIBASIC CALCIUM PHOSPHATE w/VITAMIN D. (Lilly) Dibasic calcium phosphate, anhydrous, equiv. to 500 mg. of dibasic calcium phosphate dihydrate,

Vit. D synthetic 33 I.U. (0.825 mcg.)/Pulvule. Bot. 100s.

DIBENCIL.
See: Benzathine Penicillin G. (Var Mfr.)

DIBENT-PB. (Hauck) Dicyclomine HCl 20 mg., phenobarbital 15 mg./Tab. Bot. 100s.
Use: Adjunct therapy in treatment of peptic ulcer.

DIBENZEPIN. B.A.N. 10-(2-Dimethylaminoethyl)-5-methyldibenzo[b,e][1,4]diazepin-11-one.
Use: Antidepressant.
See: Noveril hydrochloride

5H-DIBENZ[b,f]AZEPINE-5-CARBOXAMIDE. Carbamazepine, U.S.P. XXI.

5H-DIBENZ[b,f]AZEPINE-5-PROPANAMINE, 10,11-DIHYDRO-N,N-DIMETHYL-, HCl. Imipramine HCl, U.S.P. XXI.

• **DIBENZEPIN HCl.** USAN. 10-[2-Dimethylamino)ethyl]-5,10-dihydro-5-methyl-llH-dibenzo-[b,e][1,4]diazepin-11-one monohydrochloride.
Use: Antidepressant.

4-(5H-DIBENZO(a,d)CYCLOHEPTEN-5-YLIDENE)-1-METHYLPIPERIDENE HYDROCHLORIDE.
See: Cyproheptadine Hydrochloride, Syr., Tab. (Merck Sharp & Dohme)

• **DIBENZOTHIOPHENE.** USAN.
Use: Keratolytic.

(+)-1,3-DIBENZYLDECAHYDRO-2-OXOIMIDAZO[4,5-c]THIENO[1,2-a]-THIOLIUM 2-OXO-10-BORNANESULFONATE (1:1). Trimethaphan Camsylate, U.S.P. XXI.

DIBENZYLETHYLENEDIAMINE DIPENICILLIN G, U.S.P.
See: Benzethacil

DIBENZYLINE. (SmithKline) Phenoxybenzamine HCl 10 mg./Cap. Bot. 100s.
Use: Long-acting alpha adrenergic blocking agent.

• **DIBROMSALAN.** USAN. 4′, 5-Dibromosalicylanilide. Diaphene
Use: Germicide.

• **DIBUCAINE,** U.S.P. XXI. Cream, Oint., U.S.P. XXI. 2-Butoxy-N-[2-(diethylamino)ethyl]-cinchoninamide.
Use: Local anesthetic.
See: D-caine, Oint. (Century)
Dulzit, Cream (Commerce)
Nupercainal, Oint. (Ciba)
W/Benzocaine.
See: Extend, Tab. (Edward J. Moore)
W/Benzocaine, tetracaine.
See: Bonal Itch Cream, Cream (Edward J. Moore)
W/Hydrocortisone.
See: Corticaine Cream (Blue Line)
W/Dextrose.
See: Nupercaine Heavy Soln. (Ciba)
W/Sod. bisulfite.
See: Nupercainal, Cream, Oint. (Ciba)
W/Zinc oxide, bismuth subgallate, acetone sod. bisulfite.
See: Nupercainal, Oint., Supp (Ciba)

• **DIBUCAINE HYDROCHLORIDE,** U.S.P. XXI. Inj., U.S.P. XXI. 2-Butoxy-N-(2-diethylamino-ethyl) cinchoninamide HCl. (Cinchocaine, Percaine)
Use: Surface & spinal anesthesia.
See: Nupercaine HCl, Sol., (Ciba)
W/Antipyrine, hydrocortisone, polymyxin B sulfate. neomycin sulfate.
See: Otocort, Liq. (Lemmon)
W/Colistin sodium methanesulfonate, citric acid, sodium citrate.
See: Coly-Mycin M, Injectable (Warner-Chilcott)
W/Hydrocortisone.
See: Cortacaine, Cream (Meyer)

DIBUPYRONE. B.A.N. Sodium N-(2,3-dimethyl-1-phenyl-5-oxopyrazolin-4-yl)-N-isobutylamino-methanesulphonate.
Use: Analgesic.

DIBUTOLINE SULFATE. Ethyl(2-hydroxy-ethyl)-dimethylammonium sulfate (2:1) bis(dibutylcarbamate).
Use: Anticholinergic.

DI-CAL. (Kenyon) Dibasic calcium phosphate 261. mg., calcium gluconate 162 mg., Vit. D 333 I.U./Cap. Bot. 100s, 1000s.

DICALCIUM PHOSPHATE. Dibasic Calcium Phosphate, U.S.P., Monocalcium Phosphate. (Various Mfr.) **Cap.** 7.5 gr., 10 gr. **Tab.** 7.5 gr., 10 gr., 15 gr. Wafers 15 gr.
Use: Calcium supplement.
See: Irophos-D, Cap. (Lannett)
W/Cal. gluconate & Vit. D. (Various Mfr.) Cap., Tab. & Wafer.
See: Calcicaps, Tab. (Nion)
Di-Cal, Cap. (Kenyon)
W/Iron & Vit. D. (Various Mfr.)
Lilly—Pulvule, Bot. 100s.
Premo-Cap. Bot. 100s, 1000s.
W/Liver protein, vitamins, minerals.
See: Pet-A-Vite, Prep. (Vortech)
W/Methyl testosterone, ethinyl estradiol, linoleic acid, cobalt sulf, niacin, desic. liver, Mg sulf., Mn sulf., Cu sulf., Fe peptonate, pot. iodide
See: Gera-Pet, Tab. (North. Amer. Pharm.)
W/Vitamin D. (Squibb) Ca 85 mg., phosphorous 60 mg., Vit.-D. 41 I.U.

DICAL-D. (Abbott) Dibasic calcium phosphate containing calcium 116.7 mg., phosphorous 90 mg., Vit. D 133 I.U./Cap. Bot. 100s, 500s.
Use: Increase oral intake of calcium & phosphorus.

DICAL-D WITH VITAMIN C. (Abbott) Dibasic calcium phosphate containing calcium 116.7 mg., phosphorus 90 mg., Vit. D 133 I.U., ascorbic acid 15 mg./Cap. Bot. 100s.
Use: Calcium, phosphorus & Vitamin C supplement.

DICAL-D WAFERS. (Abbott) Dibasic calcium phosphate containing calcium 232 mg., phosphorus 180 mg., Vit. D 200 I.U./Wafer. Box of 51s.
Use: Calcium & phosphorus supplement.

DICAL-DEE. (Barre) Vit. D 350 I.U., dibasic calcium phosphate 4.5 gr., Cal. gluconate 3 gr./Cap. Bot. 100s, 1000s.
Use: Calcium supplement.

DICALDEL. (Faraday) Dibasic calcium phosphate 300 mg., calcium gluconate 200 mg., Vit. D 33 I.U./Cap. Bot. 100s, 250s, 500s, 1000s.
Use: Calcium supplement.

;ALTABS. (Faraday) Dibasic calcium phosphate
108 mg., Ca gluconate 140 mg., Vit. D 35 I.U./Tab.
3ot. 100s, 250s, 1000s.

;ARBOSIL. (Arch) Calcium carbonate 500
ng./Tab. 12 Rolls 12s.
Jse: Antacid.

;EN. (Mallard) Dicyclomine HCl 10 mg., sodium
chloride 9 mg., chlorobutanol hydrate 5 mg./ml.
/ial 10 ml.
Jse: Anticholinergic.

CET. (Sanford & Son) Methylbenzethonium chloride
24.4 Gm., Sod. carb. monohydrate 48.8 Gm., Sod.
nitrite 24.4 Gm., trisodium ethylenediamine tetra-acetate monohydrate 2.4 Gm. Pow. Pkg. 2.4 Gm., Box
24s.
Jse: Disinfection of dental instruments.

;HLORALANTIPYRINE. Dichloralphenazone.
Chloralpyrine. A complex of 2 mol. chloral hydrate
with 1 mol. antipyrine. Sominat.
'Isometheptene mucate, N-acetyl-p-amino-phenol.
See: Midrin, Caps. (Carnrick)

CHLORALPHENAZONE. B.A.N. A complex of
chloral hydrate and phenazone. Dichloralantipyrine
(Various Mfr.)
Use: Hypnotic.
See: Fenzol
Welldorm
'Isometheptine mucate, acetaminophen.
See: Midrin, Cap. (Carnrick)

CHLORAMINE T. P-Toluenesulfone-dichloramine
(Var. Mfr.)
Use: (1 to 5% in chlorinated paraffin) Antiseptic.

CHLOREN.
See: Mechlorethamine HCl, Sterile Inj. (Var. Mfr.)

CHLORISONE ACETATE. 9a, 11b-dichloro-dl,-4-
pregnadiene-17a,21-diol-3,20-dione-21-acetate.

CHLORMETHAZANONE. 2-(3,4-dichlorophenyl)-3-
methyl-4-metathiazanone-1-dioxide.

5-DICHLORO-m-BENZENEDISULFONAMIDE. Dichlorphenamide, U.S.P. XXI.

**I-DICHLORO-2-(o-CHLOROPHENYL)-2-(p-CHLOR-
OPHENYL)-ETHANE.** Mitotane, U.S.P. XXI.

**DICHLORO-1,1-DIFLUOROETHYL METHYL
ETHER.** Methoxyflurane, U.S.P. XXI.

ICHLORODIFLUOROMETHANE, N.F. XVI.
Use: Aerosol propellant.

CHLORODIPHENYL TRICHLOROETHANE.
See: Chlorophenothane (Var. Mfr.)

7-DICHLORO-8-HYDROXYQUINALDINE. Sterosan.

7-DICHLORO-8-HYDROXYQUINOLINE.
See: Capitrol, Liq. (Westwood)

**, 3-DICHLORO-4-(2-METHYLENEBUTYRYL)-
PHENOXY] ACETIC ACID.**
See: Ethacrynic Acid, U.S.P. XXI.

2'-DICHLORO-n-METHYL-DIETHYLAMI-NE HCl.
See: Mechlorethamine HCl, U.S.P. XXI.

CHLOROPHEN. B.A.N. Di(5-chloro-2-hydroxy-phe-
nyl) methane.
Use: Anthelmintic.
See: Antiphen

CHLOROPHENARSINE. B.A.N. 3-Amino-4-hydroxy-
phenyldichloroarsine.
Use: Antifungal agent.

DICHLOROPHENARSINE HYDROCHLORIDE, (Chlorarsen, Clorarsen, Fontarsol, Halarsol.)

DICHLOROPHENE. Didroxane. G-4, bis(5-Chloro-2-
hydroxyphenyl) methane. Related to
hexachlorophene.
W/Parachlorometaxylenol, propylparaaminobenzoate,
hexachlorophene, benzocaine.
See: Triguent, Oint. (Commerce)
W/Undecylenic acid.
See: Fungicidal Talc. (Gordon)
Onychomycetin, Liq. (Gordon)
W/Undecylenic acid, salicylic acid, hexachlorophene.
See: Podiaspray, aerosol pow. (Dalin)

• **DICHLOROTETRAFLUOROETHANE,** N.F. XVI.
1, 2-Dichlorotetrafluoroethane.
Use: Aerosol propellant.

**4, 4'-DICHLORO-3-(TRIFLUOROMETHYL)-CARBANI-
LIDE.** Cloflucarban

DICHLOROXYLENOL. B.A.N. 2,4-Dichloro-3,5-xylenol.
Use: Bactericide.

• **DICHLORPHENAMIDE.** U.S.P. XXI. Tab. U.S.P. XXI.
1,3-Benzenedisulfonamide, 4,5-di-
chloro-. 1,3-Disulfamyl-4-5-dichloro-benzene. B.A.N.
4,5-Dichlorobenzene-1,3-disulfonamide.
Use: Treatment of glaucoma.
See: Daranide, Tab. (Merck Sharp & Dohme)

N,N-DICHLOR SULFAMIDOBENZOIC ACID.
See: Halazone, Tab. (Abbott)

• **DICHLORVOS.** USAN. 2, 2-Dichlorovinyl dimethyl
phosphate.
Use: Anthelmintic; insecticide, veterinary medicine.
See: Atgard
Canogard
Equigard
Vapona

DICHOLIN. (Kenyon) Ox bile ext. $\frac{3}{8}$ gr., iron lactate
$\frac{3}{4}$ gr., calumba $\frac{3}{4}$ gr., chamomile flowers $1\frac{5}{8}$ gr.,
rhubarb $1\frac{5}{8}$ gr./Cap. Bot. 100s, 1000s.

DICHROMIUM TRIOXIDE. B.A.N. Chromium
sesquioxide.
Use: Diagnostic aid.

• **DICIRENONE.** USAN.
Use: Hypotensive.

DICKEY'S OLD RELIABLE EYE WASH. (Dickey
Drug) Berberine sulfate, boric acid, propyl parasept,
methyl parasept. Plastic dropper bot. 8 cc., 12 cc.,
1 oz.
Use: Minor eye irritations.

DICLOFENAC. B.A.N. [2-(2,6-Dichloroanilino) phenyl]-
acetic acid.
Use: Anti-inflammatory.
See: Voltarol (sodium salt)

• **DICLOFENAC SODIUM.** USAN.
Use: Anti-inflammatory.

• **DICLORALUREA.** USAN.
Use: Food additive.

• **DICLOXACILLIN.** USAN. 6-[3-(2,6-Dichlorophenyl)-
5-methyl-4-isoxazolecarboxamido]-3,3-dimethyl-7-
oxo-4-thia-1-azabicyclo[3.2.0]-heptane-2-carboxylic
acid.

Use: Antibiotic.
See: Dynapen, Cap., Susp. (Bristol)
Pathocil, Cap., Susp. (Wyeth)
Veracillin, Cap., Inj. (Ayerst)

• **DICLOXACILLIN SODIUM,** U.S.P. XXI. Capsules, Sterile, For Oral Suspension U.S.P. XXI.
Use: Antibiotic.
See: Dycill, Cap. (Beecham)
Dynapen, Cap., Sol. (Bristol)

DICODETHAL ELIXIR. (Lannett) D-methorphan HBr 10 mg./5 cc. in el. terpin hydrate. Bot. 1 pt., 1 gal.
Use: Cough preparation.

DICOLE. (Blue Cross) Docusate sodium 100 mg./Cap. Bot. 100s.
Use: Stool softener.

DICOPHANE.
See: Chlorophenothane (Var. Mfr.); DDT.

DICOUMARIN.
See: Dicumarol, Preps. (Var. Mfr.)

DICOUMAROL.
See: Dicumarol, U.S.P. XXI.

• **DICUMAROL,** U.S.P. XXI. Caps., Tab., U.S.P. XXI. 2H-1-Benzopyran-2-one 3,3′-methylenebis 4-hydroxy-3,3′-methylenebis(4-hydroxycoumarin). Dicourmarol. Dicoumarin. Bishydroxycoumarin. Melitoxin. (Abbott) Tab. 25 mg., 50 mg. Bot. 100s, 1000s; 100 mg. Bot. 1000s. (Quality Generics) Tab. 25 mg., 50 mg., Bot. 100s. (Lilly) Pulvule. 25 mg. Bot. 100s, 1000s; 50 mg. Bot. 100s.
Use: Blood anticoagulant.

DICYCLOMINE. B.A.N. 2-Diethylaminoethyl bicyclohexyl-1-carboxylate. Dicycloverine (I.N.N.)
Use: Antispasmodic.
See: Merbentyl
Wyovin [hydrochloride]

• **DICYCLOMINE HYDROCHLORIDE,** U.S.P. XXI. Caps., Inj., Syrup, Tabs., U.S.P. XXI. Bicyclohexyl-1-carboxylic acid, 2-(diethylamino) ethyl 3w534 HCl. 2-(Diethylamino)ethyl (Bicyclohexyl)-1-carboxylate hydrochloride.
Use: Antispasmodic.
See: Antispas, Inj. (Keene)
Benacol, Tab. (Cenci)
Bentyl, Amp. Syringe, Cap., Tab. & Syr. (Merrell Dow)
Cyclomine, Inj. (Tunex)
Dysaps, Tab., Liq., Inj. (Savage)
Nospaz, Vial (Reid-Provident)
Rocyclo Preps. (Robinson)
Rotyl HCl, Vial (Rocky Mtn.)
Stannitol (Standex)

W/Aluminum hydroxide, magnesium hydroxide, methylcellulose.
See: Triactin Liquid & Tab. (Norwich)

W/Phenobarbital.
See: Bentyl with Phenobarbital, Prods. (Merrell Dow)

DI-CYCLONEX. (Pasadena Research) Dicyclomine HCl 10 mg./ml. Injectable vial. Vial 10 cc.

DICYCLON-M. (Kenyon) Dicyclomine HCl 10 mg., pyr mine maleate 10 mg., pyridoxine HCl 10 mg./Tab Bot. 100s, 1000s.
Use: Antinauseant.

DICYCLON NO. 1. (Kenyon) Dicyclomine HCl 10 mg./Tab. Bot. 100s, 1000s.
Use: Antispasmodic.

DICYCLON NO. 2. (Kenyon) Dicyclomine HCl 10 m phenobarbital 15 mg./Tab. Bot. 100s, 1000s.

DICYCLON NO. 3. (Kenyon) Dicyclomine HCl 20 m phenobarbital 15 mg./Tab. Bot. 100s, 1000s.

DICYNENE. (Baxter)
Use: Hemostatic agent.
See: Ethamsylate

DICYSTEINE.
See: Cystine, Pow. (Various Mfr.)

7,8-DIDEHYDRO-4,5α-EPOXY-3-METHOXY-17-ME HYLMORPHINAN-6α-OL.
See: Codeine, U.S.P. XXI. Cryst., Pow. (Var. Mfr.)

7,8-DIDEHYDRO-4,5α-EPOXY-3-METHOXY-17-ME HYLMORPHINAN-6α-OL PHOSPHATE (1:1) (Sa Codeine Phosphate, U.S.P. XXI.

7,8-DIDEHYDRO-4,5-EPOXY-3-METHOXY-17-MET YL-MORPHINAN-6α-OL SULFATE (2:1).
See: Codeine Sulfate, U.S.P. XXI. Tab., Pow. (Va Mfr.)

7,8-DIDEHYDRO-4,5α-EPOXY-17-METHYL-MORPH NAN-3,6α-DIOL SULFATE (2:1) (SALT) PENTAH DRATE. Morphine Sulfate, U.S.P. XXI.

(±)-9,10-DIDEHYDRO-N-(1-(HYDROXY-METHYL PROPYL)-1,6-DIMETHYLERGO-LINE-8β-CARBC AMIDE MALEATE (1:1)
See: Methysergide Maleate, U.S.P. XXI. (Sandoz)

9,10-DIDEHYDRO-n-[(S)-2-HYDROXY-1-METHYLE HYL]-6-METHYLERGOLINE-8β-CARBOXAMIDE MALEATE. Ergonovine Maleate.

9,10-DIDEHYDRO-N-[(S)-1-(HYDROXY-METHYL)P OPYL]-6-METHYLERGOLINE-8β-CARBOXAMID MALEATE (1:1). Methylergonovine Maleate, U.S. XXI.

DI-DELAMINE GEL. (Commerce) Tripelennamine H diphenhydramine HCl, benzalkonium chloride, menthol in a special clear gel. Gel. Tube 1.25 oz.
Use: Relief of itching.

DI-DELAMINE SPRAY. (Commerce) Tripelennami HCl, diphenhydramine HCl, menthol and benzalkonium Cl. Spray pump 4 oz.
Use: Relief of itching due to allergies, hives, non-poisonous insect bites.

3[(O-2,6-DIDEOXY-β-D-ribo-HEXOPYRANOSYL-(1 -0-2,6-DIDEOXY-β-D-ribo-HEXOPYRANOSYL-(1 -2,6-DIDEOXY-β-D-ribo-HEXOPYRANOSYL)OXY 12, 14-DIHYDROXY-5β-CARD-20(22)-ENOLIDE. Digoxin, U.S.P. XXI.

DIDREX. (Upjohn) Benzphetamine HCl 25 mg./Tab. Bot. 100s; 50 mg./Tab. Bot. 100s, 500s.
Use: Appetite depressant.

DIDRONEL. (Norwich Eaton) Etidronate disodium 20 mg. or 400 mg./Tab. Bot. 60s.
Use: Treatment of symptomatic Paget's disease c bone and prevention and treatment of heterotopic ossification due to spinal cord injury and preventic

ɜnd treatment of heterotopic ossification following :otal hip replacement.

ΞLDRIN. B.A.N. Product containing 85 per cent of 1,2,3,4,10, 10-hexachloro-6,7-epoxy-1,4,4a,5,6,7,-3,8a-octahydro-exo-1,4-endo-5,8-dimethanona-phthalene.
Use: Treatment of arthropod infestation.

IENESTROL, U.S.P. XXI. Cream, U.S.P. XXI. Nonsteroid, synthetic estrogen. Dienoestrol. 4,4′-(Diethylideneethylene)diphenol. **Cream:** (Ortho) Dienestrol 0.01%. Tube 78 Gm. w/applicator.
Use: Estrogen therapy, atrophic vaginitis.
See: D V Cream (Merrell Dow)
D V Suppositories (Merrell Dow)
Ortho Dienestrol Cream (Ortho)
/Sulfanilamide, aminacrine HCl, allantoin.
See: AVC/Dienestrol Cream, Supp. (Merrell Dow)

ETAC MAXIMUM STRENGTH ONCE-A-DAY DIET D CAPSULES. (Menley & James) Phenylpropanolamine HCl 75 mg. Pkg. 20s, 40s.
Use: Appetite suppressant.

ETETIC COUGH SYRUP. (Eckerd) Bot. 8 oz.

ETHADIONE. B.A.N. 5,5-Diethyloxazine-2,4-dione.
Use: Analeptic agent.
See: Dietroxine (I.N.N.)
Toce

IETHANOLAMINE, N.F. XVI.
Use: Pharmaceutic acid (alkalizing agent).

ETHAZINE. B.A.N. 10-(2-Diethylaminoethyl)-Phenothiazine.
Use: Treatment of the parkinsonian syndrome.
See: Diparcol (hydrochloride)

ETHAZINE HCl. 10-(β-Diethylaminoethyl)-phenothiazine HCl. Diparcol.

ETHANOLAMINE.
See: Diolamine

ETHOXIN. Intracaine HCl

(DIETHYLAMINO)-2′, 6′-ACETOXYLIDIDE. Lidocaine, U.S.P. XXI.

(DIETHYLAMINO)-2′, 6′-ACETOXYLIDIDE HCl.
See: Lidocaine HCl, U.S.P. XXI.

(2-(DIETHYLAMINO)ETHOXY)ETHYL 1-PHENYLCYCLOPENTANECARBOXYLATE CITRATE (1:1).
See: Carbetapentane Citrate.

(DIETHYLAMINO)ETHYL p-AMINOBENZOATE HCl.
See: Procaine HCl, U.S.P. XXI.

(DIETHYLAMINO)ETHYL 4-AMINO-2-CHLOROBENZOATE MONOHYDROCHLORIDE.
See: Chloroprocaine Hydrochloride, U.S.P. XXI. (Var. Mfr.)

(DIETHYLAMINO)ETHYL 4-AMINO-2-PROPOXYBENZOATE MONOHYDROCHLORIDE.
See: Chloroprocaine Hydrochloride, U.S.P. XXI. (Var. Mfr.)

(DIETHYLAMINO)ETHYL 4-AMINO-2-PROPOXYBENZOATE MONOHYDROCHLORIDE.
See: Propoxycaine Hydrochloride, U.S.P. XXI. (Var. Mfr.)

(DIETHYLAMINO)ETHYL 3-AMINO-4-PROPOXYBENZOATE MONOHYDROCHLORIDE.
Proparacaine Hydrochloride, U.S.P. XXI.

2-(DIETHYLAMINO)ETHYL(BICYCLOHEXYL)-1-CARBOXYLATE HYDROCHLORIDE.
See: Dicyclomine Hydrochloride U.S.P. XXI. (Var. Mfr.)

2-(DIETHYLAMINO)PROPIOPHENONE HYDROCHLORIDE.
See: Diethylpropion Hydrochloride, Tab. (Var. Mfr.)

10-[2-(DIETHYLAMINO)PROPYL]PHENOTHIAZINE MONOHYDROCHLORIDE. Ethopropazine Hydrochloride, U.S.P. XXI.

DIETHYLCARBAMAZINE. B.A.N. 1-Diethyl-carbamoyl-4-methylpiperazine.
Use: Treatment of filariasis.
See: Banocide
Ethodryl
Hetrazan dihydrogen citrate

• **DIETHYLCARBAMAZINE CITRATE,** U.S.P. XXI. Tab., U.S.P. XXI. Diethylcarbamazine Dihydrogen Citrate. N, N-Diethyl-4-methyl-1-piperazine-carboxamide dihydrogen citrate. 1-Piperazinecarboxamide, N,N-diethyl-4-methyl-, 2-hydroxy-1,2,3-propanetricarboxylate. Banocide, Ethodryl.
Use: Antifilarial.

DIETHYLENEDIAMINE CITRATE. Piperazine Citrate, Piperazine Hexahydrate.
See: Antepar, Syr., Tab., Wafer (Burroughs Wellcome)

13,17alpha-DIETHYL-17-HYDROGEN-4-EN-3-ONE. Genabol.

DIETHYL(2-HYDROXYETHYL)METHYL-AMMONIUM BROMIDE α-CYCLOPENTYL-2-THIOPHENE-GLYCOLATE.
See: Penthienate Bromide, Tab. (Var. Mfr.)

DIETHYL(2-HYDROXYETHYL)METHYL-AMMONIUM BROMIDE XANTHENE-9-CARBOXYLATE.
See: Methantheline Bromide, Tab. (Var. Mfr.)

4,4′-(DIETHYLIDENEETHYLENE)DIPHENOL.
See: Dienestrol, Cream, Tab. (Var. Mfr.)

DIETHYLMALONYLUREA.
See: Barbital, Tab. (Var. Mfr.)

5,5-DIETHYL-1-METHYLBARBITURIC ACID.
See: Metharbital, Tabs. (Var. Mfr.)

3, 3-DIETHYL-5-METHYL-2,4-PIPERIDINE-DIONE.
See: Methyprylon, Preps. (Var. Mfr.)

4, 4′-(1, 2-DIETHYL-3-METHYLTRIMETHYLENE) DIPHENOL.
See: Benzestrol, Tabs. (Var. Mfr.)

N, N-DIETHYLNICOTINAMIDE.
See: Nikethamide. (Var. Mfr.)

N-N-DIETHYL-M-TOLUAMIDE. W/N-Octyl Bicycloheptene Dicarboximide, 2,3,4,5-bis(delta-2-butylene)tetrahydrofurfural, Di-n-propyl isocincho-meronate, isopropanol and other isomers.
See: Bansum, Bot. (Summers)

• **DIETHYL PHTHALATE,** N.F. XVI.
Use: Plasticizer.

DIETHYLPROPION. B.A.N. α-Diethylaminopropiophenone.
Use: Appetite suppressant.
See: Amfepramone (I.N.N.)

• **DIETHYLPROPION HCl,** U.S.P. XXI. Tab., U.S.P. XXI. 1-Phenyl-2-diethylaminopropanone-1 HCl. 2-(Diethylamino)propiophenone HCl.

Use: Anorexic.
See: D.E.P.-75
Nu-Dispoz, Tab. (Coastal)
Ro-Diet, Tab. (Robinson)
Ro-Diet Timed (Robinson)
Tenuate, Tab. (Merrell Dow)
Tepanil, Tab. (Riker)
Tepanil Ten-Tab, Tab. (Riker)

α,α′-**DIETHYL-4,4′-STILBENEDIOL.** Diethylstilbestrol, U.S.P. XXI.

(E)-αα′-DIETHYL-4,4′-STILBENEDIOL DIPROPIONATE.
See: Diethylstilbestrol Dipropionate, Preps. (Var. Mfr.)

• **DIETHYLSTILBESTROL,** U.S.P. XXI. Inj. Supp., Tab., U.S.P. XXI. Phenol 4,4′-(1,2-diethyl-1,2-ethenediyl)bis-. (Cyren A, Domestrol, Estrobene, Fonatol, New-Oestranol 1, Oestrogenine, Oestromienin, Palestrol, Synthoestrin, Stiboestroform, Stilbestrol, Synestrin) alpha, alpha′-Diethyl-4,4′-stilbenediol.
Use: Estrogen.
See: Acnestrol, Lot. (Dermik)
Mase-Bestrol, Tab. (Mason)
W/Clioquinol, sulfanilamide.
See: D.I.T.I. Creme (Dunhall)
W/Nitrofurazone, diperodon HCl.
See: Furacin-E Urethral Inserts (Eaton)
W/Sulfadiazine, clioquinol.
See: Benegyn, Vag. Insert, Cream (Vortech)

• **DIETHYLSTILBESTROL DIPHOSPHATE,** U.S.P. XXI. Inj., U.S.P. XXI.
Use: Estrogen.
See: Stilphostrol, Inj., Tab. (Miles Pharm)

DIETHYLSTILBESTROL DIPROPIONATE, a,a′-Diethyl-4, 4′ stilbenediol dipropionate. Cyren B, Estilben, Estroben DP, New-Oestranol 11, Orestol, Pabestrol D, Stilbestronate, Stilboestrol DP, Stilronate, Synestrin Amp. (Various Mfr.) Amp. in oil, 0.5 mg., 1 mg., 5 mg./cc. Tab. 0.5 mg., 1 mg., 5 mg.
Use: Estrogen.

DIETHYLTHIAMBUTENE. B.A.N. 3-Diethyl-amino-1, 1-di(2-thienyl)but-1-ene.
Use: Narcotic analgesic.
See: Themalon

• **DIETHYLTOLUAMIDE,** U.S.P. XXI. Topical Soln., U.S.P. XXI. Benzamide, N, N-diethyl-3-methyl-N, N-Diethyl-m-toluamide.
Use: Repellent (arthropod).
See: RV Pellent, Oint. (Elder)

N, N-DIETHYLVANILLAMIDE.
See: Ethamivan, Inj. (Var. Mfr.)

DIET-TRIM. (Pharmex) Phenylpropanolamine, carboxymethylcellulose, benzocaine/Tab. Bot. 21s, 90s.

DIETTS. (Image) 75 mg. timed tablet.
Use: Weight control.

DIET-TUSS. (Approved) d-Methorphan 30 mg., thenylpyramine HCl and pyrilamine maleate 80 mg., sod. salicylate 200 mg., sod. citrate 600 mg., ammonium chloride 100 mg./Fl. Oz. Bot. 4 oz.
Use: Sugar-free antihistaminic.

DI-FACTOR. (Sutliff & Case) Vit. D 133 I.U., cal. carb. 200 mg., ferrous gluconate 15 mg., Vit. B-1 2 mg., B-2 2 mg., C 30 mg., magnesium carb. 5 mg., mang. sulf. 1 mg., copper sulf. 1 mg./Tab. Bot. 100s, 1000s.
Use: Prenatal dietary supplement.

• **DIFENOXIMIDE HYDROCHLORIDE.** USAN.
Use: Antiperistaltic.

• **DIFENOXIN.** USAN. 1-(3-Cyano-3, 3-diphenyl-propyl) 4-phenylpiperidine-4-carboxylic acid.
Use: Antidiarrheal.

DIFETARSONE. B.A.N. NN′-Ethylene-1, 2-diarsanilic acid.
Use: Arsenical.
See: Bemarsal disodium salt

• **DIFLORASONE DIACETATE.** USAN. 6α, 9α-difluoro-11β, 17, 21 trihydroxy-16β methyl-pregna-1, 4-diene-3, 20-dione 17, 21 diacetate.
Use: Anti-inflammatory, antipruritic.
See: Florone, Cream, Oint. (Upjohn)
Maxiflor, Cream, Oint. (Herbert)

• **DIFLUANINE HCl.** USAN. (McNeil) 1-(2-Anilinoethyl)-4-[4, 4-bis(p-fluorophenyl)butyl]-piperazine trihydrochloride.
Use: CNS stimulant.

• **DIFLUCORTOLONE.** USAN. 6α,9-Difluoro-11β, 21-dihydroxy-16α-methylpregna-1, 4-diene-3, 20-dione.
Use: Glucocorticoid.

• **DIFLUCORTOLONE PIVALATE.** USAN.
Use: Glucocorticoid.

DIFLUMIDONE. B.A.N. 3′-Benzoyldifluoromethanesulfonanilide.
Use: Anti-inflammatory.

• **DIFLUMIDONE SODIUM.** USAN.
Use: Anti-inflammatory.

• **DIFLUNISAL,** U.S.P. XXI. Tab., U.S.P. XXI.
Use: Analgesic, anti-inflammatory.
See: Dolobid, Tab. (Merck Sharp & Dohme)

• **DIFTALONE.** USAN.
Use: Anti-inflammatory.

6α, 9-DIFLUORO-11β, 16 α, 17, 21-TETRAHYDROXY-PREGNA-1,4-DIENE-3, 20-DIONE, CYCLIC 16, 17-ACETAL WITH ACETONE. Fluocinolone Acetonide, U.S.P. XXI.

6α, 9-DIFLUORO-11β, 17, 21-TRIHYDROXY-16α-METHYL-PREGNA-1, 4-DIENE-3,20-DIONE 21 PIVALATE. Flumethazone Pivalate, U.S.P. XXI.

• **DIFLUPREDNATE.** USAN. 6α, 9-difluoro-11β, 17, 21-trihydroxypregna-1, 4-diene-3, 20-dione 21-acetate-17-butyrate.
Use: Anti-inflammatory.

DI-GEL LIQUID. (Plough) Aluminum hydroxide 282 mg., mag. hydroxide 87 mg., simethicone 20 mg./5 ml. Bot. 6 oz., 12 oz. Mint or lemon-orange.
Use: Antacid, antiflatulent.

DI-GEL TABLETS. (Plough) Aluminum hydroxide, mag carb. 282 mg., mag. hydroxide 85 mg., simethicone 25 mg./Tab. Box 30s, 60s, 90s.
Use: Antacid, antiflatulent.

DIGENZYMES. (Maurry) Ox bile ext. 130 mg., pancreatin 130 mg., papain 65 mg., duodenal

ıbstances desiccated defatted 65 mg./Tab. Bot.)0s, 1000s.
se: Colitis, faulty protein, carbohydrate, and fat gestion, gallbladder stasis.
ESTALIN. (Vortech) Activated charcoal 5.3 mg., smuth subgallate 3.8 mg., pepsin 2.0 mg., erberis 1.2 mg., papain 1.2 mg., pancreatin 0.40 g., hydrastis 0.08 mg./Tab. Bot. 100s, 1000s.
se: Digestive aid.
ESTAMIC. (Metro Med) **Tabs. #1.** Bot. 50s,)0s. **#2.** Bot. 50s, 500s. **Liq.** Bot. 8 oz., gal.
se: Flatulence and bloating.
ESTANT. (Canright) Pancreatin 5.25 gr., ox bile xt. 2 gr., pepsin 5 gr., betaine HCl 1 gr./Tab. Bot. 00s, 1000s.
se: Digestant formula.
ESTEX. (Pasadena Research) Pancreatin 130 g., iron oxbile 130 mg., prolase 3 mg., mylase 15 ng., celase 1 mg./Tab. Bot. 100s, 1000s.
se: Digestive enzymes.
ESTIVE COMPOUND. (Thurston) Betaine HCl .25 gr., pepsin 1 gr., papain 2 gr., mycozyme 2 gr., x bile 2 gr./2 Tabs. Bot. 100s, 500s.
Jse: Hypochlorhydria, achlorhydria, impaired igestive ability.
ESTOZYME. (Wolins) Pepsin 250 mg., pancreatin 00 mg., dehydrocholic acid 25 mg./Tab. Bot. 000s.
ESTOZYME TABS. (Goldline) Pancreatin, pepsin, ile salts. Bot. 1000s.
Jse: Digestive aid.
IGITALIS, U.S.P. XXI. Cap., Pow., Tab., U.S.P. XXI.
Jse: Digitalis therapy, cardiotonic.
See: Digitora, Tab. (Upjohn)
IGITALIS GLYCOSIDES.
Jse: Digitalis therapy.
See: Acylanid, Tab. (Sandoz)
Cedilanid, Tab. (Sandoz)
Cedilanid-D, Amp. (Sandoz)
Crystodigin, Tab., Amp., Vial (Lilly)
Deslanoside, Inj. (Var. Mfr.)
Digiglusin, Tab. (Lilly)
Digitaline Nativelle, Sol., Tab., Elxr. (Savage)
Digitoxin, Preps. (Var. Mfr.)
Digoxin, Preps. (Var. Mfr.)
Gitaligin, Tab. (Schering)
Gitalin, Tab. (Var. Mfr.)
Lanatoside C, Inj., Tab. (Var. Mfr.)
Lanoxin, Tab., Inj., Elix. (Burroughs Wellcome)
Purodigin, Tab., (Wyeth)
GITALIS LEAF, POWDERED.
Use: Digitalis therapy.
See: Pil-Digis, Pill (Key)
GITALIS TINCTURE.
Use: Digitalis therapy.
IGITOXIN, U.S.P. XXI. Inj., Tab., U.S.P. XXI. (Various Mfr.) Amp. (0.2 mg./cc.) 1 cc., Cap. in oil, 0.1 mg., 0.2 mg., Tab. 0.1 mg., 0.2 mg.
Use: Digitalis therapy; cardiotonic.
See: Crystodigin, Tab. (Lilly)
De-Tone 0.1, 0.2, Tab. (Scrip)
Digitaline Nativelle, Prep. (Savage)
Maso-Toxin, Tab. (Mason)
Purodigin, Tab. (Wyeth)
W/Carboxymethylcellulose & Sod.
See: Foxalin, Cap. (Standex)
DIGITOXIN, ACETYL.
Use: Digitalis therapy.
See: Acylanid, Tab. (Sandox)
α-DIGITOXIN MONOACETATE.
Use: Digitalis therapy.
See: Acetyldigitoxin, Tab. (Var. Mfr.)
DIGOLASE. (Boyle) Pancreatin 80 mg., aspergillus oryzae 15 mg., papain 3 mg., polysorbate-80 20 mg./Cap. Bot. 100s.
Use: Orally, digestive enzyme deficiencies.
• **DIGOXIN,** U.S.P. XXI. Elix., Inj., Tab. U.S.P. XXI. Cryst. glycoside isolated from lvs. of digitalis lanata. 0.25 mg./Tab. Bot. 1000s. Unit dose 100s.
Use: Digitalization; cardiotonic.
See: Lanoxin, Prep. (Burroughs Wellcome)
Masoxin, Tab. (Mason)
DIGOXIN I-125 IMUSAY. (Abbott) Digoxin diagnostic kit. 100s, 300s.
Use: Quantitative determination of serum digoxin.
DIGOXIN RIABEAD. (Abbott) Test kit 100s, 300s.
Use: Solid-phase radioimmunoassay for quantitative measurement of serum digoxin.
• **DIHEXYVERINE HYDROCHLORIDE.** USAN.
Use: Anticholinergic.
DIHISTINE D.H. (Goldline) Bot. 4 oz. pt., gal.
Use Antihistaminic, antitussive, decongestant.
DIHISTINE EXPECTORANT. (Goldline) Bot. 4 oz., pt., gal.
Use: Antitussive, decongestant, expectorant.
DIHYDAN SOLUBLE.
See: Phenytoin Sodium (Various Mfr.)
DIHYDRALLAZINE. B.A.N. 1,4-Dihydrazinophthalazine.
Use: Hypotensive.
See: Nepresol [mesylate or sulfate]
DIHYDREX CAPSULES. (Kay) Dipehnhydramine HCl 12.5 mg./5 ml. w/alcohol 14% Bot. 4 oz., 16 oz., gal.
Use: Antihistaminic.
DIHYDREX EXPECTORANT. (Kay) Diphenhydramine HCl 80 mg., ammonium chloride 12 gr., sod. citrate 5 gr., menthol 1 mg./5 ml. w/alcohol 5%. Bot. pt.
Use: Cough control.
DIHYDREX INJECTION. (Kay) Diphenhydramine HCl 10 mg./ml., or 50 mg./ml. Vial 30 ml.
Use: Antihistaminic.
DIHYDROCODEINE. Paracodin. Drocode.
Use: Antitussive & analgesic.
DIHYDROCODEINONE BITARTRATE.
Use: Narcotic.
See: Hydrocodone Bitartrate, U.S.P. XXI.
W/Caffeine, phenacetin, aspirin.
See: Drocogesic #3, Tab. (Rand)
Duradyne DHC, Liq. (Forest)
W/Caffeine, phenacetin, aspirin, promethazine HCl.
See: Synalgos-DC, Cap. (Ives)
DIHYDROCODEINONE RESIN COMPLEX.
W/Phenyltoloxamine resin complex.
See: Tussionex, Prep. (Pennwalt)

10, 11-DIHYDRO-N,N-DIMETHYL-5H-DIBENZO-[a,d]CYCLOHEPTENE-PROPYLAMINE HCl. Amitriptyline Hydrochloride, U.S.P. XXI.

DIHYDRO-DIETHYLSTILBESTROL.
See: Hexestrol, Tab. & Vial (Various Mfr.)

DIHYDROERGOCORNINE. Ergot Alk. component of Hydergine.
See: Circanol, Tab. (Riker)
Deapril-ST, Tab. (Mead Johnson)

DIHYDROERGOCRISTINE. Ergot Alk. component of Hydergine.
See: Circanol, Tab. (Riker)
Deapril-ST, Tab. (Mead Johnson)

DIHYDROERGOCRYPTINE. Ergot Alk. component of Hydergine.
See: Circanol, Tab. (Riker)
Deapril-ST, Tab. (Mead Johnson)

DIHYDROERGOTAMINE. (D.H.E. 45) (Sandoz) Dihydroergotamine mesylate. Amp.

• **DIHYDROERGOTAMINE MESYLATE,** U.S.P. XXI. Inj., U.S.P. XXI. Dihydroergotamine methanesulfonate.
Use: Treatment of migraine; antiadrenergic.
See: DHE 45, Amp. (Sandoz)
W/Scopolamine HBr, phenobarbital Sod., barbital Sod. & Sandoptal.
See: Plexonal, Tab. (Sandoz)

DIHYDROFOLLICULAR HORMONE.
See: Estradiol (Various Mfr.)

DIHYDROFOLLICULINE.
See: Estradiol (Various Mfr.)

DIHYDROHYDROXYCODEINONE. Oxycodone. (Ducodal, Eukodal, Eucodal)
Use: Narcotic, analgesic.

DIHYDROHYDROXYCODEINONE HCl or BITARTRATE. Oxycodone HCl or Bitartrate.
W/Combinations.
See: Cophene-S, Syr. (Dunhall)
Corizahist-D, Syr. (Mason)
Damason-P, Tab. (Mason)
Percobarb, Cap. (Du Pont)
Percodan, Tab. (Du Pont)
Triaprin-DC, Cap. (Dunhall)

10,11-DIHYDRO-5-(3-(METHYLAMINO)-PROPYL)-5H-DIBENZ(b,f) AZAPINE MONOHYDROCHLORIDE.
See: Desipramine Hydrochloride, U.S.P. XXI.

10,11-DIHYDRO-N-METHYL-5H-DIBENZO-(a,d)CYCLOHEPTENE-$\Delta^{5\gamma}$PROPYLAMINE HYDROCHLORIDE.
See: Nortriptyline Hydrochloride, U.S.P. XXI.

DIHYDROMORPHINONE HCl.
See: Dilaudid, Prep. (Knoll)

• **DIHYDROSTREPTOMYCIN SULFATE,** U.S.P. XXI. Boluses, Inj., Sterile, U.S.P. XXI.
Use: Antibiotic.

• **DIHYDROTACHYSTEROL,** U.S.P. XXI. Caps., Oral Soln., Tabs., U.S.P. XXI. 9, 10-Seco-5,7,22-ergostartien-3-β-ol. (Roxane) 0.2 mg./Tab. Bot. 100s. Unit dose 100s.
Use: Treatment of hypocalcemia.
See: Hytakerol, Cap. Sol. (Winthrop-Breon)

DIHYDROTESTOSTERONE. Androstane-17-beta-ol-3-one.
See: Stanolone.

DIHYDROTHEELIN.
See: Estradiol (Var. Mfr.)

DIHYDROXYACETONE.
See: Chromelin, Liq. (Summers)
QT, Liq. (Plough)
Sudden Tan, Liq. (Plough)

• **DIHYDROXYALUMINUM AMINOACETATE,** U.S.P. XXI. Magma, Tab., U.S.P. XXI. Aluminum, (glycinato-N,O)dihydroxy-,hydrate. (Glycinato)-dihydroxyaluminum hydrate. Aluminum dihydroxyaminoacetate; basic aluminum aminoacetate. (Glycinato)dihydroxyaluminum.
Use: Antacid.
See: Hyperacid, Tab. (Wolins)
W/Methscopolamine bromide, sod. lauryl sulfate & magnesium hydroxide.
See: Alu-Scop, Cap., Susp. (Westerfield)
W/Phenobarbital & atropine methyl nitrate.
See: Harvatrate A, Tab. (O'Neal)
W/Salicylsalicylic acid, aspirin.
See: Salsprin, Tab. (Seatrace)

• **DIHYDROXYALUMINUM SODIUM CARBONATE,** U.S.P. XXI. Tab., U.S.P. XXI. Aluminum sodium carbonate hydroxide. Sodium (carbonato)-dihydroxyaluminate(1-)hydrate.
Use: Antacid.
See: Rolaids, Tab. (Warner-Lambert)

1,8-DIHYDROXYANTHRANOL. Anthrolin.

1,8-DIHYDROXYANTHRAQUINONE. Dioxyanthraquinone.
See: Danthron, U.S.P. XXI.

2,5-DIHYDROXYBENZOATE SODIUM. Gentisic acid.
See: Gentisate Sodium. (Various Mfr.)

3,12-DIHYDROXYCHOLANIC ACID.
See: Desoxycholic acid. (Var. Mfr.)

DIHYDROXYESTRIN.
See: Estradiol (Various Mfr.)

DIHYDROXYFLUORANE. Fluorescein.

3,4-DIHYDROXY-α-[)ISOPROPYLAMINO)METHYL]-BENZYL ALCOHOL HCl. Isoproterenol Hydrochloride, U.S.P. XXI.

(−)-3,4-DIHYDROXY-α-[(METHYLAMINO)-METHYL-BENZYL ALCOHOL. Epinephrine, U.S.P. XXI.

DIHYDROXYPHENYLISATIN.
See: Oxyphenisatin (Var. Mfr.)

(−)-3-(3,4-DIHYDROXYPHENYL)-L-ALA-NINE.
See: Levodopa, U.S.P. XXI.

2,2′-DIHYDROXY-4-METHOXYBENZOPHEN-ONE. Dioxybenzone, U.S.P. XXI.

L-3-(3,4-DIHYDROXYPHENYL)-2-METHYLALANINE SESQUIHYDRATE. Methyldopa, U.S.P. XXI.

DIHYDROXYPHENYLOXINDOL.
See: Oxyphenisatin (Var. Mfr.)

17,21-DIHYDROXYPREGNA-1,4-DIENE-3,11,-20-TRIONE. Prednisone, U.S.P. XXI.

DIHYDROXYPROPYLTHEOPHYLLINE. Dyphylline.
See: Airet, Preps. (Norwich Eaton)
Neothylline, Tab., Elix., Inj. (Lemmon)

Ephedrine HCl, butabarbital.
See: Airet R, Tabs. (Baylor Labs.)
Guaifenesin.
See: Airet G. G., Caps. & Elix. (Baylor Labs.)
HYDROXY(STEARATO)ALUMINUM. Aluminum Monostearate, N.F. XVI.
IODOHYDROXYQUIN.
See: Iodoquinol, U.S.P. XXI.
IODOHYDROXYQUINOLINE. B.A.N. 8-Hydroxy-5,7-di-iodoquinoline.
Use: Treatment of amebiasis.
See: Diodoquin
Embequin
Floraquin
IODOHYDROXYQUINOLINE.
See: Iodoquinol, U.S.P. XXI.
-DIIODO-8-QUINOLINOL.
See: Iodoquinol, U.S.P. XXI.
-DI-IODO-THYROACETIC ACID. Diac.
SOPROMINE HCl. N,N-diisopropyl-3,3-diphenylpropylamine HCl. (Lab. for Pharmaceutical Development, Inc.)
See: Desquam-X (Westwood)
DIISOPROPANOLAMINE, N.F. XVI.
Use: Pharmaceutic aid (alkalizing agent).
SOPROPYL PHOSPHOROFLUORIDATE.
See: Isofluorophate, U.S.P. XXI.
Floropryl, Oint. (Merck Sharp & Dohme)
SOPROPYL SEBACATE.
See: Delavan, Cream (Miles Pharm)
LACAP. (Coastal) Dyphylline 100 mg., guaifenesin 100 mg., ephedrine HCl 16 mg., phenobarbital 16 mg./Cap. Bot. 100s, 1000s.
LAMINATE. Mixture of mag. carb. and dihydroxy aluminum glycinate.
LANTIN. (Parke-Davis) Phenytoin. **30′ Suspension:** 30 mg./5 ml. Bot. 8 oz. Unit dose 5 ml. **125′ Suspension:** 125 mg./5 ml. Bot. 8 oz. Unit dose 5 ml. **Infatabs:** 50 mg./Tab. Bot. 100s. Unit dose 100s.
LANTIN SODIUM. (Parke-Davis) Extended phenytoin sodium **Kapseal** 30 mg., 100 mg. Bot. 100s, 1000s. Unit dose 100s. **Amp.:** (w/propylene glycol 40%, alcohol 10%, sod. hydroxide) 100 mg./2 ml. Unit dose 10s; 250 mg./5 ml. Amp. 10s. Unit dose 10s.
Use: Anticonvulsant.
LANTIN SODIUM W/PHENOBARBITAL KAPSEAL. (Parke-Davis) Phenytoin sod. 100 mg., phenobarbital 0.25 gr. or 0.5 gr./Cap. Bot. 100s, 1000s. 0.5 gr. Unit dose 100s.
Use: Anticonvulsant w/sedative.
LATRATE SR. (Reed & Carnrick) Isosorbide dinitrate 40 mg./Sustained Release Cap. Bot. 100s.
Use: Control of angina pectoris and coronary insufficiency.
LAUDID COUGH SYRUP. (Knoll) Hydromorphone HCl 1 mg., guaifenesin 100 mg., alcohol 5%/5 cc. Bot. pts.
Use: Harassing and nonproductive coughs.

DILAUDID-HP. (Knoll) Hydromorphone 10 mg./ml. Amp. 1 × 10s.
Use: Analgesic for narcotic tolerant patients.
DILAUDID HYDROCHLORIDE. (Knoll) Hydromorphone HCl. **Amp.:** (w/sod. citrate 0.2%, citric acid sol. 0.2%): 1mg., 2mg., or 4mg./ml. Box 10s. 2 mg., Box 25s. **Tab.:** 1 mg., 3 mg. Bot. 100s. 2 mg., 4 mg. Bot. 100s, 500s. Hospital Pack 100s. **Pow.:** Vial, 15 gr. Multiple dose vial 10 ml., 20 ml. 2 mg./ml. **Rectal Supp.:** (in cocoa butter base, w/colloidal silica 1%): 3 mg. Box 6s.
Use: Analgesic.
W/Guaifenesin.
See: Dilaudid Cough Syrup. (Knoll)
DILAX. (Mission) Docusate sodium 100 mg. or 250 mg./Cap. Bot. 100s.
Use: Stool softener.
• **DILEVALOL HYDROCHLORIDE.** USAN.
Use: Antihypertensive, anti-adrenergic.
DILIN. (Hauck) Dyphylline 250 mg./ml. Vials 10 ml.
Use: Smooth muscle relaxant.
DILITHIUM CARBONATE. Lithium Carbonate, U.S.P. XXI.
DILOCAINE. (Hauck) Lidocaine HCl 1% or 2%. Bot. 50 ml.
Use: Anesthetic.
DILOCOL. (Bell Pharmacal) Hydromorphone HCl 1/10 gr., sod. citrate 20 gr., antimony pot. tartrate 1/10 gr./fl. oz. Bot. 1 pt., 1 gal.
Use: Cough depressant.
DILOMINE. (Kay) Dicyclomine HCl 10 mg./ml. Vial 10 ml.
Use: Antispasmodic.
DILOR. (Savage) **Tab.:** Dyphylline 200 mg./Tab. Bot. 100s, 1000s. Unit dose 100s. **Elixir:** Dyphylline 160 mg./15 cc. Bot. Pt., gal.
Use: Vasodilator; bronchodilator.
DILOR 400. (Savage) Dyphylline 400 mg. Bot. 100s, 1000s. Unit dose 100s.
Use: Vasodilator, bronchodilator.
DILOREX. (Tunex) Dyphylline 250 mg./ml. Vial 10cc.
Use: Vasodilator, bronchodilator.
DILOR G LIQUID. (Savage) Dyphylline 300 mg., Guaifenesin 300 mg./15 ml. Bot. pts., gals.
DILOR G TABLETS. (Savage) Dyphylline 200 mg., guaifenesin 200 mg., 400 mg./Tab. Bot. 100s, 1000s. Unit dose 100s.
DILOXANIDE. B.A.N. 4-(N-Methyldichloroacetamido) phenol.
Use: Treatment of amebiasis.
See: Entamide
Furamide [2-furoate]
• **DILTIAZEM HYDROCHLORIDE.** USAN.
Use: Vasodilator.
DIMACID. (Otis Clapp) Mg carbonate, Ca carbonate/Tab. Sugar, lactose and salt free. Bot. 100s. Safety packs 500s.
Use: Antacid.
DIMACOL. (Robins) Pseudoephedrine HCl 30 mg., dextromethorphan HBr 15 mg., guaifenesin 100 mg./Cap. or 5 cc. Alcohol content of liquid 4.75%

Caps. Bot. 100s, 500s; Pre-Pack 12s, 24s. **Liq.** Bot. pt.
Use: Expectorant, decongestant, cough suppressant.

DIMAZOLE (I.N.N.). Diamthazole, B.A.N.

• **DIMEFADANE.** USAN. N, N-Dimethyl-3-phenyl-1-indanamine.
Use: Non-narcotic analgesic.

DIMEFLINE. B.A.N. 8-Dimethylaminomethyl-7-methoxy-3-methylflavone.
Use: Respiratory stimulant.
See: Remeflin hydrochloride. (Wallace)

• **DIMEFLINE HYDROCHLORIDE.** USAN.
Use: Stimulant.

• **DIMEFOLCON A.** USAN.
Use: Contact lens material.

DIMELOR. Acetohexamide, B.A.N.

DIMENATE. (Tunex) Dimenhydrinate 50 mg./ml. Vial 10cc.
Use: Motion sickness.

DIMENEST. (Fellows) Dimenhydrinate 50 mg./cc. Vials 10 cc.
Use: Antivertigo and antiemetic agent.

• **DIMENHYDRINATE,** U.S.P. XXI. Syr., Tab., Inj., U.S.P. XXI. Beta-dimethylaminoethyl benzohydryl ether-8-chlorotheophyllinate. 8-Chlorotheophylline 2-(Diphenylmethoxy)-N, N-dimethylethylamine compound (1:1). IH-Purine-2,6-dione,8-chloro-3,7-dihydro-1,3-dimethyl-, compound with 2-(diphenylmethoxy)-N,N-dimethylethanamine (1:1). Gravol.
Use: Anti-emetic, antihistamine.
See: Dimenate, Inj. (Tunex)
Dimenest, Inj. (Fellows-Testagar)
Dimentabs, Tab. (Bowman)
Dipendrate, Tab. (Kenyon)
Dramaject, Vial (Mayrand)
Dramamine, Prep. (Searle)
Dramocen, Inj. (Central)
Dymenate, Inj. (Keene)
Eldadryl, Preps. (Elder)
Eldodram, Tab. (Elder)
Hydrate, Vial (Hyrex)
Marmine, Inj., Tab. (Vortech)
Reidamine, Inj. (Reid-Provident)
Signate, Inj. (Sig)
Trav-Arex, Cap. (Quality Generics)
Traveltabs, Tab. (Geneva Drugs)

DIMENOXADOLE. B.A.N. 2-Dimethylaminoethyl 2-ethoxy-2, 2-diphenylacetate.
Use: Narcotic analgesic.

DIMENSYN. (Advanced Care) Acetaminophen 500 mg., pamabrom 25 mg., pyrilamine maleate 15 mg./Cap. Bot. 24s, 48s.
Use: Maximum strength menstrual discomfort relief.

DIMENTABS. (Bowman) Dimenhydrinate 50 mg./Tab. Bot. 100s, 1000s
Use: Antinauseant.

DIMEPHEPTANOL. B.A.N. 6-Dimethylamino-4, 4-diphenylheptan-3-ol.
Use: Narcotic analgesic.
See: Methadol

DIMEPREGNEN. B.A.N. 3β-Hydroxy-6α, 16α-dimethylpregn-4-en-20-one.
Use: Anti-estrogen.

DIMEPROPION. B.A.N. α-Dimethylaminopropiophenone. Metamfepramone (I.N.N.)
Use: Anorexigenic.

• **DIMERCAPROL,** U.S.P. XXI. Inj. U.S.P. XXI. 2, Dimercaptol-1-propanol.
Use: Antidote to gold, arsenic, mercury poisonin metal complexing agent.
See: BAL Amp. (Hynson, Wescott & Dunning)

2, 3-DIMERCAPTOPROPANOL.
See: Dimercaprol, U.S.P. XXI.

DIMESONE. B.A.N. 9α-Fluoro- 11β, 21-dihydroxy-1 17-dimethylpregna-1, 4-diene-3, 20-dione.
Use: Anti-inflammatory steroid.

DIMETANE. (Robins) Brompheniramine maleate. **Tabs.** (4 mg.) Bot. 100s, 500s. Pre-Pack 24s.**Ext tabs:** (8 mg., 12 mg.) Bot. 100s, 500s. **Elixir:** (2 mg./5 cc.) Bot. 4 oz., 1 pt., 1 gal. **Amps.:** pH adjusted with sod. hydroxide. (10 mg./cc.) 1 cc. Box 25s.
Use: Antihistamine.
W/Phenylephrine hydrochloride, phenylpropanolami hydrochloride.
See: Dimetapp Elix., Extentabs (Robins)

DIMETANE-DC COUGH SYRUP. (Robins) Brc pheniramine maleate 2 mg., phenylpropanolamin HCl 12.5 mg., codeine phosphate 10 mg./5 ml. w/alcohol 0.95%. Bot. Pt., Gal.
Use: Antihistamine, nasal decongestant, antitussi

DIMETANE DECONGESTANT ELIXIR. (Robins) Brompheniramine maleate 2 mg., phenylephrine HCl 5 mg./5 ml. w/2.3% alcohol. Bot. 4 oz.
Use: Relief of nasal congestion due to colds and allergies.

DIMETANE DECONGESTANT TABLETS. (Robins) Brompheniramine maleate 4 mg., phenylephrine HCl 10 mg./Tab. Ctn. 24s, 48s.
Use: Nasal decongestant, antihistaminic.

DIMETAPP ELIXIR. (Robins) Brompheniramine maleate 2 mg., phenylpropanolamine HCl 12.5 mg./5 cc. alcohol 2.3% Bot., 4 oz., 8 oz., pt., gal. Dis-Co Pack 5 ml. 10 $\times$ 10s.
Use: Antihistaminic, nasal decongestant.

DIMETAPP EXTENTABS. (Robins) Brompheniramin maleate 12 mg., phenylpropanolamine HCl 75 mg./Tab. Bot. 100s, 500s. Dis-Co Pack 100s. Blis packs 12s, 24s.
Use: Antihistaminic, nasal decongestant.

DIMETAPP TABLETS. (Robins) Brompheniramine maleate 4 mg., phenylpropanolamine HCl 12.5 mg./Tab. Blisterpak 24s.
Use: Antihistaminic, nasal decongestant.

• **DIMETHADIONE.** USAN. 5, 5-Dimethyl-2, 4-oxazolidine-dione. Eupractone (Travenol).
Use: Anticonvulsant.

DIMETHAZAN. 1, 3-Dimethyl-7-(2-dimethylamino-eth xanthine.

• **DIMETHICONE,** N.F. XVI. Dimethylsiloxane polymers. dimethyl polysiloxane.
Use: Prosthetic aid, component of barrier creams.
See: Covicone, Cream (Abbott)
Silicone, Oint. (Various Mfr.)
Silicote, Prep. (Arnar-Stone)

METHICONE 350. USAN.
se: Prosthetic aid for soft tissue.
ETHINDENE. B.A.N. 2- 1-[2-(2-Dimethylaminoethyl) den-3-yl]ethyl pyridine.
se: Antihistamine.
ee: Fenostil [hydrogen maleate]
ETHINDENE MALEATE. Dimethpyrindene. 2- 1-(2-dimethyl-amino-ethyl)inden-3-yl] ethyl-pyridine aleate.
se: Antihistamine.
ee: Forhistal Maleate, Tab., Syr. (Ciba)
ETHISOQUIN. B.A.N. 3-Butyl-1-(2-dimethyla-mino-hoxy)isoquinoline. Quinisocaine (I.N.N.)
se: Antipruritic.
ee: Quotane [hydrochloride]
ETHISOQUIN HYDROCHLORIDE. 3-Butyl-1-2-(di-ethyl-amino)-ethoxy isoquinoline HCl.
se: Local anesthetic.
ee: Quotane Hydrochloride, Oint. Lot. (Menley & James)
METHISTERONE. USAN.
se: Preogestin.
ETHOLIZINE PHOSPHATE. 1-(2-Methoxy-phenyl)-(3-methoxypropyl)piperazine phosphate.
nsiv.
ETHOTHIAZINE. B.A.N. 10-(2-Dimethylamino-opyl)-2-dimethysulfamoylphenothiazine.
se: Treatment of migraine.
ee: Fonazine
Banistyl [mesylate]
ETHOXANATE. B.A.N. 2-(2-Dimethylamino-ethoxy) thyl phenothiazine-10-carboxylate.
se: Cough suppressant.
ETHOXYPHENYL PENICILLIN SODIUM.
ee: Methicillin Sod. (Var. Mfr.)
2, 6-DIMETHOXY-4-PYRIMIDINYL)SULFANIL-MIDE.
ee: Sulfadimethoxine.
-DIMETHOXY-1-VERATRYLISOQUINOLINE HY-DROCHLORIDE.
ee: Papaverine Hydrochloride, U.S.P. XXI.
ETHPYRIDENE MALEATE. Dimethindene aleate, U.S.P. XXI.
ee: Dimethindene Maleate, U.S.P. XXI.
IMETHYLAMINO)-4, 4-DIPHENYL-3-HEPTA-ONE HYDROCHLORIDE. Methadone Hydrochlo-de, U.S.P. XXI.
IMETHYLAMINO)ETHYL p-(BUTYLAMINO) BEN-OATE.
ee: Tetracaine (Var. Mfr.)
IMETHYLAMINOETHYL (1-HYDROXY-CY-LOPENTYL)PHENYLACETATE HYDROCHLO-IDE. Cyclopentolate Hydrochloride, U.S.P. XI.
IMETHYLAMINO)ETHYL 1-HYDROXY-α-PHE-YLCYCLOPENTANE-ACETATE HYDROCHLO-IDE. Cyclopentolate Hydrochloride, U.S.P. XXI.
-(2-(2-(DIMETHYLAMINO)ETHYL)-INDEN-3-yl)ET-HYL)PYRIDINE MALEATE (1:1).
See: Dimethindene Maleate, U.S.P. XXI.
2-(DIMETHYLAMINO)ETHYL) (p-METHOXYBEN-ZYL)AMINO)PYRIDINE MALEATE (1:1).
See: Pyrilamine Maleate, U.S.P. XXI.

2-((2-(DIMETHYLAMINO)ETHYL)-2-THENYLAMINO)-PYRIDINE MONOHYDROCHLORIDE.
See: Methapyrilene Hydrochloride, U.S.P. XXI.
(+)-4-(DIMETHYLAMINO)-3-METHYL-1, 2-DI-PHENYL-2-BUTANOL PROPIONATE (ESTER) HYDROCHLORIDE. Propoxyphene Hydrochloride, U.S.P. XXI.
(-)-α-4-(DIMETHYLAMINO)-3-METHYL-1, 2-DI-PHENYL-2-BUTANOL PROPIONATE (ESTER) 2-NAPHTHALENE-SULFONATE (SALT).
See: Levopropoxyphene Napsylate (Var. Mfr.)
(−)-10-(3-(DIMETHYLAMINO)-2-METHYLPROPYL)-2-METHOXYPHENOTHIAZINE.
See: Methotrimeprazine, U.S.P. XXI.
10-3-(DIMETHYLAMINO)-2-METHYLPROPYL PHENOTHIAZINE TARTRATE (2:1). Trimeprazine Tartrate, U.S.P. XXI.
DIMETHYLAMINOPHENAZONE.
See: Aminopyrine (Various Mfr.)
4, 7-BIS(DIMETHYLAMINO)-1, 4, 4a, 5, 5a, 6, 11,-12a-OCTAHYDRO-3, 10, 12, 12a-TETRAHYDROXY-1, 11-DIOXO-2-NAPHTHACENE-CARBOXAMIDE MONOHYDROCHLORIDE. Minocycline Hydrochlo-ride, U.S.P. XXI.
[4-[BIS[p-(DIMETHYLAMINO)PHENYL]-METHYL-ENE]-2, 5-CYCLOHEXADIEN-1-YLIDENE]DI-METHYLAMMONIUM CHLORIDE. Gentian Violet, U.S.P. XXI.
5-[3-(DIMETHYLAMINO)PROPYL]-10, 11-DIHYDRO-5H-DIBENZ[b,f]AZEPINE MONOHYDRO-CHLORIDE. Imipramine Hydrochloride, U.S.P. XXI.
10-(3-(DIMETHYLAMINO)PROPYL)PHENO-THIAZINE. Promethazine HCl, U.S.P. XXI.
10-(3-(DIMETHYLAMINO)PROPYL)-2-(TRIFLUORO-METHYL)PHENOTHIAZINE MONOHYDRO-CHLORIDE.
See: Triflupromazine Hydrochloride (Var. Mfr.)
DIMETHYLAMINO PYRAZINE SULFATE.
See: Ampyzine Sulfate
DIMETHYLCARBAMATE of 3-Hydroxy-1-Methyl-pyridinium Bromide.
See: Mestinon, Tab. (Roche)
N, α-DIMETHYLCYCLOHEXANEETHYLAMINE.
See: Propylhexedrine, U.S.P. XXI.
N,-DIMETHYLCYCLOPENTANEETHYLAMINE HY-DROCHLORIDE.
See: Cyclopentamine Hydrochloride, U.S.P. XXI.
N, N-DIMETHYLDIBENZ [b, e] OXEPIN-$\Delta^{11(6m)}$,-y-PROPYLAMINE HYDROCHLORIDE. Curatin.
DIMETHYLHEXESTROL DIPROPIONATE.
Promethestrol Dipropionate.
See: Meprane Dipropionate, Tab. (Reed & Carnrick)
N11-(3, 4-DIMETHYL-5-ISOXAZOLYL)SULFANIL-AMIDE. Sulfisoxazole, U.S.P. XXI.
N-(3,4-DIMETHYL-5-ISOXAZOLYL)-N-SULFANIL-YLACETAMIDE, Sulfisoxazole, Acetyl, U.S.P. XXI.
N,N-DIMETHYL-2-((o-METHYL-α-PHENYLBENZYL)-OXY)ETHYCAMINE CITRATE (1:1).
See: Orphenadrine Citrate, U.S.P. XXI.
3, 3-DIMETHYL-7-OXO-6-(2-PHENOXYL-ACETAMI-DO-4-THIA 1-AZABICYCLO[3.2.0.] HEPTANE-2-CARBOXYLIC ACID. Penicillin V, U.S.P. XXI.

(±)-1, 3-DIMETHYL-4-PHENYL-4-PIPERIDINOL PROPIONATE HYDROCHLORIDE.
See: Alphaprodine Hydrochloride, U.S.P. XXI.

2, 3-DIMETHYL-1-PHENYL-3-PYRAZOLIN-5-ONE.
See: Antipyrine, U.S.P. XXI.

N, 2-DIMETHYL-2-PHENYLSUCCINIMIDE.
See: Methsuximide, U.S.P. XXI.

DIMETHYL POLYSILOXANE.
See: Dimethicone (Var. Mfr.)
W/Benzocaine, bismuth subcarbonate, carbamide, hexachlorophene, phenylephrine HCl, pyrilamine maleate, zinc oxide.
W/Hexachlorophene, zinc oxide, pyrilamine maleate, tetracaine HCl, methyl salicylate, zirconium oxide.

N[1]-(4, 6-DIMETHYL-2-PYRIMIDINYL)-SULFANILAMIDE. Sulfamethazine, U.S.P. XXI.

• **DIMETHYL SULFOXIDE,** U.S.P. XXI. Irrigation, U.S.P. XXI. Methyl sulfoxide. DMSO
Use: Topical anti-inflammatory agent.
See: Demasorb (Squibb)
Demeso (Merck Sharp & Dohme)
Domoso (Syntex)
Dromisol (Merck Sharp & Dohme)

DIMETHYLTHIAMBUTENE. B.A.N. 3-Dimethylamino-1, 1-di-(2-thienyl)but-1-ene
Use: Narcotic analgesic.

(+)-0,0′-DIMETHYLTUBOCURARINE DIIODIDE.
See: Dimethyl Tubocurarine Iodide.

DIMETHYLTUBOCURARINE. B.A.N. Dimethyl ether of (+)-tubocurarine.
Use: Neuromuscular blocking agent.
See: Diamethine [bromide]

DIMETHYL-TUBOCURARINE IODIDE.
Use: Skeletal muscle relaxant.
See: Metocurine Iodide, U.S.P. XXI.

DIMETHYLURETHIMINE.
See: Meturedepa (Armour)

1, 3-DIMETHYLXANTHINE.
See: Theophylline, U.S.P. XXI.

3, 7-DIMETHYLXANTHINE.
See: Theobromine, Prep. (Various Mfr.)

DIMETRIDAZOLE. B.A.N. 1, 2-Dimethyl-5-nitroimidazole. Emtryl.
Use: Antiprotozoan, veterinary medicine.

DIMINAZENE. B.A.N. pp′-Diamidinodiazoamino-benzene.
Use: Antiprotozoan; bactericide, veterinary medicine.

DIMINDOL. (Blue Line) Acetaminophen 325 mg./Tab. Bot. 100s, 1000s.

DIMINDOL ELIXIR. (Blue Line) Acetaminophen 120 mg., alcohol 9%/5 ml. Bot. 4 fl. oz., pt., gal.
Use: Analgesic.

DIMOTANE HYDROGEN MALEATE.
Brampheniramine, B.A.N.

• **DIMOXAMINE HYDROCHLORIDE.** USAN.
Use: Memory adjuvant.

DIMPYLATE. B.A.N. 00-Diethyl 0-(2-isopropyl-6-methyl-pyrimidin-4-yl) phosphorothioate.
Use: Insecticide, veterinary medicine.
See: Diazinon

DIMYCOR. (Standard Drug) Pentaerythritol tetranit 10 mg., phenobarbital 15 mg./Tab. Bot. 1000s.
Use: Management of coronary insufficiency.

DINACRIN. (Winthrop Products) Isonicotinic acid, hydrazide.
Use: Antitubercular agent.

DINATE. (Seatrace) Dimenhydrinate 50 mg./ml. Vi 10 cc.

DINDEVAN.
See: Phenindione (Var. Mfr.)

DINITOLMIDE. B.A.N. 3, 5-Dinitro-o-toluamide.
Use: Antiprotozoan, veterinary medicine.
See: Zoalene

DINOL. (Seatrace) Salicylamide 200 mg., acetaminophen 300 mg./Tab. Bot. 100s, 1000s.
Use: Analgesic, antipyretic.

• **DINOPROST.** USAN. 7-[3α, 5α-Dihydroxy-2β-[hydroxy-trans-oct-1-enyl]cyclopent-1-yl]cis-hept-5 enoic acid.
Use: Smooth muscle activator.
See Prostaglandin F-$_{2\alpha}$

• **DINOPROST TROMETHAMINE,** U.S.P.XXI. Inj., U.S.P. XXI.
Use: Oxytocic (prostaglandin)
See: Prostin F2 Alpha, Amp. (Upjohn)

• **DINOPROSTONE.** USAN. 7-[3α-Hydroxy-2β-[(3S) hydroxy-trans-oct-1-enyl]-5-oxocyclopent-1-yl]-cis hept-5-enoic acid.
Use: Smooth muscle activator.
See: Prostaglandin E-2

18, 19-DINORPREGN-4-EN-20-YN-3-ONE, 13-ETH 17-HYDROXY-, (17α)-(±)-. Norgestrel, U.S.P. XXI.

DI-N-PROPYL ISOCINCHOMERONATE W/N-N-di yl-m-toluamide, N-Octyl Bicycloheptene Dicarb mide, 2, 3, 4, 5-bis (delta-2-butylene) Tetrehydrofu ral other isomers, isopropanol.
See: Bansum, Bot. (Summers)

• **DINSED.** USAN. N,N′-Ethylenebis (3-nitrobenzene fonamide)
Use: Coccidiostat.

DIOCTIN. (Janssen) Difenoxin HCl.
Use: Antiperistalic.

DIOCTO. (Purepac) Docusate sodium 100 mg. or 2 mg./Cap. Bot. 100s.
Use: Stool softener.

DIOCTYL CALCIUM SULFOSUCCINATE. Docusa Calcium, U.S.P. XXI.

DIOCTYL POTASSIUM SULFOSUCCINATE.
W/Glycerin, pot. oleate and stearate.
See: Rectalad, Liq. (Wallace)

DIOCTYL SODIUM SULFOSUCCINATE. B.A.N. Docusate Sodium, U.S.P. XXI.
Use: Non-laxative fecal softener.

DIOCTYL-ZEM. (Zemmer) Docusate sodium 60 r ext. cascara sagrada 4 mg./Tab. Bot. 100s, 100
Use: Fecal softener and peristaltic stimulant.

DIODONE INJECTION.
See: Iodopyracet injection.

DIOEZE. (Century) Dioctyl sodium sulfosuccinate 2 mg./Cap. Bot. 100s, 1000s.
Use: Laxative.

)HIPPURIC ACID I-125. USAN.
ɜe: Radioactive agent.
)HIPPURIC ACID I-131. USAN.
ɩe: Radioactive agent.
HIST. (Approved) d-Methorphan 30 mg., thenyl-
'ramine HCl 80 mg., phenylephrine HCl 20 mg.,
ɩt. tartrate 1/24 gr./oz. Bot. 4 oz.
ɜe: Antihistamine.
.AMINE. Diethanolamine.
.AX. (Century) Docusate sodium 100 mg.,
ɩsanthranol 50 mg./Cap. Bot. 30s, 100s, 1000s.
ɜe: Stool softener and laxative.
.OSTENE.
ɜe: Methandriol
·MEDICONE. (Medicone) Docusate sodium 50
g./Tab. Vials 50s.
ɜe: Fecal softener.
NEX. (Interstate) Docusate sodium 100 mg. or
ɩ0 mg./Cap. Bot. 100s, 250s, 1000s.
ɜe: Laxative.
NIN. Ethylmorphine HCl.
ɜe: Orally; cough depressant, ocular
mphagogue.
NOSIL OILY. (Picker) Propyliodone 60% in
ɜanut oil. Inj.
se: Bronchographic contrast medium.
PHYLLIN.
ɜe: Aminophylline, Prep. (Various Mfr.)
PTERIN. Pteroyldiglutamic acid, PDGA, Pteroyl-
pha-glutamylglutamic acid.
se: Treatment of neoplastic diseases.
RAPIN. (Standex) Estrogenic conjugate 0.625
g., methyl testosterone 5 mg./Tab. Bot. 100s.
j. Estrone 2 mg., testosterone 25 mg./cc. Vial 10
:.
se: Hormone therapy to promote anabolism.
SATE. (Towne) Docusate sodium Caps. 100 mg.,
50 mg./Tab. Bot. 100s.
-SOFT. (Standex) Docusate sodium 100 mg., casan-
ɩranol 30 mg./Cap. Bot. 100s.
SMIN. Buchu resin obtained from lvs. of barosma
ɜrratifolia & allied rutaceae.
STATE D. (Upjohn) Vit. D 400 I.U., calcium 343
ɩg., phosphorus 265 mg./3 Tabs. Bot. 100s.
se: Calcium w/ Vit. D and mineral therapy.
SUCCIN. (CMC) Docusate sodium. Cap. 100 mg.,
50 mg., Bot. 100s. **Syr.** Bot. pt., gal.
se: Fecal softener.
-SUL. (Vortech) Docusate sodium 100 mg./Tab. or
ap. Bot. 1000s.
se: Orally, fecal softener.
SUX CAPSULES. (Jenkins) Docusate sodium 100
ɩg./Cap. Bot. 1000s.
se: Laxative.
SUX TABS. (Jenkins) Docusate sodium 60 mg.,
anthron 40 mg./Tab. Bot. 1000s.
THRON. (Vortech) Casanthranol 30 mg., docusate
odium 100 mg./Cap. Bot. 1000s.
se: Fecal softener, laxative.
THYL. Pyrimithate, B.A.N.
OTYROSINE I-125. USAN.
se: Radioactive agent.

DIOVAL. (Keene) Estradiol valerate, 10 mg./ml. Vial 10 ml.
DIOVAL XX. (Keene) Estradiol valerate, 20 mg./ml. Vial 10 ml.
DIOVAL 40. (Keene) Estradiol valerate, 40 mg./ml. Vial 10 ml.
DIOVOCYLIN. (Ciba)
See: Estradiol, Prep. (Various Mfr.)
• **DIOXADROL HYDROCHLORIDE.** USAN.
Use: Antidepressant.
DIOXAMATE. B.A.N. 4-Carbamoyloxymethyl-2-methyl-2-nonyl-1,3-dioxolan.
Use: Treatment of the parkinsonian syndrome.
DIOXAPHETYL BUTYRATE. B.A.N. Ethyl 4-morpholino-2,2-diphenylbutyrate.
Use: Narcotic analgesic.
DIOXATHION. B.A.N. A mixture consisting essentially of cis- and trans-SS'-1,4-dioxan-2,3-diyl bis (00-diethyl phosphorodithioate).
Use: Insecticide; acaricide, veterinary medicine.
See: Delnav.
DIOXINDOL. Diacetylhydroxyphenylisatin.
DIOXYANTHRANOL.
See: Anthralin, N.F. (Various Mfr.)
DIOXYANTHRAQUINONE. 1,8-Dihydroxy-anthraquinone.
See: Danthron, U.S.P. XXI.
• **DIOXYBENZONE,** U.S.P. XXI. Dioxybenzone and Oxybenzone Cream, U.S.P. XXI. Methanone, (2-hydroxy-4-methoxyphenyl)(2-hydroxyphenyl)1.
W/Oxybenzone, benzophene.
Use: Sunscreen agent.
See: Solbar, Lot. (Person & Covey)
DIOXYLINE. (Laboratoires Franca, Canada) Benzoxiquine.
DIOXYLINE PHOSPHATE. 6,7-Dimethoxy-1-(4'-ethoxy-3'-methoxybenzyl))-3-methylisoquinoline.
Use: Smooth muscle relaxant.
See: Paveril Phosphate, Tab. (Lilly)
DI-PARALENE. Chlorcyclizine, B.A.N.
DIPARCOL HYDROCHLORIDE. Diethazine.
DIPEGYL.
See: Nicotinamide, Prep. (Various Mfr.)
DIPENDRATE. (Kenyon) Dimenhydrinate 50 mg./Tab. Bot. 100s, 1000s.
DIPENICILLIN G.
See: Benzethacil
DIPENINE BROMIDE. B.A.N. 2-Dicyclopentyl-acetoxyethyltriethylammonium bromide.
Use: Antispasmodic.
See: Diponium Bromide (I.N.N.)
DIPERODON. B.A.N. 3-Piperidinopropane-1,2-diol di(phenylcarbamate).
Use. Local anesthetic.
DIPERODON, U.S.P. XXI. Oint., U.S.P. XXI. 3-Piperidino-1,2-propanediol dicarbanilate (ester) monohydrate.
Use: Local anesthetic.
DIPERODON HYDROCHLORIDE.
Use: Anesthetic.
See: Diothane Ointment (Merrell Dow)
Proctodon, Cream (Rowell)

W/Bacitracin, neomycin sulfate, polymyxin.
See: Epimycin A, Oint. (Delta)
W/Benzalkonium chloride, ichthammol, thymol, camphor, juniper tar.
See: Boro Oint. (Scrip)
W/Cetylpyridinium chloride.
See: Cetyben, Troches (Sutliff & Case)
W/Furacin (nitrofurazone).
See: Furacin E Urethral Inserts (Eaton)
Furacin H.C. Urethral Inserts (Eaton)
W/Furacin (nitorfurazone) & Microfur (nituroxime).
See: Furacin Otic, Drops. (Eaton)
W/Hydrocortisone, polymyxin B sulfate, neomycin.
See: My Cort Otic #1, Ear Drops (Scrip)
W/Hydroxyquinoline Benzoate.
See: Diothane, Oint. (Merrell Dow)
W/Methapyrilene HCl, pyrilamine maleate, allantoin, benzocaine, menthol.
See: Antihistamine Cream (Towne)
W/Neomycin sulfate, polymyxin B sulfate.
See: Aural Acute (Saron)
W/Thimerosal, isopropyl alcohol.
See: Earobex, Ear Drops (Mallard)

DIPHEMANIL METHYLSULFATE. B.A.N. 4-Benzhydrylidene-1, 1-dimethylpiperidinium methyl-sulfate.
Use: Parasympatholytic.
See: Diphenatil

• **DIPHEMANIL METHYLSULFATE,** U.S.P. XXI. Tab., U.S.P. XXI. 4-(Diphenylmethylene)-1,1-dimethylpiperidinium methylsulfate. Diphenmethanil methylsulfate.
Use: Anticholinergic.
See: Prantal, Tab. (Schering)

DI-PHEN. (Vortech) Diphenylhydantoin sod. 1.5 gr./Cap. Bot. 1000s.
Use: Anticonvulsant in epilepsy.

DIPHENACEN-10. (Central) Diphenhydramine HCl 10 mg./ml. w/chlorobutanol 0.5%. Vial 30 ml.
Use: Antihistaminic.

DIPHENACEN-50. (Central) Diphenhydramine HCl 50 mg./ml. w/chlorobutanol 0.5%. Vial 10 mg.
Use: Antihistaminic.

DIPHENADIONE. B.A.N. 2-Diphenylacetylinedane-1,3-dione.
Use: Anticoagulant.
See: Didandin
Oragulant

DIPHENADIONE. 2-(Diphenylacetyl)-1-3, indandione.
Use: Anticoagulant.
See: Dipaxin, Tab. (Upjohn)

DIPHENADRIL. (Vitarine) Diphenhydramine HCl 75 mg., alcohol 5%/oz. Bot. 4 oz., gal.
Use: Expectorant.

DIPHENATIL.
See: Diphemanil methylsulfate

DIPHEN COUGH SYRUP. (Bay) Diphenhydramine HCl 12.5 mg./5 ml. w/alcohol 5%. Bot. 4 oz., pt., gal.
Use: Antihistaminic.

DIPHEN ELIXIR. (Bay) Diphenhydramine HCl 12.5 mg./5 ml. w/alcohol 14%. Bot. 4 oz., pt., gal.
Use: Antihistaminic.

DIPHEN-EX SYRUP. (Quality Generics) Diphenhydramine HCl 12.5 mg., alcohol 5%/5 ml. Bot. pt., ga
Use: Cough relief.

DIPHENHYDRAMINE. B.A.N. 2-Benzhydryloxyethyl dimethylamine.
Use: Antihistamine.
See: Benadryl
Histex hydrochloride

• **DIPHENHYDRAMINE CITRATE,** U.S.P. XXI.
Use: Antihistaminic.

DIPHENHYDRAMINE COMPOUND EXPECTORAN (Kay) Diphenhydramine HCl 80 mg., ammonium chloride 12 gr., sod. citrate 5 gr., menthol 1/10 gr., alcohol 5%/fl. oz. Bot. 4 oz., pt., gal.
Use: Antitussive.

DIPHENHYDRAMINE EXPECTORANT. (CMC) Diphenhydramine HCl 80 mg., ammonium chlorid 12 gr./oz. w/menthol alcohol 5%, sod. citrate. B pt., gal.

• **DIPHENHYDRAMINE HYDROCHLORIDE.** U.S.P. XXI. Cap., Elix., Inj., U.S.P. XXI. Ethanamine, 2-phenylmethoxy)-N,N-dimethyl-,HCl. 2-Diphenylmethoxy)-N,N-dimethylethylamine HCl.
Use: Antihistaminic.
See: Baramine, Prod. (Barry Martin)
Baramine Expectorant (Barry Martin)
Bax, Cap., Elix., Expect., (McKesson)
Benachior, Syr. (Jenkins)
Benadryl Hydrochloride, Prep. (Parke-Davis)
Benahist, Preps. (Keene)
Bentrac, Cap. (Kenyon)
Benylin Cough Syrup (Warner-Lambert)
Diphen-Ex, Syr. (Quality Generics)
Fenylhist, Cap. (Mallard)
Histine Prods. (Freeport)
Hyrexin, Inj. (Hyrex)
Nordryl, Prep. (North. Amer. Pharm.)
Rodryl, Inj. (Rocky Mtn.)
Rodryl-50, Inj. (Rocky Mtn.)
Rohydra, Elix. (Robinson)
SK-Diphenhydramine, Tabs., Cap. Elix. (Sm Kline)
Span-Lanin, Cap. (Scrip)
T-Dryl 10, Inj. (Tunex)
T-Dryl 50, Inj. (Tunex)
Tusstat, Expect. (Century)
W/Ammonium chloride, menthol.
See: Bentrac Expectorant, Liq. (Kenyon)
Eldadryl Expectorant, Liq. (Elder)
Fenylex, Exp. (Mallard)
Tusstat Expectorant (Century)
W/Antihistamines.
See: Symptrol, Syr., Cap., Inj. (Saron)
W/Benzethonium Cl.
See: Bendylate, Inj. (Reid-Provident)
W/Chlorobutanol.
See: Ardeben, Inj. (Burgin-Arden)
W/Pheniramine maleate pyrilamine maleate, phenylephrine HCl, phenylpropanolamine HCl.
See: Symptrol, Syr. (Saron)

Phenylephrine HCl, phenylpropanolamine HCl, potassium guaiacolsulfonate, menthol, codeine phosphate.
See: Para-Hist Antitussive, Syr., Cap. (Pharmics)
Zinc oxide.
See: Ziradryl, Lot. (Parke-Davis)
PHENIDOL. B.A.N. 1,1-Diphenyl-4-piperidino-butan-1-ol
Use: Anti-emetic.
IPHENIDOL. USAN. α,α-Diphenyl-1-piperidinebutanol.
See: Vontrol, Prep. (SmithKline)
IPHENIDOL HCl. USAN. αα-Diphenyl-1-piperidinebutanol HCl.
Use: Anti-emetic.
IPHENIDOL PAMOATE. USAN. α,α-Diphenyl-1-piperidinebutanol compound with 4,4′-methylenebis 3-hydroxy-2-naphthoic acid](2:1).
Use: Anti-emetic.
PHENMETHANIL METHYLSULFATE. 4-Diphenylmethylene-1,1-dimethylpiperidinium methylsulfate.
See: Diphemanil Methylsulfate (Var. Mfr.)
PHENOXYLATE. B.A.N. Ethyl 1-(3-cyano-3,3-diphenylpropyl)-4-phenylpiperidine-4-carboxylate.
Use: Antidiarrheal.
IPHENOXYLATE HCl, U.S.P. XXI. 4-Piperidinecarboxylic acid, 1-(3-cyano-3,3-diphenylpropyl-4-phenyl-, ethyl ester, HCl, 2,2-Diphenyl-4-(4-carbethoxy-4-phenyl-1-pyeridino)butyronitrite ethyl ester HCl. Ethyl 1-(3-Cyano-3,3 diphenyl-propyl)-4-phenylisonipecoate Hydrochloride.
Use: Antiperistaltic to treat diarrhea.
Atropine.
See: Diaction, Tab. (Boots Pharm.)
Lomotil, Tab., Liq. (Searle)
SK-Diphenoxylate, Tab. (SmithKline)
IPHENOXYLATE HYDROCHLORIDE AND ATROPINE SULFATE, U.S.P. XXI. Oral Sol., Tabs., U.S.P. XXI.
Use: Antiperistaltic.
PHENYLAN SODIUM. (Lannett) Diphenyl-hydantoin sodium 0.5 gr. & 1.5 gr./Cap. Bot. 500s, 1000s.
Use: Epilepsy.
-DIPHENYL-4-(4-CARBETHOXY-4-PHENYL-1-PYERIDINO)-BUTYRONITRITE ESTHYL ESTER HYDROCHLORIDE. Diphenoxylate Hydrochloride, U.S.P. XXI.
PHENYLHYDROXYCARBINOL. Benzhydrol HCl.
-DIPHENYLHYDANTOIN. Phenytoin, U.S.P. XXI.
PHENYLHYDANTOIN. Phenytoin, U.S.P. XXI.
Use: Anticonvulsant.
-DIPHENYLHYDANTOIN SODIUM. Phenytoin, Sodium, U.S.P. XXI.
PHENYLHYDANTOIN SODIUM. Phenytoin Sodium, U.S.P. XXI.
Use: Anticonvulsant.
PHENYLISATIN.
See: Oxyphenisatin (Var. Mfr.)
DIPHENYLMETHOXY)-N,N-DIMETHYLETHYLAMINE HYDROCHLORIDE. Diphenhydramine Hydrochloride, U.S.P. XXI.

3-DIPHENYLMETHOXYTROPANE METHANESULFONATE. Benztropine Mesylate, U.S.P. XXI.
1-(DIPHENYLMETHYL)-4-METHYLPIPERAZINE MONOHYDROCHLORIDE. Cyclizine Hydrochloride, U.S.P. XXI.
1,2-DIPHENYL-4-2-(PHENYLSULFINYL)-ETHYL-3,5-PYRAZOLIDINEDIONE. Sulfinpyrazone, U.S.P. XXI.
alpha, alpha-DIPHENYL-1-PIPERIDINEBUTANOL.
See: Vontrol, Prods.
DIPHENYLPYRALINE. B.A.N. 4-Benzhydryloxy-1-methylpiperidine.
Use: Antihistamine.
See: Histryl
Lergoban (hydrochloride)
• **DIPHENYLPYRALINE HCl,** U.S.P. XXI. Tab., U.S.P. XXI. 4-Diphenyl-methoxy-1-methypiperidine HCl.
See: Diafen, Tab. (Riker)
Hispril, Cap. (SmithKline)
W/Chlorphedianol HCl, phenylephrine HCl, guaifenesin, alcohol.
See: Acutuss Expectorant (Philips Roxane)
DIPHOSPHONIC ACID.
See: Etidronic acid
DIPHOSPHOPYRIDINE (DPN). Treating alcoholism. Under study.
DIPHOSPHOTHIAMIN. Cocarboxylase.
See: Coenzyme-B, Cap. & Inj. (Inwood)
DIPHOXAZIDE. N[1]-(b-hydroxy-b,b-diphenylpropionyl)-N[2]-acetylhdrazine. Inductin.
• **DIPHTHERIA ANTITOXIN,** U.S.P. XXI. (Squibb-Connaught) 20,000 units/Vial.
Use: I.M., S.C.; protection & treatment of diphtheria.
See: Diphtheria Toxoid, U.S.P. XXI.
• **DIPHTHERIA & TETANUS TOXOIDS,** U.S.P. XXI.
• **DIPHTHERIA & TETANUS TOXOIDS ABSORBED,** U.S.P. XXI. (Dow; Lilly, Squibb-Connaught) Vial 5 ml.
Use: Active immunizing agent.
DIPHTHERIA & TETANUS TOXOIDS ADSORBED, ALUMINUM PHOSPHATE ADSORBED. (Wyeth) Vial 5 cc. Tubex 0.5 cc. Pkg. 10s. Available in pediatric and adult strengths.
DIPHTHERIA AND TETANUS TOXOIDS, COMBINED PUROGENATED. (Lederle) Vial 5 ml. Lederject disposable syringe 10 × 0.5 ml.
DIPHTHERIA & TETANUS TOXOIDS, ALUMINUM PHOSPHATE ADSORBED, PUROGENATED. (Lederle) Adult, pediatric. Vial 5 ml.
• **DIPHTHERIA & TETANUS TOXOIDS & PERTUSSIS VACCINE,** U.S.P. XXI.
Use: Prevention against diphtheria, tetanus and pertussis.
See: Tri-immunol, Vial (Lederle)
Tri-Solgen Vial, Hyporet (Lilly)
DIPHTHERIA & TETANUS TOXOIDS & PERTUSSIS VACCINE COMBINED, ALUMINUM HYDROXIDE ADSORBED.
See: Triogen, Vial (Parke-Davis)
DIPHTHERIA & TETANUS TOXOIDS & PERTUSSIS VACCINE COMBINED, ALUMINUM PHOSPHATE-ADSORBED.
See: Tri-Immunol, Vial (Lederle)

DIPHTHERIA & TETANUS TOXOIDS & PERTUSSIS VACCINE COMBINED, ALUM PRECIPITATED.
See: Triple Antigen, Vial (Wyeth)

DIPHTHERIA TOXIN, DIAGNOSTIC. Schick Test.

DIPHTHERIA TOXIN, INACTIVATED DIAGNOSTIC.
Schick test control.

• **DIPHTHERIA TOXIN FOR SCHICK TEST,** U.S.P. XXI.
Use: Diagnostic aid (dermal reactivity indicator).
See: Diphtheria Toxin, Diagnostic

• **DIPHTHERIA TOXOID,** U.S.P. XXI.
Use: Active immunizing agent.

• **DIPHTHERIA TOXOID ADSORBED,** U.S.P. XXI. Alum. Precipitated (Antoxin-Ramon, Diphtheria Anatoxin).
Use: Active immunizing agent.

DIPHTHERIA TOXOID & PERTUSSIS VACCINE. Lilly —Vial 10 tests.

DIPHYLLINE.
See: Diazma, Vial (Pharmex)

DIPIPANONE. B.A.N.4,4-Diphenyl-6-piperidino-heptan-3-one.
Use: Narcotic analgesic.
See: Pipadone (hydrochloride)

• **DIPIVEFRIN.** USAN.
Use: Adrenergic.

• **DIPIVEFRIN HYDROCHLORIDE,** U.S.P. XXI. Ophth. Sol., U.S.P. XXI.(+)-3,4-dihydroxy-a- (methylamino) methyl benzyl alcohol 3,4-dipivalate HCl.
Use: Treatment of chronic open-angle glaucoma.
See: Propine, Sol. (Allergan))

DIPONIUM BROMIDE (I.N.N.). Dipenine Bromide, B.A.N.

DIPRENORPHINE. B.A.N. N-Cyclopropylmethyl-7,8-dihydro-7 α-(1-hydroxy-1-methylethyl)-0^6-methyl-6,14 endoethanonormorphine.
Use: Narcotic antagonist.

DIPRIDAMOLE. (Foy) Dipyridamole 25 mg./Tab. Bot. 1000s.
Use: Coronary vasodilator.

DIPROLENE OINTMENT 0.05%. (Schering) Betamethasone dipropionate 0.64 mg., in ointment base. Tubes 15 Gm., 45 Gm.
Use: Topical anti-inflammatory, anti-pruritic agent.

DIPROPHYLLINE. B.A.N. 7-(2,3-Dihydroxypropyl)-theophylline.
Use: Bronchodilator.
See: Isophylline
Neutraphylline
Silbephylline

DIPROSONE AEROSOL 0.1%. (Schering) Betamethasone dipropionate 6.4 mg. (equiv. to 5 mg. bethamethasone) in vehicle of mineral oil, caprylic-capric triglyceride w/isopropyl alcohol 10%, inert hydrocarbon propellants. (propane & isobutane). Pkg. 85 Gm.
Use: Topical anti-inflammatory

DIPROSONE CREAM 0.05%. (Schering) Betamethasone dipropionate 0.64 mg. (equiv. to 0.5 mg. betamethasone) w/mineral oil, white petrolatum, polyethylene glycol 1000 monocetyl ether, cetostearyl alcohol, phosphoric acid and monobasic sod. phosphate with 4-chloro-m-cres preservative. Tube 15 Gm., 45 Gm.
Use: Anti-inflammatory dermatological.

DIPROSONE LOTION 0.05%. (Schering) Betamethasone dipropionate 0.64 mg. (equiv. t mg. betamethasone) W/isopropyl alcohol (46.8 & purified water. Bot. 20 ml., 60 ml.
Use: Topical anti-inflammatory.

DIPROSONE OINTMENT 0.05%. (Schering) Betamethasone dipropionate 0.64 mg. (eqiv. to mg. betamethasone) in white petrolatum & min oil base. Tubes 15 Gm., 45 Gm.
Use: Topical anti-inflammatory agent.

DIPTEREX. Metriphonate, B.A.N.

• **DIPYRIDAMOLE,** U.S.P. XXI. Tab., U.S.P. XXI. 2 [di-(2-hydroxy-ethyl)-amino]-4,8-dipiperidinopyrin [5,4-d]-pyrimidine.
Use: Coronary vasodilator.
See: Persantin

• **DIPYRIDAMOLE.** USAN. 2,2′,2″-2‴,-[4,8-Dipiperidinopyrimido[5,4-d]pyrimidine-2,6-diyl)-di o]tetraethanol.
Use: Coronary dilator.
See: Persantine, Tabs. (Boehringer-Ingelheim)

• **DIPYRITHIONE.** USAN.
Use: Antibacterial, antifungal.

• **DIPYRONE.** USAN, FDA. Sodium N-(2,3-dimeth 1-phenyl-5-oxopyrazolin-4-yl)-N-methylamino-me nesulfonate. Sodium noramidopyrine methanesu fonate. Sodium phenyldimethylpyrazolon-methylamino-methane sulfonate, sodium (anti-pyrin thylamino)-methane sulfonate hydrate; methyl brin, methampyrone, 4-Sod. methanesulfonate methylamine-antipyrine.
Use: Analgesic, antipyretic.

DIRIDONE. (Premo) Phenylazo-diamino-pyridine 100 mg./Tab. Bot. 100s, 1000s.
Use: Urinary anesthetic and antiseptic.

DIROX TABLETS. (Winthrop Products) Paracetam
Use: Analgesic, antipyretic,

DISALCID. (Riker) Salsalate. **Tab.:** 500 mg., 750 mg./Tab. Bot. 100s, 500s.**Cap.:** 500 mg./Cap. E 100s.
Use: Anti-inflammatory, analgesic in arthritis.

DISAMIDE. Disulfamide, B.A.N.

DISANTHROL CAPSULES. (Lannett) Docusate sodium 100 mg., casanthranol 30 mg./Cap. Bot 100s, 1000s.
Use: Laxative.

DISCASE. (Omnis surgical) Chymopapain 5.0 units ml. Vials 5 ml.
Use Intradiscal injection for herniated lumbar intervertebral discs.

DISIPAL. (Riker) N,N-dimethyl-2-(0-methyl-α-phe benzyloxy) ethylamine. Orphenadrine HCl. Tab. mg.) Bot. 100s.
Use: Parkinsonism.

DISMISS DOUCHE. (Schering) Sodium chloride, sodium citrate, citric acid, cetaryl octoate, ceteareth-27 & fragrance. Powder for dilution. Pkg 2s, 3s.
Use: Vaginal cleanser.

SOBUTAMIDE. USAN.
se: Cardiac depressant.
ODIUM CARBONATE. Sodium Carbonate, N.F. VI.
ODIUM CHROMATE. Sodium Chromate Cr 51 ijection, U.S.P. XXI.
ODIUM 3,3′-DIOXO[Δ²,²′-BINDOLINE]-5,5′-DI-ULFONATE. Indigotindisulfonate Sodium, U.S.P. XI.
ODIUM EDATHAMIL.
ee: Edathamil Disodium (Var. Mfr.)
ODIUM EDETATE. B.A.N. Disodium dihydrogen :hylenediamine-NNN′N′-tetra-acetate.
se: Chelating agent.
ODIUM EDETATE. Disodium :hylenediaminetetraacetate.
ee: Edetate Disodium, U.S.P. XXI.
ODIUM (ETHYLENEDINITRILO)TETRA-ACETO ALCIATE(2-)HYDRATE. Edetate Calcium
ODIUM (ETHYLENEDINITRILO)TETRA-ACETO IHYDRATE. Edetate Disodium, U.S.P. XXI.
ODIUM PHOSPHATE.
ee: Sodium Phosphate, U.S.P. XXI.
ODIUM PHOSPHATE HEPTAHYDRATE. Sodium hosphate, U.S.P. XXI.
ODIUM SALT OF N-(3-CARBOXY-METHYL-THIO-ERCURI-2-METHOXY-PROPYL) CAM-HORAMIC ACID. Mercaptomerin Sodium, U.S.P. XI.
ODIUM THIOSULFATE PENTAHYDRATE.
odium Thiosulfate, U.S.P. XXI.
ODIUM VERSENATE.
ee: Edathamil Disodium (Var. Mfr.)
SOFENIN. USAN.
se: Diagnostic aid.
OLAN. (Lannett) Docusate sodium 100 mg., henolphthalein 65 mg./Cap. Bot. 100s, 500s,)00s.
se: Constipation therapy.
OLAN FORTE CAPSULES. (Lannett) asanthranol 30 mg., sod. carboxymethylcellulose)0 mg., Docusate sodium 100 mg./Cap. Bot.)0s, 500s, 1000s.
se: Laxative.
ONATE. (Lannett) Docusate sodium 60 mg., 100 g., 240 mg./Cap. **Caps.** Bot. 100s, 500s, 1000s. **ab.** 100 mg., Bot. 1000s **Liq.** 10 mg./ml. Bot. pt. **yr.** 20 mg./5 ml. Bot. pt., gal.
se: Fecal softener.
OPHROL CHRONOTABS. (Schering) exbrompheniramine maleate 6 mg., pseudo-ohedrine sulf. 120 mg./S.A. Tab. Bot. 100s.
se: Antihistamine-decongestant.
SOPYRAMIDE. USAN. 4-Di-isopropylamino-2-phe-yl-2-(2-pyridyl)butyramide.
se: Anti-arrhythmic.
ee: Rythmodan
SOPYRAMIDE PHOSPHATE, U.S.P. XXI. Caps., .S.P. XXI.
OSUL. (Drug Industries) Docusate sodium 50 g./Tab. Bot. 100s, 500s.
se: Stool softener.

DI-SOSUL FORTE. (Drug Industries) Docusate sodium 100 mg., casanthranol 30 mg./Tab. Bot. 100s, 500s.
Use: Stool softener and laxative.
DISOTATE. (Forest) Disodium edetate 150 mg./cc. Vial 20 cc.
DI-SPAZ. (Vortech) Dicyclomine HCl **Cap.** 10 mg./Cap. Bot. 100s, 1000s; **Inj.:** w/sod. chloride 0.9%, chlorobutanol 0.5%/cc. Vial 10 cc.
Use: Antispasmodic.
DISTAQUAINE.
See: Penicillin V.
DISTIGMINE BROMIDE. B.A.N. NN′-Hexamethyl-enedi-[1-methyl-3-(methylcarbamoyloxy)-pyridinium bromide].
Use: Anticholinesterase.
See: Ubretid
DISTIGMINE BROMIDE. Hexamarium bromide.
DISULANS-PLUS. (Noyes) Docusate sodium 100 mg., casanthrol 30 mg./Cap. Bot. 100s, 1000s.
Use: Stool softener with laxative.
• **DISULFIRAM,** U.S.P. XXI. Tab., U.S.P. XXI. Bis-(die-thylthiocarbamoyl)disulfide. Tetraethylthiuram Disulfide.
Use: Treatment of alcoholism.
See: Antabuse, Tab. (Ayerst)
DISULFONAMIDE.
See: Dia-Mer-Sulfonamides (Var. Mfr.)
DISULFAMIDE. B.A.N. 5-Chlorotoluene-2,4-disulfona-mide.
Use: Diuretic.
See: Disamide
DITAN. (Mallard) Phenytoin sodium 100 mg./Cap. Bot. 1000s.
Use: Anticonvulsant.
DITHIAZANINE. B.A.N. 3-Ethyl-2-[5-(3-ethyl-benzo-thiazolin-2-ylidene)penta-1,3-dienyl]benzothiazolium.
Use: Anthelmintic.
See: Delvex
Telmid (iodide)
DITHRANOL.
See: Anthralin, U.S.P. XXI. (Var. Mfr.)
D.I.T.I. CREME. (Dunhall) Iodoquinol 100 mg., sulfanilamide 500 mg., diethylstilbestrol 0.1 mg./Gm. Jar. 4 oz.
Use: Intra-vaginal infections.
D.I.T.I.-2 CREME. (Dunhall) Sulfanilamide 15.0%, aminacrine HCl 0.2%, allantoin 2.0%. Tube 5 oz.
Use: Intra-vaginal cream.
DITOPHAL. B.A.N. SS′-Diethyl dithioisophthalate.
See: Etisul
Use: Antileprotic.
DITROPAN. (Marion) Oxybutynin chloride 5 mg./Tab. Bot. 100s, 1000s. Unit dose identification paks of 100s.
Use: Relief of symptoms in voiding with neurogenic bladder.
DITROPAN SYRUP. (Marion) Oxybutynin Cl. 5 mg./5 ml. Bot. 16 oz.
Use: Relief of symptoms in voiding with neurogenic bladder.

DIUCARDIN. (Ayerst) Hydroflumethiazide 50 mg./Tab. Bot. 100s.
Use: Diuretic, antihypertensive.

DIULO. (Searle) Metolazone. 2.5 mg./Tab. Bot. 100s. 5 mg./Tab. Bot. 100s, 500s. 10 mg./Tab. Bot. 100s.
Use: Diuretic, antihypertensive.

DIUPRES. (Merck Sharp & Dohme) Chlorothiazide 250 mg. or 500 mg., reserpine 0.125 mg./Tab. Bot. 100s, 1000s.
Use: Antihypertensive.

DIURETANE #1. (Wolins) Uva ursi pow. ext. 32.4 mg., buchu leaves pow. ext. 32.4 mg., corn silk pow. ext. 32.4 mg., juniper pow. ext. 16.2 mg., caffeine 16.2 mg./Tab. Bot. 100s, 1000s.

DIURETANE #2. (Wolins) Buchu pow. ext. 65 mg., couch grass 65 mg., corn silk pow. ext. 32.5 mg., hydrangea pow. ext. 32.5 mg./Tab. Bot. 100s, 1000s.

■ **DIURETICS.**
See: Aldactazide, Tab. (Searle)
Aldactone, Tab. (Searle)
Aminophylline (Var. Mfr.)
Aquazide, Tab. (Western Research)
Benzthiazide (Var. Mfr.)
Carbamide
Carbonic Anhydrase Inhibitors
Diamox (Lederle)
Diamox, Sequels (Lederle)
Dicurin Procaine, Inj. (Lilly)
Diuril, Tab., Oral Susp. (Merck Sharp & Dohme)
Dyazide, Cap. (SmithKline)
Dyrenium, Caps. (SmithKline)
Edecrin, Tab. (Merck Sharp & Dohme)
Esidrix, Tab. (Ciba)
Exna, Tab. (Robins)
Fleet Theophylline Rectal Unit, Sol. (Fleet)
Flumethiazide
Glycerin, Liq. (Var. Mfr.)
Hydrochlorothiazide, Tab. (Var. Mfr.)
Hydroflumethiazide, Tab. (Bristol)
Hydromox, Tab. (Lederle)
Hygroton, Tab. (USV)
Lasix, Tab., Inj. (Hoechst)
Mannitol (Var. Mfr.)
Mercurial diuretics
Mersalyl and Theophylline (Var. Mfr.)
Metahydrin, Tab. (Merrell Dow)
Methazolamide (Var. Mfr.)
Methyclothiazide, Tab. (Var. Mfr.)
Naqua, Tab. (Schering)
Naquival, Tab. (Schering)
Naturetin, Tab. (Squibb)
Neothylline, Amp., Elix., Tab. (Lemmon)
Proaqua, Tab. (Reid-Provident)
Renese, Tab. (Pfizer)
Sodium Diuril, I.V. Inj., Vial (Merck Sharp & Dohme)
Sodium Edecrin, I.V. Inj., Vial (Merck Sharp & Dohme)
Theocalcin, Pow., Tab. (Knoll)
Trichlormethiazide, Tab. (Var. Mfr.)
Triticoll, Tab. (Western Research)
Urea (Var. Mfr.)
Zaroxolyn, Tab. (Pennwalt)

DIURETIC TABLETS. (Faraday) Buchu leaves 15 mg., uva ursi leaves 150 mg., juniper berries 12 mg., bone meal, parsley, asparagus/Tab. Bot. 100s.

DIURETTE INJECTION. (Ortega) Mersalyl, USP, 1 mg.; theophylline USP, 50 mg./cc. Vial 10 cc.
Use: Diuresis, especially in cardiac edema.

DIURETTS. (Faraday) Tab. Bot. 84s.
Use: Diuretic.

DIURIGEN TABLETS. (Goldline) Chlorothiazide 25 mg., or 500 mg./Tab Bot. 100s, 1000s.
Use: Diuretic.

DIURIGEN WITH RESERPINE. Chlorothiazide w/reserpine. 250 mg. or 500 mg./Tab. Bot 100s 1000s.
Use: Antihypertensive.

DIURIL. (Merck Sharp & Dohme) Chlorothiazide. U.S.P. **Tabs.:** 250 mg. Bot. 100s, 1000s; 500 mg Bot. 100s, 1000s, 5000s. Unit-dose 100s. **Oral Su** 250 Gm./5ml. w/methylparaben 0.12%, propylparaben 0.02%, benzoic acid 0.1%, alcoh 0.5%. Bot. 237 ml. **I.V. Inj.:** 0.5 Gm./Vial w/0.25 Gm. mannitol, sodium hydroxide to adjust pH, thimerosal 0.4 mg/Vial.
Use: Diuretic, antihypertensive.
W/Methyldopa.
See Aldoelor, Tab. (Merck Sharp & Dohme)
W/Reserpine.
See: Diupres, Tab. (Merck Sharp & Dohme)

DIURIL. (MSD AGVET) Chlorothiazide 2 Gm. bolus 0.25 Gm/Tab.
Use: Diuretic, veterinary medicine.

DIURIL SODIUM INTRAVENOUS. (Merck Sharp & Dohme) Chlorothiazide sodium equiv. to 0.5 Gm. chlorothiazide w/mannitol 0.25 Gm., sod. hydroxide, thimerosal 0.4 mg./vial.
Use: Diuretic, antihypertensive.

DIURSAL. (Harvey) Mersalyl 100 mg., theophylline mg./cc. Amp. 2 cc., Box 25s, 100s.
Use: Diuretic.

DIU-SCRIP. (Scrip) Hydrochlorothiazide 25 mg., mg./Tab. Bot. 1000s.

DIU-TABS. (Wisconsin) Bot. 35s, 100s.
Use: Elimination of excess water.

DIUTENSEN. (Wallace) Cryptenamine (as the tann salts) 2 mg., methyclothiazide 2.5 mg./Tab. Bot. 100s, 500s.
Use: Hypertension.

DIUTENSEN-R. (Wallace) Methyclothiazide 2.5 m reserpine 0.1 mg./Tab. Bot. 100s, 500s.
Use: Hypertension.

• **DIVALPROEX SODIUM.** USAN.
Use: Anticonvulsant.

DIVINYL OXIDE. Vinyl Ether, Divinyl Ether.
Use: Inhalation anesthetic.

DIXARIT HYDROCHLORIDE. Clonidine, B.A.N.

DIZYMES. (Recsei) Protease and amylase equiv. to 250 mg. "Lipase 3,000"/Cap. Cap. 250 mg. Bot. 100s, 500s.
Use: Digestive enzymes.

IISS. (Bowman) Meclizine HCl 25 mg/Tab. Bot. 0s, 1000s.
se: Antinauseant for motion sickness.

T. (Lederle) Demethylchlortetracycline.
e: Declomycin HCl, Prep. (Lederle)

4 CHILDREN'S COUGH CONTROL. (DeWitt) d-ethorphan. Bot. 3 oz.

8 COUGH CONTROL MEDICINE. (DeWitt) d-Me-orphan. Bot. 4 oz.

COUGH SYRUP. (Bay) Dextromethorphan HBr 10 g./5 ml. w/alcohol 5%. Bot. 4 oz. pt., gal.
se: Antitussive.

ED. (Ortega) Methylprednisolone acetate 40 or 80 g./ml. Vials 5 ml.
se: Adrenocortical steroid.

O. (Crown Zellerbach; Syntex)
e: Dimethyl sulfoxide.

K-OIL. (Doak) Tar distillate 2%, in a lanolin, mineral suspension. Pl. Bot. 8 oz.
se: Dermatologic.

K OIL FORTE. (Doak) Tar distillate 5%, Bot. 4 .
se: Dermatologic.

K TAR LOTION. (Doak) Tar distillate 5%. Bot. 4 .
se: Dermatological lotion.

K TAR SHAMPOO. (Doak) Tar distillate 3% in ampoo base. Bot. 4 oz.
se: Dermatological shampoo.

K TERSASEPTIC. (Doak) A liquid cleanser, pH 8. Bot. 4 oz., pt., gal.
se: Liquid detergent.

N'S BACKACHE SPRAY. (Jeffrey Martin) Methyl alicylate 15%, menthol 8.4%, methyl nicotinate 6%. Aerosol can 4 oz.
se: External analgesic.

N'S PILLS. (Jeffrey Martin) Magnesium salicylate 25 mg./Tab. Ctn. 24s., 48s.
se: Analgesic.

B BATH OIL. (Person & Covey) Bot. 8 oz.
se: Bath & shower for dry skin.

BELL'S SOLUTION. Sodium Borate Solution ompound.
merson) Bot. 4 oz., pt.
Stanlabs) Bot. pt.

BUTAMINE. USAN. (±)-4-[2-(3-p-Hydroxy-phenyl--methylpropylamino)ethyl]pyrocatechol.
se: Cardiac stimulant.

BUTAMINE HYDROCHLORIDE. U.S.P. XXI. For j., U.S.P. XXI.
se: Cardiac stimulant.
ee: Dobutrex, Inj. (Lilly)
Inotrex (Lilly)

BUTREX. (Lilly) Dobutamine HCl 250 mg./vial. Vial 0 ml.
se: Inotropic agent.

CA ACETATE. (Organon) Desoxycorticosterone cetate 5 mg./ml. in oil. Vial 10 ml.
se: Adrenocortical insufficiency.

OCONAZOLE. USAN.
se: Antifungal.

DOCTASE. (Purepac) Docusate sodium 100 mg., casanthranol 30 mg./Cap. Bot. 100s.
Use: Stool softener.

DOCTIENT HC. (Suppositoria) Cod liver oil, hydrocortisone acetate 10 mg., lanolin, zinc oxide, bismuth subgallate, benzocaine, /Supp. Box 12s, 100s, 1000s.
Use: Antihemorrhoidal.

DOCTYL. (Approved) Docusate sodium 100 mg./Tab. Bot. 40s, 100s, 1000s.
Use: Constipation.

DOCTYLAX. (Approved) Docusate sodium 100 mg., acetophenolisatin 2 mg., prune conc. ¾ mg./Tab. Bot. 40s, 100s, 1000s.
Use: Corrective laxative.

• **DOCUSATE CALCIUM,** U.S.P. XXI. Cap. U.S.P. XXI. 1, 4-Bis(2-ethylhexyl)sulfosuccinate, cal. salt. Calcium bis-dioctyl-sulfosuccinate.
Use: Fecal softener.
See: Surfak, Cap. (Hoechst)
Doxidan, Cap. (Hoechst)

• **DOCUSATE POTASSIUM,** U.S.P.XXI. Cap., U.S.P. XXI.
Use: Stool softener
See: Dialose, Cap. (Stuart)
Dialose Plus, Cap. (Stuart)
Kasof, Cap. (Stuart)

• **DOCUSATE SODIUM,** U.S.P. XXI. Cap., Soln., Syr., Tab., U.S.P. XXI. Aerosol OT. (Am. Cyanamid). Bis-(2-ethoxy)-S-sodium sulfosuccinate. Sodium 1, 4-Bis (2-ethylhexyl) Sulfosuccinate.
Use: Pharm. aid (surfactant); stool softener.
See: Colace, Cap., Liq., Syr. (Mead Johnson)
Coloctyl, Cap. (Vitarine)
Comfolax, Cap. (Searle)
Constab-100, Tab. (Kenyon)
Dilax, Cap. (Mission)
Diomedicone, Tab (Medicone)
Diosate Caps. (Towne)
Diosuccin, Cap., Syr. (CMC)
Dio-Sul, Cap. (Vortech)
Diosux, Cap. (Jenkins)
Disonate, Cap., Tab. Syr., Liq. (Lannett)
Doss, Super Doss, Tab. (Ferndale)
Doxinate, Cap., Liq. (Hoechst)
DSS (Parke-Davis)
Duosol, Cap. (Kirkman)
Dynoctol, Cap. (Reid-Provident)
Easy-Lax, Cap. (Walgreen)
Konsto, Cap. (Freeport)
Laxatab, Tab. (Freeport)
Liqui-Doss, Liq. (Ferndale)
Modane Soft, Cap. (Adria)
Neo-Vadrin, Cap. (Scherer)
Peri-Doss, Cap. (Ferndale)
Regul-Aid, Syr. (Quality Generics)
Regutol, Tab. (Plough)
Revac Supprettes, Supp. (Webcon)
Rodox, Caps. (Rocky Mtn.)
Softon, Cap. (Stanlabs)
Stulex, Tab. (Bowman)
Surfak, Cap. (Hoechst)

W/Ascorbic acid, ferrous fumarate.
See: Hemaspan Cap. (Bock)
W/Betaine HCl, zinc, manganese, molybdenum.
See: Hemaferrin (Western Research)
W/Bisacodyl
See: Laxadan, Supp.(Lemmon)
W/Brewer's yeast.
See: Doss or Super Doss, Tab. (Ferndale)
W/Casanthranol.
See: Calotabs, Tabs. (Calotabs)
Constiban (Quality Generics)
Diolax, Caps. (Century)
Dio-Soft (Standex)
Diothron, Cap. (Vortech)
Disanthrol, Cap. (Lannett)
Di-Sosul Forte, Tab. (Drug)
D-S-S W/Casanthranol, Cap. (Wolins)
Disulans-Plus, Cap. (Noyes)
Easy-Lax Plus, Cap. (Walgreen)
Genericace, Cap. (Fellows-Testagar)
Neo-Vadrin D-D-S, Cap. (Scherer)
Nuvac, Cap. (LaCrosse)
Peri-Colace, Cap., Syr. (Mead Johnson)
Rodox, Cap. (Rocky Mtn.)
Sodex, Cap. (Mallard)
Sofflax, Cap. (Medics)
Stimulax, Cap. (Geriatric)
Syncelax, Cap. (Blue Line)
W/Casanthranol, sodium carboxymethylcellulose.
See: Dialose Plus, Cap. (Stuart)
Disolan Forte, Cap. (Lannett)
Tri-Vac, Cap. (Rhode)
W/Cascara sagrada extract.
See: Dioctyl-Zem, Tab. (Zemmer)
W/Danthron.
See: Danthross, Cap. (Elder)
Doctate-P, Cap. (Glaxo)
Doxate-D, Tab. (Dunhall)
W/Danthron, guar gum.
See: Guarsol, Tab. (Western Research)
W/Dehydrocholic acid.
See: Dubbalax-B, Cap. (Redford)
Dubbalax-N, Cap. (Redford)
Neolax, Tab. (Central)
W/D-calcium pantothenate and acetphenolisatin.
See: Peri-Pantyl, Tab. (McGregor)
W/Cascara sagrada extract.
See: Dioctyl-Zem, Tab. (Zemmer)
W/Dorbane.
See: Dorbantyl, Cap. (Riker)
Dorbantyl Forte, Cap. (Riker)
W/Ferrous fumarate, Vit. C.
See: Hemaspan, Cap. (Bock)
Recoup, Tab. (Lederle)
W/Ferrous fumarate, vitamins.
See: Bevitone, Tab. (Lemmon)
W/Ferrous fumarate, betaine HCl, desic. liver, vitamins, minerals.
See: Hemaferrin, Tab. (Western Research)
W/Guar gum, prune concentrate.
See: D-S-S Compound, Cap. (Wolins)
W/Glycerin.
See: Rectalad Enema, Liq. (Wampole)
W/Isobornyl thiocyanoacetate.
See: Barc, Cream, Liq. (Commerce)
W/Petrolatum.
See: Milkinol, Liquid, Emulsion (Kremers-Urban)
W/Phenolphthalein.
See: Correctol, Tab. (Plough)
Disolan, Cap. (Lannett)
Feen-A-Mint, Pills (Plough)
Novalax, Cap. (Coastal)
W/Phenolphthalein, dehydrocholic acid.
See: Bolax, Cap. (Boyd)
Sarolax, Caps. (Saron)
Tripalax, Cap. (Redford)
W/Polyoxyethylene nonyl phenol, sodium edetate, and 9-aminoacridine HCl.
See: Vagisec Plus Suppositories (Schmid)
W/Psyllium.
See: Sof-Cil, Pow. (Zemmer)
W/Senna concentrate.
See: Gentlax S, Tab. (Blair)
Sarolax (Saron)
Senokap-DDS, Cap. (Purdue Frederick)
Senokot S, Tab. (Purdue Frederick)
W/Sod. propionate, propionic acid, salicylic acid.
See: Prosal, Liq. (Gordon)
W/Vitamin-mineral combination.
See: Geriplex-FS, Kapseal (Parke-Davis)
Materna 1.60., Tab. (Lederle)

DODERLEIN BACILLI.
See: Redoderlein, Vial (Fellows-Testagar)

DODICIN. B.A.N. 3,6,9-Triazaheneicosanoic acid. Dodecyldi(aminoethyl)glycine.
Use: Surface active agent.

DOFAMIUM CHLORIDE. B.A.N. 2-(N-Dodecanoyl-N-methylamino)ethyldimethyl-(phenylcarbamoyl-methyl)ammonium chloride.
Use: Antiseptic.
See: Desogen.

DoFUS. (Miller) Freeze dried *Lactobacillus acidophi*- minimum of 108,000,000 organisms/Cap. Bot. 60
Use: To restore intestinal flora.

DOGMATYL. (Laboratories Delagrange, France) Sulpiride.

DOKTORS NOSE DROPS AND SPRAY. (Scherer) Phenylephrine HCl 0.25%. Spray Bot. 0.5 oz., 1 c Drops Bot. 1 oz.
Use: Nasal decongestant.

DOLACET C-3. (Hauck) Hydrocodone bitartrate 5 m acetaminophen 500 mg./Cap. Bot. 100s, 500s. U dose 50s.
Use: Analgesic.

DOLAMIDE TABS. (Major) Chlorpropamide 100 mg or 250 mg./Tab. Bot. 100s, 500s, 1000s.
Use: Hypoglycemic agent..

DOLAMIN. (Harvey) Ammonium sulf. 0.75% with sc chlor. and benzyl alc. Amp. 10 cc.
Use: Various neuralgias. 12s, 25s, 100s.

DOLANEX ELIXIR. (Lannett) Acetaminophen 325 mg./5 ml., alcohol 23%. Bot. 4 oz., 16 oz.
Use: Analgesic.

DOLANTIN.
See: Meperidine Hydrochloride, U.S.P. XXI.

LCIN. (Dolcin) Aspirin 3.7 gr., cal. succinate 2.8 gr./Tab. Bot. 100s, 200s.
Jse: Analgesic, antipyretic.
LDRAM. (Dram) Salicylamide 7.5 gr./Tab. Bot. 100s.
Use: Analgesic.
LEAR. (Eastwood) Ear drops. Bot. 0.5 oz.
LENE AP-65. (Lederle) Propoxyphene HCl 65 mg., acetaminophen 650 mg./Tab. Bot. 100s, 500s.
Use: Analgesic.
LENE COMPOUND-65. (Lederle) Propoxyphene HCl 65 mg., aspirin 389 mg., caffeine 32.4 mg./Cap. Bot. 100s, 500s.
Use: Analgesic.
LENE PLAIN. (Lederle) Propoxyphene HCl 65 mg./Caps. Bot. 100s, 500s.
Jse: Analgesic.
LICAINE. (Reid-Provident) Lidocaine HCl 2%/cc. Vials 50cc.
LOBID. (Merck Sharp & Dohme) Diflunisal 250 mg. or 500 mg./Tab. Unit-of-use 60s. Unit-dose 100s.
Use: Non-steroidal anti-inflammatory and analgesic.
LOMITE. (Barth's) Magnesium 297 mg., calcium 474.9 mg./Tab. Bot. 100s, 500s, 1000s.
LOMITE PLUS CAPSULES. (Barth's) Magnesium 37 mg., Ca 187 mg., P 50 mg., iodine 0.25 mg./Cap. Bot. 100s, 500s, 1000s.
LOMITE TABLETS. (Quality Generics) Magnesium 396 mg., calcium 633 mg./4 Tab. Bot. 250s, 500s.
LOMITE. (Blue Cross) Calcium 426 mg., magnesium 246 mg./3 Tabs. w/guar and acacia gum. Bot. 250s.
Jse: Calcium and magnesium deficiency.
LOMITE TABLETS. (Faraday) Calcium 150 mg., magnesium 90 mg./Tab. Bot. 250s.
LONIL. (Parke-Davis)
See: Pyridium Plus, Tab. (Parke-Davis)
LOPHINE HYDROCHLORIDE. (Lilly) Methadone HCl. **Amp.:** (10 mg./ml.; sod. chloride 0.9%) 1 ml. 12s, 100s. **Vial:** (10 mg./ml.) 20 ml. (Sod. chloride 0.9%, chlorobutanol 0.5%). 1s, 25s. **Tab.:** 5 mg., Bot. 100s. 10 mg. Bot. 100s.
Jse: Narcotic, analgesic & antitussive.
LOPIRONA TABLETS. (Winthrop Products) Dipyrone with chlormezanone.
Jse: Analgesic, muscle relaxant.
LORAL. (Progressive Enterprises) Colchicine salicylate 0.1 mg., phenobarbital 8 mg., sod. p-aminobenzoate 15 mg., Vit. B-1 25 mg., aspirin 325 mg./Tab. Bot. 100s, 1000s.
Jse: Treatment of gout, arthritis & rheumatism.
LORGON. (Kenyon) Mephenesin 200 mg., salicylamide 75 mg., acetyl-p-aminophenol 75 mg., ascorbic acid 50 mg./Tab. Bot. 100s, 1000s.
Jse: Analgesic.
LOSAL.
See: Meperidine Hydrochloride (Var. Mfr.)
Demerol HCl, Prods. (Winthrop-Breon)
LPRN #3. (Bock) Codeine phosphate 30 mg., acetaminophen 400 mg., aspirin 250 mg., magnesium hydroxide 60 mg., dried aluminum hydroxide 60 mg./Tab.
Jse: Analgesic.

DOLVANOL.
See: Meperidine Hydrochloride (Var. Mfr.)
Demerol HCl, Prod. (Winthrop-Breon)
• **DOMAZOLINE FUMARATE.** USAN.
Use: Anticholingeric.
DOMEBORO. (Miles Pharm) Aluminum sulfate & cal. acetate when added to water gives therapeutic effect of Burow's. One pkg. or Tab./Pt. water approx. equiv. to 1:40 dilution. **Pkg.:** 2.2 Gm., 12s, 100s. **Tab.:** effer. Box 12s, 100s, 1000s.
Use: Externally; in inflammatory skin conditions.
DOMEBORO OTIC. (Miles Pharm) Acetic acid 2%, in an aluminum acetate solution buffered to pH of 5.0 Plas. Bot. w/otic tip 2 oz.
Use: Otitis externa.
DOMEFORM-HC. (Miles Pharm) Hydrocortisone alcohol 0.5%, clioquinol 3%, in vehicle buffered to the pH range of normal skin w/cetyl alcohol, stearyl alcohol, sod. lauryl sulfate, beeswax, glycerin, petrolatum, & methylparaben. Cream: Tube 0.5 oz.
Use: Treatment of skin infections.
DOME-PASTE BANDAGE. (Miles Pharm) Zinc oxide, calamine, glycerine & gelatin bandage. Pkg. flesh-colored 4″ × 10 yd. and 3″ × 10 yd. impregnated gauze bandage.
Use: Treatment of leg ulcers.
DOMERINE MEDICATED SHAMPOO. (Miles Pharm) Salicylic acid 2%, allantoin 0.2%, in vehicle combining surface-active wetting agents with protein condensate (pH 5.3). Bot. 4 oz.
Use: Seborrheic conditions of the scalp.
DOMESTROL.
See: Diethylstilbestrol, Prep. (Various Mfr.)
D.O.M.F.
See: Merbromin (Mercurochrome) (City Chem.)
• **DOMIODOL.** USAN.
Use: Mucolytic.
• **DOMIPHEN BROMIDE.** USAN. Dodecyldimethyl-2-phenoxyethylammonium bromide. Phenododecinium Bromide (I.N.N.).
Use: Antiseptic.
See: Bradosol
Domibrom
DOMMANATE. (Forest) Dimenhydrinate 50 mg./ml. Vial 10 ml.
• **DOMPERIDONE.** USAN.
Use: Anti-emetic.
DONATUSSIN. (Laser) **Pediatric Drops:** Guaifenesin 20 mg., chlorpheniramine maleate 1 mg., phenylephrine HCl 2 mg./ml. Drop. bot. 30 ml. **Syr.:** Dextromethorphan HBr 7.5 mg., phenylephrine HCl 10 mg., chlorpheniramine maleate 2 mg., guaifenesin 100 mg./5 ml. Bot. pt., gal.
Use: Antitussive, antihistamine, decongestant.
DONATUSSIN DC SYRUP. (Laser) Hydrocodone bitartrate 2.5 mg., phenylephrine HCl 7.5 mg., guaifenesin 50 mg./5 ml. Bot. 4 oz., pt.
Use: Cough and nasal congestion.
DONDRIL. (Whitehall) Dextromethorphan HBr 10 mg., phenylephrine HCl 5 mg., chlorpheniramine maleate 1 mg./Cap. Bot. 24s.

DONNA. (Arcum) Menthol, thymol, eucalyptol, alum exsiccated, boric acid. 4 oz., 14 oz.
Use: Antiseptic douche.

DONNACIN. (Pharmex) Phenobarbital 16.20 mg., hyoscyamine sulfate 0.1037 mg., atropine sulfate 0.194 mg., hyoscine HBr 0.0065 mg./5 cc. or Tab. **Elixir:** Bot. pt., gal. **Tab.:** Bot. 1000s.
Use: Antispasmodic.

DONNAFED Jr. (Jenkins) Ephedrine HCl 1/16 gr., belladonna ext. 1/20 gr. (total alkaloids, 0.0006 gr.), salicylamide 1.25 gr./Tab. Bot. 1000s.
Use: Coryza, rhinitis, asthmatic conditions.

DONNAGEL. (Robins) Hyoscyamine sulfate 0.1037 mg., atropine sulfate 0.0194 mg., hyoscine HBr 0.0065 mg., sod. benzoate (preservative), 60 mg., kaolin 6 Gm., pectin 142.8 mg., 30 ml. alcohol 3.8%/oz. Susp., Bot. 4 oz., 1 pt.
Use: Antidiarrheal

DONNAGEL-PG. (Robins) Po. opium 24 mg., Kaolin 6 Gm., pectin 142.8 mg., hyoscyamine sulfate 0.1037 mg., atropine sulfate 0.0194 mg., hyoscine HBr 0.0065 mg., sodium benzoate 60 mg./30 cc. alcohol 5%. Bot. 6 oz., 1 pt.
Use: Control diarrhea.

DONNA-PHENAL ELIXIR. (Quality Generics) Atropine sulfate 0.0194 mg., hyoscyamine sulfate 0.1037 mg., hyoscine HBr 0.0065 mg., phenobarbital 16.2 mg. alcohol 23%. Bot. pt., gal.
Use: Antispasmodic and sedative.

DONNAPHEN ELIXIR. (Approved) Phenobarbital 16.2 mg., hyoscyamine sulfate 0.1037 mg., atropine sulfate 0.0194 mg., hyoscine HBr 0.0065 mg./5 cc. Bot. pt., gal.

DONNAPINE TABS. (Major) Belladonnal alkaloids and phenobarbital. Bot. 1000s.
Use: Sedative, antispasmodic.

DONNA-SED LIQUID. (Vortech) Phenobarbital 16.2 mg., hyoscyamine HBr 0.1037 mg., atropine sulfate 0.0194 mg., hyoscine HBr 0.0065 mg./5 cc. Bot. 4 oz., Gal.
Use: Sedative, antispasmodic.

DONNATAL. (Robins) Tab., Cap. or 5 cc. of Elixir contains hyoscyamine sulfate 0.1037 mg., atropine sulfate 0.0194 mg., hyoscine HBr 0.0065 mg., phenobarbital 16.2 mg.,**Cap. & Tab.:** Bot. 100s, 1000s. **Elixir:** w/alcohol 23%. Bot. 4 oz., 1 pt., 1 gal. Dis-Co packs 5 ml., 100s.
Use: Sedative & antispasmodic.

DONNATAL DIS-CO UNIT DOSE PACK. (Robins) Hyoscyamine sulfate 0.1037 mg., atropine sulfate 0.0194 mg., hyoscine HBr 0.0065 mg., phenobarbital 16.2 mg. (0.25 gr.)/Tab., 5 cc. **Tab.:** Unit dose pack 100s. **Elixir:** Unit dose pack (5 cc.) 25s.
Use: Antispasmodic and sedative.

DONNATAL EXTENTABS. (Robins) Hyoscyamine sulfate 0.3111 mg., atropine sulfate 0.0582 mg., hyoscine HBr 0.0195 mg., phenobarbital 48.6 mg. (3/4 gr.)/Tab. Bot. 100s, 500s. Dis-Co pack 100s.
Use: Long-acting antispasmodic & sedative.

DONNATAL #2. (Robins) Phenobarbital 32.4 mg. (0.5 gr.), hyoscyamine sulfate 0.1037 mg., atropi[ne] sulfate 0.0194 mg., hyoscine HBr 0.0065 mg./Ta[b]. Bot. 100s, 1000s.
Use: Antispasmodic & sedative.

DONNAZYME. (Robins) Hyoscyamine sulf. 0.0518 mg., atropine sulf. 0.0097 mg., hyoscine HBr 0.0033 mg., phenobarbital 8.1 mg. (1/8 gr.), peps[in] 150 mg./Tab. in outer layer, and pancreatin 300 mg., bile salts 150 mg./Tab. in core. Bot. 100s, 500s.
Use: Functional G.I. disorders.

DONPHEN. (Lemmon) Phenobarbital 15 mg., hyoscyamine sulfate 0.1 mg., atropine sulfate 0.0[...] mg., scopolamine HBr 6 mcg./Tab. Bot. 100s, 1000s.
Use: Antispasmodic.

DON'T. (Commerce) Sucrose octa acetate, isoprop[yl] alcohol. Bot. 0.45 oz.
Use: Discourage nail biting and thumb sucking.

• **DOPAMANTINE.** USAN.
Use: Antiparkinsonian

DOPAMINE. (Astra) Dopamine. **Amp.:** 200 mg./5 m[l]. Amp. Box 10s; 400 mg./10 ml. Amp. Box 5s. **Additive Syringe:** 200 mg./5 ml. Syr. Box 1s; 4[00] mg./10 ml Syr. Box 1s.
Use: Shock treatment.

• **DOPAMINE HYDROCHLORIDE,** U.S.P. XXI. Inj., U.S.P. XXI. 4-(2-Aminoethyl)pyrocatechol HCl.
Use: Adrenergic.
Intropin, Amp. (American Critical Care)

• **DOPAMINE HYDROCHLORIDE AND DEXTROS[E] INJECTION,** U.S.P. XXI.
Use: Adrenergic, emergency treatment of low bl[ood] pressure.

DOPAMINE HCL. (Abbott) Dopamine 40 mg./ml. o[r] 80 mg./ml. Amp. 5 ml., 10 ml.
Use: Emergency treatment of low blood pressure.

DOPAR. (Norwich Eaton) Levodopa 100 mg., 250 mg./Cap. Bot. 100s. 500 mg./Cap. Bot. 100s, 1000s.
Use: For treatment of Parkinson's disease.

DOPASTAT. (Parke-Davis) Dopamine HCl 40 mg./[ml.] Vial 5 ml.
Use: Adrenergic.

• **DOPEXAMINE.** USAN.
Use: Cardiovascular agent.

• **DOPEXAMINE HYDROCHLORIDE.** USAN.
Use: Cardiovascular agent.

DOPHENCO. (Blue Line) Opium pow. 1/20 gr., ipec[ac] pow. 1/20 gr., acetophenetidin 1.5 gr., atropine sulf. 1/500 gr., acetylsalicylic acid 3 gr., campho[r] monobromated 0.5 gr., caffeine 1/8 gr./Cap. Bot. 100s, 1000s.
Use: Analgesic, antipyretic.

DOPRAM. (Robins) Doxapram HCl 20 mg./ml. w/chlorobutanol (preservative) 0.5%. Vial 20 ml.
Use: Respiratory stimulant.

DORAPHEN COMPOUND 65. (Cenci) Propoxyphen[e] HCl 65 mg., aspirin 227 mg., phenacetin 162 mg[.], caffeine 32.4 mg./Cap. Bot. 100s, 500s, 1000s.
Use: Analgesic.

RAPHEN HCL. (Cenci) Propoxyphrene HCl 65 ng./Cap. Bot. 100s, 1000s.
Jse: Analgesic.

RBANE. (3M Products) Danthron. 75 mg./Tab. 3ot. 100s, 500s, 1000s.
Jse: Constipation.

RBANTYL. (3M Products) Docusate sodium 50 ng., danthron 25 mg./Cap. Bot. 30s, 100s, 250s.
Jse: Fecal softener and laxative.

RBANTYL FORTE. (3M Products) Docusate sodium 100 mg., Danthron 50 mg./Cap. Bot. 30s, 100s, 250s.
Jse: Fecal softener and laxative.

RCOL CHILDREN'S COUGH SYRUP. (Dorsey) Dextromethorphan HBr 5 mg., pseudoephedrine HCL 15 mg., guaifenesin 50 mg./5 ml. w/alcohol 5%. Bot. 4 oz., 8 oz.
Use: Cough prep.

RICO DROPS (Winthrop Products) Paracetamol.
Use: Analgesic, antipyretic.

RICO TABLETS. (Winthrop Products) Paracetamol.
Use: Analgesic, antipyretic.

RIDEN. (USV Labs.) Glutethimide. 250 mg./Tab. Bot. 100s; 500 mg./Tab. Bot. 100s, 500s, 1000s. Strip Pkg. 100s.
Use: Nonbarbiturate hypnotic.

RIGLUTE TABS DEA. (Major) Glutethimide 0.5 Gm./Tab. Bot. 100s, 1000s.
Use: Nonbarbiturate hypnotic.

RIMIDE. (Cenci) Gluthethimide 0.5 gm./Tab. Bot. 100s, 1000s.
Use: Sedative, hypnotic.

RME. (A.V.P.) Promethazine HCl 12.5 mg., 25 mg., 50 mg./Cap. Bot. 100s.
Use: Antihistaminic.

RMEER. (Pasadena Research) Scopolamine aminoxide HBr 0.2 mg./Cap. Bot. 100s, 1000s.

RMETHAN.
See: Dextromethorphan HBr. (Var. Mfr.)

RMIN SLEEPING CAPSULES. (Randob) **25 mg.** /Cap. #3 pink Cap. Bot. 32, 72/Bot. **50 mg.**/Cap. 14 caps./carton.
Use: Assist in restful sleep.

RMIRAL.
See: Phenobarbital, Prep. (Various Mfr.)

RMONAL.
See: Barbital, Prep. (Various Mfr.)

RMUTOL. (Approved) Scopolamine aminoxide HBr 0.2 mg./Cap. Bot. 24s, 60s.
Use: OTC sedative

RCOL CHILDREN'S DECONGESTANT LIQUID. (Dorsey) Pseudophedrine HCl 15 mg. 15 ml.. Bot. 4 oz.
Use: Decongestant.

RCOL CHILDREN'S LIQUID CALCIUM SUPPLEMENT. (Dorsey) Glubionate calcium 1.8 Gm/5 ml. Bot. 4 oz.
Use: Calcium supplement.

DORCOL CHILDREN'S LIQUID COLD FORMULA. (Dorsey) Pseudoephedrine HCl 15 mg., chlorpheniramine maleate 1 mg./5 ml. Bot. 4 oz.
Use: Decongestant, antihistamine.

DORCOL FEVER AND PAIN REDUCER. (Dorsey) Acetaminophen 160 mg./5 ml. Bot. 4 oz.
Use: Analgesic, antipyretic.

• **DORSATINE HYDROCHLORIDE.** USAN.
Use: Antihistaminic.

D.O.S. CAPS. (Goldline) Dioctyl sodium sulfosuccinate SG 100 mg., or 250 mg./Cap. Bot. 100s, 1000s.
Use: Laxative..

DOSS SYRUP. (Bay) Docusate sodium 20 mg./5 ml. Bot. pt., gal.
Use: Stool softener.

DOSS W/CASANTHRANOL. (Bay) Casanthranol 30 mg., docusate sodium 60 mg./15 ml. w/alcohol 10%, cc. Bot. pt., gal.
Use: Stool softener, laxative.

• **DOTHIEPIN HCL.** USAN. 11-(3-Dimethylamino-propylidene)-6H-dibenzo[b,e]thiepin hydrochloride. Dosulepin (I.N.N.)
Use: Antidepressant.
See: Prothiaden (hydrochloride)

DOTIROL. (Winthrop Products) Ampicillin trihydrate available in Cap, Suspension, Inj. (IV, IM.).
Use: Antibiotic.

DOUBLE-A. (Edwards) Acetaminophen 325 mg., aspirin 325 mg./Tab. Bot. 100s.
Use: Arthritic conditions.

DOUBLE DANDERINE. (Medtech) Benzalkonium chloride 0.2% Bot. 10 oz.
Use: Treatment of dandruff.

DOUCHE. (Jenkins) Acid boric, borax, acid tannic, sodium salicylate, zinc sulfate, pow. alum, hydrastine HCl, thymol, w/sod. bicarbonate and acid tartaric/Tab. Bot. 1000s.

DOVAPHEN CAP. (Jenkins) Dover's powder 16.2 mg. (opium 1.62 mg.), ipecac 1.62 mg., aspirin 2.5 gr., phenacetin 1.5 gr., caffeine 1/8 gr., camphor 0.25 gr., atropine sulfate 1/1000 gr./Cap. Bot. 1000s.

DOVAPHEN JR. (Jenkins) Dover's pow. 8.1 mg., acetophenetidin 0.5 gr., atropine sulfate 1/4000 gr., salicylamide 0.5 gr., caffeine 1/10 gr./Tab. Bot. 1000s.
Use: Analgesic.

DOVER'S POWDER. Ipecac 1 part, opium 1 part, lactose 8 parts.
Use: Analgesic sedative & diaphoretic.
W/Acetophenetidin, atropine sulfate, aspirin, camphor, caffeine, sod. sulfate dried.
See: Dovium, Cap. (Hance)
W/Acetophenetidin, atropine sulfate, salicylamide, caffeine.
See: Dovaphen Jr., Tab. (Jenkins)
W/Acetophenetidin, camphor, aspirin, caffeine, atropine sulfate.
See: Analgestine, Cap. (Mallard)
W/Acetophenetidin, sodium citrate, potassium guaiacolsulfonate.
See: Doverlyn, Cap., Tab. (Davis & Sly)

W/A.P.C., & camphor monobromated.
See: Coldate, Tab. (Elder)
W/Aspirin, acetophenetidin, camphor monobromated, caffeine, atropine sulfate.
See: Asco, Cap., Tab. (Sutliff & Case)
W/Aspirin, phenacetin, camphor monobromated, caffeine.
See: Coldate, Tab. (Elder)
Doveram, Prep. (Vortech)
W/Atropine sulf., A.P.C., camphor.
See: Dasin, Cap. (Beecham-Massengill)
W/Phenacetin, aspirin, camphor, caffeine alkaloid, atropine sulfate.
See: Analgestine Forte, Cap. (Mallard)
Dovernon, Cap. (Reid-Provident)
Phenacaps, Cap. (Scrip)
W/Pheneacetin, camphor, caffeine.
See: Doverlyn Adult, Tab. (Scrip)
W/Pyrilamine maleate, racephedrine HCl, salicylamide, phenacetin.
See: Asphamal-D, Tab. (Central)
W/Sodium salicylate, potassium iodide, camphor, gelsemium tincture.
See: Ricor, Tab. (Vortech)

DOVIUM. (Hance) Dover pow. 0.5 gr., acetophenetidin 1.5 gr., atropine sulfate 1/500 gr., aspirin 2 gr., camphor 0.25 gr., caffeine ⅛ gr., sod. sulfate dried 7.5 gr./Cap. Bot. 100s, 1000s.
Use: Analgesic & antipyretic.

DOWICIL 200.
See: Derma Soap (Ferndale)

DOW-ISONIAZID. (Merrell Dow) Isoniazid 300 mg./Tab. Bot. 30s.
Use: Tuberculosis treatment.

DOXAMIN. (Fellows) Thiamine HCl 100 mg., Vit. B-6 100 mg./cc. Vial 10 cc.

DOXAPAP-N TABS. (Major) Propoxyphene napsylate and acetaminophen. Bot. 100s, 500s.
Use: Analgesic.

DOXAPHENE CAPSULES. (Major) Propoxyphene HCl 65 mg./Cap. Bot. 1000s.
Use: Analgesic.

DOXAPHENE COMPOUND 65 CAPS. (Major) Propoxyphene HCl and acetaminophen. Bot. 1000s
Use: Analgesic.

• **DOXAPRAM HYDROCHLORIDE,** U.S.P. XXI. Inj., U.S.P. XXI. 1-Ethyl-4-(2-morpholinoethyl)-3,3-diphenyl-2-pyrrolidinone HCl.
Use: Respiratory & CNS stimulant.
See: Dopram, Vial (Robins)

• **DOXAPROST.** USAN.
Use: Bronchodilator.

DOXATE. Docusate sodium.
Use: Stool softener.

• **DOXAZOSIN MESYLATE.** USAN.
Use: Antihypertensive.

DOXEPIN. B.A.N. 11-(3-Dimethylaminopropylidene)-6H-ibenz[b,e]oxepin.
Use: Antidepressant.
See: Sinequan [hydrochloride]

• **DOXEPIN HYDROCHLORIDE,** U.S.P. XXI. Caps., Oral Soln., U.S.P. XXI. N,N-Dimethyldibenz[b,e] oxepin-$\Delta^{11(6H)}$, y-propylamine hydrochloride.
Use: Psychotherapeutic drug.
See: Adapin, Cap. (Pennwalt)
Sinequan, Cap. (Roerig)

DOXIDAN. (Hoechst) Danthron 50 mg., docusate calcium 60 mg./Cap. Bot. 30s, 100s, 1000s. Unit dose 100s. Display Packs 10s.
Use: Laxative.

DOXINATE. (Hoechst) Docusate sodium. **Cap.:** 60 mg. or 240 mg./Cap. Bot. 100s. **Soln.:** 5% pediat solution. Bot. 60 ml., gal.
Use: Orally, a wetting agent that keeps the stool s

DOXOLENE NAPSYLATE. Dextropropoxyphene, B.A.N.

• **DOXORUBICIN.** USAN.
Use: Antineoplastic.

DOXORUBICIN HYDROCHLORIDE, U.S.P. XXI. Inj. U.S.P. XXI. 14-Hydroxydaunorubicin. An antibio produced by *Streptomyces peuceticus* var. caesiu
See: Adriamycin (Adria)

• **DOXPICOMINE HYDROCHLORIDE.** USAN.
Use: Analgesic.

DOXYBETASOL. B.A.N. 9α-Fluoro-11β, 17α-dihydro 16β-methylpregna-1,4-diene-3,20-dione.
Use: Corticosteroid.

DOXY-C. (Century) Doxycycline hyclate 100 mg./C Bot. 50s.
Use: Antibiotic.

DOXY-CAPS. (Edwards) Doxycycline hyclate 1 mg./Cap. Bot. 50s.
Use: Broad spectrum antibiotic.

DOXYCHEL CAPSULES. (Rachelle) Doxycycline hyclate 50 mg. or 100 mg./Cap. Bot. 50s, 500s. Unit dose 100s.
Use: Antibiotic.

• **DOXYCYCLINE.** U.S.P. XXI. For Oral Susp. U.S.P. XXI. 4-(Dimethylamino)-1,4,4a,5,5a,6,11,12a-octa dro-3,5,10,12,12a-pentahydroxy-6-methyl-1,11-dio -2-naphthacenecarboxamide.
Use: Antibiotic.
See: Vibramycin for Oral Suspension (Pfizer Laboratories)

• **DOXYCYCLINE CALCIUM ORAL SUSPENSION,** U.S.P. XXI.

• **DOXYCYCLINE HYCLATE,** U.S.P. XXI. Caps., Inj., Sterile, Tab., U.S.P. XXI. 2-Naphthacenecarbo mide, 4-(dimethyl-amino)-1,4,4a,5,5a,6,11,12a-c tahydro-3,5,10,12-12a-pentahydroxy-6-methyl-1,11 dioxo-, HCl compound with ethanol monohydrate.
Use: Antibacterial.
See: Doxy-Caps, Cap. (Edwards)
Vibra-Tabs, Tab. (Pfizer Laboratories)
Vibramycin, Cap., Tab., Vial (Pfizer Laboratories

• **DOXYLAMINE SUCCINATE,** U.S.P. XXI. Syr., Tab U.S.P. XXI. 2-[α(2-Dimethylamino-ethoxy)-α-methy benzyl]pyridine bisuccinate.
Use: Antihistamine.
See: Decapryn, Prep. (Merrell Dow)
Unisom, Tab. (Leeming Pacquin)
W/Acetominophen, ephedrine sulfate, dextromethorphan HBr, alcohol.
See: Nyquil, Liq. (Vick)
W/Dextromethorphan HBr, alcohol.
See: Consotuss Antitussive, Syr. (Merrell Dow)

'Dextromethorphan HBr, sodium citrate, alcohol.
See: Vicks Formula 44 Cough Mixture, Syr. (Vicks)
'Mercodol.
See: Mercodol w/Decapryn, Syr. (Merrell Dow)
)XY-LEMMON CAPSULES. (Lemmon) Doxycycline hyclate equiv. to 100 mg. of doxycycline base/Cap. Bot. 50s, 500s. Unit dose 100s.
Use: Anti-infective.
)XY-LEMMON TABLETS. (Lemmon) Doxycycline hyclate equiv. to 100 mg./of doxycycline base/Tab. Bot. 50s.
Use: Anti-infective.
)XY-TABS. (Rachelle) Doxycycline hyclate 100 mg./Film Coated Tab. Bot. 50s, 500s.
Use: Antibiotic.
)XY-TABS-50. (Rachelle) 50 mg./Tab. Bot. 50s.
Use: Antibiotic
AMABAN. (Mallard) Dimenhydrinate 50 mg./Tab. Bot. 1000s.
Use: Prevention and treatment of nausea & vomiting.
AMAJECT. (Mayrand) Dimenhydrinate 50 mg./ml. Vial 10 ml.
AMAL. (Galen) Phenyltoloxamine dihydrogen citrate 50 mg./Tab. Bot. 100s, 1000s.
Use: Antihistamine.
AMAMINE. (Searle) Dimenhydrinate.**Liq.** 12.5 mg./4cc. Bot. 3 oz., 1 pt. **Tab.:** 50 mg. Bot. 36s, 100s, 1000s. Unit Dose 100s. Ciba Strip 12s; 4 × 12.
Use: Motion sickness.
AMAMINE INJECTION. (Searle) Dimenhydrinate. **Amp.** 50 mg., 1cc., Carton 5s, 25s, 100s. **Vial:** 250 mg./5cc. Carton 5s, 25s, 100s.
Use: Antinauseant.
AMARIN.
See: Dramamine, Prep. (Searle)
AMILIN. (Kay) Dimenhydrinate 50 mg./ml. Vial 10 ml.
Use: Antihistamine.
AMOCEN. (Central) Dimenhydrinate 50 mg./ml. Vial 10 ml. Box 12s.
Use: Anti-emetic, antihistaminic.
AMYL.
See: Dramamine, Prep. (Searle)
ANOCHOL. (Marin) Dehydrocholic acid 200 mg., homatropine methylbromide 5 mg./Tab. Bot. 60s, 500s, 1000s.
Use: Hydrocholeretic, antispasmodic.
APOLENE. Benzalkonium Chloride, B.A.N.
AWING SALVE. (Whiteworth) Tube 1 oz.
Use: Enhances healing..
AWING SALVE with TRIQUINODIN. (Towne) Tube 2 oz.
. CALDWELL SENNA LAXATIVE. (Glenbrook) Senna 7.0%, Alcohol 4.5%. bot. 5 oz., 12 oz.
Use: Laxative.
C PERI-ANAL CREAM. (Xttrium) Lassar's paste 37.5%, anhydrous lanolin USP 37.5%, cold cream 25%. Tube 5 oz.
Use: Diaper rash.

DR. DRAKE'S COUGH MEDICINE. (Last) Dextromethorphan HBr 10 mg./5 ml. Bot. 2 oz.
Use: Antitussive cough remedy.
DREST. (Dermik) Polyvinylpyrrolidone, benzalkonium chloride 0.125%, alkylisoquinolinium bromides 0.15%, in gel base. Tubes 3.5 oz.
Use: Antiseptic hair dressing.
• **DRIBENDAZOLE,** USAN.
Use: Anthelmintic.
DRICOL MESYLATE. Amidephrine, B.A.N.
DRI-DRIP. (Coastal) Chlorpheniramine maleate 8 mg., phenylpropanolamine HC1 50 mg., atropine sulfate 1/80 gr./Cap. Bot. 100s, 500s.
Use: Treatment of cold symptoms.
DRI-DRIP LIQUID. (Coastal) Phenylephrine HC1 5 mg., phenylpropanolamine 8 mg., chlorpheniramine maleate 2 mg., alcohol 3%/5 cc. Bot. 4 oz., 16 oz.
Use: Treatment of cold symptoms.
DRI-A CAPS. (Barth's) Vit. A 10,000 I.U./Cap. Bot. 100s, 500s.
DRI A&D CAPS. (Barth's) Vit. A 10,000 I.U., D 400 I.U./Cap. Bot. 100s, 500s.
DRI-E. (Barth's) Vit. E 100 I.U./Cap. Bot. 100s, 500s, 1000s. 200 I.U./Cap. Bot. 100s, 250s, 500s. 400 I.U./Cap. Bot. 100s, 250s.
• **DRIED ALUMINUM HYDROXIDE GEL,** U.S.P. XXI.
See: Aluminum Hydroxide Gel, Dried
DRIED YEAST.
See: Yeast, dried
DRI-HIST META-KAPS. (Sutliff & Case) Chlorpheniramine maleate 8 mg., phenylpropanolamine 50 mg., atropine sulfate 0.36 mg./S.A. Cap. Bot. 100s, 1000s.
Use: Antihistaminic and sympathomimetic.
DRI-HIST NO. 2 META-KAPS. (Sutliff & Case) Pyrilamine maleate 25 mg., pheniramine maleate 10 mg., phenylpropanolamine HCl 25 mg., phenylephrine HCl 10 mg./Cap. Bot. 100s, 1000s.
DRIMINATE TABS. (Major) Dimenhydrinate 50 mg./Tab. Bot. 100s, 1000s.
Use: Treatment and prevention of motion sickness.
DRINOPHEN CAPSULES. (Lannett) Phenyl-propanolamine HCl 15 mg., acetylsalicylic acid 230 mg., acetaminophen 200 mg., caffeine 15 mg./Cap. Bot. 1000s.
Use: Analgesic.
DRINUS GRADUALS. (Amfre-Grant) Chlorpheniramine maleate 8 mg., phenylephrine HCl 20 mg., methscopolamine nitrate 2.5 mg./Cap. Bot. 30s, 250s, 1000s.
Use: Antihistamine & decongestant.
DRINUS-M GRADUALS. (Amfre-Grant) Chlorpheniramine maleate 8 mg., phenylephrine HCl 20 mg./Cap. Bot. 50s., 250s, 1000s.
Use: Antihistamine, decongestant.
DRINUS SYRUP. (Amfre-Grant) Chlorpheniramine maleate 2 mg., phenylpropanolamine 12.5 mg./5 cc. Bot. 4 oz. pt., gal.
Use: Antihistamine, decongestant.
DRISDOL. (Winthrop-Breon) Ergocalciferol (Vitamin D) 200 I.U./drop in propylene glycol solvent. Bot. 60 ml.
Use: Prevention of Vitamin D deficiency.

DRISDOL 50,000 UNIT CAPSULES. (Winthrop-Breon) Vit. D-2, 50,000 I.U./Cap. Bot. 50s.
Use: Treatment of refractory rickets, hypoparathyroidism, familial hypophosphatemia.

DRISTAN 12 HOUR. (Whitehall) Chlorpheniramine maleate 4 mg., phenylephrine HCl 20 mg./Cap. Bot. 6s, 10s, 15s.
Use: Decongestant, analgesic.

DRISTAN-AF. (Whitehall) Phenylephrine HCl 5 mg., chlorpheniramine maleate 2 mg., acetaminophen 325 mg., caffeine 16.2 mg./Tab. Tins 12s, Bot. 24s, 50s, 100s.
Use: Antihistamine, nasal decongestant, analgesic.

DRISTAN CAPSULES. (Whitehall) Phenylpropanolamine HCl 12.5 mg., chlorpheniramine maleate 2 mg., acetaminophen 325 mg./Cap. Bot. 16s, 36s, 75s.
Use: Decongestant, analgesic.

DRISTAN COUGH FORMULA. (Whitehall) Dextromethorphan HBr 7.5 mg., phenylephrine HCl 5 mg., chlorpheniramine maleate 1 mg., guaifenesin, 30 mg./5ml. w/alcohol 12%. Bot. 3 oz.
Use: Antitussive.

DRISTAN LONG LASTING NASAL MIST. (Whitehall) Oxymetazoline HCl 0.05%. Bot. 0.5 oz., 1 oz.
Use: Nasal decongestant.

DRISTAN MENTHOL NASAL MIST. (Whitehall) Phenylephrine HCl 0.5%, pheniramine maleate 0.2% Bot. 0.5 oz., 1 oz.
Use: Nasal decongestant.

DRISTAN NASAL MIST. (Whitehall) Phenylephrine HCl 0.5%, pheniramine maleate 0.2%/ml. Bot. 0.5 oz., 1 oz.
Use: Nasal decongestant

DRISTAN TABLETS. (Whitehall) Phenylephrine HCl 5 mg., chlorpheniramine maleate 2 mg., acetaminophen 325 mg./Tab. Bot. 24s, 50s, 100s.
Use: Antihistamine, oral nasal decongestant, analgesic.

DRISTAN ULTRA COLD FORMULA. (Whitehall) Acetaminophen 500 mg., pseudoephedrine HCl 30 mg., chlorpheniramine maleate 2 mg., dextromethorphan 15 mg./Tab. or Cap. Tab. Bot. 20s, 48's; Cap. Pkg. 16s, 36s; Liq. Bot. 6 oz.
Use: Relief of cold symptoms.

DRITHO-CREME. (American Dermal) Anthralin 0.1%, 0.25% or 0.5%. Tube 50 gm.
Use: Psoriasis treatment.

DRITHO-CREME HP 1.0%. (American Dermal) Anthralin 1.0%. Tube 50 Gm.
Use: Psoriasis treatment.

DRITHO-SCALP. (American Dermal) Anthralin 0.25% or 0.5%. Tube 50 gm.
Use Psoriasis treatment of scalp.

DRIXORAL. (Schering) Dexbrompheniramine maleate 6 mg., pseudoephedrine sulfate 120 mg./S.A. Tab. Box 10s, 20s, 40s. Bot. 100s.
Use: Nasal decongestant, antihistamine.

DRIZE. (Ascher) Phenylpropanolamine HCl 75 mg., chlorpheniramine maleate 12 mg./S.R. Cap. Bot. 100s.
Use: Allergic rhinitis, common cold.

• **DROBULINE.** USAN.
Use: Cardiac depressant.

DROCARBIL. Acetarsone salt of arecoline. Arecolin n-acetyl-4-hydroxy-m-arsanilate.
Use: Anthelmintic in animals.

• **DROCINONIDE.** USAN.
Use: Anti-inflammatory.

DROCODE.
See: Dihydrocodeine.

DROLBAN INJECTION. (Lilly) Dromostanolone propionate 50 mg./ml. in sesame oil q.s., phenol 0.5%. Vial 10 ml. Ctn. 10s.
Use: Metastatic carcinoma of the breast.

DROMORAN, LEVO. Levorphanol, Levorphan.
See: Levo-Dromoran, Vial, Amp., Tab. (Roche)

DROMOSTANOLONE PROPIONATE. 2α-Methylar rostan-17-(β)-0l-3-one propionate. 17 β-Hydroxy-2 methyl-5α-androstan-3-one propionate.
Use: Antineoplastic.
See: Drolban, Inj. (Lilly)

• **DRONABINOL.** USAN.
Use: Anti-emetic.

DROP CHALK. (Various Mfr.) Cal. carb., prepared. Prepared Chalk.

• **DROPERIDOL,** U.S.P. XXI. Inj., U.S.P. XXI. 1-{1-[3 (p-Fluorobenzoyl)propyl-1,2,3,6-tetrahydro-4-pyridy }-2-benzimidazolinone.
Use: Tranquilizer.
See: Inapsine, Inj. (Janssen)
W/Fentanyl citrate.
Use: Tranquilizer.
See: Innovar, Inj. (Janssen)

• **DROPRENILAMINE.** USAN.
Use: Vasodilator

DROPROPIZINE. B.A.N. 1-(2,3-Dihydroxypropyl)-4-ph nylpiperazine.
Use: Antitussive.
See: Katril
Catabex
Tussilex

DROSTANOLONE. B.A.N. 17β-Hydroxy-2α-methyl-5 androstan-3-one.
Use: Anabolic steroid.
See: Dromostanolone
Methalone
Masteril (propionate)

DROTEBANOL. B.A.N. 3,4-Dimethoxy-17-methyl-m phinan-6β, 14-diol.
Use: Analgesic; antitussive.

DROTIC STERILE OTIC SOLUTION. (Ascher) Hydrocortisone 10 mg. (1%), polymixin B Sulfate 10,000 u., neomycin 3.5 mg./ml. w/preservatives Dropper Bot. 10 ml.
Use: Otitis externa.

• **DROXACIN SODIUM.** USAN.
Use: Antibacterial.

DROXARYL. Bufexamac, B.A.N.

• **DROXIFILCON A.** USAN.
Use: Contact lens material.

DROXINE L.A. (Shear-Kershman) Dyphylline 4 mg./Tab. (long acting). Bot. 100s.
Use: Smooth muscle relaxant.

DROXOVITE. (Kay) Hydroxocobalamin, 1000 mcg./cc. Vehicle; Sodium chloride 0.82%, sodium acetate 0.10%, methylparaben 0.15%, propylparaben 0.02%, acetic acid/cc. Vial 10 cc.
Use: Pernicious anemia, megaloblastic anemia.

DROXYPROPINE. B.A.N. 1-[2-(2-Hydroxyethoxy)-ethyl]-4-phenyl-4-propionylpiperidine.
Use: Cough suppressant.

DR. SCHOLL'S ATHLETE'S FOOT GEL. (Scholl) Tolnaftate 1%. Tube 0.5 oz.
Use: Anti-fungal.

DR. SCHOLL'S ATHLETE'S FOOT POWDER. (Scholl) Tolnaftate 1%. Shaker: Plastic bottle 2.5oz. Spray: Aerosal can 3.5 oz.
Use: Anti-fungal.

DR. SCHOLL'S ATHLETE'S FOOT SPRAY. (Scholl) Tolnafatate 1%. Aerosol Can 3.5 oz.
Use: Anti-fungal.

DR. SCHOLL'S CALLOUS SALVE. (Scholl) Salicylic acid 15%. Tube 0.4 oz.
Use: Callus remover.

DR. SCHOLL'S CORN SALVE. (Scholl) Salicylic acid 15.0%. Jar 0.4 oz.
Use: Corn remover.

DR. SCHOLL'S "2" DROP CORN/CALLOUS REMOVER. (Scholl) Salicylic acid 12.6%. Bot.0.33 oz.
Use: Corn and callus remover.

DR. SCHOLL'S ONIXOL. (Scholl) Sodium sulfide 1%. Bot. 0.33 oz.
Use: Treatment of in-grown toenail

DR. SCHOLL'S PRO COMFORT JOCK ITCH SPRAY.(Scholl)Tolnaftate1%.Aerosolcan3.5oz.
Use: Anti-fungal.

DR. SCHOLL'S WART REMOVER KIT. (Scholl) Salicylic acid 17%. Bot. 3.25 oz.
Use: Wart Removal.

DR. SCHOLL'S ZINO PADS/WITH MEDICATED DISKS. (Scholl) Salicylic acid 40% or 20%. Protective pads designed for use with & without salicylic acid-impregnated disks.
Use: For removal of soft and hard corns, calluses.

DRUCON. (Standard Drug) Phenylephrine HCl 5 mg., chlorpheniramine maleate 2 mg., menthol 1 mg., alcohol 5%/5 ml. Elixir Bot. pt., gal.
Use: Relief of respiratory congestion in infants and children.

DRUCON C R. (Standard Drug) Phenylephrine HCl 25 mg., chlorpheniramine maleate 4 mg./Tab. Bot. 100s.
Use: Relief of nasal congestion of colds or allergy.

DRUCON WITH CODEINE. (Standard Drug) Codeine phosphate 10 mg., phenylephrine HCl 10 mg., chlorpheniramine maleate 2 mg., menthol 1 mg., alcohol 5%/5 ml. Bot. pt.
Use: Relief of respiratory congestion.

DRY & CLEAR ACNE MEDICATION. (Whitehall) Benzoyl peroxide 5%. Bot. 1 oz., 2 oz.
Use: Acne medication.

DRY & CLEAR CLEANSER. (Whitehall) Alcohol 50%, salicylic acid 0.5%, benzoic acid 0.5%, benzethonium Cl. 0.1%. Bot. 4 oz., 8 oz.
Use: Acne medication.

DRY & CLEAR DOUBLE STRENGTH CREAM. (Whitehall) Benzoyl peroxide 10%. Tube 1 oz.
Use: Acne medication.

DRY SKIN CREME. (Gordon) Cetyl alcohol, lubricating oils in a water soluble base. Jar 2 oz., 1 lb., 5 lb.
Use: Dry skin, moisturizer, vehicle.

DRYSOL. (Person & Covey) Aluminum C1 20% in anhydrous ethyl alcohol. Bot. 37.5 cc. Dab-O-Matic Rx in 35 ml. plastic bottle w/applicator head.
Use: Hyperhidrosis.

DRYSUM. (Summers) Two soapless, lathering detergents, alcohol, acetone, perfume. Plastic Bot. 4 oz.
Use: Shampoo.

DRYTERGENT. (C & M Pharmacal) TEA-dodecylbenzenesulfonate, boric acid, lauramide DEA, propylene glycol, purified water, color, fragrance. Bot. 8 oz., 16 oz., 1 Gal.
Use: Cleanser for acne therapy.

DRYTEX. (C & M Pharmacal) Salicylic acid 2%, benzalkonium chloride 0.1% non-ionic wetting agent, acetone, isopropyl alcohol 40%, purified water, color and perfume. Lot. Bot. 8 fl. oz.
Use: Cleanser for acne and seborrhea.

d-SEB. (Rydell) Blend of 2 synthetic detergents, parachlorometaxylenol 2%, isopropanol 7.6%. Tube 60 Gm.
Use: For cleansing of excessive skin oil or as an aid in the control of acne and pimples.

D-SINUS. (Laser) Phenylpropanolamine HC1 18 mg., acetaminophen 325 mg./Cap. Bot. 24s, 100s, 1000s.
Use: Decongestant, analgesic.

D-S-S CAPSULES. (Parke-Davis) Docusate sodium 100 mg./Cap. Bot. 100s, 1000s. Unit dose 100s.

D-S-S COMPOUND. (Wolins) Docusate sodium 100 mg., guar gum 200 mg., prune concentrate 50 mg./Cap. Bot. 1000s.

D-S-S W/CASANTHRANOL. (Wolins) Docusate sodium 100 mg., casanthranol 30 mg./Cap. Bot. 100s, 1000s.

D-S-S PLUS CAPSULES. (Parke-Davis) Docusate sodium 100 mg., casanthranol 30 mg./Cap. Bot. 100s, 1000s. Unit dose 100s.

DST. Dihydrostreptomycin.
See: Dihydrostreptomycin, Prep. (Various Mfr.)

D-TEST 200. (Burgin-Arden) Testosterone cypionate 200 mg./cc. 10 cc. vial.

D-TEST 100. (Burgin-Arden) Testosterone cypionate 100 mg./cc. 10 cc. vial.

DTIC-DOME. (Miles Pharm) Dacarbazine 100 mg., 200 mg./Vial. Vial 10 ml., 20 ml.
Use: Metastatic malignant melanoma.

DUADACIN. (Hoechst) Phenylpropanolamine HCl 12.5 mg., chlorpheniramine maleate 2.0 mg., acetaminophen 325.0 mg./Cap. Bot. 100s, 1000s. Carton 5000s. 8 paks 1000s.
Use: Cold syndrome.

DUALEX-E ELIXIR. (Scruggs) Bot. pt., gal.

DUAL-PRED. (Tunex) Prednisolone acetate 80 mg., prednisolone sodium phosphate 20 mg., sodium Cl. 6.5 mg., pectin 2 mg./ml. w/sodium acetate 0.8%, benzalkonium Cl. 0.01%.
Use: Anti-inflammatory agent.

DUAL-WET. (Alcon) Polyvinyl alcohol & duasorb water soluble polymetric system, benzalkonium chloride 0.01%, disodium edetate 0.05%. Bot. 2 oz.
Use: Wetting sol. for hard contact lens.

• **DUAZOMYCIN.** USAN. Antibiotic isolated from broth filtrates of *Streptomyces ambofaciens.*
Use: Anti-neoplastic agent.

DUAZOMYCIN A. Name used for Duazomycin.

DUAZOMYCIN B. Name used for Azotomycin.

DUAZOMYCIN C. Name used for Ambomycin.

DUBILE. (Kenyon) Ox bile ext. 1.5 gr., mixed oxidized bile acids 1.5 gr., homatropine MeBr $1/120$ gr./Tab. Bot. 100s, 1000s.

DULCAGEN SUPPOSITORIES. (Goldline) Bisacodyl 10 mg./Supp. Box 12s, 100s.
Evacuant.

DULCAGEN TABLETS. (Goldline) Bisacodyl 5 mg./Tab. Bot. 100s, 1000s.
Use: Constipation treatment..

DULCETS. (Wolins) Cetylpyridium chloride 2.5 mg., benzocaine 10 mg./oz. Bot. 10s.

DULCOLAX. (Boehringer Ingelheim) Bisacodyl. **Tab.** E.C. 5 mg. Box 4s, 24s. Bot. 100s, 1000s. Unit dose 100s. **Supp.** 10 mg. Box 2s, 4s, 8s, 50s, 500s. **Bowel Prep Kit.** 4 tablets and 1 suppository/Kit. 5 Kits/box
Use: Laxative.

DU-MIN 4. (Scrip) Chlorpheniramine maleate 4 mg., caffeine 15 mg./Tab. Bot. 100s.

DUO. (Norcliff Thayer) Surgical adhesive. Tube 0.5 oz.

DUOBARBITAL. (Wolins) Amobarbital sodium secobarbital sodium 1.5 gr. or 3 gr. Cap. Bot. 1000s.
Use: Sedative-hypnotic.

DUO-C.V.P. CAPSULES. (Armour) Bioflavonoids 200 mg./Cap. Bot. 100s, 500s.
Use: Vitamin supplement.

DUO-CYP. (Keene) Testosterone cypionate 50 mg., estradiol cypionate, 2 mg./ml. Vial 10 ml.

DUODENAL SUBSTANCE.
W/Ox bile extract, pancreatin, papain.
See: Digenzyme, Tab. (Burgin-Arden)

DUODENUM WHOLE, DESICCATED & DEFATTED.
See: Viodenum, Tab., Pow. (VioBin)
W/Ferrous gluconate, Vit. B-12, cobalt chloride.
See: Bitrinsic-E, Cap. (Elder)

DUODERM. (Convatec) Hydroactive dressings/granules, wound care covering. 6×8s, Box 5s. 8×12s, Box 5s. 4×4s, 3s.
Use: Treatment of pressure sores and leg ulcers.

DUOFILM. (Stiefel) Salicylic acid 16.7%, lactic acid 16.7% in flexible collodion. Bot. 0.5 oz.
Use: Warts, keratolytic agent.

DUO-FLOW. (CooperVision) Bot. 4 oz.
Use: Cleaning and soaking solution for hard contact lenses.

DUOGASTRONE DISODIUM SALT. Carbenoxolone, B.A.N.

DUO-IONATE. (Tunex) Testosterone cypionate 50 mg., estradiol cypionate 2 mg./ml. w/chlorobutanol 0.5% in cottonseed oil. Vial 10cc.
Use: Androgen-estrogen therapy.

DUOJECT. (Mallard) Cyanocobalamin 1000 mcg., thiamine HCl 100 mg./cc.

DUOLUBE. (Muro) Petrolatum, sterile, preservative and lanolin free. Tube 3.5 Gm.
Use: Corneal lubricating ointment.

DUO-MEDIHALER. (Riker) Isoproterenol HCl 4.0 mg., phenylephrine bitartrate 6.0 mg./ml. in an inert propellant. Oral adapter w/15 ml. Vial; Oral adapter w/22.5 ml Vial. Refill vials 15 ml. and 22.5 ml.
Use: Treatment of asthma.

DUOMINE. (Kenyon) Dextromethorphan HBr 7.5 mg., chlorpheniramine maleate 10 mg., ammonium Cl 80 mg., pot. guaiacolate 80 mg., tartar emetic 0.8 mg./5 cc. Bot. 4 oz., pt., gal.

DUOMYCIN.
See: Aureomycin, Prep. (Lederle)

DUOPRIN. (Dunhall) Acetaminophen 250 mg., salicylamide 250 mg./Tab. Bot. 30s, 100s, 250s. **Cap.** Bot. 30s, 100s, 500s.
Use: Non-salicylate analgesic.

DUOPRIN-S. (Dunhall) Acetaminophen 90 mg., salicylamide 90 mg., menthol 1 mg./5 ml. Bot. pt.
Use: Analgesic.

DUOSOL. (Kirkman) Ducosate sodium 100 mg./Cap. Bot. 100s, 1000s.
Use: Fecal softener.

DUOSCORB. (Upsher-Smith) Ascorbic acid 2 Gms./Pkt. Pkt. 50s.
Use: Renal dialysis use.

DUOTAL. (Approved) 1.5 gr.: Secobarbital sod. ¾ gr., amobarbital ¾ gr./Cap. 3 gr.: Secobarbital sod. 1.5 gr., amobarbital 1.5 gr./Cap. Bot. 100s, 500s, 1000s.

DUOTAL.
See: Guaiacol Carbonate (Various Mfr.)

DUOTRATE. (Marion) Pentaerythritol tetranitrate 30 mg./Time release Cap. Bot. 100s.
Use: Coronary vasodilation.

DUOTRATE-45. (Marion) Pentaerythritol tetranitrate 45 mg./Time release Cap. Bot. 100s.
Use: Coronary vasodilation.

DUOTRONE. (Arnar-Stone; Dunhall) Estrone 2 mg., testosterone 25 mg./cc. Vial 10 cc.

DUOVAL-P.A. (Reid-Provident) Testosterone enanthate 90 mg., estradiol valerate 4 mg./cc. Vials 10 cc. 1s, 6s, 12s.

DUOVIN-S. (Spanner) Estrone 2.5 mg., progesterone 25 mg./1 cc. Vial 10 cc.

DUO-WR, No. 1 & No. 2. (Whorton) **No. 1:** Salicylic acid, compound tincture benzoin. **No. 2:** Compound tincture benzoin, formaldehyde. Bot. 0.25 oz.
Use: Topical application in the removal of warts.

DUPHRENE. (Vale) Phenylephrine HCl 5 mg., chlorpheniramine maleate 1 mg., pyrilamine maleate 12.5 mg./Tab. Bot. 100s, 500s, 1000s.
Use: Antihistaminic.

UPLAST. (Beiersdorf) Adhesive coated elastic cloth 8"×4", Box 10 strips. 10"×5", Box 8 & 10 strips.

UPLEX SHAMPOO. (C & M Pharmacal) Sodium lauryl sulfate, lauramide DEA, purified water. Bot. pt., gal.
Use: Shampoo.

UPLEX T SHAMPOO (C & M Pharmacal) Sodium lauryl sulfate, purified water, lauramide DEA, solution of coal tar, alcohol 8.3%. Bot. pt., gal.
Use: Anti-dandruff shampoo.

UPONOL.
See: Gardinol-type Detergents (Sod. Lauryl Sulfate) (Various Mfr.)

URABOLIN-25. (Organon) Nandrolone phenpropionate 25 mg./ml. in sesame oil, w/ Benzyl alcohol 5%. Amp. 1 ml. Box 3s; Vial 5 ml.
Use: Anabolic agent.
See: Deca-Durabolin, Inj. (Organon)

URABOLIN-50. (Organon) Nandrolone phenpropionate 50 mg./ml. in sterile sesame oil w/ 10% benzyl-alcohol. Vials 2 cc.
Use: Anabolic agent.

URA-C 500. (Amfre-Grant) Vit. C 500 mg./Timed Release Cap. Bot. 100s, 500s.
Use: Vit. C deficiency.

URA-CHORION PLUS. (Pharmex) Estradiol valerate 10 mg./cc. Vial 10 cc.

URACID. (Fielding) Antacid. Bot 100s.
Use: Antacid.

URACILLIN A.S. (Lilly) Penicillin G procaine 300,000 u./ml. w/lecithin 1%, sod. citrate 4%, povidone 0.1%, w/methylparaben 0.15%, propylparaben 0.02%, benzylalcohol 1% as preservatives. Vial 10 ml. Box 1s. Traypak 100s.
Use: Antibiotic.

URADYNE. (Forest) Aspirin 230 mg., acetaminophen 180 mg., caffeine 15 mg./Tab. Bot. 100s. **Forte:** Bot. 100s. **No. 2:** Bot. 100s.

URADYNE DHC. (Forest) Dihydrocodeinone bitartrate 5 mg., acetaminophen 500 mg./Tab. Bot. 50s.
Use: Analgesic.

URA-ESTRIN. (Hauck) Estradiol cypionate 5 mg./ml. Vial 10 ml.
Use: Estrogen deficiency.

URAGEN. (Hauck) Estradiol valerate 10 mg., 20 mg., or 40 mg./ml. Vial 10 ml.
Use: Estrogen therapy.

URA-KELLIN. (Pharmex) Estrone 2 mg., potassium estrone sulfate 1 mg., sod. phosphate buffer, sod. carboxymethylcellulose 0.2%, thimerosal 1:20,000, benzyl alcohol 1.5%/cc. Vial 10 cc.
Use: Deficiency of estrogens.

URALEX. (American Urologicals) Pseudoephedrine HCl 120 mg., chlorpheniramine maleate 8 mg./Cap. Bot. 100s.
Use: Nasal decongestant, antihistaminic.

URALONE INJECTION. (Hauck) Methylprednisolone acetate 40 mg., or 80 mg./ml. Vial 10 ml.
Use: Steroid therapy.

DURALUTIN INJECTION. (Hauck) Hydroxyprogesterone 250 mg./ml. Vial 5 ml.
Use: Progestogen.

DURA-METH. (Foy) Methylprednisolone 40 mg./ml. Vials 5 ml., 10 ml.
Use: Replacement therapy in adrenocortical deficiency states.

DURAMORPH PF. (Elkins-Sinn) Morphine sulfate injection 0.5 mg./ml. or 1 mg./ml. Amp. 10 ml. Box. 10s.
Use: Narcotic analgesic for I.V., Epidural or intrathecal injection..

DURANDROL. (Pharmex) Methandriol dipropionate 50 mg./cc. Vial 10 cc.

DURANEST BASE AND HCl. Etidocaine, B.A.N.
Use: Local anesthetic.
See: Duranest HCl (Astra)

DURANEST HCl. (Astra) Etidocaine 1% w/epinephrine 1:200,000. Vial 30 ml.
Use: Local anesthetic.

• **DURAPATITE.** USAN.
Use: Prosthetic aid.

DURAPHYL. (McNeil Pharm) Anhydrous theophylline controlled released 100 mg., 200 mg., or 300 mg./Tab. Bot. 100s.
Use: Bronchodilator.

DURAPRED. (Amfre-Grant) Prednisolone acetate 100 mg./ml. Vial 10 mg.
Use: Hormone.

DURAPRED T.B.A. (Amfre-Grant) Prednisolone T-butylacetate 20 mg./ml. Vial 10 ml.
Use: Hormone.

DURAQUIN. (Parke-Davis) Quinidine gluconate 330 mg./Tab. (Sustained release). Bot. 100s. Unit dose 100s.
Use: Cardiac depressant.

DURASAL. (Seatrace) Magnesium salicylate 600 mg./Tab. Bot. 100s, 500s.
Use: Anti-arthritic, analgesic, anti-pyretic.

DURASIL. (Seatrace) Aluminum hydroxide dried gel 200 mg., magnesium trisilicate 200 mg., D-calcium pantothenate 10 mg./Tab. Bot. 100s.
Use: Dietary supplement.

DURATEARS OINTMENT. (Alcon) Tube 3.5 Gm.
Use: Ocular lubricant.

DURATEST. (Hauck) Testosterone cypionate 100 mg. or 200 mg./ml. Vial 10 ml.
Use: Androgen therapy.

DURA-TESTOSTERONE. (Pharmex) Testosterone enthanate 200 mg./cc. Vial 10 cc.

DURA-TESTRONE. (Pharmex) Testosterone enthanate 90 mg., estradiol valerate 4 mg./cc.
Use: Androgen therapy.

DURA-TESTERONE FORTE. (Pharmex) Testosterone enthanate 180 mg., estradiol valerate 8 mg./cc. Vial 10 cc.
Use: Androgen therapy.

DURATHATE INJECTION. (Hauck) Testosterone enthantate 200 mg./ml. Vial 10 ml.
Use: Androgen.

DURATHESIA. (Vortech) Procaine base 15 mg., propyl p-aminobenzoate 60 mg., benzyl alcohol 50 mg./cc. Vial 10 cc.
Use: Local anesthetic for proctologic use only.

DURATION MENTHOLATED VAPOR SPRAY. (Plough) Oxymetazoline HCl 0.05%, aromatics. Squeeze Bot. 0.5 oz.
Use: Nasal decongestant.

DURATION MILD 4-HOUR NASAL SPRAY. (Plough) Phenylephrine HCl 0.5% Bot. 0.5 oz.
Use: Nasal decongestant.

DURATION NASAL SPRAY. (Plough) Oxymethazoline HCl 0.05%. Aqueous sol. Squeeze Bot. 0.5 oz., 1 oz.
Use: Nasal decongestant.

DURATESTRIN. (Hauck) Testosterone cypionate 50 mg., estradiol cypionate 2 mg./ml. Vial 10 ml.
Use: Androgen and estrogen therapy.

DURAZYME. (Blairex) Nonionic detergent preserved w/thimerosal 0.004%, EDTA 0.100% in sterile buffered hypertonic salt sol. Bot. 30ml.
Use: Daily cleaner for contact lenses.

DUREZE OTIC DROPS. (Forest) Hydrocortisone 1%, pramoxine HCl 2%, acetic acid 2%, benzalkonium cl. 0.02% parachlorometaxylenol 0.1%. Bot. 10 cc.
Use: Ear therapy.

DURICEF. (Mead Johnson) Cefadroxil. **Tab.:** 1 Gm./Tab. Bot. 24s, 100s. **Cap.:** 500 mg./Cap. Bot. 24s, 100s, 500s. **Susp.:** 125 mg./5 ml., 250 mg./5 ml., 500 mg./ 5 ml. Bot. 50 ml., 100 ml.

DUROLENE OINTMENT. (Durel) Glyceryl monostearate, petrolatum, cholesterol, polyoxyethyl sorb. monolaurate. Jars lb., 6 lb.
Use: Ointment base.

DUROMANTEL CREAM. (Durel) Spermaceti, cetyl alcohol, stearyl alcohol, glycerine, alcohol sulfates, aluminum acetate solution, purified water, methyl and propyl parasepts. Jar lb., 6 lb.

DUROSHAM. (Durel) Soapless shampoo concentrate. Bot. 6 oz., gal.

DURRAX. (Dermik) Hydroxyzine HCl 10 mg. or 25 mg./Tab. Bot. 100s.
Use: Treatment of tension, anti-anxiety and allergic dermatoses.

DUSOTAL. (Harvey) Sod. amobarbital ¾ gr., sod. secobarbital ¾ gr./Cap. Bot. 1000s. (3 gr.) Bot. 1000s.
Use: Sedative.

• **DUSTING POWDER, ABSORBABLE,** U.S.P. XXI. Starch-derivative dusting pow.
Use: Surgical aid (glove lubricant).

DUSTING POWDER, SURGICAL.
See: B-F-I Powder (Calgon).

DUTCH DROPS. Oil of Turpentine Sulfurated.

DUTCH OIL. Oil of Turpentine Sulfurated.

DUVOID. (Norwich Eaton) Bethanechol chloride 10 mg., 25 mg., 50 mg./Tab. Bot. 100s, Unit dose cartons 100s.
Use: Nonobstructive urinary retention.

D V CREAM. (Merrell Dow) Dienestrol 0.01% w/lactose, propylene glycol, stearic acid, diglycol stearate, TEA, benzoic acid, butylated hydroxytoluene, disodium edetate, buffered w/lactic acid to an acid pH. Tube 3 oz. w/applicator.
Use: Treatment of atrophic vaginitis and kraurosis vulvae associated with menopause.

D-VASO. (Dunhall) Pentylenetetrazole 50 mg., niacin 50 mg., dimenhydrinate 25 mg./Cap. Bot. 100s, 1000s.

D-VASO-S. (Dunhall) Pentylenetetrazole 50 mg., niacin 50 mg., dimenhydrinate 25 mg., alcohol 18%, sherry wine vehicle. Bot. pt.

DWIATOL. (Kenyon) Hyoscyamine HBr 0.256 mg., hyoscine HBr 0.0144 mg., atropine sulfate 0.048 mg., phenobarbital 0.5 gr./Tab. Bot. 100s, 1000s.
Use: Antispasmodic.

DYANTOIN CAPS. (Major) Phenytoin sodium 100 mg./Cap. Bot. 100s, 1000s.
Use: Anticonvulsant.

DX [illegible] FOOT POWDER. (Amlab) Zinc undecylenate [illegible]%, Salicylic acid 1%, Benzoic acid 1%, ammonium alum 5%, boric acid 10.5% w/zinc sterate, chlorophyll, talc, kaolin, starch, calcium silicate, oil of wormwood. Cont. 2 oz.
Use: Prevent recurrence of athlete's foot.

DYAZIDE. (SmithKline) Triamterene 50 mg., hydrochlorothiazide 25 mg./Cap. Bot. 100s, 1000s. Unit dose 100s. Patient Packs 100s.
Use: Diuretic, antihypertensive.

DYCILL. (Beecham Labs) Dicloxacillin disodium 250 mg. & 500 mg./Cap. Bot. 100s.
Use: Antibiotic.

DYCLONE. (Astra) Dyclonine HCl 0.5% or 1.0% Solution. Bot. 1 oz.
Use: Topical anesthetic.

• **DYCLONINE HCl,** U.S.P. XXI. Gel, Topical Sol., U.S.P. XXI. 4′-Butoxy-3-piperidinopropiophenone HCl.
Use: Topical anesthetic.
See: Dyclone, Sol. (Astra)

W/Neomycin sulfate, polymyxin B sulfate, hydrocortisone acetate.
See: Neo-polycin HC, Oint. (Merrell Dow)

DYCOLATE. (Amfre-Grant) Dyphylline 200 mg., guaifenesin 50 mg./Tab. Bot. 100s, 1000s.
Use: Bronchodilator.

DYCOMENE. (Hance) Hydrocodone bitartrate ⅙ gr., pyrilamine maleate 1⅐ gr./Fl. Oz. Bot. 3 oz., 1 gal.
Use: Sedative for coughs due to colds.

• **DYDROGESTERONE,** U.S.P. XXI. Tabs., U.S.P. XXI. 9β, 10-α-Pregna-4,6-diene-3,20-dione. Isopregnenone.
Use: Progesterone agent.

DYES.
See: Antiseptic, Dyes. Diagnostic Agents

DYFLEX-200 TABLETS. (Econo Med) Dyphylline 200 mg./Tab. Bot. 100s.
Use: Bronchial asthma.

DYFLEX-400 TABLETS. (Econo Med) Dyphylline 400 mg./Tab. Bot. 100s, 500s.
Use: Bronchodilator for relief of acute bronchial asthma.

YFLEX-G TABLETS. (Econo Med) Dyphylline 200 mg., guaifenesin 200 mg./Tab. Bot. 100s, 1000s.
Use: Treatment of acute and chronic bronchitis.

YFLEX-G ELIXIR. (Econo Med) Dyphylline 100 mg., guaifenesin 100 mg./15 ml Bot. pt.
Use: Chronic or acute bronchitis.

YFLOS. B.A.N. Di-isopropyl phosphorofluoridate. Di-isopropyl fluorophosphonate.
Use: Treatment of glaucoma.
See: DFP

YLATE. Clonitrate.
Use: Coronary vasodilator.

YLINE. (Seatrace) Dyphylline 250 mg./ml. Vial 10 cc.

YLINE-GG LIQUID. (Seatrace) Diphylline 100 mg., guaifenesin 100 mg./5 ml. Bot. Pt., gal.
Use: Anti-asthmatic.

YLINE-GG TABLETS. (Seatrace) Diphylline 200 mg., guaifenesin 200 mg./Tab. Bot. 100s, 1000s.

DYMANTHINE HYDROCHLORIDE. USAN. N,N-dimethyloctadecylamine hydrochloride.
Use: Anthelmintic.

YMELOR. (Lilly) Acetohexamide 250 mg. or 500 mg./Tab. Bot. 50s, 200s, 500s. Blister Pkg. 10 × 10s.
Use: Maturity-onset diabetes.

YMENATE. (Keene) Dimenhydrinate, 50 mg./ml. Vial 10 ml.
Use: Motion sickness.

YNACORYL.
See: Nikethamide, Prep. (Various Mfr.)

YNAPEN. (Bristol) Sod. dicloxacillin. **Cap.:** 125 mg., 250 mg. Bot. 24s, 100s. **Susp.:** 62.5 mg./5 ml. Bot. 80 ml., 100 ml., 200 ml.
Use: Infections due to penicillinase-producing staphylococci.

YNAPLEX. (Alton) Vitamin B complex. Bot. 100s, 1000s.
Use: Dietary supplement.

YNARSAN.
See: Acetarsone, Tab.

YNOSAL. (Mallard) Acetaminophen 130 mg., aspirin 260 mg., caffeine anhydrous 16 mg./Tab. Bot. 100s.
Use: Analgesic.

Y-O-DERM. (Owen) Purified water, isopropyl alcohol, acetone, dihydroxyacetone, FD&C yellow No. 6, FD&C blue No. 1, D&C Red No. 33. Bot. 4 oz.
Use: Water-soluble vitiligo stain.

DYPHYLLINE, U.S.P. XXI. Elixir, Inj., Tab., U.S.P. XXI. 7-(2,3-Dihydroxypropyl) Theophylline, Hyphylline.
Use: Vasodilator, bronchodilator.
See: Brophylline, Inj., Granucaps (Reid-Provident)
Dilor, Prep. (Savage)
Dilorex, Inj. (Tunex)
Droxine, Tab. (Shear-Kershman)
Emfabid TD, Tab. (Saron)
Lardet, Inj. (Standex)
Neothylline, Tab. (Lemmon)
Prophyllin, Oint., Pow. (Rystan)
/Chlorpheniramine maleate, guaifenesin, dextromethorphan HBr, phenylephrine HCl.
See: Hycoff-A, Syr. (Saron)
W/Guaifenesin.
See: Bronkolate-G, Tab. (Parmed)
Dilor-G, Liq., Tab. (Savage)
Embron, Syr., Cap. (Amid)
Emfaseem, Cap., Elix., Inj. (Saron)
Neothylline GG, Liq. (Lemmon)
W/Guaifenesin, ephedrine HCl, phenobarbital.
See: Dilacap, Cap. (Coastal)

DYPHYLLINE GG ELIXIR. (Goldline) Bot. pt.
Use: Bronchodilator.

DYRENIUM. (SmithKline) Triamterene 50 mg./Cap. Bot. 100s, Unit dose 100s; 100 mg./Cap. Bot. 100s, 1000s. Unit dose 100s.
Use: Diuretic.

DYSENAID JR. (Jenkins) Paregoric 5 min., bismuth subgallate 1 gr., kaolin 1 gr., pectin ⅛ gr./Tab. Bot. 1000s.
Use: Diarrhea.

DYSPEL. (Dover) Acetaminophen, ephedrine sulfate and atropine sulfate tablets. Sugar, lactose and salt free. Unit dose Box 500s.
Use: Analgesic for minor muscle pains, cramps and dysmenorrhea.

DYVON. Metriphonate, B.A.N.

E

E-1 OPHTHALMIC SOL. (Alcon) Epinephrine bitartrate 1%, equiv. to 0.5% of base. Drop. Bot. 15 cc.
Use: Wide angle glaucoma.

EACA (Lederle) Epsilon aminocaproic acid.
Use: Antifibrinolytic agent.
See; Amicar (Lederle)

EARDRO. (Jenkins) Benzocaine 15 gm., antipyrine 0.70 gm., glycerol q.s./0.5 oz. Liq. Dropper Bot. 0.5 oz.
Use: Temporary relief of earache.

EAR DROPS. (Weeks & Leo) Carbamide peroxide 6.5% in an anhydrous glycerin base. Bot. 1 oz.
Use: Hygenic ear care.

EAR DROPS (OTC). (Quality Generics) Carbamide, glycerine, propylene, chlobutanol 0.5%. Bot. 0.5 oz.
Use: Softening wax in ear canal.

EAR DROPS (Rx). (Quality Generics) Antipyrine 3.2%, benzocaine 0.85%, glycerol. Bot. 0.5 oz.

EAR-DRY. (Scherer) Isopropyl alcohol & boric acid 2.75% Bot. 1 oz.
Use: Prevention of swimmer's ear.

EAREX EAR DROPS. (Approved) Benzocaine 0.15 Gm., antipyrine 0.7 Gm./0.5 oz. Bot. 0.5 oz.

EAR-EZE. (Hyrex) Hydrocortisone alcohol 1%, pramoxine HCl 1%, parachlorometaxylenol 0.1%. Bot. 15 ml.
Use: Antibacterial, antifungal, analgesic for ears.

EARLY DETECTOR KIT. (Warner-Lambert) In-home self-test to detect hidden blood in the stool.

EAR-OL. (Metro Med) Bot. 0.5 oz., 12s.
Use: Ear solution.

EARTHNUT OIL. Peanut Oil

EASPRIN. (Parke-Davis) Aspirin 15 gr./Enteric Coated Tab. Bot. 100s.

Use: Long-termed palliative treatment of mild to moderate pain, and inflammation of arthritic conditions.

EAST-A. (Eastwood) Lotion-therapeutic. Bot. 16 oz.

EAST-GESIC. (Eastwood) Tab. Bot. 100s.

EASTINIC. (Eastwood) Tab. Bot. 100s.

EAST-IRON. (Eastwood) Tab. Bot. 100s.

EAST-NATA. (Eastwood) Tab. Bot. 100s.

EAST-SERPINE. (Eastwood) Tab. Bot. 100s.

EASTWOOD HEMATINIC. (Eastwood) Tab. Bot. 100s.

EASY-LAX. (Walgreen) Docusate sodium 100 mg./Cap. Bot. 60s.
Use: Fecal softener.

EASY-LAX PLUS. (Walgreen) Docusate sodium 100 mg., casanthranol 30 mg./Cap. Bot. 60s.
Use: Fecal softener & laxative.

EAZOL. (Mallard) Fructose, dextrose, orthophosphoric acid. Bot. pts.
Use: Relief of upset stomach and nausea.

EBV-VCA. (Wampole-Zeus) Epstein-Barr virus, viral capsid antigen antibody test. Tests 100s.
Use: Qualitative and semi-quantitative detection of EBV antibody in human serum.

EBV-VCA IgM. (Wampole-Zeus) Epstein-Barr virus, viral capsid antigen IgM antibody Test 50s.
Use: Qualitative and semiqualitative detection of EBV-VCA IgM antibody in human serum.

ECBOLINE. Ergotoxine.

ECEE PLUS. (Edwards) Vitamin E 200 I.U., ascorbic acid 100 mg., magnesium sulfate 70 mg., zinc sulfate 80 mg./Tab. Bot. 100s.
Use: Vitamin deficiency; fibrocystic breast disease.

• **ECHOTHIOPHATE IODIDE.** U.S.P. XXI. Ophth. Sol. U.S.P. XXI. Ethanaminium, 2-[(diethoxyphosphinyl)-thio]-N,N,N-trimethyl-, iodide. (2-Mercaptoethyl)-trimethylammonium iodide S-ester with O,O-diethyl phosphorothioate. Bot. 100s.
Use: Glaucoma; cholinergic.
See: Echodide, Opth. Sol. (Alcon)
Phospholine Iodide, Pow. (Ayerst)

ECLABRON. (U.S. Ethicals) Guaithylline. 240 mg./15 ml. Bot. 120 ml.
Use: Symptomatic treatment of bronchospasms.

ECLASUFED SR. (U.S. Ethicals) Pseudoephedrine HCl.
Use: Temporary relief of nasal congestion.

ECLIPSE AFTER SUN. (Dorsey) Purified water, oleth-3 phosphate, petrolatum, cetyl esters wax, glycerin, carbomer 934, imidazolidinyl urea, benzyl alcohol, sodium hydroxide. Bot. 6 oz.
Use: Moisturizer.

ECLIPSE LIP AND FACE PROTECTANT. (Dorsey) Padimate 0, oxybenzone. SPF 15. Stick 12×0.15 oz. 24×0.15 oz.
Use: Sunscreen.

ECOLID. Chlorisondamine Chloride, B.A.N.

ECOMYTRIN. Amphomycin, B.A.N.

• **ECONAZOLE.** USAN.
Use: Antifungal.

• **ECONAZOLE NITRATE.** USAN.
Use: Antifungal.

ECONOPRED. (Alcon) Prednisolone acetate 0.125%, 0.25% or 0.5%, benzalkonium chloride 0.01% w/hydroxymethyl cellulose. Droptainer 5 ml., 10 ml.
Use: Ophthalmic anti-inflammatory.

ECONOPRED PLUS. (Alcon) Prednisolone acetate 1%, benzalkonium chloride 0.01%, w/hydroxymethyl cellulose. Droptainer 5 ml., 10 ml.

ECOSONE CREAM. (Star) Hydrocortisone 0.5% in a water-soluble cream base. Tube 1 oz.
Use: Management of allergic dermatoses.

ECOTHIOPATE IODIDE. B.A.N. S-2-Dimethylamino ethyl diethyl phosphorothioate methiodide.
Use: Treatment of glaucoma.
See: Phospholine Iodide

ECOTRIN. (Menley & James) Aspirin 325 mg./Enteric Coated Tab. Bot. 70s, 140s.
Use: Anti-inflammatory, analgesic for minor aches and pains of arthritis and rheumatism.

ECOTRIN MAXIMUM STRENGTH. (Menley & James) Aspirin 7.7 gr./Enteric coated caps. Bot. 50s, 100s.
Use: Analgesic, anti-inflammatory for minor aches and pains of arthritis and rheumatism.

ECOTRIN REGULAR STRENGTH CAPSULES. (Menley & James) Enteric-coated aspirin 5 gr./Cap Bot. 70s, 140s.
Use: Analgesic for minor aches of arthritis pain and rheumatism.

E CREAM. (Image) Vitamin E cream 3000 I.U. Tube [illegible] oz.

ECTASULE III. (Fleming) Ephedrine sulfate 15 mg., amobarbital 8 mg./T.D. Cap. Bot. 100s, 1000s.

ECTASULE JUNIOR. (Fleming) Ephedrine sulfate 30 mg., amobarbital 15 mg./T.D. Cap. Bot. 100s, 1000s.

ECTASULE SENIOR. (Fleming) Ephedrine sulfate 60 mg., amobarbital 30 mg./T.D. Cap. Bot 100s, 1000s.

ECTASULE MINUS III. (Fleming) Ephedrine sulfate 15 mg./Cap. Bot. 100s, 1000s.

ECTASULE MINUS JR. (Fleming) Ephedrine sulfate 30 mg./T.D. Cap. Bot. 100s, 1000s.

ECTASULE MINUS SR. (Fleming) Ephedrine sulfate 60 mg./T.D. Cap. Bot. 100s, 1000s.

ECTIMAR. Etisazole, B.A.N.

ECTOL. (Approved) Chlorpheniramine maleate, pyrilamine maleate, diperodon, hexachlorphene, benzalkonium, menthol, camphor. Tube 1 oz.
Use: Allergy-itching.

ECTYLUREA. B.A.N. (2-Ethylcrotonoyl)urea.
Use: Sedative.
See: Nostyn

• **ECTYLUREA.** 2-Ethyl-ciscrotonylurea.

EDATHAMIL. Edetate ethylenediaminetetraacetic acid.
See: Nullapons (General Aniline)

EDATHAMIL CALCIUM-DISODIUM. Calcium Disod Ethylenediamine tetraacetate.
See: Calcium Disodium Versenate, Amp. & Tab. (Riker)

EDATHAMIL DISODIUM. Disod. salt of ethylene diamine tetraacetic acid.
See: Endrate, Amp. (Abbott)

EDECRIN. (Merck Sharp & Dohme) Ethacrynic acid 25 mg. or 50 mg./Tab. Bot. 100s. I.V. Inj. 50 mg./Vial w/mannitol 62.5 mg, thimerosal 0.1 mg.
Use: Diuretic.

EDECRIN SODIUM INTRAVENOUS. (Merck Sharp & Dohme) Ethacrynate sod. equiv. to 50 mg. ethacrynic acid w/mannitol 62.5 mg., thimerosal 0.1 mg./Vial.
Use: Diuretic.

• **EDETATE CALCIUM DISODIUM,** U.S.P. XXI. Inj., U.S.P. XXI. Calciate (2-), [[N,N′-1,2-ethanediylbis[N-(carboxymethyl)-glycinato]](4-)-N,N′,O,O′,-O″,O‴]-, disodium, hydrate, (OC-6-21)-. Disodium (ethylenedinitrilo)tetraceto calciate (2-) hydrate.
Use: Chelating agent.
See: Calcium Disod. Versenate, Amp., Tab. (Riker)

• **EDETATE DISODIUM,** U.S.P. XXI. Inj., U.S.P. XXI. Glycine, N,N′-1,2-ethanediylbis[N-(carboxymethyl)-, disodium salt, dihydrate. Disodium (ethylenedinitrilo)tetraacetate dihydrate.
Use: Pharm. aid (chelating agent).
See: Disotate, Inj. (Fellows-Testagar)
Endrate, Amp. (Abbott)
Sodium Versenate (Riker)

W/Benzalkonium chloride, boric acid, potassium chloride, sodium carbonate anhydrous.
See: Swim-Eye Drops (Savage)

W/Phenylephrine HCl, methapyrilene HCl, benzalkonium chloride, sod. bisulfite.
See: Allerest Nasal Spray (Pharmacraft)

W/Phenylephrine HCl, benzalkonium chloride, sod. bisulfate.
See: Sinarest, Aerosol (Pharmacraft)

W/Potassium chloride, benzalkonium chloride, isotonic boric acid.
See: Dacriose (Smith, Miller & Patch)

W/Prednisolone sodium phosphate, niacinamide, sodium bisulfite, phenol.
See: P.S.P. IV. Inj. (Reid-Provident)
Solu-Pred, Vial (Kenyon)

W/Sodium thiosulfate, salicylic acid, isopropyl alcohol, propylene glycol, menthol, colloidal alumina.
See: Tinver Lotion (Barnes-Hind)

• **EDETATE DIPOTASSIUM.** USAN.
Use: Pharmaceutic aid (chelating agent).

• **EDETATE SODIUM.** USAN. Tetrasodium (ethylenedinitrilo)-tetraacetate, or tetrasodium ethylenediaminetetraacetate.
Use: Chelating agent.
See: Disodium Versenate (Riker)
Vagisec, Liq. (Julius Schmid)

• **EDETATE TRISODIUM.** USAN. Trisodium hydrogen (ethylenedinitrilo) tetraacetate, or trisodium hydrogen ethylenediaminetetraacetate.
Use: Chelating agent.

EDETIC ACID. B.A.N. Ethylenediamine-NNN′N′-tetraacetic acid.
Use: Chelating agent.
See: Versene Acid

• **EDETIC ACID,** N.F. XVI. (Ethylenedinitrilo) tetraacetic acid.
Use: Pharmaceutic aid (metal-complexing agent).

• **EDETOL.** USAN.
Use: Alkalizing agent.

EDITHAMIL.
See: Edathamil

EDOGESTRONE. B.A.N. 17-Acetoxy-3,3-ethylenedioxy-6-methylpregn-5-en-20-one.
Use: Progestational steroid.

• **EDOXUDINE.** USAN.
Use: Antiviral.

EDROFURADENE. Name used for Nifurdazil.

EDROPHONIUM CHLORIDE. B.A.N. Ethyl-(3-hydroxyphenyl)dimethylammonium chloride.
Use: Diagnosis of myasthenia gravis.

• **EDROPHONIUM CHLORIDE,** U.S.P. XXI. Inj. U.S.P. XXI. Dimethylethyl (3-hydroxyphenyl) ammonium chloride. Ethyl (m-hydroxyphenyl)di-methylammonium chloride. Benzenaminium, N-ethyl-3-hydroxy-N,N-dimethyl-, chloride.
Use: Antidote to curare principles; diagnostic aid (myasthenia gravis).
See: Tensilon Chloride, Vial (Roche)

EDTA.
See: Edathamil (Var. Mfr.)

E.E.S. (Abbott) Erythromycin ethylsuccinate representing mg. of erythromycin activity. **Tab.:** E.E.S. Chewable Tablets 200 mg. Bot. 50s; E.E.S. 400 Filmtab 400 mg. Bot. 100s; **Drops:** 100 mg./2.5 ml. when reconstituted. Bot. 50 ml.; **Granules:** 200 mg./5 ml. when reconstituted. Bot. 60 ml., 100 ml., 200 ml. Abbo-Pac.; **Liquid-200 & 400:** 200 mg./5 ml. Bot. 100 ml., pt.; 400 mg./5 ml. Bot. 100 ml., pt.
Use: Antibiotic.
See: EES Prods. (Abbott)

E.E.S. 400 FILMTAB. (Abbott) Erythromycin ethylsuccinate representing 400 mg. erythromycin activity/Tab. Bot. 100s, 500s. Unit dose 100s.
Use: Antibiotic.

E.E.S. CHEWABLE TABLETS. (Abbott) Erythromycin ethylsuccinate representing erythromycin activity of 200 mg./Chewable Tab. Bot. 50s.
Use: Antibiotic.

E.E.S. DROPS. (Abbott) Erythromycin ethyl succinate representing 100 mg. erythromycin activity/2.5 ml. when reconstituted w/water. Bot. 50 ml.
Use: Antibiotic.

E.E.S. GRANULES. (Abbott) When mixed according to directions, contains erythromycin ethyl succinate representing 200 mg. erythromycin activity/5 ml. of oral suspension. **Granules** Bot. 60 ml., 100 ml., 200 ml, Abbo-Pac.
Use: Infections susceptible to erythromycin.

E.E.S. LIQUID-200 & 400. (Abbott) Erythromycin ethylsuccinate representing 200 mg. erythromycin activity/5 ml. Bot. 100 ml., pt. 400 mg./5 ml. Bot. 100 ml., pt.

EFED. (Alto) Ephedrine sulfate 8.1 mg., secobarbital 16.2 mg./Tab. Bot. 100s, 500s.
Use: Anti-asthmatic.

EFED-II. (Alto) Caffeine 200 mg./Cap. Box 24s. Bot. 100s.
Use: Stimulant.

EFEDRON HYDROCHLORIDE. (Hyrex) Ephedrine HCl 0.6% & chlorobutanol 0.5% w/Sod. chloride, menthol & cinnamon oil in a water-soluble jelly base. Nasal-tipped collapsible tubes 20 Gm.
Use: Shrinkage of nasal mucous membranes.

EFEROL. (Forest) dl-Tocopherol acetate. Cap. (30 and 100 I.U.) Bot. 100s, 500s, 1000s. 200 & 400 I.U. Bot. 50s, 100s, 500s, 1000s. 800 I.U. Bot. 100s, 500s. Parenteral: 200 mg./cc. Vial 10 cc.
Use: Vitamin E therapy.

EFEROL OINTMENT. (Forest) d-alpha Tocopherol acetate 30 I.U./Gm. Tube 1.5 oz. Jar 2 oz., and 1 lb.

E-FEROL SPRAY. (Fellows) Alpha tocopherol equivalent to 30 I.U. Vit. E/cc. Can 6 oz.

E-FEROL SUCCINATE. (Fellows) d-alpha Tocopherol acid succinate, equiv. to Vit. E. 100 or 400 I.U./Cap. Bot. 100s, 500s, 1000s. 200 I.U./Cap. Bot. 50s, 100s, 500s, 1000s. 50 I.U./Tab. Bot. 100s, 500s, 1000s.
Use: Orally, vitamin E therapy.

E-FEROL VANISHING CREAM. (Fellows) Alpha tocopherol. Jar 2 oz.

EFFECTIN TABLETS. (Winthrop Products) Bitoltoril mesylate.
Use: Bronchodilator.

EFFERSYLLIUM INSTANT. (Stuart) Psyllium hydrocolloid 3 Gm. in rounded tsp. (7 Gm.). Sodium free. Bot. 9 oz., 16 oz. Convenient packets 12s, 24s.
Use: Effervescent natural fiber bulking agent for treatment of constipation, diverticulitis, spastic colon and colitis.

EFFICOL COUGH WHIP, SUPPRESSANT, DECONGESTANT. (Block) Phenylpropanolamine HCl 6.25 mg., dextromethorphan HBr 2.5 mg./5 ml Bot. 8 oz.
Use: Cough suppressant/decongestant.

EFFICOL COUGH WHIP, SUPPRESSANT, DECONGESTANT, ANTIHISTAMINE. (Block) Dextromethorphan HBr 2.5 mg., phenylpropanolamine HCl 6.25 mg., chlorpheniramine maleate 1 mg./5 ml. Bot. 8 oz.
Use: Decongestant/cough suppressant/antihistamine.

EFO-DINE OINTMENT. (Fougera) Povidone-iodine ointment. Foilpac 1/32 oz., Tube 1 oz. Jar 1 lb.

EFRICEL. (Softcon) Phenylephrine HCl 1/8%, w/benzalkonium chloride 1:25,000 as preservative; 2.5% w/benzalkonium chloride 1:10,000 as preservative; 10% w/benzalkonium chloride 1:10,000 as preservative. Bot. 15 cc.
Use: Produce pupil dilation.

EFRICON EXPECTORANT. (Lannett) Codeine phosphate 1 gr., phenylephrine HCl 30 mg., chlorpheniramine maleate 12 mg., ammonium chloride 8 gr., Pot. guaiacol sulf. 8 gr., Sod. citrate 5 gr./fl. oz. Bot. 1 pt., gal.
Use: Antihistaminic nasal decongestant.

EFUDEX. (Roche) Fluorouracil. **Soln:** Fluorouracil 2% or 5%, w/propylene glycol, hydroxypropyl cellulose, parabens and disodium edetate, in Drop Dispensers 10 ml. **Cream:** fluorouracil 5%, in vanishing cream base consisting of white petrolatum, stearyl alcohol, propylene glycol, polysorbate 60 and parabens, Tubes 25 Gm.
Use: Treatment of solar keratoses or multiple actinic; 5% in treatment of superfical basal cell carcinoma, when conventional methods are impractical.

EGO. (Coastal) Vitamin E 200 I.U./Tab. Bot. 100s, 500s.

EGRAINE. A protein binder from oats.

• **EGTAZIC ACID.** USAN.
Use: Pharmaceutic aid.

EHRLICH 594.
See: Acetarsone, Tab.

EHRLICH 606.
See: Arspheramine (Various Mfr.)

E-IONATE P A. (Reid-Provident) Estradiol cypionate 5 mg., chlorobutanol 0.5% in cottonseed oil/cc. Vial 10 cc. 1s, 6s, 12s.
Use: Estrogen therapy.

• **ELANTRINE.** USAN.
Use: Anticholinergic.

ELAQUA XX. (Elder) Urea 20% Tube 1.5oz.
Use: Moisturizing cream.

ELASE-CHLOROMYCETIN OINTMENT. (Parke-Davis) Fibrinolysin 10 u., desoxyribonuclease 6666 u., chloramphenicol 100 mg., thimerosal 0.04 mg. as preservative, sucrose and sod. chloride/10 Gm. Tube 10 Gm. Fibrinolysin 30 u., desoxyribonuclease 20,000 u., chloramphenicol 300 mg., thimerosal 0.12 mg./30 Gm. w/liq. petrolatum polyethylene, sucrose, sod. chloride. Tube 10 Gm., 30 Gm.

ELASE OINT. & PWD. FOR SOL. (Parke-Davis) **Pow.:** Fibrinolysin 25 u., desoxyribonuclease 15,000 u., thimerosal 0.1 mg./Vial as lyophilized powder. May be reconstituted with 10 cc. of isotonic NaCl Sol. **Oint.:** Fibrinolysin 30 u., desoxyribonuclease 20,000 u., thimerosal 0.12 mg./30 Gm. Tube. Fibrinolysin 10 u., desoxyribonuclease 6,666 u./10 Gm., thimerosal 0.04 mg. as preservative. Tube avail w/V-Applicator pkg. 6s. Ointment base of liq. petrolatum, polyethylene w/sucrose and sod. chloride. Tube 10 Gm., 30 Gm.
Use: Proteolytic enzyme combination in gynecologic complications.

• **ELASTOFILCON A.** USAN.
Use: Contact lens material.

ELAVIL. (Merck Sharp & Dohme) Amitriptyline HCl. **Tabs.:** 10 mg., Bot. 100s, 1000s; 25 mg./Tab. Bot. 100s, 1000s, 5000s; 50 mg./Tab. Bot. 100s, 1000s; 75 mg., 100 mg./Tab. Bot. 100s; 150 mg./Tab. Bot. 30s, 100s. All strengths in Unit dose 100s. **Inj.:** Vial 10 mg./ml. w/dextrose 44 mg., methylparaben 1.5 mg., propylparaben 0.2 mg./ml w/water for injection. q.s. 1 ml.
Use: Antidepressant..

ELDEC. (Parke-Davis) Vit. A 1667 I.U., C 66.7 mg., B-1 10 mg., B-2 0.87 mg., B-6 0.67 mg., Nicotinamide 16.7 mg., dl-Panthenol 10 mg., Fe 16.7 mg., Ca 66.7 mg., E 10 mg., B-12 2 mcg., Folic Acid 0.33 mg./Kapseal. Bot. 100s.
Use: Vitamin and mineral supplement.

.DECORT 1%. (Elder) Hydrocortisone 1% in a water washable cream base. Tube 0.5 oz, 1 oz.
Use: Relief of inflammatory and pruritic manifestations of corticosteroid responsive dermatoses.

.DECORT 2.5%. (Elder) Hydrocortisone 2.5% in a water washable cream base. Tube 1 oz.
Use: Relief of inflammatory and pruritic manifestations of corticosteroid responsive dermatoses.

DERCAPS. (Mayrand) Vit. A 4000 I.U., D-2 400 I.U., E 200 mg., ascorbic acid 200 mg., thiamine mononitrate 10 mg., riboflavin 5 mg., pyridoxine HCl 2 mg., niacinamide 25 mg., d-calcium pantothenate 10 mg., zinc sulfate 110 mg. magnesium sulfate 70 mg., manganese sulfate 5 mg., folic acid 1 mg./Cap. Bot. 100s.
Use: Nutritional supplement.

DER'S RVP. Red Vet. Petrolatum.
Use: Dermatoses.

.DERTONIC ELIXIR. (Mayrand) Vit. B-1 2 mg., B-2 2 mg., B-6 0.5 mg., Vit. B-12 (as cobalamin conc.) 2 mcg., d-panthenol 5 mg., niacinamide 10 mg./fl. oz. w/pentylenetetrazol, alcohol 13.5%. Bot. pt., gal.
Use: Stimulant tonic.

DO-B & C. (Canright) Vit. C 250 mg., B-1 25 mg., B-2 10 mg., niacinamide 150 mg., B-6 5 mg., d-calcium pantothenate 20 mg./Tab. Bot. 100s, 1000s.
Use: B vitamins and Vit. C deficiencies.

.DOFE. (Canright) Ferrous fumarate 225 mg./Chewable Tab. Bot. 100s, 1000s.
Use: Iron supplement.

DOFE-C. (Canright) Ferrous fumarate 225 mg., ascorbic acid 50 mg./Tab. Bot. 100s.
Use: Iron and Vit. C supplement.

DONAL. (Canright) Pentobarbital sod. 0.25 gr., hyoscyamine sulfate 0.1075 mg., atropine sulfate 0.0195 mg., hyoscine HBr. 0.0070 mg./Tab. or 5 cc. Tab. Bot. 100s, 1000s. Elix. Bot. 1 pt.
Use: Sedative spasmolytic.

DONAL-L.A. (Canright) Hyoscyamine sulfate 0.3225 mg., atropine sulfate 0.0585 mg., hyoscine HBr 0.0210 mg., pentobarbital sod. ¾ gr./Cap. Bot. 50s.
Use: Antispasmodic, sedative spasmolytic.

DONAL-S. (Canright) Hyoscyamine sulfate 0.1075 mg., atropine sulfate 0.0195 mg., hyoscine HBr 0.0070 mg., pentobarbital sod. 32.5 mg./Tab. Bot. 100s, 1000s.
Use: Antispasmodic, sedative spasmolytic.

DOPAQUE. (Elder) Hydroquinone 2% in a tinted sunblocking cream base. Tube 0.5 oz., 1 oz.
Use: Gradual bleaching of hyperpigmented skin conditions and other unwanted areas of melanin hyperpigmentation

DOPAQUE FORTE. (Elder) Hydroquinone 4% in a tinted sunblocking cream base. Tube 0.5 oz., 1 oz.
Use: Gradual bleaching of hyperpigmented skin conditions and other unwanted areas of melanin hyperpigmentation.

DOQUIN. (Elder) Hydroquinone 2% in a vanishing cream base. Tube 0.5 oz., 1 oz.
Use: Gradual bleaching of hyperpigmented skin conditions.

ELDOQUIN FORTE. (Elder) Hydroquinone 4% in vanishing cream base. Tube 0.5 oz., 1 oz.
Use: Gradual bleaching of hyperpigmented skin conditions.

ELDOQUIN LOTION. (Elder) Hydroquinone 2% in lotion base. Bot. 0.5 oz.
Use: Gradual bleaching of hyperpigmented skin conditions.

ELDOVITE. (Canright) Vitamin-mineral formula. Bot. 100s.

ELECAL. (Western Research) Calcium 250 mg., magnesium 15 mg./Tab. Bot. 1000s.

ELECTROCORTIN. Aldosterone. B.A.N.

ELECTROLYTE #48 INJECTION. Pediatric maintenance electrolyte solution. Dextrose 5% in elecatrolyte #48 w/Na 25 mEq., K 20 mEq., Mg 3 mEq., Cl 22 mEq., lactate 23 mEq., H PO_4 3 mEq./L.
Use: Water, caloric, electrolyte source for maintenance in pediatrics.

■ ELECTROLYTE THERAPY.
See: K.M.C., Amp. (Ingram)
Lytren, Ready-to-Use, Liq. (Mead Johnson)

ELEGEN-G. (Grafton) Amitryptiline 10 mg., 25 mg., 50 mg./Tab. Bot. 100s, 1000s.
Use: Antidepressant.

ELEKAP CAPSULES. (Western Research) Oyster shell calcium 250 mg., magnesium oxide 15 mg., Vit. D 133 I.U./Cap. Bot. 1000s, 10 × 10s.
Use: Dietary supplement.

ELEVITES. (Barth's) Vit. A 6000 I.U., D 400 I.U., B-1 1.5 mg., B-2 3 mg., C 60 mg., B-12 10 mcg., niacin 1 mg., E 10 I.U., malt diastase 15 mg., Fe 15 mg., Ca 381 mg., P .172 mg., citrus bioflavonoid complex 15 mg., rutin 15 mg., nucleic acid 3 mg., red bone marrow 30 mg., peppermint leaves 10 mg., wheat germ 30 mg./Tab. or Cap. Bot. 100s, 500s, 1000s.

• ELFAZEPAM. USAN.
Use: Appetite stimulant.

ELITE. (Badger) Fluoride (as sodium free) in 2% soln. Bot. 1 oz., pt.
Use: Oral fluoride.

ELIXICON SUSPENSION. (Berlex) Anhydrous theophylline 100 mg./5 ml. Bot 237 ml.
Use: Bronchial asthma treatment.

ELIXIRAL. (Vita Elixir) Phenobarbital 16.20 mg., hyoscyamine sulfate 0.1037 mg., atropine sulfate 0.194 mg., hyoscine HB 0.0065 mg./5 cc. Liq. pt., gal.
Use: Sedative, antispasmodic.

ELIXOMIN. (Cenci) Theophylline 80 mg., alcohol 20%/15 ml. Bot. Pts., Gal.
Use: Bronchial asthma treatment.

ELIXOPHYLLIN CAPSULES, DYE-FREE. (Berlex) Anhydrous theophylline 100 mg., 200 mg./Cap. 100 mg. Bot. 100s. 200 mg. Bot. 100s, 500s. Unit dose 100s.
Use: Bronchial asthma, chronic bronchitis & chronic obstructive pulmonary emphysema.

ELIXOPHYLLIN ELIXIR. (Berlex) Anhydrous theophylline 80 mg., alcohol 20%/15 ml. Bot. 473 ml., 946 ml., 3785 ml.
Use: Bronchial asthma, chronic bronchitis & chronic obstructive pulmonary emphysema.

ELIXOPHYLLIN-GG ORAL LIQUID. (Berlex) Theophylline 100 mg., guaifenesin 100 mg./15 ml. Bot. 237 ml., 473 ml.
Use: Asthma & bronchospasm associated with chronic bronchitis, emphysema.

ELIXOPHYLLIN-KI ELIXIR. (Berlex) Anhydrous theophylline 80 mg., potassium iodide 130 mg., alcohol 10%/15 ml. Bot. 237 ml., gal.
Use: Excessive tenacious mucus in chronic asthma, severe chronic and allergic bronchitis, chronic obstructive pulmonary emphysema.

ELIXOPHYLLIN SR CAPSULES. (Berlex) Anhydrous theophylline 125 mg. or 250 mg./Sustained Release Cap. Bot. 100s, 500s, 1000s. Unit dose 100s.
Use: Bronchial asthma treatment.

ELLESDINE. (Janssen) Pipenperone.
Use: Tranquilizer.

ELLIMAN'S EMBROCATION LINIMENT. (CMC) Bot. 4 oz.
Use: Muscle pain, chest colds, rheumatism, lumbago.

ELON. p-Methylaminophenol.

ELOXYL. (Elder) Benzoyl peroxide 5% and 10% in gel base. Tubes 2 oz.
Use: Acne vulgaris treatment.

ELPHEMET. (Canright) Phendimetrazine tartrate 35 mg./Tab. Bot. 100s, 1000s.
Use: Anorexiant.

ELPRECAL. (Canright) Vit. A 5000 I.U., D 400 I.U., B-1 3 mg., B-2 2 mg., B-6 0.1 mg., B-12 1 mcg., C 50 mg., E 2 I.U., Ca pantothenate 2.5 mg., niacinamide 15 mg., inositol 5 mg., choline 5 mg., Ca lactate 500 mg., ferrous sulfate 50 mg., Cu 1 mg., Mn 1 mg., Mg 2 mg., K 2 mg., Zn 0.5 mg., S 1 mg./Cap. Bot. 100s.

ELSERPINE. (Canright) Reserpine 0.25 mg./Tab. Bots. 100s, 1000s.
Use: Hypotensive-tranquilizing agent.

ELSPAR. (Merck Sharp & Dohme) Asparaginase 10,000 I.U., mannitol 80 mg./vial.
Use: Acute lymphocytic leukemia therapy.

• **ELUCAINE.** USAN.
Use: Anticholinergic.

ELVANOL. (Du Pont) Polyvinyl Alcohol.

EMAGRIN. (Otis Clapp) Salicylamide, caffeine, aspirin/Tab. Sugar, lactose and salt free. Bot. 60s, 100s.
Use: Analgesic, anti-inflammatory.

EMAGRIN FORTE. (Otis Clapp) Phenylephrine HCl, atropine sulfate, acetaminophen, caffeine/Tab. Sugar, lactose and salt free. Safety Packs 1000s. Bot. 100s, 500s. AidPaks 100s. Unit boxes 8s, 16s.
Use: Analgesic, decongestant for colds, hay fever, sinusitis relief.

EMAGRIN PROFESSIONAL STRENGTH. (Otis Clapp) Aspirin, salicylamide, caffeine. Sugar, lactose and salt free. Safety packs 500s. Medipak 200s, Aidpaks 100s, Unit boxes 10s, 20s. Bot. 1000s.
Use: Analgesic, anti-inflammatory.

EMBECHINE. Aliphatic chloroethylamine.
Use: Treatment of cancer.

EMBEQUIN. Di-iodohydroxyquinoline, B.A.N.

EMBOLEX. (Sandoz) Dihydroergotamine mesylate (DHE) 0.5 mg., heparin 5000 units/Amp. 0.7 ml. Box 20s, 100s.
Use: Prevention of post operative thrombosis and pulmonary embolism.

EMBRAMINE. B.A.N. N-2-(4-Bromo-α-methylbenzhydryloxy)ethyldimethylamine.
Use: Antihistamine.
See: Mebryl (hydrochloride).

EMBRON CAPSULES. (T.E. Williams) Dyphylline 200 mg., guaifenesin 100 mg./Cap. Bot. 100s, 1000s.
Use: Bronchodilator-expectorant.

EMITRIP TABS. (Major) Amitriptyline 10 mg. or 25 mg./Tab. Bot. 250s, 1000s;
50 mg./Tab.Bot. 250s, 1000s;
75 mg./Tab. Bot. 250s;
100 mg. or 150 mg./Tab. Bot. 250s, 1000s.
Use: Antidepressant therapy.

EMBUTRAMIDE. B.A.N. N-[2-Ethyl-2-(3-methoxyphenyl)butyl]-4-hydroxybutyramide.
Use: Narcotic analgesic.

EMCODEINE TABS. (Major) Aspirin with codeine as #2, #3, and #4. Bot. 100s, 500s.
Use: Analgesic.

EMCYT. (Roche) Estramustine phosphate sodium 1[illegible] mg. Cap. Bot. 100s.
Use: Palliative treatment of patients with metastatic and/or progressive carcinoma of the prostate.

EMDOL. (Approved) Salicylamide, para-aminobenzoic acid, sod. cal. succinate, Vit. D-1250. Bot. 10[illegible] 1000s.
Use: Arthritis, rheumatism.

EMEPRONIUM BROMIDE. B.A.N. Ethyldimethyl-methyl-3,3-diphenylpropylammonium bromide.
Use: Anticholinergic.
See: Cetiprin.

EMEROID. (Delta) Zinc oxide 5%, diperodon HCl 0.25%, bismuth subcarbonate 0.2%, pyrilamine maleate 0.1%, phenylephrine HCl 0.25%, in a petrolatum base containing codliver oil/1.25 oz. Tube 1.25 oz.
Use: Hemorrhoid relief.

EMERSAL. (Medco Lab) Ammoniated mercury 5%, salicylic acid 2.5%, castor oil 23%, liquid petrolatum, polyoxyl 40 stearate, polysorbate 80, and water. Plastic bot. 4 oz.
Use: Psoriasis of the scalp, isolated psoriatic lesions, and seborrheic dermatitis.

EMESIS. (Kenyon) Levulose and dextrose 57.6 Gm., orthophosphoric acid 0.5 Gm./100 cc. Bot. 4 oz., pt., gal.

EMERSON 1% SODIUM FLUORIDE DENTAL GEL. (Emerson) Red and plain. Bot. 2 oz.
Use: Aid in prevention of dental caries.

ETAN, 6′,7′,10,11-TETRAMETHOXY-,DIHYDRO-CHLORIDE. Emetine Hydrochloride, U.S.P. XXI.

ETE-CON. (Roerig) Benzquinamide HCl 25 mg. or 50 mg./ml. Citric acid 1%. Vial 50 mg. 10s.
Use: Antiemetic.

ETICS.
See: Apomorphine HCl
Cupric Sulf.
Ipecac Syr.

ETINE BISMUTH IODIDE.
Use: Same as Emetine HCl.

METINE HYDROCHLORIDE, U.S.P. XXI. Inj., U.S.P. XXI. Emetan, 6′, 7′, 10,11-tetramethoxy-,diHCl.
Use: Antiamebic.

ETROL. (Rorer) Oral Soln. containing balanced amounts of levulose (fructose) and dextrose (glucose) with orthophosphoric acid, stabilized at an optimal pH. Bot. 3 oz., 1 pt.
Use: Antinauseant.

FASEEM. (Saron) **Liquid:** Dyphylline 100 mg., guaifenesin 50 mg./15 ml. w/alcohol 5%. Bot. pt. **Cap.:** Dyphylline 200 mg., guaifenesin 100 mg./Cap. Bot. 100s, 1000s. Unident 100s. **Inj.** Vial 10 cc.
Use: Asthma therapy.

-GG. (Econo Med) Guaifenesin 100 mg./5 cc. Bot. Pts.
Use: Expectorant.

MILIUM TOSYLATE. USAN.
Use: Cardiac depressant.

-K-10%. (Econo Med) Potassium 40 meq./30 ml. Bot. Pts.
Use: Potassium chloride supplement.

KO BECAUSE CONTRACEPTOR. (Emko-Schering) Nonoxynol-9 (8% concentration). Contraceptor container w/applicator. Tube 10 Gm.
Use: Vaginal contraceptive.

KO PRE-FIL. (Emko-Schering) Nonoxynol-9(8% concentration). Aerosol Can 30 Gm. Refill 60 Gm.
Use: Vaginal contraceptive.

KO VAGINAL FOAM. (Emko-Schering) Nonoxynol-9 (8% concentration). Kit. Aerosol w/applicator. 45 Gm. Refill 45 Gm., 90 Gm.
Use: Vaginal contraceptive.

MOLLIA-CREME. (Gordon) Cetylalcohol, lubricating oils in water-soluble base. Jar 4 oz., 5 lbs.
Use: Non-soap cleansing agent, treatment dry skin.

MOLLIA-LOTION. (Gordon) Water-dispersable waxes, lubricating bland oils in a water-soluble lotion base. Bot. 1 oz., 4 oz., gal.
Use: Dry, scaly skin, especially over extensive areas.

MPIRIN ASPIRIN TABLETS. (Burroughs Wellcome) Aspirin 325 ml./Tab. Bot. 25s, 50s, 100s, 250s.
Use: Oral analgesic.

MPIRIN COMPOUND. (Burroughs Wellcome) Product discontinued from market.

MPIRIN WITH CODEINE. (Burroughs Wellcome) Aspirin 325 mg. with codeine phosphate 15 mg., 30 mg., 60 mg./Tab. **No. 2** codeine phosphate 15 mg. (0.25 gr.). Bot. 100s, 1000s **No. 3** codeine phosphate 30 mg. (0.5 gr.) Bot. 100s, 500s, 1000s. Dispenserpak 25s. **No. 4** codeine phosphate 60 mg. (1 gr.). Bot. 100s, 500s, 1000s. Dispenserpak 25s.
Use: Orally; analgesic & antipyretic.

EMPRACET WITH CODEINE NO. 3. (Burroughs Wellcome) Acetaminophen 300 mg., codeine phosphate 30 mg./Tab. Bot. 100s, 500s. Dispenserpak 25s.
Use: Narcotic analgesic for moderate to severe pain.

EMPRACET WITH CODEINE NO. 4. (Burroughs Wellcome) Acetaminophen 300 mg., codeine phosphate 60 mg./Tab. Bot. 100s, 500s.
Use: Narcotic analgesic for moderate to severe pain.

EMTRYL. Dimetridazole, B.A.N.

EMTRYL SOLUBLE POWDER. (Salsbury) Dimetridazole 36.4 Gm./18.2 Gm. pouch.
Use: Blackhead treatment for turkeys.

EMULAVE. (CooperCare)
See: Aveenobar Oilated (CooperCare)

EMUL-O-BALM. (Pennwalt) Menthol, camphor, methyl salicylate. Bot. 2 oz., 8 oz., gal.
Use: Topical analgesic.

EMULSOIL. (Paddock) Castor oil. Bot. 2 oz.
Use: Laxative.

E-MYCIN. (Upjohn) Erythromycin **250 mg.**/Tab. Bot. 100s, 500s. Unit-dose 100s. Unit-of-Use 40s. **333 mg.** /Tab. Bot. 100s, 500s. Unit dose 100s.
Use: Antibacterial.

E-MYCIN E. (Upjohn) Erythromycin ethylsuccinate equivalent to erythromycin 200 mg./5 ml. or 400 mg./5 ml. Bot. 500 ml.
Use: Antibiotic.

EMYLCAMATE. B.A.N. 1-Ethyl-1-methylpropyl carbamate.
Use: Tranquilizer; muscle relaxant.
See: Striatran

• **ENALAPRIL MALEATE.** USAN.
Use: Antihypertensive.

• **ENALAPRILAT.** USAN.
Use: Antihypertensive.

ENARAX (Beecham Labs) Oxyphencyclimine HCl 5 mg. or 10 mg., hydroxyzine HCl 25 mg./Tab. Bot. 60s.
Use: Anticholinergic; anti-anxiety.

E-NATURAL. (Quality Generics) Natural Vit. E Cream. Jar 2 oz.
Use: Hand, face and body care.

ENBUCRILATE. B.A.N. Butyl 2-cyanoacrylate.
Use: Surgical tissue adhesive.
See: Histoacryl

ENCAINIDE HYDROCHLORIDE. (Mead Johnson) (USAN)
Use: Investigative: Antiarrhythmic.

• **ENCAINIDE HYDROCHLORIDE.** USAN.
Use: Cardiac depressant.

ENCAPRIN-MAXIMUM STRENGTH CAPSULES. (Proctor & Gamble) Aspirin 500 mg./Cap. Bot. 50s, 100s, 200s.
Use: Arthritis pain relief, antipyretic, analgesic.

ENCAPRIN-REGULAR STRENGTH CAPSULES. Aspirin 325 mg./Cap. Bot. 75s, 100s.
Use: Arthritis pain relief, antipyretic, analgesic.

ENCARE. (Thompson Medical) Vaginal contraceptive suppository w/noroxynol-9 (2.3%).
Use: Contraceptive.

EN-CEBRIN. (Lilly) Vit. A 4000 I.U., B-1 3 mg., B-2 2 mg., niacinamide 10 mg., B-6 1.7 mg., B-12 5 mcg., pantothenic acid 5 mg., C 50 mg., D 400 I.U., Ca carbonate 250 mg., ferrous fumarate 30 mg., iodine 0.15 mg., Cu 1 mg., Mg 5 mg., Mn 1 mg., Zn 1.5 mg./Pulvule. Bot. 100s.
Use: Prenatal vitamin and mineral supplement.

EN-CEBRIN F. (Lilly) Vit. A 4000 I.U., B-1 3 mg., B-2 2 mg., nicacinamide 10 mg., B-6 2 mg., folic acid 1 mg., B-12 5 mcg., Ca pantothenate 5 mg., C 50 mg., D 400 I.U., Ca carbonate 250 mg., ferrous fumarate 30 mg., iodine 0.15 mg., Cu 1 mg., Mg 5 mg., Mn 1 mg., Zn 1.5 mg./Pulvule. Rx Pak 100s.
Use: Vitamin-mineral deficiencies associated with pregnancy and lactation.

• **ENCLOMIPHENE.** USAN.

• **ENCYPRATE.** USAN. Ethyl N-benzylcyclopropane-carbamate.
Use: Antidepressant.

END-AKE ANALGESIC CREAM. (Quality Generics) Methyl nicotinate, salicylamide, histamine dihydrochloride, dipropylene glycol salicylate, capsicum oleoresin. Tube 1.25 oz.
Use: Muscular aches, simple neuralgia.

END-A-KOFF 6-WAY COUGH SYRUP. (Quality Generics) Dextromethorphan 15 mg., guaifenesin 50 mg., chlorpheniramine maleate 2 mg., phenylephrine HCl 5 mg., acetaminophen 120 mg., alcohol 10%/2 teaspoonfuls. Bot. 4 oz.
Use: Cough-suppressant, antihistamine.

ENDAL. (UAD Labs) Phenylephrine HCl 20 mg., guaifenesin 300 mg./Timed Release Tab., dye free. Bot. 100s.
Use: Nasal decongestant.

ENDAL EXPECTORANT. (UAD Labs) Codeine phosphate 10 mg., phenylpropanolamine HCl 5 mg., phenylephrine HCl 5 mg., chlorpheniramine maleate 2 mg., guaifenesin 100 mg., alcohol 5%/5 ml. Bot. Pts.
Use: Common cold therapy.

ENDECON. (Du Pont) Acetaminophen 325 mg., phenylpropanolamine HCl 25 mg./Tab. Bot. 60s.
Use: Decongestant analgesic and antipyretic.

ENDEP. (Roche) Amitriptyline HCl 10 mg., 25 mg., 50 mg., 75 mg., 100 mg. or 150 mg./Tab. Bot. 100s, 500s; Tel-E-Dose 100s; Pak 60s (10 mg., 25 mg., 50 mg.) or 30s (75 mg., 100 mg., 150 mg.); Tray 10s.
Use: Antidepressant.

ENDOBENZILINE BROMIDE. N,N-(dimethyl)-amino-ethyl-α-(bicyclo[2.2.1]-5-neptenyl) mandelate methyl bromide.
Use: Anticholinergic.

ENDOCAINE. Pyrrocaine.
Use: Local anesthetic.

ENDOLOR. (Keene) Butalbital 50 mg., caffeine 40 mg., acetaminophen 325 mg./Cap. Bot. 100s.
Use: Analgesic, sedative.

ENDOJODIN.
See: Entodon

ENDOMYCIN. A new antibiotic obtained from culture of *Streptomyces endus.* Under study.

ENDOPHENOLPHTHALEIN. (Roche) Diacetyldioxyphenylisatin-Isacen-Bisatin.
Use: Laxative.
See: Diacetylhydroxphenylisatin, Prep. (Various Mfr.)

ENDOTUSSIN-NN. (Du Pont) Dextromethorphan HBr 10 mg., pyrilamine maleate 7.5 mg., ammonium chloride 40 mg./5 ml. w/alcohol 4%. Syrup Bot. 4 oz.
Use: Antitussive, antihistaminic.

ENDOTUSSIN-NN PEDIATRIC SYRUP. (Du Pont) Dextromethorphan HBr 5 mg., ammonium chloride 60 mg., alcohol 4%/5 ml. Syrup, Bot. 4 fl. oz.
Use: Antitussive, antihistaminic.

ENDOXANA. Cyclophosphamide, B.A.N.

• **ENDRALAZINE MESYLATE.** USAN.
Use: Antihypertensive.

• **ENDRYSONE.** USAN.
Use: Anti-inflammatory.

ENDURON. (Abbott) Methyclothiazide 2.5 mg./Tab. Bot. 100s, 1000s. 5 mg. Bot. 100s, 1000s, 5000s. Abbo-Pac 100s.
Use: Antihypertensive.

ENDURONYL. (Abbott) Methyclothiazide 5 mg., deserpidine 0.25 mg./Tab. Bot. 100s, 1000s. Abbo-Pac 100s.
Use: Antihypertensive.

ENDURONYL FORTE. (Abbott) Methyclothiazide 5 mg., deserpidine 0.5 mg./Tab. Bot. 100s, 1000s.
Use: Antihypertensive.

ENERJETS. (Chilton) Caffeine 65 mg./Loz. Pkg. 10s.
Use: CNS stimulant.

ENFAMIL. (Mead Johnson) Vit. A 2000 I.U., D 400 I.U., E 20 I.U., C 52 mg., B-1 0.5 mg., B-2 1.0 mg., B-6 0.4 mg., B-12 1.5 mcg., niacin 8 mg., Ca 440 mg., P 300 mg., folic acid 100 mcg., pantothenic acid 3 mg., inositol 30 mg., biotin 15 mcg., K-1 55 mcg., choline 100 mg., Fe 1.4 mg., K 650 mg., Cl 400 mg., Cu 0.6 mg., iodine 65 mcg., Na 200 mg., Mg 50 mg., Zn 5 mg., Mn 100 mg./Qt. Con. Liq. 13 fl. oz., Inst. Pow. 1 lb.
Use: Infant feeding formula containing vitamins and minerals.

ENFAMIL READY TO USE. (Mead Johnson) Ready-to-use Enfamil infant formula 20 kcal./fl. oz. Cans 8 fl. oz., 6-can pack; 32 fl. oz., 6 cans per case.

ENFAMIL WITH IRON. (Mead Johnson) Iron 12 mg./Qt. Pkg. Con. Liq. 13 fl. oz. 24s. Pow. 1 lb. 12s.
Use: Infant feeding.

ENFAMIL W/IRON READY TO USE. (Mead Johnson) Ready-to-use Enfamil with Iron infant formula 20 kcal./fl. oz. Cans 8 fl. oz., 6-can pack; 32 fl. oz. 6 cans per case.

'AMIL NURSETTE. (Mead Johnson) Glass ırmula bottle filled with ready-to-feed Enfamil, 20 cal./fl. oz. 4 fl. oz., 6 fl. oz., and 8 fl. oz., four ottles/sealed carton. W/Iron. Ready to use. Bot. 6 oz. 4s, 24s.

IFLURANE, U.S.P. XXI. 2-Chloro-1,1,2-trifluoroethyl .fluoromethyl ether. Ethrane (Ohio Medical)
se: Anesthetic (inhalation).

GRAN-HP. (Squibb) Vit. A 8000 I.U., D 400 I.U., B-1 .7 mg., B-2 2 mg., B-6 2.5 mg., B-12 8 mcg., iacinamide 20 mg., C 60 mg., E 30 I.U., folic acid .8 mg., Ca 650 mg., iodine 0.15 mg., Fe 18 mg., u 2 mg., Mg 100 mg./2 Tabs. Bot. 100s.
se: Vitamin and mineral supplement for pregnant r lactating women.

NILCONAZOLE. USAN.
se: Antifungal.

NISOPROST. USAN.
se: Antiulcerative.

SYL. (Person & Covey) L-Lysine monohydrochloride 34 mg. or 500mg./Tab. Bot. 100s, 250s.
Jse: Dietary supplement.

NEX OINTMENT. (Ennex) Aloe vera ext. 37.5%. **Skin Oint.:** Zinc oxide 12.5%, coal tar 1.5%, lcohol 4.5%. Tube 1 oz. **Hemorrhoidal Oint.:** Tube 1 oz.
Jse: Anti-inflammatory, astringent, antipruritic.

O. (Beecham Products) Sodium tartrate, sodium itrate. Bot. 3.5 oz., 7 oz.
Jse: Acid indigestion.

NOLICAM SODIUM. USAN.
Jse: Anti-inflammatory, antirheumatic.

OVID. (Searle) Norethynodrel and mestranol. **Tab. 5 mg.:** Norethynodrel 5 mg., mestranol 0.075 mg./Tab. Bot. 100s. **Tab. 10 mg.:** Norethynodrel 9.85 mg., mestranol 0.15 mg./Tab. Bot. 50s.
Jse: Oral contraceptive (5 mg.); endometriosis, hypermenorrhea, production of cyclic withdrawal bleeding (5 mg., 10 mg.).

OVID-E 21. (Searle) Norethynodrel 2.5 mg., mestranol 0.1 mg./Tab. Compack disp. 21s, 6×21. Refills 21s, 12×21.
Jse: Oral contraceptive.

OVIL. (Hauck) Amtriptyline HCl 10 mg./ml. Vial 10 ml.
Jse: Antidepressant.

NOXACIN. USAN.
Jse: Antibacterial.

OXOLONE. B.A.N. 3β-Hydroxy-11-oxo-olean-12-en-30-oic acid.
Use: Treatment of skin diseases.
See: Biosone

PIPRAZOLE. B.A.N. 1-(2-Chlorophenyl)-4-[2-(1-methylpyrazol-4-yl)ethyl]piperazine.
Use: Psychotropic drug.

NPIROLINE PHOSPHATE. USAN.
Use: Antimalarial.

NPROMATE. USAN.
Use: Antineoplastic.

NPROSTIL. USAN.
Use: Antisecretory, antiulcerative.

ENRICH. (Ross) Liquid food with fiber providing complete, balanced nutrition as tube feeding or oral supplement in vanilla or chocolate. Cans 8 oz.
Use: Liquid food with fiber.

ENSIDON. (Geigy) Opipramol HCl.

ENSURE. (Ross) Each 32 fl. oz. contains: Protein 35.2 Gm., fat 35.2 Gm., carbohydrate 137.2 Gm., Vit. A 2500 I.U., D 200 I.U. E 22.8 I.U., K 36 mcg., C 0.15 Gm., folic acid 0.20 mg., B-1 1.5 mg., B-2 1.7 mg., B-6 2.0 mg., B-12 6.0 mcg., niacin 20 mg., choline 0.52 Gm., biotin 0.15 mg., pantothenic acid 5.0 mg., Na 0.80 Gm., potassium 1.5 Gm., Cl 1.36 Gm., P 0.52 Gm., Mg. 0.20 Gm., iodine 0.075 mg., Mn 2.0 Gm., Cu 1.0 mg., Zn 15 mg., Ca. 0.50 Gm., Fe. 9.0 mg./32 oz. W/corn syrup solids, sucrose, corn oil, soy protein isolate, soy lecithin, carrageenan, artificial flavoring. 1000 calories/quart **Bot.:** 8 oz. Gavage set. Case 24s; **Cans:** 8 oz., 32 oz. Case 24s. **Powder:** 14 oz. cans. **Gavage Feeding Set:** 8 oz. Bot.
Use: Dietary supplement providing complete balanced nutrition for full liquid diet, liquid supplement or tube feeding.

ENSURE HN. (Ross) High nitrogen liquid food providing complete, balanced nutrition as tube feeding or oral supplement in vanilla or chocolate. Cans 8 oz., 32 oz.
Use: Nutritional supplement. High nitrogen.

ENSURE OSMOLITE. (Ross)
See: Osmolite, (Ross)

ENSURE PLUS. (Ross) Each 32 fl. oz. contains: Protein 52.0 Gm., fat 50.4 Gm., carbohyrate 189.2 Gm., Vit. A 3560 I.U., D 280 I.U., E 31.2 I.U., K 52 mcg., C 152 mg., folic acid 300 mcg., B-1 2.5 mg., B-2 2.6 mg., B-6 3.0 mg., B-12 9.0 mcg., niacin 30 mg., biotin 224 mcg., choline 500 mg., pantothenic acid 8.0 mg., Na 1.08 Gm., potassium 2.2 Gm., Cl 1.9 Gm., Ca 0.60 Gm., P 0.60 Gm., Mg 300 mg., Mn 2.0 mg., iodine 100 mcg., Cu 1.5 mg., Fe 13.5 mg., Zn 22.5 mg./32 oz. W/corn syrup solids, sodium and calcium caseinates, corn oil, sucrose, soy protein isolate, soy lecithin, carrageenan, artificial flavoring w/1420 calories/quart. Cans 8 oz.
Use: Complete dietary supplement.

ENSURE PLUS HN. (Ross) High calorie, high nitrogen liquid food providing complete balanced nutrition as tube feeding or oral supplement. Cans 8 oz.
Use: High calorie, high nitrogen nutritional supplement.

ENTAB-650. (Mayrand) Aspirin 650 mg./Enteric coated tab. Bot. 100s.
Use: Pain of arthritis and rheumatism.

ENTAMIDE. Diloxanide, B.A.N.

ENTEROTUBE. (Roche) Culture-identification method for enteriobacteriacea ACA. Test Kit 25s.

ENTEX. (Norwich Eaton) Phenylephrine HCl 5 mg., phenylpropanolamine HCl 45 mg., guaifenesin 200 mg./Cap. Bot. 100s, 500s.
Use: Decongestant.

ENTEX LA. (Norwich Eaton) Phenylpropanolamine HCl 75 mg., guaifenesin 400 mg., /T.R. Tab. Bot. 100s.
Use: Long acting decongestant.

ENTEX LIQUID. (Norwich Eaton) Phenylephrine HCl 5 mg., phenylpropanolamine HCl 20 mg., guaifenesin 100 mg./5 cc. Alcohol 5%. Elix. Bot. pt.
Use: Decongestant.

ENTIRE B W/C. (Pharmex) Vitamin B complex with Vitamin C. Cap. Bot. 100s, 1000s.

ENTODON. Propiodal, Entoidoin, Endojodin, 2-Hydroxy-trimethylene-bis-(trimethylammonium iodide)

ENTOIDOIN.
See: Entodon

ENTOZYME. (Robins) Pepsin 250 mg., pancreatin 300 mg., bile salts 150 mg./Tab. Bot. 100s, 500s.
Use: Digestant.

• **ENTSUFFEN SODIUM.** USAN.
Use: Detergent.

E.N.T. SYRUP. (Springbok) Brompheniramine maleate 4 mg., phenylephrine HCl 5 mg., phenylpropanolamine HCl 5 mg./5 ml. Bot. 16 oz., Gal.
Use: Nasal decongestant, antihistaminic.

E.N.T. TABLETS. (Springbok) Phenylephrine HCl 25 mg., phenylpropanolamine HCl 50 mg., chlorpheniramine maleate 8 mg./S.A. Tab. Bot. 100s, 500s.
Use: Nasal decongestant, antihistaminic.

ENTUSS. (Hauck) **Tab.:** Hydrocodone bitartrate 5 mg., guaifenesin 300 mg./Tab. Bot. 100s. **Liquid:** Hydrocodone bitartrate 5 mg., guaifenesin 300 mg./5 ml. Bot. 4 oz., 16 oz. Sugar, alcohol, corn and tartrazine free.
Use: Expectorant.

ENTUSS-D LIQUID. (Hauck) Hydrocodone bitartrate 5 mg., pseudoephedrine 30 mg./5 ml. Sugar, alcohol, corn and dye free. Bot. 16 oz.
Use: Nasal congestion, cough, allergies.

ENTUSS-D TABLETS. (Hauck) Hydrocone bitartrate 5 mg., pseudoephedrine HCl 30 mg., guaifenesin 300 mg./Tab. Bot. 100s
Use: Nasal congestion, cough, allergies.

ENUCLENE. (Alcon) Tyloxapol 0.25%, benzalkonium chloride 0.02%, hydroxypropyl methyl cellulose 0.85%. Soln. Drop-tainers of 15 cc.
Use: Lubricant; ocular prosthesis aid.

• **ENVIRADENE.** USAN.
Use: Antiviral.

• **ENVIROXIME.** USAN.
Use: Antiviral.

ENZACTIN CREAM. (Ayerst) Triacetin 250 mg./Gm. Tube 1 oz.
Use: Athlete's foot & other superficial fungus infections.

ENZEST. (Barth's) Seven natural enzymes and 250 mg., Ca. carbonate/Tab. Bot. 100s, 250s, 500s.

■ **ENZYMES.**
See: Alpha Chymar, Vial (Armour)
Ananase, Tab. (Rorer)
Cholinesterase (Various Mfr.)
Chymotrypsin
Cotazym, Cap. (Organon)
Diastase (Various Mfr.)
Dornavac, Vial (Merck Sharp & Dohme)
Fibrinolysin
Hyaluronidase (Various Mfr.)
Neutrapen, Vial (Riker)
Pancreatin (Various Mfr.)
Papain (Var. Mfr.)
Papase, Tab. (Warner-Chilcott)
Penicillinase (Var. Mfr.)
Pepsin (Various Mfr.)
Plasmin
Rennin (Various Mfr.)
Taka-Diastase, Prep. (Parke-Davis)
Travase, Oint. (Flint)
Tri-Cone, Cap. (Glaxo)
Thrombolysin, I.V. Inj. (Merck Sharp & Dohme)
Varidase, Prep. (Lederle)

ENZYME FORMULA #E-2. (Barth's) Amylase 30 m lipase 25 mg., bile salts 1 gr., wilzyme 10 mg., pepsin 2 gr., pancreatin 0.5 gr., Ca carbonate 4 gr./Tab. Bot. 100s, 250s.
Use: Digestive aid.

ENZYMET. (Forest) Pancreatin 300 mg., pepsin 20 mg., taurocholic acid 40 mg./Tab. Bot. 72.
Use: Indigestion.

ENZYPAN. (Norgine) Peptic potency equiv. to peps 0.009 Gm., amylolytic potency equiv. to pancreat 0.276 Gm. proteolytic potency equiv. to pancrea 0.372 Gm., lipolytic potency equiv. to pancreatin 0.370 Gm., ox bile desic. 0.056 Gm./Tab. Vial 120s, 500s.
Use: Digestive enzyme deficiencies.

• **EPHEDRINE,** U.S.P. XXI. l-α-[1-(Methylamino)-eth benzyl alcohol. (Various Mfr.) (−)-erythro-α-[1-(M thylamino)ethyl]benzyl Alcohol.
Use: Adrenergic (bronchodilator).
See: Bofedrol Inhalant (Bowman)
Racephedrine HCl (Various Mfr.)

W/Procaine.
See: Ephedrine and Procaine, Rx "A", Amp. (Lilly)

W/Pyrilamine maleate, guaifenesin, theophylline.

W/Theophylline, guaifenesin, phenobarbital.
See: Duovent, Tab. (Riker)

EPHEDRINE & AMYTAL. (Lilly) Ephedrine sulfate 2 mg. & Amytal 50 mg./Pulvule. Bot. 100s.

EPHEDRINE HYDROCHLORIDE, U.S.P. XXI. l-a-[1-(Methylamino) ethyl]benzyl alcohol hydrochloride. (−)-erythro-α-[1-(Methylamino)ethyl]-benzyl Alcol hydrochloride. (Various Mfr.); Cryst. Box 1/8 oz., 0.25 oz., 4 oz.
Use: Adrenergic (bronchodilator)

EPHEDRINE HCl W/COMBINATIONS.
See: Airet R, Tab. (Baylor)
Airet Y, Tab., Elix. (Baylor)
Amphed, Cap. (Wolins)
Anoids Rectal, Supp. (Scrip)
Asmadil-S Susp. (Reid-Provident)
Asma-lief, Tab., Susp. (Quality Generics)
Asthmacon, Cap. (CMC)
Bofedral, Liq. (Bowman)
Bronchobid, Cap. (Glaxo)
Brondilate, Tab. (Walker)
Bron-Sed, Elix. (Southern Pharm.)
Calcidrine, Syr. (Abbott)

Ceepa, Tab. (Geneva)
Codel, Syr. (Elder)
Coryza Brengle, Cap. (Mallard)
Co-Xan, Elix. (Central)
Derma Medicone (Medicone)
Derma Medicone HC, Oint. (Medicone)
Dilacap, Cap. (Coastal)
Duovent, Tab. (Riker)
Ectasule, Ectasule Minus, Cap. (Fleming)
Emphysal, Cap. (Douglas)
Epragen, Pulv. (Lilly)
Fedacaps, Cap. (Freeport)
Golacal, Syr. (Arcum)
Hemocaine, Oint. (Mallard)
Histamead E.C., Liq. (Spencer-Mead)
Kie, Tab., Syr. (Laser)
Lardet Expectorant, Tab. (Standex)
Lardet, Tab. (Standex)
Mudrane GG, Tab. (Poythress)
Mudrane, Tab. (Poythress)
Myringacaine, Liq. (Upjohn)
Panaphyllin, Susp. (Panamerican)
Phedral, Tab. (Vortech)
Pyrralan DM, Expect. (Lannett)
Quadrinal, Tab., Susp. (Knoll)
Quelidrine, Syr. (Abbott)
Quibron Plus (Mead Johnson)
Tedfern, Tab. (Ferndale)
Tedral-25, Tab. (Warner-Chilcott)
T.E.P., Tab. (Kirkman)
T-E-P Compound, Tab. (Stanlabs)
Thalfed, Tab. (Beecham Labs)
Theofed, Tab. (Sutliff-Case)
Theofedral, Tab. (Redford)
Theofenal, Susp., Tab. (Spencer-Mead)
Theo-Kaps, Caps. (Scrip)
Theo-Span, Cap. (Scrip)

EPHEDRINE HYDROCHLORIDE NASAL JELLY.
See: Efedron Hydrochloride, Oint. (Hart)

EPHEDRINE and PHENOBARBITAL. (Jenkins) Phenobarbital 0.25 gr., ephedrine HCl 3/8 gr./Tab. Bot. 1000s.

EPHEDRINE-RELATED COMPOUNDS.
See: Sympathomimetic Agents

EPHEDRINE SULFATE, U.S.P. XXI. Caps., Inj., Nasal Soln., Syrup, Tabs., U.S.P. XXI.
(−)-erythro-α-[1-(Methylamino)ethyl]-benzyl Alcohol. Benzenemethanol, α-[1-(methylamino)ethyl]-, sulfate (2:1) (salt). (Various Manufacturers). **Inj.:** (Abbott) 50 mg./1 ml. ampul.
Use: Adrenergic (bronchodilator, nasal decongestant).
Use: Adrenergic, bronchodilator.
See: Ectasule Minus, Jr. & Sr., Caps. (Fleming)
Isofedrol, Isotonic Solution (Blue Line)
Slo-Fedrin, Cap. (Dooner)

EPHEDRINE SULFATE W/COMBINATIONS
See: Asminorel (Reid-Provident)
Asminyl, Tab. (Cole)
Bifed, Cap. (Alto)
B.M.E., Elix. (Brothers)
Bronkaid, Tab. (Winthrop Consumer Products)
Bronkolixir, Elix. (Winthrop-Breon)
Bronkotabs (Winthrop-Breon)
C.P.C. Cough Syr. (Coastal)
Ectasule, Cap. (Fleming)
Ectasule Minus, Cap. (Fleming)
Ephed-Organidin, Elix. (Wallace)
Eponal, Prep. (Cenci)
Fednal, Cream (Blue Line)
Flavihist, Cap. (American Labs)
Hycoff-X, Expect. (Saron)
Iso-Asminyl, Tab. (Cole)
Luasmin, Cap. (Cooper)
Marax DF, Syr. (Roerig)
Marax, Tab., Syr. (Roerig)
Maso-Thylline, Tab. (Mason)
Neogen, Supp. (Premo)
Nyquil, Liq. (Vicks)
Pazo, Oint., Supp. (Bristol-Myers)
Pheno-Fed, Tab. (Wendt-Bristol)
PBZ w/Ephedrine, Expect, Tab. (Geigy)
PBZ Expect. w/Ephedrine and Codeine (Geigy)
Rectacort, Supp. (Century)
Thymodyne, Tab. (Noyes)
Tri-Hist-Cap (Burgin-Arden)
Va-Tro-Nol, Nose Drops (Vicks)
Wyanoids, Preps. (Wyeth)

• **EPHEDRINE SULFATE AND PHENOBARBITAL CAPSULES,** U.S.P. XXI.
Use: Adrenergic (bronchodilator).

1-EPHENAMINE PENICILLIN G. Compenamine.

EPHENYLLIN. (CMC) Theophylline 130 mg., ephedrine HCl 24 mg., phenobarbital 8 mg./Tab. Bot. 100s, 500s, 1000s.
Use: Antiasthmatic, decongestant, sedative.

EPHRINE NASAL SPRAY. (Walgreen) Phenylephrine HCl 0.5%, Bot. 20 ml.
Use: Decongestant.

EPHRINITE NO. 1. (Kenyon) Phenylephrine HCl 5 mg., prophenpyridamine 12.5 mg./Tab. Bot. 100s.

• **EPICILLIN.** USAN. 6-(D-α-Aminocyclohexa-1,4-dien-1-ylacetamido)penicillanic acid.
Use: Antibiotic.
See: Dexacillin

EPICORT LOTION. (Blue Line) Hydrocortisone 0.5% or 1%, benzalkonium chloride 0.1% in a washable base w/petrolatum, methylcellulose, glycerin, polyethylene glycol ethers & perfume. Squeeze bot. 15 cc.
Use: Anti-inflammatory.

EPIFOAM. (Reed & Carnrick) Hydrocortisone acetate 1% g. pramoxine HCl, 1% in base of propylene glycol, cetyl alcohol, PEG-100 stearate, glyceryl stearate, laureth-23, polyoxyl-40 stearate, methylparaben, propylparaben, trolamine, or hydrochloric acid to adjust pH, purified water, butane and propane inert propellant. Aerosol container 10 Gm.
Use: Corticosteroid responsive dermatoses.

EPIFORM-HC. (Delta) Hydrocortisone 1%, iodohydroxyquin 3% in cream base. Tubes 20 Gm.
Use: Dermatological disorders.

EPIFRIN STERILE OPHTHALMIC SOLUTION. (Allergan) Levo-epinephrine HCl 0.25%, 0.5%, 1% or

2%. W/benzalkonium chloride, sod. metabisulfite, edetate disodium, purified water. 0.25% also contains NaCl. Bot. w/dropper 5 ml. or 15 ml. 0.25% available 15 ml. only.
Use: Treatment of chronic simple glaucoma.

■ **EPILEPSY.**
See: Anticonvulsants.

E-PILO. (CooperVision) Pilocarpine HCl 1%, 2%, 3%, 4%, & 6%, epinephrine bitartrate 1%, benzalkonium chloride 0.01%, edetate disodium 0.01%. Bot. 10 cc. w/dropper-tip plastic vial.
Use: Treatment of chronic primary open-angle glaucoma.

• **EPIMESTROL.** USAN. 3-Methoxy-estra-1,3,5(10)-triene-16α, 17α-diol. Stimovul (Organon).
Use: Anterior pituitary activator.

EPIMYCIN A. (Delta) Polymyxin B sulfate 5000 u., bacitracin 400 u., neomycin sulfate 3.5 mg., diperodon HCl 10 mg./Gm. Oint. Tube 0.5 oz.
Use: Antibacterial ointment.

EPINAL. (Alcon) Epinephrine 0.5% or 1% as borate complex w/benzalkonium chloride 0.01%, ascorbic acid, acetylcysteine, boric acid, sod. carbonate. Dropper Bot. 7.5 cc.
Use: Treatment of open-angle glaucoma.

EPINEPHRAN.
See: Epinephrine, Prep. (Various Mfr.)

• **EPINEPHRINE,** U.S.P. XXI. Inh., Soln., Aerosol, Inj., Nasal Soln., Ophth. Soln., Sterile Oil Susp., U.S.P. XXI. (−)-3,4-Dihydroxy-alpha-[(methylamino)methyl]-benzyl Alcohol. 1,2-Benzenediol,4-[1-hydroxy-2-(methylamino)ethyl]-Inhalation. Adnephrine, adrenal, adrenamine, adrenine, epinephran, eptreman, hemisine, hemostatin, nephridine, levorenine, paranephrin, renaglandin, renalina, supra-capsulin, suprarenaline, suprarenin, renoform, renostypticin, renostyptin, styptirenal, supradin, supranephrane, surrenine, takamina, vasoconstrictine, vasotonin, hypernephrin, renaleptine, scurenaline, nieraline.
Pediatric Inj.: (Abbott) Solution 0.01 mg./ml.; 5 ml. single-dose Abboject Syr.
Use: Asthma, hay fever, acute allergic states, cardiac arrest, acute hypersensitivity reactions.
See: Asthma Meter, Aerosol (Rexall)
Asmolin, Vial (Lincoln)
Emergency Ana-Kit (Hollister-Stier).
Sus-Phrine, Inj. (Berlex)
Sus-Phrine, Amp., Vial (Berlex)
Vaponefrin Solution & Nebulizer, Vial (Fisons)
W/Benzalkonium Cl, sodium chloride, sodium metabisulfite.
See: Glaucon, Sol. (Alcon)
W/Pilocarpine HCl.
See: Epicar, Sol. (Barnes-Hind)

EPINEPHRINE, RACEMIC.
See: Asthmanefrin Solution (Norcliff-Thayer)

EPINEPHRINE-RELATED COMPOUNDS.
See: Sympathomimetic Agents

• **EPINEPHRYL BORATE.** F.D.A. Cyclic (-)-4-[l-hydrox 2-(methylamino)ethyl]-o-phenylene borate.

• **EPINEPHRYL BORATE OPHTHALMIC SOLUTION** U.S.P. XXI. (−)-3,4-Dihydroxy-α-[(methyl-amino)methyl]benzyl alcohol, cyclic 3,4-ester w/boric acid.
Use: Adrenergic (ophthalmic).
See: Epinal (Alcon)
Eppy (Barnes-Hind)

EPIOSTRIOL. B.A.N. Estra-1,3,5(10)-triene-3,16β,17β-triol. 16-epiEstriol
Use: Estrogen.
See: Actriol

EPIPEN AUTO-INJECTOR. (Center) Epinephrine injection 1:1000. Delivers dose of 0.3 mg. Pkg. 1s, 2s.
Use: Insect sting emergency.

EPIPHENETHICILLIN. L-(a-phenoxy-propionamido penicillanic acid.

• **EPIPROPIDINE.** USAN. 1,1′-Bis(2,3-epoxypropyl)-4,4′-bipiperidine. Eponate.
Use: Antineoplastic.

EPIRENAN.
See: Epinephrine (Various Mfr.)

• **EPIRIZOLE.** USAN.
Use: Analgesic, anti-inflammatory.

• **EPIRUBICIN HYDROCHLORIDE.** USAN.
Use: Antineoplastic.

EPISONE. (Delta) Hydrocortisone 10 mg. in a base containing steryl alcohol, white petrolatum, mineral oil, propylene glycol, polyoxyl 40 stearate, purified water and perserved with methyl & propyl parabens. Tube 1 oz.
Use: Steroid.

• **EPITETRACYCLINE HYDROCHLORIDE,** U.S.P. XXI.
Use: Antibiotic.

• **EPITHIAZIDE.** USAN. 3-[(2,2,2-Trifluoroethylthio)methyl]-6-chloro-3,4-dihydro-2H-1,2,4-benzothiadiazine-7-sulfonamide 1,1-dioxide.
Use: Hypotensive and diuretic.

EPITRATE. (Ayerst) Epinephrine bitartrate ophthalmic solution 2%, equiv. to 1.1% base w/chlorobutanol (chloral derivative 0.55%), sod. bisulfite, sod. chloride, polyoxypropylene-polyoxyethylene-diol, disodium edetate. Drop. Bot. 7.5 ml.
Use: Treatment of chronic simple (open-angle) glaucoma.

E-PLUS. (Drug Industries) Vit. E 100 I.U., niacin 20 mg. lemon bioflavonoid complex 25 mg., C 50 mg., B-6 2 mg., B-1 5 mg./Tab. Bot. 100s, 500s.
Use: Vitamin E therapy.

MYCIN. (Edwards) Oxytetracycline HCl 250 .../Cap. Bot. 100s.
...e: Antibiotic.

NAL. (Cenci) Theophylline 2 gr., ephedrine ...fate 3/8 gr., phenobarbital 1/8 gr./Tab. Bot. 100s, ...00s.
...e: Asthma.

NAL-G. (Cenci) Theophylline 2 gr., ephedrine sul... e 3/8 gr., phenobarbital 1/8 gr., guaifenesin 1.5 .../Tab. Bot. 100s, 1000s.
...e: Anti-asthmatic.

...OPROSTENOL. USAN.
...e: Inhibitor.

...OPROSTENOL SODIUM. USAN.
...e: Inhibitor.

...OSTANE. USAN.
...e: Interceptive.

...XYAMINOXYTROPINE TROPATE ...YDROBROMIDE. Genoscopolamine HBr, Pellets. ...M.C.)

...EPOXY-3-METHOXY-17-METHYLMORPHINAN-...ONE TARTRATE (1:1) HYDRATE (2:5). Hydroco...ne Bitartrate, U.S.P. XXI.

...3-EPOXY-1αH,5αH-TROPAN-3α-OL(−)-TRO-...ATE (ESTER)HYDROBROMIDE TRIHYDRATE. ...opolamine Hydrobromide, U.S.P. XXI.

...XYTROPINE TROPATE METHYLBROMIDE.
...e: Methscopolamine Bromide. (Various Mfr.)

...AL. (Press) 80% Saturated sol. epsom salts in ...t. form. Jar 0.5 oz., 2 oz.
...e: Drawing ointment.

...KAPRON. Aminocaproic Acid, B.A.N.

...VITE 100. (Standex) Vit. E 100 I.U./Cap. Bot. ...0s.

...VITE 200. (Standex) Vit. E 200 I.U./Cap. Bot. ...0s.

...VITE 400. (Standex) Vit. E 400 I.U./Cap. Bot. ...0s.

...VITE FORTE. (Standex) Vit. E 1000 I.U./Cap. ...t. 100s.
...e: Orally; hyaluronidase for collagen diseases.

...OM SALT.
...e: Magnesium Sulfate.

...OIN.
...e: Phenytoin Sodium (Var. Mfr.)

...AGESIC. (Wyeth) Meprobamate 200 mg., Aspirin ...5 mg./Tab. Bot. 100s. Redi-pak 25s, 100s.
...e: Relief of pain accompanied by anxiety and ...nsion.

...AL. (Searle) Aspartame. **Packets** 0.035 oz. (1 ...n.). Box 50s, 100s, 200s. **Tab.** Bot. 100s.
...e: Low calorie sweetener.

...ANIL. (Wyeth) Meprobamate 200 mg. or 400 ...g./Tab. **200 mg.:** Bot. 50s, 100s, Redipax 25s, ...0s. **400 mg.:** Bot. 100s, 500s. Redipak 100s. ...yseal 400 mg./Tab. Bot. 50s.
...e: Sedative and tranquilizing agent.

...BOLIN-50. (Vortech) Nandrolone phenpropionate ... mg./ml. Vial 2 ml. Box 1s.
...e: I.M.: androgen, anabolic agent.

...GARD. Dichlorvos, B.A.N.

EQUILET. (Mission) Calcium carbonate 500 mg./Tab. Strip packed in 50s, 100s.
Use: Antacid.

• **EQUILIN,** U.S.P. XXI. Estra-1, 3-5 (10), 7-tetraen-17 one, 3 hydroxy-3-Hydroxestra-1,3,5 (10), 7-tetraen-17-one.

EQUIMATE SODIUM SALT. Fluprostenol, B.A.N.

EQUIPERTINE CAPSULES. (Winthrop Products) Oxypertine.
Use: Anxiolytic, tranquilizer.

EQUIZOLE. (MSD AGVET) Thiabendazole: **Pellets:** 13.2%; **Powder:** 10 Gm./oz. **Suspension:** 4 Gm./oz.
Use: Anthelmintic, veterinary medicine.

EQUIZOLE A. (MSD AGVET) **Liquid:** thiabendazole 2 Gm., piperazine 2.5 Gm./oz.; **Powder:** thiabendazole 6.67 Gm., piperazine 8.33 Gm./oz.
Use: Anthelmintic, veterinary medicine.

EQUIZOLE B. (MSD AGVET) Thiabendazole 20 Gm., trichlorfon 18 Gm./package. Powder 0.42 oz. pkg.
Use: Anthelmintic & for bots, veterinary medicine.

EQVALAN. (MSD AGVET) Ivermectin injectable solution, paste: 200 mcg./Kg.
Use: Antiparasitic, veterinary medicine.

ERADACIL CAPSULES. (Winthrop Products) Rosoxacin.
Use: Antigonococcal agent.

ERASEN. (Winston) Phenobarbital 16 mg., Vit. B-1 5 mg./Tab. Bot. 100s, 1000s.
Use: Sedative w/Vit. B-1 therapy.

ERCAL. (Blue Line) Ergotamine tartrate 2 mg./Sublingual tab. 12s.

ERGAMISOL. (Janssen) Levamisole HCl.
Use: Anthelmintic (veterinary).

ERGOBEL. (Wolins) Ergotamine tartrate 0.3 mg., hyoscyamine 0.1 mg., phenobarbital 20 mg./Tab. Bot. 250s, 1000s.

ERGOCAF. (Robinson) Ergotamine tartrate, caffeine. Bot. 100s, 500s, 1000s.

ERGO CAFFEIN. (CMC) Ergotamine tartrate 1 mg., caffeine alkaloid USP 100 mg./Tab. Bot. 100s, 1000s.
Use: Terminating attacks of migraine headaches.

• **ERGOCALCIFEROL,** U.S.P. XXI. Cap., Tab., Oral Soln. U.S.P. XXI. 9, 10-Secoergosta-5,7,10(19),22-tetraen-3-ol, (3β-. Irradiated Ergosta-5,7,22-trien-3-beta-ol. Use: Vitamin D (Antirachitic).
See: Calciferol.
Drisdol, Liq., Cap. (Winthrop-Breon)
Geltabs, Cap. (Upjohn)

ERGOCORNINE. (Various Mfr.) Ergot alkaloids.
Use: Peripheral vascular disorders.

ERGOCRISTINE. (Various Mfr.) Ergot alkaloid.
Use: Vascular disorders.

ERGOCRYPTINE. (Various Mfr.) Ergot alkaloid.
Use: Peripheral vascular disorders.

ERGOLINE-8-CARBOXAMIDE,9,10-DIDE-HYDRO-N-[1-(HYDROXY-METHYL)PROPYL]-1,6-DI-METHYL-,(8β-, (Z)-2-BUTANEDIOATE (1:1) (salt). Methysergide Maleate.

ERGOMAR. (Fisons) Ergotamine Tartrate 2 mg./Sublingual Tab. Pkg. 20s.
Use: Migraine and vascular headaches.

• **ERGOLOID MESYLATES.** U.S.P. XXI. Oral Soln., Tab., U.S.P.XXI. (Lederle) **0.5 mg.:** Dihydroergocornine 0.167 mg., dihydroergocristine 0.167 mg., dihydroergocryptine 0.167 mg./0.5 mg. Sublingual Tab.; **1 mg.;** dihydroergocornine 0.333 mg., dihydroergocristine 0.333 mg., dihydro-ergocryptine 0.333 mg./1 mg. Tab. Bot. 100s, 1000s.
Use: Treatment of elderly.
See: Deapril-ST, Tab. (Mead Johnson)
Hydergine Prods. (Sandoz)

ERGOMETRINE MALEATE.
See: Ergonovine (Various Mfr.)

ERGONAL. (Vita Elixir) Ergot powder 259.2 mg., aloin 8.1 mg., apiol fluid green 290 mg., oil pennyroyal 28 mg./Cap. Bot. 24s.
Use: Oxytocic.

ERGONOVINE. (Various Mfr.) Ergobasine, erolklinine, ergometrine, ergostetrine, ergotocine.
See: Ergonovine Maleate

• **ERGONOVINE MALEATE,** U.S.P. XXI. Inj., Tab., U.S.P. XXI. 9,10-Didehydro-N-[(S)-2-hydroxy-1-methylethyl]-6-methylergoline-8β-carboxamide maleate.
Use: I.V., I.M., orally; oxytocic.
See: Ergotrate Maleate, Preps. (Lilly)

ERGOSTAT. (Parke-Davis) Ergotamine tartrate 2 mg./Sublingual Tab. Vial 24s.
Use: Migraine and cluster headache treatment.

ERGOSTEROL, ACTIVATED OR IRRADIATED.
See: Ergocalciferol, U.S.P. XXI.

ERGOSTETRINE.
See: Ergonovine. (Various Mfr.)

ERGOTAMAN-3′,6′,18-TRIONE,12′-HYDROXY-2′-METHYL-5′-(PHENYLMETHYL)-2,3-DIHYDROXYBUTANEIOATE (2:1) (SALT). Ergotamine Tartrate, U.S.P. XXI.

• **ERGOTAMINE TARTRATE,** U.S.P. XXI. Inj., Inhalation Aerosol, Tab., U.S.P. XXI. Ergotaman-3′,6′, 18-trione, 12′-hydroxy-2′-methyl-5′-(phenylmethyl)-2,3-dihydroxybutanedioate (2:1) (salt). Femergin.
Use: Analgesic (specific in migraine).
See: Ergomar, Tab. (Fisons)
Ergostat, Tab. (Parke-Davis)
Gynergen, Amp., Tab. (Sandoz)
Medihaler-Ergotamine, Vial (Riker)
W/Belladonna alkaloids, acetophenetidin & caffeine.
See: Wigraine, Tab., Supp. (Organon)
W/Belladonna alk. & pentobarbital.
See: Cafergot P-B, Supp., Tab. (Sandoz)
W/Belladonna alk. & phenobarbital.
See: Bellergal, Tab. (Dorsey)
W/Caffeine.
See: Cafergot, Tab., Supp. (Sandoz)
Ergothein, Tab. (Wolins)
W/Caffeine, homatropine methylbromide.
See: Ergotatropin, Tab. (Cole)
W/Cyclizine HCl, caffeine.
See: Migral Tab. (Burroughs Wellcome)
W/1-Hyoscyamine sulfate, phenobarbital.
See: Ergkatal, Tab. (Gilbert)
Ergobel, Tab. (Wolins)

• **ERGOTAMINE TARTRATE AND CAFFEINE SUPPOSITORIES,** U.S.P. XXI.
Use: Vascular headache.
See: Cafergot, Supp. (Sandoz)

• **ERGOTAMINE TARTRATE AND CAFFEINE TABLETS,** U.S.P. XXI.
Use: Vascular headache.
See: Cafergot, Tab. (Sandoz)
Ergocaf, Tab. (Robinson)
Ergo Caffein, Tab. (CMC)
Lanatrate, Tab. (Lannett)

ERGOTHEIN. (Wolins) Ergotamine tartrate 1 mg., caffeine 100 mg./Tab. Bot. 100s, 500s, 1000s.

ERGOT, FLUID EXTRACT. (Various Mfr.) Ergot Gm./cc. Bot. 4 oz., pt.

ERGOTIDINE.
See: Histamine (Various Mfr.)

ERGOTOCINE.
See: Ergonovine (Various Mfr.)

ERGOTRATE.
See: Ergonovine (Various Mfr.)

ERGOTRATE-H.
See: Ergonovine (Various Mfr.)

ERGOTRATE MALEATE. (Lilly) Ergonovine male **Amp.:** (0.2 mg.) 1 ml., Pkg. 6s, 100s; **Tab.:** 0.2 Bot. 100s, 1000s. Blister pkg. 10 × 10s.
Use: I.V., I.M., orally; oxytocic.

▪ **ERGOT-RELATED PRODUCTS.**
See: Cafergot, Supp., Tab. (Sandoz)
Deapril-ST, Tab. (Mead Johnson)
Cafergot P-B, Tab. & Supp. (Sandoz).
DHE-45, Amp. (Sandoz)
Ergonovine (Various Mfr.)
Ergotamine (Various Mfr.)
Ergotrate (Various Mfr.)
Gynergen, Amp., Tab. (Sandoz)
Hydergine, Sub. Tab. (Sandoz)
Hydro-Ergot, Tab. (Interstate)
Methergine, Amp., Tab. (Sandoz)
Trigot, Sublingual Tab. (Squibb)
Wigraine, Supp. & Tab. (Organon)

ERGOZIDE. (Jenkins) Carbolic acid 2.25%, ergot 2.5%, zinc oxide 10%, balsam Peru 1.25%, oil cade 0.3%. Supplied 1 lb.

ERIDIONE. (Eric, Kirk & Gary) Phenindione. 50 mg./Tab. Bot. 100s, 1000s.
Use: Anticoagulant.

ERIODICTIN.
See: Vitamin P & Rutin

• **ERIODICTYON,** N.F. XVI. Flext., Aromatic Syrup N.F. XVI.
Use: Pharmaceutic aid (flavor)
See: Vitamin P & Rutin

E-R-O. (Scherer) Propylene glycol and glycerol. w/dropper tip 15 cc.
Use: For softening and facilitating the removal ear wax.

INE. (Approved) Hexachlorophene, benzocaine,)d liver oil, allantoin, boric acid, lanolin. ıbe 1.5 oz.
se: Burn and first aid remedy.

C. (Parke-Davis) Erythromycin 250 mg./Cap. con- ining enteric-coated pellets. Bot. 100s, 500s. Unit se 100s.
se: Antibiotic.

CETTE. (Ortho) Erythromycin 20 mg./ml. Pkg. 60 edgets.
se: Topical control of acne vulgaris.

DERM. (Abbott) Erythromycin topical solution %. Bot. 60 ml.
se: Treatment of acne.

MAX. (Herbert) Erythromycin 2%. Bot. 4 oz.
se: Topical control of acne vulgaris.

PAR. (Parke-Davis) Erythromycin stearate 250 ıg./Filmseal, Bot. 100s, 500s, Unit dose 100s. 500 ıg./Filmseal. Bot. 100s.
se: Antibiotic.

PED. (Abbott) Erythromycin ethylsuccinate for ral suspension representing erythromycin activity f 400 mg./5 ml. Bot. 60, 100, 200 and 5 ml. unit ose.
se: Antibiotic.

-TAB. (Abbott) Erythromycin enteric coated 250 33 mg. or 500 mg./Tab. **250 mg.:** Bot. 100s,)0s, Unit Dose 100s. **333 mg.:** Bot. 100s. Units ose 100s. **500 mg.:** Bot. 100s. Unit Dose 100s.
se: Antibiotic.

RYTHRITYL TETRANITRATE, DILUTED, U.S.P. XI.
se: Coronary vasodilator.

RYTHRITYL TETRANITRATE TABLETS, U.S.P. XI. (Various Mfr.) Erythritol, erythrol tetranitrate, troerythrite, tetranitrin, tetranitrol.
se: Coronary vasodilator.
ee: Anginar, Tabs. (Pasadena Research Labs.)
Cardilate, Tab. (Burroughs Wellcome)
henobarbital.
ee: Cardilate-P, Tab. (Burroughs Wellcome)

THROCIN. (Abbott) Erythromycin. **Erythrocin thylsuccinate:** EES products are supplied as hewable tablets, drops, granules, Filmtab tablets, quids. **Erythrocin Lactobionate:** Injectables. **rythrocin stearate:** Filmtab tablets, 250 mg., 500 ıg. Bot. 100s.
se: Antibiotic.

THROCIN LACTOBIONATE, I.V. (Abbott) *rythromycin lactobionate,* 500 mg./vial w/benzyl cohol 90 mg.; 1 Gm./vial w/benzyl alcohol 180 ıg. Pkg. 5 & 25 vials.
se: Antibiotic.

THROCIN LACTOBIONATE PIGGYBACK. Abbott) Erythromycin lactobionate for injection, 500 ıg./dispensing vial. 5 mg./ml. of erythromycin after econstitution w/90 mg. benzyl alcohol. Sterile ophilized powder in 100 ml. dispensing vial.
se: I.V. antibiotic.

ERYTHROCIN STEARATE. (Abbott) Erythromycin stearate 250 mg./Tab. Bot. 20s, 100s, 500s. Abbo-Pac 100s; 500 mg. Bot. 100s.
Use: Antibiotic.

• **ERYTHROMYCIN,** U.S.P. XXI. Caps., Oint., Ophth. Oint., Tab., Topical Sol., U.S.P. XXI. An antibiotic from *Streptomyces erythreus.* (Upjohn) Tab.: 100 mg., Bot. 100s; 250 mg., peach color. Bot. 25s, 100s.
Use: Antibiotic.
See: Dowmycin E, Tab. (Merrell Dow)
E-Mycin, Tab. (Upjohn)
Erymax, Sol. (Herbert)
EryDerm, Sol. (Abbott)
Erythrocin, Prep. (Abbott)
Erythromycin Base Filmtab. (Abbott)
Ethril 500, Tab. (Squibb)
Ilotycin, Prep. (Dista)
Robimycin, Tab. (Robins)
RP-Mycin, Tab. (Reid-Provident)

ERYTHROMYCIN BASE FILMTAB. (Abbott) Erythromycin base 250 mg. Bot. 100s. Abbo-Pac 100s. 500 mg./Tab. Bot. 100s.
Use: Antibiotic.

• **ERYTHROMYCIN ESTOLATE,** U.S.P. XXI. Cap., Oral Susp., for Oral Susp., Tab., U.S.P. XXI. Supp., Erythromycin 2′-propionate dodecyl sulfate. Lauryl sulfate salt of the propionic acid ester of erythromycin.
Use: Antibiotic
See: Ilosone, Prep. (Dista)

ERYTHROMYCIN ESTOLATE. B.A.N. Erythromycin propionyl ester lauryl sulfate.
Use: Antibiotic.
See: Ilosone

• **ERYTHROMYCIN ETHYLSUCCINATE,** U.S.P. XXI. Inj., Tabs., for Oral Susp., Oral Susp., Sterile, U.S.P. XXI. Erythromycin 2′-(Ethylsuccinate).
Use: Antibiotic.
See: E.E.S. Prods. (Abbott)
E-mycin E, Liq. (Upjohn)
Pediamycin Prods. (Ross)
Pediazole, Liq. (Ross)
Wyamycin-E, Liq. (Wyeth)

• **ERYTHROMYCIN ETHYLSUCCINATE AND SULFISOXAZOLE ACETYL FOR ORAL SUSPENSION,** U.S.P. XXI.
Use: Antibiotic, anti-infective
See: Pediazole, Susp. (Ross)

• **ERYTHROMYCIN GLUCEPTATE, STERILE,** U.S.P. XXI.
Use: Antibacterial.
See: Ilotycin Gluceptate, Amp. (Lilly)

ERYTHROMYCIN GLUCOHEPTONATE.
See: Erythromycin Gluceptate, U.S.P. XXI.
Ilotycin Glucoheptonate, Amp. (Dista)

• **ERYTHROMYCIN LACTOBIONATE FOR INJECTION,** U.S.P. XXI.
Use: Antibacterial.
See: Erythrocin Lactobionate, Vial (Abbott)

ERYTHROMYCIN 2′-PROPIONATE DODECYL SULFATE. Erythromycin Estolate, U.S.P. XXI.

ERYTHROMYCIN PROPIONATE LAURYL SULFATE.
See: Erthromycin Estolate
Ilosone, Prep. (Dista)

• **ERYTHROMYCIN STEARATE,** U.S.P. XXI. Tabs., for Oral Susp., U.S.P. XXI.
Use: Antibacterial.
See: Dowmycin-E, Tab. (Merrell Dow)
Erythrocin Stearate Prods. (Abbott)
Erypar Filmseal, Tab. (Parke-Davis)
Ethril, Tab. (Squibb)
SK-Erthromycin, Tab. (SmithKline)
Wyamycin-S, Tab. (Wyeth)

ERYTHROMYCIN SULFATE.
Use: Antibacterial.

• **ERYTHROSINE SODIUM,** U.S.P. XXI. Topical Sol., Soluble Tab., U.S.P. XXI.
Use: Diagnostic aid (dental disclosing agent).

ESANGEN. (Blue Line) Testosterone cypionate 50 mg., estradiol cypionate 2 mg., chlorobutanol 0.5% in cottonseed oil/cc. Vial 10 cc.

ESBATAL SULPHATE. Bethanidine, B.A.N.

ESCLABRON. Guaithylline.
Use: Antiasthmatic.

ESCOT. (Reid-Provident) Bismuth aluminate 100 mg., magnesium trisilicate 160 mg., aluminum hydroxide and magnesium carbonate coprecipitate 130 mg./Cap. Bot. 100s.
Use: Antacid for heartburn, sour stomach, acid indigestion.

ESERDINE FORTE TABS. (Major) Methclothiazide w/reserpine 0.5 mg./Tab. Bot. 100s.
Use: Antihypertensive.

ESERDINE TABS. (Major) Methyclothiazide w/reserpine 0.25 mg/Tab. Bot. 100s, 250s.
Use: Antihypertensive.

ESERINE. (physostigmine as alkaloid, salicylate or sulfate salt).

ESERINE SALICYLATE (PHYSOSTIGMINE). (Alcon) 0.5%. Steri-Unit 2 cc. 24s (Mesco) 0.5%. Bot. 3.5 Gm.

ESERINE SULFATE STERILE OPHTHALMIC OINTMENT. (CooperVision) Eserine sulfate 0.25%. Tube 3.5 Gm.
Use: Treatment of primary glaucoma.

ESERINE SULFATE. Physostigmine sulfate. (Robinson) 0.25%. Tube ⅛ oz.
Use: Ophthalmic ointment for treatment of primary glaucoma.

ESGIC CAPSULES. (Gilbert) Butalbital 50 mg., caffeine 40 mg., acetaminophen 325 mg./Cap. Bot. 100s.
Use: Analgesic, sedative.

ESGIC TABLETS. (Gilbert) Butalbital 50 mg., caffeine 40 mg., acetaminophen 325 mg./Tab. Bot. 100s.
Use: Analgesic, sedative.

ESIDRIX. (Ciba) Hydrochlorothiazide 25 mg., or 50 mg./Tab. Bot. 100s, 1000s; Accu-Pak 25 mg., 50 mg. Blister units 100s; Consumer Packs 25 mg. in 100s, 50 mg. in 30s, 60s; 100 mg. Tab. Bot. 100s.
Use: Diuretic and antihypertensive.
W/Apresoline.
See: Apresoline-Esidrix, Tab. (Ciba)

ESIMIL. (Ciba) Hydrochlorothiazide 25 mg., guanethidine monosulfate 10 mg./Tab. Bot. 100s Consumer Packs of 100s; Accu-Pak 100s.
Use: Diuretic, hypertensive.

ESKACEF. Cephradine, B.A.N.

ESKALITH. (SmithKline) Lithium carbonate **Cap:** 300 mg./Cap. Bot. 100s, 500s; **Tab:** 300 mg./Tab. (scored). Bot. 100s.
Use: Control of manic episodes in manic-depressive psychosis.

ESKALITH CR. (SmithKline) Lithium carbonate 450 mg./Controlled Release Tab. Bot. 100s.
Use: Treatment of manic episodes of manic-depressive illness.

• **ESMOLOL HYDROCHLORIDE.** USAN.
Use: Antiadrenergic.

E-SON. (Eastwood) Bot. 100s.

ESOPHOTRAST. (Armour) Barium sulfate 560 mg./Gm. in cream base containing suspending agents and flavoring. Tube 1 lb. Ctn. 12s.
Use: Diagnostic agent for use in radiologic examination of esophagus.

ESOTERICA DRY SKIN TREATMENT LOTION. (Norcliff Thayer) Bot. 13 fl. oz.
Use: Skin moisturizer.

ESOTERICA MEDICATED FADE CREAM FACIAL. (Norcliff Thayer) Hydroquinone 2% padimate O 3.3%, oxybenzone 2.5% in cream base. Jar 3 oz.
Use: Skin lightener.

ESOTERICA MEDICATED FADE CREAM, FORTIFIED. (Norcliff Thayer) Hydroquinone 2%, padimate O 3.3%, oxybenzone 2.5% cream. Unscented jar 3 oz., scented jar 3 oz.
Use: Skin lightener.

ESOTERICA MEDICATED FADE CREAM, REGULAR. (Norcliff Thayer) Hydroquinone 2% cream. Jar 3 oz.
Use: Skin lightener.

ESPERSON. Desoxymethasone, B.A.N.

ESPOTABS. (Combe) Yellow phenolphthalein/Tab. Bot. 6s, 20s, 50s, 85s.
Use: Laxative.

E.S.P.R. (Wolins) N-acetyl-aminophenol 1.5 gr., salicylamide, aspirin, caffeine/Tab. Bot. 100s, 1000s.

• **ESPROQUIN HYDROCHLORIDE.** USAN.
Use: Adrenergic.

ESSENTIAL-8. Liquid amino acid protein supplement.
Use: Protein supplement.
See: Essential-8, Liquid (Medics)
Vivonex Diets, Liquid (Norwich Eaton)

ESTAQUA "S." (Kay) Estrogenic substances 2 mg./cc. Vial 30 cc.

ESTAR. (Westwood) Tar equivalent to 5% Coal Tar U.S.P. in a hydro-alcoholic gel w/alcohol 13.8%. Tube 3 oz.
Use: All tar responsive dermatoses including psoriasis & eczema.

• **ESTERIFILCON A.** USAN.
Use: Contact lens material.

ESTERIGYN. (Pasadena Research) Esterified estrogen 0.625 mg., 1.25 mg./Tab. Bot. 100s, 500s.

ILBEN.
ee: Diethylstilbestrol Dipropionate. (Various Mfr.)
INYL. (Schering) Ethinyl estradiol. Tab., coated .02 mg. & 0.05 mg.) Bot. 100s, 250s; Tab. (0.5 g.) Bot. 100s.
se: Orally; estrogen therapy.
IVIN. (Alcon) A specially processed aq. infusion *Rosa gallica* (rose petals). Bot. w/dropper 0.25 oz.
se: To relieve ocular symptoms of hay fever.
OLATE. Erythromycin.
ee: Erythromycin Propionate Lauryl Sulfate
OMUL-M LIQUID. (Riker) Aluminum hydroxide-agnesium carbonate 918 mg./15 ml. Bot. 12 oz.
OMUL-M TABLETS. (Riker) Aluminum hydroxide-agnesium carbonate 500 mg., magnesium oxide 5 mg./Tab. Bot. 100s.
OPEN.
ee: Benzylpenicillin 2-diethylaminoethyl ester HI
RA-C INJECTION. (Amfre-Grant) Estradiol cypion-e 5 mg./ml. Vial 10 ml.
se: Hormone.
RA-V. (Amfre-Grant) Estradiol vaerate 20 mg./ml. al 10 ml.
se: Hormone.
RACE. (Mead Johnson) 17β-Estradiol Micronized. or 2 mg./Tab. Bot. 100s.
se: Estrogen replacement therapy.
RACE VAGINAL CREAM. (Mead Johnson) 17β stradiol 0.1 mg./Gm. Tube 42.5 Gm.
se: Estrogen replacement therapy.
RACON. (Freeport) Conjugated estrogens 1.25 g./Tab. Bot. 1000s.
se: Menopausal syndrome.
RA-D. (Seatrace) Estradiol cypionate 5 mg./ml. Vial) cc.
TRADIOL, U.S.P. XXI. Pellets, Sterile Susp., Tab., .S.P. XXI. Estra-1,3,5(10)-triene-3,17-β-diol. Beta-stradiol, agofollin, dihydroxyestrin, dihydrotheelin, ynergon, gynoestryl. The form now known to be hysiologically active is the "beta" form rather than e "alpha" form.
se: Estrogen-replacement therapy.
ee: Aquagen, Vial, Aq. (Remsen)
Estrace, Tab. (Mead Johnson)
Femogen, Susp., Tab. (Fellows-Testagar)
Progynon, Pellets (Schering)
striol and estrone.
ee: Estro Plus, Tab., Vial (Rocky Mtn.)
Hormonin No. 1 & 2, Tab. (Carnrick)
strone, estriol.
ee: Sanestro Tab. (Sandia)
strone, pot. estrone sulfate.
ee: Tri-Estrin, Inj. (Keene)
rogesterone, testosterone, procaine HCl, procaine ase.
ee: Horm-Triad, Vial. (Bell)
esterone.
ee: Testrolix, Inj. (Vortech)
estosterone & chlorobutanol in cottonseed oil.
ee: Depo-Testadiol, Vial (Upjohn)

ESTRADIOL BENZOATE. 1,3,5(10)-Estratriene-3,17-β-diol 3-Benzoate. Estra-1,3,5,(10)-triene-3,17-diol,(17β)-,3-benzoate. Beta-estradiol benzoate, benzogynoestryl, benzoestrofol difolliculin, follicormon, follidrin. Estradiol 3-Benzoate. (Various Mfr.)
Use: Estrogen therapy.
ESTRADIOL CYCLOPENTYLPROPIONATE, Estradiol 17-beta(3-cyclopentyl)propionate. Estradiol Cypionate, U.S.P. XXI.
W/Testosterone cypionate.
See: Depo-Testadiol, Vial (Upjohn)
• **ESTRADIOL CYPIONATE,** U.S.P. XXI. Inj. U.S.P. XXI. Estradiol 17-β-(3-Cyclopentyl)propionate Estradiol 17-cyclopentanepropionate. Estra-1,3,5-(10)-triene-3,17-diol,(17 beta)-, 17-cyclopentane-propanoate.
Use: Estrogen.
See: Estradiol cyclopentylpropionate
Dep-Estradiol, Inj. (Rocky Mtn.)
Depo-Estradiol Cypionate, Inj. (Upjohn)
Depogen, Inj. (Hyrex)
D-Est, Inj. (Burgin-Arden)
Estra-C, Inj. (Amfre-Grant)
Estra-Ionate, Inj. (Tunex)
Estro-Cyp, Vial (Keene)
Estrogen-810, Inj. (Blue Line)
Estroject-L.A., Vial (Mayrand)
Hormogen Depot, Inj. (Mallard)
Span-F, Inj. (Scrip)
W/Testosterone cypionate.
See: D-Diol, Inj. (Burgin-Arden)
Dep-Tesestro, Inj. (ICN)
Dep-Testradiol, Inj. (Rocky Mtn.)
Duo-Cyp, Vial (Keene)
Duo-Ionate, Inj. (Tunex)
Duracrine, Inj. (Ascher)
Estran-C, Inj. (Amfre-Grant)
Menoject, L.A., Vial (Mayrand)
T.E. Ionate P.A., Inj. (Reid-Provident)
W/Testosterone cypionate, chlorobutanol.
See: Depo-Testadiol (Upjohn)
Esagen, Sol. (Blue Line)
Span F.M., Inj. (Scrip)
T.E. Ionate P.A., Inj. (Reid-Provident)
Testadiale-Depo, Vial (Kay)
ESTRADIOL DIPROPIONATE. Estra-1,3,5(10)-triene-3,17 β-diol dipropionate. Ovocyclin Dipropionate.
• **ESTRADIOL ENANTHATE.** USAN. Estradiol 17-enanthate.
ESTRADIOL, ETHINYL.
See: Ethinyl Estradiol
ESTRADIOL MONOBENZONATE.
See: Estradiol Benzoate
ESTRADIOL PHOSPHATE.
See: Estradurin, Secule (Ayerst)
• **ESTRADIOL UNDECYLATE.** USAN. Estradiol 17-undecanoate.
Use: Estrogen.
See: Delestrec

• **ESTRADIOL VALERATE,** U.S.P. XXI. Inj., U.S.P. XXI. Estra-1,3,5(10)-triene-3,17-diol (17β)-,17-pentano-ate. Estradiol 17-valerate.
Use: Estrogen.
See: Ardefem 10,20, Inj. (Burgin-Arden)
Delestrogen, Vial (Squibb)
Depogen, Inj. (Sig)
Dioval, Preps. (Keene)
Duratrad, Inj. (Ascher)
Estate, Inj. (Savage)
Estra-L, Inj. (Pasadena Research)
Estra-V, Inj. (Amfre-Grant)
Estraval, vial (Kay)
Estra-Vate, Inj. (Tunex)
Estravel-P.A., Estraval-2X, IM (Reid-Provident)
Femogen,L.A., Inj. (Fellows-Testagar)
Repo-Estro Med., Vial (Medics)
Retestrin, Inj. (Rocky Mtn.)
Span-Est, Inj. (Scrip)
Valergen, Inj. (Hyrex)
W/Benzyl alcohol.
See: Estate, Vial (Savage)
Reposo E-40., Vial (Paddock)
W/Chlorobutanol.
See: Estraval, Vial (Kay)
W/Hydroxyprogesterone caproate.
See: Hy-Gestradol, Inj. (Pasadena-Research)
Hylutin-Est, Inj. (Hyrex)
W/Testosterone cypionate.
See: Depo-Testadiol, Inj. (Upjohn)
W/Testosterone enanthate.
See: Ardiol 90/4, 180/8, Inj. (Burgin-Arden)
Bi-Nate, Inj. (Tunex)
Deladumone, Vial (Squibb)
Delatestadiol, Vial (Dunhall)
Duoval-P.A., I.M. (Reid-Provident)
Estran-E.V., Inj. (Amfre-Grant)
Estra-Testrin, Inj. (Pasadena Research)
Repo-Duo Med., Vial (Medics)
Retadiamone, Inj. (Rocky Mtn.)
Span-Est-Test 4, Inj. (Scrip)
Teev, Inj. (Keene)
Tesogen L.A., Inj. (Sig)
Testanate, Vial (Kenyon)
Valertest, Inj. (Hyrex)
W/Testosterone enanthate, benzyl alcohol, sesame oil.
See: Duogen L.A., Inj. (Vortech)
Repose-TE. (Paddock)
Testadiate, Vial (Kay)

ESTRADOL. (Kenyon) Ethinyl estradiol. **No. 1:** 0.02 mg./Tab. **No. 2:** 0.05 mg./Tab. Bot.
Use: Estrogen therapy.

ESTRADURIN. (Ayerst) Polyestradiol phosphate. Amp. (40 mg.) w/2 ml. sterile diluent. W/polyestradiol phosphate 40 mg., phenylmercuric nitrate 0.02 mg., sod. phosphate 5.2 mg., niacinamide 25 mg., propylene glycol 4 mg.
Use: I.M., treatment of prostatic carcinoma.

ESTRAGUARD. (Reid-Provident) Dienestrol cream 0.01%. Tube 3 oz.
Use: Estrogen vaginal therapy.

ESTRA-IONATE. (Tunex) Estradiol cypionate 5 mg./ w/chlorobutanol 0.5%, cottonseed oil. Vial 5 cc
Use: Long acting progestational agent.

ESTRA-L. (Pasadena Research) Estradiol valerate in sesame oil 20 mg. Vial 10 cc. 40 mg./ml. Vial 5 cc.

ESTRALUTIN.
See: Relutin (Reid-Provident)

• **ESTRAMUSTINE.** USAN. Estradiol 3-bis (2-chl ethyl) carbamate 17-(dihydrogen phospha disodium salt.
Use: Antineoplastic agent.
See: Emcyt, Cap. (Roche)

• **ESTRAMUSTINE PHOSPHATE SODIUM.** USAN.
Use: Antineoplastic.

ESTRAN-C. (Amfre-Grant) Testosterone cypionate mg., estradiol cypionate 2 mg./ml. Vial 10 ml.
Use: Hormone.

ESTRAN-E.V. (Amfre-Grant) Testosterone enant 90 mg., estradiol valerate 4 mg./ml. Vial 10 ml.
Use: Hormone.

ESTRATAB. (Reid-Provident) **Tab.:** Esterified estrog principally sodium estrone sulfate 0.625 mg., 1.2 mg. or 2.5 mg./Tab. Bot. 100s, 1000s. 0.3 mg./Tab. Bot. 100s.
Use: Estrogen replacement therapy.

ESTRATEST. (Reid-Provident) Esterified estrog 1.25 mg., methyltestosterone 2.5 mg./Tab. Bot. 100s, 1000s.
Use: Androgen-estrogen therapy.

ESTRATEST H.S. (Reid-Provident) Esterified estrog 0.625 mg., methyltestosterone 1.25 mg./Tab. Bo 100s.
Use: Androgen-estrogen therapy.

ESTRA-TESTRIN. (Pasadena Research) Testoster enanthate 90 mg., estradiol valerate 4 mg., benz alcohol 2%/ml. Vial 10 cc.

ESTRA-1,3,5(10)-TRIENE-3,17-DIOL,(17β)-,17-CYCLOPENTANEPROPANOATE. Estradiol Cyp ate, U.S.P. XXI.

ESTRA-1,3,5(10)-TRIENE-3,17-DIOL (17β)-,17-P TANOATE. Estradiol Valerate, U.S.P. XXI.

ESTRAVAL. (Kay) Estradiol valerate 10.0 mg., ber alcohol 2%, sesame oil/ml. Vial, 10 cc.
Use: Conditions requiring estrogen therapy.

ESTRAVAL-P.A. (Reid-Provident) Estradiol valerat mg./cc. in oil. Vial 10 cc. 1s, 6s, 12s.

ESTRAVAL-2X. (Reid-Provident) Estradiol valerate mg. ethyl oleate/cc. in sesame oil. Vial 10 cc. 1 6s, 12s.

ESTRA-VATE. (Tunex) Estradiol valerate 20 mg. w/benzyl benzoate 20%, benzyl alcohol 2%. Vi 10 cc. Estradiol valerate 40 mg./ml. w/benzyl benzoate 40%, benzyl alcohol 2%. Vial 10 cc.
Use: Amenorrhea, menopausal syndrome.

• **ESTRAZINOL HYDROBROMIDE.** USAN. dl-trans 3-Methoxy-8-aza-19-nor-17a-pregna-1,3,5-trien-2 yn-17-ol hydrobromide.
Use: Estrogen.

ESTRIN.
See: Estrone

RIOL, U.S.P. XXI.
trone, estradiol.
e: Estro Plus, Tab. (Rocky Mtn.)
ITONE NO. 1. (Kenyon) Conjugated estrogens
ine 0.625 mg., methyltestosterone 5 mg./Tab.
. 100s, 1000s.
ITONE NO. 2. (Kenyon) Conjugated estrogens
ine 1.25 mg., methyltestosterone 10 mg./Tab.
. 100s, 1000s.
OATE. (Kay) Conjugated estrogens 0.625 or
5 mg./Tab. Bot. 100s, 500s, 1000s.
e: Female hormone therapy.
OBENE DP.
e: Diethylstilbestrol Dipropionate (Various Mfr.)
OCON. (Savage) Conjugated estrogens 0.625
. or 1.25 mg./Tab.
. 100s.
e: Estrogen replenishment therapy.
O-CYP. (Keene) Estradiol cypionate 5 mg./ml. Vial
ml.
OFEM. (Pasadena Research) Estradiol
ionate 5 mg./cc. Vial 10 cc.
OFOL. (Reid-Provident) 20,000 I.U./cc. Aq. Susp.
l. 10 cc., 30 cc. In oil vials 30 cc.
ROFURATE. USAN. (1)21, 23-Epoxy-19-24-dinor-
x-chola-1,3,5(10),7,20,22-hexaene-3,17-diol-3-ace-
e; (2) 17-(3-furyl) estra-1,3,5-(10),7-tetraene-3,17β
ol-3-acetate.
e: Estrogen.
ROGENIC SUBSTANCES, CONJUGATED,
ater-soluble.) A mixture containing the sodium salts
the sulfate esters of the estrogenic substances,
ncipally estrone & equilin that are of the type
reted by pregnant mares.
eam.
e: Premarin Vaginal Cream (Ayerst)
ravenous.
e: Estroject, Vial (Mayrand)
Premarin (Ayerst)
blets.
e: Aquagen, Inj. (Remsen)
Ces (ICN)
Co-Estro, Tab. (Robinson)
Estroquin, Tab. (Sheryl)
Estrosan, Tab. (Recsei)
Evestrone, Tab. (Delta)
Femogen, Oil, Tab., Sus. (Fellows-Testegar)
Genisis, Tab. (Organon)
Menotabs, Tab. (Fleming)
Orapin (Standex)
Prelestrin, Tab. (Pasadena Research)
Premarin, Tab. (Ayerst)
Tag-39 H, Tab. (Reid-Provident)
Estradiol.
e: Makrogen Aqueous Susp. (O'Neal)
hinylestradiol.
e: Demulen, Tab. (Searle)
eprobamate.
e: Milprem, Tab. (Wallace)
PMB 200, Tab. (Ayerst)
PMB 400, Tab. (Ayerst)

W/Methyltestosterone.
See: Menotab-M #1 & 2, Tab. (Fleming)
Premarin with Methyltestosterone, Tab. (Ayerst)

ESTROGENIC SUBSTANCES IN AQUEOUS SUSPENSION. (Ayerst) Sterile estrone suspension 2 mg./ml. Vials 10 ml.
Use: Menopausal symptoms, atrophic vaginitis, kraurosis vulvae, prostatic carcinoma.

■ **ESTROGENIC SUBSTANCES MIXED.** May be a crystalline or an amorphous mixture of the naturally occurring estrogens obtained from the urine of pregnant mares.
Aq. Susp.
See: Gravigen Injection (Bluco)
Lanestrin, Vial (Lannett)
Capsules.
See: Urestrin, Cap. (Upjohn)
W/Androgen therapy, vitamins & iron, & d-desoxyephedrine HCl.
See: Mediatric, Prep. (Ayerst)
W/Methyltestosterone.
See: Premarin w/methyltestosterone, Tab. (Ayerst)
W/Testosterone
See: Andrestraq, Vial (Central)

ESTROGEN-ANDROGEN THERAPY.
See: Androgen-Estrogen Therapy

ESTROGEN-810 INJECTION. (Blue Line) Estradiol cypionate 5 mg., chlorobutanol 0.5% in cottonseed oil/cc. Vial 10 cc.

• **ESTROGENS, CONJUGATED,** U.S.P. XXI. Inj. U.S.P. XXI.
Use: Estrogen.
See: Conest, Tab. (Century)
Congens, Tab. (Blaine)
Congesterone, Tab. (Kenyon)
Estrocon, Tab. (Savage)
Ganeake, Tab. (Geneva)
Menotab, Tab. (Fleming)
PMB, Tab. (Ayerst)
Premarin, Tab., I.V. (Ayerst)
Premarin Vaginal Cream (Ayerst)
Premarin with Methyltestosterone, Tab. (Ayerst)
Sodestrin and Sodestrin-H, Tab. (Reid-Provident)
Tag-39, Tab. (Reid-Provident)
Zeste, Tab. (Ascher)

■ **ESTROGENS EQUINE.**
See: PMB, Tab. (Ayerst)
Premarin, Tab., I.V. (Ayerst)
Premarin Vaginal Cream (Ayerst)
Premarin with Methyltestosterone, Tab. (Ayerst)

• **ESTROGENS, ESTERIFIED,** U.S.P. XXI. Tabs., U.S.P. XXI.
Use: Estrogen.
See: Amnestrogen, Tab. (Squibb)
Evex, Tab. (Syntex)
Menest, Tab. (Beecham Labs)
Ms-Med, Tab. (Dunhall)

■ **ESTROGENS, NATURAL.**
Use: Estrogen.
See: Depogen, Vial (Hyrex)
Estradiol, Prep. (Various Mfr.)

Estrone, Prep. (Various Mfr.)
Estrogenic Substance (Various Mfr.)
PMB, Tab. (Ayerst)
Premarin, Tab., I.V. (Ayerst)
Premarin Vaginal Cream (Ayerst)
Premarin with Methyltestosterone, Tab. (Ayerst)

ESTROGENS, SYNTHETIC.
See: Dienestrol, Prep. (Various Mfg.)
Diethylstilbestrol, Prep. (Various Mfr.)
Hexestrol, Prep. (Various Mfr.)
Meprane, Tab. (Reed & Carnrick)
TACE, Cap. (Merrell Dow)
Vallestril, Tab. (Searle)

ESTROGESTIN A. (Harvey) Estrogenic substance 1 mg., progesterone 10 mg./cc. in peanut oil. Vial 10 ml.

ESTROGESTIN C. (Harvey) Estrogenic substance 1 mg., progesterone 12.5 mg./cc. in peanut oil. Vial 10 ml.

ESTROJECT. (Mayrand) Estrogenic substances 2 mg., 5 mg./ml. Vial 10 ml. 2 mg./ml. Vial 30 ml.

ESTROJECT-LA. (Mayrand) Estradiol cypionate 5 mg./ml. Vial 10 ml.

ESTROL. (Kay) Estrogen. Vial 10 ml. or 30 ml.
Use: Hormone supplement.

ESTROLAN. (Lannett) Estrogenic sub. natural in oil 10,000 iu./cc. Vial 30 cc.

• **ESTRONE,** U.S.P. XXI. Inj., Sterile Susp., U.S.P. XXI. 3-Hydroxy-estra-1,3,5(10)-trien-17-one. Oil Inj., Femidyn, follicular hormone, folliculin, follicunodis, cristallovar, glandubolin, hiestrone, ketohydroxy-estratriene, ketohydroxyestrin. 1 mg. equals 10,000 I.U.
Use: Estrogen
See: Bestrone Suspension, Inj. (Bluco)
Estrogenic Substances in Aqueous Suspension (Ayerst)
Follestrol, Vial, Aq. (Blue Line)
Foygen, Vial (Foy)
Gynlin, Inj. (Tunex)
Menagen, Cap. (Parke-Davis)
Menformon (A), Vial (Organon)
Nestronaq, Inj. (Noyes)
Par-Supp, Vag. Supp. (Parmed)
Propagon-S, Inj. (Spanner)
Theelin, Vial, Aq. & Oil (Parke-Davis)
W/Hydrocortisone acetate.
See: Estro-V HC, Supp. (Webcon)
W/Estradiol, pot. estrone sulfate.
Tri-Orapin (Standex)
W/Estradiol, Vit. B-12.
See: Ovest, Tab. (Trimen)
Ovulin, Inj. (Sig)
W/Estriol and estradiol.
See: Estro Plus, Tab., Vial (Rocky Mtn.)
Hormonin, Tab. (Carnrick)
W/Estrogens.
Estrogenic Mixtures, Prep. (Various Mfr.)
Estrogenic Substances, Prep. (Various Mfr.)
W/Lactose.
See: Estrovag. Supps. (Fellows-Testagar)
W/Potassium estrone sulfate.
See: Dura-Keelin, Vial (Pharmex)
Estro Plus, Inj. (Rocky Mtn.)
Gynlin R. P. Inj. (Tunex)
Mer-Estrone, Inj. (Keene)
Sodestrin, Inj. (Reid-Provident)
Spanestrin-P, Vial (Savage)
W/Progesterone.
See: Duovin-S, Inj. (Spanner)
W/Testosterone.
See: Andesterone, Vial (Lincoln)
Anestro, Inj. (Mallard)
Di-Hormone, Susp. (Paddock)
Di-Met Susp. (Organon)
Diorapin (Standex)
Dl-Steroid, Vial (Kremers-Urban)
Estratest, Tab. (Reid-Provident)
Estrone-Testosterone, Vial (Maurry)
W/Testosterone, progesterone.
See: Tripole-F, Inj. (Spanner)
W/Testosterone, sod. carboxymethylcellulose, sc chloride.
See: Tostestro, Inj. (Bowman)
W/Testosterone, vitamins.
See: Android-G, Vial (Brown)
Geratic Forte, Inj. (Keene Pharm.)
Geriamic, Tab. (Vortech)
Geritag, Inj., Cap. (Reid-Provident)
W/Testosterone, vitamin & mineral formula, amin acids.
See: Geramine, Tab. & Inj. (Brown)
W/Testosterone propionate.

ESTRONE-A. (Kay) Estrone 2 mg./ml. Vial 10 ml
Use: Estrogen.

ESTRONE SULFATE, PIPERAZINE.
See: Ogen, Tab., Vaginal Cream (Abbott).

ESTRONE SULFATE, POTASSIUM.
See: Estrogens, Vial (Med. Chem.)
Kaytron, Inj. (Pasadena Research)

ESTRONE SULFATE POT. W/ESTRONE.
See: Dura-Keelin, Vial (Pharmex)

ESTRONOL AQUEOUS. (Central) Estrone 2 mg., w/preservatives and stabilizers. Vial 10 ml., 30 For I.M. use.
Use: Estrogen therapy.

ESTRONOL-LA. (Central) Estradiol cypionate 5 w/chlorobutanol 0.5%. Vial 10 ml. Box 6s.
Use: Estrogen therapy.

• **ESTROPIPITATE,** U.S.P. XXI. Vaginal Cream, T U.S.P. XXI. Estrone hydrogen sulfate compoun with piperazine (1:1).
Use: Estrogen agent.
See: Ogen, Tab., Vag. Cream. (Abbott)

ESTRO PLUS. (Rocky Mtn.) **Inj.:** Estrone 2 mg., potassium estrone sulfate 1 mg./cc. Vial 10 cc **Tab.:** Estrone 0.7 mg., estriol 0.135 mg., estra 0.3 mg./Tab. Estrone 1.4 mg., estriol 0.27 mg. estradiol 0.6 mg./ #2 Tab. Bot. 100s.
Use: Menopausal syndrome.

ESTROQUIN TABLET. (Sheryl) 1.25 mg. of purif conjugated estrogens/Tab. Bot. 100s.

TROVIS. (Parke-Davis) Quinestrol 100 mcg./Tab. Bot. 100s.
Use: Moderate to severe vasomotor symptoms of menopause; atrophic vaginitis; kraurosis vulvae; female hypogonadism; female castration; primary ovarian failure.
TAFEDRINE HCL. USAN.
Use: Bronchodilator.
See: Mercodol w/Decapryn, Liq. (Merrell Dow)
Nethamine (Merrell Dow)
TAFILCON A. USAN.
Use: Contact lens material.
ALENT. (Roger) Ethaverine HCl 100 mg./Cap. Bot. 50s, 500s.
Use: Smooth muscle relaxant.
AMIPHYLLINE. B.A.N. 7-(2-Diethylaminoethyl)-theophylline.
Use: Smooth muscle relaxant.
See: Millophylline (camsylate)
TAPP ELIXIR. (Edwards) Brompheniramine maleate 4 mg., phenylephrine HCl 5 mg., phenylpropanolamine HCl 5 mg., alcohol 2.3%. Bot. pt., gal.
Use: Decongestant, antihistaminic.
TAZOLATE HYDROCHLORIDE. USAN.
Use: Antipsychotic.
ENZAMIDE. B.A.N. 2-Ethoxybenzamide.
Use: Analgesic.
See: Lucamid
ERNA 27 CREAM. (Revlon) Pregnenolone acetate 0.5% in cream base.
Use: Skin moisturization in aged skin.
TEROBARB. USAN.
Use: Anticonvulsant.
HABID DURACAP. (Meyer) Ethaverine HCl 150 mg./T.R. Cap. Bot. 100s.
THACRYNATE SODIUM FOR INJECTION, U.S.P. XXI. Sodium [2,3-dichloro-4-(2-methylenebutyryl)-phenoxy]acetate.
Use: Diuretic.
See: Edecrin Sodium I.V. Inj. (Merck Sharp & Dohme)
HACRYNIC ACID. B.A.N. 2,3-Dichloro-4-(2-ethylacryloyl)phenoxyacetic acid.
Use: Oral diuretic.
THACRYNIC ACID, U.S.P. XXI. Tab., U.S.P. XXI. Acetic acid, [2,3-dichloro-4-(2-methylene-1-oxobutyl)-phenoxy].
Use: Diuretic.
See: Edecrin, Tab. (Merck Sharp & Dohme)
HAMBUTOL. B.A.N. (+)-NN′-Di-(1-hydroxymethylpropyl)ethylenediamine. NN′-Ethylenedi-(2-aminobutan-1-ol).
Use: Treatment of tuberculosis.
THAMBUTOL HCl, U.S.P. XXI. Tab., U.S.P. XXI. (+)-2,2′-(Ethylenediimino)-di-1-butanol Di HCl.
Use: Antitubercular.
See: Myambutol Hydrochloride (Lederle)
HAMICORT.
See: Hydrocortamate

ETHAMIVAN. B.A.N. NN-Diethylvanillamide.
Use: Central nervous system stimulant.
See: Vandid
• **ETHAMSYLATE.** USAN. Diethylammonium 2,5-dihydroxybenzenesulfonate. Dicynene.
Use: Hemostatic.
ETHANAMINE,2-[4-(2-CHLORO-1,2-DIPHENYL-ETHENYL)-PHENOXY]-N,N-DIETHYL-,2-HYDROXY-1,2,3-PROPANE-TRICARBOXYLATE(1:1). Clomiphene Citrate, U.S.P. XXI.
ETHANAMINE,2-(DIPHENYLMETHOXY)-N,N-DIMETHYL-,HYDROCHLORIDE. Diphenhydramine Hydrochloride, U.S.P. XXI.
ETHANAMINIUM,2,2′,2″-[1,2,3-BENZENETRIYLTRIS-(OXY)]-TRIS-[N,N,N-TRIETHYL]-,TRIIODIDE. Gallamine Triethiodide, U.S.P. XXI.
ETHANAMINIUM,2-[(DIETHOXYPHOSPHINYL)THIO]-N,N,N-TRIMETHYL-,IODIDE. Echothiophate Iodide, U.S.P. XXI.
ETHANAMINIUM,2,2′-(1,4-DIOXO-1,4-BUTANEDIYL)-BIS (OXY)BIS-N,N,N-TRIMETHYL-,DICHLORIDE. Succinylcholine Chloride, U.S.P. XXI.
ETHANE,2-BROMO-2-CHLORO-1,1,1-TRI-FLUORO-. Halothane, U.S.P. XXI.
1,2-ETHANEDIAMINE,N,N-DIMETHYL-N′-(PHENYL-METHYL)-N′-2-PYRIDINYL-, Tripelennamine, Citrate or Hydrochloride, U.S.P. XXI.
1,1-ETHANEDIOL,2,2,2-TRICHLORO-. Chloral Hydrate, U.S.P. XXI.
ETHANOL. (Various Mfr.) Alcohol, anhydrous. Alcohol, U.S.P. XXI.
ETHANOL,2-[[4-[(7-CHLORO-4-QUINOLINYL)-AMINO]PENTYL]ETHYLAMINO]-, SULFATE(1:1) SALT. Hydroxychloroquine Sulfate, U.S.P. XXI.
ETHANOLAMINE. Olamine.
ETHAQUIN. (Ascher) Ethaverine HCl 100 mg./Tab. Bot. 100s, 500s, 1000s, 2500s, 5000s.
Use: Peripheral vascular insufficiency.
ETHASULFATE SODIUM. Sod. 2-Ethyl-1-hexanol sulfate.
ETHATAB. (Glaxo) Ethaverine HCl 100 mg./Tab. Bot. 100s, 500s, 5000s. Unit dose 100s.
Use: Smooth muscle relaxant.
ETHAV. (Amfre-Grant) Ethaverine HCl 100 mg./Tab. Bot. 100s, 1000s.
Use: Cardiovascular.
ETHAVERINE HYDROCHLORIDE. The ethyl analog of papaverine HCl, 6,7-diethoxy-1-(3′,4′-diethoxybenzyl) isoquinoline HCl. Diquinol HCl, Preparin HCl, Perperine HCl. The tetraethyl homolog of papaverine is 2 to 4 times more active and less than half as toxic as the parent drug. This compound is not a narcotic.
(Lincoln) Tab. (0.5 gr.) Bot. 100s, 300s.
Vial (15 mg./cc.) 10 cc.
Use: I.V., Antispasmodic.
See: Cebral, Cap. (Kenwood)
Circubid, Cap. (W. F. Merchant)
Etalent, Cap. (Roger)
Ethaquin, Tab. (Ascher)
Ethatab, Tab. (Glaxo)

Isovex, Cap. (Medics)
Neopavrin, Tab., Elix. (Savage)
Pavaspan, Cap. (Jamieson-McKames)
Roldiol, Tab. (Robinson)
Spasodil, Tab. (Rand)
(Pharmex) Vial 15 mg., 20 mg., 45 mg., 75 mg./ml.
W/Pentaerythritol tetranitrate.
Use: Intramuscular, antispasmodic.
See: Papavatral, Tab. (Kenwood)

ETHAVEROL "75". (Pharmex) Ethaverine HCl 75 mg./cc. Vial 10 cc.

ETHAVEX-100 TABLETS. (Econo Med) Ethaverine HCl 100 mg./Tab. Bot. 100s.
Use: Arterial spasmolytic for peripheral and cerebral vascular insufficiency.

• **ETHCHLORVYNOL,** U.S.P. XXI. Cap., U.S.P. XXI. 1-Chloro-3-ethyl-1-penten-4 yn-3-ol.
Use: Hypnotic, sedative.
See: Arvynol
Placidyl, Cap. (Abbott)
Serensil, Prod. (Ciba).

ETHCHLORVYNOL. B.A.N. 1-Chloro-3-ethyl-pent-1-en-4-yn-3-ol.
Use: Hypnotic; sedative.

ETHEBENECID. B.A.N. 4-Diethylsulamoylbenzoic acid.
Use: Uricosuric.
See: Urelim

ETHENOL, HOMOPOLYMER. Polyvinyl Alcohol, U.S.P. XXI.

ETHENZAMIDE. o-Ethoxybenzamide.

• **ETHER,** U.S.P. XXI. Ethyl ether
Use: General anesthetic.

ETHEREA ENVIRONMENTAL PROTECTION LOTION. (Revlon) Padimate O, Oxybenzone in lotion base. SPF #6
Use: Daytime moisturizer & sunburn preventative.

ETHIAZIDE. B.A.N. 6-Chloro-3-ethyl-3,4-dihydro-1,2,4-benzothiadiazine-7-sulfonamide 1,1-dioxide.
Use: Diuretic.

• **ETHINAMATE,** U.S.P. XXI. Cap., U.S.P. XXI. 1-Ethynylcyclohexanoyl carbamate.
Use: Hypnotic.
See: Valmid, Tab. (Dista)
Valmidate

• **ETHINYL ESTRADIOL,** U.S.P. XXI. Tab., U.S.P. XXI. 17-Ethinyl-3,17-estradiol. 19-Norpregna-1,3,5(10)-trien-20-yne-3,17-diol,(17α)-. 19-Nor-17α-pregna-1,3,5-(10)-trien-20-yne-3,17-diol.
Use: Estrogen.
See: Estinyl, Tab. (Schering)
Feminone, Tab. (Upjohn)
Lynoral, Tab. (Organon)
Menolyn, Tab. (Arcum)
Ovogyn, Tab. (Pasadena Research)

ETHINYL ESTRADIOL W/COMBINATIONS
See: Ardiatric, Tab. (Burgin-Arden)
Brevicon, Tab. (Syntex)
Demulen, Tab. (Searle)
Diatric, Tab. (Pasadena Research)
Geramine, Tab., Inj. (Brown)
Geritag, Cap. (Reid-Provident)
Gynetone, Tab. (Schering)
Halodrin, Tab. (Upjohn)
Hormox Plus, Tab. (Parmed)
Loestrin 1/20, Tab. (Parke-Davis)
Loestrin 1.5/30, Tab. (Parke-Davis)
Min-Gera, Tab. (Scrip)
Modicon 21 and 28, Tab. (Ortho)
Neosterol, Tab. (Winston)
Nordette, Tab. (Wyeth)
Norinyl, Prods. (Syntex)
Norlestrin, Tab. (Parke-Davis)
Norlestrin FE., Tab. (Parke-Davis)
Ortho-Novum 1/35, 21 and 28 (Ortho)
Os-Cal-Mone, Tab. (Marion)
Ovcon-35 Tablets (Mead Johnson)
Ovcon-50 Tablets (Mead Johnson)
Ovlin, Vial (ICN)
Ovral, Tab. (Wyeth)
Vee-Gera Basic, Cap. (Mericon)
Vimah, Vial, Tab. (Hyrex)
Viromone, Tabs. (Western Research Labs.)
Zorane, Tab. (Lederle)
Zorane 1/20, 1/50, 1.5/30 (Lederle)

ETHINYL ESTRENOL.
See: Lynestrenol (Organon)

ETHINYL ESTRADIOL AND DIMETHISTERONE TABLETS.
Use: Estrogen-progestin.

17α-ETHINYL-19-NORTESTERONE. Norethindro Acetate, U.S.P. XXI.

ETHINYL (17)-19-NORTESTOSTERONE.
See: Norlutin, Tab. (Parke-Davis)

ETHIODOL. (Savage) Ethiodized oil. Fatty acid ethy ester of poppy-seed oil w/37% iodine. Amp. 10 c Box 2s.
Use: Diagnostic agent, roentgenography.

• **ETHIODIZED OIL INJECTION,** U.S.P. XXI.
Use: Diagnostic aid (Radiopaque medium)
See: Ethiodol, Inj. (Savage)

• **ETHIODIZED OIL I-131.** USAN. Radioactive iodi addition to ethyl ester of poppyseed oil. Ethiodal-131.
Use: Anti-oncotic agent.

• **ETHIOFOS.** USAN.
Formerly gammaphos.
Use: Radioprotector

ETHIONAMIDE. B.A.N. 2-Ethylisonicotinthioamide.
Use: Treatment of tuberculosis.
See: Trescatyl

• **ETHIONAMIDE,** U.S.P. XXI. Tab., U.S.P. XXI. 2-Eth thioisonicotinamide. 4-Pyridinecarbothioamide, ethyl.
Use: Tuberculostatic.
See: Trecator S.C., Tab. (Ives)

ETHISTERONE. 17-Hydroxy-17a-pregn-4-en-20-yn-3 one.
See: Anhydrohydroxyprogesterone. (Various Mfr.)

ETHOCAINE.
See: Procaine Hydrochloride (Various Mfr.)

ETHOCYLORVYNOL. β-Chlorovinyl ethyl ethynyl c binol. Ethchlorvynol, U.S.P. XXI.

ETHODRYL.
See: Diethylcarbamazine Citrate

IOGLUCID. B.A.N. 1,2:15,16-Diepoxy-4,7,10,-13-
traoxahexadecane.
se: Antineoplastic agent.
ee: Epodyl
IOHEPTAZINE. B.A.N. Ethyl hexahydro-1-methyl-
phenylazepine-4-carboxylate.
se: Analgesic.
IOHEPTAZINE CITRATE. Ethyl Hexahydro-1-meth-
-4-phenylazepine-4-carboxylate Dihydrogen citrate.
thyl Hexahydro-1-methyl-4-phenyl-1H-azepine-4-
arboxylate Citrate (1:1)
IOHEXADIOL. Ethyl hexanediol, 2-ethylhexane-1,3-
ol, Rutgers 612. Used in Comp. Dimethyl Phthalate.
se: Insect repellent.
IOMOXANE. B.A.N. 2-Butylaminomethyl-8-ethoxy-
4-benzodioxan.
se: Adrenaline antagonist.
ION TABS. (Major) Methyclothiazide 2.5 mg. or 5
g./Tab. Bot. 100s, 1000s.
se: Antihypertensive.
'HONAM NITRATE. USAN. Ethyl 1-(1,2,3-4-tetrahy-
'o-1-naphthyl)imidazole-5-carboxylate nitrate.
se: Fungicide.
IOPROPAZINE. B.A.N. 10-(2-Diethylaminopropyl)-
henothiazine. Profenamine (I.N.N.)
se: Treatment of the parkinsonian syndrome.
ee: Lysivane (hydrochloride)
HOPROPAZINE HYDROCHLORIDE, U.S.P. XXI.
ab. U.S.P. XXI. 10H-Phenothiazine-10-ethanamine,
,N-diethyl-α-methyl-,monohydrochloride. 10-[2-(Die-
ylamino)propyl]-phenothiazine monohydrochloride.
/sivane.
se: Antiparkinsonian.
ee: Parsidol HCl, Tab. (Warner-Chilcott)
IOSALAMIDE. B.A.N. 2-(2-Ethoxyethoxy) benza-
ide.
se: Analgesic; antipyretic.
'HOSUXIMIDE, U.S.P. XXI. Cap., U.S.P. XXI. 2-Eth-
-2-methyl-succinimide.
se: Anticonvulsant.
ee: Zarontin, Cap., Syr. (Parke-Davis)
IOSUXIMIDE. B.A.N. 2-Ethyl-2-methylsuccinimide.
se: Anticonvulsant.
ee: Capitus
Emeside
Simatin
Zarontin
IOTOIN. 3-Ethyl-5-phenylhydantoin.
ee: Peganone, Tab. (Abbott)
IOTOIN. B.A.N. 3-Ethyl-5-phenylimidazoline-2,4-
one.
se: Anticonvulsant.
ee: Peganone, Tab. (Abbott)
IOVAN. Ethyl Vanillin.
'HOXAZENE HYDROCHLORIDE. USAN. 4-[(p-
thoxy-phenyl)azo]-m-phenyl-enediamine HCl 2,-4-
iamino-4′-ethoxyazobenzene hydrochloride.
se: Urinary analgesic.
ee: Serenium, Tab. (Squibb)
THOXY-2-BENZOTHIAZOLESULFONAMIDE.
thoxzolamide, U.S.P. XXI.

ETHOXZOLAMIDE. 6-Ethoxy-2-benzothiazolesulfonamide.
Use: Carbonic anhydrase inhibitor.
ETHRANE. (Ohio Medical) Enflurane.
ETHRIL. (Squibb) Erythromycin stearate 250 mg./Tab. Bot. 100s, 500s; 500 mg./Tab. Bot. 50s.
Use: Antibiotic.
ETHYBENZTROPINE. B.A.N. 3-Benzhydryloxy-8-ethylnortropane.
Use: Anticholinergic.
• **ETHYBENZTROPINE.** USAN. 3-(diphenylmethoxy)-8-ethylnortropane. Panolid. Methylbenztropine.
Use: Anticholinergic.
• **ETHYL ACETATE,** N.F. XVI.
Use: Flavor.
ETHYL AMINOBENZOATE. Anesthesin, anesthrone, benzocaine, parathesin.
Use: Surface anesthetic.
See: Benzocaine (Var. Mfr.)
ETHYL BISCOUMACETATE. B.A.N. Ethyl di(4-hydroxycoumarin-3-yl)acetate.
Use: Anticoagulant.
See: Pelentan
ETHYL BISCOUMACETATE. 3,3′-(Carboxymethylene) bis (4-hydroxycoumarin) ethyl ester. Ethyl Bis (4-hydroxy-2-oxo-2H-1-benzopyran-3-yl) acetate.
ETHYL BROMIDE. (Various Mfr.) Bromoethane.
Use: Inhalation anesthetic.
5-ETHYL-5-n-BUTYLBARBITURIC ACID.
See: Butethal (Var. Mfr.)
ETHYL CARBAMATE.
See: Urethan (Var. Mfr.)
• **ETHYLCELLULOSE,** N.F. XVI.
Use: Tablet binder.
ETHYL CHAULMOOGRATE.
Use: Hansen's disease, sarcoidosis.
• **ETHYL CHLORIDE,** U.S.P. XXI.
Chloroethane
Use: Local anesthetic.
See: Gebauer-Spra-Pak
Stratford-Cook-Spray, 100 Gm.
2-ETHYLCROTONYLUREA.
See: Ectylurea
ETHYL 1-(3-CYANO-3,3-DIPHENYLPROPYL)-4-PHENYLISO-NIPECOTATE MONOHYDROCHLORIDE. Diphenoxylate Hydrochloride, U.S.P. XXI.
• **ETHYL DIBUNATE.** USAN. Ethyl 2,7-di-t-butyl-naphthalene-1-sulfonate.
Use: Cough suppressant.
ETHYL DIIODOBRASSIDATE. Iodobrassid. Lipoiodine.
ETHYLDIMETHYLAMMONIUM BROMIDE.
See: Ambutonium Bromide
5-ETHYL-3,5-DIMETHYL-2,4-OXAZOLIDINEDIONE.
Paramethadione, U.S.P. XXI.
ETHYLENE. (Various Mfr.) Ethene.
Use: Inhalation anesthetic.
• **ETHYLENEDIAMINE,** U.S.P. XXI. Component of Aminophylline.
ETHYLENEDIAMINE SOLUTION. (67% w/v).
Use: Solvent (Aminophylline Inj.).

ETHYLENEDIAMINETETRAACETIC ACID.
See. Edathamil, EDTA (Var. Mfr.)
ETHYLENEDIAMINE TETRAACETIC ACID-DISODIUM SALT.
See: Endrate Disodium, Amp. (Abbott)
1-N-ETHYLEPHEDRINE HYDROCHLORIDE.
Use: Bronchodilator & vasoconstrictor.
See: Nethamine Hydrochloride, Prep. (Var. Mfr.)
• **ETHYLESTRENOL.** F.D.A. 19-Nor-17 alphapregn-4-en-17 beta-ol.
• **ETHYLESTRENOL.** USAN. 17α-Ethyl- 17β-hydroxy-estr-4-ene.
Use: Anabolic steroid.
See: Maxibolin, Tab., Elix. (Organon)
($\pm$)-13-ETHYL-17α-ETHYNYL-17-HYDROXYGON-4-EN-3-ONE. Norgestrel, U.S.P. XXI.
2-ETHYLHEXANE-1,3-DIOL.
See: Ethohexadiol.
ETHYLHYDROCUPREINE HCl. $0^{6'}$ Ethylhydrocupreine monohydrochloride.
Use: Antiseptic.
13-ETHYL-17-HYDROXY-18,19-DINOR,17 alpha-PREGN-4-EN-3-ONE. Genabol.
ETHYL 10-(IODOPHENYL)UNDECANOATE.
See: Iophendylate, U.S.P. XXI.
ETHYL(m-HYDROXYPHENYL)DIMETHYL-AMMONIUM CHLORIDE. Edrophonium Chloride, U.S.P. XXI.
5-ETHYL-5-ISOAMYL BARBITURIC ACID.
See: Amobarbital (Var. Mfr.)
ETHYLMETHYLTHIAMBUTENE. B.A.N. 3-Ethylmethylamino-1,1-di-(2-thienyl)but-1-ene.
Use: Narcotic analgesic.
2-ETHYL-2-METHYLSUCCINIMIDE. Ethosuximide, U.S.P. XXI.
ETHYLMORPHINE HYDROCHLORIDE. 7,8-Didehydro-4,5α-epoxy-3-ethoxy-17-methyl-morphinan-6α-ol Hydrochloride. Dionin.
Use: Narcotic.
ETHYL NITRITE SPIRIT. Ethyl nitrite. Sweet Spirit of Niter. Spirit of Nitrous Ether.
• **ETHYLNOREPINEPHRINE HCl,** U.S.P. XXI. Inj., U.S.P. XXI.
See: Bronkephrine, Amp. (Winthrop-Breon)
ETHYLESTRENOL. B.A.N. 17α-Ethylestr-4-en-17β-ol.
Use: Anabolic steroid.
See: Orabolin
• **ETHYL OLEATE,** N.F. XVI.
Use: Pharmaceutic aid (vehicle).
ETHYL OXIDE; ETHYL ETHER,
Use: Solvent.
ETHYLPAPAVERINE HCl.
See: Ethaverine HCl. (Var. Mfr.)
• **ETHYLPARABEN,** N.F. XVI. Ethyl p-Hydroxybenzoate.
Use: Pharm. aid (antifungal preservative).
ETHYL PYROPHOSPHATE. B.A.N. Tetraethyl pyrophosphate.
Use: Treatment of myasthenia gravis.
5-ETHYL-SEC-BUTYLBARBITURIC ACID.
See: Butabarbital (Var. Mfr.)
ETHYLSTIBAMINE. Astaril, neostibosan.
Use: Antimony therapy.

2-ETHYLTHIOISONICOTINAMIDE. Ethionamide, U.S.P. XXI.
ETHYL VANILLATE. Ethyl-hydroxy-methoxy-benzo
• **ETHYL VANILLIN,** N.F. XVI. 3-Ethoxy-4-hydroxyb zaldehyde.
Use: Flavor.
• **ETHYNERONE.** USAN.
Use: Progestin.
ETHYNODIOL. B.A.N. 19-Nor-17α-pregn-4-en-20-y 3β,17-diol.
Use: Progestational steroid.
• **ETHYNODIOL DIACETATE,** U.S.P. XXI. 19-Nor-1 pregn-4-en-20-yne-3B,17-diol diacetate; 17α-eth 4-estrene-3β,17β-diol diacetate.
Use: As Progesterone.
See: Ovulen, Tab. (Searle)
W/Ethinyl estradiol.
See: Demulen, Preps. (Searle)
W/Mestranol.
See: Ovulen, Tab. (Searle)
• **ETHYNODIOL DIACETATE AND ETHINYL ESTRADIOL TABLETS,** U.S.P. XXI.
Use: Oral contraceptive.
• **ETHYNODIOL DIACETATE AND MESTRANOL TABLETS,** U.S.P. XXI.
Use: Oral contraceptive.
ETHYNLESTRADIOL.
See: Ethinyl Estradiol, U.S.P. (Various Mfr.)
Mestranol (Var. Mfr.)
17α-ETHYNYLESTRADIOL 3-METHYL ETHER. M tranol, U.S.P. XXI.
ETHYNYLESTRADIOL 3-METHYL ETHER.
See: Enovid, Tab. (Searle)
N-ETHYL-2-PHENYL-N-(4-PYRIDYLMETHYL)HYD CRYLAMIDE. Tropicamide, U.S.P. XXI.
• **ETIBENDAZOLE.** USAN.
Use: Anthelmintic.
ETICYLOL. (Ciba) Ethinyl estradiol.
• **ETIDOCAINE.** USAN. ($\pm$)-2-(N-Ethylpropylamino butyro-2',6'-xylidide.
Use: Local anesthetic.
See: Duranest (base and hydrochloride)
• **ETIDRONATE DISODIUM,** U.S.P. XXI. The disoc salt of (1-Hydroxyethylidene) diphosphonic acid.
Use: Treatment of symptomatic Paget's disease bone (osteitis deformans).
See: Didronel, Tab. (Procter & Gamble)
• **ETIDRONIC ACID.** USAN. (1-Hydroxy-ethylidene) diphosphonic acid.
Use: Bone calcium regulator.
• **ETIFENIN.** USAN.
Use: Diagnostic aid.
ETIFOXINE. B.A.N. 6-Chloro-2-ethylamino-4-meth 4-phenyl-4H-3,1-benzoxazine.
Use: Tranquilizer.
• **ETINTIDINE HYDROCHLORIDE.** USAN.
Use: Antagonist.
ETISAZOLE. B.A.N. 3-Ethylamino-1,2-benzisothiaz
Use: Fungicide, veterinary medicine.
See: Ectimar
ETISUL. Ditophal, B.A.N.

TNAPA ELIXIR. (U.S. Ethicals) Acetaminophen 120 mg./5 ml. Bot. 120 ml.
Use: Anti-pyretic, analgesic for children.

ETOCRYLENE. USAN.
Use: Ultraviolet screen.

ETODOLAC. USAN.
Use: Anti-inflammatory.

ETOFORMIN HYDROCHLORIDE. USAN.
Use: Antidiabetic.

ETOMIDATE. USAN.
Use: Hypnotic.

TOMIDE HYDROCHLORIDE. Bandol. Carbiphene HCl.

TONITAZENE. B.A.N. 1-(2-Diethylaminoethyl)-2-(4-ethoxybenzyl)-5-nitrobenzimidazole.
Use: Narcotic analgesic.

TOPHYLATE. Acepifylline, B.A.N.

ETOPOSIDE. USAN.
Use: Antineoplastic.
See: Vepesid, Inj. (Bristol)

ETOPRINE. USAN.
Use: Antineoplatic.

TOQUINOL SODIUM. Name used for Actinoquinol sodium.

TORPHINE. B.A.N. 7,8-Dihydro-7α-[1(R)-hydroxy-1-methylbutyl]-0^6-methyl-6,14-endoethenomorphine.
Use: Narcotic analgesic.

TOVAL.
See: Butethal, N.F. (Various Mfr.)

ETOXADROL HYDROCHLORIDE. USAN.
Use: Anesthetic.

TOXERIDINE. B.A.N. Ethyl 1-[2-(2-hydroxyethoxy)ethyl]-4-phenylpiperidine-4-carboxylate.
Use: Narcotic analgesic.

ETOZOLIN. USAN.
Use: Diuretic.

TRAFON (2–25). (Schering) Perphenazine 2 mg. amitriptyline HCl 25 mg./Tab. Bot. 100s, 500s. Unit dose 100s.
Use: Antidepressant, tranquilizer.

TRAFON (2–10). (Schering) Perphenazine 2 mg., amitriptyline HCl 10 mg./Tab. Bot. 100s, 500s. Unit dose 100s.
Use: Tranquilizer, antidepressant.

TRAFON-A (4-10). (Schering) Perphenazine 4 mg., amitriptyline HCl 10 mg./Tab. Bot. 100s, 500s. Unit dose 100s.
Use: Tranquilizer, antidepressant.

TRAFON FORTE TABLETS (4-25). (Schering) Perphenazine 4 mg., amitriptyline HCl 25 mg./Tab. Bot. 100s, 500s. Unit dose 100s.
Use: Tranquilizer, antidepressant.

TRENOL INJECTION. (Winthrop Products) Hycanthone (as mesylate).
Use: Antibilharziasis.

ETRETINATE. USAN.
Use: Antipsoriatic.

TRYNIT. Propatyl nitrate.
Use: Coronary

TRYPTAMINE. B.A.N. 3-(2-Aminobutyl)-indole. a-Ethyltryptamine. Monase [acetate]
Use: Antidepressant.

• **ETRYPTAMINE ACETATE.** USAN. 3-(2-Aminobutyl)-indole Acetate.
Use: Central stimulant.
See: Monase (Upjohn)

ETTRIOL TRINITRATE.
See: Propatyl nitrate.

E.T. VITAMINS. (Squibb) Vit. A 5,000 I.U., D 400 I.U., E 30 I.U., C 60 mg., folic acid 0.4 mg.; thiamine 1.5 mg., riboflavin 1.7 mg., niacin 20 mg., B-6 2 mg., B-12 6 mcg/Chewable Tab. Bot. 60s.
Use: Children's chewable vitamin.

E.T. VITAMINS WITH IRON. (Squibb) Vitamin A 5,000 I.U., D 400 I.U., E 30 I.U., C 60 mg., folic acid 0.4 mg., Thiamine 1.5 mg., riboflavin 1.7 mg., niacin 20 mg., B-6 2 mg., B-12 6 mcg.; iron 18 mg./Chewable Tab. Bot. 60s.
Use: Children's chewable vitamin with iron.

ETYBENZATROPINE. Ethybenztropine.

ETYNODIOL ACETATE. Ethynodiol Diacetate.

EUBASIN.
See: Sulfapyridine (Various Mfr.)

EUCAINE HCl. 2,2,6-Trimethyl-4-piperidinol benzoate HCl.

EUCALYPTOL. 1,8-Epoxy-p-menthane.
Use: Pharmaceutic aid (flavor), antitussive, nasal decongestant.
See: Vicks Sinex, Nasal Spray (Vicks)
Vicks Va-Tro-Nol, Nose Drops (Vicks)
Vicks Prods. (Vicks)

• **EUCALYPTUS OIL,** N.F. XVI.
Use: Flavor, antitussive, nasal decongestant, expectorant, topical analgesic.
See: Vicks Prods. (Vicks)
Victors Regular & Cherry Loz. (Vicks)

EUCAPINE SYRUP. (Lannett) Ammonium chloride 10 gr., pot. guaiacol sulf. 8 gr., in white pine & wild cherry syrup. Bot. 1 pt., 1 gal.
Use: Cough expectorant.

EUCATROPINE. B.A.N. 1,2,2,6-Tetramethyl-4-piperidyl mandelate. Euphthalmine
Use: Mydriatic.

• **EUCATROPINE HYDROCHLORIDE,** U.S.P. XXI. Ophth. Soln., U.S.P. XXI. 1,2,2,6-Tetramethyl-4-piperidyl mandelate HCl. Benzeneacetic acid, alpha-hydroxy-, 1,2,2,6-tetramethyl-4-piperidinyl ester hydrochloride. (Glogau) Cryst., Bot. 1 Gm.
Use: Pharm. necessity for ophthalmic dosage form.

EUCERIN. (Beiersdorf) Emulsion of equal parts Aquaphor and water. 1 lb. jar. 5 oz. tin.

EUCODAL.
See: Oxycodone (No Mfr. currently lists)

EUCORAN.
See: Nikethamide (Various Mfr.)

EUCUPIN DIHYDROCHLORIDE.
Isoamylhydrocupreine dihydrochloride.

EUDEMINE. Diazoxide, B.A.N.

EUFLAVINE.
See: Acriflavine (Various Mfr.)

• **EUGENOL,** U.S.P. XXI. (Various Mfr.) 4-Allyl-2-methoxy-phenol. Phenol, 2-methoxy-4-(2-propenyl)-.
Use: Dental analgesic, oral anesthetic.
See: Benzodent, Oint. (Vicks)

EUKADOL.
See: Dihydrohydroxycodeinone, Preps. (No Mfr. currently lists)

EULCIN. (Leeds) Methscopolamine bromide 2.5 mg., butabarbital sod. 10 mg., aluminum hydroxide gel dried 250 mg., Mag. trisilicate 250 mg./Tab. Bot. 100s.
Use: Gastric & duodenal ulcer therapy.

EULISSIN. Decamethonium Iodide, B.A.N.

EUMYDRIN DROPS. (Winthrop Products) Atropine methonitrate.
Use: Antispasmodic.

EUNERYL.
See: Phenobarbital (Various Mfr.)

EUPHORBIA COMPOUND. (Sherwood) Euphorbia pilulifera fl. ext. 1.5 cc., lobelia tr. 2.2 cc., nitroglycerin spirit 0.29 cc., Sod. iodide 1.04 Gm., Sod. bromide 1.04 Gm., alcohol 24%/30 cc. Bot. 1 pt., 1 gal.
Use: Sedative & expectorant.

EUPHORBIA PILULIFERA.
W/Cocillana, squill, antimony potassium tartrate, senega.
See: Cylana, Syr. (Bowman)
W/Phenyl salicyate & various oils.
See: Rayderm, Oint. (Velvet Pharmacal)

EUPRACTONE. (Travenol) Dimethadione.

EUPRAX. Albution.

• **EUPROCIN HCl.** USAN. O[6']-Isopentylhydrocupreine dihydrochloride.
Use: Topical anesthetic.
See: Eucupin HCl

EUQUININE. Quinine ethyl carbonate.
Use: Orally; antimalarial & antipyretic.

EURAX CREAM. (Westwood) Crotamiton 10% in vanishing-cream base of glyceryl monostearate, lanolin, PEG 6-32, glycerin, polysorbate 80, water, benzyl alcohol, mineral oil, white wax, quaternium-15 and fragrance. Tube 60 Gm.
Use: Antipruritic & scabicide.

EURAX LOTION. (Westwood) Crotamiton 10% in emollient-lotion base of glyceryl monostearate, lanolin, PEG 6-32, glycerin, Polysorbate 80, water, benzyl alcohol, light mineral oil, Na carboxymethylcellulose, simethicone, quaternium-15 and fragrance. Bot. 60 Gm., 454 Gm.
Use: Antipruritic & scabicide.

EUTHROID. (Parke-Davis) Liotrix (sod. levothyroxine & sod. liothyronine) Tabs. 0.5 gr., 1 gr., 2 gr., & 3 gr. Bot. 100s. Tab. 1 gr. Bot. 1000s.
Use: Thyroid therapy.

EUTONYL. (Abbott) Pargyline Hydrochloride. 10 mg., 25 mg./Tab. Bot. 100s.
Use: Antihypertensive agent.

EUTRON FILMTAB. (Abbott) Pargyline HCl 25 mg., methylclothiazide 5 mg./Tab. Bot. 100s.
Use: Antihypertensive agent.

EVAC-Q-KIT. (Adria) Each kit contains: (1)**Evac-Q-Mag:** Magnesium citrate, citric acid, potassium citrate. (2) **Evac-Q-Tabs:** 2 tabs containing 2 gr. phenolphthalein/Tab. (3) **Evac-Q-Sert:** 2 Supps. containing potassium bitartrate, sodium bicarbonate/Supp. in polyethylene glycol base. (4) Patient instruction sheet.
Use: Bowel evacuant.

EVAC-Q-KWIK. (Adria) Each kit contains: **Evac-(Mag.:** Magnesium citrate, citric acid, potassium citrate in cherry-flavored base. **Evac-Q-Tabs.:** 2 Ta phenolphthalein 2 gr. **Evac-Q-Kwik Supp.:** 10 m bisacodyl.
Use: Bowel evacuant.

EVAC SUPPOSITORIES. (Burgin-Arden) Sodium bica bonate, sodium biphosphate, dioctyl sodium sulfosuccinate 50 mg./Supp.
Use: Laxative.

EVAC TABLETS. (Burgin-Arden) Guar gum 300 m danthron 50 mg., sodium 100 mg./Tab.
Use: Laxative.

EVACTOL. (Delta) Dihydroxyanthraquinone 75 mg., docusate sodium 100 mg., sodium carboxymethyl cellulose 200 mg./Cap. Pkg. 10s, Bot. 10s, 30s, 100s.
Use: Laxative.

EVAC-U-GEN. (Walker) Yellow phenolphthalein 97 mg./Tab. Pkg. 35s, Bot. 100s, 1000s, 6000s.
Use: Laxative.

EVAC-U-LAX. (Mallard) Phenolphthalein, yellow mg./Wafer. Bot. 100s.

• **EVANS BLUE,** U.S.P. XXI. Inj., U.S.P. XXI. 1,3-Nap thalenedisulfonic acid, 6,6'-[(3,3'-dimethyl[1,1'- phenyl]-4,4'-diyl)bis(azo)]bis[4-amino-5-hydroxy]-, tetrasodium salt. Azovan Blue, B.A.N. (Harvey) Pu diazo dye. Amp. (0.5%) 5 ml. 12s, 25s, 100s.
Use: Diagnostic aid, (blood-volume determination).

EVERONE. (Hyrex) Testosterone enanthate 100 mg. or 200 mg., benzyl alcohol 2%/ml. Vial 10 ml.
Use: Long acting male hormone.

EVICYL TABLETS. (Winthrop Products) Inositol hexanicotinate.
Use: Hypolipidemic, peripheral vasodilator.

EVIRON. (Delta) Ferrous fumarate 160 mg., copper mg., ascorbic acid 75 mg./Tab.
Use: Hematinic.

EVIRON FA. (Delta) Ferrous fumarate 160 mg., copper 1 mg., Vit. C 75 mg., folic acid 1.5 mg./Ta
Use: Hematinic.

EVIRON FT. (Delta) Ferrous fumarate 160 mg., copper 1 mg., Vit C 50 mg., cyanocobalamin 7.5 mcg.
Use: Hematinic.

E-VISTA. (Seatrace) Hydroxyzine HCl 50 mg./ml. V 10 cc.

E-VITABON. (Pasadena Research) Vit. E 200 I.U., C 1 mg., B-1 2 mg., B-2 2 mg., B-6 5 mg., B-12 10 mc d-panthenol 5 mg., niacinamide 10 mg./Tab. Bot. 6 100s, 500s.

E-VITAL. (Pasadena Research) d-Alpha tocopheryl su cinate 100 I.U., 200 I.U./Cap. Bot. 100s, 1000s. 400 I.U. Bot. 100s, 500s.

E-VITAL CREME. (Pasadena Research) Vit. E 100 I.U A 250 I.U., D 100 I.U., d-panthenol 0.2%, allant 0.1%/Gm. Jar 2 oz., 1 lb.

VITES. (Quality Generics) Vit. E (from dl-alpha tocopheryl acetate) 100 I.U., 200 I.U., 400 I.U., 1000 I.U./Cap. Bot. 100s.

IN NINOS TABLETS. (Winthrop Products) Aspirin.
Use: Analgesic, antipyretic.

XAPROLOL HYDROCHLORIDE. USAN.
Use: Antiadrenergic.

-AQUA. (Edward J. Moore) Ext. buchu, ext. uva ursi, ext. corn silk, ext. juniper, caffeine/Tab. Bot. 80s.
Use: Diuretic.

-CALORIC WAFERS. (Eastern Research) Carboxymethylcellulose 181 mg., methylcellulose 272 mg./Wafer. Bot. 100s, 500s, 5000s.
Use: Diet control.

CEDRIN CAPSULES. (Bristol-Myers) Aspirin 250 mg., acetaminophen 250 mg., caffeine 65 mg./Cap. Bot. 24s, 40s, 60s.
Use: Analgesic.

CEDRIN TABLETS. (Bristol-Myers) Acetaminophen 250 mg., caffeine 65 mg., aspirin 250 mg./Tab. Bot. 12s, 36s, 60s, 100s, 165s, 225s, 375s. Tins 12s.
Use: Analgesic.

CEDRIN P.M.. (Bristol-Myers) Acetaminophen 500 mg., diphenhydramine citrate 38 mg./Tab. Bot. 10s, 30s, 50s, 80s.
Use: Analgesic, sleep aid.

IDINE SKIN CLEANSER. (Xitrium) Chlorhexidine gluconate 4%. Bot. 4 oz., 8 oz., 16 oz., 32 oz., gal.
Use: Antimicrobial skin cleanser.

-LAX. (Ex-Lax) Yellow phenolphthalein 90 mg./chocolated Tab. or unflavored pill. Chocolated Tab. 6s, 18s, 48s, 72s. Unflavored pills 8s, 30s, 60s.
Use: Laxative.

-LAX EXTRA GENTLE. (Ex-Lax) Phenolphthalein 65 mg., docusate sodium 75 mg./Tab. Pkg. 24s, 48s.
Use: Laxative, stool softener.

NA. (Robins) Benzthiazide 50 mg./Tab. Bot. 100s, 500s.
Use: Diuretic, antihypertensive.

-OBESE. (Kay) Phendimetrazine tartrate 35 mg./Tab. Bot. 100s, 1000s, 5000s.
Use: Anorexigenic agent.

OCAINE. (Commerce) Methyl salicylate 25%. Tube 1.3 oz.
Use: Minor pains of arthritis and rheumatism.

OCAINE ODOR FREE. (Commerce) Triethanolamine salicylate 10%. Tube 3 oz.
Use: Relief from minor pain of arthritis, rheumatism, backache, muscular aches.

OCAINE PLUS. (Commerce) Methyl salicylate. Jar 4 oz. Tube 1.3 oz.
Use: Temporary relief of minor pain of arthritis, rheumatism, muscular aches, bursitis, neuritis.

O-KOL. (Inwood) Phenylephrine HCl 5 mg., chlorpheniramine maleate 1 mg., salicylamide 3.5 gr., phenacetin 1.5 gr., caffeine 10 mg., Vit. C 20 mg./Tab. Bot. 50s, 1000s.
Use: Antihistaminic w/analgesic.

O-KOL COUGH SYRUP. (Inwood) Dextromethorphan HBr 10 mg., cetylpyridinium chloride 0.25%, phenyltoloxamine dihydrogen citrate 25 mg., sodium citrate/5 cc. Bot. 4 oz. Also Exo-Kol Pediatric Cough Syrup available. Bot. 4 oz.
Use: Coughs.

EXO-KOL NASAL SPRAY. (Inwood) Phenylephrine HCl 0.5%, pyrilamine maleate 0.15%, cetyl-dimethyl benzyl ammonium chloride 0.04%. Bot. 1 oz.
Use: Nasal-spray. Decongestant, antihistaminic.

EXOL. Di-isobutyl ethoxy ethyl dimethyl benzyl ammonium chloride.
W/Benzocaine, menthol, calamine, pyrilamine maleate.

EXONIC OT. Dioctyl Sodium Sulphosuccinate.
Use: Laxative.

EXORBIN. (Various Mfr.) Polyamine-methylene resin.

EXPECTICO COUGH SYRUP. (Coastal) Dihydrocodeinone bitartrate 30 mg., guaifenesin 600 mg., sod. citrate 900 mg., chlorpheniramine maleate 12 mg./Fl. oz. Bot. 16 oz., gal.
Use: Antitussive, antihistaminic, expectorant.

EXPECTICO PED. COUGH SYRUP. (Coastal) Dihydrocodeinone bitartrate 15 mg., guaifenesin 300 mg., sod. citrate 450 mg., chlorpheniramine maleate 6 mg., phenylephrine HCl 12 mg./Fl. oz. Bot. 16 oz., gal.
Use: Antitussive, antihistaminic, expectorant, decongestant.

EXPECTO HIST. (Wolins) Guaifenesin 100 mg., phenylephrine HCl, chlorpheniramine maleate 1 mg./Tab. Bot. 1000s.
Use: Antihistaminic, expectorant, decongestant.

EXPECTORANT COUGH SYRUP. (Weeks & Leo) Dextromethorphan HBr 15 mg., guaifenesin 100 mg./5 ml. w/alcohol 7.125%. Bot. 6 oz.
Use: Relief of cough and chest congestion.

EXPENDABLE BLOOD COLLECTION UNIT—ACD. (Travenol) Citric acid 540 mg., sodium citrate 1.49 Gm., dextrose 1.65 Gm./67.5 ml.
Use: Anti-coagulant.

EXSEL. (Herbert) Selenium sulfide 2.5% in shampoo base. Lotion. Bot. 4 oz.
Use: Seborrheic dermatitis and tinea versicolor.

EXTEN STRONE 10. (Schlicksup) Estradiol valerate 10 mg./cc. Vial 10 cc.

EXTEND. (Edward J. Moore) Benzocaine, dibucaine. Tube 1 oz.
Use: Desensitizer.

EXTEND 12. (Robins) Dextromethorphan resin complex equivalent to 30 mg. Dextromethorphan H Br. Bot. 2 oz., 4 oz.
Use: Antitussive.

EXTENDAC. (Vitarine) Belladonna alk. 0.2 mg., phenylpropanolamine HCl 50 mg., chlorpheniramine maleate 1 mg., pheniramine maleate 12.5 mg./T.R. Cap. Pkg. 12s.
Use: Extended action cold capsules.

EXTENDRYL CHEWABLE TABLETS. (Fleming) Chlorpheniramine maleate 2 mg., phenylephrine HCl 10 mg., methscopolamine nitrate 1.25 mg./Chewable Tab. Bot. 100s, 1000s.
Use: Cold treatment.

EXTENDRYL JUNIOR. (Fleming) Chlorpheniramine maleate 4 mg., phenylephrine HCl 10 mg., methscopolamine nitrate 1.25 mg./T.D. Cap.
Use: Cold treatment.

EXTENDRYL SENIOR. (Fleming) Chlorpheniramine maleate 8 mg., phenylephrine HCl 20 mg., methscopolamine nitrate 2.5 mg./T.D. Cap. Bot. 100s, 1000s.
Use: Decongestant, cold treatment.

EXTENDRYL SYRUP. (Fleming) Chlorpheniramine maleate 2 mg., phenylephrine HCl 10 mg., methscopolamine nitrate 1.25 mg./5 cc. Bot. pt., gal.
Use: Decongestant, cold treatment.

EXTENZYME TABLETS. (Allergan) Papain, sodium chloride, sodium carbonate, sodium borate, edetate disodium.
Use: Extenzyme contact soflens protein cleaner.

EXTIL HYDROGEN MALEATE. Carbinoxamine, B.A.N.

EXTRALIN. (Lilly) Liver-stomach concentrate 50 mg./Pulvule. Bot. 84s.
Use: Pernicious anemia.

EXTRA STRENGTH ASPIRIN CAPSULES. (Walgreen) Aspirin 500 mg./Cap. Bot. 80s.
Use: Analgesic.

EXTRA STRENGTH GAS-X. (Creighton) Simethicone 125 mg./Tab. Pkg. 18s.
Use: Antiflatulent.

EXTRA STRENGTH SINUS FORMULA (Eckerd) Acetaminophen 500 mg., chlorpheniramine maleate 2 mg., pseudoephedrine HCl 30 mg./Tab. Bot. 24s.
Use: Analgesic, decongestant, antihistaminic.

EXUL. (Yorktown Products Co.) Nupra (non-hormonic, nonsteridic extract of beef organs, liver, brain, adrenals) 2000 Standard Chick units, dehydrated milk (55% fat) 14 Gm., thiamine HCl 0.6 mg., niacinamide 1.2 mg., ferrous gluconate 8.7 mg., cocoa, coconut oil, casein, sucrose, ethyl vanillin malt ext./Wafer. Bot. 25s.
Use: Gastric or duodenal ulcer.

EXZIT MEDICATED CLEANSER. (Miles Pharm) Colloidal sulfur & salicylic acid cleanser. Dome Dispensajar 4 oz.
Use: Treatment of acne.

EXZIT MEDICATED CREME & LOTION. (Miles Pharm) Colloidal sulfur & resorcinol monoacetate. Creme 1 oz., tube, lotion. Bot. 2 oz.
Use: Treatment of acne.

EYE FACE AND BODY WASH STATION. (Lavoptik) Sodium Cl. 0.49 Gm., sodaium biphosphate 0.40 Gm., sodium phosphate 0.45 Gm./100 ml. w/benzalkonium Cl 0.005%. Bot. 32 oz.
Use: Emergency wash for face and body.

EYE MO. (Winthrop Products) Boric acid, benzalconium Cl, phenelephrine HCl, zinc sulfate.
Use: Ophthalmic solution.

EYE-SED OPHTHALMIC SOLUTION. (Scherer) Boric Acid 2.17%, zinc sulfate 0.217%, chlorobutanol 0.25% in purified water. Bot. 0.5 fl. oz.
Use: Astringent eye wash for use in some common types of blepharitis, especially conjunctivitis, commonly known as pink eye.

EYE-STREAM. (Alcon) Sod. chloride, potassium chloride, calcium chloride, magnesium chloride, benzalkonium chloride 0.013% sod. citrate, sod. acetate. Bot. 1 oz., 4 oz.
Use: Foreign body irrigation, emergency flushing of eyes.

EZE PAIN. (Halsey) Acetaminophen 2.5 gr., salicylamide, caffeine/Cap. Bot. 21.
Use: Analgesic.

EZOL. (Stewart-Jackson) Butalbital 50 mg., caffeine 40 mg., acetaminophen 325 mg./Cap. Bot. 100s.
Use: Treatment of tension headache.

EZOL #3. (Stewart-Jackson) Butalbital 50 mg., caffeine 40 mg., acetaminophen 325 mg., codeine 30 mg./Tab. Bot. 100s.
Use: Treatment of mild to moderate pain.

F

FACT HOME PREGNANCY TEST KIT. (Advanced Care) 1 test per kit.
Use: Accurate test for pregnancy in 45 minutes, for use as early as 3 days after a missed period.

FACTORATE. (Armour) Antihemophilic factor (human) dried for intravenous administration only. Average potency ranges of 225 I.U., 275 I.U., 325 I.U., 375 I.U., 500 I.U., 700 I.U. and 1000 I.U. w/diluent and needles.
Use: Classical hemophilia treatment.

FACTORATE GENERATION II. (Armour) Antihemophilic factor (human) dried for I.V. administration only. 250 I.U., 500 I.U., 1000 I.U. or 1500 I.U. w/diluent and needles.
Use: Classical hemophilia treatment.

• **FACTOR IX COMPLEX,** U.S.P. XXI.
Use: Hemostatic.

FACTREL. (Ayerst) Gonadorelin HCl 100 mcg. or 500 mcg./Vial w/Ampul of 2 ml. sterile diluent.
Use: Evaluation of hypothalamic-pituitary gonadotropic function.

FALGOS TABLETS. (Winthrop Products) Acetylsalicylic acid.
Use: Analgesic, antipyretic, antiinflammatory.

FALMONOX. (Winthrop Products) Teclozan available as suspension and tablets.
Use: Intestinal amebicide.

• **FAMOTIDINE.** USAN.
Use: Antagonist (to histamine hydrogen receptors).

• **FAMOTIN HCl.** USAN. 1-[(p-Chlorophenoxy)-methyl]-3, 4-dihydroisoquinoline HCl.
Use: Antiviral.

FAMPROFAZONE. B.A.N. 4-Isopropyl-2-methyl-3-[N-methyl-N-(α-methyl-phenethyl)aminomethyl]-1-phenyl-5-pyrazolone.
Use: Analgesic; antipyretic.

• **FANETIZOLE MESYLATE.** USAN.
Use: Immunoregulator.

FANSIDAR. (Roche) Sulfadoxine 500 mg., pyrimethamine 25 mg./Tab. Box 25s.

Use: Treatment of malaria due to susceptible strains of plasmodia.

ANTHRIDONE. B.A.N. 5-(3-Dimethylaminopropyl)-phenanthridone. AGN 616 is the hydrochloride.
Use: Antidepressant.

FANTRIDONE HCl. USAN. 5-[3-(Dimethylamino)-propyl]-6(5H)-phenanthridinone monohydrochloride monohydrate.
Use: Antidepressant.

ARA-GEL ANTACID TABLETS. (Faraday) Tab. Bot. 100s.

ARAMALS. (Faraday) Vit. A 10,000 I.U., D 2,000 I.U., B-1 6 mg., B-2 4 mg., B-6 0.5 mg., folic acid 0.1 mg., C 100 mg., Ca pantothenate 5 mg., niacinamide 30 mg., E 5 I.U., B-12 3 mcg./Tab. Bot. 100s, 250s, 500s, 1000s.
Use: Vitamin supplement.

ARAMALS-M. (Faraday) Faramals plus Ca 103 mg., Co 0.1 mg., Cu 1 mg., iodine 0.15 mg., Fe 10 mg., Mg 6 mg., molybdenum 0.2 mg., P 80 mg., K 5 mg., Zn 1.2 mg./Tab Bot. 100s, 250s, 500s, 1000s.
Use: Vitamin and mineral supplement.

ARAMINS. (Faraday) Vit. B-1 20 mg., B-2 6 mg., C 40 mg., niacinamide 20 mg., Ca pantothenate 3 mg., B-6 0.5 mg., pow. whole dried liver 125 mg., dried debittered yeast 125 mg., choline dihydrogen citrate 20 mg., inositol 20 mg., dl-methionine 20 mg., folic acid 0.1 mg., B-12 10 mcg., ferrous gluconate 30 mg., dicalcium phos. 250 mg., Cu sulf. 5 mg., Mg sulf. 10 mg., Mn sulf. 5 mg., Co sulf. 0.2 mg., pot. chloride 2 mg., pot. iodide 0.15 mg. Tab. Bot. 100s, 250s, 500s, 1000s.
Use: Multiple vitamin, mineral supplement.

ARA-SIN. (Faraday) Tab. Bot. 50s.
Use: Pain relief of sinus & common colds.

ARATAC. (Faraday) Flat 10 (contac). Cap. Flat 10.

ARATOL. (Faraday) Vit. A 12,500 I.U., D 1000 I.U., B-1 20 mg., B-2 6 mg., B-6 0.5 mg., B-12 15 mcg., folic acid, 0.1 mg., niacinamide 10 mg., Ca pantothenate 3 mg., C 60 mg., E 5 I.U., choline dihydrogen citrate 20 mg., inositol 20 mg., dl-methionine 20 mg., whole dried liver 100 mg., dried debittered yeast 100 mg., dicalcium phos. 200 mg., ferrous gluconate 30 mg., pot. iodide 0.2 mg., Mg. sulf. 7.2 mg., Cu sulf. 5 mg., Mn sulf. 3.4 mg., Co sulf. 0.2 mg., pot. chloride 1.3 mg., Zn sulf. 2 mg., molybdenum 0.2 mg., in a base of alfalfa. Tab. Bot. 100s, 250s, 500s, 1000s.
Use: Vitamin, mineral supplement.

ARATUSS. (Faraday) Cough syrup. Coca-Cola base. Bot. 4 oz., 8 oz.

ARATUSS JR. (Faraday) Cough syrup. Coca-Cola base. Bot. 4 oz.
Use: Cough preparation.

ARBITAL COMPOUND CAPSULES. (Major) Butalbital, caffeine and aspirin. Bot. 100s.
Use: Analgesic, sedative.

ARBITAL COMPOUND WITH CODEINE #3. (Major) Butalbital, caffeine, aspirin and codeine 30 mg. Bot. 1000s
Use: Analgesic, sedative.

ARBITAL TABS. (Major) Butalbital. Bot. 100s.
Use: Analgesic, sedative.

FARNOQUINONE. 2-Difarnesyl-3-methyl-1, 4-naphthoquinone.

FASTIN. (Beecham Labs) Phentermine HCl 30 mg./Cap. Bot. 100s, 450s. Pack 150s. (5 × 30s).
Use: Anorexiant.

FATTIBASE. (Paddock) Preblended fatty acid suppository base composed of triglycerides of cocoanut oil and palm kernel oil. Jar 1 lb., 5 lb.
Use: Fatty acid suppository base.

FAT, UNSATURATED.
See: Arcofac, Emul. (Armour)
Lufa, Cap. (USV Pharm.)

FATTY ACIDS, UNSATURATED.
See: Fats, Unsaturated
Linolestrol, Oint. (Vortech)
Undecylenic Acid (Various Mfr.)

FAZADINIUM BROMIDE. 1,1′-Azobis(3-methyl-2-phenylimidazo[1,2-α]pyridinium bromide).
Use: Neuromuscular blocking agent.

F.C.A.H. CAPSULES. (Scherer) Chlorpheniramine maleate 4 mg., acetaminophen 162 mg., salicylamide 162 mg., atropine sulfate 0.130 mg./Cap. Bot. 100s, 500s.
Use: Antihistaminic, analgesic.

• **FEBANTEL.** USAN.
Use: Anthelmentic.

FEBERIN. (Arcum) Ferrous gluconate 3 gr., C 25 mg., B-1 2 mg., B-6 1 mg., B-2 1 mg., niacinamide 5 mg./Tab. Bot. 100s, 1000s.
Use: Iron deficiency.

FEBRAMINE HYDROCHLORIDE. Cetoxime, B.A.N.

FEBREX ELIXIR. (Pan American) Acetaminophen 125 mg./5 ml. Bot. 16 oz.
Use: Analgesic.

FEBRILE ANTIGENS. (Laboratory Diagnostics) Group O antigens (somatic) are dyed blue and group H antigens (flagellars) are dyed red for clear identification. Vials 5 ml.
Use: Detection of presence of bacterial agglutinins, bacterial infection.

FEBRIN. (Jenkins) Acetophenetidin 0.1 Gm., acid acetylsalicylic 0.12 gm., caffeine 15 mg., camphor monobromated 60 mg./Tab. Bot. 1000s.
Use: Colds and muscular soreness.

FEBRINETTS. (Jenkins) Acetophenetidin 0.5 gr., acid acetylsalicylic 1 gr., camphor monobromated 1/40 gr., caffeine 1/20 gr./Tab. Bot. 1000s.
Use: Analgesic.

FEBRINOL. (Vitarine) Acetaminophen 325 mg./Tab. Bot. 100s.
Use: Analgesic.

FE-BRONE. (Fellows) Vit. B-12 1 I.U., folic acid 1 mg., ferrous sulfate exsic. (powd.) 200 mg., ferrous sulfate exsic. (timed) 200 mg., Vit. C acid 100 mg., B-6 0.5 mg., B-1 2 mg., B-2 1 mg., Cu 0.9 mg., Zn 0.5 mg., Mn 0.3 mg./Cap. Bot. 30s, 100s, 1000s.
Use: Vitamin, mineral supplement.

FECO-T. (Blaine) Ferrous fumarate 300 mg./Tab. Bot. 100s.

FEDAHIST EXPECTORANT. (Rorer) Guaiafenesin 100 mg., pseudoephedrine HCl 30 mg., chlorpheniramine maleate 2 mg./5 ml. Nonalcoholic. Bot. 4 oz.
Use: Antihistaminic, decongestant, expectorant.

FEDAHIST GYROCAPS. (Rorer) Pseudoephedrine HCl 65 mg., chlorpheniramine maleate 10 mg./T.R. Cap. Bot. 100s.
Use: Antihistaminic, decongestant.

FEDAHIST SYRUP. (Rorer) Pseudoephedrine HCl 30 mg., chlorpheniramine maleate 2 mg./5 ml. Nonalcoholic. Bot. 4 oz.
Use: Antihistaminic, decongestant.

FEDAHIST TABLETS. (Rorer) Pseudoephedrine HCl 60 mg., chlorpheniramine maleate 4 mg./Tab. Bot. 100s.
Use: Antihistaminic, decongestant.

FEDNAL. (Blue Line) Ephedrine sulfate 1%, camphor 2.5%, menthol 0.5% in petrolatum ointment base. Tube ⅖ oz., 12S.
Use: Nasal cream.

FEDRAZIL. (Burroughs Wellcome) Pseudoephedrine HCl 30 mg., chlorcyclizine HCl 25 mg./Tab. Bot. 24s, 100s.
Use: Respiratory tract congestion.

FEDREX. (Blue Line) Ephedrine HCl, potassium guaiacolsulfonate, sodium bromide in a glycerinated and aromatized cane sugar syrup. Alcohol 3%. Bot. gal.
Use: Cough preparation.

FEDRINAL. (H.L. Moore) Ephedrine HCl 12 mg., phenobarbital 12 mg., potassium iodide 160 mg., theophylline anhydrous 31.2 mg./5 ml. Bot. Pts., Gal.
Use: Respiratory conditions.

FEEN-A-MINT GUM. (Plough)Yellow phenolphthalein 97.2mg. Chewing gum Tab. Box 5s, 16s, 40s.
Use: Laxative.

FEEN-A-MINT MINT. (Plough) Yellow phenolphthalein 97.2 mg./Mint Tab. Box 20s.
Use: Laxative.

FEET TREAT. (DeWitt) Water, stearic acid, isopropyl myristate, propylene glycol, lanolin, triethanolamine, p-Chloro-m-xylenol, menthol, mag. alum. silicate, allantoin. Bot. 8 oz.
Use: Soften hard skin & calluses.

FEET TREET CREAM. (DeWitt) Stearic acid, isoprop myristate, propylene glycol, lanolin, triethanolamine, p-Chloro-m-Xylenol, menthol, Mg. aluminum silicate, allantoin. Bot. 8 oz.
Use: Soften hard skin and calluses.

FEG-L. (Western Research) Ferrous gluconate 300 mg./Tab. Handicount 28s (36 bags of 28 tab.)

FELDENE. (Pfizer Laboratories) Piroxicam. 10 mg./Cap. Bot 100s. **20mg.**/Cap. Bot. 100s, 500s. Unit dose 100s.
Use: Osteoarthritis and rheumatoid arthritis.

FELLOBOLIC INJECTION. (Fellows) Methandriol dipropionate 50 mg./cc. Vial 10 cc.

FELLO-SED. (Fellows) Chloral hydrate 0.625 Gm., cal. bromide 0.625 Gm., atropine sulfate 0.156 mg./5 cc. Bot. 8 oz., gal.
Use: Sedative & hypnotic.

FELLOWS COMPOUND SYRUP. (Fellows) Strychnine hypophosphite 1.25 mg., quinine sulfate 3.75 mg., potassium hypophosphite 10 mg., sod. hypophosphite 10 mg., cal. hypophosphite 25 mg., manganese hypophosphite 10 mg., iron pyrophosphate 10 mg./5 cc. Bot. 7 oz., gal.

FELLOZINE. (Fellows) Promethazine HCl 25 mg., 50 mg./cc. Vial 10 cc. Amp. 1 cc., 25s.
Use: Antihistaminic.

FELSULES. (Fellows) Chloral hydrate 0.25 Gm./Cap. Bot. 100s, 500s, 0.5 Gm./Cap. Bot. 50s, 100s, 250s, 500s. Unit dose 100s.
Use: Sedative.

• **FELYPRESSIN.** USAN. 2-(Phenylalanine)-8-lysine vasopressin.
Use: Vasoconstrictor.

FELYPRESSIN. B.A.N. 2-Phenylalanine-8-lysinevasopressin.
Use: Vasoconstrictor.
See: Octapressin.

FEMAGENE. (Tennessee) Boric acid, sod. borate, lactic acid, menthol, methylbenzethonium chloride, parachlorometaxylenol, lactose, surface-active agents. Pow. 6 oz.
Use: Feminine hygiene.

FEMAZOLE TABS. (Major) Metronidazole 250 mg./Tab. Bot. 100s, 250s, 500s. 500 mg./Tab. Bot 100s.
Use: Anaerobic infections.

FEMCAPS. (Buffington) Acetaminophen, caffeine, ephedrine sulfate, atropine sulfate /Tab. Sugar, lactose and salt free Dispens-a-Kit 500s. Aidpak 100s.
Use: Temporary relief of minor menstrual pains and cramps.

FEMERGIN.
See: Ergotamine Tartrate (Various Mfr.)

FEMEZE. (Stanlabs) Acetaminophen, salicylamide, caffeine alk., ammonium chloride, Vit. B-1, homatropine HBr/Tab. Carton 14s.
Use: Analgesic: periodic pain reliever.

FEMID GREEN LABEL. (Cenci) Sod. bicarbonate, sod. borate, sod. chloride, sod. perborate, menthol. Pow. Bot. 7 oz., 15 oz.
Use: Vaginal cleansing & deodorant.

FEMID PINK LABEL. (Cenci) Sodium lauryl sulfate, aluminum ammonium sulf., boracic acid, citric acid, menthol. Pow. Bot. 7 oz.
Use: Vaginal cleansing and deodorant.

FEMIDINE. (A.V.P.) Povidone-iodine. Bot. 8 oz.
Use: Cleansing douche (dilute with water).

FEMIDYN.
See: Estrone (Various Mfr.)

FEMINONE. (Upjohn) Ethinyl estradiol. 0.05 mg./Tab. Bot. 100s.
Use: Estrogen supplement.

FEMIRON. (Beecham Products) Iron 20 mg./Tab. Bot 40s, 120s.
Use: Iron supplement.

FEMIRON MULTI-VITAMINS AND IRON. (Beecham Products) Iron 20 mg., Vit. A 5,000 I.U., D 400 I.U., B-1 1.5 mg., riboflavin 1.7 mg., niacinamide 20 mg., C

60 mg., B-6 2 mg., B-12 6 mcg., calcium pantothenate 10 mg., folic acid 0.4 mg., E 15 I.U./Tab. Bot. 35s, 60s, 90s.
Use: Iron and vitamin supplement.
:MOGEN-L.A. (Fellows) Estradiol valerate 10 mg., 20 mg./cc. Inj. 10 cc. 40 mg./cc. Inj. 5 cc.
:MOTRONE. (Bluco) Progesterone in oil 50 mg./ml. Vial 10 ml.
Use: Progestin supplement.
:MSPAN. (Fellows) Pot. estrone sulfate 1 mg., estrone 2 mg./cc. Vial 10 ml.
Use: Menopausal symptoms.
:MGUARD VAGINAL CREAM. (Reid-Provident) Sulfathiazole 3.42%, sulfacetamide 2.86%, sulfabenzamide 3.7%, urea 0.64%, w/glyceryl monostearate, cetyl alcohol, stearic acid, lecithin, peanut oil, diethylaminoethyl steramide, phosphoric acid, propylene glycol, ethoxylated cholesterol, methyl paraben, propyl paraben, purified water. Tube 2.75 oz. w/Applicator.
Use: Treatment of vaginal infections.
FENALAMIDE. USAN. (1) Ethyl N-[2-(diethylamino)-ethyl]-2-ethyl-2-phenylmalonamate; (2) Phenylethylmalonic acid monoethyl ester diethylaminoethylamide.
Use: Smooth muscle relaxant.
:NAMISAL. Phenyl aminosalicylate.
FENAMOLE. USAN. 5-Amino-1-phenyl-1H-tetrazol.
Use: Anti-inflammatory agent.
:NAPRIN TABLETS. (Winthrop Products) Aspirin, chlormezanone.
Use: Analgesic, muscle relaxanat.
:NAROL. (Winthrop Products) Chlormezanone 100 mg., 200 mg./Tab. Bot. 100s.
Use: Central relaxant and tranquilizer.
:NARSONE.
See: Carbarsone (Various Mfr.)
FENBENDAZOLE. USAN.
Use: Anthelmintic.
FENBUFEN. USAN.
Use: Anti-inflammatory.
ENCAMFAMIN. B.A.N. N-Ethyl-3-phenylbicyclo-[2.2.1]hept-2-ylamine.
Use: Central nervous system stimulant; appetite suppressant.
See: Euvitaol [hydrochloride].
ENCHLORPHOS. B.A.N. OO-Dimethyl O-(2,4,5-trichlorophenyl) phosphorothioate.
Use: Insecticide, veterinary medicine.
See: Nankor
Ronnel
Trolene.
FENCILBUTIROL. USAN.
Use: Choleretic.
FENCLOFENAC. USAN. 2-(2,4-Dichlorophenoxy)-phenylacetic acid.
Use: Anti-inflammatory.
FENCLONINE. USAN. dl-3-(p-Chlorophenyl)-alanine. Under study by Pfizer.
Use: Serotonin biosynthesis inhibitor.
FENCLORAC. USAN.
Use: Anti-inflammatory.
FENCLOZIC ACID. B.A.N. 2-(4-Chlorophenyl)-thiazol-4-ylacetic acid.
Use: Anti-inflammatory.
FEND. (Mine Safety Appliances)
A-2—Water soluble cream which forms a physical barrier to water insoluble irritants. Tube 3 oz., Jar 1 lb.
E-2—This cream combines the functions of the water soluble Fend A-2 and water insoluble Fend I-2 creams. Tube 3 oz., Jar 1 lb.
I-2—Water insoluble cream which forms a physical barrier to water soluble irritants. Tube 3 oz., Jar 1 lb.
S-2—A silicone cream which forms a barrier against a combination of water soluble and water insoluble irritants. Tube 3 oz., Jar 1 lb.
X—Industrial cold cream which rubs well into the skin and serves as a skin conditioner. Tube 3 oz., Jar 1 lb.
Use: Protective creams against irritants of industrial and household origin.
FENDOL. (Buffington) Salicylamide, caffeine, acetaminophen, phenylephrine HCl, atropine sulfate/Tab. Sugar, lactose, and salt free. Dispens-A-Kit 500s. Bot. 100s.
Use: Analgesic and decongestant for relief of the common cold symptoms.
• **FENDOSAL.** USAN.
Use: Anti-inflammatory.
• **FENESTREL.** USAN. 5-Ethyl-6-methyl-4-phenyl-3-cyclohexene-1-carboxylic acid. Under study.
Use: Nonsteroid estrogen.
FENETHYLLINE. B.A.N. 7-[2-(α-Methylphenethylamino)ethyl]theophylline.
Use: Cerebral stimulant.
• **FENETHYLLINE HYDROCHLORIDE.** USAN. 7-[2-[(α-Methylphenethyl)-amino]-ethyl]theophylline hydrochloride.
Use: Stimulant.
FENFLURAMINE. B.A.N. 2-Ethylamino-1-(3-trifluoromethylphenyl)propane. N-Ethyl-α-methyl-3-trifluoromethylphenethylamine.
Use: Appetite suppressant.
See: Ponderax [hydrochloride].
• **FENFLURAMINE HYDROCHLORIDE.** USAN. N-ethyl-α-methyl-m-(trifluoro-methyl)-phenethylamine hydro-chloride.
Use: Sympathomimetic (anorexic).
See: Pondimin, Tab. (Robins)
Pendimin, Tab.
• **FENIMIDE.** USAN. 3-Ethyl-2-methyl-2-phenylsuccinimide.
Use: Tranquilizer.
• **FENISOREX.** USAN. (±)-cis-7-Fluoro-1-phenylisochroman-3-ylmethylamine.
Use: Anorexigenic.
• **FENMETOZOLE HYDROCHLORIDE.** USAN.
Use: Antidepressant, antagonist.
• **FENMETRAMIDE.** USAN.
Use: Antidepressant.
• **FENNEL OIL.** N.F. XVI.
Use: Pharmaceutic aid (flavor).
• **FENOBAM.** USAN.
Use: Sedative.

• **FENOCTIMINE SULFATE.** USAN.
Use: Gastric antisecretory.

• **FENOLDOPAM MESYLATE.** USAN
Use: Antihypertensive.

• **FENOPROFEN.** USAN. 2-(3-Phenoxyphenyl)-propionic acid. (±)-m-Phenoxyhydratropic acid; (2) dl-2-(3-phenoxyphenyl)-propionic acid.
Use: Anti-inflammatory; analgesic.

• **FENOPROFEN CALCIUM,** U.S.P. XXI. Cap., Tab., U.S.P. XXI.
Use: Anti-inflammatory, analgesic.

FENOSTIL. B.A.N. Dimethindene.

• **FENOTEROL.** USAN. (1)3,5-Dihydroxy-α-[[(p-hydroxy-α-methylphenethyl) amino] methyl]-benzyl alcohol; (2) 1-(3,5-Dihydroxyphenyl)-2-[[1-(4-hydroxybenzyl)ethyl]amino] ethanol.
Use: Bronchodilator.

• **FENPIPALONE.** USAN.
Use: Anti-inflammatory.

FENPIPRAMIDE. B.A.N. 2,2-Diphenyl-4-piperidonobutyramide.
Use: Spasmolytic.

FENPIPRANE. B.A.N. 1-(3,3-Diphenylpropyl)-piperidine.
Use: Spasmolytic.

• **FENPRINAST HYDROCHLORIDE.** USAN.
Use: Anti-allergic bronchodilator.

• **FENPROSTALENE.** USAN.
Use: Luteolysin.

• **FENQUIZONE.** USAN.
Use: Diuretic.

• **FENRETINIDE.** USAN.
Use: Antineoplastic.

• **FENSPIRIDE HYDROCHLORIDE.** USAN.
Use: Bronchodilator, anti-adrenergic.

FENTANYL. B.A.N. 1-Phenethyl-4-(N-propionylanilino)-piperidine.
Use: Narcotic analgesic.
See: Sublimaze.

• **FENTANYL CITRATE,** U.S.P. XXI. Inj. U.S.P. XXI. N-(1-phenethyl-4-piperidyl) propionanilide citrate. Propanamide, N-phenyl-N-[1-(2-phenyl-ethyl)-4-piperidinyl]-, 2-hydroxy-1,2,3-propanetricarboxylate (1:1).
Use: Narcotic analgesic.
See: Innovar, Inj. (Janssen)
Sublimaze, Inj. (Janssen)

• **FENTIAZAC.** USAN.
Use: Anti-inflammatory.

• **FENTICLOR.** USAN. Di-(5-chloro-2-hydroxyphenyl)-sulfide.
Use: Antiseptic, fungicide.

• **FENTICONAZOLE NITRATE.** USAN.
Use: Antifungal.

FENTON ELIXIR. (Winthrop Products) Ferrous Gluconate.
Use: Hematinic, dietary supplement.

FENYLHIST. (Mallard) Diphenhydramine HCl 50 mg./Cap. 25 mg./Capsule. **Cap.:** Bot. 1000s.
Use: Antihistamine with anticholinergic and sedative effects.

FENYRAMIDOL HCl. Phenyramidol HCl.

• **FENYRIPOL HYDROCHLORIDE.** USAN. α-(2-Pyrimidinylaminomethyl) benzyl alcohol hydrochloride.
Use: Skeletal muscle relaxant.

FENZOL. Dichloralphenazone, B.A.N.

FEOCYTE. (Dunhall) Ferrous fumarate 260 mg., ferrous gluconate 65 mg., Vit. C 100 mg., B-6 2 mg., cyanocobalamin 50 mcg., copper sulf. 2 mg., desiccated liver 15 mg., ferrous sulf. 65 mg./Time Cap. Bot. 100s, 1000s. T.D. Tab. Bot. 100s, 1000s.
Use: Hematinic.

FEOCYTE INJECTABLE. (Dunhall) Peptonized iron 15 mg., B-12 200 mcg., liver inj. N.F. beef, 10 u., sodium citrate 10 mg., benzyl alcohol 2%/ml. Vial 10 ml.
Use: Hematinic.

FEOSOL CAPSULES. (Menley & James) Dried ferrous sulfate 250 mg./S.R. Cap. Bot. 30s, 100s, 500s. Unit dose 100s.
Use: Sustained release action of ferrous sulfate in the treatment of iron deficiency anemias and simple iron deficiency.

FEOSOL ELIXIR. (Menley & James) Ferrous sulfate 220 mg./5 cc. w/alcohol 5%. Bot. 16 oz.
Use: Iron-deficiency anemias and simple iron deficiency.

FEOSOL PLUS. (Menley & James) Vit. B-1 2 mg., B-12 5 mcg., B-2 2 mg., niacin 20 mg., B-6 2 mg., 50 mg., folic acid 0.2 mg., dried-ferrous sulfate 3[illegible] mg./Cap. Bot. 100s.
Use: Iron deficiency anemias and simple iron deficiency.

FEOSOL TABLETS. (Menley & James) Dried ferrous sulfate 200 mg./Tab. Bot. 100s, 1000s, Unit Dose 100s.
Use: Iron deficiency anemias and simple iron deficiency.

FEOSTAT. (Forest) Iron 50 mg./ml. Vial 10 ml.

FEOSTAT. (Forest) **Tab.:** Ferrous fumarate 100 mg., or 200 mg./Chewable Tab. Bot. 100s. **Drops:** Ferrous fumarate 45 mg./0.6 ml. Bot. 2 oz.
Use: Iron deficiency anemia.

FEOSTAT SUSPENSION. (Forest) Ferrous fumarate 100 mg./5 cc. Bot. 8 oz.
Use: Anemia.

F-E-P CREME. (Boots) Hydrocortisone 1.0%, pramoxine HCl 0.5% in cream base. Tube 15 Gm.
Use: Relief of inflammatory & pruritic dermatoses.

FE-PLUS PROTEIN. (Miller) Iron (as an iron-protein complex) 50 mg./Tab. Bot. 100s.
Use: Anemia.

FEPRAZONE. B.A.N. 4-(3-Methylbut-2-enyl)-1,2-diphenylpyrazolidine-3,5-dione.
Use: Analgesic; anti-inflammatory.

FERANCEE. (Stuart) Elemental iron 67 mg. (from 20[illegible] mg. ferrous fumarate), Vit. C 150 mg./Tab. Bot. 100s.
Use: Chewable tablet for treatment of iron deficiency anemia.

FERANCEE-HP. (Stuart) Elemental iron 110 mg. (from 330 mg. ferrous fumarate), Vit. C 600 mg./Tab. Bot. 60s.
Use: Treatment of iron deficiency anemia.

RATE-C. (Vale) Ferrous fumarate 150 mg., ascorbic acid 200 mg., docusate sodium 25 mg./Tab. Bot. 100s, 500s, 1000s.
Use: Hematinic.

RATIN. (Pasadena Research) Iron 70 mg., Vit. B-12 10 mcg., C 60 mg., B-1 5 mg., B-2 3.5 mg., B-6 1 mg., niacinamide 50 mg., Ca pantothenate 5 mg., copper 0.1 mg., liver desic. 390 mg./Tab. Bot. 100s, 1000s.

R-GEN-SOL DROPS. (Goldline) Ferrous sulfate drops. Bot. 50 ml.
Use: Dietary supplement of iron.

RGON. (Winthrop-Breon) Pure ferrous gluconate. **Tab.** 320 mg. equal to approximately 36 mg. ferrous iron/Tab. Bot. 100s, 500s, 1000s, 5000s, 50,000s. **Elixir** (6%), 300 mg./5 ml. Bot. 16 fl. oz. **Cap.** 435 mg. Bot. 30s.
Use: Hematinic.

RGON PLUS. (Winthrop-Breon) Ferrous gluconate 500 mg., vit. B-12 w/intrinsic factor conc. 0.5 u., ascorbic acid 75 mg./Caplet. Bot. 100s.
Use: Hematinic.

R-IN-SOL. (Mead Johnson) **Drops:** Elemental Iron 15 mg./0.6 ml. Bot. w/dropper 50 ml. **Syr:** 18 mg./5 ml. Bot. 16 fl. oz. **Cap:** 60 mg./Cap. Bot. 100s. **Caps.** Bot. 100s.
Use: Dietary supplement of iron.

R-IRON DROPS. (Bay) Ferrous sulfate 125 mg.,/1 cc. Bot. 50 cc.
Use: Iron supplement.

RMALOX. (Rorer) Ferrous sulfate 200 mg., magnesium and aluminum hydroxides (Maalox) 200 mg./Tab. Bot. 100s.
Use: Hematinic.

RMETONE COMPOUND CAPSULES. (Winthrop Products) Pancreatin.
Use: Pancreatic deficiency, dyspepsia.

RNCORT LOTION. (Ferndale) Hydrocortisone acetate 0.5% in lotion base. Bot. 120 ml.
Use: Anti-inflammatory, anti-pruritic.

RO-FOLIC 500. (Abbott) Ferrous sulfate 525 mg. controlled release (Equiv. to 105 mg. Iron), Vit. C 500 mg., folic acid 800 mcg./Filmtab. Bot. 100s, 500s.
Use: Iron and folic acid supplement.

RO-GRAD 500 FILMTAB. (Abbott) Vit. C 500 mg., ferrous sulfate controlled release 525 mg./Filmtab Bot. 30s, 100s, 500s. Abbo-Pac. 100s.
Use: Iron-deficiency anemias.

RO-GRADUMET FILMTAB. (Abbott) Ferrous Sulfate controlled release 525 mg./Filmtab. Bot. 100s.
Use: Treatment of iron-deficiency anemia.

ROLATE. (Pasadena Research) Ferric Cl 2.5 gr., sod. cacodylate 5 gr. in Ringer's soln./10 cc. Amp. 25s.

ROLIX. (Century) Ferrous sulfate 5 gr., alcohol 5%/10 cc. Elix. Bot. 8 oz., pint, gal.

RONATE. (Pasadena Research) Ferrous gluconate 1 gr./ml. Amp. 1 cc., 25s.

ROSAN FORTE. (Sandia) Ferrous fumarate 300 mg., liver-stomach concentrate 150 mg., Vita. B-12 w/intrinsic factor concentrate 7.5 mcg., intrinsic factor concentrate 150 mg., B-12 7.5 mcg., ascorbic acid 75 mg., folic acid 1 mg., sorbitol 50 mg./Tab. Bot. 100s.
Use: Multiple vitamin, mineral supplement.

FEROSAN SYRUP. (Sandia) Ferrous fumarate 91.2 mg., B-1 10 mg., B-6 3 mg., B-12 25 mcg./5 cc. 16 oz., gal.

FEROWEET. (Barth's) Vit. B-1 6 mg., B-2 12 mg. niacin 4 mg., Fe 30 mg., B-12 10 mcg., B-6 95 mcg., pantothenic acid 50 mcg./3 Cap. Bot. 100s, 500s, 1000s.
Use: Iron and vitamin supplement.

FERRACOMP. (Hauck) Liver 2 mcg., B-12 15 mcg., B-1 10 mg., B-2 5 mg., B-6 1 mg., Ca pantothenate 1 mg., niacinamide 10 mg., iron 31.3 mg./ml. Vial 30 ml.
Use: Hematinic & tonic.

FERRALET PLUS. (Mission) Ferrous gluconate 400 mg., ascorbic acid 400 mg., folic acid 1 mg., Vit. B-2 25 mcg./Tab. Bot. 100s.
Use: Hematinic.

FERRALYN. (Lannett) Ferrous sulf. 150 mg./Tab. E.C. Bot. 500s, 1000s.

FERRANOL. (Robinson) Ferrous fumarate 3 gr. or 5 gr./Tab. Bot. 100s, 1000s.

FERRATIHIC. (Wolins) Ferrous sulfate 200 mg., magnesium hydroxide 100 mg., aluminum hydroxide 100 mg. Bot. 100s, 1000s.
Use: Hematinic.

FER-REGULES. (Quality Generics) Ferrous fumarate 150 mg., docusate sodium 100 mg./timed rel. Cap. Bot. 100s, 1000s.
Use: Hematinic, iron deficiency anemia.

FERRIC AMMONIUM CITRATE. Ammonium iron (3+) citrate.
Use: Hematinic.

FERRIC AMMONIUM SULFATE. (Various Mfr.).
Use: Astringent & styptic.

FERRIC AMMONIUM TARTRATE. (Various Mfr.).
Use: Iron deficiency.

FERRIC-B Jr. (Jenkins) Vit. B-12 5 mcg., B-1 2 mg., C 30 mg., iron peptonate. 60 mg./Tab. Bot. 1000s.
Use: Nutritional deficiencies

FERRIC CACODYLATE. (Various Mfr.).
Use: Leukemias & iron deficiency.

FERRIC CHLORIDE. (Various Mfr.)
Use: Astringent for skin disorders.

• **FERRIC CHLORIDE Fe 59.** USAN.
Use: Radioactive agent.

FERRIC CITROCHLORIDE TINCTURE. Iron (3+) chloride citrate.
Use: Hematinic.

• **FERRIC FRUCTOSE.** USAN. Fructose iron complex with potassium (2:1).
Use: Hematinic

FERRIC GLYCEROPHOSPHATE. Glycerol phosphate iron (3+) salt.
Use: Pharmaceutic necessity.

FERRIC HYPOPHOSPHITE. Iron (3+) phosphinate.
Use: Pharmaceutic necessity.

• **FERRICLATE CALCIUM SODIUM.** USAN.
Use: Hematinic.

• **FERRIC OXIDE, RED,** N.F. XVI.
• **FERRIC OXIDE, YELLOW,** N.F. XVI.
FERRIC "PEPTONATE." (Various Mfr.)
See: Iron Peptonized.
FERRIC PYROPHOSPHATE, SOLUBLE. Iron (3+) citrate pyrophosphate.
FERRIC QUININE CITRATE, "GREEN." (Various Mfr.)
Use: For iron deficiency.
FERRIC QUININE & STRYCHNINE CITRATE. (Various Mfr.)
Use: As a tonic.
FERRIC SUBSULFATE SOLUTION. (Various Mfr.)
Use: Local use on the skin.
FERRINAL-C. (Cenci) Ferrous fumarate 3 gr., Vit. C 150 mg./Tab. Bot. 100s, 1000s.
Use: Iron deficiency anemia.
FERRINAL CHRONCAP. (Cenci) Ferrous fumarate 330 mg., thiamine chloride 5 mg./S.R. Cap. Bot. 30s, 100s.
Use: Iron deficiency anemia and dietary supplement.
FERRINAL TABLETS. (Cenci) Ferrous fumarate 3 gr./Tab. Bot. 100s, 1000s.
Use: Iron deficiency anemia.
FERRIZYME. (Abbott) Test kit 100s.
Use: Enzyme immunoassay for qualitative determination of ferritin in human serum or plasma.
FERROCHOLATE.
See: Ferrocholinate
FERROCHOLINATE. Ferrocholate. Ferrocholine. A chelate prepared by reacting equimolar quantities of freshly precipitated ferric hydroxide with choline dihydrogen citrate.
Use: Iron deficiency anemia.
See: Chel-Iron, Prep. (Kinney)
FERROCHOLINE.
See: Ferrocholinate
Kelex, Tabseal. (Nutrition)
FERRO-CYTE. (Spanner) Iron peptonate 20 mg., liver injection (20 mg./cc.) 0.25 cc., Vit. B-1 22 mg., B-2 0.5 mg., B-6 2.5 mg., B-12 30 mcg., niacinamide 25 mg., panthenol 1 mg./cc. Multiple dose vial 10 cc. For I.M. inj.
Use: Iron deficiency.
FERRODYL CHEWABLE TABLETS. (Arcum) Ferrous fumarate 320 mg., Vit. C 200 mg./Tab. Bot. 100s, 1000s.
Use: Iron deficiency.
FERROGEN. (Tunex) Ferrous gluconate 30 mg., citric acid 8.2 mg., sodium citrate 11.8 mg., folic acid 0.5 mg., liver inj. equiv. to cyanocobalamin 2.5 mcg./ml. Vial 30cc.
Use: Iron deficiency and nutritional anemias.
FERRO LEXAMIN. (Eckerd) Bot. 100s.
FERROMAX (INTRAMUSCULAR IRON). (Kenyon) Iron peptonized 100 mg., copper gluconate 0.2 mg., cobalt Cl 4 mg., pectin 10 mg./cc. Vial 10 cc.
FERRON-100 IRON DEXTRAN COMPLEX. (Vortech) Low hydroxide in complex w/ a low molecular weight dextran fraction equiv. to 100 mg. elemental iron, phenol 0.5%/ml. Vial 10 ml.
FERRONEED. (Hanlon) Ferrous gluconate 300 mg., ascorbic acid 60 mg./Cap. Bot. 100s.
FERRONEED T-CAPS. (Hanlon) Ferrous fumarate 2[illegible] mg., thiamine HCl 5 mg., ascorbic acid 50 mg./T.[illegible] Cap. Bot. 100s.
Use: Iron deficiency anemia.
FERRONEX. (Pasadena Research) Liver inj. (10 mcg./ml.) 0.2 ml., B-12 15 mcg., ferrous gluconate mg., B-1 10 mg., B-2 0.5 mg., B-6 1 mg., d-panther[illegible] 1 mg., niacinamide 50 mg., procaine 0.5%, sod. citrate 1%, phenol 0.1%, benzyl alcohol 2%/cc. Vial 30 cc.
Use: Iron deficiency and vitamin therapy.
FERRO-SEQUELS. (Lederle) Ferrous fumarate 150 m[illegible] (Equiv. to 50 mg. Elemental Iron), dioctyl sod. sulfosuccinate 100 mg./Cap. T.D. Bot. 30s, 100s, 1000s. Unit dose 10×10s.
Use: Treatment of iron deficiency anemia.
FERROSPAN CAPSULES. (Imperial Lab.) Ferrous fumarate 200 mg., ascorbic acid 100 mg./Tab. Bo[illegible] 100s, 1000s.
Use: Treatment of iron deficiency anemias.
FERROSYN INJECTION. (Standex) Cyanocabalami[illegible] 30 mcg., liver 2 mcg., ferrous gluconate 100 mg., riboflavin 1.5 mg., panthenol 2.5 mg., niacinamide 100 mg., procaine 2%. Vials 30 cc.
Use: Vitamin supplement.
FERROSYN S.C. (Standex) Iron 60 mg., Vit. B-12 mcg., Mg 0.6 mg., Cu 0.3 mg., Mn 0.1 mg., K 0.5 mg., Zn 0.15 mg./Tab. Bot. 100s, 1000s.
FERROSYN SEE TABS. (Standex) Iron 34 mg., ascorbic acid 60 mg./Tab. Bot. 100s, 1000s.
Use: Hematinic with ascorbic acid.
FERROSYN TAB. (Standex) Iron 60 mg., Vit. B-12 mcg., Mg 0.6 mg., Cu 0.3 mg., Mn 0.1 mg., K 0.5 mg., Zn 0.15 mg./Tab. Bot. 100s.
FERROUS BROMIDE. (Various Mfr.)
Use: In chorea & tuberculous cervical adenitis.
FERROUS CARBONATE MASS. Vallet's mass. (Various Mfr.).
Use: For iron deficiency.
FERROUS CARBONATE, SACCHARATED. (Variou[illegible] Mfr.)
Use: For iron deficiency.
• **FERROUS CITRATE Fe-59 INJECTION,** U.S.P. X[illegible]
Use: Radioactive agent.
• **FERROUS FUMARATE,** U.S.P. XXI. Tabs., U.S.P. XXI.
Use: Hematinic.
See: Arne-C, Chew. Tab. (Haag)
Cefera, Tab. (Haag)
Childron, Susp. (Fleming)
Eldofe, Tab. (Canright)
El-Ped-Ron, Liq. (Elder)
Farbegen, Cap. (Hickam)
Feco-T., Cap. (Blaine)
Fumasorb, Tab. (Marion)
Fumerin, Tab. (Laser)
Hemocyte, Tab., Liq. (Medics)
Ircon, Tab. (Key)
Laud-Iron, Tab., Susp. (Amfre-Grant)
Maniron, Meltab. (Bowman)

/Ascorbic Acid.
See: C-Ron, Prep. (Rowell)
Cytoferin, Tabs. (Ayerst)
Eldofe-C, Tab. (Canright)
Ferancee, Tab. (Stuart)
Ferancee-HP, Tab. (Stuart)
Ferrodyl Chewable Tab. (Arcum)
Hema-C Meta-Kaps, Cap. (Sutliff & Case)
Min-Hema Chewable, Tab. (Scrip)
/Ascorbic acid, copper sulfate.
See: Ferrobid, Cap. (Glaxo)
/Ascorbic acid, & folic acid.
See: C-Ron F.A., Tab. (Rowell)
/Docusate sodium.
See: Fer-Regules, Cap. (Quality Generics)
Ferro-Sequels, Cap. (Lederle)
/Norethindrone, mestranol.
See: Ortho Novum 1/80 Fe 28, 1/50 Fe-28, 1 mg. Fe-28, Tabs. (Ortho)
/Thiamine.
See: Arner Timesules, Caps. (Haag)
/Vitamins and minerals.
See: Cohema, Tabs. (Sutliff & Case)
Stuart Formula, Tab. (Stuart)
Stuart Prenatal, Tab. (Stuart)
Stuartnatal 1 + 1, Tab. (Stuart)
Theron, Tab. (Stuart)
Vitanate, Tab. (Century)

FERROUS GLUCONATE. U.S.P. XXI. Cap., Elixir, Tab., U.S.P. XXI. Iron (2+) Gluconate.
Use: Iron deficiency.
See: Entron, Cap., Tab. (LaCrosse)
Fergon Prods. (Winthrop-Breon)
Ferrous-G, Elix. (Kenwood)
/Ascorbic acid, desiccated liver, vitamin B complex.
See: I.L.X. w/B-12, Tab. (Kenwood)
Stuart Hematinic, Liq. (Stuart)
/Polyoxyethylene glucitan monolaurate.
See: Simron, Cap. (Merrell Dow)

:RROUS IODIDE. (Various Mfr.)
Use: In chronic tuberculosis.

:RROUS IODIDE SYRUP. (Various Mfr.)
Use: In chronic tuberculosis.

:RROUS LACTATE. (Various Mfr.)
Use: For iron deficiency.

FERROUS SULFATE, U.S.P. XXI. Tab., Dried, Syr., Oral Soln., U.S.P. XXI.
Use: Iron deficiency
See: Feosol, Spansule, Tab., Elix. (Menley & James)
Ferralyn, Cap. (Lannett)
Fero-Gradumet, Tab. (Abbott)
Ferolix, Elix. (Century)
Ferrous Sulfate Filmseals, Tab. (Parke-Davis)
Fesotyme SR, Cap. (Elder)
Irospan Cap., Tab. (Fielding)
Mol-Iron, Prods. (Schering)
Telefon, Cap. (Kenyon)
/Ascorbic acid.
See: Fero-Grad-500, Tab. (Abbott)
Mol-Iron W/Vit. C, Tab., Chronosules (Schering)
W/Ascorbic acid, folic acid.
See: Fero-Folic-500, Tab. (Abbott)
W/Cyanocobalamin, ascorbic acid, folic acid.
See: Intrin, Cap. (Merit)
W/Folic acid.
See: Folvron, Cap. (Lederle)
W/Maalox
See: Fermalox, Tab. (Rorer)

FERROUS SULFATE FILMSEALS. (Parke-Davis) Ferrous Sulfate 5 gr./d release Tab. Bot. 1000s. Unit dose 100s.
Use: Iron deficiency.

• **FERROUS SULFATE Fe 59.** USAN.
Use: Radioisotope.

FERTILITY TAPE. (Weston Labs.) Regular, extrasensitive, less-sensitive. Pkg. 60 tests.
Use: W/Fertility Testor, cervical glucose test.

FERUSAL. (Vitarine) Ferrous sulfate 325 mg./Tab.
Use: Dietary supplement.

FESTAL II. (Hoechst) Lipase 6000 U., amylase 30,000 U., protease 20,000 U./Tab. Bot. 100s, 500s.
Use: Enzymes for digestion.

FESTALAN. (Hoechst) Lipase 6,000 U., amylase 30,000 U., protease 20,000 U., in inner core/Tab.w/outer layer containing atropine methylnitrate 1 mg. Bot. 100s, 1000s.
Use: Treatment of intestinal disorders.

FESTEX. (Blue Cross) Benzalkonium Cl., diperodon HCl 0.5%, carbolic acid, ichthammol, thymol, camphor, juniper tar. Tube 1.5 oz.
Use: Drawing salve.

FETOXYLATE. B.A.N. 2-Phenoxyethyl 1-(3-cyano-3,3-diphenylpropyl)-4-phenylpiperidine-4-carboxylate.
Use: Antidiarrheal.

• **FETOXYLATE HYDROCHLORIDE.** USAN.
Use: Relaxant.

• **FEZOLAMINE FUMARATE.** USAN.
Use: Antidepressant.

FIBERMED HIGH-FIBER SNACKS. (Purdue Frederick) One serving (15 snacks) contains 5 Gm. dietary fiber. Box 8 oz.
Use: High-fiber supplement.

FIBERMED HIGH-FIBER SUPPLEMENT. (Purdue Frederick) Each supplement contains 5 Gm. dietary fiber. Box 14s. Institutional pack, Box 144s of two Supplements.
Use: High-fiber dietary supplement.

FIBRIN HYDROLYSATE.
See: Aminosol, Sol. (Abbott)

FIBROGEN (HUMAN). Partially purified fibrinogen prepared by fractionation from normal human plasma.
Use: Coagulant (clotting factor).
See: Parenogen, (I.V.) Vial (Cutter)

• **FIBRINOGEN I-125.** USAN.
Use: Diagnostic aid.

FIBRINOLYSIN (HUMAN). Plasmin. An enzyme prepared by activating a human blood plasma fraction with streptokinase.
See: Thrombolysin (Merck Sharp & Dohme)

W/Desoxyribonuclease.
See: Elase, Oint., Pow. (Parke-Davis)

FIBRINOLYSIS INHIBITOR.
See: Amicar Syr., Tab., Vial (Lederle)

FILAXIS. (Amlab) Vit. A 25000 I.U., D 1250 I.U., C 150 mg., E 5 I.U., B-1 12 mg., B-2 5 mg., B-6 0.5 mg., B-12 5 mcg., Ca pantothenate 5 mg., niacinamide 100 mg., Fe 15 mg., iodine 0.15 mg., Mg. 10 mg., K 5 mg., Ca 75 mg., P 60 mg./Tab. Bot. 30s, 100s. Available w/B-12. Bot. 30s, 60s, 100s.
Use: Therapeutic vitamin formula.

FILIBON. (Lederle) Vit. A 5000 I.U., D 400 I.U., B-1 1.5 mg., B-6 2 mg., niacinamide 20 mg., B-2 1.7 mg., B-12 6 mcg., ferrous fumarate 18 mg., iodine 150 mcg., Mg 100 mg., calcium carbonate 125 mg./Tab. Bot 100s.
Use: Prenatal care.

FILIBON F.A.. (Lederle) The basic Filibon prenatal formulation plus folic acid 1 mg/Tab. Bot. 100s.
Use: Prenatal care.

FILIBON FORTE. (Lederle) A 8,000 I.U., D 400 I.U., E 45 I.U., C 90 mg., niacinamide 30 mg., B-6 3 mg., B-1 2 mg., B-2 2.5 mg., folic acid 1 mg., B-12 12 mcg., calcium 300 mg., iron 45 mg., Mg 100 mg., iodine 200 mcg./Tab. Jar 100s.
Use: Prophylaxis of anemias of pregnancy.

FILIBON OT. (Lederle) The basic Filibon prenatal formulation plus docusate sodium 100 mg./Tab. Jar 100s.
Use: Dietary supplement during pregnancy and lactation.

• **FILIPIN.** USAN.
Use: Antifungal.

FINAC. (C & M Pharmacal) Sulfur 2% in lotion base.
Use: Anti-acne cover-up lotion.

FINAJET ACETATE. Trenbolone, B.A.N.

FIOGESIC. (Sandoz) Calurin 382 mg. equiv. to aspirin 300 mg., phenylpropanolamine HCl 25 mg., pheniramine maleate 12.5 mg., pyrilamine maleate 12.5 mg./Tab. Bot. 100s.
Use: Analgesic, sinus and nasal congestion.

FIORGEN TABS PF. (Goldline) Butabarbital, aspirin, caffeine. Bot. 100s, 1000s.
Use: Analgesic.

FIORICET. (Sandoz) Acetaminophen 325 mg., butalbital 50 mg., caffeine 40 mg./Tab. Bot. 100s, 500s. SandoPak 100s.
Use: Relief of complex tension headache.

FIORINAL. (Sandoz) Butalbital (Sandoptal) 50 mg., caffeine 40 mg., aspirin 325 mg./Tab. or Cap. **Tab.:** Bot. 100s, 1000s. Sandopak 100s. **Cap.:** Bot. 100s, 500s. Control Pak 25s.
Use: Analgesic sedative.

FIORINAL WITH CODEINE CAPSULES. (Sandoz) Butalbital (Sandoptal) 50 mg., caffeine 40 mg., aspirin 325 mg./Cap. **No. 1:** ⅛ gr. codeine phosphate. Bot. 100s **No. 2:** 0.25 gr. codeine phosphate. Bot. 100s **No. 3:** 0.5 gr. codeine phosphate. Bot. 100s. Control Pak 25s.
Use: Analgesic sedative.

FIRMDENT. (Moyco) Formerly Moy. Karaya gum 94.6%, sodium borate 5.36% Pkg. 3 oz.
Use: Denture adhesive.

FIRST AID CREAM. (Johnson & Johnson) Cetyl alcohol, glyceryl stearate, isopropyl palmitate, stearyl alcohol, synthetic beeswax. Tube 0.8 oz., 1.5 oz., 2.5 oz.
Use: Skin wound protectant.

FIRST AID CREAM. (Walgreen) Benzocaine 3%, allantoin 0.2%, benzyl alcohol 4%, phenol. 0.25%. Tube 1.5 oz.
Use: Ointment for minor cuts and burns.

FITACOL. (Standex) Atropine sulfate 0.2 mg., phenylpropanolamine 12.5 mg., chlorpheniramine maleate 0.5 mg., chlorbutanol 0.5 mg., water q.s./cc. Bot. pt.

FITACOL STANKAPS. (Standex) Belladonna alkaloidal salts 0.16 mg. (atropine sulfate 0.024 mg., scopolamine HBr 0.014 mg., hyoscyamine sulfate 0.122 mg.), phenylpropanolamine HCl 50 mg., chlorpheniramine maleate 1 mg., pheniramine maleate 12.5 mg./Cap. Bot. 100s.

523 TABLETS. (Enzyme Process) Pancreatin 200 mg 4x/Tab. Tryspin, chymoprypsin, amylase, lipase enzymes from pancreatin, raw beef pancreas. Bot. 100s, 250s.
Use: Digestive aid.

FIXODENT. (Vicks Prods) Calcium sodium poly (vinyl methyl ether-maleate) and carboxymethylcellulose sodium in a petrolatum base. Pkg. ¾ oz., 1.5 oz., 2.5 oz.
Use: Denture adhesive cream.

FLACID. (Amfre-Grant) Simethicone 25 mg., aluminum hydroxide, magnesium carbonate 282 mg., Magnesium hydroxide 85 mg./Tab. Bot. 100s, 1000s.
Use: Antacid/antiflatulents.

FLAGYL. (Searle) Metronidazole 250 mg./Tab. Bot. 100s, 250s, 500s. 1000s. Unit dose 100s; 500 mg./Tab. Bot. 100s, 500s. Unit dose 100s.
Use: Trichomonacidal agent, amebicide, anaerobic infections.

FLAGYL I.V. (Searle) Metronidazole HCl sterile lyophilized powder in single-dose vials equivalent to 500 mg. metronidazole. Cartons 10s.
Use: Anaerobic infections.

FLAGYL I.V. RTU. (Searle) Metronidazole ready-to-use, premixed, 500 mg. /100 ml. Sol. Vials: glass, Box 6s; plastic, Box 24s.
Use: Anaerobic infections.

FLATUS. (Foy) Nux vomica extract 0.25 gr., cascara extract 1 gr., ginger ¾ gr., capsicum ⅛ gr./Tab. w/asfetida qs. Bot. 1000s.
Use: Stomachic, carminative, mild laxative.

FLAV-A-D. (Kirkman) Vit. A 5000 I.U., D 1000 I.U., C 10 mg./Tab. Bot. 100s, 1000s. Also w/fluoride Bot. 100s, 1000s.
Use: Dietary supplement for children and adults.

FLAVINE.
See: Acriflavine Hydrochloride (Var. Mfr.)

FLAVINOID-C. (Barth's) **Tab.** Vit. C 150 mg., hesperidin complex 10 mg., citrus bioflavonoid 50 mg., rutin 2

mg./Tab. Bot. 100s, 500s, 1000s. **Liq:** Vit. C 100 mg., bioflavonoid complex 100 mg./5 ml. Bot. 4 oz.
FLAVODILOL MALEATE. USAN.
Use: Antihypertensive.
.AVOLUTAN.
See: Progesterone (Various Mfr.)
.AVONOID COMPOUNDS.
See: Bio-Flavonoid Cpds. Vit. P.
.AVOXATE. B.A.N. 2-Piperidinoethyl 3-methylflavone-8-carboxylate.
Use: Antispasmodic.
See: Urispas [hydrochloride]
FLAVOXATE HCl. USAN. 2-Piperidinoethyl-3-methyl-4-oxo-2-phenyl-4H-1-benzopyran-8-carboxylate HCl.
Use: Urinary antispasmodic.
See: Urispas, Tab. (SmithKline)
.AVUROL. Merbromin.
.AXEDIL TRIETHIODIDE. Gallamine triethiodide soln.
Use: Similar to curare. Relax skeletal muscle.
FLAZALONE. USAN. p-Fluoro-phenyl 4-(p-fluoro-phenyl)-4-hydroxy-1-methyl-3-piperidyl ketone. 3-(4-Fluorobenzoyl)-4-(4-fluorophenyl)-1-methylpiperidin-4-ol.
Use: Anti-inflammatory.
FLECAINIDE ACETATE. USAN.
Use: Cardiac depressant.
.EET RELIEF ANESTHETIC HEMORRHOIDAL OINTMENT. (Fleet) Pramoxine HCl 1%. Six Disposable pre-filled applicators. Tube 1 oz.
Use: Direct temporary relief of rectal pain or itching.
.EET BABYLAX. (Fleet) Glycerin 4 ml. in disposable pre-lubricated rectal applicator. 6/pkg.
Use: Pediatric laxative.
.EET BAGENEMA. (Fleet) Castile soap or Fleets bisacodyl prep.
Use: Disposable large volume enema set.
.EET BISACODYL. (Fleet) Bisacodyl. **Tab.:** 5 mg./Tab. Bot. 24s, 100s, 1000s. **Suppos.:** 10 mg./Supos. Box 4s, 50s, 100s. **Enema:** 10 mg./30 ml. Disposable enema 37 ml.
Use: Laxative
.EET BISACODYL PREP PACKETS. (Fleet) Bisacodyl 10 mg./10 ml. packet. 36 packets/box.
Use: Laxative.
.EET DETECATEST. (Fleet) Three guaiac impregnated slides. Test kit.
Use: Home occult blood test for feces.
.EET ENEMA. (Fleet) Sod. biphosphate 16 Gm., sod. phosphate 6 Gm./100 cc. Bot. w/rectal tube 4.5 oz. Pediatric size 2.25 oz.
Use: Laxative.
.EET FLAVORED CASTOR OIL EMULSION. (Fleet) 1 oz. delivers 30 ml. castor oil. Bot. 1.5 oz., 3 oz.
Use: Laxative.
.EET MINERAL OIL ENEMA. (Fleet) Mineral oil 4.5 fl. oz. in an unbreakable vinyl squeeze bottle.
Use: To soften stools.
.EET PREP KIT. (Fleet) A series of different laxative kits for use prior to barium enema, bowel surgery, proctoscopy, colonoscopy, etc. w/complete patient instruction form:
Prep Kit #1: 1.5 oz. Fleet® Phospho-Soda, 4×5 mg. Fleet® Bisacodyl Tablets, 1×10 mg. Fleet® Bisacodyl Suppository.
Prep Kit #2: 1.5 oz. Fleet® Phospho-Soda, 4×5 mg. Fleet® Bisacodyl Tablets, 1 Fleet® Bagenema set for large volume enema, including optional Castile Soap Packet.
Prep Kit #3: 1.5 oz. Fleet® Phospho-Soda, 4×5 mg. Fleet® Bisacodyl Tablets, 1×37 ml. Fleet® Bisacodyl Enema.
Prep Kit #4: 1.5 oz. Fleet® Flavored Castor Oil Emulsion, 4×5 mg. Fleet® Bisacodyl Tablets, 1×10 mg. Fleet® Bisacodyl Suppository.
Prep Kit #5: 1.5 oz. Fleet® Flavored Castor Oil Emulsion, 4×5 mg. Fleet® Bisacodyl Tablets, 1 Fleet® Bagenema set for large volume enema, including optional Castile Soap Packet.
Prep Kit #6: 1.5 oz. Fleet® Flavored Castor Oil Emulsion, 4×5 mg. Fleet® Bisacodyl Tablets, 1×37 ml. Fleet® Bisacodyl Enema.
• **FLESTOLOL SULFATE.** USAN.
Use: Anti-adrenergic.
• **FLETAZEPAM.** USAN.
Use: Relaxant.
FLETCHER'S CASTORIA. (Glenbrook) Senna equiv. 6.5%. Liq. Bot. 2.5 oz., 5 oz.
Use: Laxative for children ages 1 month to 15 yrs.
FLEX ANTI-DANDRUFF SHAMPOO. (Revlon) Zinc pyrithione 1% in liquid shampoo.
Use: Anti-Dandruff shampoo.
FLEX-CARE. (Alcon) Sterile solution of sodium Cl., sodium borate, boric acid. Bot. 12 oz., 8 oz.
Use: Soft contact lens rinsing, storage, disinfection.
FLEXERIL. (Merck Sharp & Dohme) Cyclobenzaprine HCl 10 mg./Tab. Bot. 100s. Unit-dose 100s. Unit-of-Use 30s.
Use: Short-term relief of painful muscle spasms.
FLEXOJECT. (Mayrand) Orphenadrine citrate 30 mg./ml. Vial 10 ml.
Use: Muscle relaxant.
FLEXON. (Keene) Orphenadrine citrate inj. 30 mg./ml. Vial 2 ml.
FLEXOR. (Amfre-Grant) Orphenadrine citrate 30 mg./ml. Vial 10 ml.
Use: Muscle relaxant.
FLEXSOL. (Alcon) Sterile, buffered, isotonic aqueous sol. of sodium chloride, sodium borate, boric acid, adsorbobase. Bot. 6 oz.
Use: Soft contact lens solution for disinfecting & storage.
FLINT SSD. (Flint) Silver sulfadiazine cream 1%. Jar 50 Gm., 400 Gm.
Use: Topical antibacterial.
FLINTSTONES. (Miles) Vit. A 2500 I.U., E 15 I.U., C 60 mg., folic acid 0.3 mg., B-1 1.05 mg., B-2 1.2 mg., niacin 13.5 mg., B-6 1.05 mg., B-12 4.5 mcg., D 400 I.U./Tab. Bot. 60s, 100s.
Use: Multivitamin supplement.
FLINTSTONES COMPLETE. (Miles) Vit. A 5000 I.U., D 400 I.U., E 30 I.U., C 60 mg., folic acid 0.4 mg.,

B-1 1.5 mg., B-2 1.7 mg., niacin 20 mg., B-6 2 mg., B-12 6 mcg., biotin 40 mcg., pantothenic acid 10 mg., iron 18 mg., calcium 100 mg., phosphorus 100 mg., iodine 150 mcg., magnesium 20 mg., manganese 2.5 mg., zinc 15 mg./Chewable Tab. Bot. 60s.
Use: Multivitamin and mineral supplement.

FLINTSTONES WITH EXTRA C. (Miles) Vit. A 2500 I.U., D 400 I.U., E 15 I.U., C 250 mg., folic acid 0.3 mg., B-1 1.20 mg., niacin 13.50 mg., B-6 1.05 mg., B-12 4.5 mcg./Tab. Bot. 60s.
Use: Chewable multivitamin supplement with extra vitamin C.

FLINTSTONES WITH IRON. (Miles) Vit. A 2500 I.U., E 15 I.U., C 60 mg., folic acid 0.3 mg., B-1 1.05 mg., B-2 1.2 mg., niacin 13.5 mg., B-6 1.05 mg., B-12 4.5 mcg., D 400 I.U., iron 15 mg./Tab. Bot. 60s, 100s.
Use: Multivitamin supplement with iron.

• **FLOCTAFENINE.** USAN.
Use: Analgesic.

FLORAJEN. (Jenkins) Fluoride 0.5 mg., Vit. A 4000 I.U., Vit. D 400 I.U., ascorbic acid 75 mg., Vit. B-1 2 mg., Vit. B-2 2 mg., niacinamide 18 mg., B-6 1 mg., calcium pantothenate. dextro 5 mg., cyanocobalamin 2 mcg./Tab. Bot. 100s, 500s, 1000s.

FLORANTYRONE. Gamma-Fluoranthen-8-yl-gamma-oxybutyric acid.

FLORANTYRONE. B.A.N. 4-(Fluoranthen-8-yl)-4-oxobutyric acid.
Use: Stimulation of bile acid secretion.
See: Zanchol

FLORAPLEX. (Barry-Martin) Vit. B-1 100 mg., B-2 1 mg., B-6 2 mg., niacinamide 50 mg., Ca pantothenate 2 mg./cc. Vial 30 cc.

FLORAQUIN. Di-iodohydroxyquinoline, B.A.N.

FLOR-D CHEWABLE TAB. (Derm Pharm.) Fluoride 1 mg., Vit. A 4000 I.U., D 400 I.U., C 75 mg., B-1 1.5 mg., B-2 1.8 mg., niacinamide 15 mg., B-6 1 mg., B-12 3 mcg., calcium pantothenate 10 mg./Tab. Bot. 100s.
Use: Dietary supplement.

FLOR-D DROPS. (Derm Pharm.) Fluoride 0.5 mg., Vit. A 3000 I.U., D 400 I.U., C 60 mg., B-1 1 mg., B-2 1.2 mg., niacinamide 8 mg./0.6 cc. Bot. 60 cc.
Use: Dietary supplement.

• **FLORDIPINE.** USAN.
Use: Antihypertensive.

FLORICAL. (Mericon) Sodium fluoride 8.3 mg., calcium carbonate 364 mg./Cap. Bot. 100s, 500s.
Use: Dietary supplement.

FLORIDA FOAM. (Hill) Benzalkonium chloride, aluminum subacetate, boric acid 2%. Bot. 8 oz.
Use: Soap substitute, seborrhea, fungi, acne.

FLORINEF ACETATE TABLETS. (Squibb) Fludrocortisone acetate. Tab. 0.1 mg. Bot. 100s.
Use: Treatment of Addison's disease and adrenal hypoplasia.

FLORITAL. (Cenci) Butabital 50 mg., aspirin 200 mg., phenacetin 130 mg., caffeine 40 mg./Tab. Bot. 100s.
Use: Sedative and analgesic.

FLORONE CREAM. (Dermik) Diflorasone diacetate 0.5 mg./Gm. (0.05%) w/stearic acid, sorbitan monooleate, polysorbate 60, sorbic acid, citric acid propylene glycol, and purified water. Tube 15 Gm., 30 Gm., 60 Gm.
Use: Anti-inflammatory, antipruritic, antimiotic.

FLORONE OINTMENT. (Dermik) Diflorasone diacetate 0.5 mg./Gm. (0.05%) W/polyoxypropylene 15-stearyl ether, stearic acid lanolin alcohol and white petrolatum. Tube 15 Gm 30 Gm., 60 Gm.
Use: Anti-inflammatory, antipruritic, antimiotic.

FLOROPRYL. (Merck Sharp & Dohme) Isoflurophate 0.025% in sterile ophthalmic ointment in polyethylene-mineral oil gel. Tube 3.5 Gm.
Use: Miotic, cholinesterase inhibitor for glaucoma.

FLORVITE CHEWABLE TABLETS. (Everett) Vitamins, fluoride 0.5 mg./Chewable Tab. Bot 50s, 100s.
Use: Vitamin supplement & fluoride to reduce dental caries.

FLORVITE DROPS. (Everett) Vitamins and fluoride 0.25 mg. or 0.5 mg. Bot. 50 ml.
Use: Vitamin supplement and fluoride to help reduce dental caries.

FLORVITE & IRON DROPS. (Everett) Vitamins, iron, fluoride. Bot. 50 cc.
Use: Vitamin supplement with iron & fluoride to help reduce dental caries.

FLORVITE & IRON CHEWABLE. (Everett) Vitamins, fluoride 1 mg., iron 12 mg./Chewable Tab. Bot. 100s.
Use: Reduce dental caries and iron deficiency.

FLORVITE TABLETS. (Everett) Vitamins, fluoride 1 mg./Chewable Tab. Bot. 100s, 1000s.
Use: Vitamin supplement and fluoride to help reduce dental caries.

FLOWAWAY WATER TABLETS. (DeWitt) Potassium nitrate, uva ursi, buchu leaves, caffeine. Blister paks 24s, 48s.
Use: Mild diuretic.

• **FLOXACILLIN.** USAN.
Use: Antibacterial.

• **FLOXURIDINE,** U.S.P. XXI. Sterile, U.S.P. XXI. 2'-Deoxy-5-fluorouridine.
Use: Antiviral agent.
See: FUDR, Vials (Roche)

FLUANISONE. B.A.N. 4-Fluoro-γ-[4-(2-methoxyphenyl)piperazin-1-yl]butyrophenone.
Use: Neuroleptic.

FLUAX. (Merk Sharp & Dohme) Influenza virus vaccine.
Product deleted for 1983–84.
Use: Influenza immunization.

• **FLUAZACORT.** USAN.
Use: Anti-inflammatory.

• **FLUBANILATE HYDROCHLORIDE.** USAN. Ethyl N-[2(dimethylamino)ethyl]-m-(trifluoromethyl) carbanilate HCl.
Use: Antidepressant.

• **FLUBENDAZOLE.** USAN.
Use: Antiprotozpal.

UCARBRIL. 1-Methyl-6-(trifluromethyl)carbostyril.
Use: Muscle relaxant and analgesic.

LUCINDOLE. USAN.
Use: Antipsychotic.

UCLOROLONE ACETONIDE. B.A.N. 9α,-11β-Dichloro-6α-fluoro-21-hydroxy-16α, 17α-isopropylidenedioxypregna-1,4-diene-3,20-dione.
Use: Corticosteroid.
See: Topilar Fluclorolone.

LUCLORONIDE. USAN. 9, 11β-Dichloro-6α-fluoro-16α, 17, 21-trihydroxypregna-1, 4-diene-3, 20-dione cyclic 16, 17-acetal with acetone.
Use: Glucocorticoid.

UCLOXACILLIN. B.A.N. 6-[3-(2-Chloro-6-fluorophenyl)-5-methylisoxazole-4-carboxamido]-penicillanic acid.
Use: Antibiotic.
See: Floxapen

FLUCRYLATE. USAN. 2,2,2-Trifluoro-1-methylethyl-2-cyanoacrylate.
Use: Surgical aid (tissue adhesive).

FLUCYTOSINE, U.S.P. XXI. Cap. U.S.P. XXI. 5-Fluorocytosine.
Use: Antifungal.
See: Ancobon, Cap. (Roche)

FLUCYTOSINE. USAN. 4-Amino-5-fluoro-1,2-dihydropyrimidin-2-one. 5-Fluorocytosine.
Use: Antifungal.
See: Alcobon

FLUDARABINE PHOSPHATE. USAN.
Use: Antineoplastic.

FLUDAZONIUM CHLORIDE. USAN.
Use: Anti-infective, topical.

FLUDALANINE. USAN.
Use: Antibacterial.

FLUDOREX. USAN.
Use: Anorexic, anti-emetic.

UDROCORTISONE. B.A.N. 9α-Fluoro-11β,-17α,21-trihydroxypregn-4-ene-3,20-dione. 9α-Fluorohydrocortisone. Alflorone, Florinef, and Fludrocortone are the 21-acetate
Use: Corticosteroid.

FLUDROCORTISONE ACETATE. U.S.P. XXI. Tab. U.S.P. XXI. 9-alpha-Fluorohydrocortisone. Pregn-4-ene-3,20-dione,21-(acetyloxy)-9-fluoro-11,-17-dihydroxy-, (11 beta)-. 9-Fluoro-11 beta, 17,21-trihydroxypregn-4-ene-3,20-dione 21-acetate.
Use: Adrenocortical steroid (salt-regulation).
See: Florinef Acetate, Tab. (Squibb)

FLUFENAMIC ACID. USAN. N-(α, α, α-Trifluoro-m-tolyl) anthranilic acid.
Use: Anti-inflammatory agent.

FLUFENSIAL. USAN.
Use: Analgesic.

LUGESTONE. B.A.N. 9α-Fluoro-11β,17-dihydroxypregn-4-ene-3,20-dione.
Use: Progestational steroid.
See: Flurogestone

LUIDEX. (O'Connor) Natural botanical ingredients. Tabs. Bot. 36s, 72s.
Use: Diuretic

FLUIDEX PLUS. (O'Connor) Phenylpropanolamine HCl 25 mg./Tab. natural botanical ingredients Bot. 36s, 72s.
Use: Diuretic/appetite suppressant.

FLUIDEX WITH PAMABROM. (O'Connor) Pamabrom 50 mg./Cap. Pkg 3s, 12s, 24s.
Use: Premenstrual diuretic.

FLUITRAN. Trichlormethiazide.

FLUMEDROXONE. B.A.N. 17α-Hydroxy-6α-trifluoromethylpregn-4-ene-3,20-dione.
Use: Treatment of migraine.
See: Demigran [acetate]

• **FLUMEQUINE.** USAN.
Use: Antibacterial.

• **FLUMERIDONE.** USAN.
Use: Anti-emetic.

• **FLUMETHASONE.** USAN. 6α,9α-Difluoro-11β, 17α,21-trihydroxy-16α-methylpregna-1,4-diene-3,20-dione. 6α,9α-Difluoro-16α-methylprednisolone.
Use: Corticosteroid.
See: Locorten [21-pivalate] (Ciba)

• **FLUMETHASONE PIVALATE,** U.S.P. XXI. Cream, U.S.P. XXI. 6α-9α-difluoro-16α-methylprednisolone 21 pivalate. 6α,9-Difluoro-11β,17,21-trihydroxy-16-me-thylpregna-1,4-diene-3,20-dione-21 pivalate.
Use. Steroid.

FLUMETHIAZIDE. 6-Trifluoromethyl-7-sulfamyl-1,2, 4-benzothiadiazine-1, 1-dioxide.
Use: Diuretic.
See: Rautrax, Tab. (Squibb)

FLUMETHIAZIDE. B.A.N. 6-Trifluoromethyl-1,2,4-benzothiadiazine-7-sulphonamide 1,1-dioxide.
Use: Diuretic.

• **FLUMETRAMIDE.** USAN.
Use: Relaxant.

• **FLUMEZAPINE.** USAN.
Use: Antipsychotic, neuroleptic.

• **FLUMINOREX.** USAN.
Use: Anorexic.

• **FLUMIZOLE.** USAN.
Use: Anti-inflammatory.

• **FLUNARIZINE HCl.** USAN. (E)-1-[Bis-(p-fluorophenyl) methyl]-4-cinnamyl-piperazine dihydrochloride.
Use: Vasodilator.

• **FLUNIDAZOLE.** USAN.
Use: Antiprotozoal.

• **FLUNISOLIDE,** U.S.P. XXI. Nasal Soln., U.S.P. XXI.
Use: Symptoms of seasonal and perennial rhinitis.
See: Nasalide, Liq. (Syntex)

• **FLUNISOLIDE ACETATE.** USAN. Fluoxolonate.

• **FLUNITRAZEPAM.** USAN. 5-Fluorophenyl-1,3-dihydro-1-methyl-7-nitro-2H-1,4-benzodiazepin-2-one.
Use: Hynoptic.

• **FLUNIXIN.** USAN.
Use: Anti-inflammatory, analgesic.

FLUOCINOLIDE. Fluocinonide, U.S.P. XXI.

FLUOCINOLONE. B.A.N. 6α,9α-Difluoro-11β,16α, 17α,21-tetrahydroxypregna-1,4-diene-3,20-dione. 6α,9α-Difluoro-16α-hydroxy-prednisolone. Synandone [acetonidel].
Use: Corticosteroid.
See: Synalar
Synemol, Cream (Syntex)

• **FLUOCINOLONE ACETONIDE,** U.S.P. XXI. Cream, Oint., Topical Soln. U.S.P. XXI. Pregna-1,4-diene-3,20-dione,6,9-difluoro-11,21-dihydroxy-16,17-[(1-methylethylidene)bis(oxy)], (6α,11β,-16α)-. 9a-Difluoro-16a-hydroxyprednisolone-16, 17-acetonide. 6α,9α-Difluoro-11β,16α,17,21-tetrahydroxypregna-1,4-diene-3,20-dione. Cyclic 16,-17-Acetal with Acetone.
Use: Adrenocortical steroid (topical anti-inflammatory).
Use: Glucocorticoid.
See: Fluonid, Cream, Oint., Sol. (Herbert)
Synalar, Cream, Oint., Sol. (Syntex)

W/Neomycin sulfate.
See: Neo-Synalar. (Syntex)

• **FLUOCINONIDE,** U.S.P. XXI. Cream, Gel, Oint., U.S.P. XXI. F.D.A. 6α, 9α-Difluoro-11β-16α, 17α-21-tetrahydroxypregna-1,4-diene-3,20-dione, cyclic 16, 17-acetal with acetone, 21-acetate. B.A.N. 21-Acetoxy-6α,9α-difluoro-11β-hydroxy-16α, 17α-isopropylidene-dioxypregna-1,4-diene-3,20-dione. Fluocinolone 16α, 17α-acetonide 21 acetate
Use: Corticosteroid.
See: Lidex, Cream, Oint., Soln. (Syntex)
Lidex-E, Cream (Syntex)
Metosyn
Topsyn, Gel (Syntex)

• **FLUOCORTIN BUTYL.** USAN. Butyl-6α-fluoro-11β-hydroxy-16α-methyl-3,20-dioxopregna-1,4-dien-21oate.
Use: Anti-inflammatory.

• **FLUOCORTOLONE.** USAN. 6α-Fluoro-11β,21-dihydroxy-16α-methylpregna-1,4-diene-20-dione. (Berlin) 6α-Fluoro-11β, 21-dihydroxy-16α-methylpregna-1, 4-diene-3, 20-dione.
Use: Corticosteroid.
See: Ultralanum [21-hexanoate]

• **FLUOCORTOLONE CAPROATE.** USAN.
Use: Glucocorticoid.

FLUOGEN. (Parke-Davis) Influenza virus vaccine, trivalent—Immunizing antigen, ether extracted. Vials 5 ml. The 5 ml. vial contains sufficient product to deliver ten 0.5 ml. doses.
Use: Influenza immunizing agent.

FLUONID. (Herbert) Fluocinolone Acetonide. **Cream:** 0.01%. Tube 15 Gm., 60 Gm. 0.025%. Tube 15, 60 Gm. **Ointment:** 0.025% Tube 15 Gm., 60 Gm. **Solution:** 0.01% Bot. 20 ml., 60 ml.
Use: Anti-inflammatory for corticosteroid-responsive dermatoses.

FLUOPROMAZINE. B.A.N. 10-(3-Dimethylaminopropyl)-2-trifluoromethylpiamothiazine. Triflupromazine (I.N.N.)
Use: Tranquilizer.
See: Vespral
Vesprin [hydrochloride]

• **FLUORESCEIN,** U.S.P. XXI.
Use: Diagnostic aid (corneal trauma indicator).

• **FLUORESCEIN SODIUM,** U.S.P. XXI. Ophth. Strip, Inj. U.S.P. XXI. Spiro[isoberzofuran-1(3H), 9-[9H]xanthene]-3-one, 3′6′-dihydroxy, disodium salt. (Various Mfr.) Soluble fluorescein. Bot. 1 oz.
Use: 2% sol. in diagnosis of eye conditions. (circulation time).
See: Fluor-I-Strip. (Ayerst)
Fluoreseptic, Sol. (Softcon)
Funduscein, Amp. (CooperVision)
Plak-Lite Sol. (Internat. Pharm.)

FLUORESCEIN SODIUM I.V.
See: Fluorescite, Amp. (Alcon)

FLUORESCEIN SODIUM 2% SOLUTION. (Alcon) Drop-Tainer 15 cc. Steri-Unit 2 cc. 12s; (CooperVision) Dropperette 1 cc. 10s.
Use: Diagnostic agent in ophthalmology.

FLUORESCEIN SODIUM 2%. (CooperVision) A sterile aqueous solution containing fluorescein sodium 2%. Dropperette 1 ml. Box 12s.
Use: Diagnostic for topical application.

FLUORESCITE. (Alcon) Fluorescein as Sod. salt. **10%** Sol. Amp. 5 ml. Box 12s, Disp. Syringe 5 ml., 12s; **25%** Sol. Amp. Box 12s.
Use: Diagnostic aid, injectable ophthalmic.

FLUORESEPTIC. (Softcon) A sterile, buffered solutio[n] containing fluorescein sodium 2% w/phenylmercuric borate 1:25,000 as preservative, sod. bicarbonate. Plastic container in 7.5 cc., 15 c[c].
Use: Diagnostic agent.

FLUORIDE SODIUM.
See: Dentafluor Chewable, Tab. (Western Pharm.)
Karidium, Top. Soln., Tab. (Lorvic)
Karigel, Gel (Lorvic)

■ **FLUORIDE THERAPY.**
See: Adeflor preps. (Upjohn)
Cari-Tab, Softab Tab. (Stuart)
Coral Prod. (Lorvic)
Fluorineed, Chew. Tab. (Hanlon)
Fluorinse, Liq. (Pacemaker)
Fluora, Loz. (Kirkman)
Gal-Kam, Preps. (Scherer)
Luride Preps. (Hoyt)
Mulvidren-F, Softab Tab. (Stuart)
Point Two, Rinse (Hoyt)
Poly-Vi-Flor, Drops, Tab. (Mead Johnson)
Soluvite-F, Drops (Pharmics)
Tri-Vi-Flor, Drops, Tab. (Mead Johnson)

FLUORI-METHANE SPRAY. (Gebauer) Dichlorodi[-]fluoromethane 15%, trichloromonofluoromethane 85%. Bot. 4 oz.
Use: "Painful motion" syndromes.

FLUORINEED. (Hanlon) Fluoride 1 mg./Chew. Tab. Bot. 100s, 1000s.
Use: Reduce caries in children.

FLUORINSE. (Oral-B) Sodium fluoride 0.2%. Bot. 16 oz
Use: Fluoride mouthrinse.

FLUORINSE. (Pacemaker) Fluoride mouthwash. Pack. Fluoride ion level 0.05% & 0.2%. Unit dose Bot. 32 oz. Conc. 1 oz., 4 oz., gal.

FLUOR-I-STRIP. (Ayerst) Fluorescein sodium 9 mg./ ophthalmic strip. Box. 300s.
Use: Ophthalmic diagnostic agent.

FLUOR-I-STRIP-A.T. (Ayerst) Fluorescein sodium 1 mg./ophthalmic strip. 100 envelopes, each with two sterile applicators. Box 300 (150 × 2).
Use: Application tonometry.

UORITAB. (Fluoritab) Sodium fluoride 2.2 mg. equivalent to 1 mg. of fluorine (as fluoride ion) w/inert organic filler 75.8 mg./Tab. Bot. 100s; Liq. dropper bot. (fluorine 0.25 mg./Drop) 19 cc.
Use: Fluoride supplement.

FLUOROCYTOSINE.
See: Ancobon, Cap. (Roche)

UOROGESTONE ACETATE. 9-Fluoro-11β, 17-dihydroxypregn-4-ene-3, 20-dione, 17-acetate.
Use: Progestin.

UOROHYDROCORTISONE ACETATE. 9-α-Fluorohydrocortisone.
See: Fludrocortisone Acetate (Var. Mfr.)

FLUOROMETHOLONE, U.S.P. XXI. Cream, Ophth. Susp., U.S.P. XXI. Pregna-1,4-diene-3,20-diene, 9-fluoro-11,17-dihydroxy-6-methyl-,(6α,11β)-. 6α-Methyl-9α-fluoro-21-desoxyprednisolone. 9-Fluoro-11β, 17-dihydroxy-6α-methylpregna-1, 4-diene-3, 20-dione. B.A.N. 9α-Fluoro-11β-17α-dihydroxy-6α-methylpregna-1,4-diene-3,20-dione.
Use: Glucocorticoid.
See: FML Liquifilm, Ophth. Susp. (Allergan)
Oxylone, Cream Ophth. Susp. (Upjohn)
/Neomycin sulfate.
See: Neo-Oxylone, Oint. (Upjohn)

FLUOROMETHOLONE ACETATE. USAN.
Use: Glucocorticoid, anti-inflammatory.

UOROPHENE.
Use: Antiseptic agent.

UOROPLEX TOPICAL SOLUTION AND TOPICAL CREAM. (Herbert) **Solution:** Fluorouracil 1% in a propylene glycol base. Plastic bot. W/dropper 30 ml. **Cream:** Fluorouracil 1% in emulsion base w/benzyl alcohol 0.5%, ethoxylated stearyl alcohol, mineral oil, isopropyl myristate, sodium hydroxide and purified water. Tube 30 Gm.
Use: Topical treatment of multiple actinic keratoses.

FLUOROSALAN. USAN. 3, 5-dibromo-3′-trifluoromethyl salicylanilide. Fluorophene.
Use: Antiseptic.

UOROSEPTIC. (Softcon) Fluoroscein sodium 2% 7.5 ml., 15 ml.
Use: To demonstrate surface irregularities and changes in epithelial thickness and for detecting points of pressure in fitting contact lens.

UOR-O-SOL. (Hoyt) Fluoride 1.2% with silicon dioxide abrasive. Jars 50 Gm. Carton 6s.
Use: Clean & polish teeth.

UOTHANE. (Ayerst) Halothane. Bot. 125 ml., 250 ml.
Use: Inhalation anesthetic.

UOROTHYL. Bis (2, 2, 2-trifluoroethyl) ether.
See: Flurothyl.

FLUOROURACIL, U.S.P. XXI. Cream, Inj., Topical Soln., U.S.P. XXI. 5-Fluorouracil. (Roche) Amp. 10 ml., 500 mg. Box 10s.
Use: Malignancies, antineoplastic.
See: Adrucil, Inj. (Adria)
Efudex, Sol. & Cream (Roche)
Fluoroplex, Sol., Cream (Herbert Labs.)

• **FLUOTRACEN HYDROCHLORIDE.** USAN.
Use: Antipsychotic, antidepressant.

• **FLUOXETINE.** USAN.
Use: Antidepressant.

• **FLUOXYMESTERONE,** U.S.P. XXI. Tab., U.S.P. XXI. 9-α-Fluoro-11-β-hydroxy-17-α-methyltestosterone. 9-Fluoro-11β, 17β-dihydroxy-17-methylandrost-4-en-3-one.
Use: Androgen.
See: Android-F, Tab. (Brown)
Halotestin, Tab. (Upjohn)
Ora-Testryl, Tab. (Squibb)
W/Ethinyl estradiol.
See: Halodrin, Tab. (Upjohn)

FLUOXYMESTERONE. B.A.N. 9α-Fluoro-11β, 17 β-dihy 17α-methylandrost-4-en-3-one. 9α-Fluoro-11 β-hydroxymethyltestosterone.
Use: Androgen; anabolic steroid.
See: Ultandren

FLUPENTHIXOL. B.A.N. 9- 3-[4-(2-Hydroxyethel)-piperazin-1-yl]propylidene -2-trifluoromethylthioxanthene.
Use: Tranquilizer.
See: Depixol decanoate

• **FLUPERAMIDE.** USAN.
Use: Antiperistaltic.

FLUPEROLONE. B.A.N. 9α-Fluoro-11β, 17α, 21-trihydroxy-21-methylpregna-1,4-diene-3,20-dione. 9α-Fluoro-21-methylprednisolone.
Use: Corticosteroid.
See: Methral acetate

• **FLUPEROLONE ACETATE.** USAN. 9α-Fluoro-21-methylprednisolone, 9α-Fluoro-11β,17α,21-trihydroxy-21-methylpregna-1:4-diene-3:20-dione acetate. Methral.
Use: Corticosteroid.

FLUPHENAZINE. B.A.N. 10- 3-[4-(2-Hydroxyethyl)piperazin-1-yl]propyl -2-trifluoromethylphenothiazine.
Use: Tranquilizer.
See: Modecate (decanocate)
Moditen
Prolixin (dihydrochloride)

FLUPHENAZINE DECANOATE.
See: Prolixin Decanoate, Sol. (Squibb)

• **FLUPHENAZINE ENANTHATE,** U.S.P. XXI. Inj., U.S.P. XXI. 4-(3-(2-(Trifluoromethyl)phenothiazine-10-yl)-propyl)-1-piperazine-ethanol.
Use: Tranquilizer.
See: Prolixin Enanthate Prods. (Squibb)

• **FLUPHENAZINE HYDROCHLORIDE,** U.S.P. XXI. Elixir, Inj., Oral Soln., Tab., U.S.P. XXI. 1-(2-Hydroxyethyl)-4-[3-(2-trifluoromethyl)-10H-Phenothiazinyl-propyl]-piperazine diHCl. 4-(3-(2-(Trifluoromethyl) phenothiazine-10-yl) propyl)-1-piperazine-ethanol Dihydrochloride.
Use: Tranquilizer.
See: Permitil, Prep. (Schering)
Prolixin, Tab., Elix., Vials (Squibb)

• **FLUPIRTINE MALEATE.** USAN.
Use: Analgesic.

FLUPREDNIDENE. B.A.N. 9α-Fluoro-11β-17 α,21-trihydroxy-16-methylenepregna-1,4-diene-3, 20-dione.
Use: Glucocorticosteroid.

• **FLUPREDNISOLONE.** USAN. 6αFluoro-11β, 17α, 21-trihydroxypregna-1, 4-diene-3,20-dione;b) 6α-fluoroprednisolone.
Use: Corticosteroid.
See: Alphadrol, Tab. (Upjohn)

• **FLUPREDNISOLONE VALERATE.** USAN. 6-Fluoro-11β, 17, 21-trihydroxypregna-1, 4-diene-3,20-dione 17-valerate.
Use: Glucocorticoid.

FLUPROFEN. B.A.N. 2-(2′-Fluorobiphenyl-4-yl)-propionic acid.
Use: Anti-inflammatory; analgesic.

• **FLUPROQUAZONE.** USAN.
Use: Analgesic.

FLUPROSTENOL. B.A.N. (±)-7-(1R,2R,3R,5S)-3,5-Dihydroxy-2-[(3R)-3-hydroxy-4-(3-trifluoromethylphenoxy)but-1-(E)-enyl]cyclopent-1-yl hept-5-(Z)-enoic acid.
Use: Infertility, veterinary medicine.
See: Equimate (sodium salt)

• **FLUPROSTENOL SODIUM.** USAN.
Use: Prostaglandin.

• **FLUQUAZONE.** USAN.
Use: Anti-inflammatory.

• **FLURADOLINE HYDROCHLORIDE.** USAN.
Use: Analgesic.

FLURA DROPS. (Kirkman) Sodium fluoride 2.21 mg./4 drops. (4 drops q.s. one quart provides 1 part per million of fluorine ion.) Bot. 24 ml.
Use: Prevention of dental caries.

FLURA-LOZ. (Kirkman) Sod. fluoride 2.21 mg./Lozenge. Bot. 100s, 1000s.

• **FLURANDRENOLIDE,** U.S.P. XXI. Cream, Oint., Lotion, Tape, U.S.P. XXI.
Use: Adrenocortical steroid (topical anti-inflammatory).
See: Cordran, Preps. (Dista)

FLURANDRENOLONE. 6α-Fluoro-16α-hydroxyhydrocortisone 16, 17-acetonide.
Use: Topical corticoid compound.

FLURANDRENOLONE. B.A.N. 6α-Fluoro-11β,-21-dihydroxy-16α, 17α-isopropylidenedioxypregn-4-ene-3,-20-dione. 6α-Fluoro-16α, 17α-isopropylidenedioxyhydrocortisone. Fludroxycortide (I.N.N.)
Use: Corticosteroid.
Drenison
Haelan

FLURA-PREN. (Kirkman) Vit. A 4000 I.U., D 400 I.U., B-1 3 mg., B-2 2 mg., B-6 10 mg., niacinamide 10 mg., Vit. C 100 mg., K 0.5 mg., calcium carbonate 625 mg., ferrous fumarate 125 mg., Vit. B-12 w/intrinsic factor ⅛ oral u., sodium fluoride 2.21 mg./Tab. Bot. 100s.
Use: Nutritional supplement.

FLURA-TABLETS. (Kirkman) Sod. fluoride 2.21 mg., equiv. to 1 mg. fluoride ion/Tab. Bot. 100s, 1000s.

FLURA-VITE. (Kirkman) Flavored Multiple-vitamin tablet, chewable, for children. Bot. 100s.

• **FLURAZEPAM HYDROCHLORIDE,** U.S.P. XXI. Cap., U.S.P. XXI. 7-Chloro-1-[2-(diethylamino)ethyl]-5-(o-fluorophenyl)-3,-dihydro-2H-1,4-benzodiazepin-2-one dihydrochloride. B.A.N. 7-Chloro-1-(2-diethylamino-ethyl)-5-(2-fluorophenyl)-1,3-dihydro-2H-1,4-benzodiazepin-2-one.
Use: Hypnotic.
See: Dalmane, Cap. (Roche)

• **FLURBIPROFEN.** USAN. 2-(2-Fluorobiphenyl-4-yl propionic acid.
Use: Anti-inflammatory; analgesic.

FLURESS. (Barnes-Hind) Fluorescein sodium 0.25% benoxinate HCl 0.4% in isotonic boric acid soln., chlorobutanol 1.0%. Bot. 5 cc.
Use: Applanation tonometry; disclosing agent.

• **FLURETOFEN.** USAN.
Use: Anti-inflammatory, antithrombotic.

• **FLURFAMIDE.** USAN.
Use: Enzyme inhibitor.

• **FLUROCITABINE.** USAN.
Use: Antineoplastic.

FLURO-ETHYL. (Gebauer) Ethyl chloride 25%, c chlorotetrafluoroethane 75%. Aerosol can 255 Gm.
Use: Topical anesthetic.

• **FLUROGESTONE ACETATE.** USAN.
Use: Progestin.

• **FLUROTHYL,** U.S.P. XXI. Bis (2,2,2-trifluoroethyl) ether. Hexafluorodiethyl ether. B.A.N. Di-(2,2,2-tr fluoroethyl) ether. Bis(2,2,2-trifluoroethyl)ether.
Use: Central nervous system stimulant, shock inducing agent (convulsant).
See: Indoklon

• **FLUROXENE.** USAN. 2,2,2-Trifluoroethyl vinyl ethe Fluoromar.
Use: General inhalation anesthetic.

• **FLUSPIPERONE.** USAN.
Use: Antipsychotic.

FLUSPIRILENE. USAN. 8-[4, 4-bis(p-Fluoropheny butyl]-1-phenyl-1,3,8-triazaspiro-[4.5] decan-4-on Imap (McNeil).
Use: Tranquilizer.

• **FLUTAMIDE.** USAN.

• **FLUTIAZIN.** USAN.
Use: Anti-inflammatory.

• **FLUTICASONE PROPIONATE.** USAN.
Use: Anti-inflammatory.

FLUTRA. Trichlormethiazide.
Use: Diuretic.

• **FLUTROLINE.** USAN.
Use: Antipsychotic.

• **FLUZINAMIDE.** USAN.
Use: Anticonvulsant.

FLUZONE. (Squibb-Connaught) Influenza virus vaccin Vial 5 ml. (10 doses).
Use: Prevention of influenza.

FML LIQUIFILM. (Allergan) Fluorometholone 0.1%, polyvinyl alcohol 1.4% w/benzalkonium chloride, edetate disodium, sod. chloride, sod. phosphate monobasic, monohydrate, sod. phosphate dibasic, anhydrous, polysorbate 80, purified water, sod. hydroxide to adjust pH. Dropper bot. 5 ml., 10 ml., 15 ml. Unit dose, 1 ml.
Use: Ocular anti-inflammatory.

FOAM-RICH TRAVEL PACK. (Matthew) Caps. 20s.

OCOFILCON A. USAN.
Jse: Contact lens material.

LABEE. (Vortech) Liver inj. equiv. to B-12 50 mcg., olic acid 10 mg., niacinamide 75 mg., phenol).5%/cc. Vial 10 cc.

LACINE.
See: Folic acid. (Var. Mfr.)

LATE, SODIUM.
See: Folvite, Sol. (Lederle)

LEX. (Adria) Methotrexate sodium 25 mg., 50 mg., 100 mg./Vial. For injection.
Jse: Antineoplastic.

OLIC ACID, U.S.P. XXI. Inj., Tab. U.S.P. XXI. Pteroylglutamic acid. N-[p-[[(2-Amino-4-hydroxy-6-pteridinyl)-methyl]-amino] benzoyl]-L-glutamic acid. L-Glutamic acid, N-[4-[[(2-amino-1,4-dihydro-4-oxo-6-pteridinyl)methyl]-amino]benzoyl]-. Vitamin Bc.
Jse: Vitamin therapy.
See: Folvite, Tab., Sol. (Lederle)

LIC ACID ANTAGONISTS.
See: Methotrexate Inj., Tab. (Lederle)

LIC ACID SALTS.
See: Folvite, Tab., Sol. (Lederle)

LINIC ACID. Leucovorin Calcium, U.S.P. XXI.
Various Mfg.

LIPLEX-C. (Galen) Vit. B-1 3 mg., B-2 3 mg., B-6 0.5 mg., B-12 w. intrinsic factor conc. representing 3 mcg. cyanocobalamin, Ca pantothenate 1 mg., niacinamide 5 mg., ferrous fumarate 40 mg., Cu 1 mg., yeast autolysate 1 gr., liver, whole desic. 2.67 gr., folic acid 0.05 mg./Cap. Bot. 100s.
Jse: Oral hematinic and vit. supp.

LIVER "12." (Pharmex) Vit. B-12 activity from liver inj. equiv. to cyanocobalamin 10 mcg., folic acid 1 mg., Vit. B-12 100 mcg./cc. Vial 10 cc. Univial 10 cc.

LIV-B-12 FORTE. (Rocky Mtn.) Liver inj. 10 mcg., folic acid 1 mg., B-12 100 mcg./cc. Univial 10 cc.
Use: Liver & vitamin therapy.

LLESTROL. (Blue Line) **Aq. susp.** Estrone 20,000 I.U./cc. (2 mg./cc.) & 50,000 I.U./cc. (5 mg./cc) 10 cc. **Tab.** Conjugated 1.25 mg. Bot. 100s, 1000s.
Use: Estrogen therapy.

L-LI-BEE. (Foy) Liver inj. equiv. to cyanocobalamin 10 mcg., folic acid 1 mg., cyanocobalamin 100 mcg.,/cc., phenol 0.5% pH adjusted w/sod. hydroxide and/or HCl. Vial 10 cc. multi-dose, Monovials.

LLICLE STIMULATING HORMONE, HUMAN.
Menotropins, Pergonal.

LLICORMON.
See: Estradiol Benzoate. (Various Mfr.)

LLICULAR HORMONES.
See: Estrone (Various Mfr.)

LLICULIN.
See: Estrone (Various Mfr.)

LLUTEIN. (Squibb) Chorionic gonadotropin. 10,000 units Pow. 10 ml. diluent. (W/NaCl 83 mg., sodium hydroxide, phenol 0.5%).
Use: Cryptorchidism.

LTRIN. (Vitarine) Hematinic concentrate with intrinsic factor.
Use: Hematinic.

FOLVITE. (Lederle) Folic Acid (as sodium folate).
Sol.: (Sequestrene sod. 0.2%, water for injection, sod. hydroxide, benzyl alcohol 1.5%). 5 mg./ml. Vial 10 ml. **Tab.:** 1 mg. Bot. 100s, 1000s. Unit dose 10 × 10s.
Use: Megaloblastic anemias of folate deficiency.

FOMAC FOAM. (Dermik) Salicylic acid 2% in a soap-free protein/polyvinylpyrrolidone complex system. Bot. 3 oz.
Use: Treatment for acne & oily skin.

FOMOCAINE. B.A.N. 4-(3-Morpholinopropyl)-benzyl phenyl ether.
Use: Local anesthetic.

FONATOL.
See: Diethylstilbestrol (Various Mfr.)

• **FONAZINE.** USAN. Dimethothiazine.
Use: Serotonin inhibitor

FONAZINE MESYLATE. 10-[2-Dimethylamino)propyl]-N, N-dimethylphenothiazine-2-sulfonamide methanesulfonate.
Use: Antihistamine, antiserotonin, antibradykinin.

FONTARSOL.
See: Dichlorophenarsine Hydrochloride.

FOOTWORK. (Lederle) Athlete's foot remedy containing Tolnaftate 1%. Aerosol powder 3.5 oz.; Cream 0.5 oz., 1 oz.; Powder 2.75 oz.; Sol. 10 ml.
Use: Treatment & prevention of athlete's foot, jock itch, ringworm.

FORALICON PLUS ELIXIR. (Forbes) Vit. B-12 16.7 mcg., B-6 4 mg., iron 200 mg. (equiv. to elemental iron 24 mg.), niacinamide 40 mg., folic acid 0.8 mg., sorbitol sol. q.s./15 ml. Bot. 8 oz., 16 oz.
Use: Vit. B-12, B-6, or iron deficiencies.

FORBUTOL. (Vangard) A.P.C. w/butalbital 50 mg., aspirin 200 mg., phenacetin 130 mg., caffeine 40 mg./Tab. Bot. 100s, 1000s.
Use: Headache.

FORDUSTIN. (Sween) Methylbenzethonium chloride, sodium bicarbonate, corn starch. Body pow. Plastic Bot. 9 Oz.
Use: Topical bacteriostatic.

FOR FACES ONLY. (Plough) A series of sunscreen lotions with SPF 2, 4, 6 & 15 in a non-greasy base with Padimate O and oxybenzone (SPF 15 only.)
Use: Ultraviolet sunscreen.

FORMADON SOLUTION. (Gordon) Formalin solution (10% of U.S.P. strength) in an aqueous perfumed base. Bot. 1 oz., 4 oz., 0.5 gal., gal.
Use: Bromidrosis, hyperhidrosis.

FORMADRIN. (Kenyon) Chlorpheniramine maleate 12 mg., pot. guaiacol sulfonate 8 gr., ammonium chloride 8 gr., tartar emetic 1/12 gr., dl-desoxyephedrine HCl 2 mg./oz. Bot. 4 oz.
Use: Treatment of cold symptoms.

• **FORMALDEHYDE SOLUTION,** U.S.P. XXI. A 37% aqueous solution.
Use: For poison ivy, fungus infections of the skin, hyperhidrosis & as an astringent disinfectant.

FORMALIN.
See: Formaldehyde Solution (Various Mfr.)

FORMEBOLONE. B.A.N. 2-Formyl-11α, 17β-dihydroxy-17α-methylandrosta-1,4-dien-3-one.
Use: Anabolic steroid.

FORMIC ACID.
W/Silicic acid.
See: Nyloxin, Inj. (Hyson, Westcott & Dunning)

FORMINITRAZOLE. B.A.N. 2-Formamido-5-nitrothiazole.
Use: Treatment of trichomoniasis.
See: Aroxine

• **FORMOCORTAL.** USAN. 3-(2-Chloroethoxy)-9-fluoro-11β, 16α, 17, 21-tetrahydroxy-20-oxopregna-3, 5-diene-6-carboxaldehyde, cyclic 16, 17-acetal with acetone, 21-acetate.
Use: Glucocorticoid.

FORMOCORTAL. B.A.N. 21-Acetoxy-3-(2-chloroethoxy)-9α-fluoro-6-formyl-11β-hydroxy-16α,-17α-isopropylidenedioxypregna-3,5-dien-20-one.
Use: Topical corticosteroid.
See: Deflamene

FORMULA "K." (Pharmex) Calcium gluconate 1.5 Gm., potassium chloride 4.47 Gm., Mg sulf. 60 mg./cc. Vial 30 cc.

FORMULA 44 COUGH CONTROL DISCS. (Vicks)
See: Vicks Formula 44 Cough Discs (Vicks)

FORMULA 44 COUGH MIXTURE. (Vicks)
See: Vicks Formula 44 Cough Mixture (Vicks)

FORMULA 44D DECONGESTANT COUGH MIXTURE. (Vicks)
See: Vicks Formula 44D Decongestant Cough Mixture (Vicks)

FORMULA NO. 81. (Fellows) Liver (beef) for inj. 1 mcg., ferrous gluconate 100 mg., niacinamide 100 mg., B-2 1.5 mg., panthenol 2.5 mg., B-12 3.0 mcg., procaine HCl 25/2 cc. Vial 30 cc.

FORMULA 1207. (Thurston) Iodine, liver fraction No. 2, caseinates/Tab. Bot. 100s, 250s.
Use: Dietary supplement.

FORMULA NO. 3656. (Blue Line) Phenacetin 2.5 gr., aspirin 3.5 gr., phenolphthalein 0.25 gr., caffeine 0.5 gr./Tab. Bot. 1000s.

FORMULA NO. 3948. (Blue Line) Phenobarbital 16 mg., phenacetin 162 mg., aspirin 227 mg./Tab. Bot. 1000s.

2-FORMYL-1-METHYLPYRIDINIUM CHLORIDE OXIME. Pralidoxime Chloride, U.S.P. XXI.

FORMYL TETRAHYDROPTEROYLGLUTAMIC ACID. Leucovorin Calcium, U.S.P. XXI.

FORTA-FLORA. (Barth's) Whey-lactose 90%, pectin. **Pow.** Jar 1 lb. **Wafers** Bot. 100s.

FORTAGESIC TABLETS. (Winthrop Products) Paracetamol, pentazocine.
Use: Analgesic.

FORTA. (Ross) Complete nutritional supplement in pudding base. Available in vanilla, chocolate, tapioca and butterscotch. Cans 5 oz. Case 12 x 4 pacs.
Use: Oral nutritional supplement.

FORTAZ. (Glaxo) Ceftazidime for parenteral administration. Vials 500 mg., 1 Gm., 2 Gm., 6 Gm.
Use: Beta-lactam antibiotic.

FORTERRA—OBLONG RED TAB. (Panray) Vit. A 5000 I.U., D 1000 I.U., B-1 3 mg., B-2 2.5 mg., B-6 1.5 mg., B-12 2.5 mcg., C 50 mg., niacinamide mg., cal. pantothenate 5 mg., Vit. E 3 I.U., dical. phos 747 mg., ferrous sulf. 45.56 mg., manganese sulf. 4.72 mg., zinc sulf. 3.9 mg., magnesium sulf. 54 mg., potassium sulf. 11.2 mg./Tab. Bot. 100s.
Use: Vitamin, mineral supplement.

FORTE L.I.V. (Foy) Cyanocobalamine 15 mcg. Liver injection equivalent to Vit. B-12 activity 1 mcg., ferro gluconate 50 mg., B-2 0.75 mg., panthenol 1.25 m niacinamide 50 mg., citric acid 8.2 mg., sodium citrate 118 mg./ml. w/procaine HCl 2%. Bot. 30 ml.
Use: Multivitamin supplement.

FORTRAL. (Winthrop Products) Pentazocine as solution and tablets.
Use: Analgesic.

FORTRAMIN. (Thurston) Vit. E 200 I.U., A 6000 I.U. D 600 I.U., B-1 4.5 mg., B-2 4.5 mg., B-6 4.5 mg., B-12 5 mcg., C 2.75 mg., rutin 8 mg., hesperidin complex 10 mg., lemon bioflavonoids 15 mg., d-calcium pantothenate 50 mg., para-aminobenzoic acid 7 mg., biotin 10 mg., folic acid 24 mcg., niacinamide 20 mg., desicc. liver 25 mg., Fe 3 mg., Ca 75 mg. P 34 mg., Mn 10 mg., Cu 0.5 mg., Zn 0.5 mg., iodine 0.375 mg., K 500 mg., Mg 5.0 mg./Tab. Bot. 100s, 250s.
Use: Vit. supplement.

• **FOSAZEPAM.** USAN. 7-Chloro-1-dimethylphosphinylmethyl-1,3-dihydro-5-phenyl-2H-1,4-benzodiazepin-2-one.
Use: Hypnotic.

• **FOSCARNET SODIUM.** USAN.
Use: Antiviral.

FOSFESTROL. B.A.N. trans-αα′-Diethylstilbene-4,4′-diol bis(dihydrogen phosphate).
Use: Treatment of carcinoma of the prostate.
See: Honvan (tetrasodium salt)

• **FOSFOMYCIN.** USAN.
Use: Antibacterial.

• **FOSFONET SODIUM.** USAN.
Use: Antiviral.

• **FOSPIRATE.** USAN.
Use: Anthelmintic.

FOSFREE. (Mission) Calcium lactate 250 mg., calcium gluconate 250 mg., calcium carbonate 300 mg., calcium 175.7 mg., Vit. D-2 150 I.U., Vitamin A acetate 1500 I.U., ferrous gluconate 125 mg. (iron 14.5 mg.), Vitamin B-12 2.0 mcg., C 50 mg., B-6 3.0 mg. B-1 5.0 mg., B-2 2.0 mg., niacinamide (B-3) 10 mg., calcium pantothenate (B-5) 1.0 mg./Tab. Bot. 100s
Use: Prenatal, postpartum or geriatric supplement.

• **FOSTEDIL.** USAN.
Use: Vasodilator.

FOSTEX CM. (Westwood) Sulfur 2% in a flesh-tinted greasless base. Tube 1 oz.
Use: Acne medication & cover up.

FOSTEX CREAM AND MEDICATED CLEANSER. (Westwood) Sulfur 2%, salicylic acid 2% w/soapless cleansers and wetting agents. **Cream:** tube 4 oz. **Medicated Cleanser:** plastic bot. 5 oz.
Use: Acne skin cleanser.

ƎTEX BPO GEL. (Westwood) Benzyl peroxide 5%. ube 1.5 oz.
Jse: Topical aid for control of acne.

ƎTEX MEDICATED CLEANSING BAR. Vestwood) Sulfur 2%, salicylic acid 2% in base of oapless cleansers and wetting agents. Bar 3.75 z.
Jse: Acne skin cleanser.

ƎTEX 10% BPO CLEANSING BAR. (Westwood) enzoyl peroxide 10%. Bar 3.75 oz.
se: Acne skin cleanser.

ƎTRIL. (Westwood) Sulfur 2% in greaseless base. ot. Tubes 1 oz.
se: Topical aid for control of acne.

TOTAR CREAM. (Elder) Coal tar 1.6% in emollient noisturizing cream base. Tube 3 oz. Jar 1 lb.
Jse: Chronic skin disorders.

TOTAR STIK. (Elder) Coal tar 5.0% in a ydrophilic wax base. Stick 0.5 oz.
se: Chronic skin disorders.

JR ANTIHISTAMINES. (Wolins) Pyrilamine naleate 6.25 mg., phenyltoloxamine dihydrogen itrate 6.25 mg., prophenpyridamine maleate 6.25 r./Tab. Bot. 1000s.
se: Antihistaminic.

JR-B. (Pasadena Research) Vit. B-1 100 mg., B- 10 mg., B-6 50 mg., nicotinamide 100 mg./cc. Vial 0 cc.
se: Vitamin supplement.

AY COLD TABS. (Bristol-Myers) Aspirin 324 mg., henylpropanolamine HCl 12.5 mg., hlorpheniramine maleate 2.0 mg./Tab. Bot. 15s, 6s, 60s.
Jse: Analgesic, decongestant, antihistaminic.

AY LONG ACTING NASAL SPRAY. (Bristol-Myers) Oxymetazoline HCl 0.05% in isotonic buffered soln. /0.005% thimerosal preservative. Spray Bot. 0.5 z.
se: Long acting nasal decongestant.

AY NASAL SPRAY. (Bristol-Myers) Phenylephrine ICl 0.5%, naphazoline HCl 0.05%, pyrilamine naleate 0.2% w/buffered isotonic aqueous sol., nimerosal 0.005%.
tomizer 0.5 oz., 1 oz. Mentholated 0.5 oz., 1 oz.
se: Decongestant/antihistamine.

JRSALCO. (Jenkins) Salicylic acid 0.5 gr., sod. icarbonate 3 gr., mag. salicylate 2 gr., strontium alicylate 2 gr., acetophenetidin 0.25 gr. w/methyl alicylate, pancreatin 1/40 gr., diastase 1/40 gr./Tab. ot. 1000s.
se: Treatment of rheumatic conditions.

ANE. Benzthiazide, B.A.N.

WLER'S SOLUTION. Potassium Arsenite Solution Various Mfr.)

ALIN. (Standex) Digitoxin 0.1 mg. w/Sod. arboxymethylcellulose/Cap. Bot. 100s.
se: Orally; digitalis glycoside for rapid igitalization.

GLOVE.
ee: Digitalis (Var. Mfr.)

PLEX INJECTION. (Foy) Sterile injectable sol. of ine water-soluble vitamins. Packaged as 2 separate olutions for extemporaneous combination.

FRAMYCETIN. B.A.N. An antibiotic produced by Streptomyces decaris.
See: Framygen
Soframycin (sulfate)

FRANODIL. (Winthrop Products) Ephedrine sulfate, theophylline, anhydrous, chlormezanone.
Use: Antiasthmatic.

FRANOL. (Winthrop Products) Theophylline anhydrous, ephedrine sulfate, phenobarbital, thenyldiamine HCl.
Use: Antiasthmatic.

FREAMINE III. (American McGaw) Amino acid 3%, 8.5% or 10%.
Use: Amino acid solution.

FREAMINE HBC. (American McGaw) High branched 6.9% amino acid formulation for hypercatabolic patients.

FREEZONE. (Whitehall) Salicylic acid 13.6%, alcohol 20.5%, ether 64.8% in flexible collodion base. Bot. .13 oz.
Use: Corn remover.

• **FRENTIZOLE.** USAN.
Use: Immunoregulator.

FRESH. (Pharmacraft) Aluminum chloride and aluminum chlorhydrate. **Cream:** Jar ¾ oz., 1.2 oz., **Roll-on:** 1 oz., 1.5 oz.
Use: Deodorant, antiperspirant.

FRESH n' FEMININE. (Walgreen) Benzethonium chloride 0.2% Bot. 8 oz.
Use: Cleansing douche.

• **FRUCTOSE,** U.S.P. XXI. Inj., U.S.P. XXI. (Abbott) (Cutter) 10% soln. Bot. 1000 ml.
See: Frutabs, Tab. (Pfanstiehl)

• **FRUCTOSE AND SODIUM CHLORIDE INJECTION,** U.S.P. XXI.
Use: Fluid, nutrient and electrolyte replenisher.

FRUIT-SAVER. (Stanlabs) Pow. Bot. 3 oz.

FRUSEMIDE. 4-Chloro-N-furfuryl-5-sulfamoylanthranilic acid. Lasix.

FRUSEMIDE. B.A.N. 4-Chloro-N-furfuryl-5-sulphamoylanthranilic acid. Furosemide (I.N.N.)
Use: Diuretic.
See: Lasix

FRUTABS. (Pfanstiehl) Fructose tablets. 2 Gm. Bot. 100s.
Use: Quick energy source for athletes, workers, etc.

FRUT-PAK. (Eckerd) Vitamin C 250 mg., 500 mg./Tab. Bot. 100s, 200s.
Use: Vitamin C supplement.

FTA-ABS. (Wampole-Zeus) Fluorescent treponemal antibody-absorbed test. Tests 100s.
Use: An *in vitro* diagnostic aid for confirming a positive reagin test for syphillis.

FTA-ABS/DS. (Wampole-Zeus) Fluorescent treponemal antibody absorbed test. Tests 100s.
Use: An *in vitro* diagnostic aid for confirming a positive reagin test for syphilis.

• **FUCHSIN, BASIC,** U.S.P. XXI. Basic Fuchsin is a mixture of rosaniline and pararosaniline HCl. Basic Magenta.
Use: Ingredient in Carbo-Fuchsin Sol.

FUDR. (Roche) Floxuridine. 2-Deoxy-5-fluorouridine. Vial 500 mg. 5 ml.
Use: Management of carcinoma.

FULFIL. (Bristol Oncology) Nutritionally complete high calorie formula containing 355 calories/8 fl. oz. representing 40% from fat, 38% from carbohydrates and 22% from protein. Cans 8 oz.
Use: Nutritional supplement.

FUL-GLO. (Barnes-Hind) Fluorescein sod. 0.6%. Box 300 strips.
Use: Ophthalmic strips; diagnostic agent.

FULVICIN P/G. (Schering) Griseofulvin ultramicrosize 125 mg., 165 mg., 250 mg., 330 mg./Tab. Bot. 100s.
Use: Antifungal.

FULVICIN-U/F. (Schering) Griseofulvin microsize 250 mg., 500 mg./Tab. Bot. 60s, 250s.
Use: Antifungal.

FUMAGILLIN. B.A.N. A cryst. antibiotic produced during the growth of a strain of Aspergillus fumigatus.

FUMARAL ELIXIR. (Vortech) Alcohol 5%, ferrous sulfate 5 gr./10 ml. Vial 4 oz., gal.
Use: Iron deficiency anemia.

FUMARAL SPANCAP. (Vortech) Iron 330 mg., Vitamin C 200 mg./Cap. Bot. 100s, 1000s.
Use: Iron supplement w/vitamin C.

• **FUMARIC ACID.** N.F. XVI. 2-Butenedioic acid.
Use: Acidifier.

FUMATINIC CAPSULES. (Laser) Ferrous fumarate 275 mg., Vit. C 100 mg., B-12 15 mcg., folic acid 1 mg. /Cap. Bot. 100s, 1000s.
Use: Hypochromic microcytic anemia, nutritional macrocytic anemia, nutritional macrocytic or microcytic anemia of pregnancy, tropical and nontropical sprue.

FUMATRIN-FORTE. (Reid-Provident) Elemental iron 100 mg., Vit. B-12 12 mcg., C 100 mg., B-1 3 mg., desiccated liver 100 mg., folic acid 0.5 mg./Tab. Bot. 60s, 500s.
Use: Hematinic.

FUMERIN. (Laser) Ferrous fumarate 195 mg./Tab. Bot. 100s, 1000s.
Use: Iron deficiency anemia.

FUMERON. (Vitarine) Ferrous fumarate 330 mg., Vit. B-1 5 mg./TR. Cap.
Use: Hematinic.

FUMEX. (CMC) Silver acetate 6 mg., cocarboxylase 0.025 mg., NH_4Cl 25 mg./oz. Bot. 24s.
Use: To break the smoking habit.

• **FUMOXICILLIN.** USAN.
Use: Antibacterial.

FUNDUSCEIN. (CooperVision) Sodium fluorescein injection 10%. Amp. 5 ml. 12s, 25% Amp. 3 ml. 12s.
Use: Aid in ophthalmic angiography.

FUNGACETIN OINTMENT. (Blair) Triacetin (glyceryl triacetate) 25% in a water-miscible ointment base. Tube 1 oz.
Use: Topically, fungus infections.

■ **FUNGICIDES.**
See: Aftate, Prods. (Plough)
Arcum, Preps. (Arcum)
Asterol
Basic Fuchsin (Var. Mfr.)
Coparaffinate
Desenex, Prods. (Pharmacraft)
Dichlorophene
Nifuroxime (Var. Mfr.)
Nitrofurfuryl Methyl Ether (Var. Mfr.)
Phenylmercuric Preps. (Various Mfr.)
Propionate, Sodium (Various Mfr.)
Propionic Acid (Various Mfr.)
Salicylanilide (Doak)
Undecylenic Acid (Various Mfr.)

• **FUNGIMYCIN.** USAN.
Use: Antifungal

FUNGIZONE CREAM, LOTION, OINT. (Squibb) Amphotericin B 3%, Thimerosal, titanium dioxide. **Lot.** Plastic Sq. Bot. 30 cc. **Cream & Oint.** Tube 20 Gm.
Use: Monilial infections.

FUNGIZONE INTRAVENOUS. (Squibb) Amphoteric B 50 mg., sodium desoxycholate 41 mg., sodium phosphate 25.2 mg./Vial. Lypholized.
Use: Mycotic infections.

FUNGIZONE FOR LABORATORY USE IN TISSUE CULTURE. (Squibb) Amphotericin B 50 mg., sodium desoxycholate 41 mg./vial of 20 cc.
Use: Laboratory.

FUNGOID CREME. (Pedinol) Cetyl pyridinium chlori triacetin, chloroxylenol in vanishing cream base. Tube 1 oz.
Use: Topical treatment for fungus, yeast and bacterial infections of the skin.

FUNGOID TINCTURE. (Pedinol) Cetyl pyridinium Cl triacetin, chloroxylenol, glacial acetic acid, sodiu propionate, propionic acid, isopropyl alcohol, ben alcohol, acetone, propylene glycol, eucalyptol. Bo 1 oz., pt. w/Brush applicator.
Use: Treatment of nail fungus, onychomycosis.

FUNGOID SOLUTION. (Pedinol) Cetyl pyridinium C triacetin, chloroxylenol. Plastic Dropper. Bot. 15 c
Use: Topical treatment for fungus, yeast, bacteria infections of the skin.

FUN MATES. (Vitarine) Fruit flavored multiple vitam tablets.
Use: Multivitamin supplement.

FURACIN SOLUBLE DRESSING. (Norwich Eaton) Nitrofurazone 0.2% in a water-soluble, nondryi ointmentlike base of polyethylene glycols. Jar 13 Gm., 454 Gm. Tube 28 Gm., 56 Gm.
Use: Topical application in surface infections.

FURACIN TOPICAL CREAM. (Norwich Eaton) Furacin 0.2% in a water miscible, self-emulsify cream w/glycerin, cetyl alcohol, mineral oil, an ethoxylated fatty alcohol, methylparaben, propylparaben and water. Tube 14 Gm. & 28 Gm Jar 368 Gm.
Use: Topical antibacterial agent in surface infections.

ꞮADANTIN. (Norwich Eaton) Nitrofurantoin 50 mg., 00 mg./Tab. Bot. 100s, 500s. Unit dose 100s.
Ise: Antibacterial for urinary tract infections.

ꞮADANTIN ORAL SUSPENSION. (Norwich Eaton) litrofurantoin. Bot. (5 mg./ml.) 60 ml., 470 ml.
Ise: Antibacterial for urinary tract infections.

ꞮALAN. (Lannett) Nitrofurantoin 50 mg., 100 ng./Tab. Bot. 100s, 500s, 1000s.
Ise: Urinary tract antibacterial.

ꞮALAZINE HYDROCHLORIDE. 3-Amino-6-[2-(5-itro-2-furyl)vinyl]-as-triazine hydrochloride.
Jse: Anti-microbial compound.

ꞮALTADONE. (±)-5-Morpholinomethyl-3-[(5-ni-ofurfurylidene)amino]-2-oxazolidinone.

ꞮAMIDE 2-FUROATE. Diloxanide, B.A.N.

H)-FURANONE, 3-ETHYLDIHYDRO-4-[(1-METH-'L-1H-IMIDAZOL-5-YL)METHYL]-,MONOHYDROC-ILORIDE, (3S-cis)-. OR MONONITRATE. Pilocar-ine Hydrochloride, or Nitrate. U.S.P. XXI.

ꞮANITE TABS. (Major) Nitrofurantoin 50 mg. or 00 mg./Tab. Bot. 100s.
Ise: Antibacterial for urinary infections.

ꞮANTOIN. (Vortech) Nitrofurantoin 50 mg./Tab. ot. 100s, 1000s.
Jse: Urinary tract infections.

JRAPROFEN. USAN.
Jse: Anti-inflammatory.

JRAZOLIDONE, U.S.P. XXI. Oral Susp., Tab., J.S.P. XXI. 2-Oxazolidone, 3-(((5-nitro-2 furanyl) nethyl-ene)amino). 3[(5-Nitrofurfurylidene)-amino]--oxazolidinone.
Ise: Antimicrobial agent.
ee: Furoxone Tab., Susp. (Norwich Eaton)

JRAZOLIUM CHLORIDE. USAN.
Ise: Antibacterial.

JRAZOLIUM TARTRATE. USAN.
Ise: Antibacterial.

ꞮAZOSIN HCl. 1-(4-Amino-6, 7-dimethoxy-2-quin-zolinyl)-4-(2-furoyl)piperazine monohydrochloride. Inder study.
Jse: Antihypertensive.

ꞮAZYME. (Jenkins) Nitrofurazone 0.2%. Tube. 1 z., 1 lb.
Jse: Soluble dressing.

ꞮETHIDINE. 1-(2-Tetrahydrofurfuryloxyethyl)-4-phe-ylpiperidine-4-carboxylic acid ethyl ester.

ꞮETHIDINE. B.A.N. Ethyl 4-phenyl-1-[2-(tetrahy-rofurfuryloxy)ethyl]piperidine-4-carboxylate.
Ise: Narcotic analgesic.

JRODAZOLE. USAN.
Ise: Anthelmintic.

RON. (Metro Med) Ferrous fumarate Tabs. Bot. 00s, 1000s.
Ise: Hemoglobin regeneration.

ꞮONATALFA. (Metro Med) Bot. 60s, 1000s.
Ise: Prenatal vitamins and minerals.

ꞮOSE. (Ascher) Furosemide 40 mg./Tab. Bot. 000s.
Jse: Diuretic, antihypertensive.

JROSEMIDE. U.S.P. XXI. Inj., Tab., U.S.P. XXI. 4-hloro-N-(furfuryl-)-5-sulfamoylanthranilic acid. Benzoic acid, 5-(aminosulfonyl)-4-chloro-2[(2-furanylmethyl)amino]-. (Abbot) 10 mg./ml. Injection. Single dose syr. 2 ml., 5 ml., 10 ml. Single dose vial 2 ml., 10 ml. 4 ml. partial fill single dose vial.
Use: Diuretic.
See: Lasix, Tab., Inj. (Hoechst-Roussel)

FUROXONE. (Norwich Eaton) Furazolidone. **Tab.** 100 mg./Tab. Bot. 20s, 100s. **Liq.** 50 mg./15 cc. Bot. 60 cc., 473 cc.
Use: Antimicrobial agent.

• **FURSALAN.** USAN. 3, 5-Dibromo-N-(tetrahydrofurfuryl)- salicylamide. Under study.
Use: Germicide.

FUSAFUNGINE. B.A.N. An antibiotic produced by Fusarium lateritium.

• **FUSIDATE SODIUM.** USAN. (I) Sodium 3α, 11α, 16β-trihydroxy-29-nor-$8\alpha,9\beta,13\alpha,14\beta$-dammara-17(-20),24-dien-21-oate 16-acetate. Fucidine (Squibb).
Use: Antibacterial
See: Fucidine (Squibb)

• **FUSIDIC ACID.** USAN. An antibiotic produced by a strain of Fusidium. cis-16β-Acetoxy-3α,-11 α-dihydroxy-4α,8, 14-trimethyl-18-nor-5α,-$8\alpha,9\beta,13\alpha,14\beta$-cholesta-17(20),24-dien-21-oic acid.
Use: Antibacterial.

G

G-1. (Hauck) Acetaminophen 500 mg., butalbital 50 mg., caffeine 40 mg./Cap. Bot. 100s. Unit dose 50s.
Use: Analgesic associated with nervous tension & anxiety.

G-2. (Hauck) Acetaminophen 500 mg., butalbital 50 mg., codeine phosphate 15 mg./Cap. Bot. 100s. Unit dose 50s.
Use: Analgesic.

G-3. (Hauck) Acetaminophen 500 mg., butalbital 50 mg., codeine phosphate 30 mg./Cap. Bot. 100s. Unit dose 50s.
Use: Analgesic.

G-4.
See: Dichlorophene.

G-11. (Givaudan) Hexachlorophene Pow. for mfg.
See: Hexachlorophene, U.S.P. XXI.

2/G. (Merrell Dow) Guaifenesin 100 mg./5 ml. w/alcohol 3.5%. Bot. 4 oz.
Use: Expectorant

2G/DM. (Merrell Dow) Guaifenesin 100 mg., dextromethorphan HBr 15 mg./5 ml. w/alcohol 5%. Bot. 4 oz.
Use: Expectorant, antitussive.

GACID TAB. (Arcum) Mg trisilicate 500 mg., aluminum hydroxide 250 mg./Tab. Bot. 100s, 1000s.
Use: Antacid.

GALACTOSE INJECTION. (Horton & Converse) Galactose 50% in sterile distilled water. Vial 50 cc., 1s, 12s, 25s.
Use: Diagnostic agent.

GALLAMINE. B.A.N. 1,2,3-Tri-(2-diethylamino-ethoxy)-benzene.
Use: Neuromuscular blocking agent.
See: Flaxedil (Davis & Geck)

• **GALLAMINE TRIETHIODIDE,** U.S.P. XXI. Inj. U.S.P. XXI. [v-Phenenyltris(oxyethylene)] tris[triethylammonium] Triiodide. Ethanaminium, 2,2′,2″-[1,2,3-benzenetriyltris(oxy)]tris-[N,N,N-triethyl]-,triiodide.
Use: Skeletal muscle relaxant.
See: Flaxedil (Davis & Geck)

• **GALLIUM CITRATE Ga-67 INJECTION,** U.S.P. XXI.
Use: Diagnostic aid (radiopaque medium).

GALLOCHROME.
See: Merbromin (Various Mfr.)

GALLOTANNIC ACID.
See: Tannic Acid, Preps. (Var. Mfr.)

GAMASTAN. (Cutter) Immune serum globulin (human) U.S.P. Vial 2 ml., 10 ml.
Use: Prophylaxis and attenuation of measles, poliomyelitis and viral hepatitis.

GAMAZOLE TABS. (Major) Sulfamethoxazole 500 mg./Tab. Bot. 100s.
Use: Antibacterial.

• **GAMFEXINE.** USAN. N,N-Dimethyl-γ-phenyl-cyclohexanepropylamine.
Use: Antidepressant.

GAMIMUNE. (Cutter) Immune globulin intravenous 5% in 10% maltose sterile 5 plus or minus 1% sol. of human protein stabilized w/0.1 M glycine. Single dose vial 50 or 100 ml.
Use: Immune globulin.

GAMMA BENZENE HEXACHLORIDE. B.A.N.γ-1,2,3,-4,5,6-Hexachlorocyclohexane. Lindane, U.S.P. XXI.
Use: Antiparasitic.
See: Lorexane
Quellada

GAMMAR. (Armour) Immune Serum Globulin, Human U.S.P. Vial 2 ml., 10 ml.

GAMOLENIC ACID. B.A.N. cis, cis, cis-Octadeca-6,9,-12-trienoic acid.
Use: Treatment of hypercholesterolemia.

G.A.M.P.A.K. (Fellows) Gastric mucin 10 gr., aminoacetic acid 4.5 gr., magnesium trisilicate 30 gr., aluminum hydroxide gel 31.21 gr., kaolin colloidal 194.50 gr./oz. Bot. 4 oz., 8 oz.

GAMULIN Rh. (Armour) Rho (D) Immune globulin (Human). Vials, 1 dose, Vial crossmatched material.
Use: Rh-negative mothers after delivery of an Rh-positive infant.

G AND W PRODUCTS. (G&W) G and W markets. The following products under their G & W brand name:
Aminophylline Rectal Suppos., 250 mg., 500 mg.
Aspirin Rectal Suppos., 125 mg., 300 mg., 600 mg.
Bisacodyl Suppos., 10 mg.
Glycerin Suppos., Adult and Infant Sizes
Hemorrhoidal Rectal Ointment.
Hemorrhoidal Rectal Suppos., Formula C-116 and Formula C-119.
Hemorrhoidal Rectal Suppos. w/Hydrocortisone Acetate 10 mg. or 25 mg./Suppos.
Vaginal Sulfa Cream.

GANEAKE. (Geneva) Estrogens, Conjugated 0.625 mg., 1.25 mg., 2.5 mg./Tab. Bot. 100s, 1000s.

■ **GANGLIONIC BLOCKING AGENTS.**
See: Arfonad, Amp. (Roche)
Dibenzyline HCl, Cap. (SmithKline)
Hexamethonium Chloride & Bromide (Various Mfr.)
Hydergine, Amp., Tab. (Sandoz)
Inversine, Tab. (Merck Sharp & Dohme)
Priscoline HCl, Tab., Vial (Ciba)
Regitine, Amp., Tab. (Ciba)

GANTANOL. (Roche) Sulfamethoxazole **Tab.:** 0.5 Gm./Tab. Bot. 100s, 500s. Tel-E-Dose 100s. **Su** (10%) 0.5 Gm./Tsp. Cherry flavored Bot. 1 pt.
Use: Antibacterial
W/Phenazopyridine.
See: Azo Gantanol, Tabs. (Roche) 100s, 500s.

GANTANOL DS. (Roche) Sulfamethoxazole 1 Gm./Tab. Bot. 100s. Tel-E-Dose 100s.
Use: Antibacterial.

GANTREX. (Coastal) Sulfisoxazole 500 mg./Tab. Bot. 100s, 1000s.

GANTRISIN. (Roche) Sulfisoxazole. **Ophth. Oint.** w/white petrolatum, mineral oil and phenylmercu nitrate 1:50,000. (4%) Tube ⅛ oz. **Ophth. Sol.** phenylmercuric nitrate 1:100,000 added as preservative. (40 mg./ml.) Bot. w/dropper 0.5 oz. **Tab.:** (0.5 Gm.) Bot. 100s, 500s, 1000s. Drum 5000s. Prescription Pak 100s. Tel-E-Dose 100s (× 10). **Amp.:** (5 ml.) containing 2 Gm. Gantrisin, ready-to-use solution in the form of Gantrisin dic mine 10s.
Use: Antibacterial, sulfonamide therapy.
W/Phenylazo-diamino-pyridine HCl.
See: Azo Gantrisin, Tab. (Roche)

GANTRISIN, AZO.
See: Azo Gantrisin, Tab. (Roche)

GANTRISIN, LIPO. (Roche) Acetyl Sulfisoxazole.
Use: Sulfonamide therapy.
See: Lipo Gantrisin, Susp. (Roche)

GANTRISIN DIETHANOLAMINE OPHTHALMIC SOLUTION & OINTMENT. (Roche) Both Gantrisi ophthalmic oint. & sol. are stable antibacterial pre containing 4% Gantrisin in the form of Gantrisin diethanolamine. Ophth. Oint. Tube ⅛ oz.; Sol. Bo 0.5 oz.
Use: Antibacterial, sulfonamide therapy.

GANTRISIN DIOLAMINE. (Roche) Sulfisoxazole diolamine.
Use: Sulfonamide therapy.

GANTRISIN PEDIATRIC SUSPENSION. (Roche). Acetyl Sulfisoxazole 0.5 Gm./5 ml. Bot. 4 oz., pt.
Use: Sulfonamide therapy.

GANTRISIN SYRUP. (Roche) Acetyl Sulfisoxazole C Gm./5 ml. Bot. pt.
Use: Sulfonamide therapy.

GANTRISIN TEL-E-DOSE. (Roche) Sulfisoxazole Gm./Tab. Pkg. 100s (10 strips of 10).

GARAMYCIN. (Schering) **Cream:** Gentamicin sulfat 1.7 mg. (equiv. to gentamicin base 1 mg.). Methylparaben 1 mg. and butylparaben 4 mg. as preservatives, stearic acid, propylene glycol

nonostearate, isopropyl myristate, propylene glycol, olysorbate 40, sorbitol sol., and water/Gm. Tube 5 Gm. **Oint.** Gentamicin sulfate 1.7 mg. (equiv. to entamicin base 1 mg.), methylparaben 0.5 mg., ropylparaben 0.1 mg. in petrolatum base/Gm. ube, 15 Gm.
Jse: Topical dermatologic antibiotic.
RAMYCIN INJECTABLE. (Schering) Gentamicin ulfate equiv. to 40 mg. gentamicin base, nethylparaben 1.8 mg., propylparaben 0.2 mg., as reservatives, sod. bisulfite 3.2 mg., disodium detate 0.1 mg./ml. Vials 2 ml. (80 mg.), 20 ml. 800 mg.); Syringes 1.5 ml. (60 mg.), 2.0 ml. (80 ng.); **Pediatric Inj.;** 10 mg./ml. w/methylparaben .3 mg., propylparaben 0.2 mg., sod. bisulfite 3.2 ng., edetate disodium 0.1 mg./ml. Vials 2 ml. (20 ng.)
Jse: Parenteral antibiotic.
RAMYCIN INTRATHECAL INJECTION. (Schering) Gentamicin sulfate equiv. to 2 mg./ml. gentamicin ase, 8.5 mg. Na Cl/ml: Amp. 2 ml. Box 25s.
Jse: Antibiotic.
RAMYCIN I.V. PIGGYBACK. (Schering) Gentamicin sulfate equivalent to 1 mg. gentamicin ase, 8.9 mg. sodium Cl, no preservatives. 60 mg., 0 mg. Bot. 100 ml.
Jse: Parenteral antibiotic.
RAMYCIN OPHTHALMIC OINTMENT-STERILE. Schering) Gentamicin sulfate equiv. to 3 mg., entamicin, methylparaben & propylparaben as reservatives/cc. in petrolatum base. Tube ⅛ oz.
Jse: Antibiotic.
RAMYCIN OPHTHALMIC SOLUTION, STERILE. Schering) Gentamicin sulfate equiv. to 3 mg., entamicin, disodium phosphate, monosodium hosphate, sodium chloride & benzalkonium as reservative/ml. Plastic dropper bot. 5 ml. Sterile.
Jse: Antibiotic.
RDAC. (Vitarine) Belladonna alkaloids 0.13 mg., henylpropanolamine HCl 50 mg., chlorpheniramine naleate 1 mg., pheniramine maleate 12.5 mg./S.R. ap.
Jse: Relief of nasal congestion due to common old.
RDAN. (Winthrop Products) Dipyrone.
Jse: Analgesic, antipyretic, anti-inflammatory.
RDENAL.
See: Phenobarbital. (Various Mfr.)
ARDINOL TYPE DETERGENTS. Aurinol, Cyclopon, Dreft, Drene, Duponol, Lissapol, Maprofix, Modinal, Orvus, Sandopan, Sadipan.
Jse: Detergents.
RDOL. Sod. Lauroyl Sarcosinate.
RFIELDS TEA. (Last) Senna leaf powder 68.3%. Bot. 2 oz.
Jse: Stimulant laxative.
RITABS. (Blue Cross) Iron 50 mg., B-1 5 mg., B- 5 mg., C 75 mg., niacinamide 30 mg., B-5 2 mg., B- 0.5 mg., B-12 3 mcg. Bot. 1000s.
RI-TONIC HEMATINIC. (Blue Cross) B-1 5 mg., iacinamide 100 mg., B-2 5 mg., pantothenic acid 4 mg., B-6 1 mg., B-12 6 mcg., choline bitartrate 100 mg., iron 100 mg./30 ml. Bot. 16 oz.
Use: Hematinic.
GARLIC. Allium.
Use: Intestinal antispasmodic.
See: Allimin, Tab. (Mosso)
GARLIC CAPSULES. (Miller) Garlic 115 mg./Cap. Bot. 100s.
Use: Intestinal antispasmodic.
GARLIC CONCENTRATE.
W/Parsley Concentrate.
See: Allimin, Tab. (Mosso)
GARLIC OIL.
See: Natural Garlic Oil, Cap. (Spirt)
GARLIC OIL CAPSULES. (Kirkman) Bot. 100s.
GARRATHION. Carbophenothion, B.A.N.
GARTRONE. (Eric, Kirk & Gary) Veratrum Viride Alk. 250 mg./30 cc. Vials.
Use: I.M.
GAS-EZE. (Edward J. Moore) Aluminum hydroxide, magnesium hydroxide, calcium carbonate, glycine, mannitol, oil peppermint/Tab. Bot. 50s, Pak 36s.
Use: Indigestion; gas pain.
GAS PERMEABLE DAILY CLEANSER. (Barnes-Hind) Aqueous solution nonionic cleaning agents in alkaline buffered medium w/edetate disodium 2%, thimerosal 0.004%. Bot. 35 ml.
Use: Contact lens cleaner for gas permeable lenses.
GAS PERMEABLE LENS STARTER SYSTEM. (Barnes-Hind) Daily cleanser, Bot. 3 ml. Wetting & soaking sol., Bot. 60 ml., Hydra-mat II spin cleansing unit. Kit.
Use: For gas permeable lenses.
GAS PERMEABLE WETTING & SOAKING SOLUTION. (Barnes-Hind) Sterile aqueous, isotonic sol. of low viscosity, buffered to physiological pH. Bot. 2 oz.
Use: Wetting & soaking solution.
GASTRIC MUCIN.
(Wilson)—Gran. 8 oz. & 1 lb.
Use: Orally, ulcers.
W/Mg glycinate, Al hydroxide gel.
See: Mucogel, Tab. (Inwood)
W/Magnesium trisilicate, magnesium hydroxide, aluminum hydroxide.
See: Mucotin, Tab. (Warner-Chilcott)
GASTROGRAFIN. (Squibb) Diatrizoate methyl-glucamine 66%. Sodium Diatrizoate 10%. Radiopaque medium. Bot. 4 fl. oz.
Use: Roentgenographic study of the gastrointestinal tract.
GASTRON. (Winthrop Products) Pancreatin.
Use: Pancreatic deficiency, dyspepsia.
GASTROVIST. (Berlex) Diatrizoate meglumine 660 mg., diatrizoate sodium 100 mg./ml. Bot. 100 ml.
Use: Oral radiopaque medium for radiographic examination of the GI tract.
GAS-X. (Creighton) Simethicone 80 mg./Tab. Pkg. 12s, 30s.
Use: Antiflatulent.

• **GAUZE, ABSORBENT,** U.S.P. XXI.
Use: Surgical aid.

• **GAUZE, PETROLATUM,** U.S.P. XXI.
Use: Surgical aid.

GAVISCON. (Marion) Aluminum hydroxide dried gel 80 mg., magnesium trisilicate 20 mg./Tab. Bot. 100s.Box of 30s.
Use: Antacid.

GAVISCON-2. (Marion) Aluminum hydroxide dried gel 160 mg., magnesium trisilicate 40 mg./Tab. Box of 48.
Use: Antacid.

GAVISCON LIQUID. (Marion) Aluminum hydroxide 95 mg., magnesium carbonate 412 mg./15 ml. Bot. 2 oz, 6 oz., 12 oz.
Use: Antacid.

GAYSAL-S. (Geriatric) Sodium salicylate 300 mg., acetaminophen 180 mg., aluminum hydroxide gel 60 mg./Tab. Bot. 100s, 1000s.
Use: Antiarthritic.

G.B.H. LOTION. (Century) Gamma benzene hexachloride 1%. Bot. 2 oz., pt., gal.
Use: Antaparasitic.

G.B.S. (Forest) Dehydrocholic acid 125 mg., phenobarbital 8 mg., homatropine methyl-bromide 2-5 mg./Tab.
Use: Biliary stasis & insufficiency.

GEBAUER'S 114. (Gebauer) Dichlorotetraflouroethane 100%. Can 227 Gm.
Use: Topical anesthesia for minor surgical procedures.

GEBAUER ETHYL CHLORIDE. (Gebauer) Ethyl chloride. Bot. 106 Gm. Metal tube 100 Gm.
Use: Topical anesthetic.

GEE-GEE. (Bowman) Guaifenesin 200 mg./Tab. Bot. 100s, 1000s
Use: Expectorant.

GEFARNATE. B.A.N. A mixture of steroisomers of 3,7-dimethylocta-2,6-dienyl 5,9,13-trimethyl-tetradeca-4,8,12-trienoate. Geranyl farnesylacetate. Gefarnil.
Use: Treatment of peptic ulcer.

GEL II 1.23% APF TOPICAL GEL. (Oral-B) Acidulated phosphate fluoride 1.23%. Bot. 16 oz.
Use: Topical application to aid in prevention of dental caries.

GEL II HOME TREATMENT. (Oral-B) Acidulated phosphate fluoride 0.5%. Tube 2 oz.
Use: Topical application to aid in prevention of dental caries.

GEL-A-CAP. (Kenyon) Gelatin 10 gr./Cap. Bot. 100s, 1000s.

GELADINE. (Barth's) Gelatin, protein, Vit. D/Cap. Bot. 100s, 500s.

GELAMAL. (Halsey) Magnesium-aluminum hydroxide gel. Bot. 12 oz.
Use: Antacid.

• **GELATIN,** N.F. XVI.
Use: Pharmaceutic aid.

• **GELATIN FILM, ABSORBABLE,** U.S.P. XXI.
Use: Local hemostatic.
See: Gelfilm (Upjohn)

• **GELATIN SPONGE, ABSORBABLE,** U.S.P. XXI.
Use: Local hemostatic.
See: Gelfoam, Paks (Upjohn)

GELATIN, ZINC.
See: Zinc gelatin. (Var. Mfr.)

GEL-CLEAN. (Barnes-Hind) Gel formulated with n ionic surfactant. Tube 30 Gm.
Use: Hard contact lens cleaner.

GELFILM. (Upjohn) Sterile, absorbable gelatin film. Env. 1s. 100 mm. × 125 mm. Also available as Ophth. Sterile 25 × 50 mm. Box 6s.
Use: Aid in surgical closure.

GELFOAM. (Upjohn)
STERILE SPONGES:
Size 12-3mm. 20 × 60 mm. (12 sq. cm) × 3 m
Boxes of 4 sponges in ind. envelopes.
Size 12–7 mm. 20 × 60 mm. (12 sq. cm.) × 7 mm.
Boxes of 12 sponges in ind. envelopes, and ja of 4 sponges.
Size 50. 62.5 × 80 mm. (50 sq. cm.) × 10 mm.
Boxes of 4 sponges in ind. envelopes.
Size 100. 80 × 125 mm. (100 sq. cm.) × 10 m
Boxes of 6 sponges in ind. envelopes.
Size 200. 80 × 250 mm. (200 sq. cm.) × 10 m
Boxes of 6 sponges in ind. envelopes.
Compressed size 100 (intended primarily for application in the dry state). 80 × 125 mm.
Boxes of 6 sponges in ind. envelopes.
PACKS:
Packs size 2 cm. (designed particularly for nasa packing). 2 × 40 cm. Single jar. (packing cavities).
Size 6 cm. 6 × 40 cm. Boxes of 6 sponges in i envelopes.
Use: Hemostasis in neurosurgery, otolaryngology bone surgery, malignancy, dental surgery, and abdominal surgery.

GELFOAM COMPRESSED. (Upjohn) Size 100 (12. cm. × 8 cm.) Box 6s.
Use: Topically, hemostatic.

GELFOAM DENTAL PACK. (Upjohn) Size 4, 20 m × 20 mm. × 7 mm. Jar 15 sponges. Size 2, 10 mm. × 20 mm. (2 sq. cm.) × 7 mm. Jars 15 sponges.
Use: Control bleeding.

GELFOAM POWDER. (Upjohn) Sterile Jar 1 Gm.
Use: Hemostatic.

GELFOAM PROSTATECTOMY CONES. (Upjohn) **Prostatectomy cones** (for use with Foley catheter). 13 cm. in diameter & 18 cm. in diamet Box 6s.
Use: Hemostatic for use in surgical procedures.

GEL JET GELATIN CAPSULES. (Kirkman) Bot. 1C 250s.

GEL-KAM. (Scherer) Water-free gel 0.4% stann fluoride. Cinnamon, grape, red berry, mint, non-vored and mixed fruit flavors. Bot. w/applicator t 2.3 oz., 4.3 oz., 7 oz.
Use: Prevention of decalcification and dental caries.

.OCAST. (Beiersdorf) Zinc oxide, calamine and elatin bandage. 10 yd. × 4 in. & 10 yd. × 3 in. 2s.
'se: Unna's cast dressing.

.OX LIQUID. (Xttrium) Mg. hydroxide 90 mg., uminum hydroxide-magnesium carbonate co-dried el 1.5 Gm./5 cc. Bot. 12 oz.

.OX TABLETS. (Xttrium) Aluminum hydroxide-magesium carbonate co-dried gel 400 mg./Tab. Bot. 00s, 1000s.

.PIRIN TABLETS. (Alra) Aspirin 240 mg., cetaminophen 125 mg., caffeine 32 mg., gelsinate 0 mg./Tab. Bot. 100s, 1000s. Packet 2s. Use: nalgesic.

.SAF SUPER. (Robinson) Safflower oil 750 g./Cap. Bot. 100s, 1000s. Pkg. 30s. Bulk pkg. 000s.

.SAF SUPER W/B-6. (Robinson) Safflower oil 912 g., B-6 0.5 mg./Cap. or Safflower oil 1150 mg., -6 3 mg./Cap. Bot. 100s, 250s, 1000s.

.SEMIUM. (Various Mfr.) Pkg. 1 oz.
se: For neuralgia.

\PC.
ee: APC Combinations.

.SEMIUM W/COMBINATIONS.
ee: Briacel, Tab. (Briar)
Bricor, Tab. (Briar)
Cystitol, Tab. (Briar)
Lanased, Tab. (Lannett)
Ricor, Tab. (Vortech)
Sodadide, Tab. (Scrip)
UB, Tab. (Scrip)
Urisan-P, Tab. (Sandia)
Uriseptic w/Gelsemium, Tab. (Spencer-Mead)
Uritol, Tab. (Kenyon)
Urothyn Improved, Tab. (Reid-Provident)
Urseptic, Tab. (Century)
U-Tract, Tab. (Bowman)

.SODYNE. (Blue Line) Aspirin 3.5 gr., cetophenetidin 2.5 gr., caffeine 0.5 gr./Tab. Bot. 00s, 1000s.
se: Analgesic & antipyretic.

.UMAC CHEWABLE. (Vitarine) Magnesium silicate 7.5 gr., dried aluminum hydroxide gel. 4 ./Tab.
se: Antiacid.

.USIL. (Parke-Davis) Magnesium hydroxide 200 mg., uminum hydroxide 200 mg., simethicone 25 mg./5 l. or Tab. **Susp.** Bot. 6 oz., 12 oz. **Tab.** Bot. 165s. trips in boxes 50s, 100s, 1000s.
se: Gastric hyperacidity, peptic ulcer, flatulence, atal hernia.

.USIL II. (Parke-Davis) Magnesium hydroxide 400 g., aluminum hydroxide 400 mg., simethicone 30 g./5 ml. or Tab. **Liq.:** Bot. 12 oz. **Tab.:** Strips of)s.
se: Double strength antacid for heartburn, acid digestion, peptic ulcers, hiatal hernia, peptic sophagitis.

.USIL M. (Parke-Davis) Magnesium hydroxide 200 g., aluminum hydroxide 300 mg., simethicone 25 mg./5 ml. or Tab. **Liq.:** Bot. 12 oz. **Tabs.:** Strips in boxes of 100.
Use: Peptic ulcer, heartburn, flatulence, gastric hyperacidity, hiatal hernia.

• **GEMCADIOL.** USAN.
Use: Antihyperlipoproteinemic.

• **GEMEPROST.** USAN.
Use: Prostaglandin.

• **GEMFIBROZIL,** U.S.P. XXI. Cap. U.S.P. XXI. 2,2-Dimethyl-5-(2,5-xyly-loxy) valeric acid.
Use: Treatment of hypercholesterolemia.
See: Lopid, Cap. (Parke-Davis)

GEMNISYN. (Rorer) Aspirin 325 mg., acetaminophen 325 mg./Tab. Bot. 100s.
Use: Analgesic, antipyretic, anti-inflammatory.

GEMONIL. (Abbott) Metharbital 100 mg./Tab. Bot. 100s.
Use: Grand mal, petit mal and myoclonic epilepsy & in mixed types of seizures.

GENABID T.D. CAPS. (Goldline) Papaverine 150 mg./Cap. Bot. 100s, 1000s.
Use: Smooth muscle relaxant.

GENACED TABLETS. (Goldline) Bot. 100s.
Use: Analgesic.

GENACOL TABLETS. (Goldline) Bot. 50s.
Use: Analgesic, decongestant cough reliever.

GENACOTE TABLETS. (Goldline) 5 gr./Tab. Bot. 100s.
Use: Antipyretic, anti-inflammatory.

GENAGESIC TABS. (Goldline) Propoxyphene, acetaminophen Bot. 100s, 500s.
Use: Analgesic.

GENALAC TABS. (Goldline) Calcium carbonate, glycerine Bot. 100s, 1000s.
Use: Antacid.

GENALG CREME LINIMENT. (Goldline) Bot. 2 oz.
Use: Muscle smoother.

GENALUDE TABS. (Goldline) Phendimetrazine tartrate 35 mg/Tab. Bot. 1000s.
Use: Anorexiant.

GENAMIN COLD SYRUP. (Goldline) Bot. 4 oz.
Use: Antihistamine.

GENAMIN EXPECTORANT SYRUP. (Goldline) Bot. 4 oz.
Use: Antihistamine, decongestant.

GENAPAP CHILDREN'S CHEWABLE TABS. (Goldline) Acetaminophen 80 mg./Tab. Bot. 30.
Use: Analgesic, antipyretic.

GENAPAP CHILDREN'S ELIXIR. (Goldline) Cherry flavor. Bot. 4 oz.
Use: Analgesic, antipyretic.

GENAPAP-C TABLETS. (Goldline) Bot. 100s.
Use: Multisymptom cough and cold formula.

GENAPAP DROPS. (Goldline) Acetaminophen 80 mg./0.8 ml. Bot. 0.5 oz.
Use: Infant analgesic, antipyretic.

GENAPAP EXTRA STRENGTH CAPSULES. (Goldline) Acetaminophen 500 mg./Cap. Bot. 50s, 100s.
Use: Analgesic, antipyretic.

GENAPAP TABLETS. (Goldline) Acetaminophen 325 mg./Tab. Bot. 100s.
Use: Analgesic, antipyretic.

GENAPAX. (Key) Gentian violet 5 mg./sanitary-type tampon. Box 12s.
Use: Treatment of monilial and non-specific vaginitis.

GENAPHED PLUS TABLETS. (Goldline) Bot. 24s.
Use: Decongestant.

GENAPHED TABLETS. (Goldline) Bot. 100s.
Use: Decongestant.

GENAREG TABLETS. (Goldline) Bot. 30s.
Use: Laxative.

GENASAL DECONGESTANT SPRAY.(Goldline) Bot. 0.5 oz.
Use: Nasal decongestant.

GENASEC TABLETS. (Goldline) Bot. 24s, 90s.
Use: Analgesic.

GENASOFT CAPSULES. (Goldline) Bot. 60s.
Use: Laxative.

GENASOFT PLUS CAPSULES. Bot. 60s.
Use: Laxative.

GENASONE CREAM. (Goldline) Tube 0.5 oz.
Use: Anti-inflammatory, antipruritic.

GENASPOR ANTIFUNGAL CREAM. (Goldline) Tolnaftate 1%. Bot. 15 gm.
Use: Antifungal.

GENASYME TABLETS. (Goldline) Simethicon 80 mg./Tab. Bot. 100s.
Use: High capacity antiflatulent.

GENATON LIQUID. (Goldine) Bot. 12 oz.
Use: Antacid.

GENATON TAB. (Goldline) Bot. 12 oz.
Use: Antacid.

GENATROPINE HCl. Atropine-N-oxide HCl. Aminoxytropine Tropate HCl.
See: X-tro, Cap. (Xttrium)

GENATUSS DM SYRUP. (Goldline) Bot. 4 oz.
Use: Expectorant.

GENATUSS SYRUP. (Goldline) Bot. 4 oz.
Use: Expectorant.

GENCALC 600 TABLETS. (Goldline) Calcium 600 mg./Tab. Bot. 60s.
Use: High potency calcium supplement.

GENCOLD CAPSULES. (Goldline) Bot. 10s.
Use: Nasal decongestant.

GENCOUGH. (Goldline) Bot. 3 oz.
Use: Cough mixture.

GENCOUGH-D. (Goldline) Bot. 3 oz.
Use: Antitussive, decongestant.

GENDECON TABLETS. (Goldline) Bot. 24s, 50s.
Use: Analgesic, decongestant.

GENDANE. (Goldline) Danthron tablets Bot. 100s, 1000s.
Use: Laxative.

GENEBS EXTRA STRENGTH CAPSULES. (Goldline) Acetaminophen 500 mg./Cap. Bot. 100s, 1000s.
Use: Analgesic, antipyretic.

GENEBS EXTRA STRENGTH TABLETS. (Goldline) Acetaminophen 500 mg./Tab. Bot. 100s, 1000s.
Use: Analgesic, antipyretic.

GENEBS TABLETS. (Goldline) Acetaminophen 325 mg./Tab. Bot. 100s, 1000s.
Use: Analgesic, antipyretic.

GENERBON LIQUID. (Goldline) Bot. pt., gal.
Use: Dietary supplement.

GENERICACE. (Fellows) Docusate sodium 100 mg casanthranol 30 mg./Cap. Bot. 100s, 1000s.

GENESIS B-hCG. (Wampole) Monoclonal antibody r oimmunoassay for the qualitative detection and quantitative determination of B-hCG/hCG in se and qualitative detection of B-hCG/hCG in urine. 125s.
Use: Aid in the diagnosis of pregnancy.

GENEYES DROPS. (Goldline) Bot. 0.5 oz.
Use: Eye irritations.

GENFIBER. (Goldline) Bot. 14 oz.
Use: Bulk laxative.

GENITE. (Goldline) Bot. 6 oz.
Use: Analgesic, decongestant.

GENEX CAPS. (Goldline) Phenylpropanolamine HC acetaminophen. Bot. 100s, 1000s.
Use: Anti-inflammatory, analgesic.

GEN-K POWDER. (Goldline) Potassium CL powde meq./1.5 mg. Box 30s.
Use: Potassium supplement.

GEN-K TABS. (Goldline) Effervescent potassium. 30s.
Use: Potassium supplement.

■ **GENITAL HERPES TREATMENT.**
See: Acyclovir
Zovrax Cap., Oint. (Burroughs Wellcome)

GENNA TABLETS. (Goldline) Bot. 100s
Use: Cathartic.

GENNIN TABLETS. Bot. 100s.
Use: Analgesic.

GENOPHYLLIN.
See: Aminophylline (Various Mfr.)

GENOPTIC LIQUIFILM STERILE OPHTHALMIC SOLUTION. (Allergan) Gentamicin sulfate equivalent to 3.0 mg. 0.3% gentamicin/ml. w/polyvinyl alcohol 1.4%, edetate disodium, HC NaOH to adjust pH and purified water. Disodium phosphate, monosodium phosphate, sodium Cl., benzalkonium Cl. Bot. 5 ml.
Use: Ocular antibiotic.

GENOPTIC S.O.P. STERILE OPHTHALMIC OINTMENT. (Allergan) Gentamicin sulfate equivalent to 3.0 mg. gentamicin/Gm. w/white petrolatum, methyl-paraben, propylparaben. Tube Gm.
Use: Ocular antibiotic.

GENOSCOPOLAMINE. (CMC) Scopolamine aminoxide HBr, scopolamine-N-oxide HBr, e yaminoxytropine tropate HBr. Pellets 0.5 mg. Bo 60s.
Use: Orally, hypnotic & sedative.
See: Scopodex, Pellet. (CMC)

GENPRIN TABLETS. (Goldline) Bot. 100s.
Use: Analgesic.

GENSALATE SODIUM. Sod. gentisate. (Sod. salt 2,5-dihydroxybenzoic acid)
Use: Analgesic & antipyretic.

GENSAN TABLETS. (Goldline) Bot. 100s.
Use: Analgesic.

GENSLIM C/F CAPSULES. (Goldline) Bot. 28s.
Use: Appetite suppressant.

NSLIM EXTRA STRENGTH CAPSULES.
Goldline) Bot. 20s.
Jse: Appetite suppressant.

NTACIDIN OPHTHALMIC SOLUTION.
CooperVision) Gentamicin sulfate 3 mg./ml. Bot. 5 nl.
Jse: Topical antibiotic for external eye infections.

NTACIDIN OPHTHALMIC OINTMENT.
CooperVision) Gentamicin 3 mg./Gm. Tube 3.5 im.
Jse: Topical antibiotic for treatment of external eye nfections.

NTAMICIN, B.A.N. An antibiotic produced by *Micromonospora purpurea.*
See: Cidomycin
Garamycin
Genticin (sulfate).

ENTAMICIN SULFATE, U.S.P. XXI. Cream, Oint., nj., Ophth. Oint., Ophth. Soln., Sterile, U.S.P. XXI. Schering) Produced by *Micromonospora purpurea.*
Jse: Antibacterial.
See: Apogen, Inj. (Beecham Labs)
Garamycin, Prep. (Schering)
Genoptic, Prep. (Allergan)

ENTIAN VIOLET, U.S.P. XXI. Topical Soln., Cream, U.S.P. XXI. Methylrosaniline chloride. Bismuth Violet.
Jse: Topical anti-infective.
See: Genapax, tampon. (Key)
GVS, Vag. cream & inserts. (Savage)
Surfactants.
See: Hyva, Vag. Tab. (Holland-Rantos)

NTISATE SODIUM. 5-Hydroxysalicylate sod., 2,5-dihydroxy benzoate sodium

NTLAX-B GRANULES. (Blair) Standardized senna concentrate w/guar gum. 1 Can 6 oz.
Jse: Laxative.

NTLAX S TABLETS. (Blair) Standardized senna concentrate, docusate sodium. Bot. 30s, 60s.
Jse: Treatment of constipation.

NTLE SHAMPOO. (Ulmer) Bot. 2 oz., 8 oz., gal.
Jse: Mild, neutral shampoo.

NTRAN. (Travenol) Dextran-70 6%, Sod. chloride .9%. Plastic Bot. 500 ml; Dextran-40 10% in saline. Plastic Bot. 500 ml. Dextran-40 10% w/Dextrose 5%. Plastic Bot. 500 ml.
Jse: Plasma volume expander.

NTRIM. (Goldline) Bot. 16 oz.
Jse: Meal replacement.

NTZ RECTAL WIPES. (Roxane) Pramoxine HCl %, alcloxa 0.2%, cetylpyridinium chloride 0.05%, hamamelis water (nonalcoholic) 50%. Box 7s, 20s, 00s individually wrapped disposable wipes. Dispenser 50s. Jelly, Tubes—single dose, 12s.
Jse: Anal/perianal itching and discomfort.

NUINE BAYER ASPIRIN. (Glenbrook) Aspirin 325 mg./Tab. film coated. Bot. 24s, 50s, 200s, 300s, 2s.
Jse: Analgesic, antipyretic, anti-inflammatory, antiplatelet.

NVITE. (Goldline) Bot. 130s.
Jse: Multivitamin.

GEOCILLIN. (Roerig) Carbenicillin indanyl sodium 382 mg./Tab. Bot. 100s. Unit Dose 100s.
Use: Antibiotic.

GEOPEN. (Pfipharmecs) Carbenicillin Disodium.
Vial: 1 Gm., 2 Gm., 5 Gm./Vial; Pkg. 10s.
Piggyback Vial: 2 Gm. **Bulk Pharmacy Pack:** 10 Gm., 30 Gm. for I.V. use.
Use: Antibiotic for susceptible anaerobes & gramnegative aerobes.

• **GEPIRONE HYDROCHLORIDE.** USAN.
Use: Tranquilizer.

GERALIX LIQUID. (Vortech) Vit. B-1 10 mg., B-2 5 mg., B-6 2 mg., choline bitartrate 100 mg., inositol 100 mg., Ca glycerophosphate 100 mg., Mn 1 mg., Mg 1 mg., Zn 1 mg., alcohol 15%/45 cc. Bot. 6 oz., gal.
Use: Dietary supplement.

GERA PLUS. (Towne) Iron 50 mg., B-1 5 mg., B-2 5 mg., C 75 mg., niacinamide 30 mg., Capantothenate 2 mg., B-6 0.5 mg., B-12 3 mcg./Tab. Bot. 100s.
Use: Dietary supplement.

GERAVITE. (Hauck) Lysine monohydrochloride 150 mg., B-1 1 mg., B-2 1.2 mg., niacinamide 100 mg., B-12 10 mcg./15 ml. w/alcohol 15%. Bot. 16 oz., gal.
Use: Stimulant, antidepressant, tonic.

GERI-ALL-D. (Barth's) Vit. A 10,000 I.U., D 400 I.U., B-1 7 mg., B-2 14 mg., C 200 mg., niacin 4.17 mg., B-12 25 mcg., E 50 I.U., B-6 0.35 mg., pantothenic acid 0.63 mg., plus trace minerals and other factors. 2 Cap. Bot. 1 mo., 3 mo., and 6 mo. supply of Geri-All regular and Geri-All-D.
Use: Vitamin, mineral therapy.

GERIAMIC. (Vortech) Ferrous sulfate 50 mg., B-12 3 mcg., B-1 5 mg., B-2 5 mg., B-6 0.5 mg., niacinamide 30 mg., Ca pantothenate 2 mg., C 75 mg./Tab. 100s.
Use: Vitamin.

GERIATRAZOLE. (Kenyon) Vit. B-12 50 mg., B-2 2 mg., liver-painless 2 mcg., dl-methionine 10 mg., inositol 20 mg., d-panthenol 20 mg., B-1 20 mg., B-6 5 mg., niacinamide 75 mg., pentylenetetrazole 10 mg./cc. Vial 30 cc.
Use: Vitamin (geriatric).

GERIATRIC ELIXIR. (CMC) Methamphetamine HCl 1 mg. Vit. B-1, B-2, B-6, B-12, niacinamide, Ca pantothenate choline, inositol, Fe, Cu, Ca, P/15 cc., alcohol 12% in sherry wine flavored base. Bot. Pt., Gal.
Use: CNS stimulant, vitamin therapy (geriatric).

GERIATRIC MULTIVITAMIN. (Zenith) Iron 50 mg., Vit. B-1 5 mg., B-2 5 mg., C 75 mg., niacinamide 30 mg., Ca pantothenate 2 mg., B-6 0.5 mg., B-12 3 mcg., inositol 20 mg., methionine 25 mg., choline bitartrate 25 mg., debittered brewers dried yeast 50 mg./Tab. Bot. 100s.
Use: Vitamin, mineral therapy (geriatric).

GERIATROPLEX. (Morton) Cyanocobalamin 30 mcg., liver inj. 0.1 cc. B-12 activity 2 mcg., ferrous gluconate 50 mg., B-2 1.5 mg., Ca pantothenate 2.5 mg., niacinamide 100 mg., citric acid 16.4 mg., sod. citrate 23.6 mg./2 cc. Vial 30 cc.
Use: Geriatric.

GERIBOM. (Bowman) Vit. A 10,000 I.U., D 400 I.U., B-1 5 mg., B-2 2.5 mg., B-6 1 mg., B-12 2 mcg., C 75 mg., niacinamide 40 mg., Ca pantothenate 4 mg., E 2 I.U., dicalcium phosphate anhydrous 260 mg., choline bitartrate 31.4 mg., inositol 15 mg., ferrous sulfate 102 mg., manganese sulfate dried 1.573 mg., potassium sulfate 4.458 mg., zinc sulfate dried 1.388 mg., magnesium sulfate dried 21.583 mg./Cap. Bot. 100s, 500s, 1000s.

GERI-BON. (Inwood) Vit. B-1 2 mg., B-2 2 mg., C 75 mg., niacinamide 30 mg., Ca pantothenate 2 mg., B-6 0.5 mg., B-12 3 mcg., inositol 20 mg., methionine 25 mg., choline bitartrate 25 mg., iron 50 mg., debittered brewer's yeast 50 mg./Tab. Bot. 100s.

GERIDEN. (Kenyon) Methyltestosterone 2 mg., ethinyl estradiol 0.01 mg., rutin 10 mg., Vit. C 30 mg., B-12 2 mcg., A 5000 I.U., D 500 I.U., E 2 I.U., Ca. pantothenate 3 mg., B-1 2.5 mg., B-6 0.5 mg., niacinamide 15 mg., Fe 15 mg., Cu 0.2 mg., Mn 1 mg., Mg 5 mg., K 2 mg., choline bitartrate 40 mg., PABA 10 mg., inositol 20 mg./Cap. Bot. 100s, 1000s.

GERI-DERM. (Barth's) Vit. A 400,000 I.U., D 40,000 I.U., E 200 I.U., panthenol 800 mg./4 oz. Jar 4 oz.
Use: Skin supplement.

GERIDIUM TABLETS. (Goldline) Phenazopyridine HCl 100 mg. or 200 mg./Tab. Bot. 100s, 1000s.
Use: Urinary analgesic, anti-infective.

GERIFORT PLUS. (A.P.C.) Vit. A 10,000 I.U., B-1 5 mg., B-2 6 mg., B-6 2 mg., C 75 mg., Vit. D-2 1,000 I.U., niacinamide 60 mg., Fe 10 mg., Ca 115 mg., P 83 mg., iodine 0.1 mg., Ca pantothenate 10 mg., d-alpha tocopheryl acid succinate 3 I.U., cobalamin conc. 3 mcg., choline bitartrate 70 mg., inositol 35 mg., biotin 15 mcg., Cn 0.2 mg., Mg 2 mg., Mn 0.5 mg., potassium 0.15 mg./Amcap. Bot. 100s.

GERIGARD. (Eckerd) Vit. B-1, B-2, B-6, B-12, niacinamide, Ca pantothenate, biotin, Vit. A, D, C & E, calcium, phosphorus, iron, iodine, Cu, Mg, Mn, Zn./Cap. Bot. 60s, 150s.

GERIJEN IMPROVED. (Jenkins) Testosterone 10 mg., estrone 1 mg., cyanocobalamin 50 mcg., niacinamide 50 mg., inositol 5 mg., methionine 5 mg., choline chloride 5 mg./cc., pectin 0.25%. Vial 10 cc.

GERILETS. (Abbott) Vit. A 5000 I.U., D 400 I.U., E 45 I.U., C 90 mg., folic acid 0.4 mg., B-1 2.25 mg., B-2 2.6 mg., niacin 30 mg., B-6 3 mg., B-12 9 mcg., biotin 0.45 mg., pantothenic acid 15 mg., Fe 27 mg./Tab. Bot. 100s.
Use: Vitamin, iron supplement (geriatric).

GERILITE ELIXIR. (Vitarine) Vit. B-1 5 mg., B-2 5 mg., B-6 1 mg., B-12 3 mcg., panthenol 4 mg., niacinamide 100 mg., iron 100 mg., choline bitartrate 100 mg., dl-methionine 100 mg./Fl. Oz. Bot. 12 oz.
Use: Nutritional fortifier.

GERILITE TAB. (Vitarine) Vit. B-1 5 mg., B-2 5 mg., B-6 0.5 mg., B-12 3 mcg., C 75 mg., niacinamide 30 mg., Ca pantothenate 2 mg., iron 50 mg./Tab. Bot. 100s, 250s.
Use: Dietary supplement.

GERIMED. (Fielding) Vitamin & minerals. Bot. 60s.
Use: Dietary supplement.

GERINEED. (Hanlon) Vit. A 5000 I.U., B-1 20 mg., B-2 5 mg., niacinamide 20 mg., B-6 0.5 mg., Ca pantothenate 5 mg., B-12 5 mcg., rutin 25 mg., Vit. C mg., Vit. E 10 I.U., choline 50 mg., inositol 50 m Ca lactate 1.64 mg., Fe sulfate 10 mg., Cu 1 mg iodine 0.5 mg., Mn & Mg sulfate 1 mg., pot. sulf 5 mg., Zn sulfate 0.5 mg./Cap. Bot. 100s.

GERIPAN. (Image) Bot. 100s.
Use: Vitamin supplement.

GERI-PEN ELIXIR. (Fellows) Pentylenetetrazol mg., nicotinic acid 50 mg., alcohol 5%/5 cc. Bot pt., gal.

GERI-PEN TABLETS. (Fellows) Pentylenetetrazol mg., nicotinic acid 50 mg./Tab. Bot. 100s, 1000s

GERIPLEX. (Parke-Davis) Vit. A 5000 I.U., B-1 5 m B-2 5 mg., B-12 2 mcg., nicotinamide 15 mg., Vi 50 mg., choline dihydrogen citrate 20 mg., Vit. E I.U., taka-distase 2.5 gr., ferrous sulfate 30 mg., c per sulfate 4 mg., Mang. sulfate 4 mg., zinc sulfa 2 mg., dicalcium phosphate (anhydrous) 200 mg./Kapseal Bot. 100s, 500s.
Use: Vitamin-mineral combination.

GERIPLEX-FS. (Parke-Davis) Same as Geriplex, docusate sodium 100 mg./Kapseal Bot. 100s.

GERIPLEX-FS LIQUID. (Parke-Davis) Vit. B-1 1.2 B-2 1.7 mg., B-6 1 mg., B-12 5 mcg., niacinamide mg., iron 15 mg., pluronic F-68 200 mg./30 ml., a hol 18%. Bot. 1 pt.

GERI-PLUS. (Approved) Vit. A 12,500 I.U., D 1200 B-1 15 mg., B-2 10 mg., C 75 mg., niacinamide 30 Ca pantothenate 2 mg., B-6 0.5 mg., E 5 I.U., Brew yeast 10 mg., B-12 15 mcg., iron 11.58 mg., de cated liver 15 mg., choline bitartrate 30 mg., inositol 30 mg., Ca 59 mg., Phos. 45 mg., Zn 0. mg., Fr. dicalcium phos. 200 mg., Mn 1.11, Mg. mg., enzymatic factors and amino acids/Cap. B 50s, 100s, 1000s.
Use: Geriatric formula.

GERI-PLUS ELIXIR. (Approved) Vit. B-1 25 mg., B 2 10 mg., B-6 1 mg., niacinamide 100 mg., Ca p tothenate 5 mg., B-12 20 mcg., iron ammonium cit 100 mg., choline 200 mg., inositol 100 mg., Mg chloride 2 mg., Mn citrate 2 mg., Zn acetate 2 n amino acids/Fl. Oz. Bot. pt.
Use: Supplement.

GERISOL. (Amfre-Grant) Testosterone 10 mg., estr 0.5 mg., Vit. B-12 100 mcg., liver injection 2 m thiamine HCl 50 mg., niacinamide 50 mg., ribofla sodium phosphate 1 mg., pyridoxine HCl 5 mg., panthenol 10 mg./ml. w/lidocaine HCl 2%. Vial ml.
Use: Hormone, vitamin supplement.

GERISPAN. (Robinson) Vit. A 12,500 I.U., D 1000 I.U., B-1 5 mg., B-2 2.5 mg., niacinamide 40 mg. B-6 1 mg., Ca pantothenate 4 mg., B-12 2 mcg., C mg., E 2 I.U., choline bitartrate 31.4 mg., inosito mg., Ca 75 mg., phosphorus 58 mg., Fe 30 mg., Mg 3 mg., Mn 0.5 mg., Pot. 2 mg., Zn 0.5 mg./C Bot. 100s, 1000s. Bulk Pack 5000s.
Use: Dietary supplement for older persons and convalescents.

GERITINIC. (Geriatric) Vit. A 5000 I.U., D 400 I.U., B-12 5 mcg., niacinamide 10 mg., inositol 20 choline bitartrate 30 mg., amino acetic acid 30 r

Cal. pantothenate 1 mg., desic. liver 22.4 mg., conc. yeast 22.4 mg., Pot. acetate 30 mg., ferrous sulfate 195 mg., phyllins/Tab. Bot. 42s, 500s.
Use: Nutritional anemias.

RITOL. (Beecham Products)
Liq.: Bot. 4 oz., 12 oz. **Tab.:** Bot. 14s, 40s, 100s, 180s.

RITOL COMPLETE TABLETS. (Beecham) Vit. A 5000 I.U., E 30 I.U., C 60 mg., folic acid 400 mcg., B-1 1.5 mg., B-2 1.7 mg., niacinamide 20 mg., B-6 2 mg., B-12 6 mcg., D 400 I.U., biotin 300 mcg., pantothenic acid 10 mg., Ca. 162 mg., P 125 mg., iodine 150 mcg., iron 50 mg., Mg. 100 mg., Cu 2 mg., Mn 7.5 mg., K 15 mcg., chloride 7 mg., Cr 15 mcg., molybdenum 15 mcg., selenium 15 mcg., Zn. 15 mg., N: 5 mcg., silicon 10 mcg., tin 10 mcg., vanadium 10 mcg./Tab. Bot. 14s, 40s, 100s, 180s.
Use: Dietary supplement.

RITOL LIQUID HIGH POTENCY IRON AND VITAMIN TONIC. (Beecham Products) Iron 100 mg., Vit. B-1 5 mg., B-2 5 mg., niacinamide 100 mg., panthenol 4 mg., pyridoxine 1 mg., B-12 1.5 mcg., methionine 50 mg., choline bitartrate 100 mg./oz. (Two Tablespoonfuls). Bot. 4 oz., 12 oz., 24 oz.
Use: Prevent deficiency in iron & specific vitamins.

RITONIC INJ. (Kenyon) Vit. B-12 50 mcg., d-panthenol 5 mg., niacinamide 50 mg., choline chloride mg., inositol 5 mg., methionine 5 mg., estrone 1 mg., testosterone 10 mg. Liver-painless (B-12 equiv.) mcg./cc. Vial 30 cc.
Use: B complex with hormones.

RITONIC LIQUID. (Geriatric) Thiamine chloride 1 mg., riboflavin 1 mg., Vit. B-12 3 mcg., niacinamide 10 mg., pyridoxine HCl 0.1 mg., Mag. as sulfate 1 mg., iron as ammonium citrate 35 mg., Mang. as sulfate .5 mg., Cal. as glycerophosphate 10 mg., Phos. as Cal. glycerophosphate 8 mg., Pot. as sulfate 1 mg., aminoacetic acid 60 mg., yeast conc. 125 mg., liver fraction-1 125 mg./5 cc. Bot. 8 oz., 1 gal.
Use: Nutritional deficiencies.

RIX ELIXIR. (Abbott). Vit. B-1 6 mg., B-2 6 mg., niacin 00 mg., iron 15 mg., B-6 1.64 mg., cyanocobalamin mcg./30 ml. Bot. pt.
Use: Hematinic.

RLIPO. (Kenyon) Choline bitartrate 250 mg., methionine 150 mg., inositol 100 mg., whole liver desic. 100 mg., B-cotrate 100 mg., B-1 1.5 mg., B-2 1 mg., B-6 0.1 mg., d-calcium pantothenate 2 mg., niacinamide 15 mg./3 Tabs. Bot. 100s, 1000s.

RMANIN.
See: Suramin Sodium (Naphuride Sod.)

RMICIN. (CMC) Alkylbenzyldimethyl chloride 17% Bot. pt., 1 gal. 50% Bot. gal.
Use: (diluted) Antiseptic.

R-O-FOAM. (Geriatric) Methylsalicylate 30%, benzocaine 3%, and volatile oils. Aerosol can 4 oz.
Use: Anesthetic-analgesic.

RREN. (Wren) Pentylenetetrazol 100 mg., niacin 0 mg./Tab. Bot. 100s, 1000s.
Use: Geriatric therapy.

RTEROL DEPO. (Fellows) Medroxyprogesterone acetate 50 mg., 100 mg./cc. Vial 5 cc.

GESIC. (Lexalabs) Aspirin 226.8 mg., caffeine 32.4 mg., codeine 32.4 mg./Tab. Bot. 100s.
Use: Analgesic.

• **GESTACLONE.** USAN. (1) 17β-Acetyl-6-chloro-1β, 1a,2β,8β,9α,10,11,12,13,14α-,15,16β,16a,17-tetradecahydro-10β,13β-dimethyl-3H-dicyclopropa[1,2:16,-17]cyclopenta-[a]-phenanthren-3-one.
Use: Progestin.

GESTANIN. Allylestrenol, B.A.N. (Organon)

GESTEROL 50. (Forest) Progesterone 50 mg. in aq. susp. or oil/cc. Vial 10 cc.

GESTEROL L.A. (Forest) Hydroyprogesterone caproate 125 mg./cc. Vial 10 cc. 250 mg./cc. Vial 5 cc.

GESTIN. (Dalin) Formerly G.I. 8. Bot. 4 oz., 8 oz.

• **GESTODENE.** USAN.
Use: Progestin.

GESTONEED. (Hanlon) Ca. lactate 1069 mg., Vit. C 100 mg., nicotinic acid 18 mg., Vit. B-2 2.4 mg., Vit. B-1 1.8 mg., Vit. B-6 9 mg., Vit. D 500 I.U., Vit. A 6000 I.U./Cap. Bot. 100s.
Use: Prenatal dietary supplement.

• **GESTONORONE CAPROATE.** USAN. 17-Hydroxy-19-norpregn-4-ene-3,20-dione hexanoate.
Use: Progestin.

• **GESTRINONE.** USAN.
Use: Progestin.

GESTRONOL, B.A.N. 17-Hydroxy-19-norpregn-4-ene-3,20-dione.
Use: Progestational steroid.
See: Gestonorone (I.N.N.)
Depostat hexanoate

GEVRABON. (Lederle) Vit. B-1 5 mg., B-2 2.5 mg., Vit. B-12 1 mcg., niacinamide 50 mg., Vit. B-6 1 mg., pantothenic acid 10 mg., choline 100 mg., inositol 100 mg., Zn 2 mg., iodine 100 mcg., Mg 2 mg., Mn 2 mg., Fe 15 mg./30 ml. w/alcohol 18%. Bot. 16 fl. oz., 1 gal.
Use: Vitamin & mineral deficiencies.

GEVRAL. (Lederle) Vit. A acetate 5000 I.U., B-1 1.5 mg., B-2 1.7 mg., B-6 2 mg., B-12 6 mcg., C 60 mg., E 30 I.U., niacinamide 20 mg., Ca 162 mg., P 125 mg., elemental iron 18 mg., Mg 100 mg., iodine 150 mcg./Tab. Bot. 100s.
Use: Vitamin and mineral supplement.

GEVRAL PROTEIN. (Lederle) Protein 60%, carbohydrate 27.1%, fat 2%, sodium 0.02%, Vit. A 2167 I.U., D 217 I.U., B-1 2.2 mg., B-2 2.2 mg., B-6 0.22 mg., B-12 0.87 mcg., Ca pantothenate 2.2 mg., niacinamide 6.5 mg., C 22 mg., E 4.3 I.U., choline 21 mg., inositol, 22 mg., lysine 1.1 mg., Ca 359 mg., Cu 0.4 mg., iodine 0.04 mg., Fe (as ferrous fumarate) elemental 4.3 mg., Mg 0.4 mg., Mn 0.4 mg., P 52.8 mg., Na less than 50 mg., Zn 0.22 mg., 26 Gm. alcohol 1% w/Ca caseinate, lactose, artificial flavors, malt ext., sucrose, yeast, sod. saccharin, polysorbate 80. Can. 0.5 lb., 5 lb.
Use: Therapeutic-nutritional supplement.

GEVRAL T. (Lederle) Vit. A acetate 5,000 I.U., D 400 I.U., B-1 2.25 mg., B-2 2.6 mg., B-6 3 mg., B-12 9 mcg., C 90 mg., E 45 I.U., niacinamide 30 mg., Ca 162 mg., P 125 mg., elemental iron 27 mg., Mg 100

mg., iodine 225 mcg., Cu 1.5 mg., Zn 22.5 mg./Cap. Bot. 100s.
Use: Severe vitamin deficiencies.

GG-CEN CAPSULES. (Central) Guaifenesin 200 mg./Cap. Bot. 100s.
Use: Temporary relief of dry nonproductive cough.

GG-CEN SYRUP. (Central) Guaifenesin 100 mg., alcohol 10%/5 ml. Bot. 4 oz., pt., gal.
Use: Expectorant.

G.G.I. EXPECTORANT. (Amfre-Grant) Guaifenesin 100 mg., Cal. iodide 150 mg./5 cc. Bot. 16 oz., gal.
Use: Bronchial asthma, bronchitis, pulmonary emphysema.

GG-TUSSIN. (Vitarine) Guaifenesin syrup.
Use: Expectorant.

GISPASMIN. (Winston) Phenobarbital 16 mg., magnesium hydroxyaminoacetate 250 mg., hyoscyamine sulf. 0.052 mg., hyoscine HBr 0.003 mg. atropine sulf. 0.01 mg./Tab. Bot. 100s, 1000s.
Use: Antispasmodic with sedative.

GITALIN. A cardioactive glycoside derived from digitalis purpurea.
Use: Cardiotonic.

GITALIN (AMORPHOUS).
Use: Cardiotonic.

GL-2 SKIN ADHERENT. (Gordon) Bot. pt., qt., gal. Ready to use.

G-L 7 SKIN ADHERENT. (Gordon) A plastic material which may be used full strength or diluted with 3 to 10 parts 99% isopropyl alcohol, acetone or naphtha. Pkg. pt., qt., gal.

GLANDUBOLIN.
See: Estrone (Various Mfr.)

GLAUBER'S SALT.
See: Sodium Sulfate (Var. Mfr.)

GLAUCON SOLUTION. (Alcon) Epinephrine HCl 1%, 2% w/benzalkonium chloride, 0.02% sodium chloride, 0.2% sodium metabisulfite 0.3% (as preservative). Drop. Bot. 10 ml.
Use: Glaucoma, miotic therapy.

GLAUCOSTAT. (Kinghill) Acelidine.
Use: Parasympathomimetic.

• **GLAZE, PHARMACEUTICAL,** N.F. XVI.
Use: Pharmaceutic aid (tablet coating).

• **GLEPTOFERRON.** USAN.
Use: Hematinic.

• **GLIAMILIDE.** USAN.
Use: Antidiabetic.

GLIBENCLAMIDE. B.A.N. 1- 4-[2-(5-Chloro-2-methoxybenzamido)ethyl]benzenesulphonyl-3-cyclohexylurea.
Use: Oral hypoglycemic agent.
See: Daonil
Euglucon

• **GLIBORNURIDE.** USAN. endo-1-[(IR)-(2-Hydroxy-3-bornyl)]-3-(p-tolysulfonyl) urea. Glutril.
Use: Oral hypoglycemic.

• **GLICETANILE SODIUM.** USAN.
Use: Antidiabetic.

• **GLIFLUMIDE.** USAN.
Use: Antidiabetic.

GLIM.
See: Gardinol Type Detergents (Various Mfr.)

• **GLIPIZIDE.** USAN.
Use: Antidiabetic.

GLIQUIDONE. B.A.N. 1-Cyclohexyl-3-p-[2-(3,4-dihyd 7-methoxy-4,4-dimethyl-1,3-dioxo-2(1H)-isoquinol thyl]phenylsulfonylurea.
Use: Oral hypoglycemic.

GLISOXEPIDE. B.A.N. 3-[4-(Perhydroazepin-1-ylure idosulfonyl)phenethylcarbamoyl]-5-methylis-oxazo
Use: Oral hypoglycemic agent.

GLOBIN ZINC INSULIN INJECTION. Globin zinc insulin, insulin w/globin & zinc chloride added.
Use: S.C., insulin therapy.

• **GLOBULIN, ANTI-HUMAN SERUM,** U.S.P. XXI.

GLOBULIN, GAMMA.
See: Gamma Globulin (Various Mfr.)
Poliomyelitis Immune Globulin, Human, Vial. (V Mfr.)

GLOBULIN, HEPATITIS B IMMUNE.
See: H-BIG, Vial (Abbott)

• **GLOBULIN, IMMUNE,** U.S.P. XXI.
Use: I.M., measles prophylactic & polio; passive immunizing agent.
See: Gammagee, Vial (Merck Sharp & Dohme)
Generic, Vials 2 & 10 ml. (Cutter)
Generic, Vial 2 ml. (Lederle)

• **GLOBULIN, Rho(D) IMMUNE,** U.S.P. XXI.
Use: Immunosuppressive.

GLOBULIN, POLIOMYELITIS IMMUNE. Human.
See: Poliomyelitis Immune Globulin (Var. Mfr.)

• **GLOXAZONE.** USAN. 3-Ethoxybutane-1,2-dione b thiosemicarbazone).
Use: Antiprotozoan, veterinary medicine.
See: Contrapar

GLUBIONATE CALCIUM.
See: Neo-Calglucon, Syrup (Dorsey)

• **GLUCAGON,** U.S.P. XXI. Inj., U.S.P. XXI. (Lilly) 1 unit w/1 ml. diluent. 10 units w/10 ml. diluent. Glucagon HCl 1 mg. or 10 mg. w/diluent; soln. contains lactose, glycerin 1.6% w/phenol 0.2% a preservative. Vials.
Use: Hypoglycemic shock.

GLUCAMIDE. (Lemmon) Chlorpropamide 100 mg. 250 mg./Tab. Bot. 100s, 250s, 500s.
Use: Oral hypoglycemic agent.

• **GLUCEPTATE SODIUM.** USAN.
Use: Pharmaceutic aid.

D-GLUCITOL, 1-DEOXY-1-(METHYLAMINO). Me mine, U.S.P. XXI.

d-GLUCITOL (d-Sorbitol)/Homatropine methylb mide.
See: ProBilagol, Liq. (Purdue Frederick)

■ **GLUCO-CORTICOIDS.**
See: Cortical Hormone Products.

GLUCOMETER REFLECTANCE PHOTOMETER. (Ames) Electronic meter for blood glucose testin Use at home by lay diabetics to read Dextrostix reagent strips.
Use: For blood glucose monitoring.

D-GLUCONIC ACID, CALCIUM SALT. Calcium Gluc ate, U.S.P. XXI.

.UCONIC ACID SALTS.
See: Calcium Gluconate
Ferrous Gluconate
Magnesium Gluconate
Potassium Gluconate
)-GLUCOPYRANOSIDE,β-D-FRUCTO-FURANOSY-L-. Sucrose, N.F. XVI.
;LUCOSAMINE. USAN. 2-Amino-2-deoxy-β-D-glucopyranose.
'Nystatin, oxytetracycline.
See: Terrastatin, Cap., Sol. (Pfizer)
'Tetracycline HCl, nystatin.
See: Tetrastatin Cap., Susp. (Pfizer)
'Tetracycline.
See: Tetracyn, Cap., Syr. (Roerig)
'Oxytetracycline.
See: Terramycin, Prep (Pfizer)
.UCOSE.
See: Pal-A-Dex, Pow. (Baker)
;LUCOSE ENZYMATIC TEST STRIP, U.S.P. XXI.
Use: Diagnostic aid (in vitro, reducing sugars in urine).
;LUCOSE, LIQUID, N.F. XVI. (Various Mfr.)
Cerelose, Dextrose.
Use: 5-50% sol. as nutrient; for acute hepatitis and dehydration; to increase blood volume; pharm. aid (tablet binder, coating agent).
GLUCOSE, MONOHYDRATE. Dextrose, U.S.P. XXI.
.UCOSE-40 OPHTHALMIC OINTMENT. (CooperVision) Liquid glucose 40%. Tube 3.5 Gm.
Use: Treatment of corneal edema.
.UCOSE OXIDASE. W/peroxidase, pot. iodide.
See: Diastix, Vial, Tab. (Ames)
.UCOSE POLYMERS.
See: Polycose, Pow., Liq. (Ross)
.UCOSE REAGENT STRIPS. (Ames) Seralyzer reagent strips. Bot 50s.
Use: A quantitative strip test for glucose in serum or plasma.
.UCOSE TEST.
See: Combistix (Ames),
Glucose Reagent Strips (Ames).
.UCOSE TOLERANCE TEST PREPARATION.
See: Glucola (Ames)
.UCOSOL LIQUID. (Lannett) Liq. pt., gal.
.UCOSULFONE SODIUM, INJ.
See: Sodium Glucosulfone Injection
.UCOTROL. (Roerig) Glipizide 5 mg. or 10 mg./Tab. Bot. 100s.
Use: Oral hypoglycemic.
.UCOVITE. (Vale) Ferrous gluconate 260 mg., B-1 1 mg., B-2 0.5 mg., C 10 mg./Tab. Bot. 100s, 1000s, 5000s.
.UCUROLACTONE. Gamma lactone of glucofuranuronic acid.
See: Preltron-Oral, Tab. (Pasadena Research)
.UCURONATE SODIUM.
See: Preltron, Inj. (Pasadena Research)
.U-K. (Western Research) Potassium gluconate 486 mg./Tab. Bot. 1000s.
Use: Supplement.

GLUKOR. (Hyrex) Chorionic gonadotropin 200 I.U., Vit. B-1 25 mg., glutamic acid 52.5 ppm, procaine HCl 1%/cc. Vial 10 cc., 25 cc.
Use: I.M., androgen deficiency, uterine disorders.
GLUSIDE.
See: Saccharin (Var. Mfr.)
GLUTAMATE SODIUM.
W/Niacin, Vit., Minerals.
See: L-Glutavite, Cap. (Cooper)
L-GLUTAMIC ACID, N-[4-[[(2-AMINO-1,-4-DIHYDRO-4-OXO-6-PTERIDINYL)-METHYL]AMINO]BENZOY-L]-. Folic Acid, U.S.P. XXI.
L-GLUTAMIC ACID, N-[4-][2,4-DIAMINO-6-PYERIDI-NYL)METHYL]-METHYLAMINO]BENZOYL]-. Methotrexate, U.S.P. XXI.
GLUTAMIC ACID HYDROCHLORIDE. Acidogen, aciglumin, glutasin.
Use: The hydrochloride for achlorhydria & hypochlorhydria.
See: Acidulin, Pulvules (Lilly)
W/Cellulase, Pepsin, Pancreatin, Ox Bile Extract.
See: Kanulase, Tab. (Dorsey)
GLUTAMIC ACID SALTS.
See: Calcium Glutamate (Various Mfr.)
• **GLUTARAL CONCENTRATE,** U.S.P. XXI.
Use: Disinfectant.
See: Cidex (Surgikos)
GLUTARALDEHYDE. (City Chem.) Glutaraldehyde 25% in water. Pkg. 3 kg.; (Ayerst) Sonacide Sol., Gal., 5 Gal.
GLUTEST. (Leland) Testosterone 10 mg., thiamine HCl 25 mg., glutamic acid 52.5 ppm, procaine HCl 1%, benzyl alc. 2%/cc. Vial 10 cc., 25 cc.
Use: I.M.; female climacteric.
GLUTEST. (Leland) Methyltestosterone 2 mg., thiamine mononitrate 5 mg., mono sodium glutamate 300 mg./Tab. Bot. 100s, 500s.
Use: Testosterone therapy.
GLUTETHIMIDE. B.A.N. 2-Ethyl-2-phenylglutatimide.
Use: Non-barbiturate hypnotic.
See: Doriden, Tab. (USV)
• **GLUTETHIMIDE,** U.S.P. XXI. Cap., Tab., U.S.P. XXI. Alpha-ethyl-alpha-phenyl-glutarimide. 2-Ethyl-2-phenylglutarimide.
Use: Non-barbiturate hypnotic.
See: Dorimide, Tab. (Cenci)
Doriden, Cap. (USV)
Rolathimide, Tab. (Robinson)
GLUTOFAC. (Kenwood) *Saccharomyces siccum* 390 mg., Vit C 250 mg., B-1 15 mg., B-2 10 mg., niacinamide 50 mg., B-6 50 mg., Ca-pantothenate 20 mg., Mg sulfate 70 mg., Zn 80 mg./Tab. Bot. 90s, 500s.
Use: Nutritional supplement.
GLUTOL. (Paddock) Dextrose 100 Gm./180 ml. Bot. 180 ml.
Use: Glucose tolerance test.
GLUTOSE. (Paddock) Concentrated glucose for insulin reactions. Bot. 2 oz.
Use: Hypoglycemic states.
GLUTRIL. Glibornuride, B.A.N.

• **GLYBURIDE.** USAN.
Use: Antidiabetic.
See: Diabeta (Hoechst)
Micronase, Tab. (Upjoin)

GLYCALOX. B.A.N. A polymerized complex of glycerol and aluminum hydroxide. Glucalox (I.N.N.)
Use: Treatment of gastric hyperacidity.
See: Manalox AG.

GLYCARNINE IRON.
See: Ferronord, Tab. (Cooper)

GLYCATE CHEWABLES. (Forest) Glycine 150 mg., calcium carbonate 300 mg./Tab. Bot. 100s.

• **GLYCERIN,** U.S.P. XXI. Ophth. Soln., Oral Soln., U.S.P. XXI. 1,2,3-Propanetriol.
Use: Pharm. aid.
See: Corn Huskers Lotion (Warner-Lambert)
Glyrol, Liq. (CooperVision)
Osmoglyn (Alcon)
W/Urea.
See: Kerid Ear Drops (Blair)

• **GLYCERIN SUPPOSITORIES,** U.S.P. XXI. (Various Mfr.) Glycerin, sodium stearate.
Use: Rectal evacuant; cathartic.

• **GLYCEROL, IODINATED.** USAN.
Use: Expectorant.

GLYCERYL GUAIACOLATE.
Use: Expectorant.
See: Guaifenesin, U.S.P. XXI.

GLYCERYL GUAIACOLATE CARBAMATE.
Methocarbamol.
See: Robaxin, Tab., Inj. (Robins)
Robaxin 750, Tab. (Robins)

GLYCERYL GUAIACOL ETHER.
See: Guaifenesin.

• **GLYCERYL MONOSTEARATE,** N.F. XVI. (Various Mfr.) Monostearin.
Use: Pharm. aid (emulsifying agent).

GLYCERYL-T. (Rugby) Theophylline 150 mg., guaifenesin 90 mg./Cap. Bot. 100s, 1000s.
Use: Bronchodilator.

GLYCERYL TRIACETIN. (Various Mfr.) Triacetin.
See: Enzactin, Aer., Pow., Cream (Ayerst)
Fungacetin, Oint., Liq. (Blair Labs.)

GLYCERYL TRINITRATE OINTMENT.
See: Nitrol, Oint. (Kremers-Urban)

GLYCERYL TRINITRATE TABLETS.
See: Nitroglycerin (Var. Mfr.)
Nitroglyn, Tab. (Key Corp.)

GLYCETS-ANTACID TABLETS. (Weeks & Leo) Calcium carbonate 350 mg., simethicone 25 mg./Chewable Tab. Bot. 100s.
Use: Antacid.

GLYCINATO DIHYDROXYALUMINUM HYDRATE.
See: Dihydroxyaluminum Aminoacetate, U.S.P. XXI.

• **GLYCINE,** U.S.P. XXI. Irrigation, U.S.P. XXI. Aminoacetic Acid.
Use: Myasthenia gravis treatment, irrigating solution.
W/Aluminum hydroxide-magnesium carbonate coprecipitated gel.
See: Glycogel, Tab., Susp. (Central)
W/Alum. & mag. hydroxide, mag. trisilicate, belladonna ext.mannitol, oil peppermint.
See: Gas-Eze, Tab. (Edward J. Moore)
W/Calcium Carbonate.
See: Antacid No. 6, Tab. (Bowman)
Antacid Tab. (Sutliff & Case)
Glycate Chewables, Tab. (O'Neal)
P.H. Tabs. (Scrip)
Titralac, Liq., Tab. (Riker)
Wol-Lac, Tab. (Wolins)
W/Calcium carbonate, amylolytic, proteolytic cellulolytic enzymes.
See: Co-gel, Tab. (Arco)
W/Chlortrimeton & sod. salicylate.
See: Corilin, Liq. (Schering)
W/Glutamic acid, alanine.
See: Prostall, Cap. (Metabolic Prods.)
W/Magnesium trisilicate, calcium carbonate.
See: P.H. Tabs., Chewable, Mix (Scrip)
W/Vit. B Complex, C, & iron.
See: Bironate-B, Cap. (Coastal)

GLYCINE, ALUMINUM SALT.
See: Dihydroxyaluminum Aminoacetate, U.S.P. X

GLYCINE, N-(4-AMINOBENZOYL)-. Aminohippuric Acid, U.S.P. XXI.

GLYCINE, N,N'-1,2-ETHANEDIYLBIS[N-(CARBOXYMETHYL)-], DISODIUM SALT, DIHYDRA
Edetate Disodium, U.S.P. XXI.

GLYCINE HYDROCHLORIDE. (Various Mfr.)
Use: Recommended for achlorhydria.

• **GLYCOBIARSOL.** U.S.P. XXI. Tab., U.S.P. XXI. Bismuthyl-N-Glycolylarsanilate, Chemo Puro, Pow. Mfr. (Hydrogen N-glycoloylarsanilato) oxobismuth
Use: Amebiasis, Trichomonas vaginalis, Monilia albicans.

GLYCOBIARSOL. (I.N.N.) Bismuth Glycollylarsanila B.A.N.

GLYCOCOLL. Glycine.
See: Aminoacetic Acid (Various Mfr.)

GLYCOCYAMINE. Guanidoacetic acid.

GLYCO IOPHEN SOLUTION. (Wade) Tr. iodine, phenol 2%, glycerine q.s., oil peppermint. Bot. 2 oz., 4 oz., pt., gal.
Use: Antiseptic.

• **GLYCOL DISTERATE.** USAN.
Use: Pharmaceutic aid.

GLYCOL MONOSALICYLATE.
W/Oil of mustard, camphor, menthol, methyl salicylate.
See: Musterole, Oint., Cream (Plough)

GLYCOPHENYLATE BROMIDE.
See: Mepenzolate Methylbromide.

• **GLYCOPYRROLATE,** U.S.P. XXI. Inj., Tab., U.S.P XXI. 1-Methyl-3-pyrrolidyl a-phenylcyclopentan lycolate methobromide. 3-Hydroxy-1,1-dimethylpy rolidinium bromide α-cyclopentylmandelate.
See: Robinul, Tab., Inj. (Robins)
Robinul Forte, Tab. (Robins)

GLYCOPYRRONIUM BROMIDE. B.A.N. 3-α-Cyclop tylmandeloyloxy-1,1-dimethylpyrrolidinium bromide
Use: Anticholinergic.
See: Glycopyrrolate
Robinul

YCOTUSS. (Vale) Guaifenesin 100 mg./Tab. or 5 nl. **Syr.** pt., gal. **Tabs.** 100s, 500s, 1000s.
Jse: Expectorant.

YCOTUSS-dM. (Vale) Guaifenesin 100 mg., dextromethorphan HBr 10 mg./Tab. or 5 cc. **Tab.** 00s, 500s, 1000s. **Syr.** pt., gal.
Jse: Expectorant/antitussive.

LYCYRRHIZA, U.S.P. XXI. Pure Extract, luidextract, U.S.P. XXI. Licorice root.
Jse: Flavoring agent.

LYCYRRHIZA EXTRACT, PURE, U.S.P. XXI.
Jse: Flavoring agent.

LYCYRRHIZA FLUIDEXTRACT, N.F. XVI.
Camphorated opium tincture, tartar emetic, glycerin.
See: Brown Mixture. (Bowman)
Pepsin-papain complex, pancreas, malt diastase, charcoal, ox bile.
See: Pepsocoll, Tabs. (Western Research Labs.)

YDANILE SODIUM. (1)5′-Chloro-2-[p-[(5-isobutyl-2-pyrimidinyl)sulfamoyl]-phenyl]-o-acetanilidide monosodium salt; (2) 4-[N-(5-isobutyl-2-pyrimidinyl)-sulfamoyl] phenylacetic acid-5-chloro-2-methoxyanilide sodium salt.
Jse: Oral hypoglycemic.

LYHEXAMIDE. USAN.
Jse: Antidiabetic.

YMIDINE. B.A.N. Sodium salt of 2-benzenesulfonamido-5-(2-methoxy-ethoxy)pyrimidine.
Jse: Oral hypoglycemic agent.
See: Gondafon
  Lycanol

LYMIDINE SODIUM. USAN.[N-[5-(2-Methoxyethoxy)-2-idinyl] benzene-sulfonamido]-sodium.
Jse: Oral hypoglycemic.

YMOL.
See: Petrolatum Liquid (Various Mfr.)

YNAZAN EXPECTORANT. (Scherer) Theophylline sod. glycinate, 60 mg. (equiv. to 30 mg., theophylline), guaifenesin 50 mg., sod. citrate 100 mg./5 cc. Bot. pt.
Use: Management of non-productive cough due to the common cold.

LYOCTAMIDE. USAN. 1-Cyclooctyl-3(p-tolylsulfonyl) urea.
Use: Hypoglycemic agent.

Y-O-TUSSIN. (Research Pharmacal Lab.) Guaifenesin 100 mg./tsp. Bot., gal.
Use: Cough syrup.

Y-OXIDE. (Marion) Carbamide peroxide 10% in flavored anhydrous glycerol. Plas. bot. 0.5 fl. oz., 2 fl. oz.
Use: Oral inflammation.

YOXYLDIUREIDE.
See: Allantoin (Various Mfr.)

LYPARAMIDE. USAN. 1-(p-Chlorophenylsulfonyl)-3-(p-dimethylaminophenyl) urea.
Use: Oral hypoglycemic.

YPHODYL B INJ. (Torigian) Iron cacodylate 0.020 Gm., sod. glycerophosphate 0.2 Gm., strychnine glycerophosphate 0.001 Gm./cc. Amp. 1 cc. 12s, 25s, 100s.

GLYROL. (CooperVision) Glycerin 75% v/v in a solution of citric acid and purified water. Glass Bot. 4 oz.
Use: Oral osmotic agent to reduce intraocular pressure.

GLYTABS. (Pharmics) Amino acetic acid 100 mg., calcium carbonate 300 mg., aluminum hydroxide, magnesium carbonate 200 mg./Chew. Tab. Bot. 100s, 1000s.
Use: Antacid.

GLYTINIC TABLET. (Boyle) Ferrous gluconate 3.4 gr., glycine 325 mg., B-12 2.5 mcg., B-1 1.9 mg., B-2 1.9 mg., B-6 0.56 mg., niacinamide 11.25 mg., panthenol 1.63 mg., liver desic. 1.25 gr./Tab. Bot. 100s.
Use: Potent hematinic.

GLY-TRATE. (Sutliff & Case) Nitroglycerin 2.5 mg./Meta-Kap. Bot. 100s.
Use: Management of angina pectoris.

GLYTUSS. (Mayrand) Guaifenesin 200 mg./Tab. Bot. 100s, 500s.
Use: Antitussive-expectorant.

GLYVENOL. (Ciba) Tribenoside. Not available in U.S.
Use: Venoprotective agent.

G-MYTICIN CREME AND OINTMENT. (Pedinol) Gentamicin sulfate equivalent to 1 mg. gentamicin base. Tube 15 Gm.
Use: Anti-infective.

GOLACOL. (Arcum) Codeine sulfate 30 mg., papaverine HCl 30 mg., emetine HCl 2 mg., ephedrine HCl 15 mg. syrup orange q.s./30 cc alcohol 6.25%. Bot. 4, 16 oz., gal.
Use: Cough syrup.

GOLD (Au^{198}) Colloid Radio.
Use: Antineoplastic Agent.
See: Radio Gold (Au^{198})

GOLD Au 198 INJECTION.
Use: Antineoplastic; diagnostic for liver scanning.

■ **GOLD COMPOUNDS.**
See: Aurocein-10, Vial (Christina)
  Gold Sodium Thiosulfate (Various Mfr.)
  Myochrysine, Amp. (Merck Sharp & Dohme)
  Solganal, Vial. (Schering)

GOLD, MERCAPTOBUTANEDIOATO(1-)-, DISODIUM SALT, MONOHYDRATE. Gold Sodium Thiomalate, U.S.P. XXI.

• **GOLD SODIUM THIOMALATE,** U.S.P. XXI. Inj., U.S.P. XXI. Gold, mercaptobutanedioato(1-)-, disodium salt, monohydrate. (Disodium mercaptosuccinato) gold monohydrate.
Use: Rheumatoid arthritis.
See: Myochrysine, Amp. (Merck Sharp & Dohme)

GOLD SODIUM THIOSULFATE. Sterile, Auricidine, Aurocidin, Aurolin, Auropin, Aurosan, Novacrysin, Solfocrisol & Thiochrysine.
Use: Rheumatoid arthritis.

GOLD THIOGLUCOSE.
See: Aurothioglucose, U.S.P. XXI.

GOLD, (1-THIO-d-GLUCOPYRANOSATO)-. Aurothioglucose, U.S.P. XXI.

GOLDEN BALM. (Jenkins) Methyl salicylate, menthol, camphor/Fl. oz. Bot. 3 oz., pt., gal.

GOLDEN BOUNTY VITAMIN PRODUCTS. (Squibb)
See: Squibb Golden Bounty Products.

GOLDEN-WEST COMPOUND. (Golden-West) Gentian root, licorice root, cascara sagrada, damiana leaves, senna leaves, psyllium seed, buchu leaves, crude pepsin. Box 1.5 oz.
Use: Laxative.

GOLDICIDE CONCENTRATE. (Pedinol) N-Alkyl-dimethylbenzylammonium chloride, cetyl dimethyl ammonium chloride. Bot. (Conc.) 1 oz. Ctn. 10s.
Use: Chemical disinfection of surgical and podiatry instruments.

GOLD SEAL CHEWABLE VITAMIN C. (Walgreen) Ascorbic acid 250 mg. or 500 mg./Tab.
Use: Vit. C supplement.

GOLD SEAL FERROUS GLUCONATE. (Walgreen) Iron 37 mg./Tab. Bot. 100s.
Use: Iron supplement.

GOLD SEAL TIME RELEASE FERROUS SULFATE. (Walgreen) Iron 50 mg., or 65 mg./Tab. Bot. 100s.
Use: Iron supplement.

GOLYTELY. (Braintree) Power for reconstitution containing polyethylene glycol 236 Gm., sodium sulfate 22.74 Gm., sodium bicarbonate 6.74 Gm., sodium chloride 5.86 Gm., potassium chloride 2.97 Gm. when made up to 4 liters.
Use: For bowel cleansing prior to GI examination.

■ **GOMENOL PREPARATIONS.**
Note: Products withdrawn from market.

GONACRINE.
See: Acriflavine (Various Mfr.)

GONADEX. (Continental) Chroionic gonadotropin 10,000 u w/mannitol 100 mg., benzyl alcohol 0.9%, sod. phosphate dibasic and monobasic. Vial. 10 cc.
Use: Precocious puberty.

GONADORELIN. B.A.N. L-Pyroglutamyl-L-histidyl-L-tryptophyl-L-seryl-L-tyrosyl-glycyl-L-leucyl-L arginyl-L-prolyl-L-glycinamide.
Use: Luteinizing hormone- and follicle stimulating hormone-releasing hormone.

• **GONADORELIN ACETATE.** USAN.
Use: Gonad-stimulating principle.
See: Cryptolin Prods. (Hoechst)

• **GONADORELIN HYDROCHLORIDE.** USAN.
Use: Gonad-stimulating principle.

GONADOTROPIC SUBSTANCE.
See: Gonadotropin Chorionic

• **GONADOTROPIN, CHORIONIC,** U.S.P. XXI. For Inj., U.S.P. XXI. Human Pregnancy Urine.
Use: In the female: Chronic cystic mastitis, functional sterility, dysmenorrhea, premenstrual tension, & threatened abortion. In the male: Cryptorchidism, hypogenitalism, dwarfism, impotency, enuresis.
See: Android HCG, Inj. (Brown)
Antuitrin "S", Vial (Parke-Davis)
A.P.L., Secules (Ayerst)
Chopion-Plus, Vial (Pharmex)
Corgonject, Vial (Mayrand)
Dura-Chroion Plus, Vial (Pharmex)
Follutein Powd. (Squibb)
Gonadamine 5000, Vial (Torigian)
Harvatropin, Vial (Harvey)
Libigen, Vial (Savage)
Pregnyl, Amp. (Organon)
W/Vit. B-1, glutamic acid, procaine HCl.
See: Glukor, Vial. (Brown)

GONADOTROPIN, PITUITARY ANT. LOBE.
Extracted from anterior lobe of equine pituitaries (not pregnant mare urine) (rat unit = 1 Fevold-His unit).

GONADOTROPIN SERUM. Pregnant Mare's Serum

GONADOTROPIN SPECIAL DILUENT. (Kenyon) Sc succinate 0.5%, sod. nicotinate 1.0%, glutamic a 52.5 ppm, propylparaben 0.02%, chlorobutanol 0.5%. Vial 10 cc.

GONIC. (Hauck) Chorionic gonadotropin 10,000 unit Vial 10 ml./w diluent.

GONIOSCOPIC HYDROXYPROPYL METHYLCELLULOSE.
See: Goniosol Lacrivial, Sol. (Smith, Miller & Patc

GONIOSOL. (CooperVision) Gonioscopic hydroxypropyl methylcellulose 2.5%. Bot. 15 ml.
Use: Gonioscopic examinations.

GONOZYME. (Abbott) Test kit 100s.
Use: Enzyme immunoassay for detection of *Neisseria gonorrhoeae* in urogenital swab specimens.

GOOD SAMARITAN OINTMENT. (Good Samaritan) Tin 1.7 oz.
Use: Promotes healing of irritated or burned skin.

GO PAIN. (DePree) **Cream:** Methyl salicylate, chlorobutanol, menthol, camphor, thymol. Tube 1. oz., 4 oz. **Oral Gel:** Benzocaine, eugenol. Tube 3/8 oz. **Throat spray** 4 oz.

GO PAIN EXTRA STRENGTH BALM. (DePree) Methyl salicylate Jar 3¾ oz.
Use: External analgesic.

GO-PAIN LOTION. (Eckerd) Methyl nicotinate, meth salicylate, menthol, camphor. Bot. 5 oz.

GO PAIN THROAT LOZENGES. (Eckerd) Benzocaine, menthol, eucalyptus.
Use: Sore throat pain.

GORDOBALM. (Gordon) Chloroxylenol, methyl salicylate, menthol, camphor, thymol, eucalyptus c isopropyl alcohol 16%, fast-drying gum base. Bot. oz., gal.

GORDOCHOM. (Gordon) Undecylenic acid 25%, chloroxylenol 3%, penetrating oil base. Bot. 0.5 oz 1 oz.
Use: Superficial fungus condition, calloused nail grooves.

GORDOFILM. (Gordon) Salicylic acid 16.7%, lactic acid 16.7% in flexible collodian.
Use: Keratolytic for removal of verrucae.

GORDOGESIC CREAM. (Gordon) Methyl salicylate 10% in absorbtion base. Jar 2.5 oz., 1 lb.
Use: Muscular aches, pains, and strains, simple neuralgia.

GORDOMATIC CRYSTALS. (Gordon) Sod. borate, sod. bicarbonate, sod. chloride, thymol, menthol, c of eucalyptus. Jar 8 oz., 7 lb.
Use: Aromatic, soothing foot soak.

RDOMATIC LOTION. (Gordon) Menthol, camphor, propylene glycol, isopropyl alcohol. Bot. 1 oz., 4 oz., gal.
Use: Burning aching, tired feet.
RDOMATIC POWDER. (Gordon) Menthol, thymol camphor, oil of eucalyptus, salicylic acid, alum bentonite, talc. Shaker can 3.5 oz. Can 1 lb., 5 lbs.
Use: Cooling, soothing powder.
RDOPHENE. (Gordon) Neutral coconut oil soap 15% and glycerin. Bot. 4 oz., gal.
Use: Surgical soap for office and at home use.
RDO-POOL WHIRLPOOL CONCENTRATE. (Gordon) Septi-Chlor (trichlorohydroxy diphenyl ether) broad spectrum antimicrobial and bacteriostatic agent. Bot. 4 oz., pt., gal.
Use: Water softener and de-scumming agent.
RDO-VITE A CREME. (Gordon) Vit. A 100,000 I.U. /oz. in water soluble base. Jar 0.5 oz., 2.5 oz., 4 oz., lb., 5 lb.
Use: Dry skin and fissures, treatment for diabetic and geriatric skin.
RDO-VITE A LOTION. (Gordon) Vit. A 100,000 I.U. /oz. Plastic Bot. 4 oz., gal.
Use: Treatment of diabetic and geriatric skin.
RDO-VITE E CREME. (Gordon) Vit. E 1500 I.U./oz., water soluble base. Jar 2.5 oz., lb.
Use: Skin care; helpful for dryness after surgery.
RD-UREA. (Gordon) Urea 22% or 40% in petrolatum base. Jars 1 oz.
Use: Devitalized nail tissue cleansing, loosening and debriding; non-surgical avulsion of nails.
RMEL CREAM. (Gordon) Urea 20% in emollient base. Jar 2.5 oz., 4 oz., 1 lb.
Use: Hyperkeratotic for dry skin conditions and fissures.
TAMINE. (Vita Elixir) Ergotamine tartrate 1 mg., caffeine 100 mg./Tab.
Use: Migraine therapy.
RAMICIDIN, U.S.P. XXI.
Use: Antibacterial.
/Neomycin.
See: Spectrocin Ointment (Squibb)
/Neomycin sulfate, polymyxin B sulfate, thimerosal.
See: Neo-Polycin Ophthalmic Solution (Merrell Dow)
/Neomycin sulf., polymyxin B sulf., benzocaine.
See: Tricidin, Oint. (Amlab)
/Neomycin, triamcinolone, nystatin.
See: Mycolog Cream, Oint. (Squibb)
/Polymyxin B sulfate, neomycin sulfate.
See: Neosporin, Ophth. Sol. (Burroughs Wellcome)
Neosporin-G. Cream (Burroughs Wellcome)
/Polymyxin B sulfate, neomycin sulfate & hydrocortisone acetate.
See: Cortisporin, Cream (Burroughs Wellcome)
RAMINEAE POLLENS.
See: Allergenic Extracts, Timothy and Related Pollens (Parke-Davis)
RANULEX. (Hickam) Trypsin 0.1 mg., balsam peru 72.5 mg., castor oil 650.0 mg. w/emulsifier/0.82 cc. Spray can, 2 oz., 4 oz.
Use: Wound healing.

GRAPEFRUIT DIET PLAN with DIADAX CAPSULES. (O'Connor) Natural grapefruit ext. 50 mg., phenylpropanolamine HCl 30 mg./Cap. Bot. 20s, 50s.
Use: Vitamin fortified appetite suppressant.
GRAPEFRUIT DIET PLAN with DIADAX EXTRA STRENGTH CAPSULES. (O'Connor) Natural grapefruit Ext. 100 mg., phenylpropanolamine HCl 75 mg./Cap. Bot. 10s, 24s.
Use: Vitamin fortified appetite suppressant.
GRAPEFRUIT DIET PLAN with DIADAX TABLETS. (O'Connor) Natural grapefruit ext., phenylpropanolamine HCl 10 mg./Tab. Bot. 42s, 90s.
Use: Vitamin fortified appetite suppressant.
GRATUS STROPHANTHIN.
See: Ouabain (Various Mfr.)
GRAVIGEN INJECTION. (Bluco) Estrogenic sub. in aq. susp. or oil. 20,000 u./cc. Vial 30 cc.
GRAVINEED. (Hanlon) Vit. C 100 mg., Vit. E 10 I.U., Vit. B-1 3 mg., Vit. B-2 2 mg., Vit. B-6 10 mg., Vit. B-12 5 mcg., Vit. A 4000 I.U., Vit. D 400 I.U., niacin 10 mg., folic acid 0.1 mg., iron fumarate 40 mg., Ca. 67 mg./Cap. Bot. 100s.
Use: Prenatal dietary supplement.
GRAVOL. Dimenhydrinate, B.A.N.
GREEN MINT. (Block) Urea, glycine, polysorbate 60, sorbitol, alcohol 12.2%, peppermint oil, menthol, chlorophyllin-copper complex. Bot. 7 oz., 12 oz.
Use: Mouthwash and gargle.
GREEN SOAP, U.S.P. XXI.
Use: Detergent.
GRIFULVIN V. (Ortho) Griseofulvin microsize. **Tab.:** 250 mg./Tab. Bot. 100s; 500 mg./Tab. Bot. 50s, 100s, 500s. **Susp.:** 125 mg./5 cc. Bot. 4 oz.
Use: Fungus infections of skin, hair & nails (oral).
GRILLODYNE TABLETS. (Fellows) Aspirin 3.5 gr., phenacetin 2.5 gr., caffeine alkaloid 0.5 gr., phenobarbital 0.25 gr./Tab. Bot. 1000s.
GRISACTIN. (Ayerst) Griseofulvin microsize. 125 mg./Cap. Bot. 100s; 250 mg./Cap. Bot. 100s, 500s. 500 mg./Tab. Bot. 60s.
Use: Ringworm infections.
GRISACTIN ULTRA. (Ayerst) Grisofulvin ultramicrosize 125 mg., 250 mg. or 330 mg./Tab. Bot. 100s.
Use: Ringworm infections.
• **GRISEOFULVIN,** U.S.P. XXI. Cap., Oral Susp., Tab., Ultramicrosized Tab., U.S.P. XXI. An antibiotic. 7-Chloro-4,6-dimethoxy-coumaran-3-one-2-spiro-1′-(2′-methoxy-6′-methylcyclohex-2′-en-4′-one). 7-Chloro-2′,4,6-trimethoxy-6′-methylspiro[benzofuran-2(3H), 1′-[2]-cyclohexene]-3,4′-dione. Spiro[benzofuran-2(3H)-1′-[2]cyclohexene]-3,4′-dione,7-chloro-2′,4,6-trimethoxy-6′-methyl-, (1′s-trans)-. Fulcin, Grisovin
Use: Antifungal (antibiotic).
See: Fulvicin P/G. Tab. (Schering)
Fulvicin-U/F, Tab. (Schering)
Grifulvin V, Tab., Susp. (Ortho)
Grisactin, Cap., Tab. (Ayerst)
Grisactin Ultra, Tab. (Ayerest)

GRISEOFULVIN MICROCRYSTALLINE.
See: Fulvicin U/F, Tab. (Schering)
Grifulvin V, Tab., Susp. (Ortho)
Grisactin, Cap., Tab. (Ayerst)

GRISEOFULVIN ULTRAMICROSIZE.
See: Fulvicin P/G. Tab. (Schering)
Gris-Peg Tablets (Dorsey)

GRIS-PEG TABLETS. (Herbert) Griseofulvin ultramicrosize. **125 mg.,/Tab. Bot. 100s, 500s. 250 mg.** /Tab. Bot. 100s.
Use: Oral antifungal.

GROFAS. Quindoxin, B.A.N.

GRO. (Coastal) Sterilized bone meal 16 gr., Vit. A 400 u., D 400 u., red bone marrow 20 mg./Tab. Bot. 100s.

GROUP A STREP. (Wampole-Zeus) Direct fluorescent test for group A Streptocci. 72 × 10 wells.
Use: Identification of Group A streptococci from cultures.

GROWTH HORMONE. B.A.N. Extract of human pituitaries containing predominantly growth hormone.
See: Crescormon.

G-STROPHANTHIN.
See: Ouabain. (Various Mfr.)

G-TUSSIN SYRUP. (Quality Generics) Guaifenesin 100 mg./5 cc. Bot. pt., gal.
Use: Coughs.

G-TUSSIN DM SYRUP. (Quality Generics) Guaifenesin 100 mg., dextro-methorphan HBr 15 mg., alcohol 1.-4%/5 ml. Bot. pt., gal.
Use: Expectorant.

GUAIACOHIST. (Pharmex) Potassium guaiacol-sulfonate 40 mg., sod. iodide 50 mg., chlorpheniramine maleate 5 mg./cc. Vial 30 cc.

GUAIACOL. (Various Mfr.) Methylcatechol.
Use: Chronic infections of the respiratory tract.
W/Cacodylic acid.
See:
W/Methyl Salicylate.
See: Guiatex, Oint. (Scrip)
W/Naiouli oil, eucalyptol, iodoform, camphor.
See: Guaidol Compound, Vial (Medical Chem.; Kenyon)
Kleer, Inj. (Scrip)

GUAIACOL. (Jenkins) Guaiacol 0.1 Gm., eucalyptol 0.08 Gm., iodoform 0.02 Gm., camphor 0.05 Gm., sesame oil q.s./2 cc. Vial 10 cc.
W/Methyl salicylate, menthol.
See: Guaiamen, Cream (Lannett)

GUAIACOL CARBONATE. (Various Mfr.) (Duotal).
Use: Expectorant.

GUAIACOL GLYCERYL ETHER.
See: Guaifenesin

GUAIACOL POTASSIUM SULFONATE.
See: Bronchial, Syr. (DePree)
W/Ammonium Cl, sod. citrate, benzyl alcohol, carbinoxamine maleate.
See: Clistin Expectorant, Syr. (McNeil)
W/Dextromethorphan HBr.
Bronchial DM, Syr. (DePree)
W/Dextromethorphan HBr, chlorpheniramine malea[te], ammonium Cl, tartar emetic.
See: Duomine, Syr. (Kenyon)
W/Pheniramine maleate, pyrilamine maleate, codei[ne] phosphate.
See: Tritussin Syrup (Towne)

GUAIADOL. (Medwick) Aqueous. Vial 30 cc.

GUAIADOL COMPOUND. (Medical Chem.) Naiouli [oil] 100 mg., eucalyptol 80 mg., guaiacol 100 mg., iodoform 20 mg., camphor 50 mg./2 cc. Aqueous or in oil. Vial 30 cc.

GUAIADOL COMPOUND. (Medwick) Oil. Vial 30 cc.

GUAIAJEN. (Jenkins) Phenylephrine HCl 5 mg., pyrilamine maleate 12.5 mg., guaifenesin 100 mg./Tab. Bot. 1000s.
Use: Cold symptoms.

GUAIAMEN. (Lannett) Methyl salicylate, guaiacol, menthol in greaseless base. 4 oz., 1 lb.

GUAIAMINE SOLU-CAPS. (Sutliff & Case) Caffei[ne] 32.5 mg., chlorpheniramine maleate 2 mg., phenylephrine HCl 5 mg., guaifenesin 50 mg., salicylamide 3 gr., acetaminophen 2 gr./Cap. Bot. 100s, 1000s.
Use: Colds.

GUAIANESIN.
See: Guaifenesin
Use: Expectorant.

• **GUAIAPATE.** USAN.
Use: Antitussive.

GUAIFED CAPSULES. (Muro) Guaifenesin 250 mg., pseudoephedrine HCl 120 mg./TR Cap. Bot. 100s
Use: Expectorant, decongestant.

• **GUAIFENESIN,** U.S.P. XXI. Cap., Syrup, Tab., U.S.P. XXI. Methphenoxydiol. 3-(o-methoxyphenoxy) 1,2-propanediol.
Synonyms:
Glyceryl Guaiacolate
Glyceryl Guaiacol Ether
Guaianesin
Guaifylline
Guaiphenesin, B.A.N.
Guayanesin
Use: Expectorant.
See: Anti-tuss, Liq. (Century)
Consin-GG, Syr. (Wisconsin)
Dilyn, Liq., Tab. (Elder)
2/G, Liq. (Merrell Dow)
G-100, Syr. (Bock)
GG-Cen, Syr. (Central)
Glycotuss, Tab., Syr. (Vale)
Gly-O-Tussin, Liq. (Research Pharmacal Lab.)
Glytuss, Tab. (Mayrand)
G-Tussin, Syr. (Quality Generics)
Hytuss, Tab., Cap. (Hyrex)
Robitussin, Syr. (Robins)
Tursen, Tab. (Wren)
Wal-Tussin, Syr. (Walgreen)
W/Combinations.
See: Actified C Expectorant, Liq. (Burroughs Wellcome)
Actol Exp., Syr., Tab. (Beecham Labs)
Adatuss, Syr. (W.F. Merchant)

Airet G.G., Cap., Elix. (Baylor Labs.)
Ambenyl-D, Liq. (Marion)
Anti-tuss D.M., Liq. (Century)
Antitussive Guaiacolate, Syr. (Med. Chem.)
Asbron G, Tab., Elix. (Dorsey)
Asma. Syr. (Coastal)
Bur-Tuss Expectorant (Burlington)
Brexin, Cap., Liq. (Savage)
Bri-stan, Liq. (Briar)
Bronchohist, Syr. (Sutliff & Case)
Broncholate, Cap., Elix. (Bock)
Bronchovent, Tab. (Mills)
Bronkolate-G, Tab. (Parmed)
Bronkolixir, Elix. (Winthrop-Breon)
Bronkotabs, Tab. (Winthrop-Breon)
Bro-Tane, Exp. (Scrip)
C.D.M., Expect. (Lannett)
Cerylin, Liq. (Spencer-Mead)
Cheracol-D, Syr. (Upjohn)
Chlor-Trimeton, Expect. (Schering)
Colrex, Expectorant (Rowell)
Conar-A, Susp., Tab. (Beecham Labs)
Conar Expectorant, Liq. (Beecham Labs)
Consin-DM, Syr. (Wisconsin)
Coricidin Children's Cough Syrup (Schering)
Cortane D.C., Exp. (Standex)
Dextro-Tuss GG, Liq. (Ulmer)
Diabetussin, Expect. (Research Pharm.)
Dilacap, Cap. (Coastal)
Dilaudid, Syr. (Knoll)
Dilor-G, Tab., Liq. (Savage)
Dilyn, Liq. (Elder)
Dimacol, Cap. (Robins)
Dimetane Expectorant, Liq. (Robins)
Dimetane Expectorant-DC, Liq. (Robins)
DM Plus, Liq. (West-Ward)
Donatussin, Syr. (Laser)
Duovent, Tab. (Riker)
Emfaseem, Liq., Tab. (Saron)
Entex, Caps., Liq. (Norwich Eaton)
Expectico Cough Syrup (Coastal)
Expecto Hist, Tab. (Wolins)
Fedahist, Expect. (Dooner)
Formula 44D Decongestant Cough Mixture, Syr. (Vicks)
G-100/DM, Syr. (Bock)
G-Bron Elixir (Laser)
2G/DM, Liq. (Merrell Dow)
Glycotuss-DM, Tab. (Vale)
G-Tussin-DM, Syr. (Quality Generics)
Guaiamine, Cap. (Sutliff & Case)
Guiatussin w/Codeine. Liq. (Spencer-Mead)
Guistrey Fortis, Tab. (Bowman)
Gylanphen, Tab. (Lannett)
Histussinol, Syr. (Bock)
Hycoff-A, Syr. (Saron)
Hycotuss Expect., Liq. (Du Pont)
Hylate, Tab., Syr. (Hyrex)
Isoclor. Expect. (American Critical Care)
Lanatuss, Expect. (Lannett)
Lardet Expectorant, Tab. (Standex)
Mudrane GG, Tab., Elix. (Poythress)
Neospect, Tab. (Lemmon)
Novahistine Cough Formula, Liq. (Merrell Dow)
Novahistine DMX, Liq. (Merrell Dow)
Novahistine, Expect. (Merrell Dow)
Panaphyllin, Susp. (Panamerican)
Partuss-A, Tab. (Parmed)
Partuss AC (Parmed)
Pedituss Syrup (Sutliff & Case)
Phenatuss, Liq. (Dalin)
PMP, Expect. (Schlicksup)
PMP, Syrup (Schlicksup)
Polaramine Expect. (Schering)
Poly-Histine Expect. (Bock)
Polytuss-DM, Liq. (Rhode)
P.R. Syrup, Liq. (Fleming)
Queltuss, Syr., Tab. (Westerfield)
Quibron, Cap., Liq. (Mead Johnson)
Quibron-300, Cap. (Mead Johnson)
Quibron Plus, Cap., Elix. (Mead Johnson)
Quilate, Cap. (Wolins)
Rentuss, Cap., Syr. (Wren)
Rhinex DM (Lemmon)
Robitussin AC, CF, DAC, DM, PE (Robins)
Robitussin-DM Cough Calmers, Loz. (Robins)
Rondec-DM, Syr. (Ross)
Rymed, Prods. (Edwards)
Santussin, Caps. (Sandia)
Scotcof, Liq. (Scott/Cord)
Silexin, Cough Syr. (Clapp)
Slo-Phyllin GG, Cap., Syr. (Dooner)
Sorbase Cough Syr. (Fort David)
Sorbase II Cough Syr. (Fort David)
Spen-Histine Expect. (Spencer-Mead)
Sudafed Cough Syrup (Burroughs Wellcome)
Theofed, Tab. (Sutliff & Case)
Theo-Guaia, Cap., Liq. (Sutliff & Case)
Tolu-Sed, Liq. (Scherer)
Tolu-Sed DM, Liq. (Scherer)
Trihista-Phen, Liq. (Recsei)
Tri-Histin Expect. (Recsei)
Tri-Mine, Expect. (Spencer-Mead)
Trind-DM, Liq. (Mead Johnson)
Trind, Liq. (Mead Johnson)
Tussafed, Exp. (Calvital)
Tussar-2, Syr. (Armour)
Tussend, Liq. (Merrell Dow)
Verequad, Tab., Susp. (Knoll)
Vicks Cough Syrup (Vicks)
Vicks Formula 44D Decongestant Cough Mixture, Syr. (Vicks)
Wal-Tussin DM, Syr. (Walgreen)

GUAIODOL AQUEOUS. (Kenyon) Potassium guaiacol sulf. 40 mg., sod. iodide 50 mg. in saturated aqueous naiouli, guaiacol, eucalyptol, menthol/cc. Vial 30 cc.

GUAIODOL COMPOUND. (Kenyon) Naiouli oil 0.10 Gm., eucalyptol 0.08 Gm., guaiacol 0.1 Gm., iodoform 0.02 Gm., camphor 0.05 Gm./2 cc. Vial 30 cc.

GUAIODOL-PLUS AQUEOUS. (Kenyon) Potassium guaiacolsulfonate 40 mg., sod. iodide 50 mg., chlorpheniramine maleate 5 mg., sod. bisulfite 1 mg. in saturated aqueous naiouli, guaiacol, eucalyptol, menthol/cc. Vial 30 cc.

GUAIPHENESIN. B.A.N. 3- -Methoxyphenoxy-propane-1:2-diol. Guaiacol glycerol ether.
Use: Cough suppressant.
See: Guaifenesin U.S.P. XXI.

GUAIPHENYL. (Bowman) Guaifenesin 100 mg., phenylephrine HCl 10 mg., chlorpheniramine maleate 1 mg./Tab.
Use: Decongestant, expectorant, antihistaminic.

GUAIPHOTOL. (Foy) Iodine 1/30 gr., calcium cresoate 4 gr./Tab. Bot. 1000s.
Use: Expectorant for use in bronchitis.

• **GUAITHYLLINE.** USAN. 3-(o-Methoxy-phenoxy)-1,2-propanediol w/theophylline.
Use: Antiasthmatic.

GUAMECYCLINE. B.A.N. N-(4-Guanidinoformi-midoyl-piperazin-1-ylmethyl)tetracycline.
Use: Antibiotic.

GUAMIDE.
See: Sulfaguanidine. (Various Mfr.)

• **GUANABENZ.** USAN.[(2,6-Dichlorobenzylidene)-amino] guanidine.
Use: Antihypertensive.
See: Wytensin, Tab. (Wyeth)

• **GUANABENZ ACETATE,** U.S.P. XXI. Tab., U.S.P. XXI.
Use: Antihypertensive.

GUANACLINE. B.A.N. 1-(2-Guanidinoethyl)-1,-2,3,6-tetrahydro-4-picoline.
Use: Hypotensive.

• **GUANADREL SULFATE.** USAN. (1,4-Dioxaspiro[4.5] dec-2-ylmethyl)guanidine sulfate (2:1).
Use: Antihypertensive.
See: Hylorel, Tab. (Pennwalt)

• **GUANABENZ ACETATE.** USAN.
Use: Antihypertensive.

• **GUANCYDINE.** USAN.
Use: Antihypertensive.

GUANETHIDINE. B.A.N. 1-(2-Guanidinoethyl)-azacyclo-octane.
Use: Hypotensive.
See: Ismelin sulfate, Tab. (Ciba)

• **GUANETHIDINE MONOSULFATE,** U.S.P. XXI. Tab., U.S.P. XXI. [2-(Hex-ahydro-1(2H)-azocinyl)-ethyl]-guanidine sulfate (2:1), or [2-(hexahydro-1(2H)-azocinyl)-ethyl] guanidine hydrogen sulfate.
Use: Hypotensive.
W/Hydrochlorothiazide.
See: Esimil, Tab. (Ciba)

• **GUANETHIDINE SULFATE,** U.S.P. XXI. Tab. U.S.P. XXI. Guanidine, 2-(hexahydro-1(2H)-azocinyl)ethyl-, sulfate (2:1). [2-(Hexahydro-1-(2H)-azocinyl)ethyl] guanidine sulfate.
Use: Hypotensive agent.
See: Ismelin, Tab. (Ciba)
W/Hydrochlorothiazide.
See: Esimil, Tab. (Ciba)

• **GUANFACINE HYDROCHLORIDE.** USAN.
Use: Antihypertensive.

GUANIDINE HCl. (Key) Guanidine HCl 125 mg./Tab. Bot. 100s.
Use: Parasympathetic stimulant.

GUANIDINE, [2-(HEXAHYDRO-1(2H)-AXOCINYL)-ETHYL]-, SULFATE (2:1). Guanethidine Sulfate, U.S.P. XXI.

GUANISOQUIN. 7-Bromo- 3,4-dihydro-2-(1H)-isoquinoline carboxamidine Sulfate (2:1).
Use: Antihypertensive agent.

• **GUANISOQUIN SULFATE.** USAN.
Use: Antihypertensive.

GUANOCLOR. B.A.N. [2-(2,6-Dichlorophenoxy)-ethy]aminoguanidine.
Use: Hypotensive.
See: Vatensol sulfate

• **GUANOCLOR SULFATE.** USAN.[[2-(2,6-Di-chloro phenoxy)-ethyl]amino] guanidine sulfate.
Use: Antihypertensive.
See: Vatensol

• **GUANOCTINE HYDROCHLORIDE.** USAN.
Use: Antihypertensive.

• **GUANOXABENZ.** USAN.
Use: Antihypertensive.

GUANOXAN. B.A.N. 2-Guanidinomethyl-1,4-benzodioxan.
Use: Hypotensive.
See: Envacar sulfate

• **GUANOXAN SULFATE.** USAN. (1,4-Benzodioxane-2-ylmethyl)-guanidine sulfate. Envacar.
Use: Antihypertensive.

• **GUANOXYFEN SULFATE.** USAN. (3-Phenoxypropyl guanidine sulfate.
Use: Hypotensive and antidepressant.

GUARDAL. (Morton) Vit. A 10,000 I.U., B-1 20 mg., B-2 8 mg., C 50 mg., niacinamide 10 mg., Ca d-pantothenate 5 mg., Fe 10 mg., dried whole liver 100 mg., yeast 100 mg., choline bitartrate 30 mg., B-6 0.[illegible] mg., B-12 8 mcg., mixed tocopherols 5 mg., dicalcium phosphate anhydrous 150 mg., Mg sulfate dried 7.[illegible] mg., Na 1 mg., pot. chloride 1.3 mg./Tab. Bot. 100s.

GUARDEX. (Archer-Taylor) Tube 4 oz., 1 lb., 4.5 lb.
Use: Protective cream.

• **GUAR GUM,** N.F. XVI.
Use: Pharm. aid (tablet binder; tablet disintegrant).
W/Danthron, docusate sodium.
See: Guarsol, Tab. (Western Research)
W/Docusate sodium, prune conc.
See: D-S-S Compound, Cap. (Wolins)
W/Standardized senna concentrate.
See: Gentlax B, Granules, Tab. (Blair)

GUARSOL TABLETS. (Western Research) Guar gum 300 mg., danthron 50 mg., docusate sodium 100 mg./Tab. 2 Handicount 28 (36 bags of 28).
Use: Bulk laxative, stool softener.

GUAYANESIN.
Use: Cough suppressant.
See: Guaifenesin (Various Mfr.)

GUIAMID AC EXPECTORANT. (Vangard) Guaifenesin 100 mg., codeine phosphate 10 mg./5 ml. Bot. pt., gal.
Use: Cough expectorant, depressant.

GUIAMID DM EXPECTORANT. (Vangard) Guaifenesin 100 mg., dextromethorphan HBr. 15 mg./5 ml. w/alcohol 1.4%. Bot. pt.
Use: Cough expectorant, depressant.

GUIAMID EXPECTORANT. (Vangard) Guaifenesin 100 mg./5 ml. w/alcohol 3.5%: Bot. pt., gal.
Use: Cough expectorant.

GUIAPHED ELIXIR. (Goldline) Guaifenesin, ephedrine sulfate, theophylline, phenobarital. Bot. Pt.
Use: Bronchodilator.

GUIATUSCON. (CMC) Guaifenesin 100 mg./5 cc. Vial.

GUIATUSCON. (CMC) Liq. Bot. 4 oz., pt., gal.

GUIATUSCON A.C. (CMC) Liq. Bot. 4 oz., pt., gal.

GUIATUSCON D.M. (CMC) Syr. Bot. 4 oz., pt., gal.

GUIATUSS A.C. SYRUP. (Goldline) Bot. 4 oz., pt. gal.
Use: Antitussive, expectorant.

GUIATUSS BERTUSS COUGH SYRUP. (Alton) Bot. 4 oz., 8 oz., 16 oz., gal.
Use: Cough relief.

GUIATUSS DAC SYRUP. (Goldline) Bot. Pt.
Use: Antitussive, expectorant.

GUIATUSS DM BERTUSS COUGH SYRUP. (Alton) Bot. 4 oz., 8 oz., 16 oz., gal.
Use: cough relief.

GUIATUSS D.M. SYRUP. (Goldline) Bot. 4 oz., pt., gal.
Use: Antitussive, expectorant.

GUIATUSS SYRUP. (Goldline) Bot. 4 oz., pt., gal.
Use: Antitussive.

GUIDO. (Rocky Mtn.) Camphor 0.025 Gm., guaiacol 0.05 Gm., iodoform 0.01 Gm., eucalyptol 0.04 Gm. Vial 30 cc.
Use: Expectorant.

GUISTREY FORTIS. (Bowman) Guaifenesin 100 mg., phenylephrine HCl 10 mg., chlorpheniramine maleate 1 mg./Tab. Bot. 100s, 1000s.
Use: Cold symptoms.

GULFASIN TABS. (Major) Sulfasoxazole 500 mg./Tab. Bot. 100s.
Use: Antibacterial.

GUM-ZOR. (DeWitt) Lot. Bot. 0.5 oz.

GUNCOTTON, SOLUBLE. Pyroxylin.

GUSTALAC. (Geriatric) Cal. carbonate 300 mg., defatted skim milk pow. 200 mg./Tab. Bot. 100s, 250s, 1000s.
Use: Antacid in the treatment of peptic ulcers.

GUSTASE. (Geriatric) Gerilase (standard amylolytic enzyme) 30 gm., geriprotase (standard proteolytic enzyme) 6 mg., gericellulase (standard cellulolytic enzyme) 2 mg./Tab. Bot. 42s, 100s, 500s.
Use: Digestion.

GUSTASE PLUS. (Geriatric) Phenobarbital 8 mg., homatropine methylbromide 2.5 mg., gerilase 30 mg., geriprotase 6 mg., gericellulase 2 mg./Tab. Bot. 42s, 100s, 500s.
Use: Antispasmodic and a sedative.

GUTTA PERCHA, U.S.P. XXI.
Use: Dental restoration agent.

G VITAMIN.
See: Riboflavin (Various Mfr.)

GLYNAPHEN TABLETS. (Lannett) Phenobarbital 1/8 gr., ext. hyoscyamus 1/10 gr., terpin hydrate 2 gr., guaifenesin 1 gr., calcium lactate 1 gr./Tab. Bot. 1000s.

G-WELL LOTION. (Goldline) Bot. 2 oz., pt.
Use: Scabies treatment.

G-WELL SHAMPOO. (Goldline) Bot. 2 oz., pt, gal.
Use: Pediculosis.

GYN. (Amfre-Grant) Mag. gluconate 0.5 Gm./Tab. Bot. 100s, 1000s.
Use: Antispasmodic in treatment of primary dysmenorrhea.

GYNECORT. (Combe) Hydrocortisone acetate 0.5%. Tube 0.5 oz., 1.0 oz.
Use: Pruritus vulvae.

GYNE-LOTRIMIN VAGINAL CREAM 1%. (Schering) Clotrimazole 50 mg./applicatorful. Tube 45 Gm.
Use: Vulvovaginal candidiasis.

GYNE-LOTRIMIN VAGINAL TABLETS. (Schering) Clotrimazole 100 mg./Tab. Box 7 Tab. w/applicator.
Use: Vulvovaginal candidiasis.

GYNERGON.
See: Estradiol (Various Mfr.)

GYNE-SEC. (Marlyn) Diiodohydroxyquinoline 100 mg., sulfadiazine 500 mg., sorbic acid 5 mg., stilbestrol 0.1 mg., methylbenzethonium chloride 7.5 mg., boric acid 100 mg., sod. lauryl sulfate 5 mg., lactose 300 mg., tartaric acid 5 mg./insert. Box 20s, 50s w/applicator.
Use: Vaginal infections.

GYNLIN. (Tunex) Estrone 2 mg./ml. in aq. susp. Vial 30 cc.
Use: Estrogen deficiency.

GYNLIN R.P. (Tunex) Estrone 2 mg., potassium estrone sulfate 1 mg./ml. in aq. susp. Vial 10cc.
Use: Rapid & prolonged estrogen therapy.

GYNOGEN. (Forest) Estrogenic substance 2 mg./ml. Vial 30 ml.

GYNOGEN L.A. 10. (Forest) Estradiol valerate in sesame oil 10 mg./ml. Vial 10 ml.

GYNOGEN L.A. 20. (Forest) Estradiol valerate in sesame oil 20 mg./ml. Vial 10 ml.

GYNOL II CONTRACEPTIVE JELLY. (Advanced Care) Nonxynol-9 in 2% concentration. Starter (2.85 oz. tube w/applicator) Refill (4.44 oz. tube).
Use: Contraceptive jelly for use with diaphragm.

GYNO-PETRARYL. (Janssen) Econazole nitrate.
Use: Antifungal.

H

HACHIMYCIN. B.A.N. An antibiotic produced by *Streptomyces hachijoensis.*
Use: Antibiotic used in the treatment of trichomoniasis.
See: Trichomycin

HAEMATE P. (Armour) Factor VIII (Human). Packs of 250 I.U., 500 I.U. or 1000 I.U. for Inj.
Use: Hemophilia therapy.

• **HALAZEPAM,** USAN.
Use: Sedative.
See: Paxipam, Tab. (Schering)

• **HALAZONE,** U.S.P. XXI Tab. for Soln., U.S.P. XXI. p-(Dichlorosulfamoyl)benzoic acid. (Abbott) Tab. 4 mg. Bot. 100s.
Use: Disinfectant.

• **HALCINONIDE.** U.S.P. XXI. Cream, Ointment, Topical Sol., U.S.P. XXI. Corticosteroid halcinonide. 21-Chloro-9-fluoro-11,16,17-trihydroxy-pregna-4-ene -3,20-dione, cyclic 16,17 acetal.
Use: Anti-inflammatory.
See: Halciderm Cream (Squibb)
Halog Cream Oint., Sol. (Squibb)

HALCION. (Upjohn) Triazolam 0.25 mg. or 0.5 mg./Tab. Bot. 100s. Unit dose 100s.
Use: Hypnotic for insomnia.

HALDOL. (McNeil Pharm) Haloperidol. **Tab.:** 0.5 mg., 1 mg., 2 mg./Tab. Bot. 100s, 1000s. 5 mg., 10 mg. Bot. 100s, 1000s. 20 mg. Bot. 100s. Blister Pack 10×10s in all sizes.**Conc. Soln.:** 2 mg./cc. Bot. 15 cc. 120 cc. **Inject.:** (w/methylparaben 1.8 mg. propylparaben 0.2 mg., lactic acid) ampul 5 mg./cc. Box 10×1 ml. & multidose vial of 10 ml. Prefilled Syringe 10×1 ml.
Use: Antipsychotic.

HALDRONE. (Lilly) Paramethasone acetate 1 mg./Tab. Bot. 100s. 2 mg./Tab. Bot. 100s.
Use: Steroid therapy, anti-inflammatory agent.

HALENOL. (Blue Cross) Acetaminophen 325 mg./Tab. Bot. 100s.
Use: Analgesic.

HALENOL ELIXIR. (Blue Cross) Acetaminophen 120 mg./5 ml. w/alcohol 7%. Bot. 4 oz.
Use: Analgesic for children.

HALENOL EXTRA STRENGTH CAPSULES. (Blue Cross) Acetaminophen 500 mg./Cap. Bot. 100s.
Use: Analgesic, antipyretic

HALENOL EXTRA STRENGTH TABLETS. (Blue Cross) Acetaminophen 500 mg./Tab. Bot. 100s.
Use: Analgesic, antipyretic

HALETHAZOLE. B.A.N. 5-Chloro-2-[4-(2-diethyl-amino-ethoxy)phenyl]benzothiazole.
Use: Antifungal agent.
See: Episol

HALEY'S M-O. (Winthrop Consumer Products) Mineral oil (25%) & milk of magnesia in emulsion base. Bot. 8 oz., 1 pt., 1 qt. Flavored and regular.
Use: Laxative.

HALFORT-T. (Blue Cross) Vit. C 300 mg., B-1 15 mg., B-2 10 mg., Niacin 100 mg., B-6 5 mg., B-12 4 mcg., pantothenic acid 20 mg./Tab. Bot. 100s.
Use: Vitamin supplement.

HALI-BEST. (Barth's) Vit. A 10,000 I.U., D 400 I.U./Cap. Bot. 100s, 500s.

HALIBUT LIVER OIL.
Use: Vitamin A & D deficiencies.

HALIVER OIL.
See: Halibut Liver Oil (Various Mfr.)

HALIVER OIL WITH VIOSTEROL.
See: Halibut Liver Oil with Viosterol

HALLS MENTHO-LYPTUS DECONGESTANT COUGH FORMULA. (Warner-Lambert) Dextromethorphan HBr 15 mg., phenylpropanolamine HCl 37.5 mg., menthol 14 mg., eucalyptus oil 12.7 mg./10 ml. w/alcohol 22%. Bot. 3 oz. 6 oz.
Use: Antitussive, decongestant.

HALL'S MENTHO-LYPTUS COUGH TABLETS. (Warner-Lambert) Menthol and eucalyptus oil in varying amounts. Regular, honey-lemon, cherry flavor and ice blue. Stick-Pack 9s. Bags 30s.
Use: Antitussive.

HALODRIN. (Upjohn) Fluoxymesterone 1 mg., ethinyl estradiol 0.02 mg./Tab. Bot. 100s.
Use: Androgen-estrogen therapy.

• **HALOFANTRINE HYDROCHLORIDE.** USAN.
Use: Antimalarial.

• **HALOFENATE.** USAN. 2-Acetamidoethyl (4-chlorophenyl) (3-trifluoromethylphenoxy)-acetate.
Use: Hypolipemic agent.
See: Livipas (Merck Sharp & Dohme).

HALOFUGINONE. B.A.N.DL-trans-7-Bromo-6-chloro-3-[3-(3-hydroxy-2-piperidyl)-2-acetonyl]-quinazolin-4-one.
Use: Antiprotozoan, veterinary medicine.

• **HALOFUGINONE HYDROBROMIDE.** USAN.
Use: Anti-protozoal.

HALOGAN. (Blue Cross) Chloroxylenol, acetic acid, glycerin, benzalkonium Cl. Ear drops Bot. 0.5 oz.
Use: Remove ear wax.

HALOG CREAM. (Squibb) Halcinonide 0.025% and 0.1%, in specially formulated cream base consisting of glyceryl monostearate, cetyl alcohol, myristyl stearate, isopropyl palmitate, polysorbate 60, propylene glycol and purified water. Tube 15 Gm., 30 Gm., 60 Gm., Jar 240 Gm.
Use: Topical corticosteroid therapy.

HALOG E CREAM. (Squibb) Halcinonide 0.1 mg. in hydrophylic vanishing cream base consisting of propylene glycol dimethicone 350, castor oil, cetearyl alcohol, ceteareth-20, propylene glycol stearate, white petrolatum, water. Tubes 15, 30, 60 Gm.
Use: Topical corticosteroid therapy.

HALOG OINTMENT. (Squibb) Halcinonide 0.1%, in Plastibase (plasicized hydrocarbon gel), PEG 400, PEG 6000 distearate, PEG 300, PEG 1540, and butylated hydroxy toluene. Tube 15 Gm., 30 Gm., 60 Gm., Jar 240 Gm.
Use: Anti-infammatory, antipruritic, vasoconstrictor.

HALOG SOLUTION. (Squibb) Halcinonide 0.1 mg./ml. w/edetate disodium, PEG 300, purified water and butylated hydroxy toluene as preservative. Bot. 20 ml., 60 ml.
Use: Topical corticosteroid therapy.

• **HALOPEMIDE.** USAN.
Use: Antipsychotic.

HALOPENIUM CHLORIDE. B.A.N. 4-Bromo-benzyl-3-(4-chloro-2-isopropyl-5-methyl-phenoxy)-propyldimethylammonium chloride.
Use: Antiseptic.

• **HALOPERIDOL,** U.S.P. XXI. Tab., Inj., Oral Soln. U.S.P. XXI. 4[-4-p-Chlorophenyl-4-hydroxy-piperidino]-4′-fluorobutyrophenone. Serenace Sol.
Use: Antipsychotic, tranquilizer.
See: Haldol, Tab., Conc., Inj. (McNeil)

• **HALOPERIDOL DECANOATE.** USAN.
Use: Antipsychotic.

• **HALOPREDONE ACETATE.** USAN.
Use: Anti-inflammatory.

HALOPROGESTERONE. USAN. 6α-Fluoro-17α-bromo-progesterone.
Use: Progestin.

HALOPROGIN, U.S.P. XXI. Cream, Top. Soln., U.S.P. XXI. 3-Iodo-2-propynyl-2, 4, 5-trichlorophenyl ether. Under study.
Use: Antimicrobic.
See: Halotex, Cream & Sol. (Westwood)

HALOPYRAMINE. B.A.N. 2-(4-Chloro-N-2-pyridylbenzylamino)ethyldimethylamine. Chloropyramine (I.N.N.)
Use: Antihistamine.
See: Synopen hydrochloride

HALORTON. (Vita Elixir) **#1** chlorprophenpridamine 4 mg./Time Rel. Cap; **#2** chlorprophenpridamine 8 mg./Timed Rel. Cap.; **#3** chlorprophenpridamine 12 mg./Timed Rel. Cap.
Use: Antihistaminic.

HALOTESTIN. (Upjohn) Fluoxymesterone, 2 mg./Tab. Bot. 100s; 5 mg./Tab. Bot. 100s; 10 mg./Tab. Bot. 100s. Unit-of-Use Bot. 30s.
Use: Androgenic and anabolic agent.
W/Ethinyl estradiol.
See: Halodrin, Tab. (Upjohn)

HALOTEX CREAM. (Westwood) Haloprogin 1% in water dispersible, base composed of PEG-400, PEG-4000, diethyl sebacate, polyvinylpyrrolidone. Tube 15 Gm., 30 Gm.
Use: Treatment of superficial fungal infections of the skin.

HALOTEX SOLUTION. (Westwood) Haloprogin 1% in a vehicle of diethyl sebacate w/alcohol 75%. Bot. 10 ml., 30 ml.
Use: Treatment of superficial fungal infections of the skin.

HALOTHANE, U.S.P. XXI. 2-Bromo-2-chloro-1-1,1-trifluoroethane. Fluothane.
Use: General anesthetic (inhalation).
See: Fluothane, Liq. (Ayerst)
Halothane, 250 ml. Liquid (Abbott)

HALOTUSSIN. (Blue Cross) Guaifenesin 100 mg./5 ml. Bot. 4 oz.
Use: Expectorant.

HALOTUSSIN-DM. (Blue Cross) Guaifenesin 100 mg., dextromethorphan HBr 15 mg./5 ml.
Use: Expectorant, cough suppressant.

HALOXON. B.A.N. Bis(2-chloroethyl)3-chloro-4-methylcoumarin-7-yl-phosphate.
Use: Anthelmintic, veterinary medicine.
See: Loxon

HALQUINOL. B.A.N. A mixture of the chlorinated products of 8-hydroxyquinoline containing about 65 per cent of 5,7-dichloro-8-hydroxyquinoline.
Use: Anti-infective.
See: Quixalin

HALQUINOLS. USAN. 5, 7-Dichloro-8-quinolinol; 5-chloro-8-quinolinol and 7-chloro-8-quinolinol in proportions resulting naturally from chlorination of 8-quinolinol. Trade mark, Quinolor (active ingredient of) & Tarquinor.
Use: Topical antimicrobial.

HAMA. Hydroxy-aluminum magnesium aminoacetate.

• **HAMYCIN.** USAN.
Use: Antifungal.

HANDORA CREAM. (Torch) Greaseless, water-washable cream, fatty alcohol glycerine, natural fatty acid in hydrophillic base.
Use: Restore & maintain normal skin tone when exposed to irritants.

HANG-OVER-CURE. (Silvers) Calcium carbonate, glycine, thiamine HCl, pyridoxine HCl, aspirin. Cont. 6 Tab.
Use: Hangover treatment.

HANIFORM. (Hanlon) Vit. A 25,000 I.U., D 1,000 I.U., B-1 10 mg., B-2 5 mg., C 150 mg., niacinamide 150 mg./Cap. Bot. 100s.
Use: Dietary supplement.

HANIPLEX. (Hanlon) Vit. B-1 20 mg., B-2 10 mg., B-6 1 mg., Ca pantothenate 10 mg., B-12 5 mcg., niacin 20 mg., liver conc. 50 mg., Vit. C 150 mg./Cap. Bot. 100s.
Use: Dietary supplement.

■ **HANSEN'S DISEASE.** Leprosy.
See: Diasone, Sod., Tab. (Abbott)
Ethyl Chaulmoograte (Various Mfr.)
Isoniazid (Various Mfr.)

HAPONAL. (Jenkins) Atropine sulfate 0.96 mg., hyoscine HBr 0.02 mg., hyoscyamine sulfate 0.30 mg., phenobarbital 50 mg./Cap. Bot. 1000s.
Use: Antispasmodic.

HAPONAL. (Kenyon) Atropine sulfate 0.0195 mg., hyoscine HBr 0.0065 mg., hyoscyamine sulfate 0.1040 mg., phenobarbital 0.25 gr./Tab. Bot. 100s, 1000s.
Use: Antispasmodic.

HARBOLIN. (Arcum) Hydralazine HCl 25 mg., hydrochlorothiazide 15 mg., reserpine 0.1 mg./Tab. Bot. 100s, 1000s.

HARCYTE. (Harvey) Estradiol benzoate 2.5 mg., progesterone 25 mg./cc. sesame oil. Vial 10 cc.

HARMAR. (Zemmer) Propoxyphene HCl 65 mg./Cap. Bot. 500s.

HARMONYL. (Abbott) Deserpidine 0.25 mg./Tab. Bot. 100s, 1000s.
Use: Treatment of hypertension.

HARTSHORN. Ammonium Carbonate

HARVADEN. (Harvey) Adenosine-5-monophosphoric acid 25 mg., Vit. B-12 60 mcg./cc. Vial 10 cc.
Use: I.M., neuritis and pruritus.
W/Phenobarbital. (Durst) Atropine methyl nitrate 1/60 gr., phenobarbital 0.25 gr./Tab. Bot. 100s, 1000s, 5000s.
Use: Antispasmodic with sedative.

HARVATROPIN. (Harvey) Chorionic gonadotropin 1000 I.U./cc. when diluted. Vial 10 cc., w/diluent.
Use: Treatment of cryptorchidism.

HAUGASE. (Madland) Trypsin, chymotrypsin. Bot. 50s, 250s.
Use: Enzyme therapy.

HAUTOSONE. (Fellows) Hydrocortisone 0.5% in Triusol (three polyols) 15 Gm. Box 6s.

HAVAB. (Abbott) Test kits 100s.
Use: Radioimmunoassay or enzyme immunoassay for detection of antibody to hepatitis A virus.

HAVAB-M. (Abbott) Test kits 100s. Uses radioimmunoassay or enzyme immunoassay for the detection of specific IgM antibody to hepatitis A virus in human serum or plasma.

HAYNON. Chlorpheniramine, B.A.N.

HAZOGEL BODY AND FOOT RUB. (Nortech) Witch hazel 70%, isopropanol 20% in a neutralized resin vehicle. Bot. 4 oz.
Use: Relief of topical itching; soothing body and foot rub.

H-BIG HEPATITIS B IMMUNE GLOBULIN (HUMAN). (Abbott) Hepatitis B immune globulin (human) Vials 4, 5 ml.
Use: Immune globulin.

HC DERMA-PAX. (Recsei) Hydrocortisone 0.5% in liquid base. Dropper Bot. 2 oz.
Use: Treatment of poison oak, poison ivy, insect bites, cold sores.

HC-FORM. (Recsei) Hydrocortisone 1%, clioquinol 3%, chlorobutanol 1%. Jelly 0.5 oz., 1 oz., 1 lb.
Use: Contact and atopic dermatitis.

HC-JEL. (Recsei) Hydrocortisone 1%, chlorobutanol 1%. Jelly 0.5 oz., 1 oz., 1 lb.
Use: Dermatitis, pruritus.

H-CORT. (Torch) Hydrocortisone micronized powder. Bot. 5 Gm., 10 Gm., 100 Gm.
Use: Extemporaneous prescription compounding.

HCV CREME. (Saron) Hydrocortisone alcohol 1%, clioquinol 3%. Tube 15 Gm., 45 Gm.
Use: Antibacterial, anti-inflammatory.

HEAD & CHEST CAPSULES. (Procter & Gamble) Phenylpropanolamine HCl 25 mg., guaifenesin 200 mg./Cap. Pkg. 12s, 24s.
Use: Decongestant/expectorant cold medicine.

HEAD & CHEST LIQUID. (Procter & Gamble) Phenylpropanolamine HCl 12.5 mg., guaifenesin 100 mg./5 ml. w/alcohol 5%. Bot. 4 oz., 8 oz.
Use: Decongestant, expectorant cold medicine.

HEAD & CHEST TABLETS. (Procter & Gamble) Phenylpropanolamine HCl 25 mg., guaifenesin 200 mg./Tab. Pkg. 18s, 36s.
Use: Decongestant, expectorant cold medicine.

HEAD & SHOULDERS. (Procter & Gamble) Zinc pyrithione 1% in cream or lotion detergent shampoo. **Cream** Tube 2.5 oz., 4 oz., 7 oz. **Lotion** 4 oz., 7 oz., 11 oz., 15 oz.
Use: Dandruff treatment and seborrheic dermatitis of the scalp.

HEALON. (Pharmacia) Sodium hyaluronate 10 mg./ml. Syringes 0.4, 0.75, or 2.0 ml.
Use: Surgical aid in cataract extraction, IOL implantation, corneal transplant, glaucoma filtration, retinal attachment surgery.

HEART MUSCLE DEPRESSANT.
See: Pronestyl HCl, Cap., Vial (Squibb)

HEART MUSCLE EXTRACTS, Adenosine-5-Monophosphate sodium.

HEATROL. (Cross) Sodium Cl., potassium Cl, calcium phosphate, Mg. carbonate. Safety pks. 1000s. Medipaks 200s. Aidpaks 100s. Dispensers 350s.
Use: Replacement of electrolytes lost from perspiration.

HEAVY METAL POISONING, ANTIDOTE.
See: BAL., Amp. (Hynson, Westcott & Dunning)
Calcium Disodium Versenate, Amp., Tab. (Riker)

HEB CREAM BASE. (Barnes-Hind) Washable, hypoallergenic, odorless base. Jar 1 lb.
Use: For the incorporation of many of the medicinals used in dermatology.

HEDAQUINIUM CHLORIDE. B.A.N.
Hexadecamethylenedi-(2-isoquinolinium chloride).
Use: Antifungal agent.
See: Teoquil

HEDEX CAPLETS. (Winthrop Products) Paracetamol
Use: Analgesic.

HEET LINAMENT. (Whitehall) Methyl salicylate 15%, camphor 3.6%, oloeoresin capsicum 0.025%, alcohol 70%. Bot. 2⅓ oz., 5 oz.
Use: External analgesic.

• **HEFILCON A.** USAN.
Use: Contact lens material.

• **HELFILCON B.** USAN.
Use: Contact lens material.

HEISKELL'S OINTMENT. (Guild) Pkg. 1 oz.

HEISKELL'S SKIN SOAP. (Guild) Cake 3.5 oz., 5 oz

• **HELIUM,** U.S.P. XXI.
Use: Diluent for gases.

HELMATAC. Parbendazole, B.A.N.

HEMABEX. (Barry-Martin) Vit. B-1 40 mg., B-2 16 mg., B-6 1 mg., niacinamide 20 mg., B-12 18 mcg., Ca pantothenate 10 mg., inositol 50 mg., ferric ammonium citrate 720 mg., choline dihydrogen citrate 150 mg./Fl. oz. Bot. pt., gal.
Use: Vit. B complex.

HEMA-CHEK. (Ames) Fecal occult blood test containing slide tests, developer and applicators. Pkg. 100s, 300s, 1000s.
Use: Fecal occult blood test.

HEMA-C META-KAPS. (Sutliff & Case) Ferrous fumarate 300 mg. (100 mg. iron), ascorbic acid 200 mg./long acting Granucap. Bot. 100s, 1000s.

HEMA-COMBISTIX REAGENT STRIPS. (Ames) Four way strip test of urinary pH, glucose, protein and occult blood. Strips. Bot. 100s.

HEMAFATE T.D. CAPSULES. (Knight) Bot. 60s.
Use: Sustained-action hematinic.

HEMAFERRIN TABLETS. (Western Research) Ferrous fumarate 150 mg., desiccated liver 50 mg. docusate sodium 25 mg., betaine HCl 100 mg., folic acid 0.4 mg., Vit. C 50 mg., B-6 2 mg., manganese 2 mg., B-12 5 mcg., copper 1 mg., zinc 2 mg., molybdenum 0.4 mg./Tab. 28 Pack 1000s.
Use: Non-constipating hematinic.

HEMAFOLATE. (Canright) Ferrous gluconate 293 mg., liver fraction II 250 mg., gastric sub. 100 mg., Vit. C 50 mg., B-12 10 mcg./Tab. Bot. 100s, 1000s.
Use: Hematinic agent.

HEMA-FORTE. (Stayner) Vit. B-1 5 mg., B-2 5 mg., B-6 1 mg., Ca pantothenate 2 mg., niacinamide 25 mg., liver desiccated 300 mg., iron 25 mg., inositol 25 mg., choline bitartrate 25 mg., B-12 5 mcg., C 5 mg./Tab. Bot. 100s, 1000s.
Use: B vitamin-iron supplement.

MAGLO. (Seatrace) Cyanocobalamin 15 mcg./ml. 'ial 30 cc.

MOGLOBIN REAGENT STRIPS. (Ames) Seralyzer eagent strips. Bot. 50s.
Jse: A quantitive strip test for hemoglobin in whole lood.

MALIVE LIQUID. (Barth's) Vit. B-1 3.15 mg., B-2 .33 mg., niacin 22.5 mg., B-6 0.81 mg., B-12 6 mcg., iotin 3.6 mcg., iron 60 mg., choline, inositol, liver raction No. 1, pantothenic acid./15 cc. Bot. 8 oz., !4 oz.
Jse: Iron and vitamin supplement.

MALIVE TABLETS. (Barth's) Vit. B-12 25 mcg., iron 75 mg., B-1 2.5 mg., B-2 5 mg., niacin 1.4 mg., C 30 ng., liver 240 mg., B-6, pantothenic acid, aminobenzoic acid, choline, inositol, biotin, Mg, Mn, Cu/3 Tab. Bot. 100s, 500s, 1000s.
Jse: Iron and vitamin supplement.

MANEED. (Hanlon) Hematinic B-12, intrinsic factor, ron/Cap. Bot. 100s.

IEMAPOIETIC AGENTS.
See: Iron products
Lipotropic Preparations
Liver Products
Vitamins

MASPAN. (Bock) Ferrous fumarate 330 mg., Vit. C 200 mg., docusate sodium 20 mg./Tab. Bot. 100s, 1000s.
Use: Anemia treatment.

MASTIX REAGENT STRIPS. (Ames) A cellulose strip, impregnated with a peroxide and orthotolidine. Bot. 50s.
Use: Detection hematuria and hemoglobinuria.

MAT. (Kenyon) Iron 57.4 mg., Vit. B-1 3 mg., B-2 2 mg., B-12 1 mcg., niacinamide 5 mg., liver desic. 2 gr., stomach substance 50 mg./Tab. Bot. 100s, 1000s.
Use: Hematinic.

MATEST REAGENT STRIPS. (Ames) Strontium peroxide, o-Tolidin, tartaric acid & Cal. acetate. Tab. Bot. 100s.
Use: Diagnostic aid for the test of blood in the feces.

MATINIC. (Canright) Ferrous gluconate 180 mg., liver desic. 200 mg., Vit. B-12 1 mcg., copper gluconate 0.3 mg., Vit. C 25 mg., B-1 3.3 mg./Tab. Bot. 100s, 1000s.
Use: Anemias.

MATINIC CAPSULES. (Robinson) Vit. B-1 1 mg., B-2 2 mg., iron 40 mg., Vit. B-12 1 mcg., liver desic. 200 mg./Cap. Bot. 100s, 1000s.

HEMATINICS.
See: Iron Products
Ferric Compounds
Ferrous Compounds
Liver Products
Vitamin B-12
Vitamin Products

EMATRAN. (Hauck) Iron dextran 50 mg./ml. Bot 10 ml.
Use: Hematinic.

EMATRIN. (Towne) Iron 50 mg., Vit. B-12 10 mcg., copper 2 mg., B-1 10 mg., B-2 10 mg., B-6 2 mg., C 150 mg., niacinamide 50 mg., calcium pantothenate 5 mg., liver desic. 200 mg./Captab. Bot. 60s, 100s.
Use: Hematinic.

HEMATRIN NO. 1. (Kenyon) Ferrous sulfate ex. 200 mg., desic. liver N.F. 200 mg., stomach substance 100 mg., C 50 mg., folic acid 1 mg., B-12 w/intrinsic factor conc. 0.25 I.U., B-12 N.F. (from cobalamin conc.) 6.26 mcg./Tab. Bot. 1000s.
Use: Hematinic.

HEMATRIN NO. 2. (Kenyon) Intrinsic factor w/Vit. B-12 0.5 I.U., liver stomach conc. 175 mg., Vit. B-12 conc. 10 mcg., folic acid 0.2 mg., ferrous sulfate exsic. 400 mg., Vit. C 75 mg./Cap. Bot. 100s, 1000s.
Use: Hematinic.

HEMET OINTMENT. (Blue Cross) Zinc oxide 5%, diperodon HCl 0.25%, bismuth subcarbonate 0.2%, pyrilamine maleate 0.1%, phenylephrine HCl 0.25% in petroleum base. Tube 1.5 oz.
Use: Rectal anesthetic.

HEMET SUPPOSITORIES. (Blue Cross) Bismuth subgallate, zinc oxide, boric acid, bismuth resorcin comp., balsam, benzocaine/Supp. Box. 12s.
Use: Hemorrhoid treatment.

HEMEX. (Vogarell) Ointment Tube 1.25 oz., Suppositories Box 12s.
Use: Relief of piles and minor rectal irritations.

HEMISINE.
See: Epinephrine (Various Mfr.)

HEMISUCCINOXYPREGNENOLONE, DELTA-5-Panzalone.

HEMOCAINE. (Mallard) Benzocaine 1%, phenol 1%, tannic acid 3%, thymol iodide 1%, ephedrine HCl 0.15%, zinc oxide 10%, peru balsam 2%. Jar 1 oz., 1 lb.
Use: Relief of itching and irritation from hemorrhoids.

HEMOCYTE. (U.S. Chemical) Ferrous fumarate 324 mg./Tab. Bot. 100s. Vial 10 cc.
Use: Anemia.

HEMOCYTE-F. (U.S. Chemical) Ferrous fumarate 325 mg., folic acid 1 mg./Tab.
Use: Hematinic, anti-anemic.

HEMOCYTE PLUS. (U.S. Chemical) Ferrous fumarate 324 mg., sodium ascorbate 200 mg., Vit. B-1 10 mg., B-2 6 mg., B-6 5 mg., B-12 15 mcg., Folic acid 1 mg., niacinamide 30 mg. Ca pantothenate 10 mg., Zn sulfate 80 mg., Mg sulfate 70 mg., Mn sulfate 4 mg., Cu sulfate 2 mg./Tabule. Bot. 100s.
Use: Anemia treatment.

HEMOFIL. (Hyland) Antihemophilic factor (human), method four, dried, concentrated. Vial W/Diluent. 10 ml., 30 ml.
Use: Antihemophilia therapy.

HEMOFIL T. (Hyland) Antihemophilia Factor (Human), method four, dried, heat-treated 225–375 IU/10 ml.; 450–650 IU/20 ml.; 675–999 IU/30 ml.; 1000–1600 IU/30 ml.
Use: Treatment of Hemophilia A, for prevention & control of hemorrhagic episodes.

HEMOFORM. (Spanner) Iron, arsenic, Cu. Ampul 10 cc. 100s.

HEMOGEST. (Mills) Betaine HCl 50 mg., ferrous fumarate 100 mg., folic acid 0.05 mg., zinc gluconate 5 mg., copper gluconate 10 mg., manganese gluconate 5 mg., Vit. B-1 1 mg., B-2 1 mg., B-6 0.5 mg., Vit. B-12 1 mcg., niacinamide 10 mg./Tab. Bot. 100s.
Use: Hematinic.

HEMORRHOIDAL UNISERTS. (Upsher-Smith) Bismuth subgallate 2.25%, bismuth resorcin compound 1.75%, benzyl benzoate 1.2%, peruvian balsam 1.8%, zinc oxide 11%/Suppos. Cartons 12s, 50s.
Use: Treatment of hemorrhoids.

HEMORRHOIDAL-HC UNISERTS. (Upsher-Smith) Hydrocortisone acetate 10 mg., bismuth subgallate 2.25%, bismuth resorcin compound 1.75%, benzyl benzoate 1.2%, peruvian balsam 1.8%, zinc oxide 11%/Suppos. Cartons 12s, 50s.
Use: Treatment of hemorrhoids.

HEMOSTATICS, LOCAL.
See: Absorbable Gelatin Sponge (Upjohn)
Gelfilm (Upjohn)
Gelfoam, Preps. (Upjohn)
Oxidized Cellulose
Thrombin (Various Mfr.)

■ **HEMOSTATICS, SYSTEMIC.**
See: Adrenosem Salicylate, Prep. (Beecham-Massengill)
Aquamephyton, Inj. (Merck Sharp & Dohme)
Carbazochrome Salicylate
Mephyton, Tab. (Merck Sharp & Dohme)

HEMOSTATIN.
See: Epinephrine (Various Mfr.)

HEMO-VITE. (Drug Industries) Ferrous fumarate 240 mg., Cu sulfate 1 mg., C 150 mg., B-1 5 mg., B-2 5 mg., B-6 1 mg., Ca pantothenate 10 mg., niacinamide 50 mg., folic acid 0.2 mg., intrinsic factor, B-12 0.5 I.U./Tab. Bot. 100s, 500s. Liq. Bot. pt.
Use: Vitamin supplement to treat anemias.

HEMOVITE LIQUID. (Drug Industries) Vit. B-12 crystallin 8.34 mcg., B-6 2.0 mg., ferric pyrophosphate soluble 100 mg., folic acid 0.25 mg., niacinamide 13.3 mg./5cc. Bot. 473cc
Use: Vitamin supplement to treat anemias.

HEMOZYME ELIXIR. (Barrows) Vit. B-1 5 mg., B-2 5 mg., B-6 1 mg., panthenol 4 mg., niacinamide 100 mg., B-12 3 mcg., iron 100 mg., choline bitartrate 100 mg., dl-methionine 100 mg., yeast extract and alcohol 12%/fl. oz. Bot. 12 oz.
Use: Iron tonic.

HENBANE.
See: Hyoscyamus (Various Mfr.)

HENYDIN-M. (Arcum) Thyroid desic. powd. 0.5 gr., B-1 1 mg., B-2 0.5 mg., B-6 0.5 mg., niacinamide 2.5 mg./Tab. Bot. 100s, 1000s.

HENYDIN-R. (Arcum) Thyroid desic. powd. 1 gr., B-1 2 mg., B-2 1 mg., B-6 1 mg., niacinamide 5 mg./Tab. Bot. 100s, 1000s.

HEPAHYDRIN, Tab. (Comatic) Dehydrocholic acid 3.75 Gm./Tab. Bot. 100s.

HEPANE-LS EXTRA. (Kenyon) Vit. B-12 activity 40 mcg./cc. Vial 10 cc.

■ **HEPARIN ANTAGONIST.**
See: Protamine Sulfate (Various Mfr.)

HEPARIN CALCIUM.
Use: Anticoagulant
See: Calciparine, Inj. (American Critical Care)

HEPARIN LOCK FLUSH SOLUTION. (Winthrop-Bre[illegible] 10 USP Units/1 ml. in 2 ml. cartridge or 100 USP Units/1 ml. in 2 ml. cartridge. Carpuject.
Use: Maintain patency of indwelling venipuncture device.

HEPARIN LOCK FLUSH SOLUTION. (Wyeth) Heparin sodium 10 u. or 100 u./1 ml. vial. Pkg. 5[illegible] Tubex 1 ml., 2 ml.
Use: Clearing intermittent infusion sets.

• **HEPARIN SODIUM,** U.S.P. XXI. Inj., Lock Flush Sol., U.S.P. XXI. (Upjohn) 1,000 Units/ml. Vial 10 ml., 30 ml. 5,000 Units/ml. Vial 1 ml., 10 ml. 10,0[illegible] Units/ml. Vial 1 ml., 4 ml. (Winthrop) 5,000 USP Units/1 ml. Carpuject 1 ml. fill in 2 ml. cartridge.
Use: I.M., I.V. or S.C., anticoagulant in prevention treatment of thrombosis or embolism. Note: Protamine sulfate is antidote.
See: Hepathrom, Amp., Vial (Fellows-Testagar)
Heprinar, Inj. (Armour)
Lipo-Hepin, Amp., Vial (Riker)
Lipo-Hepin/BL, Amp., Vial (Riker)
Liquaemin, Vial (Organon)
W/Choline chloride, Vit. B-12, folic acid & niacinami[illegible]
Hep-Plex, Vial (Kenyon)
W/Vit. B-12, folic acid, niacinamide, choline chloride.
See: Heparin-B, Vial (Medical Chem.)

• **HEPARIN CALCIUM,** U.S.P. XXI. Inj., U.S.P. XXI.
Use: Anticoagulant.

HEPATHROM. (Fellows) Heparin sodium. 1000 u. equals 10 mg. supplied: (1000 u./cc.) Vials Amp.1 cc., 10 cc., 30 cc. (5000 u./cc.) Amp. 1 cc., Vials 10 cc. (10,000 u./cc.) Amps. 1 cc., Vial 4 cc., 10 cc. (20,000 u./cc.) Vial 1 cc., 4, 5 & 10 cc. (40,00[illegible] u./cc.) Vials 1, 4 & 10 cc.

• **HEPATITIS B IMMUNE GLOBULIN,** U.S.P. XXI.
Use: Passive immunizing agent.
See: Hep-B-Gammagee, Inj. (Merck Sharp & Dohm[illegible]

• **HEPATITIS B VIRUS VACCINE INACTIVATED,** U.S.P. XXI.
Use: Active immunizing agent.
See: Heptavax-B (Merck Sharp & Dohme)

HEP-B-GAMMAGEE. (Merck Sharp & Dohme) Hepatit[illegible] B Immune Globulin. Vial 5 ml.
Use: Post exposure prophylaxis for those exposed to HBsAg positive materials.

HEPFOMIN R INJECTION. (Keene) Liver inj. equiv. t[illegible] Cyanocobalamin 10 mcg., folic acid 0.4 mg., cyanocobalamine 100 mcg., niacinamide 75 mg. Vial 10 ml.

HEP-FORTE. (Marlyn) Bot. 100s, 500s.
Use: Vitamin-liver dietary supplement.

HEPICEBRIN. (Lilly) Vit. B-1 2 mg., Vit. B-2 3 mg., ascorbic acid 75 mg., niacinamide 20 mg., Vit. A 5000 I.U., D 400 I.U./Tab. Pkg. 100s. Blister pkg. 10 × 10s.
Use: Vitamin deficiencies.

P-PLEX. (Kenyon) Heparin sod. 2500 u., Vit. B-12 50 mcg., choline Cl 100 mg., folic acid 2 mg., niacinamide 50 mg. in isotonic saline/cc. Vial 10 cc.

PROFAX.
See: Mucoplex (Stuart)

PTABARBITONE. B.A.N. 5-(Cyclohept-1-enyl)-5-ethylbarbituric acid.
Use: Hypnotic; sedative.
See: Medomin

PATAMINE. (American McGaw) Amino acid injection 8%. Bot. 500 ml.
Use: Nutritional support for liver diseased patients.

PTAMINOL. B.A.N. 6-Amino-2-methylheptan-2-ol.
Use: Coronary vasodilator.

HEPTANONE,6-DIMETHYLAMINO-4,4-DIPHENYL-HYDROCHLORIDE. Methadone Hydrochloride, U.S.P. XXI.

PATIC-AID. (American McGaw) Instant drinks & puddings.
Use: For hepatic disease patients.

P-LOCK. (Elkins-Sinn) Sterile heparin sodium solution in saline 10 U. or 100 U. Dosette 1 ml., 2 ml. Multiple dose vial 10 ml., 30 ml.
Use: Maintenance of patency of heparin lock catheters.

P-LOCK PF. (Elkins-Sinn) Preservative-free heparin flush sol. 10 U./ml. or 100 U./ml. Vial 1 ml.
Use: Maintenance of patency of heparin lock catheters.

PTAVAX-B. (Merck Sharp & Dohme) Hepatitis B vaccine. Vial 3 ml.
Use: Immunization against hepatitis B.

PTO. (Zenith) Meprobamate 150 mg., ethoheptazine citrate 75 mg., aspirin 250 mg./Tab.
Use: Relief of pain accompanied by anxiety and tension.

PTO-M. (Zenith) Meprobamate 200 mg., aspirin 325 mg./Tab. Bot. 50s
Use: Short term treatment of pain with anxiety.

PTUNA PLUS. (Roerig) B-1 3.1 mg., B-2 2 mg., B-6 1.6 mg., niacinamide 15 mg., calcium pantothenate 0.9 mg., B-12 5 mcg., with intrinsic factor conc. 25 mg., C 150 mg., liver des. 50 mg., ferrous sulfate, dried 311 mg., copper 1 mg., molybdenum 0.2 mg., calcium 37.4 mg., iodine 0.05 mg., manganese 0.033 mg., magnesium 2 mg., phosphorus 29 mg., potassium 1.7 mg./Cap. Bot. 100s.
Use: Fortified oral hematopoietic formulation.

EROIN. Forbidden in U.S.A. by Federal statute because of its addiction-causing nature.
See: Diacetylmorphine.

ERPECIN-L. (Campbell) Pyridoxine HCl, allantoin, octyl p-(dimethylamino)-benzoate (Padimate O), titanium dioxide in a balanced, acidic lipid system. Tube 2.5 Gm.
Use: Cold sore lip balm.

ERPLEX LIQUIFILM. (Allergan) Idoxuridine 0.1%, polyvinyl alcohol 1.4%. Plast. Bot. w/dropper 15 ml.
Use: Treatment of keratisis caused by herpes simplex virus.

HESACORB. (Jenkins) Citrus bioflavonoids comp. 100 mg., C 100 mg./Cap. Bot. 1000s.

HES-BIC. (Kenyon) Hesperidin purified 100 mg., ascorbic acid 100 mg./Cap. Hesperidin purified 200 mg., ascorbic acid 200 mg./Tab. Bot. 100s, 1000s.
Use: Hemorrhage and capillary fragility.

HESPAN INJECTION. (American Critical Care) Hetastarch 6.0 Gm., sodium chloride 0.90 Gm./100 ml. w/water for injection. Bot. 500 ml.
Use: Plasma volume expander.

HESPER BITABS. (Merrell Dow) Hesperidin complex 200 mg./Tab. Bot. 100s.

HESPER CAPSULES. (Merrell Dow) Hesperidin complex 100 mg./Cap. w/lactose, calcium stearate, gelatin Bot. 100s.

HESPERIDIN.
Use: Capillary fragility and permeability, and hemorrhage.
See: Vitamin P; also Rutin
W/Combinations.
See: A.C.N., Tab. (Person & Covey)
Acna-Vite, Cap. (Cenci)
Ceebec, Tab. (Person & Covey)
Citrobic, Tab. (Blue Line)
HesBic, Cap., Tab. (Kenyon)
Hesper Bitabs, Tab. (Merrell Dow)
Nialex, Tab. (Mallard)
Norimex-Plus, Cap. (Vortech)
Ominal, Tab. (Kenwood)
Pregent, Tab. (Beutlich)
Vita Cebus, Tab. (Cenci)

HESPERIDIN W/C. (Various Mfr.)
Use: Vitamin P and C therapy.
See: Min-Hest, Cap. (Scrip)

HESPERIDIN METHYL CHALCONE.
Use: Deficiency of Vitamin P.

HETACILLIN. B.A.N. 6-(2,2-Dimethyl-5-oxo-4-phenylimidazolidin-1-yl)penicillanic acid.
Use: Antibiotic.

• **HETACILLIN,** U.S.P. XXI. For Oral Susp., Tab., U.S.P. XXI. 6-(2,2-Dimethyl-5-oxo-4-phenyl-1-imidazolidinyl)-3, 3-dimethyl-7-oxo-4-thia-1-azabicyclo[3.2.0] heptane-2-carboxylic acid.
Use: Antibiotic.
See: Versapen, Tab., Susp., Drops (Bristol)

• **HETACILLIN POTASSIUM,** U.S.P. XXI. Cap., Intramammary Inf., Oral Susp., Tab., Sterile, U.S.P. XXI.
See: Versapen-K, Vial, Cap. (Bristol)

• **HETAFLUR.** USAN.
Use: Dental caries prophylactic.

• **HETASTARCH.** USAN.
Use: Plasma volume extender. Hespan, Inj. (American Critical Care)

• **HETERONIUM BROMIDE.** USAN. (±)-3-Hydroxy-1, 1-dimethypyrrolidinium bromide, α-phenyl-2-thiopheneglycolate. Hetrum Chloride.
Use: Anticholinergic.

HEXABAX. (Kirkman) Antibacterial skin cleanser. Bot. pt.

HEXA-BETALIN. (Lilly) Pyridoxine HCl. Vial 10 mg./ml. Ctn. 10s.
Use: Vitamin B-6 therapy.

HEXACHLORCYCLOHEXANE.
See: Benzene Hexachloride, Gamma.

γ-1,2,3,4,5,6-HEXACHLOROCYCLOHEXANE. Benzene Hexachloride, Gamma.

• **HEXACHLOROPHENE.** U.S.P. XXI. Phenol, 2,2′-methylenebis[3,4,6-trichloro-. 2.2′-Methylenebis (3,4,6-trichlorophenol). Di-(3,5,6-trichloro-2-hydroxyphenyl)methane. Hexachlorophene (I.N.N.)
Use: Antiseptic.
See: Derl
Gamophen, Leaves, Bar (Arbrook)
pHisoHex Prods. (Winthrop-Breon)
W/Soya protein complex.
See: Soy-Dome Cleanser, Liq. (Miles Pharm)

• **HEXACHLOROPHENE CLEANSING EMULSION,** U.S.P. XXI.
Use: Anti-infective, topical detergent

• **HEXACHLOROPHENE LIQUID SOAP, DETERGENT LIQUID,** U.S.P. XXI.
See: pHisoHex Liq. Prods. (Winthrop-Breon)
Use: Anti-infective, topical detergent.

HEXACOSE. Mixture of C-6 alcohols derived from oxidation of tetracosane—$C_{24}H_{50}$.
See: Hexathricin, Aerospra (Lincoln)

HEXACREST. (Nutrition) Vit. B-6 100 mg./cc., benzyl alcohol 1.5% Vial 10 cc.
Use: Source of B-6.

HEXACYCLONATE SODIUM. (Warner-Lambert) Sodium 3,3-pentamethylene-4-hydroxybutyrate. Treatment of alcoholism. Under Study.

HEXADECADROL.
See: Dexamethasone.

HEXADECANOIC ACID, 2- (2,2-DICHLOROACETYL-)AMINO-3-HYDROXY-3-(4-NITROPHENYL)PROPYL ESTER. Chloramphenicol Palmitate, U.S.P. XXI.

HEXADERM. (Amfre-Grant) Hydrocortisone free alcohol 0.5%, hexachlorophene 0.5%, menthol 0.125%. Tube 1 oz.
Use: Acute dermatosis.

HEXADERM-I.Q. (Amfre-Grant) Hydrocortisone 0.5%, hexachlorophene 0.5%, clioquinol 3%. Tube 1 oz.
Use: Antifungal, antieczematous, antibacterial.

HEXADIENOL. Hexacose.

HEXADIMETHRINE BROMIDE. B.A.N. Poly-(NNN′N′-tetra-methyl-N-trimethylenehexamethylenediammonium dibromide). Polybrene.
Use: Heparin antagonist.

HEXADROL. (Organon) Dexamethasone **Tab.:** 0.5 mg./Tab. Bot. 100s, 500s. Strips 10 x 10; 0.75 mg./Tab. Bot. 100s, 500s. Strips 10 x 10; 1.5 mg./Tab. Bot. 100s. Strips 10 x 10; 4.0 mg./Tab. Bot. 100s. Strips 10 x 10. **Elixir:** 0.5 mg./5 ml. w/alcohol 5%. Bot. 4 oz. **Cream:** 0.04% Tube 30 Gm.
Use: Corticosteroid.

HEXADROL PHOSPHATE. (Organon) Dexamethasone sodium phosphate 4 mg./ml.,10 mg./ml., 20mg./ml. w/benzyl alcohol as preservative. **4 mg./ml.:** Vial 1 ml., 5 ml. Disposable syringe 1 ml. **10 mg./ml.:** Vial 10 ml. Disposable syringe 1 ml. **20 mg./ml.:** Vial 5 ml. Disposable syringe 5 ml.
Use: Corticosteroid.

• **HEXAFLUORENIUM.** F.D.A. Hexamethylene bis-[9-fluorenyldimethylammonium ion]
Use: Muscle relaxant.

• **HEXAFLUORENIUM BROMIDE,** U.S.P. XXI. Inj., U.S.P. XXI. Hexamethyl-enebis-[fluoren-9-yldi-methyl ammonium] dibromide.
Use: Muscle relaxant; potentiator (succinylcholine).

HEXAFLUORODIETHYL ETHER. Name used for Flurothyl.

HEXAFLUORONIUM BROMIDE. Hexafluorenium bromide.

1-(HEXAHYDRO-1H-AZEPIN-1-YL)-3-(p-TOLYLSULFONYL)-UREA. Tolazamide, U.S.P. XXI.

[2-(HEXAHYDRO-1(2H)-AZOCINYL)ETHYL] GUANIDINE SULFATE. Guanethidine Sulfate, U.S.P. XXI.

1,2,2,3a,β,8,8a,β-HEXAHYDRO-1,3a,8-TRI-METHYLPYRROLO[2,3,-b]-INDOL-5YL METHYLCARBAMATE. Physostigmine, U.S.P. XXI.

HEXAHYDROXYCYCLOHEXANE.
See: Inositol, Prep. (Various Mfr.)

5,6,9,17,19,21-HEXAHYDROXY-23-METHOXY-2,4,12,15,18,20,22-HEPTAMETHYL-8-[N-(4-METHYL-1-PIPERAZINYL)-FORMIMIDOYL-2,7-(EPOXYPENTADECA]1,11,13]TRIENIMINO)NAPHTHO[2,1-b]FURAN-1,11-(2H)-DIONE 21 ACETATE. Rifampin U.S.P. XXI.

HEXAKOSE. Mixture of tetracosanes & oxidation products.
See: Hexathricin, Aerospra (Lincoln)
W/Benzethonium chloride, p-chloro-m-xylenol, ethyl p-aminobenzoate & tyrothricin.
See: Hexathricin, Aeropak (Lincoln)

HEXALOL. (Central) Atropine sulf. 0.03 mg., hyoscyamine 0.03 mg., methenamine 40.8 mg., phenyl salicylate 18.1 mg., benzoic acid 4.5 mg., methylene blue 5.4 mg./Tab. Bot. 100s, 1000s.
Use: Urinary antiseptic, antispasmodic.

HEXAMARIUM BROMIDE. (Hexamethylene bis(3-pyridyl N-methylcarbamate) dimethyl bromide.

HEXAMETHONIUM.
W/Rauwiloid.
See: Rauwiloid w/hexamethonium, Tab. (Riker)

HEXAMETHONIUM BROMIDE. B.A.N. Vegolysen. Hexamethylene (bistrimethyl ammonium) bromide.
Use: Hypotensive.

HEXAMETHONIUM CHLORIDE. (Various Mfr.) Hexamethylene (bistrimethylammonium) chloride.

HEXAMETHONIUM IODIDE. B.A.N.
Hexamethylenedi(trimethylammonium iodide).
Use: Hypotensive.
See: Hexathide

HEXAMETHONIUM TARTRATE. B.A.N.
Hexamethylenedi(trimethylammonium hydrogen tartrate).
Use: Hypotensive.
See: Vegolysen T

EXAMETHYLENAMINE.
See: Methenamine (Various Mfr.)

EXAMETHYLENAMINE MANDELATE. (CMC) 0.25, 0.5, 1.0 Gm./Tab. Bot. 100s, 1000s.
See: Mandelamine, Tab., Susp. (Parke-Davis)

EXAMETHYLENETETRAMINE.
See: Methenamine, U.S.P. XXI.
Hexamethylenetetramine Mandelate.

EXAMETHYLPARAROSANILINE CHLORIDE.
See: Bismuth Violet, Sol. (Table Rock)

EXAMETHYLROSANILINE CHLORIDE.
See: Gentian Violet

EXAMIC ACID. Cyclamic Acid, B.A.N.

EXAMINE HIPPURATE. B.A.N. A 1:1 complex of hexamine and hippuric acid.
Use: Antiseptic.
See: Hiprex

EXAMIN. (Galen) Vit. A 5000 I.U., D 400 I.U., B-1 1.5 mg., B-2 2 mg., B-6 0.1 mg., Ca pantothenate 1 mg., niacinamide 20 mg., C 37.5 mg./Cap. Bot. 100s.
Use: Vitamin deficiencies.

EXAMINE.
See: Methenamine (Various Mfr.)

EXAPROFEN. B.A.N. 2-(4-Cychlohexylphenyl)-propionic acid.
Use: Anti-inflammatory; antipyretic; analgesic.

EXAPROPYMATE. B.A.N. 1-(2-Propynyl)cyclohexanol carbamate. Merinax.
Use: Sedative hypnotic.

EXAPRADOL HCl. a-(1-Aminohexyl)benzhydrol HCl.
Use: Central nervous system stimulant.

EXASEPT. (Med. Chem.; Kenyon) Hexachlorophene 3% in high-sudsing soap-free lotion base. Bot. 5 oz., pt., gal.
Use: Skin cleanser.

EXATE. (Davis & Sly) Atropine sulfate 1/2000 gr., Ext. hyoscyamus 0.25 gr., methylene blue 1/10 gr., methanamine 0.5 gr., benzoic acid 0.5 gr., salol 0.5 gr./Tab. Bot. 1000s.
Use: Renal discomfort.

EXATHRICIN AEROSPRA. (Lincoln) Hexadienol 8 Gm., benzethonium chloride 80 mg., p-chloro m-xylenol 800 mg., tyrothricin 40 mg., ethyl-p-aminobenzoate 1.6 Gm./6 oz. Aeropak 3 oz.
Use: Topically, burns, pyodermas & fungal infections.

EXATHRICIN EPISIOTOMY AEROSPRA. (Lincoln) Hexakose (hexadienol) 4.2 Gm., p-chloro-m-xylenol 420 mg., benzethonium chloride 55 mg., ethyl-p-aminobenzoate 2.77 Gm./3 oz. can. Aerospra can 3 oz.

EXATHRICIN OTIC. (Lincoln) Benzocaine 50 mg., p-chloro-m-xylenol 40 mg., benzethonium chloride 1 mg./cc. Bot. 15 cc.
Use: Fungus infections of ear.

EXAVITAMIN. (Panray) Vit. A 5000 I.U., D 400 I.U., C 75 mg., B-1 2 mg., B-2 3 mg., nicotinamide 20 mg./Tab. Bot. 1000s.

EXAVITAMIN. (Upsher-Smith) Tab. Bot. 100s, 1000s. Unit Dose 100s.

HEXAVITAMIN CAPSULES and TABLETS, U.S.P. XXI. Vit-A 5000 I.U., B-1 2 mg., B-2 3 mg., C 75 mg., D 400 I.U., nicotinamide 20 mg./Tab. or Cap. Bot. 100s, 1000s, 5000s. (Various Mfr.)
See: Hepicebrin, Tab. (Lilly)

HEXAVITMIN TABLETS. (A.V.P.) Vit. A 5000 I.U., D 400 I.U., C 75 mg., B-1 2 mg., B-2 3 mg., niacin 20 mg./Tab. Bot. 500s.
Use: Multivitamin.

HEXAVITAMIN TABLETS, N.F. (Fellows) Vit. A 1.5 mg., D 10.0 mcg., C 75 mg., B-1 2 mg., B-2 3 mg., nicotinamide 20 mg./S.C. Tab. Bot. 1000s.

HEXAVITAMIN TABLETS. (Stanlabs) Vit. A 5000 u., D 400 u., C 75 mg., B-1 2 mg., B-2 3 mg., niacinamide 20 mg./Tab. Bot. 100s, 1000s. (Vitarine) Tab. Bot. 100s, 200s.

HEXAZOLE. B.A.N. 4-Cyclohexyl-3-ethyl-1,2,4-triazole.
Use: Central nervous system stimulant.
See: Azoman

HEXCARBACHOLINE BROMIDE (I.N.N.). Carbolinium Bromide, B.A.N.

HEXCARBACHOLINE BROMIDE. 1,6-Hexamethylenebiscarbaminoylcholine bromide.

• **HEXEDINE.** USAN. 2,6-bis(2-Ethylhexyl)hexahydro-7a-methyl-1H imidasol[1,5c]imidazole.
Use: Antibacterial.

HEXENE-OL. Hexacose.

HEXENOL. Hexacose.

HEXESTROL. Dihydro-diethylstilbestrol. Hexoestrol. Meso-3,4-bis(p-hydroxyphenyl)-n-hexane. (CMC) 3 mg./Tab. Bot. 100s, 1000s.
Use: Estrogen therapy. (200 mcg. to 3 mg. I.M.)

HEXESTROL AND PHENOBARBITAL. (Jenkins) Hexestrol 1 mg., phenobarbital 0.25 gr./Tab. Bot. 1000s.

HEXETHAL SODIUM. (Hebaral) Sod. ethylhexylbarbiturate.
Use: Sedative & hypnotic.

HEXETIDINE. B.A.N. 5-Amino-1,3-bis(beta-ethylhexyl)-5-methylhexahydropyrimide. Triocil.
Use: Bactericide; fungicide.
See: Oraldene; Sterisil

HEXOBARBITAL.
See: Sombulex, Tab. (Riker)
W/Acetaminophen, salicylamide, d-amphetamine sulfate, secobarbital sod., butabarbital sod., phenobarbital.
See: Sedragesic, Tab. (Lannett)
W/Dihydrohydroxycodeinone HCl, dihydrohydroxycodeinone terephthalate, homatropine terephthalate, aspirin, phenacetin, caffeine.
See: Percobarb, Cap. (Du Pont)
W/Dihydrohydroxycodeinone terephthalate, dihydrohydroxycodeinone HCl, homatropine terephthalate, aspirin, phenacetin, caffeine.
See: Percobarb-Demi, Cap. (Du Pont)

• **HEXOBARBITAL,** U.S.P. XXI. Tab., U.S.P. XXI. (Cyclonal Sod., Dorico Soluble, Evipan Sod., Hexanastab, Hexobarbitone Sod., Methenexyl Sod.). N-methyl-5-cyclohexenyl-5-methylbarbiturate.
Use: Sedative.
See: Sombucaps, Caps (Riker)
Percobarb, Prods (Du Pont)

• **HEXOBENDINE.** USAN. Hexobendine HCl. 1,2-Di-[N-methyl-3-(3,4,5-trimethoxybenzoyloxy)propylamino]ethane.
Use: Coronary vasodilator.

HEXOCYCLIUM METHYLSULFATE. B.A.N. N-β-Cyclohexyl-β-hydroxy-β-phenylethyl)-N′-methylpiperazine dimethylsulfate.
Use: Anticholinergic.

HEXOESTROL.
See: Hexestrol (Various Mfr.)

HEX-ON. (Sween) 30 cc., vials w/Drop top cap.
Use: Odor-antagonist.

HEXOPAL. (Winthrop Products) Inositol hexanicotinate.
Use: Hypolipidemic, peripheral vasodilator.

HEXOPRENALINE. B.A.N. NN′-Di-[2-(3,4-dihydroxyphenyl)-2-hydroxyethyl]hexamethylenediamine.
Use: Bronchodilator.

• **HEXYLCAINE HYDROCHLORIDE,** U.S.P. XXI. Topical Soln., U.S.P. XXI. 1-(Cyclohexylamino)-2-propanol benzoate (ester) HCl.
Use: Injectable (Veterinary) and local (Human) anesthetic.
See: Cyclaine Topical Solution (Merck Sharp & Dohme)

• **HEXYLENE GLYCOL,** N.F. XVI.
Use: Pharmaceutical aid.

• **HEXYLRESORCINOL,** U.S.P. XXI. Pill, U.S.P. XXI. 4-Hexylresorcinol. (Various Mfr.)
Use: Anthelmintic (intestinal roundworms and trematodes) and minor throat irritations.
See: Jayne's P.W., Tab. (Glenbrook)
Listerine Antiseptic Throat Lozenges (Warner-Lambert)
Sucrets Sore Throat Lozenge (Calgon)
W/Benzocaine, camphor, menthol.
See: Auristil, Dropule (Blue Line)

HEXYPHEN-2. (Robinson) Trihexyphenidyl HCl 2 mg./Tab. Bot. 100s.
Use: Anticholingergic, antiparkinsonian.

HEXYPHEN-5. (Robinson) Trihexyphenidyl HCl 5 mg./Tab. Bot. 100s, 1000s.
Use: Anticholinergic, antiparkinsonian.

HGP CLEANER. (CooperVision) Daily cleaner. Bot. 30 ml.
Use: For Boston II rigid gas permeable contact lenses.

H.H.R. (Towne) Hydralazine HCl 25 mg., hydrochlorothiazide 15 mg., reserpine 0.1 mg./Tab. Bot. 100s, 1000s.
Use: Hypertension treatment.

HI-BEE W/C. (Vortech) Vit. B-1 15 mg., B-2 10 mg., B-6 5 mg., C 300 mg., niacinamide 50 mg., D-calcium pantothenate 10 mg./Cap. Bot. 50s, 100s, 1000s.
Use: Vit. B & C replacement therapy.

HIBICLENS. (Stuart) Chlorhexidine gluconate 4%, isopropyl alcohol 4%, in a non alkaline base. Bot. 4 oz., 8 oz., 16 oz., 32 oz., 1 gal. Packette 15 ml.
Use: Surgical hand scrub, health-care personnel handwash, skin wound cleanser, preoperative patient skin preparation and whole body washing.

HIBICLENS SPONGE BRUSH. (Stuart) Chlorhexidine gluconate impregnated sponge-brush. Unit-of-use 22 ml. sponge-brushes.
Use: Antimicrobial skin cleanser for use in surgical handscrub.

HIBISCRUB. Chlorhexidine gluconate, B.A.N.
Use: Surgical handscrub.

HIBISTAT. (Stuart) Chlorhexidine gluconate 0.5%. **Liquid:** isopropyl alcohol 70% with emollients. Bot. 4 oz., 8 oz. **Towlettes**: Unit of use pocket-size towlettes impregnated with 5 ml. Hibistat.
Use: Germicidal hand rinse.

HIBITANE. Chlorhexidine, B.A.N.

HIBOL. (Amfre-Grant) Methandriol dipropionate 50 mg./ml. Vial 10 ml.
Use: Anabolic.

HI B & C. (Vitarine) High potency Vit. B complex with Vit. C.
Use: Dietary supplement.

HI B PLEX. (Standex) Vit. B-1 100 mg., B-2 2 mg., B-3 100 mg., panthenol 2 mg./ml. Vial 30 ml.
Use: Vitamin.

HI B WITH C. (Towne) Vit. C 300 mg., B-1 15 mg., B-2 10.2 mg., niacin 50 mg., B-6 5 mg., pantothenic acid 10 mg./Cap. Bot. 100s.
Use: Dietary supplement.

HI-COR 1.0. (C & M Pharmacal) Hydrocortisone 1.0% in a nonionic, ester-free, salt-free, paraben-free washable base. Tube 20 Gm., 1 oz. Jar 2 oz., 16 oz., 96 oz.
Use: Derma-steroid.

HI-COR-2.5. (C & M Pharmacal) Hydrocortisone 2.5% in a nonionic, ester-free, salt-free, paraben-free washable base. Tube 20 Gm., 1 oz. Jar 2 oz., 16 oz., 96 oz.
Use: Derma-steroid.

HIESTRONE.
See: Estrone (Various Mfr.)

HIGH B-12. (Barth's) Vit. B-12, desic. liver. Cap. Bot. 100s, 500s.

HIGH POTENCY COLD CAP. (Weeks & Leo) Salicylamide 325 mg., chlorpheniramine maleate 4 mg., dextromethorphan HBr. 15 mg., caffeine 16.2 mg./Tab. Bot. 18s.
Use: Colds, coughs, hay fever.

HIGH POTENCY PAIN RELIEVERS. (Weeks & Leo) Acetaminophen 300 mg., salicylamide 300 mg./Cap. Bot. 20s, 40s.
Use: Analgesic.

HIGH POTENCY VITAMINS AND MINERALS. (Burgin-Arden) Vit. A 25,000 I.U., D 400 I.U., B-1 10 mg., B-2 5 mg., C 150 mg., niacinamide 100 mg., Ca 103 mg., P 80 mg., Fe 10 mg., Vit. B-6 1 mg., B-12 5 mcg., Mg 5.5 mg., Mn 1 mg., K 5 mg., Zn 1.4 mg./Tab. Bot. 100s, fever.
Use: Multivitamin with minerals.

HIGH POTENCY VIT. CAP. (Scrip) Vit. A 25,000 I.U., D 400 I.U., B-1 10 mg., B-2 10 mg., C 200 mg., sod. ascorbate 100 mg., B-6 5 mg., Ca pantothenate 20 mg., B-12 5 mcg., E 15 I.U./Cap. Bot. 100s.

ILL-CORTAC LOTION. (Hill) Hydrocortisone 0.5%, sulfur 5%, isopropyl alcohol 5%, oat powd. 20%, zinc oxide 20% Lot. Bot. 2 oz.
Use: Acne vulgaris and acne rosacea.

ILL-SHADE LOTION. (Hill) Para-aminobenzoic acid, alcohol 65%. Sun protective factor 22.
Use: Sunscreen.

ILOMID. Tribromsalan, B.A.N.

INKLE'S PILLS. (Stanlabs) Aloin, belladonna, cascara and podophyllum. Bot. 100s, 1000s.

I-POTENCY B-COMPLEX. (Kenyon) Vit. B-1 20 mg., B-2 12 mg., B-6 2 mg., B-12 3 mcg., C 50 mg., Ca pantothenate 5 mg., folic acid 0.1 mg., niacinamide 25 mg., liver fraction II 30 mg., yeast 175 mg., iron gluconate 30 mg., iron reduced 10 mg., choline bitartrate 20 mg., inositol 20 mg., d1-methionine 20 mg./Tab. Bot. 100s, 1000s.

I-POTENCY B-COMPLEX W/C. (Zenith) Vit. C 500 mg., niacinamide 100 mg., Ca pantothenate 20 mg., B-1 15 mg., B-2 10 mg., B-6 5 mg., B-12 4 mcg./Tab. Bot. 100s.

I-POTENCY VITAMINS/MINERALS. (Zenith) Vit. B-1 15 mg., B-2 10 mg., B-6 2 mg., pantothenic acid 10 mg., niacinamide 100 mg., B-12 7.5 mcg., C 150 mg., E 5 mg., A 3 mg., D 10 mcg., Fe 15 mg., Cu 1 mg., iodine 0.15 mg., Mn 1 mg. Mg 5 mg., Zn 1.5 mg./Tab. Bot. 100s.
Use: Multivitamin with minerals.

IPPRAMINE.
See: Methenamine hippurate.

IPPUTOPE. (Squibb) Radio-iodinated sodium iodohippurate (^{131}I) Injection Bot. 1 m Ci, 2 m Ci.
Use: Diagnostic.

IPREX. (Merrell Dow) Methenamine hippurate 1 Gm./Tab. Bot. 100s.
Use: Prophylactic or long-term suppressive treatment of urinary tract infections.

I-PRO WAFERS. (Mills) Casein-lactalbumin fusion 13.3 gr., dl-methionine 5 mg., l-lysine monohydrochloride 16.7 mg., l-cystine 5 mg./Tab. Bot. 336s.

I-RIBO. (Kenyon) Vit. B-2 riboflavin-5-phos, 50 mg./cc. Vial 10 cc.

ISPRIL. (SmithKline) Diphenylpyraline HCl 5 mg./Spansule. Bot. 50s.
Use: Relief from hay fever, allergic rhinitis, urticaria.

IST-A-BALM MEDICATED LOTION. (Quality Generics) Pyrilamine maleate 0.75%, diperodon HCl 0.25%, benzalkonium chloride 0.1%, menthol, camphor. Bot. 4 oz.
Use: Anesthetic-antiseptic, antihistamine.

ISTABID DURACAP. (Glaxo) Phenylpropanolamine HCl 75 mg., chlorpheniramine maleate 8 mg./S.R. Cap. Bot. 100s.
Use: Decongestant, antihistaminic.

ISTA-C. (Eckerd) D-methorphan HBr 10 mg., phenylephrine HCl 5 mg., pyrilamine maleate 12.5 mg., Vit. C 75 mg., pot. salicylate 3.75 gr., caffeine 0.25 gr./Cap.

ISTA-C SYRUP. (Eckerd) D-methorphan 10 mg., phenylephrine HCl 2.5 mg., pyrilamine maleate 8 mg., Vit. C 30 mg., NAPAP 81 mg., glyceryl guaiacol ether 50 mg./5 cc. Bot. 3 oz.

HISTACHLOR. (Kenyon) Chlorpheniramine maleate 4 mg./Tab. Bot. 100s, 1000s.

HISTACHLOR D-8, D-12. (Kenyon) Chlorpheniramine maleate 8 mg., 12 mg./Delayed Action Tab. Bot. 1000s.

HISTACHLOR T-8, T-12. (Kenyon) Chlorpheniramine maleate 8 mg., 12 mg./Time release Cap. Bot. 100s, 1000s.

HISTACHLOR W/A.P.C. (Kenyon) Chlorpheniramine maleate 2 mg., salicylamide 3.5 gr., phenacetin 2.5 gr., caffeine 0.5 gr./Tab. Bot. 100s, 1000s.

HISTA-COMPOUND #5. (Vortech) Acetaminophen 150 mg., salicylamide 175 mg., chlorpheniramine maleate 2 mg./Tab. Bot. 100s, 1000s.
Use: Antihistaminic, analgesic.

HISTACOMP SYRUP. (Approved) Thenylpyramine HCl 80 mg., ammonium chloride 10 gr., Sod. citrate 5 gr., antimony Pot. tartrate 1/24 gr., menthol & aromatics q.s./fl. oz. Bot., Syr. 4 oz., 8 oz. Also available w/dextromethorphan. Bot. 4 oz.
Use: Allergic & asthmatic coughs.

HISTACOMP TABLETS. (Approved) Pyrilamine maleate 25 mg., aspirin 3.5 gr., phenacetin 2.5 gr., caffeine 0.5 gr./Tab. Bot. 30s, 100s, 1000s.
Use: Allergic symptoms & the common cold.

HISTACON. (Marsh-Emory) Chlorpheniramine maleate 12 mg., ephedrine hydrochloride 15 mg., atropine sulfate 0.24 mg./S.R. Tab. Bot. 100s, 1000s.
Use: Antihistaminic, decongestant.

HISTACON SYRUP. (Marsh-Emory) Chlorpheniramine maleate 3 mg., ephedrine HCl 4 mg., atropine sulfate 0.06 mg., alcohol 5%/5 cc. Bot. pt.
Use: Allergic, respiratory conditions.

HISTA-DERFULE. (Forest) Chlorpheniramine maleate 4 mg., acetaminophen 325 mg., phenylpropanolamine HCl 25 mg., powdered opium 2 mg./Cap. Bot. 100s, 1000s.
Use: Analgesic.

HISTADYL E.C. (Lilly) Codeine phosphate 60 mg., ephedrine HCl 30 mg., chlorpheniramine maleate 12 mg., ammonium chloride 660 mg., menthol 3.9 mg./30 ml. w/alcohol 5%. Bot. 4 oz., pt., gal.
Use: Antitussive, antihistaminic, decongestant, expectorant.

HISTAGESIC D.M. (Bowman) Phenylpropanolamine HCl 25 mg., chlorpheniramine maleate 4 mg., dextromethorphan HBr 10 mg, acetaminophen 324 mg./Tab. Bot. 100s, 1000s.
Use: Analgesic, decongestant, antihistaminic, antitussive.

HISTAGESIC MODIFIED. (Bowman) Acetaminophen 324 mg., phenylephrine HCl 10 mg., chlorpheniramine maleate 4 mg./Tab.
Use: Analgesic, decongestant, antihistaminic.

HISTAJECT. (Mayrand) Atropine, chlorphemiramine maleate. Vial 10 ml.

HISTAJEN. (Jenkins) Codeine phosphate 10 mg., pyrilamine maleate 12 mg., ammonium chloride 175

mg., potassium citrate 131 mg., alcohol 2%/5 cc. Syr. Bot. 3, 4 oz., gal.
Use: Common cold, hay fever.

HISTAJEN JR. (Jenkins) Chlorpheniramine maleate 1 mg., acetophenetidin 75 mg., caffeine 15 mg., salicylamide 105 mg./Tab. Bot. 1000s.
Use: Colds and allergies.

HISTALET. (Reid-Provident) **Syrup:** Pseudoephedrine HCl 45 mg., chlorpheniramine maleate 3 mg./5 ml. Bot. pt. **Forte:** Phenylephrine HCl 10 mg., pyrilamine maleate 25 mg., chlorpheniramine maleate 4 mg., phenylpropanolamine HCl 50 mg./Sustained Release Tab. Bot. 100s, 250s. **Histalet DM:** Pseudoephedrine HCl 45 mg., chlorpheniramine maleate 3 mg., dextromethorphan HBr 15 mg./5 ml. Syr. Bot. 1 pt.
Use: Treatment, common cold.

HISTALET X. (Reid-Provident) **Syrup:** Pseudoephedrine HCl 45 mg., guaifenesin 200 mg./5 ml. w/alcohol 15%. Bot. 16 oz. **Tab.:** Pseudoephedrine HCl 120 mg., guaifenesin 400 mg./Tab. Bot. 100s.
Use: Treatment of common cold, bronchitis, croup, emphysema.

HISTALOG HYDROCHLORIDE. Ametazole, B.A.N.

HISTAMIC TABS. (Metro Med) Chlorpheniramine maleate 4 mg., pseudoephedrine HCl 15 mg./Tab. Bot. 100s, 1000s.

HISTAMINE. 2-(4-Imidazolyl) ethylamine.
Use: Diagnostic agent.

HISTAMINE ACID PHOSPHATE.
See: Histamine Phosphate, U.S.P. XXI.

HISTAMINE DIHYDROCHLORIDE.
W/Methyl nicotinate, oleoresin capicum, glycomonosalicylate.
See: Akes-N-Pain Rub, Oint. (Edward J. Moore)
W/Menthol, thymol, methyl salicylate.
See: Imahist Unction (Gordon)

• **HISTAMINE PHOSPHATE,** U.S.P. XXI. Inj. U.S.P. XXI. 1H-Imidazole-4-ethanamine, phosphate (1:2). 4-(2-Aminoethyl) imidazole Bis (Dihydrogen Phosphate).
Use: S.C., I.V., allergy therapy & diagnostic aid.

HISTANTIN HYDROCHLORIDE. Chlorcyclizine, B.A.N.

HISTAPCO. (Apco) Chlorpheniramine maleate 4 mg., ipecac and opium powd. 0.25 gr., (contains opium 0.025 gr.), camphor monobromated ⅛ gr., salicylamide 2 gr., phenacetin 1.5 grs., caffeine alkaloid ⅛ gr., atropine sulfate 1/500 gr./Tab.
Use: Analgesic, antipyretic, antihistaminic, and nasal antisecretory.

HISTAQUAD. Cap. (Richlyn) Phenylpropanolamine HCl 25 mg., pyrilamine maleate 12.5 mg., pheniramine maleate 12.5 mg., phenylephrine HCl 2.5 mg./Cap. Bot. 1000s.

HISTAQUAD. Tab. (Richlyn) Pyrilamine maleate 6.25 mg., phenyltoloxamine dihydrogen citrate 6.25 mg., prophenpyridamine maleate 6.25 mg./Tab. Bot. 1000s.

HISTARON-4. (Approved) Chloroprophenpyridamine maleate 4 mg./Tab. Bot. 100s, 500s, 1000s.

HISTARON-12. (Approved) Chloroprophenpyridamine maleate 12 mg./Cap. Bot. 100s, 500s, 1000s.

HISTASPAN-D. (USV Labs.) Chlorpheniramine maleate 8 mg., phenylephrine HCl 20 mg., methscopolamine nitrate 2.5 mg.,/Cap. in sustained-release micro-dialysis cells. Bot. 100s, 1000s.
Use: Antihistaminic with decongestant.

HISTASPAN-PLUS. (USV Labs.) Chlorpheniramine maleate 8 mg., phenylephrine HCl 20 mg./Cap. in sustained-release micro-dialysis cells. Bot. 100s.
Use: Antihistaminic and decongestant for relief of nasal congestion.

HISTATAB PLUS. (Century) Chlorpheniramine maleate 2 mg., phenylephrine HCl 5 mg./Tab. Bot. 100s, 1000s.
Use: Antihistaminic, decongestant.

HISTATAPP ELIXIR. (Upsher-Smith) Brompheniramine maleate 4 mg., phenylephrine HCl 5 mg., phenylpropanolamine HCl 5 mg./5 cc. Bot. 4 oz., pt., gal.
Use: Antihistamine, nasal decongestant.

HISTATAPP T.D. (Upsher-Smith) Brompheniramine maleate 12 mg., phenylephrine HCl 15 mg., phenylpropanolamine HCl 15 mg./Tab. Bot. 100s, 500s, unit dose 100s.
Use: Antihistamine, nasal decongestant.

HISTATROL. (Center) Histamine phosphate control 1:1000 and 1:10,000. 2 ml. dropper vial 1:1000 or vial 1:100,000 intradermal.
Use: Skin test control.

HISTA-VADRIN SYRUP. (Scherer) Phenylpropanolamine HCl 20 mg., chlorpheniramine maleate 2 mg., phenylephrine HCl 2.5 mg., alcohol 2%/5 cc. Bot. pt.
Use: Upper respiratory decongestant.

HISTA-VADRIN TABLETS. (Scherer) Phenylpropanolamine HCl 40 mg., chlorpheniramine maleate 6 mg., phenylephrine HCl 5 mg./Tab. Bot. 100s.
Use: Antihistaminic-Decongestant.

HISTA-VADRIN T.D. CAPSULES. (Scherer) Phenylpropanolamine HCl 50 mg., chlorpheniramine maleate 4 mg., belladonna alkaloids 0.2 mg./Cap. Bot. 50s, 250s.
Use: Nasal congestion relief.

HISTERONE INJECTION. (Hauck) Testosterone aqueous 50 mg. or 100 mg./ml. Vial 10 ml.
Use: Androgen.

HISTEX. (Mallard) Chlorpheniramine maleate, 12 mg./T.D. Cap. Pkg. 100s, 1000s.
Use: Antihistaminic.

HISTEX HYDROCHLORIDE. Diphenhydramine, B.A.N.

• **HISTIDINE,** U.S.P. XXI. $C_6H_9N_3O_2$. L-histidine.
Use: Amino acid.

HISTINE-1. (Freeport) Diphenhydramine HCl 10 mg., alcohol 12-14%/4 cc. Bot. 4 oz.
Use: Antihistaminic with anticholingergic, antitussive, antiemetic & sedative effects.

HISTINE-2. (Freeport) Diphenhydramine HCl 12.5 mg./5 ml. w/alcohol 5%. Bot. 4 oz.
Use: Antitussive, expectorant for control of cough due to colds or allergy.

STINE-4. (Freeport) Chlorpheniramine maleate 4 mg./Tab. Bot. 1000s.
Use: Antihistaminic.

STINE-8. (Freeport) Chlorpheniramine maleate 8 mg./T.R. Tab. Bot. 1000s.
Use: Antihistaminic.

STINE-12. (Freeport) Chlorpheniramine maleate 12 mg./T.R. Tab. Bot. 1000s.
Use: Antihistminic.

STINE-25. (Freeport) Diphenhydramine HCl 25 mg./Cap. Bot. 1000s.
Use: Antihistaminic with antitussive, antiemetic, & sedative effects.

STINE-50. (Freeport) Diphenhydramine HCl 50 mg./Cap. Bot. 1000s.
Use: Antihistaminic with anticholinergic, antitussive, antiemetic, sedative effect.

STJEN CAPSULE. (Jenkins) Phenylpropanolamine HCl 25 mg., pyrilamine maleate 12.5 mg., prophenpyridamine maleate 12.5 mg., phenylephrine HCl 2.5 mg./Cap. Bot. 1000s.

STIDINE MONOHYDROCHLORIDE. Beta-4-Imidazoyl-1-amino propionic acid HCl.
Use: I.M., peptic & jejunal ulcers.

STIVITE-D. (Vitarine) Dextromethorphan HBr 30 mg., ammonium Cl 8 gr., ephedrine sulfate ⅜ gr., menthol, methapyrilene fumarate 75 mg./oz. w/alcohol (by volume) 4.8%. Bot. 4 oz.
Use: Coughs due to colds.

STOACRYL. Enbucrilate, B.A.N.

STOGESIC. (Century) Phenylpropanolamine HCl 25 mg., pyrilamine maleate 10 mg., chlorpheniramine maleate 2 mg., terpin hydrate 2.5 gr., acetaminophen 5 gr./Tab. Bot. 100s, 1000s.
Use: Cold symptoms.

STOLYN-CYL. (Berkeley Biologicals) Histoplasmin sterile filtrate from yeast cells of *Histoplasma capsulatum.* Vial 1.3 ml.
Use: Skin test.

HISTOPLASMIN, U.S.P. XXI. (Parke-Davis) An aqueous solution containing standardized sterile culture filtrate of *Histoplasma capsulatum* grown on liquid synthetic medium. Vial 1 ml. to give 10 tests.
Use: Diagnostic aid in testing for histoplasmosis.

STOR-D. (Hauck) **Timecelles:** Chlorpheniramine maleate 8 mg., phenylephrine HCl 20 mg., methscopalamine 2.5 mg./Cap. Bot. 100s, 500s. **Syrup:** chlorpheniramine maleate 2 mg., phenylephrine HCl 5 mg./5 ml. w/alcohol 2%. Bot. 16 oz.
Use: Symptoms of cold, allergy and sinusitis.

STORAL. (Merchant) Chlorpheniramine maleate 12 mg., pseudoephedrine HCl 60 mg., methscopolamine nitrate 2.5 mg./Cap. Bot. 100s.
Use: Antihistaminic, decongestant, vasoconstrictor.

STORAL LIQUID. (Merchant) Chlorpheniramine maleate 2 mg., pseudoephedrine HCl 30 mg., methscopolamine nitrate 0.5 mg., alcohol 5%/5 cc. Bot. 16 oz.
Use: Antihistamine.

HISTOSAL. (Ferndale) Pyrilamine maleate 12.5 mg., phenylpropanolamine HCl 20 mg., acetaminophen 324 mg., caffeine 30 mg./Tab. Bot. 100s.
Use: Antihistaminic, analgesic, antipyretic.

HISTOSTAB HYDROCHLORIDE OR MESYLATE. Antazoline, B.A.N.

HISTOSTAT. (Salsbury) Nitarsone.

• HISTRELIN.
Use: LHRH agonist.

HISTREY. (Bowman) Chlorpheniramine maleate 4 mg./Tab. Bot. 100s, 1000s.
Use: Antihistaminic.

HISTRYL. Diphenylpyraline, B.A.N.

HIST-SPAN. (Kenyon) Pyrilamine maleate 25 mg., phenylpropanolamine HCl 25 mg., prophenpyridamine maleate 10 mg./T.R. Cap. Bot. 100s, 1000s.

HIST-SPAN NO. 2. (Kenyon) Pyrilamine maleate 25 mg., phenylpropanolamine HCl 25 mg., prophenpyridamine maleate 10 mg., phenylephrine HCl 10 mg./T.R. Cap. Bot. 100s, 1000s.

HISTUNEX. (Tunex) Atropine sulfate 0.2 mg., chlorpheniramine 5 mg./ml. Vial 10 cc.
Use: Decongestant.

HI-TOR. (Barth's) Vit. B-12 15 mcg., niacin 1.5 mg., B-1 6 mg., B-2 12 mg., B-6 54 mcg., pantothenic acid 150 mcg., choline 3.75 mg., inositol 5.25 mg./Tab. Bot. 100s, 500s, 1000s.

HI-TOR 900. (Barth's) Vit. B-1 13.5 mg., B-2 5.2 mg., niacin 15 mg., B-6 0.6 mg., pantothenic acid 1.2 mg., biotin, B-12 2.5 mcg., iron 0.9 mg., protein 7.5 Gm., inositol 50 mg., choline 40 mg., aminobenzoic acid 0.15-2.4 mg./15 Gm. Bot. 1 lb., 3 lb.

HIWOLFIA. (Bowman) Rauwolfia 25 mg., 50 mg., or 100 mg./Tab. Bot. 100s, 1000s.
Use: Antihypertensive.

HMS LIQUIFILM. (Allergan) Medrysone 1.0%, Liquifilm (polyvinyl alcohol) 1.4%. W/benzalkonium chloride, edetate disodium, sod. chloride, pot. chloride, sod. phosphate monobasic monohydrate, sod. phosphate dibasic anhydrous, hydroxypropyl methylcellulose, purified water, sod. hydroxide or hydrochloric acid. Ophth. Susp. Dropper Bot. 5 ml., 10 ml.
Use: Ocular anti-inflammatory.

H_2OEX. (Fellows) Benzthiazide 50 mg./Tab. Bot. 100s, 1000s.
Use: Diuretic.

HOLD. (Beecham Products) Dextromethorphan HBr 7.5 mg./Loz. Plastic tube 10 loz.
Use: Cough suppressant.

HOLOCAINE HYDROCHLORIDE. (Various Mfr.) Phenacaine HCl.
Use: Topically, local anesthetic.

HOMAPIN-5. (Mission) Homatropine methylbromide 5 mg./Tab. Bot. 100s.
Use: Antispasmodic-anticholinergic.

HOMAPIN-10. (Mission) Homatropine methylbromide 10 mg./Tab. Bot. 100s.
Use: Antispasmodic-anticholinergic.

HOMARYLAMINE HYDROCHLORIDE. N-Methyl-3,4-methylenedioxyphenethylamine HCl.

HOMATROCEL. (Softcon) Sterile buffered Methulose solution containing homatropine hydrobromide 2% & 5% w/benzalkonium chloride 1:15,000, monobasic & dibasic sod. phosphate, sod. chloride. Bot. 15 cc. sterile bufopto plastic containers.
Use: Mydriatic and cycloplegic.

• **HOMATROPINE HYDROBROMIDE,** U.S.P. XXI. Ophth. Sol., U.S.P. XXI. Benzeneacetic acid, α-hydroxy-, 8-methyl-β-azabicyclo-[3.2.1]-oct-3-yl ester, HBr, endo-(±)-. 1αH, 3αH-Tropan-3α-ol mandelate (ester) HBr.
Use: Mydriatic & cycloplegic.
See: Homatrocel, Sol. (Softcon)
Murocoll, Liq. (Muro)

HOMATROPINE HYDROCHLORIDE.
Use: Topically, mydriatic & cyclopegic; anticholinergic.

• **HOMATROPINE METHYLBROMIDE,** U.S.P. XXI. Tab., U.S.P. XXI. 3α-Hydroxy-8-methyl-1αH, 5αH-tropanium bromide mandelate.
Use: Anticholinergic.
See: Mesopin, Elix., Tab. (Du Pont)
Novatrin, Liq., Tab. (Ayerst)
Sed-Tens SE, Tab. (Lemmon)

HOMATROPINE METHYLBROMIDE W/COMBINATIONS
See: Aloxed, Liq. (N. Amer.)
Aridol, Tabs. (MPL)
Atrocholin, Tab. (Blue Line)
Biloric, Caps. (Arcum)
Butabel HMB, Tab. (Saron)
DIA-Quel Liq. (Inter. Pharm.)
Digesplen, Tab., Elixir (Med. Prod.; Panamericana)
Dranochol, Tab. (Marin)
Femicin, Tab. (Norcliff Thayer)
Hepahydrin, Tab. (Comatic)
Homachol, Tab. (Lemmon)
Homapin, Tab. (Mission)
Hycodan, Tab., Pow., Syr. (Du Pont)
Hycomine Syr., Tab. (Du Pont)
Maracid, Tab. (Marin)
Matropinal, Elix., Inserts (Comatic)
Matropinal Forte, Tab. (Comatic)
Matropinal Forte, Inserts (Comatic)
Mephenesal, Tab. (Richlyn)
Mesopin-PB, Tab., Elixir (Du Pont)
Nau-Aid 15, Supp. (Scrip)
Neocholan, Tab. (Merrell Dow)
Obesa-Mead #15, Tab. (Spencer-Mead)
Obesa-Mead, Tab., Cap. (Spencer-Mead)
Obe-Slim, Tab. (Jenkins)
Pancobile, Tab. (Reid-Provident)
Panitol H.M.B., Tab. (Wesley)
Periodic, Cap. (Towne)
Probilagol, Liq. (Purdue-Frederick)
Sinulin Tablets (Carnrick)
Spasticol S.A., PB, Tab. (Key Pharm.)
Spasmatol, Tab. (Pharmed)
Stim-10/50, Tab. (Scrip)
Stopp-15, 90, Supp. (Keene)
Tapuline, Tab. (Wesley)

HOMATROPINE METHYLBROMIDE AND PHENOBARBITAL COMBINATIONS
See: Bilamide, Tab. (Norgine)
Gustase-Plus, Tab. (Geriatric)
Lanokalin, Tab. (Lannett)
Matropinal, Tab., Elix. (Comatic)
Mesopin-PB, Tab., Elix. (Du Pont)
Novatrin w/Phenob., Tab. (Ayerst)
Oxi-Barb, Tab. (Scrip)
S.B.P. Plus, Tab. (Lemmon)
Spasmed Jr., Tab. (Jenkins)

HOMICEBRIN. (Lilly) Vit. A 2500 U.S.P. units, Vit. B-1 1 mg., B-2 1.2 mg., B-6 0.8 mg., niacinamide 10 mg B-12 3 mcg., C 60 mg., D 400 U.S.P. units/5ml. w/alcohol 5%. Bot. 16 fl. oz.
Use: Vitamin deficiencies.

HOMOCHLORCYCLIZINE. B.A.N. 1-(p-Chlorobenzhydryl)-4-methylhomopiperazine. 1-(4-Chlorobenzhydrylhexahydro-4-methyl-1,4-diazepine.
Use: Antihistamine.

HOMOGENE-S. (Spanner) Testosterone 25 mg., 50 mg or 100 mg./cc. Vial 10 cc.
Use: Androgen therapy.

• **HOMOSALATE.** USAN.
Use: Ultraviolet sunscreen.
W/Combinations.
See: Coppertone, Prods. (Plough)

HOMOSULFANILAMIDE HCl.
See: Sulfbenzamine HCl, Pow. (Flint; Eaton)

HOMO-TET. (Savage) Tetanus Immune Globulin Human 250 u./cc. Vial 1 cc. Syringe, Disposable, 250 u.
Use: Biologic.

HOMPRENORPHINE. B.A.N. N-Cyclopropylmethyl-7,8-dihydro-7α-[1(R)-hydroxy-1-methylpropyl]-0³0⁶-dimethyl-endoethenonormorphine.
Use: Analgesic.

• **HOQUIZIL HCl.** USAN. 2-Hydroxy-2-methylpropyl 4-(6,7-dimethoxy-4-quinazolinyl)-1-piperazinecarboxylate monohydrochloride.
Use: Bronchodilator.

HORMOFOLLIN.
See: Estrone (Various Mfr.)

HORMOGEN-A. (Mallard) Natural estrogens 20,000 I.U./cc. Vial 30 cc.

HORMOGEN DEPOT. (Mallard) Estradiol cypionate 5 mg./cc. Vial 10 cc.

HORMOPLETE. (Key) Conjugated estrogenic substance 0.25 mg., methyltestosterone 2.5 mg., A 12,500 I.U., D 1000 I.U., B-1 10 mg., B-2 3 mg., B-6 2 mg., niacinamide 25 mg., nicotinic acid 5 mg., Ca pantothenate 5 mg., C 75 mg., E 2 I.U., B-12 2 mcg., ferrous sulfate 50 mg., pancreatin 100 mg., dl-methionine 15 mg., inositol 20 mg., choline bitartrate 40 mg., Ca 60 mg., phosphorus 30 mg., Cu 0.45 mg., Mn 0.5 mg., Pot. 2 mg., Zn 0.5 mg., Mg 3 mg./Tab. Bot. 50s, 500s.
Use: Vitamin, mineral, hormone supplement.

Homosalate w/combinations
See: Coppertone, Liq. (Plough)

HOSPITAL FOAM CLEANER. (Aeroceuticals) 0-phenylphenol 0.10%, 4-chloro-2-cyclopentyl-

henol 0.08%, lauric diethanolamide 0.20%, trie-
anolamine dodecylbenzenesulfonate 0.30%.
se: Germicidal, disinfectant foam cleaner.
SPITAL LOTION. (Paddock)
iisobutylcresoxyethoxy-ethyl dimethyl benzyl amm.
hloride, menthol, lanolin, mineral and vegetable
ils. Bot. 4 oz., 8 oz., gal.
T WEATHER" TABLETS. (Pharmex) Salt,
extrose. Tab. Bot. 100s, 1000s.
JRNAZE. (Delta) Chlorpheniramine maleate 8 mg.,
henylephrine HCl 20 mg./Cap. Bot. 100s.
se: Oral antihistaminic, decongestant.
-23. An experimental compound developed at the
asteur Institute in Paris to stop or slow the
production of the Acquired Immune Deficiency
yndrone (AIDS) virus, at least temporarily.
ACTHAR GEL. (Armour) Respiratory
orticotropin injection highly purified 40 U.S.P.
nits/1 ml. Vial 1 ml., 5 ml.; 80 U.S.P. Units/1 ml.
ial 1 ml., 5 ml.
se: I.M. or S.C. stimulation of adrenal cortex &
seases related to it.
LUBRICATING JELLY. (Holland-Rantos) Tube
oz.
se: Lubricating jelly.
-PRENATAL TABLETS. (Cenci) Comprehensive,
ell-balanced, vitamin-mineral formula. Tab. Bot. 90s,
00s.
se: Prenatal supplement.
-TYLAPRIN ELIXIR. (Cenci) Acetaminophen 120
g., alcohol 7%/5 cc. Bot. 2 oz., 4 oz.
se: Analgesic.
NEED. (Hanlon) Chloral hydrate 3¾ gr., 7.5
./Cap. Bot. 100s.
se: Sedative.
-1. (Wampole-Zeus) Herpes Simplex virus type I
st system. Tests 100s.
se: For the qualitative and semi-quantitative detec-
on of HSV-1 antibody in human serum.
-2. (Wampole-Zeus) Herpes simplex virus type II
ntibody test. Tests 100s.
se: For the qualitative and semi-quantitative detec-
on of HSV-2 antibody in human serum.
FACTORATE. (Armour) Antihemophilic factor
uman) dried, heat-treated for I.V. administration
nly. Single-dose vial w/diluent and needles.
se: Classical hemophilia treatment.
FACTORATE GENERATION II. (Armour)
ntihemophilic factor (human) dried heat treated for
V. administration only. Single dose vial w/diluent
nd needles.
se: Classical hemophilia treatment.
STAINLESS OINTMENT. (DeWitt) Ointment.
ube 1 oz.
se: Treatment hemorrhoids.
H RIABEAD. (Abbott) Human thyroid stimulating
ormone radioimmunoassay. Test units 100s.
se: Determination of concentration of human
yroid stimulating hormone in serum.
IAN ANTOHEMOPHILIC FACTOR.
ee: Antihemophilic factor

HUMAN COAGULATION. Fraction II, IX and X. B.A.N. A preparation of human blood containing coagulating factors II, IX and X.
Use: Treatment of hemophilia B deficiency.

HUMAN INSULIN. Insulin Human, U.S.P. XXI.
Use: Hypoglycemic.
See: Humulin Prods. (Lilly)

HUMAN MEASLES IMMUNE SERUM.
See: Immune Globulin, U.S.P. XXI.

HUMAN SERUM ALBUMIN.
See: Albumotope (Squibb)

HUMATIN CAPSULES. (Parke-Davis) Paromycin sulfate 250 mg./Cap. Bot. 16s.
Use: Treatment of intestinal amebiasis.

HUMIST. (Scherer) Sodium chloride 0.65%, chlorobutanol 0.35%. Bot. 15 cc, 45 cc.
Use: Nasal spray.

HUMORSOL. (Merck Sharp & Dohme) Demecarium bromide 0.125% and 0.25% ophthalmic soln. w/sod. chloride, water for injection, benzalkonium chloride 1:5,000. Sol. 5 ml. Ocumeter.
Use: Treatment of glaucoma, miotic, cholinesterase inhibitor.

HUMULIN N. (Lilly) NPH human insulin (recombinant DNA origin) 100 u./ml. Vial 10 ml.
Use: Diabetes treatment.

HUMULIN R. (Lilly) Regular human insulin (recombinant DNA origin) 100 u./ml. Vial 10 ml.
Use: Diabetes treatment.

HURRICAINE. (Beutlich) Benzocaine 20%. Liquid or Gel. Bot. 1 oz.
Use: Topical anesthetic.

HURRICAINE LIQUID PACK. (Beutlich) Benzocaine 20%. Unit dose 0.25 cc. packets. Box 50s.
Use: Topical anesthetic.

HURRICAINE TOPICAL ANESTHETIC SPRAY. (Beutlich) Benzocaine 20%. Aerosol can 2 oz.
Use: Topical anesthetic for oral or mucosal application.

HURRICAINE TOPICAL ANESTHETIC SPRAY KIT. (Beutlich) Benzocaine 20%. Aerosol can 2 oz. plus 200 disposable extension tubes.
Use: Topical anesthetic.

HU-TET. (Hyland) Tetanus immune globulin (human) sterile 16.5% soln., gamma globulin fraction of the plasma of persons who have been immunized w/tetanus toxoid. Vials and syringes 250 u.
Use: Injured persons who run the risk of tetanus infection and need the immediate protection offered by tetanus antitoxin.

HYACIDE. (Niltig) Benzethonium chloride 0.1% with sod. nitrite 0.55%. Bot. 1 oz.
Use: Germicidal solution.

HYALEX. (Miller) Magnesium salicylate 260 mg., magnesium p-aminobenzoate 163 mg., Vit. A 1500 I.U., Vit. D 100 I.U., Vit. E 3 I.U., Vit. B-12 2 mcg., pantothenic acid 5 mg., zinc 0.7 mg./Tab. Bot. 100s.
Use: Arthritis, bursitis, neuritis & rheumatism.

HYALIDASE.
See: Hyaluronidase (Various Mfr.)

• **HYALURONIDASE INJECTION,** U.S.P. XXI. Hyalidase, Hydase Enzymes which depolymerize hyaluronic acid. Hyalase, Rondase.
Use: Hypodermoclyses & promote diffusion.
See: Alidase, Vial (Searle)
Wydase, Vial (Wyeth)

• **HYALURONIDASE FOR INJECTION,** U.S.P. XXI.

HYAMAGNATE. Hydroxy-Aluminum-Magnesium-Aminoacetate, Sodium-free.

HYAMATE. (Xttrium) Buramate.
Use: Tranquilizer.

HYAMINE 10-X. (Rohm & Haas) Di-isobutyl cresoxy ethoxy ethyl dimethyl benzyl ammonium chloride.
W/Sulfur, salicylic acid.
See: Derma-Cover, Liq. (Scrip)

HYAMINE 1622. (Rohm & Haas)
See: Benzethonium Chloride U.S.P. XXI.

HYAMINE 2389. (Rohm & Haas) Mainly methyl dodecyl benzyl trimethyl ammonium chloride.
Use: Disinfection and deodorization.

HYAMINE 3500. (Rohm & Haas)
See: Benzalkonium Chloride U.S.P. XXI.

HYATAL ELIXIR. (Winsale; Kenyon) Phenobarbital 16 mg., hyoscyamine sulfate 0.1037 mg., atropine sulfate 0.0194 mg., scopolamine hyoscine HBr 0.0065 mg./5 cc. Bot. pt., gal.

HYBALAMIN. (Mallard) Crystalline hydroxocobalamin 1000 mcg./cc. Vial 10 cc.

HYBEC FORTE. (Amlab) Vit. B-1 100 mg., B-2 20 mg., B-6 2.5 mg., niacinamide 25 mg., C 200 mg., B-12 10 mcg., Ca pantothenate 5 mg., iron 10 mg., choline bitartrate 24 mg., inositol 10 mg., biotin 5 mcg., liver 50 mg., yeast 100 mg./Tab. Bot. 30s, 100s.
Use: Water-soluble-vitamin deficiencies.

HYBEPHEN ELIXIR. (Beecham Labs) Phenobarbital 15 mg., hyoscyamine sulf. 0.1277 mg., atropine sulf. 0.233 mg., scopolamine HBr 0.0094 mg./5 ml. w/alcohol 16.5%, Orange color & citris flavor. Bot. pt.
Use: Antispasmodic and sedative.

HYBEPHEN TABLETS. (Beecham Labs) Phenobarbital 15 mg., hyosyamine sulf. 0.1277 mg., atropine sulf. 0.0233 mg., scopolamine HBr 0.0094 mg./Tab. Bot. 100s.
Use: Antipasmotic and sedative.

HYBOLIN DECANOATE. (Hyrex) Nandrolone decanoate 50 mg., 100 mg./ml. Vial 2 ml.
Use: Anabolic maintenance.

HYBOLIN IMPROVED. (Hyrex) Nandrolene phenpropionate 25 mg./ml. Vial 5 ml. 50 mg./ml. Vial 2 ml.
Use: Anabolic maintenance.

HYCAL. (Beecham Labs) Calories 280, carbohydrates 49.5%, fat-not more than 0.02%, protein-not more than 0.03%, water 69 ml./3.8 fl. oz. Bot. 3.8 oz. Case 24 bot.
Use: Low-electrolyte, limited-liquid volume, high carbohydrate source of calories.

• **HYCANTHONE.** USAN. 1-[(2-(Diethylamino)-ethyl)-amino]-4-(hydroxymethyl)thioxanthen-9-one.
Use: Schistosomacide.

HYCLORITE. Sod. Hypochlorite Sol., U.S.P. XXI.

HYCODAN. (Du Pont) Hydrocodone bitartrate 5 mg., homatropine methylbromide 1.5 mg./5 ml. or Tab. Syr. Bot. 1 pt., 1 gal., Tab. Bot. 100s, 500s, 1000s
Use: Antitussive.

HYCODAPHEN. (Ascher) Hydrocodone bitartrate 5 mg., acetaminophen 500 mg./Tab. Bot. 100s.
Use: Pain relief.

HYCOFF-A-NN LIQUID. (Saron) Dextromethorpha HBr 15 mg., pseudoephedrine HCl 45 mg., dyphylline 100 mg./15 ml. Alcohol free. Bot. pt.
Use: Antitussive, decongestant, bronchodilator.

HYCOFF X-NN. (Saron) Dextromethorphan HBr 10 mg pseudoephedrine HCl 30 mg./5 ml. Alcohol and sugar free. Bot. pt.
Use: Antitussive, decongestant.

HYCOMINE. (Du Pont) Hydrocodone bitartrate 5 mg. phenylpropanolamine HCl 25 mg./5 ml. Syr. Bot. 1 pt., 1 gal.
Use: Orally, antitussive and antihistaminic.

HYCOMINE COMPOUND. (Du Pont) Hydrocodone bitartrate 5 mg., chlorpheniramine maleate 2 mg., phenylephrine HCl 10 mg., acetaminophen 250 mg., caffeine 30 mg./Tab. Bot. 100s, 500s.
Use: Antihistaminic for treatment of respiratory tra infections.

HYCOMINE PEDIATRIC. (Du Pont) Hydrocodone bitartrate 2.5 mg., phenylpropanolamine HCl 12.5 mg./5 ml. Bot. 1 pt., 1 gal.
Use: Orally, antitussive.

HYCORTOLE. (Premo) Hydrocortisone. **Cream:** 0.5% 5 Gm., 20 Gm.; 1%, 5 Gm, 20 Gm., & 4 oz. 2.5% Tube 5 Gm., 20 Gm.; **Oint.:** 1%, 2.5% Tube 5 Gm 20 Gm.

HYCOTUSS EXPECTORANT. (Du Pont) Hydrocodone bitartrate 5 mg., guaifenesin 100 mg alcohol 10% v/v/5 ml. Bot. pt.
Use: Antitussive.

HYDANTOIN DERIVATIVES.
Use: Anticonvulsant.
See: Dilantin, Prep. (Parke-Davis)
Diphenylhydantoin Sod., U.S.P.
Ethotoin
Mesantoin, Tab. (Sandoz)
Phenantoin

HYDASE.
Use: Hypodermoclyses & promote diffusion.
See: Hyaluronidase (Various Mfr.)

HYDELTRA-T.B.A. (Merck Sharp & Dohme) Prednisolone tebutate 20 mg. w/sod. citrate 1 mg., polysorbate 80-1 mg., sorbitol soln. 0.5 ml. (equiv. 450 mg. d-sorbitol), benzyl alcohol 9 mg., water injection q.s. 1 ml. Vial 1 ml., 5 ml.
Use: Corticosteroid (glucocorticoid).

HYDELTRASOL INJECTION. (Merck Sharp & Dohme) Prednisolone sodium phosphate 20 mg./ml. w/niacinamide 25 mg., sod. hydroxide to adjust pH, disodium edetate 0.5 mg., sod. bisulfite 1mg., phenol 5 mg., water for injection q.s. 1 ml. Vial 2 ml., 5 ml.
Use: Corticosteroid (glucocorticoid).

HYDELTRONE. (MSD AGVET) Prednisolone sodium phosphate and neomycin sulfate equivalent to 2.5

ng. prednisolone 21-phosphate and 3.5 mg. neomy-
:in base/Gm.
Jse: Ophthalmic ointment, veterinary medicine.
DELTRONE-T.B.A. (MSD AGVET) Prednisolone
ebutate susp. 20 mg./cc.
Jse: Anti-inflammatory agent, veterinary medicine.
DERGINE LC LIQUID CAPSULES. (Sandoz)
:rgoloid mesylates 1 mg./Cap. Bot. 100s, 500s.
SandoPak 100s 500s.
Jse: Selected symptoms in elderly patients.
DERGINE LIQUID. (Sandoz) Equal parts of
lihydroergocornine, dihydroergocristine,
lihydroergocryptine as the mesylates. (Ergoloid
Aesylates) 1 mg./ml. Bot. 100 ml. w/dropper.
Jse: Selected symptoms in elderly patients.
DERGINE, ORAL. (Sandoz) Equal parts of
lihydroergocornine, dihydroergocristine,
lihydroergocryptine (Ergoloid Mesylates). 1
ng./Tab. Bot. 100s, 500s. SandoPak (unit dose)
00s, 500s.
Jse: Selected symptoms in elderly patients.
DERGINE, SUBLINGUAL. (Sandoz) Equal parts of
lihydroergocornine, dihydroergocristine,
lihydroergocryptine as the mesylates (Ergoloid
Aesylates). 0.5 mg. and 1.0 mg./Tab. Tab. Bot.
00s, 1000s. SandoPak (unit dose) 100s.
Jse: Selected symptoms in elderly patients.
DEX. (Moore Kirk) Methamphetamine HCl 5 or 10
ng./Tab. Bot. 1000s.
Jse: For mild depression and anxiety states;
appetite control in obesity.
DEXTRAN. (Hyrex) Iron dextran complex 50
ng./ml. Vial 10 ml.
Jse: Anemia.
DORIL. (Cenci) Hydrochlorthiazide 25 or 50
ng./Tab. Bot. 100s, 1000s.
Jse: Diuretic.
DRABAMINE PHENOXYMETHYL PENICILLIN.
See: Penicillin V Hydrabamine.
DRABASE. (Summers) Hydrophilic oint. Jar. 1 lb.
DRACRYLIC ACID BETA LACTONE.
See: Propiolactone
DRAL. (Reid-Provident) **25/25:** Hydralazine HCl 25
ng., hydrochlorothiazide 25 mg./Cap. **50/50:**
Hydralazine HCl 50 mg., hydrochlorothiazide 50
ng/Cap. **100/50:** Hydralazine HCl 100 mg.,
hydrochlorothiazide 50 mg./Cap. Bot. 100s.
Jse: Anti-hypertensive.
DRALAZIDE. (Zenith) Hydralazine 25 mg.,
hydrochlorothiazide 15 mg./Tab. Bot. 100s.
Jse: Antihypertensive.
DRALAZIDE TABS. (Goldline) Bot. 100s, 1000s.
Jse: Antihypertensive.
YDRALAZINE HCl, U.S.P. XXI. Inj., Tab., U.S.P.
XXI. 1-Hydrazinophthalazine HCl. Phthalazine, 1-hy-
lrazino-, HCl.
Jse: Antihypertensive.
See: Apresoline, Amp. & Tab. (Ciba)
Dralzine, Tab. (Lemmon)
Hydralyn, Tab. (Kenyon)
W/Hydrochlorothiazide.
See: Apresazide, Cap. (Ciba)
Apresoline-Esidrix, Tab. (Ciba)
Hydralazide, Tab. (Zenith)
Hydroserpine Plus, Tab. (Zenith)
W/Reserpine.
See: Dralserp, Tab. (Lemmon)
Serpasil-Apresoline, Tab. (Ciba)
W/Reserpine, hydrochlorothiazide (Esidrix).
See: Harbolin, Tab. (Arcum)
Ser-Ap-Es, Tab. (Ciba)
Serapine, Tab. (Cenci)
Serpahyde TM, Tab. (Wolins)
Thia-Serpa-Zine, Tab. (Robinson)
Unipres, Tab. (Reid-Provident)
HYDRALLAZINE. B.A.N. 1-Hydrazinophthalazine. Hydralazine (I.N.N.) Apresoline hydrochloride.
Use: Hypotensive.
HYDRALYN. (Kenyon) Hydralazine HCl 25 mg., 50 mg./Tab. Bot. 100s, 1000s.
Use: Hypertension.
HYDRAMINE ELIXIR. (Goldline) Diphenhydramine. Bot. 4 oz. pt., gal.
Use: Cough medication.
HYDRARGAPHEN. B.A.N. 2,2′-(Binaphthalene-3-sulfonyloxyphenylmercury). Phenylmercury 2:2′-dinaphthylmethane-3:3′-disulfonate.
Use: Antiparasitic; anti-infective.
See: Penofome
Penotrane (Ward Blenkinsop in England)
HYDRASERP. (Geneva) Hydrochlorothiazide 25 mg., 50 mg., reserpine 0.1 mg./Tab. Bot. 100s, 1000s.
HYDRA-SPRAY L.A. (Vortech) Xylometazoline HC1. Bot. 20 ml.
Use: Nasal decongestant.
HYDRASTINE. (Penick) Alkaloid. Bot. 1 oz.
HYDRASTINE HYDROCHLORIDE. (Penick) Pow., Bot. 1 oz.
Use: Uterine hemostatic.
HYDRATE. (Hyrex) Dimenhydrinate 50 mg./ml. w/propylene glycol 50%, benzyl alcohol 5%. Amp. 1 ml. Boxes 25s, 100s; Vials 10 cc.
Use: Antinauseant, antihistamine.
HYDRAZIDE CAPS. (Goldline) Bot. 100s, 1000s.
Use: Antihypertensive.
I-HYDRAZINOPHTHALAZINE MONOHYDROCHLORIDE. Hydralazine Hydrochloride, U.S.P. XXI.
HYDRAZOL. (Softcon) Acetazolamide 250 mg./Tab. Bot. 100s.
Use: Carbonic anhydrase inhibitor.
HYDRAZONE. 3-(4-Methyl-piperazinyliminomethyl)rifamycin SV.
Use: Pulmonary tuberculosis.
See: Rimactane, Cap. (Ciba)
HYDREA. (Squibb) Hydroxyurea. 500 mg./Cap. Bot. 100s.
Use: Antineoplastic agent.
HYDRIL. (Blaine) Diphenhydramine HCl 80 mg., ammonium chloride 12 gr., sodium citrate 5 gr., menthol 1/10 gr., alcohol 5%/oz. Bot. 4 oz.
Use: Expectorant.

HY-DRINE. (Zemmer) Benzthiazide 50 mg./Tab. Bot. 1000s.
HYDRIODIC ACID. (Various Mfr.)
Use: Iodide therapy.
HYDRIODIC ACID SYRUP. (Lilly) Hydriodic acid 1.4 Gm./100 ml. Bot. 16 fl. oz.
HYDRIODIC ACID THERAPY.
See: Aminoacetic Acid HI
HYDRISALIC GEL. (Pedinol) Salicylic acid 6%, isopropanol, propylene glycol, hydroxypropyl cellulose. Tube 1 oz.
Use: Keratolytic.
HYDRISEA LOTION. (Pedinol) Dead sea salts concentrate 8%, sodium, potassium, calcium magnesium Chloride, propylene glycol stearate, polysorbate 40, silicone oil, coloring agent. Bot. 4 oz.
Use: Hyperkeratotic and dry skin conditioner.
HYDRISINOL CREME AND LOTION. (Pedinol) Sulfonated hydrogenated castor oil. **Cream:** Spout Cap Jar 4 oz., 1 lb. **Lotion:** Bot. 8 oz.
Use: Skin moisturizer, particularly for diabetics.
HYDRO-12. (Table Rock) Crystalline hydroxocobalamin 1000 mcg./cc. Pkg. 10 cc.
HYDRO-BAN CAPSULES. (Whiteworth) Juniper oil 10 mg., uva ursi 50 mg., buchu extract 50 mg., parsley piert extract 50 mg., iron 6 mg./Cap. Bot. 42s.
Use: Diuretic with iron.
HYDROBEXAN. (Keene) Hydroxocobalamin 1000 mcg./ml. Vial 10 ml.
HYDRO-CHLOR. (Vortech) Hydrochlorthiazide 50 mg./Tab. Bot. 100s, 1000s.
Use: Diuretic.
HYDROCHLORATE. Same as Hydrochloride.
• **HYDROCHLORIC ACID,** N.F XVI. Diluted, N.F. XVI. (Various Mfr.) Muriatic Acid), Absolute 38%. Diluted 10%.
Use: Well diluted, achlorhydria; pharm. aid (acidifying agent).
■ **HYDROCHLORIC ACID THERAPY.**
Use: Gastric acidifier.
See: Betaine HCl (Various Mfr.)
Glutamic Acid HCl (Various Mfr.)
Glycine HCl (Various Mfr.)
HYDROCHLOROSERPINE. (Freeport) Hydralazine HCl. 25 mg., Hydrochlorthiazide 15 mg., reserpine 0.1 mg./Tab. Bot. 1000s.
Use: Antihypertensive.
• **HYDROCHLOROTHIAZIDE,** U.S.P. XXI. Tab. U.S.P. XXI. 2H-1,2,4-Benzothiadiazine-7-sulfonamide, 6-chloro-3,4-dihydro-,1,1-dioxide. 6-Chloro-3,4-dihydro-2H-1,2,4-Benzothiadiazene-7-sulfonamide 1, 1-dioxide.
Use: Diuretic.
See: Chlorzide, Tab. (Foy)
Delco-Retic, Tab. (Delco)
Diu-Scrip, Cap. (Scrip)
Esidrix, Tab. (Ciba)
Hydromal, Tab. (Mallard)
HydroDiuril, Tab. (Merck Sharp & Dohme)
Hydrozide Inj. (MSD AGVET)
Hydrozide-50, Tab. (Mayrand)
Kenazide-E,-H, Tab. (Kenyon)
Oretic, Tab. (Abbott)
Ro-Hydrazide, Tab. (Robinson)
SK-Hydrochlorothiazide, Tab. (SmithKline)
Thiuretic, Tab. (Parke-Davis)
Zide, Tab. (Reid-Provident)
W/Deserpidine.
See: Oreticyl, Tab. (Abbott)
W/Guanethidine monosulfate.
See: Esimil, Tab. (Ciba)
W/Hydralazine HCl.
See: Apresazide, Cap. (Ciba)
Apresoline-Esidrix, Tab. (Ciba)
Hydralazide, Tab. (Zenith)
W/Methyldopa.
See: Aldoril, Tab. (Merck Sharp & Dohme)
W/Propranolol.
See: Inderide, Tab (Ayerst)
W/Reserpine.
See: Aquapres-R, Tab. (Castal)
Hydropine, Tab. (Wolins)
Hydropres, Tab. (Merck Sharp & Dohme)
Hydroserp, Tab. (Zenith)
Hydroserpine, Tab. (Geneva)
Hydrotensin-50, Tab. (Mayrand)
Hyperserp, Tab. (Elder)
Mallopress, Tab. (Mallard)
Serpasil-Esidrix, Tab. (Ciba)
Thia-Serp-25, Tab. (Robinson)
Thia-Serp-50, Tab. (Robinson)
W/Reserpine, Hydralazine HCl.
See: Harbolin, Tab. (Arcum)
Hydroserpine Plus, Tab. (Zenith)
SER-AP-ES, Tab. (Ciba)
Serapine, Tab. (Cenci)
Serpahyde TM, Tab. (Wolins)
Thia-Serpa-Zine, Tab. (Robinson)
Unipres, Tab. (Reid-Provident)
W/Spironolactone.
See: Aldactazide, Tab. (Searle)
W/Timolol maleate.
See: Timolide, Tab. (Merck Sharp & Dohme)
W/Triamterene.
See: Dyazide, Cap. (SmithKline)
■ **HYDROCHOLERETICS.**
See: Bile Salts (Various Mfr.)
Dehydrocholic Acid (Various Mfr.)
Desoxycholic Acid (Various Mfr.)
Ox Bile Ext. (Various Mfr.)
HYDROCIL INSTANT. (Rowell) Blond psyllium coating containing psyllium 3.5 Gm/3.7 Gm. dos[illegible] Tan granular, instant mix, sugar-free, low sodium, potassium powder. Unit dose packets. Jar 250 G[illegible]
Use: Bulk forming laxative.
HYDRO COBEX. (Pasadena Research) Hydroxocobalamin 1000 mcg. Vial 10 cc.
HYDROCODONE. B.A.N. Dihydrocodeinone (Vario[illegible] Mfr.) 7,8-Dihydro-0^3-methylnormorphine.
Use: Cough suppressant.
HYDROCODONE RESIN COMPLEX.
Use: Cough suppressant.

'Phenyltoloxamine resin complex.
See: Tussionex, Prods. (Pennwalt)

HYDROCODONE BITARTRATE, U.S.P. XXI. Tab., U.S.P. XXI. Dihydrocodeinone bitartrate. 4,5α-Epoxy-3-methoxy-17-methylmorphinan-6-one tartrate (1:1) hydrate (2:5).
Use: Antitussive.
See: Anodynos-DHC, Tab. (Berlex)
Dicodethal, Elix. (Lannett)
Combinations.
See: Vicodin, Tab. (Knoll)

DROCODONE COMP. SYRUP. (Goldline) Hydrocodone bitartrate w/homatropine methylbromide, Bot. pt. gal.
Use: Antitussive.

DROCORT. (Kenyon) Hydrocortisone 1%, clioquinol 3%, pramoxine HCl 0.5% in a cream base. Jar 20 Gm.
Use: Anti-inflammatory (topical).

DROCORTAMATE HCl. 17-Hydroxycorticosterone-21-diethylaminoaceate HCl.
Use: Anti-inflammatory (topical).
See: Ulcortar, Oint. (Ulmer)

DROCORTEX. (Kenyon) Hydrocortisone 1% in a cream base. Jar. 20 Gm.

HYDROCORTISONE, U.S.P. XXI. Cream, Sterile, Susp., Oint., Gel., Tab. Lot., Enema, U.S.P. XXI. Pregn-4-ene-3,20-dione, 11,17,21-trihydroxy-, (11β)-Hydrocortisone. 11β, 17, 21-Trihydroxypregn-4-ene-3, 20-Dione. Compound F. Cortisol. (Upjohn) Micronized non-sterile powder for prescription compounding.
Use: Anti-inflammatory (topical).
See: Acticort Lotion 100. (Cummins)
Aeroseb-HC, Aersol (Herbert)
Alphaderm, Cream (Norwich Eaton)
Caldecort Spray (Pharmacraft)
Cetacort, Lot. (Owen)
Cort-Dome, Cream, Lot., Supp. (Miles Pharm)
Cortef, Tab., Cream, Oint. (Upjohn)
Cortenema, Enema (Rowell)
Cortinal, Tube (Kenyon)
Cortril, Oint. (Pfipharmecs)
Cremesone, Cream (Dalin)
Delacort, Lot. (Mericon)
Dermacort, Cream, Lot. (Rowell)
Dermolate, Prods. (Schering)
Durel-Cort, Creme, Oint., Lot. (Durel)
Ecosone, Cream (Star)
HC Derma-Pax, Liq. (Recsei)
HI-COR-1.0, Cream, (C&M Pharmacal)
HI-COR-2.5, Cream (C&M Pharmacal)
Hycortole, Cream, Oint. (Premo)
Hydrocortex, Tube (Kenyon)
Hydrocortone, Tab. (Merck Sharp & Dohme)
Hytone, Cream, Oint., Lot. (Dermik)
Lexocort, Pow., Lot. (Lexington)
Lipo-Adrenal Cortex, Vial (Upjohn)
Maso-Cort, Lot. (Mason)
Microcort, Lotion (Alto Pharm.)
My Cort, Cream (Scrip)
Optef, Sol. (Upjohn)
Proctocort, Oint. (Rowell)
Rocort, Lot. (Rocky Mtn.)
Signef, Supp. (Fellows-Testagar)
Synacort, Cream (Syntex)
Tarcortin, Cream (Reed & Carnrick)
Texacort 25, & 50, Lot. (Cooper)
Ulcort, Cream, Lot. (Ulmer)

HYDROCORTISONE W/COMBINATIONS
See: Achromycin W/Hydrocortisone, Oint., Ophth. Oint. (Lederle)
Acrisan w/Hydrocortisone, Liq. (Recsei)
Aural Acute, Ear Drops (Saron)
Bafil, Cream. (Scruggs)
Barseb HC, Scalp Lot. (Barnes-Hind)
Barseb Thera-spray, Aerosol (Barnes-Hind)
Biscolan HC, Supp. (Lannett)
Bro-Parin, Otic Susp. (Riker)
Calmurid HC, Cream (Pharmacia)
Caquin, Cream (O'Neal, Jones, Feldman)
Carmol HC, Cream (Ingram)
Coidocort, Cream (Coast)
Cor-Tar-Quin, Cream, Lot. (Miles Pharm)
Cortef, Preps. (Upjohn)
Corticaine Cream (Glaxo)
Corticoid, Cream (Jenkins)
Cortin, Cream (C&M Pharm.)
Cortisporin, Prep. (Burroughs Wellcome)
Derma-Cover-HC, Liq., Oint. (Scrip)
Dermarex, Cream (Hyrex-Key)
Dicort, Cream, Supp. (Hickam)
Doak Oil Forte, Liq. (Doak)
Drotic No. 2, Drops (Ascher)
Durel-Cort 'V,' Cream, Oint., Lot. (Durel)
Eldecort, Cream (Elder)
Fostril HC, Lot. (Westwood)
HC-Form, Jelly (Recsei)
HC-Jel, Jelly (Recsei)
Heb-Cort., Cream, Lot. (Barnes-Hind)
Heb-Cort MC, Lot. (Barnes-Hind)
Heb-Cort. V, Cream, Lot. (Barnes-Hind)
Hexaderm, Hexaderm-I.Q., Cream (Amfre-Grant)
Hi-Cort N Cream (Blaine)
Hill-Cortac, Cream, Lot. (Hill)
Hydrocort, Tube (Kenyon)
Hydroquin, Cream, Oint. (Robinson)
Hysone, Oint. (Mallard)
Kencort, Cream (Kenyon)
Kleer, Spray (Scrip)
Lanvisone, Cream (Lannett)
Loroxide-HC, Lot. (Dermik)
Maso-Form, Cream (Mason)
Mity-quin, Cream (Reid-Provident)
Myci-Cort, Liq., Spray (Misemer)
My-Cort, Drops, Lot., Oint., Spray (Scrip)
Neocort, Oint. (H.V.P.)
Neo-Cort Dome, Cream, Lot., Drops (Miles Pharm)
Neo Cort Top, Oint. (Standex)
Neo-Domeform-HC, Cream, Lot., Susp. (Miles Pharm)
Nutracort, Cream, Gel., Lot. (Owen)
1 + 1 Creme, 1 + 1-F Creme (Dunhall)
Ophthel, Liq. (Elder).

Ophthocort, Oint. (Parke Davis)
Orlex HC Otic (Baylor)
Oto, Drops (Reid-Provident)
Otobiotic, Soln. (Schering)
Otocalm-H Ear Drops (Parmed)
Otostan H.C. (Standex)
Panhydrosone, Tab., Pow. (Panray)
Pyocidin-Otic, Sol. (Berlex)
Quinsone, Cream (Sutliff & Case)
Racet Forte, Cream (Lemmon)
Racet LCD, Cream (Lemmon)
Rectal Medicone-HC (Medicone)
Sherform-HC, Creme (Sheryl)
Stera-Form, Creme (Mayrand)
Steramine Otic, Drops (Mayrand)
Syntar HC Cream, Oint. (Elder)
Tarcortin, Cream (Reed & Carnrick)
Tar-Quin-HC, Oint. (Jenkins)
Tenda HC, Cream (Dermik)
Terra-Cortril, Prep. (Pfipharmecs)
Theracort, Lot. (C&M Pharm.)
T-Spray, Spray (Saron)
Vanoxide-HC, Lot. (Dermik)
V-Cort, Cream (Scrip)
Vioform-Hydrocortisone, Prep. (Ciba)
Vio-Hydrocort, Oint., Cream (Quality Generics)
Vytone, Cream, (Dermik)

• **HYDROCORTISONE ACETATE,** U.S.P. XXI. Sterile Susp., Lotion, Ophth. Oint., Ophth. Susp., Oint., Cream, U.S.P. XXI. Pregn-4-ene-3,20-dione, 21-(acetyloxy)-11,17-dihydroxy-, (11β)-. Hydrocortisone 21-acetate. 17-Hydroxycorticosterone-21-acetate, comp.F. (Upjohn) Micronized non-sterile powder for prescription compounding.
Use: Adrenocortical steroid (topical anti-inflammatory).
See: Anusol-HC, Supp. (Warner-Chilcott)
Biosone, Vial (Kay)
Caldecort, Cream (Pharmacraft)
Cortef Acetate, Ophth. Oint., Inj. (Upjohn)
Cortifoam, Aerosol (Reed & Carnrick)
Cortiprel, Cream (Pasadena Research)
Cortril Acetate, Aq. Susp., Oint. (Pfipharmecs)
Ferncort, Lotion (Ferndale)
Fernisone Inj., Vial (Ferndale)
Gynecort, Oint. (Combe)
Hydro-Can (Paddock)
Hydrocort, Vial (Dunhall)
Hydrocortone Acetate, Inj. (Merck Sharp & Dohme)
Hydrosone, Inj. (Sig)
My-Cort, Lot. (Scrip)
Pramosone Cream, Lot. (Ferndale)
Span-Ster, Inj. (Scrip)
Tucks-HC (Parke-Davis)

HYDROCORTISONE ACETATE W/COMBINATIONS
See: Anusol-HC, Cream, Supp. (Warner-Chilcott)
Biotic-Opth W/HC, Oint. (Scrip)
Biotres HC, Cream (Central)
Biscolan HC, Supp. (Lannett)
Carmol HC, Cream (Ingram)
Chloromycetin-Hydrocortisone Ophth. Susp. (Parke-Davis)
Coly-Mycin-S Otic, Sol. (Warner-Chilcott)
Cor-Oticin, Liq. (Maurry)
Cortaid, Cream, Lot., Oint. (Upjohn)
Cortef Acetate, Inj., Oint., Susp. (Upjohn)
Derma Medicone-HC, Oint. (Medicone)
Dicort, Supp. (Hickam)
Doctient HC, Supp. (Suppositoria)
Epifoam, Aerosol (Reed & Carnrick)
Estro-V HC, Supp. (Webcon)
Eye-Cort, Sol. (Mallard)
Furacin-HC Otic (Eaton)
Furacin HC Urethral Inserts (Eaton)
Furacort Cream (Eaton)
Komed HC, Lotion (Barnes-Hind)
Lida-Mantle HC, Cream (Miles Pharm)
Mantadil, Cream (Burroughs Wellcome)
Neo-Cortef, Preps. (Upjohn)
Neo-Hytone Cream (Dermik)
Neopolycin-HC, Oint., Ophth. Oint. (Merrell Dow)
Ophthocort, Ointment (Parke-Davis)
Ortho, Eye-Ear Drops (Vortech)
Proctofoam-HC, Aer. (Reid and Carnrick)
Pyracort, Liq. (Lemmon)
Quinsone, Oint. (Sutliff & Case)
Racet Forte, Cream (Lemmon)
Rectacort, Supp. (Century)
Rectal Medicone-HC, Supp. (Medicone)
Wyanoids HC, Suppos. (Wyeth)

• **HYDROCORTISONE AND ACETIC ACID OTIC SOLUTION,** U.S.P. XXI.
Use: Anti-inflammatory.

• **HYDROCORTISONE BUTYRATE,** U.S.P. XXI.
Use: Glucocorticoid.

• **HYDROCORTISONE CYPIONATE,** U.S.P. XXI. Ora[l] Susp. U.S.P. XXI. Hydrocortisone 21-cyclopentan[e]propionate. Hydrocortisone Cypionate.
Use: Glucocorticoid.

• **HYDROCORTISONE HEMISUCCINATE,** U.S.P. XX[I]

• **HYDROCORTISONE SODIUM PHOSPHATE,** U.S.[P.] XXI. Inj., U.S.P. XXI. Pregn-4-ene-3,20-dione, 11,1[7]-dihydroxy-21-(phosphonoxy)-, disodium salt, (11β)-. Hydrocortisone 21-(disodium phosphate). H[y]drocortisone Sodium Phosphate.
Use: Adrenocortical steroid (anti-inflammatory).

• **HYDROCORTISONE SODIUM SUCCINATE,** U.S.P. XXI. Inj., U.S.P. XXI. Pregn-4-ene-3,20-dione, 31-(3-carboxy-l-oxopropoxy)-11,17-dihydroxy-, (11β)-. H[y]drocortisone 21-(sodium succinate). Hydrocortiso[ne] Sodium Succinate.
Use: Adrenocortical steroid (anti-inflammatory).
See: A-hydroCort, Vial (Abbott)
Solu-Cortef, Vial (Upjohn)

HYDROCORTISONE DIETHYLAMINOACETATE HC[l]
See: Hydrocortamate

HYDROCORTISONE DYPROPIONATE.
See: Cortef, Fluid (Upjohn)

HYDROCORTISONE I.V.
See: A-Hydro Cort, Vial (Abbott)
Solu-Cortef, Vial (Upjohn)

HYDROCORTISONE PHOSPHATE.
See: Hydrocortone Phosphate, Inj. (Merck Sharp & Dohme)

YDROCORTISONE VALERATE, U.S.P. XXI.
ream, U.S.P. XXI.
Jse: Glucocorticoid.
See: Westcort Cream (Westwood)

DROCORTONE ACETATE SALINE SUSPENSION. Merck Sharp & Dohme) Hydrocortisone Acetate 25 ng./ml. or 50 mg./ml., w/sod. chloride 9 mg., olysorbate 80 4 mg., sod. carboxymethylcellulose mg./ml. w/benzyl alcohol 9 mg. q.s. water for njection to 1 ml. Vial 5 ml.
Jse: Corticosteroid for intra-articular, intralesional and soft tissue injection.

DROCORTONE PHOSPHATE INJECTION. (Merck Sharp & Dohme) Hydrocortisone sodium phosphate quivalent to hydrocortisone 50 mg./ml. v/creatinine 8 mg., sod. citrate 10 mg./ml. w/sod. ydroxide to adjust pH, sod. bisulfite 3.2mg., nethylparaben 1.5mg., propylparaben 0.2mg., water or injection q.s./ml. Vial 2ml. multiple dose, 10 ml. multiple dose. Disp. syringe 2 ml. single dose.
Jse: Adrenocortical steroid.

DROCORTONE TABLETS. (Merck Sharp & Dohme) Hydrocortisone 10 mg., 20 mg./Tab. Bot. 00s.
Jse: Corticosteroid (glucocorticoid).

DRO-D TABLETS. (Blue Cross) Hydrochlorothiazide 5 mg. or 50 mg./Tab. Bot. 1000s.
Jse: Diuretic.

DRODIURIL. (Merck Sharp & Dohme) Hydrochlorothiazide 25 mg./Tab. Bot. 100s, 1000s; Unit-dose 100s; 50 mg./Tab. Bot. 100s, 1000s, 000s. Unit-dose 100s; 100 mg./Tab. Bot. 100s.
Jse: Diuretic, antihypertensive.

DRO-ERGOT. (Interstate) Hydrogenated ergot alkaloids 0.5 mg. or 1.0 mg./Tab. Bot. 100s.

YDROFILCON A. USAN.
Jse: Contact lens material.

YDROFLUMETHIAZIDE, U.S.P. XXI. Tab., U.S.P. XXI. 3,4-Dihydro-6-tri-fluoromethyl-7-sulfamoylbenzo-,2,4-thiadiazine1,1 dioxide,3,4-Dihydro-6-(trifluoromethyl)-2H-1,2,4-benzo-thiadiazine-7-sulfonamide-1,1-Dioxide. Di-Ademil; Hydrenox; Naclex; Rontyl
Jse: Antihypertensive; diuretic.
See: Diucardin, Tab. (Ayerst)
Saluron, Tab. (Bristol)
Reserpine.
See: Salutensin, Tab. (Bristol)
Salutensin-Demi, Tab. (Bristol)

DROGEN DIOXIDE.
See: Hydrogen Peroxide.

YDROGEN PEROXIDE CONCENTRATE, U.S.P. XXI.

YDROGEN PEROXIDE TOPICAL SOLUTION, U.S.P. XXI. (Various Mfr.) (3%). 4 oz., 8 oz., pt.
Jse: Antiseptic.

DROGEN PEROXIDE SOLUTION 30%, Perhydrol. Hydrogen pioxide. Bot. 0.25 lb., 0.5 lb., 1 lb.
Jse: Dentistry & preparing the 3% solution.

DROGESIC. (Edwards) Hydrocodone birtartrate 7.5 ng., acetaminophen 650 mg./Tab. Bot. 100s.
Jse: Mild to moderate pain.

HYDROLOID-G SUBLINGUAL. (Major) Ergoloid mesylates: 0.5 mg./Tab. Bot. 250s; 0.1 mg./Tab. Bot. 250s, 1000s.
Use: Selected symptoms in the elderly.

HYDROLOID-G TABS. (Major) Ergoloid mesylates 1 mg./Tab. Bot. 250s, 1000s.
Use: Selected symptoms in the elderly.

HYDROMAL. (Mallard) Hydrochlorothiazide 50 mg./Tab. Bot. 1000s

HYDROMAX SYRUP. (Blue Cross) Ephedrine sulfate 6.25 mg., theophylline 32.5 mg., hydroxyzine HCl 2.5 mg./5 ml. Bot. 16 oz.
Use: Bronchodilator for use in asthma.

HYDROMORPHINOL. B.A.N. 7,8-Dihydro-14-hydroxymorphine. Numorphan Oral
Use: Narcotic analgesic.

HYDROMORPHONE. B.A.N. 7,8-Dihydromorphinone. Dilaudid hydrochloride
Use: Narcotic analgesic.

HYDROMORPHONE. 4,5-Epoxy-3-hydroxy-17-methylmorphinan-6-one.
Use: Analgesic (narcotic).

• **HYDROMORPHONE HYDROCHLORIDE,** U.S.P. XXI. Inj., Tab., U.S.P. XXI. Dihydromorphinone HCl. 4,5α-Epoxy-3-hydroxy-17-methylmorphinan-6-one HCl.
Use: Analgesic; Narcotic.
See: Dilaudid Prods. (Knoll)
W/Sod. citrate, antimony pot. tartrate and chloroform. Inj.
See: Dilocol, Liq. (Table Rock)

HYDROMORPHONE SULFATE. 4,5-Epoxy 3-hydroxy-17-methylmorphinan-6-one sulfate (2:1).
Use: Analgesic (narcotic).

HYDROMOX. (Lederle) Quinethazone 50 mg./Tab. Bot. 100s, 500s.
Use: Treatment of edema & hypertension.

HYDROMOX-R. (Lederle) Quinethazone 50 mg., reserpine 0.125 mg./Tab. Bot. 100s, 500s.

HYDROPANE. (Blue Cross) Hydrocodone bitartrate 5 mg., homatropine methylbromide 1.5 mg./5 ml. Bot. 16 oz.
Use: Cough syrup.

HYDROPEL. (C & M Pharmacal) Silicone 30%, hydrophobic starch derivative 10%, petrolatum. Jar. 2 oz., 1 lb.
Use: Protective silicone ointment.

HYDROPHILIC OINTMENT, U.S.P. XXI. Stearyl alcohol, white petrolatum, propylene glycol, sod. lauryl sulfate & water. 1 lb. jar (Fougea)

HYDROPHILIC OINTMENT BASE. Oil in water emulsion bases. (Emerson) 1 lb.
See: Aquaphilic Ointment (Medco)
Cetaphil, Cream, Lot. (Texas Pharmacal)
Dermovan, Cream (Texas Pharmacal)
Lanaphilic Ointment (Medco)
Monobase, Oint. (Torch)
Polysorb, Oint. (Savage)
Unibase, Oint. (Parke-Davis)

HYDROPINE #1. (Wolins) Hydrochlorothiazide 25 mg., reserpine 0.125 mg./Tab. Bot. 100s, 1000s.

HYDROPINE #2. (Wolins) Hydrochlorothiazide 50 mg., reserpine 0.125 mg./Tab. Bot. 100s, 1000s.

HYDROPLUS. (Reid-Provident) Hydrocholorothiazide 50 mg., reserpine 0.125 mg./Tab. Bot. 1000s.
Use: Hypertension treatment.

HYDROPRES-25 & 50. (Merck Sharp & Dohme) **25:** Hydrochlorothiazide 25 mg., reserpine 0.125 mg./Tab. **50:** Hydrochlorothiazide 50 mg., reserpine 0.125 mg./Tab. Bot. 100s, 1000s.
Use: Antihypertensive.

HYDROPRIN. (Cenci) Hydrochlorothiazide 25 mg., reserpine 0.125 mg./Tab. or 50 mg./Tab. Bot. 100s, 1000s.
Use: Hypertension treatment.

HYDROQUIN. (Robinson) Hydrocortisone 1%, clioquinol 3%. Cream: Tube 5 Gm., 20 Gm. Jar 4 oz., 8 oz., 1 lb. Ointment: Jar 4 oz., 1 lb.
Use: Adrenocortical steroid therapy.

HYDROQUIN W/COAL TAR SOLUTION. (Robinson) Hydrocortisone 0.5%, clioquinol 1%, coal tar sol. 3%. Tube 0.5 oz.

• **HYDROQUINONE,** U.S.P. XXI. Cream, Topical Soln., U.S.P. XXI. 1,4-Benzenediol.
Use: Depigmenting agent.
See: Artra Skin Tone Cream (Plough)
Black and White Bleaching Cream (Plough)
Derma-Blanch, Cream (Chattem)
Eldopaque Cream, Oint. (Elder)
Eldopaque Forte Cream, Oint. (Elder)
Eldoquin, Cream, Lot. (Elder)
Esoterica Medicated Cream Prods. (Norcliff Thayer)

HYDROQUINONE MONOBENZYL ETHER.
See: Benoquin, Oint., Lot. (Elder)

HYDROSAL. (Hydrosal Co.) A colloidal susp. of aluminum acetate 5%. **Susp.:** Bot. 16 oz., 1 gal. **Oint.:** 54 Gm., 113.4 Gm. Jars 54 Gm., 454 Gm.

HYDROSERP. (Zenith) Hydrochlorothiazide 25 mg., or 50 mg., reserpine 0.125 mg. or 0.1 mg./Tab. Bot. 100s, 1000s.
Use: Antihypertensive.

HYDROSERP-50. (Freeport) Hydrochlorothiazide 50 mg., reserpine 0.125 mg./Tab. Bot. 1000s.
Use: Antihypertensive.

HYDROSERPINE. (Geneva) Hydrochlorothiazide 25 mg., 50 mg., reserpine 0.125 mg./Tab. Bot. 100s.
Use: Antihypertensive.

HYDROSERPINE NO. 1. (Goldline) Hydrochlorothiazide 25 mg., reserpine. Bot. 100s, 1000s
Use: Antihypertensive.

HYDROSERPINE No. 1. (Zenith) Hydrochlorothiazide 25 mg., reserpine 0.125 mg./Tab. Bot. 100s, 1000s.
Use: Antihypertensive, diuretic.

HYDROSERPINE NO. 2. (Goldline) Hydrochlorothiazide 50 mg., reserpine. Bot. 100s, 1000s.
Use: Antihypertensive.

HYDROSERPINE No. 2. (Zenith) Hydrochlorothiazide 50 mg., reserpine 0.125 mg./Tab. Bot. 100s, 1000s.
Use: Antihypertensive, diuretic.

HYDROSERPINE No. 3. (Zenith) Hydrochlorothiazi 25 mg., reserpine 0.1 mg./Tab. Bot. 100s, 1000s.
Use: Antihypertensive, diuretic.

HYDROSERPINE No. 4. (Zenith) Hydrochlorothiazi 50 mg., reserpine 0.1 mg./Tab. Bot. 100s, 1000s.
Use: Antihypertensive diuretic.

HYDROSERPINE PLUS. (Zenith) Hydralazine HCl 2 mg., hydrochlorothiazide 15 mg., reserpine 0.1 mg./Tab. Bot. 100s, 1000s.
Use: Hypertension.

HYDROSOL. (Rocky Mtn.) Prednisolone 21 phosphate 20 mg./cc. Vial 10 cc.
Use: Steroid.

HYDROSONE. (Sig) Hydrocortisone acetate 25 mg. 50 mg./ml. Vial 5 mg.
Use: Anti-inflammatory.

HYDRO-T TABS. (Major) Hydrochlorothiazide: 25 mg./Tab. Bot. 100s; 50 mg./Tab. Bot. 1000s; 5000s. 100 mg./Tab. Bot. 250s, 1000s.
Use: Diuretic.

HYDROTALCITE. B.A.N. Aluminum magnesium hydroxide carbonate hydrate. Altacite.
Use: Antacid.

HYDROTENSIN-50. (Mayrand) Hydrochlorothiazide mg., reserpine 0.125 mg./Tab. Bot. 100s, 1000s.
Use: Treatment of hypertension.

HYDROTOIN CREAM. (Knight) Hydrocortisone 0.5% Tube 0.5 oz.
Use: Antifungal, antibacterial, antipruritic.

HYDROXACEN. (Central) Hydroxyzine HCl 50 mg./ml. w/benzyl alcohol 0.9%, sodium hydroxid Vial 10 ml.
Use: I.M. tranquilizer, antihistaminic.

HYDROX B-12. (Rocky Mtn.) Hydroxocobalamin 1C mcg./cc. Vial 10 cc.

HYDROXAL. (Blue Line) Aluminum hydroxide susp. Bot. 1 gal.
Use: Orally, antacid.

HYDROXAMETHOCAINE. B.A.N. 2-Dimethyl-ami ethyl 4-butylaminosalicylate. Hydroxytetracaine (I.N.N.)
Use: Local anesthetic.

HYDROXINDASOL HCl. 5-Hydroxy-1-(p-methoxy-be zyl)-2-methyltryptamine HCl.

• **HYDROXOCOBALAMIN,** U.S.P. XXI. Inj., U.S.P. XXI. α-(5,6-Dimethylbenzimidazolyl) hydroxoco mide. Vit. B 12a and B 12b. Hydrovit; Neo-Cytam
Use: Treatment of megaloblastic anemia.
See: Alphamin, Inj. (Vortech)
AlphaRedisol, Inj. (Merck Sharp & Dohme)
Alpha-Ruvite, Vial (Savage)
Cobavite L.A., Vial (Lemmon)
Droxomin, Inj. (Reid-Provident)
Droxovite, Vial (Kay)
Hydrobexan, Vial (Keene)
Rubesol-L.A. 1000, Inj. (Central)
Span-12, Inj. (Scrip)
Sytobex-H, Vial (Parke-Davis)
Twelve-Span, Vial (Foy)

4'-HYDROXYACETANILIDE. Acetaminophen, U.S.P. XXI.

HYDROXY BIS(ACETATO)ALUMINUM. Aluminum Subacetate Topical Solution, U.S.P. XXI.

DROXYAMPHETAMINE. B.A.N. 4-(2-Amino-propyl)-phenol. Paredrine.
Use: Sympathomimetic; mydriatic.

HYDROXYAMPHETAMINE HYDROBROMIDE, U.S.P. XXI. Ophth. Soln., U.S.P. XXI. dl-p-(2-Amino-propyl) phenol HBr.
Use: Adrenergic (ophthalmic).
See: Paredrine Hydrobromide, Sol. (SmithKline)

β-HYDROXYANDROST-4-EN-3-ONE HEPTANOATE, OR PROPIONATE. Testosterone Enanthate, or Propionate. U.S.P. XXI.

HYDROXYBENZAMIDE.
See: Salicylamide.

DROXYBIS(SALICYLATO)ALUMINUM DIACETATE.
See: Aluminum aspirin

DROXYCHLOROQUINE. B.A.N. 7-Chloro-4-[4-(N-ethyl-N-2-hydroxyethylamino)-1-methyl-butylamino]quinoline.
Use: Antimalarial.
See: Plaquenil sulfate (Winthrop-Breon)

HYDROXYCHLOROQUINE SULFATE, U.S.P. XXI. Tab., U.S.P. XXI. Ethanol, 2-4-(7-chloro-4-quinolinyl)-amino pentyl ethylamino-, sulfate (1:1) salt. 7-Chloro-4- 4-[ethyl(2-hydroxyethyl)-amino]-1-methyl-butylamino quinoline sulfate. 2-[[4-[(7chloro-4-quinolyl)amino]-pentyl]ethylamino]ethanol Sulfate (1:1).
Use: Antimalarial; lupus erythematosus suppressant.
See: Plaquenil, Tab. (Winthrop-Breon)

HYDROXYCORTICOSTERONE-21-ACETATE. Hydrocortisone Acetate, U.S.P. XXI.

DROXYDIONE SODIUM. 21-Hydroxy-pregnanedione sod. succinate.

DROXYDIONE SODIUM SUCCINATE. B.A.N. Sod. 21-hydroxypregnane-3,20-dione succinate. Presuren; Viadril.
Use: Anesthetic.

β-HYDROXYESTER-4-EN-3-ONE DECANOATE.
See: Deca-Durabolin, Amp., Vial (Organon)

HYDROXYETHANESULFONIC ACID, 2-HYDROXY-4,4′-STILBENEDICARBOXAMIDINE COMPOUND (2:1). Hydroxystilbamidine Isethionate, U.S.P. XXI.

HYDROXYETHYL BENZYLCARBAMATE. Buranate.

HYDROXYETHYL CELLULOSE, N.F.XVI.
Use: Topical protectant, thickening agent.

(HYDROXYETHYL)DIISOPROPYLMETHYL-AMMONIUM BROMIDE XANTHENE-9-CARBOXYLATE. Propantheline Bromide, U.S.P. XXI.

-HYDROXYETHYL)-2-METHYL-5-NITRO-MIDAZOLE. Metronidazole, U.S.P. XXI.

HYDROXY-4′, 5′,6,7-FUROCOUMARIN, AMMOIDIN, XANTHOTOXIN. Methoxsalen, U.S.P. XXI.

-HYDROXYETHYL)-4-[3-(2-TRIFLUOROMETHYL)-10-PHENOTHIAZINYL-PROPYL]-PIPERAZINE DIHYDROCHLORIDE. Fluphenazine Hydrochloride, U.S.P. XXI.

DROXYISOINDOLIN. Under study.
Use: Hypertension treatment.

17-HYDROXY-7α-MERCAPTO-3-OXO-17α-PREGN-4-ENE-21-CARBOXYLIC ACIDα-LACTONE ACETATE. Spironolactone, U.S.P. XXI.

2-HYDROXY-4-METHOXYBENZOPHENONE. Oxybenzone, U.S.P. XXI.

l-m-HYDROXY-α-[(METHYLAMINO)METHYL]-BENZYL ALCOHOL HYDROCHLORIDE. Phenylephrine Hydrochloride, U.S.P. XXI.

11,β-HYDROXY-6α-METHYLPREGN-4-ONE-3,20DIONE. (Allergan; Upjohn)

1-(HYDROXYMERCURI-¹⁹⁷Hg)-2-PROPANOL.
See: Merprane

17β-HYDROXY-17-METHYLANDROST-4-EN-3-ONE Methyltesterone, U.S.P. XXI.

17-HYDROXY-6α-METHYLPREGN-4-ENE-3,20DIONE 17 ACETATE. Medroxyprogesterone Acetate, U.S.P. XXI.

• **HYROXYPROPYL METHYLCELLULOSE PHTHALATE,** N.F. XVI.

17-β-HYDROXY-6α-METHYL-17-(1-PRO-PYNYL)-ANDROST-4-EN-3-ONE.
See: Oracon, Tab. (Mead Johnson)

N-[l-(HYDROXYMETHYL)PROPYL]-l-METHYL-D-LYSERGAMIDE BIMALEATE. Methysergide Maleate, U.S.P. XXI.

3-HYDROXY-l-METHYLPYRIDINIUM BROMIDE DIMETHYLCARBAMATE. Pyridostigmine Bromide, U.S.P. XXI.

HYDROXYMYCIN. An antibiotic substance obtained from cultures of *Streptomyces paucisporogenes.*

HYDROXYPETHIDINE. B.A.N. Ethyl 4-(3-hydroxy-phenyl)-1-methylpiperidine-4-carboxylate.
Use: Narcotic analgesic.

• **HYDROXYPHENAMATE.** USAN. 2-Hydroxy-2-phenylbutyl carbamate.
Use: Tranquilizer.

(M-HYDROXYPHENYL) TRIMETHYLAMMONIUM BROMIDE DIMETHYL CARBAMATE. Neostigmine Bromide, U.S.P. XXI.

(m-HYDROXYPHENYL) TRIMETHYL AMMONIUM METHYL SULFATE DIMETHYL CARBAMATE. Neostigmine Methylsulfate, U.S.P. XXI.

17-HYDROXY-19-NOR-17α-PREGN-4-EN-20-YN-3-,ONE ACETATE. Norethindrone Acetate, U.S.P. XXI.

17-HYDROXY-19-NOR-17α-PREGN-4-EN-20-YN-3-ONE. Norethindrone, U.S.P. XXI.

17-HYDROXYPREGN-4-ENE-3,20-DIONE HEXANOATE. Hydroxyprogesterone Caproate, U.S.P. XXI.

HYDROXYPROCAINE. B.A.N. 2-Diethylamino-ethyl 4-aminosalicylate.
Use: Local anesthetic.

HYDROXYPROGESTERONE. B.A.N. 17α-Hydroxy-pregn-4-ene-3,20-dione. Primolut Depot [hexanoate].
Use: Progestogen.

• **HYDROXYPROGESTERONE CAPROATE,** U.S.P. XXI. Inj., U.S.P. XXI. 17α-Hydrogypregn-4-ene-3,20-dione. Pregn-4-ene-3,20-dione,17-[(l)oxohexyl)-oxy]-.
Use: Progestin.
See: Delalutin, Vial (Squibb)
Hy-Gestrone, Vial (Pasadena Research)
Hylutin, Inj. (Hyrex)
Hyprogest 250, Inj. (Keene)

Hyproval-P.A., Inj. (Reid-Provident)
Pro-Depo, Inj. (Vortech)
W/Estradiol valerate.
See: Hy-Gestradol, Inj. (Pasadena Research)
Hylutin-Est., Inj. (Hyrex)

• **HYDROXYPROPYL CELLULOSE,** N.F. XVI.
Use: Topical protectant, tablet coating agent.

• **HYDROXYPROPYL METHYLCELLULOSE,** U.S.P. XXI. Ophth. Sol. U.S.P. XXI. Cellulose, 2-hydroxypropyl methyl ether. Cellulose hydroxypropyl methyl ether. The propylene glycol ether of methylcellulose available in the 2208, 2906 and 2910 forms.
Use: Suspending agent; ophth, topical protectant.
See: Anestacon (Alcon)
Econopred, Susp. (Alcon)
W/Benzalkonium chloride.
See: Goniosol (Smith, Miller & Patch)
Isopto Tears (Alcon)
Ultra Tears, Sol. (Alcon)

• **HYDROXYPROPYL METHYLCELLULOSE PHTHALATE 200731,** N.F. XVI.

• **HYDROXYPROPYL METHYLCELLULOSE PHTHALATE 200824,** N.F. XVI.

8-HYDROXYQUINOLINE COMB.
See: Ammens Medicated Powder, Spray (Bristol-Myers)
Foille, Spray, Liq., Oint. (Carbisulphoil)

8-HYDROXYQUINOLINE SULFATE. (City Chem.)
Use: As an antiseptic.
See: Oxyquinoline Sulfate (Various Mfr.)

5-HYDROXYSALICYLIC ACID. Gentisic Acid. (Various Mfg.)

HYDROXYSTEARIN SULFATE. Sulfonate hydrogenated castor oil.

HYDROXYSTILBAMIDINE. B.A.N. 4,4′-Diamidino-2-hydroxystilbene.
Use: Treatment of leishmaniasis and trypanosomiasis.

• **HYDROXYSTILBAMIDINE ISETHIONATE,** U.S.P. XXI. Sterile, U.S.P. XXI. Benzenecarboximidamide, 4-[2-[4-(aminoiminomethyl)phenyl]ethnyl]-3-hydroxy-bis(2-hydroxyethanesulfonate). 2-Hydroxy-4,4′-stilbenedicarboxamidine bis(2-hydroxyethanesulfonate)(Salt). 2-Hydroxyethanesulfonic acid, 2-hydroxy-4,4′-stilbenedicarboxamidine compound (2:1) (Merrell Dow) Amp. (225 mg.) 20 cc. Box 1s.
Use: Antileishmanial; I.V. 225 mg., may be repeated at 24-hour intervals; blastomycosis Indian kalaazar.

2-HYDROXY-4,4′-STILBENEDICARBOXAMIDINE BIS (2-HYDROXY-ETHANESULFONATE)(SALT). Hydroxystilbamidine Isethionate, U.S.P. XXI.

HYDROXYTOLUIC ACID. B.A.N. 2-Hydroxy-m-toluic acid. 3-Methylsalicylic acid.
Use: Analgesic.

6-HYDROXY-β,2,7-TRIMETHYL-5-BENZOFURANACRYLIC ACID, β-LACTONE W/4,-5,8-trimethylpsoralen. Trisoralen.

• **HYDROXYUREA,** U.S.P. XXI. Cap., U.S.P. XXI. Hydroxycarbamide (I.N.N.)
Use: Antineoplastic agent.
See: Hydrea, Cap. (Squibb)

HYDROXYZINE. B.A.N. 1-4-(Chlorobenzhydryl)-4-[2-(2-hydroxyethoxy)ethyl]piperazine-.
Use: Tranquilizer.
See: Atarax hydrochloride.
Equipose embonate.

HYDROXYZINE COMPOUND SYRUP. (Goldline) Ephedrine sulfate theophylline. Bot. pt. gal.
Use: Bronchodilator.

• **HYDROXYZINE HCl,** U.S.P. XXI. Inj., Syrup, Tab. U.S.P. XXI. 2-[2-[-4-(p-Chloro-α-phenylbenzyl-)-1-piperazinyl]ethoxy]ethanol dihydrochloride. **Inj.:** (Abbott) 100 mg./2 ml. amp. or Abboject syringe, 50 mg./10 ml. vial.
Use: Tranquilizer, antihistaminic.
See: Atarax, Syr., Tab. (Roerig)
Hyzine-50, Inj. (Hyrex)
Vistarex 50, Inj. (Tunex)
Vistazine 25, Inj. (Keene)
Vistazine 50, Inj. (Keene)
Isoject Vistaril. (Pfizer Laboratories)
W/Ephedrine sulf., theophylline.
See: Marax DF, Syr. (Roerig)
Marax Tab. (Roerig)
Theo-Drox, Tab. (Quality Generics)
W/Oxyphencyclimine HCl.
See: Vistrax 5 & 10, Tab. (Pfizer Laboratories)
W/Pentaerythritol tetranitrate.
See: Cartrax 10, 20, Tab. (Roerig)

• **HYDROXYZINE PAMOATE,** U.S.P XXI. Cap., Oral Susp., U.S.P. XXI. 1,1′-Methylene bis(2-hydroxy-3-naphthalene-carboxylic acid salt of 1-p-chlorobenzhydryl)-4-[2-2-hydroxy-ethoxyethyl]piperazine. 2-(2-(4-(piperazine. 2-(2-(4-(p-Chloro-α-phenyl-benzyl)-1-piperazinyl)ethoxy)ethanol 4,4′-Methylenebis-(3-hydroxy-2-napthoate) (1:1).
Use: Tranquilizer; antihistaminic.
See: Vistaril, Cap., Susp. (Pfizer Laboratories)

HYDROXYZINE PLUS TABLETS. (Goldline) Ephedrine sulfate, theophylline. Bot. 100s, 1000s.
Use: Bronchodilator.

HYDROZIDE. (MSD AGVET) Hydrochlorothiazide In. 25 mg./cc.
Use: Diuretic, veterinary medicine.

HYDROZIDE-Z-50. (Mayrand) Hydrochlorothlazide mg./Tab. Bot. 100s, 1000s.
Use: Treatment of hypertension.

HY-E-PLEX. (Nutrition) Nat. Vit. E 400 I.U./Cap. W Bot. 100s.

HY-FLOW. (CooperVision) Polyvinyl alcohol, hydroxythycellulose, potassium chloride, sodium chloride benzalkonium chloride 0.01%, edetate disodium 0.025%. Bot. 60 ml.
Use: Wetting solution for hard contact lenses.

HYGEFEM DOUCHE. (Blue Line) **Pow.** Benzalkonium chloride, citric acid, sod. phosphate, K alum, aromatics, excipient, colors. Bot. 4 oz., .38 oz. B 6s, 12s.
Use: Astringent and acidic vaginal douche.

HY-GESTRONE. (Pasadena Research) Hydroxyprogesterone caproate 125 mg./ml. Vial 10 cc. 250 mg./ml. Vial 5 cc.

'GIENIC POWDER.
See: Bo-Car-Al, Pow. (Calgon)
'GROTON. (USV Labs.) Chlorthalidone 25 mg., 50 mg., 100 mg./Tab. Bot. 100s, 1000s. Strip dispenser 100s. Bot. 5000s for 50 mg. and 100 mg. strengths.
Use: Diuretic, antihypertensive.
'LIDONE TABS. (Major) Chlorthalidone: 25 mg. or 50 mg./Tab. Bot. 250s; 1000s. 100 mg./Tab. Bot. 100s, 250s, 1000s.
Use: Antihypertensive.
'LOREL TABLETS. (Pennwalt) Guanadrel sulfate 10 mg. or 25 mg./Tab. Bot. 100s.
Use: Hypertension, step II therapy.
'LUTIN INJECTABLE. (Hyrex) Hydroxyprogesterone caproate in oil 250 mg./ml. Vial 5 ml.
Use: Long acting progesterone for endometriosis, infertility, amenorrhea, menstrual cycle.
IYMECROMONE. USAN.
Use: Choleretic.
'METIC. (Hyrex) Trimethobenzamide HCl 100 mg./ml. Vial 20 ml. I.M. administration.
Use: Treatment of nausea & vomiting.
'-N.B.P. OINTMENT. (Bowman) Bacitracin zinc 400 u., neomycin sulfate 5 mg., polymixin B sulfate 10,000 u./Gm. Tube ⅛ oz.
Use: Topical antibiotic.
'OSCINE AMINOXIDE HBr.
'OSCINE HYDROBROMIDE. Scopolamine HBr, U.S.P. XXI.
Use: Intestinal antispasmodic.
'OSCINE-HYOSCYAMINE-ATROPINE.
Use: Anticholinergic.
See: Atropine w/hyoscyamine w/hyoscine
'OSCINE METHOBROMIDE. B.A.N.
Use: Treatment of peptic ulcer.
See: Methscopolamine Bromide
IYOSCYAMINE, U.S.P. XXI. Tab., U.S.P. XXI. 1αH,5αH-Tropan-3α-ol(−)-tropate (ester). Levo form of atropine.
Use: Anticholinergic.
See: Bellafoline, Amp., Tab. (Sandoz)
Cysto-Spaz, Tab. (Webcon)
'OSCYAMINE-ATROPINE-HYOSCINE.
Use: Anticholinergic.
See: Atropine w/hyoscyamine w/hyoscine
IYOSCYAMINE HYDROBROMIDE, U.S.P. XXI. 1αH,5αH-Tropan-3α-ol(−)-tropate HBr. Daturine HBr. (Various Mfr.)
Use: Anticholinergic.
'Physostigmine salicylate.
See: Pyatromine-H Inj. (Kremers-Urban)
'OSCYAMINE HYDROCHLORIDE. (Various Mfr.)
'OSCYAMINE MALEATE.
See: Bellafoline, Amp., Tab. (Sandoz)
'OSCYAMINE SALTS.
Use: Anticholinergic.
'Atropine salts.
See: Atropine W/Hyoscyamine.
IYOSCYAMINE SULFATE, U.S.P. XXI. Elixir, Inj., Oral Soln., Tab., U.S.P. XXI. 1αH,5αH-Tropan-3α-ol-(−)-tropate (ester) sulfate (2:1) dihydrate.
Use: Anticholinergic.
See: Anaspaz, Tab. (Ascher)
Cystospaz-M, Cap. (Webcon)
W/Atropine sulfate, hyoscine HBr, phenobarbital.
See: Bar-Cy-Amine, Elix. (Sutliff & Case)
Bar-Cy-A, Tabs. (Sutliff & Case)
DeTal, Elix., Tab. (DeLeon)
Donnatal, Prods. (Robins)
Hyatal, Elix., Liq. (Kenyon)
Hyonal C.T., Tab. (Paddock)
Maso-Donna, Elix., Tab. (Mason)
Peece, Tab. (Scrip)
Sedamine, Tab. (Dunhall)
Spasaid, Cap. (Century)
Spasmolin, Tab. (Kenyon)
Spasquid, Elix. (Geneva)
W/Atropine sulf, hyoscine HBr, phenobarbital, pepsin, pancreatin, bile salts.
See: Donnazyme, Tab. (Robins)
W/Atropine sulfate. Scopolamine HCl, phenobarbital.
See: Ultabs, Tab. (Burlington)
W/Belladonna Alkaloids.
See: Belladonna Products
W/Butabarbital.
See: Cystospaz-SR, Cap. (Webcon)
W/Methenamine, atropine sulfate, methylene blue, salol, benzoic acid, gelsemium.
See: Uriprel, Tab. (Pasadena Research)
W/Phenobarbital.
See: Levsin/PB, Tab., Elix., Drops, Inj. (Kremers-Urban)
W/Phenobarbital, simethicone, atropine sulfate, scopolamine HBr.
See: Kinesed, Tab. (Stuart)
HYOSCYAMUS EXTRACT.
W/A. P. C.
See: Valacet Junior, Tab. (Vale)
W/A. P. C., gelsemium ext.
See: Valacet, Tab. (Vale)
HYOSCYAMUS PRODUCTS AND PHENOBARBITAL COMBINATIONS.
Use: Anticholinergic, sedative.
See: Anaspaz PB, Tab. (Pasadena Research)
Donnacin, Elixir, Tab. (Pharmex)
Donnatal, Preps. (Robins)
Elixiral, Elixir (Vita Elixir)
Floramine, Tab. (Lemmon)
Gylanphen, Tab. (Lannett)
Kinesed, Tab. (Stuart)
Neoquess, Tab. (O'Neal)
Nevrotose, Cap. (Vale)
Restophen, Tab. (Noyes)
Sedajen, Tabs. (Jenkins)
Sedatromine, Tab. (Sutliff & Case)
HYOSED T.D. (Galen) Hyoscyamine HBr 0.256 mg., hyoscine HBr 0.0144 mg., atropine sulfate 0.0480 mg., phenobarbital 32.0 mg./Timed disintegration tab. Bot. 100s, 1000s.
Use: Sedative, intestinal antispasmodic.
HY-PAM 25. (Lemmon) Hydroxyzine pamoate equivalent to 25 mg. hydroxyzine HCl/Cap. Bot. 100s, 500s, 1000s.

Use: Relief of anxiety & tension, allergic dermatoses.

HY-PAM 50. (Lemmon) Hydroxyzine pamoate equivalent to 50 mg. hydroxyzine HCl/Cap. Bot. 100s, 500s, 1000s.
Use: Relief of anxiety & tension, allergic dermatoses.

HYPAQUE-76. (Winthrop-Breon) Diatrizoate meglumine 66%, diatrizoate sodium 10%, iodine 370 mg./ml. Vials 30 ml. Box. 25s; Vials 50 ml. Box 25s, Vials 100 ml. Box. 10s; Bot. 200 ml. Box 10s; Dilution Bot. 200 ml. containing 100 ml. drug. Box 10s. Calibrated 200 ml. dilution bottle w/150 ml. Hypaque-76. Box 10s.
Use: Urography, aortography, angiography, venography, angiocardiography, arteriography, contrast enhancement of computed tomographic head imaging and intravenous digital arteriography, contrast enhancement of computed tomographic body imaging.

HYPAQUE-CYSTO. (Winthrop-Breon) Diatrizoate meglumine 30% solution. 250 ml. in 500 ml. dilution bottle. **Pediatric:** 100 ml. in 300 ml. dilution bottle.
Use: Retrograde cystourethrography.

HYPAQUE-M 75%. (Winthrop-Breon) Diatrizoate meglumine 50%, diatrizoate sodium 25%, 385 mg. iodine/ml. Vials 20 ml., 50 ml. Box 25s.
Use: Angiocardiography, angiography, aortography & urography.

HYPAQUE-M 90%. (Winthrop-Breon) Diatrizoate meglumine 60% & diatrizoate sodium 30%. Vial 50 ml. Box 25s.
Use: Angiocardiography, angiography, aortography, urography, hysterosalpingography.

HYPAQUE MEGLUMINE 30%. (Winthrop-Breon) Diatrizoate meglumine 30%. Bot. 300 ml. w/ & w/o I.V. infusion set. Vials of 100 ml. Box 10s.
Use: Infusion urography, CT scan enhancement.

HYPAQUE MEGLUMINE 60%. (Winthrop-Breon) Diatrizoate meglumine 60%. which contains 47.06% iodine. **Vial:** 20 ml. Box 25s. 30 ml. Box 25s. 50 ml. Box 25s. 100 ml. Box 10s. **Dilution Bottle:** 200 ml. w/hanger containing 150 ml. Hypaque meglumine 60%. w/10 intravenous infusion sets. Box 10s.; 200 ml. w/hanger containing 200 ml. Hypaque meglumine 60%, rubber stoppered. Box 10s; 200 ml. w/hanger containing 100 ml. Hypaque meglumine 60% w/10 intravenous infusion sets. Box 10s.
Use: Excretory urography, cerebral angiography, peripheral arteriography, venography, direct cholangiography, splenoportography, arthrography, discography, contrast enhancement of computed tomographic body imaging.

HYPAQUE (R)-131 SODIUM.
See: Sodium Diatrizoate

HYPAQUE ORAL. (Winthrop-Breon) **Powder:** Diatrizoate sodium oral powder containing 600 mg. iodine/Gm. Cans 250 Gm. Bot. 10 Gm. **Liquid:** A 41.66% solution. Bot. 120 ml.
Use: Contrast radiology of G.I. tract (orally & enema).

HYPAQUE SODIUM. (Winthrop-Breon) Diatrizoate s dium and contains 59.87% iodine. Sodium 3, diacetamido 2,4,6-triiodobenzoate.
Use: Radiopaque medium.
See: Hypaque, Prod. (Winthrop-Breon)

HYPAQUE SODIUM 20%. (Winthrop-Breon) Diatrizoa sodium 20% containing 120 mg. iodine/ml. Multidose vials 100 ml. Box 10s.
Use: Retrograde pyelography.

HYPAQUE SODIUM 25%. (Winthrop-Breon) Diatrizoa sodium 25% containing 150 mg. iodine/ml. Bot. 300 ml., w/ and w/out intravenous infusion set.
Use: Urography and CT scan enhancement.

HYPAQUE SODIUM 50%. (Winthrop-Breon) Diatrizoa sodium. **Vial:** 50% 30 ml., 20 ml. Box 25s, Vial 50 ml. Box 25s. **Dilution Bottle:** 200 ml. w/hanger containing 150 ml. Hypaque sodium 50% w/10 intravenous infusion sets; 200 ml. w/hanger containing 200 ml. Hypaque sodium 50%, rubber stoppered. Box 10s.
Use: Cerebral and peripheral angiography, aortography, excretory urography, direct cholangiography, hysterosalpingography, intraosseous venography, splenoportography.

HYPERAB. (Cutter) Rabies immune globulin (Human Vial 2 ml., 10 ml.
Use: I.M., passive immunization.

HYPERACID. (Wolins) Dihydroxyaluminum aminoacetate 0.5 Gm./Tab. Bot. 100s, 1000s.

HYPERHEP. (Cutter) Hepatitis B immune globulin (Human) Vial 250 unit, prefilled syringe 250 unit.
Use: Passive immunity, I.M.

HYPERINE. (Sutliff & Case) Reserpine 0.25 mg./Tab Bot. 100s, 1000s.
Use: Antihypertensive.

HYPEROPTO 5%. (Professional Pharmacal) Sterile 5% sodium chloride ointment. Tube 3.5 gm.
Use: Eye therapy.

HYPEROPTO OINTMENT. (Professional Pharmacal) Sodium HCl 50 mg., D.I. water 150 mg., anhydrou lanolin 150 mg., liquid petrolatum 50 mg., white petrolatum 599 mg., methyl paraben 7 mg., propyl paraben 3 mg./Gm. Tube 3.5 gm.
Use: Reducing edema.

HYPER-RAUW. (Sutliff & Case) Rauwolfia serpenti 100 mg./Tab. Bot. 100s, 1000s.
Use: Antihypertensive.

HYPERSAL. (Softcon) Sodium chloride 5%, 0.002% thimerosal, 0.05% disodium edetate. Bot. 15 ml.
Use: Reduction of corneal edema.

HYPERSTAT I.V. INJECTION. (Schering) Diazoxide 300 mg. pH adjusted to approx. 11.6 with sod. hydroxide./20 ml. Amp.
Use: Antihypertensive for hospital use only.

HYPERTEN. (Kenyon) Phenobarbital 0.25 gr., nitroglycerin 1/300 gr., sod. nitrate 1 gr., veratrum viride 3/4 gr./Tab. Bot. 100s, 1000s.
Use: Hypertension treatment.

HYPERTENSIN-CIBA. Angiotensin Amide, B.A.N.

HYPERTENSION DIAGNOSIS.
See: Regitine, Amp., Tab. (Ciba)

HYPERTENSION THERAPY.
See: Aldoclor, Tab. (Merck Sharp & Dohme)
Aldomet, Tab. (Merck Sharp & Dohme)
Aldomet Ester HCl, Amp. (Merck Sharp & Dohme)
Aldoril, Tab. (Merck Sharp & Dohme)
Alkavervir
Alseroxylon
Apresoline, Amp., Tab. (Ciba)
Apresoline, Apresoline Esidrix, Amp., Tab. (Ciba)
Arfonad, Amp. (Roche)
Blocadren, Tab. (Merck Sharp & Dohme)
Corgard, Tab. (Squibb)
Cryptenamine
Deserpidine
Dibenzyline HCl, Cap. (SmithKline)
Diupres, Tab. (Merck Sharp & Dohme)
Diutensen & Diutensen-R, Tab. (Wallace)
Dyazide, Cap. (SmithKline)
Enduron, Tab. (Abbott)
Enduronyl, Tab. (Abbott)
Enduronyl Forte, Tab. (Abbott)
Esidrix, Tab. (Ciba)
Eutonyl, Tab. (Abbott)
Eutron, Tab. (Abbott)
Exna & Exna-R, Tab. (Robins)
Hesperidin Methyl Chalcone (Various Mfr.)
Hexamethonium Chloride & Bromide (Various Mfr.)
Hydro Diuril, Tab. (Merck Sharp & Dohme)
Hydropres, Tab. (Merck Sharp & Dohme)
Hygroton, Tab. (USV)
Hyperstat, I.V. Inj. (Schering)
Inversine, Tab. (Merck Sharp & Dohme)
Lopressor, Tab. (Geigy)
Metatensin, Tab. (Merrell Dow)
Midamor, Tab. (Merck Sharp & Dohme)
Moderil, Tab. (Pfizer)
Moduretic, Tab. (Merck Sharp & Dohme)
Naturetin, Tab. (Squibb)
Naquival, Tab. (Schering)
Oretic, Tab. (Abbott)
Oreticyl, Tab. (Abbott)
Priscoline HCl, Preps. (Ciba)
Protoveratrines A & B
Raudixin, Tab. (Squibb)
Rautrax, Tab. (Squibb)
Rautrax-N, Tab. (Squibb)
Rauwolfia Serpentina (Various Mfr.)
Rauzide, Tab. (Squibb)
Regroton, Tab. (USV)
Renese-R, Tab. (Pfizer)
Rescinnamine, Tab. (Var. Mfr.)
Reserpine (Various Mfr.)
Rutin, Tab. (Various Mfr.)
Tetraethylammonium Chloride (Various Mfr.)
Timolide, Tab. (Merck Sharp & Dohme)
Vasodilators
Veratrum Alba
Veratrum Viride
Wytensin, Tab. (Wyeth)
Zaroxolyn, Tab. (Pennwalt)

HYPER-TET. (Cutter) Tetanus immune globulin (Human) U.S.P. Vial 250 u., Disp. Syringe 250 u.
Use: For immediate injection after injury.

HYPERTHYROIDISM.
See: Antithyroid agents

HYPER-ZEM. (Zemmer) Sod. nitrite 60 mg., pot. nitrate 60 mg., ox bile desic. 8 mg., sod. bicarbonate 110 mg./Tab. Bot. 100s, 1000s.
Use: Orally, vasodilator.

HYPHYLLINE. Dyphylline. (7-Dihydroxy-propyl-theophylline).
See: Neothylline, Elix., Amp., Tab. (Lemmon)

HYPLEX VARI DOSE. (Hyrex) Sterile injectable solution of Vitamins. **Sol. #1:** B-1 3 mg., B-2 3.6 mg., B-6 4 mg., niacin 40 mg., pantothenic acid 15 mg., C 100 mg., biotin 60 mcg./ml. **Sol. #2:** Vit. B-12 5 mcg., folic acid 400 mcg./ml.
Use: Multivitamin.

HYPNALDYNE. (Vortech) Phenobarbital 16.2 mg., hyoscyamine sulfate 0.104 mg., atropine sulfate 0.019 mg., scopolamine HBr 0.0065 gr./Tab. Bot. 100s, 1000s.
Use: Sedative w/antispasmodic.

HYPNOGENE.
See: Barbital (Various Mfr.)

HYPNOMIDATE. (Janssen) Etomidate.
Use: Hypnotic.

HYPNO-SED. (Jenkins) Bromisovalum 1 gr., carbromal 3 gr., thiamine mononitrate 9 mg./Tab. Bot. 1000s.

■ **HYPNOTICS.**
See: Sedatives

"HYPO."
See: Sodium Thiosulfate (Various Mfr.)

HYPO-BEE. (Towne) Vit. B-1 50 mg., B-2 20 mg., B-6 5 mg., B-12 15 mcg., niacinamide 25 mg., Ca pantothenate 5 mg., Vit. C 300 mg., E 200 I.U., iron 10 mg./Tab. Bot. 30s, 100s.

HYPOCHLORITE PREPS.
See: Antiformin
Dakin's Soln.
Hyclorite

■ **HYPOGLYCEMIC AGENTS.**
See: Chlorpropamide
Diabinese, Tab. (Pfizer)
Dymelor, Tab. (Lilly)
Orinase, Tab., Vial (Upjohn)
Phenformin HCl
Tolbutamide
Tolinase, Tab. (Upjohn)

HYPOMINS. (Pasadena Research) Vit. A 5000 I.U., D 400 I.U., C 50 mg., B-1 5 mg., B-2 5 mg., B-6 1 mg., Ca pantothenate 5 mg., niacinamide 20 mg., E 2 I.U., B-12 2 mcg., Fe 10 mg., iodine 0.1 mg., Ca 100 mg., Cu 0.2 mg./Tab. Bot. 100s, 1000s.

α-**HYPOPHAMINE.** Oxytocin.

• **HYPOPHYOSPHOROUS ACID,** N.F. XVI.
Use: Antioxidant.

HYPOTEARS. (CooperVision) Polyvinyl alcohol 1%. Bot. 15 ml. or 30 ml.
Use: Ocular lubricant.

■ **HYPOTENSIVE AGENTS.**
See: Hypertension Therapy

HypRho-D. (Cutter) Rho (D) Immune globulin (Human). Pre-filled single dose syringe. Single dose vials. Pkg. 10s.
Use: Prevent immunization of Rh-woman at time of induced or spontaneous abortion up to 12 weeks gestation.

HYPROGEST 250. (Keene) Hydroxyprogesterone caproate inj. 250 mg./ml. Vial 5 ml.
Use: I.M. Long acting progestational agent.

HYPROMELLOSE. B.A.N. A partial mixed methyl and hydroxypropyl ether of cellulose.
Use: Surface active agent.
See: Isopto

HYPROVAL P.A. (Reid-Provident). Hydroxyprogesterone caproate 250 mg., benzyl benzoate 46%, benzyl alcohol 2%, in castor oil base. Vial 5 ml.
Use: I.M. progestin therapy.

HYREX-105. (Hyrex) Phendimetrazine tartrate 150 mg./Cap. Bot. 100s.
Use: Anorexiant.

HYREXIN. (Hyrex) Diphenhydramine HCl 50 mg./cc. Vial 10 cc.
Use: Antihistamic.

HYROXON. (Kay) Hydroxyprogesterone caproate 250 mg./ml. Vial 5 ml.
Use: Progestin.

HYRUNAL. (Kenyon) Rutin 20 mg., mannitol hexanitrate 0.5 gr., phenobarbital 0.25 gr./Tab. Bot. 100s, 1000s.
Use: Hypertension.

HYRUNAL W/VERATRUM VIRIDE. (Kenyon) Phenobarbital 0.25 gr., mannitol hexanitrate 0.5 gr., rutin 10 mg., veratrum viride 100 mg./Tab. Bot. 100s, 1000s.

HYSCORBIC PLUS. (Bock) Vit. E 45 I.U., C 600 mg., folic acid 400 mcg., B-1 20 mg., B-2 10 mg., niacinamide 100 mg., B-6 10 mg., B-12 25 mcg., pantothenic acid 25 mg., copper 3 mg., zinc 23.9 mg./Tab. Bot. 60s.
Use: High potency vitamin formula.

HYSERP. (Freeport) Reserpine alkaloid 0.25 mg./Tab. Bot. 1000s.
Use: Antihypertensive.

HYSERP-SER-A-GEN. (Goldline) Reserpine, hydralazine HCl, hydrochlorothiazide. Bot. 100s, 1000s.
Use: Hypertension treatment.

HYSKON. (Pharmacia) Clear, viscid, sterile, solution of 32% dextran 70 in dextrose. Bot. 100 ml., 250 ml.
Use: Distending the uterine cavity and in irrigating and visualizing its surfaces.

HYSONE. (Mallard) Iodoquinol 3%, hydrocortisone 1% in a water soluble base w/sodium lauryl sulfate, propylene glycol, cetyl alcohol, white petrolatum, water. Oint. Tube 15 Gm.
Use: Treatment of contact or atopic dermatitis.

HYSTERONE TABS. (Major) Fluoxymesterone 10 mg./Tab. Bot. 100s.
Use: Androgenic, anabolic agent.

HYTAKEROL. (Winthrop-Breon) Dihydrotachyste (Hydrocalciferol) 0.125 mg./Cap. Bot. 50s. Sol. in oil, 0.25 mg./cc. Bot. 15 cc.
Use: Tetany therapy, hypoparathyroidism.

HYTINIC. (Hyrex) Polysaccharide-iron complex 1 mg./Cap. Bot. 50s, 500s. Unit dose 100s.
Use: Iron deficiency anemia.

HYTINIC ELIXIR. (Hyrex) Polysaccharide-iron 1 mg./Tsp. Bot. 8 oz.
Use: Iron deficiency anemia.

HYTINIC INJECTION. (Hyrex) Ferrous gluconate 30 mg., citric acid 8.2 mg., sodium citrate 11.8 mg., folic acid 0.5 mg., liver equivalent to Vit. B-12 2.5 mc
Use: Iron-vitamin therapy.

HYTONE CREAM. (Dermik) Hydrocortisone in cream base. 0.5%, Tube 1 oz.; 1%, Tube 1 oz., Jar 4 oz. 2.5% Tube 1 oz., 2 oz.
Use: Anti-inflammatory for dermatoses.

HYTONE LOTION 1%. (Dermik) Hydrocortisone 1% (10 mg./ml.). Bot. 4 oz.
Use: Anti-inflammatory for dermatoses.

HYTONE LOTION 2.5%. (Dermik) Hydrocortisone 2 1/2% (25 mg./ml.) in lotion base. Bot. 2 oz.
Use: Anti-inflammatory for dermatoses.

HYTONE OINTMENT. (Dermik) Hydrocortisone in ointment base. 0.5%. Tube 1 oz.; 1%, Tube 1 oz., 2.5%, Tube 1 oz.
Use: Anti-inflammatory for dermatoses.

HYTUSS TABLETS. (Hyrex) Guaifenesin 100 mg./Tab. Bot. 100s, 1000s.
Use: Expectorant.

HYTUSS-2X. (Hyrex) Guaifenesin 200 mg./Cap. Bo 100s, 1000s.
Use: Expectorant.

HYWOLFIA-S.C. Orange. (Jenkins) Pow. whole roo rauwolfia serpentina 50 mg./Tab. Bot. 1000s. Also red, yellow, 100 mg./Tab. Bot. 1000s.

HYZINE-50. (Hyrex) Hydroxyzine HCl 50 mg./cc. Vi 10cc.
Use: Tranquilizer, antihistaminic.

I

IBENZMETHYZIN. Name used for Procarbazine Hydrochloride.

IBERET. (Abbott) Controlled release, ferrous sulfate 525 mg., ascorbic acid 150 mg., Vit. B-12 25 mcg., B 1 6 mg., B-2 6 mg., niacinamide 30 mg., B-6 5 mg., C pantothenate 10 mg./Filmtab. Bot. 60s.
Use: Iron-deficiency anemias.

IBERET-500. (Abbott) Ascorbic acid 500 mg., controlle release ferrous sulfate 525 mg., vit. B-12 25 mcg., B-1 6 mg., B-2 6 mg., niacinamide 30 mg. B-6 5 mg Ca pantothenate 10 mg./Filmtab. Bot. 30s, 60s, 500s. Abbo-Pac.
Use: Iron deficiency anemias.

IBERET-FOLIC-500 FILMTAB. (Abbott) Controlled re lease, ferrous sulfate 105 mg., Vit. C 500 mg., niacinamide 30 mg. Ca pantothenate 10 mg.,

thiamine mononitrate 6 mg., B-2 6 mg., B-6 5 mg., folic acid 800 mcg., B-12 25 mcg./Filmtab. Bot. 60s.
Use: Iron deficiency anemia.

IBERET LIQUID. (Abbott) Elem. iron 26.25 mg., Vit. C 37.5 mg., B-12 6.25 mcg., B-1 1.5 mg., B-2 1.5 mg., niacinamide 7.5 mg., B-6 1.25 mg., dexpanthenol 2.5 mg./5 ml. Liquid Bot. 8 fl. oz.
Use: Iron deficiency anemia.

IBERET-500 LIQUID, ORAL SOLUTION. (Abbott) Elem. iron 26.25 mg., Vit. B-12 6.25 mcg., B-1 1.5 mg., B-2 1.5 mg., niacinamide 7.5 mg., dexpanthenol 2.5 mg., B-6 1.25 mg., C 125 mg./5 ml. Bot. 8 oz.
Use: Iron deficiency anemia.

IBEROL. (Abbott) B-12 12.5 mcg., Iron (as 525 mg. ferrous sulf.) 105 mg., Vit. C 75 mg., B-1 3 mg., B-2 3 mg., niacinamide 15 mg., B-6 1.5 mg., Ca pantothenate 3 mg./Filmtab. Bot. 100s.
Use: Treatment of anemias.

IBEROL-F. (Abbott) Vit. B-12 12.5 mcg., Iron (as Ferrous sulf.) 105 mg., folic acid 0.2 mg., Vit. C 75 mg., B-1 3 mg., B-2 3 mg., niacinamide 15 mg., Vit. B-6 1.5 mg., Ca pantothenate 3 mg./Filmtab. Bot. 100s.
Use: Anemias.

• **IBOPAMINE.** USAN.
Use: Dopaminergic agent (peripheral).

• **IBUFENAC.** USAN. (p-Isobutylphenyl-acetic acid).
Use: Antirheumatic (anti-inflammatory, analgesic & antipyretic).
See: Dytransin.

• **IBUPROFEN,** U.S.P. XXI. Tab., U.S.P. XXI. (3) 2-(p-Isobutyl phenyl) propionic acid; p-Isobutylhydratropic acid. 2-(4-Isobutylphenyl)propionic acid. Brufen.
Use: Anti-inflammatory.
See: Motrin, Tab. (Upjohn)
Nuprin, Tab. (Bristol-Myers)

• **IBUPROFEN ALUMINUM.** USAN.
Use: Anti-inflammatory.

ICE MINT. (Westwood) Stearic acid, syn. cocoa butter, lanolin oil, camphor, menthol, beeswax, mineral oil, sodium borate, aromatic oils, emulsifiers, water. Jar 4 oz.
Use: Cream for burning feet, chapped skin, detergent hands, sunburn.

• **ICHTHAMMOL,** U.S.P. XXI. Oint., U.S.P. XXI. Ichthynate. Isarol Oint.
Use: Mild antiseptic in skin disorders.
W/Aluminum acetate, phenol, zinc oxide, boric acid, eucalyptol.
See: Lanaburn, Oint. (Lannett)
W/Aluminum hydroxide, phenol, zinc oxide, camphor, eucalyptol.
See: Almophen, Oint. (Bowman)
W/Benzocaine, resin cerate, carbolic acid, thymol, camphor, juniper tar, hexachlorophene.
See: Boil-Ease Anesthetic Drawing Salve (Commerce)
W/Benzocaine, tetracaine, resin cerate, thymol iodide.
See: Boilaid, Oint. (Edward J. Moore)
W/Hydrocortisone acetate, benzocaine, oxyquinoline sulfate, ephedrine HCl.
See: Derma Medicone-HC (Medicone)
W/Naftalan, calamine, amber pet.
See: Naftalan, Oint. (Paddock)
W/Phenol, benzocaine, balsam peru, alum. exsic., cade oil, eucalyptus oil, carbolic acid.
See: Alucaine, Oint. (Jenkins)

ICHTHYNATE.
See: Ichthammol

• **ICTASOL.** USAN.
Use: Disinfectant.

ICTOTEST REAGENT STRIPS. (Ames) p-Nitrobenzene diazonium p-toluene sulfonate. Reagent Tab., Bot. 100s.
Use: Test for urinary bilirubin.

ICY HOT RUB. (Searle) Methyl salicylate 12%, menthol 9%. Tubes 1.25 oz, 3 oz.
Use: Counterirritant, analgesic rub.

ICY HOT BALM. (Searle) Methyl salicylate 29%, menthol 8%. Jars 3.5 oz., 7 oz.
Use: Counterirritant, analgesic balm.

IDO-CORTISTAN OINTMENT. (Standex) Hydrocortisone alcohol 10 mg., clioquinol 30 mg., methylparaben 0.5 mg., propylparaben 0.5 mg./0.5 oz. Tube 0.5 oz.

IDOTEIN. (Sig) Sod. iodide 40 mg., peptone 20 mg./ml. Vial 30 ml.

• **IDOXURIDINE,** U.S.P. XXI. Ophth. Oint., Soln., U.S.P. XXI. 5-Iodo-2′-deoxyuridine. Uridine; Dendroid; Kerecid; Ophthalmidine.
Use: Herpes simplex; antiviral.
See: Dendrid, Ophth. Sol. (Alcon)
Herplex Ophth. Soln. (Allergan)
Stoxil, Ophth. Sol., Oint. (SmithKline

• **IFOSFAMIDE.** USAN. (Mead Johnson)
Use: Investigative: Antineoplastic.

IGEPAL Co-430. (General Aniline & Film) Non-oxynol 4.

IGEPAL Co-730. (General Aniline & Film) Non-oxynol 15.

IGEPAL Co-880. (General Aniline & Film) Non-oxynol 30.

ILETIN I. (Lilly) Regular and modified insulin products.
Protamine Zinc: 40, 100 u./cc. Vial 10 cc.
Regular: 40, 100 u./cc. Vial 10 cc.
Lente: 40, 100 u./cc. Vial 10 cc.
Semilente: 40, 100 u./cc. Vial 10 cc.
Ultralente: 40, 100 u./cc. Vial 10 cc.
NPH: 40, 100 u./cc. Vial 10 cc.
Use: Diabetes.

ILETIN II. (Lilly) Special insulin products prepared from purified beef and purified pork.
Regular: 100 u./cc. Vial 10 cc.
Lente: 100 u./cc. Vial 10 cc.
NPH: 100 u./cc. Vial 10 cc.
Protamine Zinc: 100 u./cc. Vial 10 cc.
Use: Diabetes.

ILETIN II CONCENTRATED. (Lilly) Purified pork regular insulin 500 u./cc. Vial 20 cc.
Use: Diabetes.

ILIDAR PHOSPHATE. Azapetine, B.A.N.

ILOPAN. (Adria) Dexpanthenol 250 mg./cc. w/Chlorobutanol 0.5%. Amp. 2 cc. Box 25s. Stat-Pak Disp. Syringe 2 cc.
Use: Intestinal atony and distention.

ILOPAN- CHOLINE. (Adria) Ilopan 50 mg., choline bitartrate 25 mg./Tab. Bot. 100s, 500s.
Use: Antiflatulent.

ILOSONE. (Dista) Erythromycin estolate. **Cap.:** (Erythromycin base) 125 mg., 250 mg./Pulvule. 125 mg. Bot. 24s, 100s. 250 mg. Bot. 24s, 100s. Blister pkg. 10 × 10s. **Liq.:** (250 mg. or 125 mg./5 ml.) Bot. 100 ml., 16 fl. oz. **Tab:** 500 mg./Tab. Bot. 50s. **Ready-Mixed Drops. Susp.:** 100 mg./ml. Bot. 10 ml. **For Oral Susp.** 125 mg./5 ml. Bot. 60 ml.
Use: Most common bacterial infections.

ILOSONE CHEWABLE. (Dista) Erythromycin estolate 125 mg., 250 mg./Tab. Bot. 50s.
Use: Bacterial infections.

ILOTYCIN OPHTHALMIC OINTMENT. (Dista) Erythromycin 5 mg./Gm. Tube 0.12 oz., 1 Gm.
Use: Antibiotic therapy against gram-positive & gram-negative organisms.

ILOTYCIN TABS. (Dista) Erythromycin 250 mg./Tab. Bot. 24s, 100s, 500s.
Use: Antibiotic.

ILOTYCIN GLUCEPTATE I.V. (Dista) Erythromycin gluceptate. Vial. I.V. (250 mg.) 30 ml. 1s, (500 mg.) 30 ml. 1s; (1 Gm.) 30 ml. Box 1s.
Use: I.V.; antibiotic therapy.

ILOZYME. (Adria) Pancrelipase equiv. to lipase 11000 u., protease 40,000 u., amylase 40,000 u./Tab. Bot. 250s.
Use: Exocrine pancreatic insufficiency.

I.L.X. ELIXIR. (Kenwood) Liver fraction 1 98 mg., iron 102 mg., B-1 5 mg., B-2 2 mg., nicotinamide 10 mg., B-12 10 mcg./15 cc. w/alcohol 8% Bot. 12 oz.
Use: Hematinic, multivitamin. Iron & ammonium citrate 18 gr., liver fraction No. 1, 3 gr., Vit. B-1 10 mg., B-2 4 mg., nicotinamide 20 mg., Vit. B-12 20 mcg./30 cc., alcohol 8%. Bot. 12 oz.
Use: Anemias.

I.L.X. B-12 TABLETS. (Kenwood) Iron (as ferrous gluconate) 5 gr., Vit. C 60 mg., B-12 10 mcg., liver 2 gr., thiamine HCl 2 mg., riboflavin 2 mg., niacinamide 20 mg./Tab. Bot. 100s.
Use: Hematinic, multivitamin.

• **IMAFEN HYDROCHLORIDE.** USAN.
Use: Antidepressant.

IMBRETIL. Carbolonium Bromide, B.A.N.

• **IMCARBOFOS.** USAN.
Use: Anthelmintic.

IMENOL. (Sig) Guaiacol 0.10 Gm., eucalyptol 0.08 Gm., iodoform 0.02 Gm., camphor 0.05 Gm./ml. Vial 30 ml.
Use: Mucous liquefaction and respiratory antibacterial.

IMFERGEN. (Goldline) Iron dextran. Vial 10 ml.
Use: Iron deficiency.

IMFERON. (Merrell Dow) An iron-dextran complex containing 50 mg. iron/ml. Amp. 2 ml. Box 10s. Vial (w/phenol 0.5%), 10 ml. Box 2s.
Use: I.M. and I.V. therapy for iron deficiency state not amenable to oral iron therapy.

1H-IMIDAZOLE,4,5-DIHYDRO-2-(1-NAPHTHALENYL-METHYL)-MONOHYDROCHLORIDE. Naphazoline Hydrochloride, U.S.P. XXI.

IH-IMIDAZOLE-4-ETHANAMINE, PHOSPHATE (1:2). Histamine Phosphate, U.S.P. XXI.

IH-IMIDAZOLE-1-ETHANOL,2-METHYL-5-NITRO. Metronidazole, U.S.P. XXI.

2H-IMIDAZOLE-2-THIONE,1,3-DIHYDRO-1-METHYL-. Methimazole, U.S.P. XXI.

2,4-IMIDAZOLIDINEDIONE,5,5-DIPHENYL-. Phenytoin, U.S.P. XXI.

m-[N-(2-IMIDAZOLIN-2-YLMETHYL)-p-TOLUIDINO]PHENOL MONOMETHANESULFONATE (SALT). Phentolamine Mesylate, U.S.P. XXI.

2,4-IMIDAZOLIDINEDIONE,1-[[(5-NITRO-2-FURANYL)METHYLENE]AMINO]-. Nitrofurantoin, U.S.P. XXI.

• **IMIDECYL IODINE.** USAN. 1-Carboxymethylene-1-(2-ethanol)-2-alkyl(C_7 to C_{17})-2-imidazolinium chloride-tridecyl polyoxyethylene-ethanol-iodine complex.
Use: Antiseptic agent.

IMIDOCARB. B.A.N. 3,3′-Di-(2-imidazolin-2-yl)carbanilide.
Use: Antiprotozoan, veterinary medicine.

• **IMIDOCARB HCl.** USAN. 3,3′-Di-2-imidazolin-2-ylcarbanilide dihydrochloride.
Use: Antiprotozoal.

IMIDODICARBONIMIDIC DIAMIDE,N-(2-PHENYLETHYL)-MONOHYDROCHLORIDE. Phenformin Hydrochloride.

• **IMIDOLINE HYDROCHLORIDE.** USAN. 1-(m-Chlorophenyl)-3-(2-(dimethylamino)ethyl)-2-imidazolidinone hydrochloride.
Use: Tranquilizer.

• **IMIDUREA,** N.F. XVI.

• **IMILOXAN HYDROCHLORIDE.** USAN.
Use: Antidepressant.

IMIPEMIDE.
Use: Antibacterial.
See: Imipenem, USAN.

• **IMIPENEM.** USAN.
Use: Antibacterial.

• **IMIPRAMINE HCl.** U.S.P. XXI. Inj., Tab., U.S.P. XXI. 5H-Dibenz [b,f] azepine-5-propanamine, 10,11-dihydro-N,N-dimethyl-, HCl. 5-(3-Dimethyl-aminopropyl)-10,11,dihydro-5H-dibenz-(b,f) azepine HCl. Praminil. Berkomine, IA-Pram, Impamin, Iprogen, Norpramine, & Tofranil HCl salts.
Use: Antidepressant.
See: Janimine, Tab. (Abbott)
Presamine, Tab. (USV)
SK-Pramine, Tab. (SmithKline)
Tofranil, Tab., Amp. (Geigy)
W.D.D., Tab. (Reid-Provident)

IMIRON INJECTION. (Amfre-Grant) Iron dextran 50 mg./ml. Vial 10 ml.
Use: Hematinic.

IMIPRAMINE PAMOATE. bis 5-[3-(Di-methylamino) propyl]-10,11-dihydro-5H-dibenz [b,f] azapine compound (2:1) with 4,4-methylenebis-[3-hydroxy-2-naphthoic acid].
Use: Antidepressant.
See: Tofranil-PM, Cap. (Geigy)

IMMOLIN. (Schmid) Methoxypolyoxyethyleneglycol 550 laurate 5%, nonylphenoxpolyethoxyethanol 1% in creamjel emulsion base. Tube 75 Gm.
Use: Contraceptive.

IMMUGLOBIN. (Savage) Soln. of gamma globulin standardized for measles & polio antibody content. 16.5% $\pm$ 1.5% Gamma Globulin/cc. Vial 10 cc.
Use: Gamma globulin deficiency.

• **IMMUNE GLOBULIN,** U.S.P. XXI. Immune Serum Globulin Human. Gamma-globulin fraction of normal human plasma. Vial 10 cc. Tubex 1 cc., 2 cc. w/thimerosal 1:10,000.
Use: Modification of active measles, prophylaxis of hepatitis, treatment of immune deficiencies.
See: Gamastan, Vial (Cutter)
Gamimune, Vial (Cutter)
Gammagee, Vial (Merck Sharp & Dohme)
Gammar, Vial (Armour)
Generic, Vial 2 ml., 10 ml. (Merck Sharp & Dohme)
Immuglobin, Vial (Savage)

IMMUNE GLOBULIN, Rh_0 (D).
See: Gamulin Rh (Parke-Davis)
HypRho-D (Cutter)
RhoGAM (Ortho Diagnostics)

IMMUNE SERUMS.
See: Human Measles Immune Serum (Var. Mfr.)
Immune Serum Globulin (Human)

IMMUNE SERUM (ANIMAL).
See: Botulism Antitoxin, Vial (Lederle)
Diphtheria Antitoxin
Gas Gangrene Antitoxin
Tetanus Antitoxin
Tetanus Antitoxin—Gas Gangrene Combined

IMMUNE SERUM (HUMAN).
See: Hypertussis, Vial (Cutter)
Poliomyelitis Immune Globulin (Various Mfr.)

IMMUNEX CRP. (Wampole) Two-minute latex agglutination slide test for the qualitative detection of C-Reactive protein in serum. Kit 100s.
Use: An aid in the diagnosis of inflammatory conditions.

IMMUNOREX. (Barry) Treatment set of 4 serially diluted vials w/concentration of 1:60 w/v pollen units.
Use: Restore allergic balance.

IMODIUM CAPSULES. (Janssen) Loperamide 2 mg./Cap. Bot. 100s, 500s.
Use: Acute, non-specific, chronic diarrhea and reducing volume of discharge from ileostomies.

IMODIUM LIQUID. (Janssen) Loperamide 0.2 mg./ml.
Use: Control of chronic diarrhea.

IMOGAM RABIES IMMUNE GLOBULIN. (Merieux Institute) Rabies immune globulin (human) 150 I.U./ml. Vial 2 ml. or 10 ml. in tamper proof box.
Use: For post-exposure rabies treatment.

IMOLAMINE. B.A.N. 4-(2-Diethylaminoethyl)-5-imino-3-phenyl-1,2,4-oxadiazoline.
Use: Treatment of angina pectoris.
See: Angolon hydrochloride

IMOVAX RABIES VACCINE. (Merieux Institute) Merieux rabies vaccine, Wistar rabies virus strain PM-1503-3M grown in human diploid cell cultures. Tamper proof box w/1 ml. vaccine, syringe and needles.
Use: Pre & post exposure to rabies.

IMPACT. (Approved) Belladonna alkaloids 0.16 mg., phenylpropanolamine HCl 50 mg., chlorpheniramine maleate 1 mg., pheniramine maleate 12.5 mg./Cap. Pack 12s, 24s. Vial 15s, 30s, Bot. 1000s.
Use: Decongestant.

IMPREGON CONCENTRATE. (Fleming) Tetrachlorosalcylankide 2%. Bot 4 oz.
Use: Diaper rash and mold inhibitor.

IMPROMEN. (Janssen) Bromperidol decanoate.
Use: Anti-psychotic.

IMPROMEN DECANOAS. (Janssen) Bromperidol decanoate.
Use: Antipsychotic.

• **IMPROMIDINE HYDROCHLORIDE.** USAN.
Use: Diagnostic aid.

IMPROVED SINUSTAT. (Vitarine) Acetaminophen 325 mg., phenylpropanolamine HCl 25 mg., phenyltoloxamine citrate 22 mg./Tab.
Use: Temporary relief of sinus headache & nasal congestion.

IMUNIVY. (Kay) Poison ivy extract. Vial 1 ml.
Use: Prophylactic sensitization for poison ivy.

IMUNOAK. (Kay) Poison oak extract. Vial 1 ml.
Use: Prophylactic sensitization for poison oak.

IMURAN. (Burroughs Wellcome) **Tab.:** Azathioprine. 50 mg./Tab. Bot. 100s. **Inj.:** Azathioprine 100 mg./20 ml. Vial.
Use: Immunosuppression agent for renal transplantation, rheumatoid arthritis.

INACTIVATED DIAGNOSTIC DIPHTHERIA TOXIN.
See: Diphtheria Toxin for Schick Test, U.S.P. XXI.

INAPSINE. (Janssen) Droperidol 2.5 mg./ml. Amp. 2 ml., 5 ml., 10 ml. Box 10s. Multi-dose Vial w/methylparaben 1.8 mg., propylparaben 0.2 mg., lactic acid/10 cc. Box 10s.
Use: Tranquilizer.
W/Fentanyl citrate.
Use: Tranquilizer, premedication induction of anesthetic.
See: Innovar, Inj. (Janssen)

INCORPOHIST. (Blue Line) Pyrilamine maleate 10 mg., prophenpyridamine maleate 5 mg./Tab. Bot. 1000s.
Use: Triple antihistaminic.

INCREMIN W/IRON. (Lederle) l-Lysine HCl 300 mg., Vit. B-12 25 mcg., B-1 10 mg., B-6 5 mg., ferric pyrophosphate soluble 30 mg., sorbitol 3.5 Gm., alcohol 0.75%/5 cc. Syr. Bot. 4 fl. oz. & 16 fl. oz.
Use: An appetite stimulant.

• **INDACRINONE.** USAN.
Use: Antihypertensive, diuretic.

INDALITAN. Clorindione, B.A.N.

INDALONE.
See: Butopyronoxyl (Various Mfr.)

• **INDAPAMIDE.** USAN.
Use: Antihypertensive, diuretic.

• **INDECAINIDE HYDROCHLORIDE.** USAN.
Use: Cardiac depressant.

• **INDELOXAZINE HYDROCHLORIDE.** USAN.
Use: Antidepressant.

INDERAL INJECTION. (Ayerst) Propranolol HCl 1 mg./ml. Amp. 1 ml. Box 10s.
Use: Arrhythmia

INDERAL TABLETS. (Ayerst) Propranolol HCl. 10 mg., 20 mg., 40 mg., 60 mg., 80 mg. or 90 mg./Tab. Bot. 100s, 1000s. Unit dose 100s. Bot. 5000s and Unit of use 60s, 90s, 100s, 120s, for 10 mg., 20 mg., 40 mg. and 80 mg.
Use: Arrhythmia, angina pectoris, hypertension, migraine, myocardial infarcation.

INDERAL-LA. (Ayerst) Propranolol HCl 80 mg., 120 mg. or 160 mg./SR Cap. Bot. 100s, 1000s, unit dose.
Use: Angina pectoris, hypertension, migraine treatment.

INDERIDE.(Ayerst) Propranolol HCl 40 mg., hydrochlorothiazide 25 mg./Tab. Bot 100s, 1000s. Unit Dose 100s. Propranolol HCl 80 mg., hydrochlorothiazide 25 mg./Tab. Bot. 100s, 1000s. Unit Dose 100s.
Use: Hypertension management.

INDIAN GUM.
See: Karaya Gum

INDIGO CARMINE. (CMC) Sod. indigotindisulfate 0.8% Amp. 5 cc. 100s.

INDIGO CARMINE. (Hynson, Westcott & Dunning) Sod. indigotindisulfonate 8 mg./ml. Amp. 5 ml. Box 10s, 100s.
Use: Localizing ureteral orifices during cystoscopy.
See: Sod. indigotindisulfonate

• **INDIGOTINDISULFONATE SODIUM,** U.S.P. XXI. Inj., U.S.P. XXI. 1H-Indole-5-sulfonic acid, 2-(1,3-dihydro-4-oxo-5-sulfo-2H-indol-2-ylidene)-2,3-dihydro-3-oxo-, sod. salt. Indigo Carmine, Amp. (Various Mfr.)
Use: Diagnostic aid (cystoscopy).
See: Sodium Indigotindisulfonate

• **INDIUM In III OXYQUINOLINE.** USAN.
Use: Radioactive agent, diagnostic aid.

• **INDIUM In 111 PENTETRATE INJECTION,** U.S.P. XXI.
Use: Diagnostic aid for cardiac output determination.

INDOCIN. (Merck Sharp & Dohme) Indomethacin. **Cap.:** 25 mg./Cap. Bot. 100s, 1000s. Unit-dose 100s. Unit of use 100s; 50 mg./Cap. Bot. 100s. Unit-dose 100s. Unit-of-use 60s, 100s. **Suppos.:** 50 mg/Suppos. Pkg. 30s.
Use: Non-steroidal anti-inflammatory agent.

INDOCIN I.V. (Merck Sharp & Dohme) Indomethacin sodium trihydrate equivalent to 1.0 mg. indomethacin/Vial.
Use: Patent ductus arteriosus.

INDOCIN SR. (Merck Sharp & Dohme) Indomethacin 75 mg./S.R. Cap. Unit-of-Use 30s, 60s.
Use: Non-steroidal anti-inflammatory agent.

• **INDOCYANINE GREEN,** U.S.P. XXI. Sterile, U.S.P. XXI. A tricarbocyanine dye. 1H-Benz [e] indolium, 2-[7-[1,3-dihydro-1,1-dimethyl-3-(4-sulfobutyl)-2H-benz [e] indol-2-ylidene]-1,3,5-heptatrienyl]-1,1-dimethyl-3-(4-sulfobutyl)-, hydroxide, inner salt, sodium salt.
Use: Diagnostic aid.
See: Cardio-Green, Inj. (Hynson, Westcott & Dunning)

INDOGESIC. (Century) Acetaminophen 32.5 mg., butalbital 50 mg./Tab. Bot. 100s, 1000s.
Use: Analgesic, sedative.

INDOKLON. Hexafluorodiethyl ether. Flurothyl. Bis-(2, 2,2-trifluorethyl)ether.
Use: Shock inducing agent (convulsant).

• **INDOLAPRIL HYDROCHLORIDE.** USAN.
Use: Antihypertensive.

INDO-LEMMON. (Lemmon) Indomethacin 25 mg. or 50 mg./Cap. Bot. 100s, 500s.
Anti-inflammatory.

INDOMED. (Rowell) Indomethacin 25 mg. or 50 mg./Cap. Bot. 100s.
Use: Anti-inflammatory.

INDOMETH CAPS. (Major) Indomethacin 25 mg./Tab. Bot. 100s, 1000s. 50 mg./Tab. Bot. 100s, 500s.
Use: Anti-inflammatory agent.

• **INDOMETHACIN,** U.S.P. XXI. Cap., U.S.P. XXI. 1-(p-Chlorobenzoyl)-5-methoxy-2-methyl-indole-3-acetic acid.
Use: Anti-inflammatory agent (nonsteroid).
See: Indocin, Cap., S.R. Cap. (Merck Sharp & Dohme)
Indo-Lemmon, Cap. (Lemmon)
Indomed, Cap. (Rowell)

• **INDOPROFEN.** USAN.
Use: Analgesic, anti-inflammatory.

• **INDORAMIN.** USAN. N-[1-(2-Indol-3-ylethyl)-4-piperidyl]benzamide. 3-[2-(4-Benzamidopiperidino)ethyl]indole.
Use: Antihypertensive.

• **INDORAMIN HYDROCHLORIDE.** USAN.
Use: Antihypertensive.

• **INDORENATE HYDROCHLORIDE.** USAN.
Use: Antihypertensive.

• **INDOXOLE.** USAN.
Use: Antipyretic, anti-inflammatory.

• **INDRILINE HYDROCHLORIDE.** USAN.
Use: Stimulant.

INFACAPS A & D. (Lannett) Vitamin A 3000 I.U., D 800 I.U./Cap. Bot. 1000s, 5000s.

INFALYTE. (Pennwalt) Provides (per liter) sodium 50 mEq., chloride 40 mEq., bicarbonate 30 mEq., potassium 20 mEq., D-glucose 111 m.moles/24 Gm. packet to be dissolved in 32 fl. oz. of water or/6 Gm. packet to be dissolved in 8 fl. oz. of water.
Use: Oral electrolyte replenisher.

INFANTOL PINK. (Scherer) Paregoric (equivalent) contains 15 mg. opium/fl. oz w/bismuth subsalicylate, Ca carageenan, pectin, Zn phenolsulfonate, alcohol 2%. Suspension. Bot. 4 oz., 8 oz., pt.
Use: Antidiarrheal.

INFANTOVIT PLUS. (CMC) Vit. A 5000 I.U., D 1000 I.U., C 60 mg., B-1 1.5 mg., B-2 1 mg., B-6 0.5 mg., Ca pantothenate 3 mg., nicotinamide 10 mg., B-12 1 mcg., folic acid 0.05 mg./Chewable sphere. Bot. 30s, 100s, 250s, 1000s.
Use: Dietary supplement.

NFARUB CREAM. (Whitehall) Methylsalicylate 35%, menthol 10% in vanishing cream base. Tube 1.25 oz., 3.5 oz.
Use: External analgesic.

NFATUSS. (Scott/Cord) Dextromethorphan HBr 7.20 mg., chlorpheniramine maleate 1.10 mg., phenylpropanolamine HCl 4.80 mg., ammonium chloride 50.00 mg./5 cc. Bot. 4 oz., pt., gal.
Use: Cough due to colds.

NFATUSSIS. (Blue Line) Pot. citrate, squill fl. ext. ipecac syr., tolu syr., honey & alcohol. Bot. 1 pt., 1 gal.
Use: Cough, expectorant.

NFLAMASE MILD 1/8% OPHTHALMIC SOLUTION. (CooperVision) Prednisolone sod. phosphate 0.125% (equiv. to prednisolone phosphate 0.11%). Bot. 5 ml. and 10 ml. w/dropper tip.
Use: Anti-inflammatory.

NFLAMASE FORTE 1% OPHTHALMIC SOLUTION. (CooperVision) Prednisolone sod. phosphate 1.0% (equiv. to prednisolone phosphate 0.91%). Bot. 5 ml., 10 ml.
Use: Anti-inflammatory.

INFLUENZA VIRUS VACCINE, U.S.P. XXI.
Use: Active immunizing agent.
See: Fluzone, Inj. (Squibb-Connaught)

NFLUENZAE TYPE B SERUM (RABBIT) ANTIHEMOPHILUS. (Various Mfr.) The sterile suspension of formaldehyde-killed influenza virus, type A, Asian strain grown in the extra-embryonic fluid of chick eggs.
Use: Immunization.

NFLUENZA VIRUS VACCINE.
Lederle—Bivalent types A and B. A/Port Chalmers/1/73 (h3n2)-700 CCA Units, B/Hong-Kong/5/72-500 CCA Units. Vial 5 ml.
Wyeth—Types A & B Tubex Cartridge-Needle Unit 0.5cc., 10s. Vial 5 cc.
Use: Prevention of influenza.
See: Fluzone, Inj. (Squibb-Connaught)

NGADINE TABS. (Major) Guanethidine sulfate 10 mg. or 25 mg./Tab. Bot. 100s, 1000s.
Use: Antihypertensive.

NH. (Ciba) Isoniazid 300 mg./Tab. Bot.
Use: Tuberculosis treatment.
See: Rimactane/INH, Dual Pack (Ciba)

NHAL-AID. (Key)
Use: Drug delivery system for metered dose inhalers.

NNERCLEAN HERBAL LAXATIVE. (Last) Senna leaf powder, psyllium seed, buckthorne, anise seed, fennel seed. Bot. 1 oz., 2 oz.
Use: Stimulant laxative.

NNERTABS. (Last) Senna leaf powder and psyllium seed tablets. Bot. 80s, 200s.
Use: Stimulant laxative.

NNER RINSE. (Block) Sodium lauryl sulfate, sodium borate, edetate disodium, triethanolamine, ethyl alcohol, aromatics, citric acid buffer. Bot. 2 oz., 4 oz.
Use: Vaginal douche concentrate.

INNOVAR INJECTION. (Janssen) Fentanyl citrate 0.05 mg., droperidol 2.5 mg./cc. Amp. 2 cc., 5 cc. Box of 10s.
Use: Tranquilizer, analgesic

INOCOR LACTATE. (Winthrop-Breon) Amrinone lactate (base equivalent) 5 mg./ml. w/0.25 mg. sodium betabisulfite. Amp. 20 ml. Box 5s.
Use: Short term management of congestive heart failure.

INOPHYLLINE.
See: Aminophylline (Various Mfr.)

INOSIT.
See: Inositol, (Var. Mfr.)

INOSITOL. 1,2,3,5/4,6-Cyclohexanehexol. Commercial solvents (Bios 1,Hexahydroxycyclohexane, Inosit, Dambose).
Use: Alterations in lipid metabolism.
W/Choline bitartrate, vitamins, minerals.
W/Choline chloride, dl-methionine, B-12.
Cho-Meth, Vial (Kenyon)
See: Lypo-B, Vial (Rocky Mtn.)
W/Methionine, choline bitartrate, liver desic., Vit. B-12.
See: Limvic, Tab. (Briar)
W/Panthenol, choline chloride, vitamins, minerals, estrone, testosterone.
See: Geramine, Inj. (Brown)
W/Panthenol, choline chloride, vitamins, minerals, estrone, testosterone, polydigestase.
See: Geramine, Tab. (Brown)

• **INOSITOL NIACINATE.** USAN. Myo-Inositol hexanicotinate. Meso-inositol hexanicotinate, hexanicotinate. Meso-inositol hexanicotinate. Hexopal; Mesonex
Use: Peripheral Vasodilator.

INOSITOL NICOTINATE. Inositol Niacinate.

INPERSOL W/DEXTROSE. (Abbott) Dextrose 1.5%, 2.5% & 4.25% w/sodium chloride 140.5 mEq., Ca chloride 3.5 mEq., Mg chloride 1.5 mEq., sod. lactate 445 mEq./100 ml. **1.5% Dextrose:** 250 ml./500 ml.; 500 ml., 1000 ml.; 1000 ml./2000 ml.; or 1500 ml./2000 ml. partial fill single-dose container and 3000 ml. container. **2.5% Dextrose:** 250 ml./500 ml.; 500 ml./1000 ml.; 1000 ml./2000 ml.; or 1500 ml./2000 ml. partial fill single-dose container and 3000 ml. single-dose container. **4.25% Dextrose:** 250 ml./500 ml.; 500 ml./1000 ml.; 1000 ml./2000 ml.; or 1500 ml./2000 ml. partial fill single-dose container and 3000 ml. single-dose container.
Use: Peritoneal dialysis solution.

INPERSOL-LM. W/DEXTROSE. (Abbott) Inpersol-LM w/1.5% or 2.5% Dextrose. **1.5% Dextrose:** Single-dose flexible container 2000 ml. **2.5% Dextrose:** Partial fill single-dose 2000 ml./3000 ml.
Use: Peritoneal dialysis solution.

INPROQUONE. B.A.N. 2,5-Di(aziridin-1-yl)-3,6-dipropoxy-1,4-benzoquinone.
Use: Antineoplastic agent.

INSECT ANTIGEN. (Hollister-Stier) Potent extracts from whole insect body of honey bee, bumblebee, hornet, yellowjacket, wasp, mosquito, ant, flea, moth, fly, locust, and household insects. Scratch (1:10) and Intradermal (100 PNU/cc.) tests.

Use: Diagnosis and desensitizing of stinging insect venom.

INSECT ANTIGEN, STINGING 108. (Barry) Combined antigens of bumble bee, honey bee, wasp, hornet, and yellow jacket/5 cc.; three 5 cc. serial dilution vials. Vial 5 cc., 10 cc. 1:100.
Use: Hyposensitization against common insect venom reactions.

INSERFEM. (Blue Line) Iodoquinol 100 mg., benzalkonium Cl 1 mg., tartaric acid 5 mg., lactose & liquid glucose 1.1 Gm./Vag. Tab. Bot. 60s w/ or w/o plastic inserters.
Use: Vaginitis, particularly with trichomonas infection.

INSPIREASE. (Key)
Use: Drug delivery system for metered-dose inhalers.

INSTAFREEZE SPRAY. (Century) Fluorinated and chlorinated hydrocarbons. Bot. 7 oz.

INSTA-CHAR. (Kerr) **Regular:** Aqueous suspension activated charcoal 50 Gm./8 oz. **Pediatric:** Aqueous suspension activated charcoal 15 Gm/4 oz.
Use: Antidote for toxic substances.

INSTA-GLUCOSE. (ICN) Undiluted USP glucose. Unit dose tube containing 31 Gms. of liquid glucose.
Use: Insulin reactions.

INST-E-VITE. (Barth's) Vit. E 100 I.U./Cap. Bot 100s, 500s, 1000s. 200 I.U./Cap. Bot. 100s, 250s, 500s.

INSULATARD NPH. (Nordisk) Isophane purified pork insulin suspension 100 I.U./ml.
Use: Diabetes care (IDDM).

• **INSULIN.** U.S.P. XXI. Inj., U.S.P. XXI.
See: Iletin Prod. (Lilly)
Insulin Prod. (Squibb)

INSULIN. (Nordisk) Insulatard NPH Mixtard Velosulin

INSULIN. (Lilly)
Human-100 u./ml.
Isophane—40 u., 100 u./ml.
Protamine Zinc—40u., 100 u./ml.
Regular—40u., 100 u./ml.
Semilente—Zinc insulin 40 u., 100 u./ml.
Ultralente—Zinc insulin 40 u., 100 u./ml.
Lente—Zinc insulin 40 u., 100 u./ml. Vial 10 ml.
Use: Hypoglycemia.

• **INSULIN, DALANATED.** USAN.
Use: Antidiabetic.

INSULIN, GLOBIN ZINC INJECTION.
Use: Antidiabetic.

• **INSULIN HUMAN,** U.S.P. XXI. Inj., U.S.P. XXI.
Use: Antidiabetic.

• **INSULIN I-125.** USAN.
Use: Radioactive agent.

• **INSULIN I-131.** USAN.
Use: Radioactive agent.

• **INSULIN INJECTION,** U.S.P. XXI. Insulin, insulin HCl.
Use: Antidiabetic.

• **INSULIN, NEUTRAL.** USAN.
Use: Antidiabetic.

INSULIN NOVO RAPITARD. Biphasic Insulin Injection, B.A.N.

• **INSULIN, PROTAMINE ZINC SUSPENSION,** U.S.P. XXI. 40, 100 u./cc. Vials 10 cc.
Use: Antidiabetic.

• **INSULIN ZINC SUSPENSION,** U.S.P. XXI.
Use: Antidiabetic.
See: Lente Insulin, Vial (Lilly)

• **INSULIN ZINC SUSPENSION, EXTENDED,** U.S.P. XXI.
Use: Antidiabetic.

• **INSULIN ZINC SUSPENSION, PROMPT,** U.S.P. XXI.
Use: Antidiabetic, Hypoglycemic.

INTAL CAPSULES. (Fisons) Cromolyn sodium 20 mg., lactose powder 20 mg./Cap. Box 60s, 120s.
Use: Bronchial asthma inhibitor.

INTAL NEBULIZER SOLUTION. (Fisons) Cromolyn sodium 20 mg. in 2 ml. distilled water for use with a power operated nebulizer unit. Box 60s, 120s., 2 ml. ampules.
Use: Anti-asthmatic.

INTERCEPT CONTRACEPTIVE INSERTS. (Advanced Care) Nonoxynol-9 5.56% at pH 4.5. Starter 12 inserts w/applicator. Refill 12 inserts.
Use: Contraceptive insert.

INTEGRIN CAPS. (Winthrop Products) Oxypertine.
Use: Anxiolytic, tranquilizer.

• **INTERFERON.** USAN. A protein formed by the interaction of animal cells with viruses capable of conferring on animal cells resistance to virus infection. A drug derived from human white blood cells and originally used in Finland.
Note: An investigational drug in the U.S.A.
Use: Antineoplastic, antiviral. Treatment of breast cancer lymphoma, multiple melanoma & malignant melanoma

INTRADEX. Dextran, B.A.N.

INTRALIPID 10% I.V. FAT EMULSION. (KabiVitrum) I.V. fat emulsion containing soybean oil 10%, egg yolk phospholipids 1.2%, glycerin 2.25% & water for injection. I.V. Flask 100ml., 500ml.
Use: Calories & fatty acids for prolonged nutrition.

INTRALIPID 20% I.V. FAT EMULSION. (KabiVitrum) I.V. fat emulsion containing soybean oil 20%, egg yolk phospholipids 1.2%, glycerin 2.25% and water for injection. I.V. Flask 100 ml., 500 ml.
Use: Calories and fatty acids for prolonged nutrition.

INTRA-SUL. (Torigian) Sod. thiosulfate, sod. sulfide, sulfur. Amp. 2 cc. 6s, 25s, 100s.

INTRAVAL SODIUM.
See: Pentothal Sodium, Prep. (Abbott)

• **INTRAZOLE.** USAN. 1-(p-Chlorobenzoyl)-3-(1H-tetrazol-5-ylmethyl) indole.
Use: Anti-inflammatory.

• **INTRIPTYLINE HYDROCHLORIDE.** USAN.
Use: Antidepressant.

INTRON-C. (Pharmics) Ferrous fumarate 300 mg., Vit. C 500 mg./Cap. Bot. 1000s.
Use: Iron deficiency anemia.

INTROPIN 200 mg. (American Critical Care) Dopamine HCl 40 mg./ml. w/sodium bisulfite 1% as an antioxidant. Vial 5 ml. Box 20s; Amp. 5 ml. Box 20s; Prefilled additive Syr. 5 ml. Box 5s.
Use: Treatment of shock.

INTROPIN 400 mg. (American Critical Care) Dopamine HCl 80 mg./ml. w/sodium bisulfite 1% as an antioxidant. Vial 5 ml. Box 20s.; Prefilled additive Syringe 5 ml. Box 5s.
Use: Treatment of shock.

INTROPIN 800 mg. (American Critical Care) Dopamine HCl 160 mg./ml. w/sodium bisulfite 1% as an antioxidant. Vial 5 ml. Box 20s.; Prefilled additive syringe 5 ml. Box 5s.
Use: Treatment of shock.

INULIN. (American Critical Care) Purified inulin 5 Gm./50 ml. Sod. chloride 0.9%, sod. hydroxide to adjust pH. Amps. 50 ml.
Use: Diagnostic aid, kidney function, glomerular filtration rate.

INVENEX INJECTABLES. (Invenex) A wide variety of generic injectable products.

INVENOL. Carbutamide, B.A.N.

INVERSINE. (Merck Sharp & Dohme) Mecamylamine HCl. 2.5 mg./Tab. Bot. 100s.
Use: Antihypertensive.

INVERT SUGAR. (Abbott) 10% solution. Bot 1000 ml.
Use: Nutritional.
See: Emetrol, Liq. (Rorer)
Travert, Sol. (Travenol)

• **IOBENZAMIC ACID.** USAN. N-3-(3-Amino-2,4,6-triiodobenzoyl)-N-phenyl-β-alanine. Osbil. (Mallinkcrodt)
Use: Contrast medium for cholecystography.

• **IOCARMATE MEGLUMINE.** USAN.
Use: Diagnostic aid.

• **IOCARMIC ACID.** USAN. 5,5′-(Adipoyldiamino)-bis-(2,4,6-tri-iodo-N-methylisophthalamic acid). Dimer X is a sterile solution of the meglumine salt.
Use: Radio-opaque substance.

• **IOCETAMIC ACID,** U.S.P. XXI. Tab., U.S.P. XXI. N-Acetyl-N-(3-amino-2,4,6-triiodophenyl)-2-methylalanine. 3-(N-3-Amino-2,4,6-tri-iodophenyl)acetamido-2-methylpropionic acid.
Use: Diagnostic aid (radiopaque medium).

IOCON GEL. (Owen) Polyoxyethylene ethers, coal tar solution, Iopol (a cationic polymer), alcohol 1%, benzalkonium chloride in a non-ionic/amphoteric base. Tube 3.5 oz.
Use: Scalp dermatoses.

IOCORTAR. (Doak) Microfine hydrocortisone w/clioquinol 3%, solution of coal tar 3%. **Cream:** 0.5% Tube 1 oz; 1% Tube 1 oz. **Lotion:** 0.25% 4 oz.; 0.5% 1 oz.; 1% 1 oz. **Oint.:** 1% 1 oz.
Use: Dermatologic.

• **IODAMIDE.** USAN. 3-Acetamido-5-(acetamidomethyl)-2,4,6-triiodobenzoic acid. α,5-Di(acetamido)-2,-4,6-tri-iodo-m-toluic acid.
Use: Radiopaque.

• **IODAMIDE MEGLUMIDE.** USAN.
Use: Radiopaque, diagnostic aid.
W/Combinations:
See: Renovue-65, Vial (Squibb)
Renovue-Dip, Vial (Squibb)

IODEX. (Medtech) Iodine 4.7% in petrolatum ointment base. Jar 1 oz., 14 oz.
Use: Topical anti-infective.

IODEX W/METHYL SALICYLATE. (Medtech) Iodine 4.7%, methyl salicylate 4.8% in petrolatum ointment base.
Use: Local analgesic, topical anti-infective.

• **IODIDIDE, SODIUM, I-123 CAPSULES,** U.S.P. XXI.

• **IODIDE, SODIUM, I-123 TABLETS,** U.S.P. XXI.

• **IODIDE, SODIUM, I-125 CAPSULES,** U.S.P. XXI.

• **IODIDE, SODIUM, I-125 SOLUTION,** U.S.P. XXI.

• **IODIDE, SODIUM, I-131 CAPSULES,** U.S.P. XXI.

• **IODIDE, SODIUM, I-131 SOLUTION,** U.S.P. XXI.

• **IODINATED GLYCEROL.** B.A.N. A mixture of iodinated dimers of glycerol.
Use: Mucolytic expectorant.
See: Organidin, Elix., Sol., Tab. (Wampole)

• **IODINATED I-125 ALBUMIN INJECTION,** U.S.P. XXI.

• **IODINATED I-131 ALBUMIN AGGREGATED INJECTION,** U.S.P. XXI.

• **IODINATED I-131 ALBUMIN INJECTION,** U.S.P. XXI.

IODINATED HUMAN SERUM ALBUMIN.
See: Albumotope (Squibb)

• **IODINE,** U.S.P. XXI. Topical Sol., Strong Soln., Tincture, U.S.P. XXI.
Use: Topical anti-infective; source of iodine.
See: Kelp Tablets (Quality Generics)

IODINE 131: CAPSULES DIAGNOSTIC-CAPSULES THERAPEUTIC-SOLUTION THERAPEUTIC ORAL.
See: Iodotope (Squibb)

IODINE CACODYLATE, COLLOIDAL. Cacodyne Iodine.

IODINE COMBINATION.
See: Calcidrine Syr. (Abbott)

IODINE-IODOPHOR.
See: Betadine, Prep. (Purdue Frederick)
Isodine, Preps. (Blair)

IODINE POVIDONE.
See: Efodine, Oint. (Fougera)
Iodophor
Mallsol, Liq. (Mallard)

■ **IODINE PRODUCTS, ANTI-INFECTIVE.**
See: Anayodin
Betadine, Prep. (Purdue Frederick)
Chiniofon
Diodoquin, Tab. (Searle)
Diiodo-Hydroxyquinoline (Various Mfr.)
Isodine, Preps. (Blair)
Prepodyne, Sol., Scrub (West)
Quinoxyl
Surgidine, Liq. (Continental)
Vioform, Prep. (Ciba)

■ **IODINE PRODUCTS, DIAGNOSTIC.**
See: Chloriodized Oil (Var. Mfr.)
Ethyl Iodophenylundecylate (Var. Mfr.)
Iodized Oil
Iodoalphionic Acid (Various Mfr.)
Iodobrassid
Iodohippurate Sodium (Var. Mfr.)
Iodopanoic Acid (Var. Mfr.)
Iodophthalein Sodium (Various Mfr.)
Iodopyracet, Prep. (Var. Mfr.)
Lipiodol Lafay, Amp., Vial (Savage)
Methiodal Sodium (Var. Mfr.)
Pantopaque, Amp. (Lafayette)

Sodium Acetrizoate (Var. Mfr.)
Sodium Iodomethamate (Var. Mfr.)
Telepaque, Tab. (Winthrop-Breon)

■ **IODINE PRODUCTS, NUTRITIONAL.**
See: Calcium Iodobehenate (Various Mfr.)
Entodon
Hydriodic Acid (Var. Mfr.)
Iodobrassid (Various Mfr.)
Organidin, Elix., Sol., Tab. (Wampole)
Orgaphen, Elix., Tab. (Wampole)
Potassium Iodide (Various Mfr.)
Syniodin, Tab. (Blue Line)

IODINE RATION, (Barth's) Iodine (from kelp) 0.15 mg., trace minerals/Tab. Bot. 90s, 180s, 360s.

IODINE RATION. (Nion) Iodine (from kelp) 0.15 mg./3 Tab. Bot. 175s, 500s.
Use: Dietary supplement.

IODINE SOLUBLE.
See: Burnham Soluble Iodine, Sol. (Burnham)

IODINE SURFACE ACTIVE COMPLEX.
See: Ioprep, Sol. (Arbrook)

• **IODINE TINCTURE, STRONG,** U.S.P. XXI.

• **IODIPAMIDE,** U.S.P. XXI. Benzoic acid, 3,3′-[(1,6-dioxo-1,6-hexanediyl)diimino]bis[2,4,6-triiodo-. NN′-Di-(3-carboxy-2,4,6-tri-iodophenyl)-adipamide. Adipiodone (I.N.N.)
Use: Pharm. necessity for Iodipamide Meglumine Injection.

• **IODIPAMIDE MEGLUMINE INJECTION,** U.S.P. XXI. Benzoic acid, 3,3′-[(1,6-dioxo-1,6-hexanediyl)diimino] bis [2,4,6-triiodo-, compound with 1-deoxy-1-(methylamino)-d-glucitol (1:2).
Use: Diagnostic aid (radiopaque medium).

IODIPAMIDE METHYLGLUCAMINE. N,N′-Adipyl-bis(3-amino-2,4,6-triiodobenzoic acid). Also sodium salt inj.
W/Diatrizoate methylglucamine.
See: Sinografin, Vial (Squibb)

• **IODIPAMIDE SODIUM I-131.** USAN.
Use: Radioactive agent.

IODIPAMIDE SODIUM INJECTION.
See: Cholografin Sod., Sol. (Var. Mfr.)

IODIZED OIL. A vegetable oil containing not less than 38% and not more than 42% of organically combined iodine.
Use: Diagnostic aid (radiopaque, hysterosalpingography.
See: Lipiodol Lafay, Amp., Vial (Savage)

IODIZED POPPY-SEED OIL.
See: Lipiodol Lafay, Amp., Vial (Savage)

IODOALPHIONIC ACID. 3-(4-Hydroxy-3,5-Diiodo-phenyl)-2-phenylpropionic acid. Biliselectan dikol, pheniodol.

• **IODOANTIPYRINE I-131.** USAN.
Use: Radioactive agent.

IODOBEHENATE CALCIUM. Calcium iodododocosanoate.
Use: Antigoitrogenic.

IODOBRASSID. Ethyl Diiodobrassidate. Lipoiodine.

• **IODOCETYLIC ACID I-123.** USAN.
Use: Diagnostic aid.

• **IODOCHOLESTEROL I-131.** USAN.
Use: Radioactive agent.

• **IODOCHLORHYDROXYQUIN.** Clioquinol, U.S.P. XXI.

IODOCORT CREAM. (Ulmer) Hydrocortisone 1%, clioquinol 3%. Tube 20 Gm.

IODO CREAM. (Day-Baldwin) Clioquinol 3%. Tube 1 oz., Jar 1 lb.

IODOFORM. (Various Mfr.) Triiodomethane. Pow., Bot. ⅛ oz., 1 oz., 0.25 lb., 1 lb.
Use: For dressing wounds.
W/Guaiacol, eucalyptol, camphor.
See: Camusol, Vial (Central)
Guaiphoto, Vial (Foy)
Guiaform, Inj. (Vortech)
Guido, Vial (Rocky Mtn.)
Imenol, Inj. (Sig)
Kleer, Vial (Scrip)
Respirex, Vial (Savage)

IODOGENOL PEPIN. (C.M.C.) Organic iodide preparation, 1¾ oz.

IODO H-C. (Day-Baldwin) Clioquinol 3%, hydrocortisone 1%. **Oint:** Tube. 20 Gm. Jar. 1 lb. **Cream:** Tube. 20 Gm. Jar 1 lb.

• **IODOHIPPURATE SODIUM I-125.** USAN.
See: Hipputope I 125 (Squibb)

• **IODOHIPPURATE, SODIUM I-131 INJECTION,** USAN. U.S.P. XXI. Glycine, N-(2-iodo-^{131}I-benzoyl)-, sod. salt.
Use: Diagnostic aid (renal function determination).
See: Hipputope (Squibb)

IODO-HIPPURIC ACID.
See: Hipputope (Squibb)

7-IODO-8-HYDROXYQUINOLINE-5-SULFONATE, SODIUM.
See: Chiniofon, Tab. (CMC)

IODOL. 2,3,4,5-Tetraiodopyrrole.

IODO-NIACIN TABLETS. (Forest) Pot. iodide 135 mg., niacinamide HCl 25 mg./Tab. Bot. 100s, 500s, 1000s.
Use: Iodine therapy.

IODO OINTMENT. (Day-Baldwin) Clioquinol 3%. Tube 1 oz., Jar 1 lb.

IODOPANOIC ACID.
Use: Diagnostic aid (radiopaque medium).

IODOPHENE. Iodophthalein.

IODOPHENE SODIUM.
See: Iodophthalein Sodium. (Various Mfr.)

IODOPHOR.
See: Betadine, Prep. (Purdue Frederick)
Isodine, Preps. (Blair)

IODOPHTHALEIN SODIUM. Tetraiodophenolphthalein Sod., Tetraiodophthalein Sod., Tetiothalein Sod. (Antinosin, Cholepulvis, Cholumbrin, Foriod, Iodophene, Iodorayoral, Nosophene Sod., Opacin, Photobiline, Piliophen, Radiotetrane.).
Use: Radiopaque medium for cholecystography.

IODO-PRO. (Fellows) Sod. iodide 40 mg., peptone 20 mg./cc. Vial 30 cc.

IODOPROPYLIDENE GLYCEROL.
See: Organidin, Elix., Tab., Sol. (Wampole)

• **IODOPYRACET I-125.** USAN.
Use: Radioactive agent.

IODOPYRACET I-131. USAN.
Use: Radioactive agent.
See: Diodrast (R)-131

IODOPYRACET INJ. (Diatrast, Diodone, Iopyracil, Neo-Methiodal, NeoSkiodan) 3,5-Diiodo-4-oxo-1(4H)-pyridineacetic Acid 2,2-Iminodiethanol (1:1) Compound.
Use: Radiopaque medium.

IODOPYRACET COMPOUND. Diodrast.

IODOPYRACET CONCENTRATED. Diodrast

IODOPYRINE. Antipyrine "iodide."
Use: Iodides & analgesic.

IODOQUINOL, U.S.P. XXI. Tab., U.S.P. XXI. 8-Quinolinol-5,7-diiodo. Diiodohydroxyquinoline, (Embequin, Enterosept)5,7-Diiodo-8-quinolinol.
Use: Anti-amebic.
See: Floraquin (Searle)
Inserfem, Vag. Tabs. (Blue Line)
Sebaquin, Shampoo (Summers Labs.)

W/9-Aminoacridine HCl.
See: Vagitric, Cream (Elder)
Yodoxin, Tab., Pow. (Glenwood)

W/Diiodohydroxyquin
See: Panaquin, Tab. (Panray)

W/Hydrocortisone alcohol.
See: Vytone, Cream (Dermik)

W/Hydrocortisone, coal tar solution.
See: Cor-Tar-Quin, Cream, Lot. (Miles Pharm)

W/Stilbestrol, sulfadiazine, tartaric acid, boric acid, etc.
See: Gynben, Vag. Insert, Cream (ICN)
Gynben Insufflate, Pow. (ICN)

W/Sulfadiazine, diethylstilbestrol.
See: Benegyn, Vag. Insert, Cream (Vortech)

W/Surfactants.
See: Lycinate, Supp. (Hoechst)

W/Sulfanilamide, diethylstilbestrol.
See: Amide V/S, Vag Ins. (Scrip)
D.I.T.I. Creme (Dunhall)

IODOSONE CREAM. (Century) Hydrocortisone 1%, clioquinol 3%, promoxine HCl 0.5%. Tube 0.5 oz.

IODOTHIOURACIL. B.A.N. 1,2-Dihydro-5-iodo-2-thioxopyrimidin-4-one. 5-Iodo-2-thiouracil
Use: Antithyroid substance.
See: Itrumil [sodium derivative]

IODOTOPE (Diagnostic). (Squibb) Sodium Iodide-I-131 for oral use. 8,15, 30, 50, 100 u Ci/Vial of 5, 10, 15, 20 Caps.
Use: Diagnostic agent.

IODOTOPE (Therapeutic). (Squibb) Sodium Iodide I-131. 6 m Ci Caps./5, 10, 15, 20, 50, 75 m Ci solution.
Use: Therapeutic agent.

• **IODOXAMATE MEGLUMINE.** USAN.
Use: Diagnostic aid.

• **IODOXAMIC ACID.** USAN. NN'-(1,16-Dioxo-4,-7,10,-13-tetraoxahexadecane-1,16-diyl)di-(3-amino-2,4,6-tri-iodobenzoic acid).
Use: Contrast medium.

IODOXYL.
See: Sodium Iodomethamate (Var. Mfr.)

• **IOFETAMINE HYDROCHLORIDE I 123.** USAN.
Use: Diagnostic aid, radioactive agent.

• **IOGLICIC ACID.** USAN.
Use: Diagnostic aid.

• **IOGLUCOL.** USAN.
Use: Diagnostic aid.

• **IOGLUCOMIDE.** USAN.
Use: Diagnostic aid.

• **IOGLYCAMIC ACID.** USAN. 3,3-(Diglycoloyl-diimino)-bis-[2,4,6-triiodobenzoic acid]. Biligram, Bilivistan.
Use: Radiopaque (cholecystographic and cholangiographic).

• **IOGULAMIDE.** USAN.
Use: Diagnostic aid (radiopaque medium).

• **IOHEXOL.** USAN.
Use: Diagnostic aid.

IOHYDRO CREAM. (Freeport) Hydrocortisone 1%, clioquinol 3%, pramoxine HCl 0.5%/0.5 oz. Tubes 0.5 oz.
Use: Broad control of various dermatologic disorders.

• **IOMETHIN I-125.** USAN. 4-[[3-(Dimethylamino)propyl-]amino]-7-iodo-^{125} I-quinoline.
Use: Diagnostic aid (neoplasm).

• **IOMETHIN I-131.** USAN. 4-[[3-Dimethylamino)propyl-]amino]-7-iodo-^{131} I-quinoline.
Use: Diagnostic aid (neoplasm).

IONAMIN. (Pennwalt) Phentermine. Phenyl-tertiary-butylamine as resin complex 15 mg. and 30 mg./Cap. Bot. 100s, 400s.
Use: Appetite suppressant.

IONAX ASTRINGENT CLEANSER. (Owen) Isopropyl alcohol 48%, Owenethers, (polyoxyethylene ethers), acetone, salicylic acid, allantoin. Bot. 8 oz.
Use: Astringent skin cleanser.

IONAX FOAM. (Owen) Polyoxyethylene ethers, benzalkonium Cl, purified water, isobutane, propylene glycol, myristamide. DEA, PEG 1000, D&C No. 5. Aerosol cans 2.5 oz, 5 oz.
Use: Aerosol oily skin cleanser.

IONAX SCRUB. (Owen) Polyethylene granules, polyoxyethylene ethers, alcohol 10%, benzalkonium Cl. Tubes 2 oz., 4 oz.
Use: Abradant cleanser for oily skin.

IONAZE.
See: Propazolamide

ION-EXCHANGE RESINS.
See: Polyamine Methylene Resin
Resins, Sodium Removing

IONIL RINSE. (Owen) Conditioners with benzalkonium Cl in water base. Bot. 16 oz.
Use: Rinse.

IONIL SHAMPOO. (Owen) Salicylic acid, benzalkonium Cl, alcohol 12%, polyoxyethylene ethers. Plas. Bot. w/disp. cap 4 oz., 8 oz., 16 oz., 32 oz.
Use: Anti-seborrheic.

IONIL T. (Owen) A nonionic/cationic foaming shampoo w/coal tar. salicylic acid, benzalkonium chloride, alcohol 12%, polyoxyethylene ethers. Plas. bot. 4 oz., 8 oz., 16 oz., 32 oz.
Use: Anti-seborrheic.

IONOSOL B W/DEXTROSE 5%. (Abbott) Sod. chloride 180 mg., pot. chloride 100 mg., Mg chloride, anhy. 25 mg., dipotassium phosphate, anhy. 100 mg., monosodium phosphate anhy. 14 mg., sod. lactate 280 mg., dextrose 5 Gm., sod. bisulfite 30 mg./100 ml. Bot. 250 ml., 500 ml., 1000 ml.

IONOSOL B W/INVERT SUGAR 10%. (Abbott) Sod. chloride 180 mg., pot. chloride 100 mg., Mg chloride, anhy. 25 mg., dipotassium phosphate anhy. 100 mg., monosodium phosphate, anhy. 14 mg., sod. lactate 246 mg., invert sugar 10 Gm., sod. bisulfite 30 mg./100 ml. Bot. 1000 ml.

IONOSOL D-CM. (Abbott) Sod. chloride 516 mg., pot. chloride 89.4 mg., cal. chloride, anhy. 27.8 mg., Mg chloride, anhy. 14.2 mg., sod. lactate 560 mg./100 ml. Bot. 1000 ml.

IONOSOL D-CM W/DEXTROSE 5%. (Abbott) Sod. chloride 516 mg., pot. chloride 89.4 mg., cal. chloride, anhy. 27.8 mg., Mg chloride, anhy. 14.2 mg., sod. lactate 560 mg., dextrose 5 Gm., sod. bisulfite 50 mg./100 ml. Bot. 1000 ml.
Use: Duodenal use.

IONOSOL D (MODIFIED) W/INVERT SUGAR 10%. (Abbott) Sod. chloride 117 mg., pot. chloride 268 mg., cal. chloride, anhy. 25.5 mg., Mg chloride, anhy. 13.3 mg., sod. lactate 672 mg., invert sugar 10 Gm., sod. bisulfite 41.6 mg./100 ml. Bot. 1000 ml.

IONOSOL G W/DEXTROSE 10%. (Abbott) Sod. chloride 370 mg., pot. chloride 126 mg., ammonium chloride 377 mg., dextrose 10 Gm. sodium bicarbonate (buffer) 4.5 mg., sodium bisulfite 30 mg./100 ml. Bot. 1000 ml.
Use: Gastric use.

IONOSOL G W/INVERT SUGAR 10%. (Abbott) Sod. chloride 350 mg., pot. chloride 127 mg., ammonium chloride 375 mg., invert sugar 10 Gm., sod. bisulfite 60 mg., sod. bicarbonate 4.5 mg./100 ml. Bot. 1000 ml.

IONOSOL MB W/DEXTROSE 5%. (Abbott) Pot. chloride 141 mg., Mg chloride, anhy. 14.2 mg., monopotassium phosphate, anhy. 15 mg., monosodium phosphate, anhy. 21.4 mg., sod. lactate 260 mg., dextrose 5 Gm., sod. bisulfite 22 mg./100 ml. Bot. 250 ml., 500 ml., 1000 ml.

IONOSOL T W/DEXTROSE 5%. (Abbott) Sod. chloride 146 mg., pot. chloride 111 mg., monosodium phosphate, anhy. 181 mg., pot. lactate 256 mg., dextrose 5 Gm., sod. bisulfite 23 mg./100 ml. Bot. 250 ml., 500 ml., 1000 ml.

• **IOPAMIDOL.** USAN.
Use: Diagnostic aid.

• **IOPANOIC ACID,** U.S.P. XXI. Tabs. U.S.P. XXI. Benzenepropanoic acid, 3-amino-α-ethyl-2,4,6-triiodo-. 2-(3-Amino-2,4,6-tri-iodobenzyl)-butyric acid. 3-Amino-a-ethyl-2,4,6 Triiodohydrocinnamic acid.
See: Telepaque, Tab. (Winthrop-Breon)

IOPHED SYRUP. (Marsh-Emory) Ephedrine HCl 12 mg., calcium iodide hexahydrate 167 mg., chloral hydrate 300 mg./5 cc. Bot. pt.
Use: Bronchial & cardiac asthma & status asthmaticus.

• **IOPHENDYLATE,** U.S.P. XXI. Benzenedecanoic acid, iodo-t-methyl-, ethyl ester.
Use: Diagnostic aid (radiopaque medium).

• **IOPHENDYLATE INJECTION,** U.S.P. XXI. Ethiodan Myodil. Ethyl Iodophenylundecylate.
Use: Diagnostic aid (radiopaque medium).
See: Pantopaque, Amp. (LaFayette)

IOPHENOXIC ACID. Tabs. a-(2-4,6-Triiodo-3-hydroxybenxyl) butyric acid.

IOPODATE SODIUM.
See Ipodate Sodium.

IOPREP. (Surgikos) Nonylphenoxypolyethylenoxy (4) ethanol and nonylphenoxypolyethyleneoxy (15) ethanol iodine complex 5.5%, nonylphenoxypolyethyleneoxy (30) ethanol 10%. Solution provides 1% available iodine. Bot. plastic, gal.
Use: Antiseptic.

• **IOPROCEMIC ACID.** USAN.
Use: Diagnostic aid.

• **IOPRONIC ACID.** USAN.
Use: Diagnostic aid.

• **IOPYDOL.** USAN. 1-(2,3-Dihydroxypropyl)-3,5-diiodo-4(1H)-pyridone.
Use: X-ray contrast medium for bronchography.

• **IOPYDONE.** USAN. 3,5-Diiodo-4-(1H)-pyridone.
Use: X-ray contrast medium for bronchography.

• **IOSEFAMIC ACID.** USAN. 5,5′-(Sebacoyldiimino) bis[2,4,6-triiodo-N-methylisophthalamic acid]
Use: Contrast medium.

• **IOSERIC ACID.** USAN.
Use: Diagnostic aid.

• **IOSULAMIDE MEGLUMINE.** USAN.
Use: Diagnostic aid.

• **IOSUMETIC ACID.** USAN.
Use: Diagnostic aid.

• **IOTASUL.** USAN.
Use: Diagnostic aid.

• **IOTETRIC ACID.** USAN.
Use: Diagnostic aid.

• **IOTHALAMATE MEGLUMIDE AND IOTHALMATE SODIUM INJECTION,** U.S.P. XXI.

• **IOTHALAMATE MEGLUMINE INJECTION,** U.S.P. XXI. Benzoic acid, 3-(acetylamino)-2,4,6-triiodo-5-[(methylamino)carbonyl]-, compound with 1-deoxy-1-(methylamino)-d-glucitol (1:1).
Use: Diagnostic aid (radiopaque medium).

• **IOTHALAMATE SODIUM I-125.** USAN.

• **IOTHALAMATE SODIUM I-131.** USAN.

• **IOTHALAMATE SODIUM INJECTION,** U.S.P. XXI. Benzoic acid, 3-(acetylamino)-2,4,6-triiodo-5-[(methylamino)carbonyl]-, sod. salt. 5-Acetamido-2,4,6-triiodo-N-methylisophthalamic acid, sod. salt. Sod. Iothalamate.
Use: Diagnostic aid (radiopaque medium).

• **IOTHALAMIC ACID,** 3-(acetylamino)-2,4,6-triiodo-5-[(methylamino)carbonyl]-. 5-Acetamino-2,4,6-triiodo-N-methylisophthalamic acid.
Use: Radiopaque; pharm. necessity for Iothalamate Meglumine Injection, Iothalamate Meglumine and Iothalamate Sodium Injection, and Iothalamate Sodium Injection.

IOTHIOURACIL SODIUM. Sod. salt of 5-iodo-2-thiouracil.

IOTIS. (Research Pharmacal Lab.) Iodine crystals 0.03, carbamide 1%, benzyl alcohol 3%, glycerine (dehydrated) Bot. 15 cc.
Use: Chronic otitis externa.

IOTROL. USAN.
Use: Radiopaque medium.

IOTROXIC ACID. USAN.
Use: Diagnostic aid.

• **IOTYROSINE 1-131.** USAN.
Use: Radioactive agent.

• **IOXAGLATE MEGLUMINE.** USAN.
Use: Diagnostic agent (radiopaque medium).

• **IOXAGLATE SODIUM.** USAN.
Use: Diagnostic agent (radiopaque medium).

• **IOXAGLIC ACID.** USAN.
Use: Diagnostic agent (radiopaque medium).

• **IOXOTRIZOIC ACID.** USAN.
Use: Diagnostic aid.

IPATERP. (Fellows) Terpin hydrate 2 gr., ammonium chloride 1 gr., licorice extract 0.5 gr., ipecac 1/10 gr./Tab. Bot. 1000s.
Use: Antitussive, expectorant.

• **IPECAC,** U.S.P. XXI. Powd., Syr. U.S.P. XXI.
Use: Emetic.

W/Combinations
See: Balmial Cough Syrup, Syr. (Clapp)
Creozets, Loz. (Creomulsion Co.)
Derfort, Cap. (Cole)
Diatrol, Tab. (Otis Clapp)
Dophenco, Cap. (Blue Line)
Ipedote, Syrup (Panray)
Ipsatol/DM, Cough Syr. (Key)
Ipsatol, Syr. (Key)
Mallergan, Liq. (Mallard)
Neo-Bronchoid, Tab. (Moore-Kirk)
Phenatrocaps, Cap. (O'Neal)
Phenatrohist, Cap. (O'Neal)
Polyectin, Liq. (Amid)
Proclan, Preps. (Cenci)
Romilar, CF, Syr. (Block)
Rhubarb, Ipecac & Soda, Tab. (Noyes)
Rubacac, Tab. (Scrip)
Spenlaxo, Tab. (Spencer-Mead)
Terpium, Tab. (Scrip)

IPEDOTE SYRUP. (Panray) Syrup of ipecac. Bot. 30 ml.
Use: Emetic.

• **IPEXIDINE MESYLATE.** USAN.
Use: Dental caries prophylactic.

• **IPODATE CALCIUM,** U.S.P. XXI. Oral Susp., U.S.P. XXI. Benzenepropanoic acid, 3-[[(dimethylamino)methylene]amino]-2,4,6-triiodo-, calcium salt.
Use: Diagnostic aid (radiopaque medium).
See: Oragrafin cal., Granules (Squibb)

• **IPODATE SODIUM,** U.S.P. XXI. Cap., U.S.P. XXI. Benzenepropanoic acid, 3-[[(dimethylamino)-methylene] amino]-2,4,6-triiodo-, sod. salt.
Use: Diagnostic aid (radiopaque medium).
See: Bilivist, Cap. (Berlex)
Oragrafin sod., Cap., Vial (Squibb)

IPRAN HCAL TABS. (Major) Propranolol HCl 20 mg. or 40 mg./Tab. Bot. 250s; 80 mg./Tab. 100s.
Use: Arrhythmia, angina pectoris.

• **IPRATROPIUM BROMIDE.** USAN. 8-Isopropyl-3-(±)-tropoyloxy-1αH,5αH-tropanium bromide. N-Isopropylatropinium bromide.
Use: Bronchodilator.
See: Atrovent

• **IPRINDOLE.** USAN. 5-[3-(Dimethylamino)-propyl]-6,-7,8,9,10,11-hexahydro-5H-cyclo-oct[β]-indole. 5-(3-Dimethylaminopropyl)-6,7,8,9,10-11-hexahydrocyclooct[β]indole. Prondol hydrochloride.
Use: Antidepressant.

• **IPROCINODINE HYDROCHLORIDE.** USAN.
Use: Antibacterial.

IPROCLOZIDE. B.A.N. 4-Chlorophenoxy-2′-isopropylacetohydrazide.
Use: Monoamine oxidase inhibitor.

• **IPROFENIN.** USAN.
Use: Diagnostic aid.

IPRONIAZID. B.A.N. l-isonicotinyl-2-isopropylhydrazine phosphate. 2′-Isopropylisonicotinohydrazide.
Use: Monoamine oxidase inhibitor.
See: Marsilid phosphate.

• **IPRONIDAZOLE.** USAN. 2-Isopropyl-1-methyl-5-nitroimidazole. Ipropran (Hoffman-LaRoche).
Use: Antiprotozoal (Histomonas).

• **IPROPLATIN.** USAN.
Use: Antineoplastic.

IPROVERATRIL. Name used for verapamil.

• **IPROXAMINE HYDROCHLORIDE.** USAN.
Use: Vasodilator.

IPSATOL. (Key) Ipecac alkaloids 0.24 mg., ammonium chloride 22 mg./5 ml. in tolu balsam syrup base. Bot. 4 oz.
Use: Pediatric expectorant.

IPSATOL/DM. (Key) Dextromethorphan HBr 10 mg./5 ml. in addition to the Ipsatol formulation. Bot. 4 fl. oz.
Use: Antitussive, expectorant.

IRCON. (Key) Ferrous fumarate 200 mg./Tab. Bot. 100s.
Use: Hematinic.

IRCON-FA. (Key) Ferrous fumarate 250 mg., folic acid 1 mg./Tab. Bot. 100s.

IRGASAN CF3. Cloflucarban. Under study.
Use: Antiseptic.

• **IRIDIUM IR-192.** USAN.
See: Iriditope (Squibb)

IRIGATE. (Ketchum) Bot. 4 oz.
Use: Eyewash.

IRISIN. A polysaccharide found in several species of iris.

IROCAINE.
See: Procaine Hydrochloride (Various Mfr.)

IRODEX. (Keene) Iron dextran complex 50 mg./ml. Vial 10 ml.
Use: Iron deficiency anemia.

IRODEX. (Tunex) An iron-dextran complex 50 mg./ml. Vial 10cc.
Use: Iron deficiency anemia.

IROMIN-G. (Mission) Ferrous gluconate 333.3 mg. (Iron 38.6 mg.), Vit. B-12 (crystalline on resin) 2.0 mcg., C

100 mg., A acetate 4000 I.U., D-2 400 I.U., B-1 5.0 mg., B-2 2.0 mg., B-6 25 mg., niacinamide 10 mg., cal. pantothenate 1.0 mg., folic acid 0.8 mg., calcium gluconate 100 mg., calcium lactate 100 mg., calcium carbonate 70 mg. (calcium 50 mg.)/Tab. Bot. 100s.
Use: Hematic supplement.

IRON, ARSENIC AND COPPER INJ. (Torigian) Iron cacodylate 0.065 Gm., sod. cacodylate 0.15 Gm., copper sulfate 0.5 mg./5 cc. Amp. 5 cc.

IRON BILE SALTS.
See: Bilron, Pulvules (Lilly)

IRON CACODYLATE. (CMC) 0.03 Gm./cc., 1 gr./2 cc., 1 gr./5 cc. Amp. 100s.

IRON CACODYLATE. (Torigian) Metallic iron 12%, organically combined arsenic as ferric salt of dimethylarsonate. Amp. 0.5 gr. 1 cc., 25s, 100s. 1 gr. 2 cc. 5 cc., 25s, 100s.

IRON CARBONATE COMPLEX.
See: Polyferose

IRON CHOLINE CITRATE COMPLEX.
See: Chel-Iron, Tab. (Kinney)
Kelex, Tabseals. (Nutrition Control)

IRONCO-B. (Vale) Ferrous sulfate 194.4 mg., manganese sulfate 21.6 mg., dicalcium phosphate 129.6 mg., B-1 1 mg., B-2 1 mg., niacin 6.0 mg.,Vit. D 100 I.U./Tab. Bot. 100s, 500s, 1000s.

• **IRON-DEXTRAN INJECTION.,** U.S.P. XXI.
Use: Hematinic.
See: Ferrodex, Inj. (Keene Pharm.)
Hydextran, Inj. (Hyrex)
Imferon, Amp., Vial (Merrell Dow)

IRON-FOLIC ACID-LIVER. (Medwick) Vial 30 cc.

"IRON FOR WOMEN". (Pharmex) Ferrous fumarate 5 gr./Tab. Bot. 90s.

IRON (2+) FUMARATE. Ferrous Fumarate, U.S.P. XXI.

IRON (2+) GLUCONATE.
See: Ferrous Gluconate, U.S.P. XXI.

IRON OXIDE MIXTURE WITH ZINC OXIDE.
Calamine, U.S.P. XXI.

IRON PEPTONIZED.
See: Saferon, Tab. (Elder)

IRON PROTEIN COMPLEX.

• **IRON SORBITEX.** USAN. A sterile, colloidal solution of a complex of trivalent iron, sorbitol, and citric acid, stabilized with dextrin and sorbitol.
Use: Hematinic.

• **IRON SORBITEX INJECTION,** U.S.P. XXI. (Formerly iron sorbitol)
Use: Iron supplement.
See: Jectofer Amp. (Astra)

IRON SULFATE. W/Maalox.
See: Fermalox, Tab. (Rorer)

IRON w/PRO SOF SG. (Vangard) Ferrous fulmarate 150 mg., docusate sodium 100 mg./Cap. Bot. 100s.
Use: Vitamin w/stool softener.

IRON WITH VITAMIN C. (Squibb) Iron 50 mg., Vit. C 25 mg./Tab. Bot. 100s. (Formerly called Feramel)
Use: Hematinic.

IROPHOS D. (Lannett) Dicalcium phosphate anh. 330 mg., ferrous sulf. 30 mg., Vit. D 333 I.U./Cap. Bot. 500s, 1000s.
Use: Hematinic.

IROSPAN. (Fielding) Ferrous sulfate 200 mg., Vit. C 150 mg./Cap. Bot. 60s. Tab. Bot. 100s.
Use: Iron deficiency anemia.

IRRADIATED 7-DEHYDROCHOLESTEROL.
See: Activated 7-Dehydrocholesterol.

IRRADIATED ERGOSTEROL.
See: Calciferol.

IRRIGATE. (Professional Pharmacal) Boric acid 1.2%, potassium Cl. 0.38%, sodium carbonate 0.014%, benzalkonium Cl. 0.01%, disodium edetate 0.05%. Bot. 0.5 oz., 4 oz.
Use: Ocular cleanser.

ISACEN.
See: Oxyphenisatin, Prep. (Various Mfr.)

• **ISAMOXOLE.** USAN.
Use: Anti-asthmatic.

ISAVERINE HCl. Methindizate, B.A.N.

ISMELIN. (Ciba) Guanethidine monosulfate, 10 mg. and 25 mg./Tab. Bot. 100s, 1000s; Consumer Packs of 100s.
Use: Hypertension treatment.

ISMOTIC. (Alcon) Isosorbide solution.
Use: Reduce intraocular pressure.

ISO-ALCOHOLIC ELIXIR.
Use: Vehicle.

ISOAMINILE. B.A.N. (Robins) 4-Dimethylamino-2-isopropyl-2-phenylvaleronitrile. Dimyril citrate.
Use: Antitussive.

ISOAMYLHYDROCUPREINE DIHYDROCHLORIDE.
See: Eucupin Dihydrochloride

ISOAMYL NITRATE.
See: Amyl Nitrite, U.S.P. XXI.

ISOAMYNE.
See: Amphetamine (Various Mfr.)

ISO-BID. (Geriatric) Isosorbide dinitrate 40 mg./Cap. Bot. 30s, 100s, 500s.
Use: Prophylaxis in angina pectoris.

ISOBORNYL THIOCYANOACETATE, TECHNICAL.
Use: Pediculicide.
See: Barc, Liq. (Commerce)
W/Anhydrous soap.
W/Docusate sodium and related terpenes.
See: Barc, Cream (Commerce)

• **ISOBUCAINE HYDROCHLORIDE,** U.S.P. XXI. 2-Isobutylamino-2-methylpropyl benzoate HCl. 2-(Isobutylamino)-2-methyl-1-propanol benzoate (ester) HCl.
Use: Local anesthetic (dental).

• **ISOBUCAINE HCl & EPINEPHRINE INJECTION,** U.S.P. XXI.
Use: Local anesthetic (dental).

• **ISOBUTAMBEN,** USAN. Isobutyl p-aminobenzoate. Isocaine. Cycloform.
Use: As a surface anesthetic.

• **ISOBUTANE,** N.F. XVI.

)BUTYLALLYLBARBITURIC ACID.
Aspirin, phenacetin, caffeine.
See: Buff-A-Comp, Tab., Cap. (Mayrand)
Fiorinal, Cap., Tab. (Sandoz)
Lanorinal, Cap. (Lannett)
Palgesic, Tab., Cap. (Pan Amer.)
Sedagesic, Tab. (Kay)
Tenstan, Tab. (Standex)
Wolgraine, Tab. (Wolins)
'Aspirin, phenacetin, caffeine, codeine phosphate.
See: Fiorinal w/codeine, Cap. (Sandoz)

)BUTYL p-AMINOBENZOATE. Isobutamben, U.S.A.N.

SOBUTYLPHENYLACE-ACID. Ibufenac

)BUZOLE. B.A.N. 5-Isobutyl-2-(4-methoxybenzenesulphonamido)-1,3,4-thiadiazole. Glysobuzole (I.N.N.)
Use: Oral hypoglycemic agent.
See: Stabinol

)CAINE. Isobutamben, U.S.A.N.

)CAL. (Mead Johnson) Lactose-free isotonic liquid containing as a % of the calories 13% protein as casein and soy protein; 37% fat as soy oil and medium chain triglycerides; 50% carbohydrate as corn syrup solids w/vitamins and minerals for the tube fed patient. Vitamins, and minerals. Cans 8 fl. oz., 12 fl. oz., 32 fl. oz., Bot. 8 fl. oz.
Use: Complete enteral liquid diet, nutritionally balanced and lactose free to meet nutritional needs of tube fed patients.

OCAL HCN. (Mead Johnson) High calorie, nitrogen nurtitionally complete food. Protein 15%, fat 40%, carbohydrate 45%. Cans 8 fl. oz.
Use: Complete, concentrated nutrition.

ISOCARBOXAZID, U.S.P. XXI. Tab., U.S.P. XXI. 1-Benzyl[-2-(5-methyl-3-isoxazolyl-carbonyl)hydrazine. 5-Methyl-3-isoxazolecarboxylic acid 2-benzylhydrazide. 3-(2-Benzylhydrazinocarbonyl)-5-methylisoxazole. 2′-Benzyl-5-methylisoxazole-3-carbohydrazide.
Use: Antidepressant.
See: Marplan, Tab. (Roche).

OCLOR EXPECTORANT. (Fisons) Codeine phosphate 10 mg., pseudoephedrine HCl 30 mg., guaifenesin 100 mg./5 ml. Bot. Pt. Gal.
Use: Treatment of nonproductive cough with nasal and sinus congestion.

OCLOR LIQUID. (Fisons) Chlorpheniramine maleate 2 mg., pseudoephedrine HCl 30 mg./5 ml. Bot. Pt. Gal.
Use: Treatment of common cold, hay fever, allergies, sinusitis.

OCLOR TABLETS. (Fisons) Chlorpheniramine maleate 4 mg., pseudoephedrine HCl 60 mg./Tab. Bot. 100s, 500s.
Use: Treatment of common cold, hay fever, allergies, sinusitis.

OCLOR TIMESULE CAPSULES. (Fisons) Chlorpheniramine maleate 8 mg., pseudoephedrine HCl 120 mg./Cap. Bot. 100s, 500s.
Use: Treatment of common cold, hay fever, allergies, sinusitis.

ISOCOCAINE. Pseudococaine.

• **ISOCONAZOLE.** USAN.
Use: Antibacterial, antifungal.

ISO D. (Dunhall) Isosorbide dinitrate. **Cap.** 40 mg. Bot. 100s, 1000s. **Tab.** (sublingual) 5 mg. Bot. 100s.

ISODINE ANTISEPTIC SOLUTION. (Blair) Povidone-iodine. Solution: Bot. 1 oz.
Use: Topical antiseptic.

ISOEPHEDRINE HCl. d-Isoephedrine HCl.
See: Pseudoephedrine HCl.
W/Chlorpheniramine maleate.
See: Isoclor, Tab., Expect., Timesule, Liq. (Arnar-Stone)
W/Chlorprophenpyridamine maleate.
See: Isoclor, Tab. (Arnar-Stone)
W/Theophylline sodium glycinate & guaifenesin.
See: Iso-Tabs 60 Tab. (Rowell)

D-ISOEPHEDRINE SULFATE.
See: Pseudoephedrine Sulfate.

• **ISOETHARINE,** USAN. 3,4-Dihydroxy α-(l-isopropylamino-propyl)benzyl alcohol. 1-(3,4-Dihydroxyphenyl)-2-isopropylaminobutan-1-ol. Numotac hydrochloride.
Use: Bronchodilator.

• **ISOETHARINE HYDROCHLORIDE,** U.S.P. XXI.
Use: Bronchodilator.
See: Bronkosol, Sol. (Winthrop-Breon)

• **ISOETHARINE INHALATION SOLUTION,** U.S.P. XXI.
Use: Bronchodilator.

• **ISOETHARINE MESYLATE,** U.S.P. XXI. Inhalation Aerosol, U.S.P. XXI.
Use: Bronchodilator
See: Bronkometer, Aerosol (Winthrop-Breon)

ISOFEDROL. (Blue Line) Ephedrine sulfate 1% in an isotonic sol. Bot. ¾ oz.
Use: Nasal vasoconstrictor.

ISOFIL. (Seatrace) Theophylline 200 mg., noscapine 30 mg./Tab. Bot. 100s, 1000s.
Use: Long-acting bronchodilator.

• **ISOFLUPREDONE ACETATE.** USAN.
Use: Anti-inflammatory.

• **ISOFLURANE.** U.S.P. XXI.
Use: Anesthetic.

• **ISOFLUROPHATE,** U.S.P. XXI. Ophth. Oint., U.S.P. XXI. Phosphorofluoridic acid, bis(1-methylethyl)ester. Diisopropyl phosphorofluoridate.
Use: Cholinergic (ophthalmic).
See: Floropryl, Oint. (Merck Sharp & Dohme)

ISOGREGNENONE. Dydrogesterone.
See: Duphaston, Tab. (Philips Roxane)

ISO-IODEIKON.
See: Phentetiothalein Sodium (No Mfr. currently lists.)

ISOJECT. (Pfipharmecs) A purified, sterile, disposable injection system.
Permapen (benzathine pencillin G.) aqueous solution, 1,200,000 u./2 cc. 10s.
Terramycin (oxytetracycline) Intramuscular solution 250 mg./2 cc. 10s.

• **ISOLEUCINE,** U.S.P. XXI. $C_6H_{13}NO_2$, L-isoleucine. DL-Isoleucine. (Pfaltz & Bauer)—Pow. 10 Gm.
Use: Nutrient.

ISOMEPROBAMATE.
See: Carisoprodol (Var. Mfr.)

• **ISOMEROL.** USAN.
Use: Antiseptic.

ISOMETHADONE. B.A.N. 6-Dimethylamino-5-methyl-4,4-diphenylhexan-3-one.
Use: Narcotic analgesic.
See: Isoamidone

ISOMETAMIDIUM. B.A.N. 8-m-Amidinophenyl-diazoamino-3-amino-5-ethyl-6-phenylphenanthridinium chloride.
Use: Antiprotozoan, veterinary medicine.
See: Samorin HCl.

ISOMETHEPTENE BITARTRATE.
See: Tega-Nyl, Vial (Ortega)

ISOMETHEPTENE HCl. Methyl-isooctenylamine mucate or tartrate. Also available as Hydrochloride.
W/N-acetyl-p-aminophenol, dichloralphenazone.
See: Midrin, Cap. (Carnrick)

ISOMETHEPTENE MUCATE.
See: Midrin, Cap. (Carnick)
Octinum, Tab. (Knoll)

ISOMETHEPTENE TARTRATE.
See: Tri-Grain, Vial (Pharmex)

ISOMIL. (Ross) Soy protein isolate formula. Each liter contains: protein 18 g, fat 36.9 g, carbohydrate 68.0 g, Ca 0.70 g, P 0.50 g, Na 0.32 g, K 0.95 g, Cl 0.43 g, Mg 50 mg., Zn 5.0 mg., Cu 0.50 mg., Fe 12 mg., iodine 0.10 mg., Mn 0.20 mg., Vit. A 2000 IU, D 400 IU, E 20 IU, C 55 mg., B-1 0.40 mg., B-2 0.60 mg., B-6 0.40 mg., niacin 9.0 mg., folic acid 0.10 mg., B-12 3.0 mcg., pantothenic acid 5.0 mg., biotin 30 mcg., K-1 0.10 Concentrated liquid 13 fl. oz. cans; ready-to-feed (20 Cal/fl. oz.) 4 oz. and 8 oz. bottles, 8 oz. and 32 oz. cans; "as fed" 20 cal/fl. oz. Use: For milk sensitive and lactose intolerant infants and children.

ISOMIL SF. (Ross) Low osmolar sucrose free soy protein isolate formula; concentrated liquid 13 fl oz cans, ready-to-feed (20 cal/fl oz) 4 oz and 8 oz bottles, 32 oz cans; "as fed" 20 cal/fl oz; per liter: protein 20.0 Gm., fat 36.0 Gm., carbohydrate 68.0 Gm., Ca 0.70 Gm., P 0.50 Gm., Na 0.32 Gm., K 0.77 Gm., Cl 0.59 Gm., Mg 50 mg, Zn 5.0 mg, Cu 0.50 mg, Fe 12 mg, Iodine 0.10 mg, Mn 0.20 mg, Vit. A 2000 IU, D 400 IU, E 20 IU, C 55 mg, thiamine 0.40 mg, riboflavin 0.60 mg, B-6 0.40 mg, niacin 9.0 mg., folic acid 0.10 mg, B-12 3.0 mcg, pantothenic acid 5.0 mg, biotin 30 mcg, Vit. K-1 and sucrose.
Use: For milk sensitive and lactose and sucrose intolerant infants and children.

ISOMUNE-CK. (Roche) Rapid immunochemical separation method of the heart specific CK-MB isoenzyme for quantitation when used with an appropriate CK substrate reagent. 100 and 250 test kits.

ISOMUNE-LD. (Roche) Rapid immunochemical separation method of the heart specific LD-1 isoenzyme for quantitation when used with an appropriate LD substrate reagent. 40 and 100 test kits.

• **ISOMYLAMINE HCl.** USAN. 2-(Diethylamino)ethyl 1-isopentylcyclohexanecarboxylate HCl.
Use: Smooth muscle relaxant.

ISOMYN.
See: Amphetamine (Various Mfr.)

ISONATE SUBLINGAL. (Major) Isosorbide 2.5 mg. or 5 mg/Sublingal Tab. Bot. 100s, 1000s.
Use: Treatment angina pectoris.

ISONATE TABLETS. (Major) Isosorbide 5 mg., 10 mg., 20 mg. or 30 mg./Tab. Bot. 100s, 1000s.
Use: Treatment angina pectoris.

ISONATE TD-CAPS. (Major) Isosorbide 40 mg./T.D. Cap. Bot. 100s, 1000s.
Use: Treatment angina pectoris.

ISONATE T.R. TABS. (Major) Isosorbide 40 mg./TD Tab. Bot. 100s, 1000s.
Use: Treatment angina pectoris.

• **ISONIAZID,** U.S.P. XXI. Inj., Syr., Tab. U.S.P. XXI. Isonicotinic acid hydrazide, isonicotinyl hydrazide. Cotinazin; I.N.H.; Mybasan; Neumandin; Nicetal; Nydrazid; Pycazide; Rimifon; Tubomel; Vazadrine.
Use: Antibacterial (tuberculostatic).
See: Dow-Isoniazid, Tab. (Merrell Dow)
INH, Tab. (Ciba)
Laniazid, Tab. (Lannett)
Niconyl, Tab. (Parke-Davis)
Nydrazid, Tab., Inj. (Squibb)
Panzid, Tab., Pow. (Panray)
Rolazid, Tab. (Robinson)
Teebaconin, Tab., Pwd. (Consol. Mid.)
Triniad, Tab. (Kasar)
Uniad, Tab. (Kasar)
W/p-Aminosalicylic acid.
See: Di-Isopacin, Tab. (CMC)
Isopacin, Tab. (CMC)
W/Calcium paraminosalicylate.
See: Calpas-INH, Tab. (Amer. Chem. & Drug)
W/Calcium p-aminosalicylate, Vit. B-6.
See: Calpas Isoxine, Tab. (American Chem. & Drug)
Calpas-INAH-6, Tabs. (Amer. Chem. & Drug)
W/Pyridoxine HCl. (Vit. B6)
See: Niadox, Tab. (Barnes-Hind)
P-I-N Forte, Syr., Tab. (Lannett)
Teebaconin w/B6 (Consol. Mid.)
Triniad Plus 30, Tab. (Kasar)
Uniad-Plus, Tab. (Kasar)
W/Pyridoxine HCl, sodium aminosalicylate.
See: Pasna, Tri-Pack 300, Granules (Barnes-Hind)
W/Rifampin.
See: Rimactane/INH DuoPack (Ciba)
W/Sodium aminosalicylate, pyridoxine.
See: Pasna Tri-Pack, Granules (Barnes-Hind)
W/Sodium para-aminosalicylate.
See: Isopacin, Double-Isopacin, Tab. (CMC)

ƆNICOTINIC ACID HYDRAZIDE.
See: Isoniazid, U.S.P. XXI. (Var. Mfr.)
ƆNICOTINYL HYDRAZIDE.
See: Isoniazid, U.S.P. XXI. (Var. Mfr.)
ƆNIPECAINE HYDROCHLORIDE.
See: Meperidine Hydrochloride, U.S.P. XXI. (Var. Mfr.)
ƆPENTAQUINE.
Use: Curative & prophylactic in malaria.
SOPHANE INSULIN SUSPENSION, U.S.P. XXI.
Use: Hypoglycemic agent.
See: NPH Iletin, Vial (Lilly)
ƆPHYLLINE. Diprophylline, B.A.N.
ƆPREDNIDENE. B.A.N. $11\beta,17\alpha$,21-Trihydroxy-16-methylenepregna-4,6-diene-3,20-dione.
Use: ACTH inhibitor.
ƆPREGNENONE.
See: Duphaston, Tab. (Philips Roxane)
Dydrogesterone
ƆPRENALINE. B.A.N. (±)-1-(3,4-Dihydroxy-phenyl)-2-isopropylaminoethanol. Isopropylnoradrenaline.
Use: Sympathomimetic.
See: Isoproterenol HCl
SOPROPAMIDE IODIDE, U.S.P. XXI. Tab., U.S.P. XXI. (3-Carbamoyl-3,3-diphenylpropyl) diisopropylmethylammonium iodide. Tyrimide.
Use: Anticholinergic.
See: Darbid, Tab. (SmithKline)
/Prochlorperazine maleate.
See: Iso-Perazine, Cap. (Lemmon)
OPROPHENAMINE HCl. Name used for Clorprenaline HCl.
OPROPICILLIN POTASSIUM. Potassium 3,3-dimethyl-6-(2-methyl-2-phenoxypropionamido)-7-oxo-4-thia-1-azabicyclo [3.2.0]heptane-2-carboyxlate.
Use: Antibiotic.
ISOPROPOYL-α-(2-METHYLHYDRAZI-NO)-p-TOLUAMIDE HCl. Procarbazine HCl. U.S.P. XXI.
SOPROPYL ALCOHOL, U.S.P. XXI.
Use: Local anti-infective; pharm. aid (solvent).
SOPROPYL ALCOHOL, AZEOTROPIC, U.S.P. XXI.
OPROPYLARTERENOL HYDROCHLORIDE.
Use: Asthma, vasoconstrictor & allergic states.
OPROPYLARTERENOL SULFATE.
See: Isoproterenol Sulf.
(ISOPROPYLAMINO)-3-(1-NAPHTHYLOXY)-2-PROPANOL HCl. Propanolol HCl, U.S.P. XXI.
ISOPROPYL MYRISTATE, N.F. XVI.
Use: Pharm. aid (emollient)
OPROPYL-NORADRENALINE HCl.
See: Isoproterenol HCl, U.S.P. XXI.
ISOPROPYL PALMITATE, N.F. XVI.
Use: Pharmaceutic aid (oleaginous vehicle).
OPROPYL PHENAZONE. 4-Isopropyl antipyrine. Larodon
ISOPROPYL RUBBING ALCOHOL, U.S.P. XXI.
Use: Rubefacient, solvent.
OPROTERENOL.
See: Norisidrine (Abbott)
/Butabarbital, theophylline, ephedrine HCl.
See: Medihaler-Iso, Vial (Riker)

• **ISOPROTERENOL HYDROCHLORIDE,** U.S.P. XXI. Inhalation, Tab. Inj.; U.S.P. XXI. 1,2-Benzenediol,4-[1-hydroxy-2-[(1-methylethyl)-amino]ethyl]-, HCl. 3,4-Dihydroxy-α-[(isopropylamino)methylbenzyl alcohol hydrochloride. Oleudrin-Proternol. 1:5,000 5 ml and 10 ml in Univ. Add. Syr.; 1:5,000 1 mg and 2 mg pintop vials; 1:50,000 10 ml with Abboject Syr. (21G × 1 0.5").
Use: Adrenergic (bronchodilator).
See: Isuprel HCl, Prods. (Winthrop-Breon)
Norisodrine, Aerotrol, Syrup (Abbott)
Proternol, Tab. (Key Pharm.)
Vapo-Iso, Sol. (Fisons)
W/Acetylcysteine.
See: Mucomyst with Isoproterenol, Sol. (Mead Johnson)
W/Aminophylline, ephedrine sulfate, phenobarbital.
See: Asminorel, Tab. (Reid-Provident)
W/Clopane (clopentamine) HCl, propylene glycol, ascorbic acid.
See: Aerolone Compound, Sol. (Lilly)
W/Phenobarbital, ephedrine sulfate, theophylline, pot. iodide.
See: Isophed, Tab. (Jamieson-McKames)
W/Phenobarbital sod., ephedrine sulfate, theophylline hydrous.
See: Iso-asminyl, Tab. (Cole)
W/Phenylephrine bitartrate.
See: Duo-Medihaler, Vial (Riker)
• **ISOPROTERENOL INHALATION SOLUTION,** U.S.P. XXI.
Use: Bronchodilator.
• **ISOPROTERENOL HYDROCHLORIDE AND PHENYLEPHRINE BITARTRATE INHALATION AEROSOL,** U.S.P. XXI.
Use: Adrenergic (bronchodilator)
See: Duo-Medihaler, Vial (Riker)
• **ISOPROTERENOL SULFATE,** U.S.P. XXI. Inhal. Aerosol, Inhal. Sol., U.S.P. XXI.
See: Medihaler-Iso, Vial (Riker)
W/Calcium iodide (anhydrous), alcohol.
See: Norisodrine, Syr. (Abbott)
ISOPTIN IV. (Knoll) Verapamil HCl 5 mg., sodium Cl. 17 mg./2 ml. Amp. 2 ml.
Use: Calcium ion influx inhibitor.
ISOPTIN. (Knoll) Verapamil HCl 10 mg./4 ml. Amp. 4 ml.
Use: Calcium ion influx inhibitor.
ISOPTIN I.V. (Knoll) Verapamil HCl. **Single Dose Vials:** 5 mg./2 ml. and 10 mg./4 ml. **Pre-filled Syringe:** 5 mg./2 ml. and 10 mg./4 ml.
Use: Calcium ion influx inhibitor.
ISOPTIN TABLETS. (Knoll) Verapamil HCl 80 mg. or 120 mg./Tab. Bot. 100s. Unit Dose 10 × 10s.
Use: Calcium ion influx inhibitor for treatment of angina.
ISOPTO ALKALINE. (Alcon) 1% Methylcellulose sterile ophth. sol. Dropper Bot. 15 cc.
Use: Ophthalmic emollient & lubricant, artificial tears.

ISOPTO ATROPINE. (Alcon) Atropine sulfate in methylcellulose solution. Drop-tainer 0.5% and 3.0% 5 cc. 1.0% 5 cc., 15 cc.
Use: Mydriatic and cycloplegic.

ISOPTO CARBACHOL. (Alcon) Carbachol U.S.P. 0.75%, 1.5%, 2.25%, 3%, in a sterile buffered solution of 1% methylcellulose. Drop-Tainer 15 cc., 0.75%, 1.5%, 3%, 30 cc.
Use: Glaucoma, contraindications, corneal injuries.

ISOPTO CARPINE. (Alcon) Pilocarpine HCl in stable sterile 0.5% methylcellulose sol. w/isotonicity of lacrimal fluid. Bot. Drop-Tainer (0.25%, 0.5%, 1%, 2%, 3%, 4%, 5%, 6%, 8% & 10% pilocarpine HCl) 15 cc.; 0.5%, 1%, 2%, 3%, 4%, 6% 30 cc.
Use: Glaucoma.

ISOPTO CETAMIDE. (Alcon) Sod. Sulfacetamide 15% in buffered pH 7.4, 0.5% methylcellulose sol. Drop-Tainer 5 cc., 15 cc.
Use: Conjunctival infections.

ISOPTO CETAPRED. (Alcon) Sulfacetamide sod. U.S.P. 10%, prednisolone U.S.P. 0.25%, methylcellulose 0.5% in a sterile, buffered and stable suspension. Drop-Tainer 5 cc., 15 cc.
Use: Chronic and allergic blepharitis and conjunctivitis.

ISOPTO ESERINE. (Alcon) Eserine salicylate 0.25% & 0.5% in stable sterile 0.5% methyl cellulose solution. Drop-Tainer 15 cc.
Use: Treatment & control of glaucoma.

ISOPTO FRIN. (Alcon) 0.12% Phenylephrine HCl in a methylcellulose sol. Drop-Tainer 15 cc.
Use: Ocular decongestant.

ISOPTO HOMATROPINE. (Alcon) Homatropine HBr 2.0% and 5.0% in methylcellulose solution. Drop-Tainer 5 cc., 15 cc.

ISOPTO HYOSCINE. (Alcon) Hyoscine HBr 0.25% in a methylcellulose solution. Drop-Tainer 5 cc., 15 cc.

ISOPTO P-ES. (Alcon) Pilocarpine 2%, eserine salicylate 0.25%, sterile buffered, isotonic vehicle containing 0.5% methylcellulose. Plastic Drop-Tainer 15 cc.
Use: Glaucoma treatment.

ISOPTO PLAIN. (Alcon) Methylcellulose 0.5% Drop-Tainer 15 cc.
Use: Ophthalmic lubricant and emollient, artificial tears.

ISOPTO TEARS. (Alcon) Hydroxypropyl methylcellulose 0.5%, benzalkonium chloride 1:10,000. Bot. Drop-Tainer 15 cc., 30 cc.
Use: Artificial tears.

ISORDIL CHEWABLE TABLETS. (Ives) Isosorbide dinitrate 10 mg./chewable Tab. Bot. 100s. Clinipak.
Use: For angina pectoris.

ISORDIL SUBLINGUAL. (Ives) Isosorbide dinitrate 2.5 mg./Tab. Bot. 100s, 500s. Clinipak; 5 mg./Tab. Bot. 100s, 250s, 500s Clinipak; 10 mg./Tab. Bot. 100s. Clinipak.
Use: Angina pectoris and coronary insufficiency.

ISORDIL TEMBIDS. (Ives) Isosorbide dinitrate 40 mg./Tab. or Cap. **Tab.** Bot. 100s, 500s, 1000s. **Cap.** Bot. 100s., 500s.
Use: For angina pectoris.

ISORDIL TITRADOSE TABLETS. (Ives) Isosorbide dinitrate. 5 mg./Tab. Bot. 100s, 500s, 1000s. Clinipak; 10 mg./Tab. Bot. 100s, 500s, 1000s. Clinipak; 20 mg./Tab. Bot. 100s, 500s. Clinipak; 3 mg./Tab. Bot. 100s; 40 mg./Tab. Bot. 100s.
Use: Control of angina pectoris and coronary insufficiency.

ISORGEN-G. (Grafton) Isosorbide 5 mg., 10 mg./Ta Bot. 1000s.

ISOSORB-5. (Robinson) Isosorbide dinitrate oral mg./Tab. Bot. 100s, 1000s.
Use: Coronary vasodilator; anti-anginal.

ISOSORB-10. (Robinson) Isosorbide dinitrate mg./Tab. Bot. 100s, 1000s.
Use: Coronary vasodilator, anti-anginal.

• **ISOSORBIDE.** USAN.
Use: Diuretic.

• **ISOSORBIDE CONCENTRATE,** U.S.P. XXI.
Use: Diuretic.

• **ISOSORBIDE ORAL SOLUTION,** U.S.P. XXI.
Use: Diuretic.

• **ISOSORBIDE DINITRATE, DILUTE,** U.S.P. XXI. Tab., U.S.P. XXI. D-Glucitol, 1,4:3,6-dianhydro-, dinitrate.
Use: Coronary vasodilator; anti-anginal.
See: Dilatrate-SR, Cap. (Reed & Carnrick)
Iso-Bid, Cap. (Geriatric)
Iso-D, Cap., Tab. (Dunhall)
Isordil, Tab. (Ives)
Isordil Tembids Cap., Tabs. (Ives)
Isosorb Prods. (Robinson)
Nitromed, Tab. (U.S. Ethicals)
Onset, Tab. (Bock)
Sorbitrate, Tab. (Stuart)
Sorquad., Tab. (Reid-Provident)

W/Phenobarbital.
See: Isordil w/Phenobarbital, Tab. (Ives)
Sorbitrate w/Phenobarbital, Tab. (Stuart)

• **ISOSTERYL ALCOHOL.** USAN.
Use: Pharmaceutic aid.

• **ISOSULFAN BLUE.** USAN.
Use: Diagnostic aid.

ISOTEIN HN. (Sandoz Nutrition) Vanilla Flavor. Maltodextrin, delactosed lactalbumin, partially hydrogenated soy oil with BHA, fructose, medium chain triglycerides, artificial flavor, sodium caseinate, mono and diglycerides, sodium chloride, vitamins and minerals. Powder 2.9 oz. packets.
Use: Total feeding, oral or tube.

ISOTHIPENDYL. B.A.N. 10-(2-Dimethylamino-propyl)-10H-pyrido[3,2-b]-[1,4]benzothiazine.
Use: Antihistamine.
See: Nilergex
Theruhistin (HCl)

ISOTRATE. (Hauck) Isosorbide dinitrate 40 mg./Timecelle. Bot. 100s, 500s. Unit dose 50s.
Use: Coronary vasodilator.

OTRETINOIN. USAN.
se: Keratolytic.
OTRETINOIN. USAN. 13-cis-retinoic acid.
se: Treatment of severe recalcitrant cystic acne.
ee: Accutane, Cap. (Roche)
VEX. (U.S. Chemical) Ethaverine HCl. 100
g./Cap. Bot. 100s, 1000s.
se: Smooth muscle relaxant, vasorelaxant.
OXAZOLIDINONE, 4-AMINO-. Cycloserine, U.S.P.
XI.
OXEPAC. USAN.
se: Anti-inflammatory.
OXICAM. USAN.
se: Anti-inflammatory.
XSUPRINE. B.A.N. 1-(4-Hydroxyphenyl)-2-(1-meth-
-2-phenoxyethylamino)propan-1-ol.
se: Peripheral vasodilator.
ee: Dilavase
Duphaspasmin (lactate)
Duvadilan
Vasodilan
Vasotran (HCl)
OXSUPRINE HCl, U.S.P. XXI. Inj., Tab., U.S.P.
XI. 1-(p-Hydroxy-phenyl)-2-(1′-methyl-2′-phenoxy
thylamino) propanol-1 HCl. p-Hydroxy-α-[1-[(1-meth-
-2-phenoxyethyl)amino ethyl benzyl alcohol HCl.
se: Vasodilator.
ee: Rolisox-10, Tab. (Robinson)
Rolisox-20, Tab. (Robinson)
Vasodilan, Tab., Amp. (Mead Johnson)
PREL. (Winthrop-Breon) Isoproterenol HCl. Availa-
le in various dosage forms.
PREL GLOSSETS. (Winthrop-Breon) Isoproterenol
Cl 10 mg., 15 mg./Tab. Bot. 50s.
se: Bronchodilator.
PREL INHALATION SOLUTION. (Winthrop-Breon)
oproterenol HCl inhalation Sol. 1:200 and 1:100.
ot. 10 ml., 60 ml.
se: Bronchodilator
PREL MISTOMETER. (Winthrop-Breon) Iso-
roterenol HCl. Complete nebulizing unit of aerosol
oln. containing 10 ml., 15 ml. or 22.5 ml. of
oproterenol HCl w/inert propellants, alcohol 33%
nd ascorbic acid. Measured dose of approximately
31 mcg. Aerosol Unit. Bot. 10 ml., 15 ml., 22.5 ml.
efill 15 ml., 22.5 ml.
se: Bronchodilator.
PREL STERILE INJECTION. (Winthrop-Breon) Iso-
roterenol HCl 0.2 mg., lactic acid 0.12 mg.,
odium lactate 1.8 mg., sodium chloride 7 mg. and
ot more than 1 mg. sodium metabisulfite as
reservative/ml. of 1:5000 sol. **Amp.** 1 ml. Boxes
5s; 5 ml. Boxes 10s.
se: Adjunct treatment of shock, cardiac standstill,
tc.
PRENE.
ee: Isoproterenol (Var. Mfr.)
HI-KOOL. (Eckerd) Zirconium oxide 5%, ben-
ocaine, chlorobutanol, pyrilamine maleate,
enzethonium Cl, calamine, zinc oxide. Tube 1.5
z.
se: Antipruritic, local anesthetic, antihistaminic,
ntispeptic.

ITCHAWAY. (Moyco) Zinc undecylenate 20%, undecylenic acid 2%. Powder, Cans 1.5 oz.
Use: Antifungal foot powder for athlete's foot.
ITOBARBITAL.
W/Acetaminophen.
See: Panitol, Tab. (Wesley)
• **ITRACONAZOLE.** USAN.
Use: Antifungal.
ITRAMIN TOSYLATE. B.A.N. 2-Nitratoethylamine toluene-p-sulfonate.
Use: Angina pectoris; Vasodilator.
See: Nilatil
• **IVERMECTIN.** USAN. (MSD AGVET) 22,23-Dihydroaver-mectin B-1, (80% or more "a" component, 20% or less "b" component). Ivomec and Eqvalan.
Use: Antiparasitic, veterinary medicine.
IVERSAL HYDRATE. Ambazone, B.A.N.
I.V. ESTRO. (Rocky Mtn.) Potassium estrone sulfate 4 mg./cc. Vial 10 cc. Amp. 5 cc. Box 6s.
Use: I.M. or I.V. functional uterine bleeding.
IVOCORT. (Winston) Micronized hydrocortisone alcohol 5 mg./Gm. Bot. 4 oz.
Use: Dermatoses.
IVOMEC. (MSD AGVET) Ivermectin injectable solution, suspension 200 mg./Kg.
Use: Antiparasitic, veterinary medicine.
IVY-CHEX. (Bowman) Polyvinylpyrrolidone-vinyl acetate & benzylkonium chloride 1:1000 in alcohol acetone base. Aerosol can 4 oz.
Use: Treatment or prevention of poison ivy, poison oak, poison sumac dermatitis.
IVY DRY. (Ivy) Tannic acid 10%, isopropyl alcohol 12.5% Liq. 4 oz., Cream 1 oz. Super 6 oz.
Use: Relief of itching.
IVY-RID. (Mallard) Polyvinylpyrrolidone-vinylacetate, benzalkonium chloride. Spray can 3 oz.
Use: Relief of itching and discomfort of poison ivy, poison oak and poison sumac.
IZONID TABLETS. (Major) Isoniazid 300 mg./Tab. Bot. 100s.
Use: Tuberculosis treatment.

J

JACOBSON'S SOLUTION WITH VIT. A. (CMC) Benzyl alcohol 2%, benzyl cinnamate 1.6%, ethyl cinnamate 0.5% in olive oil w/Vit. A. 10,000 I.U. Amp. 1 cc. Box 12s, 50s.
Use: Resolution of localized inflammation.
JALOVIS.
See: Hyaluronidase (Various Mfr.)
JANIMINE. (Abbott) Imipramine HCl 10 mg., 25 mg., 50 mg./Tab. Bot. 100s, 1000s.
Use: Antidepressant.
JAPAN AGAR.
See: Agar (Various Mfr.)
JAPAN GELATIN.
See: Agar (Various Mfr.)
JAPAN ISINGLASS.
See: Agar (Various Mfr.)

JECTO SAL. (Mallard) Sodium thiosulfate 50 mg./ml. Vial 30 ml.
Use: Analgesic, antipyretic.

JEL DROX LIQUID. (Coastal) Aluminum hydroxide 4%, magnesium hydroxide 1%/5 cc. Bot. 12 oz., 16 oz.
Use: Antacid.

JENAMICIN. (Hauck) Gentamicin sulfate 40 mg./ml. Vial 2 ml.
Use: Antibiotic.

JEN-BALM. (Jenkins) Methyl salicylate 15%, oil of eucalyptus 3%, menthol 2%. Jar, 1 oz., 1 lb.
Use: Analgesic balm for muscular aches, bursitis.

JEN-DIRIL. (Jenkins) Hydrochlorothiazide 50 mg./Tab. Bot. 1000s.
Use: Diuretic.

JENKAPS. (Jenkins) Vit. B-1 1.5 mg., B-2 2 mg., nicotinamide 10 mg., B-6 0.1 mg., cal. pantothenate 1 mg., B-12 1 mcg., liver desiccated 50 mg. dried yeast 100 mg./Cap. Bot. 100s, 1000s.

JEN-LAX. (Jenkins) Bile salts 0.5 gr., ext. cascara sagrada 0.5 gr., phenolphthalein yellow 0.5 gr., aloin 1/8 gr., podophyllin 1/20 gr./Tab. Bot. 1000s.

JENSENEX. (Jenkins) Nicotinic acid 50 mg., salicylamide 0.3 Gm., B-12 activity 3 mcg., C 15 mg./Tab. Bot. 1000s.
Use: Geriatric energizer.

JEN-VITE. (Jenkins) Vit. A 5000 I.U., D 1000 I.U., B-1 2.5 mg., B-2 2.5 mg., nicotinamide 20 mg., B-6 1 mg., cal. pantothenate 5 mg., B-12 2 mcg., C 40 mg., E 2 I.U./Cap. Bot. 100s, 1000s.
Use: Vitamin supplement.

JERI-BATH. (Dermik) Concentrated moisturizing bath oil. Plastic Bot. 8 oz.

JERI-LOTION. (Dermik) Concentrated moisturizing lotion. Paraben free. Plastic Bot. 6 oz.

JETRIUM. Dextromoramide, B.A.N.

JIFFY. (Block) Benzocaine, menthol, eugenol in glycerin-water base with alcohol. Bot. 0.125 oz.
Use: Toothache drops.

J-LIBERTY. (J Pharmacal) Chlordiazepoxide HCl 5, 10, or 25 mg./Cap.
Use: Relief of anxiety & tension.

JOHNSON'S BABY CREAM. (Johnson & Johnson) Dimethicone 2%. Jar 6 oz. Tube 2oz.
Use: Skin protectant.

JOHNSON'S MEDICATED POWDER. (Johnson & Johnson) Bentonite, kaolin, talc, zinc oxide. Pow. Sm., Med., Lg.
Use: Diaper rash & prickly heat remedy.

• **JOSAMYCIN.** USAN.
Use: Antibacterial.

JUBALON HYDROCHLORIDE. Carbiphene, B.A.N.

JUNICOID. (Jenkins) Dextromethorphan HBr 5 mg., cocillana comp., 88 mg., pot. guaiacolsulfonate 66 mg., citric acid 22 mg./5 cc. Syr. Bot. 3 oz., 4 oz., gal.

• **JUNIPER TAR,** U.S.P. XXI. Oil of cade.
Use: Local anti-eczematic.

JUNYER-ALL. (Barth's) Vit. A 6000 I.U., D 400 I.U., B-1 3 mg., B-2 6 mg., C 120 mg., niacin 1 mg., E 12 I.U., B-12 10 mcg., Ca 217 mg., P 97.5 mg., red bone marrow 10 mg., organic iron 15 mg., iodine 0.1 m beef peptone 20 mg./2 Vit. and mineral caps. Bo 10 mo., 3 mo., 6 mo. supply.
Use: Vitamin supplement.

JUVOCAINE.
See: Procaine Hydrochloride (Various Mfr.)

K

K-10 SOLUTION. (Cenci) Pot. chloride 10% in a sug less nonalcoholic solution (20 mEq/15 cc.) Bot. gal.

K 34. Hexachlorophene.

KABIKINASE. (Kabi) Streptokinase 250,000 or 600,000 I.U./Vial.
Use: Thrombolytic agent.

KABIKINASE. (Pharmacia) Streptokinase 250,000 I.U., 600,000 I.U., 750,000 I.U./Vial. Box 10 × 5 ml.
Use: Lysis of vascular thrombi and emboli.

KAERGONA.
See: Menadione (Various Mfr.)

• **KALAFUNGIN.** USAN.
Use: Antifungal.

KALCINATE. (Kay) Calcium gluconate 1 Gm., calci D-saccharate 0.004 Gm./10 cc. Amp. 10 cc, 2 100s.

KALLIDINOGENASE. B.A.N. An enzyme that splits the kinin, kallidin, from kininogen.
Use: Vasodilator.
See: Glumorin; Depot-Glumorin

KALOL. (Jenkins) Boric acid, sodium biborate, sodium chloride, menthol, thymol, oil of eucalyptu methyl salicylate (synthetic), carbolic acid/Tab. B 1000s.

KALORY-PLUS. (Tyler) Thyroid 3 gr., amphetamine s fate 15 mg., atropine sulfate 1/180 gr., aloin 0.25 g phenobarbital 0.25 gr./Timed release cap. Bot. 100s, 1000s.
Use: Anorexient.

KAMAGEL. (Towne) Opium 15 mg., colloidal kaolin Gm., pectin 300 mg., milk of bismuth 5 ml./fl. oz. Bot. 4 oz.
Use: Antidiarrheal.

KAMFOLENE. (Wade) Camphor, menthol, methyl salicylate, oils turpentine and eucalyptus, carbolic acid 2%, calamine, zinc oxide in lanolin base. Ja oz., lb.
Use: Antiseptic.

KANALKA TABLETS. (Lannett) Phenobarbital sod. 0.25 gr., benzocaine 0.25 gr., mag. carbonate 2 g calcium carbonate 3 gr./Tab. Bot. 100s, 1000s.
Use: Antacid w/sedative.

KANAMYCIN. B.A.N. An antibiotic produced by *Streptomyces kanamyceticus.*
Use: Antibiotic.
See: Kannasyn; Kantrex (sulfate)

• **KANAMYCIN SULFATE,** U.S.P. XXI. Caps., Inj., Sterile, U.S.P. XXI. D-Streptamine, 0-3-amino deoxy-α-d-glucopyranosyl-(1→6)-0-6-amino-6-deo α-d-gluco-pyranosyl-(1→4)-2-deoxy-, sulfate (1:1).

tibiotic obtained from *Streptomycin namyceticus.*
se: Antibacterial.
e: Kantrex, Cap., Vial (Bristol)
Klebcil, Inj. (Beecham)
KEX. (Edward J. Moore) Benzocaine, tannic acid, nzyl alcohol, diisobutyl crosoxy ethoxy ethyl nethyl benzyl ammonium chloride, in propylene se. Bot. 0.5 oz. w/applicator.
e: Toothaches, teething pains, cold sores, fever sters.
TREX. (Bristol) Kanamycin sulf. **Cap.** (0.5 Gm.) ot. 20s, 100s. **Vial** (0.5 Gm./2 cc.) or (1.0 Gm./3 .) **Pediatric Inj.,** 75 mg./2 ml. **Disposable Syr.** 0 mg./2 ml.
se: Infections from gram-positive and gram-negative cteria.
ULASE. (Dorsey) Cellulase (Dorase) standardized 9 mg., pepsin 150 mg., glutamic acid HCl 200 g., lipase 1,000 U., amylase 1,000 U., protease ,000 U. ox bile extract 100 mg./Tab. Bot. 50s.
se: Digestant.
CASIL. (Jenkins) Kaolin colloidal 60 mg., calcium rbonate 0.1 Gm., magnesium trisilicate 60 mg., smuth subgallate 15 mg., papain 8 mg., atropine lphate 1/2000 gr./Tab. Bot. 1000s.
se: Antacid and adsorbent.
CHLOR 10% LIQUID. (Adria) Potassium and loride 20 mEq each, 15 cc. alcohol 5%, sugar, ccharin, flavoring, FD&C Yellow No. 5. Bot. pt., ls.
se: Potassium supplement.
CHLOR-EFF. (Adria) Elemental potassium 20 mEq d chloride 20 mEq/Tab. supplied by: potassium loride 0.6 Gm., potassium citrate 0.22 Gm., otassium bicarbonate 1 Gm., betaine HCl 1.84 m., saccharin 20 mg., artificial fruit flavor and olor/Tab. Sugar free. Carton 60s.
se: Potassium supplement.
CHLOR S-F 10% LIQUID. (Adria) Potassium 20 Eq and chloride 20 mEq/15 ml. w/saccharin, avoring, alcohol 5%. Sugar free. Bot. 4 oz., pt.
se: Potassium supplement.
OLIN, U.S.P. XXI. (Various Mfr.)
se: Adsorbent for diarrhea.
lumina gel, pectin.
ee: Kalpec, Susp. (Wyeth)
luminum hydroxide, pectin.
ee: Kao-pectin, Tab. (Wolins)
Kenpectin, Susp. & Kenpectin-P, Susp. (Kenwood)
tropine sulfate, phenobarbital.
ee: Alkasans, Tab. (Noyes)
elladonna, phenobarbital.
ee: Bellkata, Tab. (Ferndale)
ismuth compound.
ee: Kaomine, Pow. (Lilly)
ismuth subgallate.
ee: Diastop, Liq. (Elder)
ismuth subgallate, pectin, zinc phenolsulfonate pium pow.
ee: Amogel, Tab. (Vortech)
Diastay, Tab. (Elder)

W/Bismuth subgallate, Zinc phenolsulfonate, powdered opium.
See: B-K-Z Tablets, Chewable, Tab. (Sutliff and Case)
W/Bismuth subsalicylate, salol, methyl salicylate, benzocaine, pectin.
W/Calcium carbonate, magnesium trisilicate, bismuth subgallate, papain, atropine sulphate.
See: Kaocasil, Tab. (Jenkins)
W/Cornstarch, camphor, zinc oxide, eucalyptus oil.
See: Mexsana, Pow. (Plough)
W/Furazolidone, pectin.
See: Furoxone, Liq. (Eaton)
W/Hyoscyamine sulfate, sod. benzoate, atropine sulfate, hyoscine HBR, pectin.
See: Donnagel, Susp. (Robins)
W/Neomycin sulfate, pectin.
See: Pecto-Kalin, Liq. (Harvey)
W/Opium pow., bismuth subgallate, pectin, and zinc phenolsulfonate.
See: Bismuth, Pectin & Paregoric (Lemmon)
W/Opium pow., pectin, hyoscyamine sulfate, atropine sulfate, hyoscine HBr, alcohol.
See: Donnagel P.G., Susp. (Robins)
W/Paregoric, aluminum hydroxide, bismuth subcarbonate, pectin.
See: Kapinal, Tab. (Jenkins)
W/Pectin.
See: Baropectin, Susp. (Barry-Martin)
Kaopectate, Liq. (Upjohn)
Kapectin, Liq. (Approved)
Keotin, Liq. (Blue Line)
Pecto-Kalin, Susp. (Lemmon)
Pectokay Mixture (Bowman)
W/Pectin, belladonna alkaloids.
See: Kapectolin, Liq. (GMC)
W/Pectin, bismuth subcarbonate.
See: B-K-P Mixture, Liq. (Sutliff & Case)
W/Pectin, bismuth subcarbonate, belladonna.
See: Kay-Pec, Liq. (Case)
W/Pectin, bismuth subcarbonate, opium pow.
See: KBP/O, Cap. (Cole)
W/Pectin, bismuth subsalicylate.
W/Pectin, bismuth subsalicylate, paregoric, zinc sulfocarbolate.
W/Pectin, hyoscyamine sulfate, atropine sulfate, hyoscine HBr.
See: Kapigam, Liq. (Reid-Provident)
Palsorb Improved, Liq. (Hauck)
W/Pectin, pow. opium ext.
See: Keoparic, Susp. (Blue Line)
Pecto-Kalin, Susp. (Lemmon)
W/Pectin, opium powd., bismuth subgallate, zinc phenolsulfonate.
See: Cholactabs, Tab. (Philips Roxane)
B.P.P., Tab. (Lemmon)
W/Pectin, paregoric (equivalent)
See: Duosorb, Liq. (Reid-Provident)
Kaoparin, Liq. (McKesson)
Kapectin, Liq. (Approved)
Ka-Pek w/Paregoric, Liq. (APC)
Parepectolin, Susp. (Rorer)

W/Pectin, zinc phenolsulfonate.
See: Pectocel, Susp. (Lilly)
Pectocomp, Liq. (Lannett)
W/Phenobarbital, atropine sulfate, aluminum hydroxide gel.
See: Kao-Lumin, Tab. (Philips Roxane)
W/Salol, zinc sulfocarbolate, aluminum hydroxide, bismuth subsalicylate, pectin.
See: Wescola Antidiarrheal-Stomach Upset (Western Research)

KAODONNA PG SUSPENSION. (Vangard) Kaolin 6 Gm., pectin 142.8 mg., hyoscyamine sulfate 0.0137 mg., atropine sulfate 0.0194 mg., hyoscine HBr 0.0065 mg., sodium benzoate 60 mg., powdered opium 24 mg./30 ml. w/alcohol 5%. Bot. pt., gal.
Use: Antidiarrheal.

KAODONNA SUSPENSION. (Vangard) Kaolin 6 Gm., pectin 142.8 mg., hyoscyamine sulfate 0.0137 mg., atropine sulfate 0.0194 mg., hyoscine HBr 0.0065 mg., sodium benzoate 60 mg./30 ml. w/alcohol 3.8%. Bot. pt., gal.
Use: Antidiarrheal.

KAOLIN COLLOIDAL.
W/Bismuth subcarbonate.
See: Bisilad, Susp. (Central)
W/Magnesium trisilicate, aluminum hydroxide dried gel.
See: Kamadrox, Tab. (Elder)
Kathmagel, Tab. (Mason)
W/Opium, pectin, milk of bismuth.
See: Kamagel Liq. (Towne)
W/Paregoric, pectin, milk of bismuth, methyl parahydroxybenzoate, alcohol.
See: Mul-Sed, Susp. (Webcon)
W/Pectin, aromatics.
See: Paocin, Susp. (Beecham-Massengill)
W/Pectin, belladonna alkaloids.
See: Kamabel Liq. (Towne)
W/Phenobarbital, homatropine methylbromide.
See: Lanokalin, Tab. (Lannett)

KAON CL CONTROLLED RELEASE TABLETS. (Adria) Potassium chloride 500 mg./Tab. w/FD&C Yellow No. 5. Bot. 100s, 250s, 1000s.
Use: Potassium supplement.

KAON CL-10 CONTROLLED RELEASE TABLETS. (Adria) Potassium Cl 750 mg./Tab. Bot. 100s, 500s, Stat-Pak 100s.
Use: Potassium supplement.

KAON CL 20%. (Adria) Potassium and chloride 40 mEq. to potassium chloride 3 Gm., saccharin and flavoring. 15 ml. alcohol 5%. Bot. pt.
Use: Potassium supplement.

KAON ELIXIR. (Adria) 20 mEq. elemental pot. (as 4.68 Gm. pot. gluconate)/15 cc. w/aromatics, saccharin, grape and lemon-lime flavors, alcohol 5%. Unit pkg. pt., gal.
Use: Potassium supplement.

KAON TABLETS. (Adria) 5mEq. elemental potassium obtained from 1.17 Gm. potassium gluconate/S.C. Tab. Bot. 100s & 500s.
Use: Potassium supplement.

KAO-NOR ELIXIR. (Vortech) Elemental potassium mEq. as pot. gluconate 4.68 Gm./15 ml. w/saccharin, alcohol 5%. Bot. 4 oz., gal.
Use: Potassium deficiency.

KAOPECTATE. (Upjohn) Kaolin 90 gr., pectin 2 gr./oz. Bot. 8 oz., 12 oz., 16 oz., 1 gal. Unit dose pkg. 3 oz. Bilingual. Bot. 8 oz., 12 oz.
Use: Orally for symptomatic relief of diarrhea.

KAOPECTATE CONCENTRATE. (Upjohn) Kaolin 1 gr., pectin 3 gr./oz. Unit-dose 3 oz., Bot. 8 oz., 12
Use: Orally for symptomatic relief of diarrhea.

KAOPECTATE TABLET FORMULA. (Upjohn) Attapulgite 600 mg./Tab. Blister pak 12s, 20s.
Use: For the relief of diarrhea.

KAO-PECTIN. (Wolins) Aluminum hydroxide 1 gr., ka 2 gr., pectin 0.5 gr., aromatics/Tab. Bot. 1000s.

KAOPEN SUSPENSION. (Wayne) Bot. pt.

KAPECTIN. (Approved) Kaolin 90 gr., pectin 2 gr./ Bot. gal.
W/Paregoric Liq. 4 oz.
Use: Diarrhea.

KAPECTOLIN. (Goldline) Bot. gal.
Use: Antidiarrheal.

KAPECTOLIN-PG LIQUID. (Goldline) Bot. 6 oz., pt.,
Use: Antidiarrheal.

KAPECTOLIN P.G. (Century) Powdered opium 24 mg., kaolin 6 mg., pectin 142.8 mg., hyoscyamine sulfate 0.1037 mg., atropine sulfate 0.0194 mg., hyoscine hydrobromide 0.0065 mg., sodium benzoate preservative 65 mg. Bot. gal.
Use: Antidiarrheal.

KAPECTOLIN. (CMC) Kaolin 90 gr., pectin 2 gr./fl. oz. Bot. 4 oz., 8 oz., pt., gal.
Use: Antidiarrheal.
W/Belladonna. Kaolin 6000 mg., pectin 142.8 mg., hyoscyamine sulfate 0.1037 mg., atropine sulfate 0.194 mg., hyoscine HBr 0.0065 mg./fl. oz. Bot. oz., pt., gal.
W/Paregoric 6%. Bot. 4 oz., pt., gal.

KA-PEK. (A.P.C.) Kaolin 90 gr., pectin 4.5 gr./Fl. Bot. 6 oz., gal.
Use: Control of diarrhea.

KA-PEK WITH PAREGORIC. (APC) Paregoric 60 m kaolin 90 gr., pectin 4.5 gr./Fl. Oz. Bot. 4 oz.
Use: Control of diarrhea.

KAPILIN.
See: Menadione (Various Mfr.)

KAPINAL. (Jenkins) Paregoric 0.6 ml., (Pow. opium 0.0375 gr.), kaolin colloidal 0.3 Gm., aluminum hydroxide 0.12 Gm., bismuth subcarbonate 60 m pectin 60 mg., aromatics/Tab. Bot. 1000s.
Use: Antacid and adsorbent.

KARAYA GUM. (Penick) Indian Gum. Sterculia gum
See: Tri-Costivin (Prof. Lab.)
W/Frangula
See: Saraka, Gran. (Plough)
W/Psyllium seed, plantago ovata, brewers yeast.
See: Plantamucin Granules (Elder)
W/Cortex rhamni frangulae.
See: Movicol (Norgine)
W/Refined psyllium mucilloid.
See: Hydrocil regular (Rowell)

REON.
ee: Menadione (Various Mfr.)
RIDIUM. (Lorvic) **Tab.:** Sodium fluoride 2.21 mg., od. chloride 94.49 mg., disintegrant 0.5 mg./Tab. ot. 180s, 1000s. **Liq.** Sodium fluoride 2.21 mg., od. chloride 10 mg., purified water q.s./8 drops. ot. 30 ml., 60 ml.
Jse: Reduction of dental caries.
RIGEL. (Lorvic) Fluoride ion 0.5%, 0.1 molar hosphate. Gel. Bot. 30 ml., 130 ml., 250 ml.
se: Reduction of dental caries.
RIGEL-N. (Last) Fluoride ion 0.5% 0.1 molar phoshate in neutral pH. Bot. 24 ml., 130 ml.
se: Reduction of dental caries.
ASAL. USAN. Approximately $Na_8AP_2(OH_2(PO_4)_4$ vith about 30% of dibasic sodium phosphate; odium aluminum phosphate, basic.
Jse: Food additive.
SDENOL. (Edward J. Moore) Clorpactin WCS-60. Jar 0 Gm.
Jse: Germicidal mouthwash for relief of bleeding ums.
SOF. (Stuart) Docusate potassium 240 mg./Cap. ot. 30s, 60s.
se: General constipation, anorectal disorders, tool softener.
SUGAMYCIN. Under study.
Jse: Antibiotic.
VACAPS. (Blue Line) Hyoscyamus ext. ⅛ gr., opaiba mass, methylene blue, and ext. kava ava/Tab. Bot. 100s, 1000s.
VITON.
ee: Menadione, U.S.P. XXI. (Var. Mfr.)
YBOVITE "1000." (Kay) Cyanocobalamine 1000 ncg./cc. Vial 30 cc.
Jse: Vitamin B-12 supplement.
Y CIEL ELIXIR. (Berlex) Potassium chloride 1.5 m/15 ml. (20 mEq./15 ml.) w/alcohol 4%. Bot. 18 ml., 473 ml,, 3785 ml.
Jse: Potassium replacement.
Y CIEL POWDER. (Berlex) Potassium chloride. 1.5 m./Packette. (20 mEq./Packet). Box 30s, 100s, 00s.
Jse: Potassium replacement.
YEXALATE. (Winthrop-Breon) Sod. polystyrene sulonate. Jar 1 lb.
Jse: Hyperkalemia.
YPECTOL. (Kay) Kaolin 90 gr., pectin 2 gr./1 oz. ot. Pts., Gal.
Jse: Antidiarrheal.
Y POTE 10% Solution. (Vitarine) Potassium Cl. 40 nEq./30 ml. Cherry flavor.
Jse: Treatment of potassium deficiency or otassium depletion.
Y-POTE SOLUTION. (Vitarine) Pot. chloride 0.5 Gm., upplying 5 mEq. elemental potassium/5 cc. Bot. 5 z., pt., gal.
Jse: Treatment of potassium deficiency.
Y POTE SUGAR FREE. (Vitarine) Potassium Cl 30 nEq./30 ml. Citrus flavor.
Jse: Treatment of potassium deficiency or epletion.

KAYTRATE. (Kay) Pentaerythritol tetranitrate. Tab. (20 mg.) green. Bot. 100s, 1000s. Kaykaps (30 mg.) purple & yellow. Bot. 100s, 1000s.
KAYTRON. (Pasadena Research) Pot. estrone sulfate, aqueous 20 mg./2 cc. Vial 20 cc., Amp. 2 cc. 25s, 100s.
KAY-VI-C. (Kay) Vit. C 300 mg., niacinamide 100 mg., B-1 20 mg., B-2 10 mg., pyridoxine HCl 5 mg., D-calcium pantothenate 20 mg., magnesium sulfate 70 mg., zinc sulfate 80 mg./Cap. Bot. 100s, 1000s.
Use: Vitamin supplement.
K-B-PLEX. (Kay) Water-soluble or oil soluble fractions of B-complex. Vial 10 ml., 30 ml.
Use: Vitamin supplement.
KBP/O. (Forest) Kaolin 350 mg., pectin 60 mg., pow. opium 3 mg., bismuth subcarbonate 60 mg./Cap. Bot. 100s, 1000s.
Use: Diarrhea remedy.
K+CARE. (Alra)
Use: Potassium supplement.
K-C LIQUID. (Century) Kaolin 5.2 Gm., pectin 260 mg., bismuth subcarbonate 260 mg./oz. Bot. 4 oz., pt., gal.
KC-20 ELIXIR. (Scruggs) Bot. pt., gal.
KCL-20. (Western Research) Potassium chloride 1.5 Gm. (20 mEq. potassium, 20 mEq. chloride)/ Packet. Box 30s.
Use: Supplement.
K-CLORE-Y. (Kay) Potassium 20 mEq provided by potassium chloride 1.5 Gm./15 ml. w/sugar & flavoring. Bot. Pts., Gal.
Use: Potassium supplement.
K.D.C. VAGINAL CREAM. (Kenyon) Sulfanilamide 15%, 9-aminoacridine HCl 0.2%, allantoin 2% in a dispersible base containing stearic acid, diglycol, stearate, triethanolamine, propylene glycol, lactic acid, water.
KE.
See: Cortisone Acetate (Various Mfr.)
KEDRIN TABLET. (Dolcin) Analgesic compound. Bot. 100s.
Use: Analgesic without aspirin.
KEELAMIN. (Mericon) Zinc 20 mg., manganese 5 mg., copper 3 mg./Tab. Bot. 100s.
Use: Dietary supplement.
KEEP-A-WAKE. (Stayner) Vit. B-1 5 mg., B-2 2 mg., B-12 activity (cobalamin conc., 1.5 mcg.), niacinamide 10 mg., caffeine citrate 2.5 gr./Tab. Bot. 24s.
Use: Ward off drowsiness & fatigue.
KEFERON. (Kay) Ferric hydroxide, dextran 0.9% sodium Cl. Vial 2 ml., 5 ml. Amp.
Use: Iron supplement.
KEFGLYCIN. Cephaloglycin, B.A.N.
KEFLEX. (Dista) Cephalexin. **Pulvule** 250 mg., 500 mg. Bot. 20s, 100s. Blister pkg. 10 × 10s; **Tab.:** 1 Gm. Bot. 24s. Blister pkg. 100s. **For Oral Susp.** 125 mg./5 ml. Bot. 60 ml., 100 ml., 200 ml. Unit dose 5 ml. × 100s; 250 mg./5 ml. Bot. 100 ml., 200 ml. Unit dose 5 ml. × 100s.
Use: Antibiotic.

KEFLEX FOR PEDIATRIC DROPS. (Dista) Cephalexin. 100 mg./ml. Dropper Bot. 10 ml.

KEFLIN, NEUTRAL. (Lilly) Cephalothin sodium 1 Gm./10 ml., Vial 1s, 25s; 1 Gm./100 ml. Vial 10s; 2 Gm./20 ml. Vial 10s; 2 Gm./100 ml., Vial 10s; 4 Gm./50 ml., Vial 10s; 20 Gm./200 ml. Vial 6s. Faspak 1 Gm. or 2 Gm. Vial 96s.
Use: Broad-spectrum bactericidal antibiotic.

KEFZOL. (Lilly) Cefazolin sodium. 250 mg./10 ml., Vial 1s; 500 mg./10 ml., Vial 1s, 25s; 500 mg./100 ml. Vial 10s; 1 Gm./10 ml., Vial 1s, 25s; 1 Gm./100 ml., Vial 10s; 10 Gm./100 ml., Vial 6s; Redi Vial 500 mg. 1s, 10s; Redi Vial 1 Gm. 1s, 10s; Faspak 500 mg. or 1 Gm. Box 96s.
Use: Antibiotic.

KELEX. (Nutrition) Iron choline citrate 360 mg. providing approx. 40 mg. of elemental iron/Tabseal. Bot. 90s.
Use: Anemia.

KELGIN. Algin.

KELL E. (Canright) di-α Tocopheryl 100 I.U. Bot. 100s, 200 I.U. Bot. 100s, 400 I.U. Bot. 100s.

KELLOGG'S TASTELESS CASTOR OIL. (Beecham Products) Castor oil 100%. Bot. 2 oz.
Use: Laxative.

KELP. (Arcum) Tab. Bot. 100s, 1000s.

KELP. (Stanlabs) Tab. Bot. 100s.

KELP TABLETS. (Kirkman) Bot. 125s.

KELP TABLETS. (Quality Generics) Iodine 0.15 mg. Bot. 250s, 500s.

KELP TABLETS. (Faraday) Iodine from kelp 0.15 mg./Tab. Bot. 100s.

KELP-B-THIN. (Quality Generics) Vit. B-6 21 mg., soya lecithin 600 mg., iodine 225 mcg., dry cider vinegar 240 mg./6 Tabs or 6 Caps. Bot. 100s, 250s.
Use: Dietary supplement.

KELP PLUS. (Barth's) Iodine from kelp plus 16 trace minerals/Tab. Bot. 100s, 500s, 1000s.

KELP (WITH IRON) TABLETS. (Eckerd) Bot. 250s.

KEMADRIN. (Burroughs Wellcome) Procyclidine HCl 5 mg./Tab. Bot. 100s.
Use: Parkinsonism.

KEMICETINE. Chloramphenicol, B.A.N.

KEMITHAL. Thialbarbital. 5-Allyl-5-cyclohex-2-enyl-2-thiobarbituric acid.

KENACORT. (Squibb) Triamcinolone 4 mg./Tab. Bot. 100s. 8 mg./Tab. Bot. 50s.
Use: Oral corticosteroid.

KENACORT DIACETATE. (Squibb) Triamcinolone diacetate equiv. to 4 mg., triamcinolone; buffered with sodium citrate and sodium phosphate/5 cc. Bot. 120 cc.
Use: Oral corticosteroid.

KENAHIST-S.A. (Kenyon) Phenylpropanolamine HCl 50 mg., pheniramine maleate 25 mg., pyrilamine maleate 25 mg./Tab. Bot. 100s, 1000s.
Use: Cough and colds.

KENAKION. (Harriett Lane Home of Johns Hopkins Hospital) Vit. K-1 oxide.
Use: Vit. K-induced kernicterus.

KENALOG. (Squibb) Triamcinolone acetonide **0.1%** **Cream:** Tubes 15 Gm., 60 Gm., 80 Gm. Jar 240 Gm., 5.25 lb. in aqueous lotion base w/propylen glycol, cetyl and stearyl alcohols, glyceryl monostearate, sorbitan monopalmitate, polyoxyethylene sorbitan monolaurate, methylparaben, propylparaben, polyethylene glyc monostearate, simethicone and sorbic acid. **0.5%** **Cream:** Tube 20 Gm, Lot. sq. bot. 15 cc., 60 cc. **Ointment:** (w/base of polyethylene, mineral oil) Tube 15 Gm., 60 Gm., 80 Gm. Jar 240 Gm. 0.5% Tube 20 Gm., **Spray:** 6.6 mg./100 Gm. Can 23 Gm., 63 Gm.
Use: Topical corticosteroid.

KENALOG 0.025%. (Squibb) **Cream:** Tube, 15 Gm 80 Gm. Jar, 240 Gm., 5.25 lb. **Lotion:** in aqueou lotion base w/propylene glycol, cetyl and stearyl alcohols, glyceryl monostearate, sorbitan monopalmitate, polyoxyethylene sorbitan monolaurate, methylparaben, propylparaben, polyethylene glycol monostearate, simethicone a sorbic acid, tinted in an isopropyl palmitate vehic with alcohol (4.7%) Bot. 60 ml. **Ointment:** plastibase (w/base of polyethylene and mineral gel) 15, 80 & 240 Gm.
Use: Topical corticosteroid.

KENALOG H. (Squibb) Triamcinolone acetonide cream USP 0.1%. Each Gm. of cream provides mg. of triamcinolone acetonide in a specially formulated hydrophilic vanishing cream base containing propylene glycol, dimethicone 350, castor oil, cetearyl alcohol and ceteareth-20, pro lene glycol stearate, white petrolatum, purified water. Tube 15 Gm., 60 Gm.
Use: Topical corticosteroid.

KENALOG-10 INJECTION. (Squibb) Sterile triamci lone acetonide suspension 10 mg./cc., w/sod. chloride for isotonicity, 0.9% (w/v) benzyl alcoh as a preservative, 0.75% sod. carboxymethylcellulose, and 0.04% polysorbate Sod. hydroxide or HCl acid may be present to adjust pH to 5.0 to 7.5. At the time of manufactu the air in the container is replaced by nitrogen. Vial 5 cc.
Use: Anti-inflammatory, corticosteroid.

KENALOG-40 INJECTION. (Squibb). Sterile triamci lone acetonide suspension 40 mg./cc., w/sod. chloride for isotonicity, 0.9% (w/v) benzyl alcoh as a preservative, 0.75% sod. carboxymethylcellulose, and 0.04% polysorbate Sod. hydroxide or HCl acid may be present to adjust pH to 5.0 to 7.5. At the time of manufactu the air in the container is replaced by nitrogen. V 1 cc., 5 cc., 10 cc.
Use: Anti-inflammatory, corticosteroid.

KENALOG IN ORABASE. (Squibb) Triamcinolone acetonide 0.1% in Orabase. 1 mg. triamcinolone acetonide per gram. Tube 5 Gm.
Use: Dental paste.

KENAZIDE-E. (Kenyon) Hydrochlorothiazide 50 mg./Tab. Bot. 100s, 1000s.
Use: Anti-hypertensive.

AZIDE-H. (Kenyon) Hydrochlorothiazide 50 g./Tab. Bot. 100s, 1000s.
se: Anti hypertensive.
CORT. (Kenyon) Hydrocortisone 1%, clioquinol % in bland, water washable base. Jar. 1 lb.
DALL'S "COMPOUND B."
se: Corticosterone (Various Mfr.)
DALL'S "COMPOUND E."
se: Cortisone Acetate (Var. Mfr.)
DALL'S "COMPOUND F."
se: 17-Hydroxycorticosterone (Various Mfr.)
DALL'S "DESOXY COMPOUND B."
se: Desoxycorticosterone Acetate (Var. Mfr.)
ISONE DROPS. (Kenyon) Neomycin sulfate 6 g., hydrocortisone 5 mg., parachlorometaxylenol 05%, pramoxine HCl 1%, alcohol 4.8%/cc. Bot. cc.
se: Ear infections.
PECTIN-P SUSPENSION. (Kenwood) Paregoric 1 am, purified kaolin 90 gr., aluminum hydroxide 10 ., pectin 3 gr./fl. oz. w/alcohol 6%. Bot. 4 oz.
se: Treatment of diarrhea.
TONIC. (Kenyon) Vit. A 25,000 I.U., D 1000 I.U., 1 10 mg., B-2 10 mg., B-6 5 mg., B-12 5 mg., C 200 g., niacinamide 100 mg., Ca pantothenate 20 g./Cap. Bot. 1000s.
se: Multivitamin.
-TUSS. (Kenyon) Dextromethorphan HBr 10 mg., henylephrine HCl 5 mg., chlorpheniramine maleate mg., salicylamide 227 mg., phenacetin 100 mg., ffeine alkaloid 10 mg., ascorbic acid 20 mg./Tab. ot. 100s, 1000s.
se: Cough and colds.
PARIC SUSPENSION. (Blue Line) Pow. opium t. 0.514 gr., kaolin 80 gr., pectin 6 gr., alcohol %/fl. oz. Bot. 4 fl. oz., 14 fl. oz.
se: Diarrhea.
TIN. (Blue Line) Kaolin 80 gr., pectin 8 gr./oz. ot. 4 oz., 14 oz., 1 gal.
se: Orally, intestinal disturbances.
ALYT GEL. (Westwood) Salicylic acid 6% in a el base of propylene glycol w/alcohol 19.4%, droxypropyl cellulose, water. Tube 1 oz.
se: Dermatologic: Removal of excessive keratin nd adjunctive therapy for fungal infections; odiatric: Removal of excessive keratin on dorsal nd planter hyperkeratotic lesions.
ASOL. (Upsher-Smith) Therapeutic bath oil. Bot. 8 z.
I CREME. (Westwood) Cream containing water, ineral oil, talc, sorbitol, ceresin, lanolin alcohol, agnesium stearate, glyceryl oleate/propylene ycol, isopropyl myristate, methylparaben, opylparaben, fragrance, quaternium-15. Tube 2.25 z.
se: Moisturizer, emollient.
ID EAR DROPS. (Blair) Urea and glycerin in opylene glycol. Bot. w/dropper 8 ml.
se: Ear wax remover.
I FACIAL CLEANSER. (Westwood) Water, ycerin, squalane, propylene glycol, glyceryl earate, PEG-100 stearate, stearic acid, steareth-20, lanolin alcohol, magnesium aluminium silicate, cetyl alcohol, beeswax, PEG-20 sorbitan, beeswax, methylparaben, propylparaben, quaternium-15, fragrance. Bot. 4 oz.
Use: Soapless facial cleanser.

KERI FACIAL SOAP. (Westwood) Bar consisting of Na tallowate, Na cocoate, water, mineral oil, octyl hydroxystearate, fragrance, glycerin, titanium dioxide, PEG-75, lanolin oil, docusate Na, PEG-4 dilaurate, propylparaben, PEG-40 stearate, glyceryl monostearate, PEG-100 stearate, NaCl, BHT. EDTA. Bar 3.25 oz.
Use: Gentle facial skin cleanser.

KERI LIGHT LOTION. (Westwood) Water, stearyl alcohol, ceteareath-20, cetearyl octaneoate, glycerin, stearyl heptanoate, stearyl alcohol, Carbomer 934, sodium hydroxide, squalane, methylparaben, propylparaben, and fragrance. Bot. 6.5 oz. 13 oz.
Use: Moisturizer.

KERI LOTION. (Westwood) Mineral oil, lanolin oil, water, propylene glycol, glyceryl stearate PEG-100 stearate, PEG 40 stearate, PEG-4 dilaurate, laureth-4, parabens, docusate sodium, triethanolamine, quaternium 15. Carbomer 934 and fragrance. Bot. 6.5 oz., 13 oz., 20oz.
Use: Skin lubricant, moisturizer.

KEROCAINE.
See: Procaine Hydrochloride (Various Mfr.)

KERODEX. (Ayerst)
No. 51: Water-miscible, Tube 4 oz., Jar 1 lb.
No. 71: Water-repellent, Tube 4 oz., Jar 1 lb.
Use: Skin protective.

KEROHYDRIC. A de-waxed, oil-soluble fraction of lanolin.
Use: Emollient, cleanser.
See: Alpha-Keri, Soap, Spray (Westwood)
Keri, Cream, Lot., (Westwood)
W/Docusate sodium, sod. alkyl polyether sulfonate, sod. sulfoacetate, sulfur, salicylic acid, hexachlorophene.
See: Sebulex, Cream, Liq. (Westwood)

KERR INSTA-CHAR. (Kerr) **Regular:** Aqueous suspension activated charcoal 50 gm./8 oz. **Pediatric:** Aqueous suspension activated charcoal 15 Gm./4 oz. pediatric.
Use: Toxic substance antidote.

KERR TRIPLE DYE. (Kerr) Gentian violet, proflavine hemisulfate, brilliant green in water. Dispensing Bot. 15 ml.
Use: Umbilical area antiseptic.

KESSADROX. (McKesson) Magnesium-aluminum hydroxide gel. bot. 12 oz.
Use: Antacid.

KESSOTAPP ELIXIR. (McKesson) Brompheniramine maleate, phenylephrine HCl, phenylpropanolamine HCl/5 ml. Bot. pt., gal.
Use: Decongestant.

KESSO-TETRA. (McKesson) Tetracycline HCl 250 mg. or 500 mg./Cap. Bot. 100s, 1000s, 5000s.
Use: Antibiotic.

KESTRIN. (Hyrex) Estrogens 20,000 u. (2 mg.) in oil or aqueous/cc. Vial 10 cc., 30 cc. I.V. 4 mg./5 cc. Vial 5 cc.
Use: Estrogen therapy.

KESTRONE AQUEOUS. (Hyrex) 5 mg./cc. Vial 10 cc.
Use: Estrogen therapy.

KETALAR. (Parke-Davis) Ketamine HCl with sod. chloride, benzethonium chloride 0.1 mg./ml. as preservative. 10 mg./ml. Vial. 20 ml. Pkg. 10s. 50 mg./ml. Vial 50 ml. Pkg. 10s; 100 mg./ml. Vial 5 ml. Pkg. 10s.
Use: Rapid acting general anesthetic.

• **KETAMINE HCl,** U.S.P. XXI. Inj., U.S.P. XXI. (±)-2-(o-Chlorophenyl)-2-(methylamino) cyclohexanone HCl.
Use: Anesthetic.
See: Ketaject, Vial (Bristol)
Ketalar, Inj. (Parke-Davis)

• **KETANSERIN.** USAN.
Use: Serotonin antagonist.

• **KETAZOCINE.** USAN.
Use: Analgesic.

• **KETAZOLAM.** USAN.
Use: Tranquilizer.

• **KETHOXAL.** USAN.
Use: Antiviral.

• **KETIPRAMINE FUMARATE.** USAN. 5-[3-Diethylamino)propyl]-5,11-dihydro-10H-dibenz[b, f]-azepin-10-one fumarate (1:1).
Use: Antidepressant.

KETOBEMIDONE. B.A.N. 4-(3-Hydroxyphenyl)-1-methyl-4-propionylpiperidine. Cliradon.
Use: Narcotic analgesic.

KETOCHOLANIC ACID. 90% oxidized cholic acid of natural bile acids.
See: Dehydrocholic acid (Various Mfr.)

• **KETOCONAZOLE.** USAN.
Use: Antifungal.

• **KETOCONAZOLE,** U.S.P. XXI. Tab., U.S.P. XXI. 1-acetyl-4 (4-((2-2(2,4 dichlorophenyl)-2-(1-H-imidazol-1-yimethyl)-1,3-dioxolan-4-yl)methoxy) phenyl) piperazine.
Use: Broad spectrum antifungal.
See: Nizoral, Tab. (Janssen)

KETODESTRIN.
See: Estrone (Various Mfr.)

KETO-DIASTIX REAGENT STRIPS. (Ames) Dip and read reagent strip test for glucose and ketones in urine. Two test areas: glucose levels from 30 mg. to 5000 mg/dL; Ketone test (acetoacetic acid) negative 5, 40, 80, 160 mg./dL. Bot 100s. Bot. 50, 100 strips.
Use: Diagnostic and monitoring diabetic patients.

• **KETORFANOL.** USAN.
Use: Analgesic.

KETOHEXAZINE. 4, 6-Diethyl-3(2H)-pyridazinono (Lederle).
Use: Hypnotic.

KETOHYDROXYESTRATRIENE.
See: Estrone

KETOHYDROXYESTRIN.
See: Estrone (Var. Mfr.)

KETOLAN. (Galen) Mixed oxidized bile acids 180 mg., desoxycholic acid 60 mg., homatropine methylbromide 2 mg./Tab. Bot. 100s, 1000s.
Use: Hydrocholeretic, choleretic, fat emulsifier.

• **KETOPROFEN.** USAN.
Use: Anti-inflammatory.

• **KETOROLAC TROMETHAMINE.** USAN.
Use: Analgesic.

KETOSTIX REAGENT STRIPS. (Ames) Sod. nitroprusside, sod. phosphate, glycine. Stick test ketones in urine (measures acetoacetic acid) Bo 50s, 100s.
Use: Urine-ketone estimation.

• **KETOTIFEN FUMARATE.** USAN.
Use: Anti-asthmatic.

KEY-PLEX INJECTABLE. (Hyrex) Thiamine 100 Riboflavin 2 mg., pyridoxine 2 mg., panthenol 2 mg., niacinamide 100 mg./ml. Vial 30 ml.
Use: Vitamin deficiency.

KEY-PRED. (Hyrex) Prednisolone. Parenteral, mg./cc., Vial 10 cc., 30 cc.; 50 mg./cc., Vial 10 100 mg./cc., Vial 10 cc.
Use: Steroid therapy.

KEY-PRED-SP. (Hyrex) Prednisolone sodium p phate 20 mg./ml.
Use: Steroid therapy.

K-FLEX. (Kay) Orphenadrine citrate 30 mg./ml. Via ml.
Use: Treatment of Parkinson's syndrome.

K-FORTE. (O'Connor) Potassium 39 mg. (from po sium gluconate, potassium citrate and potassium chloride), Vit. C 10 mg./Tab. Bot. 90s.
Use: Potassium supplement.

K-FORTE MAXIMUM STRENGTH. (O'Connor) Po sium 99 mg., Vit. C 25 mg./Tab. Bot. 60s.
Use: Potassium supplement.

KHAROPHEN.
See: Acetarsone (Var. Mfr.)

KHELLIN. 5,8-dimethoxy-2-methyl-4′,5′-furano-6,7-chromone.
Use: Coronary vasodilator.

KIDDIE POWDER. (Gordon) Pure fine Italian talc. Can 3.5 oz.
Use: Foot powder.

KIDDIES SIALCO. (Foy) Chlorpheniramine maleate mg., phenylephrine HCl 2.5 mg., acetaminophen 62.5 mg., salicylamide 75 mg./Tab. Bot. 1000s.
Use: Analgesic, antihistaminic.

KIDDI-VITES, Improved. (Geneva) Vit. A 5000 I.U 500 I.U., B-1 1 mg., B-2 1.5 mg., B-12 2 mcg., C mg., B-6 1 mg., pantothenate 2 mg., niacinamide mg./Tab. Bot. 100s, 1000s.
Use: Multivitamin.

KIDETT. (Kay) Vit. A 5000 I.U. D 400 I.U., B-1 1.5 r B-2 1.5 mg., C 37.5 mg., Niacinamide 20 mg., B-6 mg., Ca pantothenate 1 mg., B-12 1.0 mcg., E 1 /Cap. Bot. 100s, 1000s.
Use: Vitamin supplement.

■ **KIDNEY FUNCTION AGENTS.**
See: Indigo Carmine Sol. (Var. Mfr.)
Inulin, Amp. (Arnar-Stone)
Iodohippurate, Sod.

Mannitol Sol., Amp. (Merck Sharp & Dohme)
Methylene Blue (Various Mfr.)
Phenolsulfonphthalein (Various Mfr.)

: **SYRUP.** (Laser) Pot. iodide 150 mg., ephedrine HCl 8 mg./5 ml. Syr. Bot. pt., gal.
Jse: Bronchodilator, expectorant.

IATE. Hexahydrotetra hydroxybenzoate salt, quinic acid salt.

IDER-DARE. (Sween) Bot. 16 oz., gal.
Jse: Skin care cream.

IESED. (Stuart) Phenobarbital 16 mg., hyoscyamine sulf. 0.1 mg., atropine sulf. 0.02 mg., scopolamine hydrobromide 0.007 mg./Tab. Bot. 100s.
Jse: Antispasmodic, sedative.

IEVAC. (Squibb) Sincalide 5 mcg./vial.
Jse: Diagnostic for gallbladder, pancreatic secretion and cholecystography.

ISMAN'S ASTHMA CIGARETTES & POWDER. Guild) Cigarettes 50/Pkg. Pow. 3 oz.

I WHITE. (Whiteworth) Triamcinolone acetonide.
Cream: 0.025%, 1%. Tube 15 Gm., 80 Gm.
Ointment: 1%. Tube 15 Gm., 80 Gm.
Jse: Anti-inflammatory steroid.

IKMASSAGE. (Kirkman) 8 oz., gal.

ITASAMYCIN. USAN. An antibiotic substance obtained from cultures of *Streptomyces kitasatoensis.* Under study.
Jse: Antibiotic.

ARON LOTION 2.0%. (Dermik) Salicylic acid 2%, sulfur colloid 5%, in a hydro-alcoholic suspension w/colloidal magnesium aluminum silicate, alkyl-aryl sulfonic acid salts, propylene glycol, silicone emulsion, cellulose gum, tetrasodium EDTA, 2-bromo-2-nitropropane-1,3-diol, lauric myristic diethanolamide, butyl paraben, fragrance, alcohol 13.1%. Bot. 2 oz. plas. sq.
Jse: Seborrhea, acne and related conditions.

AVIKORDAL. (U.S. Ethicals) Nitroglycerin 2.6 mg./S.R. Tab. Bot. 100s, 1000s.
Jse: Vasodilator for anginal attacks.

EBCIL. (Beecham Labs) Kanamycin sulfate 500 mg./2 ml. vial or 1 Gm./3 ml. Vial. **Ped. Inj.** 75 mg./2 ml. Vial in 10s; 500 mg./2ml. disposable syringe in 25s.
Jse: Antibiotic.

EBSIELLA PNEUMONIAE.
Haemophilus influenzae, Neisseria catarrhalis, streptococci, staphylococci, pneumococci, killed.
See: Mixed Vaccine No. 4 W/H. Influenzae (Lilly)

EER CHEWABLE. (Scrip) Phenylphrine HCl 5 mg., chlorpheniramine maleate 2 mg., d-methorphan HBr 2.5 mg., Vit. C 15 mg./Chewable Tab. Bot. 100s.

EER COMPOUND. (Scrip) Acetaminophen. 300 mg., phenylpropanolamine HCl 35 mg., caffeine 10 mg./Tab. Bot. 100s.

EER IMPROVED. (Scrip) Atropine sulfate 0.2 mg., chlorpheniramine maleate 5 mg./cc.

EER MILD. (Scrip) Phenylpropanolamine HCl 75 mg./Cap. Bot. 100s.

ENSEB. (Durel) Mild astringent and facial cleanser. Bot. 4 oz., gal.

KLER-RO LIQUID. (Ulmer) Surgical cleanser and laboratory detergent. Bot. gal.

KLER-RO POWDER. (Ulmer) Surgical cleanser and laboratory detergent. Can 2 lb., Bot. 6 lb., Drum 45 lb.

K-LOR. (Abbott) Potassium chloride equiv. to potassium 20 mEq. and chloride 20 mEq./2.6 Gm. for oral solution. Pkg. 30s, 100s. 15 mEq/2 Gm. Pkg. 100s.
Use: Potassium chloride supplement.

KLOR-10% SOLUTION. (Upsher-Smith) Potassium chloride 10%. Bot. 4 oz., pt., gal.

KLOR-CON POWDER. (Upsher-Smith) Potassium chloride for oral solution 20 mEq/Packet. Packets 1.5 Gm. Box 30s, 100s.
Use: Potassium supplement.

KLOR-CON/25 POWDER. (Upsher-Smith) Potassium Cl. for oral sol. 25 mEq./Pkt. Cartons 30s, 100s, 250s.
Use: Potassium supplement.

KLOR-CON SOLUTION. (Upsher-Smith) Potassium chloride 20% oral solution. Bot. 4 oz., pt., gal.

KLORIDE. (Amfre-Grant) K chloride 1.5 Gm./15 cc. Elix. Bot., pt., gal.
Use: Treatment of potassium deficiency.

KLORLYPTUS. (High) Chemical cpd. of eucalyptus oil & chlorine in a petroleum ointment and light oil base. **Oint.:** Jars 1 oz., 1 lb. **Oil:** Bot. 30 ml., 1 pt.
Use: Topical dressing.

KLOROMIN. (Blue Cross) Chlorpheneramine maleate 4 mg./Tab. Bot. 1000s.
Use: Decongestant.

KLORVESS EFFERVESCENT GRANULES. (Sandoz) Potassium 20 mEq. & chloride 20 mEq. supplied by KCl 1.125 Gm., potassium bicarbonate 0.5 Gm., L-lysine monohydrochloride 0.913 Gm./Packet. Box 30s.
Use: Potassium & chloride supplement.

KLORVESS EFFERVESCENT TABLETS. (Sandoz) Pot. chloride 1.125 Gm., pot. bicarb. 0.5 Gm., 1-lysine HCl 0.913 Gm./Eff. Tab. Sodium & sugar free. Pkg. 60s, 1000s.
Use: Potassium & chloride supplement.

KLORVESS LIQUID. (Sandoz) Potassium chloride 1.5 Gm., (20 mEq.)/15 ml., alcohol 0.7%. Bot. pt. Unit dose 15 ml. Box 100s.
Use: Potassium & chloride supplement.

KLOTRIX. (Mead Johnson) Potassium chloride 10 mEq. KCl/Tab. Slow-release Tab. Bot. 100s, 1000s. Unit dose 100s.
Use: Potassium supplement.

K-LYTE. (Mead Johnson) Pot. bicarbonate and citrate 25 mEq. potassium/Tab., individually wrapped effervescent tabs.; Flavors: Lime, Orange. Pkg. 30s, 100s, 250s.
Use: Treatment of potassium loss accompanying body fluid disorders.

K-LYTE/CL. (Mead Johnson) Pot. chloride 25 mEq. /Dose. Pkg. 30s, 100s, 250s; Individually wrapped effervescent tabs.; Bulk powder 225 Gm./Can. Available in citrus and fruit punch flavors.
Use: Potassium and chloride replacement therapy.

K-LYTE/CL 50. (Mead Johnson) Potassium Cl. 50 mEq/ Dose. Pkg. 30s, 100s. Available in citrus and fruit punch flavors.
Use: Potassium & chloride replacement therapy.

K-LYTE DS. (Mead Johnson) Potassium bicarbonate & citrate 50 mEq. Potassium/Effervescent Tab. Pkg. 30s, 100s, individually foil wrapped. Available in lime and orange flavors.
Use: Potassium replacement therapy, treatment of potassium loss.

KNIBEL TABLETS. (Knight) Bot. 100s, 500s.
Use: Antispasmodic.

KNIBEL T.D. CAPSULES. (Knight) Bot. 100s.
Use: Sustained action antispasmodic.

KNIHALANT SPRAY. (Knight) Bot. 20 cc.
Use: Nasal congestion.

KNIMINE T.D. CAPSULES. (Knight) Bot. 100s.
Use: Antihistamine decongestant.

KNIMINE TABLETS. (Knight) Bot. 100s.
Use: Antihistamine decongestant.

KNISED TABLETS. (Knight) Bot. 100s.
Use: Sedative.

KNISERP TABLETS. (Knight) Bot. 100s.
Use: Antihypertensive and calmative.

KNITRON TABLETS. (Knight) Bot. 100s.
Use: Hematinic.

KNITUSSIN SYRUP. (Knight) Bot. pt.
Use: Antitussive, antihistamine expectorant.

KOATE. (Cutter) Antihemophilic Factor (Human) comprises factors VIII, AHF and AHG; each 10 ml. contains approx. 250 AHF units. Vials 250u, 500u, 1000u, 1500u w/diluent.
Use: Antihemophilic.

KOATE HT. (Cutter) Antihemophilic factor, human-heat treated. Vial 250 units, 500 units, 1000 units or 1500 units w/diluent.
Use: Treatment of conditions caused by factor VIII deficiency/Hemophilia A.

KODONYL EXPECTORANT. (Blue Cross) Bromodiphenhydramine HCl 3.75 mg., diphenhydramine HCl 8.75 mg., ammonium Cl. 80 mg. potassium guaiacolsulfonate 80 mg., menthol 0.5 mg./5 ml. Bot. 16 oz.
Use: Expectorant, antihistaminic.

KOHLER HEADACHE POWDERS. (Guild) Pkg. 8s.

KOHLER ONE NIGHT CORN SALVE. (Guild)

KOLANTYL GEL. (Merrell Dow) Aluminum hydroxide 150 mg., magnesium hydroxide 150 mg./5 ml. Bot. 12 oz.
Use: Antacid.

KOLANTYL WAFERS. (Merrell Dow) Magnesium hydroxide 170 mg., aluminum hydroxide 180 mg./wafer. Box 32s.
Use: Antacid.

KOLYUM LIQUID AND POWDER. (Pennwalt) Potassium ion 20 mEq., chloride ion 3.4 mEq. from pot. gluconate 3.9 Gm., pot. chloride 0.25 Gm./15 ml. or 5 Gm. **Liquid:** Bot. pt., gal. **Powder:** Packets 5 Gm. 30s.
Use: Potassium deficiency.

KOMED LOTION. (Barnes-Hind) Sodium thiosulfate 8%, salicylic acid 2%, w/Isopropyl alcohol 25% menthol, camphor, colloidal alumina. Squeeze Bo 1.75 oz.
Use: Treatment of acne associated with oily skin.

KOMED HC. (Barnes-Hind) Hydrocortisone acetate 5%, sodium thiosulfate 8%, salicylic acid 2%, isopropyl alcohol 25%, menthol, camphor, colloid alumina, disodium edetate. Lotion, Plastic Bot. 2
Use: Acne therapy.

KOMEX. (Barnes-Hind) Sodium tetraborate deca drate. Jar 75 Gm.
Use: Aid in reducing oily skin conditions associat with acne.

KONAKION. (Roche) Phytonadione-synthetic vitami K_{-1} w/polysorbate 80, phenol, propylene glycol, s acetate, glacial acetic acid. Amp.: 1 mg./0.5 ml. Box 10s.
Use: Prevention and treatment of hypoprothrombinemia.

KONDON'S NASAL JELLY. (Kondon) Tube 20 Gm W/Ephedrine alkaloid. Tube 20 Gm.

KONDREMUL. (Fisons) Plain: Mineral oil 55% w/Iri moss, emulsion. Bot. 1 pt., 8 oz.
Use: Laxative.

W/Phenolphthalein 2.2 gr./Tbsp. Bot. 1 pt.

W/Cascara 0.66 Gm./15 cc. Bot. 14 oz.

KONSTO. (Freeport) Docusate sodium 100 mg./Ca Bot. 1000s.
Use: Fecal softener.

KONSYL POWDER. (Lafayette) Psyllium hydrophyll mucilloid.
Use: Bulk producing laxative.

KONSYL-D POWDER. (Lafayette) Psyllium hydroph mucilloid with dextrose.
Use: Bulk producing laxative.

KONYNE. (Cutter) Stable, dried, purified plasma fraction comprising coagulation factors II, VII, IX and X with a minimal amount of total protein; 500 clinical units of Factor IX/20 ml. Vials 500u, 1000 w/diluent.
Use: To correct or prevent bleeding.

KONYNE-HT. (Cutter) Factor IX complex human h treated. Vial 500 units or 1000 units w/diluent.
Use: Treatment of conditions caused by factor IX deficiency, especially Hemophilia B.

KOOL FOOT CREAM LOTION. (Wade) Menthol, camphor, acid boracic, glycerine, methyl salicylat isopropyl alcohol. Bot. 2 oz., 4 oz., pt.

KOREAN GINSENG. (Kirkman) Bot. 60s.

KORIZOL. (Sutliff & Case) Methapyrilene HCl 0.2%, Naphazoline HCl 0.05%, Cetylpyridinium chloride 0.02%, thimerosal 0.005%. Bot. w/dropper 20 cc
Use: Acute & chronic sinusitis.

KORO-FLEX. (Holland-Rantos) (Diaphragm, Arcing) I proved contouring spring natural latex diaphragm. 60-95 mm.

KOROMEX. (Holland-Rantos) **Cream:** Octoxynol 3.0%, base of purified water, propylene glycol, stea acid, sorbitan stearate, polysorbate 60, boric acid and fragrance, pH buffered and adjusted to 4.5. Tube 45 Gm. w/ or w/out measured dose applicator; refill 128 Gm. **Jelly:** Nonoxynol-9 3% base of purified water, propylene glycol, cellulose

gum, boric acid, sorbitol, starch, simethicone, fragrance, pH buffered and adjusted to 4.5. Tube 81 Gm., 126 Gm. **Foam:** Nonoxynol-9 12.5%. Aerosol can 40 Gm.
Use: Spermicide, contraceptive & vaginal lubricant with diaphragm.

ROMEX CONTRACEPTIVE CRYSTAL CLEAR GEL. (Holland-Rantos) Nonoxynol-9 2% in base of purified water, propylene glycol, cellulose gum, boric acid, sorbitol, simethicone w/pH 4.5. Tube 126 Gm. w/applicator
Use: Contraceptive for use with diaphragm.

ROMEX COIL SPRING DIAPHRAGM. (Holland-Rantos) Diaphragm made of pure latex rubber, cadmium plated coil spring is tension adjusted. As kit w/Koromex Contraceptive Jelly and Koromex Contraceptive Cream. Sizes 50 mm.-95 mm. at graduations of 5 mm.

ROMEX COMBINATION. (Holland-Rantos) Diaphragm 50-95 mm., Koromex Jelly and Cream/Kit.

ROSTATIN. (Holland-Rantos) Nystatin 100,000 u./Vaginal Tab. Boxes 15s, 30s.
Use: Vulvovaginal candidiasis.

RUM. (Geneva) Acetominophen 5 gr./Tab. Bot. 1000s.

RYZA TAB. (Fellows) Phenylephrine HCl 15 mg., phenylpropanolomine HCl 25 mg., chlorpheniramine maleate 4 mg., acetaminophen 300 mg., hyoscyamine HBr 0.134 mg., hyoscine HBr 0.008 mg., atropine sulfate 0.020 mg./Tab. Bot. 1000s.

TABARB. (Wesley) Phenobarbital 1/4 gr./Tab. Bot. 1000s.
Use: Sedative.

AVA. (Kay) Papaverine HCl 150 mg./Cap. (Kaykap) Bot. 100s, 500s, 1000s.

HEN. (Kay) Promethazine HCl 50 mg./cc. Vial 10 cc. Expect.: w/codeine, pt., gal.

HOS M.F. (Beach) Potassium acid phosphate 155 mg., sodium acid phosphate 350 mg./Tab. Bot. 100s, 500s.
Use: Acidify the urine, phosphorus supplement.

HOS NEUTRAL. (Beach) Dibasic sodium phosphate 852 mg., potassium acid phosphate 155 mg., sodium acid phosphate 130 mg./Tab. Bot. 100s, 500s.
Use: Lowers urinary calcium levels, phosphorus supplement.

HOS NO. 2 (Beach) Potassium acid phosphate 305 mg., sodium acid phosphate, anhydrous 700 mg./Tab. Bot. 100s, 500s.
Use: Urinary acidifier, phosphorus supplement.

HOS ORIGINAL. (Beach) Potassium acid phosphate 500 mg./Tab. Bot. 100s, 500s.
Use: Acidify the urine, useful in idiopathic hypercalciuria, phosphorus supplement.

SUSPENSION. (Century) Kaolin 5.2 Gm., pectin 260 mg./oz. Bot. 4 oz., pt, gal.
Use: Antidiarrheal.

KRONOFED-A-JR. (Ferndale) Pseudoephedrine HCl 60 mg., chlorpheniramine maleate 4 mg./Cap. Bot. 100s, 500s.
Use: Antihistaminic, decongestant.

KRONOFED-A KRONOCAPS. (Ferndale) Pseudoephedrine HCl 120 mg., chlorpheniramine maleate 8 mg./Cap. Bot. 100s, 500s.
Use: Antihistaminic, decongestant.

KRONOHIST KRONOCAPS. (Ferndale) Chlorpheniramine maleate 4 mg., pyrilamine maleate 25 mg., phenylpropanolamine HCl 50 mg./Cap. Bot. 100s, 1000s.
Use: Antihistaminic-decongestant.

KRUSCHEN SALTS. (CMC) Mineral spa-type supplement. Bot. 4 oz.

• **KRYPTON CLATHRATE Kr 85.** USAN.
Use: Radioactive agent.

• **KRYPTON Kr 81m,** U.S.P. XXI.
Use: Radioactive agent.

K-TAB. (Abbott) Potassium chloride (10 mEq) 750 mg./Slow Release Tab. Bot. 100s, 1000s. Abbo-Pac 100s.
Use: Potassium supplement.

K.T.V. TABLETS. (Knight) Vitamin B-12 and minerals. Bot. 50s.

KUDROX (Double Strength) SUSPENSION. (Rorer) Susp. of aluminum hydroxide & magnesium hydroxide w/ 0.13 mEq. sodium. Bot. 12 oz.
Use: Antacid.

KUTAPRESSIN INJECTION. (Rorer) Liver derivative complex. Vial 20 cc.
Use: Subcutaneous, I.M. to reduce inflammation and edema in a variety of skin conditions.

KUTRASE. (Rorer) Amylolytic enzyme 30 mg., proteolytic enzyme 6 mg., lipolytic enzyme 75 mg., cellulolytic enzyme 2 mg., phenyltoloxamine citrate 15 mg., hyoscyamine sulfate 0.0625 mg./Cap. Bot. 100s, 500s.
Use: Enzymatic digestant with antispasmodic, anticholinergic and calmative.

KU-ZYME. (Rorer) Amylolytic enzyme 30 mg., proteolytic enzyme 6 mg., lipolytic enzyme 75 mg., cellulolytic enzyme 2 mg./Cap. Bot. 100s, 500s.
Use: Enzymatic digestant.

KU-ZYME-HP. (Rorer) Lipase 8,000 u., protease 30,000 u., amylase 30,000 u./Cap. Bot. 100s.
Use: Enzymatic digestant.

KWELCOF. (Ascher) Hydrocodone bitartrate 5 mg., guaifenesin 100 mg./5 ml. Bot. Pt. Alcohol, dye, sugar, and corn products free.
Use: Antitussive, expectorant.

KWELL. (Reed & Carnrick) Lindane 1%. **Lot.** W/Glyceryl monostearate, cetyl alcohol, stearic acid, trolamine, 2-amino-2-methyl-1-propanol, methyl p-hydroxybenzoate, butyl p-hydroxybenzoate, irish moss extract. Bot. 2 oz., 16 oz. **Shampoo.** W/Polyethylene sorbitan monostearate, TEA-Lauryl sulfate, acetone and purified water. Bot. 2 oz., pt., gal. **Cream.** W/Stearic acid, lanolin, glycerin, 2-

amino-2-methyl-1-propanol, perfume and purified water. Tube 2 oz., Jar 1 lb.
Use: Topically, scabies & pediculosis.

KYODEX REAGENT STRIPS. (Kyoto) A disposable plastic reagent strip for determination of glucose in whole blood. Vial 25s.
Use: Evaluation of carbohydrate metabolism.

KYOTEST UG REAGENT STRIPS. (Kyoto) Reagent strips for glucose and ketones in urine.
Use: Diagnostic.

KYOTEST UGK REAGENT STRIP. (Kyoto) Disposable reagent strip for measurement of glucose and ketones in the urine. Vial 50s, 100s.
Use: Diagnostic.

KYOTEST UK REAGENT STRIPS. (Kyoto) Reagent strip for ketones in urine. Vial 50s.
Use: Diagnostic..

L

LA-12. (Hyrex) Hydroxocobalamin 1000 mcg./cc. Vial 10 cc.
Use: Treatment of megaloblastic anemia.

• **LABETALOL HYDROCHLORIDE.** USAN.
Use: Anti-adrenergic.
See: Trandate Inj., Tab. (Glaxo).

LABID. (Norwich Eaton) Theophylline anhydrous 250 mg./Tab. Bot. 100s.
Use: Relief of symptoms of asthma.

LABSTIX REAGENT STRIPS. (Ames) Urine screening in 30 sec. pH values, protein, glucose, ketones, occult blood. Bot. 100s.
Use: Diagnostic.

LACLEDE CLEANER. (Laclede) 2 lb. Container.
Use: Detergent for instruments and trays.

LACLEDE DISCLOSING SWAB. (Laclede) 6″ Swabs. 100s, 500s, 1000s.
Use: Dental swab.

LACLEDE PROFIE. (Laclede) Enzyme-action prophylaxis. **Paste:** Jar. 13.5 oz. **Liq.:** Bot. pt. **Tab.:** Bot. 500s.
Use: Removal of calculus.

LACLEDE ROOM DEODORIZER. (Laclede) Can 16 oz.
Use: Neutralize odors.

LACLEDE SKIN LUBRICANT. (Laclede) Tube 1.5 oz.
Use: Skin lubricant for lips, face and intra-oral use.

LACLEDE TOPI-FLUOR A.P.F. TOPICAL CREAM. (Laclede) Fluoride ion 1.23% (from sod. fluoride) in orthophosphoric acid 0.98%. Jar 50 ml., 500 ml., 1000 ml., 2000 ml.
Use: Dental cream.

LACOTEIN. (Christina) Protein digest 5% w/preservatives. Vial 30 cc. w/iodochin Vial 30 cc.
Use: I.M., nonspecific protein therapy.

LACRIL ARTIFICAL TEARS. (Allergan) Hydroxypropyl methylcellulose & gelatin A in a sterile buffered isotonic solution w/chlorbutanol 0.5%. Drop bot. 15 ml.

LACRI—LUBE S.O.P. (Allergan) White petrolatum, mineral oil, nonionic lanolin derivatives, chlorobutanol. Unit-dose 0.7 Gm. Tube 3.5 Gm., [illegible] Gm.
Use: Ocular lubricant.

LACRISERT. (Merck Sharp & Dohme) Hydroxyprop[illegible] cellulose 5 mg./Lacrisert ophthalmic insert. Pkg. contains 60 unit doses, 2 reusable applicators an[illegible] storage container.
Use: Dry eye syndromes.

LACTALBUMIN HYDROLYSATE.
See: Aminonat

LACTATED PEPSIN ELIXIR. (Parke-Davis) 1[illegible] Gm./100 ml. Alcohol 15%. Elix. Bot. 16 fl. oz.

• **LACTATED RINGER'S INJECTION,** U.S.P. XXI.

• **LACTIC ACID,** U.S.P. XXI. Propanoic acid, 2-hydroxy.
Use: Pharm. necessity for Sodium Lactate Injecti[illegible] U.S.P. XXI.

W/Sodium pyrrolidone carboxylate.
See: LactiCare (Stiefel)

LACTICARE LOTION. (Stiefel) Lactic acid 5%, sodium pyrrolidone carboxylate 2.5% in an emollient lotion base. Bot. 8 oz. 12 oz. w/pump dispenser.
Use: Dry skin treatment.

LACTINEX. (Hynson, Westcott & Dunning) *Lactobacillus acidophilus & Lactobacillus bulgaric[illegible]* mixed culture. Tab. 250 mg., Bot. 50s. Granules [illegible] Gm. pk. Box 12s.
Use: Orally, to restore intestinal flora.

LACTOBACILLUS ACIDOPHILUS. Preparation ma[illegible] from acid-producing bacterium.
Use: Antidiarrheal.
See: Bacid (Fisons)
DoFUS (Miller)

LACTOBACILLUS ACIDOPHILUS & BULGARICUS MIXED CULTURE.
See: Lactinex, Tab., Granules (Hynson, Westcott [illegible] Dunning)

LACTOBACILLUS ACIDOPHILUS, VIABLE CULTURE.
See: DoFus, Tab. (Miller)
Lactinex Granules, Tab. (Hynson, Westcott & Dunning)
Neo-Cultol, Jelly (Fisons)

LACTOCAL-F. (Laser) Vit. A 8000 I.U., D 400 I.U., E [illegible] I.U., C 100 mg., Folic acid 1 mg., B-1 3 mg., B-2 [illegible] mg., nicotinamide 20 mg., B-6 5 mg., B-12 12 mcg., [illegible] 200 mg., iodine 0.15 mg., iron 65 mg., Mg. 10 mg[illegible] Cu 2 mg., Zn 15 mg./Tab. Bot. 100s, 1000s.
Use: Vitamin and mineral supplement for pregnan[illegible] and lactation.

LACTOFLAVIN.
See: Riboflavin, U.S.P. XXI. (Var. Mfr.)

• **LACTOSE,** N.F. XVI. Milk sugar.
Use: Pharm. aid (tablet and capsule diluent).
See: Natur-Aid powder (Scott/Cord)

LACTRASE. (Rorer) Lactase 125 mg./Cap. Bot. 10[illegible]
Use: Lactose intolerance.

• **LACTULOSE,** U.S.P. XXI. Concentrate, Syr, U.S.P. XXI. 4-0-β-D-Galactopyranosyl-D-fructose. Duphal[illegible]
Use: Treatment of hepatic coma and chronic constipation.

See: Cephulac, Syr. (Merrell Dow)
Chronulac, Liq. (Merrell Dow)

ADOGAL. (Winthrop Products) Danazol.
Use: Gonadotropin inhibitor.

ADOGAR. (Winthrop Products) Danazol.
Use: Gonadotropin inhibitor.

ADY ESTHER 4 PURPOSE FACE CREAM. (Norcliff Thayer) Jar 4 oz., 8 oz.

ADY ESTHER FACE POWDER. (Norcliff Thayer) Box 1 oz.

A.E. 20. (Seatrace) Estradiol valerate 20 mg./ml. Vial 10 cc.

A.E. 40. (Seatrace) Estradiol valerate 40 mg./ml. Vial 10 cc.

LAETRILE. Substance obtained from apricot pits and thought by some to arrest certain forms of cancer. Contains amygdalin (a cyanogenic glycoside) as the major component. Currently legal in many states.

AGOL OIL. (Last) 8 Hydrooxyquinoline 0.038% in oil base. Bot. 1 oz., 2 oz., 4 oz., 16 oz.
Use: Soothing, cleansing oil.

AGOL OINTMENT. (Last) Allantoin 1%, benzocaine 5%. Jar 1 oz., 8 oz., 16 oz., 5 lb.
Use: Soothing, dressing ointment.

AKTOMOL. (Durel) Whole milk, dewaxed lanolin esters. Bot. pt., gal.
Use: Pediatric and geriatric skin conditioner, prophylatic for normal skin.

AMOTANE-X. (Myers) Trichlorethylamino-glycol-benzoate (ethylaminobenzoate-chloralhydrate derivative). Bot. 4 oz., 6 oz., 8 oz., pt., qt., gal.
Use: Antiseptic, anesthetic, antipruritic.

AMPRENE. Clofazimine, B.A.N.

ANABAC. (Lannett) Aspirin 0.3 gr., caffeine 15 mg., potassium bromide 15 mg., sodium bromide 15 mg./Tab. Bot. 1000s.

ANABARB. (Lannett) **No. 1:** Sod. amobarbital ¾ gr., sod. secobarbital ¾ gr./Cap. Bot. 500s, 1000s. **No. 2:** Sod. amobarbital 1.5 gr., sod. secobarbital 1.5 gr./Cap. Bot. 500s, 1000s.
Use: Sedative.

ANABEE-C. (Lannett) Vit. B-1 15 mg., B-1 10 mg., B-6 5 mg., niacinamide 50 mg., calcium pantothenate 10 mg., C 300 mg./Cap. Bot. 100s, 1000s.

ANABROM ELIXIR. (Lannett) 60 gr. of combined bromides of sod., pot., strontium, ammonium/fl. oz. Bot. 1 pt., 1 gal.

ANABURN OINT. (Lannett) Aluminum basic acetate, phenol, zinc oxide, boric acid, ichthammol, eucalyptol, Jar 1 lb.

ANACANE CREME. (Combe) Benzocaine, chlorothymol, resorcin. Tube 1.25 oz., 2.5 oz. Spray Can 3 oz.
Use: Topical anesthetic.

ANACILLIN. (Lannett) Penicillin G potassium 200,000 u./5 cc. Bot. 100 cc. 400,000 u./5 cc. Bot. 100 cc., 150 cc.
Use: Antibiotic.

LANACILLIN VK TABLETS. (Lannett) Potassium phenoxymethyl penicillin 400,000 u. (250 mg.), 800,000 u. (500 mg.)/Tab. Bot. 100s.
Use: Antibiotic.

LANACILLIN VK POWDER. (Lannett) Potassium phenoxymethyl penicillin 125 mg./5 cc. (200,000 u.), 250 mg./5 cc. (400,000 u.), Bot. 100 cc.

LANACORT CREAM. (Combe) Hydrocortisone acetate 0.5%. Tube 0.5 oz., 1.0 oz.
Use: Topical anti-inflammatory.

LANAMINS. (Lannett) Combination of vitamins (11)/Cap. Bot. 100s, 1000s.

LANAPHILIC OINTMENT. (Medco Lab) Sorbitol, isopropyl palmitate, stearyl alcohol, white petrolatum, oil soluble lanolin, sodium lauryl sulfate, propylene glycol, methylparaben, propylparaben. Jar 16 oz. Also available w/Urea 10% or 20%.
Use: Prescription compounding and dry skin.

LANASED. (Lannett) Atropine sulfate 0.03 mg., hyoscyamine 0.03 mg., methenamine 408 mg., methylene blue 5.4 mg., phenyl salicylate 18.1 mg., gelsemium 6.1 mg., benzoic acid 4.5 mg./Tab. Bot. 1000s.

LANATOSIDE C. B.A.N. 3-(3″-Acetyl-4″-β -glucosyl-tridigitoxosido)-digoxogenin.
Use: Myocardial stimulant.
See: Cedilanid, Tab. (Sandoz)

LANATRATE. (Lannett) Ergotamine tartrate 1 mg., caffeine alkaloid, 100 mg./Tab. Bot. 100s, 500s, 1000s.
Use: Relief of different throbbing and recurrent headaches.

LANATUSS. (Lannett) Guaifenesin 100 mg., phenylpropanolamine HCl 5 mg., chlorpheniramine maleate 2 mg., sodium citrate 197 mg., citric acid 60 mg./5 cc. Bot. pts., gal.
Use: Cough, decongestant.

LANAURINE. (Lannett) Antipyrine & Benzocaine in glycerin. Bot. 0.5 oz., 4 oz.
Use: Otitis media.

LANAVITE. (Lannett) Vitamins A 5000 I.U., D 1000 I.U., B-1 1.5 mg., B-2 2 mg., B-6 0.1 mg., C 37.5 mg., B-12 1 mcg., niacinamide 20 mg., Ca pantothenate 1 mg. E 1 I.U./Cap. Bot. 500s, 1000s.

LANAVITE DROPS. (Lannett) Vit. A 3000 I.U., D 400 I.U., B-1 1 mg., B-2 1.2 mg., niacinamide 8 mg., C 60 mg./0.6 cc. Drop. bot. 15 cc., 60 cc.

LANAZETS. (Lannett) Cetylpyridinium 1 mg., benzocaine 5 mg./Loz. Bot. 500s, 1000s.

LANES PILLS. (Last) Casanthranol 45 mg./Tab. Bot. 20s.
Use: Laxative.

LANESTRIN. (Lannett) Estrogenic sub. natural in aq. susp. 20,000 u./cc. Vial 30 cc.

LANIAZID C.T. (Lannett) Isoniazid 50 mg. Tab. Bot. 500s, 1000s. 100 mg./Tab. Bot. 100s, 500s, 1000s.
Use: Tuberculosis.

LANNATES ELIXIR. (Lannett) Sodium glycerophosphate 2 gr., calcium glycerophosphate 2 gr., phosphoric acid 1.5 min., wine base/fl. oz. Bot. pt., gal.

LANOKALIN. (Lannett) Phenobarbital 15 mg., homatropine methyl bromide 5 mg., colloidal kaolin 300 mg./Tab. Bot. 1000s.
Use: Antacid, absorbant.

• **LANOLIN,** U.S.P. XXI. Anhydrous U.S.P. XXI.
Use: Water-in-oil emulsion ointment base; absorbent ointment base.
See: Kerohydric (Westwood)
W/Coconut oil, pine oil, castor oil, cholesterols, lecithin and parachlorometaxylenol.
See: Sebacide, Liq. (Paddock)
W/Diiosbutylcresoxyethoxyethyl, dimethyl benzyl ammonium chloride, menthol.
See: Hospital Lotion (Paddock)

• **LANOLIN ALCOHOLS,** N.F. XVI.
Use: Pharmaceutic aid (ointment base ingredient).

LANOLINE. (Burroughs Wellcome) Perfumed emollient ointment. Tube 1.75 oz.
Use: Derma emollient.

LANO-LO BATH OIL. (Whorton) 8 oz.

LANOLOR. (Squibb) Cream. Jar 8 oz. Tube 2 oz.

LANOPHYLLIN ELIXIR. (Lannett) Anhydrous theophylline 80 mg., alcohol 20%/15 cc. Bot. pt., gal.

LANOPHYLLIN INJ. (Lannett) Theophylline 250 mg./cc. Inj. 10 cc. vial.

LANOPLEX ELIXIR. (Lannett) Vit. B-1 4 mg., B-6 mg., nicotinamide 40 mg., B-6 2 mg./fl. oz. Bot. pt., gal.

LANOPLEX FORTE CAPSULES. (Lannett) Vit. B-1 25 mg., B-2 12.5 mg., nicotinamide 50 mg., C 250 mg., B-6 3 mg., B-12 5 mcg., Ca pantothenate 10 mg./Cap. Bot. 100s, 500s, 1000s.

LANOPLEX INJECTION. (Lannett) Vitamins B-1 100 mg., B-2 1 mg., B-6 2 mg., niacinamide 50 mg., cal. pantothenate 10 mg., benzyl alcohol 1%, urea 10%, chlorobutanol 0.5%/cc. Vial 30 cc.

LANORINAL. (Lannett) Isobutylallybarbituric acid 50 mg., caffeine 40 mg., aspirin 200 mg., phenacetin 130 mg./Cap. or Tab. **Cap.** Bot. 100s, 1000s. **Tab.** Bot. 1000s.
Use: Tension headache.

LANOTHAL PILLS. (Lannett) Phenolphthalein 0.5 gr., aloin 0.25 gr., ipecac 1/15 gr., belladonna ext. 1/12 gr./Pill. Bot. 1000s.

LANOXICAPS. (Burroughs Wellcome) Digoxin solution in capsules. Digoxin 0.05 mg., 0.1 mg. or 0.2 mg./Cap. Bot. 100s.
Use: Digitalization, cardiotonic.

LANOXIN. (Burroughs Wellcome) Digoxin. **Tab.** 0.125 mg., Bot. 100s, 1000s; 0.25 mg., Bot. 100s, 500s, 1000s, 5000s. Unit dose 1000s. Unit of Use Bot. 100s, 0.5 mg., Bot. 100s. **Pediatric Elixir** (0.05 mg./ml.) Bot. 60 ml. **Inj.** (w/propylene glycol 40%, alcohol 10%, sod. phosphate 0.3%, anhydrous citric acid 0.08%) Amp. 0.5 mg./2 ml. Amp. 12s, 100s. **Pediatric Inj.** 0.1 mg./ml. Amp. 1 ml. 50s.
Use: Digitalization, cardiotonic.

LANTRISUL. (Lannett) Sulfamerazine, sulfadiazine, sulfamethazine 2.5 gr. each/Tab. Bot. 100s, 500s, 1000s. **Susp.** Bot. pt., gal.
Use: Triple sulfa therapy.

LANTURIL. (Winthrop Products) Oxypertine.
Use: Anxiolytic, tranquilizer.

LANUM. (Various Mfg.) Lanolin.

LANVISONE CREAM. (Lannett) Hydrocortisone 1%, clioquinol 3%. Tube 20 Gm. Jar 16 oz.

LAPAV. (Amfre-Grant) **Cap.:** Papaverine HCl 1[illegible] mg./Cap. Bot. 100s, 1000s. **Elixir:** Papaverine H[illegible] 100 mg./15 cc. Bot. 4 oz., 16 oz., 1 Gal.
Use: Relief of cerebral and peripheral ischemia.

LAPUDRINE HYDROCHLORIDE. Chlorproguanil, B.A.N.

• **LAPYRIUM CHLORIDE.** USAN.
Use: Pharmaceutic aid.

LARDET. (Standex) Phenobarbital 8 mg., theophylli[illegible] 130 mg., ephedrine HCl 24 mg./Tab. Bot. 100s.

LARDET EXPECTORANT. (Standex) Phenobarbital [illegible] mg., theophylline 130 mg., ephedrine HCl 24 mg., guaifenesin 100 mg./Tab. Bot. 100s.

LARGACTIL HYDROCHLORIDE. Chlorpromazine B.A.N.

LARGON. (Wyeth) Propiomazine HCl 20 mg./ml. w/ sodium formaldehyde sulfoxylate, sodium acetate buffer. Amp. 1 cc., 2 cc. Pkg. 25s. 20 mg./Tubex [illegible] cc., 10s.
Use: Tranquilizing agent.

LAROBEC. (Roche) Vit. B-1 15 mg., B-2 15 mg., niaci[illegible] mide 100 mg., Ca pantothenate 20 mg., B-12 5 mc[illegible] folic acid 0.5 mg., C 500 mg./Tab. Bot. 100s.
Use: Nutritional supplementation for patients und[illegible] treatment w/levodopa.

LARODOPA CAPSULES. (Roche) Levodopa 250 mg./Cap. Bot. 100s, 500s; 500 mg./Cap. Bot. 10[illegible] 500s.
Use: Treatment of Parkinson's disease and syndrome.

LARODOPA TABLETS. (Roche) Levodopa 100 mg./Tab. Bot. 100s; 250 mg./Tab. Bot. 100s, 50[illegible] 500 mg./Tab. Bot. 100s, 500s.
Use: Treatment of Parkinson's disease and syndrome.

LAROTID. (Beecham Labs) Amoxicillin. **Cap.:** 250 mg. Bot. 18s, 100s, 500s. Tel-E-Dose 100s. 500 [illegible] Bot. 18s, 50s, 500s. Tel-E-Dose 100s. **Oral Suspe[illegible] sion:** 125 mg. or 250 mg. (as trihydrate)/5 ml. B[illegible] 80 ml., 100 ml., 150 ml. **Pediatric drops:** 50 mg. (as trihydrate)/1 ml. Bot. 15 ml.

LAROXYL HYDROCHLORIDE. Amitriptyline, B.A.N.

LARYLGAN THROAT SPRAY. (Ayerst) Antipyrine 0.3%, pyrilamine maleate 0.05%, sodium capryla[illegible] 0.50%, w/alcohol 1%, methyl salicylate, benzyl alcohol 0.05%, methylparaben, propylparaben, gentian violet, menthol, isobornyl acetate, aromatics, glycerin, sod. saccharin. Bot. 28 ml. (0.94 fl. oz.)
Use: Throat spray.

LARYNEX. (Dover) Benzocaine lozenges. Sugar, lactose and salt free. Unit dose Box 500s.
Use: Sore throat relief.

• **LASALOCID.** USAN.
Use: Coccidiostat.

LASAN CREAM. (Stiefel) Anthralin 0.1%, 0.2%, or 0.4%. Tube 65 Gm.
Use: Psoriasis treatment.

LASAN HP-1 CREAM. (Stiefel) Anthralin 1%. Tube 65 Gm.
Use: Psoriasis treatment.

LASAN NASAL SPRAY. (Eastwood) Bot. 2/3 oz.

LASAN OINTMENT. (Stiefel) Anthralin 0.4% in ointment base. Tube 60 Gm.
Use: Psoriasis treatment.

LASIX. (Hoechst) Furosemide **Tab.:** 20 mg., 40 mg/Tab. Bot. 100s, 500s, 1000s. Unit Dose 100s; 40 mg./Tab. Unit of Use 100s; 80 mg./Tab. Bot. 50s. Unit Dose 100s. **Inj.:** 2 ml./Amp. Box 5s, 50s; 4 ml./Amp. Box 5s, 25s; 10 ml./Amp. Box 5s, 25s; Syringes 2 ml., 4 ml., 10 ml. Box 5s. **Oral Soln.:** Drop. Bot 60 ml.; Bot. 120 ml. w/spoon. mg./cc.
Use: Diuretic, antihypertensive.

LASSAR'S PASTE.
See: Zinc Oxide Paste, U.S.P. XXI. (Various Mfr.)

LAUDACIN. (Sutliff and Case) Opium 10 mg./15 cc. Syr. Bot. 3 oz., pt., gal.
Use: Diarrhea.

LAUDEXIUM METHYLSULFATE. B.A.N. Decamethylene-α, ω-bis-(1-(3′, 4′-dimethoxybenzyl)-1,-2,3,4-tetrahydro-6,7-dimethoxy-2-methylisoquinolinium methosulfate. Laudolissin.
Use: Neuromuscular blocking agent.

LAUD-IRON. (Amfre-Grant) Ferrous fumarate 5 gr./Tab. Bot. 100s, 1000s. Liq. Bot. 4 oz.
Use: Iron deficiency anemia.

LAUD-IRON-C. (Amfre-Grant) Ferrous fumarate 200 mg., ascorbic acid 150 mg./Gradual. Bot. 100s.

LAUD IRON FOLIC TABLETS. (Amfre-Grant) Ferrous fumarate 320 mg., folic acid 800 mcg., ascorbic acid 500 mg./Tab. Bot. 100s, 1000s.
Use: Iron supplement.

LAUD-IRON FORTE. (Federal) Ferrous fumarate 5 gr., Vit. B-12 50 mcg., B-12 w/Intrinsic Factor concentrate 0.5 I.U., C 100 mg., folic acid 1 mg., B-1 7.5 mg., B-2 5 mg., B-6 5 mg., niacinamide 25 mg., pantothenic acid 5 mg./Tab. Bot. 100s, 500s. Sol. Vial 30 cc.
Use: Hematinic.

LAUD-IRON PLUS. (Amfre-Grant) Ferrous fumarate 100 mg., B-12 5 mcg., D-sorbitol 500 mg./Chewable Tab. Bot. 100s, 1000s.
Use: Iron deficiency anemia.

LAUD-IRON SUSPENSION. (Amfre-Grant) Ferrous fumarate 100 mg./5 cc. Bot. pt.
Use: Hematinic.

LAURETH 4. USAN.
Use: Pharmaceutic aid.

LAURETH 9. USAN. Mixture of polyoxyethylene lauryl ethers having a statistical average of 9 ethylene oxide groups per molecule.
Use: Surfactant, emulsifier, spermaticide.

LAURETH 10S. USAN.
Use: Spermaticide.

LAUROCAPRAM. USAN.
Use: Pharmaceutical aid.

LAURO EYE WASH. (Otis Clapp) Boric acid, sodium chloride. Bot. 0.5 oz., 4 oz., irrigator bot.
Use: Eye wash and tear substitute.

LAUROLINIUM ACETATE. B.A.N. 4-Amino-1-dodecylquinaldinium acetate. Laurodin.
Use: Surface active agent.

LAUROMACROGOL 400. Laureth 9.

• **LAURYL ISOQUINOLINIUM BROMIDE.** USAN.
Use: Anti-infective.

LAURYL SOLUTION. (Knight) Bot. pt.
Use: Acid vaginal douche.

LAURYL SULFOACETATE.
See: Lowila, Cake, Liq., Oint. (Westwood)

LAVACOL. (Parke-Davis) Ethyl alcohol 70%. Plastic Bot. 1 pt.

LAVATAR. (Doak) Coal tar distillate 25.5% in a bath oil base. Liq. Bot. 4 oz., 1 pt.
Use: Treatment of dermatoses, and psoriasis of the scalp.

• **LAVENDER OIL,** N.F. XVI.
Use: Perfume.

LAVOPTIK EMERGENCY WASH. (Lavoptik) Eye, face, body wash. 32 oz./Emergency station.
Use: Emergency wash for eyes, face, body.

LAVOPTIK EYE WASH. (Lavoptik) Sodium chloride 0-49 Gm., sodium biphosphate 0.40 Gm., sodium phosphate 0.45 Gm./100 ml. w/benzalkonium chloride 0.005%. Bot. 6 oz.
Use: Eye wash, eye drop, irrigation liquid.

LAVORIS. (Vicks Prods) Zinc chloride, glycerin, poloxamer 407, saccharin, polysorbate 80, flavors, clove oil, alcohol, citric acid, water. Bot. 6, 12, 18, 24 fl. oz.
Use: Mouthwash and gargle.

LAXATAB. (Freeport) Danthron 75 mg., docusate sodium 100 mg., D-calcium pantothenate 25 mg./Tab. Bot. 1000s.
Use: Laxative.

LAXATIVE CAPS. (Weeks & Leo) Docusate sodium 100 mg., casathranol 30 mg./Cap. Bot. 30s, 60s.
Use: Management of chronic or temporary constipation.

■ **LAXATIVES.**
See: Agar-Gel (Various Mfr.)
Aloe (Various Mfr.)
Aloin (Various Mfr.)
Bile Salts (Various Mfr.)
Bisacodyl, Tab., Supp. (Various Mfr.)
Bisacodyl Tannex (Barnes-Hind)
Carboxymethylcellulose Sodium (Various Mfr.)
Casanthranol, Cap., Tab. (Various Mfr.)
Cascara Sagrada (Various Mfr.)
Cascara Sagrada Fluidextract, Liq. (Parke-Davis)
Cascara Tablets (Various Mfr.)
Castor Oil (Various Mfr.)
Correctol, Tab. (Plough)
Danthron, Tab. (Various Mfr.)
Docusate Sodium (Various Mfr.)
Ex-Lax, Tab., Powder (Ex-Lax. Inc.)
Feen-a-Mint, Gum, Mints (Plough)
Karaya Gum (Penick)
Liquid Petrolatum, Liq. (Var. Mfr.)
Magnesia Magma (Various Mfr.)
Maltsupex (Wallace)
Methylcellulose (Various Mfr.)

Mucilloid of Psyllium Seed W/Dextrose (Searle)
Natures Remedy (Norcliff Thayer)
Nujol, Liquid (Plough)
Oxyphenisatin Acetate (Various Mfr.)
Petrolatum, Liquid (Various Mfr.)
Petrolatum, Liquid, Emulsion (Various Mfr.)
Phenolphthalein (Various Mfr.)
Plantago ovata, Coating (Various Mfr.)
Poloxalkol, Cap., Sol. (Various Mfr.)
Prune Concentrate, Tab., Cap. (Various Mfr.)
Prune Preps. (Various Mfr.)
Psyllium Granules W/Dextrose (Med. Chem.)
Psyllium Husk Powder (Upjohn)
Psyllium Hydrocolloid, Pow. (Stuart)
Psyllium Hydrophilic Mucilloid (Various Mfr.)
Psyllium Seed, Gel, Granules (Various Mfr.)
Regutol, Tab. (Plough)
Sakara, Gran. (Plough)
Senna, Alexandrian, Liq., Tab. (Various Mfr.)
Senna, Cassia angustifolia, Tab. (Brayten)
Senna Conc., Standardized, Gran., Tab., Pow., Supp. (Various Mfr.)
Senna Fruit Extract, Liq. (Various Mfr.)
Sennosides A&B, Tab. (Dorsey)
Sodium Biphosphate (Various Mfr.)
Sodium Phosphate (Various Mfr.)

LAXOBERAL. Sodium Picosulphate, B.A.N.

LAXONALIN DIACETATE. Bisoxatin, B.A.N.

LAYOR CARANG.
See: Agar (Various Mfr.)

LC-65 DAILY CONTACT LENS CLEANER. (Allergan) Daily cleaning solution for all hard, soft (hydrophilic), Polycon and Paraperm oxygen gas permeable contact lenses. Plastic dropper bottle 0.5 oz., 2 oz.

L-CAINE. (Century) Lidocaine HCl 1% Inj.: 20, 50 ml. or 2%, 50 ml. Topical Liq. 4%, 50 cc.
Use: Local anesthetic.

L-CAINE E. (Century) Lidocaine HCl 1% or 2%, epinephrine 1:100,000/cc. Inj. 20 cc., 50 cc.
Use: Local anesthetic.

L.C.D. (Almay) Cream Modified and Soln. Alcohol extractions of crude coal tar for eczemas, psoriasis, pruritus, etc. Bot. 4 oz., 1 pt.
See: Coal Tar Topical Soln., U.S.P. XXI.

LDH REAGENT STRIP. (Ames) Seralyzer reagent strip. Bot. 25s.
Use: A quantitative strip test for LDH in serum or plasma.

LEBER TABULAE. (Paddock) Aloe 0.09 Gm., extr. rhei 0.03 Gm., myrrh 0.01 Gm., frangula 5 mg., galbanum 2 mg., olibanum 3 mg./Tab. Bot. 100s, 500s, 1000s.

LEBER TAURINE. (Paddock) Sod. salicylate 8 gr., ox bile 2.25 gr., ext cascara 1:4 4.5 gr., pancreatin 1.25 gre., pepsin 1:10,000 3/10 gr./fl. oz. Bot. pt., gal.

LEC-E-PLEX. (Barth's) Vit. E 100 I.U., 200 I.U. or 400 I.U./Cap. w/lecithin. Bot. 100s, 500s, 1000s.

• **LECITHIN,** N.F. XVI.
(Arcum) 1200 mg./Cap. Bot. 100s, 1000s. Gran.Bot. 8 oz. Pow. Bot. 4 oz.
(Barth's) 8 gr./Cap. Bot. 100s, 500s, 1000s. Gran. Can 8 oz., 16 oz. Pow. Can 10 oz.
(Cavendish) Tab. (0.5 gr.) Bot. 500s.
(CMC) 1200 mg./Cap. Bot. 100s, 1000s.
(Quality Generics) 1200 mg., Caps. 100s.
(De Pree) Cap. Bot. 100s.
(Pfanstiehl) 25 Gm., 100 Gm., 500 Gm./Pkg.
W/Choline base, cephalin, lipositol.
See: Alcolec Cap., Granules (American Lecithin)
W/Coconut oil, pine oil, castor oil, lanolin, cholesterols, parachlorometaxylenol.
See: Sebacide, Liq. (Paddock)
W/Vitamins.
See: Acletin, Cap. (Associated Concentrates)
Lec-E-Plex, Cap. (Barth's)

LEC-KELP. (Western Research) Lecithin 100 mg., ke 25 mg., Vit. B-6 3.5 mg., cider vinegar 40 mg./Ca Bot. 1000s.

LECTRO. (Guild) Bot. 4 oz.

LEDERCILLIN VK. (Lederle) Penicillin V potassium. **Sol.:** 125 mg. & 250 mg./5 ml. 100 ml., 150 ml., 200 ml. **Tab.:** 250 mg./Tab. Bot. 100s, 1000s. Uni dose 10 × 10s; 500 mg./Tab. Bot. 100s. Unit dos 10 × 10s.
Use: Antibiotic.

LEDERMYCIN. Demeclocycline, B.A.N.

LEDERPLEX CAPSULES. (Lederle) Vit. B-1 2.25 mg B-2 2.6 mg., niacinamide 30 mg., B-6 3 mg., Ca pa tothenate 15 mg., B-12 9 mcg./Cap. Bot. 100s.
Use: Anemias.

LEDERPLEX LIQUID. (Lederle) Vit. B-1 2.25 mg., B-2 2.6 mg., niacinamide 30 mg., pantothenic acid 1 mg., Vit. B-6 3 mg., B-12 9 mcg./10 ml. Bot. 12 oz
Use: Hematinic w/vitamin B complex.

LEGIONELLA. (Wampole-Zeus) Direct fluorescent te for legionella organisms.
Use: An *in vitro* diagnostic aid for the identification of various legionella bacteria in tissue specimens, sputum, cultures.

LEGIONELLA, INDIRECT. (Wampole-Zeus) Indire fluorescent antibody test for *Legionella pneumophil*
Use: An immunofluorescent procedure for the detection of *L. pneumophilia* antibodies in human serum.

• **LEMON OIL,** N.F. XVI.
Use: Pharmaceutic aid (flavor).

LENATE. (Maurry) Phenol 2.75%, iodine & potassiur iodide 3.1%, menthol 0.55%, guaifenesin, glycerol, alcohol 2.5%. Bot. 1 oz., 4 oz., 8 oz., pt.
Use: Analgesic and antiseptic.

LENETRAN. Mephenoxalone.
Use: Tranquilizer.

LENICET.
See: Aluminum Acetate, Basic (Various Mfr.)

• **LENIQUINSIN.** USAN. 6,7-Dimethoxy-4-(veratrylideneamino) quinoline. Under study.
Use: Antihypertensive.

LENIUM MEDICATED SHAMPOO. (Winthrop Products) Selenium sulphide
Use: Medicated shampoo.

• **LENPERONE.** USAN.
Use: Antipsychotic.

ENS CLEAR. (Allergan) Sterile, isotonic solution surfactant cleaner w/sorbic acid 1%, edetate disodium 0.2%. Bot. 15 ml.
Use: Soft contact lens cleanser.

ENSEN. (Geneva) Diphenhydramine HCl 25 mg., 50 mg./Cap. Bot. 1000s.

ENSINE 5. (CooperVision) Poloxamer 407, sodium chloride, potassium chloride, hydroxyethylcellulose, polyvinyl alcohol, polyethylene glycol, benzalkonium Cl 0.01%, edetate disodium 0.05%. Bot. 2 oz., 4 oz.
Use: Hard contact lens soaking, wetting & cleaning solution.

ENSINE EXTRA STRENGTH CLEANER. (CooperVision) Cleaning agent, benzalkonium Cl, edetate disodium. Bot. 1.5 fl. oz.
Use: Hard contact lens cleaner.

ENS MATE. (Alcon) Plastic Bot. 2 oz., 6 oz.
Use: All-purpose contact lens solution.

ENS PLUS. (Allergan) Sterile, preservative-free, isotonic solution of 0.9% NaCl. Aerosol cont. 8 oz.
Use: Rinsing, heat disinfection, storage of soft contact lenses; rinsing with chemical disinfection.

ENSRINS. (Allergan) Sterile preserved saline solution for heat disinfection, rinsing and storage of soft (hydrophilic) contact lenses; rinsing solution for chemical disinfection. Bot. 8 oz.

ENS-WET. (Allergan) Bot. 0.5 fl. oz.
Use: Lubricate & rewet hard & soft (hydrophilic) contact lenses.

ENTE INSULIN. Susp. of zinc insulin crystals.
See: Iletin Lente, Vial (Lilly)

ENTE INSULIN. (Squibb/Novo) Insulin zinc suspension U-40 (40 u./cc), U-80 (80 u./cc.), and U-100 (100 u./cc) in 10 cc. vials.
Use: An intermediate acting form of insulin.

ENTIZOL HYDROCHLORIDE. Amitriptyline, B.A.N.

EPROSY THERAPY.
See: Hansen's disease

EPTAZOL.
See: Pentylenetetrazol.

ERGOBAN HYDROCHLORIDE. Diphenylpyraline, B.A.N.

LERGOTRILE MESYLATE. USAN.
Use: Enzyme inhibitor.

ERTON OVULES. (Vita Elixir) Caffeine 250 mg./Cap.
Use: Stimulant.

ESTEROL. (Dram) Nicotinic acid 500 mg./Tab. Bot. 250s.
Use: Hypercholesteremia and hyperlipemia.

ETHOPHEROL. (Nutrition) Vitamin E 100 I.U./Kapule. Bot. 100s.
Use: Dietary supplement.

LETIMIDE HCl. USAN. 3-[2-(Diethylamino)-ethyl]-2H-1,3-benzoxazine-2,4-(3H)-dione monohydrochloride.
Use: Analgesic.

ETUSIN. Naphthalene-2-sulfonate ester of levopropoxyphene. Levopropoxyphene (Lilly)

LEUCINE, U.S.P. XXI. $C_6H_{13}NO_2$. L-leucine.
Use: Amino acid.

LEUCOVORIN CALCIUM, U.S.P. XXI. Inj., U.S.P. XXI. L-Glutamic acid, N-[[(2-amino-5-formyl-1,4,5,6,7,8-hexahydro-4-oxo-6-pteridinyl)-methyl]amino]benzoyl]-, calcium salt (1:1), pentahydrate. Folinic acid-S.F. Formyl tetrahydropteroylglutamic acid, a derivative of folic acid as calcium salt. (Lederle) Injection: **Amp.** 3 mg./1ml. Box 6s. **Vial** 10 mg./ml. after reconstitution w/5 ml. sterile
Use: Antagonist of aminopterin & other folic-acid antagonists. Anti-anemic (folate-deficiency); antidote to folic acid antagonists.
See: Leucorvin Calcium, Prods. (Lederle).

■ **LEUKEMIA AGENTS.**
See: Antineoplastics.

LEUKERAN. (Burroughs Wellcome) Chlorambucil 2 mg./Tab. Bot. 50s.
Use: Orally, for the treatment of chronic lymphocyctic leukemia and malignant lymphomas.

• **LEUPROLIDE ACETATE.** USAN.
Use: Antineoplastic.

LEUROCRISTINE.
See: Vincristine Sulfate (Lilly)

LEUROCRISTINE SULFATE (1:1) (SALT). Vincristine Sulfate, U.S.P. XXI.

LEVALLORPHAN, B.A.N. 1-3-Hydroxy-N-allylmorphinan.(—)-N-Allyl-3-hydroxymorphinan.
Use: Narcotic antagonist.
See: Lorfan, Vial, Amp. (Roche)

• **LEVALLORPHAN TARTRATE,** U.S.P. XXI. Inj., U.S.P. XXI. 1-3-Hydroxy-n-allylmorphinan tartrate. 17-Allylmorphinan-3-ol tartrate (1:1).
See: Lorfan, Amp., Vial (Roche)

LEVAMFETAMINE. F.D.A. (—)-α-Methylphenethylamine.

LEVAMFETAMINE.
See: Levamphetamine (Various Mfr.)

LEVAMISOLE. B.A.N. (—)-2,3,5,6-Tetrahydro-6-phenylimidazo[2,1-b]thiazole. Ketrax.
Use: Anthelmintic.

• **LEVAMISOLE HYDROCHLORIDE.** USAN.
Use: Anthelmintic.

LEVAMPHETAMINE. B.A.N. levo-Amphetamine. Levamfetamine. Cydril succinate.
Use: Sympathomimetic.

• **LEVAMPHETAMINE SUCCINATE.** USAN. (l-isomer), 1-phenyl-2-amino propane succinate. Amphetamine, levo. 1-a-methylphenethylamine succinate.
Use: Anorexiant.
See: Amodril, Cap. (North Amer. Pharmacal)

LEVARTERENOL BITARTRATE.
See: Norepinephrine Bitartate, U.S.P. XXI.

LEVIRON. (Approved) Liver desiccated 7 gr., iron and ammonium citrate 3 gr., B-1 1 mg., B-2 0.5 mg., B-6 0.5 mg., Ca pantothenate 0.3 mg., niacinamide 2.5 mg., B-12 1 mcg./Cap. Bot. 100s, 1000s.
Use: Supplement.

LEVO-AMPHETAMINE. Alginate (l-isomer) alpha-2-phenylaminopropane succinate.
See: Levamphetamine

LEVO-AMPHETAMINE SUCCINATE.
See: Pedestal, Cap. & Tab. (Len-Tag)

• **LEVOCABASTINE HYDROCHLORIDE.** USAN.
Use: Antihistaminic.

• **LEVODOPA.** U.S.P. XXI. Cap., Tab., U.S.P. XXI. L-Tyrosine, 3-hydroxy-. (—)-3-(3,4-Dihydroxyphenyl)-L-alanine. Berkdopa; Brocadopa; Veldopa
Use: Treatment of the parkinsonian syndrome.
See: Bio Dopa, Cap. (Bio-Deriv.)
Dopar, Cap. (Norwich Eaton)
Larodopa, Tab. or Cap. (Roche)
Levopa, Cap. (ICN)
Parda, Cap. (Parke-Davis)
Rio-Dopa Caps., (D.D.R. Pharm.)
W/Carbidopa
See: Sinemet, Tab. (Merck Sharp & Dohme)

LEVO-DROMORAN. (Roche) Levorphanol tartrate, levo-3-Hydroxy-n-methylmorphinan tartrate. Amp. (2 mg./ml.; methyl and propyl parabens 0.2%, sod. hydroxide) 1 ml., Box 10s. Vial (2 mg./ml.; phenol 0.45%, sod. hydroxide) 10 ml. Tab. (2 mg.) Bot. 100s.
Use: Narcotic, analgesic.

LEVO-EPINEPHRINE BITARTRATE.
See: Lyophrin, Sol. (Alcon)

• **LEVOFURALTADONE.** USAN. 1-5-Morpholinomethyl-3-[(5-nitrofurfurylidene)amino]-2-oxazolidinone.
Use: Antibacterial; antiprotozoal.

LEVOID. (Nutrition) Levothyroxine sodium 0.1 mg., or 0.2 mg./Tab. Bot. 90s, 500s. I.M. or I.V. 0.1 mg./ml. (w/sod. formaldehyde sulfoxylate 0.1%, phenol 0.5%, sod. hydroxide, glycine buffer) Vial 10 ml.
Use: Thyroid deficiencies.

• **LEVOBUNOLOL HYDROCHLORIDE.** USAN.
Use: Anti-adrenergic.

• **LEVOMETHADYL ACETATE.** USAN.
Use: Analgesic, narcotic.

LEVOMETHORPHAN. B.A.N. (—)-3-Methoxy-N-methylmorphinan.
Use: Cough suppressant.

LEVOMORAMIDE. B.A.N. (—)-1-(3-Methyl-4-morpholino-2,2-diphenylbutyryl)pyrrolidine.
Use: Narcotic analgesic.

• **LEVONANTRADOL HYDROCHLORIDE.** USAN.
Use: Analgesic.

• **LEVONORGESTREL.** U.S.P. XXI.
Use: Progestin.

• **LEVONORGESTREL AND ETHINYL ESTRADIOL TABLETS,** U.S.P. XXI.
Use: Oral contraceptive.
See: Nordette; Tab. (Wyeth)

• **LEVONORDEFRIN,** U.S.P. XXI. l-1-(1-Aminoethyl)3,4-Dihydroxy benzyl alcohol. Levonordefrin. (-)-α-(1-Aminoethyl)-3,4-dihydroxybenzyl Alcohol.
Use: Adrenergic (vasoconstrictor).

LEVOPHED BITARTRATE. (Winthrop-Breon) Norepinephrine bitartrate 1 mg./ml. w/sod. chloride, sod. metabisulfite. 2 mg./ml. Amp. 4 ml. Box 10s.
Use: To maintain blood pressure in acute hypotensive states, adjunct in treatment of cardiac arrest & profound hypotension.

LEVOPHENACYLMORPHAN. B.A.N. (—)-3-Hydroxy-N-phenacylmorphinan.
Use: Narcotic analgesic.

LEVOPROME. (Lederle) Methotrimeprazine, 20 mg./ml. w/benzyl alcohol 0.9% w/v, disodium edetate 0.065% w/v, sod. metabisulfite 0.3% w/v. Vial, 10 ml., Amps. 1 ml., 25s.
Use: Analgesic, sedative.

• **LEVOPROPOXYPHENE.** USAN. Letusin α-(—)-Dimethylamino-3-methyl-1:2-diphenyl-2-propionyloxbutane. α-(—)-1-Benzyl-3-dimethylamino-2-methyl-1-phenylpropyl propionate. Letusin napsylate.
Use: Cough suppressant.

• **LEVOPROPOXYPHENE NAPSYLATE,** U.S.P. XXI. Cap., Oral Susp., U.S.P. XXI. 2-Naphthalenesulfoni acid compound with (—)-α-[2-(dimethylamino)-1-methylethyl]-α-phenylphenethyl propionate (1:1) monohydrate. α-1-4-Dimethylamino-1,2-diphenyl-3-methyl-2-butanol propionate 2-naphthalene-sulfona hydrate. (—)-α-4-(Dimethylamino)-3-methyl-1,2-diphenyl-2-butanol Propionate (ester) 2-Naphthale sulfonate (salt).
Use: Antitussive.

• **LEVOPROPYLCILLIN POTASSIUM.** USAN. (1) Potassium 3,3-Dimethyl-7-oxo-6-(—)-(2-phenoxybutyramido)-4-thia-1-azabicyclo[3.2.0]-heptane-2-carboxylate; (2) Potassium 6-(—)-(2-phenoxybutyramido) penicillinate.
Use: Antibacterial.

LEVORENINE.
See: Epinephrine, U.S.P. XXI. (Various Mfr.)

LEVOROXINE. (Bariatric) Sodium levothyroxine 0.05 mg./Tab., red; 0.1 mg., pink; 0.2 mg., yellow; 0.3 mg., dark blue. Bot. 100s, 500s.
Use: Thyroid therapy.

LEVORPHAN TARTRATE.

LEVORPHANOL. B.A.N. (—)-3-Hydroxy-N-methylmorphinan. Levorphan. Dromoran hydrogen tartrate.
Use: Narcotic analgesic.

• **LEVORPHANOL TARTRATE,** U.S.P. XXI. Inj., Tab. U.S.P. XXI. 1-3-Hydroxy-N-methyl-morphinan bitartrate. 17-Methylmorphinan-3-ol Tartrate (1:1)
Use: Analgesic (narcotic).
See: Levo-Dromoran, Amp., Tab., Vial (Roche)

LEVOTHROID. (USV Labs.) Levothyroxine sodium. **Tab.:** 0.025 mg., 0.05 mg, 0.75 mg. 0.1 mg., 0.125 mg., 0.15 mg., 0.175 mg., 0.2 mg., 0.3 mg./Tab. Bot. 100s, 1000s. Unit dose 100s. **Inj.:** 200 mcg. o 500 mcg./6 ml. Vial.
Use: Thyroid deficiency.

• **LEVOTHYROXINE SODIUM,** U.S.P. XXI. Tabs. U.S.P. XXI. L-Tyrosine, 0-(4-hydroxy-3,5-diiodo-phenyl)-3,5-diiodo-, monosodium salt, hydrate. Sodium L 3-[4-(4-Hydroxy-3,5-diiodophenoxy)-3,5-di-iodopheny]-alanine.
Use: Thyroid hormone.
See: Cytolen, Tab. (Len-Tag)
Levoid, Tab., Vial (Nutrition Control Products)
Noroxine, Tab. (Vortech)
Synthroid, Tab., Inj. (Flint)
W/Mannitol.
See: Synthroid, Inj. (Flint)
W/Sod. liothyronine.
Use: Thyroid hormone.
See: Thyrolar, Tab. (Armour)

LEVOXADROL HYDROCHLORIDE. USAN. l-2(2,2-Diphenyl-1,3-dioxolan-4-yl) piperidine hydrochloride. levo form of dioxadrol HCl.
Use: Local anesthetic.

.EVSIN DROPS. (Rorer) Hyoscyamine sulfate 0.125 mg., phenobarbital 15 mg./ml. Bot. 15 ml.
Use: Anticholinergic, antispasmodic, sedative.

.EVSIN ELIXIR. (Rorer) Hyoscyamine sulfate 0.125 mg., phenobarbital 15 mg./5 ml. Bot. pt.
Use: Anticholinergic, antispasmodic, sedative.

.EVSIN INJECTABLE. (Rorer) Hyoscyamine sulfacte 0.5 mg./ml. Amp. 1 ml. Box 5s. Vial 10 ml.
Use: Anticholinergic, antispasmodic.

.EVSIN TABLETS. (Rorer) Hyoscyamine sulfate 0.125 mg. Phenobarbital 15 mg./Tab. Bot. 100s, 500s.
Use: Anticholinergic, antispasmodic, sedative.

.EVSINEX TIMECAPS. (Rorer) Hyoscyamine sulfate 0.375 mg./Sustained Release Cap. Bot. 100s, 500s.
Use: Anticholinergic, antispasmodic.

.EVSINEX WITH PHENOBARBITAL TIMECAPS. (Rorer) Hyoscyamine sulfate 0.375 mg., phenobarbital 45 mg./Sustained Release Cap. Bot. 100s, 500s.
Use: Anticholinergic, antispasmodic, sedative.

.EVUCAL. (Kay) Calcium levulinate 1 Gm./10 cc. Ampules 10 cc. 25s.
Use: Calcium supplement.

.EVULOSE. Fructose.

.EVULOSE-DEXTROSE.
See: Invert Sugar.

.EVULOSE W/DEXTROSE.

.EXOCORT POWDER. (Lexington) Hydrocortisone 0.1% in a talc base. Pkg. 20 Gm.
Use: Anti-inflammatory.

.EXTRON. (Lilly) Liver-stomach conc. 50 mg., iron 30 mg., Vit. B-12 (activity equiv.) 2 mcg., B-1 1 mg., B-2 0.25 mg. w/other factors of Vit. B complex present in the liver-stomach conc./Pulvule. Bot. 84s.
Use: B complex therapy.

.EXTRON FERROUS. (Lilly) Liver-stomach conc. 50 mg., ferrous sulfate, anhy., 35 mg., Vit. B-12 (activity equiv.) 2 mcg., B-1 1 mg., B-2 0.25 mg., w/other factors of Vit. B complex present in the liver-stomach conc./Pulvule. Bot. 84s.
Use: B complex therapy with iron.

.'HOMME. (Geneva) Vit. A 4000 I.U., D 400 I.U., B-1 1 mg., B-2 1.2 mg., B-12 2 mcg., Ca Pan. 5 mg., B-3 10 mg., C 30 mg., Ca 100 mg., P 76 mg., Fe 10 mg. Mn 1 mg., Mg 1 mg., Zn 1 mg. Bot. 100s.
Use: Multiple vitamin.

.I BAN SPRAY. (Pfipharmecs) Synthetic pyrethroid 0.500%, related compounds 0.065%, aromatic petroleum hydrocarbons 0.664%. Bot. 5 oz. Box 6s.
Use: Control of lice, fleas on bedding, furniture, etc. (Not to be used on humans or animals).

.IBCO-12 INJECTION. (Blue Line) Liver injection 2.0 mcg., Vit. B-12, crystalline 15.0 mcg., iron peptonate 23.0 mg., Vit. B-1 10.0 mg., B-2 0.5 mg., B-6 1.0 mg., Ca pantothenate 1.0 mg., niacinamide 10.0 mg., phenol 0.5%, benzyl alcohol 2.0%, sodium citrate 1.0%/cc. 10 cc.

LIBIDINAL. (Everett) Vit. E 200 I.U., zinc gluconate 75 mg./Cap. Bot. 60s.
Use: Dietary supplement.

LIBRAX. (Roche) Clidinium bromide (Quarzan) 2.5 mg., chlordiazepoxide HCl (Librium) 5 mg./Cap. Bot. 100s, 500s. Prescription Pak. 50s. Teledose 100s (10 strips of 10).
Use: Gastrointestinal disorders.

LIBRITABS. (Roche) Chlordiazepoxide 5 mg., 10 mg., 25 mg./Tab. Bot. 100s, 500s.
Use: Relief of anxiety, tension, withdrawal symptoms of acute alcoholism.

LIBRIUM. (Roche) Chlordiazepoxide, HCl 5 mg., 10 mg. or 25 mg./Cap. Bot. 100s, 500s; Prescription Pak. 50s; Teledose (10 strips of 10; 4 rolls of 25) in RNP (Reverse Numbered Package); Amp. 100 mg., 10s.
Use: Relief of anxiety, apprehensions and nervous tension, withdrawal symptoms of acute alcoholism.

LIBRIUM INJECTABLE. (Roche) Chlordiazepoxide HCl 100 mg./Dry filled Amp. Special I.M. Diluent, 2 ml. for I.M. benzyl alcohol 1.5%, polysorbate 80 4%, propylene glycol 20%, w/maleic acid and sodium hydroxide to adjust pH to 3. Amp. 5 ml., Box 10s.
Use: Relief of anxiety and tension, withdrawal symptoms of acute alcoholism.

LICOPLEX. (Mills) Desiccated whole bile 2 gr., dried whole pancreatic substance ¾ gr., dl-methionine 2 gr., choline bitartrate 3 gr./Tab. Bot. 100s.
Use: Bile laxative and cholagogue.

LICOPLEX DS. (Keene) Cyanocobalamin 15 mcg., liver inj. equiv. to cyanocobalamin activity 1 mcg., ferrous gluconate 25 mg., riboflavin 0.75 mg., calcium pantothenate 1.25 mg., niacinamide 50 mg. Vial 30 ml.
Use: Multivitamin.

• **LICRYFILCON A.** USAN.
Use: Contact lens material.

• **LICRYFILCON B.** USAN.
Use: Contact lens material.

LIDA-MANTLE CREME. (Miles Pharm) Lidocaine 3% in vehicle buffered to the pH range of normal skin. Tube 1 oz.
Use: Topical anesthetic.

• **LIDAMIDINE HYDROCHLORIDE.** USAN.
Use: Antiperistaltic.

LIDEX CREAM. (Syntex) Fluocinonide 0.05% w/stearyl alcohol, polyethylene glycol 8000, propylene glycol, 1,2,6-hexanetriol, citric acid.
Use: Topical steroid.

LIDEX-E. (Syntex) Fluocinonide 0.05% in aqueous emollient base of stearyl alcohol, cetyl alcohol, mineral oil, propylene glycol, sorbitan monostearate, polysorbate 60, citric acid, purified water. Tube 15 Gm., 30 Gm., 60 Gm., 120 Gm.
Use: Topical steroid.

LIDEX GEL. (Syntex) Flucinonide 0.05% in gel base of propylene glycol, propyl gallate, edetate

disodium, carbomer 940. Tube 15 Gm., 30 Gm., 60 Gm., 120 Gm.
Use: Topical corticosteroid.

LIDEX OINTMENT. (Syntex) Fluocinonide 0.05% w/Amerchol CAB, white petrolatum, propylene carbonate, propylene glycol. Cream, Ointment. Tube 15 Gm., 30 Gm., 60 Gm., 120 Gm.
Use: Topical steriod.

LIDEX SOLUTION. (Syntex) Fluocinonide 0.05%. Bot. 20 ml., 60 ml.
Use: Topical steroid.

• **LIDOCAINE,** U.S.P. XXI. Oint., Oral Topical Sol., Sterile, Topical Aerosol, U.S.P. XXI. 2-Diethylamino-2′,6′-acetoxylidide. Acetamide, 2-(diethylamino)-N-(2,6-dimethylphenyl)-
Use: Local anesthetic.

• **LIDOCAINE AND EPINEPHRINE INJECTION,** U.S.P. XXI.
Use: Local anesthetic.
See: L-Caine E, Vial (Century)
Norocaine 1%, 2% w/Epinephrine. (Vortech)
Xylocaine W/Epinephrine, Sol. (Astra)

• **LIDOCAINE HYDROCHLORIDE,** U.S.P. XXI. Inj., Jelly, Topical Sol., U.S.P. XXI. Acetamide, 2-(diethylamino)-N-(2,6-dimethylphenyl)-, HCl. 2-Diethylamino-2′,6′-acetoxylidide HCl.
Use: Cardiac depressant (anti-arrhythmic); local anesthetic.
(Abbott) **0.2%, 0.4% or 0.8%:** w/5% Dextrose. 250 ml. single-dose containers; **1% or 2%.** Abboject syringes 5 ml.; 1 Gm, 2 Gm. Vial. Premixed: 0.2%, 0.4% in 5% dextrose inj./500 ml. Flex. or glass containers. **1%:** 2 ml. or 5 ml. single-dose amp. **1.5%:** 20 ml. single-dose amp. **2%:** 10 ml./20 ml. vial (for dilution to prepare I.V. drip soln.) **5%:** w/ 7.5% Dextrose amp. 2 ml.
(CMC) 1%, 2%. Vial 50 cc.
(Maurry) 2%. Vial.
(Pharmex) 1%, 2%. Vial 50 cc.
Use; Injection for infiltration block anesthesia and I.V. drip for cardiac arrhythmias.
See: Anestacon, Liq. (Webcon)
Ardecaine 1%, 2%, Inj. (Burgin-Arden)
Dolicaine, I.M. (Reid-Provident)
L-Caine, Inj., Liq. (Century)
Nervocaine, Inj. (Keene)
Norocaine, Inj. (Vortech)
Rocaine, Inj. (Rocky Mtn.)
Stanacaine (Standex)
T-CAIN, Inj. (Tunex)
Xylocaine Hydrochloride, Prep. (Astra)
W/Benzalkonium chloride.
See: Medi-Quik, Aerosol (Lehn & Fink)
Medi-Quick Pump Spray (Lehn & Fink)
W/Benzalkonium chloride, phenol, menthol, eugenol, oil thyme, oil eucalyptus.
See: Unguentine Spray (Norwich)
W/Cetyltrimethylammonium bromide, hexachlorophene.
See: Aerosept, Aerosol (Dalin)
W/Hydrocortisone, clioquinol.
See: Bafil, Lot. (Scruggs)
Hil-20 Lotion (Reid-Provident)
W/Dextrose.
W/Methylparaben, sodium chloride.
See: Nulicaine, Vial (Kay)
W/Methyl parasept.
See: L-Caine, Inj. (Century)
W/Methyl parasept, epinephrine.
See: L-Caine-E, Inj. (Century)
W/Orthohydroxyphenyl mercuric chloride, menthol, camphor, allantoin.
See: Kip First Aid preps. (Youngs Drug)
W/Parachlorometaxylenol, phenol, zinc oxide.
See: Unguentine Plus, Cream (Norwich)
W/Polymyxin B sulfate.
See: Lidosporin, Otic Soln. (Burroughs-Wellcome)
W/Testosterone, estrone, liver inj., niacinamide, panthenol, Vit. B complex.

• **LIDOCAINE HYDROCHLORIDE AND DEXTROSE INJECTION,** U.S.P. XXI.

• **LIDOCAINE HYDROCHLORIDE AND EPINEPHRINE BITARTRATE. INJECTION,** U.S.P. XXI.

• **LIDOCAINE HYDROCHLORIDE AND EPINEPHRINE INJECTION,** U.S.P. XXI.

• **LIDOFENIN.** USAN.
Use: Diagnostic aid.

• **LIDOFILCON A.** USAN.
Use: Contact lens material.

• **LIDOFILCON B.** USAN.
Use: Contact lens material.

• **LIDOFLAZINE.** USAN. 4-[4,4-bis(p-Fluro-phenyl)-butyl]-1-piperazineaceto-2′,6′-xylidide. 4-[3-(4,4′-Difluorobenzhydryl)propyl]piperazin-1-ylacet-2′,6′-xylidide.
Use: Cardiovascular agent.

LIDOJECT-1. (Mayrand) Lidocaine HCl 1%. Vial 50 ml.
Use: Local anesthetic.

LIDOJECT-2. (Mayrand) Lidocaine HCl 2%. Vial 50 ml.
Use: Local anesthetic.

LIDOX CAPS. (Major) Chlordiazepoxide HCl, clindinium. Bot. 100s, 1000s.
Use: Tranquilizer.

LIDOXIDE. (Interstate) Chlordiazepoxide HCl 5 mg., clidinium bromide 2.5 mg./Tab. Bot. 100s, 500s.
Use: Gastrointestinal disorders.

LIFER-B. (Burgin-Arden) Cyanocobalamin 30 mcg., liver inj. 0.1 cc., ferrous gluconate 100 mg., riboflavin 1.5 mg., panthenol 2.5 mg., niacinamide 100 mg., citric acid 16.4 mg., sodium citrate 23.6 mg./cc. Vial 30 cc.

LIFE SAVER KIT. (Whiteworth) Ipecac syrup two 1 oz. Bot.; Activated charcoal powder 1 oz.; poison treatment instruction booklet.
Use: Treatment of poisonings.

LIFE SPANNER. (Spanner) Vit. A 12,500 I.U., D 400 I.U., E 5 I.U., B-1 10 mg., B-2 5 mg., B-6 2 mg., B-12 5 mcg., niacinamide 50 mg., Ca pantothenate 1 mg., biotin 10 mcg., C 100 mg., hesperidin complex 10 mg., rutin 20 mg., choline bitartrate 40 mg., inositol 30 mg., betaine anhydrous 15 mg., l-lysine monohydrochloride 25 mg., Fe 30 mg., Cu 1 mg., Mn 1 mg., K 5 mg., Ca 105 mg., P 82 mg., Mg 5.5 mg., Zn 1 mg./Cap. Bot. 100s.
Use: Nutritional supplement.

LIFIBRATE. USAN.
Use: Antihyperlipoproteinemic.

LIFOCORT-100. (Hauck) Hydrocortisone sodium succinate 100 mg./Mono-mix vial. Vial 2 ml.
Use: Glucocorticoid.

LIFOJECT. (Mayrand) Liver, folic acid, Vit. B-12. Vial 10 ml.

LIFOL-B. (Burgin-Arden) Liver Inj. 10 mcg., folic acid 1 mg., cyanocobalamin 100 mcg., phenol 0.5%/cc. Vial 10 cc.

LIFOLBEX. (Central) Cyanocobalamin 100 mcg., folic acid 1.0 mg., liver inj. 0.5 ml./ml. w/phenol 0.5%. Vial 10 cc. Box 12s.
Use: Triple antimacrocytic-anemia preparation.

LIFOLEX. (Pasadena Research) Liver inj. 10 mcg., cyanocobalamin 100 mcg., folic acid 5 mg./cc. Vial 10 cc.

LIFOMIN. (Kay) Liver, beef (equiv. to cyanocobalamin 10 mcg.), folic acid 10 mg., B-12 crystalline 100 mcg., phenol 0.5%/ cc. Multiple dose sterile vial 10 cc.

LIGNOCAINE. B.A.N. N-(Diethylaminoacetyl)-2,6-xylidine. Duncaine; Lidothesin; Lignostab; Xylocaine; Xylotox.
Use: Local anesthetic.
See: Lidocaine, Oint. U.S.P. XXI. (Various Mfr.)

LILLY BULK PRODUCTS. (Lilly) The following products are supplied by Eli Lilly under the U.S.P., N.F. or chemical name as a service to the health professions:

Ammoniated Mercury Ointment
Amyl Nitrite
Analgesic Balm
Apomorphine Hydrochloride
Aromatic Elixir
Aromatic Ammonia
Atropine Sulfate
Bacitracin Ointment
Belladonna Extract, Tablets
Belladonna Tincture
Benzoin
Boric Acid
Calcium Gluceptate
Calcium Gluconate
Calcium Gluconate with Vitamin D
Calcium Hydroxide
Calcium Lactate
Carbarsone
Cascara, Aromatic, Fluidextract
Cascara Sagrada Fluidextract
Citrated Caffeine
Cocaine Hydrochloride
Codeine Phosphate
Codeine Sulfate
Colchicine
Compound Benzoin
Dibasic Calcium Phosphate
Diethylstilbestrol
Ephedrine Sulfate
Ferrous Gluconate
Ferrous Sulfate
Folic Acid
Glucagon for Injection
Green Soap Tincture
Heparin Sodium
Histamine Phosphate
Ipecac
Isoniazid
Isopropyl Alcohol, 91%
Liver, Vials for Injection
Magnesium Sulfate
Mercuric Oxide, Yellow
Methadone Hydrochloride
Methenamine for Timed Burning
Methytestosterone
Milk of Bismuth
Morphine Sulfate
Myrrh
Neomycin Sulfate
Niacin
Niacinamide
Nitroglycerin
Opium (Deorderized)
Ox Bile Extract
Pancreatin
Papaverine Hydrochloride
Paregoric
Penicillin G Potassium
Phenobarbital
Phenobarbital Sodium
Potassium Chloride
Potassium Iodide
Powder Papers (Glassine)
Progesterone
Propylthiouracil
Protamine Sulfate
Pyridoxine Hydrochloride
Quinidine Gluconate
Quinidine Sulfate
Quinine Sulfate
Reserpine
Riboflavin
Silver Nitrate
Sodium Bicarbonate
Sodium Chloride
Sodium Iodide
Sodium Salicylate
Streptomycin Sulfate
Sulfadiazine
Sulfapyridine
Sulfur
Terpin Hydrate
Terpin Hydrate and Codeine
Testosterone Propionate
Thiamine Hydrochloride
Thyroid
Tubocurarine Chloride
Tylosterone
Whitfield's Ointment
Wild Cherry Syrup
Zinc Oxide
Zinc Oxide Paste

LIMARSOL.
See: Acetarsone (City Chemical)

LIMBITROL 5-12.5. (Roche) Chlordiazepoxide 5 mg., amitriptyline HCl 12.5 mg./Tab. Bot. 100s, 500s.

Tel-E-Dose 100s. Prescription paks 50s. Rolls (4 rolls of 25).
Use: Treatment of moderate to severe depression associated with anxiety.

LIMBITROL 10-25. (Roche) Chlordiazepoxide 10 mg., amitriptyline HCl 25 mg./Tab. Bot. 100s, 500s. Tel-E-Dose 100s. Prescription paks 50s. Rolls (4 rolls of 25).
Use: Treatment of moderate to severe depression associated with anxiety.

LIMBO. (Eckerd) All-purpose liniment for sore muscles. Bot. 4 oz.

• **LIME,** U.S.P. XXI.
Use: Pharmaceutical necessity.

• **LIME SOLUTION, SULFURATED,** U.S.P. XXI.
Use: Scabicide.

LIME SULFUR SOLUTION. Calcium polysulfide and calcium thiosulfate.
Use: Scabicide.
See: Vlem-Dome, Liq. Conc. (Miles Pharm)

LINCOCIN. (Upjohn) Lincomycin HCl 500 mg./Cap. Bot. 24s, 100s. **Pediatric.** 250 mg./Cap. Bot. 24s.
Use: Antibiotic against *staphylococci, streptococci, pneumococci.*

LINCOCIN STERILE SOLUTION. (Upjohn) Lincomycin HCl equiv. to 300 mg. lincomycin base, benzyl alcohol 9.45 mg./ml. Lincomycin HCl 600 mg., benzyl alcohol 9.45 mg./ml. Vials 2 ml., 10 ml. U-Ject. 2 ml. in 5s, 25s, 100s.
Use: Treatment of serious infections.

• **LINCOMYCIN.** USAN. Antibiotic produced by *Streptomyces lincolnensis.* Methyl 6,8-Di-deoxy-6-(1-methyl-4-propyl-L-2-pyrrolidine-carboxamido)-1-thio-D-Erythro-α-D-galacto-octopyranoside.
Use: Antibiotic-infections due to gram-positive organisms.

• **LINCOMYCIN HYDROCHLORIDE,** U.S.P. XXI. Inj., Cap., Sterile, Syrup, U.S.P. XXI. D-erythro-α-D-galacto-Octopyranoside, methyl-6,8-dideoxy-6-[[1-methyl-4-propyl-2-pyrrolidinyl)carbonyl]amino]-1-thio, HCl.
Use: Antibacterial.
See: Lincocin, Cap., Sol., Syr. (Upjohn)

• **LINDANE,** U.S.P. XXI. Cream, Lot., Shampoo, U.S.P. XXI. Gamma-benzene-hexachloride, hexachlorocyclohexane.
Fidelity Lab.—Pow. 50%, Pkg. 1 lb., 5 lb.
Imperial—Pow. 50%, Pkg. 1 lb., 4 lb.; 12%, Pkg. 1 lb., 4 lb.
Use: Pediculicide, scabicide.
See: Kwell, Cream, Lot. & Shampoo (Reed & Carnrick)

LINDORA. (Westwood) Sodium laureth sulfate, water, cocamide DEA, NaCl, lactic acid, tetra sodium EDTA, benzophenone-4, FD&C Blue #1 and fragrance. Bot. 8 oz.
Use: Soap free lathering cleanser for sensitive skin.

LINIMENTO NO. 1. (D'Franssia)
Use: Arthritis, rheumatism cold aid.

LINODIL CAPSULES. (Winthrop Products) Inositol hexanicotinate.
Use: Hypolipedemic, peripheral vasodilator.

• **LINOGLIRIDE FUMARATE.** USAN.
Use: Antidiabetic.

LINOLENIC ACID W/VIT. E.
See: Petropin, Cap. (Lannett)

LINOLESTROL. (Vortech) Jar. 1 oz., 16 oz.
Use: Allergic skin conditions.

LINUCEE TABLETS. (Fellows) Vit. B-1 15 mg., B-2 1[illegible] mg., B-6 10 mg., nicotinic acid 100 mg., pantholate 2[illegible] mg., B-12 10 mcg., biotin 50 mcg./Tab. Bot. 100s.

LIORESAL. (Geigy) Baclofen 10 mg. or 20 mg./Tab. Bot. 100s. Unit Dose 100s.
Use: Muscle relaxant, antispasmodic.

LIOTHYRONINE. B.A.N. 3-[4-(4-Hydroxy-3-iodophenoxy)-3,5-di-iodophenyl]- -alanine. (—)-Tri-iodothyronine. Cynomel and Tertroxin sodium derivative.
Use: Thyroid hormone.

• **LIOTHYRONINE I-125.** USAN.
Use: Radioactive agent.

• **LIOTHYRONINE I-131.** USAN.
Use: Radioactive agent.

LIOTHYRONINE RESIN.

• **LIOTHYRONINE SODIUM,** U.S.P. XXI., Tabs. U.S.P. XXI. L-Tyrosine, 0-(4-hydroxy-3-iodophenyl)-3,5-diiodo-, sod. salt. Sod. L-triiodo-thyronine. Sod. L-4-(3-iodo-4-hydroxphenoxy)-3,5-diiodo-phenylalanine.
Use: Thyroid hormone.
See: Cytomel, Tab. (SmithKline)

• **LIOTRIX,** U.S.P. XXI. A combination of sod. levothyroxine & sod. 1-triiodothyronine in a ratio of 4 to 1 by weight.
Use: Thyroid hormone.
See: Euthroid, Tab. (Parke-Davis)
Thyrolar, Tab. (Armour)

LIPASE. W/Amylase, Protease.
Use: Digestive enzyme.
W/Amylase, bile salts, wilzyme, pepsin, pancreatin, calcium.
See: Enzyme, Tab. (Barth's)
W/Amylase, protease, cellase, hyoscine HBr,
See: Am-Zyme, Tab. (Vortech)
W/Amylase, protease, simethicone.
See: Tri-Cone, Cap. (Meyer)
W/Alpha-amylase W-100, proteinase W-300, cellase W-100, estrone, testosterone, vitamins, minerals.
See: Geramine, Tab. (Brown)
W/Alpha-Amylase, proteinasa, cellase
See: Kutrase (Kremers-Urban)
Ku-Zyme (Kremers-Urban)
W/Amylolytic, proteolytic, cellulolytic enzymes.
See: Arco-Lase, Tab. (Arco)
W/Amylolytic, proteolytic, cellulolytic enzymes, phenobarbital, hyoscyamine sulf., atropine sulf.
See: Arco-Lase Plus, Tab. (Arco)
W/Pancreatin, protease, amylase.
See: Dizymes, Caps. (Recsei)
W/Pepsin, homatropine methyl Br, amylase, protease, bile salts.
See: Digesplen, Tab., Elix., Drops (Med. Prod. Panamericana)

LIPKOTE SPF 15 ULTRA SUNSCREEN LIPBALM. (Plough) Tube 0.15 oz.
Use: Ultraviolet sunscreen.

POCHOLINE. See: Choline dihydrogen citrate. (Various Mfr.)

PODERM. (Spirt) Pancreas, whole hog 500 mg., Vit. B-6 3 mg., Cap. Bot. 180s, 500s.
Use: Orally, treatment of psoriasis.

POFLAVANOID CAPSULES. (CooperVision) Choline, inositol, B-1, B-2, niacinamide, pantothenic acid, B-6, B-12, C, lemon bioflavanoid complex./Cap. Bot. 100s, 500s.
Use: Vitamin supplement.

PO GANTRISIN. (Roche) Acetyl Sulfisoxazole 1 Gm./5 ml. in a palatable, readily digestible vegetable oil emulsion. Bot. 16 oz.
Use: Systemic and urinary tract infections.

PO-HEPIN/BL. (Riker) Heparin sodium injection, U.S.P. aqueous. Derived from beef lung. Amp. Vial.
Use: Anticoagulant.

PO-K CAPSULES. (Marcen) Epinephrine-neutralizing factor 25 u., pancreatic lipotropic factor 1.2 mg., Cy-mucopolysaccharides 2.5 mg., choline bitartrate 100 mg., dl-methionine 50 mg., inositol 25 mg., bile extract 5 mg./Cap. Bot. 100s, 500s, 1000s.
Use: Treatment of circulatory disturbances.

PO-K INJECTABLE. (Marcen) Pancreatic lipotropic factor 1.2 mg., epinephrine-neutralizing factor 25 u., Cy-mucopolysaccharides 0.5 mg., sod. citrate 10 mg., inositol 5 mg., phenol 0.5%/cc. multidose vials 10 cc., 30 cc.
Use: Treatment of circulatory disturbances.

POLYTIC ENZYME.
/Proteolytic enzyme, amylolytic enzyme, cellulolytic enzyme, methyl polysiloxane, ox bile, betaine HCl.
See: Zymme, Cap. (Scrip)

POMUL. (Upjohn) Corn oil 10 Gm./15 ml. w/d-Alpha tocopheryl acetate, butylated hydroxy-anisole, polysorbate 80, glyceride phosphates, sod. saccharin, sod. benzoate 0.05%, benzoic acid 0.05%, sorbic acid 0.07%. Bot. pt.
Use: Underweight in the malnourished.

PO-NICIN/100 mg. (Brown) Nicotinic acid 100 mg., niacinamide 75 mg., Vit. C 150 mg., B-1 25 mg., B-2 2 mg., B-6 10 mg./Tab. Bot. 100s, 500s.
Use: Vasodilator, peripheral.

PO-NICIN/250 mg. (Brown) Nicotinic acid 250 mg., niacinamide 75 mg., Vit. C 150 mg., B-1 25 mg., B-2 2 mg., B-6 10 mg./Tab. Bot. 100s, 500s.

PO-NICIN/300 mg. Timed Caps. (Brown) Nicotinic acid 300 mg., Vit. C 150 mg., B-1 25 mg., B-2 2 mg., B-6 10 mg./T.R. Cap. Bot. 100s, 500s.

POSYN. (Abbott) Intravenous fat emulsion containing safflower oil 10%, egg phosphatides 1.2%, glycerin 2.5% in water for injection. **10%:** Single-dose containers 50 ml., 100 ml., 200 ml., or 500 ml. Syringe Pump Unit 50 ml. single-dose. **20%:** Single-dose containers 200 ml. or 500 ml. Syringe Pump Unit 25 ml. or 50 ml. single-dose.
Use: Parenteral source of essential fatty acids; parenteral nutrition.

POSYN II. (Abbott) Intravenous fat emulsion: **10%:** Emulsion consisting of 5% safflower oil, 5% soybean oil. **20%:** Emulsion of 10% safflower oil, 10% soybean oil w/1.2% egg phosphatides, 2.5% glycerin. 10% Bot. 100 ml., 200 ml., 500 ml.: 20% 200 ml., 500 ml. Bot. Syringe pump units of 25, 50 ml.
Use: Energy source and prevention of essential fatty acid deficiency.

LIPOTIN. (Galen) Ferric ammonium citrate 500 mg., Vit. B-1 12 mg., B-2 6 mg., B-6 0.6 mg., folic acid 0.5 mg., Ca pantothenate 6 mg., niacinamide 15 mg., Mg 2 mg., Mn 1 mg., Co 0.1 mg., Zn 2 mg., choline 100 mg., inositol 100 mg., alcohol 12%/fl. oz. Bot. pt.

LIPOTIN TABLETS. (Galen) Choline bitartrate 83.3 mg., dl-methionine 50 mg., inositol 33.3 mg., whole desic. liver 33.3 mg., B-cotrate 33.3 mg., Vit. B-1 0.5 mg., B-2 0.3 mg., B-6 0.03 mg., d-calcium pantothenate 1.6 mg., niacinamide 5 mg./Tab. Bot. 100s, 1000s.

LIPOTRIAD CAPSULES. (CooperVision) Vit. B-1, B-2, B-6, B-12, niacin, choline, pantothenic acid, inositol. See labeled strength. Bot. 100s, 1000s.
Use: Vitamin supplement.

LIPOTRIAD LIQUID. (CooperVision) Vit. B-1, B-6, B-12, niacin, choline, pantothenic acid, inositol, niacinamide. See labeled strength. Bot. 16 fl. oz.
Use: Vitamin supplement.

■ **LIPOTROPIC AGENTS.**
See: Betaine Products (Var. Mfr.)
Choline Products (Various Mfr.)
Cho-Meth, Vial (Med. Chem.)
Cytellin, Susp. (Lilly)
Inositol Products (Various Mfr.)
Lecithin Products (Various Mfr.)
Methionine Products (Various Mfr.)

LIPOXIDE CAPS. (Major) Chlordiazepoxde HCl 5 mg. or 10 mg./Cap. Bot. 1000s. 25 mg./Cap. Bot. 500s.
Use: Tranquilizer.

LIPOZYME TABLETS. (Inwood) Choline, methionine, and inositol 1 Gm. total/Tab. Bot. 100s.
Use: Reduction of blood cholesterol level.

LIPPES LOOP. (Ortho) Intrauterine double-S. Sizes A, B, C, D.
Use: Contraceptive.

LIQUAEMIN SODIUM. (Organon) Heparin sod. aq. sol. **Vial** (20,000 u./ml.) 1 ml., 2 ml., 5 ml. 1 ml.; (5,000 u./ml.) 1 ml., 10 ml.; (10,000 u./ml.) 1 ml., 4 ml.; (1000 u./ml.) 10 ml., 30 ml., Box 25s. (40,000 u./ml.) .
Use: I.V., Sub. Q.: Anticoagulant.

LIQUA-GEL. (Paddock) Boric acid, glycerine, propylene glycol, methylparaben, propylparaben, irish moss ext., methylcellulose. Bot. 4 oz., 16 oz.

LIQUAMAR. (Organon) Phenprocoumon 3 mg./Tab. Bot. 100s.
Use: Anticoagulant.

LIQUID ANTIDOSE. (U.S. Products) Liquid activated charcoal 40 Gm./200 ml. of suspension. Dispensing jar.
Use: Poison antidote.

LIQUI-DOSS. (Ferndale) Docusate sodium 60 mg., mineral oil. Bot. pt.
Use: Stool softener.

LIQUID LATHER. (Ulmer) Gentle wash for hands, body face, hair. Bot. 8 oz., Gal.
Use: Cleanser.

LIQUID PETROLATUM EMULSION.
See: Mineral Oil Emulsion, U.S.P. XXI.

LIQUID PRED SYRUP. (Muro) Prednisone 5 mg./5 ml. in syrup base. Bot. 120 ml., 240 ml.
Use: Anti-inflammatory.

LIQUIFILM FORTE. (Allergan) Enhanced artificial tears w/polyvinyl alcohol 3%, thimerosal 0.002%, edetate disodium in a buffered sterile, isotonic solution. Bot. 0.5 fl. oz., 1 fl. oz.
Use: Artificial tears.

LIQUIFILM TEARS. (Allergan) Polyvinyl alcohol 1.4%, chlorobutanol 0.5% w/sod. chloride and purified water. Bot. 15 ml., 30 ml.

LIQUIFILM WETTING SOLUTION. (Allergan) Polyvinyl alcohol, hydroxypropyl methylcellulose, edetate disodium, NaCl, KCl and benzalkonium chloride. Bot. 20 ml., 60 ml.
Use: Hard contact lens wetting solution.

LIQUIMAT. (Owen) Sulfur 5%, alcohol 22%, in drying make-up base. Plastic Bot. 1.5 oz. 5 Shades.
Use: Medicated cover-up for pimples, oily skin & acne.

LIQUI-NOX. (Alconox) 1 qt., 1 gal.
Use: Optimum combination of anionic and nonionic detergents and wetting agents.

LIQUIPRIN. (Norcliff Thayer) Acetaminophen 80 mg./1.66 ml. Solution. Bot. 35 ml. w/dropper.
Use: Analgesic; antipyretic.

LIQUOPHYLLINE. (Paddock) Theophylline 80 mg., alcohol 20%/15 ml. Bot. pt., 0.5 gal., gal.
Use: Asthma.

LIQUOR CARBONIS DETERGENS.
See: Coal Tar Topical Soln., U.S.P. XXI. (Various Mfr.)

LIRON B-12 1000. (Kenyon) Vit. B-12 1000 mcg., liver 2 mcg., iron peptonate 20 mg., cobalt Cl 0.2 mg., Vit. B-1 10 mg., B-6 1 mg., B-2 1 mg./cc. Vial 10 cc.

LIRON B-12 50. (Kenyon) Same formula as Liron B-12 1000, except B-12 50 mg./cc. Vial 10 cc.

LISACORT. (Fellows) Prednisone 5 mg./Tab. Bot. 100s, 1000s, 5000s.
Use: Rheumatoid arthritis and other rheumatic disorders.

• **LISINOPRIL.** USAN.
Use: Antihypertensive.

LISIUM HYDROCHLORIDE. Chlorhexidine, B.A.N.

LISTEREX SCRUB MEDICATED LOTION. (Warner-Lambert) Salicylic acid 2% lotion. Golden & Herbal. Bot. 4 oz., 8 oz.
Use: Acne cleansing scrub.

LISTERINE ANTISEPTIC. (Warner-Lambert) Thymol, eucalyptol, methyl salicylate, menthol. Bot. 3 oz., 6 oz., 12 oz., 18 oz., 24 oz., 32 oz.
Use: Oral antiseptic.

LISTERINE ANTISEPTIC THROAT LOZENGES. (Warner-Lambert) Hexylresorcinol 2.4 mg./Loz. Regular and lemon-mint flavors. Boxes 24s.
Use: Relieve minor sore throat pain.

LISTERINE MAXIMUM STRENGTH ANTISEPTIC THROAT LOZENGES. (Warner-Lambert) Hexylresorcinol 4 mg./1 oz. Box 24s.
Use: Relieve minor sore throat pain.

LISTERMINT WITH FLUORIDE. (Warner-Lambert) Sodium fluoride 0.02% w/water, alcohol, glycerin, poloxamer 407, sodium lauryl sulfate, sodium citrate, sodium saccharine, ZN chloride, citric acid, flavors and colors. Bot. 6 oz., 12 oz., 18 oz., 24 oz., 32 oz.
Use: Anticavity dental rinse & mouthwash.

LITHANE. (Miles Pharm) Lithium carbonate 300 mg./Tab. Bot. 100s, 1000s.
Use: Manic-depressive illness.

• **LITHIUM CARBONATE,** U.S.P. XXI. Cap., Tab. U.S.P. XXI. Carbonic acid, dilithium salt.
Use: Antidepressant.
See: Eskalith, Cap., Tab. (SmithKline)
Lithane, Tab. (Miles Pharm)
Lithobid, Tab. (Ciba)
Lithotabs, Tab. (Rowell)

LITHIUM CARBONATE CAPSULES AND TABLETS. (Roxane) Lithium carbonate 300 mg./Cap. or Tab. Bot. 100s, 1000s.
Use: Control of manic episodes in manic-depressive psychosis.

• **LITHIUM CITRATE,** U.S.P. XXI. Syrup U.S.P. XXI. CH_2 (COO Li) C (OH)(COOLi) CH_2 COO Li.x. $H_2O.C_6H_5Li_3O_7$ (Roxane) 8 m Eq./5 ml.
Use: Manic-depressive states.
See: Cibalith-SiLiq. (Ciba)
Lithonate-S, Liq. (Rowell)

• **LITHIUM HYDROXIDE,** U.S.P. XXI. $LiOH.x.H_2O$. Lithium hydroxide monohydrate.
Use: Manic-depressive states.

LITHOBID. (Ciba) Lithium carbonate 300 mg./Tab. (slow release). Bot. 100s, 1000s. Unit Dose 100s.
Use: Manic-depressive states.

LITHONATE. (Rowell) Lithium carbonate 300 mg./Cap. Bot. 100s, 1000s. Unit-of-use 90s. Unit dose 100s.
Use: Control of manic episodes in manic-depressive psychosis.

LITHOSTAT. (Mission) Acetohydroxamic acid 250 mg./Tab. Bot. 120s.
Use: Urease inhibitor.

LITHOTABS. (Rowell) Lithium carbonate 300 mg./Tab. Bot. 100s, 1000s. Unit dose 100s.
Use: Control of manic episodes in manic-depressive psychosis.

LIVEC. (Enzyme Process) Vit. A 5000 I.U., B-1 1.5 mg., B-2 1.7 mg., niacin 20 mg., C 60 mg., B-6 2 mg., pantothenic acid 10 mg., E 30 I.U., B-12 6 mcg., calcium 250 mg., iron 5 mg., D 400 I.U. folacin 0.075 mg./3 Tabs. Bot. 100s, 300s.
Use: Dietary supplement.

LIVER. (Lilly; CMC) Amp. inj. 2 mcg./ml. Bot. 10 ml., 2 mcg./ml. Bot. 30 ml., 10 mcg./ml. Bot. 10 ml., 20 mcg./ml. Bot. 10 ml.
See: Tonic 10 & 20. (Scrip)

LIVERBEX. (Spanner) Liver 2 mcg., B-1, B-2, B-6, B-12, niacinamide, pantothenate/cc. Vial 30 cc.

IVER, B-12 AND FOLIC ACID. (Lincoln) Vit. B-12 activity 5 mcg., cyanocobalamin 35 mcg., cyanocobalamin 5 mg., folic acid, w/phenol 5%, sodium citrate 0.25%, disodium sequestrene 0.01%, sodium bisulfite 0.025%/cc. Vial 15 cc.

IVER, B12 AND FOLIC ACID FORTE. (Lincoln) Vit. B-12 activity 10 mcg., cyanocobalamin 150 mcg., cyanocobalamin 10 mg., folic acid, w/phenol 0.5%, sodium citrate 0.5%, disodium sequestrene 0.01%, sodium bisulfite 0.05%/cc. Vial 15 cc.

IVER DESICCATED. Desic. liver substance.

IVER EXTRACT. Dry liver ext. W/Vit. B-12 & folic acid.

IVER-FOLIC ACID B-12. (Sandia; CMC) Vit. B-12 10 mcg., folic acid 10 mg., cyanocobalamin 100 mcg./cc. Vial 10 cc. (Medwick) Vit. B-12 10 mcg., folic acid 1 mg., cyanocobalamin 100 mcg./cc. Vial 30 cc.

LIVER FUNCTION AGENTS.
See: Bromsulphalein, Amp. (Hynson, Westcott and Dunning)
Iodophthalein (Various Mfr.)
Sulfobromophthalein Sodium, Amp. U.S.P. XXI. (Gotham)

IVERGRAN. (Rawl) Desiccated whole liver 9 Gm., Vit. B-1 18 mg., B-2 36 mg., niacinamide 90 mg., choline bitartrate 216 mg., B-6 3.6 mg., calcium pantothenate 3.6 mg., inositol 90 mg., biotin 6 mcg., Vit. B-12 5.4 mcg., methionine 198 mg., arginine 242 mg., cystine 72 mg., glutamic acid 675 mg., histidine 99 mg., isoleucine 333 mg., leucine 495 mg., lysine 297 mg., phenylalanine 189 mg., threonine 333 mg., tryptophan 45 mg., tyrosine 180 mg., valine 306 mg./3 Tsp. Bot. 15 oz.
Use: Nutritional supplement.

IVER INJECTION. Liver ext. for parental use. (Various Mfr.)

IVER INJECTION. (Arcum; Lederle) B-12 20 mcg./cc. Vial 10 cc.

IVER INJECTION, CRUDE. (Lilly) 2 mcg./ml. Vials 30 ml.; (Medwick) 2 mcg./cc. Vial 30 cc.; (Vortech) 2 mcg./cc. Vial 30 ml.
Use: General hematinic.

IVER-IRON-B COMPLEX WITH VITAMIN B-12. (Maurry) Liver inj. 2.0 mcg., B-12 15.0 mcg., ferrous gluconate 31.1 mg., B-1 10.0 mg., B-2 0.5 mg., B-6 1.0 mg., cal. pantothenate 1.0 mg., niacinamide 10.0 mg., d-Glucose 1.0%, chlorobutanol 0.5%, benzyl alcohol 2.0%/inj.
Use: Treat Vitamin B deficiencies and anemias.

IVER, IRON, FOLIC & COBALT. (Kenyon) Liver refined (B-12 eqv.) 10 mcg., iron peptonate 59 mg., cobalt gluconate 9 mg., folic acid 5 mg., procaine HCl 1%/2 cc. Vial 30 cc.

IVER IRON VITAMINS INJ. (Arcum) Liver inj. (10 mcg. B-12 Activity/cc.) 0.1 cc., crude liver inj. (2 mcg. B-12 Activity/cc.) 0.125 cc., green ferric ammonium citrate 20 mg., niacinamide 50 mg., Vit. B-6 0.3 mg., B-2 0.3 mg., procaine HCl 0.5%, phenol 0.5%/2 cc. Vial 30 cc.

IVER, IRON, VITAMINS. (CMC) Liver (B-12 eqv.) 1.0 mcg., iron gluconate 59 mg., B-2 0.3 mg., B-6 0.3 mg., niacinamide 50 mg./2 cc. Vial 30 cc.

LIVER, IRON, VITAMINS. (Kenyon) Liver (B-12 eqv.) 1 mcg., iron gluconate 59 mg., niacinamide 50 mg., Vit. B-2 (as 5-phos.) 0.3 mg., B-6 0.3 mg., sod. dicitrate 10 mg./2 cc. procaine HCl 1% Vial 30 cc.

LIVER, IRON & VITAMINS. (Pharmex) Liver inj. (equiv. to 1 mcg. B-12) 100 mg., B-12 5 mcg., B-2 0.3 mg., B-6 0.3 mg., niacinamide 50 mg., iron peptonate 19.5 mg., sod. citrate 1%, phenol 0.5%/3 cc. Vial 30 cc.

LIVER, IRON, VITAMINS AND AMINO ACIDS. (Kenyon) Liver B-12 Eqv., 1 mcg., ferrous gluconate 50 mg., B-2 (as 5-phos.) 0.5 mg., d-panthenol 2.5 mg., niacinamide 100 mg., dl-methionine 10 mg., choline chloride 5 mg./2 cc. Vial 30 cc.

LIVER, IRON, VITAMINS WITH B-12. (CMC) Liver (B-12 eqv.) 2 mcg., B-12 15 mcg., ferrous gluconate 20 mg., B-1 10 mg., B-2 0.5 mg., B-6 1 mg., d-panthenol 1 mg., niacinamide 10 mg., choline chloride 20 mg./cc., procaine HCl 0.5% Vial 30 cc.

LIVER, IRON, VITAMINS WITH B-12. (Kenyon) Liver (B-12 eqv.) 2 mcg., Vit. B-12 15 mcg., ferrous lactate 20 mg., B-1 10 mg., B-2 (as 5-phos.) 9.5 mg., B-6 1 mg., d-panthenol 1 mg., niacinamide 10 mg., choline chloride 0.5 mg./cc. Vial 30 cc.

LIVER-P (PAINLESS). (Vortech) Vit. B-12 activity 2; mcg./cc. Vial 10 cc.

LIVER, RAW.
W/Duodenum.
See: Jayron, Pow., Cap. (VioBin)

LIVER, REFINED. (Medwick) 20 mcg./cc. Vial 10 cc., 30 cc.

LIVER VASOCONSTRICTOR.
See: Kutapressin, Vial, Amp. (Kremers-Urban)

LIV-FER-B. (Sutliff & Case) Liver fraction No. 1 0.6 Gm., ferrous gluconate 0.06 Gm., mang. gluconate 10 mg., copper gluconate 0.001 Gm., zinc sulfate 0.003 Gm., Vit. B-1 2 mg., B-2 2 mg., B-12 2 mcg., alcohol 12%
niacinamide 10 mg., sod. citrate 0.6 Gm./Fl. oz., alcohol 12%. Elix. 6 oz., 1 pt., 1 gal.
Use: Hematinic.

LIV-FER-BLEX. (Sutliff & Case) Ferrous gluconate 0.022 Gm., liver conc. 0.227 Gm., thiamine HCl 1 mg., riboflavin 1 mg., niacin 10 mg., brewer's yeast 0.194 Gm./Tab. Bot. 100s, 1000s.
Use: Iron-deficiency anemias.

LIVIFOL. (Dunhall) Vit. B-12 activity from liver inj. equivalent to cyanocobalamin 10 mcg., folic acid 1 mg., cyanocobalamin 100 mcg./ml. Vial 10 ml.
Use: Vitamin, iron supplement.

LIVIPAS. Halofenate, B.A.N.

LIVI-PLEX FORTIFIED. (Rocky Mtn.) Vit. B-12 30 mcg., liver inj. 1.0 cc., ferrous gluconate 50 mg., riboflavin 1.5 mg., calcium pantothenate 2.5 mg., niacinamide 100 mg., citric acid 16.4 mg., sodium citrate 23.6 mg., benzyl alcohol 2%, procaine HCl 2%/2 cc. Vial 30 cc.

LIVITAMIN. (Beecham Labs) Ferrous fumarate 100 mg., Vit. B-1 3 mg., B-2 3 mg., B-6 3 mg., C 100 mg., niacinamide 10 mg., Ca pantothenate 2 mg., B-12 5

mcg., Cu 0.66 mg., desic. liver 150 mg./Cap. Bot. 100s.
Use: Iron and vitamin deficiency anemias.

LIVITAMIN CHEWABLE TABLETS. (Beecham Labs) Ferrous fumarate 50 mg., Vit. C 100 mg., B-1 3 mg., B-2 3 mg., niacinamide 10 mg., B-6 3 mg., Ca pantothenate 2 mg., cyanocobalamin 5 mcg., copper 0.33 mg./Tab. Bot. 100s.
Use: Iron and vitamin supplement.

LIVITAMIN W/INTRINSIC FACTOR. (Beecham Labs) Desic. liver 150 mg., ferrous fumarate 100 mg., B-1 3 mg., C 100 mg., B-2 3 mg., niacinamide 10 mg., B-12 5 mcg., B-6 3 mg., Ca pantothenate 2 mg., Cu 0.66 mg., B-12 w/intrinsic factor ⅓ u./Cap. Bot. 100s.
Use: Pernicious anemia & geriatrics.

LIVITAMIN LIQUID. (Beecham Labs) Iron peptonized N.F. 210 mg., liver fraction No. 1 0.5 Gm., B-1 3 mg., B-2 3 mg., niacinamide 10 mg., B-6 HCl 3 mg., pantothenic acid 2 mg., Vit. B-12 5 mcg., Cu 0.66 mg./15 cc. Bot. 8 oz., 1 pt., 1 gal.
Use: General hematinic.

LIVITAMIN PRENATAL. (Beecham Labs) Vit. D 400 USP units, A 6000 USP units, B-1 3 mg., B-2 3 mg., niacinamide 20 mg., pantothenic acid 5 mg., B-6 10 mg., C 100 mg., B-12 5 mcg., folic acid 0.5 mg., calcium 350 mg., Iron as Fe fumarate 50 mg./Tab. Bot. 100s.

LIVITOL. (CMC) Vit. A 2500 I.U., D 250 I.U., B-12 3 mcg., C 37.5 mg., folic acid 0.5 mg., iron 15 mg., cobalt 0.1 mg., copper 0.25 mg., liver fr. 250 mg., liver pow. 25 mg., gastric mucosa 75 mg./Vial. Mixovial 10 cc.
Use: Anemias.

LIVITOL INJ. W/VIT. C, B-12, IRON. (CMC) Vit. B-1 20 mg., B-2 3 mg., B-6 5 mg., B-12 20 mcg., C 100 mg., d-panthenol 5 mg., cyanocobalamin 5 mcg., ferrous gluconate 25 mg./cc. Mixovial 10 cc.

LIV-O-VITE. (Jenkins) Ferrous fumarate 3 gr. (elemental iron 1 gr.), desiccated liver 2 gr., thiamine HCl 3 mg., riboflavin 3 mg., cyanocobalamin 3 mcg./Tab. Bot. 1000s.

LIV-O-REX. (Nutrition) Liver, desiccated 1.4 gr., green iron & ammonium citrate 3 gr., B-1 1.5 mg., B-2 0.5 mg., calcium pantothenate 0.25 mg., B-6 0.15 mg., niacinamide 10 mg./Cap. Bot. 100s, 1000s.

LIVOREX W/B-12. (Reid-Provident) Liver inj. N.F. 20 mcg., iron and ammonium citrate 60 mg., niacinamide 50 mg., B-2 0.3 mg., B-6 0.3 mg., B-12 5 mcg., procaine HCl 1%/2 cc. Vials 30 cc.

LIVREX. (CMC) Liver extracts. Vit. B-12 2 mcg., 10 mcg. 20 mcg./cc.

LIVREX-BB. (CMC) Vit. B-12 activity eqv. to 10 mcg. cyanocobalamin, B-12 5 mcg., B-1 5 mg./cc.

LIVREX-BF. (CMC) Vit. B-12 activity eqv. to 2 mcg. cyanocobalamin, Vit. B-12 15 mcg., folic acid 5 mg./cc.

LIVREX-BF (5-5-25). (CMC) Cyanocobalamin 5 mcg., Vit. B-12 cryst. 25 mcg., folic acid 5 mg./cc.

LIVREX-BF (10-10-50). (CMC) Cyanocobalamin 10 mcg., Vit. B-12 50 mcg., folic acid 10 mg./cc.

LIVREX-BF (10-10-100). (CMC) Cyanocobalamin 10 mcg., B-12 100 mcg., folic acid 10 mg./cc.

LIVROBEN. (Forest) Liver 10 mcg., folic acid 0.5 mg., cyanocobalamin 100 mcg./ml. Vial 10 ml.

LIVTRINSIC. (Vitarine) Liver-stomach concentrate 240 mg., Vit. B-12 15 mcg., iron 110 mg., Vit. C 75 mg./Cap.
Use: Hematinic.

LIXOIL. (Lixoil Labs.) Sulfonated fatty oils and one or more esters of higher fatty acids. Bot. 16 oz.
Use: Dermatologic.

LKGB. (Image) Vitamins. Bot. 100s.
Use: Supplement.

LLD FACTOR.
See: Vitamin B-12, Prep. (Various Mfr.)

LMD. (Abbott) Low Molecular Weight Dextran. LMD 10% w/v in D5-W and LMD 10% w/v in Saline 0.9%, 500 ml. each.
Use: Enhancement of blood flow, plasma volume expander.

LMWD-DEXTRAN 40. (Pharmachem) Normal saline 0.9%, dextrose 10%.
Use: Plasma expander.

LOBAC. (Seatrace) Chlorzoxazone 250 mg., acetaminophen 300 mg./Cap. Bot. 40s, 100s, 1000s.
Use: Muscle relaxant, analgesic.

LOBAK TABLETS. (Winthrop Products) Chlormezanone, paracetamol 450 mg./Tab.
Use: Analgesic, tranquilizer.

LOBANA BODY LOTION. (Ulmer) Bot. 4 oz., 8 oz., 1 gal.
Use: Skin lotion.

LOBANA BODY POWDER. (Ulmer) All purpose body powder. Pkg. 8 oz.

LOBANA BODY SHAMPOO. (Ulmer) Bot. 8 oz., Gal.
Use: Hair & body cleanser.

LOBANA CONDITIONING SHAMPOO. (Ulmer) Bot. 8 oz., Gal.
Use: Shampoo for hair and scalp.

LOBANA DERM-ADE CREAM. (Ulmer) Vitamin A, D, E cream. Jar 2 oz., 8 oz.
Use: Red, irritated skin problems.

LOBANA LIQUID HAND SOAP. (Ulmer) 14 oz. dispenser, 16 oz. refill. Bot. 1 gal.
Use: cleanser.

LOBANA PERI-GARD. (Ulmer) Water-resistant ointment containing vitamin A & D. Jar 2 oz., 8 oz.
Use: Protect the skin from urine, feces or drainage.

LOBANA PERINEAL CLEANSE. (Ulmer) 4 oz. sprayer. Bot. 1 gal.
Use: Urine, feces, vomit cleanse.

LOBELIA FLUIDEXTRACT.
W/Hyoscyamus fl. ext., grindelia fl. ext., pot. iodide.
See: L.S. Mixture, Liq. (Paddock)

LOBELINE SULFATE.
See: Lobidram, Tab. (Dram)
Nikoban, Loz., Gum. (Thompson)
No-Kotin, Tab. (Walker)

• **LOBENDAZOLE.** USAN.
Use: Anthelmintic.

• **LOBENZARIT SODIUM.** USAN.
Use: Antirheumatic.

)BIDRAM. (Dram) Lobeline sulfate 2 mg./Tab. Pkg. 15s, 30s.
Use: Withdrawal symptoms of smoking.

)COID. (Owen) Hydrocortisone butyrate 0.1%. Tubes 15 Gm., 45 Gm.
Use: Topical anti-inflammatory.

LODOXAMIDE ETHYL. USAN.
Use: Anti-asthmatic, anti-allergic.

LODOXAMIDE TROMETHAMINE. USAN.
Use: Anti-asthmatic, anti-allergic.

)DRANE. (Poythress) Theophyllin anhydrous 130 mg. or 260 mg./S.R. Cap. Bot. 100s.
Use: Treatment of asthma.

)ESTRIN 21 1/20. (Parke-Davis) Norethindrone acetate 1 mg., ethinyl estradiol 20 mcg./white Tab. Petipac compacts 21 Tab.
Use: Oral contraceptive.

)ESTRIN 21 1.5/30. (Parke-Davis) Norethindrone acetate 1.5 mg., ethinyl estradiol 30 mcg./green Tab. Petipac compacts.
Use: Oral Contraceptive.

OESTRIN Fe **1/20.** (Parke-Davis) White Tab.: Norethindrone acetate 1 mg., ethinyl estradiol 20 mcg. White Tab.; Brown Tab: ferrous fumarate 75 mg./Brown Tab. (7 tabs.) Carton 5 petipac compacts of 28 Tab., carton of 5 refills 28 Tab.
Use: Oral contraceptive.

OESTRIN Fe **1.5/30.** (Parke-Davis) Green Tab.: Norethindrone acetate 1.5 mg., ethinyl estradiol 30 mcg./Green Tab. Brown Tab.: ferrous fumarate 75 mg./Brown Tab. (7 tabs.). Carton 5 petipac compacts 28 Tab., carton of 5 refills 28 tab.
Use: Oral contraceptive.

LOFEMIZOLE HYDROCHLORIDE. USAN.
Use: Anti-inflammatory.

OFENALAC. (Mead Johnson) Low phenylalanine food: Corn syrup solids 49.2%, casein hydrolysate 18.7% (enzymic digest of casein containing amino acids and small peptides & processed to remove most of the phenylalanine) corn oil 18%, modified tapioca starch 9.57%, Protein equiv. 15%, fat 18%, carbohydrate 60%, minerals (ash) 3.6%, phenylalanine 80 mg./100 Gm. pow. Vit. A 1600 I.U., D 400 I.U., E 10 I.U., C 52 mg., folic acid 100 mcg., B-1 0.5 mg., B-2 0.6 mg., niacin 8 mg., B-6 0.4 mg., B-12 2.0 mg., Biotin 0.05 mg., pantothenic acid 3 mg., Vit. K-1 100 mcg., choline 85 mg., inositol 30 mg., Ca 600 mg., P 450 mg., iodine 45 mcg., Fe 12 mg., Mg 70 mg., Cu 0.6 mg., Zn 4 mg., Mn 1 mg., Cl 450 mg., K 650 mg., Na 300 mg./qt. at normal dilution of 20 k cal/fl. oz. Can 2 0.5 lb.
Use: Dietary management of phenylketonuria.

.OFENE. (Lannett) Diphenoxylate HCl 2.5 mg., atropine sulfate 0.025 mg. Bot. 100s, 500s, 1000s.
Use: Antiperistaltic.

LOFENTANIL OXALATE. USAN.
Use: Analgesic, narcotic.

.OFEPRAMINE. B.A.N. 5- 3-[N-(4-Chlorophenacyl)methylamino]propyl -10, 11-dihydrobenz[b,f]azepine. Lopramine (I.N.N.)
Use: Antidepressant.

LOGEN LIQUID. (Goldline) Diphenoxylate HCl w/atropine sulfate. Bot. 2 oz.
Use: Treatment of diarrhea.

LOGEN TABLETS. (Goldline) Diphenoxylate HCl w/atropine sulfate. Bot. 100s, 500s, 1000s.
Use: Treatment of diarrhea.

L.O.L. LOTION. (O'Leary) Bot. 4 oz., 8 oz., 16 oz.
Use: Prevention and treatment of blackheads, enlarged pores, pimples and acne.

• **LOMETRALINE HYDROCHLORIDE.** USAN.
Use: Antipsychotic, antiparkinson.

• **LOMOFUNGIN.** USAN.
Use: Antifungal.

LOMOTIL. (Searle) Diphenoxylate HCl 2.5 mg., atropine sulfate 0.025 mg./Tab. or 5 cc. **Tabs.** Bot. 100s, 500s, 1000s, 2500s. Unit Dose 100s. **Liq.** Bot. w/dropper 2 oz.
Use: In diarrhea management as adjunctive therapy.

• **LOMUSTINE.** USAN. CCNU; NSC-79037. 1-(2-Chloroethyl)-3-cyclohexyl-1-nitrosourea.
Use: Antineoplastic.
See: CeeNu, Cap. (Bristol)

LONALAC. (Mead Johnson) High protein, low sodium powder containing as a percent of the calories: 21% protein as casein, 49% fat as coconut oil, 30% carbohydrate as lactose, Vit. A 1440 I.U., B-1 0.6 mg., B-2 2.6 mg., niacin 1.2 mg., Ca 1.69 Gm., P 1.5 Gm., Cl 750 mg., K 1.80 Gm., Na 38 mg., Mg 135 mg./qt., Pow. Can 16 oz.
Use: Low sodium, high protein supplement for use when dietary sodium restriction is prescribed.

LONG ACTING NEO-SYNEPHRINE II NOSE DROPS. (Winthrop Consumer Products) Xylometazoline HCl 0.1% Adult strength and 0.05% Child strength. Bot. 1 oz.
Use: Nasal decongestant.

LONG ACTING NEO-SYNEPHRINE II VAPOR SPRAY. (Winthrop Consumer Products) Xylometazoline HCl 0.1%. Mentholated. Spray Bot. 0.5 fl. oz.
Use: Nasal decongestant.

LONG ACTING NASAL SPRAY. (Weeks & Leo) Oxymetazoline 0.1% nasal solution. Bot. 0.75 oz.
Use: Nasal decongestant.

LONGIFENE DIHYDROCHLORIDE. Buclizine, B.A.N.

LONITEN. (Upjohn) Minoxidil 2.5 mg./Tab. Unit-of-Use Bot. 100s; 10 mg./Tab. Unit-of-Use Bot. 100s.
Use: Peripheral vasodilator used as antihypertensive.

LO/OVRAL. (Wyeth) Norgestrel 0.3 mg., ethinyl estradiol 30 mg./Tab. 6 Pilpak dispensers, 21 Tabs.
Use: Oral contraceptive.

LO/OVRAL-28. (Wyeth) 21 white tab. each containing 0.3 mg. norgestrel with 0.03 mg. ethinyl estradiol & 7 inert Tab. 6 Pilpak dispensers. 28 Tabs.
Use: Oral contraceptive.

LOPERAMIDE. B.A.N. 4-(4-p-Chlorophenyl-4- hydroxypiperidino)-NN-dimethyl-2,2-diphenyl-butyramide.
See: Imodium, Tab. (Janssen)

• **LOPERAMIDE HCL,** U.S.P. XXI. Cap., U.S.P. XXI.
Use: Antiperistaltic.
See: Imodium, Cap. (Ortho)

LOPID. (Parke-Davis) Gemfibrozil 300 mg./Cap. Bot. 100s. Lipid regulating agent.
Use: Routine treatment of elevated blood lipids for the prevention of coronary heart disease.

LOPRESSOR. (Geigy) Metoprolol tartrate. **Tab.:** 50 mg., or 100 mg./Tab. Bot. 100s, 1000s. Unit dose 100s. Gy-Pak 60s, 100s. **Ampul:** 5 mg./5 ml.
Use: Antihypertensive beta blocker for management of hypertension.

LOPRESSOR HCT. (Geigy) Metoprolol tartrate and hydrochlorothiazide tablets. **50/25 mg.:** Bot. 100s. **100/25 mg.:** Bot. 100s **100/50 mg.:** Bot. 100s.
Use: Antihypertensive beta blocker diuretic for management of hypertension.

LOPROX. (Hoechst) Ciclopirox olamine 1% in cream base. Tube 15 Gm., 30 Gm.
Use: Topical, broad-spectrum antifungal.

LOPURIN. (Boots) Allopurinol 100 mg. or 300 mg./Tab. Bot. 100s, 1000s. Unit dose 100s.
Use: Treatment of gout, uric acid nephropathy, uric acid stone formation.

LOQUA. (Quality Generics) Hydrochlorothiazide 50 mg./Tab. Bot. 100s, 1000s.
Use: Diuretic and antihypertensive.

• **LORAJMINE HYDROCHLORIDE.** USAN.
Use: Cardiac depressant.

• **LORAZEPAM.** USAN. 7-Chloro-5-(o-chlorophenyl)-1,3-dihydro-3-hydroxy-2H-1,4-benzodiazepin-2-one.
Use: Minor tranquilizer.
See: Ativan, Tab., Inj. (Wyeth)

• **LORBAMATE.** USAN.
Use: Muscle relaxant.

• **LORCAINIDE HYDROCHLORIDE.** USAN.
Use: Cardiac depressant.

LORELCO. (Merrell Dow) Probucol 250 mg./Tab. Bot. 120s.
Use: Cholesterol reducing agent.

LORFAN. (Roche) Levallorphan tartrate. 1 mg./ml. w/methyl and propyl parabens 0.2%, phenol 0.45%. Amp. 1 ml. Box 10s. Vial 10 ml.
Use: I.V. or I.M., overdosage of narcotics.

• **LORMETAZEPAM.** USAN.
Use: Sedative, hypnotic.

LOROXIDE. (Dermik) Benzoyl peroxide 5.5% w/propylene glycol, cetyl alcohol, hydroxyethylcellulose, kaolin, caramel, talc, cholesterol and related sterols, propylene glycolstearate, polysorbate 20, lanolin alcohol, propylparaben, methylparaben, tetrasodium EDTA, pH buffers, antioxidants, silicone emulsion, silica, decyl oleate, vegetable oil, purcelline oil syn., titanium dioxide, cyclohexanediamine tetraacetic acid, calcium phosphate. Lot. Bot. 25 Gm.
Use: Severe recalcitrant acne.

LORPHEN. (Geneva) **Cap.:** Chlorpheniramine maleate 8 mg., 12 mg./Cap. Bot. 100s. **Tab.** 4 mg./Tab. Bot. 100s.

LORVIC'S 2-TONE DISCLOSING SOLUTION. (Lorvic) Dropper Bot. 2 oz.

• **LORZAFONE.** USAN.
Use: Minor tranquilizer.

LO-SAL. (Glenbrook) Calcium carbonate 585 mg., magnesium hydroxide 120 mg./Tab. Boxes 2s, 12s, 36s, 48s, 96s.
Use: Antacid, low sodium.

• **LOSULAZINE HYDROCHLORIDE.** USAN.
Use: Antihypertensive.

LOTALBA CREAM. (Durel) Lotalba oint. 30%, zinc oxide 10%, sulfur pot. 5%, greaseless ointment base 55%. Jars 3 oz., lb.
Use: Acne vulgaris, acne rosacea.

LOTALBA OINTMENT. (Durel) Stabilized lotio alba, glycerine, mineral gums. Jars 3 oz., lb.
Use: Acne vulgaris, acne rosacea.

LOTAWIN CAPSULES. (Winthrop Products) Oxypertine.
Use: Anxiolytic, tranquilizer.

LOTIO ALBA. White Lotion.
Use: Acne vulgaris, seborrhea.
W/Sulfur, calamine, alcohol.
See: Sulfa-Lo, Lot. (Whorton)

LOTIO ALSULFA. (Doak) Colloidal sulfur 5%. Bot. 4 oz.
Use: Acne vulgaris, seborrhea.

LOTOCREME. (C.S. Dent) Bot. 8 oz.
Use: Body rub.

LOTRIMIN. (Schering) Clotrimazole 1%, **Cream:** Tube 15 Gm., 30 Gm., 45 Gm., 90 Gm. **Creamy Lotion:** Bot. 30 ml. **Sol:** 1% Bot. 10 ml., 30 ml.
Use: Antifungal.

LOTRISONE. (Schering) Clotrimazole 10 mg., betamethasone dipropionate/Gm. Tube 15 Gm. or 45 Gm.
Use: Topical antifungal.

LO-TROL. (Vangard) Diphenoxylate HCl 2.5 mg., atropine sulfate 0.015 mg./5 ml. Bot. 60 ml.
Use: Antidiarrheal.

LO-TROP. (Vangard) Diphenoxylate HCl 2.5 mg., atropine sulfate 0.025 mg./Tab. Bot. 100s, 1000s.
Use: Antidiarrheal.

LOTUSATE. (Winthrop-Breon) Talbutal 120 mg./Cap. Bot. 100s.
Use: Hypnotic.

LOUCEVERIN CALCIUM. Calcium 5-formyl-5, 6, 7, 8-tetrahydroteroylglutamate.

LOVE LONGER. (Youngs Drug) Benzocaine 7.5% in water soluble lubricant base. Tube 0.5 oz.
Use: Desensitizing lubricant for premature ejaculation.

LOWILA CAKE. (Westwood) Sodium lauryl sulfoacetate, dextrin, boric acid, urea, sorbitol, mineral oil, PEG 14 M, lactic acid, cellulose gum, docusate sodium, fragrance. Cake 3¾ oz.
Use: Soap-free skin cleanser.

LOW-QUEL. (Blue Cross) Diphenoxylate HCl 2.5 mg., atropine sulfate 0.025 mg./Tab. Bot. 100s.
Use: Intestinal antispasmodic.

• **LOXAPINE.** USAN. 2-Chloro-11-(4-methyl-1-piperazinyl) dibenz [b,f] [1,4] oxazepine.
Use: Tranquilizer.

XAPINE HYDROCHLORIDE.
Use: Tranquilizer
See: Daxolin Concentrate, Liq. (Miles Pharm)
Loxitane-C Oral Concentrate (Lederle)
Loxitane, Inj. (Lederle)

.OXAPINE SUCCINATE. USAN. (1)2-Chloro-11-(4-methyl-1-piperazinyl) dibenz-[b,f] [1,4]-oxazepine succinate; (2) Succinic acid compound with 2-chloro-11-(4-methyl-1-piperazinyl) dibenz-[b,f] [1,4] oxazepine.
Use: Tranquilizer.
See: Loxitane, Cap. (Lederle)

XITANE CAPSULES. (Lederle) Loxapine succinate 5 mg./Cap. Bot. 100s. Unit Dose 10 × 10s. 10 mg., 25 mg., 50 mg./Cap. Bot. 100s, 1000s. Unit Dose 10 × 10s.
Use: Tranquilizer.

XITANE-C. (Lederle) Loxapine HCl oral concentrate 25 mg./ml. 120 ml. Bot. w/dropper.
Use: Tranquilizer.

XITANE IM. (Lederle) Loxitane HCl 50 mg./ml. Vial 10 ml.
Use: Anti-psychotic.

XON. Haloxon, B.A.N.

ZOL. (USV Labs.) Indapamide 2.5 mg./Tab. Bot. 100s, 1000s. Strip dispenser 100s.
Use: Diuretic, antihypertensive.

PAM. p-Di(2-chloroethyl) amino-L-phenylalamine. An alkylating antineoplastic agent. Under study.

SARCOLYSIN.
See: Alkeran, Tab. (Burroughs Wellcome)

BAFAX. (Burroughs Wellcome) Surgical lubricant, sterile; water-soluble, non-staining. Foil wrapper 2.7 Gm., 5 Gm. Box 144s.
Use: Surgical lubricant.

BATH. (Warner-Lambert) Mineral oil, PPG-15, stearyl ether, oleth-2, nonoxynol-5; fragrance, D&C Green No. 6. Bot. 4 oz., 8 oz., 16 oz.
Use: Bath oil for dry skin.

JBINOL. (Purepac) Light, heavy, and ext. heavy mineral oil. Bot. pt., qt., gal. Ext. heavy. Bot. 8 oz., pt., qt., gal.
Use: Emollient.

JBRASEPTIC JELLY. (Guardian) Water-soluble amyl phenyl phenol complex 0.12%, phenylmercuric nitrate, 0.007%. Bellows type tubes, 10 Gm., 24s.
Use: Urethral instillation, urologic and proctologic exams.

JBRIDERM CREAM. (Warner-Lambert) Water, mineral oil, petrolatum, glycerin, glyceryl stearate, PEG-100 stearate, squalane, lanolin, lanolin alcohol, lanolin oil, cetyl alcohol, sorbitan laurate, fragrance (if scented), methylparaben, butylparaben, propylparaben, quaternium-15. Tube: scented 1.5 oz., 4 oz.; unscented 4 oz.
Use: For extremely dry skin.

JBRIDERM LOTION. (Warner-Lambert) Water, mineral oil, petrolatum, sorbitol, lanolin, lanolin alcohol, stearic acid, TEA, cetyl alcohol, fragrance (if scented), butylparaben, methylparaben, propyl paraben, sodium chloride. Bot. scented, 4 oz., 8 oz., 16 oz.; unscented 8 oz., 16 oz.
Use: For dry skin.

LUBRIN. (Upsher Smith) Lubricating vaginal suppository base containing glycerin, laureth-23, PEG 40 stearate, PEG-6-32, PEG-20, caprylic/capric triglyceride. Pkg. 5 inserts.
Use: Vaginal insert to provide vaginal lubrication for sexual intercourse.

LUCANTHONE. B.A.N. F.D.A. 1-[[2-(Diethylamino)ethyl]amino]-4-methylthioxanthen-9-one. Miracil D; Nilodin hydrochloride
Use: Treatment of filariasis and schistosomiasis.

• **LUCANTHONE HYDROCHLORIDE.** USAN. 1-[[2-(Diethylamino)ethyl] amino]-4-methylthioxanthen-9-one Monohydrochloride.
Use: Antischistosomal.

LUCOFEN HYDROCHLORIDE. Chlorphentermine, B.A.N.

LUDENS COUGH DROPS. (Luden's) Honey lemon, honey licorice, menthol, strong flavor menthol, strong flavor eucalyptus or wild cherry flavored lozenges. Square-Pack. Box. Bag.

LUDIOMIL. (Ciba) Maprotiline 25 mg., 50 mg. or 75 mg./Tab. Bot. 100s. Accu-Pak 100s.
Use: Antidepressive.

LUFA CAPSULES. (Armour) Nutrients. Bot. 100s.

LUFYLLIN. (Wallace) Dyphylline Injection. **Amp.:** (500 mg./2 ml.) Box 25s. **Elix.:** (100 mg./15 ml.; alcohol 20%) Bot. pt., gal. **Tab.:** (200 mg./Tab.) Bot. 100s, 1000s. Unit dose 100s.
Use: Bronchodilator.

LUFYLLIN-400. (Wallace) Dyphylline 400 mg./Tab. Bot. 100s, 1000s.
Use: Bronchodilator and expectorant.

LUFYLLIN-EPG. (Wallace) Ephedrine HCl 16 mg., dyphylline 100 mg., phenobarbital 16 mg., guaifenesin 200 mg./Tab. or 10 ml. **Tab.** Bot. 100s. **Elix.,** (alcohol 5.5%) Bot. pt.
Use: Bronchodilator.

LUFYLLIN-GG. (Wallace) **Tab.:** Dyphylline 200 mg., guaifenesin 200 mg./Tab. Bot. 100s, 1000s. **Elixir:** Dyphylline 100 mg., guaifenesin 100 mg., alcohol 17%/15 ml. Elix. Bot. pt., gal.
Use: Bronchodilator and expectorant.

LUGOL'S SOLUTION. Strong Iodine Solution, U.S.P. XXI. (Lyne) Iodine 5.0 Gm., pot. iodide 10 Gm., in enough purified water to make 100 ml. Bot. 15 ml. (Wisconsin) Bot. pt.

LUMINAL INJECTION. (Winthrop-Breon) Phenobarbital. 1 ml. 130 mg./Amp. Box 100s.
Use: Sedative, hypnotic, anticonvulsant.

LUMOPAQUE CAPSULES. (Winthrop Products) Tyropanoate sodium.
Use: Oral cholecystographic medium.

• **LUPITIDINE HYDROCHLORIDE.** USAN.
Use: Antegonist (to histamine hydrogen receptors, veterinary).

LUPO-TEC. (Wampole) Radioimmunoassay for the quantitative determination of antibodies to double-stranded DNA in serum. Kits 60s.
Use: Aid in diagnosis of systemic lupus erythematosus (SLE).

LUPRON INJECTION. (TAP) Leuprolide acetate 1 mg./0.2 ml. Vial 2.8 ml.
Use: Treatment of prostatic cancer.

LURAMIDE TABS. (Major) Furosemide 20 mg., 40 mg., or 80 mg./Tab. Bot. 100s, 1000's.
Use: Diuretic.

LURIDE DROPS. (Hoyt) Sodium fluoride equiv. to 0.125 mg. of fluoride/Drop. Plastic dropper bottle 30 ml.
Use: Aid in the protection against dental caries.

LURIDE-F LOZI TABLETS. (Hoyt) Sodium fluoride in Lozi base tablet available as fluoride. **0.25 mg.:** Bot. 120s; **0.5 mg.:** Bot. 120s, 1200s; **1.0 mg.:** Bot. 120s, 1000s, 5000s.
Use: Dental caries preventive.

LURIDE PROPHYLAXIS PASTE. (Hoyt) Acidulated phosphate sodium fluoride containing 0.4% fluoride ion w/silicon dioxide abrasive. Unit dose 3 Gm. Jars 50 Gm.
Use: Clean and polish teeth.

LURIDE-SF LOZI TABLETS. (Hoyt) Sodium fluoride containing 1.0 mg fluoride/Tab. Special formula with no color or flavor. Bot. 120s.
Use: Dental caries preventive.

LURIDE TOPICAL GEL. (Hoyt) Acidulated phosphate sodium fluoride containing 1.2% fluoride ion at pH 3.0 to 4.0 in gel base. Bot. 32 oz., 250 ml.
Use: Dental caries preventive.

LURIDE TOPICAL SOLUTION. (Hoyt) Acidulated phosphate sodium fluoride w/pH 3.2. Bot. 250 ml.
Use: Dental caries preventive.

LUSTOZYME. (Kenyon) Lucelzyme (cellulolytic enzyme) 1 mg., lumylzyme (amylolytic enzyme) 25 mg., luprozyme (proteolytic enzyme) 10 mg., dehydrocholic acid 100 mg., hyoscyamine HBr 0.1 mg., hyoscine HBr 0.0065 mg., atropine sulfate 0.02 mg./Tab. Bot. 100s, 1000s.
Use: Flatulence.

LUTEOGAN.
See: Progesterone (Various Mfr.)

LUTEOSAN.
See: Progesterone (Various Mfr.)

LUTOCYLOL. (Ciba) Ethisterone.

LUTOLIN-F. (Spanner) Progesterone 25 mg. or 50 mg./cc. Vial 10 cc.

LUTOLIN-S. (Spanner) Progesterone 25 mg./cc. Vial 10 cc.

• **LUTRELIN ACETATE.** USAN.
Use: Agonist.

LUTREN.
See: Progesterone (Various Mfr.)

LUTUTRIN.
See: Lutrexin, Tab. (Hynson, Westcott & Dunning)

• **LYAPOLATE SODIUM.** USAN. Sodium ethenesulfonate polymer. Peson (Hoechst).
Use: Anticoagulant.

• **LYCETAMINE.** USAN.
Use: Antimicrobial.

LYCINE HYDROCHLORIDE.
See: Betaine Hydrochloride (Various Mfr.)

LYCOLAN ELIXIR. (Lannett) Glycocoll 28 gr., lysine 100 mg. in Tokay wine base/Tbsp. Bot. pt.
Use: Geriatric vitamin.

LYDIA E. PINKHAM TABLETS. (CooperVision) 72s, 250s.

LYDIA E. PINKHAM VEGETABLE COMPOUND. (CooperVision) Bot. 8 fl. oz., 16 fl. oz.

• **LYDIMYCIN.** USAN.
Use: Antifungal.

LYMECYCLINE. B.A.N. A water-soluble combination o tetracycline, lysine and formaldehyde. Armyl; Mucomycin; Tetralysal.
Use: Antibiotic.

LYMPHAZURIN. (Hirsch) Isosulfan blue 10 mg., sodium monohydrogen phosphate 6.6 mg., potassium dihydrogen phosphate 2.7 mg./ml. Vials 5 ml.
Use: Contrast agent.

• **LYMPHOGRANULOMA VENEREUM ANTIGEN,** U.S.P. XXI. Lymphogranuloma venereum skin test antigen.
Use: Diagnostic aid (dermal reactivity indicator).

• **LYNESTRENOL.** USAN. (1) 19-Nor-17α-pregn-4-en-20-yn-17-ol; (2) 17α-Ethinyl-17β-hydroxyestr-4-ene Orgametril.
Use: Progestin.

LYNOESTRENOL. Lynestrenol.

LYOPINE. (Hyrex) Atropine sulfate lyophilized 10 mg./10 ml. vial w/diluent 10 ml.
Use: Anticholinergic, antidote to cholinesterase inhibitors.

LYPO-B. (Rocky Mtn.) Choline chloride 200 mg., dl-methionine 50 mg., inositol 100 mg., B-12 cryst. 2 mcg./2 cc. Vial 30 cc.

• **LYPRESSIN NASAL SOLUTION,** U.S.P. XXI. 8-Lysine vasopressin. Syntopressin.
Use: Antidiuretic.
See: Diapid Nasal Spray (Sandoz)

LYSERGIDE. B.A.N. NN-Diethyl-lysergamide. Lysergic acid diethylamide LSD, Delysid.
Use: Psychotomimetic.

LYSIDIN. Methyl glyoxalidin.

LYSINE. USAN.
Use: Nutrient & rapid weight gain.

• **LYSINE ACETATE,** U.S.P. XXI. $C_6H_{14}N_2O_2 \bullet C_2H_4O_2$
Use: Amino acid.

• **LYSINE MONOHYDROCHLORIDE,** U.S.P. XXI. $C_6H_{14}N_2O_2 \bullet HCl$
Use: Amino acid.
See: Enisyl, Tab. (Person & Covey).

LYSITONE. (Jenkins) l-Lysine HCl 300 mg., iron peptonate 200 mg., cobalamine conc. 10 mcg., B-1 10 mg., niacinamide 20 mg., B-2 2.5 mg., B-6 2 mg., panthenol 2 mg., d-sorbitol 1.83 Gm., alcohol 11%/Fl. Oz. Bot. 3 oz., 8 oz., gal.
Use: Reconstructive nutritional tonic.

LYSIVANE.
See: Parsidol, Tab. (Warner-Chilcott)

LYSMINS. (Miller) l-Lysine 20 mg., dl-methionine 150 mg., Cu 1.0 mg., iodine 0.015 mg., Mn 2.0 mg., Fe 10.0 mg., K 20.0 mg., Zn 2.0 mg., Mg 20.0 mg./Tab. Bot. 100s.
Use: Adults, orally as a dietary supplement.

LYSODREN. (Bristol) Mitotane. 500 mg./Tab. Bot. 100s.
Use: Inoperable adrenal cortical carcinoma.

.YSOSTAPHIN. USAN. Antibiotic derived from *Staphylococcus staphylolyticus.*
Use: Antibiotic.

'SURIDE. B.A.N. 9-(3,3-Diethylureido)-4,6,-6a,7,8,9-hexahydro-7-methylindolo[4,3-f,g]-quinoline.
Use: Prophylaxis of migraine.
See: Lysenyl.

'TEERS. (Barnes-Hind) Isotonic, viscous liquid adjusted to pH of tears. Balanced amounts of sodium and potassium ions, cellulose derivative, benzalkonium chloride 0.01% and disodium edetate 0.05%. Plas. Bot. 15 cc.
Use: Optic; artificial tear fluid.

'TREN. (Mead Johnson) Water, corn syrup solids, dextrose, Na citrate, KCl, citric acid, Na biphosphate, K citrate, Ca chloride and Mg sulfate. Ready-To-Use Bot. 8 fl. oz.
Use: Orally, electrolyte and fluid balance.

M

AAGEL. (Approved) Aluminum and Mg hydroxide. Bot. 12 oz., gal.
Use: Gastric hyperacidity.

AALOX SUSPENSION. (Rorer) Suspension of magnesium hydroxide 200 mg., and aluminum hydroxide 225 mg./5 ml. Sodium content (0.06 mEq) 1.4 mg./5 ml. Bot. 5 oz., 12 oz., 26 oz. Unit dose 15 ml., 30 ml.
Use: Antacid.

AALOX NO. 1 TABLETS. (Rorer) Magnesium hydroxide 200 mg., dried aluminum hydroxide gel 200 mg./Tab. Sodium content (0.03 mEq) 0.7 mg./Tab. Bot. 100s.
Use: Antacid.

AALOX NO. 2 TABLETS. (Rorer) Magnesium hydroxide 400 mg., dried aluminum hydroxide gel 400 mg./Tab.
Sodium content (0.06 mEq) 1.84 mg./Tab. Bot. 50s, 250s.
Strip 24s, 100s.
Use: Antacid.

AALOX PLUS SUSPENSION. (Rorer) Suspension of magnesium hydroxide 200 mg., aluminum hydroxide 225 mg., simethicone 25 mg./5 ml. Sodium content (0.05 mEq) 1.2 mg./5 ml. Bot. 12 oz. Unit dose 15 ml., 30 ml.
Use: Antacid, antiflatulent.

AALOX PLUS TABLETS. (Rorer) Magnesium hydroxide 200 mg., dried aluminum hydroxide gel 200 mg., simethicone 25 mg./Tab. Sodium content (0.03 mEq.) 0.8 mg./Tab. Bot. 50s. Strip 100s. Pocket Packs 12s. Roll Packs 12s.
Use: Antacid, antiflatulent.

AALOX TC (THERAPEUTIC CONCENTRATE). (Rorer) Suspension of magnesium hydroxide 300 mg., aluminum hydroxide 600 mg./5 ml. Sodium content (0.03 mEq.) 0.8 mg./5 ml. Bot. 12 oz.
Use: Concentrated antacid.

MAALOX TC (THERAPEUTIC CONCENTRATE) TABLETS. (Rorer) Magnesium hydroxide 300 mg., aluminum hydroxide 600 mg., sodium (0.02 mEq.) 0.5 mg./Tab. Bot. 48s.
Use: Concentrated antacid.

MACRISALB (^{131}I) INJECTION. B.A.N. Macroaggregated iodinated (^{131}I) human albumin injection.
Use: Examination of pulmonary perfusion.

MACROAGGREGATED ALBUMIN.
See: Albumotope-LS. (Squibb)

MACRODANTIN. (Norwich Eaton) Nitrofurantoin macrocrystals 50 or 100 mg./Cap. Bot. 30s, 100s, 500s, 1000s. Hospital Unit Dose 100s. 25 mg./Cap. Bot. 100s.
Use: Antibacterial for urinary tract infections.

MACRODEX. (Pharmacia) Dextran 6% w/v in normal saline and 6% w/v in 5% dextrose in water. Bot. 500 ml.
Use: Treatment of shock due to trauma, hemorrhage, burns and surgery.

MACROGOL 400. B.A.N. Polyoxyl stearate.
Use: Surface active agent.
See: Polyethylene glycol 400

MACROGOL 4000. B.A.N.
Use: Surface active agent.
See: Polyethylene glycol 4000

MACROGOL STEARATE 2000. Polyoxyl 40 Stearate.

MACROTIN W/Phenobarbital, hyoscyamus ext., caulophyllin, helonin, pulsatilla ext.
See: Tranquilans, Tab. (Noyes)

• **MAFENIDE,** USAN. α-Aminotoluene-p-sulfonamide. Marfanil [HCl], Sulfomyl [propionate], Sulfamylon [acetate].
Use: Antibacterial agent.

• **MAFENIDE ACETATE,** U.S.P. XXI. Cream, U.S.P. XXI. α-Aminotoluene-p-sulfonamide monoacetate.
See: Sulfamylon Cream (Winthrop-Breon)

• **MAFILCON A.** USAN.
Use: Contact lens material.

MAFYLON CREAM. (Winthrop Products) Mafenide acetate.
Use: Topical antibacterial agent for burns.

• **MAGALDRATE,** U.S.P. XXI. Oral Susp., Tab., U.S.P. XXI. (Ayerst) Monalium Hydrate. Aluminum Magnesium Hydroxide.
Use: Antacid.
See: Monalium Hydrate
Riopan, Tab. & Susp. (Ayerst)

MAGAN. (Adria) Magnesium salicylate (anhydrous) 545 mg./Tab. Bot. 100s, 500s.
Use: Salicylate therapy.

MAGDROX. (Vita Elixir) Magnesium hydroxide, aluminum hydroxide.
Use: Gastric antacid.

MAGLAGEL. (Kenyon) Mg-Al hydroxide gel. Bot. 12 oz., pt., gal.

MAG-LUM. (Kenyon) Magnesium trisilicate 7.5 gr., dried Al hydroxide gel 4 gr. Tab. Bot. 100s, 1000s.

MAGMA ALBA. (Durel) Sulfurated lime solution (Vleminckx's) 60.0%, saturated zinc sulfate solution 40.0%. Jars 3 oz., lb.

Use: Acne vulgaris, acne cystica, acne rosacea, rosacea-like tuberculid (Lewandowsky).

MAGMALIN SUSPENSION. (Vale) A colloidal suspension of aluminum hydroxide gel and magnesium hydroxide. Bot. pt., gal.

MAGMALIN LOZENGE. (Vale) Magnesium hydroxide 0.2 Gm., aluminum hydroxide gel, dried 0.2 Gm./Loz. Bot. 100s, 500s, 1000s.

MAGNAGEL. (Mallard) Aluminum hydroxide-magnesium carbonate 325 mg./Tab. **Tab.** Bot. 100s.
Use: Antacid.

MAGNA-GEL LIQUID. (Vortech) Magnesium-aluminum hydroxide gel. Bot. 12 oz., gal.
Use: Antacid.

MAGNALUM. (Richlyn) Magnesium hydroxide 3.75 gr., aluminum hydroxide 2 gr./Tab. Bot. 1000.
Use: Antacid.

MAGNATRIL. (Lannett) Aluminum hydroxide gel dried 4 gr., magnesium trisilicate 7 gr., magnesium hydroxide 2 gr./Tab. Bot. 50s, 100s.
Use: Antacid, adsorbant.

MAGNATRIL SUSPENSION. (Lannett) Magnesium trisilicate 4 gr., colloidal susp. of magnesium and aluminum hydroxides/5 cc. Bot. 12 fl. oz.
Use: Relief and control of pain in gastric hyperacidity and for treatment of peptic ulcer.

• **MAGNESIA TABLETS,** U.S.P. XXI.
Use: Antacid.

• **MAGNESIA & ALUMINA ORAL SUSPENSION.** U.S.P. XXI. (Philips Roxane) Oral Susp. 6 fl. oz. 25s.
Use: Antacid.
See: Maalox, Liq. (Rorer)

• **MAGNESIA & ALUMINA TABLETS,** U.S.P. XXI.
Use: Antacid.
See: Maalox, Tab. (Rorer)

MAGNESIA MAGMA. Milk of Magnesia, U.S.P. XXI.
Use: Antacid, cathartic.
See: Magnesium Hydroxide, Prep.

MAGNESIUM ACETYLSALICYLATE. Apyron, Magnespirin, Magisal, Novacetyl.
Use: Like acetylsalicylic acid.

MAGNESIUM ALUMINATE HYDRATED.
Use: Antacid.
See: Riopan, Susp., Tab. (Ayerst)

MAGNESIUM ALUMINUM HYDROXIDE.
Use: Antacid.
See: Maalox, Susp. (Rorer)
Maglagel (Kenyon)
Malogel, Gel (Quality Generics)
Medalox, Gel (Med. Chem.)
W/APC.
See: Buffadyne, Tab. (Lemmon)
W/Calcium carbonate.
See: Camalox, Susp. (Rorer)
W/Magnesium trisilicate.
See: Magnatril Susp. (Lannett)
W/Simethicone.
See: Maalox Plus, Susp. (Rorer)

• **MAGNESIUM ALUMINUM SILICATE,** U.S.P. XXI.
Use: Suspending agent.

• **MAGNESIUM CARBONATE,** U.S.P. XXI. (Baker, J. T.) Pow. 4 oz., 1 lb., 5 lb.
Use: Antacid.

• **MAGNESIUM CARBONATE AND SODIUM BICARBONATE FOR ORAL SUSPENSION,** U.S.P. XXI.
Use: Antacid.

MAGNESIUM CARBONATE W/COMBINATIONS.
Use: Antacid.
See: Alised, Tab. (Elder)
Alkets, Tab. (Upjohn)
Antacid, Tab. (Mallard)
Antacid No. 2, Tab. (Bowman)
Bismatesia, Can (Noyes)
Bufferin, Tab. (Bristol-Myers)
Buffertabs, Tab. (O'Neal)
Buffinol, Tab. (Otis Clapp)
Di-Gel, Tab., Liq. (Plough)
Dimacid, Tab. (Otis Clapp)
Dristan, Tab. (Whitehall)
Glycogel, Tab. (Central)
Glytabs, Chew. Tab. (Pharmics)
Hycidol, Pow. (Mallard)
Kanalka, Tab. (Lannett)
Magnagel, Liq., Tab. (Mallard)
Marblen, Susp., Tab. (Fleming)
Maygel, Tab. (Century)
Panacarb, Tab. (Lannett)
Ratio, Tab. (Adria)
Romach, Tab. (Ror Chem.)
Spasased, Tab. (Wolins)
Spastosed, Tab. (Vortech)

• **MAGNESIUM CHLORIDE,** U.S.P. XXI. Magnesium chloride hexahydrate.
Use: Electrolyte replenisher, pharmaceutical necessity for hemodialysis & peritoneal dialysis.
W/Pot. chloride, calcium chloride, phenol red.
See: Electrolytic Replenisher, Vial (Invenex)

• **MAGNESIUM CITRATE ORAL SOLUTION,** U.S.P. XXI. 1,2,3-Propanetricarboxylic acid, hydroxymagnesium salt (2:3).
Use: Cathartic.

• **MAGNESIUM GLUCONATE.** U.S.P. XXI. Tab., U.S.P. XXI.
Use: Magnesium deficiencies
See: Almora, Tab. (O'Neal)
Gyn, Tab. (Amfre-Grant)

MAGNESIUM GLUCONATE. (Western Research) Magnesium gluconate 500 mg./Tab. Bot. 1000s.
Use: Magnesium deficiencies.

MAGNESIUM GLYCINATE.
W/Aspirin, magnesium carbonate.
See: Buffinol, Tab. (Otis Clapp)
W/Gastric mucin; Al hydroxide gel.
See: Mucogel, Tab. (Inwood)

• **MAGNESIUM HYDROXIDE,** U.S.P. XXI.
Use: Antacid; cathartic.
See: Magnesia Magma
Milk of Magnesia

MAGNESIUM HYDROXIDE W/COMBINATIONS.
See: Aludrox, Susp., Tab., Vial (Wyeth)
Aluscop, Cap., Susp. (Westerfield)

Anachloric A, Tab. (Upjohn)
Ascriptin, Tab. (Rorer)
Ascriptin A/D, Tab. (Rorer)
Ascriptin w/Codeine, Tab. (Rorer)
Aspadine, Tab. (Vortech)
Banacid, Tab. (Buffington)
Camalox, Susp., Tab. (Rorer)
Congespirin, Tab. (Bristol-Myers)
Delcid, Susp. (Merrell Dow)
Fermalox, Tab. (Rorer)
Ferratinic, Tab. (Wolins)
4-Way Cold Tabs., Tab. (Bristol-Myers)
Gas-Eze, Tab. (Edward J. Moore)
Haley's M.O., Liq. (Winthrop Consumer Products)
Jel Drox, Liq. (Coastal)
Kamadrox Jel Liquid, Liq. (Elder)
Kolantyl, Gel, Wafer (Merrell Dow)
Kudrox, Susp., Tab. (Kremers-Urban)
Laxsil Liquid, Liq. (Reed & Carnrick)
Maalox, Susp., Tab. (Rorer)
Maalox Plus, Susp., Tab. (Rorer)
Magnatril, Susp., Tab. (Lannett)
Magoleum, Liq. (Blue Line)
Magwol #1, Tabs. (Wolins)
Mint Acid Tablets, Tab. (Kenyon)
Mylanta, Mylanta II, Liq., Tab. (Stuart)
Neutralox, Susp. (Lemmon)
Oxaine-M, Susp. (Wyeth)
Simeco, Liq. (Wyeth)
Trialka, Liq., Tab. (Commerce)
Trigelma H.M., Tab., Liq. (O'Neal)
WinGel, Liq., Tab. (Winthrop Consumer Products)

AGNESIUM NICOTINATE.
/Theobromine Mg oleate.
See: Athemol-N, Tab. (Glaxo)

AGNESIUM OROTATE.
(Nutrition) 500 mg./Tab. Bot. 100s.
See: Magora, Tab. (Miller)

MAGNESIUM OXIDE, U.S.P. XXI. Cap., Tab., U.S.P. XXI.
(Manne) 420 mg./Tab. Bot. 250s, 1000s.
(Stanlabs) 10 gr./Tab. Bot. 100s, 1000s.
Use: Pharm. aid (sorbant).
See: Mag-Ox, Tab. (Blaine)
Mag-Ox 400, Tab. (Blaine)
Niko-Mag, Cap. (Scruggs)
Oxabid, Cap. (Jamieson-McKames)
Par-Mag, Cap. (Parmed)
Uro-Mag, Cap. (Blaine)
/Calcium, Vit. D.
See: Elekap, Caps. (Western Research)
/Glutamic acid magnesium complex, N-acetyl-P-aminophenol, ascorbic acid, dl-methionine, lemon bioflavonoid complex, dl-α-tocopheryl acetate, glycine, soybean flour.
See: Ulcimins, Tab. (Miller)
/Magnesium carbonate, Ca carbonate.
See: Alkets, Tab. (Upjohn)
/Ox bile (desic.), hog bile (desic.).
See: Hyper-Cholate, Tab. (Mallard)
/Phenobarbital, atropine sulfate.
See: Magnox, Tab. (Bowman)

• **MAGNESIUM PHOSPHATE,** U.S.P. XXI.
Use: Antacid.

• **MAGNESIUM SALICYLATE.** U.S.P. XXI. Tab. U.S.P. XXI.
Use: Analgesic, antipyretic, antirheumatic.
See: Analate, Tab. (Winston)
Efficin, Tab. (Adria)
Causalin, Tab. (Amfre-Grant)
Magan, Tab. (Adria)
W/Phenyltoloxamine citrate.
See: Mobigesic, Tab. (Ascher)

• **MAGNESIUM SILICATE,** N.F. XVI.
Use: Pharmaceutic aid (tablet excipient).

• **MAGNESIUM STEARATE,** N.F. XVI.
Use: Pharmaceutic aid (lubricant).

• **MAGNESIUM SULFATE,** U.S.P. XXI. Inj. U.S.P. XXI. Epsom salt.
Use: Pow. or crystals cathartic: Inj. anticonvulsant, electrolyte replenisher.
(Abbott)—50% Amp. 2 ml. Box 25s, 100s. Abboject Syringe (20 G × 2.5″) 5 ml., 10 ml.; 12.5% in Pintop Vial, 8 ml., 20 ml.
(Atlas)—10% Amp. 10 cc. Box 100s; 1 Gm., 2 cc. Box 100s.
(Baxter)—10% Vial 10 cc., 20 cc.
(CMC)—1 Gm./2 cc., 10% Amp. 10 cc., 20 cc. 25% Amp. 10 cc. 50% Vial 30 cc.
(Quality Generics)—50% Amp. 2 cc., 100s.
(Lilly)—10% Amp. 20 cc. Box 6s, 25s; 50% 1 Gm. Amp. 2 cc., Box 12s, 100s.
(Parke-Davis)—50% Amp. 2 ml., 10s.
(Torigian)—50% Amp. 2 cc. 12s, 25s, 100s.
(Trent)—50% Amp. 2 cc., 10 cc.

• **MAGNESIUM TRISILICATE,** U.S.P. XXI. Magnesium silicate hydrate.
Use: Antacid.
See: Trisomin, Tab. (Lilly)

MAGNESIUM TRISILICATE W/COMBINATIONS.
See: Alsorb Gel C.T., Gel (Standex)
Antacid, Tab. (Panray)
Antacid, Tab. (Reid-Provident)
Antacid, Tab. (Zenith)
Antacid G, Tab. (Walgreen)
Arcodex Tablets, Tab. (Arcum)
Azolid-A, Cap. (USV)
Banacid, Tab. (Buffington)
Barosil, Susp. (Barry-Martin)
Butazolidin Alka, Cap. (Geigy)
Equilet, Tab. (Mission)
Escot, Cap. (Reid-Provident)
Gacid, Tab. (Arcum)
Gaviscon, Tab. (Marion)
Kaocasil, Tab. (Jenkins)
Kathmagel, Tab. (Mason)
Kolantyl, Wafer (Merrell Dow)
Magnased, Tab. (Century)
Magnatril, Susp., Tab. (Lannett)
Magnesil w/Calcium Carbonate, Tab. (Bowman)
Malcogel, Liq. (Upjohn)
Maracid-2, Tab. (Marin)
Marblen, Tab., Susp. (Fleming)
Mint Acid Tablets, Tab. (Kenyon)

Mucotin, Tab. (Warner-Chilcott)
Neutracomp, Tab., Liq. (CMC)
Neutralox, Liq., Tab. (Lemmon)
Noralac, Tab. (Vortech)
Pama, Tab. (Vortech)
P.H. Plus, Tab. (Scrip)
Silmagel, Tab. (Lannett)
Triactin, Tab. (Norwich)
Trigelma H.M., Tab. (O'Neal)
Trilox, Susp., Tab. (Blue Line)
Trisogel, Liq. Pulv. (Lilly)

MAGNESIUM ZINC SHAKE LOTION. (Durel) Magnesium carbonate, zinc oxide, lime water, menthol, phenol 0.5%. Bot. 8 oz., gal.
Use: Generalized and widely disseminated erythematous, vesicular and papular eruptions.

MAGNIPIN. (Kenyon) Atropine sulfate 1/500 gr., nitroglycerin 1/500 gr., magnesium sulfate 5 gr., ext. ox bile 1 gr. Tab. Bot. 100s, 1000s.

MAGOLEUM. (Blue Line) Mineral oil 25%, milk of Mag. 75%. Bot. gal.
Use: Orally, laxative & antacid.

MAGONATE. (Fleming) Magnesium gluconate 500 mg./Tab. Bot. 100s, 1000s.
Use: Magnesium deficiencies.

MAG-OX. (Blaine) Magnesium oxide 400 mg./Tab. Bot. 100s, 1000s.
Use: Antacid, calcium oxalate urinary stone prevention.

MAGSAL. (U.S. Chemical) Magnesium salicylate 600 mg., phenyltoloxamine citrate 25 mg./Tab. Bot. 100s.
Use: Analgesic, anti-arthritic, dysmenorrhea.

MAGWOL #1 TABS. (Wolins) Aluminum hydroxide gel 200 mg., magnesium hydroxide 200 mg./Tab. Bot. 100s, 1000s.

MAINTENANCE VITAMIN FORMULA W/MINERALS. (Towne) Vit. A palmitate 10,000 I.U., D 400 I.U., B-1 5 mg., B-2 2.5 mg., C 75 mg., niacinamide 40 mg., B-6 1 mg., Ca pantothenate 4 mg., B-12 2 mcg., E 2 I.U., choline bitartrate 31.4 mg., inositol 15 mg., Ca 75 mg., P 58 mg., Fe 30 mg., Mg 3 mg., Mn 0.5 mg., K 2 mg., Zn 0.5 mg./Cap. Bot. 100s.

MAIZE PRO-GEN. Arsanilic acid, B.A.N.

MAJEPTIL. Thioproperazine. Psychopharmacologic agent; pending release.

MALAGRIDE.
See: Acetarsone.

MALARAQUIN. (Winthrop Products) Chloroquine phosphate.
Use: Antimalarial agent.

MALATONIC ELIXIR. (Blue Line) Peptonized iron 8 gr., fl. ext. cascara sagrada 12 mins., fl. ext. gentian 6 mins./fl. oz. alcohol 8% Bot. gal.
Use: Iron tonic.

• **MALETHAMER.** USAN. Maleic anhydride ethylene polymer.
Use: Antidiarrheal, antiperistaltic.

• **MALIC ACID,** N.F. XVI.

MALIC ACID WITH PECTIN.
See: Mallo-Pectin, Liq. (Mallard)

MALIDONE. Aloxidone, B.A.N.

MALLAMINT. (Mallard) Calcium carbonate 420 mg./Tab. Bot. 100s.

MALLISOL. (Mallard) Povidone-iodine.
Use: Germicidal, antiseptic surgical scrub soap.

MALLOPRESS. (Mallard) Hydrochlorothiazide 25 mg., reserpine 0.125 mg./Tab. Bot. 1000s.

MAL-O-FEM 90/4 L.A. IN OIL INJ. (Fellows) Testosterone enanthate 90 mg., estradiol valerate 4 mg./cc. Vial 10 cc.

MAL-O-FEM 180/8 L.A. IN OIL INJ. (Fellows) Testosterone enanthate 180 mg., estradiol valerate 8 mg./cc. Vial 10 cc.

MAL-O-FEM. (Fellows) **Aq.**—Testosterone 25 mg., estrone 2 mg./cc. Vial 10 cc.
Use: I.M., estrogen and androgen therapy.

MAL-O-FEM CYP. (Fellows) Testosterone cypionate 5[illegible] mg., estradiol cypionate 2 mg./cc. Vial 10 cc.

MALOGEL. (Quality Generics) Magnesium-Aluminum hydroxide gel. Bot. 12 oz., gal.
Use: Adsorbent-antacid.

MALOGEN INJECTION AQUEOUS. (Fellows) Testosterone. (25 mg./cc.) 10 cc., 30 cc.; (50 mg./cc.) 10 cc.; (100 mg./cc.) 10 cc.
Use: I.M., male hormone therapy.

MALOGEN 100 L.A. IN OIL INJ. (Fellows) Testosterone enanthate 100 mg./cc. 10 cc.

MALOGEN 200 L.A. IN OIL INJ. (Fellows) Testosterone enanthate 200 mg./cc. 10 cc.

MALOGEN CYP. (Fellows) Testosterone cypionate in oil 100 mg., 200 mg./cc. Vial 10 cc.

MALONAL.
See: Barbital (Various Mfr.)

MALOTRONE AQUEOUS INJECTION. (Bluco) Testosterone, USP 25 mg., 50 mg./cc. in aq. susp. Vial 10 cc.

MALOTUSS. (Mallard) Guaifenesin 100 mg./5 cc. Bot. 3 oz.
Use: Non-narcotic expectorant cough syrup.

MALTSUPEX. (Wallace) Laxative derived from natural barley malt extract for relief of constipation in children and adults. **Liq..** Bot. 8 oz., 1 pt. **Pow.,** dry, Jar. 8 oz., lb. **Tab.** Malt Soup ext. 750 mg./Tab. Bot. 100s.
W/Psyllium seed husks.
Use: Orally, laxative.
See: Syllamalt, Pow. (Wallace)

MAMMOL OINTMENT. (Abbott) Bismuth subnitrate 40%, castor oil 30%, lanolin 22%, ceresin wax 7%, balsam peru 1%. Tube 7/8 oz., 12s.
Use: Dressing for nipples of nursing mothers.

MANALAX. (Jenkins) Phenolphthalein 0.12 Gm., atropine sulfate 0.12 mg., w. mannitol, sodium glycocholate, sodium taurocholate, ext. cascara/Tab. Bot. 100s, 1000s.
Use: Constipation.

MANCHANIL. (D'Franssia)
Use: Bleaching creme.

MANDELAMINE. (Parke-Davis) **Tab.** contains 0.25 Gm. (3¾ gr.) methenamine mandelate. Bot. 100s, 1000s. **Susp.** (250 mg./5 ml.) Bot. 4 oz., 1 pt. (500

ng./5 ml.) Bot. 8 oz., 16 oz. **Granules.** 0.5 Gm./Packet. 56s. 1.0 Gm./Packet 56s.
Jse: Urinary antiseptic.
NDELAMINE "HAFGRAMS." (Parke-Davis) Methenamine mandelate 0.5 Gm./Tab. Bot. 100s, 000s. Unit dose 100s.
Jse: Urinary antiseptic.
NDELAMINE 1 GM. (Parke-Davis) Methenamine nandelate 1 Gm./Tab. Bot. 100s, 1000s. Unit dose 00s.
NDELAMINE SUSPENSION FORTE. (Parke-Davis) Methenamine mandelate susp. 500 mg./5 cc. Bot. oz., pt.
Jse: Urinary antiseptic.
NDELETS. (Quality Generics) Methenamine nandelate 0.5 Gm. or 1.0 Gm./Tab. Bot. 100s, 000s.
NDELIC ACID.
Jse: Orally, urinary antiseptic.
NDELIC ACID SALTS.
See: Calcium mandelate (Var. Mfr.)
NDELYLTROPEINE.
See: Homatropine Salts (Var. Mfr.)
NDEX. (Vale) Methenamine mandelate 250 mg., alicylamide 120 mg., ext. belladonna 5 mg./Tab. Bot. 100s, 500s, 1000s.
Jse: Urinary antiseptic.
NDOL. (Lilly) Cefamandole nafate. Vials: **500 ng./10 ml.** Traypak: 25s; **1 Gm./10 ml.** Traypak: 25s; **1 Gm./100 ml.** Traypak: 10s; **2 Gm./20 ml.** Traypak: 10s; **2 Gm./100 ml.** Traypak: 10s; **10 Gm./100 ml.** Traypak 6s; Faspak: 1 Gm. or 2 Gm., Pkg 96s.
Jse: Antibiotic.
ANGANESE CHLORIDE, U.S.P.XXI. Inj., U.S.P. XXI.
Jse: Manganese deficiency treatment.
See: Mangatrace, Inj. (Armour)
NGANESE GLUCONATE. (Western Research) 5.45 mg./Tab. Bot. 1000s.
NGANESE GLYCEROPHOSPHATE. Glycerol phosphate manganese salt.
Jse: Pharmaceutical necessity.
NGANESE HYPOPHOSPHITE. Manganese (2+) phosphinate.
Jse: Pharmaceutical necessity.
ANGANESE SULFATE. U.S.P. XXI. Inj, U.S.P. XXI.
Thyroid, ferrous sulfate, ferrous gluconate, sod. erric pyrophosphate, ext. of nux vomica.
See: Hemocrine, Tab. (Mallard)
NGATRACE. (Armour) Manganese chloride njection containing manganese 0.1 mg./ml. Vial 10 nl. Box 25s.
Jse: Dietary supplement to I.V. Solutions for nanganese deficiency.
NIRON. (Bowman) Ferrous fumarate 3 mg./Tab. Bot. 100s, 1000s, 5000s.
Jse: Anemias.
NITERA. (Vitarine) High potency multiple vitamins.
Jse: Dietary supplement.
NIVIM. (Vitarine) Vit. A 10,000 I.U., D 1000 I.U., E I.U., B-1 20 mg., B-2 6 mg., B-12 10 mcg., B-6 0.5 mg., C 30 mg., biotin 1 mcg., niacinamide 10 mg., Ca pantothenate 3 mg., choline bitartrate 20 mg., inositol 20 mg., dl-methionine 20 mg., pd. wh. dried liver 100 mg., dried debit. yeast 100 mg., dicalcium phosphate 200 mg., ferrous gluconate 50 mg., pot. iodide 0.15 mg., Mg sulfate 7.2 mg., Cu sulfate 5 mg., Mn sulfate 3.4 mg., Zn sulfate 5 mg., pot. chloride 25 mg./Cap. Bot. 100s.
Use: Vitamin-mineral supplement.
MANN A.R.P. SOLUTION. (Mann) Bot. pt., qt., 0.5 gal., gal.
Use: Prevention of rust in sterilizers.
MANN ASTRINGENT MOUTH WASH CONCENTRATE. (Mann) Bot. 4 oz., qt., 0.5 gal., gal. Also mint flavored. Bot. qt., 0.5 gal., gal.
MANNA SUGAR.
See: Mannitol (Various Mfr.)
MANNAN. (Rugby) Purified glucomannan 500 mg./Cap. Bot. 90s.
Use: Dietary supplement.
MANN BODY DEODORANT. (Mann) Bot. 4 oz., 8 oz., pt., qt., gal.
MANN BREATH DEODORANT. (Mann) Bot. 1 oz., 4 oz., 8 oz., pt., qt., gal.
MANN EMOLLIENT. (Mann) Jar. 100 Gm.
Use: Preoperative protective application.
MANN EUGENOL U.S.P. EXTRA. (Mann) 0.25 lb., 0.5 lb., 1 lb.
Use: With zinc oxide as protective pack.
MANN GERMICIDAL SOLUTION. (Mann) Bot. gal., 6 gal. **Conc.** 12.8%. Bot. pt., qt., 0.5 gal., gal.
MANN HAND LOTION. (Mann) Twin Pack, gal.
MANN HEMOSTATIC. (Mann) Bot. 4 oz., 8 oz., pt., qt.
Use: Stop capillary bleeding.
MANN LIQUID SOAP. (Mann) Concentrated cococastile. Bot. qt., 0.5 gal., gal.
MANN LUBRICANT AND CLEANSER. (Mann) Bot. pt., qt.
MANN SUPERFATTED BAR SOAP. (Mann) Rich in lanolin. Cake. 12s.
MANN TALBOT'S IODINE. (Mann) Glycerin base. Bot. 4 oz., 8 oz., pt., qt., gal.
MANN TOPICAL ANESTHETIC. (Mann) Bot. 4 oz., 8 oz., pt., qt., gal. W/stain to indicate area treated. Bot. 4 oz., 8 oz., pt., qt.
Use: Local surface anesthetic.
MANNITE.
See: Mannitol, U.S.P. XXI.
• **MANNITOL,** U.S.P. XXI. Inj. U.S.P. XXI. Manna Sugar, D-Mannitol, Mannite.
See: Osmitrol (Travenol)
W/Aluminum hydroxide, magnesium hydroxide, glycine, calcium carbonate, oil of peppermint.
See: Gas-Eze, Tab. (Edward J. Moore)
W/Sorbitol.
See: Cystosol, Liq. (Travenol)
Cytal, Liq. (Cutter)
• **MANNITOL INJECTION,** U.S.P. XXI. (Abbott) 20%, 15%. Abbo-Vac Single dose container 500 ml.; 10%, 5%. Abbo-Vac Single dose container 1000 ml. diuretic.

Use: Diagnostic aid (renal function determination); diuretic.
See: Mannitol Solution, Amp. (Merck Sharp & Dohme)

MANNITOL HEXANITRATE.
Use: Orally, coronary vasodilator.
See: Vascunitol, Tabs. (Apco)
W/Reserpine, rutin, ascorbic acid.
See: Ruhexatal W/Reserpine, Tab. (Lemmon)

MANNITOL HEXANITRATE & PHENOBARBITAL TAB. (Bowman; Quality Generics; Jenkins; Kenyon) Mannitol hexanitrate 0.5 gr., phenobarbital 0.25 gr./Tab. Bot. 1000s. (Kenyon): Bot. 100s, 1000s.

MANNITOL HEXANITRATE WITH PHENOBARBITAL COMBINATIONS.
See: Hyrunal, Tab. (Kenyon)
Manotensin, Tab. (Dunhall)
Ruhexatal, Tab. (Lemmon)
Vascused, Tabs. (Apco)
Vermantin, Tab. (Trout)

• **MANNITOL & SODIUM CHLORIDE INJECTION,** U.S.P. XXI.
Use: Diuretic.

MANNOMUSTINE. B.A.N. 1,6-Di-(2-chloroethyl-amino)-1,6-dideoxy-D-mannitol. Degranol dihydrochloride.
Use: Antineoplastic agent.

MANOLA. (Manola Co.) Thiamine HCl 10 mg., riboflavin 3 mg., niacinamide 2.5 mg., iron citrate 3 gr., conc. sols. of glycerophosphates of Sod., Pot. & Cal. 12 min. in palatable aromatic menstruum & 15% alcohol/fl. oz. Bot. pt., 1 gal.
Use: Deficient nutrition.

MANOTENSIN. (Dunhall) Mannitol hexanitrate 32 mg., phenobarbital 16 mg./Tab. Bot. 100s, 1000s.
Use: Vasodilator.

MANOXOL OT. B.A.N. Docusate Sodium.

MANTADIL. (Burroughs Wellcome) Chlorocyclizine HCl 2%, hydrocortisone acetate 0.5%, liq. and white petrolatum, wax, methylparaben 0.25%. Cream Tubes 15 Gm.
Use: Antipruritic, anti-inflammatory, anesthetic.

MANTOMIDE. Chlorbetamide, B.A.N.

MANTOUX TEST.
See: Tuberculin, U.S.P. XXI. Test (Parke-Davis)

MANVENE. 3-Methoxy-16a-methyl-1,3,5: 10-estratriene-16B, 17B-diol.
Use: Treatment of prostatic cancer.

MANVITOL. (Vitarine) High potency Vitamin B complex w/iron and Vit. B-12, C and E. Cap. Bot. 100s.
Use: Supplement.

MANZAN. (DeWitt) Ointment Tube 1 oz., 2 oz. Supp. 12s.
Use: Antihemorrhoidal.

MAOLATE TABLETS. (Upjohn) Chlorphenesin carbamate 400 mg./Tab. Bot. 50s, 500s. Unit-Dose 100s.
Use: Muscle relaxant, mild tranquilizer.

MAPHENIDE. p-Sulphamoylbenzylamine HCl.
See: Sulfbenzamine HCl

MAPROFIX.
See: Gardinol Type Detergents (Various Mfr.)

• **MAPROTILINE.** USAN. N-Methyl-9, 10-ethanoanthracene-9(10H)-propylamine. 3-(9, 10-Dihydro-9, 10-ethanoanthracen-9-yl)propylmethylamine.
Use: Antidepressant.
See: Ludiomil, Tab. (Ciba).

• **MAPROTILINE HYDROCHLORIDE,** U.S.P. XXI. Tab., U.S.P. XXI. 9,10-Ethanoathracene-9(10H)-propanamine, N-methyl-, hydrochloride.
Use: Antidepressant.

MARACID-2. (Marin) Magnesium trisilicate 150 mg., aluminum hydroxide dried gel 90 mg., aminoacetic acid 75 mg./Tab. Bot.
Use: Antacid, adsorbant.

MARANOX. (C.S. Dent) Phenacetin 100 mg., acetaminophen 60 mg., salicylamide, caffeine/Tab. Bot.: 9 Tab. (6 white for prompt action and 3 orange for delayed action), 18 Tab. (12 white and orange).
Use: Analgesic.

MARAX DF SYRUP. (Roerig) A colorless dye free syrup containing hydroxyzine HCl 2.5 mg., ephedrine sulfate 6.25 mg., theophylline 32.5 mg., alcohol 5%/5 cc. Bot. Pt., gal.
Use: Bronchodilator.

MARAX TAB. (Roerig) Hydroxyzine HCl 10 mg., ephedrine sulf. 25 mg., theophylline 130 mg./Tab. Bot. 100s, 500s.
Use: Bronchodilator.

MARAZIDE. (Vortech) Benzthiazide 50 mg./Tab. Bot. 100s, 1000s.
Use: Diuretic.

MARAZIDE II. (Vortech) Trichloromethazide 4 mg./Tab. Bot. 100s, 1000s.
Use: Diuretic.

MARBAXIN-750. (Vortech) Methocarbamol 75[0] mg./Cap. Bot. 500s.
Use: Skeletal muscle relaxant.

MARBEC. (Marlyn) High potency B and C vitamins. **Tabs.** Bot. 100s, 1000s.

MARBLEN LIQUID. (Fleming) Magnesium carbonate 400 mg., calcium carbonate 520 mg./5 cc. Bot. pt. gal.
Use: Antacid.

MARBLEN TABLETS. (Fleming) Magnesium and calcium carbonate 21 gr./Tab. Bot. 100s, 1000s.
Use: Antacid.

MARCAINE. (Winthrop-Breon) Bupivacaine in sterile isotonic solution containing sod. chloride, pH adjusted 4.0 to 6.5 w/sod. hydroxide or hydrochloric acid.Multiple-dose vials also contain methylparaben. 1 mg./ml. as preservative . **0.25%:** Amp. 50 ml. Box 5s. Vial: single dose 10 ml., 30 ml. Box 10s; multiple dose 50 ml. Box 1s. **0.5%:** Amp. 30 ml. Box 1s. Vial: single dose 10 ml., 30 ml. Box 10s. multiple dose 50 ml. Box 1s. **0.75%:** Amp. 30 ml. Box 5s. Vial (single dose) 10 ml., 30 ml. Box 10s.
Use: Local anesthetic (injectable) for peripheral nerve block, infiltration, sympathetic block, caudal or epidural block, retrobulbar block (see package insert for complete use recommendations).

MARCAINE WITH EPINEPHRINE (1:200,000). (Winthrop-Breon) **Bupivacaine 0.25%**: with epinephrine 1:200,000: in sterile isotonic solution containing sodium chloride. Each 1 ml. contains 2.5 mg bupivacaine hydrochloride and 0.0091 mg. epinephrine bitartrate, with 0.5 mg. sodium metabisulfite, 0.001 ml. monothioglycerol, and 2 mg. ascorbic acid as antioxidants, 0.0017 ml. 60% sodium lactate buffer and 0.1 mg. edetate calcium disodium as stabilizer. In Multiple Dose Vials, each 1 ml. also contains 1 mg. methylparaben as antiseptic preservative. pH adjusted to between 3.4 and 4.5 with sodium hydroxide or hydrochloric acid. Amp. 50 ml. 5s, Single Dose Vials, 10 ml., 30 ml. 10s, Multiple Dose Vials, 50 ml. 1s. **Bupivacaine 0.5%**: with epinephrine 1:200,000: in sterile isotonic solution containing sodium chloride. Each 1 ml. contains 5 mg. bupivacaine hydrochloride and 0.0091 mg. epinephrine bitartrate, with 0.5 mg. sodium metabisulfite, 0.001 ml. monothioglycerol and 2 mg. ascorbic acid as antioxidants, 0.0017 ml. 60% sodium lactate buffer, and 0.1 mg. edetate calcium disodium as stabilizer. In Multiple Dose Vials, each 1 ml. also contains 1 mg methylparaben as antiseptic preservative. pH adjusted to between 3.4 and 4.5 with sodium hydroxide or hydrochloric acid. Amp. 3 ml. 10s, 30 ml. 5s, Single Dose Vials 10 ml., 30 ml. 10s, Multiple Dose Vials 50 ml. 1s. **Bupivacaine 0.75%**: with epinephrine 1:200,000: in sterile isotonic solution containing sodium chloride. Each 1 ml. contains 7.5 mg. bupivacaine hydrochloride and 0.0091 mg. epinephrine bitartrate with 0.5 mg. sodium metabisulfite, 0.001 ml. monothioglycerol and 2 mg. ascorbic acid as antioxidants, 0.0017 ml. 60% sodium lactate buffer and 0.1 mg. edetate calcium disodium as stabilizer. pH adjusted to between 3.4 and 4.5 with sodium hydroxide or hydrochloric acid. Amp 30 ml. 5s.
Use: Local anesthetic (injectable) for peripheral nerve block (see package insert for complete use recommendations).

MARCAINE SPINAL. (Winthrop-Breon) Bupivacaine HCl 15 mg./2 ml. (0.75%) and dextrose 165 mg./2 ml. (8.25%). Amp. 2 ml. Unit dose pak 10s.
Use: Production of subarachnoid block.

MARDON. (Geneva) Propoxyphene HCl 32 mg./Cap. Bot. 100s, 1000s. 65 mg./Cap. Bot. 100s, 500s, 1000s.

MARDON COMPOUND. (Geneva) Propoxyphene comp. 65 mg., aspirin 3.5 gr., phenacetin 2.5 gr., caffeine 0.5 gr./Cap. Bot. 100s, 500s, 1000s.

MAREZINE INJECTION. (Burroughs Wellcome) Cyclizine lactate. Amp. (50 mg./ml.) 1 ml., Box 12s.
Use: Antinauseant for motion sickness.

MAREZINE TABLETS. (Burroughs Wellcome) Cyclizine HCl 50 mg./Tab. Bot. 100s, 1000s. Box 12s.
Use: Antinauseant for motion sickness.

M/Ergotamine tartrate, caffeine.
See: Migral, Tabs. (Burroughs Wellcome)

MARFANIL.
See: Sulfbenzamine HCl (Var. Mfr.)

MARFLEX INJECTION. (Vortech) Vial 10 ml.
Use: Skeletal muscle relaxant.

MARFLEX TABLETS. (Vortech) Orphenadrine citrate 100 mg./Tab. Bot. 100s, 500s.
Use: Skeletal muscle relaxant.

MARGESIC A-C. (Vortech) Propoxyphene HCl 65 mg., aspirin 389 mg., caffeine 32.4 mg./Cap. Bot. 500s.
Use: Analgesic.

MARGESIC IMPROVED. (Vortech) Propoxyphene HCl 65 mg. Bot. 100s, 1000s.
Use: Analgesic.

MARHIST. (Marlop) Chlorpeniramine maleate 20 mg., phenylephrine HCl 2.5 mg., methscopolamine nitrate in special base/Cap. Bot. 30s, 100s. Expect. Bot. 4 oz., pt., gal.
Use: Relief of cold symptoms and hay fever symptoms.

MARION THYROID TABLETS. (Marion) Thyroid 1 gr. or 2 gr./Tab. Bot. 100s.
Use: Thyroid replacement.

MARMINE. (Vortech) Dimenhydrinate 50 mg./Tab. Bot. 1000s.
Use: Antinauseant, motion sickness.

MARMINE INJECTION. (Vortech) Dimenhydrinate 50 mg./cc. Vial 10 ml.
Use: Antinauseant, motion sickness.

MARNAL CAPSULES. (Vortech) Butalbital 50 mg., aspirin 325 mg., caffeine 40 mg./Cap. Bot. 1000s.
Use: Analgesic, sedative.

MARNAL TABLETS. (Vortech) Butabital 50 mg., aspirin 325 mg., caffeine 40 mg./Tab. Bot. 1000s.
Use: Analgesic, sedative..

MARPLAN. (Roche) Isocarboxazid 10 mg./Tab. Bot. 100s.
Use: Amine oxidase regulator, mental depression.

MARSHALL'S CUBEB CIGARETTES. (Guild) Pkg. 8s.

MARUATE-25. (Vortech) Diethylpropion HCl 25 mg./Tab. Bot. 100s, 1000s.
Use: Appetite suppressant.

MARUATE SPANTAB. (Vortech) Diethylpropion HCl 75 mg./Cap. Bot. 100s, 1000s.
Use: Anorectic.

MARZINE HYDROCHLORIDE. Cyclizine, B.A.N.

MASSE BREAST CREAM. (Advanced Care) Water, glyceryl monostearate, glycerin, cetyl alcohol, lanolin, peanut oil, Span-60, stearic acid, Tween-60, sodium benzoate, propylparaben, methylparaben, potassium hydroxide.
Use: Nipple care.

MASSENGILL FEMININE DEODORANT SPRAY. (Beecham Products) Aerosol Bot. 3 oz.
Use: Vaginal deodorant.

MASSENGILL DISPOSABLE DOUCHE. (Beecham Products) Water, alcohol, lactic acid, sodium lactate, octoxymol-9, cetylpyridium chloride, imidazolidinyl urea, disodium EDTA, fragrance, color. Bot. 6 oz.
Use: Liquid douche.

MASSENGILL LIQUID. (Beecham Products) Lactic acid, water, sodium lacate, methyl salicylate,

eucalyptol, menthol, thymol, octoxynol-9, color, alcohol. Bot. 4 oz., 8 oz.
Use: Vaginal douche.

MASSENGILL MEDICATED. (Beecham Products) Povidone iodine 0.23% when added to sanitized fluid. Bot. 6 oz.
Use: Medicated douche for vaginal therapy.

MASSENGILL POWDER. (Beecham Products) Sodium Cl., ammonium alum, PEG-8, methyl salicylate, eucalyptus oil, menthyl, thymol, phenol. Jar 4 oz., 8 oz., 16 oz., 22 oz. Packette 10s, 12s.
Use: Vaginal cleanser.

MASSENGILL VINEGAR-WATER DISPOSABLE DOUCHE. (Beecham Products) Water and vinegar solution. Bot. 6 oz.
Use: Disposable liquid douche.

MASTER FORMULA. (Barth's) Vit. A 10,000 I.U., D 400 I.U., C 180 mg., B-1 7 mg., B-2 14 mg., niacin 4.6 mg., B-6 292 mcg., pantothenic acid 210 mcg., B-12 25 mcg., biotin 2.9 mcg., E 50 I.U., calcium 800 mg., P 387 mg., iron 10 mg., iodine 0.1 mg., choline 7.78 mg., inositol 11.6 mg., aminobenzoic acid 35 mcg., rutin 30 mg., citrus bioflavonoid complex 30 mg./4 Tab. Bot. 120s, 600s, 1200s.

MASTISOL. (Ferndale) Nonirritating medical adhesive. Bot. 4 oz.
Use: Skin dressing adhesive.

MATERNA 1.60. (Lederle) Vit. A 8000 I.U., D 400 I.U., E 30 I.U., C 100 mg., folic acid 1.0 mg., B-1 3 mg., B-2 3.4 mg., B-6 4 mg., niacinamide 20 mg., B-12 12 mcg., Ca 250 mg., iodine 0.3 mg., Mg 25 mg., Fe 60 mg., Cu 2 mg., Zn 25 mg./Tab. Bot. 100s.
Use: Prenatal supplement.

MATERNAVITE CAPSULES. (Knight) Bot. 100s.
Use: Prenatal vitamin.

MATULANE. (Roche) Procarbazine HCl 50 mg./Cap. Bot. 100s.
Use: Palliative treatment of Hodgkin's disease.

MAURRY'S FUNGICIDE. (Maurry) Nitromersol 37 mg., alcohol 70-74%/oz. Bot. 1 oz., pt.
Use: External fungus infection.

MAXAFIL CREAM. (Rydell) Cinoxate 4%, methyl anthranilate 5% in cream base. Tube 1 oz.
Use: Sunscreen.

MAXAMAG SUSPENSION. (Vitarine) Magnesium hydroxide, aluminum hydroxide gel.
Use: Antacid.

MAXIBOLIN. (Organon) Ethylestrenol 2 mg./Tab. Bot. 100s. Elixir 2 mg./5 ml. Bot. 4 oz.
Use: Anabolic agent.

MAXIDEX. (Alcon) Dexamethasone 0.1% in a 0.5% solution, methylcellulose vehicle/5 cc. Bot. 5 cc. & 15 cc.
Use: Ophthalmic anti-inflammatory.

MAXIFLOR CREAM & OINTMENT. (Herbert) Diflorasone diacetate 0.05%. Tubes 15 Gm., 30 Gm., 60 Gm.
Use: Steroid-responsive dermatoses.

MAXIGESIC. (Merchant) Codeine phosphate 30 mg., acetaminophen 325 mg., promethazine HCl 6.25 mg./Cap. Bot. 100s.
Use: Analgesic.

MAXIMUM STRENGTH NO-ASPIRIN SINUS MEDICATION. (Walgreen) Acetaminophen 500 mg., pseudoephedrine HCl 30 mg./Tab. Bot. 50s.
Use: Analgesic, decongestant.

MAXITON.
See: Amphetamine (Various Mfr.)

MAXITROL OINTMENT. (Alcon) Dexamethasone 0.1%, neomycin 3.5 mg., polymyxin B sulfate 10,000 u./Gm. Tubes 3.5 Gm.
Use: Ocular infections.

MAXITROL OPHTHALMIC SUSPENSION. (Alcon) Dexamethasone 0.1%, neomycin (as sulfate) 3.5 mg., polymyxin B sulfate 10,000 u./cc. Bot. 5 cc. droptainer.
Use: Infectious ocular inflammations.

MAXZIDE. (Lederle) Hydrochlorothiazide 50 mg., triamterene 75 mg./Tab. Bot. 100s, Unit-dose 10 10s.
Use: Diuretic/antihypertensive.

MAYASEN. (Janssen) Astemizole
Use: Anti-allergenic, antihistaminic.

• **MAYTANSINE.** USAN.
Use: Antineoplastic.

MAY-VITA ELIXIR. (Mayrand) Dexpanthenol 10 mg., niacinamide 40 mg., B-6 4 mg., B-12 12 mcg., folic acid 1 mg., Fe 36 mg.; Zn 15 mg., Mn 4 mg./45 ml. w/alcohol 13%. Bot. Pts.
Use: Vitamin/mineral supplement.

MAZANOR. (Wyeth) Mazindol 1 mg./Tab. Bot. 30s.
Use: Anorectic agent.

• **MAZINDOL,** U.S.P. XXI. Tab., U.S.P. XXI. 5-(p-Chlorophenyl)-2,3-dihydro-5,H-imidazo [2,1-a]isoindol-5-ol.
Use: Anorexic; appetite suppressant.
See: Mazanor, Tab. (Wyeth)
Sanorex, Tab. (Sandoz)

MAZON MEDICATED CREAM. (Norcliff Thayer) Coal tar 0.18%, salicylic acid 1%, resorcinol 1%, benzoic acid 0.5%. Jar 1.75 oz., 3 oz.
Use: Dermatologic.

MBF. (Gerber) Meat Base Formula Liquid hypoallergenic infant feeding formula. Made from beef hearts, water, cane sugar, sesame oil, modified tapioca starch, w/tricalcium phosphate, calcium citrate, potassium chloride, iodized salt, Mg chloride, Na ascorbate, ferrous sulfate, zinc sulfate, Mn sulfate, biotin, cupric sulfate, potassium iodide and Vit. A, B-2, B-6, B-12, niacinamide, calcium pantothenate, folic acid, D, E, and K. Cans 15 oz.
Use: Hypoallergenic infant formula, specifically for milk intolerance or lactose intolerance, and other non-specific food intolerances.

M-CAPS. (Mill-Mark) Methionine 200 mg./Cap. Bot. 50s, 1000s.
Use: Diaper rash and odor control.

M-CILLIN B-400 POWDER. (Misemer) Bot. 80 cc, 1[illegible] cc.

MCT OIL. (Mead Johnson) Triglycerides of medium chain fatty acids. Lipid fraction of coconut oil; fatty acid shorter than C-8 <6%, C_8(octanoic) 67%, C_{10}(decanoic) 23%, longer than C_{10} <4%. Bot. qt.
Use: Easily absorbed dietary fat.

DP-SQUIBB. (Squibb) Technetium Tc 99 medronate. Pkg. 10 reaction vials.
Use: Bone imaging agent to delineate areas of altered osteogenesis..

EADININ. Mixture of Amoidin & Amidin alk. of Ammi Majus Linn.

EASLES CONVALESCENT SERUM.
See: Measles Immune Human Serum

EASLES IMMUNE GLOBULIN (HUMAN). Sterile soln. of gamma globulin derived from pooled normal human plasma.
Use: In conjunction with live attenuated measles virus vaccine, to attenuate symptoms.

EASLES PROPHYLACTIC SERUM.
See: Immune Serum Globulin (Human)

MEASLES & MUMPS VIRUS VACCINE LIVE, U.S.P. XXI.

EASLES, MUMPS AND RUBELLA VIRUS VACCINE LIVE, U.S.P. XXI.

EASLES AND RUBELLA VIRUS VACCINE LIVE, U.S.P. XXI.
See: M-R-Vax, Inj. (Merck Sharp & Dohme)

MEASLES VIRUS VACCINE, LIVE, U.S.P. XXI. Modified live-virus measles vaccine (Schwarz strain).
Use: One-shot vaccine for common measles (rubeola).
Use: Active immunizing agent.
See: Attenuvax, Inj. (Merck Sharp & Dohme)
Lirugen, Inj. (Merrell Dow)
M-Vac, Inj. (Lederle)
/Mumps virus vaccine, rubella virus vaccine.
See: Lirutrin, Vial (Merrell Dow)
/Rubella virus vaccine.
See: Lirubel, Vial (Merrell Dow)
M-R-Vax, Inj. (Merck Sharp & Dohme)

EASLES VIRUS VACCINE, LIVE ATTENUATED. Moraten line derived from Enders' attenuated Edmonston strain grown in cell cultures of chick embryos.
See: Attenuvax, Inj. (Merck Sharp & Dohme)
/Mumps virus vaccine, rubella virus vaccine.
See: M-M-R., Vial (Merck Sharp & Dohme)
/Rubella virus vaccine.
See: M-R-Vax, Inj. (Merck Sharp & Dohme)

EASURIN. (Winthrop-Breon) Aspirin 10 gr. in sustained-release form/Tab. Bot. 60s.
Use: Analgesic.

EBADIN. Dehydroemetine, B.A.N.

EBANAZINE. B.A.N. α-Methylbenzylhydrazine. Actomol
Use: Monoamine oxidase inhibitor.

EBARAL. (Winthrop-Breon) Mephobarbital. Tab. 0.5 gr. Bot. 250s, 1000s. 0.75 gr., 1.5 gr. Bot. 250s.
Use: Sedative, anticonvulsant for treatment petit mal and grand mal epilepsy.

MEBENDAZOLE, U.S.P. XXI. Tab., U.S.P. XXI. Methyl 5-benzoyl-2-benzimidazolecarbanate.
Use: Anthelmintic.
See: Vermox, Tab. (Janssen)

EBEVERINE. B.A.N. 4-[N-Ethyl-2-(4-methoxy-phenyl)-1-methylethylamino]butyl-3,4-dimethoxy-benzoate. Colofac; Duspatal; Duspatalin hydrochloride.

• **MEBEVERINE HYDROCHLORIDE.** USAN. 4-[Ethyl (p-methoxy-α-methyl-phenethyl) amino] butyl veratrate hydrochloride.
Use: Spasmolytic agent.

MEBEZONIUM IODIDE. B.A.N. 4,4′-Methylenedi-(cyclohexyltrimethylammonium iodide).
Use: Neuromuscular blocking agent.

MEBHYDROLIN. B.A.N. 5-Benzyl-1,2,3,4-tetrahydro-2-methyl-γ-carboline. Fabahistin napadisylate
Use: Antihistamine.

MEBINOL. Clefamide, B.A.N.

• **MEBROFENIN.** USAN.
Use: Diagnostic aid (hepatobiliary function determination).

• **MEBUTAMATE.** USAN. 2-Carbamoyloxymethyl-2,3-dimethyl carbamate. Capla.
Use: Hypotensive.

MECADOX. Carbadox, B.A.N.

MECAMYLAMINE. B.A.N. 2,2,3-Trimethyl-3-methylaminobicyclo[2.2.1]heptane. Inversine; Mevasine hydrochloride.
Use: Hypotensive.

• **MECAMYLAMINE HYDROCHLORIDE,** U.S.P. XXI. Tab., U.S.P. XXI. N, 2, 3, 3-Tetramethyl-2-norbornanamine HCl. 3-Methylaminoiso-camphane HCl. N-Methyl-di-isobornylamine HCl.
Use: Antihypertensive.
See: Inversine, Tab. (Merck Sharp & Dohme)

• **MECETRONIUM ETHYLSULFATE.** USAN.
Use: Antiseptic.

• **MECHLORETHAMINE HYDROCHLORIDE,** U.S.P. XXI. Inj. U.S.P. XXI. 2,2′-Dichloro-n-methyl-diethylamine HCl. Trituration. Dichloren.
Use: Antineoplastic.
See: Mustargen, Vial (Merck Sharp & Dohme)

MECHOL INJ. (Manne) Vial 30 cc.

MECHOL TABS. (Manne) dl B-6 5 mg., soy protein 100 mg.; Vit. B-1 5 mg.; B-2 2mg.; C 75 mg.; niacinamide 20 mg.; pantothenic acid 2 mg.; brewer's yeast 2.5 gr./Tabs. Bot. 100s, 120s, 1000s.
Use: Metabolic tonic.

MECHOLIN HCl.
See: Methacholine Chloride, U.S.P. XXI.

MECHOLYL OINTMENT. (Gordon) Methacholine Cl 0.25%, methyl salicylate 10% in ointment base. Jar 4 oz., lb., 5 lb.
Use: Minor muscular aches and pains, simple neuralgia.

MECILLINAM. B.A.N. (2S,5R,6R)-6-(Perhydro-azepin-1-ylmethyleneamino)penicillanic acid.
Use: Antibiotic.

MECLAN. (Ortho) Meclocycline sulfosalicylate cream 1%. Tube 20 Gm., 45 Gm.
Use: Acne vulgaris treatment.

MECLASTINE. Clemastine.

• **MECLIZINE HYDROCHLORIDE,** U.S.P. XXI. Tab. U.S.P. XXI. 1(p-Chloro-α-phenylbenzyl)-4-m-(methylbenzyl)piperazine 2 HCl.
Use: Antinauseant.
See: Antivert, Tab., Chewable (Roerig)

• **MECLOCYCLINE.** USAN. 7-Chloro-4-(di-methylamino)-1, 4, 4a, 5, 5a, 6, 11, 12a-octahydro-3, 5,

10, 12, 12a-pentahydroxy-6-methylene-1, 11-dioxo-2-naphthacenecarboxamide.
Use: Antibiotic.

• **MECLOCYCLINE SULFOSALICYLATE,** U.S.P. XXI. Cream, U.S.P. XXI.
Use: Antibiotic
See: Meclan, Cream (Ortho)

• **MECLOFENAMATE SODIUM,** U.S.P. XXI. Cap., U.S.P. XXI. Benjoic acid, 2-(2, 6-dichloro-3-methylphenyl) amino)-, monosodium salt, monohydrate.
Use: Anti-inflammatory.

• **MECLOFENAMIC ACID.** USAN. N-(2,6-Dichloro-m-tolyl)-anthranilic acid.
Use: Anti-inflammatory.

MECLOFENOXATE. B.A.N. 2-Dimethylamino-ethyl 4-chlorophenoxyacetate. Lucidril hydrochloride
Use: Cerebral stimulant.

MECLOMEN. (Parke-Davis) Meclofenamate sodium monohydrate equiv. to 50 or 100 mg. meclofenamic acid/Cap. Bot. 100s, 500s (100 mg.). Unit dose 100s.
Use: Non-steroidal anti-inflammatory.

• **MECLOQUALONE.** USAN. 3-(o-Chlorophenyl)-2-methyl-4 (3 H)-quinazolinone.
Use: Sedative, hypnotic.

• **MECLORISONE DIBUTYRATE.** USAN.
Use: Anti-inflammatory.

• **MECOBALAMIN.** USAN.
Use: Vitamin.

MECLOZINE. B.A.N. 1-(4-Chlorobenzhydryl)-4-(3-methylbenzyl)piperazine. Ancolan dihydrochloride.
Use: Antihistamine.

MECOBALAMIN. B.A.N. α-(5,6-Dimethylbenzimidazol-1-yl)cobamide methyl.
Use: Treatment of vitamin B-12 deficiency.

MECODRIN.
See: Amphetamine (Various Mfr.)

• **MECRYLATE.** USAN. Methyl 2-cyanoacrylate.
Use: Surgical aid (tissue adhesive).

MECYSTEINE. Methyl Cysteine.

MEDA CAP. (Circle) Acetaminophen 500 mg./Cap. Bot. 100s.
Use: Analgesic, antipyretic.

MEDA-HIST ELIXIR. (Medwick) Bot. 4 oz., pt., gal.
Use: Decongestant.

MEDA-HIST EXPECTORANT. (Medwick) Bot. 4 oz., pt., gal.
Use: Decongestant, antitussive.

MEDA-HIST DH. (Medwick) Bot. 4 oz., pt., gal.
Use: Decongestant, antitussive.

MEDALOX. (Med. Chem; Medwick) Magnesium alum. hydroxide gel. Bot. 12 oz., pt., gal.
Use: Antacid.

MED-APAP ELIXIR. (Medwick) Bot. 4 oz., pt., gal.

MEDA-TEX. (Sutliff & Case) Ethinyl estradiol 0.01 mg., methyltestosterone 2.0 mg., Vit. A 5000 I.U., D 400 I.U., E 2 I.U., C 30 mg., B-1 3 mg., B-2 2 mg., B-6 0.5 mg., B-12 1 mcg., niacinamide 20 mg., calcium pantothenate 3 mg., Fe 60 mg., Cu 1 mg., Mn 3 mg., iodine 0.15 mg., Zn 1 mg., Mg 5 mg., Ca 48 mg., P 37 mg./3 Tabs. Bot. 100s, 1000s.

MEDA-TUSS. (Medwick) Bot. 4 oz., pt., gal.

MEDA-TUSS A-C. (Medwick) Bot. 4 oz., pt., gal.

MEDA-TUSS DM. (Medwick) Bot. 4 oz., pt., gal.

MEDA-TUSS PE. (Medwick) Bot. 4 oz., pt., gal.

MEDAZEPAM. B.A.N. 7-Chloro-2,3-dihydro-1-methyl-5-phenyl-1H-1,4-benzodiazepine. Nobrium.
Use: Tranquilizer.

• **MEDAZEPAM HCl.** USAN. 7-Chloro-2, 3-dihydro-1-methyl-5-phenyl-IH-1, 4-benzodiazepine mono-HC Under study.
Use: Tranquilizer.

MEDENT. (Stewart-Jackson) Pseudoephedrine HCl 12 mg., guaifenesin 500 mg./Tab. Bot. 100s.
Use: Temporary relief of nasal congestion and nonproductive cough.

MEDI-AID FIRST AID SPRAY. (Wisconsin) Bot. 4 oz
Use: Minor cut and burn treatment.

MEDIATRIC CAPS & TABS. (Ayerst) Conjugated Estrogens 0.25 mg., methyltestosterone 2.5 mg., Vit. C 100 mg., thiamine mononitrate 10 mg., Vit. B 12 2.5 mcg., ferrous sulfate exsic. 30 mg., B-2 5 mg B-6 3 mg., niacinamide 50 mg., Ca pantothenate 2 mg., methamphetamine HCl 1 mg./Cap. & Tab. **Cap.** Bot. 100s. **Tabs.** Bot. 100s.
Use: For use in aging patients of both sexes.

MEDIATRIC LIQUID. (Ayerst) Conjugated estrogens 0.25 mg., methyltestosterone 2.5 mg., Vit. B-1 5 mg B-12 1.5 mcg., methamphetamine HCl 1 mg./15 m Bot. 1 pt.
Use: For use in aging patients of both sexes.

MEDIBRIN-T FORMULA. (Image) Multiple vitamin. Bo 100s.
Use: Supplement.

MEDICAINE CREAM. (Walgreen) Benzocaine 3%, resorcinol 2%. Tube 1.25 oz.
Use: Antipruritic.

MEDICATED HEALER. (Walgreen) Strong ammonia sol. 10%, camphor 2.7%, Bot. 6 oz.
Use: Treatment for rough hands.

MEDICATED POWDER. (Johnson & Johnson) Zinc oxide, talc, fragrance, menthol. Plastic containers oz., 6 oz., 11 oz.
Use: Minor skin irritations.

MEDI CEPTIX FIRST AID SPRAY. (Eckerd) Alcohol 3.17%, octoxynol-9 1%, benzethonium chloride 5%. Bot. 4 oz.
Use: Topical antiseptic.

MEDI-CON CAPS. (Image) Bot. 100s.
Use: Supplement.

MEDICONE DRESSING. (Medicone) Cod liver oil 12 mg., zinc oxide 125 mg., 8-hydroxyquinoline-sulfa 0.5 mg., benzocaine 5 mg., menthol 1.8 mg./Gm. w/petrolatum, lanolin, talcum, paraffin, perfume. Tube 1 oz., 3 oz.; Jar 1 lb.
Use: Antiseptic skin preparation.

MEDICONE-HC RECTAL. (Medicone) Hydrocortiso acetate 10 mg., benzocaine 2 gr., oxyquinoline sulfate 0.25 gr., zinc oxide 3 gr., menthol 1/7 gr., balsam peru 1 gr., in a cocoa butter base/Supp. Box 12s. W/out H.C. Box 12s, 24s.
Use: Anorectal inflammation, pruritus and hemorrhoids.

MEDICONET. (Medicone) Benzalkonium chloride 0.02%, ethoxylated lanolin 0.5%, methylparaben

0.15%, hamamelis water 50%, glycerin 10%. Cloth wipe. Boxes 20s.
Use: Treatment of anal discomfort as a cleanser of the affected area.

EDIGESIC PLUS. (U.S. Chemical) Butalbital 50 mg., acetaminophen 325 mg., caffeine 40 mg./Cap.
Use: Analgesic-sedative.

EDIHALER-DUO. Now Duo-Medihaler.(Riker)

EDIHALER-EPI. (Riker) Epinephrine bitartrate 7.0 mg./ml. solution. Pkg. Medihaler in inert propellant. Oral adapter w/15 ml. vial. Refill Vial 15 ml.
Use: Inhalation, bronchial asthma therapy.

EDIHALER-ERGOTAMINE. (Riker) Ergotamine tartrate 9.0 mg./ml. 0.36 mg. is delivered with each inhalation. Oral adapter w/2.5 ml. Vial.
Use: Recurrent-type headache including migrainous headache.

EDIHALER-ISO. (Riker) Isoproterenol sulfate 2.0 mg./ml. solution. Oral adapter w/15 ml. vial; Oral adapter w/22.5 ml vial. Refill vials 15 ml. and 22.5 ml.
Use: Inhalation, bronchial asthma therapy.

EDI-JECT UNIT DOSE VIALS. (Century) Tamperproof rubber stoppered vial containing 1 ml. sterile solution. Single dose use.
See: Ulti-ject disposable syringe products.
  Atropine sulfate. 0.4 mg./ml.
  Atropine sulfate. 1.2 mg./ml.
  Scopolamine HBr. 400 mcg./ml.

EDIPAK. (Geneva) First aid kit.

EDI-PHITE. (Med. Chem.) Vitamin B-1 & B-12 syrup. Bot. 4 oz., pt., gal.

EDIPLEX TABULES. (U.S. Chemical) B-complex, Vit. C, Vit. E, trace minerals, zinc/Tab. Bot. 100s.
Use: Stress, alcoholism, geriatrics.

EDIQUE EAR DROPS. (Edward J. Moore) Carbamide peroxide in anhydrous glycerol.
Use: Antiseptic ear drops.

EDIQUELL. (Warner-Lambert) Dextromethorphan HBr 15 mg./Chewy square. Pkg. 12s, 24s.
Use: Cough suppressant.

EDI-QUIK AEROSOL. (Mentholatum) Lidocaine 2.5%, benzalkonium chloride 0.1%, ethanol 38%. Aerosol 3 oz.
Use: Antiseptic, anesthetic first-aid spray.

EDI-QUICK PUMP SPRAY. (Mentholatum) Lidocaine 2.5%, benzalkonium chloride, 0.1%, ethanol 38%, isopropyl alcohol. Bot. 4 oz.
Use: Antiseptic, anesthetic first-aid spray.

EDI-SPAS ELIXIR. (Medical Chemicals; Medwick) Phenobarbital 16.2 mg., hyoscyamine sulfate 0.1037 mg., atropine sulfate 0.0194 mg., hyoscine hydrobromide 0.0065 mg., alcohol 23%/5 cc. Bot. 4 oz., pt., gal.
Use: Antispasmodic and sedative.

EDI-TAL. (Medi-Rx) Phenobarbital 16 mg., hyoscyamine sulfate 0.1037 mg., atropine sulfate 0.0194 mg., scopolamine HBr 0.0065 mg., alcohol 23%/5 cc. Bot. pt., gal. Tabs., Bot. 100s, 1000s.
Use: Antispasmodic and sedative.

EDITUSSIN-X LIQUID. (Hauck) Codeine phosphate 50 mg., ammonium chloride 520 mg., potassium guaiacolsulfonate 520 mg., pyrilamine maleate 50 mg., phenylpropanolamine HCl 50 mg., dl-desoxyephedrine HCl 2 mg., tartar emetic 5 mg., phenyltoloxamine dihydrogen citrate 30 mg./30 cc. Bot. gal., pt.
Use: Antitussive antihistaminic expectorant.

MEDI-ZINC. (Image) Zinc supplement. Bot. 100s.
Use: Supplement.

MEDIZINC. (U.S. Chemical) Zinc sulfate 220 mg./Tab.
Use: Zinc deficiencies.

MEDODORM. Chlorhexadol, B.A.N.

MEDOTAR. (Medco Lab) Coal tar 1%, polysorbate 80 0.5%, octoxynol 5, zinc oxide, starch, white petrolatum. Jar 1 lb.
Use: Psoriasis and eczema, neurodermatitis, occupational and contact dermatitis.

■ **MEDOTOPES.** (Squibb) Radiopharmaceuticals.
See: A-C-D Solution Modified (Squibb)
  Acid Citrate Dextrose Anticoagulant Solution Modified (Squibb)
  Aggregated Albumin (Squibb)
  Albumotope (Squibb)
  Angiotensin Immutope Kit (Squibb)
  Cobalt-Labeled Vitamin B-12 (Squibb)
  Cobalt Standards for Vitamin B-12 (Squibb)
  Cobatope (Squibb)
  Digoxin (^{125}I) Immutope Kit (Squibb)
  Gastrin (^{125}I) Immutope Kit (Squibb)
  Gold-198 (Squibb)
  Hipputope (Squibb)
  Human Serum Albumin (Squibb)
  Iodine 131: Capsules Diagnostic-Capsules Therapeutic-Solution Therapeutic Oral (Squibb)
  Iodinated Human Serum Albumin (Squibb)
  Iodo-hippuric Acid (Squibb)
  Macroaggregated Albumin (Squibb)
  Macrotec (Squibb)
  Minitec (Squibb)
  Phosphorus-32: Solution Oral, Therapeutic-Sodium Phosphate Solution U.S.P. for oral or IV use therapeutic or diagnostic (Squibb)
  Red Cell Tagging Solution (Squibb)
  Renotec (Squibb)
  Rose Bengal (Squibb)
  Rubratope-57: Diagnostic Capsules-Diagnostic Kit (Squibb)
  Rubratope-60: Diagnostic Capsules-Diagnostic Kit (Squibb)
  Selenomethionine (Squibb)
  Sethotope (Squibb)
  Technetium 99m (Squibb)
  Technetium 99m-Iron-Ascorbate (DTPA) (Squibb)
  Technetium 99m Sulfur Colloid Kit (Squibb)
  Tesuloid (Squibb)
  Thyrostat-FTI (Squibb)
  Thyrostat-3 (Squibb)
  Thyrostat-4 FTI (Squibb)

MEDRALONE 40. (Keene) Methylprednisolone acetate 40 mg./ml. Vial 5 ml.
Use: Anti-inflammatory.

MEDRALONE 80. (Keene) Methylprednisolone acetate 80 mg/ml. Vial 5 ml.
Use: Anti-inflammatory.

• **MEDROGESTONE.** USAN. Formerly Metrogestone. Dimethyl pregna-4, 6 diene-3, 20-dione.
Use: Oral progestin.
See: Colprone (Ayerst)

MEDROL. (Upjohn) Methylprednisolone. **Tabs.:** 2 mg. Bot. 100s; 4 mg. Bot. 30s, 100s, 500s. Unit-Dose 100s; 8 mg. Bot. 25s; 16 mg. Bot. 50s; 24 mg. Bot. 25s; 32 mg. Bot. 25s. **Dosepak:** 4 mg. Pkg. 21s. **Alternate Daypak:** 16 mg. Pkg. 14s.
Use: An anti-inflammatory corticosteroid.

MEDROL ACETATE TOPICAL. (Upjohn) Methylprednisolone acetate 2.5 mg. or 10 mg., methylparaben 4 mg., butylparaben 3 mg./Gm. 0.25% Tube 7.5 Gm., 30 Gm. ; 1% Tube 7.5 Gm., 30 Gm.
Use: Allergic dermatoses and inflammatory skin diseases.

MEDROL ENPAK. (Upjohn) Methylprednisolone acetate 40 mg. w/sod. chloride, polysorbate 80 Bot. when reconstituted as directed. Pak 6 Bot. & 1 administration unit. Refill Pk. 12s.
Use: Retention enema for adjunctive treatment of ulcerative colitis.

• **MEDRONATE DISODIUM.** USAN.
Use: Pharmaceutic aid.

• **MEDRONIC ACID.** USAN.
Use: Pharmaceutic aid.

MEDRONE. (Kay) Methylprednisolone acetate 20 mg./ml. Vial 5 ml.; 40 mg./ml. Vial 5 ml., 10 ml.; 80 mg./ml. Vial 5 ml.
Use: I.M. Glucocorticosteroid.

MEDROSPHOL Hg-197. 1-(Hydroxymercuri-197 Hg)-2-propanol.
See: Merprane

• **MEDROXALOL.** USAN.
Use: Antihypertensive.

• **MEDROXALOL HYDROCHLORIDE.** USAN.
Use: Antihypertensive.

MEDROXYPROGESTERONE. B.A.N. 17 α-Hydroxy-6α-methylpregn-4-ene-3,20-dione. Provera acetate.
Use: Progestational steroid.

• **MEDROXYPROGESTERONE ACETATE,** U.S.P.XXI. Sterile Susp., Tab., U.S.P.XXI. 17-Hydroxy-6α-methylpregn-4-ene-3, 20-dione 17-Acetate. (CMC) 50 mg., 100 mg./ml. Vial 5 ml.
See: Amen, Tab. (Carnrick)
Curretab, Tab. (Reid-Provident)
depCorlutin (Forest)
Depo-Provera, Vials (Upjohn)
P-Medrate-P.A., Inj. (Reid-Provident)
Provera, Tab. (Upjohn)

• **MEDRYSONE,** U.S.P.XXI. Ophthalmic Suspension U.S.P.XXI. 11 β-Hydroxy-6α-methylpregn-4-ene-3,20-dione.
Use: Topical anti-inflammatory agent.
See: HMS Liquifilm, Ophth. Sol. (Allergan)

MED-TANE ELIXIR. (Medwick) Brompheniramine maleate. Bot. 4 oz., pt., gal.

MED-TANE EXPECTORANT DC. (Medwick) Brompheniramine maleate. Bot. 4 oz., pt., gal.

MED-TAPP ELIXIR. (Medwick) Bot. 4 oz., pt., gal.

• **MEFENAMIC ACID.** USAN. N-(2,3-Xylyl) anthranilic acid. Ponstan.
Use: Anti-inflammatory agent.
See: Ponstel, Kapseals (Parke-Davis)

• **MEFENIDIL.** USAN.
Use: Cerebral vasodilator

• **MEFENIDIL FUMARATE.** USAN.
Use: Cerebral vasodilator

MEFENOREX HCl. USAN. N-(3-chloropropyl)-α-methylphenethylamine HCl. Under study.
Use: Anorexiant.

• **MEFEXAMIDE.** USAN.
Use: Stimulant.

• **MEFLOQUINE.** USAN.
Use: Antimalarial.

• **MEFLOQUINE HYDROCHLORIDE.** USAN.
Use: Antimalarial.

MEFOXIN. (Merck Sharp & Dohme) Sterile cefoxitin sodium 1 Gm. and 2 Gm./Vial. **1 Gm.** Vial 10 ml. 10s, 25s. Infusion bottle 100 ml. Tray 10s. Premixed I.V. Soln. in 50 ml. D5W, 24s. **2 Gm:** Vial 20 ml. 10s, 25s. Infusion bottle 100 ml. Tray 10s. Premixed I.V. Soln. in 50 ml. D5W, 24s. Bulk pkg. 10 Gm./100 ml. bottle.
Use: Broad spectrum antibiotic by I.V. or I.M. administration.

MEFRUSIDE. USAN. (FBA) 4-Chloro-N'-methyl-N'-(tetrahydro-2-methylfurfuryl)-m-benzenedisulfonamide. Baycaron.
Use: Diuretic.

MEGA-B. (Arco) Vit. B-1 100 mg., B-2 60 mg., B-6 100 mg., B-12 100 mcg., niacinamide 100 mg., folic acid 100 mcg., pantothenic acid 100 mg., d-biotin 100 mcg., PABA 100 mg./Tab. Bot. 30s, 100s, 500s.

MEGACE. (Bristol Oncology) Megestrol acetate. 20 mg., 40 mg./Tab. Bot. 100s.
Use: Palliative treatment of advanced carcinoma of the breast or endometrium.

MEGACLOR. Clomocycline, B.A.N.

MEGADOSE. (Arco) Vit. A 25,000 USP U., D 1000 USP U, C 250 mg., E 100 I.U., folic acid 400 mcg B-1 80 mg., B-2 80 mg., niacinamide 80 mg., B-6 80 mg., B-12 80 mcg., biotin 80 mcg., pantothenic acid 80 mg., choline bitartrate 80 mg., inositol 80 mg., para-aminobenzoic acid 80 mg., rutin 30 mg., citrus bioflavonoids 30 mg., betaine HCl 30 mg., glutamic acid 30 mg., hesperidin complex 5 mg., iodine 0.1 mg., Ca gluconate 10 mg., ferrous gluconate 10 mg., Mg gluconate 7 mg., Mn gluconate 6 mg., Cu gluconate 0.5 mg./Cap. Bot. 100s, 250s.
Use: Dietary supplement.

• **MEGALOMICIN POTASSIUM PHOSPHATE.** USAN.
Use: Antibacterial.

MEGATON. (Hyrex) Thiamine HCl 2.5 mg., riboflavin 2.5 mg., pyridoxine HCl 1.0 mg., Vit. B-12 5.0 mcg., dexpanthenol 5 mg., niacin 10.0 mg., ferric pyrophosphate 20 mg./30 ml. W/alcohol 15%. Bot. 16 oz.
Use: Geriatric supplement.

EGA-VITA. (Saron) Vit. C 500 mg., niacinamide 500 mg., B-6 50 mg., B-1 25 mg., B-2 10 mg., B-12 50 mcg., folic acid 150 mcg., E 200 I.U., pantothenic acid 10 mg., A 2500 I.U., D 333 I.U., magnesium oxide 50 mg., zinc sulfate 50 mg./3 Tabs. Bot. 100s.
Use: Multivitamins with minerals.

EGA-VITA HEMATINIC. (Saron) Mega-Vita formula with iron 50 mg., Vit A 1000 I.U., Cu 2 mg., Mn 1.8 mg., iodine 0.1 mg., K 10 mg./3 Tabs.
Use: Multivitamin and mineral supplement.

EGA-VITA TONIC. (Saron) Vit. B-12 25 mcg., B-6 6 mg., niacin 25 mg., aminoacetic acid 750 mg./15 ml. w/alcohol 17%.
Use: Vitamin supplement.

EGESTROL. B.A.N. 17 α-Hydroxy-6-methylpregna-4,6-diene-3,20-dione.
Use: Progestogen.

IEGESTROL ACETATE. U.S.P. XXI. Tab., U.S.P. XXI. 17 α-acetoxy-6-methylpregna-4,6-diene-3, 20-dione.
Use: Palliative treatment of advanced carcinoma of the breast or endometrium.
See: Megace (Bristol Oncology)
Pallace, Tab. (Bristol)

EGIMIDE. Bemegride, B.A.N.

EGLUMINE, U.S.P. XXI. 1-Deoxy-1-methyl-amino glucitol. 1-Methylamino-1-deoxy-D-glucitol.
Use: Pharmaceutical aid.

IEGLUMINE, DIATRIZOATE INJ., U.S.P. XXI. N-Meglumine salt of 3, 5 diacetamido-2, 4, 6-triiodo-benzoic acid. Methylglucamine Diatrizoate. D-Glucitol, 1-deoxy-1-(methylamino).
Use: Radiopaque medium.
See: Cardiografin, Vial (Squibb)
Cystografin, Vials (Squibb)
Gastrografin, Soln. (Squibb)
Hypaque-76, Inj. (Winthrop-Breon)
Hypaque-M 75%, Inj. (Winthrop-Breon)
Hypaque-M 90%, Inj. (Winthrop-Breon)
Hypaque Meglumine, Vials (Winthrop-Breon)
Reno-M-30, -60, Vial (Squibb)
Reno-M-Dip, Vial (Squibb)
/Meglumine iodipamide.
See: Sinografin, Sol. (Squibb)
/Sodium diatrizoate.
See: Gastrografin, Sol. (Squibb)
Renografin-60, Inj. (Squibb)
Renografin-76, Inj. (Squibb)
Renovist II, Inj. (Squibb)

IEGLUMINE, IODIPAMIDE INJ., U.S.P. XXI. 1-Deoxy-1-(Methyl amino) glucitol, D glucitol, 1-deoxy-1-(methylamino)
Use: Radiopaque medium.
See: Cholografin, Vial (Squibb)
/Meglumine diatrizoate.
See: Sinografin, Sol. (Squibb)

IEGLUMINE, IOTHALAMATE INJ., U.S.P. XXI. 5-Acetamido-2,4,6-triiodo-N-methylisophthalamic acid, N-methylglucamine.
/Sod. iothalamate.
Use: Radiopaque medium.

• **MEGLUTOL.** USAN.
Use: Antihyperlipoproteinemic.

MEJEPTIL.
See: Thioperazine (SmithKline)

MEJORAL-ACETAMINOPHEN. (Glendbrook) Acetaminophen 500 mg./Tab. Bot. 30s, 60s.
Use: Analgesic.

MEJORAL-ASPIRIN. (Glenbrook) Aspirin 500 mg., caffeine 30 mg./Tab. Bot. 30s, 60s.
Use: Analgesic.

MEJORALITO. (Glenbrook) Acetaminophen. **Tab.:**80 mg./Tab. Bot. 30s. **Liquid:** 80 mg./0.8 ml. Bot. 1 oz.
Use: Analgesic, antipyretic.

MEKTEC 99 AUTOMATIC LIQUID EXTRACTOR. (Imaj International) Soln. 99m Tc Sodium Pertechnetate.
Use: Radiodiagnostic.

MELADRAZINE. B.A.N. 2,4-Di(diethylamino)-6-hydrazino-1,3,5-triazine. Lisidonil (+)-tartrate
Use: Polysynaptic inhibitor.

MELANEX. (Neutrogena) hydroquinone 30 ml./ml. in solution containing 47.3% alcohol. Bot. 1 oz. w/Appliderm applicator.
Use: Hyperpigmentation.

MELARSONYL POTASSIUM. B.A.N. Dipotassium 2-[4-(4,6-diamino-1,3,5-triazin-2-ylamino)phenyl]-1,3,2-dithiarsolan-4,5-dicarboxylate. Trimelarsan
Use: Treatment of trypanosomiasis.

MELARSOPROL. B.A.N. 2-[4-(4,6-Diamino-1,3,5-triazin-2-ylamino)phenyl]-4-hydroxymethyl-1,3,2-dithiarsolan. Mel B
Use: Treatment of trypanosomiasis.

• **MELENGESTROL ACETATE.** USAN.
Use: Antineoplastic, progestin.

MELFIAT. (Reid-Provident) Phendimetrazine tartrate 35 mg./Tab. Bot. 100s, 1000s.
Use: Management of obesity.

MELFIAT 105 UNICELLES. (Reid-Provident) Phendimetrazine tartrate 105 mg./S.R. Cap. Bot. 100s.
Use: Management of obesity.

MELHORAL CHILD TABLET. (Winthrop Products) Acetylsalicylic acid.
Use: Analgesic, antipyretic.

MELITOXIN.
See: Dicumarol (Various Mfr.)

• **MELITRACEN HYDROCHLORIDE.** USAN.
Use: Antidepressant.

• **MELIZAME.** USAN.
Use: Sweetener.

MELLARIL CONCENTRATE. (Sandoz) Thioridazine HCl Solution 30 mg./ml. w/alcohol 3.0% Bot. 4 oz. Concentrate 100 mg./ml. Pk. 4 oz.
Use: Tranquilizer.

MELLARIL S. (Sandoz) Thioridazine oral suspension 25 mg./5 ml. or 100 mg./5 ml. Bot. pt.
Use: Tranquilizer.

MELLARIL TABLETS. (Sandoz) Thioridazine HCl 10 mg., 15 mg., 25 mg., 50 mg., 100 mg., 150 mg., 200 mg./Tab. Bot. 100s, 1000s. 10 mg., 15 mg., 25

mg., 50 mg., 100 mg., 200 mg./Tab. SandoPak pkgs. 100s.
Use: Tranquilizer.

MELLOBATH. (Beiersdorf) Water dispersible oil containing a lanolin fraction, polyethylene glycol oleate, light mineral oil, and perfume. Bot. 1 pt.
Use: Bath oil.

MELLOSE. Methylcellulose.

MELOIDS. (Boots) Throat pastille. Tube 0.5 oz.
Use: Hoarseness and throat irritation.

MELONEX. Metahexamide.
Use: Oral antidiabetic.

• **MELPHALAN,** U.S.P. XXI. Tabs., U.S.P. XXI. L-3-{p[bis(2-Chloroethyl)amino]phenyl} alanine. Previously Sarcolysin.
Use: Antineoplastic.
See: Alkeran, Tab. (Burroughs Wellcome)

• **MEMOTINE HCl.** USAN. 3, 4-Dihydro-1-[(p-methoxy-phen-oxy)methyl] isoquinoline HCl.
Use: Antiviral.

• **MEMOTINE HYDROCHLORIDE.** USAN.
Use: Antiviral.

• **MENABITAN HYDROCHLORIDE.** USAN.
Use: Analgesic.

• **MENADIOL SODIUM DIPHOSPHATE,** U.S.P. XXI. Inj., Tab., U.S.P. XXI. 1,4-Naphtha-lenediol,2-methyl-,bis(dihydrogen phosphate), tetrasodium salt, hexahydrate.
Use: Vitamin K therapy (Orally or I.M. 4 to 75 mg.)
See: Kappadione, Amp. (Lilly)
Synkayvite, Amp. & Tab. (Roche)

• **MENADIONE,** U.S.P. XXI. Inj., U.S.P. XXI. 2-Methyl-1,4-naphthoquinone (Menaphthone, Danitamon K, Aquinone, Aquaday, Menaquinone).
Use: Orally & I.M., Vit. K therapy.
W/Ascorbic acid.
See: Rependo, Cap. (Scruggs)
W/Ascorbic acid, hesperidin.
See: Hescor-K, Tab. (Madland)
W/Bioflavonoid citrus compound, ascorbic acid.
See: C.V.P. W/Vitamin K, Syr., Tab. (USV Pharm.)

MENADIONE DIPHOSPHATE SODIUM.
See: Menadiol Sodium Diphosphate.

MENADIONE SODIUM BISULFITE. 2-Methyl-1,4-naphthoquinone sod. bisulfite. Sodium 1,2,3,4-tetrahydro-2-methyl-1,4-dioxo-2-naphthalenesulfonate.
Use: Vit. K therapy.

MENADOXIME. B.A.N. Ammonium salt of 2-methyl-naphthaquinone-4-oxime O-carboxymethyl ether. Kapilon Soluble.
Use: Treatment of hypoprothrombinemia.

MENAPHTHENE OR MENAPHTHONE.
See: Menadione (Various Mfr.)

MENAQUINONE.
See: Menadione (Various Mfr.)

MENEST. (Beecham Labs) Esterified estrogens, conjugated estrogens (equine) 0.3 mg., 0.625/Tab. Bot. 100s. 1.25 mg./Tab. Bot. 100s, 1000s. 2.5 mg./Tab. Bot. 50s.
Use: Menopausal symptoms.

MENI-D. (Seatrace) Dimenhydrinate 25 mg., niacin 50 mg./Cap. Bot. 100s.
Use: Vertigo treatment.

• **MENINGOCOCCAL POLYSACCHARIDE VACCIN GROUP A,** U.S.P. XXI.

• **MENINGOCOCCAL POLYSACCHARIDE VACCIN GROUPS A AND C COMBINED.** U.S.P. XXI.
See: Meningovax-AC, Inj. (Merck Sharp and Dohm
W/Groups A, C, Y, W-135 Combined.
See: Menomune, Inj. (Squibb-Connaught)

MENINGOCOCCAL POLYSACCHARIDE VACCINE GROUP A, GROUP C, GROUPS A AND C COMBINED AND GROUPS A, C, Y, W-135 CO BINED.
See: Menomune Inj. (Squibb-Connaught)

• **MENINGOCOCCAL POLYSACCHARIDE VACCIN GROUP C,** U.S.P. XXI.

• **MENOCTONE.** USAN. 2-(8-Cyclohexyl-octyl)-3-droxy-1, 4-naphthoquinone. Under study.
Use: Antimalarial.

MENOGEN. (General Pharm.) Conjugated estrogens 1.25 mg./Tab. Bot. 100s.
Use: Estrogen therapy.

MENOJECT L.A. (Mayrand) Testosterone cypionate estradiol cypionate. Vial 10 ml.

MENOLYN. (Arcum) Ethinyl estradiol 0.05 mg./Tab. Bot. 100s, 1000s.
Use: Hormone therapy.

MENOMUNE. (Squibb-Connaught) Meningococcal pc saccharide vaccine, Groups A, C, Y, W-135. Vials or 50 dose w/diluent.
Use: Immunization against infection caused by *Neisseria meningitis.*

MENOMUNE-C VACCINE. Group-specific polysacc ride antigen from Neisseria meningitis, Group C. Bot. 10 & 50 dose vials.
Use: Immunization.

• **MENOTROPINS,** U.S.P. XXI. For Inj., U.S.P. XXI.
Use: Gonadotropin.
See: Pergonal

MENRIUM. (Roche) **Menrium 5-2:** Chlordiazepoxid mg., conjugated estrogens 0.2 mg./Tab. **Menriur 5-4:** Chlordiazepoxide 5 mg., conjugated estroge 0.4 mg./Tab. **Menrium 10-4:** Chlordiazepoxide mg., conjugated estrogens 0.4 mg./Tab. Bot. 100
Use: Menopause syndromes.

MENSTRESS CAPS. (Pharmex) Cap. Bot. 15s.
Use: Cramps.

MENTHALGESIC LIQUID. (Blue Line) Menthol, camphor, methyl salicylate. Bot. 2 oz. 12s, pt., ga
Use: Rubefacient liniment (external use).

MENTHALGESIC OINTMENT. (Blue Line) Chloral hydrate 1.5%, methyl salicylate 12%, menthol 1.5%, camphor 1.5% in suitable ointment base. 1 lb.

p-MENTHAN-3-OL. Menthol, U.S.P. XXI.

MENTHOL, U.S.P. XXI. Cyclohexanol, 5-methyl-2-(1 methylethyl). p-Menthan-3-ol.
Use: Topical antipruritic, local analgesic, nasal decongestant, antitussive.
See: Benzedrex Inhaler (SmithKline)
Vicks Cough Silencers, Loz. (Vicks)
Vicks Formula 44 Cough Control Discs, Loz. (Vicks)
Vicks Inhaler (Vicks)

Vicks Blue Mint, Lemon, Regular & Wild Cherry Medicated Cough Drops (Vicks)
Vicks Medi-Trating Throat Lozenges (Vicks)
Vicks Oracin Regular & Cherry, Loz. (Vicks)
Vicks Sinex, Nasal Spray (Vicks)
Vicks Vaporub, Oint. (Vicks)
Vicks Vaposteam, Liq. (Vicks)
Vicks Va-Tro-Nol, Nose Drops (Vicks)
Victors Regular & Cherry, Loz. (Vicks)
'Combinations
See: Halls Mentho-Lyptus, Prods. (Warner-Lambert)
Listerine Antiseptic, Liq. (Warner-Lambert)

:NTHOLATUM. (Mentholatum) Menthol 1.35%, camphor 9%. Tube 1 oz., 0.4 oz. Jar. 1 oz., 3 oz.
Use: External analgesic.

:NTHOLATUM DEEP HEATING LOTION. (Mentholatum) Menthol 6%, methyl salicylate 20%, lanolin derivative. Bot. 2 oz., 4 oz.
Use: External analgesic.

:NTHOLATUM DEEP HEATING RUB. (Mentholatum) Menthol 5.9%, methyl salicylate 12.7%, eucalyptus oil, turpentine oil, lanolin anhydrous. Tube 1.25 oz., 3 1/3 oz., 5 oz.
Use: External analgesic.

:NTHOLIN. (Apco) Methyl salicylate 30%, chloroform 20%, hard soap 3%, camphor gum 2.2%, menthol 0.8%, alcohol 35%. Bot. 2 oz.
Use: External application for relief of superficial muscular aches and pains.

ENTHYL VALERATE. Validol.
Use: Sedative.

ENTROLZ. (Mayer) Mayercin (Homatropine methylbromide 0.5 mg. & amm. chloride 300 mg.), caffeine alk. 32 mg., acetophenetidin 150 mg., salicylamide 225 mg. Tab. Bot. 16s.
Use: Analgesic.

MEOBENTINE SULFATE. USAN.
Use: Cardiac depressant.

EPACRINE HYDROCHLORIDE.
Use: Anthelmintic, antimalarial.
See: Quinacrine Hydrochloride, U.S.P. XXI.

EPARFYNOL. 2-Ethinylbutanol-2. Methylparafynol, methylpentynol.

MEPARTRICIN. USAN.
Use: Antifungal, antiprotozoal.

EPAVLON.
See: Meprobamate, U.S.P. XXI.

EPAZINE ACETATE & HCl. 10-[1-Methyl-3-(piperidyl)methyl] phenothiazine acetate or HCl.

MEPENZOLATE BROMIDE, U.S.P. XXI. Syrup, Tab. U.S.P. XXI. N-methyl-3-hydroxypiperidine benzilate methobromide.
Use: Anticholinergic.
See: Cantil, Tab., Liq. (Merrell Dow)
'/Phenobarbital.
See: Cantil w/phenobarbital (Merrell Dow)

EPENZOLATE METHYL BROMIDE. Mepenzolate bromide.
Use: Anticholinergic.

EPERGAN. (Wyeth) promethazine HCl 25 mg., meperidine HCl 25 mg./ 10 cc. Tubex 50 mg./2 cc. Box 10s.
Use: Analgesic and sedative.

MEPERGAN FORTIS. (Wyeth) Meperidine HCl 50 mg., promethazine HCl 25 mg./Cap. Bot. 100s.
Use: Analgesic and sedative.

• **MEPERIDINE HYDROCHLORIDE,** U.S.P. XXI. Inj., Syrup, Tab., U.S.P. XXI. (Various Mfr.) Ethyl-1-methyl-4-phenylisonipecotate hydrochloride. (Parke-Davis) 50 mg./ml., 75 mg./ml., 100 mg./ml. as 1 ml. fill in 2 ml. Steri-dose syringe. (Dolantal, Dolantin, Dolosal, Dolvanol, Endolate, Isonipecaine & Pethidine)
Use: Analgesic (narcotic).
See: Demerol Hydrochloride, Preps. (Winthrop-Breon)
W/Acetaminophen.
See: Demerol APAP, Tab. (Winthrop-Breon)
W/Promethazine HCl.
See: Mepergan, Prep. (Wyeth)

MEPHENESIN. 3-o-Tolyloxypropane-1,2-diol. Lissephen; Myanesin; Tolseram carbamate.
Use: Skeletal muscle relaxant.
See: Mervaldin, Tab. (Lannett)
Myanesin
W/Acetaminophen, Vit. C, butabarbital.
See: T-Caps, Cap. (Burlington)
W/Mephobarbital, hyoscine HBr.
See: Tranquil, Tab. (Kenyon)
W/Pentobarbital.
See: Nebralin, Tab. (Dorsey)
W/Salicylamide, butabarbital sodium.
See: Metrogesic, Tab. (Metro Med)

MEPHENESIN CARBAMATE.
See: Methoxydone

MEPHENOXALONE. 5-(o-Methoxyphenoxy-methyl-)-2-oxazolidinone.

MEPHENTERMINE. B.A.N. Nαα-Trimethyl-phenethylamine. Mephine sulfate.
Use: Hypertensive.

• **MEPHENTERMINE SULFATE,** U.S.P. XXI. Inj., U.S.P. XXI. N,α,α-Trimethyl-phenethylamine sulfate. Mephine.
Use: Vasoconstrictor and nasal decongestant. Also I.V. or I.M.
See: Wyamine Sulfate Inl. (Wyeth)
W/Phenacetin, aspirin, promethazine HCl.
See: Synalgos, Cap. (Ives)

• **MEPHENYTOIN,** U.S.P. XXI. Tab., U.S.P. XXI. 5-Ethyl-3-methyl-5-phenylhydantoin.
Use: Anticonvulsant.
See: Mesantoin, Tab. (Sandoz)

• **MEPHOBARBITAL,** U.S.P. XXI. Tab., U.S.P. XXI. 5-Ethyl-5-phenyl N-methyl-barbituric acid. 5-Ethyl-1-methyl-5-phenylbarbituric Acid.
Use: Anticonvulsant; sedative.
See: Mebaral, Tab. (Winthrop-Breon)
W/Acetaminophen.
See: Koly-Tabs (Scrip)
W/Homatropine methylbromide, atropine methylnitrate & hyoscine HBr.
W/Mephenesin, hyoscine HBr.
See: Tranquil, Tab. (Kenyon)

MEPHONE.
See: Mephentermine.

MEPHYTON. (Merck Sharp & Dohme) Phytonadione (vitamin K-1) 5 mg./Tab. Bot. 100s.
Use: Coagulation disorders.

MEPIBEN. (Schen Labs.) Methylpiperidyl benzhydryl ether.
Use: Antihistaminic.

MEPIPERPHENIDOL BROMIDE. 1-(3 Hydroxy-5-methyl-4-phenylexyl)-1-methyl piperidium bromide.
Use: Anticholinergic.

MEPIPRAZOLE. B.A.N. 1-(3-Chlorophenyl)-4-[2-(5-methylpyrazol-3-yl)ethyl]piperazine.
Use: Psychotropic agent.

MEPIVACAINE. B.A.N. 1-Methyl-2-(2,6-xylyl-carbamoyl) piperidine. Carbocaine.
Use: Local anesthetic.

• **MEPIVACAINE HCl,** U.S.P. XXI. Inj. U.S.P. XXI. dl-1-Methyl-2′,6′-pipecoloxylidide monohydrochloride. (±)-1-Methyl-2′,6′-pipecoloxylidide Hydrochloride.
Use: Local anesthetic.
See: Carbocaine, Cartridge, Vial (Cook-Waite)
Carbocaine, Vials (Winthrop-Breon)
Cavacaine, Vial (Graham)

• **MEPIVACAINE HYDROCHLORIDE AND LEVONORDEFRIN INJ.,** U.S.P. XXI.
Use: Local anesthetic.
See: Carbocaine, Cartridge, Vial (Cook-Waite)

MEPREDNISONE. 17,21-Dihydroxy-16β-methylpregna-1,4-diene-3,11,20-trione. Betaspred.
Use: Glucocorticoid.

• **MEPROBAMATE,** U.S.P. XXI. Oral Susp., Tab., U.S.P. XXI. 2-Methyl-2-n-propyl-1,3-propanediol dicarbamate. 2,2-Di(carbamoyloxymethyl)pentane. 2-Carbamoyloxymethyl-2-methylpentyl carbamate. Mepavlon.
Use: Minor tranquilizer, sedative.
See: Arcoban Tablets (Arcum)
Bamate, Tab. (Century)
Equanil Tab., Cap., (Wyeth)
Meprocon, Tab. (CMC)
Meprospan, Cap. (Wallace)
Miltown, Tab. (Wallace)
Pax-400, Tab. (Kenyon)
SK-Bamate, Tab. (SmithKline)
Tranmep, Tab. (Reid-Provident)
W/Benactyzine HCl.
See: Deprol, Tab. (Wallace)
W/Estrogens conjugated.
See: Milprem, Tab. (Wallace)
W/Ethoheptazine citrate, acetylsalicylic acid.
See: Equagesic, Tab. (Wyeth)
W/Pentaerythritol tetranitrate.
See: Miltrate, Tab. (Wallace)
Robam-Petn, Tab. (Robinson)
W/Premarin.
See: PMB-200, Tab. (Ayerst)
W/Tridihexethyl chloride.
See: Milpath, Tab. (Wallace)
Pathibamate—200, 400, Tab. (Lederle)

MEPROBAMATE, N-ISOPROPYL.
See: Carisoprodol

MEPROCHOL. B.A.N. (2-Methoxyprop-2-enyl)-trimethylammonium bromide. Esmodil.
Use: Parasympathomimetic.

MEPROCON. (CMC) Meprobamate 200 mg. or 400 mg./Tab. Bot. 100s, 500s, 1000s.
Use: Tranquilizer.

MEPROGESIC Q TABLETS. (Quantum) Meprobamate 200 mg., aspirin 325 mg./Tab. Bot. 100s, 500s.
Use: Analgesic.

MEPROLONE TABS. (Major) Methylprednisolone 4 mg./Tab. Bot. 25s, 100s.
Use: Anti-inflammatory.

MEPROSPAN. (Wallace) Meprobamate in form of coated pellets which release drug continuously for 10-12 hours. 200 mg. or 400 mg./Cap. Bot. 100s.
Use: Anxiety and tension states.

MEPROTHIXOL. B.A.N. 9-(3-Dimethylamino-propyl)-9-hydroxy-2-methoxythiaxanthen.
Use: Analgesic; anti-inflammatory.

• **MEPRYLCAINE HYDROCHLORIDE,** U.S.P. XXI. 2 Methyl-2-propylaminopropyl Benzoate HCl. 2-Meth 2-(propylamino)-1-propanol benzoate (Ester) Hydr chloride.
Use: Local anesthetic (dental).

• **MEPRYLCAINE HYDROCHLORIDE AND EPINEPHRINE INJ.,** U.S.P. XXI.
Use: Local anesthetic.

MEPTAZINOL. B.A.N. 3-Ethyl-3-(hydroxyphenyl)-1-m thylhexahydroazepine.
Use: Analgesic.

• **MEPTAZINOL HYDROCHLORIDE.** USAN.
Use: Analgesic.

MEPYRAMINE. B.A.N. N-4-Methoxybenzyl-N′N′-dimethyl-N-2-pyridylethylenediamine. 2-(N-p-Anisyl-N-2-pyridylamino)ethyldimethylamine. Anthical; Anthisan; Flavelix; Neo-antergan hydrogen maleate.
Use: Antihistamine.
See: Pyrilamine Maleate U.S.P. XXI.

MEPYRAPONE. 2-Methyl-1,2-dl-3-pyridyl-1-propane.
See: Metopirone, Tab., Amp. (Ciba)

• **MEQUIDOX.** USAN. 3-Methyl-2-quinozaline-methan 1,4-dioxide. Under study.
Use: Antibacterial.

MEQUINOLATE. Name used for Proquinolate.

MERAGIDONE SODIUM. The sodium salt of anhydro N-(beta-methoxy-gamma-hydroxymercuripropyl)-2-pyridone-5-carboxylic acid-theophylline.

• **MERALEIN SODIUM.** USAN.
Use: Topical anti-infective.
See: Sodium Meralein

MERALLURIDE. B.A.N. Equal amts. of theophylline and methoxyhydroxymercuripropyl succinylurea. [3-[3-(3-Carboxypropionyl)ureido]-2-methoxypropyl]hy oxy-mercury mixture with theophylline.
Use: Diuretic.

MERBAPHEN. 2-(Carboxymethoxy)-3-chlorophenyl (5,5-diethylbarbiturato)mercury.

MERBENTYL. Dicyclomine, B.A.N.

ERBROMIN. Disodium 2,7-dibrom-4-hydroxy-mercuri-fluorescein. (Asceptichrome, Chromargyre, Cynochrome, Flavurol, Gallochrome Mercurocol, Mercurophage, Mercurome, Planochrome)
Use: Topical antiseptic.
See: Mercurochrome, Pow., Sol. (Hynson, Westcott & Dunning)

·MERCAPTOETHYL)TRIMETHYLAMMONIUM IODIDE S-ESTER WITH O, O-DIETHYL PHOSPHOROTHIOATE. Echothiophate Iodide, U.S.P. XXI.

ERCAPTOMERIN SODIUM. Disodium salt of N-(3-carboxymethyl-thio-mercuri-2-methoxypropyl)camphoramic acid. 3-(3-Carboxy-2,2,3-trimethylaycloopentanecarboxamide)-2-methoxy propyl (hydrogen mercaptoaceto) mercury disodium salt.
Use: Diuretic.
See: Thiomerin Sodium, Inj. (Wyeth)

MERCAPTOPURINE, U.S.P. XXI. Tab., U.S.P. XXI. 6-Mercaptopurine. Purine-6-thiol. monohydrate; 6H-purine-6-thione, monohydrate.
Use: Antineoplastic.
See: Purinethol, Tab. (Burroughs Wellcome)

MERCAPTOPURINE. Mercaptopurine, U.S.P. XXI.

·3-MERCAPTOVALINE. Penicillamine, U.S.P. XXI.

ERCARBOLID. o-Hydroxy-phenylmercuric chloride.

ERCAZOLE.
See: Methimazole U.S.P. XXI.

ERCLORAN. Chlormerodrin, B.A.N.

ERCOCRESOLS.
See: Mercresin, Tr. (Upjohn)

MERCUFENOL CHLORIDE. USAN.
Use: Anti-infective.

ERCUMATILIN. 8-(2′Methoxy-3′-hydroxy-mercuri-propyl)coumarin-3-carboxylic acid. Cumertilin.

ERCUMATILIN SODIUM. 3-(3-Carboxy-2-oxo-2H-1-benzopyran-8-yl-2-methoxypropyl)hydroxymercury sodium salt compound with theophylline.
Use: Diuretic.

ERCUPROCYL. (Inwood) Mersalyl 100 mg., theophylline 50 mg., procaine borate 0.5%/cc. Amp. 2 cc. Box 100s. Vial 10 cc.
Use: Mercurial diuretic.

ERCUPURIN.
See: Mercurophylline Injection (Various Mfr.)

ERCURANINE.
See: Merbromin (City Chem.)

ERCURIAL, ANTISYPHILITICS. Mercuric Oleate Mercuric Salicylate.

MERCURIAL DIURETICS.
See: Dicurin Procaine, Vial (Lilly)
Meralluride
Mercaptomerin Sodium (Various Mfr.)
Mercumatilin
Mercupurin
Mercurophylline (Various Mfr.)
Mersalyl
Mersalyl & Theophylline, Inj. (Various Mfr.)
Mersalyn, Vial (Var. Mfr.)
Salyrgan

MERCURIC OLEATE. Oleate of mercury.
Use: Parasitic skin diseases.
W/Coal tar crude, salicylic acid, phenol & p-nitrophenol.
See: Prosol, Emulsion (Torch)
Estercol, Emulsion (less p-Nitrophenol) (Torch).

MERCURIC OXIDE OPHTHALMIC OINTMENT, YELLOW.
Use: Local anti-infective.

MERCURIC SALICYLATE. Mercury subsalicylate.
Use: Parasitic & fungous skin diseases.

MERCURIC SUCCINIMIDE. BisSuccinimidato-mercury.

MERCURIC SULFIDE, RED. W/Colloidal sulfur, urea.
See: Teenac Cream, Oint. (Elder)

MERCURIN. Sod. salt of β-methoxy-hydroxy-mercuri propylamide of camphoramic acid. Trimethylcyclopentanedicarboxylic acid. Combined with theophyline is mercurophylline sodium.

MERCUROCAL.
See: Merbromin Sol. (Premo)

MERCUROL. (Durel) Oleate of mercury 0.5%, phenol 0.5%, salicylic acid 3%, coal tar solution 1.2% in Moisturizing Hand and Body Lotion. Bot. 4 oz., pt., gal.
Use: Seborrheic dermatitis and psoriasis.

MERCUROME.
See: Merbromin Sol. (City Chem.)

MERCUROPHYLLINE SODIUM. B.A.N. Sod. salt of (beta-methoxygamma-hydroxy-mercuri-propylamide of camphoramic acid) trimethylcyclopentanedicarboxylic acid and theophylline.
Mercuzanthin Inj. Amp. 2 cc., Box 6s, 25s, 100s. Tab. Bot. 50s, 100s, 1000s.
Use: Diuretic.
See: Mercupurin. (Various Mfr.)

MERCURY-^{197} Hg,[3-[(AMINOCARBONYL)-AMINO]-2-METHOXYPROPYL]-CHLORO-. Chlormerodrin Hg 197 Injection.

• **MERCURY, AMMONIATED,** U.S.P. XXI. Oint., Ophth. Oint., U.S.P. XXI.
Use: Topical anti-infective.

MERCURY BICHLORIDE.
See: Diamond, Tab. (Lilly)

■ **MERCURY COMPOUNDS.**
See: Antiseptics, Mercurials
Mercurial, Diuretics

MERCURY-197-203.
See: Chlormerodrin (Squibb)

MERCURY OLEATE. Mercury (2+) oleate.
Pharmaceutic aid.

MERDEX. (Faraday) Docusate sodium 100 mg./Tab. Vial 60.
Use: Relief of constipation.

MERETHOXYLLINE PROCAINE.
W/Theophylline.
See: Dicurin Procaine, Vial (Lilly)

• **MERISOPROL ACETATE Hg 197.** USAN.
Use: Radioactive agent.

• **MERISOPROL ACETATE Hg 203.** USAN.
Use: Radioactive agent.

• **MERISOPROL Hg 197.** USAN.
Use: Diagnostic aid.

MERITAL CAPSULES. (Hoechst) Nomifensine maleate 50 mg./Cap. Bot. 100s.
Use: Oral anti-depressant.
MERITENE LIQUID. (Sandoz Nutrition) Vanilla Flavor: Concentrated sweet skim milk, corn syrup solids, corn oil, sodium caseinate, sucrose, artificial flavor, cellulose flour, mono & diglycerides, salt, cellulose gum, carrageenan, vitamins & minerals. Ready-to-serve 250 ml. cans.
Use: Total or supplemental feeding oral or tube.
MERITENE POWDER. (Sandoz Nutrition) Vanilla Flavor: Specially processed nonfat dry milk, corn syrup solids, sucrose, fructose, calcium caseinate, sodium chloride, natural & artificial flavors, lecithin, vitamins & minerals. Can 1 lb, 4.5 lb. 25 lb. Packets 1.14 oz.
Use: Supplemental oral or tube feedings.
MERLENATE OINTMENT. (Vortech) Phenylmercuric nitrate 1.15%, undecylenic acid 0.5% in water miscible base. Jars. 1 oz., 1 lb.
Use: Antipruritic for relief athlete's foot.
MEROCET. Cetylpyridinium Chloride, B.A.N.
MERODICEIN. Sodium meralein.
W/Saligenin.
See: Thantis, Loz. (Hynson, Westcott & Dunning)
MERPHENE. (Barry) Disinfectant concentrate. Plastic Bot. 8 oz.
MERPHYLLINE. (Seatrace) Sodium mersalyl 100 mg., theophylline 50 mg./ml. Vial 30 cc.
MERPRANE. 1-(Hydroxymercuri-197 Hg)-2-propanol.
Use: Diagnostic agent.
MERSALINE. (Standex) Mersalyl 100 mg., theophylline 50 mg./cc. Vial 30 cc.
MERSALYL. (Various Mfr.) Mersalyl Sod., Salygran, Sod. (ortho-[gamma-hydroxy- mercuri-beta-methoxy-propylcarbamyl]phenoxy) acetate.
W/Theophylline.
See: Mersaline (Standex)
W/Theophylline, methylparaben, propylparaben.
See: Meprophyl, Vial (Lemmon)
MERSALYL SODIUM & THEOPHYLLINE.
See: Mersalyl & Theophylline Inj.
MERSALYL AND THEOPHYLLINE INJECTION. (CMC) Amp. 2 cc. (Medwick) Vial 30 cc. (Metro) Mersalyl 0.2 Gm., theophylline 0.1 Gm., water for inj. q.s./2 cc. Amp. 2 cc. Box 10s, 100s. (Torigian) Amp. 2 cc. 12s, 25s, 100s. Vial 30 cc. (Reid-Provident) Mersalyl 200 mg., theophylline 100 mg./2 ml.
Use: Diuretic.
See: Aquanil (Sig.)
Mercurasol, Vial (Medics)
Mer-Im, Vial (Scrip)
Mersaline, Inj. (Standex)
Mersalyn, Vial (Bowman; Keene; Rocky Mtn.)
Mersaphyllin, Vial (Pharmex)
Theo-Syl R, Inj. (Kay)
MERSALYN. Mersalyl & Theophylline Inj.
Use: I.V. & I.M., diuretic.
See: (Bowman) Mersalyl 100 mg., theophyllin 50 mg./ml. Vial 10 cc.
(Keene) Mersalyl 100 mg., theophylline 50 mg./ml. Vials 10cc, 30cc.
(Rocky Mtn.) Mersalyl sodium 100mg., theophylline anhydrous 45 mg./ml. Vial 10cc., 30cc.
MERSAPHYLLIN. (Pharmex) Mersalyl sod. (equiv. to 40 mg. Hg) 100 mg., theophylline 50 mg./cc., methylparaben 0.18%, propylparaben 0.02%. Vial 30 cc.
MERSOL. (Century) Thimerosol tincture, N.F. 1/1000. 1 oz., 4 oz., 1 pt., 1 gal.
MERTHIOLATE. (Lilly) Thimerosal.
Aeropump: Tincture thimerosal 0.1 Gm., alcohol 50%. Bot. 6 fl. oz.
Soln.: 1:1000 4 fl. oz., 16 fl. oz., gal.
Tincture.: 1:1000 0.75 oz., 4 fl. oz., 16 fl. oz., gal. 50% alcohol.
Use: Antiseptic.
MERUVAX II. (Merck Sharp & Dohme) Lyophilized, live attenuated rubella virus of the Wistar Institute RA 27/3 strain. Each dose contains approx. 25 mcg. of neomycin. Single dose Vial 0.5 ml. 1s, 10s w/Disp. Syringe containing diluent & fitted with a 25 gauge, 5/8" needle.
W/Attenuvax.
See: M-R-Vax II, Vial (Merck Sharp & Dohme)
W/Attenuvax, Mumpsvax.
See: M-M-R II, Vial (Merck Sharp & Dohme)
W/Mumpsvax.
See: Biavax II, Vial (Merck Sharp & Dohme))
MERVALDIN. (Lannett) Formerly Proloxin.
Mephenesin. 0.5 Gm./Tab. Bot. 500s, 1000s.
Use: Muscle relaxant.
MESANTOIN. (Sandoz) (Mephenytoin) Phenantoin, 3-Methyl 5,5-phenylethylhydantoin 100 mg./Tab. Bot. 100s.
Use: Antiepileptic & anticonvulsant.
MESCOMINE.
See: Methscopolamine bromide (Var. Mfr.)
• **MESECLAZONE.** USAN.
Use: Anti-inflammatory.
• **MESIFILCON A.** USAN.
Use: Contact lens material.
• **MESORIDAZINE.** USAN. 10-[-2-(1-Methyl-2-piperidyl)ethyl]-2-(methylsulfinyl)phenothiazine. Lidanil.
Use: Tranquilizer.
• **MESORIDAZINE BESYLATE,** U.S.P. XXI. Inj., Oral Soln., Tab., U.S.P. XXI. 10-2-(1-methyl-2-piperidyl)-ethyl-2-(methylsulfinyl)phenothiazine monobenzene-sulfonate.
Use: Antipsychotic agent.
See: Serentil, Amp., Liq., Tab. (Boehringer-Ingelheim)
MESSAGE LOTION. (Sween) Bot. 8 oz., gal.
Use: Massage cream.
MESTANOLONE. B.A.N. 17 β-Hydroxy-17αmethyl-5α-androstan-3-one. Androstalone.
Use: Anabolic steroid.
• **MESTEROLONE.** USAN.
Use: Androgen.
MESTIBOL. Monomestrol.
MESTINON. (Roche) Dimethylcarbamate of 3-hydroxy-1-methyl-pyridinium bromide. Pyridostigmine bromide

60 mg./Tab. Bot. 100s, 500s. Timespan 180 mg./Tab. Bot. 100s.
Use: Myasthenia gravis treatment.

ESTINON INJECTABLE. (Roche) Pyridostigmine Br. 5 mg./ml., methyl and propyl parabens 0.2%, sodium citrate 0.02%, citric acid. Amp. 2 ml., 10s.
Use: Treatment of myasthenia gravis.

ESTINON SYRUP. (Roche) Pyridostigmine bromide 60 mg./5 ml. w/alcohol 5%. Bot. pts.
Use: Myasthenia gravis in children and infants.

MESTRANOL. U.S.P. XXI. 17 αEthynylestradiol 3-methyl ether. 3-Methoxy-19-nor-17-alpha-pregna-1,-3,5(10)-trien-20-yn-17-ol. 19 Norpregna-1,3,5(10)trien-20-yn-17-ol,3-methoxy-, (17α)-.
Use: Estrogenic compound.

'/Ethynodiol Diacetate.
See: Ovulen, Tab. (Searle)
Ovulen-21, Tab. (Searle)
Ovulen-28, Tab. (Searle)

//Norethindrone.
See: Norinyl, Tab. (Syntex)
Norinyl-1 Fe 28 (Syntex)
Ortho-Novum, Tab. (Ortho)

//Norethindrone, ferrous fumarate.
See: Ortho Novum 1/80 Fe-28, 1/50 Fe-28, 1 mg. Fe-28, Tabs. (Ortho)

V/Norethynodrel.
See: Enovid, Tab. (Searle)
Enovid-E, Tab. (Searle)
Enovid-E 21, Tab. (Searle)

IESULPHEN. B.A.N. 2,7-Dimethylthianthren. Mitigal; Sudermo.
Use: Treatment of skin infections.

MESUPRINE HYDROCHLORIDE. USAN.
Use: Vasodilator, smooth muscle relaxant.

IETABALM. (Noyes) Menthol, camphor, thymol, methyl salicylate, oils clove and cassia in a nonstaining vanishing base. Tube 1 oz., Jar 1 lb.

IETABOLIN. (Thurston) Vit. A 833 I.U., D 66 I.U., B-1 833 mcg., B-2 500 mcg., B-6 0.083 mcg., Ca pantothenate 833 mcg., niacinamide 5 mg., folic acid 0.066 mcg., niacinamide 5 mg., p-aminobenzoic acid 0.416 mcg., inositol 833 mcg., B-12 500 mcg., C 5 mg., Ca 33.1 mg., phosphorus 14.6 mg., iron 2.5 mg., iodine 0.15 mg./Tab. Bot. 100s, 500s, 1000s.
Use: Pregnancy and lactation, dietary supplement.

• **METABROMSALEN.** USAN. 3,5-Dibromosalicylanilide.
Use: Germicide.

METABUTETHAMINE HYDROCHLORIDE. 2-Isobutylaminoethyl m-aminobenzoid HCl. 2-(Isobutylamino)ethanol m-Aminobenzoate (Ester) Monohydrochloride.
Use: Local anesthetic.

METABUTOXYCAINE HYDROCHLORIDE. 2'-Diethylaminoethyl 3-Amino-2-butoxybenzoate Hydrochloride.
Use: Local anesthetic.

METACARAPHEN HYDROCHLORIDE. Netrin.

METACETAMOL. B.A.N. 3-Acetamidophenol.
Use: Analgesic.

METACORDRALONE.
See: Prednisolone. (Various Mfr.)

METACORTALONE.
See: Meticortelone, Susp. (Schering)

METACORTANDRACIN.
See: Prednisone, Tab. (Various Mfr.)

METACORTIN.
See: Meticorten, Tab. (Schering)

META-DELPHENE. Diethyltoluamide U.S.P. XXI.

METAGLYCODOL. 2-m-Chlorophenyl-3-methyl-2,3-butanediol.
Use: Central nervous system depressant.

METAHEXAMIDE. B.A.N. N-Cyclohexyl-N'-(3-amino-4-methylbenzene Sulfonyl) urea. Euglycin. Melanex.
Use: Hypoglycemic agent.

METAHYDRIN. (Merrell Dow) Trichlormethiazide 2 mg. and 4 mg./Tab. Bot. 100s.
Use: Diuretic.

• **METALOL HYDROCHLORIDE.** USAN. 4'-[Hydroxy-2-(methylamino)-propyl methanesulfonanilide hydrochloride. Under study.
Use: Andrenergic β receptor antagonist.

METALONE T.B.A. (Foy) Prednisolone tertiary butylacetate 20 mg., sod. citrate 1 mg., polysorbate 80 1 mg., d-sorbitol 450 mg./cc., benzyl alcohol 0.9% water for inj. Vial 10 ml.

METAMFEPRAMONE (I.N.N.). Dimepropion, B.A.N.

METAMUCIL. (Searle) Psyllium hydrophilic mucilloid, sodium 1 mg., potassium 31 mg./Dose. **Regular Flavor:** w/ dextrose. Pow. Pkg. 7 oz., 14 oz., 21 oz. **Orange and Strawberry Flavors:** w/flavoring, sucrose and coloring. Pow. Pkg. 7 oz., 14 oz., 21 oz.
Use: Oral laxative.

METAMUCIL INSTANT MIX. (Searle) Psyllium hydrophilic mucilloid with citric acid, sucrose, potassium bicarbonate, Na bicarbonate. Powder when combined with water forms an effervescent, flavored liquid. **Regular Flavor:** w/calcium carbonate. Cartons of 16 & 30 packets of 6.4 Gm. **Orange Flavor:** w/flavoring and coloring. Ctn. 16 and 30 packets of 6.4 Gm.
Use: Oral laxative

METANDREN. (Ciba) Methyltestosterone. **Linquet** 5 mg., 10 mg. Bot. 100s. **Tab.** 10 mg., 25 mg. Bot. 100s.
Use: Androgen therapy.

METAPHENYLBARBITURIC ACID.
See: Mebaral, Tab. (Winthrop-Breon)

METAPHYLLIN.
See: Aminophylline (Var. Mfr.)

METAPREL INHALENT SOLUTION 5%. (Dorsey) Metaproterenol sulfate 50 mg./1 ml. Bot. 10 ml. w/dropper.
Use: Bronchodilator.

METAPREL METERED DOSE INHALER. (Dorsey) Metaproterenol sulfate 225 mg., micronized powder in inert propellant/15 ml. Metered Dose Inhaler. (Approx. 0.65 mg./Inhalation).
Use: Bronchodilator

METAPREL SYRUP. (Dorsey) Metaproterenol sulfate 10 mg./5 ml. Bot. Pint.
Use: Bronchodilator.

METAPREL TABLETS. (Dorsey) Metaproterenol sulfate 10 mg., 20 mg./Tab. Bot. 100s.
Use: Oral Bronchodilator.

• **METAPROTERENOL SULFATE,** U.S.P. XXI. Inhalation Aerosol, Inhalation Soln. Syrup, Tab., U.S.P. XXI. 1,-(3,5-Dihydroxyphenyl)-2-isopropylamino-ethanol sulfate, Alupent.
Use: Bronchodilator.
See: Alupent Inhal. (Geigy)
Metaprel, Tab., Inhalation, Syr. (Dorsey)

METARAMINOL. B.A.N. (Invenex) Metaraminol bitartrate. (−)-2-Amino-1-(3-hydroxyphenyl)-propan-1-ol. 10 mg./ml. Vial 1 ml., 10 ml.
Use: Hypertensive.

• **METARAMINOL BITARTRATE,** U.S.P. XXI. Inj., U.S.P. XXI. 1-α-(1-Aminoethyl)-m-hydroxybenzyl alcohol bitartrate. Benzenemethanol, a-(1 aminoethyl)-3-hydroxy-R-(R*,R*)-2,3-dihydroxybutandioate (1:1) (salt).
Use: Sympathomimetic amine (vasopressor)
See: Aramine, Amp., Vial (Merck Sharp & Dohme)

METATENSIN. (Merrell Dow) Trichlormethiazide 2 mg. and 4 mg., each containing reserpine 0.1 mg./Tab. Bot. 100s.
Use: Antihypertensive.

• **METAXALONE.** USAN. 5-(3,5-Dimethylphenoxymethyl)-2-oxazolidinone.
Use: Skeletal muscle relaxant, tranquilizer.
See: Skelaxin, Tab. (Robins)

METAZOCINE. B.A.N. 1,2,3,4,5,6-Hexahydro-8-hydroxy-3,6, 11-trimethyl-2,6-methano-3-benzazocine.
Use: Narcotic analgesic.

METCARAPHEN HYDROCHLORIDE. 2-Diethylaminoethyl-1-(3′,4′dimethylphenyl) cyclopentanecarboxylate HCl.

METECLOPRAMIDE. 4-Amino-5-chloro-N-(2-diethylaminoethyl)-2-methoxybenzamide. Primperan is the hydrochloride.

METED SHAMPOO. (Rydell) Salicylic acid 2%, sulfur 3%, detergents 45% as liquid. Bot. 4 oz.
Use: Shampoo and cleanser.

METED 2 SHAMPOO. (Rydell) Colloidal sulfur 2.3%, salicylic acid 1%, PEG 400 5%, detergents 20%. Bot. 4 oz.
Use: Shampoo for dry, scaly dandruff.

• **METENEPROST.** USAN.
Use: Oxytoxic, prostaglandin.

METETHOHEPTAZINE. Ethyl hexahydro-1,3-dimethyl-4-phenyl-1H-azepine-4-carboxylate.
Use: Analgesic.

• **METFORMIN.** USAN. 1,1-Dimethylbiguanide. Diguanil; Glucophage; Metiguanide; Obin [HCl].
Use: Oral hypoglycemic.

METHACHOLINE BROMIDE. Mecholin bromide. (2-Hydroxypropyl)-trimethylammonium bromide acetate. Mecholyl Bromide.
Use: Cholinergic.

• **METHACHOLINE CHLORIDE,** U.S.P. XXI. (2-Hydroxypropyl)-trimethylammonium chloride acetate. Methylacetyl choline. Amechol.
Use: Cholinergic.
See: Mecholyl Chloride, Amp. (J.T. Baker)
W/Camphor, menthol & methyl salicylate.
See: Surin, Oint. (McKesson)

• **METHACRYLIC ACID COPOLYMER,** N.F. XVI.

• **METHACYCLINE.** USAN. 6-Deoxy-6-demethyl-6-methylene-5-oxytetracycline.
Use: Antibiotic.
See: Rondomycin, Cap., Syr. (Wallace)

• **METHACYCLINE HYDROCHLORIDE,** U.S.P. XXI. Cap., Oral Susp., U.S.P. XXI.
Use: Antibacterial.
See: Rondomycin, Cap., Syr. (Wallace)

METHADOL. Dimepheptanol, B.A.N.

• **METHADONE HYDROCHLORIDE,** U.S.P. XXI. Inj., Oral Concentrate, Tab., U.S.P. XXI. 6-Dimethylamino-4,4-diphenyl-3-heptanone hydrochloride. 3 Heptanone, 6-(dimethylamino)-4,4-diphenyl hydrochloride. Amidon HCl, Butalgin, Diaminon HCl, Hoechst 10820, Miadone, Physeptone HCl, Polamidon HCl.
Use: Narcotic analgesic, narcotic abstinence syndrome suppressant.
See: Dolophine Hydrochloride, Prep. (Lilly)
W/Aspirin, phenacetin, caffeine.
See: Nodalin, Tab. (Table Rock)

• **METHADYLACETATE.** USAN. 6-(Dimethylamino)-4,4-diphenyl-3-heptanol acetate (ester). 1-Ethyl-4-dimethylamino-2,2-diphenylpentyl acetate. Acetylmethadol (I.N.N.)
Use: Narcotic analgesic.

METHAGUAL. (Gordon) Guaiacol 2%, methyl salicylate 8% in petrolatum. Oint. 2 oz., lb.
Use: Minor muscular pains and strains.

METHALAMIC ACID. Name used for Iothalamic Acid, U.S.P. XXI.

METHALGEN. (Alra) Camphor, menthol, oil mustard, methyl salicylate in non-greasy cream base. Bot. 2 oz., Jar 4 oz., 1 lb.
Use: Analgesic cream.

METHALLATAL. 5-Ethyl-5-(2-methylallyl)-2-thiobarbituric acid.

METHALLENESTRIL. B.A.N. 3-(6-Methoxy-2-naphthyl)-2,2-dimethylpentanoic acid.
Use: Estrogen.

• **METHALLIBURE.** USAN. 1-Methyl-6-(1-methylallyl)-2,5-dithiobiurea.
Use: Suppression of pituitary, ovarian, and adrenal function.

• **METHALTHIAZIDE.** USAN. 3-[(Allylthio)-methyl]-6-chloro-3,4-dihydro-2-methyl-2H-1,2,4-benzothiadiazine-7-sulfonamide 1,1-dioxide.
Use: Hypotensive & diuretic.

METHAMINODIAZEPOXIDE. Chlordiazepoxide HCl, U.S.P. XXI.
See: Librium, Cap., Amp. (Roche)

METHAMOCTOL. 2-Methyl-6-(methylamino)-2-heptanol.
Use: Adrenergic.

METHAMPEX. (Lemmon) Methamphetamine HCl 10 mg./Tab. Bot. 1000s, 5000s.
Use: CNS Stimulant, anorexiant.

METHAMPHAZONE. B.A.N. 4-Amino-6-methyl-2-phenyl-3((2H)-pyridazone.
Use: Analgesic; antirheumatic.

ETHAMPHETAMINE HYDROCHLORIDE. Deoxyephedrine hydrochloride; N-α-Dimethyl-phenethylamine hydrochloride.
Use: Orally, central nervous system stimulant.
See: Desoxyn, Gradumets & Tab. (Abbott)
Methampex, Tab. (Lemmon)
Methamphetamine HCl, Tab. (Various Mfr.)
/Amobarbital; homatropine methylbromide.
See: Obe-Slim, Tab. (Jenkins)
/dl-Methamphetamine HCl, butabarbital.
See: Span-RD, Tab. (Metro Med)
/Pamabrom, pyrilamine maleate, homatropine methylbromide, hyoscyamine sulfate, scopolamine HBr.
See: Aridol, Tabs. (MPL)
/Pentobarbital sod., vitamins, minerals.
See: Fetamin, Tab. (Mission)
-METHAMPHETAMINE HCl. dl-Desoxyephedrine HCl.
See: Oxydess, Tab. (North American)
Roxyn, Tab. (Rocky Mtn.)
/d-Methamphetamine HCl, butabarbital.
See: Span-RD, Span RD-12, Tab. (Metro Med)
/Pyrilamine maleate, phenyltoloxamine dihydrogen citrate, didesoxyephedrine HCl, codeine phosphate, ammonium chloride, pot. guaiacolsulfonate, chloroform, phenylpropanolamine tartar emetic.
See: Meditussin-X Liquid (Hauck)
ETHAMPYRONE.
See: Dipyrone
ETHANAMINIUM,1-CARBOXY-N,N,N-TRIMETHYL-,HYDROXIDE, INNER SALT, COMPD. W/ 2,2,2-TRICHLORO-1,1-ETHANE-DIOL. Chloral Betaine.
ETHANAMINIUM,N-[4-[BIS[4-DIMETHYLAMINO)-PHENYL]METHYLENE]-2,5-CYCLOHEXADIEN-1-YLIDENE]-N-METHYL-, CHLORIDE. Gentian Violet, U.S.P. XXI.
ETHANDIENONE. B.A.N. 17 β-Hydroxy-17 α-methylandrosta-1,4-dien-3-one. Dianabol.
Use: Anabolic steroid.
ETHANDRIOL. Methylandrostenediol. (Various Mfr.) 17-alpha-methyl-Δ^5-androstene-3-beta, 17 beta-diol. Diolostene, Mestenediol, Methanabol. Spenbolic.
See: Anabol, Inj. (Keene Pharm.)
ETHANDRIOL DIPROPIONATE.
See: Andriol Injection (Reid-Provident)
Andronex, Inj. (Tunex)
Arbolic, Inj. (Burgin-Arden)
Crestabolic, Vial (Nutrition)
Durandrol, Vial (Pharmex)
Fellobolic, Vial (Fellows-Testagar)
Hibol, Inj. (Amfre-Grant)
Probolik (Hickam)
Robolic, Vial (Rocky Mtn.)
Steribolic, Vial (Kay)
ETHANDROSTENOLONE. Δ^1-17 α-methyltestosterone. 17 α-Methyl-17 β-hydroxyandrosta-1,4-dien-3-one. 17 β-Hydroxy-17-methylandrosta-1,4-dien-3-one.
See: Dianabol, Tab. (Ciba)

METHANONE, (2-HYDROXY-4-METHOXY-PHENYL)(2-HYDROXYPHENYL)-. Dioxybenzone, U.S.P. XXI.
METHANONE, (2-HYDROXY-4-METHOXYPHENYL)-PHENYL-. Oxybenzone, U.S.P. XXI.
METHANTHELINIUM BROMIDE. B.A.N. 2-Diethylaminoethyl xanthen-9-carboxylate methobromide. Banthine Bromide.
Use: Anticholinergic.
• **METHANTHELINE BROMIDE,** U.S.P. XXI. Sterile, Tab., U.S.P. XXI. Diethyl (2-hydroxyethyl) methyl-ammonium bromide xanthene-9-carboxylate.
Use: Parasympatholytic; anticholinergic.
See: Banthine, Vial & Tab. (Searle)
W/Phenobarbital.
See: Banthine w/Phenobarb., Tab. (Searle)
METHAPHENILENE. B.A.N. 2-(N-Phenyl-N-2-thenylamino)ethyldimethylamine. Diatrin [hydrochloride].
Use: Antihistamine.
METHAPHOR. (Borden) Protein hydrolysate (l-leucine, l-isoleucine, l-methionine, l-phenylalanine, l-tyrosine); methionine, camphor, benzethonium chloride, in Dermabase vehicle/Oint. Tube 1.5 oz.
Use: Dermatologic, amino acid preparation.
METHAPYRILENE. B.A.N. NN-Dimethyl-N′-(2-pyridyl)-N′-(2-thenyl)ethylenediamine.
NOTE: Due to recent legislation many products are being reformulated to exclude oral use of this drug.
Use: Antihistamine.
METHAPYRILENE FUMARATE. 2-[[2-(Dimethylamino)-ethyl]-2-thenylamino pyridine fumarate (2:3)
NOTE: Due to recent legislation many products are being reformulated to exclude oral use of this drug. This drug is no longer official in the U.S.P.
Use: Antihistaminic.
METHAPYRILENE HYDROCHLORIDE, 2-[[2-Diemthylamino)-ethyl]-2-thenylamino] pyridine hydrochloride. (Thenylpyramine, Teralin). Blue Line—Elixir 200 mg./fl. oz. Bot. 1 pt., 1 gal. CMC-Vial 30 cc. Kenyon-Vial 20 mg./cc.
NOTE: Due to recent legislation many products are being reformulated to exclude oral use of this drug. This drug is no longer official in the U.S.P.
Use: Antihistamine.
METHAPYRILENE HYDROCHLORIDE W/COMBINATIONS.
NOTE: Due to recent legislation many products are being reformulated to exclude oral use of this drug.
• **METHAQUALONE,** U.S.P. XXI. Tab., U.S.P. XXI. 2-Methyl-3-o-tolyl-4(3H)-quinazolinone. Melsedin, Paxidorm, Sedaquin (HCl), Melsed, Quaalude, Revonal.
Use: Tranquilizer.
See: Mequin, Tab. (Lemmon)
Parest, Cap. (Lemmon)
Quaalude, Tab. (Lemmon)
• **METHAQUALONE HYDROCHLORIDE,** U.S.P. XXI. Cap., U.S.P. XXI.

Use: Tranquilizer.
See: Optimil (Wallace)
Parest (Parke Davis)
Somnafac (CooperVision)

• **METHARBITAL,** U.S.P. XXI. Tab., U.S.P. XXI. 5,5′-Diethyl-1-methylbarbituric acid.
Use: Anticonvulsant.
See: Gemonil, Tab. (Abbott)

METHARBITONE. B.A.N. 5,5-Diethyl-1-methylbarbituric acid.
Use: Anticonvulsant.

METHAZINE. (Pharmex) Promethazine HCl 50 mg./cc. Vial 10 cc.

• **METHAZOLAMIDE,** U.S.P. XXI. Tab. U.S.P. XXI. N-(4-Methyl-2-sulfamoyl-Δ^2-1,3,4-thiadiazolin-5-ylidene)-acetamide. Acetamide, N-5-(aminosulfonyl)-3-methyl-1,3,4-thiadiazol-2(3H)-ylidene-.5-Acetylimino-4-methyl-1,3,4-thiadiazoline-2-sulfonamide.
Use: Carbonic anhydrase inhibitor.
See: Neptazane
Neptazane, Tab. (Lederle)

METH-DIA-MER SULFA TABLETS, Trisulfapyrimidines Tab., U.S.P. XXI.
Use: Triple sulfonamide therapy.
See: Buffonamide (Reid-Provident)
Chemozine, Tab. (Tennessee Pharm.)
Neotrizine, Tab. (Lilly)
Terfonyl, Susp., (Squibb)
Trionamide, Tab., (O'Neal)
Triple Sulfa, Tab. (Various Mfr.)
Triple Sulfas, Tab. (Lederle)
Trisem, Tab. (Beecham Labs)

METH-DIA-MER SULFONAMIDES.
Use: Triple sulfonamide therapy.
W/Sulfacetamide.
See: Sulfa-Plex Vaginal Cream (Rowell)
W/Sulfacetamide, hexestrol.
See: Vagi-Plex, Cream (Rowell)

METH-DIA-MER SULFONAMIDES SUSPENSION, Trisulfapyrimidines Oral Suspension, U.S.P. XXI.
Use: Triple sulfonamide therapy.
See: Chemozine, Susp. (Tennessee Pharm.)
Neotrizine, Susp. (Lilly)
Terfonyl, Susp. (Squibb)
Tri-Diazole, Liq. (Coastal)
Triple Sulfa, Susp. (CMC)
Trisem, Susp. (Beecham Labs)

METHDILAZINE, U.S.P. XXI. Tab., U.S.P. XXI. 10-(1-Methylpyrrolidin-3-ylmethyl)phenothiazine. Dilosyn (hydrochloride)
See: Tacaryl Chewable Tab. (Westwood)

• **METHDILAZINE HCl,** U.S.P. XXI. Syrup, Tab., U.S.P. XXI. 10-(1-Methyl-pyrrolidinyl)phenothiazine HCl.
Use: Antipruritic.
See: Tacaryl, Tab. (Westwood)

• **METHENAMINE,** U.S.P. XXI. Elixir, Tab., U.S.P. XXI. (Hexamethyleneamine, Cystamin, Cystogen, Hexamine, Hexamethylenetetramine.)
Use: Antibacterial (urinary).

METHENAMINE W/COMBINATIONS.
Use: Urinary tract anti-infective.
See: Cystamine, Tab. (Tennessee Pharm.)
Cysto, Tab. (Freeport)
Cystised, Tab. (Jenkins)
Cystitol, Tab. (Briar)
Cystorrhoids W/Atropine, Tab. (Noyes)
Cystrea, Tab. (Moore Kirk)
Formathyn, Tab. (Scrip)
G-U-Sist, Tab. (Freeport)
Hexalol, Tab. (Central)
Lanased, Tab. (Lannett)
UB, Tab. (Scrip)
Uralene, Tab. (Sutliff & Case)
Uramine, Tab. (Kay)
Urelief, Tab. (Rocky Mtn.)
Uricide, Tab. (Elder)
Urineaze, Tab. (Foy)
Uriprel, Tab. (Pasadena Research)
Urisan-P, Tab. (Sandia)
Urised, Tab. (Webcon)
Uriseptin, Tab. (Blaine)
Uristat, Tab. (Lemmon)
Uritabs, Tab. (Vortech)
Urithol, Tab. (O'Neal)
Uritin Modified Formula, Tab. (Wolins)
Uritrol, Tab. (Kenyon)
Uro Phosphate, Tab. (Poythress)
Urothyn Improved, Tab. (Reid-Provident)
Uro-Ves, Tab. (Mallard)
Urseptic, Tab. (Century)
UTA, Tab. (Bentex)
U-Tract, Tab. (Bowman)
U-Tran, Tab. (Scruggs)

METHENAMINE AND MONOBASIC SODIUM PHOSPHATE TABLETS, U.S.P. XXI.
Use: Antibacterial (urinary).

METHENAMINE ANHYDROMETHYLENE CITRATE.
Formanol, Uropurgol, Urotropin.

• **METHENAMINE HIPPURATE,** U.S.P. XXI. Tab., U.S.P. XXI. A 1:1 complex of methenamine and hippuric acid.
Use: Urinary antiseptic.
See: Hiprex, Tab. (Merrell Dow)
Urex, Tab.(Riker)

• **METHENAMINE MANDELATE,** U.S.P. XXI. Tab., For Oral Soln., Oral Susp.; U.S.P. XXI.
Use: Urinary antibacterial.
See: Mandacon, Tab. (Webcon)
Mandalay, Tab. (Beutlich)
Mandelamine, Tab., Susp. (Parke-Davis)
Mandelamine "Hafgram" Tab. (Parke-Davis)
Mandelets, Tab. (Quality Generics)
Methalate, Tab. (Vortech)
Methavin, Tab. (Star)
Renelate, Tab. (Fellows)
Thendelate, Tab. (Blue Line)

METHENAMINE MANDELATE W/COMBINATIONS.
Use: Antibacterial (urinary).
See: Azolate, Tab. (Amfre-Grant)
Azo-Methalate, Tab. (Vortech)
Donnasep, Tab. (Robins)

Levo-Uroqid, Tab. (Beach)
Manacid, Tab. (Hyrex)
Mandalay A.P., Tab. (Beutlich)
Mandex, Tab. (Vale)
Prov-U-Sep Forte, Tab. (Reid-Provident)
Pyrisul Plus, Tab. (Kenyon)
Renalgin, Tab. (Meyer)
Thiacide, Tab. (Beach)
Urisedamine, Tab. (Webcon)
Uritral, Cap. (Central)
Uropeutic, Tab. (Circle)
Uroqid-Acid, Tab. (Beach)

:THENOLONE. B.A.N. 17β-Hydroxy-1-methyl-5 α-androst-1-en-3-one. Primobolan acetate; Primobolan-Depot enanthate
Use: Anabolic steroid.

IETHENOLONE ACETATE. USAN. 17 β-Hydroxy-1-methyl-5 α-androst-1-en-3-one acetate. Primobolan.
Use: Anabolic agent.

IETHENOLONE ENANTHATE. USAN. 17β-Hydroxy-1-methyl-5αandrost-1-en-3-one heptanoate. Nibal injection. Primobolan.
Use: Anabolic.

:THEPONEX. (Rawl) Choline 0.54 Gm., dl-methionine 1.80 Gm., inositol 0.27 Gm., whole liver desic. 8.10 Gm., Vit. B-1 18 mg., B-2 36 mg., niacinamide 90 mg., B-6 3.6 mg., Ca pantothenate 3.6 mg., biotin 10.8 mcg., B-12 5.4 mcg. & amino acid/daily therapeutic dose. Caps. Bot. 100s, 500s.
Use: Liver disorders, diabetes.

:THEPTAZINE. Methyl hexahydro-1, 2-dimethyl-4-phenyl-1H-azepine-4-carboxylate.
Use: Analgesic.

:THERGINE. (Sandoz) Methylergonovine maleate. **Amp.** 0.2 mg./ml. w/tartaric acid 0.25 mg., NaCl 3.0 mg./ml. SandoPak 20s, 100s. **Tab:** 0.2 mg./Tab. Bot. 100s, 1000s. SandoPak pkgs. 100s.
Use: Orally, I.V. & I.M., oxytocic.

:THESTROL.
See: Promethestrol (Various Mfr.)

:THETHARIMIDE BEMEGRIDE. 3-Methyl-3-ethyl glutarimide.

IETHETOIN. USAN. 5-Ethyl-1-methyl-5-phenylimidazoline-2,4-dione. Deltoin.
Use: Anticonvulsant.

:THIBON CAPSULES. (Barrows) Choline dihydrogen citrate 278 mg., dl-methionine 111 mg., inositol 83.3 mg., B-12 2 mcg., liver conc. and liver desic. 86.6 mg./Cap. Bot. 100s.

:THICILLIN. B.A.N. 6-(2,6-Dimethoxy-benzamido)-penicillanic acid. Celbenin; Staphcillin (sodium salt)
Use: Antibiotic.

IETHICILLIN SODIUM, STERILE, U.S.P. XXI., Inj., U.S.P. XXI. Sod. 2,6-Dimethoxyphenyl penicillin. Dimethoxyphenyl pencillin sod.
Use: Antibiotic.
See:
Celbenin, Vial (Beecham Labs)
Staphcillin, Vial (Bristol)

• **METHIMAZOLE,** U.S.P. XXI. Tab., U.S.P. XXI. 1-Methylimidazole-2-thiol. Mercazole. 2H-imidazole-2-thione, 1,3-dihydro-1-methyl.
Use: Thyroid inhibitor. (5 to 20 mg.)
See: Tapazole, Tab. (Lilly)
Thiamazole (I.N.N.)

METHINDIZATE. B.A.N. 2-(1-Methyloctahydroindol-3-yl)ethyl benzilate. Present in Isaverine hydrochloride.
Use: Spasmolytic, veterinary medicine.

• **METHIODAL SODIUM,** U.S.P. XXI. Inj., U.S.P. XXI. Sod. monoiodomethanesulfonate. Abrodil, Radiographol, Diagnorenol.
Use: Radiopaque medium for urinary tract.

METHIOMEPRAZINE HCl. dl-10-(3-Dimethyl-amino-2-methylpropyl)-2-methylthiophenothiazine HCl. (SmithKline)
Use: Anti-emetic.

• **METHIONINE,** U.S.P. XXI. **Note:** Also see Racemethionine, U.S.P. XXI.
Use: Amino acid.

METHIOPLEX. (Lincoln) Methionine 25 mg., B-1 50 mg., niacinamide 100 mg., B-2 2 mg., choline 50 mg., B-6 2 mg., panthenol 2 mg., benzyl alcohol 1%, distilled water q.s./cc. Vial 30 cc.
Use: Lipotropic & vitamin therapy.

• **METHISAZONE.** USAN. N-methylisatin-β-thiosemicarbazone. 1-Methylindoline-2,3-dione 3-thiosemicarbazone. Marboran.
Use: Antiviral drug.

METHISCHOL CAPSULES. (Armour) Nutrients. Bot. 100s, 500s.

METHITURAL SODIUM. 5-(1-Methylbutyl)-5-[2-(methylthio)ethyl]-2-thiobarbituric acid sodium salt.
Use: Hypnotic; sedative.

METHIXENE. B.A.N. 9-(1-Methyl-3-piperidyl-methyl)-thiaxanthen. Tremonil (hydrochloride).
Use: Treatment of the Parkinsonian syndrome.

• **METHIXENE HYDROCHLORIDE.** USAN. l-Methyl-3-(thioxanthen-9-ylmethyl)-piperidine HCl.
Use: Antispasmodic.

METHNITE. (Kenyon) Methscopolamine nitrate 2.5 mg./Tab. Bot. 100s, 1000s.
Use: Antispasmodic.

• **METHOCARBAMOL,** U.S.P. XXI. Cap., Tab., U.S.P. XXI. 1,2-Propanediol, 3-(2-methoxy phenoxy)-, 1-carbamate. (2-Hydroxy-3-o-methoxyphenoxypropyl) carbamate. 3-(o-Methoxyphenoxy)-1,2-propanediol 1-carbamate.
Use: Skeletal muscle relaxant.
See: Delaxin, Tab. (Ferndale)
Robaxin, Tabs., Inj. (Robins)
Romethocarb, Tab. (Robinson)
S.K. Methecarbamol, Tab. (SmithKline)
W/Aspirin.
See: Robaxisal, Tab. (Robins)

METHOCEL. Methyl cellulose.

• **METHOHEXITAL,** U.S.P. XXI.
Use: Pharmaceutical necessity for Methohexital Sodium for Injection.

• **METHOHEXITAL SODIUM FOR INJECTION,** U.S.P. XXI. Alpha-(dl)-5-allyl-1-methyl-5-(1-methyl-2-penty-

nyl) barbituric sod. 2,4,6(IH,-3H,5H)-pyrimidinetrione,. 1-methyl-5-(1-methyl-2-pentynyl)-5-(2-propenyl)-, (±) monosodium salt.
Use: General anesthetic (intravenous).
See: Brevital, Amp., Pow. (Lilly)

METHOHEXITONE. B.A.N. α-5-Allyl-1-methyl-5-(1-methylpent-2-ynyl)barbituric acid.
Use: Anesthetic.
See: Brevital
Brietal

METHOIN. B.A.N. 5-Ethyl-3-methyl-5-phenylhydantoin. 5-Ethyl-3-methyl-5-phenylimidazoline-2,4-dione. Mephenytoin (I.N.N.)
Use: Anticonvulsant.
See: Mesantoin, Tab. (Sandoz)

• **METHOPHOLINE HCl.** USAN. 1-(p-Chlorophenethyl)-2-methyl-6, 7-dimethoxy-1,2,3,4-tetrahydroisoquinoline HCl.
Use: Analgesic.
See: Versidyne

METHOPTO 0.25%. (Professional Pharmacal) Methylcellulose powder 2.5 mg. (0.25% soln.), boric acid 12 mg., potassium Cl. 7.3 mg., benzalkonium Cl. 0.04 mg., glycerin 12 mg./ml. w/sodium carbonate to adjust pH and purified water. Bot. 15 or 30 ml.
Use: Tear replacement.

METHOPTO FORTE 0.5%. (Professional Pharmacal) Methylcellulose powder 5 mg. (0.5% soln.), boric acid 12 mg., potassium Cl. 7.3 mg., benzalkonium Cl. 0.4 mg., glycerin 12 mg./ml. w/sodium carbonate to adjust pH and purified water. Bot. 15 ml.
Use: Tear replacement.

METHOPTO FORTE 1%. (Professional Pharmacal) Methylcellulose powder 10 mg. (1% soln.), boric acid 12 mg., potassium Cl. 7.3 mg., benzalkonium Cl. sol 0.04 mg., glycerin 12 mg./ml. w/sodium carbonate to adjust pH and purified water. Bot. 15 ml.
Use: Tear replacement.

METHOPYRAPHONE.
See: Metopirone, Tab., Amp. (Ciba)

METHORATE. Not listed.
See: Dextromethorphan HBr

METHORBATE S.C.. (Standex) Methenamine 40.8 mg., atropine sulfate 0.03 mg., hyoscyamine sulfate 0.03 mg., salol 18.1 mg., benzoic acid 4.5 mg., methylene blue 5.4 mg./Tab. Bot. 100s.

d-METHORPHAN HBr.
See: Dextromethorphan HBr (Various Mfr.)

METHORPHINAN. •Racemorphan HBr. Dromoran.

l-METHORPHINAN LEVORPHANOL.
See: Levo-Dromoran, Amp., Tab., Vial (Roche)

METHOSERPIDINE. B.A.N. 10-Methoxydeserpidine.
Use: Hypotensive.
See: Decaserpyl

• **METHOTREXATE,** U.S.P. XXI. Tab., U.S.P. XXI. Amethopterin. 4-Amino-10-methylfolic acid. N-[p-[[(2,4-Diamino-6-pteridinyl)-methyl]-methylamino]benzoyl] glutamic acid. L-glutamic acid, N-[4-[[(2,4-diamino-6-pteridinyl)methyl] -me-thylamino]benzoyl].
Use: Leukemia in children, antineoplastic, antipsoriatic.
See: Methotrexate, Tab., Inj. (Lederle)

• **METHOTREXATE SODIUM INJECTION.** U.S.P. XXI. 4-Amino-N^{10}-methyl-pteroylglutamic acid sodium. (Lederle) 2.5 mg./ml. Vial 2 ml.; 25 mg./ml. Vial 2 ml. w/preservatives; 20 mg., 50 mg., 100 mg. Vials cryodesiccated, preservative free; 50 mg 100 mg., 200 mg. Vials; 25 mg./ml. solution preservative free.
Use: Leukemia therapy., psoriasis.
See: Methotrexate, Inj., Pow. (Lederle)
Mexate, Inj. (Bristol)

• **METHOTRIMEPRAZINE,** U.S.P. XXI. Inj., U.S.P. XX 2-Methoxy-10-(3-dimethylamino-2-methyl-propyl)phenothiazine. (—)-10-(3-(Dimethyl-amino)-2-methyl-propyl)-2-methoxyphenothiazine. Levomepromazine (I.N.N.) Veractil.
Use: Tranquilizer, non-addicting analgesic.
See: Levoprome, Amp., Vial (Lederle)

METHOXAMINE. B.A.N. 2-Amino-1-(2,5-dimethoxyphenyl)propan-1-ol. Vasoxine; Vasylox (hydrochloride).
Use: Vasoconstrictor.

• **METHOXAMINE HYDROCHLORIDE,** U.S.P. XXI. Inj., U.S.P. XXI. α-(1-Aminoethyl)-2,5-dimethoxybenzyl alcohol hydrochloride. Benzenemethanol, α-(1-aminoethyl)-2,5-dimethoxy-,hydrochloride.
Use: Sympathomimetic, adrenergic (vasopressor).
See: Vasoxyl, Inj. (Burroughs Wellcome)

• **METHOXYSALEN,** U.S.P. XXI.
Use: Topical pigmenting agent.
See: Meloxine, (Upjohn)
Oxsoralen, Cap., Lot. (Elder)

• **METHOXSALEN TOPICAL SOLUTION,** U.S.P. XXI 8-Methoxypsoralen. 8-Hydroxy-4',5',6,7-furocoumarin, ammoidin, xanthotoxin. 7H-Furo[3,2-g][1] benzopyran-7-one,2-methoxy-9-methoxy-7H-Furo[3,2-g][1] benzopyran-7-one.
Use: Topical pigmenting agent.

O-METHOXY-N,α-DIMETHYLPHENETHYLAMINE HCl. Methoxyphenamine HCl.

METHOXYDONE.
See: Mephenoxalone (Various Mfr.)

• **METHOXYFLURANE,** U.S.P. XXI. 2,2-Dichloro-1,1-difluoroethyl methyl ether.
Use: General inhalation anesthetic.
See: Penthrane, Liq. (Abbott)

METHOXYPHENAMINEI B.A.N. 1-o-Anisylethylmethylamine. Orthoxine.
Use: Bronchodilator.

9-METHOXY-7H-FURO[3,2-g][1]BENZOPYRAN-7-ONE. Methoxsalen, U.S.P. XXI.

3-METHOXY-19-NOR-17-α-PREGNA-1,3,5,(10)-TRIEN-20-YN-17-OL. Mestranol, U.S.P. XXI.

• **METHOXYPHENAMINE HYDROCHLORIDE,** U.S.P. XXI. o-Methoxy-N, α-dimethylphenethylamino HCl.
Use: Adrenergic (bronchodilator).
W/Chlorpheniramine maleate, acetophenetidin, acetylsalicylic acid, caffeine.
See: Pyrroxate, Cap., Tab. (Upjohn)

/Dextromethorphan HCl, orthoxine, sod. citrate.
See: Orthoxicol, Syr. (Upjohn)
/Dextromethorphan HBr, phenylephrine HCl, chlorpheniramine maleate.
See: Statuss, Syr., Cap. (Elder)
/Medrol.
See: Medrol, Tab. (Upjohn)

(o-METHOXYPHENOXY)-PROPANEDIOL-1,2.
See: Guaifenesin

METHOXYPHENYL GLYCERYL ETHER.
See: Guaifenesin, Guaifenesin.

ETHOXYPROMAZINE MALEATE. 10-[3-(Dimethylamino)propyl]-2-methoxyphenothiazine maleate. Tentone.
Use: CNS depressant.

METHOXYPSORALEN.
See: Methoxsalen

METHSCOPOLAMINE BROMIDE, U.S.P. XXI. Inj., Tab., U.S.P. XXI. Epoxytropine tropate methylbromide, scopolamine methylbromide, hyoscine methylbromide. 6β, 7β-Epoxy-3α-hydroxy-8-methyl-1αH, 5αH-tropanium bromide(−)-Tropate.
Use: Anticholinergic
See: Pamine, Tab., Vial (Upjohn)
Scoline, Tab. (Westerfield)
/Amobarbital.
See: Scoline-Amobarbital, Tab. (Westerfield)
/Butabarbital Sod., aluminum hydroxide gel dried & mag. trisilicate.
See: Eulcin, Tab. (Leeds Pharmacal)
/Phenobarbital.
See: Pamine PB, Prep. (Upjohn)
Synt-PB, Tab. (Scrip)
/Phenylpropanolamine HCl chlorpheniramine maleate.
See: Bobid, Cap. (Boyd)
Symptrol, Cap. (Saron)

ETHSCOPOLAMINE NITRATE. Scopolamine Methyl Nitrate, Prep. (Various Mfr.) Mescomine.
See: Allerspan, Cap. (Merit)
Aluscop, Cap., Susp. (Westerfield)
Cenahist, Cap. (Century)
Chlorpel, Cap. (Santa)
Conalsyn Chroncap, Cap. (Cenci)
Dallergy, Cap., Tab., Syr. (Laser)
Drinus Graduals, Cap. (Federal)
Drize M, Cap. (Ascher)
Extendryl, Cap., Syr., Tab. (Fleming)
Histaspan-D, Cap. (USV Labs.)
Historal, Cap., Liq. (W.F. Merchant)
Hydrochol-Plus, Tab. (Elder)
Kleer, Cap. (Scrip)
Kleer Compound, Tab. (Scrip)
Kleer-Tuss, Cap. (Scrip)
Methnite, Tab., (Kenyon)
MSC Triaminic, Tab. (Dorsey)
Narine, T.R. Cap. (Dooner)
Narspan, Cap. (Coast Labs.)
Paraspan, Cap. (Fleming)
Sanhist T.D. 12, Tab. (Sandia)
Scotnord, Tab. (Scott/Cord)
Sinaprel, Cap. (Pasadena Res.)
Sinodec, Cap. (Primedics)
Sinovan, Timed Cap. (Drug Ind.)
Sinunil, Pellsule (Misemer)
Spasmid, Elix., Tab. (Dalin)
Symptrol, Cap. (Saron)
Trisohist, Cap. (Riker)

• **METHSUXIMIDE,** U.S.P. XXI. Cap., U.S.P. XXI. N,2-Dimethyl-2-phenylsuccinamide Mesuximide (I.N.N.)
Use: Anticonvulsant.
See: Celontin Kapseal. (Parke-Davis)

METHULOSE. (Softcon) Methylcellulose 0.25% and benzalkonium chloride 1:25,000 as a preservative. Bot. 15 cc., 30 cc.
Use: Tear replacement and ophthalmic vehicle.

METHYCLODINE. (Rugby) Methyclothiazide 5 mg., deserpidine 0.25 mg./Tab. Bot. 100s.
Use: Antihypertensive, diuretic.

• **METHYCLOTHIAZIDE,** U.S.P. XXI. Tab., U.S.P. XXI. 6-Chloro-3-chloro-methyl-2-methyl-7-sulfamyl-3,4-dihydro-1,2,4-benzothiadiazine-1,1-dioxide. 6-Chloro-3-(chloromethyl)-3,4-dihydro-2-methyl-2H-1,2,4-benzothiadiazine-7-sulfonamide 1,1-Dioxide.
Use: Diuretic; antihypertensive.
See: Enduron, Tab. (Abbott) Methyclodine, Tab. (Rugby)
W/Deserpidine.
See: Enduronyl, Tab. (Abbott)
Enduronyl Forte, Tab. (Abbott)
W/Pargyline hydrochloride.
See: Eutron, Tab. (Abbott)

METHYLACETYLCHOLINE.
See: Methacholine

METHYL ALCOHOL, N.F. XVI.
Use: Pharmaceutic acid (solvent).

(−)-ERYTHRO-α-[1-(METHYLAMINO)-ETHYL]-BENZYL ALCOHOL. Ephedrine Sulfate.

METHYLAMPHETAMINE HYDROCHLORIDE & SULFATE.
See: Desoxyephedrine HCl (Var. Mfr.)

METHYLANDROSTENEDIOL.
See: Hybolin, Vial (Hyrex)
Methandriol
Methyldiol, Prep. (North American Pharm)
W/Adrenal cortex ext., Vit. B-12.
See: Geri-Ace, Inj. (Brown)
W/Carboxymethylcellulose sod., thimerosal.
See: Cenabolic, Vial (Century)
W/Pentylenetetrazol, nicotinic acid, l-lysine, dl-methionine, ethinyl estradiol, thiamine, pyridoxine, riboflavin, Vit. B-12, Vit. A, Vit. D, ascorbic acid.
See: Ardiatric, Tab. (Burgin-Arden)

• **METHYL ATROPINE NITRATE.** USAN. Atropine Methylnitrate. (Various Mfr.) 8-Methylatropinium nitrate. dl-Hyoscyamine methylnitrate.
Use: Antispasmodic.
W/Aluminum hydroxide, pectin, osmokadin, betalactose.
See: Metropectin, Tab. (Pennwalt)

W/Butabarbital, methscopolamine nitrate.
See: Scolate, Tab. (Central)
W/Oxidized bile acids, ox and hog bile ext., phenobarbital.
See: G.B.S., Tab. (O'Neal)
W/Phenobarbital & dihydroxy aluminum aminoacetate.
See: Harvatrate A, Tab. (O'Neal)

• **METHYLBENZETHONIUM CHLORIDE,** U.S.P. XXI. Lotion, Oint., Powder, U.S.P. XXI. Benzyl-dimethyl-2[2-(p-1,1,3-tetramethyl-butyl-cresoxy)ethoxy]-ethyl ammonium chloride. (p-Tertiary octyl cresoxy ethoxy ethyl dimethyl-benzyl ammonium chloride). Benzyl-dimethyl[2[2-[[4-(1,1,3,3-tetramethylbutyl)tolyl]oxy]ethoxy]-ethyl]ammonium chloride.
Use: Bactericide; Local anti-infective.
See: Ammorid, Oint. (Kinney)
Benephen, Prods. (Halsted)
Cuticura Acne Cream (Purex)
Cuticura Medicated First Aid Cream (Purex)
Diaparene Prods. (Glenbrook)
Fordustin, Pow. (Sween)
Surgi-Kleen, Liq. (Sween)
W/Cod liver oil.
See: Benephen, Prods. (Halsted)
Sween Skin Care, Cream (Sween)
W/Magnesium stearate.
See: Mennen Baby Pow. (Mennen)
W/Phenol, acetanilid, zinc oxide, calamine & eucalyptol.
See: Taloin, Oint. (Warren-Teed)
W/Phenylmercuric acetate, methylparaben.
See: Lorophyn, Supp. (Eaton)
Norforms, Aer., Supp. (Norwich)
W/Zinc oxide, calamine, eucalyptol.
See: Taloin, Tube (Warren-Teed)

METHYL BENZOQUATE. B.A.N. Methyl 7-benzyloxy-6-butyl-1,4-dihydro-4-oxoquinoline-3-carboxylate. Nequinate (I.N.N.) Statyl.
Use: Antiprotozoan, veterinary medicine.

METHYLBENZTROPINE.
See: Ethybenztropine (Sandoz)

METHYLBROMTROPIN MANDELATE.
See: Homatropine Methylbromide, U.S.P. XXI.

• **METHYLCELLULOSE,** U.S.P. XXI. Ophth. Soln., Oral Soln.,Tab.,U.S.P.XXI.Cellulosemethylether.Mellose.
Use: Suspending agent.
See: Cellothyl, Tab. (International Drug)
Cologel, Sol. (Lilly)
Isopto-Plain, Liq. (Alcon)
Melozets, Wafer (Calgon)
Methulose, Sol. (Softcon)
Syncelose, Tab. (Blue Line)
Tearisol, Sol. (Smith, Miller & Patch)
Visculose, Sol. (Softcon)
W/Benzocaine, vitamins, minerals, niacinamide.
See: Rite-Diet, Cap. (Edward J. Moore)
W/Boric acid, glycerine, propylene glycol, methylparaben, propylparaben, irish moss ext.
See: Canfield Lubricating Jelly (Paddock)
W/Carboxymethylcellulose.
See: Ex-Caloric, Wafer (Eastern Research)
W/Dicyclomine HCl, magnesium trisilicate, aluminum hydroxide-magnesium carbonate dried.
See: Triactin Tab. (Norwich)
W/Dicyclomine HCl, aluminum hydroxide & magnesium hydroxide.
See: Triactin Liq. (Norwich)
W/Phenylephrine HCl.
See: Vernacel (Professional Pharmacal)
W/Phenylephrine HCl, benzalkonium chloride.
See: Efricel ⅛% (Professional Pharmacal)
W/Polysorbate 80, boric acid.
See: Lacril Artificial Tears (Allergan)

METHYL 7(S)-CHLORO-6,7,8-TRIDEOXY-6-trans-(1-METHYL-4-PROPYL-L-2-PYRROLIDINECARBOXAMIDE)-1-THIO-L-THREO-α-D-GALACTO-OCTOPYRANOSIDE MONOHYDROCHLORIDE. Clindamycin Hydrochloride, U.S.P. XXI.

METHYLCHROMONE. B.A.N. 3-Methyl-(4H)-chromen-4-one.
Use: Coronary vasodilator.
See: Crodimyl

METHYL CYSTEINE. B.A.N. Methyl 2-amino-3-mercaptoproprionate. Mecysteine (I.N.N.) Acdrile; Visclair [hydrochloride]
Use: Vasoconstrictor.

METHYL CYSTEINE HYDROCHLORIDE. Cysteine methyl ester hydrochloride.
Use: Mucolytic agent.

METHYLDESORPHINE. B.A.N. 6-Methyl-Δ^6-deoxymorphine.
Use: Narcotic analgesic.

METHYL 6,8-DIDEOXY-6-(I-METHYL-TRANS-4-PROPYL-L-2-PYRROLIDINECARBOXAMIDE)-I-THIO-D-ERYTHRO-ALPHA-D-GALACTO-OCTOPYRANOSIDE MONOHYDROCHLORIDE MONOHYDRATE. Lincomycin Hydrochloride, U.S.P. XXI.

METHYLDIOL IN OIL. (Vortech) Methandriol dipropionate 50 mg., benzyl alcohol 5% in sesame oil/cc. Vial 10 cc.
Use: Anabolic steroid.

• **METHYLDOPA,** U.S.P. XXI. Oral Susp., Tabs. U.S.P. XXI. Levo-3-(3,4-dihydroxyphenyl)-2-methylalanine.
Use: Antihypertensive.
See: Aldomet, Tab. (Merck Sharp & Dohme)
W/Chlorothiazide.
See: Aldoclor, Tab. (Merck Sharp & Dohme)
W/Hydrochlorothiazide.
See: Aldoril, Tab. (Merck Sharp & Dohme)

• **METHYLDOPA AND HYDROCHLORTHIAZIDE TABLETS,** U.S.P. XXI.
Use: Antihypertensive.
See: Aldoril, Tab. (Merck Sharp & Dohme)

• **METHYLDOPATE HCl,** U.S.P. XXI. Inj. U.S.P. XXI. (Merck Sharp & Dohme) Ethyl ester of levo-3-(3,4-dihydroxyphenyl)-2-methylalanine HCl. l-Tyrosine, 3-hydroxy-α-methyl-,ethyl ester hydrochloride-.
Use: Anti-hypertensive agent.
See: Aldomet Ester HCl, Inj. (Merck Sharp & Dohme)

3′-METHYLENEBIS (4-HYDROXYCOUMARIN).
See: Bishydroxycoumarin (Var. Mfr.)
Dicumarol, U.S.P. XXI. (Various Mfr.)
METHYLENE BLUE, U.S.P. XXI. Inj. U.S.P. XXI. (Various Mfr.) Methylthionine chloride. 3,7-Bix-(Dimethyl-amino)phenzathionium chloride.
Use: Antimethemoglobinemic, antidote to cyanide poisoning.
See: Urolene Blue, Tab. (Star)
Wright's Stain, Liq. (Hynson, Westcott & Dunning)
METHYLENE BLUE W/COMBINATIONS.
See: Cysto, Tab. (Freeport)
Cystrea, Tab. (Moore Kirk)
G-U-Sist, Tab. (Freeport)
Hexalol, Tab. (Central)
Lanased, Tab. (Lannett)
Renalgin, Tab. (Meyer)
Uramine, Tab. (Kay)
Urineaze, Tab. (Foy)
Uriprel, Tab. (Pasadena Research)
Urised, Tab. (Webcon)
Uristat, Tab. (Lemmon)
Uritabs, Tab. (Vortech)
Uritin Modified Formula, Tab. (Wolins)
Urostat Forte, Tab. (Elder)
Urothyn Improved, Tab. (Reid-Provident)
Uro-Ves, Tab. (Mallard)
UTA, Tab. (ICN)
U-Tract, Tab. (Bowman)
2,2′-METHYLENEBIS[3,4,6-TRICHLOROPHENOL]. Hexachlorophene, U.S.P. XXI.
METHYLENE CHLORIDE, N.F. XVI.
Use: Pharmaceutic aid (solvent).
METHYLERGOMETRINE. B.A.N. N-(+)-1-(Hydroxymethyl)propyl-(+)-lysergamide.
Use: Uterine stimulant.
See: Methergin hydrogen maleate
METHYLERGONOVINE MALEATE, U.S.P. XXI. Inj., Tab., U.S.P. XXI. 9,10-Didehydro-N-[(S)-1-(hydroxymethyl) propyl]-6-methylergoline-8-carboxamide maleate (1:1).
Use: Oxytocic.
See: Methergine, Amp. & Tab. (Sandoz)
METHYLETHYLAMINO-PHENYLPROPANOL HCl.
See: Nethamine HCl. (Var. Mfr.)
METHYLGESIC. (Kay) Methyl nicotinate, methyl salicylate, menthol, camphor, dipropyleneglycol salicylate, oil of cassia, oleoresins capsicum and ginger. Lotion Bot. 4 oz., pt., gal.
Use: Analgesic, counterirritant, vasodilator.
METHYLGLUCAMINE DIATRIZOATE, INJ., A water-soluble radiopaque iodine cpd. N-methylglucamine salt of Diatrizoate.
See: Diatrizoate (Var. Mfr.)
Diatrizoate Meglumine Inj. U.S.P. XXI.
METHULGLUCAMINE IODIPAMIDE, INJ.
See: Meglumine Iodipamide, Inj. U.S.P. XXI. (Var. Mfr.)
W/Diatrizoate methylglucamine.
See: Sinografin, Vial (Squibb)

METHYLGLYOXAL-BIS-GUANYLHYDRAZONE. Methyl GAG.
METHYL 18β-HYDROXY-11,17α-DIMETHOXY-3β,20 α-YOHIMBAN-16β-CARBOXYLATE 3,4,5-TRIMETHOXYBENZOATE (ESTER)- Reserpine, U.S.P. XXI.
METHYL 3β-HYDROXY-1α-H,5αH-TROPAN-2β-CARBOXYLATE, BENZOATE (ESTER) HYDROCHLORIDE. Cocaine Hydrochloride, U.S.P. XXI.
1-METHYLIMIDAZOLE-2-THIOL. Methimazole, U.S.P. XXI.
N-METHYLISATIN BETA-THIOSEMICARBAZONE.
Under study.
Use: Smallpox protection.
• **METHYL ISOBUTYL KETONE,** N.F. XVI. 4-Methyl-2-pentanone.
Use: Pharmaceutic aid (alcohol denaturant).
METHYLISO-OCTENYLAMINE.
See: Isometheptene HCl (Var. Mfr.)
1-METHYL-D-LYSERGIC ACID BUTANOLAMIDE.
See: Sansert, Tab. (Sandoz)
METHYLMERCADONE. Name used for Nifuratel.
2-METHYL-1,4-NAPHTHOQUINONE.
See: Menadione (Var. Mfr.)
METHYL NICOTINATE.
W/Histamine dihydrochloride, oleoresin capsicum, glycomonosalicylate.
See: Akes-N-Pain Rub., Oint. (Moore)
W/methyl salicilate, menthol
See: Musterole Deep Strenght Oint. (Plough)
W/Methyl salicylate, menthol, camphor, dipropylene glycol salicylate, cassia oil, oleoresins capsium, & ginger.
See: Arthaderm, Lot. (Paddock)
Scrip-Gesic, Oint. (Scrip)
2-METHYL-5-NITROMIDAZOLE-1-ETHANOL. Metronidazole, U.S.P. XXI.
6-[(1-METHYL-4-NITROIMIDAZOL-5-YL)-THIO]PURINE. Azathioprine, U.S.P. XXI.
METHYLONE. (Paddock) Methylprednisolone acetate 40 mg./cc. Vials 5 cc.
Use: Corticosteroid.
• **METHYL PALMOXIRATE.** USAN.
See: Antidiabetic.
• **METHYLPARABEN,** N.F. XVI. (Various Mfr.) Methyl p-hydroxybenzoate. Methyl Chemosept.
Use: Pharm. aid (anti-fungal preservative).
METHYLPARAFYNOL. 3-Methyl-pentyne-1-ol-3. Oblivon, Somnesin.
METHYLPENTYNOL. B.A.N. 3-Methylpent-1-yn-3-ol. Atempol, Insomnol, Meparfynol, Methylparafynol, Oblivon, Somnesin, & Oblivon-C Carbamate.
Use: Tranquilizer.
METHYLPHENETHYLAMINE. 1-alpha-Methylphenethylamine.
See: Amphetamine HCl (Var. Mfr.)
METHYLPHENIDATE. B.A.N. Methyl α-phenyl-2-piperidylacetate.
Use: Central nervous system stimulant.
• **METHYLPHENIDATE HCl,** U.S.P. XXI. Tabs., U.S.P. XXI. Methyl a-phenyl-2-piperidine-acetate hydrochloride.

Use: Central stimulant.
See: Ritalin HCl, Tab., Vial (Ciba)

METHYLPHENIDYLACETATE HCl. Methyl 1-phenyl-2-piperidylacetate.
See: Methylphenidate HCl (Var. Mfr.)

METHYLPHENOBARBITAL. N-Methyl-5-ethyl-5-phenylbarbituric Acid.
See: Mebaral, Tab. (Winthrop-Breon)

d-METHYLPHENYLAMINE SULFATE.
See: Dextroamphetamine Sulfate, U.S.P. XXI. (Var. Mfr.)

METHYL PHENYLETHYLHYDANTOIN.
See: Mesantoin, Tab. (Sandoz)

5-METHYL-3-PHENYL-4-ISOXAZOLYL PENICILLIN. Oxacillin Sodium, U.S.P. XXI.

METHYLPHENYLSUCCINIMIDE.
See: Milontin, Kapseal, Susp. (Parke-Davis)

METHYL POLYSILOXANE.
See: Mylicon, Tab., Drops (Stuart)
Phasil, Tab. (Reed & Carnrick)
Silain, Tab. (Robins)
Simethicone

METHYLPRED-40. (Seatrace) Methylprednisolone acetate 40 mg./ml. Vial 5 cc.

• **METHYLPREDNISOLONE,** U.S.P. XXI. Tab., U.S.P. XXI. 11 α,17,21-Trihydroxy-6-α-methyl-pregna-1,4-diene-3,20-dione. Medrone, Metastab.
Use: Glucocorticoid.
See: A-Methapred, Inj. (Abbott)
Dura-Meth, Inj. (Foy)
Medralone 40, Inj. (Keene)
Medralone 80, Inj. (Keene)
Medrol, Tab. (Upjohn)
W/Neomycin sulfate.
See: Neo-Medrol, Oint. (Upjohn)
W/Sod. succinate.
See: Solu-Medrol, Vial (Upjohn)

• **METHYLPREDNISOLONE ACETATE,** U.S.P. XXI. Cream, For Enema, Sterile Susp., U.S.P. XXI. 6-α-methylprednisolone-21-acetate.
Use: Glucocorticoid.
See: Dep-med 40 Inj. (Tunex)
Depo-Medrol, Inj., Rectal (Upjohn)
Depo-Pred., Vial (Hyrex)
Medrol Preps., Cream (Upjohn)
Mepred-40, Susp. (Savage)
Mepred-80, Susp. (Savage)
Neo-Medrol, Preps. (Upjohn)
Rep-Pred, Vial (Central)

• **METHYLPREDNISOLONE ACETATE FOR ENEMA,** U.S.P. XXI.
Use: Glucocorticoid.

• **METHYLPREDNISOLONE HEMISUCCINATE,** U.S.P. XXI.
Use: Adrenocortical steroid.

• **METHYLPREDNISOLONE SODIUM PHOSPHATE.** USAN.
Use: Glucocorticoid.

• **METHYLPREDNISOLONE SODIUM SUCCINATE,** U.S.P. XXI. For Inj., U.S.P. XXI. Methylprednisolone 21-(Hydrogen Succinate) sodium salt.
Use: Adrenocorticoid steroid.
See: Solu-Medrol, Mix-O-Vial (Upjohn)

METHYLPROMAZINE. 10-(3-Dimethylaminopropyl)-2-methylphenethiazine.

METHYLPYRIMAL.
See: Sulfamerazine (Various Mfr.)

METHYLROSANILINE CHLORIDE.
Use: Anthelmintic & anti-infective.
See: Gentian Violet, U.S.P. XXI. (Various Mfr.)

• **METHYL SALICYLATE,** N.F. XVI. (Various Mfr.) Oil of wintergreen.
Use: Pharm. aid (flavor).

METHYL SALICYLATE W/COMBINATIONS.
Use: Rubefacient rub (external).
See: Analbalm, Liq. (Central)
Analgesic Balm (Various Mfr.)
Analgesic Ointment "Lannett," Oint. (Lannett)
Analgesine, Liq. (Elder)
Analgex, Oint. (Bowman)
Banalg, Liniment (Cole)
Chloral-Methylol, Oint. (Ulmer)
Chloro-Salicylate, Oint. (Kremers-Urban)
Cydonol, Lot. (Gordon)
Emul-o-balm, Liq. (Pennwalt)
Gordobalm, Oint. (Gordon)
Guaiamen, Cream (Lannett)
Listerine Antiseptic, Liq. (Warner-Lambert)
Methagul, Oint. (Gordon)
Musterole, Oint. (Plough)
Pixacol, Liq. (Pixacol)
Sloan's Linament, Liq. (Warner-Lambert)
Stimurub, Cream (Otis Clapp)
Thi-Cin, Cap. (Warren-Teed)

METHYL SULFANIL AMIDOISOXAZOLE. Sulfamethoxazole.
See: Gantanol, Tab., Susp. (Roche Lab.)

• **METHYLTESTOSTERONE,** U.S.P. XXI. Tab., Cap., U.S.P. XXI. Buccal, Tab. 17-Methyltestosterone. 17β-Hydroxy-17-methylandrost-4-en-3-one. (Anertan, Glasso-Sterandryl, Testoviron)
Use: Androgen.
See: Android-5, 10, 25, Tab. (Brown)
Arcosterone, Tabs. (Arcum)
Metandren, Linguet, Tab. (Ciba)
Neo-Hombreol-M, Tab. (Organon)
Oreton-M, Tab., Buccal Tab. (Schering)
Ostone, Tab. (Rowell)
Testred, Cap. (ICN)

METHYLTESTOSTERONE W/COMBINATIONS.
Use: Androgen.
See: Android-5, 10, 25, Tab. (Brown)
Diatric, Tab. (Pasadena Research)
Esdone, Cap., Tab. (Westerfield)
Estritone, Tab. (Kenyon)
Femogen W/Methyltestosterone, Tab. (Fellows-Testagar)
Formatrix, Tab. (Ayerst)
Geramine, Tab., Inj. (Brown)
Gera-Pet, Tab. (Vortech)
Geritag, Cap. (Reid-Provident)
Gynetone, Tab. (Schering)
Mediatric, Cap., Liq., Tab. (Ayerst)

Menotab-M #1 & 2, Tab. (Fleming)
Neosterol, Tab. (Winston)
Os-Cal-Mone, Tab. (Marion)
Premarin W/Methyltestosterone, Tab. (Ayerst)
Tylosterone, Tab., Amp. (Lilly)
Vimah, Cap. (Hyrex)
Virilon, Cap. (Star)

ETHYLTHIONINE CHLORIDE. Name used for Methylene Blue.

ETHYLTHIONINE HCl. Name used for Methylene Blue.

METHYLTHIOURACIL, U.S.P. XXI. 6-Methyl-2-thiouracil. 4-Methyl-2-thiouracil. Antibason, Methiocil.
Use: Thyroid inhibition.

ETHYL VIOLET.
See: Gentian Violet, Crystal Violet, Methylrosanaline chloride

ETHYNDAMINE. Name used for Tetrydamine.

METHYNODIOL DIACETATE. USAN.
Use: Oral progestin.

METHYPRYLON, U.S.P. XXI. Cap., Tab., U.S.P. XXI. 3,3-Diethyl-5-methyl-2,4-piperidinedione.
Use: Hypnotic.
See: Noludar, Cap. & Tab. (Roche)

ETHYRIDINE. B.A.N. 2-(2-Methoxyethyl)pyridine. Promintic.
Use: Anthelmintic, veterinary medicine.

METHYSERGIDE. USAN.
Use: Vasoconstrictor.

METHYSERGIDE MALEATE, U.S.P. XXI. Tab., U.S.P. XXI. N-[1-(Hydroxymethyl)propyl]-1-methyl-D-lysergamide bimaleate. 1-Methyl-D-lysergic acid butanolamide. (+)-9,10-Didehydro-N-[1-(hydroxymethyl)-propyl]-1,6-dimethylergoline-8β-carboxamide Maleate (1:1).
Use: Analgesic (specific in migraine).
See: Sansert, Tab. (Sandoz)

METIAMIDE. USAN. Histamine H_2 antagonist. 1-Methyl-3-[2-(5-methylimidazol-4-ylmethylthio)ethyl]thiourea.
Use: Treatment for peptic ulcer.

METIAPINE. USAN.
Use: Antipsychotic.

METICLOPINDOL. Name used for Clopidol.

METICORTEN. (Schering) Prednisone 1 mg., 5 mg./Tab. Bot. 1 mg. 100s. 5 mg. 100s.
Use: Anti-inflammatory steroid.

METI-DERM. (Schering) Prednisolone 5 mg./Gm. of cream. Tube 10 Gm., 25 Gm.
Use: Topical anti-inflammatory steroid.

METIMYD OPHTHALMIC OINT. STERILE. (Schering) Prednisolone acetate 0.5% (5 mg.), sod. sulfacetamide 10% (100 mg.) in an emollient petrolatum and mineral oil base w/methylparaben 0.5 mg., propylparaben 0.1 mg. Tube ⅛ oz.
Use: Topical ophthalmic anti-inflammatory.

METIMYD OPHTH. SUSP. STERILE. (Schering) Prednisolone acetate 5 mg., sulfacetamide sod. 100 mg./ml. Bot. dropper 5 ml.
Use: Topical ophthalmic anti-inflammatory.

• **METIOPRIM.** USAN.
Use: Antibacterial.

• **METIZOLINE.** F.D.A. 2-[(2-Methylbenzo[b]-thien-3-yl)methyl]-2-imidazoline.
Use: Nasal decongestant.
See: Benazoline.

• **METIZOLINE HYDROCHLORIDE.** USAN.
Use: Adrengeric.

• **METKEPHAMID ACETATE.** USAN.
Use: Analgesic.

• **METOCLOPRAMIDE HYDROCHLORIDE.** USAN. 4-Amino-5-chloro-n-[2-(diethyl-amino)-ethyl]-o-anisamide dihydrochloride hydrate. 4-amino-5-chloro-N-[2-(diethylamino) ethyl]-2-methoxybenzamide monohydrochloride monohydrate.
Use: Antiemetic.
See: Reglan, Amp. (Robins)

• **METOCURINE IODIDE,** U.S.P. XXI. Inj., U.S.P. XXI. (+)-O,O′-Dimethylchondro-curarine diiodide.
Use: Skeletal muscle relaxant.
See: Metubine Iodid, Vial (Lilly)

METOFOLINE. B.A.N. 1-(4-Chlorophenethyl)-1,2,3,4-tetrahydro-6,7-dimethoxy-2-methylisoquinoline.
Use: Analgesic.

METOFURONE. Name used for Nifurmerone.

• **METOGEST.** USAN.
Use: Hormone.

• **METOLAZONE.** USAN. 7-Chloro-1,2,3,4-tetrahydro-2-methyl-4-oxo-3-o-tolyl-6-quinazolinesulfonamide.
Use: Diuretic, antihypertensive.
See: Diulo, Tab. (Searle)
Zaroxolyn, Tab. (Pennwalt)

• **METOPIMAZINE.** USAN. 10-[3-(4-Carbamoyl-piperidino)propyl]-2-methanesulfonylphenothiazine.
Use: Antiemetic.

METOPIRONE. (Ciba) Metyrapone 250 mg./Tab. Bot. 18s.
Use: Diagnostic aid for pituitary function determination.

METOPON. B.A.N. Methyldihydromorphinone 7,8-Dihydro-5-methylmorphinone.
Use: Analgesic.

• **METOPRINE.** USAN.
Use: Antineoplastic.

• **METOPROLOL.** USAN. (±)-1-Isopropylamino-3-p-(2-methoxyethyl)phenoxypropan-2-ol.
Use: Beta-adrenergic blocking agent.

• **METOPROLOL TARTARATE.** USAN.
Use: Anti-adrenergic.
See: Lopressor, Tab. (Geigy)

• **METOPROLOL TARTRATE,** U.S.P. XXI. Tab., U.S.P. XXI.
Use: Beta-adrenergic blocking agent.
See: Lopressor, Tab. (Geigy)

METOQUINE.
Use: Antimalarial.
See: Quinacrine Hydrochloride (Var. Mfr.)
Atabrine HCl, Tab. (Winthrop-Breon)

• **METOQUIZINE.** USAN. 4,7-Dimethyl-9-(3,5-dimethyl-pyrazole-1-carboxamido)-4,6,6a,7,8,9,10,-10a-octahydroindolo-[4,3-fg]quinoline.
Use: Anti-ulcer agent.

METOSERPATE. B.A.N. Methyl O-methyl-18-epireserpate. Avicalm hydrochloride.
Use: Tranquilizer, veterinary medicine.

• **METOSERPATE HYDROCHLORIDE.** USAN.
Use: Sedative.

METRA. (Forest) Phendimetrazine 35 mg./Tab. Bot. 1000s.
Use: Anorexic.

METRETON OPHTHALMIC SOLUTION. (Schering) Prednisolone sodium phosphate 5.5 mg./ml. Bot. 5 ml.
Use: Topical ophthalmic anti-inflammatory.

METRIC 21. (Fielding) Metronidazole 250 mg./Tab. Bot. 100s.
Use: Antitrichomonal.

METRIPHONATE. B.A.N. Dimethyl 2,2,2-trichloro-1-hydroxyethylphosphonate. Trichlorphon. Dipterex; Dyvon; Neguvon; Tugon.
Use: Insecticide; unthelmintic, veterinary medicine.

• **METRIZAMIDE.** USAN. 2-[3-Acetamido-2, 4, 6-triiodo-5-(N-methylacetamido) benzamido]-2-deoxy-D-glucopyranose.
Use: Myelography.
See: Amipaque, Inj. (Winthrop-Breon)

• **METRIZOATE SODIUM.** USAN.
Use: Diagnostic aid (radiopaque medium).
See: Sodium metrizoate.

METROGESIC. (Metro Med) Salicylamide 325 mg., acetaminophen 162 mg., phenacetin 65 mg., Tab. Bot. 100s, 1000s. **No. 2** (w/codeine phosphate 16.2 mg.) Bot. 50s, 1000s. **No. 3** (w/codeine phosphate 32.5 mg.) Bot. 50s, 1000s.
Use: Analgesic w/Sedative.

METROGESTONE. 6,17-Dimethylpregna-4,6-diene-3, 20-dione.
Use: Oral progestin.

METRO I.V. (American McGaw) Metronidazol 500 mg./100 ml. Bot. 100 ml.
Use: Antibacterial.

METROJEN. (Jenkins) Metrate 1 mg., triple barb 12 mg. (representing 33⅓% each, pentobarbital, sod. butabarbital, sod. phenobarbital)/Tab. Bot. 1000s.
Use: Sedative, hypnotic.

METRONID. (Ascher) Metronidazole 250 mg./Tab. Bot. 100s.
Use: Amebicide, antitrichomonal.

• **METRONIDAZOLE,** U.S.P. XXI. Inj., Tab.; U.S.P. XXI. 1-(2-Hydroxethyl)-2-methyl-5-nitromidazole. 2-Methyl-5-nitromidazole-1-ethanol.
Use: Antitrichomonal.
See: Flagyl, Tab. (Searle)
Flagyl I.V., Vial (Searle)
Flagyl I.V. RTU, Vial (Searle)
Metronid, Tab. (Ascher)
Metryl, Tab. (Lemmon)

• **METRONIDAZOLE HYDROCHLORIDE.** USAN.
Use: Antibacterial.
See: Flagyl I.V. (Searle)

• **METRONIDAZOLE PHOSPHATE.** USAN.
Use: Antibacterial, antiprotozoal.

METRYL. (Lemmon) Metronidazole 250 mg./Tab. B[illegible] 100s, 250s, 500s. Unit dose 100s.
Use: Trichomonacidal agent, amebicide.

METRYL 500. (Lemmon) Metronidazole 500 mg./Ta[illegible] Bot. 50s. Unit dose 100s.
Use: Trichomonacidal agent.

METUBINE IODIDE. (Lilly) Metocurine iodide 2 mg./ml. Vial 20 ml.
Use: Skeletal-muscle relaxant.

• **METUREDEPA.** USAN. Formerly Dimethyl urethimine. Ethyl [bis(2,2-dimethyl-aziridinyl)-pho[illegible] phinyl]-carbamate. Turloc.
Use: Anti-neoplastic.

METUSSIN. (Faraday) d-Methorphan. Bot. 4 oz.
Use: Non-narcotic cough syrup.

METUSSIN JR. (Faraday) d-Methorphan. Bot. 4 oz.
Use: Children's non-narcotic cough syrup.

• **METYRAPONE,** U.S.P. XXI. Tabs. U.S.P. XXI. 2-Met[illegible] yl-1,2-di-3-pyridyl-1-propanone.
Use: Diagnostic aid (pituitary function determinatio[illegible]
See: Metopirone, Tab. (Ciba)

METYRAPONE DITARTRATE. 2-Methyl-1,2-di-3-pyr[illegible] dyl-1-propanone ditartrate. Methopyrapone
Use: Diagnostic test of pituitary function. Adrenocortical enzyme inhibitor.
See: Metopirone, Amp. (Ciba)

• **METYRAPONE TARTRATE.** USAN.
Use: Diagnostic aid.

METYRAPONE TARTRATE INJECTION. 2-methyl-1,2-di-3-pyridyl-1-propanone tartrate (1:2).
Use: Diagnostic test of pituitary function.

• **METYROSINE,** U.S.P. XXI. Cap., U.S.P. XXI. L-Tyro[illegible] sine, a-methyl-,(-)-.
Use: Antihypertensive.
See: Demser (Merck, Sharp & Dohme)

METYZOLINE. B.A.N. 3-(2-Imidazolin-2-yl-methyl)-2-methylbenzo[b]thiophene. Eunasin [hydrochloride.]
Use: Vasoconstrictor.

MEVANIN-C. (Beutlich) Vit. C 200 mg., hesperidin complex 30 mg., calcium lactate 300 mg., cyanocobalamin 1 mcg., ferrous sulfate 65 mg., folic acid 0.1 mg., Vit. A 3000 I.U., D 300 I.U., B-1 2 mg., B-2 2 mg., B-6 0.5 mg., niacin 5 mg., Cu 0.33 mg., Zn 0.40 mg., Mn 0.33 mg., Mg 1 mg., potassium 1.5 mg., iodine 0.03 mg./Cap. Bot. 90s, 450s.
Use: Vitamin & mineral supplement.

MEXATE. (Bristol) Methotrexate for injection. Vial 20 mg., 50 mg., 100 mg., 250 mg.
Use: Antineoplastic agent.

MEXENONE. B.A.N. 2-Hydroxy-4-methoxy-4′-methylbenzophenone. Uvistat.
Use: Protection of skin from sunlight.

MEXILETINE. B.A.N. 1-Methyl-2-(2,6-xylyloxy)-ethylamine.
Use: Anti-arrhythmic.

• **MEXRENOATE POTASSIUM.** USAN.
Use: Aldosterone antagonist.

MEXSANA MEDICATED POWDER. (Plough) Corn starch, kaolin, triclosan, zinc oxide. Can 3 oz., 6.25 oz., 11 oz.
Use: Topical protectant.

EXTRA. (Kenyon) Prednisolone 0.5 mg., acetylsalicylic acid 5 gr./Tab. Bot. 100s, 1000s.
Use: Arthritis.

EXTRAFOR. (Kenyon) Acetylsalicylic acid 5 gr., prednisolone 1.5 mg./Cap. Bot. 100s, 1000s.
Use: Arthritis.

EYENBERG GOAT MILK. (Jackson-Mitchell) Evaporated and powdered cans of goat milk.
Use: Cows milk allergies.

EZLIN. (Miles Pharm) Mezlocillin sodium. Vials 1 Gm., 2 Gm. 3 Gm., 4 Gm. Infusion Bot. 2 Gm., 3 Gm., 4 Gm.
Use: Broad spectrum antibiotic.

MEZLOCILLIN. USAN. 6-[D-2-(Methylsulfonyl-2-oxoimidazolin-1-ylcarboxamido)-2-phenylacetamido]penicillanic acid.
Use: Antibiotic.

MEZLOCILLIN SODIUM, STERILE, U.S.P. XXI.
Use: Antibiotic
See: Mezlin, Inj. (Miles Pharm)

G CAPSULES. (Blue Line) Vit. B-1 5 mg., Vit. A palmitate 12,500 I.U., Fe 30 mg., D 400 I.U., C 75 mg., B-2 2.5 mg., P 58 mg., niacinamide 40 mg., B-6 1 mg., B-12 2 mcg., Mg 3 mg., Ca pantothenate 4 mg., E 2 I.U., choline bitartrate 31.4 mg., inositol 15 mg., Mn 0.5 mg., K 2 mg., Zn 0.5 mg./Cap. Bot. 100s.

G-OROATE. (Miller) Mg (as magnesium orotate) 33 mg./Tab. Bot. 100s

g-PLUS PROTEIN. (Miller) Magnesium-protein complex made w/specially isolated soy protein. 133 mg./Tab. Bot. 100s.
Use: For patients deficient in magnesium.

GW. (Western Research) Magnesium gluconate 500 mg./tab. Bot. 1000s.
Use: Supplement.

-GYN. (U.S. Products) Magnesium gluconate 500 mg./Tab. Bot. 100s, 1000s.
Use: Treatment of magnesium deficiency.

IADONE.
See: Methadone HCl. (Var. Mfr.)

MIANSERIN HCl. USAN. 1,2,3,4,10,14b-Hexahydro-2-methyldibenzo[c,f]pyrazino-[1,2-a]-azepine monohydrochloride. Under study.
Use: Antiserotonin, antihistamine.

IAQUIN.
See: Camoquin, Tab. (Parke-Davis)

MIBOLERONE. USAN.
Use: Anabolic, androgen.
See: Cheque (Upjohn)

I-BON TABLETS. (Inwood) Vit. B-1 10 mg., B-2 5 mg., B-6 2 mg., pantothenic acid 10 mg., nicotinamide 30 mg., B-12 3 mcg., C 100 mg., E 5 mg., A 3 mg., D 25 mcg., Fe 1 mg., iodine 0.15 mg., Co 0.1 mg., boron 0.1 mg., Mn 1 mg., Mg 5 mg., Mo 0.2 mg., Zn (as chloride) 1.5 mg./Tab. Bot. 100s, 250s.

I-BON-T TABLETS. (Inwood) Vit. B-1 15 mg., B-2 10 mg., B-6 2 mg., pantothenic acid 10 mg., nicotinamide 100 mg., B-12 7.5 mg., C 150 mg., E 5 mg., A 25,000 I.U., D 1000 I.U., Fe 15 mg., Cu 1 mg., Mn 1 mg., Mg 5 mg., Mo 0.2 mg., Zn 1.5 mg., iodine 0.15 mg., Co 0.1 mg./Tab. Bot. 100s, 250s, 1000s.

MICASORB. W/Red Veterinary Petrolatum.
See: RV Plus, Oint. (Elder)

MICATIN. (Advanced Care) Miconazole nitrate 2%. **Cream.** Tube 0.5 oz., 1.0 oz. **Spray powder.** Aerosol 3 oz., **Powder.** Bot. 1.5 oz. **Spray Liquid Aerosol:** Bot. 3.5 oz.
Use: Treatment athlete's foot, jock itch, ringworm.

MI-CEBRIN. (Dista) Vit. B-1 10 mg., B-2 5 mg., B-6 1.7 mg., pantothenic acid 10 mg., niacinamide 30 mg., Vit. B-12 (activity equiv.) 3 mcg., C 100 mg., E 5.5 I.U., Vit. A 10,000 I.U., D 400 I.U. Also containing iron 15 mg., copper 1 mg., iodine 0.15 mg., manganese 1 mg., magnesium 5 mg., zinc 1.5 mg./Tab. Pkg. 60s, 100s, 1000s. Blister pkg. 10 × 10s.
Use: Vitamin & mineral deficiencies.

MI-CEBRIN T. (Dista) Vit. B-1 15 mg., B-2 10 mg., B-6 2 mg., pantothenic acid 10 mg., niacinamide 100 mg., B-12 7.5 mcg., C 150 mg., E 5.5 I.U., A 10,000 I.U., D 400 I.U., Fe 15 mg., Cu 1 mg., iodine 0.15 mg., Mn 1 mg., Mg 5 mg., Zn 1.5 mg./Tab. Bot. 30s, 100s, 1000s. Blister pkg. 10 × 10s.
Use: Therapeutic vitamin-minerals.

MICOFUR. Anti 5-Nitro-2-Furaldoxime, Nifuroxime.
Use: Antifungal, antibacterial (topical)
See: Tricofuron, Vaginal Pow., Supp. (Eaton)

• **MICONAZOLE,** U.S.P. XXI. Inj., U.S.P. XXI. 1-[2,4-Dichloro-β-(2,4-dichlorobenzyloxy)phenethyl]imidazole.
Use: Antifungal agent.
See: Monistat IV, Inj. (Janssen)

• **MICONAZOLE NITRATE,** U.S.P. XXI. Cream, Vaginal Suppos., U.S.P. XXI. 1-[2,4-Dichloro-β-[(2,4-dichlorobenzyl)-oxy]-phenylmethyl]imidazole mononitrate.
Use: Antifungal.
See: Monistat, Cream, (Ortho)
Monistat-Derm, Prods. (Ortho)
Nibustat Prods. (Ortho)

MICOREN. (Geigy) n-Crotonyl α-Ethylaminobutyric acid diethylamine and n-crotonyl α-propylaminobutyric acid diethylamide in aqueous solution. A respiratory stimulant; pending release.

MICRAININ. (Wallace) Meprobamate 200 mg., aspirin 325 mg./Tab. Bot. 100s.
Use: Analgesic and tranquilizer combination for treatment of muscle contraction (tension) headache.

MICRhoGAM. (Ortho Diagnostic) RH_0 (D) immune globulin (Human) micro dose. Single-dose vials. Pkg. 50s single-dose vials.
Use: Prevention of maternal Rh immunization (for up to twelve weeks).

MICRIDIUM. (Johnson & Johnson) Phenacridane (9-(p-hexyloxphenyl)-10-methyl-acridinium chloride).
Use: Skin disorders in infants and children.

MICRIN PLUS. (Johnson & Johnson) Water, S.D. alcohol 38-B, glycerin, poloxamer 407, flavor, sodium saccharin, glutamic acid buffer, cetylpyridinium chloride F.D. & C. Yellow #5 and Blue #1. Bot. 12 oz., 24 oz.
Use: Gargle & rinse.

MICROCORT. (Alto) Hydrocortisone alcohol 0.5% in water washable base. Lot. Pkg. 4 oz.
Use: Dermatoses.

MICROCULT-GC TEST. (Ames) Miniaturized culture test for the detection of *Neisseria Gonorrhoeae.* Kits for 25 tests.
Use: Diagnostic.

MICRO-K EXTENCAPS. (Robins) Potassium chloride (8 mEq) 600 mg./Cap. Bot. 100s, 500s, Dis-Co packs/100s.
Use: Potassium supplement.

MICRO-K 10 EXTENTABS. (Robins) Potassium chloride 750 mg. (10 mEq.)/Cap. Bot. 100s, 500s. Disco unit dose 100s.
Use: Potassium supplement.

MICRONASE TABLETS. (Upjohn) Glyburide 1.25 mg., 2.5 mg., or 5.0 mg./Tab. Bot. 100s. 5 mg. also available Box 100s, Bot. 500s.
Use: Lower blood glucose in type II diabetes.

MICRONEFRIN. (Bird) Racemic methylaminoethanol catechol HCl 2.25 Gm., sodium chloride, sodium bisulfite, potassium metabisulfite 0.99 Gm., chlorobutanol 0.50 Gm., benzoic acid 0.50 Gm., propylene glycol 8.0 mg./100 ml. Bot. 7.5 ml., 15 ml., 30 ml.
Use: Croup, peripheral airway diseases.

MICRONOR. (Ortho) Norethindrone 0.35 mg./Tab. Dialpak 28s.
Use: Progestin only contraceptive.

MICROSOL. (Star) Sulfamethizole 0.5 Gm. or 1.0 Gm./Tab. Bot. 100s, 1000s.
Use: Urinary antibacterial.

MICROSOL-A. (Star) Phenazopyridine 50 mg., sulfamethizole 0.5 Gm./Tab. Bot. 100s, 1000s.
Use: Urinary antibacterial for pain and burning.

MICROSTIX CANDIDA. (Ames) Box 25s.
Use: Test for Candida species in vaginal specimens.

MICROSTIX-NITRITE REAGENT STRIPS. (Ames) Box of 3 reagent strips.
Use: Dip and read test for nitrite in urine.

MICROSTIX INCUBATOR. (Ames) For use with Microstix reagent strips.

MICROSTIX-3 REAGENT STRIPS. (Ames) For immediate recognition of nitrite in urine and for semi-quantitation of bacterial growth. Bot. 25s w/25 incubation pouches.

MICROSUL. (Star) Sulfamethizole 0.5 Gm. 1.0 Gm./Tab. Bot. 100s, 1000s.
Use: Urinary tract infections.

MICROSUL-A.(Star)Sulfamethizole0.5Gm.,phenazopyridine HCl 50 mg./Tab. Bot. 100s, 1000s.
Use: Urinary tract infections.

MICROSULFON. (CMC) Sulfadiazine 0.5 Gm./Tab. Bot. 100s, 250s, 1000s.
Use: Gram-positive bacteria infections.

MICTINE. Aminometradine, B.A.N.

MICTONE 25. (Kenyon) Bethanecol Cl 25 mg./Tab. Bot. 100s, 1000s.

MICTRIN. (Econo Med) Hydrochlorothiazide 50 mg./Tab. Bot. 100s, 1000s.
Use: Diuretic.

• **MIDAFLUR.** USAN. 4-Amino-2,2,5,5-tetrakis-(trifluoromethyl)-3-imidazoline.
Use: Sedative.

MIDAHIST DH EXPECTORANT. (Vangard) Codeine phosphate 10 mg., phenylpropanolamine HCl 18.7 mg., chlorpheniramine maleate 2 mg./5 ml. w/alcohol 5%. Bot. pt., gal.
Use: Antitussive; decongestant; antihistamine.

MIDAHIST EXPECTORANT. (Vangard) Codeine phosphate 10 mg., phenylpropanolamine HCl 18.75 mg., guaifenesin 100 mg./5 ml. w/alcohol 7.5%. Bot. pt., gal.
Use: Antitussive, decongestant, expectorant.

MIDAMALINE HCl. N-(5-chloro-2-benzimidazolylmethyl)-N-phenyl-N'N'-dimethyl-ethylene-diamine HCl.
Use: Local anesthetic.

MIDAMOR. (Merck Sharp & Dohme) Amiloride 5 mg./Tab. Bot. 100s.
Use: Antikaliuretic diuretic, antihypertensive.

MIDANEED. (Hanlon) Vit. A 5000 I.U., D 500 I.U., B-1 5 mg., B-2 3 mg., B-6 0.5 mcg., B-12 5 mcg., C 10 mg., niacinamide 10 mg., Ca pantothenate 5 mg./Cap. Bot. 100s.
Use: Dietary supplement.

MIDATANE DC EXPECTORANT. (Vangard) Brompheniramine maleate 2 mg., guaifenesin 100 mg., phenylephrine HCl 5 mg., phenylpropanolamine HCl 5 mg., codeine phosphate 10 mg./5 ml. w/alcohol 3.5% Bot. pt., gal.
Use: Antihistamine, expectorant, antitussive, decongestant.

MIDATANE EXPECTORANT. (Vangard) Brompheniramine maleate 2 mg., guaifenesin 100 mg., phenylephrine HCl 5 mg., phenylpropanolamine HCl 5 mg./5 ml. w/alcohol 3.5%.
Use: Antihistamine, expectorant, decongestant.

MIDATAP TR TABLETS. (Vangard) Brompheniramine maleate 12 mg., phenylephrine HCL 15 mg., Phenylpropanolamine HCL 15 mg./Tab. Bot. 100s, 500s, 1000s.
Use: Antihistamine, Decongestant.

MIDATAP ELIXIR. (Vangard) Brompheniramine maleate 4 mg., phenylephrine HCL 5 mg., phenylpropanolamine HCL 5 mg./5 ml. w/alcohol 2.3%. Bot. pt., gal.
Use: Antihistamine, decongestant.

• **MIDAZOLAM HYDROCHLORIDE.** USAN.
Use: Injectable Anesthetic.

• **MIDAZOLAM MALEATE.** USAN.
Use: Anesthetic.

• **MIDODRINE HYDROCHLORIDE.** USAN.
Use: Antihypertensive, vasoconstrictor.

MIDOL. (Glenbrook) Cinnamedrine HCl 14.9 mg., aspirin 454 mg., and caffeine 32.4 mg./Tab. Bot. 30s, 60s. Strip pack 12s.
Use: Antispasmodic-analgesic for menstrual symptoms.

MIDRIN. (Carnrick) Isometheptene mucate 65 mg., acetaminophen 325 mg., dichloralphenazone 100 mg./Cap. Bot. 50s, 100s.
Use: Relief of migraine & tension headache.

FLEX. (Misemer) Chlorzoxazone 250 mg., acetaminophen 300 mg./Cap.
Use: Discomfort of musculoskeletal conditions.

IFOBATE. USAN.
Use: Antiatherosclerotic.

GERGOT P-B. (G&W) Ergotamine tartrate, belladonna alkaloids, caffeine, pentobarbital/Suppository. Boxes 10s.
Use: Migraine headaches.

GRADE. (Crystal) Salicylamide 3 gr., methyl-iso-octenylamide mucate 1 gr., acetaminophen 3 gr./Tab. Bot. 100s.
Use: Anti-migraine.

KAMYCIN. B.A.N. An antibiotic produced by *Streptomyces mitakoensis.* Mikamycin B is Ostreogrycin B.

LD SILVER PROTEIN.
See: Silver Protein, Mild

IILENPERONE. USAN.
Use: Antipyschotic.

LES NERVINE. (Miles) Diphenhydramine 25 mg./Tab. Pkg. 12s. Bot. 30s, 50s.
Use: Nighttime sleep aid.

IILIPERTINE. USAN. 5,6-Dimethoxy-3-[2-[4(o-methoxy-phenyl)-1-piperazinyl]ethyl]-2-methyl-indole.
Use: Tranquilizer.

LKINOL. (Rorer) Liquid petrolatum specially processed for instant aqueous mixing. Bot. 8 oz.
Use: Laxative.

IILK OF BISMUTH, U.S.P. XXI. (Various Mfr.) Bismuth hydroxide & bismuth subcarb.
Use: Orally, intestinal disturbances.
'Paregoric, kaolin & pectin, methyl parahydroxybenzoate.
See: Mul-Sed, Liq. (Webcon)

IILK OF MAGNESIA, U.S.P. XXI.
Use: Cathartic, antiacid.
See: Magnesium hydroxide.

LLAZINE. (Major) Thioridazine 10 mg./Tab. Bot. 100s; 15 mg./Tab. Bot. 100s; 25 mg./Tab. Bot. 100s, 1000s; 100 mg., 150 mg. or 200 mg./Tab. Bot. 100s, 500s.
Use: Tranquilizer.

LLICORTEN. Dexamethasone, B.A.N.

LONTIN. (Parke-Davis) Phensuximide. 0.5 Gm./Kapseal. Bot. 100s.
Use: Anticonvulsant.

LPAR. (Winthrop Products) Magnesium hydroxide, mineral oil.
Use: Laxative antacid, lubricant.

LPATH. (Wallace) Meprobamate 200 mg., tridihexethyl chloride 25 mg./Tab. Bot. 100s.
Meprobamate 400 mg., tridihexethyl chloride 25 mg./Tab. Bot. 100s, 500s.
Use: Tranquilizer and anticholinergic combination for treatment of gastrointestinal disorders.

LPREM. (Wallace) Meprobamate 200 or 400 mg., conjugated estrogens (equine) 0.45 mg./Tab. Bot. 100s.
Use: Treatment of menopausal symptoms.

IILRINONE. USAN.
Use: Cardiotonic.

MILROY ARTIFICIAL TEARS. (Milton Roy) Dr. Bot. 22 ml.
Use: Ocular lubricant and tear replacement.

MILTOWN. (Wallace) Meprobamate. Tab. 200 mg., Bot. 100s, 400 mg. Bot. 100s, 500s, 1000s. 600 mg./Tab. Bot. 100s.
Use: Tranquilizing agent.
See: Meprospan, (Wallace)

MILTRATE. (Wallace) Meprobamate 200 mg., pentaerythritol tetranitrate 10 mg. & 20 mg./Tab. Bot. 100s.
Use: Prophylactic treatment of angina pectoris.

• **MIMBANE HYDROCHLORIDE.** USAN. 1-Methylyohimbane hydrochloride.
Use: Analgesic.

• **MINAXOLONE.** USAN.
Use: Anesthetic.

MINCARD. Aminometradine. 1-Allyl-3-ethyl-6-aminotetrahydropyrimidinedione.
Use: Diuretic.

MINEPENTATE. B.A.N. 2-(2-Dimethylaminoethoxy)ethyl 1-phenylcyclopentanecarboxylate.
Use: Treatment of the Parkinsonian syndrome.

MINERAL-CORTICOIDS.
See: Desoxycorticosterone Salts (Var. Mfr.)

• **MINERAL OIL,** U.S.P. XXI.
Use: Cathartic, pharmaceutic aid (solvent, oleaginous vehicle).
See: Petrolatum, Liquid.

• **MINERAL OIL EMULSION,** U.S.P. XXI.
Use: Cathartic.

• **MINERAL OIL ENEMA,** U.S.P. XXI.
Use: Cathartic.

• **MINERAL OIL, LIGHT,** N.F. XVI.
Use: Vehicle.

MINIBEX. (Faraday) Vit. B-1 6 mg., B-2 3 mg., B-6 0.5 mg., C 50 mg., niacinamide 10 mg., Ca pantothenate 3 mg., B-12 2 mcg., folic acid 0.1 mg./Cap. Bot. 100s, 250s, 1000s.

MINI-GAMULIN Rh. (Armour) Rho (D) Immune Globulin (Human) in one-sixth the quantity contained in a standard dose.

MINIPRESS. (Pfizer Laboratories) Prazosin HCl 1 mg., 2 mg., or 5 mg./Cap. 1 mg. and 2 mg.: Bot. 250s, 1000s. Unit dose 100s; 5 mg: Bot. 250s, 500s. Unit dose 100s.
Use: Antihypertensive agent.

MINITEC. (Squibb) Sodium pertechnetate Tc 99 m generator.
Use: Radiodiagnostic.

MINITEC GENERATOR (COMPLETE WITH COMPONENTS). (Squibb) Medotopes Kit.
Use: Diagnostic agent for cancer.

MINIT-RUB. (Bristol-Myers) Methyl salicylate 15%, methol 3.5%, camphor 2.3% in anhydrous/and in base. Tubes 1.5 oz., 3 oz.
Use: Analgesic ointment.

MINIZIDE. (Pfizer Laboratories) Prazosin HCl and polythiazide **Minizide 1:** prazosin 1 mg., polythiazide 0.5 mg./Cap. **Minizide 2:** prazosin 2 mg., polythiazide 0.5 mg./Cap. **Minizide 5:** prazosin 5 mg., polythiazide 0.5 mg./Cap. Bot. 100s.
Use: Antihypertensive.

MINOCIN. (Lederle) **Cap.:** Minocycline HCl 50 mg./Cap. Bot. 100s. Unit dose 100s. 100 mg./Cap. Bot. 50s, 100s. Unit dose 10 × 10s. **I.V.:** 100 mg./Vial. **Oral Susp.:** 50 mg./5 ml. w/propylparaben 0.10%, butylparaben 0.06%, alcohol 5% v/v. Bot. 2 oz.**Tabs:** 50 mg./Tab. Bot. 100s. 100 mg./Tab. Bot. 50s.
Use: Antibiotic.

• **MINOCROMIL.** USAN.
Use: Anti-allergic.

• **MINOCYCLINE.** USAN.
Use: Antibacterial.
See: Minocyn (Lederle)

• **MINOCYCLINE HYDROCHLORIDE,** U.S.P. XXI. Cap., Oral Susp., Sterile, Tab., U.S.P. XXI. 4,7-bis-(Dimethylamino)-1,4,4a,5,5a,6,11,12a-octahydro-3, 10, 12,12a,tetrahydroxy-1,11-dioxo-2-naphthacenecarboxamide.
Use: Antibiotic.
See: Minocin, Cap., Syr., Vial (Lederle)

• **MINOXIDIL,** U.S.P. XII. Tab., U.S.P. XXI. 2,4-diamino-6-piperidinopyrimide-3-oxide.
Use: Antihypertensive peripheral vasodilator.
See: Loniten, Tab. (Upjohn)

MIN-PLEX. (Scrip) Vit. B-1 15 mg., B-2 10 mg., B-6 5 mg., nicotinamide 50 mg., calcium pantothenate 10 mg., ascorbic acid 300 mg./Cap. Bot. 100s.

MINRO-PLEX. (Mallard) Vit. A 5000 I.U., D 400 I.U., B-1 3 mg., B-2 2.5 mg., niacinamide 20 mg., B-6 1.5 mg., Ca pantothenate 5 mg., B-12 2.5 mcg., C 50 mg., E 3 I.U., Ca 215 mg., P 166 mg., Fe 13.4 mg., Mg 7.5 mg., Mn 1.5 mg., K 5 mg., Zn 1.4 mg./Cap. Bot. 50s, 1000s.

MINTEZOL. (Merck Sharp & Dohme) Thiabendazole. Susp. 500 mg./5 ml. Bot. 120 ml. Chewable Tabs. (500 mg.) Pkg. 36s.
Use: Anthelmintic.

MINT-O-FECTANT. (Lannett) Mint odor, phenol coefficient 5. Bot. pt., gal., 5 gal., 55 gal. drum.

MINURIC. Benzbromarone, B.A.N.

MIN-VITERAL. (Kay) Vit. A 5000 U.S.P. I.U., D 1000 I.U., B-1 3.0 mg., B-2 2.5 mg., nicotinamide 20 mg., B-6 0.75 mg., Ca pantothenate 5.0 mg., B-12 2.5 mcg., C 50 mg., E 3 I.U.; plus Ca, P, Fe, Mg, Mn, K, Zn. Bot. 100s, 500s, 1000s.
Use: Dietary supplement.

MIOCEL. (Softcon) Physostigmine salicylate ⅛%, pilocarpine HCl 2% and phenyl mercuric borate. 1:25,000, methylcellulose, sod. bisulfite, boric acid, sod. carbonate. Bot. dropper 5 cc., 15 cc., 30 cc.
Use: Control and treatment of glaucoma and miotic.

MIOCHOL. (CooperVision) Acetylcholine chloride 20 mg., mannitol 60 mg., sterile water for inj. 2 ml./2 cc. univial. 1:100 intraocular.
Use: Miotic in ocular surgery.

• **MIOFLAZINE HYDROCHLORIDE.** USAN.
Use: Vasodilator.

MIOSTAT INTRAOCULAR SOLUTION. (Alcon) Carbochol 0.01%. Vial 1.5 ml.
Use: Parasympathetic miotic.

MIRADON. (Schering) Anisindione 50 mg./Tab. Bot. 100s.
Use: Anticoagulant.

MIRACLE GOAT MILK. (Jackson-Mitchell) Evaporate and powdered cans of goat milk.
Use: Cows milk allergies.

MIRAFLOW. (CooperVision) Extra-strength cleaning solution. Bot. 15 ml.
Use: Hard contact lens cleaner.

MIRAL. (Geneva) Dexamethasone 0.75 mg./Tab. Bot. 100s, 1000s.

• **MIRINCAMYCIN HYDROCHLORIDE.** USAN.
Use: Antibacterial, antimalarial.

MISALOID. (Jenkins) N-acetyl-p-aminophenol 5.0 gr., salicylamide 3.0 gr., triple barb 8.0 mg., (representing 33⅓% each, pentobarbital sod., butabarbital sod., phenobarbital sod.)/Tab. Bot. 1000s.

• **MISONIDAZOLE.** USAN.
Use: Antiprotozoal *(trichomonas).*

• **MISOPROSTOL.** USAN.
Use: Anti-ulcerative.

MISSION PRENATAL. (Mission) Ferrous gluconate 333.3 mg. (iron 38.6 mg.), Vit. C 100 mg., B-1 5.0 mg., B-6 3.0 mg., B-2 2.0 mg., niacinamide 10 mg., d-calcium pantothenate 1.0 mg., B-12 2 mcg., A (acetate) 4,000 I.U., D-2 400 I.U., calcium carbonate 70 mg., calcium gluconate 100 mg., calcium lactate 100 mg. (Calcium 50 mg.) zinc 15 mg./Tab. Bot. 100s.

MISSION PRENATAL F.A. (Mission) Ferrous gluconate 333.3 mg. (iron 38.6 mg.), Vit. C 100 mg., B-1 5 mg., B-6 10 mg., B-2 2 mg., niacinamide 1[illegible] mg., B-12 2 mcg., folic acid 0.8 mg., Vit. A acetate 4000 I.U., D2 400 I.U., Ca carbonate 70 mg., Ca gluconate 100 mg., Ca lactate 100 mg., (Ca 50 mg.), d-calcium pantothenate 1 mg./Tab. Bot. 100s.
Use: Prenatal and postpartum supplement.

MISSION PRENATAL H.P. (Mission) Ferrous gluconate 333.3 mg. (iron 38.6 mg.) Vit. C 100 mg., B-1 5 mg., B-6 25 mg., B-2 2 mg., niacinamide 10 mg., Ca pantothenate 1 mg., B-12 2 mcg., folic acid 1 mg., Vit. A 4000 I.U., Vit. D 400 I.U., Ca carbonate 70 mg., Ca gluconate 100 mg., Ca lactate 100 mg./Tab. Bot. 100s.
Use: Prenatal and postpartum supplement.

MISSION PRESURGICAL. (Mission) Vit. C 500 mg., B-1 2.5 mg., B-2 2.6 mg., B-3 30 mg., B-5 16.3 mg., B-6 3.6 mg., B-12 9 mcg., A 5000 USP u., D-2 400 USP u., E 45 I.U., ferrous gluconate 233 mg., zinc 22.5 mg./Tab. Bot. 100s.
Use: Dietary supplement for pre-surgical and post-surgical patients.

MITCHUM ANTI-PERSPIRANT. (Revlon) Aluminum chlorohydrate and aluminum chloride or aluminum sesquichlorohydrate or aluminum zirconium tetrachlorohydrex. Roll-on, lotion, stick, cream, liquid, dab-on, non-aerosol spray.
Use: Anti-perspirant.

MI-THERIC. (Quality Generics) Vit. A 10,000 I.U., D 400 I.U., C 150 mg., B-1 15 mg., B-2 10 mg., B-6 2 mg., B-12 7.5 mcg., niacinamide 100 mg., pantothenic acid

10 mg., E 5 mg., iron 15 mg., Cu 1 mg., Mn 1 mg., Mg 5 mg., Zn 1.5 mg./Tab. Bot. 100s, 1000s.
Use: Vitamin-mineral therapy.

THRACIN. (Miles Pharm) Mithramycin 2,500 mcg./Vial Units of 10 vials.
Use: Antineoplastic, antihypercalcemic.

MITHRAMYCIN.
See: Plicamycin.

MITINDOMIDE. USAN.
Use: Antineoplastic.

TOBRONITOL. B.A.N. 1,6-Dibromo-1,6-dideoxy-D-mannitol. Myelobromol.
Use: Antineoplastic agent.

MITOCARCIN. USAN. Antibiotic derived from *Streptomyces* species.
Use: Antineoplastic.

TOCLOMINE. B.A.N. NN-Di-(2-chloroethyl)-4-methoxy-3-methyl-1-naphthylamine.
Use: Antineoplastic agent.

MITOCROMIN. USAN. Produced by *Streptomyces virdochromogenes.*
Use: Antineoplastic.

MITOGILLIN. USAN. An antibiotic obtained from an "unique strain" of *Aspergillus restrictus.*
Use: Antitumorigenic antibiotic.

MITOMALCIN. USAN. Produced by *Streptomyces malayensis.* Under study.
Use: Antineoplastic.

MITOMYCIN, U.S.P. XXI. For Inj., U.S.P. XXI. In literature as Mitomycin C. Antibiotic isolated from *Streptomyces caespitosis.*
Use: Antibiotic.
See: Mutamycin, Inj. (Bristol)

TOPODOZIDE. B.A.N. 2′-Ethylpodophyllohydrazide.
Use: Antineoplastic agent.

MITOSPER. USAN. Substance derived from *Aspergillus* of the *glaucus* group.
Use: Antineoplastic.

MITOTANE. U.S.P. XXI. Tabs. U.S.P. XXI. 1,1-Dichloro-2-(o-chlorophenyl)-2-(p-chlorophenyl)-ethane. Lysodren. Benzene, 1-chloro-2-[2,2-dichloro-l-(4-chlorophenyl)ethyl]-.
Use: Antineoplastic.
Lysodren, Tab. (Bristol)

TOTENAMINE. B.A.N. 5-Bromo-3-[N-(2-chloroethyl)ethylaminomethyl]benzo[b]thiophen.
Use: Antineoplastic agent.

MITOXANTRONE HYDROCHLORIDE. USAN.
Use: Antineoplastic.

TROLAN. (Robins) Calcium polycarbophil equivalent to polycarbophil 500 mg./Tab. Blister Pak 36s, 100s.
Use: Treatment of constipation and diarrhea.

TY-QUIN CREAM. (Reid-Provident) Clioquinol (3%) 30 mg., hydrocortisone (0.5%) 5 mg./Gm. Tube 20 Gm.
Use: Antifungal, antibacterial, anti-inflammatory, antipruritic.

MIXIDINE. USAN.
Use: Vasodilator (coronary).

MIXTARD. (Nordisk) Isophane purified pork insulin suspension 70% and purified pork insulin injection 30%, 100 I.U./ml.
Use: Diabetes care (IDDM).

MIXTURE 612. Dimethyl Phthalate Solution, Compound.

MLT-ASPIRIN. (Kenyon) Acetylsalicylic acid 7.5 gr./multilayered Tab. Bot. 100s, 1000s.

M-M-R II. (Merck Sharp & Dohme) Lyophilized preparation of live attenuated measles virus vaccine (Attenuvax), live attenuated mumps virus vaccine (Mumpsvax), live attenuated rubella virus vaccine (Meruvax II). See details under Attenuvax, Mumpsvax and Meruvax II. Single dose vial 1s, 10s. w/diluent.
Use: Immunization against measles, mumps and rubella.

MOBAN. (Du Pont) Molindone HCl. **Liquid**: 20 mg./ml. concentrate. Bot. 4 oz./w dropper. **Tab.**: 5 mg., 10 mg., 25 mg., 50 mg. or 100 mg./Tab. Bot. 100s.
Use: Management of manifestations of schizophrenia.

MOBENOL.
See: Tolbutamide U.S.P. XXI.

MOBIDIN. (Ascher) Magnesium salicylate, anhydrous 600 mg./Tab., Bot. 100s, 500s.
Use: Anti-arthritic agent.

MOBIGESIC. (Ascher) Magnesium salicylate 300 mg., phenyltoloxamine citrate 30 mg./ Tab. Bot. 50s, 100s. Pkg. 18's.
Use: Analgesic.

MOBISYL CREME. (Ascher) Triethanolamine salicylate in vanishing creme base. Tubes 100 Gm.
Use: Topical analgesic.

MOCCASIN BITE.
See: Antivenin, Snake, Polyvalent (Wyeth)

• **MODALINE SULFATE.** USAN. 2-Methyl-3-piperidinopyrazine monosulfate.
Use: Antidepressant.

MODANE. (Adria) Danthron 75 mg./Tab. Pkg. 10s, 30s. Bot. 100s, 1000s. Stat-Pak 100s. (10 × 10).
Use: Orally, laxative.

MODANE BULK. (Adria) Powdered mixture of equal parts of psyllium and dextrose. Container 14 oz.
Use: Bulk laxative.

MODANE LIQUID. (Adria) Danthron 37.5 mg./5 ml. Bot. 16 oz.
Use: Orally, Laxative.

MODANE MILD. (Adria) Danthron 37.5 mg./Tab. or 5 cc. Bot. 100s.
Use: Orally, laxative.

MODANE PLUS. (Adria) Danthron 50 mg., docusate sodium 100 mg./Tab. Bot. 100s, Box 30s.
Use: Laxative, stool softener.

MODANE SOFT. (Adria) Docusate sodium 120 mg./Cap. Unit. dose, Pkg. 30s.
Use: Stool Softener.

MODERIL. (Pfizer Laboratories) Rescinnamine Tab. (0.25 mg.). Bot. 100s. (0.5 mg.) Bot. 100s.
Use: Hypertension treatment.

MODICON 21. (Ortho) Norethindrone 0.5 mg., ethinyl estradiol 35 mcg./Tab. (white) Dialpak 21s.
Use: Oral contraceptive.

MODICON 28. (Ortho) Norethindrone 0.5 mg., ethinyl estradiol 35 mcg./Tab. (white) plus 7 inert Tab. Dialpak 28s.
Use: Oral contraceptive.

MODINAL.
See: Gardinol Type Detergents. (Various Mfr.)

MODUCAL. (Mead Johnson) Maltodextrin. Pow. Can 13 oz.
Use: Source of dietary carbohydrate.

MODUMATE. Arginine Glutamate, B.A.N.

MODURETIC. (Merck Sharp & Dohme) Hydrochlorthiazide 50 mg., amiloride 5 mg./Tab. Bot. 100s.
Use: Antikaliuretic diuretic, antihypertensive.

MOEBIQUIN. (CMC) Bot. 100s, 1000s.

MOEDIQUIN. (CMC) Iodoquinol 650 mg./Cap. Bot. 100s, 1000s.
Use: Amebacide.

MOENOMYCIN. Phosphorus-containing glycolipide antibiotic. Active against gram-positive organisms. Under study.

M.O., HALEY'S. (Winthrop Consumer Products)
See: Haley's M.O., Liq. (Winthrop Products)

MOLAFIL TOOTHACHE PELLETS. (DeWitt) 24s.

MOLAR PHOSPHATE.
W/Fluoride ion.
See: Coral Prod. (Lorvic)
Karigel, Gel. (Lorvic)

MOLCER. Dioctyl Sodium Sulphosuccinate, B.A.N.

• **MOLINAZONE.** USAN. 3-Morpholino-1,2,3-benzotriazin-4(3H)-one.
Use: Analgesic.

MOLINDONE. B.A.N. 3-Ethyl-6,7-dihydro-2-methyl-5-(morpholinomethyl)indol-4(5H)-one HCl.
Use: Sedative, tranquilizer, antipsychotic.

• **MOLINDONE HYDROCHLORIDE.** USAN.
Use: Antipsychotic.
See: Lidone, Cap. (Abbott)
Lidone Concentrate, Liq. (Abbott)
Moban, Tab. (Du Pont)

MOL-IRON CHRONOSULES. (Schering) Ferrous sulfate 390 mg. (78 mg. elemental iron)/Cap. Bot. 30s, 250s.
Use: Iron-deficiency anemias.

MOL-IRON LIQUID. (Schering) Ferrous sulfate 195 mg./4ml.
Use: Treatment iron-deficiency anemias.

MOL-IRON TABLETS. (Schering) Ferrous sulfate 195 mg., (equivalent 39 mg. elemental iron)/Tab. Bot. 100s.
Use: Treatment iron-deficiency anemias.
W/Vitamin C (Schering) Ferrous sulf. 195 mg., ascorbic acid 75 mg./Tab. Bot. 100s.

• **MOLSIDOMINE.** USAN.
Use: Anti-anginal, vasodilator.

MOLYCU. (Burns) Meprobamate 400 mg., copper 60 mg./ml.
Use: Molybdenum poisoning.

MOMENTUM. (Whitehall) Aspirin 500 mg., phenyltoloxamine citrate 15 mg./Tab. Bot. 24s, 48
Use: Analgesic.

MONACETYL PYROGALLOL. Eugallol. Pyrogallol Monoacetate.
Use: Keratolytic in chronic dermatitis.

MONALIUM HYDRATE. Hydrated magnesium aluminate. Magalorate.
See: Riopan, Tab. & Susp. (Ayerst)

• **MONENSIN.** USAN. (1) 2-[5-Ethyltetrahydro-5-[tetrahydro-3-methyl-5-[tetrahydro-6-hydroxy-6-(hydroxymethyl)-3,5-dimethyl-2H-pyran-2-yl]-2-furyl]-2-furyl]-9-hydroxy-β-methoxy-α,γ,2,8,-tetramethyl-1,6-dioxaspiro[4,5]decane-7-butyric acid. Coban (as sodium salt)(Lilly).
Use: Antiprotozoal; antibacterial; antifungal.

MONISTAT IV. (Janssen) Miconazole 10 mg./ml. w/PEG 40, castor oil, lactate, methylparaben, propylparaben, water. Amp. 20 ml.
Use: Antifungal.

MONISTAT 7 VAGINAL CREAM. (Ortho) Miconazole nitrate 2% in water-miscible cream. Tube 47 Gm. w/dose applicator.
Use: Local treatment of vulvovaginal candidiasis.

MONISTAT 7 VAGINAL SUPPOSITORIES. (Ortho) Miconazole nitrate 100 mg./Suppos. Pkg. 7 supp. w/applicator.
Use: Local treatment of vulvovaginal candidiasis (moniliasis).

MONISTAT-DERM CREAM. (Ortho) Miconazole nitrate 2%. w/pegoxol 7 stearate, peglicol 5 oleate, mineral oil, benzoic acid, butylated hydroxyanisole. Tube 1 oz., 15 Gm., 85 Gm.
Use: Antifungal & anticandidal.

MONISTAT-DERM LOTION. (Ortho) Miconazole nitrate 2% w/pegoxol 7 stearate, peglicol 5 oleate, mineral oil, benzoic acid, butylated hydroxyanisole. Squeeze bot. 30 ml., 60 ml.
Use: Antifungal & anti-candidal.

■ **MONO-AMINE OXIDASE INHIBITORS.**
See: Marplan, Tab. (Roche)
Nardil, Tab. (Parke-Davis)

• **MONO AND DI-ACETYLATED MONOGLYCERIDES** N.F. XVI. A mixture of glycerin esterfied mono- and di-esters of edible fatty acids followed by direct acetylation.

• **MONO AND DI-GLYCERIDES,** N.F. XVI. A mixture of mono- and di-esters of fatty acids from edible oils.
Use: Fatty acids.

MONOBASE. (Torch) Water-washable emulsion vehicle of fatty alcohols, natural wax & PEG. Consistency maintained over wide temperature range. Jar 1 lb.
Use: Ointment base for hydration of skin, vehicle for dermatological medications. Incompatible with Burow's solution.

• **MONOBENZONE,** U.S.P. XXI. Oint., U.S.P. XXI. p-(Benzyloxy)phenol.
Use: Depigmenting agent.
See: Benoquin, Oint., Lot. (Elder)

MONOBENZYL ETHER OF HYDROQUINONE.
See: Benoquin, Oint., Lot. (Elder)

MONOBROMISOVALERYLUREA.
See: Bromisovalum. (Various Mfr.)

ONO-CALAFORMULA. (Eric, Kirk & Gary) Calcium cabonate 500 mg., ferrous fumarate 90 mg., Vit. A 5000 I.U., Vit. D 400 I.U., Vit. B-1 1 mg., Vit. B-6 1 mg., Vit. B-12 3 mcg., Vit. C 50 mg., niacinamide 10 mg., Vit. B-2 1 mg., iodine 0.1 mg., Mn 1.5 mg., cobalt 0.1 mg., Cu 1 mg., Zn 1.4 mg., Mg 1 mg., K 5 mg./Tab. Bot. 30s, 100s, 180s, 1000s.
Use: Vitamin-mineral supplement.

ONOCETE SOLUTION. (Pedinol) Monochloracetic acid 80% w/color. Bot. 15 ml.
Use: Removal of verrucae.

ONOCHLOR. (Gordon) Monochloracetic acid 80%. Bot. 15 cc.
Use: Verruca cauterant.

ONOCID. (SmithKline) Cefonicid sodium 500 mg. or 1 Gm/10 ml. Vials 1 Gm./100 ml. piggyback. Pharmacy Bulk Vials equivalent to 10 Gm.
Use: Antiinfective.

ONOCYCLINE HYDROCHLORIDE.
See: Minocin I.V., Syr., Cap. (Lederle)

ONO-DIFF TEST. (Wampole) Two-minute hemagglutination slide test for the differential qualitative detection and quantitative determination of infectious mononucleosis and other heterophile antibodies in serum or plasma. Test kit 20s.
Use: An aid in the differential diagnosis of infectious mononucleosis.

ONODRAL. (Winthrop Products) Penthienate.
Use: Anticholinergic.

MONOETHANOLAMINE, N.F.XVI. 2-Aminoethanol.
Use: Pharmaceutic aid (surfactant).

ONO-GESIC TABLETS. (Central) Salicylsalicylic acid 750 mg./Tab. Bot. 100s
Use: Treatment of rheumatoid arthritis.

ONOJEL. (Sherwood) Glucose 40% in a 25 gm. unit dose.
Use: Insulin reactions.

ONOIODOMETHANESULFONATE SODIUM.
See: Methiodal Sodium, U.S.P. XXI.

ONOPAR. Stilbazium Iodide.
Use: Anthelmintic.

ONOPHEN. 2-(4-Hydroxy-3,5-diiodobenzyl)-cyclohexane carboxylic acid.
Use: Orally; cholecystography.

MONOSODIUM GLUTAMATE, N.F. XVI.

ONOSODIUM PHOSPHATE.
See: Sodium Biphosphate, U.S.P. XXI.

ONOSTEARIN. (Various Mfr.) Glyceryl monostearate.

ONO-SURE TEST. (Wampole) One-minute hemagglutination slide test for the differential qualitative detection and quantitative determination of infectious mononucleosis heterophile antibodies in serum or plasma. Kit 20s.
Use: An aid in the diagnosis of infectious mononucleosis.

ONOSYL. (Arcum) Secobarbital sod. 1 gr., butabarbital 0.5 gr./Tab. Bot. 100s, 1000s.

ONOTARD HUMAN INSULIN. (Squibb/Novo) Human insulin zinc suspension 100 Units/ml. Vial 10 ml.
Use: Human insulin (intermediate action).

MONO-TEST. (Wampole) A 2-minute hemagglutination slide test for the qualitative detection and quantitative determination of infectious mononucleosis heterophile antibodies in serum or plasma. Kits 40s, 100s.
Use: Diagnosis of infectious mononucleosis.

MONO-TEST FTB. (Wampole) Two-minute hemagglutination slide test for the qualitative detection of infectious mononucleosis heterophile antibodies using fingertip blood. Kits 10s.
Use: Aid in the diagnosis of infectious mononucleosis.

• **MONOTHIOGLYCEROL,** N.F.XVI. 3-Mercapto-1,2-propanediol.
Use: Pharmaceutic aid (preservative).

MONO-VACC. (Lincoln) Device used for vaccination against smallpox. Box 12 without vaccine or 20 sterile units with vaccine.
Use: Scarifier.

MONO-VACC TEST O.T. (Merieux Institute) 5 tuberculin units by the mantoux method. Multiple puncture disposable device. Box 25s (tamper proof).
Use: Tuberculosis screening test.

MONOXYCHLOROSENE. A stabilized, buffered, organic hypochlorous acid derivative.
See: Oxychlorosene (Guardian Chem.)

MONSEL SOLUTION. (Wade) Bot. 2 oz., 4 oz.
Use: Styptic solution.

MORANTEL. B.A.N. (E)-1,4,5,6-Tetrahydro-1-methyl-2-[2-(3-methyl-2-thienyl)vinyl]-pyrimidine.
Use: Anthelmintic, veterinary medicine.

• **MORANTEL TARTRATE.** USAN. (E)-1,4,5,6-Tetrahydro-1-methyl-2-[2(3)methyl-2-thienyl-vinyl]pyrimidine tartrate.
Use: Anthelmintic.

MORANYL.
See: Suramin Sod.

MORAZONE. B.A.N. 2:3-Dimethyl-4-(3-methyl-2-phenylmorpholinomethyl)-1-phenylpyrazol-5-one.
Use: Analgesic.

MORCO. (Archer-Taylor) Cod-liver-oil ointment w/zinc oxide, benzethonium chloride, benzocaine 1%. Suppl. 1.5 oz., 1 lb.
Use: First aid dressing.

• **MORICIZINE.** USAN.
Use: Cardiac depressant.

• **MORNIFLUMATE.** USAN.
Use: Anti-inflammatory.

MOROLINE. (Plough) Petrolatum. Jars 1.75 oz., 3.75 oz., 15 oz.
Use: Topical protectant, lubricant.

MOROXYDINE. B.A.N. 4-Morpholine-carboxymidoyl guanidine. N-(Guanidinoformimidoyl)-morpholine.
Use: Antiviral agent.

MORPEN TABS. (Major) Ibuprofen 400 mg. or 600 mg./Tab. Bot. 500s.
Use: Anti-inflammatory agent.

MORPHERIDINE. B.A.N. Ethyl 1-(2-morpholino-ethyl)-4-phenylpiperidine-4-carboxylate. Morpholino-ethyl-norpethidine.
Use: Narcotic analgesic.

MORPHINAN-6-ONE,4,5-EPOXY-3,14-DI-HYDROXY-17-(2-PROPENYL)-,HYDROCHLORIDE,(5α)-. Naloxone Hydrochloride, U.S.P. XXI.
MORPHINE ACETATE.
W/Terpin hydrate, ammonium hypophosphite & Pot. guaiacol sulfonate.
See: Broncho-Tussin Sol. (First Texas)
MORPHINE AND ATROPINE SULFATES TABLETS.
Use: Analgesic, parasympatholytic.
MORPHINE HYDROCHLORIDE. (Various Mfr.) Pow., Bot. 1 oz., 5 oz.
Use: Analgesic.
• **MORPHINE SULFATE,** U.S.P. XXI. Inj., U.S.P. XXI. (Various Mfr.) Flake or Pow. Bot. ⅛ oz., 1 oz., 5 oz., H.T. ⅛ gr., ⅙ gr., 0.25 gr., 0.5 gr., 1 gr.
Use: Narcotic, analgesic & sedative.
W/Tartar emetic, bloodroot, ipecac, squill, wild cherry.
See: Pectoral, Prep. (Noyes)
• **MORRHUATE SODIUM INJECTION.,** U.S.P. XXI.
Use: Sclerosing agent.
MOSCO. (Medtech) Salicylic acid. Jar. 0.4 oz., 0.8 oz.
Use: Corn and callus removal.
MOTILIUM. (Janssen) Domperidone maleate
Use: Antifungal.
MOTION AID ELIXIR. (Vangard) Dimenhydrinate 12.5 mg./4 ml. Bot. 10 ml.
Use: Vertigo, motion sickness.
MOTION AID TABLETS. (Vangard) Dimenhydrinate 50 mg./Tab. Bot. 100s, 1000s. Unit dose 10×10s.
Use: Vertigo, motion sickness.
■ **MOTION SICKNESS AGENTS.**
See: Antinauseants
Bucladin, Softab Tab. (Stuart)
Dramamine, Prep. (Searle)
Emetrol, Liq. (Rorer)
Marezine, Tab., Amp. (Burroughs Wellcome)
Scopolamine HBr (Various Mfr.)
• **MOTRETINIDE.** USAN.
Use: Keratolytic.
MOTRIN. (Upjohn) Ibuprofen. **300 mg.**/Tab. Bot. 500s. Unit-Of-Use 60s; **400 mg.**/Tab. Bot. 500s. Unit-of-Use Bot. 100s. Unit dose 100s; **600 mg.**/Tab. Bot. 500s. Unit-of-Use 100s. Unit Dose 100s.
Use: Anti-inflammatory agent.
MOVICOL. (Norgine) Gum karaya 3.4 Gm., cortex rhamni frangulae 0.3 Gm., Sugar 1.5 Gm./Heaping Tsp. Container 200 Gm., 500 Gm.
Use: Treatment of constipation.
• **MOXALACTAM DISODIUM.** USAN.
Use: Antibiotic
See: Moxam, Liq. (Lilly)
• **MOXALACTAM DISODIUM FOR INJECTION,** U.S.P. XXI.
Use: Anti-infective.
MOXAM. (Lilly) Moxalactam disodium Vial 1 g/10 ml. Traypak 10s; Vial 2 Gm./20 ml. Traypak 10s; Vial 10 Gm./100 ml. 6s.
Use: Antibiotic.
• **MOXAZOCINE.** USAN.
Use: Analgesic, antitussive.
MOXIPRAQUINE. B.A.N. 8- {6-[4-(3-Hydroxy-butyl)piperazin-1-yl]hexylamino} -6-methoxy-quinoline.
Use: Protozoacide.
• **MOXNIDAZOLE.** USAN.
Use: Antiprotozoal.
MOYCO FLUORIDE RINSE. (Moyco) Flavored rinse w/0.05% fluoride. Bot. 16 oz., 128 oz.
Use: As an aid in the prevention of dental caries.
M-R-VAX II. (Merck Sharp & Dohme) Live attenuated measles virus vaccine (ATTENUVAX) and live attenuated rubella virus vaccine (MERUVAX II). See details under Attenuvax and Meruvax II. Single dose Vial w/diluent. Box 1s, 10s.
Use: Immunization against measles, rubella.
MS ANTIFOAM M. (Midsil) Simethicone.
MS CONTIN. (Purdue Frederick) Morphine 30 mg./Sust. Release Tab. Bot. 50s.
Use: Prolonged relief of severe pain.
MUCILLIUM. (Robinson) Refined psyllium mucilloid & dextrose. Bot. 8 oz.
Use: Laxative.
MUCILLOID OF PSYLLIUM SEED.
W/Dextrose.
See: Metamucil, Liq. (Searle)
MUCIN.
See: Gastric Mucin (Wilson)
MUCIN, VEGETABLE.
W/Yeast or alkalized.
See: Plantamucin, Granules (Elder)
MUCODYNE. Carboxymethylcysteine, B.A.N.
MUCOGEL TABLETS. (Inwood) Gastric mucin 160 mg., magnesium glycinate 250 mg., aluminum hydroxide gel 250 mg./Tab. Bot. 100s.
Use: Peptic ulcer and hyperacidity.
MUCOMYST. (Mead Johnson) A sterile 20% solution of acetylcysteine for nebulization or direct instillation into the lung as a mucolytic agent. Approved as antidote for acetaminophen overdose w/loading dose 140 mg./Kg. body weight. Vials 4 ml. Ctn. 12s, 10 ml. Ctn. 3s with dropper, 30 ml. Ctn. 3s.
Use: Bronchopulmonary disorders, antidote acetaminophen overdose.
MUCOMYST-10. (Mead Johnson) A sterile 10% solution of acetylcysteine for nebulization or direct instillation into the lung as a mucolytic agent. Approved as antidote for acetaminophen overdose w/loading dose 140 mg./Kg. body weight. Vials 4 ml. Ctn. 12s, 10 ml. Ctn. 3s with dropper, 30 ml. Ctn. 3s.
Use: Bronchopulmonary disorders, antidote acetaminophen overdose.
MUCOPLEX. (ICN) Heprofax 750 mg., Vit. B2 1.5 mg., Vit. B12 5 mcg./Tab. Bot. 100s, 200s.
Use: Vit. B deficiencies.
MUDD. (Chattem) Natural hydrated magnesium aluminum silicate. Topical preparation.
Use: Cleansing agent.
MUDRANE. (Poythress) Aminophylline (anhydrous) 130 mg., phenobarbital 8 mg., ephedrine HCl 16 mg., Pot. iodide 195 mg./Tab. Bot. 100s, 1000s.
Use: Treatment of asthma.
MUDRANE-2. (Poythress) Potassium iodide 195 mg aminophylline (anhydrous) 130 mg./Tab. Bot. 100s.
Use: Emphysema, asthma, bronchitis, bronchiectasis.

JDRANE GG. (Poythress) Aminophylline (anhydrous) 130 mg., ephedrine HCl 16 mg., guaifenesin 100 mg., Phenobarb. 8 mg./Tab. Bot. 100s, 1000s.
Use: Bronchial asthma.

JDRANE GG-2. (Poythress) Guaifenesin 100 mg., aminophylline (anhydrous) 130 mg./Tab. Bot. 100s.
Use: Emphysema.

JDRANE GG ELIXIR. (Poythress) Theophylline 20 mg., ephedrine HCl 4 mg., guaifenesin 26 mg., phenobarbital 2.5 mg./5 cc., alcohol 20%, Bot. pt., 0.5 gal.
Use: Antiasthmatic.

JLTABOLIC. (Kenyon) Adrenal cortex ext. 50 mg., Vit. B-12 30 mcg., methylandrostenediol 10 mg., liver "pink" B-12 equiv. 10 mcg./cc. Vial 10 cc.

JLTA-GEN 12 +E. (Bowman) Vit. A 5000 I.U., D 400 I.U., B-1 2 mg., B-2 2 mg., B-6 0.5 mg., B-12 3 mcg., C 37.5 mg., E 15 I.U., folic acid 0.2 mg., nicotinamide 20 mg./Cap. Bot. 60 s, 500s, 1000s.
Use: Multiple vitamin.

JLTALAN. (Lannett) Vit. A 5,000 I.U., D 400 I.U., B-1 2.5 mg., B-2 2.5 mg., B-6 0.5 mg., B-12 2.0 mcg., C 50 mg., niacinamide 20 mg., calcium pantothenate 5 mg./Cap. Bot. 500s, 1000s.
Use: Multiple vitamin.

JLTI-B-PLEX. (Fellows) Vit. B-1 100 mg., B-2 1 mg., nicotinamide 100 mg., pantothenic acid 10 mg., B-6 10 mg./cc. Vial 10 cc., 30 cc.
Use: Multiple Vit. B deficiencies.

JLTI-B-PLEX CAPSULES. (Fellows) Vit. B-1 50 mg., B-2 5 mg., niacinamide 50 mg., Ca pantothenate 5.4 mg., B-6 0.2 mg., C 150 mg., B-12 1 mcg./Cap. Bot. 100s, 1000s.
Use: Multiple vitamin.

JLTICEBRIN. (Lilly) Vit. B-1 3 mg., B-2 3 mg., B-6 1.2 mg., pantothenic acid 5 mg., niacinamide 25 mg., Vit. B-12 (activity equiv.) 3 mcg., C 75 mg., E 6.6 I.U., Vit. A 10,000 I.U., D 400 I.U./Tab. Pkg. 100s. Blister pkg. 10 × 10s.
Use: Multiple vitamin deficiencies.

JLTIFLUOR. (Amfre-Grant) Vit. A acetate 4000 I.U., D-2 200 I.U., C 100 mg., B-1 1.2 mg., B-2 1.9 mg., niacinamide 20 mg., B-6 2 mg., folic acid 0.4 mg., cal. pantothenate 10 mg., cyanocobalamin 5 mcg., cal. carbonate 200 mg., ferrous fumarate 40 mg., sod. fluoride 2.2 mg./Tab. Bot. 100s.
Use: Dietary supplement.

JLTIFUGE CITRATE. (Blue Line) Piperazine citrate. Syr. 100 mg./cc. Bot. 4 fl. oz. 1 pt. & 1 gal. Tab. (500 mg.) Bot. 100s, 1000s.
Use: Vermifugal agent.

JLTI-GERM OIL. (Viobin) Corn, sunflower and wheat germ oils. Bot. 4 oz., 8 oz., pt., qt.

JLTI-JETS. (Kirkman) Vit. A 10,000 I.U., D-2 400 I.U., B-1 20 mg., B-2 8 mg., C 120 mg., niacinamide 10 mg., Ca pantothenate 5 mg., B-6 0.5 mg., E 50 I.U., desic. liver 100 mg., dried debittered yeast 100 mg., choline bitartrate 62 mg., inositol 30 mg., dlmethionine 30 mg., B-12 7 mcg., iron 2.6 mg., calcium (dical phos.) 58 mg., phosphorus (dical phos.) 45 mg., iodine (potassium iodide) 0.114 mg., magnesium sulf. 1 mg., copper sulf. 1.99 mg., manganese sulf. 1.11 mg., potassium chloride iodide 79 mg./Tab. Bot. 100s.
Use: Multivitamin with minerals.

MULTI-JETS-T. (Kirkman) Vit. A 25,000 I.U., D 1,000 I.U., B-1 10 mg., B-2 10 mg., B-6 2 mg., B-12 5 mcg., C 150 mg., E 5 I.U., niacinamide 100 mg., Ca pantothenate 5 mg., calcium 107 mg., phosphorus 82 Gm., Fe 15 mg., Mg 6 mg., K 5 mg., 10.15 mg., Cu 1 mg., Mn 1 mg., Zn 1.5 mg., choline bitartrate 25 mg., inositol 25 mg./Cap. Bot. 100s.
Use: Multivitamin with minerals.

MULTIPALS. (Faraday) Vit. A 5000 I.U., D 400 I.U., C 50 mg., B-1 3 mg., B-6 0.5 mg., B-2 3 mg., Ca pantothenate 5 mg., niacinamide 20 mg., B-12 2 mcg./Tab. Bot. 100s, 250s, 1000s.
Use: Multivitamin.

MULTIPALS-M. (Faraday) Vit. A 6000 I.U., D 400 I.U., B-1 3 mg., B-2 3 mg., B-6 0.5 mg., B-12 5 mcg., C 60 mg., E 2 I.U., niacinamide 20 mg., Ca pantothenate 5 mg., Fe 10 mg., Iodine 0.15 mg., Cu 1 mg., Mg 6 mg., Mn 1 mg., K 5 mg./Tab. Bot. 100s, 250s, 1000s.
Use: Multivitamin with minerals.

MULTIPLE VITAMIN MINERAL FORMULA. (Kirkman) Vit. A 5,000 I.U., D-2 400 I.U., C 50 mg., B-1 2.5 mg., B-2 2.5 mg., B-6 0.5 mg., B-12 1 mcg., niacinamide 15 mg., Ca pantothenate 5 mg., Vit. E 0.1 I.U., Ca 100 mg., Fe 7.5 mg., Mg 2.5 mg., K 2.5 mg., Zn 0.15 mg., Mn 0.5 mg., Iodine 0.07 mg./Tab. Bot. 100s.
Use: Multivitamin with minerals.

MULTIPLE VITAMINS CHEWABLE. (Kirkman) Vit. A 5,000 I.U., D 400 I.U., C 50 mg., B-1 3 mg., B-2 2.5 mg., B-6 1 mg., B-12 1 mcg., niacinamide 20 mg./Tab. Bot. 100s.
Use: Multiple vitamin.

MULTIPLE VITAMINS W/IRON. (Kirkman) Vit. A 5,000 I.U., D 400 I.U., C 50 mg., B-1 3 mg., B-2 2.5 mg., B-6 1 mg., B-12 1 mcg., niacinamide 20 mg., iron 10 mg./Tab. Bot. 100s.
Use: Multivitamin with iron.

MULTISTIX S. G. REAGENT STRIPS. (Ames) Reagent strip for urine test of pH, glucose, protein, ketones, bilirubin, blood and urobilinogen. Bot. 100s.
Use: Diagnostic aid.

MULTITEST CMI. (Merieux Institute) One disposable applicator pre-loaded with seven glycerinated liquid antigens and glycerin negative control. 10 units/box.
Use: Skin test antigens for celluar hypersensitivity.

MULTITRACE 5. (Armour) Zinc 1 mg., copper 0.4 mg., manganese 0.1 mg., chromium 4 mcg., selenium 20 mcg./ml. Boxes of 25s, 10 ml. vials.
Use: Supplement to I.V. solutions for mineral deficiency.

MULTITRACE CONCENTRATE. (Armour) Trace element mixture of zinc 5 mg., copper 1 mg., manganese 0.5 mg., chromium 10 mg./ml. Vial 1 ml. Box 25s. Vial 5 ml. Box 10s.
Use: Supplement to I.V. solutions for mineral deficiency.

MULTITRACE PEDIATRIC. (Armour) Zinc 1 mg., copper 0.1 mg., manganese 25 mcg., chromium 1 mcg./ml. Boxes of 25s 3 ml. vials.
Use: Supplement to I.V. solutions for mineral deficiency.

MULTITRACE SOLUTION. (Armour) Trace element mixture of zinc 1 mg., copper 0.4 mg., manganese 0.1 mg., chromium 4 mcg./ml. Vial 10 ml. Box 25s. Vial 30 ml. Box 10s.
Use: Supplement to I.V. solutions for mineral deficiency.

MULTI-VITAMIN. (Western Research) Vit. A 5000 I.U., D 400 I.U., B-1 1 mg., B-2 1.5 mg., B-6 1 mg., B-12 2 mcg., C 50 mg., niacinamide 10 mg., Ca pantothenate 2 mg., iron 10 mg., calcium 70 mg./Tab.

MULTI-VITAMINS CAPSULES. (Fellows) Vit. A 5,000 I.U., D 400 I.U., B-1 1.5 mg., B-2 2 mg., B-6 0.1 mg., C 37.5 mg., cal. pantothenate 1 mg., niacinamide 20 mg./Cap. Bot. 100s, 1000s, 5000s.

MULTIVITAMINS ROWELL. (Rowell) Vit. A 5000 I.U., D 400 I.U., B-1 2.5 mg., B-2 2.5 mg., C 50 mg., niacinamide 20 mg., B-6 0.5 mg., calcium pantothenate 5 mg., B-12 2 mcg., E 10 I.U./Cap. Bot. 100s, unit-dose 100s.
Use: Vitamin therapy.

MULTIZINE.
See: Trisulfapyrimidines Tab., U.S.P. XXI.

MULTOREX. (Approved) Vit. A 6000 I.U., D 1250 I.U., C 50 mg., E 5 I.U., B-1 3 mg., B-2 3 mg., B-6 0.5 mg., niacinamide 20 mg., cal. pantothenate 5 mg., B-12 5 mcg., cal. 59 mg., phos. 45 mg./Cap. Bot. 100s, 250s, 1000s.
Use: Supplement.

MULVIDREN-F. (Stuart) Fluoride 1 mg., Vit. A 4000 U., D 400 U., C 75 mg., B-1 2 mg., B-2 2 mg., B-6 1.2 mg., B-12 3 mcg., calcium pantothenate 3 mg., niacinamide 10 mg./Softab Tab. Bot. 100s.
Use: Vitamin supplement and aid in promoting development of caries-resistant teeth.

MULVITOL. (CMC) Vitamins A 5000 I.U., D 500 I.U., B-1 2.5 mg., B-2 2.5 mg., B-6 0.5 mg., B-12 1 mcg., C 37.5 mg., cal. pantothenate 5 mg., folic acid 0.1 mg., niacinamide 20 mg./Cap. Bot. 30s, 100s, 250s, 1000s.
Use: One daily. Avitaminosis.

MUMPS IMMUNE GLOBULIN, HUMAN.
See: Hyparotin, Inj. (Cutter)

• **MUMPS SKIN TEST ANTIGEN,** U.S.P. XXI. (Lilly) Antigen made from allantoic fluid of chick embryos. Vial 1 cc. (10 tests).
Use: Diagnostic aid.

MUMPSVAX. (Merck Sharp & Dohme) Live mumps virus vaccine, Jeryl Lynn strain. Single-dose vial w/diluent Pkg. 1s, 10s.
Use: Immunization against mumps.
W/Attenuvax, Meruvax II.
See: M-M-R II, Inj. (Merck Sharp & Dohme)
W/Meruvax II
See: Biavax II (Merck Sharp & Dohme).

• **MUMPS VIRUS VACCINE LIVE,** U.S.P. XXI.
Use: Active immunizing agent.
See: Mumpsvax, Inj. (Merck Sharp & Dohme)

MUMPS VIRUS VACCINE, LIVE ATTENUATED. Je Lynn (B Level) strain.
W/Measles virus vaccine, rubella virus vaccine.
See: Lirutrin, Vial (Merrell Dow)
M-M-R, Inj. (Merck Sharp & Dohme)

MURIATIC ACID.
See: Hydrochloric Acid, N.F. XVI.

MURI-LUBE. (Invenex) Mineral Oil "Light," Vial: 2 c 10 cc.,
Use: Lubricant in surgical procedures.

MURINE EYE DROPS. (Ross) Potassium chloride, sodium chloride, sodium phosphate, (monobasic and dibasic), water, glycerin, edetate disodium 0.05% and benzalkonium chloride 0.01%. Plastic dropper Bot. 0.5 oz., 1.5 oz.
Use: Soothing isotonic collyrium.

MURINE EAR DROPS. (Ross) Carbamide peroxide 6.5% in anhydrous glycerin. Bot. 0.5 oz.
Use: Softening hardened ear wax.

MURINE EAR WAX REMOVAL SYSTEM. (Ross) Carbamide peroxide 6.5% in anhydrous glycerin w/ear washing syringe. Bot. 0.5 oz. and ear wash 1 oz.
Use: Softening excessive ear wax and removal by washing with syringe.

MURINE PLUS EYE DROPS. (Ross) Tetrahydrozolir HCl with 0.05% w/boric acid, sodium borate, edetate disodium 0.1%, benzalkonium chloride 0.01%. Bot. 0.5 oz., 1.5 oz.
Use: Ophthalmic decongestant.

MURIPSIN. (Norgine) Glutamic acid HCl, 500 mg., pepsin 35 mg./Tab. Bot. 100s, 500s.
Use: Treatment of hydrochloric acid deficiencies.

MURO #128 OINTMENT. (Muro) Sodium chloride 5% in sterile ointment base. Tube 3.5 Gm.
Use: Corneal edema treatment.

MURO #128 SOLUTION. (Muro) Sodium chloride 5%. Bot. 15 ml., 30 ml.
Use: Corneal edema treatment.

MUROCEL SOLUTION. (Muro) Methylcellulose 1%. Bot. 15 ml.,
Use: Tear replacement, ophthalmic lubricant.

MUROCOLL-2. (Muro) Phenylephrine HCl 10 scopolamine HBR 0.3% Bot. 5 ml.
Use: Mydriatic, cycloplegic.

MURO'S OPCON A SOLUTION. (Muro) Naphazoline HCl 0.025% pheniramine maleate 0.3%. Bot. 15 ml.
Use: Ophthalmic anthihistaminic and decongestan

MURO'S OPCON SOLUTION. (Muro) Naphazoline HCl 0.1%. Bot. 15 ml.
Use: Ophthalmic decongestant.

MURO TEARS SOLUTION. (Muro) Hydroxypropyl methylcellulose, dextran 40. Bot. 15 ml.
Use: Ophthalmic lubricant, artificial tears.

MUSCLE ADENYLIC ACID.. (Various Mfr.) Active form of adenosine 5-monophosphate.
See: Adenosine 5-monophosphate, Prep. (Vario Mfr.)

IUSCLE RELAXANTS.
See: Curare (Various Mfr.)
Flexeril, Tab. (Merck Sharp & Dohme)
Flaxedil Triethiodide, Vial (Davis & Geck)
Lioresal, Tab. (Geigy)
Mephenesin (Various Mfr.)
Meprobamate (Various mfr.)
Metubine Iodine, Vial (Lilly)
Neostig, Tab. (Freeport)
Norflex, Tab., Inj. (Riker)
Parafon Forte, Tab. (McNeil)
P-A-V, Cap. (Amid)
Rela, Tab. (Schering)
Robaxin, Tab., Inj. (Robins)
Soma, Tab., Cap. (Wallace)
Succinylcholine Chloride (Various Mfr.)
d-Tubocurarine Chloride (Various Mfr.)

ISTARAL OIL.
See: Allyl Isothiocyanate.

ISTARGEN. (Merck Sharp & Dohme)
Mechlorethamine HCl. 10 mg./Vial w/sodium sod. chloride q.s. 100 mg./Vial. Treatment sets of 4 Vials.
Use: Parenteral administration for certain forms of neoplastic diseases.

ISTEROLE. (Plough) **Regular:** Camphor 4%, menthol 2% Jar 0.9 oz. **Extra Strength:** Camphor 5%, Menthol 3%. Jar 0.9 oz. Tube 1 oz. 2.25 oz.
Use: Analgesic rub.

ISTEROLE DEEP STRENGTH. (Plough) Methyl salicylate 30%, menthol 3%, Methyl nicotinate 0.5%. Jar 1.25 oz., Tube 3 oz.
Use: Analgesic rub.

ISTIN.
See: Mechlorethamine HCl, Sterile, U.S.P.

ISTINE. B.A.N. NN-Di-(2-chloroethyl) methylamine. Chlormethine (I.N.N.)
Use: Antineoplastic agent.

ITALIN. (Spanner) Protein and iodine. Vial 30 cc.

TAMYCIN. (Bristol) Mitomycin 5 mg., 20 mg./Vial.
Use: Antineoplastic.

VICA. (Blue Line) Vit. A palmitate 5000 I.U., Vit. D 400 I.U., B-1 1.5 mg., B-2 2 mg., nicotinamide 15 mg., C 30 mg., B-6 0.1 mg., Ca pantothenate 1 mg., Vit. B-12 1 mcg., Vit. E 1 I.U./Cap. Bot. 100s, 1000s.

IUZOLIMINE. USAN.
Use: Diuretic, antihypertensive.

V.I. (Armour) Vit. A 3 mg., D 25 mcg., E 5 mg., C 500 mg., B-1 50 mg., B-2 10 mg., niacinamide 100 mg., B-6 15 mg., dexpanthenol 25 mg./10 ml. Amp. 10 ml., 25s, 100s.
Use: I.V., infusion feeding.

V.I.-12. (Armour) **Vial 1:** Vit. A 1 mg., D 5 mcg., E 10 mg., C 100 mg., B-1 3 mg., B-2 3.6 mg., B-6 4 mg., niacinamide 40 mg., dexpanthenol 15 mg./5 ml. **Vial 2**: Biotin 60 mcg., folic acid 400 mcg., Vit. B-12 5 mgc./5 ml. Vials 1 and 2 used together. Box 25s. Ctn. 100s.Vial.
Use: I.V. infusion feeding.

V.I. CONCENTRATE. (Armour) Vit. A 3 mg., D 25 mcg., E 5 mg., C 500 mg., B-1 50 mg., B-2 10 mg., B-6 15 mg., niacinamide 100 mg., dexpanthenol 25 mg./5 ml. Vial 100s.
Use: I.V. infusion feeding.

M.V.I.-12 LYOPHILIZED. (Armour) Vit. A 1 mg., D 5 mcg., E 10 mg., C 100 mg., B-1 3 mg., B-2 3.6 mg., B-6 4 mg., B-12 5 mcg., niacinamide 40 mg., dexpanthenol 15 mg., biotin 60 mcg., folic acid 400 mcg./Vial. Box 25s. Ctn. 100s.
Use: I.V. infusion feeding.

M.V.I. PEDIATRIC. (Armour) Vit. A 0.7 mg., D 10 mcg., E 7 mg., C 80 mcg., B-1 1.2 mg., B-2 1.4 mg., B-6 1 mg., B-12 1 mcg., K 200 mcg., niacinamide 17 mg., dexpanthenol 5 mg. biotin 20 mcg., folic acid 140 mcg./Vial. Box 25s. Ctn. 100s.
Use: I.V. infusion feeding.

MYACHOL FORMULA. (Image) Multiple vitamin Bot. 100s.
Use: Supplemental.

MYADEC. (Parke-Davis) Vit. B-12 cryst. 6 mcg., B-2 10 mg., B-6 5 mg., B-1 mononitrate 10 mg., niacin 100 mg., Vit. C 250 mg., A 10,000 I.U., D 400 I.U., E 30 I.U., Fe 20 mg., iodine 0.15 mg., Mn 1.25 mg., Cu 2 mg., Zn 20 mg., Mg 100 mg., pantothenic acid 20 mg., folic acid 0.4 mg./Tab. Bot. 130s, 250s. Unit dose 100s.
Use: Nutritional agent.

MYAGEN. Bolasterone.
Use: Anabolic agent.

MYAMBUTOL. (Lederle) Ethambutol HCl Tabs. 100 mg., Bot. 100s, 1000s. 400 mg., Bot. 100s, 1000s. Unit dose 10 × 10s.
Use: Tuberculostatic.

MYANESIN.
See: Mephenesin (Various Mfr.)

MYCARTAI. (Winthrop Products) Pentaerythritol tetranitrate.
Use: Coronary vasodilator.

MYCELEX. (Miles Pharm) Clotrimazole. **Topical cream:** 1% Tube 15 Gm., 30 Gm. **Topical Soln.:** 1%. Bot. 10 ml., 30 ml.
Use: Antifungal.

MYCELEX-G. (Miles Pharm) Clotrimazole **Vag. Tab.:** 100 mg./Tab. Pkg. 7 tab. w/applicator. **Cream:** 1%. Tube 45 Gm.
Use: Vulvovaginal candidiasis treatment.

MYCHEL-S. (Rachelle) Sterile chloramphenicol sodium succinate. Vial 1 Gm./15 cc. Box 5s.
Use: Antibiotic.

MYCIFRADIN. (Upjohn) Neomycin sulfate. **Tab.** 0.5 Gm./Tab. (equivalent to 0.35 Gm neomycin). Bot. 100s, 500s. **Oral Soln.:** 125 mg./5 ml. (equivalent to 87.5 mg neomycin). Bot. pt. **Sterile Powder:** 0.5 Gm./Vial (equivalent to 0.35 Gm. neomycin) for I.M. use.
Use: Antibiotic.

MYCIGUENT. (Upjohn) Neomycin sulfate. **Cream** 5 mg./Gm. Tube 0.5 oz. **Oint.** 5 mg./Gm. Tube 0.5 oz., 1 oz., 4 oz.
Use: Antibiotic.

MYCIL, CHLORPHENESIN, B.A.N.

MYCI-SPRAY. (Misemer) Phenylephrine HCl 0.25%, pyrilamine maleate 0.15%/cc. Bot. 20cc.
Use: Nasal congestion.

MYCITRACIN. (Upjohn) Bacitracin 500 u., neomycin sulfate 5 mg., polymyxin B sulf. 5000 u./Gm. **Oint.** Tube 0.5 oz., 1 oz. Unit-Dose 1/32 oz., Box 144s. **Ophth. Oint.** Tube 3.5 Gm. w/applicator tip.
Use: Reinforced antibiotic therapy.

MYCOGEN CREAM. (Goldline) Nystatin, neomycin sulfate gramacidin w/triamcinolone Bot. 15 Gm., 30 Gm., 60 Gm., 120 gm. or 1 lb.
Use: Infected or inflamed skin.

MYCOGEN OINTMENT. (Goldline) Nystatin, neomycin sulfate. Bot. 15 Gm., 30 Gm., 60 Gm.
Use: Infected or inflamed skin.

MYCOLOG CREAM AND OINTMENT. (Squibb) Triamcinolone acetonide 1.0 mg., neomycin 2.5 mg., gramicidin 0.25 mg., nystatin 100,000 u./Gm. Ointment base: w/Plastibase (polyethylene, mineral oil). Tube 15 Gm., 30 Gm., 60 Gm., Jar 120 Gm.
Use: Infected or inflamed skin.

MYCOMIST. (Gordon) Chlorophyll, formalin, benzalkonium chloride. Bot. 4 oz., Plastic Bot. 1 oz.
Use: Fungicide to sanitize and deodorize shoes and boots.

• **MYCOPHENOLIC ACID.** USAN. (E)-6-(4-Hydroxy-6-methoxy-7-methyl-3-oxo-5-phthalanyl)-4-methyl-4-hexenoic acid.
Use: Antineoplastic.

MYCOPLASMA PNEUMONIA IFA TEST. (Wampole-Zeus) Indirect fluorescent assay for antibodies to *Mycoplasma pneumoniae.* Box 100 tests.
Use: Aid in the diagnosis of primary atypical pneumonia.

MYCOPLASMA PNEUMONIA IFA IgM TEST. (Wampole-Zeus) Indirect fluorescent assay for IgM antibodies to *Mycoplasma pneumoniae.* Box 100 tests.
Use: Aid in the diagnosis of primary atypical pneumonia.

MY-CORT LOTION. (Scrip) Hydrocortisone acetate 0.5%. Bot. 1 oz.

MY-CORT OTIC. (Scrip) Hydrocortisone free alcohol 2.5 mg., polymyxin B sulfate 2000 u., neomycin (as sulfate) 3.5 mg., diperodon HCl 5 mg./ml. Bot. 0.5 oz.

MYCOSTATIN. (Squibb) Nystatin **Tab.:** (500,000 u.) Bot. 100s. **Cr.:** 100,000 u./Gm. Tube 15 Gm., 30 Gm. **Oint.:** (100,000 u./Gm.) In PLASTIBASE (polyethylene and mineral oil). Tube 15 & 30 Gm. **Susp.:** (100,000 u./ml.) In vehicle containing sucrose 50%) Bot. w/dropper 60 ml. Unimatic 5 ml. **Vag. Tab.:** 100,000 u., lactose 0.95 Gm., ethyl cellulose, stearic acid, starch/Tab. Pkg. 15s, 30s, Unimatic Carton 50s. **Pwd.** (topical) 100,000 u./Gm. in talc. Shaker type bot. 15 Gm. 500,000 u./Gm. Vial 1 cc. for lab use.
Use: Oral, intestinal, vaginal or cutaneous moniliasis.

MYCO TRIACET CREAM & OINTMENT. (Lemmon) Nystatin 100,000 U., neomycin sulfate 2.5 mg., gramicidin 0.25 mg., triamcinolone acetonide 1 mg./Gm. **Cream:** Tube 15 Gm., 30 Gm., 60 Gm. **Ointment:** Tube 15 Gm, 30 Gm, 60 Gm.
Use: Skin infections accompanied by inflammatio

MYDFRIN 2.5%. (Alcon) Phenylephrine HCl 2.5%. Bot. 5 ml.
Use: Mydriatic.

MYDRAPRED. (Alcon) Atropine sulf. 1%, prednisolone 0.25%, in a sterile, buffered, isoton suspension. Plas. Bot. 5 cc.
Use: Mydriatic, cycloplegic, anti-inflammatory.

MYDRIACYL. (Alcon) N-Ethyl-2-phenyl-N-(4-pyridyl-methyl) hydracrylamide. Tropicamide. Bistropamic 0.5% or 1.0% Sterile aqueous solution. 15 cc. Drop-Tainer.
Use: Mydriatic-cycloplegic action.

■ **MYDRIATICS.**

Parasympatholytic Types

Atropine Salts (Various Mfr.)
Homatropine Hydrobromide (Various Mfr.)
Scopolamine Salts (Various Mfr.)

Sympathomimetic Types

Amphetamine Sulfate 3% (Various Mfr.)
Clopane HCl, Liq. (Lilly)
Ephedrine Sulfate (Various Mfr.)
Epinephrine HCl (Various Mfr.)
Neo-Synephrine HCl, Prep. (Winthrop-Breon)
Phenylephrine HCl. (Various Mfr.)

MYDRILATE HYDROCHLORIDE. Cyclopentolate, B.A.N.

MYIDONE TABS. (Major) Primidone 250 mg./Tab. Bot. 100s, 1000s.
Use: Control of seizures.

MYKINAC CREAM. (NMC Labs) Nystatin 100,000 U/Gm. Tube 15 Gm., 30 Gm.
Use: Antifungal.

MYLAGEN LIQUID. (Goldline) Bot. 12 oz., gal.
Use: Antacid, antiflatulent.

MYLANTA LIQUID. (Stuart) Magnesium hydroxide 200 mg., aluminum hydroxide 200 mg., simethico 20 mg./5 ml. Bot. 5 oz., 12 oz. Unit dose 30 ml. 100s.
Use: Antacid/antiflatulent for management of routine hyperacidity and similar gastrointestinal disorders.

MYLANTA TABLETS. (Stuart) Magnesium hydroxid 200 mg., aluminum hydroxide, dried gel 200 mg., simethicone 20 mg./Chewable Tab. Boxes 40s, 100s. Bot. 180s. Convenience pack 48s.
Use: Antacid/antiflatulent for management of routine hyperacidity and similar gastrointestinal disorders.

MYLANTA-II LIQUID. (Stuart) Magnesium hydrox 400 mg., aluminum hydroxide 400 mg., simethico 30 mg./5 ml. Bot. 5 oz., 12 oz., Unit dose 30 ml., 100s.
Use: High potency double-strength antacid/antiflatulent for management of peptic ulc and other gastrointestinal disorders related to aci hypersecretion.

MYLANTA-II TABLETS. (Stuart) Magnesium hydrox 400 mg., aluminum hydroxide 400 mg., simethico 30 mg./Chewable Tab. Box 24s, 60s.

Use: High-potency double-strength antacid/antiflatulent for management of peptic ulcer and other gastrointestinal disorders related to acid hypersecretion.

LASE 100. Alpha-amylase.
See: Diastase.

Prolase-300, dehydrocholic acid, hyoscyamine HBr, hyoscine HBr, atropine sulfate.
See: Almezyme, Cap. (Meyer)

Prolase, cellulase, calcium carbonate, magnesium glycinate.
See: Zylase Tab. (Vitarine)

LERAN. (Burroughs Wellcome) Busulfan 2 mg./Tab. Bot. 25s.
Use: Chronic myeloid leukemia.

LICON. (Stuart) Simethicone 40 mg./Chewable Tab. Bot. 100s, 500s. Unit dose 100s. **Drops.** (40 mg./0.6 ml.) Bot. 30 ml.
Use: Antiflatulent.

LICON-80. (Stuart) Simethicone 80 mg./Chewable Tab. Bot. 100s. Boxes 12s, 48s, Unit dose 100s.
Use: High-capacity antiflatulent.

O-B. (Sig) Adenosine-5-monophosphoric acid and Vit. B-12. Vial 10 ml.

OBID. (Laser) Papaverine HCl 150 mg./Cap. Bot. 100s, 1000s.
Use: Relief of ischemia.

OCALM. (Parmed) Acetaminophen 8 gr., salicylamide 2 gr., phenyltoloxamine citrate 40 mg./Tab. Bot. 100s, 1000s.
Use: Analgesic/calmative.

OCHRYSINE. (Merck Sharp & Dohme) Sterile aqueous soln. of gold sodium thiomalate 10 mg., 25 mg., 50 mg./ml. w/benzyl alcohol 0.5%. Amps. Box 6s. Vial 50 mg./ml. 10 ml.
Use: (I.M.) Rheumatoid arthritis.

ODIL.
See: Iophendylate Inj., U.S.P. XXI.

OFLEX CREME. (Adria) Trolamine salicylate 10% in a vanishing cream base. Tube 2 oz., 4 oz. Jar 8 oz., 1 lb.
Use: Topically, analgesic.

OLIN. (Hauck) Orphenadrine citrate 30 mg./ml. Vial 10 ml.
Use: Muscle relaxant.

ORGAL. Mysuran. Ambenonium chloride.
Use: Cholinergic.
See: Mytelase Chloride, Cap. (Winthrop-Breon)

OSAL. (Seatrace) Sodium thiosalicylate 50 mg./ml. Vial 30 cc.

OTALIS. (Vita Elixir) Digitalis 1.5 gr./Tab.
Use: Digitalis therapy.

OTONACHOL. (Glenwood) Bethanechol chloride 5 mg., 10 mg., 25 mg./Tab. Bot. 100s.

OTOXIN. (Vita Elixir) **#1:** Digitoxin 0.1 mg./Tab.; **#2:** digitoxin 0.2 mg./Tab.
Use: Cardiotonic.

OWN. (Emko-Schering) p-Chloro-m-xylenol 0.015% in can, 0.50% in deposited film, emollient vehicle/Spray. 3.5 oz. Hexachlorophene 0.10% in can, 1% in deposited film/Powder. Benzalkonium chloride 0.12% buffered aq. solution. Spray 2 oz.
Use: Antibacterial.

MYRALACT. B.A.N. N-(2-Hydroxyethyl)tetradecylammonium lactate.
Use: Antiseptic.

MYRIATIN DROPS. (Winthrop Products) Atropine methonitrate BP.
Use: Antispasmodic.

MYRISTICA OIL.
Use: Flavor.

MYRISTYL-γ-PICOLINIUM CHLORIDE.
See: Wet Tone, Soln. (Riker)

MYRJ 45. (ICI Americas) Mixture of free polyoxyethylene glycol and its mono- and di-stearates. *Polyoxyl 8 stearate.
Use: Surface-active agent.

MYRJ 52 and 52S. (ICI Americas) Polyoxyethylene 40 Stearate. Mixture of free polyoxyethylene glycol and its mono-and di-stearates.
Use: Surface-active agent.

MYRJ 53. (ICI Americas) Polyoxyl 50 stearate.
Use: Surface active agent.

MYROPHINE. B.A.N. 0^3-Benzyl-0^6-tetradecanoylmorphine.
Use: Narcotic analgesic.

MYSOLINE. (Ayerst) Primidone. **Tab.** 250 mg./Tab. Bot. 100s, 1000s. Unit dose 100s. 50 mg./Tab. Bot. 100s, 500s. **Susp.** 250 mg./5 ml. Bot. 8 oz.
Use: Control of grand mal, psychomotor, and focal epileptic seizures.

MYSTECLIN-F. (Squibb) Tetracycline 250 mg., amphotercin B 50 mg./Cap. Bot. 16s, 100s. Unimatic 100s.

MYSTECLIN-F SYRUP. (Squibb) Tetracycline 125 mg., potassium metaphosphate, amphotericin B 25 mg./5 ml. Bot. 240 ml.
Use: Antibiotic.

MYSURAN. Ambenonium chloride.
Use: Treatment of myasthenia gravis.
See: Mytelase Chloride, Cap. (Winthrop-Breon)

MYTELASE. (Winthrop-Breon) Ambenonium chloride 10 mg./Cap. Bot. 100s.
Use: Myasthenia gravis treatment.

MYTRATE. (Softcon) Epinephrine bitartrate 1%, 2% w/Benzalkonium chloride 1:25,000, Methulose sol., sod. bisulfite, & disod. edetate. Plastic drop bot. 15 cc.
Use: Chronic simple glaucoma.

MYTREX CREAM & OINTMENT. (Savage) Nystatin 100,000 U., neomycin sulfate 2.5 mg. neomycin base, gramicidin 0.25 mg., triamcinolone acetonide 1 mg./1 Gm. in cream or ointment base. Tube 15 Gm., 30 Gm., 60 Gm., 120 Gm.
Use: Anti-inflammatory, anti-pruritic, anti-candidal, antibacterial.

MYVEROL. (Eastman) Glyceryl monostearate.

N

NAAL. (Haag) Chloropheniramine maleate 9 mg., Phenylephrine HCl 21 mg./Cap. Bot. 50s, 250s.

NA-ANA-TAL. (Churchill) Phenobarbital 0.25 gr., phenacetin 2 gr., aspirin 3 gr., nicotinic acid 50 mg./Tab. Bot. 100s, Liquid Bot. 16 oz.
Use: Sedative-analgesic-tension.

• **NABAZENIL.** USAN.
Use: Anticonvulsant.
• **NABILONE.** USAN.
Use: Tranquilizer (minor).
• **NABITAN HYDROCHLORIDE.** USAN.
Use: Analgesic.
• **NABOCTATE HYDROCHLORIDE.** USAN.
Use: Antiglaucoma agent.
NACREM. (Jenkins) Ammonium chloride 1.5%, menthol, methyl salicylate, camphor, oil eucalyptus Tube 0.25 oz.
Use: Sinus congestion, hay fever.
• **NADIDE.** USAN. 3-Carbamoyl-1-β-D-ribofuranosylpyridinium hydroxide. Nicotinamide adenine dinucleotide. 1-(3-Carbamoylpyridinio)-βD-ribofuranoside 5-(adenosine-5′-pyrophosphate). Ensopride. Codehydrogenase I.
Use: Treat alcoholism and drug addiction.
NADINOLA FOR DRY SKIN. (Strickland) Hydroquinone 2%. Bot. 1.25 oz., 2.25 oz.
Use: Depigmenting agent for skin.
NADINOLA (DELUXE) FOR OILY SKIN. (Strickland) Hydroquinone 2%. Bot. 1.25 oz., 2.25 oz.
Use: Depigmenting agent for skin.
NADINOLA (ULTRA) FOR NORMAL SKIN. (Strickland) Hydroquinone 2%. Bot. 1.25 oz., 3.75 oz. Tube 1.85 oz.
Use: Depigmenting agent for skin.
NADISAN. Carbutamide, B.A.N.
• **NADOLOL,** U.S.P. XXI. Tab., U.S.P. XXI.
Use: Antiadrenergic.
NAEPAINE HYDROCHLORIDE. 2-(Pentylamino)-ethanol-p-aminobenzoate HCl.
Use: Local anesthetic.
NADOLOL.
Use: Antihypertensive and antiangina beta-blocker.
See: Corgard, Tab. (Squibb)
• **NAFARELIN ACETATE.** USAN.
Use: Agonist.
NAFCIL. (Bristol) Nafcillin sodium for inj. 500 mg., 1.0 Gm., 2.0 Gm./Vial; Bulk vial 10 Gm.; 500 mg., 1 Gm., 2 Gm. Piggyback vial.
Use: Anti-infective.
NAFCILLIN. B.A.N. 6-(2-Ethoxy-1-naphthamido)-penicillanic acid.
Use: Antibiotic.
See: Unipen, Vial, Cap., Pow., Tab. (Wyeth)
• **NAFCILLIN, SODIUM,** U.S.P. XXI. Caps., Inj., Oral Solution, Sterile, Tab., U.S.P. XXI. 4-Thia-1-azabicyclo[3.2.0]-heptane-2-carboxylic acid, 6-[[(2-ethoxy-1-naph-thalenyl)carbonyl]amino]-3,3-dimethyl-7-oxo-monosodium salt, monohydrate,[2S-(2α,5α,6β)]. Monosodium 6-(2-ethoxy-1-naphthamido)-3,3-dimethyl-7-oxo-4-thia-1-azabicyclo [3.2.0.] heptane-2-carboxylate monohydrate. Sodium 6-(2-ethoxy-1-naphthamido)-penicillanate.
Use: Antibiotic.
See: Nafcil, Inj. (Bristol)
Unipen, Vial, Cap., Pow., Tab. (Wyeth)
NA-FEEN. (Pacemaker) Fluoride 1 mg./Dose. Bot. Tabs. 100s, 500s, 1000s; Liq. 2 oz.
Use: Control of dental caries.
• **NAFENOPIN.** USAN. 2-Methyl-2-[p-1,2,3,4-tetrahydro-1-naphthyl)phenoxy]propionic acid.
Use: Hypolipidemic.
• **NAFIMIDONE HYDROCHLORIDE.** USAN.
Use: Anti-convulsant.
• **NAFLOCORT.** USAN.
Use: Adrenocortical steroid.
• **NAFOMINE MALATE.** USAN.
Use: Muscle relaxant.
• **NAFOXIDINE HYDROCHLORIDE.** USAN.
Use: Anti-estrogen.
• **NAFRONYL OXALATE.** USAN. 2-(Diethylamino-eth tetrahydro-α-(1-naphthyl-methyl)2-furanpropionate oxalate. Dusodril.
Use: Vasodilator.
NAFTALAN
W/Ichthyol, calamine, amber petrolatum.
See: Nagtalan, Oint. (Paddock)
• **NAFTALOFOS.** USAN.
Use: Anthelmintic.
NAFTAZONE. B.A.N. 1,2-Naphthaquinone 2-semicabazone. Haemostop
Use: Hemostatic.
NAFTIDROFURYL. B.A.N. 2-Diethylaminoethyl 2-(1-naphthylmethyl)-3-(tetrahydro-2-furyl)propionate. Praxilene [oxalate]
Use: Vasodilator.
• **NAFTIFINE HYDROCHLORIDE.** USAN.
Use: Antifungal.
NAGANOL.
See: Suramin Sodium. Naphuride Sodium.
NAGEST Times Tabs. (Leeds) Phenylpropanolamine HCl 40 mg., phenylephrine HCl 10 mg., phenyltoloxamine dihydrogen citrate 15 mg., chlorpheniramine maleate 5 mg./sustained action Tab. Bot. 50s, 100s.
Use: Decongestant-antihistamine.
NAIL-A-CAIN. (Medtech) Benzocaine 15% w/v, tanr acid 4% w/v. w/isopropyl alcohol 61%, diethyl ether 20%. Bot. 0.5 oz.
Use: Relief of pain of ingrown nails.
NAILICURE. (Purepac) Denatonium benzoate in a clear nailpolish base. Bot. 0.33 oz.
Use: Nail biting deterrent.
NAIL PLUS. (Faraday) Gelatin Cap. Bot. 100s, 200s
NAIL RITE. (Eckerd) Bot. 0.5 oz.
NAILIFE. (Quality Generics) Refined gelatin 10 gr./ Cap. Bot. 1000s. Jar 100s.
Use: Nail strengthener.
NALATE. (Kay) Sod. thiosalicylate 50 mg., sodium bisulfite 0.1%, benzyl alcohol 2%/cc. Multiple dos sterile solution 30 cc.
Use: Analgesic in arthritis or rheumatism.
• **NALBUPHINE HYDROCHLORIDE.** USAN. (−)-17-(cyclobutylmethyl)-4, 5a-epoxymorphinan-3, 6a, 14 triol, hydrochloride.
Use: Analgesic
See: Nubain, Vial (Du Pont)
NALDECON. (Bristol) Phenylephrine HCl 10 mg., phenylpropanolamine HCl 40 mg.; phenyltoloxami

citrate, 15 mg.; chlorpheniramine, 5 mg./Tab., half each ingredient in inner and half in outer layer. Bot. 100s, 500s.
Use: Hay fever, sinus, congestion.

ALDECON-CX SUSPENSION. (Bristol) Phenylpropanolamine 18 mg., guaifenesin 200 mg., codeine phosphate 10 mg./5 ml. Bot. 4 oz, 6 oz.
Use: Decongestant, expectorant, antitussive.

ALDECON-DX PEDIATRIC SYRUP. (Bristol) Phenylpropanolamine 9 mg., dextromethorphan 7.5 mg., guaifenesin 100 mg./5 ml. w/alcohol 5%. Bot. 4 oz., 16 oz.
Use: Decongestant, expectorant, antitussive.

ALDECON-EX PEDIATRIC DROPS. (Bristol) Phenylpropanolamine 9 mg., guaifenesin 30 mg./ml. w/alcohol 0.6%. Bot. 30 ml.
Use: Decongestant, expectorant.

ALDECON PEDIATRIC DROPS. (Bristol) Chlorpheniramine maleate 0.5 mg., phenyltoloxamine citrate, 2 mg., phenylpropanolamine HCl 5 mg., phenylphrine HCl 1.25 mg./1 ml. Bot. 20 ml.
Use: Decongestant.

ALDECON PEDIATRIC SYRUP. (Bristol) Chlorpheniramine maleate 0.5 mg., phenyltoloxamine citrate 2 mg., phenylpropanolamine HCl 5 mg., phenylephrine HCl 1.25 mg./5 ml. syrup. Bot. 16 oz.
Use: Decongestant.

ALDECON SYRUP. (Bristol) Chlorpheniramine maleate 2.5 mg., phenyltoloxamine citrate 7.5 mg., phenylpropanolamine 20 mg., phenylephrine HCl 5 mg./5 ml. Bot. pt.
Use: Antihistamine combinations & decongestant.

ALFON. (Dista) Fenoprofen calcium. **200** mg./Cap. Rx Pak 100s. **300** mg./Cap. Bot. 100s, 500s. 600 mg./Tab. Bot. 100s, 500s.
Use: Antiarthritic, analgesic.

NALIDIXATE SODIUM. USAN. Sodium 1-ethyl-1,4-dihydro-7-methyl-4-oxo-1,8-naphthyridine-3-carboxylate monohydrate. Under study.
Use: Antibacterial.

NALIDIXIC ACID, U.S.P. XXI. Oral Susp., Tab., U.S.P. XXI. 1-Ethyl-7-methyl-1,8-naphthyridin-4-one-3-carboxylic acid, 1-Ethyl-1,4-dihydro-7-methyl-4-oxo-1,8-naphthyridine-3-carboxylic Acid.
Use: Antibacterial.
See: NegGram, Caplet, Susp. (Winthrop-Breon)

ALLPEN. (Beecham Labs) Nafcillin sodium monohydrate 500 mg., 1 Gm., 2 Gm./Vial. Piggyback 1 Gm., 2 Gm.
Use: Antibacterial.

NALMETRENE. USAN.
Use: Antagonist to narcotics.

ALLINE HYDROCHLORIDE. (MSD AGVET) Nalorphine HCl 5 mg./cc. Injection.
Use: Narcotic antidote, veterinary medicine.

ALORPHINE. B.A.N. N-Allylnormorphine. Lethidrone [hydrobromide]
Use: Narcotic analgesic.

NALORPHINE HYDROCHLORIDE. N-Allylnormorphine HCl. 17-Allyl-7,8-didehydro-4,5-epoxymorphinan-3,6 diol hydrochlo-ride.
Use: Narcotic antagonist.

NALOXONE. B.A.N. F.D.A. (−)-17-Allyl-4,5α-epoxy-3,14-dihydroxymorphinan-6-one.
Use: Narcotic antagonist.
See: Narcan, Amp. (Du Pont)

• **NALOXONE HYDROCHLORIDE,** U.S.P. XXI. Inj. U.S.P. XXI. Morphinan-6-one, 4,5-epoxy-3,14-dihydroxy-17-(2-propenyl)-,hydrochloride.
Use: Narcotic antagonist.
See: Narcan, Amp. (Du Pont)

NALSA SPRAY. (Jenkins) Methapyrilene HCl 0.2%, naphazoline HCl 0.05%, cetyl pyridinium chloride 0.02%, thimerosal as preservative 0.005%. Spray Bot. 20 cc.

• **NALTREXONE.** USAN.
Use: Antagonist to narcotics.
See: Trexal Tab. (Du Pont).

NAMAZENE. Phenothiazine.

NAMOL XENYRATE. 2-(4-Biphenylyl) butyric acid, compound with 2-dimethyl-amino-ethanol.
See: Namoxyrate.

• **NAMOXYRATE.** USAN. 2-[4-Biphenylyl]butyric acid cpd. w/2-dimethylaminoethanol. Namol Xenyrate-previous name.
Use: Analgesic.
See: Namol Xenyrate (Warner-Chilcott)

NAMURON.
See: Cyclobarbital Calcium (Var. Mfr.)

NANROBOLIC. (Forest) Nadrolone phenpropionate 25 mg./ml. Vial 5 ml.
Use: Control of metastatic breast cancer.

NANDROBOLIC L.A. (Forest) Nandrolone decanonate 100 mg./ml. 2 ml./Vial Box 5s.

NANDROLIN. (Reid-Provident) Nandrolone phenpropionate 25 mg./ml. Vial 5 ml.
Use: Control of metastatic breast cancer.

NANDROLONE. B.A.N. 17β-Hydroxyestr-4-en-3-one. 17β-Hydroxy-19-norandrost-4-en-3-one. Nortesterone (I.N.N.)
Use: Anabolic steroid.

• **NANDROLONE CYCLOTATE.** USAN.
Use: Anabolic.

• **NANDROLONE DECANOATE,** U.S.P. XXI. Inj., U.S.P. XXI. 17β-Hydroxy-estr-4-en-3-one-decanoate.
Use: Androgen.
See: Anabolin LA-100, Vial (Alto)
Androlone-D, Inj. (Keene)
Androlone-D 50, Inj. (Keene)
Deca-Durabolin, Amp., Vial (Organon)
Hybolin Decanoate, Inj. (Hyrex)

• **NANDROLONE PHENPROPIONATE,** U.S.P. XXI. Inj. U.S.P. XXI. 19-nor-17-beta-Hydroxy-3-ketoandrost-4-ene-17-phenylpropionate. Norandrostenolone phenylpropionate. 17β-Hydroxyestr-4-en-3-one Hydrocinnamate.
Use: Androgen.
See: Anabolin IM, Vial (Alto)
Androlone, Inj. (Keene)

Androlone 50, Inj. (Keene)
Durabolin Inj. (Organon)
Hybolin Improved, Vial (Hyrex)
Nandrolin, Inj. (Reid-Provident)

NANKOR. Fenchlorphos, B.A.N.

• **NANTRADOL HCL.** USAN.
Use: Analgesic.

NAOTIN. (Drug Products) Sod. nicotinate. Amp. (equiv. to 10 mg., nicotinic acid/cc.) 10 cc., Box 25s, 100s.
Use: I.V. & I.M., nicotinic acid therapy.

• **NAPACTADINE HYDROCHLORIDE.** USAN.
Use: Antidepressant.

NAPAL. (T.E. Williams) N-Acetyl-p-aminophenol 5 gr., hyoscyamine sulfate 0.03 mg., phenyltoloxamine dihydrogen citrate 6.25 mg./Cap. Bot. 24s, 100s.
Use: Analgesic, antispasmodic, antihistaminic.

NAPAMIDE CAPS. (Major) Disopyramide phosphate 150 mg./Cap. Bot. 100s, 500s.
Use: Ventricular arrhythythmias.

NAPHAZOLINE. B.A.N. 2-(1-Naphthylmethyl)-2-imidazoline.
Use: Vasoconstrictor.

• **NAPHAZOLINE HYDROCHLORIDE,** U.S.P. XXI. Nasal Soln., Ophthalmic Soln., U.S.P. XXI. IH-Imidazole, 4,5-dihydro-2-(1-naphthalenylmethyl)-,monohydrochloride, 2-(1-Naphthylmethyl)-2-imidazoline HCl.
Use: Adrenergic.
See: Allerest Eye Drops, Soln. (Pharmacraft)
Clear Eyes, Drops (Abbott)
Naphcon, Drops (Alcon)
Privine Hydrochloride, Sol., Spray (Ciba)
Vasocon Regular, Liq. (CooperVision)
W/Antazoline phosphate, boric acid, phenylmercuric acetate, sod. chloride, sod. carbonate anhydrous.
See: Vasocon-A Ophthalmic, Sol. (CooperVision)
W/Antazoline phosphate, polyvinyl alcohol.
See: Albalon-A Liquifilm, Ophth. (Allergan)
W/Methapyrilene HCl, cetylpyridinum chloride, thimerosal.
See: Korizol, Sol. (Sutliff & Case)
Vapocyn II Nasal Spray (Reid-Provident)
W/Pheniramine maleate.
See: Naphcon A, Liq. (Alcon)
W/Phenylephrine HCl, pyrilamine maleate, phenylpropanolamine HCl.
See: 4-Way Nasal Spray (Bristol-Myers)
W/Polyvinyl alcohol.
See: Albalon, Ophth. Sol. (Allergan)
Albalon Liquifilm, Ophth. Soln. (Allergan)

NAPHCON. (Alcon) Naphazoline 0.012%. Drop-Tainer Bot. 0.5 fl. oz.
Use: Ophthalmic decongestant.

NAPHCON A. (Alcon) Naphazoline HCl 0.025%, pheniramine maleate 0.3%. Bot. 15 ml.
Use: Ocular decongestant, antihistamine.

NAPHCON FORTE. (Alcon) Naphazoline HCl 0.1%, benzalkonium chloride 0.01%, boric acid, sod. chloride, pot. chloride, disod. edetate, sod. carbonate/ml. Drop-Tainer Bot. 15 ml.
Use: Ocular decongestant.

2-NAPHTHACENECARBOXAMIDE, 4-(DIMETHYLAMINO)-1,-4,4a,5,5a,6,11,12a-OCTAHYDRO-3,5,6,10,12,12a-HEXAHYDROXY-6-METHYL-1,11-DIOXO-, MONOHYDROCHLORIDE, [4S-(4α,4aα,5α,5aα,6β,12aα)]-. Oxytetracycline Hydrochloride U.S.P. XXI.

2-NAPHTHACENECARBOXAMIDE, 4-(DIMETHYLAMINO)-1,4,4a,5,5a,6,11,12a-OCTAHYDRO-3,6,10,12,12a-PENTAHYDROXY-6-METHYL-1,11,-DIOXO-. Tetracycline, U.S.P. XXI.

2-NAPHTHACENECARBOXAMIDE, 4-(DIMETHYLAMINO)-1,4,4a,5,5a,6,11,12a-OCTAHYDRO-3,5,10,12,12a-PENTAHYDROXY-6-METHYL-1,11-DIOXO-, MONOHYDRATE. Doxycycline, U.S.P. XXI

2-NAPHTHACENECARBOXAMIDE,4,7-BIS-(DIMETHYLAMINO)-1,4,4a,5,5a,6,11,12a-OCTAHYDRO-3,10,12,12a-TETRAHYDROXY-1,11-DIOXO-, MONOHYDROCHLORIDE,[4S-(4α,4aα,5aα,12aα)]. Minocycline Hydrochloride, U.S.P. XXI.

1,4-NAPHTHALENEDIONE,2-METHYL-3-(3,7,11,15-TETRAMETHYL-2-HEXADECENYL)-,[R-[R*,R*-(E)]]-. Phytonadione, U.S.P. XXI.

1,3-NAPHTHALENEDISULFONIC ACID,6,-6′-[(3,3′-DIMETHYL[1,1′-BIPHENYL]-4,4′-DIYL)BIS(AZO)BIS 4-AMINO-5-HYDROXY]-, TETRASODIUM SALT Evans Blue, U.S.P. XXI.

NAPHTHALOPHOS. B.A.N. N-(Diethoxyphosphinyloxy)naphthalimide. Rametin.
Use: Anthelmintic, veterinary medicine.

NAPHTHONONE. (Robins) 2-(2-Hydroxynaphthy-l-)cyclohexanone.
Use: Antitussive.

O-2-NAPHTHYL m,N-DIMETHYLTHIO-CARBANILATE. Tolnaftate, U.S.P. XXI.

2-(1-NAPHTHYLMETHYL)-2-IMIDAZOLINE MONOHYDROCHLORIDE. Naphazoline Hydrochloride, U.S.P. XXI.

b-NAPHTHYL SALICYLATE. Betol, Naphthosalol, S naphthol.
Use: G.I. & G.U., antiseptic.

NAPHURIDE SODIUM. Suramin Sodium.

NAPLOPAN. (Vortech) D-pantothenyl alcohol 2 mg./ml. Vial 10 ml.
Use: Intestinal atony and distention.

NAPROSYN. (Syntex) Naproxen 250 mg./Tab. Bot. 100s, 500s. Blister pkg. 100s; 375 mg./Tab. Bot. 100s, 500s. Blister pkg. 100s; 500 mg./Tab. Bot. 100s, 500s.
Use: Non-steroid anti-inflammatory.

NAPROXEN, U.S.P. XXI. Tab., U.S.P. XXI. (+)-6-Methoxy-αmethyl-2-naphthaleneacetic acid. (+)-2-(6 Methoxy-2-naphthyl)propionic acid.
Use: Anti-inflammatory; analgesic; antipyretic.
See: Anaprox, Tab. (Syntex)
Naprosyn, Tab. (Syntex)

• **NAPROXEN SODIUM,** U.S.P. XXI. Tab., U.S.P. XXI.
Use: Anti-inflammatory, analgesic, antipyretic.

• **NAPROXOL.** USAN. (−)-6-Methoxy-β-methyl-2-naphthaleneethanol.
Use: Anti-inflammatory; analgesic; antipyretic.

APTRATE TABLETS. (Vortech) Pentaerythritol tetranitrate 10 mg., 20 mg./Tab. Alsc 20 mg., w/phenobarbital 15 mg./Tab. Bot. 1000s.
Use: Angina pectoris.

AQUA. (Schering) Trichlormethiazide 2 mg. or 4 mg./Tab. Bot. 100s, 1000s.
Use: Diuretic, hypotensive.
/Reserpine.
See: Naquival, Tab. (Schering)

AQUIVAL. (Schering) Trichlormethiazide (Naqua) 4 mg., reserpine 0.1 mg./Tab. Bot. 100s, 500s.
Use: Hypertension & diuretic.

NARANOL HCl. USAN. 8,9,10,11,11α,-12-Hexahydro-8,10-dimethyl-7 αH-naphtho[1′,2′:5,-6]pyrano-[3,2-c]pyridin-7-α-ol HCl.
Use: Tranquilizer.

NARASIN. USAN.
Use: Growth stimulant.

ARCAN. (Du Pont) Naloxone HCl. **Amp. 0.4 mg./ml.:** 1 ml. Box 10s. **Amp. 0.02 mg./ml.:** 2 ml. Box 10s.
Use: Narcotic antagonist.

ARCAN NEONATAL. (Du Pont) Naloxone HCl 0.02 mg./ml. Box 10s.
Use: Narcotic antagonist for reversal narcotic respiratory depression in neonate.

ARDELZINE. (Warner-Lambert) Psychic energizer; pending release.

ARDIL. (Parke-Davis) Phenelzine sulfate 15 mg./Tab. Bot. 100s.
Use: Anti-depressant.

ASACON. (CMC) Bot. 0.5 oz.
Use: Long acting nasal spray.

ASADENT. (Scherer) Sodium metaphosphate, glycerin, distilled water, dicalcium phosphate dihydrate, sodium carboxymethylcellulose, oil of spearmint, sodium benzoate, saccharin.
Use: Ingestible dentifrice.

ASAHIST B INJECTABLE. (Keene) Bromphpheniramine maleate 10 ml. Vial 10 ml. For IM, IV and subcutaneous administration.
Use: Decongestant and antihistamine.

ASAHIST CAPSULES. (Keene) Phenylpropanolamine HCl 40 mg., phenylephrine HCl 10 mg., chlorpheniramine maleate 12 mg./Cap. Bot. 100s.
Use: Decongestant, antihistaminic.

ASALCROM NASAL SOLUTION. (Fisons) Cromolyn sodium. Metered dose spray. Pkg. 13 ml.
Use: Anti-allergic rhinitis.

ASALIDE. (Syntex) Flunisolide 0.025% sol. Bot. 25 ml.
Use: Symptoms of seasonal and perennial rhinitis.

ASAL SALINE. (Winthrop Consumer Products) Nasal spray and drops. Sodium chloride 0.65% buffered w/phosphates and preserved . Bot. 15 ml. Spray Bot. 15 ml.
Use: Nasal moisturizer.

ASDRO. (Jenkins) Ephedrine sulfate 1%, chlorobutanol 5% with menthol, camphor, oil eucalyptus, thymol and oil red thyme. Bot. drop 0.5 oz., pt.
Use: Nose and throat drops or spray.

NASOPHEN. (Premo) Phenylephrine HCl 0.25%, 1%. Bot. 1 pt.
Use: Treatment of vasomotor rhinitis, sinusitis, allergic rhinitis, and as an adjuvant in the treatment of acute coryza.

NATABEC. (Parke-Davis) Vit. A 4000 I.U., D 400 I.U., B-1 3 mg., B-2 2 mg., B-6 3 mg., C 50 mg., B-12 5 mcg., niacinamide 10 mg., Ca carbonate 600 mg., ferrous sulfate 150 mg./Kapseal. Bot. 100s.
Use: Vitamin, iron & calcium deficiencies.

NATABEC-F.A.. (Parke-Davis) Same as Natabec, plus folic acid 0.1 mg./Kapseal. Bot. 100s.
Use: Dietary supplement during pregnancy and lactation.

NATABEC Rx. (Parke-Davis) Same as Natabec, plus folic acid 1 mg./Kapseal. Bot. 100s.

NATABEC WITH FLUORIDE. (Parke-Davis) Same formula as Natabec, plus fluoride 2.2 mg./Kapseal. Bot. 100s.
Use: Nutritional support.

NATACYN. (Alcon) Natamycin (5%) 50 mg./ml. Bot. 15 ml.
Use: Ophthalmic antifungal agent.

NATAFORT FILMSEAL. (Parke-Davis) Vit. A 6000 I.U., D 400 I.U., C 120 mg., B-1 3 mg., B-2 2 mg., B-6 15 mg., B-12 6 mcg., niacin 20 mg., Folic Acid 1 mg., E 30 I.U., Ca 350 mg., Mg. 100 mg., Zn 25 mg., Iodine 0.15 mg., Fe 65 mg./Tab. Bot. 100s.
Use: Prenatal vitamin and mineral supplement.

NATALINS. (Mead Johnson) Vit. A 8000 I.U., D 400 I.U., E 30 I.U., C 90 mg., B-1 1.7 mg., B-2 2.0 mg., B-6 4.0 mg., B-12 8 mcg., niacin 20 mg., folic acid 0.8 mg., iodine 150 mcg., Ca 200 mg., Fe 45 mg., Mg 100 mg./Tab. Bot. 100s, 1000s. Drum 36,000.
Use: Multivitamin and mineral supplement for pregnant or lactating women.

NATALINS RX. (Mead Johnson) Vit. A 8,000 I.U., D 400 I.U., E 30 I.U., C 90 mg., B-1 2.55 mg., B-2 3.0 mg., B-6 10 mg., B-12 8 mcg., niacin 20 mg., folic acid 1.0 mg., pantothenic acid 15 mg., biotin 0.05 mg., Ca 200 mg., Fe 60 mg., Mg 100 mg., Cu 2 mg., Zn 15.0 mg., iodine 150 mcg./Tab. Bot. 100s, 1000s.
Use: Multivitamin and mineral supplement for pregnant or lactating women.

• **NATAMYCIN,** U.S.P. XXI. Ophth. Susp., U.S.P. XXI. An antibiotic produced by *Streptomyces natalensis.* Pimafucin.
Use: Antibiotic.

NATA-PAR. (Pharmics) Ferrous fumarate 200 mg., C 75 mg., cal. carbonate 450 mg., A 4000 I.U., D 400 I.U., B-6 5 mg., B-1 5 mg., B-2 2 mg., niacinamide 15 mg., B-12 2.5 mcg., iodine 0.15 mg., K 0.05 mg., Mn 0.5 mg., Cu 0.25 mg., Zn 0.5 mg., Mg 1 mg./Cap. Bot. 100s, 1000s.
Use: Pregnancy and lactation.

NATAPLEX-C. (Galen) Vit. A 5000 u., D 400 u., B-1 3 mg., B-2 2 mg., B-6 e mg., C 100 mg., B-12 3 mcg., niacinamide 10 mg., folic acid 0.05 mg., Ca 575 mg., ferrous fumarate 100 mg., K.I. 0.1 mg., Mn 1 mg., Mg 1 mg., Zn 1 mg./Tab. Bot. 100s, 1000s.
Use: Vitamin-mineral supplementation during pregnancy and lactation.

NATA-SAN. (Sandia) Vit. A 4000 I.U., D 400 I.U., B-1 5 mg., B-2 4 mg., B-6 10 mg., nicotinic acid 10 mg., Vit. C 100 mg., B-12 activity 5 mcg., ferrous fumarate 200 mg. (elemental iron 65 mg.), cal. carbonate 500 mg. (calcium 196 mg.), copper (sulfate) 0.5 mg., magnesium (sulfate) 0.1 mg., manganese (sulfate) 0.1 mg., potassium (sulfate) 0.1 mg., zinc (sulfate) 0.5 mg./Tab. Bot. 100s, 1000s.

NATA-SAN F.A. (Sandia) Vit. A 4000 I.U., D 400 I.U., B-1 5 mg., B-2 4 mg., B-6 10 mg., nicotinic acid 10 mg., Vit. C 100 mg., B-12 activity 5 mcg., folic acid 1 mg., iron 65 mg., calcium 200 mg., copper (sulfate) 0.5 mg., magnesium (sulfate) 0.1 mg., manganese (sulfate) 0.1 mg., potassium (sulfate) 0.1 mg., zinc (sulfate) 0.5 mg./Tab. Bot. 100s, 1000s.

NATODINE. (Faraday) Iodine in organic form as found in kelp. 1 mg./Tab. Bot. 100s, 250s.

NATRICO. (Drug Products) Pot. nitrate 2 gr., Sod. nitrite 1 gr., nitroglycerin 0.25 gr., crataegus oxycantha 0.25 gr./Pulvoid. Bot. 100s, 1000s.
Use: Hypertension.

NATROGESTIVE. (Wolins) Sodium bicarbonate 10 gr., papain 0.5 gr., ginger, pancreatin/Tab. Bot. 1000s.

NATURACIL. (Mead Johnson) Psyllium seed husks 3.4 Gm./2 pieces Carton 24s, 40s.
Use: Bulk forming laxative.

NATUR-AID. (Scott/Cord) Lactose w/pectin-and Carob-lemon juice. Pow. 90%. Bot. 8 oz.
Use: Increase in normal intestinal flora.

NATURAL DIURETIC WATER TABLET. (Amlab) Buchu leaves 1 gr., uva ursi 1 gr., trilicum 1 gr., parsley 1 gr., juniper berries 1 gr., asparagus 1 gr., alfalfa powder 1 gr./Tab. Bot. 100s.
Use: Herbal diuretic.

NATURAL THERATAB. (Vortech) Bot. 30s, 100s.
Use: Natural & organic vitamins plus minerals.

NATURAL VITAMIN A IN OIL.
See: Oleovitamin A, U.S.P.

NATUR-"C" TABLETS. (Quality Generics) Vit. C 300 mg. Chewable Tab. Bot. 100s, 250s.
Use: Nutritional supplement.

NATURE CAL-D TABLETS. (Image) Bot. 100s.
Use: Supplement.

NATURE'S AID LAXATIVE TABS. (Walgreen) Docusate sodium 100 mg., yellow phenolphthalein 65 mg./Tab. Bot. 60s.
Use: Mild laxative & stool softener.

NATURE'S PANRAY BEE POLLEN TABLETS. (Panray) Bee pollen 500 mg./Tab. Bot. 100s.
Use: Dietary supplement.

NATURE'S PANTRY ROSE HIPS TABLETS. (Panray) Vitamin C from rose hips 500 mg., 100 mg./Tab. Bot. 100s.
Use: Dietary supplement.

NATURE'S REMEDY. (Norcliff Thayer) Aloe 100 mg., cascara sagrada 150 mg./Film coated Tab.; Foil backed blister pkg. Box 12s, 30s, 60s.
Use: Laxative.

NATURETIN. (Squibb) Bendroflumethiazide.**2.5** mg./Tab. Bot. 100s. 5 mg./Tab. Bot. 100s, 1000s. **10 mg.**/Tab. Bot. 100s.
Use: Diuretic, hypotensive.

NATURETIN W/K. (Squibb) Bendroflumethiazide 5 mg., potassium chloride 500 mg./Tab. Bot. 100s.
Use: Diuretic and hypotensive.

NATURIL. (Kenyon) Pow. ext. uva ursi 0.5 gr., pow. ext. buchu leaves 0.5 gr., pow. ext. corn silk 0.5 gr., pow. ext. juniper 0.25 gr., caffeine 0.25 gr./Tab. Bot. 100s, 1000s.

NATUR-LAX TABLETS. (Faraday) Rhubarb root, cap. aloes, ext. cascara sagrada, mandrake root, parsley, carrot/Tab. Protein coated tablets. Bot. 100s.
Use: Vegetable laxative.

NAUS-A-TORIES. (Table Rock) Pyrilamine maleate 2[illegible] mg., secobarbital 30 mg./Supp. Box 12s.
Use: Prevention or control of nausea.

NAUZINE. (Century) Dimenhydrinate 50 mg., propylene glycol 50%, benzyl alcohol 5%/cc. Inj. vial 10 cc.

NAVANE. (Roerig) Thiothixene. **Caps.** 1 mg., 2 mg., [illegible] mg. or 10 mg./Cap. Bot. 100s, 1000s. Unit dose 100s. **Liq.** 5 mg./cc. Bot. 1 oz., 4 oz. **Intramuscular solution.** Vial 2 mg./ml. Pkg. 10s.
Use: Antipsychotic agent.

NAVANE INTRAMUSCULAR FOR INJECTION. (Roerig) Thiothixene HCl 5 mg./ml. Liophylized for reconstitution with 2.2 ml. sterile water. Vial 10 cc. Pkg. 10 vials.
Use: Antipsychotic agent.

NAVANE ORAL CONCENTRATE. (Roerig) Thiothixene HCl 5 mg./ml. Bot. 1 oz., 4 oz. x/calibrated dropper.
Use: Antipsychotic.

NAVIDREX. Cyclopenthiazide, B.A.N.

NAVIDRIX (NAVIDREX, CYCLOPENTHIAZIDE). Cyclopenthiazide. 3-Cyclopentylmethyl derivative [illegible] hydrochlorothiazide.
Use: Oral diuretic.

NAVSEAST. (Eastwood) Tab. Bot. 100s.

N.B.P. OINTMENT. (Bowman) Bacitracin zinc 400 u., neomycin sulfate 5 mg., polymyxin B sulfate 10,00[illegible] u./Gm. Tube ⅛ oz., 0.5 oz.
Use: Topical antibiotic.

N.B.P. OINTMENT. (Forest) Neomycin, bacitracin, polymixin ointment. Tube ⅛ oz., 0.5 oz.
Use: Antibiotic ointment.

N-CHLORO COMPOUND ANTISEPTICS.
See: Antiseptic, N-Chloro Compounds.

N D CLEAR. (Seatrace) Chlorpheniramine maleate 8 mg., pseudoephedrine HCl 120 mg./T.D. Cap. Bot. 100s, 1000s.
Use: Antihistaminic, nasal decongestant.

N-DIETHYL META-TOLUAMIDE.
W/Red Veterinary Petrolatum.
See: RV Pellent, Oint. (Elder)

ND-GESIC. (Hyrex) Acetaminophen 300 mg., pyrilamin[illegible] maleate 12.5 mg., chlorpheniramine maleate 2 mg. phenindamine tartrate 5 mg./Tab. Bot. 100s, 1000s, 5000s.
Use: Analgesic, antihistaminic, vasoconstrictor.

ND-HIST. (Hyrex) Chlorpheniramine maleate 12 mg phenylpropanolamine HCl 40 mg., phenylephrine HCl 10 mg./long acting Cap. Bot. 100s,
Use: Antihistaminic/decongestant.

DNA. (Wampole-Zeus) Anti-native DNA test by IFA. Tests 48s.
Use: Confirmatory test for active SLE.

D-STAT. (Hyrex) Brompheniramine maleate 10 mg./ml. Vial 10 ml.
Use: Antihistaminic.

EALBARBITONE. B.A.N. 5-Allyl-5-neopentylbarbituric acid. Censedal; Nevental
Use: Hypnotic; sedative.

EBCIN. (Dista) Tobramycin sulfate. **Inj.** 80 mg./2 ml. Vial 2 ml. Box 1s, Traypak 25s; 1.2 Gm./30 ml. Vial 30 ml. 6s; 1.2 Gm./40 ml. Vial 40 ml. Traypak 6s. **Pediatric.** 20 mg./2 ml. Vial 2 ml. **Hyporets.** 80 mg./2 ml., 60 mg./1.5 ml. Box 24s.
Use: Antibiotic.

NEBRAMYCIN. USAN. A complex of antibiotic substances produced by *Streptomyces tenebrarius.*
Use: Antibacterial.

EBU-PREL. (Mahon) Isoproterenol sulf. 0.4%, phenylephrine HCl 2%, propylene glycol 10%. Liq. Vial 10 cc.
Use: Bronchial asthma.

ECHLORIN. (Interstate) Chlorpheniramine 5 mg., phenylpropanolamine 40 mg., penylephrine 20 mg., phenyltoloxamine 15 mg./Tab. Bot. 100s.
Use: Antihistaminic, decongestant.

NEDOCROMIL. USAN.
Use: Anti-allergic.

NEDOCROMIL SODIUM. USAN.
Use: Anti-allergic.

NEFAZODONE HYDROCHLORIDE. USAN. A Bristol Myers investigative drug.
Use: Antidepressant.

EFOPAM. B.A.N. 3,4,5,6-Tetrahydro-5-methyl-1-phenyl-1H-2,5-benzoxazocine.
Use: Muscle relaxant.

NEFOPAM HCl. USAN. 3,4,5,6-Tetrahydro-5-methyl-1-phenyl-1H-2,5-benzoxazocine HCl.
Use: Muscle relaxant.

EFROLAN. Clorexolone, B.A.N.

EGACIDE. (Winthrop Products) Nalidixic acid.
Use: Urinary & intestinal infections.

EGASOL SOLUTION. (O'Leary) Glyceryl ester of para-aminobenzoic acid in aq. sol., 50% isopropyl alcohol. Bot. 2 fl. oz.
Use: Sun screen.

EGATAN. (Savage) Negatol 45% in aq. sol. Bot. w/applicator 0.25 oz.

EGGRAM. (Winthrop-Breon) Nalidixic acid 1 Gm./Caplet Bot. 100s, Unit Dose Pack 100s; 500 mg./Cap. Bot. 56s, 500s, 1000s, Unit Dose Pack 100s; 250 mg./Cap. Bot. 56s, Susp. 250 mg./5 ml. Bot. pt.
Use: Treatment of urinary infections.

EGUVON. Metriphonate, B.A.N.

EISSERIA CATARRHALIS.

EMAZINE. 3-(p-Chlorophenyl)-4-imino-2-oxo-1-imidazolidine acetonitrile. Under study.
Use: Anti-inflammatory.

EMBUTAL ELIXIR. (Abbott) Pentobarbital 18.2 mg./5 ml. Alcohol 18% Bot. pt., gal.

EMBUTAL SODIUM. (Abbott) Pentobarbital sodium. **Amp.:** (100 mg./2 ml. Box 25s.) **Vial:** 50 mg./ml. Vial 20 ml., 50 ml. **Cap.:** (30 mg.) Bot. 100s, (50 mg.) Bot. 100s, 500s, 1000s. (100 mg.) Bot. 100s, 500s, 1000s, Strip Pak 100s. Abbo-Pac 100 (10 × 10). **Supp.:** (0.5 gr., 1 gr., 2 gr., 3 gr.) Box 12s.
Use: Sedative and hypnotic.

NEOARSPHENAMINE. Sod. 3,3′-diamino-4,4′-dihydroxyarsenobenzene-N-methanal sulfoxylate. (Neosalvarsan, Neoarsenobenzol).

NEO-BENZ-ALL. (Xttrium) Benzalkonium Cl 20.1%. Packet 25 ml. 15s. to make gal. of 1:750 soln. Also Aqueous Neo-Benz-All 1:750 soln. Packet 20 ml., 50s.
Use: Antiseptic, germicidal.

NEOBIOTIC. (Pfipharmecs) Neomycin sulf. 500 mg./Tab. Bot. 100s.
Use: Antibiotic.

NEO-BRONCHOID TABLETS. (Moore Kirk) Histamor (brand of pyrilamine maleate) 10 mg., phenylephrine HCl 2 mg., potassium guaiacolsulfonate 2 gr., ammonium chloride 2 gr., ipecac ⅛ gr./Tab. Bot. 1000s.
Use: Colds, coughs, allergic rhinitis and expectorant.

NEOCALAMINE. (Various Mfr.) Red ferric oxide 30 Gm., yellow ferric oxide 40 Gm., zinc oxide 930 Gm.
Use: Astringent and mild antiseptic.

NEO-CALGLUCON. (Sandoz) Glubionate calcium 1.8 benzoic acid 5.0 mg./5 ml. Syr. Bot. pt.
Use: Calcium therapy.

NEOCASTADERM. (Lannett) Resorcin, boric acid, acetone. Bot. 1 oz., 4 oz., 16 oz.
Use: Treatment of fungal infections.

NEOCET. (Vale) Pyrilamine maleate 25 mg., acetaminophen 130 mg., salicylamide 130 mg./Tab. Bot. 100s, 1000s, 5000s.
Use: Antihistaminic and analgesic.

NEOCET PEDIATRIC. (Vale) Pyrilamine maleate 12.5 mg., acetaminophen 65 mg./Tab. Bot. 100s, 1000s, 5000s.
Use: Antihistamine, analgesic.

NEO-CHOLEX. (Lafayette) Fat emulsion containing 40%/w/v pure vegetable oil. Bot. 60 cc.
Use: Produce maximum cholecystokinetic activity in roentgen study.

NEOCINCHOPHEN, B.A.N. Ethyl 6-methyl-2-phenylquinolin-4-carboxylate. Novatophan.
Use: Orally; analgesic, antipyretic & in gout.

NEO-COBEFRIN. levo-Nordefrin. 1-2, 4-dihydroxyphenyl-3-hydroxy-2-isopropylamine.
Use: Vasoconstrictor.

NEO-CORT-DOME. (Miles Pharm) Hydrocortisone alcohol 0.25%, 0.5%, or 1% w/neomycin 5 mg./Gm. Cream base: glyceryl monostearate, cetyl alcohol, lanolin, isopropyl palmitate, propylene glycol, methyl and propyl parabens. Lotion base: isopropyl myristate, isopropyl palmitate, cetyl alcohol, polyethylene glycol ricinoleate, white petrolatum, thimerosal. 0.5% Tube 0.5 oz., Dispensajar 1 oz., 4 oz., 1% Tube 0.5 oz. Lot. 0.5% Bot. 1 oz.
Use: Anti-inflammatory.

NEO-CORT-DOME, OTIC. (Miles Pharm) Hydrocortisone alcohol 10 mg., neomycin sulfate 5 mg., acetic acid 2%, vehicle buffered to the pH range of

normal skin w/glyceryl monostearate, stearic acid, propylene glycol, potassium sorbate, methyl and propyl parabens, sodium acetate. Bot. 10 cc. w/dropper.
Use: External otitis.

NEO-CORTEF CREAM. (Upjohn) Hydrocortisone acetate 10 mg. (1%), neomycin sulfate 5 mg./Gm. w/methylparaben 1 mg., butylparaben 4 mg., polysorbate 80, propylene glycol, cetyl palmitate, glyceryl monostearate, and emulsifier/Gm. When necessary, pH adjusted with sulfuric acid. Tube 20 Gm.
Use: Allergic & inflammatory skin conditions.

NEO-CORTEF OINTMENT. (Upjohn) **0.5%:** Hydrocortisone acetate 5 mg., neomycin sulfate 5 mg., methylparaben 0.2 mg., butylparaben 1.8 mg. in a bland base of white petrolatum, microcrystalline wax, mineral oil, and cholesterol/Gm. Tube 20 Gm. **1%:** Hydrocortisone acetate 10 mg., neomycin sulfate 5 mg./Gm. Oint., Tube 5 & 20 Gm. **2.5%:** Hydrocortisone acetate 25 mg., neomycin sulfate 5 mg./Gm., Oint., Tube 5 & 20 Gm.
Use: Broad range antibiotic w/anti-inflammatory effect.

NEO-CORTEF OPHTHALMIC SUSPENSION, 0.5%. (Upjohn) Hydrocortisone acetate 5 mg./ml. (0.5%), neomycin sulfate 5 mg./ml., myristyl-gamma-picolinium chloride, sodium citrate, polyethylene glycol 3350, povidone, sodium hydroxide and/or hydrochloric acid. In 5 ml. Drop Bot.
Use: Ophthalmic anti-inflammatory and antibacterial.

NEO-CORT TOP OINTMENT. (Standex) Neomycin sulfate 0.5%, hydrocortisone 1% Tube 0.5 oz.

NEO-CULTOL. (Fisons) Refined mineral oil jelly. Chocolate flavored. Bot. 6 oz.
Use: Laxative.

NEOCURB. (Pasadena Research) Phendimetrazine tartrate 35 mg./Tab. Bot. 100s, 1000s.
Use: Anorexient.

NEO-CUTONE. (Sutliff & Case) Pyrilamine maleate 1%, calamine 8%, benzocaine 3%. Lot., Container 2 oz., 1 pt., 1 gal.
Use: Topically, antihistaminic w/local anesthetic.

NEOCYLATE. (Central) Pot. salicylate 280 mg., aminobenzoic acid 250 mg./Tab. Bot. 100s, 1000s.
Use: Analgesic in rheumatic conditions.

NEOCYTEN. (Central) Orphenadrine citrate 30 mg., sodium bisulfate 1 mg., sodium Cl 2.9 mg., benzethonium Cl 0.1 mg./ml. Vial 10 ml.
Use: Skeletal muscle relaxant, antihistaminic.

NeoDECADRON OCUMETER OPHTHALMIC SOLUTION. (Merck Sharp & Dohme) Dexamethasone sod. phosphate equiv. to 1 mg. dexamethasone phosphate, neomycin sulfate equiv. to 3.5 mg. neomycin base/ml. w/creatinine, sod. citrate, sod. borate, polysorbate 80, disodium edetate, hydrochloric acid, sod. bisulfite 0.1%, benzalkonium chloride 0.02% and water for injection. q.s. 1 ml. Ocumeter ophthalmic dispenser 5 ml.
Use: Anti-inflammatory, antibacterial.

NeoDECADRON OPHTHALMIC OINTMENT. (Merck Sharp & Dohme) Dexamethasone sod. phosphate equiv. to 0.5 mg. dexamethasone phosphate, neomycin sulfate equiv. to 3.5 mg. neomycin base/Gm. w/white petrolatum and mineral oil. Tube 3.5 Gm.
Use: Anti-inflammatory, antibacterial.

NeoDECADRON TOPICAL CREAM. (Merck Sharp & Dohme) Dexamethasone sod. phosphate equiv. to 1 mg. dexamethasone phosphate, neomycin sulf. equiv. to 3.5 mg. neomycin base/Gm. w/stearyl alcohol, cetyl alcohol, mineral oil, polyoxyl 40 stearate, sorbitol soln, methyl polysilicone emul., creatinine, disodium edetate, sod. citrate, sod. hydroxide to adjust pH, purified water, methylparaben 0.15%, sod. bisulfite 0.25%, sorbic acid 0.1%. Tube 15 Gm., 30 Gm.
Use: Anti-inflammatory, antibacterial.

NEODECYLLIN. (Penick) Neomycin undecylinate.
Use: Antibacterial & antifungal.

NEO-DELTA-CORTEF OINTMENT. (Upjohn) Prednisolone acetate 5 mg., neomycin sulfate 5 mg., methylparaben 0.2 mg., butylparaben 1.8 mg./Gm., base of white petrolatum, microcrystalline wax, mineral oil, cholesterol. Tube 20 Gm.
Use: Topically, allergic dermatitis & inflammatory skin diseases.

NEO-DELTA-CORTEF OPHTHALMIC OINTMENT. (Upjohn) **0.25%:** Prednisolone acetate 2.5 mg. neomycin sulfate 5 mg./Gm. w/anhydrous lanolin, mineral oil, white petrolatum, chlorobutanol 0.65%. Tube 3.5 Gm. w/applicator tip.
Use: Eye infections.

NEO-DELTA-CORTEF OPHTHALMIC SUSPENSION (Upjohn) Prednisolone acetate 2.5 mg., neomycin sulfate 5 mg./ml. w/myristyl-gamma-picolinium chloride, sod. citrate, polyethylene glycol 3350 povidone, sod. hydroxide and/or hydrochloric acid/cc. Dropper Bot. 5 ml.
Use: Treatment of infections of the eye.

NEODEX SYRUP. (U.S. Ethicals) Dextromethorphan HBr, chlorpheniramine maleate, phenylephrine HCl, guaifenesin. Bot. 120 ml., 3840 ml.
Use: Antitussive, nasal decongestant, expectorant.

NEODRENAL.
See: Isoproterenol

NEO-DURABOLIC. (Hauck) Nandrolone decanoate. 5[illegible] mg./ml. Vial 2 ml. 200 mg./ml. Vial 1 ml.
Use: Androgen; anabolic steroid.

NEO-FLO. (Softcon) Boric acid, sodium chloride, potassium chloride and sodium carbonate preserved with benzalkonium chloride 1:15,000. Plastic squeeze bot. 30 cc., 110 cc.
Use: Ophthalmic irrigating solution.

NEO FRANOL. (Winthrop Products) Theophylline monohydrate.
Use: Bronchodilator, sedative spasmolytic.

NEOGEN. (Premo) Theophylline 3 gr., aminophylline 4 gr., ephedrine sulfate ⅜ gr., pentobarbital 1 gr., benzocaine 3 gr./Supp. Also available 0.5 strength. Box 12s.

Use: Bronchodilator, mild sedative, local anesthesia.

EO-GENIC. (Kay) Potassium estrone sulfate 1 mg., estrogenic substance 2 mg., thimerosal (preservative) 0.01%, polysorbate-80 (stabilizer) 0.15%/ml. Vial 10 cc.
Use: Menopausal syndrome, conditions involving deficiency in vaginal epithelium.

EO-GERASTAN. (Standex) Pentylenetetrazol 100 mg., nicotinic acid (niacin) 50 mg., glutamic acid 100 mg./Tab. Bot. 100s.
Use: Geriatric stimulant.

EOLAX. (Central) Docusate sodium 50 mg., dehydrocholic acid 240 mg./Tab. Bot. 100s, 1000s. Unit dose 100s.
Use: Choleretic laxative and fecal softener.

EOLOID. (Lederle) Castor oil 36.4% (emulsified) (w/w). Bot. 4 oz. Unit dose pack, 12×4 oz.
Use: Orally; laxative.

EO-MEDROL ACETATE TOPICAL. (Upjohn) Methylprednisolone acetate 2.5 mg. or 10 mg., neomycin sulfate 5 mg., methylparaben 4 mg., butylparaben 3 mg./Gm., Tube 7.5 Gm., 30 Gm.
Use: Treatment of skin lesions.

EO-MERCAZOLE. Carbimazole, B.A.N.

EO-MIST NASAL SPRAY. (A.P.C.) Phenylephrine HCl 0.50%, cetalkonium chloride 0.02%. Spray Bot. 20 cc.
Use: Decongestant, antiseptic.

EO-MIST PEDIATRIC 0.25% NASAL SPRAY. (A.P.C.) Phenylephrine HCl 0.25%, cetalkonium chloride 0.02%. Squeeze Bot. 20 cc.
Use: Decongestant, antiseptic.

EOMIXIN. (Mallard) Zinc bacitracin 400 u., neomycin 3.5 mg., polymyxin B sulfate 5,000 u. in petrolatum base/Gm. Tube 0.5 oz.

EOMYCIN. B.A.N. An antibiotic produced by a strain of *Streptomyces fradiae.* Expedil, Mycifradin, Myciguent, Neomin, Nivemycin [sulfate].

EOMYCIN BASE.
Use: Antibiotic.
/Combinations.
See: Biotic, Oint. (Scrip)
Biotic-Ophth W/HC, Oint. (Scrip)
Biotic-Opth W/HC, Oint. (Scrip)
Bro-Parin, Susp. (Riker)
Maxitrol, Oint., Susp. (Alcon)
Mycolog, Cream, Oint. (Squibb)
My Cort Otic, Ear Drops (Scrip)
Necort A.V.P., Oint. (A.V.P. Pharm.)
Neo-Cort-Dome, Cream, Lot. (Miles Pharm)
Neotal, Oint. (Mallard)
Neothalidine, Granules (Merck Sharp & Dohme)

EOMYCIN-HYDROCORTISONE CREAM. (Day-Baldwin) Neomycin 5 mg./Gm., hydrocortisone 0.5%. Tube 0.5 oz., 1 oz. W/hydrocortisone 1%. Tube 0.5 oz., 1 oz.
Use: Antibiotic, anti-inflammatory.

EOMYCIN-HYDROCORTISONE OINTMENT. (Day-Baldwin) Neomycin 5 mg./Gm., hydrocortisone 0.5%. Tube 1 oz. w/hydrocortisone 1%, 20 Gm., 1 oz.
Use: Antibiotic, anti-inflammatory.

• **NEOMYCIN PALMITATE.** USAN.
Use: Antibiotic.
See: Biozyme, Oint. (Armour)

• **NEOMYCIN AND POLYMYXIN B SULFATES, BACITRACIN, AND HYDROCORTISONE ACETATE OINTMENT,** U.S.P. XXI.
Use: Antibiotic, antifungal.

• **NEOMYCIN AND POLYMYXIN B SULFATES, BACITRACIN, AND HYDROCORTISONE ACETATE OPHTHALMIC OINTMENT,** U.S.P. XXI.
Use: Antibiotic, antifungal.

• **NEOMYCIN AND POLYMYXIN B SULFATES AND BACITRACIN OINTMENT,** U.S.P. XXI.
Use: Antibiotic.

• **NEOMYCIN AND POLYMYXIN B SULFATES AND BACITRACIN OPHTHALMIC OINTMENT,** U.S.P. XXI.
Use: Antibiotic.

• **NEOMYCIN AND POLYMYXIN B SULFATES, BACITRACIN ZINC, AND HYDROCORTISONE ACETATE OPHTHALMIC OINTMENT,** U.S.P. XXI.

• **NEOMYCIN AND POLYMYXIN B SULFATES, BACITRACIN ZINC, AND HYDROCORTISONE OINTMENT,** U.S.P. XXI.
Use: Antibiotic, anti-inflammatory.

• **NEOMYCIN AND POLYMIXIN B SULFATES, BACITRACIN ZINC, AND HYDROCORTISONE OPHTHALMIC OINTMENT,** U.S.P. XXI.
Use: Antibiotic, anti-inflammatory.

• **NEOMYCIN AND POLYMYXIN B SULFATES AND BACITRACIN ZINC OINTMENT.** U.S.P. XXI.
Use: Local anti-infective.

• **NEOMYCIN AND POLYMYXIN B SULFATES AND BACITRACIN ZINC OPHTHALMIC OINTMENT,** U.S.P. XXI.
Use: Ophthalmic antibiotic.

• **NEOMYCIN AND POLYMYXIN B SULFATES AND BACITRACIN ZINC TOPICAL AEROSOL,** U.S.P. XXI.
Use: Antibiotic.

• **NEOMYCIN AND POLYMYXIN B SULFATES AND BACITRACIN ZINC TOPICAL POWDER,** U.S.P. XXI.
Use: Antibiotic.

• **NEOMYCIN AND POLYMYXIN B SULFATES AND DEXAMETHASONE OPHTHALMIC OINTMENT,** U.S.P. XXI.
Use: Antibiotic, anti-inflammatory.

• **NEOMYCIN AND POLYMYXIN B SULFATES AND DEXAMETHASONE OPHTHALMIC SUSPENSION.** U.S.P. XXI.
Use: Antibiotic, anti-inflammatory.

• **NEOMYCIN AND POLYMYXIN B SULFATES AND GRAMICIDIN CREAM,** U.S.P. XXI.
Use: Antibiotic.

• **NEOMYCIN AND POLYMYXIN B SULFATES, GRAMICIDIN, AND HYDROCORTISONE ACETATE CREAM,** U.S.P. XXI.
Use: Antibiotic, anti-inflammatory.

• **NEOMYCIN AND POLYMYXIN B SULFATES AND GRAMICIDIN OPHTHALMIC SOLUTION,** U.S.P. XXI.
Use: Antibiotic.

• **NEOMYCIN AND POLYMYXIN B SULFATES AND HYDROCORTISONE ACETATE OPHTHALMIC SUSPENSION,** U.S.P. XXI.
Use: Antibiotic, anti-inflammatory.

• **NEOMYCIN AND POLYMIXIN B SULFATES AND HYDROCORTISONE OPHTHALMIC SUSPENSION,** U.S.P. XXI.
Use: Antibiotic, anti-inflammatory.

• **NEOMYCIN AND POLYMYXIN B SULFATES AND HYDROCORTISONE OTIC SOLUTION,** U.S.P. XXI.
Use: Antibiotic, anti-inflammatory.

• **NEOMYCIN AND POLYMYXIN B SULFATES AND HYDROCORTISONE OTIC SUSPENSION,** U.S.P. XXI.
Use: Antibiotic, anti-inflammatory.

• **NEOMYCIN AND POLYMYXIN B SULFATES OPHTHALMIC OINTMENT,** U.S.P. XXI.
Use: Antibiotic.

• **NEOMYCIN AND POLYMYXIN B SULFATES AND PREDNISOLONE ACETATE OPHTHALMIC SUSPENSION,** U.S.P. XXI.
Use: Antibiotic, anti-inflammatory.

• **NEOMYCIN AND POLYMYXIN B SULFATES SOLUTION FOR IRRIGATION.** U.S.P. XXI.
Use: Irrigating solution; topical antibacterial.

• **NEOMYCIN AND POLYMYXIN B SULFATES OPHTHALMIC SOLUTION.** U.S.P. XXI.
Use: Ophthalmic antibiotic.

• **NEOMYCIN SULFATE,** U.S.P. XXI. Cream, Oint., Ophth. Oint., Oral Soln., Sterile, Tab., U.S.P. XXI.
An antibiotic from *Streptomyces fradiae*: (Upjohn) Pow. micronized for compounding Bot. 100 Gm.
Use: Antibacterial.
See: Mycifradin Sulfate, Tab., Sol. (Upjohn)
Myciguent, Oint., & Ophth. Oint., Cream (Upjohn)
Neobiotic, Tab. (Pfizer)

W/Combinations.
See: Aural Acute (Saron)
Bacitracin Neomycin, Oint. (Various Mfr.)
Baximin, Oint. (Quality Generics)
Biotic, Oint. (Scrip)
Biotres HC, Oint. (Central)
B.N.P. Ophthalmic Oint. (Reid-Provident)
B.P.N., Oint. (Norwich)
Bro-Parin, Otic Susp. (Riker)
Coracin, Oint. (Mallard)
Cordran-N, Oint., Lot. (Dista)
Cor-Oticin, Liq. (Maurry)
Cortisporin, Prep. (Burroughs Wellcome)
Duo-Aqua-Drin, Loz. (McKesson)
Epimycin A, Oint. (Delta)
Hi-Cort N, Cream (Blaine)
Hysoquen Oint. (Reid-Provident)
Maxitrol, Ophth., Oint., Susp. (Alcon)
Mity-Mycin Ointment (Reid-Provident)
Mycifradin Sulfate Sterile, Vial (Upjohn)
Mycitracin, Oint., Ophth. Oint. (Upjohn)
My-Cort, Oint., Cream, Sol. (Scrip)
Necort, Oint. (A.V.P.)
Neo-Cort Dome, Otic Sol. (Miles Pharm)
Neo-Cortef, Preps. (Upjohn)
Neo Cort Top, Oint. (Standex)
Neo-Decadron, Ophth., Topical. (Merck Sharp Dohme)
Neo-Delta-Cortef, Preps. (Upjohn)
Neogel W/Sulfa, Tab. (Vortech)
Neo-Hydeltrasol, Oint., Sol. (Merck Sharp Dohme)
Neo-Hytone, Cream (Dermik)
Neo-Medrol, Preps (Upjohn)
Neo-Nysta-Cort, Oint. (Miles Pharm)
Neo-Oxylone, Oint. (Upjohn)
Neo-Polycin, Ophthal., Sol., Oint. (Merrell Dow)
Neosone, Ophth. Oint. (Upjohn)
Neosporin, Prep. (Burroughs Wellcome)
Neo-Thrycex, Oint. (Commerce)
Otobione Sol. (Schering)
Otoreid-HC, Liq. (Reid-Provident)
P.B.N., Oint. (Jenkins)
Spectrocin, Oint. (Squibb)
Statrol Sterile Ophthalmic Ointment (Alcon)
Tigo, Oint. (Burlington)
Tri-Bow Oint. (Bowman)
Tricidin, Oint. (Amlab)
Trimixin, Oint. (Hance)
Triple Antibiotic Ointment, Tube (Kenyon)

• **NEOMYCIN SULFATE AND BACITRACIN OINTMENT,** U.S.P. XXI.
Use: Antibiotic.

• **NEOMYCIN SULFATE AND BACITRACIN ZINC OINTMENT,** U.S.P. XXI.
Use: Antibiotic.

• **NEOMYCIN SULFATE AND DEXAMETHASONE SODIUM PHOSPHATE CREAM,** U.S.P. XXI.
Use: Antibiotic, anti-inflammatory.

• **NEOMYCIN SULFATE AND DEXAMETHASONE SODIUM PHOSPHATE OPHTHALMIC OINTMENT** U.S.P. XXI.
Use: Antibiotic, anti-inflammatory.

• **NEOMYCIN SULFATE AND DEXAMETHASONE SODIUM PHOSPHATE OPHTHALMIC SOLUTION,** U.S.P. XXI.
Use: Antibiotic, anti-inflammatory.

• **NEOMYCIN SULFATE AND FLUOCINOLONE ACETONIDE CREAM,** U.S.P. XXI.
Use: Antibiotic, anti-inflammatory.

• **NEOMYCIN SULFATE AND FLUOROMETHOLONE OINTMENT,** U.S.P. XXI.
Use: Antibiotic, anti-inflammatory.

NEOMYCIN SULFATE AND FLURANDRENOLIDE, U.S.P. XXI. Cream, Oint., U.S.P. XXI.
Use: Antibiotic, anti-inflammatory.
See: Cordran Prods. (Dista)

• **NEOMYCIN SULFATE AND GRAMICIDIN OINTMENT,** U.S.P. XXI.
Use: Antibiotic

NEOMYCIN SULFATE AND HYDROCORTISONE, U.S.P. XXI. Cream, Oint., U.S.P. XXI.
Use: Antibiotic, anti-inflammatory.

• **NEOMYCIN SULFATE AND HYDROCORTISONE ACETATE,** U.S.P. XXI. Cream, Lotion, Oint., Ophth. Oint., Ophth. Susp., U.S.P. XXI.
Use: Antibiotic, anti-inflammatory.

NEOMYCIN SULFATE AND METHYLPREDNISOLONE ACETATE CREAM, U.S.P. XXI.
Use: Antibiotic, anti-inflammatory.

NEOMYCIN SULFATE AND PREDNISOLONE ACETATE OINTMENT, U.S.P. XXI.
Use: Antibiotic, anti-inflammatory.

NEOMYCIN SULFATE AND PREDNISOLONE ACETATE OPHTHALMIC OINTMENT, U.S.P. XXI.
Use: Antibiotic, anti-inflammatory.

NEOMYCIN SULFATE AND PREDNISOLONE ACETATE OPHTHALMIC SUSPENSION, U.S.P. XXI.
Use: Antibiotic, anti-inflammatory.

NEOMYCIN SULFATE AND PREDNISOLONE SODIUM PHOSPHATE OPHTHALMIC OINTMENT, U.S.P. XXI.
Use: Antibiotic, anti-inflammatory.

NEOMYCIN SULFATE, SULFACETAMIDE SODIUM, AND PREDNISOLONE ACETATE OPHTHALMIC OINTMENT, U.S.P. XXI.
Use: Antibiotic, anti-inflammatory.

NEOMYCINSULFATEANDTRIAMCINOLONEACETONIDE OPHTHALMIC OINTMENT, U.S.P. XXI.
Use: Antibiotic, anti-inflammatory.

NEOMYCIN UNDECYLENATE. USAN.
Use: Antibacterial.
See: Neodecyllin (Penick)

EOMYCORSONE.
See: Neosone, Oint. (Upjohn)

EO-NACLEX. Bendrofluazide, B.A.N.

EO NOVALDIN. (Winthrop Products) Dipyrone.
Use: Analgesic, antipyretic, anti-inflammatory.

IEOPENYL. Clemizole Penicillin, B.A.N.

IEO PHYRIN DROPS. (Winthrop Products) Phenylephrine HCl.
Use: Nasal decongestant.
See: Phenylephrine HCl

IEO PICATYL. (Winthrop Products) Glycobiarsol.
Use: Intestinal amebicide.

NEOPLASTIC AGENTS.
See: Folic acid antagonists. Leukemia agents.

IEO-POLYCIN OINTMENT. (Merrell Dow) **Oint.:** Neomycin sulfate equiv. to 3.5 mg. neomycin base, zinc bacitracin 400 u., polymyxin B sulfate 5000 u./Gm. in special base. Tube 0.5 oz.
Use: Topical antibiotic.

IEO-PYRANISTAN. (Standex) Ascorbic acid 20 mg., phenylephrine HCl 2.5 mg., salicylamide 60 mg., acetaminophenol 60 mg., chlorpheniramine maleate 1.5 mg./Tab. Bot. 100s.
Use: Relief of sinus headache, cold symptoms.

IEOQUESS INJECTION. (Forest) Dicyclomine HCl 10 mg./ml. Vial 10 ml.

IEOQUESS TABLETS. (Forest) Hyoscyamine sulfate 0.125 mg./Tab. Bot. 100s.

IEOQUINOPHAN.
See: Neocinchophen (Various Mfr.)

IEO QUIPENYL. (Winthrop Products) Primaquine phosphate.
Use: Antimalaria agent.

IEOSAR. (Adria) Cyclophosphamide. **100 mg.:** Cyclophosphamide 100 mg., sodium Cl 45 mg./Vial. Pkg. 12s. **200 mg.:** cyclophosphamide 200 mg., sodium Cl 90 mg./Vial. Pkg. 12s. **500 mg.:** cyclophosphamide 500 mg., sodium Cl. 225 mg./Vial. Pkg 12s. **1 Gm.:** Individual cartons.
Use: Antineoplastic.

NEO-SKIODAN.
Iodopyracet, Diodrast.

NEOSPORIN AEROSOL. (Burroughs Wellcome) Aerosporin brand polymyxin B sulfate 100,000 u., neomycin sulfate 100 mg., zinc bacitracin 8000 u., dispersed in inert propellant./Containers (aerosol spray) 90 Gm. Approx. spraying time: 100 seconds.
Use: Bacterial skin infections.

NEOSPORIN CREAM. (Burroughs Wellcome) Polymyxin B sulfate and neomycin sulfate. Tube 15 Gm. Foil packets 1/32 oz. Ctn. 144s.
Use: First aid antibiotic.

NEOSPORIN-G CREAM. (Burroughs Wellcome) Polymyxin B sulfate 10,000 units, neomycin sulfate 5 mg., gramicidin 0.25 mg./Gm., liq. and white petrolatum, propylene glycol, polyoxyethylene polyoxypropylene compound, wax, methyl paraben 0.25%. Cream. Tube 15 Gm.
Use: Treatment of dermatoses.

NEOSPORIN G. U. IRRIGANT. (Burroughs Wellcome) Neomycin sulfate 40 mg., polymyxin B sulfate 200,000 u./ml. Amps. 1 ml. Box 12s, 100s. MDV 20 ml.
Use: Antibiotic irrigant.

NEOSPORIN OINTMENT. (Burroughs Wellcome) Polymyxin B sulfate 5,000 u., bacitracin zinc 400 u., neomycin sulfate 5 mg./Gm. Tube 0.5 oz., 1 oz. Foil packet 1/32 oz. Box 144s.
Use: First aid antibiotic.

NEOSPORIN OPHTHALMIC OINTMENT, STERILE. (Burroughs Wellcome) Polymyxin B sulfate 10,000 u., bacitracin zinc 400 u., neomycin sulfate 5 mg./Gm., special white petrolatum base. Tube 1/8 oz.
Use: Ocular bacterial infections.

NEOSPORIN OPHTHALMIC SOLUTION, STERILE. (Burroughs Wellcome) Polymyxin B sulfate 10,000 u., neomycin sulfate 2.5 mg., gramicidin 0.025 mg./ml., alcohol 0.5%, thimerosal 0.001%, propylene glycol, polyoxyethylene polyoxypropylene cpd., sod chloride. Bot 10 ml.
Use: Topically, eye infections.

NEOSPORIN POWDER. (Burroughs Wellcome) Polymyxin B 5000 u., zinc bacitracin 400 u., neomycin sulfate 5 mg., lactose base./Gm. Shaker vial 10 Gm.
Use: External bacterial infections.

NEO-SPRAY. (Blue Cross) Xylometazoline Solution. Bot. 0.5 oz.
Use: Nasal spray.

NEOSTEROL TABLETS. (Winston) Ethinyl estradiol 0.01 mg., methyltestosterone 2.5 mg., Vits. A, D, B Complex, C, E, B-12, minerals and lipotropes. Bot. 100s, 1000s.
Use: Vitamin, mineral, hormone, geriatric supplement.

NEOSTIBOSAN. Ethylstibamine.

NEOSTIG. (Freeport) Salicylamide 200 mg., acetaminophen 300 mg., neostigmine Br. 1.5 mg., scopolamine HBr. 0.125 mg./Tab. Bot. 1000s.
Use: Relief of pain, skeletal muscle spasm.

• **NEOSTIGMINE BROMIDE,** U.S.P. XXI. Tab., U.S.P. XXI. Benzenaminium, 3-[[(dimethylamino)-carbonyl-]oxy]-N,N,N-trimethyl-, bromide. (m-Hydroxyphenyl)-trimethylammonium bromide dimethylcarbamate.
Use: Cholinergic.
See: Prostigmin Bromide, Tab. (Roche)

• **NEOSTIGMINE METHYLSULFATE,** U.S.P. XXI. Inj., U.S.P. XXI. Benzenaminium, 3-[[(dimethylamino)carbonyl]-oxy]-N,N,N-trimethyl-, methyl sulfate. (m-Hydroxyphenyl) trimethylammonium methylsulfate dimethylcarbamate.
Use: Parasympathomimetic agent, cholinergic.
See: Prostigmin methylsulfate, Vial (Roche Lab.)

NEO-STREPSAN.
See: Sulfathiazole (Various Mfr.)

NEO-SYNALAR. (Syntex) Fluocinolone acetonide 0.025%, neomycin sulfate 0.5%, in a water washable base w/stearic acid, propylene glycol, sorbitan monostearate and monooleate, polysorbate 60 w/methylparaben and propylparaben as preservatives. Cream Tube 15 Gm., 30 Gm., 60 Gm.
Use: Infected dermatoses.

NEO-SYNEPHRINE 12 HR. (Winthrop Consumer Products) Oxymetazoline HCl 0.05%. Bot. 0.5 oz. as spray or drops.
Use: Nasal decongestant.

NEO-SYNEPHRINE HYDROCHLORIDE. (Winthrop Consumer Products) **Spray:** 0.25% children and adult, 0.5% adult. Regular in squeeze bottles of 0.5 oz. 0.5 % mentholated in squeeze bottles of 0.5 oz. **Drops:** ⅛% infant; 0.25% children and adult; 0.5% adult; 1% adult extra strength. Bot. 1 oz.; 0.25% and 1% also Bot. 16 oz. **Jelly:** 0.5%. Tube ⅝ oz.
Use: Nasal decongestant.

NEO-SYNEPHRINE HYDROCHLORIDE. (Winthrop-Breon) Phenylephrine HCl. **Amp.** 1%, 1 ml. 25s. **Ophthalmic** 2.5%, Mono-Drop Bot. 15 ml.; 10% Mono-Drop Bot. 5 ml.; 10% viscous solution, Mono-Drop Bot. 5 ml.
Use: **Amp:** vasoconstrictor; **Ophth:** vasoconstrictor & mydriatic.

NEO-SYNEPHRINE II, LONG ACTING. (Winthrop Consumer Products) Xylometazoline HCl **0.1%** Adult strength. Regular and mentholated. Spray: Bot. 0.5 oz. Drops: Bot. 1 oz. **0.05%** Child strength. Drops: Bot. 1 oz.
Use: Nasal decongestant.

NEOTAL. (Mallard) Zinc bacitracin 400 u., polymyxin B sulfate 5000 u., neomycin sulfate 5 mg., petrolatum and mineral oil base/Gm. Tube ⅛ oz.

NEO-TEARS. (Barnes-Hind) Sterile, isotonic sol. containing polyvinyl alcohol and hydroxyethylcellulose, sodium chloride, potassium chloride. Bot. 15 ml.
Use: Ophthalmic lubricating solution; artificial tear fluid.

NEO-THRYCEX OINT. (Commerce) Bacitracin, neomycin sulfate, polymyxin B sulfate. Tube 0.5 oz.
Use: Triple antibiotic ointment.

NEOTHYLLINE. (Lemmon) Dyphylline. **Tab.** (200 mg.) Bot. 100s, 1000s, (400 mg.) 100s, 500s. **Elix.** (160 mg./15 ml.) Bot. pt., gal. **Amp.** I.M. (500 mg.) Amp. 2 ml., Box 10s.
Use: Orally, diuretic vasodilator, bronchodilator and myocardial stimulant.
W/Guaifenesin & alcohol.
See: Neothylline-GG, Elix., Tab. (Lemmon)

NEOTHYLLINE-GG. (Lemon) Dyphylline 200 mg., guaifenesin 200 mg./Tab. Bot. 100s, 1000s.
Use: Bronchodilator.

NEOTRIZINE. (Lilly) Trisulfapyrimidines **Susp.:** Sulfadiazine 167 mg., sulfamerazine 167 mg., sulfamethazine 167 mg./5 ml. Bot. 16 fl. oz. **Tabs.** Sulfadiazine 167 mg., sulfamerazine 167 mg., sulfamethazine 167 mg./Tab. Bot. 100s.
Use: Orally; triple sulfonamide therapy.

NEO-TROBEX INJECTION. (Fellows) Vit. B-1 150 mg., B-6 10 mg., riboflavin 5-phosphate sod. 2 mg., niacinamide 150 mg., panthenol 10 mg., choline chloride 20 mg., inositol 20 mg./cc. Vial 30 cc.

NEOTROL. (Hance) Phenylephrine HCl 0.25%, pyrilamine maleate 0.2%, cetalkonium chloride 0.05%, tyrothricin 0.03%, phenylmercuric acetate 1:50,000. Sol., Squeeze Bot. 20 cc.
Use: Nasal congestion.

NEO-VADRIN D-S-S. (Scherer) Docusate sodium 25[illegible] mg./Cap. Bot. 100s.
Use: Stool softener.

NEO-VADRIN PROTEIN CHEWABLE TAB. (Scherer) Protein 455 mg./Tab. Bot. 250s.
Use: Dietary supplement.

NEO-VADRIN STRESS FORMULA. (Scherer) Vit. B-1 15 mg., B-2 15 mg., C 600 mg., niacinamide 100 mg., B-6 5 mg., calcium panothenate 20 mg., B-12 12 mcg., E 30 I.U., biotin 45 mcg., folic acid 0.4 mg./Tab. Bot. 60s.
Use: Multivitamin

NEO VADRIN STRESS FORMULA WITH IRON AND FOLIC ACID. (Scherer) Vit. B-1 15 mg., B-2 15 mg., niacinamide 100 mg., C 600 mg., B-6 25 mg., panothenic acid 20 mg., B-12 12 mcg., E 30 I.U., biotin 45 mcg., folic acid 0.4 mg. iron 27 mg./Tab. Bot. 60s.
Use: Dietary multivitamin supplement.

NEO-VADRIN STRESS FORMULA VITAMINS PLUS ZINC. (Scherer) Vit. E 45 I.U., C 600 mg., folic acid 400 mcg., B-1 20 mg., B-2 10 mg., B-12 25 mcg., biotin 45 mcg., pantothenic acid 25 mg., copper 3 mg., zinc 23.9 mg./Tab. Bot. 60s.
Use: Dietary multivitamin supplement.

NEO-VADRIN TIME RELEASE VIT. C. (Scherer) Vit. C 500 mg./Cap. Bot. 50s, 100s; 250 mg./Cap. Bot. 50s.
Use: Dietary supplement.

NEO-VADRIN VITAMIN B-6 TR. (Scherer) Vit. B-6. 100 mg./Cap. Bot. 100s.
Use: Pyridoxine supplement.

NEOVAL. (Blue Cross) Vit. A 10,000 I.U., D 400 I.U., B-1 10 mg., B-2 5 mg., B-6 2 mg., B-12 3 mcg., C 100

mg., E 5 mg., pantothenic acid 10 mg., niacinamide 30 mg., iron 15 mg., copper 1 mg., Mg. 5 mg., Mn 1 mg., zinc 1.5 mg., iodine 0.15 mg./Tab. Bot. 100s.
Use: Multiple vitamin and mineral supplement.

:OVAL T. (Blue Cross) Vit. A 10,000 I.U., D 400 I.U., B-1 15 mg., B-2 10 mg., B-6 2 mg., C 150 mg., B-12 7.5 mcg., E 5 mg., pantothenic acid 10 mg., E 5 mg., niacinamide 100 mg., iron 15 mg., Mg 5 mg., Mn 1 mg., zinc 1.5 mg., copper 1 mg./Tab. Bot. 1000s.
Use: High potency vitamin and mineral supplement.

:OVICAPS. (Scherer) Vit. B-1 15 mg., B-2 10 mg., B-6 5 mg., niacinamide 50 mg., C 300 mg., zinc 15 mg./Cap. Bot. 50s, 100s.
Use: Dietary supplement.

:O WHITE OINTMENT. (Whiteworth) Triple antibiotic ointment. Tube 0.5 oz., 1 oz.
Use: Antibiotic.

:OZIN. (Softcon) Phenylephrine HCl ⅛%, zinc sulf. 0.25% and benzalkonium chloride 1:25,000 as preservative. Bot. 5 fl. oz. Eye drops.
Use: Astringent, antiseptic & decongestant.

:PHRAMINE. (American McGaw) Essential amino acid injection 5.4%.
Use: For renal disease patients.

:PHRIDINE.
See: Epinephrine (Various Mfr.)

:PHROCAPS. (Fleming) Multiple vitamin. Bot. 100s.
Use: Multiple vitamin especially for dialysis patients.

:PHRON INHALANT AND VAPORIZER. (Nephron) Racemic epinephrine HCl 2.25%. Bot. 0.25 oz., 0.5 oz, or 1 oz.
Use: Inhalant for bronchial asthma.

:PHROX. (Fleming) Aluminum hydroxide 320 mg., mineral oil 10%/5 ml. Bot. pts., gal.
Use: Antacid.

EPRESOL. Dihydrallazine, B.A.N.

EPTAZANE. (Lederle) Methazolamide 50 mg./Tab. Bot. 100s.
Use: Carbonic anhydrase inhibitor, treatment of glaucoma.

NEQUINATE. USAN.
Use: Coccidiostat.

EQUINATE (I.N.N.). Methyl Benzoquate, B.A.N.

ERAVAL. Methitural Sod. 5-(1-Methylbutyl)-5-[2-(methylthio)ethyl]-2-thiobarbiturate.
Use: I.V., general anesthesia.

ERVINE. (Miles)
See: Miles Nervine

ERVOCAINE. (Keene) Lidocaine. 1%, 2%. Vial 50 ml.
Use: Local anesthetic.

ESACAINE. (Astra) **1% Conc.:** Chloroprocaine HCl 10 mg./ml. in sterile solution containing sodium bisulfite, sodium chloride w/preservatives and buffer. Vial 30 ml. **2% Conc.:** Vial 30 ml.
Use: Local anesthetic for infiltration and regional nerve block.

ESACAINE-CE. (Astra) **2% Conc.** Chloroprocaine HCl 20 mg./ml. in a sterile solution containing sodium bisulfite, sodium chloride, HCl. Vial 30 ml. **3% Conc.** Chloroprocaine HCl 30 mg./ml. in a sterile solution containing sodium bisulfite, sodium chloride, HCl. Vial 30 ml.
Use: Local anesthetic for infiltration and regional nerve block including caudal and epidural anesthesia.

NESA NINE CAP. (Standex) Vit. A 5000 I.U., D 400 I.U., C 37.5 mg., B-1 1.5 mg., B-2 2 mg., niacinamide 20 mg., B-6 0.1 mg., Ca pantothothenate 1 mg., E 2 I.U./Cap. Bot. 100s.

NESDONAL SODIUM.
See: Thiopental Sodium U.S.P. XXI.
Pentothal Sodium, Prods. (Abbott)

NESTABS. (Fielding) Prenatal vitamins and minerals. Bot. 100s.
Use: Dietary supplement.

NESTABS FA. (Fielding) Vit A 8000 U., D 400 U., E 30 U., C 120 mg., Folic acid 1 mg., thiamine 3 mg., riboflavin 3 mg., niacinamide 20 mg., pyridoxine 3 mg., B-12 8 mcg., Ca carbonate 500 mg., iodine 150 mcg., ferrous fumarate 110 mg., zinc 15 mg./Tab. Bot. 100s.
Use: Dietary supplement.

NESTREX. (Fielding) Pydridoxine 25 mg./Tab w/dextrose. Bot. 100s.
Use: Dietary supplement.

NETHAMINE. Etafedrine HCl. 1-N-ethylephedrine HCl, 2-methylethylamino-1-phenylpropanol-1 HCl.
W/Codeine phosphate, phenylephrine HCl, sodium citrate, doxylamine succinate.
See: Mercodol with Decapryn Syrup (Merrell Dow)

• **NETILMICIN SULATE,** U.S.P. XXI. Inj., U.S.P. XXI.
Use: Antibacterial
See: Netromycin (Schering)

NETRIN. Under Study.
Use: Anticholinergic.
See: Metcaraphen HCl

NETROMYCIN. (Schering) Netilmicin. **Inj.:** 100 mg/ml. Vial 1.5 ml. Box 10s, 25s. Multi-dose Vial 15 ml. Box 5s. Disposable Syringes 1.5 ml. Box 10s. **Pediatric Inj.:** 25 mg./ml. Vial 2 ml. Box 10s. **Neonatal Inj.** 10 mg./ml. Amp. 2 ml. Box 25s.
Use: Antibiotic.

NEULACTIL.
See: Pericyazine.

NEURAMATE. (Blue Cross) Meprobamate 400 mg./Tab. Bot. 100s.
Use: Tranquilizer.

NEUROSIN.
See: Calcium glycerophosphate (Various Mfr.)

NEUROSINE. (Dios) Sod. bromide 30 gr., pot. bromide 30 gr., ammonium bromide 30 gr., zinc bromide 3/5 gr., hyoscyamus ext. 3/40 gr., belladonna fl. ext. 3/40 min., cascara 3/5 gr., humulus ext. 3/5 gr., in pleasantly flavored 4% alcoholic aq. vehicle/fl. oz. Bot. 4 & 8 oz. Tabs. Bot. 50s, 100s, 200s.
Use: Antispasmodic.

NEUT [SODIUM BICARBONATE 4% ADDITIVE SOLUTION]. (Abbott) Sodium bicarbonate 0.2 Gm./5 ml. Vial (2.4 mEq. each of sodium and bicarbonate), disodium edetate anhydrous 0.05%

as stabilizer. Pintop Vials 5 ml. in 10 ml. vials. Box 25s, 100s.

NEUTRACOMP. (CMC) **Tabs.** Aluminum hydroxide 260 mg., magnesium trisilicate 488 mg./Tab. Bot. 30s, 100s, 250s, 500s, 1000s. **Liq.** 1 pt.
Use: Adsorbent, nonalkaline antacid.

NEUTRAL ACRIFLAVIN.
See: Acriflavin (Various Mfr.)

NEUTRALIN. (Dover) Calcium carbonate, magnesium oxide/Tab. Sugar, lactose and salt free. Unit dose Box 500s.
Use: Antacid.

NEUTRAL INSULIN INJECTION. B.A.N. A solution of insulin buffered at pH 7 Insulin Novo Actrapid; Nuso.
Use: Hypoglycemic agent.

NEUTRAL PROTAMINE HAGEDORN-INSULIN.
See: Insulin, N.P.H. Iletin (Lilly)

• **NEUTRAMYCIN.** USAN. A neutral macrolide antibiotic produced by a variant strain of *Streptomyces rimosus.*
Use: Antibacterial antibiotic.

NEUTRA-PHOS. (Willen) A combination of dibasic and monobasic sodium & potassium phosphates. **Powder:** Bot. 2.25 oz. reconstitutes to 1 Gal. of liquid. **Cap.:** 1.25 Gm./Cap. Bot. 48s. Each cap. reconstitutes to 2.5 oz. of solution which supplies 250 mg. phosphorus, 7.125 mEq., sodium and 7.125 mEq. potassium.
Use: Oral phosphorus supplement.

NEUTRA-PHOS-K. (Willen) A combination of monobasic & dibasic potassium phosphates. **Powder:** Bot. 2.5 oz. reconstitutes to 1 gal. of liquid. **Cap.:** 1.45 Gm./Cap. Bot. 48s. Each cap. reconstitutes to 2.5 oz. of solution which supplies 250 mg. phosphorus and 14.25 mEq. potassium.
Use: Oral phosphorus supplement sodium free.

NEUTRAPHYLLINE. Diprophylline, B.A.N.

NEUTROFLAVIN.
See: Acriflavine (Various Mfr.)

NEUTROGENA. (Neutrogena) A neutralized soap (pH 7.5) W/glycerine, triethanolamine, fatty acids. 100 Gm. Disposable Sponge Pads. Box 12s. Shampoo, Solid Bar 3.4 oz. Unscented soap, 3.5 oz.

NEUTROGENA BODY OIL. (Neutrogena) Isopropyl myristate, sesame oil, hexachlorophene 0.5%. In 8 oz. w/sponge applicator.

NEUTROGENA DISPOSABLES. (Neutrogena) Sulfur 1.5%, salicylic acid 2%, allantoin 1%/medicated pad. Pkg. 12s.
Use: Dried oily skin.

NEUTROGENA LOTION. (Neutrogena) Glycerine monostearate, triethanolamine, lactic acid, hexachlorophene 0.5%, delta and cetyl alcohol, oil in water base. In 8 oz.
Use: Emollient and protective lotion.

NEUTROGENA T/GEL. (Neutrogena) Coal tar extract equivalent to 2% crude coal tar. Bot. 4.4 oz.
Use: Treatment of scalp psoriasis, dandruff, seborrheic dermatitis and eczema.

NEVROTOSE #3. (Vale) Phenobarbital 32.4 mg., hyoscyamus 16.2 mg., passiflora ext. 16.2 mg., valerian ext. 16.2 mg., camphor monobromate 8.1 mg./Cap. Bot. 100s, 500s, 1000s.
Use: Sedative.

NEW BESEROL. (Winthrop Products) Aspirin, methocarbamol.
Use: Analgesic, tranquilizer.

NEWPHRINE. (Vitarine) Phenylephrine HCl 0.25%. Bot. 1 oz., 1%, Bot. pt.
Use: Nasal decongestant.

NEW-SKIN. (Medtech) Alcohol 6.7%, Pyroxylin solutic oil of cloves, 8-hydroxy-quinoline. Bot. 0.5 oz., 1 c Spray Bot. 1 oz. Tube: 0.09 oz.
Use: Liquid bandage.

• **NEXERIDINE HYDROCHLORIDE.** USAN.
Use: Analgesic.

NIAC. (Forest) Nicotinic acid 300 mg./S.R. Cap. Bot 100s.

NIACAL. (Bowman) Calcium lactate 324 mg., niacin 25 mg./Tab. w/peppermint flavor. Bot. 100s, 1000s.
Use: Vasodilator, calcium supplement.

NIACAMIDE.
See: Nikethamide (Various Mfr.)

• **NIACIN,** U.S.P. XXI. Inj., Tab., U.S.P. XXI. 3-Pyridin carboxylic acid.
Use: Vit. B-complex component.
See: Efacin, Tab. (Person & Covey)
Niac, Cap. (Cole)
Nicobid, Tab. (Armour)
Nico-400 (Marion)
Ni Cord XL, Caps. (Scott/Cord)
Nicotinex, Elix. (Fleming)
Nicotym, Cap. (Everett)
Ni-Span, Cap. (Vortech)
Span Niacin 300, Tab. (Scrip)
Vasotherm, Inj. (Nutrition Control Products)
Wampocap, Cap. (Wallace)

W/Pentylenetetrazol.
See: Aminobrain, Liq. (Med. Prod. Panamericana)
Atrazol, Tab., Liq. (Reid-Provident)
Gevizol (Saron)
Mentalert, Tab., Elix. (Keene Pharm.)
Nico-Metrazol, Bot. (Knoll)
Vasostim, Cap. (Dunhall)

NIACIN W/COMBINATIONS.
See: Adenocrest, Vial (Pharmex)
Antivert, Tab. (Roerig)
Ardiatric, Tab. (Burgin-Arden)
Arterine, Tab., Liq. (Paddock)
Athemol, Tab. (Meyer)
Athemol-N, Tab. (Meyer)
Benizol, Tab., Elix. (Bentex)
Benizol Plus, Elix., Tab. (ICN)
Cerebro-Nicin, Cap. (Brown)
Geroniazo, Tab., Liq. (Philips Roxane)
Geroniazol TT, Tab. (Philips Roxane)
Lipo-Nicin, Cap., Tab. (Brown)
Menic, Tab. (Geriatric)
Nascobarb Ovalet, Tab. (Mayrand)
Niapent, Tab., Elix. (Ferndale)
Norozol, Tab. (Vortech)
Pentinic, Liq. (Alto)

Phy-Vasco, Tab. (Scrip)
Senilex, Tab. (O'Neal)
Vasostim, Cap. (Dunhall)

NIACINAMIDE, U.S.P. XXI. Inj., Tab., U.S.P. XXI. 3-Pyridinecarboxamide. Nicotinic acid amide. Nicotinamide.
Use: Enzyme co-factor vitamin.
See: Niacinamide (Various Mfr.)
/Pentylenetetrazol, thiamine HCl, cyanocobalamin, alcohol.
See: Cenalene, Elix., Tab. (Central)
/Pot. iodide.
See: Iodo-Niacin, Tab. (Cole)
/Riboflavin.
See: Riboflavin & Niacinamide, Amp. (Lilly)

IACINAMIDE HI.
/Pot. iodide.
See: Iodo-Niacin, Tab. (Cole)

IALAMIDE. B.A.N. N-Benzyl-α(isonicotinoyl hydrazine)propionamide. Isonicotinic Acid 2-[2-(Benzylcarbamoyl)ethyl]hydrazide.
Use: Monoamine oxidase inhibitor; antidepressant.

IALEXO-C. (Mallard) Niacin 50 mg., Vit. C 30 mg./Tab. Bot. 100s.

IAOULI COMPOUND. (Zemmer) Benzyl alcohol 2%, guaiacol 0.1 Gm., eucalyptol 0.08 Gm., iodoform 0.02 Gm., camphor 0.05 Gm./2 cc. Vial 30 cc.

IARB SUPER. (Miller) Magnesium 100 mg., Vit. C 200 mg., niacinamide 200 mg. (as ascorbate)/Tab. Bot. 100s.

IAZIDE.(Major) Trichlormethiazide 4 mg./Tab. Bot. 1000s.
Use: Diuretic.

IAZO. Neotropin.
Use: Urinary antiseptic.

IB BASE. (Cenci) Washable self-emulsifying base especially developed for incorporation of many of the therapeutic agents used in dermatology. Pkg. 1 & 5 lbs.

IBESOL-THERAPEUTIC CAPSULES. (Table Rock) Vit. A 25,000 I.U., D-2 1000 I.U., B-1 10 mg., B-2 10 mg., B-6 2 mg., Ca pantothenate 20 mg., niacinamide 100 mg., C 300 mg., B-12 4 mcg./Cap. Bot. 30s, 100s.
Use: Therapeutic multivitamin formula.

NIBROXANE. USAN.
Use: Antimicrobial.

ICAMETATE. B.A.N. 2-Diethylaminoethyl nicotinate. Euclidan. [dihydrogen citrate].
Use: Peripheral vasodilator.

ICAMINDON.
See: Nicotinamide (Various Mfr.)

ICARB. (MSD AGVET) Nicarbazin, 25% medicated feed.
Use: Coccidiostat, veterinary medicine.

ICARBAZIN.
See: Nicarb Prods (MSD AGVET)

NICARDIPINE HYDROCHLORIDE. USAN.
Use: Vasodilator.

I' ICE. (Beecham Products) Menthol 5 mg./Lozenge in sugarless sorbitol base. Pkg. 8s, 16s.
Use: Cough lozenge.

• **NICERGOLINE.** USAN. 8β-(5-Bromonicotinoyl-oxymethyl)-10-methoxy-1,6-dimethylergoline.
Use: Vasodilator.

NICERITROL. B.A.N. Pentaerythritol tetranicotinate.
Use: Treatment of hypercholesterolemia.

NICHOLS SYPHON POWDER. (Last) Sodium bicarbonate, sodium chloride, sodium borate. 12.2 Gm pouch (add to 32 oz. water to yield isotonic sol.)

NICLOCIDE. (Miles Pharm) Niclosamide 500 mg./Chewable Tab. Box 4s.
Use: Anthelmintic.

NICLOFOLAN. 2,2'-Bis(4-chloro-6-nitrophenol). Bilevon
Use: Anthelmintic, veterinary medicine.

• **NICLOSAMIDE.** USAN. 2',5-Dichloro-4'-nitrosalicylanilide. Yomesan.
Use: Anthelmintic.
See: Niclocide, Tab. (Miles)

NICO-400. (Marion) Niacin 400 mg./Cap. Bot. 100s.
Use: Correction of nicotinic acid deficiencies.

NICOBID. (USV Labs.) Nicotinic acid 125, 250 mg., or 500 mg./Tempule time-released capsule. Bot. 100s, 500s.
Use: Vitamin supplement.

NICOBION.
See: Nicotinamide (Various Mfr.)

NICOCODINE. B.A.N. O³-Methyl-O⁶-nicotinoylmorphine.
Use: Narcotic analgesic.

NICODICODINE. B.A.N. 7,8-Dihydro-0³-methyl-O⁶-nicotinoylmorphine.
Use: Antitussive.

NICODUOZIDE. A mixture of nicothazone and isoniazid.

NICOLAR. (USV Labs.) Niacin 500 mg./Tab. Bot. 100s.
Use: For patients with hyperlipidemia who do not respond adequately to diet and weight loss.

NICOMORPHINE. B.A.N. 3,6-Dinicotinoylmorphine.
Use: Narcotic analgesic.

• **NICORANDIL.** USAN.
Use: Coronary vasodilator.

NI CORD XL CAPS. (Scott/Cord) Nicotinic acid 400 mg./Cap. Bot. 100s, 500s.

NICORETTE. (Merrell Dow) Nicotine polyacrilex 2 mg./Chewing piece. Box 96s.
Use: Temporary aid in smoking cessation program.

NICOSTROL. (U.S. Ethicals) Niacin 500 mg./Cap. Bot. 100s.
Use: Niacin deficiencies.

NICOTAMIDE.
See: Nicotinamide (Various Mfr.)

NICOTHAZONE. Nicotinaldehyde thiosemicarbazone.

NICOTILAMIDE.
See: Nicotinamide (Various Mfr.)

NICOTINAMIDE. Niacinamide, U.S.P. XXI. Vit. B-3, Aminicotin, Dipegyl, Nicamindon, Nicotamide, Nicotilamide, Nicotinic Acid Amide.

NICOTINAMIDE ADENINE DINUCLEOTIDE. Name used for Nadide.

• **NICOTINE POLACRILEX.** USAN.
Use: Smoking deterrent.
See: Nicorette (Merrell Dow)

NICOTINEX ELIXIR. (Fleming) Niacin 50 mg./5 cc. w/alcohol 14%. Bot. plastic pt., gal.

NICOTINIC ACID. Niacin, U.S.P. XXI.

NICOTINIC ACID W/COMBINATIONS.
See: Niacin W/Combinations (Various Mfr.)

NICOTINIC ACID AMIDE. Niacinamide, U.S.P. XXI.
See: Niacinamide (Various Mfr.)

• **NICOTINYL ALCOHOL.** USAN. 3-Pyridine-methanol. beta-Pyridylcarbinol.
Use: Vasodilator.

NICOTINYL TARTRATE. 3-Pyridinemethanol tatrate.
See: Roniacol Timespan. Tabs. (Roche)

NICOTYM. (Everett) Niacin 400 mg./T.R. Cap. Bot. 60s.
Use: Dietary supplement.

NICOUMALONE. B.A.N. 3-[2-Acetyl-1-(4-nitro-phenyl) ethyl]-4-hydroxycoumarin. Acenocoumarol (I.N.N.) Sinthrome
Use: Anticoagulant.

NICO-VERT. (Edwards) Niacin 50 mg., dimenhydrinate 25 mg./Cap. Bot. 100s.
Use: Nausea, dizziness.

NICOZIDE. (Premo) Isonicotinic acid hydrazide. (Isoniazid) Tab. 100 mg. Bot. 100s, 1000s.
Use: Streptomycin-resistant tuberculosis.

NIDROXYZONE. 5-Nitro-2-furaldehyde-2-(2-hydroxy-ethyl)semicarbazone.

NIERALINE.
See: Epinepherine (Various Mfr.)

• **NIFEDIPINE,** U.S.P. XXI. Cap., U.S.P. XXI. Dimethyl 1,4-dihydro-2,6-dimethyl-4-(2-nitrophenyl)pyridine-3,5 -dicarboxylate.
Use: Coronary vasodilator.
See: Procardia, Cap. (Pfizer)

NIFENAZONE. B.A.N. 2,3-Dimethyl-4-nicotinamido-1-phenyl-5-pyrazolone. Thylin
Use: Anti-inflammatory; analgesic.

NIFEREX. (Central) **Elixir:** Iron 100 mg./5 cc. polysaccharide-iron complex. Alcohol 10%. Sugar Free. Bot. 8 oz. **Tab.:** 50 mg./Tab. Bot. 100s, 1000s.
Use: Hematinic.

NIFEREX-150. (Central) Polysaccharide iron complex equiv. to iron 150 mg./Cap. Bot. 100s, 1000s.
Use: Iron deficiency anemias.

NIFEREX FORTE ELIXIR. (Central) Iron 100 mg., folic acid 1 mg., Vit. B-12 25 mcg./5 ml. Bot. 4 oz.
Use: Hematinic.

NIFEREX-150 FORTE CAPSULES. (Central) Elemental iron as polysaccharide-iron complex 150 mg., Folic acid 1 mg., Vit B-12 25 mcg./Cap. Bot. 100s, 1000s.
Use: Iron deficiency anemias.

NIFEREX-PN. (Central) **Modified Formula:** Iron 60 mg., folic acid 1 mg., Vit. C 50 mg., B-12 3 mcg., A 4000 I.U., D-2 400 I.U., thiamine mononitrate 3 mg., B-2 3 mg., B-6 2 mg., niacinamide 10 mg., Zinc sulfate 80 mg., Ca carbonate 312 mg./Tab. Bot. 100s, 1000s.
Use: Prenatal vitamin-mineral supplement.

NIFEREX W/VITAMIN C. (Central) Iron 50 mg., Vit. C 100 mg., sod. ascorbate 168.75 mg./Tab. Bot. 50s
Use: Iron deficiency anemia.

• **NIFLURIDIDE.** USAN.
Use: Ectoparasiticide.

• **NIFUNGIN.** USAN. Substance derived from *Aspergillus giganteus.*

• **NIFURADENE.** USAN. 1-[(5-Nitrofurfurylidene)-amino]-2-imidazolidinone.
Use: Antibacterial.

• **NIFURALDEZONE.** USAN. 5-Nitro-2-furaldehyde semioxamazone. Furamazone (Eaton).

• **NIFURATEL.** USAN. 5-[(Methylthio)methyl]-3-[(5-nitro furfurylidene)-amino]-2-oxazolidinone. Macmiror Magmilor, Polmiror. Under study.
Use: Antibacterial, antifungal, trichomonacidal.

• **NIFURATRONE.** USAN. N-(2-Hydroxy-ethyl)-α-(5-nitro-2-furyl)nitrone.
Use: Antibacterial.

• **NIFURDAZIL.** USAN. 1-(2-Hydroxyethyl)-3-[(5-nitrofurfurylidene)-amino]-2-imidazolidinone.
Use: Antibacterial.

NIFURETHAZONE. 5-Nitro-2-furaldehyde-2-[2-(dimethylamino)ethyl] semicarbazone.
Use: Antibacterial.

• **NIFURIMIDE.** USAN. (±-4-Methyl-1-[(5-nitro-furfurylidene)amino]-2-imidazolidinone.
Use: Antibacterial.

• **NIFURMERONE.** USAN. Chloromethyl 5-nitro-2-fufryl ketone. Metofurone.
Use: Antimycotic agent.

NIFUROXIME. 5-Nitro-2-fural-doxime. (Z)-5-Nitro-2-furaldehyde Oxime.
Use: Antifungal, antibacterial (topical), antiprotozoal.
See: Micofur
W/Furazolidone.
See: Tricofuron, Pow., Supp. (Eaton)

• **NIFURPIRINOL.** USAN.
Use: Antibacterial.

• **NIFURQUINAZOL.** USAN. 2,2'-[[2-(5-Nitro-2-furyl)-4-quinazolinyl]imino]diethanol. Under study.
Use: Antibacterial.

• **NIFURSEMIZONE.** USAN. 5-Nitro-2-furaldehyde-2-ethyl-semicarbazone.
Use: Poultry histomonostat.

• **NIFURSOL.** USAN. 3,5-Dinitrosalicylic acid (5-nitrofurfurylidene)hydrazide.
Use: Histomonocide, vet. growth stimulant.

• **NIFURTHIAZOLE.** USAN. Formic acid 2-[4-(5-nitro-2-furyl)-2-thiazolyl]hydrazide.
Use: Antibacterial (veterinary).

NIFURTIMOX. B.A.N. Tetrahydro-3-methyl-4-(5-nitrofurfurylideneamino)-1,4-thiazine 1, 1-dioxide.
Use: Treatment of trypanosomiasis.

NIGHTTIME COLD MEDICINE. (McKesson) Bot. 6 oz.
Use: Relief of cold symptoms.

NIGLYCON. (CMC) Nitroglycerine 1/25 gr./Tab. Bot. 50s.
Use: Treatment of angina.

NIGRIN. Streptonigrin.
Use: Antineoplastic.

NIGROIDS. (CMC) Throat lozenges. Box 12s.

NIHYDRAZONE. Acetic acid (5-nitrofurfurylidene) hydrazide. Veterinary.

NIKETHAMIDE. (Anacardone, Cardiamid, Cormed, Dynacoryl, Eucoran, Nicamide, Pyricardyl) N,N-Diethyl nicotinamide.
Use: Central nervous system stimulant.
See: Coramine, Amp., Liq. (Ciba)

NIKO-MAG. (Scruggs) Magnexium oxide 500 mg./Cap. Bot. 100s, 1000s.
Use: Temporary relief of constipation and gastric hyperacidity from overeating.

NIKOTIME TD CAPS. (Major) Niacin 125 mg. or 250 mg./TD Cap. Bot. 100s, 1000s.
Use: Vitamin supplement.

NILAIN. (A.V.P.) Aspirin 227 mg., acetaminophen 227 mg., caffeine 32.4 mg./Cap. Bot. 100s.
Use: Analgesic.

NILCOL ELIXIR. (Health Care Industries) Phenylpropanolamine 25 mg., chlorpheniramine maleate 2 mg., guaifenesin 100 mg., dextromethorphan; H Br. 15 mg./15 ml.
Use: Decongestant, antihistaminic, expectorant.

NILCOL TABLETS. (Health Care Industries) Phenylpropanolamine 50 mg., chlorpheniramine maleate 4 mg., guaifenesin 200 mg., dextromethorphan H Br 30 mg./Tab. Bot. 100s.
Use: Decongestant, antihistaminic, expectorant.

NILORIC. (Ascher) Dihydroergocornine, dihydroergoecristine, dihydroergocyptine osmelate equal parts to make 1 mg./Tab. Bot. 100s.
Use: Selected symptoms in elderly patients.

NILPRIN. (A.V.P. Pharmaceuticals) Acetaminophen 7.5 gr./Tab. Bot. 100s.
Use: Analgesic-antipyretic.

NILSPASM. (Parmed) Phenobarbital 50 mg., hyoscyamine sulfate 0.31 mg., atropine sulfate 0.06 mg., scopolamine hydrobromide 0.0195 mg./Tab. Bot. 100s, 1000s.
Use: Antispasmodic-sedative.

NILSTAT. (Lederle) Nystatin 500,000 u./Tab., film coated. Bot. 100s, Unit dose 100s.
Use: Treatment of *Candida albicans* infections.

NILSTAT OINTMENT & CREAM. (Lederle) Nystatin 100,000 u./Gm. **Cream base** w/Emulsifying wax, isopropyl myristate, glycerin, lactic acid, sod. hydroxide, 0.2% sorbic acid as a preservative. Tube 15 Gm. Jar 240 Gm. **Ointment base:** w/Light mineral oil, plastibase 50 W. Tube 15 Gm.
Use: Topical antibiotic.

NILSTAT ORAL SUSPENSION. (Lederle) Nystatin 100,000 u./ml. w/methylparaben 0.12%, propylparaben 0.03%, cherry flavor. Bot. 60 ml. w/dropper, 16 fl. oz..
Use: Antimycotic.

NILSTAT POWDER. (Lederle) Nystatin powder 1 or 2 billion units/Bot.
Use: Infections of the oral cavity caused by *Candida albicans.*

NILSTAT VAGINAL TABLETS. (Lederle) Nystatin 100,000 u., starch, lactose, polyvinyl pyrrolidone, sorbitol, magnesium stearate./Tab. Pkg. 15s, 30s w/applicator.
Use: Antimycotic.

NIL TUSS. (Minnesota Pharm.) Dextromethorphan HBr 10 mg., chlorpheniramine maleate 1.25 mg., phenylephrine HCl 5 mg., ammonium chloride 83 mg./tsp. Syr.: Bot. 1 pt.
Use: Cough syrup, antitussive, vasoconstrictor, antihistaminic, expectorant.

• **NILVADIPINE.** USAN.
Use: Antagonist (calcium channel).

NIL VAGINAL CREAM. (Century) Sulfanilamide 15%, 9-aminoacridine HCl 0.2%, allantoin 1.5%. Bot. 4 oz. w/applicator.

NILVERM HCl. Tetramisole, B.A.N.

• **NIMAZONE.** USAN. 3-(p-Chlorophenyl)-4-imino-2-oxo-1-imidazolidineacetonitrile.
Use: Anti-inflammatory.

• **NIMIDANE.** USAN.
Use: Acaricide.

• **NIMODIPINE.** USAN.
Use: Vasodilator.

NIMORAZOLE. B.A.N. 4-[2-(5-Nitroimidazol-1-yl)ethyl]-morpholine. Nitrimidazine. Naxogin; Nulogyl
Use: Treatment of trichomoniasis.

NIMO-TEX. (Sutliff & Case) Vit. A 5000 I.U., D 400 I.U., E 2 I.U., B-1 3 mg., B-2 2 mg., B-6 0.5 mg., B-12 1 mcg., cal. pantothenate 3 mg., niacinamide 20 mg., choline bitartrate 50 mg., inositol 10 mg., Vit. C 30 mg., ferrous sulf. 60 mg., Cu 1 mg., Mn 3 mg., iodine 0.15 mg., Mg 5 mg., Ca 48 mg., P 37 mg./Tab. Bot. 100s, 1000s.
Use: Vitamin & mineral supplement.

NINE-VITA. (Robinson) Vit. A 5000 I.U., D 1000 I.U., B-1 1.5 mg., B-2 2 mg., niacinamide 20 mg., B-6 0.1 mg., Ca pantothenate 1 mg., C 37.5 mg., E 2 I.U./Cap. Bot. 100s, 1000s. Bulk Pack 5000s.
Use: Dietary supplement.

NIODOL. (Horton & Converse) Camphor 50 mg., chlorobutanol 30 mg., eucalyptol 60 mg., guaiacol 100 mg., iodized oil 50 mg., menthol 60 mg., niaouli oil 100 mg./2 cc. Vial 30 cc. 1s, 12s, 25s.

NIONG. (US Ethicals) Nitroglycerin 2.6 mg. or 6.5 mg./Controlled Released Tab. Bot. 100s.
Use: Vasodilator for angina attacks.

NIPRIDE. (Roche) Nitroprusside, sodium, 50 mg./5 ml. Vial 5 ml.
Use: Antihypertensive.

NIRAM OINTMENT. (Guild) Pkg. 1 oz.

NIRATRON. (Progress) Chlorpheniramine maleate 4 mg./Tsp. Bot. Pts.
Use: Antihistaminic agent.

• **NIRIDAZOLE.** USAN. 1-(5-Nitrothiazol-2-yl)-imidazolidin-2-one. Ambilhar
Use: Treatment of schistosomiasis.

NIRON. (Mills) Niacinamide 150 mg., Vit. B-1 10 mg., B-2 6 mg., Vit. B-12 25 mcg., iron 30 mg./prolonged action Tab. Bot. 100s.
Use: Vitamin therapy.

NISAVAL. (Vale) Pyrilamine maleate 25 mg./Tab. Bot. 100s, 1000s.

• **NISBUTEROL MESYLATE.** USAN.
Use: Bronchodilator.

NISENTIL. (Roche) Alphaprodine HCl 40 mg./ml. Vial box. 10s. 60 mg./ml. Vial 10 ml.
Use: Obstetric analgesia.

• **NISOBAMATE.** USAN. (1) 2-(Hydroxymethyl)-2,3-dimethylpentyl isopropylcarbamate carbamate (ester); (2)2-sec-Butyl-2-methyl-1,3-propanediol carbamate isopropylcarbamate.
Use: Minor tranquilizer; sedative; hypnotic.

• **NISOLDIPINE.** USAN.
Use: Vasodilator.

• **NISOXETINE.** USAN.
Use: Antidepressant.

NI-SPAN. (Vortech) Nicotinic acid 400 mg./Cap. Bot. 100s, 1000s.
Use: Nicotinic acid deficiency.

• **NISTERIME ACETATE.** USAN.
Use: Androgen.

• **NITARSONE.** USAN. p-Nitrobenzenearsonic acid.
Use: Veterinary histomonastat.

• **NITHIAMIDE.** USAN.
Use: Antibacterial.

• **NITRAFUDAM HYDROCHLORIDE.** USAN.
Use: Antidepressant.

• **NITRALAMINE HYDROCHLORIDE.** USAN. 2-[[o-Chloro-α-(nitromethyl)benzyl]-thio] ethyl-amine HCl.
Use: Fungicide.

• **NITRAMISOLE HYDROCHLORIDE.** USAN.
Use: Anthelmintic.

• **NITRAZEPAM.** USAN. 1,3-Dihydro-7-nitro-5-phenyl-2H-1,4-benzodiazepin-2-one. Mogadon.
Use: Hypnotic, sedative.

NITRAZINE PAPER. (Squibb) Phenaphthazine. Sod. dinitrophenyl-azo-naphthol disulfonate. 15 ft. roll with dispenser & color chart.
Use: Determine pH of a solution.

NITRAZONE. (Kenyon) Nitrofurazone **Cream** 2% in a water soluble base. Tube 1 oz. **Soluble Dressing** 0.2% in a water soluble base of polyethylene glycol.

NITRE. (Eckerd) Sweet spirits. Bot. 1 oz.

• **NITRENDIPINE.**
Use: Antihypertensive.

NITREX. (Star) Nitrofurantoin 50 mg., 100 mg./Tab. Bot. 100s, 1000s.
Use: Urinary tract infections.

• **NITRIC ACID.** N.F. XVI.
Use: Pharmaceutic aid (acidifying agent).

NITRIC ACID SILVER. Silver Nitrate, U.S.P. XXI.

NITRO-BID. (Marion) Nitroglycerin 2.5 mg., 6.5 mg./T.R. Cap. Bot. 60s, 100s.
Use: Angina pectoris treatment.

NITRO-BID IV. (Marion) Nitroglycerin 5 mg./ml. Ampules or Vials: 1 ml. box of 10s; 5 ml. box of 10s; 10 ml. box of 5s.
Use: Angina pectoris treatment.

NITRO-BID 9 mg. (Marion) Nitroglycerin 9 mg./T.R. Cap. Bot. 60s, 100s.
Use: Angina pectoris treatment.

NITRO-BID OINTMENT. (Marion) Nitroglycerin (glyceryl trinitrate) 2%, lactose in lanolin and petrolatum base. Tube 20 Gm., 60 Gm. Pouch 1 Gm. in Unit dose paks of 100s.
Use: Angina pectoris treatment.

NITROCAP. (Freeport) Nitroglycerin 2.5 mg./T.R. Cap. Bot. 100s.
Use: Treatment of anginal attacks.

NITROCAP T.D. (Vortech) Nitroglycerin 2.5 mg., 6.5 mg./Cap. Bot. 100s.
Use: Angina pectoris.

NITROCELS. (Winston) Nitroglycerin 2 mg., 0.4 mg./sublingual Tab. Duopak 60s. Bot. 100s.
Use: Angina therapy.

• **NITROCYCLINE.** USAN. 4-(Dimethylamino)-1-4,4α,5,5α,6,11,12α-octahydro-3,10,12,12α-tetrahydroxy-7-nitro-1,11-dioxo-2-naphthacenecarboxamide.
Use: Antibiotic.

• **NITRODAN.** USAN.
Use: Anthelmintic.

NITRODAN. (Century) Nitrofurantoin 100 mg./Tab. Bot. 100s, 1000s.

NITRO-DIAL. (Rocky Mtn.) Nitroglycerin 2.5 mg./T.D. Cap. Bot. 50s, 250s.

NITRODISC. (Searle) Nitroglycerin. Transcustaneous nitroglycerin discs releasing 5 mg./24 hrs. or 10 mg./24 hrs. Cartons 30s.
Use: Prophylactic antianginal therapy.

NITRO-DUR TRANSDERMAL INFUSION SYSTEM. (Key) Nitroglycerin Patches 5, 10, 15 and 20 square centimeters. Box 28 patches.
Use: Cardiovascular diseases.

NITROFAN CAPS. (Major) Nitrofurantoin 50 mg. or 100 mg./Cap. Bot. 100s.
Use: Antibacterial for urinary tract infections.

NITROFOR-50. (Kenyon) Nitrofurantoin 50 mg./Tab. Bot. 100s, 1000s.

NITROFOR-100. (Kenyon) Nitrofurantoin 100 mg./Tab. Bot. 100s, 1000s.

• **NITROFURANTOIN,** U.S.P. XXI. Tab., Inj., U.S.P. XXI. 2,4-Imidazolidinedione, 1-[[(5-nitro-2-furanyl)methylene]-amino]-. 1-[(5-Nitrofurfurylidene)amino]hydantoin. 1-(5-Nitro-furfurlyideneamino)imidazoline-2,4-dione. Berkfurin; Furadantin; Urantoin
Use: Antibacterial for urinary tract infections.
See: Furadantin, Preps. (Norwich Eaton)
Furalan, Tab. (Lannett)
Furantoin, Tab. (Vortech)
Nitrex, Tab. (Star)
Nitrofor-50, Tab. (Kenyon)
Nitrofor-100, Tab. (Kenyon)
Nitrofurantoin sodium, Vial (Norwich Eaton)
Sarodant (Saron)
Trantoin, Tab. (McKesson)
Urotoin, Tab. (Scruggs)

NITROFURANTOIN MACROCRYSTALS.
Use: Antibacterial for urinary tract infections.
See: Macrodantin, Cap. (Norwich Eaton)

NITROFURASTAN. (Standex) Nitrofurazone 1 oz. Tube.
Use: Topical antibacterial agent.

• **NITROFURAZONE,** U.S.P. XXI. Cream, Oint., Topical Sol., U.S.P. XXI. 5-Nitro-2-furaldehyde semicarbazone.
Use: Bacteriostatic for surface wounds.
See: Furacin, Preps. (Norwich Eaton)
Nisept, Oint. (Blue Line)
Nitrazone, Cr., Sol. dressing (Kenyon)
Nitrofurastan, Oint. (Standex)
Nitrozone, Oint. (Century)
W/Allantoin, stearic acid.
See: Eldezol, Oint. (Elder)

1-[(5-NITROFURFURYLIDENE)AMINO]-HYDANTOIN. Nitrofurantoin, U.S.P. XXI.

NITROFURFURYL METHYL ETHER. 2-(Methyloxymethyl)-5-nitrofuran.
Use: Antifungal veterinary.

• **NITROGEN,** N.F. XVI.
Use: Pharm. aid (air displacement).

NITROGEN MONOXIDE. Laughing Gas, Nitrous Oxide.
Use: Inhalation anesthetic & analgesic.

NITROGEN MUSTARD.
See: Mustargen, Vial (Merck Sharp & Dohme)

NITROGEN MUSTARD DERIVATIVES.
See: Leukemia Agents
Leukeran, Tab. (Burroughs-Wellcome)
Mustargen HCl, Vial (Merck Sharp & Dohme)
Triethylene Melamine, Tab. (Lederle)

• **NITROGLYCERIN, DILUTED,** U.S.P. XXI.
Use: Vasodilator.

• **NITROGLYCERIN INJECTION,** U.S.P. XXI. (Abbott) 25 mg./ 1 ml. Vials 5 ml., 10 ml.
Use: Vasodilator, treatment of angina.
See: Tridil, Inj. (American Critical Care)

• **NITROGLYCERIN OINTMENT,** U.S.P. XXI.
Use: Vasodilator.

• **NITROGLYCERIN TABLETS,** U.S.P. XXI. 1,2,3-Propanetriol, trinitrate. (Various Mfr.) Glyceryl Trinitrate, Glonoin, Nitroglycerol, Trinitrin, Trinitroglycerol Tab. 1/2000 gr., 1/150 gr., 1/100 gr., Sublingual tabs. (Key) 1/100 gr., 1/400 gr., 1/200 gr., 1/400 gr./Tab. Bot. 100s, 1000s.
Use: Vasodilator.
See: Ang-O-Span, Cap. (Scrip)
Cardabid (Saron)
Corobid, Cap. (Medics)
Gly-Trate, Meta-Kap. (Sutliff & Case)
Niglycon, Tab. (Consol. Midland)
Niong, Tab. (U.S. Ethicals)
Nitrobid, Cap. (Marion)
Nitrocap T.D., Cap. (Vortech)
Nitrocels, Cap. (Winston)
Nitro-Dial, T.D. Caps. (Rocky Mtn.)
Nitrodyl, Cap. (Bock)
Nitroglyn, Tab. (Key Pharm.)
Nitrol Ointment, (Kremers-Urban)
Nitro-Lyn, Cap. (Lynwood)
Nitrong, Tab. (Wharton)
Nitrospan, Cap. (USV Labs.)
Nitrostat, Tab. (Parke-Davis)
Nitrotym, Cap. (Kenyon)
Nitro T.D., Cap. (Fleming)
Trates, Caps. (Reid-Provident)
Vasoglyn, Unicelles (Reid-Provident)
W/Butabarbital.
See: Nitrodyl-B, Cap. (Bock)
Nitrotym-Plus, Cap. (Kenyon)
W/Nicotinic acid.
See: Nitrovas, Tab. (Amfre-Grant)
W/Veratrum viride, Sod. nitrite, Pot. nitrate, aconite root.
See: Nyomin, Tab. (Elder)

NITROGLYCEROL.
See: Nitroglycerin (Various Mfr.)

NITROGLYN. (Key) Nitroglycerin 1/25 gr. (2.6 mg.), 1/10 gr. (6.5 mg.)/Tab. Bot. 100s.
Use: Angina pectoris.

NITROL IV. (Rorer) Nitroglycerin 0.8 mg. nitroglycerin/ml. Amp. 1 ml. Box 25s; 10 ml. Box 10s; 30 ml. Box 5s.
Use: Control of blood pressure in perioperative hypertension; angina pectoris.

NITROL OINTMENT. (Rorer) Nitroglycerin 2% in lanolin and petrolatum base. **Tubes:** 3 Gm., Pack 50s; 30 Gm., Pack 6s. 60 Gm., Pack 6s. **Tsar Kit:** 3 Gm., Pack 50s; 30 Gm.; 60 Gm.
Use: Coronary & peripheral vasodilator, treatment angina pectoris.

NITRO-LYN. (Lynwood) Nitroglycerin 2.5 mg./Cap. Bot. 100s.
Use: Smooth muscle relaxant; arteriole-capillary dilator.

NITROMANNITE.
See: Mannitol Hexanitrate (Various Mfr.)

NITROMANNITOL.
See: Mannitol Hexanitrate (Various Mfr.)

NITROMED. (U.S. Ethicals) Isosorbide dinitrate 20 mg. or 30 mg./Tab. Bot. 100s.
Use: Vasodilator for anginal attacks.

• **NITROMERSOL,** U.S.P. XXI. Topical Sol., Tincture, U.S.P. XXI. 4-Nitro-3-hydroxy mercuri-o-cresol anhydride. 5-Methyl-2-nitro-7-oxa-8-mercurabicyclo (4.2.0) octa-1,3,5-triene. Metaphen.
Use: Local anti-infective.

• **NITROMIDE.** USAN. 3,5-Dinitrobenzamide.
Use: Coccidiostat & antibacterial.

• **NITROMIFENE CITRATE.** USAN.
Use: Anti-estrogen.

NITRONET. (U.S. Ethicals) Nitroglycerin 2.6 mg., or 6.5/Controlled Rel. Tab. Bot. 100s.
Use: Vasodilator for anginal attacks and coronary artery disease.

NITRONG PAD-TRANSDERMAL SYSTEM. (Wharton) Nitroglycerin 2% ointment. Unit dose 7.5 mg., 15 mg., or 30 mg..
Use: Vasodilator for anginal attacks.

NITRONG TABLETS. (Wharton) Nitroglycerin 2.6 mg., 6.5 mg. or 9 mg./Controlled release Tab. Bot. 30s, 100s, 250s, 1000s.
Use: Vasodilator for anginal attacks due to coronary artery disease.

NITRONG OINTMENT. (Wharton) Nitroglycerin 2% ointment. Tube 30 Gm., 60 Gm. with dose applicator.

Use: Vasodilator for anginal attacks due to coronary artery disease.

p-NITROPHENOL.
See: Niphen, Liq. (Torch)

NITROPRESS. (Abbott) Sodium nitroprusside 50 mg./2 ml. Vial
Use: Hypotensive agent.

• **NITROSCANATE.** USAN.
Use: Anthelmintic.

NITROSPAN CAPSULES. (USV Labs.) Nitroglycerin 2.5 mg. or 6.5 mg./Sustained Release Caps. 2.5 mg./Cap. Bot. 100s; 6.5 mg./Cap. Bot. 60s.
Use: Management and treatment of anginal attacks.

NITROSTAT. (Parke-Davis) Nitroglycerin 0.15, 0.3, 0.4, and 0.6 mg./Tab. Bot. 25s, 100s.
Use: Treatment of anginal attacks.

NITROSTAT IV. (Parke-Davis) Nitroglycerin for infusion 0.8 mg./ml. Amp. 10 ml.
Use: Congestive heart failure, angina pectoris.

NITROSTAT OINTMENT. (Parke-Davis) Nitroglycerin 2%. Tubes 30 Gm., 60 Gm.
Use: Prevention and treatment of angina pectoris due to coronary artery disease.

NITROSTAT SR. (Parke-Davis) Nitroglycerin 2.5 mg., 6.5 mg., or 9 mg./SR Cap. Bot. 60s, 100s.
Use: Management, prophylaxis, or treatment of anginal attacks.

p-NITROSULFATHIAZOLE. 2-(p-Nitrophenylsulfonamide) thiazole.

NITROTYM. (Kenyon) Nitroglycerin 2.5 mg./Cap. Bot. 100s, 1000s.

NITROTYM-PLUS. (Kenyon) Nitroglycerin 2.5 mg., butabarbital 48 mg./Cap. Bot. 100s, 1000s.

NITROUS ACID, SODIUM SALT. Sodium Nitrite, U.S.P. XXI.

NITROUS ETHER.

• **NITROUS OXIDE,** U.S.P. XXI.
Use: General anesthetic (inhalation).
See: Nitrogen Monoxide.

NITROVIN. B.A.N. 1,5-Bis(5-nitro-2-furyl)penta-1,4-dien-3-one amidinohydrazone. Payzone and Panazon [hydrochloride]
Use: Growth promoter, veterinary medicine.

NITROXOLINE. B.A.N. 8-Hydroxy-5-nitroquinoline. Nibiol
Use: Antibacterial.

NITROXYNIL. B.A.N. 4-Hydroxy-3-iodo-5-nitrobenzonitrile. Trodax [meglumine salt].
Use: Anthelmintic, veterinary medicine.

NITROZONE OINTMENT. (Century) Nitrofurazone 0.2%. 4 oz., 1 lb., 5 lb.

NIVAQUINE SULFATE. Chloroquine, B.A.N.

• **NIVAZOL.** USAN. 2′-(p-Fluorophenyl-2′H-17α-pregna-2,4-dien-20-yno [3,2-c]pyrazol-17-ol.
Use: Glucocorticoid.

NIVEA OIL. (Beiersdorf) Emulsion of neutral aliphatic hydrocarbons. **Liq.** Bot. 2 oz., 4 fl. oz., 1 pt., 1 qt. **Cream** Tube 1 oz. & 2⅓ oz., Jar 4 oz., 6 oz. 1 lb. 5 lb. tin. **Soap:** bath or toilet size.
Use: Emollient.
See: Basic soap (Beiersdorf)

• **NIVIMEDONE SODIUM.** USAN.
Use: Anti-allergic.

• **NIZATIDINE.** USAN.
Use: Anti-ulcerative.

NIZORAL. (Janssen) Ketoconazole 200 mg./Tab. Bot 100s. Box of 10 strips of 10 tablets.
Use: Broad spectrum antifungal agent.

N-MULTISTIX S. G. REAGENT STRIPS. (Ames) Dip-and-read urine test for pH, protein, glucose, ketones bilirubin, blood, nitrite, urobilinogen and specific gravity. Bot. 100s.
Use: Diagnostic.

N-N COUGH SYRUP. (Vitarine) Dextromethorphan HBr 60 mg., pot. guaiacolsulfonate 390 mg., ammonium chloride 390 mg., chlorpheniramine maleate 3 mg./fl. oz. Bot. 4 oz.
Use: Antihistaminic, antitussive.

NO-ASPIRIN. (Walgreen) Acetaminophen 325 mg./Tab. Bot. 100s,
Use: Analgesic.

NO-ASPIRIN EXTRA STRENGTH. (Walgreen) Acetaminophen 500 mg./Tab. or Cap. Bot. 60s, 100s. Cap. 50s.
Use: Analgesic.

• **NOCODAZOLE.** USAN.
Use: Antineoplastic.

NOCTEC. (Squibb) Chloral hydrate. **Syrup:** 500 mg./5 ml. Bot. 1 pt., 1 gal. Bot. 100s. **Cap.:** 250 mg. or 500 mg./Cap. Bot. 100s. Unimatic 25s, 100s.
Use: Nocturnal sedation.

NODALIN. (Table Rock) Methadon HCl 2.5 mg., aspirin 3 gr., phenacetin 2 gr., caffeine ⅓ gr./Tab. Bot. 100s, 500s.
Use: Analgesic.

NODOZ, Keep Alert Tablets. (Bristol-Myers) Caffeine 100 mg./Tab. Bot. 60s. Box 15s, 36s.
Use: Stimulant.

• **NOGALAMYCIN.** USAN.
Use: Antineoplastic.

NO GEST. (Foy) Atropine sulfate 0.2 mg., phenylpropanolamine HCl 12.5 mg., chlorpheniramine maleate 5.0 mg./ml. w/benzyl alcohol 2%. Vial 10 ml.
Use: Upper respiratory decongestant.

NO-HIST CAPSULES. (Dunhall) Phenylephrine HCl 5 mg., phenylpropanolamine HCl 40 mg., pseudoephedrine HCl 40 mg./Cap. Bot. 100s.
Use: Decongestant.

NO-HIST-S SYRUP. (Dunhall) Phenylephrine HCl 5 mg., phenylpropanolamine HCl 40 mg., pseudoephedrine HCl 40 mg./5 ml. Bot. pt.
Use: Decongestant.

NOKANE. (Wren) Salicylamide 4 gr., N-acetyl-p-aminophenol 4 gr., caffeine 0.5 gr./Tab. Bot. 40s.

NOLAHIST. (Carnrick) Phenindamine tartrate 25 mg./Tab. Bot. 100s.
Use: Allergic rhinitis treatment.

NOLAMINE. (Carnrick) Chlorpheniramine maleate 4 mg., phenindamine tartrate 24 mg.,

phenylpropanolamine HCl 50 mg./Tab. Bot. 100s, 250s.
Use: Upper respiratory and nasal congestion.

IOLINIUM BROMIDE. USAN.
Use: Anti-ulcerative, antisecretory.

)LUDAR. (Roche) Methyprylon. **Tab.** 50 mg./Tab. Bot. 100s; 200 mg. Bot. 100s. **Caps.** 300 mg./Cap. Bot. 100s.
Use: Hypnotic.

)LVADEX. (Stuart) Tamoxifen citrate equivalent to 10 mg. tamoxifen/Tab. Bot. 60s, 250s.
Use: Treatment of advanced breast cancer.

)METIC. Diphenidol.
Use: Antiemetic.

)MIFENSINE. B.A.N. 8-Amino-1,2,3,4-tetrahydro-2-methyl-4-phenylisoquinoline.
Use: Thymoleptic and central nervous system stimulant.
See: Merital (Hoechst)

)NAMIN. (Western Research) Calcium 100 mg., chloride 90 mg., magnesium 50 mg., zinc 3.75 mg., iron 4.5 mg., copper 0.5 mg., iodine 37.5 mcg., potassium 100 mg., phosphorus 100 mg./Tab. Bot. 1000s.

ONE. (Forest) Heparin sodium 1000 units/ml. No preservatives. Amps 5 ml. Box 25s.
Use: Anticoagulant.

)NOXYNOL. (Ortho)
Nonylphenoxypolyethoxyethanol.
Use: Spermatocide.
See: Emko, Preps. (Emko)

NONOXYNOL 4. USAN. Nonylphenoxy-polyethyleneoxyethanol. Igepal CO-430. Under study.
Use: Nonionic surfactant.

NONOXYNOL 9. USAN. Poly (ethylene glycol) p-nonylphenyl ether. Igepal CO-630.
Use: Spermatocide.
See: Conceptrol, Cream, Gel (Ortho)
Delfen, Foam (Ortho)
Emko Prods. (Emko-Schering)
Encare, Insert (Eaton-Merz)
Gynol II, Jelly (Ortho)
Intercept, Inserts (Ortho)
Ortho-Creme, Cream (Ortho)
Ortho-Gynol, Jelly (Ortho)

NONOXYNOL 10, U.S.P. XXI.
Use: Spermatocide.

NONOXYNOL 15. USAN. Nonylphenoxy-polyethyleneoxyethanol. Igepal CO-880. Under study.
Use: Nonionic surfactant.

NONOXYNOL 30. USAN. Nonylphenoxy-polyethyleneoxyethanol. Under study.
Use: Nonionic surfactant.

ONSPECIFIC PROTEIN THERAPY.
See: Protein, Nonspecific Therapy

ONYLPHENOXYPOLYETHOXY ETHANOL.
Nonoxynol.
Use: Contraceptive agent.
See: Delfen Vaginal Foam (Ortho)
W/Benzethonium chloride.
See: Because Birth Control Foam (Emko)
Dalkon Foam (Robins)
Emko Pre-Fil, Foam (Emko)
Emko Vaginal Foam (Emko)

NORACYMETHADOL. B.A.N. α-1-Ethyl-4-methylamino-2,2-diphenylpentyl acetate.
Use: Narcotic analgesic.

• **NORACYMETHADOL HCl.** USAN. α-4, 4-Diphenyl-6-methylamino-3-heptanol acetate HCl.
Use: Analgesic agent.

NORADEX TABS. (Major) Orphenadrine citrate 100 mg./Tab. Bot. 100s, 500s.
Use: Musculoskeletal conditions.

NORADRENALINE. B.A.N. (−)-2-Amino-1-(3,4-dihydroxyphenyl)ethanol. Levarterenol (I.N.N.)
Use: Hypertensive.

NORADRYL COUGH SYRUP. (Vortech) Diphenhydramine HCl 12.5 mg./5 ml. w/alcohol 5%.
Use: Antihistaminic.

NORADRYL ELIXIR. (Vortech) Bot. 4 oz., gal.
Use: Antihistaminic.

NORADRYL EXPECTORANT. (Vortech) Bot. 4 oz., gal.
Use: Antihistaminic, expectorant.

NORALAC. (Vortech) Calcium carbonate 3.5 gr., Magnesium carbonate 2 gr./Chewable Tab. Bot. 100s.
Use: Antacid.

NORAMINIC EXPECTORANT. (Vortech) Bot. 4 oz., gal.
Use: Decongestant, expectorant.

NORAMINIC SYRUP. (Vortech) Phenylpropanolamine HCl 12.5 mg., pheniramine maleate 6.25 mg., pyrilamine maleate 6.25 mg., methylparaben 0.2%/5 cc. Bot. 4 oz., gal.
Use: Antihistaminic.

NORATUSS LIQUID. (Vortech) Potassium guaiacol sulfonate 32.4 mg., ammonium Cl 194.4 mg., terpin hydrate 32.4 mg., codeine phosphate 20 mg., ext. cocillana comp. 26.6 mg., sodium benzoate 0.1%/fl. oz. Bot. 4 oz., gal.
Use: Antitussive, expectorant.

NORAZINE HCl. (Vortech) Promazine HCl 50 mg./ml. Vial 10 ml.
Use: Tranquilizer.

• **NORBOLETHONE.** USAN. 13-Ethyl-17-hydroxy-18, 19-dinor-17αa-pregn-4-en-3-one.
Use: Anabolic.

NORBUTRINE. B.A.N. 2-Cyclobutylamino-1-(3,4-dihydroxyphenyl) ethanol.
Use: Bronchodilator.

NORCODEINE. B.A.N. N-Demethyl-O^3-methylmorphine.
Use: Narcotic analgesic.

NORCURON. (Organon) Vecuronium bromide 10 mg./5 ml. Vial 5 ml.
Use: Adjunct to general anesthesia as neuromuscular blocking agent.

NORCYCLINE. 6-Demethyl-6-deoxytetracycline. Bonomycin. Sancycline.
Use: Antibiotic.

NORDETTE-21. (Wyeth) Levonorgestrel 0.15 mg., ethinyl estradiol 0.03 mg./Tab. 6 Pilpak dispensers, 21 Tabs.
Use: Oral contraceptive.

NORDETTE-28. (Wyeth) Levonorgestrel 0.15 mg., ethinyl estradiol 0.03 mg./White Tab. (21) with inert tablets (7). 6 Pilpak dispensers, 28 tab.
Use: Oral contraceptive.

NORDRYL. (Vortech) Diphenhydramine HCl **Cap.:** Diphenhydramine HCl 25 mg. or 50 mg./Cap. Bot. 1000s. **Elix.** 10 mg./4 cc. Bot. 4 oz., gal. **Expectorant:** 80 mg., menthol 1/10 gr., ammonium chloride 12 gr., sod. citrate 5 gr., alcohol 5%/cc. 4 oz., gal. **Parenteral:** 10 mg./cc. Vial 30 cc.
Use: Anti-allergic.

NOREL PLUS CAPSULES. (U.S. Chemical) Chlorpheniramine Maleate 4 mg., phenyltoloxamine dihydrogen citrate 25 mg., phenylpropanolamine HCl 25 mg., acetaminophen 325 mg./Cap.
Use: Antihistaminic, decongestant, analgesic.

dl-NOREPHEDRINE HYDROCHLORIDE. alpha-Hydroxy-beta-aminopropylbenzene HCl.
See: Phenylpropanolamine Hydrochloride. (Various mfr.)
Propadrine, Cap., Elix. (Merck Sharp & Dohme)

• **NOREPINEPHRINE BITARTRATE,** U.S.P. XXI. Inj., U.S.P. XXI. 1,2-Benzenediol, 4-(2-amino-1-hydroxyethyl)-, 2,3-dihydroxybutanedioate (1:1) (Salt), monohydrate l-a-(Aminomethyl)3,4-dihydroxybenzyl alcohol bitartrate.
Use: Adrenergic (vasopressor).
See: Levophed Bitartrate, Sol., Amp. (Winthrop-Breon)

NORETHANDROLONE, B.A.N. 17-Alphaethyl-17-hydroxynorandrostenone, 17-Hydroxy-19-nor-17α-pregn-4-en-3-one. Nileyar
Use: Anabolic steroid.

• **NORETHINDRONE,** U.S.P. XXI. Tab., U.S.P. XXI. 19-Norpregn-4-en-20-yn-3-one, 17-hydroxy-, (17α)-. 17-Hydroxy-19-nor-17-alpha-pregn-4-en-20-yn-3-one.
Use: Progestin.
See: Micronor, Tab. (Ortho)
Norlutin, Tab. (Parke-Davis)
Nor-Qd., Tab. (Syntex)
W/Ethinyl estradiol.
See: Brevicon 21 and 28, Tab. (Syntex)
Modicon 21 and 28, Tab. (Ortho)
Ortho-Novum 21 and 28 Prods (Ortho)
Ovcon-35 Tab. (Mead Johnson)
Ovcon-50 Tab. (Mead Johnson)
W/Mestranol.
See: Norinyl, Prods. (Syntex)
Ortho-Novum Prods. (Ortho)
W/Mestranol, ferrous fumarate.
See: Norinyl-l Fe 28 Prods. (Syntex)

• **NORETHINDRONE ACETATE,** U.S.P. XXI. Tab., U.S.P. XXI. 19-Norpregn-4-en-20-yn-3-one, 17-(acetyloxy)-, (17α)-, 17α-Ethinyl-19-nortestosterone 17-Hydroxy-19-nor-17α-pregn-4-en-20-yn-3-one Acetate.
Use: Progestin.
See: Norlutate, Tab. (Parke-Davis)

• **NORETHINDRONE ACETATE AND ETHINYL ESTRADIOL TABLETS,** U.S.P. XXI.
Use: Oral contraceptive.
See: Brevicon, Tab. (Syntex)
Gestest, Tabs. (Squibb)
Loestrin, Prods. (Parke-Davis)
Norinyl, Prods. (Syntex)
Norlestrin, Prods. (Parke-Davis)

• **NORETHINDRONE AND ETHINYL ESTRADIOL TABLETS,** U.S.P. XXI.
Use: Oral contraceptive.

• **NORETHINDRONE AND MESTRANOL TABLETS** U.S.P. XXI.
Use: Oral contraceptive.

NORETHISTERONE. B.A.N. 17β-Hydroxy-19-norpreg-4-en-20-yn-3-one. 17α-Ethynyl-17β-hydroxyoestr-4-en-3-one. 17α-Ethynyl-19-nor-testosterone. Micronor; Noriday; Primolut N; Norlutin-A [acetate]
Use: Progestational steroid.
See: Norethindrone (Var. Mfr.)

• **NORETHYNODREL,** U.S.P. XXI. 17-Hydroxy-19-nor-17α-pregn-5(10)-en-20-yn-3-one.
Use: Progesterone agent.
See: Enovid, Prods (Searle)

NORFERAN. (Vortech) Iron dextran 50 mg./ml. Vial 10 ml.
Use: Anemias.

NORFLEX. (Riker) Orphenadrine citrate 100 mg./Tab. Bot. 100s, 500s.
Use: Relief of discomfort of acute painful musculoskeletal conditions.

NORFLEX INJECTABLE. (Riker) Orphenadrine citrate 60 mg., sodium bisulfite 2 mg., sodium chloride 5.8 mg., water for injection qs 2 cc. Amp. 2 cc. 6s, 50s.
Use: Relief of discomfort of acute painful musculoskeletal conditions.

• **NORFLOXACIN.** USAN.
Use: Antibacterial.

• **NORFLURANE.** USAN. 1,1,1,2-Tetrafluoroethane. Under study.
Use: Inhalation anesthetic.

NORFORMS. (Fleet) PEG 20, PEG 6, PEG 20 Palmitate, lactic acid, methylbenzethonium chloride/Supp. Regular and herbal scent. Box 6s, 12s, 24s.
Use: Vaginal deodorant suppository.

NORGESIC FORTE TABLETS. (Riker) Orphenadrine citrate 50 mg., Aspirin 770 mg., caffeine 60 mg./Tab. Bot. 100s, 500s.
Use: Relief of mild to moderate pain, acute musculoskeletal disorders.

NORGESIC TABLETS. (Riker) Orphenadrine citrate 25 mg., aspirin 385 mg., caffeine 30 mg./Tab. Bot. 100s, 500s.
Use: Relief of mild to moderate pain of acute musculoskeletal disorders.

ORGESTIMATE. USAN.
Use: Progestin.

ORGESTOMET. USAN.
Use: Progestin.

ORGESTREL. U.S.P. XXI. Tab., U.S.P. XXI. 18,19-Dinorpregn-4-en-20-yn-3-one, 13-ethyl-17-hydroxy,-(17 α)-(+)-. (±)-13-Ethyl-17-hydroxy-18, 19-dinor-17α-pregn-4-en-20-yn-3-one. (±)-13-Ethyl-17α-ethynyl-17-hydroxygon-4-en-3-one.
Use: Oral contraceptive.
See: Ovrette, Tab. (Wyeth)

ORGESTREL AND ETHINYL ESTRADIOL TABLETS, U.S.P. XXI.
Use: Oral contraceptive.
See: Lo/Ovral, Tab. (Wyeth)
Ovral-Prep. (Wyeth)

RINYL 2 MG. (Syntex) Norethindrone 2 mg., mestranol 0.1 mg./Tab. Memorette Disp. of 20s. Refill folders of 20s.
Use: Oral contraceptive, hypermenorrhea.

RINYL 1 + 35. (Syntex) Norethindrone 1 mg., ethinyl estradiol 0.035 mg./Tab. 21 & 28 day (7 inert tabs) Wallette.
Use: Oral contraceptive.

RINYL 1 + 50. (Syntex) Norethindrone 1 mg., mestranol 0.05 mg./Tab. 21 & 28 day (7 inert tabs) Wallette.
Use: Oral contraceptive.

RINYL 1 + 80 (Syntex) Norethindrone 1 mg., mestranol 0.08 mg./Tab. 21 & 28 day (7 inert tabs) Wallette.
Use: Oral contraceptive.

RISODRINE AEROTROL. (Abbott) Norisodrine HCl (isoproterenol HCl) 0.25% (2.8 mg./ml.) in inert chlorofluorohydrocarbon propellants, alcohol 33%, ascorbic acid 0.1% as preservative. Aerotrol 15 ml. Box 12s.
Use: Management of severe attacks of bronchial asthma.

RISODRINE WITH CALCIUM IODIDE SYRUP. (Abbott) Isoproterenol sulfate 3 mg., calcium iodide 150 mg./5 ml. w/alcohol 6% Bot. pt.
Use: Symptomatic control of bronchospasm and allied respiratory disorder.

RLAC. (Rowell) Vit. A 8000 I.U., D-2 400 I.U., Ca 200 mg., Iron 60 mg., C 90 mg., B-1 2 mg., B-2 2 mg., B-6 4 mg., niacinamide 20 mg., E 30 I.U., B-12 8 mcg., Folic Acid 0.4 mg., Mg 100 mg., Zn 15 mg., Cu 2 mg., iodine 0.15 mg./RoSeal. Bot. 100s.
Use: Prenatal supplement.

RLAC RX. (Rowell) Same formula as Norlac except folic acid 1 mg./Ro-Seal. Bot. 100s, 1000s. Unit-of-use 100s.
Use: Prenatal supplement for high risk of folic acid deficiency.

RLESTRIN-21 1/50 TABLETS. (Parke-Davis) Norethindrone acetate 1 mg., ethinyl estradiol 50 mcg./yellow tab. Compact 21s. Pkg. 5 compacts. Pkg. 5 refills; Ctn. 10×5 refills.
Use: Oral contraceptive.

RLESTRIN-28 1/50 TABLET. (Parke-Davis) Norethindrone acetate 1 mg., ethinyl estradiol 50 mcg./yellow tab. Compact 21 yellow, 7 white (inert) tablets. Pkg. 5 compacts. Pkg. 5 refills; Ctn. 10×5 refills.
Use: Oral contraceptive.

NORLESTRIN-21 2.5/50 TABLETS. (Parke-Davis) Norethindrone acetate 2.5 mg., ethinyl estradiol 50 mcg./pink tablet. Compact 21s. Pkg. 5 compacts. Pkg. 5 refills; Ctn. 10×5 refills.
Use: Oral contraceptive.

NORLESTRIN Fe 1/50 TABLET. (Parke-Davis) Norethindrone acetate 1 mg., ethinyl estradiol 50 mcg./yellow tab. Compact 21 yellow tablets, 7 brown 75 mg. ferrous fumarate tab. Pkg. 5 compacts. Pkg. 5 refills; ctn. 10×5 refills.
Use: Oral contraceptive.

NORLESTRIN Fe 2.5/50 TABLETS. (Parke-Davis) Norethindrone acetate 2.5 mg., ethinyl estradiol 50 mcg./pink tab. Compact 21 pink Tab., 7 brown 75 mg. ferrous fumarate Tab. Pkg. 5 compacts. Pkg. 5 refills; Ctn. 10×5 refills.
Use: Oral contraceptive.

NORLEVORPHANOL. B.A.N. (−)-3-hydroxymorphinan.
Use: Narcotic analgesic.

NOR-LIEF. (Vortech) Phenylephrine HCl 5 mg., chlorpheniramine maleate 0.5 mg., ascorbic acid 15 mg./Tab. Bot. 1000s.
Use: Antihistamine decongestant.

NORLUTATE. (Parke-Davis) Norethindrone acetate 5 mg./Tab. Bot. 50s.
Use: Amenorrhea, menstrual irregularity.

NORLUTIN. (Parke-Davis) Norethindrone, 5 mg./Tab. Bot. 50s.
Use: Control of many menstrual disorders.

NORMADERM CREAM & LOTION. (Doak) Buffered lactic acid in vanishing bases. **Cream:** jar 3¾ oz., 16 oz. **Lotion:** Bot. 4 oz., 16 oz., 128 oz.
Use: Lubricant & acid restorer for skin.

NORMAL HUMAN SERUM ALBUMIN. Albumin Human, U.S.P. XXI.

NORMATANE DC EXPECTORANT. (Vortech) Codeine phosphate 10 mg., brompheniramine maleate 2 mg., guaifenesin 100 mg., phenylephrine HCl 5 mg., phenylpropanolamine HCl 5 mg., menthol 1 mg., alcohol 3.5%/5 cc. Bot. 4 oz., gal.
Use: Antihistaminic, antitussive.

NORMATANE ELIXIR. (Vortech) Bot. 4 oz., gal.
Use: Antihistaminic, nasal decongestant.

NORMATANE EXPECTORANT. (Vortech) Brompheniramine maleate 2 mg., guaifenesin 100 mg., phenylephrine HCl 5 mg., phenylpropanolamine HCl 5 mg., menthol 1 mg., alcohol 3.5%/5 ml. Bot. 4 oz., gal.
Use: Antihistaminic, antitussive.

NORMATANE TD. (Vortech) Brompheniramine maleate 12 mg., phenylephrine HCl 15 mg., phenylpropanolamine HCl 15 mg./Tab. Bot. 100s, 1000s.
Use: Antihistaminic, decongestant.

NORMENON. Chlormadinone, B.A.N.

NORMETHADONE. B.A.N. 6-Dimethylamino-4,4-diphenylhexan-3-one.
Use: Narcotic analgesic.

NORMETHANDRONE. 17-α-methyl-19-nortestosterone. 17β-Hydroxy-17-methylestr-4-en-3-one. Methalutin. (Parke-Davis)

NOR-MIL LIQUID. (Vortech) Dipehnoxylate HCl 2.5 mg., atropine sulfate 0.025 mg./5 ml. w/ethyl alcohol 15% Bot. 2 oz.
Use: Antidiarrheal.

NOR-MIL TABLETS. (Vortech) Diphenoxylate HCl 2.5 mg./Tab. Bot. 100s, 500s, 1000s.
Use: Antidiarrheal.

NORMODYNE. (Schering). Labetalol HCl. **Inj.:** 5 mg./ml. Amp. 20 ml. (100 mg.). **Tab.:** 200 mg. 300/Tab. Bot. 100s, 500s. Unit dose 100s. Calendar paks 56s.
Use: Antihypertensive.

NORMOL. (Alcon) Sterile, isotonic solution of sodium chloride, sodium borate, boric acid. Bot. 8 oz.
Use: Soft contact lenses rinsing solution.

NORMORPHINE. B.A.N. N-Demethylmorphine.
Use: Narcotic analgesic.

NORMOSOL-M in D5-W. (Abbott) Dextrose 5 Gm., sod. chloride 234 mg., pot. acetate 128 mg., magnesium acetate 21 mg., sodium bisulfite 30 mg./100 ml. Bot. 500 ml., 1000 ml. in Abbo-Voc (glass) or LifeCare (flexible) containers.
Use: Fluid and electrolyte maintenance, I.V.

NORMOSOL-M 900 CAL. (Abbott) Dextrose 5 Gm., fructose 15 Gm., alcohol 4 ml., sodium chloride 234 mg., pot. acetate 128 mg., magnesium acetate 21 mg., sodium bisulfate 30 mg./100 ml. Bot. 1000 ml.
Use: Fluid and electrolyte maintenance, caloric source.

NORMOSOL-R; NORMOSOL-R pH 7.4; 500 ml., 1000 ml. NORMOSOL-R D5-W. (Abbott) Sod. chloride 526 mg., sod. acetate 222 mg., sod. gluconate 502 mg., pot. chloride 37 mg., magnesium chloride 14 mg. pH of Normosol-R and Normosol R in D5-W adjusted with HCl/100 ml. Bot. 1000 ml., 500 ml. in LifeCare (flexible) containers.
Use: Fluid and electrolyte replacement, I.V.

NORMOTENSIN. (Marcen) I.M. sol. for inj.: Mucopolysaccharide 20 mg., sodium nucleate 25 mg., epinephrine-neutralizing factor 25 u., sodium citrate 10 mg., inositol 5 mg., phenol 0.5%/cc. multidose vials 10 cc., 30 cc.
Use: Lowers blood pressure.

NOROCAINE. (Vortech) Lidocaine HCl 1%, 2%, W/sod. Cl and methyl parasept/cc. Vial 50 ml.
Use: Local anesthetic.

NOROCAINE 1% W/EPINEPHRINE. (Vortech) Lidocaine HCl 1%, epinephrine 1:100,000/cc. Vial 50 ml.
Use: Local anesthetic.

NOROCAINE 2% W/EPINEPHRINE. (Vortech) Lidocaine 2%, epinephrine 0.01 mg./cc. Vial 50 ml.
Use: Local anesthetic.

NOROLON. (Winthrop Products) Chloroquine phosphate.
Use: Antimalaria agent.

NOROPHYLLINE LIQUID. (Vortech) Theophylline 80 mg., alcohol 20%/15 cc. Bot. pt.
Use: Bronchial asthma, bronchitis.

NORPACE. (Searle) Disopyramide phosphate 100 mg., 150 mg./Cap. Bot. 100s, 500s, 1000s. Unit Dose 100s.
Use: Treatment of specific ventricular arrhythmia

NORPACE CR. (Searle) Disopyramide phosphate 1 mg. or 150 mg./Controlled-Release Cap. Bot. 1(500s, 1000s.
Use: Treatment of ventricular arrhythmias.

NORPANTH. (Vortech) Propantheline bromide 15 mg./Tab. Bot. 1000s.
Use: Anticholinergic.

NORPHYL. (Vita Elixir) Aminophylline 1.5 gr./Tab.
Use: Bronchial asthma, myocardial infarction.

NORPIPANONE. B.A.N. 4,4-Diphenyl-6-piperidinoh an-3-one.
Use: Analgesic.

NORPRAMIN. (Merrell Dow) Desipramine HCl. **10** mg./Tab. Bot. 100s; **25** mg./Tab. Bot. 100s, 100 Unit dose 100s; **50** mg./Tab. Bot. 100s, 1000s. U dose 100s; **75** mg./Tab. Bot. 100s; **100** mg./Tab Bot. 100s. **150** mg./Tab. Bot. 50s.
Use: Antidepressant.

NOR-PRED S. (Vortech) Prednisolone sod. phosph 20 mg./cc. Vial 10 cc.
Use: Adrenocortical steroid (anti-inflammatory).

NOR-PRED T.B.A. (Vortech) Prednisolone tertiary b acetate 20 mg., sod. citrate 1 mg., polysorbate 8 1 mg., d-sorbital 450 mg., benzyl alcohol 0.9%/ Vial 10 cc.
Use: Rheumatic arthritis.

19-NORPREGN-4-EN-20-YN-3-ONE, 17-HYDROXY-, (17α)-. Norethindrone, U.S.P. XXI.

19-NORPREGNA-1,3,5(10)TRIEN-20-YN-17-OL; 3-METHOXY-, (17α). Mestranol. U.S.P. XXI.

NOR-Q.D. (Syntex) Norethindrone 0.35 mg./Tab. D penser 42s.
Use: Progestin-only contraceptive.

NORTESTERIONATE. 19-Nortestosterone cyclopen propionate.

NOR-TET. (Vortech) Tetracycline HCl 250 mg./C orange/yellow; 500 mg./Cap. black/yellow Bot. 100s, 1000s.
Use: Antibiotic.

NORTRAN. Trifluomeprazine, B.A.N.

NORTRIPTYLINE. B.A.N. 3-(3-Methylamino-propylidene)dibenzo[a,d]cyclohepta-1,4-diene. Al gron, Altilev.
Use: Antidepressant.

• **NORTRIPTYLINE HCl,** U.S.P. XXI. Oral Sol., Cap. U.S.P. XXI. 5-(3-Methyl-aminopropylidene)-10,11-dihydro-5H-dibenzo [a,d] cycloheptene HCl. 10,11 Dihydro-N-methyl-5H-dibenzo(a,d)cycloheptene-Δ^5 γ propylamine Hydrochloride.
Use: Antidepressant.
See: Aventyl HCl, Liq., Pulvule (Lilly)
Pamelor, Cap., Liq. (Sandoz)

NORTUSSIN LIQUID. (Vortech) Guaifenesin 100 mg alcohol 3.5%/5 cc. Bot. 4 oz., gal.
Use: Expectorant.

NORTUSSIN W/CODEINE LIQUID. (Vortech) Codeine phosphate 5 mg., guaifenesin 100 mg., alcohol 3.5%/5 cc. Bot. 4 oz., gal.
Use: Antitussive, expectorant.

RVAL. Docusate sodium.

RWICH ASPIRIN. (Procter & Gamble) Aspirin 325 ng./Tab. Bot. 100s, 250s, 500s.
Jse: Pain relief of headache, minor aches and pains; antipyretic.

RWICH EXTRA STRENGTH ASPIRIN. (Procter & Gamble) Aspirin 500 mg./Tab. Bot. 150s.
Jse: Pain relief of headache, minor aches and pains; antipyretic.

RWICH GLYCERIN SUPPOSITORIES. (Fleet) Jar adult: 12s, 24s, 50s. Infant: 12s.
Jse: Laxative.

SALT SALT ALTERNATIVE. (Norcliff Thayer) Potassium Cl., potassium bitartrate, potassium glutamate, adipic acid, fumaric acid, polyethylene glycol 400, disodium inosinate. Container 11 oz.
Jse: Salt substitute.

OSCAPINE, U.S.P. XXI. Narcotine.
Jse: Antitussive.
See: Tusscapine, Susp. (Fisons)

SCAPINE HCl. l-Narcotine hydrochloride.
Jse: Antitussive.
See: Conar Prods. (Beecham Labs)
'Chlorpheniramine maleate, phenylephrine HCl, N-acetyl-p-aminophenol, salicylamide, Vit. C.
See: Noscaps, Cap. (Table Rock)
'Phenylephrine HCl.
See: Conar Liq. (Beecham Labs)
'Phenylephrine, acetylsalicylic acid, N-acetyl-p-aminophenol, caffeine, pyrilamine maleate.
See: Tussapap, Tab. (Sutliff & Case)
Phenylephrine HCl, guaifensin.
See: Conar, Expect. (Beecham Labs)

SCAPS. (Table Rock) Noscapine 7.5 mg., chlorpheniramine maleate 1 mg., phenylephrine HCl 5 mg., N-acetyl-p-aminophenol 150 mg., salicylamide 150 mg., Vit. C 20 mg./Cap. Bot. 100s, 500s.
Use: Relief of common cold.

OSIHEPTIDE. USAN.
Use: Growth stimulant.

SKOTE. (Plough) Homosalate, oxybenzone, SPF 8. Tube 7/16 oz., Jar 1 oz.
Use: Ultraviolet sunscreen.

SPAZ, IM. (Reid-Provident) Dicyclomine HCl 10 mg., sodium chloride 0.9%, chlorobutanol 0.5%, water q.s./cc. Vial 10 cc.
Use: Anticholinergic.

STRIL. (Boehringer Ingelheim) Phenylephrine HCl 0.25% or 0.5% w/benzalkonium Cl. 0.004% in buffered aqueous sol. Bot. 15 ml.
Use: Nasal decongestant.

STRILLA. (Boehringer Ingelheim) Oxymetazoline HCl 0.05% w/benzalkonium Cl. 0.02% Bot. 15 ml.
Use: Long acting nasal decongestant spray.

TENSIL MALEATE. Acepromazine, B.A.N.

VAFED. (Merrell Dow) Pseudoephedrine HCl 30 mg./5 ml., alcohol 7.5%, Bot. 4 oz.
Use: Decongestant.

VAFED A. (Merrell Dow) Pseudoephedrine HCl 30 mg., chlorpheniramine maleate 2 mg./5 ml., alcohol 5%. Bot. 4 oz.
Use: Decongestant, antihistamine.

NOVAFED A CAPSULES (Merrell Dow) Pseudoephedrine HCl 120 mg., chlorpheniramine maleate 8 mg./ controlled release capsule. Bot. 100s.
Use: Decongestant/antihistamine.

NOVAFED CAPSULES. (Merrell Dow) Pseudoephedrine HCl 120 mg./Controlled-Release Cap. Bot. 100s.
Use: Decongestant.

NOVAHISTINE COUGH & COLD FORMULA. (Merrell Dow) Dextromethorphan hydrobromide 10 mg., pseudoephedrine HCl 30 mg., chlorpheniramine maleate 2 mg./5 ml. w/alcohol 5%. Bot. 4 oz., 8 oz.
Use: Antitussive, decongestant, antihistamine for cough & cold symptoms.

NOVAHISTINE DMX. (Merrell Dow) Pseudoephedrine HCl 30 mg., dextromethorphan HBr 10 mg., guaifenesin 100 mg./5 ml. w/alcohol 10%. Bot. 4 oz., 8 oz.
Use: Antitussive, expectorant, decongestant.

NOVAHISTINE DH. (Merrell Dow) Pseudoephedrine HCl 30 mg., codeine phosphate 10 mg., chlorpheniramine maleate 2 mg./5 ml. w/alcohol 5%. Bot. 4 oz., pt.
Use: Antitussive, decongestant, antihistamine.

NOVAHISTINE ELIXIR. (Merrell Dow) Phenylephrine HCl 5 mg., chlorpheniramine maleate 2 mg./5 ml. w/alcohol 5%. Bot. 4 oz., 8 oz.
Use: Decongestant, antihistamine.

NOVAHISTINE EXPECTORANT. (Merrell Dow) Pseudoephedrine HCl 30 mg., codeine phosphate 10 mg., guaifenesin 100 mg./5 ml. w/alcohol 7.5%. Bot. 4 oz., Pt.
Use: Antitussive, decongestant, expectorant.

NOVAHISTINE FORTIS. (Merrell Dow) Phenylephrine HCl 10 mg., chlorpheniramine maleate 2.0 mg./Cap. Bot. 100s.
Use: Decongestant, antihistamine.

NOVAHISTINE L.P. (Merrell Dow) Phenylephrine HCl 20 mg., chlorpheniramine maleate 4 mg./Tab. Bot. 100s.
Use: Decongestant, antihistamine.

NOVAHISTINE TABLETS. (Merrell Dow) Phenylpropanolamine HCl 18.75 mg., chlorpheniramine maleate 2 mg./Tab. Pkg. 48s.
Use: Decongestant, antihistamine for treatment of cold and hay fever symptoms.

NOVALDIN. (Winthrop Products) Dipyrone. Available as Tabs., Amp., Drops.
Use: Analgesic, antipyretic, anti-inflammatory.

NOVAMIDON.
See: Aminopyrine (Various Mfr.)

NOVAMINE. (KabiVitrum) Amino acids injection. 8.5% in flasks of 500 ml., 1000 ml. 11.4% in flasks of 250 ml., 500 ml., 1000 ml.
Use: Source for amino acids in parenteral nutrition regimens.

NOVATOPHAN.
See: Neocinchophen (Various Mfr.)

NOVATROPINE.
See: Homatropine Methylbromide (Various Mfr.)

NOVERIL HYDROCHLORIDE. Dibenzepin, B.A.N.

NOVOBIOCIN, B.A.N. Streptonivicin. (Biotexin) An antibiotic from Streptomyces niveus and Streptomyces spheroides.
See: Albamycin, Cap. (Upjohn)

• **NOVOBIOCIN CALCIUM,** U.S.P. XXI. Oral Susp., U.S.P. XXI.
See: Cathomycin Calcium

NOVOBIOCIN MONOSODIUM SALT.
See: Sodium Novobiocin.

• **NOVOBIOCIN SODIUM,** U.S.P. XXI. Cap., U.S.P. XXI.
See: Albamycin, Cap. (Upjohn)
Cathomycin Sodium

NOVOCAIN. (Winthrop-Breon) Procaine HCl solution. **1%:** Amp. 2 ml. Box 25s, 6 ml. Box 50s; Vial 30 ml. Box 10s. **2%:** Vial 30 ml. Box 10s.
Use: Local anesthetic by infiltration injection, nerve block and other peripheral blocks.

NOVOCAIN FOR SPINAL ANESTHESIA. (Winthrop-Breon) Procaine HCl 10% solution. Amp. 2 ml. Box 25s.
Use: Spinal anesthesia.

NOVOHYDRIN. Ambuside, B.A.N.

NOXIPTYLINE, B.A.N. 3-(2-Dimethylaminoethyloxyimino)dibenzo[a,d]cyclohepta-1,4-diene.
Use: Antidepressant.

NOXYTHIOLIN. B.A.N. N-Hydroxymethyl-N′-methylthiourea. Noxyflex
Use: Antifungal agent.

NOXZEMA ACNE-12. (Noxell) Benzoyl peroxide 10%. Bot. 1 oz.
Use: Acne medicine.

NOXZEMA ANTISEPTIC SKIN CLEANSER. (Noxell) SD alcohol 63%. Bot. 4 oz., 8 oz.
Use: Oily skin cleanser.

NOXZEMA CLEAR-UPS. (Noxell) Salicylic acid 0.5% on pads. Jar 50 pad count.
Use: Acne treatment.

NOXZEMA MEDICATED SKIN CREAM. (Noxell) Menthol, camphor, clove oil, eucalyptus oil, phenol. Jar 2.5 oz., 4 oz., 6 oz., 10 oz. Tube 4.5 oz. Bot. 6 oz.
Use: Soothing sunburn pain.

NP-27 AEROSOL. (Thompson Medical) Zinc undecylenate, alcohol 20.5%. Spray Cans 4 oz.
Use: Dermatophytosis.

NP-27 CREAM. (Thompson Medical) 8-hydroxyquinoline benzoate 2.5% in cream base. Tube 1.5 oz.
Use: Antifungal for relief of athlete's foot and ringworm.

NP-27 LIQUID. (Thompson Medical) Undecylenic acid 10%, isopropyl alcohol 56%. Plastic bot. 2 oz.
Use: Dermatophytosis.

NTR NOSE DROPS. (Winthrop Consumer Products) Phenylephrine HCl.
Use: Nasal decongestant.

NTZ SOLUTION. (Winthrop Consumer Products) Oxymetazoline HCl 0.05% w/benzalkonium Cl and phenylmercuric acetate 0.002% as preservatives. Bot. 1 oz., 16 oz.; Spray Bot. 15 ml.
Use: Decongestant, antihistaminic.

NUBAIN. (Du Pont) Nalbuphine HCl **10 mg.**/ml. Ampul 1 ml., 2 ml. Vial 10 ml. **20 mg.**/ml. Ampul ml. Syringes 1 ml. calibrated. Vial 10 ml.
Use: Analgesic.

NU-BOLIC. (Seatrace) Methandriol dipropionate mg./ml. Vial 10 cc.

NUCAFED PEDIATRIC EXPECTORANT. (Beecham Labs) Codeine phosphate 10 mg., pseudoephedri HCl 30 mg., guaifenesin 100 mg./5 ml. w/alcohol 6%. Bot. Pt.
Use: Antitussive, decongestant, expectorant.

NUCITE.
See: Inositol (Various Mfr.)

■ **NUCLEIC ACID ANTAGONISTS.**
Use: Treatment certain forms of neoplastic diseases.
See: Leukeran, Tab. (Burroughs Wellcome)
Mustargen, Vial (Merck Sharp & Dohme)
Myleran, Tab. (Burroughs Wellcome)
Purinethol, Tab. (Burroughs Wellcome)
Triethylene Melamine, Tab. (Lederle)

NUCLEOSINE. (Pasadena Research) Adenosine-5′-monophosphate 25 mg., cyanocobalamin 60 mcg./cc. Vial 10 cc.

NUCOFED. (Beecham Labs) Codeine phosphate 20 mg., pseudoephedrine HCl 60 mg/5 ml. or Cap. **Liq.:** Bot. pts.; **Cap.:** Bot. 60s.
Use: Antitussive, decongestant.

NU-DISPOZ. (Coastal) Diethylpropion HCl 25 mg./Ta Bot. 100s, 1000s.

NUDIT-DEPILATORY. (Medtech) Calcium thioglycola Tube 1 oz., 2 oz., 3 oz. Brush on 1.5 oz., 2 oz. 3 oz.
Use: Depilatory cream.

NUDIT-FORTIFIED FADE CREAM. (Medtech) H droquinone Bot. 2 oz.
Use: Fade cream.

• **NUFENOXOLE.** USAN.
Use: Antiperistaltic.

nu-FLOW. (Rydell) A blend of two synthetic detergen an emollient complex, parachlorometaxylenol 2%, isopropanol 7.5% Bot. 120 ml.
Use: Concentrated, neutral, medicated shampoo.

NUGOFED EXPECTORANT. (Beecham Labs) Codeine phosphate 20 mg., pseudoephedrine HCl 60 mg., guaifenesin 200 mg./5 ml. w/alcohol 12.5%. Bot. pt.
Use: Antitussive, decongestant.

NU-IRON. (Mayrand) Polysaccharide-iron comple **Cap.:** 150 mg. elemental iron. Bot. 100s, 500s. **Elixir:** 100 mg. elemental iron/5 cc., w/alcohol 10%. Bot. 8 oz.
Use: Iron deficiency anemia.

NU-IRON PLUS ELIXIR. (Mayrand) Polysaccharide irc complex 100 mg., folic acid 1 mg., Vit B-12 25 mcg./ ml. w/alcohol 10%. Bot. 8 oz.
Use: Iron-vitamin supplement.

NU-IRON-V. (Mayrand) Polysaccharide iron 60 mg., fol acid 1 mg., ascorbic acid 50 mg., cyancobalamin 3 mcg., Vit. A 4000 I.U., D-2 400 I.U., B-1 3 mg., B-

2 3 mg., niacinamide 10 mg., Cacarbonate 312 mg., B-6 HCl 2 mg./Tab. Bot. 100s.
Use: Vitamin iron supplement.

'LEVEN. (Lemmon) Gastro-soluble layer: Pepsin 150 mg. Enteric coated inner core: pancreatic enzyme conc. 100 mg., ox bile ext. 100 mg., cellulase 10 mg./Tab. Bot. 1000s.
Use: Digestive aid.

JLICAINE. (Kay) Lidocaine HCl 10 mg. or 20 mg., methylparaben 1 mg., sodium chloride 6 mg./cc. Multiple dose sterile solution 50 cc.
Use: Minor nerve block anesthesia.

JLLAPONS. (General Aniline & Film) The whole group of chelating agents related to ethylenediaminetetraacetic acid. Pkg. according to demand.
Use: Sequestering agent.

JLLO. (Eckerd) Chlorophyllins 10 mg., ferrous sulfate 9.6 mg., Tab., Bot. 16s, 45s, 100s, 500s.
Use: Orally, to help prevent body odors, control of ileostomy and colostomy odors.

JL-TACH. (Davis & Sly) Potassium 16 mg., magnesium 13 mg., ascorbic acid 250 mg./Tab. Bot. 100s.
Use: Paroxysmal tachycardia.

JMORPHAN. (Du Pont) Oxymorphone HCl. **1 mg./ml.:** Amp. 1 ml. Box 10s, 100s. **1.5 mg./ml.:** Amp. 1 ml. Box 10s, 100s.; Vial 10 ml. Box 1s. **Rectal Suppos.:** Box 6s. 5 mg./Suppos.
Use: Relief of pain.

JMOTIZINE. (Hobart) Guaiacol 0.52 Gm., beechwood creosote 2.60 Gm., methyl salicylate 0.52 Gm./100 Gm. **Liniment** Glass Bot. 1.16 oz. Pl. Bot. 2 oz., 8 oz. **Oint.** 24 oz., 3 lb.
Use: Analgesic and decongestant.

JMOTIZINE CATAPLASM. (Hobart) Guaiacol 0.260 Gm., beechwood creosote 1.302 Gm., methyl salicylate 0.260 Gm./100 Gm. Jar. 4 oz.
Use: Relief of pain and soreness.

JMOTIZINE COUGH SYR. (Hobart) Guaifenesin 5 gr., ammonium chloride 5 gr., sodium citrate 20 gr., menthol 0.04 gr./fl. oz. Bot. 3 oz., pt., gal.

JMZIDENT. (Purepac) Benzocaine, clove oil, peppermint oil. 0.5 oz.
Use: Topical anesthetic.

JMZIT. (Purepac) Glycerin, ethyl alcohol 10%. Gel. Bot. 0.25 oz. **Lot** ¾ oz.
Use: Teething.

J-NATAL FL. (Marlyn) Vit. A acetate 2000 I.U., D 200 I.U., B-1 1.5 mg., B-2 2.5 mg., C 50 mg., nicotinamide 10 mg., d-Ca pantothenate 5 mg., B-6 5 mg., B-12 1 mcg., folic acid 0.2 mg., hesperidin 25 mg., fluoride 0.5 mg., Ca 150 mg., Fe 30 mg./Tab. Bot. 100s.
Use: Prenatal Vitamin.

JNOL.
See: Phenobarbital (Various Mfr.)

JPERCAINAL. (Ciba) **Cream.** Dibucaine 0.5%, acetone, sod. bisulfite 37%. Tube 1.5 oz. **Oint.** Dibucaine 1%, sod. bisulfite 0.5%. Tube 1 oz., 2 oz.
Use: Topically: local anesthetic, minor burns remedy. **Supp.** Zinc oxide 250 mg., bismuth subgallate 1 Gm., acetone, sod. bisulfite 0.5%. Box 12s, 24s.
Use: Hemorrhoids.

NUPERCAINE HYDROCHLORIDE. (Ciba) Dibucaine HCl Amp. 1:200, 10 mg. w/sod. chloride 10 mg., sod. phosphate monobasic 4 mg., sod. phosphate dibasic 0.9 mg./2 ml., 10s. Heavy Sol. (1:400) 5 mg., dextrose 100 mg./2 ml. Pkg. 10s. Amp. 1:1500 sod. chloride 100 mg., 20 ml. 12s.
Use: Spinal anesthetic.

NUPRIN TABLETS. (Bristol-Myers) Ibuprofen 200 mg./Tab. Blister Pak 8s. Bot. 24s, 50s, 100s.
Use: Reduction of fever, minor aches & pains.

N-URISTIX REAGENT STRIPS. (Ames) Bot 100s.
Use: Dip and read test for protein, glucose and nitrite in urine.

NURSOY. (Wyeth) Vit. A 2500 I.U., D-3 400 I.U., C 55 mg., B-1 0.67 mg., B-2 1 mg., E 9 I.U., niacin 9.5 mEq., B-6 0.4 mg., B-12 2 mcg., pantothenic acid 3 mg., K-1 0.1 mg., folic acid 50 mcg., choline 85 mg., inositol 26 mg., iodine, biotin, Ca, P, Na, K, Mg, Mn, Cl, Cu, Zn/qt. of formula. Conc. liq. Can 13 oz. Ready to feed Can 32 oz. Ready to feed Hospital Bot. 4 oz.

NU-THERA. (Kirkman) Vit. A 10,000 I.U., D 400 I.U., B-1 10 mg., B-2 5 mg., niacinamide 100 mg., B-6 1 mg., B-12 5 mcg., C 150 mg., Ca 103 mg., P 80 mg., Fe 10 mg., Mg 5.5 mg., Mn 1 mg., K 5 mg., Zn 1.4 mg./Cap. Bot. 100s.
Use: Dietary supplement for vitamin and mineral deficiency.

• **NUTMEG OIL,** N.F. XVI.
Use: Pharmaceutic aid (flavor).

NUTRACORT. (Owen) Hydrocortisone. **Cream:** 1%: Jars 2 oz., 4 oz., 1 lb., Tube 30 Gm. **Lotions:** 0.25%: 0.5%, 1%: Bot. 2 oz., 4 oz.
Use: Dermatologic anti-inflammatory.

NUTRACORT GEL. (Owen) Hydrocortisone 1.0% in vehicle of propylene glycol, alcohol 22%, hydroxypropyl cellulose and citric acid. Tube 15 gm., 60 gm.
Use: Inflammatory manifestations of corticosteroid-responsive dermatoses.

NUTRADERM. (Owen) Oil-in-water emulsion. **Lot.** Plastic Bot. 8 oz., 16 oz. **Cream:** Tube 1.5 oz., 3 oz., Jar 1 lb.
Use: Emollient.

NUTRADERM BATH OIL. (Owen) Mineral oil, PEG-4 dilaurate, lanolin oil, butylparaben, benzophenone-3, fragrance, D & C Green No. 6. Bot. 8 oz.
Use: Aid in the relief of dry, itchy skin.

NUTRAJEL. (Cenci) Aluminum hydroxide, 5 gr./5 cc. Bot. 12 oz.
Use: Antacid, duodenal ulcers.

NUTRAMAG. (Cenci) Colloidalized gel of aluminum and magnesium hydroxide. Bot. 12 oz.
Use: Antacid, nonconstipating demulcent.

NUTRAMENT LIQUID. (Drackett) Protein 16 Gm., fat 10 Gm., carbohydrates 52 Gm., and vitamins & minerals/360 calories/12.5 oz. Can 12.5 oz.
Use: Nutritional supplement.

NUTRAMIGEN. (Mead Johnson) Hypoallergenic formula that supplies 640 calories/qt. w/18 Gm. protein, 25 Gm. fat, 86 Gm. carbohydrate. Vit. A 2000 I.U., D 400 I.U., E 20 I.U., C 52 mg., folic acid 100 mcg., B-1 0.5 mg., B-2 0.6 mg., niacin 8 mg., B-6 0.4 mg., B-12 2 mcg., biotin 50 mcg., pantothenic acid 3 mg., Vit. K-1 100 mcg., choline 85 mg., inositol 30 mg., Ca 600 mg., P 400 mg., iodine 45 mcg., Fe 12 mg., Mg 70 mg., Cu 0.6 mg., Zn 5 mg., Mn 200 mcg., Cl 550 mg., K 700 mg., Na 300 mg./qt. of formula (4.9 oz. pow.), Cans 16 oz.
Use: Feeding of infants and children allergic to ordinary food proteins and/or lactose intolerant. Complete, nutritionally balanced diet.

NUTRAMIN. (Thurston) Vit. A 666 I.U., D 66 I.U., B-1 666 mcg., B-2 333 mcg., niacinamide 2 mg., folic acid 0.0444 mcg., Ca 16.6 mg., P 8.33 mg., Fe 1.33 mg., iodine 0.15 mg./Tab. Bot. 200s, 500s, 1000s.
Use: Dietary supplement.

NUTRAMIN GRANULAR. (Thurston) Vit. A 333 I.U., D 333 I.U., B-1 3.3 mg., B-2 1.6 mg., niacinamide 10 mg., folic acid 0.133 mg., Ca 250 mg., P 115 mg., Fe 6.6 mg., iodine 0.15 mg./5 Gm. Bot. 10 oz., 32 oz.
Use: Vitamin-mineral supplement.

NUTRAPLUS. (Owen) Urea 10% in emollient cream base or lotion base with preservatives. **Cream.** Tube 3 oz., Jar 1 lb.**Lot.** Bot. 8 oz., 16 oz.
Use: Moisturize dry, rough skin.

NUTRASPA BATH OIL. (Owen) Mineral oil, PEG-4 dilaurate, lanolin oil, butylparaben, benzophenone-3, fragrance, D&C green #6. Bot. 8 oz., 16 oz.
Use: Dry or pruritic skin conditions.

NUTRAVIMS. (Approved) Vit. A 6000 I.U., D 1250 I.U., C 50 mg., E 5 I.U., B-12 5 mcg., B-1 3 mg., B-2 3 mg., B-6 0.5 mg., niacinamide 20 mg., Ca pantothenate 5 mg., zinc 1.5 mg., Mn 1 mg., iodine 0.15 mg., pot. 5 mg., Mg 4 mg., iron 15 mg., Ca 59 mg., phos. 45 mg./Cap. Bot. 100s, 250s, 1000s.
Use: Daily supplement.

NUTRI-AID. (American McGaw) Complete isotonic liquid nutrition. Can 8 oz.
Use: Dietary supplement.

NUTRICOL. (Nutrition Control) Safflower oil 1530 mg., choline bitartrate 500 mg., soybean lecithin 600 mg., inositol 100 mg., natural tocopherols 20 mg., B-6 10 mg., B-12 5 mcg., panthenol 5 mg./Cap. Bot. 90s.
Use: Dietary supplement.

NUTRI-E. (Nutri Lab.) Vitamin E. Cream: 200 I.U./Gm. Jar 1 oz., 2 oz. Oil: 1 oz. Oint. 200 I.U./Gm. Tube 1 oz., 1.5 oz. Cap. 200 I.U., Bot. 80s, 400 I.U., Bot. 60s, 100s. 800 I.U., Bot. 55s.

NUTRIGANIC. (Commerce) Multi-vitamin with minerals and amino acids. Tab. Bot. 50s.
Use: Vitamin supplement.

NUTRI-PLEX TABLETS. (Faraday) Vit. B-1 5 mg., B-2 5 mg., B-6 5 mg., pantothenic acid 25 mg., B-12 12.5 mcg., niacinamide 50 mg., Fe gluconate 30 mg., choline bitartrate 50 mg., inositol 50 mg., P.A.B.A. 15 mg., C 150 mg./2 Tabs. Bot. 100s, 250s.
Use: Protein therapy.

NUTRISOURCE MODULAR SYSTEM. (Sandoz Nutrition) Individual Nutrisource modules available: protein, amino acids, amino acids-high branche chain, carbohydrate, lipid-medium chain triglyceride lipid-long branched chain triglycerides, vitamins, mi erals. Cans of liquid or powder.
Use: Complete enteral system of individual nutrien components for prescribed formula diets.

NUTRI-VAL. (Marcen) Vit. A 5000 I.U., D 500 I.U., B-1 10 mg., B-2 5 mg., B-12 activity 5 mcg., B-6 5 mc C 50 mg., hesperidin 5 mg., niacinamide 15 mg., folic acid 0.2 mg., Ca pantothenate 50 mg., cholin bitartrate 50 mg., betaine HCl 25 mg., lipo-K 0.4 m duodenum substance 50 mg., pancreas substance 50 mg., inositol 25 mg., Cy-yeast hydrolysates 50 m rutin 5 mg., 1-lysine HCl 5 mg., E 5 I.U., Ossona (glucuronic complex) 8 mg., glutamic acid 30 mg., lecithin 5 mg., iron 20 mg., iodine 0.15 mg., Ca 50 mg., P 40 mg., boron 0.1 mg., Cu 1 mg., Mn 1 mg Mg 1 mg., Pot. 5 mg., Zn 0.5 mg., biotin 0.02 mg./Cap. Bot. 100s, 500s, 1000s.
Use: Dietary supplement and absorption aid.

NUTRI-VITE NATURAL MULTIPLE VITAMIN AN MINERALS. (Faraday) Vit. A 15,000 I.U., D 400 I.U., B-1 1.5 mg., B-2 3 mg., B-12 15 mcg., niacin 50 mcg., B-6 20 mcg., choline 1.75 mg., folic acid 1 mcg., pantothenic acid 50 mcg., p-aminobenzoic ac 12 mcg., inositol 1.72 mg., C 60 mg., citrus bioflavonoids 15 mg., E 50 I.U., Fe gluconate 15 mg., Ca 192 mg., P 85 mg., iodine 0.15 mg., red bone marrow 30 mg./3 Tabs. Protein coated Tab. Bot. 100s, 250s.

NUTRIZYME. (Enzyme Process) Vit. A 5000 I.U., D 400 I.U., C 60 mg., B-1 1.5 mg., B-2 1.7 mg., niacinamide 20 mg., B-6 2 mg., pantothenate 10 mg., B-12 6 mcg., E 30 I.U., iron 10 mg., Cu 1 mg., Zn 1 mg., Folacin 0.025 mg./Tab. Bot. 90s, 250s.
Use: Dietary supplement.

NUTROFEROL PLUS. (Winthrop Products) Ferrous gluconate.
Use: Hematinic.

NUX VOMICA EXTRACT. W/Bile salts, cascara sagrada, phenolphthalein, aloin, papain.
See: Taurocolate, Tab. (Vortech)
W/Iron oxide, cinchona, vitamin B-1, alcohol.
See: Briatonic, Liq. (Briar)
W/Methyl testosterone, yohimbine HCl.
See: Climactic, Tab. (Burgin-Arden)

NUZINE OINTMENT. (Hobart) Guaiacol 1.66 Gm., oxyquinoline sulf. 0.42 Gm., zinc oxide 2.5 Gm., glycerine 1.66 Gm., lanum (anhyd.) 43.76 Gm., petrolatum 50 Gm./100 Gm. Tube 1 oz.
Use: Hemorrhoidal pain, pruritus.

NYCOFF. (Dover) Dextromethorphan HBr./Tab. Unit dose Box 500s. Sugar, lactose and salt free.
Use: Cough suppressant.

'CO-WHITE. (Whiteworth) Nystatin, neomycin, gramicidin, triamcinolone cream. Tube 15 Gm., 30 Gm., 60 Gm.
Use: Antibiotic cream.
CO-WORTH. (Whiteworth) Nystatin cream. Tube 15 Gm.
Use: Antibiotic cream.
'CRALAN. (Lannett) Vit. B-1 10 mg., calcium lactate 10 gr./Tab. Bot. 100s.
'DRANE. Beclamide. B.A.N.
DRAZID. (Squibb) Isoniazid. Tab. 100 mg., Bot. 100s, 1000s Inj. 100 mg./cc. w/chlorbutanol 0.25%, sodium hydroxide or hydrochloric acid to adjust pH. Vial 10 cc.
Use: Tuberculosis.
IYLESTRIOL. USAN. 3-Cyclopentyloxy-19-nor-17 α-pregna-1,3,5(10)-trien-20-yne-16, 17β-diol.
Use: Estrogen.
'LIDRIN HYDROCHLORIDE, U.S.P. XXI. Inj., Tab., U.S.P. XXI. p-Hydroxy-a-[1-[(1-methyl-3-phenyl-propyl)-amino]ethyl]benzyl alcohol HCl.
Use: Peripheral vasodilator.
See: Arlidin, Tab. (USV Labs.)
Rolidrin-6, Tab. (Robinson)
Rolidrin-12, Tab. (Robinson)
'LMERATE II SOLUTION CONCENTRATE. (Holland-Rantos) SD alcohol 50%, purified water, acetic acid, boric acid, polysorbate 20, nonoxynol-9, sodium acetate, FD & C Blue # 1, D & C Yellow # 10 Bo. 16 oz.
Use: Acidic cleansing douche in dilution.
'LONETS TRAVEL PACKET. (Matthew) Caps. 20s.
'QUIL. (Vicks) Dextromethorphan HBr 30 mg., pseudoephedrine HCl 60 mg., doxylamine succinate 7.5 mg., acetaminophen 1000 mg./oz. w/alcohol 25%. FDC Yellow #5 tartrazine. Bot. 6 oz., 10 oz., 14 oz.
Use: Analgesic, decongestant, antitussive, antihistaminic cold medicine.
'RAL. (Vale) Cetylpyridinium chloride 0.5 mg., benzocaine 5 mg./Lozenge w/parabens. Pkg. 100s, 1000s.
Use: Antiseptic.
'SACETOL. (Kenyon) N-Acetyl-p-aminophenol 5 gr./Tab. Bot. 100s, 1000s.
'STAFORM. (Miles Pharm) Nystatin 100,000 U., clioquinol 1% in petrolatum base w/octylphenoxyethanol, wax. Oint. Tube 0.5 oz.
Use: Moniliasis treatment.
'STAFORM-HC. (Miles Pharm) Nystaform w/hydrocortisone alcohol 1%. Bot 0.5 oz.
Use: Treatment of moniliasis.
IYSTATIN, U.S.P. XXI. Cream, For Oral Susp., Lotion, Oint., Topical Powder, Oral Susp., Tab., Vaginal Suppos., Vaginal Tab., U.S.P. XXI. An antifungal antibiotic derived from cultures of *Streptomyces noursei.*
Use: Antifungal.
See: Mycostatin Prep. (Squibb)
Nilstat, Cream, Oint., Tabs. (Lederle)
Nilstat Oral Drops (Lederle)
Nilstat Vaginal Tab. (Lederle)
Nystex, Cream, Oint. (savage)
O-V Statin, Tab. (Squibb)
W/Clioquinol
See: Nystaform, Oint. (Miles Pharm)
W/Demethylchlortetracycline.
See: Declostatin, Caps., Tab. (Lederle)
W/Gramicidin, neomycin, triamcinolone.
See: Mycolog Cream, Oint. (Squibb)
W/Neomycin base, gramicidin, triamcinolone acetonide.
See: Mycolog Cream, Oint. (Squibb)
W/Oxytetracycline, glucosamine HCl.
See: Terrastatin, Cap., Sol. (Pfizer)
W/Tetracycline phosphate buffered.
See: Achrostatin-V, Cap. (Lederle)
W/Tetracycline phosphate complex.
See: Tetrex-F, Cap. (Bristol)
• **NYSTATIN AND CLOROQUINOL OINTMENT,** U.S.P. XXI.
Use: Antifungal.
See: Nystaform, Oint. (Miles Pharm).
• **NYSTATIN, NEOMYCIN SULFATE, GRAMICIDIN AND TRIAMCINOLONE ACETONIDE,** U.S.P. XXI. Cream, Oint., U.S.P. XXI.
Use: Antifungal, antibacterial, anti-inflammatory.
See: Mycolog Prods (Squibb)
NYSTEX CREAM & OINTMENT. (Savage) Nystatin 100,000 units/Gm. Tubes 15 Gm., 30 Gm.
Use: Antifungal, antibiotic therapy.
NYSTEX ORAL SUSPENSION. (Savage) Nystatin 100,000 Units/ml. in suspension. Bot. 60 ml.
Use: Treatment of candidiasis in the oral cavity.
NYTILAX. (Mentholatum) Crystalline sennosides A & B calcium salts 12 mg./Tab. Bot. 12s, 24s.
Use: Laxative.
NYTIME COLD MEDICINE. (Rugby) Acetaminophen 1000 mg., doxylamine succinate 7.5 mg., pseudoephedrine HCl 60 mg., dextromethorphan HBr 30 mg./30 ml. w/alcohol 25%. Bot. 6 oz.
Use: Cold therapy.
NYTOL. (Block) Diphenhydramine HCl 25 mg./Tab. Bot. 16s, 32s, 72s.
Use: Sleep aid.

O

OASIS. (Zitar) Artificial saliva. Bot. 6 oz.
Use: To relieve xerostomia.
OATMEAL, GUM FRACTION.
See: Aveeno, Preps. (Cooper)
OBACIN. (Kenyon) Phendimetrazine tartrate 35 mg./Tab. Bot. 100s, 1000s.
Use: Control obesity.
OBALAN. (Lannett) Phendimetrazine tartrate 35 mg./Tab. Bot. 100s, 1000s.
Use: Treatment of obesity.
OBECALP-C. (Western Research) Placebo Capsule. Bot. 1000s.
Use: Placebo

OBECALP-T. (Western Research) Placebo Tablet. Bot. 1000s.
Use: Placebo.

OBEPAR. (Parmed) Phendimetrazine tartrate 35 mg./Tab. Bot. Bot. 100s.
Use: Appetite suppressant.

OBEPAR. (Tyler) Vit. A 3000 I.U., D 300 I.U., B-1 3 mg., B-2 2 mg., nicotinamide 10 mg., B-6 3 mg., Ca pantothenate 2 mg., B-12 3 mcg., C 37.5 mg., Ca 150 mg., Fe 5 mg., Mg 1 mg., Mn 0.1 mg., K 1 mg., Zn 0.15 mg./Cap. Bot. 100s.
Use: Phosphorus-free vitamin-mineral dietary supplement specially recommended for pregnancy.

OBERMINE. (Forest) Phentermine HCl 30 mg./Cap. Bot. 1000s.
Use: Anorexiant.

OBESITY AGENTS.
See: Anti-Obesity Agents. (Various Mfr.)

OBE-SLIM. (Jenkins) Amobarbital 50 mg., homatropine methylbromide 7.5 mg., methamphetamine 10 mg./Tab. Bot. 1000s.

OBESTIN-30. (Ferndale) Phentermine HCl 30 mg. /Cap. Bot. 100s, 1000s.
Use: Anorectic.

OBE-TITE. (Scott/Cord) Phendimetrazine tartrate 35 mg./Tab. Bot. 100s, 500s.
Use: Control of obesity.

OBETRIM-T. (Sylvania) Methamphetamine HCl 15 mg., ascorbic acid 60 mg., phenobarbital 15 mg./Tab. or Cap. **Tab.** Bot. 30s, 100s. **Cap.** Bot. 30s, 100s.
Use: Appetite control in obesity.

OBETROL. (Obetrol) Dextroamphetamine saccharate, amphetamine aspartate, amphetamine sulfate, dextroamphetamine sulf. in equal parts. Tab. 10 or 20 mg. Bot. 100s, 500s, 1000s.
Use: Treatment of obesity.

OBETROL-10 TABS. (Obetrol) Dextroamphetamine saccharate 2.5 mg., amphetamine asparate 2.5 mg., amphetamine sulfate 2.5 mg., dextroamphetamine sulfate 2.5 mg./Tab. Bot. 100s, 500s, 1000s.
Use: Treatment of obesity.

OBETROL-20 TABS. (Obetrol) Methamphetamine saccharate 5 mg., amphetamine asparate 5 mg., amphetamine sulfate 5 mg., dextroamphetamine sulfate 5 mg./Tab. Bot. 100s, 500s, 1000s.
Use: Treatment of obesity.

OBEZINE. (Western Research) Phendimetrazine tartrate 35 mg./Tab. Handicount 28 (36 bags of 28s).
Use: Anorexic.

• **OBIDOXIME CHLORIDE.** USAN. 1,1′-(Oxydimethylene)-bis-[4-formylpyridinium]dichloride dioxime.
Use: Cholinesterase reactivator.

OBLATE PLUS. (Haag) Vit. A4000 I.U., D400 I.U., B-1 3 mg., B-2 2 mg., B-6 1 mg., C50 mg., niacinamide 10 mg., B-12 2 mcg., folic acid 1 mg., calcium 230 mg., iron 30 mg., magnesium 0.15 mg., potassium 0.835 mg., iodine 0.01 mg., copper 0.15 mg., man ganese 0.05 mg., zinc 0.085 mg./Tab. Bot. 100s.

OB-NATAL. (Geneva) Prenatal multivitamins and mi rals/T.R. Tab. Bot. 100s.
Use: Prenatal, lactating dietary supplement.

OB-NATAL PLUS. (Geneva) Prenatal multivitamins a mineral. Bot. 100s.
Use: Vitamin and mineral supplement for prenata lactating women.

OBRICAL. (Canright) Ca lactate 500 mg., Vit. D 40 I.U., ferrous sulfate exsic. 35 mg., Vit. B-1 1 mg., 2 1 mg., C 10 mg./Tab. Bot. 100s, 1000s.
Use: Nutritional needs during pregnancy, rapid growth in childhood, convalescence.

OBRICAL-F. (Canright) Ferrous sulf. 50 mg., cal. lact 500 mg., Vit. D 400 I.U., B-1 1 mg., B-2 1 mg., C mg., folic acid 0.67 mg./Tab. Bot. 100s, 1000s.
Use: Vitamin & mineral supplement.

OBRITE. (Milton Roy) Contact lens and eye glass cleaner. Plastic spray Bot. 30 ml., 55 ml.

OBTUNDIA CALAMINE CREAM. (Otis Clapp) Zinc oxide, calamine, camphorated meta-cresol. Tube oz. Aidpak 0.11 oz. foilpaks, 36s. Unit box 0.11 o foilpaks, 6s.
Use: Topical antipruritic and skin protectant.

OBTUNDIA CREAM. (Otis Clapp) Camphorated me cresol, petrolatum, lanolin. Tubes 1.25 oz.; Aidpa 0.11 oz. foil pkg. Box 36s.
Use: Bactericidal, anesthetic, antifungal first aid cream.

OBTUNDIA FIRST AID SPRAY. (Otis Clapp) Camphorated meta-cresol. Aerosol can 2.5 oz.
Use: Bactericidal, fungicidal, sporicidal, anesthetic spray.

OBTUNDIA SURGICAL DRESSING. (Otis Clapp) Camphorated meta-cresol. Bot. 0.5 oz., 4 oz. Sw Pads Box 10s; Aid Packs 100s.
Use: Bactericidal, fungicidal, sporicidal, anesthetic liquid.

OB-VIT. (Scrip) Vit. A 4000 I.U., D 400 I.U., B-1 2.0 m B-2 2.0 mg., C 100 mg., calcium 400 mg., iron 115 m oyster shell calcium carbonate 500 mg., folic acid 0.1 mg., B-12 2.0 mcg./Tab. Bot. 90s.

OBY-TRIM. (Rexar) Phentermine HCl 30 mg./Cap. B 1000s
Use: Treatment of obesity.

OC-250. (Western Research) Vitamin C 250 mg./Che able Tab. Handicount 28s (36 bags of 28s).
Use: Vitamin supplement.

O-CAL-FA. (Pharmics) Iron 66 mg., calcium 200 mg., 8000 I.U., C 90 mg., D 400 I.U., B-6 4 mg., B-1 3 m B-2 2 mg., niacinamide 15 mg., B-12 2.5 mcg., fo acid 1 mg., sod. fluoride 1.1 mg., iodine 0.15 mg., manganese sulfate 0.5 mg., copper sulfate 0.25 mg., potassium iodide 0.05 mg., magnesium 1 mg zinc sulfate 0.5 mg./Tab. Bot. 100s.
Use: Vitamin & mineral supplementation.

OCCLUSAL. (GenDerm) Salicylic acid 17% in polyacrylic vehicle. Bot. 0.5 oz.
Use: Treatment & removal of common warts and plantar warts.

OCEAN. (Fleming) Sod. chloride 0.65% w/benzyl alcohol. Bot. 45 cc., pt., gal.

EAN PLUS. (Fleming) Caffeine 2.5% w/benzyl lcohol. Bot. 15 cc.
CRYLATE. USAN. Octyl 2-cyano-acrylate.
Jse: Surgical aid (tissue adhesive).
CTABENZONE. USAN. 2-Hydroxy-4-(octyloxy) ben:ophenone. Spectra-Sorb UV 531. Under study.
Jse: Sunscreen agent.
TACOSACTRIN. B.A.N. α· Corticotrophin
Jse: Corticotrophic peptide.
CTADECANOIC ACID. Oleic acid, N.F. XVI.
TADECANOIC ACID.
See: Stearic Acid, N.F. XVI.
TADECANOIC ACID, SODIUM SALT.
See: Sodium Stearate, N.F. XVI.
TADECANOIC ACID, ZINC SALT.
See: Zinc Stearate, N.F. XVI.
CTADECANOL.
See: Stearyl Alcohol, N.F. XVI.
CTANOIC ACID. USAN.
Jse: Antifungal.
TAPHONIUM CHLORIDE. B.A.N. Benzyldiethyl-2-4-(1,1,3,3-tetramethylbutyl)phenoxy]-ethylammoniu-n chloride. Octaphen; Phenoctide.
Jse: Antiseptic.
TAREX. (Approved) Vit. A 5000 I.U., D 1000 I.U., 3-1 1.5 mg., B-2 2 mg., B-6 0.1 mg., cal. pantothenate mg., niacinamide 20 mg., C 37.5 mg., E 1 I.U., 3-12 1 mcg./Cap. Bot. 100s, 1000s.
TATROPINE METHYLBROMIDE. B.A.N. Anisotropine methylbromide. 2-Propyl-pentanoylmehyltropinium bromide. 8-Methyl-O-(2-propylvaleryl)-ropinium bromide.
Jse: Anticholinergic.
See: Valpin, Elix., Tab. (Du Pont)
TAVERINE. B.A.N. 6,7-Dimethoxy-1-(3,4,5-triethoxyphenyl)isoquinoline.
Jse: Antispasmodic.
TAVIMS. (Approved) Vit. A 6000 I.U., D 1250 I.U., C 50 mg., E 5 I.U., B-1 3 mg., B-2 3 mg., B-6 0.5 mg., niacinamide 20 mg., Ca pantothenate 5 mg., B-12 5 mcg., calcium 59 mg., phosphorus 45 mg./Cap. Bot. 100s, 250s, 1000s.
CTAZAMIDE. USAN.
Jse: Analgesic.
CTENIDINE HYDROCHLORIDE. USAN.
Jse: Anti-infective, topical.
CTENIDINE SACCHARIN. USAN.
Jse: Dental plaque inhibitor.
CTICIZER. USAN. 2-Ethylhexyl diphenyl phosphate. Santicizer 141 (Monsanto). SCAN Spray-On. (Johnon & Johnson)
Jse: Pharmaceutic aid (plasticizer).
CTOCRYLENE. USAN.
Jse: Ultraviolet screen.
CTODRINE. USAN. 1,5-Dimethylhexylamine. Under study.
Jse: Vasoconstrictor, local anesthetic.
TOFOLLIN.
See: Benzestrol U.S.P. XXI.

L-threo-αD-galacto-OCTOPYRANOSIDE, METHYL 7-CHLORO-6,7,8-TRIDEOXY-6-[[(1-METHYL-4-PROPYL-2-PYRROLIDINYL)-CARBONYL]AMINO]-l-THIO, (2S-trans)-MONOHYDROCHLORIDE. Clindamycin Hydrochloride, U.S.P. XXI.
D-erythro-α-D-galacto-OCTOPYRANOSIDE, METHYL 6,8-DIDEOXY-6-[[(1-METHYL-4-PROPYL-2-PYRROLIDINYL)CARBONYL]-AMINO]-1-THIO, MONOHYDROCHLORIDE. MONOHYDRATE. Lincomycin Hydrochloride, U.S.P. XXI.
• **OCTOXYNOL 9,** N.F. XVI.
Use: Surfactant.
• **OCTRIPTYLINE PHOSPHATE.** USAN.
Use: Antidepressant.
• **OCTRIZOLE.** USAN.
Use: Ultraviolet screen.
N-OCTYL BICYALOHEPTENE DICARBOSIMIDE. W/N-N-diethyl-m-toluamide, 2,3,4,5-bis-(delta-2-butylene) tetrahydrofurfural, Di-n-propyl isocinchomeronate, other isomers, isopropanol.
See: Bansum, Bot. (Summers)
OCTYLPHENOXY POLYETHOXYETHANOL. A mono-ether of a polyethylene glycol. Igepal CA 630 (Antara).
W/Phenylmercuric acetate, methylparaben, sodium borate.
See: Lorophyn jelly, Supp. (Eaton)
W/Lactic acid, sodium lactate.
See: Jeneen premeasured liquid douche (Norwich)
OCU-BATH. (Commerce) Bot. 4 oz.
Use: Eye lotion.
OCU-DROP. (Commerce) Bot. 0.5 oz.
Use: Eye drops.
• **OCUFILCON A.** USAN.
Use: Contact lens material.
• **OCUFILCON B.** USAN.
Use: Contact lens material.
• **OCUFILCON C.** USAN.
Use: Contact lens material.
OCUMETER.
See: Decadron Phosphate, Prep. (Merck Sharp & Dohme)
Humorsol, Ophth. Sol. (Merck Sharp & Dohme)
Neo-Decadron, Prep. (Merck Sharp & Dohme)
OCURINS. (Softcon) Sod. chloride 0.85%, buffering agents, thimerosal 0.001%, disodium edetate 0.1%. Plastic squeeze Bot. 7.5 fl. oz.
Use: Opnthalmic irrigating procedures.
OCUSERT. (Ciba) Pilocarpine.
Pilo-20: Releases 20 mcg. pilocarpine/hour for one week. Pkg. 8s.
Pilo-40: Releases 40 mcg. pilocarpine/hour for one week. Pkg. 8s.
Use: Control of elevated intraocular pressure.
OC-U-ZIN Ophth. Sol. (Blue Line) (w/v) Zinc sulfate 0.25%, boric acid 2%, phenylephrine HCl 0.12%, sodium borate with benzalkonium chloride 1:10,000. Plastic squeeze Bot. 15 cc.
Use: Superficial irritations of the eye.
ODALATE. (Kenyon) Chlorpheniramine maleate 8 mg., phenylpropanolamine HCl 50 mg., atropine sulfate 0.36 mg./Cap. Bot. 100s, 1000s.

ODARA. (Lorvic) Alcohol 48%, carbolic acid less than 2%, zinc chloride, potassium iodide, glycerin, methyl salicylate, oil eucalyptus, tinct. myrrh. **Conc. Liq.** Bot. 8 oz.
Use: Mouthwash, gargle and general antiseptic.

ODONIL. (Kenyon) dl-Methionine 200 mg./Cap. Bot. 100s, 1000s.

ODOR-SCRIP. (Scrip) Dl-methionine 0.3 Gm./Cap. Bot. 100s.
Use: Treatment of diaper rash in infants.

OESTERGON.
See: Estradiol (Various Mfr.)

OESTRADIOL.
See: Estradiol (Various Mfr.)

OESTRASID.
See: Dienestrol (Various Mfr.)

OESTRIN.
See: Estrone (Various Mfr.)

OESTRIOL SUCCINATE. B.A.N. Oestra-1,3,5-(10)-triene-3,16α,17β-triol 16,17-di(hydrogen succinate).
Use: Treatment of thrombocytopenic hemorrhage.

OESTRIOL SODIUM SUCCINATE. B.A.N. Oestra-1,3,-5(10)-triene-3,16α,17β-di(sodium succinate).
Use: Treatment of thrombocytopenic hemorrhage.

OESTROFORM.
See: Estrone (Various Mfr.)

OESTROMENIN.
See: Diethylstilbestrol (Various Mfr.)

OESTROMON.
See: Diethylstilbestrol (Various Mfr.)

OFF-EZY CORN REMOVER. (Commerce) Flexible collodion, salicylic acid. Bot. 0.45 oz.
Use: Corn remover.

OFF-EZY WART REMOVER. (Commerce) Flexible collodion, salicylic acid. Bot. 0.45 oz.

O-FLEX. (Seatrace) Orphenadrine citrate 30 mg./ml. Vial 10 cc.

OFLOXACIN. USAN.
Use: Antihypertensive.

OFORNINE. USAN.
Use: Antibacterial.

OGEN. (Abbott) Estropipate. **Tab. 0.625:** 0.75 mg. Estropipate/Tab. Bot. 100s. **Tab. 1.25:** 1.5 mg. Estropipate/Tab. Bot. 100s. **Tab. 2.5:** 3 mg. Estropipate/Tab. Bot. 100s. **Tab. 5.:** 6 mg. Estropipate/Tab. Bot. 100s.
Use: Estrogen deficiency states.

OGEN VAGINAL CREAM. (Abbott) Estropipate 1.5 mg./Gm. Tube 1.5 oz. w/applicator.
Use: Atrophic vaginitis and kraurosis vulvae.

OILATUM SOAP. (Stiefel) A mild soap containing 7.5% protein-free, low viscosity, readily absorbed polyunsaturated vegetable oil. Bars 4.0 oz. or 5.8 oz./Cake. Scented or unscented.
Use: Cleansing of dry, sensitive skin.

OIL FOR USE. (DeWitt) Bot. 0.5 oz. w/dropper.
Use: Ear drops.

OIL OF CAMPHOR W/COMBINATIONS.
See: Sloan's Liniment, Liq. (Warner-Lambert)

OIL OF CLOVES W/ALCOHOL.
See: Buckley "Z.O.", Liq.(Crosby)

OIL OF PINE W/COMBINATIONS.
See: Sloan's Liniment, Liq. (Warner-Lambert)

OIL-O-SOL. (Health Care Industries) Corn oil 52%, Ca-tor Oil 40.8%, camphor 6.8%, hexylresorcinol 0.1%. Bot. 1 oz., 2 oz., 4 oz.
Use: For minor cuts, scratches, surface abrasions sunburn.

OINT-EAST OINTMENT. (Guild) Pkg. 2⅛ oz.

OINTMENT BASE, WASHABLE.
See: Absorbent Base (Upsher-Smith)
Cetaphil, Cream, Lot. (Owen)
Velvachol, Cream (Owen)

• **OINTMENT, HYDROPHILIC,** U.S.P. XXI.
Use: Pharm. aid (oil-in-water emulsion ointment bas

• **OINTMENT, WHITE,** U.S.P. XXI.
Use: Pharm. aid (oleaginous ointment base).

• **OINTMENT, YELLOW,** U.S.P. XXI.
Use: Ointment base.

• **OLAFLUR.** USAN.
Use: Dental caries prophylactic.

OLAMINE.
See: Ethanolamine

OLAQUINDOX. B.A.N. 2-(2-Hydroxyethylcarbamoyl)-3-methylquinoxaline 1,4-dioxide.
Use: Growth promoter; bactericide, veterinary medicine.

OLDEROL. (Doral) Vit. B-1 15 mg., B-2 10 mg., niacin-mide 100 mg., B-6 5 mg., B-12 4 mcg., Capantoth-nate 20 mg., folic acid 150 mcg., C 750 mg., E 3(I.U./Cap. Bot. 60s.
Use: Therapeutic vitamin supplement.

OLEANDOMYCIN. B.A.N. An antibiotic from Streptomyces antibioticus.
See: Matromycin; Romicil

OLEANDOMYCIN PHOSPHATE. Phosphate of an antibacterial substance produced by *Streptomyce antibioticus.*
Use: Infections caused by susceptible gram-positi and gram-negative organisms.

OLEANDOMYCIN SALT OF PENICILLIN.
See: Pen-M (Pfizer) Under study.

OLEANDOMYCIN, TRIACETYL. Troleandomycin US XX.

OLEIC ACID, N.F. XVI. 9-Octadecanoic acid.
Use: Pharm. aid (emulsion adjunct).

• **OLEIC ACID I-131.** USAN.
Raoleic Acid-131 (Abbott)
Use: Radioactive agent.

• **OLEIC ACID I-125.** USAN.
Use: Radioactive agent.

OLEIN OZONIDE.

OLEORESINS OF PLANTS. (Hollister-Stier) Oleoresi of plants. Applicator Vials 3 ml.
Use: Diagnosis of contact dermatitis.

OLEOVITAMIN A, Vitamin A, U.S.P. XXI.

• **OLEOVITAMIN A & D,** U.S.P. XXI. Cap., U.S.P. X
Use: Vit. A & D therapy.
See: Super-D, Perles, Liq. (Upjohn)

• **OLEOVITAMIN D, SYNTHETIC.**
Use: Vitamin D replacement therapy.
See: Viosterol in Oil.

• **OLEYL ALCOHOL,** N.F. XVI. (Z)-9-Octadecen-1-o
Use: Emulsifying agent; emollient.

VE OIL, N.F. XVI.
se: Emollient, pharm. aid (setting retardant for ental cements).

BRE EXTRA STRENGTH. (Edward J. Moore) Vit. palmitate, D, B-1, B-2, B-6, B-12, niacinamide, Ca antothenate, ascorbic acid./Tab. Bot. 50s, 100s.

EGA OIL. (Block) Methyl nicotinate, methyl alicylate, capsicum oleoresin, histamine hydrochloride, isopropyl alcohol 48%. Bot. 2.5 z., 4.85 oz.
se: External analgesic.

NIBEL. (Delta) Butabarbital 15 mg., atropine ulfate 0.0194 mg., hyoscyamine sulfate 0.1037 g., hyoscine hydrobromide 0.0065 mg., Tab. 100s.
se: Antispasmodic, antisecretory sedative.

NICOL. (Delta) Dextromethorphan HBr 15 mg., hlorpheniramine maleate 4 mg., phenylephrine HCl mg., phenindamine tartrate 4 mg., salicylamide 27 mg., acetaminophen 100 mg., caffeine alkaloid 0 mg., ascorbic acid 25 mg./Tab. Bot. 100s, Bot. t.
se: Antitussive, decongestant, antihistaminic, nalgesic.

NIHEMIN. (Delta) Iron 110 mg., C 150 mg., B-12 7.5 cg., folic acid 1.0 mg., zinc 1.0 mg., Cu 1.0 mg., n 1.0 mg., Mg 1.0 mg./Tab. or 5 ml. **Tab.** Bot. 00s., **Soln.** Bot. pt.
se: Hematinic.

NI-M TABLETS. (Blue Cross) Vitamins & Minerals r people 12 years old and older. Bot. 100s.
se: Supplement.

NINATAL. (Delta) Iron 60 mg., copper 2 mg., zinc 5 mg., Vit. A 8000 I.U., D 400 I.U. C 90 mg., Ca 00 mg., folic acid 1.5 mg., B-1 2.5 mg., B-2 3 mg., acinamide 20 mg., pyridoxine HCl 10 mg., antothenic acid 15 mg., B-12 8 mcg./Tab. Bot. 100s.
se: Vitamin-mineral supplement.

NIPEN. (Wyeth) Anhydrous ampicillin 250 g./Cap. Bot. 100s, 500s; Redipak 100s, 500 g./Cap. Bot. 100s, 500s; Redipak 100s. For oral spension 125 mg. or 250 mg./5 cc. to make 80 c., 100 cc., 150 cc., 200 cc. 500 mg./5 cc. to ake 100 cc. Drops, 100 mg./cc. Bot. w/dropper make 20 cc.
se: Antibiotic.

NIPEN-N. (Wyeth) Sod. ampicillin 125 mg., 250 mg., 00 mg., 1 Gm. or 2 Gm./Vial. Pkg. 10s. 10 m./Vial. Pkg. 1s.
se: Antibiotic.

NITABS. (Blue Cross) Vit A 5000 I.U., D 400 I.U., 50 mg., B-1 3 mg., B-2 2.5 mg., niacin 20 mg, B- 1 mg., B-12 1 mcg., pantothenic acid 0.9 mg./Tab. ot. 100s.
se: Vitamin supplement.

NITABS WITH IRON. (Blue Cross) Vit. A 5000 J., D 400 I.U., B-1 3 mg., B-2 2.5 mg., B-6 1 mg., B- 2 1 mcg., C 50 mg., niacinamide 20 mg. calcium antothenate 1 mg., iron 15 mg./Tab. Bot. 100s.
se: Multivitamin with iron.

NITRATE. (Kenyon) Vit. A 6000 I.U., D 600 I.U., E 1 mg., B-1 1.0 mg., B-2 0.1 mg., B-6 0.1 mg., C 37.5 g., B-12 1 mcg., niacinamide 15 mg., folic acid 0.067 g., hesperidin 50 mg., Ca carbonate 400 mg., iron-ferrous iodide dried 20 mg., Mg 15 mg., iodine 0.15 mg., Mn 3 mg., Zn 3 mg./3 Cap. Bot. 1000s.
Use: Vitamin mineral supplement.

OMNIZOLE. (MSD AGVET) Thiabendazole. **Boluses:** 2 Gm., 15 Gm., **Crumbles:** 6.6%; **Paste:** 43%; **Suspension:** 4 Gm./oz.
Use: Anthelmintic, veterinary medicine.

OMNIZOLE-SIX. (MSD AGVET) Thiabendazole 6 Gm./oz. Suspension.
Use: Anthelmintic, veterinary medicine.

ONCOVIN SOLUTION. (Lilly) Vincristine sulfate injection. 1 mg./ml., 2 mg./2 ml. or 5 mg./5 ml. Ctn. 10s.
Use: Treatment of acute leukemia in children.

ONDONID. Cyclofenil, B.A.N.

ONE-A-DAY ESSENTIAL. (Miles) Vit. A 5000 I.U., E 30 I.U., C 60 mg., folic acid 0.4 mg., B-1 1.5 mg., B-2 1.7 mg., niacin 20 mg., B-6 2.0 mg., B-12 6.0 mcg., K 50 mcg.; pantothenic acid 10 mg., biotin 30 mcg., D 400 I.U./Tab. Bot., 60s, 100s, 250s, 365s.
Use: Multivitamin supplement.

ONE-A-DAY MAXIMUM FORMULA. (Miles) Vit. A 5000 I.U., E 30 I.U., C 60 mg., folic acid 0.4 mg., B-1 1.5 mg., B-2 1.7 mg., niacin 20 mg., B-6 2 mg., B-12 6 mcg., K 50 mcg., D 400 I.U., pantothenic acid 10 mg., iron 18 mg., Ca 129.6 mg., P 100 mg., iodine 150 mcg., Mg 100 mg., Cu 2 mg., Cr 10 mcg., selenium 10 mcg., molybdenum 10 mcg., Mn 2.5 mg., potassium 37.5 mg., biotin 30 mcg., chloride 34 mg., Zn 15 mg./Tab. Bot. 30s, 60s, 100s.
Use: Vitamin and mineral supplement.

ONE-A-DAY PLUS EXTRA C. (Miles) Vit. A 5000 I.U., E 30 I.U., C 500 mg., Folic acid 0.4 mg., B-1 1.5 mg., B-2 1.7 mg., niacin 20 mg., B-6 2 mg., B-12 6 mcg., K 50 mcg.; pantothenic acid 10 mg., biotin 30 mcg., D 400 I.U./Tab. Bot. 60s.
Use: High potency vitamin C with 9 essential vitamins.

ONE-A-DAY STRESSGARD. (Miles) Vit. A 5000 I.U., C 600 mg., B-1 15 mg., B-2 10 mg., niacin 100 mg., D 400 I.U., E 30 I.U., B-6 5 mg., biotin 30 mcg., K 50 mc., folic acid 400 mcg., B-12 12 mcg., pantothenic acid 20 mg., iron 18 mg., zinc 15 mg., Cu 2 mg.
Use: Vitamin B complex plus C stress formula.

ONE ONLY VITAMIN TABLETS. (Robinson) Vit. A 5000 I.U., D 400 I.U., B-1 2 mg., B-2 2.5 mg., B-6 1 mg., B-12 1 mcg., niacinamide 20 mg., panthenol 1 mg./Tab. Bot. 100s, 250s, 1000s.
Use: Dietary supplement.

ONE ONLY VITAMIN TABLETS WITH IRON. (Robinson) Vit. A 5000 I.U., D 400 I.U., B-1 2 mg., B-2 2.5 mg., C 50 mg., B-6 1 mg., B-12 1 mcg., niacinamide 20 mg., calcium pantothenate 1 mg., iron 15 mg./Tab. Bot. 100s, 250s, 1000s.
Use: Dietary supplement.

1000-BC, IM OR IV. (Reid-Provident) Vit. B-1 25 mg., B-2 2.5 mg., B-6 5 mg., panthenol 5 mg., B-12 500 mcg., niacin-amide 75 mg., Vit. C 100 mg./cc.
Vial 10 cc.
Use: Vitamin supplement.

1+1 CREME. (Dunhall) Pramoxine HCl 1%, hydrocortisone 1%. Tube 1 oz.
Use: Anesthetic, anti-inflammatory.

1+1-F CREME. (Dunhall) Hydrocortisone 1%, pramoxine HCl 1%, clioquinol 3%. Tube 1 oz.
Use: Anesthetic, anti-inflammatory, anti-fungal, antibacterial.

1-2-3 OINTMENT NO. 20. (Durel) Burow's solution, lanolin, zinc oxide (Lassar's paste). Jars 1 oz., lb., 6 lb.
Use: Nummular eczema, hand eczema, and other localized eczematous processes.

1-2-3 OINTMENT NO. 21. (Durel) Burow's solution 1 part, lanolin 2, zinc oxide (Lassar's paste) 1.5, cold cream 1.5. Jars 1 oz., lb., 6 lb.
Use: Nummular eczema, hand eczema, and other localized eczematous processes.

ONOTON TABLETS. (Winthrop Products) Pancreatin, hemicellulose, oxbile extracts.
Use: Pancreatic deficiency and dyspepsia.

ONSET-5 TABLETS. (Bock) Isosorbide dinitrate 5 mg./Chewable Tab. Bot. 100s, 1000s.
Use: Cardiovascular.

ONTOSEIN.
See: Orgotein (Diagnostic Data)

OPHTHA P/S. (Misemer) Sodium sulfacetamide 100 mg., prednisolone acetate 5 mg./ml.
Use: Treatment eye infections.

OPHTHACET EYE DROPS. (Vortech) Sulfacetamide sod. 10%, methylcellulose 0.5%, boric acid with sod. bisulfite 0.1%, disodium EDTA 0.05%, thimerosal 0.01%. Bot. 0.5 oz. w/dropper.
Use: Antibacterial (ophthalmic).

OPHTHAINE HCl. (Squibb) Proparacaine 2-Diethylaminoethyl-3-amino-4-propoxybenzoate HCl 0.5%, glycerin 2.45%, chlorobutanol 0.2%, benzalkonium chloride, sod. hydroxide or hydrochloric acid to adjust pH. Sol Bot. w/dropper 15 cc.
Use: Topical anesthesia for the eye.

OPHTHALGAN. (Ayerst) Glycerin ophthalmic solution w/chlorobutanol (chloral derivative 0.55%) as preservative. Bot. 7.5 ml./Dropper screw cap.
Use: Corneal edema. Diagnostic.

OPHTHALMIC 0.5% AND 1.5%. (Quality Generics) Hydrocortisone acetate 5 mg. & 15 mg., neomycin sulfate 5 mg./Gm. Tube ⅛ oz.

OPHTHETIC STERILE OPHTHALMIC SOLUTION. (Allergan) Proparacaine HCl 0.5%, benzalkonium chloride glycerin, sodium chloride, purified. Dropper bot. 15 ml.
Use: Topical ophthalmic anesthesia.

OPHTHOCHLOR. (Parke-Davis) Chloramphenicol 5 mg./ml. in a boric acid-sod. borate buffer sol., with sod. hydroxide to adjust pH. Plastic Drop. Bot. 15 ml.
Use: Ophthalmic solution.

OPHTHOCORT. (Parke-Davis) Chloramphenicol 10 mg., hydrocortisone acetate 5 mg., polymyxin B sulfate 5,000 u./Gm. in liquid pet., polyethylene base. Tube 3.5 Gm.
Use: Ocular inflammation and infection.

OPIPRAMOL. B.A.N. 5- 3-[4-(2-Hydroxyethyl)-piperazin-1-yl]propyl -dibenz[b,f]azepine.
Use: Antidepressant.
See: Insidon dihydrochloride

• **OPIPRAMOL HYDROCHLORIDE.** USAN. 4-[3-(5H-Dibenz[b,f]azepin-5yl)-propyl]-1-piperazine-ethanol dihydrochloride.
Use: Antidepressant, tranquilizer.

• **OPIUM,** U.S.P. XXI.
Use: Pharm. necessity for powdered opium.

OPIUM ALKALOIDS, TOTAL, AS THE HYDROCHLORIDE SALT.
See: Pantopon, Amp. (Roche)

OPIUM AND BELLADONNA. (Wyeth) Powd. opium 60 mg., ext. belladonna 0.25 gr./Supp. Box 20s.

• **OPIUM POWDER.,** U.S.P. XXI.
Use: Pharmaceutical necessity for Paregoric.
W/Albumin tannate, colloidal kaolin, pectin.
See: Ekrised, Tab. (Mallard)
W/Atropine sulfate, alcohol.
See: Stopit Liq. (Scrip)
W/Belladonna extr.
See: B & O, Supp. (Webcon)
W/Bismuth subgallate, Zn phenolsulfonate, kaolin.
See: B-K-Z Tablets (Sutliff & Case)
W/Bismuth subgallate, kaolin, pectin, zinc phenolsulfonate.
See: Amogel, Tab. (Vortech)
Diastay, Tab. (Elder)
Laudacin, Liq. (Sutliff & Case)
W/Kaolin, pectin.
See: Keoparic, Susp. (Blue Line)
W/Kaolin, pectin, bismuth subcarbonate.
See: KBP/O, Cap. (Cole)
W/Kaolin, pectin, hyoscyamine sulfate, atropine sulfate, hyoscine HBr.
See: Donnagel-PG, Susp. (Robins)
W/Ipecac pow., acetophenetidin, atropine sulf., acetylsalicylic acid, camphor monobromated, caffeine.
See: Dophenco, Cap. (Blue Line)
W/Ipecac powder, phenacetin, aspirin, camphor monobromated, caffeine, anhydrous, atropine sulfate.
See: Phenatrocaps, Cap. (O'Neal)
W/Ipecac pow., phenacetin, atropine sulfate, monobromated camphor, methapyrilene HCl, salicylamide, caffeine.
See: Phenatrohist, Cap. (O'Neal)

• **OPIUM TINCTURE,** U.S.P. XXI.
W/Homatropine MBr, Pectin.
See: Dia-Quel, Liq. (I.P.C.)
W/Pectin.
See: Opecto, Elixir. (Bowman)
Parelixir, Liq. (Purdue Frederick)

OPIUM TINCTURE, CAMPHORATED.
Use: Antiperistaltic.
See: Paregoric, U.S.P. XXI.
W/Glycyrrhiza fl. ext., tartar emetic, glycerin.
See: Brown Mixture

OP-THAL-ZIN. (Alcon) Zinc sulfate 0.25%, in ste buffered solution. Drop-Tainer Bot. 0.5 oz.
Use: Ophthalmic astringent.

OPTHOCORT OINT. (Parke-Davis) Chloramphen 1%, hydrocortisone acetate 0.5%, polymyxin B ılfate 5000 u./Gm., petrolatum and polyethylene ase. Tube 3.5 Gm.

I-BON EYE DROPS. (Barrows) Phenylephrine HCl, erberine sulfate, boric acid, sodium chloride, odium bisulfite, glycerine, camphor water, eppermint water, thimerosal 0.004%. Bot. 1 oz. se: Ophthalmic sterile solution.

ICAPS. (Approved) Vit. A 32,500 I.U., D 3250 U., B-1 15 mg., B-2 5 mg., B-6 0.5 mg., C 150 mg., 5 I.U., Ca. pantothenate 3 mg., niacinamide 150 g., B-12 20 mcg., iron 11.26 mg., choline bitartrate) mg., inositol 30 mg., pepsin 32.5 mg., diastase 2.5 mg., Ca 30 mg., phos. 25 mg., Mg. 0.7 mg., . dicalcium phos. 110 mg., Mn 1.3 mg., pot. 0.68 g., Zn 0.45 mg., hesperidin comp. 25 mg., biotin) mcg., Brewer's yeast 50 mg., wheat germ oil 20 g., hydrol. yeast 81.25 mg., protein digest. 47.04 g., amino acids 34.21 mg./Cap. Bot. 30s, 60s, 0s, 1000s.
se: Multiple vitamins with minerals.

I-CLEAN. (Alcon) Thimerosal 0.004% w/surfactant nd micropolymeric beads. Bot. 12 ml., 20 ml.
se: Daily cleaning for soft & hard contact lenses.

ICROM 4%. (Fisons) Cromolyn sodium 4% phthalmic solution. Pkg. 10 ml.
se: Antiallergic for conjunctivitis.

ILETS-500. (Abbott) Vit. B-1 15 mg., B-2 10 mg., acinamide 100 mg., calcium pantothenate 20 mg., -6 5 mg., C 500 mg., A 10,000 I.U., D 400 I.U., E 30 U., B-12 12 mcg./Filmtab. Bot. 30s, 100s.

ILETS-M-500. (Abbott) Vit. C 500 mg., niacinamide 00 mg., Ca pantothenate 20 mg., B-1 15 mg., Vit. A 0,000 I.U., B-2 10 mg., B-6 5 mg., D 400 I.U., B-2 12 mcg., E 30 I.U. Fe 20 mg., Mg 80 mg., Zn .5 mg., Cu 2 mg., Mn 1 mg., iodine 0.15 g./Filmtab. Bot. 100s & 30s.
se: Vitamin-mineral therapy.

IMINE. (Schering) Azatadine maleate 1 mg./Tab. ot. 100s.
se: Antihistamine.

IMYD. (Schering) Prednisolone phos. 0.5%, sod. ılfacetamide 10%, sod. thiosulfate, tyloxapol, sodium edetate, monobasic sod. phosphate, basic sod. phosphate, sod. hydroxide to adjust H, purified water, benzalkonium chloride 0.025% nd phenylethyl alcohol 0.5% as preservatives ombined in a clear aqueous sol. Solution-Sterile. as. Drop Bot. 5 ml.
se: Steroid ophthalmic solution.

ISED SOL. (Ketchum) Zinc sulfate 0.025%, henylephrine HCl 0.12%. Bot. 15 cc.
se: Decongestant emollient-astringent.

I-ZYME ENZYMATIC CLEANER. (Alcon) Pancrea-n tablets. Pak 8s, 24s, 36s.
se: Enzymatic cleaning of contact lenses.

O-MIST. (Ketchum) Sod. propionate, sod. chloride, amphor, peppermint oil. Bot. 0.5 oz.

REX. (CMC) Eye bath Bot. 4 oz., 8 oz. Eye drops ot. 0.5 oz.

ULLE. (CMC) Sterile dressings. 24s.

ABASE. (Hoyt) Gelatin, pectin, sod. carboxy ethylcellulose in hydrocarbon gel w/polyethylene and mineral oil. 0.75 gm Packet Boxs 100s. Tube 5 Gm., 15 Gm.
Use: Oral protective paste for minor irritations of mouth and gums.

ORABASE HCA. (Hoyt) Hydrocortisone acetate 0.5% in paste base. Packets 0.75 Gm. Box 100s. Tube 5 Gm., 15 Gm.
Use: Adjunctive treatment of oral lesions.

ORABASE WITH BENZOCAINE. (Hoyt) Benzocaine 20% in paste base. Packets 0.75 Gm. Box 100s. Tube 5 Gm., 15 Gm.
Use: Topical anesthetic and emollient for oral lesions

ORABILIX SODIUM. Buniodyl, B.A.N.

ORACIN. (Vicks) **Regular** Benzocaine 6.25 mg., menthol 0.1%/Regular Loz. w/FDC Yellow #5 tartrazine. **Cherry:** Menthol 0.08%/Cherry Loz. in sorbitol base. Pkg. 18s.
Use: Cooling throat lozenges.

ORADERM LIP BALM. (Schattner) Sod. phenolate, sod. tetraborate, phenol, base containing an anionic emulsifier. ⅛ oz.
Use: Anesthetic & antiseptic.

ORADEX-C. (Commerce) Cetylpyridinium chloride 2.5 mg., benzocaine 10 mg./Troche. Bot. 10s.
Use: Antibacterial anesthetic throat troches.

ORADEXON. Dexamethasone, B.A.N.

ORAFIX MEDICATED. (Norcliff Thayer) Allantoin 0.2%, Benzocaine 2%. Tube 0.75 oz.
Use: Analgesic denture adhesive for denture sore gums.

ORAFIX ORIGINAL. (Norcliff Thayer) Denture adhesive. Tube 1.5 oz., 2.5 oz., 4 oz.

ORAFIX SPECIAL. (Norcliff Thayer) Denture adhesive. Tube 1.4 oz., 2.4 oz.

ORAFLEX. (Lilly) Benoxaprofen
Note: Withdrawn from market in 1982.

ORA-FRESH. (A.V.P.) Sugar-free non-alcoholic, non-toxic, flavored mouthwash. Unit dose cup 1 oz. Bot. 4 oz., 16 oz.
Use: Mouthwash after oral surgery.

ORAGRAFIN CALCIUM GRANULES. (Squibb) Ipodate calcium 3 Gm./8 Gm. Pkg. 25 × 1 dose pkg.
Use: Radiopaque substance.

ORAGRAFIN SODIUM CAPSULES. (Squibb) Ipodate sodium 0.5 Gm./Cap. Bot. 100s. Unimatic pkg. 100s. Card 6s. Box 25s.
Use: Radiopaque substance.

ORAGULANT. Diphenadione, B.A.N.

ORAHEMA SOLU-CAPS. (Sutliff & Case) Ferrous fumarate 200 mg., Zn 1 mg., Mn 5 mg., Cu 0.25 mg., Vit. C 30 mg., B-12 1 mcg., B-1 1 mg., B-2 1.2 mg./Solu-cap. Bot. 100s, 1000s.
Use: Multivitamin with minerals.

W/Folic acid 0.5 mg. Bot. 100s, 1000s.
Use: Nutritional supplement.

ORAHESIVE POWDER. (Hoyt) Gelatin, pectin, sodium carboxymethylcellulose. Bot. 25 Gm.
Use: Denture adhesive.

ORAHIST TR. (Vangard) Chlorpheniramine maleate 8 mg., phenylpropanolamine HCl 50 mg.,

isopropanide iodide 2.5 mg./T.R. Cap. Bot. 100s, 1000s.
Use: Antihistamine, Decongestant.

ORA-JEL. (Commerce) Benzocaine in a special base. Tube 0.2 oz., 0.5 oz.
Use: Temporary relief of toothache pain.

ORA-JEL BABY. (Commerce) Benzocaine in a special base. Tube 0.5 oz.
Use: Teething pain.

ORAJEL BRACE-AID ORAL ANESTHETIC GEL. (Commerce) Benzocaine 20%, allantoin 0.5%. Tube 0.5 oz.
Use: Relieves pain, soreness and irritations due to braces.

ORAJEL BRACE-AID ORAL HYGIENIC RINSE. (Commerce) Carbamide peroxide 10% in anhydrous glycerin. Tube 1 oz.
Use: Cleanses and disinfects sore inflamed areas.

ORA-JEL CSM. (Commerce) Benzocaine, tannic acid, benzalkonium Cl in special base. Tube 0.5 oz.
Use: Relief of minor mouth & gum irritations.

ORA-JEL D. (Commerce) Benzocaine in a special "anti-irritant" adhesive base. Tube 0.5 oz.
Use: Relief from pain of denture irritation.

ORAJEL MAXIMUM STRENGTH. (Commerce) Benzocaine in special base. Tube 1/2 oz., 3/16 oz.
Use: Relief of toothache pain.

ORAL BARIUM. (Lafayette) Contains 96% barium sulfate. Drum 100 lb.
Use: Alimentary tract radiography.

ORALCID.
See: Acetarsone

■ **ORAL CONTRACEPTIVES.**
See: Demulen, Tab. (Searle)
Enovid-E, Tabs. (Searle)
Loestrin, Prods. (Parke-Davis)
Lo/Ovral, Prods. (Wyeth)
Miconor, Tab. (Ortho)
Modicon, Prods. (Ortho)
Nordette, Tab. (Wyeth)
Norinyl, Prods. (Syntex)
Norlestrin, Prods. (Parke-Davis)
Norquen, Tab. (Syntex)
Ortho-Novum, Prods. (Ortho)
Ovcon-35, Tab. (Mead Johnson)
Ovcon-50, Tab. (Mead Johnson)
Ovral, Tabs. (Wyeth)
Ovrette, Tab. (Wyeth)
Ovulen, Tab. (Searle)

ORAL DROPS/CANKER SORE RELIEF. (Weeks & Leo) Carbamide peroxide 10% in anhydrous glycerin base. Bot. 30cc.
Use: Relief of mouth and gum irritations, canker sores, denture sores.

ORALPHYLLIN LIQUID. (CMC) Theophylline 80 mg., alcohol 20%/15 cc. Bot. pt., gal.
Use: Antiasthmatic, bronchial and coronary dilator.

ORAMIDE. (Major) Tolbutamide 0.5 Gm./Tab. Bot. 100s, 1000s.
Use: Oral hypoglycemic.

ORAMINIC II. (Vortech) Brompheniramine maleate mg./ml. Inj. vial 10 ml.
Use: Decongestant, antispasmodic.

ORAMINIC SPANCAP. (Vortech) Phenylpropanolamine HCl 75 mg., chlorpheniram maleate 12 mg. Spancap. Bot. 100s, 1000s.
Use: Decongestant, antihistaminic.

• **ORANGE FLOWER OIL,** N.F. XVI.
Use: Flavor; perfume, vehicle.

• **ORANGE FLOWER WATER,** N.F. XVI.
Use: Flavor; perfume.

ORANGE JU. C. (Image) Vitamin C 100 mg./Tab. Bot. 30s, 100s.
Use: Dietary supplement.

• **ORANGE OIL,** N.F. XVI.
Use: Flavor.

• **ORANGE PEEL TINCT., SWEET,** N.F. XVI.
Use: Flavor.

• **ORANGE SPIRIT, COMP.,** N.F. XVI.
Use: Flavor.

• **ORANGE SYRUP,** N.F. XVI.
Use: Flavored vehicle.

ORANYL. (Otis Clapp) Pseudoephedrine HCl 30 mg./Tab. Sugar, lactose and salt free. Safety pa 500s.
Use: Nasal and sinus decongestant.

ORAP. (McNeil Pharm) Pimozide 2 mg./Tab. Bot. 100s.
Use: Treatment of Tourette's Syndrome.

ORAPHEN-PD. (Comatic) Acetaminophen 120 mg ml. w/alcohol 5%. Bot. 4 oz.
Use: Analgesic, antipyretic.

ORAPIN. (Standex) Conjugated estrogen 0.625 mg 1.25 mg./Tab. Bot. 100s.

ORAPIN INJ. (Standex) Estrogenic substance 20,0 u./30 cc. Susp. aq or oil.

ORARSAN.
See: Acetarsone.

ORASONE. (Rowell) Prednisone 1 mg., 5 mg., 10 mg., 20 mg./Tab. Bot. 100s, 1000s. Unit dose 100s. Prednisone 50 mg./Tab. Bot. 100s, Unit d 100s.
Use: Steroid therapy.

ORASPAN. (Primedics) Iron fumarate 330 mg., B-1 5 mg., C 50 mg./Tab. Bot. 100s, 500s.
Use: Treatment of iron deficiency anemias.

ORA-TESTRYL. (Squibb) Fluoxymesterone. Tab. 5 n Bot. 50s.
Use: Anabolic agent.

ORATRAST. (Armour) Barium sulfate 92%, sucros 3%, sodium saccharin and approved suspending agents. Containers 25 lb.
Use: Gastrointestinal X-ray diagnosis.

ORATUSS TR. (Vangard) Ceramiphen edisylate 20 mg., chlorpheniramine maleate 8 mg., phenylpropanolamine HCl 50 mg., isopropamide iodide 2.5 mg./T.R. Cap. Bot. 100s, 500s.
Use: Antihistamine, expectorant.

ORATUSSIN. (Panray) Guaifenesin 180 mg., ephedrine HCl 65 mg., ammonium chloride 600 mg., Vit. C 100 mg., sod. citrate 500 mg., citric a 200 mg./30 cc. Bot. pt.

RAZINC. (Mericon) Zinc sulfate 220 mg./Cap. Bot. 100s, 1000s.

RBENIN. Sodium cloxacillin.
Use: Antibiotic.

RBENIN SODIUM SALT. Cloxacillin, B.A.N.

RBETIC. (Cenci) Tolbutamide 0.5 g./Tab. Bot. 200s, 1000s.
Use: Oral anti-diabetic agent.

RBIFERROUS. (Orbit) Ferrous fumarate 300 mg., Vit. B-12 12 mcg., Vit. C 50 mg., B-1 3 mg., defatted desiccated liver 50 mg./Tab. Bot. 60s, 500s.
Use: Anemias.

RBIT. (Spanner) Vit. A 6,250 I.U., D 400 I.U., B-1 3 mg., B-2 3 mg., B-6 2 mg., B-12 5 mcg., C 75 mg., niacinamide 20 mg., Ca pantothenate 10 mg., Vit. E 15 I.U., biotin 15 mcg., iron 20 mg./Tab. Bot. 100s.

RBIT WITH IRON. (Eckerd) Bot. 100s, 250s.

RCIPRENALINE. B.A.N. 1-(3,5-Dihydroxyphenyl)-2-isopropylaminoethanol.
Use: Bronchodilator.
See: Alupent (sulfate)

ORCONAZOLE NITRATE. USAN.
Use: Antifungal.

RENZYME. (Merrell Dow) Trypsin 50,000 u., chymotrypsin 4000 u./Tab. Bot. 48s. Bitabs double strength Bot. 100s.
Use: Oral enzymes for adjunctive treatment of inflammation and edema.

RETIC. (Abbott) Hydrochlorothiazide 25 mg. or 50 mg./Tab. Bot. 100s, 1000s. Strips 100s.
Use: Antihypertensive.

RETICYL 25 and 50. (Abbott) **25:** Hydrochlorothiazide 25 mg., deserpidine 0.125 mg./Tab. Bot. 100s, 1000s. **50:** Hydrochlorothiazide 50 mg., deserpidine 0.125 mg./Tab. Bot. 100s.
Use: Hypotensive.

RETICYL FORTE. (Abbott) Hydrochlorothiazide 25 mg., deserpidine 0.25 mg./Tab. Bot. 100s, 1000s.
Use: Hypotensive.

RETON METHYL. (Schering) Methyltestosterone. **Buccal Tab.** 10 mg., Bot. 100s. **Tab.** 10 mg., 25 mg., Bot. 100s.
Use: Hormone therapy.

REXIN. (Stuart) Vit. B-1 10 mg., B-6 5 mg., B-12 25 mcg./Softab Tab. Bot. 100s.
Use: Vitamin B-1, B-6 and B-12 deficiencies.

RGANIDIN. (Wallace) Iodinated glycerol. Contains virtually no inorganic iodides and no free iodine and is stable in various media including gastric juice. **Elixir** 1.2%, 60 mg./5 cc., alcohol 21.75%. Bot. pt., gal. **Soln.** 50 mg., per cc., 30 cc. dropper bottles. **Tab.** 30 mg. Bot. 100s.
Use: Mucolytic expectorant.
/Chlorpheniramine maleate & codeine phos.
See: Tussi-Organidin, Elix. (Wallace)
/Dextromethorphan HBr, chlorpheniramine maleate.
See: Tussi-Organidin DM, Elix. (Wallace)

RGATRAX. (Organon) Hydroxyzine HCl **25** mg./ml. Vial 10 ml. Disposable Syringe 1 ml. **50** mg./ml. Vial 1 ml.,
Use: Minor tranquilizer.

• **ORGOTEIN.** USAN. A group of soluble metalloproteins isolated from liver, red blood cells, and other mammalian tissues.
Use: Anti-inflammatory.

ORGOTEIN. (Diagnostic Data) Pure water soluble protein with a compact conformation maintained by 4 Gm. atoms of chelated divalent metals, produced from bovine liver as a Cu-Zn mixed chelate having superoxide dismutase activity. Ontosein, Palosein.

ORIGINAL ECLIPSE GEL. (Dorsey) Padimate 0, glyceryl PABA. SPF 10. Bot. 3 oz.
Use: Sunscreen.

ORIGINAL ECLIPSE LOTION. (Dorsey) Padimate 0, glyceryl PABA. SPF 10. Bot. 4 oz., 6 oz.
Use: Sunscreen.

ORIMUNE TRIVALENT. (Lederle) Poliovirus vaccine. Live, Oral, Trivalent. Sabin strains Types 1, 2, and 3. Dose of 0.5 ml. Dispette disposable pipette 1 dose. 10s. Pkg. 5s, 10s, 50s. Dose of 2 drops, Vial 10 doses. Pkg. 5s, 50s.

ORINASE. (Upjohn) Tolbutamide. 250 mg. & 500 mg./Tab. **250 mg.**/Tab. Bot. 100s; **500 mg.**/Tab. Bot. 200s, 500s, 1000s. Unit dose Box 100s. Unit-of-Use Bot. 50s, 100s.
Use: An oral hypoglycemic agent in the treatment of diabetes.

ORISUL. (Ciba) Sulfaphenazole. A sulfonamide under study.

ORMAZINE. (Hauck) Chlorpromazine HCl 25 mg./ml. Vial 10 ml.
Use: Tranquilizer.

• **ORMETROPRIM.** USAN. (1)2,4-Diamino-5-(6-methylveratryl)pyrimidine; (2)2,4-diamino-5-(4,5-dimethoxy-2-methylbenzyl)pyrimidine.
Use: Antibacterial.

ORNACOL. (Menley & James) Dextromethorphan HBr 30 mg., phenylpropanolamine HCl 25 mg./Cap. Pkg. 20s. Bot. 100s.
Use: Antitussive, nasal decongestant for relief of common cold and sinusitis.

ORNADE. (SmithKline) Phenylpropanolamine HCl 75 mg., chlorpheniramine maleate 12 mg./Spansule. Bot. 50s, 500s. Unit dose, 100s.
Use: Decongestant.

ORNEX. (Menley & James) Acetaminophen 325 mg., phenylpropanolamine HCl 12.5 mg./Cap. Blister Pak 24s, 48s. Bot. 100s. Dispensary Pak 800s.
Use: Temporary relief of nasal congestion, headache, aches, pains and fever due to colds, sinusitis, flu.

• **ORNIDAZOLE.** USAN.
Use: Anti-infective.

OROBEX. (Pasadena Research) Cobalamin concentrate 25 mcg./gelatin Cap. Bot. 100s, 1000s.

• **ORPANOXIN.** USAN.
Use: Anti-inflammatory.

ORPENEED VK. (Hanlon) Penicillin buffered 400,000 u./Tab. Bot. 100s.
Use: Antibiotic.

ORPHENADRINE. B.A.N. 2-(2-Methylbenzhydryloxy)-ethyldimethylamine.

Use: Treatment of the Parkinsonian syndrome.
See: Disipal, Ventromil (hydrochloride)
Norflex (citrate)

• **ORPHENADRINE CITRATE,** U.S.P. XXI. Inj., U.S.P. XXI. N,N-Dimethyl-2-(0-methyl-α-phenyl-benzyloxy)-ethylamine. N,N-Dimethyl-2-((o-methyl-α-phenylbenzyl)oxy)-ethylamine Citrate (1:1).
Use: Skeletal muscle relaxant; antihistaminic.
See: Flexon, Inj. (Keene)
Flexor, Inj. (Amfre-Grant)
Norflex, Tab., Amp. (Riker)
Orphanate, Inj. (Hyrex)
W/Aspirin, phenacetin, caffeine.
See: Norgesic, Tab. (Riker)
Norgesic Forte, Tab. (Riker)

ORPHENADRINE HYDROCHLORIDE. N,N-Dimethyl-2-(o-methyl-α-phenylbenzyloxy)ethylamine.
See: Disipal, Tab. (Riker)
W/Comb.
See: Estomul, Liq., Tab. (Riker)

ORPHENATE INJECTION. (Hyrex) Orphenadrine citrate 30 mg./ml. Vial 10 ml.
Use: Muscle relaxant.

ORTAC LIQUID. (Ion) Phenylephrine HCl 5 mg., guaifenesin 100 mg./5 ml. Bot. 4 oz.
Use: Decongestant, expectorant.

ORTAC-DM LIQUID. (Ion) Dextromethorphan 10 mg., phenylephrine HCl 5 mg., guaifenesin 100 mg./5 ml. Bot. 4 oz.
Use: cough suppressant.

ORTAL SODIUM. Sod. 5-ethyl-5-hexylbarbiturate. Hexethal sodium.

ORTEDRINE.
See: Amphetamine (Various Mfr.)

ORTHESIN.
See: Benzocaine

ORTHO ALL-FLEX DIAPHRAGM. (Ortho) Diaphragm kit (all flex arcing spring) in plastic compact, sizes 55, 60, 65, 70, 75, 80, 85, 90, 95 mm.

ORTHO DIAPHRAGM. (Ortho) Diaphragm kit, coil spring sizes 50, 55, 60, 65, 70, 75, 80, 85, 90, 95, 100, 105 mm.

ORTHOCAINE. Orthoform. (No mfr. listed).

ORTHO-CREME CONTRACEPTIVE CREAM. (Advanced Care) Nonoxynol-9 2% in nonfatty acid cream base. Tube, 70 Gm. w/measured dose applicator. Tube only 70 Gm., 115 Gm.
Use: Contraceptive cream for use with diaphragm.

ORTHO DIAPHRAGM-WHITE. (Ortho) Diaphragm kit, flat spring sizes 55, 60, 65, 70, 75, 80, 85, 90, 95 mm.

ORTHO DIENESTROL CREAM. (Ortho) Dienestrol 0.01% Tube 78 Gm. with or without applicator.
Use: Intravaginal use.

ORTHO EAR DROPS. (Vortech) Hydrocortisone acetate 15 mg., neomycin sulfate 5 mg./cc. Bot. 5 ml. w/dropper.
Use: Anti-inflammatory (otic).

ORTHOFLAVIN. (Enzyme Process) Vit. C 150 mg., E 25 mg./Tab. Bot. 100s, 250s.

ORTHOFORM. No mfr. listed. Menthyl 3-amino-4-hydroxybenzoate.
Use: Local anesthetic.
W/Tyrothricin. (Columbus) Tyrothricin 0.5 mg., tetracaine HCl 0.5%, epinephrine 1/1000 sol. 2%/Gm. Oint., Tube ⅛ oz.
Use: Eye infections.

ORTHO-GYNOL CONTRACEPTIVE JELLY. (Advanced Care) p-diisobutyl-phenoxy-polyethoxy-ethanol 1.0%, in water-dispersible jelly at pH 4.5 Tube 81 Gm. w/measured-dose applicator. Tube only 81 Gm., 126 Gm.
Use: Contraceptive jelly for use with diaphragm.

ORTHO-HYDROXYBENZOIC ACID, Salicylic Acid U.S.P. XXI.

ORTHOHYDROXYPHENYLMERCURIC CHLORIDE. (O-chloromercuriphenol)
Use: Antiseptic.
W/Benzocaine, ephedrine HCl.
See: Myrimgacaine, Liq. (Upjohn)
W/Benzocaine, parachlorometaxylenol, benzalkonium chloride and phenol.
See: Unguentine Aerosol (Norwich)
W/Benzoic acid, salicylic acid.
See: NP-27 Liq. (Norwich)

ORTHOHYDROXYPHENYLMERCURIC CHLORIDE.
W/Benzoic acid, salicylic acid, sec.-amyltricresols.
See: Salicresin, Liq. (Upjohn)
W/Zinc acetate, salicylic acid, phenol.
See: Zemacol, Medicated Skin Lotion (Norwich)

ORTHO-NOVUM 2 mg.-21. (Ortho) Norethindrone 2 mg., mestranol 100 mcg./Tab. Dialpak 21s.
Use: Oral contraceptive.

ORTHO-NOVUM 1/35-21. (Ortho) Norethindrone 1 mg., ethinyl estradiol 0.035 mg./Tab. Dialpak 21s.
Use: Oral contraceptive.

ORTHO-NOVUM 1/35-28. (Ortho) Norethindrone 1 mg., ethinyl estradiol 0.035 mg./Tab. plus 7 inert Tab. Dialpak 28s.
Use: Oral contraceptive.

ORTHO-NOVUM 1/50-21. (Ortho) Norethindrone 1 mg., mestranol 50 mcg./Tab. (yellow) Dialpak 21s.
Use: Oral contraceptive

ORTHO-NOVUM 1/50-28. (Ortho) Norethindrone 1 mg., mestranol 50 mcg./Tab. (yellow) plus 7 inert Tabs. Dialpak 28s.
Use: Oral contraceptive.

ORTHO-NOVUM 1/80-21. (Ortho) Norethindrone 1 mg., mestranol 80 mcg./Tab. (white) Dialpak 21s.
Use: Oral contraceptive.

ORTHO-NOVUM 1/80-28. (Ortho) Norethindrone 1 mg., mestranol 80 mcg./Tab. (white) plus 7 inert Tabs. Dialpak 28s.
Use: Oral contraceptive.

ORTHO-NOVUM 7/7/7/-21 TABLETS. (Ortho) White Tab: Norethindrone 0.5 mg., ethinyl estradiol 0.035 mg./Tab.; Light peach tab.: Norethindrone 0.75 mg., ethinyl estradiol 0.035 mg. /Tab.; Norethindrone 1.0 mg., ethinyl estradiol 0.035 mg./Tab. Dialpak 21s.
Use: Oral contraceptive.

ORTHO-NOVUM 7/7/7/-28 TABLETS.(Ortho) Same as Ortho-Novum 7/7/7/-21 with 7 inert (green) tabs. Dialpak 28's
Use: Oral contraceptive.

ORTHO-NOVUM 10/11-21 TABLETS. (Ortho) White Tab.: norethindrone 0.5 mg., ethinyl estradiol 0.035 mg./Tab. Peach Tab.: norethindrone 1 mg., ethinyl estradiol 0.035 mg./Tab. Dialpak 21s.
Use: Oral contraceptive.

ORTHO-NOVUM 10/11-28 TABLETS. (Ortho) White Tab.: norethindrone 0.5 mg., ethinyl estradiol 0.035 mg., Peach Tab.: norethindrone 1 mg., ethinyl estradiol 0.035 mg./Tab. Green Tab.: contains inert ingredients. Dialpak 28s.
Use: Oral Contraceptive.

ORTHO PERSONAL LUBRICANT. (Advanced Care) Greaseless, water soluble and non-staining aqueous hydrocolloid gel. Acid buffered to vaginal pH. Tube 2 oz., 4 oz.
Use: Lubricating gel.

ORTHOXICOL. (Upjohn) Dextromethorphan HBr 10 mg., methoxyphenamine HCl 17 mg./5 cc. Bot. 2 oz., 4 oz., pt.
Use: Coughs.

ORTHOXINE. Methoxyphenamine.

ORTICALM.
Use: Hypotensive and tranquilizing agent.
See: Serpasil, Prod. (Squibb)

OR TOPIC-M SUSPENSION. (Ortega) Sodium sulfacetamide 100 mg., prednisolone acetate 5 mg./ml. Bot. 5cc.
Use: Ophth. antibacterial, anti-inflammatory.

OR-TYL. (Ortega) Dicyclomine HCl 10 mg./ml. Vial 10 ml.
Use: Peptic ulcer therapy.

ORVUS.
See: Gardinol Type Detergents (Various Mfr.)

OSARSAL.
See: Acetarsone

O.S.C. (Kenyon) Calcium (oyster shell) 250 mg., Vit. D-2 125 I.U./Tab. Bot. 100s, 1000s.

OS-CAL 250. (Marion) Oyster shell powder as calcium 250 mg., Vit. D 125 I.U. and trace minerals (Cu, Fe, Mg, Mn, Zn, silica)/Tab. Bot. 100s, 240s, 500s, 1000s.
Use: Calcium & Vit. D therapy.

OS-CAL 500. (Marion) Calcium 500 mg./Tab. Bot. 60s, 120s.
Use: Calcium supplement.

OS-CAL-FORTE. (Marion) Ca 250 mg., Fe 5 mg., Cu 0.3 mg., Mg 1.6 mg., Mn 0.3 mg., iodine 0.05 mg., Zn 0.5 mg., Vit. A 1668 I.U., D 125 I.U., B-1 1.7 mg., B-2 1.7 mg., B-6 2 mg., niacinamide 15 mg., Vit. C 50 mg., E 0.83 I.U./Tab. Bot. 100s.
Use: Calcium, vitamin & mineral supplement.

OS-CAL-GESIC. (Marion) Salicylamide 400 mg., Ca 100 mg., Vit. D 50 I.U.,/Tab. Bot. 100s.
Use: Arthritis.

OS-CAL PLUS. (Marion) Ca 250 mg., Vit. D 125 I.U., A 1666 I.U., C 33 mg., B-2 0.66 mg., B-1 0.5 mg., B-6 0.5 mg., niacinamide 3.33 mg., Zn 0.75 mg., Mn 0.75 mg., Cu 0.036 mg., Fe 16.6 mg., iodine 0.036 mg./Tab. Bot. 100s.
Use: Multivitamin & Multimineral therapy.

OSMITROL. (Travenol) Mannitol in water 5%—1000 ml., 10%—500 and 1000 ml., 15%—150 and 500 ml. 20%—250 and 500 ml. Mannit-l in 0.3% NaCl, 5% —1000 ml. Mannitol in 0.45% NaCl, 20%—500 ml.
Use: Osmotic diuretic. G.U. irrigant, diagnostic use.
See: Mannitol

OSMOGLYN. (Alcon) Glycerin 50% in flavored aqueous vehicle. Plastic Bot. 6 oz.
Use: Osmotic agent for reducing intraocular pressure.

OSMOLITE. (Ross) Medical/nutritutional food for oral & tube feeding w/1000 calories/quart. Cans 8 oz., 32 oz.
Use: Oral & tube feedings especially designed for osmotic sensitive individuals.

OSMOLITE HN. (Ross) High nitrogen isotonic liquid food for oral or tube feeding. Provides complete, balanced nutrition. 1000 calories/quart. Cans 8 oz., 32 oz. Bot. 8 oz.
Use: High nitrogen isotonic liquid food.

OSPOLOT. Tetrahydro-2-(p-sulfa-molyphenyl)-1,2-thiazine-1,1-dioxide.
Use: Anticonvulsant drug; pending release.

OSSONATE CAPSULE. (Marcen) Cartilage mucopolysaccharide ext., chondroitin sulfate, 50 mg./Cap. Bot. 100s, 500s, 1000s.

OSSONATE-PLUS, CAPS. (Marcen) Ossonate-mucopolysaccharide ext. 50 mg., acetaminophen 300 mg., salicylamide 200 mg./Cap. Bot. 100s, 500s, 1000s.
Use: Prophylaxis or maintenance therapy of controlled arthritics.

OSSONATE-PLUS, INJ. (Marcen) Ossonate Cartilage mucopolysaccharide ext. 12.5 mg., casein hydrolysates 80 mg., sulfur 20 mg., sodium citrate 5 mg., benzyl alcohol 0.5%, phenol 0.5%/cc. Multidose 10 cc. vial.
Use: Skeletal muscle relaxant and pain reliever with specific antirheumatic action.

OSSONATE-75. (Marcen) Chondroitin sulfate 37.5 mg., benzylalcohol 0.5%, phenol 0.5%, sodium citrate 5 mg./cc. Vial 10 cc.
Use: Infantile and atopic eczemas, drug allergies, and dermatoses associated with intestinal toxemias.

OSTEOLATE INJECTION. (Fellows) Sodium thiosalicylate 50 mg., benzyl alcohol 2%/cc. Vial 30 cc.

OSTEON/D. (Pasadena Research) Calcium 600 mg., phosporous 400 mg., magnesium 240 mg., Vit. D 400 I.U./6 Tab. Bot. 180s.
Use: Dietary supplement.

OSTI-DERM LOTION. (Pedinol) Liquified phenol, glycerin, zinc oxide, magnesium carbonate, aluminum acetate solution, camphor water, in hydrated aluminum silicate gel. Tube 45 cc.
Use: Antipruritic, astringent.

OSTREOGRYCIN. B.A.N. Antimicrobial substances produced by *Streptomyces ostreogriseus.* (Specific substances are designated by a terminal letter; thus, Ostreogrycin B) Ostreocin is a mixture of Ostreogrycins B and G; Ostreogrycin B is Mikamycin B.

OSVARSAN.
See: Acetarsone

OTIC DOMEBORO. (Miles Pharm) Acetic acid 2%, aluminum acetate 1:10, buffered to pH 5. Soln. plastic drop. bot. 2 oz.
Use: Ear infections.

OTIC-HC. (Hauck) Chloroxylenol 1 mg., pramoxine HCl 10 mg., hydrocortisone alcohol 10 mg., benzalkonium Cl. 0.2 mg./ml. Bot. 12 ml.
Use: External ear infections.

OTIC-NEO-CORT DOME.
See: Neo-Cort Dome Otic Sol. (Miles Pharm)

OTIC-PLAIN. (Hauck) Chloroxylenol 1 mg., pramoxine HCl 10 mg., benzalkonium Cl 0.2 mg./ml. Bot. 12 ml.
Use: External ear infections.

OTIC SOLUTION NO. 1. (Foy) Hydrocortisone alcohol 10 mg., pramoxine HCl 10 mg., benzalkonium chloride 0.2 mg., acetic acid glacial 20 mg./ml. w/propylene glycol q.s.
Use: Treatment of superficial infections of the external auditory canal.

OTOBIOTIC OTIC SOLUTION. (Schering) Polymixin B and hydrocortisone in propylene glycol and glycerin vehicle w/edetate disodium, sodium bisulfite, anhydrous sodium sulfite, purified water. Bot. w/dropper 15 ml.
Use: Otitis externa.

OTOCALM-H EAR DROPS. (Parmed) Pramoxine HCl 10 mg., hydrocortisone alcohol 10%, p-Chloro-m-Xylenol 1 mg. benzalkonium chloride 0.2 mg., acetic acid glacial 20 mg., propylene glycol/ml. Bot. 10 ml.
Use: Superficial infections of the external auditory canal.

OTOCORT STERILE SOLUTION. (Lemmon) Neomycin sulfate equivalent to 3.5 mg. Neomycin base, polymyxin B sulfate 10,000 U., hydrocortisone 10 mg./1 ml. w/propylene glycol, glycerin, potassium metabisulfite and HCl. Bot. 10 ml.
Use: External ear infections.

OTOCORT STERILE SUSPENSION. (Lemmon) Neomycin sulfate equivalent to 5 mg. neomycin base, polymyxin B sulfate 10,000 U., hydrocortisone 10 mg./ml. w/cetyl alcohol, propylene glycol, polysorbate 80, thimerosal. Bot. 10 ml.
Use: External ear infections.

OTO DROPS. (Vortech) Antipyrine 870 mg., benzocaine 230 mg., chlorbutanol 1%, glycerine q.s./fl. oz. Bot. 0.5 oz. w/Dropper.
Use: Analgesic (ear drops).

OTO DROPS. (Standex) Benzocaine 0.85%, antipyrine 3.2%, glycerol q.s./0.5 oz. Bot. 0.5 oz.

OTOLGESIC. (Blue Line) Phenol 4%, benzocaine 10%, clove 4%, menthol 4%, polyethylene glycol 400. 50 min./Dropule. Pkg. 12s.
Use: Inflammation of external ear canal

OTOMYCIN-HPN. (Misemer) Polymyxin B sulfate 10,000 u., neomycin sulfate 3.5 mg., hydrocortison 10 mg./ml. Bot. 10 ml. w/dropper.
Use: Otic solution.

OTOREID-HC. (Reid-Provident) Hydrocortisone free a cohol 10 mg. (1%), polymyxin B sulfate 10,000 u., neomycin sulfate equiv. to neomycin base 3.5 mg. Dropper Bot. 10 cc.
Use: Antibiotic ear drops.

OTOSTAN H.C. (Standex) Pramoxine HCl 1.0%, hydrocortisone 1.0%, parachlorometaxylenol 0.1%, benzalkonium chloride 0.02%, acetic acid 2.0%, propylene glycol. Vial 10 cc.

OTRIVIN. (Geigy) Xylometazoline HCl **Nasal Drops:** 0.1% w/sod. chloride, phenylmercuric acetate 1:50,000. Dropper Bot. 20 ml. **Nasal Spray:** 0.1% w/pot. phosphate monobasic, pot. chloride, sod. phosphate dibasic, sod. chloride, benzalkonium chloride 1:5,000. plastic squeeze spray 15 ml. **Ped. Nasal Soln. Drops:** 0.05%. Bot. 20 ml.
Use: Nasal congestion.

OUABAIN. Card-20(22)-enolide, 3-[(6-deoxy-α-L-mannopyranosyl)-oxy]-1,5,11,14,19-pentahydroxy-, octahydrate, (1β,3β,5β,-11α)-. Ouebain octahydrate G-Strophanthin.
(Lilly)—Amp. (0.5 mg.) 2 cc., Box 12s.
(Varick)—Amp. (0.25 mg.) 1 cc., Box 6s.
Use: Cardiac glycoside therapy.

OUABAIN OCTAHYDRATE. Ouabain, U.S.P. XXI.

OUTGRO. (Whitehall) Chlorobutanol 5%, tannic acid 25%, isopropyl alcohol 83%. Bot. .13 oz.

OVARIAN EXTRACT. Aq. ext. of whole ovaries of cattle.
Use: I.M. & S.C.; estrogen therapy.

OVARIAN HORMONE, isolated from ovary.
See: Lutrexin, Tab. (Hynson, Westcott & Dunning)

OVARIAN SUBSTANCE. (Various Mfr.) Whole ovarian substance from cattle, sheep or swine.

OVCON-35. (Mead Johnson) Norethindrone 0.4 mg. ethinyl estradiol 0.035 mg./Tab. Ctn. 6×21s.
Use: Oral contraceptive.

OVCON-35, 28 day. (Mead Johnson) 21 peach tablets of norethindrone 0.4 mg. combined with ethinyl estradiol 0.035 mg., followed by 7 green inert tablets/Cart. 6×28s.
Use: Oral contraceptive.

OVCON-50. (Mead Johnson) Norethindrone 1 mg., ethinyl estradiol 0.05 mg./Tab. Ctn. 6×21s.
Use: Oral contraceptive.

OVCON-50, 28 day. (Mead Johnson) 21 yellow tablets of norethindrone 1 mg. combined with ethinyl estradiol 0.05 mg., followed by 7 green inert tablets/Cart. 6×28s.
Use: Oral contraceptive.

OVIFOLLIN.
See: Estrone (Various Mfr.)

OVLIN. (Sig) **Tabs.** Ethinylestradiol 0.02 mg., conjugated estrogens 0.2 mg./Tab. Bot. 100s, 1000s.**Injectable.** estrone 2 mg., estradiol 0.05 mg., Vit. B-12 1000 mcg./cc. Vial 30 cc.

Use: Menopause, senile vaginitis, kraurosis vulvae, pruritus vulvae, estrogen replacement therapy.

OVOCYLIN DIPROPIONATE. (Ciba) Estradiol Dipropionate.

OVOGYN. (Pasadena Research) Ethinyl estradiol 0.02 mg./Tab. Bot. 100s, 1000s. 0.05 mg./Tab. Bot. 100s, 1000s.

OVRAL. (Wyeth) Norgestrel 0.5 mg., ethinyl estradiol 0.05 mg./Tab. 6 Pilpak dispensers, 21 Tabs. Tripak 63s.
Use: Oral contraception.

OVRAL-28. (Wyeth) Norgestrel 0.5 mg., ethinyl estradiol 0.05 mg./White Tab. (21) plus inert Tabs. (7). 6 Pilpak dispenser, 21 Tabs +7 inert Tabs.
Use: Oral contraceptive.

OVRETTE. (Wyeth) Norgestrel 0.075 mg./Tab. 6 Pilpak dispensers, 28 Tabs.
Use: Oral contraception.

O-V STATIN. (Squibb) Nystatin. Oral/vaginal therapy pack containing 42 Mycostatin Oral Tabs. (500,000 u./Tab.) and 14 Mycostatin Vaginal Tabs (100,000 u./Tab.)
Use: Vaginal candidiasis.

OVULEN-21. (Searle) Ethynodiol diacetate 1 mg., mestranol 0.1 mg./Tab. Compack Disp. 21s, 6×21. 24 ×21. Refills 21s, 12×21
Use: Oral contraceptive.

OVULEN-28. (Searle) Ethynodiol diacetate 1 mg., mestranol 0.1 mg./Tab. Compack 28s: 21 active tabs, 7 placebo tabs. Compack disp. 28s, 6×28. Refills 28s, 12×28.
Use: Oral contraceptive.

OXABID. (Jamieson-McKames) Magnesium oxide 140 mg. or magnesium oxide heavy 400 mg./Cap. Bot. 100s.

OXACILLIN. B.A.N. 6-(5-Methyl-3-phenyl-4-isoxazolecarboxamido-penicillanic acid.
Use: Antibiotic.

• **OXACILLIN, SODIUM,** U.S.P. XXI. Cap., Inj., Sol., Sterile, U.S.P. XXI. 5-Methyl-3-phenyl-4-isoxazolyl penicillin. Sodium 3,3-Dimethyl-6-(5-methyl-3-phenyl-4-isoxazole-carboxamido)-7-oxocarboxylate.
Use: Antibiotic.
See: Bactocill, Cap., Vial (Beecham Labs)
Prostaphilin, Prep. (Bristol)
Sodium oxacillin

OXADIMEDINE HCl. N-(2-Benzoxazolyl)-N-benzyl-N′, N′-dimethylethylenediamine HCl.
Use: Antifibrillatory agent.

OXAFURADENE. Name used for Nifuradene.
Use: Platelet antiaggretory agent.

• **OXAGRELATE.** USAN.

OXALID. (USV Labs.) Oxyphenbutazone 100 mg./Tab. Bot. 100s, 1000s.
Use: Anti-inflammatory.

• **OXAMARIN HYDROCHLORIDE.** USAN. 6,-7-bis[2-(Diethylamino)-ethoxy]-4-methylcoumarin dihydrochloride.
Use: Systemic hemostat.

• **OXAMNIQUINE,** U.S.P. XXI. Cap., U.S.P. XXI. 6-Hydroxymethyl-2-isopropylaminomethyl-7-nitro-1,2,3,4-tetrahydroquino-line.
Use: Treatment of schistosomiasis.
See: Vansil, Cap. (Pfipharmecs)

OXANAMIDE. 2-Ethyl-3-propyl glycidamide.
Use: Tranquilizer.

• **OXANDROLONE,** U.S.P. XXI. Tab., U.S.P. XX (1) Dodecahydro-3-hydroxy-6-(hydroxy-methyl)-3,3α,-6-trimethyl-1H-benz[e]indene-7-acetic acid, α-lactone. (2) 17 β-hydroxy-17-methyl-2-oxa-5α-androstan-3-one.
Use: Anabolic.
See: Anavar, Tab. (Searle)

OXANTEL. B.A.N. 1,4,5,6-Tetrahydro-1-methyl-2-(trans-3-hydroxystyryl)pyrimidine.
Use: Anthelmintic.

• **OXANTEL PAMOATE.** USAN.
Use: Anthelmintic.

• **OXAPROTILINE HYDROCHLORIDE.** USAN.
Use: Antidepressant.

• **OXAPROZIN.** USAN. 3-(4,5-Diphenyloxazol-2-yl)-propionic acid.
Use: Anti-inflammatory.

2H-1,3,2-OXAZAPHOSPHORIN-2-AMINO, N,N-BIS-(2-CHLOROETHYL)TETRAHYDRO-, 2-OXIDE, MONOHYDRATE. Cyclophosphamide, U.S.P. XXI.

• **OXARBAZOLE.** USAN.
Use: Anti-asthmatic.

• **OXATOMIDE.** USAN.
Use: Anti-allergic, anti-asthmatic.

• **OXAZEPAM,** U.S.P. XXI. Cap., Tab., U.S.P. XXI. 7-Chloro-1,3-dihydro-3-hydroxy-5-phenyl-2H-1,4-benzodia-zepin-2-one. Serenid-D.
Use: Sedative.
See: Serax, Cap., Tab. (Wyeth)

2,4-OXAZOLIDINEDIONE,5-ETHYL-3,5-DIMETHYL-. Paramethadione, U.S.P. XXI.

2,4-OXAZOLIDINEDIONE, 3,5,5-TRIMETHYL-. Trimethadione, U.S.P. XXI.

OX BILE EXTRACT. Purified oxgall.
See: Bile Extract, Ox

OXELADIN. B.A.N. 2-(2-Diethylaminoethoxy)-ethyl 2-eethyl-2-phenylbutyrate. Pectamol citrate.
Use: Cough suppressant.

• **OXETHAZAINE.** USAN. 2-Di-(N-methyl-N-phenyl-tert. butyl-carbamoyl-methyl)-aminoethanol; N,N-bis-(N-methyl-N-phenyl-t-butyl-acetamido)-beta-hydroxethyl -amino). 2,2′-[(2-Hydroxyethyl)imino]bis-[N-(α,α-dimethylphenethyl)-N-methylacetamide]. 2-Di-[(Nαα-trimethylphenethylcarbamoyl-methyl]-amino-ethanol.
Use: Local anesthetic.

• **OXETORONE FUMARATE.** USAN.
Use: Analgesic specific for migraine.

• **OXFENDAZOLE.** USAN.
Use: Anthelmintic.
See: Synanthic (Syntex)

• **OXFENICINE.** USAN.
Use: Vasodilator.

• **OXYFILCON A.** USAN.
Use: Contact lens material.

OX GALL.
See: Bile Extract, Ox

• **OXIBENDAZOLE.** USAN.
Use: Anthelmintic.

OXIDIZED BILE ACIDS.
See: Bile Acids, Oxidized

• **OXIDIZED CELLULOSE,** U.S.P. XXI. Absorbable cellulose. Cellulosic acid.
Use: Local hemostatic.

• **OXIDOPAMINE.** USAN.
Use: Adrenergic.

• **OXIFUNGIN HYDROCHLORIDE.** USAN.
Use: Antifungal.

• **OXILORPHAN.** USAN.
Use: Antagonist to narcotics.

OXINE.
See: Oxyquinoline sulfate (Various Mfr.)

• **OXIPEROMIDE.** USAN.
Use: Antipsychotic.

OXIPOR VHC PSORIASIS LOTION. (Whitehall) Coal tar sol. 48.5%, salicylic acid 1.0%, benzocaine 2%, alcohol 81%. Bot. 1.9 oz., 4 oz.
Use: Psoriasis treatment.

• **OXIRAMIDE.** USAN.
Use: Cardiac depressant.

• **OXISURAN.** USAN. (Methyl-sulfinyl)-methyl-2-pyridyl ketone.
Use: Antineoplastic.

• **OXMETIDINE HYDROCHLORIDE.** USAN.
Use: Antagonist to histamine receptors.

• **OXMETIDINE MESYLATE.** USAN.
Use: Antagonist to histimine receptors

• **OXOGESTONE PHENPROPIONATE.** USAN. **#1:** 20β-Hydroxy-19-norpregn-4-en-3-one hydrocinnamate. **#2:** 20β-hydroxy-19-nor-4-pregnen-3-one 20-phenylpropionate.
Use: Progestogen.

OXOLAMINE. (Arcum) Crystalline hydroxycobalamin 1000 mcg./cc. Vial 10 cc.

• **OXOLINIC ACID.** USAN. 5-Ethyl-5,8-dihydro-8-oxo-1,3-dioxolo-[4,5-g]quinoline-7-carboxylic acid.
Use: Antibacterial.

OXOPHENARSINE HYDROCHLORIDE. 2-Amino-4-arsenophenol hydrochloride.

OXPENTIFYLLINE. B.A.N. 3,7-Dimethyl-1-(5-oxohexyl)xanthine. Pentoxifylline (I.N.N.).
Use: Vasodilator.
See: Trental (Hoechst)

OXPHENERIDINE. 1-(β-phenyl-β-hydroxy-ethyl)-4-carbethoxy-4-phenylpiperidine.

OXPRENOLOL. B.A.N. 1-(o-Allyloxyphenoxy)-3-isopropylaminopropan-2-ol. Trasicor hydrochloride.
Use: Beta-adrenergic receptor blocking agent.

• **OXPRENOLOL HCl.** USAN. ($\pm$) 1-[o-(Allyloxy)-phenoxy]-3-(isopropylamino)-2-propanol HCl. Trasicor. Under study.
Use: Coronary dilator.

OXSORALEN CAPSULES. (Elder) Methoxsalen. 10 mg./Cap. Bot. 30s, 100s.
Use: Symptomatic control of severe, recalcitrant, disabling psoriasis in conjunction with U.V. radiation.

OXSORALEN LOTION. (Elder) Methoxsalen 1% in a inert lotion vehicle of alcohol 71%, propylene glycol, acetone, water. Bot. 1 oz.
Use: Topical repigmenting agent in vitiligo in conjunction with U.V. light.

• **OXTRIPHYLLINE,** U.S.P. XXI. Elixir, Tab., U.S.P. XXI. Choline theophyllinate.
Use: Bronchodilator.
See: Choledyl, Tab., Elix. (Parke-Davis)
W/Guaifenesin.
See: Brondecon, Tab., Elix. (Parke-Davis)

OXY-5 ACNE-PIMPLE MEDICATION. (Norcliff Thayer) Benzoyl peroxide 5% in lotion base. Bot. 1 fl. oz.
Use: Acne treatment.

OXY-10 COVER MAXIMUM STRENGTH ACNE-PIMPLE MEDICATION. (Norcliff Thayer) Benzoyl peroxide lotion 10%. Bot. 1 oz.
Use: Acne treatment.

OXY-10 MAXIMUM STRENGTH ACNE-PIMPLE MEDICATION. (Norcliff Thayer) Benzoyl peroxide 10% in lotion base. Bot. 1 fl. oz.
Use: Acne treatment.

OXY-10 WASH ANTIBACTERIAL SKIN WASH. (Norcliff Thayer) Benzoyl peroxide 10%. Bot. 4 fl. oz.
Use: Acne treatment.

• **OXYBENZONE,** U.S.P. XXI. 2-Hydroxy-4-methoxybenzophenone. Methanone, (2-hydroxy-4-methoxyphenyl)phenyl-. Cyasorb UV 9 (Lederle).
Use: Ultraviolet screen.
W/Dioxybenzone, benzophenone.
See: Solbar, Lot. (Person & Covey)

OXYBENZONE WITH COMBINATIONS.
See: Coppertone, Prods. (Plough)
Noskote, Cream (Plough
Shade, Prods. (Plough)
Sunger, Prods. (Plough)
Super Shade, Lotion (Plough)

OXYBUPROCAINE. B.A.N. 2-Diethylaminoethyl 4-amino-3-butoxybenzoate. Novesine hydrochloride.
Use: Local anesthetic.

• **OXYBUTYNIN CHLORIDE.** USAN. 4-Diethylamino-2-butynyl-α-phenylcyclo-hexanegly-colate hydrochloride.
Use: Anticholinergic.
See: Ditropan Syrup, Tab. (Marion Lab.)
Oxybutynin Chloride. (Mead Johnson)

OXYCAP. (Hyrex) Dyphylline 200 mg., guaifenesin 200 mg./Cap. Bot. 100s, 1000s.
Use: Vasodilator, bronchodilator, expectorant.

OXYCEL. (Deseret) Cellulosic acid in absorbable hemostatic agent prepared from cellulose. Resembles ordinary surgical gauze or cotton. Pledgets 2 $\times$ 1 $\times$ 1 in. 10s. Pads 3 $\times$ 3 in. 8 ply. 10s. Strips 5 $\times$ 0.5 in. 4 ply. 18 $\times$ 2 in. 4 ply. 10s. 36 $\times$ 0.5 in. 4 ply.
Use: Hemostatic.

OXYCINCHOPHEN. B.A.N. 3-Hydroxy-2-phenyl-quinoline-4-carboxylic acid.
Use: Uricosuric.

XY-CHINOL. (Ferndale) Pot. oxyquinoline sulfate 1 gr./Tab. Bot. 100s, 1000s.
Use: Deodorizer, bacteriostatic.

OXYCHLOROSENE. USAN. Monoxychlorosene. Hydrocarbon derivative containing fourteen carbons and hypochlorous acid. The hydrocarbon chain also has a phenyl substituent which in turn holds a sulfonic acid group.
Use: Topical anti-infective.
See: Clorpactin, Prod. (Scrip)

OXYCHLOROSEN SODIUM. USAN. Sodium salt of the complex derived from hypochlorous acid and tetradecylbenzene sulfonic acid. Action of active chlorine.
Use: Topical anti-infective.

XYCLOZANIDE. B.A.N. 3,3′,5,5′,6-Pentachloro-2′-hydroxysalicylanilide. Zanil
Use: Anthelmintic, veterinary medicine.

OXYCODONE. USAN. 7,8-Dihydro-14-hydroxy-O[3]-methylmorphinone. Dihydrohydroxycodeineone Eucodal hydrochloride; Proladone pectinate.
Use. Narcotic analgesic.

OXYCODONE HCl. USAN. (1) (−)-4,5α-Epoxy-14-hydroxy-3-methoxy-17-methylmorphinan-6-one, (2) (−)-14-Hydroxydi-hydrocodeinone.
Use: Narcotic analgesic.
See: Dihydrohydroxycodeinone HCl
W/Acetaminophen & oxycodone terephthalate.
See: Percocet-5, Tab (Du Pont)
Tylox, Cap. (McNeil)

OXYETHYLATED TERTIARY OCTYLPHENOL-FORMALDEHYDE POLYMER.
See: Triton WR-1339. (Rohm & Haas)

OXYETHYLENE OXYPROPYLENE POLYMER.
See: Poloxalkol
W/Danthron, B-1, carboxymethyl cellulose.
See: Evactol, Cap. (Delta)

OXYFEDRINE. B.A.N. L-3-[(β-Hydroxy-α-methyl-phenethyl-amino]-3′-methoxypropiophenone. Ildamen hydrochloride.
Use: Coronary vasodilator.

• **OXYGEN,** U.S.P. XXI.
Use: Medicinal.

• **OXYGEN 93 PERCENT.** U.S.P. XXI.
Use: Medicinal.

OXYGEN-CARBON DIOXIDE MIXTURES.

OXYMESTERONE. B.A.N. 4,17β-Dihydroxy-17α-methylandrost-4-en-3-one. 4-Hydroxy-17α-methyl-testosterone. Oranabol
Use: Anabolic steroid.

OXYMETAZOLINE. B.A.N. 2-(4-t-Butyl-3-hydroxy-2,6-dimethylbenzyl)-2-imidazoline. Afrin and Hazol hydrochloride.
Use: Vasoconstrictor.

• **OXYMETAZOLINE HYDROCHLORIDE,** U.S.P. XXI. Nasal Soln., U.S.P. XXI. Phenol, 3-[(4,5-dihydro-1H-imidazol-2-yl-)methyl]-6-(1,1-dimethylethyl)-2,4-dimethyl-, monohydrochloride. 6-Tert-butyl-3-(2-imidazolin-2-ylmethyl)-2,4-dimethylphenol HCl.
Use: Decongestant, adrenergic.
See: Afrin, Nasal Spray, Soln. (Schering)
Duration Nasal Spray (Plough)
Duration Nose Drops (Plough)
Duration Nose Drops for Children (Plough)
St. Joseph Nasal Spray for Children (Plough)
St. Joseph Nose Drops for Children (Plough)

• **OXYMETHOLONE,** U.S.P. XXI. Tab., U.S.P. XXI. 17-beta-Hydroxy-2-(hydroxymethylene)-17-methyl-5α-androstan-3-one.
Use: Androgen.
See: Anadrol, Tab. (Syntex)

OXYMORPHONE. B.A.N. 7,8-Dihydro-14-hydroxy-morphinone. Numorphan hydrochloride.
Use: Narcotic analgesic.

• **OXYMORPHONE HCl,** U.S.P. XXI. Inj., Suppos., U.S.P. XXI. 14-Hydroxydihydromorphinone HCl. 4,5α-Epoxy-3,14-dihydroxy-17-methylmorphinan-6-one Hydrochloride.
Use: Analgesic, narcotic.
See: Numorphan Amp., Vial, Supp. (Du Pont)

OXYMYCIN. (Forest) Oxytetracycline 50 mg., lidocaine 20 mg./ml. Vial 10 ml.

• **OXYPERTINE.** USAN. 5,6-Dimethoxy-2-methyl-3-[2-(4-phenyl-1-piperazinyl-ethyl]indole. 1-[2-(5,6-Dimethoxy-2-methylindol-3-yl)ethyl]-4-phenylpiperazine. Integrin hydrochloride.
Use: Psychotropic.

• **OXYPHENBUTAZONE,** U.S.P. XXI. Tab., U.S.P. XXI. 1-(p-Hy-droxyphenyl)-2-phenyl-4-butyl-3,5-pyrazolidine-dione. Oxazolidin. 4-Butyl-1-(p-hydroxyphenyl)-2-phenyl 3,5-pyrazolidinedione monohydrate.
Use: Antiarthritic, anti-inflammatory analgesic, antipyretic.
See: Oxalid, Tab. (USV Labs.)
Tandearil, Tab. (Geigy)

OXYPHENCYCLIMINE. B.A.N. 1,4,5,6-Tetrahydro-1-methylpyrimidin-2-ylmethyl α-cyclohexylmandelate. Daricon and Naridan hydrochloride.
Use: Antispasmodic.

• **OXYPHENCYCLIMINE HCl,** U.S.P. XXI. Tab., U.S.P. XXI. 1-Methyl-1,4,5,6-tetrahydro-2-pyrimidylmethyl-alpha-cyclohexyl-alpha-phenylglycolate HCl. (1,4,5,6-Tetrahydro-1-methyl-2-pyrimidinyl)methyl α-phenyl-cyclohexane-glycolate monohydrochloride.
Use: Antispasmodic.
See: Daricon, Tab. (Beecham Labs)
W/Hydroxyzine HCl.
See: Enarax, Tab. (Beecham Labs)
Vistrax 5 & 10 Tab. (Pfizer Laboratories)
W/Phenobarbital.
See: Daricon-PB, Tab. (Beecham Labs)

OXYPHENISATIN. B.A.N. 3,3-Di-(4-hydroxyphenyl)-indolin-2-one. Bydolax; Contax diacetate.
Use: Laxative.

• **OXYPHENISATIN ACETATE.** USAN. 3,3-bis(p-Hydroxyphenyl)2-indolinone diacetate. Diacetoxydiphenylisatin, Acetphenolisatin, Acetylphenylisatin, Diacetoxyphenyloxindol, Bisatin, Phenylisatin bis-(acetoxyphenyl) oxindol.
Use: Laxative.
See: Endophenolphthalein (Roche)
Isacen (No Mfr. currently lists.)
Prulet, Tab. (Mission)
Prulet Liquitab. (Mission)

OXYPHENONIUM BROMIDE. B.A.N. Diethyl (2-hydroxyethyl-methylammonium bromide-α-phenyl cyclohexyl glycolate. 2-α-(Cyclohexyl-mandeloyloxy) ethyldiethylmethylammonium bromide.
Use: Anticholinergic.
See: Antrenyl Bromide, Tab. (Ciba)

OXYPHENUDRINE. α-{[(p-Hydroxy-α-methylphenethyl)amino]methyl}proto-catechuyl alcohol.

• **OXYPURINOL.** USAN. 4,6-Dihydroxypyrazolo(3,4-d)pyrimidine. 1H-Pyrazolo[3,4-d]pyrimidine-4,6-diol.
Use: Xanthine oxidase inhibitor.

• **OXYQUINOLINE.** USAN.
Use: Disinfectant.

OXYQUINOLINE BENZOATE. (Merck) Pkg. 1 lb. 8-Hydroxyquinoline benzoate.
W/Alkyl aryl sulfonate, disodium edetate, aminacrine HCl, copper sulfate, Na sulfate.
See: Triva, Vag. Jelly, Powd. (Boyle)
W/Benzoic acid, salicylic acid & sodium tetradecyl sulfate.
See: NP-27 Cream (Norwich)

• **OXYQUINOLINE SULFATE.** USAN. 8-Hydroxyquinoline sulfate.
Use: Disinfectant.
See: Chinosol, Tab., Pow., Vial (Vernon)

OXYQUINOLINE SULFATE W/COMBINATIONS.
See: Alochor Stypic, Liq. (Gordon)
Arnolds Rectal Supp. (Scrip)
Benzodent, Oint. (Vicks)
Dennt's Dental Poultice (C.S. Dent)
Derma Medicone Oint. (Medicone)
Derma Medicone-HC, Oint. (Medicone)
Foille, Prods. (Carbisulphoil)
Maseda Foot Powder, Pow. (Elder)
Medicone Dressing (Medicone)
Oxyzal Wet Dressing, Sol. (Gordon)
Rectal Medicone, Oint. (Medicone)
Rectal Medicone-HC, Oint. (Medicone)
Rectal Medicone Unguent, Oint. (Medicone)
Trapens, Tab. (Mills)
Triticoll, Tab. (Western Research)
Triva, Douche Pow. (Boyle)
V.A. Douche Powder (Norcliff-Thayer)
Zyanoid, Oint. (Elder)

OXY-SCRUB. (Norcliff Thayer) Abradant cleanser containing dissolving abradant particles of sodium tetraborate decahydrate. Tube 2.65 oz.
Use: Skin cleanser to open plugged pores and removing excess oil.

OXYSORALEN. 8-Hydroxy-4′,5′,6,7-furocoumarin.
See: Methoxsalen

OXYSTAT. (Hyrex) Dyphylline 250 mg./ml. Vial 10 ml.
Use: Vasodilator, bronchodilator.

OXYTETRACLOR. (Kenyon) Oxytetracycline HCl 250 mg./Cap. Bot. 100s, 1000s.
Use: Antibiotic.

• **OXYTETRACYCLINE,** U.S.P. XXI. Inj., Sterile, Tab., U.S.P. XXI.
Use: Antibiotic.
See: Oxytetraclor, Cap. (Kenyon)
Terramycin, Prod. (Pfipharmecs)
Terramycin, Prod. (Pfizer Laboratories)

• **OXYTETRACYCLINE AND NYSTATIN CAPSULES** U.S.P. XXI.
Use: Antibiotic, antifungal.

• **OXYTETRACYCLINE AND NYSTATIN FOR ORAL SUSPENSION,** U.S.P. XXI.
Use: Antibiotic, antifunal.

• **OXYTETRACYCLINE HYDROCHLORIDE AND HYDROCORTISONE OINTMENT,** U.S.P. XXI.
Use: Antibiotic, anti-inflammatory.

• **OXYTETRACYCLINE AND HYDROCORTISONE ACETATE OPTHALMIC SUSPENSION,** U.S.P. XXI
Use: Antibiotic, anti-inflammatory.

• **OXYTETRACYCLINE CALCIUM,** U.S.P. XXI. Oral Susp., U.S.P. XXI.
Use: Antibiotic.

• **OXYTETRACYCLINE HYDROCHLORIDE,** U.S.P. XXI. Cap., For Inj., Sterile, U.S.P. XXI. 5-Hydroxytetracycline HCl. An antibiotic from *Streptomyces rimosus.*
Use: Antibiotic, antirickettsial.
See: Dalimycin, Cap. (Dalin)
Oxlopar, Cap. (Parke-Davis)
Oxy-Kesso-Tetra, Cap. (McKesson)
Terramycin Hydrochloride, Preps. (Pfizer Laboratories & Pfipharmecs)
Uri-tet, Cap. (American Urologicals)
Urobiotic (Roerig)

• **OXYTETRACYCLINE AND PHENAZOPYRIDINE HYDROCHLORIDES AND SULFAMETHIZOLE CAPSULES,** U.S.P. XXI.
Use: Antibiotic; urinary analgesic antispasmodic and anti-infective.

• **OXYTETRACYCLINE HYDROCHLORIDE AND POLYMYXIN B SULFATE,** U.S.P. XXI.
Use: Antibiotic.

• **OXYTETRACYCLINE HYDROCHLORIDE AND POLYMYXIN B SULFATE OPTHALMIC OINTMENT,** U.S.P. XXI.
Use: Antibiotic.

• **OXYTETRACYCLINE HYDROCHLORIDE AND POLYMYXIN B SULFATE TOPICAL POWDER,** U.S.P. XXI.
Use: Antibiotic.

• **OXYTETRACYCLINE HYDROCHLORIDE AND POLYMYXIN B SULFATE VAGINAL TABLETS,** U.S.P. XXI.
Use: Antibiotic.

OXYTETRACYCLINE-POLYMYXIN B. Mix of oxytetracycline HCl & polymyxin B sulfate.
Use: Antibiotic.
See: Terramycin Hydrochloride w/Polymyxin B Sulfate, Oint., Tab., Pow. (Pfizer Laboratories & Pfipharmecs)

OXYTOCICS.
See: Ergot Prep.

• **OXYTOCIN INJECTION,** U.S.P. XXI.
Use: Oxytocic.
See: Pitocin, Amp. (Parke-Davis)
Syntocinon, Amp. (Sandoz)

• **OXYTOCIN NASAL SOLUTION,** U.S.P. XXI.
Use: Oxytocic.

XYTOCIN, SYNTHETIC.
See: Pitocin, Amp. (Parke-Davis)
Syntocinon, Amp. (Sandoz)
Syntocinon Nasal Spray (Sandoz)

XYZAL WET DRESSING. (Gordon) Benzalkonium chloride 1:2000, oxyquinoline sulfate, distilled water. Dropper bot. 1 oz., 4 oz.
Use: Minor infections.

YSTER SHELLS.
See: Os-Cal, Tab. (Marion)
/Vit. D-2.
See: Ostrakal, Tab. (Elder)

OZOLINONE. USAN.
Use: Diuretic.

P

1E1;P2E1;P3E1;P4E1;P6E1. (Alcon) Pilocarpine HCl 1%,2%,3%,4%,6% respectively, epinephrine bitartrate 1%. Vial plastic drop. Vial 15 cc.
Use: Management of open angle glaucoma.

-200. (Boots) Papaverine HCl 200 mg. /Cap. Bot. 100s.
Use: REief of cerebral, peripheral, and myocardial ischemia with arterial spasms & arrhythmias.

.A. (Scrip) Phenobarbital ⅛ gr., atropine sulfate 1/250 gr./Tab. Bot. 100s.

.A.A.M. (Kenyon) Acetylsalicylic acid 5 gr., para-aminobenzoic acid 5 gr., Vit. C 50 mg./Tab. Bot. 100s, 1000s.
Use: Arthritis.

ABA-"5". (Durel) P-amino benzoic acid in quick drying moisturizing base. Pl. Bot. 4 oz.
Use: Sunscreen lotion.

ABALAN. (Lannett) Potassium para-amino benzoate 5 gr., potassium salicylate 5 gr., ascorbic acid 50 mg./Tab. Bot. 100s, 1000s.

ABALATE. (Robins) Sod. salicylate 300 mg., sodium aminobenzoate 300 mg./E.C. Tab. Bot. 100s, 500s.
Use: Antirheumatic.

ABALATE-SF. (Robins) Potassium salicylate 300 mg., potassium aminobenzoate 300 mg./Tab. Bot. 100s, 500s.
Use: Antirheumatic.

ABANOL. (Elder) p-Aminobenzoic acid 5%, ethanol 70%. Bot. 4 oz.
Use: Sunburn preventative, sunscreen lotion.

ABAQUINONE CREAM. (Dermohr Pharmacal) Hydroquionone 4%, amyl dimethyl paba 3% in creamy base. Tube 1 oz.
Use: Gradual fading of "age spots".

ABASAL. (Wolins) Para-aminobenzoic acid, as sodium 5 gr., sodium salicylate 5 gr./Tab. Bot. 1000s.

ABA-SALICYLATE. (Various Mfr.) Sodium salicylate, p-aminobenzoate, Vit. C/Tab. Bot. 100s, 500s.
Use: Antirheumatic.

ABASAL N.S. (Wolins) Potassium salicylate 5 gr., potassium para-aminobenzoate 5 gr./Tab. Bot. 1000s.

ABA SODIUM. Sod. p-aminobenzoate. (Various Mfr.)
Use: Antirickettsial agent.

PABASONE. (Pinex) Sod. salicylate 5 gr., para-aminobenzoic acid 5 gr., ascorbic acid 20 mg./Tab. Bot. 100s.
Use: Arthritis, rheumatism.

P-A-C. Preparations of phenacetin, aspirin, and caffeine.
See: A.P.C. Preparations & Empirin Preparations

PACEMAKER PROPHYLAXIS PASTES WITH FLUORIDE. (Pacemaker) Silicone dioxide and diatomaceous earth, sodium fluoride 4.4%. Light abrasive, cinnamon/cherry. Medium abrasive, orange. Heavy abrasive, mint. Paste. Bot. 8 oz.

PACKER'S PINE TAR LIQUID SHAMPOO. (Rydell) Bot. 6 fl oz.
Use: Treatment of dandruff and itchy scalp.

PACKER'S PINE TAR SOAP. (Rydell) Bar 3.3 oz.
Use: Treatment of minor skin and scalp troubles.

PACLIN G. (Geneva) Penicillin G potassium 100M u., 200M u./Tab. Bot. 1000s. 250M u., 400M u./Tab. Bot. 100s, 1000s.

PACLIN VK. (Geneva) Penicillin phenoxymethyl 125 mg., 250 mg./Tab. Bot. 100s, 1000s.

P-A-C REVISED FORMULA ANALGESIC. (Upjohn) Aspirin 400 mg., caffeine 32 mg./Tab. Bot. 100s, 1000s.
Use: Analgesic.

• **PADIMATE A.** USAN.
Use: Ultraviolet screen.

• **PADIMATE O.** USAN.
Use: Ultraviolet screen.
See: Coppertone, Prods. (Plough)
Eclipse Prods. (Dorsey)
Escalol 506 (Van Dyk)
Noskote, Prods. (Plough)
Pabafilm (Owen)
Shade, Prods. (Plough)
Sunger, Prods. (Plough)
Super Shade, Prods. (Plough)
Tropical Blend Sunscreen Lotion (Plough)

PAH.
See: Sodium Aminohippurate Inj. (Var. Mfr.)

PAIN-A-LAY. (Glessner) Antiseptic, anesthetic solution. Bot. 4 oz. w/sprayer, Bot. 4 oz., 8 oz., 1 pt.
Use: Relief of sore gums, minor sore throat.

PAIN & FEVER TABLET. (Lederle) Acetaminophen 325 mg./Tab. Bot. 100s, 1000s.
Use: Analgesic, antipyretic.

PAIN EXPELLER. (Guild) Tube 2.5 oz.

PAIN EXPELLER BALM. (Guild) Tube 0.25 oz.

PAIN-EZE. (Edward J. Moore) Benzocaine, menthol, oil of peppermint. Tube ⅛ oz., 0.25 oz.
Use: Toothache and teething pain.

PAIN RELIEF OINTMENT. (Walgreen) Methylsalicylate 8.0%, menthol 7.2%. Tube 1.5 oz.
Use: Relief from pain of colds, muscle aches, neuralgia.

PAIN RELIEVERS-TENSION HEADACHE RELIEVERS. (Weeks & Leo) Acetaminophen 325 mg., phenyltoloxamine citrate 30 mg./Tab. Bot. 40s, 100s.
Use: Analgesic.

PALADAC LIQUID. (Parke-Davis) Vit. A 5000 I.U., D 400 I.U., B-1 3 mg., B-2 3 mg., B-6 1 mg., B-12 5 mcg., C

50 mg., niacinamide 20 mg., pantothenic acid 5 mg./5 ml. Bot. 4 oz., 1 pt.
Use: Multivitamin therapy.

PALADAC W/MINERALS. (Parke-Davis) Vit. A 4000 I.U., D 400 I.U., C 50 mg., E 10 I.U., B-1 3 mg., B-2 3 mg., B-6 1 mg., B-12 5 mcg., nicotinamide 20 mg., pantothenic acid 5 mg., Ca 23 mg., Fe 5 mg., P 17 mg., iodine 0.05 mg., K 2.5 mg., Mg 1 mg./Chewable Tab. Bot. 100s.
Use: Vitamin and mineral supplement.

PALAPRIN. Aloxiprin, B.A.N.

PALBAR. (Hauck) Phenobarbital 16.2 mg., atropine sulfate 0.012 mg., scopolamine HBr 0.005 mg., hyoscyamine HBr 0.18 mg./Tab. Bot. 100s, 1000s. Elixir 23% alcohol/5 cc. Bot. pt.
Use: Sedative-spasmolytic effect.

PALBAR NO. 2. (Hauck) Atropine sulfate 0.012 mg., scopolamine HBr 0.005 mg., hyoscyamine HBr 0.018 mg., phenobarbital 32.4 mg./Tab. Bot. 100s.
Use: Antispasmodic-anticholinergic.

PALESTROL.
See: Diethylstilbestrol (Various Mfr.)

PALFIUM HYDROGEN TARTRATE. Dextromoramide, B.A.N.

PALGESIC. (Pan American) Isobutylallylbarbituric acid ¾ gr., phenacetin 2 gr., aspirin 3 gr., caffeine ⅔ gr./Tab., Cap. Bot. 100s.
Use: Tension headache, as sedative-analgesic.

PALINUM.
Use: Hypnotic and sedative.
See: Cyclobarbital Calcium (Var. Mfr.)

PALMIDROL. N-(2-Hydroxyethyl)palmitamide.

PALMIRON. (Hauck) Ferrous fumarate 200 mg./Tab. Bot. 100s.
Use: Anemias.

PALMIRON-C-TABS. (Hauck) Ferrous fumarate 200 mg., ascorbic acid 120 mg., Vit. B-6 5 mg./Chewable Tab. Bot. 100s, 1000s.
Use: As hematinic.

• **PALMOXIRATE SODIUM.** USAN.
Use: Antidiabetic.

PAMABROM. 2-Amino-2-methyl-1-propanol salt of 8-bromotheophyllinate.
W/Acetaminophen.
See: Pamprin, Tab. (Chattem Labs.)
W/Acetaminophen, pyrilamine maleate.
See: Cardui, Tab. (Chattem Labs.)
Sunril, Cap. (Emko)
W/Pyrilamine maleate, homatropine methylbromide, hyoscyamine sulfate, scopolamine HBr, methamphetamine HCl.
See: Aridol, Tab.s (MPL)

• **PAMATOLOL SULFATE.** USAN.
Use: Anti-adrenergic.

PAM-B-12 INJ. (Pan American) Cyanocobalamin 1000 mcg./cc. Amp. 10 cc., 30 cc.
Use: B-12 therapy, pernicious anemia.

PAMELOR. (Sandoz) Nortriptyline HCl. **Cap.:** Nortriptyline HCl 10 mg., 25 mg. or 75 mg. base/Cap. **10 mg.** Bot. 100s, SandoPak 100s; **25 mg.:** Bot. 100s, 500s, SandoPak 100s; **75 mg.:** Bot. 100s. **Liq.:** Nortriptyline HCl equiv. to 10 mg. base/5 ml. Bot. Pts.
Use: Relief of symptoms of depression.

PAMINE. (Upjohn) Methscopolamine bromide. Tab. 2.5 mg. Bot. 100s, 500s.
Use: Antispasmodic.

PAMPRIN. (Chattem) Pamabrom 25 mg., acetaminophen 325 mg., pyrilamine maleate 12.5 mg./Tab. or Cap. Pkg. 12s, 24s, 48s.
Use: Premenstrual and menstrual symptoms.

PAMPRIN-MAXIMUM CRAMP RELIEF FORMULA (Chattem) Pamabrom 25 mg., acetaminophen 500 mg., pyrilamine maleate 15 mg./Cap. Pkg. 8s, 16s, 32s.
Use: Premenstrual and menstrual symptoms.

PAN A-C. (Eckerd) Vit. A palmitate 5000 I.U., C 150 mg., d-calcium pantothenate 25 mg./Cap. Bot. 100s, 200

PANACARB. (Lannett) Bismuth subnitrate, sod. bicarb., mag. carb., papain, diastase/Tab. Bot. 1000s.
Use: Antacid.

PANACID. (Panray) Magnesium trisilicate 500 mg., aluminum hydroxide gel 250 mg./Tab. Bot. 100s, 500s.
Use: Antacid.

PANADEINE TABLETS. (Winthrop Products) Paracetamol, codeine.
Use: Analgesic, antipyretic.

PANADEINE CO. TABLETS. (Winthrop Products) Paracetamol, codeine.
Use: Analgesic, antipyretic.

PANADO. (Winthrop Products) Paracetamol, codeine.
Use: Analgesic, antipyretic.

PANADOL. (Glenbrook) Acetaminophen 500 mg./Tab. or Cap. Bot. Tab. 2s, 30s, 60s, 100s; Cap. 10s, 24s, 48s.
Use: Analgesic, anti-pyretic.

PANADOL CHILDREN'S. (Glenbrook) Acetaminophen. **Tab.**: 80 mg./Tab. Bot. 30s. **Liquid**: 80 mg./0.8 ml. Bot. 2 oz., 4 oz. **Drops**: 80 mg./0.5 oz. Bot. 0.5 oz.
Use: Analgesic/antipyretic.

PANADYL. (Misemer) Pyrilamine maleate 25 mg., phenylpropanolamine HCl 25 mg., prophenpyridamine maleate 10 mg./Pelltab. Bot. 100s, 1000s.
Use: Decongestant, antihistaminic.

PANAFIL. (Rystan) Papain pow. 10%, urea 10%, chlorophyll water sol. 0.5%, hydrophilic base. Oint. Tube 1 oz., Jar 1 lb.
Use: For debridement and healing of skin lesions.

PANAFIL WHITE OINTMENT. (Rystan) Papain 10,000 u. enzyme activity, hydrophilic base/Gm., urea 10%. Tubes 1 oz.
Use: For debridement of skin lesions.

PANAFORT ELIXIR. (Pan American) Lysine mono HCl 800 mg., Vit. B-12 30 mcg., B-1 2 mg., B-2 12 mg., B-6 12 mg., niacinamide 100 mg., panthenol 20 mg., alcohol 5%/15 cc. Bot. 8 oz.
Use: Dietary supplement, appetite stimulant.

PANAFORT TABLETS. (Pan American) Bot. 100s.

PANAHIST. (Panray) Chlorpheniramine Maleate 4 mg. or 8 mg./Tab. Bot. 1000s.
Use: Antihistaminic

PANALGESIC. (Poythress) Methyl salicylate 55.78%, aspirin 5.32%, menthol 0.95% & camphor 2.0%, in alcohol 17% w/emollients and color. Bot. 4 oz., pt., 0.5 gal.
Use: Analgesic & counterirritant.

PANAMIN. (Panray) Aminophylline 100 mg., or 200 mg./Tab. Bot. 100s, 1000s.
Use: Bronchial dilators.

PAN-APC. (Panray) Aspirin 3.5 gr., phenacetin 2.5 gr., caffeine 0.5 gr./Tab. Bot. 1000s.
Use: Analgesic.

PANAPHYLLIN. (Pan American) Theophylline 65 mg., ephedrine HCl 12 mg., guaifenesin 50 mg./5 cc. Susp. Bot. 8 oz.
Use: Bronchodilator, vasoconstrictor, expectorant.

PANAQUIN. (Panray) Iodoquinol. 650 mg./Tab. Bot. 100s, 1000s.
Use: Amebicide.

PANASCORB. (Panray) Ascorbic acid 100 mg., 250 mg., 500 mg./Tab. Bot. 1000s.
Use: Vitamin therapy.

PANASOL. (Seatrace) Prednisone 5 mg./Tab. Bot. 100s.
Use: Adrenocortical steroid (anti-inflammatory).

PANASORB DROPS. (Winthrop Products) Paracetamol, codeine.
Use: Analgesic, antipyretic.

PANASORB ELIXIR. (Winthrop Products) Paracetamol, codeine.
Use: Analgesic, antipyretic.

PANASORB SUPPOSITORIES. (Winthrop Products) Paracetamol, codeine.
Use: Analgesic, antipyretic.

PANASORB TABLETS. (Winthrop Products) Paracetamol.
Use: Analgesic, antipyretic.

PANAZID. (Panray) Isoniazid powder 1 lb. container. Tab. 50 mg., 100 mg., 300 mg./Tab. Bot. 100s, 1000s. Injection: 1 Gm./Vial. 50 cc./Vial.
Use: Anti-tuberculostatic.

PANAZID PLUS B-6. (Panray) Isoniazid 300 mg., Vit. B-6 30 mg./Tab.; Isoniazid 100 mg., Vit. B-6 10 mg./Tab. Bot. 100s, 1000s.
Use: Anti-tuberculostatic with pyridoxine.

PANAZID TABLETS. (Panray) Isoniazid 50 mg., 100 mg., 300 mg./Tab. Bot. 100s, 1000s.
Use: Antibacterial (tuberculostatic).

PANAZON HCl. Nitrovin, B.A.N.

PAN-B-1. (Panray) Thiamin HCl 50 mg., 100 mg./Tab. Bot. 1000s.
Use: Vitamin supplement.

PAN-B-6. (Panray) Pyridoxine HCl 25 mg., 50 mg., 100 mg./Tab. Bot. 1000s.
Use: Vitamin therapy.

PANCARD. (Pan American) Pentaerythritol tetranitrate 10 mg./Tab. Bot. 100s, 500s. Also available w/phenobarbital. 20 mg./Tab. Bot. 100s.

PANCARD 30 TP. (Pan American) Pentaerythritol tetranitrate 30 mg./long-acting Panseal. Bot. 60s.
Use: Coronary vasodilator.

PANCARD 30 TPA. (Pan American) Pentaerythritol tetranitrate 30 mg., amobarbital 50 mg./long-acting Panseal. Bot. 60s.
Use: Coronary vasodilator & sedative.

PANCET. (Pan American) Propoxyphene HCl 65 mg., acetaminophen 650 mg./Tab. Bot. 100s.
Use: Analgesic.

PANCOXIN HCl. Amprolium, B.A.N.

PANCREASE. (McNeil Pharm) Enteric coated pancrelipase capsules w/Lipase 4,000 NF U., amylase 20,000 NF U., protease 25,000 NF U./Cap. Bot. 100s, 250s.
Use: Pancreatic enzyme supplement.

PANCREATIC DORNASE.
See: Dornavac for Inhalation, Vial (Merck Sharp & Dohme)

PANCREATIC ENZYME.
W/Pepsin, ox bile.
See: Nu' Leven, Nu' Leven Plus, Tab. (Lemmon)

PANCREATIC SUBSTANCE. Substance from fresh pancreas of hog or ox & contains enzymes amylopsin, trypsin & steapsin.
W/Bile extract, dl-methionine, choline bitartrate.
See: Licoplex, Tab. (Mills)
W/Bile salts, lipase.
See: Cotazym-B, Tab. (Organon)
W/Bile, whole (desic.), oxidized bile acids, homatropine methylbromide.
See: Pancobile, Tab. (Reid-Provident)
W/dl-Methionine, choline bitartrate, ox bile.
See: Cholipan, Tab. (Western Research Labs.)
W/Lipase.
See: Cotazym, Cap., Packet (Organon)

• **PANCREATIN,** U.S.P. XXI. Cap., Tab., U.S.P. XXI. Pancreatic enzymes obtained from hog or cattle pancreatic tissue.
Use: Digestant.
See: Depancol, Tab. (Warner-Chilcott)
Elzyme, Tab. (Elder)
Panteric, Tab. (Parke-Davis)

PANCREATIN W/COMBINATIONS.
See: Aro-Pepsin, Tab. (Scrip)
Bile, Anthus Comp., Cap. (Scrip)
Bilogen, Tab. (Organon)
Bocresin, Liq. (Scrip)
Calsarbain, Tab. (Sutliff & Case)
Canz, Tab. (Cole)
Diethylstilbestrol Digestive Formula, Tab. (Wolins)
Digenzyme, Tab. (Burgin-Arden)
Digestozyme, Tab. (Wolins)
Digolase, Cap. (Boyle)
Dizymes, Cap. (Recsei)
Donnazyme, Tab. (Robins)
Entozyme, Tab. (Robins)
Enzobile, Tab. (Mallard)
Enzolax, Tab. (Kay)
Enzymet, Tab. (Westerfield)
Gastroenterase, Tabs. (Wampole)
Gourmase, Cap. (Rowell)

Ilozyme, Tab. (Adria)
Konzyme, Tab. (Brunswick)
Lever Taurine, Liq. (Paddock)
Maso-Gestive, Tab. (Mason)
Nu'Leven, Tab. (Lemmon)
Nu'Leven Plus, Tab. (Lemmon)
Pepsatal, Tab. (Kenyon)
Phazyme prod., Tab. (Reed & Carnrick)
Ro-Bile, Tab. (Rowell)
Sto-Zyme, Tab. (Jalco)
Zypan, Tab. (Standard Process)

• **PANCRELIPASE,** U.S.P. XXI. Cap., Tab., U.S.P. XXI. Formerly Lipancreatin. Preparation of hog pancreas with high content of steapsin and adequate amounts of pancreatic enzymes.
Use: Pancreatic enzymes preparation; digestive aid.
See: Accelerase, Cap. (Organon)
Cotazym, Cap., Packet (Organon)
Viokase, Pow., Tab. (Viobin)
W/Mixed conjugated bile salts, cellulase.
See: Accelerase, Cap. (Organon)
Cotazym-B, Tab. (Organon)

PANCREOZYMIN. B.A.N. A hormone obtained from duodenal mucosa.
Use: Diagnostic aid.

PANCRETIDE. (Baxter) Pancreatic polypeptide in normal saline.
Use: Fibrinolytic conditions.

PANCURONIUM.
See: Poncuronium Bromide (Organon)

• **PANCURONIUM BROMIDE.** USAN. (1) 1,1′-(3α,17β-Dihydroxy-5α-androstan-2β,16β-ylene)bis-[1-methylpiperidinium]dibromide diacetate: (2) 2β,16β-dipiperidino-5α-androstane-3α, 17 β-diol diacetate dimethobromide. Pavulon (Organon).
Use: Skeletal muscle relaxant.

P AND S LIQUID. (Baker/Cummins) Bot. 4 oz., 8 oz.
Use: Shampoo.

P AND S PLUS. (Baker/Cummins) Coal tar sol. 8%, salicylic acid 2%. Tube 3.5 oz.
Use: Tar gel for psoriasis and other scaling conditions.

P AND S SHAMPOO. (Baker/Cummins) Salicylic acid 2%, lactic acid 0.5% Bot. 4 oz.
Use: Antiseborrheic shampoo.

PANEX. (Mallard) Acetaminophen 325 mg./Tab. Bot. 1000s.
Use: Analgesic.

PANFIL. (Pan American) Dyphyllin 200 mg./Tab. Bot. 100s.
Use: Treatment of bronchopulmonary insufficiency.

PANFIL-G. (Pan American) Dyphyllin 200 mg., guaifenesin 50 mg./Tab. Bot. 100s. Dyphyllin 100 mg., guaifenesin 50 mg./5 cc. Elix. Bot. pt.
Use: Treatment of bronchopulmonary insufficiency.

PANGYN. (Panray) Magnesium gluconate 0.5 mg./Tab. Bot. 100s, 1000s.
Use: Magnesium deficiencies.

PANHEMATIN. (Abbott) Hemin 313 mg./43ml. Vial 100 ml.
Use: Amelioration of recurrent attacks of acute intermittent porphyria.

PANHIST. (Panray) Chlorpheniramine 8 mg./Tab. Bot 1000s.
Use: Antihistaminic.

PANHYDROSONE. (Panray) Hydrocortisone 10 mg., 20 mg./Tab. Bot. 100s, 1000s. Powder 1 Gm., 5 Gm./Bot.
Use: Hormone.

PANIDAZOLE. B.A.N. 2-Methyl-5-nitro-1-[2-(4-pyridyl) ethyl]imidazole.
Use: Amebicide.

PANISOLONE. (Panray) Prednisolone powder 5 Gm., 1 Gm./Bot. Tab. 1 mg., 5 mg. Bot. 100s, 1000s.
Use: Adrenocortical steroid.

PANITOL. (Wesley) Allylisobutyl barbituric acid 15 mg., acetaminophen 300 mg./Tab. Bot. 100s, 1000s
Use: Tension, pain.

PANITOL H.M.B.. (Wesley) Panitol formula plus homatropine methylbromide 2.5 mg./Tab. Bot. 100s, 1000s.
Use: Gastrointestinal spasms.

PAN-KLORIDE ELIXIR. (Panray) Potassium chloride 2(meq./15 cc. Bot. 16 oz, Gal.
Use: Potassium supplement.

PANMYCIN. (Upjohn) Tetracycline HCl. **Cap.** (250 mg.) Bot. 100s, 1000s. **Tab.** 500 mg. Bot. 100s.
Use: Antibiotic therapy.

PANOL. (Forest) Dexpanthenol 250 mg./ml. Vial 10 ml.

PANOPHYLLINE FORTE. (Panray) Theophylline sodium glycinate 330 mg./15 cc. Bot. 16 oz., 1 Gal
Use: Bronchial dilators.

PANOXYL ACNE GEL. (Stiefel) Benzoyl peroxide 5%, or 10%, alcohol 20%. w/polyoxyethylene lauryl ether 6% in a hydroalcoholic gel base. Tube 2 oz., 4 oz.
Use: Antibacterial gel for treatment of acne.

PANOXYL AQ ACNE GEL. (Stiefel) Benzoyl peroxide 2.5%, 5%, or 10% with polyoxyethylene lauryl ether in an aqueous gel base. Tube 2 oz., 4 oz.
Use: Antibacterial gel for treatment of acne.

PANOXYL BAR-5. (Stiefel) Benzoyl peroxide 5% in a rich-lathering, mild surfactant cleansing base. Bar 4 oz.
Use: Acne wash.

PANOXYL BAR-10. (Stiefel) Benzoyl peroxide 10% in rich-lathering, mild surfactant cleansing base. Bar 4 oz.
Use: Acne wash.

PANPARNIT HYDROCHLORIDE. Caramiphen HCl.
Use: Parkinson's syndrome.

PANPRES. (Pan American) Hydralazine HCl 25 mg., hydrochlorothiazide 15 mg., resperine 0.1 mg./Tab. Bot. 100s.
Use: Hypertension treatment.

PANRITIS. (Pan American) Salicylamide 250 mg., acetaminophen 250 mg./Tab. Bot. 100s.
Use: Analgesic and anti-rheumatic.

PANSCOL. (Baker/Cummins) Salicylic acid 3%, lactic acid 2%, phenol (less than 1%). **Oint.:** Jar 3 oz. **Lot.:** Bot. 4 oz.
Use: Treatment and management of dry, scaling and itching skin.

ANSHAPE M TP. (Pan American) Phentermine HCl 30 mg./Cap. Bot. 60s.
Use: Anorexiant.

AN-SONE. (Panray) Prednisone powder 5 Gm., 1 Gm./Bot. Tab. 1 mg., 2.5 mg., 5 mg., Bot. 100s, 1000s.
Use: Adrenocortical steroid.

AN-TALC. (Panray) Talc 25 mg., 50 mg., 75 mg., 100 mg./Tab. Bot. 1000s.
Use: Radioimmunoassay, laboratory use only.

ANTEMIC M. (Pan American) **Tab.:** Ferrous fumarate 300 mg./Tab. Bot. 100s. **Susp.** 100 mg./5 cc. Bot. 8 oz.
Use: Iron deficiency anemia.

PANTHENOL, U.S.P. XXI. Alcohol corresponding to pantothenic acid. Pantothenol. Pantothenylol. (±)-2,4-Dihydroxy-N-(3-hydroxypropyl)-3,3-dimethylbutyramide.
Use: Treatment of paralytic ileus and postoperative distention.
See: Ilopan, Amp., Vial (Warren-Teed)
Panadon, Cream (Gordon Labs.)
Pantenyl, Vial (Kay)
Panthoderm Cream (USV Pharm)

ANTHENOL W/COMBINATIONS.
See: Android-G, Vial (Brown)
B Complex w/C, Vial (Maurry)
Benizol Plus, Elix., Tab. (ICN Pharm.)
Geramine, Inj. (Brown)
Geramine Tablets (Brown)
Geriatrazole prod., Vial (Kenyon)
Geritag, Inj. (Reid-Provident)
Ilopan-Choline, Tab. (Warren-Teed)
Life Plex, Liq. (Burgin-Arden)
Lifer-B, Liq. (Burgin-Arden)
Liva, Inj. (Vortech)
LyoB-C prod., Pkg. (Merck Sharp & Dohme)
Minoplex, Vial (Savage)
Nutricol, Cap., Inj. (Nutrition Control)
Panfort, Elix. (Panamerican)
Pantho-F, Cream (USV Pharm.)
Savaplex, Vial (Savage)
Vi-Testrogen, Vial (Pharmex)
Zentinic, Pulvules (Lilly)

ANTHODERM CREAM. (USV Labs.) Dexpanthenol 2% in water-miscible cream. Tube 1 oz., Jar 2 oz., 1 lb.
Use: Antipruritic & healing aid.

ANTIGEN. (Pasadena Research) Nonspecific antigen. Vial 10 cc.

ANTISONE. (Panray) Cortisone acetate 5 mg., 25 mg./Tab. Bot. 100s, 1000s.
Use: Anti-inflammatory agent.

ANTOCAINE.
See: Tetracaine hydrochloride. (Various Mfr.)

ANTOCRIN-F. (Spanner) Plurigland, ovarian, ant, and post. pituitary, adrenal, thyroid exts. Vial 30 cc.

ANTOPAQUE. (Alcon) Iophendylate, ethyl iodophenylundecanoate. Amp. 3 cc. 3s; 6 cc. 6s; 12 cc. 2s.
Use: Intrathecally for myelography.

PANTOPON. (Roche) Hydrochlorides of opium alkaloids w/alcohol 6%, glycerin 136 mg., methyl and propyl parabens 0.2%, acetic acid and/or sod. hydroxide to adjust pH to 3.3. Amp.: 0.33 gr/ml., Box 10s.
Use: S.C. & I.M. as an analgesic.

PANTOTHENIC ACID. As Cal. or Sod. salt.
Use: Nonspecific protein therapy.
See: Vitamin preparations.

PANTOTHENIC ACID SALTS.
See: Calcium Pantothenate
Sodium Pantothenate

PANTOTHENOL.
See: Panthenol, Prep. (Various Mfr.)

PANTOTHENYL ALCOHOL.
See: Panthenol, Prep. (Various Mfr.)

PANTOTHENYLOL.
See: Panthenol, Prep. (Various Mfr.)

PAN ULTRA. (Baker/Cummins) Benzophenone in moisturizing lotion or lipstick. Bot. 4 oz. Lipstick 4 Gm.
Use: Sun protective.

PANVITEX GERIATRIC CAPSULES. (Fellows) Safflower oil 340 mg., Vit. A 10,000 I.U., D 400 I.U., Vit. B-1 5 mg., B-6 1 mg., B-2 2.5 mg., B-12 activity 2 mcg., C 75 mg., niacinamide 40 mg., Ca pantothenate 4 mg., E 2 I.U., inositol 15 mg., choline bitartrate 31.4 mg., Ca 75 mg., P 58 mg., Fe 30 mg., Mn 0.5 mg., K 2 mg., Zn 0.5 mg., Mg 3 mg./Cap. Bot. 100s, 1000s.
Use: Vitamin and mineral supplement.

PANVITEX GERIATRIC INJ. (Fellows) Testosterone 10 mg., Vit. B-12 100 mcg., B-1 50 mg., nicotinamide 50 mg., B-6 5 mg., estrone 0.5 mg., liver inj. equiv. in B-12 activity of cyanocobalamin 2 mcg., lidocaine 20 mg., panthenol 10 mg., B-2 5 mg./cc. Vial 30 cc.

PANVITEX G.H. (Fellows) Methyl testosterone 2 mg., ethinyl estradiol 0.01 mg., Vit. A 5000 I.U., D 400 I.U., E 10 I.U., B-1 2 mg., B-2 2 mg., B-6 0.3 mg., B-12 1 mcg., C 30 mg., niacinamide 20 mg., cal. pantothenate 3 mg., choline bitartrate 40 mg., inositol 20 mg., methionine 20 mg., Fe sulfate 10 mg., Cu 0.2 mg., molybdenum 0.5 mg., Mn 1.0 mg., Zn 1.0 mg., Mg 5 mg., K 2 mg., iodine 0.15 mg./S.C. Tab. Bot. 100s, 1000s.
Use: Vitamin and mineral supplement.

PANVITEX PLUS MINERALS CAPSULES. (Fellows) Vit. A 5000 I.U., D 400 I.U., B-1 3 mg., B-2 2.5 mg., niacinamide 20 mg., B-6 1.5 mg., Ca pantothenate 5 mg., B-12 2.5 mcg., C 50 mg., E 3 I.U., Ca 215 mg., P 166 mg., Fe 13.4 mg., Mg 7.5 mg., Mn 1.5 mg., K 5 mg., Zn 1.4 mg./Cap. Bot. 100s, 1000s.
Use: Vitamin and mineral supplement.

PANVITEX PRENATAL CAPSULES. (Fellows) Ferrous fumarate 150 mg., cobalamin conc. 2 mcg., Vit. A 6,000 I.U., D 400 I.U., B-1 1.5 mg., B-2 2.5 mg., niacinamide 15 mg., B-6 3 mg., C 100 mg., calcium 250 mg., Ca pantothenate 5 mg., folic acid 0.2 mg./Cap. Bot. 100s, 1000s.
Use: Multivitamin with iron.

PANVITEX T-M. (Fellows) Vit. A 10,000 I.U., D 400 I.U., Vit. B-1 10 mg., B-6 1 mg., B-2 5 mg., B-12 5 mcg., C 150 mg., niacinamide 100 mg., Ca 103 mg., P 80 mg., Fe 10 mg., Mn 1 mg., K 5 mg., Zn 1.4 mg., Mg 5.56 mg./Cap. Bot. 100s, 1000s.
Use: Vitamin and mineral supplement.

PANWARFIN. (Abbott) Warfarin sodium 2 mg., 2.5 mg., 5 mg., 7.5 mg. and 10 mg./Tab. Bot. 100s. Abbo-Pac.
Use: Anticoagulant.

PANZYME. (Hyrex) Hyoscyamine sulfate 0.0519 mg., homatropine methylbromide 0.2885 mg., hyoscine HBr 0.0033 mg., phenobarbital 8.1 mg., pancreatin 300 mg., pepsin 150 mg./Tab. Bot. 100s, 1000s, 5000s.
Use: Functional G. I. disorders.

PAP. (Abbott) Test kit 100s.
Use: Enzyme immunoassay for measurement of prostatic acid phosphatase.

PAP. (Zenith) Phenacetin 194 mg., aspirin 162 mg., phenobarbital 16.2 mg./Cap. Also w/codeine 0.25, 0.5, 1 gr./Cap. Bot. 100s.
Use: Analgesic.

P.A.P. No. 1. (Jenkins) Phenobarbital 15 mg., acid acetylsalicylic 0.23 Gm., acetophenetidin 0.15 Gm./Tab. Bot. 1000s.
Use: Sedative and anodyne.

PAPA-CARIA. (Jenkins) Mg carbonate 100 gr., cal. carbonate 50 gr., sod. bicarbonate 120 gr., bismuth subnitrate 50 gr., cerium oxalate 25 gr., Mg trisilicate 70 gr., powd. ginger 4 gr., papain 11 gr., pancreatin 5.5 gr./oz. Pkg. 2 oz.
Use: Antacid and digestive powder.

PAPACON. (CMC) Papaverine HCl 150 mg./Cap. Bot. 30s, 100s, 500s, 1000s.
Use: Cerebral and peripheral ischemia.

• **PAPAIN.** U.S.P. XXI. Tab. for Topical Soln., U.S.P. XXI. A proteolytic substance derived from *Carlica papaya.*
Use: Proteolytic enzyme.
See: Papase, Tab. (Parke-Davis)
Softlens Enzymatic Contact Lens Cleaner (Allergan)

PAPAIN W/COMBINATIONS.
See: Baculin, Tab. (Amfre-Grant)
Bilate, Tab. (Central)
Calsarbain, Tab. (Sutliff & Case)
Cerophen, Tab. (Wendt-Bristol)
Diethylstilbestrol Digestive Formula, Tab. (Wolins)
Digenzyme, Tab. (Burgin-Arden)
Kaocasil, Tab. (Jenkins)
Natrogestive, Tab. (Wolins)
Panacarb, Tab. (Lannett)
Panafil, Oint. (Rystan)
Taurocolate, Tab. (Vortech)

PAP-A-LIX. (Freeport) n-Acetyl-aminophenol 120 mg., alcohol 10%/5 cc. Bot. 4 oz., Gal.
Use: Pediatric analgesic, antipyretic.

PAPASE. (Parke-Davis) Proteolytic enzyme from carica papaya 10,000 u./Tab. peppermint-flavored. Bot. 100s, 1000s.
Use: Symptomatology related to episiotomy.

• **PAPAVERINE HYDROCHLORIDE,** U.S.P. XXI. Inj., Tab., U.S.P. XXI. 6,7-Dimethoxy-l-veratrylisoquinoline Hydrochloride.
Use: Smooth muscle relaxant.
See: BP-Papaverine, Cap. (Burlington)
Cerebid Capsules (Saron)
Cerespan, Cap. (USV Labs.)
Cirbed, Cap. (Boyd)
Delapav, Time Cap. (Dunhall)
Lapay, Graduals (Amfre-Grant)
Myobid, Cap. (Laser)
P-200, Cap. (Boots)
Papacon, Cap. (CMC)
Papital T.R. (Zemmer)
Pap-Kaps-150 Meta-Kaps, Cap. (Sutliff & Case)
Pavabid, Cap. (Marion)
Pavacap, Unicells (Reid-Provident)
Pavacaps, Cap. (Freeport)
Pavacen Cenules, Cap. (Central)
Pavaclor, Cap. (Pasadena Research)
Pavacron, Cap. (Cenci)
Pavadel, Cap. (Canright)
Pavadyl, Cap. (Bock)
Pavakey 300, Cap. (Key)
Pavakey S.A., Cap. (Key)
Pava-lyn, Cap. (Lynwood)
Pava Par, Cap. (Parmed)
Pava-Rx, Cap. (Blaine)
Pavasule, Cap. (Jalco)
Pavatest T.D., Cap. (Fellows-Testagar)
Pavatime, Cap. (Rocky Mtn.)
Pavatym, Cap. (Everett)
Pavatran T. D. Capsules (Mayrand)
Pava-Wol, Cap. (Wolins)
Paverolan, Lanacap. (Lannett)
Pavex, Cap. (Xxtrium)
Ro-Papav, Tab. (Robinson)
Vasocap, Cap. (Keene)
Vazosan, Tab. (Sandia)

W/Codeine sulfate.
See: Copavin, Pulvule, Tab. (Lilly)

W/Codeine sulfate, aloin & Sod. salicylate.
See: Copavin Compound, Elixir (Lilly)

W/Codeine sulfate, emetine HCl, ephedrine HCl.
See: Golacol, Syr. (Arcum)

W/Phenobarbital.
See: Pavadel-PB, Cap. (Canright)

PAPAVEROLINE. B.A.N. 1-(3,4-Dihydroxybenzyl)-6,7-dihydroxyisoquinoline.
Use: Vasodilator.

PAPITAL T.R. CAPSULES. (Zemmer) Papaverine HCl 150 mg./Cap. Bot. 100s, 1000s.

PAP-KAPS-150 META-KAPS. (Sutliff & Case) Papaverine HCl 150 mg./Cap. Bot. 100s, 1000s.

PAPZANS MODIFIED. (Bowman) Acetaminophen 160 mg., phenylephrine HCl 7.5 mg., chlopheniramine maleate 1 mg./Tab. Bot. 100s, 1000s.
Use: Analgesic, decongestant, antihistaminic.

PARA-AMINOBENZOIC ACID. Aminobenzoic Acid, U.S.P. XXI.
See: Pabafilm Gel (Owen)
Paba-"5", Lot. (Durel)

Pabagel, Gel. (Owen)
Pabalate, Tab. (Robins)
Pabanol, Lot. (Elder)
Presun, Lotion, Gel (Westwood)
Protan, Liq. (Westwood)
Sunbrella, Liq. (Dorsey)
Super Shade Lotion (Plough)
W/Acetylsalicylic acid, Vit. C.
See: P.A.A.M., Tab. (Kenyon)
PARA-AMINOSALICYLIC ACID. Aminosalicylic Acid, U.S.P. XXI.
PARABAXIN. (Parmed) Methocarbamol 500 or 750 mg./Tab. Bot. 100s.
Use: Muscle skeletal relaxant.
PARABROM.
See: Pyrabrom
PARABROMIDYLAMINE.
See: Brompheniramine, Dimetane, Preps. (Robins)
PARACAIN.
See: Procaine Hydrochloride (Various Mfr.)
PARACARBINOXAMINE MALEATE. Carbinoxamine.
PARACET FORTE TABS. (Major) Chlorzazone and acetaminophen. Bot. 100s, 1000s.
Use: Skeletal muscle relaxant.
PARACETALDEHYDE.
See: Paraldehyde, U.S.P. XXI.
PARACETAMOL. B.A.N. 4-Acetamidophenol.
Use: Analgesic; antipyretic.
See: Calpol
Eneril
Febrilix
Panadol
Panok
Tabalgin
PARACHLORAMINE HYDROCHLORIDE. Meclizine HCl, U.S.P. XXI.
See: Bonine, Tab. (Pfizer)
PARACHLOROMETAXYLENOL.
Use: Phenolic antiseptic.
See: D-Seb, Liq. (Cooper)
Nu-Flow, Liq. (Cooper)
W/9-aminoacridine HCl, methyl-dodecylbenzyl-trimethyl ammonium chloride, pramoxine HCl, hydrocortisone, acetic acid.
See: Drotic No. 2, Drops (Ascher)
W/Benzocaine.
See: TPO 20 (DePree)
W/Coconut oil, pine oil, castor oil, lanolin, cholesterols, lecithin.
See: Sebacide, Liq. (Paddock)
W/Hydrocortisone, pramoxine HCl, benzalkonium chloride, acetic acid.
See: Oto Drops (Reid-Provident)
W/Hydrocortisone, pramoxine HCl, benzalkonium chloride, acetic acid, propylene glycol.
See: Otostan H.C. (Standex)
W/Lidocaine, phenol, zinc oxide.
See: Unguentine Plus, Cream (Norwich)
W/Pramoxine HCl, hydrocortisone, benzalkonium chloride, acetic acid.
See: My Cort Otic #2, Drops (Scrip)
Steramine Otic, Drops (Mayrand)
W/Resorcinol, sulfur.
See: Rezamid, Lot. (Dermik)
• **PARACHLOROPHENOL,** U.S.P. XXI. Camphorated, U.S.P XX. Phenol, 4-chloro. p-Chlorophenol.
Use: Topical antibacterial.
W/Camphor.
See: Camphorated Parachlorophenol.
PARACODIN.
See: Dihydrocodeine
PARADIONE CAPSULES. (Abbott) Paramethadione 150 mg, or 300 mg./Cap. Bot. 100s.
Use: Anticonvulsant.
PARADIONE SOLUTION. (Abbott) Paramethadione oral solution 300 mg./ml. Bot. 50 ml. w/dropper.
Use: Anticonvulsant.
PARADYNE. (Spanner) Dipyrone injection 50%. Vial 10 cc.
PARAEUSAL LIQUID. (Paraeusal) Liquid Bot. 2 oz., 6 oz., 12 oz.
Use: Cuts, burns, sunburn, minor irritations of skin.
PARAEUSAL SOLID. (Paraeusal) Ointment Jar 1 oz., 2 oz., 16 oz.
Use: Burns, bedsores, keloids, skin infection, acne.
• **PARAFFIN,** N.F. XVI.
Use: Stiffening agent.
PARAFLEX. (McNeil Pharm) Chlorzoxazone 250 mg./Tab. Bot. 100s.
Use: Skeletal muscle relaxant.
PARAFON FORTE. (McNeil Pharm) Chlorzoxazone 250 mg., acetaminophen 300 mg./Tab. Bot. 100s, 500s. Blister pack 200s.
Use: Skeletal muscle relaxant.
PARAFORM. Paraformaldehyde. (No mfr. listed)
PARAFORMALDEHYDE.
Use: Essentially the same as formaldehyde.
See: Formaldehyde (Various Mfr.)
Trioxymethylene (an incorrect term for paraformaldehyde)
PARAGLYCYLARSANILIC ACID. N-Carbamylmethyl-p-aminobenzenearsonic acid, the free acid of tryparsamide.
PARA-HIST. (Pharmics) Chlorpheniramine maleate 8 mg., phenylephrine HCl 20 mg., phenylpropanolamine HCl 30 mg./Cap. T.R. Bot. 100s.
Use: Antihistamine decongestant.
PARA-HIST ANTITUSSIVE. (Pharmics) Diphenhydramine HCl 12 mg., phenylephrine HCl 2.5 mg., phenylpropanolamine HCl 10 mg., menthol 1 mg., potassium guaiacolsulfonate 60 mg., codeine phosphate 10 mg./5 cc. Syr. Bot. pt., gal.
Use: Antitussive.
PARA-JEL. (Approved) Benzocaine 5%, cetyl dimethyl benzyl ammonium chloride. Tube 0.25 oz.
Use: Teething, toothache jel.
PARAL ORAL. (Forest) Paraldehyde 30 cc./Bot. 12s, 25s.
Use: C.N.S. depressant.
• **PARALDEHYDE,** U.S.P. XXI. Sterile, U.S.P. XXI. 1,3,5-Trioxane, 2,4,6-trimethyl-.2,4,6-Trimethyl-s-trioxane. Paracetaldehyde. Bot. 0.25 lb., 1 lb.-Amp.

Use: I.M., I.V. or Orally; Hypnotic & sedative.
See: Paral, Cap., Liq., Amp. (Fellows-Testagar)

PARAMEPHRIN.
See: Epinephrine (Various Mfr.)

• **PARAMETHADIONE,** U.S.P. XXI. Cap., Oral Soln., U.S.P. XXI. 2,4-Oxazolidinedione, 5-methyl-3,5-dimethyl-.5-Ethyl-3,5-dimethyl-2,4-oxazolidenedione.
Use: Anticonvulsant.
See: Paradione, Cap. & Sol. (Abbott)

PARAMETHASONE. B.A.N. 6α-Fluoro-11β,-17α, 21-trihydroxy-16α-methylpregna-1,4-diene-3,20-dione. 6 α-Fluoro-16α-methylprednisolone.
Use: Corticosteroid.
See: Haldrate Metilar [21-acetate]

• **PARAMETHASONE ACETATE,** U.S.P. XXI. Tab., U.S.P. XXI. 16α-Methyl-6α-fluoroprednisolone-21-acetate.6α-Fluoro-11β,17,21-trihydroxy-16α-methylpregna-1,4-diene-3,20-dione 21-Acetate.
Use: Glucorticoid.
See: Haldrone, Tab. (Lilly)

PARA-MONOCHLOROPHENOL.
See: Camphorated para-chlorophenol, Liq. (Novocol)

• **PARANYLINE HYDROCHLORIDE.** USAN.
Use: Anti-inflammatory.

• **PARAPENZOLATE BROMIDE.** USAN.
Use: Anticholinergic.

PARAROSANILINE EMBONATE. Pararosaniline Pamoate.

• **PARAROSANILINE PAMOATE.** USAN. Bis-[tris(p-Aminophenyl)methylium (4,4′-methylenebis[3-hydroxy-2-naphthoate])hydrate. Under study.
Use: Antischistosomal agent.

PARASAL SODIUM. (Panray) p-Aminosalicylate Sod. **Pow.:** Bot. 1 lb. **Tabs.:** Plain (0.5 Gm., 1 Gm.) Bot. 1000s. Lyophilized for laboratory use only 5 Gm./50 cc.
Use: Tuberculosis.

PARASITICIDE SHAMPOO. (Panray) Soap 30%, isobornyl thiocyanoacetate 5.125%, other related terpenes 1.125%. Bot. 16 oz.
Use: Antiparasitic.

■ **PARASYMPATHOLYTIC AGENTS,** Cholinergic Blocking agents.
See: Anticholinergic Agents
Antispasmodics
Mydriatics
Parkinsonism

■ **PARASYMPATHOMIMETIC AGENTS.**
See: Cholinergic Agents

PARA-THOR-MONE.
See: Parathyroid Inj. (Lilly)

PARATHYROID THERAPY. Dihydrotachysterol, U.S.P. XXI. Tachysterol.
See: Hytakerol, Sol., Cap. (Winthrop-Breon)
Parathyroid Injection (Various Mfr.)

PARA-TOX. (Eckerd) Pyrethrians 0.2%, peperonyl butoxide 2.0%, deodorized kerosene 5%.
Use: Treatment of body lice.

PARATROL LIQUID. (Walgreen) Pyrethrins 0.2%, piperonyl butoxide technical 2%, deodorized kerosene 0.8%. Bot. 2 oz.
Use: Kills head and body crab lice and eggs.

PARAXIN. Chloramphenicol, B.A.N.

PARAZONE. (Interstate) Chlorzoxazone 250 mg., acetaminophen 300 mg./Tab. Bot. 100s, 1000s.
Use: Skeletal muscle relaxant.

• **PARBENDAZOLE.** USAN. Methyl 5-butyl-2-benzimidazolecarbamate. Helmatac. Under study.
Use: Anthelmintic.

PARBUTOXATE. β-Dimethylaminoethyl-3-amino-4-butoxybenzoate.

PARCILLIN. (Parmed) Crystalline potassium penicillin G 240 mg., 400,000 u./Tab. Bot. 100s, 1000 s. Pow. for syr. 400,000/Tsp. 80 cc.
Use: Bacterial infections.

• **PARCONAZOLE HYDROCHLORIDE.** USAN.
Use: Antifungal.

PAR CREAM. (Parmed) Sulfanilamide 15%, 9-Aminoacridine HCl 0.2%, Allantoin 1.5% in a dispersible base. Tube 4 oz.
Use: Vulva, vaginal infections.

PAREDRINE. (SmithKline) Hydroxyamphetamine HBr. 1%, boric acid 2%, sod. ethyl mercurithiosalicylate 1:50,000. Bot. 0.5 oz.
Use: Ophthalmic solution; vasoconstrictor.

PAREDRINOL. p-(2-Methylaminopropyl) phenol (No Mfr. currently lists).

• **PAREGORIC.** U.S.P. XXI. (Various Mfr.)
Use: Antiperistaltic.
W/Bismuth subgallate, kaolin, pectin.
See: Dysenaid Jr., Tab. (Jenkins)
W/Glycyrrhiza fl. ext., antimony pot. tartrate.
See: Brown Mixture, Liq. (Lilly)
W/Kaolin (colloidal), aluminum hydroxide, bismuth subcarbonate, pectin.
See: Kapinal, Tab. (Jenkins)
W/Kaolin, pectin.
See: Kaoparin, Susp. (McKesson)
Kenpectin-P, Susp. (Kenwood)
Parepectolin, Susp. (Rorer)
W/Kaolin, pectin, bismuth subsalicylate, zinc sulfocarbonate.
W/Milk of bismuth, kaolin & pectin.
See: Mul-Sed, Liq. (Webcon)
W/Pectin & kaolin.
See: Parepectolin, Susp. (Rorer)
W/Zinc sulfocarbolate, phenyl salicylate, bismuth subsalicylate, & pepsin.
See: C M with Paregoric, Liq. (Beecham Labs)
Corrective Mixture with Paregoric (Beecham Labs)

PARENABOL. Boldenone undecylenate.

PAREPECTOLIN. (Rorer) Paregoric (equivalent) 3.7 ml., pectin 162 mg., kaolin 5.5 Gm./fl. oz. Susp., Bot. 4 fl. oz., 8 fl. oz.
Use: Nonspecific diarrheas.

• **PAREPTIDE SULFATE.** USAN.
Use: Antiparkinsonian.

PAR ESTRO. (Parmed) Conjugated estrogens 1.25 mg./Tab. Bot. 100s.
Use: Conjugated estrogen therapy.

PARETHOXYCAINE HCl.
W/Zirconium oxide, calamine.
See: Zotox, Spray, Cream (Commerce)

PAR-F. (Pharmics) Iron 66 mg., calcium 200 mg., Vit. C 75 mg., A 8000 I.U., D 400 I.U., B-1 5 mg., B-2 2 mg.,

3-12 2.5 mcg., B-6 5 mg. niacinamide 15 mg., iodine 0.15 mg., manganese 0.5 mg., copper 0.25 mg., zinc 0.5 mg., sodium fluoride 1.1 mg./Cap. Bot. 100s, 1000s.
Use: Vitamin and mineral supplementation.

RGEN FORTIFIED TABLETS. (Goldline) Chlorzoxazone, acetaminophen. Bot. 100s, 1000s.
Use: Skeletal muscle relaxant.

RGYLINE. B.A.N. N-Benzyl-N-methylprop-2-ynylamine.
Use: Hypotensive.
See: Eutonyl (hydrochloride)

ARGYLINE HYDROCHLORIDE, U.S.P. XXI. Tab., U.S.P. XXI. N-Methyl-N-2-propynybenzylamine hydrochloride.
Use: Antihypertensive.
See: Eutonyl, Filmtab (Abbott)
Methyclothiazide.
See: Eutron Filmtab. (Abbott)

RKELP. (Phillip R. Park) Pacific sea kelp. **Tab.:** Bot. 100s, 200s, 500s, 800s. **Gran.:** Bot. 2 oz., 7 oz., lb., 3 lb.
Use: Iodine source.

ARKINSONISM. Parasympatholytic agents.
See: Akineton, Tab., Amp. (Knoll)
Artane, Elix., Tab., Sequels (Lederle)
Caramiphen HCl
Cogentin, Tab., Amp. (Merck Sharp & Dohme)
Disipal, Tab. (Riker)
Kemadrin, Tab. (Burroughs Wellcome)
Levodopa, Cap., Tab. (Various Mfr.)
Levsin, Tab., Elix., Inj., Drops (Kremers-Urban)
Levsinex Timecaps, Cap., Syr. (Kremers-Urban)
Pagitane HCl, Tab. (Lilly)
Parsidol HCl, Tab. (Warner-Chilcott)
Phenoxene, Tab. (Merrell Dow)
Sinemet, Tab. (Merck Sharp & Dohme)
Symmetrel, Cap., Syr. (Du Pont)
Trihexyphenidyl HCl (Various Mfr.)

RLAX SYRUP. (Robinson) Docusate sodium 20 mg./5 cc. Bot. 8 oz.

RLAX. (Parmed) Danthron 75 mg. & calcium pantothenate 25 mg./Tab. Bot. 100s, 1000s.
Use: Laxative.

RLAX W/CASANTHRANOL. (Robinson) Docusate sodium 100 mg., casanthranol 50 mg./Cap. Docusate sodium 50 mg., casanthranol 25 mg./Cap. Bot. 100s, 1000s.

RLODEL. (Sandoz) Bromocriptine mesylate. **Tab.:** 2.5 mg./Tab. Bot. 30s. **Cap.:** 5 mg./Cap. Bot. 30s, 100s.
Use: Short term treatment of amenorrhea and galactorrhea, prevention of physiological lactation, Parkinson's disease.

R-MAG. (Parmed) Magnesium oxide 140 mg./Cap. Bot. 100s.

RMETH. (Parmed) Promethazine HCl 50 mg./Cap. Bot. 100s, 1000s.
Use: Allergy and motion sickness.

RMINE. (Parmed) Phentermine HCl 30 mg./Cap. Bot. 100s, 1000s.
Use: Exogenous obesity.

PARMINYL. W/Salicylamide, phenacetin, caffeine, acetaminophen.
See: Dolopar, Tab. (O'Neal)

PAR-NATAL-FA. (Parmed) Vit. A 4000 I.U., D 400 I.U., thiamine HCl 2 mg., riboflavin 2 mg., pyridoxine HCl 0.8 mg., ascorbic acid 50 mg., niacinamide 10 mg., iodine 0.15 mg., folic acid 0.1 mg., cobalamin concentrate 2 mcg., iron 50 mg., calcium 240 mg./Cap. Bot. 100s, 1000s.
Use: Vitamin & mineral supplement in pregnancy & lactation.

PAR-NATAL-RX. (Parmed) Vit. A 6000 I.U., D 400 I.U., thiamine mononitrate 1.1 mg., riboflavin 1.8 mg., pyridoxine HCl 2.5 mg., vit B-12 8 mcg., folic acid 1 mg., iron 65 mg., calcium 125 mg., ascorbic acid 60 mg., niacinamide 15 mg./Tab. Bot. 100s, 1000s.
Use: Dietary supplement during pregnancy & lactation.

PARNATE. (SmithKline) Tranylcypromine sulfate 10 mg./Tab. Bot. 100s, 1000s.
Use: Antidepressant; MAO inhibitor.

PARODONTAX DENTAL CREAM. (Edward J. Moore) Sodium dicarbonate plus five natural herbs. Tube 60 Gm.
Use: Hygenic dentifrice and aid in prevention of periodontosis & caries.

PARODYNE.
See: Antipyrine (Various Mfr.)

PAROLEINE.
See: Petrolatum Liquid (Various Mfr.)

PAROMOMYCIN. B.A.N. An antibiotic substance obtained from cultures of certain *Streptomyces* species, one of which is *Streptomyces rimosus.*
Use: Antiamebic.

• **PAROMOMYCIN SULFATE,** U.S.P XX. Caps., Syr., U.S.P. XXI.
Use: Antiamebic.

PAROTHYL. (Interstate) Meprobamate 400 mg., tridihexethyl Cl. 25 mg./Tab. Bot. 100s.
Use: Treatment of G.I. tract disorders associated with anxiety and tension.

PAROXYL.
See: Acetarsone (Var. Mfr.)

PARPANIT.
See: Caramiphen Hydrochloride (Var. Mfr.)

PARPANIT HYDROCHLORIDE. Caramiphen, B.A.N.

PARSIDOL HCl. (Parke-Davis) Ethopropazine HCl. Profenamine HCl, Lysivane, 10-(Diethylamino-1-propyl) Phenothiazine HCl. Tab. 10 mg., 50 mg., Bot. 100s.
Use: Parkinsonism.

PARSLEY CONCENTRATE.
W/Garlic conc.
See: Allimin, Tab. (Mosso)

PAR-Supp. (Parmed) Estrone 0.2 mg., lactose 50 mg./Vag. Supp. pkg. 12s.
Use: Vaginitis.

PARTEN. (Parmed) Acetaminophen 10 gr./Tab. Bot. 100s, 1000s.
Use: Antipyretic & analgesic.

PARTIAL ECLIPSE LOTION. (Dorsey) Padimate 0. SPF 5. Bot. 4 oz.
Use: Sunscreen.

PARTREX. (Parmed) Tetracycline 250 mg./Cap. Bot. 100s, 1000s.
Use: Antibacterial.

• **PARTRICIN.** USAN. Antibiotic produced by *Streptomyces aureofaciens.*
Use: Antifungal, antiprotozoal.

PARTUSS. (Parmed) Dextromethorphan hydrobromide 60 mg., pot. guaiacol sulfonate 8 gr., chlorpheniramine maleate 6 mg., ammonium Cl. 8 gr., tartar emetic 1/12 gr., chloroform 2 min./30 cc. Bot. Gal., pt., 4 oz.
Use: cough mixture.

PARTUSS "A". (Parmed) Acetaminophen 5 gr., Salicylamide 2 gr., caffeine 0.5 gr., atropine sulfate 0.12 mg., guaifenesin 100 mg., phenylpropanolamine HCl 25 mg./Tab. Bot. 1000s.
Use: Decongestant, analgesic, & expectorant.

PARTUSS A.C. (Parmed) Guaifenesin 100 mg., pheniramine maleate 7.5 mg., codeine phosphate 10.0 mg., alcohol 3.5%/5 cc. Bot 4 oz.
Use: cough suppressant and expectorant.

PARTUSS T.D. (Parmed) Acetaminophen 300 mg., salicylamide 300 mg., phenylpropanolamine HCl 60 mg., chlorpheniramine maleate 4 mg./Tab. Bot. 100s, 1000s.
Use: Decongestant.

PAR VAG SUPPOSITORY. (Parmed) Aminacrine HCl 14 mg., sulfanilamide 1.05 Gm., allantoin 140 mg./Suppository.
Use: Vaginitis treatment

P.A.S. ACID. (Kasar) Para-aminosalicylic acid 500 mg./Tab. Bot. 1000s.
Use: Tuberculosis.

PAS-C. (Hellwig) Pascorbic. p-aminosalicylic acid 0.5 Gm. with vit. C/Tab. Bot. 1000s.
Use: Tuberculosis therapy.

PASDIUM. (Kasar) Sod. aminosalicylate 0.5 Gm., 1 Gm./Tab. Bot. 1000s.
Use: Tuberculosis.

PASIBAR. (Jenkins) Acetylsalicylic acid 3.5 gr., acetophenetidin 2.5 gr., caffeine alkaloids 0.25 gr., phenobarbital 0.25 gr./Tab. Bot. 1000s. Available in blue and pink.
Use: Analgesic.

PASIJEN. (Jenkins) Passiflora 1 gr., valerian 1 gr., ext. henbane 1/8 gr. (total alkaloids 0.00019 gr.), phenobarbital 0.25 gr./Tab. Bot. 1000s.
Use: Sedative, antispasmodic.

PASKALIUM. (Glenwood) Potassium amino-salicylate. **Envules** 3 Gm. envelopes, boxes 100s. **Tab.** 0.5 Gm. Bot. 1000s. **Pow.** Bot. 100 Gm.
Use: Tuberculosis.

PASSIFLORA. Dried flowering & fruiting tops of Passiflora incarnata.
W/Phenobarbital, ext. hyoscyamus.
See: Somlyn w/Pb, Cap. (Scrip)
W/Phenobarbital, jamaica dogwood.
See: Sominol, Phenobarbital, Tab. (O'Neal)
W/Phenobarbital, valerian, hyoscyamus.
See: Aluro, Tab. (Foy)

PASTEURELLA TULARENSIS ANTIGEN. 10,000 million organisms/cc.
(Lederle)—Vial 5 cc., 20 cc.
Use: Diagnostic use for tularemia.

PATH. (Parker) Buffered neutral formalin sol. 10%. Bot. 1 gal., 5 gal. Jar 4 oz.
Use: Tissue specimen fixative.

PATHIBAMATE 200. (Lederle) Meprobamate 200 mg., tridihexethyl chloride 25 mg./Tab. Bot. 100s 1000s.

PATHIBAMATE-400. (Lederle) Meprobamate 400 m tridihexethyl chloride 25 mg./Tab. Bot. 100s, 100 Drum 5000s.
Use: Treatment of G.I. tract disorders associated with anxiety and tension.

PATHILON CHLORIDE. (Lederle) Tridihexethyl chloride 25 mg./Tab. Bot. 100s, 1000s.
Use: Anticholinergic in the treatment of peptic ulcer.
W/Meprobamate.
See: Pathibamate 200 & 400, Tabs. (Lederle)
W/Phenobarbital. Pathilon 25 mg., phenobarbital 15 mg./Tab. Bot. 100s, 1000s. (Lederle)
Use: Anticholinergic with sedative in the treatmer of peptic ulcer.

PATHOCIL. (Wyeth) Sodium dicloxacillin monohydrate. Monohydrate sodium salt of 6[3-(2, dichlorophenyl)-5-methyl-4-isoxazolyl]penicillin. 2 mg./Cap. Bot. 100s. 500 mg./Cap. Bot. 50s. Pow for oral susp. 62.5 mg./5 ml. Bot. to make 100 m
Use: Staphylococcal infection.

• **PAULOMYCIN.** USAN.
Use: Antibacterial.

PAVABID. (Marion) Papaverine HCl 150 mg./Cap. Bot. 60s, 100s, 250s, 1000s, 5000s. Unit Dose 100s.
Use: Vasodilator.

PAVABID HP. (Marion) Papaverine HCl 300 mg./Caplet. Bot. 60s.
Use: Vasodilator.

PAVACAP. (Reid-Provident) Papaverine HCl 1 mg./Unicelle. Bot. 100s, 1000s.
Use: Relief of cerebral and peripheral ischemia.

PAVACAPS. (Freeport) Papaverine HCl. 150 mg./T. Cap. Bot. 1000s.
Use: Relief of cerebral and peripheral ischemia.

PAVACEN CENULES. (Central) Papaverine HCl 150 mg./Cap. Bot. 100s, 1000s.
Use: Cerebral vasodilator.

PAVACLOR. (Pasadena Research) Papaverine HCl 150 mg. Cap. Bot. 100s.

PAVACRON CHRONCAPS. (Cenci) Papaverine HCl 150 mg./Cap. Bot. 100s, 1000s.

PAVADEL. (Canright) Papaverine HCl 150 mg./Cap. Bot. 100s, 1000s.
Use: Relief of cerebral and peripheral ischemia.

PAVADEL PB. (Canright) Papaverine HCl 150 mg., phenobarbital 45 mg./Cap. Bot. 100s.
Use: Relief of cerebral and peripheral ischemia.

/ADON ELIXIR. (Coastal) Codeine phosphate 4.8 mg., acetaminophen 11 gr., alcohol 10%/fl. z. Bot. 4 oz., pt.
'se: Analgesic.

/ADUR. (Century) Papaverine HC1 150 mg./Cap. ot. 100s, 1000s.
'se: Vasodilator, smooth muscle relaxant.

/ADYL. (Bock) Papaverine HCl 150 mg./Cap. Bot. 00s.
'se: Relief of cerebral and peripheral ischemia.

'A-LYN. (Lynwood) Papaverine HCl 150 mg./Cap. ot. 100s.
se: Smooth muscle relaxant.

/A-PAR. (Parmed) Papaverine HCl 150 mg./Cap. ot. 100s, 1000s.
se: For the relief of cerebral and peripheral chemia.

/A-RX. (Blaine) Papaverine HCl 150 mg./Timed ap. Bot. 100s.
se: Vasodilator.

/ASED. (Mallard) Papaverine HCl 150 mg./Cap. ot. 100s, 500s.

/ASPAN. (Jamieson-McKames) Ethaverine HCl 150 ng./T.R. Cap. Bot. 100s.
se: Relief of cerebral and peripheral ischemia.

/ASULE. (Misemer) Papaverine HCl 150 mg./T.D. ap.
Jse: Relief of cerebral and peripheral ischemia.

/ATEST. (Fellows) Papaverine HCl 150 mg./T.D. ap. Bot. 100s, 1000s.
Jse: Vasodilator.

VATIME. (Rocky Mtn.) Papaverine HCl 150 ng./Cap. Bot. 100s.
Jse: Vasodilator.

VATINE TABS. (Major) Papaverine 300 mg./Tab. Bot. 100s.
Jse: Vasodilator.

VATINE T.D. CAPS. (Major) Papaverine 150 ng./TD Cap. Bot. 100s, 1000s.
Jse: Vasodilator.

VATYM. (Everett) Papaverine HCl 150 mg./T.R. Cap. Bot. 100s, 1000s., unit dose 100s.
Jse: Vasodilatior.

VA-WOL. (Wolins) Papaverine HCl 150 mg./Cap. Bot. 100s, 250s, 1000s.
Jse: Relief of cerebral and peripheral ischemia.

VERINE SPANCAP. (Vortech) Papaverine HCl 150 ng./Cap. Bot. 100s, 000s.
Jse: Vasodilator.

VEROLAN. (Lannett) Papaverine 150 ng./Lanacap. Bot. 100s, 1000s.
Jse: Muscle relaxant.

VEX. (Xttrium) Papaverine HCl 150 mg./Cap. Bot. 00s.
Jse: Smooth muscle relaxant.

VRIN-T.D. (Kenyon) Papaverine HCl 150 mg./Cap. Bot. 100s, 1000s.
Jse: Vasodilator.

PAVULON. (Organon) Pancuronium bromide. 2 mg./ml. Amp. 2 ml., 5 ml. Box 25s. 1 mg./ml. Vial 10 ml. Box 25s.
Use: Muscle relaxant (surgical).

PAX-400. (Kenyon) Meprobamate 400 mg./Tab. Bot. 100s, 1000s.
Use: Tranquilizer.

PAXAREL. (Circle) Acetylcarbromal 250 mg./Tab. Bot. 100s.
Use: Sedative.

PAXIPAM. (Schering) Halazepam 20 mg. or 40 mg./Tab. Bot. 100s, 500s. Unit dose 100s.
Use: Anxiety disorders.

PAYZONE HCl. Nitrovin, B.A.N.

PAZO OINTMENT. (Bristol-Myers) Benzocaine 0.8%, zinc oxide 4%, ephedrine sulfate 0.2%, camphor 2.18%, Ointment. Tubes: 1 oz., 2 oz.
Use: Hemorrhoid medication.

PAZO SUPPOSITORY. (Bristol-Myers) Benzocaine 15.44 mg., ephedrine sulfate 3.86 mg., zinc oxide 77.2 mg., camphor 42.0/supp.
Boxes: 12s, 24s.
Use: Hemorrhoid medication.

• **PAZOXIDE.** USAN.
Use: Antihypertensive.

PB 100. (Schlicksup) Phenobarbital 1.5 gr./Tab. Bot. 1000s.

P.B.N. (Jenkins) Bacitracin 400 u., neomycin sulfate 5 mg., polymyxin B sulfate 5000 u./Gm. Tube 0.5 oz.
Use: Antibiotic ointment.

PBZ-SR. (Geigy) Tripelennamine HCl 100 mg./Tab. Sustained release. Bot. 100s.
Use: Antihistamine.

PCMX.
See: Para Chloro Meta Xylenol.

PDM. (Century) Phendimetrazine tartrate 35 mg./Tab. Bot. 1000s.
Use: Anorexic.

PEACOCK'S BROMIDES. (Natcon) **Liq.** Pot. bromide 6 gr., sod. bromide 6 gr., ammonium bromide 3 gr./5 ml. Bot. 8 oz. **Tab.** Pot. bromide 3 gr., sod. bromide 3 gr., ammonium bromide 1.5 gr./Tab. Bot. 100s.
Use: Sedative.

• **PEANUT OIL,** N.F. XVI.
Use: Pharm. aid. (solvent, oleaginous vehicle).

PECAZINE. B.A.N. 10-(1-Methyl-3-piperidylmethyl)-phenothiazine.
Use: Tranquilizer.
See: Pacatal (hydrochloride or acetate)

PECILOCIN. B.A.N. An antibiotic produced by Paecilomyces variotin banier (var. antibioticus). 1-(8-Hydroxy-6-methyldodeca-trans trans cis-2,4,6-trienoyl)-2-pyrrolidone.
See: Variotin

PECTAMOL. (British Drug House) Diethylaminoethoxyethyl-a,a-diethylphenylacetate citrate. Bot. 4, 16, 80, 160 fl. oz.
Use: Non-narcotic antitussive.

• **PECTIN,** U.S.P. XXI. (Various Mfr.)
Use: Protectant, pharmaceutic aid (suspending agent).

PECTIN W/COMBINATIONS.
See: Amogel, Tab. (Vortech)
Baropectin Susp. (Barry-Martin)
Bismuth, Pectin & Paregoric (Lemmon)
Cholactabs, Tab. (Philips Roxane)
Diastay, Tab. (Elder)
Diatrol, Tab. (Otis Clapp)
DIA-Quel, Liq. (Inter. Pharm.)
Donnagel Susp. (Robins)
Donnagel-PG, Susp. (Robins)
Dua-Pred, Inj. (Reid-Provident)
Duosorb, Liq. (Reid-Provident)
Ekrised, Tab. (Mallard)
Furoxone, Liq., Tab. (Eaton)
Infantol Pink, Liq. (Scherer)
Kamabel, Liq. (Towne)
Kao-Con, Liq. (Upjohn)
Kaolin-Bismuth Pectin Compound
Kaoparin, Susp. (McKesson)
Kaopectate, Liq. (Upjohn)
Kao-pectin, Tab. (Wolins)
Kapigam, Liq. (Reid-Provident)
Kapinal, Tab. (Jenkins)
Kenpectin prods., Susp. (Kenwood)
Keotin, Liq. (Blue Line)
KBP/O, Cap. (Cole)
Metropectin, Tab. (Pennwalt)
Mul-Sed, Susp. (Webcon)
Opecto, Elix. (Bowman)
Parelixir, Liq. (Purdue Frederick)
Parepectolin, Susp. (Rorer)
Pectocel, Liq. (Lilly)
Pectocomp, Liq. (Lannett)
Pecto-Kalin, Susp. (Lemmon)
Pectokay, Liq. (Bowman)
Pektamalt, Liq. (Warren-Teed)
Polymagma Plain Tablets (Wyeth)
Wescola Antidiarrheal-Stomach Upset (Western Research)

PECTOCOMP. (Lannett) Pectin 4 gr., kaolin 90 gr., zinc phenolsulfonate 1⅛ gr./Fl. oz. Bot. pt., gal.
Use: A supportive treatment for diarrhea and other intestinal inflammations.

PECTOKAY MIXTURE. (Bowman) Kaolin and pectin mixture. Bot. pt., gal.
Use: Antidiarrheal.

PEDAMETH. (Forest) Racemethionine. **Cap.:** 200 mg./Cap. Bot. 50s, 500s. **Liq.:** 75 mg./5 ml. Bot. pt.
Use: Control of diaper rash.

PE-DE-EM. (Bowman) Phendimetrazine tartrate 35 mg./Tab.
Use: Anorexiant.

PEDENEX. (Approved) Caprylic acid, zinc undecylenate, sod. propionate. Tube 1.5 oz. Foot powd. spray 5 oz.
Use: Athlete's foot.

PEDIACARE 1 CHILDREN'S COUGH RELIEF. (McNeil Prods) Dextromethorphan HBr 5 mg./5 ml. Bot 4 oz.
Use: Cough suppressant.

PEDIACARE 2 CHILDREN'S COLD RELIEF. (McN Prods) Pseudoephedrine HCl 15 mg., chlorpheniramine maleate 1 mg./5 ml. Bot. 4 oz.
Use: Decongestant, antihistamine.

PEDIACARE 3 CHILDREN'S COLD CHEWABLE TABLETS. (McNeil Prods) Pseudoephedrine HCl 7.5 mg., chlorpheniramine maleate 0.5 mg., dextromethorphan HBr 2.5 mg./Tab. Bot 24s.
Use: Decongestant, antihistamine, cough suppressant.

PEDIACARE 3 CHILDREN'S COLD RELIEF. (McN Prods) Pseudoephedrine HCl 15 mg., chlorpheniramine maleate 1 mg., dextromethorph HBr 5 mg./5 ml. Bot. 4 oz.
Use: Decongestant, antihistamine, cough suppressant.

PEDIACOF SYRUP. (Winthrop-Breon) Codeine ph 5.0 mg., phenylephrine HCl 2.5 mg., chlorpheniramine maleate 0.75 mg., potassium iodide 75.0 mg./5 ml. w/sodium benzoate 0.2%, alcohol 5%. Bot. 16 fl. oz.
Use: Antitussive for coughs due to colds & other upper respiratory infections.

PEDIACON. (CMC) Thiamine HCl 10 mg., B-12 cryst line 25 mg./5 cc. Bot. 4 oz., pt., gal. Same formu W/Elemental iron 30 mg./5 cc. Bot. 4 oz., pt., gal
Use: Dietary supplement.

PEDIAFLOR FLUORIDE DROPS. (Ross) Sod. Fluoride. 0.5 mg./ml. Bot. 50 ml.
Use: Fluoride supplement, prevention of dental caries.

PEDIALYTE. (Ross) Na 45 mEq, K 20 mEq, chlorid 35 mEq, citrate 30 mEq., dextrose 25 mEq/Liter. Nursing Bot. w/nipple 8 oz. Cans 32 oz. 6s. 6.2 calories/fl. oz.
Use: Oral electrolyte maintenance solution.

PEDIALYTE RS. (Ross) Sodium 75 mEq., K 20 mEq Cl 65 mEq, citrate 30 mEq, dextrose 25 Gm./L. 100 calories/L. Ready to use. Bot. 8 oz. Case 4 x 6 packs.
Use: Replacement of body water and minerals los in severe diarrhea.

PEDIAMYCIN DROPS. (Ross) Erythromycin ethylsuccinate for oral suspension 100 mg./2.5 ml Bot. 50 ml. (Dropper enclosed)
Use: Antibiotic.

PEDIAMYCIN 400. (Ross) Erythromycin ethylsuccinate oral suspension 400 mg./5 ml. Bot pt.
Use: Antibiotic.

PEDIAMYCIN LIQUID. (Ross) Erythromycin ethylsuccinate oral suspension 200 mg./5 ml. Bot pt.
Use: Antibiotic.

PEDIAMYCIN SUSPENSION. (Ross) Erythromycin ethylsuccinate for oral suspension 200 mg./5 ml., Bot., Granules reconstituted to 100 ml., 150 ml.
Use: Antibiotic.

PEDIATRIC COUGH SYRUP. (Weeks & Leo) Ammonium Cl. 300 mg., sodium citrate 600 mg./o Bot. 4 oz.

Ise: Cough relief for infants age 3 months and older.

)IATROL (B13). (Kenyon) Vit. B-12 25 mcg., B-1 10 ng./5 cc. Bot. pt., gal.

)IAZOLE SUSPENSION. (Ross) Erythromycin thylsuccinate 200 mg., sulfisoxazole acetyl 600 ng./ 5 ml. Bot. Granules reconstituted to 100 ml., 50 ml., 200 ml.

Jse: Acute otitis media caused by susceptible train of *Hemophilus influenzae* in children.

)I-BATH. (Pedinol) Collodial sulfur, Balsam peru. Bot. 6 oz.

Ise: Foot bath and soak.

)I-BOOT MIST KIT. (Pedinol) Cetyl pyridinium Cl., riacetin, chloroxylenol. Bot. 2 oz.

Jse: Fungicide, sanitizer, deodorizer for foot pparel.

)I-BORO SOAK PAKS. (Pedinol) Astringent wet ressing w/aluminum sulfate, calcium acetate, oloring agent. Box 12s, 100s.

Jse: Astringent solution for minor skin irritations.

)I-CORT V CREME. (Pedinol) Clioquinol 3%; hyrocortisone 1%, Tube 20 Gm.

Ise: Antibacterial, antifungal, antipruritic agent.

)ICRAN WITH IRON. (Scherer) Vit. B-12 (cryst.) 25 ncg., ferric pyrophosphate, soluble (elemental iron 0 mg.) 250 mg., thiamine mononitrate 10 mg., icotinamide 10 mg., alcohol 1%/5 cc. Bot. 4 oz., t.

Ise: Iron deficiency anemias.

EDICULICIDES.

See: A-200 Pyrinate (Norcliff Thayer)
Benzyl Benzoate, Preps. (Various Mfr.)
Chlorophenothane (Various Mfr.)
Cuprex, Liq. (Calgon Consumer Prods.)
DDT (Various Mfr.)
Kwell, Preps. (Reed & Carnrick)

)I-DENT CV. (Stanlabs) Sod. fluoride 2.21 mg., Vit. A 500 I.U., D-2 500 I.U., B-1 3 mg., B-2 2.5 mg., B-1 mg., B-12 1 mcg., C 75 mg., niacinamide 2.5 ng./Chewable Tab. Bot. 100s.

Ise: Aid in reducing dental caries, vitamin upplement.

)I-DRI FOOT POWDER. (Pedinol) Aluminum chlorohydroxide, zinc undecylenate, menthol, ormaldehyde. Spout Cap Bot. 2 oz.

Jse: Antiperspirant, deodorant, fungicidal foot owder.

)I-PRO FOOT POWDER. (Pedinol) Aluminum chlorydroxide, menthol, zinc undecylenate, hloroxylenol. Bot. 2 ox.

Ise: Fungicide, antiperspirant, deodorant.

)I-TOT. (Blue Cross) Bromorphan 5 mg., glyceryl uaiacolate 12.5 mg., ammonium Cl. 60 mg., odium citrate 40 mg./5 ml. Bot. 4 oz.

Ise: Cough syrup.

)ITUSS. (Sutliff & Case) N-Acetyl-p-amino-phenol 4.5 mg., sod. salicylate 129 mg., phenylephrine 2 ng., guaifenesin 20 mg./5 cc. Bot. 3 oz., 1 pt., 1 gal.

Jse: Analgesic, expectorant.

PEDI-VIT A CREME. (Pedinol) Vitamin A 100,000 units /oz. Jar 2 oz., 16 oz., 5 lb.
Use: Skin conditioner.

PEDOLATUM. (King) Salicylic acid w/sod. salicylate oint. Pkg. 0.5 oz.

PEDRIC ELIXIR. (Vale) Acetaminophen 120 mg./5ml. w/alcohol 10%. Bot. pt., gal.
Use: Analgesic.

PEDRIC SENIOR. (Vale) Acetaminophen 320 mg.
Use: Analgesic

PEDRIC WAFERS. (Vale) Acetaminophen 120 mg./Wafer. Bot. 100s, 500s, 1000s.
Use: Analgesic.

• **PEFLOXACIN.** USAN.
Use: Antibacterial.

PEGANONE. (Abbott) Ethotoin. 3-Ethyl-5-phenylhydantoin. Tab. 250 mg. Bot. 100s, 500 mg. Bot. 100s.
Use: Orally, anticonvulsant in the control of grand mal seizures.

PEGLICOL 5 OLEATE. USAN.
Use: Emulsifying agent.

P.E.G. OINTMENT. (Medco Lab) Polyethylene glycol. Jar 16 oz.
Use: Water soluble ointment base.

• **PEGOTERATE.** USAN.
Use: Suspending agent.

• **PEGOXOL 7 STEARATE.** USAN.
Use: Emulsifying agent.

PELENTAN. Ethyl Biscoumacetate. (No Mfr. currently lists)

• **PELIOMYCIN.** USAN. An antibiotic derived from *Streptomycin luteogriseus.*
Use: Antineoplastic agent.

• **PELRINONE HYDROCHLORIDE.** USAN.
Use: Cardiotonic.

• **PEMERID NITRATE.** USAN. 4-[3-(Di-methylimino)-propoxy]-1,2,2,6,6-pentamethylpiperidine dinitrate.
Use: Antitussive.

• **PEMOLINE.** USAN. 2-amino-5-phenyl-4-azolin-4-one.
Use: Childhood attention-deficit syndrome (hyperkinetic syndrome).
See: Cylert Prods. (Abbott)

PEMPIDINE. B.A.N. 1,2,2,6,6-Pentamethylpiperidine.
Use: Hypotensive.
See: Perolysen Tenormal (hydrogen tartrate)

PENAGEN-VK. (Grafton) Penicillin V 250 mg./Tab. Bot. 100s. Powder 250 mg./100 cc.
Use: Antibiotic.

PENAMECILLIN. B.A.N. Acetoxymethyl 6-phenylacetamidopenicillanate.
Use: Antibiotic.
See: Havapen

PENAMP "250", "500". (Lannett) 250 mg., 500 mg./Cap. Bot. 100s.

PENAPAR VK. (Parke-Davis) Potassium phenoxymethyl penicillin. **Tab.** 250 mg., Bot. 100s, 1000s, Unit dose 100s; 500 mg. Bot. 100s, 500s. **For oral solution** (buffered): 125 mg./5 ml. or 250 mg./5 ml. Bot. 100 ml., 200 ml.
Use: Antibiotic.

• **PENBUTOLOL.** USAN.(−)-1-tert-Butylamino-3-(2-cyclopentylphenoxy)propan-2-ol.
Use: Beta adrenergic blocking agent.

PENDECAMAINE. B.A.N. NN-Dimethyl-(3-palmitamidopropyl)glycine betaine.
Use: Surface active agent.

PENDIOMID. (Ciba) Azamethonium bromide. B.A.N.

PENECORT CREAM. (Herbert) Hydrocortisone 1% or 2.5% w/benzyl alcohol, petrolatum, stearyl alcohol, propylene glycol, isopropyl myristate, polyoxyl 40, carbome 934, sodium lauryl sulfate, edetate disodium. Tube 30 Gm., 60 Gm.
Use: Relief of inflammatory and pruritic manifestations of corticosteroid-responsive dermatoses.

PENECORT OINTMENT 2.5%. (Herbert) Hydrocortisone 2.5% in white petrolatum base. Tube 30 Gm.
Use: Relief of inflammatory and pruritic manifestations of corticosteroid-responsive dermatoses.

PENECORT TOPICAL SOLUTION 1%. (Herbert) Hydrocortisone 1% w/alcohol 51% propylene glycol, benzyl alcohol, purified water. Bot. 30 ml., 60 Gm.
Use: Relief of inflammatory pruritic manifestations of corticosteroid-responsive dermatoses.

PENETHAMATE HI.
See: Benzylpenicillin 2-diethylaminoethyl ester HI.

PENETHAMATE HYDRIODIDE. B.A.N. 2-Diethylaminoethyl 6-phenylacetamidopenicillanate hydriodide. Benzylpenicillin 2-diethylaminoethyl ester hydriodide.
Use: Treatment of respiratory tract infections.
See: Estopen

• **PENFLURIDOL.** USAN. 1-[4,4-bis(p-Flurophenyl)-butyl]-4-(4-chloro-α,α,α-trifluoro-m-tolyl)-4-piperidinol. 4-(4-Chloro-3-trifluoromethylphenyl)-1-[4,4-di-(4-fluorophenyl)butyl]piperidin-4-ol.
Use: Tranquilizer.

PENFONYLIN.
See: Pentid, Prods. (Squibb)

PENGUIN FOOT TREAT CREAM. (DeWitt) Bot. 4 oz.

• **PENICILLAMINE,** U.S.P. XXI. Caps., Tab., U.S.P. XXI. (Merck Sharp & Dohme) D-3-Mercaptovaline. Cuprimine.
Use: Metal complexing agent, cystinuria, rheumatoid arthritis.
See: Cuprimine, Caps. (Merck Sharp & Dohme)
Depen, Tab. (Wallace)

PENICILLIN. Unless clarified, it means an antibiotic substance or substances produced by growth of the molds *Penicillium notatum* or *P. chrysogenum.*
Use: Antibiotic.

PENICILLIN ALUMINUM. Aluminum 3,3-dimethyl-7-oxo-6-(2-phenylacetamido)-4-thia-1-azabicyclo-[3.2.0]-heptane-2-carboxylate.
Use: Antibiotic.

PENICILLIN CALCIUM. Calcium 3,3-dimethyl-7-oxo-6-(2-phenylacetamido)-4-thia-1-azabicyclo-[3.2.0]-heptane-2-carboxylate. U.S.P. XIII.

PENICILLIN, DIMETHOXY-PHENYL. Methicillin Sodium.
Use: Antibiotic.
See: Staphcillin, Vial (Bristol)

• **PENICILLIN G. BENZATHINE,** U.S.P. XXI. Sterile Susp., Oral Susp., Sterile, Tab. U.S.P. XXI. Benzathine penicillin G.
Use: Antibiotic.
See: Permapen, Aq. Susp. (Pfizer Laboratories)

• **PENICILLIN S BENZATHINE AND PENICILLIN G PROCAINE SUSPENSION, STERILE,** U.S.P. XXI
Use: Antibiotic.

• **PENICILLIN G, POTASSIUM,** U.S.P. XXI. Cap., Inj. for Oral Soln., Sterile, Tab., Tab. for Oral Soln., U.S.P. XXI. (Potassium Penicillin, Benzyl Penicillin Pot.)
Use: Antibiotic.
See: Arcocillin, Prep. (Arcum)
Biotic-T-500, Tab. (Scrip)
Cryspen 400, Tab. (Knight)
Deltapen, Syr., Tab. (Trimen)
G-Recillin-T, Tab. (Reid-Provident)
Hyasorb, Tab. (Key Pharm.)
K-Cillin, Prods. (Mayrand)
K-Pen, Tab. (Kay)
Lanacillin, Pow. (Lannett)
Palocillin-S, Powder (Hauck)
Palocillin-5, Tab. (Hauck)
Parcillin, Tab. (Parmed)
Pensorb, Tab. (Kenyon)
Pentids, Syr., Tab. (Squibb)
Pfizerpen, Tab., Syr. (Pfipharmecs)
Pfizerpen, Inj. (Pfizer Laboratories)
SK-Penicillin G, Tab., Sol. (SmithKline)

PENICILLIN G POTASSIUM W/COMBINATIONS.
See: Lanacillin "200,000", "400,000" (Lannett)
Pentid, Prods. (Squibb)

• **PENICILLIN G, PROCAINE, STERILE,** U.S.P. XXI. Sterile Susp., Intramammary infusion, U.S.P. XXI. Procaine Penicillin.
Use: Antibiotic.

Parenteral, aq. susp., (Procaine Penicillin, for Aq. Inj.,) Procaine Penicillin and buffered Pen. for aqueous, Inj.
See: Crysticillin A.S., Vial (Squibb)
Diurnal-Panicillin (Upjohn)
Duracillin A.S., Prep. (Lilly)
Pfizerpen-AS (Pfizer Laboratories)
Tu-Cillin, Inj. (Reid-Provident)
Wycillin, Susp. (Wyeth)

Parenteral, in oil w/aluminum monostearate. Penicillin Procaine in Oil Inj.

PENICILLIN G PROCAINE COMBINATIONS
See: Bicillin All-Purpose, Vial (Wyeth)
Bicillin C-R, Tubex (Wyeth)
Bicillin C-R 900/300 Inj. (Wyeth)
Duracillin F.A., Amp. (Lilly)
Duracillin Fortified, Vial (Lilly)

• **PENICILLIN G PROCAINE AND DIHYDROSTREPTOMYCIN SULFATE INTRAMAMMARY INFUSION,** U.S.P. XXI.
Use: Antibiotic.

• **PENICILLIN G PROCAINE AND NOVOBIOCIN SODIUM INTRAMAMMARY INFUSION,** U.S.P. XXI
Use: Antibiotic.

ENICILLIN G SODIUM FOR INJECTION, U.S.P. XXI. (Various Mfr.) Sodium Benzylpenicillin.
Use: Antibiotic.

ENICILLIN G SODIUM, STERILE, U.S.P. XXI.
Use: Antibiotic.

ENICILLIN G PROCAINE W/ALUMINUM STEARATE SUSPENSION, STERILE, U.S.P. XXI.
Use: Antibiotic.

NICILLIN HYDRABAMINE PHENOXYMETHYL. 3,3-Dimethyl-7-oxo-6-(2-phenoxyacetamido)-4-thia-1-azabicyclo[3.2.0]heptane-2-carboxylic acid compound with N,N′-bis[(1,2,3,4,-4a,9,10,10a-octahydro-7-isopropyl-1,4a-dimethyl-1-phenanthryl)methyl]ethylenediamine.
Use: Antibiotic.

NICILLIN N. Adicillin, B.A.N.
Use: Antibiotic.

NICILLIN O CHLOROPROCAINE. 6-[2-(Allylthio)acetamido]-3-3-dimethyl-7-oxo-4-thia-1-azabicyclo-[3.2.0]heptane-2-carboxylic acid compound with 2-(diethylamino)ethyl 4-amino-2-chlorbenzoate (1:1).
Use: Antibiotic.

NICILLIN O, SODIUM. Allylmercaptomethyl penicillin.
Use: Antibiotic.

NICILLIN, PHENOXYETHYL.
Use: Antibiotic.
See: Phenethicillin, Penicillin pot. 152

NICILLIN PHENOXYMETHYL BENZATHINE.
Use: Antibiotic.
See: Penicillin V Benzathine

NICILLIN PHENOXYMETHYL HYDRABAMINE.
Use: Antibiotic.
See: Penicillin V Hydrabamine

ENICILLIN V, U.S.P. XX for Oral Susp., Tab. U.S.P. XXI. Phenoxymethyl penicillin. A biosynthetic penicillin formed by fermentation, with suitable precursors of *Penicillin notatum.*
Use: Antibiotic.
See: Biotic pow. (Scrip)
Compocillin-V., Water, Susp. (Ross)
Ledercillin VK(Lederle)
Penagen-VK, Tab., Pow. (Gafton)
Pfizerpen VK (Pfipharmecs)
Robicillin-VK (Robins)
SK-Penicillin VK (SmithKline)
Uticillin VK (Upjohn)
V-Cillin, Preps. (Lilly)
V-Pen, Tab. (Century)

ENICILLIN V BENZATHINE, U.S.P. XXI. Oral Susp. U.S.P. XXI.
Use: Antibiotic.
See: Pen-Vee, Prods. (Wyeth)

NICILLIN V HYDRABAMINE. Hydrabamine phenoxymethyl penicillin.
Use: Antibiotic.
See: Compocillin-V Hydrabamine, Oral Susp. (Ross)

ENICILLIN V POTASSIUM, U.S.P. XXI. Oral Soln., Tab., U.S.P. XXI.
Use: Antibiotic.
See: Beepen VK, Tab., Syrup (Beecham Labs)
Betapen VK., Sol., Tab. (Bristol)
Biotic-V-Powder (Scrip)
Bopen, V-K, Tab. (Boyd)
Cocillin V-K, Tab. (Coastal)
Dowpen VK, Tab. (Merrell Dow)
Lanacillin VK, Tab., Pow. (Lannett)
Ledercillin VK, Oral, Sol., Tab. (Lederle)
LV, Tabs. (Elder)
Penapar VK, Tabs. or For Oral Sol'n. (Parke-Davis)
Pen-Vee-K, Sol., Tab. (Wyeth)
Pfizerpen VK, Pow., Tab. (Pfipharmecs)
Phenethicillin Pot.
Repen-VK, Tab., Oral Susp. (Reid-Provident)
Robicillin VK, Tab., Sol. (Robins)
Ro-Cillin VK, Sol., Tab. (Rowell)
Saropen-VK (Saron)
SK-Penicillin VK, Sol., Tab. (SmithKline)
Suspen, Liq. (Circle)
Uticillin VK, Tab., Sol. (Upjohn)
V-Cillin K, Tab., Oral Sol. (Lilly)
Veetids, Solution and Tabs. (Squibb)

PENICILLINASE. B.A.N. An enzyme that hydrolyzes penicillin, obtained from several strains of bacteria *(B. cereus).* Vial (1,000 u.) 20 cc. Clinical lab use only.

PENIDURAL.
Use: Antibiotic.
See: Benazthine Penicillin B.A.N.

PENNATE. (Robinson) Pentaerythritol tetranitrate. **"10":** 10 mg./Tab. Bot. 100s, 1000s. **"20":** 20 mg./Tab. Bot. 100s, 1000s. **"30":** 30 mg./Timed-caps. Bot. 100s, 500s, 1000s.
Use: Vasodilator.

PENNPHENO. (Robinson) Phenobarbital 0.25 gr., pentaerythritol 10 mg. or 20 mg./Tab. Bot. 100s, 1000s.
Use: Vasodilator.

PENOTAL. (Coastal) Phenobarbital sod. 3/8 gr., pentobarbital sod. 3/8 gr./Cap. Bot. 100s, 500s.
Use: Mild sedative.

PENOTAL ELIXIR. (Coastal) Phenobarbital sod. 1/8 gr., pentobarbital sod. 1/8 gr./5 cc., alcohol 10%. Bot. 4 oz., pt., gal.
Use: Sedative.

PENSORB. (Kenyon) Crystalline penicillin G potassium 250,000 u., buffered w. Ca carbonate/Tab. Bot. 100s, 1000s.
Use: Antibiotic.

PENSTREP. (MSD AGVET) Penicillin-dihydrostreptomycin injection and suspension. Procaine penicillin G 200,000 u., dihydrostreptomycin 0.25 Gm./cc.
Use: Antibiotic, veterinary medicine.

• **PENTABAMATE.** USAN. 3-Methyl-2,4-pentanediol dicarbamate.
Use: Tranquilizer.

PENTA-CAP #1. (Kenyon) Pentaerythritol tetranitrate 30 mg./Cap. Bot. 90s, 100s, 1000s.
Use: Vasodilator.

PENTA-CAP PLUS. (Kenyon) Pentaerythritol tetranitrate 30 mg., amobarbital 50 mg./Cap. Bot. 100s, 1000s.
Use: Vasodilator.

PENTACHLOROPHENATE SODIUM.
See: Podosan, Pow. (Doak)

PENTACOSACTRIDE. D-Ser^1-Nle^4-(Val-NH$_2$)^{25}-$\beta^{1\ 25}$-corticotrophin.
Use: Corticotrophic peptide.
See: Norleusactide (I.N.N.)

PENTACYNIUM METHYLSULPHATE. B.A.N. 4-2-[(5-Cyano-5,5-diphenylpentyl)dimethylammonio]ethyl-4-methylmorpholinium di(methylsulfate).
Use: Hypotensive.
See: Presidal

PENTAERYTHRITOL TETRANITRATE, DILUTED, U.S.P. XXI.
Use: Vasodilator.

• **PENTAERYTHRITOL TETRANITRATE,** U.S.P. XXI.
Diluted, U.S.P. XXI.
Use: Vasodilator.
See: Angijen Green, Tab. (Jenkins)
Arcotrate Nos. 1 & 2, Tab. (Arcum)
Baritrate, Tab. (Barry-Martin)
Dilac-80, Cap. (Ascher)
Duotrate, Cap. (Marion)
Duotrate-45, Cap. (Marion)
Kortrate, Cap. (Amid)
Maso-Trol, Tab. (Mason)
Metranil, Cap. (Meyer)
Naptrate, Prep. (Vortech)
Nitrin, Tab. (Vale)
Penta-Cap No. 1, Cap. (Kenyon)
Penta-E., Tab. (Recsei)
Pentafin, Granucap, Tab. (Reid-Provident)
Pentaforte-T, Tab. (Sutliff & Case)
Penta-Tal No. 1&2, Tab. (Kenyon)
Pentestan-80, Cap. (Standex)
Pentetra, Tab. (Paddock)
Pentrate T.D., Cap. (Galen)
Pentritol, Tempule. (Armour)
Pentryate, Cap., Tab. (Fellows-Testagar)
Pentryate Stronger, Cap. (Fellows-Testagar)
Pent-T-80, Cap. (Rocky Mtn.)
Pentylan, Tab. (Lannett)
Pentylan w/Phenobarbital, Tab. (Lannett)
Peritrate, Tab. (Parke-Davis)
Petro-20 mg., Tab. (Foy)
P-T-T, Cap. (La Crosse)
Rate, Cap., Tab. (Scrip)
Reithritol, Tab. (Bowman)
Tentrate, Tab. (Tennessee Pharm.)
Tetracap-30, Cap. (Freeport)
Tetracap-80, Cap. (Freeport)
Tetratab, Tab. (Freeport)
Tetratab No. 1, Tab. (Freeport)
Tranite, Cap., Tab. (Westerfield)
Vasolate, Cap. (Parmed)
Vasolate-80, Cap. (Parmed)

PENTAERYTHRITOL TETRANITRATE W/COMBINATIONS.
See: Angijen No. 3, Tab. (Jenkins)
Angijen S.C., Tab. (Jenkins)
Angitab, Tab. (Moore Kirk)
Antora-B, Cap. (Mayrand)
Arcotrate No. 3, Tab. (Arcum)
Bitrate, Tab. (Arco)
Cartrax, Tab. (Roerig)
Covap, Tab. (Blue Line)
Dimycor, Tab. (Standard Drug)
Equanitrate, Tab. (Wyeth)
Kortrate Plus, Cap. (Amid)
Maso-Trol w/Phenobarbital, Tab. (Mason)
Miltrate, Tab. (Wallace)
Papavatral, Tab. and L.A. Tab. (Kenwood)
Peaton, Tab. (O'Neal)
Penta-Cap Plus. Cap. (Kenyon)
Penta-Tal No. 3&4, Tab. (Kenyon)
Pentetra w/Phenobarbital, Tab. (Paddock)
Pentylan W/Phenobarbital, Tab. (Lannett)
Perbuzem, Tab. (Zemmer)
Peritrate W/Nitroglycerin, Tab. (Parke-Davis)
Peritrate W/Phenobarbital S.A., Tab. (Parke-Da
Petn Plus, Tab. (Saron)
Rate-10 & P.B. (Scrip)
Rate-20 & P.B. (Scrip)
Respet, Tab. (Westerfield)
Robam-Petn, Tab. (Robinson)
Tetrabarb Tab. (Blaine)
Tetratab No. 2, Tab. (Freeport)
Vasobarb, Cap. (Reid-Provident)

• **PENTAFILCON A.** USAN.
Use: Contact lens material.

PENTAFORT-T TABLETS. (Sutliff & Case) Pentae thritol tetranitrate 10 mg., 20 mg./Tab. Bot. 100s, 1000s.
Use: Vasodilator.

• **PENTAGASTRIN.** USAN. N-t-Butyloxy-carbonyl-β-alanyl-L-tryptophyl-L-methionyl-L-aspartyl-L-phenylalanine amide.
Use: Gastric acid secretion stimulant.
See: Peptavlon, Amp. (Ayerst)

PENTALAMIDE. B.A.N. 2-Pentyloxybenzamide.
Use: Treatment of fungal infections.
See: O-Pentylsalicylamide

• **PENTALYTE.** USAN.
Use: Electrolyte combination

PENTAM 300. (LyphoMed) Pentamidine isethionate 300 mg./Vial.
Use: Treatment of pneumonia due to *Pneumocys carinii.*

PENTAMETHONIUM BROMIDE. B.A.N. Pentamethylenedi(trimethylammonium bromide).
Use: Hypotensive.
See: Lytensium

PENTAMETHONIUM IODIDE. B.A.N. Pentamethylenedi(trimethylammonium iodide).
Use: Hypotensive.
See: Antilusin

PENTAMIDINE. B.A.N. 4,4'-(Pentamethylenedio dibenzamidine.
Use: Treatment of trypanosomiasis.

PENTAMETHYLENETETRAZOL.
See: Pentylenetetrazol U.S.P. (Various Mfr.)

PENTAMOXANE HCl. 2-Isoamylamino-methyl-1,4-be zodioxane HCl.
Use: Tranquilizing agent.

ENTAMUSTINE. USAN.
Jse: Antineoplastic.
PENTANEDIAMINE,N[4]-(6-CHLORO-2-METHOXY--ACRIDINYL)-N',N'-DIETHYL-,DIHYDROCHLO-RIDE, DIHYDRATE. Quinacrine Hydrochloride, .S.P. XXI.
PENTANEDIAMINE,N[4]-(7-CHLORO-4-QUINOLIN-L)-N[1],N[1]-DIETHYL-. Chloroquine, U.S.P. XXI.
PENTANEDIAMINE, N[4]-(6-METHOXY-8-QUINO-INYL)-,PHOSPHATE (1:2). Primaquine Phosphate, .S.P. XXI.
ITANOIC ACID, 4-OXO-, CALCIUM SALT (2:1), IHYDRATE. Calcium Levulinate, U.S.P. XXI.
ITAPHONATE. Dodecyltriphenylphosphonium entachlorophenolate.
Jse: Antibacterial.
ITAPIPERIDE. B.A.N. 1-Methyl-4-(3-methyl-2-phe-ylvaleryloxy)piperidine.
se: Anticholinergic.
ee: Quilene (methylsulfate)
ITAPIPERIDE METHYLSULFATE. 4'-(1'-Methyl-iperidyl)-2-phenyl-3-methyl-valerate dimethylsulfate. 'alpipamate Methylsulfate
se: Anticholinergic.
ENTAPIPERIUM METHYLSULFATE. USAN.
se: Anticholinergic.
NTAPYRROLIDINIUM BITARTRATE.
ee: Pentolinium Tartrate.
NTAQUINE. B.A.N. 8-(5-Isopropylaminopentyl-ami-o)-6-methoxyquinoline.
Jse: Antimalarial.
NTAQUINE PHOSPHATE. 8-[[5-(Isopropyl-amino)-entyl]amino]-6-methoxyquinoline phosphate.
NTARCORT. (Dalin) Hydrocortisone alcohol 0.5%, oln. coal tar 2%, clioquinol 3%, diperodone HCl .25%, Vit. A 850 I.U., D 85 I.U./Gm. Tubes: 15 im.
se: Dermatoses.
ITASODIUM BIS [4,5-DIHYDROXY-M-BEN-ENEDISULFONATO(4-)]ANTIMONATE(5-)HEPTA-YDRATE. Stibophen.
ITASODIUM COLISTINMETHANESULFONATE. terile Colistimethate Sodium, U.S.P. XXI.
ITA-STRESS. (Penta) Vit. A 10,000 I.U., D 500 I.U., -1 10 mg., B-2 10 mg., B-6 1 mg., cal. pantothenate mg., niacinamide 50 mg., C 100 mg., E 2 I.U., B-2 3.3 mcg./Cap. Bot. 90s, 1000s. Jar 250s.
Jse: Dietary supplement.
ITA-TAL. (Kenyon) Pentaerythritol tetranitrate 10 ng., 20 mg./Tab. Bot. 100s, 1000s.
NTA-TAL #3, #4. (Kenyon) Pentaerythritol tetrani-rate 10 mg., 20 mg., phenobarbital 15 mg. Tab. ot. 100s, 1000s.
NTAVALENT GAS GANGRENE. Antitoxin.
NTA-VIRON. (Penta) Cal. carbonate 500 mg., ferrous umarate 100 mg., C 50 mg., D 167 I.U., A 3.333 U., B-1 3.3 mg., B-2 3.3 mg., B-6 2 mg., cal. pantothe-ate 1.6 mg., niacinamide 16.7 mg., E 2 I.U./Cap. ot. 100s, 1000s. Jar 250s.
se: Supplement.
NTAZINE. (Century) Promethazine expectorant. ot. 4 oz., 16 oz., gal.
PENTAZINE W/CODEINE. (Century) Promethazine expectorant. Bot. 4 oz., 16 oz., gal.
PENTAZINE INJ. (Century) Promethazine 50 mg./cc. Inj. vial 10 cc.
• **PENTAZOCINE,** U.S.P. XXI. 2,6-Methano-3-benzazocin-8-ol, 1,2,3,4,5,6-hexahydro-6,11-dimethyl-3-(3-methyl-2-butenyl)-1,2,3,-4,5,6-Hexahydro-cis-6,11-dimethyl-3-(3-methyl-2-butenyl)-2,6-methano-2-benzazocin-8-ol.
Use: Analgesic.
• **PENTAZOCINE HYDROCHLORIDE,** U.S.P. XXI. Tab., U.S.P. XXI.
Use: Analgesic.
W/ Acetaminophen.
See: Talacen, Cap. (Winthrop-Breon)
• **PENTAZOCINE HYDROCHLORIDE AND ASPIRIN TABLETS,** U.S.P. XXI.
Use: Analgesic.
See: Talwin Compound, Tab. (Winthrop-Breon)
• **PENTAZOCINE LACTATE INJECTION,** U.S.P. XXI.
Use: Analgesic.
See: Talwin Injection, Inj. (Winthrop-Breon)
• **PENTAZOCINE AND NALOXONE HYDROCHLORIDE TABLETS.** U.S.P. XXI.
Use: Analgesic.
See: Talwin NX, Tab. (Winthrop Breon)
PENTESTAN 10. (Standex) Pentaerythritol tetranitrate 10 mg./Tab. Bot. 100s.
PENTESTAN 10-P. (Standex) Pentaerythritol tetranitrate 10 mg., phenobarbital 15 mg./Tab. Bot. 100s.
PENTESTAN-80. (Standex) Pentaerythritol tetranitrate 80 mg./Cap. Bot. 100s.
Use: Angina.
• **PENTETATE CALCIUM TRISODIUM.** USAN.
Use: Chelating agent.
• **PENTETATE CALCIUM TRISODIUM Yb 169.** USAN.
Use: Radioactive agent.
• **PENTETATE INDIUM DISODIUM IN 111.** USAN.
Use: Diagnostic aid, radioactive agent.
• **PENTETIC ACID.** USAN.
Use: Diagnostic aid.
PENTETRA-PARACOTE. (Paddock) Pentaerythritol tetranitrate 80 mg./Cap. Bot. 100s, 500s, 1000s. Also 30 mg./Cap., same sizes.
Use: Angina pectoris.
PENTETRAZOL. Analucin. Pentylenetetrazol
Use: Geriatric stimulant, analeptic.
PENTHIENATE. B.A.N. 2-Diethylaminoethyl α-cyclopentyl-α-(2-thienyl).
Use: Antispasmodic.
See: Monodral (methobromide)
PENTHIENATE BROMIDE. Diethyl (2-Hydroxyethyl) methylammonium bromide α-cyclopentyl-2-thiopheneglycolate.
PENTHRANE. (Abbott) Methoxyflurane; 2,2-dichloro-1, 1-difluoroethyl methyl ether. Bot. 15 ml., 125 ml.
Use: Anesthetic for obstetrics and surgery.
PENTHRICHLORAL. B.A.N. 5,5-Di(hydroxymethyl)-2-trichloromethyl-1,3-dioxan.
Use: Hypnotic; sedative.

PENTIDS. (Squibb) Potassium Penicillin G) buffered with calcium carbonate.**Tab.:** 125 mg. (200,000 u.)/Tab. Bot. 100s. **Syrup**: 125 mg. (200,000 u)/5ml. Bot. 100 ml., 200 ml.
Use: Antibiotic

PENTIDS 400. (Squibb) Potassium Penicillin G buffered with calcium carbonate. **Tab.:** 250 mg. (400,000 u.)/Tab. Bot. 100s. Unimatic 100s. **Syrup:** 250 mg. (400,000 u.)/5 ml. Bot. 100 ml., 200 ml.
Use: Antibiotic.

PENTIDS 800. (Squibb) Potassium Penicillin G 500 mg. (800,000 u.)/Tab. buffered with calcium carbonate. Bot. 30s, 100s.
Use: Antibiotic.

PENTIFYLLINE. B.A.N. 1-Hexyl-3,7-dimethyl-xanthine.
Use: Vasodilator.
See: Cosaldon

PENTINA. (Freeport) Rauwolfia serpentina, 100 mg./Tab. Bot. 1000s.
Use: Antihypertensive.

• **PENTISOMICIN.** USAN.
Use: Anti-infective.

• **PENTIZIDONE SODIUM.** USAN.
Use: Antibacterial.

• **PENTOBARITAL,** U.S.P. XXI. Elixir, U.S.P. XXI. (Various Mfr.) 5-Ethyl-5-(1-methylbutyl) barbituric acid.
See: Nembutal, Elix., Gradumets (Abbott) Penta, Tab. (Dunhall)
W/Secobarbital, butabarbital, & phenobarbital.
See: Qui-A-Zone, Tab. (Walker)

PENTOBARBITAL COMBINATIONS.
See: Cafergot-PB, Supp., Tab. (Sandoz)
Matropinal Forte, Inserts, Tab. (Comatic)
Matropinal Inserts, Elix., Tab. (Comatic)
Nembutal, Prep. (Abbott)
Neoquess, Tabs. (O'Neal)
Nipirin, Cap. (Elder)
Penotal, Cap., Elix. (Coastal)
Quad-Set, Tab. (Kenyon)
Qui-A-Zone, Tab. (Walker)
Quiess, Tab. (O'Neal)
Spasmasorb, Tab. (Hauck)
Stopp, Supp. (Keene)

• **PENTOBARBITAL, SODIUM,** U.S.P. XXI. Cap. Elixir, Inj.: U.S.P. XXI. 2,4,6,(1H,3H,5H)-Pyrimidinetrione, 5-ethyl-5-(1-methyl-butyl)-, monosodium salt. Sod. 5-Ethyl-5-(1-methylbutyl) barbiturate. Embutal.
Use: Hypnotic, sedative.
See: Maso-Pent, Tab. (Mason)
Nembutal Sodium, Prep. (Abbott)
Night-Caps, Cap. (Bowman)
Penital, Cap., Inj. (Kay)
W/Acetaminophen, salicylamide, codeine phosphate.
See: Tega-Code, Cap. (Ortega)
W/Adiphenine HCl, phamasorb, aluminum hydroxide.
See: Spasmasorb, Tab. (Hauck)
W/Atropine sulfate, hyoscine HBr, hyoscyamine sulfate.
See: Eldonal, Elix., Tab., Cap. (Canright)
W/Carbromal.
See: Carbropent, Tab. (Blue Line)
W/Ephedrine.
See: Ephedrine and Nembutal-25, Cap. (Abbott)
W/Ergotamine tartrate, caffeine alkaloid, bellafoline
See: Cafergot-P.B., Tab. (Sandoz)
W/Homatropine methylbromide, dehydrocholic acid ox bile extract.
See: Homachol, Tab. (Lemmon)
W/Phenobarbital sodium.
See: Penotal, Cap., Elix. (Coastal)
W/Pyrilamine maleate.
See: A-N-R, Rectorette (Hauck)
W/Seco-, buta-, phenobarbital.
See: Quadrabarb, Tab. (Vortech)
W/Vitamin compounds, d-methamphetamine HCl.
See: Fetamin, Tab. (Mission)

PENTOBARBITAL, SOLUBLE.
See: Pentobarbital Sodium, U.S.P.

PENTOBEE W/B-12. (Vitarine) Vit. B-1 3 mg., B-2 3 m B-6 0.3 mg., B-12 3 mcg., niacinamide 10 mg., pantothenate 3 mg./Cap. Bot. 100s, 250s.
Use: Supplement

PENTOL TABS. (Major) Pentaerythritol tetranitrate mg./Tab. Bot. 1000s; 20 mg./Tab. Bot. 100s 1000s; 80 mg. S.A. 250s, 1000s.
Use: Vasodilator.

PENTOLINIUM TARTRATE, Pentamethylene-1:5-b (1′-methylpyrrolidinium bitartrate). N,N′-Pentar thylenedi-(1-methylpyrrolidinium hydrogen tartra Pentapyrrolidinium Bitartrate.
Use: Hypotensive.

• **PENTOMONE.** USAN.
Use: Prostate growth inhibitor.

• **PENTOPRIL.** USAN.
Use: Enzyme inhibitor (angiotensin-converting).

• **PENTOSTATIN.** USAN.
Use: Potentiator.

PENTOTHAL. (Abbott) Thiopental sodium 500 mg. fliptop vial w/20 ml. water diluent; 1 Gm. fliptop w/50 ml. water diluent; 250 mg., 400 mg., and 5 mg. syringes; 5 Gm. in 250 ml. and 10 Gm. in 5C ml. Multi-Dose cont.; kits: 1 Gm./2.5%, Gm./2.5%, 5 Gm./2.5%, 2.5 Gm./2.0%, and 5 Gm./2.0%. Penthothal Rectal-susp. in AbboSert. S Single-dose syringe 250 mg., 400 mg., or 500 mg
Use: Ultra-short-acting anesthetic.

• **PENTOXIFYLLINE.** USAN. Oxpentifylline, B.A.N.
Use: Oral hemorrheologic agent for peripheral vascular disease.
See: Trental (Hoechst)

PENTRASAPAN. (Vitarine) Pentaerythritol tetranitra 80 mg./timed rel. Cap.
Use: Relief of angina.

PENTRATE T.D. (Galen) Pentaerythritol tetranitrate 30 mg./Cap. Bot. 100s.
Use: Coronary vasodilator. Sustained release.

PENTRAX SHAMPOO. (Rydell) Tar extract 8.75% w/detergents and conditioning agents. Bot. 4 oz. oz.
Use: Seborrhea, psoriasis, eczematous dermatos of scalp.

:NTRINITROL. USAN.
se: Vasodilator.
TRITOL TEMPULES. (USV Labs.) Pentaerythritol tranitrate. Timed Release Cap. 30 mg., Bot. 100s, 50s, 60 mg., Bot. 60s, 250s.
se: Antianginal used for pain of coronary artery sease.
TRYATE TABLETS. (Fellows) Pentaerythritol tranitrate 10 mg./Tab. Bot. 1000s, 5000s. 20 g./Tab. Bot. 1000s.
TRYATE TIMED CAPSULE. (Fellows) entaerythritol tetranitrate 30 mg./Cap. Bot. 30s, 00s, 1000s.
TRYATE STRONGER. (Fellows) Pentaerythritol tranitrate 80 mg./Cap. (timed relase). Bot. 30s, 00s, 1000s.
se: Angina pectoris.
T-T-80. (Rocky Mtn.) Pentaerythritol tetranitrate 80 g./Time Cap. Bot. 50s.
se: Relief of angina pectoris.
T-T-80. (Mericon) Pentaerythritol tetranitrate 80 g./T.D. Cap. Bot. 100s, 1000s.
TYLAN. (Lannett) Pentaerythritol tetranitrate 10 g./Tab. Bot. 500s, 1000s. 20 mg./Tab. Bot. 100s, 000s.
TYLAN W/PHENOBARBITAL. (Lannett) entaerythritol tetranitrate 10 mg., phenobarbital 25 gr./Tab. Bot. 100s, 500s, 1000s. **No. 2:** entaerythritol tetranitrate 20 mg., phenobarbital 15 g./Tab. Bot. 100s, 500s, 1000s.
TYLENETETRAZOL. 6,7,8,9-Tetrahydro-5-H-tet-zoloazepine. Leptazol.
se: Geriatric stimulant, analeptic.
ee: Cardiazol, Tab. (Knoll)
Cenalene-M, Tab., Elix. (Central)
Metrazol, Elix., Tab. Pow. (Knoll)
Nelex-100, Tab. (Mallard)
Nioric Modified, Tab., Elix. (Ascher)
TYLENETETRAZOL W/COMBINATIONS.
ee: Aminobrain P-T, Liq. (Med Prod. Panamericana)
Analeptone, Elix. (Reed & Carnrick)
Cerebro-Nicin, Cap. (Brown)
D-Vaso prods. (Dunhall)
Geriatrazole, Vial (Kenyon)
Gerren Tab. (Wren)
Gevizol (Saron)
Menic, Tab. (Geriatric)
Mentalert, Tab., Elix. (Keene Pharm.)
Neo-Gerastan, Tab. (Standex)
Nialex, Tab. (Mallard)
Niapent, Tab., Elix. (Ferndale)
Nicozol, Elix., Cap. (Hyrex)
Norozol, Tab. (Vortech)
Senilex, Tab. (O'Neal)
Senoral, Liq. (Kay)
Thedrazol prods. (Kenyon)
Tinaplex, Elix. (Blaine)
Tinazole, Elix. (Blaine)
Vasostim, Cap. (Dunhall)
Vita-Metrazol, Elix., Tab. (Knoll)
-VEE-K. (Wyeth) Pot. phenoxymethyl penicillin. **ab.: 125 mg.**/Tab. Bot. 36s; **250 mg.**/Tab. Bot. 100s, 500s. Redipak 100s; **500 mg.**/Tab. Bot. 100s, 500s. Redipak 100s.
Use: Penicillin susceptible organisms.
PEN-VEE K FOR ORAL SOLUTION. (Wyeth) Penicillin V potassium **250 mg.**/5 ml. Bot. 100 ml., 150 ml., 200 ml. Redipak Ctn. 20s. **125 mg.**/5 ml. Bot. 100 ml., 200 ml.
Use: Antibiotic.
• **PEPLOMYCIN SULFATE.** USAN.
Use: Antineoplastic.
• **PEPPERMINT,** N.F. XVI. Oil, Water, N.F. XVI.
Use: Pharmaceutic aid (flavor), antitussive, expectorant, nasal decongestant.
See: Vicks Prods. (Vicks)
• **PEPPERMINT OIL,** N.F. XVI.
Use: Pharmaceutic aid (flavor).
• **PEPPERMINT SPIRIT,** U.S.P. XXI.
Use: Digestive aid.
• **PEPPERMINT WATER,** N.F. XVI.
Use: Vehicle.
PEPSAMAR ESP LIQUID. (Winthrop Products) Aluminum hydroxide, glycerin.
Use: Antacid, demulcent, spasmolytic.
PEPSAMAR ESP TABLETS. (Winthrop Products) Aluminum hydroxide, magnesium hydroxide, manitol powder.
Use: Antacid, demulcent, spasmolytic.
PEPSAMAR COMP. TABLETS. (Winthrop Products) Aluminum hydroxide, magnesium hydroxide.
Use: Antacid.
PEPSAMAR HM TABLETS. (Winthrop Products) Aluminum hydroxide, starch.
Use: Antacid.
PEPSAMAR LIQUID. (Winthrop Products) Aluminum hydroxide.
Use: Antacid.
PEPSAMAR SUSPENSION. (Winthrop Products) Aluminum hydroxide magnesium hydroxide, sorbitol.
Use: Antacid, demulcent, spasmolytic.
PEPSAMAR TABLETS. (Winthrop Products) Aluminum hydroxide.
Use: Antacid.
PEPSATAL. (Kenyon) Pepsin 200 mg., pancreatin 200 mg., bile salts 100 mg., dehydrocholic acid 30 mg., desoxycholic acid 30 mg./Tab. Bot. 100s, 1000s.
PEPSICONE GEL. (Winthrop Products) Aluminum hydroxide, magnesium hydroxide, simethicone.
Use: Antacid, antiflatulent.
PEPSICONE TABLET. (Winthrop Products) Aluminum hydroxide, magnesium hydroxide, simethicone.
Use: Antacid, antiflatulent.
PEPSIN.
Use: Digestive aid.
See: Lactopepsinum, Elix. (Noyes)
PEPSIN W/COMBINATIONS.
See: Biloric, Cap. (Arcum)
Bocresin, Liq. (Scrip)
Diethylstilbestrol Digestive Formula, Tab. (Wolins)
Digesplen, Tab., Elix., Drops (Med Prod. Panamericana)
Digestozyme, Tab. (Wolins)
Donnazyme, Tab. (Robins)

Entozyme, Tab. (Robins)
Enzobile, Tab. (Mallard)
Enzylax, Tab. (Kay)
Enzymet, Tab. (Westerfield)
Foy-Nux, Tab. (Foy)
Gastroenterase, Tab. (Wallace)
Glutasyn, Cap. (Brunswick)
Gourmase, Cap. (Rowell)
Gourmase-PB, Cap. (Rowell)
Kanulase, Tab. (Dorsey)
Konzyme, Tab. (Brunswick Lab.)
Leber Taurine, Liq. (Paddock)
Maso-Gestive, Tab. (Mason)
Normacid, Tab. (Stuart)
Nu'Leven, Tab. (Lemmon)
Nu'Leven Plus, Tab. (Lemmon)
Pepsatal, Tab. (Kenyon)
Pepsin Essence
Ro-Bile, Tab. (Rowell)
Sto-Zyme, Tab. (Jalco)
Zypan, Tab. (Standard Process)

PEPSIN LACTATED, ELIXIR.
See: Peptalac, Liq. (Bowman)

PEPSIN-PAPAIN COMPLEX.
W/Pancreas, malt diastase, glycyrrhiza ext., charcoal.
See: Pepsocoll, Tabs. (Western Research Labs.)

• **PEPSTATIN.** USAN.
Use: Enzyme inhibitor.

PEPTAVLON. (Ayerst) Pentagastrin. 0.25 mg. w/sod. chloride/ml. Amp. 2 ml. Ctn. 10s.
Use: Evaluation of gastric acid secretion.

PEPTENZYME. (Reed & Carnrick) Alcohol 16%. Pleasantly aromatic. Bot. 1 pt.
Use: Pharmaceutical vehicle.

PEPTO-BISMOL LIQUID. (Procter & Gamble) Bismuth subsalicylate 1.75%. Bot. 4 oz., 8 oz., 12 oz., 16 oz.
Use: Indigestion, nausea, diarrhea, upset stomach.

PEPTO-BISMOL TABLETS. (Procter & Gamble) Bismuth subsalicylate 300 mg./Tab. Pkg. 24s, 42s, 60s.
Use: Indigestion, nausea, diarrhea, upset stomach.

PERANDREN PHENYLACETATE. (Ciba) Testosterone phenylacetate.

PERATIZOLE. B.A.N. 1-[-(2,4-Dimethylthiazol-5-yl)-butyl]-4-(4-methylthiazol-2-yl)piperazine.
Use: Antihypertensive agent.

PERBUZEM. (Zemmer) Pentaerythritol tetranitrate 10 mg., butabarbital sodium 15 mg./Tab. Bot. 100s, 1000s.
Use: Angina pectoris, hypertension.

PERCAINE.
See: Dibucaine Hydrochloride (Nupercaine HCl. Ciba)

PERCHLORETHYLENE.
See: Tetrachlorethylene, U.S.P. XXI.

PERCHLORPERAZINE.
See: Compazine, Prep. (SmithKline)

PERCOCET-5. (Du Pont) Oxycodone HCl 5 mg., acetaminophen 325 mg./Tab. Bot. 100s, 500s. Unit dose 250s.
Use: Analgesic.

PERCODAN. (Du Pont) Oxycodone HCl 4.50 mg., oxycodone terephthalate 0.38 mg., aspirin 325 mg./Tab. Bot. 100s, 500s, 1000s. Unit dose 25 1000s.
Use: Narcotic analgesic.
W/Hexobarbital.
See: Percobarb, Cap. (Du Pont)

PERCODAN-DEMI. (Du Pont) Oxycodone HCl 2.25 oxycodone terephthalate 0.19 mg., aspirin 325 mg./Tab. Bot. 100s, 500s, 1000s.
Use: Prompt, prolonged relief from pain.

PERCO-EZE. (Moyco) Oral paste.
Use: analgesic for pain of gums and mucosa.

PERCOGESIC. (Vicks) Acetaminophen 325 mg. phenyltoloxamine citrate 30 mg./Tab. Pkg. 24s. Bot. 100s. Hospital Pack Box 960s.
Use: Analgesic.

PERCOMORPH LIVER OIL. (May be blended with 50% other fish liver oils; each Gm. contains 60 I.U. Vit. A & 8500 I.U. Vit. D.)
See: Oleum Percomorphum

PERCORTEN ACETATE. (Ciba) Desoxycorticoste acetate. Vial (5 mg./ml. in oil w/chlorobutanol 0.5%) Pellets 125 mg. 1s.
Use: I.M., implantation & orally; adrenal cortex replacement therapy.

PERCORTEN PIVALATE. (Ciba) Desoxycorticosterone Pivalate. Vial (25 mg./ml.) also contains methylcellulose 10.5 mg., sod. carboxymethylcellulose 3 mg., polysorbate 80 1 mg., sod. chloride 8 mg., thimerosal 0.002%. 4 ml.
Use: I.M.; adrenocortical insufficiency.

PERCY MEDICINE. (Merrick Medicine) Bismuth subnitrate 959.0 mg., calcium hydroxide 21.9 mg./10 ml. w/alcohol 5%
Use: Relief of simple diarrhea & excess acid conditions of the stomach.

PERDIEM. (Rorer) Blend of 82% psyllium & 18% senna as active ingredients in granular form. Sodium content (0.08 mEq) 1.8 mg./rounded ts (6 Gm.). Canister 100 Gm., 250 Gm. Unit dose Gm.
Use: Relief of constipation.

PERDIEM PLAIN. (Rorer) Psyllium 100% as active ingredient in granular form. Sodium content (0.0 mEq) 1.8 mg./rounded tsp. (6 Gm.) Canisters 1 Gm., 250 Gm. Unit dose 6 Gm.
Use: Relief of constipation.

PERDILATAL HYDROCHLORIDE. Buphenin, B.A.

PERE-DIOSATE. (Towne) Docusate sodium 100 casanthranol 30 mg./Cap. Bot. 100s.
Use: Laxative.

PERESTAN. (Interstate) Docusate sodium 100 mg casanthranol 30 mg./Cap. Bot. 100s, 1000s.
Use: Laxative.

• **PERFILCON A.** USAN.
Use: Contact lens material.
See: Permalens (CooperVision)

PERGALEN.
See: Sodium Apolate

RGONAL (MENOTROPINS). (Serono) Follicle stimulating hormone (FSH) 75 I.U. and lutenizing hormone (LH) 75 I.U. Unit contains 1 Amp. product and 1 Amp. NaCl diluent.
Jse: Replacement of FSH and LH in women or men in hypogonadotropic conditions.

RGRAVA. (Arcum) Vit. A 2000 I.U., D 300 I.U., B-2 mg., B-2 2 mg., nicotinamide 10 mg., B-6 2 mg., B-12 5 mcg., C 60 mg./cal. 40 mg./Cap. Bot. 100s, 000s.
Jse: Pregnancy.

RGRAVA NO. 2. (Arcum) Vit. A 2000 I.U., D 300 I.U., B-1 2 mg., B-2 2 mg., nicotinamide 10 mg., B-2 mg., C 60 mg., cal. lactate monohydrate 200 ng., ferrous gluconate 31 mg., folic acid 0.1 ng./Cap. Bot. 100s, 1000s.
Jse: Pregnancy.

ERHEXILINE. USAN. 2-(2,2-Dicyclohexylethyl)-iperidine.
Jse: Treatment of angina pectoris.

ERHEXILINE MALEATE. USAN. 2-(2,2-Dicyclohexlethyl) piperidine maleate.
Jse: Cardiovascular agent.

RHYDROL.
See: Hydrogen Peroxide 30% (Var. Mfr.)

RIACTIN. (Merck Sharp & Dohme) Cyproheptadine HCl 4 mg./Tab. Bot. 100s.
Jse: Antipruritic, antihistaminic.

RIACTIN SYRUP. (Merck Sharp & Dohme) Cyproheptadine HCl 2 mg./5 ml. w/alcohol 5%, orbic acid 0.1%. Bot. 473 ml.
Jse: Antipruritic, antihistaminic.

RI-CARE. (Sween) Jar/2 oz., 8 oz.
Jse: Skin care ointment. Unit dose 100s.

RI-COLACE. (Mead Johnson) **Cap.:** Docusate sodium 100 mg., casanthranol 30 mg./Cap. Bot. 30s, 0s, 250s, 1000s. Unit dose 100s. **Syrup:** Docusate sodium 60 mg., casanthranol 30 mg./15 c.; ethyl alcohol 10%. Bot. 8 oz., pt.
Jse: Fecal softener and laxative.

RICOLEAST. (Eastwood) Cap. Bot. 100s.

RI-CONATE. (Cenci) Docusate sodium 100 mg., casanthranol 30 mg./Cap. Bot. 100s, 1000s.
Jse: Constipation.

RICYAZINE. B.A.N. 2-Cyano-10-[3-(4-hydroxy-iperidino)propyl]phenothiazine. Neulactil.
Jse: Tranquilizer.

RIDIN-C. (Beutlich) Hesperidin methyl chalcone 50 ng., hesperidin complex 150 mg., ascorbic acid 00 mg./Tab. Bot. 100s and 500s.
Jse: In capillary fragility.

RIES. (Xttrium) Medicated pads, w/witch hazel and lycerin. Jar 40 pads.
Jse: Hygienic wipe and local compress.

RIFOAM. (Rowell) Benzalkonium chloride 0.1%, ramoxine HCl 1.0%, allantoin 0.3%, methylparaben 0.15%, propylparaben 0.05%, witch hazel 35%, solubilized lanolin, alcohol (approx. %), water q.s. to 100%. Aerosol 1.5 oz.
Jse: Dermatologic, antipruritic, fungistatic, acteriostatic cream.

• **PERGOLIDE MESYLATE.** USAN.
Use: Dopamine agonist.

PERIHEMIN. (Lederle) Vit. B-12 5 mcg., intrinsic factor conc. 25 mg., ferrous fumarate 168 mg., folic acid 0.33 mg., ascorbic acid 50 mg./Cap. Bot. 100s.
Use: Orally; anemias.

PERIMYCIN. (Warner-Lambert) An antibiotic of the heptaene type elaborated by *Streptomyces coelicolor* variety *aminophilus.*
Use: Antifungal antibiotic.

PERI SOFCAP. (Alton) Docusate sodium with peristim. Bot. 100s, 1000s.
Use: Stool softener.

PERISTOMAL COVERING.
See: Stomahesive, Wafers (Squibb)

PERITIME-80. (Kenyon; Werner) Pentaerythritol tetra nitrate 80 mg./Cap. Bot. 100s.

PERITINIC. (Lederle) Elemental iron 100 mg., docusate sodium 100 mg., B-1 7.5 mg., B-2 7.5 mg., B-6 7.5 mg., B-12 50 mcg., C 200 mg., niacinamide 30 mg., folic acid 0.05 mg., pantothenic acid 15 mg./Tab. Bot. 60s.
Use: Hematinic-vitamin with stool softener.

PERITRATE. (Parke-Davis) Pentaerythritol tetranitrate. **Tab. 10 mg.:** Bot. 100s, 1000s. **Tab. 20 mg.:** Bot. 100s, 1000s. Unit dose 100s. **Tab. 40 mg.:** Bot. 100s. **S.A. Tab. 80 mg.** Bot. 100s, 1000s.
Use: Coronary vasodilator used in angina pectoris.

PERITRATE S.A.. (Parke-Davis) Pentaerythritol tetranitrate 80 mg. (20 mg. in immediate release layer, 60 mg. in sustained release base)/Tab. Bot. 100s, 1000s. Unit dose 100s.

PERI-WASH. (Sween) Bot. 8 oz., gal.
Use: Skin deodorizer.

• **PERLAPINE.** USAN. 6-(4-Methyl-1-piperazinyl) morphanthridine.
Use: Hypnotic.

PERLATAN.
See: Estrone (Various Mfr.)

PERMANGANIC ACID, POTASSIUM SALT.
Potassium Permanganate, U.S.P. XXI.

PERMAPEN. (Pfipharmecs) Benzathine penicillin G 1,200,000 u./cc. Disp. syringe 2 cc.
Use: Antibiotic.

PERMITIL. (Schering) Fluphenazine HCl 0.25 mg., 2.5 mg. or 5 mg./Tab. Bot. 100s; 10 mg. Tabs., Bot. 1000s
Use: Tranquilizer.

PERMITIL ORAL CONCENTRATE. (Schering) Fluphenazine HCl, 5 mg./ml. Bot. 120 ml. w. calibrated dropper. Hospital use.
Use: Tranquilizer.

PERNAVIT 1000. (Ferndale) Vit. B-12 1000 mcg./cc. Vial 10 cc., 30 cc.
Use: Hematopoietic agent.

PERNOX LOTION. (Westwood) Microfine granules of polyethylene 20%, sulfur 2%, salicylic acid in a combination of soapless cleansers & wetting agents. Bot. 6 oz.
Use: Treatment of oily skin & acne.

PERNOX MEDICATED LATHERING SCRUB CLEANSER. (Westwood) Polyethylene granules 26%, sulfur 2%, salicylic acid 1.5%. w/soapless surface active cleansers and wetting agents. Regular or lemon. Tube 2 oz., 4 oz.
Use: Therapeutic cleanser for oily skin and acne.

PERNOX SHAMPOO. (Westwood) Sodium laureth sulfate, water, lauramide DEA, quaternium 22, PEG-75 lanolin/hydrolyzed animal protein, fragrance, sodium chloride, lactic acid, sorbic acid, disodium EDTA, FD&C yellow No. 6 and blue No. 1. Bot. 8 oz.
Use: Cleanser and conditioner for oily hair.

PEROXIDASE. W/Glucose oxidase, pot, iodide.
See: Diastix Reagent Strips (Ames)

PEROXIDE, DIBENZOYL. Benzoyl Peroxide, Hydrous.

■ **PEROXIDES.**
See: Hydrogen Peroxide (Var. Mfr.)
Urea Peroxide
Zinc Peroxide

PEROXYL MOUTHRINSE. (Hoyt) Hydrogen peroxide 1.5% in mint flavored base w/ alcohol 6%. Bot. 8 oz.
Use: Mouthrinse.

• **PERPHENAZINE,** U.S.P. XXI. Inj., Oral Sol., Syrup, Tab., U.S.P. XXI. 2-Chloro-10-[3-[4-(2-hydroxyethyl)-piperazinyl]propyl]-phenothiazine. 4-(3-(2-Chloro-phenothiazin-1-yl)propyl)-1-piperazine-ethanol.
Use: Antiemetic, tranquilizer.
See: Trilafon, Prod. (Schering)
W/Amitriptyline HCl.
See: Etrafon, Prod. (Schering)
Triavil, Tab. (Merck Sharp & Dohme)

PERSADOX. (Owen) Benzoyl peroxide 5% in a base of cetyl alcohol, propylene glycol, sod. lauryl sulfate, purified water. Stearyl alcohol in cream only. **Cream** Jar 1 oz., **Lotion** Plastic Bot. 1 oz.
Use: Treatment of acne, fair or normal skin.

PERSADOX HP CREAM. (Owen) Benzoyl peroxide 10% in cetaphil base w/same ingredients as Persadox. **Cream** Jar 1 oz., **Lotion** plastic Bot. 1 oz.
Use: Treatment of acne and oily skin conditions.

PERSA-GEL. (Ortho) Benzoyl peroxide 5% and 10%. Tube 1.5 oz., or 3 oz.
Use: Acne vulgaris treatment.

PERSA-GEL W. (Ortho) Benzoyl peroxide in water-base 5% and 10%. Tube 1.5 oz., 3 oz.
Use: Topical treatment of acne vulgaris.

PERSANGUE. (Arcum) Ferrous gluconate 192 mg., C 150 mg., B-1 3 mg., B-2 3 mg., B-12 50 mcg./Cap. Bot. 100s, 500s.
Use: Iron deficiency anemias.

PERSANTIN. Dipyridamole, B.A.N.

PERSANTINE. (Boehringer Ingelheim) Dipyridamole 25 mg., 50 mg. or 75 mg./Tab. **25 mg.:** Bot. 100s, 1000s. Unit Dose 100s. Unit of Use 90s. **50 mg.:** Bot. 100s, 1000s. Unit Dose 100s. **75 mg.:** Bot. 100s.
Use: Treatment of angina pectoris.

• **PERSIC OIL,** N.F. XVI.
Use: Vehicle.

PERSISTIN. (Fisons) Aspirin 2.5 gr., salicylsalicylic acid 7.5 gr./Tab. Bot. 50s, 500s.
Use: Anti-inflammatory.

PERTECHNETIC ACID, SODIUM SALT. Sodium Pertechnetate Tc 99 m Solution.

PERTOFRANE. (USV Labs.) Desipramine hydrochloride 25 mg./Cap. Bot. 100s, 1000s. 50 mg./Cap. Bot. 100s, 1000s.
Use: Antidepressant.

PERTROPIN. (Lannett) Linolenic acid 7 min./Cap. Bot. 100s.
Use: Dietary supplement.

PERTSCAN-99m. (Abbott) Inj. Tc-99m.
Use: Radiodiagnostic.

PERTUSSIN COMPLEX D. (Chesebrough-Pond's) D tromethorphan HBr 10 mg., chlorpheniramine maleate 2 mg., phenylproanolamine, HCl 12.5 mg./5 ml. w/alcohol 9.5%. Bot. 3 oz., 6 oz.
Use: Antitussive, antihistamine, decongestant.

PERTUSSIN 8-HOUR COUGH FORMULA. (Che brough-Pond's) Dextromethorphan HBr /5 mg./5 w/alcohol 9.5%. Bot. 3 oz., 6 oz.
Use: Antitussive.

PERTUSSIN WILD BERRY COUGH SYR. (Chesebrough-Pond's) Dextromethorphan HBr mg., guaifenesin 25 mg./5 ml. w/alcohol 8.5%. 3 oz., 6 oz.
Use: Antitussive.

• **PERTUSSIS IMMUNE GLOBULIN.** U.S.P. XXI. (Cutter) A 16.5% solution of the gamma globulin fraction of blood from healthy, adult human donc hyperimmunized with pertussis vaccine. Vial 1.25 ml.
Use: Passive prevention and treatment of whoop cough.
See: Hypertussis, Vial (Cutter)

• **PERTUSSIS VACCINE,** U.S.P. XXI. (Various Mfr.)
Use: Active immunization against whooping cough.

• **PERTUSSIS VACCINE, ADSORBED,** U.S.P. XXI. Vial 7.5 cc.
Use: Active immunizing agent.

PERTUSSIS VACCINE AND DIPHTHERIA AND TETANUS TOXOIDS, COMBINED.
Use: Active immunizing agent.
See: Tri-Immunol, Vial (Lederle)
Triple Antigen, Vial (Wyeth)
Tri-Solgen, Vial, Hyporet (Lilly)

PERUVIAN BALSAM
Use: Local protectant, rubefacient.
W/Benzocaine, zinc oxide, bismuth subgallate, bori acid.
See: Anocaine, Supp. (Mallard)
W/Benzocaine, zinc oxide, 8-hydroxyquinoline ber ate, menthol. Unit of Use 90s. 50mg.: Bot. 100s, 1000s. Unit Dose 100s. 75mg.: Bot. 100s.
See: Hemorrhoidal Oint. (Towne)
W/Ephedrine sulfate, ext. belladonna, zinc oxide, boric acid, bismuth oxyiodide and subcarbonate.
See: Wyanoids, Preps. (Wyeth)

.idocaine, bismuth subgallate, Zn oxide, Al ubacetate.
ee: Xylocaine, Supp. (Astra)
Oxyquinoline sulfate, pramoxine HCl, zinc oxide.
ee: Zyanoid, Oint. (Elder)
ON. Sodium Lyapolate. Polyethenesulfonate odium.
se: Anticoagulant.
AVITE DROPS. (Vortech) Iron vitamin premix for mall animals.
AVITE TABLETS. (Vortech) Vit. A 1200 I.U., D-120 I.U., niacinamide 10 mg., B-1 1 mg., B-2 1 mg., -12 1 mcg., E 4 I.U., dicalcium phosphate anhydrous 40 mg., iron 6 mg., cobalt sulfate 0.068 mg., KI .068 mg., Cu acetate 0.156 mg./Tab. Bot. 50s.
se: Multiple vitamin for animals.
ERSON'S OINTMENT. (Peterson) Carbolic acid, amphor, tannic acid, zinc oxide. Tube w/pipe 1 oz. ar 16 oz. Can 1.4 oz., 3 oz.
se: Rectal irritation and hemorrhoids.
HADOL TABLETS. (Blue Cross) Merperidine HCl 0 mg. or 100 mg./Tab. Bot. 100s, 1000s.
se: Analgesic.
HIDINE HYDROCHLORIDE.
ee: Meperidine Hydrochloride, U.S.P. XXI.
N.
ee: Pentaerythritol tetranitrate.
RAZOLE. (Kenyon) Pentylenetetrazol 100 mg./cc. ial 30 cc.
RICHLORAL. Pentaerythritol chloral. 1,1′,1″,1‴-Neopentanetetrayl-tetraoxy)tetrakis [2,2,2-trichloro-thanol].
se: Sedative.
RO-20. (Foy) Pentaerythritol tetranitrate 20 g./Tab. Bot. 100s, 1000s.
ROGALAR. (Wyeth) Aqueous susp. of mineral oil 5%, plain. Bot. pt.
ROGALAR, PHENOLPHTHALEIN. (Wyeth) ineral oil 65%, phenolphthalein 0.3%. Bot. pt.
TROLATUM, U.S.P. XXI.
se: Ointment base.
ee: Lipkote, Stick (Plough)
TROLATUM GAUZE, U.S.P. XXI.
se: Surgical aid.
TROLATUM, HYDROPHILIC, U.S.P. XXI.
se: Absorbent ointment base; topical protectant.
ee: Lipkote, (Plough)
ROLATUM, LIQUID. Mineral Oil, U.S.P. XXI. Light ineral Oil, U.S.P. XXI. Adepsine Oil, Glymol, Liquid araffin, Parolein, White Mineral Oil, Heavy Liquid etrolatum.
se: Laxative.
ee: Clyserol Oil Retention Enema (Fuller Labs)
Fleet Mineral Oil Enema (Fleet)
Mineral Oil (Various Mfr.)
Nujol, Liq. (Plough)
Saxol (Var. Mfr.)
ROLATUM, LIQUID, EMULSION.
se: Lubricant cathartic.
ee: Milkinol, Liq. (Kremers-Urban)

W/Agar-Gel.
See: Agoral Plain, Liq. (Parke-Davis)
Petrogalar, Prep. (Wyeth)
W/Cascara.
See: Petrogalar w/Cascara, Emul. (Wyeth)
W/Docusate sodium.
See: Milkinol, Liq. (Kremers-Urban)
W/Irish moss, casanthranol.
See: Neo-Kondremul (Fisons)
W/Milk of magnesia.
See: Haley's M.O., Liq. (Winthrop Consumer Products)
Magoleum, Liq. (Blue Line)
W/Phenolphthalein.
See: Agoral, Emul. (Parke-Davis)
Petrogalar w/Phenolph., Emul. (Wyeth)
Phenolphthalein in liquid Petrolatum Emulsion.

PETROLATUM, RED VETERINARIAN. (Elder) Also known as RVP.
See: Rubrapet, Oint. (Medco)
W/Micasorb.
See: RV Plus, Oint. (Elder)
W/N-diethyl metatoluamide.
See: RV Pellent, Oint. (Elder)
W/Zinc oxide, 2-ethoxyethyl p-methoxycinnamate.
See: RV Paque, Oint. (Elder)

• **PETROLATUM, WHITE,** U.S.P. XXI.
Use: An oleaginous ointment base, topical protectant.
See: Moroline, Oint. (Plough)

PETRO-PHYLIC SOAP. (Doak) Hydrophilic Petrolatum cake 4 oz.
Use: Dry skin & infections.

PFIZER-E TABLETS. (Pfipharmecs) Erythromycin stearate 250 mg./Tab. Bot. 100s.
Use: Upper and lower respiratory, skin, and soft tissue infections.

PFIZERPEN A. (Pfipharmecs) Ampicillin. **Cap.:** 500 mg./Cap. Bot. 100s. **Oral Susp.:** 125 mg./5 cc. Bot. 100 cc., 200 cc.
Use: Antibiotic.

PFIZERPEN-AS. (Pfipharmecs) Procaine penicillin G. 3,000,000 u. in aqueous susp./Vial. Carton 5s. Multi-Vial Pack, Carton 100s.

PFIZERPEN G. (Pfipharmecs) Potassium penicillin G. **Tab.:** 200,000 u./Tab. Bot. 500s. 250,000 u./Tab. Bot. 100s. 400,000 u./Tab. Bot. 1000s.
Use: Antibiotic.

PFIZERPEN FOR INJECTION. (Pfipharmecs) Potassium penicillin G, buffered. Multi-Vial Pack: 1,000,000 u., 5,000,000 u./Vial. Carton 10s, 100s; Individual Vial: 20,000,000 u./Vial. 1s, 10s.

PFIZERPEN VK FOR ORAL SUSPENSION. (Pfipharmecs) Penicillin V potassium 125 mg./5 ml. Bot. 100 ml. 250 mg./5 ml. Bot. 200 ml.
Use: Antibiotic.

PFIZERPEN VK TABLETS. (Pfipharmecs) Penicillin V potassium 250 mg., 500 mg. (400,000 u., 800,000 u.)/Tab. **250 mg.** Bot. 100s, 1000s. **500 mg.** Bot. 100s.
Use: Antibiotic.

PGA. See: Folic Acid, U.S.P. XXI.
P.H. TABS. (Scrip) Glycine 180 mg., cal. carbonate 420 mg./Tab. Bot. 100s.
PHacid. (Baker/Cummins) Bot. 8 oz.
Use: Shampoo.
PHANODORM. Cyclobarbitone, B.A.N.
PHANQUINONE (I.N.N.). Phanquone, B.A.N.
PHANQUONE. B.A.N. 4,7-Phenanthroline-5,6-quinone. Phanquinone (I.N.N.)
Use: Treatment of amebiasis.
See: Entobex
PHARMAC-CORT. (Purepac) Hydrocortisone acetate cream 0.5%. Bot. 0.75 oz.
Use: Antipruritic.
PHARMALGEN. (Pharmacia) Freezedried hymenopteria venom/venom protein from honey bee, yellow jacket, yellow hornet white-faced hornet, wasp, mixed vespid. Diagnostic kit: 5 × 1 ml. Vial. Treatment kit: 6 × 1 ml. vial or 1 × 1.1 mg. multiple dose vial. Starter Kit: 6 × 1 ml., pre-diluted 0.01 mcg. to 100 mcg./ml.
Use: Diagnosis and treatment of Hymenoptera sting allergy.
PHARMALGEN RAST STANDARDIZED ALLERGENIC EXTRACTS-POLLENS. (Pharmacia) 100,000 allergenic units/Vial. Box 5 x 1 ml.
Use: Diagnosis & treatment of pollen allergy.
PHASPHORONE. (Metro Med) Bot. 8 oz.
Use: Oral antiseptic.
PHAZYME. (Reed & Carnrick) Simethicone 60 mg./Core Tab. Bot. 50s, 100s, 1000s.
Use: Digestant and antiflatulent.
PHAZYME-95. (Reed & Carnrick) Simethicone 95 mg./Core Tab. Bot. 100s.
Use: Digestant, antiflatulant.
PHAZYME PB. (Reed & Carnrick) Simethicone 60 mg., phenobarbital 15 mg./Core Tab. Bot. 100s, 1000s.
Use: Antiflatulent, sedative, enzyme combination.
PHEDIMETRAZINE TARTRATE.
Use: Sedative.
See: Melfiat Unicelles (Reid-Provident)
PHEDRAL. (Vortech) Phenobarbital 8 mg., theophylline 129 mg., ephedrine 24 mg./Tab. Bot. 1000s.
Use: Anti-asthmatic.
PHEMERIDE. Benzethonium Chloride, B.A.N.
• **PHEMFILCON A.** USAN.
Use: Contact lens material.
PHEMITHYN. (Davis & Sly) Benzethonium chloride monohydrate 3.17% Bot. W/measuring cap. 4 oz.
Use: Vaginal douche.
• **PHENACAINE HYDROCHLORIDE,** U.S.P. XXI. N,N′-Bis(p-ethoxy-phenyl)acetamidine HCl, monohydrate.
Use: Local anesthetic (ophthalmic).
W/Atropine, phenol, nut gall & zinc oxide.
See: Tanicaine, Oint. & Supp. (Upjohn)
W/Cod liver oil.
See: Morusan Ointment (Beecham Labs)
W/Ephedrine. (Upjohn) Phenocaine HCl 1%, epinephrine 1:25,000. Ophth. oint. Tube 1 dr.
W/Mercarbolide. (Upjohn) Holocaine HCl 2% & mercarbolide 1:3000. Ophth. oint., Tube w/applicator tip, 1 dr.
• **PHENACEMIDE,** U.S.P. XXI. Tab., U.S.P. XXI. Phenylacetylurea.
Use: Anticonvulsant.
See: Phenurone, Tab. (Abbott)
PHENACETIN. Acetophenetidin. Ethoxyacetanilide.
Use: Antipyretic, analgesic.
NOTE: The F.D.A. is currently reviewing this drug for possible withdrawal from the market due to liver and kidney toxicity. As a result, many manufacturers have already voluntarily removed this drug from their product lines. T drug is no longer official in the U.S.P.
PHENACETOPHEN. (Wolins) Aspirin 2.5 gr., phenacetin 3 gr., phenobarbital 0.25 gr./Cap. Bo 1000s.
PHENACETYLCARBAMIDE.
See: Phenurone, Tab. (Abbott)
PHENACETYLUREA.
See: Phenurone, Tab. (Abbott)
PHENACRIDANE. (9(p-Hexloxphenyl)-10-methyl-acridinium chloride.
See: Micridium (Johnson & Johnson)
PHENACTROPINIUM CHLORIDE. B.A.N. N-Phena homatropinium chloride. Trophenium.
Use: Hypotensive.
PHENACYL HOMATROPHINIUM HCl. Not availab.
PHENADOXONE. B.A.N. 6-Morpholino-4,4-dipheny heptan-3-one. Heptalgin hydrochloride.
Use: Analgesic; hypnotic.
PHENAGESIC. (Dalin) Phenylephrine HCl 10 mg., phenylpropanolamine HCl 50 mg., pyrilamine maleate 25 mg., pheniramine maleate 25 mg., acetyl-p-aminophenol 300 mg./Tab. or 5 ml. **Tab.** 50. **Syrup** without acetaminophen. Bot. 6 oz., pt.
Use: Treatment for the common cold.
PHENAGLYCODOL. B.A.N. 2-p-Chlorophenyl-3-me yl-2,3-butanediol. 2-(4-Chlorophenyl)-3-methy tane-2,3-diol.
Use: Central nervous system depressant.
See: Ultran, Pulvule, Tab. (Lilly)
W/Acetylsalicylic acid, dextro-propoxyphene.
See: Darvo-Tran, Pulvule. (Lilly)
PHENAHIST. (Robinson) Phenylephrine HCl 5 mg., chlorpheniramine maleate 2 mg., salicylamide 20 mg., caffeine 15 mg., C 20 mg., citrus bioflavonc 10 mg./Cap. Bot. 100s, 1000s. Vials 20s, Bulk Pack 5000s.
Use: Cold and hay fever symptoms.
PHENAHIST INJECTABLE. (T.E. Williams) Atropin sulfate 0.2 mg., phenylpropanolamine HCl 12.5 r chlorpheniramine maleate 5 mg./ml. Vial 10 cc.
Use: Decongestant/antihistamine.
PHENAHIST-TR CAPSULES. (T.E. Williams) Phen lephrine HCl 10 mg., phenylpropanolamine HCl mg., Chlorpheniramine maleate 12 mg./Cap. Bot 100s.
Use: Decongestant, antihistamine.
PHENALZINE DIHYDROGEN SULFATE.
See: Nardil, Tab. (Parke-Davis)

IENAMAZOLINE HCl. 2-(Anilinomethyl)-2-imidazoline HCl.
Use: Vasoconstrictor.

IENAMETH TABLETS. (Major) Promethazine 25 mg./Tab. Bot. 1000s.
Use: Antihistaminic, antiemetic.

IENAMINE ELIXIR. (Scrip) Diphenhydramine HCl 10 mg./4 cc. Bot. pt.

IENAMPROMIDE. B.A.N. N-(1-Methyl-2-piperidinoethyl)propionanilide.
Use: Analgesic.

IENANTOIN. Mephenytoin. N-Methyl-5,5-phenylethylhydantoin.
See: Mesantoin, Tab. (Sandoz)

IENAPHEN. (Robins) Acetaminophen 325 mg./Cap. Bot. 100s, 1000s.
Use: Analgesic, antipyretic.

IENAPHEN WITH CODEINE. (Robins) **No. 2:** Acetaminophen 325 mg., codeine 15 mg./Cap.; **No. 3:** Acetaminophen 325 mg., codeine 30 mg./Cap.; **No. 4:** Acetaminophen 325 mg., codeine 60 mg./Cap. Bot. 100s, 500s. Dis-Co packs 4 × 25s.
Use: Analgesic.

HENAPHEN-650 WITH CODEINE. (Robins) Codeine phosphate 30 mg., acetaminophen 650 mg./Tab. Bot. 50s. Dis-Co packs 4 × 25s.
Use: Analgesic.

HENAPHTHAZINE. Sod. dinitro phenylazonaphthol disulfonate.
See: Nitrazine paper, Roll (Squibb)

HENARSONE SULFOXYLATE. (5-Arsono-2-hydroxyanilino)methanesulfinic acid disodium salt.
Use: Antiamebic.

HENASPIRIN COMPOUND CAPSULES. (Lannett) Aspirin 3.5 gr., phenobarbital 0.25 gr./Cap. Bot. 1000s, 5000s.

HENASPIRIN COMPOUND. (Davis & Sly) Phenobarbital 0.25 gr., aspirin 3.5 gr./Cap. Bot. 1000s.

HENATIN. (Jenkins) Acetophenetidin 0.2 Gm., acid acetylsalicylic 0.25 Gm., caffeine 30 mg., camphor monobromated 0.1 Gm./Tab. Bot. 1000s.
Use: Analgesic, anodyne.

HENATIN TD CAPSULE. (Jenkins) Phenylpropanolamine HCl 50 mg., chlorpheniramine maleate 1 mg., pheniramine maleate 12.5 mg., atropine sulfate 0.025 mg., scopolamine HBr 0.014 mg., belladonna alkaloids (total) 0.16 mg., hyoscyamine sulfate 0.122 mg./Cap. Bot. 1000s.

HENATUSS. (Dalin) Codeine phosphate 10 mg., chlorpheniramine maleate 2 mg., phenylephrine HCl 5 mg., guaifenesin 100 mg., 1-menthol 1 mg./5 cc. Bot. 4 oz., pt., gal.
Use: Antitussive.

HENAZINE. (Jenkins) Phendimetrazine bitartrate 50 mg./cc. Vial 10 cc.
Use: Anorexic.

HENAZINE. (Keene) Promethazine HCl 25 mg. or 50 mg. Vial 10 ml.
Use: Antihistaminic, antiemetic, sedative.

PHENAZOCINE. B.A.N. 1,2,3,4,5,6-Hexahydro-6,11-dimethyl-3-phenethyl-2,6-methano-3-benzazocin-8-ol.
Use: Analgesic; antipyretic.
See: Narphen hydrobromide.

PHENAZOCINE HBr. 1,2,3,4,5,6-Hexahydro-8-hydroxy-6,11-dimethyl-3-phenethyl-2,6-methano-3-benzazocine HBr.
Use: Analgesic.

PHENAZODINE. (Lannett) Phenylazodiamine-pyridine HCl 0.1 Gm./Tab. Bot. 100s, 500s, 1000s.
Use: Urinary antiseptic.

PHENAZONE.
See: Antipyrine. (Various Mfr.)

PHENAZOPYRIDINE. B.A.N. 2,6-Diamino-3-phenylazopyridine. Gastrotest.
Use: Analgesic.
See: Pyridium (hydrochloride).
W/Azo-sulfisoxazole.
See: Azo-Sulfisoxazole, Tab. (Fellows-Testagar)
W/Sulfisoxazole.
See: Azocet, Tab. (O'Neal)
Azo-Urizole, Tab. (Jenkins)
G-Sox-Azo, Tab. (Scrip)

• **PHENAZOPYRIDINE HCl,** U.S.P. XXI. Tab., U.S.P. XXI. 2,6-Diamino-3-phenylazopyridine HCl.
Use: Analgesic (urinary tract).
See: Azodine, Tab. (Vortech)
Azogesic, Tab. (Century)
Azo-Pyridon, Tab. (Reid-Provident)
Azo-Standard, Tab. (Webcon)
Azo-Sulfizin (Reid-Provident)
Baridium, Tab. (Barry Martin)
Diridone, Tab. (Premo)
Phen-Azo, Tab. (Vanguard)
Phenazodine, Tab. (Lannett)
Phenyl-Idium Prods. (Quality Generics)
Pyridium, Tab. (Parke-Davis)
Uri-Pak (Westerfield)
Urodine, Tab. (Saron)

PHENAZOPYRIDINE HCl W/COMBINATIONS.
See: Azo-Cyst, Tab. (Moore Kirk)
Azo Gantanol, Tab. (Roche)
Azo Gantrisin, Tab. (Roche)
Azolate, Tab. (Amfre-Grant)
Azo-Mandelamine, Tab. (Parke-Davis)
Azo-Methalate, Tab. (Vortech)
Azosoxazole, Tab. (Quality Generics)
Azosul, Tab. (Reid-Provident)
Azosulfisoxazole (Var. Mfr.)
Azo-Sulfstat, Tab. (Saron)
Azotrex, Cap. (Bristol Labs.)
Azox, Tab. (Elder)
Buren, Tab. (Ascher)
G-Sox-Azo, Tab. (Scrip)
Mandalay A.P., Tab. (Beutlich)
Prov-U-Sep Forte, Tab. (Reid-Provident)
Pyridium Plus, Tab. (Parke-Davis)
Rosoxol-Azo, Tab. (Robinson)
Soxazo, Tab. (Sutliff & Case)
Suladyne, Tab. (Stuart)
Suldiazo, Tab. (Kay)

Sulfasol Plus, Tab. (Hyrex)
Thiosulfil-A, Tab. (Ayerst)
Thiosulfil-A Forte, Tab. (Ayerst)
Triurisul, Tab. (Sheryl)
Uridium, Tab. (Ferndale; Pharmex)
Uri-Pak, Tab. (Westerfield)
Urisan-P, Tab. (Sandia)
Uritral, Cap. (Central)
Urobiotic, Cap. (Pfizer)
Urochron, Tab. (Saron)
Urogesic, Tab. (Edwards)
Uropeutic, Tab. (Circle)
Urotrol, Tab. (Mills)
Urseptic, Tab. (Century)

PHENBENICILLIN. B.A.N. 6-(α-Phenoxyphenylacetamido)pencillanic acid. α-Phenoxybenzylpenicillin.
Use: Antibiotic.
See: Penspek [potassium salt].

• **PHENBUTAZONE SODIUM GLYCERATE.** USAN. 4-Butyl-3-hydroxy-1,2-diphenyl-3-pyrazolin-5-one sodium salt compound with glycerol.
Use: Anti-inflammatory.

PHENBUTRAZATE. B.A.N. 2-(3-Methyl-2-phenylmorpholino)ethyl 2-phenylbutryate.
Use: Appetite suppressant.

PHENCAP. (Jenkins) Phenylpropanolamine HCl 50 mg., chlorpheniramine maleate 8 mg., atropine sulfate 1/180 gr./Cap. Bot. 1000s.

• **PHENCARBAMIDE.** USAN. S-2-Diethyl-ammoethyl diphenylthiocarbamate.
Use: Spasmolytic agent.
See: Escorpal (Farben-Fabriken)

PHENCEN-50. (Central) Promethazine HCl 50 mg., disodium edetate 0.1 mg. calcium Cl. 0.04 mg., phenol 5 mg., /ml. Vial 10 ml. Box 12s.
Use: Antihistaminic, anti-emetic.

PHENCHLOR-EIGHT. (Freeport) Chlorpheniramine maleate 8 mg./T.R. Cap. Bot. 1000s.
Use: Antihistaminic.

PHENCHLOR-TWELVE. (Freeport) Chlorpheniramine maleate 12 mg./T.R. Cap. Bot. 1000s.
Use: Antihistaminic.

PHENCYCLIDINE. B.A.N. 1-(1-Phenylcyclohexyl)piperidine.
Use: Anticholinergic.

• **PHENCYCLIDINE HYDROCHLORIDE.** USAN. 1-(1-Phenylcyclohexyl)piperidine HCl.
Use: Anticholinergic.

PHENDIMETRAZINE. B.A.N. (+)-3,4-Dimethyl-2-phenylmorpholine.
Use: Appetite suppressant.
See: Plegine [tartrate].

• **PHENDIMETRAZINE TARTRATE**, U.S.P. XXI. Cap., Tab., U.S.P. XXI. d-3,4-Dimethyl-2-phenylmorpholine bitartrate.
Use: Anorexic.
See: Adipost, Cap. (Ascher)
Adphen, Tab. (Ferndale)
Anorex, Cap., Tab. (Dunhall)
Bacarate, Tab. (Reid-Provident)
B.O.F. (Saron)
Bontril PDM, Tab. (Carnrick)
Delcozine, Tab. (Delco)
Di-Ap-Trol, Tab. (Foy)
Di-Metrex, Tab. (Fellows-Testagar)
Elphemet, Tab. (Canright)
Ex-Obese, Tab. (Kay)
Limit, Tab. (Bock)
Melfiat, Tab. (Reid-Provident)
Melfiat 105, Cap. (Reid-Provident)
Minus, Tab. (Amfre-Grant)
Obacin, Tab. (Kenyon)
Obalan, Tab. (Lannett)
Obepar, Tabs. (Parmed)
Obe-Tite, Tab. (Scott/Cord)
Obezine, Tab. (Western Research)
Phenazine, Inj. (Jenkins)
Phendorex, Tab. (Wolins)
Phen-70, Tab. (Parmed)
Phentazine, Tab. (Sutliff & Case)
Phenzine, Tab. (Mallard)
Prelu-2, Cap. (Boehringer Ingelheim)
Reducto, Tab. (Arcum)
Robese "P", Tabs., Vial (Rocky Mtn.)
Ropledge, Tab. (Robinson)
Slim-Tabs, Tab. (Wesley)
SPRX 1, 2 & 3 (Reid-Provident)
Statobex, Prods. (Lemmon)
Stodex, Tab., Cap. (Jalco)
Trimtabs, Tab. (Mayrand)
Weightrol, Prep., Tab. (Vortech)

PHENDOREX. (Wolins) Phendimetrazine tartrate 35 mg./Tab. Bot. 1000s.

PHENELZINE. B.A.N. Phenethylhydrazine.
Use: Antidepressant.
See: Nardil [hydrogen sulfate].

• **PHENELZINE SULFATE,** U.S.P. XXI. Tab., U.S.P. XXI. Phenethylhydrazine sulfate. Monoamine oxidase inhibitor, betaphenylethyl-hydrazine dihydrogen sulfate.
Use: Antidepressant.
See: Nardil, Tab. (Parke-Davis)

PHENEREX. (Tunex) Promethazine HCl 50 mg./ml. Vial 10cc.
Use: Management of motion sickness, nausea, vomiting associated with pregnancy.

PHENERGAN. (Wyeth) Promethazine HCl in various dosage forms.

PHENERGAN-D. (Wyeth) Promethazine HCl 6.25 mg pseudoephedrine HCl 60 mg./Tab. Bot. 100s.
Use: Antihistaminic/decongestant.

PHENERGAN INJECTION. (Wyeth) Promethazine HC 25 or 50 mg./ml. Amp. 1 mg. Pkg. 5s, 25s.
Use: Antihistaminic.

PHENERGAN PEDIATRIC. (Wyeth) Dextromethorphan HBr 7.5 mg., promethazine HCl 5.0 mg., f ext. ipecac 0.17 min., pot. guaiacolsulfonate 44 mg., citric acid 60 mg., sod. citrate 197 mg., alcohol 7%/5 cc. Bot. 4 oz., 6 oz., pt. gal.
Use: Antitussive, antihistaminic.

ENERGAN SUPPOSITORIES. (Wyeth) romethazine HCl 12.5 mg., 25 mg., or 50 ng./Supp. Box. 12s, Redipaks.
Jse: Antihistaminic.

ENERGAN SYRUP FORTIS. (Wyeth) Promethazine ICl 25 mg./5 ml. Bot. pt.
Jse: Antihistaminic.

ENERGAN SYRUP PLAIN. (Wyeth) Promethazine ICl 6.25 mg./5 ml. Bot. 4 oz., 6 oz., 8 oz., pt., gal.
Jse: Antihistaminic.

ENERGAN TABLETS. (Wyeth) Promethazine HCl 12.5 mg., 25 mg., or 50 mg./Tab. Bot. 100s, 1000s. Redipaks.

ENERGAN VC. (Wyeth) Promethazine HCl 6.25 mg., phenylephrine HCl 5 mg./5 ml. Bot. 4 oz., 6 oz., 8 oz., pt., gal.
Use: Antihistaminic, decongestant.

ENERGAN VC WITH CODEINE. (Wyeth) Promethazine HCl 6.25 mg., codeine phosphate 10 mg., phenylephrine HCl 5 mg./5 ml. Bot. 4 oz., 6 oz., 8 oz., pt., gal.
Use: Antihistaminic, decongestant, antitussive.

ENERGAN WITH CODEINE. (Wyeth) Promethazine HCl 6.25 mg., codeine 10 mg./5 ml. Bot. 4 oz., 6 oz., 8 oz., pt., gal.
Use: Antihistaminic, antitussive.

ENERGAN WITH DEXTROMETHORPHAN. (Wyeth) Promethazine HCl 6.25 mg., dextromethorphan HBr 15 mg./5 ml. Bot. 4 oz., 6 oz., pt., gal.
Use: Antihistaminic, antitussive.

ENERHIST. (Rocky Mtn.) Promethazine HCl 25 mg., 50 mg./cc. Vial 10 cc.
Use: Antihistamine.

ENERIDINE. 1-(β-Phenyl-b-ethyl)-4-carbethoxy-4-phenylpiperidine. Ethyl 1-phenethyl-4-phenylisonipecotate.
Use: Analgesic.

ENETHICILLIN. B.A.N. 6-(α-Phenoxypropion-amido)penicillanic acid. Broxil [potassium salt].
Use: Antibiotic.

HENETHICILLIN POTASSIUM. Alpha-phenoxyethyl penicillin pot. Penicillin-152 pot.
Use: Antibiotic.
See: Chemipen

HENETHYL ALCOHOL. B.A.N. 2-Phenylethanol.
Use: Antiseptic.

PHENETHYLBIGUANIDE MONOHYDROCHLORIDE. Phenformin Hydrochloride.

HENETRON. (Lannett) Chlorpheniramine maleate 8 mg., or 12 mg./Lanacap or Lanatab. Bot. 100s, 1000s. Tabs. 4 mg., Bot. 500s, 1000s.
Use: Antihistaminic.

HENETRON COMPOUND TABLETS. (Lannett) Salicylamide 3.5 gr., phenacetin 2.5 gr., caffeine 0.5 gr., chlorprophenpyridamine maleate 2 mg./Tab. Bot. 100s, 1000s.

HENETRON INJECTABLE. (Lannett) Chlorpheniramine maleate Amp. (10 mg./cc.) 1 cc. 25s, 100s, Vial 30 cc. (100 mg./cc.) Vial 5 cc.

HENETRON SYRUP. (Lannett) Chlorpheniramine maleate 2 mg./4 cc. Bot. pt., gal.

PHENETSAL.

PHENETURIDE. B.A.N. (2-Phenylbutyryl)urea. Ethylphenacemide (I.N.N.) Benuride.
Use: Anticonvulsant.

PHENFORMIN. B.A.N. 1-Phenethylbiguanide.
Use: Oral hypoglycemic agent.
Note: Drug recalled from market 10-23-77.

PHENFORMIN HCl. Imidodicarbonimidic diamide, nN-(2-phenylethyl)-monohydrochloride. N^1-β-Phenethylbiguanide HCl.
Use: Hypoglycemic.
Note: Withdrawn from market in 1978.

PHENGLUTARIMIDE. B.A.N. 2-(2-Diethylaminoethyl)-2-phenylglutarimide. Aturbane hydrochloride.
Use: Treatment of the Parkinsonian syndrome.

PHENIFORM.
See: Phenformin HCl

PHENILAR. (Blue Cross) Dextromethorphan HBr 15 mg., guaifenesin 50 mg., chlorpheniramine maleate 2 mg., phenylephrine HCl 5 mg., acetaminophen 120 mg./10 ml. Bot. 4 oz.
Use: Cough syrup.

PHENINDAMINE. B.A.N. 1,2,3,4-Tetrahydro-2-methyl-9-phenyl-2-azafluorene. 2,3,4,9-Tetrahydro-2-methyl-9-phenyl-1H-indeno-[2,1-c]pyridine. Thephorin [hydrogentartrate].
Use: Antihistamine.

PHENINDAMINE TARTRATE. 2,3,4,9-Tetrahydro-2-methyl-9 phenyl-1 H-indeno-[2,1-c] pyridine bitartrate. 2,3,4,9-Tetrahydro-2-methyl-9-phenyl-IH-indeno-(2,1-c)pyridine Tartrate (1:1).
Use: Antihistaminic.
See: Nolahist, Tab. (Carnrick)
Thephorin, Tab. (Roche)
W/Chlorpheniramine maleate, phenylpropanolamine HCl.
See: Nolamine, Tab. (Carnrick)
W/Codeine phosphate, phenylephrine HCl, fl. ext. ipecac, pot. guaiacolsulfonate, sodium citrate, citric acid.
See: Cerose, Liq. (Ives)
W/Dextromethorphan HBr, phenylephrine, fl. ext. ipecac, pot. guaiacolsulfonate, sod. citrate, citric acid.
See: Cerose DM, Elix. (Ives)
W/Phenylephrine HCl, aspirin, caffeine, aluminum hydroxide, magnesium carbonate.
See: Dristan, Tab. (Whitehall)
W/Phenylephrine hydrochloride, caramiphen ethanedisulfonate.
See: Dondril, Tab. (Whitehall)
W/Phenylephrine HCl, chlorpheniramine maleate, drytane.
See: Comhist, Tab., Elix. (Baylor)
W/Phenylephrine HCl, chlorpheniramine maleate, belladonna alkaloids.
See: Comhist L.A., Caps. (Baylor Labs.)
W/Phenylephrine HCl, pyrilamine maleate, chlorpheniramine maleate, dextromethorphan HBr.
See: Histalet, Histalet-DM, Histalet-Forte, Syr. (Reid-Provident)

• **PHENINDIONE,** U.S.P. XXI. Tab., U.S.P. XXI. (2-Phenylindane-1,3-Dione; 2-Phenyl-1,3-indandione; Phenylindanedion, Dindevan)
Use: Anticoagulant.
See: Eridione, Tab. (Eric, Kirk & Gary)
Hedulin, Tab. (Merrell Dow)

PHEN-IODINE NO. 2. (Sutliff & Case) Iodine 0.4%, tannic acid 1.1%, phenol 5%. Ext. of witch hazel, glycerin q.s. Bot., pt., gal.
Use: Antiseptic.

PHENIODOL.
See: Iodoalphionic Acid (Var. Mfr.)

PHENIPRAZINE. B.A.N. α-Methylphenethylhydrazine. Cavodil [hydrochloride].
Use: Monoamine oxidase inhibitor.

PHENIPRAZINE HCl. (α-Methyl-phenethyl)-hydrazine monohydrochloride.
Use: Antihypertensive.

PHENIRAMINE. B.A.N. 1-Phenyl-1-(2-pyridyl)-3-dimethylaminopropane. ($\pm$)-3-Phenyl-3-(2-pyridyl)propyldimethylamine. Daneral 4-amino-salicylate; Trimeton [maleate].
Use: Antihistamine.

PHENIRAMINE MALEATE. 2-[a-[2-(Dimethylamino)ethyl]benzyl]-pyridine bimaleate. Prophenpyridamine.
Use: Antihist.
See: Inhiston, Tab. (Plough)
W/Combinations:
Allerstat, Cap. (Lemmon)
Chexit, Tab. (Dorsey)
Citra Forte, Cap., Syr. (Boyle)
Corizahist, Tab. (Mason)
Decobel, Cap. (Lannett)
Dri-Hist No. 2 Meta-Kaps (Sutliff & Case)
Fiogesic, Tab. (Sandoz)
Fitacol Stankaps (Standex)
Flavihist, Cap. (American Labs.)
Incorpohist, Tab. (Blue Line)
Kenahist-S.A., Tab. (Kenyon)
Klix Kernal Kaps, Cap. (Bowman)
Koldeze, Cap. (Scrip)
MSC Triaminic, Tab. (Dorsey)
Naso-Dex, Cap. (Commerce)
Partuss AC (Parmed)
Phenagesic, Tab., Syr. (Dalin)
Phenaphen Plus, Tab. (Robins)
Poly-Histine Caps., Elix., Lipospan (Bock)
Propahist, Cap., Tab., Syr. (Blue Line)
Pyma, Cap. (Fellows-Testagar)
Robitussin-AC, Syr. (Robins)
S.A.C., Cold Caps. (Towne)
Symptrol, Syr., Cap., Inj. (Saron)
T.A.C., Caps. (Towne)
Thor, Caps. (Towne)
Triaminic, Preps. (Dorsey)
Triaminicol, Syr. (Dorsey)
Trigelamine, Oint. (Edward J. Moore)
Tritussin, Syr. (Towne)
Triwol, Tab. (Wolins)
Tussagesic, Tab., Susp. (Dorsey)
Tussar-2, Syr. (Armour)
Ursinus, Tab. (Dorsey)
Ventilade, Syr. (Warren-Teed)
Woltac, Cap. (Wolins)

PHENISTIX REAGENT STRIPS. (Ames) Ferric and magnesium salts with cyclohexylsulfamic acid. Di and-test for phenylketonuria. Bot. 50s, 100s. F wrapped 3s.
Use: Test urine for phenylketone.

PHEN-LETS. (Jenkins) Phenylpropanolamine HCl 1 mg./Tab. Bot. 1000s.

PHENMETRAZINE. B.A.N. ($\pm$)-trans-Tetrahydro methyl-2-phenyl-1,4-oxazine. 3-Methyl-2-phenyl-m pholine. Preludin hydrochloride.
Use: Appetite suppressant.

• **PHENMETRAZINE HCl,** U.S.P. XXI. Tab., U.S.P. XXI. 3-Methyl-2-phenylmorpholine hydrochloride.
Use: Anorexic.
See: Melfiat, Tab. (Reid-Provident)
Preludin, Tab., Endurets (Boehringer Ingelheim)

• **PHENOBARBITAL,** U.S.P. XXI. Elixir, Tab., U.S.P. XXI. 2,4,6(1H,3H,%H) Pyrimidinetrione, 5-ethyl-phenyl. 5-Ethyl-5-phenylbarbituric acid. Phenyleth barbituric acid, phenylethylmalonylurea, Barbenyl, Dormiral, Duneryl, Neurobarb, Numol, Phenonyl, Somonal.
Use: Anticonvulsant, hypnotic, sedative.
See: Bar Elix., (Scrip)
Barbipil, Pill (Vortech)
Barbita, Pill (Vortech)
Henomint, Elix. (Bowman)
Hypnette, Supp., Tab. (Fleming)
Orprine, Liq. (Pennwalt)
Pheno-Square, Tab. (Mallard)
Sedadrops, Liq. (Merrell Dow)
SK-Phenobarbital, Tab. (SmithKline)
Solu-barb, Tab. (Fellows-Testagar)

PHENOBARBITAL W/AMINOPHYLLINE.
See: Aminophylline (Var. Mfr.)

PHENOBARBITAL W/ATROPINE SULFATE.
See: Atropine Sulfate (Var. Mfr.) P.A., Tab. (Scrip)

PHENOBARBITAL W/BELLADONNA.
See: Belladonna Products and Phenobarbital Combinations.

PHENOBARBITAL WITH CENTRAL NERVOUS SYSTEM STIMULANTS.
See: Amodrine, Tab. (Searle)
Arcotrate No. 3, Tab. (Arcum)
Asminyl, Tab. (Cole)
Belkatal, Tab. (Ferndale)
Bellophen, Tab. (Richlyn)
Bowdrin, Tab. (Bowman)
Bronkolixir, Elix. (Winthrop-Breon)
Bronkotab, Tab. (Winthrop-Breon)
Duovent, Tab. (Riker)
Ephenyllin, Tab. (CMC)
Luasmin, Cap. (Cooper)
Peritrate w/Phenobarbital, Tab. (Parke-Davis)
Phelantin, Cap. (Parke-Davis)
Phyldrox, Tab. (Lemmon)
Quadrinal, Susp., Tab. (Knoll)
Sedamine, Tab. (Dunhall)
Sedatromine, Tab. (Sutliff & Case)

Spabelin, Elix., Tab. (Arcum)
Synophedal, Tab. (Central)
T.E.P., Tab. (Kirkman)
T-E-P Compound, Tab. (Stanlabs)

HENOBARBITAL COMBINATIONS.
See: Aminophylline W/Phenobarbital, Combinations
Aspirin-Barbiturate, Combinations
Atropine-Hyoscine-Hyoscyamine Combinations
Atropine Sulfate w/Phenobarbital
Belladonna Ext. Combinations
Belladonna Products & Phenobarbital Combinations
Homatropine Methylbromide & Phenobarbital Combinations
Hyoscyamus Products & Phenobarbital Combinations.
Mannitol Hexanitrate w/Phenobarbital Combinations
Mephenesin & Barbiturates Combinations
Phenobarbital W/Central Nervous System Stimulants
Secobarbital Combinations
Sodium Nitrite Combinations
Theobromine W/Phenobarbital Combinations
Theophylline W/Phenobarbital Combinations
Veratrum Viride W/Phenobarbital Combinations

ᴾHENOBARBITAL W/HOMATROPINE METHYLBROMIDE.
See: Homatropine Methylbromide & Phenobarbital Combinations

ᴾHENOBARBITAL W/HYOSCYAMUS.
See: Hyoscyamus Products & Phenobarbital Combinations

ᴾHENOBARBITAL W/MANNITOL HEXANITRATE.
Use: Anticonvulsant, hypnotic, sedative.
See: Mannitol Hexanitrate w/Phenobarbital Combinations

• **PHENOBARBITAL SODIUM,** U.S.P. XXI. Inj., Sterile, Tab., U.S.P. XXI. Sodium 5-ethyl-5-phenylbarbiturate. 2,4,6(1H,3H,5H)-Pyrimidinetrione, 5-ethyl-5 phenyl, monosodium salt. (Sod. Phenylethylbarbiturate, Soluble Phenobarbital). (Various Mfr.)
Use: Anticonvulsant, hypnotic, sedative.
See: Luminal Sod., Sol. (Winthrop-Breon)

PHENOBARBITAL SODIUM IN PROPYLENE GLYCOL. Vitarine-Amp. (0.13 Gm.) 1 cc., Box 25s, 100s. (2 gr.) 1 cc., Box 25s, 100s.
Use: Anticonvulsant, hypnotic, sedative.

PHENOBARBITAL & THEOBROMINE COMBINATIONS.
See: Theobromine w/Phenobarbital Combinations

PHENOBARBITAL W/THEOPHYLLINE.
See: Theophylline w/Phenobarbital Combinations

PHENOBARBITAL W/VERATRUM VIRIDE.
See: Veratrum Viride w/Phenobarbital Combinations

PHEN-O-BEL-T. (Coastal) Phenobarbital 50 mg., hyoscyamine sulfate 0.311 mg., atropine sulfate 0.0582 mg., hyoscine HBr 0.0195 mg./T.R. Cap. Bot. 100s, 1000s.
Use: Sedative.

PHENOBUTIODIL. B.A.N. w-(2,4,6-Triiodophenoxy)-butyric acid. Vesipaque (Warner-Lambert)
Use: Radiopaque substance.
See: Biliodyl.

PHENOCTIDE. Octaphonium Chloride, B.A.N.

PHENODODECINIUM BROMIDE. Domiphen bromide, B.A.N.

PHENODYNE. (Blue Line) Aspirin 3.5 gr., acetophenetidin 2.5 gr., caffeine 0.5 gr., phenolphthalein 0.25 gr./Cap. Bot. 100s, 1000s.
Use: Orally, analgesic & antipyretic w/laxative.

PHENODYNE W/CODEINE PHOS. (Blue Line) Aspirin 3.5 gr., phenacetin 2.5 gr., phenolphthalein 0.25 gr., caffeine (hydrous) 0.5 gr., codeine phosphate 0.25 gr./Cap. Bot. 1000s. 0.5 gr./Cap. Bot. 100s, 1000s.
Use: Analgesic-antipyretic.

PHENOGESIC. (Wolins) Acetaminophen 325 mg., phenyltoloxamine 30 mg./Tab. Bot. 100s, 1000s.

PHENOJECT. (Mayrand) Promethazine HCl 25 mg., 50 mg./ml. Vial 10 ml.

• **PHENOL,** U.S.P. XXI. Liq., U.S.P. XXI. (Various Mfr.) Carbolic acid.
Use: Pharm. aid (preservative), topical antipruritic.
W/Aluminum hydroxide, zinc oxide, camphor, eucalyptol, ichthammol, thyme oil.
See: Almophen, Oint. (Bowman)
W/Benzocaine, ichthammol, balsam peru, alum exsic., oil cade, oil eucalyptus, carbolic oil.
See: Alucaine, Oint. (Jenkins)
W/Benzocaine, triclosan,
See: Solarcaine Pump Spray (Plough)
W/Dextromethorphan
See: Chloraseptic DM Lozenges (Eaton)
W/Resorcinol.
See: Black & White Ointment (Plough)
W/Resorcinol, boric acid, basic fuchsin, acetone.
See: Castellani's Paint, Liq. (Various Mfr.)

• **PHENOLATE SODIUM.** USAN.
Use: Disinfectant.

PHENOLAX. (Upjohn) Phenolphthalein 64.8 mg./Wafer. Bot. 100s.
Use: Mild laxative.

• **PHENOL, LIQUEFIED,** U.S.P. XXI.
Use: Topical antipruritic.

• **PHENOLPHTHALEIN,** U.S.P. XXI. Tab., U.S.P. XXI. (Various Mfr.) 3,3-Bis(p-hydroxyphenyl)phthalide. Pkg. 1 oz., 0.25 lb., 1 lb.
Use: Cathartic.
See: Alophen, Pill (Parke-Davis)
Espotabs, Tab. (Combe)
Evac-U-Lax, Wafer. (Mallard)
Evasof, Tab. (Lemmon)
Ex-Lax Preps. (Ex-Lax)
Feen-A-Mint, Tab. & Gum (Plough)
Phenolax, Wafers (Upjohn)

PHENOLPHTHALEIN W/COMBINATIONS.
See: Amlax, Tab. (Vortech)
Bicholate, Tab. (Blue Line)
Bilocomp, Tab. (Lannett)
Bilstan (Standex)
Correctol, Tab. (Plough)
Dibolans, Tab. (Noyes)

Disolan, Cap. (Lannett)
Evac-Q-Kit, Tab., Supp. (Warren-Teed)
Evac-U-Gen, Tab. (Walker)
Dual Formula Feen-A-Mint Pills. (Plough)
Feen-A-Mint, Gum, Mint, Pills (Plough)
Formula No. 3656, Tab. (Blue Line)
4-Way Cold Tabs. (Bristol-Myers)
Glycols, Tab. (Bowman)
Lanothal Pills (Lannett)
Laxogen, Tab. (Vortech)
Novalax, Cap. (Coastal)
Oxiphen, Tab. (Webcon)
Petrogalar W/Phenolphthalein, Liq. (Wyeth)
Petrolatum, Liq.
Phenodyne, Cap., Tab. (Blue Line)
Sarolax, Cap. (Saron)
Taurocolate, Tab. (Vortech)
Torocol, Tab. (Plessner)
Torocol Compound, Tab. (Plessner)
Tripalax, Cap. (Redford)

PHENOLPHTHALEIN IN LIQUID PETROLATUM EMULSION. (Various Mfr.)
See: Petrolatum, Liq.

• **PHENOLPHTHALEIN YELLOW.** U.S.P. XXI.
Use: Cathartic.

PHENOL RED.
See: Phenolsulfonphthalein

PHENOLSULFONATES.
See: Sulfocarbolates

PHENOLSULFONIC ACID. Sulfocarbolic acid.
Note use in Sulphodine, Tab. (Strasenburgh)

• **PHENOLSULFONPHTHALEIN,** U.S.P. XXI. Inj., U.S.P. XXI. α-Hydroxy-α,α-bis(p-hydroxyphenyl)-o-toluene-sulfonic acid)sulfone. 4,4′-(3H-2,1-Benzoxathiol-3-ylidene)-diphenol S,S-dioxide. (Various Mfr.)
Use: I.M., & I.V.; diagnostic aid. Also for renal function.

PHENOLTETRABROMOPHTHALEIN. Disulfonate Disodium.
See: Sulfobromophthalein Sodium, U.S.P. XXI.

PHENOLZINE SULFATE. β-Phenylethylhydrazine hydrogen sulfate.

PHENOMORPHAN. B.A.N. 3-Hydroxy-N-phenethylmorphinan.
Use: Narcotic analgesic.

PHENOPERIDINE. B.A.N. Ethyl 1-(3-hydroxy-3-phenylpropyl)-4-phenylpiperidine-4-carboxylate. Operidine hydrochloride.
Use: Narcotic analgesic.

PHENOTHIATAL ELIXIR. (Fellows) Phenobarbital 0.25 gr., B-1 5 mg., hyoscine HBr 0.0065 mg., atropine sulfate 0.0194 mg., hyoscyamine 0.1037 mg./5 cc. Bot. pts., gal.

PHENOTHIAZINE. Thiodiphenylamine.

PHENOTURIC. (Truett) Phenobarbital 40 mg./Tsp. Elixir, Bot. 1 pt., gals.
Use: Sedative.

PHENOXYBENZAMINE. B.A.N. 2-(N-Benzyl-2-chloroethylamino)-1-phenoxypropane. N-(2-Chloroethyl)-N-(1-methyl-2-phenoxyethyl)benzylamine. Dibenyline; Dibenzyline hydrochloride.
Use: Adrenaline antagonist.

• **PHENOXYBENZAMINE HCl,** U.S.P. XXI. Cap., U.S.P. XXI. N-Phenoxyisopropyl-N-benzyl-beta-chlorethylamine HCl. N-(2-Chloroethyl)-N-(1-methyl-2-phenoxy-ethyl)benzylamine HCl.
Use: Antihypertensive.
See: Dibenzyline, Cap. (SmithKline)

8-PHENOXYETHANOL.
See: Tridenol, Liq. (Spirt)

PHENOXYMETHYL PENICILLIN.
See: Penicillin V.

PHENOXYMETHYL PENICILLIN POTASSIUM.
See: Penicillin V potassium.

PHENOXYNATE. Mixture of phenyiphenols 17-18% octyl and related alkylphenols 2-3%.
See: Surtenol, Liq. (Guardian Chem.)

PHENOXYPROPAZINE. B.A.N. (1-Methyl-2-phenoxyethyl)hydrazine. Drazine hydrogen maleate.
Use: Monoamine oxidase inhibitor.

PHENPROBAMATE. B.A.N. 3-Phenylpropyl carbamate Gamaquil.
Use: Skeletal muscle relaxant.

• **PHENPROCOUMON,** U.S.P. XXI. Tab., U.S.P. XXI. 3-(α-Ethylbenzyl)-4-hydroxycoumarin. 4-Hydroxy-3-(1-phenylpropyl)coumarin. Marcoumar.
Use: Anticoagulant.
See: Liquamar, Tab. (Organon)

PHEN-70. (Parmed) Phendimetrazine Tartrate 70 mg./Tab. Bot. 100s, 1000s.
Use: Anorexiant.

• **PHENSUXIMIDE,** U.S.P. XXI. Cap., U.S.P. XXI. N-Methyl-2-phenylsuccinimide.
Use: Anticonvulsant.
See: Milontin, Preps. (Parke-Davis)

PHENTAL. (Geneva) Belladonna alkaloids w/phenobarbital 0.25 gr./Tab. Bot. 1000s.

PHENTAZINE. (Sutliff & Case) Phendimetrazine tartrate 35 mg./Tab. Bot. 100s, 1000s.

• **PHENTERMINE.** USAN. α,α-Dimethylphenethylamine. Phenyl-tertiarybutylamine. Duromine (an ion-exchange resin complex)
Use: Anorexiant.
See: Adipex, Tab. (Lemmon)
Adipex-8 C.T., Cap. (Lemmon)
Adipex-P, Cap. (Lemmon)
Fastin, Cap. (Beecham Labs)
Parmine, Cap. (Parmed)
Phentrol, Tab. (Vortech)
Rolaphent, Tab. (Robinson)
Tora, Tab. (Reid-Provident)
Unifast Unicelles, Cap. (Reid-Provident)
Wilpowr, Cap. (Foy)

PHENTERMINE AS RESIN COMPLEX.
See: Ionamin, Cap. (Pennwalt)

• **PHENTERMINE HYDROCHLORIDE,** U.S.P. XXI. Cap., Nasal Jelly, Tab., U.S.P. XXI. Benzeneethanamine, α,α-dimethyl-, hydrochloride.
Use: Anorexiant.

PHENTETIOTHALEIN SODIUM. Iso-lodeikon.
Use: Radiopaque medium for cholecystography & for liver function test.

HENTOLAMINE. B.A.N. 2-N-(3-Hydroxyphenyl)-p-toluidinomethyl-2-imidazoline. [Rogitine hydrochloride or mesylate].
Use: Adrenaline antagonist.
HENTOLAMINE HYDROCHLORIDE. m-[n-(2-Imidazolin-2-ylmethyl)-p-toluidino]phenol hydrochloride.
Use: Anti-adrenergic.
See: Regitine Hydrochloride, Tab. (Ciba)
•HENTOLAMINE MESYLATE, U.S.P. XXI. For Inj., U.S.P. XXI. Phenol, 3-[[(4,5-dihydro-1H-imidazol-2-yl)methyl]-(4-methyl-phenyl)amino]-, monomethanesulfonate (salt). m-[N-(2-Imidazolin-2-ylmethyl)-p-toluidino]-phenol methanesulfonate.
Use: Anti-adrenergic.
See: Regitine Inj. (Ciba)
HENTOLAMINE METHANESULFONATE.
Phentolamine mesylate, U.S.P. XXI.
HENTOLOX w/APAP. (Richlyn) Phenyltoloxamine citrate 30 mg., acetaminophen 325 mg./Tab. Bot. 1000s.
Use: Antihistaminic, analgesic.
HENTOX COMPOUND SYRUP. (Bay) Phenylpropanolamine HCl 20 mg., phenylephrine HCl 5 mg., phenytoloxamine citrate 7.5 mg., chlorpheniramine maleate 2.5 mg./5 ml. Bot. pt. gal.
Use: Decongestant, antihistaminic.
HENTRIDE-8. (Western Research) Phentermine HCl 8 mg./Tab. Handicount 28 (36 bags of 28s)
Use: Anorexic.
HENTROL. (Vortech) Phentermine HCl 8 mg./Tab. Bot. 1000s.
Use: Anorexiant.
HENTROL NO. 2. (Vortech) Phenteramine HCl 30 mg./Cap. Bot. 100s, 1000s.
Use: Anorexiant.
HENTROL NO. 4 and NO. 5. (Vortech) Phenteramine HCl 30 mg./Cap. Bot. 100s, 1000s.
Use: Anorexiant.
HENTYDRONE. 1,2,3,4-Tetrahydrofluoren-9-one.
Use: Systemic fungicide.
HENURONE. (Abbott) (Phenacemide, Phenacetylcarbamide, Phenacetylurea) Tab. 0.5 Gm., Bot. 100s.
Use: Psychomotor epilepsy, grand mal & petit mal epilepsies.
I-PHENYLACETAMIDE.
See: Acetanilid (Var. Mfr.)
PHENYLAMINOSALICYLATE. USAN. Phenyl 4 aminosalicylate. Fenamisal (I.N.N.) PhenyPAS Tebamin.
Use: Tuberculostatic.
HENYLACETYLUREA.
See: Phenurone, Tab. (Abbott)
• PHENYLALANINE, U.S.P. XXI. $C_9H_{11}NO_2$ as L-phenylalanine.
See: Phenylketonuria therapy.
-PHENYLALANINE, 4-[BIS(2-CHLOROETHYL)-AMINO-] Melphalan, U.S.P. XXI.
PHENYLALANINE MUSTARD.
See: Melphalan, U.S.P. XXI.

PHENYLAZO-DIAMINOPYRIDINE HYDROCHLORIDE.
See: Rodine, Tab. (Paddock)
PHENYLAZO SULFISOXAZOLE. (A.P.C.) Sulfisoxazole 0.5 Gm., phenylazopyridine 50 mg./Tab. Bot. 1000s.
PHENYLAZO TABLETS. (APC) Phenylazodiamino-pyridine HCl 1.5 gr./Tab. Bot. 1000s.
Use: Urinary analgesic and antiseptic.
PHENYLAZO-DIAMINO-PYRIDINE.
See: Phenazopyridine (Var. Mfr.)
PHENYLAZO-DIAMINO-PYRIDINE HCl or HBr.
See: Phenazopyridine HCl or HBr (Var. Mfr.)
• PHENYLBUTAZONE, U.S.P. XXI. Cap., Tab. U.S.P. XXI. 3,5-Pyrazolidinedione, 4-butyl-1,2-diphenyl-. 4-Butyl-1,2-diphenyl-3,5-pyrazolidinedione. 4-Butyl-1,2-diphenylpyrazolidine-3,5-dione. Benzone; Butacote; Butaphen; Butazone; Flexaz IA-But; Tetnor.
Use: Anti-inflammatory.
See: Azolid, Tab. (USV)
Butazolidin, Tab. (Geigy)
W/Aluminum hydroxide dried gel, magnesium trisilicate.
See: Azolid-A, Cap. (USV)
W/Aluminum hydroxide, mag. trisilicate.
See: Butazolidin Alka, Cap. (Geigy)
PHENYL-1-BUTYL-NORSUPRIFEN.
See: Arlidin, Tab. (USV Pharm.)
PHENYLCARBINOL.
See: Benzyl Alcohol, N.F. XVI.
PHENYLCINCHONINIC ACID. Name used for cinchophen.
PHENYLEPHRINE. B.A.N. (−)-1-(3-Hydroxyphenyl)-2-methylaminoethanol. Fenox; Neophryn; Neosynephrine hydrochloride.
Use: Vasoconstrictor; hypotensive.
See: Duo-Medihaler, Vial (Riker)
• PHENYLEPHRINE HYDROCHLORIDE, U.S.P. XXI. Inj., Nasal Soln., Ophth. Soln., U.S.P. XXI. Benzenemethanol, 3-hydroxy-α-[(methylamino)-methyl]-, hydrochloride (S)-. l-m-Hydroxy-a-[(methylamino)methyl]-benzyl alcohol hydrochloride. (Neophryn).
Use: Sympathomimetic agent, vasoconstrictor & mydriatic.
See: Alcon-Efrin, Sol. (Webcon)
Allerest Nasal Spray (Pharmacraft)
Coricidin Decongestant Nasal Mist (Schering)
Ephrine, Spray (Walgreen)
Neo-Synephrine HCl, Prep. (Winthrop Consumer Products)
Prefrin Liquifilm Ophth. Soln (Allergan)
Pyracort-D, spray (Lemmon)
Sinarest, Nasal Spray (Pharmacraft)
Super-Anahist Nasal Spray (Warner-Lambert)
W/Combinations:
See: Acotus, Liq. (Whorton)
Anodynos Forte, Tab. (Buffington)
Bellafedrol A-H, Tab. (Lannett)
Bur-Tuss Expectorant (Burlington)
C.D.M. Expect. Liq. (Lannett)
Cenahist, Cap. (Century)

Cenaid, Tab. (Century)
Chlor-Trimeton Expect. (Schering)
Chlor-Trimeton Expt. w/Codeine (Scherring)
Clistin-D, Tab. (McNeil)
Col-Decon, Tab. (Quality Generics)
Conar, Susp., Expt. (Beecham Labs)
Conar-A, Tab., Susp. (Beecham Labs)
Congespirin, Tab. (Bristol-Myers)
Coricidin Demilets (Schering)
Dallergy, Syr., Cap., Tab., Inj. (Laser)
Demazin, Syrup (Schering)
Dimetane Decongestant, Tab., Elixir (Robins)
Dimetane Expectorant, Liq. (Robins)
Dimetane Expectorant-DC, Liq. (Robins)
Dimetapp, Elix. Extentabs (Robins)
Doktors, Drops, Spray (Scherer)
Dri-Drip, Liq. (Coastal)
Drinus-M, Cap. (Amfre-Grant)
Eldatapp, Tab., Liq. (Elder)
Emagrin Forte, Tab. (Clapp)
Entex, Prods. (Norwich Eaton)
Expectico Ped. Cough Syr. (Coastal)
Eye-Gene, Sol. (Pearson)
4 Way Tab., Spray (Bristol-Myers)
Furacin Nasal Sol. (Eaton)
Histabid, Cap. (Meyer)
Histapp Prods. (Upsher-Smith)
Histospan-D, Cap. (USV)
Histospan-Plus, Cap. (USV)
Mydfrin Ophthalmic, Liq. (Alcon)
Naal, Timesule (Haag)
Na-Co-Al, Tab. (High)
Nasahist, Cap. (Keene)
Noraphen-Plus Spancap. (Vortech)
Pediacof, Syr. (Winthrop-Breon)
Phenoptic, Sol. (Muro)
Phenylzin Drops, Ophth. Sol. (CooperVision)
Prefrin-A Ophth. Soln. (Allergan)
Prefrin-Z Ophth. Soln. (Allergan)
Pyraphed, Sol. (Lemmon)
Pyristan Cap., Elix. (Arcum)
Queledrine, Syr. (Abbott)
Rhinall, Liq. (Scherer)
Rhinex DM, Tab. (Lemmon)
Rymed, Prods. (Edwards)
Sinex, Nasal Spray (Vicks)
Singlet, Tab. (Merrell Dow)
Spectab, Tab. (Reid-Provident)
Spec-T Sore Throat-Decongestant Loz. (Squibb)
Sucrets Cold Decongestant Lozenge (Calgon)
Tearefrin, Liq. (CooperVision)
Trind, Liq. (Mead Johnson)
Trind-DM, Liq. (Mead Johnson)
Tri-Ophtho, Soln. (Maurry)
T-Spray (Saron)
Turbilixir, liq. (Burlington)
Turbispan Leisurecaps, Cap. (Burlington)
Tympagesic, Liq. (Adria)
Vacon, Liq. (Scherer)
Valihist, Cap. (Clapp)
Vasocidin, Ophth. Soln. (CooperVision)
Vasosulf, Ophth. Soln. (CooperVision)

• **PHENYLETHYL ALCOHOL,** U.S.P. XXI.
Betaphenylethanol. Benzylcarbinol. (Various Mfr.) Phenethyl Alcohol.
Use: Antibacterial; preservative (ophthalmic).

beta-PHENYL-ETHYL-HYDRAZINE. Phenalzine dihydrogen sulfate.
See: Nardil, Tab. (Parke-Davis)

PHENYLETHYLMALONYLUREA.
See: Phenobarbital (Various Mfr.)

PHENYLGESIC TABS. (Goldline) Bot. 100s, 1000s.
Use: Analgesic.

PHENYLIC ACID.
See: Phenol, U.S.P. XXI.

PHENYL-IDIUM TABLETS. (Quality Generic Phenazopyridine HCl 100 mg./Tab. Bot. 100s, 1000s.
Use: Urinary tract analgesic.

PHENYL-IDIUM 200. (Quality Generics) Phenazopydine HCl 200 mg./Tab. Bot. 100s, 1000s.
Use: Urinary tract analgesic.

PHENYLINDANEDIONE. Phenindione, B.A.N.

PHENYLKETONURIA THERAPY.
See: Lofenalac, Powd. (Mead Johnson)
Phenistix Reagent Strips (Ames)

• **PHENYLMERCURIC ACETATE,** N.F. XVI. (Various Mfr.) (Acetato)phenylmercury. Bot. 1 lb., 5 lb., 10 l
Use: Preservative (bacteriostatic).

W/9-Aminoacridine HCl, sodium lauryl sulfate, succinic acid.
See: Vagiserts w/inserts, Supp. (Vortech)

W/9-Aminoacridine HCl, tyrothricin, urea, lactose.
See: Trinalis, Vag. Supp. (Webcon)

W/Benzocaine, chlorothymol, resorcin.
See: Lanacane Creme (Combe)

W/Boric acid, polyoxyethylenenonylphenol or oxyquinoline benzoate.
See: Koromex, Prep. (Holland-Rantos)

W/Methylbenzethonium chloride.
See: Norforms, Aer., Supp. (Norwich)

PHENYLMERCURIC BORATE. (F. W. Berk) Pkg. Custom packed.

W/Benzyl alcohol, benzocaine & butyl p-aminobenzoate.
See: Dermathyn, Oint. (Davis & Sly)

PHENYLMERCURIC CHLORIDE.
Chlorophenylmercury.

• **PHENYLMERCURIC NITRATE,** N.F. XVI.
(Merphenyl Nitrate, Phenmerzyl Nitrate) A.P.L.—Oint. 1:1500, 1 oz., 4 oz., 1 lb. Chicago Pharm.—Loz. w/benzocaine. Bot. 100s, 1000s. Ophth. Oint. 1:3000, Tube ⅛ oz. Sol. 1:20,000, Bot. 1 pt., 1 gal. Vaginal supp., 1:5000, Box 12s.
Use: Bacteriostatic.
See: Preparation H, Oint., Supp. (Whitehall)

W/Amyl & phenylphenol complex.
See: Lubraseptic Jelly (Guardian)

W/Undecylenic acid.
See: Bridex, Oint. (Briar)

PHENYLMERCURIC PICRATE.
Use: Germicide.

PHENYLPHENOL.
Amyl complex, phenylmercuric nitrate.
See: Lubraseptic Jelly. (Guardian)

PHENYLPROPANOLAMINE. B.A.N. 2-Amino-1-phenyl-propan-1-ol. Propadrine.
Use: Sympathomimetic.

PHENYLPROPANOLAMINE HYDROCHLORIDE, U.S.P. XXI. (±)-Norephedrine Hydrochloride. 2-Amino-1-phenyl-1-propanol (Mydriatine)
Use: Sympathomimetic.
See: Dietac Pre-Meal Diet Aid Drops (Menley & James)
Dietac Pre-Meal Diet Aid Tab. (Menley & James)
Obestat, Cap. (Lemmon)
Obestat 150, Cap. (Lemmon)
Propadrine Hydrochloride, Preps. (Merck Sharp & Dohme)
Propagest, Tab., Syr. (Carnrick)

PHENYLPROPANOLAMINE HCl W/COMBINATIONS.
See: Alclear Anti-allergy Tab. (Walgreen)
Alcon Decongestant, Tab. Liq. (Webcon)
Algecol, Tab. (Winston)
Algetuss, Liq. (Winston)
Allerest Prods. (Pharmacraft)
Allergesic, Tab. (Vitarine)
Allerstat, Cap. (Lemmon)
Amaril "D" Spancap (Vortech)
A.R.M., Tab. (Menley & James)
Bayer Prods. (Glenbrook)
Bifed, Cap. (Alto)
Blu-Hist, Cap. (Bluco)
Bowman Decongestant Compound, Inj. (Bowman)
BQ Cold Tablets (Bristol-Myers)
Breacol cough Medication, Liq. (Glenbrook)
Bur-Tuss Expectorant (Burlington)
Chexit, Tabs. (Dorsey)
Comtrex, Cap., Liq., Tab. (Bristol-Myers)
Congespirin, Liq., Tab. (Bristol-Myers)
Contac, Cap. (Menley & James)
Contac Jr., Liq. (Menley & James)
Cophene No. 2, Cap. (Dunhall)
Coricidin Children's Cough Syrup. (Schering)
Coricidin Cough Formula (Schering)
Coricidin "D" Decongestant Tablets (Schering)
Coricidin Sinus Headache Tablets (Schering)
Corzone, Syr. (Xttrium)
Dalca, Tab. (Ascher)
Daycare, Liq. (Vicks)
Decobel, Cap. (Lannett)
Decongestant, Inj. (Century)
Decongestcaps TDC, Caps. (Ulmer)
Desa-Hist Antitussive Syrup (Pharmics)
Desa-Hist AT, Tab. (Pharmics)
Desa-Hist PF, Cap. (Pharmics)
Dex-A-Diet, Prods. (O'Connor)
Dezest, Cap. (Geneva Drugs)
Dietac 12 Hour Diet Aid Cap. (Menley & James)
Dimetane Expectorant, Liq. (Robins)
Dimetane Expectorant-DC, Liq. (Robins)
Dimetapp, Elix., Extentabs (Robins)
Dorcol Pediatric Cough Syr. (Dorsey)
Dri-Drip, Cap., Liq. (Coastal)
Drinophen, Cap. (Lannett)
Eldatapp, Tab., Liq. (Elder)
Entex, Caps. (Norwich Eaton)
Entex, Liq. (Norwich Eaton)
Entex LA, Tab. (Norwich Eaton)
Fiogesic, Tab. (Sandoz)
Formula 44D Decongestant Cough Mixture, Syr. (Vicks)
4-Way Nasal Spray (Bristol-Myers)
Ginsopan, Tab., Cap. (O'Neal)
Halls Mentho-Lyptus Cough Formula, Liq. (Warner-Lambert)
Histalet Forte T.D., Tab. (Reid-Provident)
Histapp Prods. (Upsher-Smith)
Hista-Vadrin, Syr., Tab., Cap. (Scherer)
Kleer Compound, Tab. (Scrip)
Klix Kernel, Cap. (Bowman)
Koryza Tab. (Fellows-Testagar)
Leder, Prods. (Lederle)
Meditussin, Syr. (Hauck)
Meditussin-X Liquid. (Hauck)
Na-Co-Al, Tab. (High)
Naldecon, Drop, Syr., Tab. (Bristol)
Nasahist, Cap., Inj. (Keene)
Nolamine, Tab. (Carnrick)
Novahistine, Prods. (Merrell Dow)
Opasal, Cap. (Elder)
Oraminic, Prods. (Vortech)
Ornacol, Cap., Liq. (Menley & James)
Ornade, Cap. (SmithKline)
Ornex, Cap. (Menley & James)
Panadyl, Tab., Cap. (Misemer)
Partuss-A, Tab. (Parmed)
Partuss T.D., Tab. (Parmed)
Propahist, Tab., Syr., Cap., Inj. (Blue Line)
Pyristan, Cap., Elix. (Arcum)
Rhinex DM, Liq. (Lemmon)
Rohist-D, Cap., Vial (Rocky Mtn.)
Rolanade, Cap. (Robinson)
Rymed, Prods. (Edwards)
Sanhist TD, Tab., Vial (Sandia)
Santussin, Cap., Susp. (Sandia)
Sine-Aid, Tab. (McNeil)
Sine-Off, Tab. (Menley & James)
Sinarest, Tab (Pharmcraft)
Sinubid, Tabs. (Warner-Lambert)
Sinulin, Tab. (Carnrick)
Sinutab, Prods. (Warner-Lambert)
Spec-T Sore Throat-Decongestant Loz. (Squibb)
St. Joseph Cold Tablets for Children (Plough)
Sto-Caps, Cap (Jalco)
Sucrets Cold Decongestant Lozenge (Calgon)
Super-Anahist Tablets (Warner-Lambert)
Symptomax, Liq. (Reid-Provident)
Teragen, Tab. (O'Neal)
Triaminic, Preps. (Dorsey)
Triaminicin, Tab., Chewable, (Dorsey)
Triaminicol, Syr. (Dorsey)
Turbilixir, Liq. (Burlington)
Turbispan Leisurecaps, Cap. (Burlington)
Tusquelin, Syr. (Circle)

Tussagesic, Susp., Tab. (Dorsey)
Tusscaps, Cap. (Martin-Phillips)
Tuss-Ornade, Cap. (SmithKline)
Tusstrol, Liq. (Reid-Provident)
U.R.I., Cap., Liq. (ICN)
Vernate, Inj., Cap., Tab. (Reid-Provident)
Vicks Daycare, Liq. (Vicks)
Vicks Formula 44D Decongestant Cough Mixture, Syr. (Vicks)

PHENYLPROPYLMETHYLAMINE HYDROCHLORIDE. Vonedrine HCl.

PHENYL SALICYLATE. Salol.
W/Atropine sulfate, hyoscyamine, methenamine, methylene blue, gelsemium, benzoic acid.
See: Lanased, Tab. (Lannett)
Renalgin, Tab. (Meyer)
U-Tract, Tab. (Bowman)
W/Euphorbia ext. & various oils.
See: Rayderm Ointment (Velvet Pharmacal)
W/Methenamine, methylene blue, benzoic acid, hyoscyamine alkaloid, atropine sulfate.
See: Cystrea, Tab. (Moore Kirk)
Urised, Tab. (Webcon)
UTA, Tab. (ICN)
W/Methenamine, sodium biphosphate, methylene blue, hyoscyamine, alkaloid.
See: Urostat Forte, Tab. (Elder)

PHENYL-TERT-BUTYLAMINE.
See: Phentermine

PHENYLTHILONE. 2-Ethyl-2-phenyl-3,5-thiomorpholinedione.
Use: Anticonvulsant.

PHENYLTOLOXAMINE. o-Benzylphenyl-2-dimethylaminoethyl ether.

PHENYLTOLOXAMINE. B.A.N. N-2-(2-Benzylphenoxy)ethyldimethylamine.
Use: Antihistamine.

PHENYLTOLOXAMINE CITRATE. N,N-Dimethyl-2-[(alpha-phenyl-o-tolyl)oxy]ethylamine citrate.
Use: Antihistamine.
See: Volaxin Modified, Tab. (Elder)

PHENYLTOLOXAMINE CITRATE W/COMBINATIONS.
See: Col-Decon, Tab. (Quality Generics)
Conex, Liq. (Westerfield)
Conex-DA, Dual Action Tab. (Westerfield)
Conex Plus, Tab. (Westerfield)
Corzone, Syr. (Xttrium)
Dengesic, Tab. (Scott-Alison)
Euphenex, Tab. (Westerfield)
Hyptran, Tab. (Wallace)
Medache, Tab. (Organon)
Meditussin, Liq. (Hauck)
Meditussin-X, Liq. (Hauck)
Myocalm, Tab. (Parmed)
Naldecon, Prep. (Bristol)
Naldetuss, Syr. (Bristol)
Neotuss-PT, Liq. (Westerfield)
Neo-Vadrin Sinus Headache Formula, Tab. (Scherer)
Percogesic, Tab. (Du Pont)
Percogesic-C, Tab. (Du Pont)
Poly-histine Prods. (Bock)
Quadrahist, Tab. (Harvey-Pharmex)
S.A.C. Sinus, Tab. (Towne)
Scotgesic, Elix., Cap. (Scott/Cord)
Sinutab, Tab. (Warner-Lambert)
Sinutab Extra Strength, Tab. (Warner-Lambert)
Teragen, Tab. (O'Neal)
Trilamine, Cap. (Lemmon)
Tri-Synar, Tab. (Forrest)
Volaxin, Tab. (Elder)
Volaxin-A, Tab. (Elder)

PHENYLTOLOXAMINE RESIN W/COMBINATIONS.
See: Tussionex, Cap., Liq., Tab. (Pennwalt)

PHENYLZIN. (CooperVision) Zinc sulfate 0.25%, phenylephrine HCl 0.12%/Lacrivial 15 cc.
Use: Ophthalmic astringent decongestant.

PHENYRAMIDOL. B.A.N. 1-Phenyl-2-(2-pyridylamino)-ethanol. Analexin hydrochloride.
Use: Analgesic.

• **PHENYRAMIDOL HCL.** USAN. 2(β-Hydroxyphenethylamino)pyridine HCl. α-[2-Pyridylamino)-methyl]-benzyl alcohol hydrochloride.
Use: Analgesic.

PHENYTHILONE. 2-Ethyl-2-phenyl-3, 5-thiamorpholinedione.

• **PHENYTOIN,** U.S.P. XXI. Oral Susp., Tab., U.S.P. XXI. 2,4-Imidazolidinedione, 5,5-diphenyl-. 5,5-Diphenylhydantoin. Diphenylhydantoin.
Use: Anticonvulsant.
See: Dihycon, Caps. (CMC)
Dilantin Prods. (Parke-Davis)
Di-phenyl, T.R. Cap. (Drug. Ind.)
Ekko, Cap. (Fleming)
Toin, Unicelles (Reid-Provident)

• **PHENYTOIN SODIUM.** U.S.P. XXI. Extended Cap., Inj., Prompt Cap., Sterile, U.S.P. XXI. 2,4-Imidazolidinedione, 5,5-diphenyl-, monosodium salt. 5,5-Diphenylhydantoin sodium salt. Diphenylhydantoin sodium. Alepsin, Dihydan soluble, Diphentoin, Silantin Sod., Epanutin, Eptoin, Phenytoin soluble, Solantoin, Solantyl, Denyl Sod., Soluble Phenytoin (5,5-diphenyl-hydantoinate Sod.)
Use: Anticonvulsant, cardiac depressant (antiarrhythmic).
See: Dihycon, Cap. (CMC)
Dilantin Sod., Prep. (Parke-Davis)
Di-Phen, Cap. (Vortech)
Diphenylan Sod., Cap. (Lannett)
Ekko Jr. & Sr., Cap. (Fleming)

PHENZINE. (Mallard) Phendimetrazine tartrate 35 mg./Tab. Bot. 1000s.

PHERAZINE EXPECTORANT. (Blue Cross) Promethazine HCl 5 mg. ipecac 0.17 min., potassium guaiacolsulfonate 44 mg., citric acid 60 mg., sodium citrate 197 mg./5 ml. w/alcohol 7%. Bot. Pt., gal.
Use: Expectorant, antihistaminic.

PHERAZINE EXPECTORANT WITH CODEINE. (Blue Cross) Codeine phosphate 10 mg., promethazine HCl 5 mg., ipecac 0.17 min., potassium

guaiacolsulfonate 44 mg., citric acid 60 mg., sodium citrate 197 mg./5 ml. w/alcohol 7%. Bot. Pt., gal.
Use: Expectorant, antitussive, antihistaminic.

PHERAZINE EXPECTORANT WITH DEXTROMETHORPHAN. (Blue Cross) Dextromethorphan HBr 7.5 mg., promethazine HCl 5 mg., ipecac 0.17 min., potassium gualocolsulfonate 44 mg., citric acid 60 mg., sodium acid 197 mg./5 ml. w/alcohol 7%. Bot. Pt., gal.
Use: Expectorant, antihistaminic.

PHERAZINE VC EXPECTORANT. (Blue Cross) Promethazine HCl 5 mg., phenylephrine HCl 5 mg., ipecac 0.17 min., potassium guaiacolsulfonate 44 mg., citric acid 60 mg., sodium citrate 197 mg./5 ml. w/alcohol 7%. Bot. Pt., gal.
Use: Expectorant, antihistaminic, decongestant.

PHERAZINE VC EXPECTORANT WITH CODEINE. (Blue Cross) Codeine phosphate 10 mg., promethazine HCl 5 mg., phenylephrine HCl 5 mg., ipecac 0.17 min., potassium guaiacolsulfonate 44 mg., citric acid 60 mg., sodium citrate 197 mg./5 ml. Bot. Pt., gal.
Use: Expectorant, antitussive, antihistaminic, decongestant.

PHERMINE. (Fellows) Phentermine HCl 8 mg./Tab. Bot. 100s, 1000s.

PHETABAR SPACECAP. (Moore Kirk) Amobarbital 90 mg., dextroamphetamine sulfate 15 mg./timed disintegration Cap. Bot. 1000s.
Use: Combat depression; ease tension; as adjunct to diet in obesity.

PHETHARBITAL. 5,5-Diethyl-1-phenylbarbituric acid.

PHETHENYLATE. 5-Phenyl-5-(2-thienyl)hydantoinate. Also sod. salt.

PHILJECT INJECTION. (Fellows) Procaine base 75 mg., butyl-amino-benzoate 300 mg., benzyl alcohol 250 mg./5 cc. in peanut oil. Vial 5 cc.

PHILLIPS' MILK OF MAGNESIA. (Glenbrook) Magnesium hydroxide. Reg. & Mint bot. 4 oz., 12 oz., 26 oz.; Tab. 30s, 100s, 200s.
Use: Laxative, antacid.

PHILLIPS OINTMENT. (Fellows) Bismuth tribromophenate 5%. Base 1 oz., 1 lb., 5 lb.

pHisoAc-BP. (Winthrop Consumer Products) Benzoyl peroxide 10% in cream base. Tube 1 oz.
Use: Topical anti-acne agent.

pHisoDan SHAMPOO. (Winthrop Consumer Products) Sulfur 5%, sodium salicylate 0.5% w/lanolin cholesterols, entsufon sodium, petrolatum. Bot. 5 oz.
Use: Seborrhea of scalp.

pHisoDerm. (Winthrop Consumer Products) Sod. Octoxynol-3 Sulfonate, white petrolatum, water, lanolin, lanolin alcohol, sodium benzoate, Octoxynol-1, methylcellulose and lactic acid. **Regular:** Bot. 5 oz., 9 oz., 16 oz. **Dry type:** Bot. 5 oz., pt. Wall dispenser pt. **Oily type:** Bot. 5 oz., 16 oz. **Fresh Scent:** Bot. 5oz.
Use: Skin cleanser & conditioner.

PHISOHEX. (Cook-Waite) A colloidal dispersion of hexachlorophene 3% (w/w), entsufon sodium, petrolatum, lanolin cholesterols, methylcellulose, polyethylene glycol, polyethylene glycol monostearate, lauryl myristyl diethanolamide, sodium benzoate, & water. pH is adjusted with HCl acid. Bot. gal.
Use: Antiseptic detergent.

pHisoHex. (Winthrop-Breon) Entsufon sodium, hexachlorophene 3%, petrolatum, lanolin cholesterols, methylcellulose, polyethylene glycol, polyethylene glycol monostearate, lauryl myristyl diethanolamide, sod. benzoate, water, pH adjusted with hydrochloric acid. Emulsion, Bot. 5 oz., pt., gal. Wall dispensers pt. Unit packets 0.25 oz. Box 50s, Pedal operated dispenser 30 oz.
Use: Surgical scrub & antibacterial cleanser.

pHisoMed. (Winthrop Products) Hexochlorophene.
Use: Antibacterial skin cleanser.

pHisoScrub. (Winthrop-Breon) Scrub brush sponge impregnated with pHisoHex. Case of 4 dispensers, 36 u./Disp.
Use: Surgical scrub.

PHISTOL. (Kenyon) Vit. A 10,000 I.U., D 1000 I.U., B-1 5 mg., B-2 3 mg., B-6 1 mg., C 100 mg., calcium pantothenate 5 mg., niacinamide 25 mg./Cap. Bot. 100s, 1000s.

PHOLEDRINE. B.A.N. 4-(2-Methylaminopropyl)-phenol. Veritain; Veritol.
Use: Sympathomimetic.

PHOSCOLIC ACID. 2,2′-Phosphinicodilacetic acid.
Use: Adjuvant.

PHOS-FLUR ORAL RINSE SUPPLEMENT. (Hoyt) Acidulated phosphate sodium fluoride 0.05%. 1 ml fluoride/Tsp. Bot. 250 ml., 500 ml.
Use: Prevent dental caries

PHOSPHACAL-D. (Lannett) Dicalcium phosphate anh. 330 mg., Vit. D 333 I.U./Cap. Bot. 500s, 1000s.

pHOS-pHAID. (Guardian) Ammonium biphosphate 190 mg., sodium biphosphate 200 mg., sodium acid pyrophosphate 110 mg./0.5 Gm. Tab. regular or enteric coated. Bot. 90s, 500s. Also 0.25 Gm., 150s.
Use: Urinary acidifier.

PHOSPHALJEL. (Wyeth) Aluminum phosphate gel 700 mg./15 ml. Bot. 12 oz.

PHOSPHENTASIDE. Adenosine-5-monophosphate. Adenylic acid.

W/Vit. B-12, niacin.
See: Denylex Gel, Vial (Westerfield)

W/Vit. B-12, niacin, B-1.
See: Adenolin, Vial (Lincoln)

PHOSPHOLINE IODIDE. (Ayerst) Echothiophate Iodide for Ophthalmic Solution. Sterile echothiophate iodide powder w/potassium acetate 40 mg., diluent: chlorobutanol 0.5%, mannitol 1.2%, boric acid 0.06%, sod. phosphate exsic. 0.026% for preparing 0.03%, 0.06%, 0.125%, and 0.25% potencies/5 ml. of sterile eyedrops. Package: 1.5 mg. for 0.03%; 3.0 mg. for 0.06%; 6.25 mg. for 0.125%; 12.5 mg. for 0.25%.
Use: Glaucoma & accommodative esotropia.

PHOSPHOLIPIDS SOY.
See: Granulestin Conc., Granules (Associated Concentrates)

PHOSPHORATED CARBOHYDRATE SOLUTION.
See: Emetrol, Liq. (Rorer)

• **PHOSPHORIC ACID,** N.F. XVI.
Use: Solvent

• **PHOSPHORIC ACID, DILUTED,** N.F. XVI.

PHOSPHOROFLUORIDIC ACID, BIS(I-METHYLETHYL)-, ESTER. Isofluorophate, U.S.P. XXI.
Use: Solvent.

PHOSPHO-SODA. (Fleet) Sod. biphosphate 48 Gm., Sod. phosphate 18 Gm./100 cc. Bot. 1.5 oz., 3 oz., 8 oz. Flavored and unflavored.
Use: A mild saline laxative.

PHOSPHOTEC. (Squibb) Technetium Tc 99m pyrophosphate kit. 10 vials/kit.
Use: Radiodiagnostic.

PHOXIN. B.A.N. α-Diethoxyphosphinothioyloxyimino-α-phenylacetonitrile.
Use: Insecticide; anthelmintic, veterinary medicine.

PHRENILIN FORTE CAPSULES. (Carnrick) Acetaminophen 650 mg., butalbital 50 mg./Cap. Bot. 100s.
Use: Barbiturate-analgesic for relief of the symptom complex of tension headache.

PHRENILIN TABLETS. (Carnrick) Butalbital 50 mg., acetaminophen 325 mg./Tab. Bot. 100s.
Use: Barbiturate-analgesic for relief of the symptom complex of tension headache.

PHRENILIN WITH CODEINE #3. (Carnrick) Acetaminophen 325 mg., butalbital 50 mg., codeine phosphate 30 mg./Cap. Bot. 100s.
Use: Analgesic.

PHRENOTROPIN. Prothipendyl, B.A.N.

PHRESH 3.5 FINNISH CLEANSING LIQUIDE. (3M Products) Water, cocamidopropyl betaine, lactic acid, polyoxyethylene distearate, polyoxyethylene monostearate, hydroxyethyl cellulose, sodium phosphate, methylparaben. Bot. 6 oz.
Use: Soapless cleansing agent.

pH SKIN CLEANSING LOTION. (Walgreen) Alcohol 28%, boric acid 1.75%, benzoic acid 0.25%, w/thymol 0.036% eucalyptol 0.036%, thyme oil 0.036%. Bot. 16. oz.
Use: Astringent & cleanser.

PHTHALAMAQUIN. (Penick) Quinetolate.
Use: Antiasthmatic.

PHTHALAZINE, I-HYDRAZINO-, MONOHYDROCHLORIDE. Hydralazine Hydrochloride, U.S.P. XXI.

• **PHTHALOFYNE.** USAN. Mono(I-ethyl-I-methyl-2-propynyl)phthalate.

PHTHALYLSULFACETAMIDE. 4′-(Acetylsulfamoyl) phthalanilic acid. Enterosulfon.

PHTHALYLSULFATHIAZOLE. 4′-(2 Thiazolylsulfamoyl) phthalanilic acid.
Use: Antibacterial (intestinal).
See: Sulfathalidine, Tab. (Merck Sharp & Dohme)

PHYLCARDIN.
See: Aminophylline (Various Mfr.)

PHYLLINDON.
See: Aminophylline (Various Mfr.)

PHYLLOCONTIN. (Purdue Frederick) Aminophylline 225 mg./Controlled Release Tab. Bot. 100s.
Use: Relief and/or prevention of symptoms of asthma & reversible bronchospasm associated with chronic bronchitis & emphysema.

PHYLLOQUINONE. 2-Methyl-3-phytyl-1,4-naphthoquinine, Vit. K.
See: Phytonadione, U.S.P., Inj., Tab. (Var. Mfr.)
Vit. K-1 (Various Mfr.)

PHYSEPTONE. Methadone, B.A.N.

PHYSIOSOL IRRIGATION. (Abbott) Bot. 250 ml., 500 ml., 1000 ml. glass or Aqualite (semi-rigid) containers.
Use: Irrigating solution.

• **PHYSOSTIGMINE,** U.S.P. XXI. Pyrrolo [2,3-b] indol-5-ol methylcarbamate (ester), (3as-cis). 1,2,3a β,8,8a β-Hexahydro-1,3a,8-trimethyl-pyrrolo[2,3-b]-indol-5yl-methylcarbamate. An alkaloid.
Use: Parasympathomimetic agent.

• **PHYSOSTIGMINE SALICYLATE,** U.S.P. XXI. Inj., Ophth. Soln., U.S.P. XXI. Pyrrolo[2,3-b]indol-5-ol, 1,2,3,3a,8,8a-hexahydro-1,3a,8-trimethyl-, methylcarbamate (ester), (3aS-cis)-,mono(2-hydroxybenzoate). Physostigmine monosalicylate. Eserine salicylate. (Forest)—Pow., Tube 1 gr., 5 gr., 15 gr.
Use: Parasympathomimetic agent.
See: Antilirium, Amp. (Forest)
Isopto-Eserine, Ophth., Sol. (Alcon)
Miocel, Ophth. Sol. (Softcon)

W/Atropine sulfate.
See: Atrophysine, Inj. (Lannett)

W/I-Hyoscyamine HBr.
See: Phyatromine-H, Amp., Vial (Kremers-Urban)

W/Pilocarpine, methylcellulose.
See: Isopto P-ES, Soln. (Alcon)
Miocel, Sol. (Softcon)

• **PHYSOSTIGMINE SULFATE,** U.S.P. XXI. Ophth. Oint., U.S.P. XXI. Pyrrolo[2,3-b]indol-5-ol, 1,2,3,3a, 8,8a-hexahydro-1,3a,8-trimethyl-, methylcarbamate (ester), (3aS-cis)-,sulfate (2:1).
Use: Cholinergic (ophthalmic)

• **PHYTATE PERSODIUM.** USAN.
Use: Pharmaceutic aid.

• **PHYTATE SODIUM.** USAN. Sod. salt of inositolhexaphosphoric acid.

PHYTIC ACID. Inositol hexophosphoric acid.

PHYTOMENADIONE. B.A.N. 2-Methyl-3-phytyl-1,4-naphthaquinone. Vitamin K Konakion; Mephyton.
Use: Antidote to anticoagulants.
See: Phytonadione, U.S.P. (Var. Mfr.)

PHYTONADIOL SODIUM DIPHOSPHATE. Disodium salt of 2-methyl-3-phytyl-1,4-naphthohydroquinone-$0^1,0^4$-diphosphoric acid.

• **PHYTONADIONE,** U.S.P. XXI. Inj., Tabs., U.S.P. XXI. Vit. K 1,4-Naphthalenedione, 2-methyl-3-(3,7,11,-15-tetramethyl-2-hexadecenyl)-,[R-[R*,R*-(E)]]-. Phylloquinone. 2-Methyl-3-phytyl-1,4-naphthoquinone.
Use: Prothrombogenic.
See: Aquamephyton, Inj. (Merck Sharp & Dohme)
Konakion, Amp. (Roche)
Mephyton, Tab. (Merck Sharp & Dohme)

ICENADOL HYDROCHLORIDE. USAN.
Use: Analgesic
CLOXYDINE. B.A.N. NN'-Di-(p-Chlorophenylguanidinoformimidoyl)-piperazine. 1,4-Di-(4-chlorophenylguanidinoformimidoyl)piperazine.
Use: Bactericide; fungicide.
ICOTRIN DIOLAMINE. USAN.
Use: Keratolytic
CRIC ACID, TRINITROPHENOL.
See: Butesyn Picrate Ointment (Abbott)
Silver Salts (Various Prods.)
CROTOXIN. Cocculin
Use: Respiratory stimulant.
I.D.
See: Phenindione (Var. Mfr.)
FARNINE. USAN.
Use: Anti-ulcerative.
FENATE. B.A.N. Ethyl 2,2-diphenyl-3-(2-piperidyl)propionate.
Use: Analgesic.
LE-GON. (Edward J. Moore) Bismuth subgallate, balsam of peru, Zn oxide, cod liver oil in petrolatum base./Tube 1.25 oz.
Use: Rectal ointment.
LOCAR. (CooperVision) Pilocarpine HCl 0.5%, 1%, 2%, 3%, 4%, 6%. Bot. 15 ml.; Twinpack 2 × 15 ml. 0.5%, 1%, 2%, 4%, 6%; 1 ml. Dropperettes 1%, 2%, 4%. Box 12s.
Use: Miotic for treatment of glaucoma.
PILOCARPINE, U.S.P. XXI. Ocular system U.S.P. XXI.
Use: Ophthalmic cholinergic, miotic.
See: Ocusert Pilo-20 and Pilo-40 (Ciba)
PILOCARPINE HYDROCHLORIDE, U.S.P. XXI. Ophth. Soln., U.S.P. XXI. (Various Mfr.) Pilocarpine muriate.
Use: 0.5 to 2.0% sol. topically as a miotic.
(Maurry) 1%, 2%, 3%, 4%, 6%. Dropper Bot. 15 ml. (Mesco) 1%, 2%, 4%. Bot. 3.5 Gm.
See: Almocarpine (Ayerst)
Isopto-Carpine, Ophth. (Alcon)
Mi-Pilo, Sol. (Barnes-Hind)
Pilocar, Sol. (CooperVision)
Pilocel, Sol. (Softcon)
Pilomiotin, Sol. (CooperVision)
Piloptic, Soln. (Muro)
W/Epinephrine HCl.
See: E-Carpine, Inj. (Alcon)
Epicar, Ophth. Sol. (Barnes-Hind)
W/Epinephrine bitartrate, mannitol, benzalkonium chloride.
See: E-Pilo, Sol. (CooperVision)
W/Eserine salicylate, methylcellulose.
See: Isopto P-ES, Soln. (Alcon)
W/Physostigmine salicylate.
See: Miocel, Sol. (Softcon)
• **PILOCARPINE NITRATE,** U.S.P. XXI. Ophth. Soln., U.S.P. XXI. (Various Mfr.) Pow., Bot. 15 gr., ⅛ oz., 1 oz. (Mesco) 1%, 2%. Bot. 3.5 Gm.
See: P.V. Carpine (Allergan)
W/Phenylephrine HCl.
Use: Parasympathomimetic agent.
See: Pilofrin Liquifilm, Ophthalmic (Allergan)
PILOCEL. (Softcon) Pilocarpine HCl 0.25, 0.5, 1, 2, 3, 4 & 6%, buffered in methylcellulose base w/benzalkonium chloride, boric acid, sod. citrate, & pot. chloride. Bot. w/dropper 15 cc. 1%, 2%, & 4%. Also avail. in 30 cc.
Use: Ophthalmic therapy, miotic.
PILOPINE HS GEL. (Alcon) Pilocarpine HCl 4%. Tube 5 Gm.
Use: Control intraocular pressure.
PIMAFUCIN. Natamycin, B.A.N.
PIMARICIN. Natamycin, B.A.N.
PIMA SYRUP. (Fleming) Potassium iodide 5 gr./5 cc. Bot. pt., gal.
Use: Expectorant.
• **PIMETINE HYDROCHLORIDE.** USAN. 4-Benzyl-1-(2-dimethylaminoethyl)piperidine hydrochloride.
Use: Cardiovascular drug (anticholesteremic).
PIMINODINE. B.A.N. 1-(3-Phenylaminopropyl-4-phenylpiperidine-4-carboxylic acid ethyl ester. Ethyl 4-phenyl-1-(3-phenylaminopropyl)piperidine-4-carboxylate.
Use: Narcotic analgesic.
PIMINODINE ESYLATE. Ethyl 1-(30 anilinopropyl)-4-phenylisonipecotate monoethanesulfaonte.
Use: Analgesic.
PIMINODINE ETHANESULFONATE. Ethyl-4-phenyl-1-[3-(phenylamino)propyl]-piperidine-4-carboxylate ethanesulfonate.
Use: Narcotic analgesic.
• **PIMOZIDE.** USAN. 1-[1-[4,4-bis(p-Fluorophenyl)-butyl]-4-piperidyl]-2-benzimidazoline. Orap.
Use: Tranquilizer.
See: Orap, Tab. (McNeil Pharm)
P-I-N. (Lannett) Isoniazid 50 mg., Vit: B-6 1 mg./Tab. Bot. 100s, 500s, 1000s. Forte-isoniazid 100 mg., Vit. B-6 5 mg./Tab. Bot. 100s, 500s, 1000s.
Use: Treatment of tuberculosis.
• **PINACIDIL.** USAN.
Use: Antihypertiensive.
• **PINADOLINE.** USAN.
Use: Analgesic.
• **PINDOLOL.** USAN. 1-(Indol-4-yloxy)-3-isopropyl-amino)-2-propanol.
Use: Hypertension, angina, pectoris, cardiac arrhythmia.
See: Visken (Sandoz).
P-I-N FORTE SYRUP. (Lannett) Isoniazid 10 mg., pyridoxine HCl 0.5 mg./cc. Bot. pt.
• **PINE NEEDLE OIL,** N.F. XVI.
Use: Perfume; flavor.
• **PINE TAR,** U.S.P. XXI.
Use: Local antieczematic; rubefacient.
PINEX CONCENTRATE COUGH SYRUP. (Last) Dextromethorphan HBr 7.5 mg./5 ml. (after diluting 3 oz. concentrate to make 16 oz. solution). Bot. 3 oz.
Use: Antitussive.
PINEX COUGH SYRUP. (Last) Dextromethorphan HBr. 7.5 mg./5 ml. Bot. 3 oz., 6 oz.
Use: Antitussive.

PINEX REGULAR. (Pinex) Pot. guaiacolsulfonate, oil of pine & eucalyptus, ext. grindelia, alcohol 3%/30 ml. Syr. 3 oz., 8 oz. Also cherry flavored 3 oz. Super and conc. 3 oz.
Use: Antitussive.

• **PINOXEPIN HCl.** USAN.
Use: Tranquilizer.

PIOXOL. Pemoline, B.A.N.

PIPADONE HYDROCHLORIDE. Dipipanone, B.A.N.

PIPAMAZINE. B.A.N. 1-[3-(2-Chlorophenothiazin-10-yl)-propyl] isonipecotramide. 10-[3-(4-Carbamoyl-piperidino)propyl]-2-chlorophenothiazine. Mornidine.
Use: Antiemetic.

• **PIPAMPERONE.** USAN. 1′-[3-(p-Fluorobenzoyl)-propyl][1,4′-bipiperidine]-4′-carboxamide. Under study.
Use: Tranquilizer.

PIPANOL HYDROCHLORIDE. Benzhexol, B.A.N.

• **PIPAZETHATE.** USAN 2-(2-Piperidinoethoxy)-ethyl pyrido[3,2-b][1,4]benzothiazine-10-carboxylate. Selvigon hydrochloride.
Use: Cough suppressant.

PIPAZETHATE HYDROCHLORIDE. 2-(2-Piperidinoethoxy)ethyl-10-H-pyrido [3,2-b]-[1,4]benzothiazine-10-carboxylate hydrochloride.
Use: Antitussive agent.

PIPENZOLATE BROMIDE. B.A.N. 1-Ethyl-3-piperidyl benzilate methylbromide. 3-Benziloyloxy-1-ethyl-1-methylpiperidinium bromide.
Use: Anticholinergic.

• **PIPERACETAZINE,** U.S.P. XXI. Tab., U.S.P. XXI. 10-{3-[4-(2-Hydroxyethyl)piperidino]propyl} phenothiazin-2-yl methyl ketone.
Use: Tranquilizer; antipsychotic agent.
See: Quide, Tab., (Merrell Dow)

• **PIPERACILLIN SODIUM, STERILE.** U.S.P. XXI.
Use: Antibacterial.

• **PIPERAMIDE MALEATE.** USAN. 4′-[4-[3-(Dimethylamino)propyl]-1-piperazinyl]acetanilide dimaleate.
Use: Antiparasitic.

• **PIPERAZINE,** U.S.P. XXI.
Use: Anthelmintic.

PIPERAZINE CALCIUM EDETATE. B.A.N. [Dihydrogen)ethylenedinitrilo)tetraacetato]-calcium piperazine salt. Perin.
Use: Anthelmintic.

• **PIPERAZINE CITRATE,** U.S.P. XXI. Syrup, Tab., U.S.P. XXI. Piperazine, 2-hydroxy-1,2,3-propanetricarboxylate (3:2) hydrate. Piperazine citrate (3:2) hydrate. Piperazine Citrate Telra Hydrous Tripiperazine Dicitrate.
Use: Anthelmintic.
See: Antepar, Tab., Syr. (Burroughs Wellcome)
Bryrel, Syr. (Winthrop Products)
Multifuge Citrate, Tab., Syr. (Blue Line)
Pin-Tega Tabs., Syr. (Ortega)
Pipril, Liq. (Kenyon)
Ta-Verm, Syr., Tab. (Table Rock)
Vermago, Syr. (Westerfield)

• **PIPERAZINE EDETATE CALCIUM.** USAN. Dihydrogen [(ethylenedinitrilo)tetraacetato]calciate(2-) compour with piperazine (1:1). Perin.
Use: Anthelmintic.

PIPERAZINE ESTRONE SULFATE.
See: Estropipitate

PIPERAZINE HEXAHYDRATE. Tivazine.

PIPERAZINE PHOSPHATE.
Use: Anthelmintic (intestinal roundworms and trematodes).

PIPERAZINE TARTRATE.
See: Razine Tartrate, Tab. (Paddock)

PIPERIDINE PHOSPHATE.
Use: Psychiatric drug.

PIPERIDINOETHYL BENZILATE HCl. No products listed.

PIPERIDOLATE. B.A.N. 1-Ethyl-3-piperidyl dipheny lacetate.
Use: Parasympatholytic.

PIPERIDOLATE HYDROCHLORIDE. 1-Ethyl-3-piperidyl diphenylacetate HCl.
Use: Anticholinergic.

PIPEROCAINE. B.A.N. 3-(2-Methylpiperidino)-propy benzoate.
Use: Local anesthetic.

PIPEROCAINE HYDROCHLORIDE. 3-Benzoxy-1-(2-methylpiperidino) propane HCl.

PIPERONYL BUTOXIDE. B.A.N. 5-[2-(2-Butoxy-ethoxy)ethoxymethyl]-6-propyl-1,3-benzodioxole.
Use: Acaricide, veterinary medicine.

PIPEROXAN. B.A.N. 2-Piperidinomethyl-1,4-benzodioxan.
Use: Adrenergic blocking agent.

PIPEROXAN HYDROCHLORIDE. 2-(1-Piperidylmethyl)-1,4-benzodioxan HCl. Fourneau 933. Benzodioxane.
Use: Diagnosis of hypertension.

PIPERPHENIDOL HCl. 5-Methyl-4-phenyl-1-(1-piperidyl)-3-hexanol HCl.

PIPETHANATE HCl. 2-Piperidinoethyl benzilate HCl.
Use: Tranquilizer.

• **PIPOBROMAN,** U.S.P. XXI. Tab., U.S.P. XXI. 1,4-Bis(3-bromopropionyl)piperazine. Δ2,a-thiazolidine-acetate.
Use: Antineoplastic.
See: Vercyte, Tab. (Abbott)

• **PIPOSULFAN.** USAN. 1,4-Dihydracryloylpiperazine dimethanesulfonate.
Use: Antineoplastic agent.

PIPOTHIAZINE. B.A.N. 2-Dimethylsulfamoyl-10-3-[4-(2-hydroxyethyl)piperidino]propyl phenothiazine.
Use: Neuroleptic.

• **PIPOTIAZINE PALMITATE.** USAN.
Use: Antipsychotic.
See: Piportil (Ives)

PIPOXOLAN. B.A.N. 5,5-Diphenyl-2-(2-piperidinoethyl)-1,3-dioxolan-4-one.
Use: Antispasmodic.

• **PIPOXOLAN HCl.** USAN. 5,5-Diphenyl-2-(2-piperidinoethyl)-1,3-dioxolan-4-one HCl. Rowapraxin.
Use: Muscle relaxant.

PIPRACIL. (Lederle) Piperacillin sodium 2 Gm, 3 Gm. or 4 Gm./Vial; 2 Gm., 3 Gm. or 4 Gm./Infusion Bottle.
Use: Broad spectrum antibiotic.

PIPRADOL. B.A.N. α-2-Piperidylbenzhydrol.
Use: Central nervous system stimulant.

PIPRIL. (Kenyon) Piperazine citrate 0.5 Gm./5 cc. Bot. pt., gal.
Use: Anthelmintic.

PIPRINHYDRINATE. B.A.N. Diphenylpyraline salt of 8-chlorotheopylline. 4-Benzyhydryloxy-1-methylpiperidine salt of 8-chlorotheophylline. Kolton; Mepedyl.
Use: Antihistamine.

PIPROZOLIN. USAN. Ethyl 3-ethyl-4-oxo-5-piperidino Δ^2, alpha-thiazolidineacetate.
Use: Choleretic.

PIQUINDONE HYDROCHLORIDE. USAN.
Use: Antipsychotic.

PIQUIZIL HCl. USAN. Isobutyl 4-(6,7-dimethoxy-4-quinazolinyl)-1-piperazinecarboxylate monohydrochloride.
Use: Bronchodilator.

PIRACETAM. USAN. 2-Oxopyrrolidin-1-ylacetamide. Nootropyl.
Use: Cerebral stimulant.

• **PIRANDAMINE HYDROCHLORIDE.** USAN.
Use: Anti-depressant.

• **PIRAZOLAC.** USAN.
Use: Antirheumatic.

• **PIRBENICILLIN SODIUM.** USAN.
Use: Antibacterial.

PIRBUTEROL. B.A.N. 2-tert-Butylamino-1-(5-hydroxy-6-hydroxymethyl-2-pyridyl)ethanol.
Use: Bronchodilator.

• **PIRBUTEROL ACETATE.** USAN.
Use: Bronchodilator.

• **PIRBUTEROL HYDROCHLORIDE.** USAN.
Use: Bronchodilator.

• **PIRENPERONE.** USAN.
Use: Tranquilizer.

• **PIRETANIDE.** USAN.
Use: Diuretic.
Arlix Prods. (Hoechst)

• **PIRFENIDONE.** USAN.
Use: Anti-inflammatory; antipyretic.

PIRIDAZOL.
See: Sulfapyridine, Tab. (Various Mfr.)

• **PIRIDICILLIN SODIUM.** USAN.
Use: Antibacterial.

PIRIDOCAINE HCl. Beta-(2-Piperidyl) ethyl-o-aminobenzoate.

PIRIDOXILATE. B.A.N. The reciprocal salt of (5-hydroxy-4-hydroxymethyl-6-methyl-3-pyridyl)-methoxyglycolic acid with [4,5-bis(hydroxymethyl)-2-methyl-3-pyridyl] oxyglycolic acid (1:1). GLYO-6.
Use: Treatment of angina.

PIRIN-C. (Scrip) Salicylamide 450 mg., Vit. C 30 mg./Tab. Bot. 100s.

• **PIRIPROST.** USAN.
Use: Anti-asthmatic.

• **PIRIPROST POTASSIUM.** USAN.
Use: Anti-asthmatic.

PIRITON.
See: Chlorpheniramine (Var. Mfr.)

PIRITRAMIDE. B.A.N. 4-(4-Carbamoyl-4-piperidinopiperidino)-2,2-diphenylbutyronitrile. Dipodolor.
Use: Analgesic.

• **PIRLIMYCIN HYDROCHLORIDE.** USAN.
Use: Antibacterial.

• **PIRMAGREL.** USAN.
Use: Inhibitor (thromboxane synthetase).

• **PIRMENOL HYDROCHLORIDE.** USAN.
Use: Cardiac depressant.

• **PIRNABINE.** USAN.
Use: Antiglaucoma agent.

• **PIROCTONE.** USAN.
Use: Antiseborrheic.

• **PIROCTONE OLAMINE.** USAN.
Use: Antiseborrheic.

• **PIROGLIRIDE TARTRATE.** USAN.
Use: Antidiabetic.

• **PIROLATE.** USAN.
Use: Anti-asthmatic.

• **PIROLAZAMIDE.** USAN.
Use: Cardiac depressant.

PIROTHESIN HYDROCHLORIDE. Aptocaine, B.A.N.

• **PIROXICAM.** U.S.P. XXI. Cap., U.S.P. XXI. N-pyridyl-methyl-hydroxy-(benzothiazine-1 idioxide)carboxamide.
Use: Anti-inflammatory.
See: Feldene, Cap (Pfizer)

• **PIROXICAM OLAMINE.** USAN.
Use: Anti-inflammatory, analgesic.

• **PIROXIMONE.** USAN.
Use: Cardiotonic.

• **PIRPROFEN.** USAN.
Use: Anti-inflammatory.
See: Rengasil (Geigy)

• **PIRQUINOZOL.** USAN.
Use: Anti-allergic.

PIRSEAL. (Fellows) Acetylsalicylic acid 5 gr., 10 gr./Tab. Bot. 100s, 1000s.

PISO's. (Pinex) Ipecac, ammonium chloride, menthol in syrup base. Bot. 3 oz., 5 oz.
Use: Cough due to colds.

PITAYINE.
See: Quinidine, Preps. (Various Mfr.)

PITOCIN. (Parke-Davis) Oxytocin w/chlorobutanol 0.5%, acetic acid to adjust pH. Amp. (5 u.) 0.5 ml. (10 u.) 1 ml. Box 10s, Steri-dose syringe (10 u.) 1 ml. 10s.
Use: Oxytocic.

PITRESSIN. (Parke-Davis) Vasopressin w/chlorobutanol 0.5%, pH adjusted with acetic acid. Amp. 0.5 ml. (10 pressor u.) & 1 ml. (20 pressor u.) Box 10s.
Use: Prevention & control of abdominal distention.

PITRESSIN TANNATE IN OIL. (Parke-Davis) Vasopressin Tannate in peanut oil.
Amp. (5 pressor u.) 1 ml. Box 10s.
Use: Where long-continued action of Pitressin is desired; treatment of diabetes insipidus.

PITTS CARMINATIVE. (Commerce) Bot. 2 oz.
Use: Gas and colic relief.

PITUITARY, ANTERIOR. The anterior lobe of the pituitary gland supplies protein hormones classified under following headings.
See preparation of:
Corticotropin, Preps. (Var. Mfr.)
Gonadotropin, Preps. (Var. Mfr.)
Growth Hormone
Thyrotropic Principle

PITUITARY, POSTERIOR. Pituitary Extract, (Armour) Posterior. Caps ⅔ gr. Bot. 100s.

• **PITUITARY, POSTERIOR, INJECTION,** U.S.P. XXI.
See: Pituitrin, Obstetrical, Amp. (Parke-Davis)
Pituitrin, Surgical, Amp. (Parke-Davis)

PITUITARY, POSTERIOR, HORMONES.
(a) Vasopressin. Pressor principle, β-hypophamine, postlobin-V.
See: Pitressin, Amp. (Parke-Davis)
Pitressin Tannate, Amp. (Parke-Davis)
(b) Oxytocin. Oxytocic principle. α-hypophamine, postiobin-O.
See: Oxytocin, Inj.
Pitocin, Amp. (Var. Mfr.)
Syntocin, Amp. (Sandoza)

PITUITRIN-S. (Parke-Davis) Pituitary, posterior ext. 20 units/ml. Amp. 1 ml., Box 10s.
Use: Obstetrical, to stimulate uterine contraction. Surgical, prevention & control of abdominal distention.

PIVAMPICILLIN. B.A.N. Pivaloyloxymethyl 6-[D(−)-α-aminophenylacetamido]penicillinate. Pondocillin [hydrochloride.]
Use: Antibiotic.

• **PIVAMPICILLIN HYDROCHLORIDE..** USAN.
Use: Antibacterial

• **PIVAMPICILLIN PAMOATE.** USAN.
Use: Antibacterial.

• **PIVAMPICILLIN PROBENATE.** USAN.
Use: Antibacterial.

PIVAZIDE. N-Benzyl-N′-pivaloylhydrazine. Tersavid.

PIVHYDRAZINE. B.A.N. 1-Benzyl-2-pivaloyl-hydrazine.
Use: Monoamine oxidase inhibitor.

PIVMECILLINAM. B.A.N. Pivaloyloxymethyl (2S,5R,6R)-6-(perhydroazepin-1-ylmethyleneamino)-penicillanate.
Use: Antibiotic.

• **PIVOPRIL.** USAN.
Use: Antihypertensive.

PIXACOL. (Pixacol) Liquid ext. of coal tar, modified by addition of salicylic acid 1%, methylsalicylate 5%, Bot. 1 oz., 4 oz., 8 oz.
Use: Psoriasis.

PIXACREME. (Pixacol) White ointment containing ammoniated mercury 5%, phenol 2%. Jar 4 oz.
Use: Psoriasis.

PIX CARBONIS.
See: Coal Tar, Prep. (Var. Mfr.)

PIX JUNIPERI.
See: Juniper Tar, Comp. (Var. Mfr.)
Use: Sunscreen, moisturizer.

PIZOTIFEN. B.A.N. 4-(9,10-Dihydrobenzo[4,5]-cyclohepta]1,2-b]thien-4-ylidene)-1-methyl-piperidine.
Use: Prophylaxis of migraine.

• **PIZOTYLINE.** USAN. 4-(9,10-Dihydro-4H-benzo[4,5] cyclohepta]1,2-b]thien-4-ylidene)-1-methyl-piperidine
Use: Anabolic, antidepressant; migraine prophylactic.

PLACEBO CAPSULES. (Cowley) No. 3 orange red; No. 4 yellow. Bot. 1000s.
Use: Placebo.

PLACEBO TABLETS. (Cowley) 1 gr. white; 2 gr. white; 3 gr. white, red or yellow, pink, orange; 4 gr. white; 5 gr. white. Bot. 1000s.
Use: Placebo.

PLACENTA.
See: Gonadotropins, Chorionic, Inj. (Var. Mfr.)

PLACENTEX. (Roche) A latex agglutination-inhibition tube test for pregnancy sensitive to 1.01.U. of HCG per ml. of urine.

PLACIDYL. (Abbott) Ethchlorvynol. 100 mg., 200 mg./Cap. Bot. 100s. 500 mg./Cap. Bot. 100s, 500s. 750 mg./Cap. Bot. 100s. Unit dose 100s. (Abbo-Pac 500 mg., 750 mg.)
Use: Nonbarbiturate sedative or hypnotic.

• **PLAGUE VACCINE,** U.S.P. XXI. (Cutter) 2000 million killed *Pasteurella pestis*/ml. Vial 2 ml., 20 ml.
Use: S.C. vaccination, active immunizing agent.

PLANOCAINE.
See: Procaine Hydrochloride, Preps. (Var. Mfr.)

PLANOCHROME.
See: Merbromin, Sol. (Var. Mfr.)

PLANTAGO, OVATA COATING.
See: Effersyllium, Prods. (Stuart)
Konsyl, Pow. (Burton, Parsons)
L.A. Formula, Pow. (Burton, Parsons)
Metamucil, Pow. (Searle)
W/Psyllium seed, gum karaya, Brewer's yeast.
See: Plantamucin, Granules (Elder)
W/Vit. B-1.
See: Siblin, Granules (Parke-Davis)

• **PLANTAGO SEED,** U.S.P. XXI. Psyllium Seed, Plantain Seed.
Use: Fecal softener.

PLANT PROTEASE CONCENTRATE.
See: Ananase, Tab. (Rorer)

PLAQUENIL TABLET. (Winthrop Products) Hydroxycholorquine sulfate.
Use: Malaria, amebiasis.

PLASBUMIN-5. (Cutter) Normal serum albumin (Human) 5% U.S.P. fractionated from normal serum plasma, heat treated against hepatitis virus.
Albumin 12.5 Gm./250 ml. Vial 50 ml. Bot. with set 50 ml., 250 ml., 500 ml.
Use: Blood volume supporter, albumin replacement.

PLASBUMIN-25. (Cutter) Normal serum albumin (Human) 25% U.S.P. fractionated from normal serum plasma, heat treated against hepatitis virus.
Albumin 12.5 Gm./50 ml. Vial 20 ml. Bot. with set 50 ml., 100 ml.
Use: Blood volume supporter, albumin replacement.

.ASMA.
See: Normal Human Plasma (Var. Mfr.)

ASMA EXPANDERS OR SUBSTITUTES.
See: Dextran 6% & LMD 10% (Abbott)
Macrodex, Sol. (Pharmacia)

.ASMA-LYTE A INJECTION. (Travenol) Sodium 140, potassium 5, magnesium 3, chloride 98, acetate 27, gluconate 23 mEq./L w/pH adjusted to 7.4. Plastic Bot. 500 ml., 1000 ml.
Use: Fluid & electrolyte replenisher.

.ASMA-LYTE 148 INJECTION. (Travenol) Sodium 140, potassium 5, magnesium 3, Cl 98, acetate 27, gluconate 23 mEq./L. Plastic Bot. 500 ml., 1000 ml.
Use: Fluid & electrolyte replenisher.

.ASMA-LYTE M and 5% DEXTROSE INJECTION. (Travenol) Sodium 40 meq., potassium 16, calcium 5, magnesium 3, Cl 40, acetate 12, lactate 12 mEq./L. Plastic Bot. 500 ml., 1000 ml.
Use: Fluid & electrolyte replenisher.

.ASMA-LYTE R and 5% DEXTROSE INJECTION. (Travenol) Sodium 140, potassium 10, calcium 5 magnesium 3, Cl 103, acetate 47, lactate 8 mEq/L. Bot. 500 ml., 1000 ml.
Use: Fluid & electrolyte replenisher.

.ASMA-LYTE 56 and 5% DEXTROSE. (Travenol) Sodium 40, potassium 13, magnesium 3, Cl 40, acetate 16 mEq/L. Plastic Bot. 500 ml., 1000 ml.
Use: Fluid & electrolyte replenisher.

.ASMA-LYTE 148 and 5% DEXTROSE INJECTION. (Travenol) Sodium 140, potassium 5, magnesium 3, Cl 98, acetate 27, gluconate 23 mEq./L. Plastic Bot. 500 ml., 1000 ml.
Use: Fluid & electrolyte replenisher.

LASMA-LYTE 56 IN WATER. (Travenol) Sodium 40, potassium 13, magnesium 3, Cl 40, acetate 16 mEq/L. Plastic Bot. 500 ml., 1000 ml.
Use: Fluid & electrolyte replenisher.

LASMA-LYTE R INJECTION. (Travenol) Sodium 140, potassium 10, calcium 5, magnesium 3, chloride 103, acetate 47, lactate 8 mEq./L. Bot. 1000 ml.
Use: Fluid & electrolyte replenisher.

LASMANATE. (Cutter) Plasma protein fraction (Human) 5%. U.S.P. Vial 50 ml. Bot. 250 ml., 500 ml. with set.
Use: Shock. Hypoproteinemia.

LASMA PLEX. (Armour) Plasma protein fraction (human) in 5% heat treated solution. Bot. 50 ml., 250 ml., 500 ml.
Use: I.V. use for treatment of shock, burns, & hypoproteinemia.

PLASMA PROTEIN FRACTION, U.S.P. XXI. (Hyland) For the plasma protein preparation obtained from human plasma using the Cohn fractionation technic. Bot. 250 ml.
Use: Blood-volume supporter.
See: Plasmanate, Sol. (Cutter)
Plasma-Plex, Sol. (Armour)
Plasmatein (Abbott)

LASMIN. B.A.N. The proteolytic enzyme derived from the activation of plasminogen. Actase is Plasmin (Human).

PLASMINOGEN. B.A.N. The specific substance derived from plasma which, when activated, has the property of lysing fibrinogen, fibrin, and some other proteins.

PLASMOCHIN NAPHTHOATE. Pamaquine naphthoate.
Use: Malaria.

PLASMOSAN. Povidone, B.A.N.

• **PLATELET CONCENTRATE,** U.S.P. XXI.
Use: Platelet replenisher.

PLATELET FACTOR 4. (Abbott) Test kit 100s.
Use: Radioimmunoassay for quantitative measurement of total PF4 levels in plasma.

PLATINOL. (Bristol) Cisplatin 10 mg./Vial, 50 mg./Vial.
Use: Antineoplastic agent.

• **PLAURACIN.** USAN.
Use: Growth stimulant.

PLEGINE. (Ayerst) Phendimetrazine tartrate 35 mg./Tab. Bot. 100s, 1000s.
Use: Anorexiant.

PLEGISOL. (Abbott) Plegisol, cardioplegic solution. Single Dose Container 1000 ml. without sodium bicarbonate.
Use: Instillation into cardiac vasculature after buffering w/sodium bicarbonate.

PLEWIN TABLETS. (Winthrop Products) Glycobiarsol, chloroquine phosphate.
Use: Intestinal amebicide.

PLEXOLAN CREAM. (Last) Zinc oxide, lanolin. Tube 1.25 oz., 3 oz. Jar 16 oz.
Use: Protective for rough skin.

PLEXON. (Sig) Testosterone 10 mg., estrone 1 mg., liver 2 mcg., pyridoxine HCl 10 mg., panthenol 10 mg., inositol 20 mg., choline Cl 20 mg., Vit. B-12 100 mcg., procaine HCl 1%, niacinamide 100 mg., Vit. B-2 2 mg./ml. Vials 10 ml.
Use: Preventive geriatrics and nutritional deficiency.

PLIAGEL. (CooperVision) Poloxamer 407, preserved with sorbic acid 0.25%, edetate trisodium 0.5%. Bot. 25 ml.
Use: Soft contact lens cleaning solution.

• **PLICAMYCIN,** U.S.P. XXI. Inj. U.S.P.XXI. Antibiotic derived from *Streptomyces agrillaceus* & *S. tanashiensis.*
Use: Antineoplastic, antibiotic.
See: Mithracin, Pwd. (Miles Pharm)

PLOVA. (Washington Ethical) Psyllium mucilloid. Pow. Flavored 12 oz. Plain 10 0.5 oz.
Use: Bowel regulator, laxative.

PLURAVIT DROPS. (Winthrop Products) Multivitamin.
Use: Dietary supplement.

PLURI-B. (Pasadena Research) Vit. B-1 50 mg., B-2 5.0 mg., B-6 10 mg., panthenol 10 mg., niacinamide 50 mg./cc. Vial 10 cc., 30 cc. Also w/procaine HCl 1%. Vial 30 cc.
Use: Vitamin supplement, Inj.

PLURI-BEX. (Pasadena Research) Vit. B-1 100 mg., B-2 1 mg., B-6 10 mg., d-panthenol 10 mg., niacinamide 150 mg./cc. Vial 10 cc., 30 cc.
Use: Vitamin supplement.

PLUS-FACTOR TABLETS. (Sutliff & Case) Cal. carbonate 625 mg., docusate sodium 60 mg., Vit. C 50 mg., A 5000 I.U., D 400 I.U., B-1 3 mg., B-2 2 mg., B-6 2 mg., B-12 2 mcg., cal. pantothenate 5 mg., niacinamide 10 mg., iron 30 mg., Mn 1 mg., Mg 5 mg., Cu 1 mg., Zn 1.5 mg., iodine 0.15 mg./Tabs. Bot. 100s, 1000s.
Use: Pregnancy and lactation.

PMB 200. (Ayerst) Premarin (Conjugated Estrogens, U.S.P.) 0.45 mg., meprobamate 200 mg./Tab. Bot. 60s.
Use: Treatment of moderate to severe vasomotor symptoms associated with the menopause with emotional symptoms (anxiety, tension).

PMB 400. (Ayerst) Premarin (Conjugated Estrogens, U.S.P.) 0.45 mg., meprobamate 400 mg./Tab. Bot. 60s.
Use: Treatment of moderate to severe vasomotor symptoms associated with the menopause with emotional symptoms (anxiety, tension).

P.M.P. COMPOUND. (Mericon) Chlorpheniramine maleate 4 mg., phenylephrine HCl 15 mg., salicylamide 300 mg., scopolamine methylnitrate 0.8 mg./Tab. Bot. 100s, 1000s.

PMP EXPECTORANT. (Mericon) Codeine phosphate 10 mg., phenylephrine HCl 10 mg., guaifenesin 40 mg., chlorpheniramine maleate 2 mg./5 cc. Bot. gal.

P-M-Z HCl EXPECTORANT. (Sutliff & Case) Promethazine HCl 5 mg., ipecac fl. ext. 0.17 min., K guaiacolsulfonate 44 mg., citric acid anhydrous 60 mg., sod. citrate 197 mg./5 cc., alcohol 7% Bot. 4 oz., pt., gal.
W/Codeine phosphate 10 mg./5 cc. Bot. 4 oz., pt., gal.

PNEUMOCOCCAL VACCINE, POLYVALENT. Purified capsular polysaccharides from 23 penumococcal types.
Use: Vaccination against pneumococcal types.
See: Pneumovax 23, Inj. (Merck Sharp& Dohme)
Pnuimune 23, Inj. (Merck Sharp & Dohme)

PNEUMOCOCCI.
W/*Haemophilus influenzae, Neisseria catarrhalis, streptococci, Klebsiella pneumoniae, staphylococci, pneumococci,* killed.
See: Mixed Vaccine No. 4 w/H. Influenzae, Inj. (Lilly)

PNEUMONIA VACCINE, KILLED DIPLOCOCCUS.
W/*Neisseria catarrhalis, Klebsiella pneumoniae, streptococci, staphylococci.*
See: Combined Vaccine No. 4 w/Catarrhalis, Inj. (Lilly)

PNEUMONIAE VACCINE, KILLED KLEBSIELLA.
W/*Neisseria catarrhalis, Diplococcus pneumoniae, streptococci, staphylococci.*
See: Combined Vaccine No. 4 w/Catarrhalis, Inj. (Lilly)

PNEUMOVAX 23. (Merck Sharp & Dohme) Pneumococcal vaccine polyvalent 0.5 ml./dose. Vials: 5 dose, 1 dose × 5s.
Use: Immunization against pneumonia.

PNS UNNA BOOT. (Pedinol) Non-sterile gauze bandag 10 yds × 3″. Box 12s.
Use: Ambulatory procedure in treatment of leg ulcers and varicosities.

PNU-IMUNE 23. (Lederle) Pneumococcal vaccine 0 ml. dose. Vial 5 dose. Lederject disposable syring 5 × 1 dose.
Use: Vaccine against pneumococcal pneumonia.

POCHLORIN. Prophyrinic and chlorophyllic compound.
Use: Anti-hypercholesteremic agent.

PODIASPRAY. (Dalin) Undecylenic acid, salicylic aci dichlorophene. Spray-on pow. 6 oz.
Use: Fungicide-germicide.

PODIODINE. (A.V.P.) Germicidal surgical scrub and solution.

POD-BEN-25. (C & M Pharmacal) Podophyllin 25% i tincture benzoin. Bot. 1 oz.
Use: Wart removal.

PODOBEN. (Maurry) Resin podophyllum 25%, benzoin comp. 10%; isopropyl alcohol 69-72%. Bo 5 cc.
Use: Wart therapy.

• **PODOPHYLLUM,** U.S.P. XXI.
Use: Caustic.
W/Cascara sagrada, bile salts, phenolphthalein.
See: Bilstan (Standex)
W/Oxgall, cascara sagrada, dandelion root, tr. nux vomica.
See: Oxachol, Liq. (Philips Roxane)

• **PODOPHYLLUM RESIN,** U.S.P. XXI. Topical Sol., U.S.P. XXI. (Var. Mfr.) podophyllin. Pkg. 1 oz., 0.25 lb., 1 lb.
Use: Caustic.
See: Podoben, Liq. (Maurry)
W/Salicylic acid.
See: Ver-Var, Sol. (Owen)

POINT-TWO MOUTHRINSE. (Hoyt) Sodium fluoride 0.2% in a flavored neutral liquid. Bot. 120 ml.
Use: Prevention of dental caries.

POISON ANTIDOTE KIT. (Bowman) Charcoal suspension. Bot. 1.5 oz., 4s. Ipecac syrup, Bot. 0.5 oz., 2/Kit.

POISON IVY AND OAK PROPHYLAXIS. (Hollister-Stier) Allergenic extract for oral administration. Dropper Bot. 15 ml. Pkg. 3s. Strength 1:25, 1:50, 1:100.
Use: Hyposensitization of patients allergic to poison ivy and poison oak.

POISON IVY EXTRACT. (Parke-Davis) Extract from leaves of *Rhus toxicodendron* dissolved in sterile almond oil. Single dose 0.1 ml vial.
Use: Prevention of rhus dermatitis.

• **POISON IVY EXTRACT, ALUM PRECIPITATED.** USAN. An aqueous suspension of a pyridine extract of poison ivy which is precipitated with alum and adjusted to standard concentrations.
See: Aqua Ivy, Inj. (Miles Pharm)
Poisonivi, Ext. (Cutter)
Poisonok, Ext. (Cutter)

ISON IVY, OAK & SUMAC (RHUS-ALL). (Barry) Triple antigen in oil 0.2 mg./cc. Vial 5 cc.
Use: Prophylactic for hyposensitization.

ISON IVY, OAK AND SUMAC EXT.
See: Allergenic Ext., Vial (Barry)

ISON OAK EXTRACT. USAN.
Use: Anti-allergic.

ISON OAK-IVY EXTRACT. (Hollister-Stier) Poison ivy ext. & poison oak, Vial, Dropper Bot. 15 cc.
See: Ivyol, Vial (Merck Sharp & Dohme)

OLACRILLIN. USAN. Methacrylic acid with divinylbenzene. A synthetic ion-exchange resin, supplied in the hydrogen or free acid form. Amberlite IRP-64 (Rohm and Haas).
Use: Pharmaceutic aid.

OLACRILLIN POTASSIUM, N.F.XVI. A synthetic ion-exchange resin, prepared through the polymerization of methacrylic acid and divinylbenzene, further neutralized with potassium hydroxide to form the potassium salt of methacrylic acid and divinylbenzene. Supplied as a pharmaceutical-grade ion-exchange resin in a particle size of 100- to 500-mesh.
Use: Pharmaceutic aid.
See: Amberlite IRP-88 (Rohm and Haas)

LADEX TABS. (Major) Dexchlorpheniramine maleate 4 mg./Tab. Bot. 100s, 250s, 1000s; 6 mg./Tab. Bot. 100s, 1000s.
Use: Antihistaminic.

LAMETHENE RESIN CAPRYLATE. The physiochemical complex of the acid-binding ion exchange resin, polyamine-methylene resin and caprylic acid.

LARAMINE. (Schering) Dexchlorpheniramine maleate (d-isomer of Chlor-Trimeton). **Repetab:** 4 mg./Tab. Bot. 100s; 6 mg./Tab. Bot. 100s, 1000s. **Syrup:** 2 mg./5 ml. Bot. 16 oz.
Use: Antihistaminic.

LARAMINE EXPECTORANT. (Schering) Dexchlorpheniramine maleate 2 mg., pseudoephedrine sulfate 20 mg., guaifenesin 100 mg., alcohol 7.2%/5 ml. Bot. 16 oz.
Use: Antihistaminic, decongestant, antitussive.

LARGEN T.D. TABS. (Goldline) Dexchlorpheniramine maleate 4 mg. or 6 mg./Tab. Bot. 100s, 1000s.
Use: Antihistaminic.

OLDEMAN AD SUSPENSION. (Winthrop Products) Kaolin.
Use: Antidiarrheal agent.

OLDEMAN SUSPENSION. (Winthrop Products) Kaolin.
Use: Antidiarrheal agent.

OLDEMICINA SUSPENSION. (Winthrop Products) Kaolin.
Use: Antidiarrheal agent.

OLDINE METHYLSULFATE. 2-(Hydroxymethyl)-1,1-dimethyl-pyrrolidinium methylsulfate benzilate. 2-Benziloyloxymethyl-1,1-dimethylpyrrolidinium methylsulfate.
Use: Anticholinergic.

• **POLICAPRAM.** USAN.
Use: Pharmaceutic aid.

POLIDENT DENTU-GRIP. (Block) Carboxymethylcellulose gum, ethylene oxide polymer. Pkg. 0.675 oz., 1.75 oz., 3.55 oz.

POLIDEXIDE. B.A.N. Dextran cross-linked with epichlorhydrin and 0-substituted with 2-diethylaminoethyl groups, some of them quaternized with diethylaminoethyl chloride. Secholex hydrochloride.
Use: Antihypercholesterolemic agent.

• **POLIGEENAN.** USAN. 3,6-Anhydro-4-O-β-D-galactopyranosyl-α-D-galactopyranose 2,4′-bis(potassium/sodium sulfate)-(1-3′)-polysaccharide. Polysaccharide produced by limited hydrolysis of carragheen from red algae.
Use: Enzyme inhibitor.

• **POLIGNATE SODIUM.** USAN.
Use: Enzyme inhibitor.

POLI-GRIP. (Block) Karaya gum, magnesium oxide in petrolatum mineral oil base, peppermint and spearmint flavor. Tube 0.75, 1.5. 2.5 oz.
Use: Denture adhesive cream.

POLIOMYELITIS IMMUNE GLOBULIN (HUMAN). (Var. Mfr.) Prep. of gamma globulin primarily assayed for content of poliomyelitis antibodies in accordance with standard procedures licensed by National Institutes of Health.

POLIOMYELITIS VACCINE. (Purified, Salk Type IPV) (Squibb-Connaught) Amp. 5 x 1 ml. Vial 10 dose.
Use: Active immunizing for prevention of poliomyelitis.

• **POLIOMYELITIS VACCINE INACTIVATED,** U.S.P. XXI.
Use: Active immunizing agent.

• **POLIOVIRUS VACCINE LIVE ORAL,** U.S.P. XXI.
Poliovirus vaccine, live, oral, type I, II, or III.
Poliovirus vaccine, live, oral, trivalent.
Use: Active immunizing agent.
See: Orimune Trivalent I, II & III, Vial (Lederle)

POLIOVIRUS VACCINE, LIVE, ORAL, TRIVALENT.
Use: Immunization against polio strains 1, 2 & 3.
See; Orimune (Lederle)

POLIOMYELITIS VACCINE, PURIFIED. (Squibb-Connaught) Amp. 1 ml. Box 5s. Vial. 10 dose.
Use: S.C.; an active immunizing agent for the prevention of poliomyelitis.

• **POLIPROPENE 25.** USAN.
Use: Pharmaceutic aid.

POLISHED AMBERS DERMANESSE SKIN TONING CREAM. (Revlon) Hydroquinone 2%, padimate 0, oxybenzone in cream base.
Use: Skin bleaching.

POLLEN ANTIGEN, ORAL.

POLORIS POULTICES. (Block) Benzocaine, capsicum. Pkg. 5 and 12 unit.
Use: Dental pain.

• **POLOXALENE.** USAN. Liquid nonionic surfactant polymer of polyoxypropylene polyoxyethylene type.
Use: Surfactant.

POLOXALKOL. B.A.N. A polymer of ethylene oxide, propylene oxide, and propylene glycol.
Use: Surface active agent.

POLOXALKOL. Polyoxyethylene polyoxypropylene polymer.
See: Magcyl, Caps. (Elder)
W/Casanthrol.
See: Casakol, Cap. (Upjohn)
W/Phenylephrine HCl, dextrose sol.
See: Isohalent, Sol. (Elder)

• **POLOXAMER,** N.F. XVI.
Use: Surfactant.

• **POLOXAMER 182 D.** USAN.
Use: Pharmaceutic aid (suxfactant).

• **POLOXAMER 182 LF.** USAN.
Use: Food additive; pharmaceutic aid.

• **POLOXAMER 188.** USAN.
Use: Cathartic.

• **POLOXAMER 188 LF.** USAN.
Use: Pharmaceutic aid (surfactant).

• **POLOXAMER 331.** USAN.
Use: Food additive (surfactant).

POLOXAMER-IODINE.
See: Prepodyne, Sol. (West)

POLOXYL LANOLIN. B.A.N. A polyoxyethylene condensation-product of anhydrous lanolin. Aqualose.
Use: Emollient.

POLYAMINE-METHYLENE RESIN.
See: Exorbin (Var. Mfr.)

POLYAMINE RESIN.
See: Polyamine-Methylene Resin (Var. Mfr.)

POLYANETHOL SULFONATE, SODIUM.
See: Grobax, Vial (Roche Diagnostics)

POLYANHYDROGLUCOSE. Polyanhydroglucuronic acid.
See: Dextran, Inj., Sol. (Var. Mfr.)

POLYBASE. (Paddock) Preblended polyethylene glycol suppository base for incorporation of medications where a water soluble base is indicated. Jar 1 lb., 5 lb.
Use: Suppository base.

POLYBENZARSOL. Benzarsol.

POLY-BON DROPS. (Barrows) Vit. A 3000 I.U., D 400 I.U., C 60 mg., B-1 1 mg., B-2 1.2 mg., niacinamide 8 mg./0.6 cc. Bot. 50 cc.

POLYBRENE. Hexadimethrine Bromide, B.A.N.

• **POLYBUTESTER.** USAN.
Use: Surgical suture material.

• **POLYBUTILATE.** USAN.
Use: Surgical suture coating.

POLYCARBOPHIL. A synthetic, loosely crosslinked, hydrophilic resin of the polycarboxylic type. Sorboquel.
Use: Absorbent (gastrointestinal).

POLYCILLIN. (Bristol) Ampicillin trihydrate. Cap.: **250 mg.**/Cap. Bot. 100s, 500s. 1000s. **Cap.: 500 mg.** /Cap. Bot. 16s, 100s, 500s. DosaTrol 250 mg., 500 mg. Bot. 100s. **Pediatric Drops:** 100 mg./ml. Dropper Bot. 20 ml.
Use: Antibiotic.

POLYCILLIN-N. (Bristol) Sodium ampicillin 125 mg., 250 mg., 500 mg., 1 Gm., 2 Gm./Vial Pkg. 1s, 10s. Piggyback vials 500 mg., 1 Gm., 2 Gm. Bulk vial 1 Gm.
Use: Antibiotic.

POLYCILLIN ORAL SUSPENSION. (Bristol) Ampicil trihydrate. **125 mg.**/5 ml. Bot. 80 ml., 100 ml., 15 ml., 200 ml.; **250 mg.**/5 ml. Bot. 80 ml., 100 ml., 150 ml., 200 ml.; **500 mg.**/5 ml. Bot. 100 ml. 100 mg./1 ml. Bot. 20 ml. Pediatric Drops.
Use: Broad spectrum antibacterial agent.

POLYCILLIN-PRB ORAL SUSPENSION. (Bristol) Ampicillin trihydrate 3.5 Gm., probenecid 1 Gm./Bot.
Use: Treatment of uncomplicated urethral, cervica rectal or pharyngeal infections caused by N. gonorrheae in men and women.

POLYCITRA-K SYRUP. (Willen) Potassium citra monohydrate 1100 mg., citric acid monohydrate 334 mg., potassium ion 10 mEq./5 ml. Bot. 4 oz., pt.
Use: Systemic alkalizer sodium free.

POLYCITRA-LC. (Willen) Potassium citrate monohydrate 550 mg., sodium citrate dihydrate 500 mg., citric acid monohydrate 334 mg., potassium ion 5 mEq., sodium ion 5 mEq./5 ml. Bot. 4 oz., pt.
Use: Systemic alkalizer sugar free.

POLYCITRA SYRUP. (Willen) Potassium citrate monohydrate 550 mg., sodium citrate dihydrate 50 mg., citric acid monohydrate 334 mg., potassium ion 5 mEq., sodium ion 5 mEq./5 ml. Bot. 4 oz. pt.
Use: Systemic alkalizer.

POLYCOSE. (Ross) **Pow.:** Glucose polymers derived from controlled hydrolysis of corn starch. Calories 380, carbohydrate 94 Gm., moisture 6.0 Gm., Na 110 mg. K 10 mg., chloride 223 mg., Ca 30 mg., P 5 mg./100 Gm. Can 14 oz. Case 6s. **Liq.:** Calories 200, carbohydrate 50 Gm., moisture 70 Gm., ash 0.25 Gm./100 ml. Na 58 mg., K 20 mg., chloride 107 mg., Ca 30 mg., P 6 mg./100 ml. Bot. 4 oz. Case 48s.
Use: Source of calories solely from carbohydrate.

POLYCYCLINE INTRAVENOUS.
See: Bristacycline, Cap., Vial (Bristol)

• **POLYDEXTROSE.** USAN.
Use: Food additive.

POLYDINE OINTMENT. (Century) Povidone iodine in ointment base. Jar. 1 oz., 4 oz., lb.
Use: Topical anti-infective.

POLYDINE SCRUB. (Century) Povidone iodine in scrub solution. Bot. 1 oz., 4 oz., 8 oz., pt., gal.
Use: Antiseptic scrub solution.

POLYDINE SOLUTION. (Century) Povidone iodine solution. Bot. 1 oz., 4 oz., 8 oz., pt., gal.
Use: Topical anti-infective.

• **POLYDIOXANONE.** USAN.
Use: Surgical aid.

POLYECTIN. (Amid)
See: Am-Tuss Elixir

POLY ENA TEST SYSTEM FOR RNP AND SM. (Wampole-Zeus) Qualitative identification of auto antibodies to extractable nuclear antigens in human serum by gel precipitation technique. Box 48 tests.
Use: Aid in the diagnosis of SLE, MCTD, PSS, SS.

.Y ENA TEST SYSTEM FOR RNP, SM, SSA AND SB. (Wampole-Zeus) Qualitative identification of uto antibodies to extractable nuclear antigens in uman serum by gel precipitation techniques. Box 6 tests.
se: Aid in the diagnosis of SLE, MCTD, PSS, SS.

.Y ENA TEST SYSTEM FOR SSA AND SSB. Vampole-Zeus) Qualitative identification of auto anbodies to extractable nuclear antigens in human erum by gel precipitation techniques. Box 48 tests.
se: Aid in the diagnosis of SLE, MCTD, PSS, SS.

.YESTRADIOL PHOSPHATE.
ee: Estradurin, Amp. (Ayerst)

)LYETHADENE. USAN. 1,2:3,4-Diepoxybutane olymer with ethylenimine. Erythritol anhydride olyethyleneimine polymer.
se: Antacid.

)LYETHYLENE GLYCOL 300, 400, 600, 1500, 540, 4000 & 6000, N.F. XVI. Oint., N.F. XVI.
Jse: Water-soluble ointment and suppository base; ablet excipient.
ee: Carbowax (Doak Pharmacal)
P.E.G. Lotion (Medco)

)LYFEROSE. USAN. An iron carbohydrate chelate ontaining approximately 45% of iron in which the etallic (Fe) ion is sequestered within a olymerized carbohydrate derived from sucrose.
Jse: Hematinic.

LYGELINE. B.A.N. A polymer of urea and olypeptides derived from denatured gelatin.
Jse: Restoration of blood volume.

OLYGLACTIN 370 & 910. USAN. Lactic acid olyester with glycolic acid.
Jse: Synthetic absorbable suture.

OLYGLYCOLIC ACID. USAN. Poly-(oxycarbonylnethylene).
Jse: Surgical aid.
See: Dexon Sterile Suture (David & Geck)

OLYGLYCONATE. USAN.
Jse: Surgical Aid.

LYHEXANIDE. B.A.N. Poly-(1-hexamethylene-biguaide hydrochloride).
Jse: Antibacterial, veterinary medicine.

LY-HISTINE CAPSULES. (Bock) Phenyltoloxamine itrate 25 mg., pyrilamine maleate 25 mg., heniramine maleate 25mg./Cap. Bot. 100s, 1000s.
Jse: Antihistamine.

LY-HISTINE CS. (Bock) Brompheniramine maleate 2 ng., phenylpropanolamine HCl 12.5 mg., codeine hosphate 10 mg./5 ml. Bot. pt., gal.
Jse: Expectorant.

LY-HISTINE-D CAPSULES. (Bock) Phenylproolamine HCl 50 mg., phenyltoloxamine citrate 16 ng., pyrilamine maleate 16 mg., pheniramine naleate 16 mg./Cap. Bot. 100s, 1000s.
Jse: Decongestant, antihistamine.

LY-HISTINE-D ELIXIR. (Bock) Phenylpropanolanine HCl 12.5 mg., phenyltoloxamine citrate 4 mg., yrilamine maleate 4 mg., pheniramine 4 mg./5 ml. v/alcohol 4%. Bot. pt., gal.
Jse: Antihistaminic, decongestant.

POLY-HISTINE-D PEDIATRIC CAPSULES. (Bock) Phenylpropanolamine HCl 25 mg., phenyltoloxamine citrate 8 mg., pheniramine maleate 8 mg., pyrilamine maleate 8 mg./Cap.
Use: Decongestant, antihistaminic.

POLY-HISTINE-DX CAPSULES. (Bock) Pseudoephedrine HCl 120 mg., brompheniramine maleate 12 mg./Cap. Bot. 100s, 1000s.
Use: Decongestant, antihistaminic.

POLY-HISTINE ELIXIR. (Bock) Phenyltoloxamine citrate 4 mg., pyrilamine maleate 4 mg., pheniramine maleate 4 mg./5 ml. w/ alcohol 4%, Elix. Bot. pint, gal.
Use: Contact, inhalant and food allergies.

POLY-HISTINE EXPECTORANT PLAIN SYRUP. (Bock) Phenylpropanolamine HCl 12.5 mg., guaifenesin 100 mg./5 ml.
Use: Decongestant, expectorant.

• **POLYMACON.** USAN. Poly(2-hydroxyethyl methacrylate).
Use: Contact lens material.

POLYMAGMA PLAIN TABLETS. (Wyeth) Activated attapulgite 500 mg., pectin 45 mg./Tab. Bot. 50s.

• **POLYMETAPHOSPHATE P-32.** USAN.
Use: Radioactive agent.

POLYMETHINE BLUE DYE. (3,3′-Diethylhiadicarbocyanine iodide).

POLYMONINE. A formaldehyde polymer of N-methylmonoanisylamine.

POLYMOX. (Bristol) Amoxicillin. **Cap.:** 250 mg., 500 mg./Cap. Bot. 50s, 100s, 500s Dosatrol 250 mg. or 500 mg./Cap. **Oral Susp.:** 125 mg., 250 mg./5 ml. Bot. 80 ml., 150 ml. Dosatrol 125 or 250 mg./Bot. **Ped. Drops:** 50 mg./ml. Bot. 15 ml.
Use: Anti-infective.

POLYMYXIN. B.A.N. Generic term for antibiotics obtained from fermentations of various media by strains of *Bacillus polymyxa.*
Use: Polymyxins A, B & D active against susceptible gram-negative bacteria.

POLYMYXIN B. (Various Mfr.) (No Pharmaceutical Form Available) Antimicrobial substances produced by *Bacillus polymyxa.*
W/Bacitracin zinc, neomycin sulf., benzalkonium chloride.
See: Biotres, Oint. (Central)

• **POLYMYXIN B SULFATE.** U.S.P. XXI. Otic Soln., Sterile, U.S.P. XXI.
See: Aerosporin, Pow., Sol. (Burroughs Wellcome)

• **POLYMYXIN B SULFATE AND HYDROCORTISONE OTIC SOLUTION,** U.S.P. XXI.
Use: Antibiotic, anti-inflammatory.

POLYMYXIN B SULFATE STERILE. (Pfipharmecs) Polymyxin B sulfate 500,000 u./Vial for reconstitution.

POLYMYXIN B SULFATE W/COMBINATIONS.
See: Aural Acute, Drops (Saron)
Baximin, Oint. (Quality Generics)
Biotic-O, Oint. (Scrip)
Bro-Parin Otic, Susp. (Riker)
Coracin, Oint. (Mallard)

Cortisporin, Preps. (Burroughs Wellcome)
Epimycin A, Oint. (Delta)
Florotic, Liq. (Squibb)
Lidosporin, Otic Soln. (Burroughs Wellcome)
Maxitrol, Oint., Susp. (Alcon)
Mity-Mycin, Oint. (Reid-Provident)
Mycitracin, Oint., Ophth. Oint. (Upjohn)
My-Cort-Otic, Liq. (Scrip)
My-Cort-Otic #1, Drops (Scrip)
Neomixin, Oint. (Mallard)
Neo-Polycin, Oint., Ophth. Oint., Ophth. Sol. (Merrell Dow)
Neosporin, Preps. (Burroughs Wellcome)
Neosporin-G, Cream (Burroughs Wellcome)
Neosporin G.U. Irrigant, Amp. (Burroughs Wellcome)
Neotal, Oint. (Mallard)
Neo-Thrycex, Oint. (Commerce)
Ophthel, Oint. (Elder)
Ophthocort, Oint. (Parke-Davis)
Otobiotic, Soln. (Schering)
Otoreid-HC, Liq. (Reid-Provident)
P.B.N., Oint. (Jenkins)
Polysporin, Oint., Ophth. Oint. (Burroughs Wellcome)
Pyocidin-Otic Soln. (Berlex)
Statrol, Liq. (Alcon)
Statrol Sterile Ophthalmic Ointment (Alcon)
Terra-Cortril, Aerosol (Pfizer)
Terramycin, Preps. W/Polymyxin (Pfizer)
Tigo, Oint. (Burlington)
Tri-Bow, Oint. (Bowman)
Tribotic, Oint. (Burgin-Arden)
Trimixin, Oint. (Hance)
Triple Antibiotic Ointment (Kenyon)

POLYMYXIN-NEOMYCIN-BACITRACIN OINTMENT. (Various Mfr.)
Use: Antibiotic for treatment of gram-positive and gram-negative organisms.

POLY-NEO-CORT. (Robinson) Ear drops. Bot. 12.5 cc.
Use: Antibiotic ear drops.

POLYNOXYLIN. B.A.N.
Poly[methylenedi(hydroxymethyl)urea]Anaflex; Ponoxylan.
Use: Antibacterial; anti-inflammatory.

POLYNOXYLIN.
Poly[methylenedi(hydroxymethyl)urea]. Anaflex.

POLYOXYETHYLENE 8 STEARATE. Myrj 45. (ICI U.S.)., Polyoxyl 8 Stearate.

POLYOXYETHYLENE (20) SORBITAN MONOLEATE.
See: Polysorbate 80, U.S.P. XXI. (Var. Mfr.)

POLYOXYETHYLENE 20 SORBITAN TRIOLEATE. Tween 85. (ICI U.S.)., Polysorbate 85.

POLYOXYETHYLENE 20 SORBITAN TRISTEARATE. Tween 65. (ICI U.S.)., Polysorbate 65.

POLYOXYETHYLENE 40 MONOSTEARATE.
Polyoxyl 40 Stearate
See: Myrj 52 & Myrj 52S (ICI U.S.)

• **POLYOXYETHYLENE 50 STEARATE,** N.F. XVI.
Use: Surfactant; emulsifying agent.

POLYOXYETHYLENEONYLPHENOL.
W/Alkyldimethylbenzylammonium chloride, methylrosaniline chloride, polyethylene glycol ter dodecylthioether.
See: Hyva, Vag. Tab. (Holland-Rantos)

POLYOXYETHYLENE SORBITAN MONOLAURAT
Polysorbate 20, N.F. XVI.
W/Ferrous gluconate.
See: Simron, Cap. (Merrell Dow)
W/Ferrous gluconate, vitamins.
See: Simron Plus, Cap. (Merrell Dow)

POLYOXYETHYLENE LAURYL ETHER.
W/Benzoyl peroxide, ethyl alcohol.
See: Benzagel, Gel (Dermik)
Desquam-X, Prep. (Westwood)
W/Hydrocortisone, sulfur.
See: Fostril HC, Lot. (Westwood)
W/Sulfur.
See: Fostril, Lot. (Westwood)
Proseca, Oint. (Westwood)

POLYOXYETHYLENE NONYL PHENOL
W/Sodium edetate, docusate sodium, 9-aminoacrid HCl.
See: Vagisec Plus, Supp. (Schmid)

• **POLYOXYL 8 STEARATE.** USAN. Polyoxyethyler 8 stearate.
Use: Surfactant.
See: Myrj 45 (Atlas)

• **POLYOXYL 10 OLEYL ETHER,** N.F. XVI.
Use: Pharmaceutic aid (surfactant).

• **POLYOXYL 20 CETOSTEARYL ETHER,** N.F. XVI
Use: Pharmaceutic aid (surfactant).

• **POLYOXYL 35 CASTOR OIL,** N.F.XVI.

• **POLYOXYL 40 HYDROGENATED CASTOR OIL,** N.F. XVI.

• **POLYOXYL 40 STEARATE,** N.F. XVI. Macrogic Stearate 2000 (I.N.N.) Polyoxyethylene 40 monostearate.
Use: Hydrophilic oint., surfactant; surface-acti agent.
See: Myrj 52. (Atlas)
Myrj 52S. (Atlas)
W/Polyethylene glycol, chlorobutanol.
See: Blink-N-Clean (Allergan)

POLY-PRED LIQUIFILM. (Allergan) Prednisolone ac tate 0.5%, neomycin sulfate equivalent to 0.35% neomycin base, polymyxin B sulfate 10,000 u./ml. with polyvinyl alcohol 1.4%. Bot. 5 ml. dropper bo
Use: Topical anti-inflammatory anti-infective for op thalmic use.

• **POLYPROPYLENE GLYCOL,** N.F. XVI. An additio polymer of propylene oxide and water.

POLYSEPT. (Dalin) Polymyxin B sulfate 5000 u., bacitracin 400 u., neomycin sulfate 5 mg., diperodon HCl 10 mg./Gm. Tubes: 0.5 oz.
Use: Topical antibacterial therapy.

POLYSONIC LOTION. (Parker) Multi-purpose trasound lotion with high coupling efficiency. Bot. 8.5 oz., gal.
Use: For Diagnostic & therapeutic medical ultrasound.

)LYSORB HYDRATE CREAM. (Fougera) Tube 2 oz., Jar 16 oz.

'OLYSORBATE 20, N.F. XVI. (Atlas) Tween 20. Polyoxyethlene 20 sorbitan monolaurate.
Use: Surface-active agent.

'OLYSORBATE 40, N.F. XVI. (Atlas) Tween 40. Polyoxyethylene 20 sorbitan monopalmitate.
Use: Surface-active agent.

'OLYSORBATE 60, N.F. XVI. (Atlas) Tween 60. Polyoxyethylene 20 sorbitan monostearate.
Use: Surface-active agent.

'OLYSORBATE 65. USAN. (Atlas) Tween 65. Polyoxyethylene 20 sorbitan tristearate.
Use: Surface-active agent.

'OLYSORBATE 80, N.F. XVI. Polyoxyethylene (20) Sorbitan Monooleate.
Use: Surfactant.

'OLYSORBATE 85. USAN. (Atlas) Polyoxyethylene 20 sorbitan trioleate. Tween 85.
Use: Surface-active agent.

)LYSPORIN OINTMENT. (Burroughs Wellcome) Polymyxin B sulfate 10,000 u., bacitracin zinc 500 u. in special white petrolatum base/Gm. Tube 0.5 & 1 oz. Foil packet 1/32 oz. 144s. Ophth. Tube 1/8 oz.
Use: Active against gram-negative & gram-positive organisms.

)LY-STRESS THERAPEUTIC. (Xttrium) Vit. A 12,500 I.U., D 400 I.U., C 150 mg., B-1 7.5 mg., B-2 5 mg., niacinamide 75 mg., B-6 1.5 mg., B-12 3 mcg., Ca pantothenate 10 mg., Vit. E 5 I.U., phosphate 182 mg., Ca 55 mg., P 40 mg., Fe 7 mg., iodine 0.07 mg., K 2.5 mg., Cu 0.5 mg., Mn 0.5 mg., Mg 3 mg., Zn 0.7 mg./Tab. Bot. 100s, 500s.
Use: Vitamin therapy.

)LYSULFIDES. Polythionate.

)LYTABS-F CHEWABLE VITAMIN. (Major) Multivitamin w/fluoride. Bot. 100s, 1000s.
Use: Dietary supplement.

)LYTAR BATH. (Stiefel) A 25% polytar blend of four different vegetable & mineral tars in an emulsion base. Bot. 8 fl. oz.
Use: Treatment of psoriasis, eczema, pruritis.

)LYTAR SHAMPOO. (Stiefel) A neutral soap containing 1% Polytar in a surfactant shampoo. Buffered. Plastic Bot. 6 fl. oz., 12 fl. oz., gal.
Use: Treatment of psoriasis and other scalp conditions.

)LYTAR SOAP. (Stiefel) A neutral soap containing 1% Polytar. Cake 4 oz.
Use: Treatment of eczema and other skin conditions.

)LYTEF. (Ethicon) Poly(tetrafluoroethylene). PTFE.
Use: Prosthetic aid.

'OLYTHIAZIDE, U.S.P. XXI. Tab., U.S.P. XXI. 2-Methyl-3,4-dihydro-3,(2,2,2-Trifluoroethylthiomethyl)-6-chloro-7-sulfamyl-1,2,4-benzothiadiazine, 1,1-dioxide. 6-Chloro-3,4-dihydro-2-methyl-3-[[(2,2,2,-trifluoroethyl)thio]-methyl]-2H-1,2,4-Benzothiadiazine-7-sulfonamide 1,1-dioxide.
Use: Diuretic; antihypertensive.
See: Renese Tab. (Pfizer Laboratories)
W/Prazosin.
See: Minizide, Cap. (Pfizer Laboratories)
W/Reserpine
See: Renese-R, Tab. (Pfizer Laboratories)

POLYTINIC. (Pharmics) B-12 7.5 mcg., iron, elemental 100 mg., C 300 mg., B-1 5 mg., folic acid 1 mg., liver 75 mg., stomach 75 mg., intrinsic factor 1/20 u./Tab. Bot. 100s. Liq. Bot. 4 oz., 16 oz.
Use: Dietary supplement.

POLYTUSS-DM. (Rhode) Dextromethorphan HBr 15 mg., chlorpheniramine maleate 1 mg., guaifenesin 25 mg./5 ml. Bot. 4 oz., 16 oz.
Use: Cough preparation.

• **POLYURETHANE FOAM.** USAN.
Use: Prosthetic aid.

POLYVIDONE.
See: Polyvinylpyrrolidone

POLY-VI-FLOR 0.5 mg. CHEWABLE TABS. (Mead Johnson) Vit. A 2500 I.U., D 400 I.U., E 15 I.U., C 60 mg., B-1 1.05 mg., B-2 1.2 mg., niacin 13.5 mg., B-6 1.05 mg., B-12 4.5 mcg., fluoride 0.5 mg., folic acid 0.3 mg. Chewable Tab. Bot. 100s. **With Iron:** Above formula plus iron 12 mg., Cu 1 mg., Zn 10 mg./Tab. Bot. 100s.
Use: Caries prophylaxis and diet supplementation.

POLY-VI-FLOR 1 mg. CHEWABLE TABLETS. (Mead Johnson) Vit. A 2500 I.U., D 400 I.U., E 15 I.U., C 60 mg., B-1 1.05 mg., B-2 1.2 mg., niacin 13.5 mg., B-6 1.05 mg., B-12 4.5 mcg., fluoride 1 mg., folic acid 0.3 mg. Chewable Tab. Bot. 100s, 1000s. **With Iron:** Above formula plus iron 12 mg., Cu 1 mg., Zn 10 mg.
Use: Caries prophylaxis and diet supplementation.

POLY-VI-FLOR 0.25 mg. DROPS. (Mead Johnson) Vit. A 1500 I.U., D 400 I.U., E 5 I.U., C 35 mg., B-1 0.5, B-2 0.6 mg., B-6 0.4 mg., niacin 8 mg., B-12 2 mcg., fluoride 0.25 mg./1.0 ml. Drop. Bot. 50 ml.
Use: Caries prophylaxis and dietary supplement.

POLY-VI-FLOR 0.5 mg. DROPS. (Mead Johnson) Vit. A 1500 I.U., D 400 I.U., E 5 I.U., C 35 mg., B-1 0.5 mg., B-2 0.6 mg., B-6 0.4 mg., niacin 8 mg., B-12 2 mcg., fluoride 0.5 mg./1.0 ml. Drops, Bot. 30 ml., 50 ml.
Use: Caries prophylaxis and diet supplementation.

POLY-VI-FLOR 0.25 w/IRON DROPS. (Mead Johnson) Vit. A 1500 I.U., D 400 I.U., E 5 I.U., C 35 mg., B-1 0.5 mg., B-2 0.6 mg., B-6 0.4 mg., niacin 8 mg., fluoride 0.25 mg., iron 10 mg./1.0 ml. Bot. 50 ml.
Use: Caries prophylaxis, diet supplementation.

POLY-VI-FLOR 0.5 mg. W/IRON DROPS. (Mead Johnson) Vit. A 1500 I.U., D 400 I.U., E 5 I.U., C 35 mg., B-1 0.5 mg., B-2 0.6 mg., B-6 0.4 mg., niacin 8 mg., fluoride 0.5 mg., iron 10 mg./1.0 ml. Drops. Bot. 50 ml.
Use: Caries prophylaxis and diet supplementation.

POLYVINOX. B.A.N. Poly(butyl vinyl ether). Shostakovsky Balsam.
Use: Skin application.

• **POLYVINYL ACETATE PHTHALATE,** N.F. XVI.

• **POLYVINYL ALCOHOL,** U.S.P. XXI. Ethenol, homopolymer.
Use: Viscosity-increasing agent; pharm. necessity for ophthalmic solution dosage form.

See: Liquifilm Forte (Allergan)
Liquifilm Tears (Allergan)
W/Hydroxypropyl methylcellulose
See: Liquifilm Wetting Soln. (Allergan)

POLYVINYLPYRROLIDONE-IODINE COMPLEX.

POLYVINYLPYRROLIDONE, POLYVIDONE, POVIDONE.
W/Acetrizoate Sod.
See: Salpix, Vial (Ortho)

POLYVINYLPYRROLIDONE VINYLACETATE COPOLYMERS.
See: Ivy-Rid, Spray (Mallard)
W/Benzalkonium.
See: Ivy-Chex, Aerosol (Bowman)

POLY-VI-SOL CHEWABLE TABS. (Mead Johnson) Vit. A 2500 I.U., E 15 I.U., D 400 I.U., C 60 mg., B-1 1.05 mg., B-2 1.2 mg., niacin 13.5 mg., Vit. B-6 1.05 mg., B-12 4.5 mcg., folic acid 0.3 mg./Chewable Tab. Tab. Bot. 100s, 1000s. Circus Shape Tab. Bot. 24s, 100s. **With Iron:** Above formula plus iron 12 mg., Zn 8 mg./Tab. Bot. 100s, 1000s. Circus shape Tab. **With Iron and Zinc:** Bot. 100s
Use: Multivitamin and mineral supplement.

POLY-VI-SOL DROPS. (Mead Johnson) Vit. A 1500 I.U., D 400 I.U., C 35 mg., B-1 0.5 mg., B-2 0.6 mg., Vit. E 5 I.U., B-6 0.4 mg., niacin 8 mg., B-12 2 mcg./1.0 ml. Bot. 30 & 50 ml. with calibrated "Safti-Dropper."
Use: Multivitamin supplement.

POLY-VI-SOL W/IRON DROPS. (Mead Johnson) Vit. A 1500 I.U., D 400 I.U., E 5 I.U., C 35 mg., B-1 0.5 mg., B-2 0.6 mg., B-6 0.4 mg., niacin 8 mg., iron 10 mg./1.0 ml. Bot. 50 ml.
Use: Multivitamin with iron supplement.

POLYVITAMIN DROPS. . (Vitarine) Vit. A 3000 I.U., D 400 I.U., C 60 mg., B-1 1 mg., B-2 1.2 mg., niacinamide 8 mg./0.6 ml. Bot. 50 ml. w/separate dropper.

POLYVITAMINS.
See: Vitamin preparations.

PONARIS. (Jamol) Nasal emollient of mucosal lubricating and moisturizing botanical oils. Cajeput, eucalyptus, peppermint in iodized cottonseed oil. Bot. 1 oz. w/dropper.
Use: Nasal irritations.

PONDERAX HYDROCHLORIDE. Fenfluramine, B.A.N.

PONDIMIN. (Robins) Fenfluramine HCl 20 mg./Tab. Bot. 100s, 500s.
Use: Anorectic.

PONDOCILLIN HYDROCHLORIDE. Pivampicillin, B.A.N.

PONOXYLAN. Polynoxylin, B.A.N.

PONSTAN. B.A.N. Mefenamic acid.

PONSTEL KAPSEALS. (Parke-Davis) Mefenamic acid 250 mg./Cap. Bot. 100s.
Use: Analgesic.

PONTALIN. Chlorbetamide, B.A.N.

PONTOCAINE 2% AQUEOUS SOLUTION. (Winthrop-Breon) Tetracaine hydrochloride 20 mg., chlorobutanol 4 mg./ml. of 2% solution. Bot. 30 ml. Box 12s. Bot. 118 ml. Box 6s.
Use: Surface anesthesia of the nose and throat.

PONTOCAINE CREAM. (Winthrop-Breon) Tetraca hydrochloride, equivalent to 1% tetracaine hydrochloride base, in a bland, water-miscible cre with methylparaben and sodium metabisulfite as preservatives. Tube 1 oz. Pkg. 6s.
Use: Temporary relief of pain, burning and itching in skin burns and ulcers, sunburn, insect bites an hemorrhoids.

PONTOCAINE EYE OINTMENT. (Winthrop-Breon) T racaine 0.5% in a base of white petrolatum and light mineral oil. Tube 1/8 oz. Pkg. 12s.
Use: Short-term surface anesthesia of the eye.

PONTOCAINE HYDROCHLORIDE. (Winthrop-Bre Niphanoid (instantly soluble) form consisting of a network of extremely fine, highly purified particles resembling snow. Amp. 20 mg. Box 100s. 1% isotonic, isobaric solution: 10 mg. tetracaine hydrochloride, 6.7 mg. sodium chloride, and not more than 2 mg. acetone sodium bisulfite/ml. Am 2 ml. Box 25s.
Use: Spinal anesthesia.

PONTOCAINE HYDROCHLORIDE IN DEXTROSE (Hyperbaric) SOLUTIONS. (Winthrop-Breon) **0.2** Tetracaine hydrochloride 2 mg./ml. in a sterile solution containing 6% dextrose. Amp. 2 ml. 10s.
Use: saddle block (spinal anesthesia).**0.3%:** Tetracaine hydrochloride 3 mg/ml in a sterile solution containing 6% dextrose. Amp. 5 ml 10s.
Use: Spinal anesthesia (high, median and low).

PONTOCAINE OINTMENT. (Winthrop-Breon) T racaine 0.5% and menthol in an ointment consisting of white petrolatum and white wax. Tub 1 oz.
Use: Temporary relief of pain, burning and itching in hemorrhoids, skin burns and ulcers, scalds, wounds, bruises, abrasions, sunburn, ivy and othe plant poisoning and insect bites.

PONTOCAINE 0.5% SOLUTION FOR OPHTHALMOLOGY. (Winthrop-Breon) Tetracai HCl 5 mg., sodium chloride 7.5 mg., chlorobutano 4 mg./ml. of 0.5% solution. Bot. 15 ml. Pkg. 12s. Bot. 59 ml. Pkg. 6s.
Use: Short-term surface anesthesia of the eye.

POPPY-SEED OIL, the ethyl ester of the fatty aci w/iodine.
See: Lipiodol, Ascendant & Lafay, Amps., Vial (Savage)

PORCELANA SKIN BLEACHING AGENT. (Jeffrey Martin) **Regular:** Hydroquinone 2%. Jar 2 oz., 4 o **Sunscreen:** Hydroquinone 2%, octyl dimethyl PABA 2.5%. Jar 4 oz.
Use: Fading dark patches on skin.

• **PORFIROMYCIN.** USAN.
Use: Antibacterial; antineoplastic.

PORK THYROID, DEFATTED.
See: Tuloidin, Tab. (Reid-Provident)

• **POROFOCON A.** USAN.
Use: Contact lens material.

• **POROFOCON B.** USAN.
Use: Cabcurve lens (soft lenses).

PORTABIDAY. (Washington Ethical) Concentrated soln. of alkylamine lauryl sulfate, a mild detergent

with pH approx. 6 for use with Portabiday Vaginal Cleansing Kit. Bot. 3 oz.
Use: Vaginal cleansing.

RTAGEN. (Mead Johnson) A nutritionally complete dietary powder containing as a % of the calories 14%, protein as caseinate, 41% fat (86% medium chain triglycerides, 14% corn oil), 45% carbohydrate as corn syrup solids and sucrose. Vit. A 5000 I.U., D 500 I.U., E 20 I.U., C 52 mg., B-1 1 mg., B-2 1.2 mg., B-6 1.3 mg., B-12 4 mcg., niacin 13 mg., folic acid 0.1 mg., choline 85 mg., biotin 0.05 mg., Ca 600 mg., P 450 mg., Mg 130 mg., Fe 12 mg., iodine 45 mcg., Cu 1 mg., Zn 6 mg., Mn 2 mg., Cl 550 mg., Na 300 mg., K 800 mg., pantothenic acid 6.7 mg., Vit. K-1 0.1 mg./Qt. 20Kcal/Fl. oz. Can 1 lb.
Use: Nutritionally complete dietary powder containing medium chain triglycerides as its major source of fat and lactose free for use in the nutritional management of infants, children, and adults who do not efficiently digest conventional food fats or absorb long chain fatty acids.

SKINE. B.A.N. O-Propionylhyoscine. Proscopine hydrobromide.
Use: Central nervous system depressant.

STAFENE.
See: Bonamine, Tab. (Pfizer)

OSTERIOR PITUITARY INJECTION, U.S.P. XXI.
See: Pituitary, Posterior, Preps. (Various Mfr.)

STERISAN. (Kenwood) Sterilized E. coli vaccine with approximately 660 million coliform bacteria, liquefied phenol 6.67 mg., 2-ethylmercuriothio-s-benzoxazol carboxylic acid 0.33 mg./suppository in PEG base.
Use: Hemorrhoid, pruritus ani.

STLOBIN-O.
See: Pituitary, Post, Hormone (b)

STLOBIN-V.
See: Pituitary, Post., Hormone (a)

STURE. (Ayerst) Calcium phosphate 600 mg./Tab. Bot. 60s, 75s.
Use: Dietary supplement.

TABA. (Glenwood) Pot. p-aminobenzoate. **Cap.** 0.5 Gm. Bot. 250s, 1000s. **Pow.** 100 Gm., 1 lb., 5 lb. **Tab.** 0.5 Gm., Bot. 100s, 1000s. **Envule.** 2 Gm. Box 50s.
Use: Scleroderma Peyronie's dis. rheumatoid arthritis.

TABA PLUS 6. (Glenwood) Potassium p-aminobenzoate 0.5 Gm., Vit. B-6 1 mg./Tab. or Cap. **Caps.** Bot. 240s, 1000s. **Tabs.** Bot. 120s, 1000s.
Use: Antifibrosis therapy.

OTABLE-AQUA IODINE. (Wisconsin) Tab. Bot. 50s.
Use: Water purification.

OTABLE AQUA KIT. (Wisconsin) Tab. Bot. 50s with collapsible gallon container.
Use: Water purification.

OTACHLOR 10%. (Bay) Potassium Cl 20 meq./15 ml. w/alcohol 5%. Bot. pt., gal.
Use: Potassium supplement.

OTACHLOR 20%. (Bay) Potassium Cl 40 meq./15 ml. Bot. pt., gal.
Use: Potassium supplement.

POTAGE. (Lemmon) Potassium chloride 20 mEq in chicken or beef flavored base. Packets 5 Gm. Box 30s.
Use: Potassium supplement.

POTASALAN ELIXIR. (Lannett) Potassium chloride 10%. Bot. pt., gal.

• **POTASH, SULFURATED,** U.S.P. XXI.
Use: Pharmaceutic aid (source of sulfide).

POTASSIC SALINE LACTATED INJECTION.
Use: Fluid and electrolyte replenisher.

POTASSINE. (Recsei) Potassium chloride 20 mEq./15 ml. Bot. pt., gal.
Use: Potassium deficiency.

• **POTASSIUM ACETATE,** U.S.P. XXI. Inj., U.S.P. XXI. Acetic acid, potassium salt. (Various Mfr.) **Inj.:** (Abbott) 40 mEq., 20 ml. in 50 ml. Vial.
Use: Electrolyte replenisher; to avoid chloride when high concentration of pot. is needed.

POTASSIUM ACID PHOSPHATE.
See: K-Phos., Tab. (Beach)
Uro-K Tab. (Star)

POTASSIUM p-AMINOBENZOATE.
See: Potaba, Preps. (Glenwood)
W/Potassium salicylate.
See: Pabalate-SF, Tab. (Robins)
W/Pyridoxine.
See: Potaba Plus 6, Caps. or Tabs. (Glenwood)

POTASSIUM AMINOSALICYLATE.
See: Aminosalicylate potassium.

POTASSIUM p-AMINOSALICYLATE.
See: Paskalium, Preps. (Glenwood)
Teebacin Kalium, Preps. (CMC)

• **POTASSIUM ASPARTATE AND MAGNESIUM ASPARATE.** USAN.
Use: Nutrient.

• **POTASSIUM BICARBONATE,** U.S.P. XXI.
Use: Electrolyte replenisher.

• **POTASSIUM BICARBONATE EFFERVESCENT TABLETS FOR ORAL SOLUTION,** U.S.P. XXI.

• **POTASSIUM BICARBONATE AND POTASSIUM CHLORIDE FOR EFFERVESCENT ORAL SOLUTION,** U.S.P. XXI.
Use: Potassium supplement.

• **POTASSIUM BICARBONATE AND POTASSIUM CHLORIDE FOR EFFERVESCENT ORAL SOLUTION,** U.S.P. XXI.
Use: Potassium supplement.

• **POTASSIUM BICARBONATE AND POTASSIUM CHLORIDE EFFERVESCENT TABLETS FOR ORAL SOLUTION,** U.S.P. XXI.
Use: Potassium supplement.

POTASSIUM BITARTRATE.
Use: Cathartic.

POTASSIUM BROMIDE.
W/Aspirin, caffeine, sodium bromide.
See: Lanabac, Tab. (Lannett)
W/Sodium bromide, strontium bromide, ammonium bromide.
See: Lanabrom, Elix. (Lannett)

• **POTASSIUM CHLORIDE,** U.S.P. XXI. Elixir, Extended-Release Cap., Extended-Release Tab., In

Dextrose Inj., Inj., Oral Soln., For Oral Soln., U.S.P. XXI.
Use: Potassium deficiency, hypopotassemia.
Ampules:
(Abbott) **Ampules:** 20 mEq., 10 ml.; 40 mEq., 20 ml. **Pintop Vials:** 10 mEq., 5 ml. in 10 ml.; 20 mEq., 10 ml. in 20 ml.; 30 mEq., 12.5 ml. in 30 ml.; 40 mEq., 12.5 ml. in 30 ml. **Fliptop Vials:** 20 mEq., 10 ml. in 20 ml.; 40 mEq., 20 ml. in 50 ml. **Univ. Add. Syr.:** 5 mEq./5 ml., 20 mEq./10 ml., 30 mEq./20 ml., 40 mEq./20 ml. (Lilly) Amp. (40 mEq.) 20 ml., 6s, 25s.
Capsules:
See: Micro-K Extencaps, Cap. (Robins)
Liquid:
See: Cena-K, Liq. (Century)
Choice 10 and 20, Sol. (Whiteworth)
Kaochlor, Preps. (Adria)
Kaon-C1 20%, Liq. (Adria)
Kay Ciel, Elix. (Berlex)
Klor-10%, Liq. (Upsher-Smith)
Klor-Con, Liq. (Upsher-Smith)
Kloride, Eliz. (Fed. Pharm.)
Klorvess Liquid (Dorsey)
Klotrix, Tab. (Mead Johnson)
Klowess (Dorsey)
K-Lyte/C1, Tab. (Mead Johnson)
Pan-Kloride, Liq. (US. Products)
Potassine, Liq. (Recsei)
SK-Potassium Chloride, Sol. (SmithKline)
Taside, Liq. (Reid-Provident)
Powder:
See: Kaochlor-Eff, Gran. (Adria)
Kato Powder (Ingram)
Kay Ciel, Pow. (Berlex)
K-Lor, Pow. (Abbott)
K-Lyte/C1, Pow. (Mead Johnson)
Potage, Pow. (Lemmon)
Tablets:
See: Kaon Tablets, Tab. (Adria)
Kaon Controlled Release Tab. (Adria)
Klorvess Effervescent Tablets (Dorsey)
K-Tab, Tab. (Abbott)
Micro-K Extencaps (Robins)
Slow-K, Tab. (Ciba)

• **POTASSIUM CHLORIDE K 42.** USAN.
Use: Radioactive agent.

POTASSIUM CHLORIDE. (Roxane) **Oral soln.** Potassium chloride oral solution: 5%, 20 mEq./30 ml. Bot. 500 ml., 1 L, 5 L. 10%, 40 mEq./30 ml. Bot. 6 oz., 500 ml., 1 L, 5 L 20%, 80 mEq./30 ml. Bot. 500 ml., 1 L, 5 L.**Powder:** 20 mEq./4 Gm. Pkt. 30s, 100s.
Use: Hypopotassemia.

POTASSIUM CHLORIDE SOLUTION. (Lederle) Potassium chloride 10%, 20%. Sugar free. Bot. 16 oz., gal.
Use: Hypopotassemia.

POTASSIUM CHLORIDE WITH POTASSIUM GLUCONATE.
See: Kolyum, Prod. (Pennwalt)

• **POTASSIUM CHLORIDE, POTASSIUM BICARBONATE, AND POTASSIUM CITRATE EFFERVESCENT TABLETS FOR ORAL SOLUTION,** U.S.P. XXI.

• **POTASSIUM CITRATE,** U.S.P. XXI. Tripotassium Citrate.
Use: Systemic alkalizer.
W/Sod. citrate.
See: Bicitra, Liq. (Willen)
W/Sod. citrate, citric acid.
See: Polycitra-K, Liq. (Willen)
Polycitra-LC, Liq. (Willen)

• **POTASSIUM CITRATE AND CITRIC ACID ORAL SOLUTION,** U.S.P. XXI.

POTASSIUM ESTRONE SULFATE.
W/Estrone.
See: Dura-Keelin, Vial (Pharmex)
Estro Plus, Inj. (Rocky Mtn.)
Ferntheelin, Vial (Ferndale)
Mer-Estrone, Inj. (Keene Pharm.)
Sodestrin, Inj. (Reid-Provident)
Spanestrin, Vial (Savage)
W/Estrone.
See: Gynlin R P. (Tunex)
W/Estrone, estradiol.
See: R.I.P. Estrone, Inj. (Vortech)
Tri-Oraphn (Standex)
W/Micro crystalline estrone.
See: Estrones Duo-Action, Vial (Med. Chem.)

• **POTASSIUM GLUCALDRATE.** USAN.
Use: Antacid.

• **POTASSIUM GLUCONATE,** U.S.P. XXI. Elixir, Tab U.S.P. XXI. Monopotassium D-gluconate.
Use: Electrolyte replenisher.
See: Kalinate, Elix. (Bock)
Kaon, Elixir, Tab. (Warren-Teed)

POTASSIUM GLUCONATE ELIXIR. (Mills) Element potassium as potassium gluconate 20 mEq, base w/sorbitol soln./Tbs. Bot. 8 oz.

POTASSIUM GLUCONATE ELIXIR. (Philips Roxane Lederle) Potassium 40 mEq. provided by potassiu gluconate 9.36 Gm., alcohol 5%/30 ml. Bot. pt., Patient-Cup 15 ml.
Use: Replacement therapy.

POTASSIUM GLUTAMATE. The monopotassium sa of l-glutamic acid.

POTASSIUM G PENICILLIN.
See: Penicillin G Potassium, U.S.P. XXI.

• **POTASSIUM GUAIACOLSULFONATE,** U.S.P. XXI. Sulfoguaiacol. Potassium Hydroxymethoxybenzenesulfonate. Used in many cough preps.
See: Conex, Liq. (Westerfield)
Pinex Regular, Syr. (Pinex)

POTASSIUM GUAIACOLSULFONATE W/COMBINATIONS.
See: Cerose, Liq. (Ives)
Cerose-DM, Liq. (Ives)
Cervo, Liq. (Sutliff & Case)
Cetro-Cirose, Liq. (Ives)
Cheralin Syrup, Syr. (Lannett)
Cherralex, Syr. (Barre)

Cidicol, Liq. (Upjohn)
Clistin, Expect., Liq. (McNeil)
Codel, Expect. (Elder)
Codimal DH Syr. (Central)
Codimal, DM Elix., Syr. (Central)
Codimal, PH Syr. (Central)
Coditrate, Syr., Tab. (Central)
DeWitt's Cough Control Medicine, Syr. (DeWitt)
Doverlyn Children, CT Choc., Tab. (Scrip)
Efricon Expect. (Lannett)
Eucapine Syrup, Syr. (Lannett)
Formadrin, Liq. (Kenyon)
Four Red, Liq. (Mallard)
Ganerphen, Preps. (Mason)
Gomahist, Inj. (Burgin-Arden)
Gomenol, Vial (Pharmex)
Guahist, Vial (Hickam)
Guaiadol Aqueous, Inj. (Med. Chem./Bush)
Guaicohist, Vial (Pharmex)
Guaiodol-Plus, Vial (Kenyon)
Guialyn, Preps. (Scrip)
Mallergan, Liq. (Mallard)
Palodyne, Cap. (Mallard)
Para-Hist DM, Tab. (Pharmics)
Para-Hist Antitussive, Syr. (Pharmics)
Partuss, Liq. (Parmed)
Phenergan, Prods. (Wyeth)
P-M-Z HCl, Expect. (Sutliff & Case)
Proclan, Preps. (Cenci)
Pro-Expectorant, Liq. (Scrip)
Special Cough Formula S.F. 17750 (Upjohn)
Turpoin, Tab. (Mallard)
Tusquelin, Syr. (Circle)

TASSIUM HETACILLIN.
See: Versapen K, Inj., Cap. (Bristol)

OTASSIUM HYDROXIDE, N.F. XVI.
Use: Pharm. aid (alkalinizing agent).

OTASSIUM IODIDE, U.S.P. XXI. Tab., Oral Soln., U.S.P. XXI.
Use: Expectorant; antifungal; source of iodine.
See: Pima, Syr., Expect. (Fleming)
SSKI, Liq. (Upsher-Smith)

TASSIUM IODIDE W/COMBINATIONS
See: Diastix, Reagent Strips (Ames)
Elixophyllin-KI, Elix. (Berlex)
Entex K.I., Tab. (Baylor Labs.)
Heliogen, Tab. (Brown)
Iodized Lime, Tab. (Elder)
Iodo-Niacin, Tab. (Cole)
KIE, Syr., Tab. (Laser)
Kiophyllin, Tab. (Rorer)
L.S. Mixture, Liq. (Paddock)
Mudrane, Tab. (Plythress)
Mudrane-2, Tab. (Poythress)
Neo-Asmasan, Cap. (Recsei)
Quadrinal, Tab., Susp. (Knoll)
Ricor, Tab. (Vortech)
Theokin, Elix., Tab. (Knoll)
T.P.K.I., Tab. (Wendt-Bristol)
TSG Croup Liquid (Elder)
TSG-KI, Elix. (Elder)

POTASSIUM IODIDE AND NIACINAMIDE.
See: Iodo-Niacin, Tab. (Cole)

POTASSIUM MENAPHTHOSULPHATE. B.A.N.
Dipotassium 2-methyl-1,4-disulpnatonaphthalene. Vikastab [dihydrate]
Use: Vitamin K analogue.

• **POTASSIUM METAPHOSPHATE,** N.F. XVI.
Use: Buffering agent.

POTASSIUM PENICILLIN G .
Use: Antibiotic.
See: Penicillin G, Potassium U.S.P. XXI.

POTASSIUM PENICILLIN V.
Use: Antibiotic.
See: Phenoxymethyl Penicillin Potassium, U.S.P. XXI.

• **POTASSIUM PERMANGANATE,** U.S.P. XXI. Tab. for Topical Soln., U.S.P. XXI. Permanganic acid, potassium salt.
Use: Topical anti-infective.

POTASSIUM PHENETHICILLIN. Phenethicillin Potassium, U.S.P. XXI.
Use: Antibiotic.

POTASSIUM PHENOXYMETHYL PENICILLIN.
Use: Antibiotic.
See: Penicillin V Potassium, U.S.P. XXI.

• **POTASSIUM PHOSPHATE, DIBASIC,** U.S.P. XXI. Inj., U.S.P. XXI.
Use: Calcium regulator.

• **POTASSIUM PHOSPHATE, MONOBASIC,** N.F. XVI.
Dipotassium hydrogen phosphate. Solution by Various Mfr. **Inj.:** (Abbott) 15 mM, 5 ml. in 10 ml. Vial; 45m M, 15 ml. in 20 ml. Vial.
Use: Buffering agent, source of potassium.

POTASSIUM-REMOVING RESINS.
See: Kayexalate, Pow. (Winthrop-Breon)

POTASSIUM RHODANATE.
See: Pot. Thiocyanate

POTASSIUM SALICYLATE.
See: Neocylate, Tab. (Central)
W/Mephenesin, colchicine alkaloid.
W/Potassium bromide, methapyrilene HCl, vitamins.
See: Alva-Tranquil, Cap., Tab. & T.D. Tab. (Alva/Amco)
W/Potassium p-aminobenzoate.
See: Pabalate-SF, Tab. (Robins)
Pabasal N.S., Tab. (Wolins)

POTASSIUM SALT.
See: Potassium Sorbate, N.F. XVI.

• **POTASSIUM SODIUM TARTRATE,** U.S.P. XXI.
Use: Cathartic.

• **POTASSIUM SORBATE,** N.F. XVI. 2,4-Hexadienoic Acid, Potassium Salt.
Use: Preservative (antimicrobial).

POTASSIUM SULFOCYANATE. Pot. Rhodanate.
See: Pot. Thiocyanate (Var. Mfr.)

POTASSIUM THERAPY.
See: Kaon, Elixir, Tab. (Warren-Teed)
Potassium Chloride, Preps. (Various Mfr.)

POTASSIUM THIOCYANATE. Pot. sulfocyanate, Pot. Rhodanate.

POTASSIUM THIPHENCILLIN. Potassium 6-(phenylmercaptoacetamido)penicillanate.
Use: Antibiotic.

POTASSIUM TROCLOSENE. (Monsanto) Potassium dichloroisocyanurate. Dichloro-s-triazine-2,4,6(1H,3H,5H)trione Potassium derivative.
Use: Local anti-infective.

• **POTASSIUM, WARFARIN,** U.S.P. XXI. Tab., U.S.P. XXI. Potassium 3-(α-acetonylbenzyl)-4-hydroxycoumarin, Potassium Salt. Athrombin-K.
Use: Anticoagulant.
See: Athrombin-K, Tab. (Purdue-Frederick)

POVAN TABLETS. (Parke-Davis) Pyrvinium pamoate 50 mg./Tab. Bot. 50s.
Use: Control of pinworm infections.

POVIDERM OINTMENT. (Vortech) Povidone-Iodide 10% in ointment base. Tube 1 oz. Jar 1 lb.
Use: Antiseptic ointment.

POVIDERM SOLUTION. (Vortech) Povidone-Iodide 7.-5%, in liquid base. Bot. pt., Gal.
Use: Antiseptic solution.

POVIDERM SURGICAL SCRUB. (Vortech) Povidone-Iodine 5% in liquid base. Bot. 16 oz., Gal.
Use: Antiseptic scrub solution.

• **POVIDONE,** U.S.P. XXI. 2-Pyrrolidinone, 1-ethyl, homopolymer.
Use: Dispersing & suspending agent.

• **POVIDONE I-125.** USAN.
Use: Pharmaceutic aid.

• **POVIDONE I-131.** USAN.
Use: Radioactive agent.

• **POVIDONE-IODINE,** U.S.P. XXI., Topical Aerosol Soln., Oint., Cleansing Sol., Topical Soln., U.S.P. XXI. Poly(1-(2-oxo-1-pyrrolidinyl)-ethylene) Iodine Complex.
Use: Local anti-infective.
See: Betadine, Preps. (Purdue-Fredrick)
BPS, Preps. (AVP)
Efo-Dine (Fougera)
Femidine, Liq. (AVP)
Isodine, Preps. (Blair)

POVIDONE-IODINE COMPLEX.
See: Betadine, Prep. (Purdue-Frederick)
Isodine, Preps. (Blair)

POVI-DOUCHE. (Vortech) Povidone-iodine 7.5% solution. Bot. 240 ml.
Use: Cleansing douche.

POWERS' ASTHMA RELIEF. (Guild) Bot. 4 oz.

POXY COMPOUND-65. (Sutliff & Case) Propoxyphene HCl 65 mg., aspirin 227 mg., phenacetin 162 mg., caffeine 32.5 mg./Cap. Bot. 100s, 1000s.

POYALIVER STRONGER. (Fellows) Liver inj. (eqv. 10 mcg. B-12) Vit. B-12 100 mcg., folic acid 10 mcg., niacinamide 1%/cc. Vial 10 cc.

POYAMIN. (Fellows) Vit. B-12 1000 mcg./cc. Vial 10 cc., 30 cc.
Use: Hematopoietic.

POYAMIN JEL INJECTION. (Fellows) Cyanocobalamin 1000 mcg./cc. Vial 10 cc.

POYAPLEX. (Fellows) Vit. B-1 100 mg., niacinamide 100 mg., B-6 10 mg., B-2 1 mg., panthenol 10 mg., B-12 5 mcg./cc. Vial 10 cc. & 30 cc.

P.P.D. TUBERCULIN.
See: Tuberculin, Purified Protein Derivative, U.S.P. (Various Mfr.)

P.P. FACTOR (PELLAGRA PREVENTIVE FACTOR
See: Nicotinic Acid, Preps. (Var. Mfr.)

• **PPG-15 STEARYL ETHER.** USAN.
Use: Pharmaceutic aid (surfactant).

P.R. (Faraday) Acetyl-p-aminophenol 5 gr./Tab. B 30s.
Use: Pain relief.

• **PRACTOLOL.** USAN. 4′-[2-Hydroxy-3-(isopropylamino)propoxy]acetanilide.
Use: Antiadrenergic (β-receptors).

PRAENITRONA. Trolnitrate Phosphate, B.A.N.

PRAGMATAR. (Menley & James) Cetyl alcohol-coal distillate 4%, precipitated sulfur 3%, salicylic acid 3% in oil-in-water type emulsion base. Tube 1 oz
Use: Common skin disorders: dandruff, cradle ca dermatitis, eczema, itchy scaly skin, athlete's foo

PRAJMALIUM BITARTRATE. B.A.N. N-Propylajmalinium hydrogen tartrate.
Use: Treatment of heart arrhythmias.

PRALIDOXIME. B.A.N. 2-Hydroxyiminomethyl-1-methylpyridinium.
Use: Antagonist to cholinesterase inhibitors.

• **PRALIDOXIME CHLORIDE,** U.S.P. XXI. Sterile, Tabs: U.S.P. XXI. Pyridinium, 2-[(hydroxyimino)methyl]-1-methyl-,chloride. 2-Formyl-1-methylpyridinium Chloride Oxime. Pam.
Use: Anticholinergic.
See: Protopam Chloride, Tab., Vial (Ayerst)

• **PRALIDOXIME IODIDE.** USAN. 2-Pyridine aldoxime methiodide.
Use: Cholinesterase reactivator.
See: Protopam Iodide (Ayerst)

• **PRALIDOXIME MESYLATE.** USAN.
Use: Cholinesterase reactivator.

PRALIDOXIME METHIODIDE.
See: Pralidoxime Iodide (Var. Mfr.)

PRAMET FA. (Ross) Vit. A 4000 I.U., D-2 400 I.U., C 1 mg., B-1 3 mg., B-2 2 mg., B-6 5 mg., B-12 3 mc niacinamide 10 mg., Calcium pantothenate 0.92 mg., iodine 100 mcg., calcium 250 mg., copper 0.15 mg., Iron 60 mg., Folic acid 1 mg./Gradumet Bot. 100s.
Use: Prenatal vitamin/mineral supplement & for treatment of megaloblastic anemias of pregnancy

PRAMILET FA. (Ross) Vit. A 4000 I.U.; B-1 3 mg.; B-2 2 mg.; B-6 3 mg.; B-12 3 mcg.; C 60 mg.; D 400 I.U. Ca panthothenate 1 mg.; niacinamide 10 mg.; Ca 250 mg.; Cu 0.15 mg.; iodine 0.1 mg.; Fe 40 mg.; Mg 10 mg.; Zn 0.085 mg.; folic acid 1.0 mg./Filmtab. Bot. 100s.
Use: Prenatal vitamin/mineral supplement & for treatment of megaloblastic anemias of pregnancy

PRAMINIL. Imipramine, B.A.N.

PRAMIVERINE. B.A.N. 4,4-Diphenyl-N-isopropylcyclohexylamine.
Use: Spasmolytic.

PRAMOCAINE (I.N.N.). Pramoxine, B.A.N.
Use: Allergic dermatitis.

PRAMOSONE CREAM 0.5%. (Ferndale) Hydrocortisone acetate 0.5%, pramoxine HCl 1% cream base. Tube 1 oz., Jar 1 lb.
Use: Anti-inflammatory, anti-pruritic.

RAMOSONE CREAM 1%. (Ferndale) Hydrocortisone acetate 1%, pramoxine HCl 1% in cream base. Tube 1 oz. Jar. 1 lb.
Use: Anti-inflammatory, anti-pruritic.

RAMOSONE CREAM 2.5%. (Ferndale) Hydrocortisone acetate 2.5%, pramoxine HCl 1% in cream base. Tubes 1 oz., 4 oz. Jar 1 lb.
Use: Anti-inflammatory, anti-pruritic.

RAMOSONE LOTION 0.5%. (Ferndale) Hydrocortisone acetate 0.5%, pramoxine HCl 1% in lotion base. Bot. 1.5 oz., 4 oz., 8 oz., gal.
Use: Anti-inflammatory, anti-pruritic.

RAMOSONE LOTION 1%. (Ferndale) Hydrocortisone acetate 1%, pramoxine HCl 1% in lotion base. Bot. 1.25 oz., 4 oz., 8 oz.
Use: Anti-pruritic.

RAMOSONE LOTION 2.5%. (Ferndale) Hydrocortisone acetate 2.5%, pramoxine HCl 1% in lotion base. Bot 2 oz., gal.
Use: Anti-inflammatory, anti-pruritic.

RAMOSONE OINTMENT 1%. (Ferndale) Hydrocortisone acetate 1%, pramoxine HCl 1% in ointment base. Tube 1 oz., Jar 1 lb.
Use: Anti-inflammatory, anti-pruritic.

RAMOXINE. B.A.N. 4-[3-(4-Butoxyphenoxy)-propyl]-morpholine. Pramocaine (I.N.N.)
Use: Local anesthetic.

• **RAMOXINE HYDROCHLORIDE,** U.S.P. XXI. Cream, Jelly, U.S.P. XXI. 4-[3-(p-Butoxyphenoxy)-propyl]morpholine HCl.
Use: Local anesthetic.
See: Prax, Lotion (Ferndale)
Proctofoam, Aero. (Reed & Carnrick)
Tronothane HCl, Cream, Jel (Abbott)
oil, citric acid, natural & artificial flavors, mono

RAMOXINE HCl W/COMBINATIONS
See: Anti-Itch, Lot. (Towne)
Anugesic, Oint., Supp. (Parke-Davis)
Dermarex, Cream (Hyrex)
Drotic No. 2, Drops (Ascher)
Gentz, Jelly, Wipes (Philips Roxane)
My Cort Otic #2, Ear Drops (Scrip)
1 + 1 Creme, 1 + 1-F Creme (Dunhall)
Orlex HC, Otic (Baylor)
Otocalm-H Ear Drops (Parmed)
Oto Drops (Reid-Provident)
Perifoam, Aerosol (Rowell Labs.)
Proctofoam-HC, Aerosol (Reed-Carnrick)
Quada-Creme, Cream (Sutliff & Case)
Quinsone, Cream (Sutliff & Case)
Sherform-HC, Oint. (Sheryl)
Steraform Creme (Mayrand)
Steramine Otic, Drops (Mayrand)
V-Cort, Cream (Scrip)

RAMPINE. B.A.N. O-Propionylatropine, PAMN methonitrate.
Use: Treatment of peptic ulcer.

PRANOLIUM CHLORIDE. USAN.
Use: Cardiac depressant.

RAX CREAM. (Ferndale) Pramoxine HCl 1% in cream base. Tubes 1 oz. Jars 4 oz., 1 lb.
Use: Anti-pruritic.

PRAX LOTION. (Ferndale) Pramoxine HCl 1.0%. Bot. 15 ml., 120 ml.
Use: Anti-pruritic.

PRAXILENE OXALATE. Naftidrofuryl, B.A.N.

• **PRAZEPAM,** U.S.P. XXI. Cap., Tab. U.S.P. XXI. 7-Chloro-1-(cyclopropylmethyl)-1,2-dihydro-5-phenyl-2H-1,
4-benzodiazepin-2-one.
Use: Muscle relaxant.
See: Centrax, Cap. (Parke-Davis)
Vestran, Cap. (Parke-Davis)

• **PRAZIQUANTEL.** USAN. 2-Cyclohexylcarbonyl-1,3,4,6,7,11b-hexahydro-2H-pyrazino[2,1-a]-isoquinolin-4-one.
Use: Anthelmintic.

PRAZITONE. B.A.N. 5-Phenyl-5-(2-piperidyl)-methylbarbituric acid.
Use: Antidepressant.

PRAZOSIN. B.A.N. 1-(4-Amino-6,7-dimethoxy-quinazolin-2-yl)-4-(2-furyol)piperazine.
Use: Antihypertensive.
W/Polythiazide.
See: Minizide, Cap, (Pfizer Laboratories)

• **PRAZOSIN HYDROCHLORIDE,** U.S.P. XXI. Cap., U.S.P. XXI. 1-(4-Amino-6,7-dimethoxy-2-quinazoliny)-4-(2-furoyl)piperazine monohydrochloride.
Use: Antihypertensive.
See: Minipress, Cap. (Pfizer Laboratories)

PRE-17. (Standex) Vit. A 4,000 I.U., D 400 I.U., B-1 1.5 mg., B-2 2 mg., B-6 2 mg., B-12 2 mcg., C 50 mg., niacinamide 10 mg., Ca pantothenate 5 mg., Folic acid 8 mg., Fe 40 mg., calcium carbonate 240 mg./Tab. Bot. 100s.

PRECEF FOR INJECTION. (Bristol) Ceforanide 500 mg. or 1 Gm./Vials or piggyback.
Use: Anti-infective for surgical prophylaxis.

PRECISION HIGH NITROGEN DIET. (Sandoz Nutrition) Citrus Fruit Flavor: Maltodextrin, pasteurized egg white solids, sucrose, natural & artificial flavors, medium chain triglycerides, citric acid, partially hydrogenated soybean oil, polysorbate 80, mono & diglycerides, FD& C Yellow No. 5 and No. 6, vitamins & minerals. Powder 2.93 oz. Packets.
Use: Total or supplemental feeding, oral or tube.

PRECISION ISOTONIC DIET. (Sandoz Nutrition) Vanilla Flavor: Maltodextrin egg white solids, sucrose, partially hydrogenated soybean oil with BHA, natural and artificial flavor, sodium caseinate, citric acid, carrageenan, mono and diglycerides, vitamins and minerals. Individual Packets, 2.06 oz.
Use: Total or supplemental feeding, oral or tube.

PRECISION LR DIET. (Sandoz Nutrition) Orange Flavor: Maltodextrin, pasteurized egg white solids, sucrose, medium chain triglycerides, partially hydrogenated soybean oil with BHA, citric acid, natural and artificial flavors, mono and diglycerides, polysorbate 80, FD & C Yellow No.5 and No. 6, vitamins and minerals. Powder in 3 oz. packets.
Use: Total or supplemental feedings, oral or tube.

PRECORTISYL. Prednisolone, B.A.N.

PRED-5. (Saron) Prednisone 5 mg./Tab. Bot. 100s, 1000s.

PRED-A 50. (Tunex) Prednisolone acetate 50 mg./ml. Vial 10cc.
Use: Intra-articular inj.; adrenocortical insufficiency.

PRED-A 100. (Tunex) Prednisolone acetate 100 mg./ml. Vial 10cc.
Use: Intra-articular inj.; adrenocortical insufficiency.

PREDAJECT. (Mayrand) Prednisolone acetate 50 mg./ml. Vial 10 ml.
Use: Long-acting anti-inflammatory, corticosteroid.

PREDALONE 50. (Forest) Prednisolone acetate 50 mg./ml. Vial 10 ml.
Use: Anti-inflammatory.

PREDALONE T.B.A. (Forest) Prednisolone tebutate 20 mg./ml. in aqueous suspension. Vial 10 ml.

PREDAMIDE OPHTHALMIC. (Maurry) Sodium sulfacetamide 10%, prednisolone acetate 0.5%, hydroxyethylcellulose, polysobate 80, sodium thiosulfate, sodium phosphate, edetate disodium, benzalkonium Cl 0.025%. Bot. 5 ml.
Use: Anti-inflammatory, anti-bacterial.

PREDCOR INJECTION. (Hauck) Prednisolone acetate 25 mg. or 50 mg./ml. Vial 10 ml.
Use: Anti-inflammatory.

PREDCOR-TBA INJECTION. (Hauck) Prednisolone tebuate 20 mg./ml. Vial 10 ml.
Use: Anti-inflammatory.

PRED-FORTE. (Allergan) Prednisolone acetate 1%, w/benzalkonium Cl, polysorbate 80, boric acid, sod. citrate, sod. bisulfite, NaCl, edetate disodium, hydroxypropyl methylcellulose, purified water. Plastic Dropper Bot. 5 ml., 10 ml., 15 ml.
Use: Ocular anti-inflammatory.

PREDICORT-50. (Dunhall) Prednisolone acetate 50 mg./ml. Vial 10 ml.
Use: Anti-inflammatory, steroid.

PREDICORT-AP. (Dunhall) Prednisolone sodium phosphate 20 mg., prednisolone acetate 80 mg./ml. Vial 10 ml.
Use: Anti-inflammatory, steroid.

PREDICORT-RP. (Dunhall) Prednisolone sodium phosphate equivalent to prednisolone phosphate 20 mg., niacinamide 25 mg./ml. Vial 10 ml.
Use: Short-acting steroid.

PRED MILD. (Allergan) Prednisolone acetate 0.12% w/benzalkonium Cl, polysorbate 80, boric acid, sodium citrate, sodium bisulfite, NaCl, edetate disodium, hydroxypropyl methylcellulose, purified water. Bot. 5 ml., 10 ml.
Use: Ocular anti-inflammatory.

• **PREDNAZATE.** USAN.
Use: Anti-inflammatory.

PREDNELAN ACETATE. Prednisolone, B.A.N.

• **PREDNICARBATE.** USAN.
Use: Glucocorticoid.

PREDNICEN-M. (Central) Prednisone 5 mg./Tab. Bot. 100s, 1000s.

• **PREDNIMUSTINE.** USAN.
Use: Antineoplastic.

PREDNISOLAMATE. B.A.N. Prednisolone 21-diethylaminoacetate. Deltacortril DA hydrochloride.
Use: Corticosteroid.

• **PREDNISOLONE,** U.S.P. XXI. Cream, Tab., U.S.P. XXI. Pregna-1,4-diene-3,20-dione, 11,17,21-trihydroxy-, (11β)- 11β,17,21-Trihydroxypregna-1,4-dier 3,20 dione. Metacortandralone.
Use: Adrenocortical steroid (anti-inflammatory).
See: Cordrol, Tabs. (Vita Elixir)
Delta-Cortef, Tab. (Upjohn)
Fernisolone, Tab., Inj. (Ferndale)
Orasone, Tab. (Rowell)
Orasone 50, Tab. (Rowell)
Panisolone, Tab. (Panray)
Prednis, Tab. (USV Labs.)
Ster 5, Tab. (Scrip)
Sterane Injection, Vial (Pfizer Laboratories)
Sterane Tablets, Tab. (Pfipharmecs)
Ulacort, Tab. (Fellows-Testagar)
W/Aluminum hydroxide gel, dried.
See: Predoxide, Tab. (Mallard)
W/Aspirin.
See: Sarogesic, Tab. (Saron)
W/Chloramphenicol.
See: Chloroptic-P, Ophth. Oint. (Allergan)
W/Hydroxyzine HCl.
W/Neomycin sulfate.
Neo-Deltef, Drops (Upjohn)
W/Sulfacetamide sodium, methylcellulose.
See: Isopto Cetapred, Susp. (Alcon)
W/Sulfacetamide sodium.
See: Cetapred Ophthalmic Oint. (Alcon)

• **PREDNISOLONE ACETATE,** U.S.P. XXI. Sterile Susp., U.S.P. XXI. Pregna-1,4-diene-3,20-dione, 21 (acetyloxy)-11,17-dihydroxy-,(11β)-
Use: Adrenocortical steroid (anti-inflammatory).
Durapred Injection (Amfre-Grant)
Econopred, Susp. (Alcon)
Key-Pred, Inj. (Hyrex)
Nisolone, Vial (Ascher)
Pred-A 50, Inj. (Tunex)
Pred-A 100, Inj. (Tunex)
Predicort, Amp. (Dunhall)
Pred Preps. (Allergan)
Pred-Forte, Ophth. Susp. (Allergan)
Savacort-50, 100, Vial (Savage)
Sigpred, Inj. (Sig)
Steraject, Vial (Mayrand)
Sterane, Inj. (Pfizer Laboratories)
Ulacort, Inj. (Fellows-Testagar)

PREDNISOLONE ACETATE W/COMBINATIONS
See: Blephamide Liquifilm, Sol. (Allergan)
Blephamide S.O.P., Ophth, Oint. (Allergan)
Cetapred Opth. Oint. (Alcon)
Dua-Pred, Inj. (Reid-Provident)
Metimyd, Ophth. Susp., Oint. (Schering)
Neo-Delta-Cortef, Preps. (Upjohn)
Panacort R-P, Vial (Ferndale)
Prednefrin, Mild, Susp. (Allergan)
Predulose Bufopto, Sol. (Softcon)
Sulfapred, Susp. (Softcon)
Tri-Ophtho, Ophth. (Maurry)
Vasocidin Preps. (CooperVision)

PREDNISOLONE BUTYLACETATE. 1,4-Pregnadiene 3,20-dione-11β,17α,21-triol-tert-butyl-acetate.
See: Hydeltra-T.B.A., Vial (Merck Sharp & Dohme)

EDNISOLONE CYCLOPENTYLPROPIONATE. Δ^1,4-Pregnadiene-3,20-dione-11, 17a-diol-21-cyclopentylpropionate(prednisolone-21-cyclopentylpropionate).

REDNISOLONE HEMISUCCINATE, U.S.P. XXI. Pregna-1,4-diene-3,20-dione, 21-(3-carboxy-1-oxopropoxy)-11, 17-dihydroxy-, (11β)—.
Use: Adrenocortical steroid (anti-inflammatory).

REDNISOLONE SODIUM PHOSPHATE, U.S.P. XXI. Inj., Ophth. Sol.: U.S.P. XXI. Pregna-1,4-diene-3,20-dione, 11,17-dihydroxy-21-(phosphonoxy)-, disodium salt, (11)-.
Use: Adrenocortical steroid (anti-inflammatory).
See: Alto-Pred Soluble, Vial (Alto)
Hydeltrasol, Inj. (Merck Sharp & Dohme)
Hydeltrone (MSD AGVET)
Hydrosol, Inj. (Rocky Mtn.)
Inflamase Forte Ophthalmic Solution (CooperVision)
Inflamase Ophth. Solution (CooperVision)
Key-Pred SP, Inj. (Hyrex)
Liquid Pred, Inj. (Muro)
Metreton, Ophth. Sol. Sterile (Schering)
Nor-Preds, Inj. (Vortech)
P.S.P. IV (Four), Inj. (Reid-Provident)
Savacort-S, Inj. (Savage)
Sodasone, Inj. (Fellows Testagar)
Sol-Pred, Inj. (Amfre-Grant)
W/Neomycin sulf.
See: Neo-Hydeltrasol, Ophth. Sol., Ophth. Oint. (Merck Sharp & Dohme)
W/Niacinamide, disodium edetate, sodium bisulfite, phenol.
See: P.S.P. IV, Inj. (Reid-Provident)
W/Prednisolone acetate.
See: Panacort R-P, Vial (Ferndale)
Solu-Pred, Vial (Kenyon)
W/Sodium Sulfacetamide.
See: Optimyd, Sol. (Schering)
Vasocidin, Liq. (CooperVision)

REDINISOLONE SODIUM SUCCINATE FOR INJECTION, U.S.P. XXI. Pregna-1,4-diene-3-20-dione,21-(3-carboxy-1-oxopropoxy)-11,17-dihydroxy-monosodium salt, (11β)—. A hemisuccinate.
Use: Adrenocortical steroid (anti-inflammatory).

EDNISOLONE TERTIARY-BUTYLACETATE.
See: Prednisolone Tebutate, U.S.P. XXI.

EDNISOL T.B.A.. (Pasadena Research; Medwick) Prednisolone tertiary butylacetate 20 mg./ml. Vial 10 cc.

REDNISOLONE TEBUTATE SUSPENSION, STERILE, U.S.P. XXI. Pregna-1,4-diene-3,20-dione, 11,17-dihydroxy-21-(3,3-dimethyl-1-oxobutyl)oxy-, (11β)—.
Use: Adrenocorticol steroid.
See: Durapred T.B.A. Injection (Amfre-Grant)
Hydeltra-T.B.A., Vial (Merck Sharp & Dohme)
Hydeltrone—T.B.A. (MSD AGVET)
Metalone, Vial (Foy)
Rodelta T.B.A., Inj. (Rocky Mtn.)

REDNISONE, U.S.P. XXI. Syrup, Tabs., U.S.P. XXI. Pregna-1,4-diene-3,11,20-trione, 17,21-dihydroxy-. Δ 1,4-Pregnadiene-17α,21-diol-3,11-20-trione. 1-Dehydro-cortisone, Metacortandracin. 17,21-Dihydroxy-pregna-1,4-diene-3,11,20-trione.
Use: Adrenocortical steroid (anti-inflammatory)
See: Delta-Dome Tab.(Miles Pharm)
Deltasone, Tab. (Upjohn)
Keysone, Tab. (Hyrex)
Lisacort, Tab. (Fellows-Testagar)
Meticorten, Tab. (Schering)
Maso-Pred, Tab. (Mason)
Orasone, Tab. (Rowell)
Pan-Sone, Tab. (Panray)
Pred-5 (Saron)
Ropred, Tab. (Robinson)
Sarogesic, Tab. (Saron)
SK-Prednisone, Tab. (SmithKline)
Sterapred, Tab. (Mayrand)
W/Chlorpheniramine maleate.
See: Histone, Tab. (Blaine)
W/Phenylephrine HCl.
See: Prednefrin-S, Sol. (Allergan)

• **PREDNIVAL.** USAN. 11 beta, 17, 21-Trihydroxypregna-1,4-diene-3,20-dione 17 valerate.
Under study.
Use: Topical anti-inflammatory.

PREDNYLIDENE. B.A.N. 11β,17α,21-Trihydroxy-16-methylenepregna-1,4-diene-3,20-dione. Dacortilene; Decortilen.
Use: Corticosteroid.

PREDSOL DISODIUM PHOSPHATE. Prednisolone, B.A.N.

PREDULOSE. (Softcon) Prednisolone acetate 0.25%, phenylephrine HCl 0.125%, w/methyl-cellulose, methylparaben 0.04%, propylparaben 0.02%, propylene glycol, monobasic sod. phosphate, dibasic sod. phosphate, sod. thiosulfate, & polysorbate 80. Bot. 5 cc.
Use: Mild allergic & non-infectious inflammatory eye disorders.

PREFLEX. (Alcon) Isotonic, aqueous sol. of sodium phosphates, sodium chloride tyloxapol, hydroxyethylcellulose, polyvinyl alcohol. Bot. 1.5 oz.
Use: Soft contact lenses cleaning sol.

PREFRIN LIQUIFILM. (Allergan) Phenylephrine HCl 0.12%, polyvinyl alcohol 1.4%. Bot. 0.7 fl. oz.
Use: Ocular decongestant.

PREFRIN-A. (Allergan) Phenylephrine 0.12%, pyrilamine maleate 0.1%, antipyrine 0.1% w/benzalkonium chloride, sodium bisulfite, sodium citrate, boric acid, edetate disodium, purified water. Dropper Bot. 15 ml.
Use: Ocular antihistamine, decongestant.

PREFRIN-Z LIQUIFILM. (Allergan) Zinc sulfate 0.25%, phenylephrine HCl 0.12% in sterile ophthalmic solution, polyvinyl alcohol 1.4%. Bot. 0.5 fl. oz.
Use: Astringent, decongestant, sterile ophthalmic solution.

PREGESTIMIL. (Mead Johnson) Protein hydrolysate formula supplies 640 calories/qt. w/18 Gm. protein, 26 Gm. fat, 86 Gm. carbohydrate, vitamins and minerals. (Vit. A 2000 I.U., D 400 I.U., E 15 I.U., C 52 mg., folic acid 100 mcg., thiamine 0.5 mg., riboflavin 0.6 mg., niacin 8 mg., B-6 0.4 mg., B-12 2 mcg., biotin 0.05 mg., pantothenic acid 3 mg., K-1 100

mcg., choline 85 mg., inositol 30 mg., Ca 600 mg., P 400 mg., iodine 45 mcg., Fe 12 mg., Mg 70 mg., Cu 0.6 mg., Zn 4 mg., Mn 0.2 mg., chloride 550 mg., K 700 mg., Na 300 mg.)/Qt. (20 kcal/fl. oz.); Powder, cans 1 lb.
Use: Complete nutritionally balanced lactose-free hypoallergenic infant diet with readily digestible sources of protein, fat, and carbohydrate.

PREGNENINOLONE.
See: Ethisterone.

• **PREGNENOLONE.** F.D.A. 3-beta-Hydroxypregn-5-en-20-one. Synthetic steroid intermediate. 3-Hydroxy-20-keto-pregene-5.
Use: Treatment of rheumatoid arthritis.

• **PREGNENOLONE SUCCINATE.** USAN. 3-Hydroxy-5-pregnen-20-one, hydrogen succinate.
Use: Glucocorticoid.

PREGNOSIS SLIDE TEST. (Roche) Two-minute indirect test for pregnancy. Detects HCg at 1.5 to 2.5 I.U./ml. of urine.

PREGNYL. (Organon) Human chorionic gonadatrophin. Vial 10,000 I.U./Vial w/diluent. Vial 10 ml.
Use: I.M., cryptorchidism, induction of ovulation & pregnancy in anovulatory women.

PRE-INE. (Kay) Chorionic gonadotropin 10,000 I.U./Vial to be prepared. Multiple dose vial 10 cc. w/diluent.

PREJECT PREINJECTION TOPICAL ANESTHETIC. (Hoyt) Benzocaine 20% in polyethelyne glycol base. Jar 2 oz.
Use: Avoid discomfort of oral injection.

PELAMINE TABS. (Major) Tripelennamine 50 mg./Tab. Bot. 100s, 1000s.
Use: Antihistaminic.

PRELAN. (Lannett) Vit. A 4000 I.U., B-1 0.5 mg., B-2 2 mg., niacin 10 mg., B-6 3 mg., B-12 2 mcg., D 400 I.U., C 50 mg., Ca 200 mg., Fe 30 mg./Tab. Bot. 100s.
Use: Prenatal vitamin-mineral supplementation.

PRELAN F.A. TABLETS. (Lannett) Vit. A 4,000 I.U., B-1 0.5 mg., B-2 2.0 mg., niacin 10.0 mg., B-6 3.0 mg., B-12 2.0 mcg., D 400 I.U., C 50 mg., calcium 200 mg., iron 30 mg., folic acid 1 mg./Tab. Bot. 100s.
Use: Prenatal vitamin and mineral supplement.

PRELESTRIN. (Pasadena Research) Conjugated estrogens 0.625 mg., 1.25 mg./Tab. Bot. 100s, 1000s.

PRELMYCIN. (Pasadena Research) Tetracycline HCl 250 mg./Cap. Bot. 16s, 25s.

PRELTRON. (Pasadena Research) Sodium glucuronate 200 mg., 500 mg./2 cc. Amp. 25s, 100s.

PRELTRON-ORAL. (Pasadena Research) Glucuronolactone 335 mg./Tab. Bot. 100s, 1000s.

PRELU-2. (Boehringer Ingelheim) Phendimetrazine tartrate 105 mg./Cap. Bot. 100s.
Use: Anorexiant.

PRELUDIN. (Boehringer Ingelheim) Phenmetrazine HCl. **Tab.** 25 mg., Bot. 100s. **Endurets** 75 mg. Bot. 100s.
Use: Anorexiant.

PRELUS ELIXIR. (Winthrop Products) Isoproterenol HCl.
Use: Bronchodilator.

PREMARIN. (Ayerst) Conjugated Estrogens Tablets. Water-soluble conjugated estrogens derived fr[illegible] natural sources. 0.3 mg., 0.625 mg., 0.9 mg., 1.25 mg., or 2.5 mg./Tab. Bot. 100s, 1000s. 0.625 mg 1.25 mg. Unit Dose 100s. Cycle packs 21s.
Use: Moderate to severe vasomotor symptoms, atrophic vaginitis, kraurosis vulvae, female hypogonadism, etc.

PREMARIN INTRAVENOUS. (Ayerst) Conjugated Estrogens U.S.P., for Injection. Vial 25 mg./5 ml. w/diluent. (Vial also contains lactose 200 mg., so[illegible] citrate 12.5 mg., simethicone 0.2 mg. Diluent contains benzyl alcohol 2%, Water for Injection, U.S.P.
Use: Treatment of abnormal uterine bleeding due to hormonal imbalance in absence of organic pathology.

PREMARIN VAGINAL CREAM. (Ayerst) Conjugated Estrogens, U.S.P. 0.625 mg./1 Gm. w/cetyl ester wax, cetyl alcohol, white wax, glyceryl monostearate, propylene glycol monostearate, methyl stearate, phenylethyl alcohol, sod. lauryl sulfate, glycerin, mineral oil. Tube w/applicator 1. oz. (42.5 Gm.). Tube refill.
Use: Treatment of atrophic vaginitis & kraurosis vulvae.

PREMARIN W/MEPROBAMATE.
See: PMB-200 & 400, Tab. (Ayerst)

PREMARIN W/METHYLTESTOSTERONE. (Ayerst) Premarin (Conjugated Estrogens, U.S.P.) 1.25 mg methyltestosterone 10 mg./Yellow Tab. Premarin 0.625 mg., methyltestosterone 5 mg./Red Tab. B[illegible] 100s, 1000s.
Use: Moderate to severe vasomotor symptoms associated with menopause in those patients not improved by estrogens alone, postpartum breast engorgement.

W/Methyltestosterone, methamphetamine HCl & vitamins.
See: Mediatric, Cap., Liq., Tab. (Ayerst)

PREMATE-200. (Major) Meprobamate 200 mg., tridihe[illegible] ethyl Cl. 25 mg./Tab. Bot. 100s.
Use: Treatment of G.I. disorders associated with anxiety and tension.

PREMATE-400. (Major) Meprobamate 400 mg., tridihe[illegible] ethyl Cl. 25 mg./Tab. Bot. 100s.
Use: Treatment of G.I. disorders associated with anxiety and tension.

■ **PREMENSTRUAL TENSION.**
See: Motion Sickness
Pamabrom (Various Mfr.)
Pyranisamine Bromotheophyllinate (Various Mfr[illegible]

PREMESYN PMS. (Chattem) Pamabrom 25 mg., acetaminophen 500 mg., pyrilamine maleate 15 mg./Cap. Bot. 16s, 32s.
Use: Treatment of menstrual and premenstrual symptoms.

• **PRENALTEROL HYDROCHLORIDE.** USAN.
Use: Adrenergic.

ENATAL. (Kenyon) Vit. A 100 I.U., D 500 I.U., B-1 1 mg., C 25 mg., B-2 1 mg., niacinamide 3 mg., Fe 39 mg., Ca 140 mg., P 62 mg., pot. iodide 0.065 mg., Cu sulfate 1 mg., Co sulfate 1 mg., Mg oxide 10 mg., Mn sulfate 14 mg., K sulfate 11 mg., Na sulfate 0.40 mg., Zn oxide 0.40 mg., fluoride 1 mg./Tab. Bot. 100s, 1000s.
Use: Vitamin supplement.

ENATAL NO. 2. (Kenyon) Vit. A 4000 I.U., B-1 2 mg., B-2 2 mg., B-6 0.8 mg., C 50 mg., niacinamide 10 mg., iodide 0.15 mg., folic acid 0.1 mg., B-12 conc. 2 mcg., iron 50 mg., calcium 240 mg./Cap. Bot. 100s, 1000s.
Use: Vitamin supplement.

ENATE 90. (Bock) Vit. A 8000 I.U., D 400 I.U., E 30 I.U., C 200 mg., folic acid 1 mg., B-1 3 mg., B-2 3.4 mg., B-6 20 mg., B-12 12 mcg. niacinamide 20 mg., docusate sodium 50 mg., Ca 250 mg., iodine 0.15 mg., Fe 90 mg., Cu 2 mg., Zn 20 mg./Film Coated Tab. Bot. 100s, 1000s.
Use: Multivitamin, multimineral.

ENEX. (Coastal) Vit. A 500 I.U., D 400 I.U., B-1 3 mg., B-2 3 mg., B-6 10 mg., B-12 3 mcg., niacinamide 20 mg., d-calcium panthothenate 3.3 mg., Fe 42 mg., Ca 350 mg., Mn 0.33 mg., Zn 0.1 mg., Mg 0.67 mg., K 1.67 mg./Tab.
Use: Vitamin and mineral supplement.

ENISTAT. (Pharmex) Prednisolone sod. phosphate 20 mg., niacinamide 25 mg./cc. Vial 10 cc.

PRENYLAMINE. USAN. N-(3,3-Diphenylpropyl)-α-methylphenethylamine. Segontin; Synadrin lactate.
Use: Coronary vasodilator.

EPARATION H. (Whitehall) Phenylmercuric nitrate 1:10,000, live yeast cell derivative 2000 u. skin respiratory factor, shark liver oil 3%. Oint. Tube 1 oz., 2 oz. Supp. 12s, 24s, 48s.
Use: Hemorrhoids.

EPCORT CREAM. (Whitehall) Hydrocortisone 0.5%. Tube 0.5 oz., 1 oz.
Use: Topical corticosteroid.

E-PEN. (Rorer) Benzylpenicilloyl-polylysine in phosphate buffer w/sod. chloride. Amp. 0.25 ml. Single dose, sufficient for scratch and intra-dermal testing only, 5s.
Use: Skin test reagent for the detection of penicilloyl reagin associated with penicillin allergy.

EPODYNE. (West) Titratable iodine. **Solution:** 1%. Bot. pt., gal. **Scrub:** 0.75%. Bot. 6 oz., gal. **Swabs:** Saturated with sol. Pkt. 1s, Box 100s. **Swabsticks:** Saturated with sol. Pkt. 1s, Box 50s. Pkt. 3s, Box 75s.
Use: Topical antiseptic.

ESALIN. (Mallard) Aspirin 260 mg., salicylamide 120 mg., acetaminophen 120 mg., aluminum hydroxide gel dried 100 mg./Tab. Bot. 50s.

ESIDAL. Pentacynium Methylsulfate, B.A.N.

ESSOR AGENTS.
See: Sympathomimetic agents

ESSOROL. (Travenol) Metaraminol bitartrate. Vials 10 ml. (10 mg./cc.)
Use: Vasopressor.

PRESUN 4 CREAMY. (Westwood) Octyl dimethyl PABA. Bot. 4 oz.
Use: Moderate sunscreen protection, resists wash-off.

PRESUN 8 CREAMY. (Westwood) Octyl dimethyl PABA, oxybenzone. Bot. 4 oz.
Use: Sunscreen, moisturizer, resists wash-off.

PRESUN 15 CREAMY. (Westwood) Octyl dimethyl PABA, oxybenzone. Bot. 4 oz.
Use: Ultra sunscreen protection, resists wash-off.

PRESUN 8 GEL. (Westwood) PABA 5%, alcohol 55% (w/w), water, animal protein derivative, hydroxyethyl cellulose. Tube 3 oz.
Use: Sunscreen, moisturizer.

PRESUN 15 LIP PROTECTOR. (Westwood) Octyl dimethyl PABA 8%, oxybenzone 3%, mineral oil, ozokerite, petrolatum, PEG-4 dilurate, lanoline oil, propylparaben. Stick 15 oz.
Use: Sunscreen and moisturizer for lips.

PRESUN 8 LOTION. (Westwood) PABA, 55% SD alcohol 40. Bot. 4 oz., 7 oz.
Use: Moisturizer; prevention of sunburn.

PRESUN 15 LOTION. (Westwood) PABA, octyl dimethyl PABA, oxybenzone, 58% SD alcohol 40. Bot. 4 oz.
Use: Ultra sunscreen protection.

PRESUREN. Hydroxydione Sodium Succinate, B.A.N.

PRETAMAZIUM IODIDE. B.A.N. 4-(Biphenyl-4-yl)-3-ethyl-2-[4-(pyrrolidin-1-yl)styryl]thiazolium iodide.
Use: Treatment of enterobiasis.

PRETEND-U-ATE. (Vitalax) Enriched candy-appetite pacifier. Pkg. 20s.

PRETHCAMIDE. Mix. of crotethamide & cropropamide. Micoren (Geigy)

PRETTY FEET & HANDS. (Norcliff Thayer) Lotion 3 fl. oz.
Use: Rough skin remover.

PREVIDENT DISCLOSING DROPS. (Hoyt) Erythrosine sodium 1%. Bot. 1 oz.
Use: Disclosing dental plaque.

PREVIDENT DISCLOSING TABLET. (Hoyt) Erythrosine sodium 1%/Tab. Unit dose strip 1000s.
Use: Disclosing dental plaque.

PREVIDENT PROPHYLAXIS PASTE. (Hoyt) Sodium fluoride containing 1.2% fluoride ion w/pumice and alumina abrasives. Cups 2 Gm. Box 200s. Jars 9 oz.
Use: Clean and polish teeth.

PREVISION. Mestranol, U.S.P. XXI.

PREXONATE TABLETS. (Tennessee Pharm.) Vit. A acetate 5000 I.U., D 500 I.U., B-6 2 mg., B-1 5 mg., B-2 2 mg., C 100 mg., B-12 2.5 mcg., Ca pantothenate 1 mg., niacinamide 15 mg., folic acid 1 mg., Fe 45 mg., Ca 500 mg., intrinsic factor 3 mg./Tab. Bot. 100s, 1000s.
Use: Vitamin supplement.

• **PRIDEFINE HYDROCHLORIDE.** USAN.
Use: Antidepressant.

PRILOCAINE. B.A.N. N-(2-Propylaminopropionyl)-o-toluidine. 2-Propylamino-o-propionotoluidide. Citanest hydrochloride.
Use: Local anesthetic.

• **PRILOCAINE HYDROCHLORIDE,** U.S.P. XXI. Inj., U.S.P. XXI. 2-(Propylamino)-o-propionotolidide HCl.
Use: Local anesthetic.
See: Citanest Hydrochloride, Vial, Amp. (Astra)

PRIMACAINE. 2′-Diethylamino-ethyl-2-butoxy-3-aminobenzoate HCl.
Use: Dental local anesthesia.

PRIMAQUINE. B.A.N. 8-(4-Amino-1-methylbutyl-amino)-6-methoxyquinoline.
Use: Antimalarial.

• **PRIMAQUINE PHOSPHATE,** U.S.P. XXI. Tab., U.S.P. XXI. 1,4-Pentanediamine, N-(6-methoxy-8-quinolinyl)-, phosphate (1:2). (Winthrop-Breon) 8-(4-Amino-1-methylbutylamino)-6-methoxyquinoline diphosphate. Tab. 26.3 mg., Bot. 100s.
Use: Prevents relapses in nearly all cases of vivax malaria.

PRIMAR. (Amfre-Grant) Ferrous fumarate 200 mg., ascorbic acid 75 mg., folic acid 0.33 mg., pyridoxine HCl 25 mg./Tab. Bot. 100s, 1000s, 5000s.
Use: Vitamin therapy.

PRIMATENE MIST. (Whitehall) Epinephrine 0.5% w/w alcohol 34%. Bot. 0.5 oz., ¾ oz.
Use: Bronchodilator.

PRIMATENE MIST SUSPENSION. (Whitehall) Epinephrine bitartrate 0.3 mg., epinephrine bitartrate 7.0 mg./cc. Bot. ⅓ oz., 0.5 oz.
Use: Bronchodilator.

PRIMATENE M. TABLETS. (Whitehall) Theophylline 130 mg., ephedrine HCl 24.3 mg., pyrilamine maleate 16.6 mg./Tab. Bot. 24s, 60s.
Use: Oral bronchodilator.

PRIMATENE P TABLETS. (Whitehall) Theophylline 130 mg., ephedrine HCl 24 mg., phenobarbital 8 mg./Tab. Bot. 24s, 60s.
Use: Oral bronchodilator.

• **PRIMIDOLOL.** USAN.
Use: Anti-anginal; cardiac depressant.

• **PRIMIDONE,** U.S.P. XXI. Tab., Oral Susp., U.S.P. XXI. 4,6(1H,5H)-Pyrimidinedione, 5-ethyldihydro-5-phenyl-. 5-Ethyldihydro-5-phenyl-4,6(1H,5H)-pyrimidinedione. Tab. 250 mg. Bot. 100s, 1000s.
Use: Anticonvulsant.

PRIMOBOLAN ACETATE. Methenolone, B.A.N.

PRIMOLUT DEPOT HEXANOATE. Hydroxyprogesterone, B.A.N.

PRIMOSTRUM. A prep. of primiparous colostrum.

PRIMPERAN HYDROCHLORIDE. Metoclopramide, B.A.N.

PRINALGIN. Alclofenac, B.A.N.

PRINCIPEN '125' FOR ORAL SUSPENSION. (Squibb). Ampicillin trihydrate 125 mg./5 cc. Reconstitution to 80, 100, 150, 200 cc. Unimatic 125 mg./5 cc. Ctn. 25s, 100s.
Use: Broad spectrum antibiotic.

PRINCIPEN '250' FOR ORAL SUSPENSION. (Squibb). Ampicillin trihydrate 250 mg./5 cc. Reconstitution to 80, 100, 150, 200 cc.; Unimatic 5 cc./Bot. 25s. Ctn. 100s.
Use: Broad spectrum antibiotic.

PRINCIPEN '250' CAPSULES. (Squibb) Ampicillin 250 mg./Cap. Bot. 100s, 500s. Unimatic 100s.
Use: Broad spectrum antibiotic.

PRINCIPEN '500' CAPSULES. (Squibb). Ampicillin trihydrate 500 mg./Cap. Bot. 100s, 500s. Unimatic Pack 100s, 500s.
Use: Broad spectrum antibiotic.

PRINCIPEN WITH PROBENECID. (Squibb) Ampicill 389 mg., probenecid 111 mg./Cap. Bot. 9s.
Use: Treatment of uncomplicated urethral, cervica rectal, or pharyngeal infections caused by *N. gonorrhoeae* in men & women.

PRINN 0.5. (Scrip) Conjugated estrogen 0.625 mg./Tab. Bot. 100s.

PRIODERM LOTION. (Purdue Frederick) Malathion 0.5% Bot. 2 oz.
Use: Treatment of head lice & ova.

PRIORA. (Xttrium) Folic acid 0.3 mg., Vit. A 6000 I.U D 400 I.U., B-1 1.5 mg., B-2 2.5 mg., B-6 3 m niacinamide 15 mg., Ca. pantothenate 5 mg., Vit. 12 2 mcg., iron 40 mg., calcium 250 mg./Tab. Bo 100s.
Use: Phosphorus-free prenatal dietary supplement

PRIORA P.F. W/FOLIC ACID. (Xttrium) Calcium 85 mg., Vit. A 2000 I.U., D 400 I.U., C 35 mg., B-1 2 m B-2 2 mg., B-6 2 mg., niacinamide 7 mg., folic acid mg., iron 6 mg., Mn 0.12 mg./Tab. Bot. 100s, 1000
Use: Phosphorus-free prenatal dietary supplement

PRISCOLINE. (Ciba) Tolazoline Hydrochloride 25 mg./ml.; w/sod. citrate 0.65%, tartaric a acid 0.65%, chlorobutanol 0.5%. Vial 10 ml. Packages 1s.
Use: Relieves pain, promotes healing & increases blood supply to extremities.

PRISILIDENE HYDROCHLORIDE.
See: Alphaprodine HCl (Var. Mfr.)

PRISTINAMYCIN. B.A.N. An antibiotic produced by Streptomyces pristina spiralis.

PRIVADORN.
See: Bromisovalum (Var. Mfr.)

PRIVINE HYDROCHLORIDE. (Ciba) Naphazoline HC **Nasal Sol.:** 0.05%, Bot. 0.66 fl. oz. (20 ml.) w/dropper, 16 fl. oz. (473 ml.). **Nasal Spray** 0.05%, plastic squeeze bot. 0.5 fl. oz. (15 ml.).
Use: Nasal decongestant.

• **PRIZIDILOL HYDROCHLORIDE.** USAN.
Use: Antihypertensive.

PRO-50. (Dunhall) Promethazine HCl 50 mg./ml. Vial 1 ml.
Use: Antihistaminic, sedative.

PRO-ACET DOUCHE CONCENTRATE. (Pro-Acet) Lactic, citric, & acetic acids, sod. lauryl sulfate, lactose dextrose & sod. acetate. Pkg. polyethylene envelope 10 cc. Contents of 1 envelope to be diluted with 2 quarts of water.
Use: Douche 6 oz., 12 oz. Travel Packets, 10 cc.

• **PROADIFEN HYDROCHLORIDE.** USAN. 2-(Diethylamino)ethyl 2,2-diphenyl-valerate hydrochloride
Use: Drug potentiator.

PRO-AMID. (T.E. Williams) Protoveratrine A 0.2 mg./Tab. Bot. 100s, 1000s.
Use: Mild to moderate hypertension.

PROAQUA. (Reid-Provident) Benzthiazide 50 mg./Ta Bot. 100s, 500s.
Use: Diuretic.

OBALAN. (Lannett) Probenecid 0.5 Gm./Tab. Bot. 100s, 1000s.

OBAMPACIN. (Robinson) Ampicillin trihydrate 3.5 Gm., probenecid 1 Gm./Unit dose Bottle.
Use: Antibiotic, gonorrhea.

OBAMPACIN SUSPENSION. (Goldline) Bot. 60 ml.
Use: Antibiotic.

O-BANTHINE. (Searle) Propantheline Br. **7.5** mg./Tab. Bot. 100s. **15** mg./Tab. Bot. 100s, 500s. Unit dose 100s.
Use: Anticholinergic for adjunctive therapy in treatment of peptic ulcer.

O-BANTHINE W/PHENOBARBITAL. (Searle) Propantheline Br 15 mg., phenobarbital 15 mg./Tab. Bot. 100s. Unit dose 100s.
Use: Treatment of duodenal ulcer and irritable bowel syndrome.

OBARBITAL SODIUM. 5-Ethyl-5-isopropylbarbiturate sod.

OBATE. (Vita Elixir) Meprobamate 400 mg./Tab.
Use: Antianxiety & muscle relaxant.

OBEC-T. (Stuart) Vit. B-1 15 mg., B-2 10 mg., B-3 100 mg., B-6 5 mg., B-12 5 mcg., C 600 mg., Ca pantothenate 20 mg. Bot. 60s.
Use: Therapeutic B-complex with Vitamin C.

OBEN. (Richlyn) Probenecid 500 mg., colchicine 0.5 mg./Tab. Bot. 1000s.
Use: Uricosuric.

PROBENECID, U.S.P. XXI. Tabs., U.S.P. XXI. Benzoic acid, 4-[(dipropylamino)sulfonyl)]- p-(Dipropylsulfamoyl) benzoic acid.
Use: Uricosuric.
See: Benacen, Tab. (Cenci)
Benemid, Tab. (Merck Sharp & Dohme)
Benn, Tab. (Scrip)
Probalan, Tab. (Lannett)
Robenecid, Tab. (Robinson)
SK Probenecid, Tab. (SmithKline)
/Ampicillin.
See: Amcill-GC, Oral Susp. (Parke-Davis)
Polycillin-PRB, Liq. (Bristol)
Principen W/Probenecid, Cap. (Squibb)
/Ampicillin trihydrate.
See: Probampacin (Biocraft)

PROBENECID AND COLCHICINE, U.S.P. XXI.
Use: Uricosuric combination for chronic gouty arthritis.
See: Benn-C, Tab. (Scrip)
Colbenemid, Tab. (Merck Sharp & Dohme)
Robenecid w/colchicine, Tab. (Robinson)
Robenecol, Tab. (Robinson)

ROBENZAMIDE. 0-Propoxybenzamide. (Warner-Lambert)

PROBICROMIL CALCIUM. USAN.
Use: Anti-allergenic.

PROBUCOL. USAN. (1) Acetone bis(3,5-di-tertbutyl-4-hydroxyphenyl) mercaptole; (2) 4,4′-(isopropylidenedithio)-bis[2,6-di-tert-butylphenol].
Use: Anticholesteremic.
See: Lorelco, Tab. (Merrell Dow)

ROCAINAMIDE. B.A.N. 4-Amino-N-(2-diethylaminoethyl)benzamide Pronestyl.
Use: Myocardial depressant.

PROCAINAMIDE HCl. (Quality Generics)
Procainamide hydrochloride 250 mg., 500 mg./Cap. Bot. 100s, 1000s.
Use: Cardiac arrhythmia.

• **PROCAINAMIDE HYDROCHLORIDE,** U.S.P. XXI. Cap., Inj., U.S.P. XXI. Benzamide, 4-amino-N-[2-(diethylamino)ethyl]-HCl. p-Amino-N-[2-(diethylaminoethyl]benzamide HCl.
Use: Cardiac depressant in arrhythmias.
See: Procamide SR, Tab. (Rowell)
Procan SR, Tab. (Parke-Davis)
Procapan, Cap. (Panray)
Pronestyl, Cap. Vial. (Squibb)

PROCAINE ASCORBATE.

PROCAINE BASE.
W/Benzyl alcohol & propyl-p-aminobenzoate.
Use: Local anesthetic.
See: Durathesia, Inj. (Vortech)
Rectocaine, Vial (Moore-Kirk)
W/Butyl-p-aminobenzoate, benzyl alcohol, in sweet almond oil.
See: Anucaine, Amp. (Calvin)

PROCAINE BORATE. No products listed.

PROCAINE BUTYRATE. p-Aminobenzoyl-diethylaminoethanol butyrate.

• **PROCAINE HYDROCHLORIDE,** U.S.P. XXI. Inj., Sterile, U.S.P. XXI. Benzoic acid, 4-amino-, 2-(diethylamino)-ethyl ester, HCl. 2-Diethylaminoethyl p-aminobenzoate HCl. Allocaine, Bernocaine, Chlorocaine, Ethocaine, Irocaine, Kerocaine, Syncaine. (Abbott) 1% or 2% solution. Multiple-dose Vial 30 ml.
Use: Local anesthetic.
See: Anucaine, Amp. (Calvin)
Novocain, Amp., Sol. (Winthrop-Breon)
Unicaine, Vial (Kay)
W/Tetracaine and Nordefrin Hydrochlorides, Inj.

PROCAINE HYDROCHLORIDE AND LEVONORDEFRIN INJECTION.
Use: Local anesthetic.

• **PROCAINE PENICILLIN G SUSPENSION, STERILE,** U.S.P. XXI.
Use: Antibiotic.
See: Crysticillin, Vial (Squibb)
Penicillin G, Procaine (Various Mfr.)
Pfizerpen For Injection (Pfipharmecs)

• **PROCAINE, PENICILLIN G W/ALUMINUM STEARATE SUSPENSION, STERILE.,** U.S.P. XXI.
Use: Antibiotic.
See: Penicillin G Procaine with Aluminum Stearate, Sterile, U.S.P. XXI.

• **PROCAINE HYDROCHLORIDE AND EPINEPHRINE INJECTION,** U.S.P. XXI.
Use: Local anesthetic.

• **PROCAINE AND PHENYLEPHRINE HYDROCHLORIDES INJECTION,** U.S.P. XXI.
Use: Local anesthetic (dental).

• **PROCAINE AND TETRACAINE HYDROCHLORIDES AND LEVONORDEFRIN INJECTION,** U.S.P. XXI.
Use: Local anesthetic (dental).

PROCAINE, TETRACAINE AND NORDEFRIN HYDROCHLORIDES INJECTION.
Use: Local anesthetic.

PROCAINE, TETRACAINE AND PHENYLEPHRINE HYDROCHLORIDES INJECTION.
Use: Anesthetic.

PROCALAMINE INJECTION. (American McGaw) Injection of amino acid 3%, and glycerin 3% with electrolytes. Bot. 1000 ml.
Use: Amino acids.

PRO-CAL-THRON. (Vangard) Docusate calcium 60 mg., danthron 50 mg./Cap. Bot. 100s, 1000s.
Use: Stool Softener, laxative.

PROCAMIDE. (Amfre-Grant) Procainamide HCl 250 mg./Cap. Bot. 100s, 1000s.
Use: Anti-arrhythmic.

PROCAMIDE SR. (Rowell) Procainamide HCl 250 mg., 500 mg. or 750 mg./Tab. Bot. 100s.
Use: Anti-arrhythmic

PROCAN SR. (Parke-Davis) Procainamide HCl sustained release 250 mg. 500 mg. or 750 mg./Tab. Bot. 100s. Unit dose 100s.
Use: Treatment of premature ventricular contractions, ventricular tachycardia, atrial fibrillation, paroxysmal atrial tachycardia.

PRO-CAP 65. (Foy) Propoxyphene HCl 65 mg., aspirin 227 mg., phenacetin 162 mg., caffeine 32.4 mg./Cap. Bot. 500s.
Use: Analgesic.

PROCAPAN. (Panray) Procainamide HCl 0.25 mg./Cap. Bot. 100s, 1000s.
Use: Antiarrythmic.

PROCARBAZINE. B.A.N. N-4-Isopropylcarbamoylbenzyl-N'-methylhydrazine. Natulan hydrochloride.
Use: Treatment of Hodgkin's disease.

• **PROCARBAZINE HCl.,** U.S.P. XXI. Cap., U.S.P. XXI. Benzamide, N-(1-methylethyl)-4-[(2-methyl-hydrazino)methyl]-HCl. (Roche) Natulan.
Use: Cytostatic, Antineoplastic.
See: Matulane, Caps. (Roche)

PROCARDIA. (Pfizer Laboratories) Nifedipine 10 mg./Cap. Bot. 100s. 300s. Unit Dose 100s.
Use: Treatment of angina.

• **PROCATEROL HYDROCHLORIDE.** USAN.
Use: Bronchodilator.

PROCEPTION SPERM NUTRIENT DOUCHE. (Milex) Ringer type glucose douche. Bot. ample for 10 douches.
Use: Precoital douche to promote conception.

• **PROCHLORPERAZINE,** U.S.P. XXI. Suppos., U.S.P. XXI. 10H-Phenothiazine, 2-chloro-10-[3-(4-methyl-1-piperazinyl)propyl]-.
Use: Antiemetic.
See: Compazine, Preps. (SmithKline)
W/Isopropamide.
See: Iso-Perazine, Cap. (Lemmon)

• **PROCHLORPERAZINE EDISYLATE,** U.S.P. XXI. Inj., Oral Sol., Syr., U.S.P. XXI. 10H-Phenothiazine, 2-chloro-10-[3-(4-methyl-1-piperazinyl)propyl]-1,2-ethanedisulfonate (1:1).
Use: Tranquilizer, antiemetic.
See: Compazine, Preps. (SmithKline)

PROCHLORPERAZINE ETHANEDISULFONATE. Prochlorperazine Edisylate, U.S.P. XXI.
Use: Tranquilizing agent.

• **PROCHLORPERAZINE MALEATE,** U.S.P. XXI. Tabs., U.S.P. XXI. 10H-Phenothiazine, 2-chloro-10-[3-(4-methyl-1-piperazinyl)-propyl]-(Z)-2-butenedioate (1:2).
Use: Antiemetic, tranquilizer.
See: Compazine, Preps (SmithKline)

• **PROCINONIDE.** USAN.
Use: Adrenocortical steroid.

PROCLAN EXPECTORANT WITH CODEINE. (Cenci) Promethazine HCl, codeine phosphate, ipecac, potassium guaiacolsulfonate/5 cc. Bot.

PROCLAN VC EXPECTORANT WITH CODEINE. (Cenci) Codeine phosphate 10 mg., promethazine HCl 5 mg., phenylephrine HCl 5 mg., fl. ext. ipecac 0.17 min., potassium guaiacolsulfonate 44 mg., citric acid anhydrous 60 mg., sod. citrate 197 mg./cc., alcohol 7%. Bot.

• **PROCLONOL.** USAN. Bis(p-chlorophenyl)-cyclopropylmethanol. Under study.
Use: Acaricide, fungicide.

PRO COMFORT ATHLETE'S FOOT SPRAY. (Scholl) Tolnaftate 1%. Aerosol Can 4 oz.
Use: Anti-fungal.

PROCOMP-65. (Merchant) Propoxyphene HCl 65 mg., aspirin 227 mg., phenacetin 162 mg., caffeine 32.4 mg./Cap. Bot. 100s, 500s.
Use: Analgesic.

PRO CORT. (Barnes-Hind) Hydrocortisone alcohol 0.5% in cream base. Tube 1 oz.
Use: Relief of minor skin irritations.

PRO CORT M. (Barnes-Hind) Hydrocortisone alcohol 0.5% with menthol in cream base. Tube 1 oz.
Use: Relief of minor skin irritations.

PROCTALME. (Meyer) Benzocaine, chlorbutanol, neomycin, thymol iodide, ointment w/rectal applicator. Tube 1 oz.
Use: Hemorrhoids.

PROCTOCORT. (Rowell) Hydrocortisone 1% in a water-miscible base w/stearyl alcohol, polyoxyethylene 40 stearate, dibasic sodium phosphate, cetyl alcohol, isopropyl palmitate, citric acid, propylene glycol, benzyl alcohol and buffered to a pH of 5.0. Cream 30 gm. w/fingercots and rectal applicator.
Use: Treatment of severe anorectal inflammation.

PROCTOFOAM N.S. (Reed & Carnrick) Pramoxine HCl 1%. Aerosol Bot. 10 Gm. w/applicator.
Use: Inflammatory anorectal disorders.

PROCTOFOAM-HC. (Reed & Carnrick) Hydrocortisone acetate 1% and pramoxine HCl 1% in hydrophilic base of propylene glycol, ethoxylated cetyl and stearyl alcohol, polyoxyethylene-10-stearyl ether, cetyl alcohol, propyl paraben, methyl paraben, trolamine, purified water and inert propellants. Bot. aerosol container Rectal foam 10 Gm.
Use: Inflammatory anorectal disorders.

PROCTOFORM. (Fellows) Bismuth subiodide 0.125 gr., zinc oxide 2.5 gr., bismuth subcarbonate 0.9 gr., boric acid 4 gr., isobutyl-propyl-para-aminobenzoic acid 1 gr./Supp. Box 12s.
Use: Antiseptic & analgesic.

RO CUTE CREAM. (Ferndale) Silicone, hexachlorophene, lanolin. 2 oz., 1 lb.
Use: Emollient, protective, bacteriostatic.

ROCUTE LOTION. (Ferndale) Hexachlorophene, Silicone, Lanolin. Bot. 8 oz.
Use: Emollient, protective, bacteriostatic.

ROCYCLIDINE. B.A.N. 1-Cyclohexyl-1-phenyl-3-(pyrrolidin-1-yl)propan-1-ol.
Use: Treatment of the Parkinsonian syndrome.

PROCYCLIDINE HCl, U.S.P. XXI. Tab., U.S.P. XXI. α-Cyclohexyl-α-phenyl-1-pyrrolidinepropanol HCl.
Use: Skeletal muscle relaxant.
See: Kemadrin, Tab. (Burroughs Wellcome)

RO-DEPO. (Vortech) Hydroxyprogesterone caproate 250 mg., benzyl benzoate 46%, benzyl alcohol 2%, castor oil/cc. Vial 5 ml.
Use: Long acting progestational agent.

RODERM TOPICAL DRESSING. (Hickam) Aerosol topical. Each .82 cc contains castor oil 650 mg., peruvian balsam 72.5 mg. Aerosol 4 oz.
Use: Prevention of decubiti.

PRODILIDINE HCl. USAN. (1,2-Dimethyl-3-phenyl-3-pyrrolidyl propionate HCl.
Use: Analgesic.

PRODOLIC ACID. USAN.
Use: Anti-inflammatory.

RO-EST. (Burgin-Arden) Progesterone 25 mg., estrogenic substance 25,000 I.U., sodium carboxymethylcellulose 1 mg., sodium cl 0.9% benzalkonium Cl 1:10,000 sodium phosphate dibasic 0.1% in water.

RO-ESTRONE. (Pharmex) Estradiol benzoate 2.5 mg., progesterone 12.5 mg./cc. Vial 10 cc.

ROESTRONE. (Rocky Mtn.) Progesterone 25 mg., estrone 2.5 mg./cc. Vial 10 cc.

ROFAC-O. (Kay) Progesterone 100 mg., alcohol 20%. Vial 10 ml.
Use: Amenorrhea, abnormal uterine bleeding.

ROFADOL. B.A.N. 1-Methyl-3-propyl-3-(3-hydroxyphenyl)pyrrolidine.
Use: Analgesic; antitussive.

PROFADOL HCl. USAN. m-(1-Methyl-3-propyl-3-pyrrolidinyl)phenol HCl.
Use: Analgesic.

ROFAMINA.
See: Amphetamine (Various Mfr.)

ROFASI HP. (Serono) Chorionic gonadotropin 5,000 U./Vial and 10,000 U./Vial. Ctn. contains 1 vial product and 1 vial diluent (benzyl alcohol 0.9% w/water for injection).
Use: Gonad-stimulating principle.

ROFERDEX. (Fisons) Ferric hydroxide & dextran in 0.9% sodium Cl. sol. for inj. sol. equiv. 50 mg. elem. iron/ml. Amp. 2 ml., 5 ml., or 10 ml.
Use: Iron deficiency anemia by I.M. or I.V. route.

ROFENAMINE HCl. Ethopropazine HCl, B.A.N.
See: Parsidol, Tab. (Parke-Davis)

ROFESSIONAL CARE LOTION, EXTRA STRENGTH. (Walgreen) Zinc oxide 0.25% in a lotion base. Bot. 16 oz.
Use: Dry skin care.

ROFLAVINE.
Use: Topically; antiseptic.

PROFLAVINE DIHYDROCHLORIDE. 3,6-Diaminoacridine dihydrochloride.

PROFLAVINE SULFATE. 3,6-Diaminoacridine sulfate.

• **PROGABIDE.** USAN.
Use: Anticonvulsant, muscle relaxant.

PROGELAN. (Lannett) Progesterone 25 mg., 50 mg., 100 mg./cc. in oil. Vials 10 cc.

PROGELAN AQUEOUS. (Lannett) Progesterone 25 mg., 50 mg., aq. susp./cc. Vials 10 cc.

PROGENS TABS. (Major) Conjugated estrogens 0.625 mg./Tab. Bot. 100s, 1000s; 1.25 mg./Tab. Bot. 1000s; 2.5 mg./Tab. Bot. 100s, 1000s.
Use: Estrogen replacement.

PROGEST-50. (Tunex) Progesterone 50 mg./ml. w/benzyl alcohol 10% as preservative in sesame oil. Vial 10cc.
Use: Hormonal imbalances.

PROGESTAJECT-50. (Mayrand) Progesterone 50 mg./ml. in oil. Vial 10 ml.
Use: Progesterone agent.

• **PROGESTERONE,** U.S.P. XXI. Inj., Sterile Susp. U.S.P. XXI. 4-Pregnene-3,20-dione. Corpus luteum hormone. Flavolutan, Luteogan, Luteosan, Lutren.
Use: Progestin.

Aq. Susp.
See: Gesterol, Aqueous, Vial (Fellows-Testagar)
Progelan Aq., Vial (Lannett)
Prorone, Inj. (Sig)

In oil
See: Femotrone Injection (Bluco)
Gesterol, Inj. (Fellows-Testagar)
Lipo-Lutin, Amp. (Parke-Davis)
Progelan, Vials (Lannett)
Progest-50, Inj. (Tunex)
Progestin, Vial (Var. Mfr.)
Prorone, Inj. (Sig)

Tab., sublingual.

W/Estradiol benzoate.
See: Pro-Estrone, Vial (Pharmex)

W/Estradiol, testosterone, procaine HCl, procaine base.
See: Hormo-Triad, Vial (Bell)

W/Estrogenic substance.
See: Profoygen Aqueous (Foy)
Progex, Inj. (Pasadena Research)

W/Estrone.
See: Proestrone, Inj. (Rocky Mtn.)

PROGESTRONAQ-LA. (Central) Progesterone 50 mg. Vial 10 ml.
Use: Progestin.

PROGESTERONE INTRAUTERINE CONTRACEPTIVE SYSTEM, U.S.P. XXI.
Use: Contraceptive.

PROGESTERONE-LIKE.
See: Haloprogesterone
Norethynodrel

PROGESTIN. Progesterone. (Various Mfr.)

PRO-GESTIVE. (Nutrition) Pepsin 200 mg., pancreatin 200 mg., bile salts 100 mg., dehydrocholic acid 30 mg./Tab. Bot. 60s.
Use: Relief of digestive disturbances.

PROGESTIVE TABLETS. (NCP) Dehydrocholic acid 25 mg., bile salts 150 mg., pepsine 250 mg., pancreatin 300 mg./Tab. Bot. 60s.

PROGESTONE TABS. (Medroxyprogesterone 10 mg./Tab. Bot. 50s, 250s.
Use: Abnormal uterine bleeding.

PROGIATRIC. (Nutrition) Ca. L-glutamate 3 Gm., l-lysine 25 mg., C 30 mg., calcium 300 mg., iron 10 mg., vit. A 4000 I.U., B-1 1 mg., B-2 1.2 mg., B-6 1 mg., B-12 5 mcg., folic acid 25 mcg., Ca pantothenate 1 mg., niacin 50 mg./2 Tab. Bot. 90s.
Use: Dietary supplement.

• **PROGLUMIDE.** USAN. (±)-4-Benzamido-N,N-dipropylglutaramic acid. Nulsa (Wallace).
Use: Anticholinergic.

PROGLYCEM CAPSULES. (Schering) Diazoxide 50 mg., 100 mg./Cap. Bot. 100s.
Use: Management of hypoglycemia due to hyperinsulinism.

PROGLYCEM ORAL SUSPENSION. (Schering) Diazoxide 50 mg./ml. Bot. 30 ml. w/calibrated dropper.
Use: Management of hypoglycemia due to hyperinsulinism.

PROGUANIL HYDROCHLORIDE.
See: Chloroguanide Hydrochloride
Paludrine, Tab. (Ayerst)

PROHEPTAZINE. B.A.N. Hexahydro-1,3-dimethyl-4-phenyl-1H-azepin-4-ol propionate (ester).
Use: Analgesic.

PRO-HYDRO. (Mills) Protein hydrolysates (45% amino acids) 50 gr., iron 46 mg., l-lysine HCl 600 mg., dl-methione 75 mg., niacinamide 30 mg., Vit. B-1 3 mg., B-2 2 mg., B-6 2 mg., B-12 3 mcg., C 60 mg., calcium pantothenate 12 mg./6 Tab. Bot. 168s.
W/O Iron. Same formula as above without iron.
W/Vit. E. Same formula with Vit. E 30 I.U.
Use: Vitamin therapy.

PRO-ISO. (Zenith) Prochlorperazine 10 mg., isopropamide 5 mg./Cap.
Use: Treatment of gastrointestinal disorders.

PROKETAZINE DIMALEATE. Carphenazine, B.A.N.
Use: Tranquilizer.

PROKLAR. (Forest) Sulfamethizole 500 mg./Tab. Bot. 100s, 1000s. Susp. 500 mg./5 ml. Bot. 8 oz.

PROLACTIN RIA. (Abbott) Test units 50s, 100s.
Use: Quantitative measurement of total circulating human prolactin.

PROLADONE PECTINATE. Oxycodone, B.A.N.

PROLADYL. Pyrrobutamine. 1-Pyrrolidyl-3-phenyl-4-(p-chlorophenyl)-2-butene phosphate.
Use: Antihistaminic.

PROLAMINE. (Thompson Medical) Phenylpropanolamine HCl 37.5 mg./Tab.
Use: Appetite suppressant.

PROLASE. Proteolytic enzyme from *Carica papaya.*
See: Papain
W/Mylase, cellase, calcium carbonate, magnesium glycinate.
See: Zylase, Tabs. (Vitarine)
W/Mylase-100, dehydrocholic acid, hyoscine HBr, atropine sulfate.
See: Almezyme, Cap. (Meyer)

PRO-LAX. (Vangard) Natural product consisting of equal parts refined psyllium mucilloid, dextrose. Powder. Bot. 16 oz.
Use: Laxative.

PROLENE. (Ethicon) Surgical suture, nonabsorbable.

PROLENS. (Ketchum) Bot. 2 oz.
Use: Contact lens wetting and cleaning solution.

• **PROLINE,** U.S.P. XXI. $C_5H_9NO_2$ as L-proline.
Use: Amino acid.

PROLINTANE. B.A.N. 1-(α-Propylphenethyl)-pyrrolidine. 1-Phenyl-2-(pyrrolidin-1-yl)pentane. Villescon.
Use: Tonic.

• **PROLINTANE HYDROCHLORIDE.** USAN.
Use: Antidepressant.

PRO-LITE. (Devlin) Predigested liquid protein. 1 oz equals 20% to 25% minimum daily requirement. Bot. 16 oz., 32 oz.
Use: Diet supplement.

PROLIXIN. (Squibb) Fluphenazine hydrochloride. **Tabs.** 1 mg., 2.5 mg. or 5 mg./Tab. Bot. 50s, 500s. Unit dose 100s. **Elixir** 0.5 mg./ml. w/alcohol 14%. Dropper Bot. 60 ml. Bot. pt. **Inj.:** 2.5 mg./ml. Vial 5 cc., 10 cc. Unimatic syringe 1 cc. Single dose syr. 25 mg./cc. 10s.
Use: The management of manifestations of psychotic disorders, schizophrenia.

PROLIXIN DECANOATE. (Squibb) Fluphenazine decanoate 25 mg./ml. Syringe 1 ml. Vial 5 ml.
Use: Schizophrenia treatment.

PROLIXIN ENANTHATE. (Squibb) Fluphenazine enanthate 25 mg./ml. Vial 5 ml.
Use: Schizophrenia treatment.

PROLOID. (Parke-Davis) Thyroid globulin ext. Tab. 0.25 gr., 0.5 gr., 1 gr. 1.5 gr., 3 gr. Bot. 100s, 1000s. 2 gr., Bot. 100s.
Use: Myxedema, cretinism & hypothyroid states.

PROLOPRIM. (Burroughs Wellcome) Trimethoprim 100 mg. or 200 mg./Tab. Bot. 100s, Unit Dose Pack 100s.
Use: Urinary tract infections.

PROMACHLOR. (Geneva) Chlorpromazine HCl 10 mg., 25 mg., 50 mg., 100 mg., 200 mg./Tab. Bot. 100s, 1000s. 100 mg./Tab. Bot. 100s.

PROMAPAR TABLETS. (Parke-Davis) Chlorpromazine HCl 10 mg., 25 mg., 50 mg., 100 mg., 200 mg./Tab. Bot. 100s, 1000s. Unit dose 100s.

PROMAZ. (Keene) Chlorpromazine HCl 25 mg./ml. Inj. Vial 10 ml.

PROMAZINE. B.A.N. 10-(3-Dimethylaminopropyl)-phenothiazine. Sparine embonate or hydrochloride.
Use: Tranquilizer.

• **PROMAZINE HCl,** U.S.P. XXI. Inj., Oral Soln., Syrup, Tab., U.S.P. XXI. 10-(α-Dimethylamino-n-propyl) phenothiazine HCl. 10-[3-(Dimethylamino)propyl]-phenothiazine monohydrochloride.
See: Sparine, Tab., Vial, Syr. (Wyeth)

PROMENSIN. (Gotham) Progesterone 12.5 mg., Estradiol 2.5 mg./cc. in oil. Vial 5 cc.

ROMENSIN-F. (Gotham) Estradiol 2.5 mg., progesterone 12.5 mg./cc. Vial 10 cc.

ROMETH-50. (Seatrace) Promethazine HCl 50 mg./ml. Vial 10 cc.

ROMETH EXPECTORANT. (Medwick) With or without codeine. Bot. 4 oz., pt., gal.

/Dextromethorphan. Bot. 4 oz., pt., gal.

ROMETH EXPECTORANT VC. (Medwick) With or without codeine. Bot. 4 oz., pt., gal.

ROMETHASTAN. (Standex) Promethazine 25 or 50 mg./cc. Vial 10 cc.

ROMETHAZINE. B.A.N. 10(2-Dimethylamino-propyl)-phenothiazine. Phenergan hydrochloride.
Use: Antihistamine; antiemetic, sedative.

ROMETHAZINE-50. (Kenyon) Promethazine HCl 50 mg., sod. formaldehyde sulfoxylate 0.75 mg., sod. methabisulfite 0.25 mg., disodium EDTA 0.1 mg., calcium chloride 0.04 mg., phenol 5 mg., buffered with sod. acetate/cc. Vial 10 cc.

ROMETHAZINE CHLOROTHEOPHYLLINATE.
See: Promethazine Theoclate, B.A.N.

ROMETHAZINE EXPECTORANT. (Quality Generics) Promethazine HCl 5 mg., fl. ext. ipecac 0.17 min., pot. guaiacolsulfonate 44 mg., citric acid 60 mg., sodium citrate 197 mg., alcohol 7%. Pt., gal.

PROMETHAZINE HYDROCHLORIDE, U.S.P. XXI. Tab., Syr., Inj., U.S.P. XXI. 10H-Phenothiazine-10-ethanamine, N,N-trimethyl-, HCl. 10-(2-Dimethylaminopropyl)phenothiazine hydrochloride.
Use: Antihistamine, antiemetic, sedative.
See: Fellozine, Inj. (Fellows-Testagar)
K-Phen, Inj. (Kay)
Methazine, Vial (Pharmex)
Pentazine, Expect., Vial (Century)
Phenerex, Inj. (Tunex)
Phenergan, Prep. (Wyeth)
Phenerhist, Inj. (Rocky Mtn.)
Phenerject, Vial (Mayrand)
Prorex, Vial, Amp. (Hyrex)
Provigan, Inj. (Reid-Provident)
Remsed, Tab. (Du Pont)
Rolamethazine Prods. (Robinson)
Sigazine, Inj. (Sig)
Synalgos, Cap. (Ives)

ROMETHAZINE HCl W/COMBINATIONS.
Use: Antihistaminic; antiemetic.
See: Mallergan, Liq. (Mallard)
Maxigesic, Cap. (W. F. Merchant)
Mepergan, Vial, Cap. (Wyeth)
Phenergan Comp., Tab. (Wyeth)
Phenergan-D, Tab. (Wyeth)
Phenergan Pediatric, Liq. (Wyeth)
Phenergan VC Expectorant (Wyeth)
P-M-Z HCl Expectorant (Sutliff & Case)
Promethazine-50, Vial (Kenyon)
Promethazine Expectorant, Syr. (Quality Generics)
Rolamethazine Prods. (Robinson)
Synalgos, Cap. (Ives)
Synalgos-DC, Cap. (Ives)

PROMETHAZINE THEOCLATE. Promethazine salt of 8-chlorotheophylline. Promethazine chlorotheophyllinate. Avomine.
Use: Antihistamine; antiemetic; sedative.

PROMETHAZINE VC. (Bay) Promethazine HCl 6.25 mg., phenylephrine HCl 5 mg./5 ml. w/alcohol 7%. Bot. 4 oz., Pt., Gal.
Use: Antihistaminic, decongestant.

PROMETHAZINE VC WITH CODEINE. (Bay) Promethazine HCl 6.25 mg., phenylephrine HCl 5 mg., codeine 10 mg./5 ml. w/alcohol 7%. Bot. 4 oz., Pt., Gal.
Use: Antihistaminic, antitussive, decongestant.

PROMETHESTROL. B.A.N. 3,4-Di-(4-hydroxy- 3-methylphenyl)hexane. Methestrol (I.N.N.)
Use: Estrogen.

PROMETHESTROL DIPROPIONATE.
Use: Estrogen deficiency.
See: Meprane Dipropionate, Tab. (Reed & Carnrick)
W/Phenobarbital.
See: Meprane-Phenobarbital, Tab. (Reed & Carnrick)

PROMETH VC. (National) Phenylephrine HCl 5 mg., promethazine HCl 6.25 mg./5 ml. w/alcohol 7%. Bot. 4 oz., 16 oz., gal.
Use: Decongestant, antihistaminic.

PROMETOL. (Viobin) Concentrated wheat germ oil. 3 min./Cap. Bot. 100s, 250s. 10 min./Cap. Bot. 100s.

PROMINAL.
See: Mebaral, Tab. (Winthrop-Breon)

PROMINE S.R.. (Major) Procainamide. **Tab.:** 250 mg./S.R. Tab. Bot. 100s, 250s; 500 mg./S.R. Tab. Bot. 100s, 250s, 1000s; 750 mg./S.R. Tab. Bot. 100s, 250s. **Cap:** 250 mg., 375 mg. or 500 mg./S.R. Cap.
Use: Premature venticular contractions.

PROMINTIC. Methyridine, B.A.N.

PRO-MIN-VITE. (Drug Industries) Vit. A 10,000 I.U., D 1000 I.U., E 3 I.U., C 100 mg., B-1 10 mg., B-2 3 mg., B-6 2 mg., citrus bioflavonoids 25 mg., cal. pantothenate 10 mg., niacin 20 mg., B-12 2 mcg., biotin 0.1 mg., l-lysine 25 mg., iron 20 mg., Cu 0.5 mg., Mn 2 mg., molybdenum 0.5 mg., Zn 1 mg., pot. 5 mg., Mg 5 mg., iodine 0.1 mg./Tab. Bot. 100s, 500s.
Use: Geriatric dietary supplement.

PROMISE TOOTHPASTE. (Block) Potassium nitrate 5%, sodium monofluorophosphate 0.76% W/glycerin, dicalcium phosphate, dihydrate, sorbitol, sodium lauryl sulfate, hydroxyethylcellulose, silica, sodium saccharin, methyl and propyl parabens. Tube 1.0 oz., 1.6 oz., 3.0 oz.
Use: Anticaries dentifrice for sensative teeth.

PROMOX. (Suppositoria) Pramoxine HCl 1% in suppository base. Box 12s, 100s.
Use: Antihemorrhoidal.

PROMOXALAN. B.A.N. 2,2-Diisopropyl-1,3-dioxolane-4-methanol. 4-Hydroxymethyl-2,2-di-isopropyl-1,3-dioxolan.
Use: Skeletal muscle relaxant.

PROMPT. (DePree) **Spray:** Benzocaine 1.5%, parachlorometaxylenol 0.5%. Can 5 oz. **Lot.:**

Benzocaine 1%, triclosan 0.2%. Bot. 4 oz. **Tab.:** Acetaminophen 5 gr., Bot. 50s, 100s, 200s.
Use: Pain relief.

PROMPT. (Searle) Psyllium hydrophilic mucilloid and sennosides.
Use: Overnight laxative.

PROMPT BENZOCAINE CREAM. (Eckerd) Benzocaine, resorcin, chlorothymol Bot. 1.5 oz., 4 oz.
Use: Local anesthetic.

PRO-NASYL. (Progonasyl Co.) o-Iodobenzoic Acid 0.5%, triethanolamine 5.5% in a special neutral hydrophilic base compounded from oleic acid, mineral oil and vegetable oil. Bot. 15 cc., 60 cc.
Use: Treatment of sinusitis.

PRONDOL HYDROCHLORIDE. Iprindole, B.A.N.

PRONEMIA. (Lederle) Vit. B-12 15 mcg., intrinsic factor conc. 75 mg., ferrous fumarate 350 mg., ascorbic acid 150 mg., folic acid 1 mg./Cap. Bot. 100s.
Use: Hematinic.

PRONESTYL. (Squibb) Procainamide HCl. **Cap.** 0.25 Gm./Cap. Bot. 100s, 1000s. Unit dose Unimatic 100s. 375 mg./Cap. Bot. 100s. Unimatic 100s. 0.5 Gm./Cap. Bot. 100s, 1000s. Unit dose Unimatic 100s. **Inj.:** 100 mg./cc. w/benzyl alcohol 0.9%, sod. bisulfite 0.09%, sod. hydroxide or HCl. Vial 10 cc. 500 mg./cc. w/methylparaben 0.1%, propylparaben 0.2%, sod. hydroxide or HCl. Vial 2 cc. **Tab.:** 250 mg./Tab. Bot. 100s, 1000s. 375 mg./Tab. Bot. 100s. 500 mg./Tab. Bot. 100s, 1000s.
Use: Treatment of ventricular arrhythmias & related cardiac conditions.

PRONESTYL-SR. (Squibb) Procainamide HCl 500 mg./Tab. Bot. 100s. Unit dose 100s.
Use: Sustained release preparation for cardiac arrhythmias.

PRONETHALOL. B.A.N. 2-Isopropylamino-1-(2-naphthyl)-ethanol. Alderlin hydrochloride.
Use: Adrenergic beta-receptor blocking agent.

PRONETHELOL (I.C.I.) Adrenergic beta-receptor antagonist; pending release.

PRONTO-GEL. (Commerce) Tube 2 oz.
Use: Analgesic jelly.

PROPACIL TABLETS. (Quality Generics) Propylthiouracil 50 mg./Tab. Bot. 1000s.

PROPADERM 17,21-DIPROPIONATE. Beclomethasone, B.A.N.

PROPAESIN. Propyl p-Aminobenzoate. (Various Mfr.)

PROPAGEST SYRUP. (Carnrick) Phenylpropanolamine HCl 12.5 mg./5 ml. Bot. 16 oz., 4 oz.
Use: Nasal decongestant.

PROPAGEST TABLETS. (Carnrick) Phenylpropanolamine HCl 25 mg./Tab. Bot. 100s.
Use: Nasal decongestant.

PROPAGON-S. (Spanner) Estrone 2 mg./cc., 5 mg./cc. Vial 10 cc.

PROPAHIST. (Blue Line) **Tabs:** Phenylpropanolamine HCl 25 mg., pyrilamine maleate, pheniramine maleate in ratio 2:2:1/Tab. Bot. 100s, 1000s. **Syrup:** Dosage equal to one-half Tab./5 cc. Bot. pt., gal.
Use: Improve ventilation; for hay fever, nasal congestion, etc.

PROPAHIST INJ. (Blue Line) Atropine sulfate 0.2 mg., chlorpheniramine maleate 5 mg., phenylpropanolamine HCl 12.5 mg., chlorobutanol 0.5%/cc. Vial 10 cc.

PROPAHIST COMPOUND CAPSULES. (Blue Line) Phenylpropanolamine HCl 25 mg., pyrilamine maleate 10 mg., pheniramine maleate 5 mg., acetaminophen 325 mg., caffeine 30 mg./Cap. Bot. 100s, 1000s.

PROPAHIST-DM SYRUP. (Blue Line) Dextromethorphan HBr 15 mg., phenylpropanolamine HCl 12.5 mg., Incorpohist antihistamines (Pyrilamine maleate & pheniramine maleate) 12.5 mg./5 cc. Bot. 2 oz., pt., gal.

PROPAMIDINE. B.A.N. 1,3-Di-(4-amidinophenoxy)-propane. Brolene isethionate.
Use: Bactericide; fungicide.

• **PROPANE,** N.F. XVI.

PROPANEDIOL DIACETATE, 1,2.
See: VoSol, Liq. (Wampole)

1,2,3-PROPANETRIOL, TRINITRATE. Nitroglycerin Tablets, U.S.P. XXI.

• **PROPANIDID.** USAN. [4- { (Diethylcarbamoyl)-methoxy } -3-methoxyphenyl] acetic acid propyl ester Propyl 4-diethylcarbamoylmethoxy-3-methoxyphenylacetate. Epontol.
Use: Systemic anesthetic.

PROPANOLOL. 1-Isopropylamino-3-(l-napthyloxy)propan-2-ol. Propranolol.

l-PROPANONE,2-METHYL-1,2-DI-3-PYRIDINYL-. Metyrapone, U.S.P. XXI.

PROPANTHELINE. (Wolins) Propantheline Br 15 mg., phenobarbital 15 mg./Tab. Bot. 100s, 1000s.

• **PROPANTHELINE BROMIDE,** U.S.P. XXI. Sterile, Tabs., U.S.P. XXI. 2-Propanaminium, N-methyl-N-(1-methylethyl)-N-[2-](9H-xanthen-9-ylcarbonyl)oxy[ethyl]-, Br.
Use: Anticholinergic.
See: Norpanth, Tab. (Vortech)
Pro-Banthine, Prep. (Searle)
Robantaline, Tab. (Robinson)
SK-Propantheline Bromide Tab. (SmithKline)
Spastil, Tab. (Kenyon)
W/Phenobarbital.
See: Probital, Tab. (Searle)
Propantheline, Tab. (Wolins)
Robantaline with Phenobarbital (Robinson)
W/Thiopropazate dihydrochloride.
See: Pro-Banthine W/Dartal, Tab. (Searle)

PROPANYL. (Kay) Phenylpropanolamine HCl 75 mg., benzyl alcohol 2% Vial multiple dose.
Use: Nasal decongestant.

PROPA P.H. ACNE COVER-UP STICK. (Commerce) Benzoyl peroxide 10%. Stick 0.05 oz.
Use: Skin tinted acne treatment.

PROPA P.H. ACNE PADS. (Commerce) Benzoyl peroxide 5%. 60 pads/Jar.
Use: Acne medication.

ROPA PH POROX 7. (Commerce) Benzoyl peroxide 7.0%. Tube 1 oz.
Use: Pimple and acne medication.

ROPA P.H. LIQUID ACNE SOAP. (Commerce) Benzoyl peroxide 10%. Bot 4 oz.
Use: Face & body acne medication.

ROPA P.H. SUPER CLEANSER ACNE MEDICATION. (Commerce) Benzethonium Cl. 0.50%. Bot. 6 oz., 10 oz., 16 oz.
Use: Kills acne bacteria, cleans clogged pores.

PROPARACAINE HCl, U.S.P. XXI. Ophth. Soln., U.S.P. XXI. Benzoic acid, 3-amino-4-propoxy-, 2-(diethylamino)ethyl ester, HCl. Proxymetacaine, B.A.N.
Use: Anesthetic (topical, ophthalmic).
See: Alcaine Ophth. Soln. (Alcon)
Ophthaine HCl, Sol. (Squibb)
Ophthetic, Ophth. Sol. (Allergan)

PROPATYL NITRATE. USAN. 2-Ethyl-2-hydroxymethyl-1,3-propanediol trinitrate. Ettriol Trinitrate. 1,-1,1-Trisnitratomethylpropane. Etrynit; Gina. Invest. drug in U.S. but available in England.
Use: Coronary vasodilator.

ROPAZOLAMIDE. 2-Propionylamino-1,3,4-thiadiazole-5-sulfonamide. Ionaze (Lilly).

·PROPENYLANISOLE. Anethole, N.F. XVI.

PROPENZOLATE HYDROCHLORIDE. USAN. 1-Methyl-3-piperidyl-α-phenylcyclohexaneglycolate HCl.
Use: Anticholinergic.

ROPERIDINE. B.A.N. Isopropyl 1-methyl-4-phenylpiperidine-4-carboxylate.
Use: Narcotic analgesic.

ROPESIN. Name used for Risocaine.

ROPHENPYRIDAMINE.
See: Pheniramine (Var. Mfr.)

ROPHENPYRIDAMINE MALEATE.
See: Pheniramine Maleate

ROPHENPYRIDAMINE MALEATE W/COMBINATIONS.
See: Amaril-D-Spancap, Cap. (Vortech)
Four Antihistamines, Tab. (Wolins)
Histjen, Cap. (Jenkins)
Hist-Span No. 2, Cap. (Kenyon)
Nylamine, Tab. (Reid-Provident)
Panadyl, Tab., Cap. (Misemer)
Polyectin, Liq. (Amid)
Pyma, Cap. (Fellows-Testagar)
Trihistapacq Tabules, Tab. (Horton & Converse)
Tri-Hist-Cap., Cap. (Burgin-Arden)
Trimahist Elixir, Liq. (Tennessee)
Vasotus, Liq. (Sheryl)
Zerominic, Liq. (Amid)

ROPHYLLIN. (Rystan) **Powder:** Sodium propionate 1%. Box 12 packets 2.3 Gm. pwd./packet for preparation of 8 fl. oz. Jar 4 oz. bulk powder. **Oint.** Sodium propionate 5%. Tube 1 oz.
Use: Fungistatic wet dressing.

ROPICILLIN. B.A.N. 6-(α-Phenoxybutyramido)-penicillanic acid(1-Phenoxypropyl)penicillin. Brocillin & Ultrapen are the potassium salt.
Use: Antibiotic.

• PROPIKACIN. USAN.
Use: Antibacterial.

PROPINE STERILE OPTHALMIC SOLUTION. (Allergan) Dipivefrin HCl 0.1% Bot. 5 ml., 10 ml., 15 ml.
Use: Control intraocular pressure in chronic open-angle glaucoma.

PROPIODAL.
See: Entodon

• PROPIOLACTONE. USAN. 2-Oxetanone; beta-propiolactone, Betaprone. Hydracrylic acid, β-lactone.
Use: Sterilization of vaccines and tissue grafts.

• PROPIOMAZINE. USAN. 1-[10-(2-Dimethylamino-propyl)-phenothiazine-2-yl]-1-propanone. Dorevane; Indorm.
Use: Sedative.
See: Largon, Amp. (Wyeth)

• PROPIOMAZINE HYDROCHLORIDE, U.S.P. XXI. Inj., U.S.P. XXI. 1-[10-[2-(Dimethylamino)propyl]-phenothiazin-2-yl]-1-propanone HCl.
Use: Sedative.
See: Largon, Inj. (Wyeth)

• PROPIONIC ACID, N.F. XVI.
W/Sod. propionate, docusate sodium, salicylic acid.
See: Prosal, Liq. (Gordon)
Propionate-Caprylate Mixtures.

PROPIONATE-CAPRYLATE MIXTURES.
See: Sopronol, Oint., Pow., Sol. (Wyeth)

PROPIONATE COMPOUND.
See: Propion Gel (Wyeth)

PROPIONATE SALTS.
See: Copper
Potassium
Sodium
Zinc

PROPIONYL ERYTHROMYCIN LAURYL SULFATE.
See: Erythromycin Propionate Lauryl Sulfate

PROPIRAM. B.A.N. N-(1-Methyl-2-piperidinoethyl)-N-(2-pyridyl)propionamide.
Use: Analgesic.

• PROPIRAMFUMARATE. USAN. N-(1-Methyl-2-piperidinoethyl)-N-(2-pyridyl) propionamide fumarate. 1:1.
Use: Analgesic.

PROPISAMINE.
See: Amphetamine (Various Mfr.)

PROPITOCAINE. Prilocaine.
See: Citanest, Sol., Vial, Amp. (Astra)

PROPLEX. (Hyland) Factor IX Complex (Human), clotting Factor II (prothrombin), VII (proconvertin), IX (PTC, antihemophilic factor B) & X (Stuart-Prower factor) all dried & concentrated. Vial 30 ml. w/Diluent.
Use: Deficiency of factors II, VII, IX, & X.

PROPLEX SX. (Hyland) Factor IX complex, 300–1200 IU/Vial. Vial 30 ml.
Use: Treatment of points with factor IX deficiency (Hemophilia B, Christmas disease).

• PROPOFOL. USAN.
Use: Anesthetic.

PROPONADE CAPSULES. (Blue Cross)
Chlorpheniramine maleate 8 mg.,

phenylpropanolamine HCl 50 mg., isopropamide 2.5 mg./Cap. Bot. 100s.
Use: Antihistaminic, decongestant.

PROPONESIN HYDROCHLORIDE. Tolpronine, B.A.N.

PROPOQUIN. Amopyroquin HCl.
Use: Antimalarial.

PRO-POWER. (Galen) Protein hydrolysates 8.33 gr., 1-lysine HCl 100 mg., dl-methionine 12.5 mg., Vit. E 5 I.U., B-3 5 mg., B-1 0.5 mg., B-2 0.33 mg., B-5 2 mg., B-6 0.33 mg., B-12 0.5 mcg., C 10 mg.,/Cap. Bot. 90s.
Use: Vitamin supplement.

PROPOXAMIDE. o-Propoxybenzamide.

• **PROPOXYCAINE HYDROCHLORIDE,** U.S.P. XXI. 2-(Diethylamino)ethyl-4-amino-2-propoxybenzoate HCl.
Use: Local anesthetic.

• **PROPOXYCAINE AND PROCAINE HYDROCHLORIDES AND LEVONORDEFRIN INJECTION,** U.S.P. XXI.
Use: Local anesthetic (dental).

PROPOXYCAINE AND PROCAINE HYDROCHLORIDES AND NOREPINEPHRINE BITARTRATE INJECTION, U.S.P. XXI.
Use: Local anesthetic (dental).
See: Ravocaine Cartridge (Cook-Waite)

PROPOXYCHLORINOL. Toloxychlorinol.

• **PROPOXYPHENE HCl,** U.S.P. XXI. Caps. U.S.P. XXI. Benzenethanol, α[2-(dimethylamino)-1-methylethyl]-α-phenyl, propanoate (ester), HCl.
Use: Analgesic.
See: Darvon, Pulv. (Lilly)
Dolene, Cap. (Lederle)
Harmar, Cap. (Zemmer)
Myospaz, Improved, Cap. (Vortech)
Progesic, Cap. (Ulmer)
Pro-Pox 65, Cap. (Kenyon)
Ropoxy, Cap. (Robinson)
SK-65, Cap. (SmithKline)

PROPOXYPHENE HCl W/COMBINATIONS.
Use: Analgesic.
See: Bexophene, Cap. (Mallard)
Darvon Compound, Pulvule (Lilly)
Darvon Compound-65, Cap. (Lilly)
Darvon With A.S.A., Cap. (Lilly)
Dolene, AP-65, Tab. (Lederle)
Dolene Compound-65, Cap. (Lederle)
Doraphen-Comp.-65, Cap. (Cenci)
Myospaz, Cap. (Vortech)
PC-65, Cap. (Archer)
Procomp-65, Cap. (W.F. Merchant)
Pro-Pox Plus, Cap. (Kenyon)
Propoxyphene Compound 65, Cap. (Caribe, Wayne, Wolins)
Ropoxy Compound-65, Cap. (Robinson)
SK-65 APAP, Tab. (SmithKline)
SK-65 Compound, Cap. (SmithKline)
S-Pain-CPD-65, Cap. (Saron)
Stogesic, Cap. (Jalco)
Wygesic, Tab. (Wyeth)

• **PROPOXYPHENE HCl AND ACETAMINOPHEN TABLETS,** U.S.P. XXI.
Use: Analgesic.

PROPOXYPHENE HCl AND APC CAPSULES.
Use: Analgesic.
See: Darvon Compound, Cap. (Lilly)
Darvon Compound-65, Cap. (Lilly)

• **PROPOXYPHENE HCl, ASPIRIN AND CAFFEINE CAPSULES,** U.S.P. XXI.
Use: Analgesic.

• **PROPOXYPHENE NAPSYLATE,** U.S.P. XXI. Oral Susp., Tab., U.S.P. XXI.
Use: Analgesic.
See: Darvocet-N (Lilly)
Darvon-N, Tab. (Lilly)
W/Acetaminophen.
Use: Analgesic.
See: Darvocet-N, Tab. (Lilly)

• **PROPOXYPHENE NAPSYLATE AND ACETAMINOPHEN TABLETS,** U.S.P. XXI.
Use: Analgesic.

• **PROPOXYPHENE NAPSYLATE AND ASPIRIN TABLETS,** U.S.P. XXI.
Use: Analgesic.

PROPRANOLOL. B.A.N. 1-Isopropylamino-3-(1-naphthyloxy)propan-2-ol. Propanol.
Use: Beta adrenergic blocking agent.

• **PROPRANOLOL HYDROCHLORIDE,** U.S.P. XXI. Inj., Tab., U.S.P. XXI. 2-Propanol, 1-[(1-methylethyl)amino]-3-(1-naphthalenyloxy)-, HCl. Propanolol HC
Use: Antiarrhythmic agent.
See: Inderal, Tab., Inj. (Ayerst)
W/Hydrochlorthiazide.
See: Inderide, Tab. (Ayerst)

PROPYL p-AMINOBENZOATE. (Various Mfr.) Propaesin.
Use: Local anesthetic.
W/Procaine base, benzyl alcohol, phenol.
See: Durathesia, Inj. (Vortech)
Rectocaine, Vial (Moore-Kirk)

• **PROPYL GALLATE,** N.F. XVI.
Use: Pharmaceutic aid (antioxidant).

PROPYLDOCETRIZOATE. B.A.N. Propyl 3-diacetylamino-2,4,6-tri-iodobenzoate. Pulmidol.
Use: Radio-opaque substance.

• **PROPYLENE CARBONATE,** N.F. XVI.
Use: Pharmaceutical aid (gelling agent).

• **PROPYLENE GLYCOL,** U.S.P. XXI. 1-2-Propanediol.
Use: Pharmaceutical aid (humectant, solvent).

• **PROPYLENE GLYCOL ALGINATE,** N.F. XVI.
Use: Pharmaceutical aid.

• **PROPYLENE GLYCOL DIACETATE,** N.F. XVI.
Use: Pharmaceutical aid.

PROPYLENE GLYCOL MONOSTEARATE, N.F. XVI. 1,2-Propanediol monostearate.
Use: Emulsifying agent.

• **PROPYLHEXEDRINE,** U.S.P. XXI. Inhalant, U.S.P. XXI. N,α-Dimethylcyclohexaneethylamine. Evetin HCl.
Use: Adrenergic (vasoconstrictor), appetite suppressant, antihistamine.
See: Benzedrex, Inhalant (Menley & James)
Benzedrex, Inhalant (SmithKline).

• **PROPYLIODONE,** U.S.P. XXI. Sterile Oil Susp., U.S.P. XXI. 1(4H)-Pyridineacetic acid, 3,5-diiodo-4-

oxo-, propyl ester. Sterile oil Susp. (peanut oil). Sterile water susp. Propyl 3,5-di-iodo-4-oxopyridine-1-ylacetate. 3,5-Di-iodo-1-propoxycarbonylmethyl-4-pyridone. Dionosil.
Use: Radio-opaque substance.

iso-PROPYLNORADRENALINE.
See: Isoproterenol.

PROPYLPARABEN, N.F. XVI. Propyl p-hydroxybenzoate. Propyl Chemosept (Chemo Puro)
Use: Pharm. aid (antifungal preservative).

PROPYLTHIOURACIL, U.S.P. XXI. Tab., U.S.P. XXI. 4(1H)-Pyrimidinone, 2,3-dihydro-6-propyl-2-thioxo. -propyl. (Abbott) Tabs. 50 mg. Bot. 100s, 1000s. (Lilly) Tabs. 50 mg. Bot. 100s, 1000s. (Lederle) Tabs. 50 mg. Bot. 100s, 1000s. Tabs. 50 mg. Bot. 100s, 1000s, Unit dose 100s.
Use: Thyroid inhibitor.
See: Propacil Tablets (Quality Generics)

PROPYPHENAZONE. B.A.N. 4-Isopropyl-2,3-dimethyl-1-phenyl-5-pyrazolone.
Use: Analgesic.

PROQUAMEZINE. B.A.N. 10-(2,3-Bisdimethyl-aminopropyl)phenothiazine. Aminopromazine (I.N.N.) Myspamol.
Use: Bronchial spasmolytic.

PROQUAZONE. USAN. 1-Isopropyl-7-methyl-4-phenyl-2 (1H)-quinazolinone.
Use: Anti-inflammatory.

PROQUINOLATE. USAN.
Use: Coccidiostat.

PRORENOATE POTASSIUM. USAN.
Use: Aldosterone antagonist.

PROREX. (Hyrex) Promethazine HCl, 25 or 50 mg./ml. Vial 10 ml.
Use: Antihistamine, antiemetic, sedative.

PRORONE. (Sig) Progesterone 25 mg./ml. Aq. or oil susp. Vial 10 ml.
Use: Hormone therapy.

PROROXAN HYDROCHLORIDE. USAN.
Use: Anti-adrenergic.

PROSCILLARIDIN. USAN. 3β, 14β-Dihydroxy-bufa-4,20,22-trienolide 3-rhamnoside. Talusin, Tradenal.
Use: Cardiac glycoside.

PROSCOPINE HYDROBROMIDE. Poskine, B.A.N.

PROSED. (Star) Atropine sulfate 0.03 mg., hyoscyamine sulfate 0.03 mg., methenamine 40.8 mg., methylene blue 5.4 mg., phenylsalicylate 18.1 mg., benzoic acid 4.5 mg./Tab. Bot. 100s, 1000s.
Use: Urinary antispasmodic, anticholinergic, antibacterial.

PROSOBEE. (Mead Johnson) Milk free formula supplies 640 cal./qt. w/ 19.2 Gm. protein, 34 Gm. fat, 64 Gm. carbohydrate, vitamins and minerals. Vit. A 2000 I.U., D 400 I.U., E 20 I.U., C 52 mg., folic acid 100 mcg., B-1 0.5 mg., B-2 0.6 mg., niacin 8 mg., B-6 0.4 mg., B-12 2 mcg., biotin 50 mg., pantothenic acid 3 mg., K-1 100 mcg., choline 50 mg., Inositol 30 mg., Ca 600 mg., P 475 mg., Iodine 65 mcg., Fe 12 mg., Mg 70 mg., Cu 0.6 mg., Zn 5 mg., Mn 0.2 mg., chloride 520 mg., K 740 mg., Na 275 mg./Qt. (20 Kcal./fl. oz.) Concentrated liq. can 13 fl. oz.; Ready-to-use liq. can 8, 32 fl. oz. Powder, cans 14 oz.
Use: Infant food, hypoallergenic formula, lactose and sucrose free.

PRO-SOF SG 100. (Vangard) Docusate sodium 100 mg./Cap. Bot. 100s, 1000s. Unit dose 10×10s.
Use: Stool softener.

PRO-SOF SG 200. (Vangard) Docusate sodium 250 mg./Cap. Bot. 100s, 500s. Unit dose pkg. 10×10s.
Use: Laxative.

PRO-SOF SYRUP. (Vangard) Docusate sodium 20 mg./5 ml. Bot. pt.
Use: Laxative.

PRO-SOF w/CASANTHRANOL SG. (Vangard) Cansanthranol 30 mg., docusate sodium 100 mg./Cap. Bot. 100s, 1000s.
Use: Laxative.

PROSTAGLANDIN E. Dinoprostone, B.A.N.
Use: Prostaglandin.

PROSTAGLANDIN F. Dinoprost, B.A.N.
Use: Prostaglandin.

• **PROSTALENE.** USAN.
Use: Prostaglandin.

PROSTAPHLIN CAPSULES. (Bristol) Sodium oxacillin 250 mg. and 500 mg./Cap. Bot. 48s, 100s.; 250 mg., 500 mg. Dosatrol Pack 100s.
Use: Staphylococcal infections.

PROSTAPHLIN FOR INJECTION. (Bristol) Crystalline oxacillin sodium 250 mg., 500 mg., 1 Gm., 2 Gm., 4 Gm./dry filled Vial. Piggyback vials 1 Gm., 2 Gm., 4 Gm. Bulk vial 10 Gm.
Use: Treatment of infections.

PROSTAPHLIN ORAL SOLUTION. (Bristol) Sod. oxacillin reconstitute for oral soln. 250 mg./5 ml. Bot. 100 ml. Dosa-Trol Pack 25s.
Use: Orally, staphylococcal infections.

PROTHAR. (Armour) Factor IX complex (human) for I.V. administration 500 I.U., 750 I.U., or 1000 I.U. w/diluent.
Use: Factor IX deficiency (Hemophilia B).

PROTOSTAT. (Ortho) Metronidazole 250 mg. or 500 mg./Tab. 250 mg./Tab. Bot. 100s. 500 mg./Tab. Bot. 50s.
Use: Treatment of trichomoniasis, antiprotozoal.

PROSTIGMIN BROMIDE. (Roche) Neostigmine bromide. **Tab.** 15 mg., Bot. 100s, 1000s.
Use: Parasympathetic stimulant.

PROSTIGMIN METHYLSULFATE. (Roche) Injectable Neostigmine Methylsulfate, U.S.P. Amp 1:2000 w/methyl and propyl parabens 0.2%, sod. hydroxide 1 ml. Box 10s. 1:4000 w/methyl and propyl parabens 0.2%, sod. hydroxide 1 ml. Box 10s. Vial (1:1000, 1:2000 w/phenol 0.45%, sod. acetate 0.2 mg., acetic acid, sod. hydroxide) 10 ml.
Use: Parasympathetic stimulant.

PROSTIN E2. Dinoprostone, B.A.N.

PROSTIN F2 ALPHA. (Upjohn) Dinoprost tromethamine 5 mg./ml. Amp. 4 ml., 8 ml.
Use: Oxytocic.

PROSTIN VR PEDIATRIC. (Upjohn) Alprostadil 500 mcg./ml. Amp. 1 ml. Box 5s.

Use: Palliative therapy to maintain patency of the ductus arteriosus in neonates with congenital heart defects.

PROTABOLIN. (Pasadena Research) Methandriol dipropionate 50 mg./cc. Vial 10 cc.

• **PROTAMINE SULFATE,** U.S.P. XXI. Inj., for inj., U.S.P. XXI. (Lilly)-Amp. 1%, 5 cc.; 1s, 25s; 25 cc. 6s. (Upjohn)—Vial 50 mg. w/sod. chloride 45 mg., w/ph adjusted 1s, 5s, 25s; 250 mg./Vial.
Use: I.V.; heparin overdosage.

• **PROTAMINE ZINC INSULIN SUSPENSION,** U.S.P. XXI.
Use: Insulin.
See: Iletin (Insulin, Lilly)
Insulin, Protamine Zinc, Susp. (Squibb)

PROTARGIN MILD.
See: Silver Protein, Mild (Various Mfr.)

PROTARGOL. (Sterwin) Strong silver protein. Pow., Bot. 25 Gm.
Use: Topically; silver antiseptic.

PROTASE. (Kenyon) Standardized amount of ext. of proteolytic enzymes from *Carica papaya* with 10,000 u. of activity/Tab. Bot. 100s, 1000s.

PROTEASE.
W/Amylase, lipase, cellase, hyoscine HBr.
See: Am-Zyme, Tab. (Vortech)
W/Pancreatin, amylase.
See: Dizymes, Caps. (Recsei)
W/Vit. B-1, B-12.
See: Arcoret, Tab. (Arco)
W/Vit. B-1, B-12, iron.
See: Arcoret W/Iron, Tab. (Arco)

PROTECTOL MEDICATED POWDER. (Daniels) Calcium undecyclenate 15%. Bot. 2 oz.
Use: Diaper rash, chafing.

• **PROTEIN HYDROLYSATE INJ.,** U.S.P. XXI.
Use: Fluid and nutrient replenisher.
See: Amigen, Inj. (Baxter Lab.)
Aminogen, Amp., Vial (Christina)
Lacotein, Vial (Christina)
Travamin, Inj. (Travenol)
Virex, Inj. (Burgin-Arden)

PROTEIN HYDROLYSATES ORAL.
Use: Nutrient.
See: Lofenalac, Pow. (Mead Johnson)
Nutramigen, Pow. (Mead Johnson)
Pregestimil, Pow. (Mead Johnson)
Stuart Amino Acids, Pow. (Stuart)
W/Lysine HCl, methionine, niacinamide, Ca pantothenate, Vit. B complex, Vit. C, iron.
See: Pro-Hydro, Tab. (Mills)
W/Vitamin B-12.
See: Stuart Amino Acids and B-12, Tab. (Stuart)

■ **PROTEIN, NONSPECIFIC THERAPY.**
See: Lacotein, Vial (Christina)
Mucusol, Amp., Vial (Kremers-Urban)

PROTENATE. (Hyland) Plasma protein fraction (Human) 5% in buffered stabilized saline diluent. Sod. acetyltryptophanate 0.004M, sod. caprylate 0.004M, pH adjusted to neutral w/sod. bicarbonate. Vial 250 ml. and 500 ml. w/administration set.
Use: Plasma expander. Increase plasma protein & volume.

PROTENIUM. (Pasadena Research) Hydrolized gelatin w/di-tryptophane.
Caps. Bot 300s.
Use: Nutritional supplement.

PROTEOLYTIC ENZYMES.
See: Dornavac (Merck Animal Health)
Papase, Tab. (Parke-Davis)
Vardase, Prod. (Lederle)
W/Amylolytic enzyme, cellulolytic enzyme, lipolytic enzyme.
See: Arco-Lase, Tab. (Arco)
Kutrase, Cap. (Kremmers-Urban)
Kuzyme, Cap. (Kremmers-Urban)
Zymme, Cap. (Scrip)
W/Amylolytic enzyme, lipolytic enzyme, cellulolytic enzyme, belladonna ext.
See: Mallenzyme, Tab. (Mallard)
W/Amylolytic, cellulolytic enzymes, lipase, phenobarbital, hyoscyamine sulf., atropine sulf.
See: Arco-Lipase Plus, Tab. (Arco)
W/Amylolytic, cellulolytic enzymes.
See: Trienzyme, Tabs. (Fellows-Testagar)
W/Amylolytic enzyme, homatropine methylbromide, d sorbitol. (Papain.)
See: Converzyme, Liq. (Ascher)
W/Calcium carbonate, glycine, amylolytic and cellulolytic enzymes.
See: Co-Gel, Tab. (Arco)
W/Combinations
See: Butibel-zyme Tabs. (McNeil)
W/Neomycin palmitrate, hydrocortisone acetate, water-miscible base.
See: Biozyme Oint. (Armour)
W/Protease, lipase, simethicone.
See: Tri-Cone, Cap. (Meyer)
W/*Sus scrofa* Linne var. Domesticus.
See: Saromide Injection, Vial, 1.3 ml. (Saron)

PROTHAZINE. (Vortech) Promethazine HCl 25 mg., sod. formaldehyde sulfoxylate 0.75 mg., sod. metabisulfite 0.25 mg., Ca chloride 0.04 mg., phenol 5 mg./cc. Ampule 1 ml., Vial 10 ml.
Use: Antihistamine, antiemetic, sedative.

PROTHAZINE WITH CODEINE. (Vortech) Promethazine HCl 5 mg., ipecac fluid ext. 0.17 min., potassium guaiasulfonate 44 mg., citric acid 60 mg., sod. citrate 197 mg., alcohol 7%, codeine 10 mg./5 ml. Bot. 4 oz., gal.
Use: Antitussive, antihistaminic.

PROTHAZINE EXPECTORANT. (Vortech) Bot. 4 oz., gal.
Use: Antihistaminic, expectorant.

PROTHAZINE PEDIATRIC. (Vortech) Bot. 4 oz., gal.
Use: Antitussive, antihistaminic.

PROTHIADEN HYDROCHLORIDE. Dothiepen, B.A.N.

PROTHIDIUM. Pyrithidium bromide, B.A.N.

PROTHIONAMIDE. B.A.N. 2-Propylisonicotinthioamide.
Use: Treatment of tuberculosis.
See: Trevintix

PROTHIPENDYL. B.A.N. 10-(3-Dimethylaminopropyl)-pyrido[3,2-b][1,4]benzothiazine.
Use: Tranquilizer; antiemetic.
See: Phrenotropin
Tolnate [hydrochloride]

ROTHIPENDYL HCl. [(4-Dimethyl-aminopropyl-pyrido(3,2B)Benzothiazine)] HCl-monohydrate.
Use: Sedative.

ROTICULEEN. (Spanner) Vit. B-12 activity 10 mcg., folic acid 10 mg., B-12 crystalline 50 mcg., niacinamide 75 mg./cc. Multiple dose vial 10 cc. I.M. inj.

PROTIRELIN. USAN. 1-[N-(5-Oxo-L-prolyl)-L-histidyl]--prolinamide. 5-oxo-L-histidyl-L-proline amide.
Use: Thyrotrophin releasing hormone.
See: Thypinone, Inj. (Abbott)

ROTOKYLOL. B.A.N. 1-(3,4-Dihydroxyphenyl)-2-(α-methyl-3,4-methylene-dioxyphenethylamino)-ethanol.
Use: Sympathomimetic.
See: Caytine [hydrochloride]

ROTOKYLOL HCl. 3,4-Dihydroxy-α-[[[α-methyl-3,4-(methylenedioxy) phenethyl]-amino]methyl]-benzyl alcohol HCl.
Use: Adrenergic (bronchodilator).

ROTOPAM CHLORIDE. (Ayerst) Pralidoxime chloride 500 mg./Tab. Bot. 100s.; Vial 1 Gm./20 ml. **Emergency Kit:** One 1 Gm./20 ml. vial of sterile Protopam Chloride porous cake, one 20 ml. vial of sterile water for injection, U.S.P. without preservative, to be used as diluent; sterile disposable 20 ml. syringe. **Hospital package:** Six 20 ml. vials of 1 Gm. each of sterile Protopam Chloride powder, without diluent or syringe.
Use: Antidote for poisoning due to organophosphate pesticides.

ROTOSAN. (Recsei) Protein 87.5%, lactose 0.5%, fat 1.3%, ash 3.5%, sodium 0.02%. Jar 1 lb., 5 lb.
Use: Dietary supplement.

ROT-O-SEA. (Barth's) Protein 90%, containing amino acids and minerals. Bot. 100s, 500s.

ROTOTABS. (Vortech) Leucine 8.4%, lysine 6%, phenylalanine 5.8%, threonine 4%, methionine 2.1%, arginine 8.2%, isoleucine 5.8%, valine 5.8%, histidine 2.6%, tryptophan 1.1%/Tab. Bot. 100s, 1000s.
Use: Dietary supplement.

ROTOVERATRINE A.
See: Pro-Amid, Tab. (Amid)

ROTOVERATRINES A & B MALEATE.

ROTRAN PLUS. (Vangard) Meprobamate 150 mg., ethoheptazine citrate 75 mg., aspirin 250 mg./ Tab. Bot. 100s. 500s.
Use: Anti-anxiety pain reliever.

ROTRIPTYLINE. B.A.N. 7-(3-Methylaminopropyl)-1,2:-5,6-dibenzocycloheptatriene. Concordin HCl.
Use: Antidepressant.

PROTRIPTYLINE HYDROCHLORIDE, U.S.P. XXI. Tab., U.S.P. XXI. N-methyl-5H-dibenzo [α,d]cycloheptene-5-propylamine HCl.
Use: Antidepressant.
See: Vivactil, Tab. (Merck Sharp & Dohme)

ROVAL #3. (Reid-Provident) Acetaminophen 325 mg., codeine phosphate 30 mg./Tab. Bot. 100s, 500s.
Use: Analgesic.

ROVENTIL INHALER. (Schering) Metered dose aerosol unit containing albuterol in propellants. Each actuation delivers 90 mcg. of albuterol. Canister 17.0 Gm. with oral adapter. Box 1s.
Use: Bronchodilator.

PROVENTIL. (Schering) Albuterol sulfate 2 mg. or 4 mg./Tab. Bot. 100s, 500s.
Use: Relief of bronchospasm in patients with reversible obstructive airway disease.

PROVERA. (Upjohn) Medroxyprogesterone acetate 2.5 mg./Tab. Bot. 25s; 10 mg./Tab. Bot. 25s, 100s. Dosepak of 10s.
Use: Secondary amenorrhea; abnormal uterine bleeding due to hormonal imbalance.

PROVIGAN INJECTION. (Reid-Provident) Promethazine HCl 25 or 50 mg./ml. Vial 10 ml.
Use: Antihistaminic.

• **PROXAZOLE.** USAN. 5-[(2-Diethyl-amino)ethyl]-3-(α-ethyl-benzyl)-1,2,4-oxadiazole.
Use: Antispasmodic, analgesic, anti-inflammatory.

• **PROXAZOLE CITRATE.** USAN.
Use: Relaxant, analgesic, anti-inflammatory.

PROXENE. (Bowman) Propoxyphene HCl 65 mg./Cap.
Use: Analgesic.

• **PROXICROMIL.** USAN.
Use: Anti-allergic.

PROXIGEL. (Reed & Carnrick) Formerly Oxygel. Carbamide peroxide 10% in a water free gel base. Tube 1.2 oz.
Use: Oral antiseptic and cleanser.

• **PROXORPHAN TARTRATE.** USAN.
Use: Analgesic; antitussive.

PROXYMETACAINE. B.A.N. 2-Diethylaminoethyl 3-amino-4-propoxybenzoate.
Use: Local anesthetic.
See: Proparacaine
Ophthaine [hydrochloride]

PROXYPHYLLINE. B.A.N. 7-(2-Hydroxypropyl)-theophylline.
Use: Bronchodilator.
See: Brontyl
Thean

PROZINE-50. (Hauck) Promazine HCl 50 mg./ml. Vial 10 ml.
Use: Management of tension, anxiety & anti-emetic.

PRUDENTS. (Bariatric) Acetylphenylisatin 5 mg./Tab. Bot. 30s, 100s. Chewable Protein & Amino Acid
Use: Laxative.

PRULET LIQUITAB. (Mission) Phenolphthalein Liquitab. Film strip 50s.
Use: Fruit-flavored chewable laxative.

PRUNE CONCENTRATE. W/cascarin.
See: Prucara, Tab. (ICN)
W/Docusate sodium, guar gum.
See: D-S-S Compound, Cap. (Wolins)

PRUNE POWDER CONCENTRATED DEHYDRATED.
See: Diacetyldihydroxyphenylisatin
W/Cascara fl. ext. aromatic & psyllium husk pow.
See: Casyllium, Pow. (Upjohn)

PRUNE PREPS.
See: Casyllium, Granules (Upjohn)

PRUN-EVAC. (Pharmex) Bot. 30s.
Use: Laxative.

PRUNICODEINE. (Lilly) Codeine sulfate 60 mg., prunus virginiana 1.58 Gm., pinus strobus 1.05 Gm., sanguinaria 262 mg., terpin hydrate 175 mg., alcohol 25%/30 ml. Bot. 16 fl. oz.
Use: Orally; cough.

PRURILO. (Whorton) Menthol 0.25%, phenol 0.25%, calamine lotion in special lubricating base. Bot. 4 oz., 8 oz.
Use: Relief of pruritus.

PRURITOL OINTMENT. (Blue Line) Tannic acid 45 gr., zinc oxide 45 gr., balsam peru 15 gr., thymol iodide 3 gr., menthol 2 gr./oz. Tube w/rectal pipe 1.25 oz.

PSEUDODINE C COUGH SYRUP. (Bay) Triprolidine HCl 1.5 mg., pseudoephedrine HCl 30 mg., codeine phosphate 10 mg., guiafenesin 100 mg./5 ml. Bot. 4 oz., pt., gal.
Use: Expectorant, antitussive, decongestant, antihistaminic.

PSEUDODINE SYRUP. (Bay) Triprolidine HCl 1.25 mg., pseudoephedrine HCl 30 mg./5 ml. Bot. 4 oz., pt., gal.
Use: Treatment common cold, allergic rhinitis.

• **PSEUDOEPHEDRINE HYDROCHLORIDE,** U.S.P. XXI. Syrup, Tab., U.S.P. XXI. Isoephedrine HCl. α(1-Methylamino)-ethyl benzyl alcohol HCl. (+)-Pseudoephedrine HCl.
Use: Adrenergic.
See: Cenafed, Syr., Tab. (Century)
D-Feda, Cap., Syr. (Dooner)
Novafed, Cap., Liq. (Merrell Dow)
Ro-Fedrin, Tab., Syr. (Robinson)
Sinufed, Cap. (Hauck)
Sudafed, Tab., Syr. (Burroughs Wellcome)
Sudafed S.A., Cap. (Burroughs Wellcome)

PSEUDOEPHEDRINE HCl W/COMBINATIONS
See: Actified, Tab., Sry. (Burroughs Wellcome)
Actified-C Expectorant, Syr. (Burroughs Wellcome)
Ambenyl-D, Liq. (Marion)
Asmadil Unicelles (Reid-Provident)
Asthmaspan, T.D. Cap. (Wolins)
Atridine, Tab. (Interstate)
Ayr, Liq. (Ascher)
Ayrcap, Cap. (Ascher)
Brexin, Cap., Liq. (Savage)
Bronchobid, Cap. (Meyer)
Cotrol-D, Tab. (Beecham Labs)
Co Tylenol, Tab. (McNeil)
Co Tylenol Liquid Cold Formula (McNeil)
Deconamine, Cap., Tab., Elix., Syrup (Berlex)
Dimacol, Cap., Liq. (Robins)
Eldafed, Tab., Liq. (Elder)
Fedahist, Prods. (Dooner)
Fedrazil, Tab. (Burroughs Wellcome)
Historal, Cap., Liq. (W. F. Merchant)
Isoclor, Preps. (American Critical Care)
Kronofed-A, Cap. (Ferndale)
Novafed A, Liq., Cap. (Merrell Dow)
Novahistine Sinus Tablets, Tab. (Merrell Dow)
Phenergan Comp., Tab. (Wyeth)
Phenergan-D, Tab. (Wyeth)
Rhinosyn, Cap., Liq. (Comatic)
Robitussin-DAC, Liq. (Robins)
Robitussin-PE, Liq. (Robins)
Rondec D, Drops; C, Tab.; S, Syr.; T, Filmtab (Ross)
Rondec DM, Drops, Syr. (Ross)
Sinacon, Tab. (Glaxo)
Sudafed Plus, Tab., Syr. (Burroughs Wellcome)
Sudahist, Tab. (Upsher-Smith)
Suda-Proll Tab., Cap., Syr. (Quality Generics)
Triafed, Tab. (Wolins)
Triphed Tablets (Lemmon)
Triphedrine, Tab. (Redford)
Tussafed Exp. Liq. (Cavital)
Wal-Phed, Syrup, Tab. (Walgreens)

• **PSEUDOEPHEDRINE SULFATE.** U.S.P. XXI.
Use: Nasal decongestant.
See: Afrinol Repetabs (Schering)
W/Chlorpheniramine maleate.
See: Chlor-trimeton Decongestant, Tab. (Schering)
W/Dexbrompheniramine.
See: Disophrol Chronotabs, Tab. (Schering)
Drixoral S.A., Tab. (Schering)
W/Dexchlorpheniramine.
See: Polaramine Expt. (Schering)

PSEUDOMONAS POLYSACCHARIDE.
See: Piromen, Vial (Flint)

"PSEUDO-PHEDRINE". (Whiteworth) Pseudoephedrine HCl 30 mg./Tab. Bot. 100s, 1000s.
Use: Nasal decongestant.

PSEUDO PLUS. (Weeks & Leo) Pseudoephedrine HCl 60 mg., chlorpheniramine maleate 4 mg./Tab. Bot. 40s.
Use: Decongestant.

PSEUDO-PROL SYRUP. (Quality Generics) Tripolidine HCl 1.25 mg., pseudoephedrine HCl 30 mg./5 ml. Bot. Pts., Gal.
Use: Antihistamine, decongestant.

PSEUDO-PROL TABLETS. (Quality Generics) Triprolidine HCl 2.5 mg., pseudoephedrine HCl 60 mg./Tab. Bot. 100s, 1000s.
Use: Antihistaminic, decongestant.

PSILOCYBIN. B.A.N. (Sandoz) 3-(2-Dimethylaminoethyl)indol-4-yl dihydrogen phosphate.
Use: Psychotogenic agent.
See: Indocybin

PSORIASIS LOTION. (Wolins) Coal tar sol 3%, salicylic acid 1% in a greaseless lotion base. Bot. 8 oz
Use: Psoriasis.

PSORIGEL. (Owen) Coal tar sol. 7.5%, 33% alcohol in hydroalcoholic gel vehicle Tubes 4 oz.
Use: Eczema, psoriasis, & other coal tar-responsive dermatoses.

P.S.P. IV (Four). (Reid-Provident) Prednisolone sodium phosphate (equivalent to prednisolone phosphate 20 mg.), niacinamide 25 mg., EDTA disodium 0.5 mg., sod. bisulfite 1 mg., phenol 5 mg./cc. pH adjusted w/HCl acid and/or sod. hydroxide. Vial 10 cc. for IM, IV, IA or IB use.

PSYCHOTHERAPEUTIC DRUGS.
See: Ataraxic Agents

YLLIUM GRANULES.
Use: Bulk producing laxative.
'Dextrose.
See: Muci-lax, Granules (Med. Chem.)
'Senna.
See: Perdiem, Granules (Rorer)
•SYLLIUM HUSK, U.S.P. XXI.
Use: Cathartic
/Cascara fl. ext. aromatic & prune pow.
Use: Cathartic.
See: Casyllium, Pow. (Upjohn)
YLLIUM HYDROCOLLOID.
Use: Bulk producing laxative.
See: Effersyllium, Pow. (Stuart)
SYLLIUM HYDROPHILIC MUCILLOID.
Use: Bulk producing laxative.
See: Aquamucil, Liq. (Cenci)
Konsyl, Powder (Lafayette)
ucillium, Powder (Whiteworth)
/Dextrose.
See: Hydrocil Plain (Rowell)
Konsyl-D Powder (Lafayette)
V-lax, Powder (Century)
/Dextrose, casanthranol.
See: Hydrocil Fortified (Rowell)
/Docusate sodium.
See: Sof-Cil, Pow. (Zemmer)
/Oxyphenisatin acetate.
See: Plova Pow. (WEL)
/Standardized senna concentrate.
See: Senokot w/Psyllium Powder (Purdue Frederick)
SYLLIUM SEED GEL.
Use: Bulk producing laxative.
/Planta Ovata, gum Karaya, Brewer's yeast.
See: Plantamucin, Granules (Elder)
4,7-PTERIDINETRIAMINE, 6-PHENYL-. Triamterene, U.S.P. XXI.
TEROIC ACID. The compound formed by the linkage of carbon 6 of 2-amine-4-hydroxypteridine by means of a methylene group with the nitrogen of p-aminobenzoic acid.
TEROYLGLUTAMIC ACID.
See: Folic Acid, Prep. (Var. Mfr.)
TEROYLMONOGLUTAMIC ACID. Pteroylglutamic acid.
See: Folic acid, Prep. (Var. Mfr.)
TEROYLTRIGLUTAMATE SOD.
TFE. (Ethicon) Polytef.
THALOX. (Sutliff & Case) Cal. ricinoleate 65 mg., phenolphthalein 32.5 mg., sod. glycocholate 32.5 mg., sod. taurocholate 16 mg., cascara sagrada ext. 32.5 mg., aloin 8 mg./Tab. Bot. 100s, 1000s.
Use: Laxative.
ULMIDOL. Propyl Docetrizoate, B.A.N.
•ULMOCARE. (Ross) High fat, low carbohydrate liquid diet designed to reduce carbon dioxide production as tube feeding or oral supplement. Cans 8 oz.
Use: Liquid diet.

PULMOSIN. (Spanner) Guaiacol 0.10 Gm., eucalyptol 0.08 Gm., camphor 0.05 Gm., iodoform 0.02 Gm./2 cc. Multiple dose vial 30 cc. Inj. I.M.
PULMOTOL. (D'Franssia)
Use: Cough syrup.
• PUMICE, U.S.P. XXI.
Use: Abrasive (dental).
PURA. (D'Franssia) High potency Vit. E cream.
Use: For rough dry skin.
PUREBROM COMPOUND ELIXIR. (Purepac) Brompheniramine maleate 4 mg./5 ml. w/phenylephrine HCl, phenylpropanolamine HCl, alcohol. Bot. pts., gal.
Use: Antihistaminic, vasoconstrictor.
PUREBROM COMPOUND TABLETS. (Purepac) Brompheniramine maleate 12 mg./Tab. w/phenylephrine HCl, phenylpropanolamine HCl/Tab. Bot. 100s, 1000s.
Use: Antihistaminic, vasoconstrictor.
PURETANE. (Purepac) Brompheniramine maleate 2 mg., guaifenesin 100 mg., phenylephrine HCl 5 mg., phenylpropanolamine HCl 5 mg. Bot. pt.
Use: Antihistaminic, expectorant, vasoconstrictor.
PURGE. (Fleming) Castor oil Bot. 2 oz.
Use: Laxative.
PURGE EVACUANT. (Fleming) Castor oil 95%. Bot. 1 oz.
Use: Bowel evacuant.
PURIFIED OXGALL.
See: Bile Extract, Ox (Various Mfr.)
PURIFIED PROTEIN DERIVATIVE OF TUBERCULIN.
Use: Mantoux TB test.
See: Tuberculin, Old, Vial (Parke-Davis)
1H-PURINE-2,6-DIONE,8-CHLORO-3,7-DIHYDRO-1,3-DIMETHYL-, COMPOUND WITH 2-(DIPHENYLMETHOXY)-N,N-DIMETHYLETHANAMINE (1:1). Dimenhydrinate, U.S.P. XXI.
1H-PURINE-2,6-DIONE,3,7-DIHYDRO-1,3-DIMETHYL-, MONOHYDRATE. Theophylline, U.S.P. XXI.
1H-PURINE-2,6-DIONE,3,7-DIHYDRO-1,3-DIMETHYL-, COMPOUND WITH 1,2-ETHANEDIAMINE (2:1). Aminophylline, U.S.P. XXI.
1H-PURINE-2,6-DIONE,3,7-DIHYDRO-1,3,7-TRIMETHYL-. Caffeine, U.S.P. XXI.
1H-PURINE, 6-[(1-METHYL-4-NITRO-1H-IMIDAZOL-5-YL)THIO]-. Azathioprine, U.S.P. XXI.
PURINE-6-THIOL MONOHYDRATE. Mercaptopurine, U.S.P. XXI.
6H-PURINE-6-THIONE, MONOHYDRATE. Mercaptopurine, U.S.P. XXI.
6H-PURINE-6-THIONE, 2-AMINO-1,7-DIHYDRO-. Thioguanine, U.S.P. XXI.
PURINETHOL. (Burroughs Wellcome) Mercaptopurine, Tab. (50 mg.) Bot. 25s, 250s.
Use: Acute leukemia & chronic myelogenous leukemia.
PURODIGIN. (Wyeth) Digitoxin, Crystalline. **Tab.:** 0.1 mg. /Tab. Bot. 500s. 0.2 mg./Tab. Bot. 100s.
Use: Cardiac decompensation & congestive heart failure.

• **PUROMYCIN.** USAN. 3′-(L-α-Amino-p-methoxyhydrocinnamamido)-3′-deoxy-N,N-dimethyladenosine.
Use: Antibiotic.

• **PUROMYCIN HYDROCHLORIDE.** USAN.
Use: Antineoplastic; antiprotozoal.

PURPLE FOXGLOVE.
See: Digitalis, Preps. (Various Mfr.)

PURPOSE DRY SKIN CREAM. (Advanced Care) Water, white petrolatum, propylene glycol, glyceryl stearate, almond oil, sodium lactate, steareth-20, cetyl alcohol, mineral oil, ethyl esters wax, xanthan gum, steareth-2, sorbic acid, lactic acid, & fragrance. Tube 3 oz.
Use: Treatment of dry skin.

PURPOSE SHAMPOO. (Advanced Care) Water, amphoteric-19, PEG-44 sorbitan laurate, PEG-150 distearate, sorbitan laurate, boric acid, fragrance, & benzyl alcohol. Bot. 8 oz.
Use: Shampoo.

PURPOSE SOAP. (Advanced Care) Sodium and pot. salts of fatty acids, glycerin, fragrance. Bar 3.6 oz.

PURSETTES PREMENSTRUAL TABLETS. (Jeffrey Martin) Acetaminophen 500 mg., pamabrom 25 mg., pyrilamine maleate 15 mg./Tab. Bot. 24s.
Use: Relief of premenstrual period associated symptoms.

P.V. CARPINE LIQUIFILM. (Allergan) Pilocarpine nitrate 0.5%, 2%, or 4% w/polyvinyl alcohol 1.4%, sodium acetate, sodium chloride, citric acid, menthol, camphor, phenol, eucalyptol, chlorobutanol 0.5% and purified water. Dropper Bot. 15 ml.
Use: Miotic, control of intraocular pressure in glaucoma.

PVP-I OINTMENT. (Day-Baldwin) Povidoneiodine. Tube 1 oz., Jar 1 lb., Foilpac 1.5 Gm.

P-V-TUSSIN. (Reid-Provident) Hydrocodone bitartrate 2.5 mg., phenylephrine HCl 5 mg., ammonium chloride 50 mg., pyrilamine maleate 6 mg., chlorpheniramine maleate 2 mg., phenindamine tartrate 5 mg./5 cc. Bot. pt., gal.
Use: Antitussive, antihistaminic, decongestant, expectorant.

P-V TUSSIN TABLETS. (Reid-Provident) Hydrocodone bitartrate 5 mg., phenindamine tartrate 25 mg., guaifenesin 200 mg./Tab. Bot. 100s.
Use: Antitussive, decongestant, expectorant.

PYCAZIDE. Isoniazid, B.A.N.

PY-CO-PAY TOOTH POWDER. (Block) Sodium chloride, sodium bicarbonate, calcium carbonate, magnesium carbonate, tricalcium phosphate, eugenol and methyl salicylate. Can 7 oz.
Use: Dentifrice.

PYGMAL. (CMC) Tartaric acid, boric acid, Burrow's sol., glycerin, starch, talc & bentonite. Oint., Tube 1.5 oz.
Use: Antiseptic skin preparation.

PYLODATE. (Kenyon) Phenylazodiaminopyridine HCl 100 mg., methenamine mandelate 500 mg./Tab. Bot. 100s, 1000s.
Use: Urinary antiseptic.

PYLORA. (Hyrex) **No. 1:** Phenobarbital 16.2 mg., hyoscyamine sulfate 0.1037 mg., atropine sulfate 0.0194 mg., scopolamine HBr 0.0065 mg./Tab. Bo 100s, 1000s.
Use: Antispasmodic-sedative.

PYMA. (Fellows) **Cap.:** Pyrilamine maleate 50 mg., chlorpheniramine maleate 6 mg., pheniramine maleate 20 mg., phenylephrine HCl 15 mg./Timed Cap. Bot. 30s, 100s, 1000s. **Inj.:** Chlorpheniramine maleate 5 mg., phenylpropanolamine HCl 12.5 mg atropine sulfate 0.2 mg./cc. Vial 10 cc.

PYOCIDIN-OTIC SOLUTION. (Berlex) Hydrocortisone mg., polymyxin B sulfate 10,000 USP units/ml in a vehicle containing water and propylene glycol. Bot 10 ml. w/sterile dropper.
Use: Antibiotic & anti-inflammatory for otic use.

PYOPEN. (Beecham Labs). Carbenicillin disodium. 1 Gm., 2 Gm., 5 Gm./Vial. 10s; Piggyback Vials 2 Gm., 5 Gm. in 25s.; Bulk pharm pkg. 10 Gm., 20 Gm. in 25s.
Use: Antibiotic.

• **PYRABROM.** USAN. Pyrilamine 8-bromotheophylnate. Glybrom.
Use: Antihistaminic.

PYRACOL. (Davis & Sly) Pyrathyn HCl 0.08 Gm., ammonium chloride 0.778 Gm., citric acid 0.52 Gm., menthol 0.006 Gm./fl. oz. Bot. pt.

PYRACOMP COLD TABLETS. (Barry-Martin) Pyrilamine maleate 25 mg., salicylamide 3.5 gr., phenacetin 2.5 gr., caffeine 0.5 gr./Tab. Bot. 100s, 1000s.

PYRADIN. (Jenkins) Acetophenetidin 4 gr., antipyrine 1 gr., caffeine ⅛ gr., tinct. hyoscyamus 8 min. (total alkaloids .00032 gr.), tinct. gelsemium 4 min./Tab. Bot. 1000s.
Use: Analgesic, anodyne.

PYRADONE.
See: Aminopyrine (Various Mfr.)

PYRAMINYL.
See: Pyrilamine Maleate (Var. Mfr.)

PYRANEURIN INJ. (Nutrition) Vitamin B-1 100 mg., & B-6 100 mg./cc., w/benzyl alcohol 1.5%. Vial. 10 cc.
Use: B-Vitamin Inj.

PYRANILAMINE MALEATE.
See: Pyrilamine Maleate, Preps. (Var. Mfr.)

PYRANISAMINE BROMOTHEOPHYLLINATE.
See: Pyrabrom (Var. Mfr.)

PYRANISAMINE MALEATE.
See: Pyrilamine Maleate, Preps. (Var. Mfr.)

PYRANISTAN. (Standex) Chlorprophenpyridamine 60 mg./10 cc.

PYRANISTAN COMPOUND. (Standex) Chlorpheniramine maleate 2 mg., salicylamide 3.5 gr., phenacetin 2.5 gr., caffeine 0.5 gr./Tab. Bot. 100s.

PYRANISTAN CREME. (Standex) Coal tar ext. 5%, pyrilamine maleate 1%, benzocaine 2.5%, benzalkonium chloride 1%. Jar 1 oz.

PYRANISTAN STANKAPS. (Standex) Chlorpheniramine maleate 12 mg./Cap. Bot. 100s.

YRANISTAN SYRUP. (Standex) d-Methorphan HBr 30 mg., guaifenesin 75 mg., sodium citrate 150 mg., chlorpheniramine maleate 3 mg./fl. oz. Bot. pt.

YRANISTAN TAB. (Standex) Chlorpheniramine maleate 4 mg./Tab. Bot. 100s.

H-PYRANO 2,3-b 1,4 BENZODIOXIN-4-ONE, DECAHYDRO-4a,7,9-TRIHYDROXY-2-METHYL-6,8-BIS(METHYLAMINO)-,DI-HYDROCHLORIDE, PENTAHYDRATE. Sterile Spectinomycin HCl, U.S.P. XXI.

YRANTEL. B.A.N. 1,4,5,6-Tetrahydro-1-methyl-2-[trans-2-(2-thienyl)vinyl]pyrimidine. Combantrin embonate.
Use: Anthelmintic.

PYRANTEL PAMOATE, U.S.P. XXI. Oral Susp., U.S.P. XXI.
Use: Anthelmintic.
See: Antiminth, Oral Susp. (Roerig)

PYRANTEL TARTRATE. USAN. 1,4,5,6-Tetrahydro-1-methyl-2-[trans-2-(2-thienyl)vinyl]-pyrimidine Tartrate.
Use: Anthelmintic.

YRATHIAZINE HYDROCHLORIDE. (N-(2-Pyrrolidinoethyl)-phenothiazine.

PYRAZINAMIDE, U.S.P. XXI. Tabs., U.S.P. XXI. Pyrazinecarboxamide. 2-Carbamyl pyrazine. Pyrazinecarboxamide. Aldinamide, Zinamide. Pyrazinoic acid 0.5 Gm./Tab. Bot. 500s. Lederle-500 mg./Tab. Bot. 500s.
Use: Antibacterial (tuberculostatic).

YRAZINECARBOXAMIDE. Pyrazinamide, U.S.P. XXI.

YRAZODINE. (Cenci) Phenazopyridine HCl 100 mg./Cap. Bot. 100s, 1000s.
Use: Urinary tract analgesic.

PYRAZOFURIN. USAN.
Use: Antineoplastic.

YRAZOLE. Under study.
Use: Antitumor.

H-PYRAZOLE-3-ETHANAMINE, DIHYDROCHLORIDE. Betazole HCl, U.S.P. XXI.

,5-PYRAZOLIDINEDIONE, 4-BUTYL-1,2-DIPHENYL. Phenylbutazone, U.S.P. XXI.

,5-PYRAZOLIDINEDIONE, 1,2-DIPHENYL-4-2-(PHENYLSULFINYL)ETHYL-. Sulfinpyrazone, U.S.P. XXI.

YRAZOLINE.
See: Antipyrine (Various Mfr.)

H-PYRAZOLO[3,4-d]PYRIMIDIN-4-OL. Allopurinol, U.S.P. XXI.

YRBENZINDOLE.
See: Benzindopyrine hydrochloride (Var. Mfr.)

YRIBENZAMINE.
See: PBZ, Prods. (Geigy)

YRICAIN. (Jenkins) Cetylpyridium chloride 4 mg., sod. propionate 10 mg., benzocaine 5 mg./Tab. Bot. 1000s.

YRICARDYL.
See: Nikethamide, Inj. (Various Mfr.)

YRIDAMIDE. (Galen) Phenylazo-diamine pyridine HCl 50 mg., sulfacetamide 250 mg./Tab. Bot. 100s, 500s, 1000s.
Use: Urinary antiseptic.

PYRIDAMOLE TABS. (Major) Dipyridamole 25 mg./Tab. Bot. 1000s, 2500s; 50 mg. Bot. 100s, 1000s; 75 mg./Tab. Bot. 100s, 1000s.
Use: Vasodilator.

PYRIDATE TABS. (Major) Phenazopyridine 100 mg. or 200 mg./Tab. Bot. 1000s.
Use: Urinary analgesic/anti-infective.

PYRIDENE. (Approved) Phenylazo-diaminopyridine HCl 100 mg./Tab. Bot. 24s, 100s, 1000s.
Use: Urinary tract analgesic.

I(4H)-PYRIDINEACETIC ACID, 3,5-DIIODO-4-OXO-, PROPYLESTER. Propyliodone, U.S.P. XXI.

4-PYRIDINECARBOTHIOAMIDE, 2-ETHYL-. Ethionamide, U.S.P. XXI.

3-PYRIDINECARBOXAMIDE. Niacinamide, U.S.P. XXI.

PYRIDINE-3-CARBOXYLIC ACID.
See: Nicotinic Acid, Preps. (Var. Mfr.)

4-PYRIDINECARBOXYLIC ACID, HYDRAZIDE. Isoniazid, U.S.P. XXI.

PYRIDINE-BETA-CARBOXYLIC ACID DIETHYL AMIDE.
See: Nikethamide, Inj. (Various Mfr.)

3,4-PYRIDINEDIMETHANOL, 5-HYDROXY-6-METHYL-, HCl. Pyridoxine HCl, U.S.P. XXI.

3-PYRIDINEMETHANOL.
See: Roniacol, Prep. (Roche)

2-PYRIDINEPROPANAMINE, gamma-(4-CHLOROPHENYL)-N,N-DIMETHYL-,(Z)-2-BUTENEDIOATE (1:1). Chlorpheniramine Maleate, U.S.P. XXI.

PYRIDINIUM,3-//(DIMETHYLAMINO)CARBONYL/OXY-1-METHYL-, BROMIDE. Pyridostigmine Bromide, U.S.P. XXI.

PYRIDINIUM,2-/(HYDROXYIMINO)METHYL/-1-METHYL-, CHLORIDE. Pralidoxime Chloride, U.S.P. XXI.

PYRIDIUM. (Parke-Davis) Phenazopyridine HCl 100 mg. or 200 mg./Tab. Bot. 100s, 1000s. Unit dose 100s.
Use: Urinary analgesic/anti-infectant.
W/Hyoscyamine HBr & butabarbital.
See: Pyridium Plus, Tab. (Parke-Davis)

PYRIDIUM PLUS. (Parke-Davis) Formerly Dolonil. Phenazopyridine HCl 150 mg., hyoscyamine HBr. 0.3 mg., butabarbital 15 mg./Tab. Bot. 100s.
Use: Urinary analgesic, antispasmodic.

• **PYRIDOSTIGMINE BROMIDE,** U.S.P. XXI. Syr., Tabs., U.S.P. XXI. Pyridinium 3-[[(dimethylamino)-carbonyl]oxy]-1-methyl-, bromide. Dimethyl carbamic ester of 3-hydroxy-1-methylpyridinium bromide.
Use: Cholinergic.
See: Mestinon, Tab., Syr., Amp. (Roche)
Regonal (Organon)

PYRIDOX. (Oxford) **No. 1:** Pyridoxine HCl 100 mg./Tab. **No. 2:** Pyridoxine HCl 200 mg./Tab. Bot. 100s.
Use: Vitamin B-6 supplement.

PYRIDOXAL. Vit. B-6 3-Hydroxy-4-formyl-5-hydroxymethyl-2-methylpyridine.
Use: Cholinergic.

PYRIDOXAMINE. Vit. B-6. 3-Hydroxy-4-aminomethyl-5-hydroxymethyl-2-methylpyridine.

• **PYRIDOXINE HYDROCHLORIDE,** U.S.P. XXI. Inj., Tab., U.S.P. XXI. Vit. B-6. 3,4-Pyridinedimethanol, 5-hydroxy-6-methyl-, hydrochloride. Pyridoxol hydrochloride.
Use: Enzyme co-factor vitamin.
See: Beesix, Vial (Fellows-Testagar)
HexaBetalin, Amp., Tab., Vial (Lilly)
Hexavibex, Vial (Parke-Davis)
Pan B-6, Tab. (Panray)

PYRIDOXOL. 3-Hydroxy-4,5-hydroxymethyl-2-methylpyridine.
See: Pyridoxine, Vit. B-6.

PYRIDYL CARBINOL.
See: Roniacol, El. & Tab. (Roche)

4,4'-(2-PYRIDYLMETHYLENE)DIPHENOL DIACETATE (ESTER). Bisacodyl, U.S.P. XXI.

N1-2-PYRIDYLSULFANILAMIDE. Sulfapyridine, U.S.P. XXI.

PYRIHIST JR. (Evron) Same formula as Pyrihist Cough Syrup but cherry flavor. Bot. 4 fl. oz., gal.

PYRILAMINE BROMOTHEOPHYLLINATE.
See: Pyrabrom
W/2-amino-2-methyl-1-propanol.
See: Bromaleate

• **PYRILAMINE MALEATE,** U.S.P. XXI. Tab., U.S.P. XXI. 2-[[2-(Dimethylamino)ethyl](p-methoxy-benzyl)-amino]-pyridine maleate (1:1). Pyranisamine, Pyranilamine, Pyraminyl, Anisopyradamine.
Available: Cap. sustained action, Cream, Ophth. Sol., Syrup, Tablets.
Use: Antihistamine.
See: Pyma, Cap., Vial (Fellows-Testagar)
Pyristan, Cap., Elix. (Arcum)
W/Combinations.
See: Allergine, Cap. (Wolins)
Antihistamine Cream (Towne)
Anti-Itch Cream (Towne)
Cardui, Tab. (Chattem Labs.)
Corizahist, Tab. (Mason)
Coton, Syr., Tab. (Reid-Provident)
C.P.C. Cough Syrup (Coastal)
Femicin, Tab. (Norcliff Thayer)
Four Antihistamines, Tab. (Wolins)
Histjen, Cap. (Jenkins)
Hist-Span No. 2, Cap. (Kenyon)
Kenahist S.A., Tab. (Kenyon)
Miles Nervine, Tab. (Miles)
MSC Triaminic, Tab. (Dorsey)
Nasal Spray (Penta)
Prefrin-A Ophth. Sol. (Allergan)
Triwol, Tab. (Wolins)

• **PYRIMETHAMINE,** U.S.P. XXI. Tabs., U.S.P. XXI. 2,4-Pyrimidinediamine, 5-(4-chlorophenyl) 6-ethyl-.2,4-Diamino-5-(p-chlorophenyl)-6-ethyl-pyrimidine. Daraprim.
Use: Antimalarial.
See: Daraprim, Tab. (Burroughs Wellcome)
W/Sulfadoxine
See: Fansidar, Tab. (Roche)

2,4-PYRIMIDINEDIAMINE, 5-(4-CHLORO-PHENYL)-6-ETHYL. Pyrimethamine, U.S.P. XXI.

4,6(1H,5H)-PYRIMIDINEDIONE, 5-ETHYL-DIHYDRO-5-(1-METHYLBUTYL)-2-THIOXO-, MONOSODIUM SALT. Thiopental Sodium, U.S.P. XXI.

4,6(1H,5H)-PYRIMIDINEDIONE, 5-ETHYL-DIHYDRO-5-PHENYL-. Primidone, U.S.P. XXI.

2,4(1H,3H)-PYRIMIDINEDIONE, 5-FLUORO-. Fluorouracil, U.S.P. XXI.

2,4,6(1H,3H,5H)-PYRIMIDINETRIONE, 5-ETHYL 5(1)METHYLBUTYL), MONOSODIUM SALT. Pentobarbital Sodium, U.S.P. XXI.

2,4,6(1H,3H,5H)-PYRIMIDINETRIONE, 5-ETHYL-5-(3-METHYLBUTYL)-, MONOSODIUM SALT. Amobarbital Sodium, U.S.P. XXI.

2,4,6,(1H,3H,5H)-PYRIMIDINETRIONE, 5-ETHYL 5PHENYL. Phenobarbital, U.S.P. XXI.

2,4,6,(1H,3H,5H)-PYRIMIDINETRIONE, 1-METHYL-5-(1-METHYL-2-PENTYNYL)-5-(2-PROPENYL)-, (±), Monosodium salt. Methohexital Sodium for Injection, U.S.P. XXI.

2(1H)-PYRIMIDINONE, 4-AMINO-1β-D-ARABINOFURANOSYL-. Cytarabine, U.S.P. XXI.

4(1H)-PYRIMIDINONE, 2,3-DIHYDRO-6-PROPYL-2-THIOXO-. Propylthiouracil, U.S.P. XXI.

N'-2-PYRIMIDINYLSULFANILAMIDE. Sulfadiazine U.S.P. XXI.

PYRIMITHATE. B.A.N. 0-2-Dimethylamino-6-methylpyrimidin-4-y100-diethyl phosphorothioate.
Use: Insecticide, veterinary medicine.
See: Diothyl.

PYRIN-AID LIQUID. (Quality Generics) Pyrethrins 0.-2%,
piperonyl butoxide 2.0%, deodorized kerosene 0.8%. Bot. 2 oz.
Use: Kills head, body & crab lice & their eggs.

• **PYRINOLINE.** USAN.
Use: Cardiac depressant.
See: Surexin (McNeilab)

PYRISTAN. (Arcum) Phenylephrine HCl 8 mg., phenylpropanolamine HCl 15 mg., chlorpheniramine maleate 3 mg., pyrilamine maleate 10 mg./Cap. Bot. 50s, 500s. Elixir Bot. 4 oz., pt., gal.
Use: Decongestant and antihistaminic.

PYRISUL. (Kenyon) Sulfamethylthiadiazole 250 mg., phenylazodiamine pyridine 50 mg./Tab. Bot. 100s, 1000s.

PYRISUL-FORTE. (Kenyon) Sulfamethylthiadiazole 500 mg., phenylazodiamine pyridine 50 mg./Tab. Bot. 100s, 1000s.

PYRISUL PLUS. (Kenyon) Sulfamethylthiadiazole 250 mg., methenamine mandelate 250 mg., phenylazodiamine pyridine 50 mg./Tab. Bot. 100s, 1000s.

PYRITHEN.
See: Chlorothen Citrate. (Var. Mfr.)

PYRITHIDIUM BROMIDE. B.A.N. 3-Amino-8-(2-amino-1,6-dimethylpyrimidinium-4-ylamino)-6-(4-aminophenyl)-5-methylphenanthridinium dibromide.
Use: Antiprotozoan, veterinary medicine.
See: Prothidium

PYRI-THIME INJ. (Ortega) Thiamine HCl 100 mg., pyridoxine HCl 100 mg./ml. Vial 10 ml.

Use: Nausea of pregnancy, seborrheic dermatitis, thiouracil-induced granulopenia, hyperemesis gravidarum.

PYRITHIONE ZINC. USAN. Bis [1-hydroxy-2-(1H)-pyridinethionato]zinc. Zinc bis(pyridine-2-thiol 1-oxide. Zinc Omadine.
Use: Treatment of seborrhea.
See: Danex Shampoo (Herbert)
Zincon Shampoo (Lederle)

YRITINOL. B.A.N. Di(5-hydroxy-4-hydroxy-methyl-6-methyl-3-pyridylmethyl) disulfide.
Use: Cerebral neuroactivator which increases vigilance and increases or normalizes cerebral metabolism and blood flow.
See: Encephabol (Merck Sharp & Dohme)

YRODYN. (Fellows) Dipyrone 0.5 Gm./cc. Vials 30 cc.

YROGALLIC ACID OINTMENT. (Gordon) Pyrogallic acid 25% w/chlorobutanol. Jar 1.5 oz., 1 lb.
Use: Verruca therapy.

YROGALLOL. Pyrogallic acid.

YROHEP TABS. (Major) Cyproheptadine HCl 4 mg./Tab. Bot. 250s, 500s.
Use: Antipruritic, antihistaminic.

YROPHENINDANE. 1-(1-Methyl-3-pyrroli-dylmethyl)-3-phenylindane. (Mead Johnson)

PYROVALERONE HCl. USAN. 4′-Methyl-2-(1-pyrrolidinyl)valerophenone HCl.
Use: Central stimulant.

PYROXAMINE MALEATE. USAN.
Use: Antihistaminic.

PYROXYLIN, U.S.P. XXI. Soluble guncotton. Cellulose nitrate.
Use: Pharm. necessity for Collodion.

YRRALAN COMPOUND CAPSULES. (Lannett) Thenylpyramine fumarate 25 mg., acetylsalicylic acid 3.25 gr., phenacetin 2.5 gr., caffeine 0.25 gr./Cap. Bot. 100s, 500s, 1000s.
Use: Analgesic w/antihistamine.

YRRALAN EXPECTORANT. (Lannett) Thenylpyramine fumarate 80 mg., ephedrine HCl 30 mg., ammonium chloride 500 mg./fl. oz. Bot. pt., gal.

YRRALAN EXPECTORANT "DM." (Lannett) Same formula as Pyrralan Expect. w/d-methorphan HBr 10 mg./5 cc. Bot. pt., gal.
Use: Antitussive, antihistaminic, expect.

YRROBUTAMINE. B.A.N. 1-[4-(4-Chlorphenyl)-3-phenylbut-2-enyl]pyrrolidine.
Use: Antihistamine.
See: Pyronil phosphate.

PYRROBUTAMINE PHOSPHATE, U.S.P. XXI. 1-[4-(p-Chlorphenyl)-3-phenyl-2-butenyl] pyrrolidine diphosphate. 1-[α-(p-Chlorobenzyl)cinnamyl]pyrrolidine phosphate (1:2).
Use: Antihistaminic.
/Clopane HCl, Histadyl.
See: Co-Pyronil, Preps. (Lilly)

PYRROCAINE. USAN. 1-Pyrrolidine-aceto-2′,6′-xylidide. Endocaine.
Use: Local anesthetic.

PYRROCAINE HYDROCHLORIDE. 1-Pyrrolidineaceto-2′,6′-xylidide HCl.
Use: Local anesthetic (dental).

PYRROCAINE HYDROCHLORIDE AND EPINEPHRINE INJ.
Use: Local anesthetic (dental).

1-PYRROLIDINEACETO-2′,6′-XYLIDIDE MONOHYDROCHLORIDE. Pyrrocaine HCl.

2,5-PYRROLIDINEDIONE, 3-ETHYL-3-METHYL-. Ethosuximide, U.S.P. XXI.

N-(PYRROLIDINOMETHYL)TETRACYCLINE. Pyrrolidinomethyl.
See: Rolitetracycline, Inj.

2-PYRROLIDINONE, 1-ETHENYL-,HOMOPOLYMER. Povidone, U.S.P. XXI.

• **PYRROLIPHENE HYDROCHLORIDE.** USAN. d-α-Benzyl-β-methyl-α-phenyl-1-pyrrolidine-propanol acetate HCl. α-d-2-Acetoxy-1,2-dephenyl-3-methyl-4-pyrrolidinobutane HCl.
Use: Analgesic.

• **PYRROLNITRIN.** USAN. 3-Chloro-4-(3-chloro-2-nitrophenyl)pyrrole. Under study.
Use: Antifungal.

PYRROLO[2,3-b]INDOL-5-OL, 1,2,3,3a,8,8a-HEXAHYDRO-1,3a,8-TRIMETHYL-, METHYLCARBAMATE (ESTER), (3aS-cis). Physostigmine, U.S.P. XXI.

PYRROXATE. (Upjohn) Chlorpheniramine maleate 4 mg., phenylpropanolamine HCl 25 mg., acetaminophen 500 mg./Cap. Blister pkg. 24s. Bot. 500s.
Use: Relief for colds, allergies and sinus congestion.

• **PYRVINIUM PAMOATE,** U.S.P. XXI. Tab., Oral Susp., U.S.P. XXI. Quinolinium, 6-(dimethyl-amino-2-[2-(2,5-dimethyl-1-phenyl-1H-pyrrol-3-yl)ethenyl]-1-methyl-, salt with 4,4′-methyl-enebis[3-hydroxy-2-naphthalenecarboxylic]
Use: Anthelmintic.

PYTOSIN LIQUID. (Blue Line) Benzoic acid 52 gr., salicylic acid 26 gr., benzocaine 5 gr./oz., alcohol 77% Bot. 1 oz., 1 pt., 1 gal.
Use: Topical; fungicide & desquamative.

Q

Q.S. DIET AID. (Western Research) Potassium bicarbonate 70 mg., alginic acid 200 mg., methylcellulose 100 mg./Tab. Bot. 100s.
Use: Diet aid.

QT QUICK TANNING LOTION. (Plough) Padimate O, dihydroxyacetone (SPF 2). Tube 2 oz., Bot. 4 oz., 8 oz.
Use: Artificial tanner, ultraviolet sunscreen.

Q-U. (Eastwood) Cough syrup. Bot. 1 pt. With codeine Bot. 1 pt.

QUA-BID. (Quaker City Pharmacal) Papaverine HCl 150 mg./timed disintegrating Cap. Bot. 100s, 1000s.
Use: Smooth muscle relaxant.

QUADA-CREAM. (Sutliff & Case) Pramoxine HCl 1%, cetyl dimethylethyl ammonium bromide 2%,

pyrilamine maleate 1%, allantoin 0.4%. Tube 1 oz., Jar 1 lb.
Use: Antihistamine, anesthetic and antiseptic.

• **QUADAZOCINE MESYLATE.** USAN.
Use: Antagonist (opioid).

QUADRABARB. (Harvey) Secobarbital sod. 3/8 gr., penobarbital sod. 3/8 gr., butabarbital sod. 3/8 gr., phenobarbital 3/8 gr./Tab. Bot. 1000s.
Use: Sedative, hypnotic.

QUADRAHIST. (Harvey; Pharmex; Kenyon) Pyrilamine maleate, phenyltoloxamine dihydrogen citrate, prophenpyridamine maleate/Tab. (Harvey) Bot. 1000s. (Pharmex) Bot. 40s, 1000s. (Kenyon) Bot. 100s, 1000s.
Use: Antihistamine.

QUADRINAL. (Knoll) Ephedrine HCl 24 mg., phenobarbital 24 mg., theophylline calcium salicylate 130 mg., pot. iodide 320 mg./Tab. Bot. 100s, 1000s.
Use: Asthma & related allergic respiratory conditions.

QUADRINAL SUSPENSION. (Knoll) Ephedrine HCl 12 mg., phenobarbital 12 mg., theophylline calcium salicylate 65 mg., potassium iodide 160 mg./5 cc. Bot. pts.
Use: Bronchospasm and wheezing.

QUADRODIDE.
See: Quadrinal, Susp., Tab. (Knoll)

QUADRUPLE SULFONAMIDES.
See: Sulfonamides

QUAD-SET. (Kenyon) Secobarbital 25 mg., pentobarbital 25 mg., butabarbital 25 mg., phenobarbital 25 mg./Tab. Bot. 100s, 1000s.
Use: Sedative.

QUANTRIL. Benzquinamide.
Use: CNS depressant.

QUARTETS. (Eckerd) Phenylpropanolamine HCl 25 mg., chlorpheniramine maleate 2 mg., dextromethorphan HBr 15 mg., ascorbic acid 25 mg./Cap. Bot. 24s.
Use: Antihistaminic, decongestant, antitussive.

QUARZAN. (Roche) Clidinium Bromide 2.5 mg., 5 mg./Cap. Bot. 100s.
Use: Peptic ulcer disease.

• **QUAZEPAM.** USAN.
Use: Sedative; hypnotic.

• **QUAZINONE.** USAN.
Use: Cardiotonic.

• **QUAZODINE.** USAN.
Use: Cardiotonic; bronchodilator.

Q-U-CORT. (Eastwood) Cream 0.25% 0.5%, or 1%. Tube 1 oz., or 4 oz.

QUELICIN. (Abbott) Succinylcholine chloride. 50 mg./ml., 10 ml. ampul; 100 mg./ml., 10 ml. ampul; 20 mg./ml., 10 ml. fliptop vial; Quelicin-1000, 10 ml. in 20 ml. fliptop vial; Quelicin-500, 5 ml. in 10 ml. pintop vial; Quelicin-1000, 10 ml. in 20 ml. pintop vial; and 20 mg./ml. 5 ml. Abboject Syringe..
Use: Short-acting muscle relaxant.

QUELIDRINE SYRUP. (Abbott) Dextromethorphan HBr 10 mg., chlorpheniramine maleate 2 mg., ephedrine HCl 5 mg., phenylephrine HCl 5 mg., ammonium Cl 40 mg., ipecac fluid extract 0.005 cc., ethyl alcohol 2%/5 ml. Bot. 4 oz., 1 pt., 1 gal.
Use: Allergic disorders.

QUELLADA. Gamma Benzene Hexachloride, B.A.N.

QUELLS. (Stanlabs) Meclizine hydrochloride 25 mg./Chewable Tab. Box 24s.
Use: Antihistaminic.

QUELTUSS. (Forest) Dextromethorphan HBr 15 mg., guaifenesin 100 mg./Tab. or 5 ml. of Syr. **Syr.:** Bot. 4 oz., pt. **Tab.:** Bot. 100s.
Use: Cough control.

QUERCETIN. Active constituent of rutin. Quertine.

QUERTINE. Quercetin. 3,3′,4′,5,7-Pentahydroxy-flavone.
Use: Treatment of capillary fragility.

QUESTRAN. (Mead Johnson) Cholestyramine resin 4 Gm. active ingredient/9 Gm. Powder Packet. Boxes 50 packets. Can 378 Gm. (42 dose).
Use: Reduction of elevated serum low density lipoprotein (LDL) cholesterol; antipruritic for pruritus related to biliary obstruction; Primary Type II hyperlipoproteinemia.

QUIBRON. (Mead Johnson) Theophylline (anhydrous) 150 mg., guaifenesin 90 mg./Cap. or 15 ml. Liquid. **Cap.:** Bot. 100's, 1000's, Box 100's individually wrapped. **Liquid:** Bot. pt., gal.
Use: Bronchodilator for symptomatic treatment of bronchospasm.

QUIBRON-300. (Mead Johnson) Theophylline anhydrous 300 mg., guaifenesin 180 mg./Cap. Bot. 100s.
Use: Bronchodilator for symptomatic treatment of bronchospasm.

QUIBRON PLUS. (Mead Johnson) Ephedrine HCl 25 mg., theophylline (anhydrous) 150 mg., butabarbital 20 mg., guaifenesin 100 mg./Cap. or 15 ml. Elixir. **Cap.:** Bot. 100s. **Elixir:** 15% alcohol. Bot. pt., gal.
Use: Bronchodilator for symptomatic treatment of bronchospasm.

QUIBRON-T DIVIDOSE TABLETS. (Mead Johnson) Theophylline anhydrous 300 mg./Tab. Dividose design breakable into 100 mg., 150 or 200 mg. portions. Immediate release. Bot. 100s.
Use: Bronchodilator for symptomatic treatment of bronchospasm.

QUIBRON-T/SR DIVIDOSE TABLETS. (Mead Johnson) Theophylline anhydrous 300 mg./Tab. Dividose design breakable into 100 mg., 150 mg., or 200 mg. portions. Sustained release. Bot. 100s.
Use: Bronchodilator for symptomatic treatment of bronchospasm.

QUICK-K. (Western Research) Potassium bicarbonate 650 mg. (6.01 mEq.) potassium/Tab. for sol. Bot. 30s, 1000s.
Use: Supplement.

QUIDE. (Merrell Dow) Piperacetazine 10 mg. and 25 mg./Tab. Bot. 100s.
Use: Treatment of psychoses.

QUIEBAR. (Nevin) Butabarbital sodium **Spantab:** 1.5 gr./Timed Release Spantab. Bot. 50s, 500s. **Elixir** 30 mg./5 cc. Bot. pt., gal. **Tab.** 15 mg. Bot. 100s,

1000s. 30 mg. Bot. 1000s. **A.C. Cap.** Bot. 100s, 500s.
Use: Hypnotic, sedative.
IEBEL. (Nevin) Butabarbital sod. 15 mg., ext. belladonna 15 mg./Cap. Bot. 100s, 1000s. Elixir, pt., gal.
Use: Antispasmodic-sedative.
IECOF. (Nevin) Dextromethorphan HBr 7.5 mg., chlorpheniramine maleate 0.75 mg., guaiacol glyceryl ether 25.0 mg. Bot. 4 oz., pt., gal.
Use: Sugarless cough syrup.
IESS (Forest) Hydroxyzine HCl 25 mg./ml. Vial 10 ml.
IET TIME. (Whiteworth) Acetaminophen 600 mg., ephedrine sulfate 8 mg., dextromethorphan HBr 15 mg., doxylamine succinate 7.5 mg., alcohol 25 mg./30 ml. Bot. 6 oz.
Use: Analgesic, decongestant, antitussive, antihistaminic.
IET WORLD. (Whitehall) Acetaminophen 2.5 gr., aspirin 3.5 gr., pyrilamine maleate 25 mg./Tab. Bot. 12s, 30s.
Use: Analgesic.
IK-CEPT. (Laboratory Diagnostics) Slide test for pregnancy, rapid latex inhibition test. Kits: 25s, 50s, 100s.
Use: For pregnancy testing.
IK-CULT. (Laboratory Diagnostics) Slide test for fecal occult blood. Kits. 150s, 200s, 300s, and tape test.
Use: Rapid, convenient method for testing fecal specimens for occult blood.
ILATE. (Wolins) Theophylline (anhydrous) 150 mg., guaifenesin 90 mg./Cap. Bot. 100s, 1000s.
INACILLIN. B.A.N. 6-(3)Carboxyquinoxaline-2-carboxamideo)penicillanic acid.
Use: Antibiotic.
UINACRINE HYDROCHLORIDE, U.S.P. XXI. Tab., U.S.P. XXI. 1,4-Pentanediamine,N^4-(6-chloro-2-methoxy-9-acridinyl)-N^1,N^1-diethyl-, dihydrochloride, dihydrate. 6-Chloro-9- [4-(diethylamino)-1-methylbutyl]amino -2-methoxyacridine dihydrochloride. 3-Chloro-7-methoxy-9-(1-methyl-4-diethylamino-butylamino)-acridine di-HCl dihydrate.
Use: Anthelmintic.
See: Atabrine HCl, Tab. (Winthrop-Breon)
INAGLUTE DURA-TABS. (Berlex) Quinidine gluconate 324 mg./Tab. Bot. 100s, 250s, 500s. Unit dose 100s. Unit of use 90s, 120s.
Use: Cardiac arrhythmias.
INALBARBITONE SODIUM. B.A.N. Monosodium derivative of 5-allyl-5-(1-methylbutyl)-barbituric acid.
Use: Hypnotic; sedative.
See: Secobarbital Sodium
Seconal Sodium
UINALDINE BLUE. USAN. 1-Ethyl-2-[3-(1-ethyl-2(1H) quinolylidene) propenyl]-quinolinium chloride. Vernitest reagent. (Fuller)
Use: Diagnostic agent (obstetrics).
INAMINOPH TABS. (Goldline) Quinine sulfate 260 mg./Tab. Bot. 100s, 500s.
Use: Nocturnal leg cramps.

QUINAMM. (Merrell Dow) Quinine sulf. 260 mg./Tab. Bot. 100s.
Use: Prevention and treatment of nocturnal recumbency leg muscle cramps.
• **QUINAPRIL HYDROCHLORIDE.** USAN.
Use: Enzyme inhibitor (angiotensin-converting).
• **QUINAZOSIN HYDROCHLORIDE.** USAN. 2-(4-Allyl-1 piperazinyl)-4-amino-6,7-dimethoxy-quinazoline dihydrochloride.
Use: Hypotensive.
• **QUINBOLONE.** USAN. 17-beta-(1-Cyclo-penten-1-yloxy)-androsta-1,4-dien-3-one.
Use: Anabolic agent.
• **QUINDECAMINE ACETATE.** USAN. 4,4′-(Decamethylenediimino) diquinaldine diacetate dihydrate.
Use: Topical anti-infective.
• **QUINDONIUM BROMIDE.** USAN. 2,3-3α,5,6,11,12,12 α-Octahydro-8-hydroxy-1H-benzo-[α]-cyclopenta[f]-quinolizinium bromide.
Use: Cardiovascular agent.
QUINDOXIN. B.A.N. Quinoxaline 1,4-dioxide.
Use: Growth promoter, veterinary medicine.
See: Grofas
QUINE. (Rowell) Quinine sulfate 200 mg., 300 mg. 200 mg./Cap. Bot. 100s. 300 mg./Cap. Bot. 100s. Unit dose 100s.
Use: Antimalarial.
QUINESTRADOL. B.A.N. 3-Cyclopentyloxyestra-1,3,-5(10)-triene-16α,17β-diol.
Use: Estrogen.
See: Pentovis
• **QUINESTROL,** U.S.P. XXI. Tab., U.S.P. XXI. 3-(Cyclopentyloxy)-19-nor-17-α-pregna-1,3,5(10)-triene-20-yn-17-ol.
Use: Estrogen.
See: Estrovia, Tab. (Parke-Davis)
• **QUINETHAZONE,** U.S.P. XXI. Tab., U.S.P. XXI. 7-Chloro-2-ethyl-6-sulfamyl-1,2,3,4-tetra-hydro-4-quinazolinone. 7-Chloro-2-ethyl-1,2,3,4-tetrahydro-4-oxo-6-quinazolinesulfonamide. Aquamox.
Use: Diuretic.
See: Hydromox, Tab. (Lederle)
W/Reserpine.
See: Hydromox R, Tab. (Lederle)
• **QUINETOLATE.** USAN. 6-(Diethylcarbamoyl)-3-cyclohexene-1-carboxylic acid comp. with 4-((2-(dime-thylamino) ethyl)amino)6-methoxy-quinoline (2:1) Phthalamaquin (Penick).
Use: Antiasthmatic.
• **QUINFAMIDE.** USAN.
Use: Anti-amebic.
QUINGESTANOL. B.A.N. 3-Cyclopentyloxy-19-nor-17α -pregna-3,5-diene-20-yn-17-ol.
Use: Progestational steroid.
• **QUINGESTANOL ACETATE.** USAN. 3-(Cyclopentyloxy)-19-nor-17α-pregna-3,5-dien-20-yn-17-ol acetate. Under study.
Use: Progestational agent.
• **QUINGESTRONE.** USAN. 3-(Cyclopentyloxy)pregna-3,5-dien-20-one.
Use: Progestational agent.

QUINIDEX EXTENTABS. (Robins) Quinidine sulf. 300 mg./Tab. Bot. 100s, 250s. Dis-co pack of 100s.
Use: Cardiac arrhythmias.

QUINIDEX L-A.
See: Quinidex Extentabs (Robins)

• **QUINIDINE GLUCONATE,** U.S.P. XXI., Inj., U.S.P. XXI. Cinchonan-9-ol, 6′-methoxy-,(9s)-, mono-D-gluconate (salt). (Lilly) Amp. (80 mg./cc.) 10 cc.
Use: Quinidine therapy; cardiac depressant.
See: Duraquin, Tab. (Parke-Davis)
Quinaglute, Dura-Tabs. (Berlex)

QUINIDINE POLYGALACTURONATE.
See: Cardioquin Tab. (Purdue Frederick Co.)

• **QUINIDINE SULFATE,** U.S.P. XXI. Cap., Tab., U.S.P. XXI. Cinchonan-9-ol, 6′-methoxy-,(9s)-, sulfate (2:1) (salt), dihydrate.
Use: Cardiac depressant.
See: Cin-Quin (Rowell)
Maso-Quin, Tab. (Mason)
Quinidex Extentabs (Robins)
Quinora, Tab. (Key)
SK-Quinidine Sulfate, Tab. (SmithKline)

QUININE ASCORBATE. USAN.
Use: Deterrent to smoking.

QUININE BISULFATE.
Use: Orally; analgesic & antipyretic & antimalarial.

QUININE DIHYDROCHLORIDE.
Use: I.M., I.V.; antimalarial therapy.

QUININE ETHYLCARBONATE.
See: Euquinine (Various Mfr.)

QUININE GLYCEROPHOSPHATE. Quinine compound with glycerol phosphate.

• **QUININE SULFATE,** U.S.P. XXI. Cap., Tab., U.S.P. XXI. Cinchonan-9-ol, 6′-methoxy-, (8α,9R)-, sulfate (2:1) (salt) dihydrate.
Use: Antimalarial.
See: Quinamm, Tab. (Merrell Dow)
Quine, Cap. (Rowell)
W/Aminophylline.
See: Strema, Cap. (Foy)
W/Atropine sulf., emetine HCl, aconitine, camphor monobromate.
See: Coryza, Tab. (Bowman)
W/Niacin, Vit. E.
See: Myodyne, Tab. (Paddock)
W/Strychnine sulf., cinchonine sulf., cinchonidine sulf., alcohol.
See: Hospital Bitters, Liq. (Noyes)

QUININE AND UREA HYDROCHLORIDE.
Use: Sclerosing agent.

QUINISOCAINE (I.N.N.). Dimethisoquin, B.A.N.

QUINNONE CREAM. (Dermohr Pharmacal) Hydroquinone 4% in creamy base. Tube 1 oz.
Use: Temporary bleaching of darkened areas of skin.

QUINOLINIUM,6-(DIMETHYLAMINO)-2-[2-(2,5-DIMETHYL-1-PHENYL-1H-PYRROL-3-YL)ETHENYL]-1-METHYL-, SALT WITH 4,4′-METHYLENEBIS[3-HYDROXY-2-NAPHTHALENECARBOXYLIC ACID](2:1). Pyrvinium Pamoate, U.S.P. XXI.

8-QUINOLINOL, 5,7-DIIODO-. Diiodohydroxyquin, Iodoquinol, U.S.P. XXI.

QUINOPHAN.
See: Cinchophen (Various Mfr.)

QUINORA. (Key) Quinidine sulfate 200 mg., 300 mg./Tab. Bot. 100s, 1000s. Unit dose 100s.
Use: Cardiac depressant.

QUINOXYL.
See: Chiniofon

• **QUINPIROLE HYDROCHLORIDE.** USAN.
Use: Antihypertensive.

QUINPRENALINE. Quinterenol Sulfate.

QUIN-260 TABS. (Major) Quinine sulfate 260 mg./Ta Bot. 250s.
Use: Treatment of nocturnal leg cramps.

QUIN-RELEASE SR TABS. (Major) Quinidine glucona 324 mg./S.R. Tab. Bot. 250s, 500s.
Use: Cardiac arrthythmias.

QUINSONE. (Sutliff & Case) Clioquinol 30 mg., hydrocortisone acetate 10 mg., pramoxine HCl 5 mg. in base of sulfonated and polyethoxylated fat alcohols, free fatty alcohols, water/Gm. Oint. Tub 0.5 oz.
Use: Dermatologic.

• **QUINTERENOL SULFATE.** USAN. 8-Hydroxy-alph [(isopropylamino)methyl]-5-quinoline-methanol [s fate (2:1).
Use: Bronchodilator.

QUINTIOFOS. B.A.N. O-Ethyl 0-8-quinolyl phenyl-phc phonothioate.
Use: Insecticide, veterinary medicine.
See: Bacdip

• **QUINUCLIUM BROMIDE.** USAN.
Use: Antihypertensive.

• **QUIPAZINE MALEATE.** USAN. 2-(1-Piperazinyl) quinoline maleate.
Use: Oxytocic.

QUIPENYL NAPHTHOATE.
See: Pamaquine naphthoate; Plasmochin naphthoate.

QUIT. (Guild) Bot. 0.5 oz. w/applicator.
Use: For nail biting.

QUIXALIN. Halquinol, B.A.N.

QULAGEN SOFT GELATIN CAPS. (Goldline) Theophylline, glyceryl guaiacolate. Bot. 100s, 500s
Use: Bronchodilator.

Q-U-OPH. (Eastwood) Cough syrup. Bot. Pt. With c deine Pt. Cap. Bot. 100s.

Q-VEL. (Rugby) Quinine sulfate 1 gr., vitamin E 400 I.U Cap. Bot. 50s.
Use: Muscle relaxant and pain reliever for leg cramps.

R

R-3 SCREEN TEST. (Wampole) A three-minute latex eosin slide test for the qualitative detection of rheumatoid factor activity in serum. Kit 100s.
Use: An aid in the diagnosis of rheumatoid arthritis

• **RABIES IMMUNE GLOBULIN,** U.S.P. XXI.
Use: Immunizing agent (passive).

• **RABIES VACCINE.** U.S.P. XXI. (Lilly) 1 dose vial. 1.1 ml. The suspending fluid consists of 0.1%

cysteine HCl, 5% lactose, 0.2% gelatin and 0.25% dibasic potassium phosphate. Vaccine preserved w/thimerosal 1:10,000. (Lederle) 1,000 units/vial. Antirabies Serum.
Use: Immunizing agent (active).

BRO TABLETS. (Orbar) Licorice root ext., light magnesium carbonate, bismuth subnitrate, sodium bicarbonate, small amounts of frangula and calamus. Boxes 30s, 60s.
Use: Stomach distress, heartburn, indigestion.

RACEMETHIONINE, U.S.P. XXI. Cap., Tab., U.S.P. XXI. Dl-2-Amino-4-(methylthio)butyric acid.
Use: Acidifier (urinary).
See: Amurex, Cap. (Reid-Provident)
Odonil, Cap. (Kenyon)
Odor-Scrip, Cap. (Scrip)
Oradash, Cap. (Lambda)
Pedameth. Cap., Liq. (Forest)
Uranap, Cap. (Vortech)

CEMETHIONINE W/COMBINATIONS.
See: Aminomin, Vial (Pharmex)
Aminovit, Vial (Hickam)
Amodin, Inj. (Vortech)
Ardiatric, Tab. (Burgin-Arden)
Azolate, Tab. (Amfre-Grant)
Cho-Meth Vial (Kenyon)
Geriatrazole, Vial (Kenyon)
Geriatro-B, Vial (Kenyon)
Hi-Pro Wafers, Tab. (Mills)
Licoplex, Tab. (Mills)
Limvic, Tab. (Briar)
Lipo-K, Cap. (Marcen)
Lychol-B, Inj. (Burgin-Arden)
Minoplex, Vial (Savage)
Norimex-Plus, Cap. (Vortech)
Pro-Hydro, Tab. (Mills)
Vio-Geric, Tab. (Rowell)
Vio-Geric-H, Tab. (Rowell)
Vi-Testrogen, Vial (Pharmex)

CEMETHORPHAN. B.A.N. (±)-3-Methoxy-N-methylmorphinan
Use: Narcotic analgesic.
See: Dromoran (Roche)

CEMIC CALCIUM PANTOTHENATE.
See: Calcium Pantothenate, Racemic.

CEMIC DESOXY-NOR-EPHEDRINE.
See: Amphetamine (Various Mfr.)

CEMIC EPHEDRINE HCl. Racephedrine HCl.

CEMIC PANTOTHENIC ACID.
See: Vitamin, Preparations

CEMORAMIDE. B.A.N. (±)-1-(3-Methyl-4-morpholino-2,2-diphenylbutyryl)pyrrolidine.
Use: Narcotic analgesic.

CEMORPHAN HBr. B.A.N. (±)-3-Hydroxy-N-methylmorphinan.
Use: Narcotic analgesic.

CEPHEDRINE HYDROCHLORIDE. (Upjohn) dl-a-[1-(Methylamino)ethyl]benzyl alcohol hydrochloride. Cap. (3/8 gr.) Bot. 40s, 250s, 1000s. Sol. (1%) Bot. 1 fl. oz., 1 pt., 1 gal.
Use: Vasoconstrictor & nasal decongestant.
See: Ephedrine Combinations
W/Aminophylline & phenobarbital.
See: Amodrine, Tab. (Searle)
W/Theophylline sod. glycinate, phenobarbital.
See: Synophedal, Tab. (Central)

• **RACEPHENICOL.** USAN.
Use: Antibacterial.

RACET CREAM. (Lemmon) Clioquinol 3%, hydrocortisone 0.5%. W/stearic acid, cetyl alcohol, petrolatum, polyoxyl 40 stearate, sorbitol, propylene glycol, methylparaben, propylparaben, heather aroma. Tube 15 Gm., 30 Gm.
Use: Dermatologic.

RACET-1% CREAM. (Lemmon) Clioquinol 3%, hydrocortisone 1% w/steric acid, cetyl alcohol, petrolatum, polyoxyl 40 stearate, sorbitol, propylene glycol, methylparaben, propylparaben, heather aroma, water. Tube 15 Gm.
Use: Dermatologic.

RACET LCD CREAM. (Lemmon) Clioquinol 3%, hydrocortisone 1%, coal tar sol. 5% w/stearic acid, cetyl alcohol, petrolatum, polyoxyl 40 stearate, sorbitol, propylene glycol, methylparaben, propylparaben, heather aroma, rose oil, purified water. Tube 30 Gm.
Use: Dermatoses, eczema.

RACET SE. (Lemmon) Hydrocortisone 0.5%, 1.0% w/cetyl alcohol, petrolatum, polyoxyl 40 stearate, propylene glycol, sorbic acid, potassium sorbate, & purified water. Tube 15 Gm.
Use: Topical anti-inflammatory antipruritic.

RADIOACTIVE ISOTOPES.
See: Medotope, Prods. (Squibb)
Radio-Gold, Sol.
Radio-Iodinated Serum Albumin (Human)
Sodium Radio-Chromate, Inj.
Sodium Radio-Iodide, Sol.
Sodium Radio Phosphate, Sol.

RADIOACTIVE ISOTOPES.
See: Aggregated Radioiodinated Albumin, Human I-131
Chlormerodrin Hg-197, Inj.
Chlormerodrin Hg-203, Inj.
Cyanocobalamin Co-57, Cap.
Cyanocobalamin Co-60, Cap.
Gold Au-198, Inj.
Radiodinated Serum Albumin, Human I-125
Radiodinated Serum Albuminia, Human I-131
Selenomethionine Se-75, Inj.
Sodium Chromate Cr-51, Inj.
Sodium Iodide I-125, Sol., Cap.
Sodium Iodide I-131, Sol., Cap.
Sodium Phosphate P-32, Cap., Inj.
Sodium Rose Bengal I-131, Inj.
Strontium Nitrate Sr-85, Inj.
Technetium Tc-99m, Kit., Inj.
Triolein I-131, Cap., Sol.
Xenon Xe-133, Inj.

RADIOGOLD (^{198} Au), SOLUTION. Gold Au-198 Injection, U.S.P. XXI.
Use: Irradiation therapy.
See: Auretope, Vial (Squibb)

RADIO-IODIDE (^{131}I), SODIUM.
Use: Radioactive isotopes.
See: Iodotope (Squibb)
Radiocaps (Abbott)

RADIO-IODINATED (^{131}I) SERUM ALBUMIN. (Human), Iodinated I-131 Albumin Injection, U.S.P. XXI.

RADIO-IODINATED SERUM ALBUMIN (Human), (^{125}I).
See: Albumotope (^{125}I) (Squibb)

RADIO-PHOSPHATE (^{32}P), SODIUM.
Use: Radioactive isotopes.

RADIOSELENOMETHIONINE 75 Se. Selenomethionine Se 75.

RADIOTOLPOVIDONE I-131. Tolpovidone I-131.
See: Raovin (Abbott)

RAFLUOR. (Pascal Co.) Acidulated, phosphated, 1.23% sodium fluoride prep. Gel 8 oz, 16 oz., 1 qt., 1 gal. Solution 8 oz, 16 oz.
Use: Topical application by dentist to reduce tooth decay.

• **RAFOXANIDE.** USAN.
Use: Anthelmintic.

RAGUS. (Miller) Mg. 27 mg., C 100 mg., cal. 580 mg., phosphorus 450 mg., l-lysine 25 mg., dl-methionine 50 mg., A 5000 I.U., D 400 I.U., E 10 mg., B-1 20 mg., B-2 3 mg., B-6 5 mg., B-12 9 mcg., niacinamide 80 mg., pantothenic acid 5 mg., Fe 20 mg., Cu 1 mg., Mn 2 mg., K 10 mg., Zn 2 mg., Iodine 0.1 mg./3 Tabs. Bot. 100s.
Use: Dietary supplement.

RALGRO. (Commercial Solvents) Zeranol.

R A LOTION. (Medco Lab) Resorcinol 3%, calamine 6%, starch 6%, sodium borate 1.3%, alcohol 43%. Pl. bot. 4 oz., 8 oz., 16 oz.
Use: Skin medication for oily skin and acne.

RALS BENZOIN SPRAY. (Larson) Benzoin spray. Can 12 oz.
Use: Topical skin antiseptic.

RAMETIN. Naphthalophos, B.A.N.

RAMSES BENDEX. (Schmid) Flexible cushioned diaphragm; arc-ing spring. 65-90 mm. Pkg. w/Ramses Vaginal Jelly Tube 1 oz., 3 oz.
Use: Contraceptive.

RAMSES DIAPHRAGM. (Schmid) Flexible cushioned diaphragm. 50-95 mm. Pkg. diaphragm, tube of Ramses Vaginal Jelly. Pkg. diaphragm alone.
Use: Contraceptive.

RAMSES JELLY. (Schmid) Dodecoethylene glycol monolaurate 5%, boric acid 1%, glycerin, tragacanth, carboxymethylcellulose & preservative. Tube w/applicator 3 oz. Refill 3 oz., 5 oz.
Use: Contraceptive.

RANDOLECTIL. (Farbenfabriken Bayer) Butaperazine.
Use: Psychotropic agent.

R & C SPRAY III. (Reed & Carnrick) Spray containing pyrethroid (sumethrin) 0.382%, other isomers 0.018%, petroleum distillate 4.255%, Aerosol Container. 5 oz.
Use: An insecticide for use on inanimate objects infested with lice. Not for use on humans or animals.

RANESTOL. Triclofenol piperazine.
Use: Anthelmintic.

• **RANIMYCIN.** USAN.
Use: Antibacterial.

• **RANITIDINE.** USAN.
Use: Antagonist to histamine H-2 receptors.

RANTEX. (Holland-Rantos) Wipes 14s, 36s.

RAPIDAL CALCIUM SALT. Cyclobarbitone, B.A.N.

RASP. (Commerce) Bot. 3 oz.
Use: Children's cough syrup.

RASPBERRY JUICE.
Use: Flavored vehicle.

RASTINON. Tolbutamide, U.S.P. XXI.

RATIODRINE. (Metro Med) Tabs. Bot. 100s, 1000s.
Use: Obesity control.

RATTLESNAKE BITE THERAPY.
See: Antivenin, Snake Polyvalent (Wyeth)

RAUDILAN PB TABLETS. (Lannett) Rauwolfia serpentina root 50 mg., phenobarbital 15 mg./Tab. Bot. 100s, 500s, 1000s.

RAUDIXIN. (Squibb) Rauwolfia whole root. Tab. 50 mg. & 100 mg. Bot. 100s, 1000s. 100 mg. Unimat single dose carton 100s.
Use: Hypotensive & tranquilizing agent.
W/Benzydroflumethiazide, potassium chloride.
See: Rautrax-N, Tabs. (Squibb)
Rautrax-N, Modified, Tab. (Squibb)
W/Flumethiazide, pot. chloride.
See: Rautrax, Tab. (Squibb)

RAUDOLFIN. (Premo) Rauwolfia serpentina 50 mg., 100 mg./Tab. Bot. 1000s.
Use: Hypotensive agent.

RAUJA. (Table Rock) Whole root Rauwolfia serpentina 50 mg. and 100 mg./Tab. Bot. 100s, 500s.
Use: Treatment of hypertension.

RAUNEED. (Hanlon) Rauwolfia 50 mg., 100 mg./Tab. Bot. 100s.
Use: Tranquilizer.

RAUNESCINE. (Penick) An alkaloid of Rauwolfia serpentina. Under study.
Use: Tranquilizing agent.

RAUNORMINE. (Penick) 11-Desmethoxy reserpine.

RAURINE. (Westerfield) Reserpine. **Tab.** (0.1 mg., 0.25 mg.) Bot. 100s. **Delayed Action:** 0.5 mg./Ca Bot. 100s.
Use: Orally, sedative & tranquilizing agent.
W/Pentaerythritol tetranitrate.
See: Respet, Tab. (Westerfield)

RAUSERFIA. (New Eng. Phr. Co.) Rauwolfia serpentina 50 mg. or 100 mg./Tab. Bot. 100s.

RAUSERPIN. (Ferndale) Reserpine serpentina 100 mg./Tab. Bot. 100s, 1000s.
Use: Tranquilizer.

RAUTINA. (Fellows) Rauwolfia serpentina whole roo 50 & 100 mg./Tab. Bot. 1000s.
Use: Antihypertensive agent.

RAUTRAX. (Squibb) Raudixin 50 mg., flumethiazide 400 mg., pot. chloride 400 mg./Tab. Bot. 100s.
Use: Hypertension.

RAUTRAX-N. (Squibb) Standardized whole root Rauwolfia serpentina (Raudixin) 50 mg.,

bendroflumethiazide 4 mg., potassium chloride 400 mg./Cap-shaped Tab. Bot. 100s, 1000s.
Use: Hypertension.

UTRAX-N MODIFIED. (Squibb) Raudixin 50 mg., bendroflumethiazide 2 mg., KCl 400 mg./Tab. Bot. 100s.
Use: Hypertension.

UVAL. (Vale) Rauwolfia serpentina whole root 50 mg. or 100 mg./Tab. Bot. 100s, 500s, 1000s.
Use: Antihypertensive & tranquilizing agent.

UVERAT. (Kenyon) Rauwolfia serpentina whole root powder 50 mg., veratrum viride ext. eq. to total alkaloids 1.1 mg./Tab. Bot. 100s, 1000s.
Use: Hypertension.

UVERID. (Forest) Rauwolfia serpentina pwd. whole root 50 mg./Tab. Bot. 100s.
Use: Hypertension.

U-VER-TIN. (Kenyon) Rauwolfia serpentina 40 mg., veratrum viride 25 mg., rutin 20 mg., mannitol hexanitrate 30 mg./Tab. Bot. 100s, 1000s.
Use: Hypertension.

UWILOID. (Riker) Alseroxylon fraction of Rauwolfia serpentina. Tab. (2 mg.) Bot. 100s, 1000s.
Use: Hypertension.
'Hexamethonium. (Riker) Rauwiloid 1 mg., hexamethonium 250 mg./Tab. Bot. 100s.
Use: Hypertension.

UWOLFIA CANESCENS ALKALOID.
See: Harmonyl, Tab. (Abbott)

UWOLFIA SERPENTINA ACTIVE PRINCIPLES (ALKALOIDS). Deserpidine, Rescinnamine.
See: Reserpine, Inj. (Var. Mfr.)

UWOLFIA SERPENTINA ALKALOIDAL EXTRACT.
See: Alseroxylon (Var. Mfr.)

RAUWOLFIA SERPENTINA, U.S.P. XXI. Powder, Tab., U.S.P. XXI.
Use: Antihypertensive.
See: Hyper-Rauw, Tab. (Sutliff & Case)
Rau, Tab. (Scrip)
Raudixin, Tab. (Squibb)
Rauja, Tab. (Table Rock)
Raumason, Tab. (Mason)
Rauneed, Tab. (Hanlon)
Rautina, Tab. (Fellows-Testagar)
Rauval, Tab. (Vale)
Rawfola, Tab. (Foy)
Serfia, Tab. (Westerfield)
Serfolia, Tab. (Mallard)
T-Rau, Tab. (Tennessee Pharm.)
Wolfina, Tab. (Westerfield)
'Bendroflumethiazide.
See: Rautrax-N, Tab. (Squibb)
Rauzide, Tab. (Squibb)
'Bendroflumethiazide, pot. chloride (400).
See: Rautrax, Tab. (Squibb)
'Mannitol hexanitrate, rutin.
See: Maxitate W/Rauwolfia, Tab. (Pennwalt)
'Phenobarbital.
See: Raudilan PB, Tab. (Lannett)

RAUWOLSCINE. An alkaloid of *Rauwolfia canescens.* Under study.
Use: Tranquilizing agent.

RAUZIDE. (Squibb) Rauwolfia serpentina (pow.) 50 mg., bendroflumethiazide 4 mg./Tab. Bot. 100s, 1000s.
Use: Antihypertensive.

RAVOCAINE. (Cook-Waite) Propoxycaine HCl 4 mg., procaine 20 mg., levonordefrin 0.05 mg., NaCl 3 mg., acetone sodium bisulfite not more than 2 mg.; propoxycaine HCl 4 mg., procaine 20 mg., norepinephrine bitartrate equivalent to 0.033 mg. levophed base, NaCl 3 mg., acetone sodium bisulfite not more than 2 mg.; Cartridge 1.8 ml.
Use: Local anesthetic (dental).

RAWFOLA. (Foy) Rauwolfia serpentina 50 mg./Tab. Bot. 1000s.
Use: Hypotensive agent.

RAWL VITE. (Rawl) Vit. A 10,000 I.U., D 500 I.U., B-1 10 mg., B-2 5 mg., B-6 1 mg., Ca pantothenate 5 mg., nicotinamide 50 mg., C 125 mg., E 2.5 I.U./Tab. Bot. 100s.
Use: Multiple vitamin tablets.

RAWL WHOLE LIVER VITAMIN B COMPLEX. (Rawl) Whole liver 500 mg. and amino acids found in the whole liver, B-1 1 mg., B-2 2 mg., niacinamide 5 mg., choline chloride 12 mg., B-6 0.2 mg., cal. pantothenate 0.2 mg., inositol 5 mg., biotin 0.6 mcg., B-12 0.3 mcg./Cap. Bot. 100s, 500s.
Use: Deficiency of Vitamin B complex.

RAY BLOCK. (Del-Ray) Bot. 4 oz.
Use: Sunscreen.

RAY-D. (Nion) Vit. D 400 I.U., Thiamin mononitrate 1 mg. riboflavin 2 mg., niacin 10 mg., iodine 0.1 mg., calcium 375 mg., phosphorus 300 mg.,/6 Tab. Bot. 100s, 500s.
Use: Dietary supplement.

RAYDERM OINTMENT. (Velvet Pharmacal) euphorbia ext., phenyl salicylate, neatsfoot oil, olive oil, lanolin in emulsion base preserved with methyl & propylparabens Tubes 1.5 oz, Jar 1 lb.
Use: Radiation burns.

RAY-NOX. (Torch) Para-aminobenzoic acid 9.6% in a non-greasy, hydrophilic cream base. Jar 2 oz., 1 lb.
Use: Skin protection from ultraviolet rays.

• **RAYON, PURIFIED,** U.S.P. XXI.
Use: Surgical aid.

RAYTHESIN. (Raymer)
See: Propyl p-Aminobenzoate.

RAZOXANE. B.A.N. 1,2-Bis(3,5-dioxopiperazin-1-yl)propane.
Use: Antineoplastic.

RCF. (Ross) Carbohydrate free soy protein formula base—concentrated liquid, carbohydrate must be added. "as fed" 12 cal/fl oz; per liter: protein 20.0 g, fat 36.0 g, Ca 0.70 g, P 0.50 g, Na 0.32 g, K 0.77 g, Cl 0.59 g, Mg 50 mg, Zn 5.0 mg, Cu 0.50 mg, Fe 12 mg, I 0.10 mg, Mn 0.20 mg, Vit. A 2000 I.U., Vit. D 400 I.U., Vit. E 20 I.U., Vit. C 55 mg, thiamine 0.40 mg, riboflavin 0.60 mg, B-6 0.40 mg, niacin 9.0 mg., folic acid 0.10 mg, B-12 3.0 mcg, pantothenic acid 5.0 mg, biotin 30 mcg, K-1 0.10 mg.

Use: For infants unable to tolerate the amount or type of carbohydrate in conventional formulas. Carbohydrate to be added at levels appropriate for the individual infant.

REA-LO. (Whorton) Urea in water soluble moisturizing oil base. **Lotion:** 15%. Bot. 4 oz., pt. **Cream:** 30%. Jar 2 oz., 16 oz.
Use: Treatment of hyperkeratosis, dry skin conditions.

REALPHENE.
See: Acetarsone, Tab. (City Chem.)

RECINDAL. (Winthrop Products) Dextromethorphan HBr.
Use: Antitussive, decongestant.

RECORTEX. (Fellows) Adrenal cortex inj. equiv. to 100 mcg. of hydrocortisone/cc. Aqueous and lyophilized. Vial 10 cc., 50 cc.
Use: Treatment of adrenal insufficiency.

RECORTEX 2XX. (Fellows) 200 mcg./cc. Aqueous and lyophilized. Vial 10 cc., 50 cc.

RECORTEX 10X IN OIL. (Fellows) 1000 mcg./cc. Vial 10 cc.

RECOVER. (Commerce) Bot. 2.25 oz.
Use: Skin discoloration cover-up cream.

RECTACORT. (Century) Hydrocortisone acetate 10 mg., ext. belladonna 0.5%, ephedrine sulfate 0.1%, zinc oxide, boric acid, bismuth subcarbonate, balsam peru, cocoa butter. Supp. Pkg. 12s. Supp. Pkg. 12s.

RECTAL MEDICONE. (Medicone) Benzocaine 2 gr., balsam Peru 1 gr., oxyquinoline sulfate 0.25 gr., menthol 1/7 gr., zinc oxide 3 gr./Supp. Box 12s, 24s.
Use: Antiseptic & local anesthetic.

RECTAL MEDICONE-HC Suppos. (Medicone) Benzocaine 2 gr., balsam Peru 1 gr., oxyquinoline sulfate 0.25 gr., menthol 1/7 gr., zinc oxide 3 gr., hydrocortisone acetate 10 mg., cocoa butter, veg. and petrolatum oil base q.s./Supp. Box 12s.
Use: Severe anorectal inflammation.

RECTAL MEDICONE UNGUENT. (Medicone) Benzocaine 20 mg., oxyquinoline sulfate 5 mg., menthol 4 mg., zinc oxide 100 mg., balsam peru 12.5 mg., petrolatum 625 mg., lanolin 210 mg./Gm. Tubes 1.5 oz.
Use: Anorectal disorders.

RECTAL OINTMENT. (Vortech) Tube. 0.25 oz. w/applicator
Use: Antihemorrhoidal.

RECTOCAINE. (Moore Kirk) Phenol 1%, propyl-p-aminobenzoate 7%, benzyl alcohol 7%, procaine 0.5%. Amp. 5 cc.
Use: Rectally; local anesthetic.

RECTULES. (Fellows) Chloral hydrate 10 & 20 gr. Supp. in water-soluble base. Pkg. 12s.
Use: Sedative, hypnotic.

• **RED BLOOD CELLS,** U.S.P. XXI. Human red blood cells given by IV infusion.
Use: Blood replenisher.

RED CELL TAGGING SOLUTION.
See: A-C-D Solution (Squibb)

REDCEL TABLETS. (Morton) Docusate sodium 100 mg., Fe 100 mg./Tab. Bot. 100s.

RED CROSS TOOTHACHE DROPS. (Mentholatum) Eugenol 85%, alcohol 15%. Bot. 1/8 fl. oz.
Use: Topical anesthetic.

RED CROSS TOOTHACHE KIT. (Mentholatum). Complete kit containing toothache drops w/cotton pellets and tweezers.
Use: Topical anesthetic.

• **RED FERRIC OXIDE,** N.F. XVI.
Use: Pharmaceutic aid (color).

RED MERCURIC IODIDE.
Used in: Auralcaine, Liq. (Truett)

REDIPAK. (Wyeth) A special type of packaging which includes the following drugs:
Aspirin, U.S.P. 300 mg./Tab. 600 mg./Suppos.
Ativan. Lorazepam 0.5 mg., 1 mg. or 2 mg./Tab.
Chloral Hydrate 500 mg./Cap.
Codeine Sulfate Tablets. 15 mg., 30 mg., or 60 mg./Tab.
Equagesic. Meprobamate w/aspirin.
Equanil. Meprobamate 200 mg., or 400 mg./Tab.
Meperidine HCl. 50 mg./Tab.
Omnipen. Ampicillin 250 mg. or 500 mg./Cap. 25 mg./5 ml. Susp.
Penicillin G, Potassium U.S.P. 250 mg./Tab.
Pentobarbital Sod. U.S.P. 100 mg./Cap.
Pen-Vee K. Soln. Phenoxymethyl penicillin 2 mg./5 ml.
Pen-Vee K Tablets. Phenoxymethyl penicillin 2 mg., 500 mg./Tab.
Phenergan. Promethazine HCl 12.5 mg. or 25 mg./Tab.; 25 mg. or 50 mg./Suppos.
Phenobarbital. 15 mg., 30 mg., 60 mg., or 100 mg./Tab.
Secobarbital Sod. U.S.P. 100 mg./Cap.
Serax. Oxazepam 10 mg., 15 mg., 30 mg./Cap.
Unipen. Sodium nafcillin 250 mg./Cap.
Wyanoids. Suppositories.
Wygesic. Tablets.
Zactirin Compound-100. Ethoheptazine citrate w/aspirin, phenacetin and caffeine, Tabs.

REDISOL. (Merck Sharp & Dohme) Vit. B-12 (Cyanocobalamin), **Inj.:** 1000 mcg./ml. w/sod. chloride 0.83%, methylparaben 0.15%, propylparaben 0.02%, water for injection q.s. 1 ml. Vial 10 ml. **Tab.:** 50 mcg. Bot. 100s.
Use: Vitamin B-12 therapy (hematopoietic).
See also Alpha REDISOL.

REDITEMP-C. (Wyeth) Ammonium nitrate, water and special additives. Pkg. large and small sizes. 4 × 10s.
Use: For short-term topical cold application.

REDODERLEIN. (Fellows) Doederlein's bacillus (*Lactobacillus vaginalis* and *Lactobacillus crassus* 200,000/Vials (lyophilized) 5 cc. 5s.
Use: Vaginitis therapy.

REDUCTO, IMPROVED. (Arcum) Phendimetrazine bitartrate 35 mg./Tab. Bot. 100s, 1000s.

REFRESH'N. (Stanlabs) Caffeine 500 mg./Tab. Pkg. 75s.
Use: Awakener, stimulant.

REFUIN. (Roche) Under study.
Use: Antineoplastic.

GITINE. (Ciba) Phentolamine mesylate 5 mg./Vial v/mannitol 25 mg. in lyophilized form. Pkg. 2s, 6s.
Jse: Diagnostic test for pheochromocytoma.
GLAN. (Robins) Metoclopramide HCl **Inj.:** 10 ng./2 ml. Amp. 2 ml. Box 5s, 25s; 50 mg./10 ml. 3ox 25s.; Single Dose Vials 5 mg./ml. Vial 30 ml. **Syrup:** 5 mg. (as base)/5 ml. Bot. pt. Dis Co Packs 10×10s. **Tab.:** 10 mg./Tab. Bot. 100s, 500s. Dis-co Paks 100s.
Jse: Pro-motility agent for diabetic gastroparesis, prevention of nausea in emitogenic cancer chemotherapy.
GONOL. (Organon) Pyridostigmine bromide 5 ng./ml. Amp. 2 ml. Vial 5 ml. Box 25s.
Jse: Reversal agent for non-depolarizing surgical nuscle relaxants.
GROTON. (USV Labs.) Chlorthalidone 50 mg., eserpine 0.25 mg./Tab. Bot. 100s, 1000s.
Jse: Antihypertensive.
GUL-AID. (Quality Generics) **Liquid:** Docusate sodium 20 mg./5 cc. Bot. pt. **Caps.** 100 mg./Cap. 3ot. 100s, 1000s.
Jse: Laxative.
GUTOL. (Plough) Docusate sodium 100 mg./Tab. 3ox 30s, 60s, 90s.
Jse: Stool softener.
IDAMINE INJ. (Reid-Provident) Dimenhydrinate 50 ng./cc. Vial 1 ml., 10 ml.
LA. (Schering) Carisoprodol 350 mg./Tab. Bot. 100s.
Jse: Muscle relaxant.
LAXIN. A purified ovarian hormone of pregnancy obtained from sows) responsible for pubic elaxation or separation of the symphysis pubis in nammals.
See: Lutrexin, Tab. (Hynson, Westcott & Dunning)
LEFACT TRH. (Hoechst) Protirelin 0.5 mg./ml. Amp. 1 ml. Box 5s.
Jse: Diagnosis of thyroid function.
-LIEVE. (Faraday) Analgesic. Cap. 30s.
ELOMYCIN. USAN. A basic macrolide antibiotic produced by a variant strain of *Streptomyces hygroscopicus.*
Jse: Antibacterial antibiotic.
M COUGH MEDICINE. (Last) Dextromethorphan HBr 5 mg./5 ml. Bot. 3 oz., 6 oz.
Jse: Antitussive.
MEFLIN. Dimefline Hydrochloride, B.A.N.
MIVOX. (Janssen) Lorcainide HCl.
Jse: Cardiac anti-rhythmic.
MOVING CREAM. (O'Leary) Specially formulated o remove Covermark. Bot. 4 oz., 7.5 oz.
EMOXIPRIDE. USAN.
Jse: Antipsychotic.
MSED. (Du Pont) Promethazine HCl 50 mg./Tab. 3ot. 100s.
Jse: Non-barbituate sleeping agent.
NACIDIN. (Guardian) Antilithiatic agent composed of lactones, anhydrides and acid salts of edible, multivalent organic acids including gluconic and citric. Bot. 25 Gm. 6s; 300 Gm.
Use: Bladder irrigation to aid removal of stones composed of calcium and magnesium phosphate, indwelling catheter irrigation.
RENALGIN. (Glaxo) Atropine sulfate 0.03 mg., hyoscyamine 0.03 mg., methenamine 41 mg., salol 18 mg., benzoic acid 4.5 mg., methylene blue 5.4 mg./Tab. Bot. 100s, 1000s.
Use: Urinary antibacterial; antispasmodic; analgesic.
RENALTABS-S.C. (Fellows) Methenamine 40.8 mg., benzoic acid 4.5 mg., phenyl salicylate 18.1 mg., hyoscyamine sulfate 1/2000 gr., atropine sulfate 0.03 mg., methylene blue 5.4 mg., gelsemium 6.1 mg./Tab. Bot. 1000s.
RENAMIN. (Travenol) Sterile hypertonic solution of essential and non-essential amino acids. Bot. 250 ml., 500 ml.
Use: Parenteral nutritional support.
RENANOLONE. 3α-Hydroxypregnane-11,20-dione.
Use: Steroid anesthetic.
RENBU. (Wren) Butabarbital sod. 32.4 mg./Tab. Bot. 100s, 1000s.
RENELATE. (Fellows) Methenamine mandelate 1 Gm./E.C. Tab. Bot. 100s, 500s, 5000s.
Use: Urinary antiseptic.
RENESE. (Pfipharmecs) Polythiazide 1 mg., 2 mg., 4 mg./Tab. Bot. 100s, 1000s.
Use: Diuretic, antihypertensive.
RENESE-R TABLETS. (Pfipharmecs) Polythiazide 2 mg., reserpine 0.25 mg./Tab. Bot. 100s, 1000s.
Use: Antihypertensive.
RENGASIL. (Geigy) Pirprofen. Pending release.
Use: Anti-inflammatory.
RENNIN. Milk-curdling enzyme obtained from the fourth stomach of the calf.
RENOFORM.
See: Epinephrine, Preps. (Var. Mfr.)
RENOGRAFIN-60,-76. (Squibb) **-60:** Meglumine diatrizoate 52%, sod. diatrizoate 8%. Vial 10 ml., 100 ml., 10s; 30 ml., 50 ml., 25s. **-76:** Meglumine diatrizoate 66%, sod. diatrizoate 10%. Vial 20 ml., 50 ml., 25s; 100 ml., 200 ml., 10s.
Use: Contrast medium.
RENO-M-DIP. (Squibb) Meglumine diatrizoate Inj. 30% for drip infusion pyelography. Bot. 300 cc. Also w/soln. admin. sets. (Formerly Renografin-Dip)
Use: Drip infusion pyelography.
RENO-M-30. (Squibb) Meglumine diatrizoate 30%. Vial 50 cc., 100 cc. Box 25s.
Use: Retrograde pyelography.
RENO-M-60. (Squibb) Meglumine diatrizoate 60%. Vial 10 ml., 30 ml., 50 ml., 100 ml. 150 ml. Box 25s.
Use: Radiopaque contrast agent.
RENOQUID. (Glenwood) Sulfacytine 250 mg./Tab. Bot. 100s. Therapy paks 41s. Unit dose 100s.
Use: Sulfonamide therapy for urinary infection.
REN-O-SAL. (Salsbury) 3-Nitro-4-hydroxyphenylarsonic acidroxarsone 36 mg./Tab. Bot. 100s, 250s, 1000s, 10,000s.
Use: Growth promotant and coccidiosis treatment.
RENO-SED. (Vita Elixir) Methenamine 2 gr., salol 0.5 gr., methylene blue 1/10 gr., benzoic acid 1/8 gr., atropine sulfate 1/1000 gr., hyoscyamine sulfate 1/2000 gr./Tab.
Use: Genito-urinary antisepsis & sedation.

RENOVIST INJ. (Squibb) Diatrizoate methylglucamine 34.3%, sodium diatrizoate 35%, equivalent to 59.7% base which contains 62% iodine, sol. contains 37% firmly bound iodine. Vial 50 ml. Box 25s.
Use: Radiopaque medium.

RENOVIST II. (Squibb) Sodium diatrizoate 29.1%, meglumine diatrizoate 28.5%. Inj. Vial 30 cc., 60 cc. Box 25s.
Use: Radiopaque medium.

RENOVUE-65. (Squibb) Iodamide meglumide 65%, organically bound iodine 30% w/edetate disodium. Vial 50 ml.
Use: Radiopaque urographic contrast agent.

RENOVUE-DIP. (Squibb) Iodamide meglumide 24%. Infusion Bot. 300 ml.
Use: Radiopaque contrast agent for drip infusion pyelography.

RENPAP. (Wren) Acetaminophen 4 gr., salicylamide 3 gr., caffeine ⅔ gr., allylisobutylbarbituric acid ¾ gr./Tab. Bot. 100s, 1000s.

RENTUSS. (Wren) Dextromethorphan HBr 10 mg., guaifenesin 100 mg., phenylephrine HCl 5 mg., phenylpropanolamine HCl 25 mg., chlorpheniramine maleate 2 mg., acetaminophen 300 mg./Tab. Bot. 100s, 500s, 1000s. Syr: same except guaifenesin 50 mg., acetaminophen 120 mg./5 cc. pt., gal.

REPAN. (Everett) Butalbital 50 mg., caffeine 40 mg., acetaminophen 325 mg./Tab. Bot. 100s.

REPEL. (Wisconsin)
Lotion 2 oz. Non-aerosol Spray 4 oz.
Use: Insect repellent.

REPENDO. (Standex) Ascorbic acid 100 mg., menadione 0.1 mg./Cap. Bot. 100s.
Use: Treatment of capillary wall permeability.

REPEN-VK. (Reid-Provident) Penicillin V potassium 250 mg. Tab. Bot. 100s, 500s.
Use: Antibiotic.

REPODRAL SOLUTION. (Winthrop Products) Stibophen.
Use: Antibilharziasis.

REP-PRED 40. (Central) Methylprednisolone acetate 40 mg. polyethylene glycol 4000 29 mg., sodium chloride 8.7 mg./ml. Vial 5 ml.

REP-PRED 80. (Central) Methylprednisolone acetate 80 mg., polyethylene glycol 4000 28 mg., sodium chloride 8.5 mg./ml. Vial 5 ml.

REPRIEVE. (Mayer) Caffeine, alk. 32 mg., salicylamide 225 mg., B-1 50 mg., homatropine methylbromide 0.5 mg./Tab. Bot. 8s, 16s.
Use: Analgesic.

• **REPROMICIN.** USAN.
Use: Antibacterial.

• **REPROTEROL HYDROCHLORIDE.** USAN.
Use: Bronchodilator.

REPTILASE-R. (Abbott) Reptilase-R coagulation test system. Tests 10/Vial. Box 3 Vials
Use: Investigation of fibrin formation & disturbances in fibrin formation.

REQUA'S CHARCOAL TABLETS. (Requa) Wood charcoal 10 gr./Tab. Pkg. 50s. Can 125s.
Use: Flatulence, diarrhea.

RESA. (Vita Elixir) Reserpine 0.25 mg./Tab.
Use: Tranquilizing & antihypertensive agent.

RESCINNAMINE. Methyl 18β-Hydroxy-11,17 α-dimthoxy-3β20α-yohimban-16β-carboxylate 3,4,5-Trimeth-oxycinnamate (Ester). Methyl 0-(3,4,5-trimthoxy-cinnamoyl)reserpate.
Use: Tranquilizer; hypotensive.
See: Anaprel.
Cinnasil, Graduals (Amfre-Grant)
Moderil, Tab. (Pfizer Laboratories)

RESCON CAPSULES. (Ion) Methscopolamine nitrate 2.5 mg., chlorpheniramine maleate 8 mg., phenylpropanolamine 50 mg./T.R. Cap. Bot. 100s.
Use: Drying agent for excessive secretions, antihistaminic.

RESCON-GG CAPSULES. (Ion) Pseudoephedrine HCl 120 mg., chlorpheniramine maleate 8 mg., guaifenesin 200 mg./Cap. Bot. 100s.
Use: Eustachian tube decongestant.

RESCON-GG LIQUID. (Ion) Phenylephedrine HCl 5 mg., guaifenesin 100 mg./5 ml. Bot. 4 oz.
Use: Decongestant.

RESCON JR. (Ion) Pseudoephedrine HCl 60 mg., chlorpheniramine maleate 4 mg./Cap. Bot. 100s.
Use: Antihistamine, decongestant.

RESCON LIQUID. (Ion) Phenylpropanolamine HCl 12.5 mg., chlorpheniramine maleate 2 mg./5 ml. Bot. 4 oz.
Use: Decongestant, antihistaminic.

RESERJEN. (Jenkins) Reserpine 0.25 mg./Tab. Bot. 1000s.

RESERPANEED. (Hanlon) Reserpine 0.25 mg./Tab. Bot. 100s, 1000s.
Use: Tranquilizer.

• **RESERPINE,** U.S.P. XXI. Elixir, Inj. Tab., U.S.P. XXI. Yohimban-16-carboxylic acid, 11,17-dimethoxy-18-[(3,4,5-trimethoxybenzyol)oxy]-, methyl ester. Pure alkaloid from Rauwolfia serpentina.
Use: Antihypertensive.
See: Arcum R-S, Tab. (Arcum)
Broserpine, Tab. (Brothers)
De Serpa, Tabs. (De Leon)
Elserpine, Tab. (Canright)
Hyperine, Tab. (Sutliff & Case)
Maso-Serpine, Tab. (Mason)
Rauloydin, Tab. (Reid-Provident)
Raurine, Tab. (Westerfield)
Rauserpin, Tab. (Ferndale)
Reserjen, Tab. (Jenkins)
Reserpaneed, Tab. (Hanlon)
Serpalan, Tab. (Lannett)
Serpanray, Tab., Amp. (Panray)
Serpasil Preps. (Ciba)
Serpate, Tab. (Vale)
Serpena, Tab. (Haag)
Sertabs, Tab. (Table Rock)
Sertina, Tab. (Fellows-Testagar)
SK-Reserpine, Tab. (SmithKline)
Tensin (Standex)
T-Serp, Tab. (Tennessee)
Vio-Serpine, Tab. (Rowell)
Zepine, Tab. (Foy)

SERPINE W/COMBINATIONS
See: Aquapres-R, Tab. (Coastal)
Demi-Regroton, Tab. (USV Labs.)
Diupres, Tab. (Merck Sharp & Dohme)
Dralserp, Tab. (Lemmon)
Harbolin, Tab. (Arcum)
Hyd-Res-Ine, Tab. (Quality Generics)
Hydromox R, Tab. (Lederle)
Hydropres-25 or -50, Tab. (Merck Sharp & Dohme)
Hydroserp, Tab. (Zenith)
Hydroserpine, Tab. (Geneva)
Hydroserpine Plus, Tab. (Zenith)
Hydroserpine No. 1, Tab. (Zenith)
Hydroserpine No. 2,3,4, Tab. (Zenith)
Hydrotensin-Plus, Tab. (Mayrand)
Hydrotensin-50, Tab. (Mayrand)
Hyperserp, Tab. (Elder)
Mallopress, Tab. (Mallard)
Metatensin, Tab. (Merrell Dow)
Naquival, Tab. (Schering)
Regroton, Tab. (USV Labs.)
Renese-R, Tab. (Pfizer Laboratories)
Salutensin, Tab. (Bristol)
Ser-Ap-Es, Tab. (Ciba)
Serapine, Tab. (Cenci)
Serpahyde TM, Tab. (Wolins)
Serpasil-Apresoline, Tab. (Ciba)
Serpasil-Esidrix, Tab. (Ciba)
Thia-Serp-25, Tab. (Robinson)
Thia-Serp-50, Tab. (Robinson)
Thia-Serpa-Zine, Tab. (Robinson)
Unipres, Tab. (Reid-Provident)

ESERPINE AND HYDROCHLOROTHIAZIDE TABLETS. U.S.P. XXI.
Use: Antihypertensive.

ESERPINE, HYDRALAZINE HCl and HYDROCHLORTHIAZIDE, U.S.P. XXI.
Use: Antihypertensive.

SINOL MEDICINAL OINTMENT. (Mentholatum) Zinc oxide 12%, calamine 6%, resorcinol 2% in a lanolin and petrolatum base. Jar 3.5 oz., 1.25 oz.
Use: Skin protectant, analgesic.

SIN UPTAKE KIT WITH LIOTHYRONINE I-125 BUFFER SOLUTION.
See: Thyrostat-3 (Squibb)

ESINS, ANTACID.
See: Polyamine methylene Resins.

SISTON-C. (CMC) Vit. B-1 1.5 mg., B-6 0.1 mg., cal. pantothenate 1 mg., B-2 2 mg., yeast 155 mg., niacinamide 10 mg./Cap. Bot. 100s, 250s, 1000s.

SOCHIN. Chloroquine Phosphate, B.A.N.

SONIUM-A. (Winthrop Products) Sodium polystyrene sulfonate.
Use: Hyperkalemia.

SORCIN.
See: Resorcinol (Var. Mfr.)

ESORCINOL, U.S.P. XXI. Compound Ointment, U.S.P. XXI. 1,3-Benzenediol.
Use: Local antifungal; keratolytic.

ESORCINOL AND SULFUR LOTION. U.S.P. XXI.
Use: Scabicide, parasiticide, antifungal.

RESORCINOL W/COMBINATIONS
See: Acne-Aid Cream (Steifel)
Acnomel, Cake, Cream. (Menley & James)
Bicozene, Cream (Ex-Lax)
Biscolan, Supp. (Lannett)
Black and White Ointment, (Plough)
Castaderm, Prep. (Lannett)
Cenac Lotion (Central)
Clearasil, Stick (Vicks)
Derma-Cover, Liq. (Scrip)
Derma-Cover-Hc, Liq. (Scrip)
Doctient, Supp. (Suppositoria)
Doctient HC, Supp. (Suppositoria)
Exzit, Creme & Lotion (Miles Pharm)
Fusinol, Liq. (Westerfield)
Hydro Surco, Lot. (Alma)
Komed, Lot. (Barnes-Hind)
Lanacane Creme (Combe)
Mazon, Oint. (Thayer)
Mild Komed, Lot. (Barnes-Hind)
RA Lotion (Medco)
Rezamid Lotion (Dermick)
Resulin, Oint., Lot. (Almay)
Resulin-F, Cream (Almay)
Serp, Preps. (Scrip)
Tackle, Gel (Colgate-Palmolive)
Thera-Blem, Cream (Noxell)
Therac, Lot. (C & M Pharm.)
Vegoil W/Isocaine, Oint. (Philips Roxane)
Zinc Boric Lotion, Liq. (Emerson)

• **RESORCINOL MONOACETATE,** U.S.P. XXI. (Various Mfr.) Resorcin acetate.
Use: Antiseborrheic; keratolytic.
See: Euresol, Liq. (Knoll)
W/Salicylic acid, ethyl alcohol, castor oil.
See: Resorcitate w/oil, Lot. (Almay)
W/Salicylic acid, LCD, betanaphthol, castor oil, isopropyl alcohol.
See: Neomark, Liq. (C&M Pharm.)

RESORCINOLPHTHALEIN SODIUM.
See: Fluorescein Sodium, U.S.P. XXI. (Var. Mfr.)

W/Oil. Resorcinol monoacetate 1.5%, salicylic acid 1.5% castor oil 1.5%, ethyl alcohol 81%. Bot. 8 fl. oz.
Use: Scalp lotion.

RESOTREN. Cloquinate, B.A.N.

RESPAIRE-60. (Laser) Pseudoephedrine HCl 60 mg. guaifenesin 200 mg./S.R. Cap. Bot. 100s, 1000s.
Use: Decongestant, expectorant.

RESPAIRE-SR-120. (Laser) Pseudoephedrine HCl 120 mg., guaifenesin 250 mg./S.R. Cap. Bot. 100s, 1000s.
Use: Decongestant, expectorant.

RESPBID. (Boehringer Ingelheim) Theophylline anhydrous 250 mg. or 500 mg./Tab. Bot. 100s.
Use: Bronchodilator.

RESPENYL. Guaiphenesin, B.A.N.

RESPIHALER DECADRON PHOSPHATE. (Merck Sharp & Dohme)
See: Decadron phosphate, respihaler (Merck Sharp & Dohme)

RESPINOL-G TABLETS. (Misemer) Phenylephrine HCl 5 mg., phenylpropanolamine HCl 45 mg., guaifenesin 200 mg./Tab.
Use: Temporary relief of nasal congestion, respiratory allergies.

RESPINOL LA CAPSULES. (Misemer) Phenylpropanolamine HCl 75 mg., phenylephrine HCl 10 mg., guaifenesin 300 mg./L.A. Cap.
Use: Relief of symptoms of bronchitis, bronchial asthma, emphysema, sinusitis.

RESPIRATORY VACCINE. (Various Mfr.) Cold Vaccines.

RES-Q. (Boyle) Activated charcoal 50%, magnesium hydroxide 25%, tannic acid 25% (Universal antidote). Pkg. 0.5 oz.
Use: Universal antidote for accidental poisoning.

REST EASY. (Walgreen) Acetaminophen, 600 mg., ephedrine sulfate, 8 mg., d-methorphan HBr, 15 mg., doxylamine succinate 75 mg./30 ml. Bot. 6 oz.
Use: Decongestant, antihistamine, analgesic, antitussive.

RESTIME. (Stanlabs) Bot. 14s.

RESTORA. (Circle) Methyltestosterone 2.0 mg., ethinyl estradiol 0.01 mg., Vit. A 5000 I.U., D 400 I.U., E 10 I.U., B-1 2 mg., B-2 2 mg., B-6 0.3 mg., B-12 1 mcg., C30 mg., nicotinamide 20 mg., Ca panothenate 3 mg., iron 10 mg., Cu 0.2 mg., Mo 0.3 mg., Zn, Mg 5 mg., K 2 mg., iodine 0.15 mg./Cap. Bot. 100s.
Use: Vitamin, mineral supplement.

RESTORIL. (Sandoz) Temazepam 15 mg. or 30 mg./Cap. Bot. 100s, 500s. ControlPak 25s. SandoPak (unit dose) 100s.
Use: Hypnotic, sedative.

RETADIAMONE. (Rocky Mtn.) Testosterone enanthate 90 mg., estradiol valerate 4 mg./cc. Vial 10 cc. In sesame oil. Also available in double strength. Vial 5 cc.
Use: Androgen & estrogen therapy.

RETANDROS. (Rocky Mtn.) Testosterone enanthate 200 mg./cc. in sesame oil. Vial 10 cc.
Use: Androgen therapy.

RETCIN. Erythromycin, B.A.N.

RETENEMA 17-VALERATE. Betamethasone, B.A.N.

RETESTRIN. (Rocky Mtn.) Estradiol-17 valerate in sesame oil 10 mg., 40 mg./cc. Vial 10 cc.
Use: Amenorrhea, menopausal syndrome.

RETET. (Reid-Provident) Tetracycline HCl 250 mg./Cap. Bot. 100s, 1000s.
Use: Broad-spectrum antibiotic.

RETET-500. (Reid-Provident) Tetracycline HCl 500 mg./Cap. Bot. 100s.
Use: Broad-spectrum antibiotic.

RETICULEX. (Lilly) Vit. B-12 10 mcg., C 50 mg., folic acid 0.3 mg., ferrous sulfate 75 mg., liver-stomach concentrate 222 mg./Pulvule. Bot. 100s.
Use: Orally, anemias.

RETICULOGEN. (Lilly) Vit. B-1 5 mg., B-12 20 mcg./1 ml. Also sod. bisulfite 0.1%, phenol 0.5%. **Vial.** 5 ml. **Fortified:** Vit. B-1 5 mg., B-12 40 mcg./ml. Vial 5 ml.
Use: I.M.; anemias.

RETIN-A CREAM. (Ortho) Tretinoin 0.1% or 0.05% w isopropyl myristate, polyoxyl 40 stearate, stearyl alcohol, stearic acid, xanthan gum, sorbic acid, butylated hydroxytoluene. Tube 20 Gm., 45 Gm.
Use: Acne treatment.

RETIN-A GEL. (Ortho) Tretinoin 0.01% or 0.025% droxypropyl cellulose, butylated hydroxytoluene, alcohol 90% w/w. Tube 15 Gm., 45 Gm.
Use: Acne treatment.

RETIN-A LIQUID. (Ortho) Tretinoin (retinoic acid, V min A acid) 0.05%, polyethylene glycol 400, butylated hydroxytoluene, and alcohol 55%. Bot. ml.
Use: Acne treatment.

RETINOIC ACID. Tretinoin, U.S.P. XXI.
Use: Keralotytic.
See: Retin A Prods. (Ortho)

ALL TRANS-RETINOIC ACID. Tretinoin, U.S.P. XX

RETINOL. B.A.N. 3,7-Dimethyl-9-(2,6,6-trimethyl-clohex-1-enyl)nona-2,4,6,8-all-trans-tetraen-1-ol.
See: Vitamin A alcohol.

REVONAL. Methaqualone, B.A.N.

REVS CAFFEINE T.D. CAPSULES. (Vitarine) Caffe 250 mg./Cap. Bot. 15s.
Use: Combat drowsiness, fatigue, restore mental alertness.

REXAHISTINE. (Econo-Rx) Phenylephrine HCl 5 m chlorpheniramine maleate 1 mg., menthol 1 mg., sodium bisulfite 0.1%, alcohol 5%/5 ml. Bot. Gal
Use: Decongestant.

REXAHISTINE DH. (Econo-Rx) Codeine phosphate mg., phenylephrine HCl 10 mg., chlorpheniramine maleate 2 mg., menthol 1 mg., alcohol 5%/5 ml. Bot. Gal.
Use: Relief of coughs due to cold and allergy.

REXAHISTINE EXPECTORANT. (Econo-Rx) Code phosphate 10 mg., phenylephrine HCl 10 mg., chlorpheniramine maleate 2 mg., guaifenesin 100 mg., menthol 1 mg., alcohol 5%/5 ml. Bot. Gal.
Use: Expectorant.

REXIGEN. (Ion) Phendimetrazine tartrate 35 mg./T Bot. 100s.
Use: Anorexiant.

REXOLATE. (Hyrex) Sod. thiosalicylate 50 mg./cc. Vial 30 cc.
Use: Antipyretic, analgesic.

REZAMID LOTION. (Dermik) Sulfur 5%, resorcinol 2%, parachlorometaxylenol 0.5% w/alcohol 28.5 in flesh-tinted base. Bot. 2 oz.
Use: Acne, oily skin.

REZIDE. (Edwards) Reserpine 0.1 mg., hydralazine HCl 25 mg., hydrochlorothiazide 15 mg./Tab. Bot 100s, 1000s.
Use: Diuretic, antihypertensive.

RF LATEX TEST. (Laboratory Diagnostics) Latex slide test for rheumatoid factor. Kit. 100s.
Use: Rapid latex agglutination test for the qualitative screening and semi-quantitative deter nation of rheumatoid factor.

R-GEN. (Owen) Purified water, amphoteric 2, hydrolyz animal protein, lauramine oxide, methylparaben,

benzalkonium chloride, tetrasodium, EDTA, propylparaben, fragrance. Bot. 8 oz.
Use: Protein hair repair shampoo.

GEN ELIXIR. (Goldline) Iodinated glycerol. Bot. pt.
Use: Mucolytic expectorant.

HCTZ-H. (Lederle) Reserpine 0.1 mg., hydrochlorothiazide 15 mg., hydralazine HCl 25 mg./Tab. Bot. 100s, 500s.
Use: Hypertension treatment.

EABAN. (Leeming) **Tabs.:** Colloidal activated attapulgite 600 mg./Tab. Blister 12s. **Liquid:** Colloidal activated attapulgite 4.2 Gm./oz. Bot. 5.5 oz.
Use: Diarrhea treatment.

EOMACRODEX. (Pharmacia) Dextran 40. A 10% solution in normal saline or in 5% dextrose in water. Bot. 500 ml.
Use: Plasma expander, adjunctive therapy in shock, prophylaxis therapy against venous thrombosis and pulmonary embolism.

EUMASAL. (Jenkins) Sod. salicylate 5 gr., potassium iodide 1 gr., ext. gelsemium 0.25 gr., ext. cimicifuga ⅛ gr./Tab. Bot. 1000s.

EUMATEX. (Wampole) Latex agglutination test for the qualitative detection and quantitative determination of rheumatoid factor in serum.. Kit 100s.
Use: An aid in the diagnosis of rheumatoid arthritis.

EUMATON. (Wampole) Two-minute hemagglutination slide test for the qualitative and quantitative determination of rheumatoid factor in serum or synovial fluid. Test Kits 20s, 50s, 150s.
Use: An aid in the diagnosis of rheumatoid arthritis.

INALL DROPS. (Scherer) Phenylephrine HCl 0.25%. Bot. 1 oz.
Use: Nasal decongestant.

INALL SPRAY. (Scherer) Phenylephrine HCl 0.25%. Bot. 1 oz.
Use: Nasal decongestant.

INALL 10. (Scherer) Phenylephrine HCl 0.2%. Drop. Bot. 1 oz.
Use: Nasal decongestant.

INDECON. (McGregor) Phenylpropanolamine HCl 75 mg./Sustained release Cap. Dye Free. Bot 60s.
Use: Decongestant, bronchodilator.

INEX D. LAY. (Lemmon) Acetaminophen 300 mg., salicylamide 300 mg., phenylpropanolamine HCl 60 mg., chlorpheniramine maleate 4 mg./Tab. Bot. 100s, 1000s.
Use: Cold preparation.

INIHAB JR. (Bowman) Phenyelephrine HCl 2.5 mg., chlorpheniramine maleate 1 mg./Tab. Bot. 100s, 1000s.
Use: Nasal decongestant, antihistaminic.

INOCAPS. (Ferndale) Aspirin 162 mg., acetaminophen 162 mg., phenylpropanolamine HCl 20 mg./Cap. Bot. 100s.
Use: Analgesic, decongestant and antipyretic.

INOGESIC. (Vale) Phenylephrine HCl 5 mg., chlorpheniramine maleate 2 mg., salicylamide 250 mg., acetaminophen 150 mg./Tab. Bot. 100s, 500s, 1000s.

RHINOGESIC-GG. (Vale) Phenylephrine HCl 5 mg., chlorpheniramine maleate 2 mg., salicylamide 250 mg., acetaminophen 150 mg., guaifenesin 100 mg./Tab. Bot. 100s, 500s, 1000s.

RHINOGESIC JUNIOR. (Vale) Phenylephrine HCl 2 mg., Chrlorpheniramine maleate 1 mg., Salicylamide 90 mg., acetaminophen 60 mg./Tab. Bot. 100s, 500s.

RHINOLAR. (McGregor) Phenylpropanolamine HCl 75 mg., chlorpheniramine maleate 8 mg., methscopalamine nitrate 2.5 mg./Cap. Dye Free. Bot. 60s. Sustained release.
Use: Antihistaminic, decongestant, antisecretory.

RHINOLAR-EX. (McGregor) Phenylpropanolamine HCl 75 mg., chlorpheniramine maleate 8 mg./Cap. Dye Free. Bot. 60s.
Use: Antihistamine, decongestant, sustained release.

RHINOLAR-EX 12. (McGregor) Phenylpropanolamine HCl 75 mg., chlorpheniramine maleate 12 mg./Cap. Dye Free. Bot. 60s.
Use: Antihistaminic, decongestant, sustained release.

RHINOSYN. (Comatic) Pseudoephedrine HCl 120 mg., chlorpheniramine maleate 10 mg./Sust. Released Cap. Bot. 100s.
Use: Antihistamine, decongestant.

RHINOSYN-DM. (Comatic) Dextromethorphan HBr 15 mg., pseudoephedrine HCl 30 mg., chlorpheniramine maleate 2 mg./5 ml. w/alcohol 1.4%. Bot. 4 oz.
Use: Antitussive, decongestant, antihistamine.

RHINOSYN-PD. (Comatic) Chlorpheniramine maleate 2 mg., pseudoephedrine HCl 30 mg./5 ml. w/alcohol 1.2%. Bot. 4 oz.
Use: Antihistamine, decongestant.

RHINOSYN SYRUP. (Comatic) Pseudoephedrine HCl 60 mg., chlorpheniramine maleate 4 mg. /5 ml. No artificial additives. Bot. Pt.
Use: Antihistamine, decongestant.

RHINOSYN-X. (Comatic) Guaifenesin 100 mg., dextromethorphan HBr 10 mg., pseudoephedrine HCl 30 mg./5 ml. w/ alcohol 7.5%. Bot. 4 oz.
Use: Expectorant, antitussive, decongestant.

RHODANATE.
See: Potassium Thiocyanate

RHODANIDE. More commonly rhodanate, same as thiocyanate.
See: Potassium thiocyanate.

RhoGAM. (Ortho Diagnostic) Rho (D) immune globulin (human). Pkg. of single dose vials in 25s, 72s. Single Dose Vials, Pkg. 6s.
Use: Prevention of Rh hemolytic disease of the newborn.

• **RHO (D) IMMUNE GLOBULIN,** U.S.P. XXI.
See: Gamulin Rh, Vial (Parke-Davis)

RHUBAMINT ELIXIR. (Blue Line) Glycerinated, alkaline, aqueous ext. fl. rhubarb and hydrastis, spirits of cinnamon and peppermint w/potassium bicarbonate, alcohol 3%. pt., gal.

RHUBARB AND SODA MIXTURE. (Lannett) Bot. pt., gal.

RHUBARB AND SODA TABLETS. (Lannett) Tr. nux vomica 5 min., pow. rhubarb 2 gr., sod. bicarb. 5 gr., pow. ipecac 0.25 gr., oil peppermint qs./Tab. Bot. 1000s, 5000s.

RHUEX. (Kay) Zirconium oxide 4.5%, calamine 6%, zinc oxide 4%, Actamer 0.1%. Bot. 4 oz., 16 oz., gal.
Use: Itching, discomfort due to poison ivy, oak or sumac; insect bites, sunburn, and minor skin irritations.

RHULIGEL. (Lederle) Phenylcarbinol 2%, menthol 0.3%, camphor 0.3%, alcohol 31%. Tube 2 oz.
Use: Analgesic-anesthetic gel.

RHUS-ALL. (Barry) Triple antigen against poison ivy, oak or sumac. Multiple dose vial 5 cc.

RHUS TOX ANTIGEN. (Lemmon) Poison ivy extract 40 mg./ml. Vial 1 ml. Box 4s.
Use: Antigen against poison ivy.

RHUTOX LOTION. (Blue Line) Lead acetate, grindelia, echinacea in alcohol. Bot. 4 oz., 1 pt., 1 gal.
Use: Antiseptic skin preparation.

• **RIBAMINOL.** USAN. Ribonucleic acid compd. w/2-(diethylamino)-ethanole. Under study.
Use: Learning and memory enhancer.

• **RIBOFLAVIN,** U.S.P. XXI. Inj., Tab. U.S.P. XXI. Vit. B-2, Vit. G, yellow enzyme, Lactoflavin.
W/Nicotinamide. (Lilly) Riboflavin 5 mg., nicotinamide 200 mg./cc. Amp. 1 cc., Box 100s.
Use: I.M., I.V.; Vitamin B therapy.
W/Vitamins.
See: Vitamin Preparations

• **RIBOFLAVIN-5'-PHOSPHATE SODIUM,** U.S.P. XXI.

RIBOFLAVIN, METHYLOL.

• **RIBOPRINE.** USAN. N-(3-Methyl-2-butenyl) adrenosin.
Use: Antineoplastic.

RIBOTEX. (Pasadena Research) Vit. B-1 100 mg., B-2 10 mg., B-6 10 mg., niacinamide 75 mg./cc. Vial 10 cc.

RIBOZYME INJECTION. (Fellows) Riboflavin-5-Phosphate Sodium 50 mg./cc. Vial 10 cc.

RICINOLEATE, CALCIUM.
See: Pthalox, Tab. (Sutliff & Case)

RICINOLEATE SODIUM.
See: Preceptin, Gel. (Ortho)

RICOLON SOLUTION. (Winthrop Products) Ricolon concentrate.
Use: Leucocytotic preparation.

RID. (Pfipharmecs) Piperonyl butoxide 3.0%, pyrethrins 0.3%, petroleum distillate 1.2%, benzyl alcohol 2.4%. Bot. 2 oz., 4 oz.
Use: Pediculicide.

RID-A-COL. (Panray) Chlorpheniramine maleate 2 mg., aspirin 390 mg., caffeine 30 mg./Tab. Bot. 100s, 1000s.
Use: Antihistamine, analgesic.

RID-A-COL "D". (Panray) Chloraphenіramine 2 mg., aspirin 288.8 mg., caffeine 32.4 mg., phenylephrine 10 mg./Tab. Bot. 1000s.
Use: Antihistamine.

RID-A-COLD. (Panray) Chlorpheniramine maleate mg., asprin 388.8 mg., caffeine 32.4 mg./Tab. Bo 1000s.
Use: Antihistaminic.

RIDAURA CAPSULES. (SmithKline) Auranofin 3 mg./Cap. Bot. 60s.
Use: Oral gold product for management of rheumatoid arthritis.

RIFADIN. (Merrell Dow) Rifampin 150 mg. /Cap. Bo 30s. 300 mg./Cap. Bot. 30s, 60s, 100s.
Use: Antibiotic for treatment of pulmonary tuberculosis and meningococcal carriers.

RIFAMATE. (Merrell Dow) Rifampin 300 mg., isoniazid 150 mg./Cap. Bot. 60s.
Use: Pulmonary tuberculosis treatment.

• **RIFAMIDE.** USAN.
Use: Antibacterial.

RIFAMPICIN. B.A.N. 3-(4-Methylpiperazin-1-yliminomethyl)rifamycin SV.
Use: Antibiotic.
See: Rifadin.
Rimactane.

• **RIFAMPIN,** U.S.P. XXI. Cap., U.S.P. XXI. Hydrazor 3-(4-Methyl-piperazinylimino-methyl rifamycin SV.
Use: Antibacterial (tuberculostatic).
See: Rifadin, Cap. (Merrell Dow)
Rifomycin (Var. Mfr.)
Rimactane, Cap. (Ciba)

• **RIFAMPIN AND ISONIAZID CAPSULES.** U.S.P. XXI.

RIFAMYCIN. B.A.N. Rifamycin SV, an antibiotic produced by certain strains of *Streptomyces mediterranei.* 3-[[(4-Methyl-1-piperazinyl)imino]-methyl]-.
See: Rifampin, U.S.P. XXI.

• **RIFAPENTINE.** USAN.
Use: Antibacterial.

RIFOCIN-M. Rifamide, B.A.N.

RIL-SWEET. (Plough) Sodium saccharin sodium 3.3 Bot. 4 oz.
Use: Artificial sweetener.

RIMACTANE. (Ciba) Rifampin 300 mg./Cap. Bot. 3 60s, 100s.
Use: Pulmonary tuberculosis.

RIMACTANE/INH. (Ciba) Dual pack: 60 Rimactane 300 mg./Cap. & 30 Isoniazid 300 mg./Tab.
Use: Treatment of tuberculosis.

• **RIMANTADINE HCl.** USAN. Alpha-methyl-1-adama tanemethylamine HCl.
Use: Antiviral.

RIMIFON. Isoniazid, B.A.N.

RIMITEROL. B.A.N. erythro-3,4-Dihydroxy-α-(2-pipe dyl)benzyl alcohol.
Use: Bronchodilator.

• **RIMITEROL HYDROBROMIDE.** USAN. α-(3,4-Di droxy-phenyl)-2-piperidinemethanol HBr.
Use: Bronchodilator.

RIMSO-50. (Research Industries) Dimethyl sulfox 50%, water 50%. Bot. 50 ml.
Use: Interstitial cystitis intravesical instillation.

INADE. (Econo Med) Chlorpheniramine maleate 8 mg., phenylephrine HCl 20 mg., methscopolamine nitrate 2.5 mg./Cap. Bot. 120s.
Use: Common cold therapy.

INADE B.I.D. (Econo Med) Chlorpheniramine maleate 8 mg., d- isoephedrine HCl 120 mg./Sus. Rel. Cap. Bot. 100s.
Use: Relief upper respiratory congestion.

INALGIN. (Meyer) Atropine sulfate 0.03 mg., hyoscyamine 0.03 mg., gelesmium 6 mg., methenamine 41 mg., salol 18 mg., benzoic acid 4.5 mg., methylene blue 5.4 mg./Tab. Bot. 100s, 1000s.
Use: Urinary tract infections.

RINGER'S INJECTION, U.S.P. XXI. Lactated, U.S.P. XXI. (Abbott) 250 ml., 500 ml., 1000 ml. (Invenex), 250 ml., 500 ml., 1000 ml. Abbo-Vac glass or flexible containers, Vial 50 ml. Pkg. 25s. (Lilly) Amp. 20 ml. Pkg. 6s. (Cutter) Bot. 500 ml., 1000 ml.
Use: Fluid and electrolyte replenisher, irrigating solution.
/Dextrose. (Cutter) 5% solution. Bot. 1000 ml.

RINGER'S INJECTION, LACTATED, U.S.P. XXI.
Use: Fluid and electrolyte replenisher.

RINGER'S IRRIGATION, U.S.P. XXI. (Abbott) 500 ml., 1000 ml.
Use: Irrigation solution.

INOCIDIN CAPSULES. (Cenci) Phenylephrine HCl 10 mg., chlorpheniramine maleate 1 mg., pyrilamine maleate 1.5 mg., Vit. C 50 mg., caffeine 30 mg., acetophenetidin 130 mg., salicylamide 200 mg./Cap. Bot. 48s.
Use: Analgesic, antipyretic, decongestant.

INOCIDIN EXPECTORANT. (Cenci) Codeine phosphate 10.08 mg., phenylephrine HCl 10 mg., chlorpheniramine maleate 2 mg., pyrilamine maleate 6.25 mg., ammonium chloride 60 mg., sodium citrate 85 mg./5 cc. Bot. pts., gals.
Also avail. (plain) without codeine. Bot. 1 pt., gal.
Use: Antitussive, antihistaminic, decongestant, expectorant.

IOBIN. (Pasadena Research) Riboflavin 5′ phosphate sod. 50 mg./cc. Vial 10 cc.

IO-DOPA. (D.D.R. Pharm.) Levodopa 500 mg./Cap. Bot. 100s.
Use: Anti-Parkinson agent.

IOPAN. (Ayerst) Magaldrate. **Tab.:** Magaldrate 480 mg., sodium 0.1 mg./Tab. (Chew or Swallow). Pkg. 60s, 100s. Single rollpacks of 12s. **Susp.** Magaldrate 540 mg., sodium 0.1 mg. (0.004 m Eq)/5 ml. Bot. 12 oz. Individual Cups 30 ml. ea. 10 cups/Tray. 10 Trays/Packer
Use: Antacid & G.I. disturbances.

IOPAN EXTRA STRENGTH. (Ayerst) Magaldrate 1080 mg., sodium 0.3 mg./5 ml. Bot. 3 oz., 6 oz., 12 oz. Cups 30 ml. Packer 10× 10s.
Use: High potency antacid.

IOPAN PLUS. (Ayerst) **Chew Tab.:** Magaldrate 480 mg., simethicone 20 mg., sodium 0.1 mg. (0.004 m Eq)/Chew Tab. Bot. 60s., 100s. **Susp.:** Magaldrate 540 mg., simethicone 20 mg., sodium 0.1 mg. (0.004 m Eq)/5 ml. Bot. 12 oz. Individual Cups 30 ml. each. 10 cups/Tray. 10 Trays/Packer
Use: Antacid, antiflatulent.

RIOPAN PLUS EXTRA STRENGTH. (Ayerst) Magaldrate 1080 mg., simethicone 30 mg., sodium 0.3 mg./5 ml. Bot. 3 oz., 6 oz., 12 oz. Cup 30 ml. Packer 10 × 10s.
Use: High potency antacid/antiflatulent.

• **RIOPROSTIL.** USAN.
Use: Gastric antisecretory.

• **RIPAZEPAM.** USAN.
Use: Tranquilizer (minor).

• **RISOCAINE.** USAN.
Use: Anesthetic (local).

• **RISTIANOL PHOSPHATE.** USAN.
Use: Immunoregulator.

RISTOCETIN. B.A.N. An antibiotic from species of *Actinomycetes Norcardia lurida.*

RITALIN HYDROCHLORIDE. (Ciba) Methylphenidate HCl Tab. 5 mg., 10 mg., Bot. 100s, 500s, 1000s. Tab. 20 mg., Bot. 100s, 1000s. 10 mg. Accu-Pak 100s.
Use: Psychomotor stimulant.

• **RITANSERIN.** USAN.
Use: Serotonin antagonist.

RITE-DIET. (Edward J. Moore) Methylcellulose, benzocaine, Vit. A, D, B-1, B-2, C plus iron, calcium, potassium, niacinamide/Cap. Bot. 42s.

• **RITODRINE.** USAN. Erythro-p-Hydroxy-α-[1-[(p-hydroxyphenethyl)amino]ethyl] benzyl alcohol
Use: Smooth muscle relaxant.
See: Prempar hydrochloride.
Yutopar, Tab., Inj. (Astra)

• **RITODRINE HYDROCHLORIDE,** U.S.P. XXI. Inj., Tab., U.S.P. XXI.
Use: Relaxant (smooth muscle).

RIVOTRIL. Clonazepam, B.A.N.

RMS SUPPOSITORIES. (Upsher-Smith) Morphine sulfate 5 mg., 10 mg., or 20 mg./Supp. Box 12s.
Use: Narcotic analgesic.

ROAMPICILLIN. (Robinson) Ampicillin 250 mg./Tab. Bot. 100s.
Use: Antibiotic.

ROAMPICILLIN POWDER. (Robinson) Ampicillin powder 125 mg. or 250 mg./5 cc. Vials 80cc, 100cc, 150cc, 200cc.
Use: Antibiotic.

ROBAMATE. (Robinson) Meprobamate 200 mg./Tab. Bot. 100s, 400 mg./Tab. Bot. 1000s.

ROBAMOL. (Cenci) Methocarbamol 750 mg./Tab. Bot. 100s, 1000s.
Use: Musculoskeletal conditions.

ROBAM-PETN. (Robinson) Meprobamatepentaerythritol tetranitrate, Tab. Bot. 100s, 1000s.
Use: Tranquilizer-coronary vasodilator.

ROBANTALINE. (Robinson) Propantheline Bromide 15 mg./Tab. Bot. 100s, 500s, 1000s.
Use: Anticholinergic.

ROBANTALINE WITH PHENOBARBITAL. (Robinson) Propantheline bromide with phenobarbital Tab. Bot. 100s, 500s, 1000s.
Use: Anticholinergic.

ROBANUL.
See: Robinul, Preps. (Robins)

ROBARB. (Robinson) Amobarbital 0.25 gr., 0.5 gr., and 1 gr./Cap. Bot. 100s.

ROBAXIN. (Robins) Methocarbamol. **Tab.** 500 mg., Bot. 100s, 500s; Dis-Co Paks 100s. **Inj.:** 1 Gm./10 cc. of a 50% aqueous solution of polyethylene glycol 300. Single Dose Vial 10 cc. Pkg. 5s, 25s.
Use: Skeletal muscle relaxant.

ROBAXIN-750. (Robins) Methocarbamol 750 mg./Tab. **Tab.** Bot. 100s, 500s; Dis-Co Paks 100s.
Use: Skeletal muscle relaxant.

ROBAXISAL. (Robins) Methocarbamol (Robaxin) 400 mg., aspirin 325 mg./Tab. Bot. 100s, 500s. Dis-Co pack 100s.
Use: Muscle relaxant/analgesic.

ROBENECID. (Robinson) Probenecid 0.5 Gm./Tab. Bot. 100s, 1000s.
Use: Uricosuric.

ROBENECID WITH COLCHICINE. (Robinson) Colchicine 0.5 mg., probenecid 500 mg./Tab. Bot. 100s.

ROBENECOL. (Robinson) Probenecid with colchicine Tab. Bot. 100s, 1000s.
Use: Uricosuric.

ROBENIDINE. B.A.N. 1,3-Bis(4-chlorobenzyl-ideneamino)guanidine.
Use: Antiprotozoan, veterinary medicine.
See: Cycostat.

• **ROBENIDINE HYDROCHLORIDE.** USAN.
Use: Coccidiostat.

ROBESE. (Rocky Mtn.) Dextroamphetamine sulfate 5 mg./Tab. Bot. 100s, 1000s.
Use: Weight control.

ROBESE C. CAP NON-AMPHETAMINE W.C. (Rocky Mtn.) Carboxymethylcellulose 500 mg., benzocaine 9 mg., Vit. A 5000 I.U., D 400 I.U., B-1 2 mg.,- B-2 2.5 mg., niacinamide 20 mg., ascorbic acid 50 mg., B-6 1 mg., calcium pantothenate 1 mg., iron 15 mg./3 Caps. Bot. 48s, 96s.

ROBESE C. INJ. NON-AMPHETAMINE W.C. (Rocky Mtn.) Caffeine 250 mg., sodium benzoate 250 mg./2 cc. Vial 30 cc.
Use: Weight control.

ROBESE FORTE. (Rocky Mtn.) d-Amphetamine HCl 20 mg., sod. carboxymethylcellulose 2 mg., benzyl alcohol 1.5%/cc. Vial 30 cc. d-Amphetamine sulfate 15 mg., atropine sulfate 0.36 mg., aloin 16.2 mg., phenobarbital 16.2 mg./T.R. Tab. Bot. 100s.
Use: Weight control.

ROBESE "P" INJ. (Rocky Mtn.) Phenyl-propanolamine HCl 75 mg., protein hydrolysate containing amino acid 100 ml., leucine 0.415 Gm., valine 0.30 Gm., lysine 0.35 Gm., isoleucine 0.24 Gm., phenylalanine 0.28 Gm., arginine 0.15 Gm., threonine 0.18 Gm., methionine 0.22 Gm., histidine 0.12 Gm., tryptophan 0.05 Gm./cc. Vial 10 cc.

ROBESE "P" TABLETS. (Rocky Mtn.) Phendimetrazine tartrate 35 mg./Tab. Bot. 100s, 1000s.

ROBICILLIN VK. (Robins) Penicillin V Potassium 250 mg. (400,000 u.)/Tab. Bot. 100s, 1000s. 500 mg. (800,000 u.)/Tab. Bot. 100s, 500s. Oral 125 mg. (200,000 u.)/5 ml. 250 mg. (400,000 u.)/5 ml. Bot. 100 ml., 200 ml.
Use: Antibiotic.

RO-BILE. (Rowell) Pepsin 260 mg., pancreatic enzym conc. 75 mg., ox bile ext. 100 mg., dehydrocholic acid 30 mg:, belladonna ext. 8 mg./Tab. Bot. 100s
Use: Digestant.

ROBIMYCIN. (Robins) Erythromycin 250 mg./Tab. Bot. 100s, 500s.
Use: Antibiotic.

ROBINUL. (Robins) Glycopyrrolate. 1 mg./Tab. Bot. 100s, 500s.
Use: Anticholinergic.

ROBINUL-FORTE TABLETS. (Robins) Glycopyrrolat 2 mg./Tab. Bot. 100s, 500s.
Use: Anticholinergic.

ROBINUL INJECTABLE. (Robins) Glycopyrrolate 0.2 mg., benzyl alcohol (preservative) 0.9%. Vial 1 ml. Box 5s, 25s; 2 ml. Box 25s; 5 ml. Box, 25s; 20 ml. 1s.
Use: Anticholinergic.

ROBITET. (Robins) Tetracycline HCl. **Caps.** 250 mg./Cap. Bot. 100s, 1000s; 500 mg./Cap. Bot. 100s, 500s.
Use: Antibiotic.

ROBITUSSIN. (Robins) Guaifenesin 100 mg./5 ml. w/alcohol 3.5% Bot 1 oz. (4 x 25s), 4 oz., 8 oz., 1 pt., 1 gal. Dis-Co Unit Dose 5 ml., 10 ml., 15 ml. 10 10s.
Use: Expectorant.

ROBITUSSIN A-C. (Robins) Guaifenesin 100 mg., codeine phosphate 10 mg./5 cc. w/alcohol 3.5%. Bot. 2 oz., 4 oz., pt., gal.
Use: Expectorant, antitussive.

ROBITUSSIN-CF. (Robins) Guaifenesin 100 mg., phenylpropanolamine HCL 12.5 mg., dextromethorphan HBr 10 mg./5 ml. w/alcohol 4.75%. Bot. 4 oz., 8 oz., pt.
Use: Antitussive, nasal decongestant, expectorant.

ROBITUSSIN-DAC. (Robins) Guaifenesin 100 mg. pseudoephedrine HCl 30 mg., codeine phosphate 10 mg/5 ml. w/alcohol 1.4%. Bot. pt.
Use: Antitussive, nasal decongestant, expectorant.

ROBITUSSIN DIS-CO unit dose pack. (Robins) Guaifenesin 100 mg., alcohol 3.5%/5 cc. Syr. unit dose packs 5 cc., 10 cc. 15cc. (10 x 10s).
Use: Antitussive and expectorant.

ROBITUSSIN-DM. (Robins) Guaifenesin 100 mg., dextromethorphan HBr 15 mg./5 ml. w/alcohol 1.4%. Bot. 4 oz., 8 oz., pt., gal. Dis-Co Paks 5 ml., 10 ml. (10 x 10s).
Use: Antitussive, expectorant.

ROBITUSSIN-DM COUGH CALMERS. (Robins) Dextromethorphan HBr 7.5 mg., guaifenesin 50 mg./Loz. Box 16s.
Use: Antitussive, expectorant.

ROBITUSSIN NIGHT RELIEF. (Robins) Acetaminophen 1,000 mg., phenylephrine HCl 10 mg., pyrilamine maleate 50 mg., dextromethorphan HBr. 30 mg./oz. w/alcohol 25% Bot. 4 oz., 8 oz.
Use: Adult strength for relief of all cold symptoms.

BITUSSIN-PE. (Robins) Guaifenesin 100 mg., pseudoephedrine HCl 30 mg./5 ml. w/alcohol 1.4%. Bot. 4 oz., 8 oz., pt.
Use: Decongestant, expectorant.
BOLIC. (Rocky Mtn.) Methandriol dipropionate 50 mg./cc. Vial 10 cc.
BOMOL-500 TABS. (Major) Methocarbamol 500 mg./Tab. Bot. 100s, 500s.
Use: Skeletal muscle relaxant.
BOMOL-750 TABS. (Major) Methocarbamol 750 mg./Tab. Bot. 100s, 500s.
Use: Skeletal muscle relaxant.
BOMOL/ASA TABS. (Major) Methocarbamal w/ASA. Bot. 100s, 500s.
Use: Skeletal muscle relaxant.
CAINE. (Rocky Mtn.) Lidocaine HCl 1%, 2%. Vial 50 cc.
Use: Local anesthetic.
CALOSAN. (Rocky Mtn.) Calcium glycerophosphate 1%, calcium levulinate 1.5%. Vial 30 cc.
CALTROL. (Roche) Calcitriol 0.25 mcg. and 0.5 mcg./Cap. **0.25** mcg./Cap. Bot. 100s, Pak 30s; **0.5** mcg./Cap. Bot. 100s.
Use: Management of hypocalcemia in patients undergoing chronic renal dialysis.
CCAL. Benzalkonium Chloride, B.A.N.
CEPHIN. (Roche) Ceftriaxone sodium 250 mg., 500 mg. or 1 Gm./Vial to be reconstituted for IV or IM administration. Box 10s.
Use: Broad spectrum antibiotic (cephalosporin).
CHE DIAGNOSTIC SYSTEMS. (Roche) Roche laboratories markets the following line of diagnostic products:
Isomune-LD
Isomune-CK
Isomune-CK Substrate
Cardiotrol-CK Control
Placentex
Pregnosis
RIA-HCg Test Kits, (Various)
Sensi-Tex
Sensi-Chrome
Sensi-Slide
Septi-Chek
Pregnancy Test Controls
Enterotube II
Oxi/Ferm Tube
Fluram
OCHLOMETHIAZIDE. (Robinson) Trichlormethiazide 4 mg./Tab. Bot. 100s, 500s.
Use: Diuretic, antihypertensive.
OCHORIC. (Rocky Mtn.) Chorionic gonadotropin 10,000 I.U./10 cc. Univial 10 cc.
O-CHLOROZIDE. (Robinson) Chlorothiazide 250 or 500 mg./Tab. Bot. 100s, 1000s.
Use: Treatment of edema.
OCKY MOUNTAIN SPOTTED FEVER VACCINE.
Use: Active immunizing agent.
OCORT LOTION. (Rocky Mtn.) Hydrocortisone 0.5%. Bot. 4 oz.

ROCYCLO INJECTION. (Robinson) Dicyclomine HCl 10 mg./cc. Vial 10cc.
ROCYCLO-PHEN. (Robinson) Dicyclomine HCl w/phenobarbital. Tab. Bot. 100s, 500s.
Use: Anticholinergic, sedative.
ROCYCLO-10. (Robinson) Dicyclomine HCl 10 mg./Cap. Bot. 100s, 500s.
Use: Anticholinergic.
ROCYCLO-20. (Robinson) Dicyclomine HCl 20 mg./Tab. Bot. 100s, 500s.
Use: Anticholinergic.
RODELTA T.B.A. (Rocky Mtn.) Prednisolone tertiary butylacetate 20 mg./10 cc. Vial 10 cc.
RODESINE. (Rocky Mtn.) Adenosine 5 monophosphoric acid 25 mg., sod. nicotinate 20 mg., B-12 cryst. 75 mcg., benzyl alcohol 1.5%/cc. Vial 10 cc.
Use: Anti-inflammatory.
RO-DIET. (Robinson) Diethylpropion HCl 25 mg./Tab. Bot. 100s, 1000s.
Use: Anorexigenic.
RO-DIET TIMED. (Robinson) Diethylpropion HCl (time disintegration) 75 mg./Tab. Bot. 100s, 1000s.
Use: Anorexigenic.
• **RODOCAINE.** USAN.
Use: Local anesthetic.
RODOX. (Rocky Mtn.) Docusate sodium 100 mg. or 250 mg./Cap. Bot. 100s.
Use: Stool softener.
RODOX/W. (Rocky Mtn.) Docusate sodium 100 mg., casanthranol 75 mg./Cap. Bot. 100s, 1000s.
Use: Fecal softener and laxative.
RODRYL. (Rocky Mtn.) Diphenhydramine HCl 10 mg./cc. Vial 30 cc.
RODRYL-50. (Rocky Mtn.) Diphenhydramine HCl 50 mg./cc. Vial 10 cc.
Use: Antihistamine.
ROENTGENOGRAPHY.
See: Iodine Products, Diagnostic
RO-FEDRIN. (Robinson) Pseudoephedrine HCl 60 mg./Tab. Bot. 100s, 1000s.
Use: Respiratory decongestant.
RO-FEDRINE SYRUP. (Robinson) Pseudoephedrine HCl 30 mg./5 cc. Bot. pt.
Use: Respiratory decongestant.
• **ROFLURANE.** USAN. 2-Bromo-1, 1,2-trifluoroethyl methyl ether.
Use: General inhalation anesthetic.
ROGENIC. (Forest) **S.C. Tab.:** Iron 60 mg., Vit. C 100 mg., B-6 6 mg., B-12 25 mcg., desiccated liver/S.C. Tab.
Use: Multivitamin.
Dual release Tab. First release: Ferrous fumarate 40 mg., ferrous sulfate 20 mg., ferrous gluconate 7 mg., Vit. C 50 mg., cobalamin 25 mcg., B-6 5 mg., desic. liver 15 mg.; second release: ferrous fumarate 10 mg., ferrous sulfate 10 mg., ferrous gluconate 3 mg., Vit. C 20 mg., cobalamin 25 mcg., B-6 5 mg., desic. liver 15 mg./Tab. Bot. 100s. **Inj.** B-12 500 mcg., peptonized iron 20 mg., liver 10 mcg./cc. Vial 10 cc.
Use: Treatment of iron deficiency anemias.

ROGITINE. Phentolamine, B.A.N.

RO-HYDRAZIDE. (Robinson) Hydrochlorothiazide 25, 50, 100 mg./Tab. Bot. 100s, 500s, 1000s.
Use: Diuretic.

ROHIST. (Rocky Mtn.) Chloropheniramine 12 mg./T.D. Tab. Bot. 100s.

ROHIST C. (Rocky Mtn.) Chloropheniramine 100 mg./cc. Vial 10 cc.

RO-HIST. (Robinson) Tripelennamine HCl 50 mg./Tab. Bot. 100s, 1000s.

ROHIST-D. (Rocky Mtn.) Chlorpheniramine 5 mg., phenylpropanolamine HCl 12.5 mg., atropine sulfate 0.2 mg., Vit. C 100 mg./Cap. Bot. 100s. Vial 10 cc.
Use: Decongestant.

ROHIST PLUS. (Rocky Mtn.) Chlorpheniramine 12 mg., d-desoxyephedrine HCl 8 mg./T.R. Tab. Bot. 100s.
Use: Antihistamine plus stimulant, decongestant.

RO HONEY PROTEIN. (Rocky Mtn.) Protein 70%. Bot. 250s.
Use: Protein supplement.

ROHYDRA. (Robinson) **Capsules:** Diphendydramine HCl 25, 50 mg./Cap. Bot. 100s, 1000s. **Elixir:** Diphenhydramine HCl 80 mg., ammonium chloride 12 gr., sod. citrate 5 gr., menthol 0.1 gr./fl. oz. Bot. pts. gal.
Use: Allergy therapy.

ROHYDRA EXPECTORANT. (Robinson) Diphenydramine HCl. Bot. pts., gal.
Use: Allergy therapy.

RO-HYDRAZIDE. (Robinson) Hydrochlorothiazide 100 mg./Tab. Bot. 100s, 1000s.
Use: Treatment of edema.

ROLA-BEE. (Robinson) Vit. B-1 15 mg., B-2 10 mg., niacinamide 50 mg., cal. pantothenate 10 mg., C 250 mg., B-6 5 mg./Cap. Bot. 100s, 1000s.
Use: Supplement.

ROLABROMOPHEN. (Robinson) Brompehniramine maleate 4 mg./Tab. Bot. 100s, 5000s.
Use: Antihistaminic.

ROLABROMOPHEN DECONGESTANT ELIXIR. (Robinson) Brompheniramine maleate 4 mg., phenylephrine HCl 5 mg., phenylpropanolamine HCl 5 mg., alcohol 2.3%/5 ml. Bot. Pt., Gal.
Use: Rhinitis treatment.

ROLABROMOPHEN ELIXIR. (Robinson) Brompheniramine maleate 2 mg., alcohol 3%/5 ml. Bot. Pts., Gal.
Use: Antihistaminic.

ROLABROMOPHEN EXPECTORANT. (Robinson) Brompheniramine maleate 2 mg., phenylephrine HCl 5 mg., phenylpropanolamine HCl 5 mg., guaifenesin 100 mg., alcohol 3.5%/5 ml. Bot. Pt., Gal.
Use: Decongestant and expectorant.

ROLABROMOPHEN FORTE. (Robinson) Bropheniramine maleate-forte extended. Bot. 100s, 500s, 1000s.

ROLABROMOPHEN INJECTION. (Robinson) Bropheniramine maleate injection. 10 mg./cc. Vial 30 cc.; 100 mg./cc. Vial 10 cc.
Use: Antihistaminic.

ROLABROMOPHEN TIMED. (Robinson) Bropheniramine maleate time disintegration 8 mg 12 mg./Tab. Bot. 100s, 1000s.
Use: Antihistamine.

ROLAIDS ANTACID TABLETS. (Warner-Lambert) Dihydroxy aluminum sodium carbonate 334 mg./T. Regular, wintergreen and spearmint flavors. Roll 12s. Bot. 75s, 150s.
Use: Antacid.

ROLAIDS SODIUM FREE. (Warner-Lambert) Calci carbonate 317 mg., magnesium hydroxide 64 mg./Tab. Rolls 12s. Bot. 75s, 150s.
Use: Antacid.

ROLA-METHAZINE. (Robinson) Promethazine H 12.5 mg., 25 mg., 50 mg./Tab. Bot. 100s, 500s, 1000s.
Use: Antihistamine, antiemetic, sedative.

ROLA-METHAZINE EXPECTORANT PLAIN. (Rob son) Promethazine with expectorant plain. Bot. pt gal.

ROLAMETHAZINE INJECTION. (Robinson) Promethazine HCl injection 25 mg./cc. Vial 10 cc
Use: Antiemetic, antihistamine.

ROLA-METHAZINE PEDIATRIC LIQUID. (Robinso Promethazine pediatric liq. Bot. pt., gal.
Use: Antihistamine.

ROLA-METHAZINE VC EXPECTORANT. (Robinso Promethazine VC Expectorant. Bot. pt., gal.
Use: Antihistamine, decongestant, expectorant.

ROLA-METHAZINE VC EXPECTORANT WITH C DEINE. (Robinson) Promethazine VC expectora with codeine. Bot. Pts., gal.

ROLA-METHAZINE WITH CODEINE. (Robinson) Promethazine expectorant with codeine. Bot. pt., gal.
Use: Antihistamine, expectorant, antitussive.

ROLAPHENT. (Robinson) Phentermine 8 mg./Tab. Bot. 100s.
Use: Anorexiant.

ROLATHIMIDE. (Robinson) Glutethimide 0.5 Gm./Tab. Bot. 100s, 500s.
Use: Hypnotic.

ROLANADE. (Robinson) Chlorpheniramine maleate mg., phenylpropanolamine HCl 50 mg., atropine sulfate 1/180 Gr./Cap. Bot. 100s, 500s, 1000s.
Use: Cold capsules.

ROLAZID. (Robinson) Isonicotinic acid hydrazide 10 mg., 300 mg./Tab. Bot. 100s, 1000s.
Use: Antibacterial (Tuberculostatic).

ROLAZINE. (Robinson) Hydralazine HCl 25 mg. or 5 mg./Tab. Bot. 100s, 500s, 1000s.
Use: Hypotensive agent.

ROLCEDIN. (Robinson) Chlorpheniramine maleate 2 mg., salicylamide 3.5 gr., acetophenetidin 2.5 gr., caffeine 0.5 gr./Tab. Bot. 100s, 1000s.
Use: Cold symptoms.

ROLECITHIN. (Robinson) **Capsules:** Soya lecithin 259.2 mg., soy bean oil 170.2 mg., D 150 u./Cap. **Tablets:** Soya lecithin 7 gr./Tab. Bot. 100s, 250s, 1000s.

• **ROLETAMIDE.** USAN. 3′,4′,5′-Trimethoxy-3-(3-pyrr lin-1-yl) acrylophenone.
Use: Hypnotic.

ROLICAP. (Arcum) Vits. A acetate 5,000 I.U., D-2 400 I.U., B-1 3.0 mg., B-2 2.5 mg., B-6 10 mg., C 50 mg., niacinamide 20 mg., B-12 1.0 mcg./Chewable Tab. Bot. 100s, 1000s.
Use: Multiple vitamin.

ROLICTON. Amisometradine, B.A.N.

ROLICYPRAM. B.A.N. (+)-5-Oxo-N-(trans-2-phenylcyclopropyl)-L-pyrrolidine-2-carboxamide.
Use: Antidepressant.

• **ROLICYPRINE.** USAN. (+)-5-Oxo-N-(trans-2-phenylcyclopropyl)-L-2-pyrrolidinecarboxamide.
Use: Antidepressant.

ROLIDIOL. (Robinson) Ethinyl estradiol 0.02, 0.05 mg./Tab. Bot. 100s, 1000s.
Use: Estrogen therapy.

ROLIDRIN-6. (Robinson) Nylidrin HCl 6 mg./Tab. Bot. 100s, 1000s.
Use: Peripheral vasodilator.

ROLIDRIN-12. (Robinson) Nylidrin HCl 12 mg./Tab. Bot. 100s, 1000s.
Use: Peripheral vasodilator.

RO-LINOIL. (Robinson) Linolenic acid 51%, linoleic acid 17%, oleic acid 23%, stearic acid 2%, palmitic acid 7%. Cap. 200 min. Bot. 100s, 500s.
Use: Unsaturated free fatty acid diet.

• **ROLIPRAM.** USAN.
Use: Tranquilizer.

ROLISOX-10. (Robinson) Isoxsuprine HCl 10 mg./Tab. Bot. 100s.
Use: Vasodilator.

ROLISOX-20. (Robinson) Isoxsuprine HCl 20 mg./Tab. Bot. 100s.
Use: Vasodilator.

• **ROLITETRACYCLINE, STERILE,** U.S.P. XXI. Inj., U.S.P. XXI. N-(Pyrrolidinomethyl) tetracycline. 4-(Dimethylamino)-1,4,4a,5,5a,6,11,12a-octahydro-3,6,-10,12,12a-pentahydroxy-6-methyl-1,11-dioxo-N-(1-pyrrolidinylmethyl)-2-naphthacenecarboxamide. Tetrex PMT nitrate Inj. Syntetrin Inj. (Bristol) Velacycline (Squibb)
Use: Antibacterial.

• **ROLITETRACYCLINE NITRATE.** USAN. Tetrim.
Use: Antibacterial.

• **ROLODINE.** USAN. 4-(Benzylamino)-2-methyl-7H-pyrrolo-[2,3-d]-pyrimidine.
Use: Muscle relaxant.

ROLOX. (Purepac) Magnesium hydroxide, aluminum hydroxide gel. Bot. 12 oz., gal.
Use: Antacid.

ROLSERP. (Robinson) Reserpine. **Tablets:** 0.1 mg., 0.25 mg., 0.5 mg./Tab. Bot. 100s, 1000s. **Vial:** 5 mg./cc. Vial 10 cc. **Timedcaps:** 0.25 mg., 0.5 mg. or 0.75 mg./Cap. Bot. 100s, 500s, 1000s, Bulk Pack 5000s. **Elixir:** 0.25 mg./5 cc. Bot. 16 oz.

ROLUTIN. (Rocky Mtn.) Hydroxyprogesterone caproate in oil 125 mg./10 cc. Vial 10 cc.

ROLUTIN 2X. (Rocky Mtn.) Hydroxyprogesterone caproate in oil 125 mg./5 cc. Vial 5 cc.

ROLZYME. (Robinson) Pepsin 250 mg., pancreatin 200 mg., bile salts 150 mg., dehydrocholic acid 25 mg./Tab. Bot. 100s, 1000s.

ROMAPHED. (Robinson) Aminophylline, ephedrine, amobarbital. Tab. Bot. 100s, 500s, 1000s.
Use: Smooth muscle relaxant (bronchodilator).

ROMETHOCARB. (Robinson) Methocarbamol 500 mg., 750 mg./Tab. Bot. 100s, 500s.
Use: Skeletal muscle relaxant.

ROMEX COUGH & COLD CAPSULES. (APC) Guaifenesin 65 mg., dextromethorphan HBr 10 mg., chlorpheniramine maleate 1.5 mg., pyrilamine maleate 12.5 mg., phenylephrine HCl 5 mg., acetaminophen 160 mg./Cap. Bot. 21s.
Use: Decongestant.

ROMEX COUGH & COLD TABLETS. (APC) Dextromethorphan HBr 7.5 mg., phenylephrine HCl 2.5 mg., ascorbic acid 30 mg. Box 15s.
Use: Relief of cold symptoms, cough.

ROMEX TROCHES & LIQUID. (A.P.C.) **Troche:** Polymyxin B sulfate 1000 u., benzocaine 5 mg., cetalkonium chloride 2.5 mg., gramicidin 100 mcg., chlorpheniramine maleate 0.5 mg., tyrothricin 2 mg./Troche. Pkg. 10s. **Liq.** Guaifenesin 200 mg., dextromethorphan HBr 60 mg., chlorpheniramine maleate 12 mg., phenylephrine HCl 30 mg./fl. oz. Bot. 4 oz.
Use: Minor throat and mouth irritations.

ROMICIL. Oleandomycin, B.A.N.

ROMILAR III. (Block) Dextromethorphan HBr 5.0 mg., phenylpropanolamine HCl 12.5 mg./5 ml. w/alcohol 20%. Bot. 3 oz., 5 oz.
Use: Decongestant cough syrup.

ROMILAR CF. (Block) Dextromethorphan HBr 15 mg./5 ml., w/alcohol 20%. Bot. 1.75 oz., 3 oz., 5 oz.
Use: Cough suppressant.

ROMILAR, Children's Cough Syrup. (Block) Dextromethorphan HBr 2.5 mg.,. Bot. 3 oz., 6 oz.
Use: Cough therapy.

ROMINAL W/C. (Robinson) Vit. B-1 25 mg., B-2 12.5 mg., nicotinamide 75 mg., B-6 3 mg., cal. pantothenate 10 mg., C 250 mg., B-12 3 mcg./Cap. Bot. 100s.
Use: Vitamin supplement therapy.

ROMINE. (Rocky Mtn.) Dimenhydrinate 50 mg. w/propylene glycol/cc. Vial 10 cc.

ROMOTAL HYDROCHLORIDE. Tacrine, B.A.N.

ROMPUN. Xylazine, B.A.N.

RONASE. (Rowell) Tolazamide 100 mg., 250 mg. or 500 mg./Tab. Bot. 100s, 250s.
Use: Hypoglycemic agent.

RONDASE. Hyaluronidase, B.A.N.

RONDEC DROPS. (Ross) Carbinoxamine maleate 2 mg., pseudoephedrine HCl 25 mg./ml. Bot. 30 ml. with dropper.
Use: Decongestant, antihistamine for infants 1 to 17 months.

RONDEC DM DROPS. (Ross) Carbinoxamine maleate 2 mg., pseudoephedrine HCl 25 mg., dextromethorphan HBr 4 mg./ml., alcohol 0.6%. Bot. w/dropper 30 ml.
Use: Non-narcotic cough mixture.

RONDEC DM SYRUP. (Ross) Carbinoxamine maleate 4 mg., pseudoephedrine HCl 60 mg.,

dextromethorphan HBr 15 mg./5 ml. w/alcohol 0.6%. Bot. pt., 4 oz.
Use: Non-narcotic cough mixture.

RONDEC SYRUP. (Ross) Carbinoxamine maleate 4 mg., pseudoephedrine HCl 60 mg./5 ml. Syrup. Bot. 4 oz., pt.
Use: Decongestant, antihistamine for children 18 mo. and older.

RONDEC TABLET. (Ross) Carbinoxamine maleate 4 mg., pseudoephedrine HCl 60 mg./Tab. Bot. 100s, 500s.
Use: Relief of respiratory tract congestion.

RONDEC TR. (Ross) Carbinoxamine 8 mg., pseudoephedrine HCl 120 mg./S.R. Tab.
Use: Decongestant, antihistamine for 12 hour dosing.

RONDOMYCIN. (Wallace) Methacycline HCl. 150 mg. or 300 mg./Cap. **150 mg.**: Bot. 100s. **300 mg.**: Bot. 50s.
Use: Antibiotic.

RONICOTIN. (Rocky Mtn.) Nicotinic acid 500 mg./Tab. Bot. 100s, 1000s.
Use: Vasodilator.

• **RONIDAZOLE.** USAN.
Use: Antiprotozoal.

RONIL. (Rocky Mtn.) Milk sugar 3 gr./T.D. Tab. Bot. 100s.
Use: Placebo.

RONIUM. (Pasadena Research) Iron 90 mg., Vit. C 75 mg./Cap. Bot. 100s, 1000s.
Use: Hematinic.

• **RONNEL.** USAN. Fenchlorphos.
Use: Insecticide (systemic)
See: Korlan (Dow)
Trolene (Dow)

RONTYL. Hydroflumethiazide, B.A.N.

RONVET. (Geneva) Erythromycin stearate. 250 mg./Tab. Bot. 100s.

RONYL. Pemoline, B.A.N.

RO OPTHO. (Rocky Mtn.) Sodium sulfacetamide 100 mg., prednisolone 5 mg., phenylephrine HCl 0.12%/cc. Bot. 5 cc.
Use: Therapeutic eye drops.

RO-PAPAV. (Robinson) Papaverine HCl time disintegration 150 mg./Tab. Bot. 100s, 250s, 1000s.
Use: Smooth muscle relaxant.

RO-PHYLLINE. (Robinson) Theophylline 80 mg./15 ml. w/alcohol 20% in a fruit-flavored, sugar-free solution. Bot. pt., gal.
Use: Diuretic.

• **ROPITOIN HYDROCHLORIDE.** USAN.
Use: Cardiac depressant.

• **ROPIZINE.** USAN.
Use: Anticonvulsant.

ROPLEDGE. (Robinson) Phendimetrazine tartrate 35 mg./Tab. Bot. 100s, 1000s.
Use: Anorexiant.

ROPOXY. (Robinson) Propoxyphene HCl 65 mg./Cap. Bot. 100s, 500s, 1000s.
Use: Analgesic.

ROPOXY COMPOUND-65. (Robinson) Propoxypher compound. Cap. Bot. 100s, 500s.
Use: Analgesic.

ROPRED. (Robinson) Prednisone 1.0 mg., 2.5 mg., 5.0 mg., 20 mg./Tab. Bot. 100s, 500s, 1000s.
Use: Adrenocortical steroid.

RO-PRENATE. (Robinson) Prenatal vitamin and mineral. Tab. Bot. 100s, 1000s.
Use: Prenatal vitamin.

ROPREDLONE. (Robinson) Prednisolone. **Tablets:** 1 mg., 5 mg./Tab. Bot. 100s, 500s, 1000s. **Vial:** 25 mg., 50 mg., 100 mg./cc. Vial 10 cc.
Use: Adrenocortical steroid.

ROQUINE. (Robinson) Chloroquine phosphate 0.25 Gm./Tab. Bot. 100s, 500s, 1000s.

ROSA GALLICAL.
See: Estivin, Sol. (Alcon)

ROSANILINE DYES.
See: Fuchsin, Basic (Var. Mfr.)
Methylrosaniline Chloride Sol., Inj. (Var Mfr.)

• **ROSARAMICIN.** USAN.
Use: Antibacterial.

• **ROSARAMICIN BUTYRATE.** USAN.
Use: Antibacterial.

• **ROSARAMICIN PROPIONATE.** USAN.
Use: Antibacterial.

• **ROSARAMICIN SODIUM PHOSPHATE.** USAN.
Use: Antibacterial.

• **ROSARAMICIN STEARATE.** USAN.
Use: Antibacterial.

ROSCORB 5. (Rocky Mtn.) Vit. C 500 mg./Tab. Bot. 100s, 1000s.
Use: Vitamin supplement.

ROSE BENGAL.
See: Robengatope (Squibb)

• **ROSE BENGAL SODIUM I-125.** USAN.
Use: Radioactive agent.

• **ROSE BENGAL SODIUM I-131 INJECTION,** U.S.P XXI. Sodium 4,5,6,7-Tetrachloro-2′,-4′,5′,7′-tetraiodofluorescein.
Use: Diagnostic aid (hepatic function determination).

ROSE BENGAL STRIPS. (Barnes-Hind) Strips 1.3 mg Box 100 strips.
Use: Diagnostic agent for disclosing corneal injury and pathology.

ROSE-C LIQUID. (Barth's) Vit. C 300 mg., rose hip extract/Tsp. Dropper Bot. 2 oz., Bot. 8 oz.

ROSE HIPS. (Burgin-Arden) Vitamin C 300 mg., in base of sorbitol. Bot. 4 oz., 8 oz.
Use: Vitamin C supplement.

ROSE HIPS C. (Quality Generics) Vit. C 500 mg./Tab. Bot. 100s.
Use: Vitamin C therapy.

ROSE HIPS VITAMIN C. (Kirkman) Vit. C 100 mg./Tab. Bot. 100s, 250s. Vit. C 250 mg., 500 mg./Tab. Bot. 100s, 250s, 500s.
Use: Vitamin C therapy.

• **ROSE OIL,** N.F. XVI.
Use: Perfume.

• **ROSE WATER, STRONGER,** N.F. XVI.
Use: Perfume.

ROSE WATER OINTMENT, U.S.P. XXI.
Use: Emollient; ointment base.

ROSIN, U.S.P. XXI.
Use: Stiffening agent; Pharm. necessity for Zinc-Eugenol cement.

ROSOXACIN. USAN.
Use: Antibacterial.
See: Rosoxcin, Pow. (Winthrop Products)

ROSOXCIN POWDER. (Winthrop Products) Rosoxacin.
Use: Antigonoccal agent.

ROSOXOL TABLETS. (Robinson) Sulfisoxazole 500 mg./Tab. Bot. 100s, 1000s.
Use: Sulfonamide, anti-infective.

ROSOXOL-AZO. (Robinson) Sulfisoxazole, phenazopyridine HCl./Tab. Bot. 100s, 1000s.
Use: Sulfonamide, anti-infective.

ROSS SLD. (Ross) Low-residue nutritional supplement for patients restricted to a clear liquid feeding or fat malabsorption. Packet 1.3 oz. Ctn. 6s.
Use: Nutritional supplement.

RO-SULFIRAM-500. (Robinson) Disulfiram 500 mg./Tab. Bot. 50s, 500s.
Use: Treatment of alcoholism.

RO-SUPER-B TABLETS. (Robinson) Vit. B-1 50 mg., B-2 20 mg., B-6 5 mg., B-12 15 mcg., C 300 mg., liver desic. 100 mg., dried yeast 100 mg., niacinamide 25 mg., Ca pantothenate 5 mg., iron 10 mg./Tab. Bot. 100s, 250s, 1000s.
Use: Therapeutic B-complex.

ROTAZYME. (Abbott) Test kit 50s.
Use: Qualitative enzyme immunoassay for detection of rotavirus antigen in human fecal material.

ROTENSE. (Robinson) Aspirin, phenacetin, & caffeine w/allybarbituric acid/Tab. Bot. 100s, 1000s.
Use: Analgesic, sedative.

ROTERSEPT DIGLUCONATE. Chlorhexidine, B.A.N.

ROTHERAMIN. (Robinson) Vit. A 25,000 I.U., D 1000 I.U., B-1 10 mg., B-2 5 mg., niacinamide 100 mg., B-6 1 mg., B-12 5 mcg., C 150 mg., Ca 103.6 mg., phosphorus 80.2 mg., iron 10 mg., Mg 5.5 mg., Mn 1 mg., K 5 mg., Zn 1.4 mg./Cap. or Tab. Bot. 100s, 250s, 1000s.
Use: Vitamin-mineral therapy.

RO-THYRONINE. (Robinson) Liothyronine sodium 25 mcg., or 50 mcg./Tab. Bot. 100s, 500s, 1000s.
Use: Thyroid therapy.

RO-THYROXINE. (Robinson) L-thyroxine sodium 0.1 mg., 0.2 mg./Tab. Bot. 100s, 500s, 1000s.
Use: Hypothyroidism.

• **ROTOXAMINE TARTRATE.** USAN. (−)-2-[p-Chloro-α-[2-(dimethylamino)ethoxy]-benzyl pyridine tartrate (1:1).
Use: Antihistaminic.

RO-TRAN. (Robinson) Salicylamide 250 mg., powd. ext. valerian 15 mg., pwd. ext. passiflora 15 mg./Tab. Bot. 100s.
Use: Minor tensions and anxiety.

ROTRILATE. (Robinson) Trimethylcyclohexyl mandelate 200 mg./Tab. Bot. 100s, 1000s.

RO TRIM. (Rocky Mtn.) d-Amphetamine sulfate 15 mg., atropine sulfate 1/180 gr., aloin 0.25 gr., phenobarbital 0.25 gr./Cap. Bot. 100s.
Use: Weight reduction.

ROTRIM T. (Rocky Mtn.) Thyroid 3 gr./T.R. Tab. Bot. 100s.
Use: Thyroid supplement.

ROTYL HCl. (Rocky Mtn.) Dicylomine HCl 10 mg./cc. Vial 10 cc.
Use: Smooth muscle relaxant and antispasmodic.

ROVAMYCIN. Spiramycin, B.A.N.

ROVIMINS T.F.. (Rocky Mtn.) Zinc sulfate 50 mg., magnesium sulfate 50 mg., Vit. A 25,000 I.U., D 400 I.U., B-1 20 mg., B-2 30 mg., B-6 3 mg., B-12 25 mcg., Ca pantothenate 30 mg., niacinamide 100 mg., C 400 mg., E 2 I.U., managanese 3 mg., potassium sulfate 5 mg., copper oxide 1 mg., iodine 0.15 mg./Pill. Bot. 100s, 1000s.
Use: Therapeutic and stress vitamin and mineral formula.

ROXANOL ORAL SOLUTION. (Roxane) Morphine sulfate oral sol. 20 mg./ml. Bot. 30 ml. calibrated dropper.
Use: Narcotic analgesic.

ROXANOL SR TABLETS. (Roxane) Morphine sulfate 30 mg./S.R. Tab. Bot. 50s. Unit dose 25s.
Use: Narcotic analgesic.

• **ROXARSONE.** USAN. 3-Nitro-4-hydroxy-phenylarsonic acid.
Use: Coccidiostat and antibacterial.

ROXYN. (Rocky Mtn.) d-Desoxyephedrine HCl 15 mg./Tab. Bot. 100s.
Use: Weight reduction.

ROZINC. (Rocky Mtn.) Zinc sulfate 220 mg./Cap. Bot. 100s, 1000s.

RP-MYCIN. (Reid-Provident) Erythromycin, E.C. Tabs. 250 mg./Tab. Bot. 100s.
Use: Antibacterial.

R-S LOTION. (Hill) **No. 2:** Sulfur 8%, resorcinol monoacetate 4%. Bot. 2 oz.
Use: Drying medication.

RUBACELL II DIAGNOSTIC TEST. (Abbott) Passive hemagglutination procedure for the detection of antibody to rubella virus. 100 & 1000 test units.
Use: Qualitative & quantitative detection of antibody to rubella virus in serum or recalcified plasma.

RUBA-TECT. (Abbott) Rubella diagnosis test system. 100s.
Use: Hemagglutination inhibition test for the detection & quantitation of rubella antibody in serum.

RUBAZYME. (Abbott) Test kit 100s, 1000s.
Use: Enzyme immunoassay for IgG antibody to rubella virus.

RUBAZYME-M. (Abbott) Test kit 50s.
Use: Enzyme immunoassay for IgM antibody to rubella virus.

• **RUBELLA & MUMPS VIRUS VACCINE, LIVE,** U.S.P. XXI.
Use: Active immunizing agent.
See: Biavax II, Inj. (Merck Sharp & Dohme)

• **RUBELLA VIRUS VACCINE, LIVE,** U.S.P. XXI.
Use: Active immunizing agent.
See: Cendevax, Inj. (SmithKline)
Meruvax, Inj. (Merck Sharp & Dohme)
W/Measles vaccine.
See: M-R-Vax, Inj. (Merck Sharp & Dohme)
W/Measles vaccine, mumps vaccine.
See: M-M-R, Inj. (Merck Sharp & Dohme)

RUBELLA VIRUS VACCINE, LIVE ATTENUATED. Live attenuated strain of rubella virus HPV-77.
Use: Active immunizing agent.
W/Measles vaccine.
See: Lirubel, Vial (Merrell Dow)
W/Measles vaccine, mumps vaccine.
See: Lirutrin, Vial (Merrell Dow)

RUBESOL-1000. (Central) Cyanocobalamin U.S.P. 1000 mcg./ml. Vial 10 ml., 30 ml. Box 12s.

RUBICAPS. (Stanlabs) Vit. A 10,000 I.U., D 1000 I.U., B-1 16 mg., B-2 8 mg., C 100 mg., B-6 0.5 mg., B-12 6 mcg., E 1.25 I.U., niacinamide 10 mg., Ca pantothenate 5 mg., inositol 30 mg., choline bitartrate 62 mg., dl-methionine 30 mg., ferrous gluconate 30 mg., Ca 58 mg., P 45 mg., potassium iodide 0.15 mg., magnesium sulfate dried 7.2 mg., copper sulfate dried 5 mg., manganese sulfate 3.4 mg., potassium chloride 1.3 mg., liver desic. 100 mg., yeast dried 100 mg./Tab. Cartons 50s, 100s; apothecary 250s.

RUBICAPS B COMPLEX W/C. (Stanlabs) Vit. B-1 15 mg., B-2 10 mg., B-6 5 mg., C 300 mg., niacinamide 50 mg., Ca pantothenate 10 mg./Cap. Bot. 100s.
Use: Therapeutic B complex.

RUBICAPS SUPER M. (Stanlabs) Vit. A 50,000 I.U., D 1500 I.U., B-1 16 mg., B-2 10 mg., B-6 2 mg., B-12 12 mcg., C 150 mg., E 5 I.U., Ca pantothenate 10 mg., niacinamide 100 mg., rutin 10 mg., hesperidin 15 mg., biotin 20 mcg., betaine HCl 10 mg., para-aminobenzoic acid 20 mg., choline bitartrate 50 mg., inositol 20 mg., dl-methionine 20 mg., Fe 25 mg., Iodine 0.15 mg., Cu 2.5 mg., Mn 2 mg., Zn 3 mg., Mg 6 mg., Ca 58 mg., P 45 mg., K 5 mg., liver desic. 100 mg./Geltab. Bot. 100s.
Use: Therapeutic Vitamin Supplement.

• **RUBIDIUM CHLORIDE Rb 86.** USAN.
Use: Radioactive agent.

RUBRAMIN PC. (Squibb) Vit. B-12 U.S.P. (cyanocobalamin) w/benzyl alcohol 1%, sod. chloride, sod. hydroxide or HCl acid. (100 mcg./cc.; cobalt content 4 mcg./ml.) Vial 10 cc. (1000 mcg./cc.; cobalt content 40 mcg./ml.) Vial 1, 10 cc. Unimatic: 100 mcg./cc. 1 dose syringe 1s, 10s. 1,000 mcg./cc. 1 dose syringe 1s, 10s.
Use: Vitamin for various anemias.

RUBRAPET OINTMENT. (Medco Lab) Red veterinary petrolatum for light protection Jar. 16 oz.

RUBRAPLEX. (Lannett) Vitamins B-1 2.5 mg., B-2 2 mg., B-6 0.5 mg., B-12 5 mcg., cal. pantothenate 1 mg., niacinamide 20 mg./Cap. Bot. 100s, 1000s.

RUBRATOPE-57. (Squibb) Cyanocobalamin Co 57 Capsules; Solution U.S.P.

RUBRAVITE LIQUID. (Lannett) Vit. B-1 10 mg., B-12 25 mcg./5 cc. Bot. pt.

RUELENE. Crufomate, B.A.N.

RUFEN. (Boots) Ibuprofen 400 mg. or 600 mg./Tab. Bot. 100s, 500s.
Use: Relief of mild to moderate pain in rheumatoid arthritis, osteoarthritis, dysmenorrhea.

RUFEN TABS. (Goldline) Ibuprofen 400 mg. or 600 mg./Tab. Bot. 100s, 500s.
Use: Anti-inflammatory.

RUFOCROMOMYCIN. B.A.N. An antibiotic produced by *Streptomyces rufochromogenus.*

RUFOLEX. (Lannett) Vit. B-1 1.5 mg., B-2 1.5 mg., B-6 1 mg., B-12 5 mcg., C 50 mg., niacinamide 10 mg., ferrous fumarate 200 mg., d-sorbitol 200 mg., folic acid 0.25 mg./Cap. Bot. 100s.
Use: Iron & vitamin deficiencies.

RU-LETS M 500. (Rugby) Vitamin C 500 mg., niacinamide 100 mg., calcium pantothenate 20 mg., B-1 15 mg., B-2 10 mg., B-6 5 mg., A 10,000 I.U., B-12 12 mcg., D 400 I.U., E 30 I.U., Mg 80 mg., Fe 20 mg., Cu 2 mg., Zn 1.5 mg., Mn 1 mg., iodine 0.15 mg./Tab. Bot. 100s.
Use: Dietary supplement.

RUM-K-SYRUP. (Fleming) Potassium chloride 10 mEq/5 u. in butter/rum flavored base. Bot. pt., gal.
Use: Potassium supplement.

RUPHENAMIN. (Lannett) Aminophylline 100 mg., phenobarbital 15 mg., rutin 20 mg./Cap. Bot. 1000s.
Use: Cardiovascular disorders.

RUSCORB. (Robinson) **20/100:** Rutin 20 mg., C 100 mg./Tab. **50/300:** Rutin 50 mg., C 300 mg./Tab. Bot. 100s, 1000s.

RUST INHIBITOR.
See: Anti-Rust, Tab. (Winthrop-Breon)
Sodium Nitrite, Tab. (Var. Mfr.)

• **RUTAMYCIN.** USAN. From strain of *Streptomyces rutgersensis.* Under study.
Use: Antifungal antibiotic.

RUTGERS 612.
See: Ethohexadiol. (Var. Mfr.)

RUTIN. 3-Rhamnoglucoside of 5,7,3′,4′-tetrahydroxyflavonol. Eldrin, globulariacitrin, myrticalorin, oxyritin, phytomelin, rutoside, sophorin. Various Mfr.—Tab. (20, 50, 60 & 100 mg.)
Use: Vascular disorders.

RUTIN COMBINATIONS
See: Hexarutan, Tab. (Westerfield)
Hyrunal, Tab. (Kenyon)
Vio-Geric-H, Tab. (Rowell)

RUTOSIDE.
See: Rutin, Tab. (Var. Mfr.)

RU-TUSS II. (Boots) Phenylpropanolamine HCl 75 mg., chlorpheniramine maleate 12 mg./Cap. Bot. 100s.
Use: Relief of symptoms of sinus and nasal congestion.

RU-TUSS EXPECTORANT. (Boots) Codeine phosphate 59.1 mg., phenylephrine HCl 30 mg., chlorpheniramine maleate 12 mg., ammonium chloride 200 mg./30 ml. w/alcohol 5%. Bot. Pts.
Use: Expectorant, antitussive, antihistaminic, nasal decongestant.

U-TUSS LIQUID. (Boots) Phenylephrine HCl 30 mg., chlorpheniramine maleate 12 mg./30 ml. w/alcohol 5%. Bot. Pt.
Use: Relief of symptoms of hayfever, allergies, nasal congestion.

U-TUSS SUSTAINED RELEASE. (Boots) Phenylephrine HCl 25 mg., phenlypropanolamine HCl 50 mg., chlorpheniramine maleate 8 mg., hyoscyamine sulfate 0.19 mg., atropine sulfate 0.04 mg., scopolamine hydrobromide 0.01 mg./Tab. Bot. 100s, 500s.
Use: Relief of symptoms of sinus, nasal congestion.

U-TUSS TABLETS. (Boots) Bot. 100s, 500s.
Use: Decongestant, antisecretory.

U-TUSS w/HYDROCODONE. (Boots) Hydrocodone bitartrate 10 mg., phenylephrine HCl 30 mg., phenylpropanolamine HCl 20 mg., pheniramine maleate 20 mg., pyrilamine maleate 20 mg./30 ml. w/alcohol 5%. Bot. pt.
Use: Relief of symptoms of hay fever, allergies, nasal congestion & cough.

U-VERT M. (Reid-Provident) Meclizine HCl 25 mg./Tab. Bot. 100s.
Use: Antihistamine.

VP. (Elder) Red petrolatum, paraben & lanolin-free sunscreen. Oint. Tube 2 oz.
Use: Topical sunscreen ointment.

VPaba. (Elder) p-Aminobenzoic acid 5% in neutral red petrolatum-wax base/Lipstick. Stick 4.4 Gm.

V PAQUE. (Elder) Red petrolatum, zinc oxide, 2-ethoxyethyl p-methoxycinnamate in water-resistant base. Tube 0.5 oz., 1.25 oz.
Use: Opaque sunblock.

YMED. (Edwards) Phenylephrine HC1 5 mg., phenylpropanolamine HC1 45 mg., guaifenesin 200 mg./Cap. Bot. 100s.
Use: Decongestion, expectorant.

YMED-JR. (Edwards) Phenylephrine HC1 2.5 mg., phenylpropanolamine HC1 22.5 mg., guaifenesin 100 mg./Cap. Bot. 100s.
Use: Decongestion, expectorant.

YMED LIQUID. (Edwards) Phenylephrine HC1 5 mg., phenylpropanolamine HC1 20 mg., guaifenesin 100 mg./5cc. w/alcohol 5%. Bot. pt.
Use: Decongestant, expectorant.

YMED-TR. (Edwards) Phenylephrine HC1 10 mg., phenylpropanolamine HCl 75 mg., guaifenesin 300 mg./Cap. Bot. 100s.
Use: Decongestion, expectorant.

YNA. (Wallace) Chlorpheniramine 2 mg., pseudoephedrine HCl 30 mg./5 ml. Bot. 4 oz., pt.
Use: Antihistaminic, nasal decongestant.

YNA-C. (Wallace) Codeine phosphate 10 mg., pseudoephedrine HCl 30 mg., chlorpheniramine maleate 2 mg./5 ml. Bot. 4 oz., pt.
Use: Excessive coughs.

YNA-CX. (Wallace) Guaifenesin 100 mg., pseudoephedrine HCl 30 mg., codeine phosphate 10 mg./5 cc. Bot. 4 oz., pt.
Use: Dry unproductive cough.

RYNATAN. (Wallace) **Tab.:** Phenylephrine tannate 25.0 mg., chlorpheniramine tannate 8 mg., pyrilamine tannate 25 mg./Tab. Bot. 100s, 500s. **Pediatric Susp.** Phenylephrine tannate 5 mg., chlorpheniramine tannate 2 mg., pyrilamine tannate 12.5 mg./5 ml. Bot. pt., gal.
Use: Upper respiratory congestion resulting from colds, sinusitis, allergic rhinitis.

RYNATAPP. (General Pharm.) Brompheniramine maleate 4 mg., phenylephrine HCl 5 mg., phenylpropanolamine HCl 5 mg., alcohol 2.3%/5 ml. Bot. Pts.
Use: Rhinitis treatment.

RYNATUSS. (Wallace) Carbetapentane tannate 60 mg., chlorpheniramine tannate 5 mg., ephedrine tannate 10 mg., phenylephrine tannate 10 mg./Tab. Bot. 100s, 500s.
Use: Treatment of cough associated with common cold.

RYNATUSS PEDIATRIC SUSPENSION. (Wallace) Carbetapentane tannate 30 mg., chlorpheniramine tannate 4 mg., ephedrine tannate 5 mg., phenylephrine tannate 5 mg./5 ml. Susp. Bot. 8 oz., pt.
Use: Treatment of cough associated with common cold.

RYTHMOL. 2,6-bis(1-Piperidylmethyl)-4-(α,α-di-methylbenzyl)phenol dihydrobromide.
Use: Treatment of cardiac arrhythmias.

RHTHMODAN. Disopyramide, B.A.N.

RYTHROSITE. (Xttrium) Vit. B-12 12.5 mcg., intrinsic factor concentrate 10 mg., dried ferrous sulfate 200 mg., folic acid 2 mg., Vit. C 100 mg., liver desic. 50 mg./Tab. Bot. 100s, 1000s.
Use: Hematinic and vitamin supplement.

S

S-2 INHALANT & NEBULIZERS. (Nephron) Racemic epinephrine HCl 2.25%. Bot. 1 oz., 0.5 oz., 0.25 oz.
Use: Inhalant for bronchial asthma.

SAC-500. (Western Research) Vitamin C 500 mg./Timed Release Cap. Bot. 1000s.
Use: Vitamin supplement.

S.A.C. SINUS TABS. (Towne) Acetaminophen 150 mg., salicylamide 150 mg., phenylpropanolamine HCl 25 mg., phenyltoloxamine citrate 22 mg./Tab. Bot. 30s, 100s.

S-A-C TABLETS. (Lannett) Salicylamide 230 mg., acetominophen 150 mg., caffeine 30 mg./Tab. Bot. 36s, 100s, 1000s, 5000s.
Use: Muscular aches.

• **SACCHARIN,** N.F. XVI. 1,2-Benzisothiazolin-3-one-1, 1-dioxide.
(Merck)—Pkg. 1 oz., 0.25 lb., 1 lb.
(Squibb) Tabs. 0.25, 0.5 gr. Bot. 500s, 1000s; 1 gr. Bot. 1000s.
Use: Sweetening agent when sugar is contraindicated.
See: Necta Sweet, Tab. (Norwich Eaton)

• **SACCHARIN CALCIUM,** U.S.P. XXI. 1,2-Benzisothiazolin-3-one 1, 1-dioxide calcium salt hydrate (2:7)
Use: Non-nutritive sweetener.

• **SACCHARIN SODIUM,** U.S.P. XXI. Oral Soln., Tab., U.S.P. XXI. (Benzosulfimide Sod., Soluble Gluside, Soluble Saccharine) Pow., Bot. 1 oz., 0.25 lb., 1 lb. Tab. usual sizes. (Various Mfr.)
Use: Sweetening agent & test for circulation time of blood.
See: Crystallose, Crystals, Liq. (Jamieson)
Ril Sweet, Liq. (Plough)
Sucaryl, Liq., Tab. (Abbott)

SACCHARIN SOLUBLE.
See: Saccharin Sodium, Tab., Pow. (Var. Mfr.)

SACO. (Jenkins) B-12 activity 20 mcg., B-1 10 mg./Tab. Bot. 100s.
Use: Hematinic.

SACO JR. (Jenkins) B-12 activity 20 mcg., B-1 10 mg./Tab. Bot. 100s.
Use: Nutritional supplement hematinic.

SAFAPRYN. Paracetamol, B.A.N.

SAFESKIN. (C & M Pharmacal) A dermatologically acceptable detergent for patients who are sensitive to ordinary detergents. No whiteners, brighteners or other irritants. Bot. Qt.
Use: Laundry detergent for sensitive skin.

SAFE SUDS. (Ar-Ex) Hypoallergenic, all-purpose detergent for patients whose hands or respiratory membranes are irritated by soaps or detergents. pH 6.8. No enzymes, phosphates, lanolin, fillers, bleaches. Bot. 22 oz.

SAFETY-COATED ARTHRITIS PAIN FORMULA. (Whitehall) Entericcoated aspirin 500 mg./Tab. Bot. 24s, 60s.
Use: Arthritis pain.

SAFFLOWER OIL.
See: Safflower Oil Caps. (Various Mfr.)
W/Choline bitartrate, soybean lecithin, inositol, natural tocopherols, B-6, B-12, & panthenol.
See: Nutricol, Cap., Vial (Nutrition)

SAFROLE. 4-Allyl-1,2-(methylenedioxy) benzene.

SAF-T-COIL. (Schmid) Intrauterine device. Sizes 33-S, 32-S, 25-S. 1s, 6s.
Use: Contraceptive.

SALACETIN.
See: Acetylsalicylic Acid (Var. Mfr.)

SALACID 25%. (Gordon) Salicylic acid 25% In ointment base. Jar 2 oz.
Use: Keratolytic.

SALACID 60%. (Gordon) Salicylic acid 60% in ointment base. Jar 2 oz.
Use: Keratolytic.

SALACTIC FILM. (Pedinol) Salicylic acid 16.7%, lactic acid 16.7% in flexible collodian w/color. Applicator Bot. 0.5 oz.
Use: Topical removal of verrucae.

• **SALANTEL.** USAN.
Use: Anthelmintic.

SALATAR CREAM. (Lannett) Coal tar solution 5%, salicylic acid 3%. Jar 4 oz., 1 lb.

SALAZIDE TABS. (Major) Hydroflumethiazide and reserpine. Bot. 100s, 500s.
Use: Antihypertensive.

SALAZOPYRIN. Sulphasalazine, B.A.N.

SALAZOSULFAPYRIDINE (I.N.N.). Sulphasalazine, B.A.N.

SALAZOSULPHADIMIDINE. B.A.N. 4'-(4,6-Dimethylpyrimidin-2-ylsulphamoyl)-4-hydroxyazo-benzene-3-carboxylic acid.
Use: Sulfonamide.
See: Azudimidine

SALBUTAMOL. B.A.N. 1-(4-Hydroxy-3-hydroxy-methylphenyl)-2-(t-butylamino)ethanol.
Use: Bronchodilator.

SALCATONIN. B.A.N. A component of natural salmon calcitonin.
Use: Treatment of hypercalcemia and Paget's disease.

SALCEGEL. (Apco) Sodium salicylate 5 gr., calcium ascorbate 25 mg., calcium carbonate 1.0 gr., dried aluminum hydroxide gel 2.0 gr./Tab. Bot. 100s.
Use: Arthritis, rheumatoid involvements.

• **SALCOLEX.** USAN.
Use: Analgesic, anti-inflammatory.

SAL-DEX. (Scrip) Undecylenic acid 10%, salicylic acid 15%, Isopropyl alcohol 40%, propylene glycol. Bot. 15 cc.

SAL DEX BORO. (Scrip) Tannic acid 46 mg., boric acid 29 mg., salicylic acid 8 mg., isoprpyl alcohol 56%/cc. 15 cc.

SALETIN.
See: Acetylsalicylic Acid (Var. Mfr.)

• **SALETHAMIDE MALEATE.** USAN. N-[2-Di-ethyl-(amino)ethyl]-salicylamide maleate. Under study.
Use: Analgesic.

SALETO. (Mallard) Aspirin 210 mg., acetaminophen 115 mg., salicylamide 65 mg./caffeine anhydrous 16 mg./Tab. Bot. 50s, 100s, 1000s.
Use: Analgesic.

SALETO-D. (Mallard) Acetaminophen 240 mg., salicylamide 120 mg., caffeine 16 mg., phenylpropanolamine HCl 20 mg./Cap. Bot. 50s.

SALFURIDE.
See: Nifursol, B.A.N.

SAL HEPATICA TABLETS. (Chattem) Powdered Senna extract 200 mg./Tab. Bot. 30s.
Use: Laxative.

SALIBAR Jr. (Jenkins) Aspirin 2 gr., phenobarbital ⅛ gr./Tab. Bot. 1000s.
Use: Analgesic and sedative.

• **SALICYL ALCOHOL.** USAN.
Use: Local anesthetic.

SALICYLAMIDE. B.A.N. (Bryant) o-Hydroxybenzamide. Salimed
Use: Analgesic; antipyretic.
See: Amid-Sal, Tab. (Glenwood)
Doldram, Tab. (Dram)
Os-Cal-Gesic (Marion)
Salamide, Tab. (Philips Roxane)
Salrin, Tab. (Warren-Teed)

SALICYLAMIDE W/COMBINATIONS
See: A.C.A. #5, Tab. (Scrip)
A.C.D., Tab. (Philips Roxane)
Akes-N-Pain, Cap. (Edward J. Moore)
Aludine C.T. Lav., Tab. (Scrip)
Anodynos, Tab. (Buffington)
Anodynos Forte, Tab. (Buffington)
APC W/Antihistamine, Tab. (Sutliff & Case)
Arthol, Tab. (Towne)
Asco, Cap., Tab. (Sutliff & Case)
Bancaps (Westerfield)
Bancaps-C (Westerfield)
Banesin-Forte, Tab. (Westerfield)
Calm Caps, Cap. (Edward J. Moore)
Calsuxaphen, Cap., Tab. (Lannett)
Cenaid, Tab. (Century)
Centuss, MLT Tab. (Century)
Children's Cold Tab. (Towne)
Chlorphen, Tab. (Wolins)
Chlorphenwol, Cap. (Wolins)
Codalan, 1,2,3, Tab. (Lannett)
Colchek, Tab. (Creomulsion)
Coriforte, Cap. (Schering)
Dapco, Tab. (Mericon)
Decohist, Cap. (Towne)
Dengesic, Tab. (Scott-Alison)
Dodamin, Tab. (Reid-Provident)
Dolopar, Tab. (O'Neal)
Dovamide, Cap. (Philips Roxane)
Du-Min Chewable, Tab. (Scrip)
Duoprin, Tab. (Dunhall)
Duo-3X, Tab. (Med Spec)
Duramid, Tab. (O'Neal)
Emagrin, Tab. (Otis Clapp)
Emagrin Forte, Tab. (Otis Clapp)
Emersal, Liq. (Medco)
Enz-Cold, Cap. (Edward J. Moore)
Excedrin P.M., Tab. (Bristol-Myers)
F.C.A.H., Cap. (Scherer)
Femicin, Tab. (Norcliff Thayer)
Guaiamine, Cap. (Sutliff & Case)
Her-Caps, Cap. (Edward J. Moore)
Hista-Derfule, Cap. (Cole)
Hista-Compound #5 Tab. (Vortech)
Histalets, Tab., (Quality Generics)
Histalets, Tab. (Edward J. Moore)
Hi-Temp (Saron)
Hycoff Cold, Caps. (Saron)
Kiddisan, Tab. (O'Neal)
Kleer Compound, Tab. (Scrip)
Medache, Tab. (Organon)
Medigesic, Tab. (Medics)
Metrogesic, Tab. (Metro Med)
Midran, Tab. (Quality Generics)
Myocalm, Tab. (Parmed)
Neo-Pyranistan (Standex)
Nokane, Tab. (Wren)
Nosalco, Cap. (Noyes)
Nytol, Tab., Cap. (Block)
Orastin, Tab. (Commerce)
Ornex, Cap. (SmithKline)
Os-Cal-Gesic, Tab. (Marion)
Panritis, Tab. (Pan Amer.)
Parba-KS, Tab. (Elder)
Parbocyl, Tab. (Elder)
Partuss-A, Tab. (Parmed)
Partuss T.D., Tab. (Parmed)
Phenatrohist, Cap. (O'Neal)
Phenetron Compound, Tab. (Lannett)
Pirin-C, Tab. (Scrip)
P.M.P. Compound, Tab. (Mericon)
Presalin, Tab. (Mallard)
Pyradyne, Tab. (Lemmon)
Pyradyne Comp., Tab. (Lemmon)
Pyranistan Compound (Standex)
Renpap, Tab. (Wren)
Rhinex, Tab. (Lemmon)
Rinocidin, Cap. (Cenci)
S-A-C, Tab. (Lannett)
S.A.C., Preps. (Towne)
Saleto, Preps. (Mallard)
Salimeph-Forte, Tab. (Kremers-Urban)
Salipap, Tab. (Freeport)
Salocol, Tab. (Mallard)
Salphenyl, Liq., Cap. (Mallard)
Sanger Special, Tab. (Edward J. Moore)
Scotgesic, Cap., Elix. (Scott/Cord)
Sedacane, Cap. (Edward J. Moore)
Sedagesic, Tab. (Kay)
Sedalgesic, Tab. (Table Rock)
Sedragesic, Tab. (Lannett)
Sino-Comp., Tab. (Bio-Factor)
Sinulin, Tab. (Reed & Carnrick)
Sleep, Tab. (Towne)
Sominex, Cap., Tab. (J.B. Williams)
S.P.C., Prep. (Vortech)
Statomin Maleate, Tab. (Bowman)
Stopain, Tab. (Quality Generics)
Sure-Sleep, Tab. (Amer. Lab.)
Tega-code Caps (Ortega)
Teragen, Tab. (O'Neal)
Thor, Cap (Towne)
Triaprin-DC, Cap. (Dunhall)
Tri-Hist-Cap, Cap. (Burgin-Arden)
Tripac, Tab. (Person & Covey)
Tussapap, Tab. (Sutliff & Case)
Volaxin, Tab. (Elder)
Volaxin-A, Tab. (Elder)

SALICYLANILIDE. N-Phenyl salicylamide.
Use: Antifungal agent.

SALICYLATED BILE EXTRACT. Chologestin.

• **SALICYLATE MEGLUMINE.** USAN.
Use: Antirheumatic, analgesic.

SALICYLAZOSULFAPYRIDINE.
See: Sulfasalazine, U.S.P. XXI.

• **SALICYLIC ACID,** U.S.P. XXI. Collodion, Plaster, Gel, U.S.P. XXI. Benzoic acid, 2-hydroxy. Orthohydroxybenzoic acid Cryst., Pkg. 1 oz., 0.25 lb., 1 lb. Pow., Pkg. 0.25 lb., 1 lb.
Use: Keratolytic agent.
See: Calicylic, Creme (Gordon)
Listrex Scrub, Liq. (Warner-Lambert)
Salonil, Cream (Torch)
Sebulex, Cream (Westwood)

SALICYLIC ACID COMBINATIONS
See: Acnaveen, Bar (Cooper)
Acno (Cummins)
Akne Drying Lotion, Liq. (Alto)
Aromatic Foot Pow. (Gordon)
Barseb Thera-spray, aerosol (Barnes-Hind)Alt
Cuticura (Purex)
D.D.D. Prescription, Regular (Campana)
Derma-Cover, Liq. (Scrip)
Domerine Medicated Shampoo (Miles Pharm)
Duofilm, Liq. (Stiefel)
Duo-WR, Sol. (Whorton)
Estercol, Emulsion (Torch)
Exzit Cleanser (Miles Pharm)
Fibrodon, Oint. (Gordon)
Fomac Foam (Dermik)
Fostex, Cream, Liq. (Westwood)
Fostril, Cream (Westwood)
Foursalco, Tab. (Jenkins)
Fungicidal, Oint. (Gordon)
Furol Cream (Torch)
Gets-It, Liq. (Plough)
Ionax, Liq. (Owen)
Ionil, Liq. (Owen)
Ionil T, Liq. (Owen)
Keralyt, Gel (Westwood)
Klaron, Lot. (Dermik)
Komed, Lot. (Barnes-Hind)
Komed HC, Lot. (Barnes-Hind)
Lasan Pomade, Cream (Stiefel)
Lasan 2, Cream (Stiefel)
Lasan 4, Cream (Stiefel)
Maseda Foot Powder, Pow. (Elder)
Mild Komed, Lot. (Banres-Hind)
Neutrogena Disposables (Neutrogena)
NP-27 Prod. (Norwich)
Onycho-Phytex, Liq. (Unimed)
Pernox, Lot. (Westwood)
Pixacol, Bot. (Pixacol)
Podiaspray, Aerosol Pow. (Dalin)
Pragmatar, Oint. (Menley & James)
Prosal, Liq. (Gordon)
Prosol, Emulsion (Torch)
Pytosin, Liq. (Blue Line)
Resorcitate, Lot. (Almay)
Rezamid, Liq. (Dermik)
Salatar, Cream (Lannett)
Sal-Dex, Liq. (Scrip)
Salicide, Oint. (Gordon Labs.)
Salicylic Acid Soap (Stiefel)
Saligel, Gel (Stiefel)
Salsprin, Tab. (Seatrace)
Sal-Su-Tar, Oint. (ulmer)
Sebaveen, Shampoo (Cooper)
Sebucare, Liq. (Westwood)
Sebulex Shampoo, Liq. (Westwood)
Skaylos, Cream, Lot. (Ambix)
Tan-Bar-Sal, Liq. (Gordon)
Therac, Lot. (C&M Pharm.)
Therapads, Pads (Fuller)
Tinver, Lot. (Barnes-Hind)
Vanseb, Dandruff Shampoo (Herbert)
Vanseb-T Tar Shampoo (Herbert)
Verdefam, Cream, Sol. (Owen)
Vericin, Oint. (Gordon)
Ver-Var, Sol. (Owen)
Zemacol, Lotion (Norwich)

SALICYLIC ACID CREAM. (Durel) Salicylic acid 5%, in Duromantel cream.
Use: Superficial fungus infections, psoriasis, hyperkeratosis of palms and soles.

SALICYLIC ACID SOAP. (Stiefel) Neutral soap containing salicylic acid 3.5%. Cake 4 oz.
Use: Softens rough skin.

SALICYLIC ACID & SULFUR SOAP. (Stiefel) Salicylic acid 3%, sulfur 10% in neutral soap bar. Cake 4.1 oz.
Use: Anti-fungal cleansing.

• **SALICYLIC ACID TOPICAL FOAM,** U.S.P. XXI.

SALICYLSALICYLIC ACID.
Use: Analgesic.
See: Arcylate, Tab. (Hauck)
Disalcid, Tab. (Riker)
W/Aspirin.
See: Causalin, Tab. (Amfre-Grant)
Duragesic, Tab. (Meyer)
Persistin, Tab. (Fisons)

SALICYLSULPHONIC ACID. Sulfosalicylic acid. Dextrotest (Ames).

SALIGEL. (Stiefel) 5% salicylic acid in a special hydroalcoholic gel base. Tube. 2 oz.
Use: Acne therapy.

SALIGENIN. (City Chem.) Salicyl alcohol. Bot. 25 Gm., 100 Gm.
W/Merodicein.
See: Thantis, Loz. (Hyson, Westcott & Dunning)

SALIMED. Salicylamide, B.A.N.

SALINAZID. B.A.N. 2′-Salicylideneisonicotinohydrazide
Use: Treatment of tuberculosis.
See: Nupa-sal

SALINEZ NASAL DROPS. (Muro) Buffered nasal isotonic saline drop. Bot. 15 ml. w/dropper.
Use: Nasal moisturizer.

SALINEX NASAL MIST. (Muro) Buffered isotonic saline nasal mist. Bot. 50 ml.
Use: Nasal moisturizer.

SALIPAP. (Freeport) Salicylamide 5 gr., acetaminophen 5 gr./Tab. Bot. 1000s.
Use: Relief of minor aches and pains.

SALIPRAL. (Kenyon) Allylisobutyl-barbituric acid ¾ gr., aspirin 3 gr., phenacetin 2 gr., caffeine ⅔ gr./Tab. Bot. 1000s.

SALIPRAL-C. (Kenyon) Same formula as above w/Vit. C/Cap. Bot. 100s, 1000s.
Use: Sedative-analgesic.

SALITHOL LIQUID. (Madland) Balm of methyl salicylate, menthol and camphor. Bot. pt., gal. Also ointment, jar 1 & 5 lbs.
Use: Liquid analgesic balm.

SALIVART. (Westport) Carbooxymethylcellulose sodium 1 gr., sorbitol 3 gr., sodium Cl 0.084 gr., potassium Cl 0.12 gr., Ca Cl 0.015 gr., magnesium Cl 0.005 gr., potassium monohydrogen phosphate 0.034 gr./100 ml. Bot. 50 ml. aerosol spray cans.
Use: Synthetic saliva.

LMEFAMOL. B.A.N. 1-(4-Hydroxy-3-hydroxy-methylphenyl)-2-(4-methoxy-α-methylphenethylamino)ethanol.
Use: Bronchodilator.

LOCOL. (Mallard) Aspirin 210 mg., acetaminophen 115 mg., salicylamide 65 mg., caffeine anhydrous 16 mg./Tab. Bot. 100s.

LONIL. (Torch) Salicylic acid 40%, in lanolin. Jar. 1 lb.
Use: Treat hyperkeratotic plaques & callosites.

LPABA W/COLCHICINE. (Madland) Sodium salicylate 0.25 Gm., para-aminobenzoic acid 0.25 Gm., Vit. C 20 mg., colchicine 0.25 mg./Tab. Bot. 100s, 1000s.
Use: Gout and gouty arthritis.

LPHENYL. (Mallard) Salicylamide 200 mg., acetaminophen 130 mg., chlorpheniramine maleate 2 mg., phenylephrine HCl 10 mg./Cap. Bot. 100s.
Use: Analgesic, antipyretic, nasal decongestant.

L-RUB. (Mallard) Triethanolamine salicylate 10% in nongreasy base. Tube 2 oz.
Use: External rubbing creme.

SALSALATE. USAN.
Use: Antiarthritic.
See: Disalcid, tab. (Riker)

LTEN. (Wren) Salicylamide 10 gr./Tab. Bot. 100s, 1000s.

SALT SUBSTITUTES.
Use: Sodium free seasoning agent.
See: Diasal Salt (Savage)
NoSalt (Norcliff Thayer)

ALT TABLETS. (Cross) Sodium chloride 650 mg./Tab. Dispensers 500s.
Use: Replace salt lost from perspiration.

ALUPRES. Hydrochlorothiazide, B.A.N.

ALURIC. Chlorothiazide, B.A.N.

ALURON. (Bristol) Hydroflumethiazide 50 mg./Tab. Bot. 100s.
Use: Diuretic.

ALUTENSIN. (Bristol) Hydroflumethiazide 50 mg., reserpine 0.125 mg./Tab. Bot. 100s, 1000s.
Use: Antihypertensive.

ALUTENSIN-DEMI. (Bristol) Hydroflumethiazide 25 mg., reserpine 0.125 mg./Tab. Bot. 100s.
Use: Antihypertensive.

ALVARSAN.
Use: Antisyphilitic.
See: Arsphenamine (Various Mfr.)

ALVITE-B. (Faraday) Sodium chloride 7 gr., dextrose 3 gr., B-1 1 mg./Tab. Bot. 100s, 1000s.

ALYRGAN.
See: Mersalyl (Various Mfr.)

AMORIN HCl. Isometamidium, B.A.N.

ANAMYCIN. B.A.N. Actinomycin.
Use: Antineoplastic agent.

ANCHIA SILICONE PROTECTIVE CREAM. (Otis Clapp) Silicones and lanolin in greaseless cream base. Tube 3 oz. Jars 16 oz.
Use: Protective coating against industrial and medicinal chemicals.

SANCYCLINE. USAN. 6-Demethyl-6-deoxytetracycline. Formerly Norcycline.
Use: Antibiotic.
See: Bonomycin

SANDIMMUNE. (Sandoz) Cyclosporine. **Oral soln.:** 100 mg./ml. Bot. 50 ml. **Inj.:** 50 mg./ml. Amp. 5 ml. Box 10s.
Use: Prevention of rejection in kidney, liver, heart for transplants.

SANDOGLOBULIN. (Sandoz) Immune globulin 1 Gm./33 ml. reconstitution fluid; 3 Gm./100 ml. reconstitution fluid; 6 Gm./200 ml. reconstitution fluid.
Use: Immunodeficiency.

SANDOPTAL. Isobutyl allylbarbituric acid.
See: Butalbital
W/Caffeine, aspirin, phenacetin.
See: Fiorinal, Tab., Cap. (Sandoz)
W/Caffeine, aspirin, phenacetin, codeine phosphate.
See: Fiorinal w/codeine, Cap. (Sandoz)

SANDOPTAL SODIUM.
W/Sodium diethylbarbiturate, sod. phenylethylbarbiturate, scopolamine HBr, dihydroergotamine methanesulfonate.
See: Plexonal (Sandoz)

SANDOSTEN TARTRATE. Thenalidine, B.A.N.

SANESTRO. (Sandia) Estrone 0.7 mg., estradiol 0.35 mg., estriol 0.14 mg./Tab. Bot. 100s, 1000s.

SANGER HER CAPS. (Edward J. Moore) Acetaminophen 227 mg., aspirin 227 mg., caffeine arh. 32.4 mg./Cap. Bot. 18s.
Use: Menstrual pain and cramps.

SANGER SPECIAL C-12. (Edward J. Moore) Salicylamide, Co. colocynth ext., dried ferrous sulf., blue cohosh./Tab. Bot. 24s.

SANGER VAGINAL ITCH CREAM. (Edward J. Moore) Benzocaine, dibucaine, tetracaine. Tube 1.25 oz.
Use: Relief of vaginal itch.

SANGUIS. (Sig) Liver 10 mcg., B-12 100 mcg., folic acid 1 mcg./ml. Vial 10 ml.

SANHIST T.D. 5. (Sandia) Phenylpropanolamine HCl 50 mg., chlorpheniramine maleate 5 mg., ascorbic acid 100 mg./Tab. Bot. 100s, 1000s.

SANHIST T.D. 12. (Sandia) Phenylpropanolamine HCl 50 mg., chlorpheniramine maleate 12 mg., ascorbic acid 100 mg., methscopalamine nitrate 4 mg./Tab. Bot. 100s, 1000s.

SANILENS. (Ketchum) Bot. 4 oz.
Use: Contact lens soaking solution.

SANI-VESS. (Fellows) Papain, sodium bicarbonate, citric acid, tartaric acid, lactose, thymol, aromatics. Pkg. 6 oz.

SANLUOL.
See: Arsphenamine (Various Mfr.)

SANOREX. (Sandoz) Mazindol 1 mg., 2 mg./Tab. Bot. 100s.
Use: Treatment & control of obesity.

SANSERT. (Sandoz) Methysergide maleate 2 mg./Tab. Bot. 100s.
Use: Vascular headaches.

SANSPRIN. (Wolins) Acetaminophen 5 gr./Tab. Bot. 100s, 1000s.
Use: Analgesic.

SANSTRESS. (Sandia) Vit. A 25,000 I.U., Vit. D 400 I.U., B-1 10 mg., B-2 5 mg., niacinamide 100 mg., B-6 1 mg., B-12 5 mcg., C 150 mg., calcium 103 mg., phosphorus 80 mg., iron 10 mg., copper 1 mg., iodine 0.1 mg., magnesium 5.5 mg., manganese 1 mg., potassium 5 mg., zinc 1.4 mg./Cap. Bot. 100s, 1000s.
Use: Therapeutic vitamin & mineral preparation.

SANTISEPTIC LOTION. (Santiseptic) Menthol, phenol, benzocaine, zinc oxide, calamine. Bot. 4 oz.
Use: Itching and burning of eczema, hives, etc.

SANTOPHEN 1. (Monsanto) Septiphene. 4-Chloro-alpha-phenyl-o-cresol.
Use: Disinfectant.

SANTUSSIN ADULT SUSPENSION. (Sandia) Noscapine 10 mg., phenylpropanolamine HCl 12.5 mg., chlorpheniramine maleate 1.5 mg., acetaminophen (APAP) 60 mg., guiachlor compound (alcohol 12% by volume) 75 mg., guaifenesin 5 mg., ammonium chloride 70 mg./5 cc. Bot. 16 oz., gal.

SANTUSSIN CAPSULES. (Sandia) Noscapine 10 mg., phenylpropanolamine HCl 12.5 mg., chlorpheniramine maleate 1.5 mg., acetaminophen 120 mg., guaifenesin 100 mg./Cap. Bot. 100s, 1000s.

SANTUSSIN PEDIATRIC SUSPENSION. (Sandia) Noscapine 5 mg., phenylpropanolamine HCl 6.25 mg., chlorpheniramine maleate 0.75 mg., acetaminophen (APAP) 30 mg., guiachlor compound (alcohol 12% by volume) 37.5 mg./5 cc. Bot. 16 oz., gal.

SANTYL. (Knoll) Proteolytic enzyme derived from *Clostridium histolyticum.* 250 u./Gm. Oint. Tube 15 Gm., 30 Gm.
Use: Debriding dermal ulcers.

SAPONATED CRESOL SOLUTION.
See: Cresol (Var. Mfr.)

SAPONINS, WATER SOLUBLE.

• **SARALASIN ACETATE.** USAN.
Use: Antihypertensive.

SARAPIN. (High) An aqueous distillate of *Sarracenia purpurea,* pitcher plant, prepared for parenteral administration. Amps. 10 cc. 12s. Multidose Vials 50 cc.
Use: Relief of pain of neuromuscular or neuralgic origin.

SARATOGA OINTMENT. (Blair) Boric acid, zinc oxide, eucalyptol, servum preparatum & white petrolatum. Tube 1 oz., 2 oz.
Use: Relief of minor skin irritations.

L-SARCOLYSIN. Melphalan, U.S.P. XXI.

SARDO BATH OIL CONCENTRATE. (Plough) Mineral oil, isopropyl palmitate. Bot. 4 oz., 8 oz.
Use: Dry skin treatment.

SARDOETTES MOISTURIZING TOWELETTES. (Plough) Mineral oil, isopropyl palmitate, impregnated towelling material. Individual packets. Box 25s.
Use: Dry skin treatment.

SARISOL NO. 2. (Blue Cross) Sodium butabarbital 3 mg./Tab. Bot. 1000s.
Use: Sedative and hypnotic.

• **SARMOXICILLIN.** USAN.
Use: Antibacterial.

SARNA LOTION. (Stiefel) Camphor 0.5%, menthol 0.5%, phenol 0.5% in a soothing emollient base. Bot. 8 oz.
Use: Lotion for dry, itching skin.

SAROCYCLINE CAPSULES. (Saron) Tetracycline HCl. 250 mg./Cap. Bot. 100s.
Use: Antibiotic.

SARODANT. (Saron) Nitrofurantoin 50 mg./Tab. Bot. 100s, 1000s.
Use: Urinary tract antibacterial agent.

SAROFLEX. (Saron) Chlorzoxazone 250 mg., acetaminophen 300 mg./Cap.
Use: Muscle relaxant, analgesic

SAROLAX. (Saron) Docusate sodium 200 mg., phenolphthalein yellow 15 mg., dehydrocholic acid 20mg./Cap. Bot. 100s.
Use: Laxative

SAROTEN HYDROCHLORIDE. Amitriptyline, B.A.N.

• **SARPICILLIN.** USAN.
Use: Antibacterial.

S.A.S.-500. (Rowell) Sulfasalazine 500 mg./Tab. Bot. 100s, 1000s.
Use: Ulcerative colitis treatment.

S.A.S.P. (Zenith) Salicylazosulapyridine 500 mg./Tab. Bot. 100s, 500s.
Use: Ulcerative colitis.

SASTID PLAIN. (Stiefel) Sulfur 1.6%, salicylic acid 1.6%, in a surfactant cream base. Tube 2.5 oz.
Use: Cleanser; keratolytic & antiseborrheic, in management of acne.

SASTID (AL). (Stiefel) Sulfur 1.6%, Salicylic acid 1.6% w/20% aluminum oxide scrub particles. Tube 2.9 oz.
Use: Keratolytic & antiseborrheic in management of acne.

SASTID SOAP. (Stiefel) Precipitated sulfur 10%, salicylic acid 3% in a richly lathering soap base. Bar 4.1 oz.
Use: Cleanser & drying aid for acne treatment.

SATRIC. (Savage) Metronidazole. **250** mg./Tab. Bot. 100s, 250s. **500** mg./Tab. Bot. 60s.
Use: Anti-infective therapy for trichomoniasis and anaerobic bacterial infections.

SAUREX. (Enzyme Process) P 30 mg. pepsin 1:10,000 equal to 100 mg. pepesin 1:3000, betaine HCl 125 mg./Tab. Bot. 100s, 250s.
Use: Digestive aid.

SAXOL.
See: Petrolatum Liquid (Various Mfr.)

S.B.P. (Lemmon) Sodium secobarbital 50 mg., sodium butabarbital 30 mg., phenobarbital 15 mg./Tab. Bot. 1000s.
Use: Hypnotic; sedative.

SCABENE LOTION. (Stiefel) Lindane 1% in lotion base. Bot. 2 oz., 16 oz.
Use: Scabies & pediculosis treatment.

SCABENE SHAMPOO. (Stiefel) Lindane 1% in shampoo base. Bot. 2 oz., 16 oz.
Use: Treatment of pediculus capitis, phthirus pubis.

SCABICIDES.
See: Benzyl Benzoate (Var. Mfr.)
Cuprex, Liq. (Calgon)
Eurax, Cream, Lot. (Geigy)
Kwell, Lot., Cream, Shampoo (Reed & Carnrick)

SCADAN SCALP LOTION. (Miles Pharm) Cetyl trimethyl ammonium bromide (cetab) 1%, stearyl dimethyl benzyl ammonium chloride 0.1% in a nonalcoholic, nongreasy, pleasantly scented vehicle. Bot. plastic 4 oz.

SCAN. (Parker) Water soluble gel for ultrasound B scan procedures. Bot. 8 oz., gal.
Use: Ultrasound B scan procedures.

SCARLET RED. (Lilly) Oint. 5%. Tube 1 oz.

SCHAMBERG'S LOTION. (C & M Pharmacal) Menthol 0.15%, phenol 1.0% in lotion base. Bot. pt., gal.
Use: Pruritic type eczema.

• **SCHICK TEST CONTROL,** U.S.P. XXI.
Use: Diagnostic aid (dermal reactivity indicator).
See: Diphtheria Toxin, Diagnostic, Inactiv., (Var. Mfr.)

SCHIRMER TEAR TEST. (CooperVision) 10 envelopes of 5 sets.
Use: In vitro diagnostic.

SCHLESINGER'S SOLUTION.
See: Morphine HCl (Var. Mfr.)

SCLAVO BIOLOGICALS. (Sclavo) A wide variety of generic forms of biological products.

SCLAVOTEST-PPD. (Sclavo) Tuberculin purified protein derivative (PPD) multiple puncture device. 5 T.U. Box 20s, 250s.
Use: Tuberculin PPD screening.

SCLEREX. (Miller) Inositol 2 Gm., magnesium complex 34 mg., vit. C 100 mg., calcium succinate 25 mg., vit. A 2500 I.U., D 200 I.U., E 15 I.U., B-1 5 mg., B-2 2 mg., B-6 4 mg., B-12 3 mcg., niacin 10 mg., niacinamide 30 mg., pantothenic acid 7.5 mg., Fe 10 mg., Cu 1 mg., Mn 1 mg., Zn 3 mg., Iodine 0.10 mg./3 Tab. Box. 60s.
Use: Dietary supplement.

SCLEROSING AGENTS.
See: Glucose, Liq. (Var. Mfr.)
Invert Sugar (Various Mfr.)
Quinine & Urea HCl
Sodium Morrhuate, Inj. (Various Mfr.)
Sotradecol Sod., Vial (Elkins-Sinn)

SCOLINE. Suxamethonium Chloride, B.A.N.

• **SCOPAFUNGIN.** USAN.
Use: Antifungal, antibacterial.

SCOPETTES. (Birchwood) **Swabs:** 16″ Protosigmoidoscopic Swabs. Case 12s, 500s.
Junior: 8″ throat or vaginal swab. case 12s, 500s.
Sterile Junior: Same as Junior and sterile.

SCOPINE CHRONCAP. (Cenci) Scopolamine HBr 0.0195 mg., atropine sulfate 0.0582 mg., hyoscyamine sulfate 0.311 mg., phenobarbital 50.0 mg./Cap. Bot. 100s.
Use: Antispasmodic, sedative.

SCOPODEX. (CMC) Scopolamine aminoxide HBr, genoscopolamine HBr. Pellet 0.5 mg., Bot. 100s.
Use: Motion sickness.

SCOPOLAMINE. Hyoscine, l-Scopolamine, Epoxytropine tropate.
See: Hyoscine Preps. (Various Mfr.)

SCOPOLAMINE AMINOXIDE HBr.
See: Genoscopolamine, Pellets (CMC)
W/Acetylcarbromal and bromisovalum.
See: Tranquinal, Tab. (Barnes-Hind)

• **SCOPOLAMINE HYDROBROMIDE,** U.S.P. XXI. Inj., Ophth. Oint., Ophth. Soln., Tab., U.S.P. XXI.
Benzeneacetic acid, α-(hydroxymethyl)-, 9-methyl-3-oxa-9-azatricyclo [3.3.1.02,4]non-7-yl ester, hydrobromide, trihydrate. 6β, 7β-Epoxy-lαH,5αH-tropan-3α-ol($-$)-tropate(ester)hydrobromide trihydrate. Hyoscine HBr.
Use: Hypnotic & sedative, anticholinergic, mydriatic and cyclopegic.
W/Atropine sulf., ammonium benzoate, methenamine, salol.
See: Cystorrhoids W/Atropine, Tab. (Noyes)
W/Atropine and hyoscyamine.
See: Atropine sulfate table
Belladonna alkaloids
W/Butabarbital, chlorpheniramine maleate.
See: Pedo-Sol, Elix., Tab. (Warren)
W/Homatropine methylbromide, atropine sulfate, butabarbital, hyoscyamine sulfate.
See: Butabell HMB, Elix., Tabs. (Saron)
W/Hydroxypropyl methylcellulose.
See: Isopto HBr, Sol. (Alcon)
W/Hyoscyamine sulfate, atropine sulfate, phenobarbital.
See: Bar-Cy-Amine, Elix. (Sutliff & Case)
Bar-Cy, Tabs. (Sutliff & Case)
DeTal, Eliz., Tab. (DeLeon)
Donnacin, Elix., Tab. (Pharmex)
Fenatron, Prep. (Panray)
Hyonal C.T., Tab. (Paddock)
Hytrona, Tab. (Webcon)
Nilspasm, Tab. (Parmed)
Peece Kaps (Scrip)
Peece TC, Cap. (Scrip)
Scopine, Cap. (Cenci)
Sedamine, Tab. (Dunhall)
Sedapar, Tab. (Parmed)
Setamine, Tab. (Reid-Provident)
Spasaid, Cap. (Century)
Spasidon, Tab. (Haag)
Spasmolin, Tab. (Wolins)
Stannitol (Standex)
W/Pamabrom, pyrilamine maleate, homatropine methylbromide, hyoscyamine sulfate, methamphetamine HCl.
See: Aridol, Tabs. (MPL)
W/Phenylephrine, phenylpropanolamine, atropine sulfate, chlorpheniramine maleate, acetaminophen, hyoscyamine HBr.
See: Koryza Tab. (Fellows-Testagar)

SCOPOLAMINE HYDROBROMIDE COMBINATIONS.
See: Belladonna Products
Hyoscione HBr. (Var. Mfr.)

SCOPOLAMINE METHOBROMIDE.
See: Methscopolamine Bromide, Preps. (Var. Mfr.)

SCOPOLAMINE METHYLBROMIDE.
See: Methscopolamine Bromide, Preps. (Var. Mfr.)

SCOPOLAMINE METHYL NITRATE.
See: Methscopolamine Nitrate, Prep. (Var. Mfr.)

SCOPOLAMINE SALTS.
See: Belladonna Products
Hyoscine salts

SCORBEX/12. (Pasadena Research) Vit. B-1 20 mg., B-2 3 mg., B-6 5 mg., d-panthenol 75 mg., B-12 1000 mcg., C 100 mg./cc. Vial 10 cc.
Use: Vitamin supplement.

SCOTAVITE. (Scott/Cord) Vit. A 25,000 I.U., D 400 I.U., B-1 10 mg., B-2 10 mg., B-6 5 mg., B-12 5 mcg., niacinamide 100 mg., Ca pantothenate 20 mg., C 200 mg., d-alpha tocopheryl 15 I.U., acid succinate iodine 0.15 mg./Tab. Bot. 100s, 500s.
Use: Vitamin & mineral supplement.

SCOTCIL. (Scott/Cord) **Tab.:** Potassium penicillin 400,000 u. w/calcium carbonate/Tab. Bot. 100s, 500s. **Pow.** 80 cc., 150 cc.
Use: Antibiotic.

SCOTCOF. (Scott/Cord) Dextromethorphan HBr 6.85 mg., chlorpheniramine maleate 1.8 mg., phenylephrine HCl 4.4 mg., guaifenesin 66.00 mg., ammonium chloride 30.00 mg., chloroform 0.125 mg., alcohol 4.10%/5 cc. Bot. 4 oz., pt., gal.

SCOTGESIC. (Scott/Cord) **Cap.** Acetaminophen 240 mg., salicylamide 100 mg., phenyltoloxamine dihydrogen citrate 30 mg., butabarbital ⅛ gr./Cap. Bot. 100s, 500s, 1000s. **Liq.** Butabarbital 12.15 mg., acetaminophen 300 mg., salicylamide 60 mg., phenyltoloxamine citrate 30 mg./15 cc. Bot. 4 oz., pt.
Use: Analgesic.

SCOTNORD. (Scott/Cord) Chlorpheniramine maleate 8 mg., phenylephrine HCl 20 mg., methscopolamine nitrate 2.5 mg./Cap. Bot. 100s, 500s.

SCOTONIC. (Scott/Cord) Vit. B-1 10 mg., B-2 5 mg., B-6 1 mg., niacinamide 50 mg., choline chloride 100 mg., inositol 100 mg., B-12 25 mcg., calcium 19 mg., iron 50 mg., folic acid 0.15 mg., alcohol 15%, sodium benzoate 0.1%/45 cc. Bot. pt., gal.

SCOTRATE. (Robinson) Scopolamine methyl nitrate 0.5 mg./cc. Multiple dose vial 30 cc.

SCOTREX. (Scott/Cord) Tetracycline 250 mg./Cap. or 5 ml. Bot. 16s, 100s, 500s. Syr.: 2 oz., pt.

SCOTT'S EMULSION. (Beecham Products) Vit. A 5000 U., Vit. D 400 U./4 tsp. Bot. 6.25 oz., 12.5 oz.
Use: Vitamin A & D supplement.

SCOT-TUSSIN SUGAR-FREE. (Scot-Tussin) Dextromethorphan HBr 15 mg., chlorpheniramine maleate 2 mg./5 ml. Bot. 4 oz., 8 oz., 16 oz., gal.
Use: Cough cold medicine for diabetics, thyroid, high blood pressure, and heart disease patients.

SCOT-TUSSIN SUGAR-FREE 5-ACTION. (Scot-Tussin) Phenylephrine HCl 4.17 mg., pheniramine maleate 13.33 mg., sodium citrate 83.33 mg., sodium salicylate 83.33 mg., caffeine citrate 25 mg./5 ml. Non-narcotic, non-alcoholic. Bot. 4 oz., oz., 16 oz., gal.
Use: Coughs, colds, allergies.

SCOTT-TUSSIN SUGAR FREE EXPECTORANT (Scot-Tussin) Guaifenesin 100 mg./5 ml. w/alcohc 3.5%. Dye free, sodium free, and sugar free.
Use: Expectorant.

SCOT-TUSSIN WITH SUGAR. (Scot-Tussin) Phenylephrine HCl 4.17 mg., pheniramine maleate 13.3 mg., sodium citrate 83.33 mg., sodium salicylate 83.33 mg., caffeine citrate 25 mg./5 ml. Bot. 4 oz., 8 oz., 16 oz. gal.
Use: Colds, coughs, allergies.

SCOTUSS. (Scott/Cord) d-Methorphan 15 mg., chlorpheniramine maleate 1 mg., phenylephrine HCl 5 mg., phenylpropanolamine HCl 5 mg., N-acetyl-P-aminophenol 120 mg., guaifenesin 100 mg., alcohol 8.2%/5 cc. Bot. 4 oz., pt., gal.
Use: Cough due to colds.

SCOTUSS PEDIATRIC COUGH SYRUP. (Scott/Cord) Dextromethorphan HBr 7.5 mg., guaifenesin 50 mg., chlorpheniramine maleate 0.5 mg., phenylephrine HCl 2.5 mg., acetaminophen 60 mg., phenylpropanolamine HCl 2.5 mg., methylparaben 0.15%, propylparaben 0.05%/5 cc. Bot. 4 oz., pt.

SC-PLUS. (Western Research) Sodium carboxymethylcellulose 500 mg., docusate sodium 100 mg./Tab. Bot. 1000s.
Use: Bulk laxative.

SCRIP-DRI. (Scrip) Formalin soln., formaldehyde in perfumed aqueous base. Bot. 2 oz.

SCRIP SUPER DRI. (Scrip) Formalin soln. in perfumed aqueous base. Bot. 2 oz.

SCRIP-ZINC. (Scrip) Zinc sulfate 220 mg./Cap. Bot. 100s.

SCURENALINE.
See: Epinephrine, Prep. (Various Mfr.)

SCUROFORME.
See: Butyl Aminobenzoate (Various Mfr.)

S.D.M. #5. (ICI Americas) Mannitol hexanitrate 7% in lactose.
Use: Vasodilator.

S.D.M. #17. (ICI Americas) Nitroglycerin 10% in lactose.
Use: Vasodilator.

S.D.M. #23. (ICI Americas) Pentaerythritol tetranitrate 20% in lactose.
Use: Vasodilator.

S.D.M. #27. (ICI Americas) Nitroglycerin 10% in propylene glycol.
Use: Vasodilator.

S.D.M. #35. (ICI Americas) Pentaerythritol tetranitrate 35% in mannitol.
Use: Vasodilator.

S.D.M. #37. (ICI Americas) Nitroglycerin 10% in ethanol.
Use: Vasodilator.

S.D.M. #40. (ICI Americas) Isorsorbide dinitrate 25% in lactose.
Use: Vasodilator.

S.D.M. #50. (ICI Americas) Isosorbide dinitrate 50% in lactose.
Use: Vasodilator.

-DSS. (Western Research) Senna 175 mg., docusate sodium 50 mg./Tab. Bot. 1000s.
Use: Laxative.

EA GREENS. (Modern) Iodine 0.25 mg./Tab. Bot. 220s, 460s.

EALE'S LOTION-MODIFIED. (C & M Pharmacal) Sulfur 6.4%, sodium borate in lotion base. Bot. pt., gal.
Use: Acne therapy.

EA MASTER. (Barth's) Vit. A 10,000 u., D 400 u./Cap Bot. 100s, 500s.

EATRA-GESIC. (Seatrace) Aspirin 325 mg., phenyltoloxamine 20 mg./Tab. Bot. 100s, 1000s, 5000s.
Use: Analgesic, antihistaminic.

EBACIDE. (Paddock) Coconut oil, pine oil, castor oil, lanolin, cholesterols, lecithin, parachlorometaxylenol. Bot. 4 oz., pt., gal.
Use: Bactericidal sudsing skin cleanser.

EBACLEN HYDROCHLORIDE. Xenysalate, B.A.N.

EBA-LO. (Whorton) Acetone-alcohol cleanser. Bot. 4 oz.
Use: Oily skin cleanser.

EBANA SHAMPOO. (Myers) Salicylic acid 2%. Bot. 4 oz., 8 oz., pt., qt., 0.5 gal.
Use: Seborrhea, dandruff, oily skin.

EBANATAR SHAMPOO. (Myers) Salicylic acid 2%, liquor carbonis detergens 3%. Bot. 4 oz., 8 oz., pt., qt., 0.5 gal., gal.
Use: Sebhorrhea, dandruff.

EBA-NIL CLEANSER. (Owen) Cleansing mixture of alcohol 49.7%, acetone, polysorbate 20, purified water and fragrance. Bot. 8 oz., 16 oz. Towelettes, Pkg. 24s.
Use: Oily skin cleanser for acne.

EBA-NIL CLEANSING MASK. (Owen) Astringent face mask containing water, bentonite, polyethylene, SD alcohol-40, sulfated castor oil, titanium dioxide, kaolin, chromium oxide, methylparaben, fragrance. Tubes 3.5 oz.
Use: Cleanser for pimples, blackheads and oily skin.

EBAQUIN SHAMPOO. (Rydell) Iodoquinol 3% in a neutral, soapless detergent, lathering base. Bot. 4 oz.
Use: Antiseborrheic shampoo.

EBASORB. (Summers) Activated attapulgite 10%, hexachlorophene 1%, polysorbate 80 1%, colloidal sulfur 2%, salicylic acid 2%, propylene glycol. Plas. Bot. 2 oz. w/dispenser top.

EBASUM. (Summers) Polysorbate 80 1.25%, acetone 14%, isopropanol 50%. Bot. 4 oz., pt.
Use: Skin cleanser.

EBAVEEN SHAMPOO. (Rydell) Aveeno colloidal oatmeal 5%, sulfur 2%, salicylic acid 2%, emollients 4% in soap-free base. Plastic bottle 4 oz.
Use: Antiseborrheic.

EBIZON LOTION. (Schering) Sulfacetamide sod. 100 mg., methylparaben 1 mg. w/trisodium edetate, sod. thiosulfate, propylene glycol, isopropyl myristate, propylene glycol monostearate, polyethylene glycol 400 monostearate & water. Tube 3 oz., plastic squeeze.
Use: Scaling dermatoses, antibacterial.

SEBUCARE SCALP LOTION. (Westwood) Laureth-4, salicylic acid 1.5%, alcohol 61%, water, PPG 40 butyl ether, dihydroabietyl alcohol, fragrance. Bot. 4 oz.
Use: Treatment of dandruff, seborrhea capitis.

SEBULEX CREAM SHAMPOO. (Westwood) Same formula as Sebulex in a cream shampoo. Tube 4 oz.

SEBULEX SHAMPOO. (Westwood) Sulfur 2%, salicylic acid 2% in sebulytic brand of surface-active cleansers and wetting agents. Plastic bot. 4 oz., 8 oz.
Use: Therapeutic shampoo for dandruff and seborrheic dermatitis.

SEBULEX CONDITIONING SHAMPOO WITH PROTEIN. (Westwood) Sulfur 2%, salicylic acid 2%, water, sodium octoxynol-3 sulfonate, sodium lauryl sulfate, lauramide DEA, acetamide MEA, amphoteric-2, hydrolyzed animal protein, magnesium aluminum silicate, propylene glycol, methylcellulose, PEG-14 M, fragrance, disodium EDTA, docusate sodium, FD&C blue 1, D & C yellow. Bot. 4 oz., 8 oz.
Use: Therapeutic and conditioning shampoo for dandruff, seborrheic dermatitis.

SEBUTONE CREAM SHAMPOO. (Westwood) Tar equivalent to Coal Tar USP 5%, sulfur 2%, salicylic acid 2%, in sebulytic type surface-active soapless cleansers & wetting agents. Tubes 4 oz.
Use: Therapeutic shampoo for stubborn dandruff and psoriasis.

SEBUTONE THERAPEUTIC TAR SHAMPOO. (Westwood) Tar equivalent to Coal Tar USP 0.5%, sulfur 2%, salicylic acid 2%, in Sebulytic type of surface-active soapless cleansers and wetting agents. Plastic bot. 4 oz. 8 oz.
Use: Therapeutic shampoo for stubborn dandruff and psoriasis.

SECBUTOBARBITONE. B.A.N. 5-sec-Butyl-5-ethylbarbituric acid. Butabarbitone.
Use: Hypnotic; sedative.

SECHOLEX HCl. Polidexide, B.A.N.

• **SECOBARBITAL,** U.S.P. XXI. Elixir U.S.P. XXI. 5-Allyl-5-(methylbutyl)-barbituric acid. Pow., Bot. ⅛ oz., 1 oz.
Use: Hypnotic.
See: Seco-8, Cap. (Fleming)

SECOBARBITAL COMBINATIONS.
See: Amoseco, Cap. (Robinson)
Buffadyne w/Barbiturates, Tabs. (Lemmon)
Butseco, S.C.T., Tab. (Bowman)
Corovas, Preps. (Amfre-Grant)
Dusotal, Cap. (Harvey)
Efed, Syr., Tab. (Alto)
Gaysal, Tab. (Geriatric)
Monosyl, Tab. (Arcum)
Naus-A-Tories, Supp. (Table Rock)
Quad-Set, Tab. (Kenyon)
Secophen, Tab. (Mallard)
Sedalgesic, Tab. (Table Rock)
Stim 15/60, Cap. (Scrip)

SECOBARBITAL ELIXIR.
See: Seconal Elixir. (Lilly)

• **SECOBARBITAL SODIUM,** U.S.P. XXI. Cap., Inj., Sterile, U.S.P. XXI. Sod. 5-allyl-5-(1-methyl-butyl)-barbiturate. Quinalbarbitone Sodium, B.A.N.
Use: Hypnotic, sedative.
Generic Products:
(Bowman) Secobarbital sodium 1.5 gr./Tab.
(CMC)—50 mg./cc. Vial 30 cc.
(Hance)—Cap. 1.5 gr., Bot. 100s, 1000s.
(Lannett)—Cap. ¾ gr., 1.5 gr., Bot. 100s, 500s.
(Parke-Davis)—Cap. 1.5 gr. Bot. Unit dose 100s.
(Robinson) Cap. ¾ gr., 1.5 gr., Pow. 1 oz.
See: Seco-8, Cap. (Fleming)
Seconal Sodium, Prep. (Lilly)

• **SECOBARBITAL SODIUM AND AMOBARBITAL SODIUM CAPSULES,** U.S.P. XXI.
Use: Hypnotic, sedative.
See: Tuinal, Caps. (Lilly)

9,10-SECOCHOLESTA-5,7,10(19)-TRIEN-3-OL. Cholecalciferol, U.S.P. XXI.

9,10-SECOERGOSTA-5,7,10(19),22-TETRAEN-3-OL, (3 beta)-. Ergocalciferol, U.S.P. XXI.

SECONAL SODIUM. (Lilly)
Vial: 50 mg./ml. Vial. 20 ml. **Pulvules:** 50 mg. Bot. 100s, 500s. Blister pkg. 10 x 10s; 100 mg. Bot. 100s, 500s. Blister pkg. 10 x 10s. Dispenser rolls 40 x 25s unit dose pkg. **Supp.**: 30 mg., 60 mg., 120 mg., 200 mg. Pkg. 12s.
Use: Hypnotic & sedative.
W/Amytal Sod.
See: Tuinal, Cap. (Lilly)
W/Ephedrine sulfate.
See: Ephedrine & Seconal Sodium, Pulvule (Lilly)

SECRAN. (Scherer) Vit. B-12 (cryst.) 25 mcg., thiamine mononitrate 10 mg., niacinamide 10 mg., alcohol 17%/5 cc. Bot. pt.
Use: B-Vitamin deficiencies.

SECRAN/FE ELIXIR. (Scherer) Vit. B-12 (cryst.) 25 mcg., ferric pyrophosphate, soluble (elemental iron 30 mg.), thiamine mononitrate 15 mg., nicotinamide 10 mg./5 cc., alcohol 1%. Bot. pt.
Use: Iron deficiency anemia.

SECRAN PRENATAL TABS. (Scherer) Vit. A acetate 8000 u., D-2 400 I.U., E acetate 30 I.U., C 60 mg., Niacinamide 20 mg., B-2 2 mg., B-1 1.7 mg., B-6 2.5 mg., B-12 8 mcg., folic acid 1.0 mg., calcium 250 mg., magnesium 25 mg., elemental zinc 20 mg., iron 60 mg./Tab. Bot. 100s, 240s.
Use: Nutritional supplement.

SECRETIN. B.A.N. A hormone obtained from duodenal mucosa.
Use: Diagnostic aid.

SECRETIN-BOOTS. (Adria) Hormone from porcine duodenal mucosa, freeze dried sterile powder, 100 units.
Use: Diagnostic for pancreatic dysfunction.

SECRETIN-KABI. (Pharmacia) Secretin 75 cu/Vial. Box 5 x 10 ml.
Use: Diagnosis of pancreatic dysfunction.

SECTRAL. (Ives) Acebutolol HCl 200 or 400 mg./Cap. Bot. 100s. Strips of 5s.
Use: Antihypertensive.

SEDACANE. (Edward J. Moore) Acetaminophen 120 mg., salicylamide 210 mg., caffeine 30 mg., Ca gluconate 60 mg./Cap. Bot. 12.
Use: Analgesic.

SEDAFORM.
See: Chlorobutanol (Various Mfr.)

SEDAGESIC. (Kay) Isobutylallyl barbituric acid ¾ gr. aspirin 3 gr., acetophenetidin 2 gr., caffeine ⅔ gr./Tab. Bot. 100s, 1000s.
Use: Sedative, analgesic.

SEDAJEN. (Jenkins) Phenobarbital 5/16 gr., passiflora 1.5 gr., hyoscyamus ¾ gr. (total alkaloids 0.0003 gr.)/Tab. Bot. 1000s.
Use: Sedative & antispasmodic.

SEDALGESIC INSERTS. (Table Rock) Aspirin 195 mg., secobarbital 30 mg./Insert. Box 12s.
Use: Sedative, analgesic; antipyretic.

SEDALGESIC TABLETS. (Table Rock) Bromisovalum 150 mg., acetaminophen 100 mg., salicylamide 10[illegible] mg./Tab. Bot. 100s, 500s.
Use: Analgesic-sedative.

SEDAMINE. (Approved) Phosphorated carbohydrate sol. Bot. 4 oz.
Use: Anti-nausea.

SEDAMINE. (Dunhall) Hyoscyamine sulfate 0.1037 mg., atropine sulfate 0.0194 mg., hyoscine HBr 0.0065 mg., phenobarbital 16.2 mg./Tab. Bot. 100s 1000s.
Use: Antispasmodic.

SEDAPAP #3 CAPSULES. (Mayrand) Acetaminophen 500 mg., butalbital 50 mg., codeine phosphate 30 mg./Cap. Bot. 100s.
Use: Management of moderate to severe pain.

SEDAPAP-10 TABLETS. (Mayrand) Acetominophen 10 gr., butabarbital 16 mg./Tab. Bot. 100s, 500s.
Use: Analgesic, sedative.

SEDAPAR. (Parmed) Atropine sulfate 0.0195 mg., hyoscine HBr 0.0065 mg., hyoscyamine sulfate 0.1040 mg., phenobarbital 0.25 gr./Tab. Bot. 1000s.
Use: Sedative & antispasmodic.

SEDAQUIN. Methaqualone, B.A.N.

SEDATANS TABLETS. (Lannett) Tab. Bot. 100s, 1000s.

■ **SEDATIVE/HYPNOTIC AGENTS.**
See: Bromides (Var. Mfr.)
Barbiturates (Var. Mfr.)
Butisol Sodium (McNeil)
Carbamide (Urea) Compounds (Var. Mfr.)
Chloral Hydrate Preparations (Var. Mfr.)
Chlorobutanol (Var. Mfr.)
Dalmane, Caps. (Roche)
Intasedol, Elix. (Elder)
Largon, Inj. (Wyeth)
Lotusate, Cap. (Winthrop-Breon)
Noludar, Tab., Cap. (Roche)
Paraldehyde, Preps. (Var. Mfr.)
Phenergan HCl, Preps. (Wyeth)
Placidyl, Cap. (Abbott)
Plexonal, Tab. (Sandoz)
Quaalude, Tab. (Rorer)
Restoril, Cap. (Sandoz)

Valmid, Tab. (Lilly)
Vingesic, Cap. (Amid)

EDATROMINE TABLETS. (Sutliff & Case) Phenobarbital 0.25 gr., hyoscyamus 1/48 gr., belladonna 1/20 gr., atropine sulfate 1/300 gr., hyoscyamine sulfate 1/1200gr., hyoscine HBr 1/2400 gr./Tab. Bot. 100s, 1000s.
Use: Antispasmodic, sedative.

EDEVAL.
See: Barbital (Various Mfr.)

EDRAGESIC TABLETS. (Lannett) Acetaminophen 0.325 Gm., salicylamide 0.195 Gm., d-amphetamine sulfate 2.5 mg., hexobarbital 8 mg., secobarbital sod. 2.7 mg., butabarbital sod. 2.7 mg., phenobarbital 2.7 mg./Tab. Bot. 100s, 1000s.
Use: Sedative.

EDRAL. (Vita Elixir) Phenobarbital 1/8 gr., theophylline 2 gr., ephedrine 3/8 gr./Tab.
Use: Treatment of bronchial asthma, hay fever.

EDRALEX. (Kay) **Liq.** Phenobarbital 16.0 mg., hyoscyamine sulfate 0.1037 mg., atropine sulfate 0.0194 mg., scopolamine HBr 0.0065 mg./5 ml. Bot. 4 oz., 16 oz., gal.; **Tabs.** Bot. 1000s.
Use: Antispasmodic sedative.

EDS. (Pasadena Research) Phenobarbital 16 mg., hyoscyamine HBr 0.128 mg., hyoscine HBr 0.0072 mg., atropine sulfate 0.024 mg./Tab. Bot. 100s, 1000s.

SEELAZONE. USAN.
Use: Anti-inflammatory, uricosuric.

EFFIN. (Glaxo) Cephalothin sodium. Vials 1 Gm. or 2 Gm. 1 Gm./100 ml. pk. 2 Gm./100 pk. 10 Gm./100 ml. bulk.
Use: Antibiotic.

EGO LIQUID. (Pet Milk Co.) Protein 77 Gm., carbohydrate 103 Gm., fat 20 Gm., Vit. A 5000 I.U., D 400 I.U., C 100 mg., B-1 2 mg., B-2 3 mg., niacinamide 15 mg., B-6 2 mg., Ca pantothenate 10 mg., Iodine 150 mcg., K 3.5 Gm., Na 0.9 Gm., Mn 2 mg., Zn 5 mg./4 cans. Can 10 oz., Powd. Inst. mix 1 oz.
Use: Liquid diet food.

ELAN CREAM, PLAIN. (Noyes) Cetyl alcohol 12%, glyceryl stearate 2%, lanolin 0.5%, glycerin 10%, Na lauryl sulfate 1%, methyl and butyl parabens as preservatives. Jar 2 oz., 4 oz., 1 lb.
Use: Skin irritations.

ELAN WITH SILICONE. (Noyes) Cetyl alcohol 12%, glyceryl stearate 2%, lanolin anhyd. 0.5%, S-F-96 2.5%, sorbo 10%, Na lauryl sulfate 1% w/methyl, propyl, butyl parabens as preservatives. **Cream:** Jar 2 oz., 4 oz., 1 lb. **Lotion:** 8 oz., pt., gal.

ELDANE. (Merrell Dow) Terfenadine 60 mg./Tab. Bot. 100s.
Use: Non-sedating antihistamine.

ELENICEL. (Pasadena Research) Selenium yeast complex 200 mcg., Vit. C 100 mg., E 100 mg./Cap. Bot. 90s.
Use: Dietary supplement.

ELENITRACE. (Armour) Selenious acid injection containing selenium 40 mcg./1 ml. Vial 10 ml. Box 25s.
Use: Supplement to I.V. solutions for selenium deficiency.

SELENIUM. (Nion) Selenium 50 mcg./Tab. Bot. 100s.
Use: Dietary supplement.

SELENIUM DISULFIDE.
See: Selenium Sulfide, Deterg. Susp. (Var. Mfr.)

• **SELENIUM SULFIDE,** U.S.P. XXI. Lot. U.S.P. XXI.
Use: Treatment of dandruff; antifungal, antiseborrheic.
See: Exsel Lotion (Herbert)
Iosel 250, Liq. (Owen)
Selsun, Susp. (Abbott)

• **SELENOMETHIONINE Se 75 INJECTION,** U.S.P. XXI. 2-Amino-4-(methylselenyl) butyric acid (^{75}Se)
Use: Diagnostic aid (pancreas function determination).
See: Sethotope, Inj. (Squibb)

SELESTOJECT. (Mayrand) Betamethasone sodium phosphate 4 mg./ml. Vial 5 ml.
Use: Glucocorticoid.

SELORA POWDER. (Winthrop Products) Potassium chloride.
Use: Salt substitute.

SELSUN BLUE. (Ross) Selenium sulfide 1% in lotion base. Bot. 4 oz., 7 oz., 11 oz. Dry, Oily, Normal formulas.
Use: Anti-dandruff shampoo.

SELSUN SUSPENSION. (Abbott) Selenium sulfide 2.5%. Bot. 4 fl. oz.
Use: Seborrheic dermatitis of scalp and tinea versicolor.

SELVIGON HYDROCHLORIDE. Pipazethate, B.A.N.

SEMICID. (Whitehall) Nonoxynol-9 100 mg./Suppos. Box 10s, 20s.
Use: Contraceptive.

SEMILENTE INSULIN.
See: Iletin, Vial (Lilly)

• **SEMUSTINE.** USAN.
Use: Antineoplastic.

SENAGRADA TABLETS. (Blue Line) Phenolphthalein 1 gr., senna 2.5 gr., cascarin bitterless 1/6 gr./Tab. Bot. 100s, 1000s.

SENATHALIN WAFERS. (Blue Line) Phenolphthalein 1 gr., senna 2.5 gr., cascarin, bitterless 1/6 gr./Wafer. 100s, 1000s.

SENILAVITE. (Defco) Vit. A 5000 I.U., C 100 mg., B-1 2.5 mg., B-2 2 mg., nicotinamide 10 mg., B-6 1 mg., Ca pantothenate 5 mg., B-12 w/intrinsic factor conc. 0.133 I.U., ferrous fumarate 150 mg., glutamic acid HCl 150 mg., docusate sodium 50 mg./Cap. Bot. 100s.
Use: Nutritional supplement.

SENILEZOL ELIXIR. (Edwards) Vit. B-1 2.5 mg., B-2 2.5 mg., B-6 1 mg., B-12 5mcg., dexpanthenol 5 mg., niacin 10 mg., ferric pyrophosphate 20 mg. 130 ml. w/ alcohol 15% Bot. pt.
Use: Vitamin and mineral supplement.

• **SENNA,** U.S.P. XXI. Fluidextract, Syrup, U.S.P. XXI. Alexandrian.
Use: Cathartic.
See: Casafru, Liq. (Key)

SENNA CONC., STANDARDIZED.
Use: Cathartic.
See: Senokot, Gran., Tab., Supp. (Purdue Frederick)
X-Prep. Pow. (Gray)
W/Docusate sodium.
See: Gentlax S. Tab. (Blair)
Senokap-DSS, Cap. (Purdue Frederick)
Senokot S. Tab. (Purdue Frederick)
W/Guar gum.
See: Gentlax B Tab., Granules (Blair)
W/Psyllium.
See: Perdiem, Granules (Rorer)
Senokot W/Psyllium Powder (Purdue Frederick)

SENNA FRUIT EXTRACT, STANDARIZED.
Use: Cathartic.
See: Senokot Syrup (Purdue Frederick)
X-Prep, Liq. (Gray)

SENNA-GEN TABS. (Goldline) Bot. 100s, 1000s.
Use: Laxative.

SENNA POWDER COMPOUND. (Penick) Comp. licorice pow. Bot. 0.25 lb., 1 lb.
Use: Mild cathartic.

• **SENNOSIDES,** U.S.P. XXI. Tab., U.S.P. XXI.
Use: Laxative, stool softener.

SENOKAP-DSS CAPSULES. (Purdue Frederick) Docusate sodium (dioctyl sodium sulfosuccinate) 50 mg., standardized senna conc. 163 mg./Cap. Bot. 60s.
Use: Laxative, stool softener.

SENOKOT TABLETS and GRANULES. (Purdue Frederick) **Granules:** Standardized senna concentrate. Canister 2 oz., 6 oz., 12 oz. **Tabs.:** Bot. 50s, 100s, 1000s. Unit Strip Pack 100s. Box 20s.
Use: Laxative.

SENOKOT S TABLETS. (Purdue Frederick) Standardized senna concentrate w/docusate sodium. Tab. Bot. 30s, 60s, 1000s.
Use: Laxative, stool softener.

SENOKOT SUPPOSITORIES. (Purdue Frederick) Standardized senna concentrate. Pkg. 6s.
Use: Rectal laxative.

SENOKOT SYRUP. (Purdue Frederick) Standardized ext. senna fruit. Bot. 2 oz., 8 oz.
Use: Relief of constipation.

SENORAL-M. (Kay) Pentylenetetrazol 100 mg., B-1 1.67 mg., B-6 7.5 mg., cyanocobalamin 2.5 mcg. w/alcohol 15%. 5 cc. Bot. pt., gal.
Use: Analeptic in patients with mental confusion, apathy and memory defects.

SENSI-SLIDE. (Roche) Latex agglutination inhibition slide test for pregnancy (0.8IU/ml HCG) requiring only two minutes for clear-cut results. Clinical studies show 98.4 percent accuracy of test.

SENSI-TEX. (Roche) Latex agglutination-inhibition tube test for pregnancy employing a latex bound beta-human chorionic gonadotropin antigen. Will detect HCg levels to 0.25 I.U.
Use: Pregnancy test.

SENSITIVE EYES SALINE SOLUTION. (Bausch & Lomb) Sterile, preserved solution for cleaning, rinsing, heat disinfection & storing soft contact lens. Bot. 8 oz.
Use: Solution for soft contact lens.

SENSODYNE TOOTHPASTE. (Block) Glycerin, sorbitol, sodium methyl cocoyl taurate, PEG-40 stearate, strontium chloride hexahydrate 10%, methyl and propylparabens, tint. Tubes 2.1, 4.0 oz.
Use: Sensitive teeth.

SENSORCAINE. (Astra) Bupivacaine HCl 0.25%, 0.50% or 0.75%. Amp. 30 ml.
Use: Local anesthetic.

• **SEPAZONIUM CHLORIDE.** USAN.
Use: Anti-infective, topical.

• **SEPERIDOL HCl.** USAN. 4-[4-(4-Chloro-α,α,α-trifluoro-m-tolyl)-4-hydroxypiperidino]-4′-fluorobutyrophenone HCl. Under study.
Use: Neuroleptic.

SEPO. (Otis Clapp) Benzocaine. Loz. Bot. 80s. Safety pack 1000s.
Use: Salt free anesthetic for sore throat relief.

SEPP. (Marion) Isopropyl alcohol 70%, acetone 10%, iodine tincture 2%, PVP iodine solution 10%, green soap tincture, compound benzoin tincture. Carton 200 applicators.
Use: Antiseptic for skin preparation.

SEPTA. (Circle) Bacitracin 400 units, neomycin sulfate 5 mg., polymixin B sulfate 5,000 units/Gm. in ointment base. Tube 1 oz.
Use: Antibiotic.

SEPTI-CHEK. (Roche) Blood culture and simultaneous sub-culture system with three media to support clinically significant pathogens. Quick and easy assembly forms a closed system to protect sub-cultures from contamination.

SEPTILINE SOLUBLE. (Noyes) NaCl, Na borate (formed), eucalyptol, Me salicylate, thymol, menthol, chlorothymol. Wafers 100s, 1000s.

SEPTIPHENE. 4-Chloro-α-phenyl-o-cresol. Santophen 1. (Monsanto).
Use: Disinfectant.

SEPTO. (Vita Elixir) Methylbenzethonium Cl., ethanol 2%, menthol.
Use: Germicidal & antiseptic liquid.

SEPTRA. (Burroughs Wellcome) Sulfamethoxazole 400 mg., trimethoprim 80 mg./Tab. Tab. Bot. 100s, 500s. Unit dose 100s.
Use: Urinary infections, *Pneumocystis carinii pneumonitis,* otitis media, bronchitis.

SEPTRA DS. (Burroughs Wellcome) Trimethoprim 160 mg., sulfamethoxazole 800 mg./Tab. Bot. 60s. Compliance Pak 20s.
Use: Urinary infections, *Pneumocystis Carinii pneumonitis,* otitis media, bronchitis.

SEPTRA I.V. (Burroughs Wellcome) Trimethoprim 80 mg., sulfamethoxazole 400 mg./5 ml. amp. Box 10s. Multiple Dose Vials 10 ml., 20 ml.
Use: Urinary tract infection, shigellosis, *Pneumocystis Carinii pneumonitis.*

SEPTRA SUSPENSION. (Burroughs Wellcome) Trimethoprim 40 mg., sulfamethoxazole 200 mg./5 ml. Bot. 100 ml., 473 ml.

Use: Urinary tract infections , *Pneumocystis Carinii pneumonitis* and otitis media.
'PTRIN. Co-trimoxazole, B.A.N.
.QUENS. Mestranol, B.A.N.
;ERACTIDE ACETATE. USAN. Ala[26]-Gly[27]-SER[31]α^{1-39} corticotrophin acetate.
Use: Corticotrophic peptide.
See: Acthar Gel (Armour)
.RALYZER. (Ames) A system for blood chemistries and therapeutic drug assays consisting of a reflectance photometer and a series of solid-phase reagent strips.
Use: Quantitative testing from serum or plasma.
.R-AP-ES. (Ciba) Reserpine 0.1 mg., hydralazine HCl 25 mg., hydrochlorothiazide 15 mg./Tab. Bot. 100s, 1000s; Consumer Packs of 100s; Accu-Pak 100s.
Use: Hypertension.
:RAPINE TABLETS. (Cenci) Hydralazine HCl 25 mg., hydrochlorothiazide 15 mg., reserpine 0.1 mg./Tab. Bot. 100s, 1000s.
:RAX. (Wyeth) Oxazepam. **Caps.** 10 mg., 15 mg., 30 mg. Bot. 100s, 500s. 10 mg. Redipak 25s. 15 and 30 mg. Redipak 25s, 100s. **Tabs.** 15 mg., Bot. 100s.
Use: Psychotropic.
:RBIO. (Metro Med) Capsules Bot. 100s, 1000s.
Use: Hypertension.
:RC DIHYDROCHLORIDE. Betahistine, B.A.N.
:REEN. (Foy) Chlordiazepoxide HCl 5 mg., 10 mg./Cap. Bot. 500s, 1000s.
Use: Antianxeity, sedative.
:RENACE. Haloperidol, B.A.N.
:RENE. (Approved) Salicylamide 2 gr., scopolamine aminoxide HBr 0.2 mg./Cap. Bot. 24s, 60s.
Use: Tranquilizer.
:RENSIL. Ethchlorvynol, B.A.N.
:RENTIL. (Boehringer Ingelheim) Mesoridazine besylate. **Inj.** 25 mg./ml. (w/disodium edetate 0.5 mg., sod. chloride 7.2 mg., carbon dioxide gas q.s.) Amp. 20s, 100s. **Tab.** 10, 25, 50, 100 mg. Bot. 100s, 5000s. **Oral Concentrate** 25 mg./cc. Grad. dropper Bot. 4 oz.
Use: Antipsychotic.
:RFOLIA. (Mallard) Rauwolfia serpentina 100 mg./Tab. Bot. 1000s.
Use: Hypotensive agent.
:RICINASE. A proteolytic enzyme.
;ERINE, U.S.P. XXI. $C_3H_7NO_3$ as L-serine.
Use: Amino acid.
;ERMETACIN. USAN.
Use: Anti-inflammatory.
:RNYLAN. Phencyclidine., B.A.N. 1-(1-Phenycyclohexyl)-piperidine HCl.
Use: Anesthetic.
:RODEN. Thiacetazone, B.A.N.
:ROMYCIN. (Lilly) Cycloserine 250 mg./Pulvule. Bot. 40s.
Use: Pulmonary tuberculosis.
:ROPHENE. (Serono) Clomiphene citrate 50 mg./Tab. Box 30s.
Use: Induction of ovulation in selected anovulatory women.

SERPAHYDE. (Wolins) Reserpine 0.1 mg., hydralazine HCl 25 mg., hydrochlorothiazide 15 mg./Tab. Bot. 100s, 1000s.
SERPALAN TABLETS. (Lannett) Reserpine alkaloid 0.1 mg., 0.25 mg., 1.0 mg./Tab. Bot. 100s, 500s, 1000s.
SERPANRAY. (Panray) Reserpine 0.25 mg., 1 mg./Tab. Bot. 100s, 1000s.
SERPASIL. (Ciba) Reserpine. **Tab.:** 0.25 mg./Tab. Bot. 100s, 500s, 1000s. Consumer Packs of 100s; 0.1 mg./Tab. Bot. 100s, 1000s. **Amp.:** (2.5 mg./ml.) w/dimethylacetamide 0.1 ml., adipic acid 10 mg., versene 0.1 mg., benzyl alcohol 0.01 ml., polyethylene glycol 0.05 ml., ascorbic acid 0.5 mg., sod. sulfite 0.1 mg./ml. 2 ml., 5s.
Use: Antihypertensive & tranquilizing agent.
SERPASIL-APRESOLINE. (Ciba) **#1:** Reserpine 0.1 mg., hydralazine HCl 25 mg./Tab. Bot. 100s. **#2:** Reserpine 0.2 mg., hydralazine HCl 50 mg./Tab. Bot. 100s.
Use: Hypertensive disorders.
SERPASIL-ESIDRIX. (Ciba) **#1:** Reserpine 0.1 mg., hydrochlorothiazide 25 mg./Tab. **#2:** Reserpine 0.1 mg., hydrochlorothiazide 50 mg./Tab. Bot. 100s, 1000s.
Use: Mild-to-moderate hypertension.
SERPATE. (Vale) Reserpine 0.1 mg. or 0.25 mg./Tab. Bot. 100s, 500s, 1000s.
Use: Antihypertensive & tranquilizing agent.
SERPAZIDE TABLETS. (Major) Reserpine, hydralazine HCl, and hydrochlorothiazide. Bot. 100s, 1000s.
Use: Antihypertensive.
SERPENA. (Haag) Reserpine 0.25 mg./Tab. Bot. 100s, 500s, 1000s.
SERTABS. (Table Rock) Reserpine 0.25 mg., 0.5 mg./Tab. Bot. 100s, 500s.
Use: Tranquilizer and antihypertensive.
SERTINA. (Fellows) Reserpine 0.25 mg./Tab. Bot. 1000s, 5000s.
Use: Antihypertensive and ataraxic.
• **SERTRALINE HYDROCHLORIDE.** USAN.
Use: Antidepressant.
SERUM, ALBUMIN, NORMAL HUMAN.
See: Albumin Human, U.S.P. XXI. (Var. Mfr.)
SERUM, ALBUMIN, HUMAN, RADIOIODINATED.
See: Iodinated. I-125
Albumin Injection, U.S.P. XXI.
SERUM, ANTIHEMOPHILUS INFLUENZAE TYPE B (RABBIT). Antihaemophilus (influenzae Type B Serum, Rabbit). (Squibb)
SERUM, GLOBULIN (HUMAN), IMMUNE.
See: Globulin Immune Serum (Human), (Var. Mfr.)
SERUM, MEASLES IMMUNE, HUMAN.
See: Measles Virus Vaccine Live, U.S.P. XXI.
SERUM PERTUSSIS IMMUNE, HUMAN.
See: Pertussis Vaccine Adsorbed, U.S.P. XXI.
SERUTAN. (Beecham Products) Vegetable hemicellulose from Plantago Ovata. **Gran.:** Pkg. 6 oz., 18 oz. **Pow.:** 7 oz., 14 oz., 21 oz. Fruit flavored: 6 oz., 12 oz., 18 oz.
Use: Laxative.

• **SESAME OIL,** N.F. XVI.
Use: Pharm. aid (solvent).
SESTRON. N-Ethyl-3,3′-diphenyl-dipropylamine. Profenil. (Smith, Miller & Patch)
SETHADIL. Sulphaethidole, B.A.N.
SETHOTOPE. (Squibb) Selenomethionine Se 75; available as 0.25, 1.0 m C i.
• **SETOPERONE.** USAN.
Use: Antipsychotic.
SEVEN-FIFTY. (Freeport) Acetylsalicylic acid 7.5 gr./Tab. Bot. 1000s.
Use: Relief of minor aches and pains.
SEVIN. Carbaryl, B.A.N.
• **SEVOFLURANE.** USAN. Fluoromethyl 2,2,2-trifluoro-1-(trifluoromethyl)ethyl ether.
Use: Anesthetic (inhalation).
SEXOVID. Cyclofenil, B.A.N.
SHADE. (Plough) A series of waterproof sunscreen lotions with SPF 4, 6, 8, and 15 w/Padimate O and oxybenzone. Bot. 4 fl oz.
Use: Broad spectrum ultraviolet sunscreen.
SHAMPOO-ETS TRAVEL PACKET. (Matthew) Caps. 20s.
SHAPE AID. (Wolins) Benzocaine 3 mg., sodium carboxymethylcellulose 167 mg., Vit. A 1667 I.U., D2 133 I.U., B-1 0.67 mg., C 16.67 mg., B-2 0.833 mg., B-6 0.334 mg., niacinamide 6.67 mg., iron 5 mg., D-calcium pantothenate 0.334 mg./Cap. Bot. 100s, 1000s.
• **SHELLAC,** N.F.XVI.
Use: Pharmaceutic aid (tablet coating agent).
SHEPARD'S CREAM LOTION. (Dermik) Creamy lotion with no lanolin or mineral oil, for entire body. Scented or unscented. Bot. 8 oz., 16 oz.
Use: Skin dryness.
SHEPARD'S MOISTURIZING SOAP. (Dermik) Mildly scented, superfatted with lanolin. Bar 4 oz.
SHEPARD'S SKIN CREAM. (Dermik) Scented or unscented, w/no lanolin or mineral oil. Jar 4 oz.
Use: Lubricant and emollient.
SHERAMIN ELIXIR. (Blue Line) Thiamine hydrochloride, detannated sherry wine, sugar, citric acid, 0.1% w/v benzoic acid as preservative, alcohol 14%. Standardized to supply 8 mg., Vit. B-1 per fl. oz. or 27 mg. per 100 cc. Bot. pt., gal.
SHERFORM-HC CREME. (Sheryl) Hydrocortisone 1%, pramoxine HCl 0.5%, clioquinol 3%. Oint. tube 0.5 oz.
Use: Skin disorders.
SHERHIST. (Sheryl) Phenylephrine HCl, pyrilamine maleate/Tab. 100s. Liq. 1 pt.
Use: Relief of sinusitis.
SHERNATAL TABLETS. (Sheryl) Phosphorus free calcium, non-irritating iron, trace minerals and essential vitamins. Tab. 100s.
Use: Prenatal vitamin and mineral supplement.
SHERRY-JEN TONIC. (Jenkins) Vit. B-1 8 mg., B-2 4 mg., cyanocobalamin 4 mcg., nicotinamide 20 mg., Ca pantothenate 5 mg., B-6 1 mg., inositol 30 mg., choline bitartrate 60 mg., ferric ammonium citrate 60 mg., alcohol 9%/fl. oz. Bot. 4 oz., 8 oz., gal.
SHERTUS LIQUID. (Sheryl) Dextromethorphan HBr, chlorpheniramine maleate, phenylephrine HCl, ammonium chloride. Liq. 1 pt.
Use: Relief of cough and respiratory congestion.
SHIELD. (Birchwood) Pkg. 1 shield.
Use: Anorectal protective garmet.
SHOHL'S SOLUTION. Sodium Citrate and Citric Aci[d] Oral Solution, U.S.P. XXI.
Use: Systemic alkalizer.
SHOSTAKOVSKY BALSAM. Polyvinox, B.A.N.
SHUR SEAL GEL. (Milex) Nonoxynol-9 6 Gm./5 oz. pr[e-]measured pak. Box 24s.
Use: Contraceptive jelly for use with diaphragm.
SIALCO. (Foy) Chlorpheniramine maleate 4 mg., salicylamide 150 mg., acetaminophen 125 mg., phenylephrine HCl 5 mg./Tab. Bot. 100s, 500s, 1000s.
Use: Antihistaminic, analgesic, nasal decongestant.
SIBELIUM. (Janssen) Flunarizine HCl.
Use: Vasodilator.
SIBLIN. (Parke-Davis) Water-absorbent material fro[m] plantago/Tsp. Box 4 oz., 1 lb.
Use: Bulk laxative.
SIDEROL. (Doral) Chelated iron ammonium citrate 720 mg., folic acid 400 mcg., B-12 25 mcg., B-1 5 mg., B-6 1 mg., niacin 60 mg., panthenol 10 mg., PABA 6 mg., 1-lysine HCl 100 mg., inositol 10 mg., choline citrate 50 mg., methionine 6.25 mg., trace minerals: Cu, Zn, Mn., K, Mg., in base with sorbitol, liver fraction no. 1, & beef peptone/cc. Bot. 6 oz.
Use: Prevention & treatment of iron, vit. B complex, folic acide deficiencies.
SIGAMINE. (Sig) Cyanocobalamin injection 1000 mcg./cc. Vial 10 ml., 30 ml. Also Sigamine L.A. Vial 10 ml.
Use: Vit. B-12 deficiency.
SIGAZINE. (Sig) Promethazine HCl 50 mg./ml. Vial 10 ml.
Use: Antihistamine.
SIGESIC. (Rand) Cap. Bot. 100s, 1000s.
Use: Analgesic and sedative.
SIGNA CREME. (Parker) Conductive cosmetic quality electrolyte cream.
Use: High conductive electrode cream for diagnostic electrocardiograms.
SIGNA GEL. (Parker) Conductive saline electrode ge[l].
Use: Defibrillation, ECG, EMG, electrosurgery.
SIGNA PAD. (Parker) Pre-moistened electrode pads.
Use: Defibrillation, ECG, EMG, electrosurgery.
SIGNATAL C. (Sig) Calcium 230 mg., iron 49.3 mg., Vit. A 4000 I.U., D 400 I.U., B-1 2 mg., B-2 2 mg., B-6 1 mg., B-12 2 mcg., folic acid 0.1 mg., niacinamide 10 mg., Vit. C 50 mg., iodine 0.15 mg./S.C. Tab. Bot. 100s, 1000s.
Use: Pre-and postnatal dietary supplement.
SIGNATE. (Sig) Dimenhydrinate 50 mg. propylene glycol 50%, benzyl alcohol 5%/ml. Vial 10 ml.
Use: Prophylaxis and treatment of motion sickness.
SIGNEF "SUPPS". (Fellows) Hydrocortisone 15 mg./Supp. 12s. w or w/out appl.
Use: Vaginal treatment.
SIGPRED. (Sig) Prednisolone acetate. Vial 10 ml.

;TAB. (Upjohn) Vit. A 5000 I.U., D 400 I.U., B-1 10.3 ng., B-2 10 mg., C 333 mg., niacin 100 mg., B-6 6 mg., pantothenic acid 20 mg., folic acid 0.4 mg., B-12 18 mcg., Vit. E 15 I.U./Tab. Bot. 30s, 90s, 500s.
Use: Vitamin supplement.
ILAFILCON A. USAN
Use: Contact lens material.
ILAFOCON A. USAN.
Use: Contact lens material.
.AIN. (Robins) Simethicone (activated methylpolysiloxane). Tab. 50 mg. Bot. 100s.
Use: Antiflatulent.
.AIN-GEL. (Robins) Simethicone 25 mg., aluminum hydroxide 282 mg., magnesium hydroxide 285 mg./5 ml. Bot. 12 oz.
Use: Antiflatulent, antacid.
ILANDRONE. USAN. 17 β-(Trimethylsioloxy)-androst-4-en-3-one.
Use: Androgen.
.BEPHYLLINE. Diprophylline, B.A.N.
.EXIN SYRUP. (Otis Clapp) Dextromethorphan HBr and guaifenesin in sugar, salt and alcohol free vehicle. Bot. 1 oz. (12s), 4 oz., 16 oz.
Use: Antitussive, expectorant cough syrup.
.EXIN TABS. (Otis Clapp) Dextromethorphan HBr, benzocaine/Tab. Safety Pack 500s.
Use: Sore throat relief, cough suppressant, anesthetic.
.LICA GEL, N.F. XVI.
Use: Pharm. aid (suspending agent; anticaking agent; disintegrating agent;.
ILICEOUS EARTH, PURIFIED, N.F. XVI.
Use: Filtering medium.
.ICONE. (Dow Chemicals) Dimethicone. Liq., Bot. 1 oz. Bulk Pkg. Oint.
See also: Simethicone (Var. Mfr.)
'Lanolin.
See: Sanchia Silicone Protective Cream (Otis Clapp)
'Nitro-Cellulose & castor oil.
See: Covicone, Cream (Abbott)
'Triethylene glycol & mineral oil.
See: Allergex, Liq., Spray (Hollister-Stier)
ILICONE DIOXIDE, COLLOIDAL, N.F. XVI.
Use: Tablet diluent, suspending & thickening agent.
.ICONE OINTMENT. Dimethicone Dimethyl polysiloxane.
See: Covicone Cream (Abbott)
.ICONE OINTMENT NO. 2. (C & M Pharmacal) 10% high viscosity silicone in a blend of petrolatum and hydrophobic starch. Jar 2 oz., 1 lb.
Use: Protective ointment.
.ICONE POWDER. (Gordon) Talc with silicone. Pkg. 4 oz., 1 lb., 5 lb.
Use: Dusting powder to prevent tape from adhering to clothing.
.MAGEL. (Lannett) Aluminum hydroxide 2.5 gr., magnesium trisilicate 3.85 gr./Tab. Bot. 1000s, 5000s.
Use: Protective antacid.
ILODRATE USAN. Mag. aluminosilicate hydrate.
Use: Antacid.

SILTEX. (Edward J. Moore) Camphor, menthol, allantoin, tinct. benzoin in lanolin-petrolatum base. Tube 0.25 oz.
Use: Chapped lips, cold sores, fever blisters.
SILVADENE. (Marion) Silver sulfadiazine (10 mg./1Gm.) 1%, base w/white petrolatum, stearyl alcohol, isopropyl myristate, sorbitan monooleate, polyoxyl 40 stearate, propylene glycol, water, methylparaben 0.3%. Cream Jar 50 Gm., 400 Gm., 1000 Gm. Tube 20 Gm.
Use: Anti-infective.
SILVER COMPOUNDS.
See: Silver Iodide, Colloidal
Silver Nitrate, Preps. (Various Mfr.)
Silver Picrate (City Chem.)
Silver Protein, Mild (Various Mfr.)
Silver Protein, Strong (Various Mfr.)
• **SILVER NITRATE,** U.S.P. XXI. Ophth. Soln., Toughened, U.S.P. XXI. Nitric acid silver.
Use: Astringent, caustic & antiseptic.
• **SILVER NITRATE OPHTHALMIC SOLUTION,** U.S.P. XXI. (Wax Amp.)
Use: Astringent, anti-infective.
Generic Products:
(Lilly)—Amp. 1%, 100s.
(Parke-Davis)—Cap. 1%, 100s.
• **SILVER NITRATE, TOUGHENED,** U.S.P. XXI. Silver nitrate plus 4% silver chloride.
Use: Caustic.
SILVER PICRATE. (City Chem.) 1 oz.
Use: Antiseptic.
SILVER PROTEIN, MILD. Argentum Vitellinum, Cargentos, Mucleinate Mild, Protargin Mild
See: Argyrol Prods. (CooperVision)
SILVER PROTEIN, STRONG.
See: Protargol, Pow. (Sterling)
• **SILVER SULFADIAZINE.** USAN.
Use: Topical anti-infective.
See: Silvadene, Oint. (Marion)
SILVER SULFADIAZINE CREAM. (Flint) Silver sulfadiazine 1% in opaque, water-miscible cream base. Jar. 50 Gm., 400 Gm.
Use: Topical antibacterial.
SIMECO. (Wyeth) Aluminum hydroxide 365 mg., magnesium hydroxide 300 mg., simethicone 30 mg./ 5 ml. Bot. 12 oz.
Use: Antacid, antiflatulant.
• **SIMETHICONE,** U.S.P. XX, Emulsion, Oral Susp., Tab., U.S.P. XXI. Mixture of liquid dimethyl polysiloxanes with silica aerogel.
Use: Antiflatulent; pharmaceutic aid (release agent).
See: Mylicon, Tab. & Liq. (Stuart)
Mylicon-80, Tab. (Stuart)
Silain, Tab. (Robins)
Ingredients of:
Mylanta, Tab., Liq. (Stuart)
Phazyme, Tab. (Reed & Carnick)
W/Aluminum hydroxide & magnesium hydroxide
See: Di-Gel, Liq. Tab. (Plough)
Mylanta, Mylanta II, Tab. & Liq. (Stuart)
Silain-Gel, Liq. (Robins)

Simeco, Liq. (Wyeth)
Simethox, Liq. (Quality Generics)
W/Enzymes.
See: Phazyme, Tabs. (Reed & Carnrick)
Tri-Cone, Cap. (Glaxo)
W/Hyoscyamine sulfate, atropine sulfate, hyoscine HBr, butabarbital sod.
See: Sidonna, Tab. (Reed & Carnrick)
W/Hyoscyamine sulfate, atropine sulfate, scopolamine HBr & phenobarbital.
See: Kinesed, Chewable Tab. (Stuart)
W/Magnesium aluminum hydroxide
See: Maalox Plus, Susp. (Rorer)
W/Magnesium carbonate.
See: Di-Gel, Tab. & Liq. (Plough)
W/Magnesium hydroxide.
See: Laxsil, Liq. (Reed & Carnrick)
W/Magnesium hydroxide & dried aluminum hydroxide gel.
See: Maalox Plus, Tab. (Rorer)
W/Pancreatin.
See: Phazyme, Tab. (Reed & Carnrick)
Phazyme-95, Tab. (Reed & Carnrick)
W/Pancreatin, phenobarbital.
See: Phazyme-PB, Tab. (Reed & Carnrick)

SIMETHOX. (Quality Generics) Aluminum hydroxide 400 mg., magnesium hydroxide 400 mg., simethicone 30 mg./5 cc. Bot. 12 oz.
Use: Antacid, antiflatulent.

SIMILAC 13/SIMILAC 13 WITH IRON. (Ross) milk-based formula ready-to-feed. Each liter contains: protein 11.9 g, fat 23.2 g, carbohydrate 46.0 g, Ca 0.41 g, P 0.31 g, Na 0.22 g, K 0.58 g, Cl 0.41 g, Mg 32 mg, Fe 7.8 mg. (1.0 mg. in Similac 13), Zn 3.3 mg., Cu 0.39 mg., iodine 65 mcg., Mn 22 mcg., Vit. A 1625 IU, D 260 IU, E 13 IU, C 36 mg., B-1 0.42 mg., B-2 0.65 mg., niacin 4.6 mg. Eq., B-6 0.26 mg., folic acid 65 mcg., B-12 1.0 mcg., pantothenic acid 2.0 mg. Bot. 4 fl. oz.
Use: For infants requiring a dilute feeding.

SIMILAC 20/SIMILAC 20 WITH IRON. (Ross) Milk-based formula, ready-to-feed (20 cal. fl. oz.). Each liter contains: protein 15 g, fat 36.1 g, carbohydrate 72.3 g, Ca 0.51 g, P 0.39 g, Na 0.23 g, K 0.78 g, Cl 0.53 g, Mg 41 mg., Zn 5.0 mg., Cu 0.60 mg., iron 12.0 mg. (1.5 mg. in Similac 20 regular), iodine 0.10 mg., Mn 34 mcg., Vit. A 2500 IU, D 400 IU, E 20 IU, C 55 mg., B-1 0.65 mg., B-2 1.0 mg., niacin 7.0 (mg. Eq), B-6 0.40 mg., folic acid 100 mcg., B-12 1.5 mcg., pantothenic acid 3 mg. Bot. 4 fl oz; 8 fl oz; 32 fl oz;
Use: When a formula of standard dilution is desired for an infant.

SIMILAC 24 LBW. (Ross) Milk-based medium chain trigylceride low osmolar formula, ready-to-feed (24 cal./fl. oz.) Each liter contains: protein 22.0 g, fat 44.9 g, carbohydrate 84.9 g, Ca 0.73 g, P 0.56 g, Na 0.36 g, K 1.22 g, Cl 0.90 g, Mg 80 mg., Fe 3.0 mg., Zn 8.0 mg., Cu 0.80 mg., iodine 0.12 mg., Mn 41 mcg., Vit. A 2400 IU, D 480 IU, E 24 IU, C 100 mg., B-1 1.0 mg., B-2 1.2 mg., niacin 8.4 mg. B-6 0.48 mg., folic acid 120 mcg., B-12 1.8 mcg., pantothenic acid 3.6 mg. Bot. 4 fl. oz.
Use: For low-birth-weight infants who need a low molar concentrated feeding containing medium chain triglycerides.

SIMILAC 24/SIMILAC 24 WITH IRON. (Ross) Milk-based formula ready-to-feed (24 cal./fl. oz.). Each l contains: protein 22.0 g, fat 42.8 g, carbohydrate 84.9 g, Ca 0.73 g, P 0.56 g, Na 0.33 g, K 1.07 g, 0.74 g, Mg 55 mg., Fe 15 mg. (1.8 mg in Similac 24 Regular), Zn 6.0 mg., Cu 0.72 mg., iodine 0.12 mg., Mn 41 mcg., Vit. A 3000 IU, D 480 IU, E 24 IU, C 66 mg., B-1 0.78 mg., B-2 1.2 mg., niacin 8.4 n Eq, B-6 0.48 mg., folic acid 120 mcg., B-12 1.8 mc pantothenic acid 3.6 mg. Bot. 4 fl. oz.
Use: For infants who need a concentrated feedin

SIMILAC 27. (Ross) Milk-based ready-to-feed form (27 cal./fl. oz.). Each liter contains: protein 24.7 g fat 48.1 g, carbohydrate 95.5 g, Ca 0.81 g, P 0.62 g, Na 0.39 g, K 1.2 g, Cl 0.81 g, Mg 61 mg., Fe 2 mg., Zn 6.8 mg., Cu 0.81 mg., iodine 0.14 mg., M 46 mcg., Vit. A 3375 IU, D 540 IU, E 27 IU, C 74 mg., B-1 0.88 mg., B-2 1.4 mg., niacin 9.4 mg. Eq, V B-6 0.54 mg., folic acid 140 mcg., Vit. B-12 2.0 mc pantothenic acid 4.0 mg. Bot. 4 fl. oz.
Use: For low-birth-weight infants requiring a conce trated feeding.

SIMILAC 60/40 POWDER. (Ross) Milk-based form powder with 60:40 whey to casein ratio. Each lite contains (as fed 20 cal./fl. oz.): protein 15.0 g, fat 37.8 g, carbohydrate 69.0 g, Ca 0.40 g, P 0.20 g, Na 0.16 g, K 0.58 g, Cl 0.45 g, Mg 42 mg., Fe 1.5 mg., Zn 5.0 mg., Cu 0.60 mg., iodine 42 mcg., Mn 34 mcg., Vit. A 2000 IU, D 400 IU, E 17 IU, C 55 mg., B-1 0.65 mg., B-2 1.0, Niacin mg. Eq. 7.3, B-6 0.40 mg., folic acid 100 mcg., Vit. B-12 1.5 mc pantothenic acid 3.0 mg., Vit. K-1 55 mcg. Cans 1
Use: For infants requiring low electrolyte formula a calcium-to-phosphurus ratio of 2:1.

SIMILAC CONCENTRATED LIQUID/SIMILAC CONCENTRATED LIQUID WITH IRON. (Ross) 1 fl. oz. diluted 1:1 to give 20 Cal/fl. oz. See SIMILAC 20/SIMILAC 20 With Iron for compositio on "as fed" 20 cal./fl. oz. basis.

SIMILAC NATURAL CARE HUMAN MILK FORTIFIER. (Ross) Infant formula designed to be mixed with human milk or fed alternately with human milk to low-birth-weight infants. Bot. 4 oz.
Use: Feeding for low-birth-weight infants.

SIMILAC POWDER/SIMILAC POWDER WITH IRON (Ross) Milk-based formula, "as" fed (20 cal./fl. oz Each liter contains: protein 15.5 g, fat 36.1 g, carbohydrate 72.3 g, Ca 0.51 g, P 0.39 g, Na 0.30 g, K 1.1 g, Cl 0.49 g, Mg 41 mg., Fe 12.0 mg., Zn 5.0 mg., Cu 0.60 mg., iodine 0.10 mg., Mn 34 mcg Vit. A 2500 IU, D 400 IU, E 15 IU, C 55 mg., B-1 0.6 mg., B-2 1.0 mg., niacin 7.0 mg., B-6 0.40 mg., fo acid 100 mcg., B-12 1.5 mcg., K-1 27 mcg., pant thenic acid 3.0 mg. Cans 1 lb.
Use: For infants requiring standard dilution formula or one with an increased concentration.

SIMILAC SPECIAL CARE 20. (Ross) Infant Formula ready-to-feed (20 Cal./fl. oz.). Milk-based low osmol formula with 60:40 whey: casein ratio and

containing medium chain triglycerides. Each liter contains: protein 18.3 g, fat 36.7 g, carbohydrate 71.7 g, Ca 1200 mg., P 600 mg., Na 310 mg., potassium 940 mg., Cl 640 mg., Mg 83 mg., Fe 2.5 mg., Zn 10.0 mg., Cu 1.7 mg., Mn 0.08 mg., iodine 0.13 mg., Vit. A 4580 IU, D 1000 IU, E 25 IU, C 250 mg., B-1 1.7 mg., B-2 4.2 mg., niacin 34 mg., pantothenic acid 12.5 mg., B-6 1.7 mg., folic acid 0.25 mg., biotin 0.25 mg., B-12 3.7 mcg., choline 67 mg., inositol 37 mg., K-1 83 mcg. Bot. 4 fl. oz.
Use: For growing low-birth-weight infants who require only a 20 cal./fl. oz. formula.

MILAC SPECIAL CARE 24. (Ross) Infant Formula ready-to-feed (24 Cal./fl. oz.). Milk-based low osmolar formula with 60:40 whey:casein ratio and containing medium chain triglycerides. Each liter contains: protein 22.0 g, fat 44.0 g, carbohydrate 86.0 g, Ca 1440 mg., P 720 mg., Na 380, K 1120 mg., Cl 710 mg., Mg 100 mg., Fe 3.0 mg., Zn 12 mg., Cu 2.0 mg., iodine 0.150 mg., Mn 0.10 mg., Vit. A 5500 I.U., D 1200 I.U., E 30 mg., C 300 mg., B-1 2.0 mg., B-2 5.0 mg., niacin 40 mg., B-6 2.0 mg., folic acid 0.3 mg., B-12 4.5 mcg., K-1 100 mcg., pantothenic acid 15 mg., choline 80 mg., inositol 45 mg. Bot. 4 fl. oz.
Use: For growing low-birth-weight infants.

MILAC WITH WHEY AND IRON. (Ross) Iron fortified, whey-predominant-protein formula for feeding term infants. **Powder,** Cans 1 lb.; **Conc. liq.,** Cans 13 oz., Case 12s; **Ready to Feed,** Cans 32 oz.
Use: For feeding term infants.

IRON. (Merrell Dow) Iron (supplied as ferrous gluconate) 10 mg./Cap. Bot. 100s.
Use: Prevention and treatment of iron deficiency and iron deficiency anemia.

IRON PLUS. (Merrell Dow) Iron 10 mg. (supplied as ferrous gluconate), Vit. B-12 3.33 mcg., ascorbic acid 50 mg., B-6 1 mg., folic 0.1 mg./Cap. Bot. 100s.
Use: Prevention and treatment of iron deficiency and iron deficiency anemia.

IMTRAZENE. USAN. 1,4-Dimethyl-1,4-diphenyl-2-tetrazene.
Use: Antineoplastic.

IAC. (Marin) Phenacetin 150 mg., acetaminophen 150 mg., phenylpropanolamine HCl 25 mg., phenyltoloxamine citrate 22 mg./Tab. Bot. 30s, 100s.
Use: Relief sinus headache and common cold symptoms.

IAPREL. (Pasadena Research) Chlorpheniramine maleate 8 mg., phenylephrine HCl 20 mg., methscopolamine nitrate 2.5 mg./Cap. Bot. 100s, 1000s. Box 30s.

IAREST. (Pharmacraft) Acetaminophen 325 mg., chlorpheniramine maleate 2 mg., phenylpropanolamine HCl 18.7 mg./Tab. Sleeve Pack 20s, 40s, 80s.
Use: Sinus headache, congestion.

IAREST DECONGESTANT NASAL SPRAY. (Pharmacraft) Phenylephrine HCl 0.5%. Bot. 0.5 oz.
Use: Nasal decongestant.

SINAREST, EXTRA-STRENGTH. (Pharmacraft) Acetaminophen 500 mg., chlorpheniramine maleate 2 mg., phenylpropanolamine HCl 18.7 mg./Tab. Sleeve Pack 24s.
Use: Sinus headache, congestion.

SINASCOL. (Vitarine) Chlorpheniramine maleate 8 mg., phenylephrine HCl 20 mg., methscopolamine nitrate 2.5 mg./Cap.
Use: Antihistaminic and decongestant.

SINAXAR. Styramate, B.A.N.

• **SINCALIDE.** USAN.
Use: Choleretic.

SINE-AID EXTRA-STRENGTH SINUS HEADACHE CAPSULES. (McNeil Prods) Acetaminophen 500 mg., pseudoephedrine HCl 30 mg./Cap. Bot. 20s.
Use: Treatment of sinus headache, pain and congestion.

SINE-AID SINUS HEADACHE TABLETS. (McNeil Prods) Acetaminophen 325 mg., pseudoephedrine HCl 30 mg./Tab. Bot. 24s, 50s, 100s.
Use: Sinus headache pain and pressure.

SINECOD CITRATE. Butamyrate, B.A.N.

• **SINEFUNGIN.** USAN.
Use: Antifungal.

SINEMET 10/100. (Merck Sharp & Dohme) Carbidopa 10 mg., Levodopa 100 mg./Tab. Bot. 100s. Unit-dose 100s.
Use: Treatment of Parkinson's disease.

SINEMET 25/100. (Merck Sharp & Dohme) Carbidopa 25 mg., levodopa 100 mg./Tab. Bot. 100s. Unit-dose 100s.
Use: Treatment of Parkinson's disease.

SINEMET 25/250. (Merck Sharp & Dohme) Carbidopa 25 mg., levodopa 250 mg./Tab. Bot. 100s. Unit-dose 100s.
Use: Treatment of Parkinson's disease.

SINE-OFF CAPSULES WITH ACETAMINOPHEN. (Menley & James) Chlorpheniramine maleate 2.0 mg., pseudoephedrine HCl 30 mg., acetaminophen 500 mg./Cap. Pkg. 20s.
Use: Sinus headache and congestion.

SINE-OFF CAPSULES, NO DROWSINESS FORMULA. (Menley & James) Pseudoephedrine HCl 30 mg., acetaminophen 500 mg./Cap. Pkg. 20s.
Use: Sinus headache and congestion relief when drowsiness is a problem.

SINE-OFF TABLETS. (Menley & James) Chlorpheniramine maleate 2.0 mg., phenylpropanolamine HCl 12.5 mg., aspirin 325 mg. Tab. Pkg. 24s, 48s, 100s.
Use: Sinus headache & congestion.

SINEQUAN. (Roerig) Doxepin HCl **Cap.** 10 mg./Cap. Bot. 100s, 1000s. Unit dose 100s; 25 mg., 50 mg./Cap. Bot. 100s, 1000s, 5000s. Unit dose 100s; 75 mg./Cap. Bot. 100s, 1000s; Unit Dose 100s; 100 mg./Cap. Bot. 100s, 1000s. Unit Dose 100s; 150 mg./Cap. Bot. 50, 500s. Unit-dose 100s. **Oral Concentrate** 10 mg./ml. Bot. 120 ml.
Use: Psychotherapeutic drug.

SINEX. (Vicks) Phenylephrine HCl 0.5%, cetylpyridinium chloride 0.04%, camphor, menthol, eucalyptol, methyl salicylate w/thimerosal 0.001%

preservative. Nasal Spray. Plastic Squeeze Bot. 0.5 oz., 1 oz.
Use: Nasal decongestant spray.

SINEXIN. (Bowman) Acetaminophen 324 mg., phenylehrine HCl 5 mg., chlorpheniramine maleate 2 mg., caffeine 32.4 mg./Cap.
Use: Analgesic, decongestant, antihistaminic.

SINEX LONG ACTING. (Vicks) Oxymetazoline HCl 0.05% in aqueous soln. with mentholated vapors and thimerosal 0.001% Nasal spray. Bot. 0.5 oz., 1 oz.
Use: Nasal decongestant.

SINGLET. (Merrell Dow) Phenylephrine HCl 40 mg., chlorpheniramine maleate 8 mg., acetaminophen 500 mg./Tab. Bot. 100s.
Use: Decongestant, analgesic, antihistamine.

SINO-COMP. (Bio-Factor) Salicylamide 3.5 gr., caffeine 10 mg., phenylephrine HCl 5 mg., Vit. C 20 mg., chlorprophenpyridamine maleate 2 mg./Tab. Bot. 1000s.
Use: Decongestant & analgesic.

SINOCON TR. (Vangard) Phenylpropanolamine HCl 20 mg., phenylephrine HCl 5 mg., phenyltoloxamine citrate 7.5 mg., chlorpheniramine maleate 2.5 mg./Tab. Bot. 100s, 1000s.
Use: Antihistamine, decongestant.

SINODEC. (Primedics) Chlorpheniramine maleate 8 mg., phenylephrine HCl 20 mg., methscopolamine nitrate 2.5 mg./Cap. Bot. 100s, 500s.
Use: Antihistaminic.

SINO-EZE MLT. (Richlyn) Salicylamide 3.5 gr., acetaminophen 100 mg., phenylephrine HCl 5 mg., chlorpheniramine maleate 2 mg./Tab. Bot. 1000s.
Use: Sinus, colds.

SINOGRAFIN. (Squibb) Meglumine diatrizoate 40% and meglumine iodipamide 20%. Vial 10 cc.
Use: Diagnostic.

SINOPHEN. (Kay) Phenylephrine HCl 1% in buffered isotonic sol., sodium bisulfite 0.2%. Methylparaben 0.02%, propyparaben 0.01%. Bot. Pts.
Use: Nasal decongestant.

SINO-TUSSIN MLT. (Richlyn) Dextromethorphan HBr 10 mg., salicylamide 3.5 gr., acetaminophen 100 mg., phenylephrine HCl 5 mg., chlorpheniramine maleate 2 mg./Tab. Bot. 1000s.
Use: Cold therapy.

SINOVAN TIMED. (Drug Industries) Chlorpheniramine maleate 8 mg., phenylephrine HCl 20 mg., methscopolamine nitrate 2.5 mg./Cap. Bot. 100s, 1000s.
Use: Cold, hay fever, allergies.

SINTHROME. Nicoumalone, B.A.N.

SINTISONE L-STEAROYLGYLCOLATE. Prednisolone, B.A.N.

SINUADE. (Kay) Chlorpheniramine maleate 8 mg., phenylpropanolamine HCl 50 mg./Timed Release Cap. Bot. 100s, 1000s.

SINUBID. (Parke-Davis) Acetaminophen 600 mg., phenylpropanolamine HCl 100 mg., phenyltoloxamine 66 mg./Tab. Bot. 100s.
Use: Relief of common cold.

SINUCOL. (Tennessee Pharm.) Chlorpheniramine maleate 8 mg., phenylephrine HCl 20 mg., methscopolamine nitrate 2.5 mg./Cap. Bot. 100s, 500s. Parenteral. Vial 10 cc.
Use: Respiratory congestion and hypersecretion.

SINUDRAIN. (Wolins) Phenylephrine 5 mg., phenindamine 10 mg., aspirin, caffeine, aluminum hydroxide magnesium carbonate, co-dried gel/Ta Bot. 100s, 1000s.

SINUESE. (Jenkins) Pot. guaiacolsulfonate 40 mg., sod. iodide 50 mg., menthol, camphor, guaiacol, eucalyptol/cc. Vial 30 cc., 12s.

SINUFED TIMECELLE. (Hauck) Pseudoephedrine H 60 mg., guailfenesin 300 mg./Cap. Bot. 100s.
Use: Nasal decongestant.

SINUGESIC. (Vortech) Bot. 1000s.
Use: Antihistaminic, decongestant.

SINU-LETS. (Quality Generics) Acetaminophen 32 mg., phenylpropanolamine HCl 25 mg., phenyltoloxamine citrate 25 mg./Tab. Vials 36s. Bot. 100s, 1000s.
Use: Sinus headaches.

SINULIN TABLETS. (Carnrick) Phenylpropanolamine HCl 37.5 mg., chlorpheniramine maleate 2 mg., acetaminophen 325 mg., salicylamide 250 mg., homatropine methylbromide 0.75 mg./Tab. Bot. 20s, 100s. Blisters of 24s.
Use: Sinus congestion, headache.

SINUPAN. (Ion) Phenylephrine HCl 40 mg., guaifenesin 200 mg./S.R. Cap. Bot. 100s.
Use: Decongestant.

SINUS. (Zenith) Phenacetin 150 mg., acetaminophen 150 mg., phenylpropanolamine HCl 25 mg., phenyltoloxamine citrate 22 mg./Tab. Bot. 1000s.
Use: Antihistamine, decongestant.

SINUSEZE. (Amlab) Acetaminophen 325 mg., phenopropanolamine HCl 25 mg., phenyltoloxamir citrate 22 mg/Tab. Bot. 36s.
Use: Symptomatic relief of sinus symptoms.

SINUS HEADACHE TABLETS. (Eckerd) Phenylpropanolamine HCl 12.5 mg., acetaminoph 325 mg./Tab. Bot. 24s, 48s.
Use: Analgesic, decongestant.

SINUS TABLETS. (Kenyon) Phenacetin 150 mg., acetaminophen 150 mg., phenyltoloxamine dihydrogen citrate 22 mg./Tab. Bot. 100s, 1000s.

SINUS TABLETS. (Walgreen) Acetaminophen 325 mg., phenylpropanolamine HCl 25 mg., phenyltoloxamine citrate 22 mg./Tab. Bot. 30s.
Use: Analgesic, decongestant, antihistamine.

SINUS TABLETS #2. (Vitarine) Acetaminophen 32 mg., phenylpropanolamine HCl 25 mg./Tab.
Use: Temporary relief of sinus headache & congestion.

SINUSTAT. (Vitarine) Acetaminophen 325 mg., phenylpropanolamine HCl 25 mg., phenyltoloxami citrate 22 mg./Tab. Bot. 50s.
Use: Relief from the pain of sinus headaches and the common cold.

NUTAB. (Warner-Lambert) Acetaminophen 325 mg., pseudoephedrine HCl 30 mg., chlorpheniramine HCl 2 mg./Tab. Bot. 100s. Blister pack 12s, 30s.
Use: Analgesic, decongestant, antihistaminic.

NUTAB MAXIMUM STRENGTH. (Warner-Lambert) Acetaminophen 500 mg., pseudoephedrine HCl 30 mg., chlorpheniramine maleate 2 mg./Tab. or Cap. Blister pack 24s.
Use: Analgesic, decongestant, antihistaminic.

NUTAB II MAXIMUM STRENGTH NO DROWSINESS FORMULA. (Warner-Lambert) Acetaminophen 500 mg. pseudoephedrine HCl 30 mg./Tab. or Cap. Pack 24s.
Use: Analgesic, decongestant.

NUTROL. (Weeks & Leo) Phenylpropanolamine HCl 25 mg., phenyltoloxamine citrate 22 mg., acetaminophen 325 mg./Tab. Bot. 40s, 90s.
Use: Sinus headache.

NU-WOL. (Wolins) Acetaminophen 150 mg., phenacetin 150 mg., phenylpropanolamine HCl 25 mg., phenyltoloxamine citrate 22 mg./Tab. Bot. 100s, 1000s.
Use: Analgesic, decongestant, antihistaminic.

NU-WOL II. (Wolins) Acetaminophen 150 mg., phenacetin 150 mg., phenylpropanolamine HCl 25 mg./Tab. Bot. 100s, 1000s.
Use: Analgesic, decongestant.

ROIL. (Siroil) Mercuric oleate, cresol, vegetable & mineral oil. Emulsion, Bot. 8 oz.
Use: Antiseptic skin therapy.

R-O-LENE. (Siroil) Tube 4 oz.
Use: Skin softener.

SISOMICIN. USAN.
Use: Antibacterial.

SISOMICIN SULFATE, U.S.P. XXI. Inj., U.S.P. XXI.
Use: Antibacterial.

STOMETRIL. Mestranol, B.A.N.

TABS. (Canright) Lobeline Sulf. 1.5 mg., benzocaine 2 mg., aluminum hydroxide—magnesium carbonate co-dried gel 150 mg./Loz. Bot. 100s.
Use: Discourage smoking.

SITOGLUSIDE. USAN.
Use: Antiprostatic hypertrophy.

TOSTEROLS. A mixture of 80 to 90% beta-sitosterol and 10 to 20% dihydro-beta-sitosterol.
See: Cytellin, Susp. (Lilly)

XAMEEN. (Spanner) Vit. B-1 100 mg., B-6 100 mg./cc. Vial 10 cc.
Use: B vitamin therapy.

K-65. (SmithKline) Propoxyphene HCl 65 mg./Cap. Bot. 100s, 500s. Unit dose 100s.
Use: Analgesic.

K-65 APAP. (SmithKline) Propoxyphene HCl 65 mg., Acetaminophen 650 mg./Tab. Bot. 100s, 500s.
Use: Analgesic.

K-65 COMPOUND. (SmithKline) Propoxyphene HCl 65 mg., aspirin 389 mg., caffeine 32.4 mg./Cap. Bot. 100s, 500s.
Use: Analgesic.

K-AMITRIPTYLINE. (SmithKline) Amitriptyline HCl 10 mg., 25 mg., 50 mg./Tab. Bot. 100s, 1000s. 75 mg., 100 mg., 150 mg./Tab. Bot. 100s.
Use: Relief of depression, anxiety symptoms.

SK-AMPICILLIN. (SmithKline) Ampicillin **Cap.** 250, 500 mg./Cap. Bot. 24s, 100s, 500s. **Oral Susp.** 100 mg./ml. Bot. 20 ml.; 125, 250 mg./5 ml. Bot. 100 ml., 150 ml., 200 ml.
Use: Antibiotic.

SK-AMPICILLIN-N. (SmithKline) Ampicillin sodium 500 mg./Vial. Box 1s.
Use: Antibiotic.

SK-APAP W/CODEINE. (SmithKline) Acetaminophen 300 mg., codeine phosphate 15 mg./Tab. Bot. 100s. Acetaminophen 300 mg., codeine phosphate 30 mg./Tab. Bot. 100s, 1000s. Acetaminophen 300 mg., codeine phosphate 60 mg./Tab. Bot. 100s, 500s.
Use: Analgesic.

SK-BAMATE. (SmithKline) Meprobamate 200 mg., 400 mg./Tab. Bot. 100s. 400 mg. Bot. 1000s.
Use: Relief of anxiety and tension.

SK-CHLORAL HYDRATE. (SmithKline) Chloral Hydrate 500 mg./Cap. Bot. 100s.
Use: Hypnotic.

SK-CHLOROTHIAZIDE. (SmithKline) Chlorothiazide 250 mg., 500 mg./Tab. Bot. 100s, 1000s.
Use: Diuretic, antihypertensive.

SK-DEXAMETHASONE. (SmithKline) Dexamethasone 0.5 mg., 0.75 mg., 1.5 mg./Tab. Bot. 100s.
Use: Steroidal anti-inflammatory.

SK-DIPHENOXYLATE. (SmithKline) Diphenoxylate HCl 2.5 mg., atropine sulfate 0.025 mg. Bot. 100s, 1000s.
Use: Adjunctive therapy in diarrhea.

SK-DIPYRIDAMOLE. (SmithKline) Dipyridamole 25 mg./Tab. Bot. 100s, 1000s; 50 mg./Tab. Bot. 50s, 100s; 75 mg./Tab. Bot. 100s.
Use: Treatment of angina pectoris.

SK-DOXYCYCLINE HYCLATE. (SmithKline) Doxycycline hyclate 50 mg./Cap. Bot. 50s; 100 mg./Cap. Bot. 50s, 500s.
Use: Antibiotic.

SKELAXIN. (Carnrick) Metaxalone 400 mg./Tab. Bot. 100s.
Use: Skeletal muscle relaxant.

SKELAXIN. (Robins) Metaxalone 400 mg./Tab. Bot. 100s, 500s.
Use: Skeletal muscle relaxant.

■ **SKELETAL MUSCLE RELAXANTS.**
See: Anectine, Sol., Pow. (Burroughs Wellcome)
Flexeril, Tab. (Merck Sharp & Dohme)
Mephenesin (Var. Mfr.)
Metubine Iodide, Vial (Lilly)
Neostig, Tab. (Freeport)
Paraflex, Tab. (McNeil)
Parafon Forte, Tab. (McNeil)
Quelicin, Fliptop & pintop vials, Syringe w/lancet, Ampules. (Abbott)
Rela, Tab. (Schering)
Robaxin, Tab., Inj. (Robins)
Skelaxin, Tab. (Robins)
Soma, Preps. (Wallace)
Sucostrin, Vial, Amp. (Squibb)
Syncurine, Vial (Burroughs Wellcome)
Trancopal, Cap. (Winthrop-Breon)
d-Tubocurarine Chloride (Var. Mfr.)

SK-ERYTHROMYCIN. (SmithKline) Erythromycin Stearate 250 mg./Film Coated Tab. Bot. 100s, 500s. 500 mg./Tab. Bot. 100s.
Use: Antibiotic.

SK-FUROSEMIDE. (SmithKline) Furosemide 20 or 40 mg./Tab. Bot. 100s, 500s.
Use: Diuretic.

SK-HYDROCHLOROTHIAZIDE. (SmithKline) Hydrochlorothiazide 25 mg. or 50 mg./Tab. Bot. 100s, 1000s.
Use: Diuretic, antihypertensive.

SKIN CARE. (Sween) Bot. unit-dose 2 oz., 9 oz.
Use: Cream for irritated skin.

SKIN DEGREASER. (Aeroceuticals) Freon 100%. Bot. 2 oz., 4 oz.
Use: Presurgical skin degreaser.

SKIN SHIELD LIQUID BANDAGE. (Commerce) Dyclonine HCl, benzethonium Cl. Bot. 0.45 oz.
Use: Protection for cuts, bruises & scrapes.

SK-LYGEN. (SmithKline) Chlordiazepoxide HCl 5 mg., 10 mg., 25 mg./Cap. Bot. 100s, 500s.
Use: Relief of anxiety, tensions.

SK-METRONIDAZOLE. (SmithKline) Metronidazole 250 mg./Tab. Bot. 100s, 500s.
Use: Antibacterial, antiprotozoal.

SK-OXYCODONE w/ACETAMINOPHEN. (SmithKline) Oxycodone HCl 5 mg., acetaminophen 325 mg./Tab. Bot 100s, 500s.
Use: Relief of moderate to moderately severe pain.

SK-OXYCODONE w/ASPIRIN. (SmithKline) Oxycodone HCl 4.5 mg., oxycodone terephthalate 0.38 mg., aspirin 325 mg./Tab. Bot. 100s.
Use: Relief of moderate to moderately severe pain.

SK-PENICILLIN G. (SmithKline) Penicillin G Potassium 400,000 u./Tab. Bot. 100s, 1000s. 800,000 u./Tab. Bot. 100s.
Use: Antibiotic.

SK-PENICILLIN VK. (SmithKline) Penicillin V potassium. **Oral Sol.:** 125 mg., 250 mg./5 ml. Bot. 100 ml., 200 ml.; **Tab.:** 250 mg. Bot. 100s, 500s, 1000s; 500 mg. Bot. 100s.
Use: Antibiotic.

SK-PHENOBARBITAL. (SmithKline) Phenobarbital 15, 30 mg./Tab. Bot. 1000s.
Use: Sedative, hypnotic.

SK-POTASSIUM CHLORIDE. (SmithKline) Potassium chloride. 10%: Each 30 ml. contains 40 mEq. potassium chloride, alcohol 5%. **20%:** Each 30 ml. contains 80 mEq. potassium chloride, 5% alcohol. Bot. 16 oz..
Use: Treatment of hypokalemia.

SK-PRAMINE. (SmithKline) Imipramine HCl 10 mg./Tab. Bot. 100s; 25 mg./Tab. Bot. 100s, 1000s; 50 mg./Tab. Bot. 100s, 1000s.
Use: Antidepressant.

SK-PREDNISONE. (SmithKline) Prednisone 5 mg./Tab. Bot. 100s, 1000s.
Use: Adrenocortical Steroid (antiinflammatory).

SK-PROBENECID. (SmithKline) Probenecid 500 mg./Tab. Bot. 100s, 1000s.
Use: Treatment of hyperuricemia associated with gout, adjunctive therapy with antibiotics.

SK-PROPANTHELINE BROMIDE. (SmithKline) F pantheline bromide 15 mg./Tab. Bot. 100s, 1000s
Use: Adjunctive ulcer therapy for treatment of peptic ulcer.

SK-QUINIDINE SULFATE. (SmithKline) Quinidine S fate 200 mg./Tab. Bot. 100s, 500s, 1000s.
Use: Anti-arrhythmic.

SK-RESERPINE. (SmithKline) Reserpine 0.25 mg./T Bot. 1000s.
Use: Antihypertensive.

SK-SOXAZOLE. (SmithKline) Sulfisoxazole 5 mg./Tab. Bot. 100s.
Use: Antibacterial for treatment of urinary tract infections.

SK-TERPIN HYDRATE AND CODEINE ELIXIR. (Sm Kline) Terpin hydrate 85 mg., codeine 10 mg./5 r Bot. 4 oz., 16 oz.
Use: Antitussive, expectorant.

SK-TETRACYCLINE CAPSULES. (SmithKline) Te cycline HCl 250 mg./Cap. Bot. 100s, 1000s. 500 mg./Cap. Bot. 100s.
Use: Antibiotic.

SK-TETRACYCLINE SYRUP. (SmithKline) Tetracycl 125 mg./5 ml. w/methylparaben 0.12%, propylparaben 0.03%/5 ml. w/alcohol 1%. Bot. pt.
Use: Antibiotic.

SK-THIORIDAZINE HCL. (SmithKline) Thioridazine H 10, 25, or 50 mg./Tab. Bot. 100s, 1000s. 100 mg./Tab. Bot. 100s, 500s.
Use: Tranquilizer.

SK-TOLBUTAMIDE. (SmithKline) Tolbutamide 5 mg./Tab. Bot. 100s, 1000s.
Use: Antidiabetic.

SLEEP II. (Walgreen) Diphenhydramine HCl 25 mg./Tab. Bot. 16s, 32s, 72s.
Use: Sleep aid.

SLEEP CAP. (Weeks & Leo) Diphenhydramine HCl 50 mg./Cap. Vials 25s, 50s.
Use: Induce relaxed sleep.

SLEEP-EZE TABLETS. (Whitehall) Diphenhydram HCl 25 mg./Tab. Pkg. 12s, 26s, 52s.
Use: Mild sedative, soporific.

SLEEP TABS. (Towne) Scopolamine aminoxide HBr 0.2 mg., salicylamide 250 mg./Tab. Bot. 36s, 90s
Use: Sleep aid.

SLEEP TABLET. (Walgreen) Pyrilamine maleate 25 mg./Tab. Bot 32s, 72s, 16s.
Use: Sleep aid.

SLENDER. (Carnation) Skim milk, veg. oils, caseinates, vitamins, minerals. **Liquid:** 220 cal./ 1 oz. Can. **Powder:** 173 or 200 cal. mixed w/6 oz. skim or low fat milk. Pkg 1 oz.
Use: Diet food.

SLENDER-X. (Progressive Drugs) Phenylpropanolamine, methylcellulose, caffeine, vitamins/Tab. Pkg 21s, 42s, 84s. Gum 20s, 60s.

SLIMETTES. (Blue Cross) Phenylpropanolamine HC 35 mg., caffeine 140 mg./Cap. Box 20s.
Use: Appetite depressant.

LIM-FAST. (Thompson Medical) Meal replacement powder mixed with milk to replace 1, 2 or 3 meals a day.

LIM-LINE. (Thompson Medical) Benzocaine, dextrose/Chewing gum. Box 36s, 60s.

LIM PLAN PLUS WITHOUT CAFFEINE. (Whiteworth) Phenylpropanolamine HCl 75 mg./Tab. Box 40s.
Use: Appetite control.

LIM-TABS. (Wesley) Phendimetrazine tartrate 35 mg./Tab. Bot. 1000s.

LOAN'S LINIMENT. (Warner-Lambert) Capsicum oleoresin 0.62%, methyl salicylate 2.66%, oil of camphor 3.35%, turpentine oil 46.76%, oil of pine 6.74%. Bot. 2 oz., 7 oz.
Use: Counterirritant, rubefacient.

LO-BID GYROCAPS. (Rorer) Theophylline anhydrous 50 mg., 100 mg., 200 mg., or 300 mg./Timed Release Cap. Bot. 100s, 1000s. Unit dose.
Use: Bronchodilator.

LO-PHYLLIN 80 SYRUP. (Rorer) Theophylline 80 mg./15 ml. Nonalcoholic. Bot. 4 oz., pt., gal., Unit dose 15 ml.
Use: Bronchodilator.

LO-PHYLLIN GG. (Rorer) Theophylline 150 mg., guaifenesin 90 mg./Cap. or 15 ml. syrup. **Cap.** Bot. 100s. **Syr.** Bot. pt.
Use: Bronchodilator, expectorant.

LO-PHYLLIN GYROCAPS. (Rorer) Theophylline anhydrous 60 mg., 125 mg. or 250 mg./T.R. Cap. Bot. 100s, 1000s. Unit dose.
Use: Bronchodilator.

LO-PHYLLIN TABLETS. (Rorer) Theophylline anhydrous 100 mg. or 200 mg./Tab. Bot. 100s, 1000s. Unit dose.
Use: Bronchodilator.

LOW-K. (Ciba) Potassium Chloride Bot. 100s, 1000s. Accu-Pak units of 100. Consumer Packs 100s.
Use: Potassium supplement.

LOW FE. (Ciba) Dried ferrous sulfate 160 mg./Tab. Bot. 30s.
Use: Iron-deficiency anemia.

LT. (Western Research) Sodium levo-thyroxine 0.1 mg., 0.2 mg. or 0.3 mg. /Tab. Bot. 1000s.
Use: Hypothyroidism treatment.

LT LOTION. (C & M Pharmacal) Salicyclic acid 3%, lactic acid 5%, coal tar soln. 2%. Bot. 4.3 oz.
Use: Anti-dandruff lotion.

LYN-LL. (Edwards) Phendimetrazine tartrate 105 mg./T.R. Cap. Bot. 100s.
Use: Appetite suppressant.

M-A FORMULA. (Wyeth) A series of liquid feeding formulas:
Iron Fortified, Infant Formula-Powder.
Iron Fortified, Infant Formula-Ready to Feed.
Iron Fortified, Infant Formula-Liquid.
Lo-Iron, Infant Formula-Liquid.
Lo-Iron, Infant Formula-Powder.
Lo-Iron, Infant Formula-Ready to Feed.
Use: For infant feeding.

SMALL FRY CHEWABLE TABS. (Approved) Vit. A 5000 I.U., D 1000 I.U., B-12 5 mcg., B-1 3 mg., B-2 2.5 mg., B-6 1 mg., C 50 mg., niacinamide 20 mg., Cal. pantothenate 1 mg., E 1 I.U., l-lysine 15 mg., biotin 10 mg./Tab. Bot. 100s, 250s, 365s.

• **SMALLPOX VACCINE,** U.S.P. XXI. (Lederle, Avianized)—Tube 1s, 5s, 10s, vaccinations. 1 vaccination and needle in glass capillary tube. (Wyeth)—Tube 1s, 5s, 10s, vaccinations. Vaccinia Immune Globulin (Human), Inj. (Hyland)
W/Brilliant Green 1s, 10s.
Use: Active immuniziing agent.

SMURF. (Mead Johnson) Vit. A 2500 I.U., D 400 I.U., E 15 I.U., C 60 mg., Folic acid 0.3 mg., B-1 1.05 mg., B-2 1.2 mg., niacin 13.5 mg., B-6 1.05 mg., B-12 4.5 mcg.,/Tab. Bot. 60s
Use: Multivitamin and mineral supplement.

SMURF WITH IRON & ZINC. (Mead Johnson) Vit. A 2500 IU, D 400 IU, E 15 IU, C 60 mg, Folic acid 0.3 mg., B-1 1.05 mg., B-2 1.2 mg., niacin 13.5 mg., B-6 1.05 mg., B-12 4.5 mcg., iron 12 mg., zinc 8 mg./Tab. Bot. 60s.
Use: Multivitamin and mineral supplement.

SN-13, 272.
See: Primaquine Phos., U.S.P. XXI. (Var. Mfr.)

SNAKE VENOM.
Use: S.C., I.M. & orally; trypanosomiasis.
See: Antivenin. (Wyeth)

SNAP PAK ASPIRIN. (DeWitt) Aspirin 325 mg./Tab. Pak 16 Tabs.
Use: Analgesic.

SOACLENS. (Alcon) Thiomerosal 0.004%, EDTA 0.1%. Bot. 5 cc., 4 oz.
Use: Contact lens soaking and wetting solution.

SOAKARE. (Allergan) Benzalkonium chloride 0.01%, edetate disodium, NaOH to adjust pH and purified water. Bot. 4 fl. oz.
Use: Hard contact lens soaking solution.

▪ **SOAPS, GERMICIDAL.**
See: Dial, Preps. (Armour)
Fostex, Cake, Cream, Liq. (Westward)
pHisoHex, Liq. (Winthrop-Breon)
Thylox, Shampoo, Soap (Dent)

▪ **SOAP SUBSTITUTES.**
See: Acne-Dome, Cleanser (Miles Pharm)
Domerine, Shampoo (Miles Pharm)
Lowila, Cleanser (Westwood)
pHisoDerm, Preps. (Winthrop Consumer Products)

SOCYLATE. (Tunex) Sodium thiosalicylate 50 mg./ml. w/benzyl alcohol 2% as preservative. In water for injection. Vial 30cc.
Use: Analgesic, antipyretic.

• **SODA LIME,** N.F. XVI.
Use: Carbon dioxide absorbant.

SODA MINT. (Bowman) Sodium bicarbonate 5 gr., oil peppermint q.s./Tab. Bot. 100s, 1000s.

SODA MINT. (Lilly) Sodium bicarbonate 5 gr., oil peppermint q.s./Tab. Bot. 100s.

SODASONE. (Fellows) Prednisolone sod. phosphate 20 mg., niacinamide 25 mg./ml. Vial 10 ml.
Use: Adrenocortical hormone therapy.

• **SODIUM ACETATE,** U.S.P. XXI. Inj., Soln., U.S.P. XXI. Acetic acid, sodium salt, trihydrate. (Abbott) 40 mEq., 20 ml. in 50 ml. Fliptop Vial.
Use: Alkalizer; pharmaceutic acid (in solution for hemodialysis & peritoneal dialysis.)
SODIUM ACETATE & THEOPHYLLINE.
• **SODIUM ACETAZOLAMIDE.** Acetazolamide Sodium, U.S.P. XXI.
Use: Carbonic anhydrase inhibitor.
SODIUM ACETOSULFONE. Sodium 2-N-acetylsulfamyl-4,4′-diaminodiphenylsulfone.
Use: Leprostatic agent.
See: Promacetin, Tab. (Parke-Davis)
SODIUM ACETRIZOATE INJECTION, B.A.N. Sodium 3-acetamino-2,4,6-triiodobenzoate, Diaginol.
Use: Radio-opaque substance.
See: Salpix, Vial (Ortho)
SODIUM ACID PHOSPHATE.
See: Sodium Biphosphate (Various Mfr.)
SODIUM ACTINOQUINOL. 8-Ethoxy-5-quinoline sulfonic acid sodium salt.
Use: Treatment of flash burns (ophthalmic).
See: Uviban
SODIUM ALGINATE, N.F. XVI.
Use: Suspending agent.
See: Algin
Kelgin (Kelco)
SODIUM AMINOBENZOATE. Sodium p-aminobenzoate.
Use: Dermatomyositis and scleroderma.
SODIUM AMINOPTERIN. Aminopterin Sod.
SODIUM AMINOSALICYLATE.
See: Aminosalicylate Sodium, U.S.P. XXI.
SODIUM AMOBARBITAL. Amobarbital Sodium, U.S.P. XXI.
• **SODIUM AMYLOSULFATE.** USAN. Sod. salt of potato amylopectin. Depepsin.
Use: Peptic ulcer.
SODIUM ANAZOLENE. 4-[(4-Anilino-5-sulfo-1-naphthyl)azo]-5-hydroxy-2,7-naphthalene disulfonic acid trisodium salt.
Use: Diagnostic aid for blood volume and cardiac output.
SODIUM ANOXYNAPHTHONATE. B.A.N. Sodium 4′-anilino-8-hydroxy-1,1′-azonaphthalene-3,-5′,6-trisulfonate.
Use: Investigation of cardiac disease.
See: Anazolene Sodium (I.N.N.)
Coomassie Blue
SODIUM ANTIMONYLGLUCONATE. B.A.N. Sodium salt of a trivalent antimony derivative of gluconic acid.
Use: Treatment of schistosomiasis.
See: Triostam
SODIUM APOLATE. B.A.N. (Lloyd Bros.) Sodium ethenesulfonate polymer.
Use: Anticoagulant.
See: Pergalen
Peson (Hoechst)
Sod. Lyapolate
• **SODIUM ARSENATE AS 74.** USAN.
Use: Radioactive agent.

• **SODIUM ASCORBATE,** U.S.P. XXI. Monosodium L ascorbate.
Use: Pharmaceutic necessity for ascorbic acid injection.
See: Cenolate, Inj. (Abbott)
Liqui-Cee, Bot. (Arnar-Stone)
Sodascorbate, Tab. (Mosso)
Vitac Injection, Vial (Hickman)
SODIUM AUROTHIOMALATE.
See: Gold Sodium Thiosulfate, U.S.P. XXI.
• **SODIUM BENZOATE,** N.F. XVI.
Use: Pharm. aid (antifungal agent, preservative).
SODIUM BENZYLPENICILLIN. Penicillin G Sodium, U.S.P. XXI. Sodium Penicillin G.
Use: Antibiotic.
• **SODIUM BICARBONATE,** U.S.P. XXI. Inj., Oral Powder, Tabs, U.S.P. XXI. (Abbott) Injection. **4.2%** (5 mEq) Infant 10 ml. Syringe (21 G × 1.5 in. needle). **7.5%:** (44.6 mEq) 50 ml. Syringe (18 G x 1.5 in. needle) or 50 ml. Amp. **8.4%:** (10 mEq) Pediatric 10 ml. Syringe (21 G × 1.5 in. needle) o (50 mEq) 50 ml. Syringe (18 G × 1.5 in. needle) o 50 ml. Vial.
Use: Antacid, electrolyte replenisher systemical alkalizer.
W/Bismuth subcarbonate and Magnesia.
See: Anachloric A, Tab. (Upjohn)
W/Sodium Bitartrate.
See: Ceo-Two, Supp. (Beutlich)
Col-Evac, Supp. (Fellows)
W/Sodium carboxymethylcellulose, alginic acid.
See: Pretts, Tabs. (Marion)
SODIUM BIPHOSPHATE.
Use: Cathartic.
See: Sodium Phosphate Monobasic, U.S.P. XXI.
SODIUM BISMUTH TARTRATE.
See: Bismuth Sod. Tartrate, Preps.
SODIUM BISULFITE. Sulfurous acid, monosodium salt. Monosodium sulfite.
Use: Antioxidant.
• **SODIUM BORATE,** N.F. XVI.
Use: Pharm. aid (alkalizing agent).
SODIUM BUTABARBITAL.
See: Butabarbital Sodium, U.S.P. XXI.
SODIUM CALCIUMEDETATE. B.A.N. Calcium chela of the disodium salt of ethylenediamine-NNN′-N′-tetra-acetic acid.
Use: Treatment of lead poisoning.
See: Calcium Disodium Versenate.
SODIUM CALCIUM EDETATE.
See: Calcium Disodium Versenate, Amp., Tab. (Riker)
• **SODIUM CARBONATE,** N.F. XVI.
Use: Pharm aid (alkalizing agent).
SODIUM CARBOXYMETHYLCELLULOSE.
Carboxymethylcellulose Sodium, U.S.P. XXI. CMC. Cellulose Gum.
SODIUM CELLULOSE GLYCOLATE.
See: Carboxymethylcellulose, Sod. (Various Mfr.)
SODIUM CEPHALOTHIN. Cephalothin Sodium, U.S.P XXI.
Use: Antibiotic.

ODIUM CHLORIDE, U.S.P. XXI. Inhalation Soln., Inj., Bacteriostatic for Inj., Irrigation, Ophth. Soln., Tab., Tab. for Soln., U.S.P. XXI.
Use: Fluid and Irrigation, electrolyte replenisher, isotonic vehicle.
ODIUM CHLORIDE AND DEXTROSE TABLETS, U.S.P. XXI.
Use: Electrolyte and nutrient replenisher.
ODIUM CHLORIDE INJECTION, U.S.P. XXI. (Abbott) - Normal Saline 0.9% available in 150 ml., 250 ml., 500 ml. and 1,000 ml. cont.; **Partial-fills:** 50 ml. in 200 ml., 50 ml. in 300 ml., and 100 ml. in 300 ml.; **fliptop vials:** 10 ml., 20 ml., 50 ml. and 100 ml.,; **Bacteriostatic vials:** 10 ml., 20 ml. and 30 ml.; 50 mEq, 20 ml. in 50 ml. fliptop or pintop vial; 100 mEq, 40 ml. in 50 ml. fliptop vial; 50 mEq, 20 ml. univ. add. syr.; Sod. Chl. 0.45%, 500 ml. and 1,000 ml.; Sod. Chl. 5%, 500 ml.; Sodium Chloride Irrigating Sol., 250 ml., 500 ml., 1,000 ml., 3,000 ml.; (Upjohn) Sodium chloride 9 mg./ml. w/benzyl alcohol 9.45 mg. Vial 20 ml. (Winthrop-Breon) **Carpuject:** 2 ml. fill cartridge, 22 gague 1 1/4 inch needle or 25 gauge 5/8 inch needle.
Use: Fluid and irrigation, electrolyte replenisher, isotonic vehicle.
ODIUM CHLORIDE Na 22. USAN.
Use: Radioactive agent.
DIUM CHLORIDE SUBSTITUTES.
See: Salt substitutes.
DIUM CHLORIDE TABLETS, U.S.P. XXI. (Parke-Davis) Sodium chloride 15 1/2 gr./Tab. Bot. 1000s.
Use: Preparation of normal saline solution.
DIUM CHLORIDE THERAPY.
See: Thermolene, Tab. (Lannett)
Thermotabs., Tab. (Calgon)
DIUM CHLOROTHIAZIDE, FOR INJECTION. Chlorothiazide Sodium For Injection, U.S.P. XXI.
Use: Diuretic.
DIUM CHOLATE. (City Chem.) Sodium cholate Bot. 100 Gm.
ODIUM CHROMATE Cr 51 INJ., U.S.P. XXI.
Use: Diagnostic aid (blood volume determination).
See: Radio Chromate Cr 51 Sodium
ODIUM CITRATE, U.S.P. XXI. 1,2,3-Propanetricarboxylic acid, 2-hy-droxy-, trisodium salt. Trisodium citrate. Trisodium citrate dihydrate.
Use: Anticoagulant.
See: Anticoagulant Citrate Dextrose Solution, U.S.P. XXI.
Anticoagulant Citrate Phosphate Dextrose Solution, U.S.P. XXI.
ODIUM CITRATE AND CITRIC ACID ORAL SOLUTION, U.S.P. XXI. Shohl's Solution.
Use: Systemic alkalizer.
DIUM CLOXACILLIN.
See: Cloxacillin Sodium, U.S.P. XXI.
DIUM COLISTIMETHATE. Colistimethane Sodium, Sterile, U.S.P. XXI. Antibiotic produced by *Aerobacillus colistinus.*
DIUM COLISTIN METHANESULFONATE. Colistimethane Sodium, U.S.P. XXI. The sodium methanesulfonate salt of an antibiotic substance elaborated by *Aerobacillus colistinus.*
Use: Antibiotic.
• **SODIUM DEHYDROACETATE,** N.F. XVI.
Use: Pharmaceutic aid (antimicrobial preservative).
SODIUM DEXTROTHYROXINE. Sodium D-3,3′,5,5′-tetraiodothyronine. Sodium D-3-(4-(4-Hydroxy-3,5-diiodophenoxy)-3,5-diiodophenyl)-alanine.
Use: Anticholesteremic.
SODIUM DIATRIZOATE. Diatrizoate Sodium, U.S.P. XXI.
Use: Radiopaque medium.
SODIUM DIBUNATE. B.A.N. Sodium 2,7-di-t-butylnaphthalene-1-sulfonate.
Use: Cough suppressant.
See: Becantyl
SODIUM[2,3-DICHLORO-4-(2-METHYLENEBUTYRYL)-PHENOXY]ACETATE. Ethacrynate Sodium for Injection, U.S.P. XXI.
SODIUM DICLOXACILLIN. Dicloxacillin Sodium, U.S.P. XXI.
Use: Antibiotic.
SODIUM DICLOXACILLIN MONOHYDRATE.
Use: Antibiotic.
See: Pathocil, Prep. (Wyeth)
SODIUM DIHYDROGEN PHOSPHATE. Sodium Biphosphate U.S.P. XXI.
SODIUM DIMETHOXYPHENYL PENICILLIN.
See: Methicillin Sodium (Var. Mfr.)
SODIUM DIOCTYL SULFOSUCCINATE.
See: Docusate Sodium U.S.P. XXI.
SODIUM DIPHENYLHYDANTOIN. Phenytoin Sodium, U.S.P. XXI. Diphenylhydantoin Sodium.
Use: Anticonvulsant.
SODIUM DIPROTRIZOATE, B.A.N. Sodium 3,5-dipropionamide-2,4,6-triiodobenzoate.
SODIUM EDETATE, Edetate Disodium, U.S.P. XXI. Tetrasodium ethylenediaminetetraacetate.
Use: Chelating agents.
See: Vagisec products (Julius Schmid)
SODIUM ETHACRYNATE For INJ. Ethacrynate Sodium for Injection, U.S.P. XXI.
Use: Diuretic.
• **SODIUM ETHASULFATE.** USAN.
Use: Detergent.
SODIUM 6-(2-ETHOXY-1-NAPHTHAMIDO)-PENICILLANATE. Nafcillin Sodium, U.S.P. XXI.
SODIUM ETHYL-MERCURI-THIO-SALICYLATE.
See: Thimerosal, (Var. Mfr.)
Merthiolate, Prep. (Lilly)
SODIUM FEREDETATE (I.N.N.). Sodium Ironedetate, B.A.N.
SODIUM FLUORESCEIN, Fluorescein Sodium U.S.P. XXI. Resorcinolphthalein sodium.
Use: Diagnostic aid (corneal trauma indicator).
• **SODIUM FLUORIDE,** U.S.P. XXI. Oral Soln, Tab, U.S.P. XXI.
Use: Prophylactic dental caries.
See: Dentafluor, Tab., Drops (Saron)
Flura Drops, Drops (Kirkman)
Flura-Loz, Lozenge (Kirkman)
Karidium, Liq., Tab. (Lorvic)

Kari-Rinse, Liq. (Lorvic)
Luride, Tab. (Davies, Rose-Hoyt)
NaFeen, Tab., Liq. (Pacemaker)
Pediaflor, Drop (Ross)
Solu-Flur, Tab. (Robinson)
T-Fluoride, Tab. (Tennessee Pharm.)
W/Vitamins.
See: Fluorac, Tab. (USV)
Luride, Tab. & Drops (Davies, Rose-Hoyt)
Mulvidren-F, Tab. (Stuart)
So-Flo, Tab., Drop (Professional Pharm.)
W/Vit. A, D, C.
See: Cari-Tab, Softab. (Stuart)
Tri-Vi-Flor, Drops, Tab. (Mead Johnson)

SODIUM FLUORIDE SOLUTION PEDIATRIC DROPS. (Moyco) 1.0 ml. once/day 0–3 yrs. 2.0 ml. once/day over 3 yrs. Bot. 50 ml.
Use: Aid in the prevention of dental caries.

• **SODIUM FLUORIDE AND PHOSPHORIC ACID GEL,** U.S.P. XXI.

• **SODIUM FLUORIDE AND PHOSPHORIC ACID TOPICAL SOLUTION,** U.S.P. XXI.

SODIUM FOLATE. Monosodium folate.
Use: Water-soluble, hematopoietic vitamin.

SODIUM FORMALDEHYDE SULFOXYLATE, N.F. XVI. (Various Mfr.) $H_2C(OH)SO_2Na$.
Use: Reducing agent; preservative.

SODIUM-FREE SALT.
See: Co-Salt, Bot. (USV Pharm.)
Diasal, Prep. (Savage)

SODIUM GAMMA-HYDROXYBUTYRIC ACID. Under study.
Use: Anesthetic adjuvant.

SODIUM GENTISATE.
See: Gentisate, Sod.

SODIUM GLUCALDRATE. B.A.N. Sodium gluconatodihydroxyaluminate.
Use: Treatment of gastric hyperacidity.
See: Glymaxil

SODIUM GLUCASPALDRATE, B.A.N. Octasodium tetrakis (gluconato)-bis (salicylato), μ-diacetatodialuminate(III) dihydrate.
Use: Analgesic.

SODIUM GLUCOSULFONE INJ. Disodium 1,1′-[Sulfonylbis(p-phenyleneimino)]bis-[D-gluco-2,3,4,5,6-pentahydroxy-1-hexanesulfonate].
Use: Leprostatic.

SODIUM GLUTAMATE.
See: Glutamate

SODIUM GLYCEROPHOSPHATE. Glycerol phosphate sodium salt.
Use: Pharmaceutic necessity.

SODIUM GLYCOCHOLATE, A BILE SALT.
See: Bile Salts.
W/Phenolphthalein, cascara sagrada ext., sodium taurocholate, aloin.
See: Oxiphen, Tab. (Webcon)
W/Sod. nitrite, blue flag.
See: So-Nitri-Nacea, Cap. (Scrip)
W/Sod. taurocholate, sod. salicylate, phenolphthalein, bile ext., cascara sagrada ext.
See: Glycols, Tab. (Bowman)

SODIUM HEPARIN. Heparin Sodium, U.S.P. XXI.
Use: Anticoagulant.

SODIUM HEXACYCLONATE. Sodium 1-hydrox methylcyclohexaneacetate.

SODIUM HEXOBARBITAL. Sodium 5-(1-cyclohexen 1-yl)-1,5-dimethylbarbiturate.
Use: Intravenous general anesthetic.

SODIUM HYDROGEN CITRATE. (Various Mfr.)

• **SODIUM HYDROXIDE,** N.F. XVI. Caustic Soda.
Use: Pharm. aid (alkalizing agent).

SODIUM HYDROXYDIONE SUCCINATE. Sodium 2 hydroxypregnane-3,20-dione succinate.

• **SODIUM HYPOCHLORITE SOLUTION,** U.S.P. XX
Use: Local anti-infective; disinfectant.
See: Antiformin
Dakin's Soln.
Hyclorite

SODIUM HYPOPHOSPHITE. Sodium phosphinate.
Use: Pharmaceutic necessity.

SODIUM HYPOSULFITE.
See: Sodium Thiosulfate (Var. Mfr.)

SODIUM INDIGOTINDISULFONATE. Indigotindisulfonate Sodium, U.S.P. XXI. Indigo Carmine.
Use: I.V., I.M., diagnostic aid for renal function determination.

• **SODIUM IODIDE,** U.S.P. XXI. Soln., U.S.P. XXI.
Use: Iodine therapy; Pharm. necessity for Iodine Tincture.
See: Guaiadol Aqueous Sol., Vial (Medical Chem.)
Prodide (Hickam)
W/Foreign protein, benzyl alcohol, phenol.
See: I-pro, Inj. (Century)
W/Iodinated peptone.
W/Potassium guaiacolsufonate.
See: Guaiadol Aqueous, Vial (Medical Chem.)
W/Potassium guaiacolsulfonate, chlorpheniramine maleate, sodium bisulfite.
See: Gomahist, Inj. (Burgin-Arden)
W/Sulfur, sod. citrate, phenol, benzyl alcohol.
See: Sulfo-Iodide, Inj. (Marcen)

• **SODIUM IODIDE I-125 SOLUTION,** U.S.P. XXI.
Use: Diagnostic aid (thyroid function determinatior

• **SODIUM IODIDE I-131 CAPSULES & SOLUTIO** U.S.P. XXI.
Use: Diagnostic aid (thyroid function determinatio antineoplastic; thyroid inhibitor.
See: Iodotope I-131 (Squibb)
Oriodide (Abbott)
Radiocaps (R)-131 (Abbott)
Theriodide (R)-131 (Abbott)

SODIUM IODIPAMIDE. Disodium 3,3′-(Adipoyldiimino) bis-[2,4,6-triiodobenzoate].
Use: Radiopaque medium.

SODIUM ortho-IODOHIPPURATE. Iodohippurate S dium, I-131 Injection, U.S.P. XXI.
See: Hipputope (Squibb)

SODIUM IODOMETHAMATE. Disodium 1,4-dihydro-3,5-diiodo-1-methyl-4-oxo-2,6-pyridine dicarboxyla (Iodoxyl, Pyelecton, Uropac)

ODIUM IODOMETHANE SULFONATE. Methiodal Sodium, U.S.P. XXI.

ODIUM IOTHALAMATE. Iothalmate Sodium Injection, U.S.P. XXI.
Use: Radiopaque medium.

ODIUM IOTHIOURACIL. Sod. 5-iodo-2-thiouracil.

ODIUM IPODATE. Ipodate Sodium, U.S.P. XXI.
Use: Radiopaque.
See: Biloptin
Oragrafin Sodium, Cap. (Squibb)

ODIUM IRONEDETATE. B.A.N. Iron chelate of the monosodium salt of ethylenediamine-NNN'N'-tetra-acetic acid.
Use: Treatment of iron-deficiency anemia.
See: Sodium Feredetate (I.N.N.)
Sytron

ODIUM ISOAMYLETHYLBARBITURATE.
See: Amytal Sodium, Prep. (Lilly)

SODIUM LACTATE INJECTION, U.S.P. XXI. Propanoic acid, 2-hydroxy-, monosodium salt. Monosodium lactate. (Abbott) 1/6 Molar, 250 ml., 500 ml., and 1,000 ml.; 50 mEq, 10 ml. in 20 ml. fliptop vial.
Use: Fluid and electrolyte replenisher.

SODIUM LACTATE SOLUTION, U.S.P. XXI.

SODIUM LAURYL SULFATE, N.F. XVI. Sulfuric acid monododecyl ester sodium salt. Sodium monododecyl sulfate.
Use: Pharm aid (Surfactant).
See: Duponol
/Aluminum ammonium sulfate, boracic acid, citric acid, menthol.
See: Femid Green Label, Pow. (Cenci)
/9-Aminoacridine HCl, phenylmercuric acetate, succinic acid.
See: Vagiserts W/Inserts, Tab. (Vortech)
/Hydrocortisone.
See: Nutracort, Cream, Lot. (Owen)
/Danthron.
See: Alu-Scop, Cap., Susp. (Westerfield)
/Iodoquinol, phenylmercuric acetate, lactose, pot. alum., papain.
See: Baculin, Tab. (Amfre-Grant)

ODIUM LEVOTHYROXINE. Levothyroxine Sodium, U.S.P. XXI.

ODIUM LIOTHYRONINE. Liothyronine Sodium, U.S.P. XXI.
Use: Thyroid hormone.

ODIUM LYAPOLATE. Polyethylene sulfonate sodium. Peson (Hoechst). Sodium Apolate, B.A.N.
Use: Anticoagulant.

ODIUM MALONYLUREA.
See: Barbital Sod. (Various Mfr.)

ODIUM MERALEIN. (Hynson, Westcott & Dunning) Mono-sodium salt of 2,7-diiodo-4-hydroxy-mercuriresorcinsulfonphthalein. Merodicein.
Use: Local anti-infective.

ODIUM MERCAPTOMERIN. Mercaptomerin Sodium, U.S.P. XXI.
Use: Diuretic.

SODIUM METABISULFITE, N.F. XVI.

SODIUM METHIODAL. Methiodal Sodium, U.S.P. XXI. Sodium monoiodomethanesulfonate. Sodium Iodomethanesulfonate, Inj.
Use: Radiopaque medium.

SODIUM METHOHEXITAL FOR INJECTION. Methohexital Sodium for Injection, U.S.P. XXI.
Use: General anesthetic.
See: Brevital Sod., Pow. (Lilly)

SODIUM METHOXYCELLULOSE. Mixture of methylcellulose and sod. CMC

SODIUM METRIZOATE, B.A.N. Sodium 3-acetamido-2,4,6-triiodo-5-(N-methyl-acetamido) benzoate.
Use: Contrast medium.
See: Triosil

• **SODIUM MONOFLUOROPHOSPHATE,** U.S.P. XXI.

SODIUM MORRHUATE, INJ. Morrhuate Sodium Inj., U.S.P. XXI.
Use: Sclerosing agent.

SODIUM NAFCILLIN. Nafcillin Sodium, U.S.P. XXI.
Use: Antibacterial.

SODIUM NICOTINATE. Sod. pyridine-3-carboxylate (Various Mfr.)
W/Adenosine 5 monophosphoric acid.
Use: I.V., nicotinic acid therapy.
See: Rodesine, Inj. (Rocky Mtn.)

SODIUM NITRATE. (Var. Mfr.) Granules, Pkg. 1 lb.
W/Sod. nitrite, ox bile & exhinacea.
See: Hyper-Zem, Tab. (Zemmer)

• **SODIUM NITRITE,** U.S.P. XXI. Inj., U.S.P. XXI. (Various Mfr.) Gran., Bot. 0.25 lb., 1 lb.
See: Anti-Rust, Tabs. (Winthrop-Breon)
W/Sodium Thiosulfate, amyl nitrite.
Use: Vasodilator and antidote to cyanide poisoning.
See: Cyanide Antidote Pkg. (Lilly)

SODIUM NITRATE COMBINATIONS.
See: Hyperlon, Tab. (Kenyon)
Hyper-Zem, Tab. (Zemmer)
Veraphen, Tab. (Davis and Sly)
Veratrum, Tab. (Vortech)

• **SODIUM NITROPRUSSIDE,** U.S.P. XXI. Sterile, U.S.P. XXI.
Use: Hypotensive agent
See: Keto-Diastix (Ames)
Nipride, Vial (Roche)
Nitropress, Vial (Abbott)

SODIUM NORAMIDOPYRINE METHANESULFONATE. Dipyrone, B.A.N.

SODIUM NOVOBIOCIN. Sodium salt of antibacterial substance produced by *Streptomyces niveus.* Novobiocin monosodium salt.
Use: Antibiotic.
See: Albamycin, Cap., Syr., Vial (Upjohn)

• **SODIUM OXYBATE.** USAN. Sodium 4-hydroxybutyrate.
Use: Adjunct to anesthesia.

SODIUM PANTOTHENATE.
Use: Orally, dietary supplement.

SODIUM PARA-AMINOBENZOATE.
See: p-Aminobenzoate, Sod. (Various Mfr.)

SODIUM PARAAMINOHIPPURATE INJECTION.
Use: I.V., to determine kidney tubular excretion function.
SODIUM PARA-AMINOSALICYLATE.
See: p-Aminosalicylate, Sod. (Various Mfr.)
SODIUM PENICILLIN G. Penicillin G Sodium, Sterile, U.S.P. XXI. Sodium benzylpenicillin.
SODIUM PENICILLIN O. Sodium-6-[2-(allylthio)-acetamido]-3,3-dimethyl-7-oxo-4-thia-1-azabicyclo-[3.2.0]heptane-2-carboxylate.
SODIUM 3,3-PENTAMETHYLENE-4-HYDROXYBUTYRATE. Hexacyclonate Sodium. Under study.
SODIUM PENTOBARBITAL. Pentobarbital Sodium, U.S.P. XXI.
Use: Hypnotic.
SODIUM PERBORATE. Sodium Peroxyborate. Sodium peroxyhydrate.
SODIUM PEROXYBORATE.
See: Sod. Perborate. (Var. Mfr.)
SODIUM PEROXYHYDRATE.
See: Sodium Perborate (Var. Mfr.)
• **SODIUM PERTECHNETATE Tc 99 m INJECTION,** U.S.P. XXI. Pertechnetic acid, sodium salt.
Use: Diagnostic aid (brain scanning; thyroid scanning.)
See: Minitec (Squibb)
SODIUM PHENOBARBITAL. Phenobarbital Sodium, U.S.P. XXI.
Use: Anticonvulsant, hypnotic.
SODIUM PHENYLETHYLBARBITURATE.
Phenobarbital Sodium, U.S.P. XXI.
• **SODIUM PHOSPHATE,** U.S.P. XXI. Dired, Effervescent, Inj., U.S.P. XXI. Disodium hydrogen phosphate. (Abbott) 45 mM P, 15 ml. in 30 ml. fliptop vial.
Use: Cathartic, buffering agent, source of phosphate.
W/Gentamicin sulfate, monosodium phosphate, sodium chloride, benzalkonium chloride.
See: Garamycin Ophthalmic Sol. (Schering)
W/Sod. biphosphate.
See: Enemeez, Enema (Armour)
Fleet Enema (Fleet)
Phospho-Soda, Liq. (Fleet)
Saf-tip, Enemas (Fuller)
• **SODIUM PHOSPHATE, DIBASIC,** U.S.P. XXI.
• **SODIUM PHOSPHATE, DRIED,** U.S.P. XXI.
Use: Cathartic.
• **SODIUM PHOSPHATE, MONOBASIC,** U.S.P. XXI. Monosodium Phosphate. Sod. Acid Phosphate, Sod. Dihydrogen Phosphate, Sodium Biphosphate.
Use: Cathartic.
See: Travad, Enema (Flint)
W/Gentamicin sulfate, disodium phosphate, sodium chloride, benzalkonium chloride.
See: Garamycin Ophthalmic Sol. (Schering)
W/Methenamine.
See: Uro-Phosphate, Tab. (Poythress)
W/Methenamine mandelate, levo-hyoscyamine sulfate.
See: Levo-Uroquid, Tab. (Beach)
W/Methenamine, phenyl salicylate, methylene blue, hyoscyamine, alkaloid.
See: Urostat Forte, Tab. (Elder)
W/Sod. acid pyrophos, sodium bicarbonate.
See: Vacuetts, Supp. (Dorsey)
W/Sod. phosphate.
See: Enemeez Enema (Armour)
Fleet Enema (Fleet)
Phospho-Soda, Liq. (Fleet)
Saf-tip Enemas (Fuller)
• **SODIUM PHOSPHATES ENEMA,** U.S.P. XXI.
Use: Cathartic.
• **SODIUM PHOSPHATES ORAL SOLUTION,** U.S.P XXI.
Use: Cathartic.
• **SODIUM PHOSPHATE P32 SOLUTION,** U.S.P. XX Phosphoric -32P acid, disodium salt. Disodium pho phate -32P.
Use: Antineoplastic, antipolycythemic. Diagnostic. aid (ocular tumor localization.).
SODIUM PHYTATE. Nonasodium phytate: Sod. cyclohexanehexyl (hexaphosphate).
Use: Chelating agent.
SODIUM PICOSULPHATE. B.A.N. diSodium 4,4′-(2-pyridyl)methylenedi(phenyl sulfate).
Use: Laxative.
See: Laxoberal
• **SODIUM POLYPHOSPHATE.** USAN.
Use: Pharmaceutic aid.
• **SODIUM POLYSTYRENE SULFONATE,** U.S.P. XX Benzene, ethenyl-, homopolymer, sulfonated, sodiu salt. Styrene polymer, sulfonated, sodium salt.
Use: Ion exchange resin (potassium).
See: Kayexalate, Pow. (Winthrop-Breon)
• **SODIUM PROPIONATE,** N.F. XVI. 5% Soln. Eye drops (Crookes-Barnes) Lacrivial 15 cc.
Use: Preservative.
W/Chlorophyll 'a'
See: Prophyllin, Pwd., Oint. (Rystan)
W/Neomycin sulfate.
See: Otobiotic, Ear Drops (Schering)
W/Propionic acid, docusate sodium, salicylic acid.
See: Prosal, Liq. (Gordon)
W/Sod. caprylate, propionic acid & undecylenic acid.
See: Sopronol, Pwd. (Wyeth)
W/Sod. caprylate, zinc caprylate, dioctyl sod. sulfosuccinate, propionic acid.
See: Sopronol, Oint., Sol. (Wyeth)
W/Sodium chloride, methylene blue.
SODIUM PSYLLIATE.
Use: Sclerosing agent.
• **SODIUM PYROPHOSPHATE.** USAN.
Use: Pharmaceutic aid.
SODIUM RADIO CHROMATE INJ. Sod. Chromate C 51 Inj., U.S.P. XXI.
SODIUM RADIO IODIDE SOLUTION. Sodium Iodide I-131 Solution, U.S.P. XXI.
Use: Thyroid tumors, hyperthyroidism & cardiac dysfunction.
SODIUM RADIO-PHOSPHATE, P-32 Soln. Radic Phosphate P32 Solution. Sodium phosphate P-32 So lution, U.S.P. XXI.
SODIUM REMOVING RESINS.
See: Resins
SODIUM RHODANATE.
See: Sodium Thiocyanate

SODIUM RHODANIDE.
See: Sodium Thiocyanate
SODIUM SACCHARIN. Saccharin Sodium, U.S.P. XXI.
Use: Noncaloric sweetener.
SODIUM SALICYLATE, U.S.P. XXI. Tab., U.S.P. XXI.
Use: Analgesic.
See: Uracel, Tab. (Vortech)
W/Iodide. (Various Mfr.)
Use: Intravenous injection.
W/Iodide & cholchicine. (Various Mfr.)
Use: I.V., gout.
SODIUM SALICYLATE, NATURAL.
Use: Analgesic.
See: Alysine, Elixir (Merrell Dow)
SODIUM SALICYLATE COMBINATIONS.
See: Apcogesic, Tabs. (Apco)
Bisalate, Tab. (Allison)
Bufosal, Gran. (Table Rock)
Colsalide, Tab. (Vortech)
Corilin, Liq. (Schering)
Dibolans, Tab. (Noyes)
Gaysal-S, Tab. (Geriatric)
Glycols, Tab. (Bowman)
Laxogen, Tab. (Vortech)
Nucorsal, Tab. (Westerfield)
Pabalate, Tab. (Robins)
pHisoDan, Liq. (Winthrop Consumer Products)
Pedituss, Syr. (Sutliff & Case)
Ruphon, Tab. (Elder)
Ricor, Tab. (Vortech)
Salcoce, Tab. (Cole)
Thi-Cin, Cap. (Warren-Teed)
Thymaxol, Tab. (Noyes)
SODIUM SECOBARBITAL. Secobarbital Sodium, U.S.P. XXI.
Use: Hypnotic.
SODIUM SECOBARBITAL AND SODIUM AMOBARBITAL CAPSULES.
Use: Sedative.
See: Tuinal, Cap. (Lilly)
• **SODIUM STARCH GLYCOLATE,** N.F. XVI.
• **SODIUM STEARATE,** N.F. XVI. Octadecanoic acid, sodium salt.
Use: Emulsifying and stiffening agent.
• **SODIUM STEARYL FUMARATE,** N.F. XVI.
SODIUM STIBOGLUCONATE. B.A.N. Sodium salt of a pentavalent antimony derivative of gluconic acid.
Use: Treatment of leishmaniasis.
See: Pentostam
SODIUM SUCCINATE.
Use: Alkalinize urine & awaken patients following barbiturate anesthesia.
SODIUM SULAMYD Ophthalmic Oint. 10% Sterile. (Schering) Sulfacetamide sod. 10%. (100 mg.) W/Methylparaben, propylparaben, benzalkonium Cl, sorbitan monolaurate and water. Tube ⅛ oz.
Use: Ophthalmic Anti-infective.
SODIUM SULAMYD Ophthalmic Sol. 10% Sterile. (Schering) Sulfacetamide sodium 10% W/V solution with methylcellulose, sod. thiosulfate, methylparaben, propylparaben, sod. dihydrogen phosphate. Bot. 5 ml. Box 25s. 15 ml. Box 1s.
Use: Ophthalmic Anti-infective.
SODIUM SULAMYD Ophthalmic Solution 30% Sterile. (Schering) Sulfacetamide sod. 30% W/V w/sod. thiosulfate 1.5 mg., methylparaben 0.5 mg., propylparaben 0.1 mg. as preservative, sod. dihydrogen phosphate as buffer./ml. Bot. 15 ml. Box 1s.
Use: Ophthalmic Anti-infective.
SODIUM SULFABROMOMETHAZINE. Sodium N[1]-(5-Bromo-4,6-dimethyl-2-pyrimidinyl) sulfanilamide.
Use: Antibacterial.
SODIUM SULFACETAMIDE.
See: Sulfacetamide Sodium Preps. (Various Mfr.)
SODIUM SULFADIAZINE.
See: Sulfadiazine Sodium Preps. (Various Mfr.)
SODIUM SULFAMERAZINE.
See: Sulfamerazine Sodium Preps. (Various Mfr.)
SODIUM SULFAPYRIDINE.
See: Sulfapyridine Sodium Pow. (Pfaltz & Bauer)
• **SODIUM SULFATE,** U.S.P. XXI. Inj., U.S.P. XXI.
Use: Cathartic.
• **SODIUM SULFATE S 35.** USAN.
Use: Radioactive agent.
SODIUM SULFATHIAZOLE.
Use: Antibacterial.
See: Sulfathiazole Sodium, Inj. (Various Mfr.)
SODIUM SULFOACETATE. W/Sod. alkyl aryl polyether sulfonate, docusate sodium, kerohydric, sulfur, salicylic acid, hexachlorophene.
See: Sebulex, Liq., Cream (Westwood)
SODIUM SULFOBROMOPHTHALEIN. Sulfobromophthalein Sodium, U.S.P. XXI.
Use: Diagnostic aid (hepatic function determination).
SODIUM SULFOCYANATE.
See: Sodium Thiocyanate. (Var. Mfr.)
SODIUM SULFOXONE. Sulfoxone Sodium, U.S.P. XXI. Disodium sulfonylbis (p-phenyleneimino)dimethanesulfonate.
See: Diasone Sodium, Tab. (Abbott)
SODIUM SURAMIN.
See: Suramin Sodium
SODIUM TAUROCHOLATE, A BILE SALT.
See: Bile Salts.
W/Phenolphthalein, cascara sagrada ext. sodium glycocholate, aloin.
See: Oxiphen, Tab. (Webcon)
SODIUM TETRADECYL SULFATE.
See: Sotradecol, Inj. (Elkins-Sinn)
SODIUM TETRAIODOPHENOLPHTHALEIN.
See: Iodophthalein Sod. (Var. Mfr.)
SODIUM THIACETPHENARSAMIDE. The trivalent organic arsenical p-[bis-(carboxymethylmercapto)-arsino] benzamide. Ceparsolate Sodium (Abbott)
SODIUM THIAMYLAL FOR INJECTION. Thiamylal Sodium For Injection, U.S.P. XXI.
Use: General anesthetic.
See: Surital, Inj. (Parke-Davis)
SODIUM THIOCYANATE. Sodium Sulfocyanate. Sod. Rhodanide.

SODIUM THIOPENTAL.
See: Thiopental Sodium, U.S.P. XXI.

SODIUM THIOSALICYLATE.
See: Arthrolate, I.M. (Reid-Provident)
Osteolate, Vial (Fellows-Testagar)
Rexolate, Vial (Hyrex)
Socylate, Inj. (Tunex)
Thiodyne, Vial (Savage Lab.)
Thiolate (Hickam; Pharmex)
Thiosal, Inj. (Keene)
Th-Sal, Vial (Foy)

• **SODIUM THIOSULFATE,** U.S.P. XXI. Inj., U.S.P. XXI. Sod. hyposulfite. "Hypo." Thiosulfuric acid, disodium salt, pentahydrate. Disodium thiosulfate pentahydrate.
Use: For argyria, cyanide & iodine poisoning, arsphenamine reactions; prevention of spread of ringworm of feet.
W/Salicylic acid, hydrocortisone acetate, alcohol.
See: Komed HC, Lot. (Barnes-Hind)
W/Salicylic acid, isopropyl alcohol.
See: Tinver, Lotion (Barnes-Hind)
W/Salicylic acid, resorcinol, alcohol.
See: Mild Komed, Lot. (Barnes-Hind)
Komed, Lot. (Barnes-Hind)
W/Sodium nitrite, amyl nitrite.
See: Cyanide Antidote Pkg. (Lilly)

SODIUM L-THYROXINE.
See: Letter, Tab. (Armour)
Levoid, Inj., Tab. (Nutrition Control)
Roxstan, Tab. (Reid-Provident)
Synthroid, Tab., Inj. (Flint)

SODIUM TOLBUTAMIDE. Tolbutamide Sodium, U.S.P. XXI.
Use: Diagnostic aid (diabetes).

SODIUM TRICLOFOS. Sodium trichloroethylphosphate.
Use: Sedative, hypnotic.

• **SODIUM TRIMETAPHOSPHATE.** USAN.
Use: Pharmaceutic aid.

SODIUM TYROPANOATE, B.A.N. Sodium 3-butyramido-α-ethyl-2,4,6-triiodohydrocinnamate. Radiopaque.
Use: Cholecystographic agent.
See: Bilopaque, Cap. (Winthrop-Breon)

SODIUM VERSENATE. (Riker) Disodium Edetate Inj., U.S.P. 1 Gm./5 cc. 20% Amp. 15 ml. Box 5s.
See: Edathamil
Use: (I.V. infusions) Hypercalcemia.

SODIUM VINBARBITAL INJECTION.
Use: Sedative.

SODIUM WARFARIN. Warfarin Sodium, U.S.P. XXI.
Use: Anticoagulant.

SOD-LATE 10. (Schlicksup) Sodium salicylate 10 gr./Tab. Bot. 1000s.
Use: Analgesic.

SODOL TABS. (Major) Carisoprodol 350 mg./Tab. Bot. 250s.
Use: Musculoskeletal agent for muscle spasms.

SODUBEN. (Arcum) Butabarbital sodium 30 mg./Tab. Bot. 100s, 1000s.
Use: Sedative.

SOFCAPS. (Alton) Docusate sodium 100 mg., or 250 mg./Cap. Bot. 100s, 1000s.
Use: Stool softener.

SOF-CIL. (Zemmer) Psyllium mucilloid, plantago ovata dextrose, docusate sodium 10 mg./rounded teaspoonful. Pkg. 2 oz., 6 oz., 12 oz.
Use: Treatment of constipation.

SOFENOL 5. (C & M Pharmacal) Moisturizing lotion formulation. Bot. 8 oz.

SOFLENS ENZYMATIC CONTACT LENS CLEANER. (Allergan) Papain tablets for solution. W/Vials 12s, 24s, 48s. Refill 24s, 36s.
Use: Enzymatic cleansing agent for soft contact lenses.

SOFT-B-M CAPSULE. (Morton) Docusate sodium 100 mg. or 250 mg./Cap. Bot. 100s.
Use: Stool softener.

SOFT-CARE STERILE DISINFECTING SOL. (Barnes-Hind) Aqueous isotonic sol. of sodium Cl, povidone, octylphenoxy ethanols w/ borate buffer. Bot. 12 oz.
Use: Soft contact lens care.

SOFT'N SOOTHE. (Ascher) Benzocaine, menthol, moisturizers. Tube 50 Gm.
Use: Dry, itchy skin.

SOFTOL CUTICLE REMOVER. (Guild) Bot. 0.5 oz.

SOFTON. (Stanlabs) Docusate sodium 100 mg., 250 mg./Cap. Bot. 100s.
Use: Laxative, constipation aid.

SOFT MATE COMFORT DROPS. (Barnes-Hind) Sterile, aqueous, isotonic, buffered, lubricating & rewetting solution w/edetate disodium 0.1%.
Use: Soft contact lens care.

SOFT-MATE SALINE SOLUTION. (Barnes-Hind) Sterile aqueous isotonic solution of sodium chloride. Bot. 8 oz., 12 oz.
Use: Soft contact lens care.

SOFT MATE WEEKLY CLEANING SOLUTION. (Barnes-Hind) Non enzymatic surfactant cleaning solution.
Use: Soft contact lens weekly cleaner.

SOLACEN. Tybamate, B.A.N.

SOLAGEST. (Canright) Pancreatin 10.5 gr., hyoscyamine sulf. 0.072 mg., atropine sulf. 0.013 mg., hyoscine HBr 0.0047 mg., pentobarbital sod. 10.8 mg./Tab. Bot. 100s, 1000s.
Use: Antispasmodic, digestant formula.

SOLANEED. (Hanlon) Vit. A 25,000 u./Cap. Bot. 100s.

SOLAPSONE. B.A.N. Tetrasodium salt of bis-[4-(3-phenyl-1,3-disulfopropylamino)phenyl]sulfone.
Use: Antileprotic.
See: Solasulfone (I.N.N.)
Sulphetrone

SOLAQUIN. (Elder) Hydroquinone 2%, ethyl dihydroxypropyl PABA 5%, dioxybenzone 3%, oxybenzone 2%. Tube 1 oz.
Use: Skin bleaching agent with sunscreen.

SOLAQUIN FORTE CREAM. (Elder) Hydroquinone 4%, ethyl dihydroxypropyl PABA 5%, dioxybenzone 3%, oxybenzone 2% in a vanishing cream base. Tube 0.5 oz., 1 oz.
Use: Skin bleaching agent with sunscreen.

SOLAQUIN FORTE GEL. (Elder) Hydroquinone 4%, ethyl dihydroxypropyl-p-amino benzoate 5%, dioxybenzone 3% in hydroalcoholic base. Tubes 0.5 oz., 1 oz.
Use: Skin bleaching agent with sunscreen.

SOLARCAINE. (Plough)
Cream: Benzocaine 1%, triclosan. Tube 0.5 oz., 1 oz., 2 oz.
Lotion: Benzocaine 0.5%, triclosan. Bot. 3 oz., 6 oz.
Spray (aerosol): Benzocaine 9.4%, triclosan 0.18%, isopropyl alcohol 24%. Can 3 oz, 5 oz.
Use: Sunburn remedy.

SOLAR CREAM. (Doak) PABA, titanium dioxide & magnesium stearate in a flesh-colored, water-repellent base. Tube 1 oz.
Use: Protection from ultraviolet rays.

SOLARGENTUM.
See: Mild silver protein (Various Mfr.)

SOLATENE. (Roche) Beta-carotene 30 mg./cap. Bot. 100s.
Use: Ameliorate photosensitivity.

SOLBAR CREAM. (Person & Covey) Oxybenzone 3%, dioxybenzone 3%. Cream 2.5 oz.
Use: Ultraviolet protection.

SOLBAR PF PABA FREE 15. (Person & Covey) Oxybenzone 5%, octyl methoxycinnamate 7.5%. Sunscreen SPF 15. Tube 2.5 oz.
Use: PABA free sunscreen.

SOLBAR PLUS 15. (Person & Covey) Oxybenzone 6%, octyl dimethyl PABA 6%. Tube 4 oz.
Use: Sunscreen (SPF 15).

SOLFOTON. (Poythress) Phenobarbital 16 mg., dispersed on colloidal bentonite./Tab. or Cap. Bot. 100s, 500s. Tabs. 100s, 500s.
Use: Orally, mild sedation.

SOLFOTON S/C TABS. (Poythress) Phenobarbital 16 mg., bensulfoid 65 mg./sugar coated Tab. Bot. 100s.
Use: Mild sedation.

SOLGANAL. (Schering) Aurothioglucose, 50 mg., /ml. in sesame oil. Vial 10 ml.; Box 1s.
Use: I.M., gold therapy, antiarthritic.

SOLIWAX. Docusate Sodium, U.S.P. XXI. Docusate Sodium, Solasulfone (I.N.N.).

SOLPADEINE TABLETS. (Winthrop Products) Paracetamol.
Use: Analgesic.

SOL-PRED. (Amfre-Grant) Prednisolone sodium phosphate 20 mg./ml. Vial 10 ml.
Use: Hormone supplement.

SOLTICE HIGH THERM. (Chattem) Menthol, methyl salicylate, camphor, eucalyptus oil. Tube 1.25 oz.
Use: Topical analgesic balm.

SOLTICE QUICK-RUB. (Chattem) Methyl salicylate, camphor, menthol, eucalyptol. Cream. 1.5, 3¾ oz.
Use: Chest rub.

SOLU-BARB 0.25 TABLETS. (Fellows) Phenobarbital 0.25 gr./Tab. Bot. 24s.

SOLUCAP C. (Jamieson-McKames) Vit. C 1000 mg./Capsulet. Bot. 100s.

SOLUCAP E. (Jamieson-McKames) Vit. E 100 I.U., 400 I.U., or 1000 I.U./Cap. Bot. 100s.

SOLU-CORTEF. (Upjohn) **100 mg.:** Hydrocortisone sodium succinate 100mg., sodium biphosphate 0.8 mg., sodium phosphate 8.73 mg./2 ml. Vial w/or w/out ampoule bacteriostatic water for injection and benzyl alcohol 0.9% w/v. Vials 5s, 25s; Hydrocortisone sodium succinate 100 mg., sodium biphosphate 0.8 mg., sodium phosphate 8.76 mg., benzyl alcohol 18.1 mg. Mix-O-Vial 5s, 25s. **250 mg.:** Hydrocortisone sodium succinate 250 mg., sodium biphosphate 2 mg., sodium phosphate 21.8 mg., benzyl alcohol 16.4 mg./2 ml. Mix-O-Vial 1s, 5s, 25s. **500 mg.:** Hydrocortisone sodium succinate 500 mg., sodium biphosphate 4 mg., sodium phosphate 44 mg., benzyl alcohol 33.4 mg./4 ml. Mix-O-Vial 1s, 5s, 25s. **1000 mg.:** Hydrocortisone sodium succinate 1000 mg., sodium biphosphate 8 mg., sodium phosphate 88 mg., benzyl alcohol 66.9 mg./8 ml. Mix-O-Vial 1s, 5s, 10s.
Use: Anti-inflammatory corticosteroid for treatment of acute adrenal cortical insufficiency.

SOLU-EXE. (Forest) Hydroxyquinoline 0.12%, carbitol acetate 12.10%. Bot. 3 oz.

SOLU-FLUR. (Robinson) Sodium fluoride 2.21 mg./Tab. Bot. 100s, 1000s.
Use: Prophylactic dental caries.

SOLUJECT. (Mayrand) Prednisolone acetate 80 mg., prednisolone sodium phosphate 20 mg./ml. Vial 10 ml.
Use: Long-acting, short-acting anti-inflammatory.

SOLU-MEDROL. (Upjohn) **40 mg.:** Methylprednisolone sodium succinate 40 mg., lactose 25 mg., sodium biphosphate 1.6 mg., sodium phosphate 17.46 mg., benzyl alcohol 8.8 mg., water for injection q.s. 1 ml. Mix-O-Vial or Act-O-Vial 1s, 5s, 25s, 50s, 100s; Mix-O-Vial or Act-O-Vial 40 mg./1 ml. Pack 25s, 50s, 100s. **125 mg.:** Methylprednisolone sodium succinate 125 mg., sodium biphosphate 1.6 mg., sodium phosphate 17.4 mg., benzyl alcohol 17.6 mg., water for injection q.s. 2 ml. Mix-O-Vial or Act-O-Vial 1s, 5s, 25s, 50s, 100s; Mix-O-Vial or Act-O-Vial 125 mg./2 ml. Pack 25s, 50s, 100s. **500 mg.:** Methylprednisolone sodium succinate 500 mg., sodium biphosphate 6.4 mg., sodium phosphate 69.6 mg., benzyl alcohol 70.2 mg./Vial w ampoule bacteriostatic water for injection 8 ml., benzyl alcohol 9.45 mg./ml. Vials 1s, 5s, 25s. **1000 mg.:** Methylprednisolone sodium succinate 1000 mg., sodium biphosphate 12.8 mg., sodium phosphate 139.2 mg., benzyl alcohol 141 mg./Vial w ampoule bacteriostatic water for injection 16 ml., benzyl alcohol 9.45 mg./ml. Vials 1s, 5s, 25s; Vial 1000 mg. w/I.V. Administration set. Pack 1s, 5s, 25s. Vials without diluent 500 mg., 1000 mg.
Use: Treatment of emergency hypersensitivity.

SOLUMOL. (C & M Pharmacal) Petrolatum, mineral oil, cetyl-stearyl alcohol, sodium lauryl sulfate, glycerin, propylene glycol, sorbic acid, purified water. Jars 1 lb.
Use: Washable ointment base.

SOLU-PRED. (Kenyon) Prednisolone sod. phosphate equiv. to prednisolone phosphate 20 mg., niacinamide 25 mg., disodium edetate 0.5 mg., sod. bisulfite 1 mg., phenol 5 mg./cc. Vial 10 cc.

SOLUVITE-F. (Pharmics) Vit. A 3000 I.U., D 400 I.U., C 100 mg., fluoride 0.25 mg./0.6 cc. Bot. 57 cc.
Use: Fluoride therapy with vitamins.

SOLUREX. (Hyrex) Dexamethasone sodium phosphate 4 mg./ml. Vial 5 ml., 10 ml., 30 ml.
Use: Adrenocortical steroid therapy.

SOLUREX L A. (Hyrex) Dexamethasone acetate suspension 8 mg./ml. Vial 5 ml.
Use: Adrenocortical steroid therapy.

SOLU-SONE R.P. (Seatrace) Prednisolone sodium phosphate 20 mg., prednisolone acetate 80 mg./ml. Vial 10 cc.

SOLVISYN-A. (Towne) Water soluble Vit. A 10,000 u./Cap. 25,000 u./Cap. 50,000 u./Cap. Bot. 100s, 1000s.

• **SOLYPERTINE TARTRATE.** USAN. 7- 2-[4-(o-Methoxy-
phenyl)-1-piperazinyl]ethyl 5H-1,3-dioxolo[4,5-f]indole tartrate.
Use: Anti-adrenergic.

SOMA. (Wallace) Carisoprodol 350 mg./Tab. Bot. 100s, 500s, 500s Unit dose.
Use: Musculoskeletal agent for acute muscle spasms, pain & stiffness.

SOMA COMPOUND TABS. (Wallace) Carisoprodol 200 mg., aspirin 325 mg./Tab. Bot. 100s, 500s. Unit dose 500s.
Use: Analgesic with musculoskeletal agent for acute muscle spasms, pain & stiffness.

SOMA COMPOUND W/CODEINE. (Wallace) Carisoprodol 200 mg., aspirin 325 mg. codeine phosphate 16 mg./Tab. Bot. 100s.
Use: Analgesic with musculoskeletal agent for muscle spasms, pain & stiffness.

• **SOMANTADINE HYDROCHORIDE.** USAN.
Use: Antiviral.

• **SOMATREM.** USAN.
Use: Growth hormone.

• **SOMATROPIN.** USAN. Growth hormone derived from the anterior pituitary gland.
Use: Growth stimulant.

SOMILAN. Chloral Betaine, B.A.N.

SOMINEX 2. (Beecham Products) Diphenhydramine HCl 25 mg./Tab. Blister packs 16s, 32s, 72s.
Use: Mild sedative.

SOMINEX 2 PAIN RELIEF FORMULA. (Beecham Products) Diphenhydramine HCl 25 mg., acetaminophen 500 mg./Tab. Blister Pk. 16s, 32s, 72.
Use: Sleep and pain relief.

SOMNATABS. (Thurston) Pow. ext. Passiflora incarnata 3 gr., pow. ext. Piscidia erythrina 2 gr., pow. ext. Viburnum opulus 1 gr., pow. ext. hyoscyamus ⅛ gr./Tab. Bot. 50s, 100s, 500s.

SOMNESIN. Methylpentynol, B.A.N.

SOMOPHYLLIN-CRT. (Fisons) Anhydrous theophyllin[e] 100 mg., 200 mg., 250 mg., or 300 mg./Sust. Release Cap. Bot. 100s. Unit dose 100s.
Use: Bronchodilator.

SOMOPHYLLIN-DF ORAL LIQUID. (Fisons) Aminop[h]hylline 105 mg./5 ml. that provides 90 mg. theophylline base/5 ml. Dye Free. Bot. 8 oz.
Use: Bronchodilator.

SOMOPHYLLIN ORAL LIQUID. (Fisons) Aminophylline 105 mg./5 ml. that provides 90 mg. theophylline base/5 ml. w/dye. Bot. 8 oz., 32 oz.
Use: Bronchodilator.

SOMOPHYLLIN RECTAL SOLUTION. (Fisons) Aminophylline 300 mg./5 ml. Bot. 3 oz. W/18 recta[l] tips; Bot. 5 oz. W/30 rectal tips.
Use: Rectally administered bronchodilator.

SOMOPHYLLIN-T CAPSULES. (Fisons) Theophyllin[e] 100 mg., 200 mg., 250 mg./Cap. Bot. 100s.
Use: Bronchodilator.

SONACIDE. (Ayerst) Potentiated acid glutaraldehyde. Bot. 1 gal., 5 gal.,
Use: Sterilizing & disinfecting.

SONDRATE ELIXIR. (Kenyon) Chloral hydrate 1.6 Gm./Fl. oz. Bot. 4 oz., pt., gal.

SONEKAP. (Eastwood) Cap. Bot. 100s.

SONERYL.
See: Butethal (Var. Mfr.)

SONIPHEN. (Forest) Phenobarbital 16 mg., sodium nitrite 65 mg./Tab. Bot. 100s.

SOOTHE. (Walgreen) Bismuth subsalicylate 100 mg./Tsp. Bot. 9 oz.
Use: Upset stomach, nausea, simple diarrhea.

SOOTHE. (Alcon) Camphor 0.01%, phenylephrine HC[l] 0.15%, thiomerosal 0.002%/cc. Bot. 15 cc.
Use: Eye decongestant.

SOPRONOL OINTMENT. (Wyeth) Sod. propionate, sodium caprylate, zinc caprylate in ointment base. Tube 1 oz.
Use: Dermatophytosis (Athlete's foot).

SOPRONOL POWDER. (Wyeth) Sod. propionate, sodium caprylate, zinc propionate. Can 2 oz.
Use: Prophylactic fungicide.

SOPRONOL SOLUTION. (Wyeth) Sodium propionate, sodium caprylate, docusate sodium, n-propyl alcohol. Bot. 2 fl. oz.
Use: Dermatophytosis.

SOQUETTE. (Barnes-Hind) Alkyl dimethyl benzyl ammonium chloride 0.01%, disodium salt of ethylenediamine tetraacetic acid 0.20%, polyvinyl alcohol. Bot. 4 fl. oz.
Use: Soaking and storing hard contact lenses.

SORBASE COUGH SYRUP. (Fort David) Dextromethorphan HBr 10 mg., guaifenesin 100 mg./5 cc. in sorbitol base. Bot. 4 oz., pt., gal.

SORBASE II COUGH SYRUP. (Fort David) Hydrocodone bitartrate 5 mg., guaifenesin 100 mg./5 cc.

• **SORBIC ACID,** N.F. XVI.
Use: Preservative (antimicrobial).

SORBIDE T.D. (Mayrand) Isosorbide dinitrate 40 mg./T.R. Cap. Bot. 100s.
Use: Coronary vasodilator.

ORBIDE NITRATE. B.A.N. 1,4:3,6-Dianhydrosorbitol 2,5-dinitrate. Isosorbide Dinitrate (I.N.N.)
Use: Coronary vasodilator.
See: Cedocard
Vascardin

ORBIDON HYDRATE. (Gordon) Water-in-oil ointment. Jar 2 oz., 0.5 oz., 1 lb., 5 lb.
Use: Treatment of dry skin.

ORBIMACROGOL OLEATE 300.
See Polysorbate 80.

SORBINIL. USAN.
Use: Enzyme inhibitor.

SORBITAN MONOLAURATE. N.F. XVI. Mixture of laurate esters of sorbitol and its anhydrides.
Use: Surface-active agent; emulsifying agent.
See: Span 20 (ICI U.S.)

SORBITAN MONOOLEATE, N.F. XVI. Mixture of oleate esters of sorbitol and its anhydrides.
Use: Surface-active agent.
See: Span 80 (ICI U.S.)

ORBITAN MONOOLEATE POLYOXYETHYLENE DERIVATIVES.
See: Polysorbate 80, N.F. XVI.

SORBITAN MONOPALMITATE, N.F. XVI. Mixture of palmitate esters of sorbitol and its anhydrides.
Use: Surface-active agent.
See: Span 40 (ICI U.S.)

SORBITAN MONOSTEARATE, N.F. XVI. Mixture of stearate esters of sorbitol and its anhydrides.
Use: Surface-active agent.
See: Span 60 (ICI U.S.)

SORBITAN SESQUIOLEATE. USAN. Sorbitan mono-oleate and sorbitan dioleate.
Use: Surfactant.
See: Arlacel C (ICI U.S.)

• **SORBITAN TRIOLEATE.** USAN.
Use: Surfactant.
See: Span 85 (ICI U.S.)

• **SORBITAN TRISTEARATE.** USAN.
See: Span 65 (ICI U.S.)

ORBITANS.
See: Polysorbate 80, U.S.P.

• **SORBITOL,** N.F. XVI. Solution, U.S.P. XXI.
Use: Diuretic; dehydrating agent; humectant; pharmaceutic aid (sweetening agent, tablet excipient).
See: Sorbo (ICI U.S.)
W/Homatropine methylbromide.
See: Probilagol Liquid (Purdue Frederick)
W/Mannitol.
See: Sorbitol-mannitol Irrigation (Abbott)

SORBITON. (Kenyon) Vit. B-12 5 mcg., folic acid 0.1 mg., ferrous fumarate 100 mg., D-sorbitol 500 mg./Tab. Bot. 100s, 1000s.
Use: Hematinic.

SORBITRATE. (Stuart) Isosorbide dinitrate. **Oral Tab.:** 5 mg. Bot. 100s, 500s. Unit dose 100s; 10 mg. Bot. 100s, 500s. Unit Dose 100s; 20 mg, 30 mg., 40 mg. Bot. 100s. Unit Dose 100s. **Sustained Action Tab.** 40 mg. Bot. 100s. Unit Dose 100s; **Sublingual Tab.** 2.5 mg., 5 mg. Bot. 100s, 500s. Unit Dose 100s; 10 mg. Bot. 100s. Unit dose 100s.**Chewable Tab.** 5 mg. Bot. 100s, 500s. Unit Dose 100s. 10 mg. Bot. 100s. Unit Dose 100s.
Use: Prevention and treatment of angina pectoris.

SORBO. (ICI Americas) Sorbitol Solution, U.S.P. XXI.

SORBUTUSS. (Dalin) d-Methorphan HBr 10 mg., guaifenesin 100 mg., ipecac fl. ext. 0.05 min., potassium citrate 85 mg., citric acid 35 mg./5 cc. Bot. 3 oz., pt.
Use: For coughs.

SORDINOL. Clopenthixol, B.A.N.
Use: Tranquilizer.

SORETHYTAN (20) MONO-OLEATE.
See: Polysorbate 80, (Var. Mfr.)

SORETTS LOZENGES. (Lannett) Benzocaine 0.5 gr., ext. licorice 1/8 gr., menthol 1/200 gr./Loz. Bot. 500s, 1000s.
Use: Antiseptic throat lozenges.

SORMODREN. Bornaprine, B.A.N.

SOSEGON SOLUTION. (Winthrop Products) Pentazocine
Use: Analgesic.

SOSEGON SUSPENSION. (Winthrop Products) Pentazocine.
Use: Analgesic.

SOSEGON TABLETS. (Winthrop Products) Pentazocine.
Use: Analgesic.

S.O.S. FIRST AID CREAM. (Quality Generics) Benzalkonium Cl, diperodon HCl 0.5%, allantoin 0.2% in base w/eucalyptol & benzyl alcohol. Tube 1.5 oz.
Use: Antiseptic & anesthetic.

SOTACOR HCl. Sotalol, B.A.N.

SOTALOL. B.A.N. (±)-4′-(1-Hydroxy-2-isopropylamino-ethyl)methanesulf-onanilide.
Use: Beta adrenergic blocking agent.
See: Beta-Cardone
Sotacor (hydrochloride)

• **SOTALOL HYDROCHLORIDE.** USAN. 4′-[1-Hydroxy-2-(isopropylamino)-ethyl]methanesulfonanilide hydrochloride. Under study.
Use: Adrenergic β-receptor antagonist.

• **SOTERENOL HYDROCHLORIDE.** USAN.
Use: Adrenergic (bronchodilator).

SORADECOL. (Elkins-Sinn) Sodium tetradecyl sulfate 1% or 3%. Amp. 2 ml.
Use: Sclerosant for varicose veins.

SOVENTOL. Bamipine, B.A.N.

SOXA-FORTE. (Vita Elixir) Sulfisoxazole 0.5 Gm., phenazopyridine 50 mg./Tab.
Use: Sulfa therapy.

SOXA TABLETS. (Vita Elixir) Sulfisoxazole 0.5 Gm./Tab. Bot. 100s, 1000s.
Use: Treatment of infections due to hemolytic streptococci, staphylococci, gonococci.

SOXAZO TABLETS. (Sutliff & Case) Sulfisoxazole 500 mg., phenazopyridine HCl 50 mg./Tab. Bot. 100s, 1000s.

SOXO TABLETS. (Sutliff & Case) Sulfonamides 500 mg. Bot. 100s.

SOYALAC. (Loma Linda) Infant formula based on an extract from whole soybeans containing all

essential nutrients. **Ready to Serve Liquid:** Cans 32 fl. oz. **Double Strength Concentrate:** Cans 13 fl. oz. **Powder:** Cans 14 oz.
Use: Alternative and supplement to breast milk for infants, for adults and infants sensitive to animal milk

SOYALAC-i. (Loma Linda) Soy protein isolate infant formula containing no corn derivatives and a negligible amount of soy carbohydrates. Contains all essential nutrients in various forms. **Ready to Serve Liquid:** Cans 32 fl. oz. **Double Strength Concentrate:** Cans 13 fl. oz.
Use: Breast milk supplement for infant feeding, for individuals senstitive to animal milk or corn products.

SOYA LECITHIN. Soybean extract. 100s.
Use: Phosphorus therapy.
See: Neo-Vedrin (Scherer)

SOYBEAN LECITHIN.
W/Safflower oil, choline bitartrate, whole liver, inositol, methionine, natural tocopherols, B-6, B-12, panthenol.
See: Nutricol, Cap., Vial (Nutrition Control)

• **SOYBEAN OIL,** U.S.P. XXI.

SOY-DOME CLEANSER. (Miles Pharm) Hexachlorophene 3%, polyvinylpyrrolidone 1%, colloidal soy bean complex, in a bland lotion base. Squeeze Bot. w/applicator 6 oz.
Use: Antiseptic skin lotion.

SPABELIN No. 1. (Arcum) Phenobarbital 15 mg., belladonna pow. ext. 1/8 gr./Tab. Bot. 100s, 1000s.

SPABELIN NO. 2. (Arcum) Phenobarbital 30 mg., belladonna pow. ext. 1/8 gr./Tab. Bot. 100s, 1000s.

SPABELIN ELIXIR. (Arcum) Hyoscyamine sulfate 81 mcg., atropine sulfate 15 mcg., scopolamine HBr 5 mcg., phenobarbital 16.2 mg./5 cc. Bot. 16 oz., 1 gal.

SPAN 20. (ICI Americas) Sorbitan Monolaurate, N.F. XVI.

SPAN 40. (ICI Americas) Sorbitan Monopalmitate, N.F. XVI.

SPAN 60. (ICI Americas) Sorbitan Monostearate, N.F. XVI.

SPAN 65. (ICI Americas) Sorbitan tristearate. Mixture of stearate esters of sorbitol and its anhydrides.
Use: Surface active agent.

SPAN 80. (ICI Americas) Sorbitan Monooleate, N.F. XVI.

SPAN 85. (ICI Americas) Sorbitan trioleate. Mixture of oleate esters of sorbitol and its anhydrides.
Use: Surface active agent.

SPAN-AC. (Stanlabs) Box 12s.
Use: Timed release cold capsule.

SPANCAP #1. (Vortech) Dextroamphetamine sulfate 15 mg./Cap. Bot. 100s, 1000s.
Use: Central stimulant.

SPANCAP C. (Vortech) Sodium ascorbate 500 mg./Cap. Bot. 50s, 100s, 1000s.
Use: Timed Vitamin C therapy.

SPAN-FF. (Metro Med) Ferrous fumarate 5 gr./Sustained release Cap. Bot. 60s, 500s.

SPAN-NIACIN. (Scrip) Nicotinic acid 150 mg./Tab. Bot. 100s.

SPAN-RD. (Metro Med) d-Methamphetamine HCl 1 mg., dl-methamphetamine HCl 6 mg., butabarbital 3 mg./Tab. Bot. 100s, 1000s.

SPANTUSS LIQUID. (Arco) d-Methorphan HBr 15 mg chlorpheniramine maleate 4 mg., phenylephrine HC 5 mg., acetaminophen 120 mg./5 cc. Bot. 4 oz., 1 pt.
Use: Relief from cough and congestion.

SPANTUSS TABLET. (Arco) Chlorpheniramine maleate 8 mg., phenylephrine HCl 25 mg., dextromethorphan HBr 5 mg./Tab. Bot. 60s.
Use: Antihistamine, decongestant antitussive.

• **SPARFOSATE SODIUM.** USAN.
Use: Antineoplastic.

SPARINE EMBONATE, Promazine, B.A.N.

SPARINE. (Wyeth) Promazine hydrochloride.**Tab.** 10 mg., 25 mg., 50 mg., or 100 mg./Tab. Bot. 50s, 500s. 10 mg. Bot. 50s only. **Inj.** 25 mg./cc. Vial 10 cc. Tubex 1 cc., 50 mg./cc. Vial 2 cc., 10 cc. Tubex 1 cc., 2 cc. **Syrup** 10 mg./5 cc. Bot. 4 oz. **Concentrate** 30 mg./cc., dropper Bot. 4 oz.
Use: Ataraxic.

• **SPARSOMYCIN.** USAN.
Use: Antineoplastic.

• **SPARTEINE SULFATE.** USAN.
Use: Oxytocic.
W/Sod. chloride.
See: Tocosamine sulfate, Amp. (Trent)

SPARTUS. (Lederle) Vit. A 5000 I.U., E 30 I.U., C 300 mg., folic acid 400 mcg., B-1 7.5 mg., B-2 8.5 mg. niacinamide 100 mg., B-6 10 mg., B-12 30 mcg., D 400 I.U., biotin 45 mcg., pantothenic acid 25 mg., magnesium 100 mg., iodine 150 mcg., copper 2 mg., chromium 25 mcg., molybdenium 25 mcg., selenium 25 mcg., manganese 5 mg., potassium 40 mg., Ca 162 mg., P 75 mg., chloride 36.3 mg., zinc 15 mg./Tab. Bot. 60s.
Use: High potency vitamin, mineral & electrolyte supplement.

SPARTUS PLUS IRON. (Lederle) Vit. A 5000 I.U., E 30 I.U., C 300 mg., folic acid 400 mcg., B-1 7.5 mg., B-2 8.5 mg., niacinamide 100 mg., B-6 10 mg., B-12 30 mcg., D 400 I.U., biotin 45 mcg., pantothenic acid 25 mg., iodine 150 mcg., iron 27 mg., magnesium 100 mg., copper 3 mg., chromium 15 mcg., molybdenium 15 mcg., selenium 15 mcg., manganese 6 mg., potassium 15 mg., chloride 13.6 mg., zinc 15 mg., Ca 162 mg., P 75 mg./Tab. Bot. 60s.
Use: High potency vitamin, mineral & electrolyte supplement.

SPASAID. (Century) Hyoscyamine sulfate 0.30 mg., atropine sulfate 0.06 mg., hyoscine HBr 0.02 mg., phenobarbital 3/4 gr./Cap. Bot. 100s, 1000s.

SPASASED. (Wolins) Sodium phenobarbital 0.25 gr., scopolamine HBr 1/1000 gr., magnesium carbonate 5 gr./Tab. Bot. 1000s.

SPASDEL CAPSULES. (Marlop) Atropine sulfate 0.0582 mg., hyoscine HBr 0.0195 mg., hyoscyamine sulfate 0.311 mg., phenobarbital 50 mg./T.R. Cap. Bot. 100s.
Use: Antispasmodic, sedative.

PASIDON. (Haag) Phenobarbital 0.25 gr., hyoscyamine sulfate 0.1037 mg., atropine sulfate 0.0194 mg., hyoscine hydrobromide 0.0065 mg./Tab. Bot. 100s, 500s, 1000s.

PASLIN. (Blaine) Phenobarbital 16.2 mg., hyoscyamine sulfate 0.1040 mg., atropine sulfate. 0.0195 mg., scopolamine HBr 0.0065 mg./Tab. Bot. 100s, 1000s.
Use: Antispasmodic and sedative.

PASLOIDS. (Harvey) Hyoscyamine sulfate 0.1040 mg., atropine sulfate 0.0195 mg., hyoscine HBr 0.0065 mg., phenobarbital 0.25 gr./Tab. Bot. 1000s.
Use: Antispasmodic & sedative.

PASMATOL. (Pharmed) Homatropine MeBr 3 mg., pentobarbital 12 mg., mephobarbital 8 mg./Tab. Bot. 100s, 1000s.
Use: Antispasmodic.

PASMED. (Jenkins) Hyoscyamine HBr 0.1037 mg., atropine sulfate 0.0194 mg., hyoscine HBr 0.0065 mg., tri-bar (1/3 each sod. butabarb., sod. pentobarb., sod. phenobarb.) 16.2 mg./Tab. or 5 ml. **Tab.:** Bot. 1000s. **Elixir:** Bot. 4 oz., pt., gal. Alcohol 15%.
Use: Sedative and antispasmodic.

PASMED JR. (Jenkins) Homatropine methylbromide 1/96 gr., phenobarbital sod. 1/8 gr., lactose, special mint flavor/Tab. Bot. 1000s.
Use: Sedative.

PASMID. (Dalin) Methscopolamine nitrate 2.5 mg., phenobarbital 8.0 mg./Tab. or 5 cc. **Elix.:** Bot. 4 oz., pt. **Tab.:** Bot. 50s, 100s.
Use: Antispasmodic, anticholinergic.

PASMOBARB. (Wolins) Hyoscyamine HBr 0.128 mg., hyoscine HBr 0.007 mg., atropine sulfate 0.024 mg., butabarbital sodium/Tab. Bot. 1000s.
Use: Sedative and antispasmodic.

PASMODINE. (Noyes) Alcohol 4%, emulsion of infused oils lobelia, stillingia, cajeput, lavender, cassia, eucalyptol. Mixture 3 oz., pt., gal.
Use: Sugar free expectorant.

PASMOJECT. (Mayrand) Dicyclomine HCl 10 mg./ml. Vial 10 ml.
Use: Antispasmodic for G.I. spasms.

PASMOLIN. (Richlyn) Phenobarbital 16.2 mg., hyoscyamine sulfate 0.1037 mg., atropine sulfate 0.0194 mg., hyoscine HBr 0.0065 mg./Tab. Bot. 1000s
Use: Sedative and antispasmotic.

PASMOLIN. (Wolins) Hyoscyamine sulfate 0.1037 mg., hyoscyamine HBr 0.0065 mg., atropine sulfate 0.0194 mg., phenobarbital 16.2 mg./Tab., Cap. Bot. 1000s, 5000s.
Use: Sedative and antispasmodic.

PASMOLIN NO. 3 OR NO. 4 (Wolins) Phenobarbital 16.2 mg., hyoscyamine sulfate 0.1040 mg., atropine sulfate 0.0195 mg., hyoscine HBr 0.0065 mg./Cap. Bot. 1000s.
Use: Sedative and antispasmodic.

PASMOLIN TDC. (Wolins) Hyoscyamine sulfate 0.311 mg., hyoscyamine HBr 0.0195 mg., atropine sulfate 0.0582 mg., phenobarbital 50 mg./Cap. Bot. 1000s, 5000s.
Use: Antispasmodic and sedative.

SPASMOLYN. (Heun) Mephenesin 0.5 Gm./Tab. Bot. 100s.

SPASMOLYTIC AGENTS.
See: Antispasmodics

SPASMOPHEN. (Lannett) Phenobarbital 15 mg., hyoscyamine sulf. 0.1037 mg., atropine sulf. 0.0194 mg., hyoscine HBr 0.0065 mg./Tab. or 5 cc. **Tabs.** Bot. 500s, 1000s. **Liq.** Bot. pt., gal.
Use: Antispasmodic-sedative.

SPASNIL. (Rhode) Phenobarbital 15 mg., hyoscyamine sulfate 0.1037 mg., atropine sulfate 0.0194 mg., hyoscine 0.0065 mg./Tab. Bot. 100s.
Use: GI antispasmodic & sedative.

SPASNO-LIX. (Freeport) Phenobarbital 16.2 mg., hyoscyamine sulfate 0.1037 mg., atropine sulfate 0.0194 mg., hyoscine HBr. 0.0065 mg., alcohol 21-23 %/5 cc. Bot. 4 oz.
Use: Sedative, antispasmodic.

SPASODIL. (Rand) Ethaverine HCl 50 mg. & 100 mg./Tab. Bot. 100s & 1000s.
Use: Antispasmodic, vasodilator.

SPASTIL. (Kenyon) Propantheline Br 15 mg./Tab. Bot. 100s, 1000s.
Use: Antispasmodic.

SPASTOLATE. (Barry-Martin) Phenobarbital 16.2 mg., hyoscyamine sulf. 0.1037 mg., atropine sulf. 0.0194 mg., hyoscine HBr. 0.0065 mg./Tab. or 5 cc. **Tab.** Bot. 1000s. **Elix.** qt., gal.
Use: Antispasmodic w/sedative.

SPASTOSED. (Vortech) Calcium carbonate 226 mg., magnesium carbonate 162 mg./Tab. Bot. 1000s. Sodium free.
Use: Antacid.

SPASTYL. (Pharmex) Dicyclomine HCl 10 mg./cc. Vial 10 cc.

S.P.B. TABLET. (Sheryl) Therapeutic B complex formula with 300 mg. of ascorbic acid. Tabs. 100s.
Use: To replace stress-depleted vitamin reserves.

SPD. (A.P.C.) Methyl salicylate, methyl nicotinate, dipropyleneglycol salicylate, oleoresin capsicum, camphor, menthol. Cream Bot. 4 oz., Tube 1.5 oz.
Use: Relief of arthritis, rheumatism, neuralgia.

• **SPEARMINT,** N.F. XVI.
Use: Flavor.

• **SPEARMINT OIL,** N.F. XVI.
Use: Flavor.

SPECIAL FORMULA OINTMENT "RF". (Lannett) Zinc oxide 10%, boric acid 4%, starch 10%, camphor 1%, menthol 0.5% in a petrolatum-aquaphor base. Jar 1 lb.
Use: Dermatological.

SPECTAZOLE. (Ortho) Pegoxol 7 stearate, peglicol 5 oleate, mineral oil, benzoic acid, butylated hydroxyanisole. Tube 15 Gm., 30 Gm., 85 Gm.
Use: Antifungal, candidal agent.

SPECTINOMYCIN. Formerly Actinospectocin. An antibiotic isolated from broth cultures of *Streptomyces spectabilis.*
Use: Antibacterial.
See: Trobicin, Vial, Amp. (Upjohn)

• **SPECTINOMYCIN HYDROCHLORIDE, STERILE,** U.S.P. XXI. For Susp., U.S.P. XXI. An antibiotic produced by *Streptomyces spectabilis.*
Use: Antibacterial.

SPECTRA 360. (Parker) Salt free electrode gel. Tube 8 oz.
Use: T.E.N.S. application.

SPECTRA PAD FOR T.E.N.S. (Parker) Pre-moistened salt-free electrode pads.
Use: Transcutaneous electrical nerve stimulation.

SPECTROBID POWDER FOR ORAL SUSPENSION. (Roerig) Bacampicillin powder 125 mg./5 ml.
Use: Antibacterial.

SPECTROBID TABLETS. (Roerig) Bacampicillin HCl 400 mg./Tab. Bot. 100s.
Use: Antibacterial.

SPECTRO-BIOTIC. (A.P.C.) Bacitracin 400 u., neomycin sulfate 5 mg., polymyxin B sulfate 5000 u./Gm. Oint. 0.5 oz., 1 oz.
Use: Infection in cuts, wounds, etc.

SPECTROCIN. (Squibb) Neomycin sulfate equivalent to 2.5 mg. neomycin base, gramicidin 0.25 mg./Gm. Tube 0.5 oz., 1 oz.

SPECTRO-JEL. (Recsei) glycol polysiloxane. cetylpyridinium chloride, 15% v/v isopropylalcohol in methycellulose base jelly. Bot. 4 oz., pts., gal.
Use: Degerming cleansing agent in acne, diaper rash and pyodermas.

SPEC-T SORE THROAT ANESTHETIC LOZENGES. (Squibb) Benzocaine 10 mg./Loz. Box 10s.
Use: Topical oral antibacterial.

SPEC-T SORE THROAT/COUGH SUPPRESSANT LOZENGES. (Squibb) Benzocaine 10 mg., dextromethorphan HBr 10 mg.
Use: Local anesthetic & cough suppresant.

SPEC-T SORE THROAT/DECONGESTANT LOZENGES. (Squibb) Benzocaine 10 mg., phenylephrine HCl 5 mg., phenylpropranolamine HCl 10.5 mg./Loz. Pkg. 10s.
Use: Local anesthetic & decongestant.

SPEEDRIN. (Quality Generics) Buffered aspirin 5 gr. Bot. 100s, 1000s.

SPERMACETI.
Use: Stiffening agent; pharm. necessity for Cold Cream.

SPERMINE. Diaminopropyltetramethylene.

SPEROTABS—C.T. (Fellows) Amobarbital 4 mg., atropine sulfate 0.064 mg., magnesium hydroxyaminoacetate 100 mg., magnesium oxide, heavy 150 mg., aluminum hydroxide, dense 150 mg., methylcellulose 100 mg., magnesium trisilicate 150 mg., chlorophyllin, water soluble, 2 mg., benzocaine 4 mg./Tab. Bot. 1000s, 5000s.

SPERTI OINTMENT. (Whitehall) Live yeast cell derivative supplying 2,000 u. skin respiratory factor/oz. w/shark liver oil 3.0%, phenylmercuric nitrate 1:10,000. Tube 1 oz.
Use: Healing ointment.

SPHERULIN. (Berkeley Biologicals) Coccidioidin: Sterile filtrate prepared from spherules of *Coccidioides immitis.* Vial 1 ml., 1:100 equivalent. 0.5 ml., 1:10 equivalent.
Use: Skin test.

SPIDER-BITE ANTIVENIN.
See: Antivenin Crotalidae and Micrurus, U.S.P. XXI.

• **SPIPERONE.** USAN. 8-[3-(p-Fluorobenzoyl)-propyl]-1-phenyl-1,3,8-triazaspiro-[4.5]decan-4-one.
Use: Tranquilizer.

• **SPIRAMYCIN.** USAN. (Ives) Antibiotic substance from cultures of *Streptomyces ambofaciens.* Rovamycin.
Use: Antibiotic.

SPIRILENE. B.A.N. 8-[4-(4-Fluorophenyl)pent-3-enyl]-1-phenyl-1,3,8-triazaspiro[4,5]decan-4-one.
Use: Tranquilizer.

SPIROBARBITAL SODIUM. 1-Ethyl-2,4-dimethyl-8 thio-7,9-diazaspiro[4.5]decane-6,8,10-trione sodiur salt.

• **SPIROGERMANIUM HYDROCHLORIDE.** USAN.
Use: Antineoplastic.

• **SPIROMUSTINE.** USAN. Formerly spirohydantoin mustard.
Use: Anti-neoplastic.

• **SPIRONOLACTONE,** U.S.P. XXI. Tab. U.S.P. XXI. 17-Hydroxy-7α-mercapto-3-oxo-17α-pregn-4-ene-21-carboxylic acid γ-lactone 7-acetate: 3-(3-oxo-7 α-acetylthio-17β-hydroxy-4-androsten-17 α-yl) pro pionic acid γ-lactone.
Use: Diuretic.
See: Aldactone, Tab. (Searle)
W/Hydrochlorothiazide.
See: Aldactazide, Tab. (Searle)

SPIROPITAN. (Janssen) Spiperone
Use: Antipsychotic.

• **SPIROPLATIN.** USAN.
Use: Antineoplastic.

SPIROTRIAZINE HCl. 2,4-Diamino-5(p-chlorophenyl)-9-methyl-1,3,5-triazaspiro [5.5]undeca-1,3-diene HCl
Use: Anthelmintic.

• **SPIROXASONE.** USAN.
Use: Diuretic.

• **SPONGE, ABSORBABLE GELATIN,** U.S.P. XXI.
Use: Local hemostatic.

SPRAY SKIN PROTECTANT. (Morton) Isopropyl alcohol, polyvinylpyrolidine, vinyl alcohol, plasticizer & propellant. Aerosol can 6 oz.
Use: Protective skin coating.

SPREADING FACTOR.
See: Hyaluronidase (Various Mfr.)

SPRX-1. (Reid-Provident) Phendimetrazine tartrate 3[illegible] mg./Tab. Bot. 100s.
Use: Anorexic.

SPRX-3. (Reid-Provident) Phendimetrazine tartrate 3[illegible] mg./Cap. Bot. 100s.
Use: Anorexic.

SPRX 105 CAPSULES. (Reid-Provident) Phendimetrazine tartrate 105 mg./S.R. Cap. Bot. 28s, 500s.
Use: Anorexic.

S-P-T. (Fleming) Pork thyroid, desiccated. 1,2,3,[illegible] gr./Cap. Bot. 100s, 1000s.
Use: Hypothyroidism.

.Q. (MSD AGVET) Sulfaquinoxaline: 40% medicated feed. Solution 20%.
Use: Sulfonamide, veterinary medicine.

QUIBB GOLDEN BOUNTY PRODUCTS. (Squibb)
Cod Liver Oil Capsules. Cod liver oil 0.6 ml./Cap. Bot. 100s.
Use: Vitamin A & D.
Vitamin A Capsules. Vit. A 10,000 I.U./Cap. Bot. 100s.
Use: Vitamin A supplement.
Vitamin E. Vit. E 400 I.U./Cap. Bot. 60s, 90s.
Use: Vitamine E supplement.

RC EXPECTORANT. (Edwards) Hydrodone bitartrate 5 mg., pseudoephedrine HCl 60 mg., guaifenesin 200 mg. w/alcohol 12.5%. Bot. pt.
Use: Decongestant, expectorant, anti-tussive.

SKI. (Upsher-Smith) Potassium iodide oral solution 300 mg./0.3 cc. Dropper Bot. 1 oz., 8 oz.
Use: Chronic pulmonary diseases.

-SPAS. (Southern States) Pentobarbital 16.2 mg., atropine sulfate 0.0194 mg., hyoscyamine sulfate 0.1037 mg., hyoscine HBr 0.0065 mg./Tab. or 5 cc. **Liq.** Bot. pt. **Tab.** Bot. 100s, 1000s.
Use: Sedative & antispasmodic.

.T. 37. (Beecham Products) Hexylresorcinol 0.1% in glycerin aqueous solution. Bot. 5 oz., 12 oz.
Use: General antiseptic.

TABINOL. Isobuzole, B.A.N.

TABL-PLEX W/VITAMIN C. (Morton) Vit. B-1 25 mg., B-2 7.13 mg., B-6 5 mg., panthenol 5 mg., niacinamide 50 mg., Vit. C 50 mg., gentisic acid ethanolamide 2.5%, polyethylene glycol 300 10%, benzyl alcohol 2%/cc. Vial 30 cc.

TADOL. (Bristol) Butorphanol tartrate 1 mg./ml. Vial 1 ml. 2 mg./ml. disposable syringe. Vial 1 ml., 2 ml., 10 ml.
Use: Analgesic.

TAFTABS. (Modern) Fine bone flour containing calcium, phosphorus, iron, iodine, Vit. D, magnesium Tab. Bot. 85s, 160s.

TAINLESS IODIZED OINTMENT. (Day-Baldwin) Jar 1 lb.

TAINLESS IODIZED OINTMENT WITH METHYL SALICYLATE 5%. (Day-Baldwin) Jar 1 lb.

TALL. (Cenci) o-Hydroxybenzoic acid 0.5 %, thymol 0.5 %, ethyl alcohol S.D. 70%. Bot. 0.5, 2 oz. w/dropper.
Use: Earache and ear infections.

STALLIMYCIN HYDROCHLORIDE. USAN.
Use: Antibacterial.

TAMYL TABLETS. (Winthrop Products) Pancreatin.
Use: Pancreatic deficiency, dyspepsia.

TANACAINE. (Standex) Lidocaine HCl 2% Bot. 50 cc.

TANACILLIN. (Standex) Buffered penicillin 250,000 u./Tab. 500,000 u./Tab. Bot. 100s.

TANACILLIN PO. (Standex) Buffered penicillin Pow. 250,000 u. Bot. 60 cc. 500,000 u. Bot. 80 cc.

TAN-APAP. (Stanlabs) Acetaminophen 500 mg./Cap. Bot. 50s.
Use: Analgesic.

STAN A SYN. (Standex) Vit A palmitate 50,000 I.U./Cap. Bot. 100s.

STAN A SYN CREME. (Standex) Vits. A & D. 1 oz.

STAN A SYN FORTE. (Standex) Vit. A palmitate 10,000 I.U./Cap. Bot. 100s.

STAN A SYN FORTE S. (Standex) Vit. A soluble 10,000 I.U./Cap. Bot. 100s.

STAN A SYN JR. (Standex) Vit. A palmitate 25,000 I.U./Cap. Bot. 100s.

STAN A SYN S. (Standex) Vit. A soluble 50,000 I.U./Cap. Bot. 100s.

STANBACK PAIN RELIEF POWDERS. (Stanback) Aspirin 650 mg./Powder. Pkgs. 2s, 6s., 24s, 50s.
Use: Analgesic, antipyretic, anti-inflammatory.

STANBACK MAX-EXTRA STRENGTH. (Stanback) Aspirin 850 mg./powder. Pkg. 2s, 4s, & 36s.
Use: Analgesic, antipyretic, anti-inflammatory.

STANCARE. (Block) Stannous fluoride 10 mg./Tab. One tablet in 10 ml. water prepares a 0.1% solution. Box 28s, 46s.
Use: Fluoride mouth rinse.

STANDEX. (Standex) Vit. A 1333 I.U., D 133 I.U., B-1 0.33 mg., B-2 0.40 mg., C 10 mg., niacinamide 3.3 mg., Fe 3.3 mg., Ca 15 mg., P 29 mg., sod. carboxymethylcellulose 100 mg./Cap. Bot. 100s.

STANNITOL ELIXIR. (Standex) Phenobarbital 0.25 gr., hyoscyamine sulfate 0.1037 mg., atropine sulfate 0.0194 mg., scopolamine HBr 0.0065 mg., alcohol 23%/5 cc. Bot. pt.

STANNITOL INJ. (Standex) Dicyclomine HCl 10 mg./cc. Vial 10 cc.

STANNITOL TAB. (Standex) Phenobarbital 0.25 gr., atropine sulfate 0.0195 mg., hyoscine HBr 0.0065 mg., hyoscyamine sulfate 0.1040 mg./Tab. Bot. 100s.

• **STANNOUS CHLORIDE.** USAN.
Use: Pharmaceutic aid.

• **STANNOUS FLUORIDE,** U.S.P. XXI. Gel, U.S.P. XXI. Tin fluoride.
Use: Dental caries prophylactic.

STANNOUS FLUORIDE. (City Chem.) Stannous fluoride. Bot. 4 oz., lb.

• **STANNOUS PYROPHOSPHATE.** USAN.
Use: Diagnostic aid (bone imaging).

• **STANNOUS SULFUR COLLOID.** USAN.
Use: Diagnostic aid.

STANOLONE, B.A.N. Androstanolone, dihydrotestosterone, androstane-17(β)-ol-3-one. 17 β-Hydroxy-5 α-androstan-3-one.
See: Anabolex
Anabolic steroid.
Anaprotin

• **STANOZOLOL,** U.S.P. XXI. Tab., U.S.P. XXI. 17 β-Hydroxy-17 α-methylandrostano[3,2-c] pyrazole. 17-Methyl-2'H-5 α-androst-2-eno(3,2-c)pyrazol-17 β-ol. Formerly Androstanazole.
Use: Anabolic agent.
See: Stromba
Winstrol Tab. (Winthrop-Breon)

STANPRO-75. (Standex) Phenylpropanolamine 75 mg./cc. Vial 30 cc.

STANTEEN CAP. (Standex) Vit. A 5000 I.U., D 400 I.U., B-1 3 mg., B-2 2.5 mg., C 50 mg., niacinamide 20 mg., Ca 46 mg., P 35 mg., Fe 1.34 mg., B-6 1 mg., Ca pantothenate 2 mg., B-12 2 mcg., Mg 1 mg., Mn 1.5 mg., K 5 mg., Zn 1.4 mg./Cap. Bot. 100s.

STAPHAGE LYSATE (SPL). (Delmont) Phage-lysed staphylococci 120-180 million/cc. Amp. 1 cc. package 10s for inj.; multidose vials 10 cc. for other methods of administration.
Use: Prophylaxis and treatment of staphylococcal infections.

STAPHCILLIN. (Bristol) Sodium methicillin 1 Gm., equiv. to 900 mg. methicillin activity/Vial. Vial 1 Gm., 4 Gm., 6 Gm.; Piggyback vials. 1 Gm., 4 Gm.
Use: Penicillin therapy.

• **STARCH,** N.F. XVI.
Use: Dusting powder; tablet disintegrant.
See: Mexsana, Pwd. (Plough)

STARCH GLYCERITE.
Use: Emollient.

• **STARCH, PREGELATINIZED,** N.F. XVI.
Use: Pharm. aid (tablet excipient).

• **STARCH, TOPICAL,** U.S.P. XXI.
Use: Dusting powder.

STAR-OTIC. (Star) Burrows sol. 10%, acetic acid 1.0%, boric acid 1.0%. Drop bot. 15 cc.
Use: Treatment of otitis externa, bacterial & fungal infections of ear canal.

STATICIN 1.5%. (Westwood) Erythromycin 15 mg./ml. in clear solution w/alcohol 55%, propyleme glycol, Laureth-4 and fragrance. Bot. 60 ml.
Use: Topical control of acne vulgaris.

STATOBEX. (Lemmon) Phendimetrazine tartrate 35 mg./Tab. or Cap. Bot. 1000s. Green & white.
Use: Anorexiant.

STATOBEX-G. (Lemmon) Phendimetrazine tartrate 35 mg./Tab. Bot. 1000s. Green.
Use: Anorexiant.

• **STATOLON.** USAN. Antiviral agent derived from *Penicillium stoloniferum.*
Use: Antiviral agent.

STATOMIN MALEATE II. (Bowman) Chlorpheniramine maleate 2 mg., acetaminophen 324 mg., caffeine 32 mg./Tab. Bot. 1000s.
Use: Decongestant, analgesic, antihistaminic.

STATROL. (Alcon) Polymixin B sulfate 16, 250 u./ml., neomycin 3.5 mg./ml. hydroxypropyl methylcellulose 0.5%. Droptainer 5 ml.
Use: Bacterial infections of the eye.

STATROL STERILE OPHTHALMIC OINTMENT. (Alcon) Polymyxin B sulfate 10,000 U., neomycin 3.5 mg./Gm. Tube 3.5 Gm.
Use: Bacterial infections of the eye.

STA-WAKE DEXTABS. (Approved) Caffeine 1.5 gr., dextrose 3 gr./Tab. Bot. 36s, 1000s.
Use: Stimulant.

STAY-ALERT. (Edward J. Moore) Caffeine 250 mg./Cap. Bot. 12s, 18s.

STAY AWAKE CAPSULES. (Whiteworth) Caffeine 250 mg./Cap. Bot. 30s.
Use: CNS Stimulant.

STAYMINS. (Stayner) Vit. A 5000 I.U., D 500 I.U., B-1 1.5 mg., B-2 1.5 mg., niacinamide 10 mg., B-6 0. mg., C 50 mg., B-12 2 mcg./5 ml. Bot. 16 oz.
Use: Multivatimin liquid.

STAYMINS TABLETS. (Stayner) Vit. A 5000 I.U., D 500 I.U., E 1 I.U. B-1 2.5 mg., B-2 2.5 mg., B-6 0.5 mg B-12 2 mcg., C 50 mg., Ca pantothenate 5 mg niacinamide 20 mg., inositol 10 mg., choline bitartrate 10 mg./Tab. Bot. 100s, 1000s.
Use: Multivitamin tablet.

STAYNERAL TABLETS. (Stayner) Vit. A 5000 I.U., D 500 I.U., E 5 I.U., B-1 5 mg., B-2 5 mg., B-6 1 mg., C 100 mg., B-12 2 mcg., niacinamide 25 mg., Ca pantothenate 5 mg., Ca 50 mg., P 40 mg., Fe 10 mg., Mn 0.5 mg., Zn 0.1 mg., Mg 0.5 mg., Iodine 0.2 mg., Cu 0.1 mg./Tab. Bot. 100s, 1000s.
Use: Vitamin-mineral therapy.

STAY-UPS. (Faraday) Tab. Bot. 30s.
Use: To combat fatigue.

STAZE. (Commerce) Karaya gum. Tube 1.75 oz., 3.5 oz.
Use: Denture adhesive.

S-T DECONGEST. (Scot-Tussin) Phenylephrine HCl 5 mg., phenylpropanolamine HCl 5 mg., brompheniramine maleate 4 mg./5 ml. w/alcohol 2.3%. Sugar free and dye free. Bot. 8 oz., 16 oz., gal.
Use: Hay fever and allergies.

STEAPSIN.
W/Oxidized bile acids, ox bile, homatropine methylbromide.
See: Oxacholin, Tab. (Philips Roxane)

• **STEARIC ACID,** N.F. XVI. Purified, N.F. XVI. Octadecanoic acid.
Use: Pharm aid (emulsion adjunct, tablet lubricant).

• **STEARYL ALCOHOL,** N.F. XVI.
Use: Pharm aid (emulsion adjunct).

STECSOLIN. Oxytetracycline, B.A.N.

• **STEFFIMYCIN.** USAN.
Use: Antibacterial, antiviral.

STELAZINE. (SmithKline) Trifluoperazine HCl. **Tab.** 1 mg., 2 mg., 5 mg. & 10 mg., Bot. 100s, 1000s. Unit dose 100s. **Vial** 10 ml. (2 mg./ml.) Box 1s, 20s. **Oral Conc.** (10 mg./ml.) Bot. 2 fl. oz. Ctn. 12s.
Use: Tranquilizing agent.

STEMETIL. Prochlorperazine, B.A.N.

STEMULTROLIN. (Lincoln) Chorionic gonadotropin (Human) 500 I.U./cc. Vial 10 cc.
Use: Male senility.

• **STENOBOLONE ACETATE.** USAN. 17-beta-Hydroxy-2-methyl-5-alpha-androst-1-en-3-one acetate.
Use: Inj. anabolic.

STERA-FORM CREME. (Mayrand) Hydrocortisone 1% clioquinol 3%, pramoxine HCl 0.5%. Pkg. 0.5 oz.

STERAJECT. (Mayrand) Prednisolone acetate 25 mg., 50 mg./ml. Vial 10 ml.

STERAMINE OTIC. (Mayrand) Pramoxine HCl 1.0%, hydrocortisone 1.0%, parachlorometaxylenol 0.1%, benzalkonium chloride 0.02%, acetic acid 2.0% in a nonaqueous propylene glycol vehicle. Bot. 10 cc.
Use: Antibacterial, antifungal, anti-inflammatory anesthetic.

TERANE TABLETS. (Pfipharmecs) Prednisolone 5 mg./Tab. Bot. 5000s.
Use: Rheumatoid arthritis, allergies and various inflammatory skin conditions.

TERAPRED TABLETS. (Mayrand) Prednisone 5 mg./Tab. Bot. 100s, 1000s.
Use: Anti-inflammatory steroid.

TERAPRED-UNIPAK. (Mayrand) Prednisone 5 mg./Tab. Dosepak 21 tab.
Use: Anti-inflammatory steroid.

TERCULIA GUM.
See: Karaya Gum (Var. Mfr.)

V/Vit. B-1.
See: Imbicoll W/Vit. B-1 (Upjohn)

TERIBOLIC. (Kay) Methandriol dipropionate 50 mg./cc. Vial 10 cc.
Use: Anabolic steroid.

TERICOL. (Alton) Isopropyl alcohol 91% Bot. 16 oz, 32 oz., Gal.
Antibacterial, topical anti-infective.

• **STERILE AUROTHIOGLUCOSE SUSPENSION,** U.S.P. XXI. Authothioglucose Injection. Gold thioglucose. Gold, (l-thio-D-glucopyranosato)-. (l-Thio-D-glucopyranosato) gold.
Use: Antirheumatic.
See: Solganal, Vial (Schering)

• **STERILE ERYTHROMYCIN GLUCEPTATE,** U.S.P. XXI. Erythromycin monoglucoheptonate (salt). Erythromycin glucoheptonate (1:1) (salt).
Use: Antibacterial.

STERILE THIOPENTAL SODIUM. Thiopental sodium, U.S.P. XXI.
See: Pentothal Sodium, Amp. (Abbott)

STERISIL. Hexetidine, B.A.N.

STERI-UNNA BOOT. (Pedinol) Glycerin, gum acacia, zinc oxide, white petrolatum, amylum in an oil base. 10 Yds. × 3.5 in. steralized bandage.
Use: Treatment of leg ulcers, varicosities, sprains, strains & reduce swelling after surgery.

STERNEEDLE TESTING KIT FOR HEAF TUBERCULIN TEST, ALLERGY & SMALLPOX. (Panray) 1 "Sterneedle" device, 100 "Sterneedle" No. 6 cartridge, concentrated tuberculin PPD solution 'Connaught'. Vial 1 cc. Also available w/50 smallpox No. 3 and 50 TB Test cartridges No. 6./Kit. Also mass testing kit.

STEROLOX. (Kenyon) Benzethonium Cl. benzoic acid, salicylic acid, thymol, menthol, isopropyl alcohol 50%. Bot. 2 oz., pt., gal.

STEROXIN. Chlorquinaldol, B.A.N.

S-T FORTE. (Scot-Tussin) Hydrocodone bitartrate 2.5 mg., phenylephrine HCl 5 mg., phenylporpanolamine HCl 5 mg., pheniramine maleate 13.33 mg., guaifenesin 80 mg./5 ml. Regular or sugar free. Bot. pt. gal.
Use: Cough and cold treatment.

STIBAMINE GLUCOSIDE. B.A.N. Sodium 4-glucosylaminophenylstibonate.
Use: Treatment of leishmaniasis.

STIBOCAPTATE. B.A.N. Antimony(III) sodium meso-2, 3- dimercaptosuccinate.
Use: Treatment of schistosomiasis.
See: Astiban

STILBAMIDINE. B.A.N. 4, 4′-Diamidinostilbene.
Use: Treatment of trypanosomiasis.

STILBAMIDINE ISETHIONATE. 2-Hydroxyethane-sulfonic acid compound with 4, 4′-stilbenedicarboxamidine.
Use: Antiprotozoal.

• **STILBAZIUM IODIDE.** USAN. 1-Ethyl-2, 6-bis(p-1-pyrrolidinyl-styryl)-pyridinium iodide.
Use: Anthelmintic.
See: Monopar

STILBESTROL.
See: Diethylstilbestrol, U.S.P. XXI. (Various Mfr.)

STILBESTRONATE.
See: Diethylstilbestrol Dipropionate (Various Mfr.)

STILBOESTROL.
See: Diethylstilbestrol (Various Mfr.)

STILBOESTROL DP.
See: Diethylstilbestrol Dipropionate (Various Mfr.)

STILLMAN'S. (Stillman) Cream Jar. ⅞ oz., 1⅞ oz., Cream Bella Aurora: ⅞ oz.

• **STILONIUM IODIDE.** USAN.
Use: Antispasmodic.

STILPHOSTROL. (Miles Pharm) Diethylstilbestrol diphosphate. Amp. (250 mg./5 cc.) 5 cc. Box 20s. Tab. 50 mg., Bot. 50s.
Use: Inoperable prostatic carcinoma.

STILRONATE.
See: Diethylstilbestrol Dipropionate (Var. Mfr.)

STIMATE. (Armour) Desmopressin acetate 4 mcg./ml. Vial 10 ml.
Use: Treatment of mild to moderate Hemophilia A.

STIMULAX. (Geriatric) Docusate sodium 250 mg., casathranol 30 mg./Cap. Bot. 30s, 100s, 500s.
Use: Fecal softener & laxative.

STIMURUB. (Otis Clapp) Menthol, methyl salicylate, oleo resin of capsicum, in greaseless base. Tubes 36 × 0.25 oz., 1 oz., Jar. 16 oz.
Use: Relief from muscular aches, strains, sprains.

STING-EZE. (Wisconsin) Bot. 0.5 oz.
Use: After bite treatment.

STINGING INSECT ANTIGEN. (Barry) Polyvalent whole-body insect extract of wasp, hornet, bumblebee, honey bee and yellow jacket antigens/Vial. Set 3 serial dilution.

STIRIMAZOLE. B.A.N. 2-(4-Carboxystyryl)-5-nitro-1-vinylimidazole.
Use: Treatment of amebiasis, trichomoniasis, and trypanosomiasis.

• **STIRIPENTOL.** USAN.
Use: Anticonvulsant.

• **STIROFOS.** USAN.
Use: Insecticide (veterinary).

ST. JOSEPH ASPIRIN FOR ADULTS. (Plough) Aspirin 5 gr./Tab. Bot. 36s, 100s, 200s.
Use: Internal analgesic.

ST. JOSEPH ASPIRIN FOR CHILDREN. (Plough) Aspirin 1.25 gr./Tab. Bot. 36
Use: Internal analgesic.

ST. JOSEPH ASPIRIN-FREE ELIXIR FOR CHILDREN. (Plough) Acetaminophen 80 mg./2.5 ml. Alcohol and sugar free. Bot. 2 oz., 4 oz.
Use: Internal analgesic.

ST. JOSEPH ASPIRIN-FREE FOR OLDER CHILDREN. (Plough) Acetaminophen 160 mg./Tab. Bot. 30s.
Use: Internal analgesic, antipyretic.

ST. JOSEPH ASPIRIN-FREE INFANT DROPS. (Plough) Acetaminophen 80 mg./0.8 ml. dropper. Aspirin and sugar free. Bot. 0.5 oz.
Use: Internal analgesic.

ST. JOSEPH ASPIRIN-FREE TABLETS FOR CHILDREN. (Plough) Acetaminophen 80 mg./Tab. Bot. 30s.
Use: Internal analgesic.

ST. JOSEPH COLD TABLETS FOR CHILDREN. (Plough) Aspirin 81 mg., phenylpropanolamine HCl 3.125 mg./Tab. Bot. 30s.
Use: Analgesic, antipyretic, antihistaminic.

ST. JOSEPH COUGH SYRUP FOR CHILDREN. (Plough) Dextromethorphan HBr 7.5 mg./5 ml. Bot. 2 oz., 4 oz.
Use: Antitussive.

STO-CAPS. (Misemer) Chlorpheniramine maleate 8 mg., phenylpropanolamine HC1 50 mg., methscopolamine nitrate 2.5 mg./Cap.
Use: Relief of the symptoms of common cold, sinusitis, allergic rhinitis.

STOMACH SUBSTANCE DESICCATED.
W/Vit. B-12, cobalt gluconate & ferrous gluconate.

STOMAHESIVE. (ConvaTec) **Peristomal covering** gelatin, pectin, sod. CMC, polyisobutylene. Nonsterile wafers 4″ × 4″. Box 5s; 8 × 8 Box 3s. **Wafer with Surfit flange:** 4 × 4 wafer and one consists of the following flanges: 38 mm. (1.5 inch) flange. Box 5s.; 45 mm. (1¾ inch) flange. Box 5s., 57 mm. (2.25 inch) flange. Box 5s.; 70 mm. (2¾ inch) flange. Box 5s. **Surfit drainable pouch**. 10 inch or 12 inch opaque with one of the following flanges: 38 mm. (1.5 inch) flange. Box 10s.; 45 mm. (1¾ inch) flange, Box 10s.; 57 mm. (2.25 inch) flange,Box10s.;70mm.(2¾inch)flange,Box10s.
Use: To protect skin from contact with exudates from colostomy or ileostomy.

STOMAHESIVE PASTE. (ConvaTec) Peri-stomal paste. Tube 2 oz.
Use: To fill areas around stoma.

STOMAHESIVE WAFERS. (ConvaTec) Peri-stomal covering. 4 × 4s, Pkg. 5s. 8 × 8s, Box 3s.
Use: Peri-stomal covering.

STOMAHESIVE WAFER WITH SURFIT FLANGE. (ConvaTec) Peri-stomal covering with plastic fringe for attaching ostomy pouch. Box 5s.
Use: Part of two-piece ostomy care system.

STOMAL. (Foy) Phenobarbital 16.2 mg., hyoscyamine sulfate 0.1037 mg., atropine sulfate 0.0194 mg., scopolamine HBr 0.0065 mg./Tab. Bot. 1000s.
Use: Treatment of peptic ulcer.

STOOL SOFTENER. (Amblab) Docusate sodium 100 mg. and 250 mg./Cap. Bot. 100s.
Use: Stool softener.

STOOL SOFTENER. (Weeks & Leo) Docusate sodium 100 mg. or 250 mg./Cap. Bot. 30s, 100s. Calcium docusate 240 mg./Cap. Bot. 100s.
Use: Stool softener.

STOP. (Oral-B) Stannous fluoride 0.4% in water-free base. Tube 2 oz.
Use: Topical application to aid in prevention of dental caries.

STOPAYNE. (Springbok) Codeine phosphate 30 mg., promethazine HCl 6.25 mg., acetaminophen 357 mg./Cap. Bot. 100s, 500s. Unit dose 100s.
Use: Analgesic.

STOPAYNE SYRUP. (Springbok) Acetaminophen 120 mg., promethazine HCl 6.25 mg., codeine phosphate 5 mg./5 ml. Bot. 4 oz., 16 oz.
Use: Analgesic, antipyretic.

STOP-KOFF. (Stanley) Dextromethorphan HBr 15 mg., benzocaine 3 mg./soft gelatin cap. Bot. 30s.
Use: Commmon cold therapy.

STOP-ZIT. (Purepac) Denatonium benzoate in a clear nailpolish base. Bot. 0.75 oz.
Use: Thumbsucking-nail biting deterrent.

• **STORAX,** U.S.P. XXI.
Use: Pharm, necessity for Compound Benzoin Tincture.

STOVARSOL.
Use: Trichomonas vaginalis vaginitis, amebiasis & Vincent's angina.
See: Acetarsone, Tab.

STOXIL. (SmithKline) Idoxuridine. **Ophthalmic solution:** 0.1%, Thimerosal 1:50,000. 15 ml. Bot. with droppers. **Ophthalmic ointment:** 0.5%, Petrolatum base (5 mg./Gm.) Tube 4 Gm.
Use: Antiviral agent for herpetic keratitis.

STO-ZYME. (Misemer) Pancreatic enzyme 100 mg., ox bile extract 100 mg., cellulase 10 mg./Tab.
Use: Digestive enzymes.

STRAMONIUM. (Penick) Pow., Bot. 0.25 lb., 1 lb.
Use: Sedative & antispasmodic.

STREMA. (Foy) Quinine sulfate 260 mg./Cap. Bot. 100s, 500s, 1000s.

STREN-TAB. (Barth's) Vit. C 300 mg., B-1 10 mg., B-2 10 mg., niacin 33 mg., B-6 2 mg., pantothenic acid 20 mg., B-12 4 mcg./Tab. Bot. 100s, 300s, 500s.

STREPTASE I.V. (Hoechst) Streptokinase I.V. infussion. Ctn. 10 vials, 250,000 IU/vial; 10 vials 750,000 IU/vial.
Use: Thrombolytic.

STREPTOCOCCI.
W/*Haemophilus influenzae, Neisseria catarrhalis, Klebsiella pneumoniae, staphylocci, pneumococci,* killed.
See: Mixed Vaccine No. 4 W-H. Influenzae (Lilly)

STREPTOCOCCI VACCINE, KILLED.
W/*Neisseria catarrhalis, Klebsiella pneumoniae, Diplococcus pneumoniae, staphylococci.*
See: Combined Vaccine No. 4 W/Catarrhalis (Lilly)

STREPTODORNASE. B.A.N. An enzyme obtained from cultures of various strains of *Streptococcus hemolyticus.*
See: Streptokinase-Streptodornase

STREPTODUOCIN, B.A.N. A mix. of equal parts of streptomycin & dihydrostreptomycin sulfates.

Use: Antibiotic.
See: Dimycin
Mixtamycin

TREPTOHYDRAZID. Streptomyclidene isonicotinyl hydrazine sulfate. Streptonicozid, B.A.N. Streptomycin isoniazid.
Use: Tuberculosis treatment.

TREPTOKINASE. B.A.N. An enzyme obtained from cultures of various strains of *Streptococcus hemolyticus.*
See: Kabikinase
Streptase, Inj. (Hoechst)

TREPTOLYSIN O TEST. (Laboratory Diagnostics) Reagent 6 × 10 ml., buffer 6 × 40 ml., Control Serum, 6 × 10 ml. or Kit.
Use: Diagnosis of "Group A" Streptococcal infections.

TREPTOMYCIN CALCIUM CHLORIDE. Streptomycin Calcium Chloride Complex.

TREPTOMYCIN ISONIAZID.
See: Streptohydrazid

STREPTOMYCIN SULFATE INJECTION, U.S.P. XXI. Sterile. U.S.P. XXI. (Various Mfr.)
Use: Antibacterial (tuberculostatic).
V/Dihydrostreptomycin sulfate.
See: Streptoduocin, Inj. (Various Mfr.)

TREPTOMYCYLIDENE ISONICOTINYL HYDRAZINE SULFATE.
See: Streptohydrazid

TREPTONASE-B. (Wampole) Tube test for the quantitative determination of *antideoxyribonuclease-B* (ADNase-B) titers in serum. Kit 10s.
Use: Diagnosis of *Streptoccal A* sequelae.

• **STREPTONICOZID.** USAN. Streptomycylidene isonicotinyl hydrazine sulfate.
Use: Antibiotic.
See: Streptohydrazid

• **STREPTONIGRIN.** USAN. Antibiotic isolated from both filtrates of *Streptomyces flocculus.* 5-Amino-6-(7-amino-5, 8-dihydro-6-methoxy-5, 8-dioxo-2-quinolyl)-4-(2-hydroxy-3, 4-dimethoxyphenyl)-3-methylpicolinic acid.
Use: Antineoplastic agent.
See: Nigrin (Pfizer)

STREPTONIVICIN. Novobiocin, B.A.N. (Various Mfr.)

STREPTOVARICIN. An antibiotic composed of several related components derived from cultures of *Streptomyces variabilis.* Dalacin (Upjohn)

• **STREPTOZOCIN.** USAN.
Use: Antineoplastic.
See: Zanosar, Powder (Upjohn).

STREPTOZYME. (Wampole) Rapid hemagglutination slide test for the qualitative detection and quantitative determination of streptococcal extracellular antigens in serum, plasma and peripheral blood. Kits 15s, 50s, 150s
Use: An aid in the diagnosis of *Streptococcal A* sequelae.

STRESSAIDS. (Vitarine) High potency stress formula with Vit. B & C.
Use: Dietary supplement.

STRESSAIDS 600 W/IRON. (Vitarine) Vit. B-1 15 mg., B-2 15 mg., B-6 25 mg., B-12 12 mcg., C 600 mg., niacinamide 100 mg., E 30 I.U., Ca 20 mg., folic acid 400 mcg., Iron 27 mg./Tab.
Use: Dietary supplement.

STRESSAIDS 600 WITH ZINC. (Vitarine) High potency stress formula with Vit. B, C and E, and zinc.
Use: Dietary supplement.

STRESSCAPS. (Lederle) Vit. B-1 10 mg., B-2 10 mg., niacinamide 100 mg., C 300 mg., B-6 2 mg., B-12 6 mcg., folic acid 400 mcg., biotin 45 mcg., Ca pantothenate 20 mg./Cap. Bot. 30s, 100s.
Use: Vitamin B complex therapy.

STRESS COMPLEX TABLETS. (Eckerd) Vit. C 600 mg., folic acid 0.4 mg., thiamin 25 mg., riboflavin 25 mg., niacin 100 mg., B-6 15 mg., B-12 25 mg., Ca pantothenate 25 mg., Cu 4 mg., Zn 30 mg./Tab. Bot. 40s, 80s.
Use: High potency vitamin supplement.

STRESS FORMULA WITH ZINC. (Towne) Vit. E 45 I.U., C 600 mg., folic acid 400 mcg., B-1 20 mg., B-2 10 mg., niacinamide 100 mg., B-6 10 mg., B-12 25 mcg., biotin 40 mcg., pantothenic acid 25 mg., copper 3 mg., zinc 23.9 mg./Tab. Bot. 60s.
Use: Dietary supplement.

STRESSTABS 600. (Lederle) Vit. B-1 15 mg., B-2 15 mg., B-6 5 mg., B-12 12 mcg., C 600 mg., niacinamide 100 mg., Vit. E 30 I.U., calcium pantothenate 20 mg./Tab. Bot. 30s, 60s, 500s. Unit dose 100s. Unit of Use Pkg. 50 × 30s, 50 × 60s.
Use: Multivitamin.

STRESSTABS 600 WITH IRON. (Lederle) Stresstab 600 formula with Vit. B-6 5 mg., ferrous fumerate 27 mg./Tab. Bot. 30s, 60s.
Use: Multivitamin with iron.

STRESSTABS 600 WITH ZINC. (Lederle) Vit. B-1 20 mg., B-2 10 mg., B-6 5 mg., B-12 12 mcg., C 300 mg., E 30 I.U., niacinamide 100 mg., pantothenic acid 25 mg., folic acid 400 mcg., Cu 3 mg., zinc 23.9 mg./Tab. Bot. 30s, 60s.
Use: Multavitamin with zinc.

STRESSTEIN. (Sandoz Nutrition) Maltodextrin, medium chain triglycerides, L-leucine, soybean oil, L-isoleucine, L-valine, L-glutamic acid, L-arginine, L-lysine acetate, L-alanine, L-threonine, L-phenylalamine, L-aspartic acid, L-histidine, L-methionine, glycine, polyglycerol esters of fatty acids, L-serine, L-proline, sodium chloride, L-tryptophan, L-cysteine, sodium citrate, vitamins and minerals. Powder 3.4 oz. packets.
Use: Tube feeding.

STRESSVICON. (CMC) Vit. B-1 10 mg., B-2 10 mg., C 150 mg., niacinamide 100 mg., B-6 5 mg., cal. pantothenate 25 mg., B-12 10 mcg., liver conc. 50 mg., brewer's yeast 50 mg./Cap. Bot. 30s, 100s, 250s, 500s, 1000s.
Use: Therapeutic vitamins.

STRIATRAN. Emylcamate, B.A.N.

STRI-DEX B.P. (Glenbrook) Benzoyl peroxide 10%. in greaseless, vanishing cream base.
Use: Acne medication.

STRI-DEX LOTION. (Glenbrook) Salicylic acid 0.5%, alcohol 28%, sulfonated alkyl benzenes, citric acid, sodium carbonate, simethicone, water. Bot. 4 oz.
Use: Acne medication.

STRI-DEX PADS. (Glenbrook) Salicylic acid 0.5%, alcohol 28%, sulfonated alkyl benzenes, citric acid, sodium carbonate, simethicone, water. Jar 42 pads, 75 pads.
Use: Acne medication.

STROMBA AMPULES. (Winthrop Products) Stanozolol.
Use: Anabolic steroid.

STRONTIUM BROMIDE. Cryst. or Granule, Bot. 0.25 lb., 1 lb. Amp. 1 Gm./10 cc.
Use: Sedative & antiepileptic.
W/Bromides of sodium, potassium, ammonium.
See: Lanabrom, Elix. (Lannett)

• **STRONTIUM CHLORIDE Sr 85.** USAN.
Use: Radioactive agent.

STRONTIUM LACTATE TRIHYDRATE.

• **STRONTIUM NITRATE Sr 85.** USAN.
Use: Radioactive agent.

STRONTIUM SR 85 INJECTION.
Use: Diagnostic aid (bone scanning).

STROPHANTHIN. K-strophanthin.

STROPHEN. (Kenyon) Prednisone 0.75 mg., salicylamide 5 gr., alum. hydroxide gel 75 mg., Vit. C 20 mg./Tab. Bot. 100s, 1000s.
Use: Arthritis.

STRYCHNINE. (Various Mfr.) Pow., Bot. ⅛ oz., 1 oz.

STRYCHNINE SULFATE. (Various Mfr.) Cryst., Bot. ⅛ oz., 1 oz. Pow., Bot. ⅛ oz., 5 lb.
W/Thyroid ext., yohimbine HCl.
See: Andro-Medicone (Medicone)

STUART FORMULA. (Stuart) Vit. A 5000 I.U., B-1 1.5 mg., B-2 1.7 mg. niacin 20 mg., B-6 2 mg., B-12 6 mcg., C 60 mg., D 400 I.U., E 15 I.U., Ca 160 mg., Fe 18 mg., magnesium 100 mg., phos. 125 mg., folic acid 0.4 mg., iodine 150 mcg./Tab. Bot. 100s, 250s.
Use: Dietary vitamin & mineral supplement.

STUARTINIC. (Stuart) Vit. B-12 25 mcg.,B-1 6 mg., B-2 6 mg., niacinamide 20 mg., Ca pantothenate 10 mg., Vit. B-6 1 mg., C 500 mg., iron 100 mg./Tab. Bot. 60s.
Use: Hematinic; iron deficiency.

STUARTNATAL 1 + 1. (Stuart) Vit. A 8000 I.U., B-1 2.55 mg., B-2 3 mg. niacin 20 mg., B-6 10 mg., B-12 12 mcg., C 90 mg., D 400 I.U., E 30 I.U., Folic Acid 1 mg. Ca 200 mg., magnesium 100 mg., Iron 65 mg., iodine 150 mcg./Tab. Bot. 100s, 500s.
Use: Vitamin, mineral supplement in pregnancy and lactation.

STUART PRENATAL. (Stuart) Vit. A 8000 I.U., B-1 1.7 mg., B-2 2 mg., B-6 4 mg., B-12 8 mcg., C 60 mg., D 400 I.U., E 30 I.U., Niacin 20 mg., Fe 60 mg., Ca 200 mg., magnesium 100 mg., iodine 150 mcg., Folic Acid 0.8 mg./Tab. Bot. 100s, 500s.
Use: Vitamin & mineral supplement in pregnancy & lactation.

STUGERON. Cinnarizine, B.A.N.

STULEX. (Bowman) Docusate sodium 100 mg. or 25 mg./Tab. Bot. 100s, 1000s.
Use: Nonlaxative fecal softener.

STYE. (Commerce) Yellow mercuric oxide 1.0%. Tub. 0.125 oz.
Use: Minor irritation and infection of eyelid.

STYPTIRENAL.
See: Epinephrine (Various Mfr.)

STYPTO-CAINE SOLUTION. (Pedinol) Hydroxyquinoline sulphate, tetracaine HCl, aluminum Cl, aqueous glycol base. Bot. 2 oz.
Use: Hemostatic solution.

STYRAMATE, B.A.N. 1-Phenyl-1,2-ethanediol 2-carbamate. β-Hydroxyphenethyl carbamate. 2-Hydroxy-2-phenylethyl carbamate.
Use: Skeletal muscle relaxant.
See: Sinaxar

STYRENE POLYMER, SULFONATED, SODIUM SALT. Sodium Polystyrene Sulfonate, U.S.P. XXI.

STYRONATE RESINS. Ammonium and potassium salts of sulfonated styrene polymers.
Use: Conditions requiring sodium restriction.

SUAVITIL HYDROCHLORIDE. Benactyzine, B.A.N.

SUBLIMAZE. (Janssen) Fentanyl 0.05 mg./cc. Amp. 10 ml., 20 ml. Pkg. 5s.
Use: Analgesic, anesthetic agent.

SUCARYL LIQUID. (Abbott) Saccharin 1.21% (as sodium saccharin), benzoic acid 0.1%, methyl paraben 0.5% as preservative, water. Bot. 6 oz, 12 oz.
Use: Artificial sweetening agent.

SUCARYL TABLETS. (Abbott) Saccharin 12.5 mg. (equivalent to approx. 0.25 gr. sodium saccharin)/Tab. Bot. 1000s.
Use: Artificial sweetening agent.

• **SUCCIMER.** USAN.
Use: Diagnostic aid.

SUCCINATES.
See: Calcium succinate
Sodium succinate
Succinic acid

SUCCINCHLORIMIDE. N-Chlorosuccinimide.

SUCCINIC ACID.
W/9-Aminoacridine HCl, phenyl mercuric acetate, sod. lauryl acetate.
See: Vagiserts W/Inserts, Tab. (Vortech)
W/9-Aminoacridine undecylenate, N-myristyl-3-hydroxybutylamine hydrochloride, methylbenzethonium chloride.
See: Cenasert, Tab. (Central)

• **SUCCINYLCHOLINE CHLORIDE,** U.S.P. XXI. Inj., Sterile, U.S.P. XXI. Ethanaminium, 2,2′-[(1,4-dioxo-1,4-butanediyl)bis(oxy)]bis-N,NN-tri-methyl-, dichloride. Choline chloride succinate (2:1).
Use: Skeletal muscle relaxant.
See: Anectine chloride, Amp. (Burroughs Wellcome)
Quelicin, Amp., Additive Syringes, Fliptop & Pintop Vials (Abbott)
Sucostrin, Amp., Vial (Squibb)

SUCCINYLSULFATHIAZOLE. 4′-(2-Thiazolysulfamoyl)
Use: Intestinal antibacterial.

COSTRIN CHLORIDE. (Squibb) Succinylcholine chloride 20 mg./cc. w/methylparaben 0.1%, propylparaben 0.01%, sodium hydroxide or hydrochloric acid. Vial 10 cc.; For infusion 50 mg./cc. Vial. 10 cc. High potency 100 mg./cc. Vial 10 cc.
Use: Muscle relaxant.

SUCRALFATE. USAN. Beta-D-fructofuranosyl-alpha-D-glucopyranoside octakis (hydrogen sulfate) aluminum hydroxide complex.
Use: Duodenal ulcer therapy.
See: Carafate, Tab. (Marion)

JCRALOX. B.A.N. A polymerized complex of sucrose and aluminum hydroxide.
Use: Treatment of gastric hyperacidity.
See: Malalox AS

JCRETS CHILDREN'S SORE THROAT LOZENGES. (Beecham Products) Dyclonine HCl 1.2 mg./Lozenge. Cherry flavor. Tin 24s.
Use: Sore throat treatment for children 3 years and over.

JCRETS COLD DECONGESTANT LOZENGE. (Beecham Products) Phenylpropanolamine HCl 25 mg./Lozenge. Box 24s.
Use: Decongestant.

JCRETS COUGH CONTROL LOZENGE. (Beecham Products) Dextromethorphan HBr 7.50 mg./Lozenge. Tin 24s.
Use: Antitussive.

JCRETS MAXIMUM STRENGTH SORE THROAT LOZENGES. (Beecham Products) Dyclonine HCl 3 mg./Lozenge. Tin 24s.
Use: Temporary relief of minor sore throat & mouth irritation.

JCRETS SORE THROAT LOZENGE. (Beecham Products) Hexylresorcinol 2.4 mg./Loz. **Regular:** Tin 24s, 48s. **Mentholated:** Tin 24s.
Use: Minor throat irritations.

SUCROSE, N.F. XVI. Compressible, Confectioners, N.F. XVI. Saccharose. Sugar. α-D-Glucopyranoside, β-D-fructo-furanosyl-.
Use: I.V.; diuretic & dehydrating agent; pharm. aid (sweetening agent).

SUCROSE OCTAACETATE, N.F. XVI.
Use: Alcohol denaturant.

UDAFED. (Burroughs Wellcome) Pseudoephedrine HCl **Tab:** 30 mg./Tab. Box 24s, Bot. 100s, 1000s; 60 mg./Tab. Bot. 100s, 1000s. **Syr.** (30 mg./5 cc.) Bot. 4 oz., 1 pt.
Use: Decongestant of respiratory tract mucosa.
/Chlorcyclizine HCl.
See: Fedrazil, Tab. (Burroughs Wellcome)
/Codeine phosphate, acetophenetidin, aspirin, caffeine.
See: Emprazil-C, Tabs. (Burroughs Wellcome)

UDAFED COUGH SYRUP. (Burroughs Wellcome) Pseudoephedrine HCl 30 mg., dextromethorphan HBr 10 mg., guaifenesin 100 mg./5 ml. w/alcohol 2.4%. Bot. 4 oz., 8 oz.
Use: Cough treatment.

UDAFED PLUS. (Burroughs Wellcome) **Tab.:** Pseudoephedrine HCl 60 mg., chlorpheniramine maleate 4 mg./Tab. Box 24s, 48s. **Syrup:** Pseudoephedarine HCl 30 mg., chlorpheniramine maleate 2 mg./5 ml. Bot. 4 oz.
Use: Sinus & upper respiratory tract decongestant.

SUDAFED S.A. (Burroughs Wellcome) Pseudoephedrine HCl 120 mg./Sustained Action Cap. Bot. 40s, 100s. Box 10s.
Use: Nasal or eustachian tube congestion.

SUDANYL. (Dover) Pseudoephedrine HCl./Tab. Sugar, lactose and salt free. Unit dose Box 500s.
Use: Decongestant.

SUDDEN TAN LOTION. (Plough) Padimate O, dihydroxyacetone, Bot. 4 oz.
Use: Artificial tanning agent, ultraviolet sunscreen, moisturizer.

SUDERMO. Mesulphen, B.A.N.

• **SUDOXICAM.** USAN. 4-Hydroxy-2-methyl-N-thiazol-2-yl-2H-1,2-benzothiazine-3-carboxamide 1,1-dioxide.
Use: Anti-inflammatory.

SUDRIN. (Bowman) Pseudoephedrine HCl 30 mg. or 60 mg./Tab. Bot. 100s, 1000s.
Use: Nasal decongestant.

SUEDA-G. (Hyrex) Guaifenesin 250 mg., pseudoephedrine HCl 120 mg./T.R. Cap. Bot. 100s, 1000s.
Use: Expectorant, decongestant.

SUFENTA. (Janssen) Sufentanil citrate.
Use: Analgesic, anesthetic agent.

• **SUFENTANIL.** USAN.
Use: Analgesic.

• **SUFENTANIL CITRATE.** USAN.
Use: Narcotic analgesic.

SUFREX. (Janssen) Ketanserin tarfrate.
Use: Serotonin antagonist.

• **SUGAR, COMPRESSIBLE,** U.S.P. XXI.
Use: Pharm. aid (sweetening agent, tablet excipient).

• **SUGAR, CONFECTIONER'S,** U.S.P. XXI.
Use: Pharm. aid (sweetening agent; tablet excipient).

• **SULAZEPAM.** USAN. 7-Chloro-1,3-dihydro-1-methyl-5-phenyl-2H-1,4-benzodiazepine-2-thione.
Use: Tranquilizer (minor).

SULAZO. (Freeport) Sulfisoxazole 500 mg., phenylazodiaminopyridine HCl 50 mg./Tab. Bot. 1000s.
Use: Urinary tract infections complicated by pain.

• **SULBACTAM BENZATHINE.** USAN.
Use: Synergistic.

• **SULBACTAM PIVOXIL.** USAN.
Use: Inhibitor, synergist.

• **SULBENOX.** USAN.
Use: Growth stimulant (veterinary).

SUL-BLUE SHAMPOO. (Quality Generics) Selenium sulfide 1%. Bot. 4 oz.
Use: Dandruff treatment.

SULCOLON. (Lederle) Sulfasalazine 500 mg./Tab. Bot. 500s.
Use: Anti-infective, ulcerative colitis.

• **SULCONAZOLE NITRATE.** USAN.
Use: Antifungal.

SULDIAZO. (Kay) Sulfisoxazole 0.5 Gm., phenazopyridine HCl 50 mg./Tab. Bot. 100s, 1000s.
Use: Urinary tract infections.

SULF-10. (CooperVision) Na sulfacetamide 10%. Bot. 15 ml.; Dropperette 1 ml. Box 12s.
Use: External bacterial eye infections.

SULFA-10 OPHTHALMIC. (Maurry) Sodium sulfacetamide 10%, hydroxyethylcellulose, sodium borate, boric acid, disodium edetate, sodium metabisulfite, sodium thiosulfate 0.2%, chlorobutanol 0.2%, methyl paraben 0.015%. Bot. 15 ml.
Use: Antibacterial.

• **SULFABENZ.** USAN.
Use: Antibacterial, coccidiostat.

• **SULFABENZAMIDE,** U.S.P. XXI. Benzamide, N-(4-aminophenyl) sulfunyl)-N-Sulfanilylbenzamide. Sulfanilylbenzamide, N′ benzoylsulfanilamide.
See: Sultrin, Vag. Tab., Cream (Ortho)

SULFABROMETHAZINE SODIUM.
Use: Antibacterial.

SULFACARBAMIDE (I.N.N.). Sulphaurea, B.A.N.

SULFACEL-15. (Softcon) Sod. sulfacetamide 15%, methylcellulose 0.25%, methylparaben 0.05%, propylparaben 0.01%, sod. thiosulfate, monobasic and dibasic sod. phosphate, propylene glycol. Bot. 5 cc., 15 cc.
Use: External ophthalmic bacterial infections.

SULFACET. (Dermik)
See: Sulfacetamide

• **SULFACETAMIDE,** U.S.P. XXI. Acetamide, N-(4-aminophenyl) sulfonyl)-N-Sulfanilylacetamine. N-acetylsulfanilamide.
Use: Antibacterial.
See: Isopto-Cetamide, Ophth. Sol. (Alcon)

SULFACETAMIDE W/COMBINATIONS.
See: Acet-Dia-Mer Sulfonamides
Azosul, Tab. (Reid-Provident)
Cetapred, Oint. (Alcon)
Cetazine, Tab. (Bowman)
Chero-Trisulfa (V), Susp. (Vita Elixir)
Neogel W/Sulfa, Tab. (Vortech)
Sulf-10, Ophth. Soln. (CooperVision)
Sulfa-Plex Vaginal Cream (Rowell)
Sultrin, Tab., Cream (Ortho)
Triosulfon, Tab. (CMC)
Triurisul, Tab. (Sheryl)
Uridium, Tab. (Pharmex)
Urotrol, Tab. (Mills)
Vagi-Plex, Cream (Rowell)

• **SULFACETAMIDE SODIUM,** U.S.P. XXI. Ophth. Oint., Ophth. Sol., U.S.P. XXI. Acetamide, N-[(4-aminophenyl)sulfonyl]-, monosodium salt, monohydrate. N-Sulfanilylacetamide monosodium salt monohydrate.
Use: Antibacterial (Ophthalmic).
See: Bleph 10, Liquifilm (Allergan)
Centamide, Ophth. Oint. (Alcon)
Sebizon Lotion (Schering)
Sodium Sulamyd Ophthalmic Ointment 30% (Schering)
Sulf-10, Drops (Maurry)
Sulf-10, Soln. Drops (Smith, Miller & Patch)
W/Methylcellulose.
See: Sodium Sulamyd Ophth. Sol. 10% (Schering)
W/Phenylephrine HCl, methylparaben, propylparaben
See: Vasosulf, Liq. (CooperVision)
W/Prednisolone.
See: Cetapred Ophthalmic Ointment (Alcon)
Vasocidin, Soln. (CooperVision)
W/Prednisolone acetate.
See: Blephamide S.O.P., Ophth. Oint. (Allergan)
Metimyd, Ophth. Oint. and Susp. (Schering)
W/Prednisolone, methylcellulose.
See: Isopto Cetapred, Susp. (Alcon)
W/Prednisolone acetate, phenylephrine.
See: Blephamide Liquifilm Ophth. Susp. (Allergan)
Tri-Ophtho, Ophth. Drops (Maurry)
W/Prednisolone phosphate.
See: Optimyd Sol., Sterile (Schering)
W/Prednisolone sodium phosphate, phenylephrine, sulfacetamide sodium.
Vasocidia Ophth. Sol. (CooperVision)
W/Sulfur.
See: Sulfacet-R, Lot. (Dermik)

SULFACETAMIDE, SULFADIAZINE, & SULFAMERAZINE ORAL SUSPENSION.
See: Acet-Dia-Mer-Sulfonamides.

SULFACET-R LOTION. (Dermik) Sodium sulfacetamide 10%, sulfur 5%, in flesh-tinted base. Bot. 25 Gm.
Use: Treatment of acne and seborrheic dermatitis.

SULFACHLORPYRIDAZINE. B.A.N. N[1]-(6-chloro-3-pyridazinyl) sulfanilamide.
See: Cosulid
Nefrosul, Tab. (Riker)

• **SULFACYTINE.** USAN. 4-(4-Aminobenzene-sulfonamido)-1-ethyl-1,2-dihydropyrimidin-2-one. 1-Ethyl-N-sulfanilylcytosine.
Use: Antibacterial.
See: Renoquid, Tab. (Parke-Davis)

SULFADIASULFONE SODIUM. Acetosulfone sodium.

• **SULFADIAZINE,** U.S.P. XXI.; Tab., U.S.P. XXI. 2-Sulfanilamidopyridine, N′-2-pyrimidinylsulfanilamide. Benzenesulfonamide, 4-amino-N-2-pyrimidi-nyl-.
Use: Antibacterial.
See: Microsulfon, Tab. (Consolid. Mid.)

SULFADIAZINE COMBINATIONS.
See: Acet-Dia-Mer-Sulfonamides. (Various Mfr.)
Amide, Preps. (Scrip)
Benegyn, Vag. Insert, Cream (North Am. Pharm.)
Buffonamide, Liq. (Reid-Provident)
Cetazine, Tab. (Bowman)
Chemozine, Tab., Susp. (Tennessee Pharm.)
Cherasulfa, Liq, Tab. (Cenci)
Chera-Sulfa Improved, Susp. (Sutliff & Case)
Chero-Trisulfa, Susp. (Vita Elixir)
Dia-Mer-Sulfonamides (Various Mfr.)
Dia-Mer-Thia-Sulfonamide (Various Mfr.)
Gynben, Cream, Inserts (ICN)
Gynben Insufflate, Pow. (ICN)
Lantrisul, Tab., Susp. (Lannett)
Meth-Dia-Mer-Sulfonamides (Various Mfr.)
Quadetts, Tab. (Elder)

Quad-Ramoid, Susp. (Elder)
Silvadene (Marion)
Suladyne (Reid-Provident)
Suladyne, Tab. (Stuart)
Sulfajen, Cream. (Jenkins)
Sulfaloid Suspension (Westerfield)
Sul-Trio, Preps. (Kay)
Terfonyl, Liq, Tab. (Squibb)
Triosulf, Tab. (Jenkins)
Triple Sulfa, Tab. (Various Mfr.)
Trisem, Tab., Susp. (Beecham Labs)
Trisuval, Tab. (Jalco)

ULFADIAZINE AND SULFAMERAZINE. Citrasulfas.
See: Dia-Mer-Sulfonamides

SULFADIAZINE SODIUM, U.S.P. XXI. Sterile Inj., U.S.P. XXI. Benzenesulfonamide, 4-amino-N-2-pyrimidinyl-, monosodium salt. N^1-2-Pyrimidinylsulfanilamide monosodium salt.
Use: Antibacterial.
'/Sod. bicarbonate.
(Pitman-Moore)—Tab. 5 gr., Bot. 1000s; 2.5 gr., Bot. 100s, 500s, 1000s.

ULFADIAZINE, SULFAMERAZINE & SULFACETAMIDE SUSPENSION.
See: Acet-Dia-Mer-Sulfonamides
Coco Diazine (Lilly)

ULFADIMETHOXINE. Sulphadi-methoxine, B.A.N. N′-(2,6-Dimethoxy-4-pyrimidinyl) sulfanilamide.
Use: Antibacterial.

ULFADIMETINE. N^1-(2-6-Dimethyl-4-pyrimidyl) sulfanilamide. Sulfisomidine. Elkosin (Ciba)

ULFADIMIDINE.
See: Sulfamethazine

ULFADINE.
See: Sulfadimidine
Sulfamethazine
Sulfapyridine, Tab. (Various Mfr.)

SULFADOXINE, U.S.P. XXI. N^1-(5,6-dimethoxy-4-pyrimidinyl) sulfanilamide. 4-(4-Aminobenzene-sulfonamido)-5,6-dimethoxypyrimidine. Fanasil Fanzil (Roche)
Use: Antibacterial sulfonamide.
'/Pyrimethamine.
See: Fansidar, Tab. (Roche)

SULFADOXINE AND PYRIMETHAMINE TABLETS, U.S.P. XXI.
Use: Antibacterial, antimalarial.

ULFAETHIDOLE. Sulphaethicole, B.A.N. Sulfaethylthiadiazole. N^1-(5-ethyl-1,3,4-thiadiazole-2-yl) sulfanilamide. Sulfaethylthiadiazole. Sethadil.
Use: Antibacterial.

ULFAETHYLTHIADIAZOLE.
See: Sulfaethidole.

ULFAFURAZOLE. B.A.N. 5-(4-Aminobenzene-sulphonamido)-3,4-dimethylisoxazole. Gantrisin. Sulphafurazole. Sulfisoxazole

ULFAGAN. (Zenith) Sulfisoxazole 500 mg./Tab. Bot. 100s.
Use: Anti-infective.

ULFAGUANIDINE. (N-Guanylsulfanilamide; Abiguanil; Ganidan; Guamide).
Use: G.I. tract infections.

W/Sulfacetamide, neomycin sulf., atropine methyl nitrate, carob flour.
See: Neogel W/Sulfa, Tab. (Vortech)
W/Sulfamethazine, sulfamerazine & sulfadiazine.
See: Quadetts, Tab. (Elder)
Quad-Ramoid, Susp. (Elder

SULFA-GYN. (Mayrand) Sulfathiazole 3.42%, sulfacetamide 2.86%, sulfabenzamide 3.70%, urea 0.64%. Tube 85 Gm.
Use: Triple sulfa cream.

SULFAJEN CREAM. (Jenkins) Sulfamerazine 0.167 Gm., sulfadiazine 0.167 Gm., sulfamethazine 0.167 Gm./5 cc. Bot. 3 oz., 4 oz., gal.
Use: Triple sulfonamide therapy.

• **SULFALENE.** USAN. N′-(3-Methoxypyrazinyl) sulfanilamide. Sulfametopyrazine, B.A.N.
Use: Antibacterial.
See: Kelfizina (Abbott)

SULFALOID SUSPENSION. (Forest) Sulfadiazine 167 mg., sulfamerazine 167 mg., sulfamethazine 167 mg./5 ml. Bot. 2 oz., 3 oz., 4 oz., 16 oz.
Use: Antibacterial.

SULFALOID TABLETS. (Forest) Meth-Dia-Mer-Sulfonamides. Tab. 0.5 Gm. (0.167 Gm. each). Bot. 100s.
Use: Antibacterial.

• **SULFAMERAZINE,** U.S.P. XXI. Tab., U.S.P. XXI. Benzenesulfonamide, 4-amino-N-(4-methyl-2-pyrimidinyl)-. N^1-(4-Methyl-2-pyrimidinyl)-sulfanilamide. (Sumedine)
Use: Infections caused by susceptible bacteria.

SULFAMERAZINE COMBINATIONS.
Use: Antibacterial.
See: Amide, Preps. (Scrip)
Cetazine, Tab. (Bowman)
Chemozine Tab., Susp. (Tennessee Pharm.)
Cherasulfa, Liq, Tab. (Cenci)
Chera-Sulfa Improved, Susp. (Sutliff & Case)
Chero-Trisulfa-V, Susp. (Vita Elixir)
Gelazine, Liq. (Mallard)
Lantrisol, Tab., Susp. (Lannett)
Quadetts, Tab. (Elder)
Quad-Ramoid, Susp. (Elder)
Sul-Trio, Preps. (Kay)
Terfonyl, Liq, Tab. (Squibb)
Triosulfon, Tab. (CMC)
Triple Sulfa, Tab. (Various Mfr.)

SULFAMERAZINE SODIUM.
Use: Antibacterial.

SULFAMERAZINE & SULFADIAZINE.
See: Dia-Mer-Sulfonamides.

SULFAMERAZINE, SULFADIAZINE & SULFAMETHAZINE.
Use: Antibacterial.
See: Meth-Dia-Mer-Sulfonamides

SULFAMERAZINE, SULFADIAZINE & SULFATHIAZOLE.
Use: Antibacterial.
See: Dia-Mer-Thia-Sulfonamides

• **SULFAMETER.** USAN. N^1(5-methoxy-2-pyrimidinyl)-sulfanilamide. 4-Amino-N-(5-methoxy-2-pyrimidinyl) benzenesulfonamide.

Use: Antibacterial.
See: Sulla, Tab. (Robins)

• **SULFAMETHAZINE,** U.S.P. XXI.
Benzenesulfonamide, 4-amino-N-(4,6-dimethyl-2-pyrimidinyl)-. 4,6-Dimethyl-2-sulfanilamidopyrimidine. NI-(4,6-Dimethyl-2-pyrimidinyl)sulfanilamide.
Use: Antibacterial.
See: Neotrizine, Susp., Tab. (Lilly)
W/Sulfacetamide, sulfadiazine, sulfamerazine.
See: Sulfa-Plex, Vaginal Cream (Rowell)
W/Sulfadiazine, sulfamerazine.
See: Lantrisul, Tab., Susp. (Lannett)
Sulfaloid, Susp. (Westerfield)
Terfonyl, Liq, Tab. (Squibb)
Triple Sulfa, Tab. (Var. Mfr.)
W/Sulfadiazine, sulfamerazine, sodium citrate.
See: Chera-Sulfa, Cab. (Century)
Cherasulfa, Liq. Tab. (Cenci)
Triple Sulfa, Susp. (Standex)

• **SULFAMETHIZOLE,** U.S.P. XXI. Oral Susp., Tab., U.S.P. XXI. N'-(5/Methyl-1,3,4-thiadiazole-2-yl)-sulfanilamide. Methisul, Mizol, Uolueosil. Sulphamethizole.
Use: Antibacterial.
See: Bursul, Tab. (Burlington)
Microsul, Tab. (Star)
Proklar-M, Liq., Tab. (Westerfield)
Sulfasol, Tab. (Hyrex-Key)
Sulfstat, Forte, Tab. (Saron)
Sulfurine, Tab. (Table Rock)
Thiosulfil, Forte, Tab. (Ayerst)
Urifon, Tab. (Amid)

SULFAMETHIZOLE W/COMBINATIONS.
Use: Antibacterial.
See: Azosul, Tab. (Reid-Provident)
Azo Sulfstat, Tab. (Saron)
Azotrex, Cap. (Bristol)
Microsul-A, Tab. (Star)
Signasul Azopak, Tab. (Amer. Urological)
Sulfasol Plus, Tab. (Hyrex-Key)
Thiosulfil-A, Tab. (Ayerst)
Thiosulfil-A Forte, Tab. (Ayerst)
Triurisul, Tab. (Sheryl)
Urobiotic, Cap. (Pfizer)
Uropeutic, Tab. (Circle)
Urotrol, Tab. (Mills)

SULFAMETHOMIDINE. (Warner-Lambert) N'-(6-methoxy-2-methyl-4-pyrimidinyl)sulfanilamide monohydrate.
Use: Antibacterial sulfonamide.

• **SULFAMETHOXAZOLE,** U.S.P. XXI. Oral Susp., Tab., U.S.P. XXI. Sulphamethoxazole, Methyl sulfanilamidoisoxazole. 5-Methyl-3-sulfanilamido-isoxazole. N'-(5-methyl-3-isoxazolyl) sulfanilamide.
Use: Antibacterial.
See: Gantanol, Prep. (Roche)
W/Trimethoprim.
See: Bactrim, Prods. (Roche)
Septra, Tab. (Burroughs Wellcome)
Septra DS, Tab. (Burroughs Wellcome)

SULFAMETHOXAZOLE AND PHENAZOPYRIDINE HCl.
Use: Urinary antibacterial.
See: Azo-Gantanol, Tab. (Roche)

• **SULFAMETHOXAZOLE AND TRIMETHOPRIM ORAL SUSPENSION,** U.S.P. XXI.
Use: Urinary antibacterial.

• **SULFAMETHOXAZOLE AND TRIMETHOPRIM TABLETS,** U.S.P. XXI.
Use: Urinary antibacterial.

SULFAMETHOXYDIAZINE. Sulfameter
Use: Antibacterial.
See: Sulla, Tab. (Robins)

SULFAMETHOXYPYRIDAZINE, B.A.N. N[1]-(6-Methox 3-pyridazinyl) sulfanilamide. 3-(4-Aminobenzenesi fonamido)-6-methoxypyridazine.
Use: Antibacterial.
See: Kynex.
Lederkyn.

SULFAMETHOXYPYRIDAZINE ACETYL.
Use: Antibacterial.

SULFAMETHYLTHIADIAZOLE.
Use: Antibacterial.
See: Sulfamethizole, Preps.

SULFAMETIN. N[1]-(5-Methoxy-2-pyrimidinyl)sulfanil mide. (Formerly sulfamethoxydiazine)
Use: Antibacterial.
See: Sulla, Tab. (Robins)

SULFAMETOPYRAZINE. B.A.N. 2-(4-Aminobenzenesulfonamido)-3-methoxypyrazine.
Use: Antibacterial.
See: Sulfalene (I.N.N.)
Kelfizine.

SULFAMEZANTHENE.
Use: Antibacterial.
See: Sulfamethazine

• **SULFAMONOMETHOXINE.** USAN. N[1]-(6-methoxy-4-pyrimidinyl) sulfanilamide.
Use: Antibacterial sulfonamide.

• **SULFAMOXOLE.** USAN. N'-(4,5-dimethyl-2-oxa-zoly sulfanilamide.
Use: Antibacterial.

p-SULFAMOYLBENZYLAMINE HCl. Sulfbenzamide.

SULFAMYLON CREAM. (Winthrop-Breon) Mafenid acetate equiv. to 85 mg. of base/Gm. W/cetyl alcohol, stearyl alcohol, cetyl esters wax, polyoxyl 40 stearate, polyoxyl 8 stearate, glycerin, water w/methylparaben and propylparaben, sodium metabisulfite, edetate disodium. Tube 2 oz., 4 oz. Can 14.5 oz.
Use: Adjunctive therapy in second and third-degre burns.

SULFANILAMIDE. p-Aminobenzenesulfonamide.
Use: Antibacterial.

SULFANILAMIDE COMBINATIONS.
Use: Antibacterial.
See: AVC/Dienestrol Cream, Supp. (Merrell Dow)
AVC, Cream, Supp. (Merrell Dow)
D.I.T.I. Cream (Kenyon)
Femguard, Vag. Cream (Reid-Provident)
K.D.C. Vaginal Cream (Kenyon)
Par Cream (Parmed)

Sulfem Vag. Cream (Federal Pharm.)
Tricholan, Vaginal Cream (Spencer-Mead)
Vagacreme, Cream (Delta)
Vagisan Creme (Sandia)
Vagisul, Creme (Sheryl)
Vagitrol, Cream, Suppos. (Lemmon)

•**SULFANILAMIDOPYRIDINE.** Sulfadiazine, U.S.P. XXI.
Use: Antibacterial.

SULFANILATE ZINC. USAN.
Use: Antibacterial.

•**SULFANILYLACETAMIDE.**
Use: Antibacterial.
See: Sulfacetamide, Tab. (Various Mfr.)

ULFANILYLBENZANIDE.
Use: Antibacterial.
See: Sulfabenzamide

SULFANITRAN. USAN. 4′-[(p-Nitrophenyl) sulfamoyl]-acetanilide.
Use: Antibacterial.

ULFAPHENAZOLE. Sulphaphenzaole, B.A.N. N′-(1-phenyl-5-pyrazolyl) sulfanilamide. 5-(4-Aminobenzenesulphonamido)-1-phenylpyrazole.
See: Orisulf (Ciba)

ULFAPRED. (Softcon) Prednisolone acetate 0.25%, sodium sulfacetamide 10%, phenylephrine HCl 0.125%, in a sterile buffered Methulose suspension w/methylparaben 0.04%, propylparaben 0.02%, propylene glycol, monobasic and dibasic sod. phosphate, sod. thiosulfate, polysorbate 80. Plas. Bot. 5 cc., 15 cc.
Use: Allergic and inflammatory diseases of the eye.

ULFAPYRAZOLE. B.A.N. N^1-(3-Methyl-1-phenyl-pyrazol-5-yl)sulfanilamide.
Use: Sulphonamide, veterinary medicine.
See: Vesulong.

SULFAPYRIDINE, U.S.P. XXI. Tab., U.S.P. XXI. Benzenesulfonamide, 4-amino-N-2-pyridinyl-. 2-Sulfanilamidopyridine. N′-2-Pyridylsulfanilamide. (Pfaltz & Bauer) Pow., Bot. 1 lb.
Use: Dermatitic herpetiformis suppressant.

ULFAQUINOXALINE.
See: S.Q. Preps (MSD AGVET)

ULFARSPHENAMINE. Disodium-[arsenobis[6-hydroxy-m-phenylene)imino]]-dimethanesulfonate.

SULFASALAZINE, U.S.P. XXI. Tab., U.S.P. XXI. 5-[[p-(2-Pyridylsulfamoyl)-phenyl]azo]salicylic acid. 4-Hydroxy-4′-(2-pyridylsulfamoyl)azobenzene-3-carboxylic acid. Sulphasalazine, B.A.N.
Use: Antibacterial.
See: Azulfidine, Tab., Susp. (Pharmacia)
Salazopyrin.
Salicylazosulfapyridine.
Salazopyrin.
S.A.S.-50, Tab. (Rowell).
S.A.S.P., Tab. (Zenith)
Sulcolon, Tab. (Lederle)
Sulfapyridine (I.N.N.)

SULFASOMIZOLE. USAN. 5-(4-Aminobenzenesulfonamido)-3-methylisothiazole. N′-(3-methylisothiazolyl)sulfanilamide.
Use: Antibacterial sulfonamide.
See: Bidizole.

SULFASOX. (Bowman) Sulfasoxazole 500 mg./Tab. Bot. 100s, 1000s.
Use: Treatment of urinary tract infections.

SULFASYMASINE. N′-(4,6-Diethyl-S-triazin-2-yl) sulfanilamide.
Use: Antibacterial sulfonamide.

SULFA-TER-TABLETS. (A.P.C.) Trisulfapyrimidines, U.S.P. Bot. 1000s.

• **SULFATHIAZOLE,** U.S.P. XXI. Benzenesulfonamide, 4-amino-N-2-thiazolyl-N′-2-Thiazolylsulfanilamide. 2-Sulfanilamidothiazole.
Use: Antibacterial.
W/Chlorophyllin.
See: Thiaphyll Cr. (Lannett)

SULFATHIAZOLE COMBINATIONS.
See: Sultrin, Tab. & Cream (Ortho)

SULFATHIAZOLE CARBAMIDE.
See: Otosmosan, Liq. (Ayerst)

• **SULFATHIAZOLE, SULFACETAMIDE, AND SULFABENZAMIDE VAGINAL CREAM,** U.S.P. XXI.
Use: Antibacterial.

• **SULFATHIAZOLE, SULFACETAMIDE, AND SULFABENZAMIDE VAGINAL TABLETS,** U.S.P. XXI.
Use: Antibacterial.

SULFATRIM DS TABS. (Goldline) Trimeth 800 mg., sulfameth 160 mg./Tab. Bot. 100s, 500s.
Use: Antibiotic.

SULFATRIM SS TABS. (Goldline) Trimeth 400 mg., sulfameth 80 mg./Tab. Bot. 100s.
Use: Antibiotic.

SULFA TRIPLE NO. 2. (Richlyn) Sulfadiazine 162 mg., sulfamerizine 162 mg., sulfamethazine 162 mg./Tab. Bot. 1000s.
Use: Antibacterial.

• **SULFAZAMET.** USAN. N′-(3-Methyl-1-phenylpyrazol-5-yl) sulfanilamide.
Use: Antibacterial.
See: Vesulong (Ciba)

SULFBENZAMINE HYDROCHLORIDE. Mafenide HCl p-Methylaminophenyl sulfonamide HCl. Pow., Bulk.
Use: Bacteriostatic.

SULFEM VAGINAL CREAM. (Amfre-Grant) Sulfanilamide 15%, 9-aminoacridine HCl 0.2%, allantoin 1.5%. Tube 4 oz. W/applicator.
Use: Antibacterial and antifungal.

SULFHYDRYL ION.
See: Hydrosulphosol (Lientz)

• **SULFINALOL HYDROCHLORIDE.** USAN.
Use: Antihypertensive.

• **SULFINPYRAZONE,** U.S.P. XXI. Caps., Tab., U.S.P. XXI. 1,2-Diphenyl-4-(2-phenylsulphinylethyl)pyrazolidine-3,5-dione. 1,2-Diphenyl-4-(2-phenylsulfinylethyl-3,5-pyrazolidine-dione. Sulphinpyrazone, B.A.N.
Use: Uricosuric.
See: Anturane, Tab., Cap. (Ciba)

SULFISOMIDINE. Sulfadimetine. Sulphasomidine, B.A.N.

SULFISOXAZOLE. (Purepac) Sulfisoxazole 0.5 Gm./Tab. Bot. 100s, 1000s.
Use: Urinary tract infections.

• **SULFISOXAZOLE,** U.S.P. XXI. Tab., U.S.P. XXI. N'-(3,4-Dimethyl-5-isoxazolyl)sulfaniamide.
Use: Anti-infective sulfa.
See: Barazole, Tab. (Barry Martin)
Gantrisin Preps. (Roche)
G-Sox, Tab. (Scrip)
Rosoxol, Tab. (Robinson)
SK-Soxazole, Cap. (SmithKline)
Soxa, Tab. (Vita Elixir)
Sulfagan, Tab. (Zenith)
Sulfisoxazole, Tab. (Purepac)
Sulfium, Ophthalmic, Sol., Oint. (Alcon)
Sulfizin, Tab. (Reid-Provident)
Velmatrol, Tab. (Kenyon)
W/Aminoacridine HCl, allantoin.
See: Vagilia, Cream (Lemmon)
W/Phenazopyridine.
See: Azo-Gantrisin, Tab. (Roche)
Azo-Soxazole, Tab. (Quality Generics)
Azo-Sulfisoxazole, Tab. (Richlyn; Century)
Azo-Urizole, Tab. (Jenkins)
Barazole-Azo, Tab. (Barry Martin)
Rosoxol-Azo, Tab. (Robinson)
Soxazo, Tab. (Sutliff & Case)
Suldiazo, Tab. (Kay)
W/Phenylazodiaminopyridine HCl.
See: Azo-sulfisoxazole, Tab. (Vortech)
Azo-Sulfizin (Reid-Provident)
Velmatrol-A Tab. (Kenyon)

• **SULFISOXAZOLE, ACETYL,** U.S.P. XXI. Oral Susp., U.S.P. XXI. Acetamide, N-(4-amino-phenyl)sulfonyl-N-(3,4-dimethyl-5-isoxazolyl)-. N-(3,4-Dimethyl-5-isoxazolyl)-N-sulfanilylacetamide.
Use: Antibacterial.
See: Gantrisin Acetyl, Preps. (Roche)
W/Erythromycin Ethylsuccinate.
See: Pediazol, Susp. (Ross)

SULFISOXAZOLE DIETHANOLAMINE. Sulfisoxazole Diolamine.

• **SULFISOXAZOLE DIOLAMINE.** U.S.P. XXI. Inj., Ophth. Oint, Ophth. Sol. U.S.P. XXI. 2,2'-Iminodiethanol salt of N[1]-(3,4-Dimethyl-5-isoxazolyl)sulfanilamide compound with 2,2'-iminodiethanol(1:1). Gantrisin diolamine.
Use: Antibacterial.
See: Gantrisin, Ophth. Sol. & Oint. (Roche)

• **SULFOBROMOPHTHALEIN SODIUM,** U.S.P. XXI. Inj., U.S.P. XXI.
Use: Liver function test.

SULFOCARBOLATES. Salts of Phenolsulfonic Acid, Usually Ca, Na, K, Cu, Zn.

SULFOCYANATE.
See: Potassium Thiocyanate.

SULFO-GANIC. (Marcen) Thioglycerol 20 mg., sod. citrate 5 mg., phenol 0.5%, benzyl alcohol 0.5%/cc. Vial 10 cc., 30 cc.
Use: I.M., adjunctive treatment in arthritides due to sulfur metabolism disorders or deficiencies.

SULFOGUAIACOL.
See: Pot. Guaiacolsulfonate

SULFOIL. (C & M Pharmacal) Sulfonated castor oil, water. Bot. pt., Gal.
Use: Soap free cleanser for skin and hair.

SULFO-LO. (Whorton) Sublimed sulfur, freshly preci tated polysulfides of zinc, potassium, sulfate, and calamine in aqueous-alcoholic suspension. **Lotic** Bot. 4 oz., 8 oz., **Soap:** 3 oz.
Use: Treatment of acne.

SULFOMYL. Mafenide, B.A.N.

• **SULFOMYXIN.** USAN.
Use: Antibacterial.

SULFONAMIDE, DOUBLES.
See: Dia-Mer-Sulfonamides

SULFONAMIDE PREPS.
See: Acet-Dia-Mer (Various Mfr.)
Dia-Mer Sulfonamides (Various Mfr.)
Dia-Mer-Thia (Various Mfr.)
Meth-Dia-Mer, Preps. (Various Mfr.)

SULFONAMIDES, VETERINARY USE.
See: S.Q. (Merck Animal Health)
Sulfabrom (Merck Animal Health)
Sulfastrep w/streptomycin (Merck Animal Healt
Sulfathalidine (Merck Animal Health)
Sul-Thi-Zol (Merck Animal Health)

SULFONAMIDES, QUADRUPLE.
See: Quadetts, Tab. (Elder)
Quad-Ramoid, Susp. (Elder)

SULFONAMIDES, TRIPLE.
See: Acet-Dia-Mer Sulfonamides
Dia-Mer-Thia Sulfonamides
Meth-Dia-Mer Sulfonamides

SULFONES.
See: Avlosulfon, Tab. (Ayerst)
Dapsone
Diasone, Enterabs (Abbott)
Glucosulfone Sodium
Promacetin, Tab. (Parke-Davis)

SULFONETHYLMETHANE. 2,2-Bis-(ethylsulfonyl)b tane.

SULFONITHOCHOLYLGLYCINE.
See: S.L.C.G., Kit (Abbott)

SULFONMETHANE. 2,2-Bis(ethylsulfonyl)propane.

SULFONPHTHAL.
See: Phenolsulfonphthalein, Prep. (Various Mfr.)

• **SULFONTEROL HYDROCHLORIDE.** USAN.
Use: Bronchodilator.

4,4'-SULFONYLDIANILINE. Dapsone, U.S.P. XXI.

SULFONYLUREAS.
See: Diabinese, Tab. (Pfizer)
Dymelor, Tab. (Lilly)
Orinase, Tab., Vial (Upjohn)
Tolinase, Tab. (Upjohn)

SULFORCIN LOTION. (Owen) Sulfur 5%, resorcinol 2%, alcohol 11.65%, methylparaben. Bot. 4 oz., 1 oz.
Use: For acne, seborrheic dermatitis & oily skin conditions.

SULFORMETHOXINE. Name used for Sulfadoxine.

SULFORTHOMIDINE. Name used for Sulfadoxine.

JLFOSALICYLATE W/Methenamine
See: Hexalet, Tab. (Webcon)
JLFOSALYCYLIC ACID. Salicylsulphonic acid.
SULFOXONE SODIUM, U.S.P. XXI. Tab., U.S.P. XXI.
JLFOXYL LOTION REGULAR. (Stiefel) Benzoyl peroxide 5%, sulfur 2% Bot. 2 oz.
Use: Acne treatment.
JLFOXYL LOTION STRONG. (Stiefel) Benzoyl peroxide 10%, sulfur 5% Bot. 2 oz.
Use: Acne treatment.
JLFUR-8 HAIR & SCALP CONDITIONER. (Plough) Sulfur 2%, menthol 1%, triclosan 0.1%. Jar 2 oz., 4 oz., 8 oz.
Use: Antiseborrheic.
JLFUR-8 LIGHT FORMULA HAIR & SCALP CONDITIONER. (Plough) Sulfur, triclosan, menthol. Jar 2 oz., 4 oz.
Use: Antiseborrheic.
JLFUR-8 SHAMPOO. (Plough) Triclosan 0.2%. Bot. 6 oz., 12 oz.
Use: Antiseborrheic.
JLFUR, ANTIARTHRITIC.
See: Thiocyl, Amp. (Torigian)
SULFURATED LIME TOPICAL SOLUTION, U.S.P. XXI. Vleminckx Lotion.
Use: Scabicide, parasiticide.
SULFUR COMBINATIONS.
See: Acnaveen, Bar (Cooper)
Acne-Aid, Cream, Lot. (Stiefel)
Acnederm, Liq. (Lannett)
Akne Oral Kapsulets, Cap. (Alto)
Acnomel, Cake, Cream. (Menley & James)
Acno, Sol., Lot. (Cummins)
Acnotex, Liq. (C&M Pharm.)
Akne, Drying Lot. (Alto)
Antrocol, Tab., Cap. (Poythress)
Aracain Rectal Oint. (Commerce)
Clearasil, Stick (Vicks)
Derma Cover-HC, Liq. (Scrip)
Epi-clear, Lotion (Squibb)
Exzit, Preps. (Miles Pharm)
Fomac, Cream (Dermik)
Fostex, Liq. Cream, Bar (Westwood)
Fostex, Cream, Liq. (Westwood)
Fostex CM, Cream (Westwood)
Fostril, Cream (Westwood)
Furol Cream (Torch)
Hydro Surco, Lot. (Almo)
Klaron, Lot. (Dermik)
Liquimat, Liq. (Owen)
Lotio-P (Alto)
Neutrogena Disposables (Neutrogena)
Pernox, Lot. (Westwood)
pHisoDan, Liq. (Winthrop Consumer Products)
Postacne, Lot. (Dermik)
Pragmatar, Oint. (Menley & James)
Proseca, Liq. (Westwood)
Rezamid, Lot. (Dermik)
Sastid Soap (Stiefel)
Sebaveen, Shampoo (Cooper)
Sebulex Shampoo, Liq. (Westwood)
Sulfacet-R, Lot. (Dermik)
Sulfo-lo, Lot. (Wharton)
Sulforcin, Pow., Lot. (Owen)
Sulfur-8, Prods. (Plough)
Teenac, Cream (Elder)
Thera-Blem, Cream (Noxell)
Vanseb, Cream (Herbert)
Vanseb-T Tar Shampoo (Herbert)
Xerac, Oint. (Person & Covey)
• **SULFUR DIOXIDE,** N.F. XVI.
Use: Antixodant, pharmaceutic aid.
• **SULFUR OINTMENT,** U.S.P. XXI.
Use: Scabicide, parasiticide.
• **SULFUR, PRECIPITATED,** U.S.P. XXI.
Use: Scabicide; parasiticide.
See: Bensulfoid, Pow., Lot. (Poythress)
Epi-Clear, Lot. (Squibb)
Ramsdell's Sulfur Cream (Fougera)
Sulfur Soap (Steifel Labs)
SULFUR, SALICYL DIASPORAL. (Doak)
See: Diasporal, Cream (Doak)
SULFUR SOAP. (Stiefel) Precipitated sulfur 10%. Cake 4.1 oz.
Use: Acne treatment.
• **SULFUR, SUBLIMED,** U.S.P. XXI. Flowers of Sulfur.
Use: Parasiticide, scabicide.
SULFUR, TOPICAL.
See: Thylox, Liq., Soap (Dent)
• **SULFURIC ACID,** N.F. XVI.
Use: Pharmaceutic aid (acidifying agent).
SULFURINE. (Table Rock) Sulfamethizole 0.5 Gm./Tab. Bot. 100s & 500s.
Use: Treatment of urinary infections.
SULGLYCOTIDE. B.A.N. The sulfuric polyester of a glycopeptide isolated from pig duodenum.
Use: Treatment of peptic ulcer.
See: Gliptide (sodium salt)
• **SULINDAC,** U.S.P. XXI. Tab., U.S.P. XXI.
Use: Anti-inflammatory.
See: Clinoril Tab. (Merck Sharp & Dohme)
• **SULISOBENZONE.** USAN. 5-Benzoyl-4-hydroxy-2-methoxybenzenesulfonic acid.
Use: Sunscreen agent.
See: Uval Lotion (Dorsey)
Uvinul MS-40 (General Aniline & Film)
• **SULMARIN.** USAN.
Use: Hemostatic.
SULNAC. (NMC Labs) Sulfathiazol 3.42%, sulfacetamide 2.86%, sulfabenzamide 3.7%, urea 0.64% in cream base. Tube 2.75 oz.
Use: Treatment of hemophilus vaginal vaginitis.
• **SULNIDAZOLE.** USAN.
Use: Antiprotozoal.
SULOCARBILATE. 2-Hydroxyethyl-p-sulfamylcarbanilate.
• **SULOCTIDIL.** USAN.
Use: Vasodilator.
• **SULOXIFEN OXALATE.** USAN.
Use: Bronchodilator.
SULOXYBENZONE. 4-p-Anisoyl-3-hydroxybenzene sulfonic acid. 2-Hydroxy-4′-methoxy-5-sulfobenzophenone. Cyasorb UV 284 (Lederle)

SULPHABENZIDE.
See: Sulfabenzamide

SULPHALOXIC ACID. B.A.N. 4′-[(Hydroxymethylcarbamoyl)sulfamoyl]phthalanilic acid.
See: Enteromide calcium salt.

SULPHAMETHOXYDIAZINE. B.A.N. 2-p-Aminobenzenesulphonamido-5-methoxypyrimidine, 5-Methoxy-2-sulphanilamidopyrimidine Durenate.

SULPHAMOPRINE. B.A.N. 2-(4-Aminobenzenesulfonamido)-4,6-dimethoxypyrimidine.

SULPHAMOXOLE. B.A.N. 2-(4-Aminobenzenesulfonamido)-4,5-dimethyloxazole.
See: Nuprin.

SULPHAN BLUE. B.A.N. Sodium 4-(4-diethylaminobenzylidene)cyclohexa-2,5-dienylidenediethylammonium -α-benzene-2,4-disulfonate.
Use: Investigation of the cardiovascular system.
See: Blue VRS
Disulphine Blue VNS

SULPHAPROXYLINE. B.A.N. N^1-(4-Isopropoxybenzoyl)-4-aminobenzenesulfonamide.

SULPHASOMIDINE. B.A.N. 4-(4-Aminobenzenesulfonamido)-2,6-dimethylpyrimidine.
See: Sulfisomidine (I.N.N.)
Elkosin.

SULPHATHIOUREA. B.A.N. 4-Aminobenzenesulfonylthiourea.
See: Badional.

SULPHATOLAMIDE. B.A.N. 4-Aminobenzenesulphonylthiourea salt of α-amino-p-toluenesulfonamide.
See: Marbadal

SULPHAUREA. B.A.N. 4-Aminobenzesulfonylurea.
See: Euvernil
Sulfacarbamide (I.N.N.)

SULPHETRONE. Solapsone, B.A.N.

SULPHOMYXIN. Penta-(N-sulphomethyl) polymyxin B.

SULPHOMYXIN SODIUM. B.A.N. A mixture of sulfomethylated polymyxin B and sodium bisulfite.
Use: Antibiotic.
See: Thiosporin.

SULPHRIN SUSPENSION. (Muro) Sodium sulfacetamide 100 mg., prednisolone acetate 5 mg., phenylephrine HCl 0.12% Bot. 5 ml.
Use: Antibacterial and anti-inflammatory.

SULPIK. (Durel) Sulfur 5%, salicylic acid 3%, in Duromantel cream.
Use: Superficial tinea infections, seborrheic dermatitis.

SULPIK T. (Durel) Sulfur 5%, salicylic acid 3%, LCD (coal tar solution) 3%. In Duromantel Cream.
Use: Superficial tinea, infections, non-exudative forms of seborrheic dermatitis.

• **SULPIRIDE.** USAN. (1) N-[(1-ethyl-2-pyrrolidinyl)methyl]-5-sulfamoyl-o-anisamide; (2) N-[(Ethyl-1-pyrrolidinyl-2)-methyl]methoxy-2-sulfamoyl-5-benzamide. Dogmatyl (Laboratories Delagrange, France).
Use: Antidepressant.

• **SULPROSTONE.** USAN.
Use: Prostaglandin.

SUL-RAY ACNE CREAM. (Last) Sulfur 2% in cream base. Jars 1.75 oz., 6.75 oz., 20 oz.
Use: Acne medication.

SUL-RAY SHAMPOO. (Last) Sulfur shampoo 2%. Bot 8 oz.
Use: Medicated shampoo for dandruff.

SUL-RAY SOAP. (Last) Sulfur soap. Bar 3 oz.
Use: Acne medication.

• **SULTAMICILLIN.** USAN.
Use: Antibacterial.

SULTEN-10. (Muro) Sodium sulfacetamide 10%. Bot 1 ml.
Use: Opthalmic antibacteria.

• **SULTHIAME.** USAN. Formerly Sulphenytame. p-(Tetrahydro-2H-1,2-thiazin-2-yl)-benzenesulfonamide-S,-dioxide.
Use: Anticonvulsant.

SULTRIN Triple Sulfa Vaginal Tablets. (Ortho) Sulfathiazole 172.5 mg., sulfacetamide 143.75 mg., sulfabenzamide 184 mg./Vag. Tab. Pkg. 20s w/appl.
Use: Treatment of *H. vaginalis* (Gardnerella) vaginitis.

SULTRIN Triple Sulfa Cream. (Ortho) Sulfathiazole 3.42%, sulfacetamide 2.86%, sulfabenzamide 3.7%, urea 0.64%. Tube 78 Gm. with measured dose applicator.
Use: Treatment of *H. vaginalis* (Gardnerella) vaginitis.

SUL-TRIO. (Kay) Sulfadiazine 166 mg., sulfamerazine 166 mg., sulfamethazine 166 mg./5 cc. Bot. pt., gal.

SUL-TRIO MM. (Kay) Sulfadiazine 167 mg., sulfamethazine 167 mg., sulfamerazine 167 mg./Tab. Bot. 1000s.

SULVESOR LOTION. (Durel) Sulfur 2%, resorcinol 1%, neocalamine, talc, titanium dioxide, alcohol 34%. 2 oz., 4 oz., gal.
Use: Antifungal, antibacterial, keratolytic antiseborrheic.

SUMMER'S EVE DISPOSABLE DOUCHE. (Fleet) Single or twin 4.5 oz. disposable units. Regular, herbal, vinegar & water.
Use: Cleansing douche.

SUMMER'S EVE MEDICATED DISPOSABLE DOUCHE. (Fleet) Contains povidone-iodide. Single or twin 4.5 oz. disposable units.
Use: Temporary relief of minor vaginal irritation and itching.

SUMMER'S EVE VAGINAL SUPPOSITORIES. (Fleet) Box 10s w/applicator.
Use: Feminine suppository.

SUMOX. (Reid-Provident) Amoxicillin. **Cap.:** 250 mg Bot. 100s. **Pow. for oral sus.:** 125 mg./5ml. Bot. 80 cc.; 250 mg./5 ml 80 cc.
Use: Antibiotic.

SUMSCREEN. (Summers) Red petrolatum. Tube 100 Gm.
Use: Sunscreen.

SUMYCIN. (Squibb) Tetracycline HCl. **Cap.** 250 mg./Cap. Bot. 100s, 1000s. Unimatic 100s. 500 mg./Cap. Bot. 100s, 500s. Unimatic 100s. **Syr.** 125 mg., 500 mg./5 ml. Bot. 60 cc., 1 pt. **Tab.** 250 mg./Tab. Bot. 100s, 1000s. 500 mg./Tab. Bot. 100s, 500s.
Use: Antibiotic.

JNBURN REMEDY.
See: Solarcaine, Prods. (Plough)

SUNCILLIN SODIUM. USAN. 3,3-Dimethyl-7-oxo-6-[2-phenyl-D-2-(sulfoamino)acetamido]-4-thia-1-azabicyclo[3.2.0]heptane-2-carboxylic acid disodium salt.
Use: Antibacterial.

JNDOWN. (Johnson & Johnson) A series of products marketed under the Sundown name including: **Moderate** (SPF 4) padimate O 3.3%.; **Extra** (SPF 6) padimate O 3.3%, oxybenzone 1.0%; **Maximal** (SPF 8) padimate O 4.75, oxybenzone 1.75%; **Ultra** (SPF 15) padimate O 6.5%, oxybenzone 3%. Bot. 4 oz.
Use: Prevention of sunburn (sunscreen).

JNDOWN SUNBLOCK STICK. (Johnson & Johnson) Octyl dimethyl PABA 7%, oxybenzone 3%. Stick 0.35 oz.
Use: Prevention of sunburn.

JNDOWN SUNSCREEN STICK. (Johnson & Johnson) Octyl Dimethyl PABA 5.3%, oxybenzone 1.75%. Stick 0.35 oz.
Use: Prevention of sunburn.

JNICE. (Citroleum) Allantoin 0.25%, menthol 0.25%, methyl salicylate 10%/Cream. 3 oz.
Use: Burn remedy.

JNRIL. (Emko-Schering) Acetaminophen 300 mg., pamabrom 50 mg., pyrilamine maleate 25 mg./Cap. Bot. 100s.
Use: Premenstrual tension.

JNSTICK. (Rydell) Lipand face protectant containing digalloyl trioleate 2.5%in emollient base. Plas. swivel container 0.14 oz.
Use: Prevention & relief of chapping and sunburning of lips.

JPAC. (Mission) Acetaminophen 160 mg., aspirin 230 mg., caffeine 33 mg., calcium gluconate 60 mg./Tab. Filmstrips 24s, Bot. 100s, 1000s.
Use: Analgesic.

JPER AFKO-HIST. (APC) Chlorpheniramine maleate 2 mg., aspirin 230 mg., phenacetin 160 mg., caffeine 32 mg./Tab. Bot. 1000s.
Use: Antihistamine, analgesic, antipyretic.

JPER-ANAHIST. (Warner-Lambert) Acetaminophen 325 mg., pseudoephedrine HCl 30 mg./Tab. Blister Pack 30s.
Use: Decongestant, analgesic.

JPER AYTINAL TABLETS. (Walgreen) Vit. A 7,000 I.U., B-1 5 mg., B-2 5 mg., B-5 10 mg., B-6 3 mg., B-12 9 mcg., C 90 mg., pantothenic acid 10 mg., D 400 I.U., E 30 I.U., niacin 30 mg., biotin 55 mcg., folic acid 0.4 mg., iron 30 mg., Ca 162 mg., P 125 mg., iodine 150 mcg., Cu 3 mg., Mn 7.5 mg., Mg 100 mg., K 7.7 mg., Zn 24 mg., Chloride 7 mg., Cr 15 mcg., Se 15 mcg., Mo 15 mcg., choline bitartrate 1000 mcg., inositol 1000 mcg., PABA 1000 mcg., rutin 1000 mcg., yeast 12 mg. Bot. 50s, 100s, 365s.
Use: Multiple vitamins with minerals.

JPER-B. (Towne) Vit. B-1 50 mg., B-2 20 mg., B-6 5 mg., B-12 15 mcg., C 300 mg., liver desic. 100 mg., dried yeast 100 mg., niacinamide 25 mg., Ca pantothenate 5 mg., iron 10 mg./Captab. Bot. 50s, 100s, 150s, 250s.

SUPER B KAPSULES. (Pharmex) High potency Vit. B. Cap. Bot. 50s, 100s.

SUPER C-1000. (Pharmex) Vit. C 1000 mg./Tab. Bot. 100s.

SUPERCITIN SUGAR-FREE. (Vitarine) Dextromethorphan HBr 20 mg., chlorpheniramine maleate 2 mg., sod. citrate 100 mg., acetaminophen 120 mg./10 cc. Bot. 4 oz.
Use: Cough syrup.

SUPER D. (Upjohn) Vit. A 10,000 I.U., D 400 I.U./Perle. Bot. 100s.
Use: Vitamin A & D therapy.

SUPER-DECON COLD CAPSULES. (Vitarine) Salicylamide 250 mg., phenylephrine HCl 5 mg., C 50 mg., caffeine 32 mg./Cap. Vial 15s.
Use: Decongestant, antihistaminic, analgesic.

SUPER DOSS. (Ferndale) Brewer's yeast 210 mg., docusate sodium 120 mg./Tab. Bot. 100s, 1000s.
Use: Constipation.

SUPERE-PECT. (Barth's) Alpha tocopherol 400 I.U., apple pectin 100 mg./Cap. Bot. 50s, 100s, 250s.
Use: Vitamin E supplement.

SUPER "HISTA-C" CAPSULES. (Eckerd) Dextromethorphan H Br 10 mg., phenylpropanolamine HCl 12.5 mg., pyrilamine maleate 12.5 mg., acetaminophen 325 mg./Cap. Bot. 24s.
Use: Cough and cold symptoms.

SUPER "HISTA-C" SYRUP. (Eckerd) Dextromethorphan H Br 10 mg., phenylpropanolamine HCl 12.5 mg., acetaminophen 195 mg., chlorpheniramine maleate 0.66 mg./5 ml. Bot. 4 oz., 8 oz.
Use: Treatment of cough and cold symptoms.

SUPER HYDRAMIN PROTEIN POWDER. (Nion) Protein 65%, carbohydrate 21.8%, fat 1% in powder form. Cans 1 lb.
Use: Dietary supplement.

SUPER K-B-T TABLETS. (Quality Generics) Vit. B-6 50 mg., soya lecithin 1200 mg., kelp 100 mg., dry cider vinegar 240 mg./3 Tabs. Bot. 100s, 250s.

SUPERINONE. Tyloxapol.
See: Triton WR-1339 (Rohm & Haas)

SUPER MANIVIM. (Vitarine) Vit. A 33,000 I.U., D 1600 I.U., E 3.3 I.U., B-1 25 mg., B-2 12 mg., B-6 1.2 mg., B-12 25 mcg., C 150 mg., niacinamide 75 mg., cal. pantothenate 3 mg., biotin 2 mcg., cal. carbonate 100 mg., ferrous gluconate 30 mg., pot. iodide 0.15 mg., Mg sulfate 7.2 mg., Cu sulfate 5 mg., Mn sulfate 3.4 mg., pot. chloride 6.6 mg., Zn sulfate 3.2 mg., amino acids, nutrient, natural and other factors/Cap. Bot. 30s, 100s, 250s.
Use: Diet supplement, convalescence.

SUPER MANIVIM-FORMULA #46. (Vitarine) Multivitamin & multimineral supplement for adults.
Use: Dietary supplement.

SUPER NUTRI-VITES. (Faraday) Vit. A 36,000 I.U., D 400 I.U., B-1 25 mg., B-2 25 mg., B-6 50 mg., B-12 50 mcg., niacinamide 50 mg., Ca pantothenate 12.5 mg., choline bitartrate 150 mg., inositol 150 mg., betaine HCl 25 mg., PABA 15 mg., glutamic acid 25 mg., desic. liver 50 mg., C 150 mg., E 12.5 I.U., Mn gluconate 6.15 mg., bone meal 162 mg., Fe gluconate 50 mg., Cu gluconate 0.25 mg., Zn gluconate 2.2 mg., K iodide 0.1 mg., Ca 53.3 mg., P 24.3 mg., Mg gluconate 7.2 mg./Protein Coated Tab. Bot. 60s, 100s.

SUPER PLENAMINS MULTIPLE VITAMINS AND MINERALS. (Rexall) Vit. A 8000 I.U., D-2 400 I.U., Vit. B-1 2.5 mg., B-2 2.5 mg., C 75 mg., niacinamide 20 mg., B-6 1.0 mg., B-12 3.0 mcg., biotin 20 mcg., E 10 I.U., pantothenic acid 3.0 mg., liver conc. 100 mg., Fe 30 mg., Ca 75 mg., P 58 mg., Iodine 0.15 mg., Cu 0.75 mg., Mn 1.25 mg., Mg 10.0 mg., Zn 1.0 mg./Tab. Bot. 36s, 72s, 144s, 288s, 365s.
Use: Multivitamin with minerals.

SUPER POLI-GRIP/WERNET'S CREAM (Block) Carboxymethylcellulose gum, ethylene oxide polymer, petrolatum-mineral oil base. Tube 0.7, 1.4, 2.4 oz.
Use: Denture adhesive cream.

SUPPER STRESS. (Towne) Vit. C 600 mg., E 30 I.U. B-1 15 mg., B-2 15 mg., niacin 100 mg., B-6 5 mg., B-12 12 mcg., pantothenic acid 20 mg./Tab. Bot. 60s.
Use: Dietary supplement.

SUPPER STRESS PLUS IRON. (Towne) Vit. C 600 mg., E 30 I.U., B-1 15 mg., niacin 100 mg., B-6 5 mg., B-12 12 mcg., pantothenic acid 20 mg., folic acid 0.4 mg., iron 27 mg./Tab. Bot. 60s.
Use: Dietary supplement.

SUPER-T. (Towne) Vit. A palmitate 10,000 I.U., D 400 I.U., B-1 10 mg., B-2 10 mg., B-6 1 mg., B-12 6 mcg., C 200 mg., niacinamide 100 mg., Vit. E 15 I.U., Ca 103 mg., P 80 mg., Fe 10 mg., Iodine 0.1 mg., Cu 1 mg., K 5 mg., Mg 5.5 mg., Mn 1 mg., Zn 1.4 mg./Captab. Bot. 100s, 130s.

SUPER TETRO. (Wisconsin) Bot. 4 oz., 8 oz., gal.
Use: Cleanser.

SUPER THERA 46. (Faraday) Vit. A 36,000 I.U., essential vitamins, minerals, amino acids w/nutrient factors, digestive enzymes, B-12 25 mcg./Tab. Bot. 100s.

SUPER TROCHE. (Weeks & Leo) Benzocaine 5 mg., cetalkonium Cl 1 mg./Lozenge. Bot. 15s, 30s.
Use: Relief of minor sore throat & irritation.

SUPER TROCHE PLUS. (Weeks & Leo) Benzocaine 10 mg., cetalkonium Cl. 2 mg./Loz. Bot. 12s.
Use: Relief of minor sore throat & irritation.

SUPER-T WITH ZINC. (Towne) Vit. A 10,000 I.U., D 400 I.U., E 15 I.U., C 200 mg., B-1 10 mg., B-2 10 mg., B-6 5 mg., B-12 6 mcg., niacinamide 50 mg., iron 18 mg., iodine 0.1 mg., copper 2 mg., manganese 1 mg., zinc 15 mg./Cap. Bot. 130s.
Use: Dietary supplement.

SUPERVIM TABLETS. (U.S. Ethicals) Vitamins and minerals Bot. 100s.
Use: Multiple vitamin/mineral supplement.

SUPER WERNET'S POWDER. (Block) Carboxymethylcellulose gum, ethylene oxide polymer. Bot. 0.63, 1.75, 3.55 oz.
Use: Denture adhesive.

SUPER WESVITE. (Western Research) Vit. A 10,000 I.U., B-1 15 mg., B-2 15 mg., B-6 25 mg., B-12 25 mcg., C 100 mg., D 400 I.U., Vit. E 30 I.U., biotin 500 mcg., Ca 100 mg., Ca pantothenate 25 Gm., choline bitartrate 10 mg., lemon bioflavonoids 10 mg., copper 2 mg., pantothenic acid 25 mg., inositol 20 mg., iron 20 mg., magnesium 50 mg., folic acid 400 mcg., hesperidin complex 10 mg., rutin 20 mg., potassium 25 mg., molybdenum 100 mcg., manganese 6 mg., niacin 40 mg., para-amino benzoic acid 8 mg., phosphorus 52 mg., potassium iodide 0.1 mg., zinc 5 mg., iodine 100 mcg./Tab. Bot. 1000s.
Use: Vitamin-mineral and amino acid supplement.

SUPLEX. (Rocky Mtn.) Vit. B-1 100 mg., B-2 2 mg., B-6 4 mg., niacinamide 100 mg., panthenol 12 mg./cc Vial 30 cc.

SUPPORT. (Mission) Calcium caseinate, nonfat dry milk, artificial flavors, sodium bicarbonate, salt, sodium saccharin and maltol. Ca 330 mg., P 300 mg., K 244 mg., Na 81 mg., Protein 16 Gm., carbohydrate 8 Gm., Calories 99/oz. Pow. Container 10 oz.
Use: Extra nutritional support.

SUPPORT-500. (Doral) Vit. A 12,500 I.U., D 50 I.U., B-1 10 mg., B-2 5 mg., niacinamide 25 mg., B-6 2 mg., Ca-pantothenate 10 mg., C 500 mg., E 50 I.U., Mg sulfate 70 mg., Mn sulfate 4 mg., Zn 80 mg./Cap.
Use: Vitamin-mineral supplement.

SUPRA MIN. (Towne) Vit. A 10,000 I.U., D 400 I.U., E 30 I.U., C 250 mg., folic acid 0.4 mg., B-1 10 mg., B-2 10 mg., niacin 100 mg., B-6 5 mg., B-12 6 mcg., pantothenic acid 20 mg., iodine 150 mcg., iron 10 mg., magnesium 2 mg., copper 20 mg., manganese 1.25 mg./Tab. Bot. 130s.
Use: Dietary supplement.

SUPRAZINE TABS. (Major) Trifluoperazine 2 mg./Tab. Bot. 250s.; 5 mg./Tab. Bot. 250s, 1000s; 10 mg./Tab. Bot. 250s.
Use: Tranquilizer.

SUPRARENAL. Dried, partially defatted and powdered adrenal gland of cattle, sheep or swine.

SUPRINS. (Towne) Vit. A palmitate 10,000 I.U., D 400 I.U., B-1 10 mg., B-2 10 mg., B-6 5 mg., B-12 6 mcg., C 250 mg., Ca pantothenate 20 mg., niacinamide 100 mg., biotin 25 mcg., Vit. E 15 I.U., Ca 103 mg., P 80 mg., Fe 10 mg., Iodine 0.1 mg., Cu 1.0 mg., Zn 20 mg., Mn 1.25 mg./Captab. Bot. 100s.

SUPROCLONE. USAN.
Use: Sedative.

• **SUPROFEN.** USAN.
Use: Anti-inflammatory.

SURAMIN SODIUM. Hexa-Sodium bis-(m-amino-benzoyl-m-amino-p-methylbenzoyl-1-naph-thylamino-4,6,8-trisulfonate) carbamide. (Bayer 205; Germanin).

SURBEX FILMTAB. (Abbott) Thiamine mononitrate 6 mg., B-2 6 mg., nicotinamide 30 mg., B-6 2.5 mg., Ca pantothenate 10 mg., Vit. B-12 5 mcg., Filmtab. Bot. 100s.
Use: Vit. B-complex therapy.

W/Vit. C. (Abbott) Same as Surbex Filmtab, except Vit. C 250 mg./Filmtab Bot. 100s, 500s.

SURBEX-T FILMTAB. (Abbott) Vit. B-1 15 mg., B-2 10 mg., niacinamide 100 mg., Vit. B-6 5 mg., B-12 10 mcg., Ca pantothenate 20 mg., Vit. C 500 mg./Filmtab. Bot. 100s, 500s. Abbo-Pac 100s.
Use: Vitamin deficiencies.

RBEX-750 WITH IRON. (Abbott) Vit. B-1 15 mg., B-2 15 mg. B-6 25 mg., B-12 12 mcg., C 750 mg., Ca pantothenate 20 mg., E 30 I.U., niacinamide 100 mg., iron 27 mg., folic acid 0.4 mg./Tab. Bot. 50s.
Use: Vitamin & mineral supplement.

RBEX-750 WITH ZINC. (Abbott) B-1 15 mg., B-2 15 mg., B-6 20 mg., B-12 12 mcg., C 750 mg., E 30 I.U., pantothenic acid 20 mg., niacin 100 mg., folic acid 0.4 mg., zinc 22.5 mg./Tab. Bot. 50s.
Use: Vitamin & mineral supplement.

RFACAINE. (Lilly) Cyclomethycaine sulfate. **Cream** 0.5%, Tube 1 oz. **Jelly** 0.75%, Tube 5 oz. **Oint.** 1%, Tube 1 oz.

RFACE-ACTIVE AGENTS.
See: Antiseptics, Surface-Active

RFADIL. (Lilly) Cyclomethycaine and diphenhydramine. **Cream:** Diphenhydramine 2%, cyclomethycaine 0.5%. Tube 1 oz. **Lot:** Diphenhydramine 2 Gm., cyclomethycaine 0.5 Gm., benzyl alcohol 2 Gm., titanium dioxide 5 Gm./100 ml. Plastic Bot. 75 ml.
Use: Dermatitis treatment.

RFAK. (Hoechst) Docusate calcium 50 mg. or 240 mg./Cap. 50 mg., Bot. 30s, 100s; 240 mg. Bot. 30s, 100s, 500s. Unit Dose Pack 100s.

RFATHESIN SULFATE. Cyclomethycaine, B.A.N.

R-FIT FLEXIBLE PERI-STOMAL COVERING. (ConvaTec) Peri-stomal covering with stomahesive & hypo-allergenic adhesive collar. Box 5s.
Use: Part of two-piece ostomy care system.

R-FIT UREOSTOMY POUCH. (ConvaTec) Disposable ostomy pouch. Box 10s.
Use: Part of two-piece ostomy care system.

RFOL POST IMMERSION BATH OIL. (Stiefel) Mineral oil, isopropyl myristate, isostearic acid, PEG-40, sorbitan peroleate, Bot. 8 oz.
Use: Post-Immersion bath oil for dry skin.

URFOMER. USAN.
Use: Hypolipidemic.

RGASOAP. (Wade) Castile vegetable oils. Bot. qt., gal.
Use: Surgical soap.

RGEL LIQUID. (Ulmer) Patient lubricant fluid. Bot. 4 oz., 8 oz., pt., gal.

URGIBONE. USAN. Bone and cartilage obtained from bovine embryos and young calves.
Use: Prosthetic aid (internal bone splint).
See: Unilab Surgibone (Unilab)

RGICAL SIMPLEX P. (Howmedica) Methyl methacrylate 20 ml. poly 6.7 Gm., methyl methacrylate-styrene copolymer 33.3 Gm. **Powd.** 40 Gm. **Liq.** 20 ml.
Use: Bone cement.

RGICAL SIMPLEX P RADIOPAQUE. (Howmedica) Methyl methacrylate 20 ml., poly 6 Gm., methyl methacrylate-styrene copolymer 30 Gm. **Powd.** 40 Gm. **Liq.** 20 ml.
Use: Bone cement.

URGICAL SUTURE, ABSORBABLE, U.S.P. XXI.
Use: Surgical aid.

• **SURGICAL SUTURE, NONABSORBABLE,** U.S.P. XXI.
Use: Surgical aid.

SURGICEL ABSORBABLE HEMOSTAT. (Johnson & Johnson) Sterile absorbable knitted fabric prepared by controlled oxidation of regenerated cellulose. Sterile strips 2″×14″, 4″×8″, 2″×3″, 0.5″×2″.
Use: Absorbable hemostat.

SURGIDINE. (Continental) Iodine 0.8% in iodine complex. Germicide. Bot. 8 oz., gal. Foot operated dispenser 8 oz., gal.
Use: Antiseptic.

SURGI-KLEEN. (Sween) Methylbenzethonium chloride, refined coconut oil superamides, lanolin derivatives, cleansers, water soluble base. Bot. pt., gal.
Use: Topical anti-bacterial cleanser.

SURGILUBE. (Day-Baldwin) Sterile-bacteriostatic. Foil-pac: 3 Gm., 5 Gm., Tube: 5 Gm., 2 oz., 4.5 oz.
Use: Surgical lubricant.

SURGILUBE. (Fougera) Sterile surgical lubricant. Foilpac 3 Gm., 5 Gm.; Tube 5 Gm., 2 oz. 4.5 oz.
Use: Sterile surgical lubricant.

SURIN OINTMENT. (McKesson) Tube 1.25 oz.

SURITAL SODIUM. (Parke-Davis) Thiamylal sodium. **Steri-Vial:** 1 Gm., 25s; 5 Gm., 10s; 10 Gm., 10s.
Use: I.V.; short-acting anesthetic.

SURMONTIL. (Ives) Trimipramine maleate 25 mg., 50 mg. or 100 mg./Cap. Bot. 100s. Clinipaks.
Use: Antidepressant.

SUROFENE. Hexachlorophene.

SUSANO. (Blue Cross) Phenobarbital 0.25 gr., hyoscyamine sulfate 0.1037 mg., atropine sulfate 0.0194 mg., scopolamine HBr 0.0065 mg./Tab. Bot. 1000s.
Use: Sedative, antispasmotic.

SUSANO ELIXIR. (Blue Cross) Phenobarbital 0.25 gr., hyoscyamine sulfate 0.1037 mg., atropine sulfate 0.0194 mg., scopalamine HBr 0.0065 mg./5 ml. Bot. 16 oz., gal.
Use: Sedative, antispasmotic.

SUSPEN. (Circle) Penicillin V potassium 250 mg./5 ml. Bot. 100 ml.
Use: Antibiotic.

SUS-PHRINE INJECTION. (Berlex) Epinephrine 1:200 Amp. 0.3 ml., 12s, 25s. Multiple Dose Vial 5 ml., 1s.
Use: Bronchial asthma.

SUS SCROFA LINNE var DOMESTICUS.
W/Proteolytic enzyme, autolyzed.
See: Saromide Injection, Vial (Saron)

SUSTACAL HC. (Mead Johnson) High calorie nutritionally complete food. Protein 16%, fat 34%, carbohydrate 50%. Cans 8 oz. Vanilla, chocolate or eggnog.
Use: Complete, concentrated oral nutrition.

SUSTACAL LIQUID. (Mead Johnson) A vanilla, eggnog or chocolate flavored liquid containing as a % of the calories 24% protein, 21% fat, 55% carbohydrate with appropriate vitamin and mineral levels to meet 100% of the US RDA's. Cans, 8, 12 and 32 fl. oz.
Use: High protein, nutritionally complete, oral nutritional supplement, lactose free.

SUSTACAL POWDER. (Mead Johnson) Caloric distribution and nutritional value when added to milk are similar to that of Sustacal liquid except lactose. Contains vanilla: Pow. 1.9 oz. packets 4's, 3.8 lb. can; Chocolate 1.9 oz. packets 4's.
Use: High protein, nutritionally complete, oral nutritional supplement.

SUSTACAL PUDDING. (Mead Johnson) Ready-to-eat fortified pudding containing at least 15% of the US RDA's for protein, vitamins and minerals, in a 240 calorie serving. As a % of the calories protein 11%, fat 36%, carbohydrate 53%. Flavors: chocolate, vanilla, and butterscotch. Tins, 5 oz., 110 oz.
Use: Complete nutritional supplement to help increase patient acceptance of nutritional support.

SUSTAGEN. (Mead Johnson) High calorie, high protein supplement containing as a % of the calories 24% protein, 8% fat, 68% carbohydrate. Contains all known essential vitamins and minerals. Prepared from nonfat milk, corn syrup solids, powdered whole milk, calcium caseinate, and dextrose. Vanilla: Can 1, 2.5 & 5 lb. Chocolate: Can 1 lb.
Use: Complete nutrient, nutritional supplement.

SUSTAIRE . (Pfipharmecs) Theophylline 100 mg., 300 mg./Sust. Released Tab. Bot. 100s.
Use: Long acting relief of reversible bronchospasm.

• **SUTILAINS,** U.S.P. XXI. Oint., U.S.P. XXI. Proteolytic enzymes.
Use: Debriding agent.
See: Travase, Oint. (Flint)

SUVAPLEX TABLET. (Tennessee Pharm.) Vit. A 5000 I.U., D 500 I.U., B-1 2.5 mg., B-2 2.5 mg., B-6 0.5 mg., B-12 1 mcg., C 37.5 mg., Ca pantothenate 5 mg., niacinamide 20 mg., folic acid 0.1 mg./Tab. Bot. 100s.
Use: Vitamin supplement.

SUXAMETHONIUM BROMIDE. B.A.N. Bis-2-dimethylaminoethyl succinate bismethobromide 00'-Succinyldi-(2-oxyethyltrimethylammonium bromide).
Use: Neuromuscular blocking agent.
See: Brevidil M

SUXAMETHONIUM CHLORIDE, B.A.N.
See: Anectine
Brevidil M
Scoline
Succinylcholine Chloride, Inj. (Var. Mfr.)

• **SUXEMERID SULFATE.** USAN. Bis-(1,2,2,6,6-pentamethyl-4-piperidyl)succinate sulfate.
Use: Antitussive.

SUXETHONIUM BROMIDE. B.A.N. 00'-Succinyldi-[(2-oxyethyl)ethyldimethylammonium bromide].
Use: Neuromuscular blocking agent.
See: Brevidil E

SU-ZOL. (Boots) Pentylenetetrazol 50 mg., 15 ml. w/alcohol 15%. ml. Bot. 16 oz.
Use: Cerebral, respiratory stimulant.

SWAMP ROOT. Compound of various organic roots in an alcohol base.
Use: Diuretic to the kidney.

SWEEN SKIN CARE. (Sween) Methylbenzethonium chloride, cod liver oil w/Vit. A & D., keratin fractio of lanolin, water-repellent base. Jar 2 oz., 9 oz.
Use: Topical antiseptic.

SWEETA. (Squibb) Saccharin sodium and sorbitol. Bot. 24 ml., 2 oz., 4 oz.
Use: Sweetening Agent

SWEETASTE. (Purepac) Saccharin 0.25 gr., 0.5 gr., gr./Tab. w/Sodium bicarbonate. Bot. 1000s.
Use: Sugar substitute.

■ **SWEETENING AGENTS.**
See: Ril-Sweet (Plough)
Saccharin, Preps. (Various Mfr.)
Sucaryl, Preps. (Abbott)
Sweetaste, Tab. (Purepac)

SWIM EAR. (Fougera) Bot. 1 oz.
Use: Prevention of external otitis.

SWIM 'N CLEAR. (Wisconsin) Swimmers ear drops. Bot. 1.25 oz.
Use: Drops for swimmer's ear to dry up excess water.

SWIRL CLEAN. (Alcon) Display carton.
Use: Electric hard contact lens cleaner.

SWISS KRISS. (Modern) Senna leaves, herbs. Coarse cut mixture. Can 1.5 oz., 3.25 oz., Tab. 24 120s, 250s.
Use: Laxative.

SYLLACT. (Wallace) Psyllium seed husks. Pow. Bot 10 oz.
Use: Orally, laxative.

SYLLAMALT. (Wallace) Maltsupex powder 50%, psyllium seed husks 50% powder. Bot. 10 oz.
Use: Laxative.

• **SYMCLOSENE.** USAN. Trichloroisocyanuric acid.
Use: Local anti-infective.

• **SYMETINE HCl.** USAN. 4,4'-(Ethylenedioxy)-bis-[N-hexyl-N-methylbenzylamine dihydrochloride].
Use: Amebicidal compound.

SYMMETREL. (Du Pont) Amantadine HCl. **Caps.** 10 mg./Cap. Bot. 100s, 500s. Unit Dose 100s. **Syr.** 5 mg./5 ml. Bot. pt.
Use: Antiviral agent, treatment of Parkinson's disease, treatment of drug induced extrapyramidal symptoms.

■ **SYMPATHOLYTIC AGENTS.**
See: Adrenergic-Blocking Agents
D.H.E. 45, Amp. (Sandoz)
Dibenzyline, Cap. (SmithKline)
Dihydroergotamine
Ergotamine Tartrate
Gynergen, Amp., Tab. (Sandoz)

■ **SYMPATHOMIMETIC AGENTS.**
See: Adrenalin (Parke-Davis)
Adrenergic agents
Aerolate Sr. & Jr., Cap. (Fleming)
Aerolone Cpd. (Lilly)
Afrin, Preps. (Schering)
Amesec, Enseal, Pulvule (Lilly)
Aramine, Amp., Vial (Merck Sharp & Dohme)
Arlidin HCl, Tab. (USV Pharm.)
Benzedrine Sulfate, Spansule, Tab. (SmithKline)
Brethine, Amp., Tab (Geigy)

Bronkephrine, Amp., (Winthrop-Breon)
Bronkometer (Winthrop-Breon)
Bronkosol Sol. (Winthrop-Breon)
Delcobese, Tab. (Delco)
Demazin, Tab., Syr. (Schering)
Desoxyn, Gradumet, Tab. (Abbott)
Dexamyl Tab. (SmithKline)
Dexedrine, Elix. Spansule, Tab. (SmithKline)
D-Feda, Cap., Liq. (Dooner)
Didrex, Liq. Tab. (Upjohn)
Dimetapp, Elix., Tab. (Robins)
Drinus Graduals (Amfre-Grant)
Duovent, Tab. (Riker)
Ectasule Minus Sr. & Jr., Cap. (Fleming)
Ectasule III, Cap. (Fleming)
Ephedrine preps.
Epinephrine salts
Extendryl, Cap., Syr., Tab. (Fleming)
Fedrazil, Tab. (Burroughs Wellcome)
Fiogesic, Tab. (Sandoz)
Histabid, Cap., Vial (Meyer)
Isoephedrine HCl
Isuprel HCl, Preps. (Winthrop-Breon)
Levophed Bitartrate, Amp. (Winthrop-Breon)
Metaproterenol Sulfate (Var. Mfr.)
Napril, Cap. (Marion)
Neo-Synephrine HCl, Preps. (Winthrop-Breon)
Nolamine, Tab. (Carnrick)
Norisodrine Sulfate, Sol. (Abbott)
Obedrin-LA, Tab. (Beecham Labs)
Obetrol, Tab. (Obetrol)
Orthoxine, Orthoxine & Aminophylline (Upjohn)
Orthoxine HCl, Tab., Syr. (Upjohn)
Otrivin, Sol., Spray (Geigy)
Phenylephrine HCl, Preps.
Phenylpropanolamine HCl
Pseudoephedrine HCl, Syr., Tab.
Rondec DSC & T (Ross)
Slo-Fedrin & Slo-Fedrin A (Dooner)
Sudafed, Tab., Syr. (Burroughs Wellcome)
Triaminic, Prep. (Dorsey)
Triaminicol, Syr. (Dorsey)
Tussagesic, Susp., Tab. (Dorsey)
Tussaminic, Tab. (Dorsey)
Ursinus, Tab. (Dorsey)
Vasoxyl HCl Amp., Vial (Burroughs Wellcome)
Wyamine Sulfate, Amp., Vial (Wyeth)

MPTROL. (Saron) Phenylpropanolamine HCl 50 mg., chlorpheniramine maleate 8 mg.,/S.R. Cap. Bot. 50s.
Use: Decongestant, antihistaminic.

NA-CLEAR. (Pruvo) Decongestant plus Vit. C. 25 mg./Tab. Bot. 12s, 30s.
Use: Decongestant.

NACORT. (Syntex) Hydrocortisone cream. **1%:** Tube 15 Gm., 30 Gm., 60 Gm. **2.5%:** Tube 30 Gm.
Use: Topical steroid.

NACTHEN. Tetracosactrin, B.A.N. (Ciba) Cosyntropin.

NADRIN LACTATE. Prenylamine, B.A.N.

SYNALAR. (Syntex) Fluocinolone acetonide, **Cream: 0.01%** Tube 15 Gm., 30 Gm., 60 Gm., 120 Gm. Jar 425 Gm. **0.025%** Tube 15 Gm., 30 Gm., 60 Gm., 120 Gm. Jar 425 Gm. **Oint.: 0.025%:** Tube 15 Gm., 30 Gm., 60 Gm., 120 Gm. Jar 425 Gm. **Soln. 0.01%:** Bot. 20 ml., 60 ml.
Use: Topical steroid.

SYNALAR-HP. (Syntex) Fluocinolone acetonide 0.2%. **Cream** Tubes 12 Gm.
Use: Topical steroid.

SYNALGOS CAPSULES. (Ives) Aspirin 356.4 mg., caffeine 30 mg./Cap. Bot. 100s, 500s.
Use: Treatment of mild to moderate pain.

SYNALGOS-DC CAPSULES. (Ives) Dihydrocodeine bitartrate 16 mg., aspirin 356.4 mg., caffeine 30 mg./Cap. Bot. 100s, 500s.
Use: Analgesic, relaxant.

SYNANDONE ACETONIDE. Fluocinolone, B.A.N.

SYNAPP-R. (Blue Cross) Acetaminophen 325 mg., phenylpropanolamine HCl 25 mg., phenyltoloxamine citrate 22 mg./Tab. Bot. 40s.
Use: Analgesic, decongestant.

SYNATUSS-ONE. (Freeport) Guaifenesin 100 mg., dextromethorphan HBr. 15 mg., alcohol 1.4%/5 cc. Bot. 4 oz.
Use: Antitussive.

SYNCAINE.
See: Procaine Hydrochloride, Inj., Tab. (Various Mfr.)

SYNCELAX. (Blue Line) Casanthranol 30 mg., docusate sodium 100 mg./Tab. Bot. 100s, 1000s.
Use: Laxative.

SYNCELOSE. (Blue Line) Methylcellulose. Tab. 0.5 Gm., Bot. 100s, 1000s.
Use: Hydrophilic colloid laxative.

SYNCORT.
See: Desoxycorticosterone Acetate, Inj., Pellets (Various Mfr.)

SYNCORTYL.
See: Desoxycorticosterone Acetate, Inj., Pellets (Various Mfr.)

SYNDOLOR CAPSULES. (Knight) Bot. 100s, 1000s.
Use: Analgesic.

SYNEMOL. (Syntex) Fluocinolone acetonide 0.025%. Tube 15 Gm., 30 Gm., 60 Gm., 120 Gm.
Use: Topical steroid.

SYNEPHRICOL. (Winthrop Products) Paracetamol.
Use: Cold treatment.

SYNIODIN. (Blue Line) Iodine 1 gr. combined w/protein/Tab. Bot. 100s.
Use: Iodine therapy.

SYNKAYVITE. (Roche) Menadiol sodium disphosphate. **Amp.:** 5 mg. or 10 mg./1 ml. w/sodium metabisulfite 2 mg., phenol 0.45% NaCl 0.4%. Amp. 1 ml. Box 10s; 75 mg./2 ml. Amp. 2 ml. Box 10s. **Tab.** 5 mg., Bot. 100s.
Use: Synthetic Vitamin K for hemorrhagic tendency.

SYNKONIN.
See: Hydrocodone (Various Mfr.)

SYNOPEN HYDROCHLORIDE. Halopyramine, B.A.N.

SYNOPHYLATE. (Central) Theophylline sodium glycinate. **Elix.:** Theophylline 165 mg./15 ml.

w/alcohol 20%. Bot. pt., gal. **Tab.:** Theophylline 165 mg./Tab. Bot. 100s, 1000s.
Use: Vasodilator.

SYNOPHYLATE-GG. (Central) Theophylline sod. glycinate 300 mg., guaifenesin 100 mg./15 ml. or Tab. **Syr.** pt., gal. **Tabs.** Bot. 100s.
Use: Symptomatic treatment of bronchial asthma.

SYNTHALOIDS. (Buffington) Benzocaine, calcium-iodine complex/Lozenge. Salt free. Bot. 100s, 1000s. Unit boxes 8s, 16s, 24s. Dispens-A-Kit 500s. Aidpaks 100s. Medipaks 200s.
Use: Sore throat relief.

SYNTHOESTRIN.
See: Diethylstilbestrol, Preps. (Various Mfr.)

SYNTHROID. (Flint) Sodium levothyroxine 25 mcg., 50 mcg., 75 mcg., 100 mcg., 125 mcg., 150 mcg., 200 mcg., 300 mcg./Tab. Bot. 100s, 1000s. Unit Dose available in all strengths.
Use: Thyroid deficiencies.

SYNTHROID INJECTION. (Flint) Lyophilized sodium levothyroxine 100 mcg., 200 mcg., 500 mcg. w/mannitol 10 mg and tribasic sodium phosphate anhydrous 0.7 mg. Vial 10 ml.
Use: Thyroid deficiency; myxedema coma.

SYNTHROX. (Vortech) Sod. levothroxine 0.1 mg., 0.2 mg./Tab. Bot. 1000s.
Use: Thyroid deficiencies.

SYNTOCINON AMPULS. (Sandoz) A sterile aqueous sol. of synthetic oxytocin w/sodium acetate 1.0%, chlorobutanol 0.5%, alcohol 0.61%, acetic acid. Amp. (10 I.U./ml.) 1 ml. SandoPak Pkg. 20s, 100s.
Use: Induction, stimulation or management of labor and for prevention and control of postpartum hemorrhage.

SYNTOCINON NASAL SPRAY. (Sandoz) Syn. oxytocin 40 I.U./cc. w/exsic. sodium phosphate, citric acid, sodium chloride, glycerine, sorbitol, methyl & propylparaben, chlorobutanol 0.05% and Purified Water U.S.P. q.s. Squeeze bottle 2 ml. & 5 ml.
Use: Initial milk let-down.

SYNTOPRESSIN. Lypressin, B.A.N.

SYPHILIS (FTA-ABS) FLUORO KIT. (Clinical Sciences).
Use: Test for syphilis.

SYRAJEN. (Jenkins) Codeine phosphate 10.9 mg., chlorpheniramine maleate 2 mg., pot. guaiacolsulfonate 44 mg., citric acid 60 mg., sod. citrate 197 mg./5 cc. Bot. 4 oz., gal.
Use: Expectorant.

SYRCODATE. (Blue Line) Codeine phosphate 1 gr., ammonium chloride 8 gr., Sod. benzoate 4 gr., aromatics flavors in sugar syr. Bot. 4 oz., 1 gal.
Use: Sedative expectorant.

SYRIDYL A-F CAPSULES. (Fellows) N-acetyl-p-aminophenol 0.130 Gm., salicyamide 0.195 Gm., caffeine 32.5 mg., Dover's Pow. 30 mg., ascorbic acid 50 mg., chlorpheniramine maleate 2 mg., phenylephrine HCl 5 mg., opium 3.2 mg., ipecac 3.2 mg./Cap. Bot. 100s, 500s, 1000s.

SYRIDYL A-F COMPOUND. (Fellows) Phenylephrine HCl 5 mg., chlorpheniramine maleate 1.5 mg., pyrilamine maleate 6.25 mg., potassium guaiacolsulfonate 83.3 mg., sodium citrate 166.6 mg., citric acid 53.3 mg., dihydrocodeinone bitartrate 1.67 mg. alcohol 2%/5 cc. Bot. pt., gal.

SYRIDYL D MINTS. (Fellows) Phenylephrine hydrochloride 5 mg., chlorpheniramine maleate 2 mg./Tab. Bot. 100s.

SYRIDYL EXPECTORANT. (Fellows) Pheniramine maleate 7.5 mg., sodium citrate 42 mg., ammoniu chloride 104.8 mg., alcohol 6.7%/5 cc. Bot 4 oz., pt., gal.

SYROCOHIST SYRUP. (Blue Line) Codeine phosphate 20 mg., pyrilamine maleate 30 mg., pheniramine maleate 15 mg., ephedrine sulf. 75 mg., in flavored nonalcoholic syrup/30 cc. Bot. pt gal.

SYROCOHIST EXPECTORANT SYRUP. (Blue Line) Codeine phosphate 60 mg., ephedrine sulf. 75 mg pyrilamine maleate 30 mg., pheniramine maleate mg., ammonium chloride 600 mg., sod. citrate 12(mg., alcohol 4.75%/30 cc. Bot. pt., gal.

SYROSINGOPINE. B.A.N. 4-Ethoxy-carbonyl-3,5-dim thoxybenzoic acid ester of methyl reserpate. Met 18β-Hydroxy-11-17α-dimethoxy-3β, 20α-yohimban-16β-carboxylate-4-Hydroxy-3,5-dimetho benzoate Ethyl Carbonate (Ester). Methyl O-(4-eth ycarbonyloxy-3,5-dimethoxybenzoyl)reserpate.
Use: Hypotensive.
See: Isotense.
W/Hydrochlorothiazide.
Use: Hypotensive.

SYROXINE TABS. (Major) Sodium levothyroxine 0.1 mg., 0.15 mg., 0.2 mg., or 0.3 mg./Tab. Bot. 100(
Use: Thyroid deficiencies.

SYRPALTA. (Emerson) Syr. containing comb. of fru flavors. Bot. 1 pt., 1 gal.
Use: Vehicle for masking drug taste.

SYRTUSSAR. Dextromethorphan, B.A.N.

• **SYRUP,** N.F. XVI.
Use: Flavored vehicle.

SYTOBEX. (Parke-Davis) Cyanocobalamin 10 mcg./ml. w/buffer and preservatives. Vial 10 ml.
Use: Vitamin B-12 deficiency.

SYTRON. Sodium Ironedetate, B.A.N.

T

T-3 RIABEAD. (Abbott) Test kit 50s, 100s.
Use: Radioimmunoassay for qualitative measurement of total circulating serum liothyronin

T-4 RIA (peg). (Abbott) Diagnostic kit 50s, 100s, 50(
Use: For quantitative measurement of total circulating serum thyroxine.

T-4 SQUIBB. (Squibb) Radioimmune assay kit for T-4. 200 tests./kit.
Use: Radioimmune assay.

T-14. (Freeport) Cyanocobalamine 1000 mcg./ w/sodium Cl. 0.5%, benzyl alcohol 1.5%. Vials 3 cc.
Use: Treatment of vitamin B-12 deficiencies.

16. (Freeport) Pyridoxine HCl 100 mg., thiamine HCl 100 mg., benzyl alcohol 1.5%/ml. Vials 10 cc.
Use: Treatment of vitamin B-1 and vitamin B-6 deficiencies.

38. (Freeport) Testosterone cypionate 100 mg., benzyl alcohol 0.9% in cottonseed oil/cc. Vials 10 cc.
Use: Androgen replacement therapy.

81. (Freeport) Estrogenic substance 2 mg., sodium carboxymethylcellulose 2 mg., povidone 2 mg., dried sodium phosphate 2.9 mg., citric acid 2.05 mg., methylparaben 0.9 mg., propylparaben 0.1 mg., benzyl alcohol 1%/ml. Vials 30 cc.
Use: Estrogen replacement therapy.

95. (Freeport) Cyanocobalamine 1000 mcg., thiamine HCl 100 mg., sodium Cl. 0.9% benzyl alcohol 1.5%/ml. Vials 10 cc.
Use: Vitamin B-1 and B-12 replacement therapy.

100. (Freeport) Testosterone cypionate 100 mg., benzyl alcohol 0.9% in cottonseed oil/cc. Vials 10cc.
Use: Androgen replacement therapy.

846 PREDOXIDE-5. (Mallard) Prednisolone 5 mg./Tab. Bot. 1000s.

. (Wampole-Zeus) Anti-thyroid antibodies by IFA. Test 48s.
Use: A useful tool in identifying two thyroid autoantibodies in a single test.

ASA. (Haag) Acetylsalicylic acid 7.5 gr./Tab. Bot. 100s, 1000s.

BALGIN. Paracetamol, B.A.N.

BASYN. (Freeport) Chlorpheniramine maleate 2 mg., phenylephrine HCl 10 mg., acetaminophen 5 gr., salicylamide 5 gr./Tab. Bot. 1000s.
Use: Relief of muscular aches, headache, nasal congestion due to colds.

BAZONE TABS. (Major) Oxyphenbutazone 100 mg./Tab. Bot. 100s.
Use: Anti-inflammatory.

BRON. (Parke-Davis) Ferrous fumarate 304.2 mg. (representing ele. iron 100 mg.), docusate sodium 50 mg., Vit. E 30 I.U., B-1 6 mg., B-2 6 mg., niacinamide 30 mg., cal. pantothenate 10 mg., B-6 5 mg., C 500 mg., folic acid 1 mg., B-12 25 mcg./Filmseal Bot. 100s. Unit dose pkg. 100s.
Use: Nutritional supplement.

CARYL. (Westwood) Methdilazine HCl **Tab.:** 8 mg./Tab. Bot. 100s. **Syr.** 4 mg./5 ml. Bot. 16 oz.
Use: Antipruritic.

CARYL CHEWABLE TAB. (Westwood) Methdilazine, 3.6 mg./Tab. Bot. 100s.
Use: Antipruritic.

CE. (Merrell Dow) Chlorotrianisene 12 mg., 25 mg., 72 mg./Cap. (12 mg.) Bot. 28s, 100s, 500s; (25 mg.) Bot. 60s. (72 mg.) Pkg. 48s.
Use: Estrogen therapy.

CHYSTEROL.
See: Dihydrotachysterol, Tab. (Philips Roxane)

CITIN. (Ciba) Under study. Benzoctamine, B.A.N.

CKLE. (Colgate) Resorcinol 2%, benzyl alcohol 1%, menthol 0.2%, allantoin 0.2%. Clear gel. Tube 1 oz., 2 oz., 3 oz.
Use: Dermatologic.

• **TACLAMINE HYDROCHLORIDE.** USAN.
Use: Tranquilizer (minor).

TA CREAM. (C & M Pharmacal) Triamcinolone acetonide 0.025% or 0.05%. Jar 2 oz., 8 oz., 1 lb.
Use: Topical anti-inflammatory.

TACRINE. B.A.N. 9-Amino-1,2,3,4-tetrahydroacridine.
Use: Central nervous system stimulant.
See: Romotal hydrochloride.

TAGAMET. (SmithKline) Cimetidine **Tab.:** Cimetidine 200 mg. or 300 mg./Tab. Bot 100s. Single unit pkg. 100s; 400 mg./Tab. Bot. 60s. Blister card 10 × 10s. **Liquid;** Cimetidine HCl 300 mg./5 ml. Bot. 8 oz. Single-dose 5 ml. cups. Tray 10s. **Vials:** Cimetidine HCl 300 mg./2 ml. Vials 2 ml., 8 ml., 10s. **Pre-filled Syringes:** 300 mg./2 ml. Box 1s.
Use: Histamine H_2-receptor antagonist for treatment of duodenal ulcer and gastrointestinal diseases.

TAKARA. (Ladco) Aluminum, boric acid, phenol, oil of peppermint/Pow. 120 Gm. 12s. Can 3.75 oz., 8 oz.
Use: Vaginal douche.

TALACEN. (Winthrop-Breon) Pentazocine HCl 25 mg., acetaminophen 650 mg./Caplet. Bot. 100s. Unit dose 250s. (10 × 25s.)
Use: Analgesic.

TALAMPICILLIN. B.A.N. Phthalidyl 6-[D(-)-α-aminophenylacetamido] penicillinate.
Use: Antibiotic.

• **TALAMPICILLIN HYDROCHLORIDE.** USAN.
Use: Antibacterial.

TALATROL. Trometamol, B.A.N.

• **TALBUTAL,** U.S.P. XXI. Tab., U.S.P. XXI. 5-Allyl-5-sec-butylbarbituric acid.
Use: Hypnotic.
See: Lotusate, Cap. (Winthrop-Breon)

• **TALC,** U.S.P. XXI. A native hydrous magnesium silicate.
Use: Dusting powder, pharmaceutical aid.

TALC TABLETS. (U.S. Products) Talc 25 mg., 50 mg., 75 mg. or 100 mg./Tab. Bot. 1000s.
Use: Radioimmunoassay, for laboratory use only.

• **TALERANOL.** USAN.
Use: Enzyme inhibitor.

• **TALISOMYCIN.** USAN.
Use: Antineoplastic.

• **TALMETACIN.** USAN.
Use: Analgesic, antipyretic, anti-inflammatory.

• **TALNIFLUMATE.** USAN.
Use: Anti-inflammatory, analgesic.

TALOIN. (Adria) Methylbenzethonium chloride, zinc oxide, calamine, eucalyptol in a water-repellent base. Oint.: Tube 2 oz.
Use: Skin protective & antiseptic.

• **TALOPRAM HYDROCHLORIDE.** USAN.
Use: Potentiator.

• **TALOSALATE.** USAN.
Use: Analgesic, anti-inflammatory.

TALOXIMINE. B.A.N. 4-(2-Dimethylaminoethoxy)-1,2-dihydro-1-hydroxyiminophthalazine.
Use: Respiratory stimulant.

TALWIN COMPOUND. (Winthrop-Breon) Pentazocine HCl 12.5 mg., asprin 325 mg./Tab. Bot. 100s.
Use: Analgesic.

TALWIN INJECTION. (Winthrop-Breon) Pentazocine lactate injection. **Ampuls:** Uni-amp: 30 mg./1 ml. 25s; 45 mg./1.5 ml. 25s; 60 mg./2 ml. 25s. **Vial:** 30 mg./10 ml. **Uni-Nest:** 30 mg./ml. Box 25s; 60 mg./2 ml. Box 25s. **Carpuject:** 30 mg./ml. Box 10s; 45 mg./1.5 ml. Box 10s; 60 mg./2 ml. Box 10s.
Use: Analgesic.

TALWIN NX. (Winthrop-Breon) Pentazocine HCl 50 mg., naloxone 0.5 mg./Tab. Bot. 100s. Dispenser Pkg. 250s, 10 sleeve 25s. Unit dose 100s.
Use: Analgesic.

• **TAMETRALINE HYDROCHLORIDE.** USAN.
Use: Antidepressant.

• **TAMOXIFEN CITRATE,** U.S.P. XXI. Tab., U.S.P. XXI. (Z)-(4-(1,2-diphenyl-1-butenyl) phenoxy)-N,N-dime-
thylethanamine 2-hydroxy-1,2,3-propanetricarboxylate (1:1).
Use: Treatment of mammary carcinoma.
See: Nolvadex, Tab. (Stuart)

TAMP-R-TEL. (Wyeth) A tamper-resistant package for narcotic drugs which includes the following:
Codeine phosphate 30 mg., 60 mg./1 cc.
Hydromorphone HCl 1 mg., 2 mg., 3 mg., 4 mg./Tubex
Meperidine HCl 25 mg./cc. and **Promethazine HCl** 25 mg./cc. 2 cc.
Meperidine HCl 25 mg./1 cc., 50 mg./1 cc., 75 mg./1 cc., 100 mg./1 cc.
Morphine Sulfate 2mg., 4mg., 8 mg., 10 mg., 15 mg./1 cc.
Pentobarbital, Sodium 50 mg./1 cc., 100 mg./2 cc.
Phenobarbital, Sodium 30 mg., 60 mg., 130 mg./1 cc.
Secobarbital, Sodium 50 mg./1 cc., 100 mg./2 cc.

TANAC LIQUID. (Commerce) Benzalkonium Cl, benzocaine, tannic acid in a special base. Bot. 0.45 oz.
Use: Mouth sores, cold sores, fever blisters.

TANAC ROLL-ON. (Commerce) Tannic acid, benzalkonium Cl, benzocaine. Bot. 0.3 oz.
Use: Cold sores, fever blister, cracked lips.

TANAC STICK. (Commerce) Benzocaine, tannic acid, octyl dimethyl PABA, allantoin, benzalkonium Cl., emollient core & base. Stick 0.1 oz.
Use: Cold sores, fever blisters, dry lips.

TANADEX. (Commerce) Tannic acid 2.86%, phenol 1.05%, benzocaine 0,47%. Bot. 3 oz.
Use: Throat gargle.

TAN-A-DYNE. (Archer-Taylor) Tannic acid compound w/iodine. Bot. 4 oz., pt., gal.
Use: Swab and gargle concentrate.

TANBISMUTH.
See: Bismuth Tannate.

TAN CARE AFTER TANNING LOTION. (Plough) Bot. 6 oz., 10 oz.
Use: After-sun skin moisturizer

TANCOLIN. Dextromethorphan, B.A.N.

• **TANDAMINE HYDROCHLORIDE.** USAN.
Use: Antidepressant.

TANDEARIL. (Geigy) Oxyphenbutazone 100 mg./Ta Bot. 100s, 1000s. Unit Dose 100s.
Use: Anti-inflammatory, antiarthritic, analgesic, antip retic.

• **TANNIC ACID.** U.S.P. XXI. Gallotannic acid. Glycerite. Tannin.
Use: 1 to 20% solution as an astringent.
See: Amertan, Oint. (Lilly)
W/Benzocaine, benzyl alcohol, diisobutylphenoxyethoxyethyl dimethyl benzyl ammonium chloride.
See: Kankex, Liq. (Edward J. Moore)
W/Benzocaine, phenol, thymol iodide, ephedrine HC zinc oxide, peru balsam.
See: Hemocaine, Oint. (Mallard)
W/Bisacodyl.
See: Clysodrast, Packet (Barnes-Hind)
W/Boric acid, salicylic acid, isopropyl alcohol.
See: Sal Dex Boro, Liq. (Scrip)
W/Chlorobutanol, isopropyl alcohol.
See: Outgro, Sol. (Whitehall)
W/Cyanocobalamin, zinc acetate, glutathione, phen
See: Depinar, Amp. (Armour)
W/Merthiolate.
See: Amertan, Oint. (Lilly)
W/Phenol, iodine.
See: Phen-Iodine No. 2, Liq. (Sutliff & Case)
W/Salicylic acid, boric acid.
See: Tan-Bor-Sal, Liq. (Gordon)

TANNIC SPRAY. (Gebauer) Tannic acid 4.5%, chlorbutanol 1.3%, menthol less than 1%, benzocaine less than 1%. propylene glycol 33%, ethanol 60.5% Bot. 57 Gm., 114 Gm.
Use: Relief of sunburn and other minor burns.

TANPHETAMIN.
See: Dextroamphetamine tannate

TAO. (Roerig) Troleandomycin equivalent to 250 mg oleandomycin /Cap. Bot. 100s.
Use: Antibiotic therapy.

TAORYL EDISYLATE. Caramiphen, B.A.N.

TAPAL AMPULS. (Winthrop Products) Dipyrone.
Use: Analgesic, antipyretic, anti-inflammatory.

TAPAL TABLETS. (Winthrop Products) Dipyrone.
Use: Analgesic, antipyretic, anti-inflammatory.

TAPAR TABLETS. (Parke-Davis) Acetaminophen 3 mg./Tab. Bot. 100s.
Use: Analgesic.

TAPAZOLE. (Lilly) Methimazole. 1-methyl-2-merca toimidazole. Tab. (5 mg. & 10 mg.) Bot. 100s.
Use: Hyperthyroidism.

• **TAPE, ADHESIVE,** U.S.P. XXI.
Use: Surgical aid.

TA-POFF. (Ulmer) Adhesive tape remover. Bot. 1 **Aerosol.** Can 6 oz.

TAPULINE. (Wesley) Activated attapulgite 600 mg., pectin 60 mg., homatropine methylbromide 0.5 mg./Chewable Tab. Bot. 100s, 1000s.
Use: Diarrhea.

TAR.
See: Coal Tar, Preps.

TARACTAN. (Roche) Trans isomer 2-chloro-9-(3-methyl aminopropylidene) thioxanthene. **Tab.:**

Chlorprothixene 10, 25, 50 or 100 mg./Tab. Bot. 100s, 500s. **Concentrate** 100 mg./5 ml. Bot. 1 pt. **Amp.** (w/methyl and propyl parabens 0.2%.) 25 mg./2 ml., 10s.
Use: Tranquilizer.

AR DISTILLATE. (Doak) Decolorized fractional distillate of crude coal tar. Each cc. equiv. to 1 Gm. whole crude coal tar. Bot. 2 oz., 16 oz.
Use: Active ingredient for dermatologic preparations.

ARLENE LOTION. (Medco Lab) Refined crude coal tar, salicylic acid, propylene glycol. Plastic Applicator Bot. 2 oz.
Use: seborrheic dermatitis.

ARPASTE. (Doak) Coal tar, distilled 5% in zinc paste. Tube 1 oz., Jar 4 oz., w/Hydrocortisone 0.5%. Tube 1 oz.
Use: Dermatitis.

AR-QUIN-HC. (Jenkins) Hydrocortisone 0.5%, liquor carbonis detergens 3.0%, clioquinol 1.0%. Oint. Tube 0.5 oz.

ARSUM. (Summers) Coal tar 10%, salicylic acid 5%. Bot. 4 oz.
Use: Dermatologic, shampoo.

ARTAR EMETIC.
See: Antimony Potassium Tartrate, U.S.P.

TARTARIC ACID, N.F. XVI.
Use: Buffer.

ASHAN, Skin Cream. (Block) Vit. A palmitate, D-2, D-panthenol, Vit. E. Tube 1 oz.

AUROCHOLIC ACID.
V/Pancreatin, pepsin.
See: Enzymet, Tabs. (Westerfield)

AUROLIN. B.A.N. 4,4′-Methylenedi(tetrahydro-1,2,4-thiadiazine-1-dioxide).
Use: Antibacterial.
See: Tauroflex.

AUROPHYLLIN. (Vale) Ext. ox bile 32.4 mg., phenolphthalein 32.4 mg., ext. cascara sagrada 32.4 mg.,/Tab. Bot. 100s, 1000s, 5000s.

AURULTAM. B.A.N. Tetrahydro-1,2,4-thiadiazine 1,1-dioxide.
Use: Antibacterial; antifungal.

AVEGIL HYDROGEN FUMARATE. Clemastine, B.A.N.

A-VERM. (Table Rock) Piperazine citrate 100 mg./cc. Syr. Bot. 1 pt., 1 gal. Tabs. 500 mg. Bot. 100s, 500s.
Use: Anthelmintic.

AVILEN PLUS. (Table Rock) Liver solution 1 Gm., ferric pyrophosphate soluble 500 mg., Vit. B-12 24 mcg., B-1 6 mg., B-2 7.2 mg., B-6 3 mg., panthenol 3 mg., niacinamide 60 mg., l-lysine HCl 300 mg., 5% alcohol/cc. Bot. 16 oz., 1 gal.
Use: Hematinic.

AVIST. (Sandoz) Clemastine fumarate 2.68 mg./Tab. Bot. 100s.
Use: Antihistamine.

AVIST-1 TABLETS. (Sandoz) Clemastine fumarate 1.34 mg./Tab. Bot. 100s.
Use: Antihistamine.

TAVIST-D. (Sandoz) Clemastine fumarate 1.34 mg., phenylpropanolamine HCl 75 mg./Tab. Bot. 100s.
Use: Relief of allergic rhinitis symptoms.

TAXOL. (CMC) Bile Salts 1 gr., aloes ⅖ gr., hyoscyamus ext. 1/13 gr., w/pancreas, duodenum/Tab. Bot. 50s, 500s.
Use: Laxative.

TAYSTRON. (Vale) Elemental iron 15 mg., Vit. B-1 3 mg., C 20 mg., B-12 4 mcg./Tab. Bot. 100s, 500s, 1000s.
Use: Iron and vitamin supplement.

• **TAZADOLENE SUCCINATE.** USAN.
Use: Analgesic.

• **TAZIFYLLINE HYDROCHLORIDE.** USAN.
Use: Antihistaminic.

• **TAZOLOL HYDROCHLORIDE.** USAN.
Use: Cardiotonic.

TBA-PRED. (Keene) Prednisolone tebutate 10 mg./ml. susp. Vial 10 ml.
Use: Corticosteroid for intra-articular and soft tissue injection.

T-BENZETTES. (Wolins) Benzocaine 5 mg., anise flavor/Loz. Bot. 1000s.

TBZ. (MSD AGVET) Thiabendazole. **Cubes:** 3.3% thiabendazole; **Paste:** 43% thiabendazole; **Pellets:** 6.6%; **Bolus:** 2 Gm., 15 Gm.; **Suspension:** Various sizes.
Use: Anthelmintic, veterinary medicine.

TBZ-6. (MSD AGVET) Thiabendazole suspension 6 Gm./oz.
Use: Anthelmintic, veterinary medicine.

T-CAINE 1%. (Tunex) Lidocaine HCl 10 mg./ml. Vial 50cc.
Use: Infiltration & nerve block anesthesia.

T-CAINE 2%. (Tunex) Lidocaine HCl 20 mg./ml. Vial 50cc.
Use: Infiltration & nerve block anesthesia.

T.C.M. 200. (Zenith) Tridihexethyl Cl 25 mg., meprobamate 200 mg./Tab.
Use: Tranquilizer.

T.C.M. 400. (Zenith) Tridihexethyl Cl 25 mg., meprobamate 400 mg./Tab.
Use: Tranquilizer.

T-CORT. (Torch) Triamcinolone acetonide micronized powder. Bot. 1 Gm., 10 Gm.
Use: Extemporaneous prescription compounding.

T/DERM. (Neutrogena) Neutar coal tar extract 5% in oil base. Bot. 4 oz.
Use: Psoriasis treatment.

T-DRYL 10. (Tunex) Diphenhydramine HCl 10 mg./ml. Vial 30 cc.
Use: Antihistaminic.

T-DRYL 50. (Tunex) Diphenhydramine HCl 50 mg./ml. Vial 10cc.
Use: Antihistaminic.

T.D. THERALS. (Reid-Provident) Vit. A 10,000 I.U., D 400 I.U., E 5 I.U., C 100 mg., B-1 10 mg., B-2 5 mg., B-6 0.5 mg., B-12 5 mcg., niacinamide 50 mg., calcium pantothenate 5 mg., ferrous sulfate 34 mg., pot. iodide 0.13 mg., manganese sulfate 3 mg., pot. sulfate 11 mg., copper sulfate 2.8 mg., zinc sulfate

3.9 mg., magnesium sulfate 10 mg./T.R. Cap. Bot. 100s.
Use: Multiple avitaminosis therapy.

TEAR AID. (Ketchum) Vial 15 cc.
Use: Decongestant-emollient.

TEARGEN. (Goldline) Bot. 15 ml.
Use: Artificial tears.

TEARISOL. (CooperVision) An isotonic buffered aqueous sol. of hydroxypropyl methylcellulose 0.5%, edetate disodium 0.01%, benzalkonium chloride 0.01%, boric acid, sodium carbonate, potassium chloride Bot. 15 ml.
Use: Artificial tears in many eye conditions.

TEARS NATURALE. (Alcon) Duasorb water soluble polymeric system, benzalkonium chloride 0.01%, disodium edetate 0.05%. Droptainer 15 ml. & 30 ml.
Use: Artificial tear & lubricant for ocular irritation & dry eyes.

TEARS PLUS. (Allergan) Polyvinyl alcohol, povidone. Bot. 0.5 oz., 1 oz.
Use: Artificial tears.

TEATCOTE PLUS. Polyhexanide, B.A.N.

• **TEBUQUINE.** USAN.
Use: Antimalarial.

T.E.C. (Invenex) Zn 1 mg., Cu 0.4 mg., Cr. 4.0 mcg., Mn 0.1 mg. Vial 10 ml.
Use: Trace element additives for TNP therapy.

TECALDRINE. Dextromethorphan, B.A.N.

TECHENESCAN MAA. Aggregated albumin (human).
Use: Preparation of Tc 99m Aggregated Albumin (Human).

TECHNEPLEX. (Squibb) Technetium Tc 99m penetate kit. 10 vials/kit.
Use: Radiodiagnostic.

TECHNETIUM 99m-IRON-ASCORBATE-DTPA.
See: Renotec (Squibb)

• **TECHNETIUM Tc-99m ALBUMIN INJECTION,** U.S.P. XXI.
Use: Radioactive agent.

• **TECHNETIUM Tc-99m ALBUMIN AGGREGATED INJECTION,** U.S.P. XXI.
Use: Diagnostic aid (Lung scanning)

• **TECHNETIUM Tc 99m DISOFENIN INJECTION,** U.S.P. XXI.

• **TECHNETIUM Tc-99m ETIDRONATE INJECTION,** U.S.P. XXI.

TECHNETIUM Tc-99m Generat or Solution. (New England Nuclear) Pertechnetate sodium Tc 99 m.
Use: Radiodiagnostic.

• **TECHNETIUM Tc-99mFERPENTETATE INJECTION,** U.S.P. XXI.
Use: Radioactive agent.

• **TECHNETIUM Tc-99m MEDRONATE INJECTION,** U.S.P. XXI.

• **TECHNETIUM Tc-99m OXIDRONATE INJECTION,** U.S.P. XXI.

• **TECHNETIUM Tc-99m PENTETATE INJECTION,** U.S.P. XXI.
Use: Radioactive agent.

• **TECHNETIUM Tc-99m PYROPHOSPHATE INJECTION,** U.S.P. XXI.
Use: Radioactive agent.

• **TECHNETIUM Tc-99m (Pyro- and trimetra-) PHOSPHATES INJECTION,** U.S.P. XXI.
Use: Radioactive agent.

• **TECHNETIUM Tc-99m SODIUM INJECTION,** U.S. XXI.
Use: Radioactive agent.

• **TECHNETIUM Tc-99m SUCCIMER INJECTION** U.S.P. XXI.
Use: Radioactive agent.

TECHNETIUM Tc-99m SULFUR COLLOID KIT.
Use: Radioactive agent.
See: Tesuloid (Squibb)

• **TECHNETIUM Tc-99m SULFUR COLLOID INJECTION,** U.S.P. XXI.
Use: Diagnostic aid (liver scanning)

TECLOSINE. Under study.
Use: Amebacide.

TECLOTHIAZIDE. B.A.N. 6-Chloro-3,4-dihydro-3-trichloromethyl-1,2,4-benzothiadiazine-7-sulfonamide 1,1-dioxide.
Use: Diuretic.
See: Deplet potassium derivative.

• **TECLOZAN.** USAN. N,N'-(p-Phenylenedimethylene) bis]2,2-dichloro-N-(2-ethoxy-ethyl)-acetamide].
Use: Amebicide.
See: Falmonox (Winthrop Products)

TEDRAL. (Parke-Davis) **Tab.:** Theophylline 130 mg ephedrine HCl 24 mg., phenobarbital 8 mg./Tab. Bot. 24s, 100s, 1000s. Unit dose 100s. **Susp. (Pediatric):** Theophylline 65 mg., ephedrine HCl 12 mg., phenobarbital 4 mg./5 cc. Bot. 8 oz., 16 oz.
Use: Symptomatic relief in asthma.

TEDRAL-25. (Parke-Davis) Identical with Tedral except that butabarbital 25 mg. has been substituted for phenobarbital, 8 mg./Tab. Bot. 100s.
Use: Relief of bronchospasms and bronchial asthma.

TEDRAL ELIXIR. (Parke-Davis) Theophylline 32.5 mg ephedrine HCl 6 mg., phenobarbital 2 mg./5 cc. Alcohol 15%. Pediatric. Bot. pt.
Use: Bronchospasm of asthma.

TEDRAL EXPECTORANT TABLETS. (Parke-Davis Theophylline 130 mg., ephedrine HCl 24 mg., phenobarbital 8 mg., guaifenesin 100 mg./Tab. Bot 100s.
Use: Expectorant.

TEDRAL-SA. (Parke-Davis) Theophylline 180 mg ephedrine HCl 48 mg., phenobarbital 25 mg./S.A. Tab. Bot. 100s, 1000s. Unit dose 100s.
Use: Prevention of asthmatic attacks.

TEEBACIN. (CMC) Sod. p-aminosalicylate **Tab.** 0.5 Gm Bot. 500s, 1000s. 1 Gm./Tab. Bot. 500s, 1000s. **Pow.** Bot. 1 lb. Packettes. 4.18 Gm., 5.57 Gm./Packette. 100s.
Use: Tuberculosis.

TEEBACIN ACID BUFFERED. (CMC) p-Aminosalicylic acid 0.5 Gm. with magnesium glycinate & carbonate/Tab. Bot. 500s, 1000s.
Use: Tuberculosis treatment.

TEEBACONIN. (CMC) Isoniazid 100, 300 mg./Tab. Bot. 100s, 250s, 1000s. Pow. 1 lb.
Use: Tuberculosis.

TEEBACONIN W/Vit. B-6. (CMC) Isoniazid 100 mg., and 5, 10 or 50 mg. pyridoxine HCl/Tab. Bot. 100s, 500s, 1000s.
Use: Tuberculosis susceptible to isoniazid therapy.

TEEBAZONE. Tibione. 4-Acetylamino-benzaldehyde thiosemicarbazone. Under study.
Use: Antituberculosis.

TEEPHEN. (Robinson) **Capsules, Tablets:** Theophylline 2 gr., ephedrine 3/8 gr., phenobarbital 1/8 gr./Cap. or Tab. Bot. 100s, 1000s. Bulk Pack 5000s. **Suppositories:** Same formula as Caps and Tabs. Box 12s. **Suspension:** Theophylline 1 gr., ephedrine HCl 1/5 gr., phenobarbital 1/15 gr./5 cc. Bot. 8 oz.

• **TEFLURANE.** USAN. 2-Bromo-1,1,1,2-tetrafluoroethane.
Use: General inhalation anesthetic.

TEGA-ATRIC ELIXIR. (Ortega) Pentylenetetrazol 100 mg., niacin 50 mg., vit. B-1 30 mg., B-2 30 mg., B-6 10 mg., B-12 100 mcg., choline bitartrate 150 mg., inositol 100 mg./30 ml. w/alcohol 15%. Sherry wine flavor. Bot. pt., gal.
Use: Geriatric therapy.

TEGA-C-CAPS. (Ortega) Ascorbic acid 500 mg./T. R. Cap. Bot. 100s, 1000s.
Use: Dietary supplement.

TEGACID.
See: Glyceryl monostearate

TEGA-CODE M. (Ortega) Acetaminophen 300 mg., salicylamide 200 mg., codeine phosphate 30 mg./Cap. Bot. 100s, 500s.
Use: Analgesic.

TEGA CORT FORTE 1%. (Ortega) Micronized hydrocortisone alcohol 1% in water washable base. Bot. 2 oz., 4 oz.
Use: Topical lotion for relief of inflammatory dermatoses.

TEGA CORT LOTION 0.5%. (Ortega) Micronized hydrocortisone alcohol 0.5% in water washable base. Bot. 2 oz., 4 oz.
Use: Topical lotion for relief of inflammatory dermatoses.

TEGA-FLEX. (Ortega) Orphenadrine citrate 30 mg./ml. Vial 10 ml.
Use: Musculoskeletal conditions.

• **TEGAFUR.** USAN. (Mead Johnson)
Use: Antineoplastic.

TEGAMIDE. (G&W) Trimethobenzamide HCl 100 mg., or 200 mg./ Supp. Boxes 10s, 50s.
Use: Control of nausea and vomiting.

TEGA OTIC. (Ortega) Hydrocortisone alcohol 1%, pramoxine HCl 1%, parachlorometaxylenol 0.1%, benzalkonium Cl 0.02%, glacia acetic acid 20 mg./ml. Bot. 10 cc.
Use: Bacterial & fungal infection of the ear.

TEGA-PAP. (Ortega) Acetaminophen 120 mg., alcohol 10%/Tab. or 5 cc. Bot. pt., gal. Tab. Bot. 100s, 1000s.
Use: Analgesic, antipyretic.

TEGA VERT. (Ortega) Niacin 50 mg., dimenhydrinate 25 mg./Cap. Bot. 100s, 1000s.
Use: Vertigo, Meniere's syndrome.

TEGOPEN. (Bristol) Cloxacillin sodium 250 mg./Cap. Bot. 100s. 500 mg./Cap. Bot. 100s. Granules for Soln. 125 mg./5 ml. Bot. 100 ml., 200 ml.
Use: Antibiotic.

TEGRETOL. (Geigy) Carbamazepine 200 mg./Tab. Bot. 100s, 1000s, Unit Dose 100s. Gy-Pak 100s. **Chewable Tab.:** 100mg./Tab. Bot.100s. Unit dose 100s.
Use: Epilepsy; trigeminal neuralgia.

TEGRIN CREAM. (Block) Allantoin 2%, coal tar ext. 5% in cream base. Tube 2 oz., 4.4 oz.
Use: Psoriasis.

TEGRIN SHAMPOO. (Block) Tar extract 5% in cream base shampoo. Tube. 2 oz., 3.2 oz., 5 oz. Bot. 3.75 oz., 6.6 oz. **Cream** Jar 2 oz., 4.4 oz., **Lotion:** Bot. 3.75, 6.6 oz. **Soap** Bar 4.5 oz.
Use: Antiseborrheic, antidandruff.

T.E. IONATE P.A.. (Reid-Provident) Testosterone cypionate 50 mg., estradiol cypionate 2 mg., chlorobutanol 0.5%, in cottonseed oil/cc. Vial 10 cc. 1s, 6s, 12s.

TEK-CHEK. (Ames) Controls for routine urinalysis. Pkg. 4 vials.
Use: For use with Ames urinalysis strips.

TELACHLOR TD CAPS. (Major) Chlorpheniramine maleate 8 mg. or 12 mg./T.D. Tab. Bot. 1000s.
Use: Antihistaminic.

TELDRIN MAXIMUM STRENGTH CAPSULES. (Menley & James) Chlorpheniramine maleate 12 mg./Spansule. Pkg. 12s, 24s. Bot. 50s, 500s. Unit-dose 100s.
Use:Allergy relief.

TELDRIN MULTI-SYMPTOM ALLERGY RELIEVER. (Menley & James) Chlorpheniramine maleate 2 mg., acetaminophen 325 mg., pseudoephedrine HCl 30 mg./Cap. Pkg. 20s, 40s.
Use: Antihistaminic, analgesic, decongestant for hay fever and sinusitis symptoms.

TELDRIN TIMED-RELEASE ALLERGY CAPSULE. (Menley & James) Chlorpheniramine maleate 8 mg./Spansule. Pkg. 12s, 24s. Bot. 50s, 500s. Single unit pack 100s.
Use: Antihistamine for hay fever and allergy.

TELEFON. (Kenyon) Ferrous sulfate 150 mg./Cap. Bot. 100s, 1000s.

TELEPAQUE. (Winthrop-Breon) Iopanoic acid. 0.5 Gm./Tab. Envelope of 6 Tablets. Box 25 envelopes.
Use: Orally; cholecystographic medium.

TELMID IODIDE. Dithiazanine, B.A.N.

TELODRON. (Norden) Chlorpheniramine maleate.

TELOTREX. Tetracycline, B.A.N.

TEM. Tretamine, B.A.N.
See: Triethylenemelamine, Tab. (Lederle)

TEMARIL. (SmithKline) Trimeprazine tartrate. **Tab.** Trimeprazine tartrate 2.5 mg./Tab. Bot. 100s, 1000s. Single Unit Pak 100s. **Syr.** 2.5 mg./5 ml. w/alcohol 5.7%. Bot. 4 oz. **Spansule** 5 mg. Bot. 50s, Single Unit Pak, 100s.
Use: Antipruritic.

• **TEMAZEPAM.** USAN. 7-Chloro-1,3-dihydro-3-hydroxy-1-methyl-5-phenyl-2H-1,4-benzodiazepin-2-one.

Use: Minor tranquilizer.
See: Restoril, Cap. (Sandoz)

• **TEMEFOS.** USAN.
Use: Ectoparasiticide.

TEMETAN. (Nevin) Acetaminophen 324 mg./Tab. Bot. 100s, 500s. Elixir (324 mg./5 cc.) Bot. pt.
Use: Analgesic.

• **TEMODOX.** USAN.
Use: Growth stimulant.

TEMPO. (Vicks) Calcium carbonate 414 mg., aluminum hydroxide 133 mg., magnesium hydroxide 81 mg., simethicon 20 mg./Tab. Bot. 10s, 30s, 60s.
Use: Antacid, antiflatulant.

TEMPRA. (Mead Johnson) Acetaminophen. **Red drops** 80 mg./0.8 ml. Bot. w/dropper 15 ml. **Red syrup** 160 mg./5 ml. Bot. 4 oz., 1 pt. **Tab.:** 80 mg./Chewable Grape flavor Tab. Bot 30s.
Use: Relief of fever and pain.

TENDRON. (Amfre-Grant) Dexamethasone sodium phosphate 4 mg./ml. Vial 5 ml.
Use: Hormone supplement.

TENDRON L.A. (Amfre-Grant) Dexamethasone acetate 8 mg./ml. Vial 5 ml.
Use: Hormone.

• **TENIPOSIDE.** USAN.
Use: Antineoplastic.

TENOL. (Vortech) Acetaminophen 5 gr./Tab. Bot. 100s, 1000s.
Use: Analgesic.

TENOL LIQUID. (Vortech) Acetaminophen 120 mg., NAPA alcohol 7%/5 cc. Bot. 3 oz., 4 oz., Gal.
Use: Analgesic.

TENOL-PLUS. (Vortech) Acetaminophen 250 mg., aspirin 250 mg., caffeine 65 mg./Tab. Bot. 1000s.
Use: Analgesic.

TENORETIC TABLETS. (Stuart) **50 mg.:** Atenolol 50 mg., Chlorthalidone 25 mg./Tab. Bot. 100s. **100 mg.:** Atenolol 100 mg., Chlorthalidone 25 mg./Tab Bot. 100s.
Use: Antihypertensive agent.

TENORMAL HYDROGEN TARTRATE. Pempidine, B.A.N.

TENORMIN. (Stuart) Atenolol 50 mg. or 100 mg./Tab. Bot. 100s. Unit dose 100s.
Use: Antihypertensive.

TENSAWAY. (Stanlabs) Vit. B-1, B-2, B-6, niacinamide, ext. passion flower, salicylamide, scopolamine aminoxide HBr, pyrilamine maleate. Tab. Carton 30s.
Use: Nervous tension.

TENSEZE. (A.P.C.) Phenyltoloxamine citrate 88 mg., salicylamide 130 mg./Cap. Bot. 10s.
Use: Nervous tension.

TENSILON. (Roche) Edrophonium chloride. **Vial:** 10 mg./ml., w/phenol 0.45%, sodium sulfite 0.2%, sodium citrate, citric acid. Box 1s; **Amp.** 10 mg./ml., w/sodium sulfite 0.2%, sodium citrate, citric acid 1 ml. Box 10s.
Use: Curare antagonist, muscle stimulant.

TENSIN. (Standex) Reserpine 0.25 mg./Tab. Bot. 100s.

TENSOCAINE TABLETS. (Winthrop Products) Acetominophen.
Use: Analgesic, antipyretic.

TENSOLAX TABLETS. (Winthrop Products) Chlormezanone.
Use: Analgesic, muscle relaxant.

TENSOLATE. (Apco) Phenobarbital 0.25 gr., hyoscyamine sulfate 0.1037 mg., atropine sulfate 0.0194 mg., hyoscine HBr 0.0065 mg./Tab. Bot. 100s.
Use: Antispasmodic sedative, for visceral spasm.

TENSOPIN. (Apco) Phenobarbital 0.25 gr., homatropine methylbromide 2.5 mg./Tab. Bot. 100s.
Use: Antispasmodic.

TENSOR. (Crystal) Mannitol hexanitrate 30 mg., veratrum viride 100 mg., rutin 20 mg., Rauwolfia serpentina alkaloids 0.75 mg./Tab. Bot. 100s.
Use: Hypertension.

TENSTAN. (Standex) Isobutylallylbarbituric acid ¾ gr caffeine ⅔ gr., aspirin 3 gr., phenacetin 2 gr./Tab. Bot. 100s.
Use: Analgesic.

TENTRATE. (Tennessee Pharm.) Pentaerythritol tetranitrate 20 mg./Tab. Bot. 100s, 1000s.

TENUATE. (Merrell Dow) Diethylpropion HCl 25 mg./Tab. Bot. 100s.
Use: Anorectic.

TENUATE DOSPAN. (Merrell Dow) Diethylpropion HCl 75 mg./Controlled Release Tab. Bot. 100s, 250s.
Use: Anorectic.

T-E-P COMPOUND. (Stanlabs) Theophylline 2 gr. ephedrine ⅜ gr., phenobarbital ⅛ gr./Tab. Bot. 1000s.
Use: Bronchial antispasmodic.

TEOQUIL. Hedaquinium Chloride, B.A.N.

TEPANIL. (Riker) Diethylpropion HCl. Tab. 25 mg. Bot. 100s.
Use: Treatment and control of obesity.

TEPANIL TEN-TAB. (Riker) Diethylpropion 75 mg./Tab. Bot. 30s, 100s, 250s.
Use: Treatment and control of obesity.

• **TEPROTIDE.** USAN.
Use: Enzyme-inhibitor.

TEQUINOL SODIUM. Name used for Actinoquinol Sodium.

TERALASE. W/Pancreatin, polysorbate-80.
See: Digolase, Cap. (Boyle)

• **TERAZOSIN HYDROCHLORIDE.** USAN.
Use: Antihypertensive.

TERBUTALINE. B.A.N. 1-(3,5-Dihydroxyphenyl)-2-(t-butylamino)ethanol.
Use: Bronchodilator.

• **TERBUTALINE SULFATE,** U.S.P. XXI. Inj., Tab., U.S.P. XXI. a-[(tert-Butylamino)methyl]-3,5-dihydroxybenzyl alcohol sulfate.
Use: Bronchodilator.
See: Brethine, Amp., Tab. (Geigy)

TERCODRYL. (Approved) Codeine phos. ¾ gr., pyrilamine maleate 25 mg./fl. oz. Bot. 4 oz.
Use: Antihistamine.

• **TERCONAZOLE.** USAN.
Use: Antifungal.
• **TERFENADINE.** USAN.
Use: Antihistaminic.
See: Seldane, Tab. (Merrill Dow)
• **TERODILINE HYDROCHLORIDE.** USAN.
Use: Vasodilator (coronary).
TERFONYL SUSPENSION. (Squibb)
Trisulfapyrimidines 500 mg./5 ml. Bot. pt.
Use: Bacterial infections sensitive to sulfonamides.
TERFONYL TABLETS. (Squibb) Trisulfapyramidines 500 mg./Tab. sulfadiazine 0.167 Gm., sulfamerazine 0.167 Gm., sulfamethazine 0.167 Gm./Tab. Bot. 100s.
Use: Triple sulfonamide therapy.
See: Meth-Dia-Mer-Sulfonamides
TERG-A-ZYME. (Alconox) Alconox with enzyme action. Box 4 lb. Ctn. 9×4 lb., 25 lb., 50 lb., 100 lb., 300 lb.
Use: Biodegradeable detergent and wetting agent.
TERIDOL JR. (Approved) Terpin hydrate, cocillana, pot. guaiacolsulfonate, ammonium chloride. Bot. 3 oz.
Use: Children's cough syrup.
• **TEROXALENE HYDROCHLORIDE.** USAN 1-(3-Chloro-p-tolyl)-4-[6-(p-tert-pentylphenoxy)-hexyl] piperazine hydrochloride.
Use: Antischistosomal.
• **TEROXIRONE.** USAN.
Use: Antineoplastic.
TERPACOF. (Jenkins) Codeine phosphate 10 mg., terpin hydrate 88 mg./5 ml. Bot. 3 oz., gal.
Use: Cough sedative and expectorant.
TERPATE. (Geneva) Pentaerythritol tetranitrate 10 mg., 20 mg./Tab. Bot. 100s.
TERPEX JR. (Approved) d-Methorphan 25 mg., terpin hydrate, pot. guaiacolsulfonate, cocillana, ammonium chloride. Bot. 4 oz.
Use: Children's cough syrup.
TERPHAN ELIXIR. (Vale) Terpin hydrate 85 mg., dextromethorphan hydrobromide 10 mg./5 ml. w/alcohol 40% Bot. pt., gal., 3 oz.
Use: Sedative.
• **TERPIN HYDRATE,** U.S.P. XXI. Elixir, with Codeine Elixir, U.S.P. XXI. cis-p-Menthane-1,8-diol hydrate. Cryst. & Pow., Pkg. 0.25 lb., 4 oz., 1 lb.
Use: Expectorant for chronic cough.
See: Creoterp (Jenkins)
SK-Terpin Hydrate and Codeine, Liq. (SmithKline)
Terp, Liq. (Scrip)
TERPIN HYDRATE W/COMBINATIONS
See: Cerose Comp. Cap. (Ives)
Dicodethal, Elix. (Lannett)
Gylanphen, Tab. (Lannett)
Histogesic, Tab. (Century)
Ipaterp C.T., Tab. (Fellows)
Palodyne, Cap. (Mallard)
Prunicodeine, Liq. (Lilly)
S.A.C. Throat Lozenges (Towne)
Terpichlor, Tab. (Richlyn)
Terpium, Tab. (Scrip)
Toclonol Expectorant, Liq. (Cenci)
Toclonol W/Codeine, Liq. (Cenci)
Turpoin, Tab. (Mallard)
W/Dextromethorphan, phenylephrine HCl, chloropheniramine maleate, acetaminophen, ascorbic acid.
See: Cerose Compound, Cap. (Ives)
W/Dextromethorphan, phenylpropanolamine HCl, pheniramine maleate, pyrilamine maleate.
See: Tussaminic, Tab. (Dorsey)
W/Dextromethorphan, phenylpropanolamine HCl, pheniramine maleate, pyrilamine maleate, acetaminophen.
See: Chexit, Tab. (Dorsey)
Tussagesic, Tab., Liq. (Dorsey)
• **TERPIN HYDRATE AND DEXTROMETHORPHAN HYDROBROMIDE ELIXIR,** U.S.P. XXI.
Use: Expectorant, antitussive.
See: Dicodethal, Elix. (Lannett)
TERRA-CORTRIL. (Pfipharmecs)
Use: Anti-inflammatory, antibiotic.
Topical Oint.: Hydrocortisone 1%, terramycin 3% in base of mineral oil and petrolatum.
Ophth. Susp.: Hydrocortisone 15 mg. terramycin HCl 5 mg./cc. Bot. w/dropper 5 cc.
TERRAMYCIN. (Pfipharmecs) Oxytetracycline
Use: Antibiotic.
Caps.: HCl salt 250 mg./Cap. Bot. 16s, 100s, 500s. Unit-Dose Pak Box 100s.
I.M. Solution: Oxytetracycline 100 mg. or 250 mg./2 cc.w/lidocaine 2%. Amp. 5s, 100s, 50 mg./cc. Vial 10 cc. Pkg. 5s.
I.V.: HCl salt 250 mg. Vial 5s, 500 mg. Vial 5s.
Oint., Ophth. W/Polymyxin B Sulfate: Oxytetracycline HC1 5 mg.w/Polymyxin B sulfate 1 mg./Gm. Tube 1/8 oz.
Oint., Topical: Oxytetracycline HCl 30 mg. w/Polymyxin B Sulfate 10,000 u./Gm. Tube 0.5 oz., 1 oz. 12s.
Powd. Topical: Oxytetracycline HCl 30 mg. w/Polymyxin B Sulfate 1 mg./Gm. Bot. 1 oz.
Syrup: Calcium oxytetracycline (125 mg./5 cc.) Bot. 2 oz., pt.
Tab., Oral: Oxytetracycline HCl 250 mg./Tab. Bot. 100s.
Tab., Vaginal: Oxytetracycline HCl 100 mg. w/Polymyxin B sulfate 100,000 units/Tab., starch, sod. carboxymethylcellulose, lactose, Mg stearate, methyl-paraben 0.3%, propylparaben 0.07%. Box 10s.
W/Hydrocortisone.
See: Terra-Cortril (Pfipharmecs)
TERRASTATIN. (Pfipharmecs) Oxytetracycline 250 mg., nystatin 250,000 units/Cap
Use: Antibiotic, antifungal.
TERRASYL. (Zenith) Chlorpheniramine maleate 2 mg., aspirin 324 mg., caffeine/Tab. Bot. 100s.
TERSAVID. N^1-pivaloyl-N^2-benzyl-hydrazine.
Use: Monoamine oxidase inhibitor.
TERTIARY AMYL ALCOHOL.
See: Amylene Hydrate. (Various Mfr.)

4′-TERT-BUTOXYACETANILIDE.
See: Tromal (Burroughs Wellcome)

6-TERT-BUTYL-3-(2-IMIDAZOLIN-2-YLMETHYL)-2,4-DIMETHYL-PHENOL MONO-HYDROCHLORIDE. Oxymetazoline Hydrochloride, U.S.P. XXI.

TERTROXIN SODIUM DERIVATIVE. Liothyronine, B.A.N.

TESAMONE. (Dunhall) Testosterone aqueous suspension.
'25' (25 mg./ml.) Amp. 10 ml.
'50' (50 mg./ml.) Amp. 10 ml.
'100' (100 mg./ml.) Amp. 10 ml.
Use: Androgen therapy.

• **TESICAM.** USAN. 4′-Chloro-1,2,3,4-tetrahydro-1,3-dioxo-4-isoquinolinecarboxanilide.
Use: Anti-inflammatory.

• **TESIMIDE.** USAN.
Use: Anti-inflammatory.

TESLAC. (Squibb) Testolactone 50 mg./Tab. Bot. 100s.
Use: Antineoplastic agent.

TESOGEN. (Sig) Testosterone 25 mg., estrone 2 mg./ml. Vial 10 ml.
Use: Hormone therapy.

TESOGEN L.A.. (Sig) Testosterone enanthate 180 mg., 90 mg., 50 mg., estradiol valerate 8 mg., 4 mg. and 2 mg. respectively/ml. Vial 10 ml.
Use: Androgen therapy.

TESONE. (Sig) Testosterone 25 mg., 50 mg., 100 mg./ml. Vial 10 ml.
Use: Androgen hormonal therapy.

TESONE L.A. (Sig) Testosterone enanthate 200 mg./ml. Vial 10 ml.
Use: Hormonal therapy.

TESTONE L.A. IN OIL. (Vortech) Testosterone enanthate 100 mg., 200 mg., benzyl alcohol 2%/cc. Vial 10 cc.

TESSALON. (Du Pont) Benzonatate 100 mg./Perle. Bot. 100s.
Use: Antitussive.

TESTA-C INJECTABLE. (Vortech) Testosterone cypionate 200 mg., benzyl alcohol 0.9%, benzyl benzoate 20%, cottonseed oil/cc. Vial 10 cc.
Use: Androgen therapy.

TESTADIATE-DEPO. (Kay) Testosterone cypionate 50 mg., estradiol cypionate 2 mg., chlorobutanol 0.5% in cottonseed oil/cc. Vial 10 cc.
Use: Hormone therapy.

TESTANATE No. 1. (Kenyon) Testosterone enanthate 100 mg., lipophilic soln. 200 mg./cc. Vial 10 cc.

TESTANATE No. 2. (Kenyon) Testosterone enanthate 90 mg., estradiol valerate 4 mg./cc. Vial 10 cc.

TESTANATE No. 3. (Kenyon) Testosterone enanthate 180 mg., estradiol valerate 8 mg./cc. Vial 10 cc.

TES-TAPE. (Lilly) Diagnostic test for glucose in urine. Glucose oxidase, glucose peroxidase, orthotolidine. Single Pkg. 100 tests.
Use: Diagnostic agent.

TESTAQUA. (Kay) Testosterone 25 mg., 50 mg., or 100 mg./cc. Vial 10 cc.
Use: Male hormone therapy.

TESTARR GRANULES, FLAKES, PLAIN & FORTIFIED. (Fellows) Plantago seed mucilage. Also available w/thiamine. Pkg. 180 Gm., 390 Gm.
Use: Laxative.

TESTAVOL-S. (Fellows) Vitamin A palmitate. 50,000 u./Cap. Bot. 100s, 1000s.
Use: Vitamin A deficiencies.

TEST-ESTRIN. (Marlyn) **Injection** (aqueous) Multiple dose vial 10 cc. 1s, 6s, 25s, 100s.

TESTEX. (Pasadena Research) Testosterone propionate in sesame oil 25 mg., 50 mg., 100 mg./cc. Vial 10 cc.

TESIONATE 100. (Seatrace) Testosterone cypionate 100 mg./ml. Vial 10 cc.

TESIONATE 200. (Seatrace) Testosterone 200 mg./ml. Vial 10 cc.

TEST-IONATE 200. (Tunex) Testosterone cypionate 200 mg./ml. w/benzyl benzoate 20%, benzyl alcohol 0.9%, cottonseed oil. Vial 10cc.
Use: Androgen therapy.

TESTOJECT. (Mayrand) Testosterone cypionate 100 mg./ml. Vial 10 ml.
Use: Androgenic hormone

TESTOJECT-50. (Mayrand) Testosterone 50 mg./ml. Vial 10 ml.
Use: Androgenic hormone.

TESTOJECT E.P. (Mayrand) Testosterone enanthate 200 mg., testosterone propianate 25 mg./ml. Vial 1 ml.
Use: Replacement therapy for male hypogonadism.

TESTOJECT LA. (Mayrand) Testosterone cypionate 100 mg./ml. in oil. Vial 10 ml.
Use: Longacting androgenic hormone.

• **TESTOLACTONE,** U.S.P. XXI. Sterile Suspension, Tab., U.S.P. XXI. 13-Hydroxy-3-oxo-13, 17-secoandrosta-1,4-dien-17oic acid-8-lactone.
Use: Antineoplastic agent.
See: Teslac, Vial, Tab. (Squibb)

TESTOLIN. (Pasadena Research) Testosterone suspension 25 mg., 50 mg., 100 mg./cc. Vial 10 cc. 25 mg./cc. Vial 30 cc.

TESTONE L. A. (Vortech) Testosterone enanthate 100 mg., 200 mg., benzyl alcohol 2%/ml. Vial. 10 ml.
Use: Androgen therapy (long acting).

TESTONEX 50. (Tunex) Testosterone 50 mg./ml. Vial 10 cc.
Use: Androgen therapy.

TESTONEX 100. (Tunex) Testosterone 100 mg./ml. Vial 10 cc.
Use: Androgen therapy.

• **TESTOSTERONE,** U.S.P. XXI. Pellets, Sterile Susp., U.S.P. XXI. 17 β-Hydroxyandrost-4-en-3-one.
Use: Androgen.
See: Android-T, Vial (Brown)
Androlan, Vial (Lannett)
Andronaq, Aq. Susp., Vial (Central)
Depotest, Vial (Hyrex)
Dura-Testrone, Vial (Pharmex)

Homogene-S, Inj., Vial (Spanner)
Malotrone Aqueous Injection (Bluco)
Nendron, Inj. (Noyes)
Neo-Hombreol-F, Aq. Susp., Vial (Organon)
Tesone, Inj. (Sig)
Testaqua, Aq. Susp., Vial (Kay)
Testolin, Vial (Pasadena Research)
Testonex 50, Inj. (Tunex)
Textonex 100, Inj. (Tunex)
Testrone, Vial (Pharmex)

TESTOSTERONE W/COMBINATIONS
See: Andesterone, Vial (Lincoln)
Android-G Vial (Brown)
Androne, Vial (Rocky Mtn.)
Anestrol, Inj. (Mallard)
Angen, Vial (Davis & Sly)
Depo-Testadiol, Vial (Upjohn)
Di-Genik, Vial (Savage)
Di-Hormone, Susp. (Paddock)
Di-Steroid, Vial (Kremers-Urban)
Duogen, Inj. (Vortech)
Duogen, Vial (Bel-Mar)
Estrone-Testosterone, Vial (Maurry)
Estrovag-Femogen, Supp. (Fellows-Testagar)
Geramine, Tab., Inj. (Brown)
Geratic Forte, Inj. (Keene Pharm.)
Geriamic, Tab. (Vortech)
Gerihorm, Inj. (Burgin-Arden)
Glutest, Vial (Brown)
Halodrin, Tab. (Upjohn)
Hormo-Triad, Vial (Bell)
Hormox Plus, Tab. (Parmed)
Mal-O-Fem, Aq. Susp., Vial (Fellows)
Terogen, Vial (Pasadena Research)
Tesogen, Inj. (Sig)
Testrolix, Inj. (Vortech)
Testrone, Vial (Pharmex)
Tostestro, Vial (Bowman)
Vi-Testrogen, Vial (Pharmex)

TESTOSTERONE CYCLOPENTANE PROPIONATE.
Testosterone Cypionate, U.S.P. XXI.

• **TESTOSTERONE CYPIONATE,** U.S.P. XXI. Inj., U.S.P. XXI. 17-β-Hydroxyandrost-4-en-3-one cyclopentanepropionate. Androst-4-en-3-one, 17-(3-cyclopentyl-1-oxopropoxy)-, (17β-Testosterone cyclopentanepropionate.
Use: Androgen.
See: Andro-Cyp 100, Inj. (Keene)
Andro-Cyp 200, Inj. (Keene)
Androgen-860, Inj. (Blue Line)
Depo-Testosterone, Inj. (Upjohn)
Dep-Test, Inj. (Sig)
Depotest, Vial (Hyrex)
D-Test 100, 200, Inj. (Burgin-Arden)
Durandro, Inj. (Ascher)
Testa-C, Inj. (Vortech)
Testra-C, Inj. (Amfre-Grant)
Test-Ionate 200, Inj. (Tunex)
Testromed-P.A., Vial (Medics)
Testoject, Vial (Mayrand)
T-Ionate-P.A., Vial (Reid-Provident)
W/Combinations.
See: D-Diol, Inj. (Burgin-Arden)
Depotestogen, Vial (Hyrex)
Depo-Testadiol, Sol. (Upjohn)
Dep-Testradiol, Inj. (Rocky Mtn.)
Duo-Cyp (Keene)
Duo-Ionate, Inj. (Tunex)
Duracrine, Inj. (Ascher)
Esangen, Sol. (Blue Line)
Estran-C, Inj. (Amfre-Grant)
Menoject-L.A. Vial (Kay)
Span F. M., Inj. (Scrip)
Spenduo, Inj. (Spencer-Mead)
Testa-C, Inj. (Vortech)
T.E. Ionate P.A., Inj. (Reid-Provident)
Testadiate-Depo, Vial (Kay)

• **TESTOSTERONE ENANTHATE,** U.S.P. XXI. Inj., U.S.P. XXI. Androst-4-en-3-one, 17-(1-oxoheptyl)-oxy-(17β)-. Testosterone heptanoate. 17β-Hydroxyandrost-4-en-3-one heptanoate.
Use: Androgen.
See: Andryl, Inj. (Keene)
Arderone 100, 200, Inj. (Burgin-Arden)
Delatest, Inj. (Dunhall)
Delatestryl, Inj. Vial (Squibb)
Dura-Testosterone, Vial (Pharmex)
Everone 200 Mg., Vial (Hyrex)
Repo-Testro Med., Vial (Medics)
Retandros-200, Inj. (Rocky Mtn.)
Span-Test 100 & 200. (Scrip)
Tesone L. A., Inj. (Sig)
Testate, Inj. (Savage)
Testra-E, Inj. (Amfre-Grant)
Testrin-P.A., Inj. (Pasadena Research)
Testone L. A. in Oil, Inj. (Vortech)
W/Chlorobutanol.
See: Anthatest, Vial (Kay)
W/Estradiol valerate.
See: Ardiol 90/4, 180/8, Inj. (Burgin-Arden)
Bi-Nate, Inj. (Tunex)
Deladumone, Vial (Squibb)
Delatestadiol, Vial (Dunhall)
Ditate, Ditate DS, Vial (Savage)
Duoval-P.A., Inj. (Reid-Provident)
Estran-E.V., Inj., (Amfre-Grant)
Repo-Duo Med., Vial (Medics)
Repose-TE. (Paddock)
Retadiamone, Vial (Rocky Mtn.)
Span-Est-Test 4, Inj. (Scrip)
Teev, Preps. (Keene)
Testanate No. 2 & 3, Vial (Kenyon)
Valertest, Amp., Vial (Hyrex)

TESTOSTERONE HEPTANOATE.
Use: Androgen.
See: Testosterone enanthate.

• **TESTOSTERONE KETOLAURATE.** USAN.
Testosterone 3-oxododecanoate.
Use: Androgen.

• **TESTOSTERONE PHENYLACETATE.** USAN.
Perandren phenylacetate.
Use: Androgen.

• **TESTOSTERONE PROPIONATE,** U.S.P.XXI.Tab.,Inj., U.S.P.XXI.Androst-4-en-3-one,17-(1-oxopropoxy),-(17β)-. 17β-Hydroxyandrost-4-en-3-one propionate.
Use: Androgen.
See: Androlan, Vial (Lannett)
Androlin, Vial (Lincoln)
Malotrone-P Injection (Bluco)
Neo-Hombreol, Vial (Organon)
Testex, Vial (Pasadena Research)
W/Estrone.

TESTOSTROVAL-P.A. (Reid-Provident) Testosterone enanthate 200 mg./cc. In oil. Vial 5 cc. 1s, 6s, 12s.

TESTRA-C. (Amfre-Grant) Testosterone cypionate 100 mg./ml. Vial 10 ml.
Use: Hormone.

TESTRA-E. (Amfre-Grant) Testosterone enanthate 100 mg./ml. Vial 10 ml.
Use: Hormone.

TESTRAMONE. (Harvey) Testosterone 12.5 mg., Vit. B-1 10 mg., B-2 2 mg., B-6 5 mg., niacinamide 40 mg., inositol 50 mg., choline chloride 10 mg., methionine 10 mg./cc. Vial 10 ml.
Use: Androgen therapy with Vitamin B complex.

TESTRIN-P.A. (Pasadena Research) Testosterone enanthate 200 mg., benzyl alcohol 2%/cc. Vial 10 cc.

TESTRED. (ICN) Methyltestosterone 10 mg./Cap. Bot. 100s.
Use: Androgen therapy.

TESTRONE. (Pharmex) Testosterone 25 mg., estrone 2 mg./cc. Vial 10 cc.
Use: I.M.; androgen therapy.

TESTURIA. (Ayerst) Combination kit containing 5 × 20 sterile dip strips and 5 × 20 culture trays of trypticase soy agar.
Use: Diagnostic aid.

TESULOID. (Squibb) Technetium Tc 99m sulfur colloid 5 vials/kit.
Use: Radiodiagnostic.

• **TETANUS ANTITOXIN,** U.S.P. XXI. (Wyeth)—Vial 1500, 3,000, 20,000 & 40,000 u. Tubex Sterile Cartridge Needle Unit 1500, 3000, 5000 u./t.
Use: Passive immunizing agent.
See: Homo-Tet, Vial, Syringe (Savage)

TETANUS AND DIPHTHERIA TOXOIDS ADSORBED FOR ADULT USE, U.S.P. XXI.
Use: Active immunizing agent for persons over 7 yrs. old.
Generic Products:
(Squibb-Connaught) Vial 5 ml. for I.M. use.
(Lederle) Vial 5 ml.

TETANUS-DIPHTHERIA TOXOIDS ADSORBED, ALUMINUM PHOSPHATE ADSORBED. (Wyeth) Vial 5 cc. Tubex 0.5 cc.
Use: I.M., Primary immunization or maintenance in persons over 10 years old.

TETANUS AND DIPHTHERIA TOXOIDS COMBINED PUROGENATED. (Lederle) Lederject disposable syringe 10 × 0.5 ml. Vial 5 ml. New package.

• **TETANUS IMMUNE GLOBULIN,** U.S.P. XXI.
(Hyland) Gamma globulin fraction of the plasma of persons who have been hyperimmunized with tetanus toxoid, 16.5%. Vial 250 u.
Use: Prophylaxis of injured, against tetanus passive immunizing agent.
See: Gamulin-T, Vial (Merrell Dow)
Homo-Tet Vial, 1 cc. (Savage)
Hu-Tet, Vial (Hyland)
Hyper-Tet Injection Vial, 250 u. (Cutter)
Immu-Tetanus, Vial, Disp. Syr. (Parke-Davis)
T-I-Gammagee, Disp. Syr. (Merck Sharp & Dohme)

TETANUS IMMUNE GLOBULIN, HUMAN, (Wyeth) 250 u./Tubex, 1 cc. Dissolved in glycine 0.3 M; contains thimerosal 0.01%.
See: Ar-Tet, Syringe, Vial (Armour)

• **TETANUS TOXOID,** U.S.P. XXI.
(Squibb-Connaught)—Vial 7.5 ml. for I.M. or S.C. use.
(Lederle)—Vial 0.5 cc., 5 cc.
(Wyeth)—Vial 7.5 cc. Tubex 0.5 cc.
Use: Active immunizing agent against tetanus.

• **TETANUS TOXOID, ADSORBED,** U.S.P. XXI.
(Serums and Vaccines of America) 20 Lf purified tetanus toxoid, 0.01% thimerosal as preservative/ml. Box 2 ampuls of 0.5 ml. Vial 5 ml., 7.5 ml., 0.5 ml. Amp. for booster injection.
(Squibb-Connaught) Vial 5 ml. for I.M. use
(Lederle)—Vial 5 ml. Steri-Dose syringe 0.5 ml. 10s.
(Wyeth)—Vial 5 cc. Tubex 0.5 cc.
Use: Active immunizing agent against tetanus.

TETANUS TOXOID ADSORBED PUROGENATED.
(Lederle) Vial 5 ml. Disp. syringe 0.5 ml.
Use: Active immunizing agent.

• **TETANUS TOXOID, ALUMINUM PHOSPHATE ADSORBED.**
Use: Active immunizing agent.
See: (Lederle) Vial 5 cc. 10s. Lederject Disp. Syr. 10 × 0.5 cc.
(Wyeth) Vial 5 cc. Tubex 0.5 cc.

TETANUS TOXOID, ALUM PRECIPITATED.
Use: Active immunizing agent.
See: (Cutter)—Vial 5 cc.
(Lilly)—Vial 1 & 5 cc. Hyporets 0.5 cc. 10s, 100s.
(Merck Sharp & Dohme)—Vial 5 cc.

TETANUS TOXOID, FLUID.
(Lederle)—Vial 7.5 ml., 0.5 ml. 10s, 100s.
Use: Active immunizing agent.

TETANUS TOXOID FLUID PUROGENATED.
(Lederle) Lederject Disposable syringe 10 × 0.5 ml. Vial 7.5 ml.

TETANUS TOXOID PURIFIED, FLUID.
(Wyeth)—Vial 7.5 cc., Tubex 0.5 cc.
Use: Active immunizing agent.

TET-CY. (Metro Med) Tetracycline HCl 250 mg./Cap. Bot. 100s, 1000s.
Use: Antibiotic.

TETIOTHALEIN SODIUM.
See: Iodophthalein Sodium. (Var. Mfr.)

TETNOR. Phenylbutazone, B.A.N.

TETRABEAD-125. (Abbott) T-4 diagnostic kit 100s, 500s.
Use: Quantitative measurement of total circulating serum thyroxine.

TETRA-C. (Century) Tetracycline HCl 250 mg./Cap. Bot. 100s, 1000s.
Use: Antibiotic.

TETRABENAZINE. B.A.N. 1,3,4,6,7,11b-Hexahydro-3-isobutyl-9, 10-dimethoxybenzo[a] quinolizin-2-one.
Use: Tranquilizer.
See: Nitoman

4,5,6,7-TETRABROMO-3′,3″-DISULFOPHENOLPHTHALEIN DISODIUM SALT. Sulfobromophthalein Sodium, U.S.P. XXI.

• **TETRACAINE,** U.S.P. XXI. Oint., Ophth. Oint., U.S.P. XXI. 2-Dimethylaminoethyl p-butyl-aminobenzoate.
Use: Local anesthetic.

• **TETRACAINE AND MENTHOL OINTMENT,** U.S.P. XXI.
Use: Local anesthetic.

• **TETRACAINE HYDROCHLORIDE,** U.S.P. XXI. Cream, Inj., Ophth. Soln., Topical Soln., Sterile, U.S.P. XXI. 2-(Dimethyl-amino)-ethyl p-(butylamino)-benzoate HCl. Benzoic acid, 4-(butylamino)-, 2-(dimethylamino)ethyl ester, monohydrochloride.
Use: Local anesthetic, topical anesthetic, spinal anesthetic.
See: Bristacycline, Cap. (Bristol)
Pontocaine Hydrochloride Prods. (Winthrop-Breon)
W/Benzocaine, butyl aminobenzoate.
See: Cetacaine, Liq., Oint., Spray (Cetylite)
W/Hexachlorophene, dimethyl polysiloxane, methyl salicylate, pyrilamine maleate, zinc oxide.
W/Isocaine, benzalkonium Cl.
See: Isotraine Oint. (Philips Roxane)

TETRACAINE HYDROCHLORIDE 0.5%.
(Alcon) 0.5%/1 cc. Drop-Tainer, Ophth. 15 cc. Steri-Unit, 2 cc. (Cooper Vision) Dropperettes 1 ml. in 10s.

TETRACAP 250. (Circle) Tetracycline hydrochloride 250 mg./Cap. Bot. 100s.
Use: Antibiotic.

• **TETRACHLORETHYLENE,** U.S.P. XXI. Cap., U.S.P. XXI. Perchlorethylene, tetrachlorethylene.
Use: Anthelmintic (hookworms and some trematodes).

4,5,6,7-TETRACHLORO-2′,4′,5′,7′-TETRAIODOFLUORESCEIN DISODIUM SALT. Rose Bengal Sodium I-131 Injection, U.S.P. XXI.

TETRACLOR. (Kenyon) Tetracycline HCl 250 mg./Cap. Bot. 100s, 1000s.

TETRACLOR-L. (Kenyon) Tetracycline HCl 125 mg./5 cc. Bot. pt.

TETRA-CO. (Coastal) Tetracycline HCl 250 mg./Tab. Bot. 100s, 1000s. Syr. Bot. pt.

TETRA-CO 500 BID. (Coastal) Tetracycline 500 mg./Cap. Bot. 100s, 1000s.

TETRACON. (Professional Pharmacal)
Tetrahydrozoline HCl 0.5 mg., disodium edetate 1.0 mg., boric acid 12 mg., benzalkonium Cl. 0.1 mg., sodium Cl. 2.2 mg., sodium borate 0.5 mg./ml. w/water. Bot. 15 ml.
Use: Minor eye irritation.

TETRACOSACTIDE. (I.N.N.). Tetracosactrin, B.A.N.

TETRACOSACTRIN. B.A.N. $\beta^{1\text{-}24}$-Corticotrophin.
Use: Corticotrophic peptide.
See: Cortrosyn
Cosyntropin
Synacthen
Tetracosactide (I.N.N.)

• **TETRACYCLINE,** U.S.P. XXI. Boluses, Oral Susp., U.S.P. XXI. 4-(Dimethylamino)-1,4,4a,5,5a,6,11,12a-octahydro-3,-6,10,12,12a-penta hydroxy-6-methyl-1,11-dioxo-2-naphthacenecarboxamide.
Use: Antibiotic.
See: Robitet, Syr. (Robins)
Sumycin, Syrup (Squibb)
W/N-acetyl-para-amino-phenol, phenyltoloxamine citrate.
Use: Antibacterial; antiamebic; antirickettsial.
See: Paltet, Cap. (Hauck)
Tetrex, Bid Cap., Cap., Vial (Bristol)

• **TETRACYCLINE AND AMPHOTERICIN B,** U.S.P. XXI. Cap., Oral Susp., U.S.P. XXI.

• **TETRACYCLINE HYDROCHLORIDE,** U.S.P. XXI. Cap., Inj., Oint., Ophth Oint., Topical Soln., Ophth. Susp., Sterile, Tab., U.S.P. XXI.
Use: Antibiotic.
See: Achromycin, Preps. (Lederle)
Amer-Tet, Tab. (Robinson)
Amer-Tet Suspension (Robinson)
Anacel, Sol. (Softcon)
Bicycline, Caps. (Knight)
Centet 250, Tab. (Central)
Cyclopar, Cap. (Parke-Davis)
Desamycin, Cap. (Pharmics)
Fed-Mycin, Cap. (Amfre-Grant)
G-Mycin, Cap. & Syr. (Coast)
Maso-Cycline, Cap. (Mason)
Nor-Tet, Cap. (Vortech)
Partrex, Cap. (Parmed)
Retet, Cap. (Reid-Provident)
Robitet, Cap. (Robins)
Sarocycline, Cap., Inj., Syr. (Saron)
Scotrex, Caps. (Scott/Cord)
SK-Tetracycline, Cap., Syr. (SmithKline)
Sumycin, Cap., Tab., Syr. (Squibb)
Tet-Cy, Cap. (Metro)
Tetracap 250, Cap. (Circle)
Tetra-C, Cap. (Century)
Tetrachel, Cap. (Rachelle)
Tetrachor, Tetrachor-L, Cap. Liq. (Kenyon)
Tetra-Co, Cap. (Coastal)
Tetracycline HCl, Cap.
Tetracycline HCl, Preps.
Tetracyn, Cap., Inj., (Pfipharmecs)
Tetralan "250", "500", Cap. (Lannett)
Tetram and Tetram-S, Cap., Syr. (Dunhall)
Tetramax, Cap. (Rand)
Topicycline, Liq. (Proctor & Gamble)
Trexin, Cap. (A.V.P. Pharm.)
W/Citric Acid.
See: Achromycin V, Cap., Drop, Susp., Syr. (Lederle)
W/Nystatin.
See: Comycin, Cap. (Upjohn)
Tetrastatin, Cap. (Pfipharmecs)
W/Sulfamethizole, phenazopyridine HCl.
See: Azotrex, Cap. (Bristol)

• **TETRACYCLINE HYDROCHLORIDE AND NYSTATIN CAPSULES,** U.S.P. XXI.
Use: Antibiotic, antifungal.

See: Comycin, Cap. (Upjohn) Tetrastatin, Cap. (Pfipharmecs)

• **TETRACYCLINE ORAL SUSPENSION,** U.S.P. XXI.
Use: Antibiotic.
See: Brand names under Tetracycline.

• **TETRACYCLINE PHOSPHATE COMPLEX,** U.S.P. XXI. Cap., Inj., Sterile, U.S.P. XXI. A sparingly soluble complex of sodium metaphosphate and tetracycline.
Use: Antibiotic.
See: Bristrex
Tetrex, Cap., Vial (Bristol)
Tetrex-S, Ped. Drops, Syr. (Bristol)
W/Amphotericin B.
See: Mysteclin F, Cap., Drops & Syr. (Squibb)

TETRACYN. (Pfipharmecs) Tetracycline HCl. 250 mg. Cap. Bot. 100s, 1000s. 500 mg. Bot. 100s.
Use: Antibiotic.

TETRACYN I.M. (Pfipharmecs) Tetracycline HCl 100 mg./Vial 1 cc., 5s.

TETRAETHYLAMMONIUM BROMIDE (TEAB).
Use: Diagnostic & therapeutic agent in peripheral vascular disorders. Diagnostic in hypertension.

TETRAETHYLAMMONIUM CHLORIDE.
Use: Ganglionic blocking agent.

TETRAETHYLTHIURAM DISULFIDE.
See: Disulfiram

• **TETRAFILCON A.** USAN.
Use: Contact lens material.

TETRAGEN. Tetracycline, B.A.N.

2-(1,2,3,4-TETRAHYDRO-1-NAPHTHYL)-2-IMIDAZOLINE MONOHYDROCHLORIDE. Tetrahydrozoline Hydrochloride, U.S.P. XXI.

TETRAHYDROPHENOBARBITAL CALCIUM.
See: Cyclobarbital Calcium, Prep.

TETRAHYDROXYQUINONE. Name used for Tetroquinone.

TETRAHYDROZOLINE. B.A.N. 2-(1,2,3,4-Tetrahydro-1-naphthyl)-2-imidazoline.
Use: Vasoconstrictor.
See: Tetryzoline (I.N.N.)
Tyzanol hydrochloride.

• **TETRAHYDROZOLINE HYDROCHLORIDE,** U.S.P. XXI. Nasal Sol., Ophth. Sol. U.S.P. XXI. 2-(1,2,3,4-Tetrahydro-1-naphthyl)-2-imidazoline HCl.
Use: Adrenergic.
See: Murine Plus (Abbott)
Tyzine, Sol. (Key)
Visine, Sol. (Leeming)

2′,4′,5′,7′-TETRAIODOFLUORESCEIN DISODIUM SALT MONOHYDRATE. Erythrosine Sodium, U.S.P. XXI.

TETRAIODOPHENOLPHTHALEIN SODIUM.
See: Iodophthalein Sodium.

TETRAIODOPHTHALEIN SODIUM.
See: Iodophthalein Sodium.

1-3,5,3′,5′-TETRAIODOTHYRONINE SODIUM. Levothyroxine Sodium U.S.P. XXI.

TETRALAN "250". (Lannett) Tetracycline HCl 250 mg./Cap. Bot. 100s, 1000s.

TETRALAN "500". (Lannett) Tetracycline HCl 500 mg./Cap. Bot. 100s, 1000s.

TETRALYSAL. Lymecycline, B.A.N.

TETRAM. (Dunhall) Tetracycline 250 mg./Cap. Bot. 100s.
Use: Antibiotic.

TETRAMAX. (Rand) Tetracycline HCl 250 mg./Cap. Bot. 100s, 1000s.
Use: Antibacterial & antirickettsial.

TETRAMETHYLENE DIMETHANESULFONATE.
See: Busulfan, U.S.P. XXI.

1,2,2,6-TETRAMETHYL-4-PIPERIDYL MANDELATE HYDROCHLORIDE. Eucatropine Hydrochloride, U.S.P. XXI.

TETRAMETHYLTHIURAM DISULFIDE. Thiram.
Use: Antibacterial & antifungal agent.
See: Rezifilm, Aerosol (Squibb)

TETRAMISOLE. B.A.N. (±)-2,3,5,6-Tetrahydro-6-phenylimidazo[2,1-b]thiazole.
Use: Anthelmintic, veterinary medicine.
See: Nilverm hydrochloride.

• **TETRAMISOLE HYDROCHLORIDE.**USAN. ± 2,3,5,6-Tetrahydro-6-phenylimidazo [2,1-b]-thiazole HCl.
Use: Anthelmintic.
See: Ripercol (American Cyanamid)

TETRANEED. (Hanlon) Pentaerythritol tetranitrate 80 mg./Time Cap. Bot. 100s.

TETRANTOIN. 7,8-Benzo-1,3-diazaspiro(4,5)-decane-2,4-dione. 3′,4′-Dihydrospiro-[imidazolidine-4,2′(1′H)-naphthalene]-2,5-dione.
Use: Anticonvulsant.

TETRATAB. (Freeport) Pentaerythritol tetranitrate 10 mg./Tab. Bot. 1000s.
Use: Management, prophylaxis and treatment of angina attacks.

TETRATAB NO. 1. (Freeport) Pentaerythritol tetranitrate 20 mg./Tab. Bot. 1000s.
Use: Management, prophylaxis, & treatment of angina attacks.

TETRATAB NO. 2. (Freeport) Pentaerythritol tetranitrate 10 mg., phenobarbital 0.25 gr./Tab. Bot. 1000s.
Use: Prophylactic treatment of angina.

TETRATE. (Pasadena Research) Pentaerythritol tetranitrate 30, or 80 mg./Cap. Bot. 100s, 1000s.
Use: Coronary vasodilator.

TETRAZYME. (Abbott) Test kit 100s, 500s.
Use: Enzyme immunoassay for quantitative measurement of total circulating serum thyroxine (free and protein bound).

TE TREE OIL. (Metabolic Prod.) Australian oil of Melaleuca alternifolia 100% pure. Bot. 1, 4, 8, 16 oz. **Cream** Bot. 8 oz. **Oint.** Tube 1 oz., 3 oz.
Use: Antiseptic, fungistatic.

TETREX. (Bristol) Tetracycline phosphate complex equivalent to 250 mg. tetracycline HCl/Cap. Bot. 100s.
W/Sulfamethizole and phenylazo-diaminopyridine HCl.
See: Azotrex, Cap. (Bristol)

TETREX bid CAPS. (Bristol) Tetracycline phosphate complex equivalent to 500 mg., tetracycline HCl/Cap. Bot. 50s, 100s.

TETREX PMT NITRATE. Rolitetracycline, B.A.N.

• **TETROQUINONE.** USAN. Tetrahydroxy-p-benzoquinone.
Use: Treat keloids, keratolytic.
See: Kelox (Elder)

• **TETRYDAMINE.** USAN. 4,5,6,7-Tetrahydro-2-methyl-3-(methylamino)-tetrahydroindazole.
Use: Analgesic, anti-inflammatory.

TETRYZOLINE (I.N.N.). Tetrahydrozoline, B.A.N.

TETTERINE. (Shuptrine) **Oint.:** Antifungal agents in green petrolatum base. Tin 1 oz.; Antifungal agents in white petroleum base. Tube 1 oz. **Powder:** Fungicide, germicide formula powder for heat and diaper rash. Can 2.5 oz. **Soap:** Bar 3.25 oz.
Use: Treatment ringworm, athlete's foot, diaper rash and other skin conditions.

TEXACORT SCALP LOTION. (Rydell) Hydrocortisone alcohol 1%, benzalkonium chloride, alcohol 33%, propylene glycol, polysorbate 20, purified water. Dropper Bot. 1 fl. oz.
Use: Corticosteroid.

T-FLUORIDE. (Tennessee) Sodium fluoride 2.21 mg./Tab. Bot. 100s, 1000s.
Use: Dental caries and prophylactic.

T-GEN SUPPOSITORIES. (Goldline) Trimethobenzamide HCl 100 mg./Supp. pediatric. 200 mg./Supp. adults.
Box 10s, 50s.
Use: Antinausea.

T-GESIC CAPSULE. (Tennessee) Acetyl para-amino phenol 200 mg., phenacetin 2.5 gr., hyoscyamine sulfate 0.031 mg., pentobarbital 0.25 gr./Cap. Bot. 100s.
Use: Analgesic.

• **THALIDOMIDE.** USAN. a-(N-Phthalimido)glutarimide. 2-Phthalimidoglutarimide.
Use: Hypnotic, sedative.

THALITONE. (Boehringer Ingelheim) Chlorthalidone 25 mg./Tab. Bot. 100s.
Use: Diuretic.

THALLIUM 201. (Squibb) Thallous chloride Tl 201. 2.2, 6.6 nmCi/vial.
Use: Radiodiagnostic.

• **THALLOUS CHLORIDE TL-201 INJECTION,** U.S.P. XXI.
Use: Diagnostic aid (radioactive agent).

THAM SOLUTION. (Abbott) Tromethamine 18 Gm., acetic acid 2.5 Gm., in water for inj. Single-dose container.
Use: For prevention and correction of severe systemic acidosis.

THAM-E. (Abbott) Tromethamine 36 Gm., sodium Cl. 1.75 Gm., potassium Cl. 0.37 Gm./150 ml. powder. Vial for reconstitution.
Use: Systemic acidosis in life-threatening situations.

THEAMIN. Monoethanolamine salt of theophylline
See: Monotheamin, Supp. (Lilly)
W/Amobarbital.
See: Monotheamin and Amytal, Pulvule (Lilly)

THEAN. Proxyphylline, B.A.N.

THEBACON. B.A.N. O^6-Acetyl-O^3-methyl-Δ^6-morphine.
Use: Narcotic analgesic; cough suppressant.
See: Acetyldihydrocodeinone

THEDRAZOL. (Kenyon) Pentylenetetrazol 100 mg., nicotinic acid 50 mg./Tab. Bot. 100s, 1000s.
Use: Hypertension.

THEDRAZOL-L. (Kenyon) Pentylenetetrazol 100 mg., niacin 50 mg./5 cc. Bot. 4 oz., pt., gal.

THEELIN AQUEOUS SUSPENSION. (Parke-Davis) A suspension of estrone in isotonic sodium chloride solution for I.M. adm. **Steri**-Vial: 2 mg. (20,000 I.U.)/ml. Vial 10 ml.
Use: For treating symptoms associated with menopause.

THEELIN INJECTION. (Morton) Estrone suspension 2 mg. or 5 mg./ml. Vial 10 ml. For I.M. administration.
Use: Estrogen.

THEELIN IN OIL. (Morton) Natural estrogenic substance 2 mg./ml. (20,000 I.U./ml.) in oil. Vial 30 cc.
Use: Estrogen.

THEMALON. Diethylthiambutene, B.A.N.

THENALIDINE. B.A.N. 1-Methyl-4-N-(2-thenyl)-anilinopiperidine.
Use: Antihistamine.
See: Sandosten (tartrate)

THENALIDINE TARTRATE. 1-Methyl-4-(N-2-thenylanilino) piperidine tartrate.
Use: Antihistaminic; antipruritic.

THENDELATE. (Blue Line) Methenamine mandelate 0.5 gr./Tab. Bot. 100s, 1000s.

THENFADIL. Thenyldiamine, B.A.N.

• **THENIUM CLOSYLATE.** USAN. N,N-Dimethyl, N2-phenoxy-ethyl-N-2-thenylammonium p-chlorobenzenesulfonate.
Use: Canine hookworm.
See: Bancari (Burroughs Wellcome)

THENYLDIAMINE. B.A.N. 2-(N-2-Pyridyl-N-2-thenyl-amino)ethyldimethylamine.
Use: Antihistamine.
See: Thenfadil (hydrochloride)

THENYLDIAMINE HYDROCHLORIDE. 2-[(2-Dimethylaminoethyl)-3-thenyl-amino] pyridine HCl, thenyldramine chloride. Dethylandiomine.

THENYLPYRAMINE.
See: Methapyrilene Hydrochloride, Preps.

THEO-24. (Searle) Theophylline anhydrous 100 mg., 200 mg., or 300 mg./Controlled- Release Cap. Bot. 100s. Unit Dose 100s.
Use: Bronchodilator, antiasthmatic.

THEOBID. (Glaxo) Theophylline 260 mg./Timed Cap. Bot. 60s, 500s. Unit dose 100s.
Use: Bronchial asthma, chronic obstructive pulmonary disease.

THEOBID JR DURACAP. (Glaxo) Anhydrous theophylline 130 mg./Cap. Sustained release. Bot 60s, 500s.
Use: Bronchial asthma, chronic obstructive disease.

THEOBROMA OIL. Cocoa Butter, N.F. XVI.
Use: Suppository base.

THEOBROMINE WITH PHENOBARBITAL COMBINATIONS.
See: Harbolin, Tab. (Arcum)
Theocardone, Tab. (Lemmon)
T.P. KI, Tab. (Wendt-Bristol)

THEOBROMINE CALCIUM GLUCONATE.
(Bates)—Tab., Bot. 100s, 1000s. Also available w/phenobarbital.
(Grant)—Tab., Bot. 100s, 500s, 1000s.

THEOBROMINE MAGNESIUM OLEATE.
W/Magnesium nicotinate.
See: Athemol-N, Tab. (Glaxo)

THEOBROMINE SODIUM ACETATE. Theobromine calcium salt mixture with calcium salicylate.
Use: Diuretic; smooth muscle relaxant.

THEOBROMINE SODIUM SALICYLATE.
See: Doan's Pills (Purex)
W/Cal. lactate, Phenobarbital.
See: Theolaphen, Tab. (Elder)

THEOCALBITAL. (Forrest) Cal. lactate 1 gr., phenobarbital sod. 0.25 gr., theobromine 3.5 gr./Tab. Bot. 100s.
Use: Diuretic with sedative.

THEOCAP. (Glaxo) Theophylline anhydrous 200 mg./Cap. Bot. 60s, 500s.
Use: Bronchial asthma, obstructive pulmonary disease.

THEOCLEAR 80 SYRUP. (Central) Theophylline 80 mg./15 ml. Bot. Pt., Gal.
Use: Bronchodilator

THEOCLEAR L.A.-130 (Central) Theophylline 130 mg./Cenule. Bot. 100s, 1000s.
Use: Bronchodilator

THEOCLEAR L.A.-260 (Central) Theophylline 260 mg./Cenule Bot. 100s, 1000s.
Use: Bronchodilator

THEO-COL. (Quality Generics) Theophylline 150 mg., guaifenesin 90 mg./ 15 ml. Elix. w/alcohol 15%. Cap. Bot. 100s, 1000s, Elix. Bot. pt., gal.

THEOCOLATE LIQUID. (Bay) Theophylline 150 mg., guaifenesin 90 mg./15 cc. Bot. pt., gal.
Use: Bronchodilator, expectorant for treatment of bronchospasm.

THEOCOMP CAPSULES. (Barry-Martin) Aminophylline 2 gr., ephedrine sulfate 3/8 gr., amobarbital 3/8 gr./Cap. Bot. 1000s.

THEODRENALINE. B.A.N. 7-[2-(3,4,β-Trihydroxyphenethylamino)ethyl]theophylline.
Use: Analeptic.

THEO-DROX. (Quality Generics) Ephedrine sulfate 25 mg., theophylline 130 mg., hydroxyzine HCl 10 mg./Tab. Bot. 100s, 500s.
Use: Bronchodilator.

THEO-DUR SPRINKLE (Key) Anhydrous theophylline 50 mg., 75 mg., 125 mg. or 200 mg./Sust. Action Cap. Bot. 100s.
Use: Bronchodilator.

THEO-DUR TABLETS. (Key) Anhydrous theophylline 100 mg., 200 mg., 300 mg./Sust. Action Tab. Bot. 100s, 500s, 1000s, 5000s. Unit dose 100s.
Use: Bronchodilator.

THEOFED. (Sutliff & Case) Phenobarbital 8 mg., theophylline 130 mg., ephedrine HCl 24 mg., atropine sulfate 1/300 gr., pyrilamine maleate 25 mg., magnesium trisilicate 130 mg., guaifenesin 50 mg./Tab. Bot. 100s, 1000s.
Use: Diuretic, antispasmodic, sedative, bronchodilator and antihistamine.

THEOFEDRAL FORMULA. (Wolins) Phenobarbital 1/8 gr., theophylline 2 gr., ephedrine HCl 3/8 gr./Tab. Bot. 100s, 1000s, 5000s.

THEOFENAL. (Cumberland) Theophylline 130 mg., ephedrine HCl 24 mg., phenobarbital 8 mg./ Tab. Bot. 100s.
Use: Symptomatic relief in asthma.

• **THEOFIBRATE.** USAN.
Use: Antihyperlipoproteinemic.

THEOFORT. (Amfre-Grant) Theophylline sod. glycinate 320 mg./15 cc. Bot. pt., gal.
Use: Bronchial dilator.

THEOGEN. (Sig) Conjugated estrogens 2 mg./ml. Vial 10 cc., 30 cc.
Use: Menopausal syndrome.

THEOGEN I.P. (Sig) Estrone 2 mg., potassium estrone sulfate 1 mg./ml. Vial 10 ml.
Use: Estrogen therapy.

THEO-GUAIA. (Sutliff & Case) **Liq.:** Theophylline 50 mg., guaifenesin 35 mg., alcohol 20%/5 cc. Bot. pts., gals.
Use: Asthmatic disorders.

THEOLAIR. (Riker) Anhydrous theophylline 125 mg./Tab. Boxes 250s foil sealed. Bot. 100s.
Use: Relief of bronchospasm.

THEOLAIR 250. (Riker) Theophylline anhydrous 250 mg./Tab. Bot. 100s. Box 250s foil sealed.
Use: Bronchial dilator.

THEOLAIR LIQUID. (Riker) Theophylline anhydrous 80 mg./15 ml. Bot. pt.
Use: Bronchdilator.

THEOLAIR PLUS LIQUID. (Riker) Theophylline 80 mg., guaifenesin /15 ml. Bot. Pt.
Use: Relief of acute bronchial asthma.

THEOLAIR PLUS TABLETS. (Riker) **125:** Theophylline 125 mg., guaifenesin 100 mg./Tab. Bot. 100s. **250:** Theophylline 250 mg., guaifenesin 200 mg./Tab. Bot. 100s.
Use: Relief of acute bronchial asthma.

THEOLAIR-SR 200. (Riker) Theophylline anhydrous 200 mg./Tab. (slow release). Bot. 100s, 250s.
Use: Bronchial dilator.

THEOLAIR-SR 250. (Riker) Theophylline anhydrous 250 mg./Tab. (slow release). Bot. 100s, 250s.
Use: Bronchial dilator.

THEOLAIR-SR 300. (Riker) Theophylline anhydrous 300 mg./Tab. (slow release). Bot. 100s, 250s.
Use: Bronchial dilator.

THEOLAIR-SR 500. (Riker) Theophylline anhydrous 500 mg./Tab. (slow release). Bot. 100s, 250s.
Use: Bronchial dilator.

THEOLATE LIQUID. (Goldline) Theophylline, glyceryl guaiacolate. Bot. pt. gal.
Use: Bronchodilator.

HEO-LIX. (Freeport) Theophylline 80 mg., alcohol 19-20% per 15 cc. Bot. pt.
Use: Treatment of bronchial asthma, bronchitis, and cardiac dyspnea.

HEOLIXIR. (Panray) Theophylline 80 mg., alcohol 20%/15 cc. Bot. 4 oz., 8 oz., pt., gal.
Use: Bronchodilator.

HEOMER INJECTION. (Fellows) Sod. mersalyl 100 mg., theophylline 50 mg./cc. Vial 10 cc.

HEON. (Bock) Theophylline 50 mg./5 ml. w/alcohol 10%. Bot. pt., gal
Use: Bronchodilator.

HEO-ORGANIDIN. (Wallace) Theophylline anhydrous 120 mg., iodinated glycerol 30 mg./15 cc. w/alcohol 15%. Bot. pt., gal.
Use: Bronchodilator, mucolytic-expectorant combination.

HEOPHYL-225. (McNeil Pharm) Anhydrous theophylline. **Tab.:** 225 mg./Tab. Bot. 100s. **Elixir:** 225 mg./30 ml. Bot. pt.
Use: Bronchodilator.

HEOPHYL CHEWABLE TABLETS. (McNeil Pharm) Anhydrous theophylline 100 mg./Chewable Tab. Bot. 100s.
Use: Bronchodilator.

HEOPHYL-SR. (McNeil Pharm) Anhydrous theophylline 125 mg. or 250 mg./SR Cap. Bot. 100s.
Use: Bronchodilator.

THEOPHYLLINE, Cap., U.S.P. XXI. Tab., U.S.P. XXI. 1,3-Dimethylxanthine. 1H-Purine-2,6-dione,3,-7-dihydro-1,3-dimethyl-, monohydrate.
Use: Coronary vasodilator & diuretic; pharm necessity for Aminophylline Injection.
See: Accurbron, Liq. (Merrell Dow)
Aerolate, Cap., Elix. (Fleming)
Aquaphyllin, Syr. (Ferndale)
Bronkodyl, Cap., Elix. (Winthrop-Breon)
Duraphyl, Tab. (McNeil Pharm)
Elixicon, Susp. (Berlex)
Elixophyllin, Elix., Cap. (Berlex)
Elixophyllin SR, Cap. (Berlex)
Lanophyllin, Elix. (Lannett)
Lodrane, Cap. (Poythress)
Optiphyllin, Elix. (Fougera)
Oralphyllin, Liq. (Consol. Midland)
Quibron-T Dividose, Tab. (Mead Johnson)
Quibron-T/SR Dividose, Tab. (Mead Johnson)
Slo-bid, Caps. (Rorer)
Slo-Phyllin, Cap., Syr., Tab. (Dooner)
Somophyllin, Cap. (Fisons)
Theo-II, Elix. (Fleming)
Theobid, Cap. (Glaxo)
Theobid Jr, Cap. (Glaxo)
Theocap, Cap. (Glaxo)
Theoclear 80, Liq. (Central)
Theoclear L.A., Cenule (Central)
Theo-Dur, Tab. (Key)
Theolair, Tab., Liq. (Riker)
Theolair SR, Tab. (Riker)
Theolixir, Elix. (Panray)
Theospan, Cap. (Laser)
Theostat, Prods. (Laser)
Theovent Long-Acting, Cap. (Schering)

THEOPHYLLINE W/COMBINATIONS
See: Airet Y, Tab., Elix. (Baylor)
Anti-Asthma, Tab. (Panray)
Asmabar, Tab. (Blue Line)
Asma-lief, Tab., Susp. (Quality Generics)
Asma Syrup (Coastal)
Asthmaspan, Cap. (Wolins)
Ayrcap, Cap. (Ascher)
B.A. Prods. (Federal)
Broncholate, Cap., Elix. (Bock)
Bronkaid, Tab. (Brew)
Co-Xan, Liq. (Central)
Elixophyllin-KI, Elix. (Berlex)
Emphysal Cap. (Douglas)
Eponal, Tab. (Cenci)
Fedrelen, Tab. (Scrip)
Foyuretic, Vial (Foy)
Isophed, Tab. (Jamieson-McKames)
Lardet, Tab. (Standex)
Lardet Expectorant, Tab. (Standex)
Liquophylline, Liq. (Paddock)
Marax DF, Syr. (Roerig)
Marax, Tab. (Roerig)
Maso-Thyllin, Tab. (Mason)
Meprophyl, Vial (Lemmon)
Mernephria, Inj. (Paddock)
Mersaline, Inj. (Standex)
Mersaphyllin, Vial (Pharmex)
Phedral, Tab. (Vortech)
Pheno-Fed, Tab. (Wendt-Bristol)
Phyllicin, Pow. (Knoll)
Quibron, Cap., Liq.(Mead Johnson)
Quibron-300, Cap. (Mead Johnson)
Quibron Plus, Cap. (Mead Johnson)
Quilate, Cap. (Wolins)
Slo-Phyllin Gg, Cap. Syr. (Dooner)
Synate-M, Tab. (Central)
Synophylate, Liq. (Central)
Tedral SA, Tab. (Parke-Davis)
Theobid, Cap. (Glaxo)
Theocol, Cap. Liq. (Quality Generics)
Theofed, Tab. (Sutliff & Case)
Theofedral Formula, Tab. (Wolins)
Theofenal, Tab. (Cumberland)
Theolair Plus, Tab., Liq. (Riker)
Theo-Organidin, Elix. (Wampole)
Thephecon, Improved, Cap. (Marsh-Emory)
Theophylline-KI Elixir (G & W Labs)

THEOPHYLLINE WITH PHENOBARBITAL COMBINATIONS.
See: Aqualin-Plus, Supp. (Webcon)
Asma-Lief, Tab., Susp. (Quality Generics)
Asminyl, Tab. (Cole)
Bronkolixir, Elix. (Winthrop-Breon)
Bronkotab, Tab. (Winthrop-Breon)
Ceepa, Tab. (Geneva)
Chlorphen, Tab., Cap., Vial (Truxton)
Emfaseen, Cap. (Saron)
For-Az-Ma, Syr. (Vitarine)
Iso-Asminyl, Tab. (Cole)

Synophedal, Tab. (Central)
Synophylate w/Phenobarbital, Tab., (Central)
T-E-P Compound, Tab. (Stanlabs)
Thephecon Improved, Cap. (Marsh-Emory)
Thymodyne, Tab. (Noyes)
Vitaphen, Tab. (Vitarine)

THEOPHYLLINE AMINOISOBUTANOL. Theophylline w/2-amino-2-methyl-1-propanol.
See: Butaphyllamine (Var. Mfr.)

THEOPHYLLINE, 8-BROMO, AMINOISOBUTANOL.
See: Pamabrom

THEOPHYLLINE, 8-BROMO, PYRILAMINE.
See: Pyrabrom

THEOPHYLLINE-CALCIUM SALICYLATE.
W/Ephedrine HCl, phenobarbital, pot. iodide.
See: Quadrinal, Tab., Susp. (Knoll)
W/Phenobarbital, ephedrine HCl, guaifenesin.
See: Verequad, Tab., Susp. (Knoll)
W/Potassium iodide.
See: Theokin, Tab., Elix. (Knoll)

THEOPHYLLINE, 8-CHLORO, DIPHENHYDRAMINE. Dimenhydrinate, U.S.P. XXI.
See: Dramamine, Prep. (Searle)

THEOPHYLLINE CHOLINE SALT.
See: Choledyl, Tab., Elix. (Warner-Chilcott)

• **THEOPHYLLINE, EPHEDRINE HYDROCHLORIDE, AND PHENOBARBITAL TABLETS,** U.S.P. XXI.
Use: Bronchodilator, sedative.

THEOPHYLLINE ETHYLENEDIAMINE.
See: Aminophylline, Prep., (Var. Mfr.)

• **THEOPHYLLINE AND GUAIFENESIN CAPSULES,** U.S.P. XXI.
Use: Smooth muscle relaxant, expectorant.

THEOPHYLLINE MONOETHANOLAMINE.
See: Fleet Brand, Rectal (Fleet)
Monotheamin, Supp. (Lilly)

THEOPHYLLINE OLAMINE. Theophylline compound with 2-amino-ethanol (1:1).
Use: Smooth muscle relaxant.

• **THEOPHYLLINE SODIUM GLYCINATE,** U.S.P. XXI. Elixir, Tab., U.S.P. XXI.
Use: Smooth muscle relaxant.
See: Bronchobid, Cap. (Glaxo)
Synophylate, Elix., Tab. (Central)
Theofort, Elix. (Federal Pharm.)
W/Guaifenesin.
See: Asbron G, Tab., Elix. (Dorsey)
Synophylate-GG, Tab., Syr. (Central)
W/Phenobarbital.
See: Synophylate w/Phenobarbital, Tab. (Central)
W/Potassium iodide.
See: TSG-KI, Elix. (Elder)
W/Potassium iodide, ephedrine HCl, codeine phosphate.
See: TSG Croup Liquid. (Elder)
W/Racephedrine & phenobarbital.
See: Synophedal, Tab. (Central)

THEOSPAN-SR 130. (Laser) Theophylline anhydrous 130 mg./Cap. Bot. 100s, 1000s.
Use: Bronchodilator.

THEOSPAN-SR 260. (Laser) Theophylline anhydrou 260 mg./Cap. Bot. 100s, 1000s.
Use: Bronchodilator.

THEOSTAT 80 SYRUP. (Laser) Theophylline anhydrous 80 mg./15 ml. Bot. Pts., Gal.
Use: Bronchodilator.

THEO-SYL-R. (Kay) Sodium mersalyl 100 mg., theophylline 50 mg./cc. Vial 10 cc.
Use: Mercury diuretic.

THEOTABS. (Panray) Theophylline 130 mg., ephedrine HCl 25 mg., phenobarbital 8 mg./Tab. Bot. 100s, 1000s.
Use: Anti-asthmatic.

THEO-TIME SR TABS. (Major) Theophylline 100 mg 200 mg., or 300 mg./S.R. Tab. Bot. 100s, 500s.
Use: Bronchodilator.

THEOVENT LONG-ACTING. (Schering) Theophyllin anhydrous 125 mg. or 250 mg./Cap. Bot. 100s, 500s.
Use: Bronchial dilator.

THEPHECON IMPROVED CAPSULES. (Marsh-Emory Theophylline 260 mg., pseudoephedrine hydrochloride 50 mg., butabarbital 15 mg./Cap. Bot. 100s, 1000s.
Use: Bronchial dilatation.

THERA. (Zenith) Multiple vitamin tablet. Bot. 100s.

THERA-9. (Quality Generics) Vit. A 10,000 I.U., D 40 I.U., C 200 mg., B-1 10 mg., B-2 10 mg., B-6 2 mg., B 12 5 mcg., niacinamide 100 mg., calcium pantothe nate 20 mg./Tab. Jar 100s. Tin 1000s.
Use: Therapeutic formula vitamin.

THERA-9M. (Quality Generics) Vit. A 10,000 I.U., D 40 I.U., C 200 mg., B-1 10 mg., B-2 10 mg., B-6 5 mg., B 12 5 mcg., niacinamide 100 mg., Ca pantothenate 2 mg., Vit. E 5 I.U., Iodine 0.15 mg., Fe 12 mg., Cu 2 mg., Mn 1 mg., Mg 65 mg., Zn 1.5 mg./Tab. Jar 100s. Tin 1000s.
Use: Therapeutic vitamins and minerals.

THERA BATH. (Walgreen) Mineral oil 90%
Use: Dry skin care.

THERA BATH WITH VITAMIN E. (Walgreen) Mineral oil 91%, Vit E 2000 I.U./16 oz.
Use: Dry skin care.

THERA BEE CEE. (Reid-Provident) Vit. B-1 15 mg., B-2 10 mg., B-6 5 mg., niacinamide 50 mg., calcium pantothenate 10 mg., Vit. C 300 mg./Cap. Bot. 100s.
Use: Vitamin supplement.

THERABID. (Mission) Vit. C 500 mg., B-1 15 mg., B-2 10 mg., niacinamide 100 mg., Ca pantothenate 20 mg., B-6 10 mg., B-12 5 mcg., Vit. A acetate 25,000 I.U., Vit. D-2 200 I.U., E 30 I.U./Tab. Bot. 100s.

THERABLOAT. (Norden) Poloxalene.

THERABRAND. (Approved) Vit. A 25,000 I.U., D 1000 I.U., B-1 10 mg., B-2 10 mg., niacinamide 100 mg., C 200 mg., B-6 5 mg., cal. pantothenate 20 mg., B-12 5 mcg./Cap. Bot. 100s, 1000s.
Use: Vitamin therapy.

THERABRAND-M. (Approved) Vit. A 25,000 I.U., D 1000 I.U., C 200 mg., B-1 10 mg., B-2 10 mg., B-6 5 mg., niacinamide 100 mg., cal. pantothenate 20 mg., E 5

I.U., B-12 5 mcg., iodine 0.15 mg., iron 15 mg., Cu 1 mg., Ca 125 mg., Mn 1 mg., Mg 6 mg., Zn 1.5 mg./Cap. Bot. 100s, 1000s.
Use: Vitamin, mineral therapy.

HERAC. (C & M Pharmacal) Colloidal sulfur 4.0%, salicylic acid 2.35% in lotion base. Bot. 2 oz.
Use: Vanishing anti-acne lotion.

HERACAP. (Arcum) Vit. A 10,000 I.U., D 400 I.U., B-1 10 mg., B-2 5 mg., niacinamide 150 mg., C 150 mg./Cap. Bot. 100s, 1000s.
Use: Dietary supplement.

HERACAPS. (Alton) Bot. 100s 1000s.
Use: Dietary supplement.

HERACAPS M. (Alton) Bot. 100s, 1000s.
Use: Dietary supplement with minerals.

HERACEBRIN. (Lilly) Vit. A 25,000 I.U., D 1500 I.U., B-12 10 mcg., B-1 15 mg., B-2 10 mg., B-6 2.5 mg., niacinamide 150 mg., C 150 mg., pantothenic acid 20 mg., E 18.5 I.U./Pulvule. Bot. 100s.
Use: Multiple vitamin deficiencies.

HERACORT. (C & M Pharmacal) Hydrocortisone 0.25%, colloidal sulfur 4%, salicylic acid 2.35% in lotion base. Lot. Bot. 2 oz.
Use: Vanishing anti-acne lotion.

HERADAN. (Danbury) Vit. A 8,333 I.U., D 133 I.U., B-1 3.30 mg., B-2 3.30 mg., Ca pantothenate 11.70 mg., E 5 I.U., Cu 0.67 mg., Mg 41.70 mg., Fe 66.70 mg., B-12 50 mcg., folic acid 0.33 mg., C 100 mg./Tab. Bot. 100s, 1000s.
Use: Anemia treatment.

HERA-FLUR. (Hoyt) Acidulated fluoride phosphate. Fluoride ion 0.5% (from sod. fluoride 1.1%). Gel-Drops. Bot. 24 ml.
Use: Protection dental caries.

HERA-FLUR-N. (Hoyt) Neutral sodium fluoride 1.1% Bot. 24 ml., 60 ml.
Use: Protection against dental caries.

HERAFORMS. (Horton & Converse) Vit. A 25,000 I.U., D 1000 I.U., C 150 mg., B-1 10 mg., B-2 10 mg., B-6 1 mg., B-12 5 mcg., niacinamide 100 mg., cal. pantothenate 5 mg., Vit. E 5 I.U. w/minerals/Tab. Bot. 100s, 250s, 500s.
Use: Vitamin-mineral deficiencies.

HERA FORMULA. (Zenith) Vit. A 10,000 I.U., D 400 I.U., B-1 10 mg., B-2 10 mg., B-6 5 mg., B-12 5 mcg., niacinamide 100 mg., Ca pantothenate 20 mg., Vit. C 200 mg., E 15 I.U./Tab. Bot. 100s.

HERAFORTIS. (General Vitamin) Vit. A 12,500 I.U., D 1000 I.U., B-1 5 mg., B-2 5 mg., B-6 1 mg., B-12 3 mcg., niacinamide 50 mg., pantothenic acid salt 10 mg. Vit. C 150 mg., folic acid 0.5 mg./Cap. Bot. 100s, 1000s.
Use: Multivitamin therapy.

HERAGARDS M. (Eckerd) Vit. A 10,000 I.U., D 400 I.U., B-1 10 mg., B-2 10 mg., B-6 5 mg., B-12 5 mcg., niacinamide 100 mg., cal. pantothenate 20 mg., C 200 mg., E 15 I.U., w/iodine, Fe, Cu, Mn, Mg, Zn/Tab. Bot. 100s, 200s.
Use: Vitamin, mineral dietary supplement.

HERAGRAN. (Squibb) Vit. A 5,500 I.U., C 120 mg., B-1 3 mg., B-2 3.4 mg., niacin 30 mg., B-6 3 mg., B-12 9 mcg., D 400 I.U. pantothenic acid 10 mg., folic acid 0.4 mg., biotin 15.5 mcg./Tab. Bot. 30s, 60s, 100s. 180s, 1000s. Unimatic 100s. **Liquid:** 1 teaspoonful of liquid
is equiv. to 1 tablet. Bot. 4 oz. Unimatic 5 cc. 100s.
Use: Multiple vitamin.

THERAGRAN HEMATINIC. (Squibb) Theragran formula with minerals: Iodine 150 mcg., iron 27 mg., Mg. 100 mg., Cu 2 mg., Zn 15 mg., Mn 5 mg., Cr 15 mcg., Se 10 mcg., Mb 15 mcg., K 7.5 mg., Cc 7.5 mg./Tab. Bot. 90s.
Use: Multiple vitamin with minerals.

THERAGRAN-M. (Squibb) Vit. A 5,500 I.U., D 400 I.U., C 120 mg., B-1 3 mg., B-2 3.4 mg., niacinamide 30 mg., Cal. pantothenate 10 mg., Vit. B-6 3 mg., E 30 I.U., B-12 9 mcg., w/Ca, Iodine 150 mcg., Fe 27 mg., Mg 100 mg., Cu 2 mg., Zn 22.5 mg., Mn 7.5 mg., folic acid 0.4 mg., biotin 15 mcg., Cr 15 mcg., Se 10 mcg., Mo 15 mcg., K 7.5 mg./Tab. Bot. 30s, 60s, 100s, 180s, 1000s, Unimatic 100s.
Use: Multivitamin therapy with minerals.

THERA H TABS. (Major) Bot. 100s, 250s.
Use: Multivitamin and mineral supplement.

THERA-HEXAMIN. (Galen) Vit. A 25,000 I.U., D 400 I.U., B-1 10 mg., B-2 5 mg., niacinamide 100 mg., C 150 mg./Cap. Bot. 100s.
Use: Multiple vitamin deficiencies.

THERALAX SUPPOSITORIES.. (Beecham Labs) Bisacodyl 10 mg./Supp. Pkg. 50s.
Use: Laxative.

THERALETS. (Panray) Vit. A 10,000 IU., D 400 IU., E 15 IU., C 200 IU., B-1 10 mg., B-2 10 mg., Niacinamide 100 mg., pyridoxine HCl 5 mg., B-12 5 mcg., Ca pantothenate 20 mg./Cap.
Use: Vitamin supplement.

THERMODENT. (Mentholatum) Strontium Cl. 10%. Tubes.
Use: Toothpaste for sensitive teeth.

THERALETS M. (Panray) A 10,000 IU., D 400 IU., E 15 IU., C 200 mg., B-1 10 mg., B-2 10 mg., niacinamide 100 mg., B-6 5 mg., B-12 5 mcg., Ca pantothenate 20 mg., Ca 125 mg., Iodine 150 mcg., iron 12 mg., magnesium 65 mg., manganese 1 mg., Cu 2 mg., Zn 1.5 mg./Cap.
Use: Vitamin & mineral supplement.

THERALETS S.C.. (Panray) Vit. A 25,000 I.U., D 400 I.U., B-1 10 mg., B-2 5 mg., niacinamide 150 mg., C 150 mg./Tab. Bot. 1000s.
Use: Vitamin therapy.

THERAMIN. (Arcum) Vit. A 10,000 I.U., D 400 I.U., B-1 10 mg., B-2 5 mg., niacinamide 100 mg., B-6 5 mg., B-12 10 mcg., C 150 mg., cal. pantothenate 15 mg., Ca 103.6 mg., Iodine 0.1 mg., Fe 15 mg., P 80 mg., Mg 6 mg./Tab. Bot. 30s, 100s, 1000s.

THERAMIN CAPSULES. (VRC Vitamin Research) Vit. A 25,000 I.U., D 1000 I.U., B-1 10 mg., B-2 5 mg., B-6 1 mg., B-12 5 mcg., C 150 mg., niacinamide 100 mg., Ca 103.6 mg., P 80.2 mg., Fe 10 mg., Mn 0.954 mg., K 4.93 mg., Zn 1.4 mg., Mg 5.56 mg./Cap. Bot. 100s.

THERANEED. (Hanlon) Vit. A 16,000 I.U., B-1 10 mg., B-2 10 mg., B-6 2 mg., C 300 mg., Ca pantothenate 10 mg., niacinamide 10 mg., B-12 10 mcg./Cap. Bot. 100s.

THERAPALS. (Faraday) Vit. A 25,000 I.U., D 400 I.U., B-1 10 mg., B-2 5 mg., niacinamide 150 mg., B-6 0.5 mg., E 5 I.U., C 150 mg., B-12 10 mcg., Ca 103 mg., Co 0.1 mg., Cu 1 mg., Vit. K 0.15 mg., Mg 6 mg., Mn 1 mg., molybdenum 0.2 mg., P 80 mg., K 5 mg., Zn 1.2 mg./Tab. Bot. 100s, 250s, 1000s.

THERAPEUTIC B COMPLEX W/ASCORBIC ACID. (Horton & Converse) Vit. C 300 mg., niacinamide 100 mg., B-1 10 mg., B-2 6 mg., B-6 40 mg., cal. pantothenate 40 mg., Vit. B-12 activity 4 mcg./2 Caps. Bot. 100s.

THERAPEUTIC LIQUID. (Kenwood) Vit. A 10,000 I.U., D 400 I.U., E 4.5 I.U., C 150 mg., B-1 6 mg., B-2 3 mg., B-6 1 mg., niacinamide 60 mg., calcium pantothenate 6 mg., calcium 38 mg., phosphorus 29 mg., magnesium 6 mg., manganese 1 mg., potassium 5 mg./15 cc. Bot. 12 oz.
Use: High potency vitamin and mineral.

THERAPEUTIC M. (Stanlabs) Vit. A 10,000 I.U., D 400 I.U., B-1 10 mg., B-2 10 mg., B-6 5 mg., B-12 5 mcg., C 200 mg., E 15 I.U., Ca pantothenate 20 mg., niacinamide 100 mg., Cu 2 mg., Mn 1 mg., Zn 1.5 mg., Mg 65 mg., Fe 12 mg., Iodine 0.15 mg./Cap. Bot. 100s.
Use: Dietary supplement.

THERAPEUTIC V & M. (Whiteworth) Vit. A 10,000 I.U., D 400 I.U., B-1 10 mg., B-2 10 mg., B-6 5 mg., B-12 5 mcg., niacinamide 100 mg., Ca panothenate 20 mg., C 200 mg., E 15 I.U., iodine 0.15 mg., iron 12 mg., copper 2 mg., Mn 1 mg., Mg 60 mg., zinc 1.5 mg./Tab.
Use: Vitamin and mineral supplement.

THERAPEUTIC VITAMIN CAPSULES. (Lannett) Vit. A 25,000 I.U., D 1000 I.U., B-1 10 mg., B-2 5 mg., niacinamide 150 mg., C 150 mg./Cap. Bot. 100s, 500s, 1000s. Tab. Bot. 1000s.
Use: Vitamin supplement.

THERAPEUTIC VITAMIN CAPSULES AND TABLETS—IMPROVED FORMULA. (Lannett) Vit. A 25,000 I.U., D 1000 I.U., thiamine mononitrate 12.5 mg., B-2 12.5 mg., niacinamide 100 mg., B-6 5 mg., B-12 5 mcg., calcium pantothenate 25 mg., C 200 mg./Cap. Caps. 100s, 500s, 1000s. Tab. Bot. 1000s.
Use: Vitamin supplement.

THERAPEUTIC VITAMIN FORMULA W/MINERALS. (Towne) Vit. A palmitate 10,000 I.U., D 400 I.U., B-1 15 mg., B-2 10 mg., B-6 5 mg., B-12 12 mcg., C 200 mg., niacinamide 100 mg., Ca pantothenate 20 mg., Vit. E 15 I.U., Ca 103 mg., Fe 10 mg., Mn 1 mg., K 5 mg., Zn 1.5 mg., Mg 6 mg./Cap. Bot. 30s, 60s, 100s, 250s.

THERAPEUTIC VITAMIN FORMULA W/MINERALS. (Towne) Vit. A palmitate 25,000 I.U., D 1000 I.U., B-1 10 mg., B-2 5 mg., B-6 1 mg., B-12 5 mcg., C 150 mg., niacinamide 100 mg., Ca 103 mg., P 80 mg., Fe 10 mg., Iodine 0.1 mg., Mn 1 mg., K 5 mg., Cu 1 mg., Zn 1.4 mg., Mg 5.5 mg./Cap. Bot. 100s, 1000s.

THERAPEUTIC VITAMIN TABLET. (Vortech) Vit. A 10,000 I.U., D 400 I.U., B-1 10 mg., B-2 10 mg., niacinamide 100 mg., C 200 mg., B-6 5 mg., d-calcium pantothenate 20 mg., B-12 5 mcg., E 15 I.U./Tab. Bot. 100s.
Use: Multiple vitamin.

THERAPHON. (Approved) Vit. A 25,000 I.U., D 1000 I.U., B-1 10 mg., B-2 5 mg., C 150 mg., niacinamide 150 mg./Cap. Bot. 100s, 1000s.

THERAPLEX. (Kenyon) Vit. A 25,000 I.U., D 1000 I.U., B-1 10 mg., B-2 10 mg., niacinamide 150 mg., B-12 5 mcg./Tab. Bot. 100s, 1000s.

THERAPLEX-PLUS. (Kenyon) Vit. A palmitate 25,000 I.U., D 1000 I.U., B-1 10 mg., B-2 5 mg., B-6 1 mg., B-12 5 mcg., C 150 mg., niacinamide 100 mg., dical phosphate 360 mg., Ca 106 mg., P 82 mg., ferrous sulfate 34 mg., Mn sulfate 3 mg., pot. sulfate 11 mg., Zn sulfate 3.9 mg., Mg sulfate 40 mg./Cap. Bot. 100s, 1000s.

THERA-STAY. (Stayner) Vit. A 25,000 I.U., D 1000 I.U., B-1 12.5 mg., B-2 12.5 mg., niacinamide 100 mg., B-6 5 mg., cal. pantothenate 25 mg., B-12 5 mcg., C 200 mg./Cap. Bot. 100s.
Use: Vitamin therapy.

THERA-STAY "M". (Stayner) Vit. A 25,000 I.U., D 1000 I.U., B-1 10 mg., B-2 5 mg., B-6 1 mg., B-12 5 mcg., C 150 mg., niacinamide 100 mg., Ca 104 mg., P 80 mg., Fe 10 mg., Iodine 0.1 mg., Mn 1 mg., K 5 mg., Cu 1 mg., Zn 1.4 mg., Mg 5.5 mg., E 2 I.U./Cap. Bot. 100s, 500s.
Use: Vitamin-mineral therapy.

THERATINIC. (Jamieson-McKames) Vit. B-12 5 mcg., fortified iron 59 mg., niacin 50 mg., pyridoxine 0.3 mg., cyancobalamin 2 mcg., folic acid 2 mg./2 cc. w/sod. citrate 1%, phenol 0.5%, procaine HCl 1%.
Use: Hypochromic and hematopoietic anemia.

THERAVEE HEMATINIC VITAMIN. (Vangard) Vit A 2.5 mg., D 3.3 mcg., thiamine 3.3 mg., riboflavin 3.3 mg., pyridoxine HCl 3.3 mg., niacinamide 33.3 mg., calcium pantothenate 11.7 mg., Vit. E 5 mg., copper 0.67 mg., magnesium 41.7 mg., iron 66.7 mg., B-12 50 mcg., folic acid 0.33 mcg., C 100 mg./Tab. Bot. 100s. Unit dose 10×10s.
Use: Dietary supplement.

THERAVEE M VITAMIN. (Vangard) Vit A 3 mg., D 10 mcg., E 15 mg., C 200 mg., thiamine 10.3 mg., riboflav 10 mg., niacin 100 mg., B-6 4.1 mg., B-12 5 mcg., pantothenic acid 18.4 mg., iodine 150 mcg., iron 12 mg., magnesium 65 mg., copper 2 mg., zinc 1.5 mg., manganese 1 mg./Tab. Bot. 100s, 1000s. Unit dose 10×10s
Use: Dietary supplement.

THERAVEE VITAMIN. (Vangard) Vit. A 10,000 I.U., D 400 I.U., E 14 I.U., C 200 mg., Thiamine 10.3 mg., riboflavin 10 mg., niacin 100 mg., B-6 4 .1 mg., B-12 5 mcg., pantothenic acid 18.4 mg./Tab. Bot. 100s. Unit dose Pkg. 250s.
Use: Dietary supplement.

THERAVILAN CAPSULES. (Lannett) Vit. A 25,000 I.U., D 1000 I.U., B-1 10 mg., B-2 5 mg., B-6 1 mg., C

150 mg., B-12 5 mcg., niacinamide 100 mg., dicalcium phosphate anhyd. 360 mg., ferrous sulfate dried 34 mg., potassium iodide 0.133 mg., manganese sulfate dried 3 mg., cobalt sulfate 0.49 mg., potassium sulfate 11 mg., sodium molybdate 0.45 mg., copper sulfate monohydrate 2.8 mg., zinc sulfate dried 3.9 mg., magnesium sulfate dried 40 mg./Cap., Tab. Caps. Bot. 100s, 500s, 1000s. Tab. Bot. 100s, 1000s.
Use: Multivitamin with minerals.

THERAVIM CAPSULES. (Robinson) Vit. A 25,000 I.U., D 400 I.U., B-1 10 mg., B-2 5 mg., C 150 mg., niacinamide 150 mg./Cap. Bot. 50s, 100s, 500s, 1000s. Bulk Pack 5000s. W/Vit. B-12 5 mcg./Cap. Bot. 100s, 250s, 1000s.
Use: Therapeutic standard formula vitamin capsules.

THERAVIM HI-PO. (Robinson) Vit. A 25,000 I.U., D 400 I.U., B-1 10 mg., B-2 10 mg., B-6 5 mg., B-12 5 mcg., C 200 mg., E 15 I.U., niacinamide 100 mg., calcium pantothenate 20 mg./Cap. or Tab. Bot. 100s, 1000s.
Use: Therapeutic high potency vitamins.

THER-CO-MIN. (Coastal) Vit. B-1 15 mg., B-2 2 mg., B-6 2 mg., pantothenic acid (Ca pantothenate racemic) 10 mg., niacinamide 100 mg., B-12 7.5 mcg., C 150 mg., E 5 I.U., A 25,000 I.U., D 1000 I.U., Cu 1 mg., Fe 15 mg., Mn 1 mg., Zn 1.5 mg., Iodine 0.015 mg./Cap. Bot. 100s.
Use: Multivitamin with minerals.

THEREL. (La Crosse) Triethanolamine lauryl sulfate w/diglycol laurate. Bot. 8 oz., 0.5 gal.
Use: Soapless non-allergenic shampoo.

THEREVAC. (Bowman) Docusate potassium 283 mg., benzocaine/20 mg./Tube capsule w/soft soap in PEG 400 and glycerin base. , Unit 4cc., packages 4s, 12s, 50s.
Use: Disposable enema.

THEREX NO. 1. (Blue Cross) Vit A 10,000 I.U., D 400 I.U., E 15 I.U., C 200 mg., B-1 10 mg., B-2 10 mg., niacinamide 100 mg., B-6 5 mg., B-12 5 mcg., calcium pantothenate 20 mg./Tab. Bot. 100s.
Use: High potency vitamin supplement for adults.

THEREX-M. (Blue Cross) Vit. A 10,000 I.U., D 400 I.U., E 15 I.U., C 200 mg., B-1 10 mg., B-2 10 mg., niacinamide 100 mg., B-6 5 mg., B-12 5 mcg., calcium pantothenate 20 mg., iodine 150 mcg., iron 12 mg., Mg 65 mg., Cu 2 mg., zinc 1.5 mg., Mn 1 mg./Tab. Bot. 100s.
Use: Vitamin and mineral supplement.

THEREX-Z. (Blue Cross) Vit. A 10,000 I.U., D 400 I.U., E 15 I.U., C 200 mg., B-1 10 mg., B-2 10 mg., niacinamide 100 mg., B-12 5 mcg., B-6 5 mg., Ca pantothenate 20 mg., iodine 150 mcg., Cu 2 mg., iron 12 mg., Zn 22.5 mg./Tab. Bot. 100s.
Use: Vitamin, mineral supplement.

THERMA-KOOL. (Nortech) Compresses in following sizes: 3″ × 5″, 4″ × 9″, 8.5″ × 10.5″.
Use: Cold or hot compress.

THERMOLENE. (Lannett) Sodium chloride 7 gr., dextrose 3 gr., Vit. B-1 1 mg./Tab. Bot. 1000s.

THERMOLOID. (Mills) Thyroid 1 gr., 2 gr., 3 gr., 4 gr., 5 gr./Tab. Bot. 100s.
Use: Thyroid therapy.

THERMOTABS. (Beecham Products) Sod. chloride 0.45 Gm., pot. chloride 30 mg., cal. carb. 18 mg., dextrose 0.2 Gm./Tab. Bot. 100s.
Use: Heat fatigue.

THEROAL. (Vangard) Theophylline 24 mg., ephedrine HCl 24 mg., phenobarbital 8 mg./Tab. Bot. 100s, 1000s.
Use: Antiasthmatic.

THERUHISTIN. Isothipendyl, B.A.N.

THEX FORTE CAPSULES. (Medtech) Vit. C 500 mg., B-1 25 mg., B-2 15 mg., B-6 5 mg., niacinamide 100 mg., Ca pantothenate 10 mg./Cap. Bot. 60s, 100s.
Use: Saturation vitamin therapy, vitamin supplement.

THIA. (Sig) Thiamine HCl 100 mg./ml. Vial 30 ml.
Use: Thiamine deficiency.

• **THIABENDAZOLE,** U.S.P. XXI. Oral Susp., Tab. U.S.P. XXI. 1H-Benzimidazole,2-(4-thiazolyl)-2-(4-Thiazolyl)-benzimidazole.
Use: Anthelmintic.
See: Mintezol, Tab., Susp. (Merck Sharp & Dohme)

THIABENDAZOLE, VETERINARY USE. 2-(4-Thiazolyl)-1H-benzimidazole
See: Equizole (MSD AGVET)
Equizole A w/piperazine (MSD AGVET)
Equizole B w/trichlorfon (MSD AGVET)
Omnizole (MSD AGVET)
TBZ (MSD AGVET)
Thibenzole (MSD AGVET)

THIACETARSAMIDE SODIUM. Sodium mercaptoacetate S,S-diester with p-carbamoyldithiobenzenearsonous acid.
Use: Antitrichomonal.

THIACETAZONE, B.A.N. p-Acetylaminobenzaldehyde thiosemicarbamazone.
Use: Treatment of tuberculosis and leprosy.
See: Berculon A
Neustab
Seroden
Thioparamizone

THIACIDE. (Beach) Methenamine mandelate 500 mg., pot. acid phosphate 250 mg./Tab. Bot. 100s, 500s.
Use: Control of urinary infection.

THIA-DIA-MER-SULFONAMIDES. Sulfadiazine w/sulfamerazine & sulfathiazole.
See: Trionamide, Tab. (O'Neal)

THIADOX. (Barry-Martin) Thiamine HCl 100 mg., pyridoxine HCl 100 mg./cc. Vials 10 cc.

THIAHEP INJECTION. (Lannett) Liver ext. (derived from 10 U.S.P. Units injectable) 100 mg., liver ext. (derived from 10 U.S.P. Units crude liver) 100 mg., iron peptonate 20 mg., niacinamide 50 mg., pyridoxine HCl 0.3 mg., riboflavin 3 mg./2 cc. Multiple dose vial 300 cc.

THIALBARBITAL.
See: Kemithal

THIALBARBITONE. B.A.N. 5-Allyl-5-(cyclohex-2-enyl)-2-thiobarbituric acid.
Use: Anesthetic.
See: Kemithal (sodium salt)

THIAMAZOLE (I.N.N.). Methimazole, B.A.N.

THIAMBUTOSINE. B.A.N. 1-(4-Butoxyphenyl)-3-(4-dimethylaminophenyl)thiourea.
Use: Treatment of leprosy.

• **THIAMINE HYDROCHLORIDE,** U.S.P. XXI. Elixir, Inj., Tab., U.S.P. XXI. 3-[(4-amino-2-methyl-5-pyrimidinyl)-methyl]-5-(2-hydroxyethyl)-4-methyl-, chloride, monohydrochloride. Aneurine HCl, thiamine chloride, Vit. B-1 HCl. Thiazolium,
Use: Enzyme co-factor vitamin.
See: Apatate Drops (Kenwood)
Betalin S, Amp., Elixir, Tab. (Lilly)
Thia, Vial (Sig)

• **THIAMINE MONONITRATE,** U.S.P. XXI. Elixir, U.S.P. XXI. Thiazolium, 3-[(4-amino-2-methyl-5-pyrimidinyl)-methyl]-5-(2-hydroxyethyl)-4-methyl-, nitrate (salt). (Various Mfr.) Thiamine nitrate.
Use: Enzyme CD Factor Vitamin.
W/Sodium salicylate, colchicine.
See: Sodsylate, Tab. (Durst)

• **THIAMIPRINE.** USAN. 2-Amino-6-[(1-methyl-4-nitroimidazol-5-yl)thio] purine.
Use: Antileukemic.

• **THIAMPHENICOL.** USAN.
Use: Antibacterial.

• **THIAMYLAL SODIUM, FOR INJECTION,** U.S.P. XXI. Sodium 5-allyl-5-(1-methylbutyl)-2-thiobarbiturate.
Use: Anesthetic (systemic).
See: Surital Sodium, Prep. (Parke-Davis)

THIAPHYLL CREAM. (Lannett) Sulfathiazole 5%, chlorophyllin 1%. Jar 4 oz. & 1 lb.
Use: Topically to promote healing.

THIA-SERP-25. (Robinson) Hydrochlorothiazide 25 mg., reserpine alkaloid 0.125 mg./Tab. Bot. 100s, 1000s.
Use: Hypertensive disorders.

THIA-SERP-50. (Robinson) Hydrochlorothiazide 50 mg., reserpine alkaloid 0.125 mg./Tab. Bot. 100s, 1000s.
Use: Hypertensive disorders.

THIA-SERPA-ZINE. (Robinson) Reserpine alkaloid, hydrochlorothiazide, hydralazine HCl. Tab. Bot. 100s, 1000s.
Use: Hypertensive disorders.

THIA-TWELVE. (Rocky Mtn.) B-12 cryst. 1000 mcg., B-1 100 mg./cc. Vial 10 cc.
Use: Nutritional supplement.

• **THIAZESIM.** USAN. 5-(2-Dimethylaminoethyl) 2,3-dihydro-2-phenyl-1,5-benzothiazepin-4-one.
Use: Antidepressant.

THIAZESIM HCl. 5-[2-(Dimethylamino)-ethyl]-2,3-dihydro-2-phenylbenzo-1,5-thiazepin-4-(5H)-one hydrochloride.
Use: Antidepressant.

• **THIAZINAMINIUM CHLORIDE.** USAN.
Use: Antiallergic.

THIAZOLIUM, 3-[(4-AMINO-2-METHYL-5-PYRIMIDINYL)METHYL]-5-(2-HYDROXYETHYL)-4-METHYL-, CHLORIDE, MONOHYDROCHLORIDE. Thiamine Hydrochloride, U.S.P. XXI.

2-(4-THIAZOLYL)BENZIMIDAZOLE. Thiabendazole U.S.P. XXI.

THIBENZOLE "100". (MSD AGVET) Thiabendazole medicated feed: 100 Gm./lb.
Use: Anthelmintic, veterinary medicine.

THIBENZOLE "200". (MSD AGVET) Medicated feed. 200 Gm./lb.
Use: Anthelmintic, veterinary medicine.

THIENO[1′,2′:1,2]THIENO[3,4-d]IMIDAZOL-5-IUM, DECAHYDRO-2-OXO-1,3-BIS-(PHENYLMETHYL)-, SALT WITH (+)-7,7-DIMETHYL-2-OXOBICYCLO[2.2.1]HEPTANE-1-METHANESULFONIC ACID (1:1). Trimethaphan Camsylate, U.S.P. XXI.

7-(2-THIENYL ACETAMIDO) CEPHALOSPORANIC ACID, SOD. SALT. Cephalothin Sodium, U.S.P. XXI.

THIETHANOMELAMINE.
See: Tretamine, B.A.N.

THIETHYLENE THIOPHOSPHORAMIDE.
See: Thiotepa, B.A.N.

• **THIETHYLPERAZINE.** USAN. 2-Ethylthio-10-[3-(4-methylpiperazin-1-yl)propyl]phenothiazine.
Use: Central nervous system depressant.
See: Torecan

• **THIETHYLPERAZINE MALEATE,** U.S.P. XXI. Inj., Suppos., Tab., U.S.P. XXI. Torecan, 2-Ethyl-mercapto-10-[3′-(1″-methyl-piperazinyl-4″)propyl-1″]phenothiazine maleate. 2-(Ethylthio)-10-[3-(4-methyl-1-piperazinyl)propyl]phenothiazine maleate (1:2).
Use: Antiemetic.
See: Torecan, Amp., Supp., Tab. (Boehringer Ingelheim)

THIHEXINOL METHYLBROMIDE. alpha-Dithienyl-(4-dimethylamino-cyclohexyl)-carbinolmethbromide. [4-(Hydroxydi-2-thienylmethyl)cyclohexyl] trimethylammonium Bromide.
Use: Anticholinergic.

• **THIMERFONATE SODIUM.** USAN. Ethyl(hydrogen p-mercaptobenzenesulfonato)mercury sodium salt; Sodium p-[(ethylmercuri)-thio] benzenesulfonate. Sulfo-Merthiolate (Lilly).
Use: Topical anti-infective.

• **THIMEROSAL,** U.S.P. XXI. Topical Aerosol, Topical Soln., Tr., U.S.P. XXI. Sod. Ethylmercurithiosalicylate. Sodium Ethyl (Sodium o-mercaptobenzoate)mercury.
Use: Local anti-infective; pharmaceutical aid (preservative).
See: Aeroaid, Aerosol (Aeroceuticals)
Merphol Tincture 1:1000, Liq. (Bowman)
Mersol, Liq. (Century)
Merthiolate, Prep. (Lilly)

2,2-THIOBIS (4,6-dichlorophenol).
See: Bithionol.

THIOCARBANIDIN. Under study.
Use: Tuberculosis.

THIOCARLIDE. B.A.N. 1,3-Di-(4-isopentyloxyphenyl)-thiourea.

Use: Treatment of tuberculosis.
See: Isoxyl

HIOCYANATE SODIUM. Sodium thiocyanate.
Use: Hypotensive.

HIOCYL. (Torigian) Sodium thiosalicylate 100 mg./2 ml. Amp. 2 cc. Box 25s, 100s.
Use: I.M. Rheumatism.

HIODINONE. Name used for Nifuratel.

HIODIPHENYLAMINE.
See: Phenothiazine.

HIODRIL. Carboxymethylcysteine, B.A.N.

HIOFURADENE. 1[(5-Nitrofurfurylidene)-amino]-2-imidazolidinethione.

HIOGLYCEROL.
/Sod. citrate, phenol, benzyl alcohol.
See: Sulfo-ganic, Vial (Marcen)

THIOGUANINE, U.S.P. XXI. Tab. U.S.P. XXI. 6H-Purine-6-thione,2-amino-1,7-dihydro-.2-Amino-purine-6-thiol, hemihydrate. Tabloid (Burroughs Wellcome) 40 mg., Bot. 25s.
Use: Antineoplastic agent.

HIOHEXAMIDE. N-(p-Methyl-mercaptophenylsulfonyl)-N′-cyclohexylurea.
Use: Blood sugar lowering compound.

HIOISONICOTINAMIDE. Under study.
Use: Antituberculosis drug.

HIOLATE. (Hickman; Pharmex) Sod. thiosalicylate 50 mg./cc. Vial 30 cc.

HIOMERSAL. B.A.N. Sodium salt of (2-carboxyphenylthio)ethylmercury.
Sodium ethylmercurithiosalicylate
Thiomerosal
Thiomersalate
Use: Antiseptic; preservative.
See: Merthiolate

HIOMESTERONE. B.A.N. 1α,7α-Bis-(acetylthio)-17β-hydroxy-17α-methylandrost-4-en-3-one.
Use: Anabolic steroid.
See: Emdabol

HIOPARAMIZONE. Thiacetazone, B.A.N.

THIOPENTAL SODIUM, U.S.P. XXI.; Inj., U.S.P. XXI. Sodium 5-ethyl-5-(1-methylbutyl)-2-thiobarbiturate. Thiopentone sodium.
Use: Anesthetic (intravenous), anticonvulsant.
See: Pentothal Sodium, Amp. (Abbott)

HIOPHOSPHORAMIDE.
See: Thio-Tepa, Vial (Lederle)

HIOPROPAZATE. B.A.N. 10-{3-[4-(2-Acetoxy-ethyl)-piperazin-1-yl]propyl}-2-chlorophenothiazine.
Use: Tranquilizer.
See: Dartalan [hydrochloride]

THIOPROPAZATE HYDROCHLORIDE. 2-Chloro-10-{3-[(2-acetoxyethyl)-4-piperazinyl]-propyl} phenothiazine dihydrochloride.4-[3-(2-Chlorophenothiazine-10-yl)propyl]-1-piperazine ethanol Acetate Dihydrochloride.
Use: Tranquilizer.

HIOPROPERAZINE. B.A.N. 2-Dimethylsulfamoyl-10-[3-(4-methylpiperazin-1-yl)propyl]phenothiazine.
Use: Tranquilizer; antiemetic.
See: Majeptil (mesylate)

THIOPROPERAZINE MESYLATE. N,N-Dimethyl-10-[3-(4-methyl-1-piperazinyl)propyl] phenothiazine-2-sulfonamide dimethanesulfonate.
Use: Central depressant; antiemetic.

• **THIORIDAZINE,** U.S.P. XXI. Oral Susp., U.S.P. XXI. 10-[2-(1-Methyl-2-piperidyl)ethyl]-2-methylthiophenothiazine.
Use: Tranquilizer.
See: Mellaril, Susp. (Sandoz)

• **THIORIDAZINE HCl,** U.S.P. XXI. Oral Soln., Tab., U.S.P. XXI. 10-[-2-(1-Methyl-2-piperidyl)-ethyl]-2-(methylthio) phenothiazine hydrochloride. 10H-Phenothiazine, 10-[2-(1-methyl-2-piperidinyl)-ethyl]-2-(methylthio)-, monohydrochloride.
Use: Tranquilizer.
See: Mellaril, Tabs., Soln., (Sandoz)

• **THIOSALAN.** USAN. 3,4′,5-Tribromo-2-mercaptobenzanilide. Under study.
Use: Germicide.

THIOSALICYLIC ACID SALT.

THIOSTAN. (Standex) Sodium thiosalicylate 50 mg./30 cc. Bot. 1 oz.

THIOSUL. (Vortech) Thiosalicylic acid as sodium salt 50 mg., benzyl alcohol 2%/cc. Vial 30 ml.
Use: Analgesic, antipyretic.

THIOSULFIL-A. (Ayerst) Sulfamethizole 0.25 Gm., phenazopyridine HCl 50 mg./Tab. Bot. 100s, 1000s.
Use: Urinary tract infections, analgesic for initial 48 hr. treatment.

THIOSULFIL-A FORTE. (Ayerst) Sulfamethizole 0.5 Gm., phenazopyridine HCl 50 mg./Tab. Bot. 100s, 1000s.
Use: Urinary tract infections, analgesic for initial 48 hr. treatment.

THIOSULFIL DUO-PAK. (Ayerst) Combination package w. 1 bottle, Thiosulfil Forte, 40 white tablets and 1 bottle, Thiosulfil-A Forte, 16 yellow tablets.
Use: Treatment of uncomplicated urinary tract infection.

THIOSULFIL FORTE. (Ayerst) Sulfamethizole 0.5 Gm./Tab. Bot. 100s.
Use: Treatment urinary tract infections, analgesic for initial 48 hr. treatment.

• **THIOTEPA,** U.S.P. XXI. For Inj., U.S.P. XXI. Thiophosphoramide. N, Tris(1-Aziridinyl phosphine sulfide. (Lederle) Triethylenethiophosphoramide 15 mg./Vial.
Use: Antineoplastic.

THIOTEPA. (Lederle) The ethylenimine-type N, N; N''-Triethylene thiophosphoramide. Powder for reconstitution: Thiotepa powder 15 mg., Na chloride 80 mg., Na bicarbonate 50 mg./Vial. Vial 15 mg.
Use: A polyfunctional alkylating agent used in the chemotherapy of certain neoplastic diseases.

• **THIOTHIXENE,** U.S.P. XXI. Cap., U.S.P. XXI. N,N,-Dimethyl-9-(3-(4-methyl-1-piperazinyl)propylidene)thioxanthene-2-sulfonamide. As HCl salt.
Use: Psychotherapeutic agent.
See: Navane, Cap., Vial (Roerig)
Navane Concentrate Solution (Roerig)

• **THIOTHIXENE HCl,** U.S.P. XXI. Inj., Oral Soln., U.S.P. XXI.
Use: Antipsychotic.
See: Navane Hydrochloride (Pfizer)

THIOURACIL. 2-Thiouracil.
Use: Treatment of hyperthyroidism, angina pectoris, congestive heart failure.

THIOUREA. (City Chem.) Pow., Bot., 1 lb.
Use: The same as thiouracil and to stimulate granulating tissue.

THIOXANTHENE DERIVATIVE.
See: Taractan, Prep. (Roche)

THIOXOLONE. B.A.N. 6-Hydroxy-1,3-benzoxathiol-2-one.
Use: Keratolytic agent.
See: Camyna

THIPHENAMIL. F.D.A. S-[2-(Diethylamino)-ethyl]-diphenylthioacetate.

• **THIPHENAMIL HYDROCHLORIDE.** USAN. S-[2-(Diethylamino)ethyl] diphenylthioacetate HCl.
Use: Anticholinergic.
See: Trocinate, Tab. (Poythress)

• **THIPENCILLIN POTASSIUM.** USAN. (1) Potassium 3,3-dimethyl-7-oxo-6-[2-(phenylthio)acetamido]-4-thia-1-azabicyclo[3.2.0] heptane-2-carboxylate; (2) Potassium 6-(phenylmercaptoacetamido)-penicillanate.
Use: Antibacterial.

THIPYRI-12. (Sig) Vit. B-1 1000 mg., B-6 1000 mg., cyanocobalamin (B-12) 10,000 mcg., sod. chloride 0.5%, sod. bisulfite 0.1%, benzyl alcohol (as preservative) 0.9%. Univial 10 ml.

• **THIRAM.** USAN. Bis(dimethylthiocarbamoyl) disulfide.
Use: Antifungal.

THIURETIC TABLETS. (Parke-Davis) Hydrochlorothiazide Tabs. 25 mg./Tab. Bot. 100s. 50 mg./Tab. Bot. 100s, 1000s. Unit dose 10 × 10.
Use: Diuretic, antihypertensive.

THIXO-FLUR TOPICAL GEL. (Hoyt) Acidulated phosphate sodium fluoride in gel base 1.2%. Bot. 32 oz. 8 oz., 4 oz.
Use: Dental caries prevention.

• **THONZONIUM BROMIDE,** U.S.P. XXI. Hexadecyl {2-[(p-methoxybenzyl)-2-pyrimidinylamino]ethyl} dimethylammonium bromide.
Use: Detergent.

W/Colistin base, neomycin base, hydrocortisone acetate, polysorbate 80, acetic acid, sodium acetate.
See: Coly-Mycin-S, Otic, Liq. (Warner-Chilcott)

W/Isoproterenol.
See: Nebair, Aerosol (Warner-Chilcott)

W/Neomycin sulfate, gramicidin, thonzylamine HCl, phenylephrine HCl.
See: Biomydrin, Spray, Drops (Warner-Chilcott)

THONZYLAMINE. B.A.N. 2-[N-p-Anisyl-N-(pyrimidin-2-yl)amino]ethyldimethylamine.
Use: Antihistamine.
See: Neohetramine

THONZYLAMINE HYDROCHLORIDE. 2[[2-(Dimethylamino)ethyl](p-methoxybenzyl)amino]pyrimidine monohydrochloride.
Use: Antihistamine.

THOR SYRUP. (Towne) Dextromethorphan HBr 90 mg., pyrilamine maleate 22.5 mg., phenylephrine HCl 10 mg., ephedrine sulfate 15 mg., sod. citrate 325 mg., ammon. chloride 650 mg., guaifenesin 50 mg.,/fl. oz. Bot. 4 oz.

THORADEX HCl. (Cenci) Chlorpromazine 10 mg., 25 mg., 50 mg., 100 mg./Tab. Bot. 100s, 1000s.

THORAGOL. Bibenzonium Bromide, B.A.N.

THORAZINE. (SmithKline) Chlorpromazine HCl,
Tab.: (10, 25, 50, 100, 200 mg.)
Bot. 100s, 1000s. Single unit pkg. 100s.
Amp.: (25 mg. w/ascorbic acid 2 mg., sodium bisulfite 1 mg., sodium sulfite 1 mg., NaCl 6 mg./1 ml.), 1 ml., 2 ml. Box 10s, 100s, 500s. Vial: 10 ml. Box 1s, 20s, 100s.
Spansule: 30, 75, 150 & 200 mg. Bot. 50s, 100s (S.U.P.), 500s. 300 mg. Bot. 50s, 100s (S.U.P.).
Syr.: (10 mg./5 ml.) Bot. 4 oz.
Supp.: Chlorpromazine base, w/glycerin, glyceryl monopalmitate, glyceryl monostearate, hydrogenated cocoanut oil fatty acids, hydrogenated palm kernel oil fatty acids. (25, 100 mg.) Box 12. **Conc:** (30 mg./ml.) Bot. 4 oz., 1 gal. (100 mg./ml.) Bot. 8 oz.
Use: Antiemetic. Neuropsychiatric disorders.

THORETS. (Buffington) Benzocaine 18.9 mg./lozenge. Dispens-A-Kits 500s. Sugar, lactose and salt free.
Use: Sore throat relief.

THORPHAN. (Vitarine) Dextromethorphan HBr 15 mg., chlorpheniramine maleate 2 mg., phenylephrine HCl 5 mg., acetyl-p-aminophenol 120 mg., ascorbic acid 30 mg./10 cc. Bot. 4 oz.
Use: Treatment of common cold.

THOR-PROM TABS. (Major) Chlorpromazine 10 mg., 25 mg., 50 mg., or 100 mg. Tab. Bot. 100s, 1000s; 200 mg./Tab. Bot. 250s, 1000s.
Use: Antiemetic, neuropsychiatric disorders.

• **THOZALINONE.** USAN. 2-Dimethylamino-5-phenyl-2-oxazolin-4-one.
Use: Antidepressant.
See: Stimsen (Lederle)

THREACON EXPECTORANT. (CMC) Pheniramine maleate, phenylephrine HCl, guaifenesin, sod. citrate, citric acid in mentholate humectant syrup base. Bot. pt., gal.

THREE AMINE TD. (Vitarine) Phenylpropanolamine HBr 50 mg., pheniramine maleate 25 mg., pyrilamine maleate 25 mg./Time Rel. Cap.
Use: Antihistamine and decongestant.

• **THREONINE,** U.S.P. XXI. $C_4H_9NO_3$ as L-threonine.
Use: Amino acid.

THROAT DISCS. (Marion) Capsicum, peppermint, anise, cubeb, glycyrrhiza, linseed. Box 60s.
Use: Minor throat irritations.

THROAT DISCS. (Wolins) Benzocaine 5 mg., sodium propionate 10 mg./Tab. Bot. 1000s.

ROAT-EZE. (Faraday) Cetylpyridinium chloride 1:3000, cetyl dimethyl benzyl ammonium chloride 1:3000, benzocaine 10 mg./Wafer. Loz., foil wrapped. Vial 15.
Use: Anesthetic lozenge.

HROMBIN, U.S.P. XXI. Thrombin, topical, mammalian origin.
(Parke-Davis)—Thrombin, Topical (Bovine).
(Upjohn)—Vial (1000 u.) 30 ml.
Use: Local hemostatic.

ROMBINAR. (Armour) Thrombin topical. Vial 1000, 5000, 10,000, 50,000 U.S. Standard Units.
Use: Topical hemostat.

ROMBOPLASTIN.
Use: Diagnostic aid (prothrombin estimation).

ROMBOSTAT. (Parke-Davis) Prothrombin is activated by tissue thromboplastin in the presence of calcium chloride. **1000** U.S. (N.I.H.) units. Vial 10 ml. **5000** U.S. units. Vial 10 ml. and 5 ml. diluent. **10,000** U.S. units. Vial 20 ml. and 10 ml. diluent. **20,000** U.S. units. Vial 30 ml. and 20 ml. diluent.
Use: Local hemostatic.

ROPHYLLINE REAGENT STRIPS. (Ames) Seralyzer reagent strip. Bot. 25s.
Use: A quantitative strip test for theophylline in serum or plasma.

SAL. (Foy) Sodium thiosalicylate 50 mg. Vial 30 ml.
Use: Antipyretic.

URFYL NICOTINATE. B.A.N. Tetrahydrofurfuryl nicotinate. Trafuril.
Use: Topical vasodilator.

YCAL. (Mills) Thermoloid (thyroid) 2 gr., iodized calcium 2 gr., peptone 1 gr./Tab. Bot. 1000s.

YLIN. Nifenazone, B.A.N.

YLOX. (C.S. Dent) Medicated shampoo & soap, contains absorbable sulfur. Bot. 6 oz. Bar 3⅜ oz.
Use: Seborrheic dermatitis, Dandruff Control. Bot. 6 oz.

HYMOL, N.F. XVI. Phenol, 5-methyl-2-(1-methylethyl)- p-Cymen-3-ol. (Var. Mfr.) 0.25 lb., 1 lb.
Use: Antifungal, anti-infective local anesthetic, antitussive, nasal decongestant.
See: Vicks Regular & Wild Cherry Medicated Cough Drops (Vicks)
Vicks Vaporub, Oint. (Vicks)
Combinations.
See: Listerine Antiseptic, Sol. (Warner-Lambert)

YMOL IODIDE.
Use: Antifungal; anti-infective.

YMOLIDINE. (Blue Line) Phenol 0.5%, iodine, camphor, thymol in mineral oil. Liq. 1 pt., 1 gal.
Use: Topically; antiseptic.

HYMOPENTIN. USAN. Formerly thymopoietin
Use: Immunoregulator.

YMOXAMINE. B.A.N. 4-(2-Dimethylamino-ethoxy)-5-isopropyl-2-methylphenyl acetate. Moxisylyte (I.N.N.) Opilon [hydrochloride].
Use: Peripheral vasodilator.

YODATIL. Name used for Nifuratel.

THYPINONE. (Abbott) Protirelin 500 mcg./1 ml. Amp.
Use: Adjunctive agent in the diagnostic assessment of thyroid function.

THYRAR. (USV Labs.) Bovine thyroid preparation 0.5 gr., 1 gr., 2 gr./Tab. Bot. 100s.
Use: Hypothyroid states.

THYROBROM. (Mills) Brominated thyroid. Tab. or S.C. Tab. (1 gr. & 2 gr., 3 gr., 4 gr.) Bot. 1000s.
Use: Thyroid therapy.

THYROCALCITONIN. Calcitonin, B.A.N.

• **THYROGLOBULIN,** U.S.P. XXI. Tab., U.S.P. XXI. Substance obtained by fractionation of thyroid glands from hog, *Sus scrofa* Linne' var. domesticus Gray (Fam. Suidae), containing not less than 0.7% iodine.
Use: Thyroid hormone.
See: Proloid, Tab. (Parke-Davis)
Thyrar, Tab. (Armour)

• **THYROID,** U.S.P. XXI.; Tab., U.S.P. XXI.
Use: Thyroid hormone.
See: Arco Thyroid, Tab. (Arco)
Armour Thyroid, Tab. (USV Labs.)
Dathroid 0.05 & 3, Tab. (Scrip)
Delcoid, Tab. (Delco)
Marion Thyroid, Tab. (Marion)
S-P-T., Cap. (Fleming)
Thermoloid, Tab. (Mills)
Thyrocrine, Tab. (Lemmon)
Thyroid Strong, Tab. (Marion)
Thyro-Teric, Tab. (Mallard))

THYROID COMBINATIONS.
See: Andro-Medicone, Tab. (Medicone)
Foyaloid-B, Tab. (Foy)
Geramine, Vial (Brown)
Hemocrine, Tab. (Mallard)
Henydin, Prep. (Arcum)
Lotone, Tab. (Westerfield)
Thycal, Tab. (Mills)

THYROID BROMINATED.
See: Thyrobrom, Tab. (Mills)

THYROID HORMONES.
See: Liothyronine Sod.
Synthroid, Inj., Tab. (Flint)
Thyroxin (Var. Mfr.)

THYROID PREPARATIONS.
See: Proloid, Tab. (Parke-Davis)
Thyrar, Tab. (USV Labs.)
Thyrobrom, Tab. (Mills)
Thyroxin, Prep. (Var. Mfr.)

THYROID STRONG, COATED. (Marion) Thyroid hormone 0.5 gr., 2 gr., 3 gr./Tab. Bot. 100s; 1 gr./Tab. Bot. 100s, 1000s.
Use: Thyroid replacement.

THYROID STRONG, UNCOATED. (Marion) Thyroid 0.5 gr., 1 gr., or 2 gr. Bot. 100s, 1000s.
Use: Thyroid replacement.

THYROLAR. (USV Labs.) Liotrix. 0.25 gr./Tab. Bot. 100s; 0.5 gr., 1 gr., 2 gr., 3 gr./Tab. Bot. 100s, 1000s.
Use: Thyroid deficiency.

• **THYROMEDAN HYDROCHLORIDE.** USAN. 2-(Diethylamino)ethyl [3,5-diiodo-4-(3-iodo-4-methoxyphenoxy) phenyl] acetate hydrochloride.
Use: Thyromimetic.

THYROPROPIC ACID. 4-(4-Hydroxy-3-iodophenoxy)-3,5-diiodohydrocinnamic acid. Triopron (Warner Chilcott)
Use: Anticholesteremic.

THYRO-TERIC. (Mallard) Thyroid 1 gr./Tab. Bot. 1000s.

THYROTROPHIN. B.A.N. Thyrotrophic hormone. Thytropar; Thytrophin.

THYROTROPIC PRINCIPLE OF BOVINE ANTERIOR PITUITARY GLANDS.
See: Thytropar, Vial (Armour Labs.)

• **THYROXINE I-125.** USAN.
Use: Radioactive agent.

• **THYROXINE I-131.** USAN.
Use: Radioactive agent.

L-THYROXINE, SODIUM.
See: Levoid, Vial (Pharmex)
Synthroid, Tab., Inj. (Flint)

THYTROPAR. (Armour) Thyrotropin from bovine anterior pituitary glands. Thyrotropin, B.A.N. Vial 10 IU.
Use: Thyroid myxedema due to pituitary insufficiency.

THYTROPHIN. Thyrotrophin, B.A.N.

THYROZYME-II A. (Abbott) T-4 diagnostic kit. 100 & 500 test units.
Use: Quantitative measurement of unsaturated thyroxine binding globulin in serum.

TIACRILAST. USAN.
Use: Anti-allergic.

• **TIAMENIDINE HYDROCHLORIDE.** USAN.
Use: Antihypertensive.

• **TIAMULIN.** USAN.
Use: Antibacterial.

• **TIAMULIN FUMARATE.** USAN.
Use: Antibacterial.

• **TIAPAMIL HYDROCHLORIDE.** USAN.
Use: Antagonist (to calcium).

• **TIARAMIDE HYDROCHLORIDE.** USAN.
Use: Anti-asthmatic.

• **TIAZOFURIN.** USAN.
Use: Poultry coccidiostat.

• **TIAZURIL.** USAN.
Use: Coccidiostat.

• **TIBOLONE.** USAN. (1) 17-Hydroxy-7α-methyl-19-nor-17α-pregn-5(10)-en-20-yn-3-one; (2) 17α-Ethynyl-17-hydroxy-7α-methyl-5 (10)-estren-3-one.
Use: Anabolic.

• **TIBRIC ACID.** USAN. 2-Chloro-5-(cis-3,5-dimethylpiperidinosulfonyl)benzoic acid.
Use: Treatment of hyperlipemia.

• **TIBROFAN.** USAN. 4,4′,5-Tribromo-2-thiophenecarboxanilide. Under study.
Use: Disinfectant.

• **TICABESONE PROPIONATE.** USAN.
Use: Glucocorticoid.

TICAR. (Beecham Labs) Ticarcillin disodium. 1 Gm., Gm., 6 Gm./Vial in 10s. Piggyback vials 3 Gm. in 10s. Bulk Pharmacy Pkg. 20 Gm. in 10s.
Use: Antibiotic.

• **TICARBODINE,** USAN. α,α,α-Trifluoro-2,6-dime ylthio-1-piperidinecarboxy-m-toluidide. 2,6-Dimeth piperidino-3′-(trifluoromethyl)thioformanilide.
Use: Anthelmintic.

• **TICARCILLIN CRESYL SODIUM.** USAN.
Use: Antibacterial.

• **TICARCILLIN DISODIUM, STERILE,** U.S.P. XXI. 6-[2-Carboxy-2-(3-thienyl)-acetamido]penicillanic acid.
Use: Antibiotic.
See: Ticar, inj. (Beecham Labs.)

• **TICLATONE.** USAN. 6-Chloro-1,2-benzisothiazolin-3-one.
Use: Antibacterial, antifungal.
See: Landromil (Dosey).

• **TICLOPIDINE HYDROCHLORIDE.** USAN.
Use: Inhibitor (platelet).

TICON. (Hauck) Trimethobenzamide HCl 100 mg./m Vial 20 ml.
Use: Treatment postoperative nausea & vomiting.

• **TICRYNAFEN.** USAN.
Use: Diuretic, uricosuric, antihypertensive.

TIDEX. (Allison) Dextroamphetamine sulfate, 5 mg./Tab. Bot. 100s, 1000s.
Use: Obesity control.

TIDEXSOL TABLETS. (Winthrop Products) Acetominophen.
Use: Analgesic, antipyretic.

TIEMONIUM IODIDE. B.A.N. 4-[3-Hydroxy-3-phenyl-3-(2-thienyl)propyl]-4-methylmorpholinium iodide.
Use: Antispasmodic; anticholinergic.

TIGAN. (Beecham Labs) Trimethobenzamide hydrochloride.**Cap.** 100 mg. Bot. 100s, 250 mg. Bot. 100s, 500s. **Amp.** (100 mg./ml.) 2 ml. Box 10s. Vial 20 cc. **Thera-Ject** (100 mg./ml.) 2 ml. B 25s. **Supp.** 200 mg. Box 10s, 50s. **Pediatric Sup** 100 mg. Box 10s.
Use: Nausea and vomiting.

• **TIGESTOL.** USAN. (1) 19-Nor-17α-pregn-5(10)-en-20-yn-17-ol; (2) 17-α-Ethynyl-5(10)-estren-17- Under study.
Use: Progestin.

TIGLOIDINE. B.A.N. Tiglylpseudotropeine. Tiglyssin [hydrobromide]
Use: Treatment of the Parkinsonian syndrome.

TIGLYSSIN HYDROBROMIDE. Tigloidine, B.A.N.

TIGO. (Burlington) Polymixin B sulfate 5,000 u., zinc bacitracin 400 u., neomycin sulfate 5 mg./Gm. Oi Tube 0.5 oz.
Use: Triple antibiotic.

TIHIST-DP. (Vita Elixir) d-methorphan HBr 10 m pyrilamine maleate 16 mg., sodium citrate 3.3 gr./ cc
Use: Cough syrup.

TIHIST NASAL DROPS. (Vita Elixir) Pyrilamine maleate 0.1%, phenylephrine HCl 0.25%, sodium

bisulfite 0.2%, methylparaben 0.02%, propylparaben 0.01%/30cc.
Use: Nasal decongestant.

JA TABLETS. (Vita Elixir) Oxytetracycline HCl 250 mg./Tab.
Use: Antibiotic.

JA SYRUP. (Vita Elixir) Oxytetracycline HCl 125 mg./5 cc.
Use: Antibiotic.

JECT-20. (Mayrand) Trimethobenzamide HCl 100 mg./ml. Vials 20 ml.
Use: Anti-emetic.

ILETAMINE HCl, USAN. 2-(Ethylamino)-2-(2-thienyl)cyclohexanone HCl.
Use: Anesthetic; anticonvulsant.

LIDATE. B.A.N. Ethyl 2-dimethylamino-1-phenylcyclohex-3-ene-1-carboxylate.
Use: Analgesic.

ILIDINE HCl. USAN. (±)-Ethyl trans-2-(dimethylamino)-1-phenyl-3-cyclohexene-1-carboxylate HCl.
Use: Analgesic.

ILORONE HCl. USAN. 2,7-Bis[2-(diethylamino)ethoxy]fluoren-9-one dihydrochloride.
Use: Antiviral.

ME CAPS. (Weeks & Leo) Phenylpropanolamine HCl 50 mg., chlorpheniramine 4 mg., atropine sulfate 0.024 mg., scopolamine HBr 0.014 mg., hyoscyamine sulfate 0.122 mg.,/T.R. Cap. Bot. 14s, 28s.
Use: Decongestant, drying agent for colds and hay fever.

MED REDUCING AIDS-CAFFEINE FREE. (Weeks & Leo) Phenylpropanolamine HCl 75 mg./T.R. Cap. Bot. 28s, 56s.
Use: Reducing aid.

IMEFURONE. USAN.
Use: Antiatherosclerotic.

MENTIN. (Beecham Labs) Ticarcillin disodium 3 Gm., clavulanic acid 0.1 Gm. Vials 3.2 Gm.
Use: Antibacterial.

IMOBESONE ACETATE. USAN.
Use: Adrenocortical steroid.

MOLIDE. (Merck Sharp & Dohme) Timolol maleate 10 mg., hydrochlorothiazide 25 mg./Tab. Bot. 100s.
Use: Antihypertensive.

IMOLOL. USAN.
Use: Anti-adrenergic (beta-receptor).

IMOLOL MALEATE, U.S.P. XXI. Ophth. Sol., Tab., U.S.P. XXI. (S)-1-[Cl, 1-dimethyl-ethyl) amino]-3-[[4-(4 morpholinyl)-1,2,5-thiadiazol-3-yl]oxy]-2-propanol, (Z)-butenedioate (1:1) salt.
Use: Treatment of chronic open angle, aphakic and secondary glaucoma, antihypertensive, prevention of recurrent M.I.
See: Blocadren, Tab. (Merck Sharp & Dohme)
Timoptic, Oph. (Merck Sharp & Dohme)

IMOLOL MALEATE AND HYDROCHLORO-THIAZIDE TABLETS, U.S.P. XXI.
Use: Antihypertensive.
See: Timolide, Tab. (Merck Sharp & Dohme)

TIMOPTIC. (Merck Sharp & Dohme) Timolol maleate 0.25% and 0.5% solution. Ocumeter Ophthalmic Dispenser 5 ml., 10 ml., 15 ml.
Use: Treatment of chronic open angle, aphakic and secondary glaucoma; patients with elevated IOP at risk to require lowering of ocular pressure.

• **TINABINOL.** USAN.
Use: Antihypertensive.

TINACTIN. (Schering) **Soln. 1%:** Tolnaftate (10 mg./ml.) w/butylated hydroxytoluene, in nonaqueous homogeneous PEG 400. Plastic squeeze bot. 10 ml. **Cream 1%:** Tolnaftate (10 mg./Gm.) in homogeneous, nonaqueous vehicle of PEG-400, propylene glycol, carboxypolymethylene, monoamylamine, titanium dioxide and butylated hydroxytoluene. Tube 15 Gm. **Powder 1%:** Tolnaftate w/corn starch, talc. Plastic container 45 Gm. **Powd. Aerosol 1%:** Tolnaftate w/butylated hydroxytoluene, talc. polyethylene-polypropylene glycol monobutyl ether, denatured alcohol and inert propellant of isobutane. Spray can 100 Gm.
Use: Topical fungicidal agent.

TINADERM. Tolnaftate, B.A.N.

TINASTAT. (Vita Elixir) Sodium hyposulfite, benzethonium Cl./2 oz.
Use: Keratolytic lotion.

TINDAL. (Schering) Acetophenazine maleate 20 mg./Tab. Bot. 100s.
Use: Tranquilizer.

TINE TEST, OLD TUBERCULIN, Rosenthal. (Lederle)
See: Tuberculin Tine Test (Lederle)

TINE TEST, PURIFIED PROTEIN DERIVATIVE. (Lederle)
See: Tuberculin Tine Test (Lederle)

TIN FLUORIDE. Stannous Fluoride, U.S.P. XXI.

TING. (Pharmacraft) **Cream:** Benzoic acid, boric acid, zinc oxide, zinc stearate, alcohol 16%. Tube 0.9 oz., 1.8 oz. **Powder:** Boric acid, benzoic acid, zinc stearate, zinc oxide. Can 2.5 oz. **Aerosol (hydrocarbon):** Total undecylenate 19% as undecylenic acid and zinc undecylenate. Can 2.7 oz.
Use: Fungus infections, athlete's foot.

• **TINIDAZOLE.** USAN. 1-[2-(Ethylsulfonyl)-ethyl]-2-methyl-5-nitroimidazole.
Use: Antiprotozoal.
See: Fasigyn (Pfizer)
Simplotan (Pfizer)

TINSET. (Janssen) Oxatomide.
Use: Anti-allergenic, anti-asthmatic.

TINVER LOTION. (Barnes-Hind) Sodium thiosulfate 25%, salicylic acid 1%, isopropyl alcohol 10%, propylene glycol, menthol, disodium edetate, colloidal alumina.
Plastic Bot. 6 oz.
Use: Specific for tinea versicolor.

• **TIOCONAZOLE,** U.S.P. XXI.
Use: Antifungal.

• **TIODAZOSIN.** USAN.
Use: Antihypertensive.

• **TIODONIUM CHLORIDE.** USAN.
Use: Antibacterial.

T-IONATE-P.A. (Reid-Provident) Testosterone cypionate 200 mg., benzyl benzoate 20%, benzyl alcohol 0.9%, in cottonseed oil/ml. Vial 10 ml. 1s, 6s, 12s.

• **TIOPERIDONE HYDROCHLORIDE.** USAN.
Use: Antipsychotic.

TIOPHYLL. (Schaffer Lab) Iodine 0.71%, boric acid 0.61%, phenol 0.60%, viscarin 0.48%, chlorophyll 0.45%. Liq. Bot. pt. gal.
Use: Minor urinary tract infections.

• **TIOPINAC.** USAN.
Use: Anti-inflammatory, analgesic.

• **TIOTIDINE.** USAN.
Use: Antagonist.

• **TIOXIDAZOLE.** USAN.
Use: Anthelmintic.

TIP-A-LIP. (Eckerd) Metahomomethyl salicylate, allantoin, lanolin derivative, silicone, camphor, menthol, white petrolatum, mineral oil, white beeswax. Bot. 3/8 oz.
Use: Lip protectant.

TIPRAMINE TABS. (Major) Imipramine 10 mg./Tab. Bot. 250s; 25 mg. or 50 mg./Tab. Bot. 250s, 1000s.
Use: Antidepressant.

TIPRENOLOL. B.A.N. 3-Isopropylamino-1-[2-(methylthio)phenoxy]propan-2-ol.
Use: Beta adrenergic receptor blocking agent.

• **TIPRENOLOL HCl.** USAN. (±)-1-(Isopropylamino)-3-[o-(methylthio)-phenoxy]-2-propanol HCl.
Use: Anti-adrenergic (β-receptor).

• **TIPRINAST MEGLUMIDE.** USAN. A Mead Johnson investigative drug.
Use: Anti-allergenic agent.

• **TIPROPIDIL HYDROCHLORIDE.** USAN.
Use: Vasodilator.

• **TIQUINAMIDE HYDROCHLORIDE.** USAN.
Use: Anticholingeric.

TIREND. (Norcliff Thayer) Caffeine 100 mg./Tab. Bot. 12s, 25s, 50s.
Use: Stimulant.

TISSUE FIXATIVE AND WASH SOLUTION. (Wampole-Zeus) A modified Michel's tissue fixative and buffered wash solution.
Use: To facilitate the transport and processing of fresh tissue biopsies.

TIS-U-SOL. (Travenol) Pentalyte irrigation containing Na 137.5, K 6, Mg. 1,6, Cl 142, sulfate 1.6, P 1.5 (as HPO_4). Plastic Bot. 1000 ml. Bot. 1000 ml.
Use: Physiologic irrigating solution.

TITAN. (Barnes-Hind) Benzalkonium chloride, EDTA, nonionic cleaner buffers. Bot. 1 oz., 2 oz.
Use: Hard contact lens cleaning solution.

TITAN II WEEKLY CLEANING SOLUTION. (Barnes-Hind) Non-enzymatic surfactant cleaning solution.
Use: Hard contact lens weekly cleaner.

• **TITANIUM DIOXIDE,** U.S.P. XXI.
Use: Solar ray protectant.

TITICUM RIPENS.
W/Oxyquinoline sulfate, charcoal.
See: Triticoll, Tabs. (Western Research)

TITRALAC. (3M Products) **Tab.:** Cal. carb. 0.42 Gm./Tab. Bot. 9s, 40s, 60s, 100s, 500s, 1000s. **Liq.:** Cal. carb. 1.0 0.30 Gm./5 ml. Bot. 12 fl. oz.
Use: Gastric antacid.

• **TIXANOX.** USAN.
Use: Anti-allergic.

T-MATINIC. (Tennessee) Iron 100 mg., liver desic. 2(mg., stomach pwd. 100 mg., Vit. B-12 10 mcg., C mg., folic acid 1 mg./Cap. Bot. 100s, 1000s. Vial 30 cc.

TOBAVIM. (Blue Cross) Vit. A 2500 I.U., D 400 I.U. 60 mg., E 15 I.U., B-1 1.05 mg., B-2 1.2 mg., niac 13.5 mg., B-6 1.05 mg., B-12 4.5 mcg./5 ml.
Use: Vitamin supplement for children 4 years old adults.

• **TOBRAMYCIN,** U.S.P. XXI. Opth. Oint., Ophth. Soln., U.S.P. XXI. An antibiotic obtained from cultures of *Streptomyces tenebrarius.*
Use: Antibiotic.
See: Tobrex, Soln., Oint. (Alcon)

• **TOBRAMYCIN SULFATE INJECTION,** U.S.P. XXI.
See: Nebcin, Amp., Hyporet. (Lilly)

TOBREX OPHTHALMIC OINTMENT. (Alcon) Tobramycin 0.3% in sterile ointment base. Tube 3 Gm.
Use: External ophthalmic bacterial infections.

TOBREX SOLUTION. (Alcon) Tobramycin 0.3%. ophthalmic solution. Bot. 5 ml. w/dropper.
Use: Topical ophthalmic anti-infective.

TOCAINIDE. USAN.
Use: Antiarrhythmic.
See: Tonocard, Tab. (Merck Sharp & Dohme)

• **TOCAMPHYL.** USAN. 1-p, α-Dimethyl-benzyl car phorate 1:1 salt with 2,2′-iminodiethanol.
Use: Choleretic.
See: Gallogen, Tab. (Beecham-Massengill)

TOCE. Diethadione, B.A.N.

TOCLONOL EXPECTORANT. (Cenci) Carbetapentane citrate 7.25 mg., terpin hydrate 16.65 mg., menthol 0.83 mg., alcohol 7.2%, sodiu citrate 66.15 mg., citric acid 6.65 mg., glycerin 45 min./5 cc. Bot. 3 oz., 6 oz., 16 oz.
Use: Cough.

TOCLONOL W/CODEINE ELIXIR. (Cenci) Same as Toclonol Expectorant plus codeine 10 mg./5 cc. Bot. pt., gal.

TOCOPHER. (Quality Generics) Vit. E (from d-alp tocopheryl acetate conc.) 100 I.U./Cap. Bot. 100s 1000s.

TOCOPHER-400. (Quality Generics) Vit. E (d-alp tocopheryl acetate conc.) 400 I.U./Cap. Bot. 100s 1000s.

TOCOPHER-M. (Quality Generics) Vit. E (from mix tocopheryls conc.) 1000 I.U./Cap. Bot. 50s, 100s.

TOCOPHER-PLUS. (Quality Generics) Vit. E(d-alp tocopheryl acetate conc.) 200 I.U./Cap. Bot. 100s 1000s.

TOCOPHEROL-DL-ALPHA. Vitamin E, U.S.P. XXI. 7,8-Trimethyltocol, alpha-Tocopherol, dl-alpha-toc pherol, vit. E, wheat germ oil. dl-2,5,7,8-Tetrameth 2-(4′,8′,12′-trimethyltridecyl)-6-chromanol.

Cap. & Tab.:
Denamone, Cap. (3 min., 10 min.) wheat germ oil (Vio-Bin)
Ecofrol, Cap. (O'Neal)
Eprolin, Gelseal (Lilly)
Epsilan M, Cap. (Warren-Teed)
Lib-E, Cap. (AVP)
Oint.:
Myopone (Drug Prods.)
Sol.:
Aquasol E, Sol. (USV Pharm.)

OCOPHERSOLAN. USAN. (+)-α-Toco-pheryl po-yethylene glycol 1000 succinate.
Jse: Vitamin E supplement.

COPHERYL ACETATE-d-ALPHA. Vitamin E, U.S.P. XXI.
See: Aquasol E, Prods. (USV Labs.)
E-Ferol, Prep. (Fellows)
Epsilan-M, Cap. (Warren-Teed)
Lib-E-400, Cap. (AVP)
Tocopher, Cap. (Quality Generics)
Tokols, Cap. (Ulmer)
Vit. E. (Var. Mfr.)

COPHERYL ACETATES, CONC. D-ALPHA. Vitamin E, U.S.P. XXI. d-alpha-Toco-pheryl acetate.
Jse: Treatment of habitual & threatened abortion.

COPHERYL ACID SUCCINATED D-ALPHA. Vitamin E, U.S.P. XXI.
See: E-Ferol Succinate, Tab., Cap. (Fellows)
Vit. E (Var. Mfr.)

COSAMINE. (Trent) Sparteine sulfate 150 mg., sod. chl. 4.5 mg./cc. Amps. 1 cc. Box 12s, 100s.
Jse: I.M. Oxytocic.

DAY VAGINAL CONTRACEPTIVE SPONGE. (VLI) Nonoxynol-9, citric, sorbic, benzoic acid, sodium dihydrogen, citrate, sodium metabisulfite, polyurethane foam sponge. 3/pk.
Jse: Contraceptive.

DRAZOLINE. B.A.N. Ethyl 3-phthalazin-1-ylcarbazate. Binazine.
Jse: Antihypertensive.

FENACIN. B.A.N. N-Methyl-2-(2-methyl-benzhydryloxy)ethylamine. Elamol hydrochloride
Jse: Treatment of the Parkinsonian syndrome.

OFENACIN HCl. USAN. N-Methyl-2-[(o-methyl-α-phenyl-benzyl)oxy]-ethylamine HCl.
Jse: Anticholinergic.

FRANAZINE. (Geigy) Combination of imipramine and promazine. Pending release.

FRANIL. (Geigy) Imipramine HCl **Tab.** 10 mg. Bot. 100s, 1000s; 25 mg. & 50 mg. Bot. 100s, 1000s. Unit Dose 100s. Gy-Pak 100s, 1 unit (12×100); 6 units (72×100). **Amps.** 25 mg./2 cc. w/ascorbic acid 2 mg., sod. bisulfite 1 mg., sod. sulfite 1 mg. Box 10s.
Jse: Antidepressant, antienuretic.

FRANIL-PM. (Geigy) Imipramine pamoate 75 mg., 100 mg. , 125 mg. or 150 mg./Cap. Bot. 30s, 100s. 75 mg./Cap. Bot. 1000s. Unit dose 75 mg. and 150 mg. in 100s.
Jse: Antidepressant.

TOLAMIDE TABS. (Major) Tolazamide 100 mg./Tab. Bot. 100s; 250 mg./Tab. 200s, 500s; 500 mg./Tab. Bot. 100s.
Use: Hypoglycemic agent.

• **TOLAMOLOL.** USAN. 4-[2-(2-Hydroxy-3-o-tolyloxy-propylamino)ethoxy]benzamide.
Use: Beta adrenergic receptor blocking agent.

TOLANASE. Tolazamide, B.A.N.

• **TOLAZAMIDE,** U.S.P. XXI. Tabs., U.S.P. XXI. (Upjohn) 1-(Hexahydro-1-azepinyl)-3-(p-tolylsulfonyl) urea. 1-Perhydroazepin-1-yl-3-toluene-p-sulphonylurea. Tolanase. Benzenesulfonamide, N-[[(hexahydro-1H-azepin-1-yl)amino]carbonyl]-4-methyl-. 1-(Hexahydro-1H-azepin-1-yl)-3-(p-tolylsulfonyl) urea.
Use: Hypoglycemic agent.
See: Ronase, Tab. (Rowell)
Tolinase, Tab. (Upjohn)

• **TOLAZOLINE HYDROCHLORIDE,** U.S.P. XXI. Inj., Tab., U.S.P. XXI. Benzazoline HCl, 2-Benzyl-2-imidazoline HCl. Vasimid, Vasodil.
Use: Anti-adrenergic.
See: Priscoline, Prep. (Ciba)
Tazol, Tab. (Durst)
Toloxan, Tab. (Kenyon)
Tolzol, Tab. (Robinson)

• **TOLBUTAMIDE,** U.S.P. XXI. Tab. U.S.P. XXI. N-Butyl-N′-toluene-p-sulfonylurea. Benzenesulfonamide, N-[(butylamino)carbonyl]-4-methyl-. 1-Butyl-3-(p-tolylsulfonyl)urea.
Use: Hypoglycemic.
See: Orinase, Prep. (Upjohn)
SK-Tolbutamide, Tab. (SmithKline)

TOLBUTAMIDE SODIUM.
Use: Diagnostic aid (diabetes).
See: Orinase Diagnostic (Upjohn)

• **TOLCICLATE.** USAN.
Use: Antifungal.

TOLDIMFOS. B.A.N. 4-Dimethylamino-o-tolylphosphinic acid. Tonophosphan (sodium salt)
Use: Phosphorus source, veterinary medicine.

TOLECTIN. (McNeil Pharm) Tolmetin sodium 200 mg./Tab. Bot. 100s, 500s.
Use: Anti-inflammatory.

TOLECTIN DS. (McNeil Pharm) Tolmetin sodium 400 mg./Cap Bot. 100s.
Use: Anti-inflammatory.

• **TOLFAMIDE.** USAN.
Use: Enzyme inhibitor.

TOLFRINIC. (Ascher) Ferrous fumarate 600 mg., Vit. B-12 25 mcg., Vit. C 100 mg./Tab. Bot. 100s.
Use: Hemopoietic.

• **TOLIMIDONE.** USAN.
Use: Antiulcerative.

TOLINASE. (Upjohn) Tolazamide. **100 mg.**/Tab. Unit of use 100s. **250 mg.**/Tab. Unit of use 100s. Bot, 200s, 1000s. Unit Dose 100s. **500 mg.**/Tab. Unit of use 100s.
Use: Hypoglycemic agent.

• **TOLINDATE.** USAN.
Use: Antifungal.
See: Dalnate (USV Pharm.)

• **TOLIODIUM CHLORIDE.** USAN.
Use: Food additive.

• **TOLMETIN.** USAN.
Use: Anti-inflammatory.

• **TOLMETIN SODIUM,** U.S.P. XXI. Cap., Tab., U.S.P. XXI. Sodium 1-Methyl-5-p-toluoylpyrrole-2-acetic acid.
Use: Anti-inflammatory.
See: Tolectin, Tab. (McNeil).
Tolectin DS, Cap. (McNeil)

• **TOLNAFTATE,** U.S.P. XXI. Topical Aerosol Powder, Cream, Gel, Powder, Topical Soln., U.S.P. XXI. o-2-Naphthyl m,N-dimethyl-thiocarbanilate. Naphthiomate-T; Tinaderm. Carbamothoic acid, methyl(3-methylphenyl)-, 0-2-naphthalenyl ester.
Use: Topical antifungal agent.
See: Aftate, Prods. (Plough)
Tinactin, Sol., Cream, Pow., Pow. Aer. (Schering)

TOLNATE HYDROCHLORIDE. Prothipendyl, B.A.N.

TOLONIUM CHLORIDE. 3-Amino-7-dimethyl-amino-2-methyl-phenazathionium. Blutene Chloride

TOLOXAN. (Kenyon) Tolazoline HCl 25 mg./Tab. Bot. 100s, 1000s.

TOLOXYCHLORINAL. 1,1′-[[(o-Tolyloxy)-methyl]ethylenedioxy]bis[2,2,2-trichloro-ethanol].1,1′-[3-o-Tolyloxypropylenedioxy]bis (2,2,2-trichloroethanol. Propoxychlorinol
Use: Sedative.

3-o-TOLOXY-1,2-PROPANEDIOL.
See: Mephenesin, Prep. (Var.Mfr.)

TOLPENTAMIDE. B.A.N. 1-Cyclopentyl-3-toluene-p-sulfonylurea.
Use: Hypoglycemic agent.

TOLPERISONE. B.A.N. 2-Methyl-3-piperidino-1-p-tolylpropan-1-one. Mydocalm
Use: Muscle relaxant.

TOLPIPRAZOLE. B.A.N. 5-Methyl-3-[2-(4-m-tolylpiperazin-1-yl)ethyl]pyrazole.
Use: Tranquilizer.

• **TOLPOVIDONE I-131.** USAN. ω-(p-Iodobenzyl)-poly[1-(2-oxo-1-pyrrolidinyl)ethylene]-^{131}I.
Use: Differential diagnosis of source of hypoalbuminemia.
See: Raovin (Abbott)

TOLPRONINE. B.A.N. 1-(1,2,3,6-Tetrahydro-1-pyridyl)-3-o-tolyloxypropan-2-ol. Proponesin [hydrochloride]
Use: Analgesic.

TOLPROPAMINE. B.A.N. NN-Dimethyl-3-phenyl-3-p-tolypropylamine. Tylagel [hydrochloride]
Use: Antipruritic.

• **TOLPYRRAMIDE.** USAN. N-p-tolylsulfonyl-1-pyrrolidinecarboxamide. 1-Tetramethylene-3-p-tolysulfonylurea.
Use: Oral hypoglycemic

• **TOLRESTAT.** USAN.
Use: Inhibitor (aldose reductase).

TOLSERAM CARBAMATE. Mephenesin, B.A.N.

• **TOLU BALSAM,** U.S.P. XXI.
Use: Pharm. necessity for Compound Benzoin Tincture, expectorant.
See: Vicks Regular & Wild Cherry Medicated Co[illegible] Drops (Vicks)

• **TOLU BALSAM SYRUP,** N.F. XVI. (Lilly) Bot. 16 oz.
Use: Vehicle.

• **TOLU BALSAM TINCTURE,** N.F. XVI.
Use: Flavor.

TOLUIDINE BLUE O CHLORIDE.
See: Blutene Chloride

TOLU-SED (No Sugar). (Scherer) Codeine phosph[illegible] 10 mg., guaifenesin 100 mg./5 ml. w/alcohol 10[illegible] Bot. 4 oz., pt.
Use: Temporary relief of coughs due to colds, ar[illegible] minor throat irritations.

TOLU-SED DM (No Sugar). (Scherer) d-Methorp[illegible] HBr. 10 mg., guaifenesin 100 mg./5 ml. w/alcoh[illegible] 10%. Bot. 4 oz., pt.
Use: Temporary relief of cough due to the comm[illegible] cold.

TOLYCAINE. B.A.N. Methyl 2-diethylaminoacetami[illegible] m-toluate. Baycain [hydrochloride]
Use: Local anesthetic.

TOLYD. (Galen) Mephenesin 325 mg., hyoscyamin[illegible] HBr 0.1105 mg., hyoscine HBr 0.013 mg., homatropine methyl bromide 0.039 mg., sodium phenobarbital 8.1 mg./Tab. Bot. 100s, 1000s.
Use: Antispasmodic, muscle relaxant.

TOLZOL. (Robinson) Tolazoline HCl 25 mg./Tab. B[illegible] 100s, 1000s. Bulk pack 5000.

• **TOMOXETINE HYDROCHLORIDE.** USAN.
Use: Antidepressant.

TONACON. (CMC) Vit. B-1 5 mg., B-2 5 mg., B-1[illegible] mcg., B-6 1 mg., niacinamide 100 mg., panthen[illegible] mg., methionine 100 mg., choline 100 mg., iron [illegible] mg./fl. oz. Bot. pt., gal.
Use: Dietary supplement.

TONAMINE. (Kenyon) Liver, B-12 equiv. 1 mcg., ferr[illegible] gluconate 44 mg., Vit. B-2 0.5 mg., folic acid 2 mg. panthenol 2.5 mg., dl-methionine 10 mg., niacinam[illegible] 100 mg., procaine HCl 2%/2 cc. Vial 30 cc.

TONAVITE. (Apco) Vit. B-1 2 mg., niacinamide 5 [illegible] strychnine sulfate 1/60 gr., arsenous acid 1/60 gr., protochloride of mercury 1/50 gr., ex. gentian 1 gr., dried iron sulfate 2.5 gr./Tab. Bot. 100s.
Use: Tonic.

TONAVITE-M ELIXIR. (Goldline) Bot. 12 oz.
Use: Dietary supplement.

• **TONAZOCIN MESYLATE.** USAN.
Use: Analgesic.

TONBEC TABLETS. (A.V.P.) Vit. B-1 15 mg., B-2 mg., B-6 5 mg., nicotinamide 50 mg., Ca pantothen[illegible] 10 mg., ascorbic acid 300 mg./Tab. Bot. 60s.
Use: Therapeutic vitamin B and C supplement.

TONECOL. (A.V.P.) Promethazine w/expectorant a[illegible] vasoconstrictor. Bot. pt.
Use: Cough medicine.

TONECOL COUGH SYRUP. (A.V.P.) Dextromethorphan HBr 10 mg., phenylephrine HCl 5 mg., ch[illegible] pheniramine maleate 1 mg., sodium citrate 15 m[illegible] guaifenesin 25 mg./5 ml. w/alcohol 7%. Bot. 1 p[illegible]
Use: Treatment of cold symptoms, expectorant.

NELAX TABLETS. (A.V.P.) Danthron 75 mg., alcium pantothenate 25 mg./Tab. Bot. 100s, 000s.
Jse: Peristaltic stimulant, laxative.

NEX. (Vitarine) Vit. A 10,000 I.U., D 400 I.U., B-1 10 ng., B-2 5 mg., B-6 2 mg., pantothenic acid 10 mg., iacinamide 30 mg., cobalamin conc. 3 mcg., C 00 mg., alpha tocopherol 5 I.U., Fe 15 mg., Cu 1 ng., Iodine 0.15 mg., Mn 1 mg., Mg 5 mg., Zn 1.5 ng./Tab. Bot. 100s.

NEX T. (Vitarine) Vit. A 10,000 I.U., D 400 I.U., B-15 mg., B-2 10 mg., B-6 2 mg., pantothenic acid 10 ng., niacinamide 100 mg., B-12 7.5 mcg., C 150 mg., 5 I.U., Fe 15 mg., Cu 1 mg., Iodine 0.15 mg., Mn mg., Mg 5 mg., Zn 1.5 mg./Tab. Bot. 100s.

NOCARD. (Merck Sharp & Dohme) Tocainide HCl 00 mg. and 600 mg./Tab. Bot. 100s. Unit-dose 100s.
Jse: Antiarrhythmic.

NOCO. (Sutliff & Case) Strychnine sulfate 0.8 mg., hyroid 4 mg., zinc phosphide 4 mg., iron 65 mg., alcium gluconate 97 mg./Tab. Bot. 1000s.
Jse: Systemic stimulant and tonic.

NOPHOSPHAN SODIUM SALT. Toldimfos, B.A.N.

OTHACHE DROPS. (DeWitt) Oil of cloves 10%, Benzocaine 5%, creosote 4.8%, alcohol 20%, ther 207 grains/oz. Bot. 0.25 oz.
Jse: Temporary relief of pain from toothache.

P 20. (Eckerd) Benzocaine 20%, para-chlorometaxlenol 1% Tube 1.5 oz.

P BRASS ZP-11. (Revlon) Zinc pyrithione 0.5% in ream base.
Jse: Anti-dandruff hairdress.

PEX. (Vicks Prods) Benzoyl peroxide 10%. Bot. 1 oz.
Jse: Acne clearing lotion.

P-FORM. (Hoyt) Topical formfitting gel applicators. Disposible trays for topical fluoride office reatments, plus permanent trays for topical fluoride ome self treatments. Box 100s.
Jse: Topical fluoride applications in home or office.

PIC. (Syntex) 5% benzyl alcohol in greaseless gel ase containing camphor, menthol, w/30% sopropyl alcohol. Tube 2 oz.
Jse: Antipruritic.

PICAL FLUORIDE. (Pacemaker). Acidulated hosphate fluoride. Flavors: orange, bubblegum, me, raspberry, grape cinnamon. Liq. Bot. 4 oz., pt.

PICORT CREAM. (Hoechst) Desoximetasone .25% emollient cream consisting of isopropyl nyristate, cetylstearyl alcohol, white petrolatum, nineral oil, lanolin alcohol and purified water. ubes 15 Gm., 60 Gm.
Jse: Synthetic corticosteroid for relief of ermatoses.

PICORT GEL. (Hoechst) Desoximetasone 0.05% gel base. Tube 15 Gm., 60 Gm.
Jse: Synthetic corticosteroid for relief of ermatoses.

PICORT LP CREAM. (Hoechst) Desoximetasone .05%. Tubes 15 Gm, 60 Gm.
Jse: Synthetic corticosteroid for relief of ermatoses.

TOPICORT OINTMENT. (Hoechst) Desoximetasone 0.25% in ointment base. Tube 15 Gm., 60 Gm.,
Use: Synthetic corticosteroid for relief of dermatoses.

TOPICYCLINE. (Norwich Eaton) Tetracycline HCl 2.2 mg./ml. w/4-epitetracycline HCl, sodium bisulfite. Bot. 70 ml.
Use: Topical treatment of acne vulgaris.

TOPILAR. Fluclorolone Acetonide, B.A.N.

TOPOCAINE.
See: Surfacaine (Lilly)

• **TOPTERONE.** USAN.
Use: Anti-androgen.

• **TOQUIZINE.** USAN.
Use: Anticholingeric.

TORA. (Reid-Provident) Phentermine HCl 8 mg./Tab. Bot. 1000s.

TORECAN. (Boehringer Ingelheim) Thiethylperazine maleate **Tab.** 10 mg. Bot. 100s; **Amp.** 10 mg./2 cc. (w/sod. metabisfulfite 0.5 mg., ascorbic acid 2 mg. sorbitol 40 mg., carbon dioxide) Box 20s, 100s. **Supp.** 10 mg. (w/theobroma oil) Box 12s.
Use: Antiemetic and antinauseant.

TORNALATE INHALER. (Winthrop-Breon) Bitolterol mesylate metered inhaler. Bot. 16.4 Gm. w/oral inhaler. Refill 16.4 Gm.
Use: Bronchodilator for bronchial asthma and reversible bronchospasms.

TORNALATE TABLETS. (Winthrop Products) Bitolterol mesylate.
Use: Bronchodilator.

TOROFOR. (Torch) Clioquinol 3% in hydrophilic vehicle. Jar 2 oz., 1 lb.
Use: Cream anti-eczematous, antibacterial, anti-fungal, antipruritic.

TORULA YEAST, DRIED, Obtained by growing *Candida (torulopsis) utilis* yeast on wood pulp wastes (Nutritional Labs.) Conc. 100 lb. drums.
Use: Natural source of protein & Vitamin B-complex vitamins.

• **TOSIFEN.** USAN.
Use: Anti-anginal.

TOSMILEN. Demecarium Bromide, B.A.N.

TOTACILLIN. (Beecham Labs) Ampicillin trihydrate equivalent to: **Cap.** 250 mg./Cap. Bot. 500s. 500 mg./Cap. Bot. 500s. **Susp.:** 125 mg. 15 cc. Bot. 100 ml., 200 ml. 250 mg./5 cc. Bot. 100 ml., 200 ml.

TOTACILLIN-N. (Beecham Labs) Ampicillin sodium 250 mg., 500 mg., 1 Gm., 2 Gm./Vial in 10s; Piggyback vials 500 mg., 1 Gm., 2 Gm., in 25s; Bulk pharm. pkg. 10 Gm. in 25s.
Use: Antibiotic.

TOTAL. (Allergan) Polyvinyl alcohol, edetate disodium and benzalkonium chloride in a sterile buffered, isotonic solution. Bot: 2 fl. oz., 4 fl. oz.
Use: Hard contact lens all purpose solution.

TOTAL ECLIPSE ALCOHOL BASE LOTION. (Dorsey) Oxybenzone, padimate 0, glyceryl PABA. SPF 15. Bot. 4 oz.
Use: Sunscreen.

TOTAL ECLIPSE MOISTURIZING BASE LOTION. (Dorsey) Padimate 0, octyl salicylate, oxybenzone. SPF 15. Bot. 4 oz., 6 oz.
Use: Sunscreen.

TOTAQUINE, Alkaloids from Cinchona bark, 7 to 12% quinine anhydr., 70% to 80% total alkaloids (cinchonidine, cinchonine, quinidine & quinine).

TOTOMYCIN HYDROCHLORIDE. Tetracycline, U.S.P. XXI.

TOXICODENDRON QUERCIFOLIUM EXTRACT.

TOXIFERINE. (Roche) Skeletal muscle relaxant; pending release.

• **TOXIN, DIPHTHERIA FOR SCHICK TEST,** U.S.P. XXI.

TOXO. (Wampole-Zeus) *Toxoplasma* antibody test system. Tests 120s.
Use: An IFA test system for the detection of antibodies to *Toxoplasma gondii.*

• **TOXOID, DIPHTHERIA,** U.S.P. XXI.
See: Diphtheria Toxoid, Aluminum Hydroxide, Adsorbed

• **TOXOID, TETANUS ADSORBED,** U.S.P. XXI.

TOXOID MIXTURE.
See: Tri-Solgen, Vial (Lilly)

T.P.L. TROCHES. (Kasdenol) Triamite. Loz. 5 Gm. 15s.

TPM-TEST. (Wampole) Indirect hemagglutination test for the qualitative and quantitative determination of antibodies to *Toxoplasma gondii* in serum. Kits 120s,
Use: An aid in the diagnosis of toxoplasmosis.

TPN ELECTROLYTES. (Abbott) multiple electrolyte additive: 321 mg sodium chloride, 331 mg calcium chloride, 1491 mg potassium chloride, 508 mg magnesium chloride, 2420 mg. sodium acetate; 20 ml in 50 ml fliptop or pintop vial or 20 ml Univ. Add. Syr.
Use: Provides electrolytes during total parenteral nutrition.

TP TROCHES. (Edward J. Moore) Triamite. Jars 500s, Box 15s.
Use: Temporary relief of minor sore throat & mouth.

• **TRACAZOLATE.** USAN.
Use: Sedative.

TRACE. (Lorvic) Erythrosine conc. sol. Squeeze Bot. 30 ml., 60 ml. Dispenser Packets 200s.
Use: Plaque dye sol.

TRACE 28. (Lorvic) D & C Red 28 in aqueous sol. Bot. 30 ml., 60 ml.
Use: Diagnostic aid to disclose dental plaque.

TRACEPLEX. (Enzyme Process) Iron 30 mg., iodine 0.1 mg., Cu 0.5 mg., Mg 40 mg., zinc 10 mg., B-12 5 mcg./4 Tabs. Bot. 100s, 250s.
Use: Mineral supplement.

TRACO-DISCS. (Neoco; Nion) Mag. trisilicate 3 gr., Cal. carb. 7 gr./Disc. Bot. 100s.
Use: Antacid, adsorbent.

TRACRIUM INJECTION. (Burroughs Wellcome) Atracurium besylate 10 mg./ml. Amp. 5 ml. Box 10s.
Use: Surgical muscle relaxant.

TRAC TABS. (Hyrex) Atropine sulfate 0.03 mg., hyoscyamine 0.03 mg., methenamine 40.8 mg., methylene blue 5.4 mg., phenyl salicylate 18.1 m gelsemium 6.1 mg., benzoic acid 4.5 mg./Tab. B 100s, 1000s.
Use: Urinary tract infections.

TRAC TABS 2X. (Hyrex) Atropine sulfate 0.06 mg. hyoscyamine 0.06 mg., methenamine 81.6 mg., methylene blue 10.8 mg., phenyl salicylate 36.2 mg., gelsemium 12.2 mg., benzoic acid 9.0 mg./Tab. Bot. 100s, 1000s.
Use: Urinary tract infections.

TRAFURIL. Thurfyl Nicotinate, B.A.N.

• **TRAGACANTH,** N.F. XVI.
Use: Pharmaceutical aid (suspending agent).

TRAL FILMTAB. (Abbott) Hexocyclium methylsulfa 25 mg./Tab. Bot. 100s.
Use: Anticholinergic agent.

TRAL GRADUMET. (Abbott) Hexocyclium methylsulfate 50 mg./Gradumet. Bot. 100s.
Use: Anticholinergic agent in sustained release form.

TRALMAG. (Forest) Dihydroxyaluminum aminoacet 200 mg., magnesium hydroxide 150 mg., aluminu hydroxide gel 150 mg./5 ml. Bot. 12 oz.
Use: Antacid.

• **TRALONIDE.** USAN.
Use: Glucocorticoid.

• **TRAMADOL HYDROCHLORIDE.** USAN.
Use: Analgesic.

• **TRAMAZOLINE,** USAN. 2-[(5,6,7,8-Tetrahydro naphthyl)amino]-2-imidazoline.
Use: Adrenergic.

TRANCAPS. (Seatrace) Brompheniramine maleate mg., phenylephrine HCl 15 mg., phenylpropanolamine HCl 15 mg./Cap. Bot. 100s 1000s.
Use: Antihistaminic, nasal decongestant.

TRANCIN. Fluphenazine.
Use: Treat anxiety and tension.

TRANCOGESICO TABLETS. (Winthrop Products) Dipyrone, chlormezanone.
Use: Analgesic, antipyretic, muscle relaxant.

TRANCOPAL. (Winthrop-Breon) Chlormezanone mg./Cap. Bot. 100s. 200 mg./Cap. Bot. 100s, 1000s.
Use: Relaxant and tranquilizer for mild anxiety ar tension states.

TRANDATE INJECTION. (Glaxo) Labetalol HCl 5 mg./ml. Amp. 20 ml. Box 1s.
Use: Antihypertensive.

TRANDATE TABLETS. (Glaxo) Labetalol HCl 200 mg. or 300 mg./Tab. Bot. 100s, 500s. Unit dose 100s.
Use: Antihypertensive.

• **TRANEXAMIC ACID.** USAN. Trans-4-(Aminomet cyclohexanecarboxylic acid. Amstat. (lederle) Amikapron.
Use: Hemostatic.

• **TRANILAST.** USAN.
Use: Anti-asthmatic.

RANMEP. (Reid-Provident) Meprobamate 400 mg./Tab. Bot. 100s, 1000s.
Use: Relief of anxiety and tension.

RANQUIL. (Kenyon) Mephenesin 400 mg., mephobarbital 10 mg., hyoscine HBr 0.25 mg./Tab. Bot. 1000s.

RANQUIL CAPSULES. (Vortech) Pyrilamine maleate 25 mg./Cap. Bot. 42s, 1000s.
Use: Mild relaxant.

TRANQUILIZERS.
See: A-poxide, Cap. (Abbott)
Atarax, Prep. (Roerig)
Centrax, Cap. (Parke-Davis)
Compazine, Prep. (SmithKline)
Equanil, Tab., Susp. (Wyeth)
Equanil L.A., Cap. (Wyeth)
Fenarol, Tab. (Winthrop Products)
Haldol, Tab., Inj., Conc. Sol. (McNeil)
Harmonyl, Tab. (Abbott)
Librium, Cap., Ing. (Roche)
Loxitane, Prod. (Lederle)
Mellaril, Tab., Sol. (Sandoz)
Meprobamate (Various Mfr.)
Miltown, Prep. (Wallace)
Permitil, Prep. (Schering)
Proketazine Maleate, Prep. (Wyeth)
Prolixin, Prep. (Squibb)
Sparine HCl, Prep. (Wyeth)
Stelazine, Prep. (SmithKline)
Taractan, Prep. (Roche)
Thorazine HCl, Prep. (SmithKline)
Tindal, Tab. (Schering)
Trancopal, Cap. (Winthrop-Breon)
Tranxene, Cap. (Abbott)
Trilafon, Prep. (Schering)
Tybatran, Cap. (Robins)
Ultran, Prep. (Lilly)
Valium, Prep. (Roche)
Vesprin, Prep. (Squibb)
Vistaril, Prep. (Pfizer)

RANQUILS CAPSULES. (Blue Cross) Pyrilamine maleate 25 mg./Cap. Bot. 30s.
Use: Night time sleep aid.

RANQUILS TABLETS. (Blue Cross) Acetaminophen 300 mg., pyrilamine maleate 25 mg./Tab. Bot. 30s.
Use: Analgesic & night time sleep aid.

RANSACT. (Westwood) Laureth-4 6%, sulfur 2%, alcohol 37%, in greaseless gel base. Tube 1 oz.
Use: Drying & peeling of acne skin.

TRANSCAINIDE. USAN.
Use: Anti-arrhythmic, cardiac depressant.

RANSCLOMIPHENE. (E)-2-[p-(2-Chloro-1, 2-diphenylvinyl) phenoxy] triethylamine.

RANSDERM-NITRO. (Ciba) Nitroglycerin 2.5 mg., 5 mg., 10 mg. or 15 mg. **2.5 mg.:** 2.5 mg./24 hr. Pkg. 30s. **5 mg.:** 5 mg./24 hr. Pkg. 7s, 30s. **10 mg.:** 10 mg./24 hr. Pkg. 30s. **15 mg.:** 15 mg./24 hr. Pkg. 30s.
Use: Prevention and treatment of angina pectoris due to coronary artery disease.

TRANSDERM-SCOP. (Ciba) Scopolamine 0.5 mg. per 2-unit blister pkg. (programmed delivery over 3-day period).
Use: Antiemetic, antinauseant.

TRANSITHAL. Buthalitone Sodium, B.A.N.

TRANSTHYRETIN EIA. (Abbott) Test kits 100s.
Use: Enzyme immunoassay for the quantitative determination of transthyretin in human serum or plasma.

TRANXENE CAPSULES. (Abbott) Clorazepate dipotassium 3.75 mg., 7.5 mg., 15 mg./Cap. Bot. 100s, 500s. Abbo-Pac 100s.
Use: Minor tranquilizer.

TRANXENE TABLETS. (Abbott) Chlorazepate dipotassium tab. 3.75 mg., 7.5 mg or 15 mg./Tab. Bot. 100s.
Use: Mild Tranquilizer.

TRANXENE-SD. (Abbott) Chlorazepate dipotassium 22.5 mg./Tab. Bot. 100s.
Use: Minor tranquilizer.

TRANXENE-SD HALF STRENGTH TABLETS. (Abbott) Chlorazepate dipotassium 11.25 mg./Tab. Bot. 100s.
Use: Minor tranquilizer.

TRANYLCYPROMINE. B.A.N. (±)trans-2-Phenylcyclopropylamine. Parnate (sulfate)
Use: Monoamine oxidase inhibitor; antidepressant.

• **TRANYLCYPROMINE SULFATE,** U.S.P. XXI. Tab., U.S.P. XXI. Trans-dl-2-phenylcyclopropylamine sulfate (±)-trans-2-phenylcyclopropylamine sulfate (2:-1).
Use: Antidepressant.
See: Parnate, Tab. (SmithKline)

TRAPENS. (Mills) Triticum 4 gr., oxyquinoline sulf. 1/20 gr., pow. charcoal 0.5 gr./Tab., Bot. 100s.

TRASICOR. (Ciba) Oxprenolol HCl, B.A.N.

TRATES. (Reid-Provident) Nitroglycerin 2.5 mg. or 6.5 mg./Granucap. Bot. 100s.

TRAUMACAL. (Mead Johnson) Nutritionally complete formula for traumatized patients. Cans 8 oz. Vanilla flavor.
Use: Specific for nitrogen and energy needs in a limited volume for multiple trauma and major burns.

TRAUM-AID HBC. (American McGaw) Advanced high branched chain amino acids diet.
Use: For trauma & sepsis patients.

T-RAU TABLET. (Tennessee Pharm.) Rauwolfia serpentina 50 mg. or 100 mg./Tab. Bot. 100s, 1000s.
Use: Hypotensive, tranquilizer.

TRAVAMULSION 10% INTRAVENOUS FAT EMULSION. 1.1 kcal/ml. 270 mOsm/liter. Bot. 500 ml.
Use: Parenteral nutrition.

TRAVAMULSION 20% INTRAVENOUS FAT EMULSION. (Travenol) 2.0 kcal/ml. 300 mOsm/liter. Bot. 500 ml.
Use: Parenteral nutrition.

TRAV-AREX. (Quality Generics) Dimenhydrinate 50 mg./Cap. Bot. 24s, 100s, 1000s.
Use: Motion sickness.

TRAVASE. (Flint) Proteolytic enzyme ointment, from bacillus subtilis; 82,000 casein units of proteolytic activity/ Gm. Tube 14.2 Gm.
Use: Debriding agent.

TRAVASOL. (Travenol) Crystalline L-Amino acids injection 5.5%, 8.5% (with or without electrolytes). IV Bot. 500 ml., 1000 ml., 2000 ml.
Use: Parenteral nutrition.

TRAVASOL 3.5% M INJECTION WITH ELECTROLYTE #45. (Travenol) Crystalline L-Amino acids 3.5% Sol. Bot. I.V. 500 ml., 1000 ml.
Use: Parenteral nutrition.

TRAVASOL 10%. (Travenol) Crystalline L-amino acids injection 10%. Bot. 200 ml., 500 ml., 1000 ml., 2000 ml.
Use: Parenteral nutrition.

TRAVASORB HEPTATIC DIET. (Travenol) 378 kcal/Pkt. 6 pkt./Carton.
Use: Enteral nutrition.

TRAVASORB HN PEPTIDE DIET. (Travenol) High nitrogen defined peptide 333 kcal/Pkt. 6 pkt/Carton.
Use: Enteral nutrition.

TRAVSORB MCT LIQUID DIET. (Travenol) Digestible protein medium chain triglyceride diet. Cans 8 oz., 32 oz.
Use: Enteral nutrition.

TRAVASORB MCT POWDER DIET. (Travenol) Digestible protein medium chain triglyceride diet 400 kcal/Pkt. 6 pkt./Carton.
Use: Enteral nutrition.

TRAVASORB RENAL DIET. (Travenol) 467 kcal/Pkt. 6 pkt/Carton.
Use: Enteral nutrition.

TRAVASORB STANDARD DIET. (Travenol) Defined peptide diet, 333 kcal/pkt. 6 packets/Carton.
Use: Enteral nutrition.

TRAVASORB WHOLE PROTEIN LIQUID DIET. (Travenol) Lactose free complete nutrition 250 kcal/Can. Cans 8 oz.
Use: Enteral Nutrition.

TRAVEL AIDS. (Faraday) Dimenhydrinate 50 mg./Tab. Bot. 30s.
Use: Motion sickness.

TRAVEL-EZE. (Approved) Pyrilamine maleate 25 mg., hyoscine hydrobromide 0.325 mg./Tab. Pkg. 20s.
Use: Motion sickness.

TRAVEL SICKNESS. (Walgreen) Dimenhydrinate 50 mg./Tab. Bot. 24s.
Use: Nausea, dizziness, vomiting.

TRAVELTABS. (Geneva) Dimenhydrinate 50 mg./Tab. Bot. 100s.
Use: Motion sickness.

TRAVERT. (Travenol) Invert sugar injection. Sol 5% or 10% in water or Saline. Plastic Bot. 1000 ml.
W/electrolyte No. 1 Bot. 1000 cc.
W/electrolyte No. 2 Bot. 500 cc., 1000 cc.,
W/electrolyte No. 3 Bot. 1000 cc.
W/electrolyte No. 4 Bot. 250, 500 cc. Sol. (10%)
Use: Replenishment solution containing invert sugar & electrolytes.

• **TRAZODONE HYDROCHLORIDE,** USAN. 2-[3-[4-(m-Chlorophenyl)-1-piperazinyl]propyl]-1,2,4-triazol[4,3-a]pyridin-3(2H)-one monohydrochloride.
Use: Antidepressant.
See: Desyrel, Tab. (Mead Johnson)

TREATS PLUS IRON. (Eckerd) Vit. A 5000 I.U., D 400 I.U., E 15 I.U., C 75 mg., folic acid 0.4 mg., thiamin 1.9 mg., riboflavin 2.1 mg., niacin 25 mg., B-6 2.5 mg., B-12 7.5 mcg. iron 22.5 mg./Cap. B[ot.] 100s.
Use: Vitamin supplement with iron.

• **TREBENZOMINE HYDROCHLORIDE.** USAN.
Use: Antidepressant.

TRECATOR S.C. (Ives) Ethionamide. 2-Ethyl t[hi]oisonicotinamide. 250 mg./Tab. Bot. 100s.
Use: Anti-tubercular agent.

• **TRELOXINATE.** USAN.
Use: Antihyperlipoproteinemic.

TREMONIL HYDROCHLORIDE. Methixene, B.A.N.

TRENBOLONE. B.A.N. 17β-Hydroxyoestra-4,9,11-trien-3-one. Finajet (acetate).
Use: Anabolic steroid, veterinary medicine.

• **TRENBOLONE ACETATE.** USAN.
Use: Anabolic steroid for veterinary use.

TRENDAR. (Whitehall) Acetaminophen 325 mg., pamabrom 25 mg./Tab. Bot. 24s, 50s.
Use: Menstrual pain.

TRENIMON. Triaziquone, B.A.N.

TRENTADIL HYDROCHLORIDE. Bamifylline, B.A.N.

TRENTAL TABLETS. (Hoechst) Pentoxifylline 400 mg./Controlled Release Tab. Bot. 100s. Unit dose 100s.
Use: Oral hemorrheologic agent for peripheral vascular disease.

TREOSULFAN. B.A.N.L-Threitol 1,4-dimethane-sulphonate.

• **TREPIPAM MALEATE.** USAN.
Use: Sedative.

• **TRESTOLONE ACETATE.** USAN.
Use: Antineoplastic, androgen.

TRESADERM. (MSD AGVET) Thiabendazole 40 mg., dexamethasone 1 mg., neomycin 3.2 mg./ml. solution.
Use: Dermatologic solution, veterinary medicine.

TRESCATYL. Ethionamide, B.A.N.

TRETAMINE. B.A.N. 2,4,6-Tri(aziridin-1-yl)-1,3,5-tri[a]zine. Triethanomelamine; Triethylene Melamine; TEM.
Use: Antineoplastic agent.

TRETHINIUM TOSYLATE. B.A.N. 2-Ethyl-1,2,3,4-te[t]rahydro-2-methylisoquinolinium toluene-p-sulfonate.
Use: Hypotensive.

TRETHOCANOIC ACID. 3-Hydroxy-3,7,11-trimeth[yl]dodecanoic acid.
Use: Anticholesteremic.

• **TRETINOIN,** U.S.P. XXI. Cream, Gel, Topical Soln., U.S.P. XXI. 3,7-Dimethyl-9-(2,6,6-trimethylcyclohex-1-enyl)nona-2,4,6,8-all-transtetraenoic acid. All tran[s] Retinoic acid. Vit. A acid.
Use: Keratolytic.
See: Retin-A, Cream, Gel, Sol. (Ortho)

REVINTIX. Prothionamide, B.A.N.
REXAN TABLETS. (Du Pont) Naltrexone HCl 50 mg./Tab. Bot. 50s.
Use: Opioid antagonist.
REXIN. (A.V.P.) Tetracycline HCl 250 mg./Cap. Bot. 100s.
Use: Antibiotic.
RIACET CREAM. (Lemmon) Triamcinolone acetonide 0.025%, 0.1%, 0.5%. **0.025%:** Tube 15 Gm., 80 Gm.; **0.1%:** Tube 15 Gm., 80 Gm.; **0.5%:** Tube 15 Gm.
Use: Topical anti-inflammatory steroid.
TRIACETIN, U.S.P. XXI. Glyceryl triacetate.
Use: Topical antifungal.
See: Enzactin, Preps. (Ayerst)
Fungacetin, Oint. (Blair)
RIACETYLOLEANDOMYCIN. Troleandomycin.
Use: Antibiotic.
RIACORT. (Kay) Triamcinolone deacetate 40 mg./ml. Vial 5 ml.
Use: Anti-inflammatory.
RIACT LIQUID. (Winthrop Products) Aluminum, magnesium hydroxide, simethicone.
Use: Antacid, antiflatulent.
RIACT TABLETS. (Winthrop Products) Aluminum, magnesium hydroxide, simethicone.
Use: Antacid, antiflatulent.
RIAFED. (Wolins) Triprolidine HCl 2.5 mg., pseudoephedrine 60 mg./Tab. Bot. 100s, 1000s.
TRIAFUNGIN. USAN.
Use: Antifungal.
RIAM-A. (Hyrex) Triamcinolone acetonide 40 mg./ml. Vial 5 ml.
Use: Glucocorticoid.
TRIAMCINOLONE, U.S.P. XXI. Tabs., U.S.P. XXI. 9-Alpha fluoro-16-alpha hydroxy-prednisolone. 9-Fluoro-11β, 16α,17,21-tetrahydroxypregna-1,4-diene-3, 20-dione.
Use: Adrenocortical steroid (anti-inflammatory).
See: Aristocort, Tab., Syr. (Lederle)
Aristoderm, Foam (Lederle)
Aristospan, Parenteral (Lederle)
Kenacort, Tab., Syr. (Squibb)
SK-Triamcinolone, Tab. (SmithKline)
TRIAMCINOLONE ACETONIDE, U.S.P. XXI. Topical Aerosol, Cream, Oint., Dental Paste, Lotion, Sterile Susp., U.S.P. XXI. 9-α-fluoro-16-α-17-α-isopropylidenedioxy-Δ' hydrocortisone. Pregna-1,4-diene-3,20-dione,8-fluoro-11,21-dihydroxy-16-17-[(1-methylethylidene)bis(oxy)]-,(11β,16α)-. 9-Fluoro-11β,16α,17,21-tetrahydroxypregna-1,4-diene-3,20-dione cyclic 16,-17-acetal with acetone.
Use: Glucocorticoid, topical anti-inflammatory.
See: Aristocort, Cream, Oint (Lederle)
Aristoderm Foam (Lederle)
Aristogel, Gel (Lederle)
Kenalog Preps. (Squibb)
Triacet, Cream (Lemmon)
Tramacin, Cream (Johnson & Johnson)
Tri-Kort, Inj. (Keene)
/Neomycin, gramicidin, Nystatin.
See: Mycolog, Preps. (Squibb)

• **TRIAMCINOLONE ACETONIDE SODIUM PHOSPHATE.** USAN.
Use: Glucocorticoid.
• **TRIAMCINOLONE DIACETATE,** U.S.P. XXI. Sterile Susp., Syrup, U.S.P. XXI. 9-Alpha-fluoro-16-alpha-hydroxyprednisolone diacetate. 9-Fluoro-11β, 16α, 17,21-tetrahydroxy-pregna-1,4-diene-3,20-dione-16,21-diacetate.
Use: Glucocorticoid.
See: Amcort, Inj. (Keene)
Aristocort Diacetate Forte (Lederle)
Aristocort Diacetate Intralesional, Inj. (Lederle)
Cinex-40, Inj. (Tunex)
Kenacort, Syr. (Squibb)
Tracilon, Susp. (Savage)
Triam-Forte, Inj. (Hyrex)
• **TRIAMCINOLONE HEXACETONIDE,** U.S.P. XXI. Sterile Susp., U.S.P. XXI. 9-Fluoro-11β,16α,17,21-tetra hyroxypregna-1,-4-diene-3,20-dione cyclic 16, 17-acetal with acetone, 21-(3,3-dimethylbutyrate).
Use: Injectable glucocorticoid.
See: Aristospan, Prep. (Lederle)
TRIAM-FORTE. (Hyrex) Triamcinolone diacetate 40 mg./ml. Vial 5 ml.
Use: Adrenocortical steroid therapy.
TRIAMINIC. (Dorsey) Pyrilamine maleate 25 mg., pheniramine maleate 25 mg., phenylpropanolamine HCl 50 mg./Timed-release Tab. Bot. 100s, 250s.
Use: Antihistaminic.
W/Dormethan, terpin hydrate.
See: Tussaminic, Tab. (Dorsey)
TRIAMINIC ALLERGY TABLETS. (Dorsey) Phenylpropanolamine HCl 25 mg., chlorpheniramine maleate 4 mg./Tab. Blister pk. 12×24s.
Use: Decongestant, antihistamine.
TRIAMINIC CHEWABLES. (Dorsey) Phenylpropanolamine HCl 6.25 mg., chlorpheniramine maleate 0.5 mg./Tab. Blister pkg. 24s.
Use: Chewable decongestant for children.
TRIAMINIC COLD SYRUP. (Dorsey) Phenylpropanolamine HCl 12.5 mg., chlorpheniramine maleate 2 mg./5 ml. Bot. 4 oz., 8 oz.
Use: Decongestant in colds and allergies.
TRIAMINIC COLD TABLETS. (Dorsey) Phenylpropanolamine HCl 12.5 mg., chlorpheniramine maleate 2 mg./Tab. Blister pkg. Bot. 24s, 48s.
Use: Temporary relief of cold, flu, hay fever, sinusitis symptoms.
TRIAMINIC-DM COUGH FORMULA. (Dorsey) Phenylpropamolamine HCl 12.5 mg., dextromethorphan HBr 10 mg./5 ml. Bot. 4 oz., 8 oz.
Use: Antitussive, decongestant.
TRIAMINIC EXPECTORANT. (Dorsey) Phenylpropanolamine HCl 12.5 mg., guaifenesin 100 mg./5 ml. w/alcohol 5%.. Bot. 4 oz., 8 oz.
Use: Decongestant-expectorant.

TRIAMINIC EXPECTORANT W/CODEINE. (Dorsey) Phenylpropanolamine HCl 12.5 mg., codeine phosphate 10 mg., guaifenesin 100 mg./5 ml. w/alcohol 5%. Bot. 4 oz., pt.

TRIAMINIC EXPECTORANT DH. (Dorsey) Guaifenesin 100 mg., phenylpropanolamine HCl 12.5 mg., pheniramine maleate 6.25 mg., pyrilamine maleate 6.25 mg., hydrocodone bitartrate 1.67 mg./5 ml. w/alcohol 5%. Bot. 1 pt.
Use: Treatment of cough.

TRIAMINIC JUVELETS. (Dorsey) Phenylpropanolamine HCl 25 mg., pyrilamine maleate 12.5 mg., pheniramine maleate 12.5 mg./Tab. Bot. 50s.
Use: Decongestant in common cold.

TRIAMINIC ORAL INFANT DROPS. (Dorsey) Phenylpropanolamine HCl 20 mg., pheniramine maleate 10 mg., pyrilamine maleate 10 mg./ml. Dropper bot. 15 ml.
Use: Decongestant and antihistaminic action.

TRIAMINIC-12 TABLETS. (Dorsey) Phenylpropanolamine HCl 75 mg., chlorpheniramine maleate 12 mg./S.R. tab. Pkg. 10s, 20s.
Use: Decongestant, antihistaminic.

TRIAMINIC TR TABLETS. (Dorsey) Phenylpropanolamine HCl 50 mg., pheniramine maleate 25 mg., pyrilamine maleate 25 mg./T.R. Tab.
Use: Decongestant, antihistaminic.

TRIAMINICIN TABLETS. (Dorsey) Phenylpropanolamine HCl 25 mg., aspirin 450 mg., caffeine 30 mg., chlorpheniramine maleate 2 mg./Tab. Pkg. 12s, 24s, 48s, 100s. Industrial pkg. 200 × 1s.
Use: Treatment of the common cold.

TRIAMINICOL MULTI SYMPTOM COLD SYRUP. (Dorsey) Phenylpropanolamine HCl 12.5 mg., pyrilamine maleate 6.25 mg., chloropheniramine maleate 2 mg., dextromethorphan HBr 10 mg./5 ml. (cough syr.) Bot. 4 oz., 8 oz.
Use: Cough depressant & decongestant.

TRIAMINICOL MULTI-SYMPTOM COLD TABLET. (Dorsey) Phenylpropanolamine HCl 12.5 mg., chlorpheniramine maleate 2 mg., dextromethorphan HBr 10 mg./Tab. Blister pkg. 24s, 48s.
Use: Temporary relief of nasal congesion, cold, flu, bronchial irritation.

TRIAMINILONE-16,17-ACETONIDE.
See: Triamcinolone acetonide.

2,4,7-TRIAMINO-6-PHENYLPTERIDINE. Triamterene, U.S.P. XXI.

TRIAMOLONE 40. (Forest) Triamcinolone diacetate 40 mg./ml. Vial 5 ml.

TRIAMONIDE 40. (Forest) Triamcinolone acetonide 40 mg./ml. Vial 5 ml.

• **TRIAMPYZINE SULFATE.** USAN. 2-(Dimethylamino)-3,5,6-trimethylpyrazine sulfate.
Use: Anticholinergic.

• **TRIAMTERENE,** U.S.P. XXI. Caps., U.S.P. XXI. (SmithKline) 2,4,7-Triamino-6-phenyl-pteridine. 2,4,7-Pteridinetriamine,6-phenyl-Dytac.
Use: Diuretic.
See: Dyrenium, Cap. (SmithKline)
W/Hydrochlorothiazide.
Use: Diuretic.
See: Dyazide, Cap. (SmithKline)

TRIANIDE. (Seatrace) Triamcinolone acetonide 40 mg./ml. Vial 5 cc.

TRIAPRIN. (Dunhall) Acetaminophen 250 mg., salicylamide 250 mg., pentobarbital 25 mg./Caps. Bot. 100s, 500s.
Use: Analgesic, sedative.

TRIAPRIN-DC. (Dunhall) Acetaminophen 250 mg salicylamide 250 mg., dihydrocodeine bitartrate 20 mg./Cap. Bot. 100s, 500s.
Use: Analgesic, antitussive.

TRIASYN B. (Panray) Vit. B-1 2 mg., niacinamide 2 mg., B-2 3 mg./Tab. Bot. 1000s.
Use: Nutritional supplement.

TRIATROPHENE. (Lannett) Magnesium trisilicate 7.5 gr., phenobarbital 1/8 gr., atropine sulfate 1/1000 gr./Tab. Bot. 1000s.
Use: G.I. sedative.

TRIAVIL. (Merck Sharp & Dohme) Perphenazine 4 mg., amitriptyline HCl 10 mg./salmon-colored Tab perphenazine 2 mg., amitriptyline HCl 25 mg./orange Tab.; perphenazine 4 mg., amitriptyline 25 mg./yellow Tab.; perphenazine 2 mg., amitriptyline HCl 10 mg./blue Tab. Bot. 100s, 500 Unit-dose 100s. Perphenazine 4 mg., amitryptyline 5 mg./orange Tab. Bot. 60s, 100s. Unit-dose 100s.
Use: Tranquilizer, antidepressant.

TRIAZIQUONE. B.A.N. Tri(aziridin-1-yl)-1,4-benzoquinone. Trenimon
Use: Antineoplastic agent.

• **TRIAZOLAM.** USAN.
Use: Sedative, hypnotic.
See: Halcion, Tab. (Upjohn).

TRI-BAY-FLOR DROPS. (Bay) Vit. A 1500 I.U., D 4 I.U., C 35 mg., fluoride 0.5 mg./1 ml. Bot. 50 ml.
Use: Multivitamin with fluoride.

TRIBARB. (Lannett) Cap. Bot. 100s, 1000s.

• **TRIBENOSIDE.** USAN. Ethyl 3,5,6-tri-O-benzyl-D-glucofuranoside. Glyvenol Not available in U.S.
Use: Venoprotective agent.

TRI-BIOCIN. (Approved) Bacitracin 400 u., polymyxin sulfate 5000 u., neomycin 5 mg./Gm. Tube 0.5 oz
Use: Topical antibiotic.

TRI-BIOTIC OINTMENT. (Standex) Polymyxin B sulfa 5,000 u., bacitracin 400 u., neomycin sulfate 5 mg./Gm. Tube 0.5 oz.

TRIBROMOETHANOL. 2,2,2-Tribromoethanol.
Use: Anesthetic (inhalation).

TRIBROMOMETHANE. Bromoform.

• **TRIBROMSALAN.** USAN. 3,4′,5-Tribromosalicylanilide. Hilomid.
Use: Germicide.
See: Diaphene (or ASC-4) (Stecker)
Tuasol 100 (Merrell Dow)

TRI-CALSATE. (Paxton) Tri-cal. phosphate 35.5%, t sod. phosphate 12.5%, sod. citrate 52%. Aq. susp Bot. 4.5 oz., 18 oz.
Use: Antacid.

TRICETAMIDE. USAN. 3,4,5-Trimethoxybenzoylglycine diethylamide.
Use: Sedative.

RI-CHLOR. (Gordon) Trichloracetic acid 80%. Bot. 15 cc.
Use: Topical, as a caustic verruca cauterant.

RICHLORAN.
See: Trichloroethylene

TRICHLORMETHIAZIDE, U.S.P. XXI. Tab., U.S.P. XXI. 3-Dichloromethyl-6-chloro-7-sulfamyl-3,4-dihydro-1,2,4-benzothiadiazine-1,1-dioxide. 6-Chloro-3-(dichloromethyl)-3,4-dihydro-2H-1,2,4-benzothiadiazine-7-sulfonamide-1,1-Dioxide.
Use: Diuretic; antihypertensive.
See: Aquex, Tab. (Lannett)
Metahydrin, Tab. (Merrell Dow)
Naqua, Tab. (Schering)
Rochlomethiazide, Tab. (Robinson)

/Reserpine.
See: Metatensin, Tab. (Merrell Dow)
Naquival, Tab. (Schering)

RICHLORMETHINE (I.N.N.).
See: Trimustine, B.A.N.

TRICHLOROACETIC ACID, U.S.P. XXI. Acetic acid, trichloro.
Use: Topical, as a caustic.

RICHLOROBUTYL ALCOHOL.
See: Chlorobutanol

RICHLOROCARBANILIDE. W/Salicylic acid, sulfur.

1,1-TRICHLORO-2-METHYL-2-PROPANOL. Chlorobutanol, N.F. XVI.
Use: Analgesic (inhalation).

TRICHLOROMONOFLUOROMETHANE, N.F. XVI.
Use: Aerosol propellant.

RICHLORPHON. Metriphonate, B.A.N.

RICHOLINE CITRATE.
See: Choline citrate

RICHOMYCIN. Hachimycin, B.A.N.

RICHORAD. Acinitrazole, B.A.N.

RICHOTINE. (Reed & Carnrick) **Powd.** Sodium lauryl sulf., sod. perborate, chloride, aromatics. Pkg. 5, 12, 20 oz. **Liq.** Sodium lauryl sulfate, sodium borate, ethyl alcohol 8%, aromatics. Bot. 4 oz., 8 oz.
Use: Vaginal douche.

TRICIRIBINE PHOSPHATE. USAN.
Use: Antineoplastic.

TRICITRATES ORAL SOLUTION, U.S.P. XXI.

RICLOBISONIUM. Triburon, Oint. (Roche)

RICLOBISONIUM CHLORIDE.
Hexamethylenebis[dimethyl[1-methyl-3-(2,2,6-trimethylcyclohexyl)propyl]-ammonium] Dichloride.
Use: Topical anti-infective.

TRICLOCARBAN. USAN. 3,4,4′-Trichlorocarbanilide.
Use: Germicide.
See: Artra Beauty Ban (Plough)

/Clofulcarban.
See: Safeguard Bar Soap, (P & G)

TRICLOFENOL PIPERAZINE. USAN. Piperazine (1:2) with (2,4,5-trichlorophenol).
Use: Anthelmintic (nematodes).

TRICLOFOS. B.A.N. 2,2,2-Trichloroethyl dihydrogen phosphate. Tricloryl (mono-sodium salt)
Use: Hypnotic.

• **TRICLOFOS SODIUM.** USAN.
Use: Hypnotic; sedative.
See: Triclos, Tab., Liq. (Merrell Dow)

• **TRICLONIDE.** USAN.
Use: Anti-inflammatory.

TRICLORYL MONO-SODIUM SALT. Triclofos, B.A.N.

• **TRICLOSAN.** USAN. 5-Chloro-2-(2,4-dichlorophenoxy)phenol.
Use: Antibacterial
See: Clearasil Soap (Vicks)

TRI-CONE. (Glaxo) Amylase 10 mg., Prolase 10 mg., lipase 10 mg., simethicone 40 mg./Cap. Bot. 60s, 500s.
Use: Aid digestion, relieve gaseousness.

TRI-CONE PLUS. (Glaxo) Amylase 10 mg., prolase 10 mg., lipase 10 mg., simethicone 40 mg., hyoscyamine sulfate 0.025 mg./Tab. Bot. 60s, 500s.
Use: Digestion aid, antiflatulant.

TRICONOL VAGINAL CREAM. (Coastal) Sulfanilamide 15%, 9-aminoacridine HCl 0.2%, allantoin 2.0%. Tab. Bot. 100s.
Use: Vaginal infections.

TRICYCLAMOL CHLORIDE, B.A.N. 1-(3-Cyclohexyl-3-hydroxy-3-phenylpropyl)-1-methylpyrroidinium chloride. Elorine Chloride; Lergine.
Use: Anticholinergic.

TRICYLATATE HCl. 1-Methyl-3-pyrrolidylmethyl benzilate HCl.

TRIDESILON CREAM. (Miles Pharm) Desonide 0.05% in vehicle buffered to the pH range of normal skin w/glycerin, methyl paraben, sodium lauryl sulfate, aluminum acetate, cetyl stearyl alcohol, synthetic bees-wax, white petrolatum, mineral oil. Tube 15 Gm., 60 Gm. Plastic Jar 5 Gm., lb.
Use: Corticosteroid therapy.

TRIDESILON OTIC. (Miles Pharm) Desonide 0.05%, acetic acid 2% in vehicle. Bot. 10 ml.
Use: Otitis externa treatment.

TRIDEX TAB., TIMED TRIDEX CAP., TIMED TRIDEX JR. CAP. (Fellows) Changed to Daro Tab., Daro Timed Cap., Daro Jr. Timed Cap.

TRI-DIAZOLE LIQUID. (Coastal) Sulfamethazine 2.5 gr., sulfadiazine 2.5 gr., sulfamerazine 2.5 gr., sod. citrate 0.75 gr./Tsp. Bot. 16 oz.

• **TRIDIHEXETHYL CHLORIDE,** U.S.P. XXI. Inj., Tab., U.S.P. XXI. (3-Cyclohexyl-3-hydroxy-3-phenylpropyl)-tri-ethylammonium chloride.
Use: Anticholinergic.

W/Meprobamate.
See: Milpath, Tab. (Wallace)
Pathibamate, Tab. (Lederle)

W/Phenobarbital.
See: Pathilon w/Phenobarbital Tab., Cap. (Lederle)

TRIDIL 0.5 mg./ml. (American Critical Care) Nitroglycerin 0.5 mg./ml. w/alcohol 10%, water for injection, buffered with sodium phosphate. Amp. 10 ml. Box 20s.
Use: Vasodilator; anti-anginal, hypotensive.

TRIDIL 5 mg./ml. (American Critical Care) Nitroglycerin 5 mg./ml. w/alcohol 30%, propylene glycol 30%, water for injection. Amp. 5 ml., 10 ml. Vial 5 ml., 10 ml. Box 20s. Special administration set w/10 ml.Amp.
Use: Vasodilator; anti-anginal, hypotensive.

TRIDIONE. (Abbott) Trimethadione. (Troxidone). Cap. 300 mg., Bot. 100s. Dulcet Tab. 150 mg., Bot. 100s. Sol. 1.2 Gm./fl. oz., Bot. 1 pt.
Use: Epilepsy.

• **TRIENTINE HYDROCHLORIDE.** USAN.
Use: Wilson's disease therapy adjunct.

TRIENZYME. (Fellows) Amylolytic 30 mg., proteolytic 10 mg., celluloytic 3 mg./Tab. Bot. 1000s.
Use: Relief of functional digestive disorders.

TRI-ERGONE. (Quality Generics) **0.5 mg. Tab.:** Hydrogenated ergot alkaloids as dihydroergocornine 0.167 mg., dihydroergokryptine 0.167 mg., dihydroergocristine 0.167 mg./Sublingual tab. Bot: 100s, 1000s. **1.0 mg. Tab.:** Hydrogenated ergot alkaloids as dihydroergocornine 0.334 mg., dihydroergokryptine 0.334 mg., dihydroergocristine 0.334 mg./Sublingual Tab. Bot. 100s, 1000s.
Use: Selected symptoms in elderly patients.

TRI-ESTROGEN. (Rocky Mtn.) Potassium estrone sulfate 1 mg., estrone 2 mg., estradiol 0.2 mg./10 cc. Vial 10 cc.

TRIETHANOLAMINE,
See: Trolamine, N.F. XVI.

TRIETHANOLAMINE POLYPEPTIDE OLEATE CONDENSATE.
See: Cerumenex, Drops (Purdue Frederick)

TRIETHANOLAMINE SALICYLATE.
See: Aspercreme, Cream (Sperti)
Aspergel, Oint. (LaCrosse)
Myoflex, Cream (Warren-Teed)

TRIETHANOLAMINE TRINITRATE BIPHOSPHATE.
Trolnitrate Phosphate.

• **TRIETHYL CITRATE,** N.F. XVI.

TRIETHYLENEMELAMINE. Tretamine TEM. 2,4,6-Tris(1-aziridinyl)-5-triazine.
Use: Antineoplastic.

• **TRIFENAGREL.** USAN.
Use: Antithrombotic.

• **TRIFLOCIN.** USAN. 4-(α,α,α-Trifluoro-m-toluidino) nicotinic acid.
Use: Diuretic.

• **TRIFLUBAZAM.** USAN.
Use: Tranquilizer.

• **TRIFLUMIDATE.** USAN. Ethyl m-benzoyl-N-[(trifluoromethyl)sulfonyl]carbanilate.
Use: Anti-inflammatory.

• **TRIFLUPERIDOL.** USAN.
Use: Antipsychotic.

TRIFLUOMEPRAZINE. B.A.N. NN-Dimethyl-2-(2-trifluoromethylphenothiazin-10ylmethyl) propylamine. Nortran.
Use: Tranquilizer, veterinary medicine.

TRIFLUOPERAZINE. B.A.N. 10-[3-(4-Methyl-piperazin-1-yl)propyl]-2-trifluoromethylphenothiazine.
Use: Tranquilizer; antiemetic.

• **TRIFLUOPERAZINE HCl,** U.S.P. XXI. Inj., Syrup, Tab., U.S.P. XXI. 10-[3-(1-Methyl-4-piperazinyl)-propyl]-2-trifluoromethyl phenothiazine HCl. 10-(3-(4-Methyl-1-piperazinyl)propyl)-2-(trifluoromethyl)phenothiazine dihydrochloride.
Use: Tranquilizer.
See: Stelazine Inj., Liq., Tab. (SmithKline)

2,2,2-TRIFLUOROETHYL ETHER.
See: Indoklon

4-[3-[2-(TRIFLUOROMETHYL)PHENOTHIAZIN-10-YL]PROPYL]-1-PIPERAZINEETHANOL. Fluphenazine Enanthate, U.S.P. XXI.

• **TRIFLUPROMAZINE,** U.S.P. XXI. Oral Susp., XXI.
Use: Tranquilizer, antipsychotic agent.

• **TRIFLUPROMAZINE HCl,** U.S.P. XXI. Inj., Tab., U.S.P. XXI. 10-[3-Di-methylamino)propyl]-2-(trifluoromethyl)phenothiazine HCl. Fluopromazine, B.A.N.
Use: Tranquilizer, antipsychotic agent.
See: Vesprin, Prep. (Squibb)

• **TRIFLURIDINE.** USAN.
Use: Antiviral used to treat herpes simplex eye infections.
See: Viroptic (Burroughs Wellcome)
See: Viroptic Ophthalmic Soln., (Burroughs Wellcome)

TRIGELAMINE. (Edward J. Moore) Pyrilamine maleate, pheniramine maleate, chloropheniramine maleate, benzalkonium Cl, menthol. Tube. 1.25 oz.
Use: Triple antihistamine gel.

TRIGESIC. (Squibb) Acetyl-p-aminophenol 2 gr., aspirin 3.5 gr., caffeine 0.5 gr./Tab. Bot. 100s.
Use: Analgesic.

TRIGLYCERIDE REAGENT STRIP. (Ames) Seralyzer reagent strip Bot. 25s.
Use: A quantitative test for triglycerides in serum or plasma.

TRI-GRAIN. (Pharmex) Isometheptene tartrate. **Inj.** 100 mg./cc. Vial 10 cc. **Tab.** Bot. 24s, 100s.

TRIHEMIC-600. (Lederle) Vit. C 600 mg., B-12 25 mcg intrinsic factor conc. 75 mg., folic acid 1 mg., Vit. E 30 I.U., ferrous fumarate 115 mg., dioctyl sod. succinate 50 mg./Tab. Bot. 30s, 500s.
Use: Anemias.

• **TRIHEXYPHENIDYL HYDROCHLORIDE,** U.S.P. XXI. Elix., Tab. U.S.P. XXI. α-Cyclohexyl-α-phenyl-1-piperidinepropanol HCl. 1-Piperidine-propanol, α-cyclohexyl-α-phenyl-, HCl. Benzhexol, B.A.N.
Use: Anticholinergic, antiparkinsonian.
See: Artane, Elixir & Tab. (Lederle)
Hexyphen-2, Tab. (Robinson)
Hexyphen-5, Tab. (Robinson)

TRIHISTAPACQ TABULES. (Horton & Converse) Prophenpyridamine maleate 6 mg., pyrilamine maleate 8 mg., phenylpropanolamine HCl 15 mg., salicylamide 3 gr., phenacetin 2 gr., caffeine citrate 0.5 gr., ascorbic acid 100 mg., hesperidin 100 mg./Tab. Bot. 18s.
Use: Relief of headache, muscular aches and fever due to common colds.

TRI-HISTIN. (Recsei) **25 mg. Tab.:** Pyrilamine maleate 10 mg., chlorpheniramine maleate 1 mg. **50 mg. Tab.:** Pyrilamine maleate 20 mg., methapyrilene HCl 15 mg., chlorpheniramine maleate 2 mg. **100 mg. S.A. Cap.:** Pyrilamine maleate 40 mg., pheniramine maleate 25 mg. **Expectorant:** Pyrilamine maleate 5 mg., chlorpheniramine maleate 0.5 mg., guaifenesin 20 mg., phenylpropanolamine 7.5 mg., phenylephrine HCl 2.5 mg., sod. citrate 100 mg./5 cc. Bot. pt. gal. **Liquid:** Pyrilamine maleate 5 mg., chlorpheniramine maleate 0.5 mg./5 cc. Bot. pt. gal. **Tab.** Bot. 100s, 500s, 1000s. 50 mg. Bot. 1000s.**Cap.** Bot. 100s, 500s, 1000s.
Use: Triple antihistamine therapy.

W/Benzyl alcohol, chlorobutanol & isopropyl alcohol.
See: Derma-Pax, Liq. (Recsei)

W/Codeine phosphate, guaifenesin, phenylpropanolamine, phenylephrine HCl, sodium citrate.
See: Trihista-Cod., Liq. (Recsei)

W/Ephedrine HCl, aminophylline, mephobarbital.
See: Asmasan, Tab. (Recsei)

TRIHYDROGEN ORAL TABS. (Goldline) Ergoloid mesylate 1.0 mg./Tab. Bot. 100s, 500s, 1000s.
Use: Selected symptoms in the elderly.

TRIHYDROGEN S.L. TABS. (Goldline) Ergoloid mesylate 0.5 mg. or 1.0 mg./Tab. Bot. 100s, 1000s.
Use: Selected symptoms in the elderly.

TRIHYDROXYESTRINE. Trihydroxyestrin.

TRIHYDROXYETHYLAMINE. Triethanolamine.

11β,17,21-TRIHYDROXY-6-α-METHYLPREGNA-1,4-DIENE-3,20-DIONE 21-ACETATE. Methylprednisolone Acetate, U.S.P. XXI.

11β,17,21-TRIHYDROXYPREGNA-1,4-DIENE-3,20-DIONE (ANHYDROUS). Prednisolone, U.S.P. XXI.

TRI-IMMUNOL. (Lederle) Diphtheria & tetanus toxoids & pertussis vaccine combined, aluminum phosphate-adsorbed purogenated. Vial 7.5 ml.
Use: I.M., Immunization.

TRIIODOMETHANE.
See: Iodoform. (Various Mfr.)

L-TRIIODOTHYRONINE SOD.
See: Cytomel, Tab. (SmithKline)
Liothyronine Sod.

dl-TRIIODOTHYRONINE SODIUM.

3,7,12-TRIKETOCHOLANIC ACID.
See: Dehydrocholic Acid (Various Mfr.)

TRI-K. (Century) Potassium acetate 0.5 Gm., potassium bicarbonate 0.5 Gm., potassium citrate 0.5 Gm./fl. oz. Bot. pt., gal.

• **TRIKATES ORAL SOLUTION,** U.S.P. XXI.
Use: Potassium deficiency.

TRIKATES ORAL SOLUTION. (Lilly) Potassium 15 mEq. from pot. acetate, pot. bicarbonate and pot. citrate/5 ml. Bot. 16 fl. oz., gal.
Use: Potassium deficiency.

TRI-KORT. (Keene) Triamcinalone acetonide suspension 40 mg./ml. Vial 5 ml.
Use: Anti-inflammatory.

TRILAFON. (Schering) Perphenazine. **Tab.** 2, 4, 8 mg., & 16 mg. Bot. 100s, 500s. **Inj:** 5 mg./ml., w/disodium citrate 24.6 mg., sod. bisulfite 2 mg., and water for injection/ml. Amp. 1 ml. Box 100s. **Repetabs** 8 mg., Bot. 100s. **Concentrate** 16 mg./5 ml. Bot. 4 oz. w/dropper.
Use: Tranquilizer.

TRILAX. (Drug Industries) Docusate sodium 200 mg., yellow phenolphthalein 30 mg., dehydrocholic acid 20 mg./Cap. Bot. 100s, 500s.
Use: Laxative, fecal softener, choleretic.

TRILISATE LIQUID. (Purdue Frederick) Choline magnesium trisalicylate from choline salicylate 293 mg., magnesium salicylate 362 mg./ tsp. to provide 500 mg. salicylate/tsp. Bot. 8 oz.
Use: Non-steroidal anti-inflammatory, anti-arthritic.

TRILISATE TABLETS. (Purdue Frederick) Choline magnesium trisalicylate **500 mg./Tab.** of salicylate from choline salicylate 293 mg., magnesium salicylate 362 mg./Tab. Bot. 100s. **750 mg./Tab.** of salicylate from choline salicylate 400 mg. and magnesium salicylate 544 mg. Bot. 100s. 1000 mg./Tab. of salicylate from choline salicylate 587 mg., magnesium salicylate 725 mg. Bot. 60s.
Use: Non-steroidal anti-inflammatory, anti-arthritic.

TRILLEKAMIN HYDROCHLORIDE. Trimustine, B.A.N.

TRILOG. (Hauck) Triamcinolone acetonide 40 mg./ml. Vial 5 ml.
Use: Steroid therapy.

TRILONE. (Century) Triamcinalone diacetate susp. Amp. 10cc.
Use: Corticosteroid.

TRILONE. (Hauck) Triamcinolone diacetate 40 mg./ml. Vial 5 ml.
Use: Steroid therapy.

• **TRILOSTANE.** USAN.
Use: Adrenocortical suppressant.

TRILOX. (Blue Line) **Susp.,** Mag. trisilicate 75 gr., aluminum hydroxide gel 90 gr., alcohol 1%/fl. oz. Bot. 14 oz. **Tab.,** Mag. trisilicate 7.5 gr., aluminum hydroxide gel, dried 5 gr./Tab. Bot. 100s, 500s, 1000s.
Use: Gastric antacid.

TRIMAGEL TABLETS. (Quality Generics) Magnesium trisilicate 0.5 Gm., dried aluminum hydroxide gel 0.25 Gm./Tab. Bot. 100s, 500s.
Use: Gastric hyperacidity.

TRIMAHIST ELIXIR. (Tennessee Pharm.) Phenylephrine HCl 5 mg., prophenpyridamine maleate 12.5 mg., l-menthol 1 mg., alcohol 5%/5 cc. Bot. pt., gal.
Use: Antihistaminic elixir.

TRIM-AID CAPSULES. (Wolins) Sodium carboxymethylcellulose 134 mg., benzocaine 5 mg., Vit. A 1,500 I.U., D 200 I.U., B-1 1 mg., B-2 1.2 mg., niacinamide 5 mg., C 30 mg., calcium 45 mg., phosphorus 23 mg./Cap. Bot. 18s, 60s, 1000s.

TRIMAX GEL. (Winthrop Products) Aluminum, magnesium hydroxide, simethicone.
Use: Antacid, antiflatulent.

TRIMAX TABLET. (Winthrop Products) Aluminum, magnesium hydroxide, simethicone.
Use: Antacid, antiflatulent.

TRIMAZIDE CAPS. (Major) Trimethobenazamide 250 mg./Cap. Bot. 100s.
Use: Treatment of nausea and vomiting.

TRIMAZINOL. α-{[(4,6-Diaminos-triazin-2-yl)-aminol]-methyl} benzyl alcohol.
Use: Anti-inflammatory agent.

• **TRIMAZOSIN HYDROCHLORIDE.** USAN.
Use: Antihypertensive.

TRIMCAPS. (Mayrand) Phendimetrazine tartrate 105 mg./Slow-rel. Cap. Bot. 30s, 100s.
Use: Anorectic.

TRIMELARSAN. Melarsonyl Potassium, B.A.N.

TRIMEPERIDINE. B.A.N. 1,2,5-Trimethyl-4-phenyl-4-piperidyl propionate.
Use: Narcotic analgesic.

TRIMEPRAZINE. B.A.N. 10-(3-Dimethylamino-2-methylpropyl)phenothiazine. Alimemazine (I.N.N.) Vallergan.
Use: Tranquilizer; antihistamine.

TRIMEPRAZINE TARTRATE, U.S.P. XXI. Syrup, Tab., U.S.P. XXI. (±)-10-(3-Dimethylamino-2-methylpropyl)-phenothiazine tartrate (2:1) 10H-Phenothiazine-10-propanamine N,N,β-trimethyl-2,3-dihydroxybutanedioate (2:1).
Use: Anti-pruritic.
See: Temaril, Prep. (SmithKline)

TRIMETAMIDE. Trimethamide.

TRIMETAPHAN CAMSYLATE. B.A.N. 1,3-Dibenzyl-decahydro-2-oxoimidazo[4,5-c]thieno[1,2-a]-thiolium(+)-camphor-10-sulfonate.
Use: Hypotensive.
See: Arfonad.

TRIMETAZIDINE. B.A.N. 1-(2,3,4-Trimethoxybenzyl)-piperazine.
Use: Vasodilator.
See: Vastarel dihydrochloride.

• **TRIMETHADIONE,** U.S.P. XXI. Cap., Oral Soln., Tab., U.S.P. XXI. 3,5,5-Trimethyl-2,4-oxazolidinedione.
Use: Anticonvulsant.
See: Tridione, Prep. (Abbott)

TRIMETHADIONE (I.N.N.). Troxidone, B.A.N.

TRIMETHAMIDE. N-[(2-Amino-6-methyl-3-pyridyl)methyl]3,4,5-trimethoxybenzamide.
Use: Antihypertensive agent.

TRIMETHAPHAN CAMPHORSULFONATE. Trimethaphan Camsylate, U.S.P. XXI.

• **TRIMETHAPHAN CAMSYLATE,** U.S.P. XXI. Inj., U.S.P. XXI. d-3,4-(1′,3′-Dibenzyl-2′-ketoimidazolido)-1,2-trimethylenethiophanium d-camphorsulfonate. Trimethaphan camphorsulfonate. (+)-1,3-Dibenzyl-decahydro-2-oxoimidazo[4,5-c]thieno-[1,2-α]-thiolium 2-oxo-10-bornanesulfonate.
Use: Antihypertensive.
See: Arfonad, Amp. (Roche)

TRIMETHIDINIUM METHOSULFATE, B.A.N. d-(N-methyl-N-(gamma-trimethyl-ammonium-propyl))-1-methyl-8,8-di-methyl-3-azabicyclo-(3,2,1) octane dimethosulfate. 1,3,8,8-Tetramethyl-3-(3-(trimethylammonio)propyl)-3-azoniabicyclo(3.2.1)octane. Tab.
Use: Antihypertensive.

• **TRIMETHOBENZAMIDE HCl,** U.S.P. XXI. Cap., Inj., U.S.P. XXI. N- {p-[2-(Dimethylamino) ethoxy]-benzyl} -3,4,5-trimethoxybenzamide HCl.
Use: Antiemetic.
See: Tegamide, Suppos. (G & W)
Tigan, Preps. (Beecham Labs.)

TRIMETHOBENZAMIDE HYDROCHLORIDE AND BENZOCAINE SUPPOSITORIES.
Use: Antiemetic.

• **TRIMETHOPRIM,** U.S.P. XXI. Tab., U.S.P. XXI. 2,4-Diamino-5-(3,4,5-trimethoxybenzyl)pyrimidine. Syraprim.
Use: Antibacterial agent.
See: Proloprim, Tab. (Burroughs Wellcome)
Trimpex, Tab. (Roche)
W/Sulfamethoxazole.
See: Bactrim, Oral Susp. Ped. Susp., Tab. (Roche)
Septra, Tab. (Burroughs Wellcome)
Septra DS, Tab. (Burroughs Wellcome)

• **TRIMETHOPRIM SULFATE.** USAN.
Use: Antibacterial.

2,5,9-TRIMETHYL-7H-FURO[3,2-g][1]BENZOPYRAN-7-ONE. Trioxsalen, U.S.P. XXI.

3,5,5-TRIMETHYL-2,4-OXAZOLIDINEDIONE. Trimethadione, U.S.P. XXI.

2,4,6-TRIMETHYL-s-TRIOXANE. Paraldehyde, U.S.P. XXI.

1,3,7-TRIMETHYLXANTHINE. Caffeine.

TRIMETHYLENE. Cyclopropane, U.S.P. XXI.

TRIMETON. Pheniramine, B.A.N.

• **TRIMETOZINE.** USAN.
Use: Sedative.

• **TRIMETREXATE.** USAN.
Use: Antineoplastic.

TRIMETTE. (Wesley) Phenobarbital 0.25 gr., atropine sulf. 2/300 gr., dextroamphetamine sulf., 15 mg., aloin 0.25 gr./Cap. or Tab. Bot. 1000s.

TRIMEX. (Mills) Dextroamphetamine sulf. 15 mg., amobarbital 60 mg., thyroid 3 gr./Cap. Bot. 50s.
No. 2: dextroamphetamine sulf. 10 mg., amobarbital 60 mg., thyroid 2 gr./Cap. Bot. 50s.

• **TRIMIPRAMINE.** USAN. 5-[3-(Dimethylamino)-2-methylpropyl]-10,11-dihydro-5H-dibenz[b,f]-aze-pine.
Use: Antidepressant.
See: Surmontil (Ives)

• **TRIMIPRAMINE MALEATE.** USAN. 5-[3-(Di-methylamino)-2-methylpropyl]-10,11-dihydro-5H-dibenz [b,f]azepine maleate (1:1).
Use: Antidepressant.
See: Surmontil Maleate (Ives)

TRIMIXIN. (Hance) Bacitracin 200 u., polymyxin B sulfate 4000 u., neomycin sulfate 3 mg./Gm. Oint., Tube 0.5 oz.
Use: Topically, antibiotic therapy.

• **TRIMOPROSTIL.** USAN.
Use: Gastric antisecretory.

TRIMO-SAN. (Milex) Oxyquinoline sulfate, sodium lauryl sulfate 0.0084%, boric acid 1.0%, borax 0.70%. Tube 4 oz. w/boilable nylon jel Jector; 4 oz. refill tube.
Use: Restore and maintain vaginal acidity.

RIMOX. (Squibb) **Cap.:** Amoxicillin trihydrate 250 mg./Cap. Bot. 100s, 500s. Unit Dose 100s; 500 mg./Cap. Bot. 50s, 500s. Unit Dose 100s. **Oral Susp.:** 125 mg./5 ml. Bot. 80 ml., 100 ml., 150 ml. Unimatic Bot. 5 ml., Ctn. 4 × 25s. 250 mg./5 ml. Bot. 80 ml., 100 ml., 150 ml. Unimatic Bot. 5 ml., Ctn. 4 × 25s.
Use: Antibiotic.

TRIMOXAMINE HYDROCHLORIDE. USAN. α-Allyl-3,4,5-trimethoxy-N-methylphenethylamine HCl.
Use: Antihypertensive.

RIMPEX. (Roche) Trimethoprim 100 mg./Tab. Bot. 100s; Tel-E-Dose 100s; Prescription paks 20s.
Use: Treatment of initial episodes of uncomplicated urinary tract infections.

TRIMOPROSTIL. USAN.

RIMSTAT. (Laser) Phendimetrazine tartrate 35 mg./Tab. Bot. 100s, 1000s.
Use: Anorexiant.

RIMTABS. (Mayrand) Phendimetrazine tartrate 35 mg./Tab. Bot. 100s, 500s.
Use: Management of obesity.

RIMUSTINE. B.A.N. Tri-(2-chloroethyl)amine. Trichlomethine (I.N.N.) Trillekamin hydrochloride.
Use: Antineoplastic agent.

RIMYCIN OINTMENT. (Blue Cross) Polymyxin B sulfate 5000 units, bacitracin 400 units, neomycin 5 mg., diperodon HCl 10 mg./Gm. Tube 0.5 oz.
Use: Antibiotic.

RINALIN REPETABS. (Schering) Azatadine maleate 1 mg., pseudoephedrine sulfate 120 mg./Tab. Bot 100s.
Use: Long-acting antihistamine, decongestant.

RIND. (Mead Johnson) Phenylpropanolamine HCl 12.5 mg., chlorpheniramine maleate 2 mg./5 ml. w/alcohol 5%. Bot. 5 oz.
Use: Relief of cold symptoms.

RIND DM. (Mead Johnson) Phenylpropanolamine HCl 12.5 mg., dextromethorphan HBr 7.5 mg., Chlorpheniramine maleate 2 mg./5 ml. w/alcohol 5%. Bot. 5 oz.
Use: Relief of cough and cold symptoms.

RINIAD. (Kasar) Isoniazid 300 mg./Tab. Bot. 30s, 100s, 1000s.
Use: Treatment of tuberculosis.

RINIAD PLUS 30. (Kasar) Isoniazid 300 mg., pyridoxine HCl 30 mg./Tab. Bot. 30s, 100s, 1000s.

RINITRIN TABLETS.
See: Nitroglycerin Tablets, U.S.P. XXI.

RINITROPHENOL. Picric acid. 2,4,6-Trinitrophenol.
See: Picric Acid (Var. Mfr.)

RINOL HYDROCHLORIDE. Benzhexol, B.A.N.

RI-NORINYL. (Syntex) Norethindrone 1 mg. with ethinyl estradiol 0.035 mg./Tab. Norethindrone 0.5 mg. with ethinyl estradiol 0.035 mg./Tab. 21 + 28 day. (7 inert tabs) Wallette.
Use: Oral contraceptive.

TRINOTIC. (Fellows) Secobarbital 65 mg., amobarbital 40 mg., phenobarbital 25 mg./Tab. Bot. 1000s.
Use: Hypnotic.

TRINSICON CAPSULES. (Glaxo) Folic acid 0.5 mg., ascorbic acid 75 mg., iron 110 mg., special liver stomach concentrate 240 mg., cyanocobalamin 12 mcg./Cap. Bot. 60s, 500s. Unit dose 100s.
Use: Multivitamin with iron.

TRINSICON-M. (Glaxo) Ascorbic acid 75 mg., iron 110 mg., special liver stomach concentrate 240 mg., cyanocobalamin 12 mcg./Cap. Bot. 60s.
Use: Multivitamin with iron.

TRINSITRATE. (Quality Generics) Desic. liver 350 mg., B-12 activity 25 mcg., ferrous sulfate exsic. 800 mg., C 150 mg./2 Caps. Bot. 100s, 1000s.
Use: Hematinic formula.

TRIO-BAR. (Jenkins) Butabarbital sod. 33⅓%, phenobarbital sod. 33⅓%, phenobarbital sod. 33⅓%. Total barbituates 0.25 gr., ¾ gr. or 1.5 gr./Tab. Bot. 1000s.
Use: Sedative.

TRIOBEAD-125. (Abbott) T3 diagnostic kit. Test units 50s, 100s, 500s.
Use: Quantitative measure of thyroid functioning.

TRIOCIL.
See: Hexetidine

• **TRIOLEIN I-125.** USAN.
Use: Radioactive agent.

• **TRIOLEIN I-131.** USAN.
Use: Radioactive agent.

TRI-ORAPIN. (Standex) Estrone 2 mg., estradiol 0.2 mg., potassium estrone 1 mg./10 cc.

TRIOSIL. Sodium Metrizoate, B.A.N.

TRIOSTAM. Sodium Antimonylgluconate, B.A.N.

TRIOSULF. (Jenkins) Sulfadiazine 2.5 Gr., sulfamerazine 2.5 gr., sulfamethazine 2.5 gr./Tab. Bot. 1000s.

TRIOSULFON. (CMC) Sulfacetamide 0.166 Gm., sulfamethazine 0.166 Gm., sulfamerazine 0.166 Gm./Tab. Bot. 30s, 100s, 1000s.
Use: Sulfonamide therapy.

TRIOSULFON DMM. (CMC) Tab. Bot. 100s, 250s, 1000s.

TRIOXANE.
See: Trioxymethylene (Var. Mfr.)

1,3,5-TRIOXANE,2,4,6-TRIMETHYL-. Paraldehyde, U.S.P. XXI.

• **TRIOXIFEN MESYLATE.** USAN.
Use: Anti-estrogen.

• **TRIOXSALEN,** U.S.P. XXI. Tab., U.S.P. XXI. 6-Hydroxy-β,2,7-trimethyl-5-benzofuranacrylic acid,δ-lactone; 4,5,-8-trimethylpsoralen. 2,5,9-Trimethyl-7H-furo-(3,2-g)(1)benzopyran-7-one. 7H-Furo[3,2-g][1]-benzopyran-7-one, 2,5,9-trimethyl-.
Use: Pigmenting and phototherapeutic agent.
See: Trisoralen, Tab. (Elder)

TRIOXYMETHYLENE. Name is incorrectly used to denote paraformaldehyde in some pharmaceuticals.
See: Paraformaldehyde (Various Mfr.)

W/Sod. oleate, triethanolamine, docusate sodium, stearic acid & aluminum silicate.
See: Cooper Creme (Whittaker)

• **TRIPAMIDE.** USAN.
Use: Antihypertensive, diuretic.

TRIPARANOL. B.A.N. 2-(p-Chlorophenyl)-1-[p-[2-(diethylamino)ethoxy]phenyl]-1-p-tolylethanol.
Use: Blood lipid lowering agent.

TRIPELENNAMINE. B.A.N. 2-(N-Benzyl-N-2-pyridyl)ethyldimethylamine.
Use: Antihistamine.
See: Pyribenzamine citrate or hydrochloride. (Geigy)

• **TRIPELENNAMINE CITRATE,** U.S.P. XXI. Elixir U.S.P. XXI. 2-(Benzyl[2-dimethylamino-ethyl]-amino) pyridine dihydrogen citrate. 1,2-Ethanediamine, N,N-dimethyl-N′-(phenylmethyl)-N′-2-pyridinyl-,2-hydroxy-1,2,3-propanetricarboxylate (1:1).
Use: Antihistaminic.

• **TRIPELENNAMINE HYDROCHLORIDE,** U.S.P. XXI. Tab. U.S.P. XXI.
Use: Antihistaminic.
See: Pyribenzamine hydrochloride, Preps. (Geigy)
Ro-Hist, Tab. (Robinson)

TRIPHASIL-21. (Wyeth) Three drug phases in 21 day cycle: **Phase I:** 6 brown tab. Levonorgestrel 0.050 mg., ethinyl estradiol 0.030 mg. Tab. **Phase II:** 5 white tab. Levonorgestrel 0.075 mg., ethinyl estradiol 0.040 mg. Tab. **Phase III:** 10 yellow tab. Levonorgestrel 0.125 mg., ethinyl estradiol 0.30 mg./Tab.
Use: Oral contraceptive.

TRIPHASAL-28. (Wyeth) Three drug phases and one inert phase in 28 day cycle: **Phase I:** 6 brown tab. Levonorgestrel 0.050 mg., ethinyl estradiol 0.030 mg. Tab. **Phase II:** 5 white tab. Levonorgestrel 0.075 mg., ethinyl estradiol 0.040 mg. Tab. **Phase III:** 10 yellow tab. Levonorgestrel 0.125 mg., ethinylestradiol 0.030 mg./Tab. **Phase IV:** 7 inert green tablets.
Use: Oral contraceptive.

TRIPHED. (Lemmon) Triprolidine HCl 2.5 mg., pseudoephedrine HCl 60 mg./Tab. Bot. 100s, 1000s. Unit dose 100s.
Use: Allergic rhinitis, common cold symptoms.

TRI-PHEN ELIXIR. (Bay) Brompheniramine maleate 4 mg., phenylephrine HCl 5 mg., phenylpropanolamine HCl 5 mg./5 ml. w/alcohol 2.3% Bot. 4 oz., pt., gal.
Use: Antihistaminic, decongestant.

TRIPHENYLMETHANE DYES.
See: Fuchsin
Methylrosaniline Chloride

TRIPHENYLTETRAZOLIUM CHLORIDE. TTC.
See: Uroscreen (Pfizer)

TRIPHEX CAPSULES. (Tennessee Pharm.) Dextroamphetamine sulfate 15 mg., amobarbital 100 mg./Cap. Bot. 100s.

TRIPIPERAZINE DICITITRATE, HYDROUS.
See: Piperazine Citrate, U.S.P. XXI.

TRIPIRIN. (CMC) Multi-layered aspirin 7.5 gr./Tab. Bot. 24s, 100s, 1000s.

TRIPLAN-D. (Eastwood) Antibiotic ointment. Tube 0.5 oz. Jar 4 oz.

TRIPLE ANTIBIOTIC OINTMENT. (Century) Bacitracin, Neomycin and Polymixin-B in ointment base.
Use: Antibacterial ointment.

TRIPLE ANTIBIOTIC OINTMENT. (Vortech) Bacitracin 400 u., neomycin sulfate 5 mg., polymyxin B sulfate 5000 u./Tube 0.5 oz.
Use: Antibacterial ointment.

TRIPLE ANTIBIOTIC OINTMENT. (Walgreen) Bacitracin 400 u., polymyxin-B sulfate 5000 u., neomycin sulfate 5.0 mg./Gm. Tube 0.5 oz., 1 oz.
Use: Antibiotic ointment

TRIPLE ANTI-B OINTMENT. (Eckerd) Bacitracin 400 U., neomycin sulfate 5 mg., polymixin B sulfate 5000 U./Gm.
Use: Topical antibacterial.

TRIPLE BARBITURATE ELIXIR. (CMC) Phenobarbital 0.25 gr., butabarbital ⅛ gr., pentobarbital ⅛ gr./5 cc. Bot. pt., gal.
Use: Pediatric sedative.

TRIPLE BROMIDES, EFFERVESCENT TABLETS. W/Phenobarbital.
See: Palagren, Liq. (Westerfield)

TRIPLE DYE. (Kerr) Gentian violet, proflavine, hemisulfate, brilliant green in water. Dispensing Bot 15 ml.
Use: Umbilical area antiseptic.

TRIPLE DYE. (Xttrium) Brilliant green 2.29 mg., proflavine hemisulfate 1.14 mg., gentian violet 2.29 mg./ml. Bot. 30 ml.
Use: Umbilical area disinfectant.

TRIPLEN. (Interstate) Tripelennamine HCl 50 mg./Tab. Bot. 100s, 1000s.
Use: Antihistamine.

TRIPLE PASTE. (Torch) Burow's sol. 1 part, absorption base 2 parts, Lassar's zinc oxide paste 3 parts. Jar 2 oz., 1 lb.
Use: Eczemas.

TRIPLE SULFA. (Sutliff & Case) Sulfadiazine 2.5 gr., sulfamethazine 2.5 gr., sulfamerazine 2.5 gr./Tab. Bot. 100s, 1000s.
Use: Antibacterial, sulfonamide therapy.

TRIPLE SULFA. (Standex; Kenyon) Sulfadiazine 2.5 gr., sulfamethazine 2.5 gr., sulfamerazine 2.5 gr./Tab. Bot. 100s. (Kenyon) Bot. 100s, 1000s.
Use: Antibacterial, sulfonamide therapy.

TRIPLE SULFA LIQUID. (Vortech) Bot. 4 oz., Gal.
Use: Triple sulfonamide therapy.

TRIPLE SULFA SUSPENSION. (Standex) Sulfamethazine 2.5 gr., sulfadiazine 2.5 gr., sulfamerazine 2.5 gr., sodium citrate 0.75 gr./5 cc. Bot. pt.
Use: Antibacterial, sulfonamide therapy.

TRIPLE SULFA SUSPENSION. (CMC) Sulfadiazine 0.166 Gm., sulfamethazine 0.166 Gm., sulfamerazine 0.166 Gm./5 cc. Bot. pt., gal.
Use: Antibacterial, sulfonamide therapy.

TRIPLE SULFA SUSPENSION, NO. 2. (Fellows) Sulfamethazine 2.5 gr., sulfadiazine 2.5 gr., sulfamerazine 2.5 gr., sod. citrate 7.5 gr./Tsp. Bot. gal.
Use: Antibacterial, sulfonamide therapy.

TRIPLE SULFA TABLETS. (Century; Stanlabs) Sulfadiazine 2.5 gr., sulfamerazine 2.5 gr., sulfamethazine 2.5 gr./Tab. Bot. 100s, 1000s.
Use: Antibacterial, sulfonamide therapy.

RIPLE SULFA TABLETS #2-C.T. (Wolins) Sulfadiazine 166 mg., sulfamerazine 166 mg., sulfamethazine 166 mg./Tab. Bot. 100s, 1000s.
Use: Antibacterial, sulfonamide therapy.

RIPLE SULFOID. (Vale) Sulfadiazine 167 mg., sulfamerazine 167 mg., sulfamethazine 167 mg./5 ml. or Tab. Bot. pt., 2 oz. 12s. Tab. Bot. 100s, 1000s.
Use: Sulfonamide therapy.

'RIPLE SULFONAMIDE. Dia-Mer-Thia Sulfonamides. Meth-Dia-Mer Sulfonamides.
Use: Sulfonamide therapy.

'RIPLE X. (Youngs Drug) Pyrethrins 0.3%, piperonyl butoxide 3.0%, petroleum distilate 1.2%, benzyl alcohol 2.4% Bot. 2 oz, 4 oz.
Use: Pediculocide for human use, head body & pubic lice.

'RIPOLE-F. (Spanner) Testosterone 25 mg., estrone 6 mg., progesterone 25 mg./cc. Vial 10 cc.

TRIPOSED SYRUP. (Blue Cross) Triprolidine HCl 1.25 mg., pseudoephedrine HCl 30 mg./5 ml. Bot. pt., gal.
Use: Antihistaminic, decongestant.

TRIPOSED TABLETS. (Blue Cross) Triprolidine HCl 2.5 mg., pseudoephedrine HCl 60 mg./Tab. Bot. 100s, 1000s.
Use: Antihistaminic, decongestant.

TRIPOTASSIUM CITRATE.
See: Potassium Citrate, U.S.P. XXI.

TRIPROFED. (Robinson) Tiprolidine HCl w/pseudoephedrine. Bot. 100s, 1000s.
Use: Antihistamine, nasal decongestant.

TRIPROFED EXPECTORANT WITH CODEINE. (Robinson) Triprolidine HCl w/pseudoephedrine, codeine, expt., Bot. pt., gal.
Use: Antitussive, antihistaminic.

TRIPROFED SYRUP. (Robinson) Triprolidine HCl w/pseudoephedrine syrup. Bot. pts., gal.
Use: Antihistamine, nasal decongestant.

TRIPROLIDINE. B.A.N. trans 1-(2-Pyridyl)-3-(pyrrolidin-1-yl)-1-p-tolylprop-1-ene.
Use: Antihistamine.
See: Actidil hydrochloride.

• **TRIPROLIDINE HCl,** U.S.P. XXI. Syrup, Tab., U.S.P. XXI. Trans 1-4-methylphenyl)-1-(2-pyridyl)-3-pyrrolidino-prop-1-ene HCl. Trans-2-[3-(1-pyrrolidinyl)-1-(p-tolyl)-propenyl]pyri-dine hydrochloride. (E)-2-(3-(1-Pyrrolidinyl)-1-p-tolypropenyl)pyridine monohydrochloride monohydrate.
Use: Antihistiminic.
See: Actidil, Syr. (Burroughs Wellcome)
W/Codeine phosphate, pseudoephedrine HCl, guaifenesin.
See: Actifed-C Syr. (Burroughs Wellcome)

• **TRIPROLIDINE AND PSEUDOEPHEDRINE HYDROCHLORIDE SYRUP,** U.S.P. XXI.
Use: Antihistaminic, decongestant.

• **TRIPROLIDINE AND PSEUDOEPHEDRINE HYDROCHLORIDE TABLETS,** U.S.P. XXI.
Use: Antihistaminic, decongestant.
W/Pseudoephedrine.
See: Actifed, Tab., Syr. (Burroughs Wellcome)
Atridine, Tab. (Interstate)
Sudahist, Tab. (Upsher-Smith)
Suda-Prol, Tab., Cap. (Quality Generics)
Triafed, Tab. (Wolins)
Triphed, Tab. (Lemmon)
Triphedrine, Tab. (Redford)
Triprofed Preps. (Robinson)

TRIPTONE. (Commerce) Scopolamine hydrobromide 0.25 mg./Cap. Bot. 12s.
Use: Motion sickness relief.

2,4,6-TRIS(1-AZIRIDINYL)-S-TRIAZINE. Triethylenemelamine.

TRI-SOF. (Vangard) Docusate potassium 100 mg., casanthranol 30 mg./Cap. Bot. 100s, 500s.
Use: Stool softener, laxative.

TRISOL. (Buffington) Borax, sodium Cl, boric acid. Irrigator Bot. 1 oz., 4 oz.
Use: Eye wash, tear substitute.

TRISORALEN. (Elder) Trioxsalen 5 mg./Tab. Bot. 28s, 100s.
Use: Repigmentation of idiopathic vitiligo; increasing tolerance to sunlight; enhancing pigmentation.

TRISTOJECT. (Mayrand) Triamcinolone diacetate 40 mg./ml. Vial 5 ml.
Use: Anti-inflammatory corticosteroid.

TRISULFAPYRIMIDINES. Oral Susp., Tab., U.S.P. XXI.
Use: Antibacterial.
See: Meth-Dia-Mer Sulfonamides (Various Mfr.)
Neotrizine, Prep. (Lilly)
Terfonyl, Liq. Tab. (Squibb)

TRI-SYNAR. (Forrest) Belladonna ext. 4.1 mg., phenyltoloxamine 20 mg., ethaverine HCl 20 mg./Tab. Bot. 100s.
Use: Antispasmodic.

TRI-SYNAR PLUS. (Forrest) Belladonna pow. ext. 4.1 mg., phenyltoloxamine 20 mg., ethaverine HCl 12.5 mg., phenobarbital 2.03 mg., butabarbital sod. 2.025 mg., pentobarbital sod. 6.075 mg., secobarbital sod. 6.075 mg./Tab. Bot. 100s.
Use: Sedatives w/antispasmodic.

TRITANE. (Econo-Rx) Brompheniramine maleate 2 mg., guaifenesin 100 mg., phenylephrine HCl 5 mg., phenylpropanolamine HCl 5 mg., alcohol 3.5%/5 ml. Bot. Gal.
Use: Expectorant.

TRITANE DC. (Econo-Rx) Brompheniramine maleate 2 mg., guaifenesin 100 mg., phenylephrine HCl 5 mg., phenylpropanolamine HCl 5 mg., alcohol 3.5%, codeine phosphate 10 mg./5 ml. Bot. Gal.
Use: Expectorant and antitussive.

TRITHEON. Acinitrazole, B.A.N.

TRITHION. Carbophenothion, B.A.N.

• **TRITIATED WATER.** USAN.
Use: Radioactive agent.
See: Tritiotope (Squibb)

TRITICOLL. (Western Research) P.E. triticum repens 4 gr., oxyquinoline sulf. 1/20 gr., charcoal 0.5 gr./Tab. Bot. 1000s.
Use: Diuretic.

TRI-TINIC. (Vortech) Liver desic. 75 mg., stomach 75 mg., Vit. B-12 15 mcg., Fe 110 mg., folic acid 1 mg., ascorbic acid 75 mg./Cap. Bot. 30s, 100s, 1000s.
Use: Hematinic.

TRITON WR-1339. (Rohm & Haas) Oxyethylated tertiary octyl-phenol-formaldehyde polymer.

TRITUSSIN COUGH SYRUP. (Towne) Pyrilamine maleate 40 mg., pheniramine maleate 20 mg., citric acid 100 mg., codeine phosphate 58 mg./fl. oz. w/menthol and glycerin in flavored base. Bot. 4 oz.

TRIURISUL. (Sheryl) Sulfacetamide 250 mg., sulfamethizole 250 mg., phenazopyridine HCl 50 mg./Tab. Bot. 100s.
Use: Urinary Antiseptic-analgesic.

TRI-VAC. (Rhode) Docusate sodium 100 mg., casanthranol 30 mg., sodium carboxymethylcellulose 400 mg./Cap. Bot. 30s, 100s.
Use: Laxative.

TRIVA DOUCHE POWDER. (Boyle) Alkyl aryl sulfonate 35%, sod. sulfate 52.5%, oxyquinoline sulfate 2%, lactose 9.67%, disodium ethylene hydrated silica, EDTA .33% Packet 3 Gm., 24s.
Use: Douche for trichomonal and monilial infections.

TRIVA-COMBINATION. (Boyle) Oxyquinoline benzoate and sulfate, alkly aryl sulfonate, disodium ethylenediamine-tetra-acetate, 9-aminoacridine HCl, copper sulfate./3 Gm. Douche Packet 24s and Jel tube 85 Gm. w/applicator.
Use: Therapeutic vaginal douche and jelly.

TRIVA JEL. (Boyle) Oxyquinoline benzoate 7.5 mg., dodecylbenzene sulfonate 62.5 mg., disodium ethylenediamine tetra-acetate 2.5 mg., 9-aminoacridine HCl 10 mg., copper sulfate 0.063 mg., sodium sulfate 6.9 mg./5 Gm w/tragacanth, Irish moss, lanolin, glycerin, sod. bicarb, methyl-, propyl-, and butyl-parahydroxybenzoate. Tubes 85 Gm.
Use: Vulvovaginitis, monilia, trichomonas.

TRI-VERT. (T.E. Williams) Dimenhydrinate 25 mg., niacin 50 mg., pentylenetetrazol 25 mg./Cap. Bot. 100s.
Use: Motion sickness treatment.

TRI VIDA F. (Pharmics) Vit. A 3000 I.U., D 400 I.U., C 100 mg., fluoride 0.25 mg., B-6 1 mg./0.6 cc. Bot. 57 cc.
Use: Dietary supplement.

TRI-VI-FLOR 0.5 mg. DROPS. (Mead Johnson) Fluoride 0.5 mg., Vit. A 1500 I.U., D 400 I.U., C 35 mg./1.0 ml. Bot. 30, 50 ml.
Use: Caries prophylaxis and diet supplementation.

TRI-VI-FLOR 0.25 mg. DROPS. (Mead Johnson) Fluoride 0.25 mg., Vit. A 1500 I.U., D 400 I.U., C 35 mg./1.0 ml. Drop. Bot. 50 ml.
Use: Caries prophylaxis, dietary supplement.

TRI-VI-FLOR 0.25 mg. WITH IRON DROPS. (Mead Johnson) Fluoride 0.25 mg., Vit. A. 1500 I.U., D. 400 I.U., C 35 mg., iron 10 mg./1.0 ml. Drop. Bot. 50 ml.
Use: Caries prophylaxis, dietary supplement with iron.

TRI-VI-FLOR 1.0 mg. CHEWABLE TABLETS. (Mead Johnson) Fluoride 1 mg., Vit. A 2500 I.U. D 400 I.U., Vit. C 60 mg./Tab. Bot. 100s, 1000s.
Use: Carries prophylaxis and diet supplementation.

TRI-VI-SOL DROPS. (Mead Johnson) Vitamin A 2500 I.U., D 400 I.U., C 60 mg./1.0 ml. drops. Bot. 30, 50 ml. with calibrated 'Safti-dropper.
Use: Vitamin A, C and D supplement.

TRI-VI-SOL WITH IRON DROPS. (Mead Johnson) Vit A 1500 I.U., C 35 mg., D 400 I.U., iron 10 mg./1.0 ml. Bot. 50 ml.
Use: Vitamin A, C and D with iron supplement.

TRI-VITE. (Foy) Thiamine HCl 100 mg., pyridoxine HCl 100 mg., cyanocobalamine 1000 mcg./ml. Vial 10 ml.
Use: B vitamin therapy.

TRIZMA. Trometamol, B.A.N.

TROBICIN. (Upjohn) Spectinomycin HCl equivalent to spectinomycin activity: **2 Gm.**/Vial w/Ampoule of diluent containing bacteriostatic water for injection 3.2 ml., benzyl alcohol 0.945% in ampoule. **4 Gm.** /Vial w/Ampoule of diluent containing bacteriostatic water for injection 6.2 ml., benzyl alcohol 0.945%.
Use: Treatment of gonorrhea.

TROCAINE LOZENGES. (Vortech) Benzocaine 5 mg./Tab. Bot. 1000s.
Use: Anesthetic throat lozenge.

• **TROCLOSENE POTASSIUM.** USAN. (1) 1,3-Dichloro-s-triazine-2,4,6 (1H,3H,5H)trione potassium salt; (2) Potassium dichloroisocyanurate.
Use: Topical anti-infective.

TRODAX EGLUMINE SALT. Nitroxynil, B.A.N.

TROFAN. (Upsher-Smith) L-Tryptophan 0.5 Gm./Tab. Bot. 30s, 100s.
Use: Dietary supplement.

TROKETTES. (Vitarine) Cetylpyridinium chloride 1:3000, cetyldimethylbenzylammonium chloride 1:3000, benzocaine 10 mg./Troche. Pkg. 10s, Jar 15s, 1000s.
Use: Throat and mouth irritations.

• **TROLAMINE,** N.F. XVI. 2,2″,2″-Nitrilotri-ethanol Ethanol, 2,2′,2″-nitrilotris-. Triethanolamine.
Use: Pharmaceutic aid (alkalizing agent).
W/Ortho-iodobenzoic.
See: Progonasyl (Saron)

• **TROLEANDOMYCIN,** U.S.P. XXI Cap., Oral Susp., U.S.P. XXI. Triacetyloleandomycin.
Use: Antibiotic.
See: Tao (Roerig)

TROLENE. Fenchlorphos, B.A.N.

TROLNITRATE PHOSPHATE, B.A.N. Di[tri-(2-nitratoethyl)ammonium]hydrogen phosphate. Praenitrona.
Use: Vasodilator.
See: Nitretamin (Squibb)

TROMAL. Butacetin. 4′-tert-Butoxyacetanilide.
Use: Analgesic antidepressant agent.

TROMETAMOL. B.A.N. 2-Amino-2-hydroxymethyl-propane-1,3-diol. Tromethamine, Talatrol, Trizma.
Use: Treatment of gastric hyperacidity.

TROMETHAMINE, U.S.P. XXI. For Inj., U.S.P. XXI. 2-Amino-2(hydroxymethyl)-1,3-propanediol. Trometamol, B.A.N.
Use: Alkalizer.

TRONOLANE CREAM. (Ross) Pramoxine HCl 1% in cream base. Tubes 1 oz., 2 oz.
Use: Anesthetic hemorrhoidal cream.

TRONOLANE SUPPOSITORIES. (Ross) Pramoxine HCl 1% in a lubricating suppository base. Pkg. 10s, 20s.
Use: Anesthetic hemorrhoidal suppository.

TRONOTHANE HYDROCHLORIDE. (Abbott) Pramoxine HCl Jelly (1%) Tube 1 oz. Cream (1%) Tube 1 oz.
Use: Local anesthetic.

1αH,3αH-TROPAN-3α-OL MANDELATE (ESTER) HYDROBROMIDE. Homatropine Hydrobromide, U.S.P. XXI.

1αH, 5αH-TROPAN-3-α-OL (±)-TROPATE (ESTER), SULFATE (2:1)(SALT) MONOHYDRATE. Atropine Sulfate, U.S.P. XXI.

TROPHENIUM. Phenactropinium Chloride, B.A.N.

TROPH-IRON. (Menley & James) Vit. B-12 25 mcg., B-1 10 mg., iron 20 mg./5 cc. Bot. 4 fl. oz.
Use: For vitamin B-1, B-12 and iron deficiencies.

TROPHITE. (Menley & James) Vitamin B-12 25 mcg., B-1 10 mg./5 cc. or Tab.**Elixir,** Bot. 4 oz., **Tab.** Bot. 50s.
Use: For deficiencies of vitamins B-1 and B-12.

TROPICAL BLEND. (Plough) A series of products is marketed under the Tropical Blend name including: Dark Tanning Lotion (SPF 2), and Sunscreen Lotion (SPF 4). Most contain homosalate in various oil and lotion bases.

• **TROPICAMIDE,** U.S.P. XXI. Ophth. Soln., U.S.P. XXI. N-Ethyl-2-phenyl-N-(4-pyridylmethyl)hydracrylamide. Benzeneacetamide, N-ethyl-α-(hydroxymethyl)-N-(4-pyridinylmethyl)-. Formerly Bis-Tropamide.
Use: Anticholinergic, ophthalmic.
See: Mydriacyl, Drops. (Alcon)

TROPIGLINE. B.A.N. Tiglytropeine.
Use: Treatment of the Parkinsonian syndrome.

TROPINE BENZOHYDRYL ESTER METHANE-SULFONATE. (also named benztropine methane-sulfonate).

• **TROSPECTOMYCIN SULFATE.** USAN.
Use: Antibacterial.

TROVIT. (Sig) Vit. B-2 0.3 mg., B-6 1 mg., choline Cl 25 mg., panthenol 2 mg., dl-methionine 10 mg., inositol 20 mg., niacinamide 50 mg., Vit. B-12 10 mg./ml. Vial 30 ml.
Use: B-complex deficiency.

TROXERUTIN. B.A.N. 3′,4′,7-Tri-[0-(2-hydroxyethyl)]rutin.
Use: Treatment of venous disorders.

TROXIDONE. B.A.N. 3,5,5-Trimethyloxazolidine-2,4-dione.
Use: Anticonvulsant.
See: Trimethadione (I.N.N.) Tridione.

TROXONIUM TOSYLATE. B.A.N. Triethyl-2-(3:4:5-trimethoxybenzoyloxy)ethylammonium toxylate (Tosylic acid is the trivial name for p-toluenesulfonic acid).
Use: Hypotensive.

TROXYPYRROLIUM TOSYLATE. B.A.N. N-Ethyl-N-2-(3:4:5-trimethyoxybenzoyloxy)-ethyl-pyrrolidinium toxylate (Tosylic acid is the trivial name for p-toluenesulphonic acid).
Use: Hypotensive.

TRYMEX. (Savage) Triamincinolone acetonide.
Cream: 0.025% Tube. 15 Gm., Jar 80 Gm., 1 lb.; 0.1% Tube 15 Gm., Jar 80 Gm., 1 lb.; 0.5% Tube. 15 Gm. **Ointment:** 0.025% Tube. 15 Gm. Jar 80 Gm.; 0.1% 15 Tube. Jar 80 Gm.
Use: Anti-inflammatory, anti-pruritic, topical steroid.

TRYPARSAMIDE. Monosodium N-(Carbamoylmethyl)arsanilate.

TRYPSIN, CRYSTALLIZED, U.S.P. XXI. For Inhalation Aerosol, U.S.P. XXI.
Use: Proteolytic enzyme.
W/Castor oil.
See: Granulex (Hickam)
W/Chymotrypsin.
See: Chymolase, Tab. (Warren-Teed)
Chymoral, Tab. (Armour)
Orenzyme, Tab. (Merrell Dow)

TRYPTIZOL HYDROCHLORIDE. Amitriptyline HCl, U.S.P XXI.

• **TRYPTOPHAN,** U.S.P. XXI. $C_{11}H_{12}N_2O_2$ as L-tryptophan.
Use: Amino acid.

TRYSUL. (Savage) Sulfathiazole 3.42%, sulfacetamide 2.86%m sulfabenzamide 3.70%, urea 0.64%. Tube 78 Gm.
Use: Vaginitis treatment.

T-SERP TABLET. (Tennessee Pharm.) Reserpine alkaloid 0.25 mg./Tab. Bot. 100s, 1000s.
Use: Hypotensive and tranquilizer.

T-STAT. (Westwood) Erythromycin 20 mg./ml. w/alcohol 71.2%. Bot. 60 ml.
Use: Acne vulgaris treatment.

TTC. Triphenyltetrazolium Chloride.
See: Uroscreen, Tube (Pfizer)

• **TUAMINOHEPTANE,** U.S.P XXI. Inhalant, U.S.P. XXI.
Use: Adrenergic.

TUAMINOHEPTANE SULFATE. 1-Methylhexylamine sulfate (2:1).
Use: Adrenergic (vasoconstrictor)

TUBERCULIN, MONO-VACC TEST. (Lincoln) Mono-Vacc test is a sterile, disposable multiple puncture scarifier with liquid Old Tuberculin on the points. Box 25 tests.
Use: Diagnostic.

• **TUBERCULIN.** U.S.P. XXI.
Use: Diagnostic aid (dermal reactivity indicator).

TUBERCULIN PPD, STABILIZED. (Panray) Stabilized solution in sterile isotonic phosphate-buffered saline w/phenol 0.3% and Tween 80 0.0005%. 1st strength, Vial 1.0 cc.; Intermediate strength Vial 1.0 cc., 5.0 cc.; 2nd strength, concentr. Vial 1 cc.

TUBERCULIN PURIFIED PROTEIN DERIVATIVE. (Squibb-Connaught) A concentrated solution for multiple puncture testing. Vial 1 ml.
Use: For screening tuberculin activity.

TUBERCULIN PURIFIED PROTEIN DERIVATIVE.
See: Tubersol, Inj. (Squibb-Connaught)

TUBERCULIN TINE TEST. (Lederle) **Old Tuberculin (OT):** Each disposable test unit consists of a stainless steel disc, with four tines (or prongs) 2 millimeters long, attached to a plastic handle. The tines have been dip-dried with antigenic material. The entire unit is sterilized by ethylene oxide gas. The test has been standardized by comparative studies, utilizing 0.05 mg. U.S. Standard Old Tuberculin (5 International Units) or 0.0001 mg. U.S. Standard (5 International Units) by the Mantoux technique. The reliability appears to be comparable to the standard Mantoux. 100s, 500s, 1000s. **Purified Protein Derivative (PPD):** Equivalent to or more potent than 5 TU PPD Mantoux test. Tests in a jar 25s, 100s or 250s.

TUBERLATE. (Heun) Sod. p-aminosalicylate 12 gr., succinic acid 4 gr./Tab. Bot. 500s.
Use: Tuberculosis treatment.

TUBERSOL. (Squibb-Connaught) Tuberculin purified protein derivative (Mantoux) 1TU, 5 TU, or 250 TU.
Use: For the detection of tuberculosis infection.

TUBEX. (Wyeth) The following drugs are available in various Tubex sizes:
Ativan
Bicillin C-R
Bicillin Long-Acting
Chlorpromazine HCl
Codeine Phosphate
Cyanocobalamin
Dexamethasone Sodium Phosphate
Digoxin
Dimenhydrinate
Diphenhydramine HCl
Diphtheria and Tetanus Toxoids Adsorbed (Pediatric)
Epinephrine
Furosemide
Heparin Flush Kits
Heparin Lock Flush.
Heparin Sodium Solution
Hydromorphone HCl
Hydroxyzine HCl
Immune Serum Globulin (Human)
Influenza Virus Vaccine, Trivalent
Largon
Lidocaine HCL
Mepergan
Meperidine HCl
Morphine Sulfate
Oxytocin
Pentobarbital Sodium
Phenergan
Phenobarbital Sodium
Prochlorperazine Edisylate
Secobarbital Sodium
Sodium Chloride
Sparine HCl
Tetanus and Diphtheria Toxoids Adsorbed (Adult)
Tetanus Immune Globulin (Human)
Tetanus Toxoid Alum. Phos. Ad.
Tetanus Toxoid, Fluid
Thiamine Hydrochloride
Triple Antigen
Wyamine Sulfate
Wycillin

• **TUBOCURARINE CHLORIDE,** U.S.P. XXI. Inj., U.S.P. XXI. Tubocuraranium, 7′,12′-dihydroxy-6,6′-dimethoxy-2,2′,2′-trimethyl-, chloride, hydrochloride pentahydrate. d-Tubocurarine chloride. Various mfr.
Metubine Iodide (Lilly) 3 mg./ml. Amp. 10 ml.
(Abbott) 3 mg./ml. in 10 ml. fliptop vials; 15 mg. in 5 ml. Abboject Syringe.
Use: Skeletal muscle relaxant.

TUBOCURARINE CHLORIDE, DIMETHYL. Dimethyl ether of d-tubocurarine chloride.

(±)-TUBOCURARINE CHLORIDE HYDROCHLORIDE PENTAHYDRATE. Tubocurarine Chloride, U.S.P XXI.

TUBOCURARINE IODIDE, DIMETHYL. Dimethyl ether of d-tubocurarine iodide.
Use: Skeletal muscle relaxant.
See: Metubine, Vial (Lilly)

TUBOMEL. Isoniazid, B.A.N.

TUCKS. (Parke-Davis) Pads saturated with solution of witch hazel 50%, glycerin 10%, methylparaben 0.1%, benzalkonium Cl 0.003% Jar 40s, 100s.
Use: Proctologic & dermatologic disorders.

TUCKS OINTMENT AND CREAM. (Parke-Davis) Witch hazel 50% in cream or ointment base. Tube 40 Gm. w/rectal applicator.
Use: Astringent.

TUCKS TAKE-ALONGS. (Parke-Davis) Non-woven wipes saturated with solution of witch hazel 50%, glycerine 10% w/purified water, methylparaben 0.1%, benzalkonium chloride 0.003%. Box 12s.

TUGON. Metriphonate, B.A.N.

TUINAL. (Lilly) Equal parts Seconal Sod. & Amytal Sod. Pulvule **50 mg.** Bot. 100s; **100 mg.** Bot. 100s, 1000s. Blister Pkg. 10 × 10s. Dispenser rolls, 40 × 25s; **200 mg.** Bot. 100s, 1000s. Blister Pkg. 10 × 10s.
Use: Sedative & hypnotic.

TUMS. (Norcliff Thayer) Calcium carbonate 500 mg./Tab. Available in peppermint and assorted flavors in various package sizes. Rolls singles, 3-roll wraps. Bot. 75s, 150s.
Use: Antacid.

TUR-BI-KAL NASAL DROPS. (Emerson) Phenylephrine HCl in a salin solution. Dropper Bot. 1 oz., 12s.
Use: Nasal decongestant.

TURBILIXIR. (Burlington) Chlorpheniramine maleate 2 mg., phenylephrine HCl 5 mg., phenylpropanolamine HCl 5 mg./5 ml. Bot. Pts., gal.
Use: Antihistamine, decongestant.

TURBINAIRE.
See: Decadron Phosphate, Preps. (Merck Sharp & Dohme)

TURBISPAN LEISURECAPS. (Burlington) Chlorpheniramine maleate 12 mg., 1-phenylephrine HCl 15 mg., phenylpropanolamine HCl 15 mg./Sus. Rel. Cap. Bot. 30s.
Use: Antihistamine, decongestant.

TURGASEPT AEROSOL. (Ayerst) Ethyl alcohol 44.25%, essential oils 0.90%, n-alkyl (50% C-14, 40% C-12, 10% C-16) dimethyl benzylammonium Cl 0.33%, o-phenylphenol 0.25% w/propellant. Spray can 11.5 oz. in bouquet, fresh lemon, leather, citrus blossom scents.
Use: Spray disinfectant, air deodorant.

TURGEX. (Xttrium) Hexachlorophene 3% w/emulsifying agents. Aerosol Foam 6 oz. Liq. 5 oz., gal.
Use: Antibacterial.

TURPENTINE OIL W/COMBINATIONS.
See: Sloan's Liniment, Liq. (Warner-Lambert)

TUSAL. (Hauck) Sodium thiosalicylate 50 mg./ml. Vial 30 ml.
Use: Relief of muscular pains, acute gout, arthritis, rheumatic fever.

TUSANA. Dextromethorphan, B.A.N.

TUS-F. (Orbit) Dextromethorphan HBr 10 mg./5 ml. Bot. 4 oz., Pts.
Use: Antitussive, decongestant.

TUSILAN. Dextromethorphan HBr.

TUS-ORAMINIC. (Vortech) Bot. 100s, 1000s.
Use: Antitussive, decongestant.

TUSQUELIN. (Circle) Dextromethorphan HBr 15 mg., chlorpheniramine maleate 2 mg., phenylpropanolamine 5 mg., phenylephrine HCl 5 mg., fl. ext. ipecac 0.17 min., potassium guaiacolsulfonate 44 mg.,/5 ml., alcohol 5% Syrup, pt.
Use: Antitussive w/expectorant; antihistamine.

TUSREN. (Wren) Guaifenesin 200 mg./Tab. Bot. 100s, 1000s.

TUSSABAR. (Tennessee) Acetaminophen 400 mg., salicylamide 500 mg., potassium guaiacolsulfonate 120 mg., pyrilamine maleate 30 mg., ammonium chloride 500 mg., sodium citrate 500 mg., phenylephrine HCl 30 mg./oz. Bot. pt., gal.
Use: Analgesic, antipyretic, decongestant and expectorant.

TUSSABID. (Ion) Guaifenesin 200 mg., dextromethorphan HBr 30 mg./Cap. Bot. 24s, 100s.
Use: Cough relief.

TUSSACOL. (Jenkins) Dextromethorphan HBr 7.5 mg., pyrilamine maleate 8.0 mg., chlorpheniramine maleate 0.3 mg., phenylephrine HCl 5.0 mg., acetaminophen 100.0 mg., guaifenesin 50 mg./Tab. Bot. 1000s.

TUSSAFED DROPS. (Everett) Carbinoxamine maleate 2 mg., pseodoephedrine HCl 25 mg., dextromethorphan HBr 9 mg./1 ml. Bot. 30 ml. with calibrated dropper.
Use: Temporary relief of cough, nasal congestion, runny nose.

TUSSAFED SYRUP. (Everett) Dextromethorphan HBr 15 mg., pseudoephedrine HCl 60 mg., carbinoxamine maleate 4 mg./5 ml. Bot. 4 oz., 16 oz.
Use: Antitussive, decongestant, antihistamine.

TUSSAFED EXPECTORANT. (Calvital) Chlorpheniramine maleate 2 mg., pseudoephedrine HCl 30 mg., guaifenesin 100 mg./5 cc. Bot. pt., gal.
Use: Cough relief.

TUSSAGESIC TABLETS. (Dorsey) Phenylpropanolamine HCl 25 mg., pheniramine maleate 12.5 mg., pyrilamine maleate 12.5 mg., dextromethorphan HBr 30 mg., terpin hydrate 180 mg., acetaminophen 325 mg./T.R. Tab. Bot. 100s.
Use: Common cold symptoms.

TUSSAGESIC SUSPENSION. (Dorsey) Phenylpropanolamine HCl 12.5 mg., pheniramine maleate 6.25 mg., pyrilamine maleate 6.25 mg., dextromethorphan HBr 15 mg., terpin hydrate 90 mg., acetaminophen 120 mg./5 ml. Liq. Bot. pt.
Use: Common cold symptoms.

TUSSAHIST. (Defco) Codeine phosphate 10 mg., phenylpropanolamine HCl 12.5 mg., chlorpheniramine maleate 2 mg., pyrilamine maleate 7.5 mg., guaifenesin 100 mg./5 cc. Bot. 4 oz. pt., gal.
Use: Treatment of coughs.

TUSSANIL DH SYRUP. (Misemer) Phenylephrine HCl 10 mg., phenylpropanolamine HCl 5 mg., pyrilamine maleate 3.33 mg., chlorpheniramine maleate 1.66 mg., dihydrocodinone bitartrate 1.66 mg./5 ml.
Use: Symptomatic relief of colds, sinus, & allergic rhinitis.

TUSSANOL. (Tyler) Pyrilamine maleate ¾ gr., codeine phosphate 1 gr., ammonium chloride 7.5 gr., sodium citrate 5 gr., menthol 1/10 gr./fl. oz. Bot. 4 fl. oz., pt., gal.
Use: Antihistamine, antitussive.

TUSSANOL with EPHEDRINE. (Tyler) Ephedrine sulfate 2 gr., pyrilamine maleate ¾ gr., codeine phosphate 1 gr., ammonium chloride 7.5 gr., sodium citrate 5 gr., menthol 1/10 gr./30 cc. Bot. 16 fl. oz.
Use: Cough syrup. Bronchodilator, decongestant, antihistaminic.

TUSSAPAP. (Sutliff & Case) N-Acetyl-p-amino-phenol 195 mg., aspirin 130 mg., phenylephrine HCl 5 mg., noscapine 5 mg., caffeine 32.5 mg., pyrilamine maleate 12.5 mg./Tab. Bot. 100s, 1000s.
Use: Treatment of common cold.

TUSSAR-2 SYRUP. (USV Labs.) Codeine phosphate 10 mg., carbetapentane citrate 7.5 mg., chlorpheniramine maleate 2 mg., guaifenesin 50 mg., sod. citrate 130 mg., citric acid 20 mg./5 ml. w/alcohol 5%, methyl paraben 0.1%. Bot. pt.
Use: Cough suppressant.

TUSSAR DM. (USV Labs.) Dextromethorphan HBr 15 mg., chlorpheniramine maleate 2 mg., phenylephrine HCl 5 mg./5 ml. w/methylparaben 0.1% Bot. pt.
Use: Non-narcotic antitussive, antihistaminic, decongestant.

TUSSAR SF. (USV Labs.) Codeine phosphate 10 mg., carbetapentane citrate 7.5 mg., chlorpheniramine maleate 2 mg., guaifenesin 50 mg., sod. citrate 130 mg., citric acid 20 mg./5 ml., methylparaben 0.1%, alcohol 12%. Sugar free. Bot. pt.
Use: Coughs.

TUSSCAPS. (Martin-Philips) Chlorpheniramine maleate 8 mg., phenylpropanolamine 50 mg., dextromethorphan 20 mg., atropine sulfate 0.25 mg./Cap. Bot. 100s.
Use: Common cold.

TUSS-CHLORPHENADE. (Wolins) Chlorpheniramine maleate 8 mg., phenylpropanolamine HCl 50 mg., dextromethorphan 20 mg., atropine sulfate 0.36 mg./Cap. Bot. 100s, 1000s.

TUSSCIDIN EXPECTORANT. (Cenci) Guaifenesin 100 mg./5 cc. Bot. 4 oz., pt., gal.

TUSSCIDIN EXPECTORANT-D. (Cenci) Dextromethorphan HBr 15 mg., guaifenesin 100 mg./5 cc. Bot. 4 oz., pt., gal.

TUSSEND EXPECTORANT. (Merrell Dow) Pseudoephedrine HCl 60 mg., hydrocordone bitartrate 5 mg., guaifenesin 200 mg./5ml. w/ alcohol 12.5%. Bot. Pt.
Use: Antitussive, decongestant, expectorant.

TUSSEND LIQUID. (Merrell Dow) Hydrocodone bitartrate 5 mg., pseudoephedrine HCl 60 mg./5 ml. w/alcohol 5%. Bot. pt.
Use: Antitussive-decongestant.

TUSSEND TABLETS. (Merrell Dow) Hydrocodone bitartrate 5 mg., pseudoephedrine HCl 60 mg./Tab. Bot. 100s.
Use: Antitussive, decongestant.

TUSS-GENADE MODIFIED CAPS. (Goldline) Bot. 100s, 1000s.
Use: Decongestant.

TUSSGEN EXPECTORANT. (Goldline) Bot., pt., gal.
Use: Expectorant.

TUSSGEN LIQUID. (Goldline) Bot. 100s, 1000s.
Use: Antitussive, decongestant.

TUSSIDRAM. (Dram) d-Methorphan 10 mg., phenylpropanolamine 12.5 mg., guaifenesin 50 mg., chlorpheniramine maleate 2 mg./5 cc. Bot. pt.
Use: Nasal decongestion and coughs.

TUSSILEX. Dropropizine, B.A.N.

TUSSIONEX. (Pennwalt) Hydrocodone (as resin complex) 5 mg., phenyltoloxamine 10 mg. as the resin complex/Tab., Cap., 5 cc. **Tab.:** Bot. 100s, **Liq.:** Bot. 1 pt., 900 ml. **Cap.:** Bot. 50s.
Use: Antitussive.

TUSSI-ORGANIDIN LIQUID. (Wallace) Codeine phosphate 10 mg.; Organidin 30 mg./5 ml. Bot. 16 fl. oz., gal.
Use: Antitussive and expectorant combination.

TUSSI-ORGANIDIN DM LIQUID. (Wallace) Dextromethorphan HBr 10 mg., Organidin 30 mg./5 ml. Bot. pt., gal.
Use: Antitussive and expectorant combination.

TUSSIREX WITH CODEINE. (Scot-Tussin) Codeine phosphate 10 mg., pheniramine maleate 13.33 mg., phenylephrine HCl 4.17 mg., sodium citrate 83.33 mg., sodium salicylate 83.33 mg., caffeine citrate 25 mg./5 ml. With and without sugar. Bot. Pts., gal
Use: Coughs, colds.

TUSSI-R-GEN DM LIQUID. (Goldline) Bot. pt.
Use: Antitussive, expectorant.

TUSSI-R-GEN LIQUID EXPECTORANT. (Goldline) Bot pt.
Use: Expectorant.

TUSS-ORNADE LIQUID. (SmithKline) Caramiphen edisylate 6.7 mg., phenylpropanolamine HCl 12.5 mg./5 ml. w/alcohol 5%. Bot. pt.
Use: Antitussive, decongestant.

TUSS-ORNADE SPANSULE. (SmithKline) Caramiphen edisylate 40 mg., phenylpropanolamine HCl 75 mg./Cap. Bot. 50s, 500s.
Use: Antitussive, decongestant.

TUSS-ORAMINIC. (Vortech) Chlorpheniramine maleate 8 mg., phenylpropanolamine HCl 50 mg., atropine sulfate 1/180 gr., dextromethorphan HBr 20 mg./Spancap. Bot. 100s, 1000s.
Use: Antihistaminic, decongestant, antitussive.

TUSSTAT EXPECTORANT. (Century) Diphenhydramine HCl 80 mg., ammonium chloride 12 gr., sodium citrate 5 gr., menthol 1/10 gr., alcohol 5%/oz. Bot. 4 fl. oz., pt., gal.

T.V.M. (Vitarine) Vit. A 10,000 I.U., D 400 I.U., B-1 10 mg., B-2 10 mg., niacinamide 100 mg., B-6 5 mg., B-12 5 mcg., C 200 mg., d-calcium pantothenate 20 mg., E 15 I.U., Fe 12 mg., Mn 1 mg., Mg 65 mg., Iodine 0.15 mg., Cu 2 mg., Zn 1.5 mg./Captab. Bot. 100s, 250s, 1000s.

TWEEN 20, 40, 60, 80. (ICI Americas) Polysorbates, N.F. XVI.
Use: Surface active agents.

TWENDEX PB. (Allison) Dextroamphetamine sulfate 20 mg., phenobarbital 1 gr./Tab. Bot. 30s, 100s.
Use: Obesity and mood stimulant.

TWENTISEC. (Schmid) Twenty second pregnancy test. 20 tests/Kit.

TWENTY EIGHTS. (Faraday) Tab. Bot. 28s.
Use: Relief of menstrual pain.

TWIN-K-CL LIQUID. (Boots) Potassium 15 mEq., chloride 4 mEq./15 ml. Bot. 16 oz.
Use: Oral potassium therapy for treatment of hypokalemia.

TWIN-K LIQUID. (Boots) Potassium ions 20 mEq./15 ml. Bot. Pt.
Use: Treatment of hypokalemia.

TWOCAL HN HIGH NITROGEN LIQUID NUTRITION. (Ross) Water, hydrolyzed corn starch, corn oil, sodium caseinate, sucrose, sodium calcium caseinate, medium-chain trigylcerides, potassium citrate, magnesium chloride, calcium phosphate tribasic, sodium citrate, zinc sulfate, ferrous sulfate, manganese chloride, cupric sulfate, soy protein isolate, natural & artificial flavors, soy lecithin, choline chloride, ascorbic acid, alpha-tocopheryl acetate, niacinamide, calcium panothenate, pyridoxine HCl, Vit. A palmitate, thiamine chloride HCl. ribflavin, folic acid, biotin, phylloquinone, Vitamin D-3, cyanocobalamin. Can 8 oz.
Use: Complete, balanced nutrition.

TWO-CAL IM. (Fellows) Calcium glycerophosphate 10 mg., calcium levulinate 15 mg./ml. Vial 100 ml.
Use: Hypocalcemia.

2-24 COLD AND HAY FEVER TIME CAPSULE. (Walgreen) Belladonna alkaloids 0.2 mg., phenylpropanolamine HCl 50 mg., chlorpheniramine maleate 4 mg./Cap. Bot. 10s.
Use: Cold and hayfever.

2-24 TIME CAPSULE. (Walgreen) Belladonna alkaloids 0.2 mg./Cap. Bot. 10s.
Use: Antihistamine, decongestant.

TWO-DYNE CAPSULES. (Hyrex) Butalbital 50 mg., caffeine 40 mg., acetaminophen 325 mg./Cap. Bot. 100s, 1000s.
Use: Pain, nervous tension.

• **TYBAMATE.** USAN. 2-Methyl-2-propyl-trimethylene butylcarbamate carbamate. 2-(Hydroxymethyl)-2-methylpentyl butylcarbamate carbamate. 2-Carbamoyloxymethyl-2-methylpentyl butylcarbamate. Benvil; Solacen.
Use: Tranquilizer.

TYCOPAN. (Lilly) Vit. A 20,000 I.U., D 1000 I.U., B-1 10 mg., B-2 8 mg., B-6 10 mg., pantothenic acid 60 mg., niacinamide 60 mg., Vit. B-12 15 mcg., C 200 mg., E 22 I.U., biotin 0.16 mg., folic acid 0.45 mg., aminobenzoic acid 33 mg., inositol 160 mg., lipoic acid 0.3 mg., choline bitartrate 160 mg./3 Caps. Bot. 100s.
Use: Chronic alcoholism.

TYFORMIN. B.A.N. 4-Guanidinobutyramide.
Use: Oral hypoglycemic agent.
See: Augmentin hydrochloride.

TYLAGEL HYDROCHLORIDE. Tolpropamine, B.A.N.

TYLAN. Tylosin, B.A.N.

TYLENOL CHILDREN'S CHEWABLE TABLETS. (McNeil Prods) Acetaminophen 80 mg./Tab. Pkg. 30s. Hosp. 250 × 1.
Use: Analgesic, antipyretic.

TYLENOL CHILDREN'S ELIXIR. (McNeil Prods) Acetaminophen 160 mg./5 ml. Bot. 2 oz., 4 oz., pt. Unit Dose 100 × 5 ml., 100 × 10 ml.
Use: Analgesic, antipyretic.

TYLENOL EXTRA-STRENGTH ADULT LIQUID. (McNeil Prods) Acetaminophen 1000 mg./30 ml. w/alcohol 7%. Bot. 8 oz. Hosp. 8 oz.
Use: Analgesic, antipyretic.

TYLENOL EXTRA-STRENGTH. (McNeil Prods) **Tab.:** Acetaminophen 500 mg./Tab. Bot. 30s, 60s, 100s, 200s. Vial 12s. **Caps.:** Bot. 24s, 50s, 100s, 165s. Hospital Sizes: Bot. 500s. Unit dose 200 × 2, 5 × 100. **CAPLETS:** Vial 10s. Bot. 24s, 50s.
Use: Analgesic, antipyretic.

TYLENOL INFANTS' DROPS. (McNeil Prods) Acetaminophen 80 mg./0.8 ml. Bot. w/dropper 15 ml.
Use: Analgesic, antipyretic.

TYLENOL JUNIOR STRENGTH SWALLOWABLE TABLETS. (McNeil Products) Acetaminophen 160 mg./Tab. Box. 30s. Hosp. 250 × 1.
Use: Analgesic, antipyretic.

TYLENOL MAXIMUM STRENGTH SINUS MEDICATION. (McNeil Prods) Acetaminophen 500 mg., pseudoephedrine HCl 30 mg./**Cap:.** Bot. 20s, 40s. **Tab:.** Bot. 24s, 50s.
Use: Temporary relief of the pain and congestion caused by sinusitis and colds.

TYLENOL REGULAR STRENGTH. (McNeil Prods) Acetaminophen. **Tabs:** 325 mg. Tin 12s. Vial 12s. Bot. 50s, 100s, 200s, 1000s. Unit dose 1000s. Hospital Sizes: Bot. 1000s, 5000s. Drum 25,000. **Cap.:** 325 mg. Bot. 24s, 50s, 100s.
Use: Analgesic, antipyretic.
W/Carbinoxamine, phenylephrine HCl.
See: Clistin-D, Tab. (McNeil)
W/Chlorpheniramine maleate & pseudoephedrine HCl.
See: Cotylenol Cold Formula, Liq., Tab. (McNeil)
W/Chlorzoxazone.
See: Parafon Forte, Tab. (McNeil)

TYLENOL WITH CODEINE. (McNeil Pharm) **Tab.**: Acetaminophen 300 mg.with codeine phosphate. **No. 1:** codeine phosphate 7.5 mg. Bot. 100s. **No. 2:** codeine phosphate 15 mg. Bot. 100s, 500s. Unit dose 20 × 25s. **No. 3:** codeine phosphate 30 mg. Bot. 100s, 500s, 1000s. Unit dose 20 × 25s. **No. 4:** codeine phosphate 60 mg. Bot. 100s, 500s. Unit dose 20 × 25s. **Cap.**: Acetaminophen 300 mg. with codeine phosphate. **No. 3**: codeine phosphate 30 mg./Cap. Bot. 100s. Unit dose 100s. **No. 4**: codeine phosphate 60 mg./Cap. Bot. 100s. Unit dose 100s.
Use: Analgesic, antipyretic.

TYLENOL WITH CODEINE ELIXIR. (McNeil Pharm) Acetaminophen 120 mg., codeine phosphate 12 mg./5 ml. w/alcohol 7% Bot. Pts.
Use: Analgesic, antipyretic.

TYLOSIN. B.A.N. An antibiotic derived from an actinomycete resembling Streptomyces fradie. Tylan.
Use: Antibiotic, veterinary medicine.

TYLOX. (McNeil Pharm) Oxycodone HCl 5 mg., acetaminophen 500 mg./Cap. Bot. 100s unit dose 4 × 25s.
Use: Relief of moderate to severe pain.

• **TYLOXAPOL.** U.S.P. XXI. p-(1,1,3,3-Tetramethylbutyl) phenol polymer with formaldehyde and ethylene oxide.
Use: Detergent.

TYMATRO THROAT TROCHES. (Bowman) Cetylpyridinium Cl 1.5 mg., benzocaine 5 mg./Lozenge.
Use: Throat anesthetic.

TYMAZOLINE. B.A.N. 2-(5-Isopropyl-2-methylphenoxymethyl)-2-imidazoline. Pernazene hydrochloride.
Use: Vasoconstrictor.

TYMPAGESIC. (Adria) Phenylephrine HCl 0.25%, antipyrine 5%, benzocaine 5%, in propylene glycol. Liq., Bot. w/dropper 13 cc.
Use: Antihistaminic & analgesic ear drops.

• **TYPHOID VACCINE,** U.S.P. XXI.
(Wyeth)—Vial 5 cc., 10 cc., 20 cc.
Use: Active immunizing agent.

TYPHUS VACCINE.
Use: Active immunizing agent.
TYRIMIDE. Isopropamide Iodide, B.A.N.
TYROBENZ. (Mallard) Benzocaine 5 mg., cetalkonium chloride 2.5 mg., aromatics qs./Troche. Bot. 500s.
Use: Sore throat.
TYROHIST NASAL SPRAY. (Quality Generics) Pyrilamine maleate, desoxyephedrine HCl, cetalkonium chloride. Bot. 20 cc.
Use: Antihistamine, antibacterial, decongestant.
TYRO-LOZ. (Kenyon) Tyrothricin 2 mg., benzocaine 5 mg./Loz. Bot. 100s, 1000s.
Use: Sore throat.
• **TYROPANOATE SODIUM,** U.S.P. XXI. Cap., U.S.P. XXI. Sodium 3-butyramido-α-ethyl-2,4,6-triiodohydrocinnamate.
Use: Diagnostic aid (radiopaque medium-cholecystographic).
See: Bilopaque (Winthrop-Breon)
TYROPAQUE CAPS. (Winthrop Products) Tyropanoate sodium.
Use: Oral cholecystographic medium.
• **TYROSINE,** U.S.P. XXI. L-Tyrosine.
Use: Amino acid.
L-TYROSINE, 3-HYDROXY- Levodopa, U.S.P. XXI.
LEVO-TYROSINE, 3-HYDROXY-α-METHYL-, ETHYL ESTER° HYDROCHLORIDE. Methyldopate Hydrochloride, U.S.P. XXI.
L-TYROSINE,3-HYDROXY-α-METHYL-, SESQUIHYDRATE. Methyldopa, U.S.P. XXI.
L-TYROSINE, O-(4-HYDROXY-3,5-DIIODOPHENYL)-3,5-DIIODO-MONOSODIUM SALT, HYDRATE. Levothyroxine Sodium, U.S.P. XXI.
L-TYROSINE, O-(4-HYDROXY-3-IODO-PHENYL-3,5-DIIODO-, MONOSODIUM SALT. Liothyronine Sodium, U.S.P. XXI.
TYROSUM. (Summers) Isopropanol 50%, polysorbate 80 & acetone. Bot. 4 oz., 1 pt. Pkg. 24s, 50s. w/3 cc. pad. Packetts 25s, 30s.
Use: Skin cleaner.
• **TYROTHRICIN,** U.S.P. XXI. Spray. Sol., Troches: An antibiotic from *Bacillus brevis.* Tyrodac; Tyroderm.
TYROTHRICIN COMBINATIONS.
TY-TABS. (Major) Acetaminophen with codeine #2, #3 or #4. Bot. 100s, 500s, 1000s.
Use: Analgesic, antipyretic.
TYZANOL HYDROCHLORIDE. Tetrahydrozoline, B.A.N.
TYZINE NASAL SOLUTION. (Key) Tetrahydrozoline HCl 0.1% Bot. pt., oz.
Use: Nasal decongestant.
TYZINE NASAL SPRAY. (Key) Tetrahydrozoline HCl 0.1%. Bot. 0.5 oz.
Use: Nasal decongestant.
TYZINE PEDIATRIC NASAL DROPS. (Key) Tetrahydrozoline HCl 0.05%. Bot. 0.5 oz.
Use: Nasal decongestant.

U

UAA. (Econo Med) Methenamine 40.8 mg., phenyl salicylate 18.1 mg., methylene blue 5.4 mg., benzoic acid 4.5 mg., atropine sulfate 0.03 mg., hyoscyamine 0.03 mg./Tab. Bot. 100s.
Use: Antispasmodic and urinary antiseptic.
UBRETID. Distigmine Bromide, B.A.N.
UCG-BETA SLIDE MONOCLONAL II. (Wampole) Two-minute latex agglutination inhibition slide test for the qualitative detection of B-hCG/hCG (sensitivity 0.5 I.U. hCG/ml.) in urine. Kits 50s, 100s, 300s.
Use: Aid in the diagnosis of pregnancy.
UCG-BETA STAT. (Wampole) One-hour passive hemagglutination inhibition tube test for the qualitative detection and quantitative determination of B-hCG/hCG sensitivity 0.2 I.U. hCG/ml. in urine. Kits 50s, 300s.
Use: Aid in the diagnosis of pregnancy.
UCG-LYPHOTEST. (Wampole) One-hour passive hemagglutination inhibition tube test for the qualitative or quantitative determination of human chorionic gonadotropin (sensitivity 0.5-1.0 I.U. hCG/ml.) in urine. Kits 10s, 50s, 300s.
Use: Aid in the diagnosis of pregnancy.
UCG-SLIDE TEST. (Wampole) Rapid latex agglutination inhibition slide test for the qualitative detection of human chorionic gonadotropin (Sensitivity: 2 I.U. hCG/ml) in urine. Kits 30s, 100s, 300s, 1000s.
Use: Aid in the diagnosis of pregnancy.
UCG-TEST. (Wampole) Two-hour hemagglutination inhibition tube test for the determination of human chorionic gonadotropin (sensitivity 0.5 I.U. hCG/ml undiluted specimen. 1.5 I.U. hCG/ml. 1:3 diluted specimen) in urine and serum. Kits 10s, 25s, 100s, 300s.
Use: Aid in the diagnosis of pregnancy.
UCG-TITRATION SET. (Wampole) A two-hour hemagglutination inhibition tube test for the determination of human chorionic gonadotropin (Sensitivity 1 I.U. hCG/ml.) in urine or serum. Kit 45s.
Use: Aid in the diagnosis of pregnancy.
ULACORT. (Fellows) Prednisolone 5 mg./Tab. Bot. 1000s.
Use: Rheumatoid arthritis.
ULACORT (AQUASPENSION INJECTIONS). (Fellows) Prednisolone acetate 25 mg. or 50 mg./cc. Vial 10 cc.
ULBREVAL. Buthalitone Sodium, B.A.N.
ULCERIN P TABLETS. (Winthrop Products) Aluminum hydroxide.
Use: Antacid.
ULCERIN TABLETS. (Winthrop Products) Aluminum hydroxide.
Use: Antacid.
■ **ULCER THERAPY.**
See: Antacids
Anticholinergic Agents
ULTANDREN. Fluoxymesterone, B.A.N.
ULTIMA II SCIENTIFIC SUN PRODUCTS. (Revlon) Padimate O, oxybenzone in lotion, oil, & stick.
Use: Sunburn prevention.
ULTRABEX. (Approved) Vit. B-1 20 mg., C 50 mg., B-2 2 mg., B-6 0.5 mg., niacinamide 35 mg., cal. pantothenate 0.5 mg., wheat germ oil 30 mg., B-12 20 mcg., liver desic. 150 mg., Fe 11.58 mg., Ca 29 mg., P 23 mg., dicalcium phos. 100 mg., Mg 1.11

mg., Mn 1.30 mg., K 2.24 mg., Zn 0.68 mg., choline 25 mg., inositol 25 mg., pepsin 32.5 mg., diastase 32.5 mg., hesperidin 25 mg., biotin 20 mcg., hydrol. yeast 81.25 mg., protein digest 47.04 mg., amino acids 34.21 mg./Cap. Bot. 50s, 100s, 1000s.
Use: Dietary supplement.

ULTRACAIN HCl. Carticaine, B.A.N.

ULTRA CAP. (Weeks & Leo) Acetaminophen 300 mg., guaifenesin 50 mg., chlorpheniramine maleate 4 mg., phenylephrine HCl 10 mg., dextromethorphan HBr. 6 mg./Cap. Vial 18s.
Use: Cold & flu relief.

ULTRACEF CAPSULES. (Bristol) Cefadroxil 500 mg./Cap. Bot. 50s, 100s.
Use: Antibiotic, antibacterial.

ULTRACEF ORAL SUSPENSION. (Bristol) Cefadroxil 125 mg. or 250 mg./5 ml. Bot. 50 ml., 100 ml.
Use: Antibiotic, antibacterial.

ULTRACEF TABLETS. (Bristol) Cefadroxil 1 Gm./Tab. Bot. 24s.
Use: Antibiotic, antibacterial.

ULTRACORTENOL. Prednisone, B.A.N.

ULTRACORTINOL. (Ciba) Agent to suppress over-active adrenal glands. Pending release.

ULTRA-DERM BATH OIL. (Baker/Cummins) Bot. 8 oz.
Use: Skin moisturizer.

ULTRA-DERM MOISTURIZER. (Baker/Cummins) Bot. 8 oz.
Use: Moisturizing lotion.

ULTRA-DEW. (La Crosse) Therapeutic bath oil. Bot. 8 oz., 0.5 gal.
Use: Dry skin care.

ULTRAGESIC. (Stewart-Jackson) Acetaminophen 600 mg., hydrocodone bitartrate 5 mg./Tab. Bot. 100s.
Use: Relief of mild to moderate pain.

ULTRALANUM 21-HEXANOATE. Fluocortolone, B.A.N.

ULTRALENTE INSULIN.
See: Iletin (Lilly)

ULTRA MIDE 25. (Baker/Cummins) Bot. 8 oz.
Use: Moisturizing lotion.

ULTRAN. Phenaglycodol, B.A.N.

ULTRAPAQUE- C. (Lafayette) Barium sulfate 96%. Containers 100 lbs.
Use: Alimentary tract radiography.

ULTRAPEN POTASSIUM SALT.
See: Propicillin, B.A.N.

ULTRASONE. (Gordon) Ultrasonic contact cream. Bot. qt., gal. Plastic Bot. 8 oz.

ULTRA TEARS. (Alcon) Hydroxypropyl methylcellulose 1%, benzalkonium chloride 0.01%/15 cc. Drop-tainer disp. 15 cc.
Use: Artificial tears.

ULTRAZINE. (Vortech) Prochlorperazine 5 mg./ml. w/preservative & buffer. Vial 10 ml.
Use: I.M. or I.V. as antiemetic, tranquilizer.

ULTRUM. (Towne) Vitamin A 5000 I.U., E 30 I.U., C 90 mg., folic acid 400 mcg., B-1 2.25 mg., B-2 2.6 mg., niacinamide 20 mg., B-6 3 mg., B-12 9 mcg., biotin 45 mcg., D 400 I.U. pantothenic acid 10 mg., Ca 162 mg., P 125 mg., iodine 150 mcg., iron 27 mg., Mg 100 mg., Cu 3 mg., Mn 7.5 mg., K 7.5 mg., zinc 22.5 mg./Tab. Bot. 100s.
Use: Dietary supplement.

ULTRUM WITH SELENIUM. (Towne) Vit. A 5000 I.U., E 30 I.U., C 90 mg., folic acid 2.25 mg., B-1 2.25 mg., B-2 2.6 mg., niacinamide 20 mg., B-6 3 mg., B-12 9 mcg., D 400 I.U., biotin 45 mcg., pantothenic acid 10 mg., Ca 162 mg., P 125 mg., iodine 150 mcg., iron 27 mg., Mg 100 mg., Cu 3 mg., Mn 7.5 mg., K 7.7 mg., Cl 7 mg., molytdinian 15 mcg., Se 15 mcg., zinc 22.5 mg./Tab. Bot. 130 mg.
Use: Dietary supplement.

10-UNDECENOIC ACID. Undecylenic Acid, U.S.P. XXI.

10-UNDECENOIC ACID, ZINC (2+) SALT. Zinc Undecylenate, U.S.P. XXI.

UNDECOYLIUM CHLORIDE-IODINE. 1-[[(2-Hydroxyethyl) carbamoyl]methyl]-pyridimium chloride alkanoates compound with I_2 (1:1). Virac, Prep. (Ruson)
Use: Topical anti-infective.

• **UNDECYLENIC ACID.** U.S.P. XXI. Compound Oint. U.S.P. XXI. 10-Undecenoic acid. (Lannett) Cap. 0.44 Gm., Bot. 100s, 500s, 1000s. Oint. comp. N.F.
Use: Topical antifungal.
See: Desenex Liquid,
Penetrating Foam (Pharmacraft)
W/Benzethonium chloride, benzalkonium chloride, tannic acid, isopropyl alcohol.
See: Tulvex, Liq. (Commerce)
W/Dichlorophene.
See: Fungicidal Talc. (Gordon)
Onychomycetin, Liq. (Gordon)
W/Salicylic acid.
See: Sal-Dex, Liq. (Scrip)
W/Salicylic acid, benzoic acid, sulfur, dichlorophene.
See: Fungicidal Oint. (Gordon)
W/Salicylic acid, dichlorophene, hexachlorophene.
See: Podiaspray, Aerosol Pow. (Dalin)
W/Sod. propionate, sod. caprylate, propionic acid, salicylic acid, copper undecylenate.
See: Verdefam, Sol. (Texas)
W/Zinc undecylenate.
See: Cruex Cream, Spray Pow. (Pharmacraft)
Desenex, Prep. (Pharmacraft)
Ting, Aerosol (Pharmacraft)
Undoguent, Cream (Torch)

UNDECYLENIC ACID SALTS. Calcium, Copper, Zinc.

UNDE-JEN. (Jenkins) Undecylenic acid 5%, zinc undecylenate 20%. Tube 1 oz., lb.

UNDEX CREAM. (Durel) Undecylenic acid 5%, zinc undecylenate 5% in Duromantel cream.
Use: Treatment and prevention of superficial dermatomycoses.

UNDOGUENT. (Torch) Undecylenic acid 5%, zinc undecylenate 20% in a non-greasy, water-washable cream base. Jar. 2 oz., 1 lb.
Use: Antifungal, antiseptic cream.

UNDULANT FEVER DIAGNOSIS. Brucella Abortus Antigen. Brucellergen.

UNGUENTINE OINTMENT "ORIGINAL FORMULA". (Mentholatum) Phenol 1% in ointment base. Tube 1 oz.

Use: Antiseptic, anesthetic for pain relief of minor burns.

UNGUENTINE PLUS FIRST AID CREAM. (Mentholatum) Parachlorometaxylenol 2%, lidocaine HCl 2%, phenol 0.5% in a moisturizing cream base. Tube 1 oz.
Use: Antiseptic, anesthetic for sunburn, minor burns, cuts and insect bites.

UNGUENTINE SPRAY. (Mentholatum) Benzocaine, alcohol. Can 5 oz.
Use: Sunburn, minor burns, itch, cuts and scrapes.

UNGUENTUM BOSSI. (Doak) Ammoniated mercury 5%, hexamethylene tetramine sulfosalicylic acid 2%, tar distillate "Doak" 5%, Doak oil 40%, nonionic emulsifiers 5%, unguentum "Doak" 48%. Tube 2 oz. Jar 16 oz.
Use: Psoriasis.

UNIAD. (Kasar) Isoniazid 100 mg./Tab. Bot. 100s, 1000s.
Use: Tuberculosis.

UNIAD-PLUS. (Kasar) Isoniazid 100 mg. pyridoxine HCl 5 mg. or 10 mg./Tab. Bot. 1000s.
Use: Tuberculosis.

UNIBASE. (Parke-Davis) Water-absorbing oint. base. Jar 1 lb.
Use: Ointment base.

UNICAP. (Upjohn) Vit. A 5000 I.U., D 400 I.U., E 15 I.U., C 60 mg., folic acid 400 mcg., B-1 1.5 mg., B-2 1.7 mg., niacin 20 mg., B-6 2 mg., B-12 6 mcg./Tab. or Cap. **Tab.:** Bot. 90s, 120s. **Cap.** Bot. 90s, 120s, 240s, 1000s.
Use: Multivitamin.

UNICAP JUNIOR CHEWABLE. (Upjohn) Vit. A 5000 I.U., D 400 I.U., E 15 I.U., C 60 mg., folic acid 400 mcg., B-1 1.5 mg., B-2 1.7 mg., niacin 20 mg., B-6 2 mg., B-12 6 mcg./Tab. Bot. 90s, 120s.
Use: Multivitamin.

UNICAP M. (Upjohn) Vit A 5000 I.U., D 400 I.U., E 30 I.U., C 60 mg., folic acid 400 mcg. B-1 1.5 mg., B-2 1.7 mg., niacin 20 mg., B-6 2 mg., B-12 6 mcg., pantothenic acid 10 mg., iodine 150 mcg., Fe 18 mg., Cu 2 mg., Zn 15 mg., Ca 60 mg., P 45 mg., Mn 1 mg., K 5 mg./Tab. Bot. 30s, 90s, 120s, 180s, 500s.
Use: Multiple vitamins with mineral supplement.

UNICAP PLUS IRON. (Upjohn) Vit. A 5000 I.U., D 400 I.U., E 15 I.U., C 60 mg., folic acid 400 mcg., B-1 1.5 mg., B-2 1.7 mg., niacin 20 mg., B-6 2 mg., B-12 6 mcg., pantothenic acid 10 mg., iron 18 mg./Tab. Bot. 90s.
Use: Vitamin supplement with iron.

UNICAP SENIOR. (Upjohn) Vit. A 5000 I.U., D 200 I.U., E 15 I.U., C 60 mg., folic acid 400 mcg., B-1 1.4 mg., B-2 1.7 mg., niacin 16 mg., B-6 2.2 mg., B-12 3 mcg., pantothenic acid 10 mg., iodine 150 mcg., Fe 10 mg., Cu 2 mg., Zn 15 mg., Ca 100 mg., P 77 mg., Mg 30 mg., Mn 1 mg., K 5 mg./Tab. Bot. 90s, 120s.
Use: Supplement to the often deficient diet.

UNICAP T. (Upjohn) Vit. A 5000 I.U., D 400 I.U., E 30 I.U., C 500 mg., folic acid 400 mcg., B-1 10 mg., B-2 10 mg., niacin 100 mg., B-6 6 mg., B-12 8 mcg., pantothenic acid 25 mg., iodine 150 mcg., Fe 18 mg., Cu 2 mg., Zn 15 mg., Mn 1 mg., K 5 mg., Se 10 mg./Tab. Bot. 60s, 500s.
Use: Nutritional deficiencies.

UNIFAST UNICELLES. (Reid-Provident) Phentermin HCl 30 mg./Cap. Bot. 100s.
Use: Appetite suppressant.

UNILAX. (Ascher) Danthron 75 mg., docusate sodiun 150 mg./Tab. Pkg. 10s, 20s. Bot. 60s, 100s.
Use: Laxative, stool softener.

UNIMYCIN DIHYDRATE. Oxytetracycline, B.A.N.

UNIPEN. (Wyeth) Sodium nafcillin **Cap.** 250 mg. Bot. 100s. Redipak 100s. **Tab.** 500 mg. Bot. 50s. Cap. and Tab. buffered w/calcium carbonate. **Inj.** 500 mg./Vial, 10s. Buffered to make 2 cc. 1 Gm., 2 Gm. **Vial:** Piggyback Vials 1 Gm., 1.5 Gm., 2 Gm., 4 Gm. Bulk vial 10 Gm. **Oral Sol.** w/alcohol 2% 250 mg./5 cc. Bot. to make 100 cc.
Use: Treatment of infections.

UNIPHYL TABLETS. (Purdue Frederick) Theophylline 200 mg. or 400 mg./Controlled-Released Tab. Bot 60s.
Use: Relief/prevention of asthma symptoms and bronchial spasms.

UNIPRES. (Reid-Provident) Hydralazine HCl 25 mg., hydrochlorothiazide 15 mg., reserpine 0.1 mg./Tab. Bot. 100s, 1000s.
Use: Anti-hypertension.

UNISOL. (CooperVision) Sterile, preservative-free saline solution. Vials 15 ml. Box 10s, 25s.
Use: Rinsing, heat disinfection and storage of soft contact lenses.

UNISOL 4. (CooperVision) Sterile saline sol. for all soft lenses. Bot. 4 oz. Box 2s.
Use: Rinsing, heat disinfection & storage of soft lenses.

UNISOM. (Leeming) Doxylamine succcinate 25 mg./Tab. Blister 8s, 16s, 32s.
Use: Sleep aid.

UNITENSEN AQUEOUS INJECTION. (Wallace) Cryptenamine 260 CSR units/ml. w/chlorobutanol 0.5%, NaCl 0.8%. Amp. 2 ml. 5s.
Use: Hypertensive crises.

UNITENSEN TABLETS.. (Wallace) Cryptenamine 2 mg./Tab. Bot. 100s, 500s.
Use: Anti-hypertensive.

UNNA'S BOOT.
See: Zinc Gelatin, U.S.P. XXI.

UNPROCO CAPSULES. (Reid-Provident) Dextromethorphan HBr 30 mg., guaifenesin 200 mg./Cap. Bot. 100s.
Use: Antitussive, expectorant.

■ **UNSATURATED ACIDS.**
See: Fatty acids, unsaturated; fats, unsaturated.

UPLEX. (Arcum) Vit. A 5000 I.U., D 400 I.U., B-1 3 mg., B-2 3 mg., B-6 1 mg., B-12 2.5 mcg., nicotinamide 20 mg., calcium pantothenate 5 mg., Vit. C 50 mg./Cap. Bot. 100s, 1000s.
Use: Dietary supplement.

UPLEX NO. 2. (Arcum) Vit. A palmitate 10,000 I.U., D 400 I.U., B-1 5 mg., B-2 5 mg., C 100 mg., B-6 2 mg.,

B-12 3 mcg., E 2.5 I.U., niacinamide 25 mg., ca pantothenate 5 mg./Cap. Bot. 100s, 1000s.
Use: Dietary supplement.

URABETH TABS. (Major) Bethanecol 10 mg./Tab. Bot. 250s; 25 mg./Tab. Bot. 250s, 1000s; 5 mg./Tab. Bot. 100s.
Use: Parasympathomimetic.

URACEL. (Vortech) Sod. salicylate 324 mg./Tab. Bot. 1000s.
Use: Analgesic.

URACID. (Wesley) dl-Methionine 0.2 Gm./Cap. Bot. 100s, 1000s.
Use: Diaper Rash.

• **URACIL MUSTARD,** U.S.P. XXI. Cap., U.S.P. XXI. 5-[Bis(2-Chloroethyl)amino]uracil. (Upjohn) 1.0 mg./Cap. Bot. 50s.
Use: Antineoplastic.

URADAL.
See: Carbromal (Various Mfr.)

URALENE TABLETS. (Sutliff & Case) Methenamine 40.8 mg., atropine sulfate 0.03 mg., hyoscyamine sulfate 0.03 mg., salol 18.1 mg., benzoic acid 4.5 mg., methylene blue 5.4 mg./Tab. Bot. 1000s.
Use: Urinary antiseptic.

URAMINE. (Kay) Atropine sulfate 0.03 mg., hyoscyamine 0.03 mg., methenamine 40.8 mg., methylene blue 5 4 mg., phenyl salicylate 18.1 mg., benzoic acid 4.5 mg./Tab. Bot. 1000s.
Use: Urinary antiseptic.

URAMUSTINE. B.A.N. 5-Di-(2-chloroethyl) aminouracil.
Use: Antineoplastic agent.

URANAP. (Vortech) dl-Methionine 0.2 Gm./Cap. Bot. 100s.
Use: Control of diaper rash.

URANTOIN. Nitrofurantoin, B.A.N.

URAPINE TABS. (Major) Bot. 1000s.
Use: Urinary analgesic.

URDEX. (Pharmex) Phenylpropanolamine 12.5 mg., atropine sulfate 0.2 mg., chlorpheniramine 5 mg./cc. Vial 10 cc.

• **UREA,** U.S.P. XXI. Sterile U.S.P. XXI. Carbamide (Various Mfr.)
Use: Topically for dry skin.
See: Aquacare, Cream, Lot. (Herbert)
Aqucare-HP, Cream, Lot. (Herbert)
Artra Ashy Skin Cream (Plough)
Calmurid, Cream (Pharmacia)
Carmol, Cream (Ingram)
Carmol Ten Lotion (Ingram)
Elaqua 10% or 20%, Cream (Elder)
Gormel Cream (Gordon)
Nutraplus, Cream, Lot. (Owen)
Rea-lo, Lot. (Whorton)
W/Benzocaine, benzyl alcohol, p-chloro-m-xylenol, propylene glycol.
See: 20-Cain Burn Relief, Bot. (Alto)
W/Hydrocortisone acetate
See: Carmol-HC, Cream (Ingram)
W/Glycerin.
See: Kerid Ear Drops, Liq. (Blair)
W/Sulfur colloidal, red mercuric sulfide.
See: Teenac Cream, Oint. (Elder)
W/Zinc oxide, sulfur, salicylic acid, benzalkonium chloride, isopropyl alcohol.
See: Akne Drying Lotion, Bot. (Alto)

UREACIN-10 LOTION. (Pedinol) Urea 10%. Bot. 8 oz.
Use: Moisturizing and softening lotion for dry, hard, rough, hardened skin.

UREACIN-20 CREME. (Pedinol) Urea 20%. Jars 2.5 oz.
Use: Moisturizing and softening cream for dry, hard skin when extra penetration needed; eradication of plantar keratoma.

UREACIN-40 CREME. (Pedinol) Urea 40%. Jar 1 oz.
Use: Nail destruction and dissolution.

UREA PEROXIDE.

UREAPHIL. (Abbott) Sterile urea 40 Gm., citric acid 1 mg./150 ml. Bot. 150 ml.
Use: Osmotic dehydrating agent.

URECHOLINE. (Merck Sharp & Dohme) Bethanechol Chloride Inj., 5 mg./ml., Vial 1 ml. 6s. Tab. 5 mg., 10 mg., 25 mg., 50 mg. Bot. 100s. Unit-Dose 100s.
Use: Parasympathomimetic.

• **UREDEPA.** USAN. Ethyl[bis(1-aziridinyl)-phos-phinyl]-carbamate.
Use: Anti-neoplastic.
See: Avinar (Armour)

p-UREIDOBENZENEARSONIC ACID.
See: Carbarsone, U.S.P. XXI.

• **UREDOFOS.** USAN.
Use: Anthelmintic.
See: Sansalid (Beecham)

URELIEF. (Rocky Mtn.) Methenamine 2 gr., salol 0.5 gr., methylene blue 1/10 gr., benzoic acid 1/8 gr., hyoscyamine sulfate 1/2000 gr., atropine sulfate 1/1000 gr./Tab. Bot. 100s.
Use: Urinary anti-infective.

URELIM. Ethebenecid, B.A.N.

UREMIDE. (Mallard) Phenylazodiaminopyridine HCl 50 mg., sulfamethazole 250 mg./Tab. Bot. 50s.
Use: Analgesic, antibacterial, antispasmodic.

URESE. (Roerig)
See: Benzthianide.

URETHAN. Ethyl Carbamate, Ethyl Urethan, Urethane.
Use: Antineoplastic.

UREX TABLETS. (Riker) Methenamine hippurate 1 Gm./Tab. Bot. 100s, 500s.
Use: Urinary anti-infective.

URICOSURIC AGENTS.
See: Anturane, Tab., Cap. (Geigy)
Benemid, Tab. (Merck Sharp & Dohme)
Col BENEMID, Tab. (Merck Sharp & Dohme)

U.R.I. (Sig) Atropine sulfate 0.2 mg., chlorpheniramine maleate 5 mg., phenylpropanolamine HCl 12.5 mg./ml. Vial 10 ml.
Use: Symptomatic relief of colds.

URIC ACID REAGENT STRIPS. (Ames) Seralyzer reagent strip. Bot. 25s.
Use: A quantitative strip test for uric acid in serum or plasma.

URIDINAL. (Crystal) Phenylazodiamino pyridine HCl 1.5 gr./Tab. Bot. 100s.
Use: Urinary antiseptic.

URIDINAL-S. (Crystal) Tab. Bot. 100s.

4-[3-[2-(TRIFLUOROMETHYL)PHENOTHIAZIN-10-YL]PROPYL]-1-PIPERAZINEETHANOL. Fluphenazine or Enanthate Hydrochloride.

URIDINE, 2-DEOXY-5-IODO-. Idoxuridine, U.S.P. XXI.

URIDIUM. (Ferndale; Pharmex) Phenylazodiamine pyridine HCl 75 mg., sulfacetamide 250 mg./Tab. Bot. 30s, 100s, 1000s. (Ferndale) 100s.
Use: Urinary antiseptic.

URIFON. (T.E. Williams) Sulfamethizole 500 mg./Tab. Bot. 100s, 1000s.

URIFON-FORTE. (T.E. Williams) Sulfamethizole 450 mg., phenazopyridine HCl 50 mg./Cap. Bot. 100s, 1000s.

URIGEN. (Fellows) Calcium mandelate 0.2 Gm., methenamine 0.2 Gm., phenazopyridine HCl 50 mg., sodium phosphate 80 mg./Cap. Bot. 100s, 1000s.

URILENE. (Crystal) Tab. Bot. 100s.

URINARY ANTISEPTIC #2 S.C.T. (Lemmon) Atropine sulfate 0.03 mg., hyoscyamine sulfate 0.03 mg., methenamine 40.8 mg., methylene blue 5.4 mg., phenyl salicylate 18.1 mg., benzoic acid 4.5 mg./Tab. Bot. 100s, 1000s.
Use: Urinary antiseptic.

URINE.
See: Diagnostic agents

URINE SUGAR TEST.
See: Clinistix (Ames)

URIN-TEK. (Ames) Tubes, plastic caps, adhesive labels, collection cups, and disposable tube holder. Package 100×5.

URIPREL. (Pasadena Research) Methenamine 40.8 mg., atropine sulfate 0.03 mg., hyoscyamine sulfate 0.03 mg., salol 18.1 mg., benzoic acid 4.5 mg., methylene blue 5.4 mg., gelsemium 6.1 mg./Tab. Bot. 100s, 1000s.

URISAN-P. (Sandia) Atropine sulfate 0.03 mg., hyoscyamine 0.03 mg., gelsemium 6.1 mg., methenamine 40.8 mg., salol 18.1 mg., benzoic acid 4.5 mg., methylene blue 5.4 mg., phenylazodiaminopyridine HCl 100 mg./Tab. Bot. 100s, 1000s.
Use: Urinary antiseptic, analgesic.

URISED. (Webcon) Atropine sulfate 0.03 mg., hyoscyamine 0.03 mg., methenamine 40.8 mg., methylene blue 5.4 mg., benzoic acid 4.5 mg., phenyl salicylate 18.1 mg./Tab. Bot. 100s, 500s, 1000s.
Use: Relief of pain in urinary infections.

URISEDAMINE. (Webcon) Methenamine mandelate 500 mg., l-hyoscyamine 0.15 mg./Tab. Bot. 100s.
Use: G.U. antiseptic & antispasmodic.

URISEPT. (Robinson) Urinary antiseptic Tab. Bot. 100s, 1000s.

URISPAS. (SmithKline) Flavoxate HCl 100 mg./Tab. Bot. 100s. Unit Dose 100s.
Use: Urinary antispasmodic.

URISTIX REAGENT STRIPS. (Ames) Firm paper two-test strip. Proteinuria: Yellow tip-tetrabromphenol blue. Glycosuria: Red tip-glucose oxidase. Bot. 100s.
Use: Dip and read test for protein and glucose in urine.

URITABS. (Vortech) Atropine sulfate 0.03 mg., hyoscyamine 0.03 mg., methenamine 40.8 mg., salol 18.1 mg., benzoic acid 4.5 mg., methylene blue 5.4 mg./Tab. Bot. 100s, 1000s.
Use: Urinary tract antiseptic.

URITHOL. (Forest) Methenamine 40.8 mg., Methylene blue 5.4 mg., benzoic acid 4.5 mg., atropine sulfate 0.03 mg., hyoscyamine 0.03 mg., salol 18.1 mg./Tab. Bot. 100s.
Use: Cystitis, pyelitis, urethritis.

URITIN. (Richlyn) **Purple:** Methenamine 40.8 mg., atropine sulfate 0.03 mg., hyoscyamine sulfate 0.03 mg., salol 18.1 mg., benzoic acid 4.5 mg., methylene blue 5.4 mg., gelsemium 6.1 mg./Tab. Bot. 1000s.

URITIN FORMULA. (Vangard) Atropine sulfate 0.03 mg., hyoscyamine 0.03 mg., methenamine 40.8 mg., methylene blue 5.4 mg., phenyl salicylate 18.1 mg., benzoic acid 4.5 mg./Tab. Bot. 1000s.
Use: Urinary antiseptic.

URITIN MODIFIED FORMULA. (Wolins) Methenamine 40.8 mg., atropine sulfate 0.03 mg., hyoscyamine sulfate 0.03 mg., salol 18.1 mg., benzoic acid 4.5 mg., methylene blue 5.4 mg./Tab. Bot. 1000s.

URITIN TABLETS. (Goldline) Bot. 100s.

URITROL. (Kenyon) Atropine sulfate 0.03 mg., hyoscyamine 0.03 mg., gelsemium 6.1 mg., methenamine 40.8 mg., salol 18.1 mg., benzoic acid 4.5 mg., methylene blue 5.4 mg./Tab. Bot. 100s, 1000s. Double Strength Tabs. Bot. 100s, 1000s.

URIZOLE. (Jenkins) Sulfisoxazole 7.7 gr./Tab. Bot. 1000s.

UROBILISTIX REAGENT STRIPS. (Ames) p-Dimethylaminobenzaldehyde in an acid buffer. Bot. 50s, strips.
Use: Dip and read test for urine urobilinogen.

UROBIOTIC. (Roerig) Oxytetracycline as the HCl equiv. to 250 mg. oxytetracycline, sulfamethizole 250 mg., phenazopyridine HCl 50 mg./Cap. Bot. 50s. Unit-dose pack. Box 100s.
Use: Urinary tract infections.

URODINE. (Interstate) Phenazo pyridine HCl 100 mg./Tab. Bot. 1000s.
Use: Urinary analgesic and antiseptic.

URODINE. (Kenyon) Phenylazodiaminopyridine HCl 100 mg./Tab. Bot. 100s, 1000s.
Use: Urinary analgesic and antiseptic.

URODINE. (Robinson) Phenylazo-diamino-pyridine HCl 1.5 gr./Tab. Bot. 100s, 1000s.
Use: Urinary antiseptic.

UROGESIC. (Edwards) Phenazopyridine HCl 100 mg., hyoscyamine HBr 0.12 mg., atropine sulfate 0.08 mg., scopolamine HBr 0.003 mg./Tab. Bot. 100s, 500s.
Use: Analgesic for urinary tract disturbances.

■ **UROGRAPHY AGENTS.**
See: Diodrast
Iodohippurate Sodium, Inj.
Iodopyracet
Iodopyracet Compound

Methiodal, Inj.
Renografin (Squibb)
Renovist (Squibb)
Renovue (Squibb)
Sodium Acetrizoate, Inj.
Sodium Iodomethamate, Inj.

UROKINASE. USAN. Plasminogen activator isolated from human kidney tissue.
Use: Plasminogen activator.

RO-KP-NEUTRAL. (Star) Sodium (as dibasic sodium phosphate) 1361 mg., potassium 298.6 mg., phosphorous (as dibasic potassium phosphate) 1037 mg./6 Tabs. Bot. 100s.
Use: Treatment of oxalate renal calculi.

ROLENE BLUE. (Star) Methylene blue 65 mg./Tab. Bot. 100s, 1000s.
Use: Urinary antiseptic & stimulant to mucous membrane surfaces.

ROLOGIC SOL G. (Abbott) Bot. 1000 ml.
Use: Irrigating solution.

ROLUCOSIL. Sulphamethizole, B.A.N.
See: Thiosulfi, Preps. (Ayerst)

RO-MAG. (Blaine) Magnesium oxide 140 mg./Cap. Bot. 100s, 1000s.
Use: Antacid; calcium oxalate urinary stone prevention.

ROMIDE. (Edwards) Salicylamide 0.667 Gm./Tab. Bot. 100s, 500s.
Use: Prevention of calcium-containing urinary calculi.

RONAL.
See: Barbital (Various Mfr.)

RO-PHOSPHATE. (Poythress) Sod. acid phosphate 500 mg., methenamine 300 mg./S.C. Tab. Bot. 100s, 1000s.
Use: Urinary antiseptic.

ROQID-ACID. (Beach) Methenamine mandelate 350 mg., sodium acid phosphate 200 mg./Tab. Bot. 100s, 500s.
Use: Urinary acidifier, antibacterial, antiseptic.

ROQID-ACID NO. 2. (Beach) Methenamine mandelate 500 mg., sodium acid phosphate 500 mg./Tab. Bot. 100s, 500s.
Use: Urinary acidifier, antiseptic.

ROSCREEN. (Warner-Lambert) 2,3,5, Triphenyltetrazolium chloride. Individual test tubes containing dry, buffered tetrazolium reagent for in-vitro testing of urine. Each tube is calibrated at the 2 cc. level. Boxes 12s, 50s.
Use: Diagnostic agent for urinary infection.

ROTROL. (Mills) Sulfacetamide 250 mg., sulfamethizole 250 mg., phenazopyridine HCl 50 mg./Tab. Bot. 100s.
Use: Urinary tract infection and pain.

ROTROPIN NEW. Methenamine Anhydromethylene Citrate (Various Mfr.)

ROVIST CYSTO. (Berlex) Diatrizoate meglumine 300 mg., edetate calcium disodium 0.05 mg./ml. Bot.: 500 ml. dilution bot. w/300 ml. soln.
Use: Diagnostic radiopaque medium intended for instillation.

UROVIST CYSTO PEDIATRIC. (Berlex) Diatrizoate meglumine 300 mg., edetate calcium disodium 0.05 mg./ml. Bot.: 300 ml. dilution bot. w/100 ml. soln.
Use: Diagnostic radiopaque medium intended for instillation.

UROVIST MEGLUMINE DIU/CT. (Berlex) Diatrizoate meglumine 300 mg., edetate calcium disodium 0.05 mg./ml. Bot. 300 ml. Ctn. 10s.
Use: Diagnostic radiopaque medium for parenteral use.

UROVIST SODIUM 300. (Berlex) Diatrizoate sodium 500 mg., edetate calcium disodium 0.1 mg./ml. Vial 50 ml. Box 10s.
Use: Diagnostic radiopaque medium for parenteral use.

URSINUS INLAY-TABS. (Dorsey) Calcium carbaspirin (equivalent to aspirin 300 mg.), phenylpropanolamine HCl 25 mg., pheniramine maleate 12.5 mg. pyrilamine maleate 12.5 mg./Tab. Bot. 24s, 100s.
Use: Analgesic, decongestant.

URSULFADINE NO. 1. (Kenyon) Phenylazodiaminopyridine HCl 50 mg., sulfacetamide 250 mg./Tab. Bot. 100s, 1000s.

UTEN CAPSULES. Papaveroline, B.A.N.

UTICILLIN VK. (Upjohn) Penicillin V Potassium 250 mg./Tab. Bot. 1000s, 500 mg./Tab. Bot. 100s.
Use: Penicillin susceptible infections.

UTICORT GEL. (Parke-Davis) Betamethasone benzoate 0.025% in solubilized gel base. Tubes 15 Gm., 60 Gm.
Use: Relief of inflammatory manifestations of corticosteroid responsive dermatoses.

UTICORT CREAM. (Parke-Davis) Betamethasone benzoate 0.025%. Tube 15 Gm., 60 Gm.
Use: Relief of inflammatory manifestations of corticosteroid responsive dermatoses.

UTICORT LOTION. (Parke-Davis) Betamethasone benzoate 0.025%. Bot. 15 ml., 60 ml.
Use: Relief of inflammatory manifestations of corticosteroid responsive dermatoses.

UTICORT OINTMENT. (Parke-Davis) Betamethasone benzoate 0.025%. Tube 15 Gm., 60 Gm.
Use: Relief of inflammatory manifestations of corticosteroid responsive dermatoses.

UTIMOX, (Parke-Davis) Amoxicillin trihydrate **Cap.:** 250 mg., or 500mg./Cap. Bot. 100s, 500s. Unit dose 100s. **Oral susp.:** 125 mg. or 250 mg./5 ml. Bot. 80 ml, 100 ml., 150 ml., 200 ml.
Use: Antibiotic.

U-TRACT. (Bowman) Atropine sulfate 0.03 mg., hyoscyamine sulfate 0.03 mg., methenamine 40.8 mg., methylene blue 5.4 mg., phenylsalicylate 18.1 mg., benzoic acid 4.5 mg./Tab. Bot. 100s, 1000s.
Use: Treatment urinary tract infections.

U-TRAN. (Scruggs) Atropine sulfate 0.03 mg., hyoscyamine 0.03 mg., methenamine 40.80 mg., benzoic acid 4.50 mg., salol 18.10 mg., methylene blue 5.40 mg./Tab. Bot. 100s, 1000s.

U-TRI SPEC FORMULA OINTMENT. (U-Tri) Oint. Tube 4 oz., 8 oz. Jar 4 oz., 8 oz.
Use: Athletics, muscular aches and pains, colds.

UVALERAL.
See: Bromisovalum.
UVASAL POWDER. (Winthrop Products) Sodium bicarbonate, tartaric acid.
Use: Antacid.
UVA URSI. Leaves. (Sherwood Labs.) Fluid ext. Bot. pt., gal.
W/Buchu leaves, corn silk, juniper, caffeine.
See: Diuretane #1, Tab. (Wolins)
UVIBAN. Sodium Actinoquinol.
Use: Treatment of flash burns. (ophthalmic)
UVINUL MS-40. (General Aniline & Film)
See: Sulisobenzone.
UVISTAT. Mexenone, B.A.N.

V

VABRA ASPIRATOR. (CooperVision) Sterile uterine curette, diameter 3 mm., Disposable.
Use: Endometrial screening.
VACCINE, MUMPS. Mumps Virus Vaccine Live, U.S.P. XXI.
• **VACCINE, PERTUSSIS.** Pertussis Vaccine, U.S.P. XXI.
Use: Active immunizing agent.
• **VACCINE, PERTUSSIS, ADSORBED.** Pertussis Vaccine Adsorbed, U.S.P. XXI.
Use: Active immunizing agent.
See: Pertussis Vaccine, Aluminum Hydroxide Adsorbed
• **VACCINE, PERTUSSIS, ALUM PRECIPITATED.**
Use: Active immunizing agent.
See: Pertussis Vaccine, Alum Precipitated (Various Mfr.)
• **VACCINE, POLIOMYELITIS.** Poliovirus Vaccine Inactivated, U.S.P. XXI.
Use: Active immunizing agent.
• **VACCINE, RABIES (DUCK EMBRYO),** Rabies Vaccine U.S.P. XXI.
Use: Active immunizing agent.
• **VACCINE, SMALLPOX.** Smallpox Vaccine, U.S.P. XXI.
Use: Active immunizing agent.
VACCINE, WHOOPING COUGH. Pertussis Vaccine, U.S.P. XXI.
Use: Active immunizing agent.
• **VACCINIA IMMUNE GLOBULIN,** U.S.P. XXI. (Hyland) Gamma globulin fraction of serum of healthy adults recently immunized w/vaccinia virus 16.5%. Vial 5 ml.
Use: Prevention or modification of smallpox or vaccinia infections; passive immunizing agent.
VACOCIN. Under study.
Use: Antibiotic.
VACON. (Scherer) Phenylephrine HCl 0.20% with benzalkonium chloride. Nasal solution, Bot. 1 oz. Drops 1 oz.
Use: Nasal decongestant.
VAGACREME. (Delta) Sulfanilamide 12%, sulfacetamide 3%, 9-aminoacridine HCl 0.2%, allantoin 1.5%. Tube 4 oz. w/appl.
Use: Vaginitis.
VAGICREAM. (Vortech) Sulfanilamide 15%, 9-aminoacridine HCl 0.2%, allantoin 1.5%. Tube 4 oz.
Use: Vaginitis and non-specific vaginal infections.
VAGILIA CREAM. (Lemmon) Sulfisoxazole 10%, aminacrine HCl 0.2%, allantoin 2% in a water-miscible base w/stearic acid, mineral oil, polysorbate 60, sorbitan monostearate, sorbitol, methylparaben, propylparaben, purified water. Cream, Tube 90 Gm.
Use: Treatment of vaginitis and cervicitis.
VAGILLA SUPPOSITORIES. (Lemmon) Sulfisoxazole 600 mg., aminacrine HCl 12 mg., allantoin 120 mg./Supp. Box 16s.
Use: Treatment of vaginitis, cervicitis.
VAGILIA TRIPLE SULFA. (Lemmon) Sulfathiazole 3.42%, sulfacetamide 2.86%, sulfabenzamide 3.7%, urea 0.64% in cream base. Tube 78 Gm.
Use: Vaginal infection.
VAGINEX CREME. (Schmidt) Benzocaine and resorcinol in cream base.
Use: Antipruritic for feminine itching.
VAGISAN CREME. (Sandia) Sulfanilamide 15%, 9-aminoacridine HCl 0.2%, allantoin 1.5%. In a dispersible base. Tube 4 oz. w/applicator.
VAGISEC. (Schmid) Polyoxyethylene nonyl phenol, sodium ethylenediaminetetraacetate, docusate sodium. Plastic Bot. 4 oz. Liquid, Packettes, 12s.
Use: Trichomonacide.
VAGISEC PLUS SUPPOSITORIES. (Schmid) Polyoxyethylene nonyl phenol 0.175%, sodium edetate 0.022%, docusate sodium 0.0024%, 9-aminoacridine HCl 0.2%, in a polyethylene glycol base w/glycerin and citric acid. Box 28s.
VAGISUL CREME. (Sheryl) Sulfanilamide 15%, aminoacridine 0.2%, allantoin 1.5%. Tube 4 oz.
Use: Vaginitis, cervicitis and post-cauterization therapy.
VAGITROL CREAM. (Lemmon) Sulfanilamide 15%, aminacrine HCl 0.2%, allantoin 2%. w/lactose, stearic acid, cetyl alcohol, triethanolamine, sod. lauryl sulfate, glycerin, methylparaben and propylparaben as preservatives, buffered w/lactic acid to a pH of approximately 4.5. Tube 4 oz.
Use: Vaginitis treatment.
VAGITROL NEW FORMULA CREAM. (Lemmon) Sulfanilamide 15% in cream base. Tube 113 Gm.
Use: Vaginal infections.
VALACET. (Vale) Hyoscyamus 10.8 mg., aspirin 259.2 mg., caffeine anhydrous 16.2 mg., gelsemium ext. 0.6 mg./Tab. or Cap. Bot. 100s, 1000s, 5000s.
VALADOL. (Squibb) Acetaminophen. **Tabs.:** 5 gr. Bot. 100s, 500s. **Liq.:** (w/alcohol 9%) 120 mg./5 cc. Bot. 4 oz.
Use: Aspirin substitute.
VALAX. (Vale) Danthron 37.5 mg., docusate sodium 100 mg./Tab. Bot. 100s, 1000s.
Use: Laxative, fecal softener.
VALCAPS. (Roche) Diazepam 2 mg., 5 mg., 10 mg./Cap. Box 100s. Limited marketing.
Use: Anxiety disorders; tension, anxiety, apprehension and fatigue associated with psychoneurotic states; acute alcohol withdrawal; skeletal muscle spasms; etc.

VALDRENE. (Vale) Diphenhydramine HCl 50 mg./Tab. Bot. 100s, 1000s, 5000s.
Use: Antihistamine.

VALDRENE EXPECTORANT. (Vale) Diphenhydramine HCl 80 mg., ammonium chloride 778 mg., sod. citrate 324 mg., menthol 6.5 mg./30 ml. w/alcohol 5%. Syr. Bot. 3 oz., pt., gal.
Use: Antitussive.

VALERGEN. (Hyrex) Estradiol valerate 10 mg., 20 mg., 40 mg./ml. Vial 10 ml.

VALERIAN. (Lilly) Tincture, alcohol 68%. Bot. 4 fl. oz., 16 fl. oz.

W/Phenobarbital, passiflora, hyoscyamus.
See: Aluro, Tab. (Foy)

VALERTEST. (Hyrex) **No. 1:** Estradiol valerate 4 mg., testosterone enanthate 90 mg./cc. Vial 10 cc. **No. 2:** Double strength. Vial 10 cc. Amp. 2 cc., 10s.
Use: Combined estrogen and androgen therapy.

VALETHAMATE BROMIDE, 2-Diethylaminoethyl 3-methyl-2-phenylvalerate methylbromide. Di-ethyl(2-hydroxyethyl)methyl-ammonium bromide 3-methyl-2-phenylvalerate. Murel.
Use: Anticholinergic.

VALIHIST. (Otis Clapp) Phenylephrine HCl, chlorpheniramine maleate, caffeine, acetaminophen/Tab. Sugar, lactose and salt free. Safety paks 500s.
Use: Decongestant, antihistaminic and analgesic for cold, sinus amd hay fever relief.

• **VALINE,** U.S.P. XXI. $C_5H_{11}NO_2$ as L-valine.
Use: Amino acid.

L-VALINE, 3-MERCAPTO-. Penicillamine, U.S.P. XXI.

VALISONE. (Schering) Betamethasone valerate. **Cream:** 1 mg./Gm. Hydrophilic cream of water, mineral oil, petrolatum, polyethylene glycol 1000 monocetyl ether, cetostearyl alcohol, monobasic sod. phosphate, phosphoric acid, 4-chloro-m-cresol as preservative. Tube 15 Gm., 45 Gm., 110 Gm. **Oint.:** 1 mg./Gm. Base of liquid and white petrolatum and hydrogenated lanolin. Tube 15 Gm., 45 Gm. **Lotion:** 1 mg./Gm. w/isopropyl alcohol 47.5%, water slightly thickened w/carboxy vinyl polymer, pH adjusted w/sod. hydroxide. Bot. 20 ml., 60 ml. **Reduced Strength Cream 0.01%:** Hydrophilic cream of water, mineral oil, petrolatum, polyethylene glycol 1000 monocetyl ether, cetostearyl alcohol, monobasic sod. phosphate, phosphoric acid, 4-chloro-m-cresol as preservative. Tubes 15 Gm. 60 Gm.
Use: Anti-inflammatory dermatological.

VALIUM TABLETS. (Roche) Diazepam. 2 mg., 5 mg., or 10 mg./Tab. Bot. 100s, 500s. Tel-E-Dose 100s (10 ×10), (4×25) RPN (Reverse Numbered Packages); Prescription Paks 50s, 500s.
Use: Anxiety disorders; tension, anxiety, apprehension and fatigue associated with psychoneurotic states; acute alcohol withdrawal; skeletal muscle spasms; etc.

VALIUM INJECTABLE. (Roche) Diazepam 5 mg./ml. w/propylene glycol 40%, ethyl alcohol 10%, sodium benzoate, benzoic acid 5%, benzyl alcohol 1.5%. Amps. 2 ml. 10s. Vial 10 ml. Box 1s; Tel-E-Ject (Disposable syringes) 2 ml., Box 10s.
Use: Anxiety disorders; tension, anxiety, apprehension and fatigue associated with psychoneurotic states; acute alcohol withdrawal; skeletal muscle spasms; etc.

VALLERGAN. Trimeprazine, B.A.N.

VALLERGINE.
See: Promethazine HCl, U.S.P. XXI.

VALMID. (Dista) Ethinamate. Pulvule 500 mg. Bot. 100s.
Use: Nonbarbiturate sedative.

VALMIDATE. Ethinamate, B.A.N.

• **VALNOCTAMIDE.** USAN.
Use: Tranquilizer.
See: Axiquel (McNeil)

VALOID HYDROCHLORIDE. Cyclizine, B.A.N.

VALORIN. (Otis Clapp) Acetaminophen 325 mg./Tab. Sugar and salt free. Safety packs 500s. Aidpacks 100s.
Use: Analgesic, antipyretic.

VALORIN EXTRA. (Otis Clapp) Acetaminophen 500 mg./Tab. Sugar, lactose and salt free. Safety packs 500s. Aidpacks 100s.
Use: Extra strength non-aspirin analgesic, antipyretic.

VALORIN SUPER. (Otis Clapp) Acetaminophen 500 mg./Tab. Caffeine, sugar, salt, lactose free. Safety packs 500s.
Use: Maximum strength analgesic, antipyretic.

VALPIN 50. (Du Pont) Anisotropine methyl-bromide 50 mg./Tab. Bot. 100s, 1000s.
Use: Antispasmodic, anticholinergic.

VALPIN 50-PB. (Du Pont) Anisotropine methylbromide 50 mg. with phenobarbital 15 mg./Tab. Bot. 100s, 1000s.
Use: Anticholinergic.

VALPIPAMATE METHYLSULFATE.
See: Pentapiperide Methylsulfate.

• **VALPROATE SODIUM.** USAN.
Use: Anticonvulsant.

• **VALPROIC ACID,** U.S.P. XXI. Cap., Syrup, U.S.P. XXI. 2-Propylpentanoic acid.
Use: Anticonvulsant.
See: Depakene, Cap. Liq. (Abbott)

VALRELEASE. (Roche) Diazepam 15 mg./S.R. Cap. Pk 30s, Bot. 100s.
Use: Relief of anxiety.

VANADRYX TR. (Vangard) Dexbrompheniramine maleate 6 mg., psuedoephedrine sulfate 120 mg./Tab. Bot. 100s, 500s.
Use: Antihistamine, decongestant.

VANCENASE NASAL INHALER. (Schering) Metered-dose aerosol unit containing beclomethasone dipropionate in propellants. Each actuation delivers 42 mcg. Canister 16.8 Gm.w/nasal adapter.
Use: Treatment of seasonal or perennial rhinitis.

VANCERIL INHALER. (Schering) Metered-dose aerosol unit of beclomethasone dipropionate in propellants. Each actuation delivers 42 mcg. of beclomethasone dipropionate. Canister 16.8 Gm. w/oral adapter. Box 1s.
Use: Treatment of chronic bronchial asthma.

VANCOCIN HCl. (Lilly) Vancomycin HCl Vial: 500 mg./10 ml. Rubber-stoppered Vial. 10 ml. Pow. Bot. 6 Gm., 10 Gm.
Use: Severe resistant infections.

• **VANCOMYCIN HCl,** U.S.P. XXI. For Oral Soln., Sterile, U.S.P. XXI. An antibiotic from *Streptomyces orientalis.*
Use: (I.V.) Gram-positive (staph.) infection; antibacterial.
See: Vancocin HCl, Preps. (Lilly)

VANDID. Ethamivan, B.A.N.

• **VANILLA.** N.F. XVI. Tinct. N.F. XVI.
Use: Pharmaceutic acid (flavor).

VANILLAL.
See: Ethyl Vanillin.

• **VANILLIN,** N.F. XVI. 4-Hydroxy-3-methoxy-benzaldehyde.
Use: Pharmaceutic aid (flavor).

VANIROME.
See: Ethyl Vanillin.

VANODONNAL TIMECAPS. (Drug Industries) Phenobarbital 50 mg., atropine sulfate 0.0582 mg., hyoscyamine sulfate 0.311 mg., hyoscine hydrobromide 0.0195 mg./S.R. Cap. Bot. 100s.
Use: Long-acting antispasmodic and sedative.

VANOXIDE. (Dermik) Benzoyl peroxide 5% w/propylene glycol, hydroxy-ethylcellulose, FD & C color, cholesterol-sterol, cetyl alcohol, propylene glycol stearate, polysorbate 20, lanolin alcohol, propylparaben, decyl oleate, purcelline oil syn., antioxidants, vegetable oil, methylparaben, tetrasodium EDTA, buffers, cyclohexanediamine tetraacetic acid, calcium phosphate, silicone emulsion, silica. Bot. 25 Gm., 50 Gm.
Use: Severe, recalcitrant acne.

VANOXIDE-HC. (Dermik) Hydrocortisone alcohol 0.5%, benzoyl peroxide 5%/25 Gm. in lotion w/same ingredients as Vanoxide. Bot. 25 Gm.
Use: Severe, recalcitrant acne.

VANQUIN. Viprynium Embonate, B.A.N.

VANQUISH. (Glenbrook) Aspirin 227 mg., acetaminophen 194 mg., caffeine 33 mg., dried aluminum hydroxide gel, 25 mg., magnesium hydroxide 50 mg./Tab. Capsuleshaped tablets. Bot. 15s, 30s, 60s, 100s.
Use: Relief of headache, muscular aches and pains, neuralgia and neuritic pain, functional menstrual pain, minor pains of arthritis and rheumatism.

VANSEB DANDRUFF SHAMPOO. (Herbert) Sulfur 2%, salicylic acid 1%, surfactants, protein. **Cream:** Tube 3 oz. **Lotion:** Bot. 4 oz.
Use: Antidandruff, antiseborrheic.

VANSEB-T TAR SHAMPOO. (Herbert) Sulfur 2%, salicylic acid 1%, Coal Tar Solution. U.S.P. 5%, surfactants, protein. **Cream:** Tube 3 oz. **Lotion:** Bot. 4 oz.
Use: Antidandruff, antiseborrheic.

VANSIL. (Pfipharmecs) Oxaminiquine 250 mg./Cap. Bot. 24s.
Use: Schistosomicide.

VAPOCET TABLETS. (Major) Hydrocodone 5 mg. Acetaminophen 500 mg./Tab. Bot. 100s.
Use: Analgesic, antipyretic.

VAPO-ISO SOLUTION. (Fisons) Isoproterenol HCl 0.5%, sod. chloride, glycerin. Vial 10 cc.
Use: Bronchodilator.

VAPONA. Dichlorvos, B.A.N.

VAPONEFRIN SOLUTION. (Fisons) A 2.25% solution of bioassayed racemic epinephrine as HCl, chlorobutanol 0.5%. Vials 7.5, 15, 30 cc.
Use: Bronchodilator.

VAPORUB. (Vicks)
See: Vicks Vaporub (Vicks)

VAPOSTEAM. (Vicks)
See: Vicks Vaposteam (Vicks)

VARICELLA-ZOSTER IMMUNE GLOBULIN, U.S.P. XXI. A sterile buffered solution of the globulin fraction of human plasma containing 99% immunoglobulin G with traces of immunoglobulins A and M. It is derived from adult human plasma selected for high titers of varicella-zoster antibiodies.
Use: Passive immunizing agent.

VARI-FLAVORS. (Ross) Flavor packets to provide flavor variety for patients on liquid diets. Dextrose, artificial flavoring (strawberry, cherry, lemon, orange, pecan) and flavoring. Packets 1 Gm. 24s/Ctn.
Use: Liquid nutrition flavoring aid.

VARIOTIN. Pecilocin, B.A.N.

VARITOL. (Kenyon) Atropine sulfate 0.03 mg., hyoscyamine 0.03 mg., gelsemium 6.1 mg., methenamine 40.8 mg., salol 18.1 mg., benzoic acid 4.5 mg., methylene blue 5.4 mg./Tab. Bot. 100s, 1000s.

VARITOL-D.S. (Kenyon) Atropine sulfate 0.06 mg. hyoscyamine 0.06 mg., gelsemium 12.2 mg., methenamine 81.6 mg., salol 36.2 mg., benzoic acid 9 mg., methylene blue 10.8 mg./Tab. Bot. 100s, 1000s.

VASCARDIN. Sorbide Nitrate, B.A.N.

VASCORIL HYDROGEN MALEATE. Cinepazate, B.A.N.

VASULIT SULPHATE. Bamethan, B.A.N.

VASCUNITOL. (Apco) Mannitol hexanitrate 0.5 gr./Tab. Bot. 100s.
Use: Vasodilator.

VASCUSED. (Apco) Mannitol hexanitrate 0.5 gr., phenobarbital 0.25 gr./Tab. Bot. 100s.
Use: Vasodilator.

VASELINE DERMATOLOGY FORMULA CREAM. (Chesebrough-Pond's) Petrolatum, mineral oil, dimethicone. Jar 3 oz., 5.25 oz.
Use: Treatment for severe cases of dry skin.

VASELINE DERMATOLOGY FORMULA LOTION. (Chesebrough-Pond's) Petrolatum, mineral oil, dimethicon. Bot. 5.5 oz., 11 oz., 16 oz.
Use: Treatment for severe cases of dry skin.

VASELINE FIRST AID CARBOLATED PETROLEUM JELLY. (Chesebrough-Pond's) Petrolatum, chloroxylenol. Plastic Jar 1.75 oz., 3.75 oz. Plastic Tube 1 oz., 2.5 oz.
Use: Medicated antibacterial.

VASELINE PURE PETROLEUM JELLY SKIN PROTECTANT. (Chesebrough-Pond's) White petrolatum. Tubes 1 oz., 2.5 oz. Jars 1.75 oz., 3.75 oz., 7.75 oz., 13 oz.
Use: Protectant for minor skin irritations.

VASIMID.
See: Tolazoline HCl, U.S.P. XXI.

VASOCIDIN OPHTHALMIC OINTMENT. (CooperVision) Prednisolone acetate 5 mg., sulfacetamide sodium 100 mg./Gm. Tube 5 Gm.
Use: Anti-inflammatory, antibacterial.

VASOCIDIN OPHTHALMIC SOLUTION. (CooperVision) Prednisolone sodium phosphate 0.25% (equiv. to Prednisolone phosphate 0.23%), sulfacetamide sod. 10%, thimerosal 0.01%. Plastic dropper-tip squeeze bot. 5 ml., 10 ml., 15 ml.
Use: Anti-inflammatory, anti-bacterial.

VASOCLEAR. (CooperVision) Naphazoline HCl 0.02% in Lipiden polymeric system, benzalkonium Cl 0.01%, edetate disodium 0.03%. Bot. 15 ml.
Use: Decongestant eye drops.

VASOCLEAR A. (CooperVision) Naphazoline HCl 0.02%, zinc sulfate 0.25%, polyvinylalcohol 0.25%. Bot. 15 ml.
Use: Decongestant astringent lubricating eyedrops.

VASOCON-A OPHTHALMIC SOLUTION. (CooperVision) Naphazoline HCl 0.05%, antazoline phosphate 0.5%. Plastic squeeze bot. w/dropper tip 15 ml.
Use: Ocular decongestant and antihistamine.

VASOCON REGULAR. (CooperVision) Naphazoline HCl 0.1%. Bot. plastic squeeze w/dropper tip 15 ml.
Use: Topical ocular vasoconstrictor.

VASOCONSTRICTOR.
See: Epinephrine Prep.

VASODIL.
See: Tolazoline HCl, U.S.P. XXI.

VASODILAN. (Mead Johnson) Isoxsuprine HCl 10 mg./Tab. Bot. 100s, 1000s, 5000s. Unit Dose 100s. 20 mg./Tab. Bot. 100s, 500s, 1000s, 5000s. Unit dose 100s. Amp. 2 ml. (5 mg./cc.) Box 6s.
Use: Arterial insufficiency. Peripheral vascular disease. Cerebrovascular disorders.

VASODILATORS.
See: Amyl Nitrite
Apresoline, Tab., Amp. (Ciba)
Arlidin, Tab. (USV)
Cardilate, Tab. (Burroughs Wellcome)
Cyclospasmol, Tab., Cap. (Ives)
Erythrityl Tetranitrate, Tab.
Glyceryl Trinitrate, Preps.
Isordil, Tab. (Ives)
Kortrate, Cap. (Amid)
Kortrate Plus, Cap. (Amid)
Mannitol Hexanitrate
Metamine, Tab. (Pfizer)
Nisine, Elix. (Amid)
Nitroglycerin
Pentritol, Cap., Tempule (Armour)
Peritrate, Tab. (Parke-Davis)
Sodium Nitrite
Sorbitrate, Tab. (Stuart)
Vasodilan, Tab., Amp. (Mead Johnson)

■ **VASODILATORS, CORONARY.**
See: Glyceryl Trinitrate, Preps. (Various Mfr.)
Isordil, Tab. (Ives)
Khellin (Various Mfr.)
Papaverine, Inj., Tab. (Various Mfr.)
Pentaerythritol Tetranitrate, Tab.
Peritrate, Tab. (Parke-Davis)
Roniacol Elix., Tab. (Roche)
Sorbitrate, Tab. (Stuart)

VASODISTAL HYDROGEN MALEATE. Cinepazide, B.A.N.

VASOFLO. (Hauck) Papaverine HCl 150 mg./Cap. Bot 100s.
Use: Cerebral and peripheral ischemia.

VASOLATE. (Parmed) Pentaerythritol tetranitrate 30 mg./Cap. Bot. 100s, 1000s.
Use: Relief of angina pectoris.

VASOLATE-80. (Parmed) Pentaerythritol tetranitrate 80 mg./Cap. Bot. 100s, 1000s.
Use: Relief of angina pectoris.

VASOMIDE TABLETS. (Lannett) Niacin 50 mg., salicylamide 300 mg., ascorbic acid 15 mg., Vit. B-1 3 mg., dl-desoxyephedrine HCl 2.5 mg., B-12 3 mcg./Tab. Bot. 100s, 1000s.

VASOMINIC-T.D. (A.V.P.) Phenylpropanolamine HCl 50 mg., chlorpheniramine 25 mg., pyrilamine maleate 25 mg./T.R. Tab. Bot. 100s.
Use: Antihistaminic, decongestant.

• **VASOPRESSIN INJECTION,** U.S.P. XXI. beta-Hypophamine. Post. pituitary pressor hormone.
Use: Posterior pituitary hormone (antidiuretic).
See: Pitressin, Amp. (Parke-Davis)

VASOPRESSIN TANNATE INJECTION. beta-Hypophamine tannate.
See: Pitressin Tannate, Amp. (Parke-Davis)

VAS-O-SPAN. (Scrip) Papaverine 150 mg./Cap. Bot. 100s.

VASOSTIM. (Dunhall) Niacin acid 100 mg., pnetylenetetrazol 100 mg./Cap. Bot. 100s, 1000s.
Use: Cerebral stimulant.

VASOSULF. (CooperVision) Sulfacetamide sodium 15%, phenylphrine HCl 0.125%, methylparaben 0.02%, propylparaben 0.005%. Bot. 5 ml., 15 ml.
Use: Ophthalmic antibacterial/decongestant.

VASO T.D. CAPSULES. (Knight) Bot. 100s, 1000s.

VASOTHERM INJ. (Pharmex) Niacin as sod. salt 100 mg., benzyl alcohol 1.5%/cc. Vial 30 cc.
Use: Vasodilator.

VASOTRAN HYDROCHLORIDE. Isoxsuprine, B.A.N.

VASOTUS LIQUID. (Sheryl) Codeine phosphate 1/6 gr., phenylephrine HCl, prophenpyridamine maleate. Liq. 1 pt.
Use: Cough and respiratory congestion.

VASOXINE. Methoxamine, B.A.N.

VASOXYL INJECTION. (Burroughs Wellcome) Methoxamine HCl 20 mg./ml. w/citric acid anhydrous 0.3%, sodium citrate 0.3%. Vial 1 ml.
Use: Supporting, restoring, maintaining blood pressure during anesthesia.

VASTAREL DIHYDROCHLORIDE. Trimetazidine, B.A.N.

VASYLOX HYDROCHLORIDE. Methoxamine, B.A.N.

VATENSOL. Guanoclor sulfate, B.A.N.
Use: Adrenergic neuron blocking agent.

VA-TRO-NOL. (Vicks)
See: Vicks Va-Tro-Nol (Vicks)

VAZADRINE. Isoniazid, B.A.N.

VAZOSAN. (Sandia) Papaverine HCl 150 mg./Tab. Bot. 100s, 1000s.

V-CILLIN-K. (Lilly) Penicillin V potassium. **125 mg.**/Tab. Bot. 50s, 100s; **250 mg.**/Tab. Bot. 24s, 100s, 500s. **500 mg.**/Tab. Bot. 24s, 100s, 500s.
Use: Orally, penicillin therapy.

V-CILLIN-K FOR ORAL SOLUTION. (Lilly) Penicillin V potassium. 125 mg./5 ml. Bot. 5 ml. Pkg. 100s. Bot. 100, 150, 200 ml. 250 mg./5 ml. Bot. 5 ml. Pkg. 100s. Bot. 100 ml., 150 ml., 200 ml.
Use: Orally, penicillin therapy.

V-COMP TABLETS. (Eckerd) Acetaminophen 325 mg., pseudoephedrine HCl 15 mg., d-Methorphan HBr 10 mg., chlorpheniramine maleate 2 mg., guaifenesin 50 mg./Tab. Bot. 24s.
Use: Relieves cold and flu virus symptoms.

V-CORT. (Scrip) Hydrocortisone 1%, clioquinol 3%, pramoxine HCl 0.5% in a washable base. Tube 1 oz.

VDRL ANTIGEN. (Laboratory Diagnostics) VDRL antigen with buffered saline. **Vial:** Sufficient for 500 tests. **Amp.:** 10 × 0.5 ml. sufficient for 500 tests.
Use: Blood test in diagnosis of syphilis.

VDRL SLIDE TEST. (Laboratory Diagnostics) VDRL antigen. Vial 5 ml. Complete kit, reactive control, nonreactive control, 5 ml.
Use: Slide flocculation and spinal fluid test for syphilis.

VE-400. (Western Research) Vitamine E 400 I.U./Caps. Bot. 100s.
Use: Vitamin supplement.

VE-T4. (Western Research) dl-Alpha tocopheryl acetate 400 I.U./Tab. Bot. 100s.
Use: Vitamin E therapy.

• **VECURONIUM BROMIDE.** USAN.
Use: Blocking agent.

VEETIDS. (Squibb) Penicillin-V potassium. **Solution** 125 mg. or 250 mg./5 ml. Bot. 100 ml., 200 ml. **Tab.** 250 mg. or 500 mg./Tab. Bot. 100s, 1000s. Unimatic 100s.

• **VEGETABLE OIL, HYDROGENATED,** U.S.P. XXI.
Use: Pharm. aid (tablet lubricant).

VEGOLYSEN. Hexamethonium Bromide, B.A.N.

VELACYCLINE. N-Pyrrolidinomethyl tetracycline.
Use: Antibiotic.

VELBAN. (Lilly) Ext. from Vinca rosea Linn. Vinblastine sulfate, lyophilized Vial 10 mg./10 ml. Box 10s.
Use: Antineoplastic.

VELBE SULPHATE. Vinblastine, B.A.N.

VELDOPA. Levodopa, B.A.N.

VELLADA TABLETS. (Fellows) Phenobarbital 0.25 gr., ext. hyoscyamus ⅛ gr., ext. passiflora 0.25 gr., ext. valerian 0.25 gr./Tab. Bot. 1000s.

VELMATROL. (Kenyon) Sulfisoxazole 500 mg./Tab. Bot. 100s, 1000s.

VELMATROL-A. (Kenyon) Sulfisoxazole 500 mg phenylazodiaminopyridine HCl 50 mg./Tab. Bot. 100s, 1000s.
Use: Urinary antibiotic, antiseptic.

VELOSEF. (Squibb) Cephradine. **Oral Susp.:** 125 mg. or 250 mg./5 ml. Bot. 100 ml., 200 ml.**Cap.:** 250 mg., or 500 mg./Cap. Bot. 24s, 100s. Unit dose Unimatic 100s. **Inj.** (w/anhydrous sod. carbonate. Sodium equiv. to 136 mg./Gm. of cephradine) 250 mg., 500 mg., 1 Gm./Vial 2 Gm., 4 Gm./100 ml.; 2 Gm. sodium free for infusion. Bot. 200 ml.
Use: Antibiotic.

VELOSULIN. (Nordisk) Purified pork insulin injection 100 I.U./ml.
Use: Diabetes care (IDDM).

VELTANE. (Lannett) Brompheniramine maleate 4 mg./Tab. Bot. 1000s.
Use: Antihistamine.

VELTAP. (Lannett) Brompheniramine maleate 4 mg., phenylephrine HCl 5 mg., phenylpropanolamine HC 5 mg., alcohol 2.3%/5 ml. Bot. pts., gal.
Use: Upper respiratory infections.

VELVACHOL. (Owen) Hydrophilic ointment base petrolatum, mineral oil, cetyl alcohol, cholesterol, parabens, stearyl alcohol, purified water, sodium lauryl sulfate. Jar 1 lb.
Use: Hydrophilic ointment base.

VELVEDERM CLEANSER. (Torch) Sulfonated detergent with a stable emulsion of vegetable oil. Bot. 8 oz.
Use: Cleansing lotion.

VELVEDERM-HANDORA NORMALIZER. (Torch) Glycerine, fatty alcohols, fatty acid in hydrophilic base w/pH of 5.0 to 5.5. Cream 4 oz., 8 oz. jar. Lotion 8 oz. Bot.
Use: Emollient skin cream and lotion.

VELVEDERM MOISTURIZER. (Torch) Mineral oil, emulsifiers, fatty alcohol, propylene glycol, hydroxymethylcellulose and water. Bot. 4 oz.
Use: Lubricating skin lotion, vehicle for common dermatologicals.

VENESETIC.
See: Amobarbital Sodium, Preps. (Various Mfr.)

VENETHENE. No mfr. listed.

VENOMIL. (Hollister-Stier) Diagnostic 1 mcg./ml Maintenence 100 mcg./ml. Individual patient kits.
Use: Hymenoptera (stinging insect) sensitive patients.

VENSTAT. (Seatrace) Atropine sulfate 0.2 mg., chlorpheniramine maleate 5 mg./ml. Vial 10 cc.

VENTABS. (Seatrace) Acetaminophen 325 mg., phenylpropanolamine HCl 18 mg., atropine sulfate 0.15 mg./Tab. Bot. 100s, 1000s.
Use: Nasal decongestant, analgesic, anti-pyretic.

VENTHERA. (Amfre-Grant) Vit. A acetate 25,000 I.U., D-2 1000 I.U., B-1 12.5 mg., B-2 12.5 mg., niacinamide 100 mg., C 200 mg., B-6 5 mg., d-calcium pantothenate 20 mg., B-12 5 mcg., E acetate 5 I.U., biotin 1 mcg., Ca 105 mg., P 80 mg., Iodine 0.15 mg., Fe 15 mg., potassium sulfate 5 mg., copper sulfate 1

mg., manganese sulfate 1 mg., mag. oxide 6 mg., zinc sulfate 1.5 mg./Tab. Bot. 100s.
Use: Treatment of deficiencies of essential vitamins and minerals.

'ENTOLIN. (Glaxo) Albuterol sulfate 2 mg. or 4 mg./Tab. Bot. 100s, 500s.
Use: Bronchodilator.

'ENTOLIN INHALER. (Glaxo) Albuterol 90 mcg./actuation. Aerosol cannister 17 Gm. containing 200 metered inhalations. Cannister 17 Gm. w/oral adapter.

'ENTROMIL. Orphenadrine, B.A.N.

'EPESID. (Bristol) Etoposide inj. 100 mg. Vial
Use: Antineoplastic agent.

'ERACOLATE. (C-D Consumer Products) Bile salts 1.07 gr., phenolphthalein 0.5 gr., capsicum oleoresin 0.05 min., cascara ext. 1 gr./Tab. Bot. 100s.
Use: Laxative.

'ERACTIL. Methotrimeprazine, B.A.N.

VERADOLINE HYDROCHLORIDE. USAN.
Use: Analgesic.

VERAPAMIL. USAN. 5-[3,4-Di-methoxyphenethyl)methylamino]-2-(3,4-dimethoxyphenyl)-2-isopropylvaleronitrile. Isoptin. Cordilox hydrochloride.
Use: Coronary vasodilator.

VERAPAMIL HYDROCHLORIDE. USAN.
Use: Coronary vasodilator.

'ERAPHEN. (Davis & Sly) Phenobarbital 0.25 gr., veratrum viride ¾ gr., sodium nitrite 1 gr./Tab. Bot. 1000s.

'ERATRUM ALBA.
See: Protoveratrines A & B. (Various Mfr.)

'ERATRUM VIRIDE. Approx. 1 gr. equals 4 craw units.
Use: Hypertension treatment.
See: Cryptenamine
Gartrone, Vials (Eric, Kirk & Gary)
'/Sod. nitrite, aconite, nitroglycerin & pot. nitrate.
See: Nyomin, Tab. (Elder)

'ERATRUM VIRIDE WITH PHENOBARBITAL COMBINATIONS.
See: Hyperlon, Tab. (Kenyon)
Hyrunal, Tab. (Kenyon)
Verabar, Tab. (Bowman)

'ERATRUM VIRIDE UNIT.
See: C.S.R. Unit

'ERAZEPTOL. (Femco) Chlorothymol, eucalyptol, menthol, phenol, boric acid & zinc sulfate. Pow., Bot. 3 oz., 6 oz., 10 oz.
Use: Vaginal douche.

'ERAZIDE. B.A.N. 2′-Veratrylideneisonicotino-hydrazide.
Use: Treatment of tuberculosis.

'ERAZINC. (Forest) Zinc sulfate 220 mg./Cap. Bot. 100s, 1000s.
Use: Astringent.

'ERCYTE. (Abbott) Pipobroman 25 mg./Tab. Bot. 100s.
Use: Antineoplastic.

'ERDEFAM CREAM. (Owen) Sodium propionate 1%, sodium caprylate 1%, propionic acid 3%, salicylic acid 3%, undecylenic acid 2%, copper undecylenate 0.5%, vanishing cream base. Tube 1 oz.
Use: Treatment of fungal infections.

VERDEFAM SOLUTION. (Owen) Sod. propionate 2%, sod. caprylate 2%, propionic acid 3%, undecylenic acid 5%, salicylic acid 5%, copper undecylenate 0.5%, docusate sodium 0.1%, purified water, isopropyl alcohol 59%. Sol. Bot. 2 oz.
Use: Fungus infections.

VERGO OINT. (Daywell) Cal. pantothenate 8%, ascorbic acid 2%, starch. Tube 0.5 oz.
Use: Treatment of warts.

• **VERILOPAM HYDROCHLORIDE.** USAN.
Use: Analgesic.

VERIN. (Verex) Aspirin 650 mg./Time Release Tab. Bot. 100s.
Use: Treatment of arthritis.

VERI-STAPH. (Wampole-Zeus) Latex agglutination slide test for *Staphylococcus aureus*. Tests 120s.
Use: Rapid detection of both clumping factors and protein A seen in *Staphylococcus aureus* cultures.

VERITAIN. Pholedrine, B.A.N.

VERITOL. Pholedrine, B.A.N.

VERMANTIN. (Trout) Phenobarbital 0.25 gr., veratrum viride pow. ext. ⅖ gr., mannitol hexanitrate 0.5 gr., rutin ⅓ gr./Tab. Bot. 100s, 1000s.
Use: Hypertension.

VERMICIDE. (Pharmex) Tube 2 oz.
Use: Crab lice.

VERMITRATE. (Vortech) Piperazine citrate 100 mg./cc. Bot. pt., gal.

VERMIZINE. (Vortech) **Syr.** Piperazine citrate 100 mg./cc. Bot. 4 oz., pt., gal; **Tab.** 250 mg./Tab., Bot. 1000s.
Use: Treatment of pinworms & roundworms.

VERMOX. (Janssen) Mebendazole 100 mg./Tab. Box 12s.
Use: Anthelmintic.

VERNACEL. (Professional Pharmacal) Prophenpyridamine maleate 0.5%, phenylephrine HCl ⅛% in a methylcellulose solution. Plastic Bot. 15 cc., 30 cc.
Use: Ophthalmic allergic symptoms.

VERNAMYCINS. Under study.
Use: Antibiotic.

VERNATE-II.(Reid-Provident) Chlorpheniramine maleate 12 mg., phenylpropanolamine HCl 75 mg./S.R. Cap. Bot. 1000s.
Use: Treatment common cold.

VERNOLEPIN. A sesquiterpene dilactone. Under study.
Use: Against Walker carcinosarcoma 256.

• **VEROFYLLINE.** USAN.
Use: Bronchodilator, anti-asthmatic.

VERONAL SODIUM.
See: Barbital Sodium (Various Mfr.)

VERR-CANTH. (C & M Pharmacal) Cantharidin 0.7%, penederm 0.5%. Bot. 7.5 cc w/applicator tip.
Use: Topically for removal of benign epithelial growths.

VERREX. (C & M Pharmacal) Salicylic acid 30%, podophyllin 10%. Bot. 7.5cc w/applicator tip.
Use: Wart Removal.

VERRUSOL. (C & M Pharmacal) Salicylic acid 30%, podophyllin 5%, cantharidin 1%, Bot. 7.5 cc.
Use: Wart removal.

VERSACAPS. (Seatrace) Brompheniramine maleate 4 mg., pseudoephedrine HCl 60 mg., guaifenesin 300 mg./Cap. Bot. 100s, 1000s.
Use: Antihistaminic, nasal decongestant, antitussive.

VERSAL. (Suppositoria) Bismuth subgallate, Peru balsam, zinc oxide, benzyl benzoate/Supp. Box 12s, 100s, 1000s.
Use: Antihemorrhoidal.

VERSAL HC. (Suppositoria) Hydrocortisone acetate 10 mg./Supp. w/bismuth subgallate, balsam peru, zinc oxide, benzyl benzoate Box 12s, 100s, 1,000s.
Use: Antihemorrhoidal.

VERSAPEN. (Bristol) Hetacillin. **Oral Susp.:** Hetacillin equiv. to 112.5 mg., ampicillin/5 ml. Bot. 100 ml., 225 mg./5 ml. Bot. 100 ml.

VERSAPEN K. (Bristol) Potassium hetacillin equiv. to ampicillin 225/Cap. Bot. 100s.
Use: Antibiotic.

VERSA-QUAT. (Ulmer) Quaternary ammonium one-step cleaner-disinfectant-sanitizer-fungicide-virucide for general housekeeping. Bot. gal., 5 gal.
Use: Cleanser, disinfectant.

VERSENATE, CALCIUM DISODIUM.
See: Calcium Disodium Versenate, Amp. (Riker)

VERSENATE DISODIUM.
See: Disodium Versenate, Amp. (Riker)

VERSENE ACID. Edetic Acid, B.A.N.

VERSIDYNE. Methopholine. 1-(p-Chlorophenethyl)-2-methyl-6,7-dimethoxy-1,2,3,4-tetrahydroisoquinoline.
Use: Analgesic.

VERSTAT. (Saron) Pheniramine maleate 12.5 mg., nicotinic acid 50 mg./Cap.

VERSTRAN. (Parke-Davis) Prazepam.
Use: Muscle relaxant.
See: Centrax, Tab. (Parke-Davis)

VERTON ACETATE. Chlormadinone, B.A.N.

VERUCID GEL. (Ulmer) Salicylic acid. Tube 5 Gm.
Use: Wart remover.

VERV ALERTNESS CAPSULES. (APC) Caffeine 200 mg./Cap. Vial 15.
Use: Maintain physical and mental alertness.

VESICHOLINE. (Star) Bethanechol chloride 25 mg./Tab. Bot. 100s, 1000s.
Use: Non-obstructive urinary retention.

VESIPAQUE. (Warner-Lambert) Phenobutiodil.
Use: Radiopaque diagnostic aid.

VESPRAL. Fluopromazine, B.A.N.

VESPRIN. (Squibb) Triflupromazine. **10 mg./ml.:** Vial 10 ml. **20 mg./ml.:** Vial 1 ml. w/benzyl alcohol 1.5%.
Use: Tranquilizer.

VESULONG. (Ciba) Sulfazamet. Sulfapyrazole, B.A.N.

VETALAR. (Parke-Davis) Ketamine HCl 100 mg./ml. Bot. 10 ml.
Use: Anesthetic for veterinary use.

V-GAN. (Hauck) Promthazine HCl 25 or 50 mg./ml. Via 10 ml.
Use: Anti-emetic, antihistaminic.

VIACAPS. (Manne) Vit. A (soluble) 45,000 I.U., C 50(mg./Caps. Bot. 60s, 120s, 1000s.
Use: Acne therapy.

VIADRIL. Hydroxydione Sodium Succinate, B.A.N.

VI-AQUA CAPSULES. (Armour) Aqueous multip vitamins. Bot. 100s.
Use: Dietary supplement.

VI-AQUA FORTE. (Armour) Aqueous multivitamin fo mula. Bot. 100s.
Use: Dietary supplement.

VI-AQUAMIN FORTE CAPSULES. (Armour) Aqueou vitamins with minerals. Bot. 100s.
Use: Dietary supplement.

VIATRIC. (Pasadena Research) Ethinyl estradiol 0.01 mg., methyltestosterone 2.5 mg., ferrous fumarate 15 mg., l-lysine 50 mg., Vit. A 7500 I.U., D 500 I.U., E 1 7.5 mg., B-2 7.5 mg., B-6 2 mg., niacinamide 50 mg Ca pantothenate 10 mg., B-12 10 mcg., C 50 mg., ruti 15 mg., choline bitartrate 50 mg., inositol 25 mg., Vit. E 10 I.U., with trace elements/Tab. Bot. 100s, 1000s.
Use: Androgen-estrogen therapy with nutritional vita min and mineral supplements.

VIBAZINE DIHYDROCHLORIDE. Buclizine, B.A.N.

VIBEDOZ Injection. (Blue Line) Cyanocobalamin 100 mcg./ml. Benzyl alcohol 1.5%. Normal saline, sterile sol. Vial 10 ml.

VIBESATE. Polvinate 9.3%, molrosinol 3.1% with propellant.

VIBRAMYCIN. (Pfizer Laboratories) Doxycycline **Caps.** 50 mg./Cap. Bot. 50s, unit dose pak 100s, X-Pack (10 Caps.) 5s.; 100 mg./Cap. Bot. 50s, 500s unit dose pak 100s. V-Pak (5 Caps) 5s. Nine-Pak 10s **Ped. Oral Susp.** 25 mg./5 cc. Bot. 2 oz. **Syrup:** 50 mg./5 cc. Bot. oz., pt.
Use: Antibiotic.

VIBRAMYCIN INTRAVENOUS. (Pfipharmecs) Doxycycline hyclate 100 mg., ascorbic acid 480 mg./Vial, 5s; doxycycline hyclate 200 mg., ascorbic acid 960 mg./Vial, 1s.
Use: Antibiotic.

VIBRA-TABS. (Pfizer Laboratories) Doxycycline hyclat 100 mg./Tab. Bot. 50s, 500s. Unit dose Pack 100s
Use: Antibiotic.

VICAM-R. (Keene) **Sol. #1:** Vit. B-1 3 mg., B-2 3.6 mg biotin 60 mcg., niacin 40 mg., B-6 4 mg., C 100 mg pantothenic acid 15 mg./ml. **Sol #2:** Vit. B-12 5 mcg folic acid 400 mcg./ml. Vial multiple dose.
Use: Parenteral dietary supplement for I.M. injection.

VICEF. (Drug Industries) Thiamin HC1 10 mg., pyridoxine HCl 10 mg., Vit B-12 50 mcg., C 100 mg E 100 I.U., niacinamide 25 mg. folic acid 1.5 mg., ferrous fumarate 45 mg./2 Cap. Bot. 100s.
Use: Vitamin, mineral supplement.

VICHOX. (Vitarine) Vit. A 5000 I.U., D 400 I.U., C 60 mg., B-1 1.5 mg., B-2 1.7 mg., B-6 2 mg., B-12 6 mcg.

niacinamide 20 mg., E 15 I.U., folic acid 0.4 mg./Tab. Bot. 100s, 250s. w/iron. Bot. 100s.
Use: Dietary supplement.

'ICHOX w/IRON. (Vitarine) Multivitamin supplement w/iron/Chewable Tab.
Use: Dietary supplement.

'ICKS BLUE THROAT DROPS. (Vicks) Menthol in a soothing sugar base. Stick-Pack 10s. Bag 23s.
Use: Cough drop.

'ICKS CHILDRENS COUGH SYRUP. (Vicks) Dextromethorphan hydrobromide 3.5 mg., guaifenesin 50 mg./5 ml. w/alcohol 5%. Bot. 3 oz.
Use: Cough syrup.

'ICKS COUGH SILENCERS. (Vicks) Dextromethorphan HBr 2.5 mg., benzocaine 1 mg., Special Vicks Medication (menthol, peppermint oil, anethole) 0.35%/Loz. Box 13s.
Use: Cough medication.

'ICKS DAYCARE CAPSULES. (Vicks) Acetaminophen 325 mg., pseudoephedrine HCl 30 mg., guaifenesin 100 mg., dextromethorphan HBr 10 mg./Cap. Blister Pack 20's, 36's.
Use: Multi-symptom colds medicine.

'ICKS DAYCARE LIQUID. (Vicks) Acetaminophen 650 mg., dextromethorphan HBr 20 mg., pseudoephedrine HCl 60 mg., guaifenesin 100 mg./oz. w/alcohol 10%. Bot. 6 oz., 10 oz.
Use: Multi-symptom colds medicine.

'ICKS FORMULA 44 COUGH CONTROL DISCS. (Vicks) Dextromethorphan (HBr equivalent) 5 mg., benzocaine 1.25 mg., Special Vicks Medication (menthol, peppermint oil, anethole) 0.35%/Disc. Pkg. 24s.
Use: Cough medication.

'ICKS FORMULA 44. (Vicks) Dextromethorphan HBr 30 mg., doxylamine succinate 7.5 mg./10 ml. w/alcohol 10%. Bot. 3 oz., 6 oz., 8 oz.
Use: Effective strength cough mixture.

'ICKS FORMULA 44D. (Vicks) Dextromethorphan HBr 60 mg., pseudoephedrine HCl 60 mg., guaifenesin 200 mg./15 ml. Alcohol 10%. Bot. 3 oz., 6 oz., 8 oz.
Use: Cough mixture and decongestant.

'ICKS FORMULA 44M. (Vicks) Dextromethorphan HBr 30 mg., pseudoephedrine HCl 60 mg., guaifenesin 200 mg., acetaminophen 500 mg./20 ml. w/alcohol 20%. Bot. 4 oz., 8 oz.
Use: Multi-symptom cough mixture.

'ICKS HEADWAY. (Vicks) Acetaminophen 325 mg., phenylpropanolamine HC1 18.72 mg., chlorpheniramine maleate 2 mg./Tab. or Cap.**Tab.:** Bot. 20s, 40s. **Cap.:** Bot. 16s, 36s.
Use: Decongestant, analgesic, antihistaminic.

'ICKS INHALER. (Vicks) l-Desoxyephedrine 50 mg., Special Vicks Medication (menthol, camphor, methylsalicylate, bornyl acetate) 150 mg. Inhaler 0.007 oz.
Use: Nasal decongestant.

'ICKS LIFESTAGE-CHILDREN'S FORMULA. (Vicks) Vit. A 5000 I.U., D 400 I.U., E 30 I.U., C 60 mg., folic acid 0.4 mg., B-1 1.5 mg., B-2 1.7 mg., niacin 20 mg., B-6 2 mg., B-12 6 mcg., biotin 0.3 mg., pantothenic acid 10 mg., iron 9 mg./2 Chewable Tabs. Bot. 60s.
Use: Vitamin & iron supplement.

VICKS LIFESTAGE-MEN'S FORMULA. (Vicks) Vit. A 10,000 I.U., D 400 I.U., E 50 I.U., C 200 mg., folic acid 0.4 mg., B-1 10 mg., B-2 10 mg., niacin 100 mg., B-6 5 mg., B-12 6 mcg., pantothenic acid 20 mg., iodine 150 mcg., iron 18 mg., magnesium 100 mg., copper 2 mg., zinc 15 mg., manganese 1.25 mg./Tab. Bot. 30s.
Use: High potency vitamin and mineral supplement.

VICKS LIFESTAGE-STRESS FORMULA FOR MEN. (Vicks) Vit. E 45 I.U., C 500 mg., folic acid 0.4 mg., B-1 20 mg., B-2 10 mg., niacin 100 mg., B-6 10 mg., B-12 25 mcg., magnesium 100 mg., zinc 22.5 mg./Tab. Bot. 30s.
Use: High potency vitamin supplement with zinc and magnesium.

VICKS LIFESTAGE-STRESS FORMULA FOR WOMEN. (Vicks) Vit. E 45 I.U., C 500 mg., folic acid 0.4 mg., B-1 20 mg., B-2 10 mg., niacin 100 mg., B-6 10 mg., B-12 25 mcg., iron 27 mg., magnesium 100 mg., zinc 22.5 mg./Tab. Bot. 30s.
Use: High potency vitamin supplement with zinc, magnesium, & iron.

VICKS LIFESTAGE-TEEN'S FORMULA. (Vicks) Vit. A 5000 I.U., D 400 I.U., E 30 I.U., C 100 mg., folic acid 0.4 mg., B-1 15 mg., B-2 10 mg., niacin 50 mg., B-6 7.5 mg. B-12 12.5 mcg., pantothenic acid 10 mg., calcium 160 mg., phosphorus 125 mg., iron 18 mg./Tab. Bot. 30s.
Use: Vitamin & mineral supplement.

VICKS LIFESTAGE-WOMEN'S FORMULA. (Vicks) Vit. A 5000 I.U., D 400 I.U., E 30 I.U., C 100 mg., folic acid 0.4 mg., B-1 3 mg., B-2 3.4 mg., niacin 40 mg., B-6 4 mg., B-12 12 mcg., pantothenic acid 10 mg., iodine 150 mcg., iron 27 mg., magnesium 100 mg., copper 2 mg., zinc 15 mg./Tab. Bot. 60s.
Use: Vitamin & mineral supplement with iron.

VICKS NYQUIL. (Vicks) Acetaminophen 1000 mg., doxylamine succinate 7.5 mg., pseudoephedrine HCl 60 mg., dextromethorphan HBr 30 mg./oz. w/FD&C Yellow #5 tartrazine and alcohol 25%. Bot. 6 oz., 10 oz., 14 oz.
Use: Nighttime colds medicine.

VICKS ORACIN. (Vicks) Benzocaine 6.25 mg., menthol 0.1% (Regular) 0.08% (cherry) in a cooling sorbitol base/Loz. Regular or Cherry flavor. Regular flavor lozenge contains FD&C Yellow #5 tartrazine. Pkg. 18s.
Use: Cooling throat lozenge.

VICKS SINEX. (Vicks) Phenylephrine HCl 0.5%, cetylpyridinium Cl 0.04%, Special Vicks Blend of Aromatics (menthol, eucalyptol, camphor, methyl salicylate). w/thimerosal 0.001% preservative. Nasal Spray. Plastic Squeeze Bot. 0.5 oz., 1 oz.
Use: Nasal decongestant spray.

VICKS SINEX LONG-ACTING. (Vicks) Oxymetazoline HCl 0.05% in aqueous soln. containing menthol vapors and thimerosal 0.001%.. Nasal Spray. Plastic Squeeze Bot. 1 oz., 0.5 oz.
Use: Nasal decongestant spray, long acting.

VICKS THROAT DROPS. (Vicks) Menthol in soothing Vicks sugars base. Regular, wild cherry, lemon flavor. Box 13s. Bag 30s.
Use: Cough Drop.

VICKS THROAT LOZENGES. (Vicks) Benzocaine 5 mg., cetylpyridinium Cl 1.66 mg., Special Vicks Medication (menthol, eucalyptus oil, camphor). Loz. 12s.
Use: Sore throat and coughs of colds.

VICKS VAPORUB. (Vicks) Special Vicks Medication (camphor 4.73%, menthol 2.67%, spirits of turpentine 4.5%, eucalyptus oil 1.2%) 14%. Jar 1.5 oz., 3 oz. 6 oz.
Use: Decongestant vaporizing ointment.

VICKS VAPOSTEAM. (Vicks) Polyoxyethylene dodecanol 1.8%, eucalyptus oil 1.7%, camphor 6.2%, tincture of benzoin 5%, w/alcohol 55%. Bot. 4 oz., 6 oz.
Use: Steam medication, decongestant and antitussive.

VICKS VA-TRO-NOL. (Vicks) Ephedrine sulfate 0.5%, Special Vicks Aromatic Blend in an aqueous base (menthol, eucalyptol, camphor, methyl salicylate) 0.06% w/thimerosal 0.001%. Nose Drop Bot. 0.5 oz., 1 oz.
Use: Nasal decongestant, vapor-action.

VICODIN. (Knoll) Hydrocodone bitartrate 5 mg., acetaminophen 500 mg./Tab. Bot. 100s. Hospital pack 100s.
Use: Analgesic, antipyretic.

VICON-C. (Glaxo) Ascorbic acid 300 mg., niacinamide 100 mg., zinc sulfate 80 mg., magnesium sulfate 70 mg., Vit. B-1 20 mg., d-calcium pantothenate 20 mg., B-2 10 mg., B-6 5 mg./Cap. Bot. 60s, 500s. Unit dose 240s.
Use: Therapeutic vitamin-mineral complex.

VICON CHEWABLE TABLETS. (Glaxo) Vit. A 2000 I.U., E 25 I.U., C 75 mg., Zn 10 mg., Mg 35 mg., Niacinamide 12.5 mg., Thiamine 5 mg., Calcium pantothenate 5 mg., Riboflavin 2.5 mg., Mn 2 mg., pyridoxine HCl 1 mg. Bot. 60s, 500s.
Use: Vitamin deficiencies.

VICON FORTE. (Glaxo) Vit. A 8000 I.U., E 50 I.U., C 150 mg., zinc sulf. 80 mg., mag. sulf. 70 mg., niacinamide 25 mg., B-1 10 mg., calcium pantothenate 10 mg., B-2 5 mg., B-6 2 mg., B-12 10 mcg., folic acid 1 mg., manganese Cl 4 mg./Cap. Bot. 60s, 500s. Unit dose 240s.
Use: Therapeutic vitamin-mineral complex.

VICON PLUS. (Glaxo) Vit. A acetate 4000 I.U., E 50 I.U., C 150 mg., zinc sulfate 80 mg., magnesium sulf. 70 mg., niacinamide 25 mg., B-1 10 mg., d-calcium pantothenate 10 mg., B-2 5 mg., manganese chloride 4 mg., B-6 2 mg./Cap. Bot. 60s, 500s.
Use: Therapeutic vitamin-mineral complex.

VICON WITH IRON. (Glaxo) B-complex with iron, zinc, Vit. C & E. Caps. Bot. 60s, 500s.
Use: Vitamin, mineral supplement.

VICRYL SUTURES. (Ethicon) Polyglactin 910.

VICTORS. (Vicks) Special Vicks Medication (menthol, eucalyptus oil) in a soothing Vicks sugar base. Regular or Cherry flavor drops. Stick-Pack 10s, Ba 30s.
Use: Cough drop.

• **VIDARABINE PHOSPHATE.** USAN.
Use: Antiviral.

• **VIDARABINE, STERILE.** U.S.P. XXI., Conc. for Inj., Ophth. Oint., U.S.P. XXI. 9-β-D-Arabinofuranosylade nine.
Use: Antiviral.
See: Vira-A Ophthalmic, Oint. (Parke-Davis)
Vira-A Inj. (Parke-Davis)

• **VIDARABINE SODIUM PHOSPHATE.**
Use: Antiviral.

VI-DAYLIN ADC DROPS. (Ross) Vit. A 1500 I.U.; C 3 mg.; D 400 I.U./1 ml. Bot. 30 ml., 50 ml. Also available w/iron 10 mg./ml. Bot. 50 ml., w/dropper
Use: Pediatric vitamin supplement.

VI-DAYLIN ADC PLUS IRON DROPS. (Ross) Vit. 1500 I.U.; C 35 mg.; D 400 I.U.; iron 10 mg./1 ml. Bot. 50 ml. w/dropper.
Use: Vitamins A, D and C with iron.

VI-DAYLIN CHEWABLE. (Ross) Vit. A 2500 I.U., D 40 I.U., E 15 I.U., C 60 mg., folic acid 0.3 mg., B-1 1.0 mg., B-2 1.2 mg., niacin 13.5 mg., B-6 1.05 mg., B-12 4.5 mcg./Tab. Bot. 100s.
Use: Multivitamin supplement for children and adults.

VI-DAYLIN CHEWABLE W/FLUORIDE. (Ross) Fluo ride 1 mg. B-1 1.05 mg., B-2 1.2 mg., niacinamide 13. mg., B-6 1.05 mg., C 60 mg., A 2500 I.U., B-12 4. mcg., E 15 I.U., folic acid 0.3 mg., D 400 I.U./Tab. Bot. 100s.
Use: Multivitamin with fluoride supplement.

VI-DAYLIN DROPS. (Ross) Vit. A 1500 I.U., D 400 I.U E 5 I.U., C 35 mg., B-1 0.5 mg., B-2 0.6 mg., niaci 8 mg., B-6 0.4 mg., B-12 1.5 mcg./1 ml. Bot. 50 ml.
Use: Multivitamin supplement for infants and children under 4 years of age.

VI-DAYLIN/F ADC DROPS. (Ross) Vit. A 1500 I.U., 400 I.U., C 35 mg., fluoride 0.25 mg./1 ml. Bot. 50 ml.
Use: As an aid in the prevention of dental caries and as prophylaxis of vit. A, D & C deficiencies.

VI-DAYLIN/F ADC PLUS IRON DROPS. (Ross) Vit. 1500 I.U.; C 35 mg.; D 400 I.U.; iron 10 mg.; fluoride 0.25 mg./1 ml. Bot. 50 ml.
Use: Vitamins A, D and C with iron and fluoride supplement.

VI-DAYLIN/F DROPS. (Ross) Vit. A 1500 I.U., D 40 I.U., E 5 I.U., C 35 mg., B-1 0.5 mg., B-2 0.6 mg niacin 8 mg., B-6 0.4 mg., fluoride 0.25 mg./1 ml. Bo 50 ml.
Use: Aid in prevention of dental caries and prophylaxis of vitamin deficiencies in infants & children.

VI-DAYLIN/F PLUS IRON DROPS. (Ross) Fluorid 0.25 mg., Vit. A 1500 I.U., D 400 I.U., E 5 I.U., C 3 mg., B-1 0.5 mg., B-2 0.6 mg., niacin 8 mg., B-6 0. mg., iron 10 mg./ml. Bot. 50 ml.
Use: Multivitamin with fluoride and iron.

-DAYLIN LIQUID. (Ross) Vit. A 2500 I.U.; B-1 1.05 mg.; B-2 1.2 mg.; B-6 1.05 mg.; B-12 4.5 mcg.; C 60 mg.; D 400 I.U.; E 15 I.U., niacin 13.5 mg./5 ml. Bot. 8 oz., pt.
Use: Liquid multivitamin for children and adults.

-DAYLIN PLUS IRON CHEWABLE. (Ross) Vit. A 2500 I.U., D 400 I.U., E 15 I.U., C 60 mg., folic acid 0.3 mg., B-1 1.05 mg., B-2 1.2 mg., niacin 13.5 mg., B-6 1.05 mg., B-12 4.5 mcg., iron 12 mg./Tab. Bot. 100s.
Use: Multivitamin with iron.

-DAYLIN PLUS IRON DROPS. (Ross) Vit. A 1500 I.U., D 400 I.U., E 5 I.U., C 35 mg., B-1 0.5 mg., B-2 0.6 mg., niacin 8.0 mg., B-6 0.4 mg., iron 10 mg./1 ml. Bot. 50 ml.w/dropper.
Use: Multivitamin with iron for children under 4 years of age.

-DAYLIN PLUS IRON LIQUID. (Ross) Vit. A 2500 I.U., D 400 I.U., C 60 mg., E 15 I.U., B-1 1.05 mg., B-2 1.2 mg., Niacin 13.5 mg., B-6 1.05 mg., B-12 4.5 mcg., iron 10 mg./tsp. Bot. 8 oz., 16 oz.
Use: Liquid multivitamin & iron supplement for children and adults.

DEC. (Pharmics) Vit. A 5000 I.U., D 1000 I.U., C 50 mg., B-1 2 mg., B-2 2 mg., B-6 0.5 mg., d-Ca pantothenate 2 mg., nicotinamide 20 mg., B-12 2 mcg., Fe 15 mg., Iodine 15 mg., Mn 1 mg., K 5 mg., Cu (Cu sulfate) 1 mg., Zn 0.5 mg., Mg 1 mg./Cap. Bot. 100s, 1000s.
Use: Vitamin-mineral supplement.

DECON. (Vita Elixir) Vit. D 50,000 units/Cap.
Use: Dietary supplement.

-DERM SOAP. (Arthrins) Extract of Amaryllis. 10% Pkg. 1 cake. 3.5 oz. bar.
Use: Hypo-allergenic and antipruritic.

DES CT W/FLUORIDE. (Pharmics) Vit. A 4000 I.U., D 400 I.U., B-1 1 mg., B-2 1.2 mg., B-6 1.5 mg., B-12 2 mcg., C 60 mg., d-panthenol 2.5 mg., niacinamide 10 mg., E 1 I.U., sod. fluoride 2.2 mg./Tab. Bot. 100s, 1000s.
Use: Dietary supplement.

FEX. (Mallard) Liver injection, equiv. in cyanocobalamin activity 10 mcg., cyanocobalamin 100 mcg., folic acid 1 mg./cc.

/IFILCON A. USAN.
Use: Contact lens material.

FLUORINEED. (Hanlon) Vit. A 5000 I.U., D 400 I.U., C 75 mg., B-1 2 mg., B-2 3 mg., niacinamide 20 mg., fluoride 1 mg./Chew. Tab. Bot. 100s.
Use: Vitamin supplement.

'IGABATRIN. USAN.
Use: Anticonvulsant.

GANIC. (Commerce)
Vit. A: 10,000 I.U./Cap. Bot. 100s.
Vit. B Complex: Bot. 100s.
Vit. B Complex W/C and Iron: Tab. Bot. 100s.
Vit. C: 150 mg., 300 mg., 1000 mg./Tab.; Sugarless 500 mg./Tab. Bot. 100s.
Vit. E: 100, 200, 400, 600, 1000 I.U./Cap. Bot. 100s.
Lecithin: 260 mg., Vit. A & D./Cap. Bot. 100s.

GEROL ELIXIR. (Quality Generics) Iron 100 mg., Vit. B-1 100 mg., B-2 5 mg., B-6 5 mg., B-12 1 mcg., niacinamide 3 mg., panthenol 100 mg., choline bitartrate 100 mg., alcohol 12%/Fl. oz. Bot. pt.

VIGEROLAN. (Lannett) Geriatric vitamin-mineral capsule with choline, inositol, and methionine. Bot. 100s, 500s, 1000s.

VIGORAMIN THERAPEUTIC. (CMC) High potency vitamin. Cap. Bot. 30s, 100s, 250s, 1000s.

VIGOWAYNE ELIXIR. (Wayne) Bot. pt.

VIGRAN. (Squibb) **Chewable:** Vit. B-1 0.7 mg., B-2 0.8 mg., niacinamide 9 mg., B-6 0.7 mg., C 40 mg., A 2500 I.U., D 400 I.U., E 10 I.U., B-12 3 u., folic acid 0.2 mg./Chewable Tab. Bot. 60s. **Tab.:** Vit. A 5000 I.U., D 400 I.U., E 30 I.U., C 60 mg., folic acid 0.4 mg., B-1 1.5 mg., B-2 1.7 mg., niacin 20 mg., B-6 2 mg., B-12 6 mcg./Cap. Bot. 100s, Pkg. 2 bot. **Plus Iron:** B-1 1.5 mg., B-2 1.7 mg., niacinamide 20 mg., B-6 2 mg., C 60 mg., A 5000 I.U., D 400 I.U., E 30 I.U., B-12 6 mcg., folic 0.4 mg., iron (as ferrous fumarate) 27 mg./Tab. Bot. 90s.
Use: Multivitamin at least 125% of the M.D.R.

VIKASTAB DIHYDRATE. Potassium Menaphthosulphate, B.A.N.

VILEX. (Dunhall) Vit. B-1 100 mg., riboflavin phosphate sodium 1 mg., B-6 10 mg., panthenol 5 mg., niacinamide 100 mg./ml. Amp. 30 ml.
Use: Multiple Vit. B deficiency.

VILIVA. (Vita Elixir) Ferrous fumarate 3 gr.
Use: Iron therapy, anemia.

VILLESCON. Prolintane, B.A.N.

VILOXAZINE. B.A.N. 2-(2-Ethoxyphenoxymethyl)-tetrahydro-1,4-oxazine.
Use: Treatment of mental disease.
See: Vivalan hydrochloride.

• **VILOXAZINE HCL.** USAN.
Use: Antidepressant.

VIMEGA-B/C. (Pasadena Research) Vit. B-1 25 mg., B-2 15 mg., B-6 10 mg., B-12 10 mcg., niacinamide 100 mg., cal. pantothenate 50 mg., Vit. C 750 mg./Tab. Bot. 100s, 1000s, Box 30s.

VIMINAL CAPSULES. (Cenci) Vit. A 5000 I.U., D 400 I.U., B-1 3 mg., B-2 2.5 mg., niacinamide 20 mg., B-6 1.5 mg., Ca pantothenate 5 mg., B-12 2.5 mcg., C 50 mg., E 3 I.U., Ca 215 mg., P 166 mg., Fe 13.4 mg., Mg 7.5 mg., Mn 1.5 mg., K 5 mg., Zn 1.4 mg./Cap. Bot. 30s, 100s, 500s.
Use: Dietary supplement.

VIMINAL G CAPSULES. (Cenci) Vit. A 12,500 I.U., D 400 I.U., B-1 5 mg., B-2 2.5 mg., niacinamide 40 mg., B-6 1 mg., Ca pantothenate 4 mg., B-12 2 mcg., C 75 mg., E 2 I.U., choline bitartrate 31.4 mg., inositol 15 mg., Ca 75 mg., P 58 mg., Fe 30 mg., Mg 3 mg., Mn 0.5 mg., K 2 mg., Zn 0.5 mg./Cap. Bot. 30s, 100s, 500s.
Use: Geriatric vitamin.

VIMINAL T. (Cenci) Vit. A 25,000 I.U., D 400 I.U., B-1 10 mg., B-2 5 mg., niacinamide 100 mg., B-6 1 mg., B-12 5 mcg., C 150 mg., Ca 103.6 mg., P 80.2 mg., Fe 10 mg., Mg 5.5 mg., Mn 1 mg., K 5 mg., Zn 1.4 mg./Cap. Bot. 100s, 500s.
Use: Vitamin deficiencies.

VIMIN-CO. (Jenkins) Vit. A 5000 I.U., D 400 I.U., B-1 3 mg., B-2 2.5 mg., B-6 1 mg., B-12 2 mcg., C 50 mg., niacinamide 20 mg., Ca 46 mg., P 35 mg., Fe 13.4 mg., Ca pantothenate 2 mg., Mg 1 mg., Mn 1.5 mg., K 5 mg., Zn 1.4 mg./Cap. Bot. 1000s.
Use: Vitamin-mineral capsule.

VI-MIN-FOR-ALL. (Barth's) Vit. A 3 mg., D 10 mcg., C 120 mg., B-1 35 mg., B-12 15 mcg., biotin, niacin 2.33 mg., E 30 I.U., B-6, pantothenic acid, Ca 375 mg., P 180 mg., Fe 20 mg., Iodine 0.1 mg., rutin 10 mg., hesperidin-lemon bioflavonoid complex 10 mg., choline, inositol 2.4 mg., Cu 10 mcg., Mn 2 mg., Zn 110 mcg., silicone 210 mcg./Tab. 100s, 500s.
Use: Diet supplement.

VIMMS-38. (Approved) Vit. A 12,500 I.U., D 1200 I.U., B-1 15 mg., B-2 10 mg., C 75 mg., niacinamide 30 mg., Ca pantothenate 2 mg., B-6 0.5 mg., E-5 I.U., Brewer's yeast 10 mg., B-12 15 mcg., Fe 11.58 mg., desic. liver 15 mg., choline bitartrate 30 mg., inositol 30 mg., Ca 59 mg., P 45 mg., Zn 0.68 mg., Fr. dicalcium phos. 200 mg., Mn 1.11 mg., Mg 1 mg., K 0.68 mg., pepsin 16.5 mg., diastase 16.5 mg., yeast 40.63 mg., protein digest 23.52 mg., amino acids 34.22 mg./Cap. Bot. 50s, 100s, 1000s.
Use: Supplement and therapy.

VINACTANE SULFATE. (Ciba) Viomycin Sulfate.

• **VINAFOCON A.** USAN
Use: Contact lens material.

VINBARBITAL. 5-Ethyl-5-(1-methyl-1-butenyl)barbituric acid.
Use: Sedative.

VINBARBITAL SODIUM. 5-Ethyl-5-(1-methylbut-1-enyl)-barbiturate sod.
Use: Sedative.

VINBARBITONE. B.A.N. 5-Ethyl-5-(1-methylbut-1-enyl)barbituric acid.
See: Delvinal
Use: Hypnotic; sedative.

• **VINBLASTINE SULFATE,** U.S.P. XXI. Inj., Sterile, U.S.P. XXI. Vincaleukoblastine. Alkaloid extracted from *Vinca rosea* Linn.
Use: Antineoplastic.
See: Velban, Amp., Vial (Lilly)

VINCALEUKOBLASTINE, 22-OXO-, SULFATE (1:1)(SALT). Vincristine Sulfate, U.S.P. XXI.

• **VINCOFOS.** USAN.
Use: Anthelmintic.

• **VINCRISTINE SULFATE,** U.S.P. XXI. Inj., U.S.P. XXI. (Lilly) Vincaleukoblastine, 22-oxo-,sulfate (1:1)(salt) Leurocristine. An alkaloid extracted from Vinca rosea Linn.
Use: Antineoplastic.
See: Oncovin, Amp. (Lilly)

• **VINDESINE.** USAN.
Use: Antineoplastic.

• **VINDESINE SULFATE.** USAN.
Use: Antineoplastic.

• **VINEPIDINE SULFATE.** USAN.
Use: Antineoplastic.

• **VINGLYCINATE SULFATE.** USAN. 4-Deacetylvincaleukoblastine 4-(N,N-dimethylglycinate) (ester) sulfate (1:1.5)(salt).
Use: Antineoplastic.

• **VINLEUROSINE SULFATE.** USAN. Sulfate salt of an alkaloid extracted from *Vinca rosea* Linn. Also see Vinblastine.
Use: Antineoplastic.

• **VINPOCETINE.** USAN.
See: Cavinton (Abbott)

• **VINROSIDINE SULFATE.** USAN. Sulfate salt of an alkaloid extracted from *Vinca rosea* Linn. Also see Vinblastine.
Use: Antineoplastic.

VINYLACETATE-POLYVINYLPYRROLIDONE.
See: Ivy-Rid, Spray (Mallard)

VINYL ALCOHOL POLYMER. Polyvinyl Alcohol, U.S.P. XXI.

VINYLBITONE. B.A.N. 5-(1-Methylbutyl)-5-vinyl-barbituric acid.
Use: Hypnotic; sedative.

• **VINYL ETHER,** U.S.P. XXI.
Use: General anesthetic (inhalation.)
See: Vinethene, Liq.

1-VINYL-2-PYRROLIDINONE POLYMER. Povidone U.S.P. XXI.

VINYZENE. Bromchlorenone.
Use: Fungicide and bactericide.

• **VINZOLIDINE SULFATE.** USAN.
Use: Antineoplastic.

VIO-BEC. (Rowell) Vit. B-1 25 mg., B-2 25 mg., niacinamide 100 mg., Ca pantothenate 40 mg., B-6 25 mg C 500 mg./Cap. Bot. 100s.
Use: Vitamin & mineral supplement.

VIO-BEC FORTE. (Rowell) Vit. B-1 25 mg., B-2 25 mg B-6 25 mg., C 500 mg., calcium pantothenate 40 mg niacinamide 100 mg., E 30 I.U., B-12 5 mcg., folic ac 0.5 mg., Zn 25 mg., Cu 3 mg./Tab. Bot. 100s.
Use: Vitamin therapy.

VIOFORM. (Ciba) Clioquinol.
Cream: (3%) Tube 1 oz.
Oint.: (3% in petrolatum base) Tube 1 oz.
Use: Antifungal, antibacterial.

VIOFORM-HYDROCORTISONE. (Ciba) **Cream:** Clioquinol 3%, hydrocortisone 1% in water-washable base w/stearyl alcohol, cetyl alcohol, stearic acid, sod. lauryl sulfate, glycerin, petrolatum. Tubes 20 Gm. **Ointment:** Clioquinol 3%, hydrocortisone 1% in petrolatum base. Tubes 20 Gm. **Lotion:** Clioquinol 3%, hydrocortisone 1% in water-washable base w/stearic acid, cetyl alcohol, lanolin, propylene glycol, sorbitan trioleate, polysorbate 60 triethanolamine, methylparaben, propylparaben. Plastic squeeze Bot., 15 ml. **Mild Cream** Clioquinol 3%, hydrocortisone 0.5% w/ingredients included in Cream. Tube 0.5 oz., 1 oz. **Mild Ointment:** Clioquinol 3%, hydrocortisone 0.5% in petrolatum base. Tube 1 oz.
Use: Antibacterial, antifungal, antipruritic, antiinflammatory.

'IO-HYDROCORT CREAM. (Quality Generics) Hydrocortisone 10 mg., clioquinol 30 mg./Gm. Tube 5 Gm., 20 Gm.
Use: Antifungal, anti-inflammatory.

'IO-HYDROSONE CREAM. (Vortech) Hydrocortisone 0.1%, clioquinol 3%, pramoxine HCl 0.5%. Tube 0.5 oz.
Use: Relieves pain and itching associated with dermatologic disorders.

'IOKASE. (Robins) **Tab.:** Lipase 8000 u., protease 30,000 u., amylase 30,000 u./16,800 mg. Tab. Bot. 100s, 500s. **Powder:** Lipase 16,800 u., protease 70,000 u., amylase 70,000 u./0.7 Gm. (0.25 tsp.)
Use: Aid digestion.

'IOMYCIN SULFATE. STERILE, Sulfate salt of antibiotic produced by selected strains of *actinomycete* to which *Streptomyces puniceus* & *Streptomyces floridea* have been applied.
Use: Tuberculostatic, antibacterial.

'IONACTANE PANTOTHENATE-SULPHATE. Viomycin, B.A.N.

IO-PRAMOSONE CREAM. (Ferndale) Clioquinol 3%, hydrocortisone acetate 0.5%, pramoxine HCl 1.0% in cream. Bot. 1 oz.
Use: Contact or atopic dermatitis, eczema, infectious dermatitis, anti-pruritic.

IO-PRAMOSONE LOTION. (Ferndale) Clioquinol 3%, hydrocortisone acetate 0.5%, pramoxine HCl 1.0% in lotion. Bot. 1.25 oz.
4 oz.
Use: Contact or atopic dermatitis, eczema, infectious dermatitis, antipruritic.

IOSTEROL W/HALIBUT LIVER OIL. Vit. A 50,000 I.U., Vit. D 10,000 I.U./Gm.
(Abbott)—Bot. 5 cc., 20 cc., 50 cc. Cap. Vit. A 5000 I.U., D 1000 I.U.
(Ives) Cap. Vit. A 5000 I.U., D 1700 I.U.

I-PENTA INFANT DROPS. (Roche) Vit. A 5000 I.U., D 400 I.U., C 50 mg., E 2 I.U./0.6 ml. Bot. 50 ml.
Use: Progressive vitamin therapy for specific age groups.

I-PENTA MULTIVITAMIN DROPS. (Roche) Vit. A 5000 I.U. B-1 1 mg., B-2 1 mg., B-6 1 mg., C 50 mg., D 400 I.U., d-panthenol 10 mg., niacinamide 10 mg. E 2 I.U., d-biotin 30 mcg./0.6 ml. Bot. 50 ml.
Use: Progressive vitamin therapy for specific age groups.

I-PENTA F CHEWABLES. (Roche) Vit. A acetate 5000 I.U., calciferol 10 mcg., C 60 mg., B-1 1.2 mg., B-2 1.5 mg., B-6 1.2 mg., B-12 3 mcg., d-biotin 40 mcg., niacinamide 10 mg., E 2 I.U., d-calcium pantothenate 10 mg., fluoride 1 mg./chewable Tab. Bot. 100s. Available in 5 fruit flavors with matching colors.
Use: Nutritional support.

I-PENTA F INFANT DROPS. (Roche) Vit. A 5000 I.U., calciferol 10 mcg., C 50 mg., dl-alpha-tocopheryl acetate 2 mg., fluoride 0.5 mg./0.6 ml. Bot. 30 ml. w/calibrated dropper.
Use: Infant nutritional.

I-PENTA F MULTIVITAMIN DROPS. (Roche) Vit. A palmitate 5000 I.U., calciferol 10 mcg., C 50 mg., B-1 1 mg., B-2 1 mg., B-6 1 mg., dl-α-tocopheryl acetate 2 I.U., d-biotin 30 mcg., niacinamide 10 mg., d-panthenol 10 mg., fluoride 0.5 mg./0.6 ml. Bot. 30 ml. with a calibrated dropper.
Use: Nutritional supplement.

VIPRYNIUM EMBONATE. B.A.N. 6-Dimethyl-amino-2-[2-(2:5-dimethyl-1-phenyl-3-pyrrolyl)vinyl]-1-methylquinolinium embonate. (Embonic acid is adopted as the trivial name for 4:4′ methylenebis-(3-hydroxymaphthalene-2-carboxylic acid). Vanquin. Pyrvinium Pamoate.
Use: Anthelmintic.

VIRA-A FOR INFUSION. (Parke-Davis) Vidarabine for infusion 200 mg./ml. Vial 5 ml.
Use: Treatment of herpes simplex virus encephalitis.

VIRA-A OPHTHALMIC. (Parke-Davis) Vidarabine 3% in a sterile inert base. Tube 3.5 Gm.
Use: Treatment of acute keratoconjunctivitis & recurrent epithelial keratitis due to herpes simplex virus types 1 & 2.

VIRAC. (Ruson) Undecoylium chloride-iodine. Iodine complexed with a cationic detergent. Surgical sol. Bot. 2 oz., 8 oz., 1 gal.
Use: Antiseptic.

VIRACIL. (Approved) Phenylephrine HCl 5 mg., hesperidin 50 mg., thenylene HCl 12.5 mg., pyrilamine maleate 12.5 mg., C 50 mg., salicylamide 2.5 gr., caffeine 0.5 gr., sod. salicylate 1.25 gr./Cap. Bot. 16s, 36s.
Use: Cold symptoms.

VIRAMISOL. (Seatrace) Adenosine phosphate 25 mg./ml. Vial 10 cc.

VIRANOL. (American Dermal) Salicylic acid 16.7%, lactic acid 16.7% in flexible collodion vehicle. Bot. 10 ml.
Use: Removal of warts.

• **VIRIDOFULVIN.** USAN.
Use: Antifungal.

• **VIRGINIAMYCIN.** USAN. An antibiotic produced by *Streptomyces virginie.*

VIRIDIUM. (Vita Elixir) Phenylazodiaminopyridine HCl 100 mg./Tab.
Use: Genito-urinary antisepsis.

VIRILON. (Star) Methyltestosterone 10 mg./Cap. (sustained release) Bot. 100s, 1000s.
Use: Male climacteric, hypogonadal impotence, neurasthenia.

VIROMED LIQUID. (Whitehall) Acetaminophen 10 gr., pseudoephedrine HCl 30 mg., dextromethorphan HBr 20 mg., alcohol 16.63%. Bot. 6 oz.
Use: Antitussive, analgesic.

VIROMED TABLETS. (Whitehall) Aspirin 5 gr., chlorpheniramine maleate 1 mg., pseudoephedrine HCl 15 mg., dextromethorphan HBr 7.5 mg., guaifenesin 50 mg./Tab. Bot. 20s, 48s.
Use: Antitussive, analgesic.

VIROPTIC OPHTHALMIC SOLUTION. (Burroughs Wellcome) Trifluridine 1%. Bot. 7.5 ml.
Use: Herpes simplex eye infection treatment.

• **VIROXIME.** USAN.
Use: Antiviral.

VIROZYME INJECTION. (Marcen) Sodium nucleate 2.5%, phenol 0.5%, protein hydrolysate 2.5%, benzyl alcohol 0.2%. Vial 5 cc., 10 cc.
Use: Promote leukocytosis and phagocytosis.

VIRUGON. Under study. Anhydro bis-(beta-hydroxyethyl) biguanide derivative.
Use: Treatment of influenza, mumps, measles, chickenpox, and shingles.

VISALENS SOAKING & CLEANING SOLUTION. (Leeming) Sterile sol. containing cleaning agents, benzalkonium chloride, buffered sol. Bot. 4 oz.
Use: Soaking & cleaning sol. for hard contact lenses.

VISALENS WETTING SOLUTION. (Leeming) Sterile sol. containing polyvinyl alcohol with hydroxypropyl methylcellulose, edetate disodium, sodium chloride, benzalkonium chloride 1:25,000 Bot. 2 oz.
Use: Wetting agent for hard contact lenses.

VISCARIN W/IODINE, BORIC ACID, PHENOL, CHLOROPHYLL.
See: Triophyll, Liq. (Schaffer)

VISCLAIR HYDROCHLORIDE. Methyl Cysteine, B.A.N.

VISCULOSE. (Softcon) Methylcellulose 0.5%, 1% w/benzalkonium chloride 1:25,000 Bot. 15 cc.
Use: Substitute for lacrimal secretions, for patients with tear deficiencies.

VISCUM ALBUM, EXTRACT. Visnico.
Use: Vasodilator.

VISIDEX II REAGENT STRIPS. (Ames) Disposable plastic test strip with two reagent pads. Glucose oxidase reaction. Bot. 25s.
Use: Blood glucose testing using visual interpretation of test results.

VISINE. (Leeming) Tetrahydrozoline HCl 0.05%, NaCl, boric acid, sodium borate, benzalkonium chloride 0.01%, disodium ethylenediamine tetraacetate 0.1%. Dropper Bot. 0.5 oz.; Plastic bot. 0.5 oz., ¾ oz., 1 oz.
Use: Eye irritations.

VISINE AC. (Leeming) Tetrahydrozoline HCl 0.05%, zinc sulfate 0.25%, benzalkonium chloride 0.01%, NaCl, boric acid, sodium citrate, ethylene diamine tetraacetate 0.1%. Bot. 0.5 oz., 1 oz.
Use: Eye irritations accompanied by allergy and colds.

VISKEN. (Sandoz) Pindolol 5 mg. or 10 mg./Tab. Bot. 100s.
Use: Hypertension treatment.

VISNADINE. B.A.N. 10-Acetoxy-9,10-dihydro-8,8-dimethyl-9-α-methylbutyryloxy-2H,8H-benzo-[1,2-b:3,4-b']dipyran-2-one. Cardine.
Use: Coronary vasodilator.

VISTACON. (Hauck) Hydroxyzine HCl 25 mg./ml. Vial 10 ml. 50 mg/ml. Vial 10 ml.
Use: Management of tension, anxiety, psychomotor agitation.

VISTAJECT 25 & 50. (Mayrand) Hydroxyzine HCl 25 mg. or 50 mg./ml. Vial 10 ml.
Use: Relief of anxiety and tension.

VISTAREX 50. (Tunex) Hydroxyzine HCl 50 mg./ml. Vial 10cc.
Use: Anxiety, nausea, vomiting.

VISTARIL. (Pfizer Laboratories) Hydroxyzine pamoate equiv. to Hydroxyzine HCl, **Cap.:** 25, 50, 100 mg. Bot. 100s, 500s, Unit Dose 100s. **Oral susp.** 25 mg./5 cc. Bot. 120 ml., pt.
Use: Psychotherapeutic agent.

VISTARIL I.M. (Pfipharmecs) Hydroxyzine HCl 25 mg./ml. & 50 mg./ml. Vial 10 ml. Unit dose 25 mg./ml.; 50 mg./ml.; 75 mg./1.5 ml.; 100 mg./2 ml Box 10's.
Use: Ataraxic.

VISTARIL ISOJECT I.M. (Pfipharmecs) Hydroxyzine HCl 50 mg./ml. & 100 mg./2 ml. Amp. 1 ml., 2 ml.
Use: Ataraxic.

VISTAZINE 50. (Keene) Hydroxyzine HCl 50 mg./ml. Vial 10 mg./ml.
Use: Psychotherapeutic agent.

VISTRAX 5 & 10. (Pfizer Laboratories) Oxyphencyclimine 5 mg. or 10 mg., hydroxyzine 25 mg./Tab. Bot. 100s.
Use: Anticholinergic.

VITABANK. (Williams) Vit. A 5,000 I.U., E 30 I.U.,C 90 mg., folic acid 400 mcg., B-1 2.25 mg., B-2 2.6 mg niacinamide 20 mg., B-6 3 mg., B-12 9 mcg., D 40[illegible] I.U., biotin 45 mcg., pantothenic acid 10 mg., Ca 170 mg., P 130 mg., iodine 150 mcg., Fe 18 mg., Mg 100 mg., Cu 2 mg., Mn. 2.5 mg., K 7.5 mg., Zn 15 mg., selenium 25 mcg./Tab. Bot. 60s.
Use: Multivitamin with minerals.

VITABEE 1. (CMC) Thiamine **Inj.:** 100 mg./cc. Vial 1[illegible] cc., 30 cc. **Tab.:** 10 mg., 25 mg., 50 mg., 100 mg., 250 mg. Bot. 100s, 1000s.

VITABEE 2. (CMC) Riboflavin **Inj.:** 40 mg./cc. Vial 1[illegible] cc. **Tab.:** 10 mg., 25 mg., 50 mg. Bot. 100s, 1000s

VITABEE 6. (CMC) Pyridoxine HCl **Inj.:** 100 mg./cc. Vial 10 cc. **Tab.:** 10 mg., 25 mg., 50 mg., 100 mg., 250 mg. Bot. 100s, 1000s.

VITABIX. (Spanner) Vit. B-1 100 mg., B-2 2 mg., B-6 5 mg., B-12 30 mcg., niacinamide 100 mg., panthenol 10 mg./cc. 10 cc. Multiple dose vial 30 cc. Inj. I.M. or I.V.

V-I TABS. (Kenyon) Vit. A 5000 I.U., D-2 500 mg., B-1 3 mg., B-2 2.5 mg., B-6 1 mg., B-12 1 mg., C 50 mg niacinamide 20 mg., Ca pantothenate 1 mg., Fe 15 mg./Tab. Bot. 100s, 1000s.

VITA-CEBUS. (Cenci) Vit. A 10,000 I.U., D 1000 I.U., [illegible] 100 mg., B-1 5 mg., B-2 5 mg., B-6 1 mg., B-12 mcg., niacin and niacinamide 30 mg., Ca pantothenate 5 mg., E 3 mg., yeast 1 gr., liver 1 gr., hesperidin complex 10 mg., Ca 200 mg., Cu 0.75 mg., Mg 5 mg., Mn 1 mg., K 5 mg., Zn 0.3 mg./2 Tabs. Bot. 100s, 250s. Liquid, 4 oz., 8 oz.
Use: Dietary supplement.

VITACEE. (CMC) Vitamin C 100 mg. or 500 mg./2 cc Amp. 2 cc. 500 mg. Amp. 5 cc. I.M.-I.V. 1000 mg. Amp 10 cc.

VITACOMP. (Jenkins) Vit. A 5000 I.U., D 400 I.U., B-1 3 mg., B-2 2.5 mg., C 50 mg., B-6 1 mg., B-12 1 mcg niacinamide 20 mg., pantothenic acid 1 mg./Tab. Bot. 1000s.
Use: Multiple vitamin tablet.

VITACREST. (Nutrition) Vit. A 25,000 I.U., D 400 I.U. E 10 I.U., B-1 25 mg., B-2 12 mg., B-6 10 mg., B-

12 10 mcg., biotin 10 mcg., folic acid 0.1 mg., Ca pantothenate 25 mg., niacinamide 50 mg., inositol 25 mg., l-glutamic acid 10 mg., l-lysine HCl 20 mg., p-aminobenzoic acid 25 mg., C 250 mg., wheat germ oil 10 mg., brewers yeast, dried 10 mg., whole liver desic. 10 mg., soybean lecithin 50 mg., iron 10 mg., cal. carbonate 625 mg., Cu 0.2 mg., Zn 0.2 mg., Mg 10 mg., Mn 0.2 mg., K 10 mg./Cap. Bot. 100s.
Use: Therapeutic vitamin-mineral formula.

VITADYE. (Elder) F.D. & C yellow No. 5, D. & C. red. No. 40, F.D. & C. blue No. 1 dyes & dihydroxyacetone 5%. Bot. 0.5 oz., 2 oz.
Use: Cosmetic cover for hypopigmented skin.

VITAFOL. (Everett) Vitamins, folic acid, iron, calcium. Bot. 100s, 1000s.
Use: Dietary supplement

VITA ELIXIR. (Vita Elixir) Alcohol 25%, Vit. A palmitate 5000 U., D-2 500 U., iron 10 mg./45 cc. w/multivitamins & minerals.
Use: Dietary supplement.

VITAFORT. (Kessel) Vit. A 4,000 I.U., D 400 I.U., E 15 I.U., C 70 mg., folic acid 1 mg., B-1 2 mg., B-2 2 mg., niacinamide 20 mg., B-6 2 mg., B 12 5 mcg., Ca-pantothenate 10 mg./Cap. Bot. 60s.
Use: Nutritional supplement

VITAGETTS. (Vortech) Vit. A palmitate 5000 I.U., Vit. D 1000 I.U., B-1 3 mg., B-2 2.5 mg., nicotinamide 20 mg., B-6 1.5 mg., calcium pantothenate 5 mg., B-12 2.5 mcg., C 50 mg., Vit. E 3 I.U., Ca 251 mg., P 166 mg., Fe 13.4 mg., Mg 7.5 mg., Mn 1.5 mg., K 5 mg., Zn 1.4 mg./Tab. Bot. 100s, 1000s.
Use: Vitamin & mineral therapy.

VITA-GLEN. (Glenwood) Pediatric multiple vitamin. Cap. Bot. 100s.

VITA-IRON. (Century) Vit. A 5000 I.U., D 500 I.U., B-1 2 mg., B-2 2.5 mg., C 50 mg., B-6 1 mg., B-12 1 mcg., niacinamide 20 mg., Ca pantothenate 1 mg., iron 15 mg./Tab. Bot. 30s, 100s, 1000s.
Use: Multivitamin with iron.

VITA-IRON FORMULA. (Barth's) Iron 120 mg., B-1 5 mg., B-2 10 mg., C 20 mg., niacin 2 mg., B-12 25 mcg. lysine, desic. liver 200 mg., bromelain/Tab. Bot. 100s, 500s.

VITAJEN. (Jenkins) Vit. B-1 12 mg., B-2 4 mg., B-12 10 mcg., B-6 2 mg., Ca pantothenate 6 mg., nicotinic acid 40 mg./Fl. oz. Bot. 4 oz., gal.
Use: B complex supplement.

VITA-KAPS FILMTABS. (Abbott) Vit. A 5000 I.U., D 400 I.U., B-1 3 mg., B-2 2.5 mg., nicotinamide 20 mg., B-6 1 mg., C 50 mg., B-12 3 mcg./Filmtab. Bot. 100s.
Use: Dietary supplement.

VITAKAPS-M. (Abbott) Vit. A 5000 I.U., D 400 I.U., B-1 3 mg., B-2 2.5 mg., nicotinamide 20 mg., B-6 1 mg., B-12 3 mcg., C 50 mg., Fe 10 mg., Cu 1 mg., Iodine 0.15 mg., Mn 1 mg., Zn 7.5 mg./Filmtab. Bot. 100s.
Use: Multivitamin with minerals.

VITAL. (Ross) Each packet contains: Protein 12.5 Gm., fat 3.25 Gm., carbohydrates 56.5 Gm., Vit. A 1000 I.U., Vit. D 80 I.U., Vit. E 12 I.U., Vit C 18 mg., folic acid 0.08 mg., B-1 0.3 mg., B-2 0.34 mg., B-6 0.44 mg., B-12 1.2 mcg., niacin 4 mg., biotin 0.06 mg., pantothenic acid 2 mg., Vit K-1 56 mcg., choline 40 mg., Ca 200 mg., phosphorus 200 mg., Na 115 mg., potassium 350 mg., Cl 200 mg., Mg 80 mg., iodine 30 mcg., Mn 0.75 mg., Cu 0.4 mg., Zn 3 mg., Fe 3.6 mg./Packet W/glucose oligo- and poly-saccharides, enzymatically hydrolyzed proteins (soy, whey and meat), sucrose, corn starch, safflower oil. Packets 2.75-oz (79 Gm.)/Case of 72.
Use: Hydrolyzed, low-residue feeding for patients with impared gastrointestinal function.

VITAL HIGH NITROGEN. (Ross) A partially hydrolized low-residue feeding providing complete nutrition for patients with impaired gastrointestinal function. Packets 2.79 oz. Ctn. 6s.
Use: Nutritional feeding.

VITALAX. (Vitalax) Candy base, gumdrop flavored. Pkg. 20s.
Use: Laxative.

VITALITY E CAPSULES. (Quality Generics) Wheat germ oil 3 min./Cap. Bot. 100s, 1000s.

VITALITY-E "6" CAPSULES. (Quality Generics) Wheat germ oil 6 minims/Cap. Bot. 100s, 1000s.

VITALITY-E "14". (Quality Generics) Wheat germ oil 14 minims/Cap. Bot. 100s, 1000s.

VITALITY-E "20". (Quality Generics) Wheat germ oil 20 minims/Cap. Bot. 100s, 1000s.
Use: Vitamin supplement.

VITAMEL-M. (Eastwood) Liquid Bot. 16 oz.

VITAMEL WITH IRON. (Eastwood) Drops 50 cc. Chewable Tab. Bot. 100s.

• **VITAMIN A,** U.S.P. XXI. Caps., U.S.P. XXI. Oleovitamin A.
Use: Anti-xerophthalmic vitamin, emollient.

Ampules
Aquasol A Preps. (USV Pharm.)

Capsules
Acon (Du Pont)
Alphalin (Lilly)
Aquasol A (USV Labs.)
Vi-Dom-A (Miles Pharm)

Ointment
Aquasol A (USV Pharm.)
Retin-A (Johnson & Johnson)

Tablets
Dispatabs (Person & Covey)

Vials
Aquasol A (USV Labs.)

VITAMIN A, ALPHALIN. (Lilly) Vit. A. 50,000 I.U./Gelseal. Bot. 100s.
Use: Vitamin A deficiency.

VITAMIN A, WATER MISCIBLE, OR SOLUBLE. Water Miscible vitamin A.

VITAMIN Bc.
See: Folic acid (Var. Mfr.)

VITAMIN B-1. Thiamine Hydrochloride, U.S.P. XXI.

VITAMIN B-1 MONONITRATE. Thiamine mononitrate.

VITAMIN B-1 & B-12. (Pharmex) Vit. B-1 100 mg., B-12 1000 mcg./cc. Vial 10 cc.

VITAMIN B-1 W/PANCREATIN, OX BILE EXT. PEPSIN, GLUTAMIC ACID HCl.
See: Maso-Gestive, Tab. (Mason)

VITAMIN B-1 W/THYROID.
See: T & T, Tab. (Mason)

VITAMIN B-2. Riboflavin, U.S.P. XXI.

VITAMIN B-3. Niacinamide, U.S.P. XXI. Nicotinamide.

VITAMIN B-5. Calcium Pantothenate U.S.P. XXI.

VITAMIN B-6. Pyridoxine Hydrochloride, U.S.P. XXI.
See: Hexa-Betalin, Tab. (Lilly)
Hexavibex, Vial (Parke-Davis)

VITAMIN B-6 & B-1. (Pharmex) Vit. B-6 100 mg., B-1 100 mg./cc. Vial 10 cc.

VITAMIN B-8.
See: Adenosine phosphate.

VITAMIN B-12. Cyanocobalamin, U.S.P. XXI. Cobalamine.
See:
Capsules & Tablets
Redisol (Merck Sharp & Dohme)
Vials & Ampules
Bedoce (Lincoln)
Berubigen (Upjohn)
Betalin-12 (Lilly)
Cabadon-M (Reid-Provident)
Cobadoce Forte (Reid-Provident)
Crysto-Gel (Reid-Provident)
Cyano-Gel, Liq. (Maurry)
Dodex (Organon)
Poyamin (Fellows)
Redisol (Merck Sharp & Dohme)
Rhodavin (Noyes)
Rubramin (Squibb)
Ruvite 1000 (Savage)
Sigamine (Sig)
Sytobex-H (Parke-Davis)
Vibedoz, Inj. (Blue Line)
Vi-Twel, Inj. (Berlex)

W/Ferrous-sulfate, ascorbic acid, folic acid.
See: Intrin, Cap. (Merit)

W/Folic acid, niacinamide, liver.
See: Hepfomin 500 Inj. (Keene Pharm.)

W/Thiamine.
See: Cobalin, Vial (Ulmer)
Cyamine, Vial (Keene)

W/Thiamine & vitamin B-6.
See: Orexin, Tab. (Stuart)

VITAMIN B-12a & b.
See: Hydroxocobalamin (Var. Mfr.)

VITAMIN B-15. Pangamic acid, betaglucono-dimethylaminoacetic acid.
Use: Alleged to increase oxygen supply in blood. Not approved by FDA as a vitamin or drug. Illegal to sell Vitamin B-15.

VITAMIN B-17.
See Laetril.

VITAMIN B COMPLEX. Conc. ext. of dried brewer's yeast & ext. of corn processed w/*Clostridium acetobutylicum.*
See: Becotin, Pulvule (Lilly)
Betalin Complex, Amp. (Lilly)
Savaplex, Vial (Savage)

W/Estrone, testosterone.
See: Amplex, Inj. (Vortech)

VITAMIN B COMPLEX CAPSULES, N.J.F. (Quality Generics) Vit. B-1 2 mg., B-2 3 mg., B-6 1 mg. niacinamide 20 mg., dried yeast 300 mg./Cap. Bot. 100s, 1000s.

VITAMIN B COMPLEX NO. 104. (Century) Vit. B-1 10 mg., B-2 2 mg., B-6 2 mg., d-panthenol 10 mg. niacinamide 125 mg., benzyl alcohol 1%, gentisic acid ethanolamide 2.5%/Vial 30 cc.

VITAMIN B COMPLEX, BETALIN COMPLEX, ELIXIR. (Lilly) Vit. B-1 2.7 mg., B-2 1.35 mg., B-12 3 mcg., B-6 0.555 mg., pantothenic acid 2.7 mg. niacinamide 6.75 mg., liver fraction 500 mg./5 ml. w/alcohol 17%. Bot. 16 oz.
Use: Vitamin B supplement.

VITAMIN B-COMPLEX W/C. (Sutliff & Case) Vit. B-1 2.5 mg., B-2 3 mg., niacinamide 25 mg., calcium pantothenate 5 mg., B-6 2.5 mg., C 100 mg., B-12 2 mcg., brewer's yeast 240 mg./Tab. Bot. 100s, 1000s.

VITAMIN B COMPLEX W/VITAMIN C. (Century) Vit. B-1 25 mg., B-2 5 mg., B-6 5 mg., niacinamide 50 mg. panthenol 5 mg., calcium 50 mg., propethylene glycol 300 10%, gentisic acid ethanolamide 2.5%, benzyl alcohol 2%/Vial 30 cc.

VITAMIN B COMPLEX, BETALIN COMPLEX CAPSULES. (Lilly) Vit. B-1 1 mg., B-2 2 mg., B-6 0.4 mg., pantothenic acid 3.333 mg., niacinamide 10 mg., Vit. B-12 1 mcg./Pulvule. Bot. 100s.
Use: Orally, vitamin B complex deficiencies.

VITAMIN C.
See: Ascorbic Acid Preparations.

VITAMIN C, CEVALIN. (Lilly) Ascorbic acid. **250 mg.** /Tab. Bot. 100s. **500 mg.**/Tab. Bot. 100s, 500s.
Use: Vitamin C deficiency.

VITAMIN C W/COMBINATIONS.
See: Allbee C-800, Prods. (Robins)
Allbee with C, Cap. (Robins)
Allbee-T, Tab. (Robins)
Anti-therm, Tab. (Scrip)
Bejectal w/Vit. C (Abbott)
Colrex, Cap. (Rowell)
C.P.C. plus, Tab. (Coastal)
Nialexo-C, Tab. (Mallard)
Thex, Cap. (Ingram)
Thex Forte, Cap. (Ingram)
Vicon-C, Cap. (Glaxo)
Vicon Chewable, Tab. (Glaxo)
Vicon Forte, Cap. (Glaxo)
Vicon Plus, Cap. (Glaxo)
Vi-Zac, Cap. (Glaxo)
Z-BEC, Tab. (Robins)

VITAMIN C SYRUP. (Quality Generics) Vit. C 500 mg./5 cc. Bot. 4 oz.

VITAMIN D. Cholecalciferol, U.S.P. XXI.

VITAMIN D, DELTALIN. (Lilly) Vit. D 2. 50,000 Units (1.25 mg.)/Gelseal. Bot. 100s.
Use: Vitamin D deficiency.

VITAMIN D, SYNTHETIC.
See: Activated 7-Dehydro-cholesterol Calciferol

ITAMIN D-1.
See: Dihydrotachysterol.

ITAMIN D-2. Activated ergasterol, Ergocalciferol.
See: Calciferol, Prep. (Various Mfr.)
Drisdol, Liq. (Winthrop-Breon)
Viosterol (Various Mfr.)

ITAMIN D-3.
See: Activated 7-dehydrocholesterol
Calciferol Prep. for related activity

ITAMIN D-3-CHOLESTEROL. Cpd. of crystalline vitamin D-3 & cholesterol.

ITAMIN D-4.
See: Dihydrotachysterol, Prep. (Various Mfr.)

ITAMIN D CAPSULES. (Quality Generics) Vit. D 50,000 I.U./Cap. Bot. 100s, 1000s.

VITAMIN E, U.S.P. XXI. Cap., U.S.P. XXI. It may consist of: d- or dl-alpha tocopherol, d-ordl alpha tocopheryl acetate, d- or dl-alpha tocopheryl acid succinate, mixed tocopherols concentrate, or d-alpha tocopheryl acetate concentrate.
See: Aquasol E (USV)
Eprolin, Gelseal (Lilly)
E-Vites, Cap. (Quality Generics)
Pertropin Caps. (Lannett)
Solucap E. Cap. (Jamieson-McKames)
Tega-E-Cream (Ortega)
Tocopher, Prod. (Quality Generics)
Tocopherol, Prep. (Various Mfr.)
Wheat Germ Oil (Various Mfr.)

ITAMIN E, EPROLIN. (Lilly) Alpha-tocopherol, 100 units/Gelseal. Bot. 100s.
Use: Vitamin E therapy.

ITAMIN E W/QUININE SULFATE, NIACIN.
See: Myodyne, Tab. (Paddock)

ITAMIN E LOTION. (Vortech) D-alpha tocopheryl acetate (natural) 200 I.U., 1000 I.U./oz. in non-greasy emollient residual base. Bot. 1 oz., 2 oz., 4 oz., 16 oz.
Use: Dermatologic.

ITAMIN E SKIN OIL. (Quality Generics) Pure Vit. E 28,000 I.U. Bot. 1 Oz.
Use: Emollient.

ITAMIN F.
See: Fats, Unsaturated
Fatty Acids, Unsaturated

ITAMIN G.
See: Riboflavin

ITAMIN K.
See: Hykinone, Amp. (Abbott)
Menadiol, Sodium Diphosphate, Prep. (Various Mfr.)
Menadione, Prep. (Various Mfr.)
Menadione Sod. Bisulfite, Prep. (Various Mfr.)

ITAMIN K. Phytomenadione, B.A.N.

ITAMIN K-1.
See: Phytonadione, U.S.P. XXI.

ITAMIN K-3.
See: Menadione, U.S.P. XXI.

ITAMIN K OXIDE. Not available, but usually K-1 is desired.

VITAMIN M.
See: Folic Acid, U.S.P. XXI.

VITAMIN P. Citrin.
See: Bio-Flavonoid Cpds. (Various Mfr.)
Hesperidin Preps. (Various Mfr.)
Quercetin (Various Mfr.)
Rutin, Prep. (Various Mfr.)

VITAMIN T. Sesame seed factor, termite factor.
Use: Claimed to aid proper blood coagulation and promote formation of blood platelets. Not approved by FDA as an active vitamin.

VITAMIN U. Present in cabbage juice.

VITAMINS W/ANTIOBESITY AGENTS.
See: Fetamin Tab. (Mission)
Obedrin Cap. or Tab. (Massengill)

VITAMINS W/LIVER & LIPOTROPIC AGENTS.
See: Heptuna, Cap. (Roerig)
Lederplex, Preps. (Lederle)
Livitamin, Preps. (Beecham Labs)
Metheponex, Caps. (Rawl)
Methischol, Caps. (USV Pharm.)

VITAMIN, MAINTENANCE FORMULA.
See: Stuart Formula, Tab & Liq. (Stuart)
Vi-Magna, Cap. (Lederle)

VITA-MINS. (Mills) Vit. A 5000 I.U., D 200 I.U., C 30 mg., B-1 1 mg., B-2 2 mg., B-6 0.1 mg., B-12 1 mcg., d-calcium pantothenate 0.5 mg., niacinamide 20 mg., folic acid 0.1 mg., ferrous gluconate 25 mg., copper gluconate 5 mg., zinc gluconate 5 mg., manganese gluconate 5 mg./Tab. Bot. 100s.
Use: Vitamin and mineral therapy.

VITAMINS: STRESS FORMULA.
See: Cebefortis, Tab. (Upjohn)
Folbesyn, Tab., Vial (Lederle)
Probec-T, Tab. (Stuart)
Stresscaps, Cap. (Lederle)
Stresscaps With Iron (Lederle)
Stresscaps With Zinc (Lederle)
Stresstabs-600 (Lederle)
Thera-combex Kap. (Parke-Davis)

VITA NATAL. (Scot-Tussin) Folic Acid 1 mg./Tab. Bot. 100s.
Use: Vitamin therapy.

VITA NO. ONE. (Freeport) Thiamine monitrate 15 mg., riboflavin 10 mg., pyridoxine HCl 5 mg., nicotinamide 50 mg., calcium pantothenate 10 mg., ascorbic acid 300 mg./Cap. Bot. 100s.
Use: Vit. B-Complex & C deficiencies.

VITAON. (Vita Elixir) Vit. B-12 25 mcg., thiamine HCl 10 mg., ferric pyrophosphate 250 mg./5 cc.
Use: Therapeutic elixir.

VITA PLUREX FORTE. (Standex) Vit. B-1 1.5 mg., B-2 2.0 mg., B-6 0.1 mg., Ca pantothenate 1.0 mg., niacinamide 10.0 mg./Tab. Bot. 100s.

VITA PLUREX W/C CAPSULES. (Standex) Vit. B-1 15 mg., B-2 10 mg., B-6 5 mg., niacinamide 50 mg., Ca pantothenate 10 mg., Vit. C 300 mg./Cap. Bot. 100s.

VITA-PLUS B-12. (Scot-Tussin) Vit. B-12 injection 1,000 mcg./ml.
Use: Vitamin B-12 therapy.

VITA-PLUS E. (Scot-Tussin) Vit. E 400 I.U./Cap.
Use: Vitamin E therapy.

VITA-PLUS H CAPSULES. (Scot-Tussin). Bot. 100s.
Use: Hematinic.

VITA-PLUS H LIQUID. (Scot-Tussin) Vit. B-1 10 mg.; l-lysine monohydrochloride 100 mg.; B-12 25 mcg.; B-6 5 mg.; iron pyrophosphate soluble 100 mg./Tsp. Bot. 4 oz., 8 oz. pt., gal.
Use: Hematinic with B vitamins.

VITAREX. (Pasadena Research) Vit. A 25,000 I.U., D 400 I.U., B-1 15 mg., B-2 10 mg., B-6 3 mg., B-12 5 mcg., C 300 mg., niacinamide 100 mg., Ca pantothenate 20 mg., E 10 I.U., Fe 15 mg., Iodine 0.15 mg., Ca 50 mg., P 40 mg., Cu 0.1 mg., Mn 0.1 mg., Mg 5 mg., K 2 mg./Tab. Bot. 30s, 100s, 4000s.

VITA-SED. (Galen) Phenobarbital 0.5 gr., Vit. B-1 1.5 mg., B-2 2 mg., C 20 mg./Tab. Bot. 100s, 1000s.
Use: Sedative, vitamin combination.

VITA-SUP. (Kenyon) Vit. A 12,500 I.U., D 1000 I.U., B-1 5 mg., B-2 2.5 mg., B-6 1 mg., B-12 2 mcg., C 75 mg., niacinamide 40 mg., Ca pantothenate 4 mg., E 3 I.U., dical. phosphate 260 mg., choline bitartrate 31.4 mg., inositol 15 mg., liver protein fraction 25 mg., ferrous sulfate 102 mg., Mn sulfate 1.5 mg., pot. sulfate 4.5 mg., Zn sulfate 1.4 mg., Mg sulfate 21.6 mg./Cap. Bot. 100s, 1000s.

VITATONE DROPS. (Winthrop Products) Multivitamin.
Use: Dietary supplement.

VITAZIN. (Mesmer) Ascorbic acid 300 mg., niacinamide 100 mg., thiamine monoitrate 20 mg., d-Calcium pantothenate 20 mg., riboflavin 10 mg., pyridoxine HCl 5 mg., magnesium sulfate 70 mg., zinc 110 mg./Cap.
Use: Vitamin & mineral supplement.

VITA-ZOO. (Towne) Vit. A 2500 I.U., D 400 I.U., E 15 I.U., C 60 mg., folic acid 0.3 mg., B-1 1.05 mg., B-2 1.20 mg., niacin 13.50 mg., B-6 1.05 mg., B-12 4.5 mcg./Tab. Bot. 100s.
Use: Dietary supplement.

VITA-ZOO PLUS IRON. (Towne) Vit. A 2500 I.U., D 400 I.U., E 15 I.U., C 60 mg., folic acid 0.3 mg., B-1 1.05 mg., B-2 1.20 mg., niacin 13.5 mg., B-6 1.05 mg., Vit. B-12 4.5 mcg., iron 15 mg./Tab. Bot. 100s.
Use: Dietary supplement.

VI-TESTROGEN. (Pharmex) Testosterone 10 mg., estrogenic substance (natural) 1 mg., Vit. B-1 50 mg., B-2 2 mg., B-6 5 mg., panthenol 10 mg., niacinamide 100 mg., inositol 25 mg., choline chloride 25 mg., d,l-methionine 25 mg./cc, sod. carboxymethylcellulose 0.05%, procaine HCl 1%, benzyl alcohol 2%. Vial 10 cc.

VITEX-C. (Pasadena Research) Vit. B-1 10 mg., riboflavin-5′-phosphate Na 10 mg., B-6 20 mg., panthenol 20 mg., biotin 0.2 mg., C 100 mg., niacinamide 100 mg./2 cc. Amp. 2 cc., 25s, 100s. Vial 10 cc., 30 cc.
Use: Vitamin supplement for IM or IV use.

VITEXIN. (Pasadena Research) Vit. B-1 100 mg., B-2 10 mg., B-6 50 mg., d-panthenol 20 mg., niacinamide 75 mg./cc. Vial 10 cc.

VIT-MIN-I-FACT. (Sutliff & Case) Vit. A 5000 I.U., D 4(I.U., E 2 I.U., B-1 3 mg., B-2 3 mg., B-6 0.5 mg., B 12 1 mcg., niacinamide 25 mg., calcium pantothenate 5 mg., C 75 mg., Cu 1 mg., Mn 3 mg., Mg 6 mg., dicalcium phosphorous anhydrous 200 mg., K 5 mg./Tab. Bot. 100s.

VITORMAINS. (Hauck) Tab. Bot. 100s.
Use: Multiple vitamin.

VITRAMONE. (Harvey) Natural estrogenic hormone mg., w/Vit. B-1 10 mg., B-2 2 mg., B-6 5 mg., niacinamide 40 mg., inositol 50 mg., choline chloride 10 mg., methionine 10 mg./cc. 10 ml.
Use: Estrogen therapy w/Vitamin B complex.

VITRON-C. (Fisons) Ferrous fumarate 200 mg., ascorbic acid 125 mg. Tab. Bot. 100s, 1000s.
Use: Iron deficiency anemia.

VITRON-C PLUS TABLETS. (Fisons) Ferrous fumara 400 mg., Vit. C 250 mg./Tab. Bot. 30s, 100s, 500s
Use: Iron deficiency anemia.

VITRONIC LIQUID. (Coastal) Vit. B-1 5 mg., B-2 5 mg B-6 1 mg., B-12 3 mcg., iron 100 mg., nicotinic aci 100 mg., magnesium 5 mg./30 cc., alcohol 15%. Bot. pt.

VIVACTIL. (Merck Sharp & Dohme) Protriptyline HCl 5 mg./Tab. Bot. 100s. 10 mg./Tab. Bot. 100s. Unit dose 100s.
Use: Antidepressant.

VIVALAN HYDROCHLORIDE. Viloxazine, B.A.N.

VIVARIN. (Beecham Products) Caffeine. alkaloid 200 mg./Tab. Bot. 16, 40, 80.
Use: Stimulant.

VIVIKON. (Brown) Vit. B-1 5 mg., B-2 2 mg., B-6 10 mg d-panthenol 5 mg., niacinamide 10 mg., procaine HC 2%/cc. 100 cc.

VIVONEX FLAVOR PACKETS. (Norwich Eaton) Orange-pineapple, lemon-lime, strawberry, and vanilla. Pkg. 60s.
Use: Non-nutritive flavoring for Vivonex diets whe consumed as the oral feedings.

VIVONEX, HIGH NITROGEN. (Norwich Eaton) Free amino acid/complete enteral nutrition. Ten packets provide 3,000 kilocalories, 20 Gm. available nitrogen, 135 Gm. amino acids, 2.61 Gm. fat, 630 Gm. carbohydrate & full day's balanced nutrition. Calorie: nitrogen ratio is 150:1. Unflavored powder, 80 Gm. packets, Pkg. 10s.
Use: Elemental high nitrogen diet for drinking & enteral catheter feeding.

VIVONEX, STANDARD. (Norwich Eaton) Free amino acid/complete enteral nutrition. Six packets provide 1,800 kilocalories, 5.88 Gm. available nitrogen (37.08 Gm. usable protein), 2.61 Gm. fat, 407 Gm. carbohydrate, and full day's balanced nutrition. Calorie: nitrogen ratio is 300:1. Unflavored powder, 80 Gm. packets, Pkg. 6s.
Use: Elemental diet for drinking and enteral catheter feeding.

VIVONEX T.E.N. (Norwich Eaton) Elemental diet for total enteral nutrition. Pkg. 80.4 Gm. Ctn. 10s.
Use: Dietary.

VI-ZAC. (Glaxo) Vit. A 5000 I.U., C 500 mg., E 50 I.U., zinc sulfate 80 mg./Cap. Bot. 60s, 500s.
Use: Therapeutic vitamin-mineral complex.

V-LAX. (Century) Psyllium mucilloid (hydrophilic) 50%, dextrose 50%. Powder 0.25 lb., 1 lb., 5 lb.
Use: Fecal softener.

VLEMASQUE. (Dermik) Sulfurated lime topical solution 6% (Vleminck's Soln.) w/alcohol 7% in drying clay mask. Jar. 4 oz.
Use: Treatment of acne.

VLEM-DOME. (Miles Pharm) Vleminckx solution in powder form. Calcium polysulfide, calcium thiosulfate, sulfur. 4 cc. container mixed w/1 pt. water. Packets 6s.
Use: Skin conditions (acne).

VLEMINCKX'S SOLUTION. Solution of Sulfurated Lime.
Use: Antiseptic.
See: Ulmer.

VM. (Last) Vit. B-1 6 mg., B-2 4 mg., niacinamide 40 mg., iron 100 mg., calcium 188 mg. phosphorus 188mg., manganese 4 mg., alcohol 12%. Bot. 16 oz.
Use: Vitamin, mineral supplement.

V-M TAB. (Kenyon) Vit. A palmitate 5000 I.U., D-2 500 I.U., B-1 2.5 mg., B-2 2.5 mg., B-6 0.5 mg., B-12 1 mcg., C 50 mg., niacinamide 15 mg., E 0.5 I.U., d-cal. pantothenate 5 mg., iron 25 mg., Cu 0.375 mg., Mn 0.5 mg., Zn 0.15 mg., K 2.5 mg., Mg 2.5 mg., Iodine 0.05 mg./Tab. Bot. 100s, 1000s.
Use: Multivitamin with minerals.

VOCALZONES. (CMC) Menthol, myrrh, peppermint oil, licorice. Lozenges Tin 1 oz.
Use: Relief of pharyngitis.

• **VOLAZOCINE.** USAN. 3-(Cyclopropylmethyl)-1,2,3,4,-5,6-hexahydro-cis-6,11-dimethyl-2,6-methano-3-benzazocine. Under study.
Use: Analgesic.

VOLIDAN. (British Drug House) Megestrol acetate.

VOLITAL. Pemoline, B.A.N.

VOLITANE. (Trent) Parethoxycaine 0.2%, hexachlorophene 0.025%, dichlorophene 0.025%. Aerosol spray cans 3 oz.
Use: Treatment of minor burns and bites.

VOLTAROL SODIUM SALT. Diclofenac, B.A.N.

VONEDRINE HYDROCHLORIDE. Vonedrine (phenylpropylmethylamine) HCl.
Use: Nasal decongestant.

VONTROL. (SmithKline) Diphenidol 25 mg./Tab. Bot. 100s.
Use: Treatment of vertigo, nausea, & vomiting.

VORTEL. Clorprenaline HCl.
Use: Bronchodilator.

VORGHESA SUN PRODUCTS. (Revlon) Padimate O, oxybenzone in cream and gel base.
Use: Sunburn prevention.

VOSOL OTIC SOLUTION. (Wallace) Propylene glycol diacetate 3%, acetic acid 2%, benzethonium Cl 0.02%, sodium acetate 0.015% in propylene glycol. Multi-Pack 3 × 15 ml., 3 × 30 ml.
Use: Treatment of acute otitis externa.

VOSOL HC OTIC SOLUTION. (Wallace) Propylene glycol diacetate 3%, acetic acid 2%, benzethonium Cl 0.02%, sodium acetate 0.015% in propylene glycol, citric acid 0.2%, hydrocortisone 1%. Multi-Pack 3 × 10 ml.
Use: Treatment of acute otitis externa with inflammation.

VOXSUPRINE TABS. (Major) Isoxsuprine 10 mg. or 20 mg./Tab. Bot. 100s, 1000s.
Use: Arterial insufficiency.

V-TUSS EXPECTORANT. (Vangard) Hydrocodone bitartrate 5 mg., pseudoephendrine HCl 60 mg., guaifenesin 200 mg./5 ml. w/alcohol 12.5%.
Use: Decongestant, cough depressant, expectorant.

VULVAELINE. (Scrip) Zinc oxide 10%, boric acid 5%, benzoic acid 2%, carbolic acid 1.5%, salicylic acid 1%. Jar 1 lb.

V.V.S. SUPPOSITORIES. (Econo Med) Sulfisoxazole 700 mg., allantoin 140 mg., aminacrine HCl 14 mg./Supp. Box 16s.
Use: Trichomonads, monillasis.

VYTONE CREAM. (Dermik) Hydrocortisone 0.5% or 1%, iodoquinol 1% in a greaseless vehicle w/propylene glycol, glyceryl monostearate, cholesterol and related sterols, isopropyl myristate, polysorbates 20 and 60, cetyl alcohol, sorbitan monostearate, polyoxyl 40 stearate, sorbic acid, purified water. Cream 0.5% or 1% Tube 1 oz.
Use: Dermatologic.

W

WADE GESIC BALM. (Wade) Menthol 3%, methyl salicylate 12%, petrolatum base. Tube 1 oz. Jar 1 lb.
Use: Analgesic.

WADE'S DROPS. Compound Benzoin Tincture.

WAKESPAN. (Weeks & Leo) Caffeine 250 mg./T.R. Cap. Vial 15s.
Use: CNS stimulant for alertness.

WAL-FINATE ALLERGY TABS. (Walgreen) Chlorpheniramine maleate 4 mg./Tab. Bot. 50s.
Use: Antihistamine.

WAL-FINATE DECONGESTANT TABS. (Walgreen) Chlorpheniramine maleate 4 mg., pseudoephedrine sulfate 60 mg./Tab. Bot. 50s.
Use: Antihistaminic, decongestant.

WAL-FORMULA D COUGH SYRUP. (Walgreen) Dextromethorphan HBr 20 mg., phenylpropanolamine HCl 25 mg., guaifenesin 100 mg./10 ml. w/alcohol 10%. Bot. 6 oz.
Use: Nasal decongestant, expectorant, non-narcotic cough suppressant.

WALGREEN ARTIFICIAL TEARS. (Walgreen) Hydroxypropyl methylcellulose 0.5%. Bot. 0.5 oz.
Use: Lubrican for dry eyes.

WALGREEN SODA MINTS. (Walgreen) Sodium bicarbonate 300 mg./Tab. Bot. 100s, 200s,
Use: Antacid.

WALGREEN'S FINEST VIT B-6. (Walgreen) Pyridoxine HCl 50 mg./Tab. Bot. 100s.
Use: Vit B-6 supplement.

WAL-MINIC. (Walgreen) Phenylpropanolamine HCl 12.5 mg., guaifenesin 100 mg./5 ml. w/alcohol 5%. Bot. 6 oz.
Use: Expectorant decongestant.

WAL-MINIC COLD RELIEF MEDICINE. (Walgreen) Phenylpropanolamine HCl 12.5 mg., chlorpheniramine maleate 2 mg./5 ml. Bot. 6 oz.
Use: Non-alcoholic antihistamine, decongestant.

WAL-MINIC DM. (Walgreen) Phenylpropanolamine HCl 12.5 mg., dextromethorphan HBr 10 mg./5 ml. Bot. 6 oz.
Use: Non-narcotic non-alcoholic antitussive decongestant.

WAL-PHED PLUS. (Walgreen) Pseudoephedrine HCl 60 mg, chlorpheniramine maleate 4 mg./Tab. Bot. 50s.
Use: Decongestant, antihistamine.

WAL-PHED SYRUP. (Walgreen) Pseudoephedrine HCl 30 mg./5 ml. Bot. 4 oz.
Use: Decongestant.

WAL-PHED TABLETS. (Walgreen) Pseudoephedrine HCl 30 mg./Tab. Bot. 50s, 100s.
Use: Decongestant.

WAL-TUSSIN. (Walgreen) Guaifenesin 100 mg./5 ml. Bot. 4 oz.
Use: Expectorant.

WAL-TUSSIN DM. (Walgreen) Guaifenesin 100 mg., dextromethorphan HBr 15 ml./5 ml. Bot. 4 oz.
Use: Expectorant, cough suppressant.

WANS. (Webcon) Pyrilamine maleate 25 mg., pentobarbital sod. 30 mg./Children's Supp. **No. 1:** pyrilamine maleate 50 mg., pentobarb, sod. 45 mg./Supp. **No. 2:** pyrilamine maleate 50 mg., pentobarb. 100 mg./Supp. Strip 12s.
Use: Nausea.

WARFARIN, B.A.N. (Various Mfr.) Comp. 42. 3-(alpha-Acetonylbenzyl)-4-hydroxycoumarin. 4-Hydroxy-3-(3-oxo-1-phenylbutyl)coumarin.
Use: Rodenticide; anticoagulant.
See: Coumadin
Marevan (sodium derivative)

• **WARFARIN POTASSIUM,** U.S.P. XXI. Tab., U.S.P. XXI.
Use: Anticoagulant.
See: Athrombin-K, Tabs. (Purdue Frederick)

• **WARFARIN SODIUM,** U.S.P. XXI. For Inj., Tab., U.S.P. XXI. 2H-1-Benzopyran-2-one, 4-hydroxy-3-(3-oxo-1-phenylbutyl)-, sod. salt. 3-(alpha-Acetonyl-benzyl)-4-hydroxycoumarin & its sod. salt athrombin.
Use: Anticoagulant.
See: Coumadin Sodium, Tab., Inj. (Du Pont)
Panwarfin, Tab. (Abbott)

WART-AWAY. (Eckerd) Salicylic acid 13.13%, glacial acetic acid 1.8%, camphor 1.8%, castor oil 3.12%, pyroxylin 6.88%, acetone 75%. Liq. Bot. 0.5 oz.
Use: Wart removal.

WART FIX. (Last) Castor oil 100%. Bot. 0.3 fl. oz.
Use: Wart treatment.

WART-OFF. (Pfipharmecs) Salicylic acid in flexible collodion. Bot. 0.5 oz.
Use: Wart remover.

WARTGON. (Edward J. Moore) Castor oil. Tube 0.5 oz.
Use: Wart removal.

• **WATER,** U.S.P. XXI is found in the following grades of purity:
Bacteriostatic Water for Injection, U.S.P. XXI.
Purified Water, U.S.P. XXI.
Sterile Water For Inhalation, U.S.P. XXI.
Sterile Water For Injection, U.S.P. XXI.
Sterile Water For Irrigation, U.S.P. XXI.
Water, U.S.P. XXI.
Water For Injection, U.S.P. XXI.
Use: Pharmaceutic aid (Solvent), irrigation therapy, vehicle, fluid.
See: Abbott Labs. for sizes of each available.
Upjohn for sizes available.

WATERMELON SEED EXTRACT. Citrin (Table Rock)

WATERMELON SEED EXTRACT W/Phenobarbital & theobromine. Cithal (Table Rock)

WATER-MISCIBLE VITAMIN A.
See: Acon, Cap. (Du Pont)
Aquasol Vit. A, Caps. (USV Labs.)
Testavol-S, Cap. (Fellows)
Vi-Dom-A, Cap. (Miles Pharm)

• **WAX, CARNAUBA,** N.F. XVI.
Use: Pharmaceutic aid (tablet polishing agent).

• **WAX, EMULSIFYING,** N.F. XVI.
Use: Emulsifying agent, stiffening agent.

• **WAX, MICROCRYSTALLINE,** N.F. XVI.
Use: Pharmaceutic aid (stiffening agent).

• **WAX, WHITE,** U.S.P. XVI.
Use: Pharm. aid (stiffening agent)

• **WAX, YELLOW,** N.F. XVI.
Use: Stiffening agent.

WAXSOL. Docusate Sodium, U.S.P. XXI.

WAYDS. (Wayne) Docusate sodium 100 mg./Cap. Bot. 100s.
Use: Relief of constipation.

WAYDS-PLUS CAPSULES. (Wayne) Docusate w/casanthranol. Bot. 50s.
Use: Constipation.

WAYNADE T-D CAPSULES. (Wayne) Antihistamine compound. Bot. 100s.
Use: Relief of nasal congestion, runny nose.

WAYNE-E CAPSULES. (Wayne) Vit. E 100 I.U., 200 I.U./Cap. Bot. 1000s. 400 I.U./Cap. Bot. 100s.

WAYSED TABLETS. (Wayne) Bot. 100s, 1000s.

WAYVITE ELIXIR. (Wayne) Bot. pt.

WEHAMINE. (Hauck) Dimenhydrinate 50 mg./ml. Vial 1 ml., 10 ml. Box. 25s.
Use: Management of nausea, vertigo, vomiting.

WEH-LESS. (Hauck) Phendimetrazine tartrate 35 mg./Cap. Bot. 100s.
Use: Management of exogenous obesity.

WEHLESS-105 TIMECELLES. (Hauck) Phendimetrazine tartrate 105 mg./SA Cap. Bot. 100s.
Use: Anorexic.

WEHVERT. (Hauck) Meclizine HCl 25 mg./Tab. Bot. 100s, 500s.
Use: Management of nausea vomiting, and dizziness.

WEHYDRYL. (Hauck) Diphenhydramine HCl 50 mg./ml. Vials 10 ml.
Use: Antihistaminic.

WEIGHTROL TAB. (Vortech) Phendimetrazine tartrate 35 mg./Tab. Bot. 100s., 1000s.
Use: Anorexiant.

WELDERS EYE LOTION. (Weber) tetracaine, potassium chloride, boric acid, camphor, glycerin. w/disodium edetate, benzal konium chloride as preservatives. Bot. 1 oz.
Use: Relief for "welding flash" and "arc burn."

WELLCOVORIN. (Burroughs Wellcome) Leucovorin calcium 5 mg. or 25 mg./Tab. 5 mg./Tab. Bot. 100s; 25 mg./Tab. Bot. 25s.
Use: Prophylaxis and treatment of the undesired hematopoietic effects of folic acid antagonists.

WELLCOVORIN INJECTION. (Burroughs Wellcome) Leucovorin calcium 5 mg./1 ml. Amp. Box 12s. 25 mg./5 ml. Amp. Box 10s.
Use: Prophylaxis and treatment of the undesired hematopoietic effects of folic acid antagonists.

WELLDORM. Dichloralphenazone, B.A.N.

WERNET'S ADHESIVE CREAM. (Block) Carboxymethlcellulose gum, ethylene oxide polymer, petrolatum in mineral oil base. Tube 1.5 oz.
Use: Denture adhesive cream.

WERNET'S POWDER. (Block) Gum karaya, ethylene oxide polymer. Bot. 0.63, 1.75, 3.55 oz.
Use: Denture adhesive.

WES-B/C. (Western Research) Vit. B-1 15 mg., B-2 10 mg., B-6 5 mg., niacinamide 50 mg., Ca pantothenate 10 mg., Vit. C 300 mg./Cap. Bot. 1000s.

WESCOHEX. (West) Bot. 5 oz., pt., gal.
Use: Antibacterial skin cleanser.

WESMATIC FORTE TABLETS. (Wesley) Phenobarbital ⅛ gr., ephedrine sulfate 0.25 gr., chlorpheniramine maleate 2 mg., guaifenesin 100 mg./Tab. Bot. 100s, 1000s.
Use: Treatment of bronchitis and emphysema.

WESTCORT CREAM. (Westwood) Hydrocortisone valerate 0.2% in a hydrophilic base of white petrolatum, stearyl alcohol, propylene glycol, amphoteric-9, carbomer 940, sodium phosphate, sodium lauryl sulfate, sorbic acid, water. Tubes 15 Gm., 45 Gm., 60 Gm., 120 Gm.
Use: Topical anti-inflammatory.

WESTHROID. (Western Research) Thyroid 0.5 gr., 1 gr., 2 gr., 3 gr. or 4 gr./Tab. 5 gr. S.C. Tab. Handicount 28 (36 bags of 28s).
Use: Treatment of hypothyroidism.

WESTRIM. (Western Research) Phenylpropanolamine HCl 37.5 mg./Tab. Bot. 100s.
Use: Anorectic.

WESTRIM-LA 50. (Western Research) Phenlypropanolamine HCl 50 mg./Timed Release Cap. Bot. 1000s.
Use: Anorectic-decongestant.

WESTRIM-LA 75. (Western Research) Phenylpropancolamine HCl 75 mg./Timed Release Cap. Bot. 1000s.
Use: Anorectic-decongestant.

WESVITE. (Western Research) Vit. B-1 10 mg., B-2 5 mg., B-6 2 mg., pantothenic acid 10 mg., niacinamide 30 mg., B-12 3 mcg., C 100 mg., E 5 I.U., Vit. A 10,000 I.U., D 400 I.U., Fe 15 mg., Cu 1 mg., Iodine 0.15 mg., Mn 1 mg., Zn 1.5 mg./Tab. Bot. 1000s.
Use: Vitamin-mineral supplement.

WET-N-SOAK. (Allergan) Polyvinyl alochol, edetate disodium & benzalkonium chloride 0.004% in buffered, isotonic, sterile sol. Bot. 4 oz., 6 oz.
Use: Wetting and soaking sol. for hard and Polycon and Paraperm oxygen gas permeable contact lenses.

WETTING SOLUTION. (Barnes-Hind) Hydroxypropylethylcellulose 0.5%, polyvinyl alcohol 2%, benzalkonium chloride 0.004%, EDTA 0.02%, sod. chloride. Bot. 35 ml., 2 oz.
Use: Hard contact lens wetting solution.

WHEATACOL. (Eckerd) Iron, B-2, B-1, B-6, B-12, C, E, niacinamide, Ca pantothenate, calcium, phosphorus, Mg., Mn, Zn/Tab. Bot. 40s, 100s, 200s. Elix. Alcohol 12%. Bot. pt.

WHEATACOL TABLET. (Eckerd) Iron 50 mg., Vit. B-1 15 mg., B-2 7.5 mg., B-6 2 mg., B-12 5 mcg., niacinamide 40 mg., pantothenic acid 5 mg., Vit. C 100 mg., E 5 I.U., Ca 60 mg., P 44 mg., Mg 2 mg., Mn 1 mg./Tab. Bot. 100s, 200s.
Use: Vitamin and mineral supplement.

WHEATAVIMS. (Eckerd) Vit. A 10,000 I.U., D 400 I.U., E 50 I.U., C 250 mg., folic acid 0.4 mg., B-1 25 mg., B-2 25 mg., niacinamide 100 mg., B-6 5 mg., B-12 25 mcg., biotin 50 mcg., pantothenic acid 25 mg., Ca 162 mg., P 125 mg., iodine 150 mcg., Fe 27 mg., Mg 100 mg., Cu 3 mg., Zn 22.5 mg., wheatgerm 200 mg./2 Tab. Bot. 60s, 150s.
Use: Vitamin and mineral supplement.

WHEAT GERM OIL. (Viobin) **Liq.:** Bot. 4 oz., 8 oz., pt., qt., **Cap.: 3 min.** Bot. 100s, 400s; **6 min.:** Bot. 100s, 225s, 400s; **20 min.:** Bot. 100s.

WHEAT GERM OIL. (Various Mfr.)
See: Natural Wheat Germ Oil, Cap., Oint. (Spirt)
Natural Viobin Wheat Germ Oil, Liq. (Spirt)
Tocopherol Prep. (Various Mfr.)
Use: Vit. E deficiency.

WHEAT GERM OIL CAPSULES. (Robinson) Soft gelatin, oblong, clear 3,6, 14 min./Cap. 100s, 1000s.

WHEAT GERM OIL CONCENTRATE. (Thurston) Perles. 6 min. Bot. 100s.
Use: Heart disorders, heart muscle fatigue.

WHIRL-SOL. (Sween) Lipid-soluble de-waxed fraction of lanolin. Bot. 8 oz., pt.
Use: Emollient, antipruritic.

WHITE IODINE. (Pharmex) Bot. 0.5 oz.
• **WHITE LOTION,** U.S.P. XXI.
Use: Astringent; topical protectant.
See: Lotioblanc, Lotion (Arnar-Stone)
• **WHITE OINTMENT,** U.S.P. XXI.
Use: Pharmaceutic aid (oleaginous ointment base).
WHITE PRECIPITATE.
See: Ammoniated Mercury, U.S.P. XXI.
WHITFIELD'S OINTMENT. (Various Mfr.) Benzoic acid 12%, salicylic acid 6%. Tube 1 oz., 1.5 oz. Jar 1 lb.
Use: Fungicidal.
WHITSPHILL. (Torch) Salicylic acid 6%, benzoic acid 12% in hydrophilic vehicle. Jar 1 lb., 2 oz. Also avail. in half-strength.
Use: Fungus infections.
WHOOPING COUGH VACCINE.
See: Pertussis Vaccine, U.S.P. XXI.
WHORTON'S CALAMINE LOTION. (Whorton) Calamine, zinc oxide, and glycerin (U.S.P. strength) in carboxymethylcellulose lotion vehicle. Bot. 4 oz., gal.
WHORTON'S SKIN CARE CREAM. (Whorton) 5 oz., 16 oz.
WIBI LOTION. (Owen) Purified water, SD alcohol 40, glycerin, PEG-4, PEG-6-32 stearate, PEG-6-32, glycol stearate, carbomer 940, PEG-75, methylparaben, propylparaben, triethanolamine, menthol & fragrance. Bot. 8 oz., 16 oz.
Use: Dry skin lotion.
WIDOW SPIDER SPECIES ANTIVENIN (LATRODECTUS MACTANS). Antivenin, Lactrodectus mactans, U.S.P. XXI.
Use: Passive immunizing agent.
WIGRAINE. (Organon) Ergotamine tartrate 1.0 mg., caffeine 100 mg./Tab. or Supp. **Tab.** Box 20s, 100s. **Supp.** Box 12s.
Use: Migraine, vascular headache.
WIGRETTES. (Organon) Ergotamine tartrate 2 mg./Sublingual Tab. Bot. 24s.
Use: Migraine, vascular headache.
WILD CHERRY.
Use: Flavored vehicle.
WILPOWR. (Foy) Phentermine HCl. 30 mg./Cap. Bot. 100s, 500s, 1000s.
Use: Anorexiant.
WILPOR-CLEAR. (Foy) Phentermine HCl 30 mg./Cap. Bot. 1000s.
Use: Anorexiant.
WINADOL SYRUP. (Winthrop Products) Paracetemol.
Use: Analgesic, antipyretic.
WINADOL TABLETS. (Winthrop Products) Paracetamol.
Use: Analgesic, antipyretic.
WINASMA TABLETS. (Winthrop Products) Theophylline anhydrous, ephedrine sulphate, chlormezanone.
Use: Antiasthmatic.
WINASORB DROPS. (Winthrop Products) Paracetamol.
Use: Analgesic, antipyretic.
WINASORB SUSPENSION. (Winthrop Products) Paracetamol.
Use: Analgesic, antipyretic.
WINASORB SYRUP. (Winthrop Products) Paracetamol.
Use: Analgesic, antipyretic.
WINASORB TABLETS. (Winthrop Products) Paracetamol.
Use: Analgesic, antipyretic.
WINAVIT TABLETS. (Winthrop Products) Stanozolol, vitamins.
Use: Anabolic steroid with vitamins.
WINDOLOR TABLETS. (Winston) Butabarbital 15 mg., acetaminophen 200 mg., phenacetin 120 mg., caffeine 30 mg./Tab. Box. 100s, 1000s.
Use: Analgesic, antitensive.
WINGEL. (Winthrop Consumer Products) Short polymer, hexitol stabilized aluminum-magnesium hydroxide equiv. to aluminum hydroxide 180 mg. and magnesium hydroxide 160 mg./5 ml. or Tab. **Liq.:** Bot. 6 oz., 12 oz. **Tab.:** Box 50s, 100s.
Use: Antacid.
WINORYLATE SACHET. (Winthrop Products) Benorylate.
Use: Analgesic.
WINOLATE SUSPENSION. (Winthrop Products) Benorylate.
Use: Analgesic.
WINSTEROID TABLETS. (Winthrop Products) Stanozolol.
Use: Anabolic steroid.
WINSTROL. (Winthrop-Breon) Stanozolol 2 mg./Tab. Bot. 100s.
Use: Anabolic steroid.
WINTERGREEN OINTMENT. (Wisconsin) Bot. 2 oz., 1 lb.
Use: Muscle soreness, arthritis pain.
WINTHROCIN SUSPENSION. (Winthrop Products) Erythromycin sterate.
Use: Antibiotic.
WINTHROCIN TABLETS. (Winthrop Products) Erythromycin sterate.
Use: Antibiotic.
WINTODON TABLETS. (Winthrop Products) Glycobiarsol.
Use: Amebicide.
WINTOMYLON CAPS. (Winthrop Products) Nalidixic acid.
Use: Urinary, intestinal infections.
WINTOMYLON SUSPENSION. (Winthrop Products) Nalidixic acid.
Use: Urinary, intestinal infections.
WINTOMYLON TABLETS. (Winthrop Products) Nalidixic acid.
Use: Urinary, intestinal infections.
WINTON TABLETS. (Winthrop Products) Aluminum and magnesium hydroxide.
Use: Antacid, demulcent.
WINTOSIN COUGH SYRUP. (Winthrop Products) Dextromethorphan HBr.
Use: Antitussive decongestant.

WINTRAMOX CAPSULES. (Winthrop Products) Amoxicillin trihydrate.
Use: Antibiotic.

WINTRAMOX SUSPENSION. (Winthrop Products) Amoxicillin trihydrate
Use: Antibiotic.

WINTREX CAPSULES. (Winthrop Products) Tetracycline HCl.
Use: Antibiotic.

WINTROPLEX TABLETS. (Winthrop Products) Aspirin, chlormezanone.
Use: Analgesic, tranquilizer.

WITHIN MULTIVITAMIN. (Miles) Vit. A 5000 I.U., E 30 I.U., C 60 mg., folic acid 0.4 mg., B-1 1.5 mg., B-2 1.7 mg., niacin 20.0 mg., B-6 2.0 mg., B-12 6.0 mcg., K 50 mcg.; pantothenic acid 10 mg., biotin 30 mcg., D 400 I.U., iron 27 mg. Ca 300/Tab. Bot. 60s, 100s.
Use: Multivitamin supplement with iron and calcium.

WNS SUPPOSITORIES. (Winthrop Products) Sulfamylon HCl.
Use: Hemorrhoidal preparation.

WOLFINA. (Forest) Rauwolfia serpentina 100 mg./Tab. Bot. 100s.
Use: Antihypertensive, tranquilizing agent.

WOLGRAINE. (Wolins) Aspirin 3 gr., phenacetin 2 gr., caffeine ⅔ gr., isobutyl-allylbarbituric acid ¾ gr./Tab. Bot. 100s, 1000s.

WOL-LAC. (Wolins) Aminoacetic acid (glycine) 0.18 Gm., calcium carbonate 0.42 Gm./Tab. Bot. 1000s.

WOLTAC. (Wolins) Belladonna alkaloids (total 0.16 mg.) atropine sulfate 0.024 mg., scopolamine HBr 0.014 mg., hyoscyamine sulfate 0.122 mg., phenylpropanolamine HCl 50 mg., chlorpheniramine maleate 1 mg., pheniramine maleate 12.5 mg./Cap. Bot. 100s, 1000s.

WONDERFUL DREAM SALVE. (Kondon) Phenylmercuric nitrate 1:5000, oils of tar, turpentine, olive and linseed oil, rosin, burgundy pitch, camphor.

WOOD CHARCOAL TABLETS. (Cowley) 5 gr.; 10 gr./Tab. Bot. 1000s.

WOOD CREOSOTE.
See: Creosote (Various Mfr.)

WORMAL TABLETS. (Salsbury) Phenothiazine 500 mg., piperazine 50 mg., dibutyltin dilaurate 125 mg./Tab. Bot. 100s, 1000s, 10,000s.
Use: Treatment for worming poultry.

WOOL FAT. Lanolin Anhydrous.

WUN-A-VIT. (Blue Cross) Vit. A 5000 I.U., D 400 I.U., E 15 I.U., C 60 mg., folic acid 0.4 mg., B-1 1.5 mg., B-2 1.7 mg., niacin 20 mg., B-6 2 mg., B-12 6 mcg./Tab. Bot. 100s.
Use: Vitamin supplement.

WUN-A-VIT PLUS IRON. (Blue Cross) Vit. A 5000 I.U., D 400 I.U., E 15 I.U., C 60 mg., folic acid 0.4 mg., B-1 1.5 mg., B-2 1.7 mg., niacin 20 mg., B-6 2 mg., B-12 6 mcg., iron 18 mg./Tab. Bot. 100s.
Use: Vitamin supplement with iron.

WUN-TABS. (Quality Generics) Vit. A 5000 I.U., D 400 I.U., C 50 mg., B-1 2 mg., B-2 2.5 mg., B-6 1 mg., B-12 1 mcg., niacinamide 20 mg., pantothenic acid 1 mg./Cap. Bot. 250s, 1000s. Jar 100s.
Use: Multiple vitamin.

WUN-TABS W/IRON. (Quality Generics) Vit. A 5000 I.U., D 400 I.U., C 50 mg., B-1 2 mg., B-2 2.5 mg., B-6 1 mg.,
B-12 1 mcg., niacinamide 20 mg., cal. pantothenate 1 mg., iron 15 mg./Tab. Jar 100s, Bot. 1000s.
Use: Supplement.

WUN-TAB M. (Quality Generics) Vit. A 5000 I.U., D 500 I.U., C 50 mg., B-1 2.5 mg., B-2 2.5 mg., B-6 0.5 mg., B-12 2 mcg., niacinamide 20 mg., calcium pantothenate 5 mg., Ca 35 mg., Cu 1 mg., Iodine 0.15 mg., Fe 10 mg., Mn 1 mg., Mg 6 mg., K 5 mg./Tab. Bot. 1000s. Jar 100s.
Use: Dietary supplement.

W/W-ANTI-SPAS. (Whiteworth) Antispasmodic compound Bot. 16 oz.
Use: Antispasmodic.

W/W-BROMINE. (Whiteworth) Brompheniramine elixir. Bot. 16 oz., gal.
Use: Expectorant.

W/W-BROMINE DS. (Whiteworth) Brompheniramine DC. Bot. 16 oz.
Use: Expectorant.

W/W-FED LIQUID. (Whiteworth) Triprolidine w/pseudoephedrine in syrup. Bot. 16 oz., gal.
Use: Antihistaminic, decongestant.

W/W-FED TABLETS. (Whiteworth) Triprolidine w/pseudoephedrine. Tab. Bot. 100s, 1000s.
Use: Antihistaminic, decongestant.

W/W FED w/C. (Whiteworth) Triprolidine w/pseudoephedrine, codeine. Bot. 16 oz., gal.
Use: Expectorant.

W/W HISTINE DH. (Whiteworth) Phenylhistine DH elixir. Bot. 16 oz.
Use: Antihistamine.

W/W-HISTINE ELIXIR. (Whiteworth) Phenylhistine elixir. Bot. 16 oz.
Use: Antihistamine.

W/W-HISTINE EXPECTORANT. (Whiteworth) Phenylhistine expectorant. Bot. 16 oz.
Use: Antihistamine.

WYAMINE SULFATE INJECTION. (Wyeth) Mephentermine sulfate 15 mg., sod. acetate, methylparaben 1.8 mg., propylparaben 0.2 mg./cc. Vial 10 cc., Amp. 2 cc., 25s. 30 mg./cc. Vial 10 cc. Tubex 30 mg./Tubex 1 cc.
Use: I.V. or I.M.; in hypotensive states not associated with hemorrhage.

WYAMYCIN-E LIQUID. (Wyeth) Erythromycin ethylsuccinate oral susp. 200 mg., or 400 mg./5 ml. Bot. Pts.
Use: Antibacterial agent.

WYAMYCIN-S TABLETS. (Wyeth) Erythromycin stearate 250 mg./Tab. Bot. 100s, 500s. 500 mg./Tab. Bot. 100s.
Use: Antibacterial agent.

WYANOIDS. (Wyeth) Ephedrine sulfate 3 mg., w/belladonna ext. 15 mg., boric acid, zinc oxide, bismuth oxyiodide & subcarb., balsam peru & cocoa butter./Supp., Box 12s.
Use: Hemorrhoids.

WYCILLIN. (Wyeth) Penicillin G procaine susp. 300,000 u./cc. in a stabilized aqueous suspension w/sod. citrate buffer, w/v lecithin approximately 0.5%, carboxymethylcellulose 0.5%, povidone 0.5%, methylparaben 0.1%, propylparaben 0.01%. Tubex 1 cc. 10s. Vial 600,000 u./cc. Tubex 1 cc. 10s, 50s. 1,200,000 u./Tubex 2 cc. 10s. 2,400,000 u./disposable syringe 4 cc., 10s.

WYCILLIN INJECTION AND PROBENECID TABLETS. (Wyeth) Combination Pkg. containing two disposable syringes of procaine penicillin G 2,400,000 U./4 ml. size and two probenecid tablets 0.5 Gm. each.
Use: Treatment of gonorrhea.

WYDASE LYOPHILIZED. (Wyeth) Hyaluronidase. Vial 150 U.S.P. [TR]u./1 cc. 1500 U.S.P. [TR]u./10 cc.
Use: Spreading factor.

WYDASE STABILIZED SOLUTION. (Wyeth) Hyaluronidase 150 U.S.P. [TR]u. in sterile saline sol. Vial 1 cc., 10 cc. Store below 59°F., stable 3 yrs.
Use: Hypodermoclysis.

WYOVIN HYDROCHLORIDE. Dicyclomine, B.A.N.

WYGESIC. (Wyeth) Propoxyphene HCl 65 mg., acetaminophen 650 mg./Tab. Bot. 100s, 500s. Redipak 100s.
Use: Pain relief.

WYMOX. (Wyeth) Amoxicillin **Cap.:** 250 mg./Cap. Bot. 100s, 500s. 500 mg/Cap. Bot. 50s, 500s. **Oral Susp.:** 125 mg./5 ml. Bot. to make 80 ml., 100 ml., 150 ml.; 250 mg./5 ml. Bot. to make 80 ml, 100 ml., 150 ml.
Use: Ear, nose, throat, G.I. tract infections.

WYTENSIN. (Wyeth) Guanabenz acetate 4 mg./Tab. Bot. 100s, 500s. 8 mg./Tab. Bot. 100s.
Use: Antihypertensive.

WYVAC RABIES VACCINE. (Wyeth) Human diploid-cell strain subvirion antigen. Single dose Amp.
Use: Rabies vaccine.

X

• **XAMOTEROL.** USAN.
Use: Cardiac stimulant.

XANAX. (Upjohn) Alprazolam 0.25 mg., 0.5 mg. or 1 mg./Tab. Bot. 100s. Unit dose 100s. Bot. 500s.
Use: Management of anxiety disorders.

• **XANOXATE SODIUM.** USAN.
Use: Bronchodilator.

• **XANTHAN GUM,** N.F. XVI.
Use: Suspending agent.

XANTHINE DERIVATIVES.
See: Caffeine
Theobromine
Theophylline

XANTHINOL NIACINATE. USAN. 7-{2-Hydroxy-3-[(2-hydroxyethyl))methylamino]-propyl} theophylline compound with nicotinic acid.
Use: Vasodilator.
See: Complamex
Complamin

XANTHIOL HCl. 4-[3-(2-Chlorothioxanthene-9-yl)-propyl]-1-pipera zinepropanol dihydrochloride.
Use: Antinauseant.
See: Daxid (Roerig)

XANTHOCILLIN, B.A.N. Antibiotics obtained from the mycelium of Penicillium notatum (Xanthocillin X is 2:3-Diisocyano 1:4-di(p-hydroxyphenyl) buta-1:3-diene).

XANTHOTOXIN. Methoxsalen.

X-A-PAIN ANALGESIC TABLETS. (Eckerd) Acetaminophen 325 mg., phenyltoloxamine citrate 30 mg., caffeine 30 mg./Tab.
Use: Analgesic, antihistaminic.

X-DRIN. (Pharmex) **Cap.:** Bot. 72s. **Pellets:** Bot. 144s. **Tab.:** Bot. 21s, 90s.
Use: Dietary.

YELLOW FEVER VACCINE.
See: YF-VAX, Inj. (Squibb-Connaught).

XENTHIORATE HCl. 2-Diethylaminoethyl-2(4-biphenylyl)thiobutyrate HCl.

XENYSALATE, B.A.N. 2-Diethylaminoethyl 3-phenylsalicylate. Sebaclen is the hydrochloride.
Use: Treatment of seborrhea.

XERAC. (Person & Covey) Isopropyl alcohol 44%, microcrystalline sulfur 4%. Tube 1.5 oz.
Use: Acne vulgaris management.

XERAC AC. (Person & Covey) Aluminum Cl hexahydrate 6.25% in anhydrous ethanol. Bot 35 ml., 60 ml.
Use: Antiperspirant.

XERAC BP5. (Person & Covey) Benzoyl peroxide 5% in hydrogel. Tubes 1.5 oz., 3 oz.
Use: Aid in management of acne.

XERAC BP10. (Person & Covey) Benzoyl Peroxide 10% in hydrogel. Tubes 1.5 oz., 3 oz.
Use: Acne management.

XEROFORM OINTMENT 3%.
(City) Pwder. 0.25 lb., 1 lb.
(Consolidated) Jar 1 lb., 5 lb.
(Robinson) Jar. 1 lb., 5 lb.

XERO-LUBE. (Scherer) Potassium phosphate, dibasic potassium phos., magnesium chloride, potassium chloride, calcium chloride, sodium chloride, sodium fluoride, sorbitol sol., sodium carboxymethylcellulose, methyl paraben. Bot. 6 oz.
Use: Moisten & lubricate oral cavity.

YF-VAX. (Squibb-Connaught) Yellow fever vaccine. Vials 1 or 5 dose.
Use: Active immunizing agent against yellow fever.

• **XILOBAM.** USAN.
Use: Relaxant.

• **XIPAMIDE.** USAN.
Use: Antihypertensive, diuretic.

• **XORPHANOL MESYLATE.** USAN.
Use: Analgesic.

X-OTAG. (Reid-Provident) Orphenadrine citrate. **Inj.:** 30 mg./ml. Vial 10 ml.**Tab:** 100 mg./Tab. Bot. 100s.
Use: Skeletal muscle relaxant.

X-PREP BOWEL EVACUANT KIT. (Gray) Kit contains Senokot S tablets.
Use: Pre-radiographic bowel evacuant.

X-PREP BOWEL EVACUANT KIT-2. (Gray) Kit contains citralax granules.
Use: Pre-radiographic bowel evacuant.

X-PREP LIQUID. (Gray) Standardized extract of senna fruit. Bot. 2.5 oz.
Use: Pre-radiographic bowel evacuant.

X-RAY CONTRAST MEDIA.
See: Iodine Products, Diagnostic.

X SEB SHAMPOO. (Baker/Cummins) Salicylic acid 4%, coal tar solution 10% in a blend of surface active agents. Bot. 4 oz.
Use: Antiseborrheic shampoo.
Use: Itching scalp.

X SEB T. (Baker/Cummins) Coal tar sol 10%, salicylic acid 4% Bot. 4 oz.
Use: Psoriasis, dandruff, seborrheic dermatitis.

XTRACARE. (Sween) Cream. Bot. 8 oz.
Use: Foot care.

XTRA-VITES. (Barth's) Vit. A 10,000 I.U., D 400 I.U., C 150 mg., B-1 5 mg., B-2 1 mg., niacin 3.33 mg., pantothenic acid 183 mcg., B-6 250 mcg., B-12 215 mg., E 15 I.U., rutin 20 mg., citrus bioflavonoid complex 15 mg., choline 6.67 mg., inositol 10 mg., folic acid 50 mcg., biotin, aminobenzoic acid/Tab. Bot. 30s, 90s, 180s, 360s.
Use: Vitamin supplement.

X-TRO. (Xttrium) Atropine oxide hydrochloride 0.2 mg./Cap. Bot. 100s, 1000s.
W/Phenobarb. 15 mg./Cap. Bot. 100s, 1000s.
Use: Anticholinergic.

X-TROZINE CAPSULES. (Rexar) Phendimetrazine tartrate 35 mg./Cap. Bot. 1000s.
Use: Treatment of obesity.

X-TROZINE S.R. CAPSULES. (Rexar) Phendimetrazine tartrate 105 mg./S.R. Cap. Bot. 100s, 200s, 1000s.
Use: Treatment of obesity.

X-TROZINE TABLETS. (Rexar) Phendimetrazine tartrate 35 mg./Tab. Bot. 1000s.
Use: Treatment of obesity.

X-WAX. (CMC) Bot. 10 ml.
Use: Earwax remover.

• **XYLAMIDINE TOSYLATE.** USAN. N-[2-(m-Methoxyphenoxy)propyl]-2-m-tolylacetamidine mono-p-toluenesulfonate hemihydrate.
Use: Antiserotonin.

XYLAZINE. B.A.N. N-(5,6-Dihydro-4H-1,3-thiazin-2-yl)-2,6-xylidine.
Use: Analgesic, veterinary medicine.
See: Rompun

• **XYLAZINE HYDROCHLORIDE.** USAN.
Use: Analgesic, relaxant (muscle).

XYLOCAINE HYDROCHLORIDE. (Astra) Lidocaine HCl **Amp.** (1%): 2 cc., 10s; 5 cc., 10s; 30 cc., 5s; w/epinephrine 1:200,000 30 cc., 5s. (1.5%): 20 cc., 5s; w/epinephrine 1:200,000 30 cc., 5s. (2%): 2 cc., 10s; 10 cc., 5s.; w/epinephrine 1:200,000 20 cc., 5s. (4%): 5 cc., 10s. **Multi. Dose Vials.** (0.5%): 50 cc. w/epinephrine 1:200,000 50 cc. (1%): 20 cc., 50 cc. w/epinephrine 1:100,000 20 cc., 50 cc. (2%): 20 cc., 50 cc.; w/epinephrine 1:100,000 20 cc., 50 cc. **Single dose Vials:** (1%); 30 cc. (1.5%) 20 cc.; w/epinephrine 1:200,000 30 cc. (2%) w/epinephrine 1:200,000 20 cc.
Use: Local anesthetic.

XYLOCAINE HYDROCHLORIDE FOR CARDIAC ARRHYTHMIA. (Astra) **Intravenous:** lidocaine 2% Single inj. 100 mg./5 cc. amp., 10s. Continuous infusion 1 Gm./25 ml. Vial; 2 Gm./50 ml. Vial. Prefilled syringe 100 mg./5 cc. 12s. Continuous infusion prefilled syringe 1 Gm., 2 Gm.
Intramuscular: Amp. 10%, 5 ml.

XYLOCAINE HYDROCHLORIDE 4% SOLUTION. (Astra) Retrobulbar and transtracheal injection and topical use. Lidocaine Amp. 5 cc. Box 10s. Topical use only. 50 cc. Screw top Bot.

XYLOCAINE HYDROCHLORIDE FOR SPINAL ANESTHESIA. (Astra) Lidocaine HCl 1.5% & 5%, glucose 7.5%, sod. hydroxide to adjust pH. Specific gravity 1.028-1.034 Amp. 2 cc. Box 10s.

XYLOCAINE JELLY. (Astra) Lidocaine HCl 20 mg., methyl-p-hydroxbenzoate 0.7 mg., propyl-p-hydroxybenzoate 0.3 mg., sod. hydroxide, sodium carboxymethylcellulose and preservatives/Tube 30 cc.
Use: Urological.

XYLOCAINE OINTMENT. (Astra) 2.5% Lidocaine base OTC. 35 Gm./Tube. 5% Lidocaine base 35 Gm./Tube 5% Lidocaine base flavored 3.5 Gm./Tube, 10s. Jar 35 Gm. Ointment base of polyethylene glycols and propylene glycol.
Use: Topical anesthetic.

XYLOCAINE VISCOUS. (Astra) Lidocaine HCl 2%, sodium carboxymethylcellulose, flavoring agents and preservatives. Bot. 20 cc. 25s; 100 cc.; 450 cc.
Use: Anesthesia of mouth and pharynx.

• **XYLOMETAZOLINE HCl,** U.S.P. XXI. Nasal Soln., U.S.P. XXI. 2-(4-tert-Butyl-2,6-dimethyl benzyl)-2-imidazoline HCl.
Use: Adrenergic (vasoconstrictor).
See: Isohalent L.A., Liq. (Elder)
Long Acting Neo-Synephrine, Prod. (Winthrop Consumer Products)
Otrivin Spray (Geigy)
Rhinall L.A., Liq. (First Texas)
Sine-Off, Spray (Menley & James)
Vicks Sinex Long Acting, Nasal Spray (Vicks)

XYLO-PFAN. (Adria) D-xylose 25 Gm./Bot.
Use: Diagnostic agent for evaluating intestinal absorption.

XYLOPHAN D-XYLOSE TOLERANCE TEST. (Pfanstiehl) D-xylose 25 Gm./Unit dose bot. Use: Evaluation of intestinal absorption.

• **XYLOSE,** U.S.P. XXI.
Use: Diagnostic aid (intestinal function determination).

XYLOTOX. Lignocaine, B.A.N.

Y

YAGER'S LINIMENT. (Yager) Oil of turpentine and Camphor w/clove oil fragrance, emulsifier, emollient and ammonium oleate (less than 0.5% free ammonia) penetrant base.
Use: Rubefacient liniment.

YATREN.
See: Chiniofon, Tab.

YDP LICE SPRAY. (Youngs Drug) Synthetic pyrethroid in aerosol. Can. 5 oz.
Use: Control of lice on inanimate objects.

YEAST ADENYLIC ACID. An isomer of adenosine 5-monophosphate, has been found inactive.
See: Adenosine 5-Monophosphate, Preps. for active compounds.

• **YEAST, DRIED.**
Use: Protein and Vit. B Complex source.

• **YEAST TABLETS, DRIED.**
Use: Supplementary source of B complex vitamins.
See: Brewer's Yeast, Tab.

YEAST, TORULA.
See: Torula Yeast

YEAST W/IRON.
See: Natural Super Iron Yeast Powder (Spirt) (Pharmex) Bot. 200s.

YELLOW ENZYME.
See: Riboflavin (Var. Mfr.)

• **YELLOW FERRIC OXIDE,** N.F. XVI.

• **YELLOW FEVER VACCINE,** U.S.P. XXI.
Use: Active immunizing agent.
See: YF-VAX, Inj. (Squibb-Connaught)

• **YELLOW OINTMENT,** U.S.P. XXI.
Use: Pharmaceutic aid (ointment base).

• **YELLOW WAX,** N.F. XVI.
Use: Pharmaceutic aid (stiffening agent).

YF-VAX. (Squibb-Connaught) Yellow fever vaccine. Vials 1 dose or 5 dose with diluent.
Use: Active immunizing agent.

• **YITTERBIUM Yb 169 PENTETATE INJECTION,** U.S.P. XXI.

YOCON. (CMC) Yomimbine HCl 5.4 mg./Cap. Bot. 100s, 1000s.
Use: Impotency.

YODORA DEODORANT CREAM. (Norcliff Thayer) Jar 2 oz.

YODOXIN. (Glenwood) Iodoquinol 210 mg./Tab. Bot. 25s, 100s, 1000s. Pow. Bot. 25 Gm.

YOHIMBAN-16-CARBOXYLIC ACID, 11, 17-DIMETHOXY-18-[(3,4,5-TRIMETHOXY-BENZOYL)-OXY]-, METHYL ESTER. Reserpine, U.S.P. XXI.

YOHIMBINE.
W/Thyroid and strychnine.
See: Andro-Medicone, Tab. (Medicone)

YOHIMBINE HCl.
W/Methyl testosterone, nux vomica ext.
See: Climactic, Tab. (Burgin-Arden)
Rochor, Tab. (Rocky Mtn.)
W/Thyroid, strychnine sulf.
See: Andro-Medicone, Tab. (Medicone)

YOMESAN. (Farbenfabriken Bayer) Niclosamide, B.A.N. Under study.
Use: Anthelmintic.

YUTOPAR. (Astra) Ritodrine HCl. **Tab.:** 10 mg./Tab. Bot. 60s. **Inj.:** 10 mg./ml. Amp. 5 ml. Box 12s.
Use: Smooth muscle relaxant.

Z

ZACTIPAR. Paracetamol, B.A.N.

ZANIL. Oxyclozanide, B.A.N.

ZANOSAR. (Upjohn) Streptozocin sterile powder 1 Gm./Vial.
Use: Metastatic islet cell carcinoma of the pancreas.

ZANTAC INJECTION. (Glaxo) Ranitidine HCl 25 mg./ml. w/phenol 5 mg., monobasic potassium phosphate 0.96 mg., dibasic sodium phosphate 2.4 mg./ml. Vial 2 ml. Box 10s.
Use: Treatment of ulcer when oral medication unable to be used.

ZANTAC TABLETS. (Glaxo) Ranitidine HCl 150 mg./Tab. Bot. 30s, 60s. Unit dose 100s.
Use: Short term treatment of duodenal ulcer.

ZANTRYL. (Ion) Phentermine HCL 30 mg./S.R. Cap. Bot. 100s.
Use: Exogenous obesity.

ZARONTIN. (Parke-Davis) Ethosuximide. **Cap:** 250 mg./Cap. Bot. 100s. **Syrup:** 250 mg./5 ml. Bot. pt.
Use: Treatment of petit mal epilepsy.

ZAROXOLYN. (Pennwalt) Metolazone 2.5 mg., 5 mg., 10 mg./Tab. Bot. 100s, 500s, 1000s. Strip Pack 100s.
Use: Diuretic, antihypertensive.

Z-BEC. (Robins) Vit. E 45 I.U., C 600 mg., B-1 15 mg., B-2 10.2 mg., niacin 100 mg., B-6 10 mg., B-12 6 mcg., pantothenic acid 25 mg., Zn 22.5 mg./Tab. Bot. 60s, 500s; Dis-Co Packs (tabs) 100s.
Use: Nutritional supplement.

ZEASORB-AF POWDER. (Stiefel) Tolnaftate 1% in a base of talc, microporous cellulose, supersorb carbohydrate acryllic copolymer. Can 2.5 oz.
Use: Antifungal.

ZEASORB POWDER. (Stiefel) Talc, microporous cellulose, supersorb carbohydrate acrylic copolymer. Sifter-top-Cans 2.5 oz., 8 oz.
Use: Moisture absorbent.

ZEMACON LOTION. (CMC) Sulfur, zinc oxide, titanium oxide, camphor. Bot. 2 oz., pt., gal.
Use: External treatment of acne.

ZEMACON SKIN CLEANSER. (CMC) Sod. alkylaryl polyether sulfonate, lanolin cholesterols, petrolatum, hexachlorophene 3%. Bot. 4 oz., pt., gal.

EMALO. (Barre) Sulfur, ZnO, camphor, titanium oxide. Bot. 4 oz., pt., gal.

EMARINE. (Zemmer) Butabarbital sod. 16.2 mg., hyoscine HBr 0.0065 mg., hyoscyamine sulfate 0.1037, atropine sulfate 0.0194/Dr. Tab. or T.R. Cap. Cap. Bot. 100s, 1000s. **Elix.** Bot. 3 oz., pts., gal. **Tab.** Box 100s, 1000s.
Use: Antispasmodic or sedative.

EM-HISTINE. (Zemmer) Pyrilamine maleate Tab. 25 mg., Bot. 100s, 1000s.
/Butacaine. Oint: Methapyrilene HCl 2%, butacaine sulfate 1%, chlorobutanol 0.5%. Tube 1 oz.
/Codeine. Syrup: Pyrilamine maleate 16 mg., codeine phosphate 10.95 mg./5 ml. Bot. pt., gal.
/Thenylpyramine HCl 25 mg., pyrilamine maleate 12.5 mg./Cap. Bot. 100s, 1000s.
Use: Antihistaminic.

EMO LIQUID EXTRA STRENGTH. (Plough) Phenol 1.5%, methyl salicylate 0.5%. Bot. 7.5 oz.
Use: Anti-pruritic.

EMO LIQUID REGULAR STRENGTH. (Plough) Phenol 1.5%, methyl salicylate 0.4%, Bot. 7.5 oz.
Use: Anti-pruritic.

ENATE. (Reid-Provident) Vit. A 5000 I.U., D 400 I.U., E 30 I.U., C 80 mg., folic acid 1 mg., thiamine 3 mg., riboflavin 3 mg., niacin 20 mg., B-6 10 mg., B-12 12 mcg., Ca 300 mg., iodine 175 mcg., iron 65 mg., magnesium 100 mg., zinc 20 mg./Tab. Bot. 100s.
Use: Dietary supplement for pregnancy and lactation.

ZENAZOCINE MESYLATE. USAN.
Use: Analgesic.

ENDIUM. (Oral-B) Sodium fluoride 0.22%. Tube 0.9 oz., 2.3 oz.
Use: Toothpaste.

ENI B W/C. (Zenith) Vit. C 500 mg., B-1 15 mg., B-2 10 mg., B-6 5 mg., niacin 50 mg., calcium pantothenate 10 mg./Tab. Bot. 100s.

ENIVITES M. (Zenith) Vit. A 4000 I.U., D 400 I.U., B-1 1 mg., B-2 1.2 mg., B-6 2 mg., B-12 2 mcg., Ca pantothenate 5 mg., niacinamide 10 mg., C 30 mg., Ca 100 mg., P 76 mg., Fe 10 mg., Mn 1 mg., Mg 1 mg., Zn 1 mg./Tab. Bot. 100s.

ENTINIC. (Lilly) Elemental iron (as ferrous fumarate) 100 mg., folic acid 0.05 mg., Vit. B-1 7.5 mg., B-2 7.5 mg., B-6 7.5 mg., B-12 50 mcg., pantothenic acid 15 mg., niacinamide 30 mg., C 200 mg./Pulvule. Bot. 60s.
Use: Treatment of iron deficiency anemia.

ENTRON. (Lilly) Iron (as ferrous sulfate) 20 mg., Vit. B-1 1 mg., B-2 1 mg., B-6 1 mg., B-12 5 mcg., pantothenic acid 1 mg., niacinamide 5 mg., C 100 mg./5 ml./, alcohol 2%. Bot. 8 fl. oz.
Use: Liquid hematinic.

ZENTRON CHEWABLE. (Lilly) Elemental iron (as ferrous fumarate) 20 mg., B-1 1 mg., B-2 1 mg., B-6 1 mg., B-12 5 mcg., pantothenic acid 1 mg., niacinamide 5 mg., C 100 mg./Chewable tab. Bot. 50s.

ZEPHIRAN CHLORIDE. (Winthrop-Breon) Benzalkonium Chloride **Tinct.** 1:750 tinted (w/alcohol 50%, acetone 10%) Bot. 1 gal.; **Aqueous soln.** 1:750 Bot. 8 oz., 1 gal.; **Spray:** Bot. 1 fl. oz., 6 fl. oz. Use; Antiseptic; **Conc.** 17%, Bot. 4 fl. oz., 1 gal.
Use: Germicide, disinfectant.

ZEPHIRAN TOWELETTES. (Winthrop-Breon) Moist paper towels with solution of zephiran chloride 1:750. Boxes 20s, 100s, 1000s.
Use: Antiseptic skin cleanser.

ZEPHREX. (Bock) Pseudoephedrine HCl 60mg., guaifenesin 400 mg./Tab.
Use: Decongestant, expectorant.

ZEPHREX-LA. (Bock) Pseudoephedrine HCl 120 mg., guaifenesin 600 mg./Tab.
Use: Decongestant, expectorant.

ZEPINE. (Foy) Reserpine alkaloid 0.25 mg./Tab. Bot. 100s, 500s, 1000s.

• **ZERANOL.** USAN. (1) (3S, 7X)-3,4,5,6,7,8,9,10,11,12-Decahydro-7, 14,16-trihydroxy-3-methyl-1H-2-benzoxacyclotetradecin-1-one; (2) (6X, 10S)-6-(6,-10-dihyroxyundecyl)-β-resorcylic acid lactone. Ralgro (Commercial Solvents).
Use: Anabolic.

ZETAR EMULSION. (Dermik) Colloidal whole coal tar 30% (300 mg./ml.) in polysorbates. Bot. 6 oz.
Use: Generalized recalcitrant dermatoses, for the bath and for prescription compounding.

ZETAR SHAMPOO. (Dermik) Colloidal whole coal tar 1% in a shampoo. 6 oz. Plastic bottles.
Use: Antiseptic, antibacterial, antiseborrheic.

ZIDE. (Reid-Provident) Hydrochlorothiazide 50 mg./Tab. Bot. 1000s.

• **ZIDOMETACIN.** USAN.
Use: Anti-inflammatory.

• **ZILANTEL.** USAN.
Use: Anthelmintic.

ZIMCO. (Sterwin) Vanillin.

• **ZIMELDINE HYDROCHLORIDE.** USAN.
Use: Antidepressant.

• **ZIMELIDINE HYDROCHLORIDE.**
Use: Antidepressant.See: Zimeldine hydrochloride.

ZINACEF. (Glaxo) Cefuroxime sodium 750 mg. or 1.5 Gm./Vial.
Use: Antibiotic.

ZINAMIDE. Pyrazinamide, B.A.N.

ZINCATE. (Paddock) Zinc sulfate 220 mg./Cap. Bot. 100s, 500s, 1000s.
Use: Emetic and astringent.

ZINC-220. (Alto) Zinc sulfate/Cap. Bot. 100s, 1000s, 5000s, 10,000s.
Use: Dietary supplement, zinc deficiency.

• **ZINC ACETATE,** U.S.P. XXI. Acetic acid, zinc salt, dihydrate.
Use: Pharm, necessity for Zinc eugenol Cement.

ZINC BACITRACIN. Bacitracin Zinc, U.S.P. XXI.
Use: Antibiotic.

ZINC BROMIDE. W/Sodium Br., ammonium Br, potassium Br, ext. hyoscyamus, ext. belladonna.
See: Neurosine, Tab., Liq. (Dios)

• **ZINC CHLORIDE,** U.S.P. XXI. Inj., U.S.P. XXI.
Use: Astringent, desensitizer for dentin, replacement therapy.
See: Zinctrace, Inj. (Armour)

W/Formaldehyde.
See: Forma Zincol Concentrate (Ingram)

• **ZINC CHLORIDE Zn 65.** USAN.
Use: Radioactive agent.

ZINCFRIN. (Alcon) Zinc sulfate 0.25%, phenylephrine HCl 0.12% in buffered sol. Droptainer 15 cc.
Use: Astringent and ocular decongestant.

• **ZINC-EUGENOL CEMENT,** U.S.P. XXI.
Use: Dental protectant.

• **ZINC GELATIN,** U.S.P. XXI. Zinc gelatin boot. Unna's Boot.
Use: Topical protectant.

• **ZINC GELATIN IMPREGNATED GAUZE,** U.S.P. XXI.
Use: Topical protectant.

ZINC-GLENWOOD. (Glenwood) Zinc Sulfate 220 mg./Cap. Bot. 100s.

• **ZINC GLUCONATE,** U.S.P. XXI.

ZINCHLORUNDESAL. Zincundesal.

ZINC INSULIN.
See: Insulin Zinc, Prep. (Various Mfr.)

ZINCON SHAMPOO. (Lederle) Pyrithione zinc 1% w/sodium methyl cocoyltaurate, NaCl, MgAl silicate, Na cocoyl isethionate, glutaral and water w/pH adjusted. Bot. 4 oz., 8 oz.
Use: Dandruff Shampoo.

• **ZINC OXIDE,** U.S.P. XXI. Flowers of zinc.
Use: Mild astringent & antiseptic in skin diseases.
See: Calamine Preps.

W/Combinations.
See: Akne, Drying Lotion (Alto)
Almophen, Oint. (Bowman)
Anecal, Cream (Lannett)
Anocaine, Supp. (Mallard)
Anoids Rectal Supp. (Scrip)
Anugesic, Oint., Supp. (Parke-Davis)
Anulan, Vial. (Lannett)
Anusol, Oint., Supp. (Parke-Davis)
Anusol-HC, Supp. (Parke-Davis)
Aracain Rectal Oint., Supp. (Commerce)
Biscolan, Supp. (Lannett)
Bonate, Supp. (suppositoria)
Calamatum, Preps. (Blair)
Cala-Zinc-Ol, Liq. (Emerson)
Caldesene, Oint. (Pharmacraft)
Caleate HC Cream, Oint. (Elder)
Caloxide W/Benzocaine, Cream (Blue Line)
Caloxol, Oint. (Bowman)
CZO, Lot. (Elder)
Derma Medicone HC, Supp. (Medicone)
Dermatrol, Oint. (Gordon)
Desitin, Oint. (Leeming)
Diaprex, Oint. (Moss, Belle)
Doctient, Supp. (Suppositoria)
Elder Diaper Rash Oint. (Elder)
Epinephricaine, Oint. (Upjohn)
Ergophene, Oint. (Upjohn)
Hemocaine, Oint. (Mallard)
Hemorrhoidal Oint. (Towne)
Hydro Surco, Lot. (Alma)
Ladd's Paste (Paddock)
Lanaburn, Oint. (Lannett)
Lasan, Oint. (Stiefel)
Medicated Powder (Johnson & Johnson)
Medicated Foot Powder (Upjohn)
Mexsana, Pow. (Plough)
Nullo Foot Cream (DePree)
Obtundia Calamine Cream (Otis Clapp)
Pazo, Oint. & Supp. (Bristol-Myers)
Petrozin Compound Oint. (Bowman)
Pile-Gon, Oint. (Edward J. Moore)
PZM Ointment (Wendt-Bristol)
Rectal Medicone HC, Supp. (Medicone)
Rhuex, Liq. (Kay)
RVPaque, Oint. (Elder)
Saratoga, Oint. (Blair)
Schamberg, Lot. (Paddock)
Sebasorb, Lot. (Summer)
Supertah, Oint. (Purdue Frederick)
Taloin, Tube (Warren-Teed)
Ting, Cream, Pow. (Pharmacraft)
Unguentine Oint. "Original Formula" (Norwich-Eaton)
Versal, Supp. (Suppositoria)
Wyanoids, Preps. (Wyeth)
Xylocaine Supp. (Astra)
Zinc Boric Lotion, Liq. (Emerson)
Zonox Colloidal, Liq. (Scrip)

ZINC OXIDE OINTMENT, U.S.P. XXI. (Norwich Eaton) Tubes 1 oz., 2.25 oz.
Use: Protective coating for minor skin irritations.

• **ZINC OXIDE PASTE,** U.S.P. XXI.
Use: Topical protectant, astringent

• **ZINC OXIDE AND SALICYLIC ACID PASTE,** U.S.P XXI.
Use: Topical protectant; astringent.

ZINC PHENOLSULFONATE.
Use: Astringent.

W/Belladonna leaf ext., kaolin, pectin, sodium carboxymethylcellulose.
See: Gelcomul, Liq. (Commerce)

W/Bismuth subgallate, kaolin, pectin, opium pow.
See: Amogel, Tab. (Vortech)
Diastay, Tab. (Elder)

W/Bismuth subsalicylate, salol, methyl salicylate.
See: Pepto-Bismol, Liquid (Norwich Eaton)

W/Kaolin, pectin.
See: Pectocel, Liq. (Lilly)

W/Mag. trisilicate, cal. carb., bis. subcarb., cerium oxalate.
See: Bismosalicate Comp., Liq. (Blue Line)

W/Opium pow., bismuth subgallate, pectin, kaolin.
See: Bismuth, Pectin & Paregoric (Lemmon)
B.K.Z., Tab. (Sutliff & Case)

ZINC PYRITHIONE. Bis-[1-hydroxy-2(1H)-pyridineth ionato] zinc.
Use: Bactericide, fungicide, antiseborrheic.
See: Breck One, Shampoo (Breck)
Zincon, Shampoo (Lederle)
ZP-11, Liq. (Revlon)

• **ZINC STEARATE,** U.S.P. XXI. Octadecanoic acid, zinc salt.
Use: Dusting powder.
W/Combinations.
See: Ting, Cream, Pow. (Pharmacraft)

ZINC SULFANILATE. Zinc sulfanilate tetrahydrate. Nizin, Op-Isophrin-Z, Op-Isophrin-Z-M (Broemmel).
Use: Antibacterial.

• **ZINC SULFATE,** U.S.P. XXI. Inj., Ophth. Sol. U.S.P. XXI. Sulfuric acid, zinc salt (1:1), heptahydrate.
Use: Astringent (ophthalmic).
See: Bufopto Zinc Sulfate, Sol. (Softcon)
Medizinc, Tab. (Medics)
Op-Thal-Zin Ophth. (Alcon)
Scrip-Zinc, Cap. (Scrip)
Zinc-Glenwood, Cap. (Glenwood)
Zin-Cora, Caps. (Elder)
W/Boric acid, phenylephrine HCl.
See: Oc-U-Zin, Ophth. Sol. (Blue Line)
Phenylzin Drops, Ophth. Sol. (Smith Miller & Patch)
W/Calcium lactate.
See: Zinc-220, Cap. (Alto)
W/Menthol, methyl salicylate, alum, boric acid, oxyquinoline citrate.
See: Maso pH Powder (Mason)
W/Phenylephrine HCl, polyvinyl alcohol.
See: Prefrin-Z, Liquifilm (Allergan)
W/Piperocaine HCl, boric acid, potassium chloride.
See: M-Z Drops (Smith, Miller & Patch)
W/Sodium Chloride.
See: Bromidrosis Crystals (Gordon)
W/Sulfur, hexachlorophene.
See: Acnederm, Lot. (Lannett)
W/Vitamins.
See: Neovicaps TR, Cap. (Scherer)
Vicon-C, Cap. (Glaxo)
Vicon Chewable, Tab. (Glaxo)
Vicon Forte, Cap. (Glaxo)
Vicon Plus, Cap. (Glaxo)
Vi-Zac, Cap. (Glaxo)
Z-Bec, Tab. (Robins)

ZINC SULFATE BUFOPTO. (Softcon) Zinc sulfate 0.25%, benzalkonium chloride 1:25,000. Bot. 15 cc., 30 cc.
Use: Astringent, antiseptic, bacteriostatic.

ZINC SULFATE COMPOUND. (Lilly) Zinc sulfate 12.5 Gm., salicylic acid 500 mg., phenol, eucalyptol, menthol, and thymol 100 mg., boric acid 86.6 Gm./100 Gm. Bot. 4 oz.

ZINC SULFIDE, LOTION.
See: White Lotion, U.S.P.

ZINC SULFOCARBOLATE.
W/Aluminum hydroxide, pectin, kaolin, bismuth subsalicylate, salol.
See: Wescola Antidiarrheal-Stomach Upset (Western Research)

ZINCTRACE. (Armour) Zinc chloride injection containing zinc 1 mg./1 ml. Vial 10 ml. Box 25s.
Use: Supplement to I.V. solutions for zinc deficiency.

ZINCUNDESAL.
See: Zinchlorundesal

ZINC-10-UNDECENOATE.
See: Zinc Undecylenate, U.S.P. XXI.

• **ZINC UNDECYLENATE,** U.S.P. XXI. 10-Undecenoic acid, zinc (2+) salt. Zinc 10-undecenoate. (Various Mfr.)
Use: Antifungal.
W/Benzocaine, hexachlorophene.
See: Fung-O-Spray (Scrip)
W/Benzocaine, undecylenic acid, menthol.
See: Decyl-Cream LBS (Scrip)
W/Caprylic acid, sodium propionate.
See: Deso-Cream (Quality Generics)
Deso-Talc, Foot Powder (Quality Generics)
W/Undecylenic acid.
See: Cruex Cream, Spray Pow. (Pharmacraft)
Desenex, Prods. (Pharmacraft)
Ting, Aerosol (Pharmacraft)
Quinsana, Med. Oint. (Mennen)

ZINKAPS. (Ortega) Zinc sulfate 220 mg./Cap. Bot. 100s, 1000s.
Use: Zinc supplement.

• **ZINOCANAZOLE HYDROCHLORIDE.** USAN.
Use: Antifungal.

• **ZINOSTATIN.** USAN.
Use: Antineoplastic.

• **ZINTEROL HYDROCHLORIDE.** USAN.
Use: Bronchodilator.

• **ZINVIROXIME.** USAN.
Use: Antiviral.

ZIPAN-25/50. (Savage) Promethazine HCl 25 mg., 50 mg./ml. Vial 10 ml. Box 25 × 1 ml.
Use: Antihistaminic, sedative, anti-motion anticholinergic.

ZIRADRYL LOTION. (Parke-Davis) Benadryl HCl 2%, zinc oxide 2%, alcohol 2%. Bot. 6 oz.
Use: Poison ivy and related dermatitis.

ZIRCONIUM CARBONATE OR OXIDE.
See: Dermaneed, Lot. (Hanlon)
W/Benzocaine, menthol, camphor.
See: Rhulicream, Oint. (Lederle)
W/Benzocaine, menthol, camphor, calamine, pyrilamine maleate.
See: Ivarest, Cream (Carbisulphoil)
W/Benzocaine, menthol, camphor, calamine, isopropyl alcohol.
See: Rhulispray, Aerosol (Lederle)
W/Benzocaine, pyrilamine maleate, povidone.
See: Poison Ivy Cream (McKesson)
W/Calamine, zinc oxide, pyrilamine maleate.
See: Zircostan, Creme (Standex)
W/Parethoxycaine, calamine.
See: Zotox, Spray, Oint. (Commerce)

ZIRCOSTAN CREME. (Standex) Zirconium oxide 4.5%, calamine 6.0%, zinc oxide 4.0%, pyrilamine maleate 0.5%.

ZNG. (Western Research) Zinc gluconate 35 mg./Tab. Handicount 28 (36 bags of 28 tab.)
Use: Supplement.

Zn-PLUS PROTEIN. (Miller) Zinc in a zinc-protein complex made with isolated soy protein 5 mg./Tab. Bot. 100s.
Use: Dietary supplement.

ZODEAC-100. (Econo Med) Multivitamin and multi-mineral supplement with 1 mg. folic acid. Bot. 100s.
Use: Dietary supplement.

ZOALENE. Dinitolmide, B.A.N.

ZOAMIX. Dinitolmide, B.A.N.

ZODIEX. (Eckerd) Phenacetin 125 mg., salicylamide, Pamabrom 25 mg., pyrilamine maleate/Tab. Pack 24s.
Use: Premenstrual discomfort.

• **ZOFENOPRIL CALCIUM.** USAN.
Use: Enzyme inhibitor (angiotensin-converting).

• **ZOLAMINE HCl.** USAN. 2-[[2-(Dimethylamino)ethyl]-(p-methoxybenzyl)-amino]thiazole monohydrochloride.
Use: Antihistamine and local anesthetic.
W/Eucupin dihycrochloride.
See: Otodyne, Sol. (Schering)

• **ZOLAZEPAM HYDROCHLORIDE.** USAN.
Use: Sedative.

• **ZOLERTINE HYDROCHLORIDE.** USAN. 1-Phenyl-4-[2-(1H-tetrazol-5-yl)ethyl]piperazine HCl.
Use: Antiadrenergic; vasodilator.

ZOLYSE. (Alcon) Lyophilized alpha-chymotrypsin 750 units balanced salt solution 10 cc./Unit pak. 12s.
Use: Cataract surgery.

ZOMAX. (McNeil Pharm) Zomepirac sodium 100 mg./Tab. Bot. 100s.
Use: Relief of mild to moderately severe pain.

• **ZOMEPIRAC SODIUM,** U.S.P. XXI. Tab., U.S.P. XXI. Sodium 5-(4-chlorobenzoyl)-1, 4-dimethyl-1H-pyrrole-2-acetate dihydrate.
Use: Non-steroidal, anti-inflammatory and analgesic agent.
See: Zomax, Tab. (McNeil)

• **ZOMETAPINE.** USAN.
Use: Antidepressant.

ZONE-A LOTION. (UAD Labs) Hydrocortisone acetate 1%, pramoxine HCl 1%. Bot. 2 oz.
Use: For relief of the inflammatory manifestations of corticosteroid responsive dermatoses.

• **ZONISAMIDE.** USAN.
Use: Anticonvulsant.

ZONITE LIQUID DOUCHE CONCENTRATE. (Norcliff Thayer) Benzalkonium chloride 0.1%, propylene glycol, menthol, thymol in buffered solution. Bot. 8 fl. oz., 12 fl. oz.
Use: Vaginal douche.

ZONIUM CHLORIDE. (Lannett) Benzalkonium chloride 12.8%, 17%, 50%. Bot. pt., gal. 12.8%, 17% Bot. 4 oz. Also as 1:1,000, Bot. 1 pt., 1 gal.
Use: Antiseptic.

• **ZORBAMYCIN.** USAN.
Use: Antibacterial.

ZORPRIN. (Boots) Aspirin 800 mg./S.R. Tab. Bot. 100s.
Use: Treatment of rheumatoid arthritis, osteoarthritis.

• **ZORUBICIN HYDROCHLORIDE.** USAN.
Use: Antineoplastic.

ZOVIRAX CAPSULES. (Burroughs Wellcome) Acyclovir 200 mg./Cap. Bot. 100s. Unit dose 100s.
Use: Treatment of genital herpes.

ZOVIRAX OINTMENT 5%. (Burroughs Wellcome) Acyclovir 50 mg./Gm Tube 15 Gm.
Use: Management of initial herpes genitalis and mucocutaneous herpes simplex virus infections.

ZOVIRAX STERILE POWDER. (Burroughs Wellcome) Acyclovir sodium 500 mg./Vial. Vial 10 ml. ctn. 25s.
Use: Treatment of initial and recurrent mucosal & cutaneous herpes simplex.

ZOXAPHEN. (Mallard) Chlorzoxazone 250 mg., acetaminophen 300 mg./Tab. Bot. 500s.
Use: Musculoskeletal disorders.

ZOXAZOLAMINE, B.A.N. 2-Amino-5-chlorobenzoxazole. Flexin.
Use: Skeletal muscle relaxant-uricosuric.

Z-PRO-C. (Person & Covey) Elemental zinc 45 mg., ascorbic acid 100 mg./Tab. Bot. 100s.
Use: Zinc and vitamin C therapy.

Z-TEC. (Seatrace) Iron equivalent 50 mg./ml. from iron dextran complex. Vial 10 cc.

• **ZUCLOMIPHENE.** USAN.

ZYLOPRIM. (Burroughs Wellcome) Allopurinol 100 mg./Tab. Bot. 100s, 1000s, unit dose packs 100s; 300 mg./Tab. Bot. 30s, 100s, 500s, unit dose packs 100s.
Use: Antigout.

ZYLORIC. Allopurinol, B.A.N.

ZYMACAP. (Upjohn) Vit. A 5000 I.U., D 400 I.U., E 15 I.U., C 90 mg., folic acid 400 mcg., B-1 2.25 mg., B-2 2.6 mg., niacin 30 mg., B-6 3 mg., B-12 9 mcg., pantothenic acid 15 mg./Cap. Bot. 90s, 240s.
Use: Vitamin deficiencies.

ZYMENOL. (Houser) Brewer's yeast 12%, mineral oil 50%, agar q.s. Bot. 8 oz., 14 oz., Reg. or chocolate.
Use: Bowel management.

ZYMME. (Scrip) Dl-methyl polysiloxane 0.8 mg., ox bile 100 mg., pancreatin 50 mg., cellulase 0.3 mg., betaine HCl 4 gr./Cap.
Bot. 100s.
Use: Enzymatic digestive.

ZYMOWIN. (Winston) Amylolytic enzyme 25 mg., proteolytic enzyme 10 mg., cellulolytic enzyme 1 mg., dehydrocholic acid 100 mg., hyoscyamine HBr 0.1 mg., hyoscine HBr 0.0065 mg., atropine sulfate 0.02 mg./Tab. Bot. 100s, 1000s.
Use: Enzyme-antispasmodic in digestive disturbances.

ZYMOZYME TABLETS. (Inwood) Vit. A 25,000 I.U., D 2000 I.U., B-12 10 mcg., B-1 10 mg., B-2 10 mg., niacinamide 150 mg., B-6 1 mg., cal. pantothenate 10 mg., C 150 mg., D 12 I.U., rutin 25 mg., citrus bioflavonoid complex 25 mg., choline bitartrate 50 mg., inositol 25 mg., dl-methionine 25 mg., K 1 mg., nucleic acid 25 mg., yeast enzymatic hydrolysate

25 mg., glutamic acid 12.5 mg., glycine 12.5 mg., cysteine HCl 12.5 mg., iron 20 mg., Mn 1 mg., Cu 0.45 mg., Mg 1 mg., pot. 5 mg., Zn 0.5 mg./Tab. Bot. 100s.
Use: Multivitamin, mineral, lipotopic and phosphorylating therapy.

ZYNOXUN OINTMENT. (Alton) Tube 5 oz. Jar. 1 lb.
Use: Protective ointment.

ZYPAN TABLETS. (Standard Process) Pancreatin 1.5 Gm., pepsin (1:3000) 1.5 Gm., betaine HCl 2.75 Gm., ammonium chloride 0.15 Gm./Tab. Bot. 100s.
Use: Digestive aid.

Word	Abbreviation	Meaning
ana	$\overline{aa}$, aa	of each
ante cibum	a.c.	before meals or food
ad	ad	to, up to
aurio dextra	a.d.	right ear
ad libitum	ad lib.	at pleasure
aurio laeva	a.l.	left ear
ante meridiem	A.M.	morning
aqua	aq.	water
aqua destillata	aq. dest.	distilled water
aurio sinister	a.s.	left ear
aures utrae	a.u.	each ear
bis in die	b.i.d.	twice daily
bowel movement	b.m.	bowel movement
blood pressure	b.p.	blood pressure
cong	c.	a gallon
cum	$\bar{c}$	with
capsula	caps.	capsule
	cc.	cubic centimeter
compositus	comp.	compound
dies	d.	day
dilue	dil.	dilute
dispensa	disp.	dispense
divide	div.	divide
dentur tales doses	d.t.d.	give of such a dose
elixir	el.	elixir
	e.m.p.	as directed
et	et	and
	ex aq.	in water
fac, fiat, fiant	f., ft.	make, let be made
Food and Drug Administration	FDA	Food and Drug Administration
gramma	Gm., g.	gram
granum	gr.	grain
gutta	gtt.	a drop
hora	h.	hour
hora somni	h.s., hor. som.	at bedtime
	i.m., I.M	intramuscular
	i.v.	intravenous
liquor	liq.	a liquor, solution
	mcg.	microgram
	mg.	milligram
	ml.	milliliter
misce	M.	mix
more dictor	m. dict.	as directed
mixtura	mixt.	a mixture
National Formulary	N.F.	National Formulary
numerus	no.	number
nocturnal	noc.	in the night
non repetatur	non. rep.	do not repeat, no refills
octarius	O, Oct.	a pint
oculus dexter	o.d.	right eye
oculus laevus	o.l.	left eye
oculus sinister	o.s.	left eye
oculo uterque	o.u.	each eye
post cibos	p.c., post. cib.	after meals
post meridiem	P.M.	afternoon or evening
per os	p.o.	by mouth
pro re nata	p.r.n.	as needed

*The listing of commonly used abbreviations is included as an aid in interpreting medical orders.

Word	Abbreviation	Meaning
pulvis	pulv.	a powder
	q.d.	every day
quiaque hora	q.h.	every hour
quater in die	q.i.d.	four times a day
	q.o.d.	every other day
quantum sufficiat	q.s.	a sufficient quantity
	q.s. ad	a sufficient quantity to make
quam volueris	q.v.	as much as you wish
recipe	Rx	take, a recipe
repetatur	rep.	let it be repeated
sine	$\bar{s}$, s	without
secundum artem	s.a.	according to art
sataratus	sat.	saturated
signa	Sig.	label, or let it be printed
solutio	sol.	solution
	solv.	dissolve
semis	$\overline{ss}$., ss	one-half
si opus sit	s.o.s.	if there is need
statim	stat.	at once, immediately
suppositorium	supp.	suppository
syrupus	syr.	syrup
tabella	tab.	tablet
	tal.	such
	tal. dos.	such doses
ter in die	t.i.d.	three times a day
tincture	tr., tinct.	tincture
tritura	trit.	triturate
	tsp.	teaspoonful
unguentum	ung.	ointment
United States Adopted Names	USAN	official adopted names
United States Pharmacopeia	U.S.P.	United States Pharmacopeia
ut dictum	ut. dict.	as directed
while awake	w.a.	while awake

Weight Equivalents

1 grain	= 1 gr	= 64.8	milligrams
1 gram	= 1 Gm or g	= 15.432	grains
1 kilogram	= 1 Kg	= 2.20	pounds avoirdupois (lb)
1 ounce avoirdupois	= 1 oz	= 28.35	grams
1 ounce apothecary	= 1 ℥	= 31.1	grams
1 pound avoirdupois	= 1 lb	= 454.	grams

Measure Equivalents

1 milliliter	= 1 ml	= 16.23	minims (♏)
1 fluidram†	= 1 fʒ	= 3.4	ml
1 teaspoonful†	= 1 tsp	= 5.00	ml
1 tablespoonful	= 1 tbs or tbsp	= 15.	ml
1 fluidounce	= 1 f℥	= 29.57	ml
1 wineglassful	= 2 f℥	= 60.	ml
1 teacupful	= 4 f℥	= 120.	ml
1 tumblerful	= 8 f℥	= 240.	ml
1 pint	= 1 pt or O or Oct	= 473.	ml
1 liter	= 1 L	= 33.8	fluidounces (f℥)
1 gallon	= 1 gal or C or Cong	= 3785.	ml

*The listing of approximate practical equivalents is included to aid the practitioner in calculating and converting dosages among the various systems.

†Note: On prescription a fluidram is assumed to contain a teaspoonful which is 5 ml.

METRIC SYSTEM

Metric Weight					Metric Liquid Measure				
1 microgram†	μg (mcg)	=	0.000,001	g	1 microliter	μl	=	0.000,001	L
1 milligram	mg	=	0.001	g	1 milliliter	ml	=	0.001	L
1 centigram	cg	=	0.01	g	1 centiliter	cl	=	0.01	L
1 decigram	dg	=	0.1	g	1 deciliter	dl	=	0.1	L
1 gram	g	=	1.0	g	1 liter	L	=	1.0	L
1 dekagram	Dg	=	10.0	g	1 dekaliter	Dl	=	10.0	L
1 hectogram	Hg	=	100.0	g	1 hectoliter	Hl	=	100.0	L
1 kilogram	Kg	=	1000.0	g	1 kiloliter	Kl	=	1000.0	L

APOTHECARY SYSTEM

Apothecary Weight

1 grain‡	gr	= 1 gr	
1 scruple	℈	= 20 gr	
1 dram	ʒ	= 60 gr	= 3℈
1 ounce	℥	= 480 gr	= 8ʒ
1 pound	℔	= 5760 gr	= 12℥

Apothecary Liquid Measure

1 minim	♏	= 1 ♏	
1 fluidram	fʒ	= 60 ♏	
1 fluidounce	f℥	= 480 ♏	= 8 fʒ
1 pint	pt	= 7680 ♏	= 16 f℥
1 quart	qt	= 15630 ♏	= 32 f℥
1 gallon	gal	= 61440 ♏	= 8 pt℥

AVOIRDUPOIS SYSTEM

Avoirdupois Weight

1 ounce = 1 oz = 437.5 grains (gr)
1 pound = 1 lb = 16 ounces (oz) = 7000 grains (gr)

*The listing of common systems of weight and measure is included to aid the practitioner in calculating dosages.

†Note: The abbreviation μg or mcg is used for microgram in pharmacy rather than gamma (γ) as in biology.

‡Note: The grain in each of the above systems has the same value, and thus serves as a basis for the interconversion of the other units.

Glossary

Abduction—the act of drawing away from a center.
Abstergent—a cleansing application or medicine.
Acaricide—an agent lethal to mites.
Achlorhydria—the absence of hydrochloric acid from gastric secretions.
Acidifier, systemic—a drug used to lower internal body pH in patients with systemic alkalosis.
Acidifier, urinary—a drug used to lower the pH of the urine.
Acidosis—an accumulation of acid in the body.
Acne—an inflammatory disease of the skin accompanied by the eruption of papules or pustules.
Addison's Disease—a condition caused by adrenal gland destruction.
Adduction—the act of drawing toward a center.
Adenitis—a gland or lymph node inflammation.
Adjuvant—an ingredient added to a prescription which complements or accentuates the action of the primary agent.
Adrenergic—a sypathomimetic drug that activates organs innervated by the sympathetic branch of the autonomic nervous system.
Adrenocorticotropic Hormone—an anterior pituitary hormone that stimulates and regulates secretion of the adrenocortical steroids.
Adrenocortical steroid, anti-inflammatory—an adrenal cortex hormone that participates in regulation of organic metabolism and inhibits the inflammatory response to stress; a glucocorticoid.
Adrenocortical steroid, salt regulating—an adrenal cortex hormone that maintains sodium-potassium electrolyte balance by stimulating and regulating sodium retention and potassium excretion by the kidneys.
Adsorbent—an agent that binds chemicals to its surface; it is useful in reducing the free availability of toxic chemicals.
Alkalizer, systemic—a drug that raises internal body pH in patients with systemic acidosis.
Allergen—a specific substance that causes an unwanted reaction in the body.
Amblyopia—pertaining to a dimness of vision.
Amebiasis—an infection with a pathogenic ameba.
Amenorrhea—an abnormal discontinuation of the menses.
Amphiarthrosis—a joint in which the surfaces are connected by discs of fibrocartilage.
Anabolic—an agent that promotes conversion of simple substance into more complex compounds; a constructive process for the organism.
Analeptic—a potent central nervous system stimulant used to maintain vital functions during severe central nervous system depression.
Analgesic—a drug that selectively suppresses pain perception without inducing unconsciousness.
Ancyclostomiasis—the condition due to the presence of hookworms in the intestine.
Androgen—a hormone that stimulates and maintains male secondary sex characteristics.
Anemia—a deficiency of red blood cells.
Anesthetic, general—a drug that eliminates pain perception by inducing unconsciousness.
Anesthetic, local—a drug that eliminates pain perception in a limited area by local action on sensory nerves; a topical anesthetic.
Angina pectoris—a sharp chest pain starting in the heart, often spreading down the left arm. A symptom of coronary disease.
Angiography—an X-ray of the blood vessels.
Anhydrotic—a drug that checks perspiration flow systemically; an antidiaphoretic.
Anodyne—a drug which act on the sensory nervous system, either centrally or peripherally, to produce relief from pain.
Anorexiant—a drug that suppresses appetite, usually secondary to central stimulation of mood.
Anorexigenic—an agent promoting a dislike or aversion to food.
Antacid—a drug that neutralizes excess gastric acid locally.
Anthelmintic—a drug that kills or inhibits worm infestations such as pinworms and tapeworms (nematodes, cestodes, trematodes).
Antiadrenergic—a drug that prevents response to sympathetic nervous system stimulation and adrenergic drugs; a sympatholytic or sympathoplegic drug.
Antiamebic—a drug that kills or inhibits the pathogenic protozoan.*Endamoeba histolytica,* the causative agent of amebic dysentery.
Antianemic—a drug that stimulates the production of erythrocytes in normal size, number and hemoglobin content; useful in treating anemias, antidoting overdoses of anemia-causing drugs.
Antiasthmatic—an agent that relieves the spasms of asthma.
Antibacterial—a drug that kills or inhibits pathogenic bacteria, the causative agents of many systemic gastrointestinal and superficial infections.
Antibiotic—an agent produced by or derived

from living cells of molds, bacteria or other plants, which destroy or inhibit the growth of microbes.

Anticholesteremic—a drug that lowers blood plasmacholesterol levels.

Anticholinergic—a drug that prevents response to parasympathetic nervous system stimulation and cholinergic drugs; a parasympatholytic or parasympathoplegic drug.

Anticoagulant—a drug that inhibits clotting of circulating blood or prevents clotting of collected blood.

Anticonvulsant—a drug that selectively prevents epileptic seizures; a central depressant used to arrest convulsions by inducing unconsciousness.

Antidepressant—a psychotherapeutic drug that induces mood elevation, useful in treating depressive neuroses and psychoses.

Antidiabetic—a drug used to prevent the development of diabetes.

Antidote—a drug that prevents or counteracts the effects of poisons or drug overdoses, by adsorption in the gastrointestinal tract (general antidotes) or by specific systemic action (specific antidotes).

Antieczematic—a topical drug that aids in the control of exudative inflammatory skin lesions.

Antiemetic—a drug that prevents vomiting, especially that of systemic origin.

Anti-fibrinolytic—an agent (drug) that inhibits liquifaction of fibrin.

Antifilarial—a drug that kills or inhibits pathogenic filarial worms of the superfamily *Filarioidea,* the causative agents of diseases such as loaiasis.

Antiflatulant—an agent inhibiting the excessive formation of gas in the stomach or intestines.

Antifungal—a drug that kills or inhibits pathogenic fungi, the causative agents of systemic, gastrointestinal, and superficial infections.

Antihemophilic—a blood derivative containing the clotting factors absent in the hereditary disease hemophilia.

Antihistaminic—a drug that prevents response to histamine, including histamine released by allergic reactions.

Antihypercholesterolemic—a drug that lowers blood cholesterol levels, especially elevated levels sometimes associated with cardiovascular disease.

Antihypertensive—a drug that lowers blood pressure, especially diastolic blood pressure in hypertensive patients.

Anti-infective, local—a drug that kills a variety of pathogenic microorganisms and is suitable for sterilizing the skin or wounds.

Anti-inflammatory—a drug which counteracts or suppresses inflammation, and produces suppression of the pain, heat, redness and swelling of inflammation.

Antileishmanial—a drug that kills or inhibits pathogenic protozoa of the genus *Leishmania,* the causative agents of diseases such as kala-azar.

Antileprotic—an agent which fights leprosy, a generally chronic skin disease.

Antilipemic—an agent reducing the amount of circulating lipids.

Antimalarial—a drug that kills or inhibits the causative agents of malaria.

Antimetabolite—a substance that competes with or replaces a certain metabolite.

Antimethemoglobinemic—a drug that reduces non-functional methemoglobin (Fe^{+++}) to normal hemoglobin (Fe^{++}).

Antimycotic—an agent inhibiting the growth of fungi.

Antinauseant—a drug that suppresses nausea, especially that due to motion sickness.

Antineoplastic—a drug that is selectively toxic to rapidly multiplying cells and is useful in destroying malignant tumors.

Antioxidant—an agent used to reduce decay or transformation of a material from oxidation.

Antiperiodic—a drug that modifies or prevents the return of malarial fever; an antimalarial.

Antiperistaltic—a drug that inhibits intestinal motility, especially for the treatment of diarrhea.

Antipruritic—a drug that prevents or relieves itching.

Antipyretic—a drug employed to reduce fever temperature of the body; a febrifuge.

Antirheumatic—a drug that alleviates inflammatory symptoms of arthritis and related connective tissue diseases.

Antirickettsial—a drug that kills or inhibits pathogenic microorganisms of the genus Rickettsia, the causative agents of diseases such as typhus. (Chloramphenicol USP)

Antischistosomal—a drug that kills or inhibits pathogenic flukes of the genus *Schistosoma,* the causative agents of schistosomiasis.

Antiseborrheic—a drug that aids in the control of seborrheic dermatitis ("dandruff").

Antiseptic—a substance that will inhibit the growth and development of microorganisms without necessarily destroying them.

Antisialagogue—a drug which diminishes the flow of saliva.

Antispasmodic—an agent used to quiet the spasms of voluntary and involuntary muscles; a calmative or antihysteric.

Anti-syphilitic—a remedy used in the treatment of syphilis.

Antitoxin—a biological drug containing antibodies against the toxic principles of a pathogenic microorganism, used for passive immunization against the associated disease.

Antitrichomonal—a drug that kills or inhibits the pathogenic protozoan *Trichomonas vaginalis,* the causative agent of trichomonal vaginitis.

Antitrypanosomal—a drug that kills or inhibits pathogenic protozoa of the genus *Trypanosoma,* the causative agents of diseases such as West African trypanosomiasis.

Antitussive—a drug that suppresses coughing.

Antivenin—a biological drug containing antibodies against the venom of a poisonous animal, and useful in antidoting the animal's bite.

Anxiety—a feeling of apprehension, uncertainty and fear.

Aperient—a mild laxative.

Aphakic—having no crystalline lens.

Aphasia—the inability to use and/or understand written and spoken words, due to damage of cortical speech centers.

Aphonia—a whisper voice due to disease of the larynx or its innervation.

Apnea—the absence of breathing.

Areola—a pigmented ring on the skin.

Arsenical—having to do with arsenic.

Arteriosclerosis—a hardening of the arteries.

Arthritis—an inflammation of a joint.

Ascariasis—a condition caused by roundworms in the intestine.

Ascaricide—an agent that kills roundworms of the genus *Ascaris.*

Aspergillus—a fungi genus including many types of molds.

Astasia—the ability to stand up without help.

Asthma—a disease characterized by recurring breathing difficulty due to bronchial muscle constriction.

Astringent—a mild protein precipitant suitable for local application to toughen, shrink, blanch, wrinkle and harden tissue, diminish secretions, and coagulate blood.

Ataractic—an agent having a quieting, tranquilizing effect.

Ataxia—incoordination, especially of gait.

Atheroma—a fatty granular degeneration of an artery wall.

Atrophy—a wasting away.

Avitaminosis—a disease caused by lack of one or more vitamins in the diet.

Axilla—armpit.

Bacteriostatic—an agent that inhibits the growth of bacteria.

Basedow's disease—a form of hyperthyroidism, also known as Grave's disease and Parry's disease.

Biliary Colic—a sharp pain in the upper right side of the abdomen due to a gallstone impaction.

Bilirubin—a bile pigment.

Biliuria—the presence of bile in the urine.

Blood Calcium Regulator—a drug that maintains the blood level of ionic calcium, especially by regulating its metabolic disposition elsewhere.

Blood Volume Supporter—an intravenous solution whose solutes are retained in the vascular system to supplement the osmotic activity of plasma proteins.

Bradycardia—a slow heart rate.

Bright's Disease—a disease of the kidneys, including the presence of edema and excessive urine protein formation.

Bromidrosis—foul smelling perspiration.

Bronchitis—an inflammation of the bronchi.

Bronchodilator—a drug which can dilate the lumina of air passages of the lungs.

Bruit—an arterial sound audible with a stethoscope.

Buerger's Disease—a thromboangiitis obliterans inflammation of the walls and surrounding tissue of the veins and arteries.

Bursitis—an inflammation of the bursa.

Callus—a hard bonelike material developing around a fractured bone.

Calmative—a sedative.

Candidiasis—an infection by the yeastlike organism *Candida albicans.*

Carbonic Anhydrase Inhibitor—an enzyme inhibitor, the therapeutic effects of which are diuresis and reduced formation of intraocular fluid.

Carcinoma—a malignant growth.

Cardiac Depressant—a drug that depresses myocardial function so as to supress rhythmic irregularities characterized by fast rate; an antiarrythmic.

Cardiac Stimulant—a drug that increases the contractile force of the myocardium, especially in weakened conditions such as congestive heart failure; a cardiotonic.

Cardiopathy—a disease of the heart.

Caries—decay of the teeth.

Carminative—an aromatic or pungent drug that mildly irritates the gastrointestinal tract and is useful in the treatment of flatulence and colic. Peppermint Water is a common carminative.

Caruncle—a small fleshy projection on the skin.

Cathartic—a drug that promotes defecation, usually by enhancing peristalsis or by softening and lubricating the feces.

Caudal—pertains to the distal end or tail.

Caustic—a topical drug that destroys tissue on contact and is suitable for removal of abnormal skin growths.

Central Depressant—a drug that reduces the functional state of the central nervous system and with increasing dosage induces sedation, hypnosis, and general anesthesia; respiration is depressed.

Central Stimulant—a drug that increases the functional state of the central nervous system and with increasing dosage induces restlessness, insomnia, disorientation, and convulsions; respiration is stimulated.

;erebral—pertaining to the brain.
;erumen—earwax.
;hloasma—skin discoloration.
;holagogue—a drug that stimulates the emptying of the gallbladder and the flow of bile into the duodenum.
;holeciptitis—an inflammation of the gallbladder.
;holecystokinetic—an agent that promotes emptying of the gallbladder.
;holelithiasis—the presence of calculi (stones) in the gallbladder.
;holeretic—a drug that increases the production and secretion of dilute bile by the liver.
;horea—a disorder, usually of childhood, characterized by uncontrolled spasmotic muscle movements; sometimes referred to as St. Vitus' dance.
;hymotrypsin—a proteinase in the gastrointestinal tract; proposed use has been treatment of edema and inflammation.
;laudication—limping.
;limacteric—a time period in women just preceding termination of the reproductive processes.
;lonus—a spasm in which rigidity and relaxation succeed each other.
;oagulant—a drug that replaces a deficient blood factor necessary for coagulation; clotting factor.
;occidiostat—a drug used in the treatment of coccidal (protozoal) infections in animals, especially birds; used in veterinary medicine.
olitis—an inflammation of the colon.
;olloid—a disperse system of particles larger than those of true solutions but smaller than those of suspensions (1 to 100 millimicrons in size).
;ollyrium—an eyewash.
olostomy—the surgical formation of a more or less permanent opening into the colon.
orticoid—a term applied to hormones of the adrenal cortex or any substance, natural or synthetic, having similar activity.
orticosteroid—a steroid produced by the adrenal cortex.
oryza—a headcold.
ounterirritant—an agent (irritant) which causes irritation of the part to which it is applied, and draws blood away from a deep seated area.
ranial—pertaining to the skull.
repitation—the grating of a joint.
ryptitis—an inflammation of a follicle or glandular tubule, usually in the rectum.
ryptococcus—a genus of fungi which does not produce spores, but reproduces by budding.
ryptorchidism—the failure of one or both testes to descend.
utaneous—pertaining to the skin.
Cyanosis—a blue or purple skin discoloration due to oxygen deficiency.
Cycloplegia—the loss of accommodation.
Cyclopegic—a drug which paralyzes accommodation of the eye.
Cystitis—an inflammation of the bladder.
Cystourethography—the examination by x-ray of the bladder and urethra.
Cytostasis—a slowing of the movement of blood cells at an inflamed area, sometimes causing capillary blockage.
Debridement—the cutting away of dead or excess skin from a wound.
Decongestant—a drug which reduces congestion caused by an accumulation of blood.
Decubitus—the patient's position in bed; the act of lying down.
Demulcent—an agent used generally internally to sooth and protect mucous membranes.
Dermatitis—an inflammation of the skin.
Dermatomycosis—lesions or eruptions caused by fungi on the skin.
Detergent—an emulsifying agent useful for cleansing wounds and ulcers as well as the skin.
Dextrocardia—when the heart is located on the right side of the chest.
Diagnostic Aid—a drug used to determine the functional state of a body organ or the presence of a disease.
Diaphoretic—a drug used to increase perspiration; a hydrotic or sudorfice.
Diarrhea—an abnormal frequency and fluidity of stools.
Digestive Enzyme—an enzyme that promotes digestion by supplementing the naturally occurring counterpart.
Digitalization—the administration of digitalis to obtain a desired tissue level of drug.
Diplopia—double vision.
Disinfectant—an agent that destroys pathogenic microorganisms on contact and is suitable for sterilizing inanimate objects.
Distal—farthest from a point of reference.
Diuretic—a drug that promotes renal excretion of electrolytes and water, thereby increasing urine volume.
Dysarthia—difficulty in speech articulation.
Dysmenorrhea—pertaining to painful menstruation.
Dysphagia—difficulty in swallowing.
Dyspnea—difficult breathing.
Ecbolic—a drug used to stimulate the gravid uterus to the expulsion of the fetus, or to cause uterine contraction; an oxytocic.
Eclampsia—a toxic disorder occurring late in pregnancy involving hypertension, weight gain, edema and renal dysfunction.
Ectasia—pertaining to distension or stretching.Ectopic—out of place.
Ectopic—out of place; not in normal position.

Eczema—an inflammatory disease of the skin with infiltrations, watery discharge, scales and crust.
Effervescent—bubbling; sparkling; giving off gas bubbles.
Embolus—a blood clot in the blood stream lodged in a vessel, thus obstructing circulation.
Emetic—a drug that induces vomiting, either locally by gastrointestinal irritation or systemically by stimulation of receptors in the central nervous system.
Emollient—a topical drug, especially an oil or fat, used to soften the skin and make it more pliable.
Encometrium—the uterine mucous membrane.
Enteralgia—an intestinal pain.
Enterobiasis—a pinworm infestation.
Enuresis—involuntary urination, as in bedwetting.
Epidermis—the outermost layer of the skin.
Episiotomy—a surgical incision of the vulva when deemed necessary during childbirth.
Epistaxis—a nosebleed.
Erythema—redness.
Erythrocyte—a red blood cell.
Escharotic—corrosive.
Estrogen—a hormone that stimulates and maintains female secondary sex characteristics and functions in the menstrual cycle to promote uterine gland proliferation.
Etiology—the cause of a disease.
Euphoria—an exaggerated feeling of well being.
Eutonic—having normal muscular tone.
Exfoliation—a scaling of the skin.
Exophthalmos—a protrusion of the eyeballs.
Expectorant—a drug that increases secretion of respiratory tract fluid, thereby lowering its viscosity and cough-inducing irritancy and promoting its ejection.
Extension—the movement of a joint to move 2 body parts away from each other.
Exteroceptors—receptors on the exterior of the body.
Fasiculations—the visible twitching movements of muscle bundles.
Fibroid—a tumor of fibrous tissue, resembling fibers.
Filariasis—the condition of having round worm parasites reproducing in the body tissues.
Fistula—an abnormal opening leading from a body cavity to the outside of the body or to another cavity.
Flexion—the movement of a joint in which 2 moveable parts are brought toward each other.
Fungistatic—inhibiting the growth of fungi.
Furunculosis—a condition marked by the presence of boils.
Gallop Rhythm—a heart condition where 3 separate beats are heard instead of 2.
Gastralgia—a stomach pain.
Gastritis—inflammation of the stomach lining.
Gastrocele—a hernial protrusion of the stomach.
Gastrodynia—pain in the stomach, a stomach ache.
Geriatrics—a branch of medicine which treats problems peculiar to old age.
Germicidal—an agent that is destructive to pathogenic microorganisms.
Gingivitis—an inflammation of the gums.
Glaucoma—a disease of the eye evidenced by an increase in intraoccular pressure and resulting in hardness of the eye, atrophy of the retina and eventual blindness.
Glossitis—an inflammation of the tongue.
Glucocorticoid—a corticoid which increases gluconeogenesis, thereby raising the concentration of liver glycogen and blood sugar.
Glycosuria—an abnormal quantity of glucose in the urine.
Gout—a disorder which is symptomized by a high uric acid level and sudden onset recurrent arthritis.
Granulation—the formation of small round fleshy granules on a wound in the healing process.
Hematemesis—the vomiting of blood.
Hematinic—a drug that promotes hemoglobin formation by supplying a factor essential for its synthesis.
Hemiplegia—a condition in which one side of the body is paralyzed.
Hematopoietic—a drug that stimulates formation of blood cells, especially by supplying deficient vitamins.
Hemoptysis—bleeding in the lungs.
Histoplasmosis—a lung infection caused by the inhalation of fungus spores, often resulting in pneumonitis.
Hodgkin's Disease—a disease marked by chronic lymph node enlargement sometimes including spleen and liver enlargement.
Hydrocholeresis—putting out a thinner, more watery bile.
Hypercholesterolemia—the condition of having an abnormally large amount of cholesterol in the body cells.
Hemorrhage—copious bleeding.
Hemostatic—a locally acting drug that arrests hemorrhage by promoting clot formation or by serving as a mechanical matrix for a clot.
Hepatitis—an inflammation of the liver.
Hyperemia—an excess of blood in any part of the body.
Hyperesthesia—an increase in sensations.
Hyperglycemic—a drug that elevates blood glucose level, especially for the treatment of hypoglycemic states.
Hypertension—blood pressure above the normally accepted limits, high blood pressure.
Hypertriglyceridemia—an increased level of triglycerides in the blood.

Hypnotic—a central depressant which, with suitable dosage, induces sleep.
Hypodermoclysis—a subcutaneous injection with a solution.
Hypoesthesia—a diminished touch of sensation.
Hypoglycemic—a drug that promotes glucose metabolism and lowers blood glucose level, useful in the control of diabetes mellitus.
Hypokalemia—an abnormally small concentration of potassium ions in the blood.
Hyposensitize—to reduce the sensitivity to an agent, referring to allergies.
Hypotensive—a drug which diminishes tension or pressure, to lower blood pressure.
Ichthyosis—an inherited skin disease characterized by dryness and scales.
Idiopathic—denoting a disease of unknown cause.
Ileostomy—the establishment of an opening from the ileum to the outside of the body.
Immune Serum—a biological drug containing antibodies for a pathogenic microorganism, useful for passive immunization against the associated disease.
Immunizing Agent, active—an antigenic preparation (toxoid or vaccine) used to induce formation of specific antibodies against a pathogenic microorganism, which provides delayed but permanent protection against the associated disease.
Immunizing Agent, passive—a biological preparation (antitoxin, antivenin or immune serum) containing specific antibodies against a pathogenic microorganism, which provides immediate but temporary protection against the associated disease.
Impetigo—an inflammatory skin disease with isolated pustules.
Insulin—one of the hormones that regulate carbohydrate metabolism, used as replacement therapy in diabetes mellitus.
Inversion—a turning inward.
Irrigating solution—a solution for washing body surfaces and/or various body cavities.
Isoniazid—a compound effective in tuberculosis treatment.
Kakidrosis—foul smelling perspiration.
Keratitis—an inflammation of the cornea.
Keratolytic—a topical drug that softens the superficial keratin-containing layer of the skin to promote exfoliation.
Lacrimal—pertaining to tears.
Laxative—a gentle purgative medicine; a mild cathartic.
Leishmaniasis—a number of types of infections transmitted by sandflies.
Leucocytopenia—a decrease in the number of white cells.
Leucocytosis—an increased white cell count.
Leukoderma—an absence of pigment from the skin.
Libido—sexual desire or creative energy.
Leucocyte—a white blood cell.
Lipoma—a fatty tumor.
Lipotropic—a drug, especially one supplementing a dietary factor, that prevents the abnormal accumulation of fat in the liver.
Lochia—a vaginal discharge of mucus, blood and tissue after childbirth.
Lues—a plague; specifically syphilis.
Macrocyte—a large red blood cell.
Malaise—a general felling of illness.
Melasma—a darkening of the skin.
Melena—black feces from altered blood in the higher CIT.
Meninges—the membranes covering the brain and spinal cord.
Metastasis—the shifting of a disease or its symptoms from one part of the body to another.
Mastitis—an inflammation of the breast.
Miotics—agents which constrict the pupil of the eye; a myotic.
Moniliasis—an infection with any of the species of monilia types of fungi *(Candida).*
Mucolytic—an agent that can destroy or disolve mucous membrane secretions.
Myalgia—a pain in the muscles.
Myasthenia Gravis—a chronic progressive muscular weakness caused by myoneural conduction, usually spreading from the face and throat.
Myelocyte—an immature white blood cell in the bone marrow.
Myelogenous—originating in bone marrow.
Myoclonus—involuntary, sudden and rapid unpredictable jerks; faster than chorea.
Mydriatic—a drug that dilates the pupil of the eye, usually by anticholinergic or adrenergic mechanism.
Myoneural—pertaining to muscle and nerve.
Myopia—nearsightedness.
Narcotic—a drug that produces insensibility or stupor; a class of drug regulated by law.
Neonatal—pertaining to the first four weeks of life.
Neoplasm—an abnormal tissue growing more rapidly than usual showing a lack of structural organization.
Nephritis—an inflammation of the kidney.
Nephrosclerosis—a hardening of the kidney tissue.
Neuralgia—a pain extending along the course of one or more of the nerves.
Neurasthenia—nervous prostration.
Neuroglia—the supporting elements of the nervous system.
Neuroleptic—a substance that acts on the nervous system.
Neurosis—a functional disorder of the nervous system.
Nocturia—urination at night.
Normocytic—pertaining to anemia due to some defect in the blood-forming tissues.

Nuchal—the nape of the neck.
Nystagmus—a rhythmic oscillation of the eyes.
Oleaginous—oily or greasy.
Omphalitis—an inflammation of the navel in a newborn.
Onychomycosis—a ringworm or fungus infection of the nails.
Ophthalmic—pertaining to the eye.
Oral—pertaining to the mouth.
Orthopnea—a discomfort in bleeding in any but the upright sitting or standing positions.
Osmidrosis—foul smelling perspiration.
Ossification—a formation of, or conversion to, bone.
Osteomyelitis—an inflammation of the marrow of the bone.
Osteoporosis—a reduction in bone quantity; skeletal atrophy.
Otalgia—pain in the ear; an earache.
Otitis—inflammation of the ear.
Otomycosis—an ear infection caused by fungus.
Otorrhea—a discharge from the ear.
Oxytocic—a drug that selectively stimulates uterine motility and is useful in obstetrics, especially in the control of postpartum hemorrhage.
Ozochrotia—foul smelling perspiration.
Palpitations—an awareness of one's heart action.
Paget's Disease—a disease characterized by lesions around the nipple and areola found in elderly women.
Pallor—the lack of the normal red color imparted to the skin by the blood of the superficial vessels.
Parasympatholytic—See Anticholinergic.
Parasympathomimetic—See Cholinergic.
Parenteral—pertaining to the administration of a drug by means other than through the alimentary canal; subcutaneous, intramuscular or intravenous administration of drug.
Parkinsonism—a group of neurological disorders marked by hypokinesia, tremor, and muscular rigidity.
Paroxysm—a sudden recurrance of intensification of symptoms.
Pathogenic—giving origin to disease.
Pediatric—pertaining to children's diseases.
Pediculicide—an insecticide suitable for erradicating louse infestations in humans (pediculosis).
Pediculosis—an infestation with lice.
Pellagra—a condition characterized by GI disturbances, mental disorders, and skin redness and scaling.
Pernicious—particularly dangerous or harmful.
Phlebitis—an inflammation of a vein.
Pleurisy—an inflammation of the membrane surrounding the lungs and the thoracic cavity.
Pneumonia—an infection of the lungs.
Poikilocytosis—a condition in which pointed or irregularly shaped red blood cells are found in the blood.
Polydipsia—excessive thirst.
Posology—the science of dosage.
Posterior Pituitary Hormone(s)—a multifunctional hormone with oxytocic-milk ejectory, and antidiuretic-vasopressor fractions.
Progestin—a hormone that functions in the menstrual cycle and during pregnancy to promote uterine gland secretion and to reduce uterine motility.
Pronation—the act of turning the palm downward or backward.
Prophylactic—a remedy that tends to prevent disease.
Protectant—a topical drug that remains on the skin and serves as a physical barrier to the environment.
Proteolytic Enzyme—an enzyme used to liquefy fibrinous or purulent exudates.
Psoriasis—an inflammatory skin disease accompanied with itching.
Psychotherapeutic—a drug that selectively affects the central nervous system to alter emotional state. See Antidepressant; Tranquilizer.
Ptosis—a drooping or sagging of the muscle.
Pulmonary—pertaining to the lungs.
Purulent—containing or forming pus.
Pyelitis—a local inflammation of renal and pelvic cells due to bacterial infection.
Pylorospasm—a spasmodic muscle contraction of a sphincter.
Pyoderma—any skin discharge characterized by pus formation.
Radiopaque Medium—a diagnostic drug, opaque to X rays, whose retention in a body organ or cavity makes X-ray visualization possible.
Reynaud's Phenomenon—spasms of the digital arteries with blanching and numbness of the fingers, usually with another disease.
Reflex Stimulant—a mild irritant suitable for application to the nasopharynx to induce reflex respiratory stimulation.
Rheumatoid—a condition resembling rheumatism.
Rhinitis—an inflammation of the mucous membrane of the nose.
Rubefacient—a topical drug that induces mild skin irritation with erythema, sometimes used to relieve the discomfort of deep-seated inflammation.
Rubeola—a synonym popularly used for both measles and rubella.
Saprophytic—getting nourishment from dead material.
Sarcoma—a malignant tumor derived from connective tissue.
Scabicide—an insecticide suitable for the

erradication of itch mite infestations in humans (scabies).

Schistosomacide—an agent which destroys schistosomes; destructive to the trematodic parasites or flukes.

Schistosomiasis—an infection with *Schistosoma haematobium* involving the urinary tract and causing cystitis and hematuria.

Scintillation—a visual sensation manifested by an emission of sparks.

Sclerosing Agent—an irritant suitable for injection into varicose veins to induce their fibrosis and obliteration.

Scotomata—an area of varying size and shape within the visual field in which vision is absent or depressed.

Seborrhea—a condition arising from an excess secretion of sebum.

Sebum—the secretions of the fatty glands.

Sedative—a central depressant which, in suitable dosage, induces mild relaxation useful in treating tension.

Sinusitis—an inflammation of a sinus.

Skeletal Muscle Relaxant—a drug that inhibits contraction of voluntary muscles, usually by interfering with their innervation.

Smooth Muscle Relaxant—a drug that inhibits contraction of involuntary (e.g., visceral) muscles, usually by action upon their contractile elements.

Sociopath—a psychopathic person who, due to his unaccepted attitudes, is badly adjusted to society.

Spasmolytic—an agent that relieves spasms and involuntary contraction of a muscle; an antispasmodic.

Sputum—mucous spit from the mouth.

Stenosis—the narrowing of the lumen of a blood vessel.

Stomachic—a drug which is used to stimulate the appetite and gastric secretion.

Stomatitis—an inflammation of the mouth.

Subcutaneous—under the skin.

Sudorific—causing perspiration.

Superacidity—an increase of the normal acidity of the gastric secretion; hyperacidity.

Supination—the act of turning the palm forward or upward.

Suppressant—a drug useful in the control, rather than the cure, of a disease.

Surfactant—a surface active agent that decreases the surface tension between two miscible liquids; used to prepare emulsions, act as a cleansing agent, etc.

Synarthrosis (fibrous joint)—a joint in which the bony elements are united by continuous fibrous tissue.

Syncope—fainting.

Synovia—clear fluid which lubricates the joints; joint oil.

Systole—the ventricular contraction phase of a heartbeat.

Tachycardia—a rapid contraction rate of the heart.

Taeniacide—an agent used to kill tapeworms.

Taeniafuge—an agent used to expel tapeworms.

Therapeutic—A remedy for the treatment of disease.

Thoracic—pertaining to the chest.

Thyroid Hormone—a drug containing one or more of the iodinated amino acids that stimulate and regulate the metabolic rate and functional state of body tissues.

Thyroid Inhibitor—a drug that reduces excessive thyroid hormone production, usually by blocking synthesis of iodinated amino acids.

Tics—a repetitive twitching of muscles, often in the face and upper trunk.

Tinea—a fungal infection of the skin.

Tonic—an agent used to stimulate the restoration of tone to muscle tissue.

Tonometry—the measurement of tension in some part of the body.

Topical—the local external application of a drug to a particular place.

Toxoid—a modified bacterial toxin, less toxic than the original form, used to induce active immunity to bacterial pathogens.

Tranquilizer—a psychotherapeutic drug that induces emotional repose without significant sedation, useful in treating certain neuroses and psychoses.

Tremors—involuntary rhythmic tremulous movements.

Trichomoniasis—an infestation with parasitic flagellate protozoa of the genus *Trichomonas.*

Trypanosomiasis—a disease caused by protozoan flagellates in the blood.

Uricosuric—a drug that promotes renal excretion of uric acid, useful in the treatment of gout.

Urolithiasis—a condition marked by the formation of stones in the urinary tract.

Urticaria—a rash of hives generally of systemic origin.

Vaccine—a preparation containing live attenuated or dead pathogenic microorganisms, used to induce active immunity.

Vasoconstrictor—an adrenergic drug used locally in the nose to constrict blood vessels and reduce tissue congestion.

Vasodilator—a drug that relaxes vascular smooth muscles, expecially for the purpose of improving peripheral or coronary blood flow.

Vasopressor—an andrenergic drug used systemically to constrict blood vessels and raise blood pressure.

Verruca—a wart.

Vertigo—dizziness, giddiness.

Vesicant—an agent which when applied to the skin causes blistering and the formation of vesicles; an epispastic.

Visceral—pertaining to the internal organs.

Vitamin—an organic chemical essential in small amounts for normal body metabolism, used therapeutically to supplement the naturally occurring counterpart in foods.

he following new official monographs appear as changes to the U.S.P. XXI–N.F. XVI, the official ompendia published by the U.S. Pharmacopeial Convention, Inc, together in a single binding, which ecame official on January 1, 1985 as a result of (1) Supplement 1, official January 1, 1985; and (2) upplement 2, official July 1, 1985. U.S.P. consulted with the U.S. Adopted Names (USAN) Council nd also with interested parties from industry and government in deciding upon the announced names.

ew USP XXI Monographs

cetaminophen and Diphenhydramine Citrate Tablets
cetohydroxamic Acid
cetohydroxamic Acid Tablets
denine
clometasone Dipropionate
clometasone Dipropionate Cream
clometasone Dipropionate Ointment
prazolam
prazolam Tablets
prostadil
prostadil Injection
um, Ammonium
um, Potassium
moxicillin, Sterile
moxicillin for Suspension, Sterile
moxicillin Oral Suspension
mpicillin Boluses
mpicillin Soluble Powder
mpicillin Suspension, Sterile
nticoagulant Citrate Phosphate Dextrose Adenine Solution
spirin, Alumina, and Magnesia Tablets
acitracin Methylene Disalicylate, Soluble
acitracin Methylene Disalicylate Soluble Powder
acitracin Zinc Soluble Powder
aclofen
aclofen Tablets
utalbital and Aspirin Tablets
alcium Carbonate Oral Suspension
arisoprodol
arisoprodol and Aspirin Tablets
arisoprodol, Aspirin, and Codeine Phosphate Tablets
ellulose Sodium Phosphate
hlortetracycline Hydrochloride Tablets
otrimazole Lotion
metidine
metidine Tablets
tric Acid, Magnesium Oxide, and Sodium Carbonate Irrigation
oxacillin Benzathine
oxacillin Benzathine Intramammary Infusion
oxacillin Benzathine, Sterile
oxacillin Sodium Intramammary Infusion
oxacillin Sodium, Sterile
omolyn Sodium Inhalation
omolyn Sodium Nasal Solution
hydrostreptomycin Sulfate
hydrostreptomycin Sulfate Boluses
hydrostreptomycin Sulfate Injection
hydrostreptomycin Sulfate, Sterile
noprost Tromethamine
noprost Tromethamine Injection
phenhydramine Citrate
pivefrin Hydrochloride
pivefrin Hydrochloride Ophthalamic Solution
yphylline Elixir
razolidone Oral Suspension
razolidone Tablets
uanabenz Acetate
uanabenz Acetate Tablets

Halcinonide
Halcinonide Cream
Halcinonide Ointment
Halcinonide Topical Solution
Hetacillin Potassium Intramammary Infusion
Hetacillin Potassium Oral Suspension
Hetacillin Potassium Tablets
Hydrocortisone and Acetic Acid Otic Solution
Hydrocortisone Butyrate
Hydroxypropyl Methycellulose
Ketoconazole Tablets
Levonorgestrel
Levonorgestrel and Ethinyl Estradiol Tablets
Lidocaine and Epinephrine Injection
Magnesium Oxide Capsules
Magnesium Oxide Tablets
Metaproterenol Sulfate
Metaproterenol Sulfate Inhalation Aerosol
Metaproterenol Sulfate Inhalation Solution
Metaproterenol Sulfate Syrup
Metaproterenol Sulfate Tablets
Miconazole Nitrate Vaginal Suppositories
Mineral Oil Enema
Minoxidil
Minoxidil Tablets
Nadolol
Nadolol Tablets
Neomycon Sulfate and Hydrocortisone Acetate Lotion
Nitroglycerin Injection
Oxygen 93 Percent
Penicillin G Procaine Intramammary Infusion
Penicillin G Procaine and Dihydrostreptomycin Sulfate Intramammary Infusion
Penicillin G Procaine and Novobiocin Sodium Intramammary Infusion
Penicillin V Benzathine Oral Suspension Yellow Phenolphthalein
Pentazocine and Naloxone Hydrochlorides Tablets
Piroxicam
Piroxicam Capsules
Potassium Chloride, Potassium Bicarbonate and Potassium Citrate Effervescent Tablets for Oral Solution
Prednisone Syrup
Spectinomycin Hydrochloride for Suspension, Sterile
Stannous Floride Gel
Technetium Tc 99m Disofenin Injection Vincristine
Tetracycline Boluses
Tetracycline Hydrochloride and Novobiocin Sodium Tablets
Tetracycline Hydrochloride, Novobiocin, Sodium, and Prednisolone Tablets
Tetracycline Phosphate Complex and Novobiocin Sodium Capsules
Tioconazole
Valproic Acid
Valproic Acid Capsules
Valproic Acid Syrup
Vincristine
Zinc Gluconate

NEW NF XVI MONOGRAPHS

Bentonite, Purified
Cyclomethicone
Dextrin
Hexylene Glycol
Hydroxypropl Methycellulose Phthalate
Propylene Glycol Alginate
Sodium Stearyl Fumarate
Triethyl Citrate

Legend:

WC = well closed container
T = tight container
LR = light resistant container
\+ = controlled temperature
P = plastic specified
G = glass specified
C = collapsible tubes
TP = tamper-proof
In = inert atmosphere
U = unit dose

a = tablets
b = capsules
c = solution
d = syrup
e = elixir
f = cream
g = ointment
h = lotion
i = suppository
j = suspension
k = ophthalmic
l = aerosol
m = vaginal
n = lozenges
o = powder
p = enema
r = inhalation
s = nasal
t = gel
v = otic
w = intraocular solution
x = veterinary use
y = emulsion
z = tincture

Drug (Dosage Form)	WC	T	LR
Acetaminophen		X[a b e j]	
Acetaminophen and Aspirin (tab)		X	
Acetaminophen and Diphenhydramine Citrate (tab)		X	
Acetaminophen for Effervescent Oral Soln.		X	
Acetohydroxamic Acid (tab)		X	
Acetazolamide (tab)	X		
Acetic Acid Otic Soln.		X	
Acetohexamide (tab)	X		
Acetophenazine Maleate (tab)		X	
Acetylcysteine and Isoproterenol HCl Inhalation Soln.		G/P	
Acrisorcin (cream)		C	
Alcohol		X	
Dehydrated Alcohol		X	
Rubbing Alcohol		X	
Alclometasone Dipropionate		C[f g]	
Allupurinol (tab)	X		
Alprazolam	X	X[a]	X[a]
Alum	X		
Ammonium Alum	X		
Potassium Alum	X		
Alumina and Magnesia	X[a]	X[j +]	
Alumina and Magnesia and Carbonate	X[a]	X[j +]	
Alumina and Magnesium Trisilicate		X[j +]	
Aluminum Acetate Topical Soln.		X	
Aluminum Hydroxide Gel	X[a]	X[j +]	
Aluminum Phosphate Gel	X[a]	X[j +]	
Aluminum Subacetate Topical Soln.		X	
Amantadine Hydrochloride		X[b d]	
Amcinonide		X[f g]	
Amiloride HCl (tab)	X		
Amiloride HCl and Hydrochlorothiazide (tab)	X		
Aminobenzoic Acid	X[t c]	X[t c]	
Aminobenzoate Potassium	X[b a]	X[c]	
Aminocaproic Acid		X[a d]	
Aminoglutethimide (tab)	X		
Aminophylline	X[i +]	X[a]	
Aminosalicylate Calcium		X[a b]	X[a b]
Aminosalicylate Sodium (tab)		X[+]	X[+]
Aminosalicylic Acid (tab)		X[+]	X[+]
Amitriptyline HCl (tab)	X		
Aromatic Ammonia Spirit		X	X
Ammonium Chloride (tab)		X	
Amobarbital	X[a]	X[e]	
Amobarbital Sodium (cap)		X	
Amodiaquine		X	
Amodiaquine HCl (tab)		X	
Amoxicillin		X[a b j +]	
Amphetamine Sulfate (tab)		X	
Amphotericin B	X[h]	C[f g]	
Ampicillin (all dosage forms)		X	
Ampicillin Boluses		X[x]	
Ampicillin Soluble Powder		X[x]	
Ampicillin and Probenecid		X[b i]	U[j]
Amprolium		X[o c x]	
Amyl Nitrate (inhalant)		UG[+]	UG[+]
Anileridine HCl (tab)		X	X
Anthralin Ointment	X		X
Antipyrine and Benzocaine Otic Solution			X
Apomorphine HCl (tab)		X	
Ascorbic Acid		X[a c]	X[a c]
Aspirin	X[i +]	X[a b]	
Aspirin, Alumina and Magnesia (tab)		X	
Atropine Sulfate	X[a]	C[k g]	
Azothioprine (tab)			X

*The listing of container requirements for Compendial drugs is included as an aid to the practitioner in storing and dispensing.

Drug (Dosage Form)	WC	T	LR
Bacampicillin HCl		X[a,j]	
Bacitracin	X[g,+]	CTP[k,+]	
Bacitracin Methylene Disalicylate, Soluble	X[x]	X[o,x]	
Bacitracin Zinc Soluble Powder		X[x]	
Bacitracin Zinc	X[g,+]		
Bacitracin Zinc and Polymixin B Sulfate (ointment)	X	TP[k]	X
Baclofen	X[a]	X[o]	
Barium Sulfate	X[j]		
Beclomethasone Dipropionate	X		
Belladonna Extract (tab)		X	X
Belladonna (tincture)		X[+]	X[+]
Bendroflumethiazide (tab)		X	
Benoxinate HCl Opthalmic		X[c]	
Benzethonium Chloride Topical Solution (tincture)		X[c,z]	X[c,z]
Benzocaine HCl		X[f,g,+]	X[f,g,+]
Benzocaine Otic Soln		X[+]	X[+]
Benzocaine Topical		X[c,i,+]	X[c,+]
Benzoic and Salicylic Acid (ointment)	X[+]		
Cp. Benzoin Tincture		X[+]	X[+]
Benzonatate (cap)		X	X
Benzoyl Peroxide		X[h,t]	
Benzthiazide (tab)		X	
Benztropine Mesylate (tab)	X		
Benzyl Benzoate (lot)		X	X
Benzylpenicilloyl Polylysine Concentrate		X	
Bephenium Hydroxy-naphthoate Oral Suspension		X	
Beta Carotene Caps		X	X
Betaine HCl	X		
Betamethasone	X[a,d]	C[f]	
Betamethasone Benzoate (gel)		XC	
Betamethasone Dipropionate	XC[g]	X[h,l]C[f]	
Betamethasone Valerate		C[f,g]X[f,g,l]	X[h]
Bethanechol Chloride (tab)	X		
Biperiden HCl (tab)	X		
Bisacodyl	X[a,i,+]		
Milk of Bismuth	X[+]		
Bromodiphen Hydramine HCl		X[b]	X[e]
Bromocriptine Mesylate		X[a]	X[a]
Brompheniramine Maleate	X[e]	X[a]	X[e]
Busulfan (tab)	X		
Butabarbitol and Aspirin (tab)		X	
Butabarbital Sodium	X[a,b]	X[e]	

Drug (Dosage Form)	WC	T	LR
Butalbital and Aspirin (tab)		X	
Butamben	X		
Calamine (lot)		X	
Calamine, Phenolated (lot)		X	
Calciferol (cap)		X	X
Calcium Carbonate	X[a]	X[j,t]	
Calcium Carbonate and Magnesia	X[a]		
Calcium and Magnesium Carbonates	X[a]		
Calcium Gluconate (tab)	X		
Calcium Hydroxide Topical Soln.		X	
Calcium Lactate (tab)		X	
Calcium Pantothenate (tab)		X	
Calcium Phosphate, dibasic (tab)	X		
Camphor Spirit		X	
Candicidin	X[g,+]	X[m,+]	
Carbachol Soln.		X[k,w,+]	
Carbamazepine (tab)		X	
Carbamide Peroxide Topical Soln.		X[+]	X[+]
Carbenicillin Indanyl Sodium (tab)	X		
Carbidopa and Levodopa	X[a]		X[a]
Carbinoxamine Maleate (tab)		X	X
Carbol-Fuchsin Topical Soln.		X	X
Carphenazine Maleate Oral		X	X
Carboxymethyl-cellulose Sodium Paste	X[+]		
Carboxymethylcellulose Sodium (tab)		X	
Carisoprodol (tab)		X	
Carisoprodol and Aspirin (tab)	X		
Carisoprodol, Aspirin and Codeine Phosphate (tab)	X		
Cascara Sagrada Extract		X[+]	X[+]
Cascara Sagrada Fluidextract		X[+]	X[+]
Cascara (tab)		X	
Cascara, Aromatic Fluid Extract		X[+]	X[+]
Castor Oil (cap)		X[b,y,+]	
Castor oil aromatic	X		
Cefaclor		X[b,j]	
Cefadroxil		X[a,b,j]	
Cellulose Sodium Phosphate	X		
Cephalexin		X[a,b,j]	
Cephradine		X[a,b,j]	

Drug (Dosage Form)	WC	T	LR
Cetylpyridinium Chloride	X[n]	X[c]	
Charcoal, Activated	X		
Chloral Hydrate		X[b]	X[d]
Chlorambucil (tab)	X		X
Chloramphenicol (all dosage forms)		X	
Chloramphenicol Ophthalmic		CTP[c g]	
Chloramphenicol Palmitate Oral		X	X
Chloramphenicol and Hydrocortisone Acetate for Ophthalmic Susp.		X	
Chloramphenicol and Polymyxin B Sulfate Ophthalmic Oint.		CTP+	
Chloramphenicol, Polymixin B Sulfate and Hydrocortisone Acetate Ophthalmic Oint.		CTP+	
Chloramphenicol and Prednisolone Ophthalmic Oint.		CTP+	
Chlordiazepoxide (tab)		X	X
Chlordiazepoxide and Amitriptyline HCl		X[a]	X[a]
Chlordiazepoxide HCl (cap)		X	X
Chloroquine Phosphate (tab)	X		
Chlorothiazide	X[a]	X[j]	
Chlorotrianisene (cap)	X+		
Chlorophenoxamine HCl (tab)		X	X
Chlorpheniramine Maleate		X[a d]	X[d]
Chlorpromazine HCl	X[a]	X[d]	X[a]
Chlorpromazine HC1 (supp)	X+		X+
Chlorpropamide (tab)	X		
Chlorprothixene	X[a]	X[j]	X[a]
Chlortetracycline HCl	C[g]	X[b a]	C[g]X[b a]
Chlortetracycline HC1 Ophthalmic Oint.		CTP+	
Chlorthalidone (tab)	X		
Chlorzoxazone (tabs)		X	
Chlorzoxazone and Acetaminophen		X[a b]	
Cholestyramine Oral Susp.		X	
Chymotrypsin Opthalmic Soln.		UG+	
Ciclopirox Olamine Cream	C+		
Cimetidine (tab)		X+	X+
Cinoxacin	X[b]		
Cinoxate Lotion		X	X
Clemastine Fumante Tabs		X+	X+

Drug (Dosage Form)	WC	T	LR
Clindinium Bromide (cap)		X	
Clindamycin HCl (cap)		X	
Clindamycin Palmitate HCl Oral Soln.		X	
Clindamycin Phosphate Topical Soln.		X	
Clioquinol (Iodochlor-hydroxyquin)	X[o]	C[f g]	C[f g]
Clocortolone Pivalate		C[f]	C[f]
Clofibrate (cap)	X		X
Clomiphene Citrate (tab)	X		X
Clonazepam (tab)		X+	X+
Clonidine HCl (tab)	X		
Clonidin HCl and Chlorthalidone (tab)	X		
Clotrimazole	X[m]	X[c h +]	X[c +]
Clotrimazole (cream)		C+	
Cloxacillin Benzathine		X[o x]	
Cloxacillin Sodium		X[b c]	
Coal Tar		X[c g]	
Cobalamine Concentrate		X	X
Cyanocobalamin Co-57	X[b]	X[c]	X[b c]
Cyanocobalamin Co-60	X[b]	U[c]	X[b c]
Cocaine HCl Tablets for Topical	X		
Cod Liver Oil		In	
Codeine Phosphate (tab)	X		X
Codeine Sulfate (tab)	X		
Colchicine (tab)	X		X
Cold Cream		X	
Colistin Sulfate Oral Suspension		X	X
Colistin and Neomycin Sulfates and Hydrocortisone Acetate Otic Susp.		X	
Collodion		X	
Collodion, Flexible		X+	
Cortisone Acetate (tab)	X		
Cromolyn Sodium for Inhalation		X+	X+
Cromolyn Sodium Soln.		X[s]	X
Crotamiton (cream)		C	X
Cyclacillin		X[a j]	
Cyclizine HCl (tab)		X	X
Cyclobenzapine HCl (tab)	X		
Cyclomethycaine Sulfate	X[i]	C[f g t]	
Cylcopentamine HCl Soln.		X[s]	
Cyclopentolate HCl Opthalmic Soln.		X+	
Cyclophosphamide (tab)		X+	
Cycloserine HCl (tab)		X	

Drug (Dosage Form)	WC	T	LR
Cyclothiazide (tab)	X		
Cyproheptadine HCl	X[a]	X[d]	
Danazol (cap)	X		
Danthron (tab)	X		
Dapsone (tab)	X		
Decavitamin	X[a]	X[b]	X[a b]
Dehydrocholic Acid (tab)	X		
Demecarium Bromide Opthalmic Soln.		X	X
Demeclocycline Oral Susp.		X	X
Demeclocycline HCl		X[a b]	X[a b]
Demeclocycline HCl and Nystatin		X[a b]	X[a b]
Desipramine HCl		X[a b]	
Desoximetasone	C[f t +]	C[f t +]	C[f]
Desoxycorticosterone Acetate Pellets		U	
Dexamethasone	X[a]	X[e k]C[t +]	
Dexamethasone Sodium Phosphate		C[f]X[r t]	X[k]
Dexchlorpheniramine Maleate		X[a d]	X[d]
Dextroamphetamine Sulfate	X[a]	X[e b]	X[e]
Dextroamphetamine Sulfate	X[a]	X[e b]	X[e]
Dextromethorphan HBr (syr)		X	X
Dextrothyroxine Sodium (tab)	X		
Diatrizoate Meglumine and Diatrizoate Sodium Soln.		X	X
Diatrizoate Sodium Soln.		X	X
Diazepam		X[a b]	X[a b]
Diazepam Extended Release (cap)		X	X
Diazoxide	X[b]	X[j b]	X[j]
Dibucaine		XC[f g]	XC[f g]
Dichlorphenamide (tab)	X		
Dicloxacillin Sodium	X[b i]		
Dicumarol	X[a b]		
Dicyclomine HCl	X[a b]	X[d]	
Dienestrol (cream)		X	
Diethylcarbamazine Citrate (tab)		X	
Diethylpropion HCl (tab)	X		
Diethylstilbesterol	X[a]	X[i +]	
Diethyltoluamide Topical Soln.		X	
Diflunisal (tab)	X		
Digitalis		X[a b]	
Digitoxin (tab)	X		
Digoxin		X[a e +]	
Dihydrostreptomycin Sulfate Boluses		X[x]	
Dihydrotachysterol	X[b a]	X[c]	X[b a c]
Dihydroxyaluminum Aminoacetate (tab)	X		
Dihydroxyaluminum Aminoacetate Magma	X[+]		
Dihydroxyaluminum Aminoacetate	X[a]		
Dihydroxyaluminum Sodium Carbonate (tab)	X		
Dimenhydrinate	X[a]	X[d]	
Dimethisoquin HCl		X[j]	
Dimethyl Sulfoxide		X[+]	X[+]
Dinoprost Tromethamine (tab)		X	
Dioxybenzone and Oxybenzone (cream)		X	
Diperodon (ointment)		X	
Diphemanil Methyl sulfate (tab)		X	
Diphenhydramine HCl		X[b]	X[e]
Diphenhydramine Citrate		X	X
Diphenoxylate HCl and Atropine Sulfate	X[a]	X[c]	X[a c]
Diphenylpyraline HCl (tab)			X
Diphylline		X	X[a e]
Dipivefrin HCl		X[k o]	X[k o]
Dipyridamole Tabs		X	X
Disopyramide Phosphate (cap)	X		
Disulfiram (tab)		X	X
Docusate Calcium (cap)		X[+]	
Docusate Potassium (cap)		X[+]	
Docusate Sodium	X[a]	X[b + d c]	X[d]
Doxepin HCl	X[b]	X[c]	X[c]
Doxycycline for Oral Susp.		X	X
Doxycycline Calcium Oral Susp.		X	X
Doxycycline Hycolate		X[a b]	X[a b]
Doxylamine Succinate	X[a]	X[d]	X[a d]
Dusting Powder, Absorbable	X		
Dyclonine HCl Topical Soln.		X	X
Dyclonine HCl (gel)		P/G	G
Dydrogesterone (tab)	X		
Echothiophate Iodide for Ophthalmic Soln.		G[+]	
Ephedrine Sulfate	X[a]	X[b d s]	X[b d s]
Ephedrine Sulfate and Phenobarbital (cap)	X		
Epinephrine		X[k r s]	X[k r s]
Epinephrine Inhalation Aerosol		X	X
Epinephrine Bitartrate		X[k]	X[k]
Epinephrine Bitartrate Inhalation Aerosol		X	X
Epinephryl Borate Opthalmic Soln.		X	X
Ergocalciferol		X[a b c]	X[a b c]
Ergoloid Mesylates		X[c + a]	X[c + a]

Drug (Dosage Form)	WC	T	LR
Ergonovine Maleate (tab)	X		
Ergotamine Tartrate (tab)	X		
Ergotamine Tartrate Inhalation Aerosol		X	X
Ergotamine Tartrate and Caffeine	X[a]	X[i +]	X[a]
Erythrityl Tetra-nitrate (tab)		X[+]	
Erythromycin		X[a b]	
Erythromycin (oint)		CX[+]	
Erythromycin Ophthalmic Ointment		CTP[+]	
Erythromycin Topical Soln.		X	
Erythromycin Estolate		X[a b j]	
Erythromycin Estolate Oral Susp.		x[+]	
Erythromycin Ethylsuccinate		X[a j]	
Erythromycin Ethylsuccinate Oral Susp.	X[+]		
Erythromycin Ethylsuccinate and Sulfisoxazole Acety for Oral Susp.	X		
Erythromycin Stearate		X[a j]	
Erythrosine Sodium		X[a c]	X[a c]
Estradiol (tab)		X	X
Estrogens, Con-jugated (tab)	X		
Estrogens, Esteri-fied (tab)	X		
Estropipate (Pipera-zine Estrone Sulfate) (tab)	X[a]	C[m f]	
Ethacrynic Acid (tab)	X		
Ethambutol HCl (tab)	X		
Ethchlorvynol (cap)		X	X
Ethinamate (cap)		X	
Ethinyl Estradiol (tab)	X		
Ethionamide (tab)		X	
Ethopropazine HCl (tab)	X		X
Ethosuximide (cap)		X	
Ethynadiol Diacetate and Ethinyl Estradiol (tab)	X		
Ethynadiol Diacetate and Mestranol (tabs)	X		
Eucatropine HCl Opthalmic Soln.		X	
Eugenol		X	X
Fenoprofen Calcium	X[a b]		
Ferrous Fumerate (tab)		X	
Ferrous Gluconate		X[a b e]	X[a b e]

Drug (Dosage Form)	WC	T	LR
Ferrous Sulfate		X[a c d]	X[c]
Flucytosine (cap)		X	X
Fluhydrocortisone Acetate (tab)	X		
Flumethasone Pivalate (cream)		C	
Flunisolide Nasal Soln.		X[+]	X[+]
Fluocinolone Acetonide		X[c f g]	
Fluocinolone Acetate Topical Soln.		X	
Fluocinolone		C[f g t]	
Flourometholone (cream)		C	
Fluorometholone Ophthalmic Susp.		X	
Fluorouracil		X[c f +]	
Fluoxymesterone (tab)	X		X
Fluphenazine HCl		X[a c e]	X[c e]
Flurandrenolide		X[f g h]	X[f g h]
Flurandrenolide (tabs)		X[+]	
Flurazepam HCl (cap)		X	X
Folic Acid (tab)	X		
Formaldehyde Soln.		X[+]	
Furazolidone		X[j +]	X[j +]
Furosemide (tab)		X	X
Gauze (all)	X		
Gemfibrozil (cap)		X	
Gentamicin Sulfate		X[k]C[f g]	
Gentain Violet		X[c]C[f t]	
Glutaral Concentrate		X[+]	X[+]
Glutethimide	X[a b]		
Glycerin	X[i +]	X[c]	
Glycerin Ophthalmic Soln.		TPG/P	X
Glycobiarsal (tab)	X		X
Glycopyrrolate (tab)		X	
Griseofulvin		X[a b j]	
Guaifenesin		X[a b d]	
Guanabenz Acetate		X[a o]	X[a o]
Guanethidine Mono-sulfate (tab)	X		
Guanethidine Sulfate (tab)	X		
Halazone Tablets for Soln.		X	
Halcinonide	X[a f g]		
Haloperidol		X[a c]	X[a c]
Haloprogin		X[+ f]	X[f]
Haloprogin Topical Soln.		X[+]	X[+]
Halothane		G[+]	X[+]
Hetacillin		X[a j]	
Hetacillin Potassium		X[b]	[a j x]
Hexachlorophene Cleansing Emulsion		X	X
Hexachlorophene Liquid Soap		X	X
Hexavitamin		X[a b]	X[a]
Hexobarbital (tab)	X		
Hexylcaine HCl Topical Soln.		X	
Hexylresorcinol (pills)	X		

Drug (Dosage Form)	WC	T	LR
Homatropine Hydrobromide Opthalmic Soln.		X	
Homatropine Methylbromide (tab)		X	X
Hydralazine HCl (tab)		X	X
Hydrochlorothiazide (tab)	X		
Hydrocodone Bitartrate (tab)		X	X
Hydrocortisone (Cortisol)	X[a g]	X[f h p t]	
Hydrocortisone Acetate	X[f g]	X[h]	
Hydrocortisone Acetate Ophthalmic		X	
Hydrocortisone Cypionate Oral Susp.		X	X
Hydrocortisone and Acetic Acid Otic Soln.		X	X
Hydrocortisone Butyrate	X		
Hydrocortisone Acetate Lotion		X	
Hydrocortisone Valerate (cream)	X[f]		
Hydroflumethiazide (tab)		X	
Hydrogen Peroxide Topical Soln.		X	X
Hydromorphone HCl (tab)		X	X
Hydroquinone (cream)	X		X
Hydroquinone Topical Soln.		X	X
Hydroxyamphetamine HBr Opthalmic Soln.		X	X
Hydroxychloroquin Sulfate (tab)	X		
Hydroxypropyl Methylcellulose Opthalmic		X	
Hydroxyurea (cap)		X	
Hydroxyzine HCl		X[a d]	X[d]
Hydroxyzine Pamoate	X[b]	X[i]	X[i]
Hyoscyamine (tab)	X		X
Hyoscyamine Sulfate		X[a e c +]	X[a e c +]
Ibuprofen (tab)	X		
Ichthammol (ointment)		C[+]	
Idoxuridine Ophthalmic		C[g t]X[c]	X[c]
Imipramine HCl (tab)		X	
Indomethacin (cap)	X		
Iocetamic Acid (tab)		X	
Iodine (all Soln. and Tinct.)		X[+]	X[+]
Iodine, Sodium, I-123, I-125, I-131 (cap)	X		
Iodoquinol (tab)	X		
Iopanoic Acid (tab)		X	X
Ipecac Syrup		X[+]	

Drug (Dosage Form)	WC	T	LR
Ipodate Calcium for Oral Susp.	X		
Iopodate Sodium (cap)		X	
Isocarboxazide (tab)	X		
Isoetharine Inhalation Soln.		X	X
Isoetharine Mesylate Inhalation			X
Isoflurophate Opthalmic		C[g]	
Isoniazid	X[a]	X[d]	X[a d]
Isopropamide Iodide (tab)	X		
Isopropyl Alcohol (all)		X[+]	
Isoproterenol Inhalation		X	X
Isoproterenol HCl	X[a]	X[r l]	X[a r l]
Isoproterenol HCl and Phenylephrine Bitartrate Inhalation		X	X
Isoproterenol Sulfate Inhalation		X[c l]	X[c l]
Isosorbide Concentrate		X	X
Isosorbide Dinitrate (tab)	X[+]		
Isosorbide Oral (soln)		X	
Isoxsuprine HCl (tab)		X	
Kanamycin Sulfate (cap)		X	
Ketoconazole (tab)	X		
Lactic Acid		X	
Lactolose (syr/conc)		X[+]	
Lanolin		X[+]	
Lanolin, Anhydrous	X[+]		
Levodopa		X	X
Levonorgestrel	X		X
Levonorgestrel and Ethinyl Estradiol (tab)	X		
Levopropoxyphene Napsylate		X[b j +]	X[j +]
Levorphanol Tartrate (tab)	X		
Levothyroxine Sodium (tab)		X	X
Lidocaine (ointment)		X[g l]	
Lidocaine Oral Topical Soln.		X	
Lidocaine HCl Topical Soln.		X	
Lidocaine HCl Jelly		X	
Lime, Sulfurated, Topical Soln.		X	
Lincomycin HCl		X[b d]	
Lindaine		X[f h]	
Lindaine Shampoo		X	
Liothyronine Sodium (tab)		X	
Liotrix (tab)		X	
Lithium Carbonate	X[a b]		
Lithium Citrate (Syr)		X	
Loperamide HCl (cap)	X		
Lypressin Nasal Soln.		P	

Drug (Dosage Form)	WC	T	LR
Mafenide Acetate (cream)		X[+]	X[+]
Magaldrate	X[a]	X[j]	
Magnesia (tab)	X		
Magnesium Carbonate and Sodium Bicarbonate for Oral Susp.		X	
Magnesium Citrate Oral Soln.		X[+]	
Magnesium Gluconate (tab)	X		
Magnesium Oxide	X[a b]		
Magnesium Salicylate (tab)		X	
Maprotiline HCl (tab)	X		
Mazindol (tab)		X[+]	
Mebendazol (tab)	X		
Mecamylamine HCl (tab)	X		
Mechlorethamine HCl		X	X
Meclizine HCl (tab)	X		
Meclocycline Sulfosalicylate Cream		X	X
Meclofenamate Sodium (cap)		X	X
Medroxyprogesterone Acetate (tab)	X		
Medrysone Opthalmic Susp.	X	X	
Megestrol Acetate (tab)	X		X[o]
Melphalon (tab)	X		
Menadiol Sodium Diphosphate (tab)	X		X
Menpenzolate Bromide	X[a]	X[d]	X[a]
Meperidine HCl	X[a]	X[d]	X[a d]
Mephenytoin (tab)	X		
Mephobarbital (tab)	X		
Meprobamate	X[a]	X[j]	
Mercaptopurine (tab)	X		
Mercury, Ammoniated (ointment)	X	C[k]	X
Mesoridazine Besylate	X[a]	X[j +]	X[j+]
Metaproterenol Sulfate	X[a]	X[or l d]	X[or d l a]
Methacycline HCl		X[b j]	X[b j]
Methadone HCl	X[a]	X[d +]	X[d +]
Methadone HCl Oral Concentrate		X[+]	X[+]
Methantheline Bromide (tab)		X	X
Methaqualone (tab)	X		
Metharbital (tab)		X	
Methazolamide (tab)	X		
Methdilazine (tab)		X	X
Methdilazine HCl		X[a d]	X[a d]
Methenamine	X[a]	X[e]	
Methenamine and Monobasic Sodium Phosphate (tab)		X	

Drug (Dosage Form)	WC	T	LR
Methenamine Hippurate (tab)	X		
Methenamine Mandelate	X[a]	X[j]	
Methenamine Mandelate for Oral Soln.		X	
Methimazole (tab)	X		X
Methocarbamol (tab)		X	
Methotrexate (tab)	X		
Methoxsalen Topical Soln.		X	X
Methscopolamine Bromide (tab)		X	
Methsuximide (cap)		X	
Methylclothiazide (tab)	X		
Methylbenzethonium Chloride	X[e]	X[n]C[g]	
Methylcellulose	X[a]	X[c k +]	X[c +]
Methyldopa	X[a]	X[j +]	X[j +]
Methyldopa and Hydrochlorothiazide (tab)	X		
Methylergonovine Maleate (tab)		X	X
Methylphenidate HCl (tab)		X	
Methylprednisolone (tab)		X	
Methylprednisolone Acetate	X[p]	X C[f]	X[f]
Methyltestosterone	X[a b]		
Methyprylon		X[a b]	X[a b]
Methysergide Maleate (tab)		X	
Metoprolol Tartrate (tab)		X	X
Metronidazole (tab)	X		X
Metyrapone (tab)		X+	X+
Metyrosine (cap)	X		
Miconazole Nitrate		X[m i]C[f]	
Mineral Oil Emulsion		X[P Y]	
Minocycline HCl		X[a b j]	X[a b j]
Mitotane (tab)		X	X
Monobenzene Ointment		X[+]	
Minoxidil	X[O]	X[a]	
Nadolol	X[o]	X[a]	
Nafcillin Sodium		X[b c a]	X[a]
Nalidixic Acid		X[a j]	
Naphazoline HCl		X[k s]	X[k s]
Naproxen (tab)	X		
Naproxen Sodium (tab)	X		
Natamycin Ophthalmic Susp.		TP	
Neomycin Sulfate	X[g f +]	X[a c +]	X[c +]
Neomycin Sulfate Ophthalmic Oint.		TPC[+]	
Neomycin Sulfate and Bacitracin		X[g +]	X[g +]
Neomycin Sulfate Bacitracin Zinc	XC[g]		
Neomycin Sulfate and Dexamethasone Sodium Phosphate		X[f]	

Drug (Dosage Form)	WC	T	LR
Neomycin Sulfate and Dexamethasone Sodium Phosphate Ophthalmic		X[g c +]	X[g c +]
Neomycin Sulfate and Fluocinolone Acetonide		XC[f]	
Neomycin Sulfate and Fluorometholone	CX[g]		
Neomycin Sulfate and Flurandrenolide		CX[f g]	X[f g]
Neomycin Sulfate and Gramicidin	CX[g]		
Neomycin Sulfate and Hydrocortisone	CX[f g]		
Neomycin Sulfate and Hydrocortisone Otic Susp.	X		X
Neomycin Sulfate and Hydrocortisone Acetate	CX[f g h]		
Neomycin Sulfate and Hydrocortisone Acetate Ophthalmic		TP[j g]	
Neomycin Sulfate and Methylprednisolone Acetate		CX[f]	X[f]
Neomycin Sulfate and Prednisolone Acetate		X[g k]	X[g k]
Neomycin Sulfate and Prednisolone Acetate Ophthalmic Susp.		X	
Neomycin Sulfate and Prednisolone Sodium Phosphate Ophthalmic Oint.		CPT +	
Neomycin Sulfate, Sulfacetamide Sodium and Prednisolone Acetate Ophthalmic		TP[g]	
Neomycin Sulfate and Triamcinoline Acetonide Ophthalmic Oint.		TP	
Neomycin and Polymyxin B Sulfates Ophthalmic	CPT[g+]	CX[k g]	X[g +]
Neomycin and Polymyxin B Sulfate and Bacitracin Zinc	CX[g o]	CX[k g l]	X[g +]
Neomycin and Polymyxin B Sulfate and Bacitracin Zinc and Hydrocortisone Oint.	X[+]	X[k +]	
Neomycin and Polymyxin B Sulfate and Bacitracin Zinc and Hydrocortisone Acetate Oint.	CX[+]		
Neomycin and Polymyxin B Sulfates, Bacitracin and Hydrocortisone Acetate Ointment	X[g k +]		

Drug (Dosage Form)	WC	T	LR
Neomycin and Polymyxin B Sulfate and Hydrocortisone Otic Soln.		X	X
Neomycin and Polymyxin B Sulfates and Dexamethasone Ophthalmic	C[g]	X[j]	X[j]
Neomycin and Polymyxin B Sulfate and Gramicidin	CX[f]		
Neomycin and Polymyxin B Sulfate and Gramicidin Ophthalmic Soln.		X	
Neomycin and Polymyxin B Sulfates, Gramicidin and Hydrocortisone Acetate Cream	X		
Neomycin and Polymyxin B Sulfates and Hydrocortisone Ophthalmic Susp.		X[k]	X[v]
Neomycin and Polymyxin B Sulfates and Hydrocortisone Acetate Ophthalmic Susp.		X	
Neomycin and Polymyxin B Sulfates and Prednisolone Acetate Ophthalmic Susp.		X	
Neostigmine Bromide (tab)		X	
Niacin (tab)	X		
Niacinamide (tab)		X	
Nifedipine (cap)		X +	X[+]
Nitrofurantoin		X[a j]	x[a j]
Nitrofurazone		X[c f g]	X[c f g]
Nitroglycerin		G[a] +X[g]	
Nitromersol Topical Soln.		X	X
Nitromersol Tincure		X	X
Northindrone (tab)	X		
Norethindrone and Ethinyl Estradiol (tab)	X		
Norethindrone and Mestranol (tab)	X		
Norethindrone Acetate (tab)	X		
Norethindrone Acetate and Ethinyl Estradiol (tab)	X		
Norgestrel (tab)	X		
Norgestrel and Ethinyl Estradiol (Tab)	X		
Nortriptyline HCl		X[a c]	X[c]
Novobiocin Calcium Oral Susp.		X	X
Nylidrin HCl (tab)		X	
Nystatin	X[g]	X[a f h m]	X[a j m]
Nystatin Cream		XC[+]	
Nystatin Vaginal Supp.		X +	X[+]
Nystatin and Cliquinol Ointment		XC +	

Drug (Dosage Form)	WC	T	LR
Nystatin, Neomycin Sulfate, Gramicidin and Triamcinolone Acetonide		X[f,g]	
White and/or Yellow Ointment	X		
Oleovitamin A and D (cap)		X	X
Opium Powder	X		
Opium Tincture		X[+]	X[+]
Oxacillin Sodium (cap)		X[+]	
Oxamniquine (cap)		X	
Oxandrolone (tab)		X	X
Oxazepam (tab/cap)	X[a,b]		
Oxtriphylline		X[a,e]	
Oxymetazoline HCl Nasal Soln.		X	
Oxymetholone (tab)	X		
Oxymorphone HCl Suppositories	X		
Oxyphenbutazone (tab)		X	
Oxyphencyclimine HCl (tab)		X	
Oxytetracycline (tab)		X	X
Oxytetracycline Calcium Oral Susp.		X	X
Oxytetracycline and Nystatin		X[b,j,+]	X[b,j,+]
Oxytetracycline HCl and Hydrocortisone Ointment	X		X
Oxytetracycline HCl and Hydrocortisone Acetate Ophthalmic Susp.		X	X
Oxytetracycline and Phenazopyridine Hyrochlorides and Sulfamethizole (cap)		X	X
Oxytetracycline HCl and Polymyxin B Sulfate Ointment	X[g,o,m]		X[g]
Oxytetracycline HCl and Polymyxin B Ophthalmic Oint.	CX[+]		
Oxytriphylline (cap)		X[a,e]	X
Pancreatin		X[a,b,+]	
Pancrelipase		X[a,b,+]	
Papain Tablets for Topical Soln.		X[+]	x[+]
Papaverine HCl (tab)		X	
Parachlorophenol Camphorated		X	X
Paramethadione		X[b,c]	X[c]
Paramethasone Acetate (tab)	X		
Paregoric		X[+]	X[+]
Pargyline HCl (tab)	X		
Paromomycin Sulfate (cap)		X[b,d]	
Pectine	X		
Penicillamine		X[a,b]	

Drug (Dosage Form)	WC	T	LR
Penicillin G Benzathine		X[a,j]	
Penicillin G Potassium		X[a,c]	
Penicillin V		X[a,j]	
Penicillian V Benzathine		X[l,+]	
Penicillin V Potassium		X[a,c]	
Pentaerythritol Tetranitrate		X[a]	
Pentazocine HCl (tab)		X	X
Pentazocine HCl (tab)		X	X
Pentazocine HCl and Aspirin (tab)		X	X
Pentazocine and Naloxone HC1 (tab)		X	X
Pentobarbital Elixir		X	
Pentobarbital Sodium		X[b,e]	
Peppermint Spirit		X	
Perphenazine	X[c,d]	X[a]	X[c,d]
Phenacemide (tab)	X		
Phenazopyridine HCl (tab)		X	
Phendimetrazine Tartrate	X[a]	X[b]	
Phenelzine Sulfate (tab)		X[+]	X[+]
Phenindione (tab)	X		
Phenmetrazine HCl (tab)		X	
Phenobarbital	X[a]	X[e]	X[e]
Phenobarbital Sodium (tab)		X	
Phenol		X	X
Phenol Liquefied		X	X
Phenolphthalein (tab)		X	
Phenoxybenzamine HCl (cap)	X		
Phenprocoumon (tab)	X		
Phensuximide (cap)		X	
Phentermine HCl		X[b,a]	
Phenylbutazone	X[a]	X[b]	
Phenylephrine HCl Soln.		X[k,s]	X[k,s]
Phenylephrine HCl Nasal Jelly		X	
Phenytoin	X[a]	X[j,+]	
Phenytoin Sodium, Extended		X	
Phenytoin Sodium, Prompt		X	
Physostigmine Salicylate Ophthalmic Solu.		X	
Physostigmine Sulfate Ophthalmic Ointment		CTP	
Phytonadione (tab)	X		X
Pilocarpine HCl Opthalmic Soln		X	X
Pilocarpine Nitrate Ophthalmic Soln.		X	X
Piperacetazine (tab)	X		X
Piperazine Citrate (tab/syr)		X[a,d]	
Pipobroman (tab)	X		

Drug (Dosage Form)	WC	T	LR
Podophyllum Resin Topical Soln.		X +	X +
Polymyxin B Sulfate and Hydrocortisone Otic Soln.		X	X
Polythiazide (tab)		X	X
Potassium Bicarbonate Effervescent Tabs for Oral Soln.		X+	
Potassium Bicarbonate and Potassium Chloride for Effervescent Oral Soln.		X[+ o a]	
Potassium Chloride Elixir		X	X[e]
Potassium Chloride Extended Release		X[a b +]	
Potassium Chloride, Potassium Bicarbonate, and Potassium Citrate Effervescent Tablets for Oral Solu.		X +	
Potassium Citrate and Citric Acid Oral Soln.		X	
Potassium Gluconate		X[a]	X[a e]
Potassium Iodide		X[a]	X[a c]
Potassium Permanganate Tablets for Topical Soln.		X	
Povidone Iodide Topical Soln.		X +	
Povidone-Iodine Oint		X	
Povidone-Iodine Cleansing Soln.		X	
Pralidoxime Chloride (tab)	X		
Pramoxine HCl (cream)		X[f t]C[t]	
Prazepam		X[a b]	X[a b]
Prazosin HCl (cap)	X		X
Prednisolone	X[a]	X C[f]	
Prednisolone Sodium Phosphate Ophthalmic Soln.		X	X
Prednisone (tab)	X[a]	X[d]	
Primaquine Phosphate (tab)	X		X
Primadone	X[a]	X[j]	X[j]
Probenecid (tab)	X		
Probenecid and Colchicine (tab)	X		X
Procainamide HCl (cap)		X	
Procarbazine HCl (cap)		X	X
Prochlorperazine Suppositories		X	
Prochlorperazine Edisylate Syr.		X[c d]	X[c d]
Prochlorperazine Maleate (tab)	X		X
Procyclidine HCl (tab)		X+	
Promazine HCl		X[a c d]	X[a c d]
Promethazine HCl		X[a d]	X[a d]
Propantheline Bromide (tab)	X		
Proparacaine HCl Opthalmic Soln.		X	X
Propoxyphene HCl (cap)		X	
Propoxyphene HCl and Acetaminophen		X[a]	
Propoxyphene HCl, Aspirin, and Caffeine (cap)		X+	
Propoxyphene Napsylate		X[a j]	X[j]
Propoxyphene Napsylate and Acetaminophen (tab)		X+	
Propoxyphene Napsylate and Aspirin		X	
Propanolol HCl (tab)	X		X
Propylene Glycol		X	
Propylhexedrine Inhalant		X+	
Propylthiouracil (tab)	X		
Protriptylene HCl (tab)		X	
Psueodephedrine HCl		X[a d]	X[d]
Pyrantel Pamoate Oral Susp.		X	X
Pyrazinamide (tab)	X		
Pyridostigmine Bromide		X[a d]	X[d]
Pyridoxine HCl (tab)	X		
Pyrilamine Maleate (tab)	X		
Pyrimethamine (tab)		X	X
Pyrvinium Pamoate		X[a j]	X[a j]
Quinacrine HCl (tab)		X	
Quinestrol (tab)	X		
Quinethazone (tab)		X	
Quinidine Sulfate	X[a]	X[b]	X[a b]
Quinine Sulfate	X[a]	X[b]	
Racemethionine	X[a b]		X
Rauwolfia Serpentina (tab)		X	X
Reserpine		X[a e]	x[a e]
Reserpine and Hydrochlorothiazide (tab)		X	X
Reserpine, Hydralazine and Hydrochlorothiazide (tab)		X	X
Resorcinol, Compound (ointment)		X+	
Resorcinol and Sulfur (lot)		X	
Riboflavin (tab)		X	X
Rifampin (cap)		X+	X+
Rifampin and Isoniazid (cap)		X+	X+
Ritodrine HCl (tab)		X+	
Rose Water Ointment		X	X
Saccharin Sodium	X[a]	X[c]	
Salicylic Acid Collodion		X+	

Drug (Dosage Form)	WC	T	LR
Salicylic Acid Gel		XC[+]	
Salicylic Acid Plaster	X[+]		
Salicylic Acid Topical Foam		X	
Scopolamine HBr Ophthalmic		X[c]C[g]	
Scopolamine HBr (tab)		X	X
Secobarbital Elixir		X	
Secobarbital Sodium (cap)		X	
Secobarbital Sodium and Amobartibal (cap)	X		
Selenium Sulfide Lotion		X	
Senna Syrup		X[+]	
Sennosides (tab)	X		
Silver Nitrate Opthalmic Soln.		X	X
Toughened Silver Nitrate		X	X
Simethicone	X[a]	X[j v]	X[j]
Sodium Acetate Soln.		X	
Sodium Bicarbonate (tab)	X[a o]		
Sodium Bicarbonate	X		
Sodium Chloride	X[a]	X[k]	
Sodium Chloride and Dextrose	X		
Sodium Citrate and Citric Acid Oral Solution		X	
Sodium Fluoride		X[a c]	
Sodium Fluoride and Phosphoric Acid		P[c t]	
Sodium Iodide		X[c]	
Sodium Lactate Soln.	X		
Sodium Phosphate	X[p]	X[c]	
Sodium Phosphate Effervescent	X		
Sodium Salicylate (tab)	X		
Sorbitol Soln.	X		
Spironolactone (tab)		X	X
Stannous Fluoride Gel	X		
Stanozolol (tab)		X	X
Topical Starch	X		
Sulfacetamide Sodium Opthalmic	TPC[g]	X[c+]	X[c+]
Sulfadiazine (tab)	X		X
Sulfadoxine and Pyrimethamine (tab)	X		X
Sulfamerazine (tab)	X		
Sulfamethizole	X[a]	X[j]	X[j]
Sulfamethoxazole	X[a]	X[j]	X[a j]
Sulfamethoxazole and Trimethoprim	X[a]	X[j]	X[j a]
Sulfapyridine (tab)	X		X
Sulfasalazine (tab)	X		
Sulfathiaxole, Sulfacetamide and Sulfabenzamide Vaginal	C[f]X[a]		X[a f]
Sulfinpyrazone	X[a b]		

Drug (Dosage Form)	WC	T	LR
Sulfisoxazole (tab)	X		X
Sulfisoxazole Acetyl Oral Susp.		X	X
Sulfisoxazole Diolamine Opthalmic		X[g]X[c]	X[c]
Sulfoxone Sodium (tab)		X	X
Sulfur Ointment	X[+]		
Sulindac Tabs	X		
Sutilains Ointment		CX[+]	
Talbutal (tab)		X	
Talc	X		
Tamoxifen Citrate (tab)	X		X
Tape, Adhesive	X[+]		
Terbutaline (tab)		X[+]	
Terpin Hydrate Elixir		X	
Terpin Hydrate and Codeine Elixir		X	
Terpin Hydrate and Dextromethorphan HBr Elixir		X	
Testolactone (tab)		X	
Tetracaine Ophthalmic Oint.		C	
Tetracaine Oint.		C	
Tetracaine and Menthal Oint.	X	X	
Tetracaine		X[c]C[f]	X[c]
Tetracaine Ophthalmic Soln.		X	X
Tetrachlorethylene (cap)		X[x]	
Tetracycline Boluses		X[x]	
Tetracycline and Novobiocin Sodium (tab)		X[x]	
Tetracycline Novobiocin Sodium and Prednisolone (tab)		X[x]	
Tetracycline Phosphate Complex and Novobiocin Sodium (cap)		X[x]	
Tetracycline Oral Susp.		X	X
Tetracycline and Amphotericin B		X[b j]	X[b j]
Tetracycline HCl (tablet/capsule/Ophtalmic Suspension/topical solution)	X[g +]	X	X
Tetracycline HCl and Nystatin (cap)		X	X
Tetracycline Phosphate Complex (cap)		X	X
Tetrahydrozoline HCl Soln.		X[k s]	
Theophylline	X[a b]		
Theophylline, Ephedrine HCl and Phenobarbital (tab)		X	
Theophylline and Guaifenesin (cap)		X	

Drug (Dosage Form)	WC	T	LR
Theophylline Sodium Glycinate	X[a]	X[e]	
Thiabendazole		X[a j]	
Thiamine HCl		X[a e]	X[a e]
Thiamine Mononitrate Elixir		X	X
Thiethylperazine Maleate (tab)		X[a i +]	X[a i +]
Thimerosol Topical		X[c i +]	X[c i +]
Thimerosal Tincture		X[+]	X
Thioguanine (tab)		X	
Thioridazine Oral Susp.		X	X
Thioridazine HCl	X[a]	X[c +]	X[c +]
Thiothixene (cap)	X		X
Thiothixene HCl Oral Soln.		X	X
Thyroglobulin (tab)		X	
Thyroid (tab)		X	
Timolol Maleate Ophthalmic Soln.	X[a]	X	X[a]
Timolol Maleate (tab)	X		X
Timolol Maleate and Hydrochlorothiazide (tab)	X		X
Tioconazole (tab)		X	
Tobramycin Ophthalmic		X[c]CTP[g]	
Tolazamide (tab)		X	
Tolazoline HCl (tab)	X		
Tolbutamide (tab)	X		
Tolmetin Sodium	X[a]	X[b]	
Tolnaftate		X[f t o]	
Tolnaftate Topical		X[i c +]	
Tolu Balsam		X[+]	
Tranylcypromine Sulfate (tab)	X		X
Tretinoin		C[f]X[c]	X[c f t]
Triamcinolone (tab)	X		
Triamcinolone Acetonide	X[g]	X[f h]	
Triamcinolone Acetonide Topical		X[l +]	
Triamcinolone Acetonide Dental Paste		X	
Triamcinolone Diacetate (syr)		X	X
Triamterene (cap)		X	X
Trichlormethiazide (tab)		X	
Tricitrates Oral Solution		X	
Tridihexethyl (tab)	X		
Trifluoperazine HCl	X[a]	X[d]	X[a d]
Triflupromazine Oral Susp.		X	X
Triflupromazine HCl (tab)	X		X
Trihexyphenidyl HCl		X[a e]	
Trikates Oral (soln)		X	X
Trimeprazine Tartrate	X[a]	X[d]	X[a]
Trimethadione		X[a b c +]	
Trimethobenzamide HCl (cap)	X		
Trimethoprim (tab)		X	X
Trioxsalen (tab)	X		X
Tripelennamine HCl (tab)	X		
Tripelennamine Citrate Elixir		X	X
Triprolidine HCl		X[a d]	X[a d]
Triprolidine and Pseudoephedrine Hydrochlorides		X[a d]	X[a d]
Trisulfapyrimidines	X[a]	X[j +]	
Troleandomycin		X[b j +]	
Tropicamide Ophthalmic Soln.		X[+]	
Tuaminoheptane Inhalent		X[+]	
Tyropanoate Sodium (cap)		X	X
Undecylenic Acid, Compound Ointment		X	
Uracil Mustard (cap)		X	
Valproic Acid		X[bd+]	
Vancomycin HCl	X[b]	X[c]	
Vidarabine Ophthalmic Ointment		CTP[+]	
Vitamin A (cap)		X	X
Vitamin E (cap)		X	X
Vitamin E Preparation		In	X
Warfarin Potassium (tab)		X	X
Warfarin Sodium (tab)		X	X
White Lotion		X	
Xylometazoline HCl Nasal Soln.		X	X
Zinc-Eugenol Cement	X		
Zinc Gelatin (all)		X	
Zinc Gluconate (tab)	X		
Zinc Oxide (oint/paste)	X[+]		
Zinc Sulfate Ophthalmic Soln.		X	
Zomepirac Sodium (tab)	X		

Provided by Dr. Kenneth S. Alexander, Associate Professor o[f] Pharmacy, College of Pharmacy, University of Toledo.

Legend:

I = containers for sterile solids as described under injections
S = single dose
M = multiple dose
U = unspecified
P = plastic
A = type I glass
B = type II glass
C = type III glass

D = type II or III glass depending on final soln pH
IN = inert atmosphere
M = protect from moisture
LR = Light Resistant
L = Protect From Light
R = Refrigerator (2 – 8°C)
F = Freezer (– 4°C)
RT = Controlled Room Temperature
RT = controlled room temperature

Drugs	Container	Glass Type	Storage Conditions
Acetazolamide Sodium, Sterile	I	C	
Acetic Acid Irrigation	S	A,B	
Acetylcystein Soln.	S,M(P,A closure)	A	
Acetylcholine for Ophthalmic Soln.	I		
Dehydrated Alcohol Inj.	S	A	
Alcohol and Dextrose Inj.	S	A,B	
Alphaprodine HCl Inj.	S,M	A	
Aminoacetic Acid Irrigation	S	A,B	
Aminocaproic Acid Inj.	S,M	A	
Aminohipurate Sodium Inj.	S,M	A	
Aminophylline Inj.	S	A	CO_2 excluded
Amitriptyline HCl Inj.	S,M	A	
Ammonium Chloride Inj.	S,M	A,B	
Ammonium Molybdate Inj.	S,M	A,B	
Amobarbital Sodium, Sterile	I	D	
Amoxicillin, Sterile	I	C	
Amphotericin B for Inj.	I		R,L
Ampicillin, Sterile	I		
Ampicillin Sodium, Sterile	I		R,L
Anileridine Inj.	S,M	A	L
Anticoagulant Sodium Citrate Soln.	S	A,B	
Anticoagulant Citrate Dextrose Solution	S,M,P	A,B	
Anticoagulant Citrate Phosphate Dextrose Adenine Solution	S,P	A,B	
Anticoagulant Sodium Citrate Soln.	S	A,B	
Anticoagulant Heparin Soln.	S,P	A,B	
Antihemophilic Factor			R
Cryoprecipitated Antihemophilic Factor			F (-18°C)
Antirabies Serum	U		R
Antivenin (Latrodectus mectans)	S		H
Antivenin (Crotalidae) Polyvalent	S		H
Antivenin (Micrurus fulvius)	S		H
Arginine HCl Inj.	S	B	
Antirabies Serum	U		R
Ascorbic Acid Inj.	S	A,B	LR
Atropine Sulfate Inj.	S,M	A	
Aurothioglucose Susp., Sterile	S,M	A	L
Azathioprine Sodium for Inj.	I	C	RT
Azlocillin Sodium, Sterile	I		
Bacitracin, Sterile	I	D	R
Bacitracin Zinc, Sterile	I		R(cool place)
BCG Vaccine	U	A	R
Benztropine Mesylate Inj.	S,M	A	
Benzylpenicilloyl Polylysine Inj.	M		R

*The listing of container and storage requirements for sterile Compendial drugs is included as an aid to the practitioner in storing and dispensing.

Drugs	Container	Glass Type	Storage Conditions
Betamethasone Sodium, Sterile Phosphate and Betamethasone Acetate (Susp.)	M	A	
Bethanechol Chloride Inj.	S	A	
Biological Indicator for Dry Heat Sterilization, Paper Strip			L,H,M
Biological Indicator for Ethylene Oxide Sterilization, Paper Strip			L,H,M
Biological Indicator for Steam Sterilization, Paper Strip			L,H,M
Biperiden Lactate Inj.	S	A	L
Bleomycin Sulfate, Sterile	I	B	
Blood Grouping Serums (All)	U		R
Brompheniramine Maleate Inj.	S,M	A	L
Bupivacaine HCl Inj.	S,M	A	
Bupivacaine and Epinephrine Inj.	S,M	A	
Butorphanol Tartrate Inj.	S,M	A	L
Caffeine and Sodium Benzoate Inj.	S	A	
Calcium Chloride Inj.	S	A	
Calcium Gluceptate Inj.	S	A,B	
Calcium Gluconate Inj.	S	A	
Calcium Levulinate Inj.	S	A	
Capreomycin Sulfate, Sterile	I	B	R
Carbenicillin Disodium, Sterile	I	D	
Carboprost Tromethamine Inj.	S,M	A	R
Cefamandole Naftate for Inj.	I	D	
Cefamandole Sodium, Sterile	I		
Cefamandole Sodium for Inj.	I		
Cefazolin Sodium Inj.	I		F
Cefazolin Sodium, Sterile	I	B	
Cefotaxime Sodium, Sterile	I	B	
Cefoperezone Sodium, Sterile	I		
Cefoxitin Sodium, Sterile	I	B	
Ceftizoxime Sodium, Sterile	I		
Cellulose Oxidized (all)	I		L,R
Cephalothin Sodium Inj.	I		F
Cephapirin Sodium, Sterile	I	D	
Cephradine for Inj.	I		
Cephradine, Sterile	I		
Chloramphenicol Inj.	S,M		
Chloramphenicol, Sterile	I		
Chloramphenicol Sodium Succinate, Sterile	I	B	
Chlordiazepoxide HCl, Sterile	I	B	L
Chloroprocaine HCl Inj.	S,M	A	
Chloroquine HCl Inj.	S	A	
Chlorothiazide Sodium for Inj.	I	C	
Chlorphenamine Maleate Inj.	S,M	A	L
Chlorpromazine HCl Inj.	S,M	A	L
Chlorprothixene Inj.	S		L
Chlortetracycline HCl, Sterile	I		L
Cholera Vaccine	U		R
Sodium Chromate Cr51 Inj.	S,M		
Chromic Chloride Inj.	S,M	A,B	
Citric Acid, Magnesium Oxide Sodium Carbonate Irrigation	S	A,B	
Clindamycin Phosphate, Sterile	I	D	
Clindamycin Phosphate Inj.	S,M	A	
Coccidiodin			R
Codeine Phosphate Inj.	S,M	A	L
Colchicine Inj.	S	A	L
Colistemethate Sodium, Sterile	I	D	
Corticotropin Inj.	S,M	A	R
Corticotropin for Inj.	I	B	
Repository Corticotropin Inj.	S,M	A	

Drugs	Container	Glass Type	Storage Conditions
Corticotropin Zinc Hydroxide, Sterile (Susp.)	S,M	A	RT
Cortisone Acetate Susp., Sterile	S,M	A	
Cromolyn Sodium Inhalation	S(double-ended ampule)	A	
Cupric Chloride Inj.	S,M	A,B	
Cupric Sulfate Inj.	S,M	A,B	
Cyclophosphamide for Inj.	I		RT
Cyanocobalamin Inj.	S,M	A	LR
Cyclizine Lactate Inj.	S	A	
Cyclophosphamide for Inj.	I	B	RT
Cysteine HCl Inj.	S,M	A	
Cytarabine, Sterile	I	B	
Dacarbazine for Inj.	S,M, or I	A	L
Dactinomycin for Inj.	I	B	H,LR
Daunorubicin HCl for Inj.	I	B	LR
Digitoxin Inj.	S	A	avoid excessive heat
Dextrose and Sodium Chloride Inj.	S	A,B	
Diatrizoate Meglumine Inj.	S,M	A,C	L
Diatrizoate Meglumine and Diatrizoate Sodium Inj.	S	A,C	L
Diatrizoate Sodium Inj.	S,M	A,C	L
Diazepam Inj.	S,M	A	L
Diazoxide Inj.	S	A	L
Dibucaine HCl Inj.	S,M	A	L
Dicloxacillin Sodium, Sterile	I	D	
Dicyclomine HCl Inj.	S,M	A	
Diethylstilbestrol Inj.	S,M	A	LR
Digitoxin Inj.	S,M	A	L
Digoxin Inj.	S	A	LR,H
Dihydroergotamine Mesylate Inj.	S	A	avoid heat
Dimenhydrinate Inj.	S,M	A,C	
Dimercaprol Inj.	S,M	A,C	
Dimethyl Sulfate Irrigation	S		RT,L
Dinoprost Tromethamine Inj.	S,M	A	
Diphenhydramine HCl Inj.	S,M	A	L
Diphtheria Antitoxin	U		R
Diphtheria Toxoid	U		R
Diphtheria Toxoid Adsorbed	U		R
Diphtheria and Tetanus Toxoids/Adsorbed	U		R
Diphtheria and Tetanus Toxoids and Pertussis Vaccine/Adsorbed	U		R
Dobutamine HCl for Inj.	I	B	RT
Dopamine HCl Inj.	S	A	
Dopamine HCl and Dextrose Inj.	S	A,B	
Doxapram HCl Inj.	S,M	A	
Doxorubicin HCl for Inj.	I	B	
Doxycycline Hyclate, Sterile	I		L
Doxycycline Hyclate for Inj.	I	B	L
Droperidol Inj.	S,M	A	L
Dyphylline Inj.	S,M	A	RT,L
Edetate Calcium Disodium Inj.	S	A	
Edetate Disodium Inj.	S	A	
Edrophonium Chloride Inj.	S,M	A	
Emetine HCl Inj.	S	A	LR
Ephedrine Sulfate Inj.	S,M	A	LR
Epinephrine Inj.	S,M	A	LR
Epinephrine Oil Susp., Sterile	S	A,C	LR
Epinephrine Bitartrate for Ophthalmic Soln.	I		
Ergonovine Maleate Inj.	S	A	LR,R
Ergotamine Tartrate Inj.	S	A	LR
Erythromycin Ethylsuccinate Inj.	S,M	A	
Erythromycin Ethylsuccinate, Sterile	I		
Erythromycin Gluceptate, Sterile	I	D	

Drugs	Container	Glass Type	Storage Conditions
Erythromycin Lactobionate for Inj.	I	D	
Estradiol Suspension, Sterile	S,M	A	
Estradiol Cypionate Inj.	S,M	A	LR
Estradiol Valerate Inj.	S,M	A,C	LR
Estrone Inj.	S,M	A	
Estrone Suspension, Sterile	S,M	A	
Ethracrynate Sodium for Inj.	I	D	
Ethiodized Oil Inj.	S,M		LR
Ethylnorepinephrine HCl Inj.	S,M	A	LR
Evans Blue Inj.	S	A	
Fentanyl Citrate Inj.	S	A	L
Floxuridine, Sterile	M	A	L
Fluorexein Sodium Inj.	S	A	
Fluorouracil Inj.	S	A	RT,L
Fluphenazine Enanthate Inj.	S,M	A,C	L
Fluphenazine HCl Inj.	S,M	A	L
Folic Acid Inj.	S,M	A	
Fructose Inj.	S	A,B	
Fructose and Sodium Chloride Inj.	S	A,B	
Furosemide Inj.	S,M	A	LR
Gallamine Triethiodide Inj.	S,M	A	L
Gallium Citrate Ga67 Inj.	S,M		
Gallium Citrate Ga67 Inj., Sterile	I	D	
Gentamicin Sulfate Inj.	S,M	A	
Globulin Serum, Anti-Human	U		R
Glucagon for Inj.	I/S,M w/solvent	A	
Glycine Irrigation	S	A,B	
Glycopyrrolate Inj.	S,M	A	
Gold Sodium Thiomalate Inj.	S,M	A	L
Chorionic Gonadotropin for Inj.	I	D	
Haloperidol Inj.	S,M	A	L
Heparin Calcium Inj.	S,M	A	R
Heparin Lock Flush Soln.	S,M	A	
Heparin Sodium Inj.	S,M	A	
Hepatitis B Virus Vaccine Inactivated	U		R
Hetacillin Potassium, Sterile	I		
Hexafluorenium Bromide Inj.	S,M	A	L
Histamine Phosphate Inj.	S,M	A	L
Hyaluronidase Inj.	S,M	A	R
Hyaluronidase for Inj.	I	A,C	RT
Hydralazine HCl Inj.	S,M	A	
Hydrocortisone (Cortisol) Suspension, Sterile	S,M	A	
Hydrocortisone (Cortisol) Acetate Suspension, Sterile	S,M	A	
Hydrocortisone (Cortisol) Sodium Phosphate Inj.	I	C	
Hydrocortisone (Cortisol) Sodium Succinate for Inj.	I	C	
Hydromorphone HCl Inj.	S,M	A	L
Hydroxyocobalamin Inj.	S,M	A	L
Hydroxyprogesterone Caproate Inj.	S,M	A,C	
Hydroxystilbamidine Isethionate, Sterile	I	D	LR
Hydroxyzine HCl Inj.	S,M		L
Hyoscyamine Sulfate Inj.	S,M	A	
Indium In-III Pentetate Inj.	S		
Imipramine HCl Inj.	S	A	LR
Indigotindisulfonate Sodium Inj.	S	A	LR
Indocyanine Green, Sterile	I	B	
Insulin Inj.	M		R
Isophane Insulin Suspension	M		R
Insulin Zinc Suspension	M		R
Extended Insulin Zinc Suspension	M		R
Prompt Insulin Zinc Suspension	M		R

Drugs	Container	Glass Type	Storage Conditions
Protamine Zinc Insulin Suspension	M		R
Insulin Human Inj.	M		
Inulin and Sodium Chloride Inj.	S	A,B	
Iodinated I-125 Albumin Inj.	S,M		R
Iodinated I-131 Albumin Inj.	U		
Iodinated I-131 Albumin Aggregated Inj.	S,M		R
Iodohippurate Sodium I-131 Inj.	S,M		
Rose Bengal Sodium I-131 Inj.			
Iodipamide Inj.	S	A	L
Iodipamide Meglumine Inj.	S	A,C	
Iophendylate Inj.	S	A	
Iothalamate Meglumine Inj.	S	A	L
Iothalamate Meglumine and Sodium Iothalamate Inj.	S	A	L
Iothalamate Sodium Inj.	S	A	L
Ferrous Citrate Fe54 Inj.	S,M		
Iron Dextran Inj.	S,M	A,B	
Iron Sorbitex Inj.	S	A	
Isobucaine HCl and Epinephrine Inj.	S	A	
Isoniazid Inj.	S,M	A	L
Isoproterenol HCl Inj.	S	A	L
Isoxsuprine HCl Inj.	S,M	A	
Kanamycin Sulfate Inj.	S,M	A,C	
Kanamycin Sulfate, Sterile	I		
Ketamine HCl Inj.	S,M	A	L,H
Leucovorin Calcium Inj.	S	A	LR
Levallorphan Tartrate Inj.	S,M	A	
Levorphanol Tartrate Inj.	S,M	A	
Lidocaine HCl Inj.	S,M	A	
Lidocaine HCl, Sterile	I		
Lidocaine HCl and Dextrose Inj.	S	A,B	
Lidocaine HCl and Epinephrine Inj.	S,M	A	LR
Lincomycin HCl Inj.	S,M	A	
Lincomycin HCl, Sterile	I		
Magnesium Sulfate Inj.	S,M	A	
Manganese Chloride Inj.	S,M	A,B	
Manganese Sulfate Inj.	S,M	A,B	
Mannitol Inj.	S	A,B	
Mannitol and Sodium Chloride Inj.	U	D	
Measles Virus Vaccine Live	S,M		LR,R
Measles and Mumps Virus Vaccine Live	S,M		LR,R
Measles, Mumps and Rubella Virus Vaccine Live	S,M		LR,R
Measles and Rubella Virus Vaccine Live	S,M		LR,R
Mechlorethamine HCl for Inj.	I	B	
Medroxyprogesterone Acetate Susp., Sterile	S,M	A	
Menadiol Sodium Diphosphate Inj.	S	A	LR
Menadione Inj.	S,M	A	
Meningococcal Polysaccharide Vaccine (Group A)	M		R
Meningococcal Polysaccharide Vaccine (Group C)	M		R
Meningococcal Polysaccharide Vaccine (Groups A and C combined)	M		R
Meperidine HCl Inj.	S,M	A	
Mephentermine Sulfate Inj.	S,M	A	
Mepivacaine HCl Inj.	S,M	A	
Mepivacaine HCl and Levonordefrin Inj.	S,M	A	
Meprobamate Inj.	S	A	
Meprylcaine HCl and Epinephrine Inj.	S	A	L
Mesoridazine Besylate Inj.	S	A	L
Metaraminol Bitartrate Inj.	S,M	A	L
Methadone HCl Inj.	S,M	A	LR
Methantheline Bromide, Sterile	I	D	

Drugs	Container	Glass Type	Storage Conditions
Methicillin Sodium, Sterile	I		RT
Methicillin Sodium for Inj.	I		L,RT
Methiodal Sodium Inj.	S,M	A	
Methocarbamol Inj.	S	A	
Methohexital Sodium for Inj.	I	C	
Methotrexate Sodium Inj.	S,M	A	L
Methotrimeprazine Inj.	S,M	A	L
Methoxamine HCl Inj.	S,M	A	L
Methscopolamine Bromide Inj.	S,M	A	
Methydopate HCl Inj.	S	A	
Methylene Blue Inj.	S	A	
Methylergonovine Maleate Inj.	S	A	LR
Methylprednisolone Acetate Susp., Sterile	S,M	A	
Methylprednisolone Sodium Succinate for inj.	I	C	
Metocurine Iodide Inj.	S,M	A	
Metronidazole Inj.	S	A,B	
Mezlocillin Sodium, Sterile	I		
Miconazole Inj.	S	A	RT
Minocycline HCl, Sterile	I		L
Mitomycin for Inj.	I	D	L
Morphine Sulfate Inj.	S,M	A	L
Morrhuate Sodium Inj.	S,M	A	
Moxalactam Disodium for Inj.	I		
Mumps Virus Vaccine Live	S,M		LR,R
Nafcillin Sodium, Sterile	I		
Nafcillin Sodium for Inj.	I	D	
Naloxone HCl Inj.	S,M	A	L
Nandrolone Decanoate Inj.	S,M	A	L
Nandrolone Phenpropionate Inj.	S,M	A	L
Neomycin Sulfate, Sterile	I		
Neostigmine Methylsulfate Inj.	S,M		L
Netilmicin Sulfate Inj.	S,M	A	
Niacin Inj.	S,M	A	
Niacinaimide Inj.	S,M	A	
Nitroglycerin Inj.	S,M	A,B	
Norepinephrine Bitartrate Inj.	S	A	LR
Nylidrin HCl Inj.	S,M	A	
Orphenadrine Citrate Inj.	S,M	A	L
Oxacillin Sodium for Inj.	I	D	RT
Oxacillin Sodium, Sterile	I		
Oxymorphone HCl Inj.	S,M	A	L
Oxytetracycline Inj.	S,M		L
Oxytetracycline, Sterile	I		L
Oxytetracycline HCl for Inj.	I	B	L
Oxytetracycline HCl, Sterile	I		L
Papaverine HCl Inj.	S,M	A	
Paraldehyde, Sterile	S	A,B	LR,RT
Parathyroid Inj.	S,M	A,B	R
Penicillin G Benzathine, Sterile	I		
Penicillin G Benzathine Susp., Sterile	S,M	A,B	R
Penicillin G Benzathine and Penicillin G Procaine Susp., Sterile	S,M	A,C	
Penicillin G Potassium, Sterile	I	D	
Penicillin G Procaine, Sterile	I		
Penicillin G Procaine for Susp., Sterile	S,M	A,C	
Penicillin G Procaine Susp., Sterile	S,M	A,C	R
Penicillin G Procaine w/Aluminum Stearate Susp., Sterile	S,M	A,C	
Penicillin G Sodium for Inj.	I	D	
Penicillin G Sodium, Sterile	I	D	
Pentazocine Lactate Inj.	S,M	A	
Pentobarbital Sodium Inj.	S,M	A	
Perphenazine Inj.	S,M	A	L
Pertussis Vaccine	U		R

Drugs	Container	Glass Type	Storage Conditions
Pertussis Vaccine Adsorbed	U		R
Phenobarbital Sodium, Sterile	I	D	
Phenobarbital Sodium Inj.	I	D	
Phenolsulfonphthalein Inj.	S	A	
Phentolamine Mesylate for Inj.	I	B	
Phenylephrine HCl Inj.	S,M	A	L
Phenytoin Sodium, Sterile	I	C	
Phenytoin Sodium Inj.	S,M	A	RT
Physostigmine Salicylate Inj.	S	A	L
Phytonadione Inj.	S,M	A	L
Pilocarpine Ocular System	S		R
Piperacillin Sodium, Sterile	I		
Plicamycin for Inj.	I	D	L
Posterior Pituitary Inj.	S,M	A	
Poliovirus Vaccine Inactivated	U		R
Polymyxin B Sulfate, Sterile	I	D	L
Potassium Acetate Inj.	S,M	A,B	
Potassium Chloride Inj.	S,M	A,B	
Potassium Chloride in Dextrose Inj.	S	A,B	
Chromic Phosphate P32 Susp.	S,M		
Potassium Phosphates Inj.	S,M	A	
Pralidoxone Chloride, Sterile	I	B	
Prednisolone Acetate Susp., Sterile	S,M	A	
Prednisolone Sodium Phosphate Inj.	S,M	A	L
Prednisolone Sodium Succinate for Inj.	I	D	
Prednisolone Tebutate Susp., Sterile	S,M	A	
Prilocaine HCl Inj.	S,M	A	
Procainamide HCl Inj.	S,M	A	
Procaine HCl Inj.	S,M	A,B	
Procaine HCl, Sterile	I	D	
Procaine HCl and Epinephrine Inj.	S,M	A,B	LR
Procaine and Phenylephrine HCls Inj.	S,M	A	
Procaine HCl, Tetracycline HCl and Levonordefrin Inj.	S,M	A	
Prochlorperazine Edisylate Inj.	S,M	A	L
Progesterone Inj.	S,M	A,C	
Progesterone Susp., Sterile	S,M	A	
Progesterone Intrauterine Contraceptive Sys.	S		
Promazine HCl Inj.	S,M	A	L
Promethazine HCl Inj.	S,M	A	L
Propantheline Bromide, Sterile	S	D	
Propiomazine HCl Inj.	S	A	RT,L
Propoxycaine HCl, Procaine HCl and Levonordefrin Inj.	S	A	
Propoxycaine HCl, Procaine HCl and Norepinephrine Bitartrate Inj.	S,M	A	
Propranolol HCl Inj.	S	A	LR
Propyliodone Oil Susp., Sterile	S	D	LR
Protamine Sulfate Inj.	S	A	R
Protamine Sulfate for Inj.	I	D	
Protein Hydrolysate Inj.	S	A,B	H
Pyridostigmine Bromide Inj.	S	A	L
Pyridoxine HCl Inj.	S,M	A	L
Quinidine Gluconate Inj.	S,M	A	
Rabies Immune Globin	U		R
Rabies Vaccine	U		R
Reserpine Inj.	S	A	LR
Riboflavin Inj.	S,M	A	LR
Ringer's Inj.	S	A,B	
Lactated Ringer's Inj.	S	A,B	
Ritodrine HCl Inj.	S	A	RT
Rolitetracycline for Inj.	I	B	L
Rolitetracycline, Sterile	I		L
Rubella Virus Vaccine Live	S,M		LR,R

Drugs	Container	Glass Type	Storage Conditions
Rubella and Mumps Virus Vaccine Live	S,M		LR,R
Scopolomine Hydrobromide Inj.	S,M	A	LR
Secobarbital Sodium Inj.	S,M	A	L,R
Sisomicin Sulfate Inj.	S,M	A	
Secobarbital Sodium, Sterile	I	D	
Selenomethionine Se75 Inj.	U		R
Smallpox Vaccine	U		R
Sodium Acetate Inj.	S	A	
Sodium Bicarbonate Inj.	S	A	
Sodium Cholride Inhalation Soln.	S		
Sodium Chloride Inj.	S	A,B	
Sodium Chloride Inj., Bacteriostatic	S,M	A,B	
Sodium Lactate Inj.	S	A,B	
Sodium Nitrate Inj.	S	A	
Sodium Nitroprusside, Sterile	I	D	L
Sodium Pertechnetate Tc99m Inj.	S,M		R
Sodium Phosphates Inj.	S,M	A	
Sodium Sulfate Inj.	S	A	
Sodium Thiosulfate Inj.	S	A	
Spectinomycin HCl, Sterile	I	B	
Streptomycin Sulfate, Sterile	I	D	
Streptomycin Sulfate Inj.	S,M	A	
Succinylcholine Chloride, Sterile	I	D	
Succinylcholine Chloride Inj.	S,M	A,B	R
Sulfadiazine Sodium Inj.	S	A	LR
Sulfisoxazole Diolamine Inj.	S,M	A	L
Sulfobromophthalein Sodium Inj.	S	A	
Technetium Tc99m Albumin Inj.	S,M		R
Technetium Tc99m Albumin Aggregated Inj.	S,M		R
Technetium Tc99 Disofenin Inj.	S,M		In
Technetium Tc99m Etiodonate Inj.	S,M		
Technetium Tc99m Ferpentate Inj.	S,M		R,L
Technetium Tc99m Gluceptate Inj.	S,M		R
Technetium Tc99m Medronate Inj.	S,M		
Technetium Tc99m Oxidronate Inj.	S,M		
Technetium Tc99m Penetate Inj.	S,M		R
Technetium Tc99m Pyrophosphate Inj.	S,M		R
Technetium Tc99m (Pyro- and trimeta-) Phosphates Inj.	U	D	
Technetium Tc99m Succimer Inj.	S		RT,L
Technetium Tc99m Sulfur Colloid Inj.	S,M		
Terbutaline Sulfate Inj.	S	A	L,RT
Testolactone Susp., Sterile	S,M	A	
Testosterone Pellets	S		
Testosterone Susp., Sterile	S,M	A	
Testosterone Cypionate Inj.	S,M	A	L
Testosterone Enanthate Inj.	S,M	A	
Testosterone Propionate Inj.	S,M	A	
Tetanus Antitoxin	U		R
Tetanus Immune Globulin	U		R
Tetanus Toxoid	U		R
Tetanus Toxoid Adsorbed	U		R
Tetanus and Diphtheria Toxoids Adsorbed (for adult use)	U		R
Tetracaine HCl, Sterile	I	A	
Tetracaine HCl Inj.	S,M	A	R,L
Tetracycline HCl, Sterile	I		L
Tetracycline HCl for Inj.	I	B	L
Tetracycline Phosphate Complex for Inj.	I		L
Tetracycline Phosphate Complex, Sterile	I		L
Thallous Chloride Tl201 Inj.	S,M		
Thiamine HCl Inj.	S,M	A	L
Thiamylal Sodium for Inj.	I	C	
Thiethylperazine Malate Inj.	S	A	L

Drugs	Container	Glass Type	Storage Conditions
Thiopental Sodium for Inj.	I	C	
Thiotepa for Inj.	I	D	R,L
Thiothixene HCl Inj.	S	A	L
Thiothixene HCl for Inj.	I		LR
Ticarcillin Disodium, Sterile	I	D	
Tobramycin Sulfate, Sterile	I		
Tobramycin Sulfate Inj.	S,M	A	
Tolazoline HCl Inj.	S,M	A	
Tolbutamide Sodium, Sterile	I	D	
Triamcinolone Diacetate Susp., Sterile	S,M	A	
Triamcinolone Hexacetonide Susp., Sterile	S,M	A	
Tridihexethyl Chloride Inj.	S	A	
Trifluoperazine HCl Inj.	M	A	L
Trifluopromazine HCl Inj.	S,M	A	L
Trimethaphan Camsylate Inj.	S,M	A	R
Trimethobenzamide HCl Inj.	S,M	A	
Tromethamine for Inj.	I	C	
Tubocurarine Chloride Inj.	S,M		
Typhoid Vaccine	U		R
Urea, Sterile	I	D	
Vaccinia Immune Globulin	U		R
Vancomycin HCl, Sterile	I	B	
Variccila-Zoster Immune Globulin	U		R
Vasopressin Inj.	S,M	A	
Vidarabine Concentrate for Inj.	S,M	A	
Vinblastine Sulfate, Sterile	I	D	R
Vincristine Sulfate for Inj.	I	D	R
Warfarin Sodium for Inj.	I	D	LR
Bacteriostatic Water for Inj.	S,M	A,B	
Water for Inj., Sterile	S	A,B	
Water for Irrigation, Sterile	S	A,B	
Xenon Xe133 Inj.	S (totally filled)		R
Yellow Fever Vaccine	U (nitrogen filled ampuls®)		
Ytterbium Yb169 Pentetate Inj.	S		RT
Zinc Chloride Inj.	S,M	A,B	
Zinc Sulfate Inj.	S,M		

Provided by Dr. Kenneth S. Alexander, Associate Professor of Pharmacy, College of Pharmacy, University of Toledo.

Drug Product	Manufacturer	Dosage Form	Reason/Comments
Accutane	Roche	Capsule	Mucous membrane irritant
Acutrim	Ciba	Tablet	Slow release
Aerolate SR, JR, III	Fleming & Co.	Capsule	Slow release*
Afrinol	Schering	Tablet	Slow release
Aminodur	Berlex	Tablet	Slow release
Ananase	Rorer	Tablet	Enteric-coated
Artane Sequels	Lederle	Capsule	Slow release*
Arthritis Bayer Trimed-Release	Glenbrook	Capsule	Slow release
Asbron F Inlay	Sandoz	Tablet	Multiple compressed tablet
Avazyme, Avazyme-100	Wallace	Tablet	Enteric-coated
Azulfidine Entabs	Pharmacia Labs	Tablet	Enteric-coated
Belladenal-S	Sandoz	Tablet	Slow release
Bellergal-S	Sandoz	Tablet	Slow release
Bisacodyl	(Various)	Tablet	Enteric-coated
Bisco-Lax	Schein	Tablet	Enteric-coated‖
Bontril-SR	Carnrick	Capsule	Slow release*
Breonesin	Breon	Capsule	Liquid filled†
Bromphen Compund	Schein	Tablet	Slow release
Bronkodyl S-R	Breon	Capsule	Slow release
Butibel-Zyme	McNeil	Tablet	Slow release
Cama Arthritis Pain Reliever	Dorsey	Tablet	Multiple compressed tablet
Carter's Little Pills	Wallace	Tablet	Enteric-coated
Cartrax	Roerig	Tablet	Slow release
Chexit	Dorsey	Tablet	Slow release
Chlorpheniramine Maleate T-D	Lederle	Capsule	Slow release
Chlor-Trimeton Repetab	Schering	Tablet	Slow release
Choledyl SA	Parke-Davis	Tablet	Slow release
Chymoral	Armour	Tablet	Interference with enzymatic activity
Circanol	Riker	Tablet	Sublingual form
Clistin R-A	McNeil	Tablet	Slow release
Codexin	Arco	Capsule	Slow release
Combid Spansules	SKF	Capsule	Slow release
Comist	Norwich	Capsule	Slow release*
Compazine Spansule	SKF	Capsule	Slow release
Congress SR, JR	Fleming & Co	Capsule	Slow release
Constant-T	Geigy	Tablet	Slow release*
Contac	Menley & James	Capsule	Slow release*
Cotazym-S	Organon	Capsule	Enteric-coated*
CPA Time Capsules	Schein	Capsule	Slow release
Dainite-KI	Wallace	Tablet	Enteric-coated
Deconamine-SR	Berlex	Capsule	Slow release*
Decongestant S.R.	Genera	Tablet	Slow release
Depakene	Abbott[a]	Capsule	Mucous membrane irritant slow release
Dexachlor	Schein	Tablet	Slow release
Dexedrine Spansule	SKF	Capsule	Slow release
Diacin	Lemmon	Capsule	Slow release
Diamox Sequels	Lederle	Capsule	Slow release
Diatac	Menley & James	Capsule	Slow release*
Dilatrate-SR	Reed & Carnrick	Capsule	Slow release
Dimetane Extentab	A.H. Robins	Tablet	Slow release
Dimetapp Extentabs	A.H. Robins	Tablet	Slow release
Dipav 150 mg	Lemmon	Capsule	Slow release
Disobrom S.R.	Genera	Tablet	Slow release
Disophrol Chronotab	Schering	Tablet	Slow release
Donnatal Extentab	A.H. Robins	Tablet	Slow release
Donnazyme	A.H. Robins	Tablet	Enteric-coated
Drisdol	Winthrop	Capsule	Liquid filled†
Drixoral	Schering	Tablet	Slow release
Dulcolax	Boehringer Ingelheim	Tablet	Enteric coated‖

*The listing of oral dosage forms that should not be crushed is included as an aid to the practitioner in dispensing drugs and consulting with patients.

Drug Product	Manufacturer	Dosage Form	Reason/Comments
Duotrate	Marion	Capsule	Slow release
Easprin	Parke-Davis	Tablet	Enteric-coated
Ecotrin	Menley & James	Tablet	Enteric-coated*
Elixophyllin SR	Berlex	Capsule	Slow release*
E-Mycin	Upjohn	Tablet	Enteric-coated
Entex LA	Norwich	Tablet	Slow release
Entozyme	A.H. Robins	Tablet	Enteric-coated
Epsilan-M	Adria	Capsule	Taste††
Equanil	Wyeth	Tablet	Taste††
Ergomar	Fisons	Tablet	Sublingual route
Eryc	Parke-Davis	Capsule	Enteric-coated
Eskalith CR	SKF	Tablet	Slow release
Extendryl JR, SR	Fleming & Co.	Capsule	Slow release*
Fedahist	Rorer	Capsule	Slow release
Feldene	Pfizer	Capsule	Mucous membrane irritant
Feosol	Menley & James	Tablet	Enteric-coated
Feosol Spansule	Menley & James	Capsule	Slow release*
Fergon	Breon	Capsule	Slow release*
Ferroctyl	Schein	Capsule	Enteric-coated
Ferro-Grad 500 mg	Abbott[a]	Tablet	Slow release
Fero-Gradumet	Abbott[a]	Tablet	Slow release
Ferro-Sequels	Lederle	Capsule	Slow release*
Festal	Hoechst[a]	Tablet	Enteric-coated
Fiogesic	Sandoz	Tablet	Multiple comp. tab.
Fortespan	Menley & James	Capsule	Slow release
Hepicebrin	Lilly	Tablet	Enteric-coated
Histabid	Glaxo	Capsule	Slow release*
Histatapp T.D.	Upsher-Smith	Tablet	Slow release
Hydergine Sublingual	Sandoz	Tablet	Sublingual route
Hyrex-105	Hyrex	Capsule	Slow release*
Hytakerol	Winthrop	Capsule	Liquid filled†
Iberet	Abbott[a]	Tablet	Slow release
Iberet-500	Abbott[a]	Tablet	Slow release
Ilotycin	Dista	Tablet	Enteric-coated
Indocin SR	MSD	Capsule	Slow release*
Isoclor Timesule	Am. Crit. Care	Capsule	Slow release
Isordil Chew 10 mg	Ives	Tablet	Crushing prevents absorption in mouth
Isordil Sublingual	Ives	Tablet	Sublingual route
Isordil Tembid	Ives	Tablet, capsule	Slow release
Isuprel Glossets	Breon[a]	Tablet	Sublingual route
Kanulase	Dorsey	Tablet	Multiple comp. tab.
Kaon-Cl 10	Adria	Tablet	Slow release
Kaon-Cl 6.7 mEq.	Adria	Tablet	Slow release
Keff	Lemmon	Tablet	Effervescent tablet‡
Klorvess	Sandoz	Tablet	Effervescent tablet‡
Klotrix	Mead Johnson	Tablet	Slow release
K-Tab	Abbott[a]	Tablet	Slow release
Labid	Norwich	Tablet	Slow release
Laxadane	Lemmon	Tablet	Enteric-coated
Leder-BP Sequels	Lederle	Capsule	Slow release*
Leder-CC Sequels	Lederle	Capsule	Slow release*
Leder-CPI Sequels	Lederle	Capsule	Slow release*
Lithobid	Ciba-Geigy	Tablet	Slow release
Marblen	Fleming & Co.	Tablet	Diminishes prolonged effect
Measurin	Breon	Tablet	Slow release
Meprospan	Wallace	Capsule	Slow release*
Mestinon Timespan	Roche	Tablet	Slow release
Metadren Linguets	Ciba	Tablet	Sublingual
MI-Cebrin	Dista	Tablet	Enteric-coated
MI-Cebrin T	Dista	Tablet	Enteric-coated
Micro-K	A.H. Robins	Capsule	Slow release*
Modane	Adria	Capsule	Liguid in cap.
Motrin	Upjohn	Tablet	Taste‡
MSC Triaminic	Dorsey	Tablet	Enteric-coated
Multicebrin	Lilly	Tablet	Enteric-coated

Drug Product	Manufacturer	Dosage Form	Reason/Comments
Naldecon	Bristol[a]	Tablet	Slow release
ND-Hist	Hyrex	Capsule	Slow release
Neosynephrinol	Winthrop	Capsule	Slow release
Nico 400	Marion	Capsule	Slow release
Nicobid	Armour	Capsule	Slow release
Nico-Span	Key	Capsule	Slow release
Nitro-Bid	Marion	Capsule	Slow release
Nitroglycerin T-D	Lederle	Capsule	Slow release
Nitroglyn	Key	Tablet	Slow release*
Nitrolin	Schein	Capsule	Slow release
Nitrostat	Parke-Davis	Tablet	Sublingual tablet
Nitrostat SR	Parke-Davis	Capsule	Slow release
Noctec	Squibb	Capsule	Liquid form in cap.
Nolamine	Reed & Carnrick	Tablet	Slow release
Norflex	Riker	Tablet	Slow release
Novafed	Dow	Capsule	Slow release
Novafed A	Dow	Capsule	Slow release
Novahistin LP	Dow	Tablet	Slow release
Nu'Leven	Lemmon	Tablet	Enteric-coated
Obestat	Lemmon	Capsule	Slow release
Oragrafin	Squibb	Capsule	Liquid form in cap.
Ornade Spansule	SKF	Capsule	Slow release
Pabalate, Pabalate SF	A.H. Robins	Tablet	Enteric-coated
Pabirin Buffered	Dorsey	Tablet	Multiple compressed tab.
Pancrease	J & J	Capsule	Enteric-coated
Panmysin	Upjohn	Capsule	Taste
Papaverine HCl T-R	Lederle	Capsule	Slow release*
Pathilon Sequels	Lederle	Capsule	Slow release*
Pavabid	Marion	Capsule	Slow release
PBZ-SR	Geigy[a]	Tablet	Slow release
Pantritol	Armour	Capsule	Slow release
Perdiem	Rorer	Granules	Wax-coated
Peritrate SA	Parke-Davis	Tablet	Slow release
Permitil Chronotab	Schering	Tablet	Slow release
Peritrate SA	Parke-Davis	Tablet	Slow release
Phazyme	Reed & Carnrick	Tablet	Slow release
Phazyme 95	Reed & Carnrick	Tablet	Slow release
Phazyme PB	Reed & Carnrick	Tablet	Slow release
Phenergan	Wyeth	Tablet	Taste††
Phyllocontin	Purdue Frederick	Tablet	Slow release
Polaramine Repetab	Schering	Tablet	Slow release
Prelu-2	Boehringer Ingelheim	Capsule	Slow release
Preludin Endurets	Boehringer Ingelheim	Tablet	Slow release
Procan SR	Parke-Davis	Tablet	Slow release
Procardia	Pfizer	Capsule	Delays absorption¶
Prochlor-ISO	Schein	Capsule	Slow release
Proketazine Maleate	Wyeth	Tablet	Slow release
Pronestyl-SR	Squibb	Tablet	Slow release
Quadra-Hist	Schein	Tablet	Slow release
Quibron-T/SR	Mead Johnson	Tablet	Slow release
Quinaglute Dura-Tabs	Berlex	Tablet	Slow release
Quinidex Extentabs	A.H. Robins	Tablet	Slow release
Renalgin	Glaxo	Tablet	Activations§
Resaid S.R.	Genera	Capsule	Slow release*
Resaid-D S.R.	Genera	Capsule	Slow release*
Resbid	Boehringer Ingelheim	Tablet	Slow release
Rhinex D-Lay	Lemmon	Tablet	Slow release
Ritalin-SR	Ciba	Tablet	Slow release
Ro-Bile	Rowell	Tablet	Enteric-coated
Robimycin Robitab	A.H. Robins	Tablet	Enteric-coated
Roniacol Timespan	Roche	Tablet	Slow release
Roxanol-Sr	Roxane	Tablet	Slow release
Singlet	Dow	Tablet	Slow release
SK Bisacodyl	SKF	Tablet	Enteric-coated
SK-Erythromycin	SKF	Tablet	Enteric-coated
Slo-Bid Gyrocaps	Rorer	Capsule	Slow release*

Drug Product	Manufacturer	Dosage Form	Reason/Comments
Slo-Phyllin GG	Rorer	Capsule	Slow release
Slo-Phyllin Gyrocaps	Rorer	Capsule	Slow release*
Slo-FE	Ciba	Tablet	Slow release
Somophyllin-CRT	Fisons	Capsule	Slow release*
Sorbitrate S.A.	Stuart	Tablet	Slow release
Sparine	Wyeth	Tablet	Taste††
SPRX-105	Tutag[a]	Capsule	Slow release
S-P-T	Fleming	Capsule	Liquid gelatin susp.
Sudafed SA	Burroughs Wellcome	Capsule	Slow release
Sueda-G	Hyrex	Capsule	Slow release*
Sustaire	Roerig	Tablet	Slow release
Symmetrel	Dupont	Capsule	Slow release
Tamine S.R.	Genera	Tablet	Slow release
Tedral SA	Parke-Davis	Tablet	Slow release
Teldrin	Menley & James	Capsule	Slow release
Temaril Spansule	SKF	Capsule	Slow release
Tepanil	Riker	Tablet	Slow release
Tessalon Perles	Dupont	Capsule	Slow release
Theo-24	Searle	Tablet	Slow release
Theobid	Glaxo	Capsule	Slow release*
Theobid Jr.	Glaxo	Capsule	Slow release*
Theo-Dur	Key	Tablet	Slow release
Theo-Dur Sprinkle	key	Capsule	Slow release*
Theolair SR	Riker	Tablet	Slow release
Theophyl SR	Knoll	Capsule	Slow release
Theovent	Schering	Capsule	Slow release
Thorazine Spansule	SKF	Capsule	Slow release
Travist-D	Sandoz	Tablet	Multiple compressed tab.
Triaminic	Dorsey	Tablet	Enteric-coated
Triaminic-12	Dorsey	Tablet	Slow release
Triaminic TR	Dorsey	Tablet	Multiple compressed tab.
Triaminic Juvelets	Dorsey	Tablet	Slow release
Tri-Hist	Schein	Tablet	Slow release
Trilafon Repetab	Schering	Tablet	Slow release
Tuss-Ade	Schein	Capsule	Slow release
Tussagesic	Dorseu	Tablet	Enteric-coated
Tussaminic	Dorsey	Tablet	Enteric-coated
Tuss-Ornade Spansule	SKF	Capsule	Slow release
Ursinus Inlay	Dorsey	Tablet	Multiple compressed tab.
Valrelease	Roche	Capsule	Slow release
Wyamycin-S	Wyeth	Tablet	Slow release
Wygesic	Wyeth	Tablet	Taste††
Zorprin	Boots	Tablet	Slow release

The listing is included to alert the health care practitioner about oral dosage forms that should not be crushed, and to serve as an aid in consulting with patients. (Reprinted from Mitchell F: Hospital Pharmacy 20: 310, 1985)

[a]Information not obtained directly from the manufacturer.

*Capsule may be opened and the contents taken without crushing or chewing: soft food such as applesauce or pudding may facilitate administration; contents may generally be administered via nasogastric tube using an appropriate fluid such as cherry syrup.

†Capsule may be opened and the liquid contents removed for administration.

‡Effervescent tablets must be dissolved in the amount of diluent recommended by the manufacturer.

§Acid contents of the stomach may prematurely activate the ingredients.

||If the liquid capsule is crushed or the contents expressed, the active ingredient will be, in part, absorbed sublingually.

¶Antacids and/or milk may prematurely dissolve the coating of the tablet.

**Tablets are made to disintegrate under the tongue.

††The taste of the product in a liquid form would likely be unacceptable to the patient; administration via nasogastric tube should be acceptable.

LISTED IN NUMERICAL ORDER

0002
Lilly, Eli, & Co.

0003
Squibb Pharmaceutical Co.

0004
Roche Laboratories

0005
Lederle Laboratories,
Davis & Geck, American
Cyanamid Co.

0006
Merck Sharp & Dohme

0007
Smith Kline & French
Laboratories

0008
Wyeth Laboratories

0009
Upjohn Company, The

0011
Hynson, Westcott & Dunning
Inc.

0013
Warren-Teed Laboratories
Div. of Adria Laboratories, Inc.

0014
Searle & Co.

0015
Bristol Labs

0016
Pharmacia Laboratories

0017
Wampole Laboratories
Wallace Laboratories

0018
Pennwalt Corporation
Prescription Division

0021
Reed & Carnrick

0022
McKesson Laboratories

0023
Herbert Laboratories
Allergan Pharmaceuticals, Inc.

0024
Winthrop Laboratories

0025
Searle Laboratories

0026
Miles Pharmaceuticals

0028
Geigy Pharmaceuticals

0029
Beecham Laboratories

0031
Robins, A.H., Company

0032
Rowell Laboratories, Inc.

0033
Syntex Laboratories, Inc.

0034
Purdue Frederick Co., The

0035
Eaton Laboratories

0037
Wallace Laboratories

0038
Stuart Pharmaceuticals

0039
Hoechst-Roussel
Pharmaceuticals, Inc.

0041
Cooper Laboratories,
Inc.

0043
Dorsey Laboratories

0044
Knoll Pharmaceutical Co.

0045
McNeilab, Inc.

0046
Ayerst Laboratories

0047
Warner/Chilcott
Laboratories

0048
Flint Laboratories

0049
Roerig

0051
Unimed, Inc.

0052
Organon Inc.

0053
Armour Pharmaceutical
Co.

0054
Phillips Roxane Labs., Inc.

0055
Cole Pharmacal Co., Inc.

0056
Endo Labs., Inc.

0057
Breon Laboratories Inc.

0058
SMP, Div. CooperVision P.R.,
Inc.

0062
Ortho Pharmaceutical
Corporation

0063
Reid-Provident Labs., Inc.

0065
Alcon Laboratories, Inc.

0066
Dermik Laboratories, Inc.

0067
Rorer, William H., Inc.

0068
Merrell-National Labs.

0069
Pfizer Laboratories

0070
USV Laboratories Inc.

0071
Parke, Davis & Co.

0072
Westwood Pharmaceuticals,
Inc.

0073
Lakeside Laboratories

0074
Abbott Laboratories
Murine Company
Ross Laboratories

0075
USV Laboratories, Div.
USV Pharmaceutical Corp.

0076
Star Pharmaceuticals, Inc.

0078
Sandoz Pharmaceuticals

0081
Burroughs Wellcome Co.

0082
Ives Laboratories Inc.

0083
CIBA Pharmaceutical
Company

0084
American Pharmaceutical Co.

0085
Schering Corporation

0086
Carnrick Laboratories

0087
Mead Johnson & Company

0088
Marion Laboratories, Inc.
Derm-Arts Laboratories

0089
Riker Laboratories, Inc.

*The "Pharmaceutical Company Labeler Code Index" is presented to aid the practitioner in the identification of drug products. In this section the codes are listed in numerical order. Additionally, the pharmaceutical labeler codes are also listed with the alphabetical listing of Pharmaceutical Manufacturers and/or Drug Distributors.

0091
Kremers-Urban Co.

0093
Lemmon Company

0094
American Critical Care

0095
Poythress, Wm. P., & Co., Inc.

0096
Person & Covey, Inc.

0098
Kirkman Laboratories, Inc.

0105
USV (P.R.) Development Corp.

0107
Ortho Pharmaceuticals, Inc.

0109
Allergan Caribbean

0110
Tarmac Products, Inc.

0111
Emko Company, The

0112
Mitchum-Thayer, Inc.

0116
Xttrium Laboratories, Inc.

0118
Hollister-Stier Laboratories

0123
Stayner Corp.

0124
Reid-Provident Pharmaceuticals

0125
International Pharmaceutical Corporation

0126
Hoyt Laboratories

0127
Ulmer Pharmacal Co.

0128
Calgon Consumer Products Co., Inc.

0131
The Central Pharmacal Co.

0132
Fleet, C. B., Co., Inc.

0133
Zemmer Co., The
Moore Kirk Labs.

0137
Johnson & Johnson Dermatological Division

0138
Plough, Inc.

0139
Park Laboratories, Inc.

0141
Fuller Laboratories, Inc.

0142
Amfre-Grant
Ormont Drug & Chemical Co., Inc.

0143
West-ward, Inc.

0145
Stiefel Laboratories, Inc.

0147
Camall Company

0149
Norwich-Eaton Pharmaceuticals

0152
Gray Pharmaceutical Company

0154
Blair Laboratories, Inc.

0157
American Labs.
Towne, Paulsen & Co., Inc.

0158
Denver Chemical Mfg. Co., The

0159
Noyes, P.J. Co., The

0161
Cutter Laboratories, Inc.

0162
Arch Laboratories

0163
Elder, Paul B., Co.
Campbell Laboratories, Inc.

0165
Blaine Co., Inc.

0166
Mallard Inc.

0168
Fougera, E. & Co., Inc.

0171
Johnson, Matt, Co.

0172
Zenith Laboratories, Inc.

0173
Glaxo Incorporated

0175
Hartford Laboratories

0177
International Drug, Inc.

0178
Mission Pharmacal Co.

0179
Madland Laboratories, Inc.

0181
Vita Elixir Co., Inc.

0182
Generix Drug Sales Co., Inc.

0183
Dow Pharmaceuticals

0184
Medics Pharmaceutical Corp.

0185
Vitarine Co., Inc.
Laboratorios Gimenez, Inc.

0186
Astra Pharmaceutical Products, Inc.

0187
ICN Pharmaceuticals

0191
Mahon, Thomas J., Inc.
Ortega Pharmaceutical Co.

0192
Miles Laboratories, Inc.

0193
Ames Company

0195
Wharton Laboratories, Inc.

0196
Rachelle Laboratories

0197
Ex-Lax Inc.

0198
North American Pharmacal

0212
Doyle Pharmaceutical Co.

0215
Medical Chemicals, Inc.
Medwick Laboratories, Inc.

0217
Dunhall Pharmaceuticals, Inc.

0219
Humphreys Pharmacal, Inc.

0221
Dooner Laboratories, Inc.

0222
Boyle & Co.

0223
Consolidated Midland Corp.

0225
Ascher, B.F., & Co., Inc.

0228
Purepac Pharmaceutical Co.

0233
Trent Pharmaceuticals, Inc.

0234
Schmid Laboratories

0235
Pharmacraft Division
Pennwalt Corporation

0237
Webber Pharmaceuticals, U.S.A., Inc.
Fellows Medical Division

0242
Stanlabs Pharmaceutical Co.

0244
Medicone Company

0245
Upsher-Smith Laboratories, Inc.

0247
Alcon/B. P.
Burton, Parsons & Company, Inc.

0248
Brown Pharmaceutical Co., Inc., The

0249
Geriatric Pharmaceutical Corp.

0251
Spanner, G.O., Inc.

0252
Bowman Pharmaceuticals, Inc.
Bowman, Inc.

0253
Sutliff & Case Co., Inc.

0256
Fleming & Company

0258
Inwood Laboratories, Inc.

0259
Mayrand Incorporated

0261
Drug Industries Co., Inc.

0263
Rystan Co., Inc.

0267
Federal Pharmacal Corp.

0268
Center Laboratories, Inc.

0269
Roussel Corporation

0271
Palmedico, Inc.

0273
Lorvic Corp., The

0274
Scherer Laboratories, Inc.

0275
Arco Pharmaceuticals, Inc.

0276
Misemer Pharmaceuticals, Inc.

0277
Laser, Inc.

0279
Robinson Laboratory, Inc.

0281
Savage Laboratories

0282
Dalin Pharmaceuticals, Inc.

0283
Beutlich, Inc.

0284
Lexington Chemical Co., Inc.

0285
King Pharmaceutical Co., Inc.

0288
Fluoritab Corp.

0291
Westerfield

0292
Watson, T.E., Co.

0299
Owen Laboratories

0311
Almay Inc.

0314
Hyrex Pharmaceuticals
Matco Drug Company

0315
Len-Tag Co.

0316
Del-Ray Laboratories, Inc.

0317
Whorton Pharmaceuticals, Inc.
Yeager Specialty Co.

0318
Ormont Drug & Chemical Co., Inc.

0322
Merrick Medicine Co.

0323
Welty Corporation

0326
Calbio Pharmaceuticals

0327
Guardian Chemical Corp.

0329
Scruggs Pharmacal Company, Inc.

0331
Premo Pharmaceutical Labs., Inc.

0341
Parker Laboratories, Inc.

0343
Youngs Drug Products Corp.

0346
Softcon Products

0348
Lambda Pharmacal Labs., Inc.

0349
Parmed Pharmaceuticals, Inc.

0351
Kay Pharmacal Co., Inc.

0352
Schuemann Laboratories, Inc.

0357
Cumberland Mfg. Co.
Arcum Pharmaceutical Corp.

0359
Columbia Medical Co.

0362
Novocol Chemical Mfg. Co., Inc.

0365
Progressive Enterprises

0368
Bell Pharmacal Corp.

0369
Key Pharmaceuticals, Inc.

0371
Layton Laboratories

0372
Hannaway, R. T., Inc.
Scot-Tussin Pharmacal Co., Inc.

0373
Baker, J.T., Chemical Company

0374
Lyne Laboratories

0375
Corvit Pharmaceuticals

0377
Vale Chemical Co., Inc., The

0381
Carter-Glogau Laboratories

0382
Northrup Pharmaceutical Co.

0383
Hoffman Laboratories, Inc.

0385
Coast Laboratories, Inc.

0386
Gebauer Chemical Co.

0391
Lardon Labs.

0393
Salem Pharmacal

0394
Mericon Industries, Inc.

0395
Humco Laboratory, Inc.

0396
Milex Products, Inc.

0397
Jenkins Laboratories, Inc.

0398
C & M Pharmacal, Inc.
Ries-Hamly, Inc.
0411
Forbes Pharmacal, Inc.

0414
Suppositoria Labs., Inc.

0417
Hall, Don, Laboratories

0418
Pasadena Research Laboratories, Inc.

0419
Santa Pharmaceuticals, Inc.

0421
Fielding Pharmaceutical Co., The

0425
Day-Baldwin, Inc.

0427
Winston Pharmaceuticals, Inc.

0429
Merit Pharmaceutical Co., Inc.

0432
Rex Laboratory, Inc.

0436
Century Pharmaceuticals, Inc.

0444
Carr Drug Co.
Scrip, Inc.

0446
Leeds Pharmacal Corp.

0451
Muro Pharmacal Labs., Inc.

0452
Brunswick Laboratories

0454
Metro Med., Inc.

0456
O'Neal, Jones & Feldman, Inc.

0461
Yager Drug Co.

0463
Truxton, Inc.

0466
Macsil, Inc.

0467
Invenex Pharmaceuticals

0472
Barre Drug Co., Inc.

0473
Carbisulphoil Co.

0475
Berkeley Laboratories

0477
Obetrol Pharmaceuticals

0479
Burlington Pharmacal, Inc.

0482
Kenwood Laboratories, Inc.

0484
SK&F Co.

0485
Edwards Pharmacal Co.

0486
Beach Pharmaceuticals
Hill Dermaceuticals

0487
Nephron Corporation

0491
Coastal Pharmaceutical Co., Inc.

0493
Amid Laboratories, Inc.

0494
Foy Laboratories, Inc.

0496
Ferndale Laboratories, Inc.

0511
Sandia Pharmaceuticals, Inc.

0512
Marsh-Emory Laboratories, Inc.

0514
Dow B. Hickam, Inc.

0516
Glenwood Laboratories, Inc.

0517
American Quinine

0518
Advance Biofactures Corp.

0523
Acid-Eze Company, Inc.

0524
Rucker Pharmacal Co., Inc.

0526
Carlton Corp., The

0527
Lannett Co., Inc.

0529
Blue Line Chemical Co., The

0534
Aeroceuticals, Inc.

0535
Gilbert Laboratories

0538
Landry Pharmaceuticals, Inc.

0539
American Urologicals, Inc.

0543
Mosso, C. A., Co.

0544
Eastwood Pharmacal Co., Inc.

0551
Seatrace Co., The

0552
Comatic Laboratories, Inc.

0553
Hydrosal Co.

0555
Barr Laboratories, Inc.

0556
Cenci, H.R., Laboratories, Inc.

0558
Tri-State Pharmaceutical Co., Inc.

0563
Bock Pharmacal Company

0568
Baylor Laboratories, Inc.

0569
Rand Labs., Inc.

0571
Archer Pharmaceutical Co., Inc.

0572
Sheraton Laboratories, Inc.

0573
Whitehall Labs.

0574
Paddock Laboratories

0575
Cummins Pharmaceutical Co., Inc.

0576
Medical Prods. Panamericana, Inc.

0578
Jones & Vaughan, Inc.

0585
Fisons Corporation

0587
Dermakon Laboratories Division, Preston Pharmaceutics, Inc.

0588
Keene Pharmaceuticals, Inc.

0592
Jones, Ed, Inc.

0596
Canright Corp.

0597
Boehringer Ingelheim Ltd.

0598
Approved Pharmaceutical Corp.
Pharmacy Associates

0611
Jalco Pharmaceuticals, Inc.

0614
Douglas Pharmacal Industries, Inc.

0615
Vangard Laboratories

0617
Dios Chemical Co.

0618
Luyties Pharmacal Co.

0619
Walker Pharmacal Co.

0621
Wise's K.C. Homeopathic Pharmacy

0633
Inland Alkaloid Company

0638
Fray Corp.

0639
Paraeusal Co.

0641
Elkins-Sinn, Inc.

0642
Everett Laboratories, Inc.

0645
Medi-Rx Pharmaceuticals, Inc.

0648
Truett Laboratories

0653
Nejo Pharmacal Co.

0655
Bomiseco Laboratories, Inc.

0656
Tennessee Pharmaceutical Co., Inc.

0657
DDR Pharmaceutical Corp.

0659
Circle Pharmaceuticals, Inc.

0664
Bocan Drug Co.

0667
Fort David Laboratories, Inc.

0669
Lepler Laboratories, Inc.

0673
Sidal Pharmaceutical Co., Inc.

0674
General Pharmaceutical Prods., Inc.

0689
Daniels Pharmaceuticals

0692
Martin-Phillips Laboratories, Inc.

0697
Delco Chemical Co., Inc.

0698
Grafton Pharmaceutical Co.

0711
Scott-Alison Pharmaceuticals, Inc.

0713
G & W Laboratories, Inc.

0716
Standex Laboratories, Inc.

0721
Eastern Research Labs., Inc.

0727
Park Plaza Pharmaceuticals, Inc.

0731
Alto Pharmaceuticals, Inc.

0733
Laboratorios Terrier, Inc.

0734
Tablicaps, Inc.

0737
Amazol Company, The
D'Franssia Corp.

0741
Walker Corp. & Co., Inc.

0749
Mill-Mark Pharmaceuticals, Inc.

0752
Norgine Laboratories, Inc.

0758
Moffet, Inc.

0759
Chrisman Co.

0762
Rhode, J. G., Co., The

0764
Medco Supply Co.

0766
Norcliff Thayer Inc.

0777
Dista Products Co.

0781
Geneva Generics

0785
UAD Laboratories, Inc.

0793
Rals Laboratories

0795
Brothers Pharmaceuticals, Inc.

0799
Perry Laboratories, Inc.

0814
Interstate Drug Exchange

0815
Reiss Williams Company

0816
Midway Medical Co., Inc.

0823
Sheryl Pharmaceuticals, Inc.

0827
Delta Drug Corp.

0832
Western Research Laboratories, Inc.

0834
Saron Pharmacal Corp.

0835
Geneva Drugs Ltd.

0836
Virtal Pharmacal Co., Inc.

0839
Moore, H. L., Drug Exchange, Inc.

0841
Haberle Drug Co.

0849
Ingram Pharmaceutical Co.

0875
Bio-Factor Labs.

0884
Pedinol Pharmacal, Inc.

0892
Bell Therapeutic Supplies, Inc.

0893
Barry Martin Pharmaceuticals, Inc.

0897
National Magnesia Co., Inc.

0904
Major Pharmaceutical Corp.

0917
Wesley Pharmacal Co., Inc.

0919
Werner Laboratories, Inc.

0923
Whiteworth, Inc.

0928
Wolins Pharmacal Corp.

0944
Hyland Laboratories

0971
Winthrop Products, Inc.

0991
Webcon Pharmaceuticals

0992
Kahlenberg Laboratories

0993
American Felsol Co.

0995
Pfipharmecs

1016
Bluco Incorporated

1097
Rilox Company, The

1212
Brown Medicine Co.

1215
Galen Pharmaceuticals, Inc.

1237
King's Specialty Co.

1246
Thera-Medic, Inc.

1277
Morton Pharmaceuticals, Inc.

10244
Otis Clapp & Son, Inc.
Buffington Division
Cross Division

10003
A.V.P. Pharmaceuticals, Inc.

10038
Velvet Pharmcal Co.

10040
Amco Drug Products Co., Inc.

10125
Phoenix Pharmacal

10153
Bisleri Co., Inc.

10244
Otis Clapp & Son, Inc.

10310
Del Laboratories, Inc.
Commerce Drug Co., Inc.

10327
DeWitt International Corp.

10341
Doktors Laboratories, Inc.

10440
G. E. Laboratories, Inc.

10648
Larson Labs., Inc.

10651
Lavoptik Co., Inc.

10706
Manne, Kenneth A., Co.

10797
Natcon Chemical Co., Inc.

10824
Nortech Laboratories

10833
Spirt & Company
Hart Laboratories

10929
Pyro-Sana Laboratory

10945
Rasman Pharmacal Co., Inc.

10952
Recsei Laboratories

10956
Reese Chemical Co.

10973
Richards Pharmaceutical Co.

10989
ROR Pharmacal Co., Inc.

11086
Summers Laboratories, Inc.

11089
Superior Chemical International, Inc.
McGregor & Co.

11299
Torch Laboratories, Inc.

11311
Trimen Laboratories, Inc.

11312
Carbo-Fung Labs., Inc.

11365
Wade Chemical Company

11370
Warner-Lambert Company

11397
Western Pharmacal Co.

11414
Willen Drug Co.

11422
Winton, Ralph, Co.

11463
Barry Laboratories, Inc.

11489
Cunningham Distributors

11530
Stanback Co., Ltd.

11588
Jeffrey Martin, Inc.

11649
Press Chemical & Pharmaceutical Laboratories

11694
Key Company, The

11696
Dattel Pharmaceutical Co., Inc.

11701
Sween Corp.

11808
Ion Laboratories, Inc.

11853
Gaddy, R. L., Company

11868
Monticello Drug Co.

11940
Medco Lab. Inc.

11980
Allergan America

12072
Temesco

12120
Wisconsin Pharmacal Co., Inc.
Badger Pharmacal, Inc.

12126
Ivy Corp.

12136
Bird Corporation

12154
Allison Laboratories, Inc.

12336
Econo-Rx, Inc.

12359
Rawl Chemical Co., Inc.

12418
Culminal, Inc.

12434
Last, Alvin, Inc.

12620
Reaco Products, Inc.

12758
Mason Pharmaceuticals, Inc.

12766
Miller Laboratories

12805
International Chemical Laboratories

12814
Merchant, W. F., Pharmaceutical Co., Inc.

12843
Glenbrook Laboratories

12939
Marlop Pharmaceuticals, Inc.

14869
Lexalabs, Inc.

17021
Cameron Medical Corp.

17154
Danal Laboratories Inc.

17201
Leland Laboratories, Inc.

19041
Doshire, Inc.

19810
Bristol-Myers Products

21769
Reily Chemical Co.

23900
Vicks Health Care

35476
Vitacorp.

36969
Merrell-National Laboratories, Inc., (PR)

38242
Adria Laboratories Inc.
(Includes Warren-Teed Products)

41167
Chattem Laboratories

42021
Sclavo, Inc.

44081
Med-Corp, Inc.

44384
Biological Corp. of America

45800
Menley and James Laboratories

50419
Berlex Laboratories

50821
Springbrook Pharmaceuticals, Inc.

76660
Vicks Toiletry Products

0074
Abbott Laboratories
Abbott Park
North Chicago, IL 60064

0074
Abbott Consumer Products
See: Ross Laboratories.

0074
Abbott Diagnostic Products
Div. of Abbott Laboratories

0074
Abbott Hospital Products
Div. of Abbott Laboratories

0074
Abbott Pharmaceutical Products
Div. of Abbott Laboratories

0523
Acid-Eze Company, Inc.
Triangle Shopping Center
Trion, GA 30753

38242
Adria Laboratories Inc.
Div. of Erbamont Inc.
P.O. Box 16529
Columbus, OH 43216

0518
Advance Biofactures Corp.
35 Wilbur St.
Lynbrook, NY 11563

Advanced Care Products
Div. Ortho Pharmaceutical Corp.

0534
Aeroceuticals Health Care Prods.
49 John Street
Southport, CT 06490

Alberto-Culver Co.
2525 W. Armitage Ave.
Melrose Park, IL 60160

0065
Alcon Labs., Inc.
6201 S. Freeway
Box 1959
Ft. Worth, TX 76101

0065
Alcon Labs., Inc.
Surgical Products Div.
P.O. Box 1959
Ft. Worth, TX 76101

Alconox, Incorporated
215 Park Avenue, S.
New York, NY 10003

Alkalol Co.
Box 964
Taunton, MA 02780

11980
Allergan America
See: Allergan Pharmaceuticals, Inc.

0109
Allergan Caribbean
See: Allergan Pharmaceuticals, Inc.

0023
Allergan Pharmaceuticals, Inc.
2525 duPont Drive
Irvine, CA 92715

Alpern Laboratories
Subs. Lesch Corp.
414 West Lenox Ave.
Oak Park, IL 60302

Alpha Pharmaceuticals, Inc.
1336 N. Carolan St.
P.O. Box 1336
Burlingame, CA 94010

Alra Laboratories, Inc.
3850 Clearview Court
Gurnee, IL 60031

0731
Alto Pharmaceuticals, Inc.
P.O. Box 271369
Tampa, FL 33688

Alton Products Inc.
93 Border St.
W. Newton, MA 02165

10040
Amco Drug Prods. Co., Inc.
Box 10
North Olmsted, OH 44070

Amend Drug & Chemical Co., Inc.
83 Cordier St.
Irvington, NJ 07111

0094
American Critical Care
Div. American Hospital Supply Corp.
1600 Waukegan Road
McGraw Park, IL 60085

0005
American Cyanamid Co.
Agriculture Division
P.O. Box 400
Princeton, NJ 08540

American Dermal Corp.
P.O. Box 427
Somerset, NJ 08873

0993
American Felsol Company
See: T.E. Watson Co.

0157
American Labs. (Amlab)
Div. Towne, Paulsen & Co., Inc.

American Lecithin Co., Inc.
32–34 61st Street
Woodside, L.I., NY 11377

American McGaw
Div. Am. Hosp. Supply Corp.
2525 McGaw Ave.
Santa Ana, CA 92711

American Pharmaceutical Products Co.

0517
American Quinine
Hosp. Div. Natcon Chemical Co., Inc.
1 Fairchild Court
Plainview, NY 11803

0539
American Urilogicals, Inc.

0193
Ames Company
Div. Miles Labs., Inc.
P.O. Box 70
1127 Myrtle Street
Elkhart, IN 46514

0142
Amfre-Grant, Inc.
See: U.S. Products, Inc.

0493
Amid Laboratories, Inc.
See: T. E. Williams Pharmaceuticals, Inc.

0598
Approved Pharm. Corp.
1643 E. Genesee St.
Syracuse, NY 13202

Arbrook, Inc.
See: Surgikos

0162
Arch Laboratories
Div. of Norcliff Thayer Inc.
319 S. 4th Street
St. Louis, MO 63102

Archar Drug Co.
107 E. Markham St.
P.O. Box 2701
Little Rock, AR 72203

0275
Arco Pharmaceuticals, Inc.
105 Orville Drive
Bohemia, NY 11716

0357
Arcum Pharm. Corp.

Ar-Ex Products Co.
1036 W. Van Buren St.
Chicago, IL 60607

0053
Armour Pharm. Co.
Div. Revlon Health Care Group
303 South Broadway
Tarrytown, NY 10591

Arnar Stone Labs.
See: American Critical Care

0225
Ascher, B.F. & Co., Inc.
P.O. Box 827
Kansas City, MO 64141

Associated Concentrates
Div. American Lecithin Co., Inc.
P.O. Box 4056
Atlanta, GA 30302

*A Pharmaceutical Labeler Code appears before the address for each company. This code has been added as an aid in the identification of drug products.

186
stra Pharm. Products, Inc.
0 Otis street
Vestboro, MA 01581

tlas Chemical Co.
See: ICI United States Inc.

veeno Dermatologicals
See: Cooper Labs, Inc.

vicon, Inc.
Div. of Alcon Labs., Inc.
201 S. Freeway
P.O. Box 85
Fort Worth, TX 76101

0003
A.V.P. Pharmaceuticals, Inc.
829 Main Street
Clarence, NY 14031

0046
Ayerst Labs.
Div. Amer. Home Products Corp.
685 Third Ave.
New York, NY 10017

12120
Badger Pharmacal, Inc.
P.O. Box 171
Cedarburg, WI 53012

0575
Baker/Cummins
Div. of Key Pharmaceuticals, Inc.

Barnes-Hind Pharmaceuticals, Inc.
895 Kifer Rd.
Sunnyvale, CA 94086

0555
Barr Laboratories, Inc.
265 Livinston St.
Northvale, NJ 07647

0472
Barre Drug. Co., Inc.

11463
Barry Labs., Inc.
461 N.E. 27th St.
Pompano Beach, FL 33064

0893
Barry-Martin Pharmaceuticals, Inc.
5792 S. W. 8th St.
Miami, FL 33144

Barth Nutritional Supplements, Inc.
270 W. Merrick Rd.
Valley Stream, NY 11582

Bay Laboratories, Inc.
3654 West Jarvis
Skokie, IL 60076

Bausch & Lomb
Rochester, NY 14692

Baybank Drug Co., Inc.
See: Endo Labs.

0568
Baylor Laboratories Inc.
See: Norwich Eaton Pharmaceuticals

0486
Beach Pharmaceuticals
Div. of Beach Products, Inc.
P.O. Box 13447
Tampa, FL 33611

0029
Beecham Laboratories
Div. of Beecham, Inc.
501 Fifth St.
Bristol, TN 37620

Beecham Products
Div. of Beecham, Inc.
P.O. Box 1467
Pittsburgh, PA 15230

Beiersdorf, Inc.
P.O. Box 5529
South Norwalk, CT 06856

Bell & Co.
See: C. S. Dent & Co.

0368
Bell Pharmacal Corp.
P.O. Box 1968
Greenville, SC 29602

0892
Bell Therapeutic Supplies, Inc.
396 Rockaway Ave.
Valley Stream, NY 11581

Bellis' Santa Maria Drug
See: Anatox Co.

Bentex Pharmaceuticals
Div. ICN Corporation

Berkeley Biologicals
1831 Second Street
Berkeley, CA 94710

Berkeley Drug Co.
See: Alton Products Inc.

0475
Berkeley Laboratories
356 Warren Ave.
Stirling, NJ 07980

50419
Berlex Laboratories, Inc.
Subs. Schering AG
110 East Hanover Ave.
Cedar Knolls, NJ 07927

Beta Dyne Corp.
22 Park Place
New York City, NY 10007

0283
Beutlich, Inc.
7149 N. Austin Ave.
Niles, IL 60648

0875
Bio-Factor Labs.
103 South Elm St.
Marshville, NC 28103

Birchwood Laboratories, Inc.
7900 Fuller Road
Eden Prairie, MN 55344

12136
Bird Corp.
Subs. 3M Company
3101 East Alejo Road
Palm Springs, CA 92263

0165
Blaine Co.
2700 Dixie Highway
Fort Mitchell, KY 41017

0154
Blair Laboratories, Inc.
Subs. Purdue Fredrick Co.

Block Drug Co., Inc.
257 Cornelison Ave.
Jersey City, NJ 07302

1016
Bluco, Inc.
14849 W. McNichols
Detroit, MI 48235

Blue Cross
See: Halsey Drug Co., Inc.

0529
Blue Line Chemical Co., The
302 S. Broadway
St. Louis, MO 63102

0563
Bock Pharmacal Co.
5435 Highland Park Drive
St. Louis, MO 63110

0597
Boehringer Ingelheim
90 East Ridge
P.O. Box 368
Ridgefield, CT 06877

Boots Laboratories, Inc.
433 Commercial Ave.
Palisades Park, NJ 07650

11489
Boots Pharmaceuticals, Inc.
6540 Line Avenue
P.O. Box 6750
Shreveport, LA 71136

Borden Inc., Pharmaceutical Prod.
Div. Syntex Lab., Inc.
Stanford Industrial Park
Palo Alto, CA 94304

0252
Bowman Pharmaceuticals
Div. Jones Medical Industries
11710 Lackland Industrial Dr.
St. Louis, MO 63146

Boyd Pharmacal Co.
205 Mitchell St.
P.O. Box 552
Newland, NC 28657

0222
Boyle & Co. Company Pharmaceuticals
1030 S. Arroyo Parkway
Pasadena, CA 91105

Breck, John H., Inc.
Berdan Ave.
P.O. Box 325
Wayne, NJ 07470

0057
Breon Laboratories Inc.
See: Winthop-Breon Labs.

Briar Pharmacal, Inc.
See: North American Pharmacal

0015
Bristol Laboratories
Div. Bristol-Myers Co.
P.O. Box 4755
Syracuse, NY 13221

Bristol Myers Oncology Division
Bristol Laboratories
P.O. Box 4755
Syracuse, NY 13221

19810
Bristol-Myers Products
Div. Bristol-Myers Co.
345 Park Avenue
New York, NY 10154

Broemmel Pharmaceuticals
See: Riker Labs.

1212
Brown Medicine Co.
P.O. Box 3345
Knoxville, TN 37917

0248
Brown Pharmaceutical Co., The
2500 West 6th Street
Los Angeles, CA 90057

Buckley Pharmaceuticals
Subs. Schaffer Labs.

10244
Buffington
Div. of Otis Clapp & Son, Inc.

Burgin-Arden, Inc.
18220 N.E. San Rafael
Portland, OR 97230

Burleson Ointment Co.
P.O. Box 6405
Grand Rapids, MI 49506

0479
Burlington Pharmacal, Inc.
274 N. Graham
Hopedale Road, Box 3311
Burlington, NC 27215

0081
Burroughs Wellcome Co.
3030 Cornwallis Road
Research Triangle Park, NC 27709

0247
Burton, Parsons & Co., Inc.
See: Alcon/ B. P.

Bush Labs.
4200 Laclede Ave.
St. Louis, MO 63108

0128
Calgon Consumer Prod. Co., Inc.
Sub. of Merck & Co.

Calvital Pharmaceutical Corp.
679 E. 138th Street
Bronx, NY 10454

17021
Cameron Medical Corp.
2716 E. Florence Ave.
Huntington Park, CA 90255

0163
Campbell Laboratories, Inc.
P.O. Box 812, FDR Station
New York, NY 10150

Campana Corp.
Campana Bldg.
Div. of Purex Corp.
Batavia, IL 60510

Campbell Pharmaceuticals, Inc.
See: Ayerst Laboratories

0398
C and M Pharmacal, Inc.
1519 E. Eight Mile Rd.
Hazel Park, MI 48030

0574
Canfield, C.R., & Co.
See: Paddock Labs.

11312
Carbo-Fung Labs., Inc.
798 No. Coney Ave.
Azusa, CA 91702

0526
Carlton Corp., The
See: Glenwood Labs. Inc.

Carnation Co.
5045 Wilshire Blvd.
Los Angeles, CA 90036

Carnation Research Labs.
8015 Van Nuys Blvd.
Van Nuys, CA 91412

Carnrick Laboratories
Div. of G. W. Carnrick Co.
65 Horse Hill Road
Cedar Knolls, NY 07927

0444
Carr Drug Co.
101 South St.
Peoria, IL 61602

Carrtone Labs., Inc.
See: Century Labs., Inc.

0381
Carter-Glogau Laboratories
Div. of Chromalloy Pharmaceuticals, Inc.
5160 W. Bethany Home Road
Glendale, AZ 85301

Carter Products
Div. Carter-Wallace, Inc.
Half Acre Rd.
Cranbury, NJ 08512

Celebre, Ernest P., R. Ph
4500 6th St.
Kenosha, WI 53140

0556
Cenci, H. R., Laboratories, Inc.
152 N. Broadway
Fresno, CA 93701

0268
Center Laboratories
35 Channel Drive
Port Washington, NY 11050

Centerchem Pharmaceuticals, Inc.
475 Park Avenue South
New York, NY 10016

0131
Central Pharmaceuticals, Inc.
110–128 E. Third St.
P.O. Box 328
Seymour, IN 47274

0436
Century Pharmaceuticals, Inc.
10377 Hague Road
Indianapolis, IN 46256

Cetylite Industries, Inc.
9051 River Road
Pennsauken, NJ 08110

41167
Chattem Laboratories
Div. of Chattem, Inc.
1715 W. 38th St.
Chattanooga, TN 37409

Chesebrough-Pond's Inc.
Div. Professional Prods.
40 Merritt Boulevard
Trumbull, CT 06611

Chicago Pharmacal Co.
See: Conal Pharmaceuticals

Chilton Laboratories, Inc.
See: Ivy Corporation

Chromalloy Pharmaceuticals, Inc
See: Carter-Glogau Laboratories

Churchill Pharmaceuticals, Inc.
P.O. Box 8581
Richmond, VA 23226

0083
Ciba Pharmaceutical Co.
Div. of Ciba-Geigy Corp.
556 Morris Ave.
Summit, NJ 07901

0659
Circle Pharmaceuticals, Inc.
10377 Hague Road
Indianapolis, IN 46256

Citroleum Co.
1054 North Ave.
Bridgeport, CT 06606

City Chemical Corp.
132 W. 22nd St.
New York, NY 10011

10244
Clapp, Otis & Son, Inc.
See: Otis Clapp

Clark-West
Div. of Syntex Labs.

0223
CMC Pharmaceuticals
Div. of Consolidated Midland

0385
Coast Laboratories, Inc.
521 W. 17th St.
Long Beach, CA 90813

30491
Coastal Pharmaceutical Co., Inc.
2509 Granby St.
Norfolk, VA 23517

0055
Cole Pharmacal Co., Inc.
See: O'Neal, Jones and Feldman Pharmaceuticals

0552
Comatic Labs., Inc.

Combe Inc.
1101 Westchester Ave.
White Plains, NY 10604

10310
Commerce Drug Co., Inc.
Div. Del Labs, Inc.
565 Broad Hollow Rd.
Farmingdale, NY 11735

Conal Pharmaceuticals
Alcon—Specialty Products Division
P.O. Box 1959
Fort Worth, TX 76101

Connaught Laboratories, Inc.
Subs. E.R. Squibb Co.

0223
Consolidated Midland Corp.
195 E. Main St., Box 74
Brewster, NY 10509

C-D Consumer Products
P.O. Box 5716
Jacksonville, FL 32207

Continental Labs., Inc.
3106 Spring St.
P.O. Box 5242
Redwood City, CA 94063

ConvaTec
Subs. E.R. Squibb Co.
P.O. Box 4000
Princeton, NJ 08540

Cook-Waite Laboratories, Inc.
90 Park Avenue
New York, NY 10016

0058
CooperCare, Inc.
See: Oral B Labs. and Rydell Labs.

0041
Cooper Laboratories (P.R.), Inc.
P.O. Box 367
San German, PR 00753

0041
Cooper Laboratories, Inc.
Oral-B Division
305 Fairfield Avenue
Fairfield, NJ 07006

0041
Cooper Laboratories, Inc.
Dermatological Division
305 Fairfield Avenue
Fairfield, NJ 07006

0041
Cooper Laboratories, Inc.
Sparta Instrument Division
600 McCormick Street
San Leandro, CA 94577

0058
CooperVision, Inc.
Mountain View Division
455 E. Middlefield Road
Mountain View, CA 94043

0058
CooperVision Pharmaceuticals, Inc.
P.O. Box 367
San German, PR 00753

Cord Pharmaceuticals
See: Geneva Generics

B.C. Cowley Co.
P.O. Box 185
Worcester, MA 01613

Crane-Hall Corp.
659 Lofstrand Lane
P.O. Box 1531
Rockville, MD 20850

Creighton Products Corp.
Subs. Ex-Lax Pharm.

Creomulsion Co.
345 Glen Iris Dr., N.E.
Box 1214
Atlanta, GA 30301

10244
Cross
Div. of Otis Clapp & Son, Inc.

12418
Culminal, Inc.
Box 8
Union City, NJ 07087

0357
Cumberland Mfg. Co.
501 25th Avenue No.
Nashville, TN 37202

0575
Cummins Pharmaceutical Co
See: Baker/Cummins

0161
Cutter Biological
Div., Miles Labs., Inc.
2200 Powell Street
Emeryville, CA 94608

Dairy House Inc.
105 W. Adams St.
Chicago, IL 60603

0282
Dalin Pharmaceuticals, Inc.

0689
Daniels Pharmaceuticals
2527 25th Ave. N.
St. Petersburg, FL 33713

11696
Dattel Pharmaceutical Co., Inc.
4300 Houma Blvd., Suite 101
Metairie, LA 70002

Davies, Rose-Hoyt Pharmaceutical
Hoyt Labs
633 Highland Ave.
Needham, MA 02194

Davis Labs., Inc.
P.O. Box 747
Cherry Hill, NJ 08034

0005
Davis and Geck
Div. of American Cyanamid Co.

0425
Day-Baldwin Inc.

Daywell Laboratories Corp.
78Unquowa Place
P.O. Box 490
Fairfield, CT 06430

0657
DDR Pharmaceutical Corp.
8 Ditomas Ct.
Copiague, NY 11726

Defco Pharmaceuticals
7223 Canoga Ave.
P.O. Box 627
Canoga Park, CA 91305

Dekens Products
Div. of J. H. Guild Co. Inc.
Rupert, VT 05678

Del Laboratories, Inc.
565 Broad Hollow Road
Farmingdale, NY 11735

Delbay Pharmaceuticals, Inc.
See: Schering Corporation

de Leon Labs.
P.O. Box 867
Douglasville, GA 30133

Delmont Laboratories, Inc.
P.O. Box AA
Swarthmore, PA 19081

10310
Del Laboratories, Inc.
See: Commerce Drug. Co.

0316
Del-Ray Laboratories, Inc.
27-Twentieth Avenue N.W.
Birmingham, AL 35215

0827
Delta Drug Corp.
1034 Hendricks Ave.
P.O. Box 10126
Jacksonville, FL 32207

DePree Co., The
See: Eckerd Drug Co.

0587
Dermakon Laboratories
Div. Preston Pharmaceutics, Inc.
P.O. Box 8
Butler, NJ 07405

0088
Derm-Arts Labs.
See: Marion Labs., Inc.

Dermatologicals, Inc.
Div. of Day-Baldwin, Inc.

0066
Dermik Laboratories, Inc.
1777 Walton Road, Dublin Hall
Blue Bell, PA 19422

Devlin Pharmaceuticals, Inc.
700 North Sepulveda Blvd.
El Segundo, CA 90245

DeWitt Drug & Beauty Products, Inc.
See: DeWitt International Corp.

10327
DeWitt International Corp.
P.O. Box 6827
Greenville, SC 29606

0737
D'Franssia Corp.
4505 W. First St.
Los Angeles, CA 90004

Dickey Drug Co.
1009 West State St.
Bristol, VA 24201

Dillard & Co., R. Yates
See: Hyrex Co.

0617
Dios Chem. Co.
4200 Laclede Ave.
St. Louis, MO 63108

0777
Dista Products Co.
Div. of Eli Lily Co.
P.O. Box 1407
Indianapolis, IN 46206

Doak Pharmacal Co., Inc.
700 Shames Drive
P.O. Box 1023
Westbury, L.I., NY 11590

Dolcin Corporation
381 Broadway
Westwood, NJ 07675

Dome Laboratories
See: Miles Pharmaceuticals

0221
Dooner Labs., Inc.
See: William H. Rorer, Inc.

0043
Dorsey Laboratories
Div. Sandoz Inc.
N.E., U.S. 6 & Interstate 80
P.O. Box 83288
Lincoln, NE 68501

19041
Doshire, Inc.
Superon Drug Division
3441 W. Montrose
Chicago, IL 60618

Douglas Pharmaceutical Industries, Inc.
8906 Rosehill Road
Leneya, KS 66215

Dover Pharmaceutical, Inc.
Boston, MA 02139

0183
Dow Pharmaceuticals
See: Merrell Dow Pharmaceuticals

0212
Doyle Pharmaceutical Co.
See: Sandoz Nutrition

Drackett Products Co.
Div. Mead Johnson Nutritionals
201 East 4th Street
Cincinnati, OH 45201

Dram Pharmaceuticals, Inc.

0261
Drug Industries Co. Inc.
3237 Hilton Road
Ferndale, MI 48220

Drug Products Co., Inc.

Duke Labs, Inc.
See: Beiersdorf, Inc.

Dumas-Wilson & Co.
See: Mallinckrodt

0217
Dunhall Pharmaceuticals, Inc.
Highway 59 N
P.O. Box 100
Gravette, AR 72736

DuPont de Nemours, E.I., & Co., Inc.
Pharmaceutical Div.
1007 Market Street
Wilmington, DE 19898

Durst, S.F. & Co., Inc.
See: O'Neal, Jones & Feldman Pharmaceuticals

Eastern Chemical Div.
Guardian Chemical Corp.
230 Marcus Blvd.
Hauppage, NY 11787

0721
Eastern Research Lab., Inc.
302 S. Central Ave.
Baltimore, MD 21202

0544
Eastwood Pharmacal Co., Inc.

0035
Eaton Laboratories
See: Norwich-Eaton Pharmaceuticals

Eaton-Merz Laboratories
Div. Norwich-Eaton Pharmaceuticals
17 Eaton Avenue
Norwich, NY 13815

Eckerd Drug Company
8333 Bryan Dairy Road
P.O. Box 4689
Clearwater, FL 33518

Economed Pharmaceuticals, Inc.
P.O. Box 3303
Burlington, NC 27215

12336
Econo-Rx, Inc.
2 Blue Ridge St.
Blairsville, GA 30512

0485
Edwards Pharmacal Co.
100 East Hale
P.O. Drawer 129
Osceola, AR 72370

0163
Elder Pharmaceuticals
222 North Vincent Ave.
Covina, CA 91722

0641
Elkins-Sinn, Inc.
Subs. A.H. Robins Co.
2 Esterbrook Lane
P.O. Box 5483
Cherry Hill, NJ 08034

Emerson Labs.
See: Humco Laboratory

0111
Emko Co.
Div. Schering Corp.
7912 Manchester Ave.
St. Louis, MO 63143

0056
Endo Labs., Inc.
See E.I. du Pont de Nemours & Co., Inc.

Enzyme Process Co., Inc.
19727 Bahama St.
Northridge, CA 91324

Eric, Kirk & Gary, Inc.
9474 Crestfield
Westchester, OH 45069

Etherea Inc.
See: Revlon Inc.

Ever-Dry Corp.
Div. Scherer Labs., Inc.
P.O. Drawer 400009
Dallas, TX 75240

0642
Everett Laboratories, Inc.
76 Franklin Street
East Orange, NJ 07017

Ex-Lax Pharmaceutical Co., Inc
605 Third Avenue
New York, NY 10158

Factor, Max, & Co.
Sales Div.
1655 N. McCadden Pl.
P.O. Box 2323
Hollywood, CA 90028

Faraday Labs., Inc.
100 Hoffman Place
Hillside, NJ 07205

0267
Federal Pharmacal Corp.,
See: U.S. Products, Inc.

0496
Ferndale Labs, Inc.
780 W. Eight Mile Rd.
Ferndale, MI 48220

Ferring Pharmaceuticals, Inc.
See: Centerchem Products, Inc.

Fidelity Prescriptions Labs., Inc.
42 Wyoming St.
Daytona, OH 45409

0421
Fielding Pharm. Co., Inc.
8181 Big Bend
P.O. Box 13017
St. Louis, MO 63119

0274
First Texas Pharmaceuticals, Inc.
See: Scherer Labs., Inc.

0585
Fisons Corp.
Pharmaceutical Div.
Two Preston Court
Bedford, MA 01730

0132
Fleet, C.B., Co., Inc.
4615 Murray Pl.
P.O. Box 11349
Lynchburg, VA 24505

Fleming and Company
1600 Fenpark Drive
Fenton, MO 63026

0048
Flint Laboratories
Div. Travenol Labs. Inc.
One Baxter Parkway
Deerfield, IL 60015

Flow Pharmaceuticals
See: CooperVision Pharmaceuticals

0288
Fluoritab Corp.
1927 Copeman Blvd., Box 381
Flint, MI 48501

Forest Pharmaceuticals, Inc.
2510 Metro Boulevard
Maryland Heights, MO 63043

0168
Fougera, E., & Co.
Div. of BYK-Gulden, Inc.
60 Baylis Road
Melville, NY 11747

0494
Foy Laboratories Div.
Foy Industries, Inc.
351 W. Penn Ave.
Wernersville, PA 19565

Freeport Drug Co., Inc.
4677 Stenstrom Road
Rockford, IL 61109

0141
Fuller Labs., Inc.
Div. of Parke, Davis & Company
7900 Fuller Rd.
Eden Prairie, MN 55343

0713
G & W Laboratories, Inc.
111 Coolidge Street
South Plainfield, NJ 07080

11853
Gaddy, R. L. Company
511 Hart St., P.O. Box 1076
Tallahassee, FL 32302

Galen Labs., Inc.
917 McGee St.
Kansas City, MO 64106

Garret Laboratories, Inc.
77 Brook E 23
Passiac, NJ 07055

0386
Gebauer Chemical Co.
9410 St. Catherine Ave.
Cleveland, OH 44104

0028
Geigy Pharmaceuticals
Div. of Ciba-Geigy Corp.
Ardsley, NY 10502

0674
General Pharmaceutical Prods., Inc.
3205 Johnson Rd.
Steubenville, OH 43952

General Drug Co.
200 N. Fairfield Ave.
Chicago, IL. 60612

0182
Generix Drug Sales Co., Inc.
3001 N. 29th Ave.
Hollywood, FL 33020

0835
Geneva Drugs Ltd.
P.O. Box 10
Pomona, NY 10970

Gerber Products Co.
445 State St.
Fremont, MI 49412

0249
Geriatric Pharm. Corp.
397 Jericho Turnpike
Floral Park, L.I., NY 11001

0535
Gilbert Laboratories
31 Fairmount Avenue
Chester, NJ 07930

0173
Glaxo Incorporated
P.O. Box 13960
Five Moore Drive
Research Triangle Park, NC 27709

12843
Glenbrook Labs.
Div. of Sterling Drug, Inc.
90 Park Ave.
New York City, NY 10016

0516
Glenwood Labs., Inc.
83 North Summit St.
Box 518
Tenafly, NJ 07670

Golden-West, Co.
135 S. Central Street
Knoxville, TN 37902

Goldline Laboratories
1900 West Commercial Blvd.
Fort Lauderdale, FL 33309

Good Samaritan Laboratories, Inc.
P.O. Box 782
Norristown, PA 19404

Gordon Laboratories
State & Parkview Roads
Upper Darby, PA 19082

Gotham Pharm. Co., Inc.
See: Ormont Drug and Chemical Co., Inc.

Graco Pharmaceutical Co.
172 West Main St.
Meriden, CT 06450

0698
Grafton Pharmaceutical Co.

Grant Labs.
6020 Adeline Street
Oakland, CA 94608

0152
Gray Pharmaceutical Co.
Subs. Purdue Fredrick Co.

Greco Pharmacal, Inc.
See: Doak Pharmacal Co., Inc.

Grove Lab., Inc.
See: Bristol-Myers Co.

0327
Guardian Chem. Corp.
See: United-Guardian, Inc.

Guild, J. H., Co., Inc.
10 Main Street
Rupert, VT 05768

Haack Labs., Inc.
See: Lemmon Pharmacal Co.

Haag Inc.
5 South 15th St.
Richmond, VA 23219

0841
Haberle Drug Co.
See:. Bowman Pharmaceuticals, Inc.

Halsey Drug Co., Inc.
1827 Pacific St.
Brooklyn, NY 11233

Halsted Pharmaceuticals, Inc.
444 Bedford Rd.
P.O. Box 3
Pleasantville, NY 10570

Hanford, G. C., Mfr. Co.
304 Oneida St.
Post Office Box 1055
Syracuse, NY 13201

Hankscraft Co.
Div. of Gerber Products Co.
Booster Blvd.
P.O. Box 120
Reedsburg, WI 53959

Hanlon Drug Prods.
500 Church St.
Poughkeepsie, NY 12601

0372
Hannaway, R. T., Inc.
P.O. Box 8217, 50 Clemence St.
Cranston, RI 02920

Haskell, Charles C. & Co.,
Div. Arnar Stone Labs., Inc.

Hauck, W. E., Inc.
1207 Alpharetta St.
P.O. Box 1065
Roswell, GA 30075

Health Care Industries Inc.
2825 Middlebury St.
P.O. Box 878
Elkhart, IN 46515

0023
Herbert Laboratories
See: Allergan Pharmaceuticals, Inc.

Herring, Louis C., & Co.
P.O. Box 2191
2501 S. Orange Ave.
Orlando, FL 32806

0514
Hickam, Dow B., Inc.
P.O. Box 2006
Sugar Land, TX 77478

High Chemical Company
1760 N. Howard St.
Philadelphia, PA 19122

Hill Dermaceuticals
Div. of Beach Products, Inc.
P.O. Box 19283
Orlando, FL 32814

Hobart Labs., Inc.
900 N. Franklin St.
Chicago, IL 60610

0039
Hoechst-Roussel Pharmaceuticals Inc.
Div. American Hoechst Corp.
Route 202–206 North
Somerville, NJ 08876

Holland-Rantos Co., Inc.
Enterprise Avenue
P.O. Box 5147
Trenton, NJ 08638

0118
Hollister-Stier Labs.
Div. Miles Labs., Inc.
400 Morgan Lane
West Haven, CT 06516

Hope Co.
158 Saddleford Dr.
Chesterfield, MO 63017

0126
Hoyt Laboratories
Div. Colgate-Palmolive Co.
633 Highland Ave.
Needham, MA 02194

0395
Humco Laboratory, Inc.
P.O. Drawer 2550
Texarkana, TX 75501

0219
Humphreys Pharmacal, Inc.
63 Meadow Rd.
Rutherford, NJ 07070

0553
Hydrosal Co.
5927 St. Rt. 128
P.O. Box 8
Miamitown, OH 45041

Hygiene Research, Inc.
See Day-Baldwin

0944
Hyland Labs.
Div. Travenol Labs., Inc.
P.O. Box 1976
Glendale, CA 91202

0011
Hynson, Westcott & Dunning
Subs. Becton Dickinson
Charles & Chase Sts.
Baltimore, MD 21201

0314
Hyrex Pharmaceuticals
3494 Democrat Road
P.O. Box 18385
Memphis, TN 38118

ICI Americas, Inc.
3411 Silverside Road
P.O. Box 751
Wilmington, DE 19897

0187
ICN Pharmaceuticals
222 N. Vincent Ave.
Covina, CA 91722

Image Products, Inc.
See: U.S. Products, Inc.

Ingram Pharmaceuticals
See: Syntex Laboratories

0633
Inland Alkaloid Co.
4200 Laclede Ave.
St. Louis, MO 63108

Inolex Pharm.
Div. of Inolex Corp.
3 Science Rd.
Glenwood, IL 60425

12805
International Chem. Labs
185 Park Dr.
Eastchester, NY 10707

0177
International Drug, Inc.
See: C-D Consumer Products

0125
International Pharmaceutical Corporation
See: Marion Labs., Inc.

0814
Interstate Drug Exchange, Inc.
Engineers Hill
Plainview, L.I., NY 11803

0467
Invenex Laboratories
Div. Life Technologies, Inc.
5885 Lakehurst Drive
Orlando, FL 32819

0258
Inwood Laboratories, Inc.
Div. of Forest Laboratories, Inc.
300 Prospect St.
Inwood, NY 11696

11808
Ion Labs, Inc.
112 Holder Dr.
Hurst, TX 76053

0082
Ives Labs., Inc.
685 Third Ave.
New York, NY 10017

12126
Ivy Corporation
23 Fairfield Pl.
West Caldwell, NJ 07006

Jackson-Mitchell Pharmaceuticals, Inc.
P.O. Box 934
Turlock, CA 95381

Jalco
See: Misemer Pharm., Inc.

Jamieson-McKames, Inc.
3227 Morganford Road
St. Louis, MO 63116

Jamol Labs., Inc.
13 Ackerman Ave.
Emerson, NJ 07630

Janssen Pharmaceutica
Div. Johnson and Johnson
40 Kingsbridge Road
Piscataway, NJ 08854

11588
Jeffrey Martin, Inc.
410 Clermont Terrace
Union, NJ 07083

0397
Jenkins Labs., Inc.

0171
Johnson, Matt, Co.
1114 4th Street
Devils Lake, ND 58301

0137
Johnson & Johnson
Baby Products Co.
Grandview Rd.
Skillman, NJ 08558

0992
Kahlenberg Labs.
Div. T. E. Watson Co.
P.O. Box 3829
Sarasota, FL 33578

Kasdenol Corporation
50 Elm Street
Huntington, NY 11743

0351
Kay Pharmacal Co., Inc.
P.O. Box 50375
1312 N. Utica Ave.
Tulsa, OK 74150

Kedrin Pharmacals, Inc.
See: Dolcin Corp.

0588
Keene Pharmaceuticals Inc.
P.O. Box 7
333 S. Mockingbird
Keene, TX 76059

Kendall Co., The
Bauer & Black Div.
1 Federal St.
Boston, MA 02110

0482
Kenwood Labs., Inc.
490A Main Street
New Rochelle, NY 10801

Kenyon Drug Co.
Box 362
Mechanicsville, IA 52306

Kerr, Frank, Chemical Co.
43155 W. Nine Mile Rd.
P.O. Box 436
Novi, MI 48050

Ketchum Labs., Inc.
See: Steri-Med, Inc.

0369
Key Pharmaceuticals, Inc.
18425 N.W. 2nd Ave.
P.O. Box 693670
Miami, FL 33269

0285
King Pharmaceutical Co., Inc.
26 N. 77th St.
Birmingham, AL 35206

Kinney & Co., Inc.
1307 12th St.
P.O. Box 307
Columbus, IN 47201

0098
Kirkman Labs., Inc.
934 N.E. 25th Avenue
Portland, OR 97232

Klug Labs., Inc.
See: Galen Labs.

Knickerbocker Biologics Div.
See: Charles Pfizer & Co., Inc.

0044
Knoll Pharm. Co.
30 North Jefferson Rd.
Whippany, NJ 07981

Kondon Mfg. Co.
Div. Wonderful Dream Salve Corp.
P.O. Box 223
Croswell, MI 48422

0091
Kremers-Urban Co.
See: William H. Rorer

Laboratory Diagnostics Co., Inc.
Drawer 160
620 Route 520
Morganville, NJ 07751

La Cross
Div. Del Labs., Inc.

La Crosse Pharm. Co.
Div. Whittaker Corp.
1502 Miller Dr.
La Crosse, WI 54601

Lactona Prods.(Div.-
Warner-Lambert Pharm.)
201 Tabor Rd.
Morris Plains, NJ 07950

Lafayette Pharmacal, Inc.
4200 South Hulen Street
Fort Worth, TX 76109

0073
Lakeside Laboratories, Inc.
See: Richardson-Merrell Inc.

0348
Lambda Pharmacal Lab.
See: Medtech Laboratories, Inc.

0527
Lannett Co., Inc., The
9000 State Rd.
Philadelphia, PA 19136

10648
Larson Labs., Inc.
1320 Irwin Drive
Erie, PA 16505

La Salle Laboratories
Div. Del Labs., Inc.

0277
Laser, Inc.
2000 N. Main St.
P.O. Box 905
Crown Point, IN 46307

12434
Last, Alvin, Inc.
145 Palisades St.
Dobbs Ferry, NY 10522

10651
Lavoptik Co., Inc.
661 Western Av. N.
St. Paul, MN 55103

0005
Lederle Laboratories
Div. of American Cyanamid
Co.
N. Middletown Rd.
P.O. Box 500
Pearl River, NY 10965

Lee-Colbert Div.
See: Daniels, Robert and Co.

Leeming Division
Pfizer, Incorporated
100 Jefferson Road
Parsippany, NJ 07054

Lehn & Fink Products Group
Div. Sterling Drug Inc.
225 Summit Ave.
Montvale, NJ 07645

Leicy's, Inc.
1531–33 W. Market St.
Steubenville, OH 43952

17201
Leland Laboratories, Inc.
West Wade Hampton Blvd.
Greer, SC 29651

0093
Lemmon Company
P.O. Box 30
Sellersville, PA 18960

0162
Lewis-Howe Co.
319 S. 4th St.
St. Louis, MO 63102

0284
Lexington Chemical Co., Inc.
27 Jones Road
Box 609
Waltham, MA 02154

14869
Lexalabs, Inc.
P.O. Box 5234
Lenexa, KS 66215

Lif-O-Gen, Div.
Allied Healthcare Prods., Inc,
1720 Sublette Ave.
St. Louis, MO 63110

0002
Lilly, Eli & Co.
740 S. Alabama St.
Box 618
Indianapolis, IN 46206

Lincoln Labs., Inc.
Hickory Point Rd.
Box 1139
Decatur, IL 62525

Lloyd Brothers, Inc.
See: Hoechst-Roussel

Loma Linda Food Co.
11503 Pierce St.
Riverside, CA 92515

0273
Lorvic Corp., The
8810 Frost Ave.
St. Louis, MO 63134

Luden's Inc.
200 North 8th St.
Reading, PA 19603

0618
Luyties Pharmacal Co.
4200 Laclede Ave.
St. Louis, MO 63108

0466
Macsil, Inc.
1326 Frankford Ave.
Philadelphia, PA 19125

Madison Labs.
380 North St.
Teterboro, NJ 07608

0179
Madland Laboratories,
Inc.

Major Pharmaceutical Corp.
See: Michigan Pharmacal
Corp.

0166
Mallard, Inc.
3021 Wabash Ave.
Detroit, MI 48216

Mallincrodt Pharmaceutics
Div.
See: Wallace Laboratories

Maltbie Lab.
See: WTS-Pharmacraft
Div. Wallace and Tiernan

Mann Chemical Corp.
520 W. Main St.
Louisville, KY 40202

10706
Manne, Kenneth A. Co.
1522 Cleveland Ave., N.W.
P.O. Box 8649
Canton, OH 44711

Manola Company
4200 Laclede Ave.
St. Louis, MO 63108

Marin Pharmaceuticals
P.O. Box 174
Miami, FL 33144

0088
Marion Laboratories, Inc.
P.O. Box 9627
Kansas City, MO 64134

12939
Marlop Pharmaceuticals, Inc.
5752 Fieldston Road, Box 536
Bronx, NY 10471

Marlyn Company, Inc.
3071 S. Harbour Blvd.
Santa Ana, CA 92704

Marsh-Emory Laboratories, Inc.
600 Chama, N.E.
Albuquerque, NM 87108

0692
Martin-Phillips Labs.
8604 Verree Rd.
Philadelphia, PA 19115

12758
Mason Pharmaceuticals
P.O. Box 8330
1201 Dove Street, Suite 520
Newport Beach, CA 92660

Massengill, S.E., Co., The
See: Beecham Laboratories

0314
Matco Drug Company
See: Hyrex Pharmaceuticals

Maurry Biological Co., Inc.
6109 S. Western Avenue
Los Angeles, CA 90047

Mayer Lab., Inc.
701 Bridgeway Blvd.
P.O. Box 1336
Sausalito, CA 94965

0259
Mayrand, Inc.
1026 E. Lindsay St.
P.O. Box 20246
Greensboro, NC 27407

11089
McGregor & Co.
32580 Grand River Ave.
Farmington, MI 48024

0022
McKesson Laboratories
See: M.K. Laboratories, Inc.

0045
Mc Neil Consumer Products Co.
Subs. McNEILAB, Inc.
500 Office Center Drive
Fort Washington, PA 19034

Mc Neil Pharmaceutical
Subs. McNEILAB, Inc.
Spring House, PA 19477

0087
Mead Johnson & Company
2404 Pennsylvania St.
Evansville, IN 47721

11940
Medco Lab., Inc.
716 West Seventh St.
P.O. Box 864
Sioux City, IA 51102

0764
Medco Supply Co.
2410 Kilgore Ave.
Muncie, IN 47304

0244
Medicone Co.
225 Varick St.
New York, NY 10014

0184
Medics Pharmaceutical
See: U.S. Chemical Marketing Group

0645
Medi-Rx Pharmaceuticals, Inc.
45 N. Palmer
Houston, TX 77003

Medtech Laboratories, Inc.
721 Sheridan Avenue
P.O. Box 2930
Cody, WY 82414

45800
Menley & James Labs.
Subs. SmithKline Corp.
P.O. Box 8082
1500 Spring Garden St.
Philadelphia, PA 19101

Mennen Co.
Hanover Ave.
P.O. Box 1000
Morristown, NJ 07960

Mentholatum Co., The
1360 Niagara St.
Buffalo, NY 14213

12814
Merchant Pharmaceutical Co., Inc.
4 South Third St., P.O. Box 527
Warrenton, VA 22186

0006
Merck Sharp & Dohme
Div. Merck & Co., Inc.
West Point, PA 19486

Merck Sharp & Dohme AGVET
Div. Merck & Co., Inc.
P.O. Box 2000
Rahway, NJ 07065

0394
Mericon Industries, Inc.
420 S. W. Washington St.
P.O. Box 5759
Peoria, IL 61601

Merieux Institute, Inc.
1200 N.W. 78th Ave.
Suite 109
Miami, FL 33126

0429
Merit Pharmaceutical Company, Inc.
See: Scherer Labs., Inc.

0183
Merrell Dow Pharmaceuticals, Inc.
Subs. Dow Chemical Company
2110 E. Galbraith Rd.
Cincinnati, OH 45215

36969
Merrell Dow Laboratories Inc. (P.R.)
2110 E. Galbraith Rd.
Cincinnati, OH 45215

0322
Merrick Medicine Co.
P.O. Box 1489
Waco, TX 76703

Meyer Labs., Inc.
See: Glaxo Inc.

Michigan Pharmacal Corp.
531-603 Vester
Ferndale, MI 48220

0816
Midway Medical Co., Inc.
103 Samson St.
Glasgow, KY 42141

0192
Miles Laboratories, Inc.
Consumer Products Div.
1127 Myrtle Street
Elkhart, IN 46514

0026
Miles Pharmaceuticals
Div. Miles Laboratories, Inc.
400 Morgan Lane
West Haven, CT 06516

0396
Milex Products
5915 Northwest Hwy.
Chicago, IL 60631

Miller Pharmacal Group, Inc.
P.O. Box 279
245 W. Roosevelt Rd.
West Chicago, IL 60185

Mills Pharmaceuticals, Inc.

Mill-Mark Pharmaceuticals, Inc.
1090 Englewood Ave.
Buffalo, NY 14223

Milton Roy Company
Milroy Laboratories Division
P.O. Drawer 849
Sarasota, FL 33578

Minette Pharm. Corp.
3024 Genesee St.
P.O. Box 142
Buffalo, NY 14225

0276
Misemer Pharmaceuticals, Inc.
4553 South Campbell St.
P.O. Box 3177
Glenstone Sta.
Springfield, MO 65804

0178
Mission Pharmacal Co.
1325 E. Durango St.
P.O. Box 1676
San Antonio, TX 78296

M. J. Labs.
P.O. Box 432, Little River Sta.
Miami, FL 33138

M.K. Laboratories, Inc.
424Grasmere Ave.
Fairfield, CT 06430

Modern Products, Inc.
3015 W. Vera Ave.
P.O. Box 09398
Milwaukee, WI 53209

Monsanto Chemical Co.
800 North Lindbergh Boulevard
St. Louis, MO 63167

11868
Monticello Drug Co.
45 Broad St. Viaduct
Jacksonville, FL 32202

Moore, Edward J., Sons, Inc.
46–44 11th St.
Long Island City, N.Y. 11101

0839
Moore, H. L., Drug Exchange, Inc.
370 John Downey Dr.
New Britain, CT 06050

0133
Moore Kirk Labs., Inc.
Div. of the Zemmer Co.

01277
Morton Pharmaceuticals, Inc.
1625–39 N. Highland St.
P.O. Box 8037
Memphis, TN 38108

Moss Chemical Co. Inc.
183 St. Paul St.
Rochester, NY 14604

0543
Mosso, C. A. Co., Inc.
See: Health Care Industries Inc.

Moyco Industries, Inc.
S.E. Cor 21st and Clearfield Sts.
Philadelphia, PA 19132

M.P.L. Labs.
509 Washington Ave., S.
Minneapolis, MN 55401

Mulford Labs.
Div. Lemmon Pharmacal Co.
Sellersville, PA 18960

Murine Company
See: Abbott Labs., Consumer Prods. Div.

0451
Muro Pharmacal Inc.
890 East Street
Tewksbury, MA 01876

0897
National Magnesia Co., Inc.
70-36 83rd Street
Glendale, NY 11385

Neisler Labs., Inc.
See: Marion Labs., Inc.

Neoco Corp.
See: Nion Corp.

0487
Nephron Corporation
3319 Pacific Ave., P.O. Box 1974
Tacoma, WA 98401

Neutrogena Corp.
5755 W. 96th St.
Los Angeles, CA 90045.

Nevin, J. R., Co., Inc.
183 Royal Parkway West
Williamsville, NY 14221

New England Pharmaceutical Co.
14 Westerfield Rd.
Hamden, CT 06714

10797
New Skin Company
See: Medtech Laboratories, Inc.

Nion Corporation
11581 Federal Drive
El Monte, CA 91731

NMC Laboratories Inc.
See: National Magnesia Co.

0766
Norcliff Thayer Inc.
One Scarsdale Road
Tuckahoe, NY 10707

Nordisk-USA
6500 Rock Spring Drive
Bethesda, MD 20817

Norgine Laboratories, Inc.
2 Overhill Road
Scarsdale, NY 10583

Nortech Laboratories Inc.
4 Midland Avenue
Hicksville, NY 11801

0298
North American Pharm., Inc.
See: Vortech Pharm., Ltd.

0149
Norwich Eaton Pharmaceuticals
17 Eaton Ave.
Norwich, NY 13815

Novo Industries
Subs. E. R. Squibb Co.
120 Alexander St.
Princeton, NJ 08540

0362
Novocol Chemical Mfg. Co., Inc.
2911 Atlantic Ave.
Brooklyn, NY 11207

Noxell Corp.
11050 York Rd.
P.O. Box 1799
Baltimore, MD 21203

0159
Noyes, P. J. & Co.
101 Main St.
Lancaster, NH 03584

Nutrition Control Products
Div. Pharmex Inc.
2113 Lincoln St.
P.O. Box 151
Hollywood, FL 33022

Nutritional Biochemicals Corp.
26201 Miles Ave.
Cleveland, OH 44128

0477
Obetrol Pharmaceuticals
Div. of Rexar Pharmacal Corp.
396 Rockway Ave.
Valley Stream, NY 11581

O'Connor Products Co.
24400 Capitol
Redford, MI 48239

O'Neal, Jones and Feldman Pharmaceuticals
See: Forest Pharmaceuticals.

Oral-B Laboratories, Inc.
Subs. Gillette Co.
170 South Whisman Road
Mountain View, CA 94041

Orbar International Ltd.
711 S. Sleight St.
Naperville, IL 60540

Orbit Pharmaceutical Company Inc.
1304 N. 5th St.
Kansas City, KS 66101

0052
Organon Pharmaceuticals
375 Mt. Pleasant Ave.
West Orange, NJ 07052

0142
Ormont Drug & Chem. Co.
See: U.S. Products, Inc.

0191
Ortega Pharm. Co.
586 S. Edgewood Ave.
P.O. Box 6212
Jacksonville, FL 32205

0062
Ortho Diagnostic Systems Inc.
Div. Johnson and Johnson
Route 202
Raritan, NJ 08869

0062
Ortho Pharmaceutical Corp.
Route 202
Raritan, NJ 08869

0107
Ortho Pharmaceuticals, Inc.
P.O. Box 463
Manati, PR 00701

10244
Otis Clapp & Son, Inc.
143 Albany St.
Cambridge, MA 02139

0299
Owen Laboratories, Inc.
Div. of Alcon Labs., Specialty Prod. Div.
P.O. Box 1959
Ft. Worth, TX 76101

Oxford Laboratories Inc.
Dayton, VA 22821

0574
Paddock Laboratories, Inc.
3101 Louisiana Ave. North
Minneapolis, MN 55427

0271
Palmedico, Inc.
See: W. E. Hauck, Inc.

Pannett Products, Inc.
Div. of Dormin, Inc.
P.O. Box 723
Orleans, MA 02653

0318
Panray Pharmaceuticals
See: U.S. Products, Inc.

0638
Paraeusal Co.
1809 Belmont Ave.
Youngstown, OH 44504

0071
Parke-Davis
Div. Warner-Lambert Co.
201 Tabor Road
Morris Plains, NJ 07950

Parker Laboratories, Inc.
307 Washington Street
Orange, NJ 07050

0727
Park Plaza Pharmaceuticals, Inc.
11122 Walnut
Kansas City, MO 64114

0349
Parmed Pharmaceuticals
4220 Hyde Park Boulevard
Niagara Falls, NY 14305

0418
Pasadena Research Labs., Inc.
2107 E. Villa St.
Pasadena, CA 91107

Pascal Company, Inc.
2929 N. E. Northrup Way
Bellevue, WA 98004

Paschall Labs., Inc.
4116 Rainier Ave., S.
Seattle, WA 98118

Paxton, F. H. & Sons, Inc.
P.O. Box 729
Evanston, IL 60204

0884
Pedinol Pharmacal Inc.
110 Bell Street
West Babylon, NY 11704

0018
Pennwalt Corporation
Prescription Division
P.O. Box 1710
Rochester, NY 14603

Penta Products, Inc.
425 2nd St.
San Francisco, CA 94107

Perfumeria Brisas, Inc.
P.O. Box 384
Forest Hills, NY 11375

0799
Perry Labs., Inc.
14713 Gratiot St.
Detroit, MI 48205

0096
Person & Covey, Inc.
616 Allen Ave.
Glendale, CA 91201

Peterson Ointment Co.
257 Franklin St.
Buffalo, NY 14202

Pfanstiehl Labs., Inc.
1219 Glen Rock Ave.
Waukegan, IL 60085

0995
Pfipharmecs
Div. of Pfizer, Inc.
235 E. 42nd St.
New York, NY 10017

0069
Pfizer Laboratories
Div. of Pfizer, Inc.
235 E. 42nd St.
New York, NY 10017

Pharmaceutical Basics, Inc.
P.O. Box 9327
Denver, CO 80209

Pharmachem Corp.
Broad & Wood Sts.
Bethlehem, PA 18018

0016
Pharmacia Laboratories
Div. Pharmacia Inc.
800 Centennial Ave.
Piscataway, NJ 08854

0235
Pharmacraft Division
Pennwalt Corporation
P.O. Box 1710
Rochester, NY 14603

0598
Pharmacy Associates
1643 E. Genesee St.
Syracuse, NY 13201

Pharmex, Inc.
2113 Lincoln St., Box 151
Hollywood, FL 33022

Pharmics, Inc.
1878 S. Redwood Rd.
Salt Lake City, UT 84104

0054
Philips Roxane Labs.
See Roxane Laboratories, Inc.

Pixacol Company
Dept. DB
P.O. Box 29277
Parma, OH 44129

Plessner, Paul, Co., The
2232 4th Street North
St. Petersburg, FL 33704

0138
Plough, Inc.
Subs: Schering-Plough Corp.
P.O. Box 377
Memphis, TN 38151

0095
Poythress, Wm. P. & Co., Inc.
16 N. 22nd Street
Box 26946
Richmond, VA 23261

0331
Premo Pharmaceutical Labs., Inc.
111 Leuning Street
South Hackensack, NJ 07606

11649
Press Chemical & Pharmaceutical Labs.
P.O. Box 09103
584 East Whittler St.
Columbus, OH 43209

0587
Preston Pharmaceutics, Inc.
Post Office Box #8
Butler, NJ 07405

Primedics Labs.
California Division
1123 Goodrich Blvd.
Los Angeles, CA 90022

Procter and Gamble
Professional Services Division
P.O. Box 39175
Cincinnati, OH 45247

Professional Pharmacal Co.
See: Steri-Med, Inc.

Pruvo Pharmacal Co.
2018 W. Bender Rd.
Milwaukee, WI 53209

0034
Purdue Frederick Co.
100 Connecticut Ave.
Norwalk, CT 06856

0228
Purepac Pharmaceutical Co.
200 Elmora Ave.
Elizabeth, NJ 07207

0359
Quality Generics
262 Route 59
Monsey, NY 10952

0552
Comatic Labs., Inc.

Quinton, George, & Son, Inc.
Wantagh, NY 11793

0196
Rachelle Labs., Inc.
Sub. of International Rectifier Corp.
700 Henry Ford Ave.
Long Beach, CA 90801

Randob Labs., Ltd.
508 Franklin Ave.
Mt. Vernon, NY 10551

10952
Recsei Labs., The
330 S. Kellogg, Blvd. M.
Goleta, CA 93117

Redford Laboratories
See: Bay Laboratories, Inc.

0021
Reed & Carnrick Pharmaceuticals
Piscataway, NJ 08854

10956
Reese Chemical Co.
10617 Frank Ave.
Cleveland, OH 44106

0063
Reid-Provident Labs, Inc.
640 Tenth Street, N.W.
Atlanta, GA 30318

21769
Reily Chemical Co.
P.O. Box 50372
New Orleans, LA 70150

0815
Reiss Williams Company
Blair Park
Port Reading, NJ 07064

Renalab
Div. of Ries Biologicals

Republic Drug Co., Inc.
175 Great Arrow Ave.
Buffalo, NY 14207

Requa Mfg. Co., Inc.
1 Seneca Pl., Box 4008
Greenwich, CT 06830

Research Industries Corp.
Pharm. Division
1847 W. 2300 South
Salt Lake City, UT 84119

Revlon Health Care
See: USV Laboratories

Rexall Drug Co.
P.O. Box 7189
3901 N. Kingshighway Blvd.
St. Louis, MO 63115

Rexar Pharmacal Corp.
396 Rockaway Ave.
Valley Stream, NY 11581

0762
Rhode, J.G., Co.
302 S. Central Ave.
Baltimore, MD 21202

10973
Richards Pharmaceutical Co.
P.O. Box 1129
Santa Monica, CA 90406

Richlyn Laboratories
3725 Castor Ave.
Philadelphia, PA 19124

Rydell Laboratories
1525 Howe Street
Racine, WI 53403

0398
Ries-Hamly, Inc.
P.O. Box 83
Algonac, MI 48001

0089
Riker Labs., Inc.
Subs. 3M Company
19901 Nordhoff Street
Northridge, CA 91324

0031
Robins, A.H. Co.
1407 Cummings Drive
Richmond, VA 23220

0004
Roche Laboratories
Div. Hoffmann-LaRoche, Inc.
Roche Park
Nutley, NJ 07110

0049
Roerig
Div. Pfizer Pharmaceuticals
235 E. 42nd Street
New York, NY 10017

Roger Pharmacal, Inc.
P.O. Box 011022
1654 N.W. 35th St.
Miami, FL 33142

Rohm & Haas Co.
Independence Mall West
Philadelphia, PA 19105

0067
Rorer, William H., Inc.
500 Virginia Drive
Ft. Washington, PA 19034

0074
Ross Laboratories
Div. Abbott Laboratories
625 Cleveland Ave.
Columbus, OH 43216

0269
Roussel Corp.
155 E. 44th St.
New York, NY 10017

0032
Rowell Laboratories, Inc.
210 Main Street, West
Baudette, MN 56623

0054
Roxanne Laboratories, Inc.
330 Oak Street
P.O. Box 16532
Columbus, OH 43216

0524
Rucker Pharmacal Co., Inc.
6540 Line Avenue
Shreveport, LA 71106

Ruson Labs.
P.O. Box 42154
Portland, OR 97242

0263
Rystan Company, Inc.
47 Center Avenue
P.O. Box 214
Little Falls, NJ 07424

Salsbury Laboratories
2000 Rockford Road
Charles City, IA 50616

0511
Sandia Pharmaceuticals, Inc.

0212
Sandoz Nutrition
5320 W. 23 Street
Minneapolis, MN 55440

0078
Sandoz Pharmaceuticals
Div. of Sandoz Inc.
59 Route 10
E. Hanover, NJ 07936

Saron Pharmacal Corp
1640 Central Ave.
St. Petersburg, FL 33712

0281
Savage Labs., Inc.
Div. of Altana, Inc.
60 Baylis Road
Melville, Long Island, NY 11747

Schaffer Laboratories
P.O. Box 539
Arcadia, CA 91006

0274
Scherer Laboratories, Inc.
14335 Gills Road
Dallas, TX 75240

0085
Schering Corp.
Div. Schering-Plough Corp.
2000 Galloping Hill Rd.
Kenilworth, NJ 07033

0234
Schmid, Julius, Inc.
Route 46 West
Little Falls, NJ 07424

Scholl, Inc.
See: Plough, Inc.

0352
Schuemann Laboratories, Inc.
480 W. Auroa Road
Northfield, OH 44067

42021
Sclavo, Incorporated
5 Mansard Court
Wayne, NJ 07470

0711
Scott-Allison Pharmaceuticals, Inc.
581 Sagamore Avenue
Teaneck, NJ 07666

0372
Scot-Tussin Pharmacal Co., Inc.
50 Clemence St., P.O. Box 8217
Cranston, RI 02920

0444
Scrip, Inc.
101 South St.
Peoria, IL 61602

0329
Scruggs Pharmacal Co., Inc.

0014
Searle & Co.
San Juan, PR 00936

0025
Searle Laboratories
Div. Searle Pharmaceuticals Inc.
P.O. Box 5110
Chicago, IL 60680

0551
Seatrace Co.
P.O. Box 363
Gadsden, AL 35902

SeMed Pharmaceuticals
See: Beecham-Massengill Co.

Serono Laboratories, Inc.
280 Pond Street
Randolph, MA 02368

Serums and Vaccines of America
Division of Murai Laboratories, Inc.

Shear-Kershman Labs., Inc.
14500 South Outer 40 Rd.
Chesterfield, MO 63017

Shepard Laboratories
500 Virginia Dr.
Ft. Washington, PA 19034

Sherwood Laboratories, Inc.
1601 E. 361st St.
Willoughby, OH 44094

0823
Sheryl Pharmaceuticals, Inc.

Shield Laboratories
99–101 Saw Mill River Rd.
Yonkers, NY 10701

Shulton, Inc.
697 Route 46
Clifton, NY 07011

Shuptrine Company
P.O. Box 22127
Savannah, GA 31403

Sig: Pharmaceuticals, Inc.
Div. International Chemical & Nuclear Corp.
185 Park Drive
Eastchester, NY 10707

Silver's Pharmaceuticals
P.O. Box 238
Neptune Beach, FL 32233

Smalley & Williams, Inc.
806 Lexington Ave.
New York, NY 10021

0007
Smith Kline & French Company
Subsidiary of SmithKline Corp.

0007
Smith Kline & French Laboratories
Division of SmithKline Corp.

0484
SmithKline Corporation
1500 Spring Garden St.
Philadelphia, PA 19101

0058
Smith, Miller & Patch
Div. of CooperVision Pharmaceuticals Inc.

0058
Smith, Miller & Patch
Div. of Berlex Laboratories

0346
Softcon Products
Div. Warner-Lambert Co.
201 Tabor Road
Morris Plains, NJ 07950

Southern Drug & Mfg. Co.
1639 N. Highland
Memphis, TN 38108

0251
Spanner, G.O., Inc.
20 Church St.
Monclair, NJ 07042

Spence McCord
Div. of General Medical Corp.
La Crosse, WI 54601

Spencer-Mead, Inc.
270 West Merrick Road
Valley Stream, NY 11582

Sperti Drug Products, Inc.
7 Sperti Dr.
Fort Mitchell, KY 41017

10833
Spirt & Company
Subs. Hyrex Pharmaceuticals

50821
Springbok Pharmaceuticals, Inc.
12502 South Garden Street
Houston, TX 77071

0003
Squibb, E.R.
P.O. Box 4000
Princeton, NJ 08540

Squibb-Connaught
Subs. E.R. Squibb Co.

11530
Stanback Co., Ltd.
1500 S. Main St.
P.O. Box 1669
Salisbury, NC 28145

Standard Process Laboratories, Inc.
2023 West Wisconsin Ave.
Milwaukee, WI 53201

0716
Standex Laboratories
585 W. Second Ave.
Columbus, OH 43215

0242
Stanlabs Pharmaceutical Co.
Subs. Simpak Corporation

Star Pharmaceuticals, Inc.
5064 Nadina Lane
Box 4161
Atlanta, GA 30302

Stecker Chemicals, Inc.
See: Pfister Chemical Inc.

0346
Steri-Med, Inc.
P.O. Box 459
Lindenhurst, NY 11757

Stewart-Jackson Pharmacal, Inc.
P.O. Box 28701
Memphis, TN 38128

0145
Stiefel Laboratories, Inc.
2801 Ponce de Leon Blvd.
Coral Gables, FL 33134

Stillman Co., The
323 East Galena Blvd.
Aurora, IL 60507

Strassenberg Labs.
See: Pennwalt Corp.

Strickland and Co.
1400 Ragan
Memphis, TN 38101

Strubel Drugs
4500 6th St.
Kenosha, WI 53142

0038
Stuart Pharmaceuticals
Div. of ICI Americas Inc.
P.O. Box 751
Wilmington, DE 19897

11086
Summers Labs., Inc.
Morris Road
Fort Washington, PA 19034

0414
Suppositoria Labs., Inc.
135 Florida St.
Farmingdale, L.I., NY 11735

Surgikos Company
Box 130
Arlington, TX 76010

Surgitube Products Corp.
83 North Summit St.
Tenafly, NJ 07670

0253
Sutliff & Case Co., Inc.
P.O. Box 838
201 Spring St.
Peoria, IL 61603

11701
Sween Corp.

0033
Syntex Laboratories, Inc.
3401 Hillview Ave.
Stanford Industrial Park
Palo Alto, CA 94304

0033
Syntex Puerto Rico, Inc.
Humacao, PR 00661

0734
Tablicaps, Inc.

12072
Temesco
5135 Galaxy Dr., P.O. Box 16328
Jackson, MS 39206

Tender Corporation
P.O. Box 42
Littleton Industrial Park
Littleton, NH 03561

Tennessee Wholesale Drug Co.
200 Cumberland Bend.
Nashville, TN 37228

Texas Pharmacal
See: Alcon Laboratories or Parke-Davis

Thompson Medical Co., Inc.
919 Third Ave.
New York, NY 10022

3M Personal Care Products
Subs. 3M Company
19901 Nordhoff Street
Northridge, CA 91324

Three P Products Corp.
5 Cooper Street
Burlington, NJ 08018

Thurston Laboratories, Inc.
P.O. Box 8
Solana Beach, CA 92075

11299
Torch Laboratories, Inc.
P.O. Box 248
Reisterstown, MD 21136

Torigian Labs., Inc.
218–20 98th Ave.
Queens Village, NY 11429

0157
Towne, Paulsen & Co., Inc.
140 E. Duarte Rd.
Monrovia, CA 91016

Travenol Labs., Inc.
1425 Lake Cook Road
Deerfield, IL 60015

11311
Trimen Laboratories, Inc.

0558
Tri-State Pharm. Co., Inc.
See: Mismer Pharm., Inc.

0648
Truett Labs.
Div. Southwestern Drug Corp.
13450 Harry Hines Blvd.
P.O. Box 34029
Dallas, TX 75234

0463
Truxton, C.O. Inc.
1458–60 Haddon Ave.
Camden, NJ 08103

50023
Tunex Pharmaceuticals, Inc.
5909 Shelby Oaks Dr.
Suite 233
Memphis, TN 38134

0124
Tutag Pharmaceuticals
See: Reid-Provident

0785
UAD Laboratories, Inc.
6635 Highway 18, West
P.O. Box 10587
Jackson, MS 39209

0127
Ulmer Pharmacal
Div. Physicians & Hospital Supply Co.
2440 Fernbrook Lane
Plymouth, MN 55441

0051
Unimed, Inc.
35 Columbia Rd.
Somerville, NJ 08876

United-Guardian, Inc.
P.O. Box 2500
Smithtown, NY 11787

0009
Upjohn Company, The
7171 Portage Road
Kalamazoo, MI 49001

0245
Upsher-Smith Laboratories, Inc.
14905 23rd Ave. N.
Minneapolis, MN 55441

U.S. Chemical Marketing Group
203 Rio Circle
Decatur, GA 30030

U.S. Products, Inc.
16636 N.W. 54th Ave.
Miami Lakes, FL 33014

U.S. Ethicals
See: Wharton Labs., Inc.

0070
USV Laboratories Inc.
Manati, P.R. 00701